13th Edition

TOYS & PRICES 2006

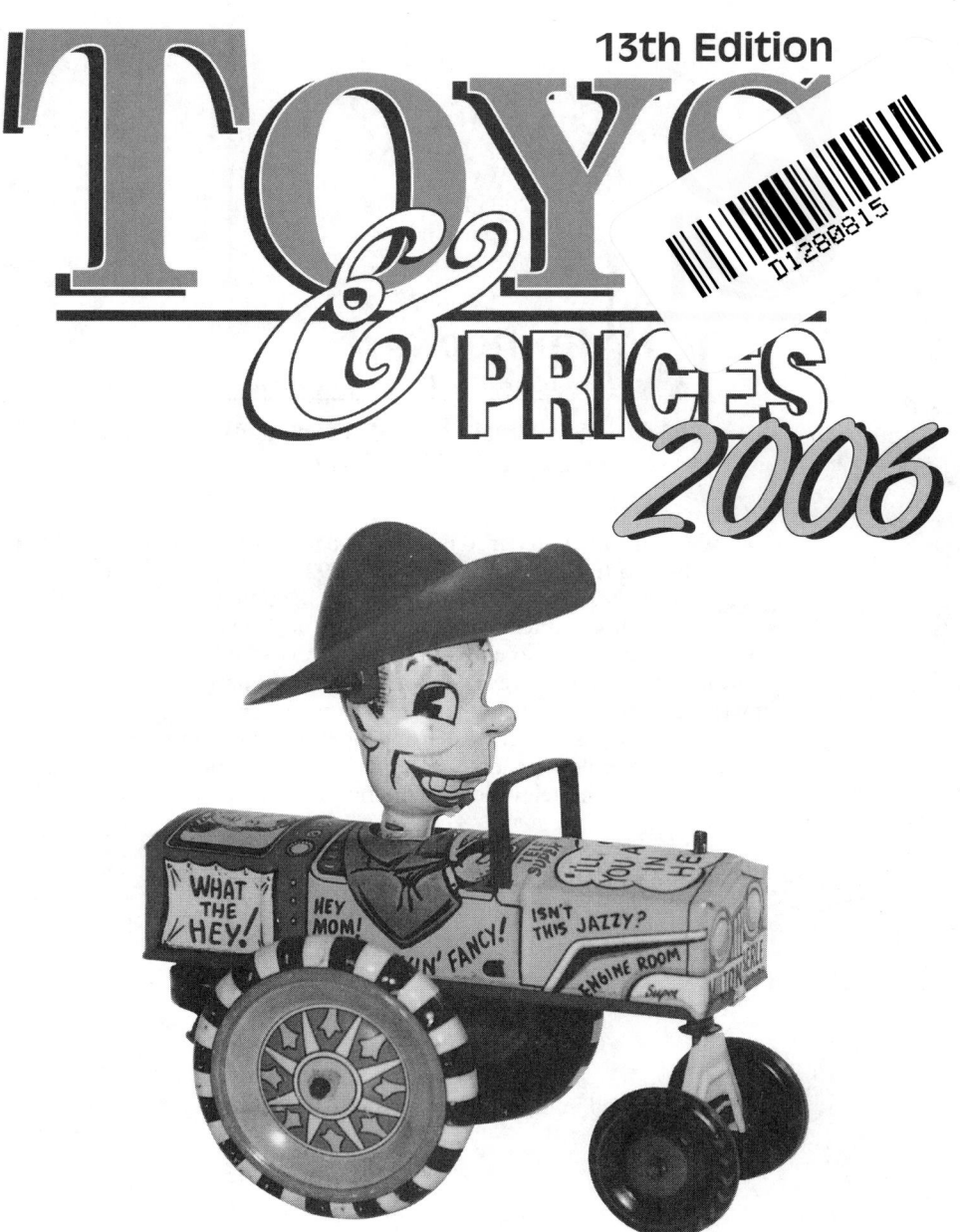

Edited by
Karen O'Brien

©2005 KP Books
Published by

kp books
An Imprint of F+W Publications

700 East State Street • Iola, WI 54990-0001
715-445-2214 • 888-457-2873

Library of Congress Catalog Number: 2005906854
ISBN: 0-89689-152-6

Designed by Sandi Morrison and Brian Brogaard
Edited by Karen O'Brien

Printed in the United States of America

CONTENTS

ON THE COVER

FRONT COVER

G.I. Joe:. . . . . .U.S. Navy Sailor, 12", Hasbro, 2001

Vehicles:. . . . . .Hot Wheels Numbered Packs, 2005 First Editions #5, Realistix, 1969 Pontiac Firebird T/A

Vehicles:. . . . . .1949-52 Tonka Wrecker

Barbie:. . . . . .Ponytail #1, Mattel, 1959

Action Figures:. . . . . . . .Transformers Generation 1 Grimlock, 1985

Lunch Boxes:. . . . . .Tom Corbett Space Cadet, Aladdin, 1954

Guns:. . . . . .Pirate Cap Pistol, Hubley, 9-1/2" long, 1940s

Games:. . . . . .The Six Million Dollar Man Game, Parker Brothers, 1975

TITLE PAGE

Vehicles:. . . . . .Milton Berle Crazy Car, tin wind-up, Marx, 1950s

BACK COVER

Action Figures:. . . . . . . .World's Greatest Super Heroes, Mr. Fantastic, Mego, 8" tall, 1975

Battery-Operated Toys:. . .Bubble Blowing Popeye, Linemar, 1950s

Robots:. . . . . .Robby Space Patrol, Nomura/TN, 1957

Lunch Boxes:. . . . . .The Bionic Woman, vinyl, 1978

Vehicles:. . . . . .Hot Wheels Redlines, Hot Heap, Mattel, 1968

Marx Play Sets:. . . . . . . .Ben Hur Play Set, Series 2000, 1959

DEDICATION

This edition is dedicated to toy shows and their producers, promoters, dealers, and patrons. Every show is an education in toy history, and every collector you meet is a potential wealth of knowledge.

Support your local toy shows!

ACKNOWLEDGMENTS

Preparing this title is a year-round endeavor that would boggle the mind of most readers, and it's a process that I could never engineer alone. I'm very grateful for the level of support this project receives from the collecting community. This book is for you, and it gets better every year because toy collectors generously share their information.

Thanks first to my family and friends for your love and support, your patience and understanding, and your not-so-gentle reminders to take a day off every now and again.

Thanks to my students, who inspire me. Thanks to all of the readers who sent in toy information and photos, and thanks to all of the toy show organizers, dealers, and attendees who "talked toys" with me as I attended shows this year. I've had so much fun—I think I need to get out to even more shows next year!

I owe a debt of thanks to the previous editors of this title, who left me a database filled with terrific toys.

The individual chapter contributors to this book are experts in their fields, and this project would not be possible without their painstaking efforts and endless patience. Thanks to Rob Barilla, Chris Fawcett, Jan Fennick, Paul Fink, Don Hultzman, John Marshall, Jack Murray, Ron O'Brien, Shawn Peterson, Randy Prasse, Edwin Price, Mark Rich, Leo Rishty, Dr. Douglas Sadecky, Mary Ann Sell, Scott Smiles, Ron Smith, John Snyder, Joe Soucy, Stuart Wells, and Michael Zarnock.

The staff of KP Books did a remarkable job in assembling this edition. Thanks to Sandi Morrison for running all of the database patterns and tackling the sizeable interior design duties, and thanks to Brian Brogaard for another spirited cover design, vivid color section, and fun-to-read chapter intros.

Thanks again to the toy division at F+W Publications for their support and continued enthusiasm. Merry Dudley, editor of Toy Cars & Models magazine, volunteered hours of data entry on this project and wrote the intro for the Vehicles chapter. Toy Shop Editor Tom Bartsch wrote the introductions for Action Figures and Character Toys. Year after year, both editors have unselfishly shared their knowledge and resources to make this a better book.

It's a privilege to work with such dedicated professionals.

My sincere thanks to you all.

Karen O'Brien
September 2005

INTRODUCTION

ATTENDING TOY SHOWS

It's no wonder I'm an advocate for attending toy shows.

Meeting toy collectors and dealers is one of the best resources available when researching the toys contained in these pages. Wandering the aisles of a toy show is an education in itself, if you're patient enough to take in the items on each table. Most dealers are happy to describe the history of the toys on their tables, because they are enthusiasts too.

Like most collectors, I've accumulated dozens of interesting stories regarding the wonderful things I've learned from asking questions of dealers. A cast-iron dealer once explained the unique features of the Kenton driver figures, and now I can spot them right away. A tin toy dealer had several Chein Drummers at his table and was kind enough to explain the differences in their lithography that occurred over time. The stories go on and on, but what shines through is an infectious love of toys.

Toy show patrons, dealers, and promoters noticed a decline in attendance during the early years of this decade, as well as a decline in the number of small, local toy shows. One collector bemoaned the loss of several shows in his area, citing the high price of gas when traveling to more remote locations. The culprit for this decline in shows and attendance is usually identified as the Internet, and one must certainly acknowledge the remarkable impact that online auctions have had on this hobby in the last ten years.

The Internet has made the "big blue marble" a small world, indeed. Collectors no longer need to wait several months for their favorite toy show to roll around. With a few clicks of the mouse, the desired toy is available via the Internet either through an online auction or courtesy of one of the many Internet storefronts that dealers are now utilizing. Fast and convenient, the Internet allows collectors to obtain toys in locations from which they might not travel.

But has the hobby paid a price for this convenience?

The fast pace of Internet collecting has added another dimension to the collecting community, and relying on it alone costs us the lost opportunity to network with other individuals. The days of finding a dealer's ad in Toy Shop and sending in a SASE with your "want list" of the toys you need are far from over. Today, people may be more likely to email that want list than reach for a stamp, but collectors are discovering a useful tool in the Internet that supplements their well-established search for toys.

"Don't put all of your eggs in one basket," is an early lesson for most children, but an appropriate directive for collectors as well. I've spoken to a number of collectors this year that cut back on the number of shows they attended to concentrate on Internet purchases. While they acknowledged that it was nice to buy specific pieces immediately from numerous states, there was a drawback in the networking opportunities that led to local acquisitions. They experienced a decline in the number of local referrals because other collectors hadn't seen them around and didn't know whether or not they were still participating in the hobby.

It's impossible to quantify the value of networking, but I'm sure all of our collections contain pieces procured because someone familiar with our interests knew we would enjoy a particular toy. A dealer who knows what you're looking for will keep an eye out for those items in his travels because he knows he'll have a guaranteed sale at the next show. Wherever they take place, these relationships are the backbone of the hobby and the foundation of our community.

Balance is the key.

Buying and selling toys is very much a community activity and to fully participate, collectors need to take advantage of every tool at their disposal. Attending toy shows, flea markets, estate sales, garage sales, and auctions coupled with regular perusal of classified advertising and Internet involvement offers collectors the widest possible exposure to the wonderful toys and people of this hobby.

Perhaps the Internet isn't the only culprit causing a decline in the number of shows in your area. The Calendar section of Toy Shop magazine carries an extensive list of toy shows every issue, so make a difference and attend a local show. Or better yet, once each year, become a dealer for a day and discover this hobby from a whole new perspective—the other side of the table.

ABOUT THE BOOK

This title continues a shift begun in previous editions to focus mainly on post-World War II toys while also including some Depression-era toys. O'Brien's Collecting Toys has also made a shift to remove its more "modern" chapters and focus on early baby boom era toys and concentrate primarily on pre-World War II toys. This separation allows both titles to enjoy a unique identity and audience.

As you can see on the Contents page, this edition is organized alphabetically by subject matter beginning with Action Figures and concluding with Western Toys. More than 31,000 toys are contained within and the number grows with each edition.

Because some popular characters fit into more than one collecting category, remember to check multiple chapters for the particular toy you're looking for. The Grizzly Adams figure featured in the color section actually has its listing in the TV Toys chapter, for example, while Charlie's Angels toys appear in both the Action Figures and TV Toys chapters.

If you are taking the plunge to participate in online auctions, this title is an excellent guide to use when setting reserve prices for your listings.

YOU ASKED FOR IT, YOU GOT IT

Hot Wheels Redlines remain popular with collectors. So popular, in fact, that I've upgraded their chapter to include prices for non-mint, loose cars. After all, these are the Redlines that we see most often at shows and in auctions.

As always, additions and upgrades were made to each chapter of the book, so look for more of your 1980s favorites in the Action Figures chapter, a re-structuring of the Tonka section listings, and improvements in the Western Toys chapter. Character Toys continue to be a favorite with readers and the chapter contains some pre- and post-World War II favorites.

BECOME A CONTRIBUTOR

Throughout the year, I receive input from regular readers of this title and that information translates into the changes made for the next edition. The advantage of being an annual title is that Toys & Prices is in a constant state of development.

Are there toys in your collection not included in these pages that you think would make good additions? Your input is encouraged. Contact me at the address below.

We are always looking for toy photos for our archives. Good quality 35mm photos or slides work the best for reproduction in print. If you have information or can donate photos of toys not pictured in these pages, please contact me at the following address:

Karen O'Brien
KP Books
700 E. State St.
Iola, WI 54990
(715) 445-4612
karen.o'brien@fwpubs.com

Enjoy your collection, and support your local toy shows!

Karen O'Brien
September 2005

This book is designed to be as easy to use as possible. The book is organized alphabetically by chapter—see Contents on p. 3. The quick-reference tabs on the side of the pages indicate the chapter. The headers at the top of each page have the chapter title followed by the section. For example, the header on page 11 reads:

Action Figures — **Aliens (Kenner, 1992-94)**

Therefore, page 11 is in the Action Figures chapter and the last section on the page is Aliens from Kenner, 1992-94.

As a general rule, individual sections override a character name. If there is a section in the book for the type of toy you're looking for, check there first. For example, if you're looking up a Superman lunch box, look first in the lunch box section. Likewise, a Yogi Bear board game will most likely appear in the postwar games section rather than in the character toys section.

The character toys section includes items that do not fit into one of our established sections or are more difficult to classify.

Also be aware that the words "figure" and "doll" are sometimes used interchangeably, although we have tried to remain consistent.

Overlap is the nature of the beast with toy classification, so if you don't find what you're looking for in one place, check a related section. For example, space-related action figures are most likely to be listed in the action figure section, but you may also find some listed in the space toys section. We're working on ways to streamline such listings to make finding items easier for readers. Your input and suggestions are welcomed.

CONDITION IS EVERYTHING

When estimating the value of a toy, you must first evaluate its condition. Mint toys in mint packaging command higher prices than well-played with toys whose boxes disappeared with the wrapping paper on Christmas day. Mint is a rare condition indeed as toys were meant to be played with by children—a group not normally disposed to the meticulous maintenance of the toys in their toy boxes, sand boxes, backyards, garages, and strewn across the living room floor.

Realistic evaluation of condition is essential, as grading standards do vary from class to class. Grading a Victorian board game is a different task than grading a Mattel Hot Wheels Redlines car.

Ultimately, the market is driven by a checkbook,

and the bottom line final value of a toy is often the last price at which it is sold. In this sense, the toy hobby, like many others, operates in a vacuum, with individual toys setting their own values. Repeated sales of specific items create precedents and establish a standard for asking prices across the market. It is by comparison of such multiple transactions that price guides such as this one are created. In the end, the value of the toy is decided by one person—the buyer.

COMMON ABBREVIATIONS

MIB or MIP *(Mint in Box, Mint in Package, C10):* Just like new, in the original package, preferably still sealed. Boxes may have been opened, but any packages inside (as with model kits) remain unopened. Blister cards should be intact, undamaged, and unopened. Factory-sealed boxes should be unopened and often command higher prices.

MNP or MNB *(Mint no Package, Mint no Box, C10):* This describes a toy typically produced in the 1960s or later in Mint condition, but missing its original package. This may also include a prototype or one-of-a-kind toy. A toy outside its original package is often referred to as "loose."

NM *(Near Mint, C9):* A toy that appears like new in overall appearance but exhibits very minor wear and does not have the original box. An exception would be a toy that came in kit form. A kit in Near Mint condition would be expected to have the original box, but the box would display some wear.

EX *(Excellent, C8):* A toy that is complete and has been played with. Signs of minor wear may be evident, but the toy is very clean and well cared for.

VG *(Very Good, C6):* A toy that obviously has been played with and shows general overall wear. Paint chipping is readily apparent. In metal toys, some minor rust may be evident. In sets, some minor pieces may be missing.

GD or G *(Good, C4):* A toy with evidence of heavy play, dents, chips, and possibly moderate rust. The toy may be missing a major replaceable component, such as a battery compartment door, or may be in need of repair. In sets, several pieces may be missing.

Action Figures

By Tom Bartsch

On the crest of a hill, G.I. Joes await to attack the collection of Bonanza characters assembled below. Meanwhile, the Marx Fighting Eagles from the Best of the West series are poised across the field to attack from the other side. Waiting for the aftermath effects is the M*A*S*H unit comprised of Hawkeye Pierce, Hunnicut, Col. Potter, and crew.

High above in the clouds, Superman and Batman of the World's Greatest Superheroes line keep watch over the whole affair while trying to make peace between the opposing sides. The adjoining village is full of characters glued to the impending battle, for their fate lies in the result. Mattel's Big Jim and Big Jeff are chatting about it on the basketball court, while Ideal's Evel Knievel gives his theory on the battle with Galoob's Inspector Gadget while playing tennis against Mego's Dr. McCoy and Dr. Zaius.

Didn't everyone's back yard have this scene played out each Saturday afternoon? No? Well, you could. Action figures have a very broad range of characters in its universe, from fictitious villains to likenesses of real-life heroes. The breadth and sheer quantity of action figures that have been produced since the 1960s is mind-boggling, and it's growing by the day. It's the strongest category in the toy market, and one every manufacturer tries to at least get a share of.

Action figures span generations, and while the original collectors are opting for Marx figures and the first G.I. Joes, today's younger collectors are going ga-ga over McFarlane's Matrix figures and the latest Peanuts creations.

EVOLVING WITH THE TIMES

When action figures first burst on the scene in 1964 with the introduction of G.I. Joe, boys finally had an answer to the fashion dolls their sisters flung in their face. Once Joe hit the scene, the floodgates started to open on the male-orientated action figure genre. What we now know as the usual suspects of the 1960s came on strong soon afterward. The goal was to capture this new audience with the notion of fully-articulated playthings holding precedence over physical activities and more stationary toys like Lincoln Logs and Monopoly. Marx, A.C. Gilbert, and Ideal soon boarded the action figure train, producing figures of spy heroes (James Bond), comic life-savers (Captain Action), and legends of the

West (Johnny West).

As we moved into the 1970s, action figure manufacturers didn't just rest on their laurels. Using the foundations of TV and films, manufacturers had all the ammunition they needed to entice a buying public and score some serious profits. The background stories were already laid out—all kids had to do was re-enact what they were watching on TV and reading in comic books. Dialogue, movements, and adventures were already ingrained in the minds of the fans who took these figures home and made the backyard their personal playground. Of course, once more and more figures entered the scene, the adventures could be intertwined, and G.I. Joe could be rounding up cattle with Johnny West or defeating the Joker with Batman. The storylines remain endless.

Today, action figures continue to be spit out with the regularity of a car on an assembly line. But the subject matter is starting to move beyond recognizable characters to U.S. fans and having more of an Asian influence. Many more anime and magna properties are now coming to North America, ushering in a new wave of collectors in the process.

There are also a lot more properties being revisited, as manufacturers are less apt to take risks in the current market. Updated versions of the Batman, Masters of the Universe, Hulk, Strawberry Shortcake, and Teenage Mutant Ninja Turtles, among others, have come into play in the last few years. While this is attributable in part to the fact that 1980s children are now able to stick large sums of money into their toy collections, it also shows how endearing these properties are 20 years down the road. Childhood memories are powerful forces.

Expect the trend of familiar figures to continue to be produced. I wouldn't even be surprised if lines like M.A.S.K. and Buck Rogers made reappearances.

TODAY'S MARKET

The purpose of *Toys & Prices* is to give toy collectors a look into the value of their toys and possibly tip them off in what will be the hit toys of   tomorrow in this ever-changing market.

The general rule of thumb with collectibles is that they are worth only what a buyer will pay. Sure, that's part of it, but we

THE TOP TEN ACTION FIGURES *(In Mint Condition)*

1. Captain Action Spider-Man costume, Ideal, 1967	$8,000
2. Captain Action Green Hornet costume, Ideal, 1967	7,500
3. Batgirl, Comic Heroine Posin' Dolls, Ideal, 1967	5,500
4. Supergirl, Comic Heroine Posin' Dolls, Ideal, 1967	4,500
5. Wonder Woman, Comic Heroine Posin' Dolls, Ideal, 1967	4,500
6. Mera, Comic Heroine Posin' Dolls, Ideal, 1967	4,500
7. Captain Action Dr. Evil Sanctuary, Ideal, 1967	3,500
8. Captain Action Dr. Evil Lab Set Display Box, Ideal, 1968	3,000
9. Captain Action Buck Rogers costume, Ideal, 1967	2,700
10. Captain Action Dr. Evil Mailer Box, Ideal, 1968	2,500

can also get a handle on what's tripping the proverbial toy trigger through market report, buying trends, and general observations at shows.

The big guns—the G.I. Nurses, Super Queens, Mego Montgomery Ward exclusives—still do and will always command several thousand dollars in the collector's market. These "Holy Grails" will forever to be the fancy of collector's dreams. But there are other toys that have attracted a pretty penny for those looking to get a piece of the past.

Among the biggest surprises today is what figures are getting once they are graded. Even figures that have just been released, like Hasbro's Original Trilogy Collection, are getting nearly triple-digit values when you can pull them off the shelf for less than $15. Grading isn't a trend that has caught on at a great length, partly because only certain action figures are getting graded at this time. These are mostly modern figures, from the 1980s to today, that are getting the grading treatment.

Outside of the graded market, there haven't been a lot of figures that have set the world on fire on the auction circuit. But that doesn't mean we can't predict what will grab some serious coin down the road. The one sure thing is that any figure that is in Excellent condition, with all its accessories and its original packaging will command top dollar nearly every time. Condition is everything these days, so those that played nice with their toys will benefit down the line if they ever decide to part with them.

2006 TRENDS

Of course, predicting what the valuable toys of tomorrow will be is no easy task. The buying public is fickle. What one deems popular today is often replaced by something else tomorrow. That's just how it works, right Pokemon fans?

Manufacturers are trying to help make these decisions for us by issuing limited-edition pieces or show exclusives that send completists running to the bank. While not diving into that realm, here are some figure lines that could be quite coveted down the road:

One of the hottest trends is action figures is actually also the simplest. Forget articulation and ultra-detail—simply put, 2-inch LEGO-like figures are all collectors need these days. From Minimates to Palz, licensed block-style figures are quite popular, and cheaply priced—two recipes for coveted collectables down the road.

As new movies based on old properties keep Hollywood glowing, the same story could be said for toys. *Willy Wonka and the Chocolate Factory, Batman Begins, Sin City, Fantastic Four,* etc., were reborn in 2005, resulting in a truckload of new toys. This also spurs interest in the original toys, and actually makes them more coveted because some collectors always prefer the vintage pieces.

When it comes to action figures from the 1960

and 1970s, the prices haven't moved all that much. But when you get into the 1980s, one thing has helped prices go through the roof—grading. Figures that would maybe bring $200 can now fetch $1,000 thanks to good condition and a grade confirming that. So if you have some original Star Wars figures in the pack and are looking for more money for them, spend a few dollars to get them slabbed and graded.

The action figure market is one of the fastest growing areas in toys. New figures are added every day, while the classic examples continue to draw interest. Because some of the original 1960s figures are so hard to find, a lot of manufacturers are trying their luck with reissues. Sometimes this hurts the value of the originals, other times it has no impact. If the figure is in good condition and has a special quality (age, rarity, accessories), you'll find a willing buyer. Based on their regularity at shows and at auction, action figures are still the backbone of the hobby. Old, new, or in between, there is a rabid fan base for all. Happy collecting!

Contributor: Tom Bartsch is the editor of Toy Shop magazine. John Marshall can be reached at www.jmuniverse.com

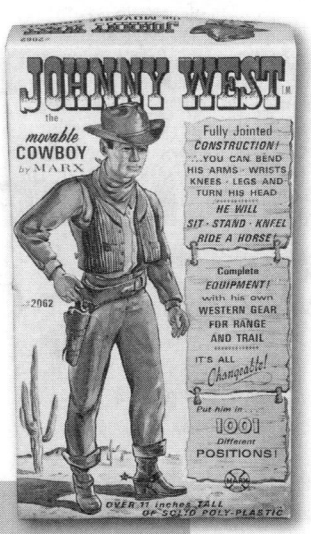

3D ANIMATION FROM JAPAN (MCFARLANE, 2000)

AKIRA

Kaneda with Motorcycle, 2000, McFarlane
  NM $3   MIP $13

Tetsuo, 2000, McFarlane
  NM $3   MIP $13

TENCHI MUYO!

Ryoko, 2000, McFarlane
  NM $3   MIP $15

TRIGUN

Vash with Stampede, 2000, McFarlane
  NM $3   MIP $13

ACTION JACKSON (MEGO, 1974)

8" FIGURES

Action Jackson, 1974, Mego, blond, brown, or black hair
  NM $15   MIP $30

Action Jackson, 1974, Mego, blond, brown, or black beard
  NM $15   MIP $30

Action Jackson, 1974, Mego, Black version
  NM $25   MIP $40

ACCESSORIES

Fire Rescue Pack, 1974, Mego
  NM $5   MIP $15

Parachute Plunge, 1974, Mego
  NM $5   MIP $15

Strap-On Helicopter, 1974, Mego
  NM $5   MIP $15

Water Scooter, 1974, Mego
  NM $5   MIP $15

OUTFITS

Air Force Pilot, 1974, Mego
  NM $7   MIP $10

Army Outfit, 1974, Mego
  NM $7   MIP $10

Aussie Marine, 1974, Mego
  NM $7   MIP $10

Baseball, 1974, Mego
  NM $7   MIP $10

Fisherman, 1974, Mego
  NM $7   MIP $10

Football, 1974, Mego
  NM $7   MIP $10

Frog Man, 1974, Mego
  NM $7   MIP $10

Hockey, 1974, Mego
  NM $7   MIP $10

Jungle Safari, 1974, Mego
  NM $7   MIP $10

Karate, 1974, Mego
  NM $7   MIP $10

Navy Sailor, 1974, Mego
  NM $7   MIP $10

Rescue Squad, 1974, Mego
  NM $7   MIP $10

Scramble Cyclist, 1974, Mego
  NM $7   MIP $10

Secret Agent, 1974, Mego
  NM $7   MIP $10

Ski Patrol, 1974, Mego
  NM $7   MIP $10

Snowmobile Outfit, 1974, Mego
  NM $7   MIP $10

Surf and Scuba Outfit, 1974, Mego
  NM $7   MIP $10

Western Cowboy, 1974, Mego
  NM $7   MIP $10

PLAY SETS

Jungle House, 1974, Mego
  NM $100   MIP $250

Lost Continent Play Set, 1974, Mego
  NM $150   MIP $350

VEHICLES

Adventure Set, 1974, Mego
  NM $40   MIP $85

Campmobile, 1974, Mego
  NM $40   MIP $85

Dune Buggy, 1974, Mego
  NM $30   MIP $60

Formula Racer, 1974, Mego
  NM $30   MIP $60

Mustang, 1974, Mego
  NM $30   MIP $60

Rescue Helicopter, 1974, Mego
  NM $40   MIP $85

Safari Jeep, 1974, Mego
  NM $40   MIP $85

Scramble Cycle, 1974, Mego
  NM $20   MIP $40

Snowmobile, 1974, Mego
  NM $15   MIP $30

ADDAMS FAMILY (PLAYMATES, 1992)

FIGURES

(Toy Shop File Photo)

Gomez, 1992, Playmates
  NM $2   MIP $6

Granny, 1992, Playmates
  NM $2   MIP $6

Lurch, 1992, Playmates
  NM $2   MIP $6

Morticia, 1992, Playmates
  NM $2   MIP $6

Pugsley, 1992, Playmates
  NM $2   MIP $6

Uncle Fester, 1992, Playmates
  NM $2   MIP $6

ADDAMS FAMILY (REMCO, 1964)

FIGURES

Lurch, 1964, Remco
  NM $150   MIP $450

Morticia, 1964, Remco
  NM $160   MIP $500

Uncle Fester, 1964, Remco
  NM $160   MIP $500

ALIEN (KENNER, 1979)

18" FIGURE

Alien, 1979, Kenner, This is the ultimate figure for Alien collectors, to be complete it must have the plastic headpiece
  NM $200   MIP $500

ALIENS (KENNER, 1992-94)

ACCESSORIES

Evac Fighter, 1992-94, Kenner
  NM $7   MIP $20

Hovertread, 1992-94, Kenner
  NM $5   MIP $20

Power Loader, 1992-94, Kenner
  NM $5   MIP $20

Stinger XT-37, 1992-94, Kenner
  NM $5   MIP $20

SERIES 1, 1992

Apone, 1992, Kenner
  NM $5   MIP $8

Bishop, 1992, Kenner, Gatlin gun, body breaks into two parts
  NM $5   MIP $8

Bull Alien, 1992, Kenner
  NM $7   MIP $8

Drake, 1992, Kenner
  NM $5   MIP $8

Gorilla Alien, 1992, Kenner
  NM $8   MIP $8

ACTION FIGURES

Hicks, 1992, Kenner
    NM $5   **MIP** $8

Queen Alien, 1992, Kenner
    NM $10   **MIP** $20

Ripley, 1992, Kenner, with Turbo Torch
    NM $5   **MIP** $15

Scorpion Alien, 1992, Kenner
    NM $7   **MIP** $15

SERIES 2, 1993

(Toy Shop File Photo)

Alien vs. Predator, 1993, Kenner, Billed as the "ultimate battle between beast and hunter."
    NM $15   **MIP** $30

Flying Queen Alien, 1993, Kenner
    NM $5   **MIP** $15

Queen Face Hugger, 1993, Kenner
    NM $5   **MIP** $15

Snake Alien, 1993, Kenner
    NM $5   **MIP** $15

SERIES 3, 1994

Arachnid Alien, 1994, Kenner
    NM $4   **MIP** $19

Atax, 1994, Kenner
    NM $4   **MIP** $15

Clan Leader Predator, 1994, Kenner
    NM $4   **MIP** $19

Cracked Tusk Predator, 1994, Kenner
    NM $4   **MIP** $11

Hudson (foreign release), 1994, Kenner
    NM $11   **MIP** $30

Invisible Predator (mail-in), 1994, Kenner
    NM $15   **MIP** $30

Kill Krab Alien, 1994, Kenner
    NM $4   **MIP** $11

King Alien, 1994, Kenner
    NM $8   **MIP** $19

Lasershot Predator (electronic), 1994, Kenner
    NM $11   **MIP** $23

Lava Predator, 1994, Kenner
    NM $4   **MIP** $11

Mantis Alien, 1994, Kenner
    NM $4   **MIP** $11

Night Cougar Alien, 1994, Kenner
    NM $4   **MIP** $11

Night Storm Predator, 1994, Kenner
    NM $4   **MIP** $11

O'Malley (foreign release), 1994, Kenner
    NM $15   **MIP** $30

Panther Alien, 1994, Kenner
    NM $4   **MIP** $11

Rhino Alien, 1994, Kenner
    NM $5   **MIP** $11

Spiked Tail Predator, 1994, Kenner
    NM $3   **MIP** $11

Stalker Predator, 1994, Kenner
    NM $3   **MIP** $11

Swarm Alien (electronic), 1994, Kenner
    NM $11   **MIP** $19

Vasquez (foreign release), 1994, Kenner
    NM $11   **MIP** $30

Wild Boar Alien, 1994, Kenner
    NM $3   **MIP** $11

ALPHA FIGHT (TOY BIZ, 1999)

5" FIGURES

Northstar & Aurora, 1999
    NM $3   **MIP** $12

Sasquatch & Vindicator, 1999
    NM $3   **MIP** $12

Snowabird & Puck, 1999
    NM $3   **MIP** $12

AMERICAN WEST (MEGO, 1973)

8" FIGURES

Buffalo Bill Cody, 1973, Mego, carded
    NM $40   **MIP** $100

Buffalo Bill Cody, 1973, Mego, boxed
    NM $40   **MIP** $75

Cochise, 1973, Mego, carded
    NM $40   **MIP** $100

Cochise, 1973, Mego, boxed
    NM $40   **MIP** $75

Davy Crockett, 1973, Mego, carded
    NM $70   **MIP** $140

Davy Crockett, 1973, Mego, boxed
    NM $70   **MIP** $110

Shadow (horse), 1973, Mego, boxed
    NM $70   **MIP** $140

Sitting Bull, 1973, Mego, carded
    NM $45   **MIP** $125

Sitting Bull, 1973, Mego, boxed
    NM $45   **MIP** $90

Wild Bill Hickok, 1973, Mego, carded
    NM $40   **MIP** $125

Wild Bill Hickok, 1973, Mego, boxed
    NM $40   **MIP** $75

Wyatt Earp, 1973, Mego, carded
    NM $40   **MIP** $125

Wyatt Earp, 1973, Mego, boxed
    NM $40   **MIP** $75

PLAY SETS

Dodge City Play Set, 1973, Mego, vinyl
    NM $100   **MIP** $200

ANGEL (MOORE ACTION COLLECTIBLES, 2002)

SERIES I

Angel, 2002, Moore Action Collectibles
    NM $5   **MIP** $14

Cordelia, 2002, Moore Action Collectibles
    NM $5   **MIP** $14

Exclusive Leather Jacket Vampire Angel, 2002, Moore Action Collectibles
    NM $5   **MIP** $15

Exclusive Short Hair Cordelia, 2002, Moore Action Collectibles, Summer Show Special
    NM $5   **MIP** $15

Exclusive Slave Cordelia, 2002, Moore Action Collectibles
    NM $5   **MIP** $15

Exclusive Vampire Angel, 2002, Moore Action Collectibles
    NM $5   **MIP** $15

Faith, 2002, Moore Action Collectibles
    NM $5   **MIP** $14

ANTZ (PLAYMATES, 1998)

FIGURES

Colonel Cutter, 1998, Playmates
    NM $2   **MIP** $4

General Mandible, 1998, Playmates
    NM $2   **MIP** $4

Princess Bala, 1998, Playmates
    NM $2   **MIP** $4

Weaver, 1998, Playmates
    NM $2   **MIP** $4

(KP Photo)

Z, 1998, Playmates, Figure includes map and helmet. Interesting to note the World Trade Center Towers on the packaging
    NM $2   **MIP** $4

ARCHIES (MARX, 1975)

FIGURES

(Toy Shop File Photo)

Archie, 1975, Marx, shown with Jughead

NM $15	MIP $75

Betty, 1975, Marx

NM $15	MIP $75

Jughead, 1975, Marx

NM $15	MIP $75

(Toy Shop File Photo)

Veronica, 1975, Marx, shown with Betty, Archie, Jughead

NM $15	MIP $75

ARMAGEDDON (MATTEL, 1998)

FIGURES

A.J. Frost, 1998, Mattel

NM $3	MIP $10

Harry Stamper, 1998, Mattel

NM $3	MIP $10

ARMY OF DARKNESS (SIDESHOW TOYS, 1998-PRESENT)

12" FIGURES

Bruce Campbell as Ash, 1998, Sideshow Toys, #1301

NM n/a	MIP $40

Evil Ash, 1998, Sideshow Toys, #1302

NM n/a	MIP $40

ASTRONAUTS (MARX, 1969)

FIGURES

(Toy Shop File Photo)

Jane Apollo Astronaut, 1969, Marx, movable, includes helmet and a variety of plastic accessories, much in the style of the "Best of the West" series

NM $65	MIP $125

Johnny Apollo Astronaut, 1969, Marx, movable

NM $125	MIP $200

Kennedy Space Center Astronaut, 1969, Marx, movable

NM $65	MIP $140

A-TEAM (GALOOB, 1984)

12" FIGURES

Mr. T, non-talking, 1984, Galoob

NM $30	MIP $65

Mr. T, talking, 1984, Galoob

NM $40	MIP $75

3-3/4" FIGURES AND ACCESSORIES

Armored Attack Adventure with B.A. Figure, 1984, Galoob, vehicle with 3-3/4" figure

NM $25	MIP $55

A-Team Four Figure Set, 1984, Galoob, 3-3/4" figures

NM $40	MIP $65

Bad Guys Figure Set: Viper, Rattler, Cobra, Python, 1984, Galoob, 3-3/4" figures on card

NM $35	MIP $60

Combat Headquarters with four A-Team figures, 1984, Galoob, 3-3/4" figures

NM $30	MIP $60

Corvette with Face Figure, 1984, Galoob, vehicle and 3-3/4" figure

NM $25	MIP $50

Interceptor Jet Bomber with Murdock, 1984, Galoob, vehicle with 3-3/4"

NM $30	MIP $60

Motorized Patrol Boat, 1984, Galoob

NM $15	MIP $35

Tactical Van Play Set, 1984, Galoob

NM $25	MIP $45

6-1/2" FIGURES AND ACCESSORIES

Amy Allen, 1984, Galoob

NM $10	MIP $30

B.A. Baracus, 1984, Galoob

NM $10	MIP $35

Cobra, 1984, Galoob

NM $6	MIP $15

Combat Attack Gyrocopter, 1984, Galoob

NM $8	MIP $20

Face, 1984, Galoob

NM $6	MIP $25

Hannibal, 1984, Galoob

NM $6	MIP $25

Murdock, 1984, Galoob

NM $8	MIP $25

Off Road Attack Cycle, 1984, Galoob

NM $8	MIP $20

Python, 1984, Galoob

NM $6	MIP $15

Rattler, 1984, Galoob

NM $6	MIP $15

Viper, 1984, Galoob

NM $6	MIP $15

AUSTIN POWERS (MCFARLANE, 1999-2000)

9" FIGURES

Austin Powers, 2000, McFarlane

NM $5	MIP $15

Dr. Evil, 2000, McFarlane

NM $5	MIP $15

(Toy Shop File Photo)

Fat Bastard, 2000, McFarlane

NM $5	MIP $30

SERIES 1

Austin in Union Jack underwear, 1999, McFarlane

NM $3	MIP $8

Austin in Union Jack Underwear, "dirty version", 1999, McFarlane

NM $5	MIP $10

Austin in velvet suit, 1999, McFarlane
> **NM** $3   **MIP** $8

Austin in velvet suit, "dirty version", 1999, McFarlane
> **NM** $5   **MIP** $10

Dr. Evil with Mr. Bigglesworth, 1999, McFarlane
> **NM** $3   **MIP** $10

Dr. Evil with Mr. Bigglesworth, "dirty version", 1999, McFarlane
> **NM** $5   **MIP** $10

Fat Bastard, 1999, McFarlane
> **NM** $25   **MIP** $35

Fat Man, 2000, McFarlane, altered version of Fat Bastard
> **NM** $5   **MIP** $15

Felicity Shagwell, 1999, McFarlane
> **NM** $3   **MIP** $8

Felicity Shagwell, "dirty version", 1999, McFarlane
> **NM** $10   **MIP** $25

Mini-Me, 1999, McFarlane
> **NM** $10   **MIP** $25

SERIES 2

Austin Powers in striped suit, 2000, McFarlane, Carnaby Street version
> **NM** $3   **MIP** $8

Austin Powers, "dirty version", 2000, McFarlane
> **NM** $3   **MIP** $10

Dr. Evil and Mini-Me with Mini-Mobile, 2000, McFarlane
> **NM** $8   **MIP** $20

Dr. Evil, Moon Mission, 2000, McFarlane
> **NM** $4   **MIP** $12

Fembot, 2000, McFarlane
> **NM** $3   **MIP** $8

Mini-Me, Moon Mission, 2000, McFarlane
> **NM** $8   **MIP** $20

Scott Evil, says "A trillion is worth more than a billion, numbnuts", 2000, McFarlane
> **NM** $3   **MIP** $10

Scott Evil, says "Get away from me, you lazy-eyed psycho", 2000, McFarlane
> **NM** $3   **MIP** $8

Vanessa Kensington, 2000, McFarlane
> **NM** $4   **MIP** $12

AUSTIN POWERS (TRENDMASTERS, 1999)

9" FIGURES

Austin Powers, 1999, McFarlane
> **NM** $4   **MIP** $12

Dr. Evil, 1999, McFarlane
> **NM** $4   **MIP** $12

Fembot, 1999, McFarlane
> **NM** $8   **MIP** $20

AUSTIN POWERS (MEZCO, 2002)

FIGURES

'70s Austin Powers, 2002, Mezco, platform shoes, oh my!
> **NM** $2   **MIP** $6

Canaby Street Austin Powers, 2002, Mezco, dressed in striped suit
> **NM** $2   **MIP** $6

Fat Bastard, 2002, Mezco, in sumo outfit
> **NM** $2   **MIP** $6

Goldmember, 2002, Mezco, comes with gold brick
> **NM** $2   **MIP** $6

Prison Dr. Evil & Mini Me, 2002, Mezco, dressed in blue prison outfits
> **NM** $2   **MIP** $6

AVENGERS (TOY BIZ, 1997-2000)

6" FIGURES

(Toy Shop File Photo)

Iron Man, 1997, Toy Biz, with "Power Converter"
> **NM** $4   **MIP** $8

Loki, 1997, Toy Biz
> **NM** $4   **MIP** $8

Scarlett Witch, 1997, Toy Biz
> **NM** $4   **MIP** $8

(Lenny Lee)

The Mighty Thor, 1997, Toy Biz, with hammer
> **NM** $4   **MIP** $8

SERIES I, 5" FIGURES

Ant-Man, 1999, Toy Biz
> **NM** $4   **MIP** $8

Captain America, 1999, Toy Biz
> **NM** $4   **MIP** $8

Ultron, 1999, Toy Biz
> **NM** $4   **MIP** $8

Vision, 1999, Toy Biz
> **NM** $4   **MIP** $8

Wasp, 1999, Toy Biz
> **NM** $4   **MIP** $8

SERIES II, 5" FIGURES

Falcon, 1999, Toy Biz
> **NM** $4   **MIP** $8

Hawkeye, 1999, Toy Biz
> **NM** $4   **MIP** $8

Kang, 1999, Toy Biz
> **NM** $4   **MIP** $8

Tigra, 1999, Toy Biz
> **NM** $4   **MIP** $8

Wonder Man, 1999, Toy Biz
> **NM** $4   **MIP** $8

SERIES III, 5" FIGURES

Ant-Man, 1999, Toy Biz
> **NM** $4   **MIP** $8

Hawkeye, 1999, Toy Biz
> **NM** $4   **MIP** $8

Iron Man, 1999, Toy Biz
> **NM** $4   **MIP** $8

Remnant I, 1999, Toy Biz
> **NM** $4   **MIP** $8

Thor, 1999, Toy Biz
> **NM** $4   **MIP** $8

SHAPE SHIFTERS

Ant-Man transforms into Armored Ant, 2000, Toy Biz
> **NM** $4   **MIP** $8

Captain America transform into American Eagle, 2000, Toy Biz
> **NM** $4   **MIP** $8

Hawykeye transforms into Armored Hawk, 2000, Toy Biz
> **NM** $4   **MIP** $8

Thor transforms into Flying Horse, 2000, Toy Biz
> **NM** $4   **MIP** $8

TEAM GIFT PACK

Hulk, Iron Man, Thor, Ant-Man/Giant Man, The Wasp, 1999, Toy Biz
> **NM** $8   **MIP** $30

BABYLON 5 (EXCLUSIVE TOY PRODUCTS, 1997)

6" FIGURES

Ambassador Delenn, 1997, Exclusive, Series I
> **NM** $3   **MIP** $7

Ambassador Delenn with Minbari Flyer, Diamond Exclusive, 1997, Exclusive, Series I
    NM $5   **MIP** $15

Ambassador Juphar Trkider, 1997, Exclusive, Series IV
    NM $3   **MIP** $7

Ambassador Kosh, 1997, Exclusive, Series II
    NM $3   **MIP** $7

Ambassador Londo Mollari, 1997, Exclusive, Series I
    NM $3   **MIP** $7

Ambassador She'Lah, 1997, Exclusive, Series IV
    NM $3   **MIP** $7

Ambassador Vlur/Nhur, 1997, Exclusive
    NM $3   **MIP** $7

Captain Elizabeth Lochley, 1997, Exclusive, Series IV
    NM $3   **MIP** $7

Captain John Sheridan, 1997, Exclusive, Series I
    NM $3   **MIP** $7

Chief Garabaldi, 1997, Exclusive, Series III
    NM $4   **MIP** $10

G'Kar, 1997, Exclusive, Series I
    NM $3   **MIP** $7

G'Kar, green outfit, Diamond Exclusive, 1997, Exclusive, Series I
    NM $5   **MIP** $15

Lennier, 1997, Exclusive, Series III
    NM $4   **MIP** $10

Lyta Alexander, 1997, Exclusive, Series III
    NM $4   **MIP** $10

Marcus Cole, 1997, Exclusive, Series II, w/White Star
    NM $4   **MIP** $10

PSI Cop Bester, 1997, Exclusive, Series IV
    NM $4   **MIP** $10

Shadow Sentient, Diamond Exclusive, 1997, Exclusive, Series III
    NM $10   **MIP** $50

Stephen Franklin, 1997, Exclusive, Series III
    NM $3   **MIP** $7

Susan Ivanova, 1997, Exclusive, Series II, w/Starfury
    NM $4   **MIP** $10

Susan Ivanova, White's Collecting Figures Exclusive, 1997, Exclusive, Series II
    NM $5   **MIP** $20

Vir Cotto, 1997, Exclusive, Series II
    NM $3   **MIP** $7

Vorlon Visitor, Diamond Exclusive, 1997, Exclusive, Series II
    NM $5   **MIP** $20

9" FIGURES

Ambassador Delenn, 1997, Exclusive, Series II
    NM $5   **MIP** $20

Ambassador G'Kar, 1997, Exclusive, Series II
    NM $5   **MIP** $20

Ambassador G'Kar, Diamond Exclusive, 1997, Exclusive, Series II
    NM $5   **MIP** $30

Ambassador Londo Mollari, 1997, Exclusive, gray hair, gold outfit
    NM $5   **MIP** $20

Chief Michael Girabaldi, 1997, Exclusive, Series III
    NM $5   **MIP** $25

John Sheridan, 1997, Exclusive, Series II
    NM $5   **MIP** $25

Lennier, Diamond Exclusive, 1997, Exclusive, Series I
    NM $5   **MIP** $25

Londo, 1997, Exclusive, Series III
    NM $5   **MIP** $25

Marcus Cole, 1997, Exclusive, Series I
    NM $5   **MIP** $20

Michael Garibaldi, 1997, Exclusive
    NM $5   **MIP** $20

Susan Ivanova, 1997, Exclusive, Series III
    NM $5   **MIP** $25

Vir Cotta, 1997, Exclusive, Series I
    NM $5   **MIP** $20

BANANA SPLITS (SUTTON, 1970)

FIGURES

Bingo the Bear, 1970, Sutton
    NM $45   **MIP** $125

Drooper the Lion, 1970, Sutton
    NM $45   **MIP** $125

Fleagle Beagle, 1970, Sutton
    NM $45   **MIP** $125

Snorky the Elephant, 1970, Sutton
    NM $45   **MIP** $125

BATMAN (MATTEL, 2003-04)

FIGURES

Arctic Shield Batman, 2004, Mattel, w/arctic shield, axe launcher
    NM $5   **MIP** $10

Battle Armor Batman, 2003, Mattel, w/ combat blade and battle armor
    NM $5   **MIP** $10

Battle Board Robin, 2003, Mattel, w/ disc missile and battle board
    NM $5   **MIP** $10

Battle Board Robin - repaint, 2004, Mattel, green vest version
    NM $10   **MIP** $20

Battle Spike Batman, 2004, Mattel, spike gauntlets, battle armor
    NM $5   **MIP** $10

Croc Armor Batman, 2004, Mattel, wing blades, claws, armor
    NM $5   **MIP** $10

Drill Cannon Batman, 2004, Mattel, cannon, 6 missiles, battle wings, claw
    NM $7   **MIP** $13

Electro-Net Batman, 2004, Mattel, 2 disks, launcher, green armor
    NM $5   **MIP** $10

Hydro-Suit Batman, 2003, Mattel, w/ dive pack, breathing mask, missile launcher
    NM $5   **MIP** $10

Ice Cannon Mr. Freeze, 2004, Mattel, w/ice cannon; version w/out goggles doubles value
    NM $7   **MIP** $14

Killer Croc, 2003, Mattel, bendable tail
    NM $10   **MIP** $20

Martial Arts Batman, 2003, Mattel, w/ dual axe staff and hand blade
    NM $5   **MIP** $10

Night Patrol Batman, 2003, Mattel, Deluxe figure w/ shield and batarang launcher
    NM $5   **MIP** $10

Quick Fire Joker, 2003, Mattel, w/ cane and gun
    NM $7   **MIP** $12

Sky Strike Batman, 2004, Mattel, Deluxe, wing pack, net missile
    NM $7   **MIP** $12

Sling Strike Nightwing, 2004, Mattel, green costume
    NM $6   **MIP** $12

Snare Strike Batman, 2004, Mattel, retractable snare rope, missile launcher
    NM $7   **MIP** $12

Stealth Armor Batman, 2003, Mattel, Deluxe, w/ stealth armor, missile launcher, jet boots
    NM $5   **MIP** $10

Tech Armor Batman, 2003, Mattel, Deluxe figure w/ laser cannon, claw arm, disc missile launcher
    NM $5   **MIP** $10

(KP Photo, Karen O'Brien collection)

Zipline Batman, 2003, Mattel, w/ zipline and batarang
    NM $5   **MIP** $10

MULTI-PACKS

Attack of the Penguin, 2004, Mattel, Animated, Batman, Penguin, Nightwing, Batgirl
    NM $15   **MIP** $30

Batman and Nightwing, 2003, Mattel, New sculpt
    NM $10   **MIP** $15

ACTION FIGURES

Batman and Nightwing, 2003, Mattel, Animated
NM $7   MIP $12

Batman and Robin, 2003, Mattel, Animated
NM $5   MIP $10

Batman and Superman, 2003, Mattel, New sculpt
NM $10   MIP $15

Batman vs. Joker, 2003, Mattel, Animated
NM $7   MIP $12

Battle Armor Batman & Quick Fire Joker, 2004, Mattel, combat blade, cane, quick-fire gun
NM $10   MIP $20

Battle Scars, Batman vs. Catwoman, 2003, Mattel, Animated
NM $7   MIP $12

Gotham City Figures, 2004, Mattel, Batman, Robin, Nightwing, exclusive silver Batgirl
NM $20   MIP $40

Gotham City Figures, Series 2, 2004, Mattel, Batman, Joker, Catwoman, Two-Face
NM $12   MIP $25

Tech Suit Batman vs. Two-Face, 2003, Mattel, Animated
NM $7   MIP $12

Zipline Batman & Battle Board Robin, 2004, Mattel, batarang, zipline, missile, battle board
NM $10   MIP $20

VEHICLES

Batcopter, 2003, Mattel, fixed Batman figure
NM $12   MIP $22

Batcycle, 2003, Mattel, fixed Batman figure
NM $10   MIP $20

Batjet, 2003, Mattel, Batman figure, 2 missiles, retractable wing
NM $10   MIP $20

Batmobile, 2003, Mattel, w/ detachable Robin Cycle, recalled
NM $10   MIP $25

Batplane, 2003, Mattel, Batman figure, 2 missiles
NM $10   MIP $20

BATMAN & ROBIN (KENNER, 1997-98)

12" FIGURES

Batgirl, 1997-98, Kenner
NM $15   MIP $35

Batman, 1997-98, Kenner
NM $13   MIP $25

Batman and Poison Ivy, 1997-98, Kenner, 2-pack, cloth outfits
NM $20   MIP $40

(Kenner)

Ice Battle Batman (WB Exclusive), 1997-98, Kenner, Includes Batarang and Bat Laser
NM $10   MIP $25

Mr. Freeze, 1997-98, Kenner
NM $10   MIP $20

Robin, 1997-98, Kenner
NM $13   MIP $23

Ultimate Batman, 1997-98, Kenner
NM $8   MIP $20

Ultimate Robin, 1997-98, Kenner
NM $8   MIP $20

5" FIGURES

Bane, 1997, Kenner, Series 1, w/double-attack axe and colossal crusher gauntlet
NM $3   MIP $8

Batgirl, 1997, Kenner, w/battle blade blaster and strike scythe
NM $3   MIP $5

Batman, Ambush Attack, 1998, Kenner, Series 2, w/Arsenal Cape and Restraint Rockets
NM $3   MIP $8

Batman, Battle Board with Ring, 1997-98, Kenner
NM $3   MIP $8

Batman, Heat Scan, 1997, Kenner, Series 1, w/opti-scope launcher and laser ray emitters
NM $3   MIP $8

Batman, Hover Attack, 1997, Kenner, Series 1, w/Blasting battle sled and sickle shields
NM $3   MIP $8

Batman, Ice Blade, 1997-98, Kenner
NM $3   MIP $8

Batman, Ice Blade with Ring, 1997-98, Kenner
NM $3   MIP $13

Batman, Laser Cape with Ring, 1997-98, Kenner
NM $3   MIP $8

Batman, Mail Away from Fuji, 1997-98, Kenner
NM $23   MIP $40

Batman, Neon Armor, 1997-98, Kenner
NM $3   MIP $8

Batman, Neon Armor with Ring, 1997-98, Kenner
NM $3   MIP $13

Batman, Rotoblade with ring, 1997-98, Kenner
NM $3   MIP $13

Batman, Sky Assault with ring, 1997-98, Kenner
NM $3   MIP $13

Batman, Snow Tracker, 1997-98, Kenner
NM $3   MIP $8

Batman, Thermal Shield with ring, 1998, Kenner, Series 2, w/Heatblast cape and flying disc blaster
NM $3   MIP $13

Batman, Wing Blast, 1997-98, Kenner
NM $3   MIP $8

Batman, Wing Blast with Ring, 1997-98, Kenner
NM $3   MIP $13

Bruce Wayne, Battle Gear, 1997, Kenner, Series 1, w/ice block armor suit and cryo claw shooter
NM $3   MIP $8

Frostbite, 1997-98, Kenner
NM $3   MIP $8

(Toy Shop File Photo)

Jungle Venom Poison Ivy, 1997, Kenner, on the left, Batgirl on right; Series 1, w/ toxic spray venom cannon and entanglement vines
NM $3   MIP $5

Mr. Freeze, Ultimate Armor with Ring, 1997, Kenner, Series 2, w/freeze-on missile
NM $5   MIP $13

Robin, Attack Wing with Ring, 1998, Kenner, Series 2, w/vertical assault cape
NM $3   MIP $8

Robin, Blade Blast, 1998, Kenner, Series 2, w/rapid deploy vine slicers and blasting battle spear
NM $3   MIP $8

Robin, Iceboard, 1997-98, Kenner
NM $3   MIP $5

Robin, Razor Skate, 1997, Kenner, Series 1, w/chopping blade launcher and ice battle armor
NM $3   MIP $5

Robin, Talon Strike, 1998, Kenner, Series 2, w/twin capture claws and roto blade
NM $3   MIP $5

Robin, Talon Strike with Ring, 1997-98, Kenner
NM $3   MIP $10

Robin, Triple Strike, 1997-98, Kenner
NM $3   MIP $5

Robin, Triple Strike with Ring, 1997-98, Kenner
    NM $3   MIP $13

ACCESSORIES

Batmobile, 1998, Kenner
    NM $8   MIP $20

Batmobile, Sonic, 1998, Kenner
    NM $8   MIP $15

Cryo Freeze Chamber, 1998, Kenner
    NM $3   MIP $8

Ice Fortress, 1998, Kenner
    NM $5   MIP $8

Ice Hammer, 1998, Kenner
    NM $10   MIP $20

Iceglow Bathammer, 1997, Kenner
    NM $25   MIP $50

Jet Blade, 1998, Kenner
    NM $8   MIP $20

NightSphere, 1998, Kenner
    NM $10   MIP $25

Wayne Manor Batcave, 1998, Kenner
    NM $23   MIP $53

DELUXE FIGURES, 1997

Batgirl with Icestrike Cycle, 1997, Kenner, w/ snow assault mode and razor wheel launcher
    NM $10   MIP $20

Batman, 1998, Kenner
    NM $5   MIP $10

Batman, Blast Wing, 1997, Kenner, w/ ice chopper hover pack and freeze-seeker missile
    NM $5   MIP $8

Batman, Rooftop Pursuit, 1997, Kenner
    NM $5   MIP $8

Mr. Freeze, Ice Terror, 1997, Kenner
    NM $5   MIP $8

Robin, 1998, Kenner
    NM $5   MIP $10

Robin, Blast Wing, 1997, Kenner
    NM $5   MIP $8

Robin, Glacier Battle, 1997, Kenner, Tandem Assault Snow Skiff and Stinger Missile
    NM $5   MIP $13

Robin, Redbird Cycle, 1997, Kenner, w/ Night strike missle and ice slice blades
    NM $10   MIP $20

FIGURES

Aerial Combat Batman, 1997, Kenner
    NM $10   MIP $20

Mr. Freeze, Iceblast, 1997, Kenner, Series 1, w/ Ice ray cannon and rocket thrusters
    NM $7   MIP $12

Mr. Freeze, Jet Wing with Ring, 1998, Kenner, Series 2, w/ Glacier assault wing and ice blaster
    NM $10   MIP $20

TWO-PACK FIGURES, 1998

A Cold Night At Gotham, 1998, Kenner
    NM $5   MIP $10

Batman vs Poison Ivy, 1998, Kenner
    NM $20   MIP $40

Brain vs. Brawn, 1998, Kenner, Batman and Bane
    NM $5   MIP $10

Challengers Of The Night, 1998, Kenner
    NM $10   MIP $15

Guardians Of Gotham, 1998, Kenner, Batman and Robin
    NM $5   MIP $10

Night Hunter Robin vs. Evil Entrapment Poison Ivy, 1998, Kenner
    NM $5   MIP $8

BATMAN 100TH EDITION FIGURE

FIGURES

(Toy Shop File Photo)

Batman, 1996, Hasbro, With diorama display stand
    NM n/a   MIP $15

BATMAN 200TH EDITION FIGURE

FIGURES

Batman, 2001, Hasbro, Batman Beyond figure w/ cloth wings
    NM $10   MIP $20

BATMAN BEYOND (HASBRO, 1999-01)

ACCESSORIES

Street-to-Sky Batmobile, 1999-01, Hasbro
    NM $10   MIP $20

FIGURES

Ballistic Blade Batman, 1999-01, Hasbro, w/ Batarang Disc Barrage
    NM $10   MIP $15

Bat Hang Batman, 1999-01, Hasbro, w/ covert Cape and Upside-down action
    NM $10   MIP $15

Blight, 1999-01, Hasbro, w/ Radiation Blaster and Plasma Missle
    NM $15   MIP $25

Covert Batman, 1999-01, Hasbro, w/ Shield Cape and Retriever Missle
    NM $7   MIP $12

Energy Strike Batman, 1999-01, Hasbro, w/ Lightning Cape and Neutron Weapons
    NM $7   MIP $12

Future Knight Batman, 1999-01, Hasbro, w/ Glide Wings and Electro Swords
    NM $10   MIP $15

Hydro-Force Batman, 1999-01, Hasbro, w/ Aqua Torpedo and Propulsion Armor
    NM $7   MIP $12

J's Gang Power Throw, 1999-01, Hasbro, Happy tosses Smirk!
    NM $7   MIP $12

Laser Batman, 1999-01, Hasbro, w/ Hyper Flight gear and Pulse Missle
    NM $7   MIP $12

Lightning Storm Batman, 1999-01, Hasbro, w/ Forcefiels and Lightning Weapons
    NM $7   MIP $12

Manta Racer Batman, 1999-01, Hasbro, w/ Surf Sled and Stinger Tail
    NM $7   MIP $12

Neon Camo Batman, 1999-01, Hasbro, Deluxe figure w/ Pump Action Launcher and combat ready canine
    NM $7   MIP $10

Power Armor Batman, 1999-01, Hasbro, w/ Anti-Gravity and Strike R.O.B.I.N.
    NM $10   MIP $15

Power Cape Batman, 1999-01, Hasbro, w/ Jet Thrusters and Sual Batarang
    NM $10   MIP $15

Sonar Strike Batman, 1999-01, Hasbro, w/ Ramjet Rocket Pack and Dual Wing Blast
    NM $7   MIP $12

Strato Defense Batman, 1999-01, Hasbro, Deluxe figure w/ Knight hunter patrol jet & Thermal disc blaster
    NM $5   MIP $10

Strikecycle Batman, 1999-01, Hasbro, Deluxe figure
    NM $5   MIP $10

Surface-to-Air Batman, 1999-01, Hasbro, w/ Converting mobile assault cape
    NM $5   MIP $10

The Jokerz, 1999-01, Hasbro, w/ Assault Hover Cycle
    NM $15   MIP $25

Tomorrow Armor Batman, 1999-01, Hasbro, Deluxe figure
    NM $7   MIP $12

BATMAN BEYOND: BATLINK (HASBRO 2000-01)

ACCESSORIES

Net Escape Playset, 2000-01, Hasbro
    NM $10   MIP $20

Netrunner Batmobile, 2000-01, Hasbro
    NM $10   MIP $15

Virtual Bat, 2000-01, Hasbro, vehicle lights up Batlink figures
    NM $7   MIP $12

ACTION FIGURES

FIGURES

Circutry Storm Batman, 2000-01, Hasbro
    NM $5   **MIP** $10

Codebuster Batman, 2000-01, Hasbro,
  w/ Optical Disk Phaser
    NM $5   **MIP** $10

Energy Surge Batman, 2000-01, Hasbro,
  w/ Batlink story on CD-ROM
    NM $5   **MIP** $10

Firewall Robin, 2000-01, Hasbro,
  w/ Anti-virus Blaster
    NM $5   **MIP** $10

Mainframe Attack Batman, 2000-01, Hasbro
    NM $5   **MIP** $10

Particle Burst Batman, 2000-01, Hasbro,
  w/ Quantimizer Batarang
    NM $7   **MIP** $12

Power Grid Batman, 2000-01, Hasbro,
  w/ 5-finger Booster Shield
    NM $5   **MIP** $10

Search Engine Batman, 2000-01, Hasbro,
  w/ Cyberscope vision
    NM $7   **MIP** $12

Virtual Joker, 2000-01, Hasbro,
  w/ Virus-tech lasers and Byte mouth
    NM $5   **MIP** $10

BATMAN BEYOND: RETURN OF THE JOKER (HASBRO, 2000)

FIGURES

Arkham Assault Joker, 2000, Hasbro,
  w/ Secret image card launcher
    NM $10   **MIP** $15

Golden Armor Batman, 2000, Hasbro
  NM $10**MIP** $15

Gotham Defender Batman, 2000, Hasbro
    NM $7   **MIP** $12

Gotham Knight Batman, 2000, Hasbro,
  w/ Jet-Booster Cape and Ion Swords
    NM $10   **MIP** $20

Rapid Switch Bruce Wayne, 2000, Hasbro,
  w/ Quick change outfit and Disk launcher
    NM $7   **MIP** $12

BATMAN FOREVER (KENNER, 1995)

ACCESSORIES

Batboat, 1995, Kenner
    NM $15   **MIP** $25

Batcave, 1995, Kenner, playset
    NM $25   **MIP** $50

Batmobile, 1995, Kenner
    NM $20   **MIP** $40

Batwing, 1995, Kenner
    NM $10   **MIP** $25

Robin Cycle, 1995, Kenner, vehicle only,
  no figure
    NM $7   **MIP** $12

Triple Action Vehicle Set, 1995, Kenner,
  Batmobile, Batwing, Batboat
    NM $20   **MIP** $40

Wayne Manor, 1995, Kenner, playset
    NM $25   **MIP** $50

FIGURES

Attack Wing Batman, 1995, Kenner,
  Deluxe figure
    NM $10   **MIP** $25

Batarang Batman, 1995, Kenner, Series 2
    NM $7   **MIP** $12

Blast Cape Batman, 1995, Kenner, Series
  1, w/ assault baldes and launching
  attack cape
    NM $10   **MIP** $15

Bruce Wayne/Batman, 1996, Kenner,
  Target Exclusive, w/ snap-on
  crimefighting armor and side swords
    NM $20   **MIP** $40

Fireguard Batman, 1995, Kenner, Series
  1, w/ spinning attack cape
    NM $10   **MIP** $15

Hydro Claw Robin, 1995, Kenner, Series 1,
  w/ aqua attack launcher and diving gear
    NM $10   **MIP** $15

Ice Blade Batman, 1995, Kenner, Series 2
    NM $7   **MIP** $12

Laser Disc Batman, 1995, Kenner, Deluxe
  figure
    NM $10   **MIP** $25

Lightwing Batman, 1995, Kenner, Deluxe
  figure w/ electra-glow wings and
  lightning launcher
    NM $10   **MIP** $25

Manta Ray Batman, 1995, Kenner, Series
  1, w/ firing sea sled and pop-out
  breathing gear
    NM $10   **MIP** $15

Martial Arts Robin, 1995, Kenner, Deluxe
  figure
    NM $10   **MIP** $15

Neon Armor Batman, 1995, Kenner, Series 2
    NM $10   **MIP** $15

Night Flight Batman, 1995, Kenner, w/
  winged backpack
    NM $10   **MIP** $20

Night Hunter Batman, 1995, Kenner, Series 1
    NM $10   **MIP** $15

Power Beacon Batman, 1995, Kenner,
  Series 2
    NM $10   **MIP** $15

Recon Hunter Batman, 1995, Kenner, Series
  2, w/ missile firing surveilance drone
    NM $10   **MIP** $15

Skyboard Robin, 1995, Kenner, Series 2,
  w/ missile blasting pursuit vehicle
    NM $10   **MIP** $15

Solar Shield Batman, 1995, Kenner, Series 2
    NM $10   **MIP** $15

Sonar Sensor Batman, 1995, Kenner,
  Series 1, w/ flying disc blaster and pop-
  up sonar scope
    NM $10   **MIP** $15

Street Biker Robin, 1995, Kenner, Series
  1, w/ launching grappling hooks and
  battle staff
    NM $10   **MIP** $15

Street Racer Batman, 1995, Kenner,
  Series 2
    NM $10   **MIP** $15

The Riddler, 1995, Kenner, Target
  Exclusive, w/ brain drain helmet, green
  figure w/ silver trim
    NM $20   **MIP** $40

The Riddler w/Brain Drain, 1995, Kenner,
  Series 1, w/ brain drain helmet, green
  figure w/ black trim
    NM $3   **MIP** $10

The Riddler w/ Question Mark Bazooka,
  1995, Kenner, Series 2, w/ question
  mark gun, black figure w/ green trim
    NM $4   **MIP** $12

The Talking Riddler, 1995, Kenner, Deluxe
  figure, says three movie phrases
    NM $10   **MIP** $20

Tide Racer Robin, 1995, Kenner, Target
  Exclusive, w/ deep dive gear and sea
  claw launcher
    NM $10   **MIP** $20

Transforming Bruce Wayne, 1995,
  Kenner, Series 1, Target Exclusive
    NM $10   **MIP** $15

Transforming Dick Grayson, 1995,
  Kenner, Series 1, w/ crime fighting suit
  and sudden reveal mask
    NM $10   **MIP** $15

Triple Strike Robin, 1995, Kenner, Series 2
    NM $7   **MIP** $12

Two-Face, 1995, Kenner, Series 1, w/ coin
    NM $10   **MIP** $15

Wing Blast Batman, 1995, Kenner,
  Series 2, w/ sudden alert bio wings
    NM $10   **MIP** $15

MULTI-PACKS

Batman v. The Riddler, 1995, Kenner,
  Batman, Riddler
    NM $20   **MIP** $40

Guardians of Gotham City, 1995, Kenner,
  Batman and Robin
    NM $20   **MIP** $40

Riddler and Two-Face, 1995, Kenner
    NM $20   **MIP** $40

BATMAN MOVIE COLLECTION (KENNER, 1997)

FIGURES

Batman v. Catwoman, 1997, Kenner,
  Batman Returns, Toys R Us
    NM $10   **MIP** $30

Batman v. Joker, 1997, Kenner, Batman
  movie, Toys R Us
    NM $10   **MIP** $30

Batman v. Riddler, 1997, Kenner, Batman
  Forever, Toys R Us
    NM $10   **MIP** $30

BATMAN RETURNS (KENNER, 1992-94)

FIGURES

Aerostrike Batman, 1993, Kenner, Series 1
NM $5   MIP $15

Air Attack Batman, 1992, Kenner, Series 1, w/ camouflage artillray gear
NM $4   MIP $15

Arctic Batman, 1992, Kenner, Series 1
NM $4   MIP $15

Batman, 16", 1992-94, Kenner
NM $25   MIP $75

Bola Strike Batman, 1992, Kenner, Toys R Us exclusive boxed figure
NM $4   MIP $15

Bruce Wayne, 1992, Kenner, Series 1, w/ quick change Batman armor
NM $10   MIP $20

Catwoman, 1992, Kenner, Series 1, w/ whipping arm action and taser gun
NM $5   MIP $15

Claw Climber Batman, 1992, Kenner, Toyr R Us exclusive boxed figure
NM $4   MIP $15

Crime Attack Batman, 1992, Kenner, Series 1
NM $4   MIP $15

Deep Dive Batman, 1992, Kenner, Series 1, w/ torpedo launching scuba gear
NM $5   MIP $15

Firebolt Batman, 1992, Kenner, Toys R Us exclusive boxed electronic figure
NM $20   MIP $40

Glider Batman, 1992-94, Kenner
NM $4   MIP $15

High Wire Batman, 1992-94, Kenner
NM $4   MIP $15

Hydrocharge Batman, 1994, Kenner, Series 2, w/ water blast missile
NM $4   MIP $15

Jungle Tracker Batman, 1994, Kenner, Series 2, w/ shoulder mount launcher
NM $4   MIP $15

Laser Batman, 1992, Kenner, Series 1
NM $4   MIP $15

Night Climber Batman, 1994, Kenner, Series 2
NM $4   MIP $15

Penguin, 1992, Kenner, Series 1
NM $15   MIP $40

Penguin Commandos, 1992, Kenner, Series 1, w/ mind control gear and missiles
NM $10   MIP $25

Polar Blast Batman, 1992, Kenner, Toys R Us exclusive boxed figure
NM $4   MIP $15

Powerwing Batman, 1992, Kenner, Series 1, wing fires missile
NM $6   MIP $15

(Toy Shop File Photo)

Robin, 1992, Kenner, Series 1, On the left, shown here with Catwoman; w/ launching grappling hook
NM $10   MIP $25

Rocket Blast Batman, 1992, Kenner, Toys R Us exclusive boxed electronic figure
NM $20   MIP $40

Shadow Wing Batman, 1992, Kenner, Series 1
NM $4   MIP $15

Sky Winch Batman, 1992, Kenner, Series 1
NM $4   MIP $15

Thunder Strike Batman, 1992-94, Kenner
NM $4   MIP $15

Thunder Whip Batman, 1992, Kenner, Series 1
NM $5   MIP $15

VEHICLES

All-Terrain Batskiboat, 1992, Kenner
NM $25   MIP $50

Bat Cycle, 1992, Kenner
NM $5   MIP $25

Batcave, 1992, Kenner
NM $40   MIP $80

Batmissle Batmobile, 1992, Kenner, removable sides reveal Batmissle
NM $50   MIP $150

Batmobile, 1992, Kenner
NM $50   MIP $150

Bat-Signal Jet, 1992, Kenner
NM $3   MIP $15

Bruce Wayne Custom Coupe, 1992, Kenner
NM $12   MIP $50

Camo Attack Batmobile, 1994, Kenner
NM $30   MIP $100

Penguin Umbrella Jet, 1992, Kenner, w/ 2 umbrella bombs
NM $15   MIP $30

Robin Jetfoil, 1992, Kenner
NM $10   MIP $25

Sky Blade, 1992, Kenner
NM $25   MIP $50

Sky Drop, 1992, Kenner, airship w/ hidden compartment
NM $15   MIP $30

BATMAN: CRIME SQUAD (KENNER, 1995-96)

ACCESSORIES

Batcycle, 1995, Kenner, Series 1 vehicle
NM $10   MIP $20

Triple Attack Jet, 1995, Kenner, Series 1, Batman: The Animated Series card
NM $7   MIP $15

FIGURES

Air Assault Batman, 1995, Kenner, Series 1, Batman: The Animated Series card
NM $5   MIP $15

Bomb Control Batman, 1996, Kenner, Series 2, The Adventures of Batman and Robin card
NM $10   MIP $25

Disaster Control Batman, 1996, Kenner, Series 2, The Adventures of Batman and Robin card
NM $10   MIP $25

Fast Pursuit Batman, 1996, Kenner, Series 2, The Adventures of Batman and Robin card
NM $10   MIP $15

Land Strike Batman, 1995, Kenner, Series 1, Batman: The Animated Series card
NM $5   MIP $15

Piranha Blade Batman, 1995, Kenner, Series 1, Batman: The Animated Series card
NM $5   MIP $15

Sea Claw Batman, 1995, Kenner, Series 1, Batman: The Animated Series card
NM $5   MIP $15

Ski Blast Robin, 1995, Kenner, Series 1, Batman: The Animated Series card
NM $5   MIP $15

Skycopter Batman, 1996, Kenner, Series 2, Deluxe figure, Batman: The Adventures of Batman and Robin
NM $15   MIP $25

Stealthwing Batman, 1995, Kenner, Series 1, Batman: The Animated Series card
NM $5   MIP $15

Supersonic Batman, 1996, Kenner, Series 2, The Adventures of Batman and Robin card
NM $10   MIP $15

Torpedo Batman, 1995, Kenner, Series 1, Batman: The Animated Series card
NM $5   MIP $15

Tri-Wing Batman, 1996, Kenner, Series 2, Deluxe figure, Batman: The Adventures of Batman and Robin, w/ Techno-glide backpack
NM $15   MIP $25

BATMAN: KNIGHT FORCE NINJAS (HASBRO, 1998-99)

FIGURES

Arsenal Cape Batman, 1999, Kenner, Series 3
NM $7   MIP $12

Batman Ally Azrael, 1998, Kenner, Series 2
NM $3   **MIP** $15

Batman vs. The Joker, 1998, Kenner, Series 1
NM $8   **MIP** $20

Fist Fury Batman, 1998, Kenner, Series 2
NM $3   **MIP** $10

Hyper Crush Robin, 1999, Kenner, Series 3
NM $7   **MIP** $12

Karate Chop Batman, 1998, Kenner, Series 1
NM $3   **MIP** $10

Knight Blade Batman, 1999, Kenner, Series 3
NM $7   **MIP** $12

Multi-Blast Batman, 1998, Kenner, rare
NM $3   **MIP** $10

Power Kick Batman!, 1998, Kenner, Series 1
NM $3   **MIP** $10

Side Strike Robin, 1998, Kenner, Series 1
NM $3   **MIP** $10

Tail Whip Killer Croc, 1998, Kenner, Series 1
NM $3   **MIP** $10

Thunder Kick Batman, 1998, Kenner, Series 2
NM $3   **MIP** $10

Tornado Blade Riddler, 1998, Kenner, Series 2
NM $3   **MIP** $10

VEHICLES

Knight Force Batmobile, 1998, Kenner
NM $5   **MIP** $15

BATMAN: LEGENDS OF BATMAN (KENNER 1994-96)

12" FIGURES

Batman vs. Catwoman, 1994-96, Kenner, figures in cloth costumes
NM $10   **MIP** $25

ACCESSORIES

Batcycle, 1994, Kenner, w/ Batman rider
NM $10   **MIP** $25

Batmobile, 1994-96, Kenner, w/ missle detonator and quick lift canopy
NM $10   **MIP** $25

Sky Bat, 1994-96, Kenner, w/ wing mount missle and menacing jaw attack
NM $20   **MIP** $40

FIGURES

Buccaneer Batman, 1996, Kenner, Series 3, w/ slamming mace actions and pirate sword
NM $7   **MIP** $12

Catwoman, 1994, Kenner, Series 1, w/ quick climb claw and capture net
NM $7   **MIP** $12

Crusader Batman, 1994, Kenner, Series 1, w/ punching action
NM $10   **MIP** $20

Crusader Robin, 1995, Kenner, Series 2, w/ firing crossbow and battle shield
NM $7   **MIP** $12

Cyborg Batman, 1994, Kenner, Series 1, w/ light-up eye and laser weapon
NM $10   **MIP** $15

Dark Rider Batman, 1994, Kenner, Series 1, featuring battle stallion
NM $15   **MIP** $30

Dark Warrior Batman, 1995, Kenner, Series 2, w/ slamming mace attack
NM $10   **MIP** $15

Desert Knight Batman, 1995, Kenner, Series 2, Deluxe figure w/ whirling scimitar swords and double battle axes
NM $20   **MIP** $40

First Mate Robin, 1996, Kenner, Series 3, blasting cannon and cutlass sword
NM $7   **MIP** $12

Flightpak Batman, 1995, Kenner, Series 2, Deluxe figure w/ battle ready jet-wing
NM $20   **MIP** $40

Future Batman, 1994, Kenner, Series 1, w/ pop-up aero-power wings
NM $10   **MIP** $15

Gladiator Batman, 1996, Kenner, Series 3, w/ spear launcher
NM $7   **MIP** $12

Knightquest Batman, 1994, Kenner, Series 1, Azrael w/ Battle wings and blazing missle
NM $10   **MIP** $20

Knightsend Batman, 1995, Kenner, Series 2, Jean-Paul Valley w/ Arial torpedo launcher
NM $10   **MIP** $20

Long Bow Batman, 1995, Kenner, Series 2, w/ arrow slinging assault
NM $7   **MIP** $12

Nightwing, 1994, Kenner, Series 1, w/ super-strike rocket launcher
NM $7   **MIP** $12

Power Guardian Batman, 1994, Kenner, Series 1, w/ real sword fighting action and shield
NM $10   **MIP** $15

Samuri Batman, 1995, Kenner, Series 2, w/ slashing sword and banner
NM $7   **MIP** $12

Silver Knight Batman, 1995, Kenner, Series 2, Deluxe figure w/ smashing battle axe and slashing sword
NM $20   **MIP** $40

The Joker, 1994, Kenner, Series 1, w/ snapping jaw
NM $10   **MIP** $15

The Laughing Man Joker, 1996, Kenner, Series 3, w/ gatling gun, pirate outfit
NM $7   **MIP** $12

The Riddler, 1995, Kenner, Series 2, w/ firing question mark ammo
NM $7   **MIP** $12

Ultra Armor Batman, 1996, Kenner, Series 3, Azrael w/ blasting battle cannon
NM $10   **MIP** $25

Viking Batman, 1995, Kenner, Series 2, w/ battle axe and shield
NM $7   **MIP** $12

MULTI-PACKS

Egyptian Batman and Egyptian Catwoman, 1994-96, Kenner
NM $10   **MIP** $20

Pirate Batman vs. Pirate Two-Face, 1994-96, Kenner
NM $10   **MIP** $20

BATMAN: LEGENDS OF THE DARK KNIGHT (KENNER, 1996-98)

ACCESSORIES

Skywing Street Bike, 1996, Kenner, w/ Batman figure
NM $20   **MIP** $35

FIGURES

Assault Gauntlet Batman, 1996, Kenner, w/ Neural pumped power and Spike strike missle gloves
NM $3   **MIP** $10

Bat Attack Batman, 1997, Kenner
NM $3   **MIP** $10

Batgirl, 1998, Kenner, w/ Knightscan wings and Batagrang
NM $5   **MIP** $15

Batman The Dark Knight, 1998, Kenner, blue and gray costume
NM $25   **MIP** $45

Batman The Dark Knight, 1998, Kenner, black costume re-issue
NM $25   **MIP** $60

Clayface, 1996-98, Kenner, Internet exclusive
NM $8   **MIP** $25

Dark Knight Detective Batman, 1996-98, Kenner, Internet exclusive
NM $20   **MIP** $40

Dive Claw Robin, 1996, Kenner, w/ Blast Attack Missle and Power Glide Wings
NM $5   **MIP** $15

Glacier Shield Batman, 1997, Kenner
NM $3   **MIP** $10

Jungle Rage Robin, 1998, Kenner, w/ Battle Staff and Utility Gauntlet
NM $3   **MIP** $10

Laughing Gas Joker, 1997, Kenner
NM $5   **MIP** $10

Lava Fury Batman, 1998, Kenner, w/ Solar arrary wings, fire swallower blast shield
NM $3   **MIP** $10

Lethal Impact Bane, 1996-98, Kenner, w/ venom-powered punch and stinger gauntlet
NM $3   **MIP** $10

Man-Bat, 1998, Kenner
NM $5   **MIP** $15

Neutral Claw Batman, 1996, Kenner
NM $5   **MIP** $10

Panther Prowl Catwoman, 1997, Kenner, w/ Battle panther exoskeleton
NM $5 MIP $15

Penguin, 1998, Kenner, w/ Spinning Attack Umbrella
NM $3 MIP $10

Shatter Blade Batman, 1996-98, Kenner, w/ Assault cape and arm swords
NM $5 MIP $10

Spline Cape Batman, 1996, Kenner
NM $5 MIP $10

Twister Strike Scarecrow, 1996, Kenner, w/ Scythe Slash attack and Nightmare glow eyes
NM $3 MIP $10

Underwater Assault Batman, 1998, Kenner
NM $3 MIP $10

BATMAN: MASK OF THE PHANTASM (KENNER, 1994)

FIGURES

Decoy Batman, 1994, Kenner
NM $10 MIP $20

Jet Pack Joker (green face), 1994, Kenner
NM $10 MIP $20

Jet Pack Joker (white face), 1994, Kenner
NM $10 MIP $20

Phantasm, 1994, Kenner
NM $15 MIP $25

Rapid Attack Batman, 1994, Kenner, also released on Batman: The Animated Series card
NM $10 MIP $20

Retro Batman, 1994, Kenner
NM $15 MIP $25

Tornado Batman, 1994, Kenner, also released on Batman: The Animated Series card
NM $10 MIP $20

Total Armor Batman, 1994, Kenner
NM $4 MIP $10

BATMAN: MISSION MASTERS (HASBRO, 1997-2002)

SERIES 1 FIGURES

Anti-Blaze Batman, 1997-2002, Hasbro, Series 1
NM $3 MIP $8

Arctic Blast Robin, 1997-2002, Hasbro, Series 1
NM $3 MIP $10

Cave Climber Batman, 1997-2002, Hasbro, Series 1
NM $3 MIP $8

Desert Attack Batman, 1997-2002, Hasbro, Series 1
NM $3 MIP $8

Glider Strike Batman, 1997-2002, Hasbro, Series 1
NM $3 MIP $8

Insect-Body Mr.Freeze, 1997-2002, Hasbro, Series 1, head detaches from body, attaches to insect legs
NM $3 MIP $10

Jungle Tracker Batman, 1997-2002, Hasbro, Series 1
NM $3 MIP $10

Mr. Freeze, 1997-2002, Hasbro, Series 1
NM $7 MIP $12

Rumble Ready Riddler, 1997-2002, Hasbro, Series 1
NM $6 MIP $15

Slalom Racer Batman, 1997-2002, Hasbro, Series 1
NM $3 MIP $8

Speedboat Batman, 1997-2002, Hasbro, Series 1
NM $3 MIP $8

SERIES 2 FIGURES

Arctic Ambush Robin, 1997-2002, Hasbro, Series 2
NM $10 MIP $20

Desert Attack Batman, 1997-2002, Hasbro, Series 2
NM $7 MIP $12

Hydro Assault Joker, 1997-2002, Hasbro, Series 2
NM $7 MIP $12

Knight Strike Batman, 1997-2002, Hasbro, Series 2
NM $7 MIP $12

Land Strike Batman, 1997-2002, Hasbro, Series 2
NM $7 MIP $12

Radar Batman, 1997-2002, Hasbro, Series 2, Deluxe figure
NM $7 MIP $12

Sea Claw Batman, 1997-2002, Hasbro, Series 2
NM $8 MIP $15

Skychopper Batman, 1997-2002, Hasbro, Series 2, Deluxe figure
NM $7 MIP $12

SERIES 3 FIGURES

Capture Cape Batman, 1997-2002, Hasbro, Series 3
NM $5 MIP $10

Firewing Batman, 1997-2002, Hasbro, Series 3
NM $7 MIP $12

Freestyle Skate Batman, 1997-2002, Hasbro, Series 3
NM $7 MIP $12

Gotham Crusader Batman, 1997-2002, Hasbro, Series 3
NM $5 MIP $10

Ground Pursuit Batman, 1997-2002, Hasbro, Series 3
NM $7 MIP $12

Highwire Zip Line Batman, 1997-2002, Hasbro, Series 3
NM $7 MIP $12

Inferno Extinction Batman, 1997-2002, Hasbro, Series 3
NM $7 MIP $12

Knight Assault Batman, 1997-2002, Hasbro, Series 3
NM $7 MIP $12

Mountain Pursuit Batman, 1997-2002, Hasbro, Series 3
NM $7 MIP $12

Quick Attack Batman, 1997-2002, Hasbro, Series 3
NM $5 MIP $10

Sky Attack Batman, 1997-2002, Hasbro, Series 3
NM $7 MIP $12

Virus Attack Mr. Freeze, 1997-2002, Hasbro, Series 3
NM $7 MIP $12

Virus Delete Batman, 1997-2002, Hasbro, Series 3
NM $5 MIP $10

SERIES 4 ACCESSORIES

B.A.T.V., 1997-2002, Hasbro, Batman all-terrain vehicle and projectile launcher w/ Batman figure
NM $10 MIP $20

Team Batcycle, 1997-2002, Hasbro, w/ Batman and Nightwing
NM $20 MIP $35

SERIES 4 FIGURES

Attack Wing Batman, 1997-2002, Hasbro, Deluxe figure w/ flight mechanized wings
NM $10 MIP $15

Battle Staff Batman, 1997-2002, Hasbro, w/ Hover Jet
NM $5 MIP $10

Jet Wing Batman, 1997-2002, Hasbro, w/ Rocket Strike Blaster
NM $5 MIP $10

Lunar Force Batman, 1997-2002, Hasbro, w/ Night Attack Wing
NM $5 MIP $10

Midnight Hunter Batman, 1997-2002, Hasbro
NM $5 MIP $10

Midnight Pursuit Batman, 1997-2002, Hasbro, w/ Night Assault Jet
NM $10 MIP $15

Midnight Rescue Batman, 1997-2002, Hasbro, w/ Strike Wing
NM $5 MIP $10

Night Assault Batman, 1997-2002, Hasbro, Deluxe figure w/ Land Runner
NM $10 MIP $15

Night Fury Robin, 1997-2002, Hasbro, w/ Triple Bolo Striker
NM $5 MIP $10

Night Shadow Batman, 1997-2002, Hasbro
NM $5 MIP $10

Night Spark Joker, 1997-2002, Hasbro, w/ Wildcard Launcher
NM $5 MIP $10

Photon Armor Batman, 1997-2002, Hasbro, w/ Shadow Blast Cape
NM $10   MIP $15

Rocket Blast Mr. Freeze, 1997-2002, Hasbro, w/ Ice Disk Launcher
NM $5   MIP $10

Shadow Blast Batman, 1997-2002, Hasbro, Deluxe figure w/ Night Charge Hoverpack
NM $10   MIP $15

Shadow Copter Batman, 1997-2002, Hasbro, Deluxe figure w/ Night Sting Missle
NM $10   MIP $15

Tunnel Racer Batman, 1997-2002, Hasbro, w/ Lightning Luge and Homing Batarang
NM $5   MIP $10

Turbo Force Nightwing, 1997-2002, Hasbro, Deluxe figure w/ Dual Mode Action Craft
NM $10   MIP $15

Velocity Storm Batman, 1997-2002, Hasbro, w/ High Speed Glider
NM $5   MIP $10

SERIES 4 MULTI-PACKS

Night Shadow Batman and Night Fury Robin, 1997-2002, Hasbro, w/ Hyper-Speed Stun Rockets and Triple Bolo Striker
NM $10   MIP $20

BATMAN: SPECTRUM OF THE BAT (HASBRO, 2000-01)

FIGURES

Fractal Armor Batman, 2000-01, Hasbro
NM $5   MIP $10

Gamma Blast Batman, 2000-01, Hasbro
NM $7   MIP $12

Infared Armor Batman, 2000-01, Hasbro
NM $7   MIP $12

Signal Hacker Batman, 2000-01, Hasbro
NM $5   MIP $10

Sonic Stun Batgirl, 2000-01, Hasbro
NM $7   MIP $12

Sub-Frequency Armor Batman, 2000-01, Hasbro
NM $5   MIP $10

Sub-Pulse Detonator Robin, 2000-01, Hasbro
NM $5   MIP $10

Technocast Catwoman, 2000-01, Hasbro
NM $5   MIP $10

Technocast Jervis Tetch, 2000-01, Hasbro, a.k.a. the Mad Hatter
NM $7   MIP $12

Terrorcast Joker, 2000-01, Hasbro
NM $10   MIP $15

Ultra-Frequency Armor Batman, 2000-01, Hasbro
NM $5   MIP $10

Ultraviolet Ambush Batman, 2000-01, Hasbro
NM $7   MIP $12

X-Ray Assailant Robin, 2000-01, Hasbro
NM $10   MIP $15

BATMAN: THE ADVENTURES OF BATMAN AND ROBIN (HASBRO, 1996-97)

DUO FORCE

Air Strike Robin, 1996, Kenner, Series 1
NM $10   MIP $20

Cycle Thruster Batman, 1997, Kenner, Series 2
NM $7   MIP $12

Hydro Storm Robin, 1997, Kenner, Series 2
NM $10   MIP $15

Mr. Freeze, 1996, Kenner, Series 1
NM $7   MIP $12

The Riddler Roto Chopper, 1997, Kenner, Series 2
NM $10   MIP $15

Turbo Surge Batman, 1996, Kenner, Series 1
NM $7   MIP $12

Vector Wing Batman, 1996, Kenner, Series 1
NM $7   MIP $12

Wind Blitz Batgirl, 1997, Kenn.er, Series 2 Sky Glider and Wave Racer
NM $10   MIP $20

MULTI-PACKS

Rogues Gallery, 1997, Kenner, Figure 8-pack w/ Catwoman, Killer Croc, Man-Bat, Poison Ivy, Scarecrow, Joker, Phantasm, Clayface
NM $50   MIP $75

SERIES 1

Bane, 1996, Kenner, w/ Body slam arm action and venom tube
NM $10   MIP $20

Hover Jet Batman, 1996, Kenner
NM $5   MIP $10

Paraglide Batman, 1996, Kenner, w/ Dive Bomb Sky Wing
NM $10   MIP $20

Pogo Stick Joker, 1996, Kenner, w/ Power Launcher
NM $5   MIP $10

Ra's Al Ghul, 1996, Kenner, w/ Strike Shooter and Combat Sword
NM $10   MIP $15

Rocketpack Batman, 1996, Kenner
NM $100   MIP $20

SERIES 1 ACCESSORIES

Nightsphere, 1996, Kenner, w/ Batman figure
NM $25   MIP $50

SERIES 2

Bola Trap Robin, 1997, Hasbro, Also released in Batman: The Animated Series figures
NM $7   MIP $12

Harley Quinn, 1997, Kenner, w/ Knockout Punching Glove and Trick Pistol
NM $15   MIP $25

Joker Machine Gun, 1997, Kenner, w/ Machine Gun and Joke-A-Matic Time Bomb
NM $10   MIP $20

BATMAN: THE ANIMATED SERIES (KENNER, 1992-95)

ACCESSORIES

AeroBat, 1992, Kenner
NM $150   MIP $30

B.A.T.V. Vehicle, 1992, Kenner
NM $10   MIP $20

Batcave, 1993, Kenner, playset
NM $50   MIP $125

Batcycle, 1992, Kenner, w/ Batman figure
NM $10   MIP $20

Batcycle, 1992, Kenner, with Nightwing
NM $10   MIP $20

Batmobile, 1992, Kenner
NM $10   MIP $65

Bat-Signal Jet, 1992, Kenner
NM $10   MIP $20

Crime Stalker, 1992, Kenner
NM $10   MIP $20

Hoverbat Vehicle, 1992, Kenner
NM $5   MIP $15

Ice Hammer, 1994, Kenner
NM $10   MIP $15

Joker Mobile, 1992, Kenner
NM $6   MIP $20

Robin Dragster, 1992, Kenner, very rare
NM $75   MIP $325

Street Jet, 1993, Kenner
NM $15   MIP $25

Turbo Batplane, 1992, Kenner
NM $6   MIP $20

FIGURES

Anti-Freeze Batman, 1994, Kenner, Series 3, w/ Firing Shield and Blaster
NM $4   MIP $10

(Lenny Lee)

Bane, 1995, Kenner, Series 4, w/ "Body Slam" action and venom tube
NM $5   MIP $10

Battle-Helmet Batman, 1995, Kenner, Mail order figure
    NM $20   **MIP** $35

Bola Trap Robin, 1994, Kenner, Series 3
    NM $7   **MIP** $12

Bruce Wayne, 1993, Kenner, Series 2
    NM $5   **MIP** $10

Catwoman, 1993, Kenner, Series 2, w/ Whipping arm action and Claw Hook
    NM $7   **MIP** $25

Clay Face, 1994, Kenner, Series 3
    NM $5   **MIP** $20

Combat Belt Batman, 1992, Kenner, Series 1
    NM $15   **MIP** $40

Cyber Gear Batman, 1995, Kenner, Series 4
    NM $15   **MIP** $25

Dick Grayson/Robin, 1994, Kenner, Series 3
    NM $5   **MIP** $15

Glider Robin, 1995, Kenner, Series 4, w/ Winged Jet Pack and Firing Claw
    NM $10   **MIP** $20

Ground Assault Batman, 1994, Kenner, Deluxe figure w/ Motorized turbo-powered ground jet
    NM $5   **MIP** $10

High-Wire Batman, 1994, Kenner, Deluxe figure w/ Quick Escape Cable Wire and Cable-Riding Action
    NM $15   **MIP** $30

Infrared Batman, 1993, Kenner, Series 2 w/ Launching Bat-Signal Disks
    NM $5   **MIP** $10

Joker, 1993, Kenner, Series 2 w/ Laughing gas spray gun
    NM $7   **MIP** $15

Killer Croc, 1994, Kenner, Series 3 w/ Power punch arm and pet crocodile
    NM $8   **MIP** $15

Knight Star Batman, 1994, Kenner, Series 3 w/ Star Blade Rocket Launcher
    NM $4   **MIP** $10

Lightning Strike Batman, 1994, Kenner, Series 3 w/ Transforming Cape Glider
    NM $4   **MIP** $10

Manbat, 1993, Kenner, Series 2
    NM $7   **MIP** $25

Mech-Wing Batman, 1994, Kenner, Deluxe figure w/ Mechanized Soaring Wings and pop-out wing action
    NM $4   **MIP** $10

Mr. Freeze, 1994, Kenner, Series 3 w/ Firing Ice Blaster
    NM $8   **MIP** $15

Ninja Robin, 1993, Kenner, Series 2 w/ chopping arm action and ninja weapons
    NM $8   **MIP** $15

Penguin, 1992, Kenner, Series 1
    NM $20   **MIP** $65

(Toy Shop File Photo)

Poison Ivy, 1994, Kenner, Series 3, w/ crossbow and Venus Flytrap weapon
    NM $20   **MIP** $30

Power Vision Batman, 1994, Kenner, Deluxe figure w/ electric light up eyes, firing missle
    NM $8   **MIP** $15

Radar Scope Batman, 1995, Kenner, Series 4
    NM $15   **MIP** $25

Rapid Attack Batman, 1994, Kenner, Series 3 w/ Escape Hook and Utility Belt
    NM $15   **MIP** $25

Riddler, 1992, Kenner, Series 1 w/ Question mark launcher
    NM $10   **MIP** $25

Robin, 1992, Kenner, Series 1 with Turbo Glider
    NM $8   **MIP** $15

Scarecrow, 1993, Kenner, Series 2
    NM $7   **MIP** $20

Sky Dive Batman, 1993, Kenner, Series 2 w/ working parachute
    NM $5   **MIP** $10

Tornado Batman, 1994, Kenner, Series 3 w/ Whirling Weapon
    NM $15   **MIP** $25

Turbojet Batman, 1992, Kenner, Series 1 w/ Firing Wrist Rocket & Pivoting Engines
    NM $7   **MIP** $15

Two Face, 1992, Kenner, Series 1
    NM $7   **MIP** $25

Ultimate Batman (16"), 1994, Kenner
    NM $25   **MIP** $75

MULTI-PACKS

Ninja Batman and Robin, 1994, Kenner, w/ Duo-power Ninja weapons
    NM $10   **MIP** $20

BATMAN: THE DARK KNIGHT COLLECTION (KENNER, 1990-91)

ACCESSORIES

Batcycle, 1990-91, Kenner
    NM $20   **MIP** $40

Batjet, 1990, Kenner
    NM $50   **MIP** $75

Batmobile, 1990-91, Kenner
    NM $50   **MIP** $75

Batwing, 1990-91, Kenner
    NM $20   **MIP** $40

Bola Bullet, 1991, Kenner
    NM $20   **MIP** $35

The Joker Cycle, 1990-91, Kenner
    NM $10   **MIP** $20

FIGURES

Blast Shield Batman, 1990-91, Kenner, Deluxe figure, boxed
    NM $12   **MIP** $25

Bruce Wayne, 1990, Kenner, Series 1, w/ quick change suit
    NM $10   **MIP** $20

Claw Climber Batman, 1990-91, Kenner, Deluxe figure, boxed
    NM $12   **MIP** $25

Crime Attack Batman, 1990, Kenner, Series 1, w/ batarang and claw
    NM $10   **MIP** $20

Iron Winch Batman, 1990, Kenner, Series 1, w/ batarang winch
    NM $10   **MIP** $20

Knockout Joker, 1991, Kenner, Series 2
    NM $15   **MIP** $50

Night Glider Batman, 1990-91, Kenner, Deluxe figure, boxed
    NM $20   **MIP** $35

Power Wing Batman, 1991, Kenner, Series 2
    NM $12   **MIP** $25

Shadow Wing Batman, 1990, Kenner, Series 1, w/ cape spreading pop-up arms and handcuffs
    NM $10   **MIP** $20

Sky Escape Joker, 1990, Kenner, Series 1, w/ whirling copter pack
    NM $15   **MIP** $25

Tec-Shield Batman, 1990, Kenner, Series 1, w/ flight pack and gold shield suit
    NM $10   **MIP** $20

Thunder Whip Batman, 1991, Kenner, Series 2
    NM $12   **MIP** $25

Wall Scaler Batman, 1990, Kenner, Series 1, w/ climbing action pack
    NM $10   **MIP** $20

BATMAN: THE NEW BATMAN ADVENTURES (HASBRO, 1997-2000)

ACCESSORIES

Batmobile, 1997-2000, fits Batman, Robin or Nightwing figure
    NM $25   **MIP** $40

Joker Toxic Lab, 2000
    NM $20   **MIP** $40

ACTION FIGURES

FIGURES

Crime Fighter Robin, 1997, Hasbro
  NM $4   **MIP** $12
Crime Solver Nightwing, 1997, Hasbro
  NM $4   **MIP** $12
Detective Batman, 1997, Hasbro
  NM $8   **MIP** $20
Force Shield Nightwing, 1998, Hasbro
  NM $3   **MIP** $8
Heavy Artillery Batman, 1998, Hasbro
  NM $3   **MIP** $8
Hydrojet Nightwing, 1998, Deluxe figure
  NM $10   **MIP** $15
Knight Glider Batman, 1998, Hasbro
  NM $3   **MIP** $8
Mad Hatter, 1997, Hasbro
  NM $5   **MIP** $10
Shatter Blade Batman, 1998, Hasbro
  NM $3   **MIP** $8
Silver Defender Batman, 1998, Deluxe figure
  NM $15   **MIP** $25
Street Strike Batman, 1998
  NM $7   **MIP** $12
The Creeper, 1998, Hasbro
  NM $3   **MIP** $8
Undercover Bruce Wayne, 1998, Hasbro
  NM $3   **MIP** $10
Wildcard Joker, 1998, Hasbro
  NM $5   **MIP** $15

MULTI-PACKS

Arkham Asylum Escape (4-pack): Batman, Two-Face, Poison Ivy, Harley Quinn, 1997-2000
  NM $30   **MIP** $45
Arkham Asylum Escape: Batman v. Two-Face, 2000
  NM $15   **MIP** $30
Batman and Robin, 2000, Wal-Mart Exclusive
  NM $15   **MIP** $30
Batman and Superman, 2000, Wal-Mart Exclusive
  NM $15   **MIP** $30
Batman Figure (4-pack): Batman, Robin, Alfred, Clayface, 1997-2000
  NM $30   **MIP** $50
Batman v. Joker, 2000, Wal-Mart Exclusive
  NM $15   **MIP** $30
Knight Force (4-pack): Batman, Robin, Nightwing, Batgirl, 1997-2000
  NM $20   **MIP** $45
World's Finest: Batman and Superman, 2001, Wal-Mart Exclusive
  NM $15   **MIP** $30

BATMAN: THE NEW BATMAN ADVENTURES (HASBRO, 1998-99)

12" FIGURES

Batgirl, 1998-99, Hasbro
  NM $10   **MIP** $30
Batman, 1998-99, Hasbro, The most valuable figure in this series
  NM $10   **MIP** $40

(Toy Shop File Photo)

Harley Quinn, 1998-99, Hasbro, Popular female comic hero
  NM $10   **MIP** $30
Joker, 1998-99, Hasbro
  NM $10   **MIP** $40
Nightwing, 1998-99, Hasbro
  NM $10   **MIP** $30
Robin, 1998-99, Hasbro
  NM $10   **MIP** $40

BATMAN: WORLD OF BATMAN (HASBRO, 2001)

FIGURES

Aqua Sled Batman, 2001, Hasbro, w/ submarine assault sled and scuba armor
  NM $7   **MIP** $12
Hover Jet Batman, 2001, Hasbro, w/ blasting battle sled
  NM $7   **MIP** $12
Plasma Glow Joker, 2001, Hasbro
  NM $10   **MIP** $15
Quick Change Bruce Wayne, 2001, Hasbro
  NM $10   **MIP** $15
Radar Scope Batman, 2001, Hasbro, w/ pulse-scan blaster
  NM $7   **MIP** $12
Rapid Attack Robin, 2001, Hasbro
  NM $7   **MIP** $12

MULTI-PACKS

Batman 2-Pack, 2001, Hasbro, Gotham City Adventures Batman and Knight Watch Batman
  NM $10   **MIP** $25

BATTLESTAR GALACTICA (MATTEL, 1978-79)

12" FIGURES

(Toy Shop File Photo)

Colonial Warrior, 1979, Mattel
  NM $30   **MIP** $85
Cylon Centurian, 1979, Mattel, Silver armor
  NM $30   **MIP** $95

3-3/4" FIGURES, SERIES 1, 1978

(Toy Shop File Photo)

Commander Adama, 1978, Mattel, With cloth robe and laser pistol, shown with Starbuck
  NM $15   **MIP** $40
Cylon Centurian, 1978, Mattel
  NM $15   **MIP** $40
Daggit (brown), 1978, Mattel
  NM $15   **MIP** $30

(Toy Shop File Photo)

Daggit (tan), 1978, Mattel, shown with Imperious Leader
  NM $15   **MIP** $30
Imperious Leader, 1978, Mattel, With red-purple cloth robe
  NM $15   **MIP** $30
Ovion, 1978, Mattel
  NM $12   **MIP** $35
Starbuck, 1978, Mattel
  NM $15   **MIP** $40

3-3/4" FIGURES, SERIES 2, 1979

Baltar, 1979, Mattel
    NM $30   **MIP** $75

(Toy Shop File Photo)

Boray, 1979, Mattel
    NM $30   **MIP** $75

Cylon Commander, 1979, Mattel
    NM $55   **MIP** $110

(Toy Shop File Photo)

Lucifer, 1979, Mattel
    NM $55   **MIP** $110

ACCESSORIES

(Toy Shop File Photo)

Lasermatic Pistol, 1978, Mattel, Barrel lights up when fired, has three different laser-firing sounds
    NM $35   **MIP** $75

VEHICLES

Colonial Scarab, 1978-79, Mattel, 1978 versions came w/ red missiles, 1979 versions didn't
    NM $25   **MIP** $75

(Toy Shop File Photo)

Colonial Stellar Probe, 1978-79, Mattel, 1978 versions came w/ red missiles, 1979 versions didn't
    NM $30   **MIP** $80

Colonial Viper, 1978-79, Mattel, 1978 editions came w/ red missiles, 1979 editions didn't
    NM $30   **MIP** $75

Cylon Raider, 1978-79, Mattel, 1978 editions came w/ red missiles, 1979 editions didn't
    NM $30   **MIP** $85

BEAVIS & BUTTHEAD (MOORE, 1998)

FIGURES

Beavis, 1998
    NM $4   **MIP** $10

Butt-head, 1998
    NM $4   **MIP** $10

Cornholio, 1998
    NM $5   **MIP** $12

BEETLEJUICE (KENNER, 1989-90)

ACCESSORIES

Creepy Cruiser, 1989-90, Kenner
    NM $3   **MIP** $13

Gross Out Meter, 1990, Kenner
    NM $7   **MIP** $15

Phantom Flyer, 1989-90, Kenner
    NM $4   **MIP** $8

Snake Mask, 1989-90, Kenner
    NM $4   **MIP** $8

Vanishing Vault, 1989-90, Kenner
    NM $5   **MIP** $10

FIGURES

Adam Maitland, 1989-90, Kenner
    NM $4   **MIP** $10

(Lenny Lee)

Exploding Beetlejuice, 1989-90, Kenner, Body flies apart to reveal bug. Also includes smaller dragon figure
    NM $3   **MIP** $5

Harry the Haunted Hunter, 1989-90, Kenner
    NM $4   **MIP** $10

Old Buzzard, 1989-90, Kenner
    NM $4   **MIP** $10

Otho the Obnoxious, 1989-90, Kenner
    NM $4   **MIP** $10

Shipwreck Beetlejuice, 1989-90, Kenner
    NM $3   **MIP** $8

Shish Kabab Beetlejuice, 1989-90, Kenner
    NM $3   **MIP** $8

Showtime Beetlejuice, 1989-90, Kenner
    NM $3   **MIP** $8

Spinhead Beetlejuice, 1989-90, Kenner
    NM $3   **MIP** $8

Street Rat, 1989-90, Kenner
    NM $4   **MIP** $10

Talking Beetlejuice, 1989-90, Kenner
    NM $18   **MIP** $38

Teacher Creature, 1989-90, Kenner
    NM $5   **MIP** $10

BEST OF THE WEST (MARX, 1965-75)

ACCESSORIES

(Toy Shop File Photo)

Buckboard with Horse and Harness, 1967-75, Marx, #4424, with Thunderbolt
    NM $100   **MIP** $225

Buckskin Horse, 1967, Marx, #2036, for 12" figures, head nods and neck bends
    NM $125   **MIP** $60

ACTION FIGURES

Circle X Ranch Playset, 1967, Marx, #5275, 22 pieces, cardboard, rare
NM $325 **MIP** $170

Comanche Horse, 1967, Marx, #1861, for 12" figures, head and leg articulation
NM $125 **MIP** $60

Covered Wagon, 1967-75, Marx, #4434, with horse and harness
NM $100 **MIP** $225

Flame Horse, 1966, Marx, #2081, for 12" figures, legs in trotting pose
NM $140 **MIP** $65

Fort Apache Playset, 1967, Marx, #1875, scaled for 12" figures
NM $400 **MIP** $200

(Toy Shop File Photo)

Pancho Pony, 1967, Marx, #1061, for 7-1/2" figures, brown with off-white mane and tail. Includes black plastic saddle and bridle
NM $50 **MIP** $75

Storm Cloud Horse, 1967, Marx, #2071, originally "Pinto", brown w/ white spots
NM $125 **MIP** $60

Thunderbolt Horse, 1965-75, Marx, #2061, most common horse produced, black version rarest
NM $75 **MIP** $125

Thundercolt Horse, 1967-69, Marx, #2031a, for use with ranch and corral sets
NM $25 **MIP** $50

FIGURES

Bill Buck, 1967, Marx, #1868, Fort Apache Fighters Series
NM $300 **MIP** $475

Captain Tom Maddox, 1967, Marx, #1865, Fort Apache Fighters, blue body, brown hair
NM $175 **MIP** $80

(Toy Shop File Photo)

Chief Cherokee, 1965, Marx, included headress, rifle, spear, Bowie knife, ceremonial mask, pipe and more
NM $150 **MIP** $200

Daniel Boone, 1965, Marx, #2060, limited articulation
NM $100 **MIP** $200

Davy Crockett, 1960s, Marx
NM $175 **MIP** $250

(Toy Shop File Photo)

Fighting Eagle, 1967, Marx, #1864, Fully poseable, includes spear, Bowie knife, hatchet, bear claw necklace, pouch and more
NM $150 **MIP** $225

(Toy Shop File Photo)

General Custer, 1967, Marx, #1866, blue molded uniform, with yellow and dark blue plastic accessories
NM $100 **MIP** $200

(Toy Shop File Photo)

Geronimo, 1967, Marx, #1863, with tan molded buckskin uniform, darker brown, yellow and medium brown plastic accessories, including Bowie knife, headband, mask, spear, rifle and more
NM $100 **MIP** $150

Geronimo and Pinto, 1967-75, Marx, #2087, mail-order set
NM $150 **MIP** $200

Geronimo w/ Storm Cloud, 1967-75, Marx, figure and horse in colored box
NM $175 **MIP** $90

Jamie West, 1967, Marx, #1062A, body molded in carmel, lt. blue, or black in Canada
NM $50 **MIP** $100

(Toy Shop File Photo)

Jane West, 1966, Marx, #2067, included white plastic clothes and accessories
NM $60 **MIP** $120

Jane West w/ Flame, 1967-75, Marx, mail-order figure and horse
NM $175 **MIP** $90

Janice West, 1967, Marx, #1067b, turquoise body, short black hair
NM $50 **MIP** $100

Jay West, 1967, Marx, #1062b, carmel body, blonde hair
NM $50 **MIP** $100

Jed Gibson, 1975, Marx, #2057c, African-American cavalry soldier, teal body, rare
NM $950 **MIP** $425

Johnny West, 1965, Marx, #2062, straight hands in 1965, curved hands 1966-75, carmel body, brown hair
NM $75 **MIP** $150

Johnny West w/ Thunderbolt, 1967-75, Marx, #2062, mail-order figure and horse
NM $175 **MIP** $90

Johnny West with Comanche, 1967, Marx, fully jointed
NM $80 **MIP** $125

Josie West, 1967, Marx, #1067a, turquoise body, blonde hair
NM $50 **MIP** $100

Princess Wildflower, 1974, Marx, #2097, included 22 accessories and gear
NM $100 **MIP** $175

(Toy Shop File Photo)

Sam Cobra, 1972, Marx, #2072, Black molded-plastic clothing and accessories
    NM $100   MIP $200

Sam Cobra w/ Thunderbolt, 1975, Marx, #4959075, mail-order figure and horse
    NM $200   MIP $90

(Toy Shop File Photo)

Sheriff Garrett, 1973, Marx, #2085, blue-molded clothing with white and blue plastic clothing and accessories included
    NM $150   MIP $200

Sheriff Garrett w/ horse, 1967-75, Marx, mail-order figure and horse, rare
    NM $300   MIP $150

Zeb Zachary, 1967-69, Marx, #1862, Fort Apache Fighters, blue body, black hair
    NM $200   MIP $300

BIG JIM (MATTEL, 1971-77)

ACCESSORIES

Baja Beast, 1973
    NM $10   MIP $75

Boat and Buggy Set, 1973
    NM $10   MIP $50

Camping Tent, 1973
    NM $5   MIP $25

Devil River Trip, 1974
    NM $15   MIP $50

Jungle Truck, 1974
    NM $15   MIP $50

Motorcross Honda, 1973
    NM $20   MIP $50

Olympic Basketball player, 1975, Mattel, Olympic series, #7374
    NM $7   MIP $12

Olympic Boxer, 1975, Mattel, Olympic series, #7348
    NM $7   MIP $12

Olympic Karate, 1975, Mattel, Olympic series, #7344
    NM $7   MIP $12

Olympic Ski Run Playset, 1975, Mattel, Olympic series, #7369
    NM $40   MIP $80

Olympic Skier, 1975, Mattel, Olympic series, #7350
    NM $7   MIP $12

Rescue Rig, 1973
    NM $20   MIP $50

Rugged Rider and Cycle Set, 1973
    NM $25   MIP $50

Sky Commander, 1974
    NM $40   MIP $75

Sport Camper, 1973
    NM $20   MIP $50

FIGURES

Big Jack, 1973
    NM $20   MIP $50

Big Jeff, 1973
    NM $20   MIP $50

Big Jim, 1971-77, Mattel, window box
    NM $20   MIP $75

Big Josh, 1973
    NM $20   MIP $50

Dr. Steel, 1975
    NM $20   MIP $50

Gold Medal Big Jack, 1975, Mattel, Olympic series
    NM $20   MIP $75

Gold Medal Big Jim, 1975, Mattel, Olympic series
    NM $20   MIP $75

Gold Medal Big Jim Olympic Boxing Match, 1975, Mattel, Olympic series, #7425
    NM $40   MIP $80

BIG JIM'S P.A.C.K. (MATTEL, 1974-77)

ACCESSORIES

Beast, 1976-77
    NM $45   MIP $100

BlitzRig, 1976-77
    NM $60   MIP $120

Frogman, 1974-77, Mattel, Double Trouble Disguise
    NM $12   MIP $40

Hard Hat Gunner, 1974-77, Mattel, Double Trouble Adventure Sets
    NM $10   MIP $40

Howler, 1976-77
    NM $30   MIP $60

LazerVette, 1976-77
    NM $45   MIP $100

Martial Arts, 1974-77, Mattel, Double Trouble Disguise
    NM $7   MIP $12

Motocross, 1974-77, Mattel, Double Trouble Disguise
    NM $7   MIP $12

S.W.A.T., 1974-77, Mattel, Double Trouble Adventure Sets
    NM $10   MIP $40

Secret Spy, 1974-77, Mattel, Double Trouble Adventure Sets
    NM $10   MIP $40

Ski Patrol, 1974-77, Mattel, Double Trouble Disguise
    NM $7   MIP $40

Swamp Patrol, 1974-77, Mattel, Sears exclusive
    NM $50   MIP $100

The Whip's Dune Buggy, 1974-77, Mattel, dune buggy vehicle
    NM $25   MIP $50

Underworld Gunner, 1974-77, Mattel, Double Trouble Adventure Sets
    NM $10   MIP $40

FIGURES

Big Jim, window box, 1974-77, Mattel, Series 2, #9258, a.k.a. "The Gold Commander," gold pants, black shirt
    NM $50   MIP $200

Big Jim, window box, 1974-77, Mattel, Series 1, #9092, a.k.a. "The Blue Commander," white pants, blue shirt
    NM $40   MIP $125

Double Trouble Commander, 1974-77, Mattel, Series 2, #9287, Face changes
    NM $75   MIP $200

Dr. Steel, window box, 1974-77, Mattel, Series 1, #7367, w/ pipe
    NM $30   MIP $100

Torpedo Fist, 1974-77, Mattel, Series 2, #9289, eye patch, hat
    NM $40   MIP $150

Warpath, window box, 1974-77, Mattel, Series 1, #9059, w/ bow, quiver, two arrows
    NM $35   MIP $150

Whip, The, window box, 1974-77, Mattel, Series 1, #9060, w/ bull whip, bolos, shinai stick, boomerangs
    NM $35   MIP $150

Zorak, 1974-77, Mattel, Series 2
    NM $50   MIP $150

BILL & TED'S EXCELLENT ADVENTURE (KENNER, 1991)

ACCESSORIES

Phone Booth, 1991, Kenner
    NM $5   MIP $10

Wild Stallyns Speaker and Tape, 1991, Kenner
    NM $3   MIP $10

FIGURES

Abe Lincoln, 1991, Kenner
    NM $7   MIP $15

Bill, 1991, Kenner
    NM $5   MIP $10

Bill & Ted Jam Session, two pack, 1991, Kenner
    NM $10   MIP $20

Billy The Kid, 1991, Kenner
    NM $5   MIP $13

Genghis Khan, 1991, Kenner
    NM $5   MIP $13

Grim Reaper, 1991, Kenner
    NM $13   MIP $25

Rufus, 1991, Kenner
    NM $5   MIP $13

Ted, 1991, Kenner
    NM $5   MIP $10

BIONIC SIX   (LJN, 1986)

ACCESSORIES

Dirt Bike, 1986, LJN
    NM $5   MIP $10

Flying Laser Throne, 1986, LJN
    NM $5   MIP $10

Laser Aero Chair, 1986, LJN
    NM $5   MIP $10

M.U.L.E.S. Van, 1986, LJN
    NM $5   MIP $10

Quad Runner, 1986, LJN, 4x4
    NM $5   MIP $10

Secret Headquarters, 1986, LJN, Super Hi-Tech Bionic Laboratory
    NM $25   MIP $50

FIGURES

Bunji, 1986
    NM $4   MIP $12

Chopper, 1986
    NM $4   MIP $12

Dr. Scarab, 1986
    NM $4   MIP $12

Eric, 1986
    NM $4   MIP $12

F.L.U.F.F.I., 1986
    NM $8   MIP $20

Glove, 1986
    NM $4   MIP $12

Helen, 1986
    NM $4   MIP $12

J.D., 1986
    NM $4   MIP $12

Jack, 1986
    NM $4   MIP $12

Klunk, 1986
    NM $4   MIP $12

Madame O, 1986
    NM $4   MIP $12

Mechanic, 1986
    NM $4   MIP $12

Meg, 1986
    NM $4   MIP $12

BIONIC WOMAN (KENNER, 1976-77)

12" FIGURES

Fembot, 1977
    NM $70   MIP $225

(Toy Shop File Photo)

Jamie Sommers, 1976, with purse
    NM $50   MIP $175

Jamie Sommers, 1976
    NM $40   MIP $150

ACCESSORIES

Beauty Salon, 1976
    NM $30   MIP $70

Carriage House, 1977
    NM $55   MIP $140

Classroom, 1976-77
    NM $100   MIP $200

Dome House, 1976-77
    NM $55   MIP $140

Sports Car, 1976
    NM $40   MIP $100

FASHIONS

Designer Budget Fashions, 1976, Kenner, Red evening gown w/ red shoes
    NM $15   MIP $30

Designer Budget Fashions, 1976, Kenner, Green dress w/ white shoes
    NM $15   MIP $30

Designer Collection, 1976, Kenner, Floral party dress w/ platform shoes
    NM $12   MIP $25

Designer Collection, 1976, Kenner, "Peach Dream," peach evinging dress w/ peach shoes
    NM $12   MIP $25

Designer Collection, 1976, Kenner, Light blue two-piece pant outfit w/ white shoes
    NM $25   MIP $45

Designer Collection, 1976, Kenner, Calico dress red/yellow w/ apron
    NM $12   MIP $25

BLACK HOLE (MEGO, 1979-80)

12" FIGURES

(Toy Shop File Photo)

Captain Holland, 1979, Mego, Shown with other figures from the Black Hole
    NM $40   MIP $75

Dr. Alex Durant, 1979, Mego
    NM $40   MIP $75

Dr. Hans Reinhardt, 1979, Mego
    NM $40   MIP $75

Harry Booth, 1979, Mego
    NM $45   MIP $85

Kate McCrae, 1979, Mego
    NM $50   MIP $95

Pizer, 1979, Mego
    NM $40   MIP $75

3-3/4" FIGURES

(Toy Shop File Photo)

Captain Holland, 1979, Mego, Shown with other figures from the Black Hole
    NM $5   MIP $25

Dr. Alex Durant, 1979, Mego
    NM $5   MIP $25

Dr. Hans Reinhardt, 1979, Mego
    NM $5   MIP $25

Harry Booth, 1979, Mego
    NM $5   MIP $25

Humanoid, 1980, Mego
    NM $200   MIP $750

Kate McCrae, 1979, Mego
    NM $5   MIP $25

Maximillian, 1979, Mego
    NM $20   MIP $75

Old B.O.B., 1980, Mego
    NM $60   MIP $200

Pizer, 1979, Mego
    NM $10   MIP $50

S.T.A.R., 1980, Mego
    NM $85   MIP $350

Sentry Robot, 1980, Mego
    NM $15   MIP $75

V.I.N.cent., 1979, Mego
    NM $15   MIP $70

ACTION FIGURES

BLACKSTAR (GALOOB, 1984)

ACCESSORIES

Ice Castle, 1984
NM $35 MIP $75

Triton, 1984
NM $25 MIP $50

Warlock, 1984
NM $25 MIP $50

FIGURES

Blackstar, 1984
NM $10 MIP $25

Blackstar with Laser Light, 1984
NM $10 MIP $35

Devil Knight with Laser Light, 1984
NM $25 MIP $45

Gargo, 1984
NM $10 MIP $35

Gargo with Laser Light, 1984
NM $10 MIP $35

Kadray, 1984
NM $10 MIP $35

Kadray with Laser Light, 1984
NM $10 MIP $35

Klone with Laser Light, 1984
NM $15 MIP $45

Lava Loc with Laser Light, 1984
NM $15 MIP $45

Mara, 1984
NM $30 MIP $60

Meuton, 1984
NM $10 MIP $35

Neptul, 1984
NM $15 MIP $50

Overlord, 1984
NM $15 MIP $45

Overlord with Laser Light, 1984
NM $15 MIP $40

Palace Guard, 1984
NM $15 MIP $40

Palace Guard with Laser Light, 1984
NM $10 MIP $35

Togo, 1984
NM $10 MIP $35

Togo with Laser Light, 1984
NM $10 MIP $35

Vizir with Laser Light, 1984
NM $10 MIP $35

White Knight, 1984
NM $10 MIP $35

BLADE (TOY BIZ, 1998)

6" FIGURES

Blade, 1998, Toy Biz
NM $10 MIP $30

Deacon Frost, 1998, Toy Biz
NM $10 MIP $30

Vampire Blade, 1998, Toy Biz
NM $8 MIP $20

Whistler, 1998, Toy Biz
NM $8 MIP $20

BLADE VAMPIRE HUNTER (TOY BIZ, 1998)

FIGURES

Blade, 1998
NM $2 MIP $8

Deacon Frost, 1998
NM $2 MIP $8

Vampire Blade, 1998
NM $2 MIP $8

Whistker, 1998
NM $2 MIP $8

BOB & DOUG MCKENZIE (MCFARLANE, 2000)

FIGURES

Bob McKenzie with half of Great White North stage set, 2000, McFarlane
NM $5 MIP $15

Doug McKenzie with half of Great White North stage set, 2000, McFarlane
NM $5 MIP $15

BONANZA (AMERICAN CHARACTER, 1966)

ACCESSOIRES

4 in 1 Wagon, 1966
NM $40 MIP $100

Ben's Palomino, 1966
NM $35 MIP $75

Hoss' Stallion, 1966
NM $35 MIP $75

Little Joe's Pinto, 1966
NM $35 MIP $75

FIGURES

Ben, 1966
NM $50 MIP $150

Ben with Palomino, 1966
NM $80 MIP $225

Hoss, 1966
NM $70 MIP $150

Hoss with Stallion, 1966
NM $70 MIP $200

Little Joe, 1966
NM $50 MIP $150

Little Joe with Pinto, 1966
NM $70 MIP $200

Outlaw, 1966
NM $50 MIP $150

BRAVESTARR (MATTEL, 1996)

FIGURES

BraveStarr and Thirty/Thirty, two-pack, 1998, Mattel
NM $15 MIP $50

Col. Borobot, 1998, Mattel
NM $7 MIP $25

Deputy Fuzz, 1998, Mattel
NM $7 MIP $25

Handle Bar, 1998, Mattel
NM $7 MIP $25

Laser-Fire BraveStarr, 1998, Mattel
NM $7 MIP $25

Laser-Fire Tex Hex, 1998, Mattel
NM $10 MIP $30

Marshal BraveStarr, 1998, Mattel
NM $7 MIP $25

Outlaw Skuzz, 1998, Mattel
NM $7 MIP $25

Sand Storm, 1998, Mattel
NM $7 MIP $25

Skull Walker, 1998, Mattel
NM $5 MIP $20

Tex Hex, 1998, Mattel
NM $10 MIP $30

Thunder Stick, 1998, Mattel
NM $10 MIP $30

BRUCE LEE (SIDESHOW TOYS, 1999)

8" FIGURES

(KP Photo)

Bruce Lee, bare chested, 1999, With stand, nunchaku and staff
NM $7 MIP $15

Bruce Lee, traditional outfit, 1999
NM $7 MIP $15

BUCK ROGERS (MEGO, 1979)

12" FIGURES

(Toy Shop File Photo)

Buck Rogers, 1979, Mego
NM $30 MIP $60

Doctor Huer, 1979, Mego
    NM $30   **MIP** $60

Draco, 1979, Mego
    NM $30   **MIP** $60

Draconian Guard, 1979, Mego, With brown and silver uniform
    NM $30   **MIP** $60

Killer Kane, 1979, Mego
    NM $30   **MIP** $60

(Toy Shop File Photo)

Tiger Man, 1979, Mego, With tattooed face and head and tiger-skin vest and clothing
    NM $30   **MIP** $125

Twiki, 1979, Mego
    NM $30   **MIP** $60

3-3/4" FIGURES

Ardella, 1979, Mego
    NM $6   **MIP** $15

Buck Rogers, 1979, Mego
    NM $35   **MIP** $60

Doctor Huer, 1979, Mego
    NM $6   **MIP** $20

Draco, 1979, Mego
    NM $6   **MIP** $20

Draconian Guard, 1979, Mego
    NM $10   **MIP** $20

Killer Kane, 1979, Mego
    NM $6   **MIP** $15

Tiger Man,, 1979, Mego
    NM $10   **MIP** $25

Twiki, 1979, Mego
    NM $20   **MIP** $45

Wilma Deering, 1979, Mego
    NM $12   **MIP** $25

3-3/4" PLAY SETS

Star Fighter Command Center, 1979, Mego
    NM $35   **MIP** $100

3-3/4" VEHICLES

Draconian Marauder, 1979, Mego
    NM $25   **MIP** $50

Land Rover, 1979, Mego
    NM $20   **MIP** $40

Laserscope Fighter, 1979, Mego
    NM $20   **MIP** $40

Star Fighter, 1979, Mego
    NM $25   **MIP** $50

Star Searcher, 1979, Mego
    NM $30   **MIP** $60

BUFFY THE VAMPIRE SLAYER (DIAMOND SELECT, 1999)

FIGURES

Prophecy Girl Buffy, 1999, Diamond Select
    NM $5   **MIP** $15

Vampiric Angel, 1999, Diamond Select
    NM $5   **MIP** $15

Willow, 1999, Diamond Select
    NM $5   **MIP** $15

BUFFY THE VAMPIRE SLAYER (MOORE ACTION COLLECTIBLES, 1999-PRESENT)

SERIES I

Angel, 1999, Moore Action Collectibles
    NM $5   **MIP** $15

Buffy, 1999, Moore Action Collectibles, blue shirt and black pants, Moore Action Collectibles Exclusive
    NM $10   **MIP** $30

Buffy, 1999, Moore Action Collectibles
    NM $5   **MIP** $15

Master, The, 1999, Moore Action Collectibles
    NM $5   **MIP** $15

Willow, 1999, Moore Action Collectibles
    NM $5   **MIP** $15

SERIES II

3-Pack, 2000, Moore Action Collectibles, Buffy, Giles, Oz
    NM $10   **MIP** $30

Buffy, red leather pants, 2000
    NM $3   **MIP** $12

Exclusive Entertainment Earth Oz, 2000, Moore Action Collectibles
    NM $6   **MIP** $15

Exclusive MAC's Fiesta Giles, 2000, Moore Action Collectibles
    NM $6   **MIP** $15

Exclusive Spike, 2000, Moore Action Collectibles
    NM $6   **MIP** $15

Exclusive Toy Fare Season 2 hair Buffy, 2000, Moore Action Collectibles
    NM $6   **MIP** $15

Exclusive Vampire Spike, 2000, Moore Action Collectibles
    NM $6   **MIP** $15

Exclusive Werewolf Oz, 2000, Moore Action Collectibles
    NM $6   **MIP** $15

Giles, 2000
    NM $3   **MIP** $12

Oz, 2000
    NM $3   **MIP** $12

(KP Photo)

Spike, 2000, Moore Action Collectibles, In black trenchcoat. Includes gravesite stand
    NM $3   **MIP** $12

SERIES III

3-Pack, 2001, Moore Action Collectibles, Cordelia, Xander, Cheerleader Cordelia
    NM $15   **MIP** $36

Cordelia, 2001, Moore Action Collectibles
    NM $5   **MIP** $13

Exclusive Cheerleader Cordelia, 2001, Moore Action Collectibles
    NM $5   **MIP** $15

Exclusive Cordelia T1, 2001, Moore Action Collectibles, Summer Show Special
    NM $5   **MIP** $15

Exclusive Military Xander, 2001, Moore Action Collectibles
    NM $5   **MIP** $15

Xander, 2001, Moore Action Collectibles
    NM $5   **MIP** $13

SERIES IV

Drusilla, 2002, Moore Action Collectibles
    NM $5   **MIP** $14

Exclusive Bunny Anya, 2002, Moore Action Collectibles
    NM $5   **MIP** $15

Exclusive Vampire Drusilla, 2002, Moore Action Collectibles
    NM $5   **MIP** $15

Geltleman #2, 2002, Moore Action Collectibles, Tilted head
    NM $5   **MIP** $14

Gentleman #1, 2002, Moore Action Collectibles, Straight head
    NM $5   **MIP** $14

BUFFY THE VAMPIRE SLAYER (SIDESHOW TOYS, 1998-PRESENT)

12" FIGURES

Angel, 2004, Sideshow Toys, #2006, "Becoming"
    NM n/a   **MIP** $40

Buffy Summers, 1998, Sideshow Toys, #2001, from the television series
    NM n/a   **MIP** $30

Buffy Summers, 2004, Sideshow Toys, #2005, "Graduation Day"
NM n/a   MIP $40

Buffy/Gentlemen, 1998, Sideshow Toys, #2000, four figures from "Hush" Season 4
NM n/a   MIP $120

Gentlemen, 1998, Sideshow Toys, #20002R, three Gentlemen figures from "Hush"
NM n/a   MIP $90

BUG'S LIFE, A (MATTEL, 1998)

FIGURES

Enemy Hopper, 1998, Mattel
NM $2   MIP $5

Enemy Molt, 1998, Mattel
NM $2   MIP $5

Francis & Slim, 1998, Mattel
NM $2   MIP $5

Hang Glider Flik, 1998, Mattel
NM $2   MIP $5

Inventor Flik, 1998, Mattel
NM $2   MIP $5

Princess Atta, 1998, Mattel
NM $2   MIP $5

Tuck & Roll, 1998, Mattel
NM $2   MIP $5

Warrior Flik, 1998, Mattel
NM $2   MIP $5

BUTCH AND SUNDANCE: THE EARLY DAYS (KENNER, 1979)

ACCESSORIES AND VEHICLES

Bluff, Butch's horse, 1979, Kenner
NM $20   MIP $50

Mint Wagon, 1979, Kenner
NM $25   MIP $60

Saloon Play Set, 1979, Kenner
NM $45   MIP $110

Spurs, Sundance's horse, 1979, Kenner
NM $20   MIP $50

FIGURES

Butch Cassidy, 1979, Kenner
NM $12   MIP $30

Marshall LeFors, 1979, Kenner
NM $12   MIP $30

O.C. Hanks, 1979, Kenner
NM $12   MIP $30

Sheriff Bledsoe, 1979, Kenner
NM $12   MIP $30

Sundance Kid, 1979, Kenner
NM $12   MIP $30

CADILLACS AND DINOSAURS (TYCO, 1994)

FIGURES

Hammer Terhune, 1994, Tyco
NM $2   MIP $5

Hannah Dundee, 1994, Tyco
NM $4   MIP $10

Hermes, 1994, Tyco
NM $2   MIP $5

Jack Cadillac Tenrec, 1994, Tyco
NM $2   MIP $5

Jungle Fighting Jack Tenrec, 1994, Tyco
NM $3   MIP $8

Kentrosaurus, 1994, Tyco
NM $5   MIP $15

Mustapha Cairo, 1994, Tyco
NM $2   MIP $5

Snake Eyes, 1994, Tyco
NM $5   MIP $15

Vice Terhune, 1994, Tyco
NM $3   MIP $8

Zeke, 1994, Tyco
NM $2   MIP $5

CAPTAIN & TENNILLE (MEGO, 1970s)

FIGURES

Daryl Dragon (Captain), 1977, Mego, Model No. 7501
NM $55   MIP $125

(Toy Shop File Photo)

Toni Tennille, 1977, Mego, Features a stand and "fully washable hair…wash and blow dry on cool setting." Interesting choice for an action figure, but after KISS, why not?
NM $55   MIP $125

CAPTAIN ACTION (IDEAL, 1966-68)

12" FIGURES

Captain Action, 1966, 1966, Ideal, with red-shirted Lone Ranger on box
NM $200   MIP $500

Captain Action, 1966, 1966, Ideal, with blue-shirted Lone Ranger on box
NM $200   MIP $500

Captain Action, 1966, 1966, Ideal, photo box
NM $300   MIP $900

Captain Action, 1967, 1967, Ideal, parachute offer on box
NM $275   MIP $700

Dr. Evil, 1967, 1967, Ideal, photo box
NM $250   MIP $450

Dr. Evil, Lab Set Display Box, 1967, Ideal, all Dr. Evil accessories plus white lab coat, blue/red thought-control helmet, reducer wand w/prism, gun, hypnotic eye (eyelid often missing), Dr. Ling mask
NM $1000   MIP $3000

Dr. Evil, Mailer box version of lab set, 1968, Ideal
NM $1000   MIP $2500

9" FIGURES

Action Boy, 1967, 1967, Ideal
NM $275   MIP $900

Action Boy, 1968, 1968, Ideal, with space suit
NM $350   MIP $1100

ACCESSORIES

Action Cave Carrying Case, 1967, 1967, Ideal, vinyl
NM $400   MIP $700

Directional Communicator Set, 1966, 1966, Ideal
NM $110   MIP $300

Dr. Evil Sanctuary, 1967, 1967, Ideal
NM $2500   MIP $3500

Jet Mortar, 1966, 1966, Ideal, two shells
NM $110   MIP $300

Parachute Pack, 1966, 1966, Ideal, silver boots, orange helmet, working (sometimes) parachute
NM $100   MIP $225

Power Pack, 1966, 1966, Ideal, Jet pack w/handles; silver helmet, gloves and boots, CA belt w/o slit for sword
NM $125   MIP $250

Quick Change Chamber, 1967, 1967, Ideal, Sears Exclusive, cardboard
NM $750   MIP $900

Silver Streak Amphibian, 1967, 1967, Ideal
NM $800   MIP $1200

Silver Streak Garage, 1966-68, Ideal, Sears Exclusive, with Silver Streak Vehicle
NM $1500   MIP $2000

Survival Kit, 1967, 1967, Ideal, twenty pieces; orange vest
NM $125   MIP $275

Vinyl Headquarters Carrying Case, 1967, 1967, Ideal, Sears Exclusive
NM $200   MIP $500

Weapons Arsenal, 1966, 1966, Ideal, ten pieces
NM $110   MIP $225

ACTION BOY COSTUMES

Aqualad, 1967, 1967, Ideal
NM $300   MIP $900

Robin, 1967, 1967, Ideal, included gloves, Batarangs, boots, uniform, face mask, suction cups for climbing buildings
NM $300   MIP $1200

Superboy, 1967, 1967, Ideal
NM $300   MIP $1000

CAPTAIN ACTION COSTUMES

(Toy Shop File Photo)

Aquaman, 1966, 1966, Ideal, costume, mask, yellow flippers, trident, seashell w/strap, yellow belt, lance-like sword, yellow/silver knife; Photo shows Batman, Captain America, Aquaman, and Superman
> **NM** $160　　**MIP** $600

Aquaman, 1967, 1967, Ideal, with flasher ring, 1966 accessories
> **NM** $180　　**MIP** $950

Batman, 1966, 1966, Ideal, costume, 2-piece mask, batarang, blue cape, utility belt and boots, blue flashlight w/hook, drill, rope w/reel and hook
> **NM** $225　　**MIP** $700

Batman, 1967, 1967, Ideal, with flasher ring, 1966 accessories
> **NM** $250　　**MIP** $1100

(Toy Shop File Photo)

Buck Rogers, 1967, 1967, Ideal, with flasher ring, silver suit, mask, black boots and gloves, black belt/shoulder harness, 2 blue rocket packs, blue helmet, canteen, raygun, flashlight
> **NM** $450　　**MIP** $2700

Captain America, 1966, 1966, Ideal, red, white, blue costume, mask, red boots, white belt w/gun holster, laser pistol, laser rifle, shield (red, white and blue w/star in middle)
> **NM** $220　　**MIP** $900

Captain America, 1967, 1967, Ideal, with flasher ring, 1966 accessories
> **NM** $225　　**MIP** $1200

Flash Gordon, 1966, 1966, Ideal, white spacesuit with helmet, silver boots, space pistol, propellant gun, belt and mask
> **NM** $200　　**MIP** $600

Flash Gordon, 1967, 1967, Ideal, with flasher ring, 1966 accessories
> **NM** $225　　**MIP** $800

Green Hornet, 1967, 1967, Ideal, with flasher ring, green trench coat, mask, black pants, white scarf, black hat w/green band, yellow gas mask, shoulder holster, pistol, tv w/phone, gold pocket watch, black cane w/removable handle
> **NM** $2000　　**MIP** $7500

Lone Ranger, 1966, 1966, Ideal, red shirt, black pants, white hat, mask, black belt w/2 holsters, 2 silver pistols, rifle, black boots w/spurs
> **NM** $200　　**MIP** $700

Lone Ranger, 1967, 1967, Ideal, blue shirt (1967 only), with flasher ring, 1966 accessories
> **NM** $500　　**MIP** $1000

(Toy Shop File Photo)

Phantom, 1966, 1966, Ideal, purple uniform, black boots, knife, rifle, two pistols, double-rig holster, mask, brass knuckles
> **NM** $225　　**MIP** $775

Phantom, 1967, 1967, Ideal, with flasher ring, 1966 accessories
> **NM** $250　　**MIP** $900

(Toy Shop File Photo)

Sgt. Fury, 1966, 1966, Ideal, camo uniform, bearded mask, moustache mask, clean-shaven mask, black boots, helmet, walkie-talkie, bandolier, machine gun, 3 grenades, .45 pistol
> **NM** $200　　**MIP** $800

Spider-Man, 1967, 1967, Ideal, with flasher ring, red/blue uniform, spider mask, red boots, yellow spider, web fluid tank w/shoulder strap and hoses, "web" sword, flashlight, grappling hook
> **NM** $550　　**MIP** $8000

Steve Canyon, 1966, 1966, Ideal, green flight suit, black boots, mask, blue cap, white flight helmet, parachute pack, oxygen mask, green belt/holster, pistol, knife
> **NM** $200　　**MIP** $700

(Toy Shop File Photo)

Steve Canyon, 1967, 1967, Ideal, with flasher ring, 1966 accessories
> **NM** $225　　**MIP** $850

Superman, 1966, 1966, Ideal, costume, mask, red boots, yellow belt, green Kryptonite, yellow shackles and chain, Krypto, Phantom Zone Projector
> **NM** $200　　**MIP** $700

Superman, 1967, 1967, Ideal, with flasher ring, 1966 accessories
> **NM** $225　　**MIP** $1100

Tonto, 1967, 1967, Ideal, with flasher ring, brown costume, headband w/feather, moccasins, brown belt, brown quiver and boe, gun, knife, four arrows (each has different color feather: red, blue, yellow, green), Taka the eagle
> **NM** $375　　**MIP** $1100

CAPTAIN ACTION (PLAYING MANTIS, 1998-99)

FIGURES AND COSTUMES

Captain Action, 1998-99, Playing Mantis
> **NM** $15　　**MIP** $20

Dr. Evil, 1998-99, Playing Mantis
> **NM** $15　　**MIP** $20

Flash Gordon, 1998-99, Playing Mantis
> **NM** $15　　**MIP** $20

Green Hornet, 1998-99, Playing Mantis, Kay-Bee exclusive
> **NM** $15　　**MIP** $25

Kabai Singh, 1999, Playing Mantis, outfit only, for Dr. Evil
> **NM** $10　　**MIP** $20

Kato, 1998-99, Playing Mantis, Kay-Bee exclusive
> **NM** $15　　**MIP** $20

ACTION FIGURES

Action Figures — *Chaos! (Moore Action Collectibles, 1997-present)*

ACTION FIGURES

(Playing Mantis)

Lone Ranger, 1998-99, Playing Mantis, Photo shows Lone Ranger and Tonto
NM $15   MIP $25

Ming the Merciless, 1998-99, Playing Mantis
NM $15   MIP $35

The Phantom, 1999, Playing Mantis
NM $10   MIP $20

Tonto, 1998-99, Playing Mantis
NM $15   MIP $25

CAPTAIN POWER AND THE SOLDIERS OF THE FUTURE (MATTEL, 1987-88)

ACCESSORIES

Dread Stalker, 1988, Mattel
NM $8   MIP $15

Interlocker Throne, 1987, Mattel
NM $10   MIP $20

Magna Cycle, 1988, Mattel
NM $12   MIP $25

Phantom Striker, 1987, Mattel
NM $12   MIP $25

Power Base, 1987, Mattel
NM $25   MIP $50

Power Jet XT-7, 1987, Mattel
NM $20   MIP $50

Power on Energizer with figure, 1987, Mattel
NM $5   MIP $15

Trans-Field Base Station, 1988, Mattel
NM $15   MIP $30

Trans-Field Communication Station, 1988, Mattel
NM $10   MIP $20

Wind-Up Soaron Beam Deflector, 1988, Mattel
NM $10   MIP $20

FIGURES, SERIES I

Blastarr Ground Guardian, 1987, Mattel
NM $5   MIP $15

Captain Power, 1987, Mattel
NM $10   MIP $20

Lord Dread, 1987, Mattel
NM $5   MIP $15

Lt. Tank Ellis, 1987, Mattel
NM $10   MIP $20

Major Hawk Masterson, 1987, Mattel
NM $5   MIP $15

Soaron Sky Sentry, 1987, Mattel
NM $5   MIP $15

FIGURES, SERIES II

Col. Stingray Johnson, 1988, Mattel
NM $12   MIP $25

Cpl. Pilot Chase, 1988, Mattel
NM $10   MIP $20

Dread Commander, 1988, Mattel
NM $45   MIP $90

Dread Trooper, 1988, Mattel
NM $45   MIP $90

Sgt. Scout Baker, 1988, Mattel
NM $10   MIP $20

Tritor, 1988, Mattel
NM $15   MIP $35

CAPTAIN SCARLETT (PEDIGREE, 1967)

12" FIGURE

Captain Scarlet, 1967, Pedigree
NM $500   MIP $1200

CAPTAIN SCARLETT (VIVID IMAGINATIONS, 1993-94)

12" FIGURES

Captain Black, 1993-94
NM $25   MIP $50

Captain Scarlett, 1993-94
NM $25   MIP $50

3-3/4" FIGURES

Captain Black, 1993-94
NM $3   MIP $8

Captain Blue, 1993-94
NM $3   MIP $8

Captain Scarlett, 1993-94
NM $4   MIP $10

Colonel White, 1993-94
NM $3   MIP $8

Destiny Angel, 1993-94
NM $5   MIP $12

Lieutenant Green, 1993-94
NM $3   MIP $8

CENTURIONS (KENNER, 1986)

ACCESSORIES

Power Pack, 1986, Kenner, Series 1
NM $5   MIP $10

FIGURES

Ace McCloud, 1986, Kenner, Series 1, Air operations expert
NM $7   MIP $12

Dr. Terror, 1986, Kenner, Series 1, Evil genius
NM $7   MIP $12

Hacker, 1986, Kenner, Series 1, Dr. Terror's Henchman
NM $7   MIP $12

Jake Rockwell, 1986, Kenner, Series 1, Land operations expert
NM $7   MIP $12

Max Ray, 1986, Kenner, Series 1, Sea operations expert
NM $7   MIP $12

VEHICLES

Detonator, 1986, Kenner, Series 1
NM $10   MIP $20

Skybolt, 1986, Kenner, Series 1
NM $10   MIP $20

Strafer, 1986, Kenner, Series 1
NM $10   MIP $20

Tidal Blast, 1986, Kenner, Series 1
NM $10   MIP $20

Wild Weasel, 1986, Kenner, Series 1
NM $10   MIP $20

CHAOS! (MOORE ACTION COLLECTIBLES, 1997-PRESENT)

SERIES I, 12" FIGURES

Lady Death, 1997-present
NM $10   MIP $30

Royal Lady Death, 1997-present
NM $10   MIP $30

SERIES I, FIGURES

Evil Earnie, 1997-present
NM $3   MIP $12

Evil Ernie, glow in the dark, 1997-present
NM $8   MIP $25

Lady Death, 1997-present
NM $3   MIP $12

Lady Death, chrome, 1997-present
NM $10   MIP $30

Lady death, glow in the dark, 1997-present
NM $10   MIP $30

Lady Demon, 1997-present
NM $3   MIP $12

Lady Demon, glow in the dark, 1997-present
NM $10   MIP $30

Purgatori, 1997-present
NM $3   MIP $12

Purgatori, metallic, 1997-present
NM $8   MIP $25

SERIES II, FIGURES

Cremator, 1997-present
NM $8   MIP $20

Cremator, 1997-present
NM $3   MIP $12

Lady Death in Battle Armor, 1997-present
NM $3   MIP $12

Lady Death, Azure, 1997-present
NM $10   MIP $30

Lady Death, bronze, 1997-present
NM $10   MIP $30

ACTION FIGURES

CHARLIE'S ANGELS (HASBRO, 1977)

8-1/2" FIGURES

(Toy Shop File Photo)

Jill — Farrah Fawcett, 1977, Hasbro
NM $50   **MIP** $100

Kelly — Jaclyn Smith, 1977, Hasbro
NM $40   **MIP** $75

Kris — Cheryl Ladd, 1977, Hasbro
NM $40   **MIP** $75

(Toy Shop File Photo)

Sabrina — Kate Jackson, 1977, Hasbro
NM $40   **MIP** $75

Sabrina, Kris, and Kelly Gift Set, 1977, Hasbro
NM $75   **MIP** $200

ACCESSORIES

Adventure Van, 1977, Hasbro, "Headquarters on Wheels"
NM $25   **MIP** $50

CHARLIE'S ANGELS (JAKKS PACIFIC, 2000)

FIGURES

Alex, 2000, JAKKS Pacific, Played by Lucy Liu in "Charlie's Angels"
NM n/a   **MIP** $30

(KP Photo)

Dylan Saunders, 2000, JAKKS Pacific, Model of Drew Barrymore's character in "Charlie's Angels" movie
NM n/a   **MIP** $30

Natalie, 2000, JAKKS Pacific, Played by Cameron Diaz in "Charlie's Angels"
NM n/a   **MIP** $30

CHiPs (MEGO, 1979)

3-3/4" FIGURES AND ACCESSORIES

Jimmy Squeaks, 1979, Mego
NM $5   **MIP** $15

Jon, 1979, Mego
NM $10   **MIP** $20

Launcher with Motorcycle, 1979, Mego
NM $25   **MIP** $50

Motorcycle, boxed, 1979, Mego
NM $5   **MIP** $30

Ponch, 1979, Mego
NM $8   **MIP** $20

Sarge, 1979, Mego
NM $10   **MIP** $30

Wheels Willie, 1979, Mego
NM $5   **MIP** $15

8" FIGURES AND ACCESSORIES

Jon, 1979, Mego
NM $20   **MIP** $50

Motorcycle, 1979, Mego
NM $30   **MIP** $75

Ponch, 1979, Mego
NM $15   **MIP** $40

Sarge, 1979, Mego
NM $25   **MIP** $50

CHUCK NORRIS KARATE KOMMANDOS (KENNER, 1986-87)

6" FIGURES

Chuck Norris Battle Gear, 1986, Kenner
NM $8   **MIP** $15

Chuck Norris Kung Fu Training, 1986, Kenner
NM $6   **MIP** $12

Chuck Norris Undercover Agent, 1986, Kenner
NM $8   **MIP** $15

Kimo, 1986, Kenner
NM $6   **MIP** $12

Ninja Master, 1986, Kenner
NM $6   **MIP** $12

Ninja Serpent, 1986, Kenner
NM $6   **MIP** $12

Ninja Warrior, 1986, Kenner
NM $6   **MIP** $12

Super Ninja, 1986, Kenner
NM $6   **MIP** $12

Tabe, 1986, Kenner
NM $6   **MIP** $12

VEHICLES

Karate Corvette, 1986, Kenner
NM $15   **MIP** $25

CLASH OF THE TITANS (MATTEL, 1980)

FIGURES

Calibos, 1980, Mattel, Lord of the Marsh
NM $20   **MIP** $50

Charon, 1980, Mattel, Ferryman of the River Styx
NM $30   **MIP** $75

Kraken, 1980, Mattel, Sea Monster
NM $75   **MIP** $250

Pegasus, 1980, Mattel
NM $25   **MIP** $75

Perseus, 1980, Mattel, Hero Son of Zeus
NM $20   **MIP** $50

Perseus and Pegasus, two-pack, 1980, Mattel
NM $50   **MIP** $105

Thallo, 1980, Mattel, Captain of the Guard
NM $20   **MIP** $50

COMIC ACTION HEROES (MEGO, 1975-78)

3-3/4" FIGURES

Aquaman, 1975, Mego
NM $30   **MIP** $75

Batman, 1975, Mego
NM $20   **MIP** $75

Captain America, 1975, Mego
NM $20   **MIP** $75

Green Goblin, 1975, Mego
NM $22   **MIP** $125

Hulk, 1975, Mego
NM $20   **MIP** $50

Joker, 1975, Mego
NM $20   **MIP** $75

(Toy Shop File Photo)

Penguin, 1975, Mego, Shown here with Robin
NM $20   **MIP** $75

Robin, 1975, Mego, Shown on previous page with The Penguin. Many of the components of Mego action figures were interchangeable, allowing the company to release almost limitless variations of popular figures
NM $20   MIP $65

Shazam, 1975, Mego
NM $20   MIP $75

Spider-Man, 1975, Mego
NM $20   MIP $75

Superman, 1975, Mego
NM $20   MIP $65

Wonder Woman, 1975, Mego
NM $20   MIP $65

ACCESSORIES

Batcopter, 1975-78, Mego, w/ Batman figure
NM $50   MIP $100

Batmobile, 1975-78, Mego, w/ Batman and Robin figures
NM $75   MIP $150

Collapsing Tower (with Invisible Plane & Wonder Woman), 1975, Mego
NM $100   MIP $200

Exploding Bridge with Batmobile, 1975, Mego
NM $100   MIP $200

Fortress of Solitude with Superman, 1975, Mego
NM $100   MIP $200

Mangler, 1975, Mego
NM $125   MIP $300

Spidercar, 1975-78, Mego, w/ Spiderman and Green Goblin figures
NM $100   MIP $300

COMIC HEROINE POSIN' DOLLS (IDEAL, 1967)

12" BOXED FIGURES

(KP Photo, Joe Desris collection)

Batgirl, 1967, Ideal, Purple gloves, boots, cape and mask
NM $1500   MIP $5500

(Toy Shop File Photo)

Mera, 1967, Ideal
NM $1000   MIP $4500

Supergirl, 1967, Ideal
NM $1000   MIP $4500

(Toy Shop File Photo)

Wonder Woman, 1967, Ideal
NM $1000   MIP $4500

COMMANDER POWER (MEGO, 1975)

FIGURE WITH VEHICLE

Commander Power with Lightning Cycle, 1975, Mego
NM $20   MIP $40

COMMANDO (DIAMOND, 1985)

18" FIGURES

Arnold Schwarzenegger, black box, 1985
NM $80   MIP $200

Arnold Schwarzenegger, red box, 1985
NM $80   MIP $300

3-3/4" FIGURES

Blaster, 1985
NM $10   MIP $25

Chopper, 1985
NM $10   MIP $25

Lead Head, 1985
NM $10   MIP $25

Matrix, 1985
NM $40   MIP $150

Psycho, 1985
NM $10   MIP $25

Sawbones, 1985
NM $10   MIP $25

Spex, 1985
NM $10   MIP $25

Stalker, 1985
NM $10   MIP $25

6" FIGURES

Blaster, 1985
NM $15   MIP $40

Chopper, 1985
NM $15   MIP $40

Lead Head, 1985
NM $15   MIP $40

Matrix, 1985
NM $35   MIP $90

Pyscho, 1985
NM $15   MIP $40

Sawbones, 1985
NM $15   MIP $40

Spex, 1985
NM $15   MIP $40

Stalker, 1985
NM $15   MIP $40

CONAN (HASBRO, 1994)

FIGURES, ASST. I

Conan the Adventurer with Star Metal Slash, 1994, Hasbro
NM $2   MIP $6

Conan the Warrior with Slashing Battle Action, 1994, Hasbro
NM $2   MIP $6

Wrath-Amon with Serpent Slash, 1994, Hasbro
NM $2   MIP $6

Zulu with Dart Firing Crossbow, 1994, Hasbro
NM $2   MIP $6

FIGURES, ASST. II

Conan the Exlporer with Two-fisted Chopping Action, 1994, Hasbro
NM $2   MIP $6

Greywolf with Cyclone Power Punch, 1994, Hasbro
NM $2   MIP $6

Ninja Conan with Katana Chop, 1994, Hasbro
NM $2   MIP $6

Skulkur with Zombie Tornado Slash, 1994, Hasbro
NM $2   MIP $6

CONAN (REMCO, 1984)

FIGURES

Conan The Warrior, 1984
NM $15   MIP $40

Devourer Of Souls, 1984
NM $15   MIP $40

Jewel Man, 1984
NM $15   MIP $40

ACTION FIGURES

Throth Amon, 1984
   NM $15   MIP $40

CONEHEADS (PLAYMATES, 1995)

FIGURES

(Playmates Toys)

Agent Seedling, 1998, Playmates, Shown here with group of figures in the series
   NM $2   MIP $4
Beldar in flight uniform, 1998
   NM $2   MIP $4
Beldar in street clothes, 1998
   NM $2   MIP $4
Connie, 1998
   NM $2   MIP $4
Prymaat in flight uniform, 1998
   NM $2   MIP $4
Prymaat in street clothes, 1998
   NM $2   MIP $4

CONGO (KENNER, 1995)

FIGURES

(KP Photo)

Amy, 1995, Shown here with a group of Congo figures
   NM $3   MIP $5

(KP Photo)

Blastface, 1995, Shown here with Congo figure group
   NM $3   MIP $5
Bonecrucher, Deluxe, 1995
   NM $4   MIP $8
Kahega, 1995
   NM $2   MIP $4
Karen Ross, 1995
   NM $2   MIP $4
Mangler, 1995
   NM $2   MIP $4

Monroe, 1995
   NM $2   MIP $4
Monroe, Deluxe, 1995
   NM $4   MIP $8
Peter Elliot, 1995
   NM $2   MIP $4

VEHICLES
Net trap Vehicle, 1995
   NM $4   MIP $8
Trail Hacker Vehicle, 1995
   NM $4   MIP $8

DANGER GIRL (MCFARLANE, 1999)

FIGURES
Abbey Chase, 1999
   NM $8   MIP $20
Major Maxim, 1999
   NM $3   MIP $8
Natalia Kassle, 1999
   NM $8   MIP $20
Sydney Savage, 1999
   NM $8   MIP $20

DC COMICS SUPER HEROES (TOY BIZ, 1989)

FIGURES
Aquaman, 1989, Toy Biz
   NM $5   MIP $10
Batman, 1989, Toy Biz
   NM $3   MIP $10
Bob The Goon, 1989, Toy Biz
   NM $5   MIP $10
Flash, 1989, Toy Biz
   NM $4   MIP $10
Flash II with Turbo Platform, 1989, Toy Biz
   NM $5   MIP $10
Green Lantern, 1989, Toy Biz
   NM $8   MIP $20
Hawkman, 1989, Toy Biz
   NM $8   MIP $20
Joker, no forehead curl, 1989, Toy Biz
   NM $3   MIP $10
Joker, with forehead curl, 1989, Toy Biz
   NM $5   MIP $10
Lex Luthor, 1989, Toy Biz
   NM $3   MIP $8
Mr. Freeze, 1989, Toy Biz
   NM $4   MIP $10
Penguin, long missile, 1989, Toy Biz
   NM $8   MIP $20
Penguin, short missile, 1989, Toy Biz
   NM $8   MIP $30
Penguin, umbrella-firing, 1989, Toy Biz
   NM $3   MIP $8
Riddler, 1989, Toy Biz
   NM $4   MIP $8

Superman, 1989, Toy Biz
   NM $15   MIP $35
Two Face, 1989, Toy Biz
   NM $15   MIP $20
Wonder Woman, 1989, Toy Biz
   NM $8   MIP $15

DEFENDERS OF THE EARTH (GALOOB, 1985)

FIGURES
Flash Gordon, 1985
   NM $8   MIP $25
Garaz, 1985
   NM $8   MIP $25
Lothar, 1985
   NM $8   MIP $25
Mandrake, 1985
   NM $8   MIP $25
Ming, 1985
   NM $8   MIP $20
Phantom, The, 1985
   NM $10   MIP $30

VEHICLES
Claw Copter, 1985
   NM $8   MIP $25
Flash Swordship, 1985
   NM $8   MIP $25
Garax Swordship, 1985
   NM $8   MIP $25
Phantom Skull Copter, 1985
   NM $10   MIP $35

DICK TRACY (PLAYMATES, 1990)

FIGURES, LARGE

(Toy Shop File Photo)

Breathless Mahoney, 1990, Based on the movie, shown here with the Dick Tracy figure
   NM $25   MIP $50
Dick Tracy, 1990
   NM $25   MIP $50

FIGURES, SMALL

Al "Big Boy" Caprice, 1990, Photo with The Blank, Dick Tracy, Influence, Lips Manlis, and Sam Catchem
    NM $8   MIP $15

(Toy Shop File Photo)

Blank, The, 1990
    NM $50   MIP $150

(Toy Shop File Photo)

Brow, The, 1990, Photo with Mumbles, Flattop, Shoulders
    NM $6   MIP $12

Dick Tracy, 1990
    NM $8   MIP $15

(Toy Shop File Photo)

Flattop, 1990, Playmates, Includes Tommy gun and bullwhip
    NM $6   MIP $12

Influence, 1990
    NM $6   MIP $12

Itchy, 1990
    NM $8   MIP $15

Lips Manlis, 1990
    NM $6   MIP $12

Mumbles, 1990
    NM $6   MIP $12

Pruneface, 1990
    NM $6   MIP $12

Rodent, The, 1990
    NM $8   MIP $15

Sam Catchem, 1990
    NM $6   MIP $12

Shoulders, 1990
    NM $6   MIP $12

Steve the Tramp, 1990
    NM $6   MIP $12

DIE-CAST SUPER HEROES (MEGO, 1979)

6" FIGURES

Batman, 1979, Mego
    NM $30   MIP $125

Hulk, 1979, Mego
    NM $25   MIP $75

Spider-Man, 1979, Mego
    NM $30   MIP $125

Superman, 1979, Mego
    NM $30   MIP $95

DOCTOR WHO (DAPOL, 1988-95)

FIGURES

Ace with bat and pack, 1988-95
    NM $4   MIP $8

Cyberman, 1988-95
    NM $4   MIP $8

Dalek, black and gold, with friction drive, 1988-95
    NM $5   MIP $10

Dalek, black and silver, with friction drive, 1988-95
    NM $5   MIP $10

Dalek, gold, with friction drive, 1988-95
    NM $5   MIP $10

Dalek, gray and black, with friction drive, 1988-95
    NM $5   MIP $10

Dalek, gray and black, with friction drive, 1988-95
    NM $5   MIP $10

Dalek, red and black, with friction drive, 1988-95
    NM $5   MIP $10

Dalek, red and gold, with friction drive, 1988-95
    NM $5   MIP $10

Dalek, white and gold, with friction drive, 1988-95
    NM $5   MIP $10

Doctor Who (2nd) Pat Troughton, 1988-95
    NM $5   MIP $10

Doctor Who (3rd), Jon Pertwee, 1988-95
    NM $5   MIP $10

Doctor Who (4th), Tom Baker, 1988-95
    NM $4   MIP $8

Doctor Who (7th) with brown coat, 1988-95
    NM $5   MIP $10

Doctor Who (7th) with gray coat, 1988-95
    NM $5   MIP $10

Early Cybermen, 1988-95
    NM $5   MIP $10

Ice Warrior, 1988-95
    NM $4   MIP $8

K9 with motor action, 1988-95
    NM $5   MIP $10

Master, The, 1988-95
    NM $4   MIP $8

Mel, blue shirt, 1988-95
    NM $4   MIP $8

Mel, pink shirt, 1988-95
    NM $4   MIP $8

Melkur, 1988-95
    NM $5   MIP $10

Sea Devil with cloth outfit, 1988-95
    NM $5   MIP $10

Silurian, 1988-95
    NM $4   MIP $8

Silurian, armored, 1988-95
    NM $4   MIP $8

Sontaran Captain with helmet, 1988-95
    NM $5   MIP $10

Tetrap, 1988-95
    NM $5   MIP $10

Time Lords, brown, 1988-95
    NM $5   MIP $10

Time Lords, burgundy, 1988-95
    NM $5   MIP $10

Time Lords, gray, 1988-95
    NM $5   MIP $10

Time Lords, off-white, 1988-95
    NM $5   MIP $10

PLAYSETS

Anniversary playset, 1988-95, Dapol
    NM $25   MIP $60

Doctor Who (3rd) Play Set, 1988-95
    NM $20   MIP $55

Doctor Who playset w/ Console, 1988, Dapol
    NM $100   MIP $200

VEHICLES AND ACCESSORIES

Dalek Play Set, 1988-95, 4 figures
    NM $20   MIP $40

Tardis with flashing light, 1988-95
    NM $25   MIP $50

DOCTOR WHO (DENYS FISHER, 1976)

FIGURES

(Corey LeChat)

Cyberman, 1976, Denys Fisher, Very 1930s-looking robotic figure from the BBC-TV series. Called "The Threat from the Outerworld" on the box

NM $250   MIP $500

Dalek, 1976

NM $250   MIP $600

Doctor Who (4th), 1976

NM $100   MIP $225

(Corey LeChat)

Giant Robot, 1976, Denys Fisher, Gray plastic robot from the BBC-TV series

NM $165   MIP $300

(Corey LeChat)

K-9, 1976, Palitoy, Looking much like today's toy robot dogs, this Talking K-9 could say a variety of phrases by pressing the control panel on his back

NM $150   MIP $300

Leela, 1976, Denys Fisher

NM $200   MIP $300

VEHICLES

(Corey LeChat)

Tardis play set, 1976, Denys Fisher, Plastic model of the time-travelling

police call box as seen in the popular BBC-TV series

NM $150   MIP $300

DOCTOR WHO (PALITOY, 1976)

FIGURES

(Corey LeChat)

Dalek, Talking, 1976, Palitoy, Shown on the right

NM $100   MIP $150

(Corey LeChat)

K-9, Talking, 1976, Palitoy

NM $150   MIP $250

DUKES OF HAZZARD (MEGO, 1981-82)

3-3/4" CARDED FIGURES

Bo Duke, 1981-82, Mego

NM $8   MIP $15

Boss Hogg, 1981-82, Mego

NM $8   MIP $20

Cletus, 1981-82, Mego

NM $15   MIP $30

Cooter, 1981-82, Mego

NM $15   MIP $30

Coy Duke, 1981-82, Mego

NM $15   MIP $30

Daisy Duke, 1981-82, Mego

NM $12   MIP $25

Luke Duke, 1981-82, Mego

NM $8   MIP $20

Rosco Coltrane, 1981-82, Mego

NM $15   MIP $30

Uncle Jesse, 1981-82, Mego

NM $15   MIP $30

Vance Duke, 1981-82, Mego

NM $15   MIP $30

3-3/4" FIGURES WITH VEHICLES

Boss Hogg's Cadillac, 1981, Mego, w/ Boss Hogg figure

NM $40   MIP $80

Daisy Jeep with Daisy, 1981, boxed, 1981-82, Mego

NM $25   MIP $50

General Lee Car with Bo and Luke, 1981, boxed, 1981-82, Mego

NM $25   MIP $50

Police Car, 1981, Mego, w/ Sheriff Roscoe P. Coltrane

NM $40   MIP $80

8" CARDED FIGURES

(Toy Shop File Photo)

Bo Duke, 1981-82, Mego

NM $15   MIP $30

Boss Hogg, 1981-82, Mego

NM $20   MIP $40

Coy Duke (card says Bo), 1981-82, Mego

NM $25   MIP $50

Daisy Duke, 1981-82, Mego

NM $25   MIP $50

(Lenny Lee)

Luke Duke, 1981-82, Mego

NM $15   MIP $30

Vance Duke (card says Luke), 1981-82, Mego

NM $25   MIP $50

DUNE (LJN, 1984)

FIGURES

Baron Harkonnen, 1984, LJN

NM $20   MIP $40

Feyd, 1984, LJN

NM $20   MIP $40

Paul Atreides, 1984, LJN

NM $20   MIP $40

Rabban, 1984, LJN

NM $20   MIP $40

Sardauker Warrior, 1984, LJN
    NM $25   MIP $50

Stilgar the Freman, 1984, LJN
    NM $20   MIP $40

VEHICLES

Sand Crawler, 1984, LJN
    NM $20   MIP $40

Sand tracker, 1984, LJN
    NM $20   MIP $40

Sandworm, 1984, LJN
    NM $25   MIP $50

Spice Scout, 1984, LJN
    NM $25   MIP $50

DUNGEONS & DRAGONS (LJN, 1983-84)

MONSTERS

Dragonne, 1983, LJN
    NM $20   MIP $40

Hook Horror, 1983, LJN
    NM $20   MIP $40

Tiamat, 1983, LJN
    NM $90   MIP $200

MOUNTS

Bronze Dragon, 1983, LJN
    NM $20   MIP $40

Destrier, 1983, LJN
    NM $15   MIP $30

Nightmare, 1983, LJN
    NM $15   MIP $30

PLAY SETS

Fortress of Fangs, 1983, LJN
    NM $65   MIP $130

SERIES I, 3-3/4" FIGURES, 1983

Elkhorn, 1983, LJN
    NM $15   MIP $30

Kelek, 1983, LJN
    NM $15   MIP $30

Melf, 1983, LJN
    NM $15   MIP $35

Mercion, 1983, LJN
    NM $15   MIP $35

Peralay, 1983, LJN
    NM $15   MIP $30

Ringlerun, 1983, LJN
    NM $15   MIP $30

Strongheart, 1983, LJN
    NM $15   MIP $30

Warduke, 1983, LJN
    NM $15   MIP $30

Zarak, 1983, LJN
    NM $15   MIP $30

SERIES I, 5" FIGURES, 1983

Northlord, 1983, LJN
    NM $20   MIP $45

Ogre King, 1983, LJN
    NM $20   MIP $45

Young Male Titan, 1983, LJN
    NM $15   MIP $30

SERIES II, 3-3/4" FIGURES, 1984

Bowmarc, 1984, LJN
    NM $40   MIP $90

Deeth, 1984, LJN
    NM $55   MIP $120

Drex, 1984, LJN
    NM $55   MIP $120

Elkhorn, 1984, LJN
    NM $20   MIP $50

Grimsword, 1984, LJN
    NM $30   MIP $70

Hawkler, 1984, LJN
    NM $50   MIP $100

Strongheart, 1984, LJN
    NM $20   MIP $45

Warduke, 1984, LJN
    NM $20   MIP $45

Zarak, 1984, LJN
    NM $20   MIP $45

Zorgar, 1984, LJN
    NM $60   MIP $120

SERIES II, 5" FIGURES, 1984

Mandoom, 1984, LJN
    NM $60   MIP $120

Mettaflame, 1984, LJN
    NM $60   MIP $120

Northland, 1984, LJN
    NM $50   MIP $100

Ogre King, 1984, LJN
    NM $65   MIP $130

Young Male Titan, 1984, LJN
    NM $50   MIP $100

E.T. THE EXTRA-TERRESTRIAL (LJN, 1982-83)

FIGURES

E.T and Elliot with bike, 1982-83, LJN
    NM $10   MIP $20

E.T. with dress and hat, 1982-83, LJN
    NM $6   MIP $12

E.T. with robe, 1982-83, LJN
    NM $6   MIP $12

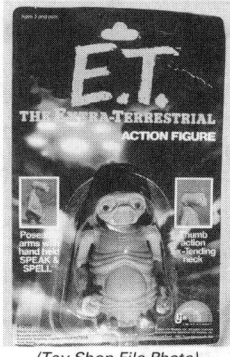

(Toy Shop File Photo)

E.T. with Speak and Spell, 1982-83, LJN, Thumb-operated switch on E.T.'s back extends neck
    NM $6   MIP $12

E.T., talking, 1982-83, LJN
    NM $15   MIP $35

E.T., walking, 1982-83, LJN
    NM $12   MIP $25

EARTHWORM JIM (PLAYMATES, 1995)

FIGURES

Bob, 1995, Playmates
    NM $5   MIP $12

Earthworm Jim with Battle Damage, 1995, Playmates
    NM $5   MIP $8

(Playmates Toys)

Earthworm Jim with Pocket Rocket, 1995, Playmates, Figure with small turbo-driven vehicle (looks a bit like a Gee-Bee racer)
    NM $5   MIP $8

Earthworm Jim with Snott, 1995, Playmates
    NM $5   MIP $8

Hench Rat with Evil Cat, 1995, Playmates
    NM $5   MIP $10

Monstrous Peter Puppy, 1995, Playmates
    NM $5   MIP $8

Peter Puppy, 1995, Playmates
    NM $5   MIP $8

Princess What's-Her-Name, 1995, Playmates
    NM $7   MIP $12

Psycrow with Major Mucus, 1995, Playmates
    NM $4   MIP $8

ACTION FIGURES

EMERGENCY (LJN, 1973)

FIGURES

John, 1973, LJN
     NM $35   **MIP** $100

Roy, 1973, LJN
     NM $35   **MIP** $100

PLAY SETS

Fire House Play Set, 1973, LJN
     NM $100   **MIP** $250

VEHICLES

Rescue Truck, 1973, LJN
     NM $100   **MIP** $300

EVEL KNIEVEL (IDEAL, 1973-74)

FIGURES

Evel Knievel, 1973-74, Ideal, red suit
     NM $20   **MIP** $50

Robby Knievel, 1973-74, Ideal
     NM $25   **MIP** $60

VEHICLES AND ACCESSORIES

Arctic Explorer set, 1973-74, Ideal
     NM $35   **MIP** $75

Chopper, 1973-74, Ideal
     NM $35   **MIP** $75

Evel Knievel Canyon Stunt Cycle, 1973-74, Ideal
     NM $40   **MIP** $80

Evel Knievel Dragster, 1973-74, Ideal
     NM $50   **MIP** $110

Evel Knievel Stunt and Crash Car, 1973-74, Ideal
     NM $45   **MIP** $100

Evel Knievel Stunt Cycle, 1973-74, Ideal
     NM $35   **MIP** $100

Explorer Set, 1973-74, Ideal
     NM $20   **MIP** $40

Racing Set, 1973-74, Ideal
     NM $20   **MIP** $40

Rescue Set, 1973-74, Ideal
     NM $20   **MIP** $40

Road and Trail Set, 1973-74, Ideal
     NM $50   **MIP** $125

Scramble Van, 1973-74, Ideal
     NM $30   **MIP** $100

Skull Canyon Play Set, 1973-74, Ideal
     NM $50   **MIP** $125

Stunt Stadium, 1973-74, Ideal
     NM $40   **MIP** $100

Tail Bike, 1973-74, Ideal
     NM $35   **MIP** $60

EXOSQUAD (PLAYMATES, 1993-95)

EXOCONVERTING SERIES

J.T. Marsh with Exoconverting E-frame, 1993-94
     NM $8   **MIP** $15

EXOWALKING SERIES

Marsala with ExoWalking E-frame, 1993-94
     NM $8   **MIP** $15

GENERAL PURPOSE E-FRAMES WITH FIGURE, ORIGINAL SERIES

(KP Photo, Brian Brogaard collection)

Alec DeLeon with Field Communications, 1993-95
     NM $8   **MIP** $15

J.T. Marsh with Aerial Attack E-Frame, 1993-95
     NM $8   **MIP** $15

Pheaton with Command E-Frame, 1993-95
     NM $8   **MIP** $15

Typhonus with High Speed Stealth E-Frame, 1993-95
     NM $8   **MIP** $15

GENERAL PURPOSE E-FRAMES WITH FIGURE, SECONDARY SERIES

Draconis with Interrogator E-frame, 1994
     NM $8   **MIP** $15

Jinx Madison with Fire Warrior E-frame, 1994
     NM $8   **MIP** $15

Jonas Simbacca with Pirate Captain E-frame, 1994
     NM $8   **MIP** $15

Nara Burns with Reconnaissance E-frame, 1994
     NM $8   **MIP** $15

Peter Tanaka with Samurai E-frame, 1994
     NM $8   **MIP** $15

(KP Photo, Brian Brogaard collection)

Rita Torres with Field Sergeant E-frame, 1994
     NM $8   **MIP** $15

Sean Napier with police Enforcer E-frame, 1994
     NM $8   **MIP** $15

Wolf Bronski with Ground Assault E-frame, 1994
     NM $8   **MIP** $15

GENERAL PURPOSE E-FRAMES WITH FIGURE, THIRD SERIES

(KP Photo, Brian Brogaard collection)

J.T. Marsh with Gridiron Command E-frame, 1995
     NM $8   **MIP** $15

Kaz Takagi with Gorilla E-frame, 1995
     NM $8   **MIP** $15

Marsala with Sub-Sonic Scout E-frame, 1995
     NM $8   **MIP** $15

Wolf Bronski with Medieval Knight E-frames, 1995
     NM $8   **MIP** $15

JUMPTROOPS

Captain Avery Butler, 1993-94
     NM $4   **MIP** $8

Gunnery Sergeant Ramon Longfeather, 1993-94
     NM $4   **MIP** $8

Lance Corporal Vince Pelligrino, 1993-94
     NM $4   **MIP** $8

Lieutenant Colleen O'Reilly, 1993-94
     NM $4   **MIP** $8

LIGHT ATTACK E-FRAMES

Livanus with Troop Transport E-frame, 1993-94

    NM $12   **MIP** $25

Maggie Weston with Field Repair E-frame, 1993-94

    NM $12   **MIP** $25

(KP Photo, Brian Brogaard collection)

Marsala with rapid Assault E-frame, 1993-94

    NM $12   **MIP** $25

Shiva with Amphibious Assault E-frame, 1993-94

    NM $12   **MIP** $25

MINI EXO-COMMAND BATTLE SETS

Alec DeLeon and Phaeton with Vesta Space Port Battleset, 1995

    NM $4   **MIP** $8

J.T. Marsh and Typhonus with Resolute II Hangar Battleset, 1995

    NM $4   **MIP** $8

Phaeton and J.T. Marsh with Olympus Mons Command Ship Bridge Battleset, 1995

    NM $4   **MIP** $8

NEO WARRIORS

Neo Cat, 1993-94

    NM $4   **MIP** $8

Neo Lord, 1993-94

    NM $4   **MIP** $8

ROBOTECH SERIES, 3" FIGURES

Excaliber, 1995

    NM $2   **MIP** $4

Gladiator, 1995

    NM $2   **MIP** $4

RaidarX, 1995

    NM $2   **MIP** $4

Spartan, 1995

    NM $2   **MIP** $4

ROBOTECH SERIES, 7" FIGURES

Excaliber MK VI, 1995

    NM $5   **MIP** $10

Gladiator Destroid, 1995

    NM $5   **MIP** $10

RaidarX, 1995

    NM $5   **MIP** $10

Spartan Destroid, 1995

    NM $5   **MIP** $10

Zentraedi Power Armor Botoru Battalion, 1995

    NM $5   **MIP** $10

Zentraedi Power Armor Quadrono Battalion, 1995

    NM $5   **MIP** $10

ROBOTECH SERIES, VEHICLES

VeriTech Hover Tank, 1995

    NM $12   **MIP** $24

VF-IS Veritech Fighter, 1995, Playmates

    NM $8   **MIP** $15

SPACE SERIES

Exocarrier Resolute II, 1993-94, with Mini E-frames

    NM $12   **MIP** $25

Kaz Takagi, 1993-94, with ExoFighter Space E-frame

    NM $12   **MIP** $25

Thrax, 1993-94, with NeoFighter Space E-frame

    NM $12   **MIP** $25

SPECIAL MISSION E-FRAMES

Alec DeLeon, 1993-94, with All-Terrain Special Mission E-frame

    NM $8   **MIP** $15

J.T. Marsh, 1993-94, with Deep Space Special Mission E-frame

    NM $8   **MIP** $15

Typhonus, 1993-94, with Deep Submergence Special Mission E-frame

    NM $8   **MIP** $15

Wolf Ronski, 1993-94, with Subterranean Special Mission E-frame

    NM $8   **MIP** $15

EXTREME GHOSTBUSTERS (TRENDMASTERS, 1997-98)

FIGURES

Eduardo, 1997

    NM $2   **MIP** $4

Eduardo, Deluxe edition, 1997

    NM $2   **MIP** $4

Egon, 1997

    NM $2   **MIP** $4

Egon, Deluxe edition, 1997

    NM $2   **MIP** $4

House Ghost, 1997

    NM $2   **MIP** $4

Kylie, 1997

    NM $2   **MIP** $4

Kylie, Deluxe edition, 1997

    NM $2   **MIP** $4

Mouth Critter, 1997

    NM $2   **MIP** $4

Roland, 1997

    NM $2   **MIP** $4

Roland, Deluxe edition, 1997

    NM $2   **MIP** $4

Sam Hain, 1997

    NM $2   **MIP** $4

Slimer, 1997

    NM $2   **MIP** $4

VEHICLES AND ACCESSORIES

Ecto 1, 1997

    NM $12   **MIP** $24

Eduardo with Motorcycle, 1998

    NM $4   **MIP** $8

Roland and Gyro-Copter, 1998

    NM $4   **MIP** $8

FANTASTIC FOUR (TOY BIZ, 1995)

10" BOXED FIGURES

Dr. Doom, 1995, Toy Biz

    NM $6   **MIP** $12

Human Torch, 1995, Toy Biz

    NM $6   **MIP** $12

Silver Surfer, 1995, Toy Biz

    NM $10   **MIP** $15

The Thing, 1995, Toy Biz

    NM $6   **MIP** $12

5" FIGURES

Annihilus, 1995, Toy Biz

    NM $3   **MIP** $10

Attuma, 1995, Toy Biz

    NM $3   **MIP** $10

Black Bolt, 1995, Toy Biz

    NM $3   **MIP** $10

Blastaar, 1995, Toy Biz

    NM $3   **MIP** $10

Dr. Doom, 1995, Toy Biz

    NM $3   **MIP** $10

Dragon Man, 1995, Toy Biz

    NM $3   **MIP** $10

Firelord, 1995, Toy Biz

    NM $3   **MIP** $10

Gorgon, 1995, Toy Biz

    NM $3   **MIP** $10

Human Torch, 1995, Toy Biz

    NM $3   **MIP** $10

Invisible Woman, 1995, Toy Biz

    NM $10   **MIP** $20

Mole Man, 1995, Toy Biz

    NM $5   **MIP** $10

Mr. Fantastic, 1995, Toy Biz

    NM $3   **MIP** $10

ACTION FIGURES

Namor the Sub-Mariner, 1995, Toy Biz
  NM $3   **MIP** $10

Silver Surfer, 1995, Toy Biz
  NM $6   **MIP** $10

Super Skrull, 1995, Toy Biz
  NM $3   **MIP** $10

Terrax, 1995, Toy Biz
  NM $3   **MIP** $10

Thanos, 1995, Toy Biz
  NM $3   **MIP** $10

Thing, 1995, Toy Biz
  NM $5   **MIP** $10

Thing II, 1995, Toy Biz
  NM $5   **MIP** $10

Triton, 1995, Toy Biz
  NM $3   **MIP** $10

ELECTRONIC 14" FIGURES

Galactus, 1995, Toy Biz
  NM $10   **MIP** $40

Talking Thing, 1995, Toy Biz
  NM $10   **MIP** $20

VEHICLES

Fantasticar, 1995, Toy Biz
  NM $15   **MIP** $35

Mr. Fantastic Sky Shuttle, 1995, Toy Biz
  NM $7   **MIP** $15

The Thing's Sky Cycle, 1995, Toy Biz
  NM $7   **MIP** $15

FLASH GORDON (MEGO, 1976)

9" FIGURES

Dale Arden, 1976, Mego
  NM $35   **MIP** $85

Dr. Zarkow, 1976, Mego
  NM $55   **MIP** $110

Flash Gordon, 1976, Mego
  NM $55   **MIP** $110

Ming the Merciless, 1976, Mego
  NM $30   **MIP** $85

PLAY SETS

Flash Gordon Play Set, 1976, Mego
  NM $55   **MIP** $125

FLASH GORDON (MATTEL, 1979)

FIGURE SETS

Bad Guys Set, 1979, Mattel, 3 figures:
Ming, Lizard Woman, Beastman,
JCPenny exclusive
  NM $30   **MIP** $75

Sears Set #1, 1979, Mattel, four figures:
Dr. Zarkhov, Ming, Vultan, Beastman,
#59353, Sears exclusive
  NM $30   **MIP** $75

Sears Set #2, 1979, Mattel, four figures:
Flash, Thun, Arak, Lizard Woman,
#59357, Sears exclusive
  NM $30   **MIP** $75

FIGURES

Beastman, 1979, Mattel, Series 2, no
accessories
  NM $5   **MIP** $12

Captain Arak, 1979, Mattel, Series 3, no
accessories
  NM $7   **MIP** $14

Dr. Zarkhov, 1979, Mattel, Series 2, no
accessories
  NM $5   **MIP** $12

Flash Gordon, 1979, Mattel, Series 1,
white gun
  NM $5   **MIP** $12

Lizard Woman, 1979, Mattel, Series 1,
white staff
  NM $5   **MIP** $12

Ming the Merciless, 1979, Mattel, Series 1,
white gun
  NM $5   **MIP** $12

Thun, the Lion Man, 1979, Mattel, Series 1,
white staff
  NM $5   **MIP** $12

Vultan, 1979, Mattel, Series 3, detachable
wings
  NM $10   **MIP** $22

VEHICLES

Ming's Shuttle, 1979, Mattel, plastic,
scarce, includes blue cannon
  NM $30   **MIP** $75

Rocket Ship, 1979, Mattel, plastic
inflatable ship, detachable cockpit,
orange nose cone cannon
  NM $25   **MIP** $55

FLINTSTONES (MATTEL, 1994)

FIGURES

Betty and Bamm Bamm, 1994, Mattel
  NM $1   **MIP** $2

Big Shot Fred, 1994, Mattel
  NM $1   **MIP** $2

Evil Cliff Vandercave, 1994, Mattel
  NM $1   **MIP** $2

Filling Station Barney, 1994, Mattel
  NM $1   **MIP** $2

Hard Hat Fred, 1994, Mattel
  NM $1   **MIP** $2

Lawn Bowling Barney, 1994, Mattel
  NM $1   **MIP** $2

Licking Dino, 1994, Mattel
  NM $1   **MIP** $2

Wilma and Pebbles, 1994, Mattel
  NM $1   **MIP** $2

GARGOYLES   (KENNER, 1995)

ACCESSORIES

Gargoyle Castle, 1995, Kenner
  NM $20   **MIP** $40

Night Striker, 1995, Kenner
  NM $10   **MIP** $20

Rippin' Rider Cycle, 1995, Kenner
  NM $7   **MIP** $12

FIGURES

Battle Goliath, 1995, Kenner
  NM $3   **MIP** $15

Broadway, 1995, Kenner
  NM $3   **MIP** $15

Bronx, 1995, Kenner
  NM $3   **MIP** $15

Brooklyn, 1995, Kenner
  NM $4   **MIP** $15

Claw Climber Goliath, 1995, Kenner
  NM $3   **MIP** $15

Demona, 1995, Kenner
  NM $4   **MIP** $15

Lexington, 1995, Kenner
  NM $3   **MIP** $15

Mighty Roar Goliath, 1995, Kenner
  NM $5   **MIP** $15

Power Wing Goliath, 1995, Kenner
  NM $5   **MIP** $15

Quick Strike Goliath, 1995, Kenner
  NM $3   **MIP** $15

Steel Clan Robot, 1995, Kenner
  NM $3   **MIP** $15

Stone Armor Goliath, 1995, Kenner
  NM $5   **MIP** $15

Strike Hammer Macbeth, 1995, Kenner
  NM $3   **MIP** $15

Xanatos, 1995, Kenner
  NM $3   **MIP** $15

GENERATION X (TOY BIZ, 1995-96)

FRESHMAN, 5" FIGURES

Chamber, 1995
  NM $2   **MIP** $6

Emplate, 1995, Toy Biz
  NM $2   **MIP** $6

Jubilee, 1995, Toy Biz
  NM $2   **MIP** $6

Penance, 1995, Toy Biz
  NM $2   **MIP** $6

Phalanx, 1995, Toy Biz
  NM $2   **MIP** $6

Skin, 1995, Toy Biz
  NM $2   **MIP** $7

SOPHOMORE, 5" FIGURES

Banshee, 1996, Toy Biz
  NM $3   **MIP** $8

Marrow, 1996, Toy Biz
  NM $3   **MIP** $8

Mondo, 1996, Toy Biz
  NM $3   **MIP** $8

Protector, The, 1996, Toy Biz
  NM $3   **MIP** $8

White Queen, 1996, Toy Biz
  NM $3   **MIP** $8

GHOST RIDER (TOY BOZ, 1995)

10" FIGURES

Blaze, 1995
    NM $4   **MIP** $8

Ghost Rider, 1995
    NM $4   **MIP** $8

Vengence, 1995
    NM $4   **MIP** $8

5" FIGURES

Blackout, 1995
    NM $2   **MIP** $6

Blaze, 1995
    NM $2   **MIP** $6

Ghost Rider, 1995
    NM $2   **MIP** $6

Skinner, 1995
    NM $2   **MIP** $6

Vengence, 1995
    NM $2   **MIP** $6

Zarathos, 1995
    NM $2   **MIP** $6

FLAMIN' STUNT CYCLES WITH MOLDED-ON FIGURES

Blaze, 1995
    NM $4   **MIP** $8

Ghost Rider, 1995
    NM $4   **MIP** $8

Vengeance, 1995
    NM $4   **MIP** $8

PLAY SETS

Ghost Rider Play Set, 1995
    NM $8   **MIP** $20

SPIRIT OF VENGEANCE MOTORCYCLES AND FIGURES

Blaze, 1995, Toy Biz
    NM $4   **MIP** $8

Ghost Rider, 1995, Toy Biz
    NM $4   **MIP** $8

Vengence, 1995
    NM $4   **MIP** $8

GHOSTBUSTERS (KENNER, 1986-91)

1986

Bad to the Bone Ghost, 1986-91, Kenner
    NM $5   **MIP** $15

Banshee Bomber Gooper Ghost with Ecto-Plazm, 1986-91, Kenner
    NM $5   **MIP** $15

Bug-Eye Ghost, 1986-91, Kenner
    NM $5   **MIP** $15

Ecto-1, 1986-91, Kenner
    NM $35   **MIP** $80

Egon Spengler & Gulper Ghost, 1986-91, Kenner, 5-1/4" tall
    NM $6   **MIP** $15

Firehouse Headquarters, 1986-91, Kenner
    NM $25   **MIP** $50

Ghost Pooper, 1986-91, Kenner
    NM $5   **MIP** $10

Ghost Zapper, 1986-91, Kenner
    NM $5   **MIP** $15

Gooper Ghost Sludge Bucket, 1986-91, Kenner
    NM $5   **MIP** $15

Gooper Ghost Squisher with Ecto-Plazm, 1986-91, Kenner
    NM $5   **MIP** $15

H2 Ghost, 1986-91, Kenner
    NM $5   **MIP** $15

Peter Venkman & Grabber Ghost, 1986-91, Kenner
    NM $6   **MIP** $15

Proton Pack, 1986-91, Kenner
    NM $20   **MIP** $40

Ray Stantz & Wrapper Ghost, 1986-91, Kenner
    NM $6   **MIP** $15

Slimer Plush Figure, 1986-91, Kenner
    NM $20   **MIP** $35

Slimer with Pizza, 1986-91, Kenner
    NM $20   **MIP** $40

Stay-Puft Marshmallow Man Plush, 1986-91, Kenner, plush
    NM $15   **MIP** $30

Winston Zeddmore & Chomper Ghost, 1986-91, Kenner
    NM $7   **MIP** $18

1988

Brain Blaster Ghost Haunted Human, 1986-91, Kenner
    NM $5   **MIP** $15

Ecto-2 Helicopter, 1986-91, Kenner
    NM $5   **MIP** $15

Fright Feature Egon, 1986-91, Kenner
    NM $5   **MIP** $15

Fright Feature Janine Melnitz, 1986-91, Kenner
    NM $5   **MIP** $15

Fright Feature Peter, 1986-91, Kenner
    NM $5   **MIP** $15

Fright Feature Ray, 1986-91, Kenner
    NM $5   **MIP** $15

Fright Feature Winston, 1986-91, Kenner
    NM $5   **MIP** $15

Gooper Ghost Slimer, 1986-91, Kenner
    NM $12   **MIP** $25

Granny Gross Haunted Human, 1986-91, Kenner
    NM $5   **MIP** $15

Hard Hat Horror Haunted Human, 1986-91, Kenner
    NM $5   **MIP** $15

Highway Haunter, 1986-91, Kenner
    NM $10   **MIP** $20

Mail Fraud Haunted Human, 1986-91, Kenner
    NM $5   **MIP** $15

Mini Ghost Mini-Gooper, 1986-91, Kenner
    NM $5   **MIP** $10

Mini Ghost Mini-Shooter, 1986-91, Kenner
    NM $5   **MIP** $10

Mini Ghost Mini-Trap, 1986-91, Kenner
    NM $5   **MIP** $10

Pull Speed Ahead Ghost, 1986-91, Kenner
    NM $5   **MIP** $15

Terror Trash Haunted Human, 1986-91, Kenner
    NM $5   **MIP** $15

Tombstone Tackle Haunted Human, 1986-91, Kenner
    NM $5   **MIP** $15

X-Cop Haunted Human, 1986-91, Kenner
    NM $5   **MIP** $15

1989

Dracula, 1986-91, Kenner
    NM $5   **MIP** $15

Ecto-3, 1986-91, Kenner
    NM $5   **MIP** $15

Fearsome Flush, 1986-91, Kenner
    NM $5   **MIP** $10

Frankenstein, 1986-91, Kenner
    NM $3   **MIP** $15

Hunchback, 1986-91, Kenner
    NM $3   **MIP** $15

Mummy, 1986-91, Kenner
    NM $3   **MIP** $15

Screaming Hero Egon, 1986-91, Kenner
    NM $5   **MIP** $15

Screaming Hero Janine Melnitz, 1986-91, Kenner
    NM $5   **MIP** $15

Screaming Hero Peter, 1986-91, Kenner
    NM $5   **MIP** $15

Screaming Hero Ray, 1986-91, Kenner
    NM $5   **MIP** $15

Screaming Hero Winston, 1986-91, Kenner
    NM $5   **MIP** $15

Slimer with Proton Pack, red or blue, 1986-91, Kenner, red or blue
    NM $15   **MIP** $35

Super Fright Egon with Slimy Spider, 1986-91, Kenner
    NM $5   **MIP** $15

Super Fright Janine with Boo Fish Ghost, 1986-91, Kenner
    NM $5   **MIP** $15

Super Fright Peter Venkman & Snake Head, 1986-91, Kenner
    NM $5   **MIP** $15

Super Fright Ray, 1986-91, Kenner
    NM $5   **MIP** $15

Super Fright Winston Zeddmore & Meanie Wienie, 1986-91, Kenner
    NM $5   **MIP** $15

ACTION FIGURES

Wolfman, 1986-91, Kenner
NM $5   MIP $15

Zombie, 1986-91, Kenner
NM $5   MIP $15

1990

Ecto Bomber with Bomber Ghost, 1986-91, Kenner
NM $5   MIP $15

Ecto-1A with Ambulance Ghost, 1986-91, Kenner
NM $20   MIP $40

Ghost Sweeper, 1986-91, Kenner, vehicle in box
NM $5   MIP $15

Gobblin' Goblin Nasty Neck, 1986-91, Kenner
NM $6   MIP $15

Gobblin' Goblin Terrible Teeth, 1986-91, Kenner, boxed action figure
NM $6   MIP $15

Gobblin' Goblin Terror Tongue, 1986-91, Kenner, boxed action figure
NM $6   MIP $15

Slimed Hero Egon, 1986-91, Kenner
NM $5   MIP $15

Slimed Hero Louis Tully & Four Eyed Ghost, 1986-91, Kenner
NM $5   MIP $15

Slimed Hero Peter Venkman & Tooth Ghost, 1986-91, Kenner
NM $5   MIP $15

Slimed Hero Ray Stantz & Vapor Ghost, 1986-91, Kenner
NM $5   MIP $15

Slimed Hero Winston, 1986-91, Kenner, boxed action figure
NM $5   MIP $15

1991

Ecto-Glow Egon, 1986-91, Kenner
NM $10   MIP $30

Ecto-Glow Louis Tully, 1986-91, Kenner
NM $10   MIP $30

Ecto-Glow Peter, 1986-91, Kenner
NM $10   MIP $30

Ecto-Glow Ray, 1986-91, Kenner
NM $10   MIP $30

Ecto-Glow Winston Zeddmore, 1986-91, Kenner
NM $10   MIP $30

GHOSTBUSTERS, FILMATION (SCHAPER, 1986)

FIGURES

Belfry and Brat-A-Rat, 1986, Schaper
NM $10   MIP $15

Bone Troller, 1986, Schaper
NM $10   MIP $15

Eddie, 1986, Schaper
NM $10   MIP $15

Fangster, 1986, Schaper
NM $10   MIP $15

Fib Face, 1986, Schaper
NM $10   MIP $15

Futura, 1986, Schaper
NM $10   MIP $15

Ghost Popper Ghost Buggy, 1986, Schaper
NM $20   MIP $40

Haunter, 1986, Schaper
NM $10   MIP $15

Jake, 1986, Schaper
NM $10   MIP $15

Jessica, 1986, Schaper
NM $10   MIP $15

Mysteria, 1986, Schaper
NM $10   MIP $15

Prime Evil, 1986, Schaper
NM $10   MIP $15

Scare Scooter Vehicle, 1986, Schaper
NM $10   MIP $20

Scared Stiff, 1986, Schaper
NM $6   MIP $15

Tracy, 1986, Schaper
NM $10   MIP $15

VEHICLES

Time Hopper Vehicle, 1986, Schaper
NM $10   MIP $15

GODZILLA (TRENDMASTERS, 1998-PRESENT)

FIGURES

Baby X Baby Godzilla, 1998-Present
NM $3   MIP $8

Capture Net Phillipe, 1996-Present
NM $2   MIP $8

Claw Slashing Baby Godzilla, 1996-Present
NM $3   MIP $6

Combat Claw Godzilla, 1996-Present
NM $8   MIP $16

Double Blast O'Neil, 1998-present
NM $3   MIP $7

Fang Bite Godzilla, 1998-present
NM $3   MIP $7

Grapple Gear Nick, 1998-present
NM $3   MIP $7

Hammer Tail Baby Godzilla Hatchling, 1998-present
NM $3   MIP $7

Living Godzilla, 1998-present
NM $10   MIP $25

Monster Claw Baby Godzilla Hatching, 1998-present
NM $3   MIP $7

Nuclear Strike Godzilla vs. Hornet Jet, 1998-present
NM $3   MIP $7

Power Shield Jean-Luc, 1998-present
NM $3   MIP $7

Razor Bite Godzilla, 1998-present
NM $10   MIP $25

Razor Fang Baby Godzilla, 1998-present
NM $3   MIP $7

Shatter Blast Godzilla vs. Rocket Launcher, 1998-present
NM $3   MIP $7

Shatter Tail Godzilla, 1998-present
NM $7   MIP $15

Spike Jaw Baby Godzilla Hatchling, 1998-present
NM $3   MIP $7

Supreme Godzilla, 1998-present
NM $15   MIP $30

Tail Thrasher Baby Godzilla, 1998-present
NM $3   MIP $7

Thunder Tail Godzilla, 1998-present
NM $7   MIP $15

Ultimate Godzilla, 1998-present
NM $12   MIP $30

Ultra Attack Animal, 1998-present
NM $3   MIP $7

VEHICLES

All-Terrain Vehicle with figure, 1998-present
NM $7   MIP $15

Apache Attack Copter, 1998-present
NM $10   MIP $20

Battle Bike with figure, 1998-present
NM $7   MIP $15

Battle Blaster with figure, 1998-present
NM $7   MIP $15

Combat Cannon with figure, 1998-present
NM $7   MIP $15

Thunderblast Tank, 1998-present
NM $7   MIP $15

GODZILLA WARS (TRENDMASTERS, 1996)

FIGURES

Battra, 1996
NM $4   MIP $8

Biollante, 1996
NM $4   MIP $8

Gigan, 1996
NM $4   MIP $8

Moguera, 1996
NM $5   MIP $10

Space Godzilla, 1996
NM $5   MIP $10

Supercharged Godzilla, 1996
NM $4   MIP $8

GODZILLA: KING OF THE MONSTERS

10" FIGURES

Ghidorah, 1995
NM $4   MIP $10

Ghidorah, walking, 1995
NM $6   MIP $12

Godzilla, 1995
NM $4   MIP $10

Godzilla, walking, 1995
NM $7   MIP $15

Mecha-Ghidora, 1995
    NM $6   **MIP** $12

Mecha-Godzilla, 1995
    NM $6   **MIP** $12

Mothra, 1995
    NM $8   **MIP** $16

Rodan, 1995
    NM $4   **MIP** $10

4-6" FIGURES

Biollante, 1995
    NM $4   **MIP** $8

Ghidorah, boxed, 1995
    NM $4   **MIP** $8

Ghidorah, carded, 1995
    NM $5   **MIP** $10

Gigan, 1995
    NM $5   **MIP** $10

Godzilla, boxed, 1995
    NM $4   **MIP** $8

Mecha-Ghidorah, boxed, 1995
    NM $4   **MIP** $8

Mecha-Ghidorah, carded, 1995
    NM $3   **MIP** $6

Mecha-Godzilla, boxed, 1995
    NM $4   **MIP** $8

Mecha-Godzilla, carded, 1995
    NM $3   **MIP** $6

Moguera, 1995
    NM $4   **MIP** $10

Mothra, boxed, 1995
    NM $5   **MIP** $10

Mothra, carded, 1995
    NM $4   **MIP** $8

Rodan, boxed, 1995
    NM $4   **MIP** $8

Rodan, carded, 1995
    NM $3   **MIP** $6

FIGURES

Battra, 1995
    NM $4   **MIP** $8

GREATEST AMERICAN HERO, THE (MEGO, 1981)

VEHICLES

Convertible Bug with Ralph and Bill figures, 1981, Mego
    NM $150   **MIP** $450

HAPPY DAYS (MEGO, 1978)

FIGURES

Fonzie, boxed, 1978, Mego
    NM $30   **MIP** $100

Fonzie, carded, 1978, Mego
    NM $30   **MIP** $75

Potsie, carded, 1978, Mego
    NM $30   **MIP** $75

(Lenny Lee)

Ralph, carded, 1978, Mego
    NM $30   **MIP** $75

Richie, carded, 1978, Mego
    NM $30   **MIP** $75

PLAY SETS

Fonzie's Garage Play Set, 1978, Mego
    NM $60   **MIP** $150

VEHICLES

Fonzie's Jalopy, 1978, Mego
    NM $40   **MIP** $80

Fonzie's Motorcycle, 1978, Mego
    NM $40   **MIP** $80

HE-MAN 2ND ANIMATED SERIES (MATTEL, 1989-1992)

ACCESSORIES

Electronic Terror Punch, 1992, Mattel
    NM $4   **MIP** $10

Electronic Thunder Punch, 1992, Mattel
    NM $4   **MIP** $10

Power Sword, 1989, Mattel
    NM $10   **MIP** $20

Rocket Disk Power Pack, 1989, Mattel
    NM $4   **MIP** $8

Sagitar (Tharkus), 1991, Mattel, creature
    NM $10   **MIP** $20

Skull Staff, 1991, Mattel
    NM $10   **MIP** $20

Turbo Tormentor, 1989, Mattel
    NM $4   **MIP** $8

FIGURES

Artilla (Weaponstronic), 1991, Mattel, Series 3
    NM $5   **MIP** $15

Battle Blade Skeletor, 1992, Mattel, Series 4
    NM $5   **MIP** $12

Battle Punching He-Man, 1990, Mattel, Series 2
    NM $5   **MIP** $15

Butthead, 1991, Mattel, Series 3
    NM $5   **MIP** $15

Disk of Doom Skeletor, 1990, Mattel, Series 2
    NM $5   **MIP** $15

Flipshot (Icarius), 1989, Mattel, Series 1
    NM $5   **MIP** $25

Flogg (Brakk), 1989, Mattel, Series 1
    NM $5   **MIP** $25

He-Man, 1989, Mattel, Series 1
    NM $6   **MIP** $12

He-Man with Flogg, 1989, Mattel, Series 1
    NM $7   **MIP** $18

He-Man with Skeletor, 1989, Mattel, Series 1
    NM $7   **MIP** $20

He-Man with Slush Head, 1989, Mattel, Series 1
    NM $7   **MIP** $20

Hoove, 1990, Mattel, Series 2
    NM $5   **MIP** $15

Hydron, 1989, Mattel, Series 1
    NM $5   **MIP** $25

Kalamarr, 1989, Mattel, Series 1
    NM $6   **MIP** $12

Karatti, 1991, Mattel, Series 3
    NM $6   **MIP** $12

Kayo (Tartarus), 1990, Mattel, Series 2
    NM $5   **MIP** $15

Lizorr, 1990, Mattel, Series 2
    NM $5   **MIP** $15

Missile Armor Flipshot Hook 'em Flogg, 1992, Mattel
    NM $5   **MIP** $12

Nocturna, 1990, Mattel, Series 2
    NM $5   **MIP** $15

Optikk, 1990, Mattel, Seires 2
    NM $5   **MIP** $15

Quakke (Earthquake), 1991, Mattel, Series 3
    NM $5   **MIP** $15

Skeletor, 1989, Mattel, Series 1
    NM $6   **MIP** $12

Slush Head (Kalamarr), 1989, Mattel, Series 1
    NM $5   **MIP** $25

Spin-Fist Hydron, 1992, Mattel, Series 4
    NM $5   **MIP** $12

Spinwit (Tornado), 1991, Mattel, Series 3
    NM $5   **MIP** $15

Staghorn, 1991, Mattel, Series 3
    NM $5   **MIP** $15

Thunder Punch He-Man, 1992, Mattel, Series 4
    NM $5   **MIP** $12

Too-Tall Hoove, 1992, Mattel, Series 4
    NM $5   **MIP** $12

Tuskador (Insyzor), 1991, Mattel, Series 3
    NM $5   **MIP** $15

Vizar, 1990, Mattel, Series 2
    NM $5   **MIP** $15

PLAY SETS

Nordor, 1990, Mattel
    NM $100   **MIP** $250

Starship Eternia, 1989, Mattel
    NM $100   **MIP** $250

VEHICLES

Astrosub, 1989, Mattel
 NM $10 MIP $20

Battle Bird, 1991, Mattel
 NM $10 MIP $20

Bolajet, 1989, Mattel
 NM $10 MIP $20

Doomcopter (Skullcopter), 1991, Mattel
 NM $10 MIP $20

Dreadwing (Shuttlepod), 1989, Mattel
 NM $5 MIP $15

Sagitar, 1989-91, Mattel
 NM $6 MIP $14

Terrorclaw (Terrapod), 1989, Mattel
 NM $5 MIP $15

Terrortread (Dreadtread), 1991, Mattel
 NM $10 MIP $20

HE-MAN REISSUES (MATTEL, 2000-01)

ACCESSORIES

He-Man with Battle Cat, 2000, Mattel, Series 1
 NM $20 MIP $50

Skeletor with Panthor, 2000, Mattel, Series 1
 NM $20 MIP $50

FIGURES

Battle Armor He-Man, 2001, Mattel, Series 2
 NM $5 MIP $15

Battle Armor Skeletor, 2001, Mattel, Series 2
 NM $5 MIP $15

Beast Man, 2000, Mattel, Series 1
 NM $5 MIP $15

Buzz Off, 2001, Mattel, Series 2
 NM $5 MIP $15

Clawful, 2001, Mattel, Series 2
 NM $5 MIP $15

Evil-Lyn, 2000, Mattel, Series 1
 NM $5 MIP $15

Faker, 2000, Mattel, Series 1
 NM $5 MIP $17

He-Man, 2000, Mattel, Series 1
 NM $10 MIP $20

Man-At-Arms, 2000, Mattel, Series 1
 NM $5 MIP $15

Mer-Man, 2000, Mattel, Series 1
 NM $5 MIP $15

Skeletor, 2000, Mattel, Series 1
 NM $10 MIP $20

Stratos, 2001, Mattel, Series 2
 NM $5 MIP $15

Teela, 2000, Mattel, Series 1
 NM $5 MIP $15

Trap Jaw, 2000, Mattel, Series 1
 NM $5 MIP $15

Tri-Klops, 2000, Mattel, Series 1
 NM $5 MIP $15

Zodac, 2001, Mattel, Series 2
 NM $5 MIP $15

GIFTSETS

Figure 10-pack, JC Penney exclusive, 2001, Mattel, Series 2
 NM $75 MIP $150

Figure 5-pack w/ exclusive Moss Man, 2001, Mattel, Series 2
 NM $25 MIP $50

Figure 5-pack w/ exclusive Prince Adam, 2001, Mattel, Series 2
 NM $25 MIP $50

HERCULES: THE LEGEND CONTINUES (TOY BIZ, 1995-97)

DELUXE 10" FIGURES

Hercules and Xena, 1995-96, ToyBiz
 NM $20 MIP $40

FIGURES

Ares, Detachable Weapons of War, 1995-96, ToyBiz
 NM $3 MIP $5

Centaur, Bug Horse Kick, 1995-96, ToyBiz
 NM $3 MIP $5

Hercules I, Iron Spiked Spinning Mace, 1995-96, ToyBiz
 NM $3 MIP $5

Hercules II, Archery Combat Set, 1995-96, ToyBiz
 NM $3 MIP $5

Hercules III, Herculean Assault Blades, 1995-96, ToyBiz
 NM $3 MIP $6

Hercules with Chain Breaking Strength, 1995-96, ToyBiz
 NM $3 MIP $5

Hercules, Swash Buckling, 1995-96, ToyBiz
 NM $3 MIP $5

Iolaus, Catapult Battle Gear, 1995-96, ToyBiz
 NM $3 MIP $5

Minotaur, Immobilizing Sludge Mask, 1995-96, ToyBiz
 NM $3 MIP $6

Mole-Man, Exploding Body, 1995-96, ToyBiz
 NM $3 MIP $5

She-Demon, Stone Strike Tail, 1995-96, ToyBiz
 NM $4 MIP $8

Xena, Warrior Princess Weaponry, 1995-96, ToyBiz
 NM $5 MIP $25

MONSTERS

Cerberus, 1995-96, ToyBiz
 NM $4 MIP $10

Echidna, 1995-96, ToyBiz
 NM $4 MIP $10

Graegus, 1995-96, ToyBiz
 NM $4 MIP $10

Hydra, 1995-96, ToyBiz
 NM $4 MIP $10

Labyrinth Snake, 1995-96, ToyBiz
 NM $4 MIP $10

Stymphalian Bird, 1995-96, ToyBiz
 NM $4 MIP $10

PLAY SETS

Hercules Tower of Power Play Set, 1995-96, ToyBiz
 NM $4 MIP $10

HERCULES: THE LEGENDARY JOURNEYS (TOY BIZ, 1995-97)

DELUXE 10" FIGURES

Hercules with bladed shield and sword dagger, 1997, ToyBiz
 NM $8 MIP $20

Xena with two sets of body armor, 1997, ToyBiz
 NM $8 MIP $20

LEGENDARY WARRIOR TWIN PACKS, 5" FIGURES

Hercules and Iolaus, 1997, ToyBiz
 NM $8 MIP $20

Hercules and Xena, 1997, ToyBiz
 NM $8 MIP $20

Xena and Gabrielle, 1997, ToyBiz
 NM $10 MIP $40

LEGENDARY WARRIORS, 5" FIGURES

Hercules, Mace Hurling Hercules, 1997, ToyBiz
 NM $3 MIP $8

Iolaus, Catapult Back-pack Iolaus, 1997, ToyBiz
 NM $4 MIP $12

Nessus, Leg Kicking Centaur, 1997, ToyBiz
 NM $3 MIP $8

Xena, Temptress Costume Xena, 1997, ToyBiz
 NM $4 MIP $12

MONSTERS, 6" FIGURES

Cerberus, 1997, ToyBiz
 NM $3 MIP $10

Graegus, 1997, ToyBiz
 NM $3 MIP $10

Hydra, 1997, ToyBiz
 NM $3 MIP $10

MT. OLYMPUS GAMES, 5" FIGURES

Atlanta, Spear Shooting Weaponry Rack, 1997, ToyBiz
 NM $4 MIP $12

Hercules, Discus Launcher, 1997, ToyBiz
 NM $3 MIP $8

Mesomorph, Shield Attack Action, 1997, ToyBiz
 NM $3 MIP $8

Salmoneus, Light-up Olympic Torch, 1997, ToyBiz
NM $3   MIP $8

HEROES OF THE AMERICAN REVOLUTION (BONANZA, 1970S)

FIGURES

Benjamin Franklin, Bonanza
NM $10   MIP $25

Daniel Boone, Bonanza
NM $10   MIP $25

George Washington, Bonanza
NM $10   MIP $25

John Paul Jones, Bonanza
NM $10   MIP $25

Marquis de Lafayette, Bonanza
NM $10   MIP $25

Nathan Hale, Bonanza
NM $10   MIP $25

Patrick Henry, Bonanza
NM $10   MIP $25

Paul Revere, Bonanza
NM $10   MIP $25

Thomas Jefferson, Bonanza
NM $10   MIP $25

HONEY WEST (GILBERT, 1965)

ACCESSORIES

Formal Outfit, 1965, 1965
NM $55   MIP $110

Honey West Accessory Set, 1965, Gilbert, telephone purse, lipstick, handcuffs and telescope
NM $45   MIP $85

Honey West Accessory Set, 1965, Gilbert, cap-firing pistol, binoculars, shoes and glasses
NM $45   MIP $85

Karate Outfit, 1965, Gilbert
NM $50   MIP $100

Pet Set with Ocelot, 1965, Gilbert
NM $60   MIP $100

Secret Agent Outfit, 1965, Gilbert
NM $50   MIP $95

FIGURES

Honey West Doll, 1965, Gilbert
NM $175   MIP $325

HOOK (MATTEL, 1991-92)

DELUXE FIGURES

Captain Hook, Skull Armor, 1991-92
NM $10   MIP $25

Lost Boy Attack Croc, 1991-92
NM $8   MIP $18

Pete Pan, Learn to Fly, 1991-92
NM $10   MIP $25

FIGURES

Captain Hook, Multi-blade, 1991-92
NM $4   MIP $10

Captain Hook, Swiss Army, 1991-92
NM $8   MIP $18

Captain Hook, Tall Terror, 1991-92
NM $4   MIP $10

Lost Boy Ace, 1991-92
NM $3   MIP $10

Lost Boy Ruffio, 1991-92, Mattel
NM $3   MIP $10

Lost Boy Thud Butt, 1991-92
NM $8   MIP $18

Peter Pan, Air Attack, 1991-92
NM $4   MIP $10

Peter Pan, Battle Swing, 1991-92
NM $5   MIP $15

Peter Pan, Food Fighting, 1991-92
NM $5   MIP $15

Peter Pan, Swashbuckling, 1991-92
NM $4   MIP $10

Pirate Bill Jukes, 1991-92
NM $4   MIP $10

Pirate Smee, 1991-92
NM $5   MIP $12

VEHICLES

Lost Boy Attack Raft, 1991-92
NM $8   MIP $20

Lost Boy Strike Tank, 1991-92
NM $8   MIP $20

INCREDIBLE HULK, THE (TOY BIZ, 1996-97)

6" FIGURES

Abomination, Toxic Blaster, 1996
NM $5   MIP $12

Gray Hulk Battle Damaged, 1996
NM $4   MIP $10

Leader, Anti-Hulk Armor, 1996
NM $4   MIP $10

Savage Hulk, Transforming Action, 1996
NM $4   MIP $10

She Hulk, Gamma Cross Bow, 1996
NM $5   MIP $12

OUTCASTS, 5" FIGURES

Battle Hulk, Mutant Outcast, 1997
NM $2   MIP $6

Chainsaw, Gamma Outcast Bat, 1997
NM $3   MIP $7

Leader-Hulk Metamorphosized, Gargoyle Sidekick, 1997
NM $3   MIP $7

Two-Head, Gamma Outcast Kangaroo-Rat, 1997
NM $3   MIP $7

Wendingo, Gamma Outcast Rattlesnake, 1997
NM $3   MIP $7

PLAY SETS

Gamma Ray Trap, 1997
NM $3   MIP $10

Steel Body Trap, 1997
NM $3   MIP $10

SMASH AND CRASH, 5" FIGURES

Battle-Damaged Hulk with Restraints and Smash Out Action, 1997
NM $3   MIP $8

Doc Samson, Omega with Missile Firing Action, 1997
NM $3   MIP $8

Incredible Hulk, Crash out Action, 1997
NM $3   MIP $8

Leader, Evil Robot Drone with Missile Firing Action, 1997
NM $3   MIP $8

Zzzax with Energy Trap, 1997
NM $3   MIP $8

TRANSFORMATIONS, 6" FIGURES

(KP Photo)

Absorbing Man, Breakaway Safe and Wrecking Ball, 1997, Includes accessories
NM $3   MIP $8

Hulk 2099, Futuristic Clip-on Weapons, 1997
NM $3   MIP $8

(KP Photo)

Maestro, Fallen Hero Armor, 1997, Includes Captain America's broken shield, and a belt featuring the masks of Iron Man and other Marvel characters

NM $3   MIP $8

Smart Hulk, Gamma Blaster Backpack, 1997

NM $3   MIP $8

INDEPENDENCE DAY (TRENDMASTERS, 1996)

FIGURES

Alien Attacker Pilot, 1996, Trendmasters
NM $5   MIP $10

Alien in Bio Chamber, 1996, Trendmasters
NM $8   MIP $12

Alien Science Officer, 1996, Trendmasters
NM $5   MIP $10

Alien Shock Trooper, 1996, Trendmasters
NM $5   MIP $10

Alien Supreme Commander, 1996, Trendmasters
NM $15   MIP $25

David Levinson, 1996, Trendmasters
NM $5   MIP $10

President Thomas Whitmore, 1996, Trendmasters
NM $5   MIP $10

Steve Hiller, 1996, Trendmasters
NM $5   MIP $10

Ultimate Alien Commander, 1996, Trendmasters, FAO Schwarz Exclusive
NM $20   MIP $35

Weapons Expert, 1996, Trendmasters
NM $10   MIP $20

Zero Gravity, 1996, Trendmasters
NM $8   MIP $15

INDIANA JONES (TOYS MCCOY, 1999)

12" FIGURES

Arabian Horse, 1999
NM $150   MIP $450

Indiana Jones, 1999
NM $250   MIP $750

INDIANA JONES AND THE TEMPLE OF DOOM (LJN, 1984)

FIGURES

(Toy Shop File Photo)

Giant Thugee, 1984, LJN, On the right
NM $45   MIP $75

(Toy Shop File Photo)

Indiana Jones, 1984, LJN, Shown in the center
NM $65   MIP $150

(Toy Shop File Photo)

Mola Ram, 1984, LJN, On the left. These figures didn't enjoy as much popularity at the time, probably reflecting the public's mood about the film
NM $55   MIP $80

INDIANA JONES, THE ADVENTURES OF (KENNER, 1982-1983)

12" FIGURES

(Toy Shop File Photo)

Indiana Jones, 12", 1982-83, Kenner, Includes leather jacket, fedora, bullwhip and pistol, Model No. 46000
NM $150   MIP $300

4" FIGURES

Belloq, 1982-83, Kenner
NM $25   MIP $65

Belloq in Ceremonial Robe Carded, 1982-83, Kenner
NM $20   MIP $500

Belloq in Ceremonial Robe, mail away, 1982-83, Kenner
NM $20   MIP $45

Cairo Swordsman, 1982-83, Kenner
NM $15   MIP $40

German Mechanic, 1982-83, Kenner
NM $25   MIP $75

Indiana Jones in German Uniform, 1982-83, Kenner
NM $25   MIP $90

Indiana Jones with whip, 1982-83, Kenner, Includes fedora, leather jacket and pistol, too
NM $75   MIP $200

(Lenny Lee)

Marion Ravenwood, 1982-83, Kenner, Includes small monkee
NM $100   MIP $350

Sallah, 1982-83, Kenner
NM $30   MIP $90

(Lenny Lee)

Toht, 1982-83, Kenner, Fully poseable, black plastic overcoat and hat. Packaging has mail-in offer for ceremonial Beloq figure
NM $15   MIP $40

PLAY SETS

(Toy Shop File Photo)

Map Room Play Set, 1982-83, Kenner
NM $35   MIP $90

Streets of Cairo Play Set, 1982-83, Kenner
NM $35   MIP $90

Well of Souls Play Set, 1982-83, Kenner
NM $50   MIP $125

VEHICLES AND ACCESSORIES

Arabian Horse, 1982-83, Kenner
　　NM $75　　**MIP** $250

Convoy Truck, 1982-83, Kenner
　　NM $75　　**MIP** $150

INHUMANOIDS (HASBRO, 1986)

EARTH CORPS

Auger, 1986, Hasbro, helmet, drill
　　NM $5　　**MIP** $12

Dr. Derek Bright, 1986, Hasbro, helmet, movable claws
　　NM $5　　**MIP** $12

Herc Armstrong, 1986, Hasbro, helmet, grappling hook arm
　　NM $5　　**MIP** $12

Liquidator, 1986, Hasbro, helmet, water shooting backpack
　　NM $5　　**MIP** $12

INHUMANOIDS

D. Compose, 1986, Hasbro, opening ribcage
　　NM $12　　**MIP** $25

Metlar, 1986, Hasbro, Inhumanoid leader
　　NM $12　　**MIP** $25

Tendrill, 1986, Hasbro, movable tentacles
　　NM $12　　**MIP** $25

MUTORES, GRANITES

Granites, 1986, Hasbro, rock-like, tan
　　NM $6　　**MIP** $12

Granok, 1986, Hasbro, rock-like, gray
　　NM $6　　**MIP** $12

MUTORES, REDWOODS

Redlen, 1986, Hasbro, tree-like, yellow
　　NM $6　　**MIP** $12

Redsun, 1986, Hasbro, tree-like, orange-brown
　　NM $6　　**MIP** $12

The Redwoods, 1986, Hasbro, tree-like, gray
　　NM $6　　**MIP** $12

MUTROES, MAGNOKOR

Magnokor, 1986, Hasbro, splits into Crygen and Pyre
　　NM $7　　**MIP** $20

VEHICLES

Terrascout, 1986, Hasbro, movable gun, scanner
　　NM $12　　**MIP** $25

Trappeur, 1986, Hasbro, movable claw, grapping hook, hovercraft
　　NM $12　　**MIP** $25

INSPECTOR GADGET (GALOOB, 1984)

12" FIGURE

Inspector Gadget, 1984, Galoob
　　NM $55　　**MIP** $110

INSPECTOR GADGET (TIGER TOYS, 1992)

FIGURES

Dr. Claw, 1992, Tiger Toys
　　NM $8　　**MIP** $20

Inspector Gadget that Falls Apart, 1992, Tiger Toys
　　NM $5　　**MIP** $15

Inspector Gadget that Squirts Water, 1992, Tiger Toys
　　NM $5　　**MIP** $15

Inspector Gadget with Expanding Arms, 1992, Tiger Toys
　　NM $4　　**MIP** $12

Inspector Gadget with Expanding Legs, 1992, Tiger Toys
　　NM $5　　**MIP** $15

Inspector Gadget with Snap Open Hat, 1992, Tiger Toys
　　NM $5　　**MIP** $15

Inspector Gadget with Telescopic Neck, 1992, Tiger Toys
　　NM $5　　**MIP** $15

MAD Agent with Bazooka, 1992, Tiger Toys
　　NM $8　　**MIP** $20

Penny and Brain, 1992, Tiger Toys
　　NM $8　　**MIP** $20

VEHICLES

Gadgetmoile, 1992, Tiger Toys
　　NM $10　　**MIP** $30

IRON MAN (TOY BIZ, 1995-96)

5" FIGURES, 1995

Blacklash, Nunchaku and Whip-cracking Action, 1995
　　NM $3　　**MIP** $8

Blizzard, Ice-Fist Punch, 1995
　　NM $7　　**MIP** $15

Century, Cape and Battle Staff, 1995
　　NM $3　　**MIP** $8

Dreadknight, Firing Lance Action, 1995
　　NM $3　　**MIP** $8

Grey Gargoyle, Stone Hurling Action, 1995
　　NM $3　　**MIP** $8

Hawkeye, Bow and Arrow, 1995
　　NM $7　　**MIP** $15

Hulkbuster Iron Man, Removable Armor, 1995
　　NM $3　　**MIP** $8

Iron Man Arctic Armor, Removable Armor and Launching Claw Action, 1995
　　NM $3　　**MIP** $8

Iron Man Hologram, 1995, Toy Biz
　　NM $3　　**MIP** $8

Iron Man Space Armor, Power-lift Space Pack, 1995, Toy Biz
　　NM $3　　**MIP** $8

Iron Man Stealth Armor, 1995, Toy Biz
　　NM $3　　**MIP** $8

Iron Man, Hydro Armor, 1995
　　NM $4　　**MIP** $10

Iron Man, Plasma Cannon Missile Launcher, 1995
　　NM $3　　**MIP** $8

Mandarin, Light-up Power Rings, 1995
　　NM $3　　**MIP** $8

Modok, Energy Brain Blasts, 1995, Toy Biz
　　NM $3　　**MIP** $8

Spider-Woman, Psisonic Web Hurling Action, 1995
　　NM $7　　**MIP** $15

Titanium Man, Retractable Blade Action, 1995
　　NM $5　　**MIP** $12

Tony Stark, Armor Carrying Suitcase, 1995
　　NM $3　　**MIP** $8

US Agent, Firing Shield Action, 1995
　　NM $15　　**MIP** $35

War Machine, Shoulder-Mount Cannons, 1995
　　NM $3　　**MIP** $8

Whirlwind, Whirling Battle Action, 1995
　　NM $5　　**MIP** $12

5" FIGURES, 1996

Crimson Dynamo, 1996
　　NM $3　　**MIP** $8

Iron Man Inferno Armor, 1996
　　NM $3　　**MIP** $8

Iron Man Lava Armor, 1996
　　NM $3　　**MIP** $8

Iron Man Magnetic Armor, 1996
　　NM $3　　**MIP** $8

Iron Man Radiation Armor, 1996
　　NM $3　　**MIP** $8

Iron Man Samurai Armor, 1996
　　NM $3　　**MIP** $8

Iron Man Subterranean Armor, 1996
　　NM $3　　**MIP** $8

War Machine 2, 1996
　　NM $4　　**MIP** $10

DELUXE 10" FIGURES

Iron Man, 1995
　　NM $4　　**MIP** $12

Mandarin, 1995
　　NM $4　　**MIP** $12

War Machine, 1995
　　NM $4　　**MIP** $12

DELUXE DRAGONS

Argent, 1995
　　NM $7　　**MIP** $15

Aureus, 1995
　　NM $7　　**MIP** $15

FinFang Foom, 1995
　　NM $7　　**MIP** $15

ACTION FIGURES

ISLAND OF MISFIT TOYS

FIGURES

Abominable Snowman, 2002, Playing Mantis
    NM n/a   **MIP** $8

Clarice, 2002, Playing Mantis, Includes two racoons and two rabbits
    NM n/a   **MIP** $8

(KP Photo)

Hermey, 2002, Playing Mantis, With a hat, book, tools and two of Bumble's teeth
    NM n/a   **MIP** $8

(KP Photo)

Rudolph, 2002, Playing Mantis, Features a light-up nose and includes misfit doll
    NM n/a   **MIP** $8

(KP Photo)

Sam, 2002, Playing Mantis, With removeable hat, banjo and umbrella
    NM n/a   **MIP** $8

(KP Photo)

Santa Claus, 2002, Playing Mantis, Features a removeable hat, toy bag and spotted elephant
    NM n/a   **MIP** $8

(KP Photo)

Yukon Cornelius, 2002, Playing Mantis, In familiar bright orange hat, blue jacket and snowshoes. Includes knife, pick and hammer
    NM n/a   **MIP** $8

JAMES BOND SECRET AGENT 007 (GILBERT, 1965)

12" FIGURES

James Bond, 1965, Gilbert, Sean Connery likeness from "Dr. No.", white shirt, swimming trunks, goggles, snorkel, fins, gun
    NM $150   **MIP** $360

Odd Job, 1965, Gilbert, in white judo outfit w/blackbelt and headband, bowler hat
    NM $125   **MIP** $250

4" FIGURES

Domino, 1965, Gilbert, light blue shirt, blue pants
    NM $10   **MIP** $20

Dr. No, 1965, Gilbert, in white lab coat
    NM $10   **MIP** $20

Goldfinger, 1965, Gilbert
    NM $10   **MIP** $25

James Bond #1, 1965, Gilbert, in white tuxedo w/gun
    NM $10   **MIP** $20

James Bond #2, 1965, Gilbert, in black scuba outfit, Model No. 16503
    NM $10   **MIP** $20

James Bond Casual, 1965, Gilbert, in blue shirt, blue pants
    NM $10   **MIP** $20

Largo, 1965, Gilbert
    NM $10   **MIP** $20

M, 1965, Gilbert
    NM $10   **MIP** $20

Moneypenny, 1965, Gilbert
    NM $10   **MIP** $20

Odd Job, 1965, Gilbert, throwing bowler
    NM $10   **MIP** $20

ACCESSORIES

Action Toys Dr. No's Dragon Tank and Largo's Hydrofoil/Yacht, 1965, Gilbert, Model No. 16543
    NM $15   **MIP** $30

Secret Agent Gun Case and Bullet Shield "M"s Desk, 1965, Gilbert, both in one package, Model No. 16543
    NM $12   **MIP** $24

Spy Wrist Watch w/Decoder, 1965, Gilbert, with Secret Sighting lenses & World Time Guide
    NM $75   **MIP** $135

FIGURE SETS

Action Toy Set #5, 1965, Gilbert, includeds M, Moneypenny, Bond in tux
    NM $25   **MIP** $50

Movie Characters Set, 1965, Gilbert, 10 characters
    NM $300   **MIP** $600

VEHICLES

Aston Martin DB5, 1965, Gilbert, battery-operated, working ejection seat, 11" long
    NM $160   **MIP** $275

JAMES BOND: MOONRAKER (MEGO, 1979)

12" FIGURES

Drax, 1979, Mego
    NM $150   **MIP** $200

Holly, 1979, Mego
    NM $150   **MIP** $200

James Bond, 1979, Mego
    NM $125   **MIP** $150

James Bond, deluxe version, 1979, Mego
    NM $350   **MIP** $500

Jaws, 1979, Mego
    NM $300   **MIP** $500

JOHNNY HERO (ROSKO, 1965-68)

13" FIGURES

Johnny Hero, 1965-68
    NM $65   **MIP** $100

Johnny Hero, Olympic Hero, 1965-68
          NM $65   MIP $100

Outfits, 1965-68
          NM $40   MIP $75

JONNY QUEST (GALOOB, 1996)

ACCESSORIES

Cyber Copter, 1996, Galoob
          NM $5   MIP $15

Quest Porpoise with Deep Sea Jonny, 1996, Galoob
          NM $5   MIP $15

Quest Rover, 1996, Galoob
          NM $5   MIP $15

QUEST WORLD FIGURES

Cyber Cycle Jonny Quest, 1996, Galoob
          NM $5   MIP $10

Cyber Jet Race, 1996, Galoob
          NM $5   MIP $10

Cyber Suit Hadji, 1996, Galoob
          NM $5   MIP $10

Cyber Trax Surd, 1996, Galoob
          NM $5   MIP $10

REAL WORLD FIGURES

Deep Sea Race Bannon & Hadji, 1996, Galoob
          NM $4   MIP $8

Jungle Commando Dr. Quest & Ezekiel Rage, 1996, Galoob
          NM $4   MIP $8

Night Stryker Jonny Quest & Jessie, 1996, Galoob
          NM $5   MIP $10

Shuttle Pilot Jonny Quest & Race Bannon, 1996, Galoob
          NM $4   MIP $8

X-Treme Action Jonny Quest & Hadji, 1996, Galoob
          NM $4   MIP $8

KISS (MCFARLANE, 1997)

6" FIGURES

(McFarlane Toys)

Ace Frehley with album, 1997, McFarlane, Series 1, Shown with his other bandmates
          NM $7   MIP $15

Ace Frehley with letter stand, 1997, McFarlane, Series 1
          NM $5   MIP $10

Gene Simmons with album, 1997, McFarlane, Series 1
          NM $7   MIP $15

Gene Simmons with letter base, 1997, McFarlane, Series 1
          NM $5   MIP $10

Paul Stanley with album, 1997, McFarlane, Series 1
          NM $7   MIP $15

Paul Stanley with letter stand, 1997, McFarlane, Series 1
          NM $5   MIP $10

Peter Criss with album, 1997, McFarlane, Series 1
          NM $7   MIP $15

Peter Criss with letter stand, 1997, McFarlane, Series 1
          NM $5   MIP $10

KISS (MEGO, 1978)

12" BOXED FIGURES

Ace Frehley, 1978, Mego
          NM $100   MIP $260

(Toy Shop File Photo)

Gene Simmons, 1978, Mego, With accurate face make-up and realistic "wild" hair
          NM $110   MIP $260

(Toy Shop File Photo)

Paul Stanley, 1978, Mego, Another in Mego's series--they wisely made the boxes interchangeable. The package shown appears to have been autographed. Face make-up is accurate, and figure also features realistic "wild" hair
          NM $100   MIP $260

Peter Criss, 1978, Mego, Editor's note: Three cheers for drummers!
          NM $100   MIP $260

KISS: ALIVE (MCFARLANE, 2000)

FIGURES

(KP Photo)

Ace, 2000, McFarlane, Series 4, Figure includes guitar and amp
          NM $3   MIP $8

(KP Photo)

Gene, 2000, McFarlane, Series 4, Includes figure, amp, guitar and candleabra
          NM $3   MIP $8

(KP Photo)

Paul, 2000, McFarlane, Series 4, Includes guitar and amp
          NM $3   MIP $8

(KP Photo)

Peter, 2000, McFarlane, Series 4, Includes drumkit
          NM $3   MIP $8

KISS: KISS CREATURES (MCFARLANE, 2002)

FIGURES

Deluxe boxed set, 2002, McFarlane, included full drum kit
    NM $20   **MIP** $45

Space Ace, 2002, McFarlane
    NM $5   **MIP** $15

The Demon, 2002, McFarlane
    NM $5   **MIP** $15

The Fox, 2002, McFarlane
    NM $5   **MIP** $15

The Starchild, 2002, McFarlane
    NM $5   **MIP** $15

KISS: PSYCHO CIRCUS (MCFARLANE, 1998)

FIGURES

(McFarlane Toys)

Ace Frehley with Stiltman, 1998, McFarlane, Series 2, Includes two figures, Stiltman with base and skull-topped stilts
    NM $5   **MIP** $10

(McFarlane Toys)

Gene Simmons with Ring Master, 1998, McFarlane, Series 2, Each poseable figure includes staff
    NM $5   **MIP** $10

(McFarlane Toys)

Paul Stanley with The Jester, 1998, McFarlane, Series 2
    NM $5   **MIP** $10

(McFarlane Toys)

Peter Criss with Animal Wrangler, 1998, McFarlane, Series 2
    NM $5   **MIP** $10

KISS: PSYCHO CIRCUS TOUR (MCFARLANE, 1999)

FIGURES

Ace Frehley, 1999, McFarlane, Series 3
    NM $4   **MIP** $8

(McFarlane Toys)

Gene Simmons, 1999, McFarlane, Series 3, Fierce-looking Gene with black bass guitar
    NM $4   **MIP** $8

(McFarlane Toys)

Paul Stanley, 1999, McFarlane, Series 3, Paul includes flying-V guitar
    NM $4   **MIP** $8

Peter Criss, 1999, McFarlane, Series 3
    NM $4   **MIP** $8

LARA CROFT (PLAYMATES, 1999)

FIGURES

Lara in Area 51 outfit, 1999, Playmates
    NM $10   **MIP** $20

Lara in jungle outfit, 1999, Playmates
    NM $10   **MIP** $20

Lara in wet suit, 1999, Playmates
    NM $10   **MIP** $20

talking Lara, 1999, Playmates
    NM $15   **MIP** $30

LAVERNE AND SHIRLEY (MEGO, 1978)

12" BOXED FIGURES

Laverne and Shirley, 1978, Mego
    NM $60   **MIP** $150

Lenny and Squiggy, 1978, Mego
    NM $90   **MIP** $150

LEGENDS OF THE WEST (EXCEL, 1974)

FIGURES

Buffalo Bill Cody, 1974, Excel Toy Co., hat, gun, and holster
    NM $25   **MIP** $50

Cochise, 1974, Excel Toy Co., rifle
    NM $25   **MIP** $50

Davy Crockett, 1974, Excel Toy Co.
    NM $25   **MIP** $50

Deadwood Dick, 1974, Excel Toy Co., rarest figure in series
    NM $30   **MIP** $70

Jesse James, 1974, Excel Toy Co.
    NM $25   **MIP** $50

Wild Bill Hickok, 1974, Excel Toy Co., gun, holster
    NM $25   **MIP** $50

Wyatt Earp, 1974, Excel Toy Co., gun, holster
    NM $25   **MIP** $50

LONE RANGER (HUBLEY, 1973)

Lone Ranger, 1973, Hubley, w/hat, mask, 2-guns and holster rig, scarf, Model No. 23620
    NM $30   **MIP** $65

Silver, 1973, Hubley, w/stand, saddle, halter, bit, reins, martingale, girth, stirrups, poseable and rears up, No. 27625, Model No. 23625
    NM $20   **MIP** $45

Tonto, 1973, Hubley
    NM $25   **MIP** $60

ACTION FIGURES

LONE RANGER RIDES AGAIN (GABRIEL, 1979)

FIGURES

(Toy Shop File Photo)

Butch Cavendish, 1979, Gabriel, Figure shown here with Smoke, Butch's horse
    NM $40   **MIP** $75

Dan Reid, 1979, Gabriel
    NM $25   **MIP** $60

Little Bear with Hawk, 1979, Gabriel
    NM $25   **MIP** $60

(Toy Shop File Photo)

Lone Ranger, 1979, Gabriel, Figure includes revolvers, hat, mask, scarf. Shown here with Silver
    NM $20   **MIP** $60

Red Sleeves, 1979, Gabriel
    NM $25   **MIP** $60

(Toy Shop File Photo)

Tonto, 1979, Gabriel, Includes buckskin cloth outfit. Shown here with Scout. The horses in this series were fully poseable and included stands
    NM $20   **MIP** $60

LONE RANGER, LEGEND OF (GABRIEL, 1982)

FIGURES

Buffalo Bill Cody, 1982, Gabriel
    NM $10   **MIP** $25

Butch Cavendish, 1982, Gabriel
    NM $10   **MIP** $20

General Custer, 1982, Gabriel
    NM $10   **MIP** $20

Lone Ranger, 1982, Gabriel
    NM $15   **MIP** $30

Lone Ranger with Silver, 1982, Gabriel
    NM $25   **MIP** $50

Scout, 1982, Gabriel
    NM $10   **MIP** $20

Silver, 1982, Gabriel
    NM $15   **MIP** $30

Smoke, 1982, Gabriel
    NM $10   **MIP** $25

Tonto, 1982, Gabriel
    NM $7   **MIP** $15

Tonto with Scout, 1982, Gabriel
    NM $25   **MIP** $50

LORD OF THE RINGS (TOY VAULT, 1998-99)

FIGURES

Balrog, 1999, Toy Vault
    NM $7   **MIP** $13

(KP Photo)

Frodo in Lorien, 1999, Toy Vault, Includes dagger, belt, pack walking stick and cloak. A nicely done toy, and interesting to see a version of Frodo that exists before release of the movies
    NM $7   **MIP** $13

(KP Photo)

Frodo in the Barrow Downs, 1999, Toy Vault, In white cermonial cloak with gold highlights
    NM $8   **MIP** $18
(KP Photo)

Frodo the Hobbit, 1999, Toy Vault, Includes cloak, sword, pack, belt and blanket
    NM $8   **MIP** $14

(KP Photo)

Gandalf the Wizard, 1999, Toy Vault, In gray cloth robe, includes hat, food pouch, pipeweed pouch, staff, belt, sword and scabbard
    NM $7   **MIP** $13

Gimli in Battle, 1999, Toy Vault
    NM $7   **MIP** $13

Gimli of the Fellowship, 1999, Toy Vault
    NM $8   **MIP** $18

Gimli in Lorien, 1999, Toy Vault
    NM $7   **MIP** $13

Gollum, 1999, Toy Vault
    NM $7   **MIP** $13

Gollum the Fisherman, 1999, Toy Vault
    NM $7   **MIP** $13

(KP Photo)

Ugluk at War, 1999, Toy Vault, Fierce Orc with sword, helmet, dagger and shield
NM $7   **MIP** $13

(KP Photo)

Ugluk on the Hunt, 1999, Toy Vault
NM $7   **MIP** $13
(KP Photo)

Ugluk the Orc, 1999, Toy Vault, Figure in gold armor. Includes medicine bottle, sword, dagger and helmet
NM $7   **MIP** $13

LORD OF THE RINGS (KNICKERBOCKER, 1979)

CREATURES

Charger of the Ringwraith, 1979, Knickerbocker
NM $40   **MIP** $125

Frodo's Horse, 1979, Knickerbocker
NM $40   **MIP** $100

Ringwraith, 1979, Knickerbocker
NM $100   **MIP** $250

FIGURES

Aragorn, 1979, Knickerbocker
NM $35   **MIP** $100

Frodo, 1979, Knickerbocker
NM $35   **MIP** $100

Gandalf, 1979, Knickerbocker
NM $35   **MIP** $100

Gollum, 1979, Knickerbocker
NM $35   **MIP** $100

Samwise, 1979, Knickerbocker
NM $35   **MIP** $100

LOST IN SPACE (TRENDMASTERS, 1998)

9" CLASSIC FIGURES

Cyclops, 1998, Trendmasters
NM $25   **MIP** $50

Don West, 1998, Trendmasters
NM $10   **MIP** $20

Dr. Smith, 1998, Trendmasters
NM $20   **MIP** $40

Judy Robinson, 1998, Trendmasters
NM $10   **MIP** $20

Robot B9, 1998, Trendmasters
NM $25   **MIP** $50

Tybo the Carrot Man, 1998, Trendmasters
NM $20   **MIP** $40

Will Robinson, 1998, Trendmasters
NM $15   **MIP** $30

FIGURES

(Lenny Lee)

Battle Armor Don West, 1998, Trendmasters, Includes blaster rifle and magnet attack micro-spider
NM $4   **MIP** $8

Cryo Chamber Judy Robinson, 1998, Trendmasters
NM $4   **MIP** $8

(Lenny Lee)

Cryo Chamber Will Robinson, 1998, Trendmasters, With chamber, camera and magnet attack micro-spiders
NM $4   **MIP** $8

(Lenny Lee)

Cryo-Suit Dr. Judy Robinson, 1998, Trendmasters, With accessories and magnet attack micro-spider
NM $4   **MIP** $8

Cyclops, 1998, Trendmasters
NM $25   **MIP** $60

(Lenny Lee)

Dr. Smith, sabotage action, 1998, Trendmasters, Includes rifle, magnet attack micro-spider and accessories
NM $7   **MIP** $15

Future Smith, 1998, Trendmasters
NM $5   **MIP** $10

Judy Robinson, 1998, Trendmasters
NM $7   **MIP** $15

(Lenny Lee)

Proteus Armor Dr. Smith, 1998, Trendmasters, With rifle, and magnet attack micro-spider
NM $4   **MIP** $8

ACTION FIGURES

(Lenny Lee)

Proteus Armor John Robinson, 1998, Trendmasters, Includes micro-spider and accessories
NM $4   MIP $8

Will Robinson, 1998, Trendmasters
NM $7   MIP $15

PLAY SETS

(Lenny Lee)

Bubble Fighter, 1998, Trendmasters, Fighter ship as seen in the beginning of the movie. Features: swiveling cockpit, missile launchers, ejecting bubble section and breakaway battle damage
NM n/a   MIP $80

Classic Jupiter 2 play set, 1998, Trendmasters
NM $50   MIP $100

(Lenny Lee)

Jupiter 2 play set, 1998, Trendmasters, Ship fits action figure in cockpit and features: pop-out hyperspace struts, missile launchers, "battle damage" and more magnet-attack micro spiders
NM $25   MIP $75

LOST WORLD OF THE WARLORD (REMCO, 1983)

ACCESSORIES AND TEAMS

Warpult, 1983
NM $15   MIP $30

Warteam with Arak, 1983
NM $25   MIP $75

Warteam with Deimos, 1983
NM $25   MIP $75

Warteam with Manchitse, 1983
NM $25   MIP $75

Warteam with Mikola, 1983
NM $25   MIP $75

FIGURES

Arak, 1983
NM $13   MIP $30

Deimos, 1983
NM $15   MIP $38

Hercules, 1983
NM $13   MIP $30

Manchiste, 1983
NM $15   MIP $38

Mikola, 1983
NM $15   MIP $38

Warlord, 1983
NM $8   MIP $25

LOVE BOAT (MEGO, 1982)

4" FIGURES

Captain Stubing, 1982, Mego
NM $10   MIP $20

Doc, 1982, Mego
NM $10   MIP $20

Gopher, 1982, Mego
NM $10   MIP $20

Isaac, 1982, Mego
NM $10   MIP $20

Julie, 1982, Mego
NM $10   MIP $25

Vicki, 1982, Mego
NM $10   MIP $25

ACCESSORIES

Love Boat Playset, 1982, Mego
NM $150   MIP $300

M*A*S*H (DURHAM, 1973)

8" FIGURES

B.J., 1973, Durham, 8"
NM $35   MIP $75

Hawkeye, 1973, Durham, 8"
NM $20   MIP $50

Hot Lips, 1973, Durham, 8"
NM $20   MIP $50

M*A*S*H (TRISTAR, 1982)

3-3/4" FIGURES AND VEHICLES

B.J., 1982, Tristar, 3-3/4" tall
NM $5   MIP $15

Colonel Potter, 1982, Tristar, 3-3/4" figure on car
NM $5   MIP $15

Father Mulcahy, 1982, Tristar, 3-3/4" figure on car
NM $5   MIP $15

Hawkeye, 1982, Tristar, 3-3/4" figure on car
NM $5   MIP $15

Hawkeye with Ambulance, 1982, Tristar
NM $15   MIP $35

Hawkeye with Helicopter, 1982, Tristar
NM $8   MIP $35

Hawkeye with Jeep, 1982, Tristar
NM $10   MIP $35

Hot Lips, 1982, Tristar, 3-3/4" figure on car
NM $10   MIP $35

Klinger, 1982, Tristar, 3-3/4" figure on car
NM $5   MIP $15

Klinger in Drag, 1982, Tristar, 3-3/4" figure on car
NM $15   MIP $35

M*A*S*H Figures Collectors Set, 1982, Tristar
NM $26   MIP $65

Winchester, 1982, Tristar, 3-3/4" tall
NM $5   MIP $15

M.A.S.K. (KENNER, 1985-88)

ADVENTURE PACKS

Coast Patrol, 1986
NM $8   MIP $20

Jungle Challenge, 1986
NM $8   MIP $20

Rescue Mission, 1986
NM $8   MIP $20

T-Bob, 1986
NM $8   MIP $20

Venom's Revenge, 1986
NM $8   MIP $20

M.A.S.K. VEHICLES

Billboard Blast with Dusty Hayes, 1987, Series 3
NM $10   MIP $30

Bulldog with Boris Bushkin, 1987, Series 3
NM $15   MIP $45

Bullet with Ali Bombay, 1987, Series 3
NM $15   MIP $45

Buzzard with Miles Mayhem and Maximus Mayhem, 1987, Series 3
NM $15   MIP $45

Collector, 1987, Kenner, Series 3
NM $10   MIP $30

Condor with Brad Turner, 1985, Series 1
NM $10   MIP $30

Firecracker with Hondo Mac Lean, 1985, Series 1
NM $10   MIP $30

Firefly with Julio Lopez, 1986, Series 2
NM $10   MIP $30

Gator with Dirty Hayes, 1985, Series 1
NM $10   MIP $30

Goliath with Matt Tracker, 1987, Series 3
NM $15   MIP $45

Hurricane with Hondo Mac Lean, 1986, Series 2
NM $10   MIP $30

Iguana with Lester Sludge, 1987, Series 3
NM $10   MIP $30

Manta with Vanessa Warfield, 1987, Series 3
NM $15   MIP $45

Meteor with Ace Riker, 1987, Series 3
NM $10   MIP $25

Pit Stop Catapult with Sly Rax, 1987, Series 3
NM $10   MIP $30

Raven with Calhoun Burns, 1986, Series 2
NM $10   MIP $30

Razorback with Brad Turner, 1987, Series 3
NM $10   MIP $30

Rhino with Bruce Sato and Matt Tracker, 1985, Series 1
NM $15   MIP $45

Slingshot with Ace Riker, 1986, Series 2
NM $10   MIP $30

Thunder Hawk with Matt Tracker, 1985, Series 1
NM $15   MIP $45

Volcano with Matt Tracker and Jacques LaFleur, 1986, Series 2
NM $15   MIP $45

Wildcat with Clutch Hawks, 1987, Series 3
NM $10   MIP $35

MYSTERY ADVENTURE PACKS

Arctic Assault, 1988, Kenner
NM $10   MIP $20

Glider Strike, 1988, Kenner
NM $5   MIP $10

Racing Arena, 1988, Kenner
NM $5   MIP $10

Sea Attack, 1988, Kenner
NM $10   MIP $20

PLAY SETS

Boulder Play Set, 1985, Series 1
NM $40   MIP $120

SPLIT SECONDS M.A.S.K. VEHICLES

Afterburner with Dusty Hanes, 1988, Series 4
NM $20   MIP $55

Detonator, 1988, Series 4
NM $10   MIP $30

Dynamo with Bruce Sato, 1988, Series 4
NM $15   MIP $55

Fireforce, 1988, Series 4
NM $10   MIP $30

Jackal with Bruno Shepherd, 1988, Kenner, Series 4
NM $10   MIP $30

Skybolt, 1988, Kenner, Series 4
NM $10   MIP $30

Stiletto, 1988, Kenner, Series 4
NM $10   MIP $30

Wolfbeast with Miles Mayhem, 1988, Kenner, Series 4
NM $10   MIP $30

SPLIT SECONDS V.E.N.O.M. VEHICLES

Barracuda with Bruno Shepherd, 1988, Series 4
NM $15   MIP $55

Vandal with Floyd Malloy, 1988, Series 4
NM $10   MIP $30

V.E.N.O.M. VEHICLES

Jackhammer with Cliffhanger, 1985, Series 1
NM $10   MIP $30

Outlaw with Miles Mayhem and Nash Gorey, 1986, Series 2
NM $15   MIP $50

Piranha with Sly Rax, 1985, Series 1
NM $10   MIP $25

Stinger with Bruno Shepherd, 1986, Series 2
NM $10   MIP $35

Switchblade with Miles Mayhem, 1985, Series 1
NM $15   MIP $50

Vampire with Floyd Malloy, 1986, Series 2
NM $10   MIP $30

MAD MONSTER SERIES (MEGO, 1974)

8" FIGURES

The Dreadful Dracula, 1974, Mego
NM $80   MIP $160

The Horrible Mummy, 1974, Mego
NM $40   MIP $90

The Human Wolfman, 1974, Mego
NM $75   MIP $150

(Toy Shop File Photo)

The Monster Frankenstein, 1974, Mego, With glow-in-the-dark eyes and hands
NM $50   MIP $100

ACCESSORIES

Mad Monster Castle, vinyl, 1974, Mego
NM $300   MIP $600

MAJOR MATT MASON (MATTEL, 1967-70)

FIGURES

(Toy Shop Photo File)

Callisto, 1967, Mattel, #6331, friend from Jupiter
NM $100   MIP $250

(Toy Shop File Photo)

Captain Lazer, 1967, Mattel, #6330, blue plastic w/ silver trim, friend from Mars
NM $125   MIP $300

Doug Davis, 1967, Mattel, yellow figure
NM $100   MIP $300

(Corey LeChat)

Jeff Long, 1967, Mattel, blue figure
　　　　NM $150　　MIP $550

Major Matt Mason, 1967, Mattel, white figure
　　　　NM $75　　MIP $225

Scorpio, 1970, Mattel, rare
　　　　NM $350　　MIP $850

Sergeant Storm, 1967, Mattel, red figure
　　　　NM $100　　MIP $400

Space Mission Team, 1969, Mattel, Four-pack w/ MMM, Callisto, Doug Davis, and Sgt. Storm
　　　　NM $350　　MIP $625

VEHICLES AND ACCESSORIES

Astro Trac Missile Convoy Set, 1968, Mattel, #6327, Sears exclusive set
　　　　NM n/a　　MIP n/a

Astro-Trak, 1967, Mattel, #6302, vehicle
　　　　NM $50　　MIP $150

Doug Davis w/ Cat Trac, 1968, Mattel, #6333, figure w/ red/orange vehicle
　　　　NM $80　　MIP $150

Firebolt Space Cannon, 1968, Mattel, #6340, accessory
　　　　NM $45　　MIP $125

Firebolt Space Cannon Super Action Set, 1968, Mattel, #6341, w/ Major Matt Mason, Sgt. Storm, and Captain Lazer
　　　　NM n/a　　MIP n/a

Gamma Ray-Gard Pak, 1969, Mattel, #6342, accessory
　　　　NM $30　　MIP $100

Jeff Long w/ Cat Trac, 1968, Mattel, #6332, figure w/ white vehicle
　　　　NM $80　　MIP $150

Lunar Base Command Set, 1969, Mattel, #6353, largest boxed set of the series
　　　　NM $250　　MIP $500

Major Matt Mason w/ Cat Trac, 1968, Mattel, #6318, figure w/ red/orange vehicle
　　　　NM $80　　MIP $155

Major Matt Mason w/ Moonsuit, 1967, Mattel, #6303, w/ jet pack, space sled, moon suit and tools
　　　　NM $100　　MIP $300

Mobile Launch Pad, 1968, Mattel, #6328, Sears exclusive
　　　　NM n/a　　MIP n/a

Moon Suit Pak, 1967, Mattel, #6301, accessory
　　　　NM $35　　MIP $100

Reconojet Pak, 1968, Mattel, #6320, accessory
　　　　NM $25　　MIP $75

Rocket Launch Pak, 1967, Mattel, #6305, accessory
　　　　NM $25　　MIP $75

Satellite Launch Pak, 1968, Mattel, #6306, accessory
　　　　NM $25　　MIP $75

Satellite Locker, 1968, Mattel, #6322, carry case
　　　　NM $30　　MIP $80

Sgt. Storm w/ Cat Trac, 1968, Mattel, #6319, figure w/ white vehicle
　　　　NM $80　　MIP $150

Space Bubble, 1969, Mattel, #6345, vehicle
　　　　NM n/a　　MIP n/a

Space Crawler, 1967, Mattel, #6304, vehicle, battery op
　　　　NM n/a　　MIP n/a

Space Crawler Action Set, 1967, Mattel, #6311, w/ MMM, Space Crawler, jet pack, and space sled
　　　　NM n/a　　MIP n/a

Space Discovery Set, 1969, Mattel, #6355, w/ Doug Davis, Callisto, Space Crawler, Space Bubble, Space Power Suit
　　　　NM n/a　　MIP n/a

Space Power Suit, 1969, Mattel, #6336, accessory
　　　　NM $30　　MIP $110

Space Power Suit Pak, 1969, Mattel, #6344, accessory
　　　　NM n/a　　MIP n/a

Space Probe Pak, 1967, Mattel, #6307, accessory
　　　　NM $25　　MIP $75

Space Shelter Pak, 1968, Mattel, #6321, accessory
　　　　NM $25　　MIP $75

Space Station & Space Crawler Deluxe Action Set, 1967, Mattel, #6310, play set
　　　　NM n/a　　MIP n/a

Space Station Set, 1967, Mattel, #6308, play set, three decks
　　　　NM $150　　MIP $350

Space Travel Pak, 1969, Mattel, #6347, w/ Jet propulsion pack, space sled, rifle, chemical tanks
　　　　NM n/a　　MIP n/a

Spaceship Carry Case, 1967, Mattel, #6316, accessory
　　　　NM $25　　MIP $50

Star Seeker, 1970, Mattel, #6357, vehicle
　　　　NM $85　　MIP $180

Star Seeker Walk in Space Set, 1970, Mattel, #6386, space walk feature
　　　　NM n/a　　MIP n/a

Super Power Set, 1970, Mattel, #6379, MMM figure, Cat Trac, Space Power Suit, Supernaut Power Limbs, rare set
　　　　NM n/a　　MIP n/a

Supernaut Power Limbs Pak, 1968, Mattel, #6343, accessory
　　　　NM $30　　MIP $110

Talking Command Console, 1969, Mattel, #5157, accessory, says nine commands
　　　　NM $80　　MIP $150

Talking Flying Major Matt Mason, 1970, Mattel, #6378, figure, talking jet pack, XRG-1 Reentry Glider
　　　　NM n/a　　MIP n/a

Talking Major Matt Mason, 1970, Mattel, #6362, figure with talking jet pack
　　　　NM n/a　　MIP n/a

Uni-Tred & Space Bubble, 1969, Mattel, #6339, vehicle
　　　　NM $95　　MIP $175

Uni-Tred Space Hauler, 1969, Mattel, #6346, vehicle set
　　　　NM n/a　　MIP n/a

XRG-1 Reentry Glider, 1969, Mattel, #6360, vehicle
　　　　NM $150　　MIP $395

XRG-1 Reentry Gliser w/ Major Matt Mason, 1969, Mattel, #6361, glider with figure
　　　　NM n/a　　MIP n/a

MAN FROM U.N.C.L.E. (GILBERT, 1965)

FIGURES

Illya Kuryakin, 1965, 1965, Black sweater, pants and shoes, spring loaded arm
　　　　NM $200　　MIP $400

(Toy Shop File Photo)

Napoleon Solo, 1965, 1965, Plastic, white shirt, black pants and shoes, spring loaded arm to shoot pistol
　　　　NM $145　　MIP $325

MARS ATTACKS! (TRENDMASTERS, 1997)

FIGURES

Martian Ambassador, 1997, Trendmasters, 6" figure
　　　　NM $6　　MIP $12

Martian Leader, 1997, Trendmasters, 6" figure

    NM $6   **MIP** $12

Martian Spy Girl, 1997, Trendmasters, 6" figure; talking version

    NM $45   **MIP** $65

Martian Spy Girl, 1997, Trendmasters, 6" figure

    NM $35   **MIP** $70

Martian Trooper, 1997, Trendmasters, 6" figure

    NM $8   **MIP** $15

MARVEL FAMOUS COVERS (TOY BIZ, 1997-98)

8" FIGURES

(Toy Shop File Photo)

Aunt May, 1997, Toy Biz, Mail-away exclusive, with tied bandana around neck

    NM $15   **MIP** $40

Captain America, 1998, Toy Biz

    NM $8   **MIP** $20

Cyclops, 1999, Toy Biz

    NM $5   **MIP** $15

Dark Phoenix, 1998, Toy Biz

    NM $4   **MIP** $12

Dr. Doom, 1998, Toy Biz

    NM $4   **MIP** $12

Green Goblin, 1997, Toy Biz

    NM $15   **MIP** $25

Magneto, 1999, Toy Biz

    NM $5   **MIP** $15

Nightcrawler, 1999, Toy Biz

    NM $5   **MIP** $15

Rogue, 1999, Toy Biz

    NM $5   **MIP** $15

Spider-Man, red and black costume, 1997, Toy Biz

    NM $15   **MIP** $40

Storm, 1997, Toy Biz

    NM $12   **MIP** $25

Thor, 1998, Toy Biz

    NM $4   **MIP** $12

Wolverine, 1997, Toy Biz

    NM $10   **MIP** $30

MARVEL MILESTONE, 8" FIGURES

Black Widow, 1998, Toy Biz

    NM $3   **MIP** $8

Daredevil, 1998, Toy Biz

    NM $3   **MIP** $8

Falcon, 1998, Toy Biz

    NM $3   **MIP** $8

Mr. Sinister, 1998, Toy Biz

    NM $3   **MIP** $8

MARVEL FAMOUS COVERS AVENGERS ASSEMBLE (TOY BIZ, 1999)

8" FIGURES

Hawkeye, 1999, Toy Biz

    NM $5   **MIP** $15

Hulk, 1999, Toy Biz

    NM $5   **MIP** $15

Iron man, 1999, Toy Biz

    NM $5   **MIP** $15

Vision, 1999, Toy Biz

    NM $5   **MIP** $15

MARVEL GOLD (TOY BIZ, 1998)

FIGURES

Black Panther, 1998, Toy Biz

    NM $8   **MIP** $16

Captain Marvel, 1998

    NM $8   **MIP** $16

Iron Fist, 1998

    NM $10   **MIP** $20

Marvel Girl, 1998, Toy Biz

    NM $8   **MIP** $16

Moon Knight, 1998, Toy Biz

    NM $8   **MIP** $16

Power Man, 1998, Toy Biz

    NM $8   **MIP** $16

Vision, 1998, Toy Biz

    NM $8   **MIP** $16

MARVEL SHAPE SHIFTERS (TOY BIZ, 1999)

7" FIGURES

Hulk forms into Dino Beast, 1999

    NM $3   **MIP** $7

Rhino forms into Racing Rhino, 1999

    NM $3   **MIP** $7

Sabretooth forms into Sabretooth Tiger, 1999

    NM $3   **MIP** $7

Spider Sense Spider-Man forms into Spider-Bat, 1999

    NM $3   **MIP** $7

MARVEL SHAPE SHIFTERS II (TOY BIZ, 1999)

7" FIGURES

Captain America forms into American Eagle, 1999

    NM $3   **MIP** $7

Colossus forms into Cyborg Gorilla, 1999

    NM $3   **MIP** $7

Kraven forms into Mighty Lion, 1999

    NM $3   **MIP** $7

Thor forms into Winged Stallion, 1999

    NM $3   **MIP** $7

MARVEL SHAPE SHIFTERS WEAPONS (TOY BIZ, 1999)

DELUXE FIGURES

Apocalypse forms into Gattling Gun, 1999

    NM $3   **MIP** $7

Iron Man forms into Battle Axe, 1999

    NM $3   **MIP** $7

Punisher forms into Power Pistol, 1999

    NM $3   **MIP** $7

Spider-Man forms into Wrist Blaster, 1999

    NM $3   **MIP** $7

MARVEL SPECIAL EDITION SERIES (TOY BIZ, 1998)

12" FIGURES

Dr. Octopus, 1998

    NM $3   **MIP** $7

Punisher, 1998

    NM $3   **MIP** $7

Spider-Woman, 1998

    NM $3   **MIP** $7

MARVEL SUPER HEROES (TOY BIZ, 1990-92)

SERIES 1, 1990

Captain America, 1990-92, Toy Biz

    NM $10   **MIP** $20

Daredevil, 1990-92, Toy Biz

    NM $15   **MIP** $40

Doctor Doom, 1990-92, Toy Biz

    NM $10   **MIP** $25

Doctor Octopus, 1990-92, Toy Biz

    NM $10   **MIP** $25

Hulk, 1990-92, Toy Biz

    NM $5   **MIP** $15

Punisher (cap firing), 1990-92, Toy Biz

    NM $5   **MIP** $15

Silver Surfer, 1990-92, Toy Biz

    NM $10   **MIP** $30

Spider-Man (suction cups), 1990-92, Toy Biz

    NM $5   **MIP** $20

SERIES 2, 1991

Green Goblin (back lever), 1990-92, Toy Biz
  NM $15   **MIP** $40

Green Goblin (no lever), 1990-92, Toy Biz
  NM $10   **MIP** $25

Iron Man, 1990-92, Toy Biz
  NM $10   **MIP** $25

Punisher (machine gun sound), 1990-92, Toy Biz
  NM $5   **MIP** $15

Spider-Man (web climbing), 1990-92, Toy Biz
  NM $15   **MIP** $35

Spider-Man (web shooting), 1990-92, Toy Biz
  NM $10   **MIP** $30

Thor (back lever), 1990-92, Toy Biz
  NM $15   **MIP** $40

Thor (no lever), 1990-92, Toy Biz
  NM $10   **MIP** $25

Venom, 1990-92, Toy Biz
  MIP $20

SERIES 3, 1992

Annihilus, 1990-92, Toy Biz
  NM $5   **MIP** $15

Deathlok, 1990-92, Toy Biz
  NM $5   **MIP** $15

Human Torch, 1990-92, Toy Biz
  NM $5   **MIP** $15

Invisible Woman, catapult, 1990-92
  NM $5   **MIP** $15

(Toy Shop File Photo)

Invisible Woman, vanishing, 1990-92, Toy Biz, turns from color uniform to translucent
  NM $75   **MIP** $150

Mister Fantastic, 1990-92, Toy Biz
  NM $5   **MIP** $15

Silver Surfer (chrome), 1990-92, Toy Biz
  NM $5   **MIP** $15

Spider-Man (ball joints), 1990-92, Toy Biz
  NM $5   **MIP** $15

Spider-Man (web tracer), 1990-92, Toy Biz
  NM $5   **MIP** $15

Thing, 1990-92, Toy Biz
  MIP $15

Venom (tongue flicking), 1990-92, Toy Biz
  NM $15   **MIP** $20

TALKING HEROES

Cyclops, 1990-92, Toy Biz
  NM $10   **MIP** $20

Hulk, 1990-92, Toy Biz
  NM $10   **MIP** $20

Magneto, 1990-92, Toy Biz
  NM $10   **MIP** $20

Punisher, 1990-92, Toy Biz
  NM $10   **MIP** $20

Spider-Man, 1990-92, Toy Biz
  NM $10   **MIP** $20

Venom, 1990-92, Toy Biz
  NM $10   **MIP** $25

Wolverine, 1990-92, Toy Biz
  NM $10   **MIP** $20

MARVEL SUPER HEROES COSMIC DEFENDERS (TOY BIZ, 1992-93)

FIGURES

Annihilus, 1992-93, Toy Biz
  NM $5   **MIP** $15

Deathlok, 1992-93, Toy Biz
  NM $5   **MIP** $15

Human Torch, 1992-93, Toy Biz
  NM $5   **MIP** $15

Invisible Woman, vanishing color action, 1992-93, Toy Biz
  NM $50   **MIP** $150

Mr. Fantastic, 1992-93, Toy Biz
  NM $8   **MIP** $20

Silver Surfer, 1992-93, Toy Biz
  NM $4   **MIP** $12

Spider-Man, enemy tracking tracer, 1992-93, Toy Biz
  NM $8   **MIP** $20

Spider-Man, multi-jointed, 1992-93, Toy Biz
  NM $5   **MIP** $15

MARVEL SUPER HEROES SECRET WARS (MATTEL, 1984-85)

4" FIGURES

Baron Zemo, 1984-85, Mattel
  NM $15   **MIP** $35

(Lenny Lee)

Captain America, with secret shield, 1984-85, Mattel, includes figure, shield and mini comic book
  NM $10   **MIP** $25

Constrictor (foreign release), 1984-85, Mattel
  NM $30   **MIP** $75

Daredevil, 1984-85, Mattel
  NM $15   **MIP** $35

(Lenny Lee)

Doctor Doom, 1984-85, Mattel, shown at left with Kang
  NM $10   **MIP** $20

(Lenny Lee)

Doctor Octopus, 1984-85, Mattel, Spidey's nemesis with mechanical arms and shield
  NM $10   **MIP** $20

Electro (foreign release), 1984-85, Mattel
  NM $30   **MIP** $75

Falcon, 1984-85, Mattel
  NM $20   **MIP** $40

Hobgoblin, 1984-85, Mattel
  NM $30   **MIP** $60

Ice Man (foreign release), 1984-85, Mattel
  NM $30   **MIP** $75

Iron Man, 1984-85, Mattel
  NM $20   **MIP** $35

(Lenny Lee)

Kang, 1984-85, Mattel, shown at right
    NM $10   **MIP** $20

Magneto, 1984-85, Mattel
    NM $10   **MIP** $20

Spider-Man, black outfit, 1984-85, Mattel
    NM $25   **MIP** $50

Spider-Man, red and blue outfit, 1984-85, Mattel
    NM $20   **MIP** $40

(Toy Shop File Photo)

Three-Figure Set, 1984-85, Mattel, includes DareDevil, Spidey (in black costume) and Captain America
    NM $40   **MIP** $90

Two-Figure Set, 1984-85, Mattel
    NM $25   **MIP** $50

Wolverine, black claws, 1984-85, Mattel
    NM $25   **MIP** $75

(Toy shop File Photo)

Wolverine, silver claws, 1984-85, Mattel
    NM $25   **MIP** $40

ACCESSORIES

Secret Messages Pack, 1984-85, Mattel
    NM $1   **MIP** $5

Tower of Doom, 1984-85, Mattel
    NM $20   **MIP** $35

VEHICLES

Doom Copter, 1984-85, Mattel
    NM $10   **MIP** $35

Doom Copter with Doctor Doom, 1984-85, Mattel
    NM $15   **MIP** $55

Doom Cycle, 1984-85, Mattel
    NM $6   **MIP** $20

Doom Cycle with Doctor Doom, 1984-85, Mattel
    NM $10   **MIP** $40

Doom Roller, 1984-85, Mattel
    NM $10   **MIP** $20

Doom Star Glider with Kang, 1984-85, Mattel
    NM $15   **MIP** $30

Freedom Fighter, 1984-85, Mattel
    NM $10   **MIP** $30

Star Dart with Spider-Man (black outfit), 1984-85, Mattel
    NM $25   **MIP** $50

Turbo Copter, 1984-85, Mattel
    NM $10   **MIP** $40

Turbo Cycle, 1984-85, Mattel
    NM $5   **MIP** $20

MARVEL'S MOST WANTED (TOY BIZ, 1998)

6" FIGURES

Blink, 1998
    NM $3   **MIP** $7

Spat and Grovel, 1998
    NM $3   **MIP** $7

X-Man, 1998
    NM $3   **MIP** $7

MASTERS OF THE UNIVERSE (MATTEL, 1981-1988)

12" FIGURES (ITALIAN)

Megator, 1987
    NM $300   **MIP** $1000

Tytus, 1987
    NM $400   **MIP** $1200

ACCESSORIES

Battle Bones Carrying Case, 1984
    NM $10   **MIP** $20

Battle Cat, 1982
    NM $15   **MIP** $50

Battle Cat with Battle Armor He-Man, 1984
    NM $50   **MIP** $125

Battle Cat with He-Man, 1982
    NM $50   **MIP** $150

Beam Blaster and Artillery, 1987
    NM $25   **MIP** $60

Bionatops, 1987, Mattel, creature
    NM $25   **MIP** $45

He-Man and Wind Raider, 1982, Mattel
    NM $10   **MIP** $25

Jet Sled, 1986
    NM $5   **MIP** $15

Mantisaur, 1986
    NM $15   **MIP** $25

(Toy Shop File Photo)

Megalaser, 1986, While this weapon didn't fire any projectiles, it had a blast-effect action and fit warriors in the series
    NM $5   **MIP** $15

(Lenny Lee)

Monstroid Creature (The Evil Horde), 1986, Mattel, Creature grabs warriors in pincers and whirls them around--pretty neat!
    NM $30   **MIP** $75

Night Stalker, 1984
    NM $15   **MIP** $30

Night Stalker with Jitsu, 1984
    NM $40   **MIP** $75

Panthor, 1983
    NM $25   **MIP** $50

Panthor with Battle Armor Skeletor, 1984
    NM $35   **MIP** $125

Panthor with Skeletor, 1983
    NM $40   **MIP** $150

Ring of caps for Thunder Punch He-Man, 1985, Mattel
    NM $2   **MIP** $6

Road Ripper w/ Battle Armor He-Man, 1984, Mattel
    NM $20   **MIP** $40

Screech, 1983
    NM $15   **MIP** $40

Screech with Skeletor, 1983
    NM $40   **MIP** $70

Screeech w/ Battle Armor Skeletor, 1984, Mattel
    NM $20   **MIP** $40

Slime Vat, 1986, Mattel
    NM $2   **MIP** $6

Stilt Stalkers, 1986
    NM $5   **MIP** $20

Stridor Armored Horse, 1984
    NM $10   **MIP** $30

ACTION FIGURES

Stridor with Fisto, 1984
NM $30   MIP $75

(Lenny Lee)

Weapons Pak, 1984, Included laser guns, body armor, battle axe, shield, sword and more
NM $5   MIP $15

Zoar, 1983
NM $15   MIP $30

Zoar with Teela, 1983
NM $40   MIP $120

FIGURES

Battle Armor He-Man, 1984
NM $15   MIP $40

Battle Armor Skeletor, 1984
NM $15   MIP $40

Beast Man, 1982
NM $25   MIP $70

Blade, 1987
NM $25   MIP $70

(KP Photo)

Blast-Attak, 1987, Limbs actually fly off the figure during battle
NM $20   MIP $40

Buzz-Off, 1984
NM $25   MIP $40

Buzz-Saw Hordak (The Evil Horde), 1987
NM $15   MIP $40

Clamp Champ, 1987
NM $15   MIP $45

Clawful, 1984
NM $20   MIP $45

Dragon Blaster Skeletor, 1985
NM $25   MIP $75

Dragon Blaster Skeletor, 1985, Mattel
NM $20   MIP $40

(KP Photo)

Dragstor (The Evil Horde), 1986, Mattel, Ripcord (like the SST's series) makes this "transforming evil warrior vehicle" pursue the good guys
NM $15   MIP $40

Evil-Lyn, 1983
NM $25   MIP $50

(KP Photo)

Extendar, 1986, With extending arms, legs, head and torso
NM $15   MIP $35

Faker, 1983, Mattel
NM $30   MIP $120

Faker II, 1987
NM $20   MIP $70

Fisto, 1984
NM $10   MIP $40

Flying Fists He-Man, 1986
NM $25   MIP $75

Grizzlor (The Evil Horde), 1985
NM $15   MIP $40

Grizzlor, black, 1985
NM $75   MIP $150

Gwildor, 1987, figure from Masters of the Universe movie
NM $15   MIP $75

He-Man, original, 1982, 1983
NM $40   MIP $130

Hordak (The Evil Horde), 1985
NM $20   MIP $40

Horde Trooper, 1986
NM $20   MIP $40

Hurricane Hordak, 1986
NM $15   MIP $60

Jitsu, 1984
NM $20   MIP $45

King Hiss (Snake Men), 1986
NM $20   MIP $45

(KP Photo)

King Randor, 1987, With scepter and mini comic book
NM $30   MIP $75

Kobra Kahn (Snake Men), 1984, 1986
NM $10   MIP $35

Leech (The Evil Horde), 1985
NM $10   MIP $35

Man-At-Arms, 1982, Mattel
NM $20   MIP $40

Man-E-Faces, 1983
NM $25   MIP $50

Man-E-Faces, five extra weapons, 1983
NM $75   MIP $175

Mantenna (The Evil Horde, 1985
NM $25   MIP $40

Mekaneck, 1983
NM $20   MIP $40

Mer-Man, 1982
NM $25   MIP $50

Modulok (The Evil Horde), 1985
NM $15   MIP $35

Mosquitor (The Evil Horde), 1987
NM $25   MIP $45

Moss Man, 1985
NM $10   MIP $40

Multi-Bot (The Evil Horde), 1986
NM $20   MIP $40

Ninjor, 1987
NM $35   MIP $80

ACTION FIGURES

Orko, 1984
    NM $20   **MIP** $50

Prince Adam, 1984
    NM $20   **MIP** $60

Ram-Man, 1983
    NM $20   **MIP** $60

(Toy Shop File Photo)

Rattlor (Snake Men), 1986, With translucent plastic "snake staff" and mini comic book
    NM $10   **MIP** $35

Rattlor, red neck, 1986
    NM $10   **MIP** $30

(Lenny Lee)

Rio Blast, 1986, Mattel, An "old West" warrior with hidden weapons. Includes comic book
    NM $25   **MIP** $40

Roboto, 1985
    NM $15   **MIP** $35

Rokkon (Comet Warrior, 1986
    NM $15   **MIP** $35

Rotar (Energy Zoids), 1987
    NM $35   **MIP** $70

Saurod, 1987, figure from Masters of the Universe movie
    NM $30   **MIP** $70

Scare Glow, 1987
    NM $35   **MIP** $75

Skeletor, original, 1982, 1983
    NM $35   **MIP** $110

Snake Face (Snake Men), 1987
    NM $25   **MIP** $45

Snout Spout, 1986
    NM $15   **MIP** $40

Sorceress, 1987
    NM $25   **MIP** $70

Spikor, 1985
    NM $15   **MIP** $40

(KP Photo)

Sssqueeze (Snake Men), 1987, Mattel, Traps warriors in "slither-hold" grip. Includes serpent
    NM $25   **MIP** $45

Stinkor, 1985
    NM $15   **MIP** $35

Stonedar (Comet Warriors), 1986
    NM $15   **MIP** $35

Stratos, blue wings, 1982, Mattel
    NM $25   **MIP** $75

Stratos, red wings, 1982
    NM $25   **MIP** $75

Sy-klone, 1985
    NM $20   **MIP** $40

Teela, 1982
    NM $25   **MIP** $65

Terror Claws Skeletor, 1986
    NM $25   **MIP** $75

Thunder Punch He-Man, 1985, Mattel
    NM $15   **MIP** $35

Thunder Punch He-man, 1985
    NM $25   **MIP** $60

Trap Jaw, 1983
    NM $30   **MIP** $85

Tri-Klops, 1983
    NM $30   **MIP** $40

Tung Lashor (Snake Men), 1986
    NM $10   **MIP** $45

Twistoid (Energy Zoids), 1987
    NM $30   **MIP** $75

Two-Bad, 1985
    NM $10   **MIP** $30

Webstor, 1984
    NM $10   **MIP** $30

Whiplash, 1984
    NM $10   **MIP** $25

Zodac, 1982, Mattel
    NM $25   **MIP** $50

GIFTSETS

Battle for Eternia, 1983, Mattel, Skeletor, Panthor, Man-E-Faces
    NM $45   **MIP** $80

Battle for Eternia, 1984, Mattel
    NM $50   **MIP** $90

Evil Horde, 1986, Mattel, Hordak, Leech, Mantenna
    NM $60   **MIP** $110

Evil Warriors, 1983, Mattel, Skeletor, Beast Man, Faker
    NM $40   **MIP** $90

Evil Warriors, 1984, Mattel, Battle Armor Skeletor, Webstor, Mer-Man
    NM $45   **MIP** $85

Evil Warriors, 1985, Mattel, Stinkor, Webstor, Whiplash
    NM $60   **MIP** $85

Flying Fist He-Man and Terror Claws Skeletor, 1986, Mattel
    NM $75   **MIP** $140

Heroic Warriors, 1983, Mattel, He-Man, Teela, Ram-Man
    NM $45   **MIP** $85

Heroic Warriors, 1984, Mattel, Battle Armor He-Man, Man-At-Arms, Man-E-Faces
    NM $45   **MIP** $80

Heroic Warriors, 1985, Mattel, Mekaneck, Buzz-Off, Moss-Man
    NM $60   **MIP** $90

Jet Sled w/ He-Man, 1986, Mattel
    NM $45   **MIP** $85

Mantisaur w/ Hordak, 1986, Mattel
    NM $35   **MIP** $55

GRAYSKULL DINOSAUR SERIES

Bionatops, 1987, Mattel
    NM $35   **MIP** $85

Turbodaltyl, 1987, Mattel
    NM $25   **MIP** $60

Tyrantisaurus Rex, 1987, Mattel
    NM $75   **MIP** $135

LASER FIGURES

Laser Light Skeletor, 1988, Mattel
    NM $75   **MIP** $250

Laser Power He-Man, 1988, Mattel
    NM $75   **MIP** $250

MAIL AWAY FIGURES

Savage He-Man (Wonder Bread Exclusive), 1982, Mattel
    NM $200   **MIP** $500

METEORBS

Astro Lion, 1987, Mattel
    NM $15   **MIP** $30

Comet Cat, 1987, Mattel
    NM $15   **MIP** $30

Cometroid, 1987, Mattel
    NM $15   **MIP** $30

Crocobite, 1987, Mattel
       NM $15   MIP $30

Dinosorb, 1987, Mattel
       NM $15   MIP $30

Gore-illa, 1987, Mattel
       NM $15   MIP $30

Orbear, 1987, Mattel
       NM $15   MIP $30

Rhinorb, 1987, Mattel
       NM $15   MIP $30

Tuskor, 1987, Mattel
       NM $15   MIP $30

Ty-Gyr, 1987, Mattel
       NM $15   MIP $30

OVERSEAS ACCESSORIES

Cliff Climber, 1987, Mattel
       NM $25   MIP $75

Scubattack, 1987, Mattel
       NM $25   MIP $75

Tower Tools, 1987, Mattel
       NM $25   MIP $75

PLAY SETS

Castle Grayskull, 1982, Mattel
       NM $75   MIP $165

Eternia, 1986, Mattel
       NM $350   MIP $700

Fright Zone, 1985, Mattel
       NM $45   MIP $125

Point Dread and Talon Fighter, 1983, Mattel
       NM $15   MIP $35

(Lenny Lee)

Slime Pit, 1986, Mattel, Slime oozes from top of pit to trap warriors. The set included real Slime, which actually must have made for a very cool effect on the figures.
       NM $25   MIP $75

(Toy Shop File Photo)

Snake Mountain, 1984, Mattel, Snake Pit went quite well with the Slime Pit for play value.
       NM $50   MIP $150

VEHICLES

Attack Trak, 1983, Mattel
       NM $25   MIP $75

Bashasaurus, 1985, Mattel
       NM $25   MIP $50

Battle Ram, 1982, Mattel
       NM $30   MIP $75

Blaster hawk, 1986, Mattel
       NM $25   MIP $60

(Lenny Lee)

Dragon Walker, 1984, Mattel, Open-cockpit vehicle that sideways "walks"
       NM $20   MIP $45

Fright Fighter, 1986, Mattel
       NM $15   MIP $45

Hordak w/ Grizzlor, 1985, Mattel
       NM $10   MIP $30

Land Shark, 1985, Mattel
       NM $15   MIP $35

Land Shark w/ Battle Armor Skeletor, 1985, Mattel
       NM $25   MIP $45

Laser Bolt, 1986, Mattel
       NM $15   MIP $40

Point Dread, 1983, Mattel
       NM $25   MIP $75

Road Ripper, 1983, Mattel, He-Man's motorcycle-type vehicle, ripcord-powered
       NM $10   MIP $30

Roton, 1984, Mattel
       NM $10   MIP $30

Spydor, 1985, Mattel
       NM $25   MIP $50

Wind Raider, 1982, Mattel
       NM $15   MIP $60

MASTERS OF THE UNIVERSE (MATTEL, 2002-03)

ACCESSORIES

Bat Fight-Pack, 2003, Mattel
       NM $4   MIP $8

Battle Cat, 2002, Mattel
       NM $5   MIP $12

Battle Raptor, 2003, Mattel
       NM $7   MIP $15

Eagle Fight-Pack, 2003, Mattel
       NM $4   MIP $8

He-Man's Sword, 2002, Mattel
       NM $7   MIP $12

Panthor, 2002, Mattel
       NM $5   MIP $12

Samurai Battlecat, 2003, Mattel
       NM $10   MIP $20

DELUXE FIGURES

Battle Sound He-Man, 2002, Mattel, Series 1
       NM $5   MIP $12

Battle Sound Skeletor, 2002, Mattel, Series 1
       NM $5   MIP $12

Samauri Man-At-Arms, 2003, Mattel
       NM $7   MIP $15

Samurai He-Man, 2003, Mattel
       NM $7   MIP $15

Samurai Skeletor, 2003, Mattel
       NM $7   MIP $15

FIGURES

Battle Glove Man-At-Arms, 2003, Mattel, Series 4
       NM $5   MIP $15

Beast Man, 2002, Mattel, Series 1
       NM $5   MIP $10

Buzz-Off, 2003, Mattel, Series 4
       NM $2   MIP $6

Evil-Lyn, 2003, Mattel, Series 3
       NM $2   MIP $6

Faker, 2003, Mattel, Toy Fare Exclusive
       NM $10   MIP $20

Fire Armor Skeletor, 2003, Mattel, Series 3
       NM $5   MIP $10

He-Man, 2002, Mattel, Series 1
       NM $5   MIP $10

Ice Armor He-Man, 2003, Mattel, Series 4
       NM $2   MIP $6

Jungle Attack He-Man, 2002, Mattel, Series 2
       NM $5   MIP $10

Makaneck, 2002, Mattel, Series 2
       NM $5   MIP $10

Man-At-Arms, 2002, Mattel, Series 1
       NM $5   MIP $10

Man-E-Faces, 2003, Mattel, Series 4
       NM $2   MIP $6

Martial Arts He-Man, 2003, Mattel, Series 4
       NM $2   MIP $6

Mega-Punch He-Man, 2003, Mattel, Series 4
       NM $2   MIP $6

Mer-Man, 2002, Mattel, Series 1
       NM $5   MIP $10

Orko, 2003, Mattel, Series 3
       NM $5   MIP $15

Prince Adam, 2003, Mattel, Series 4
       NM $5   MIP $15

Ram Man, 2002, Mattel, Series 2
       NM $5   MIP $10

Skeletor, 2002, Mattel, Series 1
       NM $5   MIP $10

Smash Blade He-Man, 2003, Mattel, Series 3
       NM $2   MIP $6

Spin Blade Skeletor, 2003, Mattel, Series 2
    NM $2   **MIP** $6

Stratos, 2002, Mattel, Series 1
    NM $5   **MIP** $10

Sy-Klone, 2003, Mattel, Series 4
    NM $5   **MIP** $15

Teela, 2003, Mattel, Series 3
    NM $5   **MIP** $15

Trapjaw, 2003, Mattel, Series 2
    NM $2   **MIP** $6

Tri-Klops, 2003, Mattel, Series 2
    NM $2   **MIP** $6

Two-Bad, 2003, Mattel, Series 3
    NM $2   **MIP** $6

Whiplash, 2003, Mattel, Series 3
    NM $2   **MIP** $6

GIFTSETS

Armor Skeletor, 2003, Mattel
    NM $10   **MIP** $20

He-Man vs. Skeletor, 2002, Mattel, figure 2-pack
    NM $10   **MIP** $20

Wolf Armor He-Man & Snake, 2003, Mattel
    NM $10   **MIP** $20

MINI FIGURES

He-Man, 2002, Mattel
    NM $2   **MIP** $6

Heroes vs. Villians Giftpack, 2002, Mattel, w/ exclusive Beastman
    NM $7   **MIP** $12

Man-At-Arms, 2002, Mattel
    NM $2   **MIP** $6

Mekaneck, 2002, Mattel
    NM $2   **MIP** $6

Mer-Man, 2002, Mattel
    NM $2   **MIP** $6

Skeletor, 2002, Mattel
    NM $2   **MIP** $6

Stratos, 2002, Mattel
    NM $2   **MIP** $6

PLAY SETS

Castle Grayskull, 2002, Mattel
    NM $25   **MIP** $50

VEHICLES

Attack Squid, 2003, Mattel
    NM $10   **MIP** $20

Bashin' Beetle, 2002, Mattel
    NM $7   **MIP** $15

Battle Hawk, 2002, Mattel
    NM $7   **MIP** $15

Battle Ram Chariot, 2002, Mattel
    NM $7   **MIP** $15

Battle Tank, 2002, Mattel
    NM $10   **MIP** $20

Terrordactyl, 2002, Mattel
    NM $7   **MIP** $15

War Whale, 2003, Mattel
    NM $10   **MIP** $20

MATRIX, THE (MCFARLANE, 2003)

SERIES 1 FIGURES

(KP Photo, Brian Brogaard Collection)

Morpheus, 2003, McFarlane, w/gun and sword
    NM $5   **MIP** $12

(KP Photo, Brian Brogaard collection)

Neo, 2003, McFarlane
    NM $5   **MIP** $10

Neo in Chateau, 2003, McFarlane, Deluxe boxed set
    NM $10   **MIP** $17

(KP Photo, Brian Brogaard collection)

Trinity, 2003, McFarlane
    NM $5   **MIP** $10

(KP Photo, Karen O'Brien collection)

Twin 1, 2003, McFarlane
    NM $5   **MIP** $12

(KP Photo, Karen O'Brien collection)

Twin 2, 2003, McFarlane
    NM $5   **MIP** $12

SERIES 2 FIGURES

A.P.U. Deluxe Boxed Set, 2003, McFarlane, w/Mifune
    NM $15   **MIP** $30

Agent Smith, fight scene, 2003, McFarlane, in suit
    NM $5   **MIP** $12

(KP Photo, Brian Brogaard collection)

Morpheus, seated, 2003, McFarlane, w/red chair, telephone stand and phone
    NM $5   **MIP** $12

Neo, fight scene, 2003, McFarlane, backdrop of Smiths
    NM $5   **MIP** $12

(KP Photo, Brian Brogaard collection)

Neo, real world, 2003, McFarlane, w/different heads
    NM $5   **MIP** $12

Niobe, 2003, McFarlane
  NM $5   **MIP** $12

Sentinel Deluxe Boxed Set, 2003, McFarlane, fully articulated tentacles, whew!
  NM $20   **MIP** $40

(KP Photo, Karen O'Brien collection)

Trinity, 2003, McFarlane, falling scene
  NM $5   **MIP** $12

McFarlane Music (McFarlane, 1999-02)

FIGURES

Alice Cooper, 2000, McFarlane
  NM $3   **MIP** $13

Angus Young, 2001, McFarlane, AC/DC guitarist
  NM $6   **MIP** $12

Iron Maiden's Eddie: from "Killers", 2002, McFarlane, based on the album artwork
  NM $6   **MIP** $12

Iron Maiden's Eddie: from "Peace of Mind", 2002, McFarlane, based on the album artwork
  NM $6   **MIP** $12

Janis Joplin, 2000
  NM $5   **MIP** $15

Jerry Garcia, 2001, McFarlane
  NM $6   **MIP** $12

Jim Morrison, 2001, McFarlane
  NM $6   **MIP** $12

Metallica: Boxed Set, 2001, McFarlane, pose from "And Justice for All"
  NM $17   **MIP** $35

Metallica: James Hetfield, 2001, McFarlane, pose from "And Justice for All"
  NM $6   **MIP** $12

Metallica: Jason Newsted, 2001, McFarlane, pose from "And Justice for All"
  NM $6   **MIP** $12

Metallica: Kirk Hammett, 2001, McFarlane, pose from "And Justice for All"
  NM $6   **MIP** $12

Metallica: Lars Ulrich, 2001, McFarlane, pose from "And Justice for All"
  NM $6   **MIP** $12

(KP Photo)

Ozzie Osbourne, 1999, McFarlane, Fairly buff Ozzy figure holding cross and dead bat with dead bats and doves at his feet. Includes church window diorama backdrop
  NM $5   **MIP** $15

(KP Photo)

Rob Zombie, 2000, Figure with mechanical arms includes "Zombie" base
  NM $5   **MIP** $15

Metal Gear Solid (McFarlane, 1998)

FIGURES

(McFarlane Toys)

Liquid Snake, 1998, McFarlane, With pistol and machine gun rifle
  NM $4   **MIP** $8

(McFarlane Toys)

Meryl Silverburgh, 1998, McFarlane, With pistol, bayonet, grappling hook and machine gun
  NM $4   **MIP** $8

(McFarlane Toys)

Ninja, 1998, McFarlane, Multi-colored figure with sword
  NM $4   **MIP** $8

(McFarlane Toys)

Psycho Mantis, 1998, McFarlane, Includes bust, vase, crystal ball and detailed figure
  NM $4   **MIP** $8

(McFarlane Toys)

ACTION FIGURES

Revolver Ocelot, 1998, McFarlane, Detailed gunslinger figure includes two pistols

> **NM** $4   **MIP** $8

(KP Photo)

Sniper Wolf, 1998, McFarlane, With rifle and snarling wolf figure

> **NM** $4   **MIP** $8

(McFarlane Toys)

Solid Snake, 1998, McFarlane, Includes a variety of weapons and accessories; rifle, pistol, infra-red goggles and more

> **NM** $4   **MIP** $8

(McFarlane Toys)

Vulcan Raven, 1998, McFarlane, With multi-barreled weapon and barrel-shaped pack

> **NM** $4   **MIP** $8

MICRONAUTS (MEGO, 1976-80)

ACCESSORIES

Karrio, 1979, Mego, carrying case

> **NM** $10   **MIP** $20

ALIEN INVADERS CARDED

Antron, 1979, Mego

> **NM** $20   **MIP** $100

Centaurus, 1980, Mego, also a foreign release

> **NM** $50   **MIP** $200

Kronos, 1980, Mego, also a foreign release

> **NM** $35   **MIP** $200

Lobros, 1980, Mego, also a foreign release

> **NM** $35   **MIP** $200

Membros, 1979, Mego

> **NM** $20   **MIP** $100

Repto, 1979, Mego

> **NM** $20   **MIP** $100

ALIEN INVADERS VEHICLES

Alphatron, 1979, Mego, vehicle w/ figure

> **NM** $5   **MIP** $10

Betatron, 1979, Mego, vehicle w/ figure

> **NM** $5   **MIP** $10

Gammatron, 1979, Mego, vehicle w/ figure

> **NM** $5   **MIP** $10

Hornetroid, 1979, Mego, vehicle for Antron

> **NM** $20   **MIP** $40

Hydra, 1976, Mego

> **NM** $7   **MIP** $15

Mobile Exploration Lab, 1976, Mego, largest of the vehicles

> **NM** $17   **MIP** $35

Solarion, 1978, Mego, rare

> **NM** $15   **MIP** $30

Star Searcher, 1978, Mego

> **NM** $15   **MIP** $40

Taurion, 1978, Mego

> **NM** $11   **MIP** $22

Terraphant, 1979, Mego, vehicle for Membros

> **NM** $20   **MIP** $40

BOXED FIGURES

Andromeda, 1977, Mego

> **NM** $10   **MIP** $25

Baron Karza, 1977, Mego

> **NM** $15   **MIP** $30

Biotron, 1976, Mego

> **NM** $10   **MIP** $25

Force Commander, 1977, Mego

> **NM** $10   **MIP** $25

Giant Acroyear, 1977, Mego

> **NM** $10   **MIP** $25

Megas, 1981, Mego, foreign release

> **NM** $10   **MIP** $25

Microtron, 1976, Mego

> **NM** $15   **MIP** $45

Nemesis Robot, 1978, Mego

> **NM** $15   **MIP** $30

Oberon, 1977, Mego

> **NM** $20   **MIP** $45

Phobos Robot, 1978, Mego

> **NM** $12   **MIP** $25

CARDED FIGURES

Acroyear, 1976, Mego, red, blue, orange

> **NM** $10   **MIP** $20

Acroyear II, 1977, Mego, red, blue, orange

> **NM** $15   **MIP** $30

Galactic Defender, 1978, Mego, white, yellow

> **NM** $15   **MIP** $30

Galactic Warrior, 1976, Mego, red, blue, orange

> **NM** $12   **MIP** $25

Pharoid with Time Chamber, 1977, Mego, blue, red, gray

> **NM** $18   **MIP** $35

Space Glider, 1976, Mego, blue, green, orange

> **NM** $15   **MIP** $30

Time Traveler, 1976, Mego, solid plastic, yellow, orange

> **NM** $15   **MIP** $30

Time Traveler, 1976, Mego, clear plastic, yellow, orange

> **NM** $15   **MIP** $30

MICROPOLIS PLAY SETS

Galactic Command Center, 1978, Mego

> **NM** $40   **MIP** $95

Interplanetary Headquarters, 1978, Mego

> **NM** $40   **MIP** $95

Mega City, 1978, Mego, largest of the micro cities, 500+ pieces

> **NM** $40   **MIP** $95

Microrail City, 1978, Mego

> **NM** $40   **MIP** $95

PLAY SETS

Astro Station, 1976, Mego

> **NM** $25   **MIP** $50

Rocket Tubes, 1978, Mego, 2 versions, deluxe and standard

> **NM** $45   **MIP** $90

Stratstation, 1976, Mego

> **NM** $30   **MIP** $65

VEHICLES

Aquatron, 1977, Mego, two pontoons, detachable motor

> **NM** $10   **MIP** $20

Battle Cruiser, 1977, Mego

> **NM** $30   **MIP** $60

Crater Cruncher with figure, 1976, Mego, Time Traveler included

> **NM** $15   **MIP** $35

Galactic Cruiser, 1976, Mego

> **NM** $15   **MIP** $35

Hydro Copter, 1976, Mego

> **NM** $10   **MIP** $25

Neon Orbiter, 1977, Mego

> **NM** $6   **MIP** $20

Photon Sled, 1976, Mego

> **NM** $10   **MIP** $25

Rhodium Orbiter, 1977, Mego
NM $10   MIP $30

Thorium Orbiter, 1977, Mego
NM $10   MIP $25

Ultronic Scooter with figure, 1976, Mego,
Time Traveler included
NM $15   MIP $45

Warp Racer with figure, 1976, Mego, Time
Traveler included
NM $15   MIP $45

MIGHTY MORPHIN POWER RANGERS (BANDAI, 1993-95)

3" FIGURES

Black Ranger, 1995, Bandai
NM $5   MIP $15

Blue Ranger, 1995, Bandai
NM $5   MIP $15

Pink Ranger, 1995, Bandai
NM $5   MIP $15

Red Ranger, 1995, Bandai
NM $5   MIP $15

Yellow Ranger, 1995, Bandai
NM $5   MIP $15

5" FIGURES WITH THUNDER BIKES

Black Ranger, 1995, Bandai
NM $6   MIP $15

Blue Ranger, 1995, Bandai
NM $6   MIP $15

Pink Ranger, 1995, Bandai
NM $6   MIP $15

Red Ranger, 1995, Bandai
NM $6   MIP $15

Yellow Ranger, 1995, Bandai
NM $6   MIP $15

8" ALIENS, 1993

Baboo, 1993, Bandai
NM $8   MIP $20

Bones, 1993, Bandai
NM $8   MIP $20

Finster, 1993, Bandai
NM $8   MIP $20

Goldar, 1993, Bandai
NM $8   MIP $20

King Sphinx, 1993, Bandai
NM $8   MIP $20

Putty Patrol, 1993, Bandai
NM $8   MIP $20

Squatt, 1993, Bandai
NM $8   MIP $20

8" FIGURES, 1993

Black Ranger, 1993, Bandai
NM $7   MIP $20

Blue Ranger, 1993, Bandai
NM $7   MIP $20

Pink Ranger, 1993, Bandai
NM $10   MIP $20

Red Ranger, 1993, Bandai
NM $5   MIP $20

Yellow Ranger, 1993, Bandai
NM $10   MIP $20

8" MOVIE FIGURES, 1995

Black Ranger, 1995, Bandai, metallic
NM $6   MIP $15

Blue Ranger, 1995, Bandai, metallic
NM $6   MIP $15

Pink Ranger, 1995, Bandai, metallic
NM $6   MIP $15

Red Ranger, 1995, Bandai, metallic
NM $6   MIP $15

White Ranger, 1995, Bandai, metallic
NM $6   MIP $15

Yellow Ranger, 1995, Bandai, metallic
NM $6   MIP $15

ACTION FEATURE EVIL SPACE ALIENS, 5-1/2" FIGURES, 1994

Dark Knight, 1994, Bandai
NM $6   MIP $15

Eye Guy, 1994, Bandai
NM $6   MIP $15

Minotar, 1994, Bandai
NM $6   MIP $15

Mutaytus, 1994, Bandai
NM $6   MIP $15

Pudgy Pig, 1994, Bandai
NM $6   MIP $15

Rita Repulsa, 1994, Bandai
NM $6   MIP $15

Snizard Lips, 1994, Bandai
NM $6   MIP $15

Spidertron, 1994, Bandai
NM $6   MIP $15

AUTO-MORPHIN POWER RANGERS, 5-1/2" FIGURES, 1994

Black Ranger, 1994, Bandai
NM $3   MIP $15

Blue Ranger, 1994, Bandai
NM $3   MIP $15

Green Ranger, 1994, Bandai
NM $3   MIP $15

Pink Ranger, 1994, Bandai
NM $3   MIP $15

Red Ranger, 1994, Bandai
NM $2   MIP $15

Yellow Ranger, 1994, Bandai
NM $3   MIP $15

DELUXE EVIL SPACE ALIENS, 8" FIGURES, 1994

Evil Eye, 1994, Bandai
NM $7   MIP $15

Goo Fish, 1994, Bandai
NM $7   MIP $15

Guitardo, 1994, Bandai
NM $7   MIP $15

Lord Zedd, 1994, Bandai
NM $8   MIP $18

Pirantus Head, 1994, Bandai
NM $7   MIP $15

Pudgy Pig, 1994, Bandai
NM $7   MIP $15

Putty Patrol, 1994, Bandai
NM $7   MIP $15

Rhino Blaster, 1994, Bandai
NM $7   MIP $15

Socaddillo, 1994, Bandai
NM $7   MIP $15

KARATE ACTION FIGURES, 1994

Black Ranger, 1994, Bandai
NM $6   MIP $12

Blue Ranger, 1994, Bandai
NM $6   MIP $12

Pink Ranger, 1994, Bandai
NM $8   MIP $16

Red Ranger, 1994, Bandai
NM $5   MIP $10

Yellow Ranger, 1994, Bandai
NM $8   MIP $16

POWER RANGERS FOR GIRLS

Kimberly, 1995, Bandai
NM $10   MIP $20

Kimberly/Trini Set, 1995, Bandai
NM $20   MIP $40

Trini, 1995, Bandai
NM $10   MIP $20

ZORDS, 1993

Dragon Dagger, 1993, Bandai
NM $20   MIP $50

Dragon Zord with Green Ranger, 1993, Bandai
NM $25   MIP $55

MegaZord, 1993, Bandai
NM $15   MIP $30

MegaZord Deluxe, 1993, Bandai
NM $20   MIP $40

Titanus the Carrier Zord, 1993, Bandai
NM $35   MIP $75

ZORDS, 1994

MegaZord, black/gold, limit. ed., 1994, Bandai
NM $50   MIP $100

Power Cannon, 1994, Bandai
NM $15   MIP $35

Power Dome Morphin Set, 1994, Bandai
NM $20   MIP $50

Red Dragon Thunder Zord, 1994, Bandai
NM $25   MIP $45

ACTION FIGURES

Saba (White Sword), 1994, Bandai
      NM $15   **MIP** $30

Thunder Zord Assault Team, 1994, Bandai
      NM $25   **MIP** $45

TOR the Shuttle Zord, 1994, Bandai
      NM $30   **MIP** $60

Ultra Thunder Zord, 1994, Bandai
      NM $35   **MIP** $70

White Tiger Zord with White Ranger,
1994, Bandai
      NM $25   **MIP** $50

MODERN HORROR CLASSICS (SIDESHOW TOYS, 1998-PRESENT)

12" FIGURES

Freddy Krueger, 2003, Sideshow Toys, #7302
      NM n/a   **MIP** $40

Furnace Environment, 2003, Sideshow Toys, #6606
      NM n/a   **MIP** $40

Furnace/ Freddy Combo Pack, 2003, Sideshow Toys, #6606R, Freddy and the Furnace
      NM n/a   **MIP** $75

Jason Voorhees, 2003, Sideshow Toys, #7301
      NM n/a   **MIP** $40

Leatherface - Texas Chainsaw Massacre, 2003, Sideshow Toys, #7303
      NM n/a   **MIP** $40

Michael Myers - Halloween, 2003, Sideshow Toys, #7304
      NM n/a   **MIP** $40

MONSTERS (McFARLANE, 1997-2002)

FIGURES

Dracula, 2002, McFarlane
      NM $5   **MIP** $20

Frankenstein, 2002, McFarlane
      NM $5   **MIP** $20

Mummy, 2002, McFarlane
      NM $5   **MIP** $20

Sea Creature, 2002, McFarlane
      NM $5   **MIP** $20

VooDoo Queen, 2002, McFarlane
      NM $5   **MIP** $20

Werewolf, 2002, McFarlane
      NM $5   **MIP** $20

SERIES 1, PLAY SETS WITH 4" FIGURES

Dracula and Bat, 1997, McFarlane, Includes Dracula, coffin, masouleum, "bat" figure and accessories
      NM $5   **MIP** $20

(McFarlane Toys)

Frankenstein and Igor, 1997, McFarlane, Hunchbacked Igor in lab coat and monster figure on upright table
      NM $8   **MIP** $20

(McFarlane Toys)

Hunchback, Quasimodo and Gargoyle, 1997, McFarlane, Includes catapult-topped bell tower and two figures
      NM $5   **MIP** $15

Werewolf and Victim, 1997, Kenner
      NM $5   **MIP** $15

SERIES 2, PLAY SETS WITH 4" FIGURES

(McFarlane Toys)

Dr. Frankenstein, 1998, McFarlane, Set includes re-animation bed, gruesome Frankenstein monster figure, Dr. F in lab coat. Includes various lab instruments
      NM $6   **MIP** $12

(McFarlane Toys)

The Mummy, 1998, McFarlane, Includes sarcophogus, Anubis figure, jars, and Mummy
      NM $6   **MIP** $12

(McFarlane Toys)

The Phantom of the Opera, 1998, McFarlane, Great detail--includes pipe organ, inspector and phantom figures
      NM $6   **MIP** $12

(McFarlane Toys)

The Sea Creature, 1998, McFarlane, Set includes diver in old-fashioned dive suit and attacking sea creature
      NM $6   **MIP** $12

MORK AND MINDY (MATTEL, 1980)

FIGURES

Mindy, 1980, Mattel
      NM $20   **MIP** $45

Mork from Ork with egg, 1980, Mattel

NM $20   MIP $45

(Toy Shop File Photo)

Mork with Talking Spacepack, upside down, 1980, Mattel, Talking Mork says, "Nano, Nano and 7 other crazy things"

NM $20   MIP $50

MOVIE MANIACS (McFarlane, 1998-2004)

18" FIGURES

(KP Photo, Merry Dudley collection)

Ash, 2001, McFarlane, from Army of Darkness

NM $10   MIP $25

Edward Scissorhands, 2002, McFarlane

NM $10   MIP $25

Freddy Krueger from "Nightmare on Elm Street", 2000, McFarlane

NM $10   MIP $25

Leatherface, 2001, McFarlane, from Texas Chainsaw Masacre

NM $10   MIP $25

Michael Myers, "Halloween", 2000, McFarlane

NM $10   MIP $25

SERIES 1

Eve, "Species II", 1998, McFarlane

NM $4   MIP $8

(McFarlane Toys)

Freddy Krueger, "Nightmare on Elm Street", 1998, McFarlane, Classic Freddy with red-striped sweater, fedora and extended claws

NM $5   MIP $15

Freddy Krueger, gorey, "Nightmare on Elm Street", 1998, McFarlane

NM $5   MIP $15

Jason, "Friday the 13th", 1998, McFarlane

NM $4   MIP $8

(McFarlane Toys)

Jason, gory, "Friday the 13th", 1998, McFarlane, Detailed figure includes machete

NM $10   MIP $30

Leatherface, "The Texas Chainsaw Massacre", 1998, McFarlane

NM $15   MIP $25

Leatherface, gory, "The Texas Chainsaw Massacre", 1998, McFarlane

NM $25   MIP $45

Patrick, "Species II", 1998, McFarlane

NM $4   MIP $8

SERIES 2

Chucky and Tiffany, "Bride of Chucky", 1999, McFarlane

NM $8   MIP $20

Chucky, "Child's Play", 1999, McFarlane

NM $5   MIP $15

(KP Photo)

Eric Draven, "The Crow", 1999, McFarlane, With black guitar and crow figure

NM $5   MIP $15

(KP Photo)

Ghostface, "Scream", 1999, McFarlane, Detailed Scream figure with knife and cellphone, movie-poster stand

NM $5   MIP $15

(KP Photo)

Michael Myers, "Halloween", 1999, McFarlane, Michael Myers figure with knife and movie-poster stand

NM $5   MIP $15

(KP Photo)

Norman Bates, "Psycho", 1999, McFarlane, Norman in "mother" outfit and wig with knife, includes movie-poster stand

NM $5   MIP $15

ACTION FIGURES

(KP Photo)

Pumkinhead, "Pumpkinhead", 1999, McFarlane, Figure includes movie-poster stand

NM $5   MIP $15

SERIES 3

(KP Photo)

Ash, "Army of Darkness", 2000, McFarlane, Great Bruce Campbell likeness with chainsaw hand, rifle and movie-poster stand

NM $5   MIP $15

(KP Photo)

Blair Monster, "The Thing", 2000, McFarlane, Highly detailed figure with movie stand

NM $5   MIP $15

(KP Photo)

Edward Scissorhands, "Edward Scissorhands", 2000, McFarlane, Very detailed likeness with movie-poster stand

NM $3   MIP $12

(KP Photo)

Fly, The, "The Fly", 2000, McFarlane, Brindle-pattern figure with movie-poster stand

NM $3   MIP $10

King Kong, "King Kong", 2000, McFarlane, Deluxe figure

NM $10   MIP $25

Norris Creature, "The Thing", 2000, McFarlane

NM $5   MIP $15

Norris Spider, "The Thing", 2000, McFarlane

NM $5   MIP $15

(KP Photo)

Shaft, "Shaft", 2000, McFarlane, Figures with "The Thing" movie stand

NM $3   MIP $10

(KP Photo)

Snake Plissken, "Escape From L.A.", 2000, McFarlane, Figure with rifle and movie-poster stand

NM $3   MIP $10

SERIES 4

Blair Witch, "Blair Witch Project", 2001, McFarlane

NM $5   MIP $15

Candyman, 2001, McFarlane

NM $5   MIP $15

(KP Photo, Brian Brogaard collection)

Evil Ash, 2001, McFarlane, from "Army of Darkness"

NM $5   MIP $15

Freddy Krueger, 2001, McFarlane, from "Nightmare on Elm Street"

NM $5   MIP $15

Jaws Deluxe Boxed Set, 2001, McFarlane

NM $15   MIP $30

T-1000, 2001, McFarlane, T2

NM $5   MIP $15

T-800, 2001, McFarlane, T2

NM $5   MIP $15

SERIES 5

Alien and Predator Deluxe Boxed Set, 2002, McFarlane

NM $15   MIP $30

Djinn, 2002, McFarlane, from "Wishmaster"

    NM $5   **MIP** $10

Jason X, 2002, McFarlane

    NM $5   **MIP** $10

Lord of Darkness, 2002, McFarlane, from "Legend"

    NM $5   **MIP** $15

Sarah Connor, 2002, McFarlane

    NM $5   **MIP** $15

T-800 Endoskeleton, 2002, McFarlane

    NM $5   **MIP** $15

(KP Photo, Brian Brogaard collection)

Tooth Fairy, 2002, McFarlane, from "Darkness Falls"

    NM $5   **MIP** $10

SERIES 6

(KP Photo, Brian Brogaard collection)

Alien Queen, 2003, McFarlane, large set, w/Ripley

    NM $10   **MIP** $30

Dog Alien, 2003, McFarlane

    NM $5   **MIP** $15

Predator, 2003, McFarlane

    NM $5   **MIP** $15

(KP Photo, Brian Brogaard collection)

Predator the Hunter, 2003, McFarlane

    NM $5   **MIP** $15

Warrior Alien, 2003, McFarlane

    NM $5   **MIP** $15

SERIES 7

12" Leatherface, 2004, McFarlane, from Texas Chainsaw Massacre

    NM $10   **MIP** $30

Colonial Marine Corporal Hicks, 2004, McFarlane, from Aliens

    NM $5   **MIP** $15

Erin, 2004, McFarlane, from Texas Chainsaw Massacre

    NM $5   **MIP** $15

Leatherface, 2004, McFarlane, from Texas Chainsaw Massacre

    NM $5   **MIP** $15

Old Monty, 2004, McFarlane, from Texas Chainsaw Massacre

    NM $5   **MIP** $15

Robocop, 2004, McFarlane, from film

    NM $5   **MIP** $15

Sherrif Hoyt, 2004, McFarlane, from Texas Chainsaw Massacre

    NM $5   **MIP** $15

MUPPETS (PALISADES, 2002-04)

12" FIGURES

Mega Animal, 2003, Palisades

    NM $10   **MIP** $20

Mega Beaker, 2003, Palisades

    NM $10   **MIP** $20

Mega Gonzo, 2004, Palisades, in tuxedo

    NM $10   **MIP** $20

EXCLUSIVES

(KP Photo, Merry Dudley collection)

"Invisible Spray" Fozzie, 2004, Palisades, exclusive2002 San Diego Comicon excludive; from Muppets in Space

    NM $5   **MIP** $12

(KP Photo, Karen O'Brien collection)

Animal Tour 2003, 2003, Palisades, convention special, didn't come w/drumsticks

    NM $12   **MIP** $25

PLAY SETS

Electric Mayhem, 2002, Palisades, w/Animal

    NM $15   **MIP** $30

Muppet Labs, 2002, Palisades, w/ Beaker

    NM $10   **MIP** $20

Pigs in Space, 2002, Palisades

    NM $10   **MIP** $20

Swedish Kitchen, 2002, Palisades, w/ the Swedish Chef

    NM $10   **MIP** $20

SERIES 01 FIGURES

Dr. Bunsen Honeydew, 2002, Palisades

    NM $6   **MIP** $15

Dr. Teeth, 2002, Palisades

    NM $8   **MIP** $18

Kermit the Frog, 2002, Palisades

    NM $6   **MIP** $12

Miss Piggy, 2002, Palisades

    NM $6   **MIP** $12

SERIES 02 FIGURES

Crazy Harry, 2002, Palisades

    NM $5   **MIP** $10

Floyd Pepper, 2002, Palisades

    NM $5   **MIP** $12

Fozzie Bear, 2002, Palisades

    NM $5   **MIP** $10

Gonzo the Great, 2002, Palisades

    NM $5   **MIP** $10

SERIES 03 FIGURES

Lew Zealand, 2002, Palisades

    NM $5   **MIP** $9

Rowlf, 2002, Palisades

    NM $5   **MIP** $10

Scooter, 2002, Palisades

    NM $5   **MIP** $9

Zoot, 2002, Palisades

    NM $7   **MIP** $15

SERIES 04 FIGURES

Dr. Strangepork, 2002, Palisades
  NM $5   MIP $9

Link Hogthrob, 2002, Palisades
  NM $5   MIP $9

(KP Photo, Merry Dudley collection)

Mr. Samuel Arrow, 2002, Palisades
  NM $5   MIP $9

Rizzo the Rat, 2002, Palisades
  NM $5   MIP $9

SERIES 05 FIGURES

Gonzo & Camilla, 2003, Palisades
  NM $5   MIP $9

Janice, 2003, Palisades
  NM $7   MIP $12

Muppet Newsman, 2003, Palisades
  NM $5   MIP $9

Pepe, 2003, Palisades
  NM $5   MIP $9

SERIES 06 FIGURES

Clifford, 2003, Palisades
  NM $4   MIP $8

Patrol Bear, 2003, Palisades
  NM $4   MIP $8

Statler, 2003, Palisades
  NM $4   MIP $8

Waldorf, 2003, Palisades
  NM $4   MIP $8

SERIES 07 FIGURES

Beauregard, 2004, Palisades
  NM $4   MIP $8

Captain Smollet & Polly, 2004, Palisades,
  Kermit as sea captain
  NM $4   MIP $8

Frog Scout Robin, 2004, Palisades
  NM $4   MIP $8

Johnny Fiama, 2004, Palisades, available
  w/3 different jacket colors, silver,
  pinstripe, maroon
  NM $6   MIP $12

SERIES 08 FIGURES

Dr. Phil Van Neuter, 2004, Palisades
  NM $4   MIP $8

Marvin Suggs, 2004, Palisades
  NM $4   MIP $8

Movie Usher Scooter, 2004, Palisades
  NM $4   MIP $8

Sam the Eagle, 2004, Palisades
  NM $4   MIP $8

SERIES 09 FIGURES

Classic Sweedish Chef, 2004, Palisades
  NM $4   MIP $8

Lips, 2004, Palisades
  NM $4   MIP $8

Pops, 2004, Palisades
  NM $4   MIP $8

Steppin' Out Fozzie (Tuxedo Fozzie),
  2004, Palisades, w/Chucky, the dummy
  NM $4   MIP $8

NIGHTMARE BEFORE CHRITSTMAS (HASBRO, 1993)

FIGURES

Behemouth, 1993, Hasbro
  NM $35   MIP $80

Evil Scientist, 1993, Hasbro
  NM $50   MIP $150

Jack Skellington, 1993, Hasbro
  NM $40   MIP $100

Jack Skellington as Santa, 1993, Hasbro
  NM $35   MIP $80

Lock, Shock and Barrel, 1993, Hasbro
  NM $75   MIP $250

Mayor, 1993, Hasbro
  NM $45   MIP $125

Oogie Boogie, 1993, Hasbro
  NM $75   MIP $250

Sally, 1993, Hasbro
  NM $40   MIP $100

Santa, 1993, Hasbro
  NM $75   MIP $250

Werewolf, 1993, Hasbro
  NM $40   MIP $100

NOBLE KNIGHTS (MARX, 1968)

FIGURES

(Toy Shop File Photo)

Black Knight, Sir Cedric, 1968, Marx,
  #2082, with removeable helmet, shield
  and accessories, a UK figure
  NM $250   MIP $550

(Toy Shop File Photo)

Gold Knight, Sir Gordon, 1968, Marx, #5366,
  like the black knight, this figure had
  molded-on armor, but included a variety
  of plastic accessories such as shield,
  helmet and sword, Sir Percival in UK
  NM $75   MIP $150

Silver Knight, Sir Stuart, 1968, Marx,
  #5364, Sir Roland in UK
  NM $75   MIP $150

HORSES

Bravo Armor Horse, 1968, Marx, #5371,
  Gold Knight's horse, chestnut color,
  Victor in UK
  NM $75   MIP $150

Valiant Armor Horse, 1968, Marx, Black
  Knight's horse, gray color, UK only
  NM $200   MIP $400

Valor Armor Horse, 1968, Marx, #5391,
  Silver Knight's horse, palomino color,
  Valour in UK, Big Valor on 1970 packaging
  NM $75   MIP $150

ONE MILLION B.C. (MEGO, 1976)

FIGURES

Dimetrodon, 1976, Mego, boxed
    NM $100   MIP $250

Grok, 1976, Mego, carded
    NM $25   MIP $50

Hairy Rhino, 1976, Mego, boxed
    NM $125   MIP $300

Mada, 1976, Mego, carded
    NM $25   MIP $50

Orm, 1976, Mego, carded
    NM $25   MIP $50

Trag, 1976, Mego, carded
    NM $25   MIP $50

Tribal Lair, 1976, Mego, boxed
    NM $100   MIP $200

Tribal Lair Gift Set (five figures), 1976, Mego, boxed
    NM $200   MIP $400

Tyrannosaur, 1976, Mego, boxed
    NM $125   MIP $300

Zon, 1976, carded, 1976, Mego, carded
    NM $25   MIP $50

OUTER SPACE MEN (COLORFORMS, 1968)

FIGURES

Alpha 7 / Man from Mars, 1968, Colorforms
    NM $150   MIP $450

(Toy Shop File Photo)

Astro-Nautilus / Man from Neptune, 1968, Colorforms, A freaky-looking dude that is similar to the work done on today's hit show Futurama.
    NM $300   MIP $750

Colossus Rex / Man from Jupiter, 1968, Colorforms
    NM $300   MIP $800

Commander Comet / Man from Venus, 1968, Colorforms
    NM $200   MIP $500

(Toy Shop File Photo)

Electron / Man from Pluto, 1968, Colorforms, A flexible figure that packs heat, and by the looks of things, can shoot lightning from his head. Striking!
    NM $200   MIP $500

(Toy Shop File Photo)

Orbitron / Man from Uranus, 1968, Colorforms, An unfortunately-named, but neat toy nonetheless. Looking very much like the Metaluna Mutant in "This Island Earth," Orbitron was a bendable figure that included a blaster pistol
    NM $200   MIP $600

Xodiac / Man from Saturn, 1968, Colorforms
    NM $200   MIP $500

PEE-WEE'S PLAYHOUSE (MATCHBOX, 1988)

5" FIGURES

Chairry, 1988, Matchbox
    NM $9   MIP $23

Conky, 1988, Matchbox
    NM $11   MIP $30

Cowboy Curtis, 1988, Matchbox
    NM $9   MIP $23

Globey and Randy, 1988, Matchbox
    NM $9   MIP $23

Jambi and Puppetland Band, 1988, Matchbox
    NM $11   MIP $26

King of Cartoons, 1988, Matchbox
    NM $8   MIP $19

Magic Screen, 1988, Matchbox
    NM $6   MIP $15

Miss Yvonne, 1988, Matchbox
    NM $15   MIP $30

Pee-Wee Herman, 1988, Matchbox
    NM $6   MIP $15

Pee-Wee Herman with Scooter, 1988, Matchbox
    NM $9   MIP $23

Pterri, 1988, Matchbox
    NM $8   MIP $19

Reba, 1988, Matchbox
    NM $9   MIP $26

Ricardo, 1988, Matchbox
    NM $8   MIP $19

PLAY SETS

Pee-Wee's Playhouse, 1988, Matchbox, w/Scooter, Floory, Clockey, Mr. Window, Dancing Flowers; working front door, fridge, swinging wall; includes platform, island couch, tv console, kitchen table and bench
    NM $50   MIP $175

PLANET OF THE APES (HASBRO, 1999)

12" FIGURES

Cornelius, 1999, Hasbro
    NM $8   MIP $20

Dr. Zaius, 1999, Hasbro
    NM $8   MIP $20

Dr. Zira, 1998, Hasbro
    NM $10   MIP $20

General Ursus, 1999, Hasbro
    NM $8   MIP $20

Gorilla Sergeant, 1998, Hasbro
    NM $10   MIP $20

Gorilla Soldier, 1998, Hasbro, Diamond Previews exclusive
    NM $15   MIP $30

Taylor, 1998, Hasbro
    NM $10   MIP $20

7" FIGURES

Commander Taylor, 1999, Hasbro
    NM $2   MIP $6

Cornelius, 1999, Hasbro
    NM $2   MIP $6

Dr. Zaius, 1999, Hasbro
    NM $2   MIP $6

Gorilla Sergeant, 1999, Hasbro
    NM $2   MIP $6

Gorilla Soldier, 1999, Hasbro
    NM $2   MIP $6

Zira, 1999, Hasbro
    NM $2   MIP $6

PLANET OF THE APES (MEGO, 1973-75)

8" FIGURES

Astronaut, 1973, Mego, boxed
NM $50   **MIP** $250

Astronaut, 1975, Mego, carded
NM $50   **MIP** $100

Astronaut Burke, 1975, Mego, carded
NM $50   **MIP** $100

Astronaut Burke, 1975, Mego, boxed
NM $50   **MIP** $250

Astronaut Verdon, 1975, Mego, boxec
NM $50   **MIP** $250

Astronaut Verdon, 1975, Mego, carded
NM $50   **MIP** $125

Cornelius, 1973, Mego, boxed
NM $40   **MIP** $200

Cornelius, 1975, Mego, carded
NM $40   **MIP** $100

Dr. Zaius, 1973, Mego, boxed
NM $40   **MIP** $200

Dr. Zaius, 1975, Mego, carded
NM $40   **MIP** $100

Galen, 1975, Mego, carded
NM $40   **MIP** $100

Galen, 1975, Mego, boxed
NM $40   **MIP** $200

General Urko, 1975, Mego, boxed
NM $50   **MIP** $250

General Urko, 1975, Mego, carded
NM $50   **MIP** $250

General Ursus, 1975, Mego, boxed
NM $50   **MIP** $250

General Ursus, 1975, Mego, carded
NM $50   **MIP** $250

Soldier Ape, 1973, Mego, boxed
NM $50   **MIP** $250

Soldier Ape, 1975, Mego, carded
NM $50   **MIP** $200

Zira, 1973, Mego, boxed
NM $30   **MIP** $200

Zira, 1975, Mego, carded
NM $30   **MIP** $100

ACCESSORIES

(Toy Shop File Photo)

Action Stallion, 1975, Mego, brown, motorized, remote-controlled
NM $50   **MIP** $100

Battering Ram, 1975, Mego, boxed
NM $20   **MIP** $40

Dr. Zaius' Throne, 1975, Mego, boxed
NM $20   **MIP** $40

Jail, 1975, Mego, boxed
NM $20   **MIP** $40

PLAY SETS

Forbidden Zone Trap, 1975, Mego, boxed
NM $90   **MIP** $200

Fortress, 1975, Mego, boxed
NM $85   **MIP** $200

Treehouse, 1975, Mego, boxed
NM $75   **MIP** $200

Village, 1975, Mego, boxed
NM $85   **MIP** $200

VEHICLES

Catapult and Wagon, 1975, Mego, boxed
NM $75   **MIP** $150

PLANET OF THE APES - MOVIE (HASBRO 2001)

12" FIGURES

Attar, 2001, Hasbro
NM $5   **MIP** $15

Leo, 2001, Hasbro
NM $5   **MIP** $15

FIGURES

Ape Commander, 2001, Hasbro
NM $2   **MIP** $5

Ari, 2001, Hasbro
NM $2   **MIP** $5

Attar, 2001, Hasbro
NM $2   **MIP** $5

Daena, 2001, Hasbro
NM $2   **MIP** $5

General Thade w/ Horse, 2001, Hasbro
NM $5   **MIP** $15

Krull, 2001, Hasbro
NM $2   **MIP** $5

Leo, 2001, Hasbro
NM $2   **MIP** $5

Limbo, 2001, Hasbro
NM $2   **MIP** $5

Pericles, 2001, Hasbro
NM $2   **MIP** $5

POCKET SUPER HEROES (MEGO, 1976-79)

3-3/4" FIGURES

Aquaman, white card, 1976, Mego
NM $50   **MIP** $100

Batman, red card, 1976, Mego
NM $20   **MIP** $75

Batman, white card, 1976, Mego
NM $20   **MIP** $125

Captain America, white card, 1976, Mego
NM $50   **MIP** $100

General Zod, red card, 1979, Mego
NM $5   **MIP** $25

Green Goblin, white card, 1976, Mego
NM $50   **MIP** $150

Hulk, 1976, white card, 1976, Mego
NM $15   **MIP** $40

(Toy Shop File Photo)

Hulk, 1979, red card, 1979, Mego, Shown on right with Robin
NM $15   **MIP** $30

Jor-El (Superman), red card, 1979, Mego
NM $10   **MIP** $20

Lex Luthor (Superman), red card, 1979, Mego
NM $10   **MIP** $20

(Toy Shop File Photo)

Robin, red card, 1979, Mego, Shown on left with Hulk
NM $20   **MIP** $60

Robin, white card, 1976, Mego
NM $20   **MIP** $100

Spider-Man, red card, 1979, Mego
NM $15   **MIP** $50

Spider-Man, white card, 1976, Mego
NM $15   **MIP** $100

Superman, white card, 1976, Mego
NM $15   **MIP** $75

Superman, red card, 1979, Mego
NM $15   **MIP** $40

Wonder Woman, white card, 1979, Mego
NM $20   **MIP** $75

ACCESSORIES

Batcave, 1981, Mego
NM $120   **MIP** $300

VEHICLES

Batmachine, 1979, Mego
NM $40   **MIP** $100

Batmobile, 1979, Mego, with Batman and Robin
NM $80   **MIP** $200

Spider-Car, 1979, Mego, with Spider-Man and Hulk
NM $30   **MIP** $75

Spider-Machine, 1979, Mego
NM $40   **MIP** $100

POWER RANGERS IN SPACE (BANDAI, 1998)

ACTION ZORDS, 5" FIGURES

Astro Megaship, 1998, Bandai
NM $2   MIP $6

Astro Megazord, 1998, Bandai
NM $2   MIP $6

Delta Megazord, 1998, Bandai
NM $2   MIP $6

Mega Tank, 1998, Bandai
NM $2   MIP $6

Mega Winger, 1998, Bandai
NM $2   MIP $6

ASTRO RANGER, 5" FIGURES

Black Ranger, 1998, Bandai
NM $2   MIP $6

Pink Ranger, 1998, Bandai
NM $2   MIP $6

Red Ranger, 1998, Bandai
NM $2   MIP $6

Red Ranger, 1998, Bandai
NM $2   MIP $6

Silver Ranger, 1998, Bandai
NM $2   MIP $6

Yellow Ranger, 1998, Bandai
NM $2   MIP $6

BATTLIZED POWER RANGERS, 5" FIGURES

Black Ranger, 1998, Bandai
NM $2   MIP $6

Blue Ranger, 1998, Bandai
NM $2   MIP $6

Red ranger, 1998, Bandai
NM $2   MIP $6

Silver, 1998, Bandai
NM $2   MIP $6

EVIL SPACE ALIENS, 5" FIGURES

Craterite, 1998, Bandai
NM $2   MIP $6

Ecliptor, 1998, Bandai
NM $2   MIP $6

STAR POWER RANGERS IN SPACE, 5" FIGURES

Blue Ranger, 1998, Bandai
NM $2   MIP $6

Green Ranger, 1998, Bandai
NM $2   MIP $6

Pink Ranger, 1998, Bandai
NM $2   MIP $6

Red Ranger, 1998, Bandai
NM $2   MIP $6

Yellow Ranger, 1998, Bandai
NM $2   MIP $6

POWER RANGERS TURBO (BANDAI, 1997)

EVIL SPACE ALIENS, 5" FIGURES

Amphibitor, 1997, Bandai
NM $2   MIP $6

Chromite, 1997, Bandai
NM $2   MIP $6

Divatox, 1997, Bandai
NM $2   MIP $6

Elgar, 1997, Bandai
NM $2   MIP $6

Griller, 1997, Bandai
NM $2   MIP $6

Hammeron, 1997, Bandai
NM $2   MIP $6

Rygog, 1997, Bandai
NM $2   MIP $6

Visceron, 1997, Bandai
NM $2   MIP $6

REPEAT TURBO RANGERS, 5" FIGURES

Blue Ranger, 1997, Bandai
NM $2   MIP $6

Green Ranger, 1997, Bandai
NM $2   MIP $6

Pink Ranger, 1997, Bandai
NM $2   MIP $6

Red Ranger, 1997, Bandai
NM $2   MIP $6

Yellow Ranger, 1997, Bandai
NM $2   MIP $6

TURBO CARTS WITH 4" FIGURE

Cart with Blue Turbo Ranger, 1997, Bandai
NM $3   MIP $8

Cart with Green Turbo Ranger, 1997, Bandai
NM $3   MIP $8

Cart with Pink Turbo Ranger, 1997, Bandai
NM $3   MIP $8

Cart with Red Turbo Ranger, 1997, Bandai
NM $3   MIP $8

Cart with Yellow Turbo Ranger, 1997, Bandai
NM $3   MIP $8

TURBO RANGERS, 5" FIGURES, EACH ACTIVATED WITH KEY

Blue Turbo Ranger, 1997, Bandai
NM $2   MIP $6

Green Turbo Ranger, 1997, Bandai
NM $2   MIP $6

Pink Turbo Ranger, 1997, Bandai
NM $2   MIP $6

Red Turbo Ranger, 1997, Bandai
NM $2   MIP $6

Yellow Turbo Ranger, 1997, Bandai
NM $2   MIP $6

TURBO SHIFTER, 5" FIGURES

Blue Ranger, 1997, Bandai
NM $2   MIP $6

Green Ranger, 1997, Bandai
NM $2   MIP $6

Pink Ranger, 1997, Bandai
NM $2   MIP $6

Red Ranger, 1997, Bandai
NM $2   MIP $6

Yellow Ranger, 1997, Bandai
NM $2   MIP $6

POWER RANGERS ZEO (BANDAI, 1996)

AUTO MORPHIN, 5-1/2" FIGURES

Blue, 1996, Bandai
NM $2   MIP $6

Gold Warrior, 1996, Bandai
NM $2   MIP $6

Green, 1996, Bandai
NM $2   MIP $6

Pink, 1996, Bandai
NM $2   MIP $6

Red, 1996, Bandai
NM $2   MIP $6

Yellow, 1996, Bandai
NM $2   MIP $6

EVIL SPACE ALIENS, 5-1/2" FIGURES

Cogs, 1996, Bandai
NM $2   MIP $6

Drill Master, 1996, Bandai
NM $2   MIP $6

Mechanizer, 1996, Bandai
NM $2   MIP $6

Quadfighter, 1996, Bandai
NM $2   MIP $6

Silo, 1996, Bandai
NM $2   MIP $6

ZEO JET CYCLES WITH FIGURE

Cycle with Blue Zeo Ranger III, 1996, Bandai
NM $2   MIP $6

Cycle with Gold Zeo Ranger, 1996, Bandai
NM $2   MIP $6

Cycle with Green Zeo Ranger IV, 1996, Bandai
NM $2   MIP $6

Cycle with Pink Zeo Ranger I, 1996, Bandai
NM $2   MIP $6

Cycle with Red Zeo Ranger V, 1996, Bandai
NM $2   MIP $6

Cycle with Yellow Zeo Ranger II, 1996, Bandai
NM $2   MIP $6

ZEO POWER ZORDS, 5-1/2" FIGURES

1-2 Punching Action Red Battlezord, 1996, Bandai
NM $2   MIP $6

Auric the Conqueror Zord, 1996, Bandai
NM $2   MIP $6

Power Sword Action Zeo Megazord, 1996, Bandai
NM $2   MIP $6

Pyramidas, 1996, Bandai
NM $2   MIP $6

Super Zeo Megazord, 1996, Bandai
NM $2   MIP $6

Warrior Wheel, 1996, Bandai
NM $2   MIP $6

ZEO RANGERS, 5-1/2" FIGURES

Blue Zeo Ranger III, 1996, Bandai
NM $2   MIP $6

Gold Zeo Ranger, 1996, Bandai
NM $2   MIP $6

Green Zeo Ranger IV, 1996, Bandai
NM $2   MIP $6

Pink Zeo Ranger I, 1996, Bandai
NM $2   MIP $6

Red Zeo Ranger V, 1996, Bandai
NM $2   MIP $6

Yellow Zeo Ranger II, 1996, Bandai
NM $2   MIP $6

ZEO RANGERS, 8" FIGURES

Blue Zeo Ranger III, 1996, Bandai
NM $3   MIP $8

Gold Zeo Ranger, 1996, Bandai
NM $3   MIP $8

Green Zeo Ranger IV, 1996, Bandai
NM $3   MIP $8

Pink Zeo Ranger I, 1996, Bandai
NM $3   MIP $8

Red Zeo Ranger V, 1996, Bandai
NM $3   MIP $8

Yellow Zeo Ranger II, 1996, Bandai
NM $3   MIP $8

PULSAR (MATTEL, 1976)

FIGURES

Hypnos, 1976, Mattel, no circulatory system, spinning disk in chest
NM $45   MIP $95

Pulsar the Ultimate Man of Adventure, 1976, Mattel, exposed chest shows veins with "blood" pumping through
NM $15   MIP $30

PLAYSET

Life Systems Center Playset, 1976, Mattel
NM $25   MIP $50

PUPPETMASTER (FULL MOON TOYS, 1997-PRESENT)

FIGURES

Blade, 1997-present, Full Moon
NM $8   MIP $20

Blade, blood splattered, 1997-present, Full Moon
NM $25   MIP $85

Blade, bullet-eyed (Troll & Joad), 1997-present, Full Moon
NM $15   MIP $40

Blade, gold, 1997-present, Full Moon
NM $8   MIP $20

Blade, red Japanese Exclusive, 1997-present, Full Moon
NM $15   MIP $40

Jester, 1997-present, Full Moon
NM $3   MIP $12

Jester, gold, 1997-present, Full Moon
NM $8   MIP $20

Jester, Japanese Exclusive, Carse of Jester, 1997-present, Full Moon
NM $3   MIP $12

Jester, Previews Exclusive, 1997-present, Full Moon
NM $8   MIP $20

Leech Woman, 1997-present, Full Moon
NM $3   MIP $12

Leech Woman, gold, 1997-present, Full Moon
NM $8   MIP $20

Leech Woman, Japanese Exclusive, Geisha Leech Woman, 1997-present, Full Moon
NM $3   MIP $12

Leech Woman, Previews Exclusive, 1997-present, Full Moon
NM $8   MIP $20

Mephisto, 1997-present, Full Moon
NM $3   MIP $12

Mephisto, clear, 1997-present, Full Moon
NM $5   MIP $15

Mephisto, Japanese Exclusive, death Mephisto, 1997-present, Full Moon
NM $8   MIP $20

Mephisto, Previews Exclusive, 1997-present, Full Moon
NM $8   MIP $20

Pinhead, 1997-present, Full Moon
NM $3   MIP $12

Pinhead, gold, 1997-present, Full Moon
NM $8   MIP $20

Pinhead, Halloween 1999, 1999, Full Moon
NM $8   MIP $20

Pinhead, Japanese Exclusive, Pinhead in the Dark, 1997-present, Full Moon
NM $8   MIP $25

Pinhead, Previews Exclusive, 1997-present, Full Moon
NM $8   MIP $20

Sixshooter, 1997-present, Full Moon
NM $8   MIP $20

Sixshooter, 1997-present, Full Moon
NM $8   MIP $20

Sixshooter, Japanese Exclusive, DOA Sixshooter, 1997-present, Full Moon
NM $10   MIP $30

Sixshooter, Troll & Joad edition, 1997-present, Full Moon
NM $10   MIP $30

Torch, 1997-present, Full Moon
NM $3   MIP $12

Torch, gold, 1997-present, Full Moon
NM $8   MIP $20

Torch, Japanese Exclusive, Camouflage Torch, 1997-present, Full Moon
NM $8   MIP $20

Torch, Previews Exclusive, 1997-present, Full Moon
NM $8   MIP $20

Totem, 1997-present, Full Moon
NM $3   MIP $12

Totem, 1998 San Diego Comicon, 1997-present, Full Moon
NM $15   MIP $45

Totem, gold, 1997-present, Full Moon
NM $5   MIP $15

Totem, Japanese Exclusive, Evil Spirit Totem, 1997-present, Full Moon
NM $10   MIP $35

Totem, Preview Exclusive, 1997-present, Full Moon
NM $8   MIP $20

Tunneler, 1997-present, Full Moon
NM $3   MIP $12

Tunneler, Australian Exclusive, 1997-present, Full Moon
NM $15   MIP $45

Tunneler, gold, 1997-present, Full Moon
NM $8   MIP $20

Tunneler, Japanese Exclusive, Cruel Sgt. Tunneler, 1997-present, Full Moon
NM $15   MIP $45

Tunneler, Previews Exclusive, 1997-present, Full Moon
NM $8   MIP $20

RAMBO (COLECO, 1985)

FIGURES

Black Dragon, 1985, Coleco, Series 1
NM $4   MIP $10

Chief, 1985, Coleco, Series 2
NM $8   MIP $15

Colonel Troutman, 1985, Coleco, Series 1
NM $4   MIP $8

Dr. Hyde, 1985, Coleco, Series 2
NM $10   MIP $23

ACTION FIGURES

General Warhawk, 1985, Coleco, Series 1
    NM $4   **MIP** $10

Gripper, 1985, Coleco, Series 1
    NM $4   **MIP** $10

K.A.T., 1985, Coleco, Series 1
    NM $5   **MIP** $10

Mad Dog, 1985, Coleco, Series 2
    NM $4   **MIP** $10

Nomad, 1985, Coleco, Series 1
    NM $8   **MIP** $13

(Toy Shop File Photo)

Rambo, 1985, Coleco, Series 1
    NM $5   **MIP** $13

Rambo with Fire Power, 1985, Coleco, Series 2
    NM $5   **MIP** $13

Sergeant Havoc, 1985, Coleco, Series 1
    NM $4   **MIP** $10

Snakebite, 1985, Coleco, Series 2
    NM $10   **MIP** $20

T.D. Jackson, 1985, Coleco, Series 2
    NM $10   **MIP** $20

Turbo, 1985, Coleco, Series 1
    NM $4   **MIP** $10

White Dragon, 1985, Coleco, Series 1
    NM $4   **MIP** $10

X-Ray, 1985, Coleco, Series 2
    NM $10   **MIP** $20

PLAY SETS

S.A.V.A.G.E. Strike Headquarters, 1985, Coleco, Series 1
    NM $25   **MIP** $55

VEHICLES

Defender 6x6, 1985, Coleco, Series 1
    NM $15   **MIP** $30

S.A.V.A.G.E. Strike Cycle, 1985, Coleco, Series 1
    NM $10   **MIP** $20

Skyfire Assault Copter, 1985, Coleco, Series 1
    NM $15   **MIP** $30

Skywolf Assault Jet, 1985, Coleco, Series 1
    NM $15   **MIP** $25

Swamp Dog, 1985, Coleco, Series 1
    NM $10   **MIP** $20

RESIDENT EVIL

SERIES II

(KP Photo)

Alexia, 2002, Palisades, Bug-winged figure with "leafy" hair
    NM $8   **MIP** $12

(KP Photo)

Claire Redfield, 2002, Palisades, Figure includes dagger and pistol
    NM $8   **MIP** $12

Mr. X, 2002, Palisades, Black jacket and uniform, dark gray skin, glowing eyes
    NM $8   **MIP** $12

(KP Photo)

Zombie Cop, 2002, Palisades, Mauled policeman with terrifying ? on a leash…
    NM $8   **MIP** $12

RESIDENT EVIL (TOY BIZ, 1998)

5" FIGURES

Chris Redfield and Cerberus, 1998
    NM $5   **MIP** $15

Hunter and Chimera, 1998
    NM $3   **MIP** $8

Jill Valentine and Web Spinner, 1998
    NM $3   **MIP** $8

Maggot Zombie and Forrest Speyer, 1998
    NM $3   **MIP** $8

Tyrant, 1998
    NM $3   **MIP** $8

ROBIN HOOD AND HIS MERRY MEN (MEGO, 1974)

FIGURES

Friar Tuck, 1974, Mego
    NM $25   **MIP** $60

Little John, 1974, Mego
    NM $65   **MIP** $150

Robin Hood, 1974, Mego
    NM $90   **MIP** $300

Will Scarlett, 1974, Mego
    NM $75   **MIP** $275

ROBIN HOOD PRINCE OF THIEVES (KENNER, 1991)

ACCESSORIES

Battle Wagon, 1991, Kenner
    NM $15   **MIP** $30

Bola Bomber, 1991, Kenner
    NM $5   **MIP** $10

Net Launcher, 1991, Kenner
    NM $5   **MIP** $10

Sherwood Forest Play Set, 1991, Kenner
    NM $30   **MIP** $60

FIGURES

Azeem, 1991, Kenner
    NM $7   **MIP** $15

(Lenny Lee)

Friar Tuck, with Battle Staff, 1991, Kenner, with fabric road
    NM $15   **MIP** $30

ACTION FIGURES

Little John, 1991, Kenner
NM $7   MIP $15

Robin Hood, Crossbow, 1991, Kenner
NM $5   MIP $18

Robin Hood, Crossbow, Costner Head, 1991, Kenner
NM $7   MIP $20

Robin Hood, Long Bow, 1991, Kenner
NM $8   MIP $17

Robin Hood, Long Bow, Costner Head, 1991, Kenner
NM $10   MIP $20

Sheriff of Nottingham, 1991, Kenner
NM $5   MIP $15

The Dark Warrior, 1991, Kenner
NM $8   MIP $20

Will Scarlett, 1991, Kenner
NM $8   MIP $20

ROBOCOP AND THE ULTRA POLICE (KENNER, 1989-90)

FIGURES

Ace Jackson, 1989-90, Kenner
NM $5   MIP $15

Anne Lewis, 1989-90, Kenner
NM $5   MIP $15

Birdman Barnes, 1989-90, Kenner
NM $8   MIP $15

Chainsaw, 1989-90, Kenner
NM $5   MIP $15

Claw Callahan, 1989-90, Kenner
NM $7   MIP $15

Dr. McNamara, 1989-90, Kenner
NM $5   MIP $15

Ed-260, 1989-90, Kenner
NM $10   MIP $25

Headhunter, 1989-90, Kenner
NM $5   MIP $15

Nitro, 1989-90, Kenner
NM $5   MIP $15

RoboCop, 1989-90, Kenner
NM $9   MIP $20

RoboCop Night Fighter, 1989-90, Kenner
NM $6   MIP $20

RoboCop, Gatlin' Gun, 1989-90, Kenner
NM $15   MIP $30

Scorcher, 1989-90, Kenner
NM $6   MIP $15

Sgt. Reed, 1989-90, Kenner
NM $6   MIP $15

Toxic Waster, 1989-90, Kenner
NM $10   MIP $20

Wheels Wilson, 1989-90, Kenner
NM $6   MIP $15

VEHICLES

Robo-1, 1989-90, Kenner
NM $10   MIP $25

Robo-Command with figure, 1989-90, Kenner, with figure
NM $10   MIP $30

Robo-Copter, 1989-90, Kenner
NM $15   MIP $35

Robo-Cycle, 1989-90, Kenner
NM $5   MIP $10

Robo-Hawk, 1989-90, Kenner
NM $10   MIP $35

Robo-Jailer, 1989-90, Kenner
NM $15   MIP $40

Robo-Tank, 1989-90, Kenner
NM $10   MIP $35

Skull-Hog, 1989-90, Kenner
NM $5   MIP $10

Vandal-1, 1989-90, Kenner
NM $5   MIP $20

ROBOTECH (MATCHBOX, 1986)

11-1/2" FIGURES

Dana Sterling, 1986
NM $20   MIP $50

Lisa Hayes, 1986
NM $20   MIP $50

Lynn Minmei, 1986
NM $20   MIP $50

Rick Hunter, 1986
NM $20   MIP $50

3-3/4" FIGURES

Bioroid Terminator, 1986
NM $5   MIP $15

Corg, 1986
NM $8   MIP $20

Dana Sterling, 1986
NM $12   MIP $30

Lisa Hayes, 1986, Matchbox
NM $7   MIP $12

Lisa Hayes, 1986, Center figure, shown with Roy Fokker and Zor Prime
NM $8   MIP $20

Lunk, 1986
NM $8   MIP $20

Max Sterling, 1986
NM $8   MIP $20

Micronized Zentraedi, 1986, Matchbox
NM $7   MIP $12

Miriya, black, 1986
NM $25   MIP $65

Miriya, red, 1986
NM $8   MIP $20

Rand, 1986
NM $5   MIP $12

Rick Hunter, 1986
NM $10   MIP $25

Robotech Master, 1986
NM $5   MIP $12

Rook Bartley, 1986
NM $20   MIP $50

Roy Fokker, 1986, At left, shown with Lisa Hayes and Zor Prime
NM $12   MIP $30

Scott Bernard, 1986
NM $12   MIP $37

Zor Prime, 1986, Matchbox
NM $8   MIP $15

6" FIGURES

Breetai, 1986
NM $8   MIP $20

Dolza, 1986
NM $5   MIP $15

Exedore, 1986
NM $8   MIP $20

Khryon, 1986
NM $8   MIP $20

Miriya, 1986
NM $8   MIP $20

8" FIGURES

Armoured Zentraedi Warrior, 1986
NM $8   MIP $20

VEHICLES AND ACCESSORIES

Armoured Cyclone, 1986
NM $8   MIP $20

Bioroid Hover Craft, 1986
NM $10   MIP $25

Bioroid Invid Fighter, 1986, Matchbox
NM $20   MIP $40

Dana's Hover Cycle, 1986
NM $12   MIP $35

Excaliber MkVI, 1986, Matchbox
NM $25   MIP $45

Gladiator, 1986, Matchbox
NM $20   MIP $40

Invid Scout Ship, 1986
NM $12   MIP $30

Invid Shock Trooper, 1986, Matchbox
NM $15   MIP $30

Raidar X, 1986, Matchbox
NM $20   MIP $40

SDF-1 Playset, 1986, Matchbox
   NM $200 MIP $400

Spartan, 1986, Matchbox
   NM $20 MIP $40

Tactical Battle Pod, 1986
   NM $12 MIP $30

Veritech Fighter, 1986
   NM $15 MIP $40

Veritech Hover Tank, 1986
   NM $15 MIP $40

Zentraedi Officer's Battle pod, 1986
   NM $12 MIP $35

Zentraedi Powered Armor, 1986, Matchbox, Botoru or Quadrono Battalion
   NM $25 MIP $45

ROCKY HORROR PICTURE SHOW (VITAL TOYS, 2000)

FIGURES

(KP Photo)

Columbia, Series 1, 2000, Vital Toys, Gold sequined hat and jacket, silver sequined top
   NM n/a MIP n/a

(KP Photo)

Frank N Furter, Series 1, 2000, Vital Toys, Very detailed likeness of Rocky Horror's famous character
   NM n/a MIP n/a

Riff Raff, Series 1, 2000, Vital Toys, Detailed figure with yellow hair and face with proper white pallor
   NM n/a MIP n/a

SEA DEVILS (MATTEL, 1970)

FIGURES

Commander Chuck Carter, 1970, Mattel, orange wetsuit, mask, diving gear, sea jet, motor
   NM $80 MIP $150

Kretar and Zark, 1970, Mattel, sea creature and shark
   NM $80 MIP $150

Rick Riley, 1970, Mattel, black wetsuit, mask, diving gear, sea jet, motor
   NM $80 MIP $150

SET

Search and Rescue Set, 1970, Mattel, Commander Carter, Aqualander, Sea Jet, motor, diving gear
   NM $100 MIP $200

SECTAURS (COLECO, 1985)

FIGURE SETS

Genral Spydrax and Spiderflyer, 1985, Coleco
   NM $15 MIP $35

Pinsor and Battle Beetle, 1985, Coleco, weapons belt, pistol, sword, axe, shield
   NM $15 MIP $35

Prince Dargon and Dragonflyer, 1985, Coleco, 2 pistols w/holsters, sword, shield, bag, Slazor
   NM $15 MIP $35

Skulk and Trancula, 1985, Coleco
   NM $15 MIP $35

FIGURES

Mantor with Rapplor, 1985, Coleco
   NM $5 MIP $15

Night-Fighting Dargon with Parafly, 1985, Coleco, night-vision trinoculars, gun, knife, double holsters
   NM $5 MIP $15

Skito with Toxcid, 1985, Coleco, gun, sword, holster, shield
   NM $5 MIP $15

Waspax with Wingid, 1985, Coleco
   NM $5 MIP $15

Zak and Bitaur, 1985, Coleco, gun, Slazor, holster, shield
   NM $5 MIP $15

PLAYSETS

The Hyve, Forbidden Fortress, 1985, Coleco
   NM $25 MIP $50

SHE-RA PRINCESS OF POWER (MATTEL, 1984-86)

CREATURES

Arrow, 1984, Mattel, #9721, Bow's horse, blue
   NM $15 MIP $40

Clawdeen, 1985, Mattel, #9627, Catra's large cat
   NM $15 MIP $40

Crystal Moonbeam, 1985, Mattel, #2434
   NM $15 MIP $45

Crystal Sun Dancer, 1985, Mattel, #2435
   NM $15 MIP $45

Crystal Swift Wind, 1985, Mattel, #2433
   NM $15 MIP $45

Enchanta, 1984, Mattel, #9681, She-Ra's swan
   NM $15 MIP $40

Royal Swift Wind, 1986, Mattel, #3050
   NM $15 MIP $40

Sea Harp, 1985, Mattel, #2902, She-Ra's Sea Horse
   NM $15 MIP $40

Silver Storm, 1986, Mattel, #3150
   NM $15 MIP $40

Storm, 1984, Mattel, #9722, Catra's horse
   NM $15 MIP $40

Swift Wind, 1984, Mattel, #9191, She-Ra's horse, pink
   NM $15 MIP $40

FASHIONS

Blue Lightning, 1986, Mattel, #2833
   NM $5 MIP $12

Colorful Secret, 1986, Mattel, #2837
   NM $5 MIP $12

Deep Blue Secret, 1984, Mattel, #2836
   NM $5 MIP $12

Fit To Be Tied, 1984, Mattel, #2825
   NM $5 MIP $12

Flight of Fancy, 1984, Mattel, #2828
   NM $5 MIP $12

Flower Power, 1984, Mattel, #2835
   NM $5 MIP $12

Frosty Fur, 1986, Mattel, #2831
   NM $5 MIP $12

Heart of Gold, 1986, Mattel, #2838
   NM $8 MIP $20

Hidden Gold, 1986, Mattel, #2832
   NM $5 MIP $12

Hold on to Your Hat, 1984, Mattel, #2826
   NM $5 MIP $12

Ready in Red, 1984, Mattel, #2827
   NM $5 MIP $12

Reflections in Red, 1986, Mattel, #2834
   NM $5 MIP $12

Rise and Shine, 1984, Mattel, #2824
   NM $5 MIP $12

Secret Messanger, 1986, Mattel, #2830
   NM $5 MIP $12

Veils of Mystery, 1984, Mattel, #2829
NM $5   MIP $12

Windy Jumper, 1986, Mattel, #2839
NM $5   MIP $12

FIGURE SETS

Bow and Arrow, 1984, Mattel, #9817
NM $20   MIP $50

Catra and Clawdeen, 1985, Mattel, #2746
NM $25   MIP $65

Catra and Storm, 1984, Mattel, #5047
NM $25   MIP $60

Defenders of Good, 1985, Mattel, #1052,
She-Ra, Perfuma, and Sweet Bee
NM $35   MIP $70

Peekablue and Moonbeam, 1985, Mattel,
#2900
NM $20   MIP $50

She-Ra and Swift Wind, 1984, Mattel
NM $25   MIP $60

Starburst She-Ra and Crystal Swift Wind,
1985, Mattel, #2898
NM $35   MIP $75

Sweet Bee and Crystal Sundancer, 1985,
Mattel, #2901
NM $25   MIP $65

FIGURES

Angella, 1984, Mattel, #9186
NM $8   MIP $15

Bow, 1984, Mattel, #9183, bow, shield
NM $8   MIP $20

Bubble Power She-Ra, 1986, Mattel, #3023
NM $15   MIP $40

Castaspella, 1984, Mattel, #9187
NM $8   MIP $15

Catra, 1984, Mattel, #9184, tail, mask, shield
NM $10   MIP $45

Double Trouble, 1984, Mattel, #9185
NM $8   MIP $15

Entrapta, 1985, Mattel, #2636
NM $8   MIP $15

Flutterina, 1985, Mattel, #2453
NM $8   MIP $15

Frosta, 1984, Mattel, #9189
NM $8   MIP $15

Glimmer, 1984, Mattel, #9188
NM $8   MIP $15

Kowl, 1984, Mattel, #9190
NM $8   MIP $15

Loo-Kee, 1986, Mattel, #1969
NM $8   MIP $15

Mermista, 1985, Mattel, #2454
NM $8   MIP $15

Netossa, 1986, Mattel, #1835
NM $10   MIP $24

Peekablue, 1985, Mattel, #2452
NM $8   MIP $15

Perfuma, 1985, Mattel, #2455
NM $8   MIP $15

Scratchin' Sound Catra, 1985, Mattel, #2451
NM $15   MIP $55

She-Ra, 1984, Mattel, #9182, helmet,
shield, sword
NM $10   MIP $45

Shower Power Catra, 1986, Mattel, #3021
NM $15   MIP $40

Spinnerella, 1986, Mattel, #3053
NM $8   MIP $15

Starburst She-Ra, 1985, Mattel, #2450
NM $12   MIP $40

Sweet Bee, 1985, Mattel, #2635
NM $15   MIP $40

PLAYSETS

Crystal Castle, 1984, Mattel, #9193, 30+
pieces
NM $30   MIP $60

Crystal Falls, 1985, Mattel, #2456
NM $25   MIP $50

SHOGUN WARRIORS (MATTEL, 1979)

24" FIGURES

Daimos, 1979, Mattel, #2988, shooting
fist, calf missile launchers
NM $75   MIP $150

Dragun, 1979, Mattel, #9858, fires
shurikan and axes
NM $75   MIP $150

Gaiking, 1979, Mattel, eye launchers,
shooting fist
NM $75   MIP $150

Godzilla, 1979, Mattel, fire tongue,
shooting fist
NM $100   MIP $200

Godzilla (2nd figure), 1979, Mattel, fire
tongue, shooting fist
NM $150   MIP $200

Great Mazinga, 1979, Mattel, #9860,
swords, missile fingers
NM $75   MIP $150

Raydeen, 1979, Mattel, #9859, shield,
shooting fist
NM $75   MIP $150

Rodan, 1979, 38" wingspan
NM $150   MIP $300

2-IN-1 FIGURES

Daimos, 1979, Mattel, #2992, die-cast, leg
cannons, shooting fists
NM $75   MIP $150

Danguard, 1979, Mattel, #2729, die-cast,
para-wing, shooting arms and head
NM $75   MIP $150

Gaiking, 1979, Mattel, #2728, die-cast
NM $75   MIP $150

Grandizer, 1979, Mattel, #2994, die-cast,
shooting fists, sickles
NM $75   MIP $150

Raydeen, 1979, Mattel, #2727, die-cast
NM $75   MIP $150

Voltus V, 1979, Mattel, #2993, die-cast,
changes to battle tank
NM $75   MIP $150

3" FIGURES

17, 1979, Mattel, #2997, Series 2
NM $10   MIP $25

Combattra, 1979, Mattel, #2512, Series 1
NM $10   MIP $25

Dangard, 1979, Mattel, #2995, Series 2
NM $10   MIP $25

Dragun, 1979, Mattel, #2515, Series 1
NM $10   MIP $25

Gaiking, 1979, Mattel, #2514, Series 1
NM $10   MIP $25

Grandizer, 1979, Mattel, #2517, Series 1
NM $10   MIP $25

Great Mazinga, 1979, Mattel, #2516, Series 1
NM $10   MIP $25

Leopaldon, 1979, Mattel, #2996, Series 2
NM $10   MIP $25

Poseidon, 1979, Mattel, #2513, Series 1
NM $10   MIP $25

Voltez V, 1979, Mattel, #2994, Series 2
NM $10   MIP $25

5" FIGURES

Dragun, 1979, Mattel, #2106, die-cast,
w/ 3 axes
NM $75   MIP $175

Dragun (2nd figure), 1979, Mattel, #2106,
die-cast, w/ 2 axes
NM $75   MIP $150

Great Mazinga, 1979, Mattel, #2103, die-
cast, knees bend
NM $85   MIP $175

Great Mazinga (2nd figure), 1979, Mattel,
#2103, die-cast, knees don't bend much
NM $75   MIP $150

Poseidon, 1979, Mattel, #2104, die-cast,
moveable shins
NM $75   MIP $150

Poseidon (second figure), 1979, Mattel,
#2104, die-cast, shins don't move
NM $75   MIP $125

Poseidon (third figure), 1979, Mattel, #2105,
die-cast, four yellow safety missiles
NM $75   MIP $125

Raider, 1979, Mattel, #2105, die-cast,
knees bend
NM $75   MIP $150

Raider (second figure), 1979, Mattel,
#2105, die-cast, knees don't bend
NM $75   MIP $125

VEHICLES

Bazoler, 1979, Mattel, #2690
NM $30   MIP $55

Combatra Vehicle #3 Battle Tank, 1979,
Mattel, #2622
NM $70   MIP $140

Daimos Truck, 1979, Mattel, #2990
NM $125   MIP $275

Dangard Launcher, 1979, Mattel, #2699
    NM $30   **MIP** $55

Grand Car, 1979, Mattel, #2696
    NM $30   **MIP** $55

Grandizer Saucer, 1979, Mattel, #8998, European release
    NM $75   **MIP** $135

Heli-Capter, 1979, Mattel, #2695
    NM $35   **MIP** $60

Jetcar, 1979, Mattel, #2698
    NM $30   **MIP** $55

Kargosaur, 1979, Mattel, #2694, rare
    NM $175   **MIP** $310

Kondar, 1979, Mattel, #2693
    NM $30   **MIP** $55

Liabe, 1979, Mattel, #2734
    NM $100   **MIP** $200

Nessar, 1979, Mattel, #2691
    NM $25   **MIP** $50

Rydoto, 1979, Mattel, #2900
    NM $25   **MIP** $55

Schicon Jet, 1979, Mattel, #2732
    NM $40   **MIP** $80

Shigcon Tank, 1979, Mattel, #2731
    NM $40   **MIP** $85

Sky Arrow, 1979, Mattel, #2733
    NM $40   **MIP** $80

Sky Jet, 1979, Mattel, #2697
    NM $25   **MIP** $50

Solar Saucer, 1979, Mattel, #2520
    NM $50   **MIP** $95

Varitank, 1979, Mattel, #2519
    NM $25   **MIP** $50

Vertilift, 1979, Mattel, #2521
    NM $25   **MIP** $50

SILVER SURFER (TOY BIZ, 1997-98)

COSMIC POWER ALIEN FIGHTERS

Adam Warlock with Cosmic Skull Space Racer, 1998
    NM $3   **MIP** $8

Cosmic Silver Surfer and Pip the Troll, 1998
    NM $3   **MIP** $8

Galactus with Silver Surfer in Cosmic Orb, 8" figure, 1998
    NM $3   **MIP** $8

Ivar and Ant Warrior with Alien Annihilator, 1998
    NM $3   **MIP** $8

Molten Lava Silver Surfer with Eyeball Alien Space Racer, 1998
    NM $3   **MIP** $8

Ronan the Accussor with Tree Root Space Racer, 1998
    NM $3   **MIP** $8

Solar Silver Surfer & Draconian Warrior, 1998
    NM $3   **MIP** $8

Super Nova with Flaming Bird, 1998
    NM $3   **MIP** $8

FIGURES

Beta Ray Bill, Thunder Hammer, 1997
    NM $3   **MIP** $10

Classic Silver Surfer with Cosmic Surf Board, 1997
    NM $3   **MIP** $10

Meegan Alien, Galactic Weapon Seeker, 1997
    NM $3   **MIP** $10

Nova, Poseable Flaming Hair, 1997
    NM $3   **MIP** $10

INFINITY GAUNTLET SERIES, 10" FIGURE

Silver Surfer, 1997
    NM $5   **MIP** $15

SILVERHAWKS (KENNER, 1987)

ACCESSORIES

Super Attack Bird Sky-Shadow, 1987, Kenner, 20" wingspan
    NM $20   **MIP** $40

Super Attack Bird Stronghold, 1987, Kenner, 20" wingspan
    NM $20   **MIP** $40

Super Attack Bird Tallyhawk, 1987, Kenner, 25" wingspan
    NM $20   **MIP** $40

FIGURES

Bluegrass, 1988, Kenner, w/Hot Licks, guitar transforms, new uniform
    NM $6   **MIP** $12

Condor, 1988, Kenner, w/Jet Stream
    NM $6   **MIP** $12

Copper Kidd, 1988, Kenner, w/Laser Disks
    NM $6   **MIP** $12

Hardware, 1988, Kenner, w/Prowler
    NM $6   **MIP** $12

Mon-Star, 1988, Kenner, w/Laser Lance
    NM $6   **MIP** $12

Moon Stryker, 1988, Kenner, w/Tail-Spin
    NM $6   **MIP** $12

Quicksilver, 1988, Kenner, w/Tallyhawk, black uniform
    NM $6   **MIP** $12

Steelwill, 1988, Kenner, w/Steamer
    NM $6   **MIP** $12

Windhammer, 1988, Kenner, w/Tuning Fork
    NM $6   **MIP** $12

FIGURES, BAD

Buzz Saw, 1987, Kenner, w/Shredator
    NM $6   **MIP** $12

Mo-Lec-U-Lar, 1987, Kenner, w/Volt-Ure
    NM $6   **MIP** $12

Mon-Star, 1987, Kenner, w/Sky Shadow
    NM $6   **MIP** $12

Mumbo-Jumbo, 1987, Kenner, w/Airshock
    NM $6   **MIP** $12

FIGURES, GOOD

Bluegrass, 1987, Kenner, w/Side Man, converts from hawk to guitar
    NM $6   **MIP** $12

Copper Kidd, 1987, Kenner, w/May-Day
    NM $6   **MIP** $12

Flashback, 1987, Kenner, w/Backlash
    NM $6   **MIP** $12

Hotwing, 1987, Kenner, w/Gyro
    NM $6   **MIP** $12

Quicksilver, 1987, Kenner, w/Tallyhawk
    NM $6   **MIP** $12

Stargazer, 1987, Kenner, w/Sly-Bird
    NM $6   **MIP** $12

Steelheart, 1987, Kenner, w/Rayzor
    NM $6   **MIP** $12

Steelwill, 1987, Kenner, w/Stronghold
    NM $6   **MIP** $12

PLAYSETS

Hawkhaven, 1987, Kenner, hawk-shaped fortress on asteroid
    NM $25   **MIP** $55

VEHICLES

Copper Racer, 1988, Kenner, friction motor, for Copper Kidd
    NM $10   **MIP** $20

Maraj, 1987, Kenner, holds five figures
    NM $25   **MIP** $55

Sky-Runner, 1988, Kenner, for Mon-Star
    NM $10   **MIP** $20

Sprinthawk, 1988, Kenner, for Quicksilver
    NM $10   **MIP** $20

SIMPSONS (MATTEL, 1990)

FIGURES

Bart, 1990, Mattel
    NM $10   **MIP** $30

Bartman, 1990, Mattel
    NM $10   **MIP** $30

Homer, 1990, Mattel
    NM $10   **MIP** $35

Lisa, 1990, Mattel
    NM $15   **MIP** $40

Maggie, 1990, Mattel
    NM $15   **MIP** $40

Marge, 1990, Mattel
    NM $10   **MIP** $30

Nelson, 1990, Mattel
    NM $10   **MIP** $30

Sofa Set, 1990, Mattel
    NM $10   **MIP** $40

SIMPSONS (PLAYMATES, 1999-2004)

ALL STAR VOICES

Brad Goodman, 2002, Playmates, by Albert Brooks
    NM $4   **MIP** $8

Fat Tony, 2002, Playmates, by Joe Mantegna
NM $4   MIP $8

Herb Powell, 2002, Playmates, by Danny DeVito
NM $4   MIP $8

Lionel Hutz, 2002, Playmates, by Phil Hartman
NM $4   MIP $8

Troy McClure, 2002, Playmates, by Phil Hartman
NM $4   MIP $8

ENVIRONMENTS

Aztec Theater, 2003, Playmates, w/McBain,
NM $8   MIP $16

Bart's Treehouse, 2003, Playmates, w/ Military Bart
NM $10   MIP $20

Bowl-A-Rama, 2001, Playmates, w/ Pin Pal Apu
NM $10   MIP $20

Burns Manor, 2002, Playmates, w/ P.J. Burns
NM $8   MIP $15

Comic Book Shop, 2001, Playmates, w/ Comic Book Guy
NM $10   MIP $20

Court Room, 2002, Playmates, w/ Judge Snyder
NM $8   MIP $15

Doctor's Office, 2002, Playmates, w/ Dr. Nick Riviera
NM $8   MIP $15

First Church of Springfield, 2001, Playmates, w/ Reverend Lovejoy
NM $10   MIP $20

Krusty Burger, 2002, Playmates, w/ Pimply Faced Teen
NM $10   MIP $20

Krustylu Studios, 2001, Playmates, w/ Sideshow Bob
NM $10   MIP $20

Kwik-E-Mart, 2000, Playmates, w/ Apu
NM $8   MIP $20

Living Room, 2000, Playmates, w/ Marge and Maggie
NM $10   MIP $45

Military Antique Shop, 2003, Playmates, w/Herman
NM $8   MIP $16

Noiseland Arcade, 2001, Playmates, w/ Jimbo Jones
NM $10   MIP $20

Nuclear Power Plant, 2000, Playmates, w/ Homer
NM $10   MIP $45

Nuclear Power Plant Lunch Room, 2004, Playmates, w/Frank Grimes
NM $8   MIP $16

Police Station, 2002, Playmates, w/ Officer Eddie
NM $10   MIP $20

Retirement Castle, 2002, Playmates, w/ Jasper
NM $10   MIP $20

Simpson's Family Kitchen, 2002, Playmates, w/ Muumuu Homer
NM $10   MIP $20

Springfield DMV, 2002, Playmates, w/Selma Bouvier
NM $8   MIP $16

Springfield Elementary, 2000, Playmates, w/ Principal Skinner
NM $10   MIP $20

Springfield Elementary School Cafeteria, 2002, Playmates, w/ Lunchlady Doris
NM $10   MIP $20

Town Hall, 2001, Playmates, w/ Mayor Quimby
NM $10   MIP $20

EXCLUSIVES

All-Star Voices 2-Pack #1, 2002, Playmates, Toys R Us, Lurleen Lumpkin, Colonel Homer
NM $10   MIP $20

All-Star Voices 2-Pack #2, 2002, Playmates, Toys R Us, Jacques, Bowling Marge
NM $10   MIP $20

Barney Gumble, 2002, Playmates, Target, Wave 2
NM $7   MIP $12

Be-Sharp Apu, 1999-2004, Playmates, Playmates mail-in
NM $12   MIP $25

Be-Sharp Barney, 1999-2004, Playmates, Playmates mail-in
NM $12   MIP $25

Be-Sharp Homer, 1999-2004, Playmates, Playmates mail-in
NM $20   MIP $45

Be-Sharp Skinner, 1999-2004, Playmates, Playmates mail-in
NM $12   MIP $25

Bongo Comics 3-Pack, 1999-2004, Playmates, Homer as Ingestible Bulk, Edna Krabappel as Vampiredna, Apu as Captain Kwik
NM $9   MIP $18

Boxing Homer, 2001, Playmates, ToyFare
NM $10   MIP $20

Convention Comic Book Guy, 2001, Playmates, ToyFare
NM $15   MIP $30

Cooder, 1999-2004, Playmates, Playmates mail-in
NM $12   MIP $25

Evil Krusty Doll, 2001, Playmates, Diamond, talks
NM $10   MIP $20

Family Christmas, 2001, Playmates, Toys R Us
NM $20   MIP $40

Family New Years, 2002, Playmates, Toys R Us
NM $10   MIP $20

High School Prom, 2002, Playmates, Diamond, Homer and Marge
NM $10   MIP $20

Homer Simpson, 2002, Playmates, Target, Wave 1
NM $7   MIP $12

KBBL Radio, 2002, Playmates, Diamond
NM $10   MIP $20

Llewellyn Sinclair, 1999-2004, Playmates, Playmates mail-in
NM $12   MIP $25

Lunar Base Environment, 2001, Playmates, Diamond
NM $10   MIP $20

Mainstreet Environment, 2002, Playmates, Toys R Us
NM $20   MIP $40

Moe Szyslak, 2002, Playmates, Target, Wave 2
NM $7   MIP $12

Moe's Tavern Environment, 2003, Playmates, Diamond
NM $10   MIP $20

Mr. Burns, 2002, Playmates, Target, Wave 1
NM $7   MIP $12

Pin Pal Moe, 2001, Playmates, ToyFare
NM $10   MIP $20

Pin Pal Mr. Burns, 2001, Playmates, ToyFare
NM $15   MIP $30

Radio Active Homer, 2000, Playmates, ToyFare Exclusive, w/radioactive plate of donuts, glow, helmet, glowing tongs
NM $50   MIP $200

Radioactive Homer, 2000, Playmates, ToyFare
NM $35   MIP $70

Treehouse of Horror I, 2000, Playmates, Toys R Us, Springfield Cemetary
NM $50   MIP $100

Treehouse of Horror II, 2001, Playmates, Toys R Us, Alien Ship
NM $50   MIP $100

Treehouse of Horror III, 2002, Playmates, Toys R Us, Ironic Punishment
NM $40   MIP $80

Treehouse of Horror IV, 2003, Playmates, Toys R Us, Collector's Lair; Bart as Stretch Dude, Lisa as Clobber Girl, Comic Book Guy as The Collector, Lucy Lawless as Xena
NM $15   MIP $30

Treehouse of Horrors, 2000, Playmates, Toys R Us Exclusive
NM $25   MIP $75

SERIES 01 FIGURES

Bart, 1999, Playmates, Series 1
NM $6   MIP $20

Grandpa, 1999, Playmates, Series 1
NM $10   MIP $30

Homer, 1999, Playmates, Series 1
NM $8   MIP $20

Krusty, 1999, Playmates, Series 1
NM $10   MIP $30

Lisa, 1999, Playmates, Series 1
      NM $10   **MIP** $30

Mr. Burns, 1999, Playmates, Series 1
      NM $10   **MIP** $20

SERIES 02 FIGURES

Barney, 2000, Playmates, Series 2
      NM $6   **MIP** $20

Chief Wiggum, 2000, Playmates, Series 2
      NM $6   **MIP** $20

Ned Flanders, 2000, Playmates, Series 2
      NM $6   **MIP** $20

Pin Pal Homer, 2000, Playmates, Series 2
      NM $6   **MIP** $20

Smithers, 2000, Playmates, Series 2
      NM $5   **MIP** $15

Sunday Best Bart, 2000, Playmates, Series 2
      NM $3   **MIP** $10

SERIES 03 FIGURES

Kamp Krusty Bart, 2000, Playmates, Series 3
      NM $5   **MIP** $9

Milhouse, 2000, Playmates, Series 3
      NM $5   **MIP** $10

Moe, 2000, Playmates, Series 3
      NM $7   **MIP** $15

Nelson, 2000, Playmates, Series 3
      NM $5   **MIP** $10

Otto, 2000, Playmates, Series 3
      NM $5   **MIP** $10

Sunday Best Homer, 2000, Playmates, Series 3
      NM $5   **MIP** $9

SERIES 04 FIGURES

Casual Homer, 2001, Playmates, Series 4
      NM $5   **MIP** $10

Groundskeeper Willie, 2001, Playmates, Series 4
      NM $5   **MIP** $10

Itchy and Scratchy, 2001, Playmates, Series 4
      NM $5   **MIP** $10

Lenny, 1999-2004, Series 4
      NM n/a   **MIP** n/a

Patty, 2001, Playmates, Series 4
      NM $5   **MIP** $10

Ralph Wiggum, 2001, Playmates, Series 4
      NM $5   **MIP** $10

SERIES 05 FIGURES

Bartman, 2001, Playmates, Series 5
      NM $5   **MIP** $10

Bumble Bee Man, 2001, Playmates, Series 5
      NM $7   **MIP** $12

Captain McCallister, 2001, Playmates, Series 5
      NM $5   **MIP** $10

Kent Brockman, 2001, Playmates, Series 5
      NM $5   **MIP** $10

Martin, 2001, Playmates, Series 5
      NM $5   **MIP** $10

Sideshow Mel, 2001, Playmates, Series 5
      NM $5   **MIP** $10

SERIES 06 FIGURES

Bleeding Gums Murphy, 2001, Playmates, Series 6
      NM $5   **MIP** $10

Carl, 2001, Playmates, Series 6
      NM $4   **MIP** $8

Dr. Hibbert, 2001, Playmates, Series 6
      NM $5   **MIP** $10

Isotopes Mascot Homer, 2001, Playmates, Series 6
      NM $4   **MIP** $8

Professor Frink, 2001, Playmates, Series 6
      NM $5   **MIP** $10

Snake, 2001, Playmates, Series 6
      NM $5   **MIP** $10

SERIES 07 FIGURES

Cletus, 2001, Playmates, Series 7
      NM $5   **MIP** $10

Dolph, 2001, Playmates, Series 7
      NM $5   **MIP** $10

Hans Moleman, 2001, Playmates, Series 7
      NM $4   **MIP** $8

Mrs. Krabappel, 2001, Playmates, Series 7
      NM $4   **MIP** $8

Officer Lou, 2001, Playmates, Series 7
      NM $4   **MIP** $8

Officer Marge, 2001, Playmates, Series 7
      NM $4   **MIP** $8

SERIES 08 FIGURES

Daredevil Bart, 2002, Playmates, Series 8
      NM $4   **MIP** $8

Kearney, 2002, Playmates, Series 8
      NM $4   **MIP** $8

Ragin' Willie, 2002, Playmates, Series 8
      NM $4   **MIP** $8

Sherri and Terri, 2002, Playmates, Series 8
      NM $4   **MIP** $8

Superintendent Chalmers, 2002, Playmates, Series 8
      NM $4   **MIP** $8

Uter, 2002, Playmates, Series 8
      NM $4   **MIP** $8

SERIES 09 FIGURES

Busted Krusty the Clown, 2002, Playmates, Series 9
      NM $4   **MIP** $8

Disco Stu, 2002, Playmates, Series 9
      NM $4   **MIP** $8

Prison Sideshow Bob, 2002, Playmates, Series 9
      NM $4   **MIP** $8

Rod and Todd Flanders, 2002, Playmates, Series 9
      NM $4   **MIP** $8

Sunday Best Grandpa, 2002, Playmates, Series 9
      NM $4   **MIP** $8

SERIES 10 FIGURES

Hank Scorpio, 2002, Playmates, Series 10
      NM $5   **MIP** $10

Marvin Monroe, 2002, Playmates, Series 10
      NM $4   **MIP** $8

Resort Smithers, 2002, Playmates, Series 10
      NM $4   **MIP** $8

Scout Leader Flanders, 2002, Playmates, Series 10
      NM $4   **MIP** $8

Stonecutter Homer, 2002, Playmates, Series 10
      NM $4   **MIP** $8

Sunday Best Marge and Maggie, 2002, Playmates, Series 10
      NM $4   **MIP** $8

Wendell, 2002, Playmates, Series 10
      NM $4   **MIP** $8

SERIES 11 FIGURES

Blue Haired Lawyer, 2002, Playmates, Series 11
      NM $4   **MIP** $8

Gil, 2002, Playmates, Series 11
      NM $4   **MIP** $8

Kirk VanHouten, 2002, Playmates, Series 11
      NM $4   **MIP** $8

Larry Burns, 2002, Playmates, Series 11
      NM $4   **MIP** $8

Plow King Barney, 2002, Playmates, Series 11
      NM $4   **MIP** $8

Rainier Wolfcastle, 2002, Playmates, Series 11
      NM $4   **MIP** $8

SERIES 12 FIGURES

Database, 2003, Playmates, Series 12
      NM $4   **MIP** $8

Don Vittorio, 2003, Playmates, Series 12
      NM $4   **MIP** $8

Luann VanHouten, 2003, Playmates, Series 12
      NM $4   **MIP** $8

Moe, 2003, Playmates, Series 12, re-release
      NM n/a   **MIP** n/a

Mr. Burns, 2003, Playmates, Series 12, re-release
      NM n/a   **MIP** n/a

Mr. Largo, 2003, Playmates, Series 12
      NM $4   **MIP** $8

Mr. Plow Homer, 2003, Playmates, Series 12
      NM $4   **MIP** $8

Number 1, 2003, Playmates, Series 12
      NM $4   **MIP** $8

SERIES 13 FIGURES

Dr. Stephan Hawking, 2003, Playmates, Series 13
      NM $4   **MIP** $8

Freddy Quimby, 2003, Playmates, Series 13
NM $4   MIP $8

Helen Lovejoy, 2003, Playmates, Series 13
NM $4   MIP $8

Legs, 2003, Playmates, Series 13
NM $4   MIP $8

Princess Kashmir, 2003, Playmates, Series 13
NM $4   MIP $8

Tuxedo Krusty the Clown, 2003, Playmates, Series 13
NM $4   MIP $8

SERIES 14 FIGURES

Groundskeeper Willie in kilt, 2003, Playmates, Series 14
NM $4   MIP $8

Louie, 2003, Playmates, Series 14
NM $4   MIP $8

Luigi, 2003, Playmates, Series 14
NM $4   MIP $8

Miss Botz, 2003, Playmates, Series 14
NM $4   MIP $8

Miss Hoover, 2003, Playmates, Series 14
NM $4   MIP $8

Sarcastic Man, 2003, Playmates, Series 14
NM $4   MIP $8

SERIES 15 FIGURES

Brandine, 2004, Playmates, Series 15
NM $4   MIP $8

Comic Book Guy, 2004, Playmates, Series 15, re-release
NM $4   MIP $8

Deep Space Homer, 2004, Playmates, Series 15
NM $4   MIP $8

Handsome Moe, 2004, Playmates, Series 15, re-release
NM $4   MIP $8

Manjula, 2004, Playmates, Series 15
NM $4   MIP $8

Octuplets, 2004, Playmates, Series 15
NM $4   MIP $8

SERIES 16 FIGURES

Agnes Skinner, 2004, Playmates, Series 16
NM $4   MIP $8

Artie Ziff, 2004, Playmates, Series 16
NM $4   MIP $8

Benjamin and Gary, 2004, Playmates, Series 16
NM $4   MIP $8

Brain Freeze Bart, 2004, Playmates, Series 16
NM $4   MIP $8

Doug, 2004, Playmates, Series 16
NM $4   MIP $8

Evil Homer, 2004, Playmates, Series 16, also called Devil Homer
NM $7   MIP $15

VEHICLES

Elementary School Bus, 2002, Playmates, interactive
NM $6   MIP $12

Family Car, 2001, Playmates
NM $7   MIP $14

SIX MILLION DOLLAR MAN (KENNER, 1975-78)

ACCESSORIES

Backpack Radio, 1975-78, Kenner
NM $10   MIP $25

Bionic Cycle, 1975-78, Kenner
NM $10   MIP $20

Bionic Mission Vehicle, 1975-78, Kenner
NM $25   MIP $25

Bionic Transport, 1975-78, Kenner
NM $10   MIP $45

Bionic Video Center, 1975-78, Kenner
NM $35   MIP $100

Critical Assignment Arms, 1975-78, Kenner
NM $15   MIP $45

Critical Assignment Legs, 1975-78, Kenner
NM $15   MIP $45

Dual Launch Drag Set with 4" Steve Austin Bionic Bigfoot figure, 1975-78, Kenner
NM $45   MIP $80

Flight Suit, 1975-78, Kenner
NM $15   MIP $30

Mission Control Center, 1975-78, Kenner
NM $25   MIP $75

Mission to Mars Space Suit, 1975-78, Kenner
NM $15   MIP $30

OSI Headquarters, 1975-78, Kenner
NM $30   MIP $70

OSI Undercover Blue Denims, 1975-78, Kenner
NM $15   MIP $30

Porta-Communicator, 1975-78, Kenner
NM $20   MIP $50

Tower & Cycle Set, 1975-78, Kenner
NM $25   MIP $50

Venus Space Probe, 1975-78, Kenner
NM $125   MIP $275

FIGURES

Bionic Bigfoot, 1975-78, Kenner, Must have the chestplate to be complete
NM $75   MIP $175

Maskatron, 1975-78, Kenner, 3 faces, 2 arms
NM $40   MIP $150

Oscar Goldman, 1975-78, Kenner, Wearing familiar checked jacket and carrying exploding briefcase, should Steve Austin's secrets fall into the wrong hands
NM $50   MIP $100

Steve Austin with biosonic arm, 1975-78, Kenner
NM $75   MIP $300

Steve Austin with engine block, 1975-78, Kenner
NM $50   MIP $150

Steve Austin with girder, 1975-78, Kenner
NM $60   MIP $150

SLAP SHOT (McFARLANE, 2000)

FIGURES

(KP Photo)

Jack Hanson, 2000, McFarlane Toys, From movie "Slap Shot." Includes detailed figure and rink diorama
NM $5   MIP $10

(McFarlane Toys)

Jeff Hanson, 2000, McFarlane Toys, Detailed figure with hockey rink base and background
NM $5   MIP $10

(Toy Shop File Photo)

Steve Hanson, 2000, McFarlane Toys, Part of the trio of figures from the movie "Slap Shot."
NM $5   MIP $10

SLEEPY HOLLOW (McFARLANE, 1999)

FIGURES

Crone, 1999, McFarlane Toys
NM $3   MIP $10

Headless Horseman, 1999, McFarlane Toys
NM $3   MIP $10

Headless Rider and Horse box set, 1999, McFarlane Toys
NM $8   MIP $20

Ichabod Crane, 1999, McFarlane Toys
NM $3   MIP $10

SPACE:1999 (MATTEL, 1976)

FIGURES

(Corey LeChat)

Commander Koenig, 1976, Mattel, Shown at center with Bergman and Russell
NM $30   MIP $60

Dr. Russell, 1976, Mattel
NM $30   MIP $60

Professor Bergman, 1976, Mattel
NM $30   MIP $60

Zython Alien, 1976, Mattel
NM $100   MIP $300

PLAY SETS

Eagle Playset with three 3" figures, 1976, Mattel
NM $150   MIP $300

Moonbase Alpha Deluxe Playset with three figures, 1976, Mattel
NM $75   MIP $200

Moonbase Alpha Playset, 1976, Mattel
NM $35   MIP $80

SPACE:1999 (PALITOY, 1975)

FIGURES

Alan Carter, 1975, Palitoy
NM $200   MIP $425

Captain Koenig, 1975, Palitoy
NM $150   MIP $250

Captain Zantor, 1975, Palitoy
NM $75   MIP $160

Mysterious Alien, 1975, Palitoy
NM $75   MIP $160

Paul Morrow, 1975, Palitoy
NM $175   MIP $300

SPAWN (McFARLANE, 1994-PRESENT)

13" FIGURES

Angela, 1996
NM $10   MIP $25

Medieval Spawn, Kay Bee Exclusive, 1997
NM $10   MIP $25

Spawn, 1996
NM $10   MIP $25

ACCESSORIES

Spawn Alley Play Set, 1994-96, McFarlane
NM $15   MIP $50

Spawnmobile, 1994-96, McFarlane
NM $12   MIP $40

Violator Monster Rig, 1994-96, McFarlane
NM $12   MIP $45

MCFARLANE TOYS COLLECTOR'S CLUB EXCLUSIVES

Cogliosto, 1994
NM $5   MIP $15

Terry Fitzgerald, 1994
NM $5   MIP $15

Todd the Artist, 1994
NM $5   MIP $15

Wanda and Cyan, 2000
NM $3   MIP $13

SERIES 01, 1994 (TODD TOYS PACKAGING)

Clown, clown head, 1994
NM $6   MIP $20

Clown, Kay Bee Exclusive, 1994
NM $3   MIP $10

Clown, monster head, 1994, McFarlane
NM $6   MIP $10

Medieval Spawn, black armor, 1994
NM $5   MIP $25

Medieval Spawn, Kay Bee Exclusive, 1994
NM $5   MIP $15

Medieval Spawn, blue armor, 1994, McFarlane
NM $5   MIP $20

Overtkill, dark green, 1994
MNP $5   MIP $15

Overtkill, Kay Bee Exclusive, 1996
MNP $3   MIP $12

Overtkill, turquoise, 1994, McFarlane
NM $7   MIP $20

Spawn, Club Exclusive, blue body, 1997
NM $8   MIP $20

Spawn, Club Exclusive, green body, 1997
NM $8   MIP $20

Spawn, Diamond Exclusive, 1994
NM $45   MIP $120

Spawn, full mask, 1994, McFarlane
NM $5   MIP $25

Spawn, Kay Bee Exclusive, 1995
NM $10   MIP $30

Spawn, Spawn No. 50 premium (Worm Head), 1996
NM $50   MIP $150

Spawn, unmasked (Hamburger Head), first card, 1994, McFarlane
NM $15   MIP $40

Tremor, dark green costume, 1994
NM $5   MIP $15

Tremor, Kay Bee Exclusive, 1996
NM $3   MIP $12

Tremor, orange skin, 1994, McFarlane
NM $8   MIP $15

Violator, 1994, McFarlane
NM $5   MIP $20

Violator, chrome card, 1994
NM $8   MIP $20

Violator, club version, 1997
NM $8   MIP $20

Violator, green card, 1994
NM $5   MIP $15

Violator, Kay Bee Exclusive, 1996
NM $4   MIP $12

Violator, mail-order, 1995
NM $20   MIP $75

Violator, red card, 1994
NM $5   MIP $15

SERIES 02, 1995

Angela, 1995, McFarlane
NM $5   MIP $25

Angela, Club Exclusive, blue, 1997, McFarlane
NM $8   MIP $20

Angela, Club Exclusive, pewter, 1997, McFarlane
NM $8   MIP $20

(KP Photo)

Angela, gold headpiece with gold and purple costume, 1995, McFarlane, Includes sword, belt and accessories
NM $20   MIP $50

Angela, Kay Bee Exclusive, 1997, McFarlane
 NM $3   **MIP** $12

Angela, McFarlane Toy Collector's Club Exclusive, 1996, McFarlane
 NM $12   **MIP** $35

Angela, silver headpiece with silver and blue costume, 1995, McFarlane
 NM $10   **MIP** $25

Badrock, blue, 1995, McFarlane, With firing missiles
 NM $10   **MIP** $25

Badrock, red pants, 1995, McFarlane
 NM $3   **MIP** $12

(McFarlane Toys)

Chapel, blue/black pants, 1995, McFarlane, Includes gun and jagged-edge sword
 NM $6   **MIP** $20

Chapel, green khaki pants, 1995, McFarlane
 NM $3   **MIP** $12

(McFarlane Toys)

Commando Spawn, 1995, McFarlane, Black and red uniform, includes weapons and headset
 NM $7   **MIP** $20

(McFarlane Toys)

Malebolgia, 1995, McFarlane, Highly-detailed figure
 NM $30   **MIP** $60

Pilot Spawn, black costume, 1995, McFarlane, Black uniform with red highlights, includes jet pack and dagger
 NM $8   **MIP** $20

Pilot Spawn, Kay Bee Toys, 1997, McFarlane
 NM $3   **MIP** $12

Pilot Spawn, white "Astronaut Spawn", 1995, McFarlane
 NM $5   **MIP** $16

SERIES 03, 1995

Cosmic Angela, 1995, McFarlane
 NM $5   **MIP** $15

Cosmic Angela, McFarlane Collector's Club Exclusive, 1997, McFarlane
 NM $5   **MIP** $15

Cosmic Angela, No. 62 Spawn and No. 9 Curse of Spawn, Diamond Exclusive, 1997, McFarlane
 NM $25   **MIP** $100

Curse, The, 1995, McFarlane
 NM $5   **MIP** $15

Curse, The, McFarlane Collector's Club Exclusive, 1997, McFarlane
 NM $5   **MIP** $15

Ninja Spawn, 1995, McFarlane
 NM $7   **MIP** $15

Ninja Spawn, McFarlane Collector's Club Exclusive, 1997, McFarlane
 NM $5   **MIP** $15

Redeemer, 1995, McFarlane
 NM $5   **MIP** $15

Redeemer, McFarlane Collector's Club Exclusive, 1997, McFarlane
 NM $5   **MIP** $15

Spawn II, 1995, McFarlane
 NM $10   **MIP** $15

Spawn II, McFarlane Collector's Club Exclusive, 1997, McFarlane
 NM $5   **MIP** $15

Vertebreaker, 1995, McFarlane
 NM $10   **MIP** $25

Vertebreaker, gray or black body, Exclusive available through various store, 1996, McFarlane
 NM $5   **MIP** $15

Vertebreaker, McFarlane Collector's Club Exclusive, 1997, McFarlane
 NM $5   **MIP** $15

Violator II, 1995, McFarlane
 NM $10   **MIP** $20

Violator II, McFarlane Collector's Club Exclusive, 1997, McFarlane
 NM $5   **MIP** $15

SERIES 04, 1996

Clown II, black guns, 1996, McFarlane
 NM $6   **MIP** $20

Clown II, neon orange guns, 1996, McFarlane
 NM $3   **MIP** $12

Cy-Gor, gold trim, 1996, McFarlane
 NM $4   **MIP** $15

Cy-Gor, purple trim, 1996, McFarlane
 NM $4   **MIP** $15

Cy-Gor, Target Exclusive, 1996, McFarlane
 NM $5   **MIP** $15

Exo-Skeleton Spawn, black and gray exo-skeleton, 1996, McFarlane
 NM $5   **MIP** $20

Exo-Skeleton Spawn, Target Exclusive, 1997, McFarlane
 NM $5   **MIP** $15

Exo-Skeleton Spawn, white and light gray bones and white costume, 1996, McFarlane
 NM $8   **MIP** $20

Future Spawn, red trimmed, 1996, McFarlane
 NM $10   **MIP** $15

Maxx, The, FAO Schwarz Exclusive, 1996, McFarlane
 NM $15   **MIP** $40

Maxx, The, with black Isz, 1996, McFarlane
 NM $15   **MIP** $40

Maxx, The, with white Isz, 1996, McFarlane
 NM $10   **MIP** $35

Shadowhawk, black with silver trim, 1996, McFarlane
 NM $4   **MIP** $15

Shadowhawk, gold with gray trim, 1996, McFarlane
 NM $3   **MIP** $10

She-Spawn, black mask, 1996, McFarlane
 NM $5   **MIP** $20

She-Spawn, red face mask, 1996, McFarlane
 NM $5   **MIP** $20

SERIES 05, 1996

Nuclear Spawn, green skin, 1996, McFarlane
 NM $3   **MIP** $10

Nuclear Spawn, orange skin, 1996, McFarlane
 NM $4   **MIP** $15

Overtkill II, flesh colored with gray trim, 1996, McFarlane
 NM $5   **MIP** $15

Overtkill II, silver with gold trim, 1996, McFarlane
 NM $5   **MIP** $15

Tremor II, orange with red blood, 1996, McFarlane
 NM $3   **MIP** $10

Tremor II, purple with green bloob, 1996, McFarlane
 NM $3   **MIP** $10

Vandalizer, FAO Schwarz Exclusive, 1996, McFarlane
 NM $10   **MIP** $25

Vandalizer, gray skinned with black trim, 1996, McFarlane
 NM $3   **MIP** $10

Vandalizer, tan skinned with brown trim, 1996, McFarlane
    NM $3   **MIP** $10

Viking Spawn, 1996, McFarlane
    NM $5   **MIP** $25

Widow Maker, black and red with flesh-colored body, 1996, McFarlane
    NM $5   **MIP** $15

Widow Maker, purple and rose outfit, gray body, 1996, McFarlane
    NM $8   **MIP** $20

SERIES 06, 1996

Alien Spawn, black with white, 1996, McFarlane
    NM $5   **MIP** $15

Alien Spawn, white with black, 1996, McFarlane
    NM $3   **MIP** $10

Battleclad Spawn, black costume, 1996, McFarlane
    NM $5   **MIP** $20

Battleclad Spawn, tan sections, 1996, McFarlane
    NM $4   **MIP** $12

Freak, The, purplish flesh with brown and silver weapons, 1996, McFarlane
    NM $3   **MIP** $10

Freak, The, tan flesh, 1995, McFarlane
    NM $5   **MIP** $15

Sansker, black and yellow, 1996, McFarlane
    NM $3   **MIP** $10

Sansker, brown and tan, 1996, McFarlane
    NM $5   **MIP** $15

Superpatriot, metallic blue arms and legs, 1996, McFarlane
    NM $3   **MIP** $10

Superpatriot, silver arms and legs, 1996, McFarlane
    NM $3   **MIP** $10

Tiffany the Amazon, green trim, 1996
    NM $5   **MIP** $15

Tiffany the Amazon, McFarlane Collector's Club Exclusive, 1998
    NM $8   **MIP** $25

Tiffany the Amazon, red trim, 1996, McFarlane
    NM $5   **MIP** $15

SERIES 07, 1997

Crutch, green goatee, 1977, McFarlane
    NM $5   **MIP** $15

Crutch, purple goatee, 1997
    NM $3   **MIP** $10

(McFarlane Toys)

Mangler, The, 1997, McFarlane, Figure includes skull-topped staff
    NM $5   **MIP** $15

(McFarlane Toys)

No-Body, 1997, McFarlane, Detailed robotic figure containing smaller "No-Body" inside
    NM $5   **MIP** $15

(McFarlane Toys)

Sam and Twitch, 1997, McFarlane, Sam with donut and pistol, Twitch with rifle
    NM $5   **MIP** $15

Scourge, 1997, McFarlane
    NM $5   **MIP** $15

Spawn III, with owl and bat, 1997, McFarlane
    NM $8   **MIP** $25

(KP Photo)

Spawn III, with wolf and bat, 1997, McFarlane, Figure also includes "spring up action cape"
    NM $8   **MIP** $25

(McFarlane Toys)

Zombie Spawn, tan skin with red tunic, 1997, McFarlane, Figure includes chainsaw and large machine-gun rifle
    NM $3   **MIP** $10

SERIES 08, 1997

Curse of the Spawn, 1997
    NM $5   **MIP** $15

Gate keeper, 1997
    NM $4   **MIP** $12

Grave Digger, 1997
    NM $4   **MIP** $12

Renegade, tan flesh, 1997
    NM $4   **MIP** $12

Rotarr, 1997
    NM $4   **MIP** $12

Sabre, 1997
    NM $4   **MIP** $12

SERIES 09, 1997

Goddess, The, 1997
    NM $4   **MIP** $12

Manga Clown, 1997
    NM $4   **MIP** $12

Manga Curse, 1997
    NM $4   **MIP** $12

Manga Ninja Spawn, 1997
    NM $4   **MIP** $12

Manga Spawn, 1997
    NM $5   **MIP** $15

Manga Violator, 1997
    NM $4   **MIP** $12

SERIES 10, MANGA 2, 1998

Cybertooth, 1998, McFarlane
    NM $4   **MIP** $15

Manga Cyber Violator, 1998, McFarlane
    NM $4   **MIP** $8

Manga Dead Spawn, 1998, McFarlane
    NM $4   **MIP** $8

Manga Freak, 1998, McFarlane
    NM $4   **MIP** $8

Manga Overkill, 1998, McFarlane
    NM $4   **MIP** $8

Manga Samurai Spawn, 1998, McFarlane
    NM $4   **MIP** $8

SERIES 11, DARK AGES, 1998

Horrid, The, 1998, McFarlane, Two figures; one winged human-type (larger) and the other, a small skeletal figure with weapon

NM $3   **MIP** $8

(KP Photo)

Ogre, The, 1998, McFarlane, Large Ogre figure controlled by smaller figure riding on shoulders. Also includes war club

NM $5   **MIP** $15

(KP Photo)

Raider, The, 1998, McFarlane, Centaur figure with battle armor, double-edged pike/axe, string of defeated skulls

NM $3   **MIP** $8

(KP Photo)

Skull Queen, The, 1998, McFarlane, Figure includes battle axes, flying skeletal warrior

NM $4   **MIP** $12

Spawn The Black Knight, 1998, McFarlane

NM $5   **MIP** $15

(KP Photo)

Spellcaster, The, 1998, McFarlane, Includes battle axe, shield and helmet

NM $4   **MIP** $15

SERIES 12, 1998

BottomLine, 1998, McFarlane

NM $5   **MIP** $15

Creech, The, 1998, McFarlane

NM $5   **MIP** $20

Cy-Gor II, 1998, McFarlane, Deluxe boxed figure

NM $5   **MIP** $25

Heap, The, 1998, McFarlane

NM $5   **MIP** $15

Re-Animated Spawn, 1998, McFarlane

NM $5   **MIP** $15

Spawn IV, 1998, McFarlane

NM $5   **MIP** $15

TopGun, 1998, McFarlane

NM $5   **MIP** $15

SERIES 13, CURSE OF THE SPAWN, 1999

Curse of the Spawn II, 1999, McFarlane

NM $5   **MIP** $10

Desiccator, 1999, McFarlane, Deluxe boxed figure

NM $7   **MIP** $12

Hatchet, 1999, McFarlane

NM $5   **MIP** $10

Medusa, 1999, McFarlane

NM $5   **MIP** $10

Priest and Mr. Obersmith, 1999, McFarlane

NM $5   **MIP** $10

Raenius, 1999, McFarlane

NM $5   **MIP** $10

Zeus, 1999, McFarlane

NM $5   **MIP** $10

SERIES 14, DARK AGES 2, 1999

Iguantus and Tuskadon, 1999

NM $5   **MIP** $15

(McFarlane Toys)

Mandarin Spawn the Scarlet Edge, 1999, A double-edged sword that is twice the size of the figure. Who wants one? I do.

NM $5   **MIP** $15

Necromancer, 1999

NM $5   **MIP** $15

Spawn the Black Heart, 1999

NM $5   **MIP** $15

Tormentor, 1999

NM $5   **MIP** $15

Viper King, 1999

NM $5   **MIP** $15

SERIES 15, TECHNO SPAWN, 1999

Code Red, 1999

NM $5   **MIP** $15

Cyber Spawn, 1999

NM $5   **MIP** $15

Gray Thunder, 1999

NM $3   **MIP** $10

Iron Express, 1999

NM $3   **MIP** $10

Steel Trap, 1999

NM $3   **MIP** $10

Warzone, 1999

NM $3   **MIP** $10

SERIES 16, NITRO RIDERS, 2000

Spawn: After Burner, 2000, 5-1/4" figure and 9x4-1/4" cycle

NM $3   **MIP** $10

Spawn: Eclipse 5000, 2000, 5-1/2" figure and 9-1/2x5-1/2" cycle

NM $3   **MIP** $10

Spawn: Flash Point, 2000, 5-1/4" figure and 9x4-1/2" cycle

NM $3   **MIP** $10

Spawn: Green Vapor, 2000, 5-1/4" figure and 9-1/2x5-1/2" cycle

NM $3   **MIP** $10

SERIES 17, SPAWN CLASSIC, 2001

(KP Photo)

Al Simmons, 2001, McFarlane, Includes stand, machine gun, pistol and accessories
    NM $3   **MIP** $8

(KP Photo)

Clown III, 2001, McFarlane, Includes wrapped body and stretcher
    NM $3   **MIP** $8

Malebogia II, 2001, McFarlane
    NM $3   **MIP** $8

(KP Photo)

Medieval Spawn II, 2001, McFarlane, Includes chain, sword and accessories
    NM $5   **MIP** $15

(KP Photo)

Spawn V, 2001, McFarlane, With stand
    NM $5   **MIP** $15

Tiffany II, 2001, McFarlane, Includes swords, knives, pike, battle staff, accessories and stand
    NM $5   **MIP** $15

SERIES 18, INTERLINK 6, 2001

(KP Photo)

HD-1, 2001, McFarlane
    NM $3   **MIP** $10

LA-6, 2001, McFarlane
    NM $3   **MIP** $10

LL-4, 2001, McFarlane
    NM $3   **MIP** $10

(KP Photo)

RA-5, 2001, McFarlane
    NM $3   **MIP** $10

(KP Photo)

RL-3, 2001, McFarlane
    NM $3   **MIP** $10

(KP Photo)

TS-2, 2001, McFarlane
    NM $3   **MIP** $10

SERIES 19, DARK AGES SPAWN: THE SAMURAI WARS, 2001

Dojo, 2001, McFarlane
    NM $5   **MIP** $10

Jackyl Assassin, 2001, McFarlane
    NM $5   **MIP** $10

Jyaaku the Nightmare, 2001, McFarlane, Deluxe boxed figure
    NM $7   **MIP** $12

Lotus the Angel Warrior, 2001, McFarlane
    NM $5   **MIP** $10

(KP Photo, Brian Brogaard collection)

Samurai Spawn, 2001, McFarlane
    NM $5   **MIP** $10

Scorpion Assassin, 2001, McFarlane
    NM $5   **MIP** $10

SERIES 20, SPAWN CLASSIC 2, 2001

Clown IV, 2001, McFarlane
NM $5   MIP $10

Domina, 2001, McFarlane
NM $5   MIP $10

Medieval Spawn III, 2001, McFarlane
NM $5   MIP $10

Overtkill III, 2001, McFarlane
NM $5   MIP $10

Spawn VI, 2001, McFarlane
NM $5   MIP $10

Violator III, 2001, McFarlane
NM $5   MIP $10

SERIES 21, ALTERNATE REALITIES, 2002

Alien Spawn, 2002, McFarlane
NM $7   MIP $12

Pirate Spawn, 2002, McFarlane
NM $7   MIP $12

Raven Spawn, 2002, McFarlane
NM $7   MIP $12

She Spawn, 2002, McFarlane
NM $7   MIP $12

Spawn VII, 2002, McFarlane
NM $7   MIP $12

Wings of Redemption Spawn, 2002, McFarlane
NM $10   MIP $20

SERIES 22, DARK AGES SPAWN: THE VIKING AGE, 2002

Berserker the Troll, 2002, McFarlane
NM $7   MIP $12

Bluetooth, 2002, McFarlane
NM $7   MIP $12

Dark Raider, 2002, McFarlane
NM $7   MIP $12

Skullsplitter, 2002, McFarlane
NM $7   MIP $12

Spawn the Bloodaxe, 2002, McFarlane
NM $7   MIP $12

Spawn the Bloodaxe and Thunderhoof, 2002, McFarlane, Deluxe boxed set
NM $10   MIP $22

Valkerie, 2002, McFarlane
NM $7   MIP $15

SERIES 23, MUTATIONS, 2003

Al Simmons, 2003, McFarlane
NM $5   MIP $10

Kin, 2003, McFarlane
NM $5   MIP $10

Malebolgia, 2003, McFarlane
NM $5   MIP $10

Spawn, 2003, McFarlane
NM $5   MIP $10

Warrior Lilith, 2003, McFarlane
NM $5   MIP $10

SERIES 23.5, SPAWN REBORN

Clown IV, 2003, McFarlane, from Series 20
NM $5   MIP $10

Curse of the Spawn II, 2003, McFarlane, from Series 13
NM $5   MIP $10

Domina, 2003, McFarlane, from Series 20
NM $5   MIP $10

(KP Photo, Brian Brogaard collection)

Raven Spawn, 2003, McFarlane, from Series 21
NM $5   MIP $10

Redeemer, 2003, McFarlane, from Series 03
NM $5   MIP $10

Wings of Redemption Spawn, 2003, McFarlane, from Series 21
NM $5   MIP $10

SERIES 24, THE CLASSIC COMIC COVERS, 2003

Hellspawn i.001, 2003, McFarlane
NM n/a   MIP $10

Spawn i.039, 2003, McFarlane
NM n/a   MIP $10

Spawn i.043, 2003, McFarlane
NM n/a   MIP $10

Spawn i.064, 2003, McFarlane
NM n/a   MIP $10

Spawn i.088, 2003, McFarlane
NM n/a   MIP $10

Spawn i.109, 2003, McFarlane
NM n/a   MIP $10

SERIES 25, CLASSIC COMIC COVERS 2

Creech Cl.001, 2004, McFarlane
NM n/a   MIP $10

Redeemer I.117, 2004, McFarlane
NM n/a   MIP $10

Sam and Twitch STI.022, 2004, McFarlane
NM n/a   MIP $10

Spawn HSI.005, 2004, McFarlane
NM n/a   MIP $10

Spawn HSI.011, 2004, McFarlane
NM n/a   MIP $10

Spawn I.095, 2004, McFarlane
NM n/a   MIP $10

SERIES 26, ART OF SPAWN

Curse 2, 2004, McFarlane, Spawn Bible art
NM $5   MIP $10

Spawn the Black Knight, 2004, McFarlane, Dark Ages Issue 1 cover art
NM $5   MIP $10

Spawn v. Cy-Gor, 2004, McFarlane, Issue 57 cover art
NM $5   MIP $10

Spawn, Issue 7, 2004, McFarlane
NM $5   MIP $10

Spawn, Issue 8, 2004, McFarlane
NM $5   MIP $10

Tiffany 3, 2004, McFarlane, Issue 45 art
NM $5   MIP $10

Tremor 3, 2004, McFarlane, Spawn Bible art
NM $5   MIP $10

SERIES 27, ART OF SPAWN

Clown 5, 2005, McFarlane, original art
NM $5   MIP $10

Spawn v. Al Simmons, 2005, McFarlane, deluxe boxed setfd
NM $10   MIP $25

Spawn, Issue 119, 2005, McFarlane, interior art
NM $5   MIP $10

Spawn, Issue 131, 2005, McFarlane, cover art
NM $5   MIP $10

Spawn, Issue 85, 2005, McFarlane, cover art
NM $5   MIP $10

Vandalizer 2, 2005, McFarlane, original art
NM $5   MIP $10

Wanda 2, 2005, McFarlane, Issue 65 interior art
NM $5   MIP $10

SERIES 28, REGENERATED

Commando Spawn 2, 2005, McFarlane
NM n/a   MIP n/a

Cyber Spawn 2, 2005, McFarlane
NM n/a   MIP n/a

Grave Digger 2, 2005, McFarlane
NM n/a   MIP n/a

Lotus Warrior Angel 2, 2005, McFarlane
NM n/a   MIP n/a

Mandarin Spawn 2, 2005, McFarlane
NM n/a   MIP n/a

Spawn v. Urizen, 2005, McFarlane, deluxe boxed set
NM n/a   MIP n/a

Zombie Spawn 2, 2005, McFarlane
NM n/a   MIP n/a

SPAWN: THE MOVIE (MCFARLANE, 1997)

DELUXE FIGURES

Attack Spawn, 1997, McFarlane
NM $10   MIP $30

(McFarlane Toys)

Malebolgia, 1997, McFarlane, Detailed figure includes skull-topped staff
NM $10   MIP $30

(McFarlane Toys)

Violator, 1997, McFarlane, From the Spawn Deluxe Boxed Set, highly-detailed figure
NM $10   MIP $30

FIGURES

Al Simmons, 1997, McFarlane, With rifle and mobile rocket launcher
NM $4   MIP $10

(McFarlane Toys)

Burnt Spawn, 1997, McFarlane, With rifle and femur-bone handled shovel
NM $4   MIP $10

(McFarlane Toys)

Clown, 1997, McFarlane, Truly terrifying figure in referee shirt and pale blue face makeup
NM $4   MIP $10

(McFarlane Toys)

Jason Wynn, 1997, McFarlane, With rifle, headset and accessories
NM $4   MIP $10

(McFarlane Toys)

Jessica Priest, 1997, McFarlane, With rifle and accessories
NM $4   MIP $10

PLAY SETS

(McFarlane Toys)

Final Battle, 1997, McFarlane, Spawn with creature crashing through house diorama
NM $10   MIP $20

(McFarlane Toys)

Graveyard, 1997, McFarlane, Includes two figures and open grave
NM $10   MIP $20

(McFarlane Toys)

Spawn Alley, 1997, McFarlane, Set includes Spawn, alley backdrop and creature
NM $10   MIP $20

SPIDER-MAN ELECTRO-SPARK (TOY BIZ, 1997)

5" FIGURES

Captain America, 1997
NM $5   MIP $15

Electro, 1997
NM $3   MIP $8

Electro-Shock Spidey, 1997
NM $3   MIP $8

Electro-Spark Spider-Man, 1997
NM $3   MIP $8

Steel-Shock Spider-Man, 1997
NM $3   MIP $8

SPIDER-MAN SNEAK ATTACK (TOY BIZ, 1998)

BUG BUSTERS, 5" FIGURES

Jack O'Lantern and Bug Eye Blaster, 1998
NM $3   MIP $8

Silver Sable and Beetle Basher, 1998
NM $3   MIP $8

Spider-Man and Spider Stinger, 1998
NM $3   MIP $8

Vulture and Jaw Breaker, 1998
NM $3   MIP $8

SHAPE SHIFTERS, 7" FIGURES

Lizard forms into Mutant Alligator, 1998
NM $2   MIP $6

Spider-Man forms into Monster Spider, 1998

> NM $2   MIP $6

Venom forms into 3-Headed Serpent, 1998

> NM $2   MIP $6

STREET WARRIORS, 5" FIGURES

Scarecrow with Pitchfork Projectile, 1998

> NM $2   MIP $6

Spider-Sense Peter Parker, 1998

> NM $2   MIP $6

Street War Spider-Man, 1998

> NM $2   MIP $6

Vermin with Rat-firing Fire Hydrant, 1998

> NM $2   MIP $6

WEB FLYERS, 5" FIGURES

Carnage, 1998

> NM $2   MIP $6

Copter Spider-Man, 1998

> NM $2   MIP $6

Hobgoblin, 1998

> NM $2   MIP $6

Spider-Man, 1998

> NM $2   MIP $6

SPIDER-MAN SPECIAL EDITION SERIES (TOY BIZ, 1998)

12" FIGURES

Black Cat, 1998

> NM $10   MIP $30

Spider-Man, 1998

> NM $8   MIP $25

Venom, 1998

> NM $8   MIP $25

SPIDER-MAN SPIDER FORCE (TOY BIZ, 1997)

5" FIGURES

Beetle with Transforming Beetle Armor, 1997

> NM $2   MIP $6

Cybersect Spider-Man with Transforming Cyber Spider, 1997

> NM $2   MIP $6

Swarm with Transforming Bee Action, 1997

> NM $2   MIP $6

Tarantula with Transforming Tarantula Armor, 1997

> NM $2   MIP $6

Wasp with Transforming Wasp Armor, 1997

> NM $2   MIP $6

SPIDER-MAN SPIDER POWER (TOY BIZ, 1999)

SERIES I, 5" FIGURES

Slime Shaker Venom, 1999

> NM $2   MIP $6

Spider Sense Spider-Man, 1999

> NM $2   MIP $6

Street Warrior Spider-Man, 1999

> NM $2   MIP $6

Triple Threat Spider-Man, 1999

> NM $2   MIP $6

SERIES II, 5" FIGURES

Doctor Octopus, 1999

> NM $2   MIP $6

Flip and Swing Spider-man, 1999

> NM $2   MIP $6

J. Jonah Jameson, 1999

> NM $2   MIP $6

Spider Sense Peter Parker, 1999

> NM $2   MIP $6

SPIDER-MAN VAMPIRE WARS (TOY BIZ, 1996)

5" FIGURES

Air-Attack Spider-Man, 1997

> NM $3   MIP $8

Anti-Vampire Spider-Man, 1997

> NM $3   MIP $8

Blade-The Vampire Hunter, 1997

> NM $3   MIP $10

Morbius Unbound, 1997

> NM $3   MIP $10

Vampire Spider-Man, 1997

> NM $3   MIP $8

SPIDER-MAN VENOM (TOY BIZ, 1996-97)

ALONG CAME A SPIDER, 6" FIGURES

Bride of Venom and Vile the Spider, 1997

> NM $3   MIP $10

Phage and Pincer the Spider, 1997

> NM $3   MIP $8

Spider-Carnage and Spit the Spider, 1997

> NM $3   MIP $8

Venom the Symbiote and Riper the Spider, 1997

> NM $3   MIP $8

PLANET OF THE SYMBIOTES, 6" FIGURES

Hybrid, pincer Wing Action, 1997

> NM $3   MIP $8

Lasher, Tentacle Whipping Action, 1997

> NM $3   MIP $8

Riot, Launching Attack Arms, 1997

> NM $3   MIP $8

Venom the Madness, Surprise Attack Heads, 1997

> NM $3   MIP $8

PLANET OF THE SYMBIOTES, DELUXE 6" FIGURES

Hybrid, Pincer Wing Action, 1996

> NM $3   MIP $8

Lasher, Tentacle Whipping Action, 1996

> NM $3   MIP $8

Riot, Launcing Attack Arms, 1996

> NM $3   MIP $8

Scream, Living Tendril Hair, 1996

> NM $3   MIP $8

Venom the Madness, Surprise Attack Heads, 1996, Toy Biz

> NM $3   MIP $8

SPIDER-MAN WEB FORCE (TOY BIZ, 1997)

5" FIGURES

Daredevil, Transforming Web Tank Armor, 1997

> NM $2   MIP $6

Lizard, Transforming Swamp Rider, 1997

> NM $2   MIP $6

Vulture, Transforming Vuture-Bot, 1997

> NM $2   MIP $6

Web Commando Spidey, Transforming Web Copter, 1997

> NM $2   MIP $6

Web Swamp Spidey, Transforming Web Swamp Seeker Armor, 1997

> NM $2   MIP $6

SPIDER-MAN WEB TRAPS (TOY BIZ, 1997)

5" FIGURES

Future Spider-Man with Snapping Cocoon Trap, 1997

> NM $2   MIP $6

Monster Spider-Man with Grappling Spider Sidekick, 1997

> NM $2   MIP $6

Rhino with Rotating Web Snare, 1997

> NM $2   MIP $6

Scorpion with Whipping Tail Attacker trap, 1997

> NM $3   MIP $8

Spider-Man with Pull-string Web Trap, 1997

> NM $2   MIP $6

SPIDER-MAN: THE NEW ANIMATED SERIES (TOY BIZ, 1994-96)

15" TALKING FIGURES

Spider-Man, 1994-96, Toy Biz

> NM $12   MIP $25

Venom, 1994-96, Toy Biz

> NM $12   MIP $25

ACTION FIGURES

2-1/2" DIE-CAST FIGURES

Spider-Man vs. Carnage, 1994-96, Toy Biz
NM $2   MIP $4

Spider-Man vs. Dr. Octopus, 1994-96, Toy Biz
NM $2   MIP $4

Spider-Man vs. Hobgoblin, 1994-96, Toy Biz
NM $2   MIP $4

Spider-Man vs. Venom, 1994-96, Toy Biz
NM $2   MIP $4

5" FIGURES

Alien Spider Slayer, 1994-96, Toy Biz
NM $3   MIP $8

Battle-Ravaged Spider-Man, 1994-96, Toy Biz
NM $3   MIP $10

Cameleon, 1994-96, Toy Biz
NM $4   MIP $12

Carnage, 1994-96, Toy Biz
NM $5   MIP $15

Carnage II, 1994-96, Toy Biz
NM $4   MIP $12

Carnage II, 1996, Toy Biz, Series 6
NM $5   MIP $10

Dr. Octopus, 1994-96, Toy Biz
NM $4   MIP $12

(KP Photo, Brian Brogaard collection)

Green Goblin, 1994-96, Toy Biz
NM $5   MIP $15

Hobgoblin, 1994-96, Toy Biz
NM $4   MIP $12

Kingpin, 1994-96, Toy Biz
NM $5   MIP $15

Kraven, 1994-96, Toy Biz
NM $4   MIP $12

Lizard, 1994-96, Toy Biz
NM $5   MIP $15

Man-Spider, 1996, Toy Biz, Series 6
NM $5   MIP $10

Morbius, 1994-96, Toy Biz
NM $4   MIP $12

(KP Photo, Brian Brogaard collection)

Mysterio, 1994-96, Toy Biz, Series 4
NM $3   MIP $12

Nick Fury, 1994-96, Toy Biz, Series 5
NM $3   MIP $12

Peter Parker, 1994-96, Toy Biz
NM $5   MIP $15

Prowler, 1994-96, Toy Biz
NM $3   MIP $12

Punisher, 1994-96, Toy Biz, The recognizable man in black (and white)
NM $3   MIP $12

Rhino, 1994-96, Toy Biz
NM $6   MIP $25

Scorpion, 1994-96, Toy Biz
NM $5   MIP $15

Shocker, 1994-96, Toy Biz
NM $4   MIP $15

Smythe, 1994-96, Toy Biz
NM $5   MIP $12

(KP Photo, Brian Brogaard collection)

Spider-Man 2099, 1996, Toy Biz, Series 7
NM $6   MIP $12

(KP Photo, Brian Brogaard collection)

Spider-Man in Black Costume, 1994-96, Toy Biz
NM $3   MIP $12

Spider-Man Octo, 1996, Toy Biz, Series 6
NM $5   MIP $10

(KP Photo, Brian Brogaard collection)

Spider-Man Six Arm, 1994-96, Toy Biz
NM $3   MIP $12

Spider-Man with Parachute Web, 1994-96, Toy Biz
NM $3   MIP $12

Spider-Man with Spider Armor, 1994-96, Toy Biz
NM $3   MIP $15

Spider-Man with Web Cannon, 1996, Toy Biz, Series 6
NM $9   MIP $18

Spider-Man with Web Parachute, 1994-96, Toy Biz
NM $8   MIP $15

Spider-Man with Web Racer, 1994-96, Toy Biz
NM $5   MIP $15

Spider-Man with Web Shooter, 1994-96, Toy Biz
NM $5   MIP $15

Spider-Man, multi-jointed, 1994-96, Toy Biz
NM $3   MIP $15

Spider-Sense Spider-Man, 1994-96, Toy Biz
NM $3   MIP $12

Symbiotic Venom Attack, 1994-96, Toy Biz
NM $3   MIP $12

Tombstone, 1996, Toy Biz, Series 6
NM $5   **MIP** $10

Venom, 1994-96, Toy Biz
NM $4   **MIP** $15

Venom II, 1994-96, Toy Biz
NM $3   **MIP** $12

Vulture, 1994-96, Toy Biz
NM $5   **MIP** $15

ACCESSORIES

Daily Bugle Play Set, 1994-96, Toy Biz
NM $10   **MIP** $15

DELUXE 10" FIGURES

Carnage, 1994-96, Toy Biz
NM $8   **MIP** $20

Dr. Octopus, 1994-96, Toy Biz
NM $7   **MIP** $15

Hobgoblin, 1994-96, Toy Biz
NM $7   **MIP** $15

Kraven, 1994-96, Toy Biz
NM $7   **MIP** $15

Lizard, 1994-96, Toy Biz
NM $7   **MIP** $15

Myserio, 1994-96, ToyBiz
NM $7   **MIP** $15

Punisher, 1994-96, ToyBiz
NM $7   **MIP** $15

Spider-Man Spider Sense, 1994-96, Toy Biz
NM $7   **MIP** $15

Spider-Man with suction cups, 1994-96, Toy Biz
NM $7   **MIP** $15

Spider-Man, Armor, 1994-96, ToyBiz
NM $7   **MIP** $15

Spider-Man, Sensational, 1994-96, ToyBiz
NM $7   **MIP** $15

Spider-Man, Silver Web, 1994-96, ToyBiz
NM $7   **MIP** $15

Spider-Man, Spider Armor, 1994-96, ToyBiz
NM $7   **MIP** $15

Spider-Man, Super Posable, 1994-96, ToyBiz
NM $7   **MIP** $15

Spider-Man, wall hanging, 1994-96, Toy Biz
NM $7   **MIP** $15

Venom, 1994-96, Toy Biz
NM $7   **MIP** $15

Venom, Dark Blue, 1994-96, ToyBiz
NM $7   **MIP** $15

Vulture, 1994-96, Toy Biz
NM $10   **MIP** $20

PROJECTORS

Hobgoblin, 1994-96, Toy Biz
NM $5   **MIP** $15

Lizard, 1994-96, Toy Biz
NM $5   **MIP** $15

Spider-Man, 1994-96, Toy Biz
NM $5   **MIP** $15

Venom, 1994-96, Toy Biz
NM $5   **MIP** $15

VEHICLES

Hobgoblin Wing Bomber, 1994-96, Toy Biz
NM $10   **MIP** $25

Smythe Battle Chair Attack Vehicle, 1994-96, Toy Biz
NM $15   **MIP** $40

Spider-Man Wheelie Cycle, 1994-96, Toy Biz
NM $7   **MIP** $15

Spider-Man's Cycle (radio-controlled), 1994-96, Toy Biz
NM $15   **MIP** $30

Tri-Spider Slayer, 1994-96, Toy Biz
NM $10   **MIP** $25

SPORTS PICKS (McFARLANE, 2000)

NHPLA FIGURES

Curtis Joseph, 2000
NM $3   **MIP** $10

Patrick Roy, 2000
NM $3   **MIP** $10

Paul Kariya, 2000
NM $3   **MIP** $10

Ray Bourque, 2000
NM $3   **MIP** $10

Steve Yzerman, 2000
NM $3   **MIP** $10

Tony Amonte, 2000
NM $3   **MIP** $10

STAR TREK (MEGO, 1974-80)

CARDED FIGURES

Andorian, 1976, Mego
NM $300   **MIP** $650

Captain Kirk, 1974, Mego
NM $25   **MIP** $50

Cheron, 1975, Mego, Black and white face and uniform
NM $85   **MIP** $175

Dr. McCoy, 1974, Mego, Medical tricorder pack
NM $35   **MIP** $75

Gorn, 1975, Mego
NM $80   **MIP** $180

(Corey LeChat)

Klingon, 1974, Mego, Black boots, brown plastic body armor, brown tunic
NM $25   **MIP** $50

Lt. Uhura, 1974, Mego
NM $50   **MIP** $135

Mr. Spock, 1974, Mego, tricorder, communicator, phaser, belt
NM $25   **MIP** $50

Mugato, 1976, Mego
NM $275   **MIP** $500

Neptunian, 1975, Mego
NM $100   **MIP** $225

Romulan, 1976, Mego
NM $600   **MIP** $1000

Scotty, 1974, Mego
NM $35   **MIP** $80

Talos, 1976, Mego
NM $275   **MIP** $500

The Keeper, 1975, Mego
NM $75   **MIP** $175

PLAY SETS

Mission to Gamma VI, 1974-80, Mego
NM $300   **MIP** $700

U.S.S. Enterprise Bridge, 1974-80, Mego
NM $100   **MIP** $275

STAR TREK ALIEN COMBAT (PLAYMATES, 1999)

FIGURES

Borg Drone, 1999, Playmates
NM $15   **MIP** $25

Klingon Warrior, 1999, Playmates
NM $15   **MIP** $25

STAR TREK COLLECTOR ASSORTMENT (PLAYMATES, 1999)

FIGURES

Andorian Ambassador, 1999, Playmates
NM $5   **MIP** $10

Captain Janeway, 1999, Playmates
NM $5   **MIP** $10

Counselor Troi, 1999, Playmates
NM $5   **MIP** $10

Dr. McCoy, 1999, Playmates
NM $5   **MIP** $10

Ensign Chekov, 1999, Playmates
NM $5   **MIP** $10

Geordi LaForge, 1999, Playmates
NM $5   **MIP** $10

Gorn Captain, 1999, Playmates
NM $5   **MIP** $10

Khan, 1999, Playmates
NM $5   **MIP** $10

Lieutenant Sulu, 1999, Playmates
NM $5   **MIP** $10

Lieutenant Uhura, 1999, Playmates
NM $5   **MIP** $10

Locutus of Borg, 1999, Playmates
    NM $5   MIP $10

Mr. Spock, 1999, Playmates
    NM $5   MIP $10

Mugatu, 1999, Playmates
    NM $5   MIP $10

Q, 1999, Playmates
    NM $5   MIP $10

Scotty, 1999, Playmates
    NM $5   MIP $10

Seven of Nine, 1999, Playmates
    NM $5   MIP $10

STAR TREK COLLECTOR SERIES (PLAYMATES, 1994-95)

9-1/2" BOXED FIGURES

Borg, 1995, Playmates, #6069
    NM $10   MIP $25

Captain Benjamin Sisko, 1995, Playmates, #16188
    NM $10   MIP $25

Captain Benjamin Sisko (Command Edition), 1994, Playmates, #6067
    NM $10   MIP $25

Captain Jean-Luc Picard (Command Edition), 1994, Playmates, #6066
    NM $10   MIP $25

Captain Jean-Luc Picard (Movie Edition), 1994, Playmates, #6288
    NM $10   MIP $25

Captain Jean-Luc Picard, Dress Uniform, 1995, Playmates, #6289
    NM $10   MIP $25

Captain Kirk (Command Edition), 1994, Playmates, #6068
    NM $10   MIP $25

Captain Kirk (Movie Edition), 1994, Playmates, #6288
    NM $10   MIP $25

Captian Christopher Pike, 1995, Playmates, #16183
    NM $10   MIP $25

Chief Miles O'Brien, 1995, Playmates, #16182
    NM $10   MIP $20

Commander Riker, 1995, Playmates, #6285
    NM $10   MIP $25

Data (Movie Edition), 1995, Playmates, #6284
    NM $10   MIP $25

Dr. Beverly Crusher, 1995, Playmates, #6282
    NM $10   MIP $25

Dr. Leonard McCoy, 1995, Playmates, #6292
    NM $10   MIP $25

Ensign Pavel Chekov, 1995, Playmates, #16185
    NM $10   MIP $25

Geordi La Forge (Movie Edition), 1994, Playmates, #6287
    NM $10   MIP $25

Guinan, 1995, Playmates, #6283
    NM $10   MIP $25

Lt. Cmdr. Deanna Troi, 1995, Playmates, #6281
    NM $10   MIP $25

Lt. Cmdr. Montgomery Scott, 1995, Playmates, #6293
    NM $10   MIP $25

Lt. Cmdr. Worf in DS9 uniform, 1995, Playmates, #6295
    NM $10   MIP $25

Lt. Hikaur Sulu, 1995, Playmates, #16184
    NM $10   MIP $25

Lt. Jadzia Dax, 1995, Playmates, #16186
    NM $10   MIP $25

Lt. Uhura, 1995, Playmates, #6294
    NM $10   MIP $25

Lt. Worf in Ritual Klingon Attire, 1995, Playmates, #6286
    NM $10   MIP $25

Major Kira Nerys, 1995, Playmates, #16189
    NM $10   MIP $20

Mr. Spock, 1995, Playmates, #6291
    NM $10   MIP $25

Q in Judges Robes, 1995, Playmates, #16187
    NM $10   MIP $25

Romulan Commander, 1995, Playmates, #16181
    NM $10   MIP $20

STAR TREK ELECTRONIC DISPLAY ASSORTMENT (PLAYMATES, 1999)

FIGURES

Captain Kirk, 1999, Playmates
    NM $20   MIP $40

Captain Picard, 1999, Playmates
    NM $20   MIP $40

Commander Riker, 1999, Playmates
    NM $20   MIP $40

Lieutenant Commander Data, 1999, Playmates
    NM $20   MIP $40

Lieutenant Worf, 1999, Playmates
    NM $20   MIP $40

Mr. Spock, 1999, Playmates
    NM $20   MIP $40

STAR TREK MILLENNIUM COLLECTOR'S SET (PLAYMATES, 1999)

FIGURES

Captain Janeway/Commander Chakotay, 1999, Playmates
    NM $15   MIP $40

Captain Kirk/Mr. Spock, 1999, Playmates
    NM $15   MIP $40

Captain Picard/Commander Riker, 1999, Playmates
    NM $15   MIP $40

Captain Sisko/, 1999, Playmates
    NM $15   MIP $40

STAR TREK V (GALOOB, 1989)

BOXED FIGURES

Captain Kirk, 1989, Galoob
    NM $10   MIP $25

Dr. McCoy, 1989, Galoob
    NM $10   MIP $25

Klaa, 1989, Galoob
    NM $10   MIP $25

Mr. Spock, 1989, Galoob
    NM $10   MIP $25

Sybok, 1989, Galoob
    NM $10   MIP $25

STAR TREK: CLASSIC MOVIE FIGURES (PLAYMATES, 1995)

FIGURES

Admiral Kirk, 1995, Playmates, #6451, "ST:TMP"
    NM $6   MIP $12

Cmdr. Kruge, 1995, Playmates, #6459, "STIII:TSFS"
    NM $6   MIP $12

Cmdr. Spock, 1995, Playmates, #6452, "ST:TMP"
    NM $6   MIP $12

Dr. McCoy, 1995, Playmates, #6453, "ST:TMP"
    NM $6   MIP $12

General Chang, 1995, Playmates, #6458, "STVI:TUC"
    NM $7   MIP $15

Khan, 1995, Playmates, #6456, "STII:TWOK"
    NM $10   MIP $20

Lt. Saavik, 1995, Playmates, #6460, "STII:TWOK" Kirstie Alley likeness
    NM $7   MIP $14

Lt. Sulu, 1995, Playmates, #6454, "ST:TMP"
    NM $6   MIP $12

Lt. Uhura, 1995, Playmates, #6455, "ST:TMP"
    NM $6   MIP $12

Martia, 1995, Playmates, #6457, "STVI:TUC"
    NM $10   MIP $20

STAR TREK: DEEP SPACE NINE (PLAYMATES, 1994-95)

SERIES 1

Chief Miles O'Brien, 1994, Playmates, #6204
    NM $6   MIP $12

Cmdr. Benjamin Sisko, 1994, Playmates, #6201
    NM $5   MIP $10

Cmdr. Gul Ducat, 1994, Playmates, #6207
    NM $8   MIP $15

ACTION FIGURES

Dr. Julian Bashir, 1994, Playmates, #6208
    NM $10   **MIP** $22

Lt. Jadzia Dax, 1994, Playmates, #6205
    NM $8   **MIP** $16

Major Kira Nerys, 1994, Playmates, #6206
    NM $5   **MIP** $10

Morn, 1994, Playmates, #6210
    NM $6   **MIP** $12

Odo, 1994, Playmates, #6202
    NM $6   **MIP** $12

Quark, 1994, Playmates, #6203
    NM $6   **MIP** $12

SERIES 2

Captain Jean-Luc Picard, 1995, Playmates, #6245, DS9 uniform
    NM $4   **MIP** $8

Chief Miles O'Brien, dress uniform, 1995, Playmates, #6226
    NM $5   **MIP** $10

Chief Miles O'Brien, duty uniform, 1995, Playmates, #6244
    NM $5   **MIP** $10

Cmdr. Benjamin Sisko, dress uniform, 1995, Playmates, #6220
    NM $5   **MIP** $10

Dr. Julian Bashir, duty uniform, 1995, Playmates, #6243
    NM $5   **MIP** $10

Jake Sisko, 1995, Playmates, #6235
    NM $5   **MIP** $10

Lt. Jadzia Dax, duty uniform, 1995, Playmates, #6242
    NM $5   **MIP** $10

Lt. Thomas Riker, 1995, Playmates, #6246, DS9 uniform
    NM $6   **MIP** $12

Q, 1995, Playmates, #6247, DS9 uniform
    NM $6   **MIP** $12

Rom w/ Nog, 1995, Playmates, #6241
    NM $7   **MIP** $14

Tosk, 1995, Playmates, #6237
    NM $5   **MIP** $10

Vedek Bareil, 1995, Playmates, #6236
    NM $8   **MIP** $16

STAR TREK: FIRST CONTACT (PLAYMATES, 1996)

5" FIGURES

Borg, 1996, Playmates, #16108
    NM $8   **MIP** $15

Data, 1996, Playmates, #16104
    NM $5   **MIP** $10

Deanna Troi, 1996, Playmates, #16106
    NM $5   **MIP** $10

Dr. Beverly Crusher, 1996, Playmates, #16107
    NM $6   **MIP** $12

Geordi LaForge, 1996, Playmates, #16103
    NM $5   **MIP** $10

Jean-Luc Picard, 1996, Playmates, #16101
    NM $5   **MIP** $10

Jean-Luc Picard in space suit, 1996, Playmates, #16115
    NM $6   **MIP** $12

Lily, 1996, Playmates, #16110
    NM $8   **MIP** $15

William Riker, 1996, Playmates, #16102
    NM $5   **MIP** $10

Worf, 1996, Playmates, #16105
    NM $5   **MIP** $10

Zefram Cochrane, 1996, Playmates, #16109
    NM $5   **MIP** $10

9" FIGURES

Data, 1996, Playmates, #16133
    NM $12   **MIP** $18

Jean-Luc Picard, 1996, Playmates, #16131
    NM $12   **MIP** $18

Jean-Luc Picard in 21st century outfit, 1996, Playmates, #16153
    NM $15   **MIP** $23

William Riker, 1996, Playmates, #16132
    NM $12   **MIP** $18

Zefram Cochrane, 1996, Playmates, #16134
    NM $18   **MIP** $25

STAR TREK: GENERATIONS (PLAYMATES: 1995)

5" FIGURES

Admiral James T. Kirk, 1995, Playmates, #6911
    NM $7   **MIP** $14

B'Etor, 1995, Playmates, #6928
    NM $7   **MIP** $14

Captain James T. Kirk in spacesuit, 1995, Playmates, #6930
    NM $8   **MIP** $15

Captain Jean-Luc Picard, 1995, Playmates, #6918
    NM $5   **MIP** $10

Cmdr. Deanna Troi, 1995, Playmates, #6920
    NM $5   **MIP** $10

Dr. Beverly Crusher, 1995, Playmates, #6924
    NM $7   **MIP** $14

Dr. Soran, 1995, Playmates, #6925
    NM $6   **MIP** $12

Guinan, 1995, Playmates, #6927
    NM $7   **MIP** $14

Lt. Cmdr. Data, 1995, Playmates, #6921
    NM $5   **MIP** $10

Lt. Cmdr. Geordi LaForge, 1995, Playmates, #6923
    NM $7   **MIP** $14

Lt. Cmdr. William Riker, 1995, Playmates, #6919 should be a Commander
    NM $5   **MIP** $10

Lt. Cmdr. Worf, 1995, Playmates, #6922
    NM $5   **MIP** $10

Lt. Cmdr. Worf in 19th Century outfit, 1995, Playmates, #6931
    NM $6   **MIP** $12

Lursa, 1995, Playmates, #6929
    NM $7   **MIP** $14

Montgomery Scott, 1995, Playmates, #6914
    NM $12   **MIP** $25

Pavel A. Chekov, 1995, Playmates, #6916
    NM $12   **MIP** $25

9" FIGURES

Captain James T. Kirk, 1995, Playmates, #6142
    NM $20   **MIP** $40

Captain Jean-Luc Picard, 1995, Playmates, #6141
    NM $10   **MIP** $20

Lt. Cmdr. Data, 1995, Playmates, #6143
    NM $10   **MIP** $20

Lt. Cmdr. Geordi LaForge, 1995, Playmates, #6144
    NM $10   **MIP** $20

STAR TREK: INSURRECTION (PLAYMATES, 1998)

12" FIGURES

Captain Picard, 1998, Playmates, #65071
    NM $7   **MIP** $14

Data, 1998, Playmates, #65074
    NM $7   **MIP** $14

Geordi LaForge, 1998, Playmates, #65504
    NM $7   **MIP** $14

William Riker, 1998, Playmates, #65072
    NM $7   **MIP** $14

Worf, 1998, Playmates, #65073
    NM $7   **MIP** $14

9" FIGURES

Anji, 1998, Playmates, #65358
    NM $5   **MIP** $10

Counselor Troi, 1998, Playmates, #65355
    NM $8   **MIP** $15

Data, 1998, Playmates, #65356
    NM $8   **MIP** $15

Geordi LaForge, 1998, Playmates, #65354
    NM $8   **MIP** $15

Jean-Luc Picard, 1998, Playmates, #65351
    NM $8   **MIP** $15

Ru' Afo, 1998, Playmates, #65357
    NM $8   **MIP** $15

William Riker, 1998, Playmates, #65352
    NM $5   **MIP** $10

Worf, 1998, Playmates, #65353
    NM $8   **MIP** $15

STAR TREK: MIXED SETS (PLAYMATES, 1996-97)

SERIES 1

Captain Jean Luc Picard, 1996, Playmates, #6442, "Tapestry," limited to 1701 figures
NM $150   MIP $275

Christine Chapel, 1996, Playmates, #6447
NM $5   MIP $10

Cmdr. Benjamin Sisko, 1996, Playmates, #6445, "Crossover"
NM $5   MIP $10

Grand Negus Zek, 1996, Playmates, #6444
NM $5   MIP $10

Janice Rand, 1996, Playmates, #6449
NM $5   MIP $10

Worf, Governor of H'Atoria, 1996, Playmates, #6437, "All Good Things"
NM $5   MIP $10

SERIES 2

Admiral William Riker, 1996, Playmates, #16034, "All Good Things"
NM $4   MIP $8

Captain Kirk, casual, 1996, Playmates, #16031
NM $5   MIP $10

Jem Haddar, 1996, Playmates, #16032
NM $5   MIP $10

Lt. Cmdr. Worf, 1996, Playmates, #16033, DS9 Strategic Operations Officer
NM $4   MIP $8

Lt. Natasha Yar, 1996, Playmates, #16043, "Yesterday's Enterprise," limited to 1701 figures
NM $75   MIP $150

Security Chief Odo, 1996, Playmates, #6446, "Necessary Evil"
NM $5   MIP $10

SERIES 3

Captain Christopher Pike, 1996, Playmates, #6448, "The Cage"
NM $5   MIP $10

Elim Garak, 1996, Playmates, #16035, DS9 Tailor
NM $4   MIP $8

Lt. Reginald Barclay, 1996, Playmates, #16044, "Projections," limited to 3000 figures
NM $60   MIP $120

Mr. Spock, 1996, Playmates, #16038, "The Cage"
NM $5   MIP $10

Talosian Keeper, 1996, Playmates, #16039, "The Cage"
NM $5   MIP $10

Vina, The Orion Slave Girl, 1996, Playmates, #16040, "The Cage"
NM $20   MIP $40

SERIES 4

Captain Benjamin Sisko, 1997, Playmates, #16021, bald head
NM $4   MIP $8

Captain Kurn, 1997, Playmates, #16020, "Sons of Mogh"
NM $4   MIP $8

Dr. Beverly Crusher, 1997, Playmates, #16047, movie "Generations," limited to 10,000 figures
NM $12   MIP $25

Gorn Captain, 1997, Playmates, #16041, "Arena"
NM $7   MIP $15

Seska as Cardassian, 1997, Playmates, #16022, ST:Voy "Maneuvers"
NM $4   MIP $8

Tom Paris Mutated, 1997, Playmates, #16023, ST:Voy "Threshold"
NM $4   MIP $8

SERIES 5

Captain Kirk in Environmental Suit, 1997, Playmates, #16048, "The Tholian Web"
NM $6   MIP $12

Dr. McCoy in dress uniform, 1997, Playmates, #16155, "Journey to Babel," limited to 10,000 figures
NM $15   MIP $30

Harry Mudd, 1997, Playmates, #16154, "I, Mudd" and "Mudd's Women"
NM $5   MIP $10

Professor Data, 1997, Playmates, #16152, "All Good Things"
NM $5   MIP $10

The Mugatu, 1997, Playmates, #16042, "A Private Little War"
NM $6   MIP $12

STAR TREK: SPACE TALK SERIES (PLAYMATES, 1995)

SPACE TALK SERIES

Borg, 1995, Playmates
NM $5   MIP $20

Picard, 1995, Playmates
NM $5   MIP $10

Q, 1995, Playmates
NM $5   MIP $20

Riker, 1995, Playmates
NM $5   MIP $10

STAR TREK: STARFLEET ACADEMY (PLAYMATES, 1996)

FIGURES

Cadet Geordi LaForge, 1996, Playmates
NM $8   MIP $15

Cadet Jean-Luc Picard, 1996, Playmates
NM $8   MIP $15

Cadet William Riker, 1996, Playmates
NM $8   MIP $15

Cadet Worf, 1996, Playmates
NM $8   MIP $15

STAR TREK: THE MOTION PICTURE (MEGO, 1979-81)

12" BOXED FIGURES

Arcturian, 1979, Mego
NM $40   MIP $125

Captain Kirk, 1979, Mego
NM $40   MIP $75

Decker, 1979, Mego
NM $45   MIP $115

Ilia, 1979, Mego
NM $40   MIP $75

Klingon, 1979, Mego
NM $40   MIP $125

Mr. Spock, 1979, Mego
NM $40   MIP $75

3-3/4" CARDED FIGURES

Acturian, 1980, Mego, Series 2, Light tan uniform
NM $75   MIP $150

Betelgeusian, 1980, Mego, Series 2
NM $75   MIP $150

Captain Kirk, 1979, Mego, Series 1
NM $12   MIP $35

Decker, 1979, Mego, Series 1
NM $12   MIP $35

Dr. McCoy, 1979, Mego, Series 1, White shirt, gray pants
NM $12   MIP $35

Ilia, 1979, Mego, Series 1
NM $10   MIP $20

Klingon, 1980, Mego, Series 2
NM $75   MIP $150

Megarite, 1980, Mego, Series 2
NM $75   MIP $150

Mr. Spock, 1979, Mego, Series 1, Dark gray uniform as seen in movie
NM $12   MIP $35

Rigellian, 1980, Mego, Series 2
NM $75   MIP $150

Scotty, 1979, Mego, Series 1
NM $12   MIP $35

Zatanite, 1980, Mego, Series 2
NM $75   MIP $150

PLAY SETS

U.S.S. Enterprise Bridge, 1980, Mego
NM $45   MIP $105

ACTION FIGURES

STAR TREK: THE NEXT GENERATION (GALOOB, 1988-89)

ACCESSORIES

Enterprise, 1989, Galoob, die-cast vehicle
NM $10 MIP $35

Ferengi Fighter, 1989, Galoob, vehicle
NM $15 MIP $50

Galileo Shuttle, 1989, Galoob, vehicle
NM $15 MIP $50

Phaser, 1989, Galoob, role playing toy
NM $20 MIP $40

SERIES 1 FIGURES

Data, blue face, 1988, Galoob
NM $50 MIP $85

Data, brown face, 1988, Galoob
NM $30 MIP $50

Data, flesh face, 1988, Galoob
NM $12 MIP $30

Data, spotted face, 1988, Galoob
NM $12 MIP $30

Geordi La Forge, 1988, Galoob
NM $5 MIP $15

Jean-Luc Picard, 1988, Galoob
NM $5 MIP $15

Lt. Worf, 1988, Galoob
NM $5 MIP $15

Tasha Yar, 1988, Galoob
NM $8 MIP $22

William Riker, 1988, Galoob
NM $5 MIP $15

SERIES 2 FIGURES

Antican, 1989, Galoob
NM $25 MIP $65

Ferengi, 1989, Galoob
NM $25 MIP $65

Q, 1989, Galoob
NM $25 MIP $65

Selay, 1989, Galoob
NM $25 MIP $65

STAR TREK: THE NEXT GENERATION (PLAYMATES, 1992-96)

SERIES 1

Borg, 1992, Playmates, #6055
NM $8 MIP $15

Captain Jean-Luc Picard, 1992, Playmates, #6011
NM $8 MIP $15

Commander Riker, 1992, Playmates, #6014
NM $8 MIP $14

Counselor Deanna Troi, 1992, Playmates, #6016
NM $12 MIP $20

Ferengi, 1992, Playmates, #6052
NM $8 MIP $20

Gowron the Klingon, 1992, Playmates, #6053
NM $10 MIP $20

Lt. Commander Data, 1992, Playmates, #6012
NM $8 MIP $15

Lt. Commander Geordi LaForge, 1992, Playmates, #6015
NM $8 MIP $20

Lt. Worf, 1992, Playmates, #6013
NM $8 MIP $15

Romulan, 1992, Playmates, #6051
NM $12 MIP $25

SERIES 2

Admiral McCoy, 1993, Playmates, #6028, with card or space cap
NM $5 MIP $12

Ambassador Spock, 1993, Playmates, #6027, with card or space cap
NM $5 MIP $12

Benzite, 1993, Playmates, #6057, with card or space cap
NM $6 MIP $12

Borg, 1993, Playmates, #6077, with card or space cap
NM $5 MIP $10

Cadet Wesley Crusher, 1993, Playmates, #6021, with card or space cap
NM $6 MIP $12

Captain Jean-Luc Picard, 1993, Playmates, #6071, with card or space cap
NM $6 MIP $12

Captain Scott (Scotty), 1993, Playmates, #6029, with card or space cap
NM $5 MIP $10

Commander Sela, 1993, Playmates, #6056, with card or space cap
NM $6 MIP $12

Commander William Riker, 1993, Playmates, #6074, with card or space cap
NM $6 MIP $12

Counselor Deanna Troi, 1993, Playmates, #6076, with card or space cap
NM $6 MIP $10

Dathon, 1993, Playmates, #6060, with card or space cap
NM $7 MIP $15

Dr. Beverly Crusher, 1993, Playmates, #6019, with card or space cap
NM $6 MIP $10

Guinan, 1993, Playmates, #6020, with card or space cap
NM $7 MIP $12

K'Ehleyr, 1993, Playmates, #6059, with card or space cap
NM $6 MIP $12

Klingon Warrior Worf, 1993, Playmates, #6024, with card or space cap
NM $7 MIP $12

Locutus, 1993, Playmates, #6023, with card or space cap
NM $6 MIP $10

Lore, 1993, Playmates, #6022, with card or space cap
NM $7 MIP $12

Lt. Cmdr. Geordi LaForge in Dress Uniform, 1993, Playmates, #6026, with card or space cap
NM $7 MIP $15

Lt. Commander Data, 1993, Playmates, #6072, with card or space cap
NM $6 MIP $10

Lt. Geordi LaForge, 1993, Playmates, #6075, with card or space cap
NM $7 MIP $15

Lt. Worf, 1993, Playmates, #6073, with card or space cap
NM $6 MIP $12

Q, red shirt, 1993, Playmates, #6058, with card or space cap
NM $7 MIP $15

Vorgon, 1993, Playmates, #6061, with card or space cap
NM $8 MIP $15

SERIES 3

Ambassador Sarek, 1994, Playmates, #6042, Canadian release
NM $5 MIP $12

(KP Photo, Karen O'Brien collection)

Captain Jean-Luc Picard as Dixon Hill, 1994, Playmates, #6050
NM $5 MIP $12

Captain Picard as Romulan, 1994, Playmates, #6032
NM $3 MIP $12

Captain Picard, red duty uniform, 1994, Playmates, #6942
NM $3 MIP $12

Commander Riker, Malcorian, 1994, Playmates, #6034, 7th season episode
NM $3 MIP $12

Dr. Noonian Soong, 1994, Playmates, #6038
NM $5 MIP $12

Ensign Ro, 1994, Playmates, #6044
NM $8 MIP $15

Ensign Wesley Crusher, 1994, Playmates, #6943
NM $5 MIP $12

(Lenny Lee)

Esoqq, 1994, Playmates, #6049, Fearsome-looking alien includes; knife, food ration, communicator, collector card
  NM $15 **MIP** $55

Gowron in Ritual Klingon attire, 1994, Playmates, #6945
  NM $8 **MIP** $20

Hugh Borg, 1994, Playmates, #6037
  NM $5 **MIP** $12

Lt. Barclay, 1994, Playmates, #6045
  NM $5 **MIP** $12

Lt. Cmdr. Data as Romulan, 1994, Playmates, #6031
  NM $5 **MIP** $12

Lt. Cmdr. Data, dress uniform, 1994, Playmates, #6941
  NM $5 **MIP** $12

Lt. Cmdr. Data, red "Redemption" outfit, 1994, Playmates, #6947, JC Penney exclusive, rare
  NM $60 **MIP** $125

(Lenny Lee)

Lt. Cmdr. Deanna Troi, 1994, Playmates, #6035, 6th season uniform, includes a stand, laptop computer, tricorder, PADD and accessories
  NM $3 **MIP** $12

Lt. Cmdr. Geordi La Forge as Tarchannen III alien, 1994, Playmates, #6033
  NM $5 **MIP** $12

Lt. Thomas Riker, 1994, Playmates, #6946
  NM $10 **MIP** $25

Lwaxana Troi, 1994, Playmates, #6041, Canadian release
  NM $3 **MIP** $12

(KP Photo)

Q, in judge's robe, 1993, Playmates, #6042, Q as he appears in "Mission to Farpoint," Next Gen's first episode, and "All Good Things," their last. Includes scroll, scepter, lion statue and gavel
  NM $6 **MIP** $10

Worf in Starfleet rescue outfit, 1994, Playmates, #6036
  NM $8 **MIP** $12

SERIES 4

Ambassador Sarek, 1995, Playmates, #6968
  NM $5 **MIP** $10

Captain Jean-Luc Picard as Locutus, 1995, Playmates, #6986, Supernova Series
  NM $10 **MIP** $22

Captain Jean-Luc Picard in "All Good Things", 1995, Playmates, #6974, Picard is older
  NM $7 **MIP** $15

Dr Beverly Crusher, duty uniform, 1994, Playmates, #6961
  NM $5 **MIP** $15

Dr. Noonian Soong, 1995, Playmates, #6982
  NM $5 **MIP** $10

Ensign Ro Laren, 1995, Playmates, #6981
  NM $5 **MIP** $10

Lt. Cmdr. Data in 1940s attire, 1995, Playmates, #6979, Holodeck Series
  NM $7 **MIP** $15

Lt. Cmdr. Data in movie uniform, 1995, Playmates, #6962
  NM $5 **MIP** $10

Lt. Cmdr. Geordi LaForge in movie uniform, 1995, Playmates, #6960
  NM $5 **MIP** $10

Lt. Natasha Yar, 1994, Playmates, #6965
  NM $5 **MIP** $15

Lt. Worf in Ritual Klingon attire, 1995, Playmates, #6985, Supernova Series
  NM $10 **MIP** $20

Lwaxana Troi, 1995, Playmates, #6967
  NM $5 **MIP** $10

Nausicaan, 1994, Playmates, #6969
  NM $5 **MIP** $15

SERIES 5

Borg, 1995, Playmates, #6441, Interstellar Action Series
  NM $7 **MIP** $15

Counselor Troi as Durango, 1995, Playmates, #6438, "A Fist Full of Datas"
  NM $5 **MIP** $10

Dr. Beverly Crusher in 1940s attire, 1995, Playmates, #6435, "The Big Goodbye"
  NM $5 **MIP** $10

Dr. Katherine Puylaski, 1995, Playmates, #6428
  NM $5 **MIP** $10

Geordi LaForge, 1995, Playmates, #6433, "All Good Things"
  NM $7 **MIP** $12

Lt. Geordi LaForge, 1995, Playmates, #6443, Interstellar Action Series
  NM $7 **MIP** $15

Picard as Galen, 1995, Playmates, #6432, "The Gambit"
  NM $5 **MIP** $10

Sheriff Worf, 1995, Playmates, #6434, "A Fist Full of Datas"
  NM $7 **MIP** $12

The Traveler, 1995, Playmates, #6436
  NM $5 **MIP** $10

(KP Photo, Karen O'Brien collection)

Vash, 1995, Playmates, #6436
  NM $5 **MIP** $10

STAR TREK: VOYAGER (PLAYMATES, 1995-96)

FIGURES

Captain Kathryn Janeway, 1996, Playmates, #6481
  NM $15 **MIP** $25

Chakotay the Maquis, 1996, Playmates, #16466
  NM $8 **MIP** $15

Cmdr. Chakotay, 1996, Playmates, #6482
  NM $5 **MIP** $10

Doctor, 1996, Playmates, #6486
  NM $8 **MIP** $15

En. Harry Kim, 1996, Playmates, #6484
  NM $8 **MIP** $15

En. Seska, 1996, Playmates, #16460
  NM $5 **MIP** $10

Kazon, 1996, Playmates, #16462
  NM $5 **MIP** $10

ACTION FIGURES

Kes the Ocampa, 1996, Playmates, #6488
    NM $12   **MIP** $18

Lt. B'Elanna Torres, 1996, Playmates, #6485
    NM $15   **MIP** $25

Lt. Carey, 1995, Playmates, #16461
    NM $7   **MIP** $15

Lt. Tom Paris, 1996, Playmates, #6483
    NM $5   **MIP** $10

Lt. Tuvok, 1996, Playmates, #6487
    NM $5   **MIP** $10

Neelix the Telaxian, 1996, Playmates, #6489
    NM $5   **MIP** $10

Torres as Klingon, 1995, Playmates, #16465
    NM $7   **MIP** $15

Vidiian, 1995, Playmates, #16463
    NM $7   **MIP** $15

VEHICLES

U.S.S. Voyager, 1995, Playmates, #6479
    NM $15   **MIP** $30

STAR TREK: WARP FACTOR (PLAYMATES, 1997-98)

SERIES 1

Captain Benjamin Sisko, 1997, Playmates, #65107, DS9 "Trials and Tribbleations"
    NM $7   **MIP** $14

Captain Koloth, 1997, Playmates, #65111, DS9 "Trials and Tribbleations"
    NM $5   **MIP** $10

Chief Miles O'Brien, 1997, Playmates, #65106, DS9 "Trials and Tribbleations," limited to 10,000
    NM $8   **MIP** $16

Constable Odo, 1997, Playmates, #65109, DS9 "Trials and Tribbleations"
    NM $5   **MIP** $10

Dr. Julian Bashir, 1997, Playmates, #65110, DS9 "Trials and Tribbleations"
    NM $7   **MIP** $14

Lt. Cmdr. Jadzia Dax, 1997, Playmates, #65108, DS9 "Trials and Tribbleations"
    NM $7   **MIP** $14

SERIES 2

Captain Beverly Picard, 1997, Playmates, #65112, "All Good Things"
    NM $5   **MIP** $10

Ilia Probe, 1997, Playmates, #65102, ST:TMP
    NM $5   **MIP** $10

Leeta the Dabo Girl, 1997, Playmates, #65102, DS9
    NM $5   **MIP** $10

Sisko as a Klingon, 1997, Playmates, #65101, DS9 "Apocalypse Rising"
    NM $4   **MIP** $8

Swarm Alien, 1997, Playmates, #65104, ST:YOY "The Swarm"
    NM $5   **MIP** $10

SERIES 3

Cadet Beverly Howard Crusher, 1997, Playmates, #65117
    NM $4   **MIP** $8

Cadet Data, 1997, Playmates, #65116
    NM $4   **MIP** $8

Cadet Deanna Troi, 1997, Playmates, #65115
    NM $4   **MIP** $8

Edith Keeler, 1997, Playmates, #65114, "City on the Edge of Forever"
    NM $4   **MIP** $8

Mr. Spock, 1997, Playmates, #65105, "Mirror, Mirror"
    NM $5   **MIP** $10

SERIES 4

Andorian, 1998, Playmates, #65120, "Whom Gods Destroy"
    NM $4   **MIP** $8

Intendant Kira, 1998, Playmates, #65124, DS9 "Crossover"
    NM $4   **MIP** $8

Kang, 1998, Playmates, #65123, DS9 "Blood Oath"
    NM $4   **MIP** $8

Keiko O'Brien, 1998, Playmates, #65121
    NM $4   **MIP** $8

Trelane, 1998, Playmates, #65122, "The Squire of Gothos"
    NM $4   **MIP** $8

SERIES 5

Borg Queen, 1998, Playmates, #65130, ST:FC
    NM $5   **MIP** $10

James Kirk, 1998, Playmates, #65128, "City on the Edge of Forever"
    NM $5   **MIP** $10

Mr. Spock, 1998, Playmates, #65129, "City on the Edge of Forever"
    NM $5   **MIP** $10

Seven of Nine, 1998, Playmates, #65131, ST:VOY "The Gift"
    NM $5   **MIP** $10

STARGATE (HASBRO, 1994)

FIGURES

Anubis, 1998, Hasbro
    NM $2   **MIP** $4

(Lenny Lee)

Col. O'Neil, 1998, Hasbro, Group shot
    NM $2   **MIP** $4

Daniel Jackson, 1994, Hasbro
    NM $2   **MIP** $5

Horus, Attack Pilot, 1998, Hasbro
    NM $2   **MIP** $4

Horus, Palace Guard, 1998, Hasbro
    NM $2   **MIP** $4

Lt. Kawalsky, 1998, Hasbro
    NM $2   **MIP** $4

Ra, 1998, Hasbro
    NM $2   **MIP** $4

Skaara, 1998, Hasbro
    NM $2   **MIP** $4

STARSKY AND HUTCH (MEGO, 1976)

FIGURES

Captain Dobey, 1976, Mego
    NM $25   **MIP** $50

Chopper, 1976, Mego, In cable-knit sweater and dark pants
    NM $25   **MIP** $45

Huggy Bear, 1976, Mego
    NM $25   **MIP** $50

Hutch, 1976, Mego
    NM $20   **MIP** $45

Starsky, 1976, Mego
    NM $20   **MIP** $45

VEHICLES

Car, 1976, Mego
    NM $85   **MIP** $195

STREET FIGHTER (HASBRO, 1994)

12" FIGURES

Blanka, 1994
    NM $15   **MIP** $25

Colonel Guile, 1994, Hasbro
    NM $15   **MIP** $25

General Bison, 1994, Hasbro
    NM $15   **MIP** $25

Ryu Hoshi, 1994, Hasbro
    NM $15   **MIP** $25

SUPER HERO BEND 'N FLEX (MEGO, 1974-75)

5" FIGURES

Aquaman, 1974-75, Mego
    NM $30   **MIP** $120

Batgirl, 1974-75, Mego
    NM $50   **MIP** $120

Batman, 1974-75, Mego
    NM $35   **MIP** $90

Captain America, 1974-75, Mego
    NM $35   **MIP** $90

Catwoman, 1974-75, Mego
    NM $70   **MIP** $175

Joker, 1974-75, Mego
    NM $40   **MIP** $150

Mr. Mxyzptlk, 1974-75, Mego
    NM $40   **MIP** $125

Penguin, 1974-75, Mego
    NM $40   **MIP** $150

Riddler, 1974-75, Mego
    NM $60   **MIP** $150

Robin, 1974-75, Mego
    NM $30   **MIP** $75

Shazam, 1974-75, Mego
    NM $50   **MIP** $125

Spider-Man, 1974-75, Mego
    NM $50   **MIP** $125

Supergirl, 1974-75, Mego
    NM $70   **MIP** $175

Superman, 1974-75, Mego
    NM $30   **MIP** $75

Tarzan, 1974-75, Mego
    NM $25   **MIP** $60

Wonder Woman, 1974-75, Mego
    NM $50   **MIP** $100

ACCESSORIES

Carry Case, 1974-75, Mego, red vinyl case w/ red plastic handle, "World's Greatest Super Heroes" logo
    NM $40   **MIP** $85

SUPER POWERS (KENNER, 1984-86)

5" FIGURES

Aquaman, 1984, Kenner
    NM $15   **MIP** $45

Batman, 1984, Kenner
    NM $35   **MIP** $75

(Lenny Lee)

Braniac, 1984, Kenner, chrome plastic figure, includes free mini comic book
    NM $15   **MIP** $30

Clark Kent, mail-in figure, 1986, Kenner
    NM $50   **MIP** $75

Cyborg, 1986, Kenner
    NM $150   **MIP** $300

(Toy Shop File Photo)

Cyclotron, 1986, Kenner
    NM $35   **MIP** $75

(Toy Shop File Photo)

Darkseid, 1985, Kenner, gray and blue figure with "Power Action Raging Motion"
    NM $5   **MIP** $15

Desaad, 1985, Kenner
    NM $10   **MIP** $30

Dr. Fate, 1985, Kenner
    NM $35   **MIP** $80

Firestorm, 1985, Kenner
    NM $15   **MIP** $35

(Lenny Lee)

Flash, 1984, Kenner, figure has power action legs that simulate the Flash's lightning-speed running style
    NM $10   **MIP** $25

Golden Pharaoh, 1986, Kenner
    NM $50   **MIP** $125

Green Arrow, 1985, Kenner, with bow
    NM $25   **MIP** $55

Green Lantern, 1984, Kenner, with lantern
    NM $30   **MIP** $60

Hawkman, 1984, Kenner
    NM $25   **MIP** $65

Joker, 1984, Kenner
    NM $15   **MIP** $30

Kalibak, 1985, Kenner
    NM $5   **MIP** $15

(Lenny Lee)

Lex Luthor, 1984, Kenner, has "Power Action Nuclear Punch"
    NM $5   **MIP** $15

(Lenny Lee)

Mantis, 1985, Kenner, figure has "Power Action Pincer Thrust" and includes a free comic book
    NM $10   **MIP** $30

Martian Manhunter, 1985, Kenner
    NM $15   **MIP** $45

Mister Miracle, 1986, Kenner
    NM $60   **MIP** $145

Mr. Freeze, 1986, Kenner
    NM $25   **MIP** $65

(Lenny Lee)

Orion, 1986, Kenner, with "Power Action Astro Punch"

NM $25   MIP $65

(Lenny Lee)

Parademon, 1985, Kenner, includes mini-comic book

NM $15   MIP $35

(Lenney Lee)

Penguin, 1984, Kenner

NM $20   MIP $40

(Lenny Lee)

Plastic Man, 1986, Kenner

NM $65   MIP $150

Red Tornado, 1985, Kenner

NM $35   MIP $85

Robin, 1984, Kenner

NM $25   MIP $50

(Toy Shop File Photo)

Samurai, 1986, Kenner

NM $45   MIP $95

Shazam (Captain Marvel), 1986, Kenner, bright-colored figure, very "cartoony" look

NM $25   MIP $65

Steppenwolf, in mail-in bag, 1985, Kenner

NM $15   MIP $20

Steppenwolf, on card, 1985, Kenner

NM $15   MIP $75

Superman, 1984, Kenner

NM $20   MIP $35

Tyr, 1986, Kenner, with yellow attached "Power Action Rocket Launcher"

NM $40   MIP $75

(Lenny Lee)

Wonder Woman, 1984, Kenner

NM $15   MIP $40

ACCESSORIES

Collector's Case, 1984, Kenner, 11-1/4" x 10" x 3-3/4"

NM $20   MIP $40

PLAY SETS

Hall of Justice, 1984, Kenner

NM $75   MIP $175

VEHICLES

Batcopter, 1986, Kenner

NM $40   MIP $125

Batmobile, 1984, Kenner

NM $50   MIP $150

Darkseid Destroyer, 1985, Kenner

NM $25   MIP $50

Delta Probe One, 1985, Kenner

NM $15   MIP $30

Justice Jogger, wind-up, 1986, Kenner

NM $20   MIP $40

Kalibak Boulder Bomber, 1985, Kenner

NM $10   MIP $25

Lex-Soar 7, 1984, Kenner

NM $10   MIP $25

Supermobile, 1984, Kenner

NM $15   MIP $30

SUPERMAN: MAN OF STEEL (KENNER, 1995-96)

FIGURES

Blast Hammer Steel, 1995, Kenner, Deluxe

NM $5   MIP $10

Conduit, 1995, Kenner

NM $4   MIP $8

Laser Superman, 1995, Kenner

NM $4   MIP $8

Lex Luthor, 1995, Kenner

NM $15   MIP $20

Power Flight Superman, 1995, Kenner

NM $4   MIP $8

Solar Suit Superman, 1995, Kenner

NM $5   MIP $10

Steel, 1995, Kenner

NM $4   MIP $8

Street Guardian Superman, 1995, Kenner

NM $4   MIP $8

Superboy, 1995, Kenner

NM $5   MIP $10

Ultra Heat Vision Superman, 1995, Kenner

NM $5   MIP $10

Ultra Shield Superman, 1995, Kenner

NM $4   MIP $8

MULTI-PACKS

Cyber-Link Superman & Cyber-Link Batman, 1995, Kenner, Wal-Mart exclusive

NM $10   MIP $20

Hunter-Prey Superman v. Doomsday, 1995, Kenner

NM $6   MIP $12

Superman v. Massacre, 1995, Kenner

NM $6   MIP $12

VEHICLES

Kryptonian Battle Suit, 1995, Kenner

NM $10   MIP $20

Superboy VTOL Cycle, 1995, Kenner

NM $7   MIP $15

Superman Matrix Conversion Coupe, 1995, Kenner, Silver w/ Clark Kent

NM $10   MIP $20

SUPERMAN: THE ANIMATED SERIES (KENNER, 1995-96)

FIGURES

Anti-Kryptonite Superman, 1995, Kenner, Series 3

NM $6   MIP $12

Brainiac, 1995, Kenner, Series 1

NM $5   MIP $10

Capture Claw Superman, 1995, Kenner, Series 2
NM $7   MIP $15

Capture Net Superman, 1995, Kenner, Series 1
NM $5   MIP $10

City Camo Superman, 1995, Kenner, Deluxe
NM $6   MIP $12

Cyber Crunch Superman, 1996, Kenner, European release
NM $10   MIP $20

Darkseid, 1995, Kenner, Series 2
NM $15   MIP $30

Deep Dive Superman, 1995, Kenner, Series 1
NM $5   MIP $10

Electro Energy Superman, 1995, Kenner, Series 2
NM $7   MIP $15

Evil Bizzaro, 1995, Kenner, Series 3
NM $15   MIP $30

Flying Superman, 1995, Kenner, Deluxe, a glider
NM $6   MIP $12

Fortress of Solitude Superman, 1995, Kenner
NM $10   MIP $20

Kryptonite Escape Superman, 1995, Kenner, Deluxe
NM $7   MIP $15

Lex Luthor, 1995, Kenner, Series 1
NM $6   MIP $12

Metallo, 1995, Kenner, Series 3, Diamond
NM $10   MIP $20

Mission Masters 3: Quick Change Superman, 1999, Hasbro, Wal-Mart exclusive
NM $7   MIP $15

Neutron Star Superman, 1995, Kenner, Series 1
NM $50   MIP $10

Power Swing Superman, 1995, Kenner, Series 3
NM $8   MIP $16

Quick Change Superman, 1995, Kenner, Series 1
NM $5   MIP $10

Strong Arm Superman, 1995, Kenner, Series 3
NM $6   MIP $12

Supergirl, 1995, Kenner, Series 3, Diamond
NM $7   MIP $14

Tornado Force Superman, 1995, Kenner, Series 3
NM $8   MIP $16

Ultra Shield Superman, 1995, Kenner
NM $5   MIP $10

Vision Blast Superman, 1995, Kenner, Deluxe
NM $7   MIP $15

X-Ray Vision Superman, 1995, Kenner
NM $5   MIP $10

MULTI-PACKS

Battle for Metropolis, 1999, Hasbro, Toys R Us exclusive, Superman, Lois Lane, Lex Luthor, Brainiac,
NM $10   MIP $20

Super Heroes v. Super Villians, 1995, Kenner, Superman, Supergirl, Bizzaro, Metallo
NM $10   MIP $22

PLAY SETS

Metropolis Bank, 1995, Kenner, w/ Superman figure, foreign release
NM $25   MIP $50

VEHICLES

Superman Conversion Coupe, 1995, Kenner, Red w/ Clark Kent
NM $10   MIP $20

TEENAGE MUTANT NINJA TURTLES (PLAYMATES, 1988-92)

GIANT TURTLES, 1991

Donatello, 1991, Playmates
NM $20   MIP $40

Leonardo, 1991, Playmates
NM $20   MIP $40

Michaelangelo, 1991, Playmates
NM $20   MIP $40

Raphael, 1991, Playmates
NM $20   MIP $40

GIANT TURTLES, 1992

Bebop, 1992, Playmates
NM $20   MIP $40

Movie Don, 1992, Playmates
NM $20   MIP $40

Movie Leo, 1992, Playmates
NM $20   MIP $40

Movie Mike, 1992, Playmates
NM $20   MIP $40

Movie Raph, 1992, Playmates
NM $20   MIP $40

Rocksteady, 1992, Playmates
NM $20   MIP $40

SERIES 01, 1988

April O'Neil, no stripe, 1988, Playmates
NM $50   MIP $100

Bebop, 1988, Playmates
NM $3   MIP $8

Donatello, 1988, Playmates
NM $8   MIP $20

Donatello, with fan club form, 1988, Playmates
NM $12   MIP $50

Foot Soldier, 1988, Playmates
NM $8   MIP $20

Leonardo, 1988, Playmates
NM $8   MIP $20

Leonardo, with fan club form, 1988, Playmates
NM $12   MIP $50

Michaelangelo, 1988, Playmates
NM $8   MIP $20

Michaelangelo, with fan club form, 1988, Playmates
NM $12   MIP $50

Raphael, 1988, Playmates
NM $8   MIP $20

Raphael, with fan club form, 1988, Playmates
NM $12   MIP $50

Rocksteady, 1988, Playmates
NM $8   MIP $20

Shredder, 1988, Playmates
NM $8   MIP $20

Splinter, 1988, Playmates
NM $8   MIP $20

SERIES 02, 1989

Ace Duck, hat off, 1989, Playmates
NM $5   MIP $40

Ace Duck, hat on, 1989, Playmates
NM $5   MIP $15

April O'Neil, blue stripe, 1989, Playmates
NM $12   MIP $30

(Toy Shop File Photo)

Baxter Stockman, 1989, Playmates, A man who had a nasty run-in with a bug.
NM $10   MIP $25

Genghis Frog, black belt, 1989, Playmates
NM $5   MIP $15

Genghis Frog, black belt, bagged weapons, 1989, Playmates
NM $5   MIP $30

Genghis Frog, yellow belt, 1989, Playmates
NM $30   MIP $75

Krang, 1989, Playmates
NM $5   MIP $15

SERIES 03, 1989

Casey Jones, 1989, Playmates
NM $5   MIP $15

General Traag, 1989, Playmates
NM $5   MIP $15

(Toy Shop File Photo)

Leatherhead, 1989, Playmates, Way too much sun for this guy.
NM $25   MIP $50

Metalhead, 1989, Playmates, carded
NM $5   MIP $15

Rat King, 1989, Playmates
NM $5   MIP $15

Usagi Yojimbo, 1989, Playmates
NM $5   MIP $15

SERIES 04, 1990

Mondo Gecko, 1990, Playmates
NM $5   MIP $15

Muckman and Joe Eyeball, 1990, Playmates
NM $5   MIP $15

Scumbag, 1990, Playmates
NM $5   MIP $15

Wingnut & Screwloose, 1990, Playmates
NM $5   MIP $15

SERIES 05, 1990

Fugitoid, 1990, Playmates
NM $5   MIP $15

Slash, black belt, 1990, Playmates
NM $3   MIP $25

Slash, purple belt, red "S", 1990, Playmates
NM $25   MIP $75

Triceraton, 1990, Playmates
NM $5   MIP $15

SERIES 06, 1990

Mutagen Man, 1990, Playmates
NM $5   MIP $15

Napoleon Bonafrog, 1990, Playmates
NM $5   MIP $15

Panda Khan, 1990, Playmates
NM $5   MIP $15

SERIES 07, 1991

April O'Neil, 1991, Playmates
NM $25   MIP $125

April O'Neil, "Press", 1991, Playmates
NM $10   MIP $20

Pizza Face, 1991, Playmates
NM $5   MIP $15

Ray Fillet, purple body, red "V", 1991, Playmates, purple torso, red V
NM $10   MIP $25

Ray Fillet, red body, maroon "V", 1991, Playmates, red torso, maroon V
NM $10   MIP $30

Ray Fillet, yellow body, blue "V", 1991, Playmates, yellow torso, blue V
NM $10   MIP $15

SERIES 08, 1991

Don The Undercover Turtle, 1991, Playmates
NM $5   MIP $15

Leo the Sewer Samurai, 1991, Playmates
NM $5   MIP $15

Mike the Sewer Surfer, 1991, Playmates
NM $5   MIP $15

Raph the Space Cadet, 1991, Playmates
NM $5   MIP $15

SERIES 09, 1991

Chrome Dome, 1991, Playmates, carded
NM $5   MIP $15

Dirt Bag, 1991, Playmates, carded
NM $5   MIP $15

Ground Chuck, 1991, Playmates
NM $5   MIP $15

Storage Shell Don, 1991, Playmates
NM $5   MIP $15

Storage Shell Leo, 1991, Playmates
NM $5   MIP $15

Storage Shell Michaelangelo, 1991, Playmates
NM $5   MIP $15

Storage Shell Raphael, 1991, Playmates
NM $5   MIP $15

SERIES 10, 1991

Grand Slam Raph, 1991, Playmates
NM $5   MIP $15

Hose 'em Down Don, 1991, Playmates
NM $5   MIP $15

Lieutenant Leo, 1991, Playmates
NM $5   MIP $15

Make My Day Leo, 1991, Playmates
NM $5   MIP $15

Midshipman Mike, 1991, Playmates
NM $5   MIP $15

Pro Pilot Don, 1991, Playmates
NM $5   MIP $15

Raph the Green Teen Beret, 1991, Playmates
NM $5   MIP $15

Slam Dunkin' Don, 1991, Playmates
NM $5   MIP $15

Slapshot Leo, 1991, Playmates
NM $5   MIP $15

T.D. Tossin' Leonardo, 1991, Playmates
NM $5   MIP $15

SERIES 11, 1992

Rahzer, black nose, 1992, Playmates
NM $5   MIP $15

Rahzer, red nose, 1992, Playmates
NM $7   MIP $25

Skateboard'n Mike, 1992, Playmates
NM $5   MIP $15

Super Shredder, 1992, Playmates
NM $5   MIP $15

Tokka, brown trim, 1992, Playmates
NM $9   MIP $25

Tokka, gray trim, 1992, Playmates
NM $5   MIP $15

SERIES 12, 1992

Movie Don, 1992, Playmates
NM $5   MIP $15

Movie Leo, 1992, Playmates
NM $5   MIP $15

Movie Mike, 1992, Playmates
NM $5   MIP $15

Movie Raph, 1992, Playmates
NM $5   MIP $15

Movie Splinter, no tooth, 1992, Playmates
NM $5   MIP $15

Movie Splinter, with tooth, 1992, Playmates
NM $25   MIP $75

VEHICLES AND ACCESSORIES

Flushomatic, 1988-92, Playmates
NM $4   MIP $10

Foot Cruiser, 1988-92, Playmates
NM $14   MIP $35

Foot Ski, 1988-92, Playmates
NM $4   MIP $10

Mega Mutant Killer Bee, 1988-92, Playmates
NM $3   MIP $8

Mega Mutant Needlenose, 1988-92, Playmates
NM $8   MIP $20

Mike's Pizza Chopper Backpack, 1988-92, Playmates
NM $4   MIP $10

Mutant Sewer Cycle with Sidecar, 1988-92, Playmates
NM $4   MIP $10

Ninja Newscycle, 1988-92, Playmates
NM $5   MIP $12

Oozey, 1988-92, Playmates
NM $4   MIP $10

Pizza Powered Sewer Dragster, 1988-92, Playmates
NM $5   MIP $15

Pizza Thrower, 1988-92, Playmates
NM $14   MIP $35

Psycho Cycle, 1988-92, Playmates
NM $10   MIP $25

Raph's Sewer Dragster, 1988-92, Playmates
NM $6   MIP $16

Raph's Sewer Speedboat, 1988-92, Playmates
NM $5   MIP $12

Retrocatapult, 1988-92, Playmates
NM $4   MIP $10

Retromutagen Ooze, 1988-92, Playmates
NM $2   MIP $4

Sewer Seltzer Cannon, 1988-92, Playmates
NM $4   MIP $10

Sludgemobile, 1988-92, Playmates
NM $7   MIP $18

Technodrome, 1988-92, Playmates
NM $24   MIP $60

Toilet Taxi, 1988-92, Playmates
NM $5   MIP $12

Turtle Blimp, green vinyl, 1988-92,
Playmates, green vinyl
NM $12   MIP $30

Turtle Party Wagon, 1988-92, Playmates
NM $16   MIP $40

Turtle Trooper Parachute, 1988-92,
Playmates
NM $4   MIP $10

Turtlecopter, 1988-92, Playmates
NM $16   MIP $40

WACKY ACTION, 1991

Breakfightin' Raphael, 1988-92, Playmates
NM $5   MIP $15

Creepy Crawlin' Splinter, 1988-92,
Playmates
NM $5   MIP $15

Headspinnin' Bebop, 1988-92, Playmates
NM $5   MIP $15

Machine Gunnin' Rocksteady, 1988-92,
Playmates
NM $5   MIP $15

Rock & Roll Michaelangelo, 1988-92,
Playmates
NM $5   MIP $15

Sewer Swimmin' Don, 1988-92, Playmates
NM $5   MIP $15

Slice 'n Dice Shredder, 1988-92, Playmates
NM $10   MIP $25

Sword Slicin' Leonardo, 1988-92, Playmates
NM $8   MIP $15

Wacky Walkin' Mouser, 1988-92, Playmates
NM $10   MIP $20

TERMINATOR 3 (MCFARLANE, 2003)

FIGURES

12" T-850 Terminator, 2003, McFarlane,
w/ sound chip
NM $15   MIP $30

T-850 Terminator, 2003, McFarlane
NM $7   MIP $15

T-850 Terminator w/ Coffin, 2003,
McFarlane
NM $7   MIP $15

T-850 vs. T-X, 2003, McFarlane, Deluxe
Boxed Set
NM $15   MIP $30

T-X Terminatrix, 2003, McFarlane
NM $7   MIP $15

T-X Terminatrix Endoskeleton, 2003,
McFarlane
NM $7   MIP $15

THIS IS SPINAL TAP (SIDESHOW TOYS, 2000)

FIGURES

David St. Hubbins, 2000
NM $10   MIP $25

Derek Smalls, 2000
NM $10   MIP $25

Nigel Tufnel, 2000
NM $10   MIP $25

THUNDERCATS (LJN, 1985-87)

6" FIGURES

Ben-Gali, 1985-87
NM $75   MIP $200

Capt. Cracker, 1985-87
NM $15   MIP $40

Capt. Shiner, 1985-87
NM $15   MIP $40

Cheetara, 1985-87
NM $30   MIP $70

Cheetara and Wilykit, 1985-87
NM $45   MIP $100

Grune the Destroyer, 1985-87
NM $10   MIP $30

Hachiman, 1985-87
NM $15   MIP $40

Jackalman, 1985-87
NM $15   MIP $35

Jaga, 1986, LJN, Series 3, w/ Sword of
Omens and Helmet, rare
NM $70   MIP $145

Lion-O, 1985-87
NM $30   MIP $70

Lion-O and Snarf, 1985-87
NM $25   MIP $60

Lynx-O, 1985-87
NM $30   MIP $75

Mongor, 1985-87
NM $30   MIP $75

Monkian, 1985-87
NM $10   MIP $35

Mumm-ra, 1985-87
NM $10   MIP $35

Panthro, 1985-87
NM $30   MIP $70

Pumyra, 1985-87
NM $25   MIP $75

Ratar-O, 1985-87
NM $10   MIP $30

Safari Joe, 1985-87
NM $10   MIP $35

Snowman of Hook Mountain, 1985-87
NM $15   MIP $40

S-S-Slithe, 1985-87
NM $15   MIP $40

Tuska Warrior, 1985-87
NM $10   MIP $35

Tygra, 1985-87
NM $30   MIP $70

Tygra and Wilykat, 1985-87
NM $25   MIP $60

Vultureman, 1985-87
NM $10   MIP $30

ACCESSORIES

Astral Moat Monster, 1986, LJN
NM $15   MIP $50

Laser Sabers Backpacks, 1986, LJN, Evil,
red pack w/ black strap
NM $5   MIP $10

Laser Sabers Backpacks, 1986, LJN, Evil,
black pack w/ red strap
NM $5   MIP $10

Laser Sabers Backpacks, 1986, LJN,
Good, orange pack w/ blue strap
NM $5   MIP $10

Laser Sabers Backpacks, 1986, LJN,
Good, blue pack w/ red strap
NM $5   MIP $10

Luna-Lasher, 1986, LJN
NM $7   MIP $15

Stilt Runner, 1986, LJN
NM $7   MIP $15

Sword of Omens, 1986, LJN, role playing
toy for kids
NM $20   MIP $50

Thunder Wings, 1986, LJN
NM $7   MIP $15

Tongue-A-Saurus, 1986, LJN
NM $40   MIP $80

BERSERKERS

Cruncher, 1985-87
NM $15   MIP $40

Hammerhead, 1985-87
NM $15   MIP $40

Ram-Bam, 1985-87
NM $15   MIP $40

Top-Spinner, 1985-87
NM $15   MIP $40

COMPANIONS

Berbil Belle, 1985-87
NM $15   MIP $50

Berbil Bert, 1986, LJN
NM $15   MIP $50

Berbil Bill, 1985-87
NM $15   MIP $50

Ma-Mut, 1985-87
NM $10   MIP $45

Snarf, 1985-87
NM $10   MIP $45

Wilykat, 1985-87
    NM $15   **MIP** $50

Wilykit, 1985-87
    NM $15   **MIP** $50

DELUXE FIGURES

Luna-Laser Mumm-Ra, 1986, LJN
    NM $75   **MIP** $185

Thunderwings Lion-O, 1986, LJN
    NM $75   **MIP** $185

PLAY SETS

Cat's Lair, 1986, LJN
    NM $100   **MIP** $225

Mumm-Ra's Tomb Fortress, 1986, LJN, w/ Mumm-Ra
    NM $35   **MIP** $75

RAM-PAGERS

Driller, the, 1985-87
    NM $25   **MIP** $75

Mad Bubbler, The, 1985-87
    NM $25   **MIP** $75

Stinger, The, 1985-87
    NM $25   **MIP** $75

VEHICLES

Hovercat, 1986, LJN
    NM $10   **MIP** $20

Mutant Fistpounder, 1986, LJN
    NM $20   **MIP** $45

Mutant Nose Diver, 1986, LJN
    NM $15   **MIP** $32

Mutant Skycutter, 1986, LJN
    NM $15   **MIP** $32

Thunderclaw, 1986, LJN
    NM $12   **MIP** $25

Thundertank, 1986, LJN
    NM $20   **MIP** $40

THUNDERCATS: MINIATURES (KID WORKS, 1986)

ACCESSORIES

Mutant 4-Pack, 1986, LJN, four figures
    NM $20   **MIP** $40

Snowman and Snowmeow, 1986, LJN
    NM $10   **MIP** $20

Thundercats 4-Pack, 1986, LJN, four figures
    NM $20   **MIP** $40

Weapons Pack, 1986, LJN
    NM $5   **MIP** $10

FIGURES

Cheetara, 1986, LJN
    NM $4   **MIP** $8

Grune, 1986, LJN
    NM $3   **MIP** $5

Hachiman, 1986, LJN
    NM $2   **MIP** $6

Jackalman, 1986, LJN
    NM $2   **MIP** $6

Lion-O, 1986, LJN
    NM $4   **MIP** $8

Monkian, 1986, LJN
    NM $2   **MIP** $6

Mumm-Ra, 1986, LJN
    NM $4   **MIP** $8

Panthro, 1986, LJN
    NM $4   **MIP** $8

Ratar-O, 1986, LJN
    NM $3   **MIP** $5

Reptilian, 1986, LJN
    NM $2   **MIP** $6

S-S-Slithe, 1986, LJN
    NM $2   **MIP** $6

Tuska Warrior, 1986, LJN
    NM $2   **MIP** $6

Tygra, 1986, LJN
    NM $4   **MIP** $8

Vulturman, 1986, LJN
    NM $2   **MIP** $6

PLAY SETS

Cat's Lair, 1986, LJN
    NM $15   **MIP** $35

Eye of Thundera, 1986, LJN
    NM $7   **MIP** $14

Mumm-Ra's Crypt, 1986, LJN
    NM $20   **MIP** $40

TICK, THE (BANDAI, 1994-95)

ACCESSORIES

(Bandai)

Steel Box, 1994, Bandai, Figure-sized box with "Really, Really Dangerous!" and "Unsafe" in yellow type
    NM $6   **MIP** $20

SERIES I, FIGURES

Bounding Tick, 1994, Bandai
    NM $6   **MIP** $10

Death Hug Dean, 1994, Bandai
    NM $6   **MIP** $10

Exploding Dyne-Mole, 1994, Bandai
    NM $4   **MIP** $10

Fluttering Arthur, 1994, Bandai
    NM $6   **MIP** $10

Grasping El Seed, 1994, Bandai
    NM $6   **MIP** $10

Growing Dinosaur Neil, 1994, Bandai
    NM $6   **MIP** $10

(KP Photo)

Man Eating Cow, 1994, Bandai, Brown and white cow with moving jaw (and a set of teeth!)
    NM $10   **MIP** $25

Pose Striking Die Fledermaus, 1994, Bandai
    NM $10   **MIP** $25

Projectile Human Bullet, 1994, Bandai
    NM $6   **MIP** $10

Sewer Spray Sewer Urchin, 1994, Bandai
    NM $6   **MIP** $10

SERIES II, FIGURES

Color Changing Chameleon, 1995, Bandai
    NM $10   **MIP** $25

Hurling Stop Sign Tick, 1995, Bandai
    NM $6   **MIP** $10

Propellerized Skippy the Dog, 1995, Bandai
    NM $6   **MIP** $10

Sliming Mucus Tick, 1995, Bandai
    NM $8   **MIP** $15

Thrakkorzog, 1995, Bandai
    NM $8   **MIP** $15

Twist and Chop American Maid, 1995, Bandai
    NM $10   **MIP** $22

TOMB RAIDER (PLAYMATES, 1999)

12" FIGURE

Talking Lara Croft, 1999, Playmates
    NM $8   **MIP** $25

9" FIGURES

Lara Croft in Area 51 outfit with hand guns and an M-16, on base, 1999
    NM $8   **MIP** $20

Lara Croft in jungle outfit with two guns, on base, 1999
    NM $8   **MIP** $20

(Playmates Toys)

Lara Croft in wet suit with harpoon and two pistols, on base, 1999, Detailed figure with stand
NM $8   MIP $20

ADVENTURES OF LARA CROFT, 6" FIGURES

Lara Croft escapes a Bengal, on diorama base, 1999
NM $3   MIP $10

Lara Croft escapes the yeti, on diorama base, 1999
NM $3   MIP $10

Lara Croft faces a Bengal, on diorama base, 1999
NM $3   MIP $10

TOTAL CHAOS (MCFARLANE, 1996-97)

SERIES 1, FIGURES

Al Simmons, 1996, McFarlane
NM $5   MIP $15

Al Simmons, blue uniform, 1996
NM $3   MIP $12

Al Simmons, red uniform with "Spawn" on visor, available through convention, 1997
NM $15   MIP $45

Conqueror, 1996
NM $5   MIP $15

Dragon Blade vs. Conqueror, Puzzle Zoo Exclusive, 1997
NM $6   MIP $18

Dragon Blade, black tunic, 1996
NM $4   MIP $12

Dragon Blade, white tunic, 1996, McFarlane
NM $5   MIP $15

(KP Photo)

Gore, 1996, McFarlane, With harpoon-launching arm and bomb-dropping parrot figure
NM $5   MIP $15

Hoof, black body with khaki armor, 1996
NM $3   MIP $12

(Lenny Lee)

Hoof, gray body with brown armor, 1996, McFarlane, With rotating and firing missile launcher
NM $5   MIP $15

Thorax, black and yellow, 1996
NM $3   MIP $12

Thorax, green and red, 1996, McFarlane
NM $4   MIP $12

Thresher, light blue skin, 1996, McFarlane
NM $5   MIP $15

Thresher, violet skin, 1996
NM $3   MIP $10

SERIES 2, FIGURES

Blitz, 1997
NM $3   MIP $10

Brain Drain, 1997
NM $3   MIP $10

Corn Boy, 1997
NM $3   MIP $10

Poacher, 1997
NM $3   MIP $10

Quartz, 1997
NM $3   MIP $10

Smuggler, 1997
NM $3   MIP $10

TOTAL JUSTICE (KENNER, 1996)

FIGURES

Aquaman, black armor, 1996, Kenner
NM $5   MIP $8

(Kenner)

Aquaman, with Hydro-Blasting Spear, gold armor, 1996, Kenner
NM $7   MIP $8

Batman, 1996, Kenner, With flight armor and glider cape
NM $5   MIP $15

Batman, Fractal Armor, 1986, Kenner
NM $8   MIP $17

Black Lightning, 1996, Kenner
NM $7   MIP $8

(Kenner)

Darkseid, 1996, Kenner, With omega-effect capture claw
NM $5   MIP $8

(Kenner)

Despero, 1996, Kenner, With galactic body blow attack

NM $5   MIP $8

(Kenner)

Flash, The, 1996, Kenner, With velocity power suit

NM $5   MIP $8

Green Arrow, 1996, Kenner

NM $5   MIP $8

(Kenner)

Green Lantern, 1996, Kenner

NM $5   MIP $8

(Kenner)

Hawkman, 1996, Kenner, With talon

NM $5   MIP $8

Huntress, 1996, Kenner

NM $5   MIP $12

Parallax, 1996, Kenner

NM $5   MIP $8

(Kenner)

Robin, 1996, Kenner, With spinning razor disc and battle staff

NM $5   MIP $12

(Kenner)

Superman, 1996, Kenner, With shield and kryptonite ray emitter

NM $5   MIP $8

TOY STORY (THINKWAY, 1996)

5" FIGURES

Alien, 1996, Thinkway
NM $5   MIP $15

Boxer Buzz, 1996, Thinkway
NM $4   MIP $8

Crawling Baby Face, 1996, Thinkway
NM $3   MIP $9

Fighting Woody, 1996, Thinkway
NM $3   MIP $9

Flying Buzz (Rocket), 1996, Thinkway
NM $4   MIP $8

Hamm, 1996, Thinkway
NM $4   MIP $8

Karate Buzz, 1996, Thinkway
NM $4   MIP $8

Kicking Woody, 1996, Thinkway
NM $4   MIP $8

Quick-Draw Woody, 1996, Thinkway
NM $4   MIP $8

Rex, 1996, Thinkway
NM $4   MIP $8

Super Sonic Buzz, 1996, Thinkway
NM $3   MIP $9

LARGE FIGURES

Talking Buzz Lightyear, 1996, Thinkway
NM $15   MIP $50

Talking Woody, 1996, Thinkway
NM $15   MIP $60

TRANSFORMERS (KENNER, 1984-1995)

GENERATION 1, SERIES 1, 1984

Bluestreak, blue, 1984, Kenner
NM $100   MIP $350

Bluestreak, silver, 1984, Kenner
NM $90   MIP $250

Brawn, 1984, Kenner
NM $10   MIP $45

Bumblebee, red, 1984, Kenner
NM $40   MIP $100

Bumblebee, yellow, 1984, Kenner
NM $20   MIP $50

Cliffjumper, red, 1984, Kenner
NM $10   MIP $40

Cliffjumper, yellow, 1984, Kenner
NM $20   MIP $50

Gears, 1984, Kenner
NM $10   MIP $40

Hound, 1984, Kenner
NM $100   MIP $275

Huffer, 1984, Kenner
NM $10   MIP $40

Ironhide, 1984, Kenner
 NM $75 MIP $250

Jazz, 1984, Kenner
 NM $75 MIP $250

(Lenny Lee)

Megatron, 1984, Kenner, Deception Leader turns from handgun to robot
 NM $100 MIP $300

Mirage, 1984, Kenner
 NM $90 MIP $250

Optimus Prime with gray or blue roller, 1984, Kenner
 NM $100 MIP $300

Prowl, 1984, Kenner
 NM $80 MIP $225

Ratchet with cross, 1984, Kenner
 NM $75 MIP $150

Ratchet without cross, 1984, Kenner
 NM $75 MIP $200

Sideswipe, 1984, Kenner
 NM $100 MIP $275

Skywarp, 1984, Kenner
 NM $50 MIP $125

Soundwave and Buzzsaw, 1984, Kenner
 NM $50 MIP $125

Starscream, 1984, Kenner
 NM $75 MIP $225

Sunstreaker, 1984, Kenner
 NM $100 MIP $275

Thundercracker, 1984, Kenner
 NM $50 MIP $120

Trailbreaker, 1984, Kenner
 NM $75 MIP $150

Wheeljack, 1984, Kenner
 NM $90 MIP $250

Windcharger, 1984, Kenner
 NM $20 MIP $50

GENERATION 1, SERIES 2, 1985

(KP Photo, Karen O'Brien collection)

Astrotrain, 1985, Kenner
 NM $50 MIP $95

Barrage, 1985, Kenner
 NM $20 MIP $55

Beachcomber, 1985, Kenner
 NM $10 MIP $40

Blaster, 1985, Kenner
 NM $20 MIP $50

Blitzwing, 1985, Kenner
 NM $25 MIP $60

Bombshell, 1985, Kenner
 NM $8 MIP $25

Bonecrusher, 1985, Kenner
 NM $10 MIP $40

Brawn, 1985, Kenner
 NM $8 MIP $20

Brawn with Minispy, 1985, Kenner
 NM $10 MIP $40

Bumblebee with Minispy, yellow, 1985, Kenner
 NM $20 MIP $50

Bumblebee, red, 1985, Kenner
 NM $10 MIP $30

Bumblebee, yellow, 1985, Kenner
 NM $10 MIP $30

Chop Shop, 1985, Kenner
 NM $10 MIP $55

Cliffjumper with Minispy, red, 1985, Kenner
 NM $50 MIP $125

Cliffjumper, red, 1985, Kenner
 NM $8 MIP $20

Cliffjumper, yellow, 1985, Kenner
 NM $10 MIP $30

Cosmos, 1985, Kenner
 NM $8 MIP $20

Dirge, 1985, Kenner
 NM $40 MIP $100

Gears, 1985, Kenner
 NM $10 MIP $30

Gears with Minispy, 1985, Kenner
 NM $10 MIP $30

Grapple, 1985, Kenner
 NM $50 MIP $125

(Toy Shop File Photo)

Grimlock, 1985, Kenner
 NM $20 MIP $125

Hoist, 1985, Kenner
 NM $50 MIP $125

Hook, 1985, Kenner
 NM $10 MIP $40

Huffer, 1985, Kenner
 NM $10 MIP $30

Huffer with Minispy, 1985, Kenner
 NM $10 MIP $40

Inferno, 1985, Kenner
 NM $40 MIP $100

Jazz, 1985, Kenner
 NM $45 MIP $110

(Lenny Lee)

Jetfire, 1985, Kenner, Red and white pieces transform from folding-wing jet bomber to robot
 NM $100 MIP $325

Kickback, 1985, Kenner
 NM $8 MIP $25

Long Haul, 1985, Kenner
 NM $10 MIP $40

Mixmaster, 1985, Kenner
 NM $10 MIP $40

Omega Supreme, 1985, Kenner
 NM $75 MIP $200

Optimus Prime, 1985, Kenner
 NM $75 MIP $250

Perceptor, 1985, Kenner
 NM $40 MIP $100

Powerglide, 1985, Kenner
 NM $8 MIP $20

Ramjet, 1985, Kenner
 NM $40 MIP $80

Ransack, 1985, Kenner
 NM $20 MIP $55

Red Alert, 1985, Kenner
 NM $60 MIP $175

Roadbuster, 1985, Kenner
 NM $50 MIP $100

Scavenger, 1985, Kenner
 NM $10 MIP $40

Scrapper, 1985, Kenner
 NM $10 MIP $40

Seaspray, 1985, Kenner
 NM $8 MIP $20

Shockwave, 1985, Kenner
 NM $75 MIP $200

Shrapnel, 1985, Kenner
 NM $8 MIP $25

Skids, 1985, Kenner
 NM $60 MIP $175

Slag, 1985, Kenner
 NM $40 MIP $100

Sludge, 1985, Kenner
 NM $40 MIP $100

Smokescreen, 1985, Kenner
 NM $50 MIP $150

Snarl, 1985, Kenner
NM $40   **MIP** $100

Thrust, 1985, Kenner
NM $40   **MIP** $80

Tracks, 1985, Kenner
NM $60   **MIP** $175

Venom, 1985, Kenner
NM $20   **MIP** $55

Warpath, 1985, Kenner
NM $8   **MIP** $20

Whirl, 1985, Kenner
NM $50   **MIP** $150

Windcharger, 1985, Kenner
NM $20   **MIP** $50

Windcharger with Minispy, 1985, Kenner
NM $20   **MIP** $50

GENERATION 1, SERIES 3, 1986

Air Raid, 1986, Kenner
NM $10   **MIP** $30

Air Raid with patch, 1986, Kenner
NM $10   **MIP** $30

Beachcomber, 1986, Kenner
NM $5   **MIP** $15

Beachcomber with patch, 1986, Kenner
NM $8   **MIP** $20

Blades, 1986, Kenner
NM $10   **MIP** $30

Blades, plastic chest, 1986, Kenner
NM $10   **MIP** $30

Blast Off, metal treads, 1986, Kenner
NM $10   **MIP** $30

Blast Off, plastic chest, 1986, Kenner
NM $10   **MIP** $30

Blurr, 1986, Kenner
NM $30   **MIP** $80

Blurr with poster, 1986, Kenner
NM $20   **MIP** $60

Brawl, metal treads, 1986, Kenner
NM $10   **MIP** $30

Brawl, plastic treads, 1986, Kenner
NM $10   **MIP** $30

Breakdown, 1986, Kenner
NM $10   **MIP** $35

Breakdown with patch, 1986, Kenner
NM $10   **MIP** $40

Broadside, 1986, Kenner
NM $20   **MIP** $60

Broadside with poster, 1986, Kenner
NM $20   **MIP** $50

Bumblebee, 1986, Kenner
NM $5   **MIP** $15

Bumblebee with patch, 1986, Kenner
NM $20   **MIP** $50

Cosmos, 1986, Kenner
NM $5   **MIP** $15

Cosmos with patch, 1986, Kenner
NM $8   **MIP** $20

Dead End, 1986, Kenner
NM $10   **MIP** $40

Dead End with patch, 1986, Kenner
NM $10   **MIP** $40

Divebomb with poster, plastic body, 1986, Kenner
NM $30   **MIP** $80

Divebomb, metal body, 1986, Kenner
NM $30   **MIP** $80

Divebomb, plastic body, 1986, Kenner
NM $40   **MIP** $100

Drag Strip, 1986, Kenner
NM $10   **MIP** $40

Drag Strip with patch, 1986, Kenner
NM $10   **MIP** $40

Fireflight, 1986, Kenner
NM $10   **MIP** $30

Fireflight with patch, 1986, Kenner
NM $10   **MIP** $30

First Aid, 1986, Kenner
NM $10   **MIP** $30

First Aid, plastic chest, 1986, Kenner
NM $10   **MIP** $30

Groove, 1986, Kenner
NM $10   **MIP** $30

Groove, silver chest, 1986, Kenner
NM $10   **MIP** $30

Headstrong, metal body, 1986, Kenner
NM $40   **MIP** $100

Hot Rod with poster, plastic toes, 1986, Kenner
NM $100   **MIP** $250

Hot Rod, metal toes, 1986, Kenner
NM $50   **MIP** $150

Hot Spot, 1986, Kenner
NM $10   **MIP** $40

Hubcap, 1986, Kenner
NM $5   **MIP** $15

Hubcap with patch, 1986, Kenner
NM $5   **MIP** $15

Kup, plastic tires and wheels, 1986, Kenner
NM $20   **MIP** $60

Kup, rubber tires and metal wheels, 1986, Kenner
NM $20   **MIP** $60

Motormaster, 1986, Kenner
NM $25   **MIP** $75

Octane, 1986, Kenner
NM $30   **MIP** $75

Octane with poster, 1986, Kenner
NM $20   **MIP** $50

Onslaught, 1986, Kenner
NM $10   **MIP** $40

Outback, 1986, Kenner
NM $5   **MIP** $15

Outback with patch, 1986, Kenner
NM $5   **MIP** $15

Pipes, 1986, Kenner
NM $5   **MIP** $15

Pipes with patch, 1986, Kenner
NM $5   **MIP** $15

Powerglide, 1986, Kenner
NM $5   **MIP** $15

Powerglide with patch, 1986, Kenner
NM $8   **MIP** $20

Rampage, metal body, 1986, Kenner
NM $20   **MIP** $75

Rampage, plastic body, 1986, Kenner
NM $20   **MIP** $75

Razorclaw, metal body, 1986, Kenner
NM $20   **MIP** $75

Razorclaw, plastic body, 1986, Kenner
NM $20   **MIP** $75

Rodimus Prime, metal toes, 1986, Kenner
NM $50   **MIP** $130

Rodimus Prime, plastic toes, 1986, Kenner
NM $50   **MIP** $130

Sandstorm, metal or plastic toes, 1986, Kenner
NM $50   **MIP** $150

Sandstorm, plastic toes, 1986, Kenner
NM $30   **MIP** $75

Seaspray, 1986, Kenner
NM $5   **MIP** $15

Seaspray with patch, 1986, Kenner
NM $8   **MIP** $20

Silverbolt, 1986, Kenner
NM $10   **MIP** $40

Skydive, 1986, Kenner
NM $10   **MIP** $30

Skydive with patch, 1986, Kenner
NM $10   **MIP** $30

Slingshot, 1986, Kenner
NM $10   **MIP** $30

Slingshot with patch, 1986, Kenner
NM $10   **MIP** $30

Springer, metal or plastic front, 1986, Kenner
NM $50   **MIP** $100

Streetwise, 1986, Kenner
NM $10   **MIP** $35

Swerve, 1986, Kenner
NM $5   **MIP** $15

Swerve with patch, 1986, Kenner
NM $5   **MIP** $15

Swindle, gray plastic chest, 1986, Kenner
NM $10   **MIP** $30

Swindle, metal treads, 1986, Kenner
NM $10   **MIP** $30

Tailgate, 1986, Kenner
NM $5   **MIP** $15

Tailgate with patch, 1986, Kenner
NM $5   **MIP** $15

Tantrum with poster, plastic body, 1986, Kenner
NM $30   **MIP** $80

Tantrum, metal body, 1986, Kenner
NM $40   **MIP** $100

Tantrum, plastic body, 1986, Kenner
NM $30   **MIP** $80

Vortex, metal treads, 1986, Kenner
    NM $10   **MIP** $30

Vortex, plastic chest, 1986, Kenner
    NM $10   **MIP** $30

Warpath, 1986, Kenner
    NM $5   **MIP** $15

Warpath with patch, 1986, Kenner
    NM $8   **MIP** $20

Wheelie, 1986, Kenner
    NM $5   **MIP** $15

Wheelie with patch, 1986, Kenner
    NM $5   **MIP** $15

Wildrider, 1986, Kenner
    NM $10   **MIP** $40

Wildrider with patch, 1986, Kenner
    NM $10   **MIP** $40

Wreck-gar, 1986, Kenner
    NM $20   **MIP** $60

Wreck-gar with poster, 1986, Kenner
    NM $30   **MIP** $80

GENERATION 1, SERIES 3, 1987

Headstrong, plastic body, 1987, Kenner
    NM $30   **MIP** $80

GENERATION 1, SERIES 4, 1987

Afterburner, 1987, Kenner
    NM $8   **MIP** $25

Afterburner with decoy, 1987, Kenner
    NM $10   **MIP** $30

Air Raid, 1987, Kenner
    NM $5   **MIP** $15

Air Raid with decoy, 1987, Kenner
    NM $10   **MIP** $35

Apeface, 1987, Kenner
    NM $20   **MIP** $55

Battletrap, 1987, Kenner
    NM $8   **MIP** $25

Blades with decoy, plastic chest, 1987, Kenner
    NM $8   **MIP** $20

Blades, plastic chest, 1987, Kenner
    NM $5   **MIP** $15

Blast Off with decoy, plastic chest, 1987, Kenner
    NM $8   **MIP** $25

Blot with decoy, 1987, Kenner
    NM $8   **MIP** $20

Blurr, 1987, Kenner
    NM $50   **MIP** $150

Brainstorm, 1987, Kenner
    NM $20   **MIP** $50

Brawl with decoy, plastic treads, 1987, Kenner
    NM $8   **MIP** $20

Breakdown with decoy, 1987, Kenner
    NM $8   **MIP** $20

Chase, 1987, Kenner
    NM $8   **MIP** $20

Chase with decoy, 1987, Kenner
    NM $8   **MIP** $35

Chromedome, 1987, Kenner
    NM $30   **MIP** $75

(KP photo, Karen O'Brien collection)

Computron Gift Set, 1987, Kenner, all five Technobots in one boxed set
    NM $200   **MIP** $550

Crosshairs, 1987, Kenner
    NM $50   **MIP** $150

Cutthroat with decoy, 1987, Kenner
    NM $8   **MIP** $35

Cyclonus, 1987, Kenner
    NM $50   **MIP** $130

Dead End with decoy, 1987, Kenner
    NM $8   **MIP** $20

Doublecross, 1987, Kenner
    NM $20   **MIP** $45

Drag Strip with decoy, 1987, Kenner
    NM $8   **MIP** $20

Fireflight, 1987, Kenner
    NM $5   **MIP** $15

Fireflight with decoy, 1987, Kenner
    NM $8   **MIP** $20

First Aid with decoy, plastic chest, 1987, Kenner
    NM $8   **MIP** $20

First Aid, plastic chest, 1987, Kenner
    NM $5   **MIP** $15

Flywheels, 1987, Kenner
    NM $8   **MIP** $25

Fortess Maximus, 1987, Kenner
    NM $300   **MIP** $900

Freeway, 1987, Kenner
    NM $8   **MIP** $20

Freeway with decoy, 1987, Kenner
    NM $10   **MIP** $35

Goldbug, 1987, Kenner
    NM $8   **MIP** $20

Goldbug with decoy, 1987, Kenner
    NM $10   **MIP** $35

Groove with decoy, silver chest, 1987, Kenner
    NM $8   **MIP** $20

Groove, silver chest, 1987, Kenner
    NM $5   **MIP** $15

Grotusque, 1987, Kenner
    NM $20   **MIP** $45

Hardhead, 1987, Kenner
    NM $20   **MIP** $50

Highbrow, 1987, Kenner
    NM $20   **MIP** $50

Hot Rod, 1987, Kenner
    NM $100   **MIP** $300

Kup, 1987, Kenner
    NM $50   **MIP** $150

Lightspeed, 1987, Kenner
    NM $8   **MIP** $20

Lightspeed with decoy, 1987, Kenner
    NM $8   **MIP** $25

Mindwipe, 1987, Kenner
    NM $20   **MIP** $50

Misfire, 1987, Kenner
    NM $30   **MIP** $80

Nosecone, 1987, Kenner
    NM $8   **MIP** $25

Nosecone with decoy, 1987, Kenner
    NM $10   **MIP** $30

Pointblank, 1987, Kenner
    NM $30   **MIP** $70

Repugnus, 1987, Kenner
    NM $20   **MIP** $45

Rippersnapper with decoy, 1987, Kenner
    NM $8   **MIP** $20

Rollbar, 1987, Kenner
    NM $10   **MIP** $35

Rollbar with decoy, 1987, Kenner
    NM $8   **MIP** $20

Scourge, 1987, Kenner
    NM $50   **MIP** $130

Searchlight, 1987, Kenner
    NM $8   **MIP** $20

Searchlight with decoy, 1987, Kenner
    NM $10   **MIP** $35

Sinnertwin with decoy, 1987, Kenner
    NM $8   **MIP** $20

Skullcruncher, 1987, Kenner
    NM $20   **MIP** $50

Skydive, 1987, Kenner
    NM $5   **MIP** $15

Skydive with decoy, 1987, Kenner
    NM $10   **MIP** $35

Slingshot, 1987, Kenner
    NM $5   **MIP** $15

Slingshot with decoy, 1987, Kenner
    NM $10   **MIP** $35

Slugslinger, 1987, Kenner
    NM $30   **MIP** $80

Snapdragon, 1987, Kenner
    NM $20   **MIP** $55

Strafe, 1987, Kenner
    NM $8   **MIP** $20

Strafe with decoy, 1987, Kenner
    NM $10   **MIP** $35

Streetwise, 1987, Kenner
    NM $5   **MIP** $15

Streetwise with decoy, 1987, Kenner
    NM $8   **MIP** $20

Sureshot, 1987, Kenner
    NM $30   **MIP** $70

Swindle with decoy, gray plastic chest, 1987, Kenner
    NM $8   **MIP** $25

Triggerhappy, 1987, Kenner
NM $30   MIP $80

Vortex with decoy, plastic chest, 1987, Kenner
NM $8   MIP $25

Weirdwolf, 1987, Kenner
NM $20   MIP $50

Wideload, 1987, Kenner
NM $8   MIP $20

Wideload with decoy, 1987, Kenner
NM $10   MIP $35

Wildrider with decoy, 1987, Kenner
NM $8   MIP $20

GENERATION 1, SERIES 5, 1988

Afterburner, 1988, Kenner
NM $5   MIP $15

Backstreet, 1988, Kenner
NM $5   MIP $15

Blot, 1988, Kenner
NM $8   MIP $20

Bomb-burst, clear insert, 1988, Kenner
NM $20   MIP $60

Bugly, 1988, Kenner
NM $20   MIP $60

Carnivac, 1988, Kenner
NM $10   MIP $40

Catilla, 1988, Kenner
NM $20   MIP $50

Chainclaw, 1988, Kenner
NM $10   MIP $40

Cindersaur, 1988, Kenner
NM $4   MIP $10

Cloudburst, clear insert, 1988, Kenner
NM $20   MIP $50

Crankcase, 1988, Kenner
NM $5   MIP $15

Cutthroat, 1988, Kenner
NM $8   MIP $20

Darkwing, 1988, Kenner
NM $20   MIP $50

Dogfight, 1988, Kenner
NM $5   MIP $15

Dreadwind, 1988, Kenner
NM $20   MIP $50

Fangry, 1988, Kenner
NM $20   MIP $50

Finback, 1988, Kenner
NM $20   MIP $65

Fizzle, 1988, Kenner
NM $4   MIP $15

Flamefeather, 1988, Kenner
NM $4   MIP $10

Getaway, 1988, Kenner
NM $10   MIP $40

Groundbreaker, 1988, Kenner
NM $20   MIP $65

Gunrunner, 1988, Kenner
NM $20   MIP $55

Guzzle, 1988, Kenner
NM $4   MIP $15

Horri-bull, 1988, Kenner
NM $20   MIP $50

Hosehead, 1988, Kenner
NM $20   MIP $50

Iguanus, 1988, Kenner
NM $10   MIP $40

Joyride, 1988, Kenner
NM $10   MIP $40

Landfill, 1988, Kenner
NM $8   MIP $20

Landmine, clear insert, 1988, Kenner
NM $10   MIP $40

Lightspeed, 1988, Kenner
NM $5   MIP $15

Nautilator, 1988, Kenner
NM $10   MIP $30

Needlenose, 1988, Kenner
NM $10   MIP $30

Nightbeat, 1988, Kenner
NM $20   MIP $60

Nosecone, 1988, Kenner
NM $5   MIP $15

Overbite, 1988, Kenner
NM $10   MIP $30

Override, 1988, Kenner
NM $5   MIP $15

Quake, 1988, Kenner
NM $10   MIP $30

Quickmix, 1988, Kenner
NM $8   MIP $25

Rippersnapper, 1988, Kenner
NM $8   MIP $20

Roadgrabber, 1988, Kenner
NM $20   MIP $55

Ruckus, 1988, Kenner
NM $5   MIP $15

Scoop, 1988, Kenner
NM $8   MIP $25

Seawing, 1988, Kenner
NM $10   MIP $30

Sinnertwin, 1988, Kenner
NM $8   MIP $20

Siren, 1988, Kenner
NM $20   MIP $50

Sizzle, 1988, Kenner
NM $4   MIP $15

Skalor, 1988, Kenner
NM $10   MIP $30

Skullgrin, clear insert, 1988, Kenner
NM $20   MIP $50

Sky High, 1988, Kenner
NM $10   MIP $40

Slapdash, 1988, Kenner
NM $10   MIP $40

Snarler, 1988, Kenner
NM $20   MIP $50

Sparkstalker, 1988, Kenner
NM $4   MIP $10

Spinister, 1988, Kenner
NM $10   MIP $30

Splashdown, 1988, Kenner
NM $20   MIP $50

Squeezeplay, 1988, Kenner
NM $20   MIP $50

Strafe, 1988, Kenner
NM $5   MIP $15

Submarauder, clear insert, 1988, Kenner
NM $20   MIP $50

Tentakil, 1988, Kenner
NM $10   MIP $30

Waverider, clear insert, 1988, Kenner
NM $20   MIP $50

Windsweeper, 1988, Kenner
NM $5   MIP $15

GENERATION 1, SERIES 6, 1989

Air Strike Patrol, 1989, Kenner
NM $3   MIP $10

Airwave, 1989, Kenner
NM $8   MIP $20

Battle Patrol, 1989, Kenner
NM $3   MIP $10

Birdbrain, 1989, Kenner
NM $5   MIP $15

Bludgeon, 1989, Kenner
NM $10   MIP $30

Bomb-burst, 1989, Kenner
NM $10   MIP $30

Bristleback, 1989, Kenner
NM $5   MIP $15

Cloudburst, 1989, Kenner
NM $10   MIP $30

Crossblades, 1989, Kenner
NM $10   MIP $40

Doubleheader, 1989, Kenner
NM $8   MIP $20

Erector, 1989, Kenner
NM $5   MIP $15

Flattop, 1989, Kenner
NM $5   MIP $15

Greasepit, 1989, Kenner
NM $8   MIP $20

Groundshaker, 1989, Kenner
NM $10   MIP $30

Hot House, 1989, Kenner
NM $8   MIP $20

Ironworks, 1989, Kenner
NM $8   MIP $20

Landmine, 1989, Kenner
NM $20   MIP $50

Longtooth, 1989, Kenner
NM $8   MIP $20

Octopunch, 1989, Kenner
NM $8   MIP $20

Off Road Patrol, 1989, Kenner
NM $3   MIP $10

Overload, 1989, Kenner
    NM $5   **MIP** $15

Pincher, 1989, Kenner
    NM $8   **MIP** $20

Race Car Patrol, 1989, Kenner
    NM $3   **MIP** $10

Rescue Patrol, 1989, Kenner
    NM $3   **MIP** $10

Roadblock, 1989, Kenner
    NM $20   **MIP** $50

Roughstuff, 1989, Kenner
    NM $5   **MIP** $15

Scowl, 1989, Kenner
    NM $5   **MIP** $15

Skullgrin, 1989, Kenner
    NM $10   **MIP** $35

Skyhammer, 1989, Kenner
    NM $20   **MIP** $50

Skyhopper, 1989, Kenner
    NM $10   **MIP** $30

Slog, 1989, Kenner
    NM $5   **MIP** $15

Sports Car Patrol, 1989, Kenner
    NM $3   **MIP** $10

Stranglehold, 1989, Kenner
    NM $8   **MIP** $20

Submarauder, 1989, Kenner
    NM $10   **MIP** $30

Thunderwing, 1989, Kenner
    NM $10   **MIP** $40

Vroom, 1989, Kenner
    NM $10   **MIP** $40

Waverider, 1989, Kenner
    NM $10   **MIP** $30

Wildfly, 1989, Kenner
    NM $5   **MIP** $15

GENERATION 1, SERIES 7, 1990

Air Patrol, 1990, Kenner
    NM $4   **MIP** $10

Astro Squad, 1990, Kenner
    NM $5   **MIP** $15

Axer, 1990, Kenner
    NM $8   **MIP** $20

Banzai-Tron, 1990, Kenner
    NM $8   **MIP** $20

Battle Squad, 1990, Kenner
    NM $5   **MIP** $15

Blaster, 1990, Kenner
    NM $4   **MIP** $12

Bumblebee, 1990, Kenner
    NM $4   **MIP** $12

Cannon Transport, 1990, Kenner
    NM $8   **MIP** $20

Construction Patrol, 1990, Kenner
    NM $4   **MIP** $10

Constructor Squad, 1990, Kenner
    NM $5   **MIP** $15

Devastator, 1990, Kenner
    NM $4   **MIP** $12

Erector, 1990, Kenner
    NM $5   **MIP** $12

Flattop, 1990, Kenner
    NM $5   **MIP** $12

Grimlock, 1990, Kenner
    NM $4   **MIP** $12

Gutcruncher, 1990, Kenner
    NM $10   **MIP** $45

Hot Rod Patrol, 1990, Kenner
    NM $4   **MIP** $10

Inferno, 1990, Kenner
    NM $8   **MIP** $20

Jackpot, 1990, Kenner
    NM $4   **MIP** $12

Jazz, 1990, Kenner
    NM $4   **MIP** $12

Kick-Off, 1990, Kenner
    NM $8   **MIP** $20

Krok, 1990, Kenner
    NM $4   **MIP** $12

Mainframe, 1990, Kenner
    NM $4   **MIP** $12

Megatron, 1990, Kenner
    NM $20   **MIP** $60

Metro Squad, 1990, Kenner
    NM $5   **MIP** $15

Military Patrol, 1990, Kenner
    NM $4   **MIP** $10

Missile Launcher, 1990, Kenner
    NM $8   **MIP** $20

Monster Trucks Patrol, 1990, Kenner
    NM $4   **MIP** $10

Overload, 1990, Kenner
    NM $5   **MIP** $12

Over-Run, 1990, Kenner
    NM $8   **MIP** $20

Prowl, 1990, Kenner
    NM $8   **MIP** $20

Race Track Patrol, 1990, Kenner
    NM $4   **MIP** $10

Rad, 1990, Kenner
    NM $4   **MIP** $12

Rollout, 1990, Kenner
    NM $4   **MIP** $12

Roughstuff, 1990, Kenner
    NM $5   **MIP** $12

Shockwave, 1990, Kenner
    NM $8   **MIP** $20

Skyfall, 1990, Kenner
    NM $8   **MIP** $20

Snarl, 1990, Kenner
    NM $8   **MIP** $20

Soundwave, 1990, Kenner
    NM $5   **MIP** $15

Sprocket, 1990, Kenner
    NM $10   **MIP** $35

Tanker Truck, 1990, Kenner
    NM $8   **MIP** $20

Treadshot, 1990, Kenner
    NM $4   **MIP** $12

Wheeljack, 1990, Kenner
    NM $10   **MIP** $35

GENERATION 2, SERIES 1, 1993

Afterburner, 1993, Kenner
    NM $3   **MIP** $12

Bonecrusher, orange, 1993, Kenner
    NM $5   **MIP** $17

Bonecrusher, yellow, 1993, Kenner
    NM $3   **MIP** $12

Bumblebee, 1993, Kenner
    NM $5   **MIP** $15

Deluge, changes colors, 1993, Kenner
    NM $5   **MIP** $15

Drench, changes colors, 1993, Kenner
    NM $5   **MIP** $15

Eagle Eye, 1993, Kenner
    NM $3   **MIP** $12

Gobots, changes colors, 1993, Kenner
    NM $5   **MIP** $15

Grimlock, dark blue, 1993, Kenner
    NM $8   **MIP** $20

Grimlock, silver, 1993, Kenner
    NM $20   **MIP** $65

Grimlock, turquoise, 1993, Kenner
    NM $35   **MIP** $100

Hook, orange, 1993, Kenner
    NM $5   **MIP** $15

Hook, yellow, 1993, Kenner
    NM $3   **MIP** $12

Hubcap, 1993, Kenner
    NM $5   **MIP** $15

Inferno, 1993, Kenner
    NM $8   **MIP** $25

Jazz, 1993, Kenner
    NM $35   **MIP** $100

Jetstorm, changes colors, 1993, Kenner
    NM $5   **MIP** $15

Long Haul, orange, 1993, Kenner
    NM $5   **MIP** $15

Long Haul, yellow, 1993, Kenner
    NM $3   **MIP** $12

Mixmaster, orange, 1993, Kenner
    NM $5   **MIP** $15

Mixmaster, yellow, 1993, Kenner
    NM $3   **MIP** $12

Ramjet, missiles grouped, 1993, Kenner
    NM $8   **MIP** $20

Ramjet, missiles separate, 1993, Kenner
    NM $10   **MIP** $35

Rapido, 1993, Kenner
    NM $3   **MIP** $12

Scavenger, orange, 1993, Kenner
    NM $5   **MIP** $15

Scavenger, yellow, 1993, Kenner
    NM $3   **MIP** $12

ACTION FIGURES

Scrapper, orange, 1993, Kenner
NM $5   MIP $15

Scrapper, yellow, 1993, Kenner
NM $5   MIP $15

Seaspray, 1993, Kenner
NM $5   MIP $15

Sideswipe, 1993, Kenner
NM $8   MIP $25

Skram, 1993, Kenner
NM $5   MIP $15

Slag, green, 1993, Kenner
NM $8   MIP $30

Slag, red, 1993, Kenner
NM $20   MIP $55

Slag, silver, 1993, Kenner
NM $20   MIP $55

Snarl, green, 1993, Kenner
NM $20   MIP $55

Snarl, red, 1993, Kenner
NM $8   MIP $30

Snarl, silver, 1993, Kenner
NM $20   MIP $55

Starscream, missiles grouped, 1993, Kenner
NM $8   MIP $20

Starscream, missiles separate, 1993, Kenner
NM $10   MIP $35

Terradive, 1993, Kenner
NM $5   MIP $15

Turbofire, 1993, Kenner
NM $5   MIP $15

Windbreaker, 1993, Kenner
NM $5   MIP $15

Windrazor, 1993, Kenner
NM $5   MIP $15

GENERATION 2, SERIES 2, 1994

Air Raid, 1994, Kenner
NM $5   MIP $15

Blast Off, 1994, Kenner
NM $5   MIP $15

Brawl, 1994, Kenner
NM $8   MIP $20

Electro, 1994, Kenner
NM $5   MIP $15

Fireflight, 1994, Kenner
NM $5   MIP $15

Jolt, 1994, Kenner
NM $5   MIP $15

Leadfoot, 1994, Kenner
NM $3   MIP $12

Manta Ray, 1994, Kenner
NM $3   MIP $12

Megatron, purple and black camouflage, 1994, Kenner
NM $5   MIP $15

Onslaught, 1994, Kenner
NM $10   MIP $40

Optimus Prime, red and white, 1994, Kenner
NM $10   MIP $30

Powerdive, black rotors, 1994, Kenner
NM $8   MIP $20

Powerdive, red rotors, 1994, Kenner
NM $3   MIP $12

Ransack, black rotors, 1994, Kenner
NM $8   MIP $20

Ransack, red rotors, 1994, Kenner
NM $3   MIP $12

Sizzle, 1994, Kenner
NM $5   MIP $15

Skydive, 1994, Kenner
NM $5   MIP $15

Slingshot, 1994, Kenner
NM $5   MIP $15

Swindle, 1994, Kenner
NM $5   MIP $15

Volt, 1994, Kenner
NM $5   MIP $15

Vortex, 1994, Kenner
NM $5   MIP $15

GENERATION 2, SERIES 3, 1995

Air Raid, 1995, Kenner
NM $2   MIP $6

Blowout, 1995, Kenner
NM $3   MIP $10

Bumblebee, 1995, Kenner
NM $3   MIP $10

Dirtbag, 1995, Kenner
NM $3   MIP $12

Double Clutch, 1995, Kenner
NM $3   MIP $10

Firecracker, 1995, Kenner
NM $3   MIP $10

Frenzy, 1995, Kenner
NM $3   MIP $10

Gearhead, clear, 1995, Kenner
NM $3   MIP $10

Gearhead, solid, 1995, Kenner
NM $3   MIP $10

High Beam, 1995, Kenner
NM $3   MIP $10

Hooligan, 1995, Kenner
NM $2   MIP $6

Ironhide, 1995, Kenner
NM $3   MIP $10

Jetfire, 1995, Kenner
NM $2   MIP $6

Megatron, 1995, Kenner
NM $3   MIP $10

Mirage, 1995, Kenner
NM $3   MIP $10

Motormouth, clear, 1995, Kenner
NM $3   MIP $10

Motormouth, solid, 1995, Kenner
NM $3   MIP $10

Optimus Prime, 1995, Kenner
NM $3   MIP $10

Roadblock, 1995, Kenner
NM $3   MIP $12

Sideswipe, 1995, Kenner
NM $3   MIP $10

Skyjack, 1995, Kenner
NM $2   MIP $6

Soundwave, 1995, Kenner
NM $3   MIP $10

Space Case, 1995, Kenner
NM $2   MIP $6

Strafe, 1995, Kenner
NM $2   MIP $6

TRANSFORMERS: BEAST WARS (KENNER, 1996-1999)

BASIC BEAST, 1996

Airazor, 1996, Kenner
NM $10   MIP $30

Armordillo, 1996, Kenner
NM $5   MIP $15

Claw Jaw, 1996, Kenner
NM $8   MIP $25

Drill Bit, 1996, Kenner
NM $8   MIP $25

Iguanus, 1996, Kenner
NM $10   MIP $30

Insecticon, 1996, Kenner
NM $5   MIP $15

Lazorbeak, 1996, Kenner
NM $8   MIP $25

Rattrap, 1996, Kenner
NM $15   MIP $50

Razorbeast, 1996, Kenner
NM $15   MIP $45

Razorclaw, 1996, Kenner
NM $10   MIP $30

Snapper, 1996, Kenner
NM $8   MIP $20

Snarl, 1996, Kenner
NM $8   MIP $25

Terrorsaur, 1996, Kenner
NM $15   MIP $50

BASIC BEAST, 1997

Powerpinch, 1997, Kenner
NM $8   MIP $25

Spittor, 1997, Kenner
NM $8   MIP $25

BASIC FUZORS, 1998

Air Hammer, 1998, Kenner
NM $5   MIP $15

Bantor, 1998, Kenner
NM $3   MIP $8

Buzzclaw, 1998, Kenner
NM $3   MIP $8

Noctorro, 1998, Kenner
NM $3   MIP $8

Quickstrike, 1998, Kenner
    NM $5   **MIP** $15

Terragator, 1998, Kenner
    NM $4   **MIP** $12

BASIC TRANSMETAL 2, 1999

Optimus Minor, 1999, Kenner
    NM $8   **MIP** $25

Scarem, 1999, Kenner
    NM $3   **MIP** $8

Sonar, 1999, Kenner
    NM $3   **MIP** $8

Spittor, 1999, Kenner
    NM $3   **MIP** $10

COMIC 2-PACK, 1996

Megatron, 1996, Kenner
    NM $15   **MIP** $50

Optimus Primal, 1996, Kenner
    NM $15   **MIP** $50

DELUXE BEAST, 1996

Blackarachnia, 1996, Kenner
    NM $40   **MIP** $115

Bonecrusher, 1996, Kenner
    NM $15   **MIP** $50

Buzz Saw, 1996, Kenner
    NM $25   **MIP** $75

Cheetor, blue eyes, 1996, Kenner
    NM $50   **MIP** $150

Cheetor, red eyes, 1996, Kenner
    NM $40   **MIP** $120

Cybershark, 1996, Kenner
    NM $30   **MIP** $90

Dinobot, 1996, Kenner
    NM $40   **MIP** $110

Jetstorm, 1996, Kenner
    NM $15   **MIP** $45

Rhinox, 1996, Kenner
    NM $40   **MIP** $110

Tarantulas, 1996, Kenner
    NM $40   **MIP** $125

Tigatron, 1996, Kenner
    NM $30   **MIP** $100

Waspinator, 1996, Kenner
    NM $40   **MIP** $125

Wolfang, 1996, Kenner
    NM $40   **MIP** $110

DELUXE BEAST, 1997

Grimlock, 1997, Kenner
    NM $25   **MIP** $75

K-9, 1997, Kenner
    NM $8   **MIP** $25

Manterror, 1997, Kenner
    NM $15   **MIP** $50

Retrax, 1997, Kenner
    NM $8   **MIP** $25

DELUXE FUZORS, 1998

Injector, 1998, Kenner
    NM $4   **MIP** $12

Silverbolt, 1998, Kenner
    NM $8   **MIP** $25

Sky Shadow, 1998, Kenner
    NM $4   **MIP** $12

Torca, 1998, Kenner
    NM $3   **MIP** $10

DELUXE TRANSMETAL 2, 1999

Iguanus, 1999, Kenner
    NM $3   **MIP** $10

Jawbreaker, 1999, Kenner
    NM $3   **MIP** $10

Ramulus, 1999, Kenner
    NM $5   **MIP** $15

Scourge, 1999, Kenner
    NM $4   **MIP** $12

DELUXE TRANSMETALS, 1998

Airazor, 1998, Kenner
    NM $8   **MIP** $20

Cheetor, 1998, Kenner
    NM $8   **MIP** $25

Rattrap, 1998, Kenner
    NM $10   **MIP** $30

Rhinox, 1998, Kenner
    NM $15   **MIP** $35

Tarantulas, 1998, Kenner
    NM $8   **MIP** $20

Terrorsaur, 1998, Kenner
    NM $5   **MIP** $15

Waspinator, 1998, Kenner
    NM $8   **MIP** $25

MEGA BEAST, 1996

B'Boom, 1996, Kenner
    NM $8   **MIP** $25

Polar Claw, 1996, Kenner
    NM $20   **MIP** $65

Scorponok, 1996, Kenner
    NM $15   **MIP** $45

MEGA BEAST, 1997

Inferno, 1997, Kenner
    NM $15   **MIP** $45

Transquito, 1997, Kenner
    NM $8   **MIP** $20

MEGA TRANSMETAL 2, 1999

Blackarachnia, 1999, Kenner
    NM $15   **MIP** $45

Cybershark, 1999, Kenner
    NM $5   **MIP** $15

MEGA TRANSMETALS, 1998

Megatron, 1998, Kenner
    NM $8   **MIP** $20

Optimus Primal, 1998, Kenner
    NM $8   **MIP** $25

Scavenger, 1998, Kenner
    NM $5   **MIP** $15

SUPER BEAST, 1998

Optimal Optimus, 1998, Kenner
    NM $8   **MIP** $20

ULTRA BEAST, 1996

Megatron, 1996, Kenner
    NM $15   **MIP** $50

Optimus Primal, 1996, Kenner
    NM $20   **MIP** $60

ULTRA TEAM, 1997

Magnaboss (Maximal Team)—Ironhide, Silverbolt, Prowl, 1997, Kenner
    NM $8   **MIP** $25

Tripredacus (Predacon Team)-Ram Horn, Sea Clamp, Cicadacon, 1997, Kenner
    NM $8   **MIP** $25

ULTRA TRANSMETAL 2, 1999

Megatron, 1999, Kenner
    NM $8   **MIP** $25

Tigerhawk, 1999, Kenner
    NM $5   **MIP** $15

ULTRA TRANSMETALS, 1998

Depth Charge, 1998, Kenner
    NM $8   **MIP** $20

Rampage, 1998, Kenner
    NM $8   **MIP** $25

VIDEO PACK-IN, 1998

Airazor, 1998, Kenner
    NM $8   **MIP** $25

Razorclaw, 1998, Kenner
    NM $8   **MIP** $25

TRON (TOMY, 1981)

FIGURES

Flynn, 1981, Tomy, disk
    NM $15   **MIP** $50

Sark, 1981, Tomy, red figure w/disk
    NM $15   **MIP** $50

Tron, 1981, Tomy, disk
    NM $15   **MIP** $65

Warrior, 1981, Tomy, red figure w/staff
    NM $15   **MIP** $55

VEHICLES

Light Cycle, 1981, Tomy, red or yellow
    NM $25   **MIP** $55

ACTION FIGURES

TUFF TALKIN' WRESTLERS (TOY BIZ, 1999)

FIGURES

Goldberg/Kevin Nash, 1999, Toy Biz
    NM $20   **MIP** $40

Sting/Diamond Dallas Page, 1999, Toy Biz
    NM $20   **MIP** $40

UNIVERSAL MONSTERS (REMCO, 1979)

8" FIGURES

Creature From the Black Lagoon, 1979
    NM $75   **MIP** $200

Dracula, 1979
    NM $40   **MIP** $100

Frankenstein, 1979
    NM $20   **MIP** $40

Mummy, The, 1979
    NM $20   **MIP** $40

Phantom of the Opera, 1979
    NM $100   **MIP** $250

Wolfman, The, 1979
    NM $55   **MIP** $130

UNIVERSAL MONSTERS (SIDESHOW TOYS, 1998-PRESENT)

1/4 SCALE

Frankenstein, 2004, Sideshow Toys, #7102, limited to 1,000
    NM n/a   **MIP** $225

Vampyre - Count Orlock, 1998, Sideshow Toys, #7101R, limited to 700
    NM $ **MIP** $150

12" FIGURES

Bela Lugosi as Bela the Gypsy, 1998, Sideshow Toys, #4412
    NM n/a   **MIP** $30

Bela Lugosi as Dracula, 1998, Sideshow Toys, #4405
    NM n/a   **MIP** $40

Bela Lugosi as Frankenstein, 1998, Sideshow Toys, #4410
    NM n/a   **MIP** $30

Bela Lugosi as Murder Legendre, 1998, Sideshow Toys, #7002
    NM n/a   **MIP** $40

Boris Karloff as the Monster from Bride of Frankenstein, 1998, Sideshow Toys, #4413
    NM n/a   **MIP** $40

Boris Karloff as The Mummy, 1998, Sideshow Toys, #4418R
    NM n/a   **MIP** $40

Creature from the Black Lagoon, 2003, Sideshow Toys, #4423
    NM n/a   **MIP** $75

Dwight Frye as Fritz, 1998, Sideshow Toys, #4406, from Frankenstein
    NM n/a   **MIP** $30

Dwight Frye as Renfield, 1998, Sideshow Toys, #4411
    NM n/a   **MIP** $30

Elsa Lanchester as Bride of Frankenstein, 1998, Sideshow Toys, #4414
    NM n/a   **MIP** $40

Frankenstein Monster, 1998, Sideshow Toys, #4416R, Son of Frankenstein
    NM n/a   **MIP** $40

Glenn Strange as Frankenstein, 1998, Sideshow Toys, #4409
    NM n/a   **MIP** $30

Henry Hill as Werewolf of London, 1998, Sideshow Toys, #4421R
    NM n/a   **MIP** $40

Lon Chaney as Frankenstein, 1998, Sideshow Toys, #4408
    NM n/a   **MIP** $30

Lon Chaney as the Vampire, 1998, Sideshow Toys, #4404, London After Midnight
    NM n/a   **MIP** $30

Lon Chaney Jr. as Larry Talbot, 1998, Sideshow Toys, #4407
    NM n/a   **MIP** $40

Lon Chaney Sr. as Phantom, 1998, Sideshow Toys, #4403
    NM n/a   **MIP** $40

Max Schreck as Vampyre, 1998, Sideshow Toys, #7001
    NM n/a   **MIP** $30

Phantom of the Opera Mask of the Red Death, 1998, Sideshow Toys, #4415R
    NM n/a   **MIP** $40

The Creature from The Creature Walks Among Us, 1998, Sideshow Toys, #4419R
    NM n/a   **MIP** $40

The Mole Man from The Mole People, 1998, Sideshow Toys, #4422R
    NM n/a   **MIP** $40

Wolfman, The, 2000, Sideshow Toys
    NM $8   **MIP** $30

SERIES I, 8" FIGURES

(KP Photo)

Creature from the Black Lagoon, special edition, 2001, Sideshow Toy, Fully poseable translucent figure
    NM $10   **MIP** $15

Frankenstein, 1998-Present, Sideshow Toy
    NM $6   **MIP** $15

Mummy, The, 1998-Present, Sideshow Toy
    NM $8   **MIP** $20

(KP Photo)

Wolfman, The, 1998-Present, Sideshow Toy, With log base and trap. Packaged in movie-poster style box
    NM $8   **MIP** $20

SERIES II, 8" FIGURES

(KP Photo)

Bride of Frankenstein, 1998-Present, Sideshow Toys, Detailed figure with stand
    NM $8   **MIP** $20

(KP Photo)

Creature From the Black Lagoon, 1998-Present, Sideshow Toys, Realistic-looking gilled Creature with stand (showing abandoned harpoon gun)
    NM $8   **MIP** $20

(KP Photo)

Phantom of the Opera, 1998-Present, Sideshow Toys, Highly-detailed figure with stand

NM $8   MIP $20

SERIES III, 8" FIGURES

(KP Photo)

Hunchback of Notredame, 1998-present, Sideshow Toys, Detailed figure with purple cloak, scepter and green crown

NM $7   MIP $15

Invisible Man, 1998-present, Sideshow Toys

NM $7   MIP $15

(KP Photo)

Metaluna Mutant, 1998-present, Sideshow Toys, Blue-gray detailed alien from "This Island Earth." A neat figure

NM $7   MIP $15

SERIES IV, 8" FIGURES

(KP Photo)

Mole People, The, 2000, Sideshow Toys, Fun-looking figure--even includes mushroom accessories!

NM $5   MIP $15

(KP Photo)

Son of Frankenstein, 2000, Sideshow Toys, Figure with fabric outer garment and replaceable arm

NM $5   MIP $15

(KP Photo)

Werewolf of London, 2000, Sideshow Toys, With cap, scarf and flower

NM $5   MIP $15

SILVER SCREEN EDITION

Boris Karloff as Frankenstein, 1998, Sideshow Toys, #44012R

NM n/a   MIP $40

Frankenstein, 2000, Sideshow Toys, Series 1

NM $5   MIP $15

Lon Chaney as Phantom of the Opera, 1998, Sideshow Toys, #44032R

NM n/a   MIP $40

Lon Chaney in London After Midnight, 1998, Sideshow Toys, #44042R

NM n/a   MIP $40

Lon Chaney Jr. as The Wolf Man, 1998, Sideshow Toys, #44022R

NM n/a   MIP $40

Max Schreck as Vampyre, 1998, Sideshow Toys, #70012R

NM n/a   MIP $40

Mummy, The, 2000, Sideshow Toys, Series 1

NM $5   MIP $15

Wolfman, The, 2000, Sideshow Toys, Series 1

NM $5   MIP $15

UNIVERSAL MONSTERS: HASBRO SIGNATURE SERIES (HASBRO, 1998)

FIGURES

Bride of Frankenstein, The, 1998, Hasbro

NM $10   MIP $25

Creature from the Black Lagoon, 1998, Hasbro, Series 2

NM $10   MIP $20

Frankenstein, 1998, Hasbro

NM $10   MIP $25

Mummy, The, 1998, Hasbro

NM $10   MIP $25

Phantom of the Opera, 1998, Hasbro, Series 2

NM $10   MIP $20

Son of Dracula, 1998, Hasbro, Series 2

NM $10   MIP $20

The Invisible Man, 1998, Hasbro, Series 2
NM $10   MIP $20

Wolf Man, The, 1998, Hasbro
NM $10   MIP $25

VAULT, THE (TOY BIZ, 1998)

6" FIGURES

Stegron, 1998, Marvel
NM $3   MIP $6

Typhoid Mary, 1998, Marvel
NM $3   MIP $6

Ultron, 1998, Marvel
NM $3   MIP $6

VIKINGS (MARX, 1960S)

FIGURES

(Toy Shop File Photo)

Brave Erik the Viking, 1970-72, Marx, #5430, lime-green outfit, blonde hair, blue eyes - like many Marx figures, this too had a molded-uniform with other plastic accessories and clothing included in the package
NM $125   MIP $300

Mighty Viking Horse, 1970-72, Marx, #5381, Palomino for Erik, Brown for Odin, 11-piece vinyl tack set, wheels in hooves, nodding heads
NM $125   MIP $300

Odin the Viking Chieftan, 1970-72, Marx, #5440, molded carmel outfit, brown hair, full beard
NM $125   MIP $300

VOLTRON (LJN, 1984)

Battling Black Lion, 1984, LJN
NM $7   MIP $15

Black Lion, 1984, LJN, Motorized Lion Force
NM $7   MIP $15

Blue Lion & Red Lion, 1984, LJN, Motorized Lion Force
NM $7   MIP $15

Green Lion & Yellow Lion, 1984, LJN, Motorized Lion Force
NM $7   MIP $15

Lion Force Fortress, 1984, LJN
NM $15   MIP $35

Radio-Controlled Voltron, 1984, LJN
NM $10   MIP $20

Voltron Assembler - Lion Force, 1984, LJN, disassembles
NM $7   MIP $15

Voltron Assembler - Vehicle Team, 1984, LJN, disassembles
NM $7   MIP $15

Voltron Assembler Gift Set, 1984, LJN, both Lion Force and Vehicle Team assemblers
NM $10   MIP $20

Voltron Motorized, 1984, LJN, w/ Motorized Black, Blue, Red, Green & Yellow Lions
NM $20   MIP $40

VOLTRON (MATCHBOX, 1985-86)

3-3/4" FIGURES

Doom Commander, 1985-86, Matchbox
NM $5   MIP $15

Haggar the Witch, 1985-86, Matchbox
NM $5   MIP $15

Hunk, 1985-86, Matchbox
NM $8   MIP $20

Keith, 1985-86, Matchbox
NM $8   MIP $20

King Zarkon, 1985-86, Matchbox
NM $5   MIP $15

Lance, 1985-86, Matchbox
NM $5   MIP $15

Pidge, 1985-86, Matchbox
NM $5   MIP $15

Prince Lotor, 1985-86, Matchbox
NM $8   MIP $20

Princess Allura, 1985-86, Matchbox
NM $8   MIP $20

Robeast Mutilor, 1985-86, Matchbox
NM $4   MIP $10

Robeast Scorpious, 1985-86, Matchbox
NM $4   MIP $12

Voltron Robot, 1985-86, Matchbox
NM $10   MIP $30

FIGURES

Skull Scavenger, 1985-86, Matchbox, pilot of the Skull Tank
NM $7   MIP $15

GIFT SETS

Deluxe Gift Set I, 1985-86, Matchbox, Warrior
NM $65   MIP $225

Deluxe Gift Set II, 1985-86, Matchbox, Gladiator
NM $55   MIP $200

Deluxe Gift Set III, 1985-86, Matchbox, Lion
NM $55   MIP $200

MINIATURES

Voltron I, 1985-86, Matchbox, die-cast
NM $15   MIP $30

Voltron II, 1985-86, Matchbox, die-cast
NM $15   MIP $30

Voltron III, 1985-86, Matchbox, die-cast
NM $15   MIP $30

VEHICLES

Coffin of Darkness, 1985-86, Matchbox
NM $8   MIP $20

Coffin of Doom, 1985-86, Matchbox
NM $8   MIP $20

Doom Blaster, 1985-86, Matchbox
NM $12   MIP $25

Skull Tank, 1985-86, Matchbox
NM $12   MIP $25

Zorkon Zapper, 1985-86, Matchbox
NM $12   MIP $25

WALTONS (MEGO, 1975)

8" FIGURES

Grandma and Grandpa, 1975, Mego
NM $25   MIP $50

John Boy and Ellen, 1975, Mego
NM $25   MIP $50

Mom and Pop, 1975, Mego
NM $25   MIP $50

ACCESSORIES

Barn, 1975, Mego
NM $50   MIP $100

Country Store, 1975, Mego
NM $50   MIP $100

Truck, 1975, Mego
NM $40   MIP $80

PLAY SETS

Farm House, 1975, Mego
NM $75   MIP $150

Farm House with Six Figures, 1975, Mego
NM $150   MIP $300

WARRIOR BEASTS, THE (REMCO, 1983)

FIGURES

Craven, 1983
NM $15   MIP $50

Gecko, 1983
NM $15   MIP $60

Guana, 1983
NM $15   MIP $50

Hydraz, 1983
NM $15   MIP $60

Ramar, 1983
NM $15   MIP $50

Skullman, 1983
NM $25   MIP $90

Snake Man, 1983
NM $25   MIP $90

Stegos, 1983
NM $15   MIP $50

Wolf Warrior, 1983
NM $30   MIP $90

Zardus, 1983
NM $15   MIP $50

WCW BASH AT THE BEACH (TOY BIZ, 2000)

6" FIGURES

Diamond Dallas Page, 2000, Toy Biz
NM $3   MIP $8

Goldberg, 2000, Toy Biz
NM $3   MIP $8

Hulk Hogan, 2000, Toy Biz
NM $3   MIP $8

Lex Luger, 2000, Toy Biz
NM $3   MIP $8

Sting, 2000, Toy Biz
NM $3   MIP $8

WCW COLLECTOR SERIES (TOY BIZ, 2000)

12" FIGURES

Goldberg, 2000, Toy Biz
NM $5   MIP $15

Hulk Hogan, 2000, Toy Biz
NM $5   MIP $15

Sting, 2000, Toy Biz
NM $5   MIP $15

WCW CYBORG WRESTLERS (TOY BIZ, 2000)

6" FIGURES

Bret Hart, 2000, Toy Biz
NM $3   MIP $8

Goldberg, 2000, Toy Biz
NM $3   MIP $8

Kevin Nash, 2000, Toy Biz
NM $3   MIP $8

Sid Vicious, 2000, Toy Biz
NM $3   MIP $8

Sting, 2000, Toy Biz
NM $3   MIP $8

WCW NITRO ACTIVE WRESTLERS (TOY BIZ, 2000)

6" FIGURES

Buff Bagwell, 2000, Toy Biz
NM $3   MIP $8

Goldberg, 2000, Toy Biz
NM $3   MIP $8

Jeff Jarrett, 2000, Toy Biz
NM $3   MIP $8

Sid Vicious, 2000, Toy Biz
NM $3   MIP $8

Vampiro, 2000, Toy Biz
NM $3   MIP $8

WCW POWER SLAM WRESTLERS I (TOY BIZ, 2000)

6" FIGURES

Goldberg, 2000, Toy Biz
NM $3   MIP $8

Hak, 2000, Toy Biz
NM $3   MIP $8

Hulk Hogan, 2000, Toy Biz
NM $3   MIP $8

Rodman, 2000, Toy Biz
NM $3   MIP $8

Sid Vicious, 2000, Toy Biz
NM $3   MIP $8

WCW POWER SLAM WRESTLERS II (TOY BIZ, 2000)

6" FIGURES

Buff Bagwell, 2000, Toy Biz
NM $3   MIP $8

Kanyon, 2000, Toy Biz
NM $3   MIP $8

Kevin Nash, 2000, Toy Biz
NM $3   MIP $8

Roddy Piper, 2000, Toy Biz
NM $3   MIP $8

Sting, 2000, Toy Biz
NM $3   MIP $8

WCW S.L.A.M. FORCE (TOY BIZ, 2000)

6" FIGURES

Benoit with comic book, 2000, Toy Biz
NM $3   MIP $8

Bret Hart with comic book, 2000, Toy Biz
NM $3   MIP $8

Goldberg with comic book, 2000, Toy Biz
NM $3   MIP $8

Kevin Nash with comic book, 2000, Toy Biz
NM $3   MIP $8

Sting with comic book, 2000, Toy Biz
NM $3   MIP $8

WCW THUNDER SLAM TWIN PACKS (TOY BIZ, 2000)

6" FIGURES

Bam Bam Bigelow and Goldberg, 2000, Toy Biz
NM $3   MIP $10

Kevin Nash and Scott Hall, 2000, Toy Biz
NM $3   MIP $10

Sting and Bret Hart, 2000, Toy Biz
NM $3   MIP $10

WCW WORLD CHAMPIONSHIP WRESTLING RING FIGHTERS (TOY BIZ, 1999)

6" FIGURES

Booker T, 1999
NM $3   MIP $10

Bret Hart, 1999
NM $3   MIP $10

Chris Benoit, 1999
NM $3   MIP $10

Scott Steiner, 1999
NM $3   MIP $10

WCW WORLD CHAMPIONSHIP WRESTLING SMASH 'N SLAM (TOY BIZ, 1999)

6" FIGURES

Hollywood Hogan, 1999
NM $5   MIP $15

Kevin Nash, 1999
NM $5   MIP $15

Macho Man Randy Savage, 1999
NM $4   MIP $12

Scott Hall, 1999
NM $5   MIP $15

WCW WORLD CHAMPIONSHIP WRESTLING SMASH 'N SLAM II (TOY BIZ, 1999)

6" FIGURES

D.D.P., 1999
NM $3   MIP $10

Giant & Rey Mysterio Jr., 1999
NM $3   MIP $10

Goldberg & Masked Wrestler, 1999
NM $3   MIP $10

Lex Luger, 1999
NM $3   MIP $10

Sting, 1999
NM $3   MIP $10

WCW/NWO RING MASTERS (TOY BIZ, 1998)

6" FIGURES

Bret Hart, 1999
NM $3   MIP $10

Chris Jericho, 1999
NM $3   MIP $10

Goldberg, 1999
NM $3   MIP $10

Lex Luger, 1999
NM $3   MIP $10

WCW/NWO SLAM 'N CRUNCH (TOY BIZ, 1998)

6" FIGURES

Buff Bagwell, 1999
    NM $3   MIP $10

Goldberg, 1999
    NM $3   MIP $10

Konnan, 1999
    NM $3   MIP $10

Sting, 1999
    NM $3   MIP $10

WCW/NWO TWO PACKS (TOY BIZ, 1999)

BATTLE OF THE GIANTS, 6" FIGURES

Giant vs. Kevin Nash, 1999
    NM $3   MIP $10

CLASH OF THE CHAMPIONS, 6" FIGURES

Sting vs. Hollywood Hogan, 1999
    NM $5   MIP $15

GRIP 'N FLIP WRESTLERS II, 6" FIGURES

Kevin Nash vs. Bret Hart, 1999
    NM $3   MIP $10

Scott Steiner vs. Rick Steiner, 1999
    NM $3   MIP $10

Sting vs. Lex Luger, 1999
    NM $3   MIP $10

GRIP 'N FLIP WRESTLERS, 6" FIGURES

Chris Jericho vs. Dean Malenko, 1999, Toy Biz
    NM $3   MIP $10

Goldberg vs. Hollywood Hogan, 1999, Toy Biz
    NM $5   MIP $15

Raven vs. Diamond Dallas Page, 1999
    NM $3   MIP $10

POWER AND BEAUTY, 6" FIGURES

Macho Man & Elizabeth, 1999
    NM $3   MIP $10

WELCOME BACK, KOTTER (MATTEL, 1976)

FIGURES

Barbarino, 1976
    NM $40   MIP $80

Epstein, 1976
    NM $20   MIP $50

Horshback, 1976
    NM $20   MIP $50

Mr. Kotter, 1976
    NM $20   MIP $50

Washington, 1976
    NM $20   MIP $50

PLAY SETS

Welcome Back Kotter Play Set, Deluxe, 1976
    NM $50   MIP $150

Welcome Back, Kotter Play Set, 1976
    NM $40   MIP $100

WETWORKS (MCFARLANE, 1995-96)

SERIES 1

Dane, 1995
    NM $3   MIP $10

Dozer, 1995
    NM $3   MIP $10

Grail, 1995
    NM $3   MIP $10

Mother-One, 1995
    NM $5   MIP $15

Vampire, dark green, 1995
    NM $5   MIP $15

Vampire, gray, 1995
    NM $5   MIP $15

Werewolf, light blue, 1995
    NM $5   MIP $15

Werewolf, reddish brown, 1995
    NM $8   MIP $20

SERIES 2

Assasin One, blue, 1996
    NM $3   MIP $10

Assasin One, red, 1996
    NM $3   MIP $10

Blood Queen, all black, 1996
    NM $8   MIP $20

Blood Queen, all black with red trim, 1996
    NM $8   MIP $20

Delta Commander, flesh tones, 1996
    NM $3   MIP $10

Delta Commander, gold, 1996
    NM $3   MIP $10

Frankenstein, brown, 1996
    NM $3   MIP $10

Frankenstein, green, 1996
    NM $3   MIP $10

Mendoza, flesh colored, 1996
    NM $3   MIP $10

Mendoza, half gold, 1996
    NM $3   MIP $10

Pilgrim, flesh tones, 1996
    NM $5   MIP $15

Pilgrim, gold, 1996
    NM $8   MIP $20

WHERE THE WILD THINGS ARE (MCFARLANE, 2000)

FIGURES

Aaron, 2000
    NM $4   MIP $15

Bernard, 2000
    NM $4   MIP $15

Emil, 2000
    NM $4   MIP $15

Max and Goatboy, 2000
    NM $4   MIP $15

Moishe, 2000
    NM $4   MIP $15

Tzippy, 2000
    NM $4   MIP $15

WITCHBLADE (MOORE ACTION COLLECTIBLES, 1998-PRESENT)

SERIES I, FIGURES

Ian Nottingham, 1998-present
    NM $3   MIP $12

Kenneth Irons, 1998-present
    NM $3   MIP $12

Medieval Witchblade, 1998-present
    NM $3   MIP $12

Sara Pezzini/Witchblade, 1998-present
    NM $3   MIP $12

SERIES II, FIGURES

(Moore Action Collectibles)

Aspen Mathews/Fathom, 1998-present, A ripped dude with a mutant right hand.
    NM $3   MIP $12

(Moore Action Collectibles)

Sara Pezzini, 1998-present, In red dress, with matching boots.
    NM $3   **MIP** $12

WIZARD OF OZ (MEGO, 1974)

4" BOXED FIGURES

Munchkin Dancer, 1974, Mego
    NM $75   **MIP** $150
Munchkin Flower Girl, 1974, Mego
    NM $75   **MIP** $150
Munchkin General, 1974, Mego
    NM $75   **MIP** $150
Munchkin Lollipop Kid, 1974, Mego
    NM $75   **MIP** $150
Munchkin Mayor, 1974, Mego
    NM $75   **MIP** $150

8" BOXED FIGURES

Cowardly Lion, 1974, Mego
    NM $25   **MIP** $60
Dorothy with Toto, 1974, Mego
    NM $25   **MIP** $60
Glinda the Good Witch, 1974, Mego
    NM $25   **MIP** $60
Scarecrow, 1974, Mego
    NM $25   **MIP** $60
Tin Woodsman, 1974, Mego
    NM $25   **MIP** $60
Wicked Witch, 1974, Mego
    NM $50   **MIP** $100
Wizard of Oz, 1974, Mego
    NM $35   **MIP** $250

PLAY SETS

Emerald City, 1974, Mego, Play set with seven 8" figures
    NM $125   **MIP** $350
Emerald City with Wizard of Oz, 1974, Mego, Play set with Wizard of Oz
    NM $45   **MIP** $100

Munchkin Land, 1974, Mego
    NM $150   **MIP** $300
Witch's Castle, Sears Exclusive, 1974, Mego
    NM $250   **MIP** $450

WIZARD OF OZ (MULTI-TOYS, 1989)

50TH ANNIVERSARY, 12" FIGURES

Cowardly Lion, 1989, Multi-Toys
    NM $5   **MIP** $15
Dorothy and Toto, 1989, Multi-Toys
    NM $5   **MIP** $15
Glinda, 1989, Multi-Toys
    NM $5   **MIP** $15

(Toy Shop File Photo)

Scarecrow, 1989, Multi-Toys, Shown with Wicked Witch
    NM $5   **MIP** $15
Tin Man, 1989, Multi-Toys
    NM $5   **MIP** $15
Wicked Witch, 1989, Multi-Toys
    NM $5   **MIP** $15
Wizard, 1989, Multi-Toys
    NM $5   **MIP** $15

WONDER WOMAN SERIES (MEGO, 1977-80)

FIGURES

(Toy Shop File Photo)

Major Steve Trevor, 1978, 1977-80, Mego, Left, in white suit
    NM $26   **MIP** $65

(Toy Shop File Photo)

Nubia, 1978, 1977-80, Mego
    NM $40   **MIP** $100
Queen Hippolyte, 1978, 1977-80, Mego
    NM $40   **MIP** $100
Wonder Woman with Diana Prince Outfit, 1978, 1977-80, Mego
    NM $100   **MIP** $200
Wonder Woman with Fly Away Action, 1977-80, Mego
    NM $125   **MIP** $250

WORLD'S GREATEST SUPER KNIGHTS (MEGO, 1975)

8" FIGURES

Black Knight, 1975
    NM $90   **MIP** $355

(Toy Shop File Photo)

Ivanhoe, 1975, In full body armor
    NM $65   **MIP** $275
King Arthur, 1975
    NM $60   **MIP** $200
Sir Galahad, 1975
    NM $80   **MIP** $300
Sir Lancelot, 1975
    NM $80   **MIP** $300

WORLD'S GREATEST SUPER PIRATES (MEGO, 1974)

FIGURES

Blackbeard, 1974
    NM $200   **MIP** $500
Captain Patch, 1974
    NM $175   **MIP** $300

Jean Lafitte, 1974
NM $250   MIP $550

Long John Silver, 1974
NM $250   MIP $550

WORLD'S GREATEST SUPER-HEROES (MEGO, 1972-78)

12-1/2" FIGURES

Amazing Spider-Man, 1978, 1972-78, Mego
NM $40   MIP $100

Batman, 1978, 1972-78, Mego, magnetic
NM $100   MIP $250

Batman, 1978, 1972-78, Mego
NM $60   MIP $125

Captain America, 1978, 1972-78, Mego
NM $75   MIP $200

Hulk, 1978, 1972-78, Mego
NM $30   MIP $100

Robin, magnetic, 1978, 1972-78, Mego
NM $125   MIP $250

Spider-Man, 1972-78, Mego, web shooting
NM $75   MIP $150

Superman, 1972-78, Mego
NM $50   MIP $125

8" FIGURES

Aquaman, 1972, Mego, carded
NM $50   MIP $150

Aquaman, 1972, Mego, Solid box, no window
NM $50   MIP $800

Aquaman, 1972, Mego, boxed
NM $50   MIP $150

Batgirl, 1973, Mego, boxed
NM $125   MIP $300

Batgirl, 1973, Mego, carded
NM $125   MIP $250

Batman, 1972, Mego, removable mask, Kresge card only
NM $200   MIP $750

Batman, 1972, Mego, painted mask, boxed
NM $60   MIP $150

Batman w/ removable cowl, 1972, Mego, Solid box, no window
NM $125   MIP $1000

Batman, fist fighting, 1975, Mego, boxed
NM $150   MIP $450

Batman, painted mask, 1972, Mego, carded
NM $60   MIP $150

Batman, removable mask, 1972, Mego, boxed
NM $200   MIP $600

Bruce Wayne, 1974, Mego, boxed, Montgomery Ward Exclusive
NM $1200   MIP $2000

Captain America, 1972, Mego, carded
NM $60   MIP $150

Captain America, 1972, Mego, boxed
NM $60   MIP $200

Catwoman, 1973, Mego, boxed
NM $150   MIP $350

Catwoman, 1973, Mego, carded
NM $150   MIP $2000

Clark Kent, 1974, Mego, boxed, Montgomery Ward Exclusive
NM $1200   MIP $2000

Conan, 1975, Mego, boxed
NM $150   MIP $400

Conan, 1975, Mego, carded
NM $150   MIP $500

Dick Grayson, 1974, Mego, boxed, Montgomery Ward Exclusive
NM $1200   MIP $2000

Falcon, 1974, Mego, boxed
NM $60   MIP $150

Falcon, 1974, Mego, carded
NM $60   MIP $1500

Green Arrow, 1973, Mego, boxed, with hat, belt and bow and arrow accessories
NM $150   MIP $450

Green Arrow, 1973, Mego, carded
NM $150   MIP $2000

Green Goblin, 1974, Mego, boxed
NM $90   MIP $275

Green Goblin, 1974, Mego, carded
NM $90   MIP $2000

Human Torch, Fantastic Four, 1975, Mego, boxed
NM $25   MIP $90

Human Torch, Fantastic Four, 1975, Mego, carded
NM $25   MIP $50

Incredible Hulk, 1974, Mego, carded
NM $20   MIP $50

Incredible Hulk, 1974, Mego, boxed
NM $20   MIP $100

Invisible Girl, Fantastic Four, 1975, Mego, boxed
NM $30   MIP $150

Invisible Girl, Fantastic Four, 1975, Mego, carded
NM $30   MIP $60

Iron Man, 1974, Mego, boxed
NM $75   MIP $125

Iron Man, 1974, Mego, carded
NM $75   MIP $450

Isis, 1976, Mego, boxed
NM $75   MIP $250

Isis, 1976, Mego, carded
NM $75   MIP $125

Joker, 1973, Mego, boxed
NM $60   MIP $200

Joker, 1973, Mego, carded
NM $60   MIP $150

Joker, fist fighting, 1975, Mego, boxed
NM $150   MIP $600

Lizard, 1974, Mego, carded
NM $100   MIP $2000

Lizard, 1974, Mego, boxed
NM $75   MIP $200

Mr. Fantastic, Fantastic Four, 1975, Mego, boxed
NM $30   MIP $140

Mr. Fantastic, Fantastic Four, 1975, Mego, carded
NM $30   MIP $60

Mr. Mxyzptlk, open mouth, 1973, Mego, boxed
NM $50   MIP $75

Mr. Mxyzptlk, open mouth, 1973, Mego, carded
NM $50   MIP $150

Mr. Mxyzptlk, smirk, 1973, Mego, boxed
NM $60   MIP $150

Penguin, 1973, Mego, boxed
NM $60   MIP $150

Penguin, 1973, Mego, carded
NM $60   MIP $125

Peter Parker, 1974, Mego, boxed, Montgomery Ward Exclusive
NM $1200   MIP $2000

Riddler, 1973, Mego, boxed
NM $100   MIP $250

Riddler, 1973, Mego, carded
NM $100   MIP $2000

Riddler, 1975, Mego, fist fighting, boxed
NM $150   MIP $600

Robin, 1972, Mego, painted mask, boxed
NM $60   MIP $150

Robin, 1972, Mego, painted mask, carded
NM $60   MIP $90

Robin, 1972, Mego, removable mask, boxed
NM $250   MIP $750

Robin, 1972, removable mask, solid box
NM $250   MIP $1500

Robin, 1975, Mego, fist fighting, boxed
NM $125   MIP $450

Shazam, 1972, Mego, boxed
NM $75   MIP $200

Shazam, 1972, Mego, carded
NM $75   MIP $150

Spider-Man, 1972, Mego, carded
NM $20   MIP $50

Spider-Man, 1972, Mego, boxed
NM $20   MIP $100

Supergirl, 1973, Mego, boxed
NM $300   MIP $450

Supergirl, 1973, Mego, carded
NM $300   MIP $450

Superman, 1972, Mego, boxed
NM $50   MIP $200

Superman, 1972, Mego, carded
NM $50   MIP $125

Superman, 1972, Mego, Solid box, no window
NM $50   MIP $800

Tarzan, 1972, Mego, boxed
NM $50   MIP $150

Tarzan, 1976, Mego, Kresge card only
NM $60   MIP $225

Thing, Fantastic Four, 1975, Mego, boxed
NM $40   MIP $150

Thing, Fantastic Four, 1975, Mego, carded
NM $40   MIP $60

Thor, 1975, Mego, boxed
NM $150   MIP $400

Thor, 1975, Mego, carded
NM $150   MIP $450

Wonder Woman, 1972-78, Mego, boxed
NM $100   MIP $350

Wonder Woman, 1972-78, Mego, Kresge card only
NM $100   MIP $450

Wondergirl, 1972-78, Mego, carded
NM $125   MIP $400

ACCESSORIES

Super Hero Carry Case, 1973, Mego
NM $40   MIP $100

Supervator, 1974, Mego
NM $60   MIP $120

PLAY SETS

Aquaman vs. the Great White Shark,
1978, Mego, rare
NM $500   MIP $1000

Batcave Play Set, 1974, Mego, vinyl
NM $150   MIP $300

Batman's Wayne Foundation Penthouse,
1977, Mego, fiberboard
NM $600   MIP $1000

Hall of Justice, 1976, Mego, vinyl
NM $125   MIP $250

SUPERMAN SERIES

General Zod, 1978, Mego
NM $50   MIP $100

Jor-El, 1978, Mego
NM $50   MIP $100

Lex Luthor, 1978, Mego
NM $50   MIP $100

Superman, 1978, Mego
NM $50   MIP $125

TEEN TITANS,
6-1/2" FIGURES

Aqualad, 1976, Mego
NM $175   MIP $350

Kid Flash, 1976, Mego
NM $175   MIP $450

Speedy, 1976, Mego
NM $300   MIP $500

Wondergirl, 1976, Mego
NM $200   MIP $450

VEHICLES

Batcopter, 1974, Mego, on display card
NM $55   MIP $110

Batcopter, 1974, Mego, boxed
NM $75   MIP $150

Batcycle, 1974, Mego, blue, carded
NM $75   MIP $135

Batcycle, 1974, Mego, blue, boxed
NM $75   MIP $170

Batcycle, 1975, Mego, black, carded
NM $60   MIP $150

Batcycle, 1975, Mego, black, boxed
NM $75   MIP $185

Batmobile, 1974, Mego, photo box
NM $75   MIP $395

Batmobile, 1974, Mego, carded
NM $50   MIP $120

Batmobile, 1974, artwork box
NM $75   MIP $325

Batmobile and Batman, 1972-78, Mego
NM $40   MIP $100

Captain Americar, 1976, Mego
NM $125   MIP $275

Green Arrowcar, 1976, Mego
NM $175   MIP $350

Jokermobile, 1976, Mego
NM $150   MIP $400

Mobile Bat Lab, 1975, Mego
NM $125   MIP $400

Spidercar, 1976, Mego
NM $50   MIP $125

WWF (JAKKS PACIFIC, 1997-PRESENT)

2-TUFF, SERIES 1

D.O.A., 1997-present
NM $4   MIP $12

Goldust and Marlena, 1997-present
NM $4   MIP $12

HHH and Chyna, 1997-present
NM $4   MIP $12

Truth Commission, 1997-present
NM $4   MIP $12

2-TUFF, SERIES 2

Brian Christopher and Jerry Lawler,
1997-present
NM $4   MIP $15

D-Lo Brown and Kama, 1997-present
NM $4   MIP $15

Kurrgan and Jackyl, 1997-present
NM $4   MIP $15

New Age Outlaws, 1997-present
NM $4   MIP $15

2-TUFF, SERIES 3

Kane and Mankind, 1997-present
NM $4   MIP $15

Legion of Doom 2000, 1997-present
NM $4   MIP $15

Rocky Maivia (The Rock) and Owen Hart,
1997-present
NM $8   MIP $20

Stone Cold Steve Austin/Undertaker,
1997-present
NM $4   MIP $15

2-TUFF, SERIES 4

Billy Gunn and Val Venis, 1997-present
NM $3   MIP $12

Mankind and The Rock, 1997-present
NM $3   MIP $12

**Stone Cold Steve Austin and Big
Bossman,** 1997-present
NM $3   MIP $12

Undertaker and Kane, 1997-present
NM $3   MIP $12

2-TUFF, SERIES 5

Debra and Jarrett, 1997-present
NM $3   MIP $10

Road Dogg and Billy Gunn, 1997-present
NM $3   MIP $10

Stone Cold Steve Austin and The Rock,
1997-present
NM $8   MIP $20

Undertaker and Viscera, 1997-present
NM $3   MIP $10

BEST OF 1997,
SERIES 1

Ahmed Johnson, 1997-present
NM $3   MIP $10

Bret Hart, 1997-present
NM $3   MIP $10

British Bulldog, 1997-present
NM $3   MIP $10

Owen Hart, 1997-present
NM $5   MIP $15

Stone Cold Steve Austin, 1997-present
NM $3   MIP $12

Undertaker, 1997-present
NM $3   MIP $10

BEST OF 1997,
SERIES 2

Crush, 1997-present
NM $3   MIP $10

Goldust, 1997-present
NM $3   MIP $10

HHH, 1997-present
NM $3   MIP $10

Ken Shamrock, 1997-present
NM $3   MIP $10

Marc Mero, 1997-present
NM $3   MIP $10

Rocky Maivia (The Rock), 1997-present
NM $5   MIP $15

Shawn Michaels, 1997-present
NM $3   MIP $10

Undertaker, 1997-present
NM $3   MIP $10

BEST OF 1998,
SERIES 1

8-Ball, 1997-present
NM $3   MIP $8

Blackjack Bradshaw, 1997-present
    NM $3   **MIP** $8

Brian Christopher, 1997-present
    NM $3   **MIP** $8

Chyna, 1997-present
    NM $3   **MIP** $8

Shawn Michaels, 1997-present
    NM $3   **MIP** $8

Skull, 1997-present
    NM $3   **MIP** $8

Stone Cold Steve Austin, 1997-present
    NM $4   **MIP** $10

Vader, 1997-present
    NM $3   **MIP** $8

BEST OF 1998, SERIES 2

Dan Severn, 1997-present
    NM $3   **MIP** $8

Dude Love, 1997-present
    NM $3   **MIP** $8

HHH, 1997-present
    NM $3   **MIP** $8

Jeff Jarrett, 1997-present
    NM $3   **MIP** $8

Ken Shamrock, 1997-present
    NM $3   **MIP** $8

Mark Henry, 1997-present
    NM $3   **MIP** $8

Stone Cold Steve Austin, 1997-present
    NM $4   **MIP** $10

Undertaker, 1997-present
    NM $3   **MIP** $8

BONE CRUNCHIN' BUDDIES, SERIES 1

Dude Love, 1997-present
    NM $5   **MIP** $15

Shawn Michaels, 1997-present
    NM $5   **MIP** $15

Stone Cold Steve Austin, 1997-present
    NM $5   **MIP** $15

Undertaker, 1997-present
    NM $5   **MIP** $15

BONE CRUNCHIN' BUDDIES, SERIES 2

Animal, 1997-present
    NM $5   **MIP** $15

Hawk, 1997-present
    NM $5   **MIP** $15

Rock, The, 1997-present
    NM $8   **MIP** $20

Stone Cold Steve Austin, 1997-present
    NM $5   **MIP** $15

Undertaker, 1997-present
    NM $5   **MIP** $15

BONE CRUNCHIN' BUDDIES, SERIES 3

HHH, 1997-present
    NM $5   **MIP** $15

Kane, 1997-present
    NM $5   **MIP** $15

Rock, The, 1997-present
    NM $8   **MIP** $20

Stone Cold Steve Austin in shirt and pants, 1997-present
    NM $5   **MIP** $15

Stone Cold Steve Austin in tights and vest, 1997-present
    NM $5   **MIP** $15

Undertaker, 1997-present
    NM $5   **MIP** $15

FULLY LOADED, SERIES 1

Al Snow, 1997-present
    NM $3   **MIP** $8

Billy Gunn, 1997-present
    NM $3   **MIP** $8

Hunter Hearst Hemsley, 1997-present
    NM $3   **MIP** $8

Kane, 1997-present
    NM $3   **MIP** $8

Road Dog Jesse James, 1997-present
    NM $3   **MIP** $8

Rocky Maivia (The Rock), 1997-present
    NM $5   **MIP** $15

FULLY LOADED, SERIES 2

Road Dog Jesse James, 1997-present
    NM $2   **MIP** $6

Rock, The, 1997-present
    NM $5   **MIP** $15

Shane McMahon, 1997-present
    NM $2   **MIP** $6

Stone Cold Steve Austin, 1997-present
    NM $3   **MIP** $10

Test, 1997-present
    NM $2   **MIP** $6

X Pac, 1997-present
    NM $3   **MIP** $8

GRUDGE MATCH

Brian Christopher vs. TAKA, 1997-present
    NM $5   **MIP** $15

Dan Severn vs. Ken Shamrock, 1997-present
    NM $5   **MIP** $15

HHH vs. Owen Hart, 1997-present
    NM $5   **MIP** $15

HHH vs HBK, 1997-present
    NM $5   **MIP** $15

Jeff Jarrett vs. X Pac, 1997-present
    NM $5   **MIP** $15

Kane vs. Undertaker, 1997-present
    NM $5   **MIP** $15

Marc Mero vs. Steve Blackman, 1997-present
    NM $5   **MIP** $15

Mark Henry vs. Vader, 1997-present
    NM $5   **MIP** $15

McMahon vs. Stone Cold Steve Austin, 1997-present
    NM $5   **MIP** $15

Road Dog Jesse James vs. Al Snow, 1997-present
    NM $5   **MIP** $15

Sable vs. Luna Vachon, 1997-present
    NM $5   **MIP** $15

Shamrock vs. Billy Gunn, 1997-present
    NM $5   **MIP** $15

Shawn Michaels vs. Stone Cold Steve Austin, 1997-present
    NM $8   **MIP** $20

Stone Cold Steve Austin vs. The Rock, 1997-present
    NM $8   **MIP** $20

LEGENDS, SERIES 1

Andre the Giant, 1997-present
    NM $3   **MIP** $12

Captian Lou Albano, 1997-present
    NM $3   **MIP** $12

Classie Freddie Blassie, 1997-present
    NM $3   **MIP** $12

Jimmy Snuka, 1997-present
    NM $3   **MIP** $12

LIVEWIRE, SERIES 1

Chyna, 1997-present
    NM $3   **MIP** $8

Ken Shamrock, 1997-present
    NM $3   **MIP** $8

Mankind, 1997-present
    NM $3   **MIP** $8

Stone Cold Steve Austin, 1997-present
    NM $4   **MIP** $10

Undertaker, 1997-present
    NM $3   **MIP** $8

Vader, 1997-present
    NM $3   **MIP** $8

LIVEWIRE, SERIES 2

Marc Mero, 1997-present
    NM $2   **MIP** $6

Mark Henry, 1997-present
    NM $2   **MIP** $6

Rock, The, 1997-present
    NM $5   **MIP** $15

Shawn Michaels, 1997-present
    NM $2   **MIP** $6

Val Venis, 1997-present
    NM $2   **MIP** $6

X Pac, 1997-present
    NM $2   **MIP** $6

ACTION FIGURES

MANAGER, SERIES 1

Backlund and Sultan, 1997-present
NM $3   MIP $12

Bearer and Mankind, 1997-present
NM $3   MIP $12

Mason and Crush, 1997-present
NM $3   MIP $12

Sable and Mero, 1997-present
NM $3   MIP $12

MAXIMUM SWEAT, SERIES 1

HHH, 1997-present
NM $3   MIP $8

Kane, 1997-present
NM $3   MIP $8

Rock, The, 1997-present
NM $5   MIP $15

Shawn Michaels, 1997-present
NM $3   MIP $8

Stone Cold Steve Austin, 1997-present
NM $3   MIP $10

Undertaker, 1997-present
NM $3   MIP $8

MAXIMUM SWEAT, SERIES 2

Billy Gunn, 1997-present
NM $2   MIP $6

Edge, 1997-present
NM $2   MIP $6

Ken Shamrock, 1997-present
NM $2   MIP $6

Road Dogg Jesse James, 1997-present
NM $2   MIP $6

Stone Cold Steve Austin, 1997-present
NM $3   MIP $10

Undertaker, 1997-present
NM $2   MIP $6

MAXIMUM SWEAT, SERIES 3

Big Bossman, 1997-present
NM $2   MIP $6

Billy Gunn, 1997-present
NM $2   MIP $6

Gangrel, 1997-present
NM $2   MIP $6

Mankind, 1997-present
NM $2   MIP $6

Rock, The, 1997-present
NM $5   MIP $15

Stone Cold Steve Austin, 1997-present
NM $3   MIP $10

RINGSIDE, SERIES 1

Referee, 1997-present
NM $3   MIP $8

Sable, 1997-present
NM $3   MIP $8

Sunny, 1997-present
NM $3   MIP $8

Vince McMahon, 1997-present
NM $3   MIP $8

RINGSIDE, SERIES 2

Honky Tonk Man, 1997-present
NM $2   MIP $6

Jim Cornette, 1997-present
NM $2   MIP $6

Jim Ross, 1997-present
NM $2   MIP $6

Referee, 1997-present
NM $2   MIP $6

Sgt. Slaughter, 1997-present
NM $2   MIP $6

Vince McMahon, 1997-present
NM $2   MIP $6

RIPPED AND RUTHLESS, SERIES 1

Goldust, 1997-present
NM $3   MIP $8

Mankind, 1997-present
NM $3   MIP $8

Stone Cold Steve Austin, 1997-present
NM $4   MIP $10

Undertaker, 1997-present
NM $3   MIP $8

RIPPED AND RUTHLESS, SERIES 2

HHH, 1997-present
NM $3   MIP $10

Kane, 1997-present
NM $5   MIP $15

Sable, 1997-present
NM $5   MIP $15

Shawn Michaels, 1997-present
NM $3   MIP $10

S.T.O.M.P., SERIES 1

Ahmed Johnson, 1997-present
NM $3   MIP $8

Brian Pillman, 1997-present
NM $3   MIP $8

Crush, 1997-present
NM $3   MIP $8

Ken Shamrock, 1997-present
NM $3   MIP $8

Stone Cold Steve Austin, 1997-present
NM $3   MIP $10

Undertaker, 1997-present
NM $3   MIP $8

S.T.O.M.P., SERIES 2

Chyna, 1997-present
NM $3   MIP $8

Mosh, 1997-present
NM $3   MIP $8

Owen Hart, 1997-present
NM $3   MIP $8

Rocky Maivia (The Rock), 1997-present, Jakks Pacific
NM $5   MIP $15

Stone Cold Steve Austin, 1997-present
NM $3   MIP $10

Thrasher, 1997-present
NM $3   MIP $8

S.T.O.M.P., SERIES 3

Animal, 1997-present
NM $3   MIP $8

Hawk, 1997-present
NM $3   MIP $8

Kane, 1997-present
NM $3   MIP $8

Marc Mero, 1997-present
NM $3   MIP $8

Sable, 1997-present
NM $3   MIP $8

Undertaker, 1997-present
NM $3   MIP $8

S.T.O.M.P., SERIES 4

Billy Gunn, 1997-present
NM $2   MIP $6

Chyna, 1997-present
NM $2   MIP $6

HHH, 1997-present
NM $2   MIP $6

Road Dog Jesse James, 1997-present
NM $2   MIP $6

Stone Cold Steve Austin, 1997-present
NM $3   MIP $8

X Pac, 1997-present
NM $2   MIP $6

SHOTGUN SATURDAY NIGHT, SERIES 1

Animal, 1997-present
NM $3   MIP $8

Hawk, 1997-present
NM $3   MIP $8

Henry O. Godwinn, 1997-present
NM $3   MIP $8

Phineas I. Godwinn, 1997-present
NM $3   MIP $8

Rocky Maivia (The Rock), 1997-present
NM $5   MIP $15

Savio Vega, 1997-present
NM $3   MIP $8

Stone Cold Steve Austin, 1997-present
NM $3   MIP $10

Undertaker, 1997-present
NM $3   MIP $8

SHOTGUN SATURDAY NIGHT, SERIES 2

Billy Gunn, 1997-present
NM $2   MIP $6

Jeff Jarrett, 1997-present
NM $2   MIP $6

Kane, 1997-present
NM $2   MIP $6

Road Dog Jesse James, 1997-present
NM $2   MIP $6

Sable, 1997-present
NM $3   MIP $8

Shawn Michaels, 1997-present
NM $2   MIP $6

SIGNATURE, SERIES 1

Animal, 1997-present
NM $3   MIP $8

Goldust, 1997-present
NM $3   MIP $8

Hawk, 1997-present
NM $3   MIP $8

Hunter Hearst Hemsley, 1997-present
NM $3   MIP $8

Mankind, 1997-present
NM $3   MIP $8

Stone Cold Steve Austin, 1997-present
NM $5   MIP $15

SIGNATURE, SERIES 2

Billy Gunn, 1997-present
NM $3   MIP $8

Dude Love, 1997-present
NM $3   MIP $8

Kane, 1997-present
NM $3   MIP $8

Road Dog Jesse James, 1997-present
NM $3   MIP $8

Shawn Michaels, 1997-present
NM $3   MIP $8

Undertaker, 1997-present
NM $3   MIP $8

SIGNATURE, SERIES 3

Edge, 1997-present
NM $3   MIP $8

HHH, 1997-present
NM $2   MIP $6

Jackie, 1997-present
NM $3   MIP $8

Rock, The, 1997-present
NM $5   MIP $15

Stone Cold Steve Austin, 1997-present
NM $5   MIP $15

Undertaker, 1997-present
NM $3   MIP $8

SUNDAY NIGHT HEAT

Billy Gunn, 1997-present
NM $3   MIP $8

Road Dog Jesse James, 1997-present
NM $3   MIP $8

Rock, The, 1997-present
NM $5   MIP $15

Sable, 1997-present
NM $2   MIP $6

Stone Cold Steve Austin, 1997-present
NM $3   MIP $10

Undertaker, 1997-present
NM $3   MIP $8

SUPERSTARS, SERIES 1

Bret Hart, 1997-present
NM $8   MIP $20

Diesel, 1997-present
NM $10   MIP $40

Goldust, 1997-present
NM $8   MIP $20

Razor Ramon, 1997-present
NM $15   MIP $50

Shawn Michaels, 1997-present
NM $5   MIP $15

Undertaker, 1997-present
NM $8   MIP $20

SUPERSTARS, SERIES 2

Bret Hart, 1997-present
NM $5   MIP $15

Owen Hart, 1997-present
NM $8   MIP $30

Shawn Michaels, 1997-present
NM $5   MIP $15

Ultimate Warrior, 1997-present
NM $8   MIP $30

Undertaker, 1997-present
NM $10   MIP $30

Vader, 1997-present
NM $5   MIP $15

SUPERSTARS, SERIES 3

Ahmed Johnson, 1997-present
NM $3   MIP $10

Bret Hart, 1997-present
NM $3   MIP $10

British Bulldog, 1997-present
NM $5   MIP $15

Diesel, reissue, 1997-present
NM $5   MIP $15

Goldust, reissue, 1997-present
NM $5   MIP $15

Mankind, 1997-present
NM $3   MIP $10

Shawn Michaels, 1997-present
NM $3   MIP $10

Sycho Sid, 1997-present
NM $3   MIP $10

SUPERSTARS, SERIES 4

Farooq, 1997-present
NM $3   MIP $10

Hunter Hearst Hemsley, 1997-present
NM $3   MIP $10

Jerry The King Lawler, 1997-present
NM $3   MIP $10

Justin Hawk Bradshaw, 1997-present
NM $3   MIP $10

Stone Cold Steve Austin, 1997-present
NM $5   MIP $15

Vader, 1997-present
NM $3   MIP $10

SUPERSTARS, SERIES 5

Flash Funk, 1997-present
NM $3   MIP $10

Ken Shamrock, 1997-present
NM $3   MIP $10

Rocky Maivia, 1997-present
NM $3   MIP $10

Savio Vega, 1997-present
NM $3   MIP $10

Stone Cold Steve Austin, 1997-present
NM $5   MIP $15

Sycho Sid, 1997-present
NM $3   MIP $10

SUPERSTARS, SERIES 6

HHH, 1997-present
NM $3   MIP $10

Jeff Jarrett, 1997-present
NM $2   MIP $6

Marc Mero, 1997-present
NM $2   MIP $6

Mark Henry, 1997-present
NM $2   MIP $6

Owen Hart, 1997-present, Jakks Pacific
NM $5   MIP $15

Steve Blackman, 1997-present
NM $2   MIP $6

SUPERSTARS, SERIES 7

Dr. Death Steve Williams, 1997-present
NM $2   MIP $6

Edge, 1997-present
NM $2   MIP $6

Stone Cold Steve Austin, 1997-present
NM $3   MIP $10

Undertaker, 1997-present
NM $3   MIP $10

Val Venis, 1997-present
NM $2   MIP $6

X Pac, 1997-present
NM $3   MIP $8

SUPERSTARS, SERIES 8

Big Boss Man, 1997-present
NM $2   MIP $6

Ken Shamrock, 1997-present
NM $2   MIP $6

Rock, The, 1997-present
NM $5   MIP $15

Shane McMahon, 1997-present
    NM $2   **MIP** $6

Shawn Michaels, 1997-present
    NM $2   **MIP** $6

SUPERSTARS, SERIES 9

Bob Holly, 1997-present
    NM $2   **MIP** $6

Christian, 1997-present
    NM $2   **MIP** $6

Gangrel, 1997-present
    NM $2   **MIP** $6

Paul Wright, 1997-present
    NM $2   **MIP** $6

Undertaker with robe, 1997-present
    NM $2   **MIP** $6

Vince McMahon, 1997-present
    NM $2   **MIP** $6

TAG TEAM, SERIES 1

Godwinns, 1997-present
    NM $4   **MIP** $15

Headbangers, 1997-present
    NM $4   **MIP** $15

Legion of Doom, 1997-present
    NM $4   **MIP** $15

New Blackjacks, 1997-present
    NM $4   **MIP** $15

TITAN TRON LIVE

Kane, 1997-present
    NM $2   **MIP** $6

Mankind, 1997-present
    NM $2   **MIP** $6

Road Dogg Jesse James, 1997-present
    NM $2   **MIP** $6

Rock, The, 1997-present
    NM $5   **MIP** $15

Stone Cold Steve Austin, 1997-present
    NM $3   **MIP** $10

Undertaker, 1997-present
    NM $2   **MIP** $6

WWF WORLD WRESTLING FEDERATION (HASBRO, 1990-94)

FIGURES

1-2-3 Kid, 1994, Hasbro
    NM $15   **MIP** $38

Adam Bomb, 1994, Hasbro
    NM $10   **MIP** $18

Akeem, 1990, Hasbro
    NM $15   **MIP** $38

Andre the Giant, 1990, Hasbro
    NM $25   **MIP** $75

Ax, 1990, Hasbro
    NM $5   **MIP** $15

Bam Bam Bigelow, 1994, Hasbro
    NM $6   **MIP** $15

Bart Gunn, 1994, Hasbro
    NM $10   **MIP** $18

Berzerker, 1993, Hasbro
    NM $3   **MIP** $8

Big Bossman with Jailhouse Jam, 1992, 1992, Hasbro
    NM $4   **MIP** $8

Big Bossman, 1990, 1990, Hasbro
    NM $4   **MIP** $8

Billy Gunn, 1994, Hasbro
    NM $10   **MIP** $18

Bret "Hitman" Hart with Hart Attack, 1992, 1992, Hasbro
    NM $5   **MIP** $13

Bret Hart, 1993 mail-in, 1993, Hasbro
    NM $38   **MIP** n/a

Bret Hart, 1994, 1994, Hasbro
    NM $4   **MIP** $8

British Bulldog with Bulldog Bash, 1992, 1992, Hasbro
    NM $4   **MIP** $8

Brutus "The Barber" Beefcake with Beefcake Flattop, 1992, 1992, Hasbro
    NM $6   **MIP** $13

Brutus the Barber, 1990, 1990, Hasbro
    NM $6   **MIP** $13

Bushwackers, two-pack, 1990-94, Hasbro
    NM $5   **MIP** $10

Butch Miller, 1994, Hasbro
    NM $3   **MIP** $8

Crush, 1993, 1993, Hasbro
    NM $6   **MIP** $13

(Hasbro)

Crush, 1994, 1994, Hasbro, Made mincemeat out of his opponents.
    NM $3   **MIP** $8

Demolition, two-pack, 1990-94, Hasbro
    NM $10   **MIP** $23

Doink the Clown, 1994, Hasbro
    NM $4   **MIP** $8

Dusty Rhodes, 1991, Hasbro
    NM $63   **MIP** $150

Earthquake, 1991, Hasbro
    NM $8   **MIP** $15

Earthquake with Aftershock, 1992, Hasbro
    NM $4   **MIP** $13

El Matador, 1993, Hasbro
    NM $3   **MIP** $8

Fatu, 1994, Hasbro
    NM $3   **MIP** $8

Giant Gonzales, 1994, Hasbro
    NM $3   **MIP** $8

Greg "the Hammer" Valentine with Hammer Slammer (1992), 1992, Hasbro
    NM $5   **MIP** $15

Hacksaw Jim Duggan, 1991, 1991, Hasbro
    NM $3   **MIP** $8

Hacksaw Jim Duggan, 1994, 1994, Hasbro
    NM $3   **MIP** $8

Honky Tonk Man, 1991, Hasbro
    NM $13   **MIP** $25

Hulk Hogan with Hulkaplex, 1992, 1992, Hasbro
    NM $5   **MIP** $10

Hulk Hogan, 1990, 1990, Hasbro
    NM $6   **MIP** $13

Hulk Hogan, 1991, 1991, Hasbro
    NM $5   **MIP** $10

Hulk Hogan, 1993, mail-in, 1993, Hasbro
    NM $38   **MIP** $50

Hulk Hogan, 1993, no shirt, 1993, Hasbro
    NM $5   **MIP** $10

I.R.S., 1993, Hasbro
    NM $4   **MIP** $8

Jake the Snake Roberts, 1990, Hasbro
    NM $5   **MIP** $10

Jim Neidhart, 1993, Hasbro
    NM $3   **MIP** $8

Jimmy Superfly Snuka, 1991, Hasbro
    NM $6   **MIP** $13

Kamala, 1993, Hasbro
    NM $5   **MIP** $13

Koko B. Ware with Bird Man Bounce, 1992, 1992, Hasbro
    NM $10   **MIP** $30

Legion of Doom, two-pack, 1990-94, Hasbro
    NM $10   **MIP** $20

Lex Luger, 1994, Hasbro
    NM $8   **MIP** $15

Ludwig Borga, 1994, Hasbro
    NM $20   **MIP** $35

Luke Williams, 1994, Hasbro
    NM $5   **MIP** $15

Macho Man Randy Savage with Macho Masher, 1992, 1992, Hasbro
    NM $15   **MIP** $35

Macho Man, 1990, 1990, Hasbro
    NM $12   **MIP** $25

Macho Man, 1991, 1991, Hasbro
    NM $15   **MIP** $35

Macho Man, 1993, 1993, Hasbro
    NM $7   **MIP** $15

Marty Jannetty, 1994, Hasbro
    NM $5   **MIP** $15

Mountie, 1993, Hasbro
    NM $6   **MIP** $15

ACTION FIGURES

Mr. Perfect with Perfect Plex, 1992, 1992, Hasbro
NM $8 MIP $20

Mr. Perfect with Texas Twister, 1992, 1992, Hasbro
NM $15 MIP $35

Mr. Perfect, 1994, 1994, Hasbro
NM $12 MIP $25

Nailz, 1993, Hasbro
NM $12 MIP $25

Nasty Boys, two-pack, 1990-94, Hasbro
NM $15 MIP $80

Owen Hart, 1993, Hasbro
NM $15 MIP $45

Papa Shango, 1993, Hasbro
NM $7 MIP $15

Razor Ramon, 1993, 1993, Hasbro
NM $15 MIP $30

(Hasbro)

Razor Ramon, 1994, 1994, Hasbro, A bad dude who often sported toothpick in his mouth.
NM $9 MIP $18

Repo Man, 1993, Hasbro
NM $7 MIP $15

Ric Flair, 1993, Hasbro
NM $7 MIP $15

Rick Martel, 1993, Hasbro
NM $5 MIP $15

Rick Rude, 1990, Hasbro
NM $15 MIP $30

Rick Steiner, 1994, Hasbro
NM $9 MIP $18

Ricky "The Dragon" Steamboat with Steamboat Springer, 1992, 1992, Hasbro
NM $7 MIP $15

Rockers, two-pack, 1990-94, Hasbro
NM $10 MIP $20

Rowdy Roddy Piper, 1991, Hasbro
NM $15 MIP $30

Samu, 1994, Hasbro
NM $5 MIP $15

Scott Steiner, 1994, Hasbro
NM $8 MIP $18

Sgt. Slaughter with Sgt.'s Salute, 1992, 1992, Hasbro
NM $15 MIP $30

Shawn Michaels, 1993, 1993, Hasbro
NM $10 MIP $25

(KP Photo)

Shawn Michaels, 1994, 1994, Hasbro, Shown here with group of figures from the series
NM $6 MIP $15

Sid Justice, 1993, Hasbro
NM $6 MIP $15

Skinner, 1993, Hasbro
NM $6 MIP $15

Smash, 1990, Hasbro
NM $12 MIP $25

Tatanka, 1993, 1993, Hasbro
NM $7 MIP $15

Tatanka, 1994, 1994, Hasbro
NM $7 MIP $15

Ted Diabiase, 1990, 1990, Hasbro
NM $10 MIP $20

Ted Diabiase, 1991, 1991, Hasbro
NM $7 MIP $15

Ted Diabiase, 1994, 1994, Hasbro
NM $7 MIP $15

Texas Tornado with Texas Twister, 1992, 1992, Hasbro
NM $10 MIP $50

Typhoon with Tidal Wave, 1992, 1992, Hasbro
NM $15 MIP $30

Ultimate Warrior with Warrior Wham, 1992, 1992, Hasbro
NM $20 MIP $40

Ultimate Warrior, 1990, 1990, Hasbro
NM $12 MIP $25

Ultimate Warrior, 1991, 1991, Hasbro
NM $10 MIP $20

Undertaker with Graveyard Smash, 1992, 1992, Hasbro
NM $9 MIP $18

Undertaker, 1993, mail-in, 1993, Hasbro
NM $25 MIP $50

Undertaker, 1994, 1994, Hasbro
NM $15 MIP $25

Virgil, 1993, Hasbro
NM $7 MIP $15

Warlord, 1993, Hasbro
NM $6 MIP $15

Yokozuna, 1994, Hasbro
NM $15 MIP $30

XENA WARRIOR PRINCESS (TOY BIZ, 1998-99)

6" FIGURES

Callisto Warrior Goddess with Hope, 1999
NM $3 MIP $10

Grieving Gabrielle, 1999
NM $3 MIP $10

Xena Conqueror of Nations, 1999
NM $3 MIP $10

Xena Warrior Huntress, 1999
NM $3 MIP $10

SERIES I, 12" FIGURES

Callisto, 1998
NM $8 MIP $25

Gabrielle, 1998
NM $8 MIP $25

Xena, 1998
NM $8 MIP $25

SERIES II, 12" FIGURES

Ares, 1999
NM $8 MIP $25

Gabrielle Amazon Princess, 1999
NM $8 MIP $25

Roman Xena, 1999
NM $8 MIP $25

Warlord Xena, 1999
NM $8 MIP $25

SERIES III, 12" FIGURES

Empress Gabrielle, 1999
NM $8 MIP $25

Shamaness Xena, 1999
NM $8 MIP $25

Xena the Evil Warrior, 1999
NM $8 MIP $25

X-FILES (MCFARLANE, 1998)

FIGURES

Fireman with Cryolitter, 1998, McFarlane
NM $10 MIP $25

Mulder in Arctic wear, 1998, McFarlane
NM $4 MIP $8

Mulder with docile alien, 1998, McFarlane
NM $4 MIP $8

Mulder with Human Host and Cryopod Chamber, 1998, McFarlane
NM $4 MIP $8

Mulder with victim, 1998, McFarlane
NM $4 MIP $8

Primitive Man with Attack Alien, 1998, McFarlane
NM $4 MIP $8

Scully in Arctic wear, 1998, McFarlane
  NM $4 MIP $8

Scully with docile alien, 1998, McFarlane
  NM $4 MIP $8

(Lenny Lee)

Scully with Human Host and Cryopod Chamber, 1998, McFarlane, Agent Scully in parka. Bases of human hosts snap together to form a row--just like in the movie
  NM $4 MIP $8

Scully with Victim, 1998, McFarlane
  NM $4 MIP $8

X-MEN (TOY BIZ, 1991-96)

FIGURES

Ahab, 1994, Toy Biz
  NM $5 MIP $15

Apocalypse I, 1991, Toy Biz
  NM $7 MIP $15

Apocalypse I, 1993, Toy Biz
  NM $4 MIP $15

Apocolypse, 1996, Toy Biz
  NM $3 MIP $12

Archangel, 1991, Toy Biz
  NM $7 MIP $15

Archangel, 1996, Toy Biz
  NM $3 MIP $8

Archangel II, 1995, Toy Biz
  NM $4 MIP $15

Banshee I, 1992, Toy Biz
  NM $7 MIP $15

Battle Ravaged Wolverine, 1995, Toy Biz
  NM $4 MIP $8

Beast, 1994, Toy Biz
  NM $10 MIP $20

Bishop II, 1993, Toy Biz
  NM $7 MIP $15

Bishop II, 1996, Toy Biz
  NM $3 MIP $8

Blob, 1995, Toy Biz
  NM $5 MIP $15

Cable Cyborg, 1995, Toy Biz
  NM $4 MIP $15

Caliban, 1995, Toy Biz
  NM $4 MIP $15

Cameron Hodge, 1995, Toy Biz
  NM $4 MIP $15

Captive Sabretooth, 1995, Toy Biz
  NM $4 MIP $15

Colossus, 1991, Toy Biz
  NM $10 MIP $20

Colossus, 1993, Toy Biz
  NM $6 MIP $15

Colossus, 1996, Toy Biz
  NM $3 MIP $8

Corsair, 1995, Toy Biz
  NM $3 MIP $15

Cyclops, 1996, Toy Biz
  NM $3 MIP $8

Cyclops I, blue, 1991, Toy Biz
  NM $10 MIP $20

Cyclops I, stripes, 1991, Toy Biz
  NM $5 MIP $15

Cyclops II, 1993, Toy Biz
  NM $5 MIP $15

Deadpool, 1995, Toy Biz
  NM $6 MIP $15

Domino, 1995, Toy Biz
  NM $5 MIP $15

Forge, 1992, Toy Biz
  NM $10 MIP $22

Gambit, 1992, Toy Biz
  NM $10 MIP $20

Gambit, 1993, Toy Biz
  NM $7 MIP $15

Gladiator, 1995, Toy Biz
  NM $3 MIP $15

Havok, 1995, Toy Biz
  NM $4 MIP $15

Ice Man, 1992, Toy Biz
  NM $20 MIP $45

Ice Man II, 1995, Toy Biz
  NM $4 MIP $15

Juggernaut, 1991, Toy Biz
  NM $10 MIP $25

Juggernaut, 1993, Toy Biz
  NM $4 MIP $15

Lady Deathstrike, 1996, Toy Biz
  NM $3 MIP $10

Magneto, 1996, Toy Biz
  NM $3 MIP $8

Magneto I, 1991, Toy Biz
  NM $6 MIP $15

Magneto II, 1992, Toy Biz
  NM $5 MIP $15

Morph, 1994, Toy Biz
  NM $10 MIP $20

Mr. Sinister, 1992, Toy Biz
  NM $7 MIP $15

Nightcrawler, 1993, Toy Biz
  NM $10 MIP $25

Nimrod, 1995, Toy Biz
  NM $5 MIP $15

Omega Red, 1993, Toy Biz
  NM $6 MIP $15

Omega Red II, 1996, Toy Biz
  NM $3 MIP $8

Phoenix, 1995, Toy Biz
  NM $10 MIP $25

Polaris, 1996, Toy Biz
  NM $3 MIP $8

Professor X, 1993, Toy Biz
  NM $6 MIP $15

Raza, 1994, Toy Biz
  NM $3 MIP $15

Sabretooth, 1996, Toy Biz
  NM $3 MIP $8

Sauron, 1992, Toy Biz
  NM $3 MIP $15

Savage Land Wolverine, 1996, Toy Biz
  NM $3 MIP $8

Spiral, 1995, Toy Biz
  NM $4 MIP $15

Storm, 1991, Toy Biz
  NM $20 MIP $40

Strong Guy, 1993, Toy Biz
  NM $3 MIP $15

Sunfire, 1995, Toy Biz
  NM $4 MIP $15

Trevor Fitzroy, 1994, Toy Biz
  NM $3 MIP $15

Tusk, 1992, Toy Biz
  NM $5 MIP $15

Warstar, 1995, Toy Biz
  NM $6 MIP $15

Weapon X, 1996, Toy Biz
  NM $3 MIP $8

Wolverine, 1996, Toy Biz
  NM $3 MIP $10

Wolverine Fang, 1995, Toy Biz
  NM $4 MIP $15

Wolverine I, 1991, Toy Biz
  NM $10 MIP $20

Wolverine I, 1993, Toy Biz
  NM $7 MIP $15

Wolverine II, 1992, Toy Biz
  NM $7 MIP $15

Wolverine III, 1992, Toy Biz
  NM $12 MIP $25

Wolverine V, 1993, Toy Biz
  NM $7 MIP $15

Wolverine, space armor, 1995, Toy Biz
  NM $6 MIP $15

Wolverine, street clothes, 1994, Toy Biz
  NM $5 MIP $15

X-Cutioner, 1995, Toy Biz
  NM $4 MIP $15

X-MEN (TOY BIZ, 1996-98)

AGE OF APOCALYPSE, 5" FIGURES, 1996

Apocalypse, Removable Armor and Transforming Limbs, 1996
NM $3   MIP $8

Cyclops, Cybernetic Guardian and Laser Blaster, 1996
NM $2   MIP $6

Gambit, Blast-throwing Action, 1996
NM $2   MIP $6

Magneto, Removable Helmet and Shrapnel, 1996
NM $2   MIP $6

Sabretooth, Wild Child Sidekick Figure, 1996
NM $2   MIP $6

Weapon X, Interchangeable Weaponry, 1996
NM $2   MIP $6

CLASSICS, LIGHT-UP WEAPONS, 5" FIGURES, 1996

Gambit, Light-up Plasma Energy Weapon, 1996
NM $3   MIP $10

Juggernaut, Light-up Jewel Weapon, 1996
NM $3   MIP $10

Nightcrawler, Light-up Sword, 1996
NM $3   MIP $10

Psylock, light-up Psychic Knife, 1996
NM $3   MIP $10

Wolverine Stealth, Light-up Plasma Weapon, 1996
NM $3   MIP $10

MISSLE FLYERS, 5" FIGURES, 1997

Apocalypse, Trap-door Chest, 1997
NM $3   MIP $8

Bishop, Fold-out Armor Wing Blasters, 1997
NM $3   MIP $8

Cable, Attack Wings, 1997
NM $3   MIP $8

Shard, Spring Loaded Firing Wing Extensions, 1997
NM $3   MIP $8

Wolverine, Head Launching Bird of Prey, 1997
NM $3   MIP $8

MONSTER ARMOR, 5" FIGURES, 1997

Cyclops with Snap-on Cyclaw Armor, 1997
NM $2   MIP $6

Mr. Sinister with Snap-on Cyber Tech Armor, 1997
NM $2   MIP $6

Mystique with Snap-on She-Beast Armor, 1997
NM $2   MIP $6

Rogue with Snap-on Leech Bat Armor, 1997
NM $2   MIP $6

Wolverine with Snap-on Fangor Armor, 1997
NM $2   MIP $6

NEW MUTANTS, 5" FIGURES, 1998

Magik, 1998
NM $2   MIP $6

Warlock, 1998
NM $2   MIP $6

Wolfsbane, 1998
NM $2   MIP $6

NINJA FORCE, 5" FIGURES, 1997

Dark Nemesis with Spear Shooting Staff, 1997
NM $3   MIP $8

Ninja Sabretooth with Clip-on Claw Armor, 1997
NM $3   MIP $8

Ninja Wolverine with Warrior Assault Gear, 1997
NM $3   MIP $8

Psylocke with Extending Power Sword, 1997
NM $3   MIP $8

Space Ninja Deathbird with Fold-Out Ninja Wings, 1997
NM $3   MIP $8

ONSLAUGHT, 6" FIGURES, 1997

Apocalypse Rising, Ozymandias, 1997
NM $3   MIP $11

Jean Grey, Psychic Claw, 1997
NM $3   MIP $11

Onslaught, Ultimate Power Armor, 1997
NM $3   MIP $10

Wolverine Unleashed, Franklin Richards, 1997
NM $3   MIP $10

ROBOT FIGHTERS, 5" FIGURES, 1997

Cyclops, Apocalypse Droid with Gattling Gun Arm, 1997
NM $3   MIP $8

Gambit, Attack Robot Droid with Projectile Missile, 1997
NM $3   MIP $8

Jubilee, Grabbing Sentinel Hand with Projectile Finger, 1997
NM $4   MIP $12

Storm, Spinning Weather Station with Lightning Projectile, 1997
NM $4   MIP $12

Wolverine, Slashing Sabretooth Droid with Missile Claw, 1997
NM $3   MIP $8

SAVAGE LAND, 5" FIGURES, 1997

Angel with Wing Flapping Sauron-Dino, 1997
NM $2   MIP $6

Kazar with Jumping Zabu Tiger, 1997
NM $2   MIP $6

Magneto with Water Spitting Amphibious, 1997
NM $2   MIP $6

Savage Storm with Head Ramming Colossus Dino, 1997
NM $2   MIP $6

Savage Wolverine with Jaw Chomping Crawler-Rex, 1997
NM $2   MIP $6

SECRET WEAPON FORCE BATTLE BASES, 5" FIGURES, 1998

Cyclops with War Tank Blaster, 1998
NM $2   MIP $6

Jean Grey with Catapult Tank Blaster, 1998
NM $2   MIP $6

Magneto Battle Base, 1998
NM $2   MIP $6

Omega with Spinning Rocket Blaster, 1998
NM $2   MIP $6

Wolverine Battle Base, 1998
NM $2   MIP $6

Wolverine with Claw Cannon Blaster, 1998
NM $2   MIP $6

SECRET WEAPON FORCE FLYING FIGHTERS, 5" FIGURES, 1998

Cyclops with High-Flying Hazard Gear, 1998
NM $3   MIP $8

Jean Grey with Fire Bird Flyer, 1998
NM $3   MIP $8

Maggot with Expanding Assault Wings, 1998
NM $3   MIP $8

Mr. Sinister with Bio-Tech Attack Wings, 1998
NM $3   MIP $8

SECRET WEAPON FORCE POWER SLAMMERS, 5" FIGURES, 1998

Gambit with Rapid Fire Card Cannon Slammer, 1998
NM $2   MIP $6

Master Mold with Rapid Fire Sentinels, 1998
NM $2   MIP $6

Rogue with Double Barrel Slammer, 1998
NM $3   MIP $8

Wolverine with Rapid Fire Disk Slammer, 1998
NM $2   MIP $6

SECRET WEAPON FORCE SHAPE SHIFTERS, 7" FIGURES, 1998

Juggernaut forms into Titanic Tank, 1998
NM $2   MIP $6

Morph forms into Mega Missile, 1998
NM $2   MIP $6

Wolverine forms into Mutant Wolf, 1998
NM $2   MIP $6

SECRET WEAPON FORCE SUPER SHOOTER, 5" FIGURES, 1998

Apocalypse, 1998
NM $3   MIP $10

Beast, 1998
NM $3   MIP $8

Colossus, 1998
NM $3   MIP $8

Wolverine, 1998
NM $3   MIP $8

SHATTERSHOT, 5" FIGURES, 1996

Age of Apocalypse Beast, Wind-up Chain Saw, 1996
NM $2   MIP $6

Archangel, Wing-flapping Action, 1996
NM $2   MIP $6

Colossus, Super Punch Gauntlets, 1996
NM $2   MIP $6

Lady Death Strike, Transforming Reaver Armor, 1996
NM $2   MIP $6

Patch Wolverine, Total Assault Arsenal, 1996
NM $2   MIP $6

SPECIAL EDITION SERIES, 12" FIGURES, 1998

Gambit, 1998
NM $8   MIP $25

Storm, 1998
NM $8   MIP $25

Wolverine, 1998
NM $8   MIP $25

X-MEN 2099 (TOY BIZ, 1996)

5" FIGURES

Bloodhawk, 1996
NM $2   MIP $6

Breakdown, Dominick Sidekick Figure, 1996
NM $2   MIP $6

Brimstone Love, 1996
NM $2   MIP $6

Halloween Jack, 1996
NM $2   MIP $6

Junkpile, Snap-on Battle Armor, 1996
NM $2   MIP $6

La Lunatica, Futuristic Jai-Lai, 1996
NM $2   MIP $6

Meanstreak, 1996
NM $2   MIP $6

Metalhead, 1996
NM $2   MIP $6

Shadow Dancer, 1996
NM $2   MIP $6

Skullfire, Glowing Fire Skeleton, 1996
NM $2   MIP $6

X-MEN VS. STREET FIGHTER (TOY BIZ, 1998)

5" FIGURES

Apocalypse vs. Dhalism, 1998
NM $2   MIP $6

Cyclops vs. M. Bison, 1998
NM $5   MIP $12

Gambit vs. Cammy, 1998
NM $2   MIP $6

Juggernaut vs. Chunu, 1998
NM $2   MIP $6

Magneto vs. Ryu, 1998
NM $5   MIP $12

Rogue vs. Zangief, 1998
NM $2   MIP $6

Sabretooth vs. Ken, 1998
NM $5   MIP $12

Wolverine vs. Akuma, 1998
NM $5   MIP $12

X-MEN/X-FORCE (TOY BIZ, 1991-96)

DELUXE 10" FIGURES

Cable, 1995
NM $8   MIP $18

Kane, 1995
NM $8   MIP $18

Shatterstar, 1995
NM $8   MIP $18

FIGURES

Arctic Armor Cable, 1996, Toy Biz
NM $3   MIP $8

Avalanche, 1995, Toy Biz
NM $3   MIP $8

Black Tom, 1994, Toy Biz
NM $5   MIP $15

Black Tom, 1995, Toy Biz
NM $5   MIP $15

Blob, The, 1995, Toy Biz
NM $5   MIP $15

Bonebreaker, 1994, Toy Biz
NM $3   MIP $15

Bridge, 1992, Toy Biz
NM $5   MIP $15

Brood, 1993, Toy Biz
NM $4   MIP $15

Cable Cyborg, 1995, Toy Biz
NM $3   MIP $8

Cable I, 1992, Toy Biz
NM $6   MIP $15

Cable II, 1993, Toy Biz
NM $4   MIP $15

Cable III, 1993, Toy Biz
NM $4   MIP $15

Cable IV, 1994, Toy Biz
NM $3   MIP $15

Cable Stealth, 1996, Toy Biz
NM $3   MIP $8

Cable V, 1994, Toy Biz
NM $5   MIP $15

(KP Photo)

Cannonball, pink, 1993, Toy Biz
NM $15   MIP $35

Cannonball, purple, 1993, Toy Biz
NM $10   MIP $20

Commando, 1995, Toy Biz
NM $3   MIP $8

Deadpool, 1992, Toy Biz
NM $15   MIP $35

Deadpool, 1995, Toy Biz
NM $3   MIP $10

Domino, 1995, Toy Biz
NM $3   MIP $10

Exodus, 1995, Toy Biz
NM $3   MIP $8

Forearm, 1992, Toy Biz
NM $10   MIP $20

Genesis, 1995, Toy Biz
NM $3   MIP $8

Gideon, 1992, Toy Biz
NM $5   MIP $15

ACTION FIGURES

Grizzly, 1993, Toy Biz
NM $5   MIP $15

Kane I, 1992, Toy Biz
NM $7   MIP $15

Kane II, 1993, Toy Biz
NM $4   MIP $15

Killspree, 1994, Toy Biz
NM $7   MIP $15

Killspree II,, 1996, Toy Biz
NM $4   MIP $8

Krule, 1993, Toy Biz
NM $3   MIP $15

Kylun, 1994, Toy Biz
NM $3   MIP $15

Longshot, 1994, Toy Biz
NM $7   MIP $15

Mojo, 1995, Toy Biz
NM $3   MIP $8

Nimrod, 1995, Toy Biz
NM $3   MIP $8

Pyro, 1994, Toy Biz
NM $5   MIP $15

Quark, 1994, Toy Biz
NM $3   MIP $15

Random, 1994, Toy Biz
NM $3   MIP $15

Rictor, 1994, Toy Biz
NM $3   MIP $15

Rogue, 1994, Toy Biz
NM $10   MIP $25

Sabretooth I, 1992, Toy Biz
NM $7   MIP $15

Sabretooth II, 1994, Toy Biz
NM $6   MIP $15

Shatterstar I, 1992, Toy Biz
NM $4   MIP $12

Shatterstar II, 1994, Toy Biz
NM $4   MIP $12

Shatterstar III, 1996, Toy Biz
NM $3   MIP $8

Silver Samurai, 1994, Toy Biz
NM $3   MIP $15

Slayback, 1994, Toy Biz
NM $3   MIP $15

Stryfe, 1992, Toy Biz
NM $10   MIP $25

Sunspot, 1994, Toy Biz
NM $3   MIP $15

Urban Assault, 1995, Toy Biz
NM $3   MIP $8

Warpath I, 1992, Toy Biz
NM $7   MIP $15

Warpath II, 1994, Toy Biz
NM $5   MIP $15

X-Treme, 1994, Toy Biz
NM $5   MIP $15

X-MEN: EVOLUTION (TOY BIZ, 2001-02)

5" FIGURES

Battle Ravaged Wolverine, 2001-02, Toy Biz, Series 3, w/ Sabretooth
NM $5   MIP $10

Cyclops, 2001-02, Toy Biz, Series 1
NM $5   MIP $10

Juggernaut, 2001-02, Toy Biz, Series 3
NM $5   MIP $10

Logan, 2001-02, Toy Biz, w/ hat and "X" base
NM $4   MIP $8

Magneto, 2001-02, Toy Biz, Series 3
NM $4   MIP $8

Nightcrawler, 2001-02, Toy Biz, Series 1
NM $5   MIP $10

Nightcrawler II, 2001-02, Toy Biz, Series 3
NM $4   MIP $8

Ninja Wolverine, 2001-02, Toy Biz, Series 2
NM $5   MIP $10

Sabretooth, 2001-02, Toy Biz, Series 1
NM $5   MIP $10

Spyke, 2001-02, Toy Biz, Series 2
NM $4   MIP $8

Storm, 2001-02, Toy Biz, Series 2
NM $5   MIP $10

The Blob, 2001-02, Toy Biz, Series 2
NM $4   MIP $8

Toad, 2001-02, Toy Biz, Series 1
NM $4   MIP $8

Wolverine, 2001-02, Toy Biz, Series 1
NM $5   MIP $10

8" FIGURES

Cyclops, 2001-02, Toy Biz
NM $6   MIP $12

Toad, 2001-02, Toy Biz
NM $6   MIP $12

Wolverine, 2001-02, Toy Biz
NM $6   MIP $12

VEHICLES

Logan Battle Cycle, 2001-02, Toy Biz, w/ Logan
NM $5   MIP $10

Sabretooth Battle Cycle, 2001-02, Toy Biz, w/ Sabretooth
NM $5   MIP $10

Wolverine Battle Cycle, 2001-02, Toy Biz, w/ Wolverine
NM $5   MIP $10

X-MEN: THE MOVIE (TOY BIZ, 2000)

FIGURES

Cyclops, 2000, Toy Biz
NM $3   MIP $10

Jean Grey, 2000, Toy Biz
NM $5   MIP $12

Logan, 2000, Toy Biz
NM $3   MIP $10

Magneto, 2000, Toy Biz
NM $3   MIP $10

Mystique, 2000, Toy Biz
NM $3   MIP $10

Professor X, 2000, Toy Biz
NM $4   MIP $12

Rogue, 2000, Toy Biz
NM $3   MIP $10

Sabretooth, 2000, Toy Biz
NM $3   MIP $10

Storm, 2000, Toy Biz
NM $4   MIP $12

Toad, 2000, Toy Biz
NM $3   MIP $10

Wolverine, 2000, Toy Biz
NM $3   MIP $10

TWO PACKS

Logan and Rogue, 2000, Toy Biz
NM $5   MIP $15

Magneto and Logan, 2000, Toy Biz
NM $5   MIP $15

Wolverine and Sabre, 2000, Toy Biz
NM $5   MIP $15

X-MEN: X2, X-MEN UNITED (TOY BIZ, 2003)

12" FIGURES

Nightcrawler, 2003, Toy Biz
NM $6   MIP $12

Wolverine, 2003, Toy Biz
NM $6   MIP $12

5"3 FIGURES

Cyclops, 2003, Toy Biz
NM $4   MIP $8

Logan, 2003, Toy Biz
NM $4   MIP $8

Nightcrawler, 2003, Toy Biz
NM $4   MIP $8

Wolverine, 2003, Toy Biz
NM $4   MIP $8

VEHICLES

X-Jet, 2003, Toy Biz, w/ Wolverine figure
NM $7   MIP $15

YELLOW SUBMARINE (McFARLANE, 1999-2004)

SERIES 1, 1999

George with Yellow Submarine, 1999, McFarlane
NM $3   MIP $10

John with Jeremy, 1999, McFarlane
NM $3   MIP $10

Paul with Captain Fred, 1999, McFarlane
    NM $3   **MIP** $10

Paul with Glove and Love base, 1999, McFarlane
    NM $4   **MIP** $12

Ringo with Blue Meanie, 1999, McFarlane
    NM $3   **MIP** $10

SERIES 2, SGT. PEPPER'S LONELY HEARTS CLUB BAND, 2000

George with Snapping Turk, 2000, McFarlane
    NM $3   **MIP** $8

(McFarlane Toys)
John with Bulldog, 2000, McFarlane
    NM $3   **MIP** $8

(McFarlane Toys)
Paul with Sucking Monster, 2000, McFarlane
    NM $3   **MIP** $9

(McFarlane Toys)
Ringo with Apple Bonker, 2000, McFarlane
    NM $3   **MIP** $8

SERIES 3, 2004

George with Blue Meanie, 2004, McFarlane
    NM $3   **MIP** $10

John with Love and Glove base, 2004, McFarlane
    NM $3   **MIP** $10

Paul with Jeremy, 2004, McFarlane
    NM $3   **MIP** $10

Ringo with Yellow Submarine, 2004, McFarlane
    NM $3   **MIP** $10

YOUNGBLOOD (MCFARLANE, 1995)

FIGURES

Crypt, 1995, McFarlane
    NM $5   **MIP** $10

Die Hard, 1995, McFarlane
    NM $4   **MIP** $8

Dutch, 1995, McFarlane
    NM $4   **MIP** $8

Sentinel, 1995, McFarlane
    NM $4   **MIP** $8

Shaft, 1995, McFarlane
    NM $4   **MIP** $8

Troll, 1995, McFarlane
    NM $10   **MIP** $22

ZORRO (GABRIEL, 1982)

FIGURES

Amigo, 1982, Gabriel
    NM $10   **MIP** $22

Captain Ramon, 1982, Gabriel
    NM $10   **MIP** $22

Picaro, 1982, Gabriel
    NM $15   **MIP** $32

Sergeant Gonzales, 1982, Gabriel
    NM $10   **MIP** $22

Tempest, 1982, Gabriel
    NM $10   **MIP** $22

Zorro, 1982, Gabriel
    NM $15   **MIP** $22

Advertising Toys

By Karen O'Brien

Advertising characters are a part of our daily lives. Much the way athletic teams adopt mascots, advertisers create endearing characters to represent everything from breakfast cereal to tires. In addition to product packaging, they appear in television commercials, radio spots, print ads, and on billboards. Some of the ad characters of today have been around for more than 100 years. Aunt Jemima, known for her pancake mixes and maple syrups, is a good example. She was first created for advertising pancake flour at the 1893 Columbian Exposition in Chicago, Illinois. Nancy Green, an African-American woman from Chicago, was hired to portray Aunt Jemima and demonstrate the pancake mix at the Fair. She was such a hit that police had to control the crowds. Soon after, a paper doll was released as a promotional item. The character is such a part of Americana, that parent company Quaker Oats once issued a press release to alert the country that Aunt Jemima was receiving a more "modern" hairdo.

Many companies followed the trend to adopt lovable characters. Kellogg's has long delighted collectors with a wide variety of premiums. A 1920s Kellogg's premium was a set of Goldilocks and the Three Bears dolls where the consumer received a piece of fabric with the image of the doll printed and was to cut, stuff, and sew the doll themselves. Decades before they became cartoons, cereal pixies Snap, Crackle, and Pop were first offered as make-your-own-dolls in the early 1940s.

Food-related characters seem to be the most popular with collectors. Although several popular characters have nothing to do with food, for example, Reddy Kilowatt (Reddy Communications), Bibendum a.k.a. The Michelin Man (Michelin Tires), and Speedy (Alka-Seltzer), food-related characters including, Elsie the Cow (Borden's dairy products), Quisp (Quaker Oats), and Mr. Peanut (Planter's Peanuts), dominate the collecting scene.

2006 TRENDS

For 2006, keep an eye on vinyl, plastic, and PVC figures from the 1950s and 1960s. Popular at shows and online auctions, their affordability and availability allow collectors to amass a variety of their favorite characters without spending a small fortune. Popular characters are also holding their value. The Pillsbury Doughboy,

Cracker Jack, Frankenberry, Boo Berry, Count Chocula, Tony the Tiger, the Jolly Green Giant are recognized by multiple generations and that longevity will ensure their future collectibility.

Also keep an eye on crossover collectibles like the plastic Roy Rogers mug once offered by Quaker Oats.

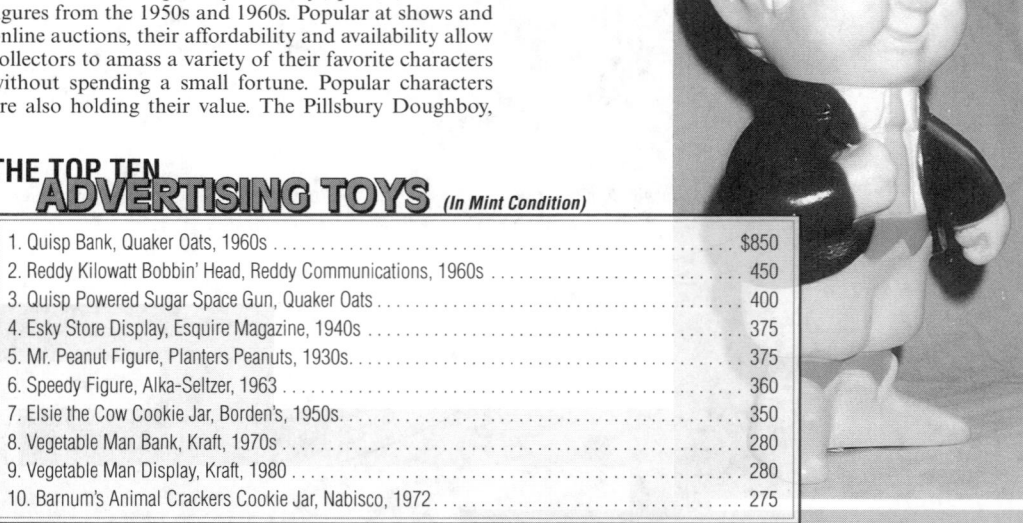

THE TOP TEN ADVERTISING TOYS *(In Mint Condition)*

1. Quisp Bank, Quaker Oats, 1960s	$850
2. Reddy Kilowatt Bobbin' Head, Reddy Communications, 1960s	450
3. Quisp Powered Sugar Space Gun, Quaker Oats	400
4. Esky Store Display, Esquire Magazine, 1940s	375
5. Mr. Peanut Figure, Planters Peanuts, 1930s	375
6. Speedy Figure, Alka-Seltzer, 1963	360
7. Elsie the Cow Cookie Jar, Borden's, 1950s	350
8. Vegetable Man Bank, Kraft, 1970s	280
9. Vegetable Man Display, Kraft, 1980	280
10. Barnum's Animal Crackers Cookie Jar, Nabisco, 1972	275

7-ELEVEN

Big Bite Figures, 1987, 7-Eleven, 3-1/2"
hot dog men holding snacks
EX $10   **NM** $15   **MIP** $25

7-UP

Spot Wind-Up, 1990, 7-Up, 3" red circular
figure w/sunglasses
EX $8   **NM** $12   **MIP** $15

AIR INDIA

Air India Man Figure, 1973, Air India,
4-1/2" statue of man wearing turban
standing on flying carpet
EX $10   **NM** $20   **MIP** $25

ALKA-SELTZER

Speedy, 2003, Funko, Wacky Wobbler,
#6012
EX $3   **NM** $7   **MIP** $12

Speedy Figure, 1963, Alka-Seltzer, 5-1/2"
vinyl boy holding Alka-Seltzer figure
EX $280   **NM** $310   **MIP** $360

ALPO

Dan the Dog Cookie Jar, 1980s, Alpo, 7"
ceramic gray and white sheep dog
EX $35   **NM** $50   **MIP** $70

Dan the Dog Wind-Up, 1979, Alpo, 3"
wind-up figure of shaggy gray dog
walking on his front paws
EX $10   **NM** $15   **MIP** $25

AMERICAN HOME FOOD PRODUCTS

Marky Maypo Figure, 1960, American
Home Food Products, 9" vinyl figure
EX $35   **NM** $45   **MIP** $55

AUNT JEMIMA SYRUP

Aunt Jemima Doll, 1950s, Aunt Jemima
Syrup, 13" cloth doll wearing red
checkered dress
EX $60   **NM** $70   **MIP** $90

Salt & Pepper Shakers, Aunt Jemima Syrup,
Aunt Jemima and Uncle Mose, plastic
EX $15   **NM** $30   **MIP** $50

BASKIN ROBBINS

Pinky the Spoon Figure, 1993, Baskin
Robbins, 5" bendable figure
EX $4   **NM** $5   **MIP** $10

BAZOOKA

Bazooka Joe, 2003, Funko, Wacky
Wobbler, #6028, 8"
EX $3   **NM** $7   **MIP** $12

Bazooka Joe Doll, 1973, Bazooka, 19"
plush boy pirate
EX $20   **NM** $25   **MIP** $30

BEATRICE FOODS

Clark Bar Figure, 1960s, Beatrice Foods,
8-1/2" vinyl boy holding a Clark bar
wearing a striped shirt
EX $200   **NM** $225   **MIP** $275

BEECH-NUT

Fruit Stripe Gum Figure, 1967, Beech-Nut,
7-1/2" bendable man shaped like a pack
of gum riding a motorcycle
EX $150   **NM** $200   **MIP** $225

BOB'S BIG BOY

Big Boy, Funko, Wacky Wobbler, 8"
EX $3   **NM** $7   **MIP** $15

Big Boy Bank, Funko, Bank w/ black or blue
shoes, 8"
EX $3   **NM** $7   **MIP** $15

Dolly Doll, 1978, Bob's Big Boy, 14" cloth
girl doll w/Dolly nametag
EX $15   **NM** $25   **MIP** $30

Nodder, 1960s
EX $15   **NM** $30   **MIP** $45

Nugget Doll, 1978, Bob's Big Boy, 10"
cloth dog doll w/"Nugget" on collar
EX $15   **NM** $25   **MIP** $30

BORDEN'S

Elsie the Cow Cookie Jar, 1950s,
Borden's, 12" Elsie w/her head popping
out of barrel
EX $275   **NM** $300   **MIP** $350

Elsie the Cow Doll, 1950s, Borden's, 12"
plush cow that moos when shaken
EX $55   **NM** $75   **MIP** $90

Elsie the Cow Lamp, 1947, Borden's,
electric lamp, ceramic
EX $150   **NM** $175   **MIP** $225

Elsie the Cow pull toy, 1944, Wood
Commodities Co., wooden, "The Cow
that Jumped over the Moon"
EX $25   **NM** $50   **MIP** $100

BRADFORD HOUSE RESTAURANTS

Bucky Bradford Figure, 1960s, Bradford
House Restaurants, 9-1/2" blond
pilgrim boy holding dish that reads "It's
Yum Yum Time"
EX $27   **NM** $33   **MIP** $40

BURGER KING

Burger King doll, 1980, Knickerbocker,
"Magical Burger King", 20"
EX $10   **NM** $20   **MIP** $40

Burger King stuffed toy, 1972, smiling,
beardless, 15"
EX $7   **NM** $15   **MIP** $32

Burger King stuffed toy, 1977, hands on
hips, w/ beard, 13"
EX $10   **NM** $20   **MIP** $35

CAMPBELL

Campbell's Kid Doll, 1950s, Campbell, 9-
1/2" vinyl jointed cheerleader wearing a
white shirt w/"C" in middle
EX $45   **NM** $65   **MIP** $80

Campbell's Kid Doll, 1973, Campbell, 16"
blonde girl w/red hair
EX $25   **NM** $35   **MIP** $40

Campbell's Kid Figure, 1950s, Campbell,
7" boy chef doll w/"C"on hat and spoon
in his hand
EX $40   **NM** $50   **MIP** $65

Campbell's Kid Figure, 1970s, Campbell,
7" vinyl Campbell boy w/blue overalls
EX $30   **NM** $40   **MIP** $50

Christmas Ornament, 1989, Campbell,
ball ornament w/picture of Campbell Kid
dressed as Santa
EX $5   **NM** $10   **MIP** $15

Wizard of O's Figure, 1978, Campbell,
7-1/2" vinyl wizard w/Spaghetti O's on
his hat and bow tie
EX $20   **NM** $30   **MIP** $35

CHAMPION AUTO STORES

Champ Man Figure, 1991, Champion Auto
Stores, 6" bendable man; head is a flag
EX $7   **NM** $10   **MIP** $15

CHICKEN DELIGHT INTERNATIONAL

Chicken Delight Bank, 1960s, Chicken
Delight International, 6" yellow and red
chicken holding a tray of biscuits
EX $85   **NM** $125   **MIP** $150

CHIQUITA

Chiquita Banana Doll, 1974, Chiquita, 16"
plush dancing banana w/fruit on its head
EX $18   **NM** $20   **MIP** $25

COCA-COLA

Sprite - Lucky Lymon, 1990, Coca-Cola,
7-1/2", vinyl, talking doll
EX $15   **NM** $25   **MIP** $35

Sprite Boy, 2003, Funko, Wacky Wobbler,
#5065
EX $3   **NM** $7   **MIP** $12

CRACKER JACK

Cracker Jack and Bingo, 1996, Borden, 16"
doll, 100th anniversary of Cracker Jack
EX n/a   **NM** $20   **MIP** $40

Cracker Jack and Bingo, 2000, Funko,
Wacky Wobbler
EX $3   **NM** $12   **MIP** $25

Cracker Jack Doll, 1974, Borden, 15" plush
sailor holding small box of Cracker
Jacks snacks
EX $15   **NM** $20   **MIP** $25

Cracker Jack Doll, 1980, Vogue Dolls,
vinyl and cloth
EX $7   **NM** $20   **MIP** $40

CREST TOOTHPASTE

Sparkle Telephone, 1980s, Crest
Toothpaste, 11" blue and silver
snowman-type character
EX $27   **NM** $38   **MIP** $44

CURAD

Taped Crusader Figure, 1977, Curad,
7-1/2" male cartoon superhero
EX $65   **NM** $75   **MIP** $85

CURITY

Miss Curity Display, 1950s, Curity, 18"
plastic store display of a nurse on a base
EX $125   NM $150   MIP $185

DEL MONTE

Clown Bank, Del Monte, colorful, smiling
clown
EX $6   NM $11   MIP $22

DOUGLAS OIL COMPANY

Freddy Fast Figure, 1976, Douglas Oil
Company, 7" freckled face boy; hat says
"Freddy Fast"
EX $90   NM $110   MIP $130

DOW BRANDS

Scrubbing Bubble Brush, 1980s, Dow
Brands, 3-1/2" light blue scrub brush
EX $10   NM $12   MIP $15

ESQUIRE MAGAZINE

Esky Store Display, 1940s, Esquire
Magazine, 11" old man dressed in a
tuxedo standing on an Esquire magazine
EX $300   NM $350   MIP $375

ESSO

Esso Tiger Figure, 1960s, Esso, 8-1/2"
plastic tiger
EX $20   NM $25   MIP $30
Esso Tiger Garbage Can, 1970s, Esso, 10"
metal garbage can w/picture of the Esso
tiger
EX $15   NM $20   MIP $30
Little Oil Drop bank, 1958, plastic, red or
white, 6-1/2"
EX $25   NM $50   MIP $100

EVEREADY BATTERIES

Energizer Bunny Plush, Eveready
Batteries, 22" plush
EX $17   NM $42   MIP $68
Eveready Cat Bank, 1981, Eveready
Batteries, black cat w/Eveready battery
on side
EX $10   NM $15   MIP $20

FACIT ADDING MACHINES

Facit Man Figure, 1964, Facit Adding
Machines, 4" man wearing yellow outfit
w/black wizard hat
EX $20   NM $25   MIP $30

FLORIDA CITRUS DEPARTMENT

Florida Orange Bird Hat, 1970s, Florida
Citrus Department, child's-size hat
w/visor, pictures Orange Bird on front
and back
EX $10   NM $15   MIP $20
Florida Orange Bird Nodder, 1970s,
Florida Citrus Department, 7" plastic
EX $50   NM $60   MIP $75
Florida Orange Bird Stick Pin, 1980s,
Florida Citrus Department, metal,
depicts the Florida Orange Bird
EX $5   NM $10   MIP $15

FUNNY FACE DRINK

Choo Choo Cherry Ramp Walker, 1971,
Funny Face Drink, 3" round, red figure
w/conductor's hat
EX $73   NM $95   MIP $120
Funny Face Mugs, 1969, Funny Face Drink,
3" mugs of Funny Face characters, each
EX $9   NM $13   MIP $17
Goofy Grape Pitcher, 1973, Funny Face
Drink, 10" pitcher of smiling, purple
character wearing lime green captain's hat
EX $75   NM $95   MIP $125
Lefty Lemon Frisbee, 1980s, Funny Face
Drink, plastic w/picture of Lefty Lemon
EX $5   NM $10   MIP $12

GENERAL MILLS

Boo Berry Bank, Funko, bank, no moving
parts, 8"
EX $3   NM $7   MIP $15
Boo Berry Figure, 1975, General Mills,
7-1/2" white and light blue ghost w/hat
and bow tie
EX $78   NM $97   MIP $124
Cereal Card Game, 1981, General Mills,
card game w/different cereal characters
EX $10   NM $15   MIP $20
Count Chocula, 2000, Funko, Wacky Wobbler
EX $3   NM $7   MIP $15
Count Chocula Figure, 1975, General
Mills, 7-1/2" vinyl vampire
EX $70   NM $85   MIP $110
Franken Berry, 2000, Funko, Wacky Wobbler
EX $3   NM $7   MIP $15

(Toy Shop File Photo)

Frankenberry Figure, 1975, General Mills,
8" vinyl pink Frankenstein
EX $72   NM $100   MIP $140
Fruit Brute Figure, 1975, General Mills, 8"
vinyl werewolf w/striped shirt
EX $75   NM $90   MIP $120
Lucky Charms, 2000, Funko, Wacky Wobbler
EX $3   NM $7   MIP $15
Lucky Charms Leprechaun Doll, 1978,
General Mills, 17" plush
EX $20   NM $25   MIP $30
Monster Cereal Pencil Case, 1980s,
General Mills, 8" x 5", vinyl case

featuring Count Chocula, Frankenberry
and Boo Berry
EX $10   NM $15   MIP $20
Trix Rabbit, 2000, Funko, Wacky Wobbler
EX $3   NM $7   MIP $12
Trix Rabbit Figure, 1977, General Mills, 9"
vinyl white rabbit
EX $32   NM $44   MIP $56

GERBER PRODUCTS

Gerber Boy figure, 1985, Gerber Products,
8" vinyl boy w/baseball cap turned
sideways that reads "I'm a Gerber Kid"
EX $25   NM $27   MIP $30

GOOD HUMOR

Good Humor Bar, 1975, Good Humor, 8"
vinyl ice cream bar w/a bite out of it
EX $175   NM $200   MIP $275

GRANDMA'S COOKIES

Grandma Bank, 1988, Grandma's
Cookies, 7-1/2" hard plastic Grandma
wearing a blue dress
EX $25   NM $30   MIP $35

H.P. HOOD

Harry Hood Figure, 1981, H.P. Hood,
7-1/2" delivery man w/"Hood"
inscription on chest
EX $55   NM $70   MIP $80

HEINZ

Aristocrat Tomato, 1939, Heinz, 6"
Aristocrat Tomato bust wearing top hat
EX $150   NM $200   MIP $225

HERSHEY'S

(Toy Shop File Photo)

Hershey's Chocolate Figure, 1987,
Hershey's, 4-1/2" bendable candy bar
shaped like a man
EX $6   NM $9   MIP $12

HOSTESS

Twinkie the Kid, 2000, Funko, Wacky
Wobbler
EX $3   NM $7   MIP $12

HUSH PUPPIES

Hush Puppies Figure, 1970s, Hush
Puppies, 8" tan and brown basset hound
EX $20   NM $25   MIP $35

ICEE

ICEE Bear Figure, 1970s, ICEE, 8" vinyl polar bear drinking an ICEE
EX $30   NM $35   MIP $40

INSTY-PRINTS

Insty-Prints Wizard Figure, 1980s, Insty-Prints, 9" vinyl figure of wizard dressed in red outfit w/moons and stars
EX $75   NM $100   MIP $135

IRON FIREMAN FURNACE

Iron Fireman Figure, 1943, Iron Fireman Furnace, 5" metal man shoveling coal
EX $65   NM $75   MIP $85

KAHN'S WIENERS

Beefy Frank Figure, 1980, Kahn's Wieners, 5-1/2" vinyl figural hot dog mustard dispenser
EX $15   NM $18   MIP $22

KEEBLER COMPANY

(Toy Shop File Photo)

Ernie the Keebler Elf Figure, 1974, Keebler Company, 7" figure of Ernie wearing oange and yellow hat and green jacket
EX $20   NM $30   MIP $35

Ernie the Keebler Elf Mug, 1972, Keebler Company, 3" plastic figural mug
EX $8   NM $12   MIP $15

KELLOGG'S

Coppertone, 1998, Kellogg's, Coppertone Beach Set: Coppertone girl, black dog, drawstring tote, suntan lotion, towel, radio and umbrella; Madame Alexander, the set
EX $25   NM $50   MIP $100

Dig 'Em Bendy Figure, 1970, Kellogg's, 3-1/2" bendable frog figure w/"Dig 'Em" on shirt
EX $10   NM $15   MIP $25

Dig 'Em Doll, 1973, Kellogg's, 16" smiling frog w/baseball hat wearing shirt that reads "Dig Em"
EX $15   NM $20   MIP $30

Dig 'Em Slide Puzzle, 1979, Kellogg's, 4" plastic squares that make a scene when put together
EX $8   NM $10   MIP $15

Milton The Toaster Figure, 1980, Kellogg's, 5" white, smiling toaster
EX $50   NM $70   MIP $90

Newton the Owl License Plate, 1973, Kellogg's, 5" x 7" plastic license plate w/Newton the Owl; made in several colors
EX $5   NM $8   MIP $10

Rice Krispie Dolls, 1998, Kellogg's, Snap, Crackle and Pop, the set
EX $100   NM $150   MIP $200

Rice Krispies Dolls, 1998, Kellogg's, 8" Snap, Crackle, Pop; Madame Alexander, each
EX $20   NM $40   MIP $65

Rice Krispies Towel, 1972, Kellogg's, 20 x 38" towel featuring Snap, Crackle and Pop!
EX $10   NM $20   MIP $25

Snap, Crackle and Pop Figures, 1975, Kellogg's, 7-1/2" vinyl, arms at side, each
EX $20   NM $25   MIP $30

Snap, Crackle and Pop Figures, 1975, Kellogg's, 7-1/2" vinyl, arms extended, each
EX $25   NM $30   MIP $35

Snap, Crackle and Pop Hand Puppets, 1950s, Kellogg's, cloth body and vinyl head, each
EX $25   NM $35   MIP $40

Snap, Crackle and Pop vinyl figures, 1984
EX $7   NM $14   MIP $20

Tony the Tiger bank, 1970s, plastic, 8-1/2"
EX $10   NM $20   MIP $30

Tony the Tiger Cookie Jar, 1968, Kellogg's, 7" plastic
EX $70   NM $95   MIP $125

Tony the Tiger Figure, 1974, Kellogg's, 7-1/2" vinyl tiger
EX $45   NM $60   MIP $75

Tony the Tiger stuffed doll, 1973, 14"
EX $10   NM $20   MIP $30

Tony Tiger, 2003, Funko, Wacky Wobbler, #6009
EX $3   NM $7   MIP $12

Toucan Sam Backpack, 1983, Kellogg's, 12" blue backpack that pictures Toucan Sam sitting on a schoolhouse
EX $15   NM $20   MIP $25

Toucan Sam Figure, 1984, Kellogg's, 3" plastic jointed figure w/blue body and multi-colored beak
EX $12   NM $15   MIP $20

Toucan Sam Wallet, 1984, Kellogg's, plastic w/picture of Toucan Sam
EX $10   NM $15   MIP $20

KENDALL COMPANY

Curad Taped Crusader Figure, 1977, Kendall Company, 7-1/2" vinyl figure
EX $65   NM $75   MIP $85

KEN-L-RATION

Ken-L-Ration Wall Pockets, 1960s, Ken-L-Ration, 3" pair of plastic wall pockets; cat's head and a dog's head
EX $40   NM $50   MIP $65

KENTUCKY FRIED CHICKEN

Colonel Sanders, Funko, Wacky Wobbler
EX $3   NM $7   MIP $15

Colonel Sanders bank, 1965, vinyl, 12-1/2"
EX $15   NM $30   MIP $45

Colonel Sanders bank, 1977, plastic, red, 9"
EX $10   NM $20   MIP $30

Colonel Sanders Nodder, 1960s, Kentucky Fried Chicken, 7" plastic nodder of Colonel holding bucket of chicken
EX $70   NM $85   MIP $100

KIDDIE CITY TOY STORE

Kaycee Kangaroo Figure, 1980s, Kiddie City Toy Store, vinyl kangaroo w/baby in pouch
EX $40   NM $55   MIP $65

KRAFT

Cheesasaurus Rex Figure, 1990s, Kraft, 5-1/2" orange dinosaur figures wearing different outfits
EX $4   NM $7   MIP $10

Mr. Wiggle Hand Puppet, 1966, Kraft, 6" red rubber
EX $150   NM $185   MIP $225

(Toy Shop File Photo)

Vegetable Man Bank, 1970s, Kraft, 8" vegetable man w/tomato for a head and a celery body
EX $205   NM $260   MIP $280

Vegetable Man Display, 1980, Kraft, 3' plastic vacuuform store display of Vegetable Man
EX $155   NM $230   MIP $280

LABATT'S BREWERY

Labatt's Beer Man Figure, 1972, Labatt's Brewery, 6" man standing next to wood barrel
EX $25   NM $35   MIP $45

ADVERTISING TOYS

MAGIC CHEF

(Toy Shop File Photo)

Magic Chef Figure, 1980s, Magic Chef, 7"
chef dressed in tuxedo and chef's hat
EX $15   **NM** $20   **MIP** $25

McDONALD'S

Big Mac hand puppet, 1973, 12"
EX $7   **NM** $14   **MIP** $25

Big Mac vinyl doll, 1976, Remco, 6-1/2"
EX $10   **NM** $20   **MIP** $30

Collector Series glasses, 1975-76, 6 in
series: Big Mac, Hamburglar, Mayor
McCheese, Ronald McDonald,
Grimmace, Captain Crook
EX $6   **NM** $10   **MIP** $15

Hamburglar stuffed doll, 1971, removable
cape
EX $7   **NM** $14   **MIP** $25

Hamburglar stuffed doll, 1972, removable
cape
EX $7   **NM** $14   **MIP** $25

Ronald McDonald stuffed doll, 1971
EX $10   **NM** $20   **MIP** $30

Ronald McDonald stuffed doll, 1977
EX $7   **NM** $14   **MIP** $22

MICHELIN TIRES

Mr. Bib Figure, 1980s, Michelin Tires, 12"
plastic figure w/Michelin sash across chest
EX $35   **NM** $45   **MIP** $55

MISTER SOFTEE

Mister Softee, 2000, Funko, Wacky
Wobbler, vanilla, chocolate, strawberry
EX $3   **NM** $7   **MIP** $15

MOHAWK CARPET COMPANY

Mohawk Tommy Doll, 1970, Mohawk Carpet
Company, 16" stuffed doll of a little boy
marked "Mohawk Tommy" across front
EX $10   **NM** $15   **MIP** $20

NABISCO

Barnum's Animal Crackers Cookie Jar,
1972, Nabisco, ceramic, shaped like a
box of animal crackers
EX $175   **NM** $225   **MIP** $275

Chips Ahoy Girl Figure, 1983, Nabisco,
4-1/2" vinyl figure of girl w/Chips Ahoy
cookie on her head and in her hand
EX $15   **NM** $18   **MIP** $20

(Toy Shop File Photo)

Fig Newton Girl Figure, 1983, Nabisco,
4-1/2" girl w/Fig Newton on her head
EX $17   **NM** $21   **MIP** $25

Nabisco Thing, 1996, Nabisco, 5" multi-
colored bendable figure w/Nabisco logo
for its head
EX $5   **NM** $10   **MIP** $15

Oreo Cookie Girl Figure, 1983, Nabisco,
4-1/2" vinyl figure of girl w/Oreo Cookie
on head and in her hand
EX $15   **NM** $18   **MIP** $20

NESTLE'S

(Toy Shop File Photo)

Quik Bunny Doll, 1976, Nestle's, 24" plush
rabbit w/letter "Q" on his chest
EX $27   **NM** $38   **MIP** $44

Quik Bunny Figure, 1991, Nestle's, 6"
bendable brown and tan rabbit w/the
letter "Q" hanging from his neck
EX $3   **NM** $7   **MIP** $10

NOVOTEL HOTEL

Dophi Figure, 1990s, Novotel Hotel, 4-1/2"
bendable dolphin figures; set of four
produced each year
EX $5   **NM** $8   **MIP** $10

OSCAR MAYER FOODS

Hot Wheels Wienermobile, Oscar Mayer
Foods, die-cast Wienermobile
EX $2   **NM** $4   **MIP** $6

Little Oscar Puppet, Oscar Mayer Foods,
thin plastic, theme song on back
EX $5   **NM** $8   **MIP** $10

Wienermobile, 1950s, Oscar Mayer
Foods, 11" car; Little Oscar pops up
when car is rolled
EX $100   **NM** $125   **MIP** $150

(Toy Shop File Photo)

Wienermobile Bank, Oscar Mayer Foods,
plastic
EX $10   **NM** $15   **MIP** $35

Wienermobile Beanbag, 1998, Oscar
Mayer Foods, 7" plush beanbag
EX $3   **NM** $5   **MIP** $8

PEPPERIDGE FARM

Goldfish Plush, 1970s, Pepperidge Farm,
16" plush figure
EX $15   **NM** $20   **MIP** $25

PILLSBURY

Biscuit the Cat Puppet, 1974, Pillsbury, 2-
1/2" vinyl cat finger puppet
EX $18   **NM** $25   **MIP** $30

Grandpopper & Grandmommer Figures,
1974, Pillsbury, 5" vinyl pair of figures
EX $85   **NM** $128   **MIP** $155

Green Giant stuffed doll, 1966
EX $10   **NM** $20   **MIP** $45

Jolly Green Giant Figure, 1970s,
Pillsbury, 9-1/2" vinyl green man
wearing loincloth of leaves
EX $85   **NM** $100   **MIP** $125

Little Sprout Figure, 1970s, Pillsbury,
6-1/2" vinyl green figure w/leaves on
head and body
EX $10   **NM** $15   **MIP** $25

Little Sprout Inflatable Figure, 1976,
Pillsbury, 24" vinyl
EX $25   **NM** $30   **MIP** $35

Little Sprout Salt and Pepper Shakers,
1988, Pillsbury, 3" ceramic figural shakers
EX $25   **NM** $30   **MIP** $35

Poppie Fresh figure, 1971, Pillsbury,
vinyl, all white
EX $10   **NM** $12   **MIP** $15

Poppin' Fresh Doll, 1972, Pillsbury, white
velour doll w/hat and scarf
EX $20   **NM** $25   **MIP** $30

Poppin' Fresh Figure, 1971, Pillsbury,
6-1/2" vinyl white baker w/blue eyes and
blue dot on hat
EX $10   **NM** $12   **MIP** $15

Sprout stuffed doll, 1970, small eyes
EX $7   **NM** $15   **MIP** $25

Sprout vinyl doll, 1996, w/ Pasta Accents
sash
EX $5   **NM** $10   **MIP** $16

PIZZA HUT

Pizza Hut Pete Bank, 1969, Pizza Hut,
7-1/2" plastic
EX $20   **NM** $35   **MIP** $50

PIZZA TIME THEATRE

Chuck E. Cheese Bank, 1980s, Pizza Time Theatre, 6-1/2" plastic
EX $8 NM $12 MIP $15

PLANTERS PEANUTS

Mr. Peanut Bank, Planters Peanuts, plastic, rare, orange, hat twists off to get to coins
EX n/a NM $70 MIP $155

Mr. Peanut Bank, Planters Peanuts, plastic, tan, hat twists off to get to coins
EX n/a NM $20 MIP $45

Mr. Peanut Bank, 1950s, Planters Peanuts, plastic, pink, 8-1/2" tall, hat twists off to get to coins
EX n/a NM $20 MIP $40

Mr. Peanut Bank, 1991, Planters Peanuts, 75th Birthday edition; black, yellow, white; base says "Mr. Peanut"
EX n/a NM $10 MIP $20

(Toy Shop File Photo)

Mr. Peanut Doll, 1967, Planters Peanuts, 21" pillow doll
EX $15 NM $20 MIP $35

Mr. Peanut Figure, 1930s, Planters Peanuts, 8-1/2" painted wood figure w/hat and cane
EX $275 NM $300 MIP $375

Mr. Peanut Figure, 1992, Planters Peanuts, 8-1/2" yellow and black plastic
EX $15 NM $20 MIP $32

Mr. Peanut Lamp, 1950s, Planters Peanuts, plastic figure of Mr. Peanut, bulb fits inside
EX n/a NM $60 MIP $125

Mr. Peanut Pinback Button, Planters Peanuts, celluloid
EX n/a NM $12 MIP $25

Mr. Peanut Wind-Up, 1984, Planters Peanuts, 3" yellow peanut man w/traditional hat and cane
EX $20 NM $25 MIP $30

Mr. Peanut Wind-Up Walker, 1950s, Planters Peanuts, black and yellow plastic, 8-1/2" tall, wind-up motor
EX n/a NM $75 MIP $150

Mr. Peanut Wind-Up Walker, 1950s, Planters Peanuts, red plastic, 8-1/2" tall, wind-up motor
EX n/a NM $75 MIP $150

Mr. Peanut's Peanut Wagon, 1950s, Pyro, plastic, 2-1/8" tall, premium, red and yellow
EX n/a NM $75 MIP $150

Stake Truck, 1950s, Pyro, plactic, 1-1/2" tall, premium, red, blue and yellow
EX n/a NM $65 MIP $115

POST CEREAL

California Raisins PVC Figure, 1987, Post Cereal, 2" male raisin playing drums
EX $5 NM $7 MIP $10

California Raisins Wind-Up, 1987, Post Cereal, 4" female raisin w/tambourine
EX $5 NM $7 MIP $10

Sugar Bear Doll, 1970s, Post Cereal, 12" plush brown bear w/blue "Sugar Bear" shirt
EX $20 NM $25 MIP $35

Sugar Bear Doll, 1988, Post Cereal, 12" plush bear w/blue "Sugar Bear" shirt
EX $15 NM $20 MIP $25

PROCTOR & GAMBLE

24 Hour Bug, 1970s, Proctor & Gamble, 7" spotted green bug
EX $50 NM $65 MIP $80

Hawaiian Punch Doll, 1983, Proctor & Gamble, 15" plush Punchy w/red hair and blue and white striped shirt
EX $20 NM $22 MIP $25

Hawaiian Punch Radio, 1970s, Proctor & Gamble, 6" figural radio of Punchy
EX $25 NM $35 MIP $45

Mr. Clean Figure, 1961, Proctor & Gamble, 8" bald man wearing white clothes w/earring; arms are folded
EX $85 NM $100 MIP $135

PURINA CHUCK WAGON

Chuck Wagon, 1975, Purina Chuck Wagon, 8" vinyl team of horses and checker board covered wagon
EX $30 NM $35 MIP $40

QUAKER OATS

Cap'n Crunch, Funko, Wacky Wobbler
EX $3 NM $7 MIP $15

Cap'n Crunch Bank, 1969, Quaker Oats, 8" captain wearing blue outfit and sword
EX $45 NM $65 MIP $85

Cap'n Crunch stuffed doll, 1978
EX $5 NM $10 MIP $20

Jean LaFoote Bank, 1975, Quaker Oats, 8" vinyl pirate wearing green suit and purple hat
EX $60 NM $85 MIP $125

Quake Cereal Doll, 1965, Quaker Oats, 9" man w/raised arms and letter "Q" across chest
EX $85 NM $95 MIP $125

Quaker Oats figure mug, plastic
EX $15 NM $25 MIP $35

Quisp, Funko, Wacky Wobbler
EX $3 NM $7 MIP $15

Quisp Bank, 1960s, Quaker Oats, 6-1/2" papier-mâché
EX $500 NM $750 MIP $850

Quisp Cereal Doll, 1965, Quaker Oats, 10" doll w/pink body, green clothes and letter "Q" across stomach
EX $70 NM $85 MIP $125

Quisp Powered Sugar Space Gun, Quisp Cereal/Quaker, 7" long, red, mail away premium
EX $150 NM $250 MIP $400

R.J. REYNOLDS

(Toy Shop File Photo)

Joe Camel Can Cooler, 1991, R.J. Reynolds, 4" vinyl
EX $7 NM $13 MIP $19

RAID

(Toy Shop File Photo)

Raid Bug, 1989, Raid, plush green bug
EX $22 NM $30 MIP $40

Raid Bug Radio, 1980s, Raid, Raid bug in standing position w/clock on one side and radio on the other
EX $70   NM $200   MIP $135

Raid Bug Wind-Up, 1983, Raid, 4" yellow and green angry bug
EX $40   NM $50   MIP $70

RALSTON PURINA

Meow Mix Cat, 1976, Ralston Purina, 4-1/2" vinyl yellow cat w/black stripes
EX $20   NM $25   MIP $30

RECKITT & COLMAN

Mr. Bubble Figure, 1990, Reckitt & Colman, 8" pink vinyl
EX $20   NM $30   MIP $35

REDDY COMMUNICATIONS

Reddy Kilowatt, 2000, Funko, Wacky Wobbler
EX $3   NM $7   MIP $15

Reddy Kilowatt Bobbin' Head, 1960s, Reddy Communications, 6-1/2" Reddy wearing cowboy outfit
EX $225   NM $275   MIP $450

Reddy Kilowatt Figure, 1961, Reddy Communications, 6" plastic figure w/lightbulb for head and lightning bolts for body
EX $150   NM $185   MIP $225

RITALIN

Ritalin Man Statue, 1970s, Ritalin, 7" smiling plastic statue w/hat
EX $58   NM $67   MIP $78

SEA HOST

Clem the Clam Push Puppets, 1969, Sea Host, 4" fish push puppets; four different fish were issued
EX $15   NM $30   MIP $40

SHOP RITE

Scrunchy Bear Doll, 1970s, Shop Rite, 16" plush bear w/Shop-Rite shirt
EX $20   NM $25   MIP $30

SMILE ORANGE DRINK

Drink Smile Statue, 1930s, Smile Orange Drink, 8" plaster statue of character w/orange for head; "Drink Smile" written across base
EX $150   NM $200   MIP $250

SMITH KLINE & FRENCH LAB

Tagamet Figure, 1989, Smith Kline & French Lab, 2-1/2" bendable pink figure standing on base
EX $15   NM $20   MIP $25

SONY

Sony Boy Figure, 1960s, Sony, 4" vinyl boy wearing yellow "Sony" shirt
EX $150   NM $200   MIP $225

SQUIRT BEVERAGE

Squirt Doll, 1961, Squirt Beverage, 17" vinyl boy w/blond hair and removable clothing; "Squirt" written across shirt
EX $100   NM $150   MIP $175

STARKIST

Charlie the Tuna Doll, 1970, Starkist, 15" pull string talking doll
EX $40   NM $50   MIP $80

Charlie the Tuna Figure, 1973, Starkist, 7-1/2" vinyl Charlie; arms pointed down
EX $50   NM $70   MIP $90

Charlie the Tuna Radio, 1970, Starkist, 6" radio
EX $50   NM $60   MIP $90

Charlie the Tuna Scale, 1972, Starkist, oval shaped bathroom scale w/Charlie the Tuna
EX $50   NM $65   MIP $80

Charlie Tuna, Funko, Wacky Wobbler
EX $3   NM $7   MIP $15

STERLING DRUG

Diaparene Baby Doll, 1980, Sterling Drug, 5" baby w/movable arms and legs; baby wears diaper
EX $35   NM $40   MIP $50

TASTYKAKE

Tastykake Baker Doll, 1974, Tastykake, 13" pillow doll wearing chef outfit
EX $15   NM $20   MIP $25

TONY'S PIZZA

Mr. Tony Figure, 1972, Tony's Pizza, 8" vinyl Italian pizza chef
EX $30   NM $35   MIP $40

TOYS R US

Geoffrey Doll, 1967, Toys R Us, 2-1/2" plush Geoffrey wearing red and white striped shirt
EX $20   NM $25   MIP $50

Geoffrey Flashlight, 1989, Toys R Us, 8-1/2" plastic figural flashlight of Geoffrey the Giraffe
EX $8   NM $10   MIP $12

TRAVELODGE

Sleepy Bear Squeeze Toy, 1970s, Travelodge, 5-1/2" bear wearing pajamas
EX $25   NM $30   MIP $35

TROPICANA

Tropic-Ana Doll, 1977, Tropicana, 17" pillow doll of Hawaiian girl
EX $15   NM $20   MIP $25

U.S. FORESTRY DEPARTMENT

Smokey the Bear bank, Norcrest, ceramic, 6" tall, Smokey sitting with hand on hat
EX n/a   NM $10   MIP $22

Smokey the Bear bank, 1980s, plastic
EX $7   NM $14   MIP $25

Smokey the Bear Bendy, 1967, U.S. Dept. of Agriculture, bendable Smokey
EX n/a   NM $5   MIP $10

Smokey the Bear Boxcar, Lionel, 60th anniversary boxcar rolling stock, #52334
EX n/a   NM $55   MIP $85

Smokey the Bear Comic book, 1960, Western Printing & Lithographing Co., "The True Story of Smokey the Bear," first edition 1960
EX n/a   NM $7   MIP $14

Smokey the Bear figure, 1976, Dakin, plastic, w/ shovel
EX $20   NM $30   MIP $45

Smokey the Bear Little Golden Book, 1955, cover reads, "Smokey the Bear"
EX n/a   NM $10   MIP $15

Smokey the Bear nodder, 1960s
EX $30   NM $65   MIP $100

Smokey the Bear Pinback Button, 1970s, brown & yellow, reads, "Join Smokey's Campaign, Prevent Forest Fires"
EX n/a   NM $7   MIP $15

Smokey the Bear Puppet, 1960s, Ideal
EX n/a   NM $10   MIP $20

Smokey the Bear soaky, 1965, Colgate-Palmolive
EX $10   NM $20   MIP $30

Smokey the Bear stuffed animal, 1960s
EX $25   NM $50   MIP $75

Smokey the Bear stuffed animal, 1960s, Ideal, Smokey in coveralls
EX n/a   NM $10   MIP $20

Smokey the Bear stuffed animal, 1972, Knickerbocker, 6-3/4" tall; box reads, "The Official Smokey Bear"
EX n/a   NM $10   MIP $20

Smokey the Bear stuffed animal, 1985, Three Bears, Inc., 9-1/2" tall, Model No. SB-12-1
EX n/a   NM $10   MIP $25

Woodsy Owl Bank, 1970s, U.S. Forestry Department, 8-1/2" ceramic figural bank
EX $100   NM $125   MIP $150

U.S. POSTAL SERVICE

Mr. ZIP Statue, 1960s, U.S. Postal Service, 6-1/2" wood statue w/mailbag and pop-up hat
EX $150   NM $180   MIP $225

WONDER BREAD

Fresh Guy Figure, 1975, Wonder Bread, 4" smiling loaf of bread w/polka dots, smiling face and "Wonder" on side
EX $100   NM $150   MIP $175

Barbie

By Sharon Korbeck

THE MODEST BEGINNINGS OF A TEEN-AGE MODEL

In 1959, a blond female with a very adult body made a lot of men blush. Of course, she was only 11-1/2 inches tall.

While she initially created shock waves in the mainly male toy industry, that didn't stop the toy world from soon embracing the spirit of what we now fondly just call Barbie.

Mattel's fashion doll icon still captures the essence of little girls' imaginations and dreams—and that's exactly what creator Ruth Handler intended.

Since the doll's introduction, Barbie has seen cosmetic changes (like hairstyle, facial expression, slight changes in body style and even a tattoo!) and more major changes (literally dozens of careers, computer technological advances, etc.). Through it all, however, Barbie has come out ahead of the competitors. Today, Mattel sells roughly $2 billion in Barbie dolls per year.

Barbie's beginnings are well-documented; her birth happened smack in the middle of a strong 1950s postwar economy.

It was then that the Barbie doll came as an inspiration to Mattel co-founder Handler as she watched her young daughter, Barbara, playing with paper dolls.

Barbara and her friends liked to play make-believe with the dolls, imagining them in roles as college students, cheerleaders, and adults with careers.

Handler immediately recognized that playing and pretending about the future was an important part of growing up. In researching the marketplace, she discovered a void and was determined to fill the niche with a three-dimensional fashion doll. Her all-male design staff, however, harbored doubts.

Several designs later, Mattel introduced Barbie, the Teen-Age Fashion Model, to skeptical buyers at New York's annual Toy Fair in 1959. Never before had they seen a doll so completely unlike the baby and toddler dolls popular at the time. A major point of controversy was Barbie's ample bosom. Actually, the contention was that the doll had breasts . . . period.

With fashion and teenage lifestyle trends evolving at a startling rate, the hundreds of people who have worked to keep Barbie current have had their hands full as styles changed from Paris couture to the inspired elegance of the Jacqueline Kennedy years to a more free-flowing, youthful look.

Mattel's design and development staff have remained current by identifying trends that relate to the lives of American teenagers. Barbie has been called an "evergreen" property, an adjective infrequently used in the toy industry. Far too often, toys and the whims of the fickle buying public are fleeting. But unlike decades of toys lost in the attics of memory, Mattel's Barbie has surpassed probably even Handler's expectations.

A COLLECTOR'S DREAM

Barbie's charm as a children's toy may have been immediate, but it wasn't until decades later that collectors started paying more attention. Collectors who had grown up with Barbie wanted to reclaim her. There was, after all, plenty to recapture—the memories of playing with dolls with friends, Barbie's fabulous fancy outfits, dream dates with Ken and, who could forget, Barbie's well-appointed dream house!

Because Barbie dolls were well-loved and played-with, many of the 1959 and early 1960s dolls are found today in less-than-perfect shape. That's why examples of the earliest Barbie dolls regularly command hundreds, even thousands, of dollars each. Having original boxes and clothing increases a doll's value.

Collectors today are interested in both vintage and newer, collector-edition dolls. Collecting is no small hobby. Full-time dealers make their livings off Barbie, and several publications exist solely to cover what's new in Barbie's world.

Nostalgia and investment potential are perhaps the two biggest motivators for Barbie collectors. And investment potential has proven itself over the last decades, especially for 1960s dolls.

BARBIE TODAY: MARKET TRENDS

Vintage dolls, particularly early 1960s issues and Ponytails from 1959, remain hard find in Mint in Box condition. Those with original boxes, accessories, and clothing remain the Holy Grail with collectors.

While it may not be difficult to find a 1960s brunette Bubblecut in Good condition, finding a rare variation (such as one with side-parted hair or with a hard-to-find hair color like brownette) is more challenging . . . and that doll will likely be more valuable than more common ones from the same time period.

The most investment-savvy way to collect Barbie dolls is to focus on early 1960s dolls; they tend to appreciate more in value than newer dolls, especially because supply and condition has diminished over the years.

THE TOP TEN BARBIE ITEMS *(In Mint Condition)*

1. Ponytail Barbie #2, brunette, Mattel, 1959	$6,500
2. Ponytail Barbie #1, brunette, Mattel, 1959	5,500
3. Ponytail Barbie #1, blonde, Mattel, 1959	5,000
4. Ponytail Barbie #2, blonde, Mattel, 1959	5,000
5. Roman Holiday, Barbie Vintage Fashions, Mattel, 1959-66	4,800
6. Gay Parisienne, Barbie Vintage Fashions, Mattel, 1959-66	4,000
7. Pan Am Stewardess, Barbie Vintage Fashions, Mattel, 1959-66	4,000
8. Easter Parade, Barbie Vintage Fashions, Mattel, 1959-66	4,000
9. Barbie's Sport Plane, Barbie vehicles, Mattel, 1964	3,500
10. Barbie's Airplane, Barbie vehicles, Mattel, 1964	3,500

Loose, naked, or damaged vintage Barbie dolls; most of those from the 1970s to today will have very little or no collectible value. Some 1960s dolls may have value in any condition because of their rarity.

Recent auction prices for vintage 1959 and 1960s dolls have remained steady, with a few peaks and valleys. In 2003, a pristine Ponytail Barbie #1 sold for more than $25,000 at a California auction, but that's unusual. Other, more realistic, prices noted have included $8,700 (paid in 2000 for a brunette Ponytail #1). A more common price for a Mint in Box example of the first Barbie doll is $2,000 and $3,500. Lesser condition #1 dolls, or those without original boxes, will bring only a fraction (50 percent or less) of those spectacular prices.

Other vintage dolls worthy of picking up include the 1966 Color Magic dolls (with hair that could change colors), Swirl Ponytails (with their swept-back hairstyle still intact) and any early African-American doll (like Black Francie or the first Black Barbie).

Some limited-edition series dolls from the last 10 years are worthy of note since they have shown some appreciation in value. For example, the Harley-Davidson series of Barbie and Ken dolls, begun in the late 1990s, has consistently held its value or increased over the past five years.

In the last five years, however, collector edition Barbie dolls have generated interest at retail, but prices have not soared (or, in some cases, increased at all) on the secondary market.

Generating the most collector attention in the past few years has been the Fashion Model collection, which debuted in 2000. The dolls are made of a revolutionary Silkstone material, a durable material which feels like porcelain but remains unbreakable. The series started off racy with Lingerie #1, with slinky underwear and decidedly retro-looking face. Obviously targeted at a sophisticated adult collector market, the series was a huge success; since then six Lingerie dolls and several other dolls in the series have been made, many selling out at dealers nationwide. In early 2003, however, Mattel announced the end of the Lingerie series, cowering to protests nationwide about the doll's risqué appearance. The cancellation of the series may lead collectors who got in on the series late searching the secondary market for the earliest Lingerie dolls.

On the retail market, Mattel and Barbie suffered some blows in 2003-04. Up-and-coming trendy dolls like MGA's Bratz targeted a younger, hipper audience and succeeded in taking market share from Mattel's "pink aisle."

Mattel aimed to recoup its popularity by issuing dolls based on familiar and trendy characters (such as Catwoman or the film property Grease). Mattel's hip and edgy Cali Girl and Mod Circle lines played up a fresh, new look (bare midriff, surf garb, trendy clothes, funky hairstyles)

Buying tip for 2006: Odds and ends. Look for the oddball pieces others might overlook, such as Barbie hangers, official Mattel Barbie clothing, vintage pilgrim shoes, and tiny accessories like hats or purses. Individually, these small pieces can help complete a set, so some collectors will pay well to acquire that one missing shoe, briefcase, or scarf. Also, look for the paper inserts that came with 1960s dolls. They included illustrations of Barbie fashions and are coveted by Barbie historians and enthusiasts.

Buying tip for 2006: Don't avoid auctions. Some entry-level collectors are afraid to bid in auctions for fear they will be outbid. True Barbie rarities may still command stratospheric prices, but buyers may be surprised at what they CAN afford. Many more common dolls, fashions, and accessories sell for reasonable price and can be a great place to begin, or add to, a collection.

Collector Alert: Not every doll in a series is a winner in collectors' eyes and not every series will maintain its popularity.

TIPS FOR COLLECTING

Although many Barbie dolls increase in value, others do not. Here are some tips for smart collecting:

• Avoid regular issue dolls (also known as pink box dolls or play dolls). These are the ones that generally retail in toy stores for less than $15. These have limited investment potential. Buy them because you like them, not because you expect them to increase in value.

• Look for limited-edition exclusives. Certain dolls are "exclusives" because they are made only for one retail outlet, like Target or FAO Schwarz. Many of these dolls have increased in value; others, however, show less success. Harley-Davidson Barbie, exclusive to Toys R Us, for example, was next to impossible to find in stores. Its secondary market prices immediately soared to $250 or more. Now, the first edition Harley Barbie could bring $800 or more.

• Look for dolls in the best possible condition. Dolls in top condition command higher prices than dolls in poor condition. And watch for original boxes, apparel, and even tiny accessories. They can all add value to a doll.

• Dig carefully through big boxes of loose dolls. Loose, naked, or damaged vintage Barbie dolls from the 1970s to today, have very little or no collectible value. Dolls from the 1960s in the same condition may be worth something to collectors; for example, even a naked or slightly damaged Color Magic or Miss Barbie doll from the 1960s could bring $100 or more.

• Don't be fooled by dates! Barbie dolls have distinct markings on their buttocks, but remember that the date on a doll is likely the date the doll's body style was copyrighted, NOT necessarily the date the doll was made. Therefore, dolls with a 1960s date may actually be made in the 1990s. Plenty of books exist with photos of dolls and markings, making it more accurate to identify your doll.

• Don't overlook licensed Barbie products. Mattel licenses the Barbie name to companies which make paper dolls, clothing, cases, watches, lunch boxes, and other collectibles. Anything with the Barbie name is collectible but not necessarily valuable.

• Buy the less-than-obvious choices. Lots of collectors are looking for dolls and fashions. Look for the more disposable items bearing the Barbie name: think boxes of bandages or Jell-O or other items meant to be consumed and discarded. The packaging will be a great find years down the road.

RESOURCES FOR COLLECTORS

Barbie collectors are never alone. They give a positive and impressive meaning to the word "network" since they find so many ways to communicate with each other. Books, magazines, Web sites, and clubs are plentiful. While not a complete list, here is a look at some of the "best bets" for Barbie collectors today.

PUBLICATIONS

Several publications cater to doll lovers; one is specifically devoted to Barbie doll fans. Check out these fine print resources.

Barbie Bazaar magazine
Murat-Caviale, Inc.
5617 Sixth Avenue
Kenosha, WI 53140
(414) 658-1004
www.barbiebazaar.com

Doll Reader
6405 Flank Dr.
Harrisburg, PA 17112-2753
www.dollreader.com

Toy Shop
700 E. State St.

Iola, WI 54990

(715) 445-2214

www.toyshopmag.com

AUCTION HOUSES

Collectors often turn to auction houses to buy and sell Barbie dolls, accessories and collections. Two of the major doll auction venues are

McMasters Harris Doll Auctions
P.O. Box 1755
Cambridge, OH 43725
(800) 842-3526
www.mcmastersauctions.com

Theriault's, The Doll Masters
P.O. Box 151
Annapolis, MD 21401
(301) 224-3655
www.theriaults.com

CLUBS

Literally hundreds of clubs, ranging from local and regional to national and international, exist to serve avid collectors. It's unknown if a complete and up-to-date list has ever been compiled, but the other Barbie resources listed on this page are the best bets for locating other collectors and clubs. For more information on Mattel's official Barbie Collector's Club, visit their Web site at www.barbiecollectibles.com or call (800) 491-7503.

WEB SITES

This list could be endless, especially with all the dealer, retail, secondary market, and fan sites out there. The best bet for surfing through the sites more successfully is to search the Internet under the keywords "Barbie," "Barbie doll [or dolls]," "Barbie collectibles," "Mattel's Barbie" or other appropriate terms.

Mattel Toys / Barbie Collectibles
www.barbiecollectibles.com

BOOKS

Books on America's favorite fashion doll icon are plentiful as well. A library search or visit to www.bn.com or www.amazon.com will also reveal more complete lists of Barbie books. Here are some favorites.

The Best of Barbie
Sharon Korbeck (2001, Krause Publications)

The Ultimate Barbie Doll Book
Marcie Melillo (revised edition, 2004, Krause Publications)

The Collectible Barbie Doll, Second Edition
Janine Fennick (1999, Running Press/Courage)

Fashion Doll Price Guide 2000-2001 (2000, Portfolio Press)

Collector's Compass Barbie Doll (2000, Martingale & Company)

The Story of Barbie Doll, Second Edition
Kitturah B. Westenhouser (1999, Collector Books)

The Collectors Encyclopedia of Barbie Dolls and Collectibles
Sibyl DeWein and Joan Ashabraner (1994 ed., Collector Books)

Contemporary Barbie
Jane Sarasohn-Kahn (1997, Antique Trader Books)

Identifying Barbie Dolls: The New Compact Study Guide and Identifier
Janine Fennick (1998)

The Barbie Doll Years: A Comprehensive Listing and Value Guide of Dolls and Accessories
Patrick C. Olds and Joyce L. Olds (2000, Collector Books)

Face of the American Dream: Barbie Doll 1959-1971
Christopher Varaste (1999, Hobby House)

Contributor: Sharon Korbeck is the author of *The Best of Barbie* (2001, Krause Publications). Besides spoiling her nieces with additions to their Barbie collections, Sharon is working on a fine collection of tin game boards. Jan Fennick has been an avid doll collector since she was very small. In 1987, an interest in 1960s pop culture and fashion lead her take her childhood Barbie dolls out of storage and her life hasn't been the same since. A combination of her love of writing and her involvement in the world of dolls as both a buyer and seller produced three books on Barbie doll collecting plus numerous articles and columns for such publications as *Barbie Bazaar, White's Guide to Collecting Figures, Beckett's Hot Toys, Doll Reader, Toy Shop* and the annual Krause Publications *Toys & Prices* as well as CollectingChannel.com. She's been a member of both the Delaware Valley and Long Island Fashion Doll Collectors Clubs and souvenir program chair person for the 1996 and the 2005 National Barbie Doll Collectors Convention. She's never met a fashion doll she didn't like. She may be reached at: *Toys & Prices*, Krause Publications, 700 E. State St., Iola, WI 54990.

ACCESSORIES

COLORFORMS SETS

Barbie Sport Fashion, 1975, Colorforms
MNP $4   MIP $8

Barbie's 3-D Fashion Theatre, 1970, Colorforms
MNP $9   MIP $20

Dress-Up Kit New Living Barbie, 1970, Colorforms
MNP $10   MIP $38

Malibu Barbie, 1972, Colorforms
MNP $7   MIP $20

MISCELLANEOUS

Barbie & Ken Wipe Away Cloths, 1964
MNP $100   MIP $280

Barbie and Ken Hangers, 1960s, SPP, plastic hangers in bag w/cardboard backing
MNP $20   MIP $35

Barbie Beauty Kit, 1961, Roclar
MNP $100   MIP $200

Barbie Bubble Bath, 1961, Roclar
MNP $45   MIP $100

Barbie Carry-All Wallet, 1963, SPP
MNP $145   MIP $255

Barbie Disco Record Player, 1976
MNP $85   MIP $160

Barbie Dresser Accessories, 1962
MNP $175   MIP $300

Barbie Ge-Tar, 1963, Mattel
MNP $200   MIP $400

Barbie Hair Fair, 1966, Mattel
MNP $75   MIP $145

Barbie Mattel-A-Phone, 1968
MNP $75   MIP $140

Barbie Nurse Kit, 1962, Pressman, tin litho box
MNP $100   MIP $275

Barbie Powder Mitt, 1961
MNP $75   MIP $140

Barbie Pretty Up Time, 1960s, brush/comb/mirror set
MNP $50   MIP $125

Barbie Record, 1965, Columbia Records
MNP $70   MIP $120

Barbie Store Display, 1980, Mattel
MNP $10   MIP $30

Barbie Wig Wardrobe, 1960s, Mattel, doll head w/three wigs
MNP $75   MIP $150

Barbie, Ken, Midge Pencil Case, 1964, SPP
MNP $100   MIP $260

Barbie's Dog Snowball, 1990s, Arco/Mattel
MNP $20   MIP $35

Francie Electric Drawing Table, 1966
MNP $65   MIP $130

Jack and Jill magazine advertisements, 1960s
MNP $15   MIP $35

Jigsaw Puzzle, 1963-65, Whitman
MNP $30   MIP $60

Jumbo Trading Cards, 1962, Dynamic, complete set
MNP $225   MIP $365

Record Player, 1961, Emenee
MNP $700   MIP $950

Record Tote, 1961, Ponytail, vinyl, several colors
MNP $75   MIP $180

Vanity Fair Transistor Radio, 1962, Vanity Fair
MNP $700   MIP $1350

Wine Set, 1986
MNP $40   MIP $75

PAPER DOLLS

Barbie and Ken Cut-Outs, 1962, Whitman, pink cover, Model No. 1971
MNP $50   MIP $135

Barbie and Ken Paper Dolls, 1970, Whitman, Model No. 1986
MNP $35   MIP $60

Barbie and Skipper, 1964, Whitman, Model No. 1957
MNP $50   MIP $125

Barbie Costume Dolls, 1964, Whitman, Model No. 1976
MNP $60   MIP $125

Barbie Cut-Outs, 1962, Model No. 1963
MNP $55   MIP $125

Barbie Doll Cut-Outs, 1963, Whitman, Model No. 1962
MNP $45   MIP $95

Barbie Dolls and Clothes, 1969, Model No. 1976
MNP $35   MIP $70

Barbie Has a New Look Paper Dolls, 1967, Whitman, Model No. 1996
MNP $40   MIP $100

Barbie Paper Dolls, boxed, 1967, Whitman, Model No. 4701
MNP $20   MIP $60

Barbie, Christie and Stacey, 1968, Whitman, Model No. 1978
MNP $35   MIP $80

Barbie, Ken and Midge Paper Dolls, 1963, Whitman, Model No. 1976
MNP $50   MIP $90

Barbie, Two Magic Dolls w/stay-on clothes, 1969, Model No. 4763
MNP $30   MIP $70

Barbie's Travel Wardrobe, boxed, 1964, Model No. 4616
MNP $50   MIP $125

Francie and Casey Paper Dolls, 1967, Whitman, Model No. 1986
MNP $30   MIP $60

Francie Paper Dolls, 1967, Whitman, Model No. 1094
MNP $40   MIP $80

Malibu Barbie Paper Dolls, 1972, Whitman, Model No. 1994
MNP $20   MIP $45

Meet Francie Paper Dolls, 1966, Whitman, Model No. 1980
MNP $35   MIP $80

Midge Cut-Outs, 1963, Whitman, Model No. 1962
MNP $45   MIP $90

P.J. Cover Girl Paper Dolls, 1971, Whitman, Model No. 1981
MNP $20   MIP $40

Skipper Paper Dolls, 1965, Whitman, Model No. 1984
MNP $25   MIP $50

Skooter Paper Dolls, 1965, Whitman, Model No. 1985
MNP $35   MIP $95

Tutti, boxed, 1967, Model No. 4622
MNP $30   MIP $60

Twiggy Paper Dolls, 1967, Whitman, Model No. 1999
MNP $25   MIP $48

STRUCTURES

Barbie and Ken Little Theatre, 1964, Mattel, Model No. 4090
MNP $175   MIP $350

Barbie Café Today, 1971, Mattel, Model No. 4973
MNP $150   MIP $350

Barbie Fashion Stage, 1971, Mattel, Model No. 1148
MNP $50   MIP $85

Barbie Goes to College, 1964, Mattel, Model No. 4093
MNP $225   MIP $500

Barbie's Dream House, 1962, Mattel, Model No. 816
MNP $75   MIP $250

Barbie's Dream Kitchen, 1965, Mattel, Model No. 4095
MNP $300   MIP $500

Barbie's New Dream House, 1964, Mattel, Model No. 4092
MNP $75   MIP $225

Fashion Shop, 1962, Mattel, Model No. 817
MNP $150   MIP $400

Francie and Casey Studio House, 1967, Mattel, Model No. 1026
MNP $60   MIP $90

Francie House, 1966, Mattel, Model No. 3302
MNP $75   MIP $125

Jamie's Penthouse (Sears), 1971, Mattel, Model No. 31122
MNP $200   MIP $425

Quick Curl Boutique, 1973, Mattel, Model No. 8665
MNP $40   MIP $80

Skipper's Dream Room, 1965, Mattel, Model No. 4094
MNP $250   MIP $500

Skipper's Schoolroom, 1965, Mattel
MNP $300   MIP $500

Tutti Ice Cream Stand, 1967, Model No. 3363
MNP $130   MIP $225

Tutti's and Todd's Playhouse, 1966
MNP $75   MIP $125

TIMEPIECES

Barbie Personal Photo Clock, 1964, Bradley/Elgin
MNP $500   MIP $600

Barbie Starbright Boudoir Clock, 1964, Bradley/Elgin
MNP $600   MIP $700

Broken Heart Wristwatch, 1964, Bradley/Elgin
MNP $300   MIP $400

Brokn' Heart Pendant, 1965, Bradley/Elgin
MNP $400   MIP $500

Curly Bangs Pendant, 1963-64, Bradley/Elgin
MNP $150   MIP $400

Curly Bangs Wristwatch, 1963-64, Bradley/Elgin
MNP $125   MIP $300

Midge Wristwatch, 1964, Bradley/Elgin
MNP $300   MIP $450

Skipper Wristwatch, 1964, Bradley/Elgin
MNP $300   MIP $450

Swirl Ponytail Wristwatch, 1964, Bradley/Elgin
MNP $150   MIP $300

VEHICLES

Allan's Mercedes Roadster, 1964, Irwin, Model No. 5348
MNP $150   MIP $575

Barbie and Ken and Midge Convertible, 1964, Irwin
MNP $125   MIP $200

Barbie's Airplane, 1964, Irwin
MNP $1000   MIP $3500

Barbie's Austin-Healey, 1964, Irwin, lavender, Montgomery Wards Exclusive
MNP $800   MIP $1000

Barbie's Austin-Healey Convertible, 1962, Irwin, coral
MNP $125   MIP $450

(KP Photo)

Barbie's Speedboat, 1964, Irwin, Shown with Ken at the helm
MNP $100   MIP $1800

Barbie's Sport Plane, 1964, Irwin
MNP $1800   MIP $3500

Ken's Hot Rod, 1963, Irwin, blue
MNP $175   MIP $350

Skipper's Speedboat, 1965, Irwin
MNP $1450   MIP $1850

Skipper's Sports Car, 1965, Irwin
MNP $175   MIP $400

VINYL CASES

Barbie & Francie Case, 1967, SPP
MNP $35   MIP $50

Barbie & Skipper Case, 1964, Mattel, assorted colors - blue or gold most common
MNP $20   MIP $35

Barbie & Stacey Sleep & Keep Case, 1969, Sears Exclusive, Model No. 5023
MNP $75   MIP $100

Barbie Double Case, 1961, Ponytail, various illustrations/colors
MNP $15   MIP $30

Barbie Double Case, 1963, SPP, various illustrations/colors
MNP $12   MIP $25

Barbie Goes Travelin' Case, 1965, SPP
MNP $100   MIP $325

Barbie Single Case, 1961, Ponytail, various illustrations/colors
MNP $10   MIP $20

Barbie Single Case, 1963, SPP, various illustrations/colors
MNP $7   MIP $15

Barbie Train Case, 1961, SPP
MNP $45   MIP $70

Fashion Queen Case, 1963, SPP
MNP $75   MIP $125

Hatbox-Style Cases, 1961, Mattel, assorted styles
MNP $20   MIP $50

Ken Cases (U.S. versions), 1961, Ponytail
MNP $12   MIP $25

Midge Cases (U.S. versions), 1963
MNP $20   MIP $45

Miss Barbie Case, 1964, SPP
MNP $75   MIP $150

Skipper Cases (U.S. versions), 1964
MNP $12   MIP $25

DOLLS

BARBIE & FRIENDS

All American Barbie, 1991, Mattel, Model No. 9423
MNP $4   MIP $15

All American Christie, 1991, Mattel, Model No. 9425
MNP $4   MIP $20

All American Ken, 1991, Mattel, Model No. 9424
MNP $4   MIP $10

All American Kira, 1991, Mattel, Model No. 9427
MNP $4   MIP $15

All American Teresa, 1991, Mattel, Model No. 9426
MNP $4   MIP $20

All Star Ken, 1981, Mattel, Model No. 3553
MNP $7   MIP $15

All Stars Barbie, 1989, Mattel, Model No. 9099
MNP $5   MIP $20

All Stars Christie, 1989, Mattel, Model No. 9352
MNP $5   MIP $15

All Stars Ken, 1989, Mattel, Model No. 9361
MNP $5   MIP $15

All Stars Midge, 1989, Mattel, Model No. 9360
MNP $5   MIP $20

All Stars Teresa, 1989, Mattel, Model No. 9353
MNP $5   MIP $20

(KP Photo)

Allan, bendable leg, 1965, Mattel, Model No. 1010
MNP $125   MIP $250

Allan, straight leg, 1964, Mattel, Model No. 1000
MNP $30   MIP $85

American Beauties Mardi Gras Barbie, 1988, Mattel, Model No. 4930
MNP $20   MIP $35

American Beauty Queen, 1991, Mattel, Model No. 3137
MNP $5   MIP $15

American Beauty Queen, black, 1991, Mattel, Model No. 3245
MNP $5   MIP $15

Angel Face Barbie, 1982, Mattel, Model No. 5640
MNP $8   MIP $30

Animal Lovin' Barbie, black, 1989, Mattel, Model No. 4828
    MNP $5   **MIP** $15

Animal Lovin' Barbie, white, 1989, Mattel, Model No. 1350
    MNP $5   **MIP** $15

Animal Lovin' Ken, 1989, Mattel, Model No. 1351
    MNP $5   **MIP** $10

Animal Lovin' Nikki, 1989, Mattel, Model No. 1352
    MNP $7   **MIP** $15

Astronaut Barbie, black, 1985, Mattel, Model No. 1207
    MNP $20   **MIP** $30

Astronaut Barbie, white, 1985, Mattel, Model No. 2449
    MNP $25   **MIP** $40

Babysitter Courtney, 1991, Mattel, Model No. 9434
    MNP $4   **MIP** $10

Babysitter Skipper, 1991, Mattel, Model No. 9433
    MNP $4   **MIP** $10

Babysitter Skipper, black, 1991, Mattel, Model No. 1599
    MNP $4   **MIP** $8

Baggie Casey, blond (sold in plastic bag), 1975, Mattel, Model No. 9000
    MNP $100   **MIP** $200

Ballerina Barbie on Tour, gold, 1st version, 1976, Mattel, Model No. 9613
    MNP $45   **MIP** $75

Ballerina Barbie, 1st version, 1976, Mattel, Model No. 9093
    MNP $20   **MIP** $50

Ballerina Cara, 1976, Mattel, Model No. 9528
    MNP $25   **MIP** $50

Barbie & Her Fashion Fireworks, 1976, Mattel, Model No. 9805
    MNP $20   **MIP** $60

Barbie & the Beat, 1990, Mattel, Model No. 3751
    MNP $5   **MIP** $15

Barbie & the Beat Christie, 1990, Mattel, Model No. 2752
    MNP $5   **MIP** $15

Barbie & the Beat Midge, 1990, Mattel, Model No. 2754
    MNP $6   **MIP** $15

Barbie Hair Happenings (department store exclusive, red hair), 1971, Mattel, Model No. 1174
    MNP $300   **MIP** $800

(KP Photo)

Barbie with Growin' Pretty Hair, 1971, Mattel, Model No. 1144
    MNP $125   **MIP** $300

Bathtime Fun Barbie, 1991, Mattel, Model No. 9601
    MNP $3   **MIP** $10

Bathtime Fun Barbie, black, 1991, Mattel, Model No. 9603
    MNP $3   **MIP** $10

Beach Blast Barbie, 1989, Mattel, Model No. 3237
    MNP $3   **MIP** $10

Beach Blast Christie, 1989, Mattel, Model No. 3253
    MNP $4   **MIP** $10

Beach Blast Ken, 1989, Mattel, Model No. 3238
    MNP $4   **MIP** $10

Beach Blast Miko, 1989, Mattel, Model No. 3244
    MNP $4   **MIP** $10

Beach Blast Skipper, 1989, Mattel, Model No. 3242
    MNP $4   **MIP** $10

Beach Blast Steven, 1989, Mattel, Model No. 3251
    MNP $4   **MIP** $10

Beach Blast Teresa, 1989, Mattel, Model No. 3249
    MNP $5   **MIP** $10

Beautiful Bride Barbie, 1978, Mattel, Model No. 9907
    MNP $50   **MIP** $80

Beauty Secrets Barbie, 1st issue, 1980, Mattel, Model No. 1290
    MNP $12   **MIP** $65

Beauty Secrets Christie, 1980, Mattel, Model No. 1295
    MNP $12   **MIP** $65

Beauty, Barbie's Dog, 1979, Mattel, Model No. 1018
    MNP $12   **MIP** $30

Bendable Leg "American Girl" Barbie, short hair, 1965, Mattel, Model No. 1070
    MNP $400   **MIP** $1200

Bendable Leg "American Girl" Barbie, Color Magic Face, 1966, Mattel, Model No. 1070
    MNP $800   **MIP** $1700

Bendable Leg "American Girl" Barbie, long hair, 1965, Mattel, Model No. 1070
    MNP $800   **MIP** $1800

Bendable Leg "American Girl" Barbie, side-part long hair, 1966, Mattel, Model No. 1070
    MNP $1700   **MIP** $2500

Bendable Leg "American Girl" Barbie, Swirl Ponytail or Bubblecut hairstyle, 1965, Mattel, Model No. 1070
    MNP $1000   **MIP** $2800

Benetton Barbie, 1991, Mattel, Model No. 9404
    MNP $10   **MIP** $25

Benetton Christie, 1991, Mattel, Model No. 9407
    MNP $10   **MIP** $25

Benetton Marina, 1991, Mattel, Model No. 9409
    MNP $10   **MIP** $25

Black Barbie, 1980, Mattel, Model No. 1293
    MNP $30   **MIP** $75

(KP Photo)

Brad, bendable leg, 1970, Mattel, Model No. 1142
    MNP $65   **MIP** $175

Brad, talking, 1970, Mattel, Model No. 1114
    MNP $65   **MIP** $200

Bubblecut Barbie Sidepart, all hair colors, 1961, Mattel, Model No. 850
    MNP $425   **MIP** $900

Bubblecut Barbie, blond, brunette, titian, 1962, Mattel, Model No. 850
    MNP $75   **MIP** $200

BARBIE

(KP Photo)

Bubblecut Barbie, brownette, 1961, Mattel, Model No. 850
MNP $500   MIP $850

Bubblecut Barbie, white ginger, 1962, Mattel, Model No. 850
MNP $250   MIP $600

Busy Barbie, 1971, Mattel, Model No. 3311
MNP $100   MIP $200

Busy Francie, 1971, Mattel, Model No. 3313
MNP $125   MIP $350

Busy Ken, 1971, Mattel, Model No. 3314
MNP $60   MIP $145

(KP Photo)

Busy Steffie, 1971, Mattel, Model No. 3312
MNP $85   MIP $225

Calgary Olympic Skating Barbie, 1987, Mattel, Model No. 4547
MNP $25   MIP $45

California Dream Barbie, 1988, Mattel, Model No. 4439
MNP $5   MIP $15

California Dream Christie, 1988, Mattel, Model No. 4443
MNP $6   MIP $10

California Dream Ken, 1988, Mattel, Model No. 4441
MNP $8   MIP $10

California Dream Midge, 1988, Mattel, Model No. 4442
MNP $3   MIP $10

California Dream Skipper, 1988, Mattel, Model No. 4440
MNP $13   MIP $10

California Dream Teresa, 1988, Mattel, Model No. 4403
MNP $15   MIP $10

Carla, European exclusive, 1976, Mattel, Model No. 7377
MNP $65   MIP $120

Casey, Twist and Turn, 1967, Mattel, Model No. 1180
MNP $75   MIP $275

Chris, titian, blond, brunette (Tutti's friend), 1967, Mattel, Model No. 3570
MNP $65   MIP $200

Christie, talking, 1970, Mattel, Model No. 1126
MNP $80   MIP $325

Christie, Twist N Turn, 1970, Mattel, Model No. 1119
MNP $80   MIP $325

Coach Ken & Tommy, white or black, 2000, Mattel
MNP $7   MIP $15

(KP Photo)

Color Magic Barbie, Golden Blonde, 1966, Mattel, Model No. 1150
MNP $400   MIP $1500

Color Magic Barbie, Midnight Black, 1966, Mattel, Model No. 1150
MNP $1100   MIP $2800

Cool City Blues: Barbie, Ken, Skipper, 1989, Mattel, Model No. 4893
MNP $20   MIP $30

Cool Shavin' Ken, 1996, Mattel, Model No. 15469
MNP $5   MIP $10

Cool Times Barbie, 1989, Mattel Model No. 3022
MNP $5   MIP $15

Cool Times Christie, 1989, Mattel, Model No. 3217
MNP $5   MIP $10

Cool Times Ken, 1989, Mattel, Model No. 3219
MNP $5   MIP $10

Cool Times Midge, 1989, Mattel, Model No. 3216
MNP $7   MIP $10

Cool Times Teresa, 1989, Mattel, Model No. 3218
MNP $5   MIP $10

Cool Tops Courtney, 1989, Mattel, Model No. 7079
MNP $7   MIP $10

Cool Tops Kevin, 1989, Mattel, Model No. 9351
MNP $5   MIP $10

Cool Tops Skipper, black, 1989, Mattel, Model No. 5441
MNP $5   MIP $10

Cool Tops Skipper, white, 1989, Mattel, Model No. 4989
MNP $7   MIP $10

Corduroy Cool Barbie, 2000, Mattel, Model No. 24658
MNP $5   MIP $10

Costume Ball Barbie, black, 1991, Mattel, Model No. 7134
MNP $6   MIP $15

Costume Ball Barbie, white, 1991, Mattel, Model No. 7123
MNP $6   MIP $15

Costume Ball Ken, black, 1991, Mattel, Model No. 7160
MNP $6   MIP $10

Costume Ball Ken, white, 1991, Mattel, Model No. 7154
MNP $6   MIP $15

Crystal Barbie, black, 1984, Mattel, Model No. 4859
MNP $10   MIP $25

Crystal Barbie, white, 1984, Mattel, Model No. 4598
MNP $10   MIP $25

Crystal Ken, black, 1983, Mattel, Model No. 9036
MNP $15   MIP $25

Crystal Ken, white, 1983, Mattel, Model No. 4898
MNP $8   MIP $30

Dance Club Barbie, 1989, Mattel, Model No. 3509
MNP $5   MIP $20

Dance Club Devon, 1989, Mattel, Model No. 3513
MNP $5   MIP $20

Dance Club Kayla, 1989, Mattel, Model No. 3512
MNP $5   MIP $20

Dance Club Ken, 1989, Mattel, Model No. 3511
MNP $5   MIP $20

Dance Magic Barbie, 1990, Mattel, Model No. 4836
> **MNP** $7   **MIP** $15

Dance Magic Barbie, black, 1990, Mattel, Model No. 7080
> **MNP** $7   **MIP** $15

Dance Magic Ken, 1990, Mattel, Model No. 7081
> **MNP** $6   **MIP** $10

Dance Magic Ken, black, 1990, Mattel, Model No. 7082
> **MNP** $6   **MIP** $10

Day-to-Night Barbie, black, 1985, Mattel, Model No. 7945
> **MNP** $10   **MIP** $40

Day-to-Night Barbie, Hispanic, 1985, Mattel, Model No. 7944
> **MNP** $17   **MIP** $45

Day-to-Night Barbie, white, 1985, Mattel, Model No. 7929
> **MNP** $10   **MIP** $45

Day-to-Night Ken, black, 1984, Mattel, Model No. 9018
> **MNP** $8   **MIP** $35

Day-to-Night Ken, white, 1984, Mattel, Model No. 9019
> **MNP** $8   **MIP** $35

Dentist Barbie, 1997, Mattel, Model No. 17255
> **MNP** $15   **MIP** $20

Doctor Barbie, 1988, Mattel, Model No. 3850
> **MNP** $8   **MIP** $25

Doctor Ken, 1988, Mattel, Model No. 4118
> **MNP** $5   **MIP** $20

Dolls of the World Princess of China, 2002, Mattel, Model No. 53368
> **MNP** $10   **MIP** $25

Dolls of the World Princess of India, 2000, Mattel, Model No. 28374
> **MNP** $8   **MIP** $20

Dolls of the World Princess of Ireland, 2002, Mattel, Model No. 53367
> **MNP** $10   **MIP** $20

(Mattel Photo)
Dolls of the World Princess of South Africa, 2003, Mattel, Model No. 56218
> **MNP** $10   **MIP** $20

Dolls of the World Princess of the Danish Court, 2003, Mattel, Model No. 56216
> **MNP** $10   **MIP** $20

Dolls of the World Princess of the French Court, 2000, Mattel, Model No. 28372
> **MNP** $8   **MIP** $20

Dolls of the World Princess of the Incas, 2000, Mattel, Model No. 28373
> **MNP** $8   **MIP** $20

Dolls of the World Princess of the Nile, 2002, Mattel, Model No. 53369
> **MNP** $10   **MIP** $20

Dolls of the World Princess of the Portuguese Empire, 2003, Mattel, Model No. 56217
> **MNP** $10   **MIP** $20

Dolls of the World/International Arctic, 1997, Mattel, Model No. 16495
> **MNP** $20   **MIP** $25

Dolls of the World/International Australian, two box variations, 1993, Mattel, Model No. 3626
> **MNP** $10   **MIP** $25

Dolls of the World/International Austrian, 1999, Mattel, Model No. 21553
> **MNP** $15   **MIP** $25

Dolls of the World/International Brazillian, 1990, Mattel, Model No. 9094
> **MNP** $15   **MIP** $35

Dolls of the World/International Canadian, 1988, Mattel, Model No. 4928
> **MNP** $15   **MIP** $35

Dolls of the World/International Chilean, 1998, Mattel, Model No. 18559
> **MNP** $10   **MIP** $20

Dolls of the World/International Chinese, 1994, Mattel, Model No. 11180
> **MNP** $10   **MIP** $20

Dolls of the World/International Czechoslovakian, 1991, Mattel, Model No. 7330
> **MNP** $20   **MIP** $35

Dolls of the World/International Dutch, 1994, Mattel, Model No. 11104
> **MNP** $10   **MIP** $30

Dolls of the World/International English, 1992, Mattel, Model No. 4973
> **MNP** $12   **MIP** $35

Dolls of the World/International Eskimo, 1982, Mattel, Model No. 3898
> **MNP** $30   **MIP** $50

Dolls of the World/International Eskimo, 1991, Mattel, Model No. 9844
> **MNP** $8   **MIP** $30

Dolls of the World/International French, 1997, Mattel, Model No. 16499
> **MNP** $10   **MIP** $20

Dolls of the World/International German, 1987, Mattel, Model No. 3188
> **MNP** $25   **MIP** $40

Dolls of the World/International German, 1995, Mattel, Model No. 12598
> **MNP** $10   **MIP** $25

Dolls of the World/International Ghanaian, 1996, Mattel, Model No. 15303
> **MNP** $15   **MIP** $25

Dolls of the World/International Gift Set (Chinese, Dutch, Kenyan), 1994, Mattel, Model No. 12043
> **MNP** $30   **MIP** $70

Dolls of the World/International Gift Set (Irish, German, Polynesian), 1995, Mattel, Model No. 13939
> **MNP** $30   **MIP** $65

Dolls of the World/International Gift Set (Japanese, Indian, Norwegian), 1996, Mattel, Model No. 15283
> **MNP** $30   **MIP** $60

Dolls of the World/International Greek, 1986, Mattel, Model No. 2997
> **MNP** $30   **MIP** $50

Dolls of the World/International Iceland, 1987, Mattel, Model No. 3189
> **MNP** $30   **MIP** $50

Dolls of the World/International Indian, 1982, Mattel, Model No. 3897
> **MNP** $30   **MIP** $50

Dolls of the World/International Indian, 1995, Mattel, Model No. 14451
> **MNP** $12   **MIP** $25

(KP Photo)

Dolls of the World/International Irish, 1984, Mattel, Model No. 7517
> **MNP** $20   **MIP** $45

Dolls of the World/International Irish, 1995, Mattel, Model No. 12998
> **MNP** $10   **MIP** $25

Dolls of the World/International Italian, 1980, Mattel, Model No. 1601
> **MNP** $65   **MIP** $125

Dolls of the World/International Italian, 1993, Mattel, Model No. 2256
> **MNP** $10   **MIP** $35

Dolls of the World/International Jamaican, silver earrings, 1992, Mattel, Model No. 4647
> **MNP** $12   **MIP** $30

(KP Photo)

(KP Photo)

(KP Photo)

Dolls of the World/International Japanese, 1984, Mattel, Model No. 9481
MNP $25   MIP $40

Dolls of the World/International Japanese, 1996, Mattel, Model No. 14163
MNP $10   MIP $20

Dolls of the World/International Kenyan, 1994, Mattel, Model No. 11181
MNP $10   MIP $25

Dolls of the World/International Korean, 1988, Mattel, Model No. 4929
MNP $15   MIP $40

Dolls of the World/International Malaysian, 1991, Mattel, Model No. 7329
MNP $10   MIP $30

Dolls of the World/International Mexican, 1989, Mattel, Model No. 1917
MNP $15   MIP $25

Dolls of the World/International Mexican, 1995, Mattel, Model No. 14449
MNP $10   MIP $15

Dolls of the World/International Moroccan, 1999, Mattel, Model No. 21507
MNP $15   MIP $25

Dolls of the World/International Native American #1, two box versions, 1993, Mattel, Model No. 1753
MNP $12   MIP $30

Dolls of the World/International Native American #2, 1994, Mattel, Model No. 11609
MNP $10   MIP $25

Dolls of the World/International Native American #3, 1995, Mattel, Model No. 12699
MNP $10   MIP $20

Dolls of the World/International Nigerian, 1990, Mattel, Model No. 7376
MNP $15   MIP $25

Dolls of the World/International Norwegian, pink flowers, limited to 3,000, 1996, Mattel, Model No. 14450
MNP $12   MIP $50

Dolls of the World/International NW Coast Native American Barbie, 2000, Mattel, Model No. 24671
MNP $12   MIP $20

Dolls of the World/International Oriental, 1981, Mattel, Model No. 3262
MNP $35   MIP $60

Dolls of the World/International Parisian, 1980, Mattel, Model No. 1600
MNP $50   MIP $50

Dolls of the World/International Parisian, 1991, Mattel, Model No. 9843
MNP $8   MIP $30

Dolls of the World/International Peruvian, 1986, Mattel, Model No. 2995
MNP $30   MIP $40

Dolls of the World/International Peruvian, 1999, Mattel, Model No. 21506
MNP $15   MIP $25

Dolls of the World/International Polish, 1998, Mattel, Model No. 18560
MNP $15   MIP $25

Dolls of the World/International Polynesian, 1995, Mattel, Model No. 12700
MNP $10   MIP $25

Dolls of the World/International Puerto Rican, 1997, Mattel, Model No. 16754
MNP $15   MIP $25

Dolls of the World/International Royal, 1980, Mattel, Model No. 1602
MNP $50   MIP $75

Dolls of the World/International Russian, 1989, Mattel, Model No. 1916
MNP $20   MIP $25

Dolls of the World/International Russian, 1997, Mattel, Model No. 16500
MNP $20   MIP $30

Dolls of the World/International Scottish, 1981, Mattel, Model No. 3263
MNP $50   MIP $70

Dolls of the World/International Scottish, 1991, Mattel, Model No. 9845
MNP $8   MIP $40

Dolls of the World/International Spanish, 1983, Mattel, Model No. 4031
MNP $40   MIP $55

Dolls of the World/International Spanish, 1992, Mattel, Model No. 4963
MNP $12   MIP $30

Dolls of the World/International Spanish, 2000, Mattel, Model No. 24670
MNP $12   MIP $25

Dolls of the World/International Swedish, 1983, Mattel, Model No. 4032
MNP $25   MIP $40

Dolls of the World/International Swedish, 2000, Mattel, Model No. 24672
MNP $12   MIP $25

Dolls of the World/International Swiss, 1984, Mattel, Model No. 7451
MNP $30   MIP $45

Dolls of the World/International Thai, 1998, Mattel, Model No. 18561
MNP $10   MIP $25

Dramatic New Living Barbie, 1970, Mattel, Model No. 1116
MNP $65   MIP $200

Dramatic New Living Skipper, 1970, Mattel, Model No. 1117
MNP $50   MIP $125

Dream Bride, 1992, Mattel, Model No. 1623
MNP $10   MIP $25

Dream Date Barbie, 1983, Mattel, Model No. 5868
    MNP $10   **MIP** $20

Dream Date Ken, 1983, Mattel, Model No. 4077
    MNP $10   **MIP** $20

Dream Glow Barbie, black, 1986, Mattel, Model No. 2242
    MNP $12   **MIP** $30

Dream Glow Barbie, Hispanic, 1986, Mattel, Model No. 1647
    MNP $25   **MIP** $50

Dream Glow Barbie, white, 1986, Mattel, Model No. 2248
    MNP $12   **MIP** $40

Dream Glow Ken, black, 1986, Mattel, Model No. 2421
    MNP $13   **MIP** $20

Dream Glow Ken, white, 1986, Mattel, Model No. 2250
    MNP $13   **MIP** $15

Dream Time Barbie, pink, 1985, Mattel, Model No. 9180
    MNP $10   **MIP** $20

Earring Magic Barbie, blond, 1993, Mattel, Model No. 7014
    MNP $15   **MIP** $20

(KP Photo)

Earring Magic Ken, 1993, Mattel, Model No. 2290
    MNP $15   **MIP** $30

Fabulous Fur Barbie, 1983, Mattel, Model No. 7093
    MNP $20   **MIP** $65

Fashion Jeans Barbie, 1981, Mattel, Model No. 5313
    MNP $15   **MIP** $65

Fashion Jeans Ken, 1982, Mattel, Model No. 5316
    MNP $12   **MIP** $25

Fashion Photo Barbie, two versions, 1978, Mattel, Model No. 2210
    MNP $20   **MIP** $60

Fashion Photo Christie, 1978, Mattel, Model No. 2324
    MNP $20   **MIP** $60

Fashion Photo P.J., 1978, Mattel, Model No. 2323
    MNP $35   **MIP** $70

Fashion Play Barbie, 1983, Mattel, Model No. 7193
    MNP $10   **MIP** $20

Fashion Play Barbie, 1987, Mattel, Model No. 4835
    MNP $10   **MIP** $20

Fashion Play Barbie, 1990, Mattel, Model No. 9429
    MNP $2   **MIP** $20

Fashion Play Barbie, 1991, Mattel, Model No. 9629
    MNP $2   **MIP** $20

Fashion Play Barbie, black, 1991, Mattel, Model No. 5953
    MNP $2   **MIP** $15

Fashion Play Barbie, Hispanic, 1990, Mattel, Model No. 5954
    MNP $2   **MIP** $15

Fashion Queen Barbie, 1963, Mattel, Model No. 870
    MNP $80   **MIP** $300

Feelin' Fun Barbie, two versions, white, 1st issue, 1988, Mattel, Model No. 1189
    MNP $5   **MIP** $10

Flight Time Barbie, black, 1990, Mattel, Model No. 9916
    MNP $5   **MIP** $10

Flight Time Barbie, white, 1990, Mattel, Model No. 9584
    MNP $5   **MIP** $15

Flight Time Ken, 1990, Mattel, Model No. 9600
    MNP $5   **MIP** $10

Fluff, 1971, Mattel, Model No. 1143
    MNP $100   **MIP** $225

Francie with Growin' Pretty Hair, 1971, Mattel, Model No. 1129
    MNP $75   **MIP** $175

Francie, bendable leg, blond, brunette, 1966, Mattel, Model No. 1130
    MNP $95   **MIP** $350

Francie, Hair Happenins, 1970, Mattel, Model No. 1122
    MNP $95   **MIP** $350

Francie, straight leg, brunette, blond, 1966, Mattel, Model No. 1140
    MNP $95   **MIP** $350

Francie, Twist N Turn, "Black Francie" 1st issue, red hair, 1967, Mattel, Model No. 1100
    MNP $750   **MIP** $1150

Francie, Twist N Turn, "Black Francie" 2nd issue, black hair, Mattel, Model No. 1100
    MNP $750   **MIP** $1500

(KP Photo)

Francie, Twist N Turn, blond or brunette, "No Bangs", 1967, Mattel, Model No. 1170
    MNP $650   **MIP** $1300

Francie, Twist N Turn, blond or brunette, long hair with bangs, 1969, Mattel, Model No. 1170
    MNP $75   **MIP** $400

Francie, Twist N Turn, blond or brunette, short hair, 1969, Mattel, Model No. 1170
    MNP $75   **MIP** $450

Free Moving Barbie, 1974, Mattel, Model No. 7270
    MNP $50   **MIP** $100

Free Moving Cara, 1974, Mattel, Model No. 7283
    MNP $65   **MIP** $125

Free Moving Ken, 1974, Mattel, Model No. 7280
    MNP $50   **MIP** $75

Free Moving P.J., 1974, Mattel, Model No. 7281
    MNP $50   **MIP** $85

Funtime Barbie, black, 1987, Mattel, Model No. 1739
    MNP $5   **MIP** $10

Funtime Barbie, white, 1987, Mattel, Model No. 1738
    MNP $5   **MIP** $10

Funtime Ken, 1987, Mattel, Model No. 7194
    MNP $7   **MIP** $10

Garden Party Barbie, 1989, Mattel, Model No. 1953
    MNP $8   **MIP** $15

Gift Giving Barbie, 1986, Mattel, Model No. 1922
    MNP $5   **MIP** $25

Gift Giving Barbie, 1989, Mattel, Model No. 1205
    MNP $5   **MIP** $20

Gold Medal Olympic Barbie Skater, 1975, Mattel, Model No. 7262
    MNP $20   **MIP** $75

BARBIE

BARBIE

Gold Medal Olympic Barbie Skier, 1975, Mattel, Model No. 7264
    MNP $20   **MIP** $75

Gold Medal Olympic P.J. Gymnast, 1975, Mattel, Model No. 7263
    MNP $20   **MIP** $85

Gold Medal Olympic Skier Ken, 1975, Mattel, Model No. 7261
    MNP $20   **MIP** $65

Gold Medal Olympic Skipper, 1975, Mattel, Model No. 7274
    MNP $20   **MIP** $65

Golden Dreams Barbie, two versions, 1981, Mattel, Model No. 1974
    MNP $15   **MIP** $50

Golden Dreams Christie, 1981, Mattel, Model No. 3249
    MNP $15   **MIP** $50

Great Shapes Barbie, black, 1984, Mattel, Model No. 7834
    MNP $5   **MIP** $10

Great Shapes Barbie, w/Walkman, 1984, Mattel, Model No. 7025
    MNP $12   **MIP** $15

Great Shapes Barbie, white, 1984, Mattel, Model No. 7025
    MNP $5   **MIP** $10

Great Shapes Ken, 1984, Mattel, Model No. 7310
    MNP $5   **MIP** $10

Great Shapes Skipper, 1984, Mattel, Model No. 7417
    MNP $5   **MIP** $10

Groom Todd, 1982, Mattel, Model No. 4253
    MNP $15   **MIP** $45

Growin' Pretty Hair Barbie, 1971, Mattel, Model No. 1144
    MNP $150   **MIP** $350

Growing Up Ginger, 1977, Mattel, Model No. 9222
    MNP $30   **MIP** $125

(KP Photo)

Growing Up Skipper, 1977, Mattel, Model No. 7259
    MNP $30   **MIP** $100

Happy Birthday Barbie, 1981, Mattel, Model No. 1922
    MNP $8   **MIP** $25

Happy Birthday Barbie, 1984, Mattel, Model No. 1922
    MNP $8   **MIP** $20

Happy Birthday Barbie, 1991, Mattel, Model No. 9561
    MNP $8   **MIP** $10

Happy Birthday Barbie, black, 1991, Mattel, Model No. 9561
    MNP $8   **MIP** $10

Hawaiian Barbie, 1975, Mattel, Model No. 7470
    MNP $25   **MIP** $60

Hawaiian Barbie, 1977, Mattel, Model No. 7470
    MNP $30   **MIP** $70

Hawaiian Fun Barbie, 1991, Mattel, Model No. 5040
    MNP $3   **MIP** $10

Hawaiian Fun Christie, 1991, Mattel, Model No. 5044
    MNP $3   **MIP** $10

Hawaiian Fun Jazzie, 1991, Mattel, Model No. 9294
    MNP $3   **MIP** $10

Hawaiian Fun Ken, 1991, Mattel, Model No. 5041
    MNP $3   **MIP** $10

Hawaiian Fun Kira, 1991, Mattel, Model No. 5043
    MNP $3   **MIP** $10

Hawaiian Fun Skipper, 1991, Mattel, Model No. 5042
    MNP $3   **MIP** $10

Hawaiian Fun Steven, 1991, Mattel, Model No. 5045
    MNP $3   **MIP** $10

Hawaiian Ken, 1979, Mattel, Model No. 2960
    MNP $13   **MIP** $50

Hawaiian Ken, 1984, Mattel, Model No. 7495
    MNP $7   **MIP** $30

High School Chelsie, 1989, Mattel, Model No. 3698
    MNP $5   **MIP** $20

High School Dude, Jazzie's boyfriend, 1989, Mattel, Model No. 3600
    MNP $5   **MIP** $20

High School Jazzie, 1989, Mattel, Model No. 3635
    MNP $5   **MIP** $20

High School Stacie, 1989, Mattel, Model No. 3636
    MNP $5   **MIP** $20

(KP Photo)

Hispanic Barbie, 1980, Mattel, Model No. 1292
    MNP $15   **MIP** $65

Hollywood Nails Barbie, white or black, 1999, Mattel
    MNP $7   **MIP** $15

Hollywood Nails Teresa, white or black, 1999, Mattel
    MNP $7   **MIP** $15

Home Pretty Barbie, 1990, Mattel, Model No. 2249
    MNP $8   **MIP** $15

Homecoming Queen Skipper, black, 1988, Mattel, Model No. 2390
    MNP $8   **MIP** $10

Homecoming Queen Skipper, white, 1988, Mattel, Model No. 1952
    MNP $12   **MIP** $10

Horse Lovin' Barbie, 1983, Mattel, Model No. 1757
    MNP $10   **MIP** $25

Horse Lovin' Ken, 1983, Mattel, Model No. 3600
    MNP $8   **MIP** $20

Horse Lovin' Skipper, 1983, Mattel, Model No. 5029
    MNP $8   **MIP** $20

Hot Stuff Skipper, 1984, Mattel, Model No. 7927
    MNP $5   **MIP** $10

Ice Capades Barbie, 50th Anniversary, black, 1990, Mattel, Model No. 7348
    MNP $5   **MIP** $25

Ice Capades Barbie, 50th Anniversary, white, 1990, Mattel, Model No. 7365
    MNP $5   **MIP** $30

Ice Capades Ken, 1990, Mattel, Model No. 7375
    MNP $5   **MIP** $20

Inline Skating Barbie, 1996, Mattel, Model No. 15473
    MNP $5   **MIP** $20

Inline Skating Ken, 1996, Mattel, Model No. 15474
    MNP $5   **MIP** $20

Inline Skating Midge, 1996, Mattel, Model No. 15475

MNP $5   MIP $20

Island Fun Barbie, 1988, Mattel, Model No. 4061

MNP $3   MIP $10

Island Fun Christie, 1988, Mattel, Model No. 4092

MNP $3   MIP $10

Island Fun Ken, 1988, Mattel, Model No. 4060

MNP $3   MIP $10

Island Fun Skipper, 1988, Mattel, Model No. 4064

MNP $3   MIP $10

Island Fun Steven, 1988, Mattel, Model No. 4093

MNP $3   MIP $10

Island Fun Teresa, 1988, Mattel, Model No. 4117

MNP $3   MIP $10

Jazzie Workout, 1989, Mattel, Model No. 3633

MNP $5   MIP $10

Jewel Girl Barbie, Christie, Teresa (new body style, belly button), 2000, Mattel

MNP $5   MIP $15

Jewel Secrets Barbie, black, two box versions, 1987, Mattel, Model No. 1756

MNP $6   MIP $40

Jewel Secrets Barbie, white, two box versions, 1987, Mattel, Model No. 1737

MNP $6   MIP $40

Jewel Secrets Ken, black, 1987, Mattel, Model No. 3232

MNP $6   MIP $20

Jewel Secrets Ken, rooted hair, 1987, Mattel, Model No. 1719

MNP $6   MIP $20

Jewel Secrets Skipper, 1987, Mattel, Model No. 3133

MNP $6   MIP $20

Jewel Secrets Whitney, 1987, Mattel, Model No. 3179

MNP $8   MIP $25

Julia, talking, first issue with straight hair, 1969, Mattel, Model No. 1128

MNP $85   MIP $250

Julia, talking, second issue, Afro hair, 1969, Mattel, Model No. 1128

MNP $85   MIP $250

Julia, Twist N Turn, one-piece nurse dress, 2nd issue, 1969, Mattel, Model No. 1127

MNP $100   MIP $250

Julia, Twist N Turn, two-piece nurse outfit, 1st issue, 1969, Mattel, Model No. 1127

MNP $125   MIP $300

Ken, bendable leg, brunette, 1965, Mattel, Model No. 750

MNP $155   MIP $300

Ken, flocked hair, brunette, blond, 1961, Mattel, Model No. 750

MNP $50   MIP $100

Ken, painted hair, brunette, blond, 1962, Mattel, Model No. 750

MNP $45   MIP $100

Ken, talking, 1970, Mattel, Model No. 1124

MNP $50   MIP $125

Kevin, 1991, Mattel, Model No. 9325

MNP $5   MIP $10

Kissing Barbie, 1979, Mattel, Model No. 2597

MNP $8   MIP $40

Kissing Christie, 1979, Mattel, Model No. 2955

MNP $10   MIP $40

Lights & Lace Barbie, 1991, Mattel, Model No. 9725

MNP $4   MIP $10

Lights & Lace Christie, 1991, Mattel, Model No. 9728

MNP $4   MIP $10

Lights & Lace Teresa, 1991, Mattel, Model No. 9727

MNP $4   MIP $10

(KP Photo)

Live Action Barbie, 1970, Mattel, Model No. 1155

MNP $60   MIP $150

Live Action Barbie Onstage, 1970, Mattel, Model No. 1152

MNP $75   MIP $250

Live Action Christie, 1970, Mattel, Model No. 1175

MNP $60   MIP $350

Live Action Ken, 1970, Mattel, Model No. 1159

MNP $55   MIP $150

Live Action Ken on Stage, 1970, Mattel, Model No. 1172

MNP $40   MIP $150

Live Action P.J., 1970, Mattel, Model No. 1156

MNP $65   MIP $250

Live Action P.J. on Stage, 1970, Mattel, Model No. 1153

MNP $75   MIP $175

Lovin' You Barbie, 1983, Mattel, Model No. 7072

MNP $20   MIP $50

Magic Curl Barbie, black, 1982, Mattel, Model No. 3989

MNP $8   MIP $20

Magic Curl Barbie, white, 1982, Mattel, Model No. 3856

MNP $10   MIP $25

Magic Moves Barbie, black, 1985, Mattel, Model No. 3137

MNP $15   MIP $25

Magic Moves Barbie, white, 1985, Mattel, Model No. 2126

MNP $15   MIP $25

(KP Photo)

Malibu Barbie, 1971, Mattel, Model No. 1067

MNP $15   MIP $50

Malibu Barbie (Sunset), 1975, Mattel, Model No. 1067

MNP $15   MIP $30

Malibu Christie, 1975, Mattel, Model No. 7745

MNP $10   MIP $50

Malibu Francie, 1971, Mattel, Model No. 1068

MNP $15   MIP $50

Malibu Ken, 1976, Mattel, Model No. 1088

MNP $8   MIP $25

Malibu P.J., 1975, Mattel, Model No. 1087

MNP $5   MIP $50

Malibu Skipper, 1977, Mattel, Model No. 1069

MNP $8   MIP $45

Midge, bendable leg, blond, brunette, titian, 1965, Mattel, Model No. 1080

MNP $200   MIP $425

Midge, straight leg, blond, brunette, titian, 1963, Mattel, Model No. 860

MNP $50   MIP $125

Miss Barbie (sleep eyes), 1964, Mattel, Model No. 1060
      MNP $300   **MIP** $1200

(KP Photo)

Mod Hair Ken, 1972, Mattel, Model No. 4224
      MNP $45   **MIP** $65

Music Lovin' Barbie, 1985, Mattel, Model No. 9988
      MNP $10   **MIP** $20

Music Lovin' Ken, 1985, Mattel, Model No. 2388
      MNP $10   **MIP** $20

Music Lovin' Skipper, 1985, Mattel, Model No. 2854
      MNP $10   **MIP** $20

My First Barbie, 1991, Mattel, Model No. 9942
      MNP $3   **MIP** $25

My First Barbie, aqua and yellow dress, 1981, Mattel, Model No. 1875
      MNP $10   **MIP** $20

My First Barbie, black, 1990, Mattel, Model No. 9943
      MNP $5   **MIP** $20

My First Barbie, Hispanic, 1991, Mattel, Model No. 9944
      MNP $3   **MIP** $15

My First Barbie, pink checkered dress, 1983, Mattel, Model No. 1875
      MNP $5   **MIP** $25

My First Barbie, pink tutu, black, 1987, Mattel, Model No. 1801
      MNP $5   **MIP** $15

My First Barbie, pink tutu, white, 1987, Mattel, Model No. 1788
      MNP $5   **MIP** $15

My First Barbie, white, 1990, Mattel, Model No. 9942
      MNP $4   **MIP** $15

My First Barbie, white dress, black, 1984, Mattel, Model No. 9858
      MNP $7   **MIP** $15

My First Barbie, white dress, white, 1984, Mattel, Model No. 1875
      MNP $5   **MIP** $20

My First Barbie, white tutu, black, 1988, Mattel, Model No. 1281
      MNP $6   **MIP** $10

My First Barbie, white tutu, Hispanic, 1988, Mattel, Model No. 1282
      MNP $6   **MIP** $10

My First Barbie, white tutu, white, 1988, Mattel, Model No. 1280
      MNP $5   **MIP** $10

My First Ken, 1st issue, 1989, Mattel, Model No. 1389
      MNP $4   **MIP** $15

My First Ken, Prince, 1990, Mattel, Model No. 9940
      MNP $4   **MIP** $15

New Look Ken, 1976, Mattel, Model No. 9342
      MNP $23   **MIP** $65

Newport Barbie, two versions, 1974, Mattel, Model No. 7807
      MNP $25   **MIP** $125

Nurse Whitney, 1987, Mattel, Model No. 4405
      MNP $15   **MIP** $30

Ocean Friends Barbie, 1996, Mattel, Model No. 15430
      MNP $5   **MIP** $10

Ocean Friends Ken, 1996, Mattel, Model No. 15430
      MNP $5   **MIP** $10

Ocean Friends Kira, 1996, Mattel, Model No. 15431
      MNP $5   **MIP** $10

Olympic Gymnast, blond, 1996, Mattel, Model No. 15123
      MNP $10   **MIP** $20

P.J., talking, 1970, Mattel, Model No. 1113
      MNP $65   **MIP** $250

P.J., Twist N Turn, 1970, Mattel, Model No. 1118
      MNP $75   **MIP** $300

Party Treats Barbie, 1989, Mattel, Model No. 4885
      MNP $8   **MIP** $25

Peaches n' Cream Barbie, black, 1984, Mattel, Model No. 9516
      MNP $8   **MIP** $40

Peaches n' Cream Barbie, white, 1984, Mattel, Model No. 7926
      MNP $8   **MIP** $45

Perfume Giving Ken, black, 1989, Mattel, Model No. 4555
      MNP $6   **MIP** $20

Perfume Giving Ken, white, 1989, Mattel, Model No. 4554
      MNP $6   **MIP** $20

Perfume Pretty Barbie, black, 1989, Mattel, Model No. 4552
      MNP $8   **MIP** $20

Perfume Pretty Barbie, white, 1989, Mattel, Model No. 4551
      MNP $8   **MIP** $20

Perfume Pretty Whitney, 1987, Mattel, Model No. 4557
      MNP $8   **MIP** $20

Pink n' Pretty Barbie, 1982, Mattel, Model No. 3551
      MNP $12   **MIP** $45

Pink n' Pretty Christie, 1982, Mattel, Model No. 3554
      MNP $10   **MIP** $40

Playtime Barbie, 1984, Mattel, Model No. 5336
      MNP $5   **MIP** $10

(KP Photo)

Ponytail Barbie #1, blond, 1959, Mattel, Model No. 850
      MNP $2000   **MIP** $5000

(KP Photo)

Ponytail Barbie #1, brunette, 1959, Mattel, Model No. 850
      MNP $2500   **MIP** $5500

Ponytail Barbie #2, blond, 1959, Mattel, Model No. 850
      MNP $2500   **MIP** $5000

Ponytail Barbie #2, brunette, 1959, Mattel, Model No. 850
      MNP $3000   **MIP** $6500

Ponytail Barbie #3, blond, 1960, Mattel, Model No. 850
      MNP $350   **MIP** $900

Ponytail Barbie #3, brunette, 1960, Mattel, Model No. 850
      MNP $400   **MIP** $1000

Ponytail Barbie #4, blond, 1960, Mattel, Model No. 850
      MNP $200   **MIP** $500

Ponytail Barbie #4, brunette, 1960, Mattel, Model No. 850
      MNP $300   **MIP** $400

Ponytail Barbie #5, blond, 1961, Mattel, Model No. 850
    MNP $150   **MIP** $350

Ponytail Barbie #5, brunette, 1961, Mattel, Model No. 850
    MNP $225   **MIP** $400

Ponytail Barbie #5, titian, 1961, Mattel, Model No. 850
    MNP $250   **MIP** $500

Ponytail Barbie #6, blond, 1962, Mattel, Model No. 850
    MNP $150   **MIP** $400

Ponytail Barbie #6, brunette, 1962, Mattel, Model No. 850
    MNP $150   **MIP** $400

Ponytail Barbie #6, titian, 1962, Mattel, Model No. 850
    MNP $150   **MIP** $400

Ponytail Swirl Style Barbie, blond, 1964, Mattel, Model No. 850
    MNP $300   **MIP** $600

Ponytail Swirl Style Barbie, brunette, 1964, Mattel, Model No. 850
    MNP $300   **MIP** $600

Ponytail Swirl Style Barbie, platinum, 1964, Mattel, Model No. 850
    MNP $500   **MIP** $1200

Ponytail Swirl Style Barbie, titian, 1964, Mattel, Model No. 850
    MNP $300   **MIP** $600

Pose n' Play Skipper (baggie), 1973, Mattel, Model No. 1117
    MNP $20   **MIP** $55

Pretty Changes Barbie, 1978, Mattel, Model No. 2598
    MNP $8   **MIP** $30

Pretty Party Barbie, 1983, Mattel, Model No. 7194
    MNP $12   **MIP** $25

(KP Photo)

Quick Curl Barbie, 1972, Mattel, Model No. 4220
    MNP $20   **MIP** $80

Quick Curl Cara, 1974, Mattel, Model No. 7291
    MNP $20   **MIP** $60

Quick Curl Deluxe Barbie, 1976, Mattel, Model No. 9217
    MNP $20   **MIP** $75

Quick Curl Deluxe Cara, 1976, Mattel, Model No. 9219
    MNP $20   **MIP** $60

Quick Curl Deluxe P.J., 1976, Mattel, Model No. 9218
    MNP $20   **MIP** $50

Quick Curl Deluxe Skipper, 1976, Mattel, Model No. 9428
    MNP $20   **MIP** $50

Quick Curl Francie, 1972, Mattel, Model No. 4222
    MNP $20   **MIP** $55

Quick Curl Kelley, 1972, Mattel, Model No. 4221
    MNP $20   **MIP** $75

(KP Photo)

Quick Curl Miss America, blond, 1974, Mattel, Model No. 8697
    MNP $35   **MIP** $75

Quick Curl Miss America, brunette, 1973, Mattel, Model No. 8697
    MNP $45   **MIP** $125

Quick Curl Skipper, 1974, Mattel, Model No. 4223
    MNP $20   **MIP** $50

Ricky, 1965, Mattel, Model No. 1090
    MNP $55   **MIP** $125

Rocker Barbie, 1st issue, 1986, Mattel, Model No. 1140
    MNP $7   **MIP** $30

(KP Photo)

Rocker Barbie, 2nd issue, 1987, Mattel, Model No. 3055
    MNP $7   **MIP** $20

Rocker Dana, 1st issue, 1986, Mattel, Model No. 1196
    MNP $7   **MIP** $30

Rocker Dana, 2nd issue, 1987, Mattel, Model No. 3158
    MNP $7   **MIP** $15

Rocker Dee-Dee, 1st issue, 1986, Mattel, Model No. 1141
    MNP $7   **MIP** $25

Rocker Dee-Dee, 2nd issue, 1987, Mattel, Model No. 3160
    MNP $7   **MIP** $15

Rocker Derek, 1st issue, 1986, Mattel, Model No. 2428
    MNP $7   **MIP** $25

Rocker Derek, 2nd issue, 1987, Mattel, Model No. 3173
    MNP $7   **MIP** $15

Rocker Diva, 1st issue, 1986, Mattel, Model No. 2427
    MNP $7   **MIP** $35

Rocker Diva, 2nd issue, 1987, Mattel, Model No. 3159
    MNP $7   **MIP** $15

Rocker Ken, 1st issue, 1986, Mattel, Model No. 3131
    MNP $7   **MIP** $35

Rollerskating Barbie, 1980, Mattel, Model No. 1880
    MNP $8   **MIP** $50

BARBIE

Rollerskating Ken, 1980, Mattel, Model No. 1881
      MNP $8   **MIP** $40

Safari Barbie, 1983, Mattel, Model No. 4973
      MNP $8   **MIP** $20

Scott, 1979, Mattel, Model No. 1019
      MNP $15   **MIP** $60

Sea Lovin' Barbie, 1984, Mattel, Model No. 9109
      MNP $8   **MIP** $20

Sea Lovin' Ken, 1984, Mattel, Model No. 9110
      MNP $8   **MIP** $20

Secret Messages Barbie, white or black, 2000, Model No. 26422
      MNP $7   **MIP** $10

Sensations Barbie, 1987, Mattel, Model No. 4931
      MNP $5   **MIP** $10

Sensations Becky, 1987, Mattel, Model No. 4977
      MNP $5   **MIP** $10

Sensations Belinda, 1987, Mattel, Model No. 4976
      MNP $5   **MIP** $10

Sensations Bobsy, 1987, Mattel, Model No. 4967
      MNP $5   **MIP** $10

Sit 'n Style Barbie, 2000, Mattel, Model No. 23421
      MNP $7   **MIP** $10

Ski Fun Barbie, 1991, Mattel, Model No. 7511
      MNP $6   **MIP** $15

Ski Fun Ken, 1991, Mattel, Model No. 7512
      MNP $6   **MIP** $15

Ski Fun Midge, 1991, Mattel, Model No. 7513
      MNP $6   **MIP** $25

(KP Photo)

Skipper, bendable leg, brunette, blond, titian, 1965, Mattel, Model No. 1030
      MNP $60   **MIP** $150

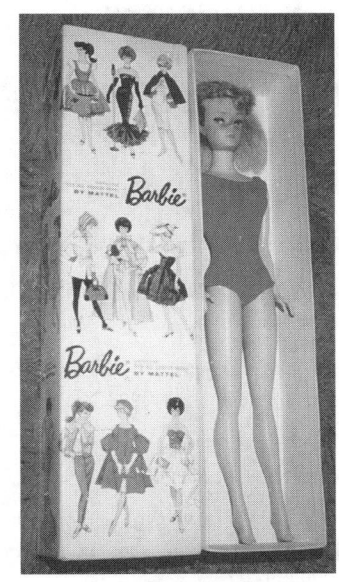

Skipper, straight leg, brunette, blond, titian, 1964, Mattel, Model No. 950
      MNP $30   **MIP** $125

Skipper, straight leg, reissues, brunette, blond, titian, 1971, Mattel, Model No. 950
      MNP $125   **MIP** $400

Skipper, Twist N Turn, blonde or brunette, curl pigtails, 1969, Mattel, Model No. 1105
      MNP $75   **MIP** $225

Skipper, Twist N Turn, blonde, brunette, red hair, long straight hair, 1968, Mattel, Model No. 1105
      MNP $75   **MIP** $225

(KP Photo)

Skooter, bendable leg, brunette, blond, titian, 1966, Mattel, Model No. 1120
      MNP $75   **MIP** $300

Skooter, straight leg, brunette, blond, titian, 1965, Mattel, Model No. 1040
      MNP $30   **MIP** $125

Snowboard Barbie, 1996, Mattel, Model No. 15408
      MNP $10   **MIP** $20

Sparkle Barbie, 1996, Mattel, Model No. 15419
      MNP $10   **MIP** $20

Sport 'n Shave Ken, 1980, Mattel, Model No. 1294
      MNP $8   **MIP** $40

Stacey, talking, blonde or red hair, side ponytail, 1968, Mattel, Model No. 1125
      MNP $175   **MIP** $425

Stacey, Twist and Turn, blonde or red hair, long ponytail with spit curls, 1968, Mattel, Model No. 1165
      MNP $150   **MIP** $425

Stacey, Twist N Turn, blonde or red hair, short rolled flip, 1969, Mattel, Model No. 1165
      MNP $175   **MIP** $425

Standard Barbie, blond, brunette, long straight hair with bangs, 1967, Mattel, Model No. 1190
      MNP $175   **MIP** $450

Standard Barbie, centered eyes, 1971, Mattel, Model No. 1190
      MNP $300   **MIP** $500

Standard Barbie, titian, long straight hair with bangs, 1967, Mattel, Model No. 1190
      MNP $250   **MIP** $450

Stars & Stripes Air Force Barbie, 1990, Mattel, Model No. 3360
      MNP $15   **MIP** $20

BARBIE

(KP Photo)

Stars & Stripes Army Barbie, white or black, 1993, Mattel, Model No. 1234/5618
MNP $10   MIP $20

Stars & Stripes Marine Corps Barbie, white or black, 1992, Mattel, Model No. 7549/7594
MNP $10   MIP $20

(KP Photo)

Stars & Stripes Navy Barbie, white or black, 1991, Mattel, Model No. 9693/9694
MNP $10   MIP $20

Stars 'n Stripes Air Force Ken, white or black, 1994, Mattel, Model No. 11554/11555
MNP $15   MIP $20

Stars 'n Stripes Air Force Thunderbirds Barbie, white or black, 1994, Mattel, Model No. 11552/11553
MNP $15   MIP $20

Stars 'n Stripes Army Ken, white or black, 1993, Mattel, Model No. 1237/5619
MNP $15   MIP $20

Stars 'n Stripes Marine Corps Ken, black or white, 1992, Mattel, Model No. 5352/7574
MNP $20   MIP $20

Style Magic Barbie, 1989, Mattel, Model No. 1283
MNP $5   MIP $20

Style Magic Christie, 1989, Mattel, Model No. 1288
MNP $5   MIP $20

Style Magic Skipper, 1989, Mattel, Model No. 1915
MNP $10   MIP $20

Style Magic Whitney, 1989, Mattel, Model No. 1290
MNP $5   MIP $20

Summit Barbie, Asian, 1990, Mattel, Model No. 7029
MNP $10   MIP $15

Summit Barbie, black, 1990, Mattel, Model No. 7028
MNP $12   MIP $15

Summit Barbie, Hispanic, 1990, Mattel, Model No. 7030
MNP $10   MIP $15

Summit Barbie, white, 1990, Mattel, Model No. 7027
MNP $8   MIP $15

Sun Gold Malibu Barbie, black, 1983, Mattel, Model No. 7745
MNP $5   MIP $15

Sun Gold Malibu Barbie, Hispanic, 1985, Mattel, Model No. 4970
MNP $3   MIP $20
(KP Photo)

Sun Gold Malibu Barbie, white, 1983, Mattel, Model No. 1067
MNP $5   MIP $15

Sun Gold Malibu Ken, black, 1983, Mattel, Model No. 3849
MNP $3   MIP $15

Sun Gold Malibu Ken, Hispanic, 1985, Mattel, Model No. 4971
MNP $3   MIP $20

Sun Gold Malibu Ken, white, 1983, Mattel, Model No. 1088
MNP $3   MIP $15

Sun Gold Malibu P.J., 1983, Mattel, Model No. 1187
MNP $5   MIP $15

Sun Gold Malibu Skipper, 1983, Mattel, Model No. 1069
MNP $5   MIP $15

Sun Lovin' Malibu Barbie, 1978, Mattel, Model No. 1067
MNP $5   MIP $20

Sun Lovin' Malibu Ken, 1978, Mattel, Model No. 1088
MNP $5   MIP $20

Sun Lovin' Malibu P.J., 1978, Mattel, Model No. 1187
MNP $5   MIP $20

Sun Lovin' Malibu Skipper, 1978, Mattel, Model No. 1069
MNP $5   MIP $20

Sun Valley Barbie, 1974, Mattel, Model No. 7806
MNP $20   MIP $130

Sun Valley Ken, 1974, Mattel, Model No. 7809
MNP $20   MIP $100

Sunsational Malibu Barbie, 1982, Mattel, Model No. 1067
MNP $6   MIP $25

Sunsational Malibu Barbie, Hispanic, 1982, Mattel, Model No. 4970
MNP $8   MIP $25

Sunsational Malibu Christie, 1982, Mattel, Model No. 7745
MNP $6   MIP $20

(KP Photo)

Sunsational Malibu Ken, black, 1981, Mattel, Model No. 3849
MNP $15   MIP $35

Sunsational Malibu P.J., 1982, Mattel, Model No. 1187
MNP $6   MIP $30

Sunsational Malibu Skipper, 1982, Mattel, Model No. 1069
MNP $5   MIP $35

Sunset Malibu Christie, 1973, Mattel, Model No. 7745
MNP $20   MIP $65

Sunset Malibu Francie, 1971, Mattel, Model No. 1068
MNP $25   MIP $65

Sunset Malibu Ken, 1972, Mattel, Model No. 1088
MNP $15   MIP $50

Sunset Malibu P.J., 1971, Mattel, Model No. 1187
MNP $10   MIP $50

Sunset Malibu Skipper, 1971, Mattel, Model No. 1069
MNP $20   MIP $50

Super Hair Barbie, black, 1987, Mattel, Model No. 3296
MNP $8   MIP $15

Super Hair Barbie, white, 1987, Mattel, Model No. 3101
MNP $8   MIP $15

Super Sport Ken, 1982, Mattel, Model No. 5839
MNP $8   MIP $15

BARBIE

Super Talk Barbie, 1994, Mattel, Model No. 12290
    MNP $10   **MIP** $15

Super Teen Skipper, 1978, Mattel, Model No. 2756
    MNP $7   **MIP** $20

Supersize Barbie, 1977, Mattel, Model No. 9828
    MNP $60   **MIP** $150

Supersize Bride Barbie, 1977, Mattel, Model No. 9975
    MNP $100   **MIP** $250

Supersize Christie, 1977, Mattel, Model No. 9839
    MNP $75   **MIP** $250

Supersize Super Hair Barbie, 1979, Mattel, Model No. 2844
    MNP $85   **MIP** $125

Superstar Ballerina Barbie, 1976, Mattel, Model No. 4983
    MNP $20   **MIP** $60

Superstar Barbie, 1977, Mattel, Model No. 9720
    MNP $15   **MIP** $70

Superstar Barbie, 1988, Mattel, Model No. 1604
    MNP $45   **MIP** $95

Superstar Barbie 30th Anniversary, black, 1989, Mattel, Model No. 1605
    MNP $6   **MIP** $35

Superstar Barbie 30th Anniversary, white, 1989, Mattel, Model No. 1604
    MNP $8   **MIP** $25

Superstar Christie, 1977, Mattel, Model No. 9950
    MNP $20   **MIP** $75

Superstar Ken, 1978, Mattel, Model No. 2211
    MNP $17   **MIP** $75

Superstar Ken, black, 1989, Mattel, Model No. 1550
    MNP $5   **MIP** $30

Superstar Ken, white, 1989, Mattel, Model No. 1535
    MNP $7   **MIP** $50

Superstar Malibu Barbie, 1977, Mattel, Model No. 1067
    MNP $10   **MIP** $35

Sweet 16 Barbie, 1974, Mattel, Model No. 7796
    MNP $25   **MIP** $125

Sweet Roses P.J., 1983, Mattel, Model No. 7455
    MNP $15   **MIP** $25

Swimming Champion Barbie, 2000, Mattel, Model No. 24590
    MNP $7   **MIP** $15

Talk With Me Barbie, 1997, Mattel, with software, Model No. 17350
    MNP $25   **MIP** $40

Talking Barbie, chignon with nape curls, blonde, brunette, titian, 1970, Mattel, Model No. 1115
    MNP $150   **MIP** $500

(KP Photo)

Talking Barbie, side ponytail with spit curls, blonde or brunette, 1968, Mattel, Model No. 1115
    MNP $100   **MIP** $425

Talking Busy Barbie, 1972, Mattel, Model No. 1195
    MNP $100   **MIP** $300

Talking Busy Ken, 1972, Mattel, Model No. 1196
    MNP $70   **MiP** $160

(KP Photo)

Talking Busy Steffie, 1972, Mattel, Model No. 1186
    MNP $150   **MIP** $350

Talking Ken, 1969, Mattel, Model No. 1111
    MNP $60   **MIP** $175

Teacher Barbie, painted on panties, black, 1996, Mattel, Model No. 13915
    MNP $15   **MIP** $20

Teacher Barbie, painted on panties, white, 1996, Mattel, Model No. 13914
    MNP $15   **MIP** $25

Teen Dance Jazzie, 1989, Mattel, Model No. 3634
    MNP $7   **MIP** $20

Teen Fun Skipper Cheerleader, 1987, Mattel, Model No. 5893
    MNP $5   **MIP** $15

Teen Fun Skipper Party Teen, 1987, Mattel, Model No. 5899
    MNP $5   **MIP** $15

Teen Fun Skipper Workout, 1987, Mattel, Model No. 5889
    MNP $5   **MIP** $15

Teen Jazzie (Teen Dance), 1989, Mattel, Model No. 3634
    MNP $4   **MIP** $35

Teen Looks Jazzie Cheerleader, 1989, Mattel, Model No. 3631
    MNP $4   **MIP** $20

Teen Looks Jazzie Workout, 1989, Mattel, Model No. 3633
    MNP $4   **MIP** $20

Teen Scene Jazzie, two box versions, 1991, Mattel, Model No. 5507
    MNP $5   **MIP** $35

Teen Sweetheart Skipper, 1988, Mattel, Model No. 4855
    MNP $5   **MIP** $25

Teen Talk Barbie, 1992, Mattel, Model No. 5745
    MNP $15   **MIP** $25

Teen Talk Barbie, "Math is Tough" variation, 1992, Mattel, Model No. 5745
    MNP $50   **MIP** $275

Teen Time Courtney, 1988, Mattel, Model No. 1950
    MNP $5   **MIP** $10

Teen Time Skipper, 1988, Mattel, Model No. 1951
    MNP $5   **MIP** $10

Tennis Barbie, 1986, Mattel, Model No. 1760
    MNP $5   **MIP** $20

Tennis Ken, 1986, Mattel, Model No. 1761
    MNP $5   **MIP** $20

(KP Photo)

Todd, 1967, Mattel, Model No. 3590
    MNP $70   **MIP** $200

Tracy Bride, 1983, Mattel, Model No. 4103
    MNP $8   **MIP** $45

Tropical Barbie, black, 1986, Mattel, Model No. 1022

> **MNP** $3   **MIP** $10

Tropical Barbie, white, 1986, Mattel, Model No. 1017

> **MNP** $3   **MIP** $10

Tropical Ken, black, 1986, Mattel, Model No. 1023

> **MNP** $3   **MIP** $10

Tropical Ken, white, 1986, Mattel, Model No. 4060

> **MNP** $3   **MIP** $10

Tropical Miko, 1986, Mattel, Model No. 2056

> **MNP** $3   **MIP** $10

Tropical Skipper, 1986, Mattel, Model No. 4064

> **MNP** $3   **MIP** $10

Truly Scrumptious, standard, 1969, Mattel, Model No. 1107

> **MNP** $175   **MIP** $400

Truly Scrumptious, talking, 1969, Mattel, Model No. 1108

> **MNP** $175   **MIP** $450

Tutti, all hair colors, floral dress w/yellow ribbon, 1967, Mattel, Model No. 3580

> **MNP** $45   **MIP** $150

(KP Photo)

Tutti, all hair colors, pink, white gingham suit, hat, 1966, Mattel, Model No. 3550

> **MNP** $50   **MIP** $170

Tutti, Germany, 1978, Mattel, Model No. 8128

> **MNP** $40   **MIP** $125

Twiggy, 1967, Mattel, Model No. 1185

> **MNP** $95   **MIP** $300

Twirley Curls Barbie, black, 1983, Mattel, Model No. 5723

> **MNP** $10   **MIP** $25

Twirley Curls Barbie, Hispanic, 1982, Mattel, Model No. 5724

> **MNP** $10   **MIP** $25

Twirley Curls Barbie, white, 1982, Mattel, Model No. 5579

> **MNP** $10   **MIP** $25

Twist N Turn Barbie, blonde, brunette, red hair with centered eyes, 1971, Mattel, Model No. 1160

> **MNP** $175   **MIP** $600

Twist N Turn Barbie, flip hair, blonde or brunette, 1969, Mattel, Model No. 1160

> **MNP** $95   **MIP** $450

Twist N Turn Barbie, light blonde, blonde, light brown, brunette, 1967, Mattel, Model No. 1160

> **MNP** $90   **MIP** $450

Twist N Turn Barbie, long straight hair with bangs, red hair, 1967, Mattel, Model No. 1160

> **MNP** $175   **MIP** $600

UNICEF Barbie, Asian, 1989, Mattel, Model No. 4774

> **MNP** $5   **MIP** $10

UNICEF Barbie, black, 1989, Mattel, Model No. 4770

> **MNP** $5   **MIP** $10

UNICEF Barbie, Hispanic, 1989, Mattel, Model No. 4782

> **MNP** $5   **MIP** $10

UNICEF Barbie, white, 1989, Mattel, Model No. 1920

> **MNP** $5   **MIP** $10

University Barbie, 1997, Mattel, many schools offered

> **MNP** $8   **MIP** $15

(KP Photo)

Walk Lively Barbie, 1971, Mattel, Model No. 1182

> **MNP** $75   **MIP** $200

Walk Lively Ken, 1971, Mattel, Model No. 1184

> **MNP** $40   **MIP** $150

Walk Lively Miss America Barbie, brunette, 1971, Mattel, Model No. 3200

> **MNP** $95   **MIP** $200

Walk Lively Steffie, 1971, Mattel, Model No. 1183

> **MNP** $75   **MIP** $300

Walking Jamie, 1970, Mattel, Model No. 1132

> **MNP** $175   **MIP** $400

Wedding Fantasy Barbie, black, 1989, Mattel, Model No. 7011

> **MNP** $7   **MIP** $20

Wedding Fantasy Barbie, white, 1989, Mattel, Model No. 2125

> **MNP** $7   **MIP** $20

Wedding Party Allan, 1991, Mattel, Model No. 9607

> **MNP** $7   **MIP** $20

Wedding Party Barbie, 1991, Mattel, Model No. 9608

> **MNP** $7   **MIP** $20

Wedding Party Kelly & Todd, 1991, Mattel, Model No. 9852

> **MNP** $15   **MIP** $25

Wedding Party Ken, 1991, Mattel, Model No. 9609

> **MNP** $7   **MIP** $20

Wedding Party Midge, 1991, Mattel, Model No. 9606

> **MNP** $7   **MIP** $15

Western Barbie, 1980, Mattel, Model No. 1757

> **MNP** $8   **MIP** $40

Western Fun Barbie, black, 1989, Mattel, Model No. 2930

> **MNP** $5   **MIP** $15

BARBIE

Western Fun Barbie, white, 1989, Mattel, Model No. 9932
MNP $5   MIP $15

Western Fun Ken, 1989, Mattel, Model No. 9934
MNP $5   MIP $15

Western Fun Nia, 1989, Mattel, Model No. 9933
MNP $5   MIP $15

Western Ken, 1981, Mattel, Model No. 3600
MNP $7   MIP $40

Western Skipper, 1982, Mattel, Model No. 5029
MNP $8   MIP $30

Wet 'n Wild Barbie, 1990, Mattel, Model No. 4103
MNP $8   MIP $15

Wet 'n Wild Christie, 1989, Mattel, Model No. 4121
MNP $3   MIP $10

Wet 'n Wild Ken, 1989, Mattel, Model No. 4104
MNP $3   MIP $10

Wet 'n Wild Kira, 1989, Mattel, Model No. 4120
MNP $3   MIP $10

Wet 'n Wild Skipper, 1989, Mattel, Model No. 4138
MNP $3   MIP $10

Wet 'n Wild Steven, 1989, Mattel, Model No. 4137
MNP $3   MIP $10

Wet 'n Wild Teresa, 1989, Mattel, Model No. 4136
MNP $3   MIP $10

Wig Wardrobe Midge, 1965, Mattel, Model No. 1009
MNP $200   MIP $500

Working Woman Barbie, black or white, 1999, Mattel
MNP $7   MIP $10

COLLECTORS' EDITIONS, STORE EXCLUSIVES, GIFT SETS

1 Modern Circle Barbie, 2003, Mattel
MNP $20   MIP $30

1 Modern Circle Barbie (Evening Wear), 2004, Mattel
MNP n/a   MIP $40

1 Modern Circle Ken, 2003, Mattel
MNP $20   MIP $30

1 Modern Circle Ken (Evening Wear), 2004, Mattel
MNP n/a   MIP $40

1 Modern Circle Melody, 2003, Mattel
MNP $20   MIP $30

1 Modern Circle Melody (Evening Wear), 2004, Mattel
MNP n/a   MIP $40

1 Modern Circle Simone, 2003, Mattel
MNP $20   MIP $30

1 Modern Circle Simone (Evening Wear), 2004, Mattel
MNP n/a   MIP $40

40th Anniversary Barbie, white or black, 1999, Mattel, Model No. 21384/22336
MNP $25   MIP $40

40th Anniversary Gala, 1999, Mattel, "bumblebee"
MNP $30   MIP $90

40th Anniversary Ken, black, 2001, Mattel, Model No. 52967
MNP $15   MIP $35

40th Anniversary Ken, white, 2001, Mattel, Model No. 50722
MNP $15   MIP $35

All American Barbie & Starstepper, 1991, Mattel, Model No. 3712
MNP $12   MIP $35

American Stories #1 American Indian, 1996, Mattel, Model No. 14612
MNP $7   MIP $10

American Stories #2 American Indian, 1997, Mattel, Model No. 17313
MNP $7   MIP $10

American Stories Civil War Nurse, 1996, Mattel, Model No. 14612
MNP $7   MIP $10

American Stories Colonial Barbie, 1995, Mattel, Model No. 12578
MNP $7   MIP $10

American Stories Patriot Barbie, 1997, Mattel, Model No. 17312
MNP $7   MIP $10

American Stories Pilgrim Barbie, 1995, Mattel, Model No. 12577
MNP $7   MIP $10

American Stories Pioneer Barbie, 1995, Mattel, Model No. 12680
MNP $7   MIP $10

American Stories Pioneer Shopkeeper, 1996, Mattel, Model No. 14756
MNP $7   MIP $10

Ames Country Looks Barbie, 1993, Mattel, Model No. 5854
MNP $8   MIP $20

Ames Denim 'N Lace Barbie, 1992, Mattel, Model No. 2452
MNP $10   MIP $25

Ames Hot Looks Barbie, 1992, Mattel, Model No. 5756
MNP $10   MIP $20

Ames Ice Cream Barbie, 1998, Mattel, Model No. 19280
MNP $8   MIP $15

Ames Lady Bug Fun Barbie, 1997, Mattel, Model No. 17695
MNP $5   MIP $15

Ames Party in Pink, 1991, Mattel, Model No. 2909
MNP $10   MIP $20

Ames Strawberry Party Barbie, 1999, Mattel, Model No. 22895
MNP $8   MIP $10

Angel Lights Barbie, 1993, Mattel
MNP $40   MIP $65

Angels of Music Harpist Angel, black or white, 1998, Mattel
MNP $35   MIP $50

Angels of Music Heartstring Angel, black or white, 1999, Mattel
MNP $40   MIP $50

Anne Klein Barbie, 1997, Mattel, Model No. 17603
MNP $35   MIP $50

Applause Barbie Holiday, 1991, Mattel, Model No. 3406
MNP $20   MIP $20

Applause Style Barbie, 1990, Mattel, Model No. 5313
MNP $10   MIP $20

Armani Barbie, 2003, Mattel
MNP $75   MIP $150

Artist Series, Reflections of Light Barbie, Renoir, 1999, Mattel, Model No. 23884
MNP $40   MIP $60

Artist Series, Sunflower Barbie, Van Gogh, 1998, Mattel, Model No. 19366
MNP $40   MIP $60

Artist Series, Water Lily Barbie, Monet, 1997, Mattel, Model No. 17783
MNP $50   MIP $60

Avon Blushing Bride Barbie, white or black, 2000, Mattel
MNP $10   MIP $20

Avon Exotic Intrigue, 2004, Mattel, Blonde, Hispanic, African American
n/a n/a

Avon Fruit Fantasy Barbie, blonde, 1999, Mattel
MNP $10   MIP $20

Avon Fruit Fantasy Barbie, brunette, 1999, Mattel
MNP $15   MIP $20

Avon Lemon-Lime Barbie, 1999, Mattel, Model No. 20318
MNP $10   MIP $20

Avon Mrs. P.F.E. Albee, 1997, Mattel, Model No. 17690
MNP $15   MIP $45

Avon Mrs. P.F.E. Albee #2, 1998, Mattel, Model No. 20330
MNP $15   MIP $45

Avon Representative Barbie, black, white, Hispanic, 1999, Mattel
MNP $20   MIP $50

Avon Snow Sensation, black or white, 1999, Mattel
MNP $15   MIP $30

Avon Spring Blossom, black, 1996, Mattel, Model No. 15202
MNP $5   MIP $10

Avon Spring Blossom, white, 1996, Mattel, Model No. 15201
MNP $5   MIP $10

Avon Spring Petals Barbie, black, 1997, Mattel, Model No. 16871
MNP $5   MIP $10

Avon Spring Petals Barbie, blond or brunette, 1997, Mattel, Model No. 10746/16872

    MNP $5   **MIP** $10

Avon Spring Tea Party Barbie, black, Mattel

    MNP $10   **MIP** $20

Avon Spring Tea Party Barbie, blond or brunette, Mattel, Model No. 18658

    MNP $10   **MIP** $20

Avon Strawberry Sorbet Barbie, 1999, Mattel, Model No. 20317

    MNP $5   **MIP** $15

Avon Timeless Silhouette Barbie, white or black, 2001, Mattel

    MNP $10   **MIP** $25

Avon Victorian Skater Barbie, white or black, 2000, Mattel

    MNP $10   **MIP** $35

Avon Winter Rhapsody Barbie, black, Mattel, Model No. 16354

    MNP $15   **MIP** $30

Avon Winter Rhapsody Barbie, blond or brunette, Mattel, Model No. 16353/16873

    MNP $15   **MIP** $30

Avon Winter Splendor Barbie, black, 1998, Mattel, Model No. 19358

    MNP $20   **MIP** $40

Avon Winter Splendor Barbie, white, 1998, Mattel, Model No. 19357

    MNP $15   **MIP** $35

Avon Winter Velvet, black, 1996, Mattel, Model No. 15587

    MNP $10   **MIP** $25

Avon Winter Velvet, white, 1996, Mattel, Model No. 15571

    MNP $10   **MIP** $25

B Mine Barbie, 1993, Mattel, Model No. 11182

    MNP $7   **MIP** $10

Back To School, 1993, Mattel, Model No. 3208

    MNP $15   **MIP** $35

Back to School, 1997, Mattel

    MNP $5   **MIP** $10

Badgley Mischka Bride, 2004, Mattel

    MNP n/a   **MIP** $140

Ballerina Barbie as Juliet, 2004, Mattel

    MNP n/a   **MIP** $35

Ballerina Barbie as Titania, 2004, Mattel

    MNP n/a   **MIP** $35

Ballerina Barbie Peppermint Candy Cane, 2003, Mattel

    MNP $10   **MIP** $30

Ballerina Dreams Barbie, 2000, Mattel, Model No. 20676

    MNP $5   **MIP** $12

Ballerina on Tour Gift Set, 1976, Mattel, Model No. 9613

    MNP $25   **MIP** $125

Ballet Lessons Barbie, black or white, 2000, Mattel

    MNP $5   **MIP** $12

Ballroom Beauties, Midnight Waltz, 1996, Mattel, Model No. 15685

    MNP $35   **MIP** $50

Ballroom Beauties, Moonlight Waltz Barbie, 1997, Mattel, Model No. 17763

    MNP $40   **MIP** $50

Ballroom Beauties, Starlight Waltz Barbie, 1995, Mattel, Model No. 14070

    MNP $35   **MIP** $50

Barbie 2000, white or black, 2000, Mattel, Model No. 27409/27410

    MNP $20   **MIP** $40

Barbie 2001, black or white, 2001, Mattel, Model No. 50842/50841

    MNP $15   **MIP** $40

Barbie 2002, (white or black), 2002, Mattel, Model No. 53975/53976

    MNP $20   **MIP** $40

Barbie 2003, White or African American, 2003, Mattel

    MNP $15   **MIP** $40

Barbie and Friends: Ken, Barbie, P.J., 1983, Mattel, Model No. 4431

    MNP $25   **MIP** $75

Barbie and Ken as Arwen & Aragorn in Lord of the Rings: Return of the King, 2004, Mattel

    MNP n/a   **MIP** $100

Barbie and Ken Camping Out, 1983, Mattel

    MNP $25   **MIP** $65

Barbie and Ken Tennis Gift Set, 1962, Mattel, Model No. 892

    MNP $400   **MIP** $900

Barbie and Krissy Magical Mermaids, black or white, 2000, Mattel

    MNP $15   **MIP** $30

Barbie as DC Comics Bat Girl, 2004, Mattel

    MNP $10   **MIP** $20

Barbie as DC Comics Catwoman, 2004, Mattel

    MNP $10   **MIP** $20

Barbie as DC Comics Catwoman, 2004, Mattel, comic book store exclusive

    MNP n/a   **MIP** $80

Barbie as DC Comics Super Girl, 2004, Mattel

    MNP $10   **MIP** $20

Barbie as Elle Woods from Legally Blonde 2, 2003, Mattel

    MNP $15   **MIP** $24

Barbie as Galadriel in Lord of the Rings: Fellowship of the Ring, 2004, Mattel

    MNP n/a   **MIP** $40

Barbie Beautiful Blues Gift Set, 1967, Mattel, Model No. 3303

    MNP $1600   **MIP** $3000

Barbie Collector's Club Café Society, 1998, Mattel, Model No. 18892

    MNP $50   **MIP** $125

Barbie Collector's Club Club Couture, 2000, Mattel, Model No. 26068

    MNP $25   **MIP** $65

Barbie Collector's Club Embassy Waltz, 1999, Mattel, Model No. 23386

    MNP $45   **MIP** $100

Barbie Collector's Club French Quarter Barbie Fashion, 2003, Mattel

    MNP $15   **MIP** $25

Barbie Collector's Club Grand Premiere, 1997, Mattel, Model No. 16498

    MNP $100   **MIP** $200

Barbie Collector's Club Holiday Treasures 1999, 1999, Mattel

    MNP $75   **MIP** $125

Barbie Collector's Club Holiday Treasures 2000, 2000, Mattel, Model No. 27673

    MNP $35   **MIP** $75

Barbie Collectors Club Hollywood Divine Blonde, 2004, Mattel, LE 3000 pcs

    MNP n/a   **MIP** $50

Barbie Collectors Club Hollywood Divine Brunette, 2004, Mattel, LE 4000 pcs

    MNP n/a   **MIP** $50

Barbie Collectors Club Melrose Morning Fashion, 2004, Mattel

    MNP n/a   **MIP** $25

Barbie Collector's Club Midnight Tuxedo, white or black, 2001, Mattel

    MNP $25   **MIP** $65

Barbie Collectors Club Nod for Mod, 2004, Mattel

    MNP n/a   **MIP** $40

Barbie Collector's Club Noir et Blanc Barbie, African American, 2003, Mattel

    MNP $40   **MIP** $60

Barbie Collector's Club Noir et Blanc Barbie, White, 2003, Mattel

    MNP $40   **MIP** $60

Barbie Millicent Roberts Matinee Today, 1996, Mattel, Model No. 16079

    MNP $22   **MIP** $60

Barbie Millicent Roberts Perfectly Suited, 1997, Mattel, Model No. 17567

    MNP $30   **MIP** $45

Barbie Millicent Roberts Pinstripe Power, 1998, Mattel, Model No. 19791

    MNP $30   **MIP** $50

Barbie's Round the Clock Gift Set, Bubblecut, 1964, Mattel, Model No. 1013

    MNP $1000   **MIP** $2500

Barbie's Sparkling Pink Gift Set, Bubblecut, 1964, Mattel, Model No. 1011

    MNP $1000   **MIP** $2400

Barbie's Wedding Party Gift Set, 1964, Mattel, Model No. 1017

    MNP $1000   **MIP** $2400

Beauty Secrets Barbie Pretty Reflections Gift Set, 1979, Mattel, Model No. 1702

    MNP $40   **MIP** $100

Best Buy Detective Barbie, 2000, Mattel, Model No. 24189

    MNP $8   **MIP** $17

Bill Blass Barbie, 1997, Mattel, Model No. 17040

    MNP $35   **MIP** $50

(KP Photo)

Billions of Dreams Barbie, 1997, Mattel, Model No. 17641
  MNP $150 **MIP** $275

(KP Photo)

Billy Boy Feelin' Groovy Barbie, 1986, Mattel, Model No. 3421
  MNP $75 **MIP** $125

(KP Photo)

Billy Boy Le Nouveau Theatre de la Mode Barbie, 1985, Mattel, Model No. 6279
  MNP $100 **MIP** $200

Birds of Beauty #1 Peacock Barbie, 1998, Mattel, Model No. 19365
  MNP $32 **MIP** $50

Birds of Beauty #2 Flamingo Barbie, 1999, Mattel, Model No. 22957
  MNP $40 **MIP** $50

Birds of Beauty #3 Swan Barbie, 2000, Mattel, Model No. 27682
  MNP $40 **MIP** $50

Birthday Fun at McDonald's Gift Set, 1994, Mattel, Model No. 11589
  MNP $15 **MIP** $35

Birthday Wishes #1, black or white, 1999, Mattel, Model No. 21128/21509
  MNP $15 **MIP** $35

Birthday Wishes #2, black or white, 2000, Mattel, Model No. 24667/24668
  MNP $20 **MIP** $40

Birthday Wishes #3, black or white, 2001, Mattel
  MNP $10 **MIP** $35

Birthday Wishes 2005, 2005, Mattel, peach or blue dress
  MNP n/a **MIP** $30

Birthday Wishes Barbie African American, 2004, Mattel
  MNP n/a **MIP** $30

Birthday Wishes Barbie Blonde, 2004, Mattel
  MNP n/a **MIP** $30

Birthday Wishes Barbie Brunette, 2004, Mattel
  MNP n/a **MIP** $30

Birthday Wishes Barbie Redhead, 2004, Mattel
  MNP n/a **MIP** $30

BJ's Fantastica Barbie, 1993, Mattel, Model No. 3196
  MNP $15 **MIP** $40

BJ's Festiva, 1993, Mattel
  MNP $15 **MIP** $40

BJ's Golden Waltz, blonde or red, 1999, Mattel
  MNP $10 **MIP** $25

BJ's Rose Bride Barbie, 1996, Mattel, Model No. 15987
  MNP $15 **MIP** $20

BJ's Sparkle Beauty, 1997, Mattel
  MNP $15 **MIP** $20

Bloomingdale's Barbie at Bloomingdale's, 1996, Mattel, Model No. 16290
  MNP $15 **MIP** $35

Bloomingdale's Calvin Klein Barbie, 1996, Mattel
  MNP $20 **MIP** $35

Bloomingdale's Donna Karan, blond, 1995, Mattel, Model No. 14452
  MNP $35 **MIP** $50

Bloomingdale's Donna Karan, brunette, 1996, Mattel, Model No. 14452
  MNP $35 **MIP** $50

Bloomingdale's Oscar de la Renta, 1998, Mattel, Model No. 20376
  MNP $30 **MIP** $45

Bloomingdale's Ralph Lauren, 1997, Mattel, Model No. 15950
  MNP $30 **MIP** $45

Bloomingdale's Savvy Shopper, Nicole Miller, 1994, Mattel, Model No. 12152
  MNP $25 **MIP** $45

Bob Mackie 45th Anniversary Barbie, 2004, Mattel, White, black hair, LE 1000 pcs
  MNP n/a **MIP** $100

Bob Mackie 45th Anniversary Barbie, 2004, Mattel, White or African American
  MNP n/a **MIP** $60

Bob Mackie Designer Gold, 1990, Mattel, Model No. 5405
  MNP $200 **MIP** $325

Bob Mackie Empress Bride, 1992, Mattel, Model No. 4247
  MNP $275 **MIP** $500

Bob Mackie Fantasy Goddess of Africa, 1999, Mattel, Model No. 22044
  MNP $120 **MIP** $175

(KP Photo)

Bob Mackie Fantasy Goddess of Asia, 1998, Mattel, Model No. SA415
  MNP $80 **MIP** $125

Bob Mackie Fantasy Goddess of the Americas, 2000, Mattel, Model No. 25859
  MNP $100 **MIP** $125

Bob Mackie Fantasy Goddess of the Arctic, 2001, Mattel, Model No. 50840
  MNP $75 **MIP** $125

Bob Mackie Goddess of the Moon, 1996, Mattel, Model No. 14105
  MNP $40 **MIP** $65

Bob Mackie Goddess of the Sun, 1995, Mattel, Model No. 14056
  MNP $40 **MIP** $65

Bob Mackie Jewel Essence Amethyst Aura, 1997, Mattel, Model No. 15522
  MNP $40 **MIP** $100

BARBIE

Bob Mackie Jewel Essence Diamond Dazzle, 1997, Mattel, Model No. 15519
MNP $40   MIP $100

Bob Mackie Jewel Essence Emerald Embers, 1997, Mattel, Model No. 15521
MNP $40   MIP $100

Bob Mackie Jewel Essence Ruby Radiance, 1997, Mattel, Model No. 15520
MNP $40   MIP $100

Bob Mackie Jewel Essence Sapphire Splendor, 1997, Mattel, Model No. 15523
MNP $40   MIP $100

Bob Mackie Madame du Barbie, 1997, Mattel, Model No. 17934
MNP $100   MIP $225

Bob Mackie Masquerade Ball, 1993, Mattel, Model No. 10803
MNP $175   MIP $275

(KP Photo)

Bob Mackie Neptune Fantasy, 1992, Mattel, Model No. 4248
MNP $350   MIP $500

Bob Mackie Platinum, 1991, Mattel, Model No. 2703
MNP $250   MIP $350

(KP Photo)

Bob Mackie Queen of Hearts, 1994, Mattel, Model No. 12046
MNP $125   MIP $200

Bob Mackie Red Carpet, Brunette Brilliance, 2003, Mattel, Model No. B0585
MNP $50   MIP $125

Bob Mackie Red Carpet, Radiant Redhead, 2002, Mattel, Model No. 55501
MNP $100   MIP $125

Bob Mackie Starlight Splendor, 1991, Mattel, Model No. 2704
MNP $200   MIP $375

Bowling Champ Barbie, 2000, Mattel, Model No. 25871
MNP $15   MIP $30

Bridal Collection Millennium Wedding, white, black or Hispanic, 2000, Mattel, Model No. 27674
MNP $25   MIP $50

Burberry Barbie, 2001, Mattel, Model No. 29421
MNP $25   MIP $40

Byron Lars Cinnabar Sensation, black or white, 1999, Mattel, Model No. 19848
MNP $35   MIP $95

Byron Lars In the Limelight, 1997, Mattel, Model No. 17031
MNP $40   MIP $250

Byron Lars Indigo Obsession, 2000, Mattel, Model No. 26935
MNP $25   MIP $65

Byron Lars Moja Barbie, 2001, Mattel, Model No. 50826
MNP $40   MIP $175

Byron Lars Nne, 2004, Mattel
MNP n/a   MIP $80

Byron Lars Plum Royale, 1998, Mattel, Model No. 23478
MNP $40   MIP $95

Byron Lars Tatu, 2003, Mattel
MNP $50   MIP $80

Caroling Fun Barbie, 1995, Mattel, Model No. 13966
MNP $8   MIP $10

Casey Goes Casual Gift Set, 1967, Mattel, Model No. 3304
MNP $800   MIP $1650

Celebration Barbie 2000, white or black, 2000, Mattel
MNP $15   MIP $45

Celebrity Lucy L.A. at Last, 2003, Mattel
MNP $25   MIP $40

Celestial Collection #1 Evening Star, 2000, Mattel, Model No. 27690
MNP $20   MIP $30

Celestial Collection #2 Morning Sun, 2000, Mattel, Model No. 27688
MNP $20   MIP $30

Celestial Collection #3 Midnight Moon Princess, 2000, Mattel, Model No. 27689
MNP $20   MIP $30

Children's Collector Series Belle (Beauty and the Beast), 2000, Mattel, Model No. 24673
MNP $15   MIP $30

Children's Collector Series Cinderella, 1997, Mattel, Model No. 16900
MNP $15   MIP $30

Children's Collector Series Little Bo Peep, 1995, Mattel, Model No. 14960
MNP $40   MIP $75

Children's Collector Series Rapunzel, 1995, Mattel, Model No. 13016
MNP $15   MIP $35

Children's Collector Series Sleeping Beauty, 1998, Mattel
MNP $15   MIP $35

Children's Collector Series Snow White, 1999, Mattel, Model No. 21130
MNP $15   MIP $35

Chocolate Obsession Barbie, 2005, Mattel
MNP n/a   MIP $35

Christian Dior 50th Anniversary, 1997, Mattel, The New Look, Model No. 16013
MNP $35   MIP $125

Christian Dior Barbie, 1995, Mattel, Model No. 13168
MNP $50   MIP $75

Chuck E. Cheese Barbie, 1996, Mattel, Model No. 14615
MNP $15   MIP $30

City Seasons Autumn in London, 1999, Mattel, Model No. 22257
MNP $20   MIP $40

City Seasons Autumn in Paris, 1998, Mattel, Model No. 19367
MNP $18   MIP $40

(KP Photo)

City Seasons Spring in Tokyo, 1999, Mattel, Model No. 19430
MNP $25   MIP $40

City Seasons Spring in Tokyo, Internet Exclusive, 1999, Mattel, Model No. 23499
MNP $30   MIP $50

City Seasons Summer in Rome, 1999, Mattel, Model No. 19431
MNP $25   MIP $40

City Seasons Winter in Montreal, 1999, Mattel, Model No. 22258
MNP $20   MIP $40

(KP Photo)

City Seasons Winter in New York, 1998, Mattel, Model No. 19429
MNP $18   MIP $40

Classic Ballet Flower Ballerina, 2001, Mattel, Model No. 28375
MNP $10   MIP $25

Classic Ballet Marzipan, 1999, Mattel, Model No. 20581
MNP $15   MIP $25

(Mattel Photo)

Classic Ballet Peppermint Candy Cane, 2003, Mattel, Model No. 57578
MNP $10   MIP $25

Classic Ballet Snowflake, 2000, Mattel, Model No. 25642
MNP $15   MIP $25

(KP Photo)

Classic Ballet Sugar Plum Fairy, 1997, Mattel, Model No. 17056
MNP $15   MIP $30

Classic Ballet Swan Ballerina, 2002, Mattel, Model No. 53867
MNP $10   MIP $25

Classic Ballet Swan Lake, black or white, 1998, Mattel, Model No. 18509/18510
MNP $15   MIP $25

Classique Benefit Ball Barbie, 1992, Mattel, Model No. 1521
MNP $40   MIP $70

Classique City Style Barbie, 1993, Mattel, Model No. 10149
MNP $30   MIP $50

Classique Evening Extravaganza, 1994, Mattel, Model No. 11622
MNP $25   MIP $50

Classique Evening Extravaganza, black, 1994, Mattel, Model No. 11638
MNP $25   MIP $50

Classique Evening Sophisticate, 1998, Mattel, Model No. 19361
MNP $18   MIP $35

Classique Midnight Gala, 1995, Mattel, Model No. 12999
MNP $25   MIP $50

Classique Opening Night Barbie, 1993, Mattel, Model No. 10148
MNP $30   MIP $60

Classique Romantic Interlude Barbie, 1997, Mattel, Model No. 17136
MNP $15   MIP $40

Classique Romantic Interlude Barbie, black, 1997, Mattel, Model No. 17137
MNP $15   MIP $40

Classique Starlight Dance, 1996, Mattel, Model No. 15461
MNP $20   MIP $40

Classique Starlight Dance, black, 1996, Mattel, Model No. 15819
MNP $20   MIP $40

Classique Uptown Chic Barbie, 1994, Mattel, Model No. 11623
MNP $25   MIP $50

Coca-Cola #5 (majorette), 2002, Mattel, Model No. 53974
MNP $20   MIP $40

Coca-Cola Barbie #1, carhop, 1999, Mattel, Model No. 22831
MNP $20   MIP $65

Coca-Cola Barbie #2, 2000, Mattel, Model No. 24637
MNP $25   MIP $59

Coca-Cola Barbie #3, Cheerleader, 2001, Mattel
MNP $15   MIP $50

Coca-Cola Fashion Classic #1, Soda Fountain Sweetheart, 1996, Mattel
MNP $50   MIP $125

Coca-Cola Fashion Classic #2, After the Walk, 1997, Mattel, Model No. 17341
MNP $46   MIP $60

Coca-Cola Fashion Classic #3, Summer Daydreams, 1998, Mattel, Model No. 19739
MNP $30   MIP $60

Coca-Cola Ken, 2000, Mattel, Model No. 25678
MNP $100   MIP $250

Coca-Cola Party, 1999, Mattel, Model No. 22964
MNP $5   MIP $15

Coca-Cola Picnic, 1998, Mattel, Model No. 19626
MNP $5   MIP $15

Coca-Cola Splash, 2000, Mattel, Model No. 22590
MNP $5   MIP $15

Coca-Cola, Disney Teddy & Doll Convention, brunette, limited to 1,500, Mattel
MNP $45   MIP $95

Collectors' Request Color Magic Barbie Giftset, 2004, Mattel
MNP n/a   MIP $50

Collectors' Request Commuter Set, 1999, Mattel, Model No. 21510
MNP $25   MIP $65

Collector's Request Evening Splendour Barbie, 2005, Mattel
MNP n/a   MIP $50

Collectors' Request Gay Parisienne, 2003, Mattel, Model No. 57610
MNP $25   MIP $50

Collectors' Request Gold 'N Glamour, 2002, Mattel, Model No. 54185
MNP $20   MIP $50

Collector's Request Open Road Barbie, 2004, Mattel
MNP n/a   MIP $55

Collector's Request Plantation Barbie, 2004, Mattel
MNP n/a   MIP $50

Collectors' Request Sophisticated Lady, 1999, Mattel, Model No. 24930
MNP $25   MIP $65

Collectors' Request Suburban Shopper, 2000, Mattel
MNP $15   MIP $45

Collectors' Request Twist N Turn Smasheroo, brunette, 1998, Mattel, Model No. 18941
MNP $25   MIP $40

Collectors' Request Twist N' Turn Smasheroo, red hair, 1998, Mattel, Model No. 23258
MNP $25   MIP $50

Cool Collecting Barbie, 2000, Mattel, Nostalgic Toys, Model No. 25525
MNP $25   MIP $40

Couture Collection Portrait in Taffeta Barbie, 1996, Mattel, Model No. 15528
MNP $65   MIP $100

Couture Collection Serenade in Satin Barbie, 1997, Mattel, Model No. 17572
MNP $65   MIP $100

Couture Collection Symphony in Chiffon, 1998, Mattel, Model No. 21295
MNP $65   MIP $100

Cracker Barrel Country Charm Barbie, 2001, Mattel
MNP $5   MIP $15

Cynthia Rowley Barbie, 2005, Mattel
    MNP n/a   **MIP** $80

Dance Club Barbie Gift Set, 1989, Mattel, Model No. 4917
    MNP $25   **MIP** $60

Dance Magic Gift Set Barbie & Ken, 1990, Mattel, Model No. 5409
    MNP $15   **MIP** $35

Dance Sensation Barbie Gift Set, 1984, Mattel, Model No. 9058
    MNP $15   **MIP** $40

David's Bridal Unforgettable Barbie, 2004, Mattel, Blonde, Hispanic, African American
    MNP n/a   **MIP** $45

Democratic National Convention Delegate Barbie, 2000, Mattel
    MNP $25   **MIP** $150

Designer Spotlight by Heather Fonesca, 2004, Mattel
    MNP n/a   **MIP** $50

Designer Spotlight, Katiana Jimenez, 2003, Mattel, Model No. B0836
    MNP $20   **MIP** $40

Diva Collection, All that Glitters, 2002, Mattel, Model No. 55426
    MNP $20   **MIP** $40

Diva Collection, Gone Platinum (white or black), 2002, Mattel, Model No. 52739/53868
    MNP $20   **MIP** $40

Diva Collection, Red Hot (white or black), 2003, Mattel, Model No. 56707/56708
    MNP $20   **MIP** $40

Dolls of the World Princess of Ancient Greece, 2004, Mattel
    MNP n/a   **MIP** $20

Dolls of the World Princess of Ancient Mexico, 2004, Mattel
    MNP n/a   **MIP** $20

Dolls of the World Princess of Cambodia, 2004, Mattel
    MNP n/a   **MIP** $20

Dolls of the World Princess of England (Tudor Rose), 2004, Mattel
    MNP n/a   **MIP** $20

Dolls of the World Princess of Imperial Russia, 2005, Mattel
    MNP n/a   **MIP** $20

Dolls of the World Princess of the Korean Court, 2005, Mattel
    MNP n/a   **MIP** $20

Dolls of the World Princess of the Navajo, 2004, Mattel
    MNP n/a   **MIP** $20

Dolls of the World Princess of the Renaissance, 2005, Mattel
    MNP n/a   **MIP** $20

Duchess Emma Barbie, 2004, Mattel
    MNP n/a   **MIP** $80

Easter Magic Barbie, 2003, Mattel
    MNP $8   **MIP** $15

Empress Sissy, Barbie as, 1996, Mattel, Model No. 15846
    MNP $35   **MIP** $60

Enchanted Mermaid, 2002, Mattel, Model No. 53978
    MNP $100   **MIP** $250

Enchanted Seasons #1 Snow Princess, 1994, Mattel, Model No. 11875
    MNP $40   **MIP** $125

Enchanted Seasons #2 Spring Bouquet, 1995, Mattel, Model No. 12989
    MNP $30   **MIP** $60

Enchanted Seasons #3 Autumn Glory, 1996, Mattel, Model No. 15204
    MNP $30   **MIP** $60

Enchanted Seasons #4 Summer Splendor, 1997, Mattel, Model No. 15683
    MNP $30   **MIP** $60

Enchanted World of Fairies, Fairy of the Forest, 2000, Mattel, Model No. 25639
    MNP $25   **MIP** $49

Enchanted World of Fairies, Fairy of the Garden, 2001, Mattel
    MNP $15   **MIP** $45

Escada Barbie, 1996, Mattel, Model No. 15948
    MNP $40   **MIP** $65

(KP Photo)

Essence of Nature #1 Water Rhapsody, 1998, Mattel, Model No. 19847
    MNP $40   **MIP** $90

Essence of Nature #2 Whispering Wind, 1999, Mattel, Model No. 22834
    MNP $40   **MIP** $80

Essence of Nature #3 Dancing Fire, 2000, Mattel, Model No. 26327
    MNP $35   **MIP** $80

(Mattel Photo)

FAO Schwarz American Beauty, Barbie as George Washington, 1996, Mattel, Model No. 17557
    MNP $35   **MIP** $65

(Mattel Photo)

FAO Schwarz American Beauty, Statue of Liberty, 1996, Mattel, Model No. 14684
    MNP $40   **MIP** $65

FAO Schwarz Barbie & Ken Tango Gift Set, 2002, Mattel
    MNP $40   **MIP** $100

FAO Schwarz Barbie Fashion Model Collection Chantaine, 2003, Mattel, LE 600 pcs
    MNP $400   **MIP** $600

FAO Schwarz Bob Mackie Lady Liberty, 2000, Mattel, limited to 15,000
    MNP $75   **MIP** $125

FAO Schwarz Bob Mackie Le Papillon, 1999, Mattel, Model No. 23276
    MNP $70   **MIP** $175

FAO Schwarz Circus Star Barbie, 1995, Mattel, Model No. 13257
    MNP $35   **MIP** $70

FAO Schwarz City Seasons Summer in San Francisco, blond, 1998, Mattel, Model No. 19363
    MNP $40   **MIP** $95

FAO Schwarz City Seasons Summer in San Francisco, red hair, Mattel
MNP $200   MIP $750

FAO Schwarz Exclusive Joyeux Barbie, 2004, Mattel, LE redheaded
MNP $200   MIP $300

FAO Schwarz Fashion Model Fashion Designer Barbie, 2002, Mattel
MNP $50   MIP $85

FAO Schwarz Fashion Model Fashion Editor, 2000, Mattel
MNP $50   MIP $90

FAO Schwarz Floral Signature #1 Antique Rose, 1996, Mattel, limited to 10,000, Model No. 15814
MNP $50   MIP $150

FAO Schwarz Floral Signature #2 Lily Barbie, 1997, Mattel, limited to 10,000, Model No. 17556
MNP $50   MIP $145

FAO Schwarz Golden Greetings Barbie, 1989, Mattel, Model No. 7734
MNP $65   MIP $150

FAO Schwarz Golden Hollywood Barbie, white or black, 1999, Mattel
MNP $55   MIP $75

FAO Schwarz Jeweled Splendor (125th Anniversary), 1995, Mattel, Model No. 14061
MNP $75   MIP $175

FAO Schwarz Madison Ave. Barbie, 1992, Mattel, Model No. 1539
MNP $75   MIP $125

FAO Schwarz Mann's Chinese Theatre Barbie, white or black, 2000, Mattel, Model No. 24636/24998
MNP $35   MIP $50

FAO Schwarz Night Sensation, 1991, Mattel, Model No. 2921
MNP $25   MIP $50

(KP Photo)

FAO Schwarz Phantom of the Opera Gift Set, 1998, Mattel, Model No. 20377
MNP $60   MIP $100

FAO Schwarz Rockettes Barbie, 1993, Mattel, Model No. 2017
MNP $65   MIP $100

FAO Schwarz Shopping Spree, 1994, Mattel, Model No. 12749
MNP $5   MIP $15

FAO Schwarz Silver Screen Barbie, 1994, Mattel, Model No. 11652
MNP $65   MIP $100

FAO Schwarz Winter Fantasy, 1990, Mattel, Model No. 5946
MNP $60   MIP $100

FAO Schwarz, Barbie at FAO, 1997, Mattel, Model No. 17298
MNP $12   MIP $25

Fashion Model 45th Anniversary Barbie & Ken Giftset, 2004, Mattel
MNP n/a   MIP $160

Fashion Model A Model Life Gift Set, 2003, Mattel
MNP $50   MIP $99

Fashion Model Capucine Barbie, 2003, Mattel
MNP $75   MIP $180

Fashion Model Chinoiserie Red Midnight, Fan Club Exclusive, 2004, Mattel
MNP n/a   MIP $175

Fashion Model Chinoiserie Red Moon, 2004, Mattel
MNP n/a   MIP $50

Fashion Model Collection 45th Anniversary Barbie, African American, 2004, Mattel
MNP n/a   MIP $50

Fashion Model Collection 45th Anniversary Barbie, Blonde, 2004, Mattel
MNP n/a   MIP $50

Fashion Model Collection Ken Fashion Insider Gift Set, 2003, Mattel
MNP $50   MIP $99

Fashion Model Collection Midnight Mischief Fashion, 2003, Mattel
MNP $15   MIP $50

Fashion Model Collection New England Escape Giftset, 2004, Mattel, fashion
MNP n/a   MIP $60

Fashion Model Collection Pajama #2 Redhead, 2005, Mattel
MNP n/a   MIP $40

Fashion Model Collection Sunday Best Barbie, African American, 2003, Mattel
MNP $30   MIP $60

Fashion Model Lingerie #6, 2003, Mattel
MNP $25   MIP $50

Fashion Model Shinoiserie Red Sunset, Barbie Bazaar Exclusive, 2004, Mattel
MNP n/a   MIP $125

Fashion Model The Spa Getaway Gift Set, 2004, Mattel
MNP n/a   MIP $99

Fashion Model Trend Setter Barbie, 2004, Mattel
MNP n/a   MIP $65

Fashion Model, Capucine, 2003, Mattel, Model No. B0146
MNP $75   MIP $150

Fashion Model, Continental Holiday Gift Set, 2002, Mattel, Model No. 55497
MNP $50   MIP $100

Fashion Model, Delphine Barbie, 2000, Mattel, Model No. 26929
MNP $35   MIP $65

Fashion Model, Dusk to Dawn, 2001, Mattel, Model No. 29654
MNP $50   MIP $125

Fashion Model, In The Pink, 2001, Mattel, Model No. 27683
MNP $75   MIP $200

Fashion Model, Lingerie #1, blond, 2000, Mattel, Model No. 26930
MNP $60   MIP $175

Fashion Model, Lingerie #2, brunette, 2000, Mattel, Model No. 26931
MNP $60   MIP $175

Fashion Model, Lingerie #3, black hair, 2001, Mattel, Model No. 29651
MNP $40   MIP $150

Fashion Model, Lingerie #4, 2002, Mattel, Model No. 55498
MNP $20   MIP $50

(Mattel Photo)

Fashion Model, Lingerie #5 (black), 2002, Mattel, Model No. 56120
MNP $20   MIP $50

Fashion Model, Lingerie #6, redhead, 2003, Mattel, Model No. 56948
MNP $25   MIP $50

Fashion Model, Lisette, 2001, Mattel, Model No. 29650
MNP $45   MIP $70

Fashion Model, Maria Therese (bride), 2002, Mattel, Model No. 55496
MNP $50   MIP $125

Fashion Model, Model Life Gift Set, 2003, Mattel, Model No. B0147
MNP $50   MIP $100

Fashion Model, Provencale, 2002, Mattel, Model No. 50829
MNP $50   MIP $150

Fashion Queen Barbie & Her Friends, 1964, Mattel, Model No. 863
MNP $1000   MIP $2400

Fashion Queen Barbie & Ken Trousseau Gift Set, 1964, Mattel, Model No. 864
MNP $1200   MIP $2800

Fashion Savvy #1 Tangerine Twist, 1997, Mattel, Model No. 17860
MNP $14   MIP $45

Fashion Savvy #2 Uptown Chic, 1998, Mattel, Model No. 19632
MNP $20   MIP $45

BARBIE

BARBIE

Ferrari Barbie #1, Scuderia, racing outfit, 2001, Mattel, Model No. 25636
  MNP $30 **MIP** $65

Ferrari Barbie #2, red dress, 2001, Mattel, Model No. 29608
  MNP $15 **MIP** $45

Festive Season, 1998, Mattel
  MNP $5 **MIP** $15

Fire and Ice (white or black), 2002, Mattel, Model No. 53511/53863
  MNP $20 **MIP** $40

Flowers in Fashion Orchid Barbie, 2001, Mattel, Model No. 50319
  MNP $25 **MIP** $65

Flowers in Fashion Rose Barbie, 2001, Mattel
  MNP $25 **MIP** $65

Francie Rise n' Shine Gift Set, 1971, Mattel, Model No. 1194
  MNP $600 **MIP** $1200

Francie Swingin' Separates Gift Set, 1966, Mattel, Model No. 1042
  MNP $700 **MIP** $1500

Fun to Dress Barbie Gift Set, 1993, Mattel, Model No. 3826
  MNP $8 **MIP** $15

Gap Barbie and Kelly Gift Set, 1997, Mattel, Model No. 18547
  MNP $15 **MIP** $45

Gap Barbie and Kelly Gift Set, black, 1997, Mattel, Model No. 18548
  MNP $15 **MIP** $45

Gap Barbie, black, 1996, Mattel, Model No. 16450
  MNP $20 **MIP** $60

Gap Barbie, white, 1996, Mattel, Model No. 16449
  MNP $30 **MIP** $60

Garden of Flowers Rose Barbie, 1999, Mattel, Model No. 22237
  MNP $25 **MIP** $50

General Mills Winter Dazzle, black, 1997, Mattel
  MNP $5 **MIP** $20

General Mills Winter Dazzle, white, 1997, Mattel, Model No. 18456
  MNP $5 **MIP** $20

Givenchy Barbie, 2000, Mattel, Model No. 24635
  MNP $40 **MIP** $80

Goddess of Beauty Barbie, 2000, Mattel, Model No. 27286
  MNP $25 **MIP** $65

Goddess of Spring Barbie, 2000, Mattel, Model No. 28112
  MNP $25 **MIP** $65

Goddess of Wisdom Barbie, 2001, Mattel
  MNP $25 **MIP** $65

Graduation Barbie Class of 1996, 1996, Mattel
  MNP $5 **MIP** $15

Graduation Barbie Class of 1997, 1997, Mattel
  MNP $5 **MIP** $10

Graduation Barbie Class of 1998, white or black, 1998, Mattel
  MNP $5 **MIP** $10

Graduation Barbie Class of 2000, black box, 2000, Mattel
  MNP $5 **MIP** $15

Graduation Barbie Class of 2000, blue box, 2000, Mattel
  MNP $5 **MIP** $15

Grand Entrance Barbie (white or black), 2002, Mattel, Model No. 53841/53842
  MNP $20 **MIP** $50

Grand Entrance Barbie, white or black, 2001, Mattel
  MNP $25 **MIP** $65

Grand Ole Opry #1 Country Rose Barbie, 1997, Mattel, Model No. 17782
  MNP $40 **MIP** $80

Grand Ole Opry #2 Rising Star Barbie, 1998, Mattel, Model No. 17864
  MNP $50 **MIP** $100

Grand Ole Opry Barbie and Kenny Country Duet, 1999, Mattel, Model No. 23498
  MNP $55 **MIP** $75

Grease Barbie 2 as Sandy Olsson, 2004, Mattel
  MNP n/a **MIP** $30

Grease Barbie as Sandy Olsson, 2003, Mattel
  MNP $20 **MIP** $40

Great Eras #01, Gibson Girl, 1993, Mattel, Model No. 3702
  MNP $25 **MIP** $75

Great Eras #02, Flapper, 1993, Mattel, Model No. 4063
  MNP $25 **MIP** $75

(Mattel Photo)

Great Eras #03, Egyptian Queen, 1994, Mattel, Model No. 11397
  MNP $20 **MIP** $65

Great Eras #04, Southern Belle, 1994, Mattel, Model No. 11478
  MNP $20 **MIP** $65

Great Eras #05, Medieval Lady, 1995, Mattel, Model No. 12791
  MNP $25 **MIP** $50

Great Eras #06, Elizabethan Queen, 1995, Mattel, Model No. 12792
  MNP $25 **MIP** $50

Great Eras #07, Grecian Goddess, 1996, Mattel, Model No. 15005
  MNP $35 **MIP** $50

Great Eras #08, Victorian Lady, 1996, Mattel, Model No. 14900
  MNP $35 **MIP** $50

Great Eras #09, French Lady, 1997, Mattel, Model No. 16707
  MNP $35 **MIP** $50

Great Eras #10, Chinese Empress, 1997, Mattel, Model No. 16708
  MNP $35 **MIP** $50

Great Fashions of the 20th Century #1, Promenade in the Park, 1998, Mattel, 1910s, Model No. 18630
  MNP $20 **MIP** $65

Great Fashions of the 20th Century #2, Dance 'til Dawn, 1998, Mattel, 1920s, Model No. 19631
  MNP $30 **MIP** $50

Great Fashions of the 20th Century #3, Steppin Out Barbie, 1999, Mattel, 1930s, Model No. 21531
  MNP $30 **MIP** $50

Great Fashions of the 20th Century #4, Fabulous Forties, 2000, Mattel, 1940s, Model No. 22162
  MNP $25 **MIP** $50

(KP Photo)

Great Fashions of the 20th Century #5, Nifty Fifties, 2000, Mattel, 1950s, Model No. 27675
  MNP $25 **MIP** $50

BARBIE

(KP Photo)

Great Fashions of the 20th Century #6, Groovy Sixties, 2000, Mattel, 1960s, Model No. 27676
MNP $25   MIP $50

Great Fashions of the 20th Century #7, Peace & Love 70s Barbie, 2000, Mattel, 1970s, Model No. 27677
MNP $15   MIP $50

Groliers Book Club The Front Window Barbie, 2000, Mattel, Model No. 27968
MNP $10   MIP $35

Hallmark Fair Valentine Barbie, 1998, Mattel
MNP $20   MIP $40

Hallmark Holiday Memories Barbie, 1995, Mattel, Model No. 14108
MNP $15   MIP $25

Hallmark Holiday Sensation Barbie, 1999, Mattel, Model No. 19792
MNP $15   MIP $25

Hallmark Holiday Traditions Barbie, 1997, Mattel, Model No. 17094
MNP $15   MIP $25

Hallmark Holiday Voyage Barbie, 1998, Mattel
MNP $15   MIP $25

Hallmark Sentimental Valentine Barbie, 1997, Mattel
MNP $15   MIP $25

Hallmark Sweet Valentine Barbie, 1996, Mattel, Model No. 14880
MNP $15   MIP $25

Hallmark Victorian Elegance Barbie, 1994, Mattel, Model No. 12579
MNP $25   MIP $50

Hallmark Yuletide Romance Barbie, 1996, Mattel, Model No. 15621
MNP $15   MIP $25

Halloween Enchantress Barbie, 2004, Mattel
MNP n/a   MIP $20

Halloween Glow Barbie, White or African American, 2002, Mattel
MNP $10   MIP $25

Halloween Maskerade Barbie, 2004, Mattel
MNP $10   MIP $20

Hanae Mori Barbie, 2000, Mattel
MNP $50   MIP $75

Happy Birthday Barbie Gift Set, 1985, Mattel
MNP $20   MIP $40

(KP Photo)

Happy Holidays 1988, 1988, Mattel, Model No. 1703
MNP $75   MIP $325

Happy Holidays 1989, 1989, Mattel, Model No. 3253
MNP $50   MIP $125

Happy Holidays 1990, 1990, Mattel, Model No. 4098
MNP $25   MIP $80

Happy Holidays 1990, black, 1990, Mattel, Model No. 4543
MNP $20   MIP $60

Happy Holidays 1991, 1991, Mattel, Model No. 1871
MNP $40   MIP $75

Happy Holidays 1991, black, 1991, Mattel, Model No. 2696
MNP $40   MIP $60

(KP Photo)

Happy Holidays 1992, 1992, Mattel, Model No. 1429
MNP $30   MIP $65

Happy Holidays 1992, black, 1992, Mattel, Model No. 2396
MNP $30   MIP $50

(KP Photo)

Happy Holidays 1993, 1993, Mattel, Model No. 10824
MNP $30   MIP $60

Happy Holidays 1993, black, 1993, Mattel, Model No. 10911
MNP $30   MIP $40

(KP Photo)

Happy Holidays 1994, 1994, Mattel, Model No. 12155
MNP $30   MIP $75

Happy Holidays 1994, black, 1994, Mattel, Model No. 12156
MNP $30   MIP $50

Happy Holidays 1995, 1995, Mattel, Model No. 14123
MNP $20   MIP $45

Happy Holidays 1995, black, 1995, Mattel, Model No. 14124
MNP $20   MIP $40

(KP Photo)

Happy Holidays 1996, white or black, 1996, Mattel, Model No. 15646
MNP $30   MIP $35

(KP Photo)

Happy Holidays 1997, 1997, Mattel, Model No. 17832
MNP $5   MIP $25

Happy Holidays 1997, black, 1997, Mattel, Model No. 17833
MNP $5   MIP $25

(KP Photo)

Happy Holidays 1998, white or black, 1998, Mattel, Model No. 20200/20201
MNP $10   MIP $25

Hard Rock Café Barbie, 2003, Mattel
MNP n/a   MIP n/a

Hard Rock Café Barbie 2, 2004, Mattel
MNP n/a   MIP $75

Harrods/Hamleys West End Barbie, 1996, Mattel, Model No. 17590
MNP $20   MIP $40

Harvey Nichols Special Edition (limited to 250), 1995, Mattel, Model No. 0175
MNP $500   MIP $900

Hills Blue Elegance Barbie, 1992, Mattel, Model No. 1879
MNP $12   MIP $40

Hills Evening Sparkle, 1990, Mattel, Model No. 3274
MNP $10   MIP $35

Hills Moonlight Rose, 1991, Mattel, Model No. 3549
MNP $7   MIP $30

Hills Party Lace Barbie, 1989, Mattel, Model No. 4843
MNP $15   MIP $35

Hills Polly Pocket Barbie, 1994, Mattel, Model No. 12412
MNP $12   MIP $25

Hills Sea Pearl Mermaid Barbie, 1995, Mattel, Model No. 13940
MNP $8   MIP $35

Hills Sidewalk Chalk Barbie, 1998, Mattel, Model No. 19784
MNP $10   MIP $25

Hills Teddy Fun Barbie, 1996, Mattel, Model No. 15684
MNP $10   MIP $25

Holiday Angel #1, black, 2000, Mattel, Model No. 28080
MNP $20   MIP $50

Holiday Angel #1, white, 2000, Mattel, Model No. 26914
MNP $20   MIP $50

Holiday Angel #2, black, 2001, Mattel, Model No. 29770
MNP $15   MIP $45

Holiday Angel #2, white, 2001, Mattel, Model No. 29769
MNP $15   MIP $45

Holiday Celebration Barbie 2002, 2002, Mattel
MNP $30   MIP $70

Holiday Celebration Barbie 2004, 2004, Mattel, Blonde or African American
MNP n/a   MIP $40

Holiday Dreams Barbie, 1994, Mattel, Model No. 12192
MNP $10   MIP $20

Holiday Hostess Barbie, 1993, Mattel, Model No. 10280
MNP $25   MIP $50

Holiday Season, 1996, Mattel, Model No. 15581
MNP $5   MIP $15

Holiday Singing Sisters Gift Set, 2000, Mattel
MNP $15   MIP $50

Holiday Surprise Barbie, white or black, 2000, Mattel
MNP $5   MIP $15

Holiday Treats Barbie, 1997, Mattel
MNP $5   MIP $12

Hollywood Hair Deluxe Gift Set, 1993, Mattel, Model No. 10928
MNP $15   MIP $35

Hollywood Legends Dorothy (Wizard of Oz), 1995, Mattel, Model No. 12701
MNP $20   MIP $75

Hollywood Legends Eliza Doolittle (My Fair Lady), green coat, 1996, Mattel, Model No. 15498
MNP $30   MIP $50

Hollywood Legends Eliza Doolittle (My Fair Lady), lace ball gown, 1996, Mattel, Model No. 15500
MNP $30   MIP $75

Hollywood Legends Eliza Doolittle (My Fair Lady), pink, 1996, Mattel, Model No. 15501
MNP $30   MIP $60

Hollywood Legends Eliza Doolittle (My Fair Lady), white lace gown w/parasol, 1996, Mattel, Model No. 15497
MNP $30   MIP $75

Hollywood Legends Glinda (Wizard of Oz), 1996, Mattel, Model No. 14901
MNP $35   MIP $65

Hollywood Legends Ken as Cowardly Lion (Wizard of Oz), 1996, Mattel, Model No. 16573
MNP $35   MIP $60

Hollywood Legends Ken as Henry Higgins (My Fair Lady), 1996, Mattel, Model No. 15499
MNP $25   MIP $45

Hollywood Legends Ken as Rhett Butler, 1994, Mattel, Gone With the Wind, Model No. 12741
MNP $25   MIP $45

Hollywood Legends Ken as Scarecrow (Wizard of Oz), 1996, Mattel, Model No. 16497
MNP $35   MIP $50

Hollywood Legends Ken as Tin Man (Wizard of Oz), 1996, Mattel, Model No. 14902
MNP $15   MIP $25

Hollywood Legends Maria (Sound of Music), 1995, Mattel, Model No. 13676
MNP $20   MIP $50

Hollywood Legends Marilyn Monroe, pink, 1997, Mattel, Gentlemen Prefer Blondes, Model No. 17451
MNP $20   MIP $45

Hollywood Legends Marilyn Monroe, red, 1997, Mattel, Gentlemen Prefer Blondes, Model No. 17452
MNP $20   MIP $45

Hollywood Legends Marilyn Monroe, white, 1997, Mattel, Seven Year Itch, Model No. 17155
MNP $20   MIP $45

Hollywood Legends Scarlett O'Hara, black/white dress, 1993, Mattel, Gone With the Wind, Model No. 13254
MNP $25   MIP $50

(KP Photo)

Hollywood Legends Scarlett O'Hara, green velvet curtain, 1994, Mattel, Gone With the Wind, Model No. 12045
MNP $25   MIP $50

Hollywood Legends Scarlett O'Hara, green/white silk dress, 1995, Mattel, Gone With the Wind, Model No. 12997
    MNP $25   **MIP** $45

Hollywood Legends Scarlett O'Hara, red velvet dress, 1994, Mattel, Gone With the Wind, Model No. 12815
    MNP $25   **MIP** $50

Hollywood Movie Star, Between Takes, 2000, Mattel, Model No. 27684
    MNP $15   **MIP** $25

Hollywood Movie Star, By the Pool, 2000, Mattel, Model No. 27684
    MNP $15   **MIP** $25

Hollywood Movie Star, Day in the Sun, 2000, Mattel, Model No. 2000
    MNP $15   **MIP** $25

Hollywood Movie Star, Hollywood Cast Party, 2001, Mattel, Model No. 50825
    MNP $15   **MIP** $25

Hollywood Movie Star, Hollywood Premiere, 2000, Mattel, Model No. 26914
    MNP $15   **MIP** $25

Hollywood Movie Star, Publicity Tour, 2001, Mattel
    MNP $15   **MIP** $25

Home Shopping Club Evening Flame, 1991, Mattel, Model No. 1865
    MNP $70   **MIP** $125

Home Shopping Club Golden Allure Barbie, 1999, Mattel
    MNP $5   **MIP** $30

Home Shopping Club Premiere Night, 1999, Mattel
    MNP $5   **MIP** $30

I Dream of Jeannie Barbie, 2001, Mattel
    MNP $15   **MIP** $45

I Love Lucy Sales Resistance, 2004, Mattel
    MNP n/a   **MIP** $35

Japanese Living Eli, 1970, Mattel, Foreign
    MNP $700   **MIP** $1400

JCPenney Enchanted Evening, 1991, Mattel, Model No. 2702
    MNP $20   **MIP** $40

JCPenney Evening Elegance, 1990, Mattel, Model No. 7057
    MNP $20   **MIP** $40

JCPenney Evening Enchantment, 1998, Mattel, Model No. 19783
    MNP $25   **MIP** $40

JCPenney Evening Majesty, 1997, Mattel, Model No. 17235
    MNP $10   **MIP** $25

JCPenney Evening Sensation, 1992, Mattel, Model No. 1278
    MNP $12   **MIP** $35

JCPenney Golden Winter, 1993, Mattel, Model No. 10684
    MNP $12   **MIP** $35

JCPenney Night Dazzle, 1994, Mattel, Model No. 12191
    MNP $15   **MIP** $35

JCPenney Original Arizona Jean Co. Barbie #1, 1996, Mattel, Model No. 15441
    MNP $12   **MIP** $25

JCPenney Original Arizona Jean Co. Barbie #2, 1997, Mattel, Model No. 18020
    MNP $12   **MIP** $25

JCPenney Original Arizona Jean Co. Barbie #3, 1998, Mattel, Model No. 19873
    MNP $12   **MIP** $25

JCPenney Royal Enchantment, 1995, Mattel, Model No. 14010
    MNP $25   **MIP** $35

JCPenney Winter Renaissance, 1996, Mattel, Model No. 15570
    MNP $10   **MIP** $25

JCPenney/Sears Evening Recital Barbie, Stacie, Kelly and Tommy, 2000, Mattel, Model No. 27954
    MNP $15   **MIP** $42

Jubilee Series, Crystal Jubilee, limited to 20,000, 1999, Mattel, Model No. 21923
    MNP $150   **MIP** $275

Jubilee Series, Gold Jubilee, limited to 5,000, 1994, Mattel, Model No. 12009
    MNP $300   **MIP** $500

Jubilee Series, Pink Jubilee, limited to 1,200, 1989, Mattel, Model No. 3756
    MNP $800   **MIP** $2000

Jude Deveraux, The Raider, Barbie and Ken Gift Set, 2003, Mattel
    MNP $40   **MIP** $80

Juicy Couture Giftset, 2004, Mattel
    MNP n/a   **MIP** $99

Julia Simply Wow Gift Set, 1969, Mattel
    MNP $400   **MIP** $1500

Just for You Barbie, 2003, Mattel, Model No. B0151
    MNP $10   **MIP** $35

Kate Spade Barbie, 2004, Mattel
    MNP n/a   **MIP** $80

K-B Fantasy Ball Barbie, 1997, Mattel, Model No. 18594
    MNP $10   **MIP** $20

K-B Fashion Avenue Barbie, 1998, Mattel, Model No. 20782
    MNP $8   **MIP** $15

K-B Glamour Barbie, black, 1997, Mattel
    MNP $10   **MIP** $20

K-B Starlight Carousel Barbie, 1998, Mattel, Model No. 19708
    MNP $10   **MIP** $20

Keepsake Treasures, Barbie and Curious George, 2001, Mattel
    MNP $15   **MIP** $30

Keepsake Treasures, Barbie and the Tale of Peter Rabbit, 1998, Mattel, Model No. 19360
    MNP $15   **MIP** $40

Keepsake Treasures, Peter Rabbit 100th Anniversary Barbie, 2002, Mattel, Model No. 53872
    MNP $20   **MIP** $40

Kelly & Tommy as Alice and the Mad Hatter, 2003, Mattel
    MNP $10   **MIP** $20

Kelly and Friends Wizard of Oz Gift Set, 2003, Mattel
    MNP $15   **MIP** $30

Kelly as the Witches from Wizard of Oz, 2004, Mattel
    MNP n/a   **MIP** $30

Kelly Nostalgic Favorites Gift Set, 2003, Mattel
    MNP $15   **MIP** $30

Kelly Princess of the World Collction, Dutch, Scottish, Spanish, 2005, Mattel
    MNP n/a   **MIP** $20

Ken as Legolas in the Lord of the Rings: Fellowship of the Ring, 2004, Mattel
    MNP n/a   **MIP** $40

Kissing Barbie Gift Set, 1978, Mattel, Model No. 2977
    MNP $25   **MIP** $65

Kmart March of Dimes Walk America Barbie & Kelly Gift Set, 1999, Mattel, Model No. 20843
    MNP $15   **MIP** $25

Kmart March of Dimes Walk America Barbie, black or white, 1998, Mattel, Model No. 18506/18507
    MNP $10   **MIP** $24

Kmart Peach Pretty Barbie, 1989, Mattel, Model No. 4870
    MNP $10   **MIP** $30

Kmart Pretty in Purple, black, 1992, Mattel, Model No. 3121
    MNP $12   **MIP** $25

Kmart Pretty in Purple, white, 1992, Mattel, Model No. 3117
    MNP $12   **MIP** $25

K-mart Route 66 Barbecue Bash, 2000, Mattel
    MNP $8   **MIP** $25

K-mart Very Berry Barbie, white or black, 2000, Mattel
MNP $5   MIP $10

Kool-Aid Barbie, 1996, Mattel
MNP $15   MIP $40

Kool-Aid Wacky Warehouse Barbie I, 1993, Mattel, Model No. 10309
MNP $25   MIP $60

Kool-Aid Wacky Warehouse Barbie II, 1994, Mattel, Model No. 11763
MNP $25   MIP $50

Kraft Treasures Barbie, 1992, Mattel
MNP $30   MIP $55

L.E. Festival Holiday Barbie (540 made), 1994, Mattel
MNP $500   MIP $900

Lady Camille Barbie, 2003, Mattel
MNP $45   MIP $80

Life Ball Barbie #1, Vivienne Westwood, 1998, Mattel
MNP $200   MIP $400

Life Ball Barbie #2, Christian LaCroix, 1999, Mattel
MNP $200   MIP $400

Little Debbie #1, 1993, Mattel, Model No. 10123
MNP $25   MIP $40

Little Debbie #2, 1996, Mattel, Model No. 14616
MNP $15   MIP $25

Little Debbie #3, 1998, Mattel, Model No. 16352
MNP $15   MIP $20

Little Debbie #4, 1999, Mattel, Model No. 24977
MNP $10   MIP $20

Living Barbie Action Accents Gift Set, 1970, Mattel, Model No. 1585
MNP $500   MIP $1500

Lounge Kitty, 2004, Mattel, Black or White
MNP n/a   MIP $40

Loving You Barbie Gift Set, 1983, Mattel, Model No. 7583
MNP $45   MIP $100

Macy's Anne Klein Barbie, 1997, Mattel, Model No. 17603
MNP $25   MIP $40

Macy's City Shopper, Nicole Miller, 1996, Mattel, Model No. 16289
MNP $25   MIP $40

Mademoiselle Isabelle Barbie, 2002, Mattel
MNP $45   MIP $80

Magic & Mystery, Morgan LeFay and Merlin, 2000, Mattel, Model No. 27287
MNP $50   MIP $75

Magic & Mystery, Tales of the Arabian Nights, 2001, Mattel, Model No. 50827
MNP $40   MIP $65

Major League Baseball Chicago Cubs, 1999, Mattel, Model No. 23883
MNP $20   MIP $35

Major League Baseball Los Angeles Dodgers, 1999, Mattel, Model No. 23882
MNP $20   MIP $11

Major League Baseball New York Yankees, 1999, Mattel, Model No. 23881
MNP $20   MIP $11

Make-A-Valentine Barbie, white or black, 1999, Mattel
MNP $5   MIP $15

Malibu Barbie "The Beach Party," w/case, 1979, Mattel, Model No. 1703
MNP $17   MIP $35

Malibu Ken Surf's Up Gift Set, 1971, Mattel, Model No. 1248
MNP $75   MIP $200

Marie Antoinette Barbie, 2003, Mattel
MNP $125   MIP $200

Masquerade Gala #1, Illusion, 1997, Mattel, Model No. 18667
MNP $50   MIP $100

Masquerade Gala #2, Rendezvous, 1998, Mattel, Model No. 20647
MNP $40   MIP $60

Masquerade Gala #3, Venetian Opulence, 2000, Mattel, Model No. 24501
MNP $30   MIP $50

(Mattel Photo)

Mattel Festival 35th Anniversary (3,500 made), 1994, Mattel
MNP $50   MIP $150

Mattel Festival 35th Anniversary Gift Set (975 made), 1994, Mattel, Model No. 11591
MNP $70   MIP $100

Mattel Festival Banquet, blond, 1994, Mattel
MNP $75   MIP $125

Mattel Festival Banquet, brunette, 1994, Mattel
MNP $75   MIP $125

Mattel Festival Banquet, red hair, 1994, Mattel
MNP $75   MIP $125

Mattel Festival Doctor, brunette (1,500 made), 1994, Mattel, Model No. 11160
MNP $35   MIP $60

Mattel Festival Gymnast (1,500 made), 1994, Mattel, Model No. 11921
MNP $35   MIP $60

Mattel Festival Happy Holiday, 1994, Mattel, Model No. 12155
MNP $200   MIP $450

Mattel Festival Haute Couture, rainbow (500 made), 1994, Mattel
MNP $75   MIP $200

Mattel Festival Haute Couture, red velvet (480 made), 1994, Mattel
MNP $75   MIP $200

Mattel Festival Night Dazzle, brunette (420 made), 1994, Mattel, Model No. 12191
MNP $100   MIP $300

Mattel Festival Snow Princess, brunette (285 made), 1994, Mattel, Model No. 12905
MNP $500   MIP $1000

Meijers Hula Hoop, 1997, Mattel, Model No. 18167
MNP $10   MIP $20

Meijers Ice Cream, 1998, Mattel, Model No. 19820
MNP $10   MIP $20

Meijers Ladybug Fun, 1997, Mattel, Model No. 17695
MNP $10   MIP $20

Meijers Shopping Fun, 1993, Mattel, Model No. 10051
MNP $10   MIP $20

Meijers Something Extra, 1992, Mattel, Model No. 0863
MNP $10   MIP $20

Mervyns Ballerina Barbie, 1983, Mattel, Model No. 4983
MNP $30   MIP $75

Mervyns Fabulous Fur, 1986, Mattel, Model No. 7093
MNP $25   MIP $65

Midge's Ensemble Gift Set, 1964, Mattel, Model No. 1012
MNP $1200   MIP $3150

Millennium Bride, limited to 10,000, 1999, Mattel, Model No. 24505
MNP $150   MIP $300

Mix n' Match Gift Set, 1962, Mattel, Model No. 857
MNP $800   MIP $1850

Model of the Moment Daria Celebutante, 2004, Mattel, Blonde
MNP n/a   MIP $50

Model of the Moment Marisa Pretty Yound Thing, 2004, Mattel, Latina
MNP n/a   MIP $50

Model of the Moment Nichelle Urban Hipster, 2004, Mattel, African American
MNP n/a   MIP $50

(KP Photo)

Montgomery Wards (mail order box),
1972, Mattel, Model No. 3210
MNP $30   MIP $500

(KP Photo)

Montgomery Wards Barbie (pink box),
1972, Mattel, Model No. 3210
MNP $350   MIP $650

My First Barbie Gift Set, 1991, Mattel,
Model No. 2483
MNP $8   MIP $20

My First Barbie Gift Set, pink tutu, 1986,
Mattel, Model No. 1979
MNP $15   MIP $35

My First Barbie Gift Set, pink tutu, 1987,
Mattel, Model No. 5386
MNP $18   MIP $40

**My First Barbie, pink tutu, Zayre's
Hispanic,** 1987, Mattel, Model
No. 1875
MNP $8   MIP $45

NASCAR Barbie #1, Kyle Petty #44, 1998,
Mattel, Model No. 20442
MNP $5   MIP $15

NASCAR Barbie #2, Bill Elliott #94, 1999,
Mattel, Model No. 22954
MNP $5   MIP $20

**National Convention A Date with Barbie
Doll in Atlanta,** 1998, Mattel
MNP $100   MIP $350

**National Convention Barbie in the Old
West,** 2000, Mattel
MNP $85   MIP $225

**National Convention We Girls Can Do
Anything Right Barbie,** 1999, Mattel
MNP $85   MIP $225

**National Convention, Barbie and the
Bandstand,** 1996, Mattel, Pennsylvania
MNP $225   MIP $450

**National Convention, Barbie Around the
World Festival,** 1985, Mattel, Michigan
MNP $125   MIP $300

**National Convention, Barbie Convention
1980,** 1980, Mattel, New York
MNP $125   MIP $350

**National Convention, Barbie Forever
Young,** 1989, Mattel, California
MNP $125   MIP $300

**National Convention, Barbie Loves a
Fairytale,** 1991, Mattel, Nebraska
MNP $150   MIP $250

**National Convention, Barbie Loves New
York,** 1984, Mattel, New York
MNP $125   MIP $275

National Convention, Barbie Ole, 1995,
Mattel, New Mexico
MNP $225   MIP $400

**National Convention, Barbie Wedding
Dreams,** 1992, Mattel, New York
MNP $50   MIP $200

National Convention, Barbie's Pow Wow,
1983, Mattel, Arizona
MNP $125   MIP $350

National Convention, Barbie's Reunion,
1986, Mattel, Arizona
MNP $125   MIP $275

**National Convention, Beach Blanket
Barbie,** 1997, Mattel, California
MNP $225   MIP $375

**National Convention, Christmas With
Barbie,** 1987, Mattel, Oklahoma
MNP $125   MIP $300

**National Convention, Come Rain or
Shine,** 1988, Mattel, Washington
MNP $125   MIP $250

**National Convention, Deep in the Heart
of Texas,** 1990, Mattel, Texas
MNP $125   MIP $250

**National Convention, Michigan
Entertains Barbie,** 1982, Mattel,
Michigan
MNP $125   MIP $275

**National Convention, The Magic of
Barbie,** 1994, Mattel, Alabama
MNP $175   MIP $375

**National Convention, We Are Family,
2004,** 2004, Mattel
MNP n/a   MIP $200

**National Convention, You've Come a
Long Way,** 1993, Mattel, Maryland
MNP $225   MIP $450

**New Lifestyles of the West Western
Plains,** 1999, Mattel, Model No. 23205
MNP $40   MIP $80

Nolan Miller #1, Sheer Illusion, 1998,
Mattel, Model No. 20662
MNP $45   MIP $75

Nolan Miller #2, Evening Illusion, 1999,
Mattel, Model No. 23495
MNP $55   MIP $80

Nostalgic 35th Anniversary Gift Set, 1994,
Mattel, Model No. 11591
MNP $50   MIP $75

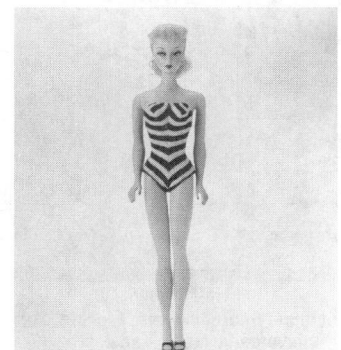

Nostalgic 35th Anniversary, blond, 1994,
Mattel, Model No. 11590
MNP $25   MIP $50

Nostalgic 35th Anniversary, brunette,
1994, Mattel, Model No. 11782
MNP $40   MIP $65

**Nostalgic Reproductions, Busy Gal
Barbie,** 1995, Mattel, Model No. 13675
MNP $25   MIP $40

**Nostalgic Reproductions, Enchanted
Evening Barbie, blond,** 1996, Mattel,
Model No. 14992
MNP $25   MIP $30

**Nostalgic Reproductions, Enchanted
Evening, brunette,** 1996, Mattel, Model
No. 15407
MNP $25   MIP $30

(KP Photo)

Nostalgic Reproductions, Fashion Luncheon, 1997, Mattel, Model No. 17382
MNP $25   MIP $40

Nostalgic Reproductions, Francie Wild Bunch, 1997, Mattel, Model No. 17601
MNP $20   MIP $50

(KP Photo)

Nostalgic Reproductions, Francie, 30th Anniversary, 1996, Mattel, Model No. 14808
MNP $20   MIP $35

Nostalgic Reproductions, Silken Flame, blond or brunette, 1998, Mattel
MNP $15   MIP $25

Nostalgic Reproductions, Solo in the Spotlight, blond or brunette, 1995, Mattel, Model No. 13534/13820
MNP $12   MIP $20

Nostalgic Reproductions, Wedding Day, blond, 1997, Mattel
MNP $10   MIP $20

Nursery Rhymes, Barbie Had a Little Lamb, 1999, Mattel, Model No. 21740
MNP $20   MIP $40

Nutcracker Barbie, 1992, Mattel, Model No. 5472
MNP $85   MIP $225

Ocean Friends Gift Set, 1996, Mattel, Model No. 16442
MNP $20   MIP $45

Olympic Barbie Gift Set, 1996, Mattel, Model No. 16443
MNP $15   MIP $30

On Parade Gift Set, Barbie, Ken, Midge, 1964, Mattel, Model No. 1014
MNP $800   MIP $2300

Osco Picnic Pretty, 1993, Mattel, Model No. 3803
MNP $15   MIP $25

Oshagatsu Barbie, 1995, Mattel, Model No. 14024
MNP $20   MIP $50

P.J.'s Swinging Silver Gift Set, 1970, Mattel, Model No. 1588
MNP $700   MIP $1500

Pace Party Sensations Barbie, 1990, Mattel
MNP $15   MIP $50

Pace Very Violet Barbie, 1992, Mattel
MNP $15   MIP $50

Paint 'N Dazzle Deluxe Gift Set, 1993, Mattel, Model No. 10926
MNP $17   MIP $35

Paul Frank Barbie, blue pajamas, 2004, Mattel
MNP n/a   MIP $60

(Mattel Photo)

Peanuts, Barbie and Snoopy, 2002, Mattel, Model No. 55558
MNP $15   MIP $25

Peppermint Princess Barbie, Winter Princess Collection, 1995, Mattel, Model No. 13598
MNP $35   MIP $50

Picture Pockets Barbie, Christie, Kira or Teresa, 2000, Mattel
MNP $5   MIP $11

Pink & Pretty Barbie Gift Set, 1982, Mattel, Model No. 5239
MNP $35   MIP $90

Pink Splendor, 1995, Mattel, Model No. 16091
MNP $150   MIP $200

Poodle Parade, 1996, Mattel, Model No. 15280
MNP $25   MIP $40

Pop Culture Barbie as That Girl, 2003, Mattel
MNP $20   MIP $40

Pop Culture James Bond 007 Barbie & Ken Gift Set, 2003, Mattel
MNP $40   MIP $75

(KP Photo)

Pop Culture, Barbie & Ken as Morticia & Gomez Addams, 2000, Mattel, Model No. 27276
MNP $40   MIP $65

Pop Culture, Barbie and Ken as Lily and Herman Munster, 2001, Mattel, Model No. 50544
MNP $25   MIP $175

Pop Culture, Barbie as Samantha from Bewitched, 2002, Mattel, Model No. 53510
MNP $20   MIP $30

Pop Culture, Barbie as That Girl, 2003, Mattel, Model No. 56705
MNP $20   MIP $30

Pop Culture, Barbie as Wonder Woman, 2000, Mattel, Model No. 24638
MNP $20   MIP $40

Pop Culture, Barbie Loves Elvis Gift Set, 1997, Mattel, Model No. 17450
MNP $30   MIP $55

Pop Culture, Barbie Loves Frankie Sinatra Gift Set, 1999, Mattel, Model No. 22953
MNP $30   MIP $50

(Mattel Photo)

Pop Culture, James Bond 007 Ken and Barbie, 2003, Mattel, Model No. B0150
MNP $30   MIP $75

(Mattel Photo)

Pop Culture, Malibu Barbie, 2002, Mattel, Model No. 56061
MNP $10   MIP $20

(KP Photo)

Pop Culture, Star Trek Barbie and Ken, 1996, Mattel, Model No. 15006
MNP $15   MIP $25

(Mattel Photo)

Pop Culture, Starring Barbie in King Kong, 2003, Mattel, Model No. 56737
MNP $20   MIP $40

Pop Culture, X-Files Barbie and Ken, 1998, Mattel
MNP $20   MIP $50

Pretty Changes Barbie Gift Set, 1978, Mattel, Model No. 2598
MNP $35   MIP $75

Pretty Hearts Barbie, 1992, Mattel, Model No. 2901
MNP $7   MIP $15

Pretty Pairs Angie N' Tangie, 1970, Mattel, Foreign, Model No. 1135
MNP $125   MIP $250

Pretty Pairs Lori N' Rori, 1970, Mattel, Foreign, Model No. 1133
MNP $125   MIP $250

Pretty Pairs Nan N' Fran, 1970, Mattel, Foreign, Model No. 1134
MNP $125   MIP $250

Princess and the Pea Barbie, 2001, Mattel, Model No. 28800
MNP $15   MIP $35

Princess Series, Rapunzel, 2002, Mattel, Model No. 53973
MNP $20   MIP $40

Queen Elizabeth I Barbie, 2004, Mattel
MNP n/a   MIP $200

Radio Shack Earring Magic, 1991, Mattel, came with software package, Model No. 25192
MNP $20   MIP $40

Red Romance Barbie, 1993, Mattel, Model No. 3161
MNP $7   MIP $15

Republican National Convention Delegate Barbie, 2000, Mattel
MNP $25   MIP $150

Romantic Bride Barbie, black, 2001, Mattel, Model No. 29439
MNP $15   MIP $45

Romantic Bride Barbie, blond, 2001, Mattel, Model No. 29438
MNP $15   MIP $45

Royal Jewels Countess of Rubies, 2001, Mattel
MNP $40   MIP $100

Royal Jewels Duchess of Diamonds, 2001, Mattel
MNP $40   MIP $100

Royal Jewels Empress of Emeralds, 2000, Mattel, Model No. 25680
MNP $50   MIP $100

Royal Jewels Queen of Sapphires, 2000, Mattel, Model No. 24924
MNP $50   MIP $100

Russell Stover Easter, 1996, Mattel, Model No. 14956
MNP $10   MIP $25

Russell Stover Easter, 1997, Mattel, Model No. 17091
MNP $5   MIP $15

Russell Stover Easter (w/Easter basket), 1996, Mattel, Model No. 14617
MNP $10   MIP $25

Sam's Club 50s Fun Barbie, 1996, Mattel, Model No. 15820
MNP $20   MIP $40

Sam's Club 60s Fun Barbie, blond, 1997, Mattel, Model No. 17252
MNP $15   MIP $25

Sam's Club 60s Fun Barbie, red hair, 1997, Mattel, Model No. 17693
MNP $10   MIP $28

Sam's Club 70s Fun Barbie, blond, 1998, Mattel, Model No. 19928
MNP $12   MIP $25

Sam's Club 70s Fun Barbie, brunette, 1998, Mattel, Model No. 19929
MNP $15   MIP $30

Sam's Club Barbie Sisters' Celebration, Barbie and Krissy, 2000, Mattel
MNP $10   MIP $25

Sam's Club Bronze Sensation Barbie, 1998, Mattel, Model No. 20022
MNP $25   MIP $40

Sam's Club Dinner Date Barbie, blond, 1998, Mattel, Model No. 19016
MNP $8   MIP $15

Sam's Club Dinner Date Barbie, red hair, 1998, Mattel, Model No. 19037
MNP $9   MIP $20

Sam's Club Festiva Barbie, 1993, Mattel, Model No. 10339
MNP $15   MIP $35

Sam's Club Jewel Jubilee Barbie, 1991, Mattel, Model No. 2366
MNP $25   MIP $60

Sam's Club Party Sensation Barbie, 1990, Mattel, Model No. 9025
MNP $20   MIP $50

Sam's Club Peach Blossom Barbie, 1992, Mattel, Model No. 7009
MNP $20   MIP $40

Sam's Club Season's Greetings Barbie, 1994, Mattel, Model No. 12384
MNP $25   MIP $60

Sam's Club Sweet Moments Barbie, 1997, Mattel, Model No. 17642
MNP $12   MIP $20

Sam's Club Wedding Fantasy Barbie Gift Set, 1993, Mattel, Model No. 10924
MNP $30   MIP $70

Sam's Club Winter Fantasy Barbie, blond or brunette, 1997, Mattel, Model No. 17249/17666
MNP $10   MIP $20

Sam's Club Winter's Eve Barbie, 1995, Mattel, Model No. 13613
MNP $12   MIP $25

School Spirit Barbie, 1996, Mattel
MNP $5   MIP $10

Schooltime Barbie 1995, 1995, Mattel
MNP $5   MIP $10

Schooltime Barbie 1998, 1998, Mattel
MNP $5   MIP $10

Sears 100th Celebration Barbie, 1986, Mattel, Model No. 2998
MNP $20   MIP $75

Sears Barbie Twinkle Town Set, 1969, Mattel, Model No. 1866
  MNP $800   MIP $1600

Sears Blossom Beautiful Barbie, 1992, Mattel, Model No. 3817
  MNP $100   MIP $275

Sears Blue Starlight, 1997, Mattel, Model No. 17125
  MNP $15   MIP $30

Sears Dream Princess, 1992, Mattel, Model No. 2306
  MNP $25   MIP $50

Sears Enchanted Princess, 1993, Mattel, Model No. 10292
  MNP $35   MIP $60

Sears Evening Enchantment, 1989, Mattel, Model No. 3596
  MNP $10   MIP $40

Sears Evening Flame, 1996, Mattel, Model No. 15533
  MNP $15   MIP $30

Sears Holiday Celebration Barbie 2004 (red dress), 2004, Mattel, Blonde or African American
  MNP n/a   MIP $40

Sears Lavender Surprise, 1990, Mattel, Model No. 9049
  MNP $8   MIP $35

Sears Lavender Surprise, black, 1990, Mattel, Model No. 5588
  MNP $8   MIP $30

Sears Lilac and Lovely Barbie, 1988, Mattel, Model No. 7669
  MNP $10   MIP $45

Sears Perfectly Plaid Gift Set, 1971, Mattel, Model No. 1193
  MNP $800   MIP $1500

Sears Pink Reflections, 1998, Mattel, Model No. 19130
  MNP $10   MIP $25

Sears Ribbons and Roses Barbie, 1995, Mattel, Model No. 13011
  MNP $10   MIP $50

Sears Silver Sweetheart Barbie, 1994, Mattel, Model No. 12410
  MNP $17   MIP $50

Sears Skooter Cut n' Button Gift Set, 1967, Mattel, Model No. 1036
  MNP $150   MIP $650

Sears Southern Belle, 1991, Mattel, Model No. 2586
  MNP $10   MIP $40

Sears Star Dream Barbie, 1987, Mattel, Model No. 4550
  MNP $10   MIP $60

Sears Winter Sports, 1975, Mattel, Model No. 9042
  MNP $65   MIP $115

Seasons Sparkle Barbie, 2003, Mattel
  MNP $8   MIP $15

Secret Hearts Gift Set, 1993, Mattel, Model No. 10929
  MNP $17   MIP $35

See's Candy Barbie, white or black, 2000, Mattel
  MNP $15   MIP $45

Service Merchandise Blue Rhapsody, 1991, Mattel, Model No. 1364
  MNP $35   MIP $75

Service Merchandise City Sophisticate, 1994, Mattel, Model No. 12005
  MNP $20   MIP $85

Service Merchandise Definitely Diamonds, 1998, Mattel, Model No. 20204
  MNP $45   MIP $95

Service Merchandise Dream Bride, black or white, 1997, Mattel, Model No. 17933/17153
  MNP $10   MIP $25

Service Merchandise Evening Symphony, 1998, Mattel, Model No. 19777
  MNP $10   MIP $25

Service Merchandise Ruby Romance, 1995, Mattel, Model No. 13612
  MNP $15   MIP $35

Service Merchandise Satin Nights, two earring versions, 1992, Mattel, Model No. 1886
  MNP $20   MIP $50

Service Merchandise Sea Princess, 1996, Mattel, Model No. 15531
  MNP $15   MIP $30

Service Merchandise Sparkling Splendor, 1993, Mattel, Model No. 10994
  MNP $17   MIP $40

Sharin Sisters Gift Set, 1992, Mattel, Model No. 5716
  MNP $12   MIP $25

Sharin Sisters Gift Set, 1993, Mattel, Model No. 10143
  MNP $12   MIP $25

Shopko/Venture Blossom Beauty, 1991, Mattel, Model No. 3142
  MNP $10   MIP $40

Shopko/Venture Party Perfect, 1992, Mattel, Model No. 1876
  MNP $12   MIP $35

Skipper Party Time Gift Set, 1964, Mattel, Model No. 1021
  MNP $100   MIP $550

Skipper Swing 'a' Rounder Gym Gift Set, 1972, Mattel, Model No. 1172
  MNP $100   MIP $400

Snap 'N Play Gift Set (Snap 'N Play Deluxe), 1992, Mattel, Model No. 2262
  MNP $12   MIP $35

Society Hound Barbie, 2001, Mattel
  MNP $20   MIP $40

(Mattel Photo)

Sophisticated Wedding (white or black), 2002, Mattel, Model No. 53370/53371
  MNP $20   MIP $50

Spiegel Golden Qi-Pao Barbie, 1998, Mattel, Model No. 20866
  MNP $30   MIP $65

Spiegel Regal Reflections, 1992, Mattel, Model No. 4116
  MNP $75   MIP $150

Spiegel Royal Invitation, 1993, Mattel, Model No. 10969
  MNP $35   MIP $75

Spiegel Shopping Chic, 1995, Mattel, Model No. 14009
  MNP $35   MIP $60

Spiegel Sterling Wishes, 1991, Mattel, Model No. 3347
  MNP $45   MIP $100

Spiegel Summer Sophisticate, 1996, Mattel, Model No. 15591
  MNP $20   MIP $45

Spiegel Theatre Elegance, 1994, Mattel, Model No. 12077
  MNP $50   MIP $75

Spiegel Winner's Circle, 1997, Mattel, Model No. 17441
  MNP $35   MIP $50

Splash 'N Color Barbie Gift Set, 1997, Mattel
  MNP $10   MIP $20

Spring Bouquet Barbie, 1993, Mattel, Model No. 3477
  MNP $10   MIP $20

Spring Parade Barbie, 1992, Mattel, Model No. 7008
  MNP $15   MIP $25

Spring Parade Barbie, black, 1992, Mattel, Model No. 2257
  MNP $15   MIP $25

BARBIE

(Mattel Photo)

Storybook Favorites, Alice and Mad Hatter (Kelly and Tommy), 2003, Mattel, Model No. 57577
MNP $10   MIP $20

Storybook Favorites, Goldilocks and the Three Bears (Kelly), 2001, Mattel, Model No. 29605
MNP $8   MIP $20

Storybook Favorites, Hansel & Gretel (Kelly and Tommy), 2000, Mattel, Model No. 28535
MNP $5   MIP $17

(Mattel Photo)

Storybook Favorites, Little Red Riding Hood (Kelly and Tommy), 2002, Mattel, Model No. 52899
MNP $10   MIP $20

(Mattel Photo)

Storybook Favorites, Mickey and Minnie Mouse (Kelly and Tommy), 2002, Mattel, Model No. 55502
MNP $10   MIP $20

Storybook Favorites, Raggedy Ann and Andy (Kelly and Tommy), 2000, Mattel, Model No. 24639
MNP $5   MIP $17

Style Set Bohemian Glamour Barbie, 2003, Mattel
MNP $25   MIP $50

Style Set Exotic Beauty Barbie, 2002, Mattel
MNP $25   MIP $50

Style Set Exotic Beauty Barbie Limited Edition, 2002, Mattel, w/ Treasure Hunt jewelry
MNP $35   MIP $65

(Mattel Photo)

Style Set, Exotic Beauty, 2003, Mattel, Model No. B0149
MNP $20   MIP $50

Style Set, Society Girl (white or black), 2002, Mattel, Model No. 56203/56204
MNP $20   MIP $50

Sweet Spring Barbie, 1992, Mattel, Model No. 3208
MNP $10   MIP $20

Sydney 2000 Olympic Pin Collector, black or white, 2000, Mattel, Model No. 25644/26302
MNP $20   MIP $30

Target 35th Anniversary Barbie, black, 1997, Mattel, Model No. 176608
MNP $10   MIP $24

Target 35th Anniversary Barbie, white, 1997, Mattel, Model No. 16485
MNP $10   MIP $20

Target Baseball Date Barbie, 1993, Mattel, Model No. 4583
MNP $10   MIP $30

Target City Style #1, 1996, Mattel, Model No. 15612
MNP $8   MIP $15

Target City Style #2, 1997, Mattel, Model No. 17237
MNP $10   MIP $20

Target Club Wedd Barbie, black, 1998, Mattel, Model No. 20423
MNP $10   MIP $20

Target Club Wedd Barbie, blond or brunette, 1998, Mattel, Model No. 19717/19718
MNP $10   MIP $20

Target Cute'n Cool, 1991, Mattel, Model No. 2954
MNP $8   MIP $30

Target Dazzlin' Date Barbie, 1992, Mattel, Model No. 3203
MNP $10   MIP $25

Target Easter Bunny Fun Barbie & Kelly, 1999, Mattel, Model No. 21720
MNP $15   MIP $25

Target Easter Egg Hunt, 1998, Mattel, Model No. 19014
MNP $15   MIP $25

Target Easter Egg Party, white or black, 2000, Mattel
MNP $15   MIP $25

Target Easter Garden Hunt Barbie and Kelly, 2001, Mattel
MNP $10   MIP $25

Target Easter Garden Kelly as Bunny, 2003, Mattel
MNP $8   MIP $15

Target Easter Garden Melody as Flower, 2003, Mattel
MNP $8   MIP $15

Target Easter Garden Melody as Lamb, 2003, Mattel
MNP $8   MIP $15

Target Easter Garden Nikki as Chick, 2003, Mattel
MNP $8   MIP $15

Target Easter Garden Tamika as Chick, 2003, Mattel
MNP $8   MIP $15

Target Gold and Lace Barbie, 1989, Mattel, Model No. 7476
MNP $10   MIP $30

Target Golden Evening, 1991, Mattel, Model No. 2587
MNP $6   MIP $45

Target Golf Date Barbie, 1993, Mattel, Model No. 10202
MNP $10   MIP $25

Target Halloween Fortune Barbie, 2003, Mattel
MNP $10   MIP $25

Target Halloween Fun Barbie & Kelly, white or black, 1999, Mattel, Model No. 23460
MNP $15   MIP $25

Target Halloween Fun Li'l Friends of Kelly, 1999, Mattel, Model No. 23796
MNP $15   MIP $25

Target Halloween Goo-tiful Barbie, 2004, Mattel
MNP n/a   MIP $20

Target Halloween Party Barbie & Ken, pirates, 1998, Mattel, Model No. 19874
MNP $20   MIP $40

Target Halloween Party Belinda as Black Cat, 2003, Mattel
MNP $8   MIP $20

Target Halloween Party Deidre (Pumpkin), 2000, Mattel, Model No. 28310
MNP $5   MIP $15

Target Halloween Party Deirdre as Pumpkin, 2002, Mattel
    MNP $8   **MIP** $15

Target Halloween Party Deirdre as Pumpkin, 2003, Mattel
    MNP $8   **MIP** $15

Target Halloween Party Jenny (Pumpkin), 2000, Mattel, Model No. 28308
    MNP $5   **MIP** $15

Target Halloween Party Jenny as Genie, 2002, Mattel
    MNP $8   **MIP** $20

Target Halloween Party Jenny as Witch, 2003, Mattel
    MNP $8   **MIP** $20

Target Halloween Party Kayla (Ghost), 2000, Mattel, Model No. 28307
    MNP $5   **MIP** $15

Target Halloween Party Kelly (Alien), 2000, Mattel, Model No. 28306
    MNP $5   **MIP** $15

Target Halloween Party Kelly as Pumpkin, 2002, Mattel
    MNP $8   **MIP** $20

Target Halloween Party Kelly as Spider, 2003, Mattel
    MNP $8   **MIP** $20

Target Halloween Party Kelly as Witch, 2004, Mattel, White or African American
    MNP n/a   **MIP** $10

Target Halloween Party Kerstie as Pumpkin, 2004, Mattel
    MNP n/a   **MIP** $10

Target Halloween Party Lorena as Witch, 2002, Mattel
    MNP $8   **MIP** $20

Target Halloween Party Melody as Tiger, 2004, Mattel
    MNP n/a   **MIP** $10

Target Halloween Party Nikki as Pumpkin, 2003, Mattel
    MNP $8   **MIP** $20

Target Halloween Party Nikkie as Ghost, 2004, Mattel
    MNP n/a   **MIP** $10

Target Halloween Party Tommy (Cowboy), 2000, Mattel, Model No. 28309
    MNP $5   **MIP** $15

Target Halloween Party Tommy as Dragon, 2003, Mattel
    MNP $8   **MIP** $20

Target Halloween Party Tommy as Scarecrow, 2002, Mattel
    MNP $8   **MIP** $20

Target Halloween Party Tommy as Vampire, 2004, Mattel
    MNP n/a   **MIP** $10

Target Happy Halloween Barbie & Kelly, 1997, Mattel, Model No. 17238
    MNP $30   **MIP** $60

Target Party Pretty Barbie, 1990, Mattel, Model No. 5955
    MNP $6   **MIP** $25

Target Pet Doctor Barbie, brunette, 1996, Mattel, Model No. 16458
    MNP $15   **MIP** $30

Target Pretty in Plaid Barbie, 1992, Mattel, Model No. 5413
    MNP $15   **MIP** $30

Target Purrfectly Halloween Barbie, 2002, Mattel
    MNP $10   **MIP** $25

Target Soccer Kelly & Tommy, 1999, Mattel
    MNP $8   **MIP** $20

Target Steppin' Out Barbie, 1995, Mattel, Model No. 14110
    MNP $8   **MIP** $20

Target Valentine Barbie, 1996, Mattel, Model No. 15172
    MNP $8   **MIP** $20

Target Valentine Date Barbie, 1998, Mattel, Model No. 18306
    MNP $8   **MIP** $20

Target Valentine Kelly and Friend, 2001, Mattel
    MNP $5   **MIP** $15

Target Valentine Lil Heart Kelly, Jenny or Balinda, 2003, Mattel
    MNP $8   **MIP** $15

Target Valentine Romance Barbie, 1997, Mattel, Model No. 16059
    MNP $8   **MIP** $20

Target Valentine Style Barbie, black, 1999, Mattel, Model No. 22150
    MNP $8   **MIP** $18

Target Valentine Style Barbie, white, 1999, Mattel, Model No. 20465
    MNP $8   **MIP** $15

Target Wild Style Barbie, 1992, Mattel, Model No. 0411
    MNP $10   **MIP** $24

Target With Love Barbie, 2000, Mattel
    MNP $8   **MIP** $15

Target Xhilaration Barbie, white or black, 1999, Mattel
    MNP $15   **MIP** $35

Tennis Star Barbie & Ken, 1988, Mattel, Model No. 7801
    MNP $18   **MIP** $40

The Waltz Barbie & Ken Gift Set, 2003, Mattel
    MNP $80   **MIP** $150

Tiff Pose N' Play, 1972, Mattel, Foreign, Model No. 1199
    MNP $125   **MIP** $350

Timeless Sentiments Angel of Hope, 1999, Mattel, Model No. 22955
    MNP $25   **MIP** $50

Timeless Sentiments Angel of Joy, white or black, 1998, Mattel, Model No. 19633/20929
    MNP $25   **MIP** $50

Timeless Sentiments Angel of Peace, 1999, Mattel, Model No. 24240
    MNP $25   **MIP** $50

Timeless Sentiments Angel of Peace, black, 1999, Mattel, Model No. 24241
    MNP $25   **MIP** $50

Todd Oldham (Designer), 1999, Mattel
    MNP $35   **MIP** $70

(KP Photo)

Together Forever, Romeo & Juliet, 1998, Mattel, Model No. 19364
    MNP $50   **MIP** $100

(KP Photo)

Together Forever, King Arthur and Queen Guinevere, 1999, Mattel, Model No. 23880
    MNP $50   **MIP** $100

Tommy as Elvis, 2004, Mattel
    MNP $10   **MIP** $25

Toys R Us 101 Dalmatians Barbie, black, 1999, Mattel, Model No. 17601
    MNP $12   **MIP** $20

(KP Photo)

Toys R Us 101 Dalmatians Barbie, white, 1997, Mattel, Model No. 17248
MNP $15   MIP $28

Toys R Us 35th Anniversary Midge, Senior Prom, 1998, Mattel, Model No. 18976
MNP $25   MIP $40

Toys R Us Astronaut Barbie, black, 1994, Mattel, Model No. 12150
MNP $15   MIP $45

Toys R Us Astronaut Barbie, white, 1994, Mattel, Model No. 12149
MNP $15   MIP $45

Toys R Us Barbie as DC Comics Bat Girl w/Batcycle, 2004, Mattel
MNP $10   MIP $30

Toys R Us Barbie for President, 1992, Mattel, Model No. 3722
MNP $17   MIP $65

Toys R Us Barbie for President, 2000, Mattel, Model No. 3940
MNP $5   MIP $18

Toys R Us Barbie Renaissance Rose Gift Set, 2000, Mattel, Model No. 28633
MNP $15   MIP $35

Toys R Us Bath Time Skipper, 1992, Mattel, Model No. 7970
MNP $12   MIP $25

Toys R Us Beauty Pagent Skipper, 1991, Mattel, Model No. 9342
MNP $10   MIP $25

Toys R Us Bicyclin' Barbie, black or white, 1995, Mattel
MNP $15   MIP $25

Toys R Us Birthday Fun Kelly Gift Set, 1996, Mattel
MNP $15   MIP $28

Toys R Us Cool 'N Sassy, black, 1992, Mattel, Model No. 4110
MNP $10   MIP $20

Toys R Us Cool 'N Sassy, white, 1992, Mattel, Model No. 1490
MNP $10   MIP $20

Toys R Us Crystal Splendor, black, 1996, Mattel, Model No. 15137
MNP $10   MIP $25

Toys R Us Crystal Splendor, white, 1996, Mattel, Model No. 15136
MNP $12   MIP $25

Toys R Us Dream Date Barbie, 1982, Mattel, Model No. 9180
MNP $7   MIP $30

Toys R Us Dream Date Ken, 1982, Mattel, Model No. 4077
MNP $5   MIP $30

Toys R Us Dream Date P.J., 1982, Mattel, Model No. 5869
MNP $8   MIP $40

Toys R Us Dream Date Skipper, 1990, Mattel, Model No. 1075
MNP $10   MIP $25

Toys R Us Dream Time Barbie, 1988, Mattel, Model No. 9180
MNP $10   MIP $30

Toys R Us Dream Wedding Gift Set, black, 1993, Mattel, Model No. 10713
MNP $22   MIP $45

Toys R Us Dream Wedding Gift Set, white, 1993, Mattel, Model No. 10712
MNP $20   MIP $45

Toys R Us Faerie Queen of Ireland, 2004, Mattel
MNP $10   MIP $30

Toys R Us Fashion Brights Barbie, white or black, 1992, Mattel, Model No. 1882/4112
MNP $10   MIP $20

Toys R Us Fashion Fun Barbie Gift Set, 1999, Mattel
MNP $15   MIP $25

(KP Photo)

Toys R Us Firefighter Barbie, white or black, 1995, Mattel, With yellow uniform and hat and dalmatian puppy, Model No. 13553/13472
MNP $10   MIP $25

Toys R Us Gardening Fun Barbie & Kelly Gift Set, 1997, Mattel, Model No. 17242
MNP $12   MIP $23

Toys R Us Got Milk? Barbie, white or black, 1996, Mattel, Model No. 15721/15122
MNP $8   MIP $20

Toys R Us Gran Gala Teresa, 1997, Mattel, Model No. 17239
MNP $8   MIP $15

Toys R Us Harley-Davidson Barbie #1, 1997, Mattel, Model No. 17692
MNP $150   MIP $325

Toys R Us Harley-Davidson Barbie #2, 1998, Mattel, Model No. 20441
MNP $75   MIP $160

Toys R Us Harley-Davidson Barbie #3, 1999, Mattel, Model No. 22256
MNP $50   MIP $90

Toys R Us Harley-Davidson Barbie #4, 2000, Mattel, Model No. 25637
MNP $50   MIP $90

Toys R Us Harley-Davidson Barbie #5, black, 2001, Mattel, Model No. 29208
MNP $45   MIP $70

Toys R Us Harley-Davidson Barbie #5, white, 2001, Mattel, Model No. 29207
MNP $45   MIP $70

(KP Photo)

Toys R Us Harley-Davidson Ken #1, 1999, Mattel, Model No. 22255
MNP $50   MIP $90

Toys R Us Harley-Davidson Ken #2, 2000, Mattel, Model No. 25638
MNP $15   MIP $55

Toys R Us I'm A Toys R Us Kid Barbie, white or black, 1998, Mattel, Model No. 18895/21040
MNP $15   MIP $30

Toys R Us International Pen Friend Barbie, 1995, Mattel, Model No. 13558
MNP $7   MIP $16

Toys R Us Love to Read Barbie, 1993, Mattel, Model No. 10507
MNP $12   MIP $40

Toys R Us Malt Shop Barbie, 1993, Mattel, Model No. 4581
MNP $10   MIP $25

Toys R Us Moonlight Magic Barbie, black, 1993, Mattel, Model No. 10609
MNP $15   MIP $55

Toys R Us Moonlight Magic Barbie, white, 1993, Mattel, Model No. 10608
MNP $15   MIP $65

Toys R Us My Size Bride Barbie, red hair, 1995, Mattel, Model No. 15649
MNP $60   MIP $135

Toys R Us Native Spirit Barbie Spirit of the Sky, 2003, Mattel
MNP $20   MIP $50

Toys R Us Native Spirit Barbie Spirit of the Water, 2002, Mattel
MNP $25   MIP $50

Toys R Us Olympic Gymnast Barbie, red hair, box w/o special edition marking, 1996, Mattel, Model No. 15725
MNP $15   MIP $30

BARBIE

Toys R Us Oreo Fun Barbie, 1997, Mattel, Model No. 18511
    MNP $8   **MIP** $18

Toys R Us Paleontologist Barbie, white or black, 1997, Mattel, Model No. 17240/17241
    MNP $12   **MIP** $24

Toys R Us Party Time Barbie, white or black, 1994, Mattel, Model No. 12243
    MNP $10   **MIP** $20

Toys R Us Pepsi Spirit Barbie, 1989, Mattel, Model No. 4869
    MNP $18   **MIP** $70

Toys R Us Pepsi Spirit Skipper, 1989, Mattel, Model No. 4867
    MNP $15   **MIP** $65

Toys R Us POG Barbie, 1995, Mattel, Model No. 13239
    MNP $7   **MIP** $15

(KP Photo)

Toys R Us Police Officer Barbie, black, 1993, Mattel, Model No. 10689
    MNP $15   **MIP** $65

Toys R Us Police Officer Barbie, white, 1993, Mattel, Model No. 10688
    MNP $15   **MIP** $70

Toys R Us Purple Passion, black, 1995, Mattel, Model No. 13554
    MNP $10   **MIP** $30

Toys R Us Purple Passion, white, 1995, Mattel, Model No. 13555
    MNP $10   **MIP** $30

Toys R Us Radiant in Red Barbie, black, 1992, Mattel, Model No. 4113
    MNP $12   **MIP** $55

Toys R Us Radiant in Red Barbie, white, 1992, Mattel, Model No. 1276
    MNP $12   **MIP** $55

Toys R Us Sapphire Sophisticate, 1997, Mattel, Model No. 16692
    MNP $12   **MIP** $25

Toys R Us School Fun, 1991, Mattel, Model No. 2721
    MNP $6   **MIP** $40

Toys R Us School Spirit Barbie, black, 1993, Mattel, Model No. 10683
    MNP $10   **MIP** $30

Toys R Us School Spirit Barbie, white, 1993, Mattel, Model No. 10682
    MNP $10   **MIP** $25

Toys R Us Share A Smile Barbie, 1997, Mattel, Model No. 17247
    MNP $7   **MIP** $15

Toys R Us Share A Smile Becky, 1997, Mattel, Model No. 15761
    MNP $15   **MIP** $28

Toys R Us Share A Smile Christie, 1997, Mattel, Model No. 17372
    MNP $7   **MIP** $15

Toys R Us Show and Ride Barbie, 1988, Mattel, Model No. 7799
    MNP $10   **MIP** $35

Toys R Us Sign Language Barbie, white or black, 2000, Mattel
    MNP $8   **MIP** $20

Toys R Us Society Style Emerald Elegance, 1994, Mattel, Model No. 12322
    MNP $15   **MIP** $40

Toys R Us Society Style Emerald Enchantment, 1997, Mattel, Model No. 17443
    MNP $25   **MIP** $50

Toys R Us Society Style Sapphire Dream, 1995, Mattel, Model No. 13256
    MNP $50   **MIP** $70

Toys R Us Space Camp Barbie, white or black, 1999, Mattel, Model No. 22435/22246
    MNP $12   **MIP** $28

Toys R Us Spellbound Lover (Iseult), 2005, Mattel
    MNP n/a   **MIP** $30

Toys R Us Spirit of the Earth Barbie, 2001, Mattel
    MNP $25   **MIP** $75

Toys R Us Spots 'N Dots Barbie, 1993, Mattel, Model No. 10491
    MNP $12   **MIP** $35

Toys R Us Spots 'N Dots Teresa, 1993, Mattel, Model No. 10885
    MNP $12   **MIP** $40

Toys R Us Spring Parade Barbie, white or black, 1992, Mattel, Model No. 7008/2257
    MNP $15   **MIP** $30

Toys R Us Sunflower Barbie, 1995, Mattel, Model No. 13488
    MNP $9   **MIP** $20

Toys R Us Sunflower Teresa, 1995, Mattel, Model No. 13489
    MNP $9   **MIP** $20

Toys R Us Sweet Romance, 1991, Mattel, Model No. 2917
    MNP $8   **MIP** $30

Toys R Us Sweet Roses, 1989, Mattel, Model No. 7635
    MNP $7   **MIP** $25

Toys R Us The Bard, 2004, Mattel
    MNP n/a   **MIP** n/a

Toys R Us Totally Hair Courtney, 1992, Mattel, Model No. 1433
    MNP $10   **MIP** $25

Toys R Us Totally Hair Skipper, 1992, Mattel, Model No. 1430
    MNP $10   **MIP** $25

Toys R Us Totally Hair Whitney, 1992, Mattel, Model No. 7735
    MNP $20   **MIP** $40

Toys R Us Travelin' Sisters Gift Set, 1995, Mattel, Model No. 14073
    MNP $30   **MIP** $65

Toys R Us Vacation Sensation Barbie, blue, 1986, Mattel, Model No. 1675
    MNP $10   **MIP** $40

Toys R Us Vacation Sensation Barbie, pink, 1989, Mattel, Model No. 1675
    MNP $12   **MIP** $48

Toys R Us Wedding Fantasy Barbie & Ken Gift Set, 1997, Mattel, Model No. 17243
    MNP $20   **MIP** $45

Toys R Us Winter Fun Barbie, 1990, Mattel, Model No. 5949
    MNP $10   **MIP** $40

Toys R Us/FAO Schwarz Sea Holiday Barbie #1, with lip gloss, 1993, Mattel
    MNP $15   **MIP** $30

Toys R Us/FAO Schwarz Sea Holiday Barbie #2, with lip gloss, 1993, Mattel
    MNP $15   **MIP** $24

Toys R Us/FAO/JCPenney, Winter Sports Barbie, 1995, Mattel
    MNP $15   **MIP** $30

Toys R Us/FAO/JCPenney, Winter Sports Ken, 1995, Mattel
    MNP $15   **MIP** $30

Trail Blazin' Barbie, 1991, Mattel, Model No. 2783
    MNP $10   **MIP** $25

Tree Trimming Barbie, white or black, 1999, Mattel
    MNP $5   **MIP** $15

Trend Forecaster Barbie, 1999, Mattel, Model No. 22833
    MNP $20   **MIP** $45

Tropical Barbie Deluxe Gift Set, 1985, Mattel, Model No. 2996
    MNP $20   **MIP** $45

Tutti and Todd Sundae Treat Set, 1966, Mattel, Model No. 3556
    MNP $150   **MIP** $350

Tutti Me n' My Dog, 1966, Mattel, Model No. 3554
    MNP $150   **MIP** $350

Tutti Nighty Night Sleep Tight, 1965, Mattel, Model No. 3553
    MNP $100   **MIP** $300

Twirley Curls Barbie Gift Set, 1982, Mattel, Model No. 4097
    MNP $30   **MIP** $85

Twist and Turn Far Out Barbie, 1999, Mattel, Model No. 21911
MNP $20   MIP $40

Vera Wang #1, bride, 1998, Mattel, Model No. 19788
MNP $75   MIP $150

Vera Wang #2, lavender dress, 1999, Mattel, Model No. 23027
MNP $55   MIP $140

Versace Barbie, 2004, Mattel
MNP $70   MIP $140

Versus by Versace Barbie, 2004, Mattel
MNP $25   MIP $80

Very Violet Barbie, 1992, Mattel, Model No. 1859
MNP $10   MIP $20

Victorian Barbie with Cedric Bear, 2000, Mattel
MNP $25   MIP $59

Victorian Tea Orange Pekoe Barbie, 2000, Mattel, Model No. 25507
MNP $110   MIP $220

Walking Jamie Strollin' in Style Gift Set, 1972, Mattel, Model No. 1247
MNP $300   MIP $600

Wal-Mart 25th Year Pink Jubilee Barbie, 1987, Mattel, Model No. 4589
MNP $20   MIP $50

Wal-Mart 35th Anniversary Barbie, black or white, Mattel, Model No. 17616/17245
MNP $10   MIP $24

Wal-Mart 35th Anniversary Teresa, 1997, Mattel, Model No. 17617
MNP $12   MIP $25

Wal-Mart Anniversary Star Barbie, 1992, Mattel, Model No. 2282
MNP $15   MIP $30

Wal-Mart Ballroom Beauty, 1991, Mattel, Model No. 3678
MNP $8   MIP $30

Wal-Mart Bathtime Fun Barbie, 1991, Mattel, Model No. 9601
MNP $5   MIP $25

Wal-Mart Country Bride, 1995, Mattel, Model No. 13014
MNP $8   MIP $15

Wal-Mart Country Bride, black, 1995, Mattel, Model No. 13015
MNP $8   MIP $15

Wal-Mart Country Bride, Hispanic, 1995, Mattel, Model No. 13016
MNP $8   MIP $15

Wal-Mart Country Western Star Barbie, black or Hispanic, 1994, Mattel, Model No. 12096
MNP $12   MIP $30

Wal-Mart Country Western Star Barbie, white, 1994, Mattel, Model No. 12097
MNP $10   MIP $25

Wal-Mart Dream Fantasy, 1990, Mattel, Model No. 7335
MNP $8   MIP $35

Wal-Mart Exclusive Zodiac Barbie, 2004, Mattel, Aries, Taurus, Gemini, Cancer, Leo, Virgo
MNP n/a   MIP $20

Wal-Mart Frills and Fantasy Barbie, 1988, Mattel, Model No. 1374
MNP $7   MIP $45

Wal-Mart Jewel Skating Barbie, 1999, Mattel, Model No. 23239
MNP $6   MIP $12

Wal-Mart Lavender Look Barbie, 1989, Mattel, Model No. 3963
MNP $7   MIP $30

Wal-Mart Portrait in Blue Barbie, black, 1998, Mattel, Model No. 19356
MNP $10   MIP $20

Wal-Mart Portrait in Blue Barbie, white, 1998, Mattel, Model No. 19355
MNP $8   MIP $18

Wal-Mart Pretty Choices Barbie, black, 1997, Mattel, Model No. 18018
MNP $8   MIP $18

Wal-Mart Pretty Choices Barbie, blond or brunette, 1997, Mattel, Model No. 17971/18019
MNP $8   MIP $18

Wal-Mart Puzzle Craze Barbie, white or black, 1998, Mattel, Model No. 20164/20165
MNP $6   MIP $14

Wal-Mart Puzzle Craze Teresa, 1998, Mattel, Model No. 20166
MNP $6   MIP $14

Wal-Mart Shopping Time Barbie, black or white, 1997, Mattel, Model No. 18231/18230
MNP $7   MIP $15

Wal-Mart Shopping Time Teresa, 1997, Mattel, Model No. 18232
MNP $7   MIP $15

Wal-Mart Skating Star Barbie, 1996, Mattel, Model No. 15510
MNP $10   MIP $15

Wal-Mart Star Skater Barbie, white or black, 2000, Mattel
MNP $5   MIP $15

Wal-Mart Superstar Barbie, black, 1993, Mattel, Model No. 10711
MNP $15   MIP $40

Wal-Mart Superstar Barbie, white, 1993, Mattel, Model No. 10592
MNP $15   MIP $30

Wal-Mart Sweet Magnolia Barbie, black, white or Hispanic, 1996, Mattel, Model No. 15653/15652/15654
MNP $9   MIP $15

Wal-Mart the Birthstone Collection, 2003, Mattel, 12 different dolls
MNP $10   MIP $25

Wal-Mart Tooth Fairy #1, 1994, Mattel, Model No. 11645
MNP $7   MIP $20

Wal-Mart Tooth Fairy #2, 1995, Mattel, Model No. 11645
MNP $5   MIP $20

Wal-Mart Tooth Fairy #3, 1998, Mattel, Model No. 17246
MNP $6   MIP $14

Walt Disney World Animal Kingdom Barbie, white or black, 1998, Mattel, Model No. 20363/20989
MNP $15   MIP $30

Walt Disney World Barbie 25th Anniversary, 1996, Mattel, Model No. 16525
MNP $15   MIP $30

Walt Disney World Disney Fun 1994, 1994, Mattel, Model No. 11650
MNP $15   MIP $50

Walt Disney World Disney Fun 1995, 1995, Mattel, Model No. 13533
MNP $15   MIP $40

Walt Disney World Disney Fun 1997, 1997, Mattel, Model No. 17058
MNP $8   MIP $20

Walt Disney World Millennium Barbie, white or black, 2000, Mattel
MNP $5   MIP $15

Walt Disney World Resort Vacation Barbie, Ken, Tommy, Kelly, 1998, Mattel, Model No. 20315
MNP $35   MIP $80

Walt Disney World Toontown Stacie, 1994, Mattel, Model No. 11587
MNP $15   MIP $30

Warner Bros. Barbie Loves Tweety, 1999, Mattel, Model No. 21632
MNP $8   MIP $22

Warner Bros. Scooby-Doo Barbie, 2001, Mattel, Model No. 27966
MNP $5   MIP $15

Wedding Fantasy Gift Set, 1993, Mattel, Model No. 10924
MNP $50   MIP $125

Wedding Flower Blushing Orchid Bride, 1997, Mattel
MNP $100   MIP $200

Wedding Flower Romantic Rose Bride, 1996, Mattel
MNP $100   MIP $220

Wedding Party Gift Set, six dolls, 1991, Mattel, Model No. 9852
MNP $45   MIP $125

Wedgwood Barbie #1, blue dress, 2000, Mattel, Model No. 25641
MNP $40   MIP $80

Wedgwood Barbie #2, pink dress, black, 2001, Mattel, Model No. 50824
MNP $30   MIP $85

Wedgwood Barbie #2, pink dress, white, 2001, Mattel, Model No. 50823
MNP $30   MIP $85

Wessco Carnival Cruise Barbie, 1997, Mattel, Model No. 15186
MNP $25   MIP $40

Wessco International Traveler #1, 1995, Mattel, Model No. 13912
  MNP $35 MIP $60

Wessco International Traveler #2, 1996, Mattel, Model No. 16158
  MNP $25 MIP $50

Western Chic Barbie, 2002, Mattel, Model No. 55487
  MNP $20 MIP $50

Western Fun Gift Set Barbie & Ken, 1989, Mattel, Model No. 5408
  MNP $12 MIP $30

Western Fun Gift Set Barbie & Ken, 1990, Mattel, Model No. 5408
  MNP $12 MIP $30

Western Plains Barbie, 2000, Mattel
  MNP $40 MIP $95

Winn-Dixie Party Pink Barbie, 1989, Mattel, Model No. 7637
  MNP $7 MIP $25

Winn-Dixie Pink Sensation, 1990, Mattel, Model No. 5410
  MNP $6 MIP $20

Winn-Dixie Southern Beauty, 1991, Mattel, Model No. 3284
  MNP $10 MIP $25

Winter Concert Barbie, 2002, Mattel
  MNP $40 MIP $80

Winter Princess #1 Winter Princess, 1993, Mattel, Model No. 10655
  MNP $35 MIP $175

Winter Princess #2 Evergreen Princess, 1994, Mattel, Model No. 12123
  MNP $35 MIP $100

Winter Princess #3 Peppermint Princess, 1995, Mattel, Model No. 13598
  MNP $35 MIP $175

Winter Princess #4 Jewel Princess, 1996, Mattel, Model No. 15826
  MNP $35 MIP $175

Winter Princess #5 Midnight Princess, 1997, Mattel, Model No. 17780
  MNP $35 MIP $175

Woolworth's Special Expressions, black, blue dress, 1991, Mattel, Model No. 2583
  MNP $4 MIP $10

Woolworth's Special Expressions, black, peach dress, 1992, Mattel, Model No. 3200
  MNP $5 MIP $30

Woolworth's Special Expressions, black, pink dress, 1990, Mattel, Model No. 5505
  MNP $4 MIP $10

Woolworth's Special Expressions, black, white dress, 1989, Mattel, Model No. 7326
  MNP $5 MIP $20

Woolworth's Special Expressions, blue dress, pastel print, 1993, Mattel, Model No. 10048
  MNP $5 MIP $15

Woolworth's Special Expressions, pink dress, 1990, Mattel, Model No. 5504
  MNP $3 MIP $20

Woolworth's Special Expressions, white, 1989, Mattel, Model No. 4842
  MNP $5 MIP $20

Woolworth's Special Expressions, white, blue dress, 1991, Mattel, Model No. 2582
  MNP $4 MIP $15

Woolworth's Special Expressions, white, peach dress, 1992, Mattel, Model No. 3197
  MNP $5 MIP $20

Woolworth's Sweet Lavender Barbie, black or white, 1992, Mattel, Model No. 2523/2522
  MNP $12 MIP $28

Workin' Out Barbie Gift Set, 1997, Mattel
  MNP $10 MIP $25

XO Valentine Barbie, 2003, Mattel
  MNP $8 MIP $15

XXXOOO Barbie Doll, 2000, Mattel
  MNP $8 MIP $20

MATTEL DOLLS, NON-BARBIE

Audrey Hepburn, Breakfast At Tiffany's, black dress, 1998, Mattel
  MNP $30 MIP $50

Audrey Hepburn, Pink Princess, 1998, Mattel
  MNP $25 MIP $40

Betty Boop #1 Glamour Girl, 2001, Mattel, Model No. 29733
  MNP $15 MIP $25

Bob Mackie Cher, 2001, Mattel, Model No. 29049
  MNP $15 MIP $40

Buffy and Mrs. Beasley, 1968, Mattel, Model No. 3577
  MNP $125 MIP $275

Chatty Cathy, 1999 reissue, 1999, Mattel, Model No. 23782
  MNP $50 MIP $100

Chatty Cathy, Holiday, 1999, Mattel, Model No. 23783
  MNP $50 MIP $125

(Mattel Photo)

Clark Gable as Rhett Butler, 2002, Mattel, Model No. 53854
  MNP $30 MIP $70

Coca-Cola Holiday Series, Santa Claus, 1999, Mattel, Model No. 23288
  MNP $25 MIP $60

Daytime Drama, Erica Kane #1, 1998, Mattel
  MNP $20 MIP $50

Daytime Drama, Erica Kane #2, 1999, Mattel
  MNP $20 MIP $45

Daytime Drama, Marlena Evans, 1999, Mattel
  MNP $20 MIP $45

Elizabeth Taylor as Cleopatra, 1999, Mattel
  MNP $35 MIP $60

Elizabeth Taylor in Father of the Bride, 2000, Mattel, Model No. 26836
  MNP $30 MIP $70

Elvis Presley #1, 1998, Mattel, Model No. 20544
  MNP $20 MIP $50

Elvis Presley #2 The Army Years, 1999, Mattel, Model No. 21912
  MNP $20 MIP $50

(Mattel Photo)

Elvis Presley #4 King of Rock 'N Roll, 2002, Mattel, Model No. 53869
  MNP $20 MIP $40

Flapper Minnie Mouse, 2001, Mattel, Model No. 29734
  MNP $30 MIP $60

Frank Sinatra The Recording Years, 2001, Mattel
  MNP $15 MIP $35

Great Villains, Captain Hook (Peter Pan), 1999, Mattel
  MNP $30 MIP $75

Great Villains, Cruella DeVil, Power in Pinstripes, 1996, Mattel, Model No. 16295
  MNP $35 MIP $75

Great Villains, Cruella DeVil, Ruthless in Red, 1997, Mattel
  MNP $35 MIP $75

Great Villains, Evil Queen (Snow White), 1998, Mattel, Model No. 18626
MNP $30   MIP $75

Great Villains, Maleficent (Sleeping Beauty), 1999, Mattel
MNP $25   MIP $75

Great Villains, Ursula (Little Mermaid), 1997, Mattel, Model No. 17575
MNP $30   MIP $75

I Love Lucy, Be a Pal, 2002, Mattel, Model No. 52737
MNP $20   MIP $40

I Love Lucy, Job Switching, 1999, Mattel, Model No. 21268
MNP $20   MIP $35

I Love Lucy, Lucy and Ricky 50th Anniversary Dolls, 2000, Mattel
MNP $25   MIP $75

(Mattel Photo)

I Love Lucy, Lucy Gets a Paris Gown, 2003, Mattel, Model No. B0313
MNP $20   MIP $40

I Love Lucy, Lucy's Italian Movie, 2000, Mattel, Model No. 25527
MNP $20   MIP $40

I Love Lucy, Vitameatavegemin, 1998, Mattel
MNP $25   MIP $45

Jolly Holiday Mary Poppins, 2000, Mattel
MNP $20   MIP $40

Marilyn Monroe, 2002, Mattel, Model No. 53873
MNP $20   MIP $35

Rosie O'Donnell, 1999, Mattel
MNP $10   MIP $25

Tinker Bell, 2001, Mattel, Model No. 29735
MNP $20   MIP $40

Vivien Leigh Scarlett O'Hara #1 Barbecue at Twelve Oaks, 2001, Mattel, Model No. 29910
MNP $25   MIP $45

Vivien Leigh Scarlett O'Hara #2 Peachtree St. Drapery Dress, 2001, Mattel, Model No. 29771
MNP $25   MIP $45

PORCELAIN BARBIES

30th Anniversary Ken, 1991, Mattel, Model No. 1110
MNP $40   MIP $65

30th Anniversary Midge, 1993, Mattel, Model No. 7957
MNP $40   MIP $65

30th Anniversary Skipper, 1994, Mattel, Model No. 11396
MNP $50   MIP $100

Benefit Performance Barbie, 1988, Mattel, Model No. 5475
MNP $150   MIP $350

Blue Rhapsody, first porcelain Barbie, 1986, Mattel, Model No. 1708
MNP $200   MIP $450

Blushing Orchid Bride Barbie, 1997, Mattel, Model No. 16962
MNP $75   MIP $175

Bob Mackie Celebration of Dance Charleston, 2001, Mattel
MNP $100   MIP $300

Bob Mackie Celebration of Dance Tango, 1999, Mattel, Model No. 23451
MNP $150   MIP $200

Crystal Rhapsody, blond, Presidential Porcelain Barbie collection, 1992, Mattel, Model No. 1553
MNP $100   MIP $300

Crystal Rhapsody, brunette, Presidential Porcelain Barbie collection, 1993, Mattel, Model No. 10201
MNP $100   MIP $600

Enchanted Evening Barbie, 1987, Mattel, Model No. 3415
MNP $125   MIP $200

Faberge Imperial Elegance Barbie, limited to **15,000,** 1999, Mattel, Model No. 19816
MNP $150   MIP $250

Gay Parisienne, blond, 1991, Mattel, Model No. 9973
MNP $225   MIP $400

Gay Parisienne, brunette, 1991, Mattel, Model No. 9973
MNP $75   MIP $125

Gay Parisienne, red hair, 1991, Mattel, Model No. 9973
MNP $225   MIP $400

Gold Sensation, Gold and Silver Porcelain Barbie Set, 1993, Mattel, Model No. 10246
MNP $175   MIP $350

Holiday Porcelain #1, Holiday Jewel, 1995, Mattel, Model No. 14311
MNP $55   MIP $125

Holiday Porcelain #2, Holiday Caroler, 1996, Mattel, Model No. 15760
MNP $60   MIP $100

Holiday Porcelain #3, Holiday Ball, 1997, Mattel, Model No. 18326
MNP $50   MIP $100

Holiday Porcelain #4, Holiday Gift, 1998, Mattel, Model No. 20128
MNP $50   MIP $100

Mattel's 50th Anniversary Barbie, 1995, Mattel, Model No. 14479
MNP $75   MIP $150

Mint Memories, Victorian Tea Porcelain Collection, 1999, Mattel
MNP $100   MIP $215

Plantation Belle, blond, Porcelain Treasures Collection, 1992, Mattel, Model No. 7526
MNP $100   MIP $300

Plantation Belle, red, Porcelain Treasures Collection, 1992, Mattel, Model No. 5351
MNP $50   MIP $125

Presidential Porcelain Evening Pearl Barbie, 1996, Mattel
MNP $95   MIP $225

Romantic Rose Bride, 1995, Mattel, Model No. 14541
MNP $75   MIP $175

Royal Splendor, Presidential Porcelain Collection, 1993, Mattel, Model No. 10950
MNP $100   MIP $250

Silken Flame Barbie, brunette, Porcelain Treasures Collection, 1993, Mattel, Model No. 1249
MNP $50   MIP $75

Silken Flame, blond, 1993, Mattel, Model No. 11099
MNP $150   MIP $250

Silver Starlight, Gold and Silver Porcelain Barbie Set, 1994, Mattel, Model No. 11875
MNP $175   MIP $350

Solo in the Spotlight, 1990, Mattel, Model No. 7613
MNP $50   MIP $75

Sophisticated Lady, 1990, Mattel, Model No. 5313
MNP $75   MIP $125

Star Lily Bride Barbie, Wedding Flower Collection, 1995, Mattel, Model No. 12953
MNP $125   MIP $250

Wedding Day Barbie, 1989, Mattel, Model No. 2641
MNP $150   MIP $250

(Mattel Photo)

Wizard of Oz Cowardly Lion, 2002, Mattel, Model No. 54180
MNP $50   MIP $150

Wizard of Oz Dorothy, 2000, Mattel, Model No. 26834

> **MNP** $70   **MIP** $150

Wizard of Oz Scarecrow, 2001, Mattel, Model No. 29190

> **MNP** $50   **MIP** $150

Wizard of Oz Tin Man, 2001, Mattel, Model No. 29676

> **MNP** $50   **MIP** $150

Wizard of Oz Wicked Witch, 2000, Mattel, Model No. 26835

> **MNP** $70   **MIP** $150

Wizard of Oz Winged Monkey, 2001, Mattel, Model No. 29476

> **MNP** $50   **MIP** $150

FASHIONS

BARBIE VINTAGE FASHIONS 1959-1966

Aboard Ship, Mattel, Model No. 1631

> **MNP** $125   **MIP** $250

After Five, Mattel, Model No. 934

> **MNP** $50   **MIP** $100

American Airlines Stewardess, Mattel, Model No. 984

> **MNP** $50   **MIP** $175

Apple Print Sheath, Mattel, Model No. 917

> **MNP** $25   **MIP** $100

Ballerina, Mattel, Model No. 989

> **MNP** $45   **MIP** $150

Barbie Arabian Nights, Mattel, Model No. 0874

> **MNP** $100   **MIP** $275

Barbie Baby-Sits, 1963, Mattel, Model No. 953

> **MNP** $100   **MIP** $275

Barbie in Hawaii, Mattel, Model No. 1605

> **MNP** $65   **MIP** $250

Barbie in Holland, Mattel, Model No. 0823

> **MNP** $50   **MIP** $175

Barbie in Japan, Mattel, Model No. 0821

> **MNP** $125   **MIP** $425

Barbie in Mexico, Mattel, Model No. 0820

> **MNP** $100   **MIP** $250

Barbie in Switzerland, Mattel, Model No. 0822

> **MNP** $75   **MIP** $225

Barbie Learns to Cook, Mattel, Model No. 1634

> **MNP** $150   **MIP** $500

Barbie Skin Diver, Mattel, Model No. 1608

> **MNP** $30   **MIP** $100

Barbie-Q Outfit, Mattel, Model No. 962

> **MNP** $50   **MIP** $140

Beau Time, Mattel, Model No. 1651

> **MNP** $175   **MIP** $500

Beautiful Bride, Mattel, Model No. 1698

> **MNP** $400   **MIP** $2100

Benefit Performance, Mattel, Model No. 1667

> **MNP** $450   **MIP** $1375

Black Magic, Mattel, Model No. 1609

> **MNP** $75   **MIP** $250

Bride's Dream, Mattel, Model No. 947

> **MNP** $75   **MIP** $200

Brunch Time, Mattel, Model No. 1628

> **MNP** $110   **MIP** $350

Busy Gal, Mattel, Model No. 981

> **MNP** $125   **MIP** $250

Busy Morning, Mattel, Model No. 956

> **MNP** $150   **MIP** $275

Campus Sweetheart, Mattel, Model No. 1616

> **MNP** $400   **MIP** $1600

Candy Striper Volunteer, Mattel, Model No. 0889

> **MNP** $175   **MIP** $365

Career Girl, Mattel, Model No. 954

> **MNP** $70   **MIP** $225

Caribbean Cruise, Mattel, Model No. 1687

> **MNP** $65   **MIP** $200

Cheerleader, Mattel, Model No. 0876

> **MNP** $50   **MIP** $170

Cinderella, Mattel, Model No. 0872

> **MNP** $125   **MIP** $425

Club Meeting, Mattel, Model No. 1672

> **MNP** $95   **MIP** $375

Coffee's On, Mattel, Model No. 1670

> **MNP** $70   **MIP** $150

(KP Photo)

Commuter Set, Mattel, Model No. 916

> **MNP** $500   **MIP** $1500

Country Club Dance, Mattel, Model No. 1627

> **MNP** $125   **MIP** $400

Country Fair, Mattel, Model No. 1603

> **MNP** $45   **MIP** $165

Crisp 'n Cool, Mattel, Model No. 1604

> **MNP** $30   **MIP** $150

Cruise Stripes, Mattel, Model No. 918

> **MNP** $35   **MIP** $165

Dancing Doll, Mattel, Model No. 1626

> **MNP** $175   **MIP** $450

Debutante Ball, Mattel, Model No. 1666

> **MNP** $400   **MIP** $1200

Dinner At Eight, Mattel, Model No. 946

> **MNP** $75   **MIP** $225

Disc Date, Mattel, Model No. 1633

> **MNP** $125   **MIP** $295

Dog n' Duds, Mattel, Model No. 1613

> **MNP** $125   **MIP** $325

Dreamland, Mattel, Model No. 1669

> **MNP** $110   **MIP** $200

Drum Majorette, Mattel, Model No. 0875

> **MNP** $60   **MIP** $200

(KP Photo)

Easter Parade, Mattel, Shown on a Ponytail #3 doll, Model No. 971
MNP $950   MIP $4000

(KP Photo)

Enchanted Evening, Mattel, Seen here on a Bubblecut Barbie, Model No. 983
MNP $100   MIP $300

Evening Enchantment, Mattel, Model No. 1695
MNP $250   MIP $500

Evening Gala, Mattel, Model No. 1660
MNP $110   MIP $350

Evening Splendor, Mattel, Model No. 961
MNP $75   MIP $300

Fabulous Fashion, Mattel, Model No. 1676
MNP $250   MIP $525

Fancy Free, Mattel, Model No. 943
MNP $15   MIP $65

Fashion Editor, Mattel, Model No. 1635
MNP $225   MIP $650

Fashion Luncheon, Mattel, Model No. 1656
MNP $450   MIP $1200

Fashion Shiner, Mattel, Model No. 1691
MNP $90   MIP $220

Floating Gardens, Mattel, Model No. 1696
MNP $175   MIP $500

Floral Petticoat, Mattel, Model No. 921
MNP $20   MIP $50

Formal Occasion, Mattel, Model No. 1697
MNP $150   MIP $500

Fraternity Dance, Mattel, Model No. 1638
MNP $175   MIP $575

Friday Night Date, Mattel, Model No. 979
MNP $50   MIP $225

Fun At The Fair, Mattel, Model No. 1624
MNP $95   MIP $285

Fun n' Games, Mattel, Model No. 1619
MNP $110   MIP $300

Garden Party, Mattel, Model No. 931
MNP $47   MIP $150

Garden Tea Party, Mattel, Model No. 1606
MNP $50   MIP $175

Garden Wedding, Mattel, Model No. 1658
MNP $195   MIP $650

(KP Photo)

Gay Parisienne, Mattel, Shown here on a Ponytail #1, Model No. 964
MNP $1100   MIP $4000

Gold 'n Glamour, Mattel, Model No. 1647
MNP $600   MIP $1600

Golden Elegance, Mattel, Model No. 992
MNP $175   MIP $350

Golden Evening, Mattel, Model No. 1610
MNP $95   MIP $250

Golden Girl, Mattel, Model No. 911
MNP $65   MIP $150

Golden Glory, Mattel, Model No. 1645
MNP $175   MIP $425

Graduation, Mattel, Model No. 945
MNP $48   MIP $95

Guinevere, Mattel, Model No. 0873
MNP $125   MIP $300

Here Comes The Bride, Mattel, Model No. 1665
MNP $400   MIP $995

Holiday Dance, Mattel, Model No. 1639
MNP $275   MIP $595

Icebreaker, Mattel, Model No. 942
MNP $50   MIP $100

International Fair, Mattel, Model No. 1653
MNP $250   MIP $500

Invitation To Tea, Mattel, Model No. 1632
MNP $265   MIP $525

It's Cold Outside, brown, Mattel, Model No. 0819
MNP $30   MIP $110

It's Cold Outside, red, Mattel, Model No. 0819
MNP $40   MIP $165

Junior Designer, Mattel, Model No. 1620
MNP $150   MIP $350

Junior Prom, Mattel, Model No. 1614
MNP $275   MIP $600

Knit Hit, Mattel, Model No. 1621
MNP $125   MIP $225

Knit Separates, Mattel, Model No. 1602
MNP $70   MIP $160

Knitting Pretty, blue, Mattel, Model No. 957
MNP $65   MIP $150

Knitting Pretty, pink, Mattel, Model No. 957
MNP $75   MIP $300

Let's Dance, Mattel, Model No. 978
MNP $50   MIP $175

Little Red Riding Hood & The Wolf, Mattel, Model No. 0880
MNP $175   MIP $450

London Tour, Mattel, Model No. 1661
MNP $125   MIP $400

Lunch Date, Mattel, Model No. 1600
MNP $45   MIP $125

Lunch On The Terrace, Mattel, Model No. 1649
MNP $175   MIP $325

Lunchtime, Mattel, Model No. 1673
MNP $150   MIP $285

Magnificence, Mattel, Model No. 1646
MNP $350   MIP $595

Masquerade, Mattel, Model No. 944
MNP $50   MIP $175

Matinee Fashion, Mattel, Model No. 1640
MNP $320   MIP $525

Midnight Blue, Mattel, Model No. 1617
MNP $375   MIP $800

(KP Photo)

Miss Astronaut, Mattel, Shown here with re-constructed helmet, Model No. 1641
MNP $395   MIP $650

Modern Art, Mattel, Model No. 1625
MNP $300   MIP $550

Mood For Music, Mattel, Model No. 940
MNP $70   MIP $150

Movie Date, Mattel, Model No. 933
MNP $30   MIP $50

Music Center Matinee, Mattel, Model No. 1633
MNP $325   MIP $600

Nighty Negligee, Mattel, Model No. 965
    MNP $30   **MIP** $75

On The Avenue, Mattel, Model No. 1644
    MNP $200   **MIP** $525

(KP Photo)

Open Road, Mattel, The Mattel Road Map included with this outfit is especially hard to find, Model No. 985
    MNP $150   **MIP** $350

Orange Blossom, 1961, Mattel, Model No. 987
    MNP $40   **MIP** $150

Outdoor Art Show, Mattel, Model No. 1650
    MNP $195   **MIP** $500

Outdoor Life, Mattel, Model No. 1637
    MNP $75   **MIP** $275

Pajama Party, Mattel, Model No. 1601
    MNP $20   **MIP** $50

(KP Photo)

Pan Am Stewardess, Mattel, Very rare fashion shown on American Girl doll, Model No. 1678
    MNP $1500 **MIP** $4000

Party Date, Mattel, Model No. 958
    MNP $85   **MIP** $175

Patio Party, Mattel, Model No. 1692
    MNP $100   **MIP** $325

Peachy Fleecy, Mattel, Model No. 915
    MNP $50   **MIP** $100

Photo Fashion, Mattel, Model No. 1648
    MNP $125   **MIP** $375

Picnic Set, Mattel, Model No. 967
    MNP $205   **MIP** $410

Pink Moonbeams, Mattel, Model No. 1694
    MNP $85   **MIP** $300

Plantation Belle, Mattel, Model No. 966
    MNP $175   **MIP** $350

Poodle Parade, Mattel, Model No. 1643
    MNP $500   **MIP** $950

Pretty As A Picture, Mattel, Model No. 1652
    MNP $175   **MIP** $450

Print Aplenty, Mattel, Model No. 1686
    MNP $75   **MIP** $275

Rain Coat, Mattel, Model No. 949
    MNP $30   **MIP** $75

Reception Line, Mattel, Model No. 1654
    MNP $350   **MIP** $500

Red Flare, Mattel, Model No. 939
    MNP $35   **MIP** $150

(KP Photo)

Registered Nurse, Mattel, Seen here on Midge, Model No. 991
    MNP $65   **MIP** $175

Resort Set, Mattel, Model No. 963
    MNP $65   **MIP** $175

Riding In The Park, Mattel, Model No. 1668
    MNP $175   **MIP** $595

(KP Photo)

Roman Holiday, Mattel, Shown on Ponytail #4 Barbie doll, Model No. 968
    MNP $750   **MIP** $4800

Satin n' Rose, Mattel, Model No. 1611
    MNP $190   **MIP** $375

Saturday Matinee, Mattel, Model No. 1615
    MNP $525   **MIP** $900

Senior Prom, Mattel, Model No. 951
    MNP $75   **MIP** $200

Sheath Sensation, Mattel, Model No. 986
    MNP $80   **MIP** $150

Shimmering Magic, Mattel, Model No. 1664
    MNP $350   **MIP** $1600

Silken Flame, Mattel, Model No. 977
    MNP $50   **MIP** $125

Singing In The Shower, Mattel, Model No. 988
    MNP $65   **MIP** $130

Skater's Waltz, Mattel, Model No. 1629
    MNP $125   **MIP** $395

Ski Queen, Mattel, Model No. 948
    MNP $65   **MIP** $150

Sleeping Pretty, Mattel, Model No. 1636
    MNP $85   **MIP** $350

Sleepytime Gal, Mattel, Model No. 1674
    MNP $95   **MIP** $220

Slumber Party, Mattel, Model No. 1642
    MNP $95   **MIP** $260

(KP Photo)

Solo In The Spotlight, Mattel, Seen here on a Ponytail #4 doll, Model No. 982
    MNP $95   **MIP** $300

Sophisticated Lady, Mattel, Model No. 993
    MNP $150   **MIP** $300

Sorority Meeting, Mattel, Model No. 937
    MNP $75   **MIP** $180

Sporting Casuals, Mattel, Model No. 1671
    MNP $60   **MIP** $165

Stormy Weather, Mattel, Model No. 0949
    MNP $50   **MIP** $95

(KP Photo)

Student Teacher, Mattel, Model No. 1622
    MNP $235   **MIP** $400

Studio Tour, Mattel, Model No. 1690
    MNP $110   **MIP** $250

Suburban Shopper, Mattel, Model No. 969
    MNP $100   **MIP** $300

Sunday Visit, Mattel, Model No. 1675
    MNP $175   **MIP** $450

Sunflower, Mattel, Model No. 1683
    MNP $75   **MIP** $245

Sweater Girl, Mattel, Model No. 976
    MNP $75   **MIP** $175

Sweet Dreams, pink, Mattel, Model No. 973
    MNP $200   **MIP** $425

Sweet Dreams, yellow, Mattel, Model No. 973
    MNP $35   **MIP** $125

Swingin' Easy, Mattel, Model No. 955
    MNP $95   **MIP** $245

Tennis Anyone, Mattel, Model No. 941
    MNP $35   **MIP** $150

Theatre Date (1963), 1963, Mattel, Model No. 1612
    MNP $75   **MIP** $175

Theatre Date (1964), 1964, Mattel, Model No. 959
    MNP $75   **MIP** $200

Travel Togethers, Mattel, Model No. 1688
    MNP $75   **MIP** $240

Under Fashions, Mattel, Model No. 1655
    MNP $175   **MIP** $500

Undergarments, Mattel, Model No. 919
    MNP $25   **MIP** $65

Underprints, Mattel, Model No. 1685
    MNP $55   **MIP** $225

Vacation Time, Mattel, Model No. 1623
    MNP $95   **MIP** $240

Wedding Day Set, Mattel, Model No. 972
    MNP $150   **MIP** $350

White Magic, Mattel, Model No. 1607
    MNP $95   **MIP** $275

Winter Holiday, Mattel, Model No. 975
    MNP $82   **MIP** $165

FRANCIE VINTAGE FASHIONS 1966

Checkmates, Mattel, Model No. 1259
    MNP $65   **MIP** $140

Clam Diggers, Mattel, Model No. 1258
    MNP $100   **MIP** $250

Concert In The Park, Mattel, Model No. 1256
    MNP $75   **MIP** $250

Dance Party, Mattel, Model No. 1257
    MNP $150   **MIP** $250

First Formal, Mattel, Model No. 1260
    MNP $80   **MIP** $175

First Things First, Mattel, Model No. 1252
    MNP $55   **MIP** $100

Fresh As A Daisy, Mattel, Model No. 1254
    MNP $65   **MIP** $140

Fur Out, 1966, Mattel, Model No. 1262
    MNP $195   **MIP** $400

Gad-About, Mattel, Model No. 1250
    MNP $75   **MIP** $220

Go Granny Go, 1966, Mattel, Model No. 1267
    MNP $85   **MIP** $200

Hip Knits, 1966, Mattel, Model No. 1265
    MNP $100   **MIP** $200

It's A Date, Mattel, Model No. 1251
    MNP $70   **MIP** $125

Leather Limelight, 1966, Mattel, Model No. 1269
    MNP $125   **MIP** $255

Orange Cozy, 1966, Mattel, Model No. 1263
    MNP $170   **MIP** $235

Polka Dots N' Raindrops, Mattel, Model No. 1255
    MNP $35   **MIP** $100

Quick Shift, 1966, Mattel, Model No. 1266
    MNP $90   **MIP** $180

Shoppin' Spree, Mattel, Model No. 1261
    MNP $75   **MIP** $140

Style Setters, 1966, Mattel, Model No. 1268
    MNP $95   **MIP** $260

Swingin' Skimmy, 1966, Mattel, Model No. 1264
    MNP $95   **MIP** $245

Tuckered Out, Mattel, Model No. 1253
    MNP $55   **MIP** $125

KEN VINTAGE FASHIONS 1961-1966

American Airlines Captain #1, Mattel, Model No. 0779
    MNP $205   **MIP** $300

Army and Air Force, Mattel, Model No. 797
    MNP $135   **MIP** $245

BARBIE

(KP Photo)

Best Man, Mattel, Seen on Allan doll, Model No. 1425
      MNP $700   **MIP** $1100

Business Appointment, Mattel, Model No. 1424
      MNP $800   **MIP** $1150

Campus Corduroys, Mattel, Model No. 1410
      MNP $20   **MIP** $65

Campus Hero, Mattel, Model No. 770
      MNP $35   **MIP** $95

Casuals, striped shirt, Mattel, Model No. 0782
      MNP $70   **MIP** $100

Casuals, yellow shirt, Mattel, Model No. 782
      MNP $40   **MIP** $65

College Student, Mattel, Model No. 1416
      MNP $190   **MIP** $400

Country Clubbin', Mattel, Model No. 1400
      MNP $40   **MIP** $85

Dr. Ken, Mattel, Model No. 793
      MNP $55   **MIP** $130

Dreamboat, Mattel, Model No. 785
      MNP $40   **MIP** $95

Drum Major, Mattel, Model No. 0775
      MNP $75   **MIP** $175

Fountain Boy, Mattel, Model No. 1407
      MNP $230   **MIP** $325

Fraternity Meeting, Mattel, Model No. 1408
      MNP $25   **MIP** $55

Fun On Ice, Mattel, Model No. 791
      MNP $55   **MIP** $105

Going Bowling, Mattel, Model No. 1403
      MNP $20   **MIP** $35

Going Huntin', Mattel, Model No. 1409
      MNP $50   **MIP** $100

Graduation, Mattel, Model No. 795
      MNP $35   **MIP** $65

Here Comes The Groom, Mattel, Model No. 1426
      MNP $1000   **MIP** $1400

Hiking Holiday, Mattel, Model No. 1412
      MNP $100   **MIP** $210

Holiday, Mattel, Model No. 1414
      MNP $48   **MIP** $100

In Training, Mattel, Model No. 780
      MNP $30   **MIP** $50

Jazz Concert, Mattel, Model No. 1420
      MNP $135   **MIP** $250

(KP Photo)

Ken A Go Go, Mattel, This outfit even included a mod-hair wig to make the rather staid Ken look hip, Model No. 1423
      MNP $500   **MIP** $700

Ken Arabian Nights, Mattel, Model No. 0774
      MNP $100   **MIP** $200

Ken In Hawaii, Mattel, Model No. 1404
      MNP $100   **MIP** $195

Ken In Holland, Mattel, Model No. 0777
      MNP $155   **MIP** $250

Ken In Mexico, Mattel, Model No. 0778
      MNP $150   **MIP** $250

Ken In Switzerland, Mattel, Model No. 0776
      MNP $150   **MIP** $200

Ken Skin Diver, Mattel, Model No. 1406
      MNP $30   **MIP** $50

King Arthur, Mattel, Model No. 0773
      MNP $225   **MIP** $375

Masquerade (Ken), Mattel, Model No. 794
      MNP $60   **MIP** $145

Mountain Hike, Mattel, Model No. 1427
      MNP $150   **MIP** $300

Mr. Astronaut, Mattel, Model No. 1415
      MNP $395   **MIP** $650

Off To Bed, Mattel, Model No. 1413
      MNP $82   **MIP** $150

Play Ball, Mattel, Model No. 792
      MNP $55   **MIP** $110

Rally Day, Mattel, Model No. 788
      MNP $66   **MIP** $130

Roller Skate Date, w/hat, Mattel, Model No. 1405
      MNP $40   **MIP** $125

Roller Skate Date, w/slacks, Mattel, Model No. 1405
      MNP $40   **MIP** $150

Rovin' Reporter, Mattel, Model No. 1417
      MNP $175   **MIP** $295

Sailor, Mattel, Model No. 796
      MNP $65   **MIP** $120

Saturday Date, Mattel, Model No. 786
      MNP $40   **MIP** $105

Seein' The Sights, Mattel, Model No. 1421
      MNP $195   **MIP** $455

Ski Champion, Mattel, Model No. 798
      MNP $85   **MIP** $155

Sleeper Set, blue, Mattel, Model No. 0781
      MNP $60   **MIP** $120

Sleeper Set, brown, Mattel, Model No. 781
      MNP $38   **MIP** $70

Special Date, Mattel, Model No. 1401
      MNP $70   **MIP** $145

Sport Shorts, Mattel, Model No. 783
      MNP $20   **MIP** $55

Summer Job, Mattel, Model No. 1422
      MNP $290   **MIP** $475

Terry Togs, Mattel, Model No. 784
      MNP $60   **MIP** $90

The Prince, Mattel, Model No. 0772
      MNP $285   **MIP** $375

The Yachtsman, no hat, Mattel, Model No. 789
      MNP $45   **MIP** $90

The Yachtsman, w/hat, Mattel, Model No. 0789
      MNP $235   **MIP** $475

Time For Tennis, Mattel, Model No. 790
      MNP $70   **MIP** $140

Time To Turn In, Mattel, Model No. 1418
      MNP $80   **MIP** $175

Touchdown, Mattel, Model No. 799
      MNP $55   **MIP** $125

Tuxedo, Mattel, Model No. 787
      MNP $125   **MIP** $245

TV's Good Tonight, Mattel, Model No. 1419
      MNP $110   **MIP** $250

Victory Dance, Mattel, Model No. 1411
MNP $60   MIP $135

RICKY FASHIONS 1965-1966

Let's Explore, Mattel, Model No. 1506
MNP $35   MIP $85

Lights Out, Mattel, Model No. 1501
MNP $55   MIP $100

Little Leaguer, Mattel, Model No. 1504
MNP $65   MIP $95

Saturday Show, Mattel, Model No. 1502
MNP $45   MIP $70

Skateboard Set, Mattel, Model No. 1505
MNP $55   MIP $100

Sunday Suit, Mattel, Model No. 1503
MNP $45   MIP $65

SKIPPER VINTAGE FASHIONS 1964-1966

Ballet Class, Mattel, Model No. 1905
MNP $60   MIP $135

Can You Play?, Mattel, Model No. 1923
MNP $60   MIP $125

Chill Chasers, Mattel, Model No. 1926
MNP $55   MIP $100

Cookie Time, Mattel, Model No. 1912
MNP $85   MIP $150

Country Picnic, Mattel, Model No. 1933
MNP $300   MIP $450

Day At The Fair, Mattel, Model No. 1911
MNP $120   MIP $200

Dog Show, Mattel, Model No. 1929
MNP $190   MIP $300

Dreamtime, Mattel, Model No. 1909
MNP $60   MIP $125

Dress Coat, Mattel, Model No. 1906
MNP $60   MIP $80

Flower Girl, Mattel, Model No. 1904
MNP $80   MIP $150

Fun Time, Mattel, Model No. 1920
MNP $100   MIP $200

Happy Birthday, Mattel, Model No. 1919
MNP $355   MIP $500

Junior Bridesmaid, Mattel, Model No. 1934
MNP $285   MIP $475

Land & Sea, Mattel, Model No. 1917
MNP $90   MIP $155

Learning To Ride, Mattel, Model No. 1935
MNP $185   MIP $275

Let's Play House, Mattel, Model No. 1932
MNP $125   MIP $250

Loungin' Lovelies, Mattel, Model No. 1930
MNP $55   MIP $125

Masquerade (Skipper), Mattel, Model No. 1903
MNP $80   MIP $155

Me N' My Doll, Mattel, Model No. 1913
MNP $150   MIP $260

Outdoor Casuals, Mattel, Model No. 1915
MNP $85   MIP $135

Platter Party, Mattel, Model No. 1914
MNP $75   MIP $125

Rain Or Shine, Mattel, Model No. 1916
MNP $50   MIP $90

Rainy Day Checkers, Mattel, Model No. 1928
MNP $155   MIP $300

Red Sensation, Mattel, Model No. 1901
MNP $65   MIP $125

School Days, Mattel, Model No. 1907
MNP $60   MIP $130

School Girl, Mattel, Model No. 1921
MNP $200   MIP $295

Ship Ahoy, Mattel, Model No. 1918
MNP $155   MIP $275

Silk N' Fancy, Mattel, Model No. 1902
MNP $60   MIP $125

Skating Fun, Mattel, Model No. 1908
MNP $48   MIP $110

Sledding Fun, Mattel, Model No. 1936
MNP $155   MIP $275

Sunny Pastels, Mattel, Model No. 1910
MNP $60   MIP $125

Tea Party, Mattel, Model No. 1924
MNP $185   MIP $300

Town Togs, Mattel, Model No. 1922
MNP $95   MIP $170

Under-Pretties, Mattel, Model No. 1900
MNP $25   MIP $50

What's New At The Zoo?, Mattel, Model No. 1925
MNP $50   MIP $120

TUTTI FASHIONS 1966

Puddle Jumpers, Mattel, Model No. 3601
MNP $20   MIP $45

Sand Castles, Mattel, Model No. 3603
MNP $55   MIP $98

Ship Shape, Mattel, Model No. 3602
MNP $55   MIP $90

Skippin' Rope, Mattel, Model No. 3604
MNP $55   MIP $95

BARBIE

Battery-Operated Toys

By Karen O'Brien

Battery-operated toys are the distant cousins of late 19th century automatons. Combining motion with bright tin lithography, quality craftsmanship, and prices the masses could afford, the battery-powered toys produced following World War II brought a new type of toy into American households—toys that moved under their own power.

Japanese companies delving into tin lithography began replacing wind-up and friction motors with the more reliable battery power source. The results were toys capable of complex and compound motions such as walking, lifting, drumming, and even dancing. The innovative designs and ingenuity employed in their creation make battery-operated toys valuable today for their motion, design, humorous outlook, and nostalgia.

Identifying the manufacturer of a particular toy without the box can be difficult. Many companies uses only initials to mark toys and others didn't mark them at all. Major manufacturers from the 1940s through the 1960s include, Marx, Linemar (Marx's Japanese subsidiary), Alps, Marusan, Yonezawa, Bandai, Ashai Toy, Toy Nomura, and Modern Toy. Marx is identified by a circle with an "X" containing the company name; Alps shows a mountain top with the name "Alps" underneath; Marusan used the initials "SAN"; Yonezawa used the initial "Y" in a leaf; Bandai used the initial "B" in a diamond; and Toy Nomura used the initials "TN."

VALUE AND 2006 TRENDS

It's difficult to find most battery-operated toys in Mint condition in original boxes. They are highly susceptible to deterioration, even if in storage, due to climate and the delicate nature of materials used to create them. Tin rusts, battery compartments corrode, and fabric fades.

Having the original box intact greatly increases the toy's desirability to collectors, as instructions were often printed on the box and manufacturers information is frequently located there.

Battery-operated toys of popular characters including Disney and Popeye will command higher prices as they have an appeal to a wider range of collectors. These toys will certainly remain popular among collectors.

The complexity of the toy also determines value. A toy with three or more actions will generally be worth more than a toy that performs only one action. Even though they may be nice display pieces, toys that don't work command much less. Restored toys should always be represented as such.

This price guide lists toys in Good, Excellent, and Mint in Box conditions. To receive a MIB designation, a toy should be operational, clean, free of rust or corrosion, and have the original box. Note that those in Good condition will exhibit wear, but will still be operational. Lesser condition toys and those that are not operational are not graded here, but should not be dismissed as they may be useful for parts.

Contributor: Leo Rishty and Don Hultzman. Mr Rishty and Mr. Hultzman may be contacted in care of: Toys & Prices, KP Books, 700 E. State St., Iola, WI 54990.

THE TOP TEN BATTERY-OPERATED TOYS (In Mint Condition)

1. Smoking Popeye, Linemar, 1950s	$3,500
2. Bubble Blowing Popeye, Linemar, 1950s	2,750
3. Mickey the Magician, Linemar, 1960s	2,550
4. Gypsy Fortune Teller, Ichida, 1950s	2,250
5. Smoking Spaceman, Linemar, 1950s	2,000
6. Drumming Mickey Mouse, Linemar, 1950s	1,900
7. Main Street, Linemar, 1950s	1,500
8. Nutty Nibs, Linemar, 1950s	1,400
9. Kooky-Spooky Whistling Tree, Marx, 1950s	1,225
10. Tarzan, Marusan, 1966	1,200

BATTERY-OPERATED TOYS

ABC Fairy Train, 1950s, MT, 14-1/2" long
EX $90 NM $120 MIP $180

Accordion Player Bunny, 1950s, Alps, 12" tall, 9" long
EX $280 NM $420 MIP $560

Air Cargo Prop-Jet Airplane, 1960s, Marx, Seaboard World Airlines, 12" long, 14-1/2" wingspan
EX $200 NM $375 MIP $480

Air Control Tower, 1960s, Bandai, 11" tall, 37" span
EX $230 NM $325 MIP $475

Air Defense Truck w/Pom-Pom Gun, 1950s, Linemar, 14" long
EX $160 NM $225 MIP $320

Aircraft Carrier, 1950s, Marx, 20" long, six actions
EX $325 NM $480 MIP $650

Alley, the Exciting New Roaring Stalking Alligator, 1960s, Marx, 17-1/2" long
EX $190 NM $255 MIP $355

American Airlines DC-7, 1960s, Linemar, 17-1/2" long, 19" wingspan
EX $210 NM $330 MIP $435

American Airlines Electra, 1950s, Linemar, 18" long, 19-1/2" wingspan
EX $200 NM $315 MIP $430

American Airlines Flagship Caroline, 1950s, Linemar, 18" long, 19-1/2" wingspan
EX $200 NM $325 MIP $425

Anti-Aircraft Unit No. 1, 1950s, Linemar, 12-1/2" long
EX $150 NM $235 MIP $300

Army Radio Jeep—J1490, 1950s, Linemar, 7-1/4" long
EX $100 NM $150 MIP $200

(KP Photo)

Arthur A-Go-Go, 1960s, Alps, 10" tall
EX $200 NM $300 MIP $410

Atomic Rocket X-1800, 1960s, MT, 9" long
EX $165 NM $245 MIP $345

B-58 Hustler Jet, 1950s, Marx, 21" long, 12" wingspan
EX $500 NM $750 MIP $1025

Ball Blowing Clown, 1950s, TN, w/2 balls and "mystery action"
EX $100 NM $150 MIP $225

Ball Playing Dog, 1950s, Linemar, 9"
EX $110 NM $175 MIP $225

Barber Bear, 1950s, Linemar, 9-1/2" tall
EX $325 NM $425 MIP $575

Barking Boxer Dog, 1950s, Marx, 7" long
EX $50 NM $85 MIP $125

Barney Bear Drummer, 1950s, Alps, 11" tall
EX $135 NM $200 MIP $250

Barnyard Rooster, 1950s, Marx, 10" tall
EX $100 NM $150 MIP $200

(KP Photo)

Bartender, 1960s, TN, 6 actions - shakes Martini, drinks, face turns red, puckers lips, smoke shoots out ears, 11-1/2" tall
EX $65 NM $85 MIP $125

Bear the Cashier, 1950s, MT, 7-1/2" tall
EX $200 NM $300 MIP $400

Bengali—The Exciting New Growling, Prowling Tiger, 1961, Linemar, 18-1/2" long
EX $175 NM $285 MIP $375

Big John, 1960s, Alps, 12" tall
EX $75 NM $100 MIP $150

Big John the Indian Chief, 1960s, TN, 12-1/2" tall
EX $125 NM $170 MIP $225

Big Max & Conveyor, 1958, Remco, 7" tall
EX $125 NM $165 MIP $250

Bimbo the Clown, 1950s, Alps, 9-1/4" tall
EX $250 NM $375 MIP $550

Blushing Gunfighter, 1960s, Y Co., 11" tall
EX $100 NM $160 MIP $200

Blushing Willie, 1960s, Y Co., 4 actions - pours real water, drinks, eyes spin, hair stands up, 10" tall
EX $65 NM $90 MIP $140

Bobby the Drumming Bear, 1950s, Alps, 10" tall
EX $225 NM $325 MIP $450

Bongo Player, 1960s, Alps, 10" tall
EX $80 NM $120 MIP $170

(KP Photo)

Bongo the Drumming Monkey, 1960s, Alps, 9-1/2" tall
EX $80 NM $120 MIP $165

Brave Eagle, 1950s, TN, 11" tall
EX $95 NM $140 MIP $215

Brewster the Rooster, 1950s, Marx, 9-1/2" tall
EX $120 NM $200 MIP $255

Bubble Blowing Bear, 1950s, MT, 9-1/2" tall
EX $175 NM $260 MIP $350

Bubble Blowing Boy, 1950s, Y Co., 7" tall
EX $150 NM $225 MIP $300

(KP Photo)

Bubble Blowing Monkey, 1950s, Alps, 5 actions, 10" tall
EX $140 NM $190 MIP $285

Bubble Blowing Popeye, 1950s, Linemar, 11-3/4" tall
EX $1350 NM $1850 MIP $2750

Bubbling Bull, 1950s, Linemar, 8" tall
EX $100 NM $175 MIP $225

Bunny the Magician, 1950s, Alps, 14-1/2" tall
EX $275 NM $460 MIP $550

Burger Chef Dog, 1950s, Y Co., 9" tall, dog cooking w/frying pan
EX $165 NM $250 MIP $325

Busy Housekeeper, 1950s, Alps, 8-1/2" tall
EX $225 NM $325 MIP $400

Busy Secretary, 1950s, Linemar, 7-1/2" tall
EX $190 NM $275 MIP $375

Busy Shoe Shining Bear, 1950s, Alps, 10" tall
EX $150   NM $225   MIP $275

Cabin Cruiser with Outboard Motor, 1950s, Linemar, 12" long
EX $125   NM $200   MIP $250

Calypso Joe, 1950s, Linemar, 11" tall
EX $300   NM $450   MIP $600

Camera Shooting Bear, 1950s, Linemar, 11" tall
EX $475   NM $700   MIP $950

Cappy the Baggage Porter Dog, 1960s, Alps, 12" tall
EX $150   NM $200   MIP $285

Caterpillar, 1950s, Alps, 16" long
EX $60   NM $105   MIP $155

Central Choo Choo, 1960s, MT, 15" long
EX $45   NM $65   MIP $90

Charlie the Drumming Clown, 1950s, Alps, 9-1/2" tall
EX $155   NM $230   MIP $310

(KP Photo)

Charlie Weaver, 1962, TN, 12"
EX $80   NM $110   MIP $155

Charm the Cobra, 1960s, Alps, 6" tall
EX $110   NM $185   MIP $260

Chee Chee Chihuahua, 1960s, Mego, 8" tall
EX $45   NM $65   MIP $90

(KP Photo)

Chef Cook, 1960s, Y Co., 11-1/2" tall
EX $150   NM $250   MIP $325

Chippy the Chipmunk, 1950s, Alps, 12" long
EX $75   NM $135   MIP $175

Circus Elephant, 1950s, TN, w/ball and umbrella
EX $50   NM $100   MIP $150

Circus Fire Engine, 1960s, MT, 11" long
EX $125   NM $210   MIP $270

Clancy the Great, 1960s, Ideal, 19-1/2" tall
EX $100   NM $170   MIP $235

Climbing Donald Duck on Friction Fire Engine, 1950s, Linemar, 12" long
EX $580   NM $875   MIP $1200

Clown Circus Car, 1960s, MT, 8-1/2" long
EX $125   NM $200   MIP $265

Clown on Unicycle, 1960s, MT, 10-1/2" tall
EX $225   NM $375   MIP $475

Coney Island Penny Machine, 1950s, Remco, 13" tall
EX $125   NM $140   MIP $250

Coney Island Rocket Ride, 1950s, Alps, 13-1/2" tall
EX $425   NM $650   MIP $850

Cragstan 2-Gun Sheriff, 1950s, Cragstan, remote control, two guns
EX $50   NM $100   MIP $150

Cragstan Beep Beep Greyhound Bus, 1950s, Cragstan, 20" long
EX $150   NM $200   MIP $250

(KP Photo)

Cragstan Crapshooter, 1950s, Y Co., 9-1/2" tall
EX $125   NM $175   MIP $225

Cragstan Crapshooting Monkey, 1950s, Alps, 9" tall
EX $125   NM $175   MIP $225

Cragstan Mother Goose, 1960s, Y Co., 8-1/4" tall
EX $100   NM $150   MIP $200

Cragstan Playboy, 1960s, Cragstan, 13" tall
EX $95   NM $165   MIP $200

Cragstan Roulette, A Gambling Man, 1960s, Y Co., 9" tall
EX $175   NM $250   MIP $350

Crawling Baby, 1940s, Linemar, 11" long
EX $40   NM $60   MIP $80

Daisy, the Jolly Drumming Duck, 1950s, Alps, 9" tall
EX $150   NM $225   MIP $300

(KP Photo)

Dancing Merry Chimp, 1960s, Kuramochi, 11" tall
EX $100   NM $150   MIP $225

Dandy, the Happy Drumming Pup, 1950s, Alps, 8-1/2" tall
EX $100   NM $150   MIP $225

Dennis the Menace, 1950s, Rosko, 9" tall, with xylophone
EX $170   NM $235   MIP $315

Disney Acrobats, 1950s, Linemar, 9" tall; Mickey, Donald, and Pluto
EX $575   NM $880   MIP $1175

Disney Fire Engine, 1950s, Linemar, 11" long
EX $550   NM $775   MIP $1000

Disneyland Fire Engine, 1950s, Linemar, 18" long
EX $375   NM $575   MIP $800

Dolly Dressmaker, 1950s, TN, 7-1/2" tall
EX $225   NM $325   MIP $450

Donald Duck, 1960s, Linemar, 8" tall
EX $250   NM $375   MIP $475

Doxie the Dog, 1950s, Linemar, 9" long
EX $30   NM $40   MIP $50

(KP Photo)

Drinking Captain, 1960s, S & E, 12" tall
EX $100   NM $150   MIP $200

Drummer Bear, 1950s, Alps, 10" tall
EX $140   NM $210   MIP $280

Drumming Mickey Mouse, 1950s, Linemar, 10" tall
EX $900   NM $1425   MIP $1900

Drumming Polar Bear, 1960s, Alps, 12"
EX $80   NM $120   MIP $160

Ducky Duckling, 1960s, Alps, 8"
EX $45   NM $70   MIP $100

El Toro, Cragstan Bullfighter, 1950s, TN, 9-1/2" long
EX $115   NM $170   MIP $235

Feeding Bird Watcher, 1950s, Linemar, 9" tall
EX $300   NM $480   MIP $625

Fido the Xylophone Player, 1950s, Alps, 8-3/4" tall
EX $150   NM $230   MIP $310

Flintstone Yacht, 1961, Remco, 17" long
EX $100   NM $155   MIP $210

Frankenstein Monster, 1960s, TN, 14" tall
EX $150   NM $225   MIP $300

Frankie the Rollerskating Monkey, 1950s, Alps, 12"
EX $125   NM $200   MIP $275

Fred Flintstone Bedrock Band, 1962, Alps, 9-1/2" tall
EX $365   NM $550   MIP $700

Fred Flintstone Flivver, 1960s, Marx, 7" long
EX $450   NM $675   MIP $900

Fred Flintstone on Dino, 1961, Marx, 22"
EX $550   NM $775   MIP $1000

Friendly Jocko, My Favorite Pet, 1950s, Alps, 8" tall
EX $110   NM $175   MIP $245

(KP Photo)

Gino, Neapolitan Balloon Blower, 1960s, Tomiyama, 10" tall
EX $150   NM $200   MIP $250

Girl with Baby Carriage, 1960s, TN, 8" tall
EX $120   NM $175   MIP $235

Godzilla Monster, 1970s, Marusan, 11-1/2" tall
EX $185   NM $265   MIP $350

(KP Photo)

Good Time Charlie, 1960s, MT, 12" tall
EX $125   NM $170   MIP $225

Grandpa Panda Bear, 1950s, MT, 9" tall
EX $125   NM $200   MIP $270

(KP Photo)

Great Garloo, 1960s, Marx, 23" tall green monster
EX $385   NM $500   MIP $725

Green Caterpillar, 1950s, Daiya, 19-1/2" long
EX $150   NM $225   MIP $300

Gypsy Fortune Teller, 1950s, Ichida, 12" tall, twenty cards
EX $1200   NM $1750   MIP $2250

Happy & Sad Face Cymbal Clown, 1960s, Y Co., 10" tall
EX $170   NM $250   MIP $320

Happy Fiddler Clown, 1950s, Alps, 9-1/2" tall
EX $270   NM $380   MIP $475

Happy Naughty Chimp, 1960s, Daishin, 9-1/2" tall
EX $75   NM $100   MIP $150

Happy Santa One-Man Band, 1950s, Alps, 9" tall
EX $125   NM $200   MIP $270

Hippo Chef, 1960s, Y Co., 10" tall
EX $140   NM $235   MIP $325

Hobo Clown with Accordion, 1950s, Alps, 10-1/2" tall
EX $300   NM $425   MIP $600

Hong Kong Rickshaw, 1960s, PMC Co., all plastic, made in Hong Kong
EX $60   NM $95   MIP $150

Hoop Zing Girl, 1950s, Linemar, 11-1/2" tall
EX $145   NM $225   MIP $295

Hoopy the Fishing Duck, 1950s, Alps, 10" tall
EX $275   NM $400   MIP $550

Hooty the Happy Owl, 1960s, Alps, 9" tall
EX $80   NM $115   MIP $165

Hungry Baby Bear, 1950s, Y Co., 9-1/2" tall
EX $200   NM $300   MIP $400

Hungry Cat, 1960s, Linemar, 9" tall
EX $300   NM $495   MIP $765

Hungry Hound Dog, 1950s, Y Co., 9-1/2" tall
EX $200   NM $300   MIP $400

Hy-Que, the "Speak no Evil, See No Evil, Hear No Evil" Monkey, 1960s, TN, 6 actions, shake his hand and he raises arms, 17" tall
EX $175   NM $300   MIP $500

Ice Cream Baby Bear, Vanilla, 1950s, MT, 9-1/2"
EX $225   NM $335   MIP $425

(KP Photo)

Indian Joe, 1960s, Alps, 12" tall
EX $90   NM $135   MIP $175

Jocko the Drinking Monkey, 1950s, Linemar, 11" tall
EX $125   NM $170   MIP $220

Jo-Jo the Flipping Monkey, 1970s, TN, 10" tall
EX $45   NM $65   MIP $100

Jolly Bambino, 1950s, Alps, 9" tall
EX $265   NM $400   MIP $525

Jolly Bear Peanut Vendor, 1950s, TN, 8" tall
EX $250   NM $375   MIP $500

Jolly Daddy, 1950s, Marusan, 8-3/4" tall
EX $165   NM $250   MIP $325

Jolly Drummer Chimpy, 1950s, Alps, 9" tall
EX $75   NM $125   MIP $150

Jolly Pianist, 1950s, Marusan, 8" tall
EX $100   NM $170   MIP $225

Jolly Santa on Snow, 1950s, Alps, 12-1/2" tall
EX $160   NM $260   MIP $320

Josie the Walking Cow, 1950s, Daiya, 14" long
EX $170   NM $220   MIP $315

Jumbo the Bubble Blowing Elephant, 1950s, Y Co., 7-1/4" tall
EX $80   NM $120   MIP $165

Jungle Jumbo [Elephant], 1950s, B-C Toy Co., walks & bellows, remote control
EX $80   NM $145   MIP $210

Jungle Trio, 1950s, Linemar, 8" tall
EX $475   NM $730   MIP $975

BATTERY-OPERATED TOYS

King Zor, 1962, Ideal, blue plastic dinosaur, 30" long
EX $300　　NM $500　　MIP $750

Kissing Couple, 1950s, Ichida, 10-3/4" long
EX $160　　NM $225　　MIP $320

Knitting Grandma, 1950s, TN, 8-1/2" tall
EX $185　　NM $280　　MIP $375

Kooky-Spooky Whistling Tree, 1950s, Marx, 14-1/4" tall
EX $600　　NM $900　　MIP $1225

Lambo Elephant, 1950s, Alps, 16" long with trailer
EX $220　　NM $340　　MIP $465

Linemar Music Hall, 1950s, Linemar, 8" tall
EX $130　　NM $170　　MIP $230

Lion, 1950s, Linemar, 9" long
EX $75　　NM $105　　MIP $150

Loop the Loop Clown, 1960s, TN, 10" tall
EX $60　　NM $120　　MIP $175
(don Hultzman and Ron Chojnacki)

Mac the Turtle, 1960s, Y Co., 8" tall
EX $125　　NM $185　　MIP $250

Magic Man Clown, 1950s, Marusan, 11" tall
EX $250　　NM $350　　MIP $500

Magic Snowman, 1950s, MT, 11-1/4" tall
EX $135　　NM $185　　MIP $260

Main Street, 1950s, Linemar, 19-1/2" long
EX $750　　NM $1100　　MIP $1500

Major Tooty, 1960s, Alps, 14" tall
EX $105　　NM $155　　MIP $220

Mambo the Jolly Drumming Elephant, 1950s, Alps, 9-1/2" tall
EX $150　　NM $225　　MIP $300

Marching Bear, 1960s, Alps, 10" tall
EX $125　　NM $185　　MIP $250

Marshal Wild Bill, 1950s, Y Co., 10-1/2" tall
EX $185　　NM $275　　MIP $360

Marvelous Mike, 1950s, Saunders, 17" long
EX $160　　NM $250　　MIP $325

Maxwell Coffee-Loving Bear, 1960s, TN, 10" tall
EX $150　　NM $200　　MIP $260

(KP Photo)

McGregor, 1960s, Rosko, 12" tall
EX $150　　NM $200　　MIP $295

Mew-Mew Walking Cat, 1950s, MT, three actions, remote control
EX $75　　NM $125　　MIP $150

Mickey the Magician, 1960s, Linemar, 10" tall
EX $1150　　NM $1725　　MIP $2550

Mighty Kong, 1950s, Marx, 11" tall
EX $295　　NM $430　　MIP $575

Mischievous Monkey, 1950s, MT, 18" tall
EX $200　　NM $300　　MIP $425

Miss Friday the Typist, 1950s, TN, 6 actions, 8" tall
EX $225　　NM $325　　MIP $425

Motorcycle Cop, 1950s, Daiya, 10-1/2" long, 8-1/4" tall
EX $425　　NM $650　　MIP $850

Mr. MacPooch, 1950s, Marusan, 8" tall
EX $155　　NM $215　　MIP $300

Mr. Traffic Policeman, 1950s, A-I, 14" tall
EX $230　　NM $360　　MIP $475

Mumbo Jumbo, 1960s, Alps, 9-3/4" tall
EX $120　　NM $180　　MIP $220

Musical Bear, 1950s, Linemar, 10" tall
EX $275　　NM $400　　MIP $550

Musical Jackal, 1950s, Linemar, 10" tall
EX $150　　NM $325　　MIP $850

Musical Jolly Chimp, 1960s, Daishin, 10-1/2" tall, plays cymbals, glares w/ eyes, shows teeth and chatters
EX $30　　NM $60　　MIP $110

Musical Marching Bear, 1950s, Alps, 11" tall
EX $195　　NM $325　　MIP $550

NASA Space Capsule, 1950s, four actions
EX $200　　NM $300　　MIP $425

Nutty Mad Indian, 1960s, Marx, 12" tall
EX $125　　NM $175　　MIP $225

Nutty Nibs, 1950s, Linemar, 11-1/2" tall
EX $700　　NM $1050　　MIP $1400

Odd Ogg, 1962, Ideal, large plastic turtle-frog creature
EX $100　　NM $190　　MIP $350

Ol' Sleepy Head RIP, 1950s, Y Co., 9" tall
EX $185　　NM $295　　MIP $385

Panda Bear, 1970s, MT, 10" long
EX $50　　NM $75　　MIP $100

Pat the Roaring Elephant, 1950s, Y Co., 9" long
EX $150　　NM $225　　MIP $300

Peppermint Twist Doll, 1950s, Haji, 12" tall
EX $185　　NM $285　　MIP $375

Peppy Puppy, 1950s, Y Co., 8" long
EX $70　　NM $95　　MIP $120

Pet Turtle, 1960s, Alps, 7" long
EX $85　　NM $130　　MIP $170

Pete the Space Man, 1960s, Bandai, 5" tall
EX $75　　NM $105　　MIP $150

Peter the Drumming Rabbit, 1950s, Alps, 13" tall
EX $160　　NM $230　　MIP $315

Phantom Raider, 1963, Ideal, 33", freighter turned warship
EX $70　　NM $135　　MIP $220

(KP Photo)

Picnic Bear, 1950s, Alps, 5 actions - pours real water, 10" tall
EX $150　　NM $175　　MIP $225

Picnic Bunny, 1950s, Alps, 10" tall
EX $130　　NM $170　　MIP $225

Picnic Monkey, 1950s, Alps, 10" tall
EX $120　　NM $175　　MIP $225

Picnic Poodle, 1950s, STS, 7" long
EX $45　　NM $70　　MIP $95

Pierrot Monkey Cycle, 1950s, MT, 8" tall
EX $250　　NM $375　　MIP $525

Piggy Cook, 1950s, Y Co., 9-1/2" tall
EX $155　　NM $250　　MIP $340

Pinkee the Farmer, 1950s, MT, 9-1/2" long
EX $110　　NM $170　　MIP $225

Pipie the Whale, 1950s, Alps, 12" long
EX $175　　NM $245　　MIP $365

Pistol Pete, 1950s, Marusan, 10-1/4" tall
EX $275　　NM $485　　MIP $550

Playful Puppy w/Caterpillar, 1950s, MT, 5" tall
EX $110　　NM $165　　MIP $225

Polar Bear, 1970s, Alps, 8" long
EX $70　　NM $105　　MIP $140

Popcorn Eating Bear, 1950s, MT, 9" tall
EX $135　　NM $190　　MIP $250

Rambling Ladybug, 1960s, MT, 8" long
EX $65　　NM $95　　MIP $130

Reading Bear, 1950s, Alps, 9" tall
EX $160　　NM $235　　MIP $325

Rembrandt the Monkey Artist, 1950s, Alps, 8" tall
EX $210　　NM $300　　MIP $425

Ricki the Begging Poodle, 1950s, Rock Valley, 9" long
EX $35　　NM $50　　MIP $65

Roarin' Jungle Lion, 1950s, Marx, 16" long
EX $175　　NM $130　　MIP $320

Rock 'N Roll Monkey, 1950s, Rosko, 13" tall
EX $195　　NM $280　　MIP $375

Rocking Chair Bear, 1950s, MT, 10" tall
EX $135　　NM $190　　MIP $250

Roller Skater, 1950s, Alps, 12" tall
EX $175　　NM $250　　MIP $350

Root Beer Counter, 1960s, K Co., 8" tall
EX $150   NM $225   MIP $300

Sam the Shaving Man, 1960s, Plaything Toy, 11-1/2" tall
EX $150   NM $225   MIP $300

Sammy Wong the Tea Totaler, 1950s, TN, 10" tall
EX $150   NM $225   MIP $325

Santa Claus on Handcar, 1960s, MT, 10" tall
EX $125   NM $200   MIP $250

Santa Claus on Reindeer Sleigh, 1950s, MT, 17" long
EX $400   NM $600   MIP $800

Santa Claus on Scooter, 1960s, MT, 10" tall
EX $130   NM $185   MIP $250

Santa Copter, 1960s, MT, 8-1/2" high
EX $100   NM $150   MIP $200

Saxophone Playing Monkey, 1950s, Alps, 9-1/2" tall
EX $250   NM $375   MIP $500

Serpent Charmer, 1950s, Linemar, 7" tall
EX $335   NM $435   MIP $700

Shaggy the Friendly Pup, 1960s, Alps, 8" long
EX $40   NM $55   MIP $80

Shoe Maker Bear, 1960s, TN, 8-1/2" tall
EX $150   NM $225   MIP $300

Shoe Shine Bear, 1950s, TN, 9" tall
EX $175   NM $250   MIP $350

Shoe Shine Joe, 1950s, Alps, 11" tall, monkey w/pipe polishing a shoe
EX $175   NM $235   MIP $325

Shoe Shine Monkey, 1950s, TN, 9" tall
EX $175   NM $235   MIP $325

Shooting Gorilla, 1950s, MT, 12" tall
EX $200   NM $275   MIP $400

Shutterbug Photographer, 1950s, TN, 9"tall
EX $575   NM $775   MIP $950

Skating Circus Clown, 1950s, TPS, 6" tall
EX $500   NM $710   MIP $950

Skiing Santa, 1960s, MT, 12" tall
EX $170   NM $250   MIP $330

Skipping Monkey, 1960s, TN, 9-1/2" tall
EX $50   NM $65   MIP $100

Slalom Game, 1960s, TN, 15-1/4" long
EX $110   NM $170   MIP $235

Sleeping Baby Bear, 1950s, Linemar, 9"long
EX $275   NM $385   MIP $500

Sleepy Pup, 1960s, Alps, 9" long
EX $45   NM $75   MIP $95

Slurpy Pup, 1960s, TN, 6-1/2" long
EX $50   NM $75   MIP $100

Smoking Bunny, 1950s, Marusan, 10-1/2" tall
EX $125   NM $190   MIP $260

Smoking Elephant, 1950s, Marusan, 8-3/4" tall
EX $135   NM $185   MIP $240

Smoking Grandpa in Rocker, 1950s, Marusan, 8" tall, 4 actions
EX $200   NM $350   MIP $450

Smoking Popeye, 1950s, Linemar, 9" tall
EX $1775   NM $2275   MIP $3500

Smoking Spaceman, 1950s, Linemar, 12" tall
EX $1000   NM $1500   MIP $2000

Smoky Bear, 1950s, Marusan, 9" tall
EX $250   NM $335   MIP $500

Sneezing Bear, 1950s, Linemar, 9" tall
EX $180   NM $240   MIP $365

Snoopy Sniffer, 1960s, MT, 8" long
EX $50   NM $80   MIP $105

Spanking Bear, 1950s, Linemar, 9" tall
EX $180   NM $300   MIP $375

Struttin' Sam, 1950s, Haji, 10-1/2" tall
EX $225   NM $335   MIP $450

Sunday Driver, 1950s, MT, 10" long
EX $70   NM $110   MIP $150

Super Susie, 1950s, Linemar, 9" tall
EX $500   NM $750   MIP $1100

Suzette the Eating Monkey, 1950s, Linemar, 8-3/4" tall
EX $400   NM $550   MIP $825

Switchboard Operator, 1950s, Linemar, 7-1/2" tall
EX $450   NM $625   MIP $950

Tarzan, 1966, Marusan, 13" tall
EX $600   NM $900   MIP $1200

Teddy Bear Swing, 1950s, TN, 17" tall
EX $300   NM $410   MIP $600

Teddy the Artist, 1950s, Y Co., 8-1/2" tall
EX $350   NM $525   MIP $800

Teddy the Boxing Bear, 1950s, Y Co., 9" tall
EX $145   NM $225   MIP $285

Teddy the Rhythmical Drummer, 1960s, Alps, 11" tall
EX $100   NM $165   MIP $220

Teddy-Go-Kart, 1960s, Alps, 10-1/2" long
EX $100   NM $165   MIP $200

(KP Photo)

Telephone Bear, 1950s, Linemar, 7-1/2" tall
EX $225   NM $300   MIP $425

Telephone Bear with Rocking Chair, 1950s, MT, 10" tall
EX $225   NM $300   MIP $425

Television Spaceman, 1960s, Alps, 14-1/2" tall
EX $445   NM $660   MIP $900

Tinkling Trolley, 1950s, MT, 10-1/2" long
EX $145   NM $205   MIP $265

Tom and Jerry Choo Choo, 1960s, MT, 10-1/4" long
EX $175   NM $255   MIP $340

Tom and Jerry Handcar, 1960s, MT, 7-3/4" long
EX $160   NM $270   MIP $350

Tom-Tom Indian, 1961, Y Co., 10-1/2" tall
EX $100   NM $140   MIP $175

Topo Gigio Playing the Xylophone, 1960s, TN
EX $400   NM $625   MIP $850

Traveler Bear, 1950s, Linemar, 8" tall
EX $160   NM $240   MIP $320

Trumpet Playing Bunny, 1950s, Alps, 10" tall
EX $185   NM $280   MIP $375

Trumpet Playing Monkey, 1950s, Alps, 9" tall
EX $175   NM $265   MIP $350

Tubby the Turtle, 1950s, Y Co., 7" long
EX $60   NM $95   MIP $125

Tumbles the Bear, 1960s, Yanoman, 8-1/2" tall
EX $95   NM $140   MIP $190

Twirly Whirly, 1950s, Alps, 13-1/2" tall
EX $400   NM $600   MIP $800

Walking Bear with Xylophone, 1950s, Linemar, 10" tall
EX $270   NM $405   MIP $520

Walking Elephant, 1950s, Linemar, 8-1/2" tall
EX $100   NM $150   MIP $225

Walking Esso Tiger, 1950s, Marx, 11-1/2" tall
EX $200   NM $300   MIP $400

Walking Itchy Dog, 1950s, Alps, 9" long
EX $55   NM $85   MIP $120

Western Locomotive, 1950s, MT, 10-1/2" long
EX $50   NM $75   MIP $100

Windy the Elephant, 1950s, TN, 9-3/4" tall
EX $150   NM $200   MIP $300

Yeti the Abominable Snowman, 1960s, Marx, 12" tall
EX $350   NM $485   MIP $750

Yo-Yo Clown, 1960s, Alps, 9" tall
EX $180   NM $255   MIP $380

Yo-Yo Monkey, 1960s, YM, 12" tall
EX $125   NM $185   MIP $250

Yo-Yo Monkey, 1960s, Alps, 9" tall
EX $135   NM $205   MIP $275

Yummy Yum Kitty, 1950s, Alps, 9-1/2" tall
EX $250   NM $400   MIP $500

Zero Fighter Plane, 1950s, Bandai, 15" wingspan
EX $170   NM $240   MIP $340

Character Toys

By Tom Bartsch

Ever meet someone and remark to a friend, "Wow, that was quite the character?" Well, toy collectors do that all the time, usually when referring to their character toys. It's that memory of the character that makes them want a piece of memorabilia that reminds them of that character, be it a record, paper doll or jigsaw puzzle.

From comic books to television shows to movies and more, characters have been a part of our lives for many years. And many times these same characters have appeared as toys. The sheer volume of character toys outweighs any other collecting category by far, simply because you can find the likeness of characters almost anywhere—soakies, clothes, books, glasses, costumes, ornaments, banks, etc. Because of these factors, character toys are among the most popular collectibles on the market, a major representation of which you will find in the following pages.

Looking at this mass of pages, it's a wonder where to begin collecting in this field. Easy. Most collectors pick a particular favorite character and focus on items bearing his or her likeness. With most of these characters, focusing on just one will more than fill a display case. Some characters have an unbelievable following—and licensing power. Other collectors will narrow their range to a group of characters from the same show or a band of superheroes. Your other challenge in all of this will be finding all the goodies that are out there. As you can see, some of the characters have a long history of entertaining the masses and being depicted on toys. The best course of action is to do your homework and always ask a lot of questions.

AN ENDLESS ARRAY OF FUN

The beauty of character toys is that they are not limited to action figures or die-cast vehicles. If you like Superman, you can pick up a comic book, a Superman member ring, candy, or a million other things. Prices can range from under a dollar to several hundred thousand dollars for his first appearance in a comic book (Action Comics #1, 1938). Editor's note: For the current value of that comic and thousands of others, consult The *Standard Catalog of Comic Books* 4th edition, (KP Books, 2005).

However, many of the character's toys are very similar. The key to finding out which one is worth

hundreds and which one is worth $50 is in the details. For starters, find out the name of the manufacturer. Then check out the details of the item. Sometimes the difference in valuable samples compared to average-priced ones is the color or an accessory. For instance, a 1970s Horsman Alice in Wonderland doll might fetch $65 Mint. A 1951 Duchess Alice in Wonderland doll can bring more than $200 Mint. Do your research before taking the plunge. Also, many character toys were reproduced over a number of years. Seen how long the character toy you see was produced and in how many versions. You might be able to find a cheaper version or the more expensive one, depending on your collecting wants.

The massive amount of product seems to be on the upswing these days, with almost every film or movie bearing related collectibles to help fuel the marketing beast. Today's leading character toys include SpongeBob Squarepants, Buffy the Vampire Slayer, Harry Potter, The Simpsons, and Asian influences like Astro Boy, Love Hina, and Yu-Gi-Oh! However, don't even ignore the evergreen favorites of Superman, Popeye (this category is exploding on the auction front in 2004), James Bond, and sci-fi characters like the Lost In Space robot.

Will these new toys on the block someday approach the prices of some of the older favorites? Maybe, but their popularity now is a good starting point to making that future a reality.

Contributor: Tom Bartsch is the Editor of *Toy Shop* magazine. John K. Snyder, Jr. is President of Diamond International Galleries and is a leading expert on comic character collectibles. He serves as a pricing advisor to *Hake's Price Guide to Character Toys, The Overstreet Comic Book Price Guide, The Overstreet Comic Book Grading Guide, The Overstreet Toy Ring Price Guide, Tomart's Radio Premiums Price Guide*, Krause Publication's *Radio Premiums Price Guide, Toys & Prices, O'Brien's Collecting Toys*, and the *Original Comic Art Price Guide*.

THE TOP TEN CHARACTER TOYS (In Mint Condition)

1. Superman Club Member Ring, 1940	$75,000
2. Superman Milk Defense Club Ring, 1941	25,000
3. Little Orphan Annie Altascope Ring, Quaker, 1942	22,000
4. Superman Trading Cards, Gum Inc., 1940	20,000
5. Batman Play Set, Ideal, 1966	12,000
6. Superman Bubblegum Badge, Fo-Lee Gum Co., 1948	10,000
7. Mickey Mouse Lionel Circus Train, Lionel, 1935	10,000
8. Donald Duck Bicycle, Shelby, 1949	8,000
9. Superman Patch, 1939	6,000
10. Doc Savage Medal of Honor Award, 1930s	6,000

101 DALMATIANS

ACCESSORIES

101 Dalmatians Snow Dome, 1961, Marx, 3" x 5" x 3-1/2" tall
  EX $35   **NM** $65   **MIP** $110

FIGURES

Dalmatian Pups Figures, 1960s, Enesco, 4-1/2" tall, set of three
  EX $25   **NM** $50   **MIP** $160

Lucky Figure, 1960s, Enesco, 4" tall
  EX $35   **NM** $65   **MIP** $100

TOY

101 Dalmatians Wind-Up, 1959, Linemar
  EX $125   **NM** $250   **MIP** $500

Lucky Squeeze Toy, Dell, 7" tall, squeakers in the bottom
  EX $10   **NM** $20   **MIP** $50

ALICE IN WONDERLAND

ACCESSORIES

Clock Radio, 1970s, General Electric, features characters on face
  EX $20   **NM** $40   **MIP** $85

Film Viewer, 1950s, Tru-Vue, viewer and filmstrip
  EX $30   **NM** $60   **MIP** $100

Handbag, 1950s, ACME Briefcase, child's red leather shoulder bag
  EX $30   **NM** $80   **MIP** $120

Handbag, 1950s, Salient, child's pink vinyl shoulder bag, Alice w/rocking fly
  EX $30   **NM** $80   **MIP** $120

Hatbox, 1950s, Neevel, Caterpillar or Tea Party graphics
  EX $55   **NM** $100   **MIP** $150

Picture Frame, 1970s, Dexter-Mahnke, cloth picture frame, featuring Mad Tea Party
  EX $20   **NM** $35   **MIP** $60

Record Player, 1951, RCA Victor, 45 rpm
  EX $75   **NM** $225   **MIP** $400

School Bag, 1950s, ACME Briefcase, fabric and leather
  EX $30   **NM** $100   **MIP** $150

Soap Set, 1951
  EX $40   **NM** $120   **MIP** $250

Wall Decor, 1951, Dolly Toy, #260 contains Alice, Mad Hatter, March Hare and a lamp
  EX $50   **NM** $100   **MIP** $200

Wall Plaque, 1974, Leisuramics, bisque, oval shape, featuring TweedleDee and TweedleDum
  EX $20   **NM** $40   **MIP** $60

Wall Plaque, 1974, Leisuramics, bisque, oval shape, featuring Mad Hatter
  EX $20   **NM** $40   **MIP** $75

BANK

Alice Bank, 1950s, Leeds, figural
  EX $100   **NM** $200   **MIP** $275

BOOK

Alice in Wonderland and Cinderella Book, 1950s, Collins, Great Britain version
  EX $25   **NM** $60   **MIP** $120

Alice in Wonderland Book, 1950s, Whitman, #2074 Cozy Corner Book, green endpapers
  EX $30   **NM** $60   **MIP** $100

Alice in Wonderland Book, 1950s, Whitman, #10426, without gold backing
  EX $30   **NM** $70   **MIP** $150

Alice in Wonderland Book, 1950s, Whitman, #10426, Big Golden Book, gold foil backing
  EX $50   **NM** $100   **MIP** $175

Alice in Wonderland Book, 1951, Whitman, Sandpiper Book w/dust jacket
  EX $50   **NM** $100   **MIP** $200

Alice in Wonderland Book, 1951, Dell Publishing, #331
  EX $35   **NM** $75   **MIP** $175

Alice in Wonderland Book, 1951, Whitman, #426, Big Golden Book
  EX $50   **NM** $100   **MIP** $175

Alice in Wonderland Classic Series with Disney Book, 1950s, Whitman, #2140 Lewis Carroll text w/Disney dust jacket
  EX $50   **NM** $100   **MIP** $200

Alice in Wonderland Paint Book, 1951, Whitman, #2167
  EX $55   **NM** $110   **MIP** $225

Alice in Wonderland Punch-Out Book, 1951, Whitman, #2164
  EX $80   **NM** $200   **MIP** $350

Alice in Wonderland Sticker Fun, 1950s, Whitman, #2193 stencil and coloring book
  EX $30   **NM** $60   **MIP** $100

(KP Photo)

Alice Meets the White Rabbit Book, 1951, Whitman, #D-19, Little Golden Book
  EX $15   **NM** $45   **MIP** $80

(KP Photo)

Mad Hatter's Tea Party Book, 1951, Whitman, #D-23 Little Golden Book
  EX $15   **NM** $45   **MIP** $60

Unbirthday Party Book, The, 1974, Whitman, #22, Walt Disney Showcase
  EX $8   **NM** $15   **MIP** $30

CANDY TIN

Candy Tin, 1950s, Edward Sharp and Sons, Great Britain English Toffee Tin
  EX $125   **NM** $250   **MIP** $325

COLLECTIBLE

Alice Snow Dome, 1961, Marx, 3" tall featuring Alice and the White Rabbit in front of tree
  EX $15   **NM** $35   **MIP** $100

Caterpillar Figure, 1956, Hagen-Renaker
  EX $200   **NM** $400   **MIP** $600

Mad Hatter Snow Dome, 1980s, New England Collectors Society, crystal, Mad Hatter, St. Patrick's Day
  EX $15   **NM** $25   **MIP** $50

Mad Hatter Teapot, 1950s, Regal
  EX $500   **NM** $1000   **MIP** $1600

Pitcher, 1950s, Regal, King of Hearts
  EX $200   **NM** $375   **MIP** $650

Plaque, 1970s, Disneyland, wooden, w/Alice and live flowers
  EX $15   **NM** $25   **MIP** $50

Salt and Pepper Shakers, 1950s, Regal, featuring TweedleDee and TweedleDum
  EX $150   **NM** $300   **MIP** $525

Salt and Pepper Shakers, 1950s, Regal, blue or white featuring Alice
  EX $150   **NM** $300   **MIP** $500

Tea Cake Box, 1980s, TDL, w/a Mad Tea Party lid
  EX $10   **NM** $15   **MIP** $30

Tea Cup and Saucer, 1986, TDL, ceramic, Mad Tea Party
  EX $60   **NM** $120   **MIP** $200

Thimble, 1980s, New England Collectors Society, Mad Hatter and Alice
  EX $5   **NM** $15   **MIP** $25

Vase, 1960s, Enesco, featuring Alice's head
  EX $75   **NM** $150   **MIP** $250

CHARACTER TOYS

White Rabbit Creamer, 1950s, Regal
EX $175   **NM** $350   **MIP** $500

White Rabbit Sugar Bowl, 1950s, Regal
EX $200   **NM** $400   **MIP** $600

COLORING BOOK

Alice in Wonderland Big Coloring Book, 1951, Whitman, #301 Big Golden, Model No. 301
EX $75   **NM** $150   **MIP** $225

Alice in Wonderland Coloring Book, 1974, Whitman, #1049
EX $5   **NM** $20   **MIP** $40

COOKIE JAR

Alice Cookie Jar, Regal, 13-1/2" tall
EX $375   **NM** $1000   **MIP** $1650

Alice Cookie Jar, 1950s, Leeds, printed in relief
EX $150   **NM** $300   **MIP** $425

Looking Glass Cookie Jar, Fred Roberts, raised characters on the body of the jar w/a mirror lid
EX $200   **NM** $450   **MIP** $725

COSTUMES

Alice Costume, 1950s, Ben Cooper, costume made until 1970s
EX $50   **NM** $100   **MIP** $200

Mad Hatter Costume, 1950s, Ben Cooper, costume made until 1970s
EX $30   **NM** $60   **MIP** $120

March Hare Costume, 1950s, Ben Cooper, costume made until 1970s
EX $30   **NM** $60   **MIP** $120

DOLLS

Alice Doll, 1950s, Gund, flat vinyl, stuffed
EX $50   **NM** $125   **MIP** $200

Alice Doll, 1951, Duchess, #739, 7-1/2" tall
EX $80   **NM** $200   **MIP** $300

Alice Doll, 1951, Duchess, 12-1/2" tall
EX $100   **NM** $225   **MIP** $350

Alice Doll, 1970s, Horsman, Alice has a castle on her apron
EX $20   **NM** $45   **MIP** $90

Alice Doll, 1970s, Pedigree, Great Britain
EX $20   **NM** $40   **MIP** $75

Alice Doll, 1970s, Horsman, #1071, Walt Disney Classics
EX $20   **NM** $35   **MIP** $75

Cheshire Cat Doll, 1970s, Disneyland, plush
EX $10   **NM** $25   **MIP** $60

Dormouse Doll, 1950s, Lars/Italy, stuffed
EX $160   **NM** $330   **MIP** $550

Mad Hatter Doll, 1950s, Gund, plush
EX $125   **NM** $275   **MIP** $425

Mad Hatter Doll, 1950s, Gund, flat vinyl, stuffed
EX $40   **NM** $90   **MIP** $150

March Hare Doll, 1950s, Gund, plush
EX $175   **NM** $350   **MIP** $600

March Hare Doll, 1950s, Gund, flat vinyl, stuffed
EX $50   **NM** $60   **MIP** $135

Queen of Hearts Doll, 1950s, Gund, flat vinyl, stuffed
EX $40   **NM** $80   **MIP** $150

TweedleDee and TweedleDum Dolls, 1950s, Gund, flat vinyl, stuffed, each
EX $75   **NM** $150   **MIP** $225

TweedleDee and TweedleDum Dolls, 1980s, TDL, plush, each
EX $15   **NM** $30   **MIP** $60

Walrus Doll, 1950s, Lars/Italy, stuffed
EX $200   **NM** $500   **MIP** $675

White Rabbit Doll, 1950s, Gund, flat vinyl, stuffed
EX $50   **NM** $125   **MIP** $175

White Rabbit Doll, 1950s, Gund
EX $110   **NM** $300   **MIP** $450

White Rabbit Doll, 1970s, Sears, plush w/ waistcoat and umbrella
EX $12   **NM** $25   **MIP** $50

White Rabbit Doll, 1970s, Disneyland, large, plush w/ yellow spectacles
EX $12   **NM** $25   **MIP** $50

White Rabbit Doll, 1970s, Disneyland, small w/ black spectacles
EX $10   **NM** $20   **MIP** $40

White Rabbit Doll, 1974, Buena Vista/Disney, plush
EX $50   **NM** $100   **MIP** $150

White Rabbit Doll, 1980s, TDL, plush
EX $10   **NM** $25   **MIP** $50

FIGURES

Alice Figure, 1950s, Marx, painted w/"Holland" stamped on the bottom
EX $40   **NM** $75   **MIP** $120

Alice Figure, 1950s, Aldon Industries, plastic, cut-out standup
EX $50   **NM** $110   **MIP** $150

Alice Figure, 1951, Shaw
EX $120   **NM** $300   **MIP** $725

Alice Figure, 1956, Hagen-Renaker
EX $200   **NM** $400   **MIP** $600

Alice Figure, 1980s, Sears, Magic Kingdom Collection, bone china
EX $15   **NM** $25   **MIP** $35

Alice Figure, 1984, Bully, Germany, PVC, wearing a blue or red dress, each
EX $10   **NM** $15   **MIP** $20

Disneyland Figures Set, 1960s, United China, large set, each piece
EX $15   **NM** $30   **MIP** $60

Disneyland Figures Set, 1970s, United China, small figures, each piece
EX $10   **NM** $15   **MIP** $30

Dormouse Figure, 1951, Shaw
EX $130   **NM** $225   **MIP** $400

Mad Hatter Figure, 1950s, Marx, painted w/ "Holland" stamped on the bottom
EX $20   **NM** $35   **MIP** $75

Mad Hatter Figure, 1950s, Sydney Pottery, large size, sold only in Australia
EX $250   **NM** $425   **MIP** $600

Mad Hatter Figure, 1951, Shaw
EX $65   **NM** $200   **MIP** $350

Mad Hatter Figure, 1956, Hagen-Renaker
EX $150   **NM** $300   **MIP** $425

Mad Hatter Figure, 1980s, Schmid, playing xylophone
EX $20   **NM** $40   **MIP** $75

Mad Hatter/March Hare Figure, 1980s, TDL, Mad Hatter, March Hare w/saxophone
EX $20   **NM** $40   **MIP** $60

March Hare Figure, 1950s, Marx, painted w/ "Holland" stamped on the bottom
EX $15   **NM** $30   **MIP** $60

March Hare Figure, 1950s, Sydney Pottery, large size, sold only in Australia
EX $200   **NM** $400   **MIP** $600

March Hare Figure, 1951, Shaw
EX $170   **NM** $320   **MIP** $500

March Hare Figure, 1956, Hagen-Renaker
EX $110   **NM** $275   **MIP** $450

Queen of Hearts Figure, 1950s, Marx, painted w/ "Holland" stamped on the bottom
EX $12   **NM** $25   **MIP** $50

Queen of Hearts Figure, 1980s, Sears, Magic Kingdom Collection, bone china
EX $15   **NM** $25   **MIP** $35

TweedleDee Figure, 1950s, Sydney Pottery, large size, sold only in Australia
EX $200   **NM** $400   **MIP** $575

TweedleDee Figure, 1951, Shaw
EX $70   **NM** $150   **MIP** $235

TweedleDum Figure, 1950s, Sydney Pottery, large size, sold only in Australia
EX $200   **NM** $400   **MIP** $575

TweedleDum Figure, 1951, Shaw
EX $70   **NM** $150   **MIP** $235

Walrus Figure, 1950s, Sydney Pottery, large size, sold only in Australia
EX $160   **NM** $375   **MIP** $550

Walrus Figure, 1951, Shaw
EX $110   **NM** $250   **MIP** $425

White Rabbit Figure, Italy, 5-1/2" tall, ceramic
EX $15   **NM** $35   **MIP** $60

White Rabbit Figure, 1950s, Marx, painted w/ "Holland" stamped on the bottom
EX $12   **NM** $25   **MIP** $50

White Rabbit Figure, 1951, Shaw
EX $65   **NM** $140   **MIP** $250

White Rabbit Figure, 1980s, Sears, Magic Kingdom Collection, bone china
EX $12   **NM** $25   **MIP** $50

GAMES

Adventures in Costumeland Game, 1980s, Walt Disney World, created for Disney costume division members,

game board and pieces in a small vinyl garment bag
EX $75   **NM** $150   **MIP** $200

Alice in Wonderland Card Game, 1980s, Thos. De LaRue
EX $10   **NM** $20   **MIP** $35

Bridge Card Game, 1950s, Whitman, two decks of cards
EX $35   **NM** $75   **MIP** $175

Canasta Card Game, 1950s, Whitman, two Canasta decks of White Rabbit cards
EX $50   **NM** $100   **MIP** $150

Queen of Hearts Card Game, 1975, Edu-Cards
EX $20   **NM** $35   **MIP** $65

GLASSWARE

Alice and White Rabbit Mug, 1991, TDL/Daiichi Seimei, promo piece
EX $25   **NM** $40   **MIP** $65

Alice Mug, 1970s, Disney
EX $12   **NM** $20   **MIP** $40

Glass, 1970s, Pepsi Cola, featuring Alice, part of Wonderful World of Disney set
EX $10   **NM** $20   **MIP** $35

Glasses, 1951, Libbey, eight styles released for film opening, each
EX $40   **NM** $60   **MIP** $120

Mad Tea Party/Cheshire Cat Mug, 1988, Applause, Cheshire Cat handle w/Tea Party on the mug
EX $12   **NM** $18   **MIP** $30

MUSIC BOX

Music Box, 1980s, Disneyland, Wooden box features Alice and White Rabbit "I'm Late"
EX $30   **NM** $60   **MIP** $100

Music Box, 1980s, TDL, plastic, tea cup rotates
EX $45   **NM** $80   **MIP** $150

Music Box, 1980s, TDL, ceramic teacup
EX $45   **NM** $80   **MIP** $150

PAPER DOLLS

Alice Paper Dolls, 1972, Whitman, #4712
EX $25   **NM** $50   **MIP** $80

Alice Paper Dolls, 1976, Whitman, #1948
EX $20   **NM** $40   **MIP** $75

PAPER GOODS

Alice Stationery and Notepad, 1970s, Pak-Well, #77065 w/a fan card cover
EX $10   **NM** $20   **MIP** $35

Cheshire Cat Costume Pattern, 1951, McCall's
EX $25   **NM** $40   **MIP** $75

Fan Card, 1951, Walt Disney, premium sent to fans who wrote letters to studio
EX $30   **NM** $50   **MIP** $75

Fan Card, 1951, Walt Disney, original release w/1973 invitation to studio screening
EX $40   **NM** $60   **MIP** $80

Mad Hatter Costume Pattern, 1951, McCall's
EX $20   **NM** $35   **MIP** $55

March Hare Costume Pattern, 1951, McCall's
EX $20   **NM** $35   **MIP** $60

Poster, 1958, Disneyland, Alice attraction
EX $400   **NM** $700   **MIP** $1000

Poster, 1980s, Walt Disney World, costume division poster featuring Cheshire Cat
EX $20   **NM** $40   **MIP** $65

Ticket, 1970s, Disneyland, employee screening ticket featuring Cheshire Cat
EX $10   **NM** $15   **MIP** $25

PREMIUMS

Bread Labels, 1950s, NBC, 12 different styles, each
EX $25   **NM** $40   **MIP** $80

Bread Seal Poster, 1950s, NBC
EX $40   **NM** $60   **MIP** $100

Bread Stickers, 1974, Continental Baking/Wonder, five styles, each
EX $5   **NM** $10   **MIP** $15

Cards, 1951, Royal Desserts, 16 different cards on the back of dessert packages, each
EX $20   **NM** $35   **MIP** $70

Cereal Box with Record, 1956, General Mills, Wheaties
EX $400   **NM** $500   **MIP** $600

Magic Picture Kit Set, 1974, Jiffy Pop, set of four
EX $12   **NM** $25   **MIP** $50

Poster, 1980, Kraft, Disneyland 25th Anniversary Family Reunion
EX $15   **NM** $30   **MIP** $65

RECORD

Record/Little Nipper Giant Storybook, 1951, RCA Victor, LY-437, 33, 45, or 78 rpm, each
EX $80   **NM** $120   **MIP** $160

TOY

Alice Disneykin, 1950s, Marx, hard plastic
EX $10   **NM** $25   **MIP** $50

Alice Disneykin, 1950s, Marx, unpainted, soft plastic
EX $10   **NM** $20   **MIP** $40

Alice Marionette, 1950s, Peter Puppet, comes in two different boxes, one "Alice in Wonderland" the other Peter Puppet Disney
EX $70   **NM** $225   **MIP** $425

Balloons, 1951, Oak Rubber, four different designs
EX $12   **NM** $20   **MIP** $50

Balloons, 1951, Eagle Rubber
EX $12   **NM** $20   **MIP** $50

Blocks, 1950s, Chad Valley, five cylindrical tin blocks w/color graphics
EX $75   **NM** $150   **MIP** $300

Child's Vanity, 1950s, Neevel, illustrated w/film scenes
EX $70   **NM** $120   **MIP** $200

Disneykin Play Set, 1950s, Marx
EX $200   **NM** $400   **MIP** $650

Jingle Ball, 1951, Vanguard
EX $12   **NM** $25   **MIP** $50

Mad Hatter Disneykin, 1950s, Marx
EX $25   **NM** $45   **MIP** $85

Mad Hatter Disneykin, 1950s, Marx, unpainted, soft plastic
EX $10   **NM** $16   **MIP** $30

Mad Hatter Hand Puppet, 1960s, hand puppet w/cloth body
EX $40   **NM** $75   **MIP** $100

Mad Hatter Marionette, 1950s, Peter Puppet
EX $100   **NM** $150   **MIP** $275

Mad Hatter Nodder, 1950s, Marx
EX $100   **NM** $250   **MIP** $375

Mad Hatter Snap Eeze, 1950s, Marx
EX $15   **NM** $30   **MIP** $50

Make-Up Kit, 1951, Hasbro
EX $25   **NM** $55   **MIP** $100

March Hare Disneykin, 1950s, Marx, unpainted and soft plastic
EX $12   **NM** $18   **MIP** $35

March Hare Marionette, 1950s, Peter Puppet
EX $100   **NM** $150   **MIP** $250

March Hare Snap Eeze, 1950s, Marx
EX $15   **NM** $20   **MIP** $50

March Hare Twistoy, 1950s, Marx
EX $15   **NM** $20   **MIP** $50

Molding Set, 1951, Model Craft
EX $50   **NM** $100   **MIP** $200

Molding Set, 1952, Great Britain, similar to Model Craft set
EX $60   **NM** $120   **MIP** $210

Puppet Theatre, 1950s, Peter Puppet
EX $125   **NM** $200   **MIP** $300

Puzzle, 1951, Jaymar, Tea Party scene
EX $50   **NM** $90   **MIP** $150

Puzzle, 1951, Jaymar, Alice and Rabbit
EX $50   **NM** $90   **MIP** $150

Puzzle, 1951, Jaymar, Alice under a tree
EX $50   **NM** $90   **MIP** $150

Puzzle, 1951, Jaymar, Croquet cast scene
EX $50   **NM** $90   **MIP** $150

Puzzle, 1979, Stafford/England, wooden, Great Britain Tea Party
EX $10   **NM** $25   **MIP** $40

Puzzle, 1980s, TDL, #18, Mad Tea Party and Cast
EX $5   **NM** $10   **MIP** $25

Queen of Hearts Disneykin, 1950s, Marx
EX $30   **NM** $55   **MIP** $85

Queen of Hearts Disneykin, 1950s, Marx, unpainted, soft plastic
EX $15   **NM** $20   **MIP** $35

Ramp Walker, 1950s, Marx, Mad Hatter and White Rabbit
EX $40   **NM** $80   **MIP** $100

CHARACTER TOYS

Rubber Stamp Set, 1970s, Multiprint, Italy, #177
EX $20   NM $30   MIP $55

Rubber Stamp Set, 1989, All Night Media
EX $10   NM $15   MIP $25

(KP Photo)

Sewing Cards, 1951, Whitman
EX $40   NM $75   MIP $125

Sewing Kit, 1951, Hasbro, 7" sewing machine and 5" doll, all plastic
EX $50   NM $100   MIP $150

TV Scene, White Rabbit and March Hare, 1950s, Marx
EX $30   NM $65   MIP $100

View-Master Set, 1970s, GAF, three reels, Disney
EX $12   NM $25   MIP $40

Wallet, 1950s, Salient, vinyl, featuring Mad Tea Party
EX $30   NM $60   MIP $100

Wallet, 1950s, Salient, vinyl, featuring White Rabbit
EX $30   NM $60   MIP $100

White Rabbit Disneykin, 1950s, Marx
EX $30   NM $60   MIP $85

White Rabbit Disneykin, 1950s, Marx, unpainted and soft plastic
EX $10   NM $20   MIP $35

White Rabbit Ears, 1980s, TDL
EX $10   NM $20   MIP $35

White Rabbit Rolykin, 1950s, Marx
EX $20   NM $40   MIP $70

WATCH

Alice Wristwatch, 1950s, U.S. Time, Alice peeking through pink flowers and a plastic statue
EX $400   NM $750   MIP $1000

Alice Wristwatch, 1950s, U.S. Time, came w/ ceramic statue
EX $400   NM $750   MIP $1000

Alice Wristwatch, 1990s, Alba, Japan, gold tone face
EX $15   NM $30   MIP $60

Tea Cup Wristwatch, 1950s, U.S. Time, picture of Mad Hatter w/ an overlay
EX $450   NM $850   MIP $1100

AMOS AND ANDY

ACCESSORIES

Amos and Andy Card Party, 1930, A.M. Davis, 6" x 8", score pads and tallies
EX $50   NM $100   MIP $200

Contest Winner Check, 1936, Pepsodent, $2.00 winner's check for contest
EX $1500   NM $1650   MIP $2000

Stock Certificate, 1930s, Bogus Taxi Company, premium
EX $300   NM $400   MIP $450

TOY

Puzzle, 1932, Pepsodent, 8-1/2" x 10", pictured Amos, Andy and other characters
EX $100   NM $200   MIP $300

ANDY GUMP

ACCESSORIES

Brush and Mirror, 4" diameter, red on ivory colored surface of brush
EX $65   NM $125   MIP $200

TOY

Chester Gump Playstone Funnies Mold Set, 1940s
EX $100   NM $150   MIP $200

Chester Gump/Herby Nodders, 1930s, ceramic 2-1/4" string nodders, each
EX $125   NM $250   MIP $375

ARCHIES

ACCESSORIES

Archie Halloween Costume, 1969, Ben Cooper
EX $50   NM $75   MIP $100

TOY

Archies Paper Dolls, 1969, Whitman
EX $25   NM $50   MIP $100

Jalopy, 1975, Marx, 12", plastic
EX $80   NM $150   MIP $275

(KP Photo)

Puzzle, 1960s, Jaymar, "Swinging Malt Shop"
EX $40   NM $60   MIP $100

ATOM ANT AND FRIENDS

TOY

Atom Ant Kite, 1960s, Roalex
EX $40   NM $80   MIP $150

Atom Ant Punch-Out Set, 1966, Whitman
EX $100   NM $175   MIP $325

Atom Ant Push Puppet, 1960s, Kohner
EX $40   NM $65   MIP $90

Atom Ant Puzzle, 1966, Whitman
EX $40   NM $80   MIP $100

Atom Ant Soaky, 1966, Purex
EX $30   NM $70   MIP $100

Morocco Mole Bubble Club Soaky, 1960s, Purex, 7" hard plastic
EX $30   NM $70   MIP $100

Squiddly Diddly Bubble Club Soaky, 1960s, Purex, 10-1/2" hard plastic
EX $30   NM $70   MIP $100

Winsome Witch Bubble Club Soaky, 1960s, Purex, 10-1/2" hard plastic
EX $30   NM $70   MIP $100

BABES IN TOYLAND

DOLL

Cadet Doll, Gund, 15-1/2" tall, fabric
EX $40   NM $80   MIP $150

TOY

Babes in Toyland Go Mobile Friction Car, 1961, Linemar, 4" x 5" x 6"
EX $150   NM $300   MIP $450

Babes in Toyland Hand Puppets, Gund, Silly Dilly Clown, Soldier, or Gorgonzo, each
EX $50   NM $100   MIP $150

Babes in Toyland Twist 'N Bend Toy, 1963, Marx, 4" tall flexible toy w/Private Valiant holding a baton
EX $10   NM $25   MIP $50

Babes in Toyland Wind-Up Toy, 1950s, Linemar, tin
EX $200   NM $400   MIP $500

Puzzle, 1961, Jaymar
EX $20   NM $45   MIP $65

BAMBI

ACCESSORIES

Bambi Prints, 1947, New York Graphic Society, 11" x 14" framed
EX $25   NM $50   MIP $100

Lamp, Bambi and Thumper
EX $150   NM $275   MIP $400

Throw Rug, 1960s, 21" x 39", Bambi and Thumper
EX $30   NM $60   MIP $100

Thumper Ashtray, 1950s, Goebel, 4" tall
EX $75   NM $150   MIP $200

Wristwatch, 1949, US Time
EX $150   NM $275   MIP $425

BANK

Flower Bank, 1940s, 5" x 5" x 7" tall, plaster
EX $75   NM $125   MIP $250

Thumper Bank, 1950s, Leeds, ceramic, figural
EX $75   NM $100   MIP $185

BOOK

Bambi Book, 1942, Grosset and Dunlap, black and white illustrations
EX $40   **NM** $70   **MIP** $100

Big Little Book, 1942, #1469
EX $50   **NM** $125   **MIP** $175

Thumper Book, 1942, Grosset and Dunlap, color and black/white illustrations
EX $40   **NM** $80   **MIP** $125

DOLL

Thumper Doll, 16" tall, plush
EX $15   **NM** $30   **MIP** $75

TOY

Bambi Soaky, Colgate-Palmolive
EX $15   **NM** $40   **MIP** $75

Thumper Pull Toy, 1942, Fisher-Price, #533, 7-1/2" x 12", wood and metal, Thumper's tail rings the bell
EX $100   **NM** $250   **MIP** $400

Thumper Soaky, 1960s, Colgate-Palmolive
EX $25   **NM** $60   **MIP** $100

BARNEY GOOGLE

DOLL

Barney Google Doll, 1922, Schoenhut, 8-1/2" tall, wood and wood composition
EX $500   **NM** $1000   **MIP** $1250

Spark Plug Doll, 1922, Schoenhut, 9" long x 6-1/2" tall, jointed wood construction w/fabric
EX $500   **NM** $1000   **MIP** $1250

FIGURE

Barney Google and Spark Plug Figurines, 3" x 3", bisque, on white bisque pedestal
EX $200   **NM** $350   **MIP** $475

TOY

Barney Google and Spark Plug, 1920s, Nifty, 7-1/2" tall, wind-up
EX $750   **NM** $1500   **MIP** $2200

Spark Plug in Bathtub, 1930, 5" long die-cast, white
EX $200   **NM** $350   **MIP** $500

Spark Plug Pull Toy, 10" x 8" tall, wood
EX $150   **NM** $250   **MIP** $400

Spark Plug Squeaker Toy, 1923, 5" long, rubber w/squeaker in mouth
EX $100   **NM** $200   **MIP** $300

Spark Plug Toy, 1920s, 5" tall, wood, on wheels
EX $125   **NM** $250   **MIP** $350

BATMAN

ACCESSORIES

Batcoin Lot, 1966, Space Magic Limited, Four 1-1/2" diameter metal coins, each depicting a scene featuring Batman and Robin battling villains
EX $30   **NM** $75   **MIP** $100

Batman and Robin Society Membership Button, 1966, Button World, full color litho metal button featuring Batman and Robin and the words "Charter Member-Batman and Robin Society"
EX $15   **NM** $25   **MIP** $35

Batman Candy Box, 1966, Phoenix Candy, 2-1/2" x 3-1/2" x 1", several color scenes
EX $100   **NM** $150   **MIP** $250

Batman Cereal Box, 1966, Kellogg's, w/Yogi Bear on front
EX $1000   **NM** $1750   **MIP** $2500

Batman Crazy Foam, 1974
EX $20   **NM** $40   **MIP** $100

Batman Dinner Set, 1966, ceramic; three pieces
EX $40   **NM** $70   **MIP** $175

Batman Fork, 1966, Imperial, 6" stainless steel w/embossed figure of Batman, w/"Batman" engraved towards the bottom
EX $15   **NM** $30   **MIP** $60

Batman Halloween Costume, 1965, Ben Cooper, plastic Halloween mask and purple and yellow cape, several versions, some feature logo on chest
EX $40   **NM** $75   **MIP** $120

(KP Photo)

Batman Helmet and Cape Set, 1966, Ideal, blue hard plastic cowl shaped helmet and soft blue vinyl cape w/drawstring
EX $250   **NM** $450   **MIP** $650

Batman Lamp, Vanity Fair, Made in Taiwan
EX $50   **NM** $100   **MIP** $220

(KP Photo)

Batman Pencil Box, 1966, Empire Pencil, gun-shaped pencil box w/set of Batman pencils
EX $30   **NM** $55   **MIP** $125

Batman Pillow, 1966, 10" x 12" w/1940s logo
EX $20   **NM** $40   **MIP** $75

Batman Wastepaper Basket, 1966, 10" tall, color tin litho
EX $30   **NM** $60   **MIP** $125

Batmobile AM Radio, 1970s, Bandai
EX $50   **NM** $100   **MIP** $200

Beach Towel, 1966, 34" x 58" white, Batman hitting a crook
EX $40   **NM** $95   **MIP** $180

Cake Decoration, 1960s, 2" hard plastic figure of Robin or Batman, each
EX $8   **NM** $15   **MIP** $30

Cake Decorations, 1966, Space Magic Limited, 4" plastic one dimensional figures of Batman, Robin and old 1940s Batman logo
EX $20   **NM** $40   **MIP** $70

Catwoman Iron-On Patch, 1966, Catwoman w/the words "Batkids Fan Club"
EX $20   **NM** $50   **MIP** $80

Charm Bracelet, 1966, on card
EX $50   **NM** $85   **MIP** $150

Child's Dinner Plate, 1966, Boontonware, 7" plastic w/image of Batman and Robin
EX $15   **NM** $30   **MIP** $60

Christmas Ornament, 1989, Presents
EX $5   **NM** $10   **MIP** $20

Coins, 1966, Transogram, plastic, set
EX $50   **NM** $75   **MIP** $120

Costume Patterns, 1960s, McCalls, patterns for making Batman, Robin, and Superman costumes, paper envelope, each
EX $15   **NM** $35   **MIP** $75

Inflatable TV Chair, 1982
EX $10   **NM** $20   **MIP** $35

Joker Cereal Bowl, 1966, Sun Valley, 5" hard plastic
EX $15   **NM** $30   **MIP** $55

Lapel Pin, 1966, Mamsell, 2" bat-shaped metal, black w/yellow eyes
EX $20   **NM** $35   **MIP** $60

Mug, 1966, 5" clear plastic; color wrap around sheet
EX $30   **NM** $60   **MIP** $100

Paper Mask, 1943, newspaper premium, announced first newspaper comic
EX $1500   **NM** $2200   **MIP** $3000

Pennant, 1966, 11 x 29" white felt, illustration of the Dynamic Duo swinging on ropes w/the Bat-signal in the background
EX $80   **NM** $150   **MIP** $250

Robin Character Sponge, 1966, Epic, 5"
EX $10   **NM** $30   **MIP** $80

Robin Iron-on Patch, 1966, 2-1/2" diameter patch, Batkids Fan Club
EX $12   **NM** $35   **MIP** $60

Robin Ornament, 1989, Presents
    EX $5   **NM** $13   **MIP** $20

Robin Placemat, 1966, 13" x 18" vinyl
    EX $35   **NM** $80   **MIP** $110

Sip-A-Drink Cup, 1966, British, 6" tall, white plastic
    EX $50   **NM** $100   **MIP** $200

(KP Photo)

Talking Alarm Clock, 1975, Janex, plastic clock w/Bat logo on face
    EX $75   **NM** $100   **MIP** $180

ACTION FIGURES

Batman Bendy Figure, 1960s, Diener, on card
    EX $35   **NM** $65   **MIP** $90

Batman Figure, 1966, Ideal, 3" yellow plastic, detachable gray plastic cape
    EX $12   **NM** $25   **MIP** $50

(KP Photo)

Batman Figure, 1988, Applause, 15" tall w/stand
    EX $15   **NM** $25   **MIP** $45

Batman Figure, 1989, Billiken, 8" on card
    EX $8   **NM** $15   **MIP** $30

Batman Figure, 1989, Bully, 7" bendy
    EX $8   **NM** $15   **MIP** $25

Batman Figure, 1989, Presents, 15-1/2" tall vinyl and cloth figure on base, 1970s logo, metal stand
    EX $20   **NM** $40   **MIP** $75

Batman Figure, 1989, Takara/Japan
    EX $40   **NM** $80   **MIP** $150

Batman Figure and Parachute, 1966, CDC, 11" x 9" card, metallic blue figure of Batman and working parachute
    EX $40   **NM** $75   **MIP** $150

Batman Flying Figure on String, 1973, Ben Cooper, 6" rubber figure of Batman w/rubber cape
    EX $12   **NM** $25   **MIP** $50

Batman Inflated Gliding Figure, 1966, Ideal, 16" soft plastic inflatable Batman w/free flowing cape and hard plastic cable rail
    EX $40   **NM** $60   **MIP** $125

Batman on a String Figure, 1966, Fun Things, 4" rubber, flexible arms, legs and removable cape
    EX $20   **NM** $30   **MIP** $60

Joker Figure, Presents, 15" vinyl figure
    EX $10   **NM** $20   **MIP** $40

Joker Figure, 1966, Ideal, 3" blue plastic
    EX $20   **NM** $30   **MIP** $50

Joker Figure, 1988, Applause, vinyl w/stand
    EX $10   **NM** $20   **MIP** $40

Robin Figure, Presents, cloth and vinyl, on base
    EX $10   **NM** $20   **MIP** $35

Robin Figure, 1966, Ideal, 3" plastic, detachable yellow plastic cape
    EX $15   **NM** $30   **MIP** $50

Robin Figure, 1970s, Palitoy, 8" figure on card
    EX $20   **NM** $40   **MIP** $80

Robin Figure, 1988, Applause, vinyl w/stand
    EX $10   **NM** $20   **MIP** $35

Robin on a String Figure, Ben Cooper, 4" tall, rubber
    EX $10   **NM** $25   **MIP** $50

BANK

Batman Bank, 1966, 7" tall glazed china figural bank depicts Batman w/hands on hip
    EX $90   **NM** $120   **MIP** $160

Batman Bank, 1989, figural bank given away w/Batman Cereal
    EX $6   **NM** $12   **MIP** $25

Joker Bank, 1974, Mego, plastic
    EX $30   **NM** $60   **MIP** $125

Robin Bank, 1966, ceramic bank depicts Robin removing mask, 7" tall
    EX $80   **NM** $110   **MIP** $150

BOOK

Batman 3-D Comic Book, 1966, DC Comics, 9" x 11" comic w/3-D pages and glasses
    EX $200   **NM** $500   **MIP** $1000

Batman Annual, 1965-66, 8" x 10" hardback annual contains reprinted stories from 1950s Batman and Detective Comics
    EX $25   **NM** $50   **MIP** $85

Batman Comic Book and Record Set, 1966, Golden Records, 33-1/3 rpm record, full size Batman comic book, official Batman membership card w/secret Batman code on back
    EX $60   **NM** $125   **MIP** $175

Batman vs. the Joker Book, 1966, Signet, 160-page paperback
    EX $10   **NM** $20   **MIP** $30

Dot-To-Dot and Coloring Book, 1967, Vasquez Brothers, Batman w/Robin the Boy Wonder, printed in the Phillipines, 20 pages
    EX $30   **NM** $50   **MIP** $100

From Alfred to Zowie! Book, 1966, Golden Press
    EX $10   **NM** $20   **MIP** $35

Paint-By-Number Book, 1966, Whitman
    EX $20   **NM** $40   **MIP** $85

Sticker Fun with Batman Book, 1966, Watkins-Strathmore, 8" x 11" softbound w/stickers
    EX $15   **NM** $50   **MIP** $110

Three Villains of Doom Book, 1966, Signet, 160 pages
    EX $10   **NM** $40   **MIP** $85

CLOTHING

Child's Belt, 1960s, elastic w/bronze logo buckle
    EX $22   **NM** $40   **MIP** $90

Child's Mittens, 1973, children's blue plastic vinyl, raised illustration of Batman and logo
    EX $12   **NM** $25   **MIP** $50

Child's Pajamas, 1966, Wormser, light blue, two piece pajamas, full color Batman logo on chest
    EX $200   **NM** $450   **MIP** $900

FOOD PRODUCTS

Batman "Punch-O" Drink Mix, 1966, small paper packet
    EX $25   **NM** $40   **MIP** $75

Batman Cereal Box, 1989, Ralston
    EX $20   **NM** $30   **MIP** $60

Batman Crusader Sundae Fudgesicle, 1966, Popsicle, 7" white and brown paper wrapper
    EX $10   **NM** $20   **MIP** $30

Bread Wrapper, 1966, New Century Bread, plastic
    EX $25   **NM** $45   **MIP** $85

Candy Cigarettes, 1960s, made in England
    EX $30   **NM** $60   **MIP** $90

Chocolate Milk Carton, 1966, Reiter and Hart, one-quart carton in yellow, red and brown, features front and back panels of Batman in action poses
    EX $100   **NM** $200   **MIP** $400

Jelly Jar, 1966, W.H. Marvin, 5"-6" glass jar w/color label, "Bat" Pure Apple Jelly
EX $200   **NM** $400   **MIP** $600

Slam Bang Ice Cream Carton, 1966, Cabarrus Creamery, features Batman and Robin on side panels
EX $20   **NM** $45   **MIP** $60

GAMES

Batman Arcade Game, 1989, Bluebox, electronic
EX $75   **NM** $120   **MIP** $165

Batman Pinball Game, 1960s, Marx, tin litho w/plastic casing
EX $35   **NM** $90   **MIP** $175

Batman Target Game, 1966, Hasbro, tin litho target w/plastic revolver and rubber-tipped darts
EX $75   **NM** $100   **MIP** $200

GLASSWARE

Batman Drinking Glass, 1976, Pepsi, 7" tall glass tumbler, all Batman characters, each
EX $10   **NM** $20   **MIP** $30

Coffee Mug, 1966, Anchor-Hocking, milk glass, action pose of Batman on one side and the Bat logo on the opposite side
EX $15   **NM** $30   **MIP** $50

Drinking Glass, 1989, 5", made in France
EX $10   **NM** $25   **MIP** $40

MAGAZINE

Life Magazine, 1966, March 11, 1966 issue, Adam West as Batman on cover
EX $50   **NM** $70   **MIP** $100

TV Guide, 1966, TV Guide, March 26-April 1 issue, photo cover of Adam West as Batman
EX $120   **NM** $250   **MIP** $385

MODEL KIT

Catwoman Returns, 1990s, Horizon, vinyl model kit
EX $10   **NM** $20   **MIP** $40

Penguin Returns Model Kit, Horizon
EX $10   **NM** $20   **MIP** $40

PAINT SET

Batman Cast and Paint Set, 1960s, plaster casting mold and paint set
EX $50   **NM** $100   **MIP** $200

Batman Paint by Number Set, 1965, Hasbro, five pre-numbered sketches, ten oil paint vials and brush
EX $50   **NM** $100   **MIP** $200

Batman Super Powers Stain and Paint Set, 1984
EX $15   **NM** $30   **MIP** $70

Sparkle Paint Set, 1966, Kenner, paint and six pre-numbered sketches of Batman
EX $50   **NM** $100   **MIP** $175

PAPER GOODS

Batman and Robin Valentine, 1966
EX $10   **NM** $30   **MIP** $60

Batman Lobby Display, 1989, Warner Bros., Michael Keaton cardboard stand up
EX $125   **NM** $200   **MIP** $250

Batman Lucky Charm Display Card, 1966, 4" x 4" paper display card used in bubble gum machines, card shows Bat logo and red "Be protected—Get your Batman lucky charm now"
EX $12   **NM** $35   **MIP** $70

Batman Postcards, 1966, Dexter Press, set of eight postcards w/Carmine Infantino artwork
EX $40   **NM** $100   **MIP** $160

Batman Postcards, 1966, Dexter Press, three full-color postcards, each taken from a comic panel from Batman comics, each
EX $8   **NM** $15   **MIP** $30

Batman Returns Display, 1992, Warner Bros.
EX $50   **NM** $90   **MIP** $160

Batman Returns Lobby Display, 1992, Warner Bros., Michael Keaton life-size cardboard stand up
EX $125   **NM** $200   **MIP** $325

Batmobile Display Sign, 1969, Burry's, 34" x 48" die-cut 3-D plastic story display, raised images of Batman, Robin, and Batmobile, bright orange w/yellow lettering
EX $600   **NM** $1000   **MIP** $1500

Button Display Card, 1966, full color display card used in bubble gum machines which offered Batman buttons
EX $30   **NM** $60   **MIP** $100

Costume Store Poster, 1966, Ben Cooper, 12" x 24", yellow
EX $80   **NM** $160   **MIP** $220

Flicker Pictures Display Card, 1966, bubble gum machine display card
EX $10   **NM** $25   **MIP** $50

Glow-in-the Dark Poster, 1966, Ciro Art, 18" x 14" poster of Batman and Robin swinging across Gotham City
EX $50   **NM** $100   **MIP** $150

Official Bat-Signal Stickers, 1966, Alan-Whitney
EX $10   **NM** $20   **MIP** $35

Party Hat, 1972, Amscan/Canadian, 7" child's cardboard hat depicts Batman and Robin
EX $8   **NM** $15   **MIP** $30

PLAYSET

Batcave Play Set, 1974, Mego, vinyl
EX $200   **NM** $400   **MIP** $600

(KP photo, Karen O'Brien collection)

Batman and Robin playset, 1973, Ideal, "Fantastic Batcave, Gotham Museum, Wayne Manor," vinyl fold-over w/cardboard figures
EX n/a   **NM** $25   **MIP** $50

(KP Photo)

Batman Play Set, 1966, Ideal, eleven pieces including characters and vehicles
EX $3000   **NM** $8000   **MIP** $12000

(KP Photo)

Batman Switch and Go Play Set, 1966, Mattel, 9" plastic Batmobile, forty feet of track, figures, etc.
EX $175   **NM** $450   **MIP** $750

Magic Magnetic Gotham City Play Set, 1966, Remco, cardboard city, character figures
EX $300   **NM** $700   **MIP** $1000

PUPPET

Batman and Robin Hand Puppets, 1966, Ideal, 12" soft vinyl head, plastic body, each
EX $100   **NM** $200   **MIP** $300

(KP Photo)

Batman Push Puppet, 1966, Kohner, 3" plastic w/push button on bottom
EX $25   **NM** $50   **MIP** $100

Batman String Puppet, 1977, Madison
  EX $35   **NM** $75   **MIP** $160

Robin Push Puppet, 1966, Kohner, 3"
  plastic, push button on bottom
  EX $40   **NM** $85   **MIP** $150

PUZZLE

(KP Photo)

Frame Tray Puzzle, 1966, Whitman,
  11" x 14", Batman and Robin thwarting
  the Joker
  EX $20   **NM** $40   **MIP** $80

RECORD

Batman and Superman Record Album,
  1969-71, Wonderland, 45 rpm record
  Batman theme song from the 1966
  television show and "The Superman Song"
  EX $20   **NM** $75   **MIP** $100

Batman Record, 1966, SPC, 45 rpm,
  sleeve shaped like Batman's head; also
  available in Robin, Joker, Penguin,
  Riddler and Batmobile versions
  EX $15   **NM** $50   **MIP** $100

Batman Soundtrack Record, 1966, 20th
  Century Fox, mono and stereo versions,
  each
  EX $60   **NM** $150   **MIP** $275

Catwoman's Revenge Record, 1975, Power
  Records, 33-1/3 rpm story record
  EX $10   **NM** $25   **MIP** $60

Joker Record, 1966, SPC, 45 rpm, sleeve
  shaped like Joker's head
  EX $20   **NM** $50   **MIP** $90

RINGS

Bat Ring, 1966, yellow plastic, originally
  for a gumball machine
  EX $20   **NM** $40   **MIP** $65

Batman/Robin Flicker-Flasher Ring,
  1966, Vari-Vue, silver plastic base
  EX $10   **NM** $20   **MIP** $25

**Riddler/Batman Punching Riddler
  Flicker-Flasher Ring**, 1966, Vari-Vue,
  silver plastic base
  EX $10   **NM** $25   **MIP** $45

**Robin/Dick Grayson Flicker-Flasher
  Ring**, 1966, Vari-Vue, silver plastic base
  EX $10   **NM** $25   **MIP** $45

TOY

Bat Bomb, 1966, Mattel
  EX $75   **NM** $100   **MIP** $210

Batman Batarang Bagatelle, 1966, Marx,
  throw at targets
  EX $15   **NM** $35   **MIP** $65

Batman Cartoon Kit, 1966, Colorforms
  EX $25   **NM** $55   **MIP** $85

Batman Kite, 1982, Hiflyer
  EX $8   **NM** $15   **MIP** $35

Batman Radio Belt and Buckle, 1966
  EX $60   **NM** $125   **MIP** $200

**Batman Superfriends Lite Brite Refill
  Pack**, 1980
  EX $5   **NM** $15   **MIP** $25

Batman Superhero Stamp Set, 1970s
  EX $10   **NM** $25   **MIP** $60

(KP Photo)

Batman Trace-a-Graph, 1966, Emenee
  EX $50   **NM** $100   **MIP** $200

(KP Photo)

Batman Utility Belt, 1960s, Ideal
  EX $1500   **NM** $3500   **MIP** $5750

Batman Wind-Up, 1989, Billiken, Tin litho
  EX $25   **NM** $50   **MIP** $100

Batman Yo-Yo, 1989, SpectraStar
  EX $10   **NM** $20   **MIP** $35

(KP Photo)

Batphone, 1966, Marx
  EX $100   **NM** $175   **MIP** $350

Batscope Dart Launcher, 1966, Tarco
  EX $25   **NM** $45   **MIP** $100

Bat-Troll Doll, 1966, Wish-Nik, vinyl,
  dressed in a blue felt Batman outfit
  w/cowl and cape
  EX $125   **NM** $200   **MIP** $350

Cave Tun-L, 1966, New York Toy, 26" x 26"
  x 2" tunnel
  EX $700   **NM** $1500   **MIP** $2350

Escape Gun, 1966, Lincoln, red plastic
  spring-loaded pistol w/Batman decal,
  two separate firing barrels
  EX $75   **NM** $150   **MIP** $225

Give-A-Show Projector Cards, 1960s,
  Kenner, four slide cards in box
  EX $10   **NM** $30   **MIP** $60

Gotham City Stunt Set, 1989, Tonka
  EX $15   **NM** $55   **MIP** $85

(KP Photo)

Joker Wind-up, 1989, Billiken, Tin litho
  EX $50   **NM** $100   **MIP** $185

Joker Yo-Yo, 1989, SpectraStar
  EX $10   **NM** $20   **MIP** $45

Projector Gun, 1989, Toy Biz
  EX $15   **NM** $30   **MIP** $70

Puppet Theater Stage, 1966, Ideal,
  marketed by Sears, 19" x 11" x 20"
  cardboard stage w/hand puppets
  EX $200   **NM** $400   **MIP** $675

Ray Gun, 1960s, 7" long blue and black
  futuristic space gun w/bat sights and
  bats on handgrip
  EX $125   **NM** $350   **MIP** $450

Rubber Stamp Set, 1966, Kellogg's, 2" x
  5" hard black plastic case, set of six
  plastic stamps plus ink pad: Batman,
  Robin, Batmobile, Joker, Riddler and
  Penguin
  EX $60   **NM** $100   **MIP** $160

Shooting Arcade, 1970s, AHI, graphics of
  Joker, Catwoman and Penguin
  EX $35   **NM** $100   **MIP** $175

VEHICLES

Bat Cycle, 1989, Toy Biz
  EX $10   **NM** $30   **MIP** $60

Bat Machine, 1979, Mego
  EX $30   **NM** $75   **MIP** $120

(KP Photo)

Batboat, 1987, Duncan
EX $10   NM $30   MIP $70

Batboat Pullstring Toy, Eidai, made in Japan
EX $60   NM $140   MIP $200

Batman Flying Copter, 1966, Remco, 12" plastic w/guide-wire control
EX $50   NM $120   MIP $210

Batman Road Race Set, 1960s, slot car racing set
EX $150   NM $300   MIP $550

Batman Slot Car, 1966, Magicar (England), 5" long Batmobile being driven by Batman and Robin in illustrated display window box
EX $150   NM $325   MIP $550

(KP Photo)

Batmobile, Apollo (Japan), radio-controlled
EX $60   NM $125   MIP $260

Batmobile, Matsushiro, radio-controlled
EX $60   NM $125   MIP $260

Batmobile, 1960s, Simms, plastic car on card
EX $20   NM $50   MIP $100

Batmobile, 1972, AHI, 11" long tin litho battery-operated mystery action car w/blinking light and jet engine noise
EX $75   NM $150   MIP $300

Batmobile, 1974, Azrak-Hamway, battery operated
EX $50   NM $100   MIP $210

Batmobile, 1977, Duncan, 12" x 8" on card
EX $25   NM $50   MIP $100

Batmobile, 1980s, Aoshinu (Japan), motorized
EX $30   NM $60   MIP $150

Batmobile, 1980s, Bandai, pullback vehicle w/machine guns
EX $25   NM $60   MIP $135

Batmobile, 1989, Toy Biz, remote control
EX $12   NM $30   MIP $65

Batmobile, 1989, Rich Man's Toys, remote control
EX $85   NM $160   MIP $350

Batmobile Motorized Kit, 1980s, Aoshinu (Japan), smaller snap kit
EX $20   NM $35   MIP $75

Batwing, 1980s, Toy Biz
EX $15   NM $30   MIP $60

(KP Photo)

Joker Van, 1989, Ertl, die-cast vehicle on card
EX $5   NM $20   MIP $40

Robin Shuttle, 1979, Mego, sized for British-made Mego figures, in box
EX $20   NM $40   MIP $90

Super Accelerator Batmobile, 1970s, AHI, on card
EX $25   NM $60   MIP $120

Turbine-Sound Batmobile, 1989, Toy Biz
EX $10   NM $15   MIP $25

WATCH

Batman Returns Watch, 1989, Consort, gray or yellow Bat logo
EX $20   NM $40   MIP $80

Batman Wristwatch, 1991, Quintel, digital
EX $10   NM $15   MIP $35

Catwoman Watch, 1991, Quintel, digital
EX $10   NM $20   MIP $50

Catwoman Watch, 1991, Consort, Batman Returns
EX $10   NM $20   MIP $60

Joker Wristwatch, 1980s, Fossil
EX $25   NM $65   MIP $120

Joker Wristwatch, 1989, Quintell, digital
EX $10   NM $20   MIP $60

Video Game Watch, 1989, Tiger, w/alarm
EX $8   NM $20   MIP $40

BETTY BOOP

DOLL

Betty Boop Doll, 1930s, Cameo products, wood w/composition head
EX $400   NM $800   MIP $1200

Betty Boop Doll, 1986, M-Toy, 12" vinyl jointed
EX $20   NM $30   MIP $70

Betty Boop Doll Clothing, 1986, M-Toy, outfits for 12" dolls high fashion boutique, each
EX $7   NM $15   MIP $30

FIGURE

Betty Boop Figure, 1980s, 3" PVC figure, eight different poses and outfits, each
EX $5   NM $10   MIP $20

Betty Boop Figure, 1988, NJ Croce, 9" bendy
EX $7   NM $20   MIP $30

TOY

Betty Boop Delivery Truck, 1990, Schylling, tin litho
EX $15   NM $30   MIP $60

Betty Boop Wacky Wobbler, 2000, Funko, nodder
EX $6   NM $12   MIP $25

BLONDIE AND DAGWOOD

ACCESSORIES

Blondie Paint Set, 1946, American Crayon
EX $75   NM $150   MIP $275

Blondie's Peg Board Set, 1934, King Features, 9" x 15-1/2", multi-colored pegs, hammer, cut-outs of Dagwood, Blondie, etc.
EX $100   NM $200   MIP $350

Blondie's Presto Slate, 1944, Presto, 10" x 13" illustration of Blondie and Dagwood and other characters
EX $50   NM $80   MIP $110

Dagwood Marionette, 1945, 14"
EX $100   NM $225   MIP $375

Dagwood's Solo Flight Airplane, 1935, Marx, 12" wingspan, plane 9" in length
EX $750   NM $1200   MIP $1550

Lucky Safety Card, 1953, 2" x 4" cards, Dagwood offers safety tips
EX $10   NM $55   MIP $80

BOOK

Blondie Paint Book, 1947, Whitman
EX $60   NM $150   MIP $250

DOLL

Blondie Paper Dolls, 1944, Whitman
EX $100   NM $225   MIP $400

Blondie Paper Dolls, 1955, Whitman
EX $40   NM $125   MIP $225

FIGURE

Blondie Figure, 1940s, 2-1/2" tall, lead
EX $30 **NM** $75 **MIP** $150

Dagwood and Kids Figures, 1944, King Features, Dagwood, Alexander, and Cookie, each
EX $50 **NM** $85 **MIP** $150

PUZZLE

Puzzle, 1930s, Featured Funnies
EX $75 **NM** $125 **MIP** $175

BUGS BUNNY

ACCESSORIES

Bugs Bunny Charm Bracelet, 1950s, brass charms of Bugs Bunny, Tweety, Sniffles, Fudd, etc.
EX $40 **NM** $80 **MIP** $125

Bugs Bunny Chatter Chum, 1982, Mattel
EX $10 **NM** $25 **MIP** $50

Bugs Bunny Clock, 1972, Litech, 12" x 14"
EX $35 **NM** $100 **MIP** $185

Bugs Bunny Mini Snow Dome, 1980s, Applause
EX $5 **NM** $15 **MIP** $35

Bugs Bunny Musical Ge-Tar, 1977, Mattel
EX $30 **NM** $70 **MIP** $110

Bugs Bunny Night Light, 1980s, Applause
EX $5 **NM** $10 **MIP** $15

Bugs Bunny Talking Alarm Clock, 1974, Janex, battery-operated
EX $50 **NM** $100 **MIP** $175

Bugs Bunny Wristwatch, 1978, Lafayette
EX $50 **NM** $120 **MIP** $180

BANK

Bugs Bunny Bank, 1940s, 5-3/4" x 5-1/2", pot metal, figure on base
EX $70 **NM** $140 **MIP** $260

Bugs Bunny Bank, 1971, Dakin, on a basket of carrots
EX $15 **NM** $30 **MIP** $60

COSTUME

Bugs Bunny Costume, 1960s, Collegeville, mask and costume
EX $25 **NM** $50 **MIP** $85

DOLL

Bugs Bunny Talking Doll, 1971, Mattel
EX $50 **NM** $110 **MIP** $180

FIGURE

Bugs Bunny Bendy, 1980s, Applause, 4" tall
EX $5 **NM** $15 **MIP** $30

Bugs Bunny Figure, 1971, Dakin, 10" tall
EX $10 **NM** $35 **MIP** $75

Bugs Bunny Figure, 1975, Warner Bros., 5-1/2" tall, ceramic, holding carrot
EX $30 **NM** $70 **MIP** $120

Bugs Bunny Figure, 1975, Warner Bros., 2-3/4" tall, ceramic
EX $15 **NM** $30 **MIP** $75

Bugs Bunny Figure, 1976, Dakin, yellow globes in "Cartoon Theater" box
EX $15 **NM** $35 **MIP** $75

Bugs Bunny in Uncle Sam Outfit, 1976, Dakin, distributed through Great America Theme Park, Illinois
EX $25 **NM** $70 **MIP** $110

TOY

Bugs Bunny Colorforms Set, 1958, Colorforms
EX $15 **NM** $50 **MIP** $100

Bugs Bunny Soaky, soft rubber
EX $10 **NM** $30 **MIP** $60

CALIFORNIA RAISINS

ACCESSORIES

California Raisins Chalkboard, 1988, Rose Art
EX $7 **NM** $15 **MIP** $40

California Raisins Clay Factory, 1988, Rose Art
EX $15 **NM** $45 **MIP** $75

California Raisins Crayon By Number, 1988, Rose Art
EX $15 **NM** $35 **MIP** $70

TOY

California Raisins Colorforms Play Set, 1987, Colorforms
EX $10 **NM** $30 **MIP** $65

California Raisins Wind-Up Walkers, 1987, Rasta
EX $6 **NM** $15 **MIP** $35

CAPTAIN AMERICA

ACCESSORIES

Captain America Club Kit, 1941, includes two badges (copper and bronze), card, envelope
EX $1500 **NM** $2500 **MIP** $3500

FIGURE

Captain America Bendy Figure, 1966, Lakeside, 6", rubber
EX $50 **NM** $85 **MIP** $150

TOY

Captain America Rocket Racer, 1984, Buddy L, Secret Wars remote controlled battery operated car
EX $75 **NM** $150 **MIP** $200

(KP Photo)

Captain America Scooter, 1967, Marx, 4", yellow plastic friction toy w/figure
EX $200 **NM** $350 **MIP** $450

Hand Puppet, 1960s, Ideal, box reads, "Super Hero TV Favorites"
EX $15 **NM** $30 **MIP** $60

CAPTAIN MARVEL

ACCESSORIES

Adventures of Captain Marvel Ink Blotter/Ruler, 1940s, Republic/Fawcett, 6" blotter w/ruler advertises the 12-part serial, theatre premium
EX $200 **NM** $625 **MIP** $825

Captain Marvel Booklet, 1940s, Fawcett
EX $50 **NM** $100 **MIP** $350

Captain Marvel Button, 1940s, celluloid, pinback
EX $30 **NM** $95 **MIP** $150

Captain Marvel Club Button, 1941, tin litho, showing Captain Marvel in bust 3/4 view, w/"Shazam" in lightning bolts at bottom
EX $30 **NM** $95 **MIP** $150

Captain Marvel Club Felt Shoulder Patches, 1940s, Fawcett, Captain Marvel diving towards Earth, yellow
EX $200 **NM** $475 **MIP** $675

Captain Marvel Club Felt Shoulder Patches, 1940s, Fawcett, Captain Marvel diving towards Earth, blue
EX $50 **NM** $100 **MIP** $200

Captain Marvel Club Membership Card, 1940s, Fawcett
EX $50 **NM** $75 **MIP** $120

Captain Marvel Code Finder, 1943
EX $225 **NM** $475 **MIP** $675

Captain Marvel Felt Pennant, 1940s, Fawcett, yellow, shows Captain Marvel flying
EX $100 **NM** $190 **MIP** $300

Captain Marvel Felt Pennant, 1940s, Fawcett, blue, shows Captain Marvel flying
EX $100 **NM** $135 **MIP** $200

Captain Marvel Film Viewer Gun, 1940s, gun-shaped movie viewer w/film strips from Paramount series
EX $125 **NM** $250 **MIP** $425

Captain Marvel Flannel Patch, 1940s, Fawcett
EX $50 **NM** $80 **MIP** $175

Captain Marvel Glow Pictures, 1940s, Fawcett, set of four
EX $350 **NM** $750 **MIP** $1000

Captain Marvel Iron-Ons, 1950s, Fawcett, sheet
EX $30 **NM** $60 **MIP** $100

Captain Marvel Jr. Wristwatch, 1940s, blue band, round dial w/blue costumed Jr., no box issued
EX $400 **NM** $850 **MIP** $1200

Captain Marvel Key Chain, 1940s, Fawcett
EX $60 **NM** $125 **MIP** $175

Captain Marvel Magic Dime Register Bank, 1948, Fawcett, available in three colors
EX $200 **NM** $425 **MIP** $650

Captain Marvel Magic Flute, 1940s, on die-cut card, shows Captain Marvel on side
EX $60　　NM $100　　MIP $160

(KP Photo)

Captain Marvel Magic Lightning Box, 1940s, Fawcett
EX $50　　NM $100　　MIP $175

Captain Marvel Magic Membership Card, 1940s, Fawcett
EX $40　　NM $60　　MIP $100

Captain Marvel Magic Picture, 1940s, Reed and Associates, paper, shows Billy Batson "transforming" into Captain Marvel
EX $50　　NM $80　　MIP $160

Captain Marvel Magic Whistle, 1948, Fawcett, seed company premium, picture of Captain Marvel on both sides, on card
EX $60　　NM $120　　MIP $175

Captain Marvel Neck Tie, 1940s, Fawcett
EX $60　　NM $150　　MIP $250

Captain Marvel Overseas Cap, 1940s, rare
EX $400　　NM $800　　MIP $1000

Captain Marvel Paint Set, 1940s, paint set w/five chalk figurines
EX $500　　NM $1100　　MIP $1600

Captain Marvel Paper Horn, 1940s, Fawcett
EX $20　　NM $40　　MIP $75

Captain Marvel Patch, 1940s, Fawcett
EX $30　　NM $75　　MIP $150

Captain Marvel Pinback Pattern, 1940s, Fawcett, pattern for original pinback
EX $15　　NM $30　　MIP $100

Captain Marvel Portrait, 1940s, Whiz Comics/Fawcett
EX $75　　NM $125　　MIP $250

Captain Marvel Portrait, 1940s, Republic, different version than Whiz Comics portrait
EX $75　　NM $150　　MIP $250

Captain Marvel Power Siren, 1940s, Fawcett
EX $60　　NM $125　　MIP $175

Captain Marvel Secret Code Sheet, 1940s, Fawcett
EX $15　　NM $30　　MIP $75

Captain Marvel Skull Cap, 1940s
EX $125　　NM $500　　MIP $700

Captain Marvel Soap, 1947, Fawcett, three illustrated bars in box
EX $300　　NM $600　　MIP $800

(KP Photo)

Captain Marvel Stationary, 1940s, Fawcett, paper and envelopes in box
EX $150　　NM $250　　MIP $400

Captain Marvel Suspenders, 1940s, Fawcett
EX $50　　NM $125　　MIP $185

Captain Marvel Sweater, 1940s, white or off-white, red Captain Marvel logo
EX $60　　NM $300　　MIP $400

Captain Marvel Tattoo Transfers, 1940s, Fawcett
EX $30　　NM $110　　MIP $200

Captain Marvel Tie Bar, 1940s, on card
EX $40　　NM $65　　MIP $150

Captain Marvel Wristwatch, 1948, in box, shows Captain Marvel holding an airplane
EX $400　　NM $900　　MIP $1350

Captain Marvel, Jr. Booklet, 1940s, Fawcett
EX $25　　NM $50　　MIP $100

(KP Photo)

Fawcett's Comic Stars Christmas Tree Ornaments, 1940s, Fawcett, metal star-shaped ornaments w/art of Captain Marvel and Hoppy
EX $25　　NM $45　　MIP $100

(KP Photo)

Mary Marvel Illustrated Soap, 1947, Fawcett, three soap bars in box
EX $300　　NM $500　　MIP $700

Mary Marvel Patch, 1940s, Fawcett
EX $150　　NM $300　　MIP $450

Mary Marvel Pin, 1940s, Fawcett, fiberboard
EX $50　　NM $150　　MIP $250

Mary Marvel Stationery, 1940s, Fawcett, boxed
EX $100　　NM $200　　MIP $400

(KP Photo)

Mary Marvel Wristwatch, 1948, in box
EX $400　　NM $900　　MIP $1300

Membership Secret Code Card, 1940s, Fawcett
EX $150　　NM $250　　MIP $400

Rocket Raider, 1940s, Fawcett, paper airplane in envelope
EX $20　　NM $40　　MIP $70

COMIC

Boy Who Never Heard of Captain Marvel Mini Comic, 1940s, Bond Bread
EX $40　　NM $100　　MIP $210

Captain Marvel and Billy's Big Game Mini Comic, 1940s
EX $90　　NM $250　　MIP $410

Captain Marvel Meets the Weatherman Mini Comic, 1940s, Bond Bread, Bond Bread premium
EX $50　　NM $110　　MIP $185

Giveaway Comics #1, Captain Marvel and the Lt. of Safety, 1950, Danger Flies a Kite
EX $400　　NM $800　　MIP $1300

Giveaway Comics #2, Captain Marvel and the Lt. of Safety, 1950, Danger Takes to Climbing
EX $400　　NM $800　　MIP $1300

Giveaway Comics #3, Captain Marvel and the Lt. of Safety, 1951, Danger Smashes Street Lights
EX $400   **NM** $800   **MIP** $1300

FIGURE

Captain Marvel Comic Hero Punch-Outs, 1942, Lowe, cardboard figures
EX $75   **NM** $200   **MIP** $375

Captain Marvel Sirocco Figurine, 1940s, Fawcett
EX $1500   **NM** $3000   **MIP** $4000

Mary Marvel Figurine, 5"
EX $500   **NM** $1250   **MIP** $2000

PUZZLE

Captain Marvel Puzzle, 1940s, Reed and Associates, in envelope
EX $50   **NM** $350   **MIP** $425

Captain Marvel Puzzle, 1941, Fawcett, in box
EX $40   **NM** $200   **MIP** $375

TOY

Captain Marvel Beanbags, 1940s, Captain Marvel, Mary Marvel or Hoppy, each
EX $75   **NM** $175   **MIP** $325

Captain Marvel Beanie, 1940s, cap shows image of Captain Marvel flying toward word "Shazam," blue
EX $175   **NM** $350   **MIP** $600

Captain Marvel Beanie, 1940s, girls' cap shows image of Captain Marvel flying toward word "Shazam," pink, rare
EX $750   **NM** $1500   **MIP** $2000

(KP Photo)

Captain Marvel Buzz Bomb, 1950s, Fawcett, paper airplane in envelope
EX $25   **NM** $85   **MIP** $150

(KP Photo)

Captain Marvel Jr. Ski Jump, 1947, Reed and Associates, paper, in envelope
EX $10   **NM** $20   **MIP** $65

Captain Marvel Jr. Statuette, 1940s, Fawcett, hand-painted plastic
EX $500   **NM** $1500   **MIP** $2500

Captain Marvel Lightning Race Cars, 1940s, Automatic Toy Co., set of four cars w/ wind-up keys; green, yellow, orange or blue; rare
EX $2000   **NM** $3000   **MIP** $4000

Captain Marvel Statuette, 1940s, Fawcett, hand-painted plastic, shows Captain Marvel standing w/arms crossed, on base w/name engraved
EX $1000   **NM** $2500   **MIP** $4000

Mary Marvel Statuette, 1940s, Fawcett, hand-painted plastic
EX $500   **NM** $1750   **MIP** $3000

CAPTAIN MIDNIGHT

ACCESSORIES

Better Little Book, 1942, Chicago Sun Syndicate, "Captain Midnight and the Moon Woman," #1452
EX $30   **NM** $80   **MIP** $120

Better Little Book, 1944, Whitman, "Captain Midnight and Sheik Jomk Khan," #1402
EX $30   **NM** $80   **MIP** $120

Captain Midnight Badge Brass, 1930s, gold, wings and words "Flight Commander," fying cross
EX $90   **NM** $210   **MIP** $400

(KP Photo)

Captain Midnight Cup, plastic, 4" tall, "Ovaltine-The Heart of a Hearty Breakfast"
EX $30   **NM** $70   **MIP** $150

Captain Midnight Map, 1940, Skelly Oil, 11" x 17"
EX $450   **NM** $750   **MIP** $1200

Captain Midnight Membership Manual, 1930s, Secret Squadron official code and manual guide
EX $55   **NM** $125   **MIP** $275

Captain Midnight Secret Society Decoder, 1949, w/key
EX $85   **NM** $180   **MIP** $375

Decoder, 1948, radio premium, copper disc w/ signal mirror
EX $15   **NM** $30   **MIP** $60

Medal of Membership, 1940, Flight Patrol Spinner coin
EX $20   **NM** $40   **MIP** $70

Mug w/ handle, 1952, Ovaltine, sticker says "Ovaltine-The Heart of a Hearty Breakfast"
EX $15   **NM** $30   **MIP** $60

Photo-matic Code-O-Graph, 1942, radio show premium, brass badge
EX $20   **NM** $40   **MIP** $70

Whistle, 1947, Code-A-Graph Decoder, radio premium
EX $15   **NM** $30   **MIP** $65

CARTOON/COMIC CHARACTERS

ACCESSORIES

Beetle Bailey Comic Strip Stamper Set, 1981, Ja-Ru, 7 stampers, book, crayon
EX $8   **NM** $25   **MIP** $60

Beetle Bailey Gun Set, 1981, Ja-Ru, cord gun and target
EX $10   **NM** $40   **MIP** $90

Daffy Dog Poster, 10" x 13", The Morning After
EX $10   **NM** $17   **MIP** $30

Dan Dunn Pinback Button, 1930s, 1-1/4"
EX $50   **NM** $200   **MIP** $375

Doggie Daddy Metal Trivet, 1960s, says "You have to work like a dog to live like one"
EX $15   **NM** $35   **MIP** $70

Dudley Do-Right Jigsaw Puzzle, 1975, Whitman, Dudley and Snidley
EX $15   **NM** $35   **MIP** $75

Easy Show Movie Projector Films, 1965, Kenner, numerous cartoon characters, each film
EX $8   **NM** $15   **MIP** $30

Favorite Funnies Printing Set, 1930s, #4004, Orphan Annie, Herby, and Dick Tracy, six stamps, pad, paper and instructions
EX $75   **NM** $175   **MIP** $275

Geoffrey Jack-in-the-Box, 1970s, Toys R Us, jack-in-the-box
EX $20   **NM** $40   **MIP** $80

Hair Bear Bunch Mug, 1978, Square Bear figural mug
EX $5   **NM** $13   **MIP** $20

Hair Bear Bunch Wristwatch, 1972, medium gold tone case, base metal back, articulated hands, red leather snap down band
EX $30   **NM** $70   **MIP** $150

Harold Teen Playstone Funnies Mold Set, 1940s
EX $40   **NM** $100   **MIP** $200

Herman and Katnip Punch Out Kite, 1960s, Saalfield, folds into a kite
EX $12   **NM** $30   **MIP** $75

Josie and the Pussycats Paper Doll Book,
1971, Whitman, Model No. 1982
EX $25   **NM** $50   **MIP** $100

Little Audrey Dress Designer Kit, 1962,
Saalfield, die cut doll and accessories in
illustrated box
EX $60   **NM** $125   **MIP** $185

**Little Audrey Shoulder Bag Leathercraft
Kit,** 1961, Jewel
EX $75   **NM** $150   **MIP** $200

Little Lulu Dish, 1940s, 5-1/2" hand
painted ceramic, pictures of Lulu, Tubby
and her friends
EX $100   **NM** $200   **MIP** $350

Nancy Music Box, 1968, United Feature,
ceramic
EX $80   **NM** $150   **MIP** $225

Supercar Molding Color Kit, 1960s,
Sculptorcraft, set of rubber plaster casting
models of vehicle and show characters,
including Mike Mercury, Beaker and
Popkiss, Jimmy and Mitch, Masterspy
EX $150   **NM** $300   **MIP** $445

**Winnie Winkle Playstone Funnies Mold
Set,** 1940s
EX $30   **NM** $75   **MIP** $150

BANK

Andy Panda Bank, 1977, Walter Lantz, 7"
tall, hard plastic
EX $12   **NM** $40   **MIP** $85

Little Lulu Bank, 8" tall hard plastic w/black
fire hydrant
EX $60   **NM** $125   **MIP** $185

Scrappy Bank, 3" x 3-1/2" metal, embossed
illustration of Scrappy and his dog
EX $150   **NM** $300   **MIP** $425

BOOK

Little Lulu Paint Book, 1944, Whitman
EX $100   **NM** $200   **MIP** $300

DOLL

Bloom County Opus Doll, 1986, 10" tall,
plush, penguin Opus wearing a Santa
Claus cap
EX $10   **NM** $30   **MIP** $75

Chilly Willy Doll, 1982, Walter Lantz,
plush
EX $7   **NM** $25   **MIP** $60

Dudley Do-Right Doll, 1972, Wham-O,
bendy
EX $20   **NM** $40   **MIP** $80

Hagar the Horrible Doll, 1983, 12" tall
EX $12   **NM** $22   **MIP** $70

King Leonardo Doll, 1960s, Holiday Fair,
cloth plush dressed in royal robe
EX $75   **NM** $100   **MIP** $200

FIGURE

Alfred E. Neuman Figurine, 1960s, base
says "What Me Worry?"
EX $70   **NM** $140   **MIP** $225

Cadbury the Butler Figure, 1981, DFC,
3-1/2" figure from Richie Rich
EX $7   **NM** $20   **MIP** $35

Wonder Woman Figure, Presents, 14" tall
cloth and vinyl figure on base
EX $9   **NM** $25   **MIP** $50

PUZZLE

Katzenjammer Kids Jigsaw Puzzle,
1930s, 9-1/2" x 14", Featured Funnies
EX $100   **NM** $200   **MIP** $325

Little Lulu Puzzles, 1973, Whitman, four
frame tray puzzles
EX $30   **NM** $60   **MIP** $100

Rosie's Beau Puzzle, 1930s, 9-1/2" x 14",
Featured Funnies
EX $50   **NM** $85   **MIP** $150

Smilin' Jack Puzzle, 1930s, 9-1/2" x 14",
Featured Funnies
EX $100   **NM** $150   **MIP** $200

TOY

Breezley Soaky, 1967, Purex, 9" tall, plastic
EX $25   **NM** $60   **MIP** $110

Henry on Trapeze Toy, G. Borgfeldt, 6" x
9", celluloid, wind-up, jointed Henry
suspended from trapeze
EX $400   **NM** $700   **MIP** $1200

Mush Mouse Pull Toy, 1960s, Ideal, pull
toy w/vinyl figure
EX $40   **NM** $100   **MIP** $180

Peter Potamus Soaky, 11" tall
EX $20   **NM** $40   **MIP** $80

Touche Turtle Soaky, 1960s, lying down
EX $15   **NM** $40   **MIP** $75

Touche Turtle Soaky, 1960s, standing
EX $25   **NM** $60   **MIP** $110

Yipee Pull Toy, 1960s, Ideal, w/vinyl
figures of Yipee, Yapee and Yahoee
EX $40   **NM** $80   **MIP** $150

CASPER THE FRIENDLY GHOST

ACCESSORIES

Casper Figure Lamp, 1950, Archlamp, 17"
tall
EX $75   **NM** $175   **MIP** $275

Casper Light Shade, 1960s
EX $70   **NM** $100   **MIP** $175

Casper Night Light, 1975, Duncan, 6-1/2" tall
EX $15   **NM** $40   **MIP** $75

COSTUME

Casper Costume, Collegeville, "Ghostland"
costume, #216
EX $45   **NM** $70   **MIP** $110

Casper Halloween Costume, 1960s,
Collegeville, mask and costume
EX $20   **NM** $40   **MIP** $90

DOLL

Casper Doll, 7-3/4" tall squeeze doll holds
black spotted puppy
EX $30   **NM** $65   **MIP** $125

Casper Doll, 1960s, 15" cloth
EX $30   **NM** $60   **MIP** $125

Casper Doll, 1972, Sutton and Sons,
rubber squeeze doll w/logo
EX $20   **NM** $30   **MIP** $60

Casper the Friendly Ghost Talking Doll,
1961, Mattel, 15" tall, terry cloth, plastic
head w/a pull string voice box
EX $75   **NM** $175   **MIP** $250

PUZZLE

Casper Jigsaw Puzzle, 1988, Ja-Ru
EX $4   **NM** $10   **MIP** $20

TOY

Casper Hand Puppet, 1960s,
Commonwealth Toys, all fuzzy, ribbon
says "Casper the Friendly Ghost"
EX $15   **NM** $30   **MIP** $60

Casper Hand Puppet, 1960s, 8" tall, cloth
and plastic head
EX $20   **NM** $40   **MIP** $100

Casper Pull Toy, 1950s, red wheels, paper
litho of cartoon Casper on wood, arms
play xylophone when pulled
EX $50   **NM** $125   **MIP** $250

Casper Soaky, 1960s, Colgate-Palmolive,
10" tall
EX $20   **NM** $55   **MIP** $90

Casper Spinning Top, 1960s, blue top
w/figure of Casper inside
EX $25   **NM** $60   **MIP** $90

Casper Wind-Up Toy, 1950s, Linemar, tin
EX $300   **NM** $500   **MIP** $850

Wacky Wobbler, 2001, Funko, nodder
EX $5   **NM** $10   **MIP** $25

Wendy the Good Witch Soaky, 1960s,
Colgate-Palmolive
EX $20   **NM** $55   **MIP** $90

CHARLIE CHAPLIN

ACCESSORIES

Charlie Chaplin Pencil Case, 8" long
EX $50   **NM** $100   **MIP** $200

Charlie Chaplin Wristwatch, 1972,
Bubbles/Cadeaux, Swiss, large chrome
case, black and white dial, articulated
sweep cane second hand, black leather
band
EX $45   **NM** $100   **MIP** $225

Charlie Chaplin Wristwatch, 1985,
Bradley, oldies series, quartz, large
black plastic case and band, sweep
seconds, shows Chaplin as Little Tramp
EX $20   **NM** $50   **MIP** $100

DOLL

Charlie Chaplin Cloth Doll, patterned fabric
EX $225   **NM** $375   **MIP** $475

Charlie Chaplin Doll, 11-1/2" tall, wind-up
EX $500   **NM** $1000   **MIP** $1500

FIGURE

Charlie Chaplin Figure, 2-1/2" tall, lead
EX $60   **NM** $175   **MIP** $325

Charlie Chaplin Figure, 8-1/2" tall, tin
w/cast iron feet, wind-up
EX $600   NM $1100   MIP $1750

TOY

Charlie Chaplin Toy, 4" tall, spring
mechanism tips his hat when string is
pulled
EX $100   NM $175   MIP $300

CHIPMUNKS

ACCESSORIES

Chipmunks Toothbrush, 1984, battery-
operated
EX $10   NM $25   MIP $50

Chipmunks Wallet, 1959, vinyl
EX $40   NM $80   MIP $120

DOLL

Alvin Doll, 1963, Knickerbocker, 14" tall
plush w/vinyl head
EX $30   NM $70   MIP $120

TOY

Chipmunks Bean Bags, 1998, three in set,
talking
EX $20   NM $40   MIP $60

Chipmunks Soaky, 1960s, 10" tall, Alvin,
Simon, or Theodore, each
EX $10   NM $40   MIP $80

CINDERELLA

ACCESSORIES

Cinderella Alarm Clock, Westclox, 2-1/2"
x 4-1/2" x 4" tall
EX $70   NM $125   MIP $275

Cinderella Bank, 1950s, ceramic,
Cinderella holding magic wand
EX $40   NM $75   MIP $150

Cinderella Charm Bracelet, 1950, golden
brass link w/five charms, Cinderella,
Fairy Godmother, slipper, pumpkin
coach and Prince
EX $40   NM $80   MIP $150

Cinderella Molding Set, 1950s, Model
Craft, set of character molds in
illustrated box
EX $40   NM $100   MIP $200

Cinderella Musical Jewelry Box, mahogany
music box plays "So This Is Love"
EX $20   NM $40   MIP $85

Cinderella Wristwatch, 1950, US Time
EX $225   NM $450   MIP $750

Cinderella Wristwatch, 1958, Timex,
Cinderella and castle, pink leather band
EX $150   NM $350   MIP $650

Fairy Godmother Pitcher, 7" tall figural
pitcher
EX $22   NM $50   MIP $100

Gus/Jaq Serving Set, 1960s, Westman,
creamer, pitcher and sugar bowl
EX $50   NM $100   MIP $200

DOLL

Cinderella Doll, 11" tall, blue stain ballgown
w/white bridal gown, glass slippers,
holding Little Little Golden Book
EX $20   NM $40   MIP $120

Cinderella Doll, Horsman, 8" tall in illustrated
box
EX $30   NM $75   MIP $175

Cinderella Paper Dolls, 1965, Whitman
EX $50   NM $100   MIP $175

Gus Doll, 1950s, Gund, 13" tall, gray doll
w/dark red shirt and green felt hat
EX $75   NM $150   MIP $250

FIGURE

Cinderella Figurine, 5" tall, plastic
EX $10   NM $20   MIP $50

Cinderella Figurine, 5" tall, ceramic
EX $20   NM $40   MIP $100

PUZZLE

Cinderella Puzzle, 1960s, Jaymar
EX $15   NM $30   MIP $60

TOY

Cinderella Soaky, 1960s, 11" tall, blue
EX $15   NM $40   MIP $80

Cinderella Wind-Up Toy, 1950, Irwin, 5"
tall, Cinderella and Prince dancing
EX $75   NM $225   MIP $350

Prince Charming Hand Puppet, 1959,
Gund, 10" tall
EX $25   NM $50   MIP $100

CRUSADER RABBIT

ACCESSORIES

Crusader Rabbit Paint Set, 1960s, 13" x 19"
EX $90   NM $135   MIP $200

BOOK

Crusader Rabbit Book, 1958, Wonder Book
EX $30   NM $60   MIP $100

Crusader Rabbit in Bubble Trouble Book,
1960, Whitman
EX $30   NM $60   MIP $95

Crusader Rabbit Trace and Color Book,
1959, Whitman
EX $55   NM $110   MIP $175

TOY

Crusader Rabbit Soaky, 1960s, Purex
EX $50   NM $100   MIP $150

DANGER MOUSE

ACCESSORIES

Danger Mouse ID Set, 1985, Gordy
EX $10   NM $15   MIP $50

Danger Mouse Pendant Necklace, 1986,
Gordy
EX $10   NM $15   MIP $50

DOLL

Danger Mouse Doll, 1988, Russ, 15" tall
EX $40   NM $60   MIP $100

DENNIS THE MENACE

ACCESSORIES

Dennis the Menace Giant Mischief Kit,
1950s, Hasbro
EX $60   NM $110   MIP $210

Dennis the Menace Paint Set, 1954,
Pressman, paints, crayons, brush and
trays
EX $40   NM $100   MIP $185

BOOK

Dennis the Menace and Ruff Book, 1959,
Whitman, Little Golden Book
EX $10   NM $18   MIP $40

Dennis the Menace and Ruff Book Ends,
1974, ceramic
EX $30   NM $65   MIP $125

PUZZLE

Dennis the Menace TV Show Puzzle,
1960, Whitman
EX $20   NM $40   MIP $60

TOY

Dennis the Menace Colorforms Set, 1961,
Colorforms
EX $15   NM $45   MIP $90

Dennis the Menace Tiddley Winks, 1961,
Whitman
EX $25   NM $45   MIP $90

DEPUTY DAWG

DOLL

Deputy Dawg Doll, 1960s, Ideal, 14" tall,
cloth w/plush arms and vinyl head
EX $75   NM $135   MIP $195

FIGURE

Deputy Dawg Figure, 1977, Dakin, 6" tall,
plastic body w/vinyl head
EX $30   NM $55   MIP $100

TOY

Deputy Dawg Soaky, 1966, 9-1/2" tall, plastic
EX $15   NM $45   MIP $80

DICK TRACY

ACCESSORIES

Air Detective Bracelet, 1938
EX $500   NM $625   MIP $825

Air Detective Cap, 1938, Quaker
EX $200   NM $400   MIP $600

Bonny Braids Store Contest Card, 1951,
5-1/2" x 5-1/2"
EX $25   NM $65   MIP $125

Candy Box, 1940s, Novel Package, box
w/cartoons and story on back; comic
strips on bottom
EX $150   NM $275   MIP $385

Christmas Tree Light Bulb, 1930s, early painted figure of Dick Tracy
EX $40   NM $90   MIP $100

Detective Club Pin, 1942, yellow, tab back
EX $25   NM $50   MIP $90

Dick Tracy Jr. Detective Agency Tie Clasp, 1930s, silver or brass, each
EX $75   NM $125   MIP $200

(KP Photo)

Dick Tracy Lamp, 1950s, painted ceramic bust of Tracy in black coat, yellow hat and red tie
EX $1500   NM $2000   MIP $3500

Dick Tracy Mask, 1933, Philadelphia Inquirer, paper
EX $200   NM $350   MIP $450

Dick Tracy Picture, 1940s, Pillsbury, part of set of eight, each 7" x 10" in mat, shows Tracy and Junior
EX $60   NM $130   MIP $250

Dinnerware Set, 1950s, Homer Laughlin, bowl, dinner plate, and mug
EX $70   NM $150   MIP $300

Dinnerware Set, 1980s, Zak Designs, plate, cup, bowl
EX $10   NM $15   MIP $30

Hat, 1940s, Miller Bros. Hat, wool fedora, blue/gray
EX $50   NM $100   MIP $175

Secret Service Patrol Bracelet, 1938, Quaker, chain bracelet w/small head of Dick Tracy and Junior and four leaf clover
EX $100   NM $150   MIP $250

Sparkle Plenty Christmas Tree Lights, 1940s, Mutual Equipment, seven-light set
EX $30   NM $65   MIP $125

Sparkle Plenty Christmas Tree Lights, 1940s, Mutual Equipment, 15-light set
EX $40   NM $90   MIP $175

Super 8 Color Film, 1965, Republic, b/w cartton "Trick or Treat"
EX $10   NM $25   MIP $50

Wall Clock, 1990s, 16" x 20" battery power quartz, face shows Disney movie Tracy talking into wrist radio
EX $15   NM $20   MIP $40

Wallpaper Section, 1950s, shows comic strip scenes of Tracy and seven other characters
EX $15   NM $40   MIP $75

BADGE

Air Detective Member Badge, 1938, Quaker, brass, wing shape
EX $90   NM $125   MIP $175

Detective Club Crime Stoppers Badge, 1940s, Guild
EX $30   NM $60   MIP $100

Dick Tracy Crime Stopper Badge, 1960s, star shape giveaway badge from WGN "9 Official Dick Tracy Crimestopper" TV Badge
EX $30   NM $65   MIP $125

Dick Tracy Detective Club Belt Badge with belt, premium
EX $35   NM $150   MIP $350

Secret Service Patrol Badge, 1938, Quaker, Sergeant
EX $40   NM $100   MIP $225

Secret Service Patrol Badge, 1938, Quaker, 2nd year chevron
EX $10   NM $30   MIP $60

Secret Service Patrol Badge, 1938, Quaker, Lieutenant
EX $50   NM $185   MIP $350

Secret Service Patrol Badge, 1938, Quaker, Inspector General, brass, 2-1/2"
EX $350   NM $650   MIP $950

Secret Service Patrol Badge, 1938, Quaker, brass girl's division badge
EX $20   NM $50   MIP $100

Secret Service Patrol Badge, 1938, Quaker, brass Captain badge
EX $75   NM $185   MIP $375

BANK

(KP Photo)

Sparkle Plenty Bank, 1940s, Jayess, 12" tall, base features a medallion of Dick Tracy as Godfather
EX $150   NM $300   MIP $525

BOOK

Ace Detective Book, 1943, Whitman
EX $30   NM $60   MIP $150

Adventures of Dick Tracy and Dick Tracy Jr. Book, 1933, Whitman, 320 pages, hardcover Big Little Book
EX $500   NM $1000   MIP $1500

Adventures of Dick Tracy the Detective Book, 1933, Whitman, first of Big Little Book series, hardcover
EX $850   NM $1400   MIP $2200

Booklet, 1934, Big Thrill Chewing Gum, five different premium books, eight pages, each
EX $75   NM $100   MIP $130

Capture of Boris Arson Book, The, 1935, Pleasure Books, pop-up book
EX $200   NM $400   MIP $750

Detective Dick Tracy and the Spider Gang Book, 1937, Whitman, 240 pages, Big Little Book
EX $75   NM $150   MIP $200

Dick Tracy and His G-Men Book, 1941, Whitman, 432 pages, Big Little Book, hardcover w/flip pictures
EX $75   NM $150   MIP $200

Dick Tracy and the Bicycle Gang Book, 1948, Whitman, 288 pages, Big Little Book, hardcover
EX $60   NM $120   MIP $180

Dick Tracy and the Boris Arson Gang Book, 1935, Whitman, 432 pages, Big Little Book, hardcover
EX $75   NM $150   MIP $200

Dick Tracy and the Hotel Murders Book, 1937, Whitman, 432 pages, hardcover Big Little Book
EX $60   NM $125   MIP $180

Dick Tracy and the Invisible Man Book, 1939, Whitman, Quaker premium, 132 pages, softcover Big Little Book
EX $100   NM $250   MIP $350

Dick Tracy and the Mad Killer Book, 1947, Whitman, 288 pages, hardcover Big Little Book
EX $40   NM $90   MIP $150

Dick Tracy and the Mystery of the Purple Cross Book, 1938, Whitman, 320 pages, Big Big Book, hardcover
EX $200   NM $400   MIP $800

Dick Tracy and the Phantom Ship Book, 1940, Whitman, 432 pages, hardcover Big Little Book
EX $45   NM $90   MIP $170

Dick Tracy and the Racketeer Gang Book, 1936, Whitman, 432 pages, hardcover Big Little Book
EX $60   NM $125   MIP $180

Dick Tracy and the Stolen Bonds Book, 1934, Whitman, 320 pages, hardcover, Big Little Book
EX $60   NM $125   MIP $180

Dick Tracy and the Tiger Lilly Gang Book, 1949, Whitman, 288 pages, hardcover Big Little Book
EX $35   NM $80   MIP $140

Dick Tracy and the Wreath Kidnapping Case Book, 1945, Whitman, 432 pages, hardcover Big Little Book
EX $40   NM $90   MIP $150

Dick Tracy and Yogee Yamma Book, 1946, Whitman, 352 pages, hardcover Big Little Book
EX $35   NM $80   MIP $135

Dick Tracy Encounters Facey Book, 1967, Whitman, 260 pages, hardcover Big Little Book, cover price 39 cents
EX $10   NM $15   MIP $30

Dick Tracy From Colorado to Nova Scotia Book, 1933, Whitman, 320 pages, hardcover Big Little Book
EX $50   NM $100   MIP $175

Dick Tracy in Chains of Crime Book, 1936, Whitman, 432 pages, hardcover, Big Little Book
EX $50   NM $100   MIP $180

(KP Photo)

Dick Tracy Junior Detective Kit Book, 1962, Golden Press, punchout book of Tracy tools, including badges, revolver, wrist radio
EX $25   NM $50   MIP $100

Dick Tracy Little Golden Book, 1962, Golden Press, features characters from the TV show
EX $20   NM $30   MIP $60

Dick Tracy Meets a New Gang Book, 1939, Whitman, Quaker premium, 132 pages, softcover Big Little Book
EX $100   NM $200   MIP $375

Dick Tracy on the High Seas Book, 1939, Whitman, 432 pages, hardcover Big Little Book
EX $50   NM $100   MIP $180

Dick Tracy on the Trail of Larceny Lu Book, 1935, Whitman, 432 pages, hardcover Big Little Book
EX $50   NM $100   MIP $175

Dick Tracy on Voodoo Island Book, 1944, Whitman, 352 pages, hardcover Big Little Book
EX $40   NM $75   MIP $150

Dick Tracy Out West Book, 1933, Whitman, 300 pages, hardcover, Big Little Book
EX $50   NM $100   MIP $180

(KP Photo)

Dick Tracy Paint Book, 1930s, Saalfield, 96 pages
EX $100   NM $200   MIP $400

Dick Tracy Returns Book, 1939, Whitman, 432 pages, hardcover Big Little Book, Republic movie serial tie-in
EX $50   NM $100   MIP $180

Dick Tracy Solves the Penfield Mystery Book, 1934, Whitman, 320 pages, hardcover, Big Little Book
EX $50   NM $100   MIP $180

Dick Tracy Special FBI Operative Book, 1943, Whitman, 432 pages, hardcover, Big Little Book
EX $40   NM $75   MIP $150

Dick Tracy Super Detective Book, 1941, Whitman
EX $35   NM $65   MIP $135

Dick Tracy the Man with No Face Book, 1938, Whitman, 432 pages, hardcover, Big Little Book
EX $50   NM $100   MIP $175

Dick Tracy the Super Detective Book, 1939, Whitman, 432 pages, hardcover Big Little Book
EX $50   NM $100   MIP $180

Dick Tracy vs. Crooks in Disguise Book, 1939, Whitman, 352 pages, hardcover, Big Little Book w/flip pictures
EX $50   NM $100   MIP $180

Dick Tracy's Ghost Ship Book, 1939, Whitman, Quaker premium, 132 pages, softcover Big Little Book
EX $100   NM $200   MIP $375

Secret Code Book, 1938, Quaker, premium
EX $50   NM $100   MIP $175

Secret Detective Methods and Magic Tricks Book, 1939, Quaker, cereal premium
EX $75   NM $175   MIP $250

BUTTON

Detective Button, 1930s, celluloid pinback w/portrait, newspaper premium
EX $25   NM $50   MIP $90

Dick Tracy and Little Orphan Annie Button, Genung Promo
EX $1000   NM $2400   MIP $3000

Pep Flintheart Pin, 1945, Kellogg's, tin litho button
EX $10   NM $20   MIP $45

Secret Service Patrol Member Button, 1938, Quaker, 1-1/4" blue and silver, pinback
EX $20   NM $45   MIP $90

COMIC BOOK

Dick Tracy Comic Book, 1947, Popped Wheat Cereal, premium
EX $6   NM $10   MIP $20

Dick Tracy in 3-D Comic Book, 1986, Blackthorne, Ocean Death Trap
EX $4   NM $8   MIP $15

Motorola Presents Dick Tracy Comic Book, 1953, Motorola, premium comic book w/paper mask and vest
EX $50   NM $100   MIP $175

DOLL

Bonny Braids Doll, 1950s, 6" tall, plastic, walking wobble doll
EX $30   NM $75   MIP $150

Bonny Braids Doll, 1951, Ideal, 14" tall w/toothbrush
EX $90   NM $180   MIP $375

Bonny Braids Doll, 1952, Ideal, 8" tall, crawls when wound
EX $80   NM $170   MIP $325

Dick Tracy Doll, 1930s, 13" tall, composition, grey trench coat w/moveable head and mouth that operates w/back pull string, gray or yellow coat
EX $200   NM $450   MIP $700

Little Honey Moon Doll, 1965, Ideal, 16" space baby, bubble helmet and outfit w/white pigtails, doll sitting on half a moon w/stars in the background
EX $200   NM $350   MIP $500

Sparkle Plenty Doll, 1947, Ideal, 12" tall
EX $125   NM $250   MIP $450

FIGURES

B.O. Plenty Figure, 1950s, Marx, Famous Comic Figures series, waxy cream, pink, 60mm tall
EX $20   NM $40   MIP $65

Blank Figure, The, 1990, Playmates, figure w/gun and hat w/featureless face attached
EX $60   NM $100   MIP $150

Breathless Mahoney Figure, 1990, Applause, 14" tall
EX $5   NM $10   MIP $20

Dick Tracy Figure, 1940s, Professional Art, 7" unpainted, detailed white chalk figure or painted
EX $80   NM $200   MIP $375

Dick Tracy Figures, 1950s, Marx, Famous Comic Figures series, several characters, each
EX $40   NM $75   MIP $150

Dick Tracy Nodder, 1960s, 6-1/2" tall, ceramic nodding head bust
EX $350   NM $800   MIP $1200

Gravel Gertie Figure, 1950s, Marx, Famous Comic Figures series
EX $12   NM $20   MIP $40

Sparkle Plenty Figure, 1950s, Marx, Famous Comic Figures series
EX $10   NM $15   MIP $50

Steve the Tramp Figure, 1990, Playmates, discontinued
EX $10   NM $20   MIP $40

GAME

Dick Tracy Bingo, Lock Them Up in Jail and Harmonize with Tracy Game, 1940s, object of each is to roll BBs into

different holes on the face of a glass framed game card for points
EX $45   **NM** $90   **MIP** $160

Dick Tracy Crime Stopper Game, 1963, Ideal, workstation contains crime indicator dial, decoder knobs, criminal buttons, clue cards and holders and clue windows
EX $40   **NM** $90   **MIP** $180

Dick Tracy Pinball Game, 1967, Marx, 14 x 24", shows characters from TV show pilot
EX $40   **NM** $90   **MIP** $175

Dick Tracy Pop-Pop Game, 1980s, Ja-Ru, Diet Smith and Flattop are targets
EX $10   **NM** $15   **MIP** $25

GUN

.45 Special Water Handgun, 1950s, Tops Plastics, plastic
EX $50   **NM** $100   **MIP** $160

Automatic Target Range Gun, 1967, Marx, BB gun mounted in an enclosed plastic shooting gallery
EX $60   **NM** $125   **MIP** $300

Dick Tracy Jr. Click Pistol #78, 1930s, Marx, aluminum
EX $75   **NM** $175   **MIP** $350

Luger Water Gun, 1971, Larami
EX $15   **NM** $35   **MIP** $90

Pop Gun, 1944, Tip Top Bread, 7-1/2" x 4-1/2" paper pop gun, premium
EX $50   **NM** $100   **MIP** $195

(KP Photo)

Power Jet Squad Gun, 1962, Mattel, 29" long cap and water rifle
EX $60   **NM** $120   **MIP** $220

Rapid Fire Tommy Gun, 1940s, Parker Johns, 20" long tommy gun w/Tracy on stock
EX $250   **NM** $400   **MIP** $600

Siren Pistol, 1930s, Marx, pressed steel, 8-1/2" long
EX $150   **NM** $425   **MIP** $675

Sub-Machine Gun, 1950s, Tops Plastics, 12" long, red, green or blue, water gun "holds over 500 shots on one filling," Dick Tracy decal on magazine
EX $100   **NM** $200   **MIP** $350

PIN

Bonny Braids Pin, 1951, Charmore, 1-1/4" figure plastic pin on full color card
EX $20   **NM** $60   **MIP** $100

Pep B.O. Plenty Pin, 1945, Kellogg's, tin litho button
EX $20   **NM** $30   **MIP** $50

Pep Chief Brandon Pin, 1945, Kellogg's, tin litho button
EX $10   **NM** $15   **MIP** $30

Pep Dick Tracy Pin, 1945, Kellogg's, tin litho button
EX $25   **NM** $45   **MIP** $80

Pep Flattop Pin, 1945, Kellogg's, tin litho button
EX $20   **NM** $35   **MIP** $60

Pep Gravel Gertie Pin, 1945, Kellogg's, tin litho button
EX $20   **NM** $35   **MIP** $50

Pep Junior Tracy Pin, 1945, Kellogg's, tin litho button
EX $10   **NM** $20   **MIP** $40

Pep Pat Patten Pin, 1945, Kellogg's, tin litho button
EX $10   **NM** $20   **MIP** $35

Pep Tess Trueheart Pin, 1945, Kellogg's, tin litho button
EX $12   **NM** $20   **MIP** $35

Secret Service Patrol Leader Pin, 1938, Quaker, litho bar pin, Patrol Leader, rare
EX $600   **NM** $1000   **MIP** $1200

RECORD

Dick Tracy Original Radio Broadcast Album, 1972, Coca-Cola, presents the cast from "The Case of the Firebug Murders" radio show
EX $20   **NM** $60   **MIP** $80

Flattop Story Double Record Set, 1947, Mercury Records, record, book, comics
EX $65   **NM** $125   **MIP** $225

RING

Dick Tracy Monogram Ring, 1938, Quaker, ring shows initials only, no Tracy name or picture
EX $175   **NM** $400   **MIP** $600

Dick Tracy Ring, 1940s, Miller Bros. Hat, enameled portrait
EX $60   **NM** $100   **MIP** $200

Dick Tracy Service Patrol Ring, 1966, premium
EX $20   **NM** $40   **MIP** $60

Secret Compartment Ring, 1938, Quaker, removable cover picturing Tracy and good luck symbols
EX $100   **NM** $200   **MIP** $300

TOY

Auto Magic Picture Gun, 1950s, 6-1/2" x 9" metal picture gun and filmstrip
EX $30   **NM** $100   **MIP** $175

(KP Photo)

Automatic Police Station, 1950s, Marx, tin litho police station and car
EX $500   **NM** $800   **MIP** $1500

(Scott Smiles)

B.O. Plenty Walker, 1940s, Marx, holds Sparkle Plenty
EX $175   **NM** $300   **MIP** $500

B.O. Plenty Wind-Up, 1940s, Marx, 8-1/2" tall holding baby Sparkle, litho tin, walks, hat tips up and down when key is wound
EX $150   **NM** $300   **MIP** $700

(KP Photo)

Baby Sparkle Plenty Paper Dolls, 1948, Saalfield, #1510, on cover, Baby Sparkle is standing by a clothes line
EX $22   **NM** $75   **MIP** $150

(KP Photo)

Baking Set, 1937, Pillsbury, cookie cutter, six press-out sheets w/pictures of Dick Tracy and his pals
EX $75   **NM** $150   **MIP** $245

Big Boy Figure, 1990, Playmates
EX $6   **NM** $12   **MIP** $25

Black Light Magic Kit, 1952, Stroward, ultra-violet bulb, cloth, invisible pen, brushes and fluorescent dyes
EX $75   **NM** $125   **MIP** $250

(KP Photo)

Bonny Braids Paper Dolls, 1951, Saalfield, #1559, Dick Tracy's new daughter and Tess
EX $50   NM $100   MIP $200

Bonny Braids Stroll Toy, 1951, Charmore, tin litho, Bonny doll in carriage
EX $35   NM $80   MIP $175

Camera Dart Gun, 1971, Larami, 8mm camera-shaped toy w/dart-shooting viewer
EX $30   NM $70   MIP $150

Coloring Set, 1967, Hasbro, six pre-sketched, numbered pictures to color, w/pencils
EX $30   NM $70   MIP $140

Crimestopper Club Kit, 1961, Chicago Tribune, premium kit containing badge, whistle, decoder, magnifying glass, fingerprinting kit, ID card, crimestopper textbook
EX $35   NM $60   MIP $100

(KP Photo)

Crimestopper Play Set, 1970s, Hubley, Dick Tracy cap gun, holster, handcuffs, wallet, flashlight, badge and magnifying glass
EX $35   NM $70   MIP $50

Crimestoppers Set, 1973, Larami, handcuffs, nightstick and badge
EX $12   NM $25   MIP $50

Decoder Card, Post Cereal, cereal premium, red or green
EX $30   NM $50   MIP $100

Detective Club Belt, 1937, leather w/secret pouch
EX $75   NM $225   MIP $400

Detective Kit, 1944, Dick Tracy Junior Detective Manual, Secret Decoder, ruler, Certificate of Membership and badge
EX $175   NM $400   MIP $700

Dick Tracy Braces, 1940s, Deluxe, Chicago Tribune premium, suspenders on colorful card
EX $50   NM $100   MIP $185

(KP Photo)

Dick Tracy Braces for Smart Boys and Girls, 1950s, Deluxe, Police badge, metal handcuffs, whistle, suspenders w/a Dick Tracy badge as a holder and magnifying glass
EX $50   NM $100   MIP $175

(KP Photo)

Dick Tracy Candid Camera, 1950s, Seymour Sales, w/50mm lens, plastic carrying case and 127 film
EX $60   NM $125   MIP $200

Dick Tracy Cartoon Kit, 1962, Colorforms
EX $20   NM $45   MIP $90

Dick Tracy Crime Lab, 1980s, Ja-Ru, click pistol, fingerprint pad, badge and magnifying glass, available in orange and bright yellow
EX $8   NM $15   MIP $30

Dick Tracy Crime Stoppers Laboratory, 1955, Porter Chemical, 60 power microscope, fingerprint pack, glass slides and magnifying glass and textbook
EX $150   NM $250   MIP $450

Dick Tracy Detective Club Wrist Radios, 1945, Gaylord
EX $85   NM $180   MIP $375

(KP Photo)

Dick Tracy Detective Set, 1930s, Pressman, color graphics of Junior and Dick Tracy, ink roller, glass plate, and Dick Tracy fingerprint record paper
EX $150   NM $225   MIP $400

Dick Tracy Figure, Lakeside, bendy
EX $15   NM $30   MIP $50

Dick Tracy Hand Puppet, 1961, Ideal, 10-1/2", fabric and vinyl, w/record
EX $35   NM $80   MIP $150

Dick Tracy Jr. Bombsight, 1940s, Miller Bros. Hat, cardboard
EX $50   NM $80   MIP $175

Dick Tracy Play Set, 1973, Ideal, contains 18 cardboard figures that measure 3-1/2" to 5" tall, w/carrying case
EX $50   NM $120   MIP $225

Dick Tracy Play Set, 1982, Placo, plastic dart gun, targets of different villians and a set of handcuffs
EX $10   NM $30   MIP $50

Dick Tracy Puzzle, 1952, 11" x 14" frame tray
EX $25   NM $85   MIP $150

Dick Tracy Soaky, 1965, Colgate-Palmolive, 10" tall
EX $25   NM $60   MIP $100

Dick Tracy Sparkle Paints, 1963, Kenner, paints, brushes and six pictures to paint
EX $25   NM $50   MIP $100

Dick Tracy Target, 1941, Marx, 10" square tin litho w/"Recovery" and "Rescuing" points on front and bullseye target on back
EX $75   NM $200   MIP $325

Dick Tracy Target Game, 1940s, Marx, 17" circular cardboard target, w/dart gun and box
EX $150   NM $350   MIP $525

(KP Photo)

Dick Tracy Target Set, 1969, Larami, red, green or blue; shoots rubber bands
EX $15   NM $35   MIP $75

Dick Tracy's Two-in-One Mystery Puzzle, 1958, Jaymar, one puzzle shows the crime and the other the solution
EX $30   NM $60   MIP $120

Famous Funnies Deluxe Printing Set, 1930s, 14 stamps, paper and stamp pad, in illustrated box
EX $80   NM $125   MIP $225

Favorite Funnies Printing Set, 1935, Stampercraft, features Tracy and other cartoon characters
EX $80   NM $110   MIP $180

Film Strip Viewer, 1948, Acme, viewer and two films in colorful illustrated box
EX $100   NM $175   MIP $225

(KP Photo)

Film Strip Viewer, 1964, Acme, viewer w/two boxes of film, on card, jumbo movie style
EX $20   **NM** $45   **MIP** $90

Film Viewer, 1973, Larami, mini color televiewer w/two paper filmstrips
EX $10   **NM** $20   **MIP** $50

Fingerprint Set, 1933, Pressman, microscope, fingerprint pad, magnifying glass and badge
EX $150   **NM** $300   **MIP** $475

Flashlight, 1939, Quaker, red, green, and black; bullet shaped w/shield tag, pocket size
EX $60   **NM** $175   **MIP** $300

Flashlight, 1939, Quaker, 3" pen light, black
EX $50   **NM** $120   **MIP** $250

Flashlight, 1961, Bantam Lite, metal wrist light
EX $25   **NM** $55   **MIP** $150

Handcuffs, 1946, John Henry, metal toy handcuffs on display header card
EX $25   **NM** $55   **MIP** $110

Hemlock Holmes Hand Puppet, 1961, Ideal, includes record
EX $40   **NM** $90   **MIP** $175

Hingees "Dick Tracy and his Friends to Life" Punch-outs, 1944, Reed and Associates, 6-1/2" tall figures, Tess Trueheart, Chief Brandon, Junior, Pat Patton and Tracy
EX $25   **NM** $75   **MIP** $125

Joe Jitsu Hand Puppet, 1961, Ideal, 10-1/2", fabric and vinyl, includes record
EX $45   **NM** $150   **MIP** $250

Junior Detective Kit, 1944, Sweets Company, certificate, secret code dial, wall chart, file cards and tape measure
EX $70   **NM** $250   **MIP** $425

Junior Dick Tracy Crime Detection Folio, 1942, radio premium, contained detective's notebook, decoder w/three mystery sheets, and puzzle
EX $70   **NM** $200   **MIP** $425

Mobile Commander, 1973, Larami, toy telephone w/plastic connecting tube, plastic gun and badge
EX $20   **NM** $40   **MIP** $100

Offical Holster Outfit, 1940s, Classy Products, leather holster w/painted Tracy profile
EX $150   **NM** $300   **MIP** $450

Playstone Funnies Kasting Kit, 1930s, Allied, molds for casting figures of Tracy and other characters
EX $40   **NM** $80   **MIP** $150

Police Whistle No. 64, Marx, tin
EX $20   **NM** $40   **MIP** $80

Puzzle, "Dick Tracy's New Daughter", 1951, Saalfield, tray puzzle of Bonny Braids
EX $22   **NM** $65   **MIP** $125

Puzzle, "The Bank Holdup", 1960s, Jaymar, triple-thick interlocking pieces featuring the TV cartoon
EX $20   **NM** $65   **MIP** $110

Puzzles, Dick Tracy Big Little Book Picture Puzzles, 1938, Whitman, 8" x 10" x 2" contains two puzzles of BLB scenes
EX $250   **NM** $350   **MIP** $550

Secret Code Writer and Pencil, 1939
EX $100   **NM** $150   **MIP** $275

Secret Detector Kit, 1938, Quaker, Secret Formula Q-11 and negatives
EX $200   **NM** $400   **MIP** $600

Secret Service Phones, 1938, Quaker, cardboard phones, walkie talkie type
EX $100   **NM** $200   **MIP** $340

Shoulder Holster Set, 1950s, J. Hapern, leather holster w/Dick Tracy's profile
EX $45   **NM** $90   **MIP** $185

Sparkle Plenty Islander Ukette, 1950, Styron, musical instrument, junior size, w/instruction book
EX $60   **NM** $130   **MIP** $300

Sparkle Plenty Washing Machine, 1940s, Kalon Radio, 12" tall tin litho, pictured outside on tub is Gravel Gertie doing the wash as B.O. Plenty holds baby Sparkle
EX $125   **NM** $200   **MIP** $400

Talking Phone, 1967, Marx, green w/ivory handle, battery-operated w/10 different phrases
EX $35   **NM** $75   **MIP** $125

Transistor Radio Receivers, 1961, American Doll and Toy, shoulder holster and secret ear plug w/two transistor radio receivers
EX $40   **NM** $80   **MIP** $160

(KP Photo)

Two-Way Electronic Wrist Radios, 1950s, Remco, 2-1/2" x 9 1/2" x 13-1/2", plastic battery-operated wrist radios
EX $80   **NM** $150   **MIP** $250

Two-Way Wrist Radios, 1960s, American Doll and Toy, plastic w/power pack, battery-operated
EX $50   **NM** $100   **MIP** $185

Two-Way Wrist Radios, 1990, Ertl, battery-operated
EX $15   **NM** $20   **MIP** $30

Wrist Band AM Radio, 1976, Creative Creations, w/earphone and two mercury batteries; box shows Tracy and Flattop
EX $30   **NM** $65   **MIP** $150

(KP Photo)

Wrist Radio, 1947, Da-Myco Products, crystal set w/receiver on a leather band, 30" wires and connectors for aerial and ground, no batteries, no tubes and no electric
EX $350   **NM** $500   **MIP** $750

Wrist TV, 1980s, Ja-Ru, paper roll of cartoon strips are threaded through the TV viewer
EX $10   **NM** $20   **MIP** $40

VEHICLE

(KP Photo)

Convertible Squad Car, 1948, Marx, 20", friction power w/flashing lights
EX $300   **NM** $450   **MIP** $800

Copmobile, 1963, Ideal, 24" long, white and blue plastic, battery-operated w/a microphone w/amplified speaker on top
EX $100   **NM** $200   **MIP** $400

Dick Tracy Car, 1950s, Marx, 6-1/2" long, light blue w/machine gun pointing out of the front window
EX $125   **NM** $275   **MIP** $475

Get Away Car, 1990, Playmates
EX $15   **NM** $25   **MIP** $50

(KP Photo)

Space Coupe, 1968, Aurora, assembly required, all plastic
EX $150   **NM** $350   **MIP** $600

WATCH

Dick Tracy Two-Way Wristwatch, 1990, Playmates, watch w/no radio function
EX $4   **NM** $7   **MIP** $20

CHARACTER TOYS

Dick Tracy Wristwatch, 1937, New Haven, oblong, round, or square face, in box
EX $300 NM $600 MIP $1000

Dick Tracy Wristwatch, 1959, Bradley
EX $50 NM $100 MIP $210

Dick Tracy Wristwatch, 1981, Omni, digital; police car box
EX $15 NM $40 MIP $90

Dick Tracy Wristwatch with Animated Gun, 1951, New Haven
EX $200 NM $450 MIP $750

DISNEY

ACCESSORIES

Disney Figure Golf Balls, set of twelve
EX $12 NM $23 MIP $35

Disney Filmstrips, 1940s, Craftman's Guild, 13 color filmstrips
EX $95 NM $180 MIP $275

Disney Tin Tray, Ohio Art, 8" x 10", pictures Mickey and Minnie Mouse, Goofy, Horace, Pluto, Donald Duck and Clarabelle
EX $25 NM $50 MIP $85

Disney World Globe, 1950s, Rand McNally, 6-1/2" metal base, 8" diameter w/Disney characters
EX $60 NM $125 MIP $200

Disneyland Ashtray, 1950s, 5" diameter, china, w/Tinker Bell and castle
EX $20 NM $65 MIP $150

Disneyland Electric Light, 1950s, Econlite, picture of Disney characters leaving a bus on a drum base
EX $45 NM $80 MIP $235

Disneyland Felt Banner, 1960s, Disney, "The Magic Kingdom," 24-1/2" red/white/blue coat of arms
EX $25 NM $60 MIP $90

(KP Photo)

Disneyland Give-A-Show Projector Color Slides, 1960s, 112 color slides
EX $85 NM $140 MIP $250

Disneyland Metal Craft Tapping Set, 1950s, Pressman
EX $25 NM $40 MIP $100

Disneyland Miniature License Plates, 1966, Marx, 2" x 4" plates w/Mickey, Minnie and Pluto, or Snow White, Donald and Goofy, each
EX $12 NM $23 MIP $35

Disneyland Pen, 1960s, 6" long w/a picture of a floating riverboat
EX $15 NM $25 MIP $40

Duck Tales Travel Tote, 1980s, travel agency premium
EX $5 NM $20 MIP $35

Fantasia Bowl, 1940, Vernon Kilns, 12" diameter and 2-1/2" tall, pink bowl w/a winged nymph from Fantasia
EX $150 NM $300 MIP $475

Fantasia Cup and Saucer Set, 1940, Vernon Kilns, 6-1/4" diameter saucer and 2" tall cup
EX $70 NM $160 MIP $235

Fantasia Musical Jewelry Box, 1990, Schmid Bros., box features Mickey and plays "The Sorcerer's Apprentice"
EX $30 NM $55 MIP $90

Figural Light Switch Plates, Monogram, hand-painted switch plates: Goofy, Donald, Mickey, on card, each
EX $6 NM $12 MIP $25

Happy Birthday/Pepsi Placemats, 1978, Pepsi, set of four mats
EX $15 NM $35 MIP $60

Lap Trays, 1960s, Hasko, set of four: Donald, Goofy and Pluto, Peter Pan, and the Seven Dwarfs
EX $35 NM $65 MIP $150

Silly Symphony Lights, Noma, set of eight
EX $100 NM $150 MIP $375

BANK

Color Television Bank, 1950s, Linemar, 4" x 4-1/2", tin, Mickey or Donald on side panels, litho screen rotates
EX $200 NM $400 MIP $600

Disneyland Haunted House Bank, 1960s, Japanese
EX $35 NM $65 MIP $225

Second National Duck Bank, Chein, 3-1/2" tall x 7" long
EX $100 NM $200 MIP $375

BOOK

Robin Hood of the Range Better Little Book, 1942, Whitman
EX $20 NM $50 MIP $100

Toby Tyler Circus Playbook, 1959, Whitman, punch-out character activity book
EX $25 NM $50 MIP $100

Walt Disney's Clock Cleaners Book, 1938, Whitman, linen-like illustrated book
EX $85 NM $175 MIP $250

FIGURES

Aristocats Thomas O'Malley Figure, 1967, Enesco, 8" tall ceramic
EX $30 NM $65 MIP $125

Fantasia Figure, Vernon Kilns, half-woman, half-zebra centaur
EX $85 NM $180 MIP $400

Fantasia Unicorn Figure, 1940s, Vernon Kilns, ceramic black-winged unicorn
EX $75 NM $110 MIP $250

Johnny Tremain Figure and Horse, 1957, Marx, plastic, 9-1/2" tall horse and 5-1/2" tall Johnny
EX $80 NM $120 MIP $225

Jose Carioca Figure, Marx, 2" tall, plastic
EX $30 NM $55 MIP $80

Jose Carioca Figure, 1960s, Marx, 5-1/2" tall plastic, wire arms and legs
EX $50 NM $110 MIP $200

GAME

Disneyland Bagatelle, 1970s, Wolverine, large game w/Disneyland graphics
EX $15 NM $25 MIP $100

Walt Disney's Game/Parade/Academy Award Winners, American Toy Works, 15 games for all ages
EX $60 NM $120 MIP $185

PUZZLE

Black Hole Puzzle, 1979, Whitman, jigsaw puzzle, V.I.N.C.E.N.T. or Cygnus
EX $15 NM $30 MIP $85

Disney "Sea Scouts" Puzzle, 1930s, Williams Ellis
EX $100 NM $175 MIP $225

Disneyland Puzzle, 1956, Whitman, frame tray
EX $20 NM $50 MIP $100

TOY

Carousel, Linemar, 7" tall w/3" figures, wind-up
EX $200 NM $350 MIP $500

Casey Jr. Disneyland Express Train, 1950s, Marx, 12" long, tin, wind-up
EX $200 NM $300 MIP $550

Character Molding and Coloring Set, 1950s, red rubber molds of Bambi, Thumper, Dumbo, Goofy, Flower and Jose Carioca to make plaster figures
EX $35 NM $75 MIP $150

Disney Rattle, 1930s, Noma, 4" tall w/Mickey and Minnie, Donald and Pluto carrying a Christmas tree
EX $100 NM $150 MIP $300

Disney Shooting Gallery, 1950s, Welso Toys, 8" x 12" x 1-1/2" tin target w/molded figures of Mickey, Donald, Goofy and Pluto
EX $75 NM $150 MIP $300

Disney Treasure Chest Set, 1940s, Craftman's Guild, red plastic film viewer and filmstrips in blue box designed like a chest
EX $70 NM $145 MIP $210

Disneyland Auto Magic Picture Gun and Theater, 1950s, battery-operated metal gun w/oval filmstrip
EX $50 NM $90 MIP $150

Disneyland F.D. Fire Truck, Linemar, 18" long, battery-operated, moveable, Donald Duck fireman climbs the ladder
EX $250 NM $400 MIP $600

Early Settlers Log Set, 1960s, Halsam, log building set based on Disneyland's Tom Sawyer's Island
EX $40   **NM** $75   **MIP** $150

Horace Horsecollar Hand Puppet, 1950s, Gund
EX $30   **NM** $75   **MIP** $150

Jose Carioca Wind-Up Toy, 1940s, France, 3-1/2" x 5" x 7-1/2" tall
EX $100   **NM** $300   **MIP** $450

Nautilus Expanding Periscope, 1954, Pressman, inspired by 20,000 Leagues Under the Sea, 19" long
EX $75   **NM** $160   **MIP** $250

(KP Photo)

Nautilus Wind-Up Submarine, 1950s, Sutcliffe/England
EX $150   **NM** $250   **MIP** $475

Official Santa Fe and Disneyland R.R. Scale Model Train, 1966, Tyco, HO scale, electric
EX $200   **NM** $350   **MIP** $600

Pecos Bill Wind-Up Toy, 1950s, Marx, 10" tall, riding his horse Widowmaker and holding a metal lasso
EX $75   **NM** $200   **MIP** $400

Sand Pail and Shovel, 1930s, Ohio Art, features pie-eyed Mickey selling cold drinks to Pluto, Minnie and Clarabelle
EX $35   **NM** $110   **MIP** $275

Walt Disney Movie Viewer and Cartridge, 1972, Action Films, #9312 w/the cartridge "Lonesome Ghosts"
EX $10   **NM** $16   **MIP** $35

Walt Disney's Character Scramble, 1940s, Plane Facts, 10 cardboard figures, 6" tall
EX $30   **NM** $70   **MIP** $175

Walt Disney's Realistic Noah's Ark, 1940s, W.H. Greene, 6" x 7" x 18" Ark, 101 2" animals, and 4" human figures on cardboard
EX $150   **NM** $350   **MIP** $700

Walt Disney's Silly Symphony Bells, Noma, Christmas tree bells
EX $60   **NM** $125   **MIP** $275

Walt Disney's Snap-Eeze Set, 1963, Marx, 12-1/2" x 15" x 1" box w/12 flat plastic figures
EX $60   **NM** $115   **MIP** $275

Walt Disney's Television Car, Marx, 8" long, friction toy lights up a picture on the roof when motor turns
EX $500   **NM** $750   **MIP** $1500

DOC SAVAGE

ACCESSORIES

Club Card, 1930s
EX $150   **NM** $200   **MIP** $300

Club Kit, 1975, comics premium; includes card, button and mailer
EX $40   **NM** $75   **MIP** $150

Club Mailer for Pin, 1930s
EX $250   **NM** $300   **MIP** $400

Club Pin, 1930s, Pulp premium, brass
EX $100   **NM** $225   **MIP** $375

Medal of Honor Award, 1930s, brass
EX $2000   **NM** $3600   **MIP** $6000

DONALD DUCK

ACCESSORIES

Donald Duck Alarm Clock, 1950s, Glen Clock/Scotland, 5-1/2" x 5-1/2" x 2", Donald pictured w/blue bird on his hand
EX $150   **NM** $300   **MIP** $675

Donald Duck Alarm Clock, 1960s, Bayard, 2" x 4-1/2" x 5"
EX $125   **NM** $275   **MIP** $600

Donald Duck Lamp, 1940s, 9" tall, china, Donald holding an axe standing next to a tree trunk
EX $150   **NM** $275   **MIP** $425

Donald Duck Lamp, 1970s, Dolly Toy, Donald on a tug boat
EX $75   **NM** $150   **MIP** $250

Donald Duck Light Switch Cover, 1976, Dolly Toy, plastic, Donald on a boat
EX $5   **NM** $10   **MIP** $25

Donald Duck Music Box, 1971, Anri, Donald w/guitar, plays "My Way"
EX $75   **NM** $100   **MIP** $200

Donald Duck Pinback, 1930s, Wanna Fight movie premium
EX $250   **NM** $650   **MIP** $875

Donald Duck Pinback, 1935, Jackets premium, cello
EX $250   **NM** $650   **MIP** $875

Donald Duck Soap, Disney, figural castile soap
EX $40   **NM** $70   **MIP** $140

Donald Duck Toothbrush Holder, 1930s, bisque, figural
EX $200   **NM** $450   **MIP** $725

Donald Duck Umbrella Holder, 1930s, 3-1/4" tall
EX $100   **NM** $200   **MIP** $350

Donald Duck WWI Pencil Box, Dixon, 5" x 8-1/2" x 1-1/4" deep, Donald flying a plane, holding a tomahawk
EX $50   **NM** $125   **MIP** $250

Ludwig Von Drake Wonderful World of Color Pencil Box, 1961, Hasbro, box shows Ludwig and the nephews
EX $25   **NM** $55   **MIP** $85

Uncle Scrooge Wallet, 1970s, 3" x 4", Uncle Scrooge tossing coins
EX $20   **NM** $40   **MIP** $85

BANK

Donald Duck Bank, 1938, Crown Toy, 6" tall, composition, movable head
EX $150   **NM** $400   **MIP** $600

Donald Duck Bank, 1940s, 5-1/2" x 6" x 7-1/2" tall, china, Donald seated holding a coin in one hand
EX $75   **NM** $200   **MIP** $325

Donald Duck Bank, 1940s, 4-1/2" x 4-1/2" x 6-1/2" tall, ceramic, Donald holding a rope w/a large brown fish by his side
EX $50   **NM** $100   **MIP** $250

Donald Duck Telephone Bank, 1938, N.N. Hill Brass, 5" tall w/cardboard figure
EX $85   **NM** $225   **MIP** $375

DOLL

Donald Duck Doll, 1938, Knickerbocker, 17" tall, red jacket, black plush hat, Donald as drum major
EX $550   **NM** $1250   **MIP** $1700

Donald Duck Doll, 1976, Mattel, talking doll
EX $75   **NM** $250   **MIP** $425

Huey, Dewey and Louie Dolls, 1950s, Gund, set of three 8" tall dolls
EX $65   **NM** $125   **MIP** $350

Louie Doll, 1940s, Gund, 8" tall, white/light green plush
EX $40   **NM** $70   **MIP** $115

FIGURES

Donald Duck Figure, Seiberling, 6" tall, hollow rubber w/squeaker in the base
EX $175   **NM** $260   **MIP** $500

Donald Duck Figure, Seiberling, 6" tall, solid rubber w/movable head
EX $175   **NM** $260   **MIP** $500

Donald Duck Figure, Seiberling, 5" tall, rubber
EX $175   **NM** $260   **MIP** $500

Donald Duck Figure, 1930s, Japanese, celluloid, long-billed Donald
EX $100   **NM** $350   **MIP** $650

Donald Duck Figure, 1950s, Dell, 7" tall, rubber
EX $75   **NM** $150   **MIP** $250

Donald Duck Fun-E-Flex Figure, 1930s, Fun-E-Flex, wooden Donald on red sled w/rope
EX $100   **NM** $200   **MIP** $500

Donald Duck Nodder, 1960s, 5-1/2" tall on green base
EX $50   **NM** $150   **MIP** $200

Ludwig Von Drake Figure, 1961, Marx, 3" tall, from the "Snap-Eeze" collection
EX $10   **NM** $20   **MIP** $40

CHARACTER TOYS

TOY

Carpet Sweeper, 1930s, Ohio Art, 3" w/wooden handle, Donald Duck and Minnie Mouse
EX $50   **NM** $125   **MIP** $250

Crayon Box, 1946, Transogram, tin, pictures Donald and Mickey
EX $30   **NM** $55   **MIP** $150

Donald and Donna Duck, 1937, Fisher-Price, 14" long, wooden, rare, Donald plays xylophone, Donna glides back and forth w/rubber wings, Donna became Daisy hence its rarity
EX $2000   **NM** $3500   **MIP** $5000

Donald Duck and Pluto Car, Sun Rubber, 6-1/2" long, hard rubber, blue
EX $50   **NM** $125   **MIP** $375

Donald Duck Bicycle, 1949, Shelby
EX $2500   **NM** $4500   **MIP** $8000

Donald Duck Camera, 1950s, Herbert-George, 3" x 4" x 3"
EX $60   **NM** $150   **MIP** $300

Donald Duck Car, 1950s, Sun Rubber, 2-1/2" x 3-1/2" x 6-1/2", rubber
EX $40   **NM** $110   **MIP** $375

Donald Duck Driving Pluto Toy, 9" long, wind-up, celluloid
EX $500   **NM** $800   **MIP** $1600

Donald Duck Dump Truck, 1950s, Linemar
EX $150   **NM** $275   **MIP** $525

Donald Duck Funnee Movie Set, 1940, Transogram, box features Donald, Mickey, and the nephews
EX $75   **NM** $200   **MIP** $300

Donald Duck Funnee Movie Set, 1949, Irwin, hand-crank viewer and four films in box
EX $85   **NM** $150   **MIP** $250

Donald Duck Marionette, 1950s, Peter Puppet, 6-1/2" tall
EX $50   **NM** $150   **MIP** $250

Donald Duck Paint Box, 1938, Transogram
EX $40   **NM** $120   **MIP** $275

Donald Duck Projector, 1950s, Stephens, projector w/four films
EX $55   **NM** $125   **MIP** $250

Donald Duck Puppet, 1960s, Pelham Puppets, 10" tall, hollow composition
EX $40   **NM** $75   **MIP** $200

Donald Duck Push Puppet, 1950s, Kohner, sailor Donald
EX $30   **NM** $100   **MIP** $160

Donald Duck Push Toy, 1950s, Gong Bell
EX $35   **NM** $60   **MIP** $100

Donald Duck Puzzle, 1940s, Jaymar, frame tray
EX $50   **NM** $100   **MIP** $175

Donald Duck Ramp Walker, 1950s, Marx, 1-1/4" x 3-1/2" x 3" tall, Donald is pulling red wagon w/his nephews
EX $110   **NM** $175   **MIP** $325

Donald Duck Sand Pail, 1939, Ohio Art, 4-1/2" tall, tin, Donald at beach playing tug-of-war w/his two nephews
EX $60   **NM** $120   **MIP** $300

Donald Duck Sand Pail, 1950s, Ohio Art, 3-1/2" tall, tin, Donald in life preserver fighting off seagulls
EX $65   **NM** $175   **MIP** $300

Donald Duck Scooter, 1960s, Marx, tin wind-up, 4" x 4" x 2"
EX $150   **NM** $250   **MIP** $350

Donald Duck Skating Rink Toy, 1950s, Mettoy, 4" diameter, Donald is skating while other Disney characters circle the rink
EX $40   **NM** $70   **MIP** $160

Donald Duck Sled, 1935, S.L. Allen, 36" long wooden slat and metal runner sled w/character decals, Donald and nephews
EX $400   **NM** $650   **MIP** $1200

Donald Duck Snow Shovel, Ohio Art, wood, tin, litho
EX $60   **NM** $130   **MIP** $250

Donald Duck Soaky, 1950s, 7" tall
EX $15   **NM** $50   **MIP** $100

Donald Duck Squeeze Toy, 1960s, Dell, 8" tall, rubber
EX $15   **NM** $40   **MIP** $80

Donald Duck Tea Set, Ohio Art, 7-1/2" tray, 2-1/4" diameter cups, saucers
EX $100   **NM** $175   **MIP** $250

Donald Duck the Drummer, 1940s, Marx, 5" x" 7 x 10" tall, Donald beats on a metal drum
EX $300   **NM** $500   **MIP** $725

Donald Duck Toy, Schuco, 5-1/2" tall, wind-up w/a bellows, quacking sound
EX $350   **NM** $700   **MIP** $1000

Donald Duck Toy Raft, 1950s, Ideal, 2" tall, blue plastic raft w/yellow sail w/Donald looking through a telescope
EX $400   **NM** $75   **MIP** $110

Donald Duck Trapeze Toy, Linemar, 5" tall, celluloid, wind-up
EX $60   **NM** $200   **MIP** $600

Donald Duck Watering Can, 1938, Ohio Art, 6" tall, tin litho
EX $25   **NM** $75   **MIP** $175

Donald Duck Wind-Up, 1972, Durham Plastic, 6-1/2" tall, hard plastic
EX $15   **NM** $40   **MIP** $85

Donald Tricycle Toy, 1950s, Linemar, tin
EX $500   **NM** $800   **MIP** $1200

Ludwig Von Drake in Go Cart, 1960s, Linemar, tin and plastic
EX $115   **NM** $250   **MIP** $500

Ludwig Von Drake Mug, 1961, 3-1/2" white china
EX $15   **NM** $20   **MIP** $50

Ludwig Von Drake Squeeze Toy, 1961, Dell, 8" tall, rubber
EX $10   **NM** $20   **MIP** $50

Ludwig Von Drake Tiddly Winks, 1961, Whitman
EX $10   **NM** $20   **MIP** $60

WATCH

Daisy Duck Wristwatch, 1948, US Time
EX $275   **NM** $550   **MIP** $875

Donald Duck Wristwatch, 1940s, US Time
EX $275   **NM** $550   **MIP** $950

DR. DOOLITTLE

FIGURES

Dr. Doolittle Figure, 1967, Mattel, 5" tall w/parrot
EX $15   **NM** $30   **MIP** $50

Dr. Doolittle Figure, 1967, Mattel, 7" tall
EX $15   **NM** $35   **MIP** $75

TOY

Dr. Doolittle Giraffe-in-the-Box, jack-in-the-box
EX $50   **NM** $100   **MIP** $200

DR. SEUSS

ACCESSORIES

Mattel-O-Phone, 1970, Mattel
EX $40   **NM** $75   **MIP** $225

DOLL

Cat in the Hat Doll, 1983, Coleco, plush
EX $10   **NM** $40   **MIP** $90

Grinch Doll, 1983, Coleco
EX $55   **NM** $110   **MIP** $300

Horton the Elephant Doll, 1983, Coleco
EX $25   **NM** $65   **MIP** $135

(KP Photo)

Lorax Doll, 1983, Coleco
EX $25   **NM** $65   **MIP** $135

Star-Bellied Sneetch Doll, 1983, Coleco
EX $40   **NM** $70   **MIP** $140

Talking Cat in the Hat Doll, 1970, Mattel
EX $60   **NM** $175   **MIP** $300

Talking Hedwig Doll, 1970, Mattel
EX $50   **NM** $125   **MIP** $250

Talking Horton Doll, 1970, Mattel
EX $60   **NM** $175   **MIP** $350

(KP Photo)

Thidwick the Moose Doll, 1983, Coleco
   EX $15   **NM** $40   **MIP** $90

(KP Photo)

Yertle the Turtle Doll, 1983, Coleco,
   12" plush
   EX $15   **NM** $45   **MIP** $100

TOY

Cat in the Hat Ge-Tar, 1970, Mattel
   EX $40   **NM** $110   **MIP** $220

Cat in the Hat Jack-in-the-Box, 1969, Mattel
   EX $100   **NM** $180   **MIP** $310

Cat in the Hat Riding Toy, 1983, Coleco
   EX $25   **NM** $50   **MIP** $135

Cat in the Hat Rocking Toy, 1983, Coleco
   EX $25   **NM** $50   **MIP** $135

Cat in the Hat Talking Puppet, 1970,
   Mattel, vinyl head
   EX $75   **NM** $125   **MIP** $300

DUMBO

ACCESSORIES

Dumbo Christmas Ornament, 2" porcelain
   bisque, 50th anniversary
   EX $8   **NM** $15   **MIP** $35

Dumbo Milk Pitcher, 1940s, 6" tall
   EX $65   **NM** $110   **MIP** $250

DOLL

Dumbo Doll, 12" plush
   EX $10   **NM** $20   **MIP** $50

FIGURES

Dumbo Figure, Dakin
   EX $12   **NM** $25   **MIP** $50

TOY

Dumbo Roll Over Wind-Up Toy, 1941,
   Marx, 4" tall, tin w/tumbling action
   EX $175   **NM** $350   **MIP** $675

Dumbo Squeeze Toy, 1950s, Dell, 5" tall
   EX $15   **NM** $30   **MIP** $75

ELMER FUDD

ACCESSORIES

Elmer Fudd Mini Snow Dome, 1980s,
   Applause
   EX $10   **NM** $20   **MIP** $35

Elmer Fudd Mug, 1980s, Applause, figural
   EX $5   **NM** $10   **MIP** $20

FIGURES

Elmer Fudd Figure, 1950s, metal 5", on
   green base w/his name embossed,
   Elmer in hunting outfit
   EX $55   **NM** $125   **MIP** $275

Elmer Fudd Figure, 1968, Dakin, 8" tall
   EX $20   **NM** $60   **MIP** $100

Elmer Fudd Figure, 1971, Dakin, in a red
   hunting outfit
   EX $30   **NM** $70   **MIP** $125

Elmer Fudd Figure, 1977, Dakin, Fun Farm
   EX $18   **NM** $33   **MIP** $65

TOY

Elmer Fudd Pull Toy, 1940s, Brice Toys,
   9", wooden, Elmer in fire chief's car
   EX $100   **NM** $225   **MIP** $400

FELIX THE CAT

ACCESSORIES

Felix Cartoon Lamp Shade, 6" tall
   EX $75   **NM** $150   **MIP** $250

Felix Flashlight, 1960s, contains whistle
   EX $50   **NM** $200   **MIP** $325

Felix Pencil Case, 1950s
   EX $25   **NM** $75   **MIP** $120

(KP Photo)

Felix Sip-a-Drink Cup, 5" tall
   EX $15   **NM** $25   **MIP** $60

DOLL

Felix Doll, 1920s, 8" tall, wood, fully jointed
   EX $200   **NM** $350   **MIP** $750

Felix Doll, 1920s, 13" tall, jointed arms
   EX $200   **NM** $350   **MIP** $750

FIGURES

Felix Figure, 1920s, Schoenhut, 4" tall,
   wood, leather ears, stands on a white
   wood base
   EX $200   **NM** $400   **MIP** $675

GAME

Felix Manual Dexterity Game, 1920s,
   German, 2", round, metal
   EX $100   **NM** $175   **MIP** $325

TOY

Felix on a Scooter, 1924, Nifty, tin wind-up
   EX $500   **NM** $800   **MIP** $1000

Felix Punching Bag, 1960s, 11" tall
   inflatable bobber
   EX $25   **NM** $60   **MIP** $110

Felix Soaky, 1960s, 10" tall, blue plastic
   EX $20   **NM** $60   **MIP** $100

Felix Soaky, 1960s, 10" tall, red plastic
   EX $20   **NM** $60   **MIP** $100

Felix Soaky, 1960s, 10" tall, black plastic
   EX $15   **NM** $50   **MIP** $90

Felix Squeak Toy, 1930s, 6" tall, soft rubber
   EX $35   **NM** $110   **MIP** $185

Felix the Cat Pull Toy, 1920s, Nifty, 5-1/2"
   tall, 8" long, tin, cat is chasing two red
   mice on the front of the cart, litho
   pictures of Felix on side
   EX $400   **NM** $750   **MIP** $1000

WATCH

Felix Wristwatch, 1960s
   EX $65   **NM** $150   **MIP** $275

FERDINAND THE BULL

BANK

Ferdinand Savings Bank, Crown Toy, 5"
   tall, wood composition w/silk flower
   w/metal trap door
   EX $50   **NM** $100   **MIP** $250

BOOK

Ferdinand the Bull Book, 1938, Whitman,
   linen picture book
   EX $75   **NM** $125   **MIP** $225

DOLL

Ferdinand Doll, 1938, Knickerbocker, 5" x 9"
   x 8-1/2" tall, joint composition w/cloth tail
   and flower stapled in his mouth
   EX $100   **NM** $210   **MIP** $375

FIGURES

Ferdinand Figure, 9" tall, plastic
   EX $20   **NM** $35   **MIP** $150

CHARACTER TOYS

Ferdinand Figure, 3-1/2" bisque
EX $15   NM $40   MIP $110

Ferdinand Figure, 1930s, Seiberling, 3" x 5-1/2" x 4" tall, rubber
EX $75   NM $110   MIP $225

Ferdinand Figure, 1938, Delco, 4-1/2" tall, ceramic, bull seated w/a purple garland around his neck
EX $75   NM $110   MIP $225

Ferdinand Figure, 1940s, Disney, composition
EX $125   NM $200   MIP $350

TOY

Ferdinand Hand Puppet, 1938, Crown Toy, 9-1/2" tall
EX $75   NM $110   MIP $230

Ferdinand Toy, 1940, Knickerbocker, wood composition w/jointed head and legs w/flower in his mouth
EX $125   NM $175   MIP $325

FLIPPER

TOY

Flipper Halloween Costume, 1964, Collegeville
EX $20   NM $40   MIP $125

Flipper Magic Slate, 1960s, Lowe
EX $12   NM $24   MIP $75

Flipper Model Kit, 1965, Revell
EX $17   NM $35   MIP $100

Flipper Puzzle, 1960s, Whitman, several variations, each
EX $12   NM $22   MIP $50

Flipper Ukelele, 1968, Mattel
EX $12   NM $22   MIP $60

FOGHORN LEGHORN

FIGURES

Foghorn Leghorn Figure, 1970, Dakin, 6-1/4" tall
EX $22   NM $45   MIP $100

Foghorn Leghorn Figure, 1980s, Applause, PVC
EX $3   NM $50   MIP $75

TOY

Foghorn Leghorn Hand Puppet, 1960s, 9", fabric w/vinyl head
EX $20   NM $75   MIP $150

FONTAINE FOX

TOY

Powerful Katrinka Toy, 1923, 5-1/2" tall, wind-up, pushing Jimmy in a wheelbarrow
EX $1200   NM $1500   MIP $2000

Toonerville Trolley, Nifty, miniature, 2" tall
EX $250   NM $350   MIP $525

Toonerville Trolley, 3" tall
EX $200   NM $350   MIP $450

Toonerville Trolley, 4" tall, red pot metal
EX $500   NM $800   MIP $1450

Toonerville Trolley, 1922, 7-1/2" tall, wind-up
EX $750   NM $1000   MIP $1500

GARFIELD

BANK

Garfield Chair Bank, 1981, Enesco
EX $12   NM $25   MIP $80

Garfield Figure Bank, 1981, Enesco, 4-3/4"
EX $12   NM $24   MIP $70

FIGURES

Garfield Easter Figure, 1978, Enesco
EX $7   NM $20   MIP $50

Garfield Figure, 1978, Enesco, Garfield as graduate
EX $6   NM $12   MIP $40

MUSIC BOX

Garfield Music Box, 1981, Enesco, Garfield dancing
EX $50   NM $75   MIP $150

GASOLINE ALLEY

ACCESSORIES

Skeezix Stationery, 1926, 6" x 8-1/2"
EX $50   NM $75   MIP $125

Uncle Walt and Skeezix Pencil Holder, F.A.S., 5" tall, bisque
EX $125   NM $200   MIP $325

FIGURES

Skeezix Comic Figure, 1930s, 6" chalk statue
EX $30   NM $50   MIP $100

Uncle Walt and Skeezix Figure Set, bisque, Uncle Walt, Skeezix, Herby and Smitty
EX $125   NM $250   MIP $400

GOOFY

ACCESSORIES

Goofy Night Light, 1973, Horsman, green, figural
EX $16   NM $30   MIP $45

Goofy Toothbrush, 1970s, Pepsodent
EX $5   NM $10   MIP $40

DOLL

Goofy Doll, 1970s, 5" x 6" x 13" tall, fabric and vinyl, laughing doll
EX $50   NM $100   MIP $200

FIGURES

Goofy Figure, Marx, Snap-Eeze figure
EX $15   NM $35   MIP $50

Goofy Figure, Arco, bendy
EX $10   NM $15   MIP $25

Goofy Lil' Headbobber, Marx
EX $50   NM $100   MIP $160

Goofy Rolykin, Marx
EX $25   NM $50   MIP $75

Goofy Twist 'n Bend Figure, 1963, Marx, 4" tall
EX $11   NM $20   MIP $30

TOY

Goofy Car, Spain, vinyl head Goofy drives tin litho car
EX $50   NM $100   MIP $150

Goofy Safety Scissors, 1973, Monogram, on card
EX $5   NM $10   MIP $20

Goofy with Bump 'n Go Action Lawn Mower, 1980s, Illfelder, 3-1/2" x 10" x 11", plastic figure pushing lawn mower w/silver handle
EX $40   NM $70   MIP $125

WATCH

Backwards Goofy Wristwatch, Pedre, silver case 2nd edition
EX $40   NM $75   MIP $225

Backwards Goofy Wristwatch, 1972, Helbros
EX $325   NM $650   MIP $1000

GUMBY

ACCESSORIES

(KP Photo)

Gumby Adventure Costume, 1960s, Lakeside, fireman, cowboy, knight and astronaut, each
EX $25   NM $50   MIP $90

FIGURES

Gumby Figure, 1980s, large, foam rubber
EX $20   NM $40   MIP $100

Gumby Figure, 1980s, Applause, 12" tall, poseable
EX $10   NM $20   MIP $40

Gumby Figure, 1980s, Applause, 5-1/2" bendy, three styles
EX $5   NM $10   MIP $30

Pokey Figure, 1960s, Lakeside
EX $20   NM $40   MIP $95

TOY

Adventures of Gumby Electric Drawing Set, 1966, Lakeside
EX $22   NM $50   MIP $125

Gumby Colorforms Set, 1988, Colorforms
EX $8   NM $12   MIP $50

Gumby Hand Puppet, 1965, Lakeside, 9" tall w/vinyl head
EX $15   NM $40   MIP $90

Gumby Modeling Dough, 1960s, Chemtoy
EX $25   NM $50   MIP $90

Gumby's Jeep, 1960s, Lakeside, yellow tin litho, Gumby and Pokey's names are printed on seat
EX $150 **NM** $250 **MIP** $400

Pokey Modeling Dough, 1960s, Chemtoy
EX $25 **NM** $50 **MIP** $90

HAPPY HOOLIGAN

ACCESSORIES

Happy Hooligan Songsheet, 1905, newspaper premium
EX $100 **NM** $150 **MIP** $250

TOY

Happy Hooligan Nesting Toys, Anri, 4" tall, wooden set of four nesting pieces
EX $100 **NM** $150 **MIP** $350

Happy Hooligan Toy, 1932, Chein, 6" tall, wind-up, walking figure
EX $350 **NM** $450 **MIP** $750

HECKLE AND JECKLE

BOOK

Heckle and Jeckle Story Book, 1957, Wonder Book
EX $30 **NM** $50 **MIP** $75

FIGURES

Heckle and Jeckle Figures, 7" soft foam figures
EX $25 **NM** $70 **MIP** $135

Little Roquefort Figure, 1959, 8-1/2" tall, wood
EX $20 **NM** $40 **MIP** $80

TOY

Heckle and Jeckle Skooz-It Game, 1963, Ideal, cylindrical container
EX $40 **NM** $80 **MIP** $125

HUCKLEBERRY HOUND

BANK

Huckleberry Hound Bank, 1960, Knickerbocker, 10" tall, hard plastic figural
EX $30 **NM** $60 **MIP** $100

Huckleberry Hound Bank, 1980, Dakin, 5" tall figural bank of Huck sitting
EX $20 **NM** $40 **MIP** $80

DOLL

Huckleberry Hound Doll, 1959, Knickerbocker, 18" plush, vinyl hands and face
EX $60 **NM** $125 **MIP** $175

Mr. Jinks Doll, 1959, Knickerbocker, 13" tall, plush, vinyl face
EX $50 **NM** $110 **MIP** $230

Pixie and Dixie Dolls, 1960, Knickerbocker, 12" tall, each
EX $25 **NM** $45 **MIP** $100

FIGURES

Hokey Wolf Figure, 1961, Marx, TV-Tinykin
EX $15 **NM** $40 **MIP** $85

Hokey Wolf Figure, 1970, Dakin
EX $30 **NM** $75 **MIP** $150

Huckleberry Hound Figure, Dakin, 8" tall
EX $25 **NM** $50 **MIP** $90

Huckleberry Hound Figure, 1960s, 6" tall, glazed china
EX $20 **NM** $40 **MIP** $100

Huckleberry Hound Figure, 1961, Marx, TV-Tinykins
EX $15 **NM** $25 **MIP** $60

Huckleberry Hound Figure Set, 1961, Marx, TV-Tinykins
EX $50 **NM** $80 **MIP** $125

TOY

Huckleberry Hound Go-Cart, 1960s, Linemar, 6-1/2" tall, friction
EX $100 **NM** $200 **MIP** $375

Huckleberry Hound Wind-Up Toy, 1962, Linemar, 4" tall, tin
EX $175 **NM** $350 **MIP** $500

Mr. Jinks Soaky, 1960s, Purex, 10" tall, Pixie and Dixie, hard plastic
EX $15 **NM** $35 **MIP** $75

Pixie and Dixie Magic Slate, 1959
EX $30 **NM** $50 **MIP** $80

WATCH

Huckleberry Hound Wristwatch, 1965, Bradley, chrome case, wind-up mechanism, gray leather band, face shows Huck in full view
EX $100 **NM** $150 **MIP** $300

HUMPTY DUMPTY

ACCESSORIES

Humpty Dumpty Bubble Bath, 1960s, Avon, figural plastic container
EX $7 **NM** $30 **MIP** $85

Humpty Dumpty Figural Soap, 1990s, Avon
EX $3 **NM** $6 **MIP** $20

Humpty Dumpty Magazine, 1960s
EX $3 **NM** $7 **MIP** $25

Humpty Dumpty Potato Chip Tin, 1990s, large blue and gold tin
EX $7 **NM** $15 **MIP** $40

FIGURE

Humpty Dumpty Figure, 1950s, Marx, Fairy Tale series, plastic
EX $5 **NM** $10 **MIP** $40

Humpty Dumpty Game, 1981, Orchard Toys, British matching game
EX $8 **NM** $15 **MIP** $50

PUZZLE

Humpty Dumpty Puzzle, 1970s, wood frame tray puzzles, several varieties
EX $5 **NM** $15 **MIP** $40

TOY

Humpty Dumpty Crib Toy, 1980s, Mattel, plastic, sits on crib rail
EX $4 **NM** $8 **MIP** $25

Humpty Dumpty Musical Toy, 1960s, Alladin Plastics, plastic, record inside toy
EX $15 **NM** $30 **MIP** $70

Humpty Dumpty Pull Toy, 1970s, Fisher-Price, plastic, several color variations
EX $5 **NM** $10 **MIP** $30

INDIANA JONES

ACCESSORIES

Indiana Jones Backpack, Pepsi
EX $20 **NM** $45 **MIP** $90

Indiana Jones The Legend Mug
EX $5 **NM** $10 **MIP** $15

Last Crusade Button, Pepsi, retailer button
EX $5 **NM** $15 **MIP** $30

Patch, 1990
EX $10 **NM** $20 **MIP** $40

Temple of Doom Calendar
EX $5 **NM** $10 **MIP** $30

Temple of Doom Storybook, hardbound
EX $7 **NM** $20 **MIP** $30

TOY

(KP Photo)

Indiana Jones 3-D View-Master Gift Set, View-Master
EX $20 **NM** $35 **MIP** $75

JAMES BOND

ACCESSORIES

007 Flicker Rings, 1967, set of 11
EX $75 **NM** $110 **MIP** $220

007 Video Disc Promo Kit, 1980s, RCA, disc, poster, pamphlet
EX $15 **NM** $30 **MIP** $60

Bond Golf Tees, 1987, British, six tees and pencil in leather pouch
EX $8 **NM** $15 **MIP** $30

James Bond Alarm Clock, painting of Roger Moore in center
EX $20 **NM** $40 **MIP** $100

James Bond B.A.R.K. Attache Case With Box, 1965, Multiple Toys, 007 luger, missles, hideaway pistol and rocket launching device, case and gun bears 007 logo
EX $1000 **NM** $1500 **MIP** $3000

James Bond Jr. Bath Towel
EX $10   NM $20   MIP $20

James Bond Parachute Set, 1984, Imperial, orange and green parachutist figures
EX $12   NM $35   MIP $80

James Bond Ring, 1964, glass oval w/photo of Sean Connery
EX $10   NM $25   MIP $40

James Bond Wall Clock, 1981, large clock w/painting of Roger Moore in action
EX $25   NM $45   MIP $100

View to a Kill Michelin Button, Bond on large size pinback w/Midas man
EX $5   NM $12   MIP $25

ACTION FIGURES

James Bond Jr. Action Ninja figure, Hasbro
EX $8   NM $15   MIP $80

James Bond Jr. Buddy Mitchell figure, Hasbro
EX $5   NM $10   MIP $30

James Bond Jr. Capt. Walker D. Plank figure, Hasbro
EX $3   NM $6   MIP $20

James Bond Jr. Dr. Derange figure, Hasbro
EX $3   NM $6   MIP $25

James Bond Jr. Dr. No. figure, Hasbro
EX $3   NM $6   MIP $25

James Bond Jr. figure, Hasbro, w/pistol
EX $3   NM $8   MIP $35

James Bond Jr. figure, Hasbro, w/scuba gear
EX $3   NM $8   MIP $35

James Bond Jr. Gordo Leiter figure, Hasbro
EX $4   NM $10   MIP $40

James Bond Jr. I.Q. figure, Hasbro, w/weapon device
EX $3   NM $6   MIP $25

James Bond Jr. Jaws figure, Hasbro
EX $5   NM $12   MIP $40

James Bond Jr. Odd Job figure, Hasbro
EX $6   NM $15   MIP $50

BOOK

Bond Pocket Diary, 1988, British leather bound
EX $5   NM $15   MIP $40

James Bond Jr. Sticker Book
EX $3   NM $6   MIP $20

COSTUME

Moonraker Halloween Costume, 1979, mask of Roger Moore and space suit costume
EX $30   NM $75   MIP $150

DOLL

(KP Photo)

Odd Job Action figure, 1965, Gilbert, 12" doll in karate outfit, w/derby
EX $300   NM $550   MIP $750

FIGURES

Jaws figure, 1979, Mego
EX $135   NM $300   MIP $600

GAME

Goldfinger II Role Playing Game
EX $6   NM $15   MIP $40

James Bond Computer Game "The Stealth Affair", 1990, based on Licence to Kill
EX $15   NM $30   MIP $70

James Bond Jr. Karate Punch Target Game, gun w/boxing glove and targets of villain
EX $8   NM $15   MIP $45

(KP Photo)

James Bond Secret Service Game, 1965, Spears
EX $150   NM $275   MIP $625

James Bond Tarot Game, 1973
EX $15   NM $30   MIP $70

James Bond Video Game, 1983, Coleco
EX $15   NM $25   MIP $60

Moonraker Spanish Card Game, 33 cards w/different color stills
EX $15   NM $30   MIP $70

The James Bond Box, 1965, rare game played w/dice
EX $50   NM $100   MIP $200

Thunderball Balloon Target Game, 1965
EX $40   NM $95   MIP $200

GUN

(KP Photo)

James Bond Harpoon Gun (Thunderball), 1960s, Lone Star, box illustrated w/undersea fight scene graphics
EX $125   NM $250   MIP $400

PUPPETS

Odd Job Puppet, Gilbert, plastic hand puppet
EX $250   NM $500   MIP $750

PUZZLE

Goldfinger Puzzle, 1965, Milton Bradley, Bond and Golden Girl
EX $25   NM $55   MIP $120

(KP Photo)

Goldfinger Puzzle, 1965, Milton Bradley, Bond's Bullets Blaze
EX $20   NM $40   MIP $95

Spy Who Loved Me Puzzle, Milton Bradley, several scenes, each
EX $20   NM $40   MIP $90

STICKERS

007 Bullet Hole Stickers, 1987, simulated bullet holes, magnetic license holder
EX $6   NM $15   MIP $40

TOY

(KP Photo)

007 Dart Gun, 1984, Imperial, photo of Roger Moore
EX $15   NM $35   MIP $100

007 Exploding Cigarette Lighter, Coibel
EX $12   NM $30   MIP $100

007 Exploding Coin, Coibel, on blister pack
EX $6   NM $20   MIP $50

007 Exploding Pen, Coibel, on blister pack
EX $6   NM $20   MIP $50

007 Exploding Spoon, Coibel, on blister pack
EX $6   NM $20   MIP $50

007 Radio Trap, 1966, Multiple Toys, radio w/secret business cards
EX $50   NM $105   MIP $220

007 Submachine Gun, 1984, Imperial, photo of Roger Moore
EX $10   NM $30   MIP $100

007 Toy Pistol, Edgemark
EX $5   NM $15   MIP $50

Electric Drawing Set, 1965, Lakeside, plastic tracing board, pencils, sharpener, adventure sheets
EX $55   NM $110   MIP $250

James Bond Disguise Kit, 1965, Gilbert
EX $40   NM $85   MIP $200

James Bond Disguise Kit #2, 1965, Gilbert
EX $40   NM $85   MIP $200

James Bond Hand Puppet, 1965, Gilbert
EX $45   NM $100   MIP $175

James Bond Hideaway Pistol, 1985, Coibel
EX $40   NM $90   MIP $170

James Bond Jr. CD Player/Weapons Kit, Hasbro
EX $10   NM $20   MIP $60

James Bond Jr. Crime Fighter Set, includes handcuffs, watch and walkie-talkie
EX $5   NM $15   MIP $50

James Bond Jr. Ninja Play Set, throw stars, nunchukas and badge
EX $8   NM $15   MIP $60

James Bond Jr. Ninja Wrist Weapon Set
EX $5   NM $10   MIP $50

(KP Photo)

James Bond Secret Attache Case, 1965, MPC, box is rare
EX $1000   NM $1500   MIP $3000

James Bond Sting Pistol, Coibel, 8-shot cap pistol and booklet from On Her Majesty's Secret Service
EX $20   NM $40   MIP $120

Living Daylights German Pistol, 1980s, Wicke, 25-shot cap gun
EX $12   NM $30   MIP $90

May Day Pistol, 1985
EX $12   NM $30   MIP $75

(KP Photo)

Thunderball Puzzle, 1965, Milton Bradley, several pictures, each
EX $20   NM $45   MIP $95

Thunderball Set, 1965, Gilbert
EX $40   NM $105   MIP $220

Tuxedo Outfit, 1965, Gilbert
EX $50   NM $110   MIP $230

VEHICLES

James Bond Aston Martin, 1965, Gilbert, 12", battery operated
EX $150   NM $300   MIP $575

James Bond Aston Martin Slot Car, 1965, Gilbert
EX $75   NM $150   MIP $325

James Bond Jr. Corvette, Hasbro
EX $15   NM $35   MIP $90

James Bond Jr. Scum Shark Mobile, Hasbro
EX $10   NM $15   MIP $40

James Bond Jr. Sub Cycle, Hasbro
EX $10   NM $15   MIP $40

James Bond Jr. Vehicles, Ertl, S.C.U.M. Helicopter, Bond's car and van; set of three
EX $20   NM $65   MIP $150

James Bond Roadrace Set, 1965, Gilbert, scenery tracks, Aston Martin and other cars
EX $350   NM $600   MIP $1000

Licence to Kill Car Set, Matchbox, jeep, seaplane, oil tanker, and copter
EX $25   NM $50   MIP $125

Living Daylights Record Mobile, 1980s
EX $5   NM $20   MIP $50

(KP Photo)

Moonraker Shuttle and Drax Copter Jr.'s, Corgi, set of two
EX $15   NM $35   MIP $80

Multi-Action Aston Martin, 1960s, friction operated car for Agent 711
EX $90   NM $200   MIP $400

(KP Photo)

Octopussy Gift Set, plane, truck and horse trailer
EX $35   NM $100   MIP $200

WATCHES

James Bond Pocket Watch, 1981, Roger Moore on face
EX $40   NM $80   MIP $175

JUNGLE BOOK

ACCESSORIES

Jungle Book Dinner Set, vinyl placemat, bowl, plate and cup
EX $10   NM $20   MIP $70

Jungle Book Utensils, fork and spoon w/melamine handles
EX $5   NM $12   MIP $50

DOLL

Baloo Doll, 12" tall, plush
EX $10   NM $50   MIP $120

FIGURES

Mowgli Figure, 1967, Holland Hill, 8", vinyl
EX $20   NM $40   MIP $90

Shere Kahn Figure, 1965, Enesco, 5" tall, ceramic
EX $20   NM $40   MIP $85

CHARACTER TOYS

TOY

Jungle Book Carrying Case, 1966, Ideal, 5" x 14" x 8"
EX $25 **NM** $60 **MIP** $150

Jungle Book Fun-L Tun-L, 1966, New York Toy, 108" x 24"
EX $40 **NM** $70 **MIP** $150

Jungle Book Magic Slate, 1967, Watkins-Strathmore
EX $10 **NM** $25 **MIP** $75

Jungle Book Sand Pail and Shovel, 1966, Chein, tin litho, illustrated w/Jungle Book characters
EX $25 **NM** $60 **MIP** $120

Jungle Book Tea Set, 1966, Chein, tin litho, plates, saucers, tea cups and serving tray
EX $35 **NM** $75 **MIP** $140

Mowgli's Hut Mobile and Figures, 1968, Multiple Toymakers, 2" x 3" x 3" mobile w/Baloo and King Louis figures
EX $35 **NM** $100 **MIP** $150

WATCH

Mowgli/Baloo Wristwatch, digital, clear plastic band
EX $5 **NM** $10 **MIP** $30

LADY AND THE TRAMP

DOLL

Lady Doll, 1955, Woolikin, 5" x 8" x 8-1/2", light tank w/burnt orange accents on face, ears, stomach and tail, plastic eyes, nose and a white silk ribbon around neck
EX $75 **NM** $150 **MIP** $300

Perri Doll, 1950s, Steiff, 6" tall, plush
EX $40 **NM** $85 **MIP** $175

Tramp Doll, 1955, Schuco, 8" tall, brown w/a white underside and face, hard plastic eyes and nose
EX $100 **NM** $175 **MIP** $375

FIGURES

Lady and Tramp Figures, 1955, Marx, Lady is 1-1/2" tall and white, Tramp is 2" tall and tan
EX $30 **NM** $75 **MIP** $150

TOY

Modeling Clay, 1955, Pressman
EX $30 **NM** $120 **MIP** $185

Puzzle, 1954, Whitman, 11" x 15", frame tray
EX $20 **NM** $35 **MIP** $75

Toy Bus, 1966, Modern Toys/Japan, 3-1/2" x 4" x 14" long
EX $20 **NM** $40 **MIP** $90

LAUREL AND HARDY

BANK

(KP Photo)

Oliver Hardy Bank, 1974, Play Pal, 13-1/2" tall, plastic
EX $15 **NM** $30 **MIP** $85

Stan Laurel Bank, 1972, 15" tall, vinyl figural bank
EX $22 **NM** $50 **MIP** $95

Stan Laurel Bank, 1974, Play Pal, 13-1/2" tall, plastic
EX $15 **NM** $30 **MIP** $85

FIGURES

Oliver Hardy Figure, 1974, Dakin, 7-1/2" tall
EX $60 **NM** $120 **MIP** $175

Stan Laurel Figure, 1974, Dakin, 8" tall
EX $60 **NM** $120 **MIP** $130

TOY

Laurel and Hardy Die-Cut Puppets, 1970s, Larry Harmon, moveable, each
EX $25 **NM** $125 **MIP** $275

Laurel and Hardy Die-Cut Puppets, 1982, Dell, soft vinyl, each
EX $20 **NM** $75 **MIP** $175

Laurel and Hardy TV Set, 1976, w/paper filmstrips
EX $25 **NM** $50 **MIP** $125

Oliver Hardy Doll, Dakin, 5" tall wind-up dancing/shaking vinyl doll
EX $35 **NM** $50 **MIP** $125

LITTLE MERMAID

ACCESSORIES

Ariel Jewelry Box, 5-3/4" x 4-1/2", musical
EX $10 **NM** $16 **MIP** $40

Ariel Toothbrush, battery operated w/holder
EX $10 **NM** $16 **MIP** $35

Flounder and Ariel Faucet Cover, plastic
EX $6 **NM** $10 **MIP** $30

Flounder Pillow, 14" x 24" shaped like Flounder
EX $8 **NM** $13 **MIP** $35

Little Mermaid Purse, 6" diameter, vinyl, canteen style purse
EX $6 **NM** $12 **MIP** $30

Little Mermaid Snow Globe, 4" water globe
EX $10 **NM** $16 **MIP** $40

Under the Sea Jewelry Box, 4" mahogany, musical
EX $20 **NM** $35 **MIP** $75

DOLL

Eric Doll, 9-1/2" tall in full dress uniform
EX $10 **NM** $16 **MIP** $35

Flounder Doll, 15" plush fish
EX $10 **NM** $16 **MIP** $35

Scuttle Doll, 15" seagull, plush
EX $12 **NM** $20 **MIP** $40

Sebastian Doll, 16" crab, plush
EX $10 **NM** $16 **MIP** $35

FIGURES

Little Mermaid Figures, Applause, several PVC characters, each
EX $2 **NM** $5 **MIP** $12

LITTLE ORPHAN ANNIE

ACCESSORIES

Beetleware Mug, 1933, Ovaltine
EX $25 **NM** $70 **MIP** $120

Beetleware Mug, 1935, Ovaltine
EX $35 **NM** $80 **MIP** $150

ID Bracelet, 1934, Ovaltine
EX $25 **NM** $60 **MIP** $150

Little Orphan Annie Altascope Ring, 1942, Quaker, premium, only eight known to exist
EX $8500 **NM** $12000 **MIP** $22000

Little Orphan Annie and Sandy Ashtray, 1930s, 3" tall, ceramic
EX $100 **NM** $200 **MIP** $400

Little Orphan Annie and Sandy Toothbrush Holder, 1930s, bisque
EX $100 **NM** $160 **MIP** $350

Little Orphan Annie Clothespins, 1938, Gold Medal, clothesline and pulley
EX $20 **NM** $40 **MIP** $80

Little Orphan Annie Glassips, 1936, drinking straws
EX $500 **NM** $600 **MIP** $750

Little Orphan Annie Mug, 1930, Ovaltine, Uncle Wiggily
EX $40 **NM** $100 **MIP** $200

Little Orphan Annie Music Box, 1970, N.Y. News, figural
EX $25 **NM** $60 **MIP** $100

Little Orphan Annie Periscope, 1942, Quaker, offered in handbook
EX $400 **NM** $600 **MIP** $750

Little Orphan Annie Stamper, 1941, Quaker, premium, w/wood handle; secret guard
EX $600 **NM** $1000 **MIP** $1200

Round Decoder Pin, 1936, Ovaltine
  EX $30   NM $130   MIP $220

Secret Compartment Decoder Pin, 1936, Ovaltine
  EX $20   NM $150   MIP $325

Shake-Up Mug, 1931, Ovaltine
  EX $30   NM $75   MIP $140

Sunburst Decoder Pin, 1937, Ovaltine
  EX $30   NM $75   MIP $180

BOOK

Little Orphan Annie and Chizzler Book, 1930s, Big Little Book
  EX $25   NM $75   MIP $160

Little Orphan Annie and the Gooneyville Mystery Book, 1947, Whitman
  EX $20   NM $100   MIP $180

Little Orphan Annie and the Haunted House Comic Book, 1928, Cupples and Leon
  EX $60   NM $150   MIP $300

Little Orphan Annie Bucking the World Comic Book, 1929, Cupples and Leon, hardcover
  EX $60   NM $150   MIP $310

Little Orphan Annie in the Circus Comic Book, 1927, Cupples and Leon, 9" x 7", 86 pages
  EX $60   NM $150   MIP $310

Little Orphan Annie Shipwrecked Comic Book, 1931, Cupples and Leon, 9" x 7", 86 pages
  EX $60   NM $120   MIP $310

(KP Photo)

Radio Annie's Secret Society Booklet, 1936, 6" x 9"
  EX $40   NM $65   MIP $160

Radio Annie's Secret Society Manual, 1938, 6" x 9", 12 pages
  EX $60   NM $100   MIP $185

DOLL

Annie Doll, 1982, Knickerbocker, 10" doll without locket
  EX $2   NM $7   MIP $20

Annie Doll, 1982, Knickerbocker, 10" tall, w/two dresses and removable heart locket
  EX $5   NM $12   MIP $30

Daddy Warbucks Doll, 1982, Knickerbocker
  EX $10   NM $50   MIP $90

Little Orphan Annie and Sandy Dolls, 1930, Famous Artists Syndicate, 9-3/4" tall, each
  EX $90   NM $150   MIP $300

Little Orphan Annie Doll, 1973, Well Toy, 7" tall
  EX $15   NM $20   MIP $60

Miss Hannigan Doll, 1982, Knickerbocker
  EX $5   NM $10   MIP $30

Molly Doll, 1982, Knickerbocker
  EX $5   NM $10   MIP $30

Punjab Doll, 1982, Knickerbocker
  EX $5   NM $15   MIP $50

Snow White Paper Dolls, 1938, rare red cover version; Ovaltine Annie premium
  EX $800   NM $1200   MIP $2000

FIGURES

Annie Figures, 1982, Knickerbocker, six figures, 2" tall, each
  EX $2   NM $5   MIP $10

Little Orphan Annie Figure, 1940s, 1-1/2" tall, lead
  EX $20   NM $40   MIP $80

Sandy Figure, 1940s, 3/4" tall, lead
  EX $20   NM $55   MIP $120

GAME

Little Orphan Annie Light Up the Candles Game, Ovaltine, 3-1/2" x 5", premium
  EX $125   NM $175   MIP $350

Little Orphan Annie Rummy Cards, 1937, Whitman, 5" x 6", colored silhouettes of Annie on the back
  EX $60   NM $90   MIP $175

TOY

Little Orphan Annie Colorforms Set, 1970s, Colorforms
  EX $10   NM $20   MIP $50

Little Orphan Annie Costume, 1930s, mask and slip-over paper dress w/belt
  EX $300   NM $450   MIP $525

Little Orphan Annie Cut-Outs, 1960s, Miller Toys, Sandy, Grunts the Pig, Pee Wee the Elephant
  EX $50   NM $100   MIP $200

Little Orphan Annie Punch-Outs, 1944, King, Larson, McMahon, 3-D punch-outs of Annie, Sandy, Punjab and Daddy Warbucks
  EX $75   NM $125   MIP $175

Little Orphan Annie Stove, 1930s, electric version, 8" x 9", gold metal, litho plates, functional oven doors and back burner
  EX $150   NM $250   MIP $375

Little Orphan Annie Stove, 1930s, non-electric model, gold-brass lithographed labels of Annie and Sandy, oven doors functional
  EX $150   NM $250   MIP $375

Pastry Set, 1950s, Transogram, Model No. 3993
  EX $20   NM $40   MIP $75

Puzzle, Novelty Dist., Famous Comics
  EX $35   NM $100   MIP $210

LOONEY TUNES

BANK

Daffy Duck Bank, 1980s, Applause, figural
  EX $10   NM $20   MIP $50

(KP Photo)

Sylvester and Tweety Bank, 1972, vinyl
  EX $15   NM $25   MIP $90

Tasmanian Devil Bank, 1980s, Applause
  EX $10   NM $20   MIP $70

DOLL

Tasmanian Devil Doll, 1971, Mighty Star, 13" tall, plush
  EX $20   NM $40   MIP $100

Tweety Doll, 1969, Dakin, 6", moveable head and feet
  EX $10   NM $25   MIP $80

FIGURE

Daffy Duck Figure, 1968, Dakin, 8-1/2" tall
  EX $15   NM $25   MIP $80

Daffy Duck Figure, 1970s, Dakin
  EX $15   NM $30   MIP $90

Daffy Duck Figure, 1980s, Applause, 4" bendy
  EX $10   NM $20   MIP $60

Sylvester Figure, 1971, Dakin, Sylvester on a fish crate
  EX $15   NM $25   MIP $80

Sylvester Figure, 1976, Dakin, Cartoon Theater
  EX $11   NM $22   MIP $60

FIGURES

Pepe Le Pew Figure, 1971, Dakin, 8" tall
  EX $25   NM $50   MIP $100

Speedy Gonzales Figure, Dakin, 5", vinyl
  EX $10   NM $20   MIP $60

CHARACTER TOYS

Speedy Gonzales Figure, 1970, Dakin, 7-1/2" tall, vinyl
EX $15   NM $25   MIP $65

Sylvester and Tweety Figures, 1975, Warner Bros., 6" tall
EX $10   NM $16   MIP $50

Sylvester Figure, 1950, Oak Rubber, 6", rubber
EX $40   NM $80   MIP $135

Sylvester Figure, 1969, Dakin
EX $15   NM $25   MIP $70

Tasmanian Devil Figure, 1989, Superior, 7", plastic, on base
EX $5   NM $15   MIP $50

Tweety Figure, 1971, Dakin, on bird cage
EX $14   NM $25   MIP $70

Tweety Figure, 1971, Dakin, Goofy Gram, holding red heart
EX $15   NM $25   MIP $70

Tweety Figure, 1976, Dakin, Cartoon Theater
EX $15   NM $25   MIP $70

TOY

Bugs Bunny Hand Puppet, 1940s, Zany, rubber head
EX $60   NM $125   MIP $200

Elmer Fudd Hand Puppet, 1940s, Zany, rubber head
EX $30   NM $70   MIP $150

Foghorn Leghorn Hand Puppet, 1940s, Zany, rubber head
EX $45   NM $85   MIP $175

Pepe Le Pew Goofy Gram, 1971, Dakin
EX $25   NM $50   MIP $100

Sylvester Hand Puppet, 1940s, Zany, rubber head
EX $60   NM $125   MIP $200

Sylvester Soaky, Colgate
EX $10   NM $30   MIP $70

Tweety Hand Puppet, 1940s, Zany, rubber head
EX $60   NM $125   MIP $200

Tweety Soaky, 1960s, Colgate, 8-1/2", plastic
EX $10   NM $30   MIP $70

MAGILLA GORILLA

ACCESSORIES

Magilla Gorilla Cereal Bowl, MB Inc.
EX $10   NM $35   MIP $90

Magilla Gorilla Plate, 1960s, 8" diameter, plastic
EX $7   NM $20   MIP $50

BOOK

Magilla Gorilla Book, 1964, Golden, Big Golden Book
EX $12   NM $30   MIP $70

DOLL

Magilla Gorilla Doll, 1960s, 11" tall, cloth body, hard arms and legs, hard plastic head
EX $125   NM $225   MIP $400

Magilla Gorilla Doll, 1966, Ideal, 18-1/2" plush w/vinyl head
EX $135   NM $250   MIP $450

TOY

Droop-A-Long Coyote Soaky, 1960s, Purex, 12", plastic
EX $20   NM $45   MIP $90

Droop-A-Long Hand Puppet, Ideal, vinyl head
EX $25   NM $60   MIP $135

Magilla Gorilla Cannon, 1964, Ideal
EX $60   NM $90   MIP $200

Magilla Gorilla Pull Toy, 1960s, Ideal, w/vinyl figure
EX $75   NM $150   MIP $250

Magilla Gorilla Puppet, Ideal
EX $40   NM $110   MIP $210

Magilla Gorilla Push Puppet, 1960s, Kohner, brown plastic figure in pink shorts and shoes, yellow base
EX $25   NM $55   MIP $110

Punkin' Puss Soaky, 1960s, Purex, 11-1/2" tall, plastic
EX $20   NM $50   MIP $85

Ricochet Rabbit Hand Puppet, 1960s, Ideal, 11", vinyl head
EX $35   NM $65   MIP $125

Ricochet Rabbit Soaky, 1960s, Purex, 10-1/2" tall, plastic
EX $30   NM $70   MIP $140

MARY POPPINS

ACCESSORIES

Mary Poppins Pencil Case, 1964, vinyl w/zipper top
EX $10   NM $22   MIP $60

DOLL

Mary Poppins Doll, 1964, Gund, 11-1/2" tall, bendable
EX $75   NM $150   MIP $300

FIGURES

Mary Poppins Figure, 8" tall, ceramic
EX $20   NM $40   MIP $90

PUZZLE

Mary Poppins Puzzle, 1964, Jaymar, frame tray
EX $8   NM $20   MIP $50

TOY

Mary Poppins Manicure Set, 1964, Tre-Jur
EX $20   NM $45   MIP $95

Mary Poppins Paper Dolls, 1973, Whitman, w/magic tote bag, Model No. 1977
EX $40   NM $75   MIP $120

Mary Poppins Tea Set, 1964, Chein, tin, creamer, plates, place settings, cups, serving tray
EX $60   NM $110   MIP $200

MICKEY AND MINNIE MOUSE

ACCESSORIES

Mickey and Donald Alarm Clock, 1960s, Jerger/Germany, 2-1/2" x 5" x 7"; metal case, dark brass finish, 3-D plastic figures of Mickey and Donald on either side
EX $70   NM $140   MIP $210

Mickey and Minnie and Donald Throw Rug, 26" x 41", Mickey and Minnie in an airplane w/Donald parachuting
EX $60   NM $120   MIP $210

Mickey and Minnie Carpet, 27" x 41", Peg Leg Pete is lassoed by Mickey; all characters in western outfits
EX $130   NM $225   MIP $360

Mickey and Minnie Snow Dome, 1970s, Monogram, 3" x 4" x 3" tall, Mickey and Minnie w/a pot of gold at the end of the rainbow
EX $12   NM $25   MIP $50

Mickey and Minnie Toothbrush Holder, 4-1/2" tall, bisque, toothbrush holes are located behind their heads
EX $120   NM $200   MIP $400

Mickey and Minnie Toothbrush Holder, 2-1/2" x 4" x 3-1/2", Mickey and Minnie on sofa w/Pluto at their feet
EX $130   NM $210   MIP $425

Mickey and Minnie Trash Can, 1970s, Chein, 13" tall tin litho, Mickey and Minnie fixing a flat tire on one side, other side shows Mickey feeding Minnie soup
EX $25   NM $80   MIP $160

Mickey and Pluto Ashtray, 3" x 4" x 3" tall, ceramic, Mickey and Pluto playing banjos while sitting on the edge of the ashtray
EX $250   NM $400   MIP $625

Mickey Mouse Alarm Clock, 1960s, Bayard, 2" x 4-1/2" x 4-1/2" tall, 1930s style Mickey w/movable head that ticks off the seconds
EX $100   NM $200   MIP $350

Mickey Mouse Alarm Clock, 1975, Bradley, travel alarm, large red cube case, shut off button on top, separate alarm wind, in sleeve box
EX $30   NM $55   MIP $100

Mickey Mouse Alarm Clock, 1988, House Martin, 5" x 7" x 2"
EX $11   NM $20   MIP $50

Mickey Mouse Ashtray, 3-1/2" tall, wood composition figure of Mickey
EX $75   NM $150   MIP $310

Mickey Mouse Beanie, 1950s, blue/yellow felt hat w/Mickey on front
EX $200   NM $350   MIP $500

Mickey Mouse Christmas Lights, 1930s, Noma, eight lamps w/holiday decals of characters
EX $125   NM $225   MIP $375

Mickey Mouse Clock, 1970s, Elgin, 10" x 15" x 3", electric wall clock
EX $12   **NM** $25   **MIP** $50

Mickey Mouse Club Coffee Tin, 1950s, illustrated lid promotes the club, tin included MM badge
EX $50   **NM** $100   **MIP** $200

Mickey Mouse Club Mousketeer Handbag, Connecticut Leather, leather/vinyl crafting set
EX $45   **NM** $60   **MIP** $125

Mickey Mouse Club Plastic Plate, 1960s, Arrowhead, 9" diameter, clubhouse w/Goofy, Pluto and Donald wearing mouse ears and sweaters w/club emblems
EX $16   **NM** $30   **MIP** $45

Mickey Mouse Club Toothbrush, 1970s, Pepsodent
EX $4   **NM** $7   **MIP** $30

Mickey Mouse Cup, 1950s, Cavalier, 3" tall, silver-plated cup w/a 2-1/2" opening
EX $25   **NM** $50   **MIP** $100

Mickey Mouse Electric Table Radio, 1960s, General Electric, 4-1/2" x 10-1/2" x 6" tall
EX $50   **NM** $150   **MIP** $225

Mickey Mouse Lamp, 1935, Soreng-Manegold, 10-1/2" tall
EX $200   **NM** $350   **MIP** $600

Mickey Mouse Map of the United States, 1930s, Dixon, 9-1/4" x 14"
EX $100   **NM** $250   **MIP** $425

Mickey Mouse Night Light, 1938, Disney, 4" tall, tin
EX $100   **NM** $200   **MIP** $300

Mickey Mouse Pencil Box, 1930s, Dixon, 5-1/2" x 10-1/2" x 1-1/4", Mickey in a gymnasium
EX $60   **NM** $125   **MIP** $275

Mickey Mouse Pencil Box, 1930s, Dixon, Mickey ready to hitch Horace to a carriage in which Minnie is sitting
EX $100   **NM** $150   **MIP** $300

Mickey Mouse Pencil Box, 1937, Dixon, 5-1/2" x 9" x 3/4", Mickey, Goofy and Pluto riding a rocket
EX $100   **NM** $150   **MIP** $300

Mickey Mouse Pencil Box, 1937, Dixon, 5" x 8-1/2" x 1-1/4", Mickey is a circus ringmaster and Donald riding a seal
EX $100   **NM** $150   **MIP** $300

Mickey Mouse Pencil Holder, 1930s, Dixon, 4-1/2" tall
EX $100   **NM** $150   **MIP** $300

Mickey Mouse Pencil Sharpener, 3" tall, celluloid, sharpener located on base
EX $65   **NM** $125   **MIP** $250

Mickey Mouse Pencil Sharpener, 1960s, Hasbro, shape of Mickey's head, pencil goes into mouth
EX $12   **NM** $25   **MIP** $50

Mickey Mouse Pitcher, 1930s, Germany, 2" x 3" diameter, china, white w/green shading around the base, Mickey on each side
EX $75   **NM** $150   **MIP** $325

Mickey Mouse Radio, 1934, Emerson, wood composition cabinet w/designs of Mickey playing musical instruments
EX $2000   **NM** $3200   **MIP** $6000

Mickey Mouse Radio, 1970s, Philgee
EX $20   **NM** $40   **MIP** $80

Mickey Mouse Record Player, 1970s, General Electric, playing arm is the design of Mickey's arm
EX $60   **NM** $125   **MIP** $175

Mickey Mouse Throw Rug, 1935, Alex. Smith Carpet, 26" x 42"
EX $130   **NM** $250   **MIP** $400

Mickey Mouse Transistor Radio, 1950s, Gabriel, 6-1/2" x 7" x 1-1/2"
EX $40   **NM** $80   **MIP** $160

Mickey Mouse Wall Clock, 1978, Elgin, 9" diameter dial, 15" long, shaped like oversize watchband, "50 Happy Years" logo on dial
EX $30   **NM** $60   **MIP** $90

Minnie Mouse Alarm Clock, 1970s, Bradley, pink metal electric two-bell clock w/articulated hands
EX $25   **NM** $50   **MIP** $85

Minnie Mouse Clock, 1970s, Phinney-Walker, 8" diameter by 1-1/2" deep, plastic, "Behind Every Great Man, There is a Woman!"
EX $40   **NM** $70   **MIP** $125

BANK

Mickey Mouse Band Leader Bank, Knickerbocker, 7-1/2" tall, plastic
EX $10   **NM** $25   **MIP** $50

Mickey Mouse Bank, 1930s, 2" x 3" x 2-1/4", tin, shaped like a treasure chest w/Mickey and Minnie on the "Isle of the Thrift"
EX $200   **NM** $300   **MIP** $520

Mickey Mouse Bank, 1930s, 2-1/2" x 6", shaped like a mailbox w/Mickey holding an envelope
EX $150   **NM** $250   **MIP** $425

Mickey Mouse Bank, 1934, German, 2-1/2" x 3", tin, bright yellow bank shaped like a beehive, Mickey approaching door holding a honey jar in one arm and key to open the door in the other
EX $400   **NM** $750   **MIP** $1000

Mickey Mouse Bank, 1938, Crown Toy, 6" tall, composition, key locked trap door on base, w/figure standing next to treasure chest and head is movable
EX $175   **NM** $250   **MIP** $500

Mickey Mouse Bank, 1950s, 5" x 5-1/2" x 6", china, shaped like Mickey's head w/slot between his ears
EX $30   **NM** $70   **MIP** $160

Mickey Mouse Bank, 1960s, Wolverine, 1-1/2" x 5-1/2" x 1" tall, plastic
EX $50   **NM** $60   **MIP** $125

Mickey Mouse Bank, 1970s, Transogram, 5" x 7-1/2" x 19" tall, plastic w/Mickey standing on a white chest
EX $15   **NM** $25   **MIP** $40

Mickey Mouse Bank, 1978, Fricke and Nacke, 3" x 5" x 7" tall, embossed image of Mickey in front, side panels have Minnie, Goofy, Donald and Pluto
EX $15   **NM** $25   **MIP** $175

Mickey Mouse Club Bank, 1970s, Play Pal Plastics, 4-1/2" x 6" x 11-1/2" tall, vinyl
EX $16   **NM** $30   **MIP** $60

Mickey Mouse Gumball Bank, 1968, Hasbro
EX $15   **NM** $40   **MIP** $90

Mickey Mouse Telephone Bank, 1938, N.N. Hill Brass, 5" tall w/cardboard figure of Mickey
EX $130   **NM** $275   **MIP** $450

BOOK

(KP Photo)

Adventures of Mickey Mouse Book, 1931, David McKay, full color illustrations, softcover
EX $100   **NM** $275   **MIP** $525

Mickey Mouse Activity Book, 1936, Whitman, 40 pages
EX $100   **NM** $150   **MIP** $325

Mickey Mouse Club Fun Box, 1957, Whitman, box includes stamp book, club scrapbook, six coloring books and four small gameboards
EX $45   **NM** $85   **MIP** $175

Mickey Mouse Has a Busy Day Book, 1937, Whitman, 16 pages
EX $50   **NM** $100   **MIP** $210

Mickey Mouse in Giantland Book, 1934, David McKay, 45 pages, hardcover
EX $75   **NM** $150   **MIP** $300

Mickey Mouse Presents a Silly Symphony Book, 1934, Whitman, Big Little Book
EX $100   **NM** $175   **MIP** $350

DOLL

Mickey and Minnie Dolls, 1940s, Gund, 13" tall, each
EX $300   **NM** $500   **MIP** $1000

(KP Photo)

Mickey Mouse Club Mouseketeer Doll,
1960s, Horsman, 8" tall, denim outfit
EX $35　　NM $75　　MIP $200

Mickey Mouse Doll, Knickerbocker, 5" x 7"
x 12" tall, fabric, Mickey in checkered
shorts and green jacket w/white felt
flower stapled to it
EX $400　　NM $650　　MIP $1000

Mickey Mouse Doll, 1930s, 4" x 7" x 10-1/2"
tall, movable arms and legs, swivel head,
black velveteen body and red felt pants
EX $750　　NM $1200　　MIP $2000

Mickey Mouse Doll, 1935, Knickerbocker,
11" tall, stuffed w/removable shoes and
jointed head, red shorts
EX $200　　NM $350　　MIP $600

Mickey Mouse Doll, 1950s, Schuco, 10" tall
EX $110　　NM $225　　MIP $400

Mickey Mouse Doll, 1960s, Gund, 12",
Mickey as fireman
EX $30　　NM $55　　MIP $90

Mickey Mouse Doll, 1970s, Hasbro,
4" x 5-1/2" x 7-1/2" tall, talks
EX $20　　NM $40　　MIP $60

Mickey Mouse Doll, 1972, Horsman,
3" x 10" x 12" tall, talking doll, says five
different phrases
EX $20　　NM $40　　MIP $70

Minnie Mouse Doll, 1935, Knickerbocker,
14" tall, stuffed, cloth, polka-dot skirt
and lace pantaloons
EX $400　　NM $750　　MIP $1000

Minnie Mouse Doll, 1940s, Petz, 10" tall
EX $135　　NM $260　　MIP $500

FIGURES

Mickey Mouse Figure, 4" tall, bisque,
dressed in a green nightshirt
EX $40　　NM $80　　MIP $140

Mickey Mouse Figure, composition, part
of the Lionel Circus Train Set
EX $150　　NM $200　　MIP $375

Mickey Mouse Figure, 1930s, Seiberling,
6-1/2" tall, rubber
EX $100　　NM $200　　MIP $375

Mickey Mouse Figure, 1930s, Goebel, 3-1/2"
tall, in a hunting outfit reading a book
EX $45　　NM $100　　MIP $185

Mickey Mouse Figure, 1930s, Seiberling,
3-1/2" tall, black hard rubber
EX $60　　NM $112　　MIP $275

Mickey Mouse Figure, 1930s, 3" tall,
bisque, holding a parade flag and sword
EX $60　　NM $125　　MIP $210

Mickey Mouse Figure, 1930s, 3" tall,
bisque, plays saxophone
EX $60　　NM $125　　MIP $210

Mickey Mouse Figure, 1930s, Seiberling,
3-1/2" tall, latex
EX $100　　NM $175　　MIP $300

Mickey Mouse Figure, 1970, Marx, 6" tall,
vinyl
EX $10　　NM $20　　MIP $40

Mickey Mouse Fun-E-Flex Figure, 1930s,
Fun-E-Flex, 7", bendy
EX $350　　NM $475　　MIP $750

Minnie Mouse Figure, 1958, Ingersoll, 5-
1/2" tall, plastic
EX $35　　NM $60　　MIP $125

Minnie Mouse Fun-E-Flex Figure, 1930s,
Fun-E-Flex, 5", bendy
EX $130　　NM $250　　MIP $375

GAME

Mickey Mouse Bean Bag Game, 1930s,
Marks Bros.
EX $100　　NM $130　　MIP $240

Mickey Mouse Club Magic Divider,
1950s, Jacmar, arithmetic game
EX $30　　NM $55　　MIP $100

Mickey Mouse Club Magic Subtractor,
1950s, Jacmar, arithmetic game
EX $11　　NM $20　　MIP $60

MUSIC BOX

Mickey Mouse Music Box, 4-1/2" x 5" x 7",
plays "It's a Small World," Mickey in
conductor's uniform standing on cake
EX $20　　NM $35　　MIP $100

Mickey Mouse Music Box, Schmid, 3" x 6"
x 7-1/2" tall, bisque, Spirit of '76, plays
"Yankee Doodle;" Mickey, Goofy and
Donald are dressed as Revolutionary
War Minutemen
EX $60　　NM $120　　MIP $220

Mickey Mouse Music Box, 1970s, Schmid,
3-1/2" x 5-1/2", plays "Mickey Mouse Club
March," ceramic, Mickey in western
clothes standing next to a cactus
EX $35　　NM $60　　MIP $125

Mickey Mouse Music Box, 1970s, Japan,
4" x 6" tall, china, plays "Side by Side,"
Mickey is brushing a kitten in a washtub
EX $15　　NM $25　　MIP $90

Mickey Mouse Music Box, 1971, Anri, 5"
x 3-1/2", plays "If I Were Rich Man"
EX $50　　NM $90　　MIP $180

Minnie Mouse Music Box, 1970s, Schmid,
3-1/2" diameter, plays "Love Story"
EX $25　　NM $40　　MIP $150

TOY

Crayons, 1946, Transogram
EX $30　　NM $60　　MIP $100

Mickey and Donald Jack-in-the-Box,
1966, Lakeside, Donald pops out
EX $100　　NM $175　　MIP $300

Mickey and Minnie Flashlight, 1930s,
Usalite Co., 6" long, Mickey leading
Minnie through the darkness guided by
flashlight and Pluto
EX $50　　NM $85　　MIP $150

Mickey and Minnie Sand Pail, Ohio Art, 5"
x 5", tin, Mickey, Minnie, Pluto and
Donald in boat looking across water at
castle, w/swivel handle
EX $100　　NM $160　　MIP $340

Mickey and Minnie Sled, 1935, S.L. Allen,
32" long, wooden slat sled, metal
runners, "Mickey Mouse" decal on
steering bar
EX $400　　NM $550　　MIP $800

Mickey and Minnie Tea Set, 1930s, Ohio
Art, 5" x 8", pitcher pictures Mickey at
piano and cups picture Mickey, Pluto
and Minnie
EX $125　　NM $200　　MIP $350

Mickey and Minnie Tray, 1930s, Ohio Art,
5-1/2" x 7-1/4", tin, Mickey and Minnie
in rowboat
EX $75　　NM $125　　MIP $225

Mickey and Three Pigs Spinning Top,
Lackawanna, 9" diameter, tin
EX $50　　NM $100　　MIP $200

Mickey Mouse Baby Gift Set, 1930s,
silver-plated cup, fork, spoon, cup and
napkin holder
EX $100　　NM $200　　MIP $350

Mickey Mouse Band Drum, 1936, 7" x 14"
diameter, cloth mesh and paper drum
heads
EX $250　　NM $350　　MIP $500

Mickey Mouse Band Sand Pail, 1938,
Ohio Art, 6" tall, tin, pictures of Mickey
Mouse, Minnie, Horace, Pluto, and
Clarabelle the cow parading down street
EX $125　　NM $225　　MIP $350

Mickey Mouse Band Spinning Top,
9" diameter
EX $40　　NM $80　　MIP $175

Mickey Mouse Boxed Lantern Slides,
1930s, Ensign, 5" x 6" x 2", cartoons:
Traffic Troubles, Gorilla Mystery,
Cactus Kid, Castaway, Delivery Boy,
Fishin' Around, Firefighters, Moose
Hunt and Mickey Steps Out
EX $160　　NM $325　　MIP $500

Mickey Mouse Bubble Buster Gun, 1936,
Kilgore, 8" long, cork gun
EX $75　　NM $150　　MIP $250

Mickey Mouse Bump-N-Go Spaceship,
1980s, Matsudaya, battery operated tin

litho w/clear dome, has six flashing lights, rotating antenna
EX $35   **NM** $65   **MIP** $150

Mickey Mouse Camera, 1960s, Ettelson, 3" x 3" x 5"
EX $18   **NM** $40   **MIP** $100

Mickey Mouse Camera, 1970s, Child Guidance, 4" x 7" x 7"
EX $12   **NM** $25   **MIP** $100

Mickey Mouse Camera, 1970s, Helm Toy, 2" x 5" x 4-1/2", Mickey in engineer's uniform riding on top of the train
EX $13   **NM** $25   **MIP** $85

Mickey Mouse Car, 1970s, Polistil, 2" x 4" x 1-1/2" tall plastic car w/rubber figure, Mickey in driver's seat
EX $30   **NM** $55   **MIP** $125

Mickey Mouse Cardboard House, 1930s, O.B. Andrews, 14" x 12" x 13" tall
EX $200   **NM** $350   **MIP** $500

Mickey Mouse Chatty Chums, 1979, Mattel
EX $8   **NM** $15   **MIP** $40

Mickey Mouse Club Magic Kit, 1950s, Mars Candy, two 8" x 20" punch-out sheets
EX $75   **NM** $100   **MIP** $160

Mickey Mouse Club Marionette, 1950s, 3" x 6-1/2" x 13-1/2" tall, composition figure of a girl w/black felt hat and mouse ears
EX $300   **NM** $425   **MIP** $600

Mickey Mouse Club Mousketeer Ears, Kohner, 7" x 12-1/2"
EX $11   **NM** $20   **MIP** $40

Mickey Mouse Club Newsreel with Sound, 1950s, Mattel, 4" x 4-1/2" x 9" tall, orange box, plastic projector w/two short filmstrips, record, cardboard screen, cartoons "Touchdown Mickey" and "No Sail"
EX $100   **NM** $170   **MIP** $300

Mickey Mouse Club Rhythm Makers Set, Emenee
EX $100   **NM** $200   **MIP** $350

(KP Photo)

Mickey Mouse Colorforms Set, 1976, Colorforms, 8" x 12-1/2" x 1", Spirit of '76
EX $10   **NM** $30   **MIP** $75

Mickey Mouse Dart Gun Target, 1930s, Marks Brothers, 10" target, dart gun and suction darts
EX $125   **NM** $250   **MIP** $400

Mickey Mouse Dinner Set, 1930s, Empresa Electro, china, 2" creamer, 3-4-1/2" plates and 3-5" plates, 7" long dish, two oval platters
EX $350   **NM** $500   **MIP** $750

Mickey Mouse Dominoes, Halsam, Mickey and Pluto on dominoes
EX $80   **NM** $100   **MIP** $180

Mickey Mouse Drum, 1930s, Ohio Art, 6" diameter
EX $200   **NM** $350   **MIP** $500

Mickey Mouse Electric Casting Set, 1930s, Home Foundary, 9-1/2" x 16" x 2"
EX $125   **NM** $200   **MIP** $400

Mickey Mouse Fire Engine, Sun Rubber, 7" long, rubber, push toy
EX $75   **NM** $150   **MIP** $275

(KP Photo)

Mickey Mouse Fire Truck with Figure, Sun Rubber, 2-1/2" x 6-1/2" x 4", Mickey driving and mold-in image of Donald standing on the back holding onto his helmet
EX $75   **NM** $150   **MIP** $275

Mickey Mouse Jack-In-the-Box, 1970s, 5-1/2" square tin litho box shows Mickey, Pluto, Donald and Goofy, Mickey pops out
EX $25   **NM** $50   **MIP** $100

Mickey Mouse Lionel Circus Train, 1935, Lionel, five cars w/Mickey, 30" train, 84 inches of track, circus tent, Sunoco station, truck, tickets, Mickey composition statue
EX $5000   **NM** $7500   **MIP** $10000

Mickey Mouse Lionel Circus Train Handcar, Lionel, metal, 9" long w/6" tall composition/rubber figures of Mickey and Minnie
EX $600   **NM** $1000   **MIP** $1500

Mickey Mouse Magic Slate, 1950s, Watkins-Strathmore, 8-1/2" x 14" tall
EX $15   **NM** $30   **MIP** $90

Mickey Mouse Marbles, Monarch, marbles and Mickey bag, on card
EX $10   **NM** $20   **MIP** $60

Mickey Mouse Mechanical Pencil, 1930s, head of Mickey on one end and decal of Mickey walking on other side of pencil
EX $100   **NM** $175   **MIP** $300

Mickey Mouse Mechanical Robot, Gabriel
EX $70   **NM** $125   **MIP** $150

Mickey Mouse Mousegetar, 1960s, 10" x 30" x 2-1/2" black plastic
EX $40   **NM** $85   **MIP** $175

Mickey Mouse Movie Projector, 1934, Keystone, 5-1/2" x 11-1/2" x 11" tall for 8mm movies
EX $275   **NM** $500   **MIP** $800

Mickey Mouse Movie-Fun Shows, 1940s, Mastercraft, 7-1/2" square by 4" deep, animated action movies
EX $106   **NM** $212   **MIP** $325

Mickey Mouse Musical Money Box, 1970s, 3" x 6", tin box w/Mickey, Pluto, Donald and Goofy
EX $30   **NM** $55   **MIP** $90

Mickey Mouse Old Timers Fire Engine, 1980s, Matsudaya, red, tin and plastic fire truck w/Mickey at the wheel
EX $40   **NM** $70   **MIP** $125

Mickey Mouse Picture Gun, 1950s, Stephens, 6-1/2" x 9-1/2" x 3", metal, lights to show filmstrips
EX $65   **NM** $125   **MIP** $250

Mickey Mouse Play Tiles, 1964, Halsam, 336 tiles
EX $15   **NM** $25   **MIP** $50

Mickey Mouse Print Shop Set, 1930s, Fulton Specialty, 6-1/2" x 6-1/2", ink pad, stamper, metal tweezers, wooden tray
EX $125   **NM** $250   **MIP** $350

Mickey Mouse Pull Toy, Toy Kraft, 7" x 22" x 8" tall, horse cart drawn by wooden horses
EX $450   **NM** $600   **MIP** $1100

Mickey Mouse Pull Toy, 1935, N.N. Hill Brass, 14" tall, wood and metal
EX $250   **NM** $400   **MIP** $650

Mickey Mouse Puppet Forms, 1960s, Colorforms
EX $10   **NM** $25   **MIP** $60

Mickey Mouse Riding Toy, 1930s, Mengel, 6" x 17" x 16" tall
EX $800   **NM** $1200   **MIP** $1750

Mickey Mouse Rodeo Rider, 1980s, Matsudaya, plastic wind-up, cowboy Mickey rides a bucking bronco
EX $25   **NM** $45   **MIP** $75

Mickey Mouse Rolykin, Marx, 1-1/2" tall, ball bearing action
EX $12   **NM** $20   **MIP** $70

Mickey Mouse Rub 'N Play Magic Transfer Set, 1978, Colorforms
EX $15   **NM** $30   **MIP** $80

Mickey Mouse Safety Blocks, 1930s, Halsam, nine blocks
EX $175   **NM** $300   **MIP** $450

Mickey Mouse Sand Pail, 1938, Ohio Art, 6" tall, tin, Mickey, Donald and Goofy playing golf
EX $125   **NM** $225   **MIP** $400

Mickey Mouse Sand Pail, 1938, Ohio Art, 3" tall, tin
EX $80   **NM** $150   **MIP** $300

Mickey Mouse Sand Shovel, Ohio Art, 10" long, tin
EX $35   **NM** $70   **MIP** $175

Mickey Mouse Saxophone, 1930s, 16" tall
EX $150   **NM** $250   **MIP** $400

Mickey Mouse Scissors, Disney, 3" long, child's scissors w/Mickey figure
EX $20   **NM** $35   **MIP** $100

Mickey Mouse Serving Tray, 1960s, 11" diameter, tin
EX $11   **NM** $35   **MIP** $70

Mickey Mouse Sewing Cards, 1978, Colorforms, 7-1/2" x 12" cut-out card designs of Mickey, Minnie, Pluto, Clarabelle, Donald Duck and Horace
EX $10   **NM** $20   **MIP** $85

Mickey Mouse Sled, 1930s, Flexible Flyer, 18" x 30" x 6" tall, wood
EX $800   **NM** $1200   **MIP** $2000

Mickey Mouse Squeeze Toy, 1950s, Dell, rubber, Mickey as hitchhiking hobo
EX $35   **NM** $75   **MIP** $160

Mickey Mouse Squeeze Toy, 1950s, Sun Rubber, 10" tall, rubber
EX $25   **NM** $50   **MIP** $110

Mickey Mouse Squeeze Toy, 1960s, Dell, 8" tall
EX $15   **NM** $30   **MIP** $70

Mickey Mouse Stamp Pad, 1930s, 3" long
EX $75   **NM** $150   **MIP** $250

Mickey Mouse Steamboat, 1988, Matsudaya, wind-up plastic steamboat w/Mickey as Steamboat Willie, runs on floor as smokestacks go up and down, box says "60 Years w/You"
EX $30   **NM** $60   **MIP** $135

Mickey Mouse Tea Set, Wolverine, plastic
EX $50   **NM** $175   **MIP** $175

Mickey Mouse Tea Set, 1930s, 3" saucer, 2" pitcher, 2-1/2" sugar bowl each piece shows Mickey and Minnie in a rowboat
EX $125   **NM** $250   **MIP** $350

Mickey Mouse Tractor, Sun Rubber, 5" long, rubber
EX $85   **NM** $200   **MIP** $400

Mickey Mouse Tricycle Toy, 1932, Steiff, 8-1/2" x 7", wood and metal frame, action movement
EX $1500   **NM** $3300   **MIP** $5000

Mickey Mouse Twirling Tail Toy, 1950s, Marx, 3" x 5-1/2" x 5-1/2" tall, w/a built-in key, metal tail spins around as the toy vibrates
EX $120   **NM** $225   **MIP** $400

Mickey Mouse Utensils, 1947, Wm. Rogers and Son, 6" fork and 5-1/2" spoon
EX $75   **NM** $100   **MIP** $185

Mickey Mouse Viewer, 1940s, Craftsmen's Guild, film viewer w/12 films
EX $85   **NM** $150   **MIP** $300

Mickey Mouse Wash Machine, Ohio Art, 8" tin litho w/Mickey and Minnie Mouse pictured doing their wash
EX $150   **NM** $350   **MIP** $550

Mickey Mouse Water Globes, 1970s, 3" x 4-1/2" x 5" tall, three dimensional plastic figures of Mickey seated w/a plastic water globe between his legs
EX $25   **NM** $50   **MIP** $150

Mickey Mouse Watering Can, 1938, Ohio Art, 6" tin litho
EX $100   **NM** $175   **MIP** $325

Mickey Mouse Wind-Up Musical Toy, 1970s, Illco, 6" tall, plays "Lullaby and Goodnight," 3-D figure of Mickey in red pants and yellow shirt
EX $25   **NM** $35   **MIP** $75

Mickey Mouse Wind-Up Toy, 1978, Gabriel, plastic transparent figure of Mickey w/visible metal gears
EX $10   **NM** $20   **MIP** $60

Mickey Mouse Wind-Up Trike, 1960s, Korean, tin litho trike w/plastic Mickey w/flag and balloon on handle, bell on back
EX $100   **NM** $175   **MIP** $300

Mickey Mouse Yarn Sewing Kit, 1930s, Marks Bros., seven cards, yarn, needle
EX $40   **NM** $165   **MIP** $300

Mickey's Air Mail Plane, 1940s, Sun Rubber, 3-1/2" x 6" long, 5" wingspan, rubber
EX $150   **NM** $300   **MIP** $500

Minnie Mouse Car, 1979, Matchbox
EX $5   **NM** $15   **MIP** $45

Minnie Mouse Choo-Choo Train Pull Toy, 1940s, Linemar, 3" x 8-1/2" x 7" tall, green metal base and green wooden wheels
EX $125   **NM** $250   **MIP** $450

Minnie Mouse Hand Puppet, 1940s, 11" tall, white on red polka-dot, fabric hard cover and a pair of black and white felt hands
EX $55   **NM** $135   **MIP** $225

Minnie Mouse Rocker, 1950s, Marx, tin wind-up, rocker moves back and forth w/gravity motion of her head and ears
EX $250   **NM** $480   **MIP** $720

Minnie with Bump-n-Go Action Shopping Cart, 1980s, Illfelder, 4" x 9-1/2" x 11-1/2" tall, plastic, battery operated Minnie pushing cart
EX $30   **NM** $55   **MIP** $80

Mouseketeer Cut-Outs, 1957, Whitman, figures and accessories
EX $60   **NM** $125   **MIP** $200

Mouseketeer Fan Club Typewriter, 1950s, lithographed tin
EX $75   **NM** $125   **MIP** $225

Puzzle, 1930s, Marks Brothers, 10" x 12", Mickey polishing the boiler on his "Mickey Mouse R.R." train engine and Minnie waving from the cab
EX $55   **NM** $110   **MIP** $250

Puzzle, 1957, Whitman, Adventureland, 11" x 15" frame tray; Mickey, Minnie, Donald and his nephew in boat surrounded by jungle beasts
EX $10   **NM** $40   **MIP** $80

Puzzle, 1960s, Jaymar, Pluto's Wash and Scrub Service
EX $15   **NM** $40   **MIP** $80

Spinning Top, 1930s, Fritz Bueschel, 7" diameter, 7" tall, Mickey, Minnie, a nephew, Donald and Horace playing a musical instrument
EX $100   **NM** $175   **MIP** $350

Spinning Top, 1950s, Chein, tin litho, features Mickey in cowboy outfit and other characters
EX $60   **NM** $140   **MIP** $280

WATCH

50 Years with Mickey Wristwatch, 1983, Bradley, small round chrome case, inscription and serial number on back
EX $45   **NM** $85   **MIP** $200

Mickey and Pluto Wristwatch, 1980, Bradley, LCD quartz, black vinyl band
EX $20   **NM** $45   **MIP** $110

Mickey Mouse Pocket Watch, 1930s, Ingersoll, 2" diameter
EX $1200   **NM** $2000   **MIP** $3500

Mickey Mouse Pocket Watch, 1970s, Bradley
EX $50   **NM** $100   **MIP** $250

Mickey Mouse Pocket Watch, 1976, Bradley, 3-1/2" x 4-1/2" x 3/4", Mickey in his Bicentennial outfit
EX $75   **NM** $175   **MIP** $300

Mickey Mouse Pocket Watch, 1988, Lorus, #2202, quartz, small gold bezel, gold chain and clip fob, articulated hands
EX $25   **NM** $50   **MIP** $100

Mickey Mouse Wristwatch, two-gun Mickey, saddle tan western style band
EX $25   **NM** $45   **MIP** $90

Mickey Mouse Wristwatch, 1939, Ingersoll, rectangular w/standard second hand between Mickey's legs
EX $225   **NM** $425   **MIP** $900

(KP Photo)

Mickey Mouse Wristwatch, 1958, Timex, electric
EX $140   **NM** $300   **MIP** $550

Mickey Mouse Wristwatch, 1960s, Timex, large round case, stainless back, articulated hands, red vinyl band
EX $50   **NM** $80   **MIP** $160

Mickey Mouse Wristwatch, 1970s, Bradley, white plastic case, watch on pendant, bubble crystal, articulated hands, gold chain
EX $25   **NM** $60   **MIP** $135

Mickey Mouse Wristwatch, 1970s, Bradley, 2-1/2" x 6" x 2-1/2", plastic case, white dial w/Mickey playing tennis, the second hand has a tennis ball on the end of it
EX $35   **NM** $75   **MIP** $175

Mickey Mouse Wristwatch, 1978, Bradley, commemorative edition
EX $65   **NM** $130   **MIP** $300

Mickey Mouse Wristwatch, 1983, Bradley, medium black octagonal case, articulated hands, no numbers on face, in plastic window box
EX $25   **NM** $260   **MIP** $400

Mickey Mouse Wristwatch, 1984, Bradley, medium white case, articulated hands, black face, sweep seconds, white vinyl band, in plastic window box
EX $20   **NM** $40   **MIP** $80

Minnie Mouse Wristwatch, 1958, Timex, small round chrome case, stainless back, articulated hands, yellow vinyl band
EX $75   **NM** $150   **MIP** $275

Minnie Mouse Wristwatch, 1978, Bradley, gold case, sweep seconds, red vinyl band, articulated hands
EX $16   **NM** $35   **MIP** $70

MIGHTY MOUSE

ACCESSORIES

Charm Bracelet, 1950s, brass charms of Gandy Goose, Terry Bear, Mighty Mouse and other Terrytoon characters
EX $75   **NM** $125   **MIP** $200

(KP Photo)

Mighty Mouse Sneakers, 1960s, Randy Co., children's, graphics on box, picture on sneakers
EX $75   **NM** $125   **MIP** $200

DOLL

Mighty Mouse Doll, 1942, rubber head, yellow suit w/red cape
EX $750   **NM** $1000   **MIP** $1350

Mighty Mouse Doll, 1942, rubber head, wearing red suit
EX $750   **NM** $1100   **MIP** $1500

Mighty Mouse Doll, 1950s, Ideal, 14" tall, stuffed, cloth
EX $50   **NM** $100   **MIP** $250

FIGURES

Mighty Mouse Figure, 1950s, 9-1/2" rubber, squeaks
EX $20   **NM** $60   **MIP** $150

Mighty Mouse Figure, 1977, Dakin, hard and soft vinyl figure
EX $30   **NM** $60   **MIP** $125

Mighty Mouse Figure, 1978, Dakin, Fun Farm
EX $35   **NM** $70   **MIP** $135

GAME

Mighty Mouse Ball Game, 1981, Ja-Ru
EX $5   **NM** $12   **MIP** $50

TOY

Mighty Mouse Cinema Viewer, 1979, Fleetwood, w/four strips
EX $10   **NM** $30   **MIP** $75

Mighty Mouse Dynamite Dasher, 1981, Takara
EX $50   **NM** $110   **MIP** $275

Mighty Mouse Flashlight, 1979, Dyno, 3-1/2" figural light
EX $50   **NM** $80   **MIP** $120

Mighty Mouse Hit the Claw Target Set, Parks
EX $100   **NM** $150   **MIP** $275

Mighty Mouse Make-a-Face Sheet, 1958, Towne, w/dials to change face parts
EX $40   **NM** $80   **MIP** $160

Mighty Mouse Mighty Money, 1979, Fleetwood
EX $20   **NM** $55   **MIP** $85

Mighty Mouse Money Press, 1981, Ja-Ru, stampers, pads and money
EX $8   **NM** $15   **MIP** $30

Mighty Mouse Movie Viewer, 1980, Chemtoy
EX $10   **NM** $15   **MIP** $50

Mighty Mouse Picture Play Lite, 1983, Janex
EX $8   **NM** $15   **MIP** $40

Mighty Mouse Wallet, 1978, Larami
EX $15   **NM** $35   **MIP** $80

Puzzle, tray puzzle; Mighty Mouse and his TV Pals
EX $20   **NM** $35   **MIP** $80

Puzzle, 1979, Fleetwood, Mighty Mouse/Heckle and Jeckle
EX $45   **NM** $90   **MIP** $140

WATCH

Mighty Mouse Wristwatch, 1979, Bradley, chrome case
EX $40   **NM** $60   **MIP** $100

MISCELLANEOUS CHARACTERS

ACCESSORIES

Amy Carter Paper Dolls, 1970s, Toy Factory, 14" cardboard doll w/accessories
EX $15   **NM** $30   **MIP** $60

Holly Hobbie Wristwatch, 1982, Bradley, small gold tone case, base metal back, yellow plastic band
EX $5   **NM** $10   **MIP** $50

Jimmy Carter Radio, peanut-shaped transistor radio
EX $20   **NM** $45   **MIP** $125

Kennedy Kards, 1960s, red, white, and blue playing cards w/cartoon artwork
EX $10   **NM** $20   **MIP** $50

Little King Lucky Safety Card, 1953, New York Journal, 2" x 4" cards, Little King warns of safety
EX $15   **NM** $30   **MIP** $75

Mr. Potato Head Ice Pops, 1950s, Hasbro, plastic molds for freezing treats, in box
EX $16   **NM** $35   **MIP** $80

Sandra Dee Paper Dolls, 1959, Saalfield, two cardboard dolls w/outfits
EX $30   **NM** $75   **MIP** $150

Tuesday Weld Paper Dolls, 1960, Saalfield, two cardboard dolls w/outfits
EX $30   **NM** $60   **MIP** $135

Uncle Don's "Puzzy and Sizzy" Membership Card, 1950s
EX $20   **NM** $50   **MIP** $75

Willie Whopper Pencil Case, 1930s, green w/illustrations of Willie, Pirate and his gal
EX $80   **NM** $125   **MIP** $200

BANK

Sir Reginald Play-N-Save Bank, 1960s, 7" tall plastic lion and hunter, on a 15" green plastic base, the hunter fires the coin into the lion's mouth
EX $45   **NM** $125   **MIP** $180

DOLL

Hardy Boys Dolls, 1979, Kenner, 12" tall Joe Hardy (Shaun Cassidy) or Frank Hardy (Parker Stevenson)
EX $20   **NM** $40   **MIP** $90

FIGURES

Bruce Lee Figure, 1986, Largo, 8" w/weapon
EX $20   **NM** $40   **MIP** $100

Diamond Jim Figure, 1930s, 5-1/2" tall
EX $30   **NM** $80   **MIP** $160

George Bush Figure, 7" tall
EX $8   **NM** $20   **MIP** $40

Lyndon Johnson Figure, 1960s, Remco
EX $17   **NM** $35   **MIP** $60

Patton Figure, Excel Toy, poseable doll w/clothing and accessories
EX $20   **NM** $40   **MIP** $80

Prince Charles of Wales Figure, 1982, Goldberger, 13" tall, dressed in palace guard uniform
EX $18   **NM** $35   **MIP** $70

Sylvester Stallone Rambo Figure, 1986, 18" tall, poseable figure
EX $10   **NM** $20   **MIP** $40

TOY

Bonzo Scooter Toy, 7" scooter w/6" Bonzo, wind-up
EX $185   **NM** $400   **MIP** $600

Daktari Puzzle, 1967, Whitman, 100 pieces
EX $10   **NM** $30   **MIP** $100

Evel Knievel Stunt Stadium, 1974, Ideal, large vinyl case w/accessories
EX $50   **NM** $100   **MIP** $200

Jimmy Carter Wind-Up Walking Peanut, 5" tall
EX $10   **NM** $22   **MIP** $50

Joan Palooka Stringless Marionette, 1952, Nat'l Mask and Puppet, 12-1/2" tall "daughter of Joe Palooka" doll comes w/pink blanket and birth certificate
EX $75   **NM** $110   **MIP** $235

Komic Kamera Film Viewer Set, 1950s, 5" long, Dick Tracy, Little Orphan Annie, Terry and the Pirates and The Lone Ranger
EX $40   **NM** $100   **MIP** $175

Mr. and Mrs. Potato Head Set, 1960s, Hasbro, cars, boats, shopping trailer, etc.
EX $25   **NM** $55   **MIP** $110

Mr. Potato Head Frankie Frank, 1966, Hasbro, companion to Mr. Potato Head, w/accessories
EX $20   **NM** $40   **MIP** $90

Mr. Potato Head Frenchy Fry, 1966, Hasbro, companion to Mr. Potato Head, w/accessories
EX $20   **NM** $40   **MIP** $90

Red Ranger Ride 'Em Cowboy, 1930s, Wyandotte, tin wind-up rocker
EX $350   **NM** $500   **MIP** $750

Ringling Bros. and Barnum and Bailey Circus Play Set, 1970s, vinyl, w/animals, trapeze personnel, clowns and assorted circus equipment
EX $25   **NM** $50   **MIP** $125

Rin-Tin-Tin Magic Erasable Pictures, 1955, Transogram
EX $75   **NM** $135   **MIP** $260

Space Ghost Puzzle, 1967, Whitman
EX $20   **NM** $55   **MIP** $110

MOON MULLINS

ACCESSORIES

Moon Mullins and Kayo Toothbrush Holder, 4" tall, bisque
EX $100   **NM** $150   **MIP** $250

Moon Mullins Playstone Funnies Mold Set, 1940s
EX $40   **NM** $80   **MIP** $160

FIGURE

Moon Mullins Figure Set, bisque, Uncle Willie, Kayo, Moon Mullins and Emmy, 2-1/4" to 3-1/2"
EX $150   **NM** $300   **MIP** $550

TOY

Moon Mullins and Kayo Railroad Handcar Toy, 1930s, Marx, 6" long, wind-up, both figures bendable arms and legs
EX $475   **NM** $750   **MIP** $1300

Puzzle, 1930s, 9-1/2" x 14", Featured Funnies
EX $20   **NM** $60   **MIP** $140

MR. MAGOO

ACCESSORIES

Mr. Magoo Drinking Glass, 1962, 5-1/2" tall
EX $10   **NM** $25   **MIP** $50

DOLL

Mr. Magoo Doll, 1962, Ideal, 5" tall, vinyl head w/cloth body
EX $75   **NM** $125   **MIP** $250

Mr. Magoo Doll, 1970, Ideal, 12" tall
EX $50   **NM** $75   **MIP** $120

FIGURES

Mr. Magoo Figure, Dakin, 7" tall
EX $40   **NM** $90   **MIP** $180

TOY

Mr. Magoo Car, 1961, Hubley, 7-1/2" x 9" long, metal, battery-operated
EX $350   **NM** $450   **MIP** $700

Mr. Magoo Hand Puppet, 1960s, vinyl head, cloth body
EX $35   **NM** $80   **MIP** $145

Mr. Magoo Puzzle, 1978, Warren, frame tray
EX $10   **NM** $20   **MIP** $50

Mr. Magoo Soaky, 1960s, Palmolive, 10" tall, vinyl and plastic
EX $20   **NM** $50   **MIP** $90

MUTT AND JEFF

BANK

Mutt and Jeff Bank, 5" tall, cast iron, two piece construction held together by screw in the back
EX $150   **NM** $200   **MIP** $325

BOOK

Big Little Book, Whitman, Mutt and Jeff, #1113
EX $35   **NM** $75   **MIP** $140

Mutt and Jeff Caroon Book, 1910, Ball Publications, 68 pages
EX $300   **NM** $500   **MIP** $900

DOLL

Mutt and Jeff Dolls, 1920s, 8" x 6-1/2" tall, composition hands and heads w/heavy cast iron feet, movable arms and legs, fabric clothing; pair
EX $225   **NM** $400   **MIP** $750

FIGURES

Mutt and Jeff Figures, 1911, A. Steinhardt and Bros, ceramic, w/a coin inserted into base; pair
EX $120   **NM** $225   **MIP** $425

NIGHTMARE BEFORE CHRISTMAS

ACCESSORIES

Beach Towel, Fashion Victim
EX $22   **NM** $29   **MIP** $40

Brass Keychain, Disney, Jack Skellington's Tombstone
EX $3   **NM** $8   **MIP** $20

Buttons, set of 12 featuring logo, characters, etc.
EX $15   **NM** $20   **MIP** $75

Comforter, Wamsutta, twin size featuring Lock, Shock and Barrel
EX $45   **NM** $55   **MIP** $100

Drawstring Bag, Jack Skellington on front
EX $10   **NM** $15   **MIP** $25

Jack Soaky, glow head
EX $20   **NM** $35   **MIP** $75

Mug, Selandia, 16 oz. acrylic mug w/floating snowflakes and glitter
EX $5   **NM** $10   **MIP** $30

Mug, Selandia, 10 oz. acrylic mug w/floating snowflakes and glitter
EX $5   **NM** $10   **MIP** $30

Mylar Balloons, Anagram, five variations, each
EX $10   **NM** $15   **MIP** $35

Pencil, Whirly Sally or Whirly Jack
EX $4   **NM** $10   **MIP** $25

Purse, multi-compartment w/mirror
EX $10   **NM** $25   **MIP** $75

PVC Figure on Drinking Straws, Jack or Sally
EX $3   **NM** $7   **MIP** $10

Sunglasses, Jet Vision Limited
EX $12   **NM** $15   **MIP** $30

Tumbler, Selandia, 7 oz., acrylic
EX $10   **NM** $13   **MIP** $20

ACTION FIGURES

Magic Action Figures, Applause, set of three; 4" figures has its own action when rolled
EX $20   **NM** $30   **MIP** $60

BOOK

Pop-Up Book
EX $20   **NM** $45   **MIP** $90

CLOTHING

Bandanna, Fashion Victim, two styles: Jack or Lock, Shock and Barrel
EX $5   **NM** $15   **MIP** $45

Baseball Caps, Fashion Victim, three styles: Fishbone w/metal keychain; Lock, Shock and Barrel; or Jack "Bone Daddy"
EX $8   **NM** $10   **MIP** $20

Boxer Shorts, Stanley DeSantis, Lock, Shock and Barrel or Jack styles; cotton
EX $6   NM $8   MIP $12

Silk Necktie, many styles/patterns
EX $15   NM $22   MIP $45

Vest, Fashion Victim, Lock, Shock and Barrel or Jack styles
EX $12   NM $15   MIP $40

DOLL

Lock, Shock and Barrel Dolls, Applause, set of three; 6" cloth and vinyl dolls
EX $25   NM $60   MIP $120

Oogie Boogie Doll, Applause, 16"; makes farting noise when squeezed
EX $15   NM $40   MIP $90

Sally Doll, Hasbro, removable limbs
EX $100   NM $250   MIP $425

(KP Photo)

Santa Claus Doll, Applause, 10" plush
EX $10   NM $30   MIP $60

Santa Puppet Doll, Hasbro
EX $25   NM $50   MIP $85

Talking Jack Doll, Hasbro
EX $50   NM $130   MIP $360

FIGURE

Glow Oogie Boogie Figure, Applause, PVC figure
EX $7   NM $25   MIP $45

FIGURES

Jack Figure, Hasbro, bendy on card
EX $6   NM $20   MIP $40

Jack in Coffin Figure, Applause, 12"
EX $30   NM $100   MIP $325

Lock, Shock and Barrel Figures, Applause, set of three, 3" PVC figures
EX $10   NM $30   MIP $60

Mayor Figure, Hasbro, bendy on card
EX $10   NM $30   MIP $60

Sally Figure, Hasbro, bendy on card
EX $15   NM $40   MIP $80

Sally in Coffin Figure, Applause, 12"
EX $125   NM $250   MIP $500

Santa Jack Figure, Hasbro, bendy on card
EX $6   NM $12   MIP $25

GAME

Handheld Video Game, Tiger
EX $25   NM $35   MIP $80

GLASSWARE

Cookie Jar, Treasure Craft, ceramic; Jack on Tombstone
EX $100   NM $250   MIP $400

JEWELRY

Pin, Oopsa Daisy, several character styles, pewter
EX $10   NM $18   MIP $30

Rhinestone Pin, Oopsa Daisy, red stones featuring Jack Skellington
EX $40   NM $65   MIP $100

Rhinestone Pin, white stones featuring Jack Skellington
EX $30   NM $55   MIP $85

KITE

Sky Floater Kite, Spectra Star
EX $5   NM $15   MIP $50

MUSIC BOX

Mayor Wind-Up Music Box, Schmid, head spins while music plays "What's This?"
EX $60   NM $125   MIP $225

ORNAMENTS

Wooden Ornaments, Kurt S. Adler, set of 10; 4" to 6" tall; individually packaged
EX $20   NM $65   MIP $80

PAPER GOODS

Bionic Airwalker Balloon, Anagram, featuring Jack Skellington; over 7" tall
EX $15   NM $20   MIP $50

Bookmarks, OSP Publishing, set of eight styles including wallet cards
EX $10   NM $15   MIP $30

Gift Bags, Cleo, five styles available
EX $6   NM $10   MIP $20

Greeting Cards, set of six featuring various characters
EX $15   NM $35   MIP $85

Notepad, Beach, 75-sheet pad featuring Lock, Shock and Barrel
EX $3   NM $5   MIP $20

Partyware, Beach, 65 pieces
EX $14   NM $16   MIP $35

Postcard Book, 30 full-color postcards
EX $5   NM $20   MIP $60

Stickers, Gibson, featuring movie characters
EX $2   NM $6   MIP $15

Video Release Poster, Touchstone, 24" x 36"
EX $15   NM $50   MIP $75

STORE DISPLAY

Cardboard Store Display, Applause, over 6" wide
EX $150   NM $200   MIP $300

TATTOOS

Temporary Tattoos, US Kids
EX $2   NM $4   MIP $10

TOY

Kaleidoscope, C. Bennett Scopes
EX $20   NM $35   MIP $90

WRISTWATCH

Wristwatch, Timex, six styles available, each
EX $10   NM $40   MIP $90

YO-YO

Yo-Yo, Spectra Star
EX $10   NM $25   MIP $45

ACCESSORIES

Lucy Candlestick Holder, Hallmark, 7-1/4" figural composition
EX $15   NM $21   MIP $60

Snoopy Snippers Scissors, 1975, Mattel, plastic, Model No. 7410
EX $30   NM $45   MIP $70

Snoopy Toothbrush, 1972, Kenner, Snoopy on doghouse holder, Model No. 30301
EX $15   NM $30   MIP $50

Vaporizer/Humidifier, Milton Bradley, plastic, 13" x 16", Snoopy on doghouse
EX $45   NM $75   MIP $110

BANK

Peanuts Banks, 1970, United Features, set of five
EX $60   NM $100   MIP $200

Snoopy Bank, 1968, United Feature, 7" figural bank
EX $15   NM $35   MIP $90

BOOKS

Peanuts Projects, 1963, Determined, activity book
EX $30   NM $45   MIP $75

Peanuts Trace and Color, 1960s, Saalfield, five book set, Model No. 6122
EX $35   NM $50   MIP $125

Peanuts: A Book to Color, Saalfield, cover features Snoopy and Charlie Brown on skateboard, Model No. 4629
EX $25   NM $45   MIP $150

Speak Up, Charlie Brown Talking Storybook, 1971, Mattel, cardboard w/vinyl pages, Model No. 4812
EX $75   NM $150   MIP $200

COSTUMES

Charlie Brown Costume, Collegeville, w/mask
EX $15   NM $30   MIP $100

Snoopy as Flying Ace Costume, Collegeville, w/mask
EX $15   NM $30   MIP $100

CHARACTER TOYS

Snoopy Costume, Collegeville, w/mask
EX $12 **NM** $25 **MIP** $100

Woodstock Costume, Collegeville, w/mask
EX $12 **NM** $25 **MIP** $75

DOLL

Peppermint Patty Doll, 14" tall, cloth
EX $10 **NM** $20 **MIP** $60

Tub Time Snoopy Doll, 1980s, Knickerbocker, rubber, Model No. 0539
EX $15 **NM** $35 **MIP** $70

DOLLS

Charlie Brown Doll, 1958, Hungerford Plastics, 8-1/2" plastic
EX $60 **NM** $125 **MIP** $250

Charlie Brown Doll, 1970s, Determined, plastic; wearing baseball gear
EX $60 **NM** $100 **MIP** $200

Charlie Brown Doll, 1976, Ideal, removable clothing, Model No. 1412-6
EX $30 **NM** $70 **MIP** $140

Charlie Brown Pocket Doll, 1968, Boucher, 7", Model No. 800
EX $20 **NM** $32 **MIP** $100

Dolls, 1960s, Simon Simple, 7-1/2", Charlie Brown, Lucy, or Linus
EX $20 **NM** $50 **MIP** $100

Dress Me Belle Doll, 1983, Knickerbocker, Belle wearing pink dress w/blue dots, Model No. 1581
EX $15 **NM** $40 **MIP** $70

Dress Me Snoopy Doll, 1983, Knickerbocker, Snoopy wearing blue jeans and red/yellow shirt, Model No. 1580
EX $15 **NM** $40 **MIP** $70

Linus Doll, 1958, Hungerford Plastics, 8-1/2" plastic
EX $50 **NM** $100 **MIP** $225

Linus Doll, 1976, Ideal, removable clothing, Model No. 1414-2
EX $55 **NM** $100 **MIP** $215

Linus Pocket Doll, 1968, Boucher, 7", Model No. 801
EX $15 **NM** $25 **MIP** $60

Lucy Doll, 1958, Hungerford Plastics, 8-1/2" plastic
EX $50 **NM** $90 **MIP** $175

Lucy Doll, 1976, Ideal, removable clothing, Model No. 1411-8
EX $30 **NM** $60 **MIP** $125

Lucy Pocket Doll, 1968, Boucher, 7" open mouth, Model No. 802
EX $15 **NM** $25 **MIP** $50

Lucy Pocket Doll, 1968, Boucher, 7" smiling, Model No. 802
EX $15 **NM** $30 **MIP** $60

Peppermint Patty Doll, 1976, Ideal, removable clothing, Model No. 1413-4
EX $30 **NM** $45 **MIP** $70

Pigpen Doll, 1958, Hungerford Plastics, 8-1/2" plastic
EX $65 **NM** $100 **MIP** $175

Playmate Snoopy Doll, 1971, Determined, 6" plush, Model No. 819
EX $10 **NM** $20 **MIP** $70

Sally Doll, 1958, Hungerford Plastics, 6-1/2" plastic
EX $65 **NM** $100 **MIP** $175

Schroeder and Piano Doll, 1958, Hungerford Plastics, 7" plastic
EX $175 **NM** $275 **MIP** $450

Snoopy as Astronaut Doll, Knickerbocker, 5" vinyl
EX $75 **NM** $150 **MIP** $225

Snoopy as Astronaut Doll, 1969, Determined, 9", rubber head, plastic body, Model No. 808
EX $75 **NM** $150 **MIP** $225

Snoopy as Astronaut Doll, 1977, Ideal, 14" plush w/helmet and space suit, Model No. 1441-5
EX $200 **NM** $300 **MIP** $400

Snoopy as Magician Doll, 1977, Ideal, 14" plush w/cape, hat, and mustache, Model No. 1448-0
EX $110 **NM** $180 **MIP** $250

Snoopy as Rock Star Doll, 1977, Ideal, 14" plush w/wig, shoes and microphone, Model No. 1446-4
EX $115 **NM** $200 **MIP** $280

Snoopy Autograph Doll, 1971, Determined, 10-1/2", Model No. 838
EX $20 **NM** $25 **MIP** $60

Snoopy Doll, Ideal, 7" rag doll
EX $8 **NM** $20 **MIP** $60

Snoopy Doll, 1958, Hungerford Plastics, 7" plastic
EX $60 **NM** $100 **MIP** $225

Snoopy Doll, 1970s, Determined, plastic jointed
EX $25 **NM** $40 **MIP** $90

Snoopy Doll, 1971, Determined, 15" plush, felt eyes, eyebrows, and nose; red tag around neck
EX $25 **NM** $45 **MIP** $95

Snoopy Paper Dolls, 1976, Determined, w/10 outfits
EX $20 **NM** $40 **MIP** $75

Snoopy Pocket Doll, 1968, Boucher, 7" w/Flying Ace outfit, Model No. 803
EX $20 **NM** $35 **MIP** $80

GAME

Lucy Tea Party Game, 1972, Milton Bradley, Model No. 4129
EX $25 **NM** $50 **MIP** $100

Snoopy Snack Attack Game, 1980, Gabriel, Model No. 70345
EX $25 **NM** $40 **MIP** $75

Snoopy's Pound-A-Ball Game, 1980, Gabriel/Child Guidance, Model No. 51702
EX $35 **NM** $65 **MIP** $90

Table Top Snoopy Game, 1980s, Nintendo, Model No. SM-73
EX $65 **NM** $125 **MIP** $160

Tabletop Hockey, 1972, Munro Games
EX $65 **NM** $125 **MIP** $160

Tell Us a Riddle, Snoopy Game, 1974, Colorforms, Model No. 2397
EX $20 **NM** $55 **MIP** $100

MUSIC BOX

Linus Music Box, Anri, wood, Linus in pumpkin patch on cover, plays "Who Can I Turn To?"
EX $100 **NM** $150 **MIP** $200

Lucy and Charlie Brown Music Box, 1971, Anri, 4", each character beside large mushroom, plays "Rose Garden", Model No. 81973
EX $100 **NM** $175 **MIP** $250

Lucy Music Box, 1969, Anri, 6-1/2", Lucy behind psychiatrist booth, plays "Try to Remember", Model No. 819400
EX $100 **NM** $250 **MIP** $325

Lucy Music Box, 1971, Anri, 5", Lucy w/mushrooms on ground, plays "Love Story", Model No. 81981
EX $100 **NM** $250 **MIP** $325

Peanuts Music Box, 1972, Schmid, 8" wooden ferris wheel box/bank, plays "Spinning Wheel", Model No. 277408
EX $175 **NM** $600 **MIP** $375

Peanuts Music Box, 1984, Schmid, 8", ceramic, characters revolve around Christmas tree, plays "Joy to the World", Model No. 253724
EX $100 **NM** $200 **MIP** $325

Peanuts Music Box, 1985, Schmid, ceramic, characters piled on car, "Clown Capers", plays "Be a Clown", Model No. 289052
EX $85 **NM** $120 **MIP** $200

Schroeder Music Box, 1971, Anri, 5", Schroeder at the piano, plays "Beethoven's Emperor's Waltz", Model No. 819030
EX $110 **NM** $150 **MIP** $275

Snoopy as Astronaut Music Box, 1970s, Schmid
EX $25 **NM** $40 **MIP** $100

Snoopy Music Box, 1974, Aviva, 6", Snoopy w/hobo pack w/Woodstock, plays "Born Free"
EX $30 **NM** $45 **MIP** $100

Snoopy Music Box, 1979, Aviva, 8", Snoopy on doghouse shaped box, roof is removable lid, plays "Candy Man", Model No. 214
EX $50 **NM** $90 **MIP** $150

Snoopy Music Box, 1982, Aviva, ceramic heart-shaped base w/Snoopy and Woodstock hugging on top, plays "Love Makes the World Go Round", Model No. 215
EX $30 **NM** $60 **MIP** $100

Snoopy Music Box, 1984, Schmid, 7" ceramic, Snoopy and Woodstock on seesaw, plays "Playmates", Model No. 253709
EX $100 **NM** $125 **MIP** $175

Snoopy Music Box, 1984, Quantasia, ceramic Snoopy and musical note on base, plays "Fur Elise", Model No. 141017
EX $50   **NM** $65   **MIP** $85

Snoopy Music Box, 1985, Quantasia, plastic, Snoopy in boat inside waterglobe, plays "Blue Hawaii", Model No. 141020
EX $20   **NM** $40   **MIP** $75

Snoopy Music Box, 1986, Schmid, 6" ceramic, Snoopy as Lion Tamer, plays "Pussycat, Pussycat", Model No. 289053
EX $60   **NM** $85   **MIP** $150

Snoopy Music Box, 1986, Schmid, 7-1/2" ceramic, Snoopy next to Christmas tree, plays "O, Tannenbaum", Model No. 159101
EX $125   **NM** $175   **MIP** $250

PUZZLES

Puzzle, 1971, Determined, eight-panel cartoon strip, 1,000 pieces, Model No. 711-2
EX $15   **NM** $25   **MIP** $60

Puzzle, 1971, Determined, four "Love Is" scenes, 1,000 pieces, Model No. 711-4
EX $25   **NM** $40   **MIP** $80

Puzzle, 1973, Milton Bradley, Schroeder, Charlie Brown, Snoopy, and Lucy on baseball mound, Model No. 4383-3
EX $10   **NM** $22   **MIP** $60

Puzzle, 1979, Playskool, six pieces, Snoopy leaning on bat, Model No. 230-27
EX $5   **NM** $10   **MIP** $40

RADIOS

Snoopy and Woodstock Radio, 1970s, Determined, plastic, two-dimensional doghouse, Model No. 354
EX $30   **NM** $50   **MIP** $100

Snoopy Bank Radio, 1978, Concept 2000, plastic, Snoopy dancing, Model No. 4442
EX $65   **NM** $100   **MIP** $150

Snoopy Doghouse Radio, 1970s, Determined, plastic
EX $60   **NM** $85   **MIP** $140

Snoopy Hi-Fi Radio, 1977, Determined, three-dimensional Snoopy wearing headphones, plastic, Model No. 405
EX $60   **NM** $125   **MIP** $200

Snoopy Radio, 1970s, Determined, figural radio, Snoopy on green grass, plastic
EX $20   **NM** $40   **MIP** $85

Snoopy Radio, 1975, Determined, plastic two-dimensional, Model No. 351
EX $30   **NM** $65   **MIP** $150

Snoopy Radio, 1977, Determined, plastic square radio w/Snoopy pointing to dial
EX $30   **NM** $65   **MIP** $150

Snoopy, Woodstock, and Charlie Brown Radio, 1970s, Concept 2000, two-dimensional plastic, Model No. 4443
EX $20   **NM** $35   **MIP** $80

Snoopy's Spaceship AM Radio, 1978, Concept 2000, plastic, Model No. 4443
EX $75   **NM** $125   **MIP** $250

TOY

Batter-Up Snoopy Colorforms, 1979, Colorforms
EX $10   **NM** $35   **MIP** $60

Big Quart-O-Snoopy Bubbles, 1970s, Chemtoy
EX $9   **NM** $13   **MIP** $20

Camp Kamp Play Set, 1970s, Child Guidance, rubber camp building w/characters, Model No. 1683
EX $75   **NM** $100   **MIP** $150

Charlie Brown Deluxe View-Master Gift Pak, 1970s, GAF/View-Master, cylindrical container holds seven reels and viewer, Model No. 2380
EX $40   **NM** $75   **MIP** $100

(KP Photo)

Charlie Brown Nodder, 1960s, Japanese, 5-1/2" tall, bobbing head
EX $125   **NM** $200   **MIP** $350

Charlie Brown Punching Bag, 1970s, Determined
EX $15   **NM** $30   **MIP** $60

Charlie Brown Push Puppet, 1977, Ideal
EX $20   **NM** $45   **MIP** $85

Charlie Brown's All-Star Dugout Play Set, 1970s, Child Guidance, Model No. 1636
EX $20   **NM** $40   **MIP** $75

Charlie Brown's Backyard Play Set, 1970s, Child Guidance
EX $20   **NM** $40   **MIP** $80

Chirping Woodstock, 1977, Aviva, plastic w/electronic sound, Model No. 477
EX $18   **NM** $25   **MIP** $80

Electronic Snoopy Playmate, 1980, Romper Room/Hasbro, Model No. 830
EX $80   **NM** $125   **MIP** $200

Express Station Set, 1977, Aviva, Snoopy riding locomotive, Model No. 988
EX $40   **NM** $60   **MIP** $100

Joe Cool Punching Bag, 1976, Ideal, Model No. 5530-1
EX $20   **NM** $30   **MIP** $60

Joe Cool Push Puppet, 1977, Ideal
EX $20   **NM** $40   **MIP** $100

Kaleidorama, 1979, Determined, Model No. 4961
EX $20   **NM** $35   **MIP** $65

Lucy Nurse Push Puppet, 1977, Ideal
EX $20   **NM** $35   **MIP** $75

Lucy's Winter Carnival Colorforms, 1973, Colorforms, Model No. 7400
EX $20   **NM** $40   **MIP** $70

Official Peanuts Baseball, 1969, Wilson, illustrated w/characters
EX $40   **NM** $100   **MIP** $150

Parade Drum, 1969, Chein, large tin drum features characters in director's chairs, Model No. 1798
EX $100   **NM** $165   **MIP** $250

Peanuts Deluxe Play Set, 1975, Determined, includes Lucy's psychiatrist booth and three action figures, Model No. 575
EX $100   **NM** $200   **MIP** $300

Peanuts Drum, 1974, Chein, tin, features characters w/instruments, Model No. 1713
EX $85   **NM** $120   **MIP** $200

Peanuts Kindergarten Rhythm Set, 1972, Chein, four percussion instruments, Model No. 327
EX $100   **NM** $160   **MIP** $240

Peanuts Magic Catch Puppets, 1978, Synergistics, four characters w/Velcro balls
EX $10   **NM** $20   **MIP** $60

Peanuts Pelham Puppets, 1979, Pelham/Tiderider, 7"-8" Charlie Brown, Snoopy or Woodstock
EX $45   **NM** $90   **MIP** $180

Peanuts Puppets Display, 1979, Pelham/Tiderider, display theater
EX $350   **NM** $550   **MIP** $800

Peanuts Show Time Finger Puppets, 1977, Ideal, several rubber character puppets, Model No. 5379-3
EX $25   **NM** $35   **MIP** $70

Peanuts Skediddler Clubhouse Set, 1970, Mattel, three rubber skediddlers, Snoopy, Lucy, Charlie Brown, Model No. 3803
EX $125   **NM** $185   **MIP** $275

Peanuts Stackables, 1979, Determined, four hard rubber figures, Model No. 8642
EX $18   **NM** $25   **MIP** $35

Peanuts Tea Set, 1961, one tray, two plates, two cups, four small plates
EX $40   **NM** $60   **MIP** $100

Piano, 1960s, Ely, wood w/characters on top
EX $165   **NM** $275   **MIP** $425

Picture Maker, 1971, Mattel, plastic character stencils, Model No. 4153
EX $45   **NM** $65   **MIP** $90

Push and Play with the Peanuts Gang, 1970s, Child Guidance, plastic w/rubber characters, Model No. 1700
EX $30   **NM** $50   **MIP** $100

Push 'N' Fly Snoopy, 1980, Romper Room/Hasbro, pull toy featuring Snoopy the Flying Ace, Model No. 824
EX $12　　**NM** $20　　**MIP** $60

Rowing Snoopy, 1981, Mattel, Model No. 3478
EX $20　　**NM** $40　　**MIP** $90

Schroeder's Piano, 1970s, Child Guidance, Model No. 1701
EX $75　　**NM** $150　　**MIP** $300

See 'N' Say Snoopy Says, 1969, Mattel, Model No. 4864
EX $40　　**NM** $80　　**MIP** $125

Snoopy Action Toys, 1977, Aviva, wind-up Snoopy as drummer or boxer
EX $25　　**NM** $45　　**MIP** $70

Snoopy and Charlie Brown Copter, 1979, Aviva/Hasbro, plastic, Model No. 600
EX $15　　**NM** $25　　**MIP** $50

Snoopy and his Flyin' Doghouse, 1974, Mattel, Model No. 8263
EX $60　　**NM** $100　　**MIP** $175

Snoopy Color 'N' Recolor, 1980, Avalon, Model No. 742
EX $30　　**NM** $50　　**MIP** $80

Snoopy Copter Pull Toy, 1980, Romper Room, sound and action toy, Model No. 822
EX $6　　**NM** $10　　**MIP** $25

Snoopy Deep Diver Submarine, 1980s, Knickerbocker, plastic, Model No. 0553
EX $35　　**NM** $55　　**MIP** $70

Snoopy Drive-In Movie Theater, 1975, Kenner, Model No. 39570
EX $95　　**NM** $160　　**MIP** $300

Snoopy Express, 1977, Aviva, mechanical wind-up train, wood, includes track, tunnel, and signs, Model No. 922
EX $20　　**NM** $55　　**MIP** $90

Snoopy Express, 1982, Aviva, mechanical wind-up train, plastic, Model No. 70911
EX $20　　**NM** $35　　**MIP** $50

Snoopy Family Car, 1978, Aviva, Model No. 2700
EX $40　　**NM** $70　　**MIP** $90

Snoopy Gravity Raceway, 1977, Aviva, Model No. 990
EX $40　　**NM** $70　　**MIP** $120

Snoopy Gyro Cycle, 1982, Aviva/Hasbro, plastic friction toy, Model No. 70440
EX $20　　**NM** $50　　**MIP** $100

Snoopy High Wire Act, 1973, Monogram/Mattel, Model No. 6661
EX $25　　**NM** $45　　**MIP** $70

Snoopy in the Music Box, 1969, Mattel, metal jack-in-the-box, Model No. 4747
EX $15　　**NM** $30　　**MIP** $100

Snoopy is Joe Cool Model Kit, 1971, Monogram/Mattel, Snoopy rides surfboard, Model No. 7502
EX $40　　**NM** $80　　**MIP** $140

Snoopy Jack-in-the-Box, 1980, Romper Room/Hasbro, plastic doghouse jack-in-the-box, Model No. 818
EX $8　　**NM** $15　　**MIP** $40

Snoopy Magician Push Puppet, 1977, Ideal
EX $15　　**NM** $35　　**MIP** $80

Snoopy Marionette, 1979, Pelham/Tiderider, 27", Pelham Puppets, Model No. DP10
EX $300　　**NM** $475　　**MIP** $700

Snoopy Movie Viewer, 1975, Kenner, Model No. 35900
EX $15　　**NM** $25　　**MIP** $60

Snoopy Musical Ge-tar, 1969, Mattel, crank handle, Model No. 4715
EX $30　　**NM** $60　　**MIP** $120

Snoopy Musical Guitar, 1980, Aviva, plastic, crank handle, Model No. 444
EX $15　　**NM** $35　　**MIP** $70

Snoopy Nodder, 1960s, Japanese, 5-1/2" tall, bobbing head
EX $45　　**NM** $100　　**MIP** $225

Snoopy Paint-by-Number Set, 1980s, Craft House, 12" x 16"
EX $10　　**NM** $20　　**MIP** $50

Snoopy Phonograph, 1979, Vanity Fair, features picture of dancing Snoopy, Model No. 66
EX $100　　**NM** $130　　**MIP** $175

Snoopy Playhouse, 1977, Determined, plastic doghouse w/furniture, Snoopy, and Woodstock, Model No. 120
EX $50　　**NM** $80　　**MIP** $150

Snoopy Playland, 1978, Aviva, Snoopy in bus and six other characters, Model No. 888
EX $60　　**NM** $80　　**MIP** $125

Snoopy Radio-Controlled Doghouse, 1980, Aviva, Model No. 988
EX $35　　**NM** $60　　**MIP** $125

Snoopy Radio-Controlled Fire Engine, 1980, Aviva, w/Woodstock transmitter, Model No. 988
EX $50　　**NM** $75　　**MIP** $120

Snoopy Sheriff Push Puppet, 1977, Ideal
EX $20　　**NM** $30　　**MIP** $80

Snoopy Sign Mobile, 1970s, Avalon, Model No. 262
EX $50　　**NM** $80　　**MIP** $160

Snoopy Skediddler and His Sopwith Camel, 1969, Mattel, w/carrying case, Model No. 4954
EX $250　　**NM** $400　　**MIP** $500

Snoopy Slugger, 1979, Playskool, ball, bat and cap, Model No. 411
EX $20　　**NM** $40　　**MIP** $85

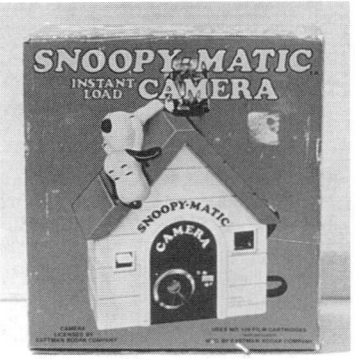

Snoopy Soaper, 1975, Kenner, gold soap dispenser w/Snoopy on top, Model No. 30700
EX $20　　**NM** $50　　**MIP** $85

Snoopy Tea Set, 1970, Chein, metal, features tray, plate, cups, and saucers, Model No. 276
EX $100　　**NM** $175　　**MIP** $250

Snoopy the Critic, 1977, Aviva, Snoopy and Woodstock on doghouse w/microphone, Model No. 222
EX $120　　**NM** $250　　**MIP** $300

Snoopy the Flying Ace Push Puppet, 1977, Ideal
EX $20　　**NM** $30　　**MIP** $90

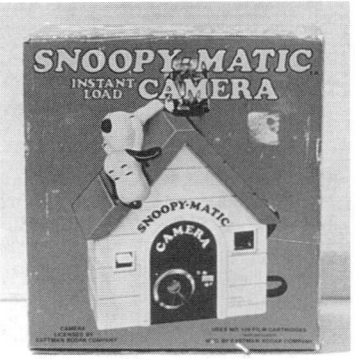

Snoopy-Matic Instant Load Camera, 1970s, Helm Toy, uses 110 film, Model No. 975
EX $95　　**NM** $150　　**MIP** $225

Snoopy's Beagle Bugle, 1970s, Child Guidance, plastic, Model No. 1730
EX $55　　**NM** $80　　**MIP** $120

Snoopy's Bubble Blowing Bubble Tub, 1970s, Chemtoy
EX $20　　**NM** $45　　**MIP** $60

Snoopy's Dog House, 1978, Romper Room/Hasbro, Snoopy walks on roof, Model No. 815
EX $20　　**NM** $45　　**MIP** $90

Snoopy's Dream Machine, 1979, DCS, w/blinking lights
EX $95　　**NM** $155　　**MiP** $220

Snoopy's Dream Machine, 1980, DCS, small version, no blinking lights, laminated cardboard, Model No. 417-M
EX $55   **NM** $80   **MIP** $120

Snoopy's Fantastic Automatic Bubble Pipe, 1970s, Chemtoy, Model No. 126
EX $5   **NM** $12   **MIP** $30

Snoopy's Good Grief Glider, 1970s, Child Guidance, spring load launcher, Model No. 1775
EX $50   **NM** $75   **MIP** $120

Snoopy's 'Lectric Comb and Brush, 1975, Kenner, Model No. 30900
EX $35   **NM** $50   **MIP** $70

(KP Photo)

Snoopy's Pencil Sharpener, 1974, Kenner, Model No. 3550
EX $25   **NM** $50   **MIP** $100

Snoopy's Shape Register, 1980, Gabriel/Child Guidance, plastic cash register, Model No. 51740
EX $30   **NM** $60   **MIP** $90

Snoopy's Soft House, 1980, Knickerbocker, soft cloth house, Model No. 0573
EX $25   **NM** $40   **MIP** $75

Snoopy's Stunt Spectacular, 1978, Child Guidance, Snoopy on motorcycle, Model No. 1750
EX $35   **NM** $50   **MIP** $90

Snoopy's Swim and Sail Club, 1970s, Child Guidance, characters and water vehicles, Model No. 1710
EX $45   **NM** $75   **MIP** $120

Snoopy's Take-a-Part Doghouse, 1980, Gabriel/Child Guidance, Model No. 51705
EX $15   **NM** $30   **MIP** $60

Spinning Top, Ohio Art, 5", Snoopy and the Gang
EX $10   **NM** $30   **MIP** $80

Spinning Top, 1960s, Chein, faces of Snoopy, Charlie Brown, Lucy, and Linus, Model No. 263
EX $40   **NM** $75   **MIP** $150

Stack-Up Snoopy, 1980, Romper Room/Hasbro, Model No. 818
EX $10   **NM** $13   **MIP** $25

Super Cartoon Maker, 1970, Mattel, molds to make character figures, Model No. 4696
EX $80   **NM** $130   **MIP** $180

Swimming Snoopy, 1970s, Concept 2000, Model No. 106
EX $15   **NM** $40   **MIP** $80

Talking Peanuts Bus, 1967, Chein, metal, chracters seen in windows, Model No. 261
EX $300   **NM** $500   **MIP** $800

Tell Time Clock, 1980s, Concept 2000, three styles: Snoopy, Woodstock or Charlie Brown
EX $15   **NM** $25   **MIP** $60

Woodstock Climbing String Action, 1977, Aviva/Hasbro, plastic, Model No. 667
EX $15   **NM** $28   **MIP** $60

Yankee Doodle Snoopy, 1975, Colorforms, Model No. 756
EX $20   **NM** $35   **MIP** $70

VEHICLES

Formula-1 Racing Car, 1978, Aviva, 11-1/2" plastic w/Woodstock or Snoopy, Model No. 950
EX $80   **NM** $125   **MIP** $185

Schroeder's Piano, Aviva
EX $30   **NM** $60   **MIP** $100

Snoopy and Woodstock in Wagon, Aviva, green die-cast w/white wheels, Model No. 72060
EX $10   **NM** $15   **MIP** $25

Snoopy and Woodstock on Skateboard, Aviva
EX $10   **NM** $15   **MIP** $25

Snoopy as Beagle Scout in Bus, 1983, Hasbro, die-cast
EX $4   **NM** $10   **MIP** $25

Snoopy as Flying Ace in Wagon, Aviva, yellow die-cast w/red wheels, Model No. 72057
EX $10   **NM** $20   **MIP** $45

Snoopy as Joe Cool in Wagon, Aviva, purple die-cast w/orange wheels, Model No. 72055
EX $10   **NM** $15   **MIP** $30

Snoopy Biplane, 1977, Aviva, die-cast, Snoopy as Flying Ace, Model No. 2024
EX $30   **NM** $50   **MIP** $90

Snoopy Emergency Set, Hasbro, Snoopy in three vehicles
EX $20   **NM** $50   **MIP** $90

Snoopy Family Car, 1977, Aviva, die-cast convertible, 2-1/4", Model No. 2028
EX $35   **NM** $55   **MIP** $90

Snoopy Handfuls, Hasbro, twin pack; characters in die-cast racers
EX $15   **NM** $35   **MIP** $60

Snoopy in Tow Truck, 1983, Hasbro, die-cast
EX $5   **NM** $10   **MIP** $30

Snoopy Racing Car Stickshifter, 1978, Aviva, Model No. 975
EX $90   **NM** $150   **MIP** $210

Snoopy Slot Car Racing Set, 1977, Aviva, Model No. XL500
EX $75   **NM** $120   **MIP** $220

Woodstock in Ice Cream Truck, Aviva, friction vehicle
EX $6   **NM** $9   **MIP** $15

WATCHES

Charlie Brown Wristwatch, 1970s, Determined, Charlie Brown in baseball gear, yellow face, black band
EX $65   **NM** $200   **MIP** $325

Lucy Wristwatch, 1970s, Timex, small chrome case, articulated arms, sweep seconds, white vinyl band
EX $35   **NM** $100   **MIP** $200

Lucy's Watch Wardrobe, 1970s, Determined, white face, comes w/blue, white, and pink bands
EX $60   **NM** $100   **MIP** $175

Snoopy Hero Time Watch, 1970s, Determined, Snoopy in dancing pose, red band
EX $75   **NM** $150   **MIP** $300

Snoopy Wristwatch, 1969, Determined, Snoopy in dancing pose, silver or gold case, various colors
EX $70   **NM** $140   **MIP** $275

Snoopy Wristwatch, 1970s, Lafayette Watch, Snoopy dancing, Woodstock is the second hand, silver case w/red face and black band
EX $70   **NM** $140   **MIP** $275

Snoopy Wristwatch, 1970s, Timex, gold bezel, tennis ball circles Snoopy on clear disk, articulated hands holding racket, denim background and band
EX $60   **NM** $90   **MIP** $175

PETER PAN

ACCESSORIES

Peter Pan Charm Bracelet, 1974
EX $30   **NM** $50   **MIP** $100

Peter Pan Map of Neverland, 1953, 18" x 24", collectors issue for users of Peter Pan Beauty Bar
EX $250   **NM** $400   **MIP** $600

Tinker Bell Pincushion, 1960s, w/1-1/2" tall Tinker Bell figure, in clear plastic display can
EX $25   **NM** $40   **MIP** $125

DOLL

Peter Pan Doll, 1953, Ideal, 18" tall
EX $100   **NM** $200   **MIP** $500

Peter Pan Doll, 1953, Duchess Doll, 11-1/2" tall, brown trim fabric shoes, green mesh stockings w/flocked outfit, hat w/a large red feather, shiny silver white metal dagger in belt, eyes, arms and head move
EX $175   **NM** $350   **MIP** $700

Tinker Bell Doll, 1953, Duchess Doll, 8" tall, flocked green outfit w/a pair of large white fabric wings w/gold trim, eyes open and close, jointed arms and head moves
EX $150   **NM** $300   **MIP** $600

Wendy Doll, 1953, Duchess Doll, 8" tall, full purple length skirt w/purple bow in

back of dress, eyes open and close, jointed arms and head moves
EX $150 **NM** $275 **MIP** $525

FIGURES

Captain Hook Figure, 8" tall, plastic
EX $10 **NM** $20 **MIP** $50

Peter Pan Baby Figure, 1950s, Sun Rubber
EX $70 **NM** $125 **MIP** $250

Peter Pan Paper Dolls, 1952, Whitman, 11 die-cut cardboard figures
EX $100 **NM** $175 **MIP** $300

Tinker Bell Figure, 1960s, Sutton, 7" tall, plastic and rubber figure
EX $25 **NM** $50 **MIP** $100

TOY

Captain Hook Hand Puppet, 1950s, Gund, 9" tall
EX $35 **NM** $70 **MIP** $175

Peter Pan Hand Puppet, 1953, Oak Rubber, rubber
EX $30 **NM** $70 **MIP** $160

Peter Pan Nodder, 1950s, 6" tall
EX $125 **NM** $250 **MIP** $400

Peter Pan Push Puppet, 1950s, Kohner, 6" tall, green and flesh colored beads, plastic head, light green plastic hat
EX $25 **NM** $50 **MIP** $110

Peter Pan Sewing Cards, 1952, Whitman
EX $15 **NM** $30 **MIP** $70

Puzzle, 1950s, Jaymar, frame tray puzzle shows Peter, Wendy, John and Michael flying over Neverland
EX $20 **NM** $42 **MIP** $90

PHANTOM

ACCESSORIES

Oil Paint by Numbers Set, 1967, Hasbro
EX $225 **NM** $320 **MIP** $550

Phantom 2040 Rubber Ball, 1995, Unice
EX $12 **NM** $17 **MIP** $30

Phantom Binoculars, 1976, Larami
EX $120 **NM** $155 **MIP** $225

Phantom Candy Jar, 1996, KFS, plastic w/figural lid
EX $12 **NM** $22 **MIP** $70

Phantom Club Rubber Stamper Skull Ring, 1950s
EX $500 **NM** $800 **MIP** $1200

Phantom Costume, 1950s, Ben Cooper
EX $175 **NM** $225 **MIP** $350

Phantom Costume, 1970s, Collegeville
EX $70 **NM** $90 **MIP** $150

Phantom Puffy Magnet, 1975, Hanna-Barbera
EX $40 **NM** $50 **MIP** $70

Phantom Squirt Camera, 1976, Larami
EX $100 **NM** $120 **MIP** $225

Playing Cards, 1990, Bulls Dist., Swedish
EX $16 **NM** $25 **MIP** $60

Playing Cards, 1990, John Sands
EX $16 **NM** $25 **MIP** $60

Rub-On Transfer Set, 1967, Hasbro
EX $100 **NM** $120 **MIP** $200

BOOK

Phantom Giant Games Book, 1968, World Distributors
EX $80 **NM** $125 **MIP** $200

COSTUME

Phantom Costume, 1989, Character Costumes
EX $40 **NM** $55 **MIP** $80

FIGURE

Phantom Figure, 1980s, 6" dark blue PVC figure
EX $25 **NM** $35 **MIP** $60

Phantom Figure, 1990s, 6" purple PVC figure
EX $12 **NM** $30 **MIP** $60

Phantom Figure, 1996, Street Players, 4" action figure w/skull throne or horse
EX $10 **NM** $20 **MIP** $40

Phantom Figures, 1990, Spain, 3-1/2", two pieces, purple PVC
EX $10 **NM** $20 **MIP** $40

Syrocco Figure, 1944, Pillsbury Mills, brown
EX $700 **NM** $1000 **MIP** $1600

Syrocco Figure, 1944, Pillsbury Mills, purple
EX $500 **NM** $900 **MIP** $1400

TOY

Phantom 2040 Carded Toys, 1995, Ja-Ru, sword, crossbow, gun or whistle light
EX $8 **NM** $12 **MIP** $30

Phantom Archery Set, 1976, Larami, bow, arrows, animals
EX $100 **NM** $125 **MIP** $220

Phantom Dagger Set, 1976, Larami, knife and sheath
EX $100 **NM** $120 **MIP** $250

Phantom Desert Survival Kit, 1976, Larami, canteen and Thermos bottle
EX $80 **NM** $120 **MIP** $200

Phantom Jungle Play Set, 1976, Larami, figure, palm trees, animals
EX $110 **NM** $160 **MIP** $325

Phantom Pathfinder Set, 1976, Larami, compass, canteen, binoculars, case
EX $80 **NM** $120 **MIP** $185

Phantom Pinback, 1940s, club member cello, Australia
EX $300 **NM** $750 **MIP** $1000

Phantom Safari Set, 1976, Larami, figure, truck, trailer, animals
EX $130 **NM** $180 **MIP** $275

Phantom Water Pistol, 1974, Nasta, w/holster
EX $70 **NM** $90 **MIP** $160

Phantom Water Pistol, 1974, Nasta
EX $80 **NM** $120 **MIP** $175

PINK PANTHER

ACCESSORIES

Pink Panther Memo Board, write on/wipe off memo board
EX $5 **NM** $10 **MIP** $25

BOOK

Pink Panther and The Fancy Party Book, Golden
EX $5 **NM** $10 **MIP** $30

Pink Panther and The Haunted House Book, Golden
EX $5 **NM** $10 **MIP** $35

Pink Panther at Castle Kreep Book, Whitman
EX $5 **NM** $10 **MIP** $35

Pink Panther at The Circus Sticker Book, 1963, Golden
EX $10 **NM** $20 **MIP** $50

Pink Panther Coloring Book, 1976, Whitman, cover shows Pink Panther roasting hot dogs
EX $10 **NM** $20 **MIP** $50

FIGURES

Pink Panther Figure, 1971, Dakin, 8" tall, w/legs open
EX $25 **NM** $50 **MIP** $100

Pink Panther Figure, 1971, Dakin, 8" tall, w/legs closed
EX $25 **NM** $50 **MIP** $100

GAME

Pink Panther Pool Game, 1980s, Ja-Ru
EX $10 **NM** $20 **MIP** $40

MUSIC BOX

Pink Panther Music Box, 1982, Royal Orleans, Christmas limited edition
EX $60 **NM** $80 **MIP** $150

Pink Panther Music Box, 1983, Royal Orleans, Christmas limited edition
EX $60 **NM** $80 **MIP** $150

Pink Panther Music Box, 1984, Royal Orleans, Christmas limited edition
EX $60 **NM** $80 **MIP** $150

TOY

Pink Panther Motorcycle, 2-1/2" plastic
EX $7 **NM** $15 **MIP** $50

Pink Panther One-Man Band, 1980, Illco, 10" tall, battery-operated, plush body w/vinyl head
EX $35 **NM** $70 **MIP** $100

Pink Panther Putty, 1970s, Ja-Ru
EX $4 **NM** $7 **MIP** $10

Pink Panther Wind-Up, 3" tall, plastic, walking wind-up w/trench coat and glasses
EX $20 **NM** $40 **MIP** $60

Puzzle, 1960s, Whitman, 100 pieces, several pictures available, each
EX $20 **NM** $35 **MIP** $60

PINOCCHIO AND JIMINY CRICKET

ACCESSORIES

Jiminy Cricket Toothbrush Set, 1950s, Dupont, plastic wall hanging Jiminy holds a toothbrush
EX $30 **NM** $55 **MIP** $90

Pinocchio Paperweight and Thermometer, 1940, Plastic Novelties
EX $30 **NM** $60 **MIP** $100

Pinocchio Plastic Cup, 1939, Safetyware, 2-3/4" tall, plastic
EX $35 **NM** $70 **MIP** $110

Pinocchio Snow Dome, 1970s, Disney, 3" x 4-1/2" x 5" tall, Pinocchio holds plastic dome between hands and feet
EX $20 **NM** $50 **MIP** $100

BANK

Pinocchio Bank, 1939, Crown Toy, 5" tall, wood composition w/metal trap door on back
EX $150 **NM** $300 **MIP** $450

Pinocchio Bank, 1960s, Play Pal Plastics, 11-1/2" tall, plastic
EX $15 **NM** $25 **MIP** $50

Pinocchio Bank, 1970s, Play Pal Plastics, 7" x 7" x 10" tall, vinyl, 3-D molded head of Pinocchio
EX $10 **NM** $20 **MIP** $50

BOOK

Pinocchio Book, 1939, Whitman, 96 pages
EX $40 **NM** $80 **MIP** $135

Pinocchio Book, 1939, Grosset and Dunlap, 9-1/2" x 13", laminated cover
EX $60 **NM** $125 **MIP** $200

Pinocchio Book, 1940, Big Little Book
EX $50 **NM** $100 **MIP** $200

Pinocchio Book Set, 1940, Whitman, 8-1/2" x 11-1/2", set of six books, 24 pages each
EX $200 **NM** $400 **MIP** $600

Pinocchio Cut-Out Book, 1940, Whitman
EX $125 **NM** $250 **MIP** $400

Pinocchio Paint Book, 1939, Disney, 11" x 15", heavy paper cover
EX $75 **NM** $150 **MIP** $300

Walt Disney Tells the Story of Pinocchio Book, 1939, Whitman, 4-1/4" x 6-1/2" paperback, 144 pages
EX $50 **NM** $80 **MIP** $140

Walt Disney's Pinocchio Book, 1939, Random House, 8-1/2" x 11-1/2", hardcover
EX $50 **NM** $100 **MIP** $180

DOLL

Jiminy Cricket Doll, 1940, Ideal, wooden jointed
EX $200 **NM** $400 **MIP** $750

Pinocchio and Jiminy Cricket Dolls, 1962, Knickerbocker, 6" tall, vinyl, titled "Knixies", each
EX $40 **NM** $60 **MIP** $110

Pinocchio Doll, 1939, Ideal, 12" tall w/wire mesh arms and legs
EX $225 **NM** $450 **MIP** $775

Pinocchio Doll, 1940, Ideal, 8" tall, wood composition head, others are jointed wood
EX $110 **NM** $250 **MIP** $550

Pinocchio Doll, 1940, Ideal, 10" tall, wood composition head, jointed arms and legs attached to body
EX $120 **NM** $300 **MIP** $600

Pinocchio Doll, 1940, Ideal, 19-1/2" tall, composition
EX $600 **NM** $950 **MIP** $1200

Pinocchio Doll, 1940, Knickerbocker, 3-1/2" x 4" x 9-1/2" tall, jointed composition doll w/movable arms and head
EX $600 **NM** $950 **MIP** $1200

FIGURES

Figaro Figure, 1940, Multi-Wood Products, 3" tall, wood composition
EX $65 **NM** $110 **MIP** $240

Figaro Figure, 1940s, Knickerbocker, composition, movable limbs and head
EX $120 **NM** $200 **MIP** $350

Gepetto Figure, 1940, Multi-Wood Products, 5-1/2" tall, wood composition
EX $55 **NM** $100 **MIP** $180

Gideon Figure, Multi-Wood Products, 5" tall
EX $40 **NM** $70 **MIP** $200

Honest John Figure, Multi-Wood Products, 2-1/2" x 3" base w/a 7" tall figure
EX $300 **NM** $400 **MIP** $500

Jiminy Cricket Figure, Marx, 3-1/2" x 4-3/4" tall, Snap-Eeze, white plastic base w/movable arms and legs
EX $30 **NM** $55 **MIP** $95

Jiminy Cricket Figure, 1940s, Ideal, wood jointed, hand painted
EX $200 **NM** $300 **MIP** $500

Lampwick Figure, 1940, Multi-Wood Products, 5-1/2" tall, wood composition
EX $80 **NM** $120 **MIP** $240

Pinocchio Figure, Crown Toy, 9-1/2" tall, jointed arms
EX $60 **NM** $110 **MIP** $275

Pinocchio Figure, 1940, Multi-Wood Products, 5" tall, wood composition
EX $80 **NM** $125 **MIP** $240

GAME

Pin the Nose on Pinocchio Game, 1939, Parker Brothers, 15-1/2" x 20"
EX $60 **NM** $120 **MIP** $210

MUSIC BOX

Pinocchio Music Box, plays "Puppet on a String"
EX $18 **NM** $35 **MIP** $85

TOY

Jiminy Cricket Hand Puppet, 1950s, Gund, 11" tall
EX $30 **NM** $60 **MIP** $140

Jiminy Cricket Marionette, 1950s, Pelham Puppets, 3" x 6" x 10" tall, dark green head with, large eyes, gray felt hat
EX $75 **NM** $160 **MIP** $350

Jiminy Cricket Ramp Walker, 1960s, Marx, 1" x 3" x 3" tall, pushing a bass fiddle
EX $80 **NM** $140 **MIP** $270

Jiminy Cricket Soaky, 7" tall bottle
EX $15 **NM** $50 **MIP** $80

Pinocchio and Jiminy Push Puppet, 1960s, Marx, 2-1/2" x 5" x 4" tall, double puppet
EX $30 **NM** $45 **MIP** $100

Pinocchio Color Box, Transogram, also known as paint box
EX $18 **NM** $35 **MIP** $80

Pinocchio Crayon Box, 1940s, Transogram, 4-1/2" x 5-1/2" x 1/2" deep, tin
EX $18 **NM** $35 **MIP** $85

Pinocchio Hand Puppet, Crown Toy, 9" tall, composition
EX $25 **NM** $45 **MIP** $70

Pinocchio Hand Puppet, 1950s, Gund, 10" tall, w/squeaker
EX $40 **NM** $75 **MIP** $150

Pinocchio Hand Puppet, 1962, Knickerbocker
EX $25 **NM** $50 **MIP** $85

Pinocchio Push Puppet, 1960s, Kohner, 5" tall
EX $15 **NM** $25 **MIP** $75

Pinocchio Soaky
EX $20 **NM** $40 **MIP** $85

Pinocchio Tea Set, 1939, Ohio Art, tin tray, plates, saucers, serving platter, cups, bowls and smaller plates
EX $175 **NM** $250 **MIP** $400

Pinocchio Walker, 1939, Marx, 9" tall, tin, animated eyes, rocking action
EX $375 **NM** $750 **MIP** $1000

Pinocchio Wind-Up Toy, Linemar, 6" tall, tin wind-up, arms and legs move
EX $200 **NM** $300 **MIP** $500

Puzzle, 1960s, Jaymar, 5" x 7", "Pinocchio's Expedition"
EX $12 **NM** $22 **MIP** $50

WATCH

Jiminy Cricket Wristwatch, 1948, US Time, Birthday Series
EX $250 **NM** $450 **MIP** $750

CHARACTER TOYS

PLUTO

ACCESSORIES

Pluto Alarm Clock, 1955, Allied, 4" x 5-1/2" x 10" tall, eyes and hands shaped like dog bones, glow in the dark
EX $100   NM $200   MIP $325

Pluto Purse, 1940s, Gund, 9" x 14" x 2"
EX $25   NM $55   MIP $100

BANK

Pluto Bank, 1940s, Disney, 4" x 4-1/2" x 6-1/2", ceramic
EX $60   NM $100   MIP $200

Pluto Bank, 1970s, Animal Toys Plus, 9" tall vinyl, Pluto standing in front of a doghouse
EX $20   NM $35   MIP $85

FIGURES

Pluto Figure, 1930s, Seiberling, 7" tall, rubber
EX $90   NM $120   MIP $200

Pluto Figure, 1930s, Seiberling, 3-1/2" long, rubber
EX $90   NM $120   MIP $200

Pluto Fun-E-Flex Figure, 1930s, Fun-E-Flex, wood
EX $50   NM $85   MIP $160

Pluto Pop-Up Critter Figure, 1936, Fisher-Price, wooden, Pluto standing on base 10-1/2" long
EX $100   NM $160   MIP $225

TOY

Pluto Hand Puppet, 1950s, Gund, 9" tall
EX $15   NM $35   MIP $80

Pluto Lantern Toy, 1950s, Linemar
EX $250   NM $350   MIP $500

Pluto Pop-A-Part Toy, 1965, Multiple Toymakers, 9" long, plastic
EX $20   NM $35   MIP $50

Pluto Push Toy, 1936, Fisher-Price, 8" long, wood
EX $150   NM $200   MIP $320

Pluto Rolykin, Marx, 1" x 1" x 1-1/2" tall, ball bearing action
EX $15   NM $35   MIP $70

Pluto Sports Car, Empire, 2" long
EX $10   NM $20   MIP $50

Pluto the Acrobat Trapeze Toy, Linemar, 10" tall, metal, celluloid, wind-up
EX $120   NM $250   MIP $350

Pluto the Drum Major, 1950s, Marx/Linemar, tin, mechanical
EX $300   NM $450   MIP $750

POPEYE

ACCESSORIES

60th Anniversary Candle Box, 1989, Presents, metal, heart shaped, #P5979
EX $5   NM $12   MIP $30

Bell, 1980, Vandor, Popeye on top, ceramic
EX $15   NM $20   MIP $35

Belt Buckle, U.S. Spinach Growers, Strength thru Spinach
EX $8   NM $20   MIP $40

Belt Buckle, 1973, Pyramid Belt, Popeye w/sailor hat
EX $10   NM $20   MIP $50

Belt Buckle, 1980, Lee, Popeye w/spinach
EX $8   NM $15   MIP $35

Blinky Cup, Beacon Plastics
EX $8   NM $15   MIP $25

Bookends, 1980, Vandor, ceramic, Popeye and Brutus
EX $20   NM $45   MIP $100

Bowl, 1971, Deka, oval, plastic
EX $10   NM $20   MIP $50

Bowl, 1979, National Home Products, plastic
EX $6   NM $12   MIP $25

Bowl, 1980, Vandor, ceramic, 1 of 3
EX $8   NM $18   MIP $40

Cabinet, mirrored
EX $75   NM $100   MIP $175

Candy, 1980, Alberts, bonbons
EX $6   NM $10   MIP $15

Candy Box, 1960, Phoenix Candy, Popeye and his pals
EX $20   NM $50   MIP $100

Candy Cigarettes, 1959, Primrose Confectionery - England
EX $15   NM $35   MIP $100

Candy Sticks, 1989, Hearst, red box
EX $6   NM $15   MIP $30

Candy Sticks, 1990, World Candies, 48 count
EX $6   NM $15   MIP $25

Cereal Bowl, 1979, National Home Products
EX $8   NM $20   MIP $45

Cereal Box, 1987, Cocoa-Puffs, w/gum
EX $25   NM $50   MIP $75

Charm Bracelet, 1990, Peter Brams, silver or gold
EX $10   NM $20   MIP $40

Chocolate Mold, 1940s, metal, Popeye
EX $35   NM $90   MIP $150

Chocolate Mold, 1991, Turmic Plastics, plastic, Popeye
EX $3   NM $6   MIP $10

Christmas Lamp Shades, 1930s, General Electric, set of ten
EX $150   NM $250   MIP $450

Christmas Light Covers, 1929, General Electric Textolite, "Cheers"
EX $125   NM $250   MIP $450

Christmas Ornament, 1981, Bully, Bluto
EX $8   NM $15   MIP $40

Christmas Ornament, 1981, Bully, Dufus
EX $8   NM $15   MIP $40

Christmas Ornament, 1987, Presents, Alice the Goon, Swee'Pea, Wimpy, Popeye, Olive Oyl or Brutus, each
EX $8   NM $15   MIP $40

Christmas Ornament, 1989, Presents, Season's Greetings
EX $8   NM $15   MIP $40

Christmas Tree Lamp Set, 1935, General Electric
EX $100   NM $300   MIP $500

Circus Man Film, 1950s, Brumberger, 8mm
EX $20   NM $30   MIP $60

Clothes Brush, 1929, KFS, wooden, black or brown
EX $30   NM $100   MIP $250

Color Markers, 1990, Sanrio, six
EX $2   NM $5   MIP $10

Comb and Brush, 1979, KFS
EX $8   NM $25   MIP $60

Cookie Jar, 1965, McCoy, ceramic white-suited Popeye
EX $200   NM $310   MIP $475

Cook's Catch-All, 1980, KFS, ceramic, Wimpy
EX $10   NM $20   MIP $50

Cup, 1940s, New Zealand, Popeye on skis, ceramic
EX $18   NM $40   MIP $80

Dice, 1990, w/Popeye head
EX $2   NM $5   MIP $15

Dish, 1940s, New Zealand, ceramic, Popeye and Olive
EX $30   NM $50   MIP $100

Dish Set, 1964, Boontonware, three piece plastic
EX $30   NM $45   MIP $90

Egg Cup, 1940s, Japan, Popeye sitting at table w/spinach
EX $30   NM $65   MIP $125

Egg Cup and Mug, 1989, Magna, Great Britain
EX $15   NM $40   MIP $75

Film Card, 1959, Tru-Vue, T-28
EX $8   NM $20   MIP $60

Freezicles, 1980, Imperial
EX $5   NM $15   MIP $20

Indian Fighter Film, Atlas Films, 8mm
EX $5   NM $10   MIP $20

Jackknife, 1940s, Imperial, green Popeye on pearl handle
EX $150   NM $250   MIP $350

Jeep Wall Plaque, ceramic
EX $6   NM $12   MIP $50

King of the Jungle Film, 1960s, Atlas Films, 8mm
EX $5   NM $10   MIP $30

Knapsack, 1979, Fabil
EX $10   NM $15   MIP $30

Kooky Straw, 1980, Imperial
EX $4   NM $10   MIP $20

Lamp, 1940s, boat w/Popeye light bulb
EX $500   NM $1000   MIP $1500

Life Raft, 1979, KFS, large, blue
EX $10   NM $20   MIP $40

Magic Eyes Film Card, 1962, Tru-Vue, set of three
EX $15   NM $25   MIP $60

Mini Hurricane Lamp, 1989, Presents, P5981-1993, 60th year
EX $4   NM $10   MIP $30

Mini Memo Board, 1980, Freelance
EX $5   NM $10   MIP $15

Mirror, 1978, Freelance, Popeye lifting weights
EX $7   NM $15   MIP $35

Mirror, 1979, Freelance, Olive w/mirror
EX $7   NM $15   MIP $35

Mirror Rattle, 1979, Cribmates
EX $8   NM $13   MIP $30

Mug, 1950s, Schmid, ceramic
EX $10   NM $20   MIP $40

Music Lovers Film, 1960s, Atlas Films, 8mm
EX $8   NM $15   MIP $20

Musical Mug, 1982, KFS, ceramic
EX $10   NM $20   MIP $35

Musical Rattle, 1979, Cribmates
EX $8   NM $15   MIP $30

(KP Photo)

Olive Oyl and Swee'Pea Hot Water Bottle, 1970, Duarry
EX $75   NM $100   MIP $200

Olive Oyl and Swee'Pea Snow Globe, 1989, Presents, several styles
EX $7   NM $15   MIP $40

Olive Oyl and Swee'Pea Telephone Shoulder Rest, 1982, Comvu
EX $6   NM $15   MIP $40

Olive Oyl and Swee'Pea Thermometer, 1981, KFS
EX $8   NM $13   MIP $20

Olive Oyl Cup, 1977, Coke, Coke Kollect-A-Set
EX $4   NM $10   MIP $30

Olive Oyl Hairbrush, 1979, Cribmates, musical
EX $8   NM $20   MIP $60

Olive Oyl Mug, 1950s, Schmid, musical ceramic
EX $15   NM $40   MIP $80

Olive Oyl Mug, 1980, Vandor, ceramic
EX $8   NM $15   MIP $25

Olive Oyl Wall Plaque, ceramic
EX $3   NM $7   MIP $20

Paper Party Blowouts, 1988, Gala/James River
EX $2   NM $4   MIP $10

Paperweight, 1937, "Popeye Eats Del Monte Spinach"
EX $100   NM $175   MIP $250

Pencil Case, 1936, Eagle, beige, #9027
EX $75   NM $125   MIP $250

Pencil Case, 1950s, Hassenfeld Bros., red
EX $35   NM $75   MIP $150

Pencil Case, 1990, Sanrio
EX $5   NM $10   MIP $20

Pencil Sharpener, 1929, KFS, orange celluloid
EX $40   NM $75   MIP $125

Pig for a Friend Mug, 1980, Vandor, ceramic
EX $6   NM $12   MIP $50

Playing Cards, 1988, Presents, metal box, #P5998, two decks, 60th year
EX $4   NM $10   MIP $25

Popeye Alarm Clock, 1967, Smiths, British
EX $100   NM $180   MIP $320

Popeye and Betty Boop Film, 1935, Exclusive Films, 8mm film
EX $15   NM $25   MIP $50

Popeye and Cast Cigar Box
EX $25   NM $45   MIP $90

Popeye and Olive Oyl Suspenders, 1979, KFS, blue
EX $6   NM $12   MIP $25

Popeye and Swee'Pea Snow Globe, 1989, Presents, several varieties
EX $5   NM $10   MIP $25

Popeye Apron, 1990, Chester
EX $4   NM $8   MIP $15

Popeye Beach Set, 1950s, Peer Products/KFS, plastic rowboat, accessories
EX $25   NM $50   MIP $100

Popeye Charm, solid gold
EX $100   NM $150   MIP $200

Popeye Charm, silver w/ dangly parts
EX $20   NM $30   MIP $60

Popeye Charm, 1930s, celluloid
EX $40   NM $60   MIP $100

Popeye Cup, 1979, Deca Plastics, plastic
EX $5   NM $10   MIP $25

Popeye Cup, 1989, Popeye Picnic, plastic
EX $1   NM $2   MIP $5

Popeye Cup and Saucer, 1930s, Japan
EX $40   NM $85   MIP $185

Popeye Glass, 1977, Coke, Coke Kollect-A-Set
EX $4   NM $10   MIP $25

Popeye Hot Water Bottle, 1970, Duarry
EX $40   NM $90   MIP $175

(KP Photo)

Popeye Lamp, 1940s, telescope w/Popeye at base
EX $225   NM $350   MIP $575

Popeye Lamp, 1959, Alan Jay, Popeye w/legs folded holding spinach
EX $75   NM $100   MIP $210

(KP Photo)

Popeye Mechanical Pencil, 1929, Eagle, 10-1/2" long illustrated pencil w/box
EX $50   NM $75   MIP $150

Popeye Night Light, Arrow Plastic
EX $8   NM $13   MIP $20

Popeye Picture, KFS-Sears, silver foil
EX $10   NM $20   MIP $40

Popeye Pin, Popeye at steering wheel, stick pin
EX $5   NM $12   MIP $35

Popeye Popcorn, 1949, Purity Mills, in can
EX $65   NM $100   MIP $150

Popeye Snow Globe, 1960s, KFS, Popeye holds globe between legs
EX $25   NM $45   MIP $100

Popeye Thimble, 1990
EX $4   NM $7   MIP $10

Popeye Toothbrush Holder, Vandor, 5"tall, figural
EX $10   NM $15   MIP $30

Popeye Toothbrush Set, 1980s, Nasta, holds two toothbrushes
EX $6   NM $15   MIP $25

Popeye Utensils, 1970s, Arrow Plastic, spoon and fork
EX $8 **NM** $15 **MIP** $30

Popeye Wall Hanging, 1979, Amscan, 42", jointed
EX $8 **NM** $13 **MIP** $20

Popeye Writing Tablet, 1929, KFS, Popeye w/spinach hypo
EX $75 **NM** $100 **MIP** $185

Popeye/Olive Oyl/Swee'Pea Lamp Shade, 1950s
EX $50 **NM** $75 **MIP** $185

Popeye/Olive Oyl/Wimpy Decals, 1935, IGS Stores
EX $25 **NM** $40 **MIP** $85

Punching Bag Film, 1950s, Brumberger, 8mm
EX $8 **NM** $15 **MIP** $30

Rain Boots, 1950s, KFS, spinach power
EX $15 **NM** $30 **MIP** $60

Record Player, 1960s, Emerson, Dynamite Music Machine
EX $50 **NM** $100 **MIP** $170

Secret Message Pen, 1981, Gordy
EX $6 **NM** $12 **MIP** $30

Sketchbook, 1960, Japan
EX $15 **NM** $25 **MIP** $60

Sleeping Bag, 1979, KFS
EX $15 **NM** $35 **MIP** $65

Soap Dispenser, 1970s, Woolfoam
EX $15 **NM** $25 **MIP** $35

Soap on a Rope, KFS, white, shaped like Popeye's head
EX $15 **NM** $25 **MIP** $60

Soap Set, 1930s, Kerk Guild, Olive Oyl, Swee'Pea, and Popeye soap figures
EX $200 **NM** $400 **MIP** $600

Stationery, 1989, Presents, metal box, heart-shaped note paper, #P5976
EX $6 **NM** $10 **MIP** $20

Storage Box, 1990, Sanrio, smoke colored
EX $6 **NM** $10 **MIP** $15

Sunday Funnies Soda Can, 1970s, Flavor Valley
EX $8 **NM** $15 **MIP** $25

Suspenders, 1970s, red, white and blue w/plastic emblems
EX $10 **NM** $20 **MIP** $35

Swee'Pea Cup, 1977, Coke, Coke Kollect-A-Cup
EX $4 **NM** $7 **MIP** $12

Swee'Pea Egg Cup, 1980, Vandor, ceramic
EX $10 **NM** $20 **MIP** $35

Swee'Pea Night Light, 1978, Presents, bone china
EX $20 **NM** $30 **MIP** $60

Swee'Pea Snow Globe, 1989, Presents, several styles
EX $10 **NM** $15 **MIP** $30

Swee'Pea Wall Plaque, 1950s, ceramic
EX $12 **NM** $35 **MIP** $70

Swee'Pea's Lemonade Stand Television Film, 1950s, Zaboly
EX $12 **NM** $25 **MIP** $60

Training Cup, 1971, Deka
EX $8 **NM** $13 **MIP** $30

Transistor Radio, 1960s, Philgee
EX $35 **NM** $60 **MIP** $100

Trash Can, 1980s, KFS
EX $10 **NM** $30 **MIP** $50

Trinket Box, 1980, Vandor, Popeye laying on top, ceramic
EX $10 **NM** $16 **MIP** $30

Trinket Box, 1980, Vandor, Popeye's head in preserver, ceramic
EX $10 **NM** $18 **MIP** $35

TV Tray, 1979, KFS
EX $8 **NM** $15 **MIP** $30

Umbrella, 1979, KFS, blue and white
EX $20 **NM** $35 **MIP** $80

Wagon Works Film, 1960s, Atlas Films, 8mm
EX $6 **NM** $10 **MIP** $25

Wallet, 1978, Larami
EX $8 **NM** $20 **MIP** $50

Wallet, 1990, Sanrio
EX $6 **NM** $10 **MIP** $20

Wallet, 1991, Presents, P-5432, tri-fold
EX $6 **NM** $10 **MIP** $20

Whistle Candy, 1989, Alberts
EX $6 **NM** $10 **MIP** $20

Wimpy Cup, 1977, Coke, Coke Kollect-A-Set
EX $4 **NM** $7 **MIP** $10

Wimpy Magnet
EX $6 **NM** $10 **MIP** $15

Wimpy Thermometer, 1981, KFS
EX $10 **NM** $15 **MIP** $25

Write on/Wipe Off Board, 1979, Freelance
EX $10 **NM** $20 **MIP** $40

BADGE

Popeye and Swee'Pea Flicker Badge, 1960s, Varivue
EX $10 **NM** $20 **MIP** $50

Popeye and Wimpy Flicker Badge, 1960s, Varivue
EX $10 **NM** $20 **MIP** $50

BANK

60th Anniversary Bank, 1988, Presents, metal, P5988
EX $15 **NM** $30 **MIP** $60

Brutus Mini Bank, 1979, KFS
EX $10 **NM** $20 **MIP** $50

(KP Photo)

Daily Dime Bank, 1956, KFS
EX $60 **NM** $150 **MIP** $260

(KP Photo)

Daily Quarter Bank, 1950s, Kalon, 4-1/2" tall, metal
EX $150 **NM** $300 **MIP** $500

(KP Photo)

Dime Register Bank, 1929, KFS, square, window shows total deposits
EX $175 **NM** $300 **MIP** $525

Knockout Bank, 1935, Straits
EX $500 **NM** $800 **MIP** $1300

Olive Oyl Bank, 1940s, cast iron
EX $200 **NM** $300 **MIP** $500

Olive Oyl Mini Bank, 1979, KFS
EX $15 **NM** $30 **MIP** $60

Popeye Bank, ceramic, Popeye in light blue cap
EX $5 **NM** $10 **MIP** $30

Popeye Bank, 1940s, Popeye w/life preserver
EX $100 **NM** $150 **MIP** $300

Popeye Bank, 1940s, 9" cast iron
EX $175 **NM** $250 **MIP** $375

Popeye Bank, 1970s, Play Pal, plastic, Popeye sitting on rope
EX $10   NM $30   MIP $55

Popeye Bank, 1972, Play Pal, shape of Popeye's head, plastic
EX $15   NM $30   MIP $65

Popeye Bank, 1979, Renz, beige bust
EX $12   NM $25   MIP $60

Popeye Bank, 1980, Leonard, silver, Popeye sitting
EX $15   NM $30   MIP $60

Popeye Bank, 1980, Vandor, ceramic, Popeye sitting on rope
EX $12   NM $25   MIP $50

Popeye Bank, 1980, Vandor, ceramic
EX $130   NM $260   MIP $525

Popeye Bank, 1990, Sanrio, w/padlock
EX $5   NM $10   MIP $25

Popeye Bank, 1990, Mexico, ceramic bust
EX $20   NM $35   MIP $50

Popeye Bank, 1991, Presents, vinyl, Popeye w/removable pipe
EX $6   NM $12   MIP $25

Popeye Mini Bank, 1979, KFS
EX $10   NM $20   MIP $40

Spinach Can Bank, 1975, KFS, blue can w/raised characters
EX $20   NM $40   MIP $80

Swee'Pea Bank, 1980, Vandor, 6-1/2" figural
EX $80   NM $125   MIP $200

Swee'Pea Mini Bank, 1979, KFS
EX $20   NM $40   MIP $90

BOOK

60th Anniversary Collection Book, 1990, Hawk Books
EX $20   NM $40   MIP $60

Adventures of Popeye Book, 1934, Saalfield
EX $75   NM $175   MIP $400

Big Surprise Book, 1976, Wonder Books
EX $5   NM $15   MIP $40

Captain George Presents Popeye Book, 1970, Memory Lane
EX $10   NM $25   MIP $55

Danger Ahoy! Book, 1969, Whitman, Big Little Book
EX $5   NM $15   MIP $35

Deep Sea Danger Book, 1980, Whitman, Big Little Book
EX $2   NM $6   MIP $20

Fun Booklets, 1980, Spot-O-Gold, set of 10
EX $20   NM $40   MIP $80

Ghost Ship to Treasure Island Book, 1967, Whitman, Big Little Book
EX $8   NM $15   MIP $45

Giant 24 Big Picture Coloring Book, 1981, Merrigold Press
EX $6   NM $12   MIP $50

Giant Paint Book, 1937, Whitman, blue or red
EX $100   NM $175   MIP $300

Great Big Popeye Paint and Crayon Book, 1937, McLoughlin Bros.
EX $125   NM $250   MIP $400

Hag of the Seven Seas Pop-Up Book, 1935, Blue Ribbon Books
EX $200   NM $350   MIP $600

House that Popeye Built Book, 1960, Wonder Books
EX $8   NM $25   MIP $55

In a Sock for Susan's Sake Book, 1940, Whitman, Big Little Book
EX $30   NM $75   MIP $180

In Quest of Poopdeck Pappy Book, 1937, Whitman, Big Little Book
EX $30   NM $75   MIP $180

Jiffy Pop Fun 'N Games Booklet, 1980, Spot-O-Gold
EX $6   NM $12   MIP $30

Little Pops the Ghost Book, 1981, Random House
EX $5   NM $10   MIP $30

Little Pops the Magic Flute Book, 1981, Random House
EX $5   NM $10   MIP $30

Little Pops the Spinach Burgers Book, 1981, Random House
EX $5   NM $10   MIP $30

Little Pops the Treasure Hunt Book, 1981, Random House
EX $5   NM $10   MIP $30

Mix or Match Storybook, 1981, Random House
EX $8   NM $15   MIP $30

Olive Oyl and Swee'Pea Wash Up Book, 1980, Tuffy Books
EX $4   NM $10   MIP $25

Paint with Water Book, 1981, Whitman
EX $3   NM $6   MIP $20

Painting and Crayon Book, 1960, England
EX $15   NM $25   MIP $80

Popeye Activity Pad, 1982, Merrigold Press
EX $3   NM $7   MIP $15

Popeye All Picture Comic Book, 1942, Whitman, Big Little Book
EX $50   NM $100   MIP $200

Popeye and his Jungle Pet Book, 1937, Whitman
EX $50   NM $100   MIP $200

Popeye and Swee'Pea Coloring Book, 1970, Whitman, 1056-31
EX $7   NM $15   MIP $50

Popeye and the Deep Sea Mystery Big Little Book, 1939, Whitman
EX $50   NM $100   MIP $200

Popeye and the Jeep Book, 1937, Whitman, Big Little Book
EX $50   NM $100   MIP $200

Popeye and the Pet Book, 1987, Peter Haddock, book three of four
EX $3   NM $5   MIP $25

Popeye and the Time Machine Book, 1990, Quaker, mini comic
EX $3   NM $5   MIP $25

Popeye Book, 1980, Random House, hardcover, based on movie
EX $4   NM $8   MIP $20

Popeye Calls on Olive Oyl Book, 1937, Whitman, 8-1/2" x 9-1/2"
EX $50   NM $80   MIP $180

Popeye Climbs a Mountain Book, 1983, Wonder Books
EX $3   NM $7   MIP $20

Popeye Color and Recolor Book, 1957, Jack Built, color, wipe and color again
EX $25   NM $50   MIP $120

Popeye How to Draw Cartoons Book, 1939, Joe Musial/D. McKay
EX $100   NM $150   MIP $300

Popeye in Puddleburg Book, 1934, Saalfield, Big Little Book
EX $50   NM $100   MIP $200

Popeye Learn and Play Activity Book, 1985, Allen Canning
EX $2   NM $5   MIP $10

Popeye Meets his Rival Book, 1937, Whitman, 8-1/2" x 11-1/2"
EX $50   NM $100   MIP $200

Popeye on Rocket Coloring Book, 1980, Whitman - France
EX $8   NM $15   MIP $40

Popeye on Safari Book, 1990, Quaker, mini comic
EX $2   NM $4   MIP $8

Popeye Paint Book, 1932, McLoughlin Bros., blue
EX $100   NM $150   MIP $325

Popeye Paint Coloring Book, 1951, Whitman
EX $25   NM $60   MIP $140

Popeye Pop-Up Book, 1981, Random House
EX $6   NM $12   MIP $40

Popeye Punch-Out Play Book, 1961, Whitman
EX $12   NM $22   MIP $45

Popeye Puppet Show Book, 1936, Pleasure Books
EX $75   NM $125   MIP $200

Popeye Sees the Sea Book, 1936, Whitman, Big Little Book
EX $50   NM $100   MIP $200

Popeye Song Folio Book, 1936, Famous Music, Z
EX $50   NM $90   MIP $160

Popeye Stay in Shape Book, 1980, Tuffy Books
EX $6   NM $10   MIP $20

Popeye Surprise Present Book, 1987, Peter Haddock
EX $6   NM $10   MIP $20

Popeye the Movie Book, 1980, Avon Printing
EX $6   NM $10   MIP $25

(KP Photo)

Popeye the Sailor Man Book, 1942, Whitman, Big Little Book
EX $40   **NM** $90   **MIP** $180

Popeye vs. Bluto the Bad Book, 1990, Quaker, mini comic
EX $2   **NM** $4   **MIP** $10

Popeye with his Friends Book, 1937, Whitman
EX $50   **NM** $100   **MIP** $200

Popeye's Adventure Book, 1958, Purnell, England
EX $15   **NM** $30   **MIP** $80

Popeye's Ark Book, 1936, Saalfield, Big Little Book
EX $50   **NM** $100   **MIP** $200

Puzzle Party Book, 1979, Cinnamon House
EX $6   **NM** $12   **MIP** $25

Quest for the Rainbird Book, 1943, Whitman, Big Little Book
EX $40   **NM** $75   **MIP** $120

Race to Pearl Peak Book, 1982, Golden
EX $6   **NM** $10   **MIP** $20

S.S. Funboat Coloring Book, 1981, Merrigold Press
EX $5   **NM** $10   **MIP** $40

Sailor and the Spinach Stalk Coloring Book, 1982, Whitman, 1150-1
EX $6   **NM** $15   **MIP** $30

Scott Fun 'N Games Booklet, 1980, Spot-O-Gold, set of five
EX $10   **NM** $20   **MIP** $40

The Outer Space Zoo Book, 1980, Golden
EX $6   **NM** $12   **MIP** $30

Thimble Theatre Book, 1935, Whitman, Big Big Book
EX $200   **NM** $350   **MIP** $650

What! No Spinach? Book, 1981, Golden
EX $6   **NM** $10   **MIP** $25

Wimpy in Back to his First Love Book, eight pages
EX $6   **NM** $10   **MIP** $15

Wimpy the Hamburger Eater Book, 1938, Whitman, Big Little Book
EX $50   **NM** $100   **MIP** $200

Wimpy Tricks Popeye and Roughhouse Book, 1937, Whitman
EX $50   **NM** $100   **MIP** $200

Wimpy Tricks Popeye Book, 1937, Whitman
EX $50   **NM** $90   **MIP** $180

Wimpy What's Good to Eat? Book, 1980, Tuffy Books
EX $6   **NM** $12   **MIP** $30

BUTTON

Bluto Button, 1979, Lisa Frank, 2", Bluto getting socked
EX $2   **NM** $7   **MIP** $15

Brutus Button, 1980, Factors, 3", movie
EX $2   **NM** $5   **MIP** $10

Brutus Button, 1983, Mini Media, 1", "I'm Mean"
EX $2   **NM** $5   **MIP** $10

Brutus Button, 1985, Strand, 3", "Gonna Eat You for Breakfast"
EX $3   **NM** $6   **MIP** $12

Brutus Button, 1985, Strand, 3", "Ya Little Runt"
EX $2   **NM** $5   **MIP** $10

Button, 1930s, Offset Gravure, 1", New York Evening Journal
EX $50   **NM** $80   **MIP** $135

Button, 1983, Mini Media, 1", "No Wimps"
EX $3   **NM** $7   **MIP** $15

Olive Oyl Button, 1946, Pep
EX $8   **NM** $25   **MIP** $45

Olive Oyl Button, 1980, Factors, 3"
EX $2   **NM** $4   **MIP** $8

Olive Oyl Button, 1983, Mini Media, 1", "More than just a pretty face"
EX $2   **NM** $4   **MIP** $8

Popeye and Olive Oyl Button, 1970s, 1-1/2", "I Love You"
EX $5   **NM** $10   **MIP** $22

Popeye and Olive Oyl Button, 1980, Lisa Frank, 1", cowboy Popeye and Indian Olive
EX $5   **NM** $10   **MIP** $20

Popeye Button, 1946, Pep
EX $15   **NM** $35   **MIP** $65

Popeye Button, 1950s, KFS, 1", Famous Studios
EX $20   **NM** $40   **MIP** $100

(KP Photo)

Popeye Button, 1959, Lowe, sew-on card
EX $12   **NM** $20   **MIP** $60

Popeye Button, 1960s, KMOX TV, 1", S.S. Popeye
EX $5   **NM** $15   **MIP** $65

Popeye Button, 1980, Factors, 3", movie
EX $2   **NM** $4   **MIP** $10

Popeye Button, 1985, Strand, 3", several styles
EX $3   **NM** $6   **MIP** $20

Popeye Button, 1989, KFS, 3", marine conservation
EX $2   **NM** $4   **MIP** $10

Popeye Button, 1990, S. Cruz, 2", Santa Cruz boardwalk
EX $2   **NM** $4   **MIP** $10

Swee'Pea Button, 1980, Lisa Frank, 1", Swee'Pea w/Jeep
EX $2   **NM** $5   **MIP** $12

Wimpy Button, 1946, Pep
EX $10   **NM** $20   **MIP** $50

Wimpy Button, 1979, Lisa Frank, 2"
EX $3   **NM** $8   **MIP** $15

Wimpy Button, 1985, Strand, 3", "Must Go Home and Water the Ducks"
EX $3   **NM** $8   **MIP** $15

DOLL

Brutus Doll, 1985, Presents, small
EX $12   **NM** $25   **MIP** $75

Brutus Doll, 1985, Presents, large with tag
EX $20   **NM** $50   **MIP** $120

Chimes Doll, 1950s, J. Swedlin, gray plush body, chimes
EX $20   **NM** $50   **MIP** $100

Jeep Doll, 1985, Presents, two sizes
EX $10   **NM** $25   **MIP** $80

Olive Oyl Doll, 9" vinyl sqeeze doll, Olive w/ Swee'Pea
EX $15   **NM** $40   **MIP** $100

Olive Oyl Doll, 1950s, Rempel, small
EX $25   **NM** $50   **MIP** $120

Olive Oyl Doll, 1960s, Dakin, 8" tall
EX $25   **NM** $50   **MIP** $120

Olive Oyl Doll, 1970s, Dakin, hard plastic w/ removable clothes
EX $20   **NM** $40   **MIP** $100

Olive Oyl Doll, 1970s, Dakin, Cartoon Theatre, in box
EX $25   **NM** $50   **MIP** $120

Olive Oyl Doll, 1979, Uneeda, removable clothing
EX $15   **NM** $30   **MIP** $80

Olive Oyl Doll, 1985, Presents, Christmas, large
EX $14   **NM** $30   **MIP** $65

Olive Oyl Doll, 1985, Presents, small
EX $10   **NM** $18   **MIP** $45

Olive Oyl Doll, 1990, Presents, small molded plastic, musical # P5948
EX $10   **NM** $20   **MIP** $40

Olive Oyl Doll, 1990, Toy Toons
EX $4   **NM** $9   **MIP** $20

Olive Oyl Doll, 1991, Presents, small molded plastic, # P5966
EX $4   **NM** $8   **MIP** $25

Olive Oyl Doll, 1991, Presents, Christmas, small
EX $8   NM $13   MIP $30

Poopdeck Pappy Doll, 1985, Presents, with tag
EX $35   NM $75   MIP $200

Popeye Doll, 23" china
EX $200   NM $350   MIP $500

Popeye Doll, 1935, Cameo
EX $250   NM $500   MIP $800

Popeye Doll, 1936, Stack, 12" tall, wood jointed, w/ pipe
EX $225   NM $475   MIP $775

Popeye Doll, 1950s, Chicago Herald American
EX $30   NM $85   MIP $250

Popeye Doll, 1950s, Rempel, small
EX $20   NM $45   MIP $120

Popeye Doll, 1950s, Woolikin, white plush
EX $30   NM $65   MIP $180

Popeye Doll, 1950s, Chad Valley, 7" tall, squeaks
EX $20   NM $55   MIP $140

Popeye Doll, 1957, Sears/Cameo, 13" in box
EX $300   NM $600   MIP $1000

Popeye Doll, 1958, Gund, 20" tall
EX $55   NM $110   MIP $250

Popeye Doll, 1960s, Quaker, 12" cloth
EX $20   NM $40   MIP $100

Popeye Doll, 1960s, 9" vinyl squeeze doll, Popeye w/Swee'Pea
EX $15   NM $30   MIP $100

Popeye Doll, 1968, Lakeside, 12" tall, sponge rubber
EX $15   NM $30   MIP $100

Popeye Doll, 1970s, Dakin, Cartoon Theatre, in box
EX $30   NM $60   MIP $150

Popeye Doll, 1970s, Dakin, hard plastic w/removable clothes
EX $20   NM $60   MIP $150

Popeye Doll, 1974, Dakin, squeaks
EX $15   NM $30   MIP $85

Popeye Doll, 1979, Uneeda
EX $20   NM $40   MIP $90

Popeye Doll, 1979, Uneeda, 16" tall
EX $22   NM $45   MIP $100

Popeye Doll, 1983, Etone, 8" plush
EX $7   NM $15   MIP $40

Popeye Doll, 1985, Presents, small
EX $8   NM $13   MIP $40

Popeye Doll, 1985, Presents, small doll w/pipe molded into hand
EX $10   NM $15   MIP $45

Popeye Doll, 1990, Presents, small molded plastic, musical #P5949
EX $10   NM $15   MIP $35

Popeye Doll, 1990, Toy Toons
EX $7   NM $15   MIP $40

Sea Hag Doll, 1985, Presents
EX $30   NM $75   MIP $225

Swee'Pea Doll, 1979, Uneeda
EX $10   NM $20   MIP $70

Swee'Pea Doll, 1985, Presents, large
EX $15   NM $30   MIP $80

Swee'Pea Doll, 1985, Presents, small
EX $12   NM $25   MIP $60

Swee'Pea Doll, 1991, Presents, small molded plastic, # P5968
EX $10   NM $15   MIP $40

Swee'Pea Doll, 1991, Presents, Christmas, small
EX $10   NM $20   MIP $60

Wimpy Doll, 1950s, KFS, rubber
EX $40   NM $75   MIP $135

Wimpy Doll, 1985, Presents, holding a hamburger
EX $50   NM $100   MIP $200

FIGURES

Bluto Figure, Cristallerie Antonio, Italian crystal
EX $15   NM $35   MIP $85

Brutus Figure, 1962, Japan Olympics, wood, Brutus in barrel
EX $75   NM $180   MIP $350

Brutus Figure, 1981, Bully, pink shirt
EX $7   NM $15   MIP $30

Brutus Figure, 1984, Comic-Spain, Brutus w/club
EX $4   NM $7   MIP $15

Brutus Figure, 1990, Presents, PVC
EX $2   NM $3   MIP $10

Brutus Figure, 1991, KFS-Hearst, wood
EX $4   NM $7   MIP $12

Character Figures, 1980, Spoontiques, two 1" figures: Jeep lifting tail, Swee'Pea w/feet showing, each
EX $10   NM $25   MIP $50

Character Figures, 1980, Spoontiques, 2" figures: Popeye w/barbell, Popeye w/parrot, Olive walking, Popeye flexing muscles, Popeye w/spinach, each
EX $10   NM $20   MIP $40

Character Figures, 1981, Spoontiques, pewter, three 1" figures: Olive w/hands clasped, Popeye w/muscles, Jeep standing, each
EX $10   NM $25   MIP $50

Character Figures, 1991, Popeye's Chicken, blue plastic, several characters available
EX $2   NM $5   MIP $10

Dufus Figure, 1981, Bully, w/hand on stomach
EX $8   NM $15   MIP $28

Jeep Figure, 1991, KFS-Hearst, wood
EX $7   NM $20   MIP $50

Olive Oyl Figure, Cristallerie Antonio, Italian crystal
EX $10   NM $15   MIP $50

Olive Oyl Figure, 1940, KFS, 8" tall
EX $70   NM $140   MIP $350

Olive Oyl Figure, 1940s, lead
EX $15   NM $30   MIP $100

Olive Oyl Figure, 1940s, 5" wooden jointed
EX $75   NM $165   MIP $400

Olive Oyl Figure, 1950s, Multiple Toymakers, 2" tall
EX $15   NM $40   MIP $75

Olive Oyl Figure, 1974, Ben Cooper, rubber
EX $20   NM $40   MIP $85

Olive Oyl Figure, 1980, KFS, arms clamped together, hanging figure
EX $5   NM $10   MIP $30

Olive Oyl Figure, 1980, Amscan, large bendy
EX $6   NM $12   MIP $30

Olive Oyl Figure, 1981, Bully, w/hands clasp
EX $8   NM $15   MIP $30

Olive Oyl Figure, 1981, Bully, holding flower
EX $8   NM $15   MIP $30

Olive Oyl Figure, 1984, Comics Spain, PVC, Olive w/flower
EX $6   NM $10   MIP $20

Olive Oyl Figure, 1986, Comics Spain, 6" bendy
EX $6   NM $10   MIP $20

Olive Oyl Figure, 1988, Jesco, small bendy
EX $2   NM $4   MIP $12

Olive Oyl Figure, 1988, Jesco, large bendy
EX $3   NM $6   MIP $18

Olive Oyl Figure, 1990, Presents, 3" tall, plastic
EX $2   NM $5   MIP $10

Olive Oyl Figure, 1990, Presents, PVC
EX $2   NM $5   MIP $10

Olive Oyl Figure, 1990, Chester, 10", Olive w/rolling pin
EX $10   NM $25   MIP $50

Olive Oyl Figure, 1990, Mexico, ceramic
EX $10   NM $25   MIP $50

Olive Oyl Figure, 1991, KFS-Hearst, wood
EX $5   NM $10   MIP $20

Popeye Figure, Cristallerie Antionio Imperatore, Italian crystal
EX $20   NM $30   MIP $60

Popeye Figure, Dakin, 8" tall w/ spinach can
EX $22   NM $45   MIP $100

Popeye Figure, 1930s, 12" tall, chalk, w/ pipe and hat, ashtray base
EX $100   NM $250   MIP $350

Popeye Figure, 1930s, 5" tall, wood jointed, held together w/string
EX $100   NM $200   MIP $400

Popeye Figure, 1940s, celluloid w/ wooden feet
EX $75   NM $125   MIP $225

Popeye Figure, 1940s, lead
EX $25   NM $50   MIP $100

Popeye Figure, 1944, Sirocco-KFS, 5", wood
EX $70   NM $120   MIP $220

Popeye Figure, 1950s, England, 7", bendy, yellow pants
EX $30   NM $60   MIP $170

Popeye Figure, 1950s, plastic, Popeye on four wheels w/telescope
EX $25   NM $50   MIP $130

Popeye Figure, 1950s, Japan, celluloid
EX $40   NM $75   MIP $150

Popeye Figure, 1960s, Combex, rubber, Popey w/ a can of spinach
EX $20   NM $40   MIP $90

Popeye Figure, 1962, Japan Olympics, wood, Popeye at bat
EX $150   NM $325   MIP $550

Popeye Figure, 1968, Lakeside, miniflex
EX $10   NM $25   MIP $70

Popeye Figure, 1969, Lakeside, superflex
EX $10   NM $25   MIP $60

Popeye Figure, 1970, Duncan, 8" tall
EX $20   NM $40   MIP $70

Popeye Figure, 1970s, ceramic, removeable head Popeye
EX $30   NM $60   MIP $100

Popeye Figure, 1974, Ben Cooper, rubber
EX $8   NM $15   MIP $40

Popeye Figure, 1978, Bronco, bendy
EX $6   NM $10   MIP $25

Popeye Figure, 1979, Imperial
EX $6   NM $10   MIP $20

Popeye Figure, 1980, Amscan, small bendy
EX $4   NM $7   MIP $14

Popeye Figure, 1980, Amscan, large bendy
EX $6   NM $12   MIP $20

Popeye Figure, 1981, Bully, several variations
EX $9   NM $18   MIP $30

Popeye Figure, 1984, Comics Spain, PVC, Popeye w/ spinach
EX $5   NM $10   MIP $20

Popeye Figure, 1986, Comics Spain, 6" bendy, white pants
EX $3   NM $6   MIP $20

Popeye Figure, 1988, Jesco, bendy
EX $6   NM $10   MIP $25

Popeye Figure, 1988, Jesco, small bendy
EX $2   NM $5   MIP $15

Popeye Figure, 1990, Mexico, ceramic
EX $7   NM $15   MIP $35

Popeye Figure, 1990, Presents, PVC
EX $1   NM $4   MIP $8

Popeye Figure, 1990, Presents, 3" tall, plastic
EX $2   NM $3   MIP $6

Popeye Figure, 1990, Chester, 10", ceramic, Popeye w/spinach
EX $6   NM $10   MIP $30

Popeye Figure, 1991, KFS-Hearst, wood
EX $8   NM $12   MIP $25

Popeye Galley Steward Figure, 1980, KFS, ceramic
EX $10   NM $22   MIP $50

Swee'Pea Figure, ceramic, one of five
EX $5   NM $15   MIP $45

Swee'Pea Figure, Cristallerie Antonio Imperatore, Italian crystal
EX $15   NM $30   MIP $50

Swee'Pea Figure, 1984, Comics Spain, PVC, Swee'Pea w/cake
EX $4   NM $8   MIP $20

Swee'Pea Figure, 1984, Presents, PVC
EX $2   NM $4   MIP $10

Swee'Pea Figure, 1990, Presents, 3" tall, plastic
EX $5   NM $10   MIP $20

Wimpy Figure, Cristallerie Antonio Imperatore, Italian crystal
EX $25   NM $40   MIP $75

Wimpy Figure, 1940s, lead
EX $15   NM $30   MIP $80

Wimpy Figure, 1944, Sirocco-KFS, 5", wood
EX $60   NM $90   MIP $200

Wimpy Figure, 1950s, Buitoni, premium
EX $40   NM $70   MIP $150

Wimpy Figure, 1981, Bully, yellow hat
EX $6   NM $12   MIP $25

Wimpy Figure, 1984, Comics Spain, Wimpy w/hamburger
EX $7   NM $15   MIP $30

Wimpy Figure, 1990, Presents, PVC
EX $2   NM $5   MIP $10

GAME

Adventures of Popeye Game, 1957, Transogram
EX $50   NM $80   MIP $160

Boxing Game, 1981, Harmony
EX $7   NM $15   MIP $40

Jumbo Card Game, 1978, House of Games
EX $10   NM $20   MIP $35

Jumbo Trading Card Game, 1960s, Dynamic Toy
EX $15   NM $30   MIP $60

Magic Play Around Game, 1960s, Amsco
EX $20   NM $45   MIP $100

Pocket Pin Ball, 1983, Nintendo/Ja-Ru, holes
EX $5   NM $10   MIP $20

Pocket Pin Ball, 1983, Nintendo/Ja-Ru, cups
EX $5   NM $10   MIP $20

Popeye Arcade Game, 1980, Parker Bros., card game
EX $5   NM $10   MIP $25

(KP Photo)

Popeye Ball Toss Game, 1950s, KFS
EX $50   NM $75   MIP $160

Popeye Bingo, 1929, Bar Zim
EX $75   NM $100   MIP $200

Popeye Break-A-Plate Game, 1963, Combex
EX $30   NM $80   MIP $150

Popeye Fishing Game, 1962, Transogram, magnetic
EX $15   NM $30   MIP $80

Popeye Fishing Game, 1980, Fleetwood
EX $5   NM $10   MIP $25

Popeye Games, 1960s, Ed-U-Card, set of four games
EX $15   NM $30   MIP $60

Popeye Hammer Game, 1960s, Holgate
EX $70   NM $140   MIP $280

Popeye Menu Pinball Game, 1935, Durable Toy and Novelty
EX $100   NM $175   MIP $275

Popeye Mini Tennis Game, 1970s, Nordic
EX $10   NM $15   MIP $30

Popeye Nail-On Game, 1963, Colorforms
EX $20   NM $45   MIP $100

Popeye Party Game, 1937, Whitman, posters, paper pipes, game box
EX $50   NM $85   MIP $170

Popeye Pinball Game, 1983, Ja-Ru
EX $6   NM $10   MIP $25

(KP Photo)

Popeye Pipe Toss Game, 1935, Rosebud Art, small version w/wooden pipe
EX $50   NM $120   MIP $210

Popeye Playing Card Game, 1934, Whitman, 5" x 7", green box
EX $50   NM $85   MIP $160

Popeye Playing Card Game, 1938, Whitman, blue box
EX $40   NM $70   MIP $150

Popeye Playing Card Game, 1983, Parker Bros.
EX $6   NM $10   MIP $30

Popeye Ring Toss Game, 1957, Transogram
EX $32   NM $65   MIP $135

Popeye Ring Toss Game, 1980, Fleetwood
EX $6   NM $10   MIP $25

Popeye Shipwreck Game, 1933, Einson-Freeman
EX $75   NM $125   MIP $250

Popeye Spinach Target Game, 1960s, Gardner
EX $40   NM $75   MIP $120

CHARACTER TOYS

Popeye the Juggler Bead Game, 1929, Bar-Zim, 3-1/2" x 5", covered w/glass
EX $40   NM $60   MIP $120

Popeye Video Game, 1983, Nintendo
EX $12   NM $20   MIP $30

Popeye/Olive Oyl/Wimpy Skill Games, 1965, Lido
EX $10   NM $16   MIP $40

Popeye's Gang Pinball Game, 1970s, MSS
EX $13   NM $25   MIP $50

Popeye's Lucky Jeep Game, 1936, Northwestern Products
EX $100   NM $175   MIP $300

Popeye's Peg Board Game, 1934, Bar Zim
EX $100   NM $200   MIP $375

Popeye's Sliding Boards and Ladders, 1958, Warren Built-Rite
EX $12   NM $25   MIP $80

Popeye's Spinach Hunt Game, 1976, Whitman
EX $11   NM $22   MIP $50

Popeye's Three Game Set, 1956, Built-Rite
EX $20   NM $40   MIP $90

Popeye's Tiddly Winks, 1948, Parker Bros.
EX $20   NM $40   MIP $100

Popeye's Treasure Map Game, 1977, Whitman
EX $12   NM $25   MIP $50

Popeye's Where's Me Pipe Game
EX $30   NM $50   MIP $90

Puzzle Game, 1978, Waddington's House of Games
EX $10   NM $20   MIP $40

Ring the Bell with Hammer Game, 1960s, Harett-Gilmar
EX $25   NM $42   MIP $70

Ring Toss Stand-Up Game, 1958, Transogram
EX $15   NM $30   MIP $70

Roly Poly and Cork Gun Game, 1958, Knickbocker
EX $60   NM $120   MIP $210

Rub 'N Win Party Game, 1980, Spot-O-Gold
EX $5   NM $10   MIP $25

Skeet Shoot Game, 1950, Irwin
EX $75   NM $125   MIP $185

Skoozit Pick-A-Puzzle Game, 1966, Ideal
EX $15   NM $35   MIP $70

Water Ball Game, 1983, Nintendo, one basket
EX $6   NM $10   MIP $25

LUNCH BOX

Mini Lunch Box, 1990, Sanrio, plastic
EX $4   NM $10   MIP $25

MUSIC BOX

Brutus Music Box, 1980, KFS, Brutus dancing
EX $10   NM $15   MIP $40

Brutus Music Box, 1989, Presents, #P5984
EX $8   NM $17   MIP $45

Music Box, 1980, Vandor, revolving Popeye spanks Swee'Pea, ceramic
EX $20   NM $45   MIP $100

Music Box, 1980, Vandor, revolving Olive w/Popeye dancing, ceramic
EX $20   NM $45   MIP $100

Music Box, 1980, Vandor, Wimpy on top of hamburger, ceramic
EX $20   NM $45   MIP $100

Olive Oyl Music Box, 1980, KFS, Olive dancing
EX $8   NM $20   MIP $50

Olive Oyl Music Box, 1989, Presents, #P5983
EX $8   NM $20   MIP $50

Popeye and Olive Oyl Music Box, Schmid, 8-1/4" figural box
EX $50   NM $100   MIP $180

Swee'Pea Music Box, 1980, KFS, Swee'Pea dancing
EX $8   NM $15   MIP $50

Swee'Pea Music Box, 1989, Presents, #P5986
EX $8   NM $15   MIP $50

Wimpy Music Box, 1989, Presents, #P5985
EX $8   NM $15   MIP $40

PIN

Pin, 1935, JCPenney, Back to School Days w/Popeye
EX $20   NM $40   MIP $90

RECORD

Fleas A Crowd Record, 1962, Peter Pan, 78 rpm
EX $10   NM $25   MIP $50

Olive Oyl on Troubled Waters Record, 1976, Peter Pan, 45 rpm
EX $7   NM $20   MIP $40

Original Radio Broadcasts Record, 1977, Golden Age, 33 rpm
EX $7   NM $25   MIP $60

Picture Disc Record, 1948, Record of America, 78 rpm
EX $25   NM $50   MIP $100

Picture Disc Record, 1982, Peter Pan, 33 rpm
EX $6   NM $10   MIP $25

Pollution Solution Record, 1970s, Peter Pan, 45 rpm
EX $5   NM $10   MIP $35

Popeye and Friends Record, 1981, Merry Records, 33 rpm
EX $3   NM $10   MIP $25

Popeye French Record, 1981, Polygram, 45 rpm
EX $7   NM $15   MIP $35

Popeye in the Movies Record, Peter Pan, 33 rpm w/book
EX $6   NM $15   MIP $35

Popeye Launches His New Song Hits Record, 1958, Peter Pan, 45 rpm
EX $15   NM $30   MIP $80

Popeye on Parade/Strike Me Pink Record, 1950s, Cricket, 45 rpm
EX $12   NM $25   MIP $60

Popeye Record, 1977, Peter Pan, 33 rpm, four stories, #1114
EX $6   NM $15   MIP $30

Popeye the Ladies Man Record, 33 rpm
EX $8   NM $15   MIP $35

Popeye the Movie Soundtrack Record, 1980, Paramount
EX $6   NM $15   MIP $30

Popeye the Sailor Man and His Friends Record, 1960s, Golden, 33 rpm
EX $8   NM $15   MIP $30

Popeye the Sailor Man Record, 1959, Golden, 45 rpm
EX $7   NM $15   MIP $30

Popeye the Sailor Man Record, 1960, Diplomat Records, 33 rpm
EX $7   NM $15   MIP $35

Popeye the Sailor Man Record, 1976, Peter Pan, 33 rpm
EX $7   NM $15   MIP $35

Popeye's Favorite Sea Shanties Record, 1960, RCA Camden
EX $10   NM $25   MIP $50

Popeye's Favorite Sea Songs Record, 1959, Peter Pan, 45 rpm
EX $10   NM $25   MIP $60

Popeye's Favorite Stories Record, 1960, RCA Camden, 33 rpm
EX $10   NM $20   MIP $40

Popeye's Songs About...... Record, 1961, Golden, 33 rpm
EX $8   NM $18   MIP $35

Six Popeye Songs Record, 1950s, Wonderland Records, 45 rpm
EX $8   NM $30   MIP $70

Song and Story Skin Diver Record, 1964, KFS
EX $10   NM $20   MIP $40

Songs of Health Record, 1960s, Golden, 45 rpm
EX $6   NM $10   MIP $25

Songs of Safety Record, 1960s, Golden, 45 rpm
EX $6   NM $10   MIP $25

Whale of a Tale Record, 1981, Peter Pan, 45 rpm
EX $6   NM $10   MIP $20

RING

Candy Rings, 1989, Alberts
EX $6   NM $15   MIP $25

Popeye and Oscar Flicker Ring, blue
EX $8   NM $20   MIP $35

Popeye and Swee'Pea Flicker Ring, blue
EX $8   NM $15   MIP $35

Popeye and Wimpy Flicker Ring, blue
EX $8   NM $15   MIP $35

TOY

Apprentice Printer, 1970s, MSS
EX $6   NM $20   MIP $40

Ball and Jacks Set, MSS
EX $6   NM $12   MIP $3035

Ball and Paddle, BC
EX $6   NM $15   MIP $35

Balloon Pump, 1957, inflato-pump
EX $40   NM $60   MIP $120

Barber Shop, 1970s, Larami
EX $5   NM $15   MIP $30

Baseball, 1983, Ja-Ru
EX $10   NM $20   MIP $40

Beach Boat, 1980, H.G. Industries, red or yellow
EX $5   NM $10   MIP $35

Biffbat-Fly Back Paddle, 1935
EX $75   NM $100   MIP $175

Billion Bubbles, 1984, Larami
EX $4   NM $8   MIP $15

Blackboard, 1962, Bar Zim
EX $20   NM $40   MIP $85

Bluto's Road Roller, 1980, Lesney/Matchbox, CS-14, 2-3/4" x 2-7/8"
EX $8   NM $18   MIP $50

Bop Bag, 1981, Miner Industries
EX $8   NM $15   MIP $30

Boxing Gloves, 1960s, Everlast
EX $35   NM $60   MIP $150

Brutus Dog Toy, 1986, Petex
EX $6   NM $12   MIP $25

Brutus Figure Painting Kit, 1980, Avalon
EX $8   NM $15   MIP $35

Brutus Hand Puppet, 1960s, Gund
EX $25   NM $60   MIP $120

Brutus Hi-Pop Ball, 1981, Ja-Ru
EX $6   NM $10   MIP $20

Brutus Hookies, 1977, Tiger
EX $5   NM $18   MIP $50

Brutus Horse and Cart, 1938, Marx, celluloid, w/Brutus, horse, and cart
EX $500   NM $825   MIP $1050

Brutus in Jeep, 1950s, tiny plastic car
EX $15   NM $35   MIP $80

Brutus Jump-Up, 1970s, Imperial
EX $8   NM $20   MIP $40

Brutus Painting Kit, 1980, Avalon
EX $8   NM $15   MIP $25

Brutus Soaky, 1960s, Colgate-Palmolive
EX $15   NM $35   MIP $80

Brutus Sports Car, 1950s, tiny plastic car
EX $15   NM $35   MIP $75

Brutus Wind-Up Toy, 1980, Durham
EX $5   NM $10   MIP $25

Bubble Blower, 1958, Transogram
EX $15   NM $35   MIP $90

Bubble Blower Boat, 1984, Larami
EX $7   NM $15   MIP $40

Bubble Blowing Popeye, 1950s, Linemar
EX $550   NM $1000   MIP $1650

Bubble Blowing Train, 1970s, Hong Kong, pink
EX $10   NM $20   MIP $60

Bubble 'N Clean, 1960s, Woolfoam
EX $20   NM $45   MIP $75

Bubble Pipe, 1960s, KFS, yellow w/red end
EX $15   NM $30   MIP $80

Bubble Pipe, 1985, Ja-Ru
EX $5   NM $12   MIP $35

Bubble Set, 1936, Transogram, two wooden pipes, tray, soap in 5" x 7-1/2" box
EX $100   NM $200   MIP $300

Bubble Shooter, 1980s, Ja-Ru, orange or yellow body
EX $5   NM $10   MIP $30

Bubbleblaster, 1980, Carlin Playthings
EX $10   NM $15   MIP $30

Bubbles Blaster, 1984, Larami
EX $5   NM $10   MIP $20

Bubbles with Dip Pow Bubbles, 1986, MSS
EX $5   NM $10   MIP $20

Cap Gun, 1981, Ja-Ru
EX $10   NM $25   MIP $60

Chain Bubbles Maker, 1984, Larami, red Popeye
EX $6   NM $10   MIP $20

Chalk, 1936, American Crayon, white, 18 pieces
EX $50   NM $90   MIP $125

Change Purse, 1990, Sanrio
EX $5   NM $10   MIP $20

Checker Board, 1959, Ideal
EX $20   NM $35   MIP $90

Chinese Jump Rope, MSS
EX $4   NM $12   MIP $25

Colorforms Birthday Party Set, 1961, Colorforms
EX $25   NM $70   MIP $110

Colorforms Movie Version, 1980, Colorforms
EX $7   NM $15   MIP $30

Color-Me Stickers, 1983, Diamond Toymakers
EX $5   NM $12   MIP $25

Color-Vue Pencil-by-Numbers, 1979, Hasbro
EX $10   NM $20   MIP $35

Construction Trucks, 1981, Larami
EX $6   NM $15   MIP $30

(KP Photo)

Crayons, 1933, American Crayon, 12 giant crayons
EX $50   NM $75   MIP $150

Crayons, 1950s, American Crayon
EX $20   NM $35   MIP $80

Crayons, 1958, Dixon, 12 giant crayons
EX $20   NM $35   MIP $80

Dockside Presto Magix, 1980, APC
EX $3   NM $6   MIP $12

Double Action Water Gun Set, MSS
EX $10   NM $20   MIP $40

Drawing Board, 1978, KFS, slate w/rope attached
EX $8   NM $16   MIP $40

Drawing Desk, 1980, Carlin Playthings
EX $10   NM $20   MIP $60

Duck Shoot, 1980s, Ja-Ru
EX $5   NM $15   MIP $30

Erase-O-Board and Magic Screen Set, 1957, Hassenfeld Bros.
EX $50   NM $90   MIP $180

Film Projector, Cinexin-Spain, 8mm w/13 movies
EX $85   NM $140   MIP $250

Finger Puppet Family, 1960s, Denmark Plastics
EX $25   NM $50   MIP $100

Flashlight, 1960s, Bantam-Lite, three color, wrist light
EX $10   NM $20   MIP $40

Flashlight, 1983, Larami, blue, yellow, or red
EX $7   NM $15   MIP $30

Foto-Fun Printing Kit, 1958, Fun Bilt
EX $32   NM $65   MIP $130

Funny Color Foam, 1983, Creative Aerosol
EX $5   NM $15   MIP $60

(KP Photo)

Funny Face Maker, 1962, Jaymar
EX $15   NM $30   MIP $70

Funny Films Viewer, 1940s, Acme
EX $50   NM $75   MIP $120

Funny Fire Fighters, 1930s, Marx, celluloid figures, Popeye on ladder and Bluto drives fire truck--both figures wear boxing gloves
EX $1250   NM $2500   MIP $3500

(KP Photo)

Give-A-Show Projector, Kenner, projector w/slides
EX $75   NM $100   MIP $180

Gumball Dispenser, 1983, Superior Toys, pocket pack
EX $10   NM $20   MIP $40

Gumball Machine, 1968, Hasbro, 6", shape of Popeye's head
EX $30   NM $50   MIP $100

Gumball Machine, 1983, Superior Toys, Popeye eating spinach
EX $10   NM $20   MIP $45

Gumball Machine, 1983, Superior Toys, Popeye gives Olive flowers
EX $10   NM $20   MIP $45

Halloween Bucket, 1979, Renz, shaped like Popeye's head, red, yellow or blue
EX $10   NM $20   MIP $40

Harmonica, 1973, Larami
EX $15   NM $40   MIP $90

Hat and Pipe, 1950s, Empire Plastics
EX $40   NM $60   MIP $110

Holster Set, 1960s, Halco
EX $90   NM $150   MIP $250

Horseshoe Magnets, 1984, Larami
EX $5   NM $15   MIP $30

Hunting Knife, 1973, Larami
EX $20   NM $50   MIP $85

ID Set, 1982, Gordy
EX $5   NM $15   MIP $40

Jack-in-the-Box, 1961, Mattel
EX $60   NM $120   MIP $210

Jack-in-the-Box, 1979, Nasta
EX $25   NM $50   MIP $100

Jack-in-the-Box, 1983, Nasta
EX $20   NM $40   MIP $85

Jeep Lucky Spinner, 1936, KFS, on card
EX $250   NM $400   MIP $600

Kaleidoscope, 1979, Larami
EX $10   NM $25   MIP $85

Kazoo and Harmonica, 1979, Larami
EX $8   NM $20   MIP $35

Kazoo Pipe, 1934, Northwestern Products
EX $75   NM $125   MIP $200

Kazoo Pipe, 1960s, Peerless Playthings, yellow
EX $15   NM $30   MIP $60

Kite, 1980, Sky-Way, inflatable
EX $6   NM $12   MIP $25

Kite, 1980, Sky-Way, regular
EX $4   NM $8   MIP $25

Lantern, 1950s, Linemar, 7-1/2" tall, battery operated, light in belly
EX $130   NM $275   MIP $525

Magic Glow Putty, FC Famous Toys
EX $6   NM $10   MIP $15

Magic Slate, 1959, Lowe
EX $20   NM $40   MIP $90

Magic Slate Paper Saver, 1981, Whitman
EX $4   NM $8   MIP $25

Make-A-Picture Premium, 1934, Quaker
EX $100   NM $175   MIP $250

Marble, 1940s
EX $8   NM $20   MIP $50

Marble Set, 1935, Akro Agate, #116
EX $1000   NM $1500   MIP $2200

Marble Set, 1980, Imperial
EX $12   NM $25   MIP $70

Marble Shooter, 1940s, milk glass container
EX $35   NM $50   MIP $100

Metal Tapping Set, 1950s, Carlton Dank
EX $25   NM $50   MIP $120

Metal Target Set, 1983, Ja-Ru
EX $8   NM $18   MIP $60

Metal Whistle, 1981, Ja-Ru
EX $5   NM $12   MIP $35

Micro-Movie, 1990, Fascinations, Popeye-Ali Baba
EX $4   NM $8   MIP $15

Miniature Train Set, 1980, Larami
EX $8   NM $15   MIP $60

Model Kit, 1970s, Carto, Popeye and Olive Oyl
EX $25   NM $60   MIP $120

Modeling Clay, 1936, American Crayon
EX $75   NM $125   MIP $200

Motor Friend, 1976, Nasta
EX $10   NM $20   MIP $50

Muscle Builder Bluto, 1980, Carlin Playthings
EX $6   NM $12   MIP $25

Muscle Builder Popeye, 1980, Carlin Playthings
EX $6   NM $12   MIP $30

My Popeye Coloring Kit, 1957, American Crayon
EX $50   NM $100   MIP $175

Official Popeye Pipe, 1958, 5" stem w/2" bowl, battery operated, "It lites, it toots"
EX $45   NM $100   MIP $200

Old Time Wild West Train, 1984, Larami
EX $5   NM $20   MIP $70

Olive Oyl Bike Bobbers, 1960s, KFS
EX $15   NM $25   MIP $60

Olive Oyl Costume, 1950s, Collegeville
EX $40   NM $75   MIP $120

Olive Oyl Costume, 1976, Ben Cooper
EX $10   NM $20   MIP $70

Olive Oyl Figure Painting Kit, 1980, Avalon
EX $6   NM $12   MIP $20

Olive Oyl Foam Toy, 1979, Cribmates
EX $8   NM $15   MIP $35

Olive Oyl Hand Puppet, 1960s, Gund, comic strip body
EX $30   NM $75   MIP $150

Olive Oyl Hi-Pop Ball, 1981, Ja-Ru
EX $5   NM $10   MIP $40

Olive Oyl Hookies, 1977, Tiger
EX $4   NM $10   MIP $30
EX $12   NM $30   MIP $70

Olive Oyl Jump-Up, Imperial
EX $5   NM $10   MIP $20

Olive Oyl Marionette, 1950s, Gund, 11-1/2" tall
EX $70   NM $120   MIP $210

Olive Oyl Painting Kit, 1980, Avalon
EX $5   NM $10   MIP $25

Olive Oyl Push Puppet, 1960s, Kohner, 4" tall, plastic
EX $15   NM $35   MIP $75

Olive Oyl Sports Car, 1950s, tiny plastic car
EX $15   NM $35   MIP $80

Olive Oyl Squeak Toy, 1979, Cribmates, on a stick
EX $5   NM $13   MIP $30

Olive Oyl Squeeze Toy, 1950s, Rempel, vinyl
EX $30   NM $60   MIP $120

Olive Oyl Swim Ring, 1979, Wet Set-Zee Toys
EX $5   **NM** $10   **MIP** $25

Olive Oyl Tiles, 1970s, Italy, 3" x 5" w/stand
EX $12   **NM** $25   **MIP** $50

Olive Oyl Toboggan, 1979, KFS
EX $6   **NM** $15   **MIP** $35

Olive Oyl's Convertible, 1980, Lesney/Matchbox, CS-15, 2-3/4" x 2-7/8"
EX $12   **NM** $30   **MIP** $75

Paint 'N Puff Set, 1979, Art Award, two versions
EX $6   **NM** $12   **MIP** $35

Pick-Up Sticks, 1957, Lido
EX $20   **NM** $40   **MIP** $80

Pirate Island Presto Magix, 1980, American Pub.
EX $10   **NM** $20   **MIP** $25

Plane and Parachute, 1980, Fleetwood
EX $8   **NM** $15   **MIP** $35

Play Money, 1930s, color bucks-framed
EX $12   **NM** $35   **MIP** $80

Play Money, 1970, The Toy House
EX $5   **NM** $10   **MIP** $30

Pool Table, 1984, Larami
EX $5   **NM** $10   **MIP** $25

Pop Maker and Son, 1987, Ja-Ru
EX $2   **NM** $4   **MIP** $15

Pop Pistol, 1984, Larami
EX $4   **NM** $10   **MIP** $40

Popeye Air Mattress, 1979, Zee Toys
EX $8   **NM** $20   **MIP** $25

Popeye and Brutus Punch Me Bop Bag, 1960s, Dartmore
EX $15   **NM** $30   **MIP** $60

Popeye and Olive Oyl Sand Set, 1950s, Peer Products, bucket, shovel
EX $20   **NM** $50   **MIP** $125

Popeye and Olive Oyl Toy Watch, 1970s, Unknown, flicker
EX $6   **NM** $12   **MIP** $30

Popeye and Shark Swim Ring, 1960s, Laurel Star-Japan
EX $10   **NM** $25   **MIP** $35

Popeye and Wimpy Walk-A-Way Toy, 1964, Marx
EX $25   **NM** $50   **MIP** $120

Popeye Arcade, 1980, Fleetwood
EX $6   **NM** $12   **MIP** $25

Popeye at the Wheel, 1950s, Woolnough, musical
EX $150   **NM** $300   **MIP** $625

Popeye Ball, rubber kick ball
EX $7   **NM** $13   **MIP** $30

Popeye Bathtub Toy, 1960s, Stahlwood, floating boat
EX $20   **NM** $40   **MIP** $90

Popeye Bend-I-Face, 1967, Lakeside
EX $15   **NM** $35   **MIP** $65

Popeye Bingo, 1980, Nasta
EX $6   **NM** $10   **MIP** $20

Popeye Blow Me Down Airport, 1935, Marx
EX $1600   **NM** $2300   **MIP** $3000

Popeye Bubble Liquid, 1970s, M. Shimmel Sons, shaped like Popeye w/necktie similar to a sailor's knot
EX $8   **NM** $15   **MIP** $25

Popeye Car, 1980, Vandor, Popeye and Olive in blue or pink car
EX $20   **NM** $45   **MIP** $100

Popeye Carnival, 1965, Toymaster
EX $75   **NM** $100   **MIP** $250

Popeye Coloring Set, 1960s, Hasbro, numbered, w/pencils
EX $12   **NM** $30   **MIP** $70

Popeye Costume, 1950s, Collegeville
EX $40   **NM** $75   **MIP** $120

Popeye Costume, 1980s, Collegeville
EX $9   **NM** $18   **MIP** $40

Popeye Costume, 1984, Ben Cooper
EX $7   **NM** $15   **MIP** $35

Popeye Dog Toy, 1986, Petex
EX $3   **NM** $6   **MIP** $10

Popeye Figure Painting Kit, 1980, Avalon
EX $4   **NM** $8   **MIP** $20

Popeye Finger Rings, 1949, Post Toasties
EX $20   **NM** $50   **MIP** $125

Popeye Flicker Badge, 1960s, Varivue, Popeye eating spinach
EX $8   **NM** $15   **MIP** $35

Popeye Flickers, 1960s, Sonwell
EX $8   **NM** $15   **MIP** $35

Popeye Ge-tar, 1960s, Mattel, 14" long, shaped like Popeye's face, plays "I'm Popeye the Sailor Man"
EX $30   **NM** $60   **MIP** $125

Popeye Glow Putty, 1984, Larami
EX $3   **NM** $6   **MIP** $10

Popeye Goes Swimming Colorforms, 1963, Colorforms
EX $15   **NM** $35   **MIP** $75

Popeye Goes to School Television, 1950s, Zaboly
EX $30   **NM** $50   **MIP** $100

Popeye Hand Puppet, 1950s, Gund, plush
EX $15   **NM** $40   **MIP** $100

Popeye Hand Puppet, 1960s, Gund, Popeye's head on cloth body
EX $20   **NM** $50   **MIP** $120

Popeye Hi-Pop Ball, 1981, Ja-Ru
EX $4   **NM** $8   **MIP** $25

Popeye Jump-Up, 1970s, Imperial
EX $8   **NM** $20   **MIP** $50

Popeye Magic Play Around, 1950s, Amsco, characters w/magnetic bases that slide across play set
EX $35   **NM** $70   **MIP** $150

Popeye Marionette, Create-Japan, wood
EX $100   **NM** $200   **MIP** $425

Popeye Marionette, 1950s, Gund, 11-1/2" tall
EX $75   **NM** $150   **MIP** $325

Popeye Mini Winder, 1980, Durham
EX $4   **NM** $10   **MIP** $30

Popeye Model Kit, 1964, Tokyo Plamo, #808
EX $60   **NM** $120   **MIP** $250

Popeye on Tricycle, Linemar, 4-1/2", tin wind-up w/celluloid arms and legs, bell rings behind Popeye
EX $350   **NM** $750   **MIP** $1000

Popeye One Man Band, 1980s, Larami
EX $6   **NM** $10   **MIP** $30

Popeye Paddle Ball, 1984, Larami, w/color photo of Popeye
EX $7   **NM** $15   **MIP** $40

Popeye Paint and Crayon Set, 1934, Milton Bradley
EX $75   **NM** $150   **MIP** $300

Popeye Paint By Numbers, 1960s, Hasbro
EX $12   **NM** $25   **MIP** $75

Popeye Paint Set, 1933, American Crayon, 6", tin
EX $75   **NM** $150   **MIP** $300

Popeye Paint-By-Numbers, 1981, Hasbro
EX $8   **NM** $13   **MIP** $30

Popeye Painting Kit, 1980, Avalon
EX $6   **NM** $10   **MIP** $25

Popeye Pencil-By-Numbers, 1979, Hasbro
EX $10   **NM** $25   **MIP** $60

Popeye Peppy Puppet, 1970, Kohner
EX $12   **NM** $25   **MIP** $50

Popeye Pipe, 1940s, red wooden
EX $20   **NM** $40   **MIP** $100

Popeye Pipe, 1958, Micro-Lite-KFS
EX $12   **NM** $30   **MIP** $100

Popeye Pipe, 1970, Edmonton Pipe, figural head
EX $15   **NM** $25   **MIP** $60

Popeye Pipe, 1970s, MSS, plastic, white
EX $8   **NM** $20   **MIP** $50

Popeye Pipe, 1970s, KFS, plastic kazoo, red and blue
EX $6   **NM** $20   **MIP** $50

Popeye Pipe, 1980, Harmony
EX $6   **NM** $10   **MIP** $20

Popeye Pistol, Delcast, Super mini cap w/24 caps No. 807-BB
EX $15   **NM** $30   **MIP** $80

Popeye Pistol, 1935, Marx
EX $400   **NM** $800   **MIP** $1300

Popeye Play Set, 1979, Cribmates, Popeye, Olive Oyl, and Swee'Pea squeak toys, mirror, rattle and pillow
EX $15   **NM** $30   **MIP** $60

Popeye Presto Paints, 1961, Kenner
EX $15   **NM** $50   **MIP** $70

Popeye Pull Toy, 1950s, Metal Masters, 10-1/2" x 11-1/2", xylophone, wood w/paper litho labels, metal wheels
EX $150   **NM** $225   **MIP** $500

Popeye Puppet, Kohner, pull string, Popeye jumps
EX $10   **NM** $15   **MIP** $30

Popeye Push Puppet, 1960, Kohner, 4" tall
EX $20　　NM $45　　MIP $90

(KP Photo)

Popeye Sailboat, 1976, KFS
EX $9　　NM $15　　MIP $60

Popeye Service Station, 1979, Larami
EX $8　　NM $25　　MIP $70

Popeye Soaky, 1960s, Colgate-Palmolive
EX $15　　NM $40　　MIP $75

(KP Photo)

Popeye Soaky, 1987, KFS, British
EX $12　　NM $20　　MIP $45

Popeye Sparkler, 1959, Chein
EX $90　　NM $125　　MIP $200

Popeye Speed Boat, 1981, Harmony
EX $10　　NM $16　　MIP $40

Popeye Speedboard Pull Toy, 1960s
EX $175　　NM $375　　MIP $700

Popeye Sports Car, 1950s, Linemar
EX $225　　NM $425　　MIP $800

Popeye Squeeze Toy, 1950s, Rempel, 8" tall, vinyl
EX $25　　NM $50　　MIP $120

Popeye Squeeze Toy, 1979, Cribmates, Popeye on a stick
EX $8　　NM $15　　MIP $40

Popeye Supergyro, 1980s, Larami
EX $6　　NM $10　　MIP $25

Popeye the Pilot, 1940s, Chein, tin wind-up airplane, 8" long, 8" wingspan
EX $750　　NM $1200　　MIP $1600

Popeye the Weatherman Colorforms, 1959, Colorforms
EX $20　　NM $50　　MIP $120

Popeye Tiles, 1970s, Italy, 3" x 5" w/stand
EX $15　　NM $35　　MIP $70

Popeye Toboggan, 1979, KFS
EX $6　　NM $10　　MIP $30

Popeye Train Pull Toy, Larami
EX $150　　NM $250　　MIP $450

Popeye Train Set, 1973, Larami
EX $6　　NM $15　　MIP $50

Popeye Transit Company Moving Van, 1950, Linemar, tin
EX $550　　NM $900　　MIP $1300

Popeye Tricky Trapeze, 1970, Kohner
EX $15　　NM $35　　MIP $80

Popeye Tricky Walker, 1960s, Jaymar, plastic
EX $10　　NM $25　　MIP $60

Popeye Tricycling, 1950s, Linemar
EX $400　　NM $650　　MIP $1000

Popeye Tug and Dingy Pull Toy, 1950s, Fisher-Price, wood
EX $135　　NM $225　　MIP $375

Popeye Tugboat, 1961, Ideal, inflatable
EX $15　　NM $35　　MIP $70

(KP Photo)

Popeye TV Cartoon Kit, 1966, Colorforms
EX $20　　NM $40　　MIP $80

Popeye TV Magic Putty, 1970s, MSS
EX $6　　NM $10　　MIP $15

Popeye Water Colors, 1933, American Crayon
EX $25　　NM $60　　MIP $110

Popeye Water Sprinkler, 1960s, KFS, w/rubbber head
EX $15　　NM $25　　MIP $40

Popeye's Official Wallet, 1959, KFS
EX $10　　NM $30　　MIP $70

Popeye's Spinach Wagon, 1980, Lesney/Matchbox, CS-13, 2-3/4" x 2-7/8"
EX $8　　NM $15　　MIP $40

Popeye's Submarine, 1973, Larami
EX $10　　NM $30　　MIP $60

Popsicle Harmonica, 1929, Czech
EX $100　　NM $200　　MIP $375

Punch Ball, 1970s, National Latex
EX $10　　NM $20　　MIP $50

Punch'Em Talking Rattle Toy, 1950s, Sanitoy
EX $15　　NM $35　　MIP $85

Punching Bag, 1960s, Dartmore
EX $15　　NM $30　　MIP $60

Puppetforms, 1950s, Colorforms
EX $25　　NM $40　　MIP $80

Puzzle, 1932, Saalfield, Popeye in Four
EX $50　　NM $100　　MIP $250

Puzzle, 1945, Jaymar, 22" x 13-1/2", Popeye
EX $40　　NM $100　　MIP $200

Puzzle, 1959, England, 120 pieces, "What a Catch"
EX $25　　NM $55　　MIP $80

Puzzle, 1960s, Roalex, tile
EX $20　　NM $35　　MIP $50

Puzzle, 1962, Tower Press, wood, Popeye
EX $10　　NM $16　　MIP $30

Puzzle, 1973, Larami, magnetic
EX $6　　NM $15　　MIP $40

Puzzle, 1976, American Pub. Corp., 5-1/2" round can
EX $10　　NM $20　　MIP $35

Puzzle, 1977, Opera Mundi, tile, "Popeye's Riddle"
EX $11　　NM $18　　MIP $30

Puzzle, 1978, Waddington's House of Games, 27" x 18" floor puzzle
EX $8　　NM $15　　MIP $35

Puzzle, 1981, Ja-Ru, comic
EX $6　　NM $12　　MIP $30

Puzzle, 1987, Illco, 11 pieces, Olive 3-D
EX $6　　NM $10　　MIP $20

Puzzle, 1987, Illco, 11 pieces, Popeye 3-D
EX $6　　NM $10　　MIP $20

Puzzle, 1987, Ja-Ru, Popeye and Son TV show
EX $5　　NM $10　　MIP $20

Puzzle, 1989, Ja-Ru, "Birthday Cake and Ice Cream"
EX $6　　NM $10　　MIP $20

Puzzle, 1989, Ja-Ru, boating and dancing
EX $6　　NM $10　　MIP $20

Puzzle, 1991, Jaymar, 12 pieces, Popeye holding turkey
EX $6　　NM $10　　MIP $20

Puzzle, 1991, Jaymar, 12 pieces, Popeye gang swimming
EX $6　　NM $10　　MIP $20

Puzzle, 1991, Jaymar, Christmas scene, inlaid, 12 pieces
EX $6　　NM $10　　MIP $20

Puzzle, 1991, Jaymar, 63 pieces, Popeye blowing candles
EX $6　　NM $10　　MIP $20

Puzzle, 1991, Jaymar, 63 pieces, jumbo, Popeye rescues Olive
EX $6　　NM $10　　MIP $20

Puzzle, 1991, Jaymar, 63 pieces, jumbo, Popeye's boat
EX $6　　NM $12　　MIP $25

Puzzle, 1991, Jaymar, 63 pieces, jumbo, Popeye and Olive surfing
EX $6   NM $10   MIP $20

Race Set, 1989, Ja-Ru
EX $6   NM $12   MIP $35

Road Building Set, 1979, Larami
EX $6   NM $12   MIP $35

Roller Skating Popeye, 1950s, Linemar
EX $150   NM $225   MIP $350

Roly Poly Popeye, 1940s, w/beaded arms and celluloid
EX $100   NM $175   MIP $300

Sailboats, 1981, Larami
EX $6   NM $10   MIP $25

Sailor's Knife, 1981, Ja-Ru
EX $10   NM $20   MIP $45

Screen-A Show Projector, 1973, Denys Fisher
EX $35   NM $90   MIP $160

Sea Hag Hand Puppet, 1987, Presents
EX $15   NM $35   MIP $110

Shaving Kit, 1979, Larami
EX $6   NM $10   MIP $35

Sling Darts, KFS
EX $20   NM $35   MIP $70

Soapy Popeye Boat, 1950s, Kerk Guild
EX $200   NM $300   MIP $500

Squirt Face, 1981, Ja-Ru
EX $6   NM $10   MIP $20

Stitch-A-Story, KFS
EX $12   NM $20   MIP $35

Sun-Eze Pictures, 1962, Tillman Toy
EX $10   NM $25   MIP $60

Sunglasses, 1980s, Larami, red, yellow, or blue
EX $6   NM $10   MIP $20

Super Race with Launcher, 1980, Fleetwood
EX $6   NM $12   MIP $25

Surf Rider, 1979, Wet Set-Zee Toys
EX $10   NM $25   MIP $65

Swee'Pea Bean Bag, 1974, Dakin
EX $10   NM $25   MIP $65

Swee'Pea Hand Puppet, 1960s, Gund, bonnet on head, cloth body decorated w/baby lambs
EX $15   NM $40   MIP $100

Swee'Pea Hand Puppet, 1987, Presents
EX $8   NM $25   MIP $70

Swee'Pea Hi-Pop Ball, 1981, Ja-Ru
EX $6   NM $12   MIP $30

Swee'Pea Squeak Toy, 1970s, frowning or smiling
EX $12   NM $25   MIP $75

Swirler Flying Barrel Toy, 1980, Imperial
EX $8   NM $15   MIP $30

Talking View-Master Set, 1962, GAF, old type
EX $12   NM $25   MIP $70

Tambourine, 1980s, Larami
EX $6   NM $10   MIP $20

Tambourine, 1990, Santa Cruz
EX $6   NM $10   MIP $20

Target Ball, 1981, Ja-Ru
EX $6   NM $10   MIP $20

Telephone, 1982, Comvu
EX $15   NM $30   MIP $70

Telescope, 1973, Larami
EX $10   NM $25   MIP $60

Thimble Theatre Cut-Outs, 1950s, Aldon
EX $50   NM $85   MIP $140

Toy Watch, 1987, Sekonda-Japan, comic strip band
EX $30   NM $50   MIP $100

Trace and Color, 1980, Fleetwood
EX $6   NM $10   MIP $20

Trumpet Bubble Blower, 1984, Larami, pink or yellow pan
EX $6   NM $12   MIP $25

Tube-A-Loonies, 1973, Larami, five small tubes on card
EX $6   NM $15   MIP $35

Turn-A-Scope, 1979, Larami
EX $6   NM $20   MIP $50

TV Set with Three Film Scrolls, 1957
EX $12   NM $20   MIP $50

View-Master Set, 1959, GAF, "The Hunting Bird"
EX $8   NM $15   MIP $40

View-Master Set, 1959, Sawyers, three reels
EX $15   NM $30   MIP $80

View-Master Set, 1959, GAF, "The Fish Story"
EX $8   NM $15   MIP $40

View-Master Set, 1962, GAF, three pack
EX $8   NM $15   MIP $50

Whistling Flashlights, 1960s, Bantam-Lite, six w/display
EX $300   NM $500   MIP $800

Whistling Wing Ding, 1950s, Mego
EX $20   NM $40   MIP $80

Wimpy Dog Toy, 1986, Petex
EX $8   NM $13   MIP $25

Wimpy Hand Puppet, 1950s, Gund, fabric hand cover, vinyl squeaker head and voice
EX $15   NM $50   MIP $120

Wimpy Hand Puppet, 1960s, Gund, cloth body
EX $15   NM $40   MIP $80

Wimpy Hand Puppet, 1987, Presents
EX $8   NM $13   MIP $90

Wimpy Ring, 1949, Post Toasties
EX $12   NM $45   MIP $110

Wimpy Squeeze Toy, 1950s, Rempel, vinyl
EX $20   NM $40   MIP $80

Wimpy Squeeze Toy, 1979, Cribmates
EX $12   NM $20   MIP $40

Wimpy Tugboat, 1961, Ideal, inflatable
EX $20   NM $40   MIP $60

Wood Slate, 1983, Ja-Ru
EX $6   NM $15   MIP $40

WATCH

Popeye Wristwatch, 1938, New Haven
EX $1500   NM $2500   MIP $4000

Popeye Wristwatch, 1964, Bradley, #308, green case
EX $115   NM $210   MIP $375

Popeye Wristwatch, 1979, Bradley
EX $60   NM $110   MIP $170

Popeye Wristwatch, 1987, Unique, Popeye's head pops open, digital
EX $12   NM $30   MIP $80

Popeye Wristwatch, 1990, KFS-Japan, Popeye in ship's wheel
EX $40   NM $80   MIP $130

Popeye Wristwatch, 1991, Armitron
EX $20   NM $35   MIP $80

PORKY PIG

BANK

Porky Pig Bank, 1930s, bisque, orange, blue, and yellow
EX $60   NM $120   MIP $225

DOLL

Porky Pig Doll, 1950, Gund, 14" tall
EX $60   NM $120   MIP $225

Porky Pig Doll, 1960s, Mattel, 17", cloth, vinyl head
EX $15   NM $35   MIP $85

Porky Pig Doll, 1968, Dakin, 7-3/4" tall in black velvet jacket
EX $15   NM $35   MIP $85

FIGURES

Porky and Petunia Figures, 1975, Warner Bros., 4-1/2" tall
EX $9   NM $16   MIP $50

TOY

Porky Pig Soaky
EX $15   NM $35   MIP $75

Porky Pig Umbrella, 1940s, hard plastic 3" figure on end, Porky and Bugs printed in red cloth
EX $100   NM $150   MIP $200

QUICK DRAW McGRAW

ACCESSORIES

Cereal Box, 1960, Kellogg's
EX $250   NM $400   MIP $600

BANK

Baba Looey Bank, 1960s, Knickerbocker, 9" tall, vinyl, plastic head
EX $16   NM $32   MIP $80

Quick Draw McGraw Bank, 1960, 9-1/2", plastic, orange, white, and blue
EX $40   NM $75   MIP $150

BOOK

Quick Draw McGraw Book, 1960, Whitman
EX $30   NM $45   MIP $90

DOLL

Auggie Doggie Doll, 1959, Knickerbocker, 10" tall, plush w/vinyl face
EX $40   NM $85   MIP $150

Baba Looey Doll, 1959, Knickerbocker, 20" tall, plush w/vinyl donkey ears and sombrero
    NM $125   MIP $250

Blabber Doll, 1959, Knickerbocker, 15" tall, plush w/vinyl face
EX $50   NM $100   MIP $180

Quick Draw McGraw Doll, 1959, Knickerbocker, 16", plush w/vinyl face, cowboy hat
EX $150   NM $300   MIP $450

Scooper Doll, 1959, Knickerbocker, 20", plush w/vinyl face
EX $75   NM $100   MIP $175

TOY

Auggie Doggie Soaky, 1960s, Purex, 10" tall, plastic
EX $15   NM $45   MIP $90

Blabber Soaky, 1960s, Purex, 10-1/2" tall, plastic
EX $18   NM $45   MIP $100

Quick Draw McGraw Moving Target Game, 1960s, Knickerbocker
EX $125   NM $175   MIP $300

Quick Draw Mold and Model Cast Set, 1960
EX $75   NM $100   MIP $150

RAGGEDY ANN AND ANDY

ACCESSORIES

Raggedy Ann/Andy Wastebasket, 1972, tin
EX $8   NM $20   MIP $60

BANK

Raggedy Andy Bank, Play Pal, 11"
EX $15   NM $20   MIP $50

Raggedy Ann Bank, 1974, Play Pal, 11"
EX $15   NM $20   MIP $50

BOOK

Camel with the Wrinkled Knees Book, 1924
EX $125   NM $200   MIP $350

Raggedy Ann Coloring Book, 1968
EX $6   NM $12   MIP $50

Raggedy Ann/Andy Paper Doll Book, 1974, Whitman, #1962
EX $15   NM $25   MIP $75

FIGURES

Raggedy Andy Figure, 1970s, rubber/wire, 4" tall
EX $5   NM $10   MIP $35

TOY

Raggedy Andy Puppet, 1975, Dakin, cloth
EX $20   NM $35   MIP $70

Raggedy Ann Puppet, 1975, Dakin, cloth
EX $20   NM $35   MIP $70

Raggedy Ann/Andy Record Player, square, cardboard
EX $45   NM $100   MIP $175

Raggedy Ann/Andy Record Player, 1950s, plastic, heart shaped
EX $100   NM $150   MIP $275

ROAD RUNNER AND WILE E. COYOTE

ACCESSORIES

Road Runner and Coyote Lamp, 1977, 12-1/2", figures standing on base
EX $40   NM $100   MIP $250

Road Runner Costume, 1960s, Collegeville
EX $30   NM $50   MIP $100

Wile E. Coyote Night Light, 1980s, Applause
EX $20   NM $45   MIP $90

BANK

Road Runner Bank, standing on base
EX $8   NM $15   MIP $50

DOLL

Road Runner Doll, 1971, Mighty Star, 13" tall
EX $12   NM $30   MIP $90

Wile E. Coyote Doll, 1970, Dakin, on explosive box
EX $40   NM $75   MIP $150

Wile E. Coyote Doll, 1971, Mighty Star, 18" tall, plush
EX $40   NM $75   MIP $150

FIGURES

Road Runner Figure, Dakin, plastic, Cartoon Theater
EX $18   NM $50   MIP $125

Road Runner Figure, 1968, Dakin, 8-3/4" tall
EX $18   NM $50   MIP $125

Road Runner Figure, 1971, Dakin, Goofy Gram
EX $15   NM $50   MIP $125

Wile E. Coyote and Road Runner Figures, 1979, Royal Crown, 7" tall, each
EX $15   NM $30   MIP $85

Wile E. Coyote Figure, 1968, Dakin, 10" tall
EX $30   NM $75   MIP $180

Wile E. Coyote Figure, 1971, Dakin, Goofy Gram, fused bomb in right hand
EX $20   NM $50   MIP $125

Wile E. Coyote Figure, 1976, Dakin, Cartoon Theater
EX $18   NM $32   MIP $100

TOY

Road Runner Hand Puppet, 1970s, Japanese, 10", vinyl head
EX $8   NM $20   MIP $60

Wile E. Coyote Hand Puppet, 1970s, Japanese, 10" vinyl head
EX $10   NM $20   MIP $60

ROCKY

DOLL

Apollo Creed Doll, 1983, Phoenix Toys, 8" tall
EX $5   NM $10   MIP $25

Clubber Lang Doll, 1983, Phoenix Toys, 8" tall
EX $6   NM $12   MIP $35

Rocky Balboa Doll, 1983, Phoenix Toys, 8" tall
EX $7   NM $15   MIP $35

ROGER RABBIT

ACCESSORIES

Baby Herman and Roger Rabbit Mug, Applause
EX $5   NM $8   MIP $15

Jessica Zipper Pull
EX $5   NM $10   MIP $15

BOOK

Paint with Water Book, Golden, #1702
EX $6   NM $12   MIP $30

Trace and Color Book, Golden, #2355
EX $5   NM $10   MIP $30

DOLL

Benny the Cab Doll, 1988, Applause, 6" long
EX $6   NM $12   MIP $30

Roger Rabbit Doll, Applause, 8-1/2" tall
EX $7   NM $15   MIP $60

Roger Rabbit Doll, Applause, 17" tall
EX $10   NM $30   MIP $125

FIGURES

Baby Herman Figure, 1987, LJN, 6" figure on card
EX $9   NM $20   MIP $35

Baby Herman Figure, 1988, LJN, ceramic
EX $9   NM $15   MIP $35

Boss Weasel Figure, 1988, LJN, 4" bendable
EX $4   NM $10   MIP $20

Eddie Valiant Figure, 1988, LJN, 4", flexible
EX $5   NM $10   MIP $20

Judge Doom Figure, 1988, LJN, 4" bendable
EX $4   NM $8   MIP $24

Roger Rabbit Figure, 1988, LJN, 4" bendable
EX $4   NM $10   MIP $30

Smart Guy Figure, 1988, LJN, flexible
EX $4   NM $8   MIP $15

GAME

Dip Flip Game, LJN
EX $8   NM $15   MIP $30

Who Framed Roger Rabbit Game, 1988, Milton Bradley low production run
EX $75   NM $125   MIP $200

TOY

Animates, 1988, Doom, Roger, Eddie and Smart Guy, each
EX $5   **NM** $8   **MIP** $15

Benny the Cab, LJN
EX $20   **NM** $40   **MIP** $75

Eddie Valiant Animate, 1988, LJN, 6" tall, bendable
EX $4   **NM** $8   **MIP** $15

Jessica License Plate
EX $6   **NM** $12   **MIP** $20

Judge Doom Animate, 1988, LJN, 6" tall poseable
EX $6   **NM** $12   **MIP** $25

Paint-A-Cel Set, Benny the Cab and Roger pictures
EX $8   **NM** $15   **MIP** $60

Roger Rabbit Animate, 1988, LJN, 6" poseable
EX $4   **NM** $10   **MIP** $20

Roger Rabbit Blow-Up Buddy, 36" tall
EX $6   **NM** $12   **MIP** $30

Roger Wacky Head Puppets, Applause, hand puppets
EX $6   **NM** $12   **MIP** $50

Roger Wind-Up, 1988, Matsudaya
EX $18   **NM** $35   **MIP** $100

Talking Roger in Benny the Cab, 17" tall
EX $12   **NM** $35   **MIP** $100

WATCH

Roger Rabbit Bullet Hole Wristwatch, 1987, Shiraka, white case and leather band, in plastic display box
EX $40   **NM** $85   **MIP** $160

Roger Rabbit Silhouette Wristwatch, 1987, Shiraka, large gold case, black band
EX $35   **NM** $80   **MIP** $160

ROOTIE KAZOOTIE

BOOK

Little Golden Book, 1953, Simon & Schuster, Rootie Kazootie Detective
EX $10   **NM** $20   **MIP** $60

Little Golden Book, 1954, Simon & Schuster, Rootie Kazootie Baseball Star, #190
EX $10   **NM** $20   **MIP** $60

Little Golden Book, 1955, Simon & Schuster, Rootie Kazootie Joins the Circus
EX $10   **NM** $20   **MIP** $60

BUTTON

Rootie Kazootie Club Button, 1950s, 1" tin litho
EX $18   **NM** $42   **MIP** $80

TOY

Rootie Kazootie Doll, 1950s, Effanbee, cloth body, vinyl head and hands
EX $75   **NM** $125   **MIP** $200

Rootie Kazootie Drum, 1950s, 8" diameter drum, Rootie on the drum head
EX $40   **NM** $75   **MIP** $150

Rootie Kazootie Fishing Tackle Box, 1950s, RK Inc., tin litho, bright graphics
EX $15   **NM** $30   **MIP** $70

RUFF AND REDDY

BOOK

Ruff and Reddy Go To A Party Tell-A-Tale Book, 1958, Whitman
EX $15   **NM** $35   **MIP** $70

TOY

Ruff and Reddy Draw Cartoon Set Color, Wonder Art
EX $50   **NM** $85   **MIP** $175

Ruff and Reddy Magic Rub-Off Picture Set, 1958, Transogram
EX $45   **NM** $80   **MIP** $175

SECRET SQUIRREL

TOY

Secret Squirrel Bubble Club Soaky, 1960s, Purex
EX $20   **NM** $35   **MIP** $90

Secret Squirrel Push Puppet, 1960s, Kohner, plastic figure in white coat, blue hat holding binoculars
EX $20   **NM** $40   **MIP** $80

Secret Squirrel Puzzle, 1967, frame tray
EX $15   **NM** $30   **MIP** $65

Secret Squirrel Ray Gun
EX $25   **NM** $50   **MIP** $100

SHIRLEY TEMPLE

ACCESSORIES

Doll Buggy, 1935, F.A. Whitney Carriage, wicker, hubcaps are labeled Shirley Temple
EX $300   **NM** $400   **MIP** $625

Doll Trunk, 18" tall w/"Our Little Girl" decal on the side, photo of Shirley
EX $100   **NM** $200   **MIP** $375

Doll Wardrobe Trunk, 20" heavy cardboard/wood steamer trunk for 18" doll, leather strap, metal latch w/lock and key, two drawers, and four cardboard hangers
EX $120   **NM** $200   **MIP** $375

Hair Ribbon and Band, 1934, Ribbon Mills, Several colors/styles
EX $15   **NM** $30   **MIP** $80

Hanger, cardboard; picture of Shirley Temple, came w/all outfits
EX $15   **NM** $25   **MIP** $60

Pen and Pencil Set, 1930s, David Kahn
EX $90   **NM** $140   **MIP** $250

Pin, Reliable, "The World's Darling/Genuine Shirley Temple, A Reliable Doll"
EX $65   **NM** $80   **MIP** $100

Purse, 1950s, red, white, and black w/Shirley Temple lettering
EX $30   **NM** $40   **MIP** $80

Stand Up and Cheer Doll Trunk, 1934
EX $125   **NM** $200   **MIP** $400

Texas Ranger/Cowgirl Gun, Came w/Texas Ranger outfit
EX $35   **NM** $70   **MIP** $200

BOOK

Composition Book, 1935, Western
EX $25   **NM** $50   **MIP** $100

My Life and Times by Shirley Temple Book, 1936, Saalfield, Big Little Book #116, Model No. 116
EX $30   **NM** $85   **MIP** $180

Scrap Book, 1935, Saalfield, #1714, Model No. 1714
EX $60   **NM** $85   **MIP** $185

Shirley Temple at Play Book, 1935, Saalfield, #1712, Model No. 1712
EX $40   **NM** $50   **MIP** $140

Shirley Temple Five Books About Me, 1936, Saalfield, Just a Little Girl, Twinkletoes, On the Movie Lot, In Starring Roles, and Little Playmate, #1730, Model No. 1730
EX $90   **NM** $150   **MIP** $250

Shirley Temple in The Littlest Rebel, 1935, Saalfield, Big Little Book, #1595, Model No. 1595
EX $20   **NM** $60   **MIP** $140

Shirley Temple My Book to Color, 1937, Saalfield, #1768, Model No. 1768
EX $35   **NM** $50   **MIP** $120

Shirley Temple Pastime Box, 1937, Saalfield, Four activity books: Favorite Puzzles, Favorite Games, Favorite Sewing Cards, and Favorite Coloring Book, #1732, Model No. 1732
EX $55   **NM** $125   **MIP** $220

Shirley Temple Scrap Book, 1936, Saalfield, #1722, Model No. 1722
EX $65   **NM** $85   **MIP** $200

Shirley Temple Scrap Book, 1937, Saalfield, #1763, Model No. 1763
EX $50   **NM** $85   **MIP** $200

Shirley Temple Story Book, 1935, Saalfield, #1726, Model No. 1726
EX $25   **NM** $40   **MIP** $120

Shirley Temple Treasury Book, 1959, Random House
EX $20   **NM** $30   **MIP** $75

Shirley Temple with Lionel Barrymore in The Little Colonel, 1935, Saalfield, Big Little Book, #1095, Model No. 1095
EX $20   **NM** $60   **MIP** $140

Shirley Temple's Blue Bird Coloring Book, 1939, Saalfield
EX $35   **NM** $65   **MIP** $150

Shirley Temple's Busy Book, 1958, Saalfield, Activity book, #5326, Model No. 5326
EX $40   **NM** $50   **MIP** $80

Shirley Temple's Favorite Poems, 1936,
Saalfield, #1720, Model No. 1720
EX $20   **NM** $60   **MIP** $90

The Story of Shirley Temple Book, 1934,
Saalfield, Big Little Book, #1089, Model
No. 1089
EX $20   **NM** $35   **MIP** $140

DOLL

Blue Bird Doll, 1939, 20" composition
EX $800   **NM** $1000   **MIP** $1600

Blue Bird Doll, 1939, 18", felt skirt and
vest, organdy blouse and apron w/blue
bird appliques
EX $910   **NM** $1025   **MIP** $1600

Bright Eyes Doll, 1936, 13" composition,
plaid dress, leather shoes
EX $610   **NM** $700   **MIP** $1100

Captain January Doll, Ideal, 22", dark blue
sailor suit w/white trim
EX $700   **NM** $910   **MIP** $1500

Captain January Doll, 1936, 16", green
pique w/silk ribbons
EX $650   **NM** $750   **MIP** $1300

Captain January Doll, 1936, 13", white
sailor suit, red bow tie, white hat,
original pin
EX $600   **NM** $700   **MIP** $1300

Captain January Doll, 1936, 18", cotton sailor
suit w/anchor applique and red silk tie
EX $650   **NM** $750   **MIP** $1400

Captain January Doll, 1936, Ideal, 20",
blue floral print, cotton school dress
w/ruffled collar
EX $725   **NM** $800   **MIP** $1450

Captain January Doll, 1957, Ideal, 12",
vinyl head, dark blonde hair, plastic
body, arms and legs
EX $175   **NM** $225   **MIP** $400

Curly Top Doll, 1935, 16" composition;
different versions available
EX $675   **NM** $750   **MIP** $1200

Curly Top Doll, 1935, Ideal, 11", pink
organdy dress
EX $875   **NM** $1050   **MIP** $1500

Curly Top Doll, 1935, 18" composition,
mohair hair, hazel eyes
EX $600   **NM** $685   **MIP** $1100

Curly Top Doll, 1935, 11", dotted swiss
dress, blue silk ribbons
EX $600   **NM** $685   **MIP** $1200

Curly Top Doll, 1935, 18", pleated dotted
swiss w/blue silk ribbons, red or lavender
EX $600   **NM** $700   **MIP** $1200

Heidi Doll, 1937, 18", striped cotton skirt,
black velveteen top w/red braid, apron,
mohair pigtails w/red ribbons
EX $950   **NM** $1075   **MIP** $1650

Heidi Doll, 1957, Ideal, 12", vinyl head,
dark blonde hair and plastic body, arms
and legs
EX $200   **NM** $285   **MIP** $400

Heidi Doll, 1960-61, 17"
EX $250   **NM** $325   **MIP** $450

Little Colonel Doll, 13", taffeta outfit,
variations in the collar, ruffles and
pantaloons
EX $775   **NM** $900   **MIP** $2000

Little Colonel Doll, Alexander, 13", pink hat
w/ruffle, pink dress and bloomers
EX $475   **NM** $575   **MIP** $1600

Little Colonel Doll, 20", blue organdy,
bonnet w/pink feather
EX $925   **NM** $1100   **MIP** $2200

Little Colonel Doll, 13", variations in
pantaloons, bonnets and shoes
EX $775   **NM** $900   **MIP** $2000

Little Colonel Doll, 1934, 13", light blue
dress w/bonnet, pantaloons and shoes
w/buckles
EX $775   **NM** $900   **MIP** $2000

Little Colonel Doll, 1934, 18", pink organdy
dress, bonnet, white pantaloons
EX $775   **NM** $900   **MIP** $2000

Little Colonel Doll, 1934, Ideal, 13",
smiling, pink hat w/feather and dress
and bloomers
EX $775   **NM** $900   **MIP** $2000

Littlest Rebel Doll, 1935, 13",
yellow/brown dress, white ruffled collar,
yellow shoes
EX $775   **NM** $900   **MIP** $2000

Littlest Rebel Doll, 1935, 16", polka dot
outfit, pantaloons, gray felt hat
EX $625   **NM** $700   **MIP** $1500

Littlest Rebel Doll, 1935, 18", cotton and
organdy outfit
EX $675   **NM** $725   **MIP** $1500

Littlest Rebel Doll, 1935, 22", red/white
cotton dress w/organdy collar
EX $775   **NM** $900   **MIP** $2000

Poor Little Rich Girl Doll, 1936, 18", pique
sunsuit w/matching tam
EX $325   **NM** $750   **MIP** $1500

Poor Little Rich Girl Doll, 1936, 13", sailor
dress w/white trim and matching tam
EX $275   **NM** $375   **MIP** $1200

Poor Little Rich Girl Doll, 1936, 13", blue
silk pajamas
EX $325   **NM** $750   **MIP** $1500

Rebecca of Sunnybrook Farm Doll, 1957,
12" vinyl, blue bib overalls, blue polka
dot blouse, straw hat
EX $125   **NM** $230   **MIP** $400

Rebecca of Sunnybrook Farm Doll, 1957, 12"
vinyl, red felt jumper and plastic purse
EX $175   **NM** $230   **MIP** $400

Rebecca of Sunnybrook Farm Doll, 1957,
12" vinyl, blue bib overalls w/plaid
blouse, black low shoes
EX $125   **NM** $185   **MIP** $300

Rebecca of Sunnybrook Farm Doll, 1957,
Ideal, 12", vinyl head, dark blonde hair,
plastic body, arms and legs
EX $175   **NM** $230   **MIP** $400

Shirley Temple Baby, 16", mohair wig,
flirty eyes
EX $525   **NM** $800   **MIP** $2100

Shirley Temple Baby, 20", composition
head, arms and legs, cloth body
EX $700   **NM** $975   **MIP** $2300

Shirley Temple Baby, Ideal, 18", painted
hair, chubby toddler body w/dimpled
cheeks, flirty eyes, dressed in pink
organdy w/silk ribbons
EX $600   **NM** $925   **MIP** $1850

Shirley Temple Doll, Reliable (Ideal/Canada),
13", yellow organdy dress, silk ribbon
EX $460   **NM** $760   **MIP** $1500

Shirley Temple Doll, Made in Japan, 8"
composition w/pink silk undies
EX $175   **NM** $210   **MIP** $400

Shirley Temple Doll, 27" composition
w/pink taffeta, bonnet and pantaloons
EX $850   **NM** $1250   **MIP** $2600

Shirley Temple Doll, 22" composition
w/facial molding
EX $600   **NM** $800   **MIP** $1500

Shirley Temple Doll, 20" composition
w/facial molding
EX $500   **NM** $750   **MIP** $1500

Shirley Temple Doll, 18" composition
w/facial molding
EX $525   **NM** $700   **MIP** $1400

Shirley Temple Doll, 16", black velveteen
coat and hat
EX $180   **NM** $350   **MIP** $1400

Shirley Temple Doll, 16", light blue
organdy w/pink hemstitching and silk
ribbons
EX $275   **NM** $575   **MIP** $1400

Shirley Temple Doll, 13", pleated pique
w/ white applique
EX $275   **NM** $550   **MIP** $1350

Shirley Temple Doll, Ideal, 22" jointed,
composition body, blonde mohair, hazel
glass eyes, open mouth, red/white polka
dot dress
EX $225   **NM** $500   **MIP** $1350

Shirley Temple Doll, Ideal, 19" vinyl, twinkle
eyes, dressed in pink nylon, black purse
EX $180   **NM** $340   **MIP** $600

Shirley Temple Doll, 16" composition
EX $375   **NM** $675   **MIP** $1350

Shirley Temple Doll, 1934, Ideal, 18", light
pink organdy
EX $475   **NM** $650   **MIP** $1500

Shirley Temple Doll, 1934, Ideal, 18",
pleated pale green, pink, or blue dress,
embroidered collar and pink silk ribbon
EX $520   **NM** $675   **MIP** $1200

Shirley Temple Doll, 1935, 18" facial
molding doll w/mohair wig (parted in the
center), light complexion, outfit from
"Curly Top"
EX $260   **NM** $525   **MIP** $1500

Shirley Temple Doll, 1957, 12", vinyl,
molded hands and feet, synthetic rooted
wig, pink slip trimmed w/lace
EX $125   **NM** $225   **MIP** $500

CHARACTER TOYS

Shirley Temple Doll, 1957, 12" vinyl, molded hands and feet, synthetic rooted wig, two piece slip/undies
EX $110   **NM** $225   **MIP** $475

Shirley Temple Doll, 1957, 12" vinyl, pink/blue nylon dress w/daisy appliques, hat, purse
EX $125   **NM** $250   **MIP** $500

Shirley Temple Doll, 1958, 15" vinyl, red nylon dress w/floral detailing at collar, hair ribbon, purse
EX $110   **NM** $210   **MIP** $375

Shirley Temple Doll, 1958, Ideal, 15" vinyl, yellow nylon dress trimmed w/lace and ribbon around skirt
EX $175   **NM** $320   **MIP** $550

Shirley Temple Doll, 1958-59, Ideal, 17" vinyl, brown twinkle eyes, pink/blue dress
EX $210   **NM** $320   **MIP** $700

Shirley Temple Doll, 1960, 15" vinyl, blue jumper w/red/white gingham blouse and pocket facing
EX $100   **NM** $200   **MIP** $375

Shirley Temple Doll, 1960s, 17", yellow party dress, white purse w/Shirley Temple lettering
EX $225   **NM** $325   **MIP** $700

Shirley Temple Doll, 1960s, Ideal, 17", yellow nylon dress and Twinkle Eyes wrist tag
EX $210   **NM** $320   **MIP** $700

Shirley Temple Doll, 1972, Ideal/Hong Kong, 16", vinyl, red polka dot dress, Stand Up and Cheer
EX $155   **NM** $185   **MIP** $300

Shirley Temple Doll, 1972, Ideal/Hong Kong, 15" vinyl manufactured for Montgomery Ward's
EX $175   **NM** $210   **MIP** $375

Stand Up and Cheer Doll, 11" composition, short rayon dress w/blue polka dots
EX $675   **NM** $925   **MIP** $1600

Stand Up and Cheer Doll, 1934, 11", dotted red, blue, or green organdy dress w/silk ribbon
EX $450   **NM** $675   **MIP** $1500

Stand Up and Cheer Doll, 1934, 13" composition, dotted organdy green dress
EX $150   **NM** $200   **MIP** $600

Stowaway Doll, 1936, 20", two-piece linen w/brass buttons
EX $650   **NM** $825   **MIP** $2000

Stowaway Doll, 1936, 25", pink taffeta, mohair hair
EX $700   **NM** $950   **MIP** $2100

Texas Ranger Doll, 17", plaid shirt, leather vest w/trim
EX $550   **NM** $700   **MIP** $1500

Texas Ranger Doll, 20", plaid shirt, leather vest w/trim, chaps, holster, and metal gun
EX $700   **NM** $950   **MIP** $2000

Texas Ranger/Cowgirl Doll, 11", plaid cotton shirt, leather vest, chaps, holster, metal gun, felt 10 gallon hat w/"Ride 'Em Cowboy" printed band
EX $450   **NM** $750   **MIP** $2000

Wee Willie Winkie Doll, 1937, 18", long sleeve cotton jacket, two pockets and six brass buttons, plaid wool skirt, tan belt w/brass buckle
EX $700   **NM** $1050   **MIP** $2100

Wee Willie Winkie Doll, 1957, Ideal, 12", vinyl head, dark blonde hair, plastic body, arms and legs
EX $190   **NM** $250   **MIP** $475

DOLL CLOTHING

Baby Take A Bow Dress, 1934, red cotton, red polka dots on collar and reverse on the bottom w/silk ribbons, fits 16" doll
EX $85   **NM** $95   **MIP** $150

Ballerina Outfit, 1957-58, blue/green nylon and tulle, flower hair piece; fits 12" vinyl doll
EX $80   **NM** $85   **MIP** $120

Bright Eyes Dress, 1934, fits 16" dolls, several colors variations
EX $85   **NM** $90   **MIP** $140

Bright Eyes Outfit, white corduroy coat and hat w/original pin, fits 16" doll
EX $100   **NM** $150   **MIP** $240

Captain January Outfit, 1936, red or green pleated pique, silk ribbons; fits a 16" doll
EX $85   **NM** $95   **MIP** $160

Coat and Hat, velveteen coat and hat w/red buttons; fits 16" doll
EX $80   **NM** $90   **MIP** $130

Coat and Hat, 1958, Ideal, red corduroy coat and hat, fits 12" doll
EX $60   **NM** $70   **MIP** $95

Curly Top Dress, 1935, striped cotton dress, fits 20" doll
EX $85   **NM** $95   **MIP** $160

Dimples Outfit, 1936, heavy felt jacket w/red trim; fits 16" doll
EX $85   **NM** $95   **MIP** $160

Dress, light blue organdy; fits 16" doll
EX $85   **NM** $95   **MIP** $160

Dress, 1958, Ideal, nylon w/loop details; fits 12" doll
EX $65   **NM** $80   **MIP** $110

Dress, Jacket, and Purse, 1959, nylon
EX $65   **NM** $75   **MIP** $100

Jumper and Blouse, 1959, Ideal, blue velveteen jumper w/floral applique, cotton blouse
EX $60   **NM** $70   **MIP** $100

Jumpsuit, red w/white flowers
EX $80   **NM** $85   **MIP** $120

Jumpsuit, red/white checkered
EX $35   **NM** $40   **MIP** $70

Littlest Rebel Dress, 1935, yellow/brown, fits an 18" doll
EX $150   **NM** $185   **MIP** $500

Littlest Rebel Outfit, checkered dress, rick rack ribbon on sleeves, lace collar and apron
EX $85   **NM** $110   **MIP** $450

Nightcoat and Cap, 1958-59, Ideal, flannel; fits 12" doll
EX $60   **NM** $70   **MIP** $100

Our Little Girl Outfit, 1935, blue or white pique, white dog appliques, fits 16" doll
EX $85   **NM** $100   **MIP** $220

Our Little Girl Outfit, 1935, red or blue dress w/music appliques, matching hat, fits 16" doll
EX $85   **NM** $100   **MIP** $220

Polka Dot Dancing Dress, 1935, blue organdy w/matching hat and sunsuit
EX $85   **NM** $90   **MIP** $150

Poor Little Rich Girl Outfit, 1935, blue sailor dress, fits 16" doll
EX $90   **NM** $100   **MIP** $160

Poor Little Rich Girl Outfit, 1935, pique and organdy dress, fits 16" doll
EX $90   **NM** $100   **MIP** $160

Poor Little Rich Girl Outfit, 1936, pleated red plaid w/white collar, fits 16" doll
EX $90   **NM** $100   **MIP** $160

Rain Cape and Umbrella, plaid red or blue rain cape w/hood and matching umbrella; fits 18" doll
EX $80   **NM** $100   **MIP** $185

Stowaway Outfit, 1936, red or blue pique, fits 16" doll
EX $90   **NM** $125   **MIP** $275

Wee Willie Winkie Outfit, 1937, pique outfit and tam, slip/undies; fits 16" doll
EX $125   **NM** $160   **MIP** $285

Wool Coat, fits 18" dolls, from Little Miss Marker
EX $60   **NM** $90   **MIP** $190

PAPER DOLLS

Paper Doll Book, 1976, Whitman, #1986, Model No. 1986
EX $8   **NM** $15   **MIP** $50

Paper Dolls, 1934, Saalfield, four 8" dolls and 30 outfits; first licensed set, #2112, Model No. 2112
EX $175   **NM** $350   **MIP** $600

Paper Dolls, 1958, Saalfield, #4435, Model No. 4435
EX $35   **NM** $50   **MIP** $170

Paper Dolls, 1959, Saalfield, 18" folding doll w/easel, costumes, and accessories, #5110, Model No. 5110
EX $10   **NM** $40   **MIP** $120

Shirley Standing Doll, 1935, Saalfield, cardboard doll on platform and different outfits, #1719, Model No. 1719
EX $150   **NM** $250   **MIP** $475

Shirley Temple Dolls and Dresses, 1960, Saalfield, Two dolls w/different outfits, #1789, Model No. 1789
EX $12   **NM** $20   **MIP** $50

PHOTOGRAPH

Promo Photo, 8" x 10" photo of Shirley w/facsimile autograph, came w/all composition dolls and outfits
EX $30   **NM** $45   **MIP** $75

PLAYING CARDS

Bridge Cards, 1934, U.S. Playing Card
EX $40   **NM** $60   **MIP** $90

SLEEPING BEAUTY

ACCESSORIES

Sleeping Beauty Alarm Clock, 1950s, Phinney-Walker, 2-1/2" x 4" x 4-1/2" tall, Sleeping Beauty surrounded by three birds and petting a rabbit
EX $75   **NM** $125   **MIP** $250

Sleeping Beauty Doll Crib Mattress, 1960s, 9" x 17", Sleeping Beauty and the fairies
EX $15   **NM** $25   **MIP** $50

BOOK

Sleeping Beauty Sticker Fun Book, 1959, Whitman
EX $15   **NM** $30   **MIP** $75

TOY

Fairy Godmother Hand Puppets, 1958, set of three: 10-1/2" tall, Flora, Merryweather, and Fauna, each
EX $75   **NM** $125   **MIP** $250

King Huber/King Stefan Hand Puppets, 1956, Gund, 10" tall, molded rubber heads w/fabric hand cover
EX $30   **NM** $75   **MIP** $150

Puzzle, 1958, Whitman, 11-1/2" x 14-1/2", Three Good Fairies circling around a baby in a crib
EX $15   **NM** $35   **MIP** $80

Puzzle, 1958, Whitman, 11-1/2" x 14-1/2", Sleeping Beauty w/Prince Phillip and Three Good Fairies circling
EX $15   **NM** $35   **MIP** $80

Puzzle, 1958, Whitman, 11-1/2" x 14-1/2", Sleeping Beauty w/forest animals
EX $15   **NM** $35   **MIP** $80

Sleeping Beauty Jack-In-The-Box, 1980s, Enesco, Princess Aurora, wooden box, plays "Once Upon A Dream"
EX $65   **NM** $125   **MIP** $250

Sleeping Beauty Magic Paint Set, Whitman
EX $25   **NM** $50   **MIP** $90

Sleeping Beauty Squeeze Toy, 1959, Dell, 4" x 4" x 5" tall, rubber, Sleeping Beauty w/rabbit
EX $30   **NM** $60   **MIP** $90

SMOKEY BEAR

BANK

Smokey Bank, 6" tall, china
EX $50   **NM** $100   **MIP** $175

BOOK

Smokey Bear and the Campers Book, 1961, Golden
EX $10   **NM** $20   **MIP** $50

Smokey Bear Coloring Book, 1958, Whitman
EX $25   **NM** $40   **MIP** $75

DOLL

Smokey Doll, 1950s, Ideal, 15" plush, vinyl face
EX $100   **NM** $175   **MIP** $350

FIGURES

Smokey Bobbing Head Figure, 1960s, 6-1/4" tall
EX $100   **NM** $250   **MIP** $450

Smokey Figure, 1971, Dakin, figure on a tree stump
EX $30   **NM** $75   **MIP** $185

TOY

Smokey Bear Record, Peter Pan, 45 rpm
EX $5   **NM** $15   **MIP** $35

Smokey Soaky, 1960s, 9" tall, plastic
EX $10   **NM** $25   **MIP** $60

WATCH

Smokey Wristwatch, 1960s, Hawthorne
EX $75   **NM** $150   **MIP** $300

SNOW WHITE AND THE SEVEN DWARFS

ACCESSORIES

Doc Lamp, 1938, LaMode Studios, 8" tall, plaster
EX $150   **NM** $300   **MIP** $500

Dopey Lamp, 1940s, 9" tall, ceramic base w/Dopey
EX $125   **NM** $275   **MIP** $475

Pencil Box, Venus Pencil, 3" x 8" x 1"
EX $75   **NM** $125   **MIP** $200

Radio, 1938, Emerson, 8" x 8" w/characters on cabinet
EX $1400   **NM** $3000   **MIP** $4500

Snow White Lamp, 1938, LaMode Studios, 8-1/2" tall
EX $200   **NM** $350   **MIP** $600

Snow White Mirror, 1940s, 9-1/2", plastic handle
EX $30   **NM** $100   **MIP** $200

Snow White Table Quoits, 1930s, Chad Valley, 9-1/2" x 21" x 1-1/4" deep
EX $125   **NM** $225   **MIP** $375

BANK

Dime Register Bank, 1938, Disney, holds up to five dollars
EX $150   **NM** $350   **MIP** $500

Dopey Bank, 1938, Crown Toy, 7-1/2" tall, wood composition
EX $100   **NM** $200   **MIP** $375

Dopey Dime Register Bank, 1938, Disney, holds up to $5
EX $200   **NM** $350   **MIP** $550

BOOK

Snow White and the Seven Dwarfs Book, 1938, Whitman, Big Little Book
EX $25   **NM** $80   **MIP** $200

Snow White Paper Dolls, 1938, Whitman, 10" x 15" x 1-1/2", blue
EX $200   **NM** $450   **MIP** $850

DOLL

Bashful Doll, 1930s, Ideal
EX $100   **NM** $200   **MIP** $450

Doc Doll, 1930s, Ideal
EX $100   **NM** $200   **MIP** $450

Dopey Doll, Krueger, 14" tall
EX $100   **NM** $220   **MIP** $450

Dopey Doll, 1930s, Ideal
EX $90   **NM** $200   **MIP** $425

Dopey Doll, 1938, Knickerbocker, 11" tall composition
EX $150   **NM** $350   **MIP** $800

Dopey Doll, 1938, Chad Valley, cloth body
EX $55   **NM** $150   **MIP** $350

Dopey Ventriloquist Doll, 1938, Ideal, 18" tall
EX $160   **NM** $325   **MIP** $775

Grumpy Doll, 1938, Knickerbocker, 11" tall, composition
EX $100   **NM** $350   **MIP** $750

Happy Doll, 1930s, 5-1/2" tall, composition, holding a silver pick w/a black handle
EX $50   **NM** $175   **MIP** $400

Sneezy Doll, Krueger, 14" tall
EX $125   **NM** $250   **MIP** $600

Snow White and the Seven Dwarfs Dolls, 1940s, Deluxe, 22" Snow White and 7" dwarfs
EX $1000   **NM** $1500   **MIP** $2500

Snow White Doll, Horsman, 8", in illustrated box
EX $25   **NM** $50   **MIP** $125

Snow White Doll, 1938, Ideal, 3-1/2" x 6-1/2" x 16" tall, fabric face and arms, red/white dress w/dwarf and forest animal design
EX $500   **NM** $1000   **MIP** $1500

Snow White Doll, 1939, Knickerbocker, 3" x 7" x 3-1/2", composition w/movable arms and legs
EX $275   **NM** $550   **MIP** $1100

Snow White Doll, 1940, Knickerbocker, 12" tall, composition
EX $250   **NM** $500   **MIP** $1000

FIGURES

Dopey Figure, 1960s, ceramic figure and barrel
EX $15   **NM** $30   **MIP** $100

Seven Dwarfs Figures, 1938, Seiberling, 5-1/2", rubber
EX $450   **NM** $600   **MIP** $850

GAME

Seven Dwarfs Target Game, 1930s, Chad Valley, 6-1/2" x 11-1/2" target, spring locked gun
EX $250   **NM** $300   **MIP** $500

CHARACTER TOYS

CHARACTER TOYS

TOY

Baby Rattle, 1938, Krueger, Snow White at piano, Dwarfs playing instruments
EX $150   NM $250   MIP $400

Dopey Rolykin, Marx, 2"
EX $35   NM $75   MIP $125

Dopey Soaky, 1960s, 10" tall
EX $11   NM $30   MIP $80

Dopey Walker, 1938, Marx, 9" tall, tin, rocking walker
EX $300   NM $650   MIP $1000

Happy Toy, YS Toys (Taiwan), battery operated, Happy fries eggs
EX $50   NM $120   MIP $300

Ironing Board, Wolverine, tin board and cover
EX $15   NM $30   MIP $80

Puzzle, 1960s, Jaymar, 11" x 14"
EX $20   NM $35   MIP $65

Puzzles, 1938, Whitman, set of two
EX $100   NM $200   MIP $400

(KP Photo)

Refrigerator, 1970s, Wolverine, 15", tin, single door, white and yellow depicting Snow White
EX $25   NM $60   MIP $150

Safety Blocks, 1938, Halsam, 7-1/2" x 14-1/2"
EX $50   NM $150   MIP $350

Sand Pail, 1938, Ohio Art, 8", tin, Snow White plays hide-n-seek w/the dwarfs
EX $100   NM $200   MIP $400

Sled, 1938, S. L. Allen, 40" long wood slat and metal runner sled w/character decals
EX $250   NM $600   MIP $1000

Snow White Marionette, 1930s, Tony Sarg/Alexander, 12-1/2" tall
EX $100   NM $300   MIP $600

Snow White Model Making Set, 1930s, Sculptorcraft
EX $100   NM $250   MIP $525

Snow White Sewing Set, 1940s, Ontex
EX $30   NM $100   MIP $200

Snow White Sink, 1960s, Wolverine, tin
EX $15   NM $30   MIP $75

Snow White Soaky
EX $15   NM $40   MIP $80

Tea Set, 1930s, Wadeheath, white china, teapot, cups, saucers, and creamer
EX $175   NM $350   MIP $600

Tea Set, 1937, Ohio Art, plates, cups, tray, saucers
EX $175   NM $350   MIP $500

Tea Set, 1960s, Marx, teapot, five saucers, large plates and tea cups
EX $40   NM $70   MIP $175

SPORTS

DOLL

Dorothy Hamill Doll, 1975, Ideal, 11-1/4" tall
EX $30   NM $55   MIP $100

Evel Knievel Doll, Ideal, 6" tall
EX $20   NM $35   MIP $100

Julius Erving (Dr. J) Doll, 1974
EX $20   NM $40   MIP $100

Wayne Gretzky Doll, Mattel, 12" tall
EX $25   NM $50   MIP $80

WATCH

Muhammed Ali Wristwatch, 1980, Bradley, chrome case, sweep seconds, brown leather band, face shows Ali in trunks and gloves, w/signature beneath
EX $100   NM $175   MIP $300

STEVE CANYON

BOOK

Steve Canyon's Interceptor Station Punch Out, 1950s, Golden
EX $75   NM $100   MIP $160

TOY

Steve Canyon Costume, 1959, Halco
EX $25   NM $60   MIP $185

Steve Canyon's Membership Card and Badge, 1/2" x 4" Milton Caniff membership card for the Airagers, Morse code on back, 3" tin litho color badge w/gold feathers w/Steve's face centered
EX $100   NM $150   MIP $220

SUPERHEROES

ACCESSORIES

Aquaman Halloween Costume, 1967, Ben Cooper
EX $35   NM $55   MIP $100

Captain America Halloween Costume, 1967, Ben Cooper
EX $100   NM $200   MIP $375

Comic Book Tattoos, 1967, Topps, Aquaman, Wonder Woman, Superman, or Batman
EX $20   NM $30   MIP $80

Flash Glass, 1978, Pepsi
EX $20   NM $40   MIP $70

Green Lantern Halloween Costume, 1967, Ben Cooper
EX $100   NM $175   MIP $300

Hawkman Button, 1966, Button World, 3", "Hawkman Superhero Club"
EX $20   NM $30   MIP $60

Justice League of America Display Card, 1970, Fleer, cardboard display from inside gumball machine
EX $30   NM $45   MIP $85

Mr. Bubble Superfriends Box, 1984, bubble bath box features Superman, Wonder Woman, Batman, and Robin
EX $20   NM $30   MIP $85

Spider-Man Button, 1966, Button World, 3", "Superhero Club"
EX $15   NM $35   MIP $75

Spider-Man Crazy Foam, 1974, American Aerosol
EX $10   NM $30   MIP $50

Wonder Woman Glass, 1978, Pepsi, 6"
EX $10   NM $25   MIP $45

Wonder Woman Record, 1977, Peter Pan Records, 33-1/3" rpm record w/comic book
EX $10   NM $30   MIP $50

BOOKS

Aquaman Scourge of the Sea Book, 1968, Whitman, Big Little Book
EX $15   NM $30   MIP $65

Spider-Man Coloring Book, 1983, Marvel Books, oversized, "The Arms of Doctor Octopus"
EX $10   NM $20   MIP $50

GAMES

Marvel Superheroes Card Game, 1978, Milton Bradley
EX $20   NM $30   MIP $90

TOY

Amazing Spider-Car, 1976, Mego, 10" long, red plastic
EX $40   NM $75   MIP $120

Aquaman Jigsaw Puzzle, 1968, Whitman, 100 pieces; Aquaman and Mera
EX $20   NM $40   MIP $70

Marvel Superheroes Colorforms Set, 1983, Colorforms
EX $10   NM $20   MIP $60

Marvel Superheroes Easy Show Projector, 1967, Kenner, projector and three cartridges
EX $150   NM $300   MIP $450

Marvel Superheroes Puzzle, 1967, Milton Bradley, 100 pieces
EX $40   NM $80   MIP $175

Marvel Superheroes Sparkle Paint Set, 1967, Kenner
EX $40   NM $80   MIP $175

Marvel World Adventure Play Set, 1975, Amsco, w/stand-up scenes and figures
EX $100   NM $200   MIP $350

Spider-Man Hand Puppet, 1976, Imperial, 9", vinyl head, plastic body
EX $15   NM $35   MIP $90

TOYS

Spider-Man Friction Vehicle, 1968, Marx, tin litho w/Spider-Man figure at wheel
EX $150   **NM** $300   **MIP** $500

SUPERMAN

ACCESSORIES

Children's Dish Set, 1966, Boontonware, 7" plate, 5-1/2" bowl, 3-1/2" cup, all white plastic w/Superman image
EX $50   **NM** $100   **MIP** $150

Fan Card, 1942, 7" x 10", shows full color Superman in hands on hips pose, reads, "Best wishes from your friend Superman"
EX $400   **NM** $700   **MIP** $1000

Fan Card, 1950s, National Comics, 5" x 7" promo b/w post card w/signature "Best Wishes, George Reeves"
EX $75   **NM** $150   **MIP** $200

Hair Brush, 1940, Monarch, wood, full length decal of Superman, brush came in handle and no-handle styles w/box
EX $100   **NM** $175   **MIP** $350

Hair Brush, 1976, Avon, Superman handle, illustrated box
EX $15   **NM** $25   **MIP** $50

Junior Defense League of America Membership Certificate, 1940s, Superman, Inc., Superman Bread premium, red/blue print and Superman bust and logo on paper, "signed" by Clark Kent
EX $600   **NM** $1000   **MIP** $1250

Membership Certificate, 1965, last year of club
EX $175   **NM** $350   **MIP** $500

Original Radio Broadcasts Record, 1977, Nostalgia Lane, old Superman radio teleplays, in illustrated sleeve showing chain breaking pose in color and b/w strip panels
EX $10   **NM** $25   **MIP** $50

Patch, 1939, 5-1/2" diameter fabric premium patch, shows 3/4 profile of Superman breaking chains off chest, Supermen of America -- Action Comics
EX $1000   **NM** $4000   **MIP** $6000

Patch, 1940s, 3-1/2" round patch shows chain breaking pose
EX $750   **NM** $2000   **MIP** $5000

Patch, 1942, Superman Bread, cardboard shield
EX $1000   **NM** $1500   **MIP** $2500

Patch, 1970s, cloth diamond-shaped patch of "S" logo in gold/red, several sizes, each
EX $5   **NM** $10   **MIP** $20

Patch, 1970s, rectangular white patch w/green border shows full color Superboy running toward viewer
EX $20   **NM** $40   **MIP** $70

Patch, 1970s, rectangular white cloth patch w/green border shows full color Supergirl flying
EX $5   **NM** $10   **MIP** $20

Patch, 1970s, triangular orange cloth patch w/red border shows Superman flying over desert scene
EX $5   **NM** $10   **MIP** $20

Patch, 1973, diamond-shaped cloth patch shows Superman standing against vertical red/white stripes, wide yellow border has stars and reads "Superman Junior Olympics"
EX $5   **NM** $10   **MIP** $20

Pen, 1947, Jaffe, red/blue pen on illustrated card
EX $300   **NM** $450   **MIP** $750

Pencil Box, 1966, Mattel
EX $25   **NM** $50   **MIP** $75

Pencil Holder, 1940s, Superman, Inc., hollow holder in shape of large pencil, illustrated on shaft w/red and blue on white images and Superman-Tim Club logos
EX $500   **NM** $850   **MIP** $1250

Pennant, 1940s, yellow pennant w/Superman image and raised logo
EX $500   **NM** $800   **MIP** $1500

Pennant, 1973, 35th anniversary item, felt pennant has Amazing World of Superman logo and reads "Metropolis, Illinois, Home of Superman", came in two sizes, each
EX $12   **NM** $25   **MIP** $85

Pillow, 1960s, 12" square felt pillow w/color art of flying Superman
EX $35   **NM** $65   **MIP** $100

Pin, 1940s, Kellogg's, 7/8" round pin w/black/red/blue bust of Superman, most common pin in Pep Cereal series of late 1940s
EX $12   **NM** $25   **MIP** $60

Record and Club Membership Kit, 1966, 33-1/3 rpm record of the original comic, Superman Club card, shoulder patch and 1" tin litho club button, in 12" square illustrated box
EX $100   **NM** $150   **MIP** $200

Super Candy and Toy, 1967, Phoenix Candy, boxed candy w/a small toy inside each box
EX $50   **NM** $75   **MIP** $135

Superman 3-D Cut-Out Picture, 1950s, Kellogg's, 4-1/2 x 6-1/2" premium framed cut-out of Superman from the back of cereal box, reads "Best Wishes From Your Friend Superman"
EX $60   **NM** $80   **MIP** $100

Superman Candy, 1940, Leader Novelty Candy, boxed candy w/punch-out trading cards on box back and coupons redeemable for Superman items, red box, front shows chain-breaking pose
EX $750   **NM** $1000   **MIP** $1500

Superman Christmas Card, 1940s, 4" x 5", Superman Brings You Christmas Greetings, shows him flying w/small tree in hands
EX $50   **NM** $150   **MIP** $300

Superman Cigarette Lighter, 1940s, Dunhill, battery-operated table-top lighter has chrome finish figure standing on black base
EX $750   **NM** $1000   **MIP** $1500

Superman Crazy Foam, 1970s, American Aerosol, spray bath soap in full color illustrated can
EX $25   **NM** $50   **MIP** $75

Superman Cup, 1984, Burger King, one of four in set w/figural handles, others are Batman, Wonder Woman and Darkseid
EX $5   **NM** $7   **MIP** $10

Superman Figurine, 1966, Ideal, 3" tall hard plastic painted or unpainted figure on base, removable cape, part of Justice League series
EX $35   **NM** $65   **MIP** $85

Superman Figurine, 1984, Craft Master, solid figurine and paint set, on illustrated card
EX $25   **NM** $50   **MIP** $80

Superman Hood Ornament, 1940s, Lee, chrome finish, shows Superman in stylized running pose w/box
EX $500   **NM** $2000   **MIP** $3000

Superman Junior Defense League Pin, 1940s, die cut pin in shape of flying Superman holding banner aloft, gold finish pin w/red/white/blue detailing
EX $75   **NM** $150   **MIP** $250

Superman Krypto-Raygun Filmstrips, 1940s, Daisy, extra boxed films for Krypto-Raygun, each
EX $25   **NM** $50   **MIP** $100

Superman Mug, 1950s, left handed mug, shows Superman on front and name across cape in back, handle has arrow and star
EX $75   **NM** $150   **MIP** $250

Superman Mug, 1966, white glass, red and blue logo w/Superman image, reverse picture is Superman breaking chain
EX $20   **NM** $40   **MIP** $65

Superman of Metropolis Award Certificate, 1973, premium given out during Metropolis, Illinois' 1973 35th anniversary of Superman celebration
EX $20   **NM** $40   **MIP** $75

Superman Phone Booth Radio, 1978, Vanity Fair, battery operated AM radio of green British-style booth has color bas-relief Superman exiting
EX $35   **NM** $75   **MIP** $175

Superman Planter, 1970s, 3" diameter painted ceramic
EX $5   **NM** $10   **MIP** $25

Superman Radio, 1973, transistor radio made in punch-out shape of Superman from waist up
EX $50   **NM** $75   **MIP** $200

Superman Record Player, 1978, latching box briefcase type record player illustrated on all sides in full color, also features b/w origin strip on back
EX $55   **NM** $100   **MIP** $200

Superman School Bag, 1950s, Acme, red/blue fold-over clasp vinyl bag,

CHARACTER TOYS

screened full color Superman figure, black plastic handle and shoulder strap
EX $100   NM $200   MIP $450

Superman Soaky, 1965, Colgate Palmolive, 10" soap bottle, shows him standing w/hands at sides
EX $20   NM $40   MIP $100

Superman Soaky, 1978, Avon, 9-1/2" bubble bath bottle, Superman stands atop building
EX $30   NM $40   MIP $65

Superman Song Record, 1950s, A.A. Records, 6" two-song, 45 rpm record in sleeve, other song is "Tarzan Song", Model No. 723
EX $25   NM $50   MIP $100

Superman Statue, 1940s, 15" tall, crude painted plaster carnival prize
EX $300   NM $450   MIP $600

Superman Statue, 1942, Syracuse Ornament, 5-1/2" tall composition statue of Superman in hands on hips pose, finished in brown patina w/red/black highlights
EX $1000   NM $2000   MIP $3500

Superman Telephone, 1979, ATE, plastic phone w/large figure of Superman in hands on hips pose standing over key pad, receiver hangs up into back of his cape, illustrated box
EX $150   NM $600   MIP $1000

Superman Toothbrush, 1970s, Janex, figural, battery operated
EX $20   NM $35   MIP $65

Superman Towels, 1970s, G.H. Wood, children's sponge towels, illustrated
EX $12   NM $25   MIP $60

Superman Wall Clock, 1978, New Haven, plastic and cardboard battery operated framed wall clock showing Superman fighting alien shaceship
EX $30   NM $60   MIP $150

Superman Wallet, 1950s, Croyden, brown, color embossed flying Superman and logo
EX $100   NM $175   MIP $375

Superman Wallet, 1960s, brown leather
EX $25   NM $40   MIP $70

Superman's Christmas Adventure Record, 1940s, Decca, set of three 78 rpm records in illustrated sleeves
EX $150   NM $500   MIP $900

Superman-Tim Club Membership Card, 1940s, Superman, Inc., blue/red or red/black card
EX $150   NM $200   MIP $325

Superman-Tim Club Press Card, 1940s, blue/red card for identifying self as an Official Reporter for club
EX $150   NM $225   MIP $350

Superman-Tim Club Redbacks, 1940s, Superman, Inc., red on white imprinted coupons styled to look like money, denominations of $1, $5 and $10 "redbacks", each
EX $10   NM $20   MIP $35

Superman-Tim Magazine, 1940s, 5" x 7" monthly store premium, each
EX $50   NM $75   MIP $150

Supermen of America Membership Certificate, 1948, 8-1/2" x 11", signed by "Clark Kent"
EX $75   NM $150   MIP $350

Utensil Set, 1966, Imperial Knife, stainless steel spoon and fork set w/Superman on the handles, on 4-1/2 x 10" illustrated card
EX $50   NM $100   MIP $200

Wall Banner, 1966, 16" x 25" w/hanging rod at top, shows large central picture of Superman in front of city skyline and two lower panels of him smashing rocks and flying through space
EX $40   NM $85   MIP $175

ACTION FIGURES

(KP Photo)

Energized Superman Figure, 1979, Remco, 12" tall battery operated hard body figure, in box
EX $35   NM $65   MIP $185

Flying Superman, 1950s, Kellogg's, plastic premium, 5" x 6-1/2", toy only
EX $50   NM $100   MIP $200

Flying Superman, 1950s, Kellogg's, premium, 5" x 6-1/2", rubber band propelled, w/instruction sheet and mailer
EX $150   NM $200   MIP $350

Flying Superman, 1955, Transogram, 12-1/2" tall molded plastic figure propelled by "super flight launcher", a rubber band attached to a pistol grip holder, on illustrated card
EX $75   NM $125   MIP $250

Superman Figure, Chemtoy, rubber, three different poses, on card, each
EX $25   NM $40   MIP $50

Superman Figure, Fun Things, 6" rubber figure on card
EX $9   NM $16   MIP $30

Superman Figure, Palitoy, 8" figure on card
EX $35   NM $65   MIP $120

Superman Figure, 1979, Japan, plastic body w/soft vinyl head, movable arms and head, in illustrated window box
EX $40   NM $60   MIP $90

BANK

Superman Bank, 1949, 9-1/2" painted ceramic shows youthful looking Superman standing on a cloud
EX $300   NM $500   MIP $800

Superman Bank, 1974, bust of Superman
EX $50   NM $75   MIP $125

Superman Dime Register Bank, 1940s, 1/2" x 2-1/2" x 2-1/2" yellow tin, front shows full color Superman breaking chains off chest, held $5 in dimes
EX $200   NM $300   MIP $525

BOOKS

Adventures of Superman Book, 1942, Random House, 4" x 5-1/2" armed services edition
EX $150   NM $225   MIP $475

Adventures of Superman Book, 1942, Random House, 6-1/2" x 9" hardcover by George Lowther, no dust jacket
EX $100   NM $200   MIP $350

Adventures of Superman Book, 1942, Random House, 6-1/2" x 9" hardcover, 220 pages, author George Lowther, full color dust jacket
EX $500   NM $800   MIP $1250

Book and Record Set, 1947, Musette Records, The Magic Ring
EX $100   NM $150   MIP $200

Book and Record Set, 1947, Musette Records, The Flying Train
EX $40   NM $100   MIP $200

Book, With Superman at the Gilbert Hall of Science, 1948, Gilbert, 32-page promo catalog for Gilbert's Erector Sets and other toys, illustrated w/Superman
EX $75   NM $100   MIP $175

Superman Book and Record Set, 1970s, Peter Pan, two stories w/record
EX $5   NM $10   MIP $15

Superman Cut-Outs, 1940, Saalfield, red cover, lighter paper than blue book, non-perforated cut-outs
EX $1500   NM $3000   MIP $4500

Superman Cut-Outs, 1940, Saalfield, perforated figures, heavy stock paper, blue cover
EX $1500   NM $3000   MIP $4500

Superman Paint-by-Number Book, 1966, Whitman, 11"x 13-1/2", 40 pictures plus coloring guide on back cover
EX $15   NM $50   MIP $100

Superman Pop-Up Book, 1979, Random House, hardcover, full color
EX $15   NM $30   MIP $60

Superman Press-Out Book, 1966, Whitman, punch out, assemble and hang scenes and characters
EX $20   NM $35   MIP $85

(KP Photo)

Superman Scrap Book, 1940, Saalfield, cover shows Superman flying over mountains toward stylized S.O.S. transmission
EX $75   NM $150   MIP $450

Superman To The Rescue Coloring Book, 1964, Whitman, cover shows Superman rescuing woman, Model No. 1001
EX $25   NM $50   MIP $100

Superman Workbook, 1940s, DC Comics, English grammar workbook
EX $200   NM $500   MIP $825

BUTTONS

Superman Button, 1966, WABC Radio, radio premium button for "It's a Bird, It's a Plane..." production, shows faceless Superman w/"WABC 77" across chest
EX $100   NM $150   MIP $300

Superman Club Button, 1966, 3-1/2" celluloid button, shows 3/4 profile thigh-up view of Superman in hands on hips pose, reads, "Official Member Superman Club"
EX $10   NM $20   MIP $30

Superman Muscle Building Club Button, 1954, Peter Puppets Playthings, part of Golden Muscle Building set, full color bust in sunburst circle in white button, reads "Superman Muscle Building Club"
EX $50   NM $150   MIP $250

Superman-Tim Club Button, 1940s, Superman, Inc., two different, both say Superman-Tim Club and have red/blue lettering and images on white background
EX $50   NM $75   MIP $120

CLOTHING

Superman Beanie, 1940s, hat w/two-color Superman embossed images on brim
EX $750   NM $900   MIP $1650

Superman Belt, 1940s, Pioneer, clear plastic w/color images and round brass buckle in box
EX $300   NM $500   MIP $700

Superman Belt, 1940s, Pioneer, brown leather w/Superman images and rectangular buckle, in box
EX $300   NM $500   MIP $750

Superman Belt, 1950s, Kellogg's, 28" long red plastic, aluminum "S" symbol buckle in red/yellow
EX $100   NM $250   MIP $425

Superman Belt Buckle, 1940s, square metal buckle shows red/blue chain breaking pose
EX $100   NM $150   MIP $425

Superman Moccasins, 1940s, Penobscot Shoe, leather moccasins w/Superman chain breaking pose on toe upper
EX $350   NM $750   MIP $2000

Superman Necktie, 1940s
EX $100   NM $200   MIP $350

Superman Necktie Set, 1940s, boxed set of two ties, small tie shows Superman standing w/arms crosses, larger tie shows Superman landing
EX $500   NM $1000   MIP $1500

Superman Suspenders, 1948, Pioneer, elastic, illustrated box
EX $350   NM $500   MIP $900

COMIC BOOKS

3-D Adventures of Superman Comic Book, 1950s, DC Comics, w/3-D goggles
EX $150   NM $250   MIP $850

Action Comics #1, 1938, DC Comics Top 9.2, first appearance of Superman
EX $125000   NM $350000   MIP $500000

Mini Comic Book, 1955, Kellogg's, cereal premium, #1, The Superman Time Capsule
EX $75   NM $100   MIP $225

Mini Comic Book, 1955, Kellogg's, cereal premium, #1-A, Duel in Space
EX $75   NM $100   MIP $210

Mini Comic Book, 1955, Kellogg's, cereal premium, #1-B, Supershow of Metropolis
EX $75   NM $100   MIP $200

Superman's Christmas Adventure Comic Book, 1940, Macy's, 1940 Macy's holiday premium
EX $1500   NM $2500   MIP $4000

Superman's Christmas Play Book, 1944, department store premium
EX $400   NM $600   MIP $1250

DOLLS

Super Babe Doll, 1947, Imperial Crown Toy, 15" tall, rubber skin, movable arms and legs, sleep eyes, composition head
EX $1000   NM $1500   MIP $2500

Superman Doll, Knickerbocker, 20" tall plush in box
EX $12   NM $25   MIP $40

Superman Doll, 1940, Ideal, 13-1/2" tall, wood jointed body w/composition head, movable head, arms and legs, ball knob hands
EX $750   NM $1000   MIP $2000

Superman Doll, 1977, Toy Works, 25-1/2" tall, cloth, w/cape
EX $12   NM $25   MIP $40

GAMES

Superman Action Game, 1940s, American Toy Works, wood and cardboard wartime game, Superman holds tottering bridge and kids shoot darts at tanks on bridge, Model No. 530
EX $1000   NM $1500   MIP $2500

Superman City Game, 1966, Remco, board game w/magnetic figures and buildings
EX $500   NM $750   MIP $1500

Superman Electronic Question and Answer Quiz Machine, 1966, Lisbeth Whiting Co., battery operated quiz game in full color illustrated box
EX $50   NM $100   MIP $225

Superman Official Eight-Piece Junior Quoit Set, 1940s, game in illustrated box includes wood and rubber game pieces, instruction booklet and membership card for "Superman Official Sports Club"
EX $75   NM $100   MIP $150

Superman Pinball Game, 1978, Bally, full-sized arcade game
EX $500   NM $750   MIP $1000

Superman Tilt Track, 1966, Kohner, marble skill game, in illustrated window box
EX $65   NM $95   MIP $175

PUZZLES

Puzzle, 1940, Saalfield, 300 pieces, 12 x 16", Superman w/Muscles Like Steel
EX $375   NM $500   MIP $750

Puzzle, 1940, Saalfield, 300 pieces, 12 x 16", Superman the Man of Tomorrow
EX $375   NM $500   MIP $750

Puzzle, 1940, Saalfield, 500 pieces, 16 x 20", Superman Stands Alone
EX $375   NM $500   MIP $850

Puzzle, 1940, Saalfield, 300 pieces, 12 x 16", Superman Shows his Super Strength
EX $375   NM $500   MIP $750

Puzzle, 1940, Saalfield, 300 pieces, 12 x 16", Superman Saves the Streamliner
EX $375   NM $500   MIP $750

Puzzle, 1940, Saalfield, 500 pieces, 16 x 20", Superman Saves a Life
EX $375   NM $500   MIP $850

Puzzle, 1966, Whitman, 150 pieces, 14" X 18", Superman
EX $12   NM $25   MIP $50

Puzzle, 1966, Whitman, two frame tray puzzles: one shows Superman fighting space robot, other shows him flying past manned rocket ship in outer space, each
EX $25   NM $50   MIP $85

Puzzle, 1973, APC
EX $10   NM $15   MIP $25

Puzzles, 1940, Saalfield, set of six small puzzles w/ 42 pieces each
EX $800   NM $1300   MIP $2000

Puzzles, 1940, set of three Superman puzzles
EX $750   NM $1000   MIP $1500

RINGS

Superman Crusader Ring, 1940s, brass or silver finish ring shows forward facing bust of Superman
EX $75   **NM** $120   **MIP** $250

Superman Member Ring, 1940, red paint on top of gold finish
EX $25000   **NM** $40000   **MIP** $75000

Superman Milk Defense Club Ring, 1941, gold finish hidden compartment ring, face is embossed milk companies initial, different initials known, lightning bolt and eyeball symbol, compartment shows Superman decal image
EX $5000   **NM** $15000   **MIP** $25000

Superman Milk Defense Club Ring, 1941, Different Milk Companies Sponsors, gold finish hidden compartment ring, face is embossed w/"S", lightning bolt and Superman bust, compartment shows Superman image, b/c of restrike none are found in MIP condition
EX $5000   **NM** $20000   **MIP** n/a

Superman Ring, 1978, Nestle's, premium ring, gold finish w/white circle center and yellow/red diamond "S" logo in middle
EX $20   **NM** $40   **MIP** $70

Superman-Tim Club Ring, 1940s, bronze finish metal ring w/embossed image of Superman in flight, w/initials S and T near his feet
EX $1500   **NM** $3000   **MIP** $4000

TOY

Bicycle Siren, 1970s, Empire
EX $10   **NM** $20   **MIP** $50

Bubble Gum Badge, 1948, Fo-Lee Gum Corp., shield-shaped brass finish badge shows a variant of the chain breaking pose inside a sun burst pattern ringed w/stars
EX $4000   **NM** $7000   **MIP** $10000

Cinematic Picture Pistol, 1940, Daisy, non-electric, film is viewed through view in back of gun, metal gun w/one pre-loaded 28 scene Superman film, Model No. 96
EX $300   **NM** $900   **MIP** $1800

Crayon-by-Numbers Set, 1954, Transogram, 16 crayons and 44 action scenes
EX $100   **NM** $200   **MIP** $400

(KP Photo)

EX $20   **NM** $40   **MIP** $75

Dangle Dandies Mobile, 1955, Kellogg's, set of eight cut outs on boxes of Rice Krispies and Corn Flakes
EX $75   **NM** $100   **MIP** $200

Film Viewer, 1947, Acme, 1-1/2" x 6-1/2" wide boxed set of hand-held viewer and two films
EX $200   **NM** $500   **MIP** $700

Film Viewer, 1947, 1-1/2" x 4" x 6-1/2" wide boxed set of hand-held viewer and six films
EX $350   **NM** $550   **MIP** $800

Film Viewer, 1965, plastic hand viewer w/two boxes of film, on illustrated card
EX $25   **NM** $40   **MIP** $85

Flying Noise Balloon, 1966, Van Dam, oversized balloon makes noise in flight, Superman illustration on balloon and card
EX $12   **NM** $23   **MIP** $50

Jumbo Movie Viewer, 1950s, Acme, blue/yellow plastic viewer w/35 mm "theatre size" film, on illustrated card, w/one filmstrip
EX $125   **NM** $200   **MIP** $350

Kryptonite Rock, 1970s, glow-in-the-dark rocks sold as kryptonite chunks, in illustrated box
EX $10   **NM** $15   **MIP** $25
(Danny Fuchs)

Krypto-Raygun Film Viewer, 1940, Daisy, battery-operated metal projector gun, seven Superman filmstrips, illustrated box, No. 94
EX $1000   **NM** $1600   **MIP** $3000

Movie Viewer, 1940, Acme Plastics, tortoise shell plastic, and three individually boxed Superman films, in large full color die-cut box
EX $450   **NM** $850   **MIP** $1200

Movie Viewer, 1947, Acme Plastics, black plastic viewer, white knob and two individually boxed Superman films, in red/blue die-cut box
EX $175   **NM** $450   **MIP** $675

Movie Viewer, 1948, Acme Plastics, red plastic viewer and three individually boxed Superman films, in small full color die-cut box
EX $150   **NM** $400   **MIP** $600

Movie Viewer, 1950s, Acme, black/red plastic viewer w/two individually boxed Superman films
EX $90   **NM** $150   **MIP** $300

Official Magic Kit, 1956, Bar-Zim, magic balls, disappearing cards, multiplying corks, vanishing trick, shell game, balancing belt and directions, in illustrated box
EX $350   **NM** $750   **MIP** $1500

Official Superman Costume, 1954, Ben Cooper, blue/red suit w/red/yellow monogram and belt, in box
EX $140   **NM** $260   **MIP** $425

Official Superman Krypto-Raygun Film Viewer, 1940, Daisy, includes raygun, battery, bulb, lens and one film strip, in illustrated box
EX $800   **NM** $1400   **MIP** $2000

Official Superman Playsuit, 1954, Funtime Playwear, rayon outfit, red cap w/screened Superman image, navy and red suit w/5" gold monogram and belt
EX $200   **NM** $400   **MIP** $625

Official Superman Playsuit, 1970, Ben Cooper, cloth suit in illustrated box
EX $20   **NM** $40   **MIP** $70

Official Superman Two-Piece Kiddie Swim Set, 1950s, set of rubber swim fins and goggles w/Superman's image or "S" symbol, in box
EX $50   **NM** $150   **MIP** $250

Paint-by-Numbers Watercolor Set, 1954, Transogram, 16 watercolors and 44 action scenes
EX $75   **NM** $200   **MIP** $375

(KP Photo)

Super Heroes String Puppets, 1978, Madison, string controlled cloth and vinyl marionette
EX $25   **NM** $75   **MIP** $150

Superman and Supergirl Push Puppets, 1968, Kohner, set of two: 5-1/4" on bases, in window box
EX $350   **NM** $600   **MIP** $1000

Superman Back-a-Wack, 1966, Dell, blue plastic paddle w/gold imprinted "S" logo and name, elastic string and red ball, on illustrated card, Model No. 1194
EX $50   **NM** $100   **MIP** $150

Superman Balloon, 1966, small balloon w/centered image
EX $5   **NM** $15   **MIP** $35

Superman Costume, 1950s, red pants and tie-on cape, blue shirt w/red, blue and yellow "S" emblem on chest, yellow belt
EX $100   **NM** $300   **MIP** $425

Superman Figure, Presents, 15" vinyl/cloth figure on base
EX $25   **NM** $40   **MIP** $60

Superman Golden Muscle Building Set, 1954, Peter Puppets Playthings, handles, springs, hand grippers, jump rope, wall hooks, measuring tape, progress chart, membership certificate and button, illustrated box
EX $700   **NM** $1000   **MIP** $1600

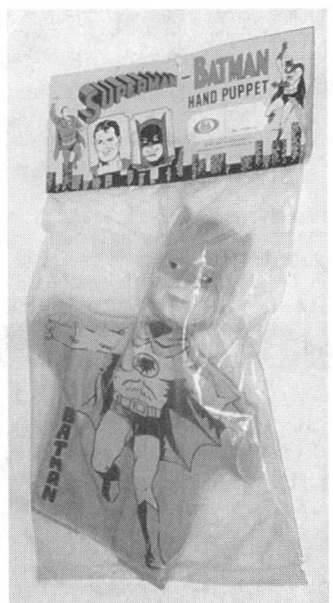
(KP Photo)

Superman Hand Puppet, 1966, Ideal, 11",
cloth body, vinyl head
EX $50   NM $75   MIP $120

Superman II View-Master Set, three reels,
based on film, Model No. L46
EX $5   NM $10   MIP $35

(KP Photo)

Superman III View-Master Set, three
reels, based on film, Model No. 4044
EX $5   NM $10   MIP $30

Superman Junior Horseshoe Set, 1950s,
Super Swim, four rubber horseshoes,
two rubber bases and two wood pegs
and Official Sports Club card and rules
for sportsmanship
EX $75   NM $150   MIP $300

Superman Junior Swim Goggles, 1950s,
Super Swim, plastic lenses, rubber
goggles w/red strap, "S" logo and
membership card for Superman Safety
Swim Club
EX $50   NM $125   MIP $225

Superman Kite, 1966, Pressman
EX $50   NM $75   MIP $135

Superman Kite, 1982, Hiflyer
EX $5   NM $10   MIP $35

Superman Krypton Rocket, 1954,
Kellogg's, 2" x 9" x 9-1/2" water powered
rocket w/"Krypton generating pump," in
mailer box
EX $150   NM $325   MIP $425

Superman Krypton Rocket, 1956, Park
Plastics, 2" x 9" x 9-1/2" water powered
rocket w/Krypton generating pump,
reserve fuel tank and Krypton Rocket, in
illustrated box, same as Kellogg's rocket
but in mass market packaging w/added
fuel tank
EX $150   NM $325   MIP $425

Superman Paint Set, 1940, American Toy
Works, three brushes, small palette,
water cup, 14 different paints and four
b/w cartoon panels, in 11" x 14-1/2"
color illustrated box
EX $400   NM $800   MIP $1250

Superman Paint Set, 1940s, American Toy
Works, box shows Superman flying up
toward upper right corner of box,
w/pallet and brushes at lower right,
"Paint Set" inside pallet
EX $400   NM $800   MIP $1250

Superman Paint Set, 1940s, American Toy
Works, larger version, shows
Superman in front of pallet background
EX $400   NM $800   MIP $1250

Superman Play Set, 1973, Ideal, self-
contained vinyl covered full color snap-
close case opens to three backdrops,
Fortress of Solitude, Daily Planet and
villain's hideout, for staging action
scenes w/supplied color punch-outs
EX $50   NM $75   MIP $175

Superman Playsuit, 1940, Fishback, red
and blue imprinted blue smock shirt and
pants w/tie-on red cape
EX $200   NM $500   MIP $1250

Superman Pogo Stick, 1977, 48" w/a vinyl
bust on top
EX $50   NM $100   MIP $225

Superman Push Puppet, 1966, Kohner, 5-
1/4" on base, in window box
EX $50   NM $75   MIP $110

Superman Roller Skates, 1975, Larami,
plastic w/color bust of Superman
shaped around front of each skate, in
illustrated window box
EX $20   NM $50   MIP $100

Superman Rub-Ons, 1966, Hasbro, magic
picture transfers in box illustrated
w/picture of Superman flying
EX $50   NM $100   MIP $150

Superman Senior Rubber Horseshoe Set,
1950s, in box
EX $75   NM $125   MIP $200

Superman Senior Swim Goggles, 1950s,
Super Swim, plastic lenses, rubber
goggles w/red strap, "S" logo on bridge,
membership card for Superman Safety
Swim Club
EX $40   NM $80   MIP $175

Superman Sky Hero, 1977, Marx, rubber
band glider w/color Superman image,
on card, Model No. 9310
EX $25   NM $40   MIP $85

Superman Space Satellite Launcher Set,
1950s, Kellogg's, premium set of
generic plastic gun w/firing "satellite
wheel" and illustrated instruction sheet,
in mailer box
EX $300   NM $600   MIP $1000

Superman Stamp Set, 1965, set of six
wood-backed character stamps
EX $25   NM $50   MIP $200

Superman Super Watch, 1967, Toy
House, plastic toy watch w/moveable
hands, watch "case" is large "S" chest
symbol, on illustrated card
EX $25   NM $50   MIP $150

Superman Tank, 1958, Linemar, large
battery operated tin, 3-D Superman w/a
cloth cape, in illustrated box
EX $1200   NM $2500   MIP $3500

Superman the Movie View-Master Set,
1979, three reels, based on film, Model
No. J78
EX $5   NM $10   MIP $30

Superman Utility Belt, 1979, Remco,
illustrated window box, decoder glasses,
kryptonite detector, nonworking watch,
handcuffs, ring, decoder map, press card
and secret message
EX $50   NM $150   MIP $275

Superman Water Gun, 1967, Multiple
Toymakers, 6" plastic, Model No. 484
EX $50   NM $100   MIP $200

Toy Wristwatch, 1950s, Germany, non-
working toy watch, blue plastic band,
rectangular case w/full color full
standing pose on white dial
EX $35   NM $65   MIP $200

Trick Picture Sun Camera, 1950s, Made in
Japan, when left in the sun for two minutes,
the camera "develops" a picture of
Superman fighting a space monster
EX $75   NM $150   MIP $250

TRADING CARDS

Superman II Trading Cards, 1981, Costa
Rican, set of 88 cards, complete set
EX $18   NM $35   MIP $50

Superman II Trading Cards, 1981, Topps,
set of 88 cards, complete set
EX $20   NM $30   MIP $40

Superman III Trading Cards, 1983, Topps,
set of 99 cards, complete set
EX $5   NM $10   MIP $15

Superman the Movie Trading Cards,
1978, Topps, set of 77 cards, first issue
EX $7   NM $13   MIP $20

Superman the Movie Trading Cards,
1979, Topps, set of 88 cards, second
issue
EX $12   NM $25   MIP $35

Superman the Movie Trading Cards,
1979, French, set of 180 cards
EX $18   NM $35   MIP $50

CHARACTER TOYS

Superman the Movie Trading Cards, 1979, OPC, set of 132 cards
EX $12   NM $25   MIP $35

Superman Trading Cards, 1940, Gum Inc., 2-1/2" x 3-1/4" cards, set of 72
EX $7500   NM $15000   MIP $20000

Superman Trading Cards, 1940, Gum Inc., 2-1/2" x 3-1/4" cards, each
EX $75   NM $125   MIP $275

Superman Trading Cards, 1966, Topps, set of 66 cards, George Reeves TV series scenes
EX $90   NM $165   MIP $350

Superman Trading Cards, 1966, Topps, set of 66 cards, shows George Reeves TV series scenes, each card
EX $5   NM $7   MIP $10

Superman Trading Cards Display Box, 1966, Topps, 2" x 4" x 8" display box of 24 unopened packs, box shows George Reeves bust
EX $500   NM $750   MIP $1350

Superman Trading Cards Wrapper, 1940, Gum Inc., 4-1/2" x 6" waxed paper
EX $500   NM $650   MIP $900

WATCHES

Superman Supertime Wristwatch, 1950s, National Comics, gray band, stamped red "S" logo, silver western style buckle, full color hands on hips pose inside chrome finish case, second hand, even-hour numbers around face, in full color box
EX $750   NM $1250   MIP $2500

Superman Wristwatch, 1939, New Haven Clock Boxed, flattened oval face, shows color image of standing Superman from knees up, leather band
EX $2000   NM $3500   MIP $5000

Superman Wristwatch, 1940s, New Haven Clock, squared-oval faced watch, leather band, dial shows Superman standing, hands on hips, in illustrated box
EX $2000   NM $3500   MIP $5000

Superman Wristwatch, 1959, Bradley, dial shows Superman flying over city, second hand, chrome finish case
EX $750   NM $1000   MIP $1750

Superman Wristwatch, 1977, gold bezel, stainless back, blue leather band, face shows Superman flying upward from below
EX $35   NM $65   MIP $200

Superman Wristwatch, 1986, Una-Donna, plastic case and band, several color and face illustrations, each
EX $10   NM $20   MIP $75

TARZAN

ACCESSORIES

Bracelet, 1934, drink more milk radio premium
EX $1500   NM $3500   MIP $5000

Jungle Map, 1933, radio premium
EX $500   NM $1000   MIP $1500

Poster, 1933, Paper Mills, three masks; premium
EX $500   NM $800   MIP $1200

Tarzan Flasher Ring, 1960s, Vari-Vue
EX $10   NM $20   MIP $50

Tarzan Party Set, 1977, Amscan
EX $10   NM $25   MIP $60

FIGURES

Figure, 1950s, 2-1/2" tall, celluloid, French
EX $750   NM $1000   MIP $1550

Kala Ape Figure, 1984, Dakin, 3" tall
EX $10   NM $15   MIP $30

Young Tarzan Figure, 1984, Dakin, 4", bendable
EX $10   NM $15   MIP $30

THREE LITTLE PIGS

ACCESSORIES

Three Little Pigs Cuff Bracelet, 1930s, 1/2" x 2-1/4", wolf blowing down a house w/pig running away
EX $350   NM $500   MIP $750

GAME

Who's Afraid of the Big Bad Wolf Game, 1930s, Parker Brothers
EX $200   NM $350   MIP $600

TOY

Puzzle, 1940s, Jaymar, 7" x 10" x 2"
EX $100   NM $200   MIP $300

Three Little Pigs Sand Pail, 1930s, Ohio Art, 4-1/2", tin
EX $100   NM $200   MIP $450

Three Little Pigs Soaky Set, 1960s, Drew Chemical, 8" tall each: Three Little Pigs and the Big Bad Wolf
EX $70   NM $125   MIP $275

WATCH

Big Bad Wolf Pocket Watch Box, 1934, Ingersoll
EX $2000   NM $3300   MIP $5000

TOM AND JERRY

BANK

Tom and Jerry Bank, 1980, Gorham, 6" tall
EX $20   NM $35   MIP $80

FIGURES

Jerry Figure, 1973, Marx, 4" tall
EX $15   NM $25   MIP $70

Tom and Jerry Figure Set, 1975, walking, Tom, Jerry, and Droopy
EX $25   NM $50   MIP $125

Tom Figure, 1973, Marx, 6" tall
EX $15   NM $30   MIP $70

TOY

Puzzles, Whitman, four frame tray puzzles
EX $20   NM $35   MIP $90

Tom and Jerry Go Kart, 1973, Marx, plastic, friction drive
EX $50   NM $75   MIP $150

Tom and Jerry on Scooter, 1971, Marx, plastic friction drive
EX $30   NM $50   MIP $90

WATCH

Tom and Jerry Wristwatch, 1985, Bradley, quartz, oldies series, small white plastic case and band, sweep seconds, face shows Tom squirting Jerry w/hose
EX $15   NM $35   MIP $90

TONY THE TIGER

ACCESSORIES

Cookie Jar, 1960s, Kellogg's, plastic, figural
EX $25   NM $70   MIP $120

Radio, 1980s, plastic, figural
EX $20   NM $45   MIP $80

BANK

Figural Bank, 1967, Kellogg's
EX $30   NM $45   MIP $90

FIGURES

Inflatable Tiger, 1950s, Kellogg's
EX $7   NM $20   MIP $35

Plush Tiger, 1970s, Kellogg's
EX $10   NM $25   MIP $75

TOP CAT

FIGURES

Top Cat Figure, 1961, Marx, TV-Tinykins, plastic
EX $20   NM $35   MIP $70

TOY

Top Cat Soaky, 1960s, 10" tall, vinyl
EX $25   NM $45   MIP $90

Viewmarx Micro-Viewer, 1963, Marx, plastic
EX $40   NM $60   MIP $120

WINNIE THE POOH

ACCESSORIES

Lamp, 1964, Dolly Toy, 7" tall
EX $35   NM $90   MIP $200

Radio, 1970s, Thilgee, 5" x 6" x 1-1/2" tall
EX $45   NM $90   MIP $135

Winnie the Pooh Button, 1960s, 3-1/2" celluloid
EX $10   NM $25   MIP $60

Winnie the Pooh Snow Globe, 5-1/2", musical
EX $15   NM $35   MIP $80

DOLL

Winnie the Pooh and Christopher Robin Dolls, 1964, Horsman, Winnie the Pooh 3-1/2" tall and Christopher 11" tall, set
EX $100   NM $175   MIP $350

Winnie the Pooh Doll, 1960s, 12" tall
EX $40   NM $60   MIP $120

TOY

Jack-In-The-Box, 1960s, Carnival Toys
EX $40   NM $60   MIP $120

Kanga and Roo Squeak Toy, 1966, Holland Hill, vinyl
EX $20   NM $40   MIP $80

Magic Slate, 1965, Western Publishing, 8-1/2" x 13-1/2"
EX $30   NM $50   MIP $120

Puzzle, 1964, Whitman, frame tray
EX $10   NM $30   MIP $70

WIZARD OF OZ

ACCESSORIES

Christmas Ornaments, 1977, Bradford Novelty, 4-1/2" tall, Dorothy, Scarecrow, Tin Man, Cowardly Lion, each
EX $5   NM $10   MIP $30

Christmas Ornaments, 1989, Presents, cloth and vinyl: Dorothy, Scarecrow, Tin Man, Cowardly Lion, Glinda and Wicked Witch, each
EX $8   NM $10   MIP $20

Cookie Jar, 1990, Clay Art, white w/relief figures of characters
EX $50   NM $100   MIP $175

Crayon Box, 1975, Cheinco, rectangular, metal
EX $5   NM $10   MIP $30

Erasers, 1989, Applause, set of six: figural, Scarecrow, Cowardly Lion, Dorothy, Wicked Witch, Tin Man, Glinda, set
EX $15   NM $20   MIP $40

Give-A-Show Projector Slides, 1968, Kenner, 35 color slides, five different shows
EX $20   NM $40   MIP $100

Magnets, 1987, Grynnen Barrett, six character magnets in box
EX $6   NM $10   MIP $15

Magnets, 1989, Vanderbilt Products, several characters available, each
EX $2   NM $3   MIP $5

Pails, 1950s, Swift and Company, Oz Peanut Butter, red and yellow and red, yellow and white tin
EX $25   NM $40   MIP $100

Scarecrow Night Light, 1989, Hamilton Gifts, 7", unpainted bone china
EX $10   NM $15   MIP $25

Snack 'N Sip Pals, 1989, Multi Toys, 12 red and white striped straws w/detachable character figures
EX $4   NM $7   MIP $25

Stationery, 1939, Whitman, 10 sheets and envelopes, w/character illustations
EX $175   NM $300   MIP $500

Tin, 1989, Multi Toys, 8" x 10" x 2", illustrated w/Emerald City and characters
EX $8   NM $15   MIP $35

Trash Can, 1975, Chein, oval metal
EX $20   NM $35   MIP $70

Wall Decorations, 1967, Shepard Press, 20 punch-out decorations
EX $20   NM $35   MIP $65

BANK

Cowardly Lion Bank, 1960s, ceramic, red nose
EX $30   NM $75   MIP $160

Dorothy Bank, 1960s, ceramic, blue dress w/brown wicker basket
EX $30   NM $60   MIP $160

Scarecrow Bank, 1960s, ceramic
EX $30   NM $50   MIP $135

Tin Man Bank, 1960s, ceramic, silver
EX $30   NM $70   MIP $150

BOOK

Cut and Make Masks, 1982, Dover, eight cut-out color masks
EX $5   NM $10   MIP $30

Dorothy and Friends Visit Oz Book, 1967, Curtis Candy, candy premium
EX $8   NM $20   MIP $45

Dorothy Meets the Wizard Book, 1967, Curtis Candy, candy premium
EX $15   NM $30   MIP $65

(KP Photo)

Jack Pumpkinhead and the Sawhorse of Oz Book, 1939, Rand McNally, hardcover, also contains "Tik Tok and the Gnome King of Oz"
EX $100   NM $200   MIP $400

Little Dorothy and Toto of Oz Book, 1939, Rand McNally, hardcover, also contains "The Cowardly Lion and the Hungry Tiger"
EX $110   NM $250   MIP $500

Little Golden Book Series, 1951, The Road to Oz, The Emerald City of Oz, and The Tin Woodman of Oz, each
EX $8   NM $20   MIP $70

Mask Book, 1990, Watermill Press, four paper masks
EX $3   NM $10   MIP $30

Return To Oz Little Golden Books, 1985, Western, Dorothy Returns to Oz, Escape from the Witch's Castle, Dorothy in the

Ornament Room, Dorothy Saves the Emerald City, each
EX $2   NM $5   MIP $10

Scarecrow and the Tin Man Book, 1904, G. W. Dillingham
EX $300   NM $600   MIP $850

Scarecrow and the Tin Man Book, 1946, Perks Publishing, black and yellow pictures
EX $30   NM $60   MIP $120

Tales of the Wizard of Oz Coloring Book, 1962, Whitman, art from animated TV show
EX $15   NM $20   MIP $70

The Tin Woodsman and Dorothy Book, 1967, Curtis Candy, candy premium
EX $12   NM $40   MIP $80

The Wonderful Cut-Outs of Oz Book, 1985, Crown, 35 figures to cut out
EX $7   NM $15   MIP $50

Wizard of Oz Book, 1975, Western, #310-32, Little Golden Book
EX $5   NM $10   MIP $40

Wizard of Oz Christmas Book, 1968, Gimbel's, New York department store premium
EX $20   NM $50   MIP $100

Wizard of Oz Color-By-Number Book, 1962, Karas Publishing, #A-116, Twinkle Books series
EX $10   NM $30   MIP $70

Wizard of Oz Paint Book, 1939, Whitman
EX $200   NM $400   MIP $600

Wizard of Oz Paper Dolls, 1976, Whitman
EX $7   NM $15   MIP $50

Wizard of Oz Sticker Fun Book, 1976, Whitman
EX $6   NM $12   MIP $35

COMIC BOOK

Tales of the Wizard of Oz Comic Book, 1962, Dell, #1306
EX $10   NM $15   MIP $50

Wizard of Oz Comic Book, 1956, Dell, Dell Junior Treasury, #5
EX $12   NM $40   MIP $100

Wizard of Oz Comic Book, 1957, Dell, Classic Illustrated Jr., #535
EX $6   NM $20   MIP $60

DOLL

Cowardly Lion Doll, 1971, M-D Tissue, cloth, light brown body w/white snout
EX $10   NM $20   MIP $40

Cowardly Lion Doll, 1984, Ideal, 9", Character Dolls series
EX $20   NM $40   MIP $90

Cowardly Lion Doll, 1988, Presents, vinyl
EX $20   NM $40   MIP $90

Cowardly Lion Doll, 1989, Largo Toys, rag doll
EX $8   NM $18   MIP $50

Dandy Lion Doll, 1962, Artistic, 14" tall, cloth and vinyl
EX $35   NM $85   MIP $175

Doodle Dolls, 1979, Whiting, three dolls: cardboard parts, yarn, Styrofoam balls, fabric
EX $8   NM $20   MIP $40

Dorothy and Toto Doll, 1984, Ideal, 9", Character Dolls series
EX $20   NM $40   MIP $80

Dorothy Doll, 1939, Ideal, 18", Judy Garland, blue checked jumper, open and close brown eyes
EX $1000   NM $1750   MIP $3000

Dorothy Doll, 1939, Sears, 15-1/2", Judy Garland, red or blue checked jumper w/black pin curls
EX $800   NM $1500   MIP $2500

Dorothy Doll, 1939, Ideal, 15-1/2", Judy Garland, blue checked jumper, open and close brown eyes
EX $700   NM $1300   MIP $2200

Dorothy Doll, 1939, Ideal, 13", Judy Garland, blue checked jumper, open and close brown eyes
EX $600   NM $900   MIP $1350

Dorothy Doll, 1971, M-D Tissue, cloth, stuffed, yellow hair, orange jumper
EX $10   NM $20   MIP $60

Dorothy Doll, 1984, Effanbee, 14-1/2" tall, vinyl, Judy Garland, blue dress and hair ribbons, ruby slippers, Legend Series
EX $45   NM $100   MIP $150

Dorothy Doll, 1988, Presents, vinyl, blue checkered jumper, white blouse, red slippers, yellow brick road base
EX $20   NM $35   MIP $80

Dorothy Doll, 1989, Largo Toys, Judy Garland
EX $8   NM $20   MIP $60

Dorothy Doll, 1991, Madame Alexander, 8", blue checked jumper w/white blouse, basket w/Toto and red shoes, Storyland Dolls series
EX $20   NM $40   MIP $80

Glinda Doll, 1989, Presents, vinyl, pink dress w/pink crown and wand, yellow brick road base
EX $20   NM $40   MIP $90

Jack Pumpkinhead Doll, 1924, Oz Doll and Toy, 13"
EX $750   NM $1300   MIP $2000

Lollipop Guild Boy Doll, 1989, Presents, vinyl, plaid shirt, green shorts and striped socks, on a yellow brick road base
EX $20   NM $40   MIP $80

Lullabye League Girl Doll, 1989, Presents, vinyl, pink ballerina dress and slippers w/hat on a yellow brick road base
EX $20   NM $40   MIP $80

Mayor of Munchkinland Doll, 1989, Presents, vinyl, black suit and shoes on a yellow brick road base
EX $20   NM $40   MIP $80

Patchwork Girl Doll, 1924, Oz Doll and Toy, 13"
EX $150   NM $300   MIP $600

Rusty the Tin Man Doll, 1962, Artistic Toy Company, 14" tall, cloth and vinyl
EX $35   NM $60   MIP $150

Scarecrow Doll, 1924, Oz Doll and Toy, 13"
EX $800   NM $1400   MIP $2200

Scarecrow Doll, 1971, M-D Tissue, cloth, stuffed, frowning, blue pants and red and white plaid jacket
EX $10   NM $15   MIP $40

Scarecrow Doll, 1984, Ideal, 9", Character Dolls series
EX $25   NM $40   MIP $75

Scarecrow Doll, 1988, Presents, vinyl, brown pants, green shirt, and black hat and shoes, on a yellow brick road base
EX $25   NM $40   MIP $85

Scarecrow Doll, 1989, Largo Toys, rag doll
EX $9   NM $15   MIP $60

Scarecrow Talkin' Patter Pillow Doll, 1968, Mattel, cloth, pull-string, says 10 phrases, dark blue pants and sleeves, white gloves, black boots
EX $50   NM $100   MIP $200

Socrates the Scarecrow Doll, 1962, Artistic, 14" tall, cloth and vinyl
EX $30   NM $70   MIP $160

Strawman Doll, 1939, Ideal, 17", Ray Bolger, tan or pink pants, black or navy jacket
EX $600   NM $1000   MIP $1800

Tin Man Doll, 1924, Oz Doll and Toy, 13"
EX $800   NM $1200   MIP $2000

Tin Man Doll, 1971, M-D Tissue, cloth, stuffed, gray body, blue eyes, red heart
EX $8   NM $20   MIP $50

Tin Man Doll, 1984, Ideal, 9", Character Dolls series
EX $20   NM $35   MIP $75

Tin Man Doll, 1988, Presents, vinyl, silver body w/a heart clock on chaint, on a yellow brick road base
EX $20   NM $35   MIP $75

Tin Man Doll, 1989, Largo Toys, rag doll
EX $10   NM $15   MIP $40

Toto Doll, 1988, Presents, 5-1/2" plush
EX $15   NM $30   MIP $75

Wicked Witch Doll, 1989, Presents, vinyl, black dress and hat, green face and hands holding broom on a yellow brick road base
EX $25   NM $40   MIP $100

Wizard of Oz Dolls, 1985, Effanbee, 11-1/2", Dorothy, Scarecrow, Tin Man, Cowardly Lion, each
EX $15   NM $22   MIP $70

Wizard of Oz Live! Dolls, Applause, cloth, three different sizes, each
EX $8   NM $15   MIP $40

FIGURES

Jack Pumpkinhead Figure, 1985, Heart and Heart, Return to Oz, 3"-4" tall, plastic jointed
EX $35   NM $55   MIP $100

Munchkins Figures, 1988, Presents, PVC, 1-3/4" to 2-3/4": Mayor, Lollipop Guild Boy, Sleepyhead Girl, Lady, Soldier and Ballerina, each
EX $5   NM $10   MIP $35

(KP Photo)

Oz-Kins Figures, 1967, Aurora, plastic Burry Biscuit premium: set of 10
EX $50   NM $100   MIP $220

Scarecrow Figure, 1939, Artisans Studio, 4", wood composition
EX $100   NM $250   MIP $550

Scarecrow Figure, 1968, 15", ceramic, painted or unpainted
EX $20   NM $50   MIP $110

Scarecrow Figure, 1984, Dalen Products, 6' inflatable
EX $12   NM $20   MIP $60

Scarecrow Figure, 1985, Heart and Heart, Return to Oz, 3"-4" tall, plastic jointed
EX $30   NM $45   MIP $100

Tik Tok Figure, 1985, Heart and Heart, Return to Oz, 3"-4" tall, plastic jointed
EX $35   NM $55   MIP $105

Tin Man Figure, 1939, Artisans Studio, 4", wood composition
EX $100   NM $250   MIP $500

Tin Man Figure, 1968, 15", ceramic, painted or unpainted
EX $20   NM $30   MIP $80

Tin Man Figure, 1985, Return to Oz, 3"-4" tall, plastic jointed
EX $20   NM $35   MIP $100

Wizard of Oz Figures, 1967, Multiple Toymakers, 6" tall, bendy, several characters, on card
EX $16   NM $30   MIP $75

Wizard of Oz Figures, 1988, Presents, 3-3/4": Dorothy, Scarecrow, Tin Man, Cowardly Lion, Wicked Witch, Glinda, each
EX $4   NM $6   MIP $15

Wizard of Oz Figures, 1989, Presents, six figures on musical bases, each
EX $10   NM $12   MIP $25

Wizard of Oz Figures, 1989, Multi Toys, 4" poseable figures, set of six
EX $15   NM $25   MIP $50

Wizard of Oz Figures, 1989, Just Toys, several characters, bendy, each
EX $4   NM $6   MIP $15

Wizard of Oz Squeak Toy, 1939, Burnstein, 7" tall, hollow rubber, several characters
EX $200   NM $300   MIP $500

GAME

Game of The Wizard of Oz, 1939, Whitman
EX $300   NM $400   MIP $700

Return to Oz Game, 1985, Golden Press
EX $8   NM $13   MIP $30

Wizard of Oz Dart Game, 1939, Dart Board Equipment, board illustrated w/yellow brick road and circular targets of Oz characters, w/three darts
EX $500   NM $800   MIP $1200

MUSIC BOX

Cowardly Lion Music Box, 1983, Schmid
EX $20   NM $35   MIP $60

Dorothy Music Box, 1983, Schmid, plays "Over the Rainbow"
EX $25   NM $40   MIP $65

Scarecrow Music Box, 1983, Schmid
EX $20   NM $35   MIP $60

Tin Man Music Box, 1983, Schmid
EX $20   NM $35   MIP $60

TOY

Carpet Sweeper, 1939, Bissell, child-sized
EX $150   NM $225   MIP $375

Cast 'N Paint Set, 1975, makes six 6" figures
EX $15   NM $25   MIP $75

Chalkboard, 1975, Roth American, wood frame, steel stand w/chalk, chalk holder and eraser
EX $16   NM $27   MIP $75

Cowardly Lion Costume, 1975, Ben Cooper, costume and mask
EX $15   NM $25   MIP $60

Cowardly Lion Costume, 1989, Collegeville, plastic mask and vinyl bodysuit
EX $10   NM $15   MIP $30

Cowardly Lion Costume, 1989, Collegeville, deluxe
EX $20   NM $40   MIP $75

Cowardly Lion Mask, 1939, Newark Mask Company, linen, hand painted
EX $60   NM $90   MIP $160

Cowardly Lion Mask, 1983, Don Post Studios, rubber
EX $35   NM $55   MIP $90

Cowardly Lion Wind-Up, 1975, Durham Industries, on illustrated card
EX $20   NM $30   MIP $60

(KP Photo)

Decoupage Kit, 1975, two wooden plaques, scenes based on film
EX $15   NM $25   MIP $60

Dorothy Costume, 1975, Ben Cooper, costume and mask
EX $15   NM $25   MIP $70

Dorothy Costume, 1989, Collegeville, deluxe, includes red metallic glitter chips for shoes
EX $20   NM $40   MIP $85

Dorothy Costume, 1989, Collegeville, plastic mask and vinyl bodysuit
EX $8   NM $15   MIP $40

Dorothy Squeak Toy, 1939, Burnstein, 7", hollow rubber
EX $150   NM $300   MIP $500

Fun Shades, 1989, Multi Toys, children's sunglasses w/character images
EX $5   NM $8   MIP $20

Glinda Squeak Toy, 1939, Burnstein, 7", hollow rubber
EX $150   NM $300   MIP $450

Glinda's Magic Wand, 1989, Multi Toys, battery operated wand w/red glitter star on end, lights up, on illustrated card
EX $5   NM $10   MIP $30

Magic Picture Kit, 1968, Jiffy Pop Popcorn
EX $5   NM $25   MIP $70

Magic Slate, 1961, Lowe, art based on animated TV show
EX $12   NM $30   MIP $80

Magic Slate, 1976, Whitman
EX $6   NM $12   MIP $40

Magic Slate, 1985, Western, Return to Oz
EX $4   NM $10   MIP $35

Magic Slate, 1989, Western
EX $3   NM $6   MIP $30

Magic Story Cloth, 1978, Raco, 38" x 44" plastic sheet, eight crayons and sponge
EX $6   NM $12   MIP $35

Off to See the Wizard Colorforms, 1967, Colorforms
EX $25   NM $50   MIP $100

(KP Photo)

Off to See the Wizard Dancing Toys, 1967, Marx, mechanical, dancing Tin Man, the Cowardly Lion and the Scarecrow, Montgomery Ward's Exclusive, each
EX $100   NM $150   MIP $250

Off to See the Wizard Flasher Rings, 1967, Vari-Vue, gumball machine prizes, silver painted resin, gold painted, dark or light blue plastic, each
EX $10   NM $20   MIP $30

Off to See the Wizard Hand Puppet, 1968, Mattel, talking, four vinyl heads on finger tips, Toto and Cowardly Lion on thumb pad, ten phrases
EX $30   NM $45   MIP $100

Paint by Number 'N Frame Set, 1969, Hasbro, 16" x 18", two plastic frames, 18 watercolors, brush and eight pictures to paint
EX $20   NM $30   MIP $90

Paint by Number Set, 1968, Craft Master, six paints, brush, picture of Tin Man, Cowardly Lion, or the Scarecrow
EX $20   NM $35   MIP $95

Paint by Number Set, 1973, Hasbro, six oil paint vials and brush
EX $6   NM $20   MIP $50

Paint by Number Set, 1979, Craft House, two 10" x 14" panels, 15 colors, brush and instructions
EX $10   NM $20   MIP $50

Paint by Number Set, 1989, Art Award, three different versions
EX $6   NM $10   MIP $20

Paint with Crayons Set, 1989, Art Award, four pictures based on MGM film characters, in illustrated box
EX $5   NM $10   MIP $20

Paper Dolls, 1975, The Toy Factory, Dorothy, Tin Man, Scarecrow, Cowardly Lion and Toto, clothes and accessories
EX $10   NM $20   MIP $60

Playing Cards, 1988, Presents, tin holds two decks
EX $5   NM $10   MIP $40

Puppet Theatre, 1965, Proctor and Gamble, cardboard theater designed for P and G puppets
EX $100   NM $175   MIP $300

Puzzle, 1960s, Haret-Gilmar, 10" x 14" puzzle in canister
EX $15 **NM** $30 **MIP** $70

Puzzle, 1976, Whitman, frame tray
EX $4 **NM** $8 **MIP** $35

Puzzle, 1976, American Puzzle Company, 200 piece puzzle in canister
EX $15 **NM** $30 **MIP** $50

Puzzle, 1984, Effanbee, in canister
EX $8 **NM** $15 **MIP** $40

Puzzle, 1985, Crisco Oil, Return to Oz, mail away premium, 200 piece puzzle
EX $30 **NM** $50 **MIP** $80

Puzzle, 1989, Western, frame tray, 100 pieces, Glinda and Dorothy in Munchkinland
EX $5 **NM** $10 **MIP** $35

Puzzle, 1990, Milton Bradley, 1000 piece jigsaw featuring the 1989 Norman James Company poster
EX $6 **NM** $15 **MIP** $30

Puzzles, 1932, Reilly and Lee, set #2, two softcover editions of Tik-Tok and Jack Pumpkinhead and the Sawhorse, plus 25 piece puzzles
EX $250 **NM** $500 **MIP** $850

Puzzles, 1932, Reilly and Lee, #1, two softcover editions of the Scarecrow and the Tin Man, Ozma and the Little Wizard, plus two puzzles, in box
EX $225 **NM** $475 **MIP** $800

Puzzles, 1960s, Jaymar, set of four, 100 pieces each, each
EX $15 **NM** $30 **MIP** $90

Puzzles, 1960s, Jaymar, frame tray
EX $10 **NM** $20 **MIP** $65

Puzzles, 1967, Whitman, set of three: Peter Pan, Alice in Wonderland and The Wizard of Oz, in box
EX $12 **NM** $18 **MIP** $60

Puzzles, 1977, Doug Smith, 17" x 22" each, frame tray
EX $10 **NM** $20 **MIP** $50

Puzzles, 1985, Golden Press, frame tray, Return to Oz characters
EX $3 **NM** $5 **MIP** $15

Return to Oz Hand Puppets, 1985, Welch's Jelly, Scarecrow, Gump, or Tik-Tok, Return to Oz promotion
EX $20 **NM** $40 **MIP** $60

Rubber Stamps, 1989, set of 11 characters in plastic case
EX $10 **NM** $15 **MIP** $30

Rubber Stamps, 1989, Multi Toys, 12 figural stampers
EX $4 **NM** $6 **MIP** $15

Rubber Stamps, 1989, 18 character stamps
EX $12 **NM** $20 **MIP** $35

Scarecrow Costume, 1967, Ben Cooper
EX $30 **NM** $40 **MIP** $75

Scarecrow Costume, 1968, Ben Cooper, battery-operated light-up mask
EX $30 **NM** $40 **MIP** $75

Scarecrow Costume, 1989, Collegeville, plastic mask and vinyl bodysuit
EX $6 **NM** $12 **MIP** $30

Scarecrow Costume, 1989, Collegeville, deluxe, includes straw
EX $20 **NM** $35 **MIP** $50

Scarecrow Mask, 1939, Newark Mask, linen, hand painted
EX $100 **NM** $150 **MIP** $250

Scarecrow Mask, 1983, Don Post Studios, rubber
EX $40 **NM** $60 **MIP** $90

Scarecrow Wind-Up, 1975, Durham Industries, on illustrated card
EX $20 **NM** $30 **MIP** $75

Scarecrow-in-the-Box, 1967, Mattel, jack-in-the-box
EX $40 **NM** $60 **MIP** $120

Showboat Play Set, 1962, Remco, pink plastic showboat w/oversized central stage area, four different plays, scenery, players and scripts
EX $75 **NM** $100 **MIP** $175

Stand-Up Rub-Ons, 1968, Hasbro, three full color transfer sheets, character outline sheets of 10 characters
EX $20 **NM** $30 **MIP** $75

Stitch a Story Set, 1973, Hasbro, two framed pictures, thread and embroidery needle
EX $10 **NM** $15 **MIP** $35

Tea Set, 1970s, Ohio Art, 30-piece set, red and yellow plastic
EX $40 **NM** $60 **MIP** $120

Tin Man Costume, 1961, Halco, costume and mask
EX $20 **NM** $35 **MIP** $90

Tin Man Costume, 1968, Ben Cooper
EX $20 **NM** $30 **MIP** $65

Tin Man Costume, 1975, Ben Cooper, costume and mask
EX $15 **NM** $25 **MIP** $55

Tin Man Costume, 1989, Collegeville, plastic mask and vinyl bodysuit
EX $6 **NM** $10 **MIP** $25

Tin Man Costume, 1989, Collegeville, deluxe
EX $20 **NM** $35 **MIP** $70

Tin Man Mask, 1939, Newark Mask, linen, hand painted
EX $100 **NM** $150 **MIP** $250

Tin Man Mask, 1983, Don Post Studios, rubber
EX $35 **NM** $55 **MIP** $85

Tin Man Robot, 1969, Remco, 21-1/2" tall, battery operated, lifts legs and swings arms as he walks
EX $125 **NM** $200 **MIP** $325

Tin Man Wind-Up, 1975, Durham Industries
EX $25 **NM** $50 **MIP** $100

Toy Watch, 1940s, tin, Scarecrow and the Tin Man on either side of non-working dial
EX $75 **NM** $125 **MIP** $175

Vinyl Stick-On Play Set, 1989, Multi Toys, 10 vinyl stickers w/Emerald City background, on header card
EX $4 **NM** $6 **MIP** $10

Water Guns, 1976, Durham, heads of Scarecrow, Tin Man, or Cowardly Lion, water squirts out of nose, each
EX $15 **NM** $30 **MIP** $70

Wicked Witch Mask, 1975, Ben Cooper
EX $6 **NM** $12 **MIP** $25

Wicked Witch Squeak Toy, 1939, Burnstein, 7", hollow rubber
EX $250 **NM** $400 **MIP** $600

Wizard of Oz Costume, 1961, Halco, costume and mask
EX $20 **NM** $35 **MIP** $75

Wizard of Oz Hand Puppets, 1965, Proctor and Gamble, plastic
EX $8 **NM** $15 **MIP** $40

Wizard of Oz Hand Puppets, 1989, Presents, several characters available, each
EX $8 **NM** $15 **MIP** $35

Wizard of Oz Hand Puppets, 1989, Multi Toys, set of six on blister cards, each
EX $6 **NM** $12 **MIP** $50

Wizard of Oz Wind-Ups, 1989, Multi Toys, 50th anniversary editions, several characters, each
EX $4 **NM** $8 **MIP** $25

Wizard Squeak Toy, 1939, Burnstein, 7", hollow rubber
EX $175 **NM** $300 **MIP** $500

WATCH

Oz Time Wristwatch, 1989, Macy's, 50th anniversary premium, round face w/Emerald City, black plastic band
EX $30 **NM** $50 **MIP** $100

Wizard of Oz Pocket Watch, 1980s, Westclock, silver finish case, four characters on dial
EX $20 **NM** $35 **MIP** $85

Wizard of Oz Wristwatch, 1989, EKO, child's LCD, red face in round yellow case, plastic band shows yellow brick road and Emerald City
EX $15 **NM** $25 **MIP** $60

Wizard of Oz Wristwatch, 1989, EKO, quartz, illustrated face showing Emerald City, black plastic band
EX $15 **NM** $25 **MIP** $60

WOODY WOODPECKER

ACCESSORIES

Alarm Clock, 1959, Columbia Time, Woody's Cafe
EX $100 **NM** $200 **MIP** $400

Lamp, 1971
EX $30 **NM** $60 **MIP** $135

Wrist Watch, 1940s, in box
EX $750 **NM** $1000 **MIP** $1500

BOOK

Woody Woodpecker's Fun-o-Rama Punch-Out Book, 1972
EX $20   NM $30   MIP $60

TOY

Paper Dolls, 1968, Saalfield, Woody Woodpecker and Andy Panda
EX $30   NM $50   MIP $90

Playing Cards, 1950s, two decks in a carrying case
EX $40   NM $65   MIP $100

Woody Woodpecker Hand Puppet, 1963, Mattel, pull-string voice box
EX $50   NM $90   MIP $135

Woody Woodpecker Nodder, 1950s
EX $75   NM $125   MIP $200

YOGI BEAR

ACCESSORIES

Coat Rack, 1979, Wolverine, 48", red wood, Yogi and Boo Boo cut out in front, growth chart on back
EX $40   NM $70   MIP $100

Hot Water Bottle, 1966
EX $25   NM $50   MIP $75

Safety Scissors, 1973, Monogram, on card
EX $4   NM $7   MIP $15

BANK

Yogi Bear Bank, 1960s, Knickerbocker, 22", figural
EX $40   NM $75   MIP $150

Yogi Bear Bank, 1980, Dakin, 7", figural
EX $6   NM $15   MIP $50

BOOK

Snagglepuss Sticker Fun Book, 1963, Whitman
EX $15   NM $30   MIP $80

Yogi vs. Magilla for President Coloring Book, 1964, Whitman, Model No. 1144
EX $35   NM $70   MIP $125

DOLL

Boo Boo Doll, 1960s, Knickerbocker, 9-1/2" tall, plush
EX $30   NM $60   MIP $120

Cindy Bear Doll, 1959, Knickerbocker, 16", plush w/vinyl face
EX $40   NM $70   MIP $140

Yogi Bear Doll, 1959, Knickerbocker, 16" plush w/vinyl face
EX $75   NM $150   MIP $300

Yogi Bear Doll, 1959, Knickerbocker, 10" tall
EX $125   NM $250   MIP $400

Yogi Bear Doll, 1960s, Knickerbocker, 19" plush
EX $75   NM $150   MIP $300

Yogi Bear Doll, 1962, 6", soft vinyl w/movable arms and head
EX $75   NM $125   MIP $200

Yogi Bear Stuff and Lace Doll, 1959, Knickerbocker, items to make a 13" x 5" doll
EX $30   NM $60   MIP $125

Yogi Squeeze Doll, 1979, Sanitoy, 12", vinyl
EX $10   NM $35   MIP $75

FIGURES

Character Figures, 1960, 12" tall, Yogi, Boo Boo, and Ranger Smith, each
EX $30   NM $60   MIP $90

Snagglepuss Figure, 1970, Dakin
EX $30   NM $75   MIP $140

Yogi Bear Figure, 1960s, Knickerbocker, 9" tall, plastic
EX $25   NM $50   MIP $120

Yogi Bear Figure, 1961, Marx, TV-Tinykins
EX $20   NM $35   MIP $80

Yogi Bear Figure, 1970, Dakin, 7-3/4" tall
EX $20   NM $35   MIP $80

GAME

Yogi Bear and Pixie and Dixie Game Car, Whitman, 7-1/2" pile on game in car
EX $30   NM $60   MIP $120

Yogi Score-A-Matic Ball Toss Game, 1960, Transogram
EX $50   NM $100   MIP $150

TOY

Bubble Pipe, 1963, Transogram, Yogi Bear figural pipe
EX $20   NM $35   MIP $50

Magic Slate, 1963
EX $20   NM $40   MIP $75

Snagglepuss Soaky, 1960s, Purex, 9" tall, vinyl/plastic
EX $20   NM $40   MIP $90

Yogi Bear and Cindy Push Puppet Set, 1960s, Kohner, boxed set of two
EX $60   NM $125   MIP $250

Yogi Bear Cartoonist Stamp Set, 1961, Lido
EX $30   NM $70   MIP $100

Yogi Bear Friction Toy, 1960s, Yogi in yellow tie and green hat, illustrated red box
EX $100   NM $150   MIP $275

Yogi Bear Ge-Tar, 1960s, Mattel
EX $55   NM $100   MIP $160

Yogi Bear Hand Puppet, Knickerbocker
EX $20   NM $35   MIP $75

Yogi Bear Paint 'em Pals, 1978, Craft Master, paint-by-number set
EX $15   NM $30   MIP $75

Yogi Bear Push Puppet, 1960s, Kohner
EX $35   NM $45   MIP $90

WATCH

Yogi Bear Wristwatch, 1963
EX $80   NM $125   MIP $250

Yogi Wristwatch, 1967, Bradley, medium base metal case, shows Yogi w/hobo sack on stick, black vinyl band
EX $80   NM $120   MIP $250

YOSEMITE SAM

ACCESSORIES

Mini Snow Dome, 1980s, Applause
EX $9   NM $16   MIP $25

Musical Snow Dome, 1980s, Applause
EX $15   NM $30   MIP $50

FIGURES

Yosemite Sam Figure, 1968, Dakin, 7" tall
EX $20   NM $40   MIP $80

Yosemite Sam Figure, 1971, Dakin, on treasure chest
EX $20   NM $40   MIP $80

Yosemite Sam Figure, 1978, Dakin, Fun Farm
EX $15   NM $25   MIP $60

TOY

Yosemite Sam Nodder, 1960s, 6-1/4", bobbing head and spring mounted head
EX $125   NM $175   MIP $350

CHARACTER TOYS

Fisher-Price

For nostalgic collectors, Fisher-Price toys conjure images of youth with their colorful paper lithography on sturdy wooden toys. More than seventy years after the production of their first toys, Fisher-Price is still the first choice of parents seeking safe, well-made toys for their children. And collectors couldn't be happier.

Founded by Herman Fisher, Irving Price, and Helen Schelle, in 1930 in East Aurora, New York, the company was determined to bring toys with a matchless charm and inherent quality to children. Sixteen toys were introduced in 1931 including Granny Doodle and Doctor Doodle, a pair of charming ducks that would initiate the use of animal characters as a staple in the Fisher-Price line.

Most collectors are familiar with the look of vintage Fisher-Price toys with their crisp, colorful paper lithography on wooden toys. Fisher-Price quickly realized the value of licensing and in 1935 the company issued the Walt Disney Mickey Mouse Band, featuring Mickey and Pluto. That piece alone can command more than $2,000 in MIB condition. Other Disney characters and Popeye also became favorites and are very desirable in today's market. Musical toys, especially items featuring bells or xylophones, became perennial favorites.

The Fisher-Price Play Family Little People appeared as early as 1959 in a yellow wooden Safety School Bus. With bodies made of wood, the Play Family could be removed from their vehicles. Their body styles and compositions have changed through the years. Today, the Little People are about three times the size of the originals and are made of plastic.

Fisher-Price is currently a subsidiary of Mattel. The company continues to produce Little People play sets in a variety of themes, and has expanded its line to include outdoor playground and riding toys, apparel, and books.

2006 Trends

Collecting vintage Fisher-Price, particularly pre-1950s pieces, can be costly, because it is difficult to find older pieces in premium condition. Collectors shouldn't pass up the modern plastic toys. Younger collectors are beginning to seek the plastic toys of their youth, especially Little People play sets and musical radios, clocks, and televisions. Adventure play sets featuring articulated figures and realistic vehicles and accessories will probably become even more popular in the next few years as crossover collecting from action figures continues. The musical toys are still fairly easy to find and can range from $5 to $30. The most common toys, including the Chatter Telephone and Corn Popper, were heavily played-with and most often found in less than Mint condition.

Note: Many Fisher-Price toys had several variations, which often means several different values. The date on the toy may only be a copyright date, which may be earlier than the actual date of manufacture. For more information on Fisher-Price toys, see *Fisher-Price: Historical, Rarity, and Value Guide 1931-Present 3rd edition* by Bruce R. Fox and John J. Murray, (Krause Publications, 2002).

Contributor: John J. Murray is the president of Toy Town USA Foundation of East Aurora, New York. He is the co-author of *Fisher-Price: Historical, Rarity, and Value Guide 1931-Present 3rd edition*, Krause Publications, 2002. He may be reached at Box 52, Spring Brook, New York, 14140.

PLASTIC

ADVENTURE PEOPLE SETS

Aero-Marine Search Team, 1979, Model No. 323
EX $25   NM $45   MIP $80

Alpha Probe, 1980, Model No. 325
EX $40   NM $50   MIP $135

Alpha Star, 1983, Model No. 326
EX $30   NM $50   MIP $95

Construction Workers, 1976, Model No. 352
EX $10   NM $20   MIP $30

Cycle Racing Team, 1977, Model No. 356
EX $10   NM $20   MIP $30

Daredevil Skydiver, 1976, Model No. 354
EX $7   NM $14   MIP $20

Daredevil Sport Van, 1978, Model No. 318
EX $40   NM $75   MIP $100

Deep Sea Diver, 1980, Model No. 358
EX $10   NM $20   MIP $30

Dune Buster, 1979, Model No. 322
EX $25   NM $50   MIP $75

Farm Fun, green tractor w/yellow wheels, farmer, hay, dog, chicken, yellow trailer, Model No. 2448
EX n/a   NM $10   MIP $20

Firestar 1, 1980, Model No. 357
EX $10   NM $20   MIP $30

Motocross Team, 1983, Model No. 335
EX $15   NM $30   MIP $45

Mountain Climbers, 1976, Model No. 351
EX $15   NM $30   MIP $45

Northwoods Trailblazer, 1977, Model No. 312
EX $25   NM $65   MIP $110

Rescue Copter, 1975, Model No. 305
EX $20   NM $45   MIP $70

Rescue Team, 1976, Model No. 350
EX $10   NM $20   MIP $30

Rescue Truck, 1975, Model No. 303
EX $20   NM $45   MIP $70

Safari, 1975, Model No. 304
EX $60   NM $85   MIP $115

Scuba Divers, 1976, Model No. 353
EX $10   NM $20   MIP $30

Sea Explorer, 1976, Model No. 310
EX $20   NM $40   MIP $60

Sea Shark, 1981, Model No. 334
EX $20   NM $45   MIP $70

Sport Plane, 1975, Model No. 306
EX $20   NM $45   MIP $70

Super Speed Racer, 1976, Model No. 308
EX $15   NM $30   MIP $50

T.V. Action Team, 1977, Model No. 309
EX $60   NM $75   MIP $140

Wheelie Dragster, 1981, with driver, Model No. 333
EX $15   NM $20   MIP $35

White Water Kayak, 1977, Model No. 355
EX $10   NM $20   MIP $30

Wilderness Patrol, 1976, Model No. 307
EX $50   NM $75   MIP $105

HUSKY PLAY SETS

Dozer Loader, 1980, Model No. 329
EX $15   NM $30   MIP $50

Farm Set, 1981, Model No. 331
EX $15   NM $30   MIP $55

Fire Pumper, 1983, Model No. 336
EX $20   NM $40   MIP $65

Firefighters, 1979, Model No. 321
EX $15   NM $30   MIP $50

Highway Dump Truck, 1980, Model No. 328
EX $15   NM $30   MIP $50

Hook & Ladder, 1979, Model No. 319
EX $15   NM $30   MIP $50

Load Master Dump, 1984, Model No. 327
EX $15   NM $30   MIP $45

Police Patrol Squad, 1981, Model No. 332
EX $20   NM $40   MIP $65

Power & Light Service Rig, 1983, Model No. 339
EX $20   NM $40   MIP $65

Power Tow Truck, 1982, Model No. 338
EX $20   NM $40   MIP $65

Race Car Rig, 1979, Model No. 320
EX $15   NM $30   MIP $50

Rescue Rig, 1981, Model No. 337
EX $20   NM $40   MIP $65

Rodeo Rig, 1980, with figure and horses, Model No. 330
EX $15   NM $30   MIP $50

LITTLE PEOPLE

3-Car Circus Train, 1979, three-car train, engine w/silver imprinted headlight, green or blue cage car w/lion litho, red caboose, light blue engineer, short ringmaster, and a red clown w/pointed yellow hat, Model No. 991
EX $25   NM $40   MIP $65

4-Car Circus Train, 1973, four-car train, engine w/paper headlight litho, blue or green car w/giraffe litho, blue or green flat car w/lion litho, red caboose, elephant, monkey, lion, giraffe, tan bear, short, light blue engineer, red clown w/pointed yellow hat, and a short ringmaster, Model No. 991
EX $25   NM $40   MIP $60

A-Frame, 1974, A-frame house w/removable door and sidewalk, three-rung white ladder, two sets of yellow bunk beds, two yellow lounge chairs, grill, two white picnic benches, white table w/steak litho, two yellow captain chairs, four-seat jeep, dad, mom, boy, girl and Lucky the dog, Model No. 990
EX $35   NM $40   MIP $80

Airport, 1972, large fold out airport base, white/turquoise jet, orange/yellow helicopter, four-car tram front car, two luggage cars, fuel car, two white/green two seat cars w/luggage rack, two green hat boxes, two yellow pieces of luggage, cardboard hanger parts box, dad, mom, boy, girl, stewardess, African-American pilot w/turquoise base, Model No. 996
EX $35   NM $65   MIP $110

Airport, 1986, airport building, blue and yellow copter, large blue and yellow plane, four captain chairs, two orange coffee tables, green and white two-seat car w/luggage rack, one brown and one blue suitcase, three-car tram, tan bald man, short light blue blond stewardess, short pilot, mom, boy and girl, Model No. 2502
EX $25   NM $50   MIP $85

Airport Crew, 1983, green pilot, black pilot w/blue body, and a tall light blue stewardess, Model No. 678
EX $4   NM $7   MIP $15

Amusement Park, 1963, large vinyl mat, tunnel/bridge, four-chair swing ride, single-seat swing ride, merry-go-round, four-piece train, two small single-seat cars (no holes for gas), two small single-seat boats, two small boats, straight-sided Little People including two blue boys, two mauve girls, two green boys and a black dog w/yellow or white ears, Model No. 932
EX $175   NM $250   MIP $500

Bath and Utility Sets, 1971, toilet, sink, tub, captains chair, sewing machine, washer, dryer, all wooded family consisting of a dad, mom, boy and a girl; many color variations exist, Model No. 725
EX $12   NM $35   MIP $60

Beauty Salon, 1990, small beauty salon connects w/No. 2454 and No. 2455; set comes w/one pink and white car w/a luggage rack and a girl, Model No. 2453
EX $7   NM $12   MIP $25

Boat Rig, 1981, blue and white truck and trailer w/snap on gray boat holder, blue and white speedboat, one man w/white body and blue ca and one dark blue worker, Model No. 345
EX $5   NM $12   MIP $25

Brown Roof House, 1980, fold-open house w/a garage, green and white car, one double bed, two twin beds, four captain chairs, one round table, two lounge chairs, one coffee table, dad, mom, boy, girl, and Lucky the dog, Model No. 952
EX $25   NM $35   MIP $45

Car and Camper, 1980, 15-pieces, white and red four-seat SUV, white and red pop-up camper w/yellow canvas tent inside, yellow clam carrier w/litho on top, green and yellow boat that sits on top of jeep, two green lounge chairs, grill, green table w/steak litho, motorcycle, dad, mom, boy and girl, Model No. 992
EX $25   NM $45   MIP $75

Castle, 1974, 21-pieces, castle w/attached flag, pink dragon, oone brown and one black horse, white or yellow horse armor, white or yellow scalloped horse harness, castle coach, two short red or yellow thrones, two tall red or yellow

thrones, two red or yellow twin beds w/crown headboard, one red or yellow double bed w/crwon headboard, one red or yellow round table w/medievil-style litho, plastic knight, woodsman, king, queen, prince, princess and a cardboard parts box; reissued in 1987 w/no flag and all plastic people, Model No. 993
EX $60   **NM** $125   **MIP** $200

Change-a-Tune Carousel, 1981, three records labeled A-B-C, two boys and a girl, Model No. 170
EX $25   **NM** $50   **MIP** $70

Choo-Choo Train, 1963, small wood and plastic train engine w/three, three straight-sided Little People and a Lucky the dog, Model No. 719
EX $25   **NM** $35   **MIP** $50

Circus Clowns, 1983, three different clowns, on card, Model No. 675
EX $4   **NM** $7   **MIP** $15

Crazy Clown Brigade, 1983, large clown car, two white crooked hoses, two white crooked ladders, white hose reel, and small green bathtub w/wheels, clown feet, tall blue clown w/white or yellow tie, and a short black clown w/a red fireman hat, Model No. 657
EX $35   **NM** $50   **MIP** $70

Cruise Boat, 1988, S.S. Tadpole, small ship, one-piece chair w/fishing pole, one yellow life preserver, short blue sea captain w/white beard, blond boy w/green base boy, Model No. 2524
EX $15   **NM** $25   **MIP** $40

Decorator Set, 1970, double bed, two twin beds, T.V., checkerboard litho round table, two stuffed chairs, coffee table, all wooden family consisting of a dad, mom, boy and a girl; many color variations exist, Model No. 728
EX $13   **NM** $35   **MIP** $60

Drive In Movie, 1990, small drive in movie building w/movie screen connects w/No. 2453 and No. 2455; set comes w/one white and yellow car w/a luggage rack and a boy, Model No. 2454
EX $7   **NM** $12   **MIP** $25

Dump Truckers, 1965, dumping station w/three slots for trucks, three trucks of different shape and color, three balls in wood or plastic, three light or dark blue straight-sided boys (one smiling, one frowning, and one w/freckles), Model No. 979
EX $45   **NM** $70   **MIP** $120

Express Train, 1987, three-car train, flat car, caboose, solid yellow one-seat car w/luggage rack, one yellow and one blue suitcase, dad, mom, light blue engineer and Lucky the dog, Model No. 2581
EX $10   **NM** $17   **MIP** $35

Farm, 1986, barn base w/mooing door, silo, four pieces of fence, tractor, cart, white harness, white trough, red chicken, white chicken, horse, cow, pig, jointed dog, sheep, dad w/cowboy hat, mom, boy w/cowboy hat and a girl, Model No. 2501
EX $20   **NM** $50   **MIP** $80

Farm family on card, 1983, dark red woman w/blond hair, tall green dad w/white hat and yellow scarf, and a blue girl w/blond hair, Model No. 677
EX $4   **NM** $7   **MIP** $15

Ferris Wheel, 1966, ferris wheel base winds up plays music, three Little People and Lucky the dog; first year versions come w/straight-sided Little People, Model No. 969
EX $35   **NM** $75   **MIP** $110

Ferry Boat, 1979, w/pull string and wheels, white and blue speed boat, two yellow life preservers, two two-seat cars, orange and black man w/o mustache, blue mom w/blond hair, tall blue captain, Model No. 932
EX $25   **NM** $45   **MIP** $70

Fire Engine, 1969, wooden truck and a fireman, Model No. 720
EX $12   **NM** $24   **MIP** $40

Fire Pumper, 1983, long red fire engine w/two yellow braces, w/two firemen, Model No. 336
EX $15   **NM** $35   **MIP** $65

Fire Station, 1980, fire house building, gray fire training tower, two yellow connecting ladders, two barricades, ambulance, fire truck w/ladder, fire chief car, two yellow truck braces, two black connecting fire hoses, two black rubber hoses, two yellow truck braces, three fireman and one dalmatian dog, Model No. 928
EX $45   **NM** $60   **MIP** $80

Fire Truck, 1989, large red and white truck w/cherry picker and attached yellow hose, red fire hydrant, two firemen and one dalmatian, Model No. 2361
EX $7   **NM** $12   **MIP** $25

Floating Marina, 1987, floating marina building w/two boats slips, orange seaplane, one yellow life preserver, detachable clear lighthouse dome, orange boat, red and white boat w/steering wheel, short blue captain w/white beard, boy and girl, Model No. 2582
EX $10   **NM** $17   **MIP** $35

Fun Jet, 1970, plane w/red wings and tail, one green and one yellow suitcase, w/dad, mom, boy and a girl, Model No. 183
EX $25   **NM** $45   **MIP** $75

Garage, 1970, two-story building, elevator and car ramps, car grease rack, four single-seat cars in red, blue, green, yellow, and three little boys and one little girl, Model No. 930
EX $25   **NM** $60   **MIP** $90

Garage, 1986, two-story building, elevator and car ramps, fire hydrant, pay phone, gas pump, three single-seat cars, and three little boys and one little girl, Model No. 2504
EX $25   **NM** $50   **MIP** $80

Garage Squad, 1983, three workers, Model No. 679
EX $4   **NM** $7   **MIP** $15

Gas Station, 1990, small gas station building connects w/No. 2453 and No. 2454; set comes w/one red and white car w/a luggage rack and a boy, Model No. 2455
EX $7   **NM** $12   **MIP** $25

Goldilocks and the Three Bears, 1967, playhouse w/yellow key attached, w/mama bear, papa bear, baby bear, and blue girl w/blond braids, Model No. 151
EX $35   **NM** $75   **MIP** $130

Happy Hoppers, 1969, push toy playset w/three Little People that pop up and down as toy is pushed; value may fluctuate depending on version of Little People, Model No. 121
EX $15   **NM** $25   **MIP** $50

Helicopter Rig, 1981, green and white truck and trailer w/gray snap-on compass, gold one-seat helicopter, one tall blue pilot and one worker w/tan base, Model No. 344
EX $5   **NM** $12   **MIP** $25

Hospital, Children's, 1976, building w/fold down door and elevator and white ambulance, turquoise plastic pieces include stretcher, x-ray, scale, two chairs, two beds, large sink, baby cradle; white plastic pieces include wheelchair, operating table, privacy screen; white baby without bib, white nurse w/white mask, doctor, African-American doctor, dad, mom and girl, Model No. 931
EX $65   **NM** $85   **MIP** $110

House, 1969, fold-open house w/yellow roof and attached garage, car w/hook, one double bed, two twin beds, four captain chairs, one round table, two lounge chairs, one coffee table, yellow stairs w/closet and litho, blue cardboard moving van parts box, dad, mom, boy, girl and Lucky the dog; complete w/moving van add $100-200 to total value, Model No. 952
EX $25   **NM** $55   **MIP** $90

Houseboat, 1972, blue base boat w/wheels and fold open lid, two yellow lounge chairs, two yellow life preservers, two red captain chairs, red lobster litho table, yellow grill, white/blue speedboat, white-bodied dad w/blue hat, mom, boy, girl and Lucky the dog, Model No. 985
EX $25   **NM** $40   **MIP** $75

Indy Race Rig, 1983, yellow and white truck w/trailer, red Indy-type racecar, w/dad engineer and a driver w/a black body and helmet, Model No. 347
EX $5   **NM** $12   **MIP** $25

Jetliner, 1981, green/white yellow plane, one brown and one blue suitcase, w/dad, mom, boy, and a girl, Model No. 182
EX $15   **NM** $30   **MIP** $50

Jetliner, 1986, large yellow and blue plane, one blue and one brown suitcase, dad, mom, boy and girl, Model No. 2360
EX $15   **NM** $30   **MIP** $55

Jetport, 1981, 22-pieces, airport building, blue and yellow copter, large blue and yellow plane, four captain chairs, two

FISHER-PRICE

orange coffee tables, green and white two-seat car w/luggage rack, one brown and one blue suitcase, three-car tram, tan bald man, light blue short stewardess w/blond hair, short pilot, mom, boy and girl, Model No. 933

EX $25   **NM** $35   **MIP** $50

Kitchen Set, 1970, 12-pieces, stove, sink, fridge, litho table, four captain chairs, all wooden family consisting of a dad, mom, boy and a girl; many color variations exist, Model No. 729

EX $12   **NM** $35   **MIP** $50

Lacing Shoe, 1970, shoe w/mostly brown litho and wheels, special lace, mom wearing glasses w/regular shaped body, two yellow triangle-shaped girls w/different faces, two square red boys w/different faces, and a dog w/marshmallow-shaped base, Model No. 146

EX $35   **NM** $45   **MIP** $80

Lift & Load Depot, 1977, building, green and yellow dump truck, fork lift, scoop loader, yellow sling, four brown pallets, two brown crates, two gray crates, two black barrels, orange scoop bucket attached to building, and one African-American and two white workers w/light blue bodies and orange hardhats, Model No. 942

EX $20   **NM** $40   **MIP** $60

Lift & Load Lumber Yard, 1979, small lumber yard building w/yellow ramp, green and yellow lift truck, truck and trailer, six pieces of wood lumber (two square, two long rectangular, two short rectangular), four brown pallets, one white and one African-American worker w/light blue bodies and orange hardhats, Model No. 944

EX $15   **NM** $30   **MIP** $45

Lift & Load Railroad, 1978, train depot building w/track section, seven-piece track (makes an oval), two-piece train (engine winds up), orange sling, two gray crates, two black barrels, four brown pallets, orange ramp, green/yellow lift truck, one white and one Afrrican-American worker w/light blue body and orange hardhats, tall light blue train engineer w/mustache, Model No. 943

EX $35   **NM** $50   **MIP** $80

Little Mart, 1987, small shopping mart building, red tow truck w/orange hook, orange shopping cart, brown bag of groceries, two-seat car w/solid greenback, yellow pay phone, dad, mom, policewoman and Lucky the dog, Model No. 2580

EX $10   **NM** $25   **MIP** $50

Little People Construction Set, 1985, orange and yellow dump truck, scoop loader, bulldozer, two black barrels, one gold-cone barricade, one brown crate, two yellow w/black stripes road barricades, two white and one African-American construction workers, Model No. 2352

EX $7   **NM** $12   **MIP** $25

Little Riders, 1976, plane, rocking horse, tricycle, wagon, train, w/boy and girl, Model No. 656

EX $10   **NM** $25   **MIP** $50

Little Trucks, 1981, orange and yellow scoop loader, bulldozer, dump truck, lift truck, one brown pallet, one gray crate, w/two light blue construction workers and two green construction workers, Model No. 397

EX $12   **NM** $17   **MIP** $35

Main Street, 1986, large building of main street w/a pull up background, two blue ramps, yellow two-seat taxi, blue mailbox, parking meter, pay phone, red fire hydrant, red stop sign, yellow turning stop light, yellow-and-black striped road diverter, mail truck, seven plastic letters, small one-seat fire truck, shopkeeper, fireman, mom, mailman, and a little girl, Model No. 2500

EX $17   **NM** $45   **MIP** $80

McDonald's, 1990, McDonald's restaurant w/pull-out playground, one blue and white two-seat car, one brown trash can, one McDonald's sign, french fry cart, Ronald McDonald, Hamburglar, mom, yellow boy w/black molded hair and girl, Model No. 2552

EX $27   **NM** $85   **MIP** $150

Merry-Go-Round, 1972, merry-go-round playset base, w/mom, two boys and a girl, Model No. 111

EX $35   **NM** $60   **MIP** $110

Mini Boat Set, 1969, car w/hook, boat w/two holes in bottom, V-shaped trailer, straight yellow body boy w/cap, and a straight-sided Lucky, Model No. 685

EX $50   **NM** $80   **MIP** $120

Mini Camper Set, 1969, car and trailer same as mini boat, wood camper marked "Fisher Price," straight yellow body boy w/cap, and a straight-sided Lucky the dog, Model No. 686

EX $50   **NM** $75   **MIP** $120

Mini Snowmobile, 1971, snowmobile w/detachable sled, turquoise boy red cap, turquoise girl w/red hair and Lucky the dog, Model No. 705

EX $20   **NM** $40   **MIP** $60

Mini Van, 1969, w/five Little People-dad, mom, girl, boy, and a dog, Model No. 141

EX $5   **NM** $10   **MIP** $25

More Sesame Street Characters, 1977, Boxed set showing Sesame Street scenes comes w/Roosevelt Franklin, Grover, Sherlock Hemlock, Prairie Dawn, The Count, Harry Monster, and Snuffleupagus, Model No. 940

EX $35   **NM** $80   **MIP** $135

Musical Lacing Shoe, 1964, wind-up musical shoe w/wheels and special lace, and three straight-sided people w/red bases, all w/different facial imprints (girl, two different boys), Model No. 991

EX $45   **NM** $65   **MIP** $110

Neighborhood, 1989, pull apart two-piece building connected by tree, attached

basketball hoop w/ball, yellow five-rung ladder, two twin beds w/teddy bear imprint, one bed w/quilt imprint, one lounge chair, modular kitchen insert, modular bathroom insert, two-seat car, turquoise pool, one round table, two captain chairs, dad, mom, boy, girl and Lucky the dog, Model No. 2551

EX $17   **NM** $25   **MIP** $40

New School, 1988, school house building w/pull-out playground, red stop sign, small school bus, yellow skateboard, white flag, chalk, orange and blue jump rope, white drum, red-bodied woman teacher w/glasses, boy, African-American girl, Asian-American boy, and orange-bodied girl w/glasses, Model No. 2550

EX $17   **NM** $35   **MIP** $70

(John Murray, Photo by Ross MacKearnin)

Nifty Station Wagon, 1960, wooden car w/wood top and two plastic braces on top, w/four large straight wooden figures, blue dad, green mom, yellow cone-shaped boy, and a black dog w/white ears and a ribbed body. The people from this set are similar in design to the people from the No. 990-984 Safety School Bus, Model No. 234

EX $175   **NM** $325   **MIP** $675

Nursery School, 1978, flat base w/dividing rooms and plastic edges, cardboard roof/play area, gold bus w/apple, double sink, stove, toilet, bathroom sink, slide, merry-go-round, blue easel, teeter totter, four captain chairs, round arts-and-craft table, dad, mom, African-American boy and two girls, Model No. 929

EX $20   **NM** $45   **MIP** $70

Nursery Sets, 1972, changing table, highchair, cradle, rocking horse, playpen, stroller, dad, mom, girl and a baby; many color variations exist, Model No. 761

EX $8   **NM** $13   **MIP** $20

Off-Shore Cargo Base, 1979, one large rectangular and square black floats, crane, tan cargo hold, helicopter landing pad, cargo hold cover, tug boat, helicopter, white and blue barge, two gold feed bags, two sections of pipe, two crates, mesh cargo net, two black tow chains, red diver, tall blue captain, and one white and one African-American worker w/light green bodies and yellow hardhats, Model No. 945

EX $20   **NM** $40   **MIP** $60

Pampers Promotional, 1988 only, yellow mini van w/family, green body boy and red cap exclusive to the set

EX $5   **NM** $10   **MIP** $25

Patio Set, 1970, flowered umbrella table, pool w/imprint, four captain chairs, BBQ grill, all wooden family consisting of a dad, mom, boy and a girl; many color variations exist, Model No. 726

EX $13   **NM** $35   **MIP** $55

Play Family Animal Circus, 1974, two yellow ladders, red hoop, yellow trapeze, blue tub (base w/clown on cardboard litho), yellow elephant stand, w/bear, monkey, lion, blue elephant, giraffe, short ringmaster and red clown, Model No. 135

EX $17   **NM** $35   **MIP** $50

Play Family Camper, 1972, green flatbed truck, white removable camper, green boat w/litho inside, boat sits on top of camper, yellow/red umbrella table, four red captain chairs, grill, yellow motorcycle, red table w/hot dog litho, toilet, sink, red ladder, dad, mom, boy, girl and Lucky the dog, Model No. 994

EX $25   **NM** $45   **MIP** $85

Play Family Farm, 1968, barn base w/mooing door, silo, four pieces of fence, tractor, cart, white harness, white trough, red chicken, white chicken, horse, cow, pig, jointed dog, sheep, dad w/cowboy hat, mom, boy w/cowboy hat, and a girl; many variations exist, Model No. 915

EX $25   **NM** $40   **MIP** $75

Play Family Lacing Shoe, 1965, shoe w/mostly black litho and blue base, special lace, w/large all-wood mom wearing glasses, two-yellow triangle-shaped girls w/different faces, two square red boys w/different faces, and a dog w/marshmallow-shaped base, Model No. 136

EX $35   **NM** $75   **MIP** $120

Play Family Tow Truck and Car, 1969, tow truck, car w/hook, and a straight body yellow boy w/cap, Model No. 718

EX $20   **NM** $35   **MIP** $55

Playground, 1986, green base playground w/spring rides and a slide, orange and yellow swing, orange and yellow merry-go-round, blue climbing cube, boy and girl, Model No. 2525

EX $10   **NM** $20   **MIP** $30

Rooms—Sears Exclusive, 1971, flat base w/divided rooms, yellow fridge, yellow double sink, yellow stove w/litho, green table w/formal setting, four green captain chairs, white tub, scale, toilet, sink, red or blue couch, two red or blue twin beds, red or blue T.V. w/litho puppet, red or blue coffeetable, red and blue stuffed chair, turquoise umbrella table, two yellow captain chairs, turquoise or yellow grill, white cotton drawstring bag, all wooden family consisting of a green bald man, blue mom w/blond hair, orange bald boy, red girl w/blond hair and Lucky the dog, Model No. 909

EX $180   **NM** $250   **MIP** $350

Safety School Bus, 1959, First version-yellow school bus w/stop sign on the drivers side and a flat nose, wooden top piece reads "Fisher Price," six removable people w/litho on wooden bodies; Second version-four removable

people and two that are fixed in the back, as the bus moves the fixed people bounce up and down, Model No. 983

EX $150   **NM** $400   **MIP** $675

Safety School Bus, 1961, yellow school bus w/stop sign on the drivers side and a flat nose, five tall wooden people, the people from this bus are similar in design to the people from the No. 990 Safety School Bus and the No. 234 Nifty Station wagon, Model No. 984

EX $150   **NM** $2755   **MIP** $475

Safety School Bus, 1962, yellow school bus w/stop sign on the drivers side and a flat nose, five tall wooden people; the people from this bus and similar in design to the people from the No. 984 Safety School Bus and the No. 234 Nifty Station wagon, Model No. 990

EX $75   **NM** $560   **MIP** $300

School, 1971, schoolhouse building w/bell and pull down sidewall w/chalkboard, four green or yellow student desks, one green or yellow teachers desk w/chair, green and yellow swing, merry-go-round, green or yellow slide, numbers tray, letter tray w/letters A-Z and extra P, S, T, N, R, I, and E letters, chalk box, eraser, blue teacher w/blond hair, two boys and two girls, Model No. 923

EX $25   **NM** $50   **MIP** $90

School Bus, 1965, five Little People kids, and one dog. There have been many variations of the School bus over the years years; all brown dog from first issue is worth $30-50 in Excellent condition, Model No. 192

EX $55   **NM** $125   **MIP** $175

Sesame Street Characters, 1976, boxed set showing Sesame Street scenes comes w/Ernie, Bert, Cookie Monster, Susan, Gordon, Mr. Hooper, Big Bird and Oscar in his can, Model No. 939

EX $35   **NM** $80   **MIP** $135

Sesame Street Clubhouse, 1977, clubhouse w/bird nest and shaker board and attached tire swing, yellow slide, three barrels (red, blue, yellow), yellow cable drum, black and red jump rope, two-seat wagon, Big Bird, Roosevelt Franklin, Grover, The Count, Bert, and Ernie, Model No. 937

EX $45   **NM** $110   **MIP** $195

Sesame Street House, 1975, brownstone fold-out building, Sesame Street lamppost, mailbox w/litho, garbage truck, five-rung white ladder, newsstand, fire hydrant on gray triangle, soda fountain stand, T.V. showing Grover, sofa, table w/pork chop litho, two captain chairs, two twin beds marked "B" and "E," chalk box, eraser, Big Bird's nest, coffeetable, Bert, Ernie, Mr. Hooper, Big Bird, Cookie Monster, Susan, Gordon, and Oscar in his can, Model No. 938

EX $60   **NM** $125   **MIP** $195

Snorkey Fire Engine, 1960, fire truck w/white base and blue wheels and yellow boom, w/four firemen w/green

bases, red arms and hats, and a black dog exclusive to this set, Model No. 168

EX $150   **NM** $225   **MIP** $425

Snorkey Fire Engine, 1961, fire truck w/red base, black wheels and a yellow boom, w/four firemen w/white bases, red arms and hats, Model No. 169

EX $150   **NM** $225   **MIP** $400

Swimming Pool, 1986, swimming pool base, black stand-up grill, diving board, slide, lifeguard stand w/white life preserver, two lounge chairs (one orange and one yellow), umbrella table w/base shaped to fit in hole, boy, and a girl, Model No. 2526

EX $10   **NM** $20   **MIP** $30

Village, 1973, large fold out village base, connecting bridge and traffic light, six letters, one yellow single bed, small fire engine, red and blue police car, mail truck, four yellow captain chairs, umbrella table, green and white one-seat car w/luggage rack, white and green back-to-back two-seat car, phone booth, yellow grill, dentist chair, barber chair, yellow couch and coffeetable, African-American doctor, white doctor, fireman, mailman w/gray base, policewoman, mom, boy, girl and Lucky the dog, Model No. 997

EX $35   **NM** $55   **MIP** $80

Western Town, 1982, building w/shaker board, tan or green buckboard, tan or green stagecoach w/removable red top, one brown and one black horse, two brown harnesses, brown saddle, gray crate, green hatbox luggage, four-pieces fence, blue sheriff w/star badge on chest, red sod-buster man w/black hat and mustache, Native American w/chest markings on front, yellow lady w/green hat, Model No. 934

EX $25   **NM** $55   **MIP** $90

Westerners, 1983, tall ringmaster, Native American w/headdress, and a green cowboy w/ten-gallon hat, on card, Model No. 676

EX $4   **NM** $7   **MIP** $15

Zoo, 1984, zoo base, tree, orange and yellow parrots, vulture, black and orange monkeys, orange cabaña, black seal, blue elephant, yellow lion cub, hippo, gorilla, mountain goat, four food trays, two green benches, one green table, three car tram, dad, mom, girl, boy, and a zookeeper w/safari-style hat, Model No. 916

EX $35   **NM** $70   **MIP** $110

WOODEN

NONE

Allie Gator, 1960, w/ plastic flippers on wooden wheels, Model No. 653

EX $45   **NM** $140   **MIP** $175

Amusement Park, 1963, 20-pieces, chair ride, musical merry-go-round, play swing, choo-choo, play people and more, Model No. 932

EX $125   **NM** $310   **MIP** $585

Baby Chick Tandem Cart, 1953, Easter only, Model No. 50
EX $50   NM $75   MIP $110

Barky Buddy, 1934, blue and yellow military uniform, red hat, red wheels, Model No. 150
EX $450   NM $1100   MIP $2000

Barky Dog, 1958, black and white w/ red wheels, Model No. 462
EX $110   NM $145   MIP $220

Barky Puppy, 1931, blue wheels, oilcloth ears, pipecleaner and wooden ball tail, Model No. 103
EX $550   NM $1000   MIP $2000

Big Bill Pelican, 1961, opening bill, cardboard fish the first three years of release (add $25 if present), light blue feet, Model No. 794
EX $95   NM $135   MIP $195

Big Performing Circus, 1932, included nine figures, original retail price was $2.75, Model No. 250
EX $450   NM $900   MIP $1800

Blackie Drummer, 1939, bear in parade uniform strikes bass drum w/ right arm and cymbal w/ left arm, Model No. 785
EX $550   NM $800   MIP $1300

Bonny Bunny Wagon, 1959, Easter release, bunny pulling wagon, light blue wheels, Model No. 318
EX $30   NM $55   MIP $90

(John Murray, Photo by Ross MacKearnin)

Boom Boom Popeye, 1937, Popeye and Sweatpea, two mallets hit litho drum, unpainted wheels, Model No. 491
EX $600   NM $1100   MIP $1600

Bossy Bell, 1959, bell, light blue wheels, yellow tail and horns, Model No. 656
EX $50   NM $80   MIP $110

Bouncing Bunny Wheelbarrow, 1939, bell on head, Model No. 727
EX $450   NM $750   MIP $1300

Bouncy Racer, 1960, driver w/ helmet bounces and arms move as pulled, large red plastic wheels, Model No. 8
EX $40   NM $75   MIP $125

(John Murray. Photo by Russ MacKearnin)

Bucky Burro, 1955, yellow burro that bucks, spring tail, driver w/ sombrero, Model No. 166
EX $225   NM $375   MIP $495

Buddy Bronc, 1938, cowboy bounces on horse, Model No. 430
EX $275   NM $450   MIP $975

Buddy Bullfrog, 1959, offered w/ checkered pants in last year, croaking noise, jumping action, top hat, Model No. 728
EX $85   NM $120   MIP $185

Bunny Basket Cart, 1957, woven basket, Model No. 301
EX $30   NM $45   MIP $80

Bunny Basket Cart, 1960, plastic basket, Model No. 303
EX $30   NM $55   MIP $85

Bunny Bell Cart, 1941, two mallets strike bell, yellow wheels, cart in front of bunny, Model No. 520
EX $125   NM $250   MIP $550

Bunny Bell Cart, 1954, two mallets strike bell, light blue wheels, cart behind bunny, Model No. 604
EX $45   NM $80   MIP $160

Bunny Cart, 1948, white bunny pulls cylindrical cart w/ metal rim, Model No. 5
EX $75   NM $100   MIP $165

Bunny Drummer, 1942, two mallets hit painted wood disk or metal bell, yellow wagon in front of bunny, red wheels, Model No. 512
EX $150   NM $225   MIP $550

Bunny Drummer, 1946, two mallets hit metal bell, yellow cart in front of bunny, red wheels, Model No. 505
EX $150   NM $225   MIP $550

Bunny Egg Cart, 1949, new for 1949, forerunner of the No. 406 Bunny Cart, Model No. 404
EX $40   NM $95   MIP $155

Bunny Egg Cart, 1950, bunny pulling cart-sides are colorful eggs, dark blue/purple wheels, Model No. 28
EX $100   NM $160   MIP $225

Bunny Engine, 1954, train w/ bell and bunny engineer, blue w/ yellow wheels, Model No. 703
EX $45   NM $85   MIP $160

Bunny Push Cart, 1957, bunny pushes cart, six light blue wheels, Model No. 303
EX $40   NM $80   MIP $120

Bunny Racer, 1942, yellow and blue "racecar" w/ red wood wheels, wooden axles during WWII, Model No. 474
EX $125   NM $235   MIP $475

Busy Bunny Cart, 1936, bunny pulls 7" cart, Easter release, Model No. 719
EX $300   NM $600   MIP $1000

Butch the Pup, 1951, yellow wheels, tail wags, felt ears, Model No. 333
EX $50   NM $70   MIP $110

Buzzy Bee, 1950, first use of acetate (form of plastic) in a Fisher-Price toy, two spring antennae, Model No. 325
EX $25   NM $45   MIP $70

Campbell Kids Farm Truck, 1954, swayed back and forth, paper vegetable cut-outs, Model No. 845
EX $145   NM $300   MIP $750

Cash Register, 1960, three numbered coins, plastic keys pop up characters, Model No. 972
EX $55   NM $115   MIP $195

Chatter Monk, 1957, monkey w/ jumping action, wooden hat, vinyl tail, chatter sound, Model No. 798
EX $85   NM $125   MIP $175

Chatter Telephone, 1962, same as the Talk-Back Telephone of 1961, red plastic handle, blue wheels, wooden wheels through 1966, Model No. 747
EX $30   NM $45   MIP $65

Choo-Choo Local, 1936, push toy, 18" stick, six wheels, steel bell, Model No. 517
EX $350   NM $850   MIP $1800

Chubby Chief, 1932, elephant on bicycle w/ steel bell, retailed for $1, Model No. 110
EX $450   NM $950   MIP $2000

Chuggy Pop-Up, 1955, red train, yellow wheels, pop-up engineer, metal boiler, realistic sound, Model No. 616
EX $85   NM $125   MIP $170

Circus Wagon, 1942, Ringmaster's arms move up and down and pipes play, blue wheels, Model No. 156
EX $525   NM $750   MIP $1100

Concrete Mixer Truck, 1959, mixing drum rotates and pops, plastic grille, lithographed sides, Model No. 926
EX $150   NM $300   MIP $485

Corn Popper, 1957, red and blue push toy, Model No. 785
EX $35   **NM** $95   **MIP** $175

Corn Popper, 1963, push toy, variations of this toy endured through 1990, Model No. 788
EX $15   **NM** $30   **MIP** $50

Cotton Tail Cart, 1940, upright bunny pulls red cart, legs rotate, clicking sound, yellow wheels, Model No. 525
EX $150   **NM** $400   **MIP** $675

Cowboy Chime, 1951, New version of old Dandy Dobbin, western pony head and litho saddle graphics attached to stick. Metal musical hush chime base had cowboy and indian graphics, Model No. 700
EX $110   **NM** $285   **MIP** $475

(John Murray. Photo by Russ MacKearnin)

Dandy Dobbin, 1941, 14-1/2" long, 12-1/4" high, riding horse w/ red seat, green or yellow wheels, braided cord bridle, Model No. 765
EX $285   **NM** $375   **MIP** $565

Dapper Donald Duck, 1936, Model No. 460
EX $175   **NM** $425   **MIP** $650

Dashing Dobbin, 1938, riding horse, blue or red versions, braided cord bridle, 150lb capacity, Model No. 742
EX $450   **NM** $650   **MIP** $900

Ding Dong Duckey, 1949, Easter release, duck's head turned side to side and concealed wires played a tune as pulled, Model No. 724
EX $175   **NM** $225   **MIP** $425

Dinkey Engine, 1959, "chug-chug" sound, pistons moved, plastic cowcatcher and cab, Model No. 642
EX $35   **NM** $50   **MIP** $95

Dizzy Dino, 1931, Pop-Up Kritters, dinosaur on banjo paddle, pulley system used 50lb test fish line, retailed for $1, Model No. 407
EX $250   **NM** $400   **MIP** $800

(John Murray. Photo by Russ MacKearnin)

Dizzy Donkey, 1939, Pop-Up Kritters, donkey on blue paddle, black ears, Model No. 433
EX $85   **NM** $130   **MIP** $175

(John Murray, Photo by Ross MacKearnin)

Doc & Dopey Dwarfs, 1938, each has hammer that hits stump, red wheels, Model No. 770
EX $875   **NM** $1750   **MIP** $2600

Doctor Doodle, 1931, styled by Margaret Evans Price, blue wheels, black topcoat and hat, orange bill, Model No. 100
EX $600   **NM** $950   **MIP** $1500

Doctor Doodle, 1940, green wheels, waddle, lower bill moves with clicker as quacking sound, Model No. 477
EX $300   **NM** $450   **MIP** $675

Dogcart Donald, 1936, Pluto pulls Donald in cart, Model No. 149
EX $600   **NM** $1400   **MIP** $2500

Doggy Racer, 1942, black wheels, arms "turned" the steering wheel, Model No. 7
EX $150   **NM** $300   **MIP** $525

(John Murray, Photo by Ross MacKearnin)

Donald Duck & Nephews, 1941, w/ two nephews Huey and Louie, red wheels, Model No. 479
EX $425   **NM** $575   **MIP** $875

(John Murray, Photo by Ross MacKearnin)

Donald Duck Cart, 1937, unpainted wheels, red cart behind Donald, Easter release, Model No. 500
EX $350   **NM** $675   **MIP** $1200

Donald Duck Cart, 1940, red wheels, blue base, Easter release, chick can behind Donald, Model No. 469
EX $200   **NM** $450   **MIP** $775

(John Murray. Photo by Russ MacKearnin)

Donald Duck Cart, 1942, swinging arms, concealed voice, blue cart behind Donald in red outfit, red wheels, Model No. 544
EX $275   **NM** $350   **MIP** $485

Donald Duck Cart, 1954, orange flip-flop feet, quack-quack sound, flowers litho on blue and yellow cart behind Donald, Model No. 605
EX $125   **NM** $250   **MIP** $425

Donald Duck Choo-Choo, 1940, yellow wheels, blue base, red engineer's hat, steel bell, 9-1/2" long in 1940, 8-1/2" long in 1941, Model No. 450
EX $300   **NM** $400   **MIP** $675

(John Murray, Photo by Ross MacKearnin)

Donald Duck Choo-Choo, 1942, yellow wheels, red base, blue engineer's hat, steel bell, Model No. 450
EX $95   **NM** $200   **MIP** $325

FISHER-PRICE

Donald Duck Delivery, 1936, long-billed Donald in front of pink cart w/ blue wheels, Model No. 715
EX $350   NM $750   MIP $1100

Donald Duck Drum Major, 1940, red wheels, green base, Donald holding green baton, Model No. 550/463
EX $150   NM $350   MIP $725

Donald Duck Drum Major, 1948, blue wheels, red base, Donald holding yellow baton, Model No. 432/532
EX $85   NM $175   MIP $325

(John Murray. Photo by Russ MacKearnin)

Donald Duck Drummer, 1949, two mallets, arms move to strike red drum, red wheels, blue base, Model No. 454
EX $285   NM $325   MIP $475

Donald Duck Pop-Up, 1938, red paddle, rubber bill, oilcloth wings, Model No. 425
EX $325   NM $650   MIP $1100

Donald Duck Xylophone, 1938, red wheels, blue base, blue hat, two arms hold mallets to strike xylophone when pulled, Model No. 185
EX $475   NM $700   MIP $925

(John Murray, Photo by Ross MacKearnin)

Donald Duck Xylophone, 1946, red wheels, green base, blue hat (different from No. 185), two arms hold mallets that strike xylophone when pulled, Model No. 177
EX $350   NM $450   MIP $675

Dopey Dwarf, 1939, blue wheels, red base, two mallets move hit drum when pulled, Model No. 770
EX $350   NM $650   MIP $1375

Doughboy Donald, 1942, 13-3/4" long, soldier outfit, two mortars, Pluto pulling green base w/ red wheels, Model No. 744
EX $550   NM $1000   MIP $2375

Drummer Bear, 1931, yellow wheels, blue base, black hat, Model No. 102
EX $550   NM $1000   MIP $2000

Ducky Cart, 1948, duck pulls cylinder-shaped cart w/ red wheels, Model No. 6
EX $45   NM $85   MIP $165

Ducky Cart, 1950, litho yellow duck w/ blue background, red wheels, Model No. 51
EX $45   NM $85   MIP $125

Ducky Daddles, 1941, yellow duck w/ blue wheels, exclusive for F.W. Woolworth Company, Model No. 14
EX $35   NM $90   MIP $165

Ducky Daddles, 1942, predecessor of Snap Quack, waddle, movable feet, head turns side to side, quacks, Model No. 148
EX $175   NM $300   MIP $625

Dumbo Circus Racer, 1941, rubber arms turned steering wheel, 10-3/4" long, Model No. 738
EX $450   NM $1000   MIP $2000

Easter Bunny, 1936, pink and white, Model No. 490
EX $125   NM $350   MIP $600

(John Murray, Photo by Ross MacKearnin)

Elsie's Dairy Truck, 1948, F-P's second advertising toy, based on Borden's Elsie the Cow, truck driven by her son Beauregard, movable arms struck nickel bell on grille, came with two glass square bottles (add $50 for each bottle), Model No. 745
EX $525   NM $725   MIP $975

Farmer in Dell Music Box, 1962, formerly #764, red crank/handle on side, Model No. 763
EX $30   NM $65   MIP $130

Farmer in the Dell Music Box Barn, 1960, crank, strap, Swiss music box, Model No. 764
EX $25   NM $65   MIP $135

Farmer in the Dell TV Radio, 1963, spring anetnnae, white handle, Model No. 166
EX $25   NM $35   MIP $60

Fido Zilo, 1955, movable arms w/ mallets to strike four nickel keys, red wheels, Model No. 707
EX $90   NM $130   MIP $165

Fire Truck, 1959, red truck w/ yellow grille & ladder, driver bounces and turns when pulled, Model No. 630
EX $35   NM $55   MIP $110

(John Murray. Photo by Russ MacKearnin)

Fuzzy Fido, 1941, spring wire tail, offset green wheels caused waddling, Model No. 444
EX $225   NM $325   MIP $450

Gabby Duck, 1952, blue wheels, yellow duck, orange bill opens, waddling motion, quacks, Model No. 767
EX $55   NM $80   MIP $225

Gabby Goofies, 1956, first version, red Daddy Goofy w/ three ducklings, twirling acetate wings, Model No. 775
EX $40   NM $60   MIP $80

Gabby Goofies, 1963, final version, blue Mama Goofy w/ three ducklings, Model No. 777
EX $20   NM $30   MIP $45

Gabby Goose, 1936, red wheels, sailor suit, concealed voice, Model No. 120
EX $400   NM $750   MIP $1100

Galloping Horse & Wagon, 1948, horse pulling red wagon w/ yellow wheels, Model No. 737
EX $150   NM $325   MIP $475

Gold Star Stagecoach, 1954, two horses pull stagecoach, driver sways side to side, two mail pouches, Model No. 175
EX $285   NM $390   MIP $625

Golden Gulch Express, 1961, red and green train, spring mounted indian on the tender, Model No. 191
EX $110   NM $145   MIP $225

Go'N Back Jumbo, 1931, Walky-Balky Back-Up Toys, wind up w/ removable key, oilcloth ears, pipecleaner tail, styled by Evans Price, designed by Edward Savage, Model No. 360
EX $450   NM $900   MIP $1200

Granny Doodle, 1931, felt bonnet, orange wheels, orange bill, Model No. 101
EX $600   NM $1000   MIP $1500

Granny Doodle & Family, 1933, duck followed by two baby ducks, green wheels, Model No. 101
EX $650   NM $1500   MIP $2000

Happy Helicopter, 1953, litho teddy bear pilot, yellow wheels and propellers, Model No. 498
EX $150   NM $200   MIP $300

Happy Hippo, 1962, vinyl ears, spring tail, storage inside for other toys, Model No. 151
EX $115   **NM** $170   **MIP** $230

Hot Diggety, 1934, wind up, hat, painted face, heavy metal dancing feet, Model No. 800
EX $600   **NM** $1200   **MIP** $1800

Howdy Bunny, 1939, orange "running" legs, green base, red wheels, Model No. 757
EX $300   **NM** $650   **MIP** $975

Huckleberry Hound Zilo, 1961, Sears exclusive, Model No. 711
EX $175   **NM** $475   **MIP** $800

Huffy Puffy Train, 1958, engine, coal car, cattle car, caboose, yellow wheels, "chug-chug" sound, Model No. 999
EX $110   **NM** $150   **MIP** $225

Humpty Dump Truck, 1963, big yellow wheels, two characters, Model No. 145
EX $40   **NM** $90   **MIP** $160

Humpty Dumpty, 1957, smiling face one side, crying face on the other, bells for hands, could roll along on arms or feet, Model No. 757
EX $265   **NM** $350   **MIP** $425

Husky Dump Truck, 1961, big orange tires, two characters, Model No. 145
EX $30   **NM** $85   **MIP** $140

Jack-n-Jill TV Radio, 1959, Swiss music box, winding knob, spring aerial, Model No. 148
EX $25   **NM** $65   **MIP** $110

Jingle Giraffe, 1956, blue wheels, spring tail, nickeled bell, Model No. 472
EX $150   **NM** $275   **MIP** $385

Jolly Jumper, 1954, red wheels w/ green feet, googly eyes, Model No. 450
EX $35   **NM** $60   **MIP** $100

Jolly Jumper, 1963, green frog, big yellow wheels, mouth opens "croak" sound, Model No. 793
EX $25   **NM** $50   **MIP** $80

(John Murray, Photo by Ross MacKearnin)

Juggling Jumbo, 1958, crank pops five colored wooden balls through circular acetate trunk, spring tail, vinyl ears, Model No. 735
EX $235   **NM** $300   **MIP** $425

Jumbo Jitterbug, 1940, Pop-Up Kritter, movable trunk & legs, oilcloth ears, blue paddle, Model No. 422
EX $65   **NM** $150   **MIP** $375

Jumbo Rolo, 1951, blue elephant pedals tricycle, six colored balls rattle in cage behind tricycle, Model No. 755
EX $235   **NM** $300   **MIP** $425

Junior Circus, 1963, 22-pieces in reusable container, Model No. 902
EX $75   **NM** $350   **MIP** $395

(John Murray. Photo by Russ MacKearnin)

Katy Kackler, 1954, wings and feet move up and down, "cluck-cluck-squawk" sound, red wheels, first of three versions, Model No. 140
EX $80   **NM** $120   **MIP** $175

Kicking Donkey, 1937, large rubber ears, red wheels, rope tail, Model No. 175
EX $400   **NM** $850   **MIP** $1300

(John Murray, Photo by Ross MacKearnin)

Kitty Bell, 1950, cat's arms rotate ball that strikes bell, blue base, yellow wheels, Model No. 499
EX $125   **NM** $170   **MIP** $285

Lady Bug, 1961, two spring antennae, red shell, "twirp-twirp" sound, Model No. 658
EX $35   **NM** $70   **MIP** $100

Leo the Drummer, 1952, red base, yellow wheels, two spring "sticks" to strike drum, Model No. 480
EX $235   **NM** $285   **MIP** $390

Looky Chug-Chug, 1949, engine and coal car, red wheels, nickel bell, moving pistons, Model No. 161
EX $125   **NM** $225   **MIP** $375

(John Murray, Photo by Ross MacKearnin)

Looky Fire Truck, 1950, three firemen, moving eyes, nickel bell, red truck w/ yellow wheels, Model No. 7
EX $125   **NM** $160   **MIP** $240

(John Murray. Photo by Russ MacKearnin)

Lop-Ear Looie, 1934, Pop-Up Kritter, mouse, retailed for 25 cents; paddle in red, blue, yellow or green, Model No. 415
EX $225   **NM** $335   **MIP** $450

Lucky Monk, 1932, monkey in orange cart w/ blue wheels, felt hat, sound, retailed for $1, Model No. 109
EX $350   **NM** $850   **MIP** $1700

Merry Mousewife, 1962, red wheels, sweeps broom, yellow tail and hat, Model No. 662
EX $60   **NM** $90   **MIP** $125

Merry Mutt, 1949, red base, blue wheels, two nicleded 3" xylophone keys, two spring mallets, Model No. 473
EX $85   **NM** $125   **MIP** $155

Mickey Mouse Band, 1935, first Disney-themed release, blue base, yellow wheels, Mickey and Pluto, push toy w/ 18" stick, Model No. 530
EX $750   **NM** $1500   **MIP** $2800
(John Murray. Photo by Russ MacKearnin)

Mickey Mouse Choo-Choo, 1938, blue base, yellow wheels, Mickey w/ long-billed red hat, nickel bell, Model No. 432
EX $750   **NM** $1125   **MIP** $1500

Mickey Mouse Drummer, 1941, red base, blue wheels, Mickey's arms move and mallets hit metal-topped drum, Model No. 476
EX $257   **NM** $350   **MIP** $475

Mickey Mouse Puddle Jumper, 1953, yellow wheels, car sways, Mickey bounces side to side, Model No. 310
EX $125   **NM** $200   **MIP** $275

(John Murray, Photo by Ross MacKearnin)

Mickey Mouse Safety Patrol, 1956, Mickey the motorcycle cop pulls cart,

yellow wheels, hands swing reading "STOP" and "GO", Model No. 733
EX $265   **NM** $400   **MIP** $575

Mickey Mouse Xylophone, 1939, band outfit, blue base, yellow wheels, 5-key xylophone, arms hold mallets, Model No. 798
EX $575   **NM** $800   **MIP** $1250

Mickey Mouse Xylophone, 1942, w/out band outfit, Model No. 798
EX $275   **NM** $500   **MIP** $925

Mickey Mouse Zilo, 1963, last Sears exclusive xylophone, last Disney pull-toy, Mickey in band outfit, 3 xylophone keys, Model No. 714
EX $165   **NM** $350   **MIP** $675

Molly Moo-Moo, 1956, red wheels, head "moo"ves up and down, spring tail, Model No. 190
EX $65   **NM** $225   **MIP** $400

Moo-oo Cow, 1958, black and white cow, vinyl ears, pink wheels, spring tail, Model No. 155
EX $125   **NM** $170   **MIP** $230

Mother Goose, 1964, orange plastic wheels, blue scarf on head, Model No. 164
EX n/a   **NM** $40   **MIP** $75

Mother Goose Music Cart, 1955, yellow goose pulls red cart, feet flip flop as pulled, Model No. 784
EX $35   **NM** $70   **MIP** $145

Music Box Sweeper, 1961, final version, Swiss music box, steel yoke, Model No. 131
EX $40   **NM** $65   **MIP** $120

(John Murray, Photo by Ross MacKearnin)

Musical Elephant, 1948, Model No. 145
EX $165   **NM** $325   **MIP** $700

Musical Push Chime, 1950, Model No. 722
EX $35   **NM** $50   **MIP** $125

Musical Sweeper, 1950, Model No. 100
EX $65   **NM** $135   **MIP** $235

Musical Sweeper, 1953, Model No. 225
EX $40   **NM** $65   **MIP** $160

Musical Tick Tock Clock, 1962, Model No. 997
EX $25   **NM** $45   **MIP** $90

(John Murray. Photo by Russ MacKearnin)

Nosey Pup, 1956, Model No. 445
EX $25   **NM** $60   **MIP** $95

Patch Pony, 1963, Model No. 616
EX $20   **NM** $35   **MIP** $50

Perky Pot, 1958, Model No. 686
EX $85   **NM** $110   **MIP** $155

(John Murray, Photo by Ross MacKearnin)

Peter Bunny Cart, 1939, Model No. 472
EX $100   **NM** $235   **MIP** $425

Peter Bunny Engine, 1941, Model No. 715
EX $85   **NM** $225   **MIP** $475

Peter Bunny Engine, 1949, Model No. 721
EX $150   **NM** $275   **MIP** $425

Peter Pig, 1959, Model No. 479
EX $35   **NM** $50   **MIP** $90

Pinky Pig, 1956, first version, wooden eyes, Model No. 695
EX $40   **NM** $70   **MIP** $110

Pinky Pig, 1958, Model No. 695
EX $35   **NM** $90   **MIP** $140

Pinocchio Express, 1939, Model No. 720
EX $650   **NM** $850   **MIP** $1300

Playful Puppy, 1961, Model No. 625
EX $55   **NM** $70   **MIP** $100

Playland Express, 1962, Model No. 192
EX $105   **NM** $140   **MIP** $195

(John Murray, Photo by Ross MacKearnin)

Plucky Pinocchio, 1939, Model No. 494
EX $450   **NM** $725   **MIP** $1100

Pluto Pop-Up, 1936, Model No. 440
EX $70   **NM** $135   **MIP** $185

Pony Chime, 1962, Model No. 137
EX $40   **NM** $70   **MIP** $95

Pony Express, 1941, Model No. 733
EX $110   **NM** $250   **MIP** $585

Poodle Zilo, 1962, Model No. 739
EX $50   **NM** $110   **MIP** $185

Pop 'N Ring, 1959, Model No. 809
EX $40   **NM** $65   **MIP** $135

Popeye, 1935, red base, yellow wheels, Model No. 700
EX $700   **NM** $1750   **MIP** $2500

Popeye Cowboy, 1937, Model No. 705
EX $700   **NM** $1650   **MIP** $2300

Popeye Spinach Eater, 1939, Model No. 488
EX $650   **NM** $1300   **MIP** $1600

(John Murray. Photo by Russ MacKearnin)

Popeye the Sailor, 1936, unpainted wheels, arms strike bell attached to steering wheel, green boat-shaped base, Model No. 703
EX $850   **NM** $1475   **MIP** $2100

Prancing Horses, 1937, Model No. 766
EX $400   **NM** $975   **MIP** $1800

Pudgy Pig, 1962, Model No. 478
EX $40   **NM** $60   **MIP** $85

Puffy Engine, 1951, Model No. 444
EX $50   **NM** $70   **MIP** $110

Pull-A-Tune Xylophone, 1957, Model No. 870
  EX $45 **NM** $80 **MIP** $110

Pushy Doddle, 1933, Model No. 507
  EX $550 **NM** $1350 **MIP** $2000

Pushy Elephant, 1934, Model No. 525
  EX $450 **NM** $975 **MIP** $1800

Pushy Piggy, 1932, first push toy, Model No. 500
  EX $700 **NM** $1500 **MIP** $2300

Quacko Duck, 1939, Model No. 300
  EX $60 **NM** $110 **MIP** $175

Quacky Family, 1946, Model No. 799
  EX $75 **NM** $130 **MIP** $185

(John Murray. Photo by Russ MacKearnin)

Queen Buzzy Bee, 1962, Model No. 444
  EX $25 **NM** $45 **MIP** $70

Rabbit Cart, 1950, Model No. 52
  EX $35 **NM** $70 **MIP** $125

Racing Bunny Cart, 1938, Model No. 723
  EX $150 **NM** $295 **MIP** $425

Racing Ponies, 1936, Model No. 760
  EX $450 **NM** $850 **MIP** $1300

Racing Pony, 1933, Model No. 705
  EX $500 **NM** $1000 **MIP** $1500

(John Murray, Photo by Ross MacKearnin)

Racing Rowboat, 1952, Model No. 730
  EX $235 **NM** $280 **MIP** $390

Raggedy Ann & Andy, 1941, 12" long, green base, red wheels, arms attached to mallet that hits drum between them, Model No. 711
  EX $1000 **NM** $2300 **MIP** $3875

Rattle Ball, 1959, Model No. 682
  EX $20 **NM** $30 **MIP** $40

Riding Horse, 1940, Model No. 254
  EX $400 **NM** $625 **MIP** $975

Rock-A-Bye Bunny Cart, 1940, Model No. 788
  EX $175 **NM** $425 **MIP** $775

Rock-A-Stack, 1960, Model No. 627
  EX $15 **NM** $40 **MIP** $70

Roller Chime, 1953, Model No. 123
  EX $85 **NM** $120 **MIP** $155

Rolling Bunny Basket, 1961, Model No. 310
  EX $35 **NM** $65 **MIP** $110

Rooster Cart, 1938, Model No. 469
  EX $110 **NM** $325 **MIP** $675

Safety School Bus, 1959, first appearance of "Play Family" figures, Model No. 983
  EX $300 **NM** $450 **MIP** $700

Safety School Bus, 1962, Model No. 990
  EX $80 **NM** $175 **MIP** $295

Scotty Dog, 1933, Model No. 710
  EX $350 **NM** $850 **MIP** $1500

Shaggy Zilo, 1960, Model No. 738
  EX $90 **NM** $120 **MIP** $180

Skipper Sam, 1934, Model No. 155
  EX $850 **NM** $2100 **MIP** $3800

Sleepy Sue (Turtle), 1962, Model No. 495
  EX $55 **NM** $75 **MIP** $90

Smokie Engine, 1960, Model No. 642
  EX $45 **NM** $70 **MIP** $90

(John Murray, Photo by Ross MacKearnin)

Snoopy Sniffer, 1938, Model No. 180
  EX $130 **NM** $290 **MIP** $475

Snoopy Sniffer, 1958, Model No. 180
  EX $50 **NM** $115 **MIP** $235

Snorky Fire Engine, 1960, four fireman figures included, Model No. 168
  EX $185 **NM** $300 **MIP** $425

Sonny Duck Cart, 1941, Model No. 410
  EX $75 **NM** $200 **MIP** $425

Space Blazer, 1953, Model No. 750
  EX $375 **NM** $525 **MIP** $725

(John Murray. Photo by Russ MacKearnin)

Squeaky the Clown, 1958, Model No. 777
  EX $250 **NM** $325 **MIP** $475

Stake Truck, 1960, Model No. 649
  EX $40 **NM** $80 **MIP** $160

Streamline Express, 1935, Model No. 215
  EX $900 **NM** $1700 **MIP** $2400

Strutter Donald Duck, 1941, Model No. 510
  EX $125 **NM** $275 **MIP** $485

Struttin' Donald Duck, 1939, Model No. 900
  EX $450 **NM** $975 **MIP** $1500

Sunny Fish, 1955, Model No. 420
  EX $100 **NM** $200 **MIP** $395

Suzie Seal, 1961, Model No. 460
  EX $25 **NM** $40 **MIP** $85

Tabby Ding Dong, 1939, Model No. 730
  EX $350 **NM** $925 **MIP** $1450

(David W Mapes Inc)

Tailspin Tabby, 1931, Model No. 400
  EX $225 **NM** $610 **MIP** $1000

Tailspin Tabby Pop-Up, 1947, Model No. 600
  EX $145 **NM** $170 **MIP** $225

Talk-Back Telephone, 1961, Model No. 747
  EX $75 **NM** $165 **MIP** $225

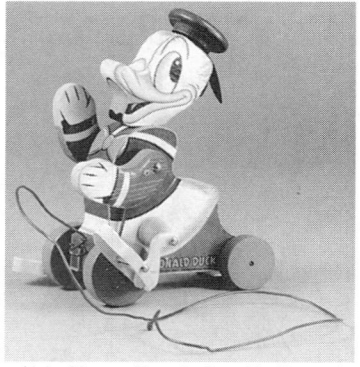
(John Murray, Photo by Ross MacKearnin)

Talking Donald Duck, 1955, Model No. 765
  EX $100 **NM** $140 **MIP** $195

(John Murray, Photo by Ross MacKearnin)

Talky Parrot, 1963, Model No. 698
  EX $145   **NM** $180   **MIP** $260

Tawny Tiger, 1962, Model No. 654
  EX $115   **NM** $130   **MIP** $180

Teddy Bear Parade, 1938, Model No. 195
  EX $850   **NM** $1400   **MIP** $1750

Teddy Choo-Choo, 1937, Model No. 465
  EX $200   **NM** $475   **MIP** $825

Teddy Drummer, 1936, Model No. 775
  EX $300   **NM** $695   **MIP** $1400

Teddy Station Wagon, 1942, Model No. 480
  EX $150   **NM** $300   **MIP** $475

Teddy Tooter, 1940, Model No. 150
  EX $200   **NM** $475   **MIP** $985

Teddy Tooter, 1957, Model No. 712
  EX $225   **NM** $275   **MIP** $395

Teddy Trucker, 1949, Model No. 711
  EX $100   **NM** $225   **MIP** $395

Teddy Xylophone, 1948, Model No. 752
  EX $250   **NM** $300   **MIP** $425

(John Murray. Photo by Russ MacKearnin)

Teddy Zilo, 1950, Model No. 777
  EX $60   **NM** $130   **MIP** $225

Ten Little Indians TV Radio, 1961, Model No. 159
  EX $25   **NM** $45   **MIP** $60

This Little Pig, 1963, Model No. 910
  EX $20   **NM** $35   **MIP** $50

Thumper Bunny, 1942, Model No. 533
  EX $225   **NM** $575   **MIP** $800

Timber Toter, 1957, Model No. 810
  EX $50   **NM** $100   **MIP** $150

Timmy Turtle, 1953, Model No. 150
  EX $85   **NM** $135   **MIP** $180

Tiny Teddy, 1955, Model No. 634
  EX $40   **NM** $75   **MIP** $110

Tiny Tim, 1957, Model No. 496
  EX $35   **NM** $70   **MIP** $120

Tip-Toe Turtle, 1962, Model No. 773
  EX $30   **NM** $45   **MIP** $80

Toot Toot Engine, 1962, Model No. 641
  EX $30   **NM** $45   **MIP** $85

Tow Truck, 1960, Model No. 615
  EX $45   **NM** $70   **MIP** $160

Toy Wagon, 1951, Model No. 131
  EX $240   **NM** $325   **MIP** $450

Trotting Donald Duck, 1937, Model No. 741
  EX $550   **NM** $825   **MIP** $1800

Tuggy Turtle, 1959, Model No. 139
  EX $95   **NM** $130   **MIP** $185

(John Murray, Photo by Ross MacKearnin)

Uncle Timmy Turtle, 1956, Model No. 125
  EX $50   **NM** $120   **MIP** $150

Waggy Woofy, 1942, Model No. 437
  EX $100   **NM** $185   **MIP** $300

Walt Disney's Carnival, 1936, Model No. 483
  EX $325   **NM** $850   **MIP** $2400

Walt Disney's Easter Parade, 1936, Model No. 475
  EX $450   **NM** $1250   **MIP** $2400

Walt Disney's Mickey Mouse, 1936, Model No. 209
  EX $250   **NM** $400   **MIP** $800

Walt Disney's Pluto-the-Pup, 1936, Model No. 210
  EX $225   **NM** $450   **MIP** $800

Whistling Engine, 1957, Model No. 617
  EX $75   **NM** $115   **MIP** $185

Wiggily Woofer, 1957, Model No. 640
  EX $85   **NM** $120   **MIP** $185

Winky Blinky Fire Truck, 1954, Model No. 200
  EX $55   **NM** $110   **MIP** $185

Woodsy-Wee Circus, 1931, Model No. 201
  EX $500   **NM** $1400   **MIP** $2500

Woofy Wagger, 1947, Model No. 447
  EX $45   **NM** $140   **MIP** $265

Woofy Wowser, 1940, Model No. 700
  EX $100   **NM** $325   **MIP** $475

Ziggy Zilo, 1958, Model No. 737
  EX $50   **NM** $100   **MIP** $185

FISHER-PRICE

Games

B oard and card games have only recently developed a devoted following among toy collectors. Games are the traditional playthings, and they were treated with indifference as compared to thousands of other items that are now considered highly collectible. The entire value of the game was in the playing, in how much fun they provided, and how much social interaction they afforded. They were casually played, their parts cheerfully smudged, crumpled, and misplaced. Once their fun quotient was exhausted, games were just as casually tossed in to closets, attics, or the trash.

While the idea of games as collectibles is fairly recent, the field is making up for that oversight with a vengeance. This is particularly true in the three most visible groupings—Victorian games, sports games, and character/television-related games.

Victorian games are loosely defined as those produced between the Civil War and World War I. The premier marque of Victorian games belongs to McLoughlin Bros., which produced many beautifully illustrated games. McLoughlin was eventually purchased by Milton Bradley in 1920, which reissued many games under the Milton Bradley name. As would be expected, these reissues have only a fraction of the value of McLoughlin originals.

Another noteworthy game maker was Parker Brothers, which since 1883 has produced many games that rival the beauty and collectibility of McLoughlin items. However, if you do come across a Victorian game in your search, it will most likely be a Milton Bradley product, by far the most prolific manufacturer of the age.

POSTWAR GAMES

Many collectors consider World War II as the breaking point between antique and modern games. However, this turning point can be defined just as logically as the pre-and post-television age.

Character games particularly lend themselves to the theory of television classification. Games released before the television era evolved from Victorian nursery rhymes and fairy tales, such as McLoughlin's Little Goldenlocks and the Three Bears (1890) and Milton Bradley's Little Jack Horner (1910). These preschool subjects were supplemented by popular comic characters like Winnie Winkle, The Katzenjammer Kids, Chester Gump, and Dick Tracy, along with literary entries such as Paker Brothers' classic Wonderful Game of Oz (1921) and Kerk Guild's A.A. Milne's Winnie the Pooh Game

(1931). Disney character games are good examples of items that bridged the gap between the pre- and post-television eras.

Television games of the 1950s saw a general decline in the quality of materials while increasing the reliance on character affiliation. Games like Lowell's Gunsmoke (1950), Milton Bradley's Annie Oakley (1950), and Parker Brothers' Bing Crosby—Call Me Lucky (1954) set a different standard for game production and marketing. Television-based games of the 1950s and 1960s are currently the most eagerly sought of all modern games. Their values reflect that demand, as witnessed by the Top 10 list included at the end of this chapter introduction.

2006 TRENDS

Today's television, film, and cartoon character games from the 1960s and later remain strong bets for future appreciation. Games in genres like science fiction have enjoyed better-than-normal appreciation; expect this trend to continue.

While most Victorian and modern character games are sought primarily for box and board art, many games have been designed to fulfill the mission of having fun and will do so no matter what their age. Nostalgic games played in the 1970s that bring back good memories form the past are now bringing a premium. Mystery Date, Park and Shop, Star Reporter, and Battling Tops sell for over $100. Condition and completeness are important for games to achieve top value.

The Internet has altered the perception of rarity in collector games. Games that had large production runs over many years have declined in value. Some rare games with cross-collectible interest have soared in price—especially items with prominent sports figures and historic personalities.

The Association of Game and Puzzle Collectors offers lots of information and possibilities for networking. Visit their Web site at: www.agpc.org

Editor's Note: Since experts agree that so few Mint examples of prewar games exist, the prewar section in this edition lists only two grades—Good and Excellent. Excellent is the highest grade generally applied to prewar games in auction catalogs and dealer price lists. This is particularly true of Victorian games.

Contributor: Paul Fink. Planes soar, trains roar, and cars race across the covers of the games in Paul Fink's collection of transportation games. From the 1880s thru the 1940s, games of motion and movement hold heightened excitement. After more than 25 years of collecting, Fink has most of the games that he wants. Now he is still out buying at shows and markets, but mainly for other collectors. He is one of the few dealers who specializes in selling just board games and puzzles. His Web site is www.gamesandpuzzles.com

THE TOP TEN Pre-War GAMES (In Mint Condition)

1. Zimmer Baseball Game, McLoughlin Bros., 1885	28,000
2. Bulls and Bears, McLoughlin Bros., 1896	13,000
3. New Parlor Game of Baseball, Sumner, 1896	10,000
4. Darrow Monopoly, Charles Darrow, 1934	9,000
5. The Champion Baseball Game, Schultz, 1889	6,800
6. Little Fireman Game, McLoughlin Bros., 1897	6,000
7. Teddy's Ride from Oyster Bay to Albany, Jesse Crandall, 1899	5,500
8. Golf, Schoenhut, 1900	5,000
9. Egerton R. Williams Popular Indoor Baseball Game, Hatch, 1886	5,000
10. Great Mails Baseball Game, Walter Mails Baseball Game, 1919	4,100

THE TOP TEN Post-War GAMES (In Mint Condition)

1. Elvis Presley Game, Teen Age Games, 1957	$4,000
6. Challenge of the Yankees, Hasbro, 1960s	1,800
2. Red Barber's Big League Baseball Game, G&R Anthony, 1950s	1,700
3. Munsters Masquerade Game, Hasbro, 1965	1,000
4. Munsters Drag Race Game, Hasbro, 1965	1,000
5. Munsters Picnic Game, Hasbro, 1965	1,000
7. Creature From the Black Lagoon, Hasbro, 1963	750
8. Willie Mays "Say Hey," Toy Development, 1954	700
9. Jonny Quest Game, Transogram, 1964	700
10. Mickey Mouse Haunted Bagatelle, 1950s	550

PREWAR GAMES

BOARD GAMES

21st Century Football, 1930s, Kerger
  EX $55   NM $90   MIP n/a

400 Game, The, 1890s, J.H. Singer
  EX $100   NM $150   MIP n/a

A&P Relay Boat Race Coast-to-Coast, 1930s, A&P
  EX $30   NM $40   MIP n/a

ABC Baseball Game, 1910s
  EX $430   NM $715   MIP n/a

ABC, Game of, 1914
  EX $60   NM $100   MIP n/a

Abcdarian, The, 1899, Chaffee & Selchow
  EX $40   NM $100   MIP n/a

Across the Channel, 1926, Wolverine
  EX $50   NM $85   MIP n/a

Across the Continent, 1892, Parker Brothers
  EX $100   NM $175   MIP n/a

Across the Continent, 1922, Parker Brothers
  EX $250   NM $500   MIP n/a

Across the Sea Game, 1930, Gabriel
  EX $60   NM $100   MIP n/a

Across the Yalu, 1905, Milton Bradley
  EX $95   NM $175   MIP n/a

Add-Too, 1940, All-Fair
  EX $5   NM $15   MIP n/a

Admiral Byrd's South Pole Game Little America, 1930s, Parker Brothers
  EX $250   NM $600   MIP n/a

Admirals, The Naval War Game, 1939, Merchandisers
  EX $75   NM $120   MIP n/a

ADT Delivery Boy, 1890, Milton Bradley
  EX $120   NM $250   MIP n/a

ADT Messenger Boy (Small Version), 1915, Milton Bradley
  EX $40   NM $70   MIP n/a

Advance And Retreat, Game of, 1900s, Milton Bradley
  EX $95   NM $225   MIP n/a

Aero-Chute, 1940, American Toy Works
  EX $75   NM $150   MIP n/a

Aeroplane Race, 1922, Wolverine
  EX $60   NM $95   MIP n/a

After Dinner, 1937, Frederick H. Beach (Beachcraft)
  EX $10   NM $20   MIP n/a

Air Base Checkers, 1942, Einson-Freeman
  EX $20   NM $30   MIP n/a

Air Mail, The, 1930, Archer Toy
  EX $75   NM $125   MIP n/a

Air Mail, The Game of, 1927, Milton Bradley
  EX $50   NM $80   MIP n/a

(KP Photo)

Air Ship Game, The, 1904, McLoughlin Bros.
  EX $425   NM $700   MIP n/a

Air Ship Game, The, 1912, McLoughlin Bros.
  EX $300   NM $600   MIP n/a

Airplane Speedway Game, 1941, Lowe
  EX $20   NM $30   MIP n/a

(KP Photo)

Akins Real Baseball, 1915, Akins
  EX $450   NM $750   MIP n/a

Aldjemma, 1944, Corey Games
  EX $30   NM $45   MIP n/a

Alee-Oop, 1937, Royal Toy
  EX $15   NM $25   MIP n/a

Alexander's Baseball, 1940s
  EX $245   NM $400   MIP n/a

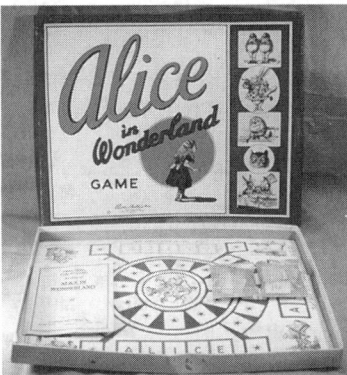

(KP Photo)

Alice in Wonderland, 1930s, Parker Brothers
  EX $60   NM $125   MIP n/a

Alice In Wonderland, Game of, 1923, Stoll & Edwards
  EX $50   NM $75   MIP n/a

All American Basketball, 1941, Corey Games
  EX $55   NM $65   MIP n/a

All American Football, 1935
  EX $35   NM $55   MIP n/a

All-American Big Boy Baseball Game, 1920s, Rosensteel-Pulich
  EX $200   NM $500   MIP n/a

All-American Football, 1925, Parker Brothers
  EX $100   NM $165   MIP n/a

All-Star Baseball Game, 1935, Whitman
  EX $100   NM $165   MIP n/a

Alpha Baseball Game, 1930s, Redlich
  EX $100   NM $150   MIP n/a

Alpha Football Game, 1940s, Replica
  EX $70   NM $115   MIP n/a

Amateur Golf, 1928, Parker Brothers
  EX $145   NM $245   MIP n/a

Ambuscade, Constellations And Bounce, 1877, McLoughlin Bros.
  EX $100   NM $175   MIP n/a

American Boy Game, 1920s, Milton Bradley
  EX $85   NM $125   MIP n/a

American Derby, 1931, Henschel
  EX $55   NM $90   MIP n/a

American Football Game, 1930, Ace Leather Goods
  EX $70   NM $115   MIP n/a

American Revolution, The New Game of The, 1844, Lorenzo Burge
  EX $960   NM $1600   MIP n/a

American Sports, 1880s
  EX $110   NM $180   MIP n/a

America's Football, 1939, Trojan Games
  EX $55   NM $90   MIP n/a

America's Yacht Race, 1904, McLoughlin Bros.
  EX $350   NM $750   MIP n/a

Amusing Game of Innocence Abroad, The, 1888, Parker Brothers
  EX $75   NM $200   MIP n/a

(KP Photo)

Ancient Game of the Mandarins, The, 1923, Parker Brothers
EX $45 **NM** $75 **MIP** n/a

Andy Gump, His Game, 1924, Milton Bradley
EX $45 **NM** $75 **MIP** n/a

Anex-A-Gram, 1938, Embossing
EX $20 **NM** $40 **MIP** n/a

Animal & Bird Lotto, 1926, All-Fair
EX $15 **NM** $20 **MIP** n/a

Arena, 1896, Bliss
EX $200 **NM** $300 **MIP** n/a

Athletic Sports, 1900, Parker Brothers
EX $145 **NM** $350 **MIP** n/a

Attack, Game of, 1889, Bliss
EX $800 **NM** $1200 **MIP** n/a

Authors, 1861, Whipple & Smith
EX $100 **NM** $300 **MIP** n/a

Authors, 1890s, J.H. Singer
EX $25 **NM** $50 **MIP** n/a

Auto Game, The, 1906, Milton Bradley
EX $150 **NM** $300 **MIP** n/a

Auto Race Electro Game, 1929, Knapp Electric & Novelty
EX $125 **NM** $210 **MIP** n/a

Auto Race Game, 1925, Milton Bradley
EX $200 **NM** $325 **MIP** n/a

Auto Race Jr., 1925, All-Fair
EX $100 **NM** $150 **MIP** n/a

Auto Race, Army, Navy, Game Hunt (four game set), 1920s, Wilder
EX $75 **NM** $125 **MIP** n/a

Auto Race, Game Of, 1920s, Orotech
EX $50 **NM** $75 **MIP** n/a

Automobile Race, Game of the, 1904, McLoughlin Bros.
EX $650 **NM** $1200 **MIP** n/a

Auto-Play Baseball Game, 1911, Auto-Play
EX $425 **NM** $700 **MIP** n/a

Aydelott's Parlor Baseball, 1910
EX $225 **NM** $375 **MIP** n/a

Babe Ruth National Game of Baseball, 1929, Keiser-Fry
EX $550 **NM** $910 **MIP** n/a

Babe Ruth's Baseball Game, 1926, Milton Bradley
EX $400 **NM** $700 **MIP** n/a

Babe Ruth's Official Baseball Game, 1940s, Toytown
EX $300 **NM** $500 **MIP** n/a

Baby Barn Yard, 1940s, B.L. Fry Products
EX $15 **NM** $25 **MIP** n/a

Bagatelle, Game of, 1898, McLoughlin Bros.
EX $300 **NM** $450 **MIP** n/a

Bagdad, The Game of The East, 1940, Clover Games
EX $25 **NM** $40 **MIP** n/a

Bambino (Baseball, Chicago World's Fair), 1933, Johnson Store Equipment
EX $295 **NM** $490 **MIP** n/a

Bambino Baseball Game, 1940, Mansfield-Zesiger
EX $145 **NM** $250 **MIP** n/a

Bamboozle, or The Enchanted Isle, 1876, Milton Bradley
EX $75 **NM** $125 **MIP** n/a

Bang, Game of, 1903, McLoughlin Bros.
EX $100 **NM** $200 **MIP** n/a

Banner Lye Checkerboard, 1930s, Geo E. Schweig & Son
EX $15 **NM** $20 **MIP** n/a

Barage, 1941, Corey Games
EX $50 **NM** $100 **MIP** n/a

Barney Google and Spark Plug Game, 1923, Milton Bradley
EX $75 **NM** $150 **MIP** n/a

Baron Munchausen Game, The, 1933, Parker Brothers
EX $50 **NM** $60 **MIP** n/a

Base Hit, 1944, Games
EX $75 **NM** $100 **MIP** n/a

Baseball, 1942, Lowe
EX $15 **NM** $25 **MIP** n/a

Baseball & Checkers, 1925, Milton Bradley
EX $100 **NM** $200 **MIP** n/a

Baseball Dominoes, 1910, Evans
EX $250 **NM** $400 **MIP** n/a

Baseball Game, 1930, All-Fair
EX $150 **NM** $300 **MIP** n/a

Baseball Game & G-Man Target Game, 1940, Marks Brothers
EX $150 **NM** $225 **MIP** n/a

Baseball Game, New, 1885, Clark & Martin
EX $165 **NM** $275 **MIP** n/a

Baseball Wizard Game, 1916, Morehouse
EX $265 **NM** $450 **MIP** n/a

Baseball, Game of, 1886, J.H. Singer
EX $600 **NM** $1000 **MIP** n/a

Basilinda, 1890, Horsman
EX $105 **NM** $175 **MIP** n/a

Basketball, 1942, Lowe
EX $15 **NM** $25 **MIP** n/a

Basketball Game, Official, 1940, Toy Creations
EX $45 **NM** $75 **MIP** n/a

Battle Checkers, 1925, Pen Man
EX $15 **NM** $50 **MIP** n/a

Battle Game, The, 1890s, Parker Brothers
EX $120 **NM** $200 **MIP** n/a

Battle of Ballots, 1931, All-Fair
EX $85 **NM** $150 **MIP** n/a

Battle of Manila, 1899, Parker Brothers
EX $600 **NM** $1200 **MIP** n/a

Bear Hunt, Game of, 1923, Milton Bradley
EX $45 **NM** $70 **MIP** n/a

Beauty And The Beast, Game of, 1905, Milton Bradley
EX $45 **NM** $75 **MIP** n/a

Bee Gee Baseball Dart Target, 1935s, Bee Gee
EX $70 **NM** $115 **MIP** n/a

Bell Boy Game, The, 1898, Chaffee & Selchow
EX $425 **NM** $700 **MIP** n/a

Belmont Park, 1930, Marks Brothers
EX $75 **NM** $100 **MIP** n/a

Bengalee, 1940s, Advance Games
EX $20 **NM** $35 **MIP** n/a

Benny Goodman Swings, 1930s, Toy Creations
EX $50 **NM** $100 **MIP** n/a

Benson Football Game, The, 1930s, Benson
EX $85 **NM** $140 **MIP** n/a

Bible Boys, 1901, Zondervan
EX $10 **NM** $15 **MIP** n/a

Bible Characters, 1890s, Decker & Decker
EX $10 **NM** $25 **MIP** n/a

Bible Lotto, 1933, Goodenough and Woglom
EX $10 **NM** $15 **MIP** n/a

(KP Photo)

Bible Quotto, 1932, Goodenough and Woglom
EX $6 **NM** $10 **MIP** n/a

Bible Rhymes, 1933, Goodenough and Woglom
EX $10 **NM** $15 **MIP** n/a

Bicycle Game, 1896, Donaldson Brothers
EX $205 **NM** $350 **MIP** n/a

(KP Photo)

Bicycle Game, The New, 1894, Parker Brothers
EX $400 **NM** $500 **MIP** n/a

Bicycle Race, 1910, Milton Bradley
EX $125   NM $250   MIP n/a

Bicycle Race Game, The, 1898, Chaffee & Selchow
EX $430   NM $700   MIP n/a

(KP Photo)

Bicycle Race, A Game for the Wheelmen, 1891, McLoughlin Bros.
EX $600   NM $1000   MIP n/a

Bicycling, The Merry Game of, 1900, Parker Brothers150
EX $200   NM $275   MIP n/a

Big Apple, 1938, Rosebud Art
EX $20   NM $40   MIP n/a

Big Bad Wolf Game, 1930s, Parker Brothers
EX $50   NM $90   MIP n/a

Big Business, 1936, Parker Brothers
EX $25   NM $50   MIP n/a

Big Business, 1937, Transogram
EX $25   NM $50   MIP n/a

Big League Basketball, 1920s, Baumgarten
EX $145   NM $300   MIP n/a

Big Six: Christy Mathewson Indoor Baseball Game, 1922, Piroxloid
EX $500   NM $800   MIP n/a

Big Ten Football Game, 1936, Wheaties
EX $55   NM $90   MIP n/a

Bike Race Game, The, 1930s, Master Toy
EX $20   NM $50   MIP n/a

Bild-A-Word, 1929, Educational Card & Game
EX $5   NM $20   MIP n/a

Billy Whiskers, 1923, Saalfield
EX $30   NM $75   MIP n/a

Billy Whiskers, 1924, Russell
EX $45   NM $75   MIP n/a

Bilt-Rite Miniature Bowling Alley, 1930s, Atwood Momanus
EX $70   NM $115   MIP n/a

Bing Miller Base Ball Game, 1932, Ryan
EX $750   NM $2000   MIP n/a

Bingo, 1925, Rosebud Art
EX $15   NM $20   MIP n/a

Bingo or Beano, 1940s, Parker Brothers
EX $5   NM $10   MIP n/a

Bird Lotto, 1940s, Gabriel
EX $10   NM $20   MIP n/a

Black Beauty, 1921, Stoll & Edwards
EX $40   NM $65   MIP n/a

Black Falcon of The Flying G-Men, The, 1939, Ruckelshaus
EX $300   NM $500   MIP n/a

Black Sambo, Game of, 1939, Gabriel
EX $90   NM $200   MIP n/a

Blackout, 1939, Milton Bradley
EX $40   NM $75   MIP n/a

Blockade, 1941, Corey Games
EX $50   NM $95   MIP n/a

Blondie Goes To Leisureland, 1935, Westinghouse
EX $20   NM $35   MIP n/a

Blow Football Game, 1912
EX $30   NM $50   MIP n/a

Blox-O, 1923, Lubbers & Bell
EX $10   NM $20   MIP n/a

Bluff, 1944, Games of Fame
EX $15   NM $25   MIP n/a

Bo Bang & Hong Kong, 1890, Parker Brothers
EX $275   NM $450   MIP n/a

Bo McMillan's Indoor Football, 1939, Indiana Game
EX $60   NM $125   MIP n/a

Bo Peep, The Game of, 1890, J.H. Singer
EX $200   NM $350   MIP n/a

Boake Carter's Star Reporter, 1937, Parker Brother75s
EX $75   NM $100   MIP n/a

Bomb The Navy, 1940s, Pressman
EX $20   NM $40   MIP n/a

Bombardment, Game of, 1898, McLoughlin Bros.
EX $100   NM $250   MIP n/a

Bombs Away, 1944, Toy Creations
EX $75   NM $150   MIP n/a

Bookie, 1931, Bookie Games
EX $55   NM $90   MIP n/a

Boston Baseball Game, 1906, Boston Game
EX $495   NM $825   MIP n/a

Boston Globe Bicycle Game of Circulation, 1895, Boston Globe
EX $55   NM $90   MIP n/a

Boston-New York Motor Tour, 1920s, American Toy
EX $60   NM $100   MIP n/a

Bottle-Quoits, 1897, Parker Brothers
EX $50   NM $85   MIP n/a

Bottoms Up, 1934, Embossing
EX $20   NM $45   MIP n/a

Bowl 'em, 1930s, Parker Brothers
EX $20   NM $35   MIP n/a

Bowling Board Game, 1896, Parker Brothers
EX $350   NM $575   MIP n/a

Box Hockey, 1941, Milton Bradley45
EX $35   NM $60   MIP n/a

Boxing Game, The, 1928, Stoll & Edwards
EX $85   NM $140   MIP n/a

Boy Scouts, 1910s, McLoughlin Bros.
EX $125   NM $200   MIP n/a

Boy Scouts in Camp, McLoughlin Bros.
EX $175   NM $300   MIP n/a

Boy Scouts Progress Game, 1924, Parker Brothers
EX $225   NM $300   MIP n/a

Boy Scouts, The Game of, 1926, Parker Brothers
EX $200   NM $350   MIP n/a

Boys Own Football Game, 1900s, McLoughlin Bros.
EX $325   NM $900   MIP n/a

Bradley's Circus Game, 1882, Milton Bradley
EX $60   NM $150   MIP n/a

Bradley's Telegraph Game, 1900s, Milton Bradley
EX $85   NM $125   MIP n/a

Bradley's Toy Town Post Office, 1910s, Milton Bradley
EX $90   NM $150   MIP n/a

Bringing Up Father Game, 1920, Embee Distributing
EX $75   NM $125   MIP n/a

Broadway, 1917, Parker Brothers
EX $90   NM $160   MIP n/a

Brownie Auto Race, 1920s, Jeanette Toy & Novelty
EX $100   NM $195   MIP n/a

Brownie Horseshoe Game, 1900s, M.H. Miller
EX $30   NM $50   MIP n/a

Brownie Ring Toss, 1920s, M.H. Miller
EX $30   NM $50   MIP n/a

Buck Rogers and His Cosmic Rocket Wars Game, 1934, Lutz & Scheinkman, Inc.
EX $400   NM $700   MIP n/a

Buck Rogers Game of the 25th Century, 1934, Lutz & Sheinkman, Inc., 13 x 18" board
EX $400   NM $700   MIP n/a

Buck Rogers Siege of Gigantica Game, 1934, Lutz & Scheinkman, Inc., 3 boards, 40 cards, 12 wooden pegs
EX $600   NM $1500   MIP n/a

Bucking Bronco, 1930s, Transogram
EX $30   NM $50   MIP n/a

Buffalo Bill, The Game of, 1898, Parker Brothers
EX $250   NM $400   MIP n/a

Buffalo Hunt, 1898, Parker Brothers
EX $175   NM $250   MIP n/a

Bugle Horn or Robin Hood, Game of, 1895, McLoughlin Bros.
EX $250   NM $500   MIP n/a

Bugville Games, 1915, Animate Toy
EX $75   NM $125   MIP n/a

Bulls and Bears, 1896, McLoughlin Bros.
EX $9000   NM $13000   MIP n/a

(KP Photo)

Bulls and Bears, 1936, Parker Brothers
EX $75   NM $200   MIP n/a

Bunker Golf, 1932
EX $115   NM $195   MIP n/a

Bunny Rabbit, or Cottontail & Peter, The Game of, 1928, Parker Brothers
EX $85   NM $145   MIP n/a

Buried Treasure, The Game of, 1930s, Russell
EX $35   NM $60   MIP n/a

Buster Brown at Coney Island, 1890s, J. Ottmann Lith.
EX $225   NM $500   MIP n/a

Buster Brown Hurdle Race, 1890s, J. Ottmann Lith.
EX $300   NM $600   MIP n/a

Buying and Selling Game, 1903, Milton Bradley
EX $100   NM $200   MIP n/a

Cabby, 1940, Selchow & Righter
EX $30   NM $60   MIP n/a

Cabin Boy, 1910, Milton Bradley
EX $50   NM $100   MIP n/a

Cadet Game, The, 1905, Milton Bradley
EX $100   NM $200   MIP n/a

Cake Walk Game, The, 1900s, Parker Brothers
EX $750   NM $2000   MIP n/a

Cake Walk, The, 1900s, Anglo American
EX $750   NM $2000   MIP n/a

Calling All Cars, 1938, Parker Brothers
EX $25   NM $30   MIP n/a

Camelot, 1950s, Parker Brothers
EX $20   NM $25   MIP n/a

Canoe Race, 1910, Milton Bradley
EX $35   NM $60   MIP n/a

Capital Cities Air Derby, The, 1929, All-Fair
EX $200   NM $400   MIP n/a

Captain and the (Katzenjammer) Kids, 1940s, Milton Bradley
EX $50   NM $100   MIP n/a

Captain Hop Across Junior, 1928, All-Fair
EX $100   NM $250   MIP n/a

Captain Kidd and His Treasure, 1896, Parker Brothers
EX $225   NM $400   MIP n/a

Captain Kidd Junior, 1926, Parker Brothers
EX $50   NM $75   MIP n/a

(KP Photo)

Captive Princess, 1880, McLoughlin Bros.
EX $135   NM $225   MIP n/a

(KP Photo)

Captive Princess, 1899, McLoughlin Bros.
EX $65   NM $150   MIP n/a

Captive Princess, Tournament And Pathfinders, Games of, 1888, McLoughlin Bros.
EX $75   NM $200   MIP n/a

Capture The Fort, 1914, Valley Novelty Works
EX $45   NM $75   MIP n/a

Car Race and Game Hunt, 1920s, Wilder
EX $75   NM $165   MIP n/a

Cargo For Victory, 1943, All-Fair
EX $75   NM $125   MIP n/a

Cargoes, 1934, Selchow & Righter
EX $50   NM $75   MIP n/a

Carl Hubbell Mechanical Baseball, Gotham
EX $100   NM $300   MIP n/a

(KP Photo)

Carnival, The Show Business Game, 1937, Milton Bradley
EX $50   NM $100   MIP n/a

Casey on the Mound, 1940s, Kamm Games
EX $200   NM $400   MIP n/a

Cat, 1915, Carl F. Doerr
EX $15   NM $25   MIP n/a

Cat, Game of, 1900, Chaffee & Selchow
EX $150   NM $300   MIP n/a

Catching Mice, Game of, 1888, McLoughlin Bros.
EX $150   NM $275   MIP n/a

Cats And Dogs, 1929, Parker Brothers
EX $100   NM $225   MIP n/a

Cavalcade, 1930s, Selchow & Righter
EX $40   NM $60   MIP n/a

Century Ride, 1900, Milton Bradley
EX $150   NM $250   MIP n/a

Century Run Bicycle Game, The, 1897, Parker Brothers
EX $210   NM $300   MIP n/a

Champion Baseball Game, The, 1889, Schultz
EX $4100   NM $6800   MIP n/a

Champion Game of Baseball, The, 1910s, Proctor Amusement
EX $75   NM $100   MIP n/a

Champion Road Race, 1934, Champion Spark Plugs
EX $20   NM $40   MIP n/a

Championship Baseball Parlor Game, 1914, Grebnelle Novelty
EX $225   NM $500   MIP n/a

Championship Fight Game, 1940s, Frankie Goodman
EX $20   NM $50   MIP n/a

Champs, The Land of Brawno, 1940, Selchow & Righter
EX $30   NM $50   MIP n/a

Characteristics, 1845, Ives
EX $180   NM $300   MIP n/a

Charge, The, 1898, E.O. Clark
EX $300   NM $500   MIP n/a

Charlie Chan, The Great Charlie Chan Detective Game, 1937, Milton Bradley
EX $300   NM $550   MIP n/a

(KP Photo)

Charlie McCarthy Game of Topper, 1938, Whitman
EX $20   NM $45   MIP n/a

Charlie McCarthy Put and Take Bingo Game, 1938, Whitman
EX $30   NM $45   MIP n/a

Charlie McCarthy's Flying Hats, 1938, Whitman
EX $25   NM $40   MIP n/a

Chasing Villa, 1920, Smith, Kline & French
EX $65   NM $180   MIP n/a

Checkered Game of Life, 1860, Milton Bradley
EX $250   NM $400   MIP n/a

Checkered Game of Life, 1866, Milton Bradley
EX $150   NM $300   MIP n/a

GAMES

Checkered Game of Life, 1911, Milton Bradley
EX $75   NM $150   MIP n/a

Checkers & Avion, 1925, American Toy Works
EX $30   NM $50   MIP n/a

Chee Chow, 1939, Gabriel
EX $15   NM $25   MIP n/a

Cheerios Bird Hunt, 1930s, General Mills
EX $15   NM $25   MIP n/a

Cheerios Hook The Fish, 1930s, General Mills
EX $15   NM $25   MIP n/a

Chessindia, 1895, Clark & Sowdon
EX $55   NM $95   MIP n/a

Chester Gump Game, 1938, Milton Bradley
EX $65   NM $125   MIP n/a

Chester Gump Hops over the Pole, 1930s, Milton Bradley
EX $75   NM $125   MIP n/a

Chevy Chase, 1890, Hamilton-Myers
EX $75   NM $125   MIP n/a

Chicago Game Series Baseball, 1890s, Doan
EX $1175   NM $1950   MIP n/a

China, 1905, Wilkens Thompson
EX $50   NM $85   MIP n/a

Chin-Chow and Sum Flu, 1925, Novitas Sales
EX $6   NM $10   MIP n/a

Ching Gong, 1937, Gabriel
EX $20   NM $25   MIP n/a

Chiromagica, or The Hand of Fate, 1901, McLoughlin Bros.
EX $300   NM $450   MIP n/a

Chivalry, 1925, Parker Brothers
EX $75   NM $125   MIP n/a

Chocolate Splash, 1916, Willis G. Young
EX $50   NM $75   MIP n/a

Christmas Goose, 1890, McLoughlin Bros.
EX $750   NM $1500   MIP n/a

Christmas Jewel, Game of the, 1899, McLoughlin Bros.
EX $250   NM $600   MIP n/a

Christmas Mail, 1890s, J. Ottmann Lith.
EX $390   NM $550   MIP n/a

Chutes And Ladders, 1943, Milton Bradley
EX $15   NM $30   MIP n/a

Cinderella, 1923, Stoll & Edwards
EX $40   NM $95   MIP n/a

Circus Game, 1914
EX $75   NM $125   MIP n/a

Citadel, 1940, Parker Brothers
EX $40   NM $60   MIP n/a

Cities, 1932, All-Fair
EX $15   NM $20   MIP n/a

City of Gold, 1926, Zulu Toy
EX $150   NM $250   MIP n/a

Classic Derby, 1930s, Doremus Schoen
EX $30   NM $50   MIP n/a

Clipper Race, 1930, Gabriel
EX $25   NM $75   MIP n/a

Clown Tenpins Game, 1912
EX $60   NM $100   MIP n/a

Coast to Coast, 1940s, Master Toy
EX $15   NM $25   MIP n/a

Cock-A-Doodle-Doo Game, 1914
EX $60   NM $100   MIP n/a

Cocked Hat, Game of, 1892, J.H. Singer
EX $100   NM $200   MIP n/a

College Baseball Game, 1890s, Parker Brothers
EX $450   NM $750   MIP n/a

College Boat Race, Game of, 1896, McLoughlin Bros.
EX $600   NM $900   MIP n/a

Colors, Game of, 1888, McLoughlin Bros.
EX $150   NM $225   MIP n/a

Columbus, 1892, Milton Bradley
EX $775   NM $1300   MIP n/a

(KP Photo)

Combination Board Games, 1922, Wilder
EX $40   NM $50   MIP n/a

Comical Animals Ten Pins, 1910, Parker Brothers
EX $185   NM $310   MIP n/a

Coney Island Playland Park, 1940, Vitaplay Toy
EX $54   NM $90   MIP n/a

Conflict, 1942, Parker Brothers
EX $50   NM $75   MIP n/a

Construction Game, 1925, Wilder
EX $500   NM $1500   MIP n/a

Coon Hunt Game, The, 1903, Parker Brothers
EX $450   NM $1200   MIP n/a

Corn & Beans, 1875, E.G. Selchow
EX $50   NM $85   MIP n/a

Corner The Market, 1938, Whitman
EX $25   NM $40   MIP n/a

Cortella, 1915, Atkins
EX $25   NM $45   MIP n/a

Cottontail and Peter, The Game of, 1922, Parker Brothers
EX $75   NM $150   MIP n/a

Country Club Golf, 1920s, Hustler Toy
EX $75   NM $125   MIP n/a

Country Store, The, 1890s, J.H. Singer
EX $100   NM $200   MIP n/a

Covered Wagon, 1927, Zulu Toy
EX $55   NM $85   MIP n/a

Cowboy Game, The, 1898, Chaffee & Selchow
EX $400   NM $700   MIP n/a

Crash, The New Airplane Game, 1928, Nucraft Toys
EX $30   NM $70   MIP n/a

Crazy Traveller, 1908, Parker Brothers
EX $40   NM $50   MIP n/a

Crime & Mystery, 1940s, Frederick H. Beach (Beachcraft)
EX $15   NM $25   MIP n/a

Criss Cross Words, 1938, Alfred Butts
EX $90   NM $150   MIP n/a

Crooked Man Game, 1914
EX $45   NM $75   MIP n/a

Cross Country, 1941, Lowe
EX $15   NM $20   MIP n/a

Cross Country Marathon, 1920s, Milton Bradley
EX $75   NM $150   MIP n/a

Cross Country Marathon Game, 1930s, Rosebud Art
EX $100   NM $200   MIP n/a

Cross Country Racer, 1940, Automatic Toy
EX $45   NM $75   MIP n/a

Cross Country Racer (w/wind-up cars), 1940s
EX $75   NM $130   MIP n/a

Crossing the Ocean, 1893, Parker Brothers
EX $75   NM $175   MIP n/a

Crow Hunt, 1904, Parker Brothers
EX $40   NM $60   MIP n/a

(KP Photo)

Crusade, 1930s, Gabriel
EX $27   NM $45   MIP n/a

Crusaders, Game of the, 1888, McLoughlin Bros.
EX $150   NM $300   MIP n/a

Cuckoo, A Society Game, 1891, J.H. Singer
EX $75   NM $150   MIP n/a

Curly Locks Game, 1910, United Game
EX $75   NM $125   MIP n/a

Cycling, Game of, 1910, Parker Brothers
EX $150   NM $300   MIP n/a

Daisy Clown Ring Game, 1927, Schacht Rubber
EX $9   NM $15   MIP n/a

Daisy Horseshoe Game, 1927, Schacht Rubber
EX $9   NM $15   MIP n/a

Danny McFayden's Stove League Baseball Game, 1920s, National Game
EX $295   NM $490   MIP n/a

Darrow Monopoly, 1934, Charles Darrow
EX $6000   NM $9000   MIP n/a

Day at the Circus, Game of, 1898, McLoughlin Bros.
EX $300   NM $400   MIP n/a

Deck Derby, 1920s, Wolverine
EX $36   NM $60   MIP n/a

Decoy, 1940, Selchow & Righter
EX $45   NM $60   MIP n/a

Defenders of The Flag Game, 1920s
EX $24   NM $40   MIP n/a

Democracy, 1940, Toy Creations
EX $50   NM $75   MIP n/a

Department Store, Game of Playing, 1898, McLoughlin Bros.
EX $750   NM $1500   MIP n/a

Derby Day, 1930, Parker Brothers
EX $45   NM $60   MIP n/a

Derby Steeple Chase, 1888, McLoughlin Bros.
EX $150   NM $250   MIP n/a

Detective, The Game of, 1889, Bliss
EX $1200   NM $2000   MIP n/a

Dewey's Victory, 1900s, Parker Brothers
EX $120   NM $200   MIP n/a

Diamond Game of Baseball, The, 1894, McLoughlin Bros.
EX $1275   NM $2150   MIP n/a

Diamond Heart, 1902, McLoughlin Bros.
EX $150   NM $225   MIP n/a

Diceball, 1938, Ray-Fair
EX $90   NM $145   MIP n/a

Dicex Baseball Game, The, 1925, Chester S. Howland
EX $195   NM $325   MIP n/a

Dick Tracy Detective Game, 1933, Einson-Freeman
EX $75   NM $150   MIP n/a

Dick Tracy Detective Game, 1937, Whitman
EX $40   NM $100   MIP n/a

Discretion, 1942, Volume Sprayer
EX $30   NM $45   MIP n/a

District Messenger Boy, Game of, 1886, McLoughlin Bros.
EX $300   NM $500   MIP n/a

District Messenger Boy, Game of, 1904, McLoughlin Bros.
EX $80   NM $200   MIP n/a

Dog Race, 1937, Transogram
EX $20   NM $40   MIP n/a

Dog Show, 1890s, J.H. Singer
EX $125   NM $300   MIP n/a

Dog Sweepstakes, 1935, Stoll & Einson
EX $45   NM $75   MIP n/a

Donald Duck's Own Party Game, 1938, Parker Brothers
EX $40   NM $100   MIP n/a

(KP Photo)

Double Game Board (Baseball), 1925, Parker Brothers
EX $40   NM $65   MIP n/a

Double Header Baseball, 1935, Redlich
EX $145   NM $250   MIP n/a

Dreamland Wonder Resort Game, 1914, Parker Brothers
EX $400   NM $800   MIP n/a

Drive 'n Putt, 1940s, Carrom Industries
EX $50   NM $90   MIP n/a

Drummer Boy Game, The, 1890s, Parker Brothers
EX $250   NM $500   MIP n/a

Dubble Up, 1940s, Gabriel
EX $15   NM $25   MIP n/a

Dudes, Game of the, 1890, Bliss
EX $225   NM $400   MIP n/a

Durgin's New Baseball Game, 1885, Durgin & Palmer
EX $425   NM $700   MIP n/a

Eagle Bombsight, 1940s, Toy Creations
EX $75   NM $150   MIP n/a

East is East and West is West, 1920s, Parker Brothers
EX $100   NM $200   MIP n/a

Easy Money, 1936, Milton Bradley
EX $35   NM $45   MIP n/a

Ed Wynn The Fire Chief, 1937, Selchow & Righter
EX $45   NM $75   MIP n/a

Eddie Cantor's Tell It To The Judge, 1930s, Parker Brothers
EX $30   NM $45   MIP n/a

E-E-YAH Base Ball Game, 1900s, National Games
EX $600   NM $1800   MIP n/a

Election, 1896, Fireside
EX $20   NM $35   MIP n/a

Electric Baseball, 1935, Einson-Freeman
EX $35   NM $60   MIP n/a

Electric Football, 1930s, Electric Football
EX $55   NM $90   MIP n/a

Electric Magnetic Baseball, 1900
EX $175   NM $295   MIP n/a

Electric Questioner, 1920, Knapp Electric & Novelty
EX $20   NM $35   MIP n/a

Electric Speed Classic, 1930, Pressman
EX $390   NM $650   MIP n/a

Electro Gameset, 1930, Knapp Electric & Novelty
EX $30   NM $45   MIP n/a

Elementaire Musical Game, 1896, Theodore Presser
EX $20   NM $35   MIP n/a

Ella Cinders, 1944, Milton Bradley
EX $30   NM $60   MIP n/a

Elmer Layden's Scientific Football Game, 1936, Cadaco
EX $20   NM $60   MIP n/a

(KP Photo)

Elsie the Cow Game, The, 1941, Selchow & Righter
EX $40   NM $80   MIP n/a

Enchanted Forest Game, 1914
EX $120   NM $200   MIP n/a

Endurance Run, 1930, Milton Bradley
EX $75   NM $150   MIP n/a

Errand Boy, The, 1891, McLoughlin Bros.
EX $200   NM $350   MIP n/a

Ethan Allen's All-Star Baseball Game, 1942, Cadaco-Ellis
EX $150   NM $400   MIP n/a

Evening Parties, Game of, 1910s, Parker Brothers
EX $180   NM $300   MIP n/a

Fairyland Game, 1880s, Milton Bradley
EX $60   NM $95   MIP n/a

Fan-i-Tis, 1913, C.W. Marsh
EX $110   NM $180   MIP n/a

(KP Photo)

Fan-Tel, 1937, Schoenhut
EX $20   NM $30   MIP n/a

Farmer Jones' Pigs, 1890, McLoughlin Bros.
EX $165   NM $200   MIP n/a

Fashionable English Sorry Game, The, 1934, Parker Brothers
EX $30   NM $50   MIP n/a

Fast Mail Game, 1910, Milton Bradley
EX $125   NM $200   MIP n/a

Fast Mail Railroad Game, 1930s, Milton Bradley
EX $75   NM $125   MIP n/a

Favorite Steeple Chase, 1895, J.H. Singer
EX $200   NM $350   MIP n/a

Ferdinand The Bull Chinese Checkers Game, 1930s
EX $60   NM $100   MIP n/a

Fibber McGee, 1936, Milton Bradley
EX $25   NM $30   MIP n/a

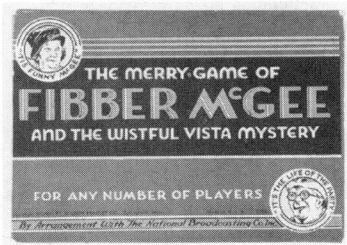
(KP Photo)

Fibber McGee and The Wistful Vista Mystery, 1940, Milton Bradley
EX $30   NM $45   MIP n/a

Fig Mill, 1916, Willis G. Young
EX $50   NM $75   MIP n/a

Finance, 1937, Parker Brothers
EX $25   NM $35   MIP n/a

(KP Photo)

Finance And Fortune, 1936, Parker Brothers
EX $20   NM $35   MIP n/a

Fire Alarm Game, 1899, Parker Brothers
EX $1300   NM $2300   MIP n/a

Fire Department, 1930s, Milton Bradley
EX $125   NM $250   MIP n/a

Fire Fighters Game, 1909, Milton Bradley
EX $120   NM $150   MIP n/a

Flag Travelette, 1895, Archarena
EX $45   NM $100   MIP n/a

Flapper Fortunes, 1929, Embossing
EX $30   NM $45   MIP n/a

Flight To Paris, 1927, Milton Bradley
EX $100   NM $200   MIP n/a

Fling-A-Ring, 1930s, Wolverine
EX $20   NM $35   MIP n/a

Flip It, 1925, American Toy Works
EX $40   NM $60   MIP n/a

Flip It, 1940, Deluxe Game
EX $20   NM $30   MIP n/a

Flip It, Auto Race & Transcontinental Tour, 1920s, Deluxe Game
EX $35   NM $90   MIP n/a

Flivver, 1927, Milton Bradley
EX $150   NM $250   MIP n/a

Flowers, Game of, 1899, Cincinnati Game
EX $30   NM $50   MIP n/a

Flying Aces, 1940s, Selchow & Righter
EX $50   NM $125   MIP n/a

Flying the Beam, 1941, Parker Brothers
EX $50   NM $80   MIP n/a

Flying the United States Airmail, 1929, Parker Brothers
EX $200   NM $400   MIP n/a

Fobaga (football), 1942, American Football
EX $50   NM $80   MIP n/a

Follow the Stars, 1922, Watts
EX $225   NM $375   MIP n/a

Foot Race, The, 1900s, Parker Brothers
EX $50   NM $75   MIP n/a

Football, 1930s, Wilder
EX $50   NM $80   MIP n/a

Football Game, 1898, Parker Brothers
EX $295   NM $495   MIP n/a

Football Knapp Electro Game Set, 1929, Knapp Electric & Novelty
EX $125   NM $205   MIP n/a

Football, The Game of, 1895, George A. Childs
EX $75   NM $125   MIP n/a

Football-As-You-Like-It, 1940, Wayne W. Light
EX $85   NM $145   MIP n/a

Fore Country Club Game of Golf, 1929, Wilder
EX $125   NM $200   MIP n/a

Fortune, 1938, Parker Brothers
EX $40   NM $50   MIP n/a

Fortune Teller, The, 1905, Milton Bradley
EX $35   NM $65   MIP n/a

Fortune Telling & Baseball Game, 1889
EX $85   NM $140   MIP n/a

Fortune Telling Game, 1934, Whitman
EX $50   NM $100   MIP n/a

Forty-Niners Gold Mining Game, 1930s, National Games
EX $25   NM $40   MIP n/a

Foto World, 1935, Cadaco
EX $90   NM $150   MIP n/a

Foto-Electric Football, 1930s, Cadaco
EX $35   NM $50   MIP n/a

Foto-Finish Horse Race, 1940s, Pressman
EX $30   NM $45   MIP n/a

Fox and Geese, 1903, McLoughlin Bros.
EX $75   NM $150   MIP n/a

Fox and Hounds, 1900, Parker Brothers
EX $85   NM $140   MIP n/a

Fox Hunt, 1905, Milton Bradley
EX $30   NM $40   MIP n/a

Fox Hunt, 1930s, Lowe
EX $20   NM $30   MIP n/a

Foxy Grandpa Hat Party, 1906, Selchow & Righter
EX $70   NM $100   MIP n/a

Frisko, 1937, Embossing
EX $20   NM $30   MIP n/a

Frog He Would a Wooing Go, The, 1898, McLoughlin Bros.
EX $1200   NM $1600   MIP n/a

Frog School Game, 1914
EX $75   NM $150   MIP n/a

Frog Who Would a Wooing Go, The, 1920s, United Game
EX $60   NM $125   MIP n/a

Fun at the Circus, 1897, McLoughlin Bros.
EX $360   NM $600   MIP n/a

(KP Photo)

Fun at the Zoo, A Game, 1902, Parker Brothers
EX $150   NM $250   MIP n/a

(KP Photo)

Fun Kit, 1939, Frederick H. Beach (Beachcraft)
EX $15   NM $20   MIP n/a

Fut-Ball, 1940s, Fut-Bal
EX $35   NM $60   MIP n/a

Game of Baseball, 1886, McLoughlin Bros.
EX $1500   NM $2000   MIP n/a

Game of Friendly Fun, 1939, Milton Bradley
EX $50   NM $145   MIP n/a

(KP Photo)

Games You Like To Play, 1920s, Parker Brothers
EX $50   NM $100   MIP n/a

Gang Busters Game, 1938, Lynco
EX $150   NM $250   MIP n/a

Gang Busters Game, 1939, Whitman
EX $50   NM $100   MIP n/a

General Headquarters, 1940s, All-Fair
EX $75   NM $100   MIP n/a

Geographical Lotto Game, 1921
EX $20   NM $30   MIP n/a

Geography Game, 1910s, A. Flanagan
EX $15   NM $25   MIP n/a

Ges It Game, 1936, Knapp Electric & Novelty
EX $20   NM $25   MIP n/a

Get The Balls Baseball Game, 1930
EX $20   NM $30   MIP n/a

(KP Photo)

Glydor, 1931, All-Fair
EX $125   NM $225   MIP n/a

G-Men Clue Games, 1935, Whitman
EX $85   NM $150   MIP n/a

Go Bang, 1898, Milton Bradley
EX $100   NM $150   MIP n/a

Go to the Head of the Class, 1938, Milton Bradley
EX $15   NM $20   MIP n/a

Going To The Fire Game, 1914, Milton Bradely
EX $90   NM $150   MIP n/a

Gold Hunters, The, 1900s, Parker Brothers
EX $85   NM $175   MIP n/a

Goldenlocks & The Three Bears, 1890, McLoughlin Bros.
EX $500   NM $800   MIP n/a

Golf Tokalon Series, The Game of, 1890s, E.O. Clark
EX $400   NM $700   MIP n/a

Golf, A Game of, 1930, Milton Bradley
EX $145   NM $245   MIP n/a

Golf, Game of, 1896, McLoughlin Bros.
EX $500   NM $715   MIP n/a

Golf, The Game of, 1898, J.H. Singer
EX $400   NM $600   MIP n/a

Golf, The Game of, 1905, Clark & Sowdon
EX $325   NM $550   MIP n/a

Gonfalon Scientific Baseball, 1930, Pioneer Game
EX $110   NM $180   MIP n/a

Good Old Aunt, The, 1892, McLoughlin Bros.
EX $100   NM $200   MIP n/a

Good Old Game of Innocence Abroad, The, 1888, Parker Brothers
EX $125   NM $300   MIP n/a

Good Things To Eat Lotto, 1940s, Gabriel
EX $15   NM $25   MIP n/a

(KP Photo)

Goose Goslin Scientific Baseball, 1935, Wheeler Toy
EX $600   NM $1000   MIP n/a

Goose, The Jolly Game of, 1851, J.P. Beach
EX $750   NM $1250   MIP n/a

Goosey Gander, Or Who Finds the Golden Egg, Game of, 1890, J.H. Singer
EX $675   NM $1150   MIP n/a

Goosy Goosy Gander, 1896, McLoughlin Bros.
EX $300   NM $500   MIP n/a

Graham McNamee World Series Scoreboard Baseball Game, 1930, Radio Sports
EX $225   NM $400   MIP n/a

Grand National Sweepstakes, 1937, Whitman
EX $20   NM $50   MIP n/a

Grande Auto Race, 1920s, Atkins
EX $75   NM $150   MIP n/a

Graphic Baseball, 1930s, Northwestern Products
EX $165   NM $275   MIP n/a

Great American Baseball Game, The, 1906, William Dapping
EX $145   NM $250   MIP n/a

Great American Flag Game, The, 1940, Parker Brothers
EX $40   NM $60   MIP n/a

Great American Game, 1910, Neddy Pocket Game
EX $145   NM $250   MIP n/a

Great American Game of Baseball, The, 1907, Pittsburgh Brewing
EX $145   NM $250   MIP n/a

Great American Game, Baseball, The, 1923, Hustler Toy
EX $150   NM $275   MIP n/a

(KP Photo)

Great American Game, The, 1925, Frantz
EX $110   NM $250   MIP n/a

Great American War Game, 1899, J.H. Hunter
EX $600   NM $1000   MIP n/a

Great Family Amusement Game, The, 1889, Einson-Freeman
EX $20   NM $35   MIP n/a

Great Horse Race Game, The, 1925, Selchow & Righter
EX $70   NM $115   MIP n/a

Gregg Football Game, 1924, Albert A. Gregg
EX $175   NM $285   MIP n/a

Greyhound Racing Game, 1938, Rex Manufacturing
EX $15   NM $25   MIP n/a

Gumps at the Seashore, The, 1930s, Milton Bradley
EX $75   NM $123   MIP n/a

Gym Horseshoes, 1930, Wolverine
EX $30   NM $45   MIP n/a

Gypsy Fortune Telling Game, The, 1895, Milton Bradley
EX $75   NM $100   MIP n/a

Halma, 1885, Horsman
EX $25   NM $50   MIP n/a

Halma, 1885, Milton Bradley
EX $25   NM $50   MIP n/a

Hand of Fate, 1901, McLoughlin Bros.
EX $1500   NM $2500   MIP n/a

Happy Family, The, 1910, Milton Bradley
EX $15   NM $25   MIP n/a

Happy Hooligan Bowling Type Game, 1925, Milton Bradley
EX $150   NM $325   MIP n/a

Hardwood Ten Pins Wooden Game, 1889
EX $60   NM $100   MIP n/a

Hare & Hound, 1895, Parker Brothers
EX $200   NM $400   MIP n/a

Hare and Hounds, 1890, McLoughlin Bros.
EX $200   NM $325   MIP n/a

Harlequin, The Game of The, 1895, McLoughlin Bros.
EX $150   NM $300   MIP n/a

Harold Teen Game, 1930s, Milton Bradley
EX $75   NM $100   MIP n/a

Heedless Tommy, 1893, McLoughlin Bros.
EX $350   NM $700   MIP n/a

Hel-Lo Telephone Game, 1898, J.H. Singer
EX $200   NM $400   MIP n/a

Helps to History, 1885, A. Flanagan
EX $20   NM $35   MIP n/a

Hen that Laid the Golden Egg, The, 1900, Parker Brothers
EX $105   NM $175   MIP n/a

Hendrik Van Loon's Wide World Game, 1935, Parker Brothers
EX $35   NM $50   MIP n/a

Hening's In-Door Game of Professional Baseball, 1889, Inventor's
EX $525   NM $875   MIP n/a

Heroes of America, 1920, Educational Card & Game
EX $20   NM $35   MIP n/a

Hialeah Horse Racing Game, 1940s,
Milton Bradley
EX $40   NM $50   MIP n/a

Hickety Pickety, 1924, Parker Brothers
EX $20   NM $40   MIP n/a

Hide and Seek, Game of, 1895,
McLoughlin Bros.
EX $1500   NM $2000   MIP n/a

Hippodrome Circus Game, 1895, Milton
Bradley
EX $175   NM $300   MIP n/a

Hippodrome, The, 1900s, E.O. Clark
EX $150   NM $200   MIP n/a

Hit and Run Baseball Game, 1930s,
Wilder
EX $150   NM $325   MIP n/a

Hit That Line, 1930s, LaRue Sales
EX $100   NM $165   MIP n/a

Hi-Way Henry, 1928, All-Fair
EX $600   NM $1500   MIP n/a

Hockey, Official, 1940, Toy Creations
EX $50   NM $75   MIP n/a

Hold The Fort, 1895, Parker Brothers
EX $150   NM $350   MIP n/a

Hold Your Horses, 1930s, Klauber Novelty
EX $10   NM $20   MIP n/a

Home Baseball Game, 1897, McLoughlin
Bros.
EX $900   NM $1700   MIP n/a

Home Defenders, 1941, Saalfield
EX $15   NM $25   MIP n/a

Home Diamond, The Great Baseball
Game, 1925, Phillips
EX $175   NM $295   MIP n/a

Home Games, 1900s, Martin
EX $105   NM $175   MIP n/a

Home Run King, 1930s, Selrite
EX $275   NM $450   MIP n/a

Home Run with Bases Loaded, 1935, T.V.
Morrison
EX $205   NM $350   MIP n/a

Honey Bee Game, 1913, Milton Bradley
EX $50   NM $85   MIP n/a

Hood's Spelling School, 1897, C.I. Hood
EX $20   NM $35   MIP n/a

Hoop-O-Loop, 1930, Wolverine
EX $20   NM $30   MIP n/a

Hornet, 1941, Lowe
EX $30   NM $45   MIP n/a

Horse Race, 1943, Lowe
EX $10   NM $20   MIP n/a

Horse Racing, 1935, Milton Bradley
EX $35   NM $60   MIP n/a

Horses, 1927, Modern Makers
EX $45   NM $75   MIP n/a

Hounds & Hares, 1894, J.W. Keller
EX $35   NM $60   MIP n/a

How Good Are You?, 1937, Whitman
EX $10   NM $15   MIP n/a

Howard H. Jones Collegiate Football,
1932, Municipal Service
EX $65   NM $100   MIP n/a

Huddle All-American Football Game, 1931
EX $100   NM $165   MIP n/a

Hunting Hare, Game of, 1891,
McLoughlin Bros.
EX $205   NM $350   MIP n/a

Hunting the Rabbit, 1895, Clark & Sowdon
EX $70   NM $115   MIP n/a

Hunting, The New Game of, 1904,
McLoughlin Bros.
EX $500   NM $800   MIP n/a

Hurdle Race, 1905, Milton Bradley
EX $75   NM $150   MIP n/a

Hymn Quartets, 1933, Goodenough and
Woglom
EX $10   NM $15   MIP n/a

Ice Hockey, 1942, Milton Bradley
EX $60   NM $85   MIP n/a

Improved Geographical Game, The,
1890s, Parker Brothers
EX $35   NM $55   MIP n/a

In and Out the Window, 1940s, Gabriel
EX $20   NM $35   MIP n/a

India, 1940, Parker Brothers
EX $15   NM $20   MIP n/a

India Bombay, 1910s, Cutler & Saleeby
EX $15   NM $25   MIP n/a

India, An Oriental Game, 1890s,
McLoughlin Bros.
EX $65   NM $100   MIP n/a

India, Game of, 1910s, Milton Bradley
EX $15   NM $40   MIP n/a

Indianapolis 500 Mile Race Game, 1938,
Shaw
EX $350   NM $575   MIP n/a

Indians and Cowboys, 1940s, Gabriel
EX $40   NM $50   MIP n/a

In-Door Baseball, 1926, E. Bommer
Foundation
EX $100   NM $180   MIP n/a

Indoor Football, 1919, Underwood
EX $145   NM $250   MIP n/a

Indoor Horse Racing, 1924, Man-O-War
EX $70   NM $115   MIP n/a

Inside Baseball Game, 1911, Popular
Games
EX $300   NM $500   MIP n/a

(KP Photo)

Intercollegiate Football, 1923, Hustler Toy
EX $175   NM $245   MIP n/a

International Automobile Race, 1903,
Parker Brothers
EX $700   NM $900   MIP n/a

International Spy, Game of, 1943, All-Fair
EX $65   NM $90   MIP n/a

Jack and Jill, 1890s, Parker Brothers
EX $55   NM $150   MIP n/a

Jack and Jill, 1909, Milton Bradley
EX $50   NM $75   MIP n/a

Jack and the Bean Stalk, 1895, Parker
Brothers
EX $110   NM $175   MIP n/a

Jack and the Bean Stalk, The Game of,
1898, McLoughlin Bros.
EX $550   NM $900   MIP n/a

Jack Spratt Game, 1914
EX $45   NM $75   MIP n/a

Jack-Be-Nimble, 1940s, Embossing
EX $20   NM $35   MIP n/a

Jackie Robinson Baseball Game, 1940s,
Gotham
EX $425   NM $900   MIP n/a

Jackpot, 1943, B.L. Fry Products
EX $15   NM $25   MIP n/a

Japan, The Game of, 1903, J. Ottmann
Lith.
EX $180   NM $300   MIP n/a

Japanese Games of Cash and Akambo,
1881, McLoughlin Bros.
EX $150   NM $250   MIP n/a

Jeep Board, The, 1944, Lowe
EX $15   NM $20   MIP n/a

Jeffries Championship Playing Cards, 1904
EX $35   NM $55   MIP n/a

Jig Chase, 1930s, Game Makers
EX $20   NM $30   MIP n/a

Jig Race, 1930s, Game Makers
EX $20   NM $30   MIP n/a

Jockey, 1920s, Carrom Industries
EX $35   NM $60   MIP n/a

GAMES

John Gilpin, Rainbow Backgammon and Bewildered Travelers, 1875, McLoughlin Bros.
EX $150   NM $300   MIP n/a

Johnny Get Your Gun, 1928, Parker Brothers
EX $75   NM $100   MIP n/a

Jolly Pirates, 1938, Russell
EX $20   NM $35   MIP n/a

Journey to Bethlehem, The, 1923, Parker Brothers
EX $95   NM $160   MIP n/a

Jumpy Tinker, 1920s, Tinker Toys
EX $20   NM $30   MIP n/a

Jungle Hunt, 1940s, Rosebud Art
EX $30   NM $50   MIP n/a

Junior Baseball Game, 1915, Benjamin Seller
EX $100   NM $165   MIP n/a

Junior Basketball Game, 1930s, Rosebud Art
EX $55   NM $125   MIP n/a

Junior Bicycle Game, The, 1897, Parker Brothers
EX $250   NM $350   MIP n/a

Junior Combination Board, 1905, McLoughlin Bros.
EX $20   NM $30   MIP n/a

Junior Football, 1944, Deluxe Game
EX $30   NM $45   MIP n/a

Junior Motor Race, 1925, Wolverine
EX $40   NM $70   MIP n/a

Kan-Oo-Win-It, 1893, McLoughlin Bros.
EX $345   NM $575   MIP n/a

Kate Smith's Own Game America, 1940s, Toy Creations
EX $40   NM $60   MIP n/a

Keeping Up with the Jones', 1921, Parker Brothers
EX $50   NM $85   MIP n/a

Keeping Up with the Jones', The Game of, 1921, Phillips
EX $75   NM $100   MIP n/a

Kellogg's Baseball Game, 1936, Kellogg's
EX $25   NM $35   MIP n/a

Kellogg's Boxing Game, 1936, Kellogg's
EX $35   NM $55   MIP n/a

Kellogg's Football Game, 1936, Kellogg's
EX $25   NM $40   MIP n/a

Kellogg's Golf Game, 1936, Kellogg's
EX $25   NM $40   MIP n/a

Kentucky Derby Racing Game, 1938, Whitman
EX $20   NM $40   MIP n/a

Kilkenny Cats, The Amusing Game of, 1890, Parker Brothers
EX $250   NM $600   MIP n/a

Kings, 1931, Akro Agate
EX $55   NM $95   MIP n/a

King's Quoits, New Game of, 1893, McLoughlin Bros.
EX $300   NM $450   MIP n/a

Kitty Kat Cup Ball, 1930s, Rosebud Art
EX $50   NM $75   MIP n/a

Klondike Game, 1890s, Parker Brothers
EX $400   NM $625   MIP n/a

Knockout, 1937, Scarne Games
EX $55   NM $90   MIP n/a

Knute Rockne Football Game, Official, 1930, Radio Sports
EX $200   NM $400   MIP n/a

Ko-Ko the Clown, 1940, All-Fair
EX $20   NM $30   MIP n/a

Kriegspiel Junior, 1915, Parker Brothers
EX $50   NM $80   MIP n/a

La Haza, 1923, Supply Sales
EX $10   NM $20   MIP n/a

Lame Duck, The, 1928, Parker Brothers
EX $60   NM $100   MIP n/a

Land and Sea War Games, 1941, Lowe
EX $40   NM $65   MIP n/a

Lasso the Jumping Ring, 1912
EX $60   NM $100   MIP n/a

Le Choc, 1919, Milton Bradley
EX $50   NM $85   MIP n/a

League Parlor Base Ball, 1889, Bliss
EX $600   NM $1000   MIP n/a

Leap Frog Game, 1900, McLoughlin Bros.
EX $165   NM $275   MIP n/a

Leap Frog, Game of, 1910, McLoughlin Bros.
EX $100   NM $150   MIP n/a

Lee at Havana, 1899, Chaffee & Selchow
EX $100   NM $200   MIP n/a

Leslie's Baseball Game, 1909, Perfection Novelty
EX $145   NM $250   MIP n/a

Let's go to College, 1944, Einson-Freeman
EX $30   NM $45   MIP n/a

Let's Play Games, Golf, 1939, American Toy Works
EX $50   NM $80   MIP n/a

Let's Play Polo, 1940, American Toy Works
EX $45   NM $75   MIP n/a

Letter Carrier, The, 1890, McLoughlin Bros.
EX $150   NM $300   MIP n/a

Letters, 1878, Horsman
EX $30   NM $45   MIP n/a

Letters or Anagrams, 1890s, Parker Brothers
EX $25   NM $40   MIP n/a

Lew Fonseca Baseball Game, The, 1920s, Carrom Industries
EX $525   NM $875   MIP n/a

Library of Games, 1938, American Toy Works
EX $15   NM $20   MIP n/a

Life in the Wild West, 1894, Bliss
EX $300   NM $500   MIP n/a

Life of the Party, 1940s, Rosebud Art
EX $25   NM $35   MIP n/a

Life's Mishaps & Bobbing 'Round the Circle, 1891, McLoughlin Bros.
EX $150   NM $200   MIP n/a

Light Horse H. Cooper Golf Game, 1943, Trojan Games
EX $175   NM $295   MIP n/a

(KP Photo)

Limited Mail & Express Game, The, 1894, Parker Brothers
EX $200   NM $275   MIP n/a

Lindy Hop-Off, 1927, Parker Brothers
EX $300   NM $400   MIP n/a

Literature Game, 1897, L.J. Colby
EX $15   NM $25   MIP n/a

Little Black Sambo, Game of, 1934, Einson-Freeman
EX $100   NM $150   MIP n/a

Little Bo-Beep Game, 1914
EX $60   NM $100   MIP n/a

Little Boy Blue, 1910s, Milton Bradley
EX $50   NM $85   MIP n/a

Little Colonel, 1936, Selchow & Righter
EX $50   NM $100   MIP n/a

Little Cowboy Game, The, 1895, Parker Brothers
EX $200   NM $600   MIP n/a

Little Fireman Game, 1897, McLoughlin Bros.
EX $4000   NM $6000   MIP n/a

Little Jack Horner Golf Course, 1920s
EX $145   NM $250   MIP n/a

Little Jack Horner, A Game, 1910s, Milton Bradley
EX $45   NM $75   MIP n/a

Little Nemo Game, 1914
EX $500   NM $1000   MIP n/a

(KP Photo)

Little Orphan Annie Game, 1927, Milton Bradley
EX $125   NM $200   MIP n/a

GAMES

Little Red Riding Hood, 1900, McLoughlin Bros.
EX $300   NM $500   MIP n/a

Little Shoppers, 1915, Gibson Game
EX $150   NM $300   MIP n/a

Little Soldier, The, 1900s, United Game
EX $125   NM $160   MIP n/a

London Bridge, 1899, J.H. Singer
EX $100   NM $150   MIP n/a

London Game, The, 1898, Parker Brothers
EX $165   NM $275   MIP n/a

Lone Ranger Game, The, 1938, Parker Brothers
EX $40   NM $60   MIP n/a

Looping the Loop, 1940s, Advance Games
EX $25   NM $40   MIP n/a

Los Angeles Rams Football Game, 1930s, Zondine
EX $175   NM $295   MIP n/a

Lost Diamond, Game of, 1896, McLoughlin
EX $200   NM $250   MIP n/a

Lost in the Woods, 1895, McLoughlin Bros.
EX $660   NM $900   MIP n/a

(KP Photo)

Lotto, 1932, Milton Bradley
EX $6   NM $10   MIP n/a

Lou Gehrig's Official Playball, 1930s, Christy Walsh
EX $525   NM $875   MIP n/a

Lowell Thomas' World Cruise, 1937, Parker Brothers
EX $75   NM $250   MIP n/a

Luck, The Game of, 1892, Parker Brothers
EX $60   NM $100   MIP n/a

Lucky 7th Baseball Game, 1937, All-American
EX $100   NM $250   MIP n/a

Mac Baseball Game, 1930s, Mc Dowell
EX $145   NM $250   MIP n/a

Macy's Pirate Treasure Hunt, 1942, Einson-Freeman
EX $20   NM $35   MIP n/a

Madrap, The New Game of, 1914
EX $45   NM $75   MIP n/a

Magic Race, 1942, Habob
EX $55   NM $90   MIP n/a

Magnetic Jack Straws, 1891, Horsman
EX $20   NM $35   MIP n/a

Magnetic Treasure Hunt, 1930s, American Toy Works
EX $15   NM $25   MIP n/a

(KP Photo)

Mail, Express or Accommodation, Game of, 1895, McLoughlin Bros.
EX $800   NM $1200   MIP n/a

Mail, Express or Accommodation, Game of, 1920s, Milton Bradley
EX $135   NM $175   MIP n/a

Major League Ball, 1921, National Game Makers
EX $325   NM $550   MIP n/a

Major League Base Ball Game, 1912, Philadelphia Game
EX $650   NM $1000   MIP n/a

Man Hunt, 1937, Parker Brothers
EX $200   NM $350   MIP n/a

Man in the Moon, 1901, McLoughlin Bros.
EX $2000   NM $3000   MIP n/a

Mansion of Happiness, 1843, Ives
EX $300   NM $400   MIP n/a

Mansion of Happiness, 1864, Ives
EX $150   NM $200   MIP n/a

Mansion of Happiness, The, 1895, McLoughlin Bros.
EX $510   NM $800   MIP n/a

Marathon Game, The, 1930s, Rosebud Art
EX $85   NM $150   MIP n/a

Marriage, The Game of, 1899, J.H. Singer
EX $200   NM $300   MIP n/a

Match 'em, 1926, All-Fair
EX $12   NM $20   MIP n/a

Mathers Parlor Baseball Game, 1909, McClurg
EX $50   NM $100   MIP n/a

Meet the Missus, 1937, Fitzpatrick Brothers
EX $45   NM $75   MIP n/a

Mental Whoopee, 1936, Simon & Schuster
EX $10   NM $15   MIP n/a

Merry Hunt, The, Singer
EX $250   NM $400   MIP n/a

Merry Steeple Chase, 1890s, J. Ottmann Lith.
EX $45   NM $100   MIP n/a

Merry-Go-Round, 1898, Chaffee & Selchow
EX $2000   NM $2500   MIP n/a

Messenger Boy Game, 1910, J.H. Singer
EX $100   NM $200   MIP n/a

Messenger, The, 1890, McLoughlin Bros.
EX $175   NM $300   MIP n/a

Mexican Pete - I Got It, 1940s, Parker Brothers
EX $25   NM $40   MIP n/a

Mickey Mouse Baseball, 1936, Post Cereal
EX $55   NM $90   MIP n/a

Mickey Mouse Big Box of Games & Things To Color, 1930s
EX $45   NM $75   MIP n/a

Mickey Mouse Circus Game, 1930s, Marks Brothers
EX $180   NM $300   MIP n/a

Mickey Mouse Coming Home Game, 1930s, Marks Brothers
EX $125   NM $200   MIP n/a

Mickey Mouse Roll'em Game, 1930s, Marks Brothers
EX $90   NM $150   MIP n/a

Midget Auto Race, 1930s, Cracker Jack
EX $10   NM $15   MIP n/a

Midget Speedway, Game of, 1942, Whitman
EX $55   NM $90   MIP n/a

Miles at Porto Rico, 1899, Chaffee & Selchow
EX $150   NM $250   MIP n/a

Miniature Golf, 1930s, Miniature Golf
EX $35   NM $60   MIP n/a

Miss Muffet Game, 1914
EX $60   NM $100   MIP n/a

Mistress Mary, Quite Contrary, 1905, Parker Brothers
EX $60   NM $105   MIP n/a

Modern Game Assortment, 1930s, Pressman
EX $25   NM $40   MIP n/a

Moneta: "Money Makes Money," Game of, 1889, F.A. Wright
EX $90   NM $150   MIP n/a

Monkey Shines, 1940, All-Fair
EX $20   NM $30   MIP n/a

Monopolist, Mariner's Compass And Ten Up, 1878, McLoughlin Bros.
EX $350   NM $600   MIP n/a

Monopoly, 1935, Parker Brothers
EX $35   NM $75   MIP n/a

Monopoly Jr. Edition, 1936, Parker Brothers
EX $20   NM $30   MIP n/a

Moon Mullins Automobile Race, 1927, Milton Bradley
EX $150   NM $200   MIP n/a

(KP Photo)

Mother Goose Bowling Game, 1884, Charles M. Crandall
EX $510   NM $850   MIP n/a

Mother Goose, Game of, 1921, Stoll & Edwards
EX $30   NM $50   MIP n/a

Mother Hubbard Game, 1914
EX $60   NM $100   MIP n/a

Motor Boat Race, An Exciting, 1930, American Toy Works
EX $150   NM $300   MIP n/a

(KP Photo)

Motor Cycle Game, 1905, Milton Bradley
EX $350   NM $600   MIP n/a

Motor Race, 1922, Wolverine
EX $90   NM $150   MIP n/a

Movie Inn, 1917, Willis G. Young
EX $45   NM $75   MIP n/a

Movie Millions, 1938, Transogram
EX $100   NM $250   MIP n/a

Movie-Land Lotto, 1920s, Milton Bradley
EX $45   NM $75   MIP n/a

Moving Picture Game, The, 1920s, Milton Bradley
EX $70   NM $120   MIP n/a

Mr. Ree, 1937, Selchow & Righter
EX $40   NM $75   MIP n/a

Mutuels, 1938, Mutuels
EX $85   NM $150   MIP n/a

My Word, Horse Race, 1938, American Toy Works
EX $60   NM $100   MIP n/a

Mythology, Game of, 1884, Peter G. Thompson
EX $65   NM $75   MIP n/a

Napoleon, Game of, 1895, Parker Brothers
EX $600   NM $800   MIP n/a

National Derby Horse Race, 1938, Whitman
EX $20   NM $35   MIP n/a

National Game of Baseball, The, 1900s
EX $500   NM $875   MIP n/a

National Game of the American Eagle, The, 1844, Ives
EX $1500   NM $2500   MIP n/a

National Game, The, 1889, National Game
EX $875   NM $1450   MIP n/a

(KP Photo)

National League Ball Game, 1890, Yankee Novelty
EX $350   NM $575   MIP n/a

Naval Maneuvers, 1920, McLoughlin Bros.
EX $800   NM $1200   MIP n/a

Navigator, 1938, Whitman
EX $45   NM $75   MIP n/a

Navigator Boat Race, 1890s, McLoughlin Bros.
EX $115   NM $195   MIP n/a

(KP Photo)

Nebbs on the Air, A Radio Game, 1930s, Milton Bradley
EX $75   NM $125   MIP n/a

Nebbs, Game of the, 1930s, Milton Bradley
EX $40   NM $75   MIP n/a

Neck and Neck, 1929, Embossing
EX $25   NM $40   MIP n/a

Neck and Neck, 1930, Wolverine
EX $75   NM $100   MIP n/a

Nellie Bly, 1898, J.H. Singer
EX $200   NM $300   MIP n/a

New Baseball Game, 1885, Clark & Martin
EX $165   NM $275   MIP n/a

New Parlor Game of Baseball, 1896, Sumner
EX $5000   NM $10000   MIP n/a

New York Recorder Newspaper Supplement Baseball Game, 1896
EX $430   NM $715   MIP n/a

Newsboy, Game of the, 1890, Bliss
EX $1200   NM $2000   MIP n/a

NFL Strategy, 1935, Tudor
EX $45   NM $70   MIP n/a

Nine Men Morris, 1930s, Milton Bradley
EX $15   NM $20   MIP n/a

Nineteenth Hole Golf Game, 1930s, Einson-Freeman
EX $85   NM $140   MIP n/a

Nip & Tuck Hockey, 1928, Parker Brothers
EX $115   NM $195   MIP n/a

No-Joke, 1941, Volume Sprayer
EX $12   NM $20   MIP n/a

Nok-Out Baseball Game, 1930, Dizzy & Daffy Dean
EX $350   NM $575   MIP n/a

North Pole Game, The, 1907, Milton Bradley
EX $200   NM $500   MIP n/a

Object Lotto, 1940s, Gabriel
EX $15   NM $25   MIP n/a

Obstacle Race, 1930s, Wilder
EX $70   NM $115   MIP n/a

Ocean to Ocean Flight Game, 1927, Wilder
EX $75   NM $100   MIP n/a

Office Boy, The, 1889, Parker Brothers
EX $200   NM $300   MIP n/a

Official Radio Baseball Game, 1930s, Toy Creations
EX $50   NM $75   MIP n/a

Official Radio Basketball Game, 1939, Toy Creations
EX $25   NM $50   MIP n/a

Official Radio Football Game, 1940, Toy Creations
EX $25   NM $50   MIP n/a

Old Hunter & His Game, 1870
EX $175   NM $295   MIP n/a

Old Maid, 1898, Chaffee & Selchow
EX $75   NM $100   MIP n/a

(KP Photo)

Old Maid & Old Bachelor, The Merry Game of, 1898, McLoughlin Bros.
EX $300   NM $500   MIP n/a

Old Maid or Matrimony, Game of, 1890, McLoughlin Bros.
EX $300   NM $500   MIP n/a

Old Mother Goose, 1898, Chaffee & Selchow
EX $105   NM $175   MIP n/a

Old Mother Hubbard, Game of, 1890s, Milton Bradley
EX $60   NM $80   MIP n/a

Old Mrs. Goose, Game of, 1910, Milton Bradley
EX $50   NM $85   MIP n/a

Oldtimers, 1940, Frederick H. Beach (Beachcraft)
EX $15   NM $20   MIP n/a

Ollo, 1944, Games Of Fame
EX $15   NM $25   MIP n/a

Olympic Runners, 1930, Wolverine
EX $125   NM $175   MIP n/a

On the Mid-Way, 1925, Milton Bradley
EX $90   NM $150   MIP n/a

One Two Button Your Shoe, 1940s, Master Toy
EX $15   NM $25   MIP n/a

Open Championship Golf Game, 1930s, Beacon Hudson
EX $45   NM $75   MIP n/a

Opportunity Hour, 1940, American Toy Works
EX $20   NM $35   MIP n/a

Ot-O-Win Football, 1920s, Ot-O-Win Toys & Games, W. Planchette
EX $55   NM $90   MIP n/a

Ouija, plywood, 1920, William Fuld
EX $60   NM $100   MIP n/a

Our Defenders, 1944, Master Toy
EX $20   NM $40   MIP n/a

Our National Ball Game, 1887, McGill & DeLany
EX $500   NM $750   MIP n/a

Our No. 7 Baseball Game Puzzle, 1910, Satisfactory
EX $110   NM $180   MIP n/a

Our Union, 1896, Fireside Game
EX $25   NM $40   MIP n/a

Outboard Motor Race, The, 1930s, Milton Bradley
EX $75   NM $100   MIP n/a

Overland Limited, The, 1920s, Milton Bradley
EX $100   NM $150   MIP n/a

Owl and the Pussy Cat, The, 1900s, E.O. Clark
EX $210   NM $350   MIP n/a

Pana Kanal, The Great Panama Canal Game, 1913, Chaffee & Selchow
EX $65   NM $110   MIP n/a

Panama Canal Game, 1910, Parker Brothers
EX $200   NM $400   MIP n/a

Pan-Cake Tiddly Winks, 1920s, Russell
EX $55   NM $100   MIP n/a

Par Golf Card Game, 1920, National Golf Services
EX $115   NM $195   MIP n/a

Par, The New Golf Game, 1926, Russell
EX $115   NM $195   MIP n/a

Parcheesi, 1880s, H.B. Chaffee
EX $50   NM $75   MIP n/a

Parker Brothers Post Office Game, 1910s, Parker Brothers
EX $105   NM $175   MIP n/a

Parlor Base Ball, Game of, 1892, McLoughlin
EX $1400   NM $2200   MIP n/a

Parlor Baseball Game, 1908, Mathers
EX $200   NM $325   MIP n/a

Parlor Croquet, 1940, Pressman
EX $15   NM $25   MIP n/a

Parlor Football Game, 1890s, McLoughlin Bros.
EX $700   NM $1100   MIP n/a

Parlor Golf, 1897, Chaffee & Selchow
EX $55   NM $90   MIP n/a

Pat Moran's Own Baseball Game, 1919, Smith, Kline & French
EX $325   NM $400   MIP n/a

Patent Parlor Bowling Alley, 1899, Thomas Kochka
EX $70   NM $115   MIP n/a

Pedestrianism, 1879
EX $350   NM $700   MIP n/a

Peg at my Heart, 1914, Willis G. Young
EX $20   NM $45   MIP n/a

Peg Baseball, 1915, Parker Brothers
EX $75   NM $150   MIP n/a

(KP Photo)

Peg Baseball, 1924, Parker Brothers
EX $50   NM $75   MIP n/a

Peggy, 1923, Parker Brothers
EX $35   NM $55   MIP n/a

Peg'ity, 1925, Parker Brothers
EX $10   NM $25   MIP n/a

Pegpin, Game of, 1929, Stoll & Edwards
EX $25   NM $45   MIP n/a

Pe-Ling, 1923, Cookson & Sullivan
EX $25   NM $45   MIP n/a

Pennant Puzzle, 1909, L.W. Hardy
EX $250   NM $400   MIP n/a

Pennant Winner, 1930s, Wolverine
EX $175   NM $225   MIP n/a

Penny Post, 1892, Parker Brothers
EX $150   NM $350   MIP n/a

Peter Pan, 1927, Selchow & Righter
EX $150   NM $200   MIP n/a

Peter Peter Pumpkin Eater, 1914, Parker Brothers
EX $60   NM $125   MIP n/a

Peter Rabbit Game, 1910, Milton Bradley
EX $55   NM $95   MIP n/a

Peter Rabbit Game, 1940s, Gabriel
EX $45   NM $75   MIP n/a

Philadelphia Inquirer Baseball Game, The, 1896
EX $145   NM $250   MIP n/a

Philo Vance, 1937, Parker Brothers
EX $90   NM $175   MIP n/a

(KP Photo)

Phoebe Snow, Game of, 1899, McLoughlin Bros.
EX $150   NM $300   MIP n/a

Piggies, The New Game, 1894, Selchow & Righter
EX $330   NM $550   MIP n/a

Pigskin, 1940, Parker Brothers
EX $20   NM $40   MIP n/a

Pigskin, Tom Hamilton's Football Game, 1934, Parker Brothers
EX $25   NM $45   MIP n/a

Pilgrim's Progress, Going To Sunday School, Tower of Babel, 1875, McLoughlin Bros.
EX $120   NM $250   MIP n/a

Pinafore, 1879, Fuller Upham
EX $45   NM $125   MIP n/a

Pinch Hitter, 1930s
EX $110   NM $180   MIP n/a

Pines, The, 1896, Fireside Game
EX $15   NM $25   MIP n/a

Pinocchio Pitfalls Marble Game, 1940
EX $30   NM $50   MIP n/a

Pinocchio Ring The Nose Game, 1940
EX $20   NM $30   MIP n/a

Pioneers of the Santa Fe Trail, 1935, Einson-Freeman
EX $25   NM $40   MIP n/a

Pirate & Traveller, 1936, Milton Bradley
EX $20   NM $45   MIP n/a

Pirate Ship, 1940, Lowe
EX $15   NM $25   MIP n/a

Pla-Golf Board Game, 1938, Pla-Golf
EX $775   NM $1300   MIP n/a

Play Ball, 1920, National Game
EX $145   NM $250   MIP n/a

Play Football, 1934, Whitman
EX $55   NM $90   MIP n/a

Play Hockey Fun with Popeye & Wimpy, 1935, Barnum
EX $205   NM $350   MIP n/a

Pocket Baseball, 1940, Toy Creations
EX $15   NM $25   MIP n/a

Pocket Edition Major League Baseball Game, 1943, Anderson
EX $85   NM $140   MIP n/a

Pocket Football, 1940, Toy Creations
EX $25   NM $40   MIP n/a

Polar Ball Baseball, 1940, Bowline Game
EX $90   NM $145   MIP n/a

Pool, Game of, 1898
EX $700   NM $1175   MIP n/a

Posting, A Merry Game of, 1890s, J.H. Singer
EX $180   NM $300   MIP n/a

Pro Baseball, 1940
EX $70   NM $115   MIP n/a

Professional Game of Base Ball, 1896, Parker Bros.
EX $500   NM $1500   MIP n/a

Psychic Baseball Game, 1935, Parker Brothers
EX $100   NM $200   MIP n/a

Quarterback, 1914, Littlefield
EX $100   NM $165   MIP n/a

Rabbit Hunt, Game of, 1870, McLoughlin Bros.
EX $150   NM $250   MIP n/a

GAMES

Race for the Cup, 1910s, Milton Bradley
  EX $225   **NM** $350   **MIP** n/a

Race, The Game of the, 1860s
  EX $425   **NM** $715   **MIP** n/a

Races, The Game of the, 1844, William Crosby
  EX $850   **NM** $1400   **MIP** n/a

Racing Stable, Game of, 1936, D & H Games
  EX $115   **NM** $195   **MIP** n/a

Radio Game, 1926, Milton Bradley
  EX $75   **NM** $150   **MIP** n/a

Raggedy Ann's Magic Pebble Game, 1941, Milton Bradley
  EX $50   **NM** $90   **MIP** n/a

Rainy Day Golf, 1920, Selchow & Righter
  EX $75   **NM** $100   **MIP** n/a

Rambles, 1881, American
  EX $195   **NM** $275   **MIP** n/a

Razz-O-Dazz-O Six Man Football, 1938, Gruhn & Melton
  EX $60   **NM** $100   **MIP** n/a

Realistic Baseball, 1925, Realistic Game & Toy
  EX $205   **NM** $350   **MIP** n/a

Realistic Golf, 1898, Parker Brothers
  EX $875   **NM** $1450   **MIP** n/a

Red Riding Hood, Game of, 1898, Chaffee & Selchow
  EX $200   **NM** $350   **MIP** n/a

Red Ryder Target Game, 1939, Whitman
  EX $100   **NM** $150   **MIP** n/a

Rex and the Kilkenny Cats Game, 1892, Parker Brothers
  EX $100   **NM** $150   **MIP** n/a

Ring-A-Peg, 1885, Horsman
  EX $25   **NM** $45   **MIP** n/a

Rip Van Winkle, 1890s, Clark & Sowdon
  EX $175   **NM** $225   **MIP** n/a

Rival Policemen, 1896, McLoughlin Bros.
  EX $2000   **NM** $3500   **MIP** n/a

Road Race, Air Race (Two-game set), 1928, Wilder
  EX $100   **NM** $150   **MIP** n/a

Robinson Crusoe, Game of, 1909, Milton Bradley
  EX $30   **NM** $75   **MIP** n/a

Roll-O Football, 1923, Supply Sales
  EX $35   **NM** $60   **MIP** n/a

Roll-O Golf, 1923, Supply Sales
  EX $35   **NM** $60   **MIP** n/a

Roll-O Junior Baseball Game, 1922, Roll-O
  EX $325   **NM** $550   **MIP** n/a

Roll-O-Motor Speedway, 1922, Supply Sales
  EX $65   **NM** $110   **MIP** n/a

Roly Poly Game, 1910
  EX $30   **NM** $50   **MIP** n/a

Rose Bowl Championship Football Game, 1940s, Lowe
  EX $40   **NM** $80   **MIP** n/a

Rough Riders, The Game of, 1898, Clark & Sowdon
  EX $225   **NM** $350   **MIP** n/a

Roulette Baseball Game, 1929, W. Barthonomae
  EX $115   **NM** $195   **MIP** n/a

Round the World Game, 1914, Milton Bradley
  EX $75   **NM** $125   **MIP** n/a

(KP Photo)

Round the World with Nellie Bly, 1890, McLoughlin Bros.
  EX $210   **NM** $300   **MIP** n/a

Royal Game of Kings and Queens, 1892, McLoughlin Bros.
  EX $375   **NM** $500   **MIP** n/a

Rube Bressler's Baseball Game, 1936, Bressler
  EX $130   **NM** $215   **MIP** n/a

Rube Walker & Harry Davis Baseball Game, 1905
  EX $875   **NM** $1450   **MIP** n/a

Rummy Football, 1944, Milton Bradley
  EX $35   **NM** $60   **MIP** n/a

Runaway Sheep, 1892, Bliss
  EX $165   **NM** $275   **MIP** n/a

Saratoga Horse Racing Game, 1920, Milton Bradley
  EX $40   **NM** $75   **MIP** n/a

Saratoga Steeple Chase, 1900, J.H. Singer
  EX $250   **NM** $400   **MIP** n/a

Scout, The, 1900s, E.O. Clark
  EX $105   **NM** $175   **MIP** n/a

GAME OF SCOUTING
FOR BOY SCOUTS

(KP Photo)

Scouting, Game of, 1930s, Milton Bradley
  EX $200   **NM** $250   **MIP** n/a

Scrambles, 1941, Frederick H. Beach (Beachcraft)
  EX $15   **NM** $20   **MIP** n/a

Shadow Game, The, 1940s, Toy Creations
  EX $1000   **NM** $1500   **MIP** n/a

Shopping, Game of, 1891, Bliss
  EX $1500   **NM** $2000   **MIP** n/a

Shufflebug, Game of, 1921
  EX $20   **NM** $30   **MIP** n/a

Siege of Havana, The, 1898, Parker Brothers
  EX $180   **NM** $250   **MIP** n/a

Sippa Fish, 1936, Frederick H. Beach (Beachcraft)
  EX $5   **NM** $10   **MIP** n/a

Skating Race Game, The, 1900, Chaffee & Selchow
  EX $600   **NM** $1000   **MIP** n/a

Skeezix and the Air Mail, 1930s, Milton Bradley
  EX $65   **NM** $100   **MIP** n/a

Skeezix Visits Nina, 1930s, Milton Bradley
  EX $65   **NM** $125   **MIP** n/a

Ski-Hi New York to Paris, 1927, Cutler & Saleeby
  EX $50   **NM** $100   **MIP** n/a

GAME OF SKIPPY
LICENSED BY PERCY CROSBY

(KP Photo)

Skippy, Game of, 1932, Milton Bradley
  EX $75   **NM** $100   **MIP** n/a

Skirmish at Harper's Ferry, 1891, McLoughlin Bros.
  EX $450   **NM** $1200   **MIP** n/a

Skor-It Bagatelle, 1930s, Northwestern Products
  EX $145   **NM** $250   **MIP** n/a

Sky Hawks, 1931, All-Fair
  EX $120   **NM** $200   **MIP** n/a

Skyscraper, 1937, Parker Brothers
  EX $250   **NM** $400   **MIP** n/a

Slide Kelly! Baseball Game, 1936, B.E. Ruth
  EX $70   **NM** $115   **MIP** n/a

Slugger Baseball Game, 1930, Marks Brothers
  EX $110   **NM** $180   **MIP** n/a

Smitty Game, 1930s, Milton Bradley
  EX $200   **NM** $300   **MIP** n/a

Smitty Speed Boat Race Game, 1930s, Milton Bradley
  EX $50   **NM** $100   **MIP** n/a

Snake Game, 1890s, McLoughlin Bros.
  EX $2000   **NM** $3000   **MIP** n/a

Snap Dragon, 1903, H.B. Chaffee
  EX $135   **NM** $225   **MIP** n/a

Sniff, 1940s, The Embossing Co.
  EX $20   **NM** $30   **MIP** n/a

GAMES

Snow White and the Seven Dwarfs, 1938, Milton Bradley
EX $75   NM $150   MIP n/a

Snow White and the Seven Dwarfs, 1938, Parker Brothers
EX $125   NM $200   MIP n/a

Snug Harbor, 1930s, Milton Bradley
EX $50   NM $85   MIP n/a

Socko the Monk, The Game of, 1935, Einson-Freeman
EX $15   NM $25   MIP n/a

Soldier Boy Game, 1914, United Game
EX $80   NM $150   MIP n/a

Soldier's Cavalry, McLouglin Bros.
EX $150   NM $300   MIP n/a

Soldiers on Guard
EX $300   NM $500   MIP n/a

Speculation, 1885, Parker Brothers
EX $40   NM $65   MIP n/a

Speed Boat, 1920s, Parker Brothers
EX $100   NM $140   MIP n/a

Speed Boat Race, 1926, Wolverine
EX $70   NM $115   MIP n/a

Speed King, Game Of, 1922, Russell
EX $150   NM $200   MIP n/a

Speedem Junior Auto Race Game, 1929, All-Fair
EX $70   NM $125   MIP n/a

Speedway Motor Race, 1920s, Smith, Kline & French
EX $145   NM $250   MIP n/a

Spider's Web, Game of, 1898, McLoughlin Bros.
EX $100   NM $150   MIP n/a

Squails, 1870s, Adams
EX $100   NM $150   MIP n/a

Squails, 1877, Milton Bradley
EX $50   NM $75   MIP n/a

Stanley in Africa, 1891, Bliss
EX $1000   NM $2000   MIP n/a

Star Basketball, 1926, Star Paper Products
EX $125   NM $205   MIP n/a

Star Ride, 1934, Einson-Freeman
EX $250   NM $300   MIP n/a

Stars on Stripes Football Game, 1941, Stars & Stripes Games
EX $55   NM $70   MIP n/a

Steeple Chase, 1890, J.H. Singer
EX $200   NM $300   MIP n/a

Steeple Chase & Checkers, 1910, Milton Bradley
EX $55   NM $90   MIP n/a

Steeple Chase, Game of, 1900s, E.O. Clark
EX $100   NM $200   MIP n/a

Steeple Chase, Game of, 1910s, Milton Bradley
EX $40   NM $65   MIP n/a

Steeple Chase, Improved Game of, 1890s, McLoughlin Bros.
EX $195   NM $325   MIP n/a

Steps to Health Coke Game, 1938, CDN
EX $40   NM $70   MIP n/a

Sto-Auto Race, 1920s, Stough
EX $65   NM $110   MIP n/a

Stock Exchange, 1936, Parker Brothers
EX $100   NM $300   MIP n/a

Stock Exchange, The Game of, 1940s, Stox
EX $40   NM $65   MIP n/a

Stop & Go, 1936, Einson-Freeman
EX $25   NM $50   MIP n/a

Stop and Go, 1928, All-Fair
EX $100   NM $125   MIP n/a

Stop and Shop, 1930, All-Fair
EX $75   NM $100   MIP n/a

Stop, Look, and Listen, Game of, 1926, Milton Bradley
EX $40   NM $75   MIP n/a

Sto-Quoit, 1920s, Stough
EX $10   NM $15   MIP n/a

Strat: The Great War Game, 1915, Strat Game
EX $25   NM $45   MIP n/a

Strategy, Game of, 1891, McLoughlin Bros.
EX $240   NM $400   MIP n/a

Strategy, Game of Armies, 1938, Corey Games
EX $55   NM $125   MIP n/a

Stratosphere, 1930s, Parker Brothers
EX $100   NM $150   MIP n/a

Stratosphere, 1936, Whitman
EX $125   NM $300   MIP n/a

Street Car Game, The, 1890s, Parker Brothers
EX $200   NM $300   MIP n/a

Strike Out, 1920s, All-Fair
EX $175   NM $295   MIP n/a

Strike-Like, 1940s, Saxon Toy
EX $55   NM $90   MIP n/a

Stubborn Pig, Game of the, Milton Bradley
EX $100   NM $200   MIP n/a

Stunt Box, 1941, Frederick H. Beach (Beachcraft)
EX $12   NM $20   MIP n/a

Submarine Drag, 1917, Willis G. Young
EX $50   NM $100   MIP n/a

Substitute Golf, 1906, John Wanamaker
EX $400   NM $700   MIP n/a

Suffolk Downs, 1930s, Corey Game
EX $65   NM $100   MIP n/a

Susceptibles, The, 1891, McLoughlin Bros.
EX $325   NM $700   MIP n/a

Sweep, 1929, Selchow & Righter
EX $25   NM $40   MIP n/a

Sweeps, 1930s, E.E. Fairchild
EX $25   NM $60   MIP n/a

Sweepstakes, 1930s, Haras
EX $55   NM $90   MIP n/a

Swing A Peg, 1890s, Milton Bradley
EX $30   NM $45   MIP n/a

T.G.O. Klondyke, 1899, J.H. Singer
EX $150   NM $250   MIP n/a

Table Golf, 1909, McClurg
EX $15   NM $25   MIP n/a

Tackle, 1933, Tackle Game
EX $70   NM $115   MIP n/a

Tait's Table Golf, 1914, John Tait
EX $350   NM $575   MIP n/a

Take It And Double, 1943, Frederick H. Beach (Beachcraft)
EX $20   NM $35   MIP n/a

Take It or Leave It, 1942, Zondine Game
EX $25   NM $35   MIP n/a

Tak-Tiks, Basketball, 1939, Midwest Products
EX $15   NM $25   MIP n/a

Teddy's Bear Hunt, 1907, Bowers & Hard
EX $700   NM $900   MIP n/a

Teddy's Ride from Oyster Bay to Albany, 1899, Jesse Crandall
EX $3000   NM $5500   MIP n/a

Tee Off, 1935, Donogof
EX $115   NM $195   MIP n/a

Telegrams, 1941, Whitman
EX $40   NM $75   MIP n/a

Telegraph Boy, Game of the, 1888, McLoughlin Bros.
EX $350   NM $500   MIP n/a

Telepathy, 1939, Cadaco-Ellis
EX $65   NM $110   MIP n/a

Tell Bell, The, 1928, Knapp Electric & Novelty
EX $75   NM $100   MIP n/a

Ten Pins, 1920, Mason & Parker
EX $35   NM $60   MIP n/a

Tennis & Baseball, 1930, All Fair
EX $70   NM $115   MIP n/a

Terry and the Pirates, 1930s, Whitman
EX $75   NM $100   MIP n/a

Tete-A-Tete, 1892, Clark & Sowdon
EX $40   NM $100   MIP n/a

They're Off, Race Horse Game, 1930s, Parker Brothers
EX $15   NM $30   MIP n/a

Thorobred, 1940s, Lowe
EX $55   NM $90   MIP n/a

Thorton W. Burgess Animal Game, 1925, Saalfield
EX $400   NM $600   MIP n/a

Three Bears, 1910s, Milton Bradley
EX $20   NM $50   MIP n/a

Three Blind Mice, Game of, 1930s, Milton Bradley
EX $25   NM $45   MIP n/a

Three Little Kittens, 1910s, Milton Bradley
EX $60   NM $100   MIP n/a

Three Little Pigs Game, 1933, Einson-Freeman
EX $55   NM $95   MIP n/a

Three Little Pigs, The Game of the, 1933, Kenilworth Press
EX $100   NM $165   MIP n/a

GAMES

Three Men in a Tub, 1935, Milton Bradley
    EX $40   **NM** $65   **MIP** n/a

Three Men on a Horse, 1936, Milton Bradley
    EX $20   **NM** $50   **MIP** n/a

Three Point Landing, 1942, Advance Games
    EX $35   **NM** $60   **MIP** n/a

Thrilling Indoor Football Game, 1933, Cronston
    EX $70   **NM** $115   **MIP** n/a

Through The Clouds, 1931, Milton Bradley
    EX $75   **NM** $125   **MIP** n/a

Through the Locks to the Golden Gate, 1905, Milton Bradley
    EX $125   **NM** $225   **MIP** n/a

Ticker, 1929, Glow Products
    EX $50   **NM** $100   **MIP** n/a

Tiddley Golf Game, 1928, Milton Bradley
    EX $125   **NM** $200   **MIP** n/a

Tiddley Winks Game, 1920s, Wilder
    EX $15   **NM** $35   **MIP** n/a

Tiger Hunt, Game of, 1899, Chaffee & Selchow
    EX $270   **NM** $450   **MIP** n/a

Tiger Tom, Game of, 1920s, Milton Bradley
    EX $30   **NM** $75   **MIP** n/a

Ting-A-Ling, The Game of, 1920, Stoll & Edwards
    EX $25   **NM** $45   **MIP** n/a

Tinkerpins, 1916, Toy Creations
    EX $55   **NM** $80   **MIP** n/a

Tipit, 1929, Wolverine
    EX $15   **NM** $20   **MIP** n/a

Tip-Top Boxing, 1922, LaVelle
    EX $200   **NM** $300   **MIP** n/a

Tit for Tat Indoor Hockey, 1920s, Lemper Novelty
    EX $45   **NM** $75   **MIP** n/a

Tit-Tat-Toe, 1929, The Embossing
    EX $15   **NM** $25   **MIP** n/a

Tit-Tat-Toe, Three in a Row, 1896, Austin & Craw
    EX $45   **NM** $75   **MIP** n/a

To the Aid of your Party, 1942, Leister Game
    EX $15   **NM** $25   **MIP** n/a

Tobagganing at Christmas, Game of, 1899, McLoughlin Bros.
    EX $1200   **NM** $2000   **MIP** n/a

Toboggan Slide, 1890s, J.H. Singer
    EX $200   **NM** $325   **MIP** n/a

Toboggan Slide, 1890s, Hamilton-Myers
    EX $225   **NM** $385   **MIP** n/a

Toll Gate, Game of, 1890s, McLoughlin Bros.
    EX $280   **NM** $500   **MIP** n/a

Tom Hamilton's Pigskin, 1935, Parker Brothers
    EX $40   **NM** $50   **MIP** n/a

Tom Sawyer and Huck Finn, Adventures of, 1925, Stoll & Edwards
    EX $70   **NM** $150   **MIP** n/a

Tom Sawyer on the Mississippi, 1935, Einson-Freeman
    EX $100   **NM** $200   **MIP** n/a

Tom Sawyer, The Game of, 1937, Milton Bradley
    EX $75   **NM** $100   **MIP** n/a

Toonerville Trolley Game, 1927, Milton Bradley
    EX $100   **NM** $200   **MIP** n/a

Toonin Radio Game, 1925, All-Fair
    EX $150   **NM** $350   **MIP** n/a

Top-Ography, 1941, Cadaco
    EX $20   **NM** $35   **MIP** n/a

Topsy Turvey, Game of, 1899, McLoughlin Bros.
    EX $150   **NM** $250   **MIP** n/a

Tortoise and the Hare, 1922, Russell
    EX $45   **NM** $60   **MIP** n/a

Toto, The New Game, 1925, Baseball Toto Sales
    EX $55   **NM** $90   **MIP** n/a

Touchdown, 1937, Cadaco
    EX $65   **NM** $110   **MIP** n/a

Touchdown Football Game, 1920s, Wilder
    EX $100   **NM** $165   **MIP** n/a

Touchdown or Parlor Football, Game of, 1897, Union Mutual Life
    EX $85   **NM** $140   **MIP** n/a

Touchdown, The New Game, 1920, Hartford
    EX $70   **NM** $115   **MIP** n/a

Tourist, A Railroad Game, 1900s, Milton Bradley
    EX $150   **NM** $325   **MIP** n/a

Tournament, 1858, Mayhew & Baker
    EX $180   **NM** $300   **MIP** n/a

Town Hall, 1939, Milton Bradley
    EX $20   **NM** $30   **MIP** n/a

Toy Town Bank, 1910, Milton Bradley
    EX $90   **NM** $150   **MIP** n/a

Toy Town Conductors Game, 1910, Milton Bradley
    EX $105   **NM** $175   **MIP** n/a

Toy Town Telegraph Office, 1910s, Parker Brothers
    EX $100   **NM** $150   **MIP** n/a

Trackle-Lite, 1940s, Saxon Toy
    EX $55   **NM** $90   **MIP** n/a

Traffic Hazards, 1939, Trojan Games
    EX $30   **NM** $75   **MIP** n/a

Trailer Trails, 1937, Offset Gravure
    EX $35   **NM** $75   **MIP** n/a

Train for Boston, 1900, Parker Brothers
    EX $600   **NM** $800   **MIP** n/a

Transatlantic Flight, Game of the, 1925, Milton Bradley
    EX $250   **NM** $400   **MIP** n/a

Transport Pilot, 1938, Cadaco
    EX $45   **NM** $90   **MIP** n/a

Trap-A-Tank, 1920s, Wolverine
    EX $75   **NM** $125   **MIP** n/a

Traps & Bunkers, 1926?, Milton Bradley
    EX $75   **NM** $125   **MIP** n/a

Travel, The Game of, 1894, Parker Brothers
    EX $200   **NM** $350   **MIP** n/a

Treasure Hunt, 1940, All-Fair
    EX $20   **NM** $50   **MIP** n/a

Treasure Island, 1923, Stoll & Edwards
    EX $75   **NM** $125   **MIP** n/a

Treasure Island, 1934, Stoll & Einson
    EX $60   **NM** $90   **MIP** n/a

Treasure Island, Game of, 1923, Gem
    EX $40   **NM** $65   **MIP** n/a

Triangular Dominoes, 1885, Frank H. Richards
    EX $35   **NM** $60   **MIP** n/a

Trilby, 1894, E.I. Horsman
    EX $270   **NM** $450   **MIP** n/a

Trip Around the World, A, 1920s, Parker Brothers
    EX $25   **NM** $45   **MIP** n/a

Trip Round the World, Game of, 1897, McLoughlin Bros.
    EX $400   **NM** $800   **MIP** n/a

Trip to Washington, 1884, Milton Bradley
    EX $100   **NM** $175   **MIP** n/a

Triple Play, 1930s, National Games
    EX $12   **NM** $20   **MIP** n/a

Trolley Ride, The Game of the, 1890s, Hamilton-Myers
    EX $210   **NM** $350   **MIP** n/a

Trunk Box Lotto Game, 1890s, McLoughlin Bros.
    EX $15   **NM** $25   **MIP** n/a

Tumblin Five Acrobats, 1925, Doremus Schoen
    EX $12   **NM** $20   **MIP** n/a

Turn Over, 1908, Milton Bradley
    EX $75   **NM** $100   **MIP** n/a

Turnover, 1898, Chaffee & Selchow
    EX $50   **NM** $85   **MIP** n/a

Tutoom, Journey to the Treasures of Pharoah, 1923, All-Fair
    EX $175   **NM** $250   **MIP** n/a

Twentieth Century Limited, 1900s, Parker Brothers
    EX $125   **NM** $175   **MIP** n/a

Ty Cobb's Own Game of Baseball, 1920s, National Novelty
    EX $350   **NM** $650   **MIP** n/a

GAMES

U.S. Postman Game, 1914
    EX $60   NM $100   MIP n/a

U-Bat-It, 1920s, Schultz Star
    EX $70   NM $115   MIP n/a

Uncle Jim's Question Bee, 1938, Kress
    EX $10   NM $20   MIP n/a

Uncle Sam at War with Spain, Great Game of, 1898, Rhode Island Game
    EX $400   NM $600   MIP n/a

Uncle Sam's Baseball Game, 1890, J.C. Bell
    EX $525   NM $875   MIP n/a

(KP Photo)

Uncle Sam's Mail, 1893, McLoughlin Bros.
    EX $225   NM $350   MIP n/a

Uncle Wiggily's New Airplane Game, 1920s, Milton Bradley
    EX $50   NM $150   MIP n/a

Van Loon Story of Mankind Game, The, 1931, Kerk Guild
    EX $50   NM $85   MIP n/a

Vanderbilt Cup Race, 1906, Bowers & Hard
    EX $2000   NM $2500   MIP n/a

Varsity Football Game, 1942, Cadaco-Ellis
    EX $45   NM $75   MIP n/a

Varsity Race, 1899, Parker Brothers
    EX $425   NM $725   MIP n/a

Vassar Boat Race, The, 1899, Chaffee & Selchow
    EX $700   NM $900   MIP n/a

Vest Pocket Checker Set, 1929, Embossing
    EX $15   NM $25   MIP n/a

Vest Pocket Quoits, 1944, Colorful Creations
    EX $25   NM $45   MIP n/a

Victo, 1943, Spare Time
    EX $20   NM $25   MIP n/a

Victory, 1920s, Klak New Haven
    EX $105   NM $175   MIP n/a

Vignette Author, 1874, E.G. Selchow
    EX $35   NM $60   MIP n/a

Visit of Santa Claus, Game of the, 1899, McLoughlin Bros.
    EX $800   NM $1500   MIP n/a

Visit to the Farm, 1893, Bliss
    EX $300   NM $500   MIP n/a

Vox-Pop, 1938, Milton Bradley
    EX $20   NM $30   MIP n/a

Voyage Around the World, Game of, 1930s, Milton Bradley
    EX $150   NM $200   MIP n/a

Wachter's Parlor Base Ball (bagatelle), 1925, Wachter
    EX $145   NM $250   MIP n/a

Walk the Plank, 1925, Milton Bradley
    EX $75   NM $125   MIP n/a

Walking the Tightrope, 1897, McLoughlin Bros.
    EX $125   NM $250   MIP n/a

Walking the Tightrope, 1920, Milton Bradley
    EX $50   NM $100   MIP n/a

Walt Disney's Game Parade, 1930s
    EX $30   NM $50   MIP n/a

(KP Photo)

Walter Johnson Baseball Game, 1930s
    EX $195   NM $325   MIP n/a

Waner's Baseball Game, 1930s, Waner's Baseball Game
    EX $250   NM $500   MIP n/a

Wang, Game of, 1892, Clark & Sowdon
    EX $45   NM $65   MIP n/a

War of Nations, 1915, Milton Bradley
    EX $75   NM $200   MIP n/a

Ward Cuff's Football Game, 1938, Continental Sales
    EX $125   NM $200   MIP n/a

Watch on De Rind, 1931, All-Fair
    EX $400   NM $650   MIP n/a

(KP Photo)

Waterloo, 1895, Parker Brothers
    EX $325   NM $550   MIP n/a

Watermelon Frolic, 1900, Horsman
    EX $135   NM $225   MIP n/a

Watermelon Patch, 1940s, Craig Hopkins
    EX $25   NM $45   MIP n/a

Way to the White House, The, 1927, All-Fair
    EX $150   NM $200   MIP n/a

(KP Photo)

We, The Magnetic Flying Game, 1928, Parker Brothers
    EX $100   NM $200   MIP n/a

West Point, 1902, Ottoman
    EX $125   NM $300   MIP n/a

What's My Name?, 1920s, Jaymar
    EX $15   NM $25   MIP n/a

Whippet Race, 1940s, Pressman
    EX $20   NM $35   MIP n/a

Whirlpool Game, 1890s, McLoughlin Bros.
    EX $85   NM $150   MIP n/a

White Wings, 1930s, Glevum Games
    EX $45   NM $70   MIP n/a

Wide Awake, Game of, 1899, McLoughlin Bros.
    EX $200   NM $400   MIP n/a

Wide World and a Journey Round It, 1896, Parker Brothers
    EX $165   NM $275   MIP n/a

Wild West Cardboard Game, 1914
    EX $90   NM $150   MIP n/a

Wild West, Game of the, 1889, Bliss
    EX $1000   NM $1700   MIP n/a

Wilder's Football Game, 1930s, Wilder
    EX $100   NM $150   MIP n/a

Win, Place & Show, 1940s, 3M
    EX $25   NM $40   MIP n/a

Winko Baseball, 1940, Milton Bradley
    EX $45   NM $70   MIP n/a

(KP Photo)

Winnie Winkle Glider Race Game, 1930s, Milton Bradley
    EX $100   NM $175   MIP n/a

Winnie-The-Pooh Game, 1933, Parker Brothers
    EX $75   NM $150   MIP n/a

Winnie-The-Pooh Game, A. A. Milne's, 1931, Kerk Guild
    EX $50   NM $85   MIP n/a

Witzi-Wits, 1926, All-Fair
    EX $150   NM $250   MIP n/a

Wizard, The, 1921, Fulton Specialty
    EX $15   NM $25   MIP n/a

Wonderful Game of Oz (pewter pieces), 1921, Parker Brothers
    EX $800   NM $1500   MIP n/a

GAMES

(KP Photo)

Wonderful Game of Oz (wooden pieces), 1921, Parker Brothers
EX $300 **NM** $500 **MIP** n/a

Wordy, 1938, Pressman
EX $25 **NM** $45 **MIP** n/a

World Flyers, Game of the, 1926, All-Fair
EX $200 **NM** $300 **MIP** n/a

World Series Baseball Game, 1940s, Radio Sports
EX $205 **NM** $350 **MIP** n/a

World Series Parlor Baseball, 1916, Clifton E. Hooper
EX $150 **NM** $250 **MIP** n/a

World's Championship Baseball, 1910, Champion Amusement
EX $175 **NM** $295 **MIP** n/a

World's Championship Golf Game, 1930s, Beacon Hudson
EX $145 **NM** $250 **MIP** n/a

World's Columbian Exposition, Game of the, 1893, Bliss
EX $600 **NM** $1000 **MIP** n/a

World's Educator Game, 1889, Reed
EX $250 **NM** $400 **MIP** n/a

(KP Photo)

World's Fair Game, 1939, Milton Bradley
EX $90 **NM** $150 **MIP** n/a

World's Fair Game, The, 1892, Parker Brothers
EX $800 **NM** $1400 **MIP** n/a

(KP Photo)

WPA, Work, Progress, Action, 1935, All-Fair
EX $100 **NM** $200 **MIP** n/a

Wyntre Golf, 1920s, All-Fair
EX $175 **NM** $300 **MIP** n/a

X-Plor-US, 1922, All-Fair
EX $100 **NM** $150 **MIP** n/a

Yacht Race, 1890s, Clark & Sowdon
EX $200 **NM** $350 **MIP** n/a

Yacht Race, 1930s, Pressman
EX $100 **NM** $150 **MIP** n/a

Yachting, 1890, J.H. Singer
EX $125 **NM** $175 **MIP** n/a

Yale Harvard Football Game, 1922, LaVelle
EX $200 **NM** $300 **MIP** n/a

Yale Harvard Game, 1890, McLoughlin Bros.
EX $1500 **NM** $2000 **MIP** n/a

Yale-Princeton Football Game, 1895, McLoughlin Bros.
EX $1500 **NM** $2000 **MIP** n/a

Ya-Lo Football Card Game, 1930s
EX $85 **NM** $140 **MIP** n/a

Yankee Doodle!, 1940, Cadaco-Ellis
EX $20 **NM** $30 **MIP** n/a

Yankee Doodle, A Game of American History, 1895, Parker Brothers
EX $285 **NM** $475 **MIP** n/a

Yankee Trader, 1941, Corey Games
EX $45 **NM** $75 **MIP** n/a

Young Athlete, The, 1898, Chaffee & Selchow
EX $425 **NM** $700 **MIP** n/a

You're Out! Baseball Game, 1941, Corey Games
EX $35 **NM** $65 **MIP** n/a

Yuneek Game, 1889, McLoughlin Bros.
EX $300 **NM** $600 **MIP** n/a

Zimmer Baseball Game, 1885, McLoughlin Bros.
EX $20000 **NM** $28000 **MIP** n/a

(KP Photo)

Zippy Zepps, 1930s, All-Fair
EX $500 **NM** $800 **MIP** n/a

Zip-Top, 1940, Deluxe Game
EX $35 **NM** $45 **MIP** n/a

Zoo Hoo, 1924, Lubbers & Bell
EX $125 **NM** $150 **MIP** n/a

(KP Photo)

Zoom, Original Game of, 1940s, All-Fair
EX $45 **NM** $60 **MIP** n/a

Zulu Blowing Game, 1927, Zulu Toy
EX $50 **NM** $100 **MIP** n/a

CARD GAMES

ABC, 1900s, Parker Brothers
EX $25 **NM** $40 **MIP** n/a

Airship Game, The, 1916, Parker Brothers
EX $30 **NM** $50 **MIP** n/a

Allegrando, 1884, Theodore Presser
EX $20 **NM** $30 **MIP** n/a

Allie-Patriot Game, 1917, McDowell And Mellor
EX $30 **NM** $50 **MIP** n/a

American History, The Game of, 1890s, Parker Brothers
EX $50 **NM** $90 **MIP** n/a

American League Fan Craze Card Game, 1904, Fan Craze
EX $1950 **NM** $3250 **MIP** n/a

American National Game Baseball, 1909, American National Game Co.
EX $75 **NM** $200 **MIP** n/a

Amusing Game of Conundrums, 1853, John McLoughlin
EX $750 **NM** $1300 **MIP** n/a

Amusing Game of the Corner Grocery, 1890s
EX $50 **NM** $100 **MIP** n/a

Anagrams, 1885, Peter G. Thompson
EX $10 **NM** $30 **MIP** n/a

Apple Pie, 1895, Parker Brothers
EX $40 **NM** $60 **MIP** n/a

Armstead's Play Ball, 1910s, Austin
EX $200 **NM** $500 **MIP** n/a

Astronomy, 1905, Cincinnati Game
EX $20 **NM** $30 **MIP** n/a

Auction Letters, 1900, Parker Brothers
EX $30 **NM** $50 **MIP** n/a

Authors Illustrated, 1893, Clark & Sowdon
EX $30 **NM** $50 **MIP** n/a

Authors, Game of Standard, 1890s, McLoughlin Bros.
EX $25 **NM** $60 **MIP** n/a

(KP Photo)

Authors, The Game of, 1890s, Parker
Brothers
EX $15   NM $35   MIP n/a

Avilude, 1873, West & Lee
EX $45   NM $75   MIP n/a

Balance The Budget, 1938, Elten Game
EX $45   NM $75   MIP n/a

Bally Hoo, 1931, Gabriel
EX $40   NM $65   MIP n/a

Baseballitis Card Game, 1909,
Baseballitis Card
EX $125   NM $205   MIP n/a

Basketball Card Game, 1940s,
Warren/Built-Rite
EX $20   NM $35   MIP n/a

Batter Up, Game of, 1908, Fenner Game
EX $150   NM $200   MIP n/a

Betty Boop Coed Bridge, 1930s
EX $50   NM $75   MIP n/a

Bible ABCs and Promises, 1940s, Judson
Press
EX $15   NM $25   MIP n/a

Bible Authors, 1895, Evangelical Pub.
EX $20   NM $35   MIP n/a

Bible Cities, 1920s, Nellie T. Magee
EX $15   NM $25   MIP n/a

Bicycle Cards, 1898, Parker Brothers
EX $150   NM $200   MIP n/a

Big League Baseball Card Game, 1940s,
State College Game Lab
EX $35   NM $60   MIP n/a

Billy Bump's Visit To Boston, 1888, Parker
Brothers
EX $25   NM $40   MIP n/a

Bird Center Etiquette, 1904, Home Game
EX $25   NM $50   MIP n/a

Birds, Game of, 1899, Cincinnati Game
EX $25   NM $50   MIP n/a

Black Cat Fortune Telling Game, The,
1897, Parker Brothers
EX $95   NM $175   MIP n/a

Block, 1905, Parker Brothers
EX $25   NM $35   MIP n/a

Blondie Playing Card Game, 1941, Whitman
EX $30   NM $50   MIP n/a

Bo Peep Game, 1895, McLoughlin Bros.
EX $40   NM $65   MIP n/a

Botany, 1900s, G.H. Dunston
EX $50   NM $100   MIP n/a

Bourse, or Stock Exchange, 1903, Flinch
Card
EX $35   NM $50   MIP n/a

Boy Scouts, The Game of, 1912, Parker
Brothers
EX $75   NM $125   MIP n/a

Buck Rogers in the 25th Century, 1936,
All-Fair, 35 full-color cards plus
instruction card
EX $300   NM $500   MIP n/a

Bugle Horn or Robin Hood, 1850s,
McLoughlin Bros.
EX $400   NM $600   MIP n/a

Bunco, 1904, Home Game
EX $10   NM $30   MIP n/a

Buster Brown at the Circus, 1900s,
Selchow & Righter
EX $100   NM $250   MIP n/a

Camouflage, The Game of, 1918, Parker
Brothers
EX $20   NM $50   MIP n/a

Captain Jinks, 1900s, Parker Brothers
EX $30   NM $55   MIP n/a

Characters, A Game of, 1889, Decker &
Decker
EX $10   NM $20   MIP n/a

Charlie Chan Game, 1939, Whitman
EX $30   NM $75   MIP n/a

**Charlie McCarthy Question and Answer
Game,** 1938, Whitman
EX $40   NM $65   MIP n/a

Charlie McCarthy Rummy Game, 1938,
Whitman
EX $20   NM $35   MIP n/a

Chestnut Burrs, 1896, Fireside Game
EX $35   NM $65   MIP n/a

Cinderella, 1895, Parker Brothers
EX $55   NM $90   MIP n/a

Cinderella, 1905, Milton Bradley
EX $40   NM $60   MIP n/a

Cinderella, 1921, Milton Bradley
EX $15   NM $25   MIP n/a

Cinderella or Hunt the Slipper, 1887,
McLoughlin Bros.
EX $75   NM $105   MIP n/a

**City Life, or The Boys of New York, The
Game of,** 1889, McLoughlin Bros.
EX $200   NM $400   MIP n/a

Cock Robin, 1895, Parker Brothers
EX $40   NM $75   MIP n/a

**Cock Robin and His Tragical Death, Game
of,** 1885, McLoughlin Bros.
EX $65   NM $105   MIP n/a

**Columbia's Presidents and Our Country,
Game of,** 1886, McLoughlin Bros.
EX $150   NM $300   MIP n/a

Comic Conversation Cards, 1890,
J. Ottmann Lith.
EX $100   NM $200   MIP n/a

**Comic Leaves of Fortune-The Sibyl's
Prophecy,** 1850s, Charles Magnus
EX $500   NM $900   MIP n/a

Comical Game of "Who," The, 1910s,
Parker Brothers
EX $20   NM $30   MIP n/a

Comical Game of Whip, The, 1920s, Russell
EX $20   NM $45   MIP n/a

Comical History of America, 1924, Parker
Brothers
EX $40   NM $75   MIP n/a

Comical Snap, Game of, 1903,
McLoughlin Bros.
EX $40   NM $65   MIP n/a

Commanders of Our Forces, The, 1863,
E.C. Eastman
EX $150   NM $225   MIP n/a

Commerce, 1900s, J. Ottmann Lith.
EX $60   NM $100   MIP n/a

Competition, or Department Store, 1904,
Flinch Card
EX $100   NM $200   MIP n/a

**Conquest of Nations, or Old Games With
New Faces, The,** 1853, Willis P. Hazard
EX $100   NM $175   MIP n/a

Costumes and Fashions, Game of, 1881,
Milton Bradley
EX $80   NM $225   MIP n/a

County Fair, The, 1891, Parker Brothers
EX $45   NM $75   MIP n/a

**Cousin Peter's Trip to New York, Game
of,** 1898, McLoughlin Bros.
EX $45   NM $75   MIP n/a

Crow Cards, 1910, Milton Bradley
EX $9   NM $15   MIP n/a

Defenders of the Flag, 1922, Stoll & Edwards
EX $35   NM $65   MIP n/a

Derby Day, 1900s, Parker Brothers
EX $30   NM $50   MIP n/a

Dewey at Manila, 1899, Chaffee & Selchow
EX $150   NM $225   MIP n/a

Dick Tracy Playing Card Game, 1934,
Whitman
EX $50   NM $75   MIP n/a

**Dick Tracy Super Detective Mystery Card
Game,** 1937, Whitman
EX $65   NM $90   MIP n/a

Din, 1905, Horsman
EX $25   NM $45   MIP n/a

Dixie Land, Game of, 1897, Fireside
EX $50   NM $70   MIP n/a

Doctor Busby Card Game, 1910
EX $35   NM $55   MIP n/a

Doctor Quack, Game of, 1922, Russell
EX $25   NM $40   MIP n/a

Doctors and the Quack, 1890s, Parker
Brothers
EX $45   NM $75   MIP n/a

Donald Duck Game, 1930s, Whitman
EX $15   NM $30   MIP n/a

Donald Duck Playing Game, 1941, Whitman
EX $25   NM $40   MIP n/a

Double Eagle Anagrams, 1890,
McLoughlin Bros.
EX $35   NM $75   MIP n/a

Double Flag Game, The, 1904,
McLoughlin Bros.
EX $75   NM $100   MIP n/a

Down the Pike with Mrs. Wiggs at the St. Louis Exposition, 1904, Milton Bradley
EX $50   NM $75   MIP n/a

Dr. Busby, 1890s, J.H. Singer
EX $60   NM $75   MIP n/a

Dr. Busby, 1900s, J. Ottmann Lith.
EX $60   NM $75   MIP n/a

(KP Photo)

Dr. Busby, 1937, Milton Bradley
EX $20   NM $50   MIP n/a

Dr. Fusby, Game of, 1890s, McLoughlin
Bros.
EX $125   NM $200   MIP n/a

Egerton R. Williams Popular Indoor Baseball Game, 1886, Hatch
EX $2500   NM $5000   MIP n/a

Elite Conversation Cards, 1887,
McLoughlin Bros.
EX $35   NM $90   MIP n/a

Excursion to Coney Island, 1880s, Milton
Bradley
EX $100   NM $250   MIP n/a

Excuse Me!, 1923, Parker Brothers
EX $15   NM $25   MIP n/a

Famous Authors, 1910, Parker Brothers
EX $40   NM $50   MIP n/a

Famous Authors, 1943, Parker Brothers
EX $10   NM $15   MIP n/a

Fan Craze Card Game, Generic, 1904, Fan
Craze
EX $100   NM $150   MIP n/a

Fan Craze Card Game, Name Players,
1904, Fan Craze
EX $1500   NM $2000   MIP n/a

Favorite Art, Game of, 1897, Parker Brothers
EX $40   NM $65   MIP n/a

Ferdinand Card Game, 1938, Whitman
EX $25   NM $65   MIP n/a

Five Hundred, Game of, 1900s, Home Game
EX $20   NM $35   MIP n/a

Flags, 1899, Cincinnati Game
EX $20   NM $40   MIP n/a

Flinch, 1902, Flinch Card
EX $10   NM $15   MIP n/a

Foolish Questions, 1920s, Wallie Dorr
EX $50   NM $75   MIP n/a

Fortune Telling, 1920s, All-Fair
EX $40   NM $50   MIP n/a

Fortune Telling Game, 1930s, Stoll &
Edwards
EX $35   NM $55   MIP n/a

Fortune Telling Game, The, 1890s, Parker
Brothers
EX $40   NM $65   MIP n/a

Fortunes, Game of, 1902, Cincinnati Game
EX $55   NM $95   MIP n/a

Fox and Geese, The New, 1888,
McLoughlin Bros.
EX $45   NM $75   MIP n/a

Foxy Grandpa at the World's Fair, 1904,
J. Ottmann Lith.
EX $150   NM $200   MIP n/a

Fractions, 1902, Cincinnati Game
EX $20   NM $30   MIP n/a

Frank Buck's Bring 'em Back Alive Game,
1937, All-Fair
EX $40   NM $75   MIP n/a

Gamevelope, 1944, Morris Systems
EX $20   NM $35   MIP n/a

Gavitt's Stock Exchange, 1903, W.W. Gavitt
EX $35   NM $65   MIP n/a

Geographical Cards, 1883, Peter G.
Thompson
EX $35   NM $65   MIP n/a

Geography up to Date, 1890s, Parker
Brothers
EX $35   NM $60   MIP n/a

George Washington's Dream, 1900s,
Parker Brothers
EX $45   NM $75   MIP n/a

G-Men, 1936, Milton Bradley
EX $35   NM $55   MIP n/a

Goat, Game of, 1916, Milton Bradley
EX $15   NM $35   MIP n/a

Gold Rush, The, 1930s, Cracker Jack
EX $20   NM $50   MIP n/a

Golden Egg, 1850s, McLoughlin Bros.
EX $450   NM $750   MIP n/a

Golden Egg, The, 1845, R.H. Pease
EX $165   NM $275   MIP n/a

Golliwogg, 1907, Milton Bradley
EX $200   NM $300   MIP n/a

Good Old Game of Corner Grocery, The,
1900s, Parker Brothers
EX $40   NM $60   MIP n/a

Good Old Game of Dr. Busby, 1900s,
Parker Brothers
EX $55   NM $85   MIP n/a

Good Old Game of Dr. Busby, 1920s,
United Game
EX $25   NM $50   MIP n/a

Grandmama's Improved Arithmetical Game, 1887, McLoughlin Bros.
EX $50   NM $75   MIP n/a

Grandmama's Improved Geographical Game, 1887, McLoughlin Bros.
EX $55   NM $65   MIP n/a

Grandmama's Sunday Game: Bible Questions, Old Testament, 1887,
McLoughlin Bros.
EX $35   NM $60   MIP n/a

Grandma's Game of Useful Knowledge,
1910s, Milton Bradley
EX $20   NM $65   MIP n/a

Great Battlefields, 1886, Parker Brothers
EX $150   NM $250   MIP n/a

Great Composer, The, 1901, Theodore
Presser
EX $35   NM $55   MIP n/a

Great Mails Baseball Game, 1919, Walter
Mails Baseball Game
EX $2475   NM $4100   MIP n/a

Guess Again, The Game of, 1890s,
McLoughlin Bros.
EX $75   NM $120   MIP n/a

Gypsy Fortune Telling Game, 1909,
McLoughlin Bros.
EX $100   NM $175   MIP n/a

H.M.S. Pinafore, 1880, McLoughlin Bros.
EX $300   NM $600   MIP n/a

Have-U It?, 1924, Selchow & Righter
EX $15   NM $25   MIP n/a

Heads and Tails, 1900s, Parker Brothers
EX $30   NM $50   MIP n/a

Hens and Chickens, Game of, 1875,
McLoughlin Bros.
EX $125   NM $175   MIP n/a

Hey What?, 1907, Parker Brothers
EX $20   NM $35   MIP n/a

Hidden Titles, 1908, Parker Brothers
EX $20   NM $35   MIP n/a

Historical Cards, 1884, Peter G. Thompson
EX $25   NM $75   MIP n/a

History up to Date, 1900s, Parker Brothers
EX $35   NM $65   MIP n/a

Hokum, 1927, Parker Brothers
EX $10   NM $20   MIP n/a

Hollywood Movie Bingo, 1937, Whitman
EX $50   NM $75   MIP n/a

Home Diamond, 1913, Phillips
EX $150   NM $225   MIP n/a

Home History Game, 1910s, Milton Bradley
EX $40   NM $60   MIP n/a

Hood's War Game, 1899, C.I. Hood
EX $40   NM $65   MIP n/a

Hoot, 1926, Saalfield
EX $100   NM $200   MIP n/a

House that Jack Built, 1900s, Parker
Brothers
EX $55   NM $75   MIP n/a

House that Jack Built, The, 1887,
McLoughlin Bros.
EX $75   NM $100   MIP n/a

Household Words, Game of, 1916,
Household Words Game
EX $50   NM $85   MIP n/a

How Silas Popped the Question, 1915,
Parker Brothers
EX $20   NM $30   MIP n/a

I Doubt It, 1910, Parker Brothers
EX $35   NM $55   MIP n/a

Illustrated Mythology, 1896, Cincinnati Game
EX $25   NM $50   MIP n/a

Improved Historical Cards, 1900, McLoughlin Bros.
EX $35   NM $55   MIP n/a

Industries, Game of, 1897, A.W. Mumford
EX $25   NM $55   MIP n/a

Ivanhoe, 1886, Parker Brothers
EX $55   NM $75   MIP n/a

Japanese Oracle, Game of, 1875, McLoughlin Bros.
EX $100   NM $200   MIP n/a

Joe "Ducky" Medwick's Big Leaguer Baseball Game, 1930s, Johnson-Breier
EX $125   NM $200   MIP n/a

Johnny's Historical Game, 1890s, Parker Brothers
EX $55   NM $75   MIP n/a

Jumping Frog, Game of, 1890, J.H. Singer
EX $75   NM $125   MIP n/a

Just Like Me, Game of, 1899, McLoughlin Bros.
EX $75   NM $100   MIP n/a

Kings, The Game of, 1845, Josiah Adams
EX $150   NM $250   MIP n/a

Komical Konversation Kards, 1893, Parker Brothers
EX $30   NM $60   MIP n/a

Lawson's Baseball Card Game, 1910
EX $100   NM $175   MIP n/a

Lawson's Patent Game of Baseball, 1884, Lawson's Card
EX $500   NM $1000   MIP n/a

Letters Improved for the Logomachist, 1878, Noyes & Snow
EX $50   NM $100   MIP n/a

Library of Games, 1939, Russell
EX $55   NM $75   MIP n/a

Lindy Flying Game, 1927, Parker Brothers
EX $30   NM $40   MIP n/a

Lindy Flying Game, The New, 1927, Nucraft Toys
EX $45   NM $60   MIP n/a

Lion & the Eagle, or the Days of '76, 1883, E.H. Snow
EX $75   NM $125   MIP n/a

Little Orphan Annie Rummy Cards, 1937, Whitman
EX $45   NM $75   MIP n/a

Lost Heir, Game of the, 1910, Milton Bradley
EX $30   NM $40   MIP n/a

Lost Heir, The Game of, 1893, McLoughlin Bros.
EX $45   NM $65   MIP n/a

Major League Baseball Game, 1900s, Parker Brothers
EX $50   NM $150   MIP n/a

Make A Million, 1934, Rook Card
EX $35   NM $50   MIP n/a

Mayflower, The, 1897, Fireside Game
EX $25   NM $50   MIP n/a

Mickey Mouse Bridge Game, 1935, Whitman
EX $35   NM $55   MIP n/a

Mickey Mouse Old Maid Game, 1930s, Whitman
EX $35   NM $65   MIP n/a

Mother Hubbard, 1875, McLoughlin Bros.
EX $75   NM $125   MIP n/a

Movie-Land Keeno, 1929, Wilder
EX $75   NM $150   MIP n/a

Musical Lotto, 1936, Tudor Metal Products
EX $35   NM $65   MIP n/a

Mythology, 1900, Cincinnati Game
EX $55   NM $75   MIP n/a

Napoleon LaJoie Baseball Game, 1913, Parker Brothers
EX $150   NM $500   MIP n/a

National American Baseball Game, 1910, Parker Brothers
EX $130   NM $200   MIP n/a

National Baseball Game, The, 1913, National Baseball Playing Card
EX $700   NM $1200   MIP n/a

Nations or Quaker Whist, Game of, 1898, McLoughlin Bros.
EX $75   NM $110   MIP n/a

Nations, Game of, 1908, Milton Bradley
EX $30   NM $65   MIP n/a

Naughty Molly, 1905, McLoughlin Bros.
EX $75   NM $100   MIP n/a

Nosey, The Game of, 1905, McLoughlin Bros.
EX $250   NM $450   MIP n/a

(KP Photo)

Oh, Blondie!, 1940s
EX $30   NM $45   MIP n/a

Old Curiosity Shop, 1869, Novelty Game
EX $200   NM $300   MIP n/a

Old Maid, 1890s, J.H. Singer
EX $75   NM $100   MIP n/a

Old Maid Card Game, 1889
EX $20   NM $50   MIP n/a

Old Maid Fun Full Thrift Game, 1940s, Russell
EX $30   NM $50   MIP n/a

Old Maid, Game of, 1870, McLoughlin Bros.
EX $75   NM $125   MIP n/a

Old Maid, with Characters from Famous Nursery Rhymes, 1920s, All-Fair
EX $30   NM $50   MIP n/a

Oliver Twist, The Good Old Game of, 1888, Parker Brothers
EX $150   NM $225   MIP n/a

Our Bird Friends, 1901, Sarah H. Dudley
EX $20   NM $30   MIP n/a

Our National Life, 1903, Cincinnati Game
EX $35   NM $65   MIP n/a

Patch Word, 1938, All-Fair
EX $15   NM $20   MIP n/a

Paws & Claws, 1895, Clark & Sowdon
EX $60   NM $90   MIP n/a

Pepper, 1906, Parker Brothers
EX $20   NM $35   MIP n/a

Peter Coddle and his Trip to New York, 1890s, J.H. Singer
EX $35   NM $50   MIP n/a

(KP Photo)

Peter Coddle tells of his Trip to Chicago, 1890, Parker Brothers
EX $30   NM $50   MIP n/a

Peter Coddle, Improved Game of, 1900, McLoughlin Bros.
EX $35   NM $55   MIP n/a

Peter Coddles, 1890s, J. Ottmann Lith.
EX $25   NM $55   MIP n/a

Peter Coddle's Trip to New York, 1925, Milton Bradley
EX $20   NM $35   MIP n/a

Peter Coddle's Trip to New York, The Game of, 1888, Parker Brothers
EX $40   NM $50   MIP n/a

Peter Coddle's Trip to the World's Fair, 1939, Parker Brothers
EX $50   NM $85   MIP n/a

Pinocchio Playing Card Game, 1939, Whitman
EX $55   NM $75   MIP n/a

Psychic Baseball, 1927, Psychic Baseball
EX $75   NM $125   MIP n/a

Real Baseball Card Game, 1900, National Baseball
EX $180   NM $275   MIP n/a

Red Riding Hood and the Wolf, The New Game, 1887, McLoughlin Bros.
EX $75   NM $120   MIP n/a

Rex, 1920s, J. Ottmann Lith.
EX $20   NM $40   MIP n/a

Robinson Crusoe for Little Folks, Game of, 1900s, E.O. Clark
EX $35   NM $65   MIP n/a

Roodles, 1912, Flinch Card
EX $15   NM $35   MIP n/a

(KP Photo)

Rook, 1906, Rook Card Co.
EX $10   NM $15   MIP n/a

Roosevelt at San Juan, 1899, Chaffee & Selchow
EX $150   NM $350   MIP n/a

Sabotage, 1943, Games Of Fame
EX $25   NM $45   MIP n/a

Skippy, A Card Game, 1936, All-Fair
EX $30   NM $60   MIP n/a

Skit Scat, 1905, McLoughlin Bros.
EX $50   NM $85   MIP n/a

Snap, 1883, Horsman
EX $45   NM $65   MIP n/a

Snap, Game of, 1892, McLoughlin Bros.
EX $40   NM $85   MIP n/a

Snap, Game of, 1910s, Milton Bradley
EX $20   NM $35   MIP n/a

Snap, The Game of, 1905s, Parker Brothers
EX $25   NM $40   MIP n/a

Stage, 1904, C.M. Clark
EX $50   NM $100   MIP n/a

Star Baseball Game, 1941, W.P. Ulrich
EX $70   NM $115   MIP n/a

Take-Off, 1930s, Russell
EX $25   NM $45   MIP n/a

Three Bears, The, 1922, Stoll & Edwards
EX $30   NM $50   MIP n/a

Three Merry Men, 1865, Amsdan
EX $75   NM $100   MIP n/a

Tom Barker Card Game, 1913
EX $1400   NM $2300   MIP n/a

Toot, 1905, Parker Brothers
EX $75   NM $110   MIP n/a

Totem, 1873, West & Lee
EX $45   NM $75   MIP n/a

Touring, 1906, Wallie Dorr
EX $50   NM $75   MIP n/a

Touring, 1926, Parker Brothers
EX $20   NM $30   MIP n/a

(KP Photo)

Traits, The Game of, 1933, Goodenough and Woglom
EX $20   NM $35   MIP n/a

Trip through our National Parks: Game of Yellowstone, A, 1910s, Cincinnati Game
EX $20   NM $45   MIP n/a

Trips of Japhet Jenkens & Sam Slick, 1871, Milton Bradley
EX $20   NM $35   MIP n/a

Trolley, 1904, Snyder Brothers
EX $45   NM $75   MIP n/a

Trolley Came Off, The, 1900s, Parker Brothers
EX $45   NM $75   MIP n/a

Twenty Five, Game of, 1925, Milton Bradley
EX $10   NM $15   MIP n/a

United States History, The Game of, 1903, Parker Brothers
EX $50   NM $65   MIP n/a

Venetian Fortune Teller, Game of, 1898, Parker Brothers
EX $100   NM $125   MIP n/a

Verborum, 1883, Peter G. Thompson
EX $35   NM $65   MIP n/a

Walt and Skeezix Gasoline Alley Game, 1927, Milton Bradley
EX $50   NM $100   MIP n/a

War and Diplomacy, 1899, Chaffee & Selchow
EX $85   NM $125   MIP n/a

War of Words, 1910, McLoughlin Bros.
EX $35   NM $60   MIP n/a

What Would You Do?, 1933, Geo E. Schweig & Son
EX $15   NM $25   MIP n/a

When My Ship Comes In, 1888, Parker Brothers
EX $55   NM $75   MIP n/a

Where do you Live?, 1890s, J.H. Singer
EX $55   NM $75   MIP n/a

Where's Johnny?, 1885, McLoughlin Bros.
EX $100   NM $175   MIP n/a

Which is It? Speak Quick or Pay, 1889, McLoughlin Bros.
EX $65   NM $150   MIP n/a

Whip, The Comical Game of, 1930, Russell
EX $20   NM $40   MIP n/a

Who is the Thief?, 1937, Whitman
EX $35   NM $55   MIP n/a

Wogglebug Game of Conundrums, The, 1905, Parker Brothers
EX $300   NM $600   MIP n/a

Worth While, 1907, Doan
EX $25   NM $40   MIP n/a

Wyhoo!, 1906, Milton Bradley
EX $40   NM $60   MIP n/a

Yankee Pedlar, Or What Do You Buy, 1850s, John McLoughlin
EX $725   NM $1200   MIP n/a

(KP Photo)

Yellowstone, Game of, 1895, Fireside Game
EX $75   NM $100   MIP n/a

Young Folks Historical Game, 1890s, McLoughlin Bros.
EX $45   NM $65   MIP n/a

Young Peddlers, Game of the, 1859, Mayhew & Baker
EX $125   NM $175   MIP n/a

Young People's Geographical Game, 1900s, Parker Brothers
EX $35   NM $55   MIP n/a

Zoom, 1941, Whitman
EX $10   NM $20   MIP n/a

DEXTERITY

Golf, 1900, Schoenhut
EX $2700   NM $5000   MIP n/a

SKILL/ACTION GAMES

400, Aristocrat of Games, The, 1933, Morris Systems
EX $15   NM $25   MIP n/a

Aero Ball, 1940s, Game Makers
EX $30   NM $75   MIP n/a

(KP Photo)

Animal Bingo, Baldwin Manufacturing
EX $40   NM $75   MIP n/a

Bag of Fun, 1932, Rosebud Art
EX $5   NM $10   MIP n/a

Balloonio, 1937, Frederick H. Beach
EX $10   NM $20   MIP n/a

Bambino, 1934, Bambino Products
EX $100   NM $125   MIP n/a

Bang Bird, 1924, Doremus Schoen
EX $20   NM $30   MIP n/a

Barber Pole, 1908, Parker Brothers
EX $50   NM $75   MIP n/a

Barn Yard Tiddledy Winks, 1910s, Parker Brothers
EX $40   NM $60   MIP n/a

Bases Full, 1930
  EX $45   **NM** $70   **MIP** n/a

Basket Ball, 1929, Russell
  EX $150   **NM** $350   **MIP** n/a

Battles, or Fun For Boys, Game of, 1889, McLoughlin Bros.
  EX $750   **NM** $2000   **MIP** n/a

(KP Photo)

Bean-Em, 1931, All-Fair
  EX $400   **NM** $600   **MIP** n/a

Bingo, 1929, All-Fair
  EX $10   **NM** $15   **MIP** n/a

Bobb, Game of, 1898, McLoughlin Bros.
  EX $250   **NM** $500   **MIP** n/a

Bomber Ball, 1940s, Game Makers
  EX $50   **NM** $100   **MIP** n/a

Bottle Imps, Game of, 1907, Milton Bradley
  EX $100   **NM** $200   **MIP** n/a

Bowling Alley, 1921, N.D. Cass
  EX $20   **NM** $35   **MIP** n/a

Bow-O-Winks, 1932, All-Fair
  EX $75   **NM** $100   **MIP** n/a

Boy Hunter, The, 1925, Parker Brothers
  EX $60   **NM** $100   **MIP** n/a

Brownie Character Ten Pins Game, 1890s
  EX $1000 **NM** $2000   **MIP** n/a

Brownie Kick-In Top, 1910s, M.H. Miller
  EX $35   **NM** $60   **MIP** n/a

Bula, 1943, Games Of Fame
  EX $30   **NM** $45   **MIP** n/a

Bull in the China Shop, 1937, Milton Bradley
  EX $20   **NM** $40   **MIP** n/a

Busto, 1931, All-Fair
  EX $100   **NM** $200   **MIP** n/a

Buzzing Around, 1924, Parker Brothers
  EX $40   **NM** $65   **MIP** n/a

Cat and Witch, 1940s, Whitman
  EX $25   **NM** $65   **MIP** n/a

Cavalcade Derby Game, 1930s, Wyandotte
  EX $50   **NM** $85   **MIP** n/a

Chinaman Party, 1896, Selchow & Righter
  EX $75   **NM** $130   **MIP** n/a

Click, 1930s, Akro Agate
  EX $50   **NM** $85   **MIP** n/a

Clown Winks, 1930s, Gabriel
  EX $15   **NM** $25   **MIP** n/a

(KP Photo)

Combination Tiddledy Winks, 1910, Milton Bradley
  EX $10   **NM** $30   **MIP** n/a

Cones & Corns, 1924, Parker Brothers
  EX $39   **NM** $65   **MIP** n/a

Conette, 1890, Milton Bradley
  EX $25   **NM** $50   **MIP** n/a

Cows In Corn, 1889, Stirn & Lyon
  EX $150   **NM** $250   **MIP** n/a

Crazy Traveller, 1920s, Parker Brothers
  EX $25   **NM** $50   **MIP** n/a

Crickets In The Grass, 1920s, Madmar Quality
  EX $35   **NM** $50   **MIP** n/a

Crow Hunt, 1930, Parker Brothers
  EX $50   **NM** $65   **MIP** n/a

Crows in the Corn, 1930, Parker Brothers
  EX $45   **NM** $75   **MIP** n/a

Deck Ring Toss Game, 1910
  EX $30   **NM** $50   **MIP** n/a

Dig, 1940, Parker Brothers
  EX $2   **NM** $5   **MIP** n/a

Dim Those Lights, 1932, All-Fair
  EX $500   **NM** $1000   **MIP** n/a

Disk, 1900s, Madmar Quality
  EX $35   **NM** $55   **MIP** n/a

Diving Fish, 1920s, C.E. Bradley
  EX $20   **NM** $30   **MIP** n/a

Dodging Donkey, The, 1920s, Parker Brothers
  EX $45   **NM** $75   **MIP** n/a

Donkey Party, 1887, McLoughlin Bros.
  EX $75   **NM** $150   **MIP** n/a

Down and Out, 1928, Milton Bradley
  EX $30   **NM** $60   **MIP** n/a

Faba Baga or Parlor Quiots, 1883, Morton E. Converse
  EX $40   **NM** $65   **MIP** n/a

Fairies' Cauldron Tiddledy Winks Game, The, 1925, Parker Brothers
  EX $35   **NM** $50   **MIP** n/a

Fascination, 1890, Selchow & Righter
  EX $35   **NM** $50   **MIP** n/a

Fiddlestix, 1937, Plaza
  EX $10   **NM** $15   **MIP** n/a

Fish Pond, 1890, E.O. Clark
  EX $50   **NM** $125   **MIP** n/a

Fish Pond, 1920s, Wilder
  EX $25   **NM** $60   **MIP** n/a

Fish Pond Game, Magnetic, 1891, McLoughlin Bros.
  EX $150   **NM** $300   **MIP** n/a

Fish Pond, Game of, 1910s, Wescott Brothers
  EX $30   **NM** $50   **MIP** n/a

Fish Pond, New and Improved, 1890s, McLoughlin Bros.
  EX $150   **NM** $250   **MIP** n/a

Fish Pond, The Game of, 1890, McLoughlin Bros.
  EX $100   **NM** $175   **MIP** n/a

Fishing Game, 1899, Martin
  EX $30   **NM** $65   **MIP** n/a

Five Little Pigs, 1890s, J.H. Singer
  EX $50   **NM** $100   **MIP** n/a

Five Wise Birds, The, 1923, Parker Brothers
  EX $25   **NM** $50   **MIP** n/a

Flap Jacks, 1931, All-Fair
  EX $125   **NM** $250   **MIP** n/a

Flash, 1940s, Pressman
  EX $20   **NM** $50   **MIP** n/a

Flitters, 1899, Martin
  EX $45   **NM** $75   **MIP** n/a

Floor Croquet Game, 1912
  EX $60   **NM** $100   **MIP** n/a

Four and Twenty Blackbirds, 1890s, McLoughlin Bros.
  EX $750   **NM** $1500   **MIP** n/a

Four Dare Devils, The, 1933, Marx, Hess & Lee
  EX $40   **NM** $65   **MIP** n/a

Gee-Wiz Horse Race, 1928, Wolverine
  EX $50   **NM** $85   **MIP** n/a

Genuine Steamer Quoits, 1924, Milton Bradley
  EX $15   **NM** $25   **MIP** n/a

(KP Photo)

Happitime Bagatelle, 1933, Northwestern Products
  EX $30   **NM** $45   **MIP** n/a

GAMES

Happy Landing, 1938, Transogram
 EX $30   **NM** $45   **MIP** n/a

Hop-Over Puzzle, 1930s, Pressman
 EX $20   **NM** $35   **MIP** n/a

Hungry Willie, 1930s, Transogram
 EX $20   **NM** $50   **MIP** n/a

Hunting in the Jungle, 1920s, A. Gropper
 EX $30   **NM** $45   **MIP** n/a

(KP Photo)

Indoor Golf Dice, 1920s, W.P. Bushell
 EX $20   **NM** $35   **MIP** n/a

Jack Straws, The Game of, 1901, Parker Brothers
 EX $20   **NM** $40   **MIP** n/a

Jamboree, 1937, Selchow & Righter
 EX $50   **NM** $75   **MIP** n/a

Japanese Ball Game, 1930s, Girard
 EX $35   **NM** $65   **MIP** n/a

Japanola, 1928, Parker Brothers
 EX $35   **NM** $60   **MIP** n/a

Jaunty Butler, 1932, All-Fair
 EX $100   **NM** $150   **MIP** n/a

Jav-Lin, 1931, All-Fair
 EX $175   **NM** $225   **MIP** n/a

Jolly Clown Spinette, 1932, Milton Bradley
 EX $30   **NM** $45   **MIP** n/a

Jolly Robbers, 1929, Wilder
 EX $50   **NM** $75   **MIP** n/a

Jumping Jupiter, 1940s, Gabriel
 EX $30   **NM** $50   **MIP** n/a

Jungle Hunt, 1940, Gotham Pressed Steel
 EX $30   **NM** $45   **MIP** n/a

Jungle Jump-Up Game, 1940s, Judson Press
 EX $30   **NM** $45   **MIP** n/a

Katzenjammer Kids Hockey, 1940s, Jaymar
 EX $40   **NM** $65   **MIP** n/a

Katzy Party, 1900s, Selchow & Righter
 EX $70   **NM** $120   **MIP** n/a

Kindergarten Lotto, 1904, Strauss
 EX $50   **NM** $80   **MIP** n/a

Knockout Andy, 1926, Parker Brothers
 EX $35   **NM** $75   **MIP** n/a

Kuti-Kuts, 1922, Regensteiner
 EX $20   **NM** $30   **MIP** n/a

Leaping Lena, 1920s, Parker Brothers
 EX $100   **NM** $200   **MIP** n/a

(KP Photo)

Lid's Off, The, 1937, American Toy Works
 EX $35   **NM** $75   **MIP** n/a

Little Orphan Annie Bead Game, 1930s
 EX $20   **NM** $35   **MIP** n/a

Little Orphan Annie Shooting Game, 1930s, Milton Bradley
 EX $100   **NM** $200   **MIP** n/a

Lone Ranger Hi-Yo Silver!! Target Game, 1939, Marx
 EX $75   **NM** $125   **MIP** n/a

Mammoth Conette, 1898, Milton Bradley
 EX $90   **NM** $150   **MIP** n/a

Marble Muggins, 1920s, American Toy
 EX $125   **NM** $200   **MIP** n/a

Mar-Juck, 1923, Regensteiner
 EX $20   **NM** $30   **MIP** n/a

Meteor Game, 1916, A.C. Gilbert
 EX $25   **NM** $45   **MIP** n/a

Mickey Mouse Miniature Pinball Game, 1930s, Marks Brothers
 EX $20   **NM** $35   **MIP** n/a

Mickey Mouse Shooting Game, 1930s, Marks Brothers
 EX $120   **NM** $200   **MIP** n/a

Mickey Mouse Skittle Ball Game, 1930s, Marks Brothers
 EX $60   **NM** $100   **MIP** n/a

Mickey Mouse Soldier Target Set, 1930s, Marks Brothers
 EX $60   **NM** $100   **MIP** n/a

Mumbly Peg, 1920s, All-Fair
 EX $15   **NM** $20   **MIP** n/a

Old Time Shooting Gallery, 1940, Warren-Built-Rite
 EX $15   **NM** $25   **MIP** n/a

Our Gang Tipple Topple Game, 1930, All-Fair
 EX $200   **NM** $350   **MIP** n/a

Peeza, 1935, Toy Creations
 EX $25   **NM** $45   **MIP** n/a

Pike's Peak or Bust, 1890s, Parker Brothers
 EX $100   **NM** $150   **MIP** n/a

Ping Pong, 1902, Parker Brothers
 EX $100   **NM** $175   **MIP** n/a

Pinocchio Target Game, 1938, American Toy Works
 EX $90   **NM** $150   **MIP** n/a

Pinocchio the Merry Puppet Game, 1939, Milton Bradley
 EX $55   **NM** $95   **MIP** n/a

(KP Photo)

Pitch Em, The Game of Indoor Horse Shoes, 1929, Wolverine
 EX $25   **NM** $35   **MIP** n/a

(KP Photo)

Pop the Hat, 1930s, Milton Bradley
 EX $35   **NM** $50   **MIP** n/a

Ranger Commandos, 1942, Parker Brothers
 EX $35   **NM** $60   **MIP** n/a

Red Ryder "Whirli-Crow" Target Game, 1940s, Daisy
 EX $150   **NM** $250   **MIP** n/a

Ride 'em Cowboy, 1939, Gotham Pressed Steel
 EX $25   **NM** $45   **MIP** n/a

Ring My Nose, 1926, Milton Bradley
 EX $75   **NM** $100   **MIP** n/a

Ring Scaling, 1900, Martin
 EX $25   **NM** $45   **MIP** n/a

Shuffle-Board, The New Game of, 1920, Gabriel
 EX $50   **NM** $85   **MIP** n/a

Simba, 1932, All-Fair
EX $100   NM $175   MIP n/a

Smitty Target Game, 1930s, Milton Bradley
EX $40   NM $75   MIP n/a

Snap-Jacks, 1940s, Gabriel
EX $15   NM $25   MIP n/a

Snow White and the Seven Dwarfs, 1938,
American Toy Works
EX $150   NM $250   MIP n/a

Spin 'em Target Game, 1930s, All Metal
Product
EX $25   NM $40   MIP n/a

Spin It, 1910s, Milton Bradley
EX $20   NM $50   MIP n/a

Stak, International Game of, 1937, Marks
Brothers
EX $30   NM $40   MIP n/a

Stax, 1930s, Marks Brothers
EX $12   NM $20   MIP n/a

Superman Action Game, 1940, American
Toy Works
EX $60   NM $100   MIP n/a

Table Croquet, 1890s, Milton Bradley
EX $25   NM $50   MIP n/a

Tactics, 1940, Northwestern Products
EX $25   NM $45   MIP n/a

Tiddledy Wink Tennis, 1890, E.I. Horsman
EX $45   NM $75   MIP n/a

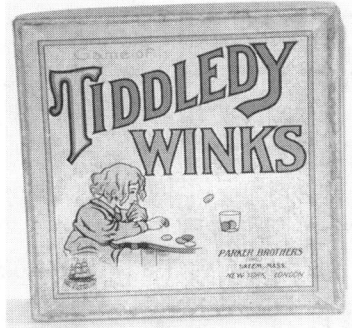

(KP Photo)

Tiddledy Winks, Game of, 1910s, Parker
Brothers
EX $20   NM $40   MIP n/a

Tinker Toss, 1920s, Toy Creations
EX $25   NM $40   MIP n/a

Tip the Bellboy, 1929, All-Fair
EX $150   NM $250   MIP n/a

Tip Top Fish Pond, 1930s, Milton Bradley
EX $20   NM $45   MIP n/a

Toss-O, 1924, Lubbers & Bell
EX $15   NM $25   MIP n/a

Touchdown, 1930s, Milton Bradley
EX $150   NM $250   MIP n/a

Toy Town Target with Repeating Pistol,
1911, Milton Bradley
EX $55   NM $95   MIP n/a

Traps and Bunkers, A Game of Golf,
1930s, Milton Bradley
EX $25   NM $40   MIP n/a

Wa-Hoo Pick-Em Up Sticks, 1936,
Doremus Schoen
EX $15   NM $25   MIP n/a

Walt Disney's Ski Jump Target Game,
1930s, American Toy Works
EX $175   NM $295   MIP n/a

Walt Disney's Uncle Remus Game,
1930s, Parker Brothers
EX $60   NM $125   MIP n/a

Washington's Birthday Party, 1911, Russell
EX $55   NM $95   MIP n/a

Watermelon Patch Game, 1896,
McLoughlin Bros.
EX $1000   NM $2000   MIP n/a

Wonder Tiddley Winks, 1899, Martin
EX $20   NM $45   MIP n/a

TABLETOP GAMES

AUTO RACING

No. 300 Electric Auto Racing, 1948-49,
Tudor
EX $50   NM $100   MIP n/a

**No. 530 Tru-Action Electric Sports Car
Race,** 1959-65, Tudor
EX $25   NM $55   MIP n/a

**No. 590 Mickey Mouse Electric Treasure
Hunt Game,** 1963-64, Tudor
EX $40   NM $85   MIP n/a

BASEBALL

No. 550 Tru-Action Electric Baseball,
1950-58, Tudor
EX $30   NM $75   MIP n/a

No. 550 Tru-Action Electric Baseball,
1958-63, Tudor
EX $25   NM $60   MIP n/a

No. 555 Tru-Action Electric Baseball,
1964-88, Tudor, square field
EX $22   NM $50   MIP n/a

BASKETBALL

Gotham Pass 'N Shoot Basketball, 1968,
Gotham Pressed Steel Co.
EX $20   NM $55   MIP n/a

Gotham Pro Basketball, 1950s, Gotham
Pressed Steel Co.
EX $15   NM $45   MIP n/a

No. 475 Magnetic Baseball, 1964-67, Tudor
EX $20   NM $45   MIP n/a

No. 480 NBPA Game, 1968-70, Tudor
EX $30   NM $75   MIP n/a

No. 480 NBPA Game, 1971, Tudor
EX $15   NM $40   MIP n/a

No. 575 Tru-Action Electric Basketball,
1957-58, Tudor
EX $30   NM $70   MIP n/a

No. 575 Tru-Action Electric Basketball,
1959-63, Tudor
EX $25   NM $55   MIP n/a

No. G-660 Gotham All Star Basketball,
1947, Gotham Pressed Steel Co.
EX $20   NM $50   MIP n/a

FOOTBALL

G-890 Dick Butkus, 1972, Gotham
EX $30   NM $75   MIP n/a

No. G-1400, 1965-67, Gotham
EX $30   NM $60   MIP n/a

No. G-1440, 1962-64, Gotham
EX $35   NM $70   MIP n/a

No. G-1503, 1968, Gotham
EX $33   NM $70   MIP n/a

No. G-1503-S NFL Big Bowl, 1965-67,
Gotham
EX $50   NM $125   MIP n/a

No. G-1506 NFL Players Association,
Gotham
EX $25   NM $60   MIP n/a

No. G-1512 Super Dome, 1969-71, Gotham
EX $45   NM $110   MIP n/a

No. G-1550 Yankee Stadium Grandstand,
1962-64, Gotham
EX $40   NM $80   MIP n/a

No. G-812 Joe Namath, 1969-71, Gotham
EX $35   NM $75   MIP n/a

No. G-812 Joe Namath, 1972, Gotham
EX $35   NM $85   MIP n/a

No. G-818 Roman Gabriel Model,
1969-71, Gotham
EX $25   NM $65   MIP n/a

No. G-818 Roman Gabriel Model, 1972,
Gotham
EX $25   NM $55   MIP n/a

**No. G-880 Gotham All-Star Electric
Football,** 1956-58, Gotham
EX $30   NM $70   MIP n/a

**No. G-880 Gotham All-Star Electric
Football,** 1959-61, Gotham
EX $25   NM $50   MIP n/a

No. G-882, 1965-67, Gotham
EX $18   NM $50   MIP n/a

No. G-883, 1968, Gotham
EX $15   NM $40   MIP n/a

No. G-883, 1972, Gotham
EX $10   NM $20   MIP n/a

**No. G-890 Gotham Official NFL Electric
Football,** 1962-64, Gotham
EX $20   NM $45   MIP n/a

No. G-895 NFL Players Association,
1969-71, Gotham
EX $22   NM $50   MIP n/a

**No. G-940 Gotham Electro Magnetic
Football,** 1954-55, Gotham
EX $38   NM $80   MIP n/a

Tudor Electronic Football, 1965, Tudor
EX $15   NM $35   MIP n/a

Tudor Tru-Action Electric Football, 1949,
Tudor
EX $25   NM $40   MIP n/a

HOCKEY

Bobby Hull, 1960s, Munro
EX $125   NM $275   MIP n/a

Bobby Hull, 1970s, Munro
EX $75   NM $155   MIP n/a

GAMES

Bobby Orr, late 1960s-early 1970s, Munro
EX $125 NM $265 MIPn/a

Canadian, late 1960s, Eagle
EX $75 NM $145 MIPn/a

Canadian Hockey Master, 1963, Munro, #976
EX $100 NM $225 MIPn/a

City Series, early 1970s, Coleco
EX $100 NM $210 MIPn/a

Foster Hewitt, 1950s, Reliable
EX $125 NM $235 MIPn/a

Hockey games, 1940s-50s, Cresta, various games
EX $200 NM $500 MIPn/a

Hot Shot, late 1960s, Munro
EX $60 NM $125 MIPn/a

Hot Shot, mid 1960s, Munro
EX $75 NM $160 MIPn/a

National, early 1960s, Eagle
EX $125 NM $200 MIPn/a

NHL All-Pro Hockey, 1969, Tudor
EX $25 NM $60 MIPn/a

NHPLA, 1969, Tudor
EX $75 NM $135 MIPn/a

No. 5100 Pro Stars, mid 1960s-early 1970s, Coleco
EX $65 NM $125 MIPn/a

No. 5160-80 Pro Stars, late 1960s-early 1970s, Coleco
EX $75 NM $165 MIPn/a

No. 730 NHL All-Star Hockey, 1968, Tudor
EX $25 NM $50 MIPn/a

No. G1200, 1950s-1960s, Gotham
EX $75 NM $155 MIPn/a

No. G-200, 1930s-1950s, Gotham
EX $125 NM $350 MIPn/a

Official Hockey Night, early 1960s, Eagle
EX $150 NM $325 MIPn/a

Official NHL, 1969-71, Coleco
EX $150 NM $500 MIPn/a

Olympic, 1964, Eagle
EX $200 NM $500 MIPn/a

Pee Wee, late 1950s, Eagle
EX $150 NM $260 MIPn/a

Playmaker, early 1960s, Eagle
EX $150 NM $250 MIPn/a

Playoff, early 1960s, Eagle
EX $125 NM $225 MIPn/a

Power Play, early 1960s, Eagle
EX $125 NM $200 MIPn/a

Power Play, late 1950s, Eagle
EX $125 NM $230 MIPn/a

Power Play, late 1960s, Coleco
EX $100 NM $185 MIPn/a

Pro Series, mid 1950s-early 1960s, Eagle
EX $125 NM $225 MIPn/a

Stanley Cup, mid 1960s, Eagle
EX $150 NM $275 MIPn/a

Stanley Cup, Beliveau, late 1960s, Coleco
EX $125 NM $235 MIPn/a

HORSE RACING

Horse and Harness Race Game, 1963-64, Tudor, combined game
EX $20 NM $50 MIPn/a

No. 525 Horse Race Game, 1950-58, Tudor
EX $25 NM $65 MIPn/a

No. 525 Horse Race Game, 1959-61, Tudor, grooved plastic track
EX $22 NM $55 MIPn/a

No. 525 Tru-Action Electric Horse Race Game, 1962, Tudor, plastic track, no grooves
EX $20 NM $40 MIPn/a

No. 526 Harness Race Game, 1962, Tudor
EX $20 NM $45 MIPn/a

Tru-Action Races Game, 1965-67, Tudor
EX $35 NM $75 MIPn/a

TRACK AND FIELD

No. 528 Track and Field Meet, 1963-64, Tudor
EX $35 NM $85 MIPn/a

No. 528 Tru-Action Races, 1965-67, Tudor
EX $35 NM $90 MIPn/a

No. 528 Tudor Track, 1962, Tudor, plastic track
EX $15 NM $45 MIPn/a

POSTWAR GAMES

BOARD GAMES

$10,000 Pyramid Game, The, 1974, Milton Bradley
EX $8 NM $15 MIP $20

$20,000 Pyramid Game, The, 1975, Milton Bradley
EX $8 NM $15 MIP $20

$25,000 Pyramid, 1980s, Cardinal Industries
EX $10 NM $15 MIP $25

$64,000 Question Quiz Game, 1955, Lowell
EX $12 NM $25 MIP $30

1-2-3 Game Hot Spot!, 1961, Parker Brothers
EX $6 NM $15 MIP $20

1863, Civil War Game, 1961, Parker Brothers
EX $20 NM $30 MIP $40

2 For The Money, 1955, Lowell
EX $10 NM $15 MIP $20

20,000 Leagues Under the Sea, 1950s, Gardner
EX $20 NM $30 MIP $50

221 B Baker Street, 1978, John Hansen
EX $2 NM $6 MIP $10

25 Ghosts, 1969, Lakeside
EX $15 NM $25 MIP $40

3 Up, 1972, Lakeside
EX $3 NM $7 MIP $12

300 Mile Race, 1955, Warren
EX $15 NM $20 MIP $40

36 Fits, 1966, Watkins-Strathmore
EX $12 NM $30 MIP $40

4 Alarm Game, 1963, Milton Bradley
EX $18 NM $40 MIP $65

4000 A.D. Interstellar Conflict Game, 1972, House of Games
EX $8 NM $20 MIP $35

(KP Photo)

77 Sunset Strip, 1960, Lowell
EX $30 NM $40 MIP $50

99, The Game of, 1969, Broman-Percepta Corp.
EX $8 NM $15 MIP $25

Abbott & Costello Who's On First?, 1978, Selchow & Righter
EX $5 NM $10 MIP $15

ABC Monday Night Football Roger Staubach Edition, 1973, Aurora
EX $15 NM $25 MIP $35

ABC Sports Winter Olympics, 1987, Mindscape
EX $10 NM $15 MIP $25

Acquire (plastic tiles), 1968, 3M
EX $12 NM $30 MIP $45

Acquire (wood tiles), 1963, 3M
EX $35 NM $75 MIP $100

Across the Board Horse Racing Game, 1975, MPH
EX $8 NM $20 MIP $35

Across the Continent (cars), 1960, Parker Brothers
EX $20 NM $30 MIP $40

Across the Continent (trains), 1952, Parker Brothers
EX $20 NM $30 MIP $40

Action Baseball, 1965, Pressman
EX $20 NM $30 MIP $40

Addams Family, 1965, Ideal
EX $65 NM $85 MIP $125

Addams Family, 1973, Milton Bradley
EX $15 NM $20 MIP $30

Admirals, 1973, Parker Brothers (U.K.)
EX $10 NM $25 MIP $35

Advance To Boardwalk, 1985, Parker Brothers
EX $5 NM $15 MIP $20

Adventure in Science, An, 1950, Jacmar
EX $20 NM $30 MIP $50

Agent Zero-M Spy Detector, 1964, Mattel
EX $30 NM $50 MIP $80

Aggravation, 1970, Lakeside
EX $5 NM $10 MIP $15

Air Assault on Crete, 1977, Avalon Hill
EX $3 NM $10 MIP $15

Air Charter, 1970, Waddington
EX $10 NM $25 MIP $35

GAMES

Air Empire, 1961, Avalon Hill
EX $40   NM $100   MIP $160

Air Race Around the World, 1950s, Lido
EX $12   NM $30   MIP $50

Air Traffic Controller, 1974, Schaper
EX $12   NM $30   MIP $40

Airline, 1985, Mulgara Products
EX $4   NM $10   MIP $15

Airline: The Jet Age Game, 1977, MPH Games
EX $6   NM $15   MIP $25

Alfred Hitchcock "Why?", 1965, Milton Bradley
EX $10   NM $20   MIP $30

Alfred Hitchcock Presents Mystery Game "Why", 1958, Milton Bradley
EX $20   NM $35   MIP $55

(KP Photo)

Alien, 1979, Kenner
EX $15   NM $45   MIP $50

All American Football, 1969, Cadaco
EX $5   NM $10   MIP $20

(KP Photo)

All In The Family, 1972, Milton Bradley
EX $10   NM $20   MIP $30

All My Children, 1985, TSR
EX $5   NM $10   MIP $20

All Pro Baseball, 1969, Ideal
EX $20   NM $35   MIP $55

All Pro Basketball, 1969, Ideal
EX $10   NM $25   MIP $35

All Pro Football, 1967, Ideal
EX $8   NM $20   MIP $30

All Star Baseball, 1960s, Cadaco-Ellis
EX $30   NM $65   MIP $125

All Star Baseball, 1970s, Cadaco-Ellis
EX $10   NM $25   MIP $45

All Star Baseball, 1989, Cadaco
EX $5   NM $12   MIP $20

All Star Baseball Fame, 1962, Cadaco-Ellis
EX $15   NM $25   MIP $40

All Star Basketball, 1950s, Gardner
EX $55   NM $90   MIP $135

All Star Electric Baseball & Football, 1955, Harett-Gilmar
EX $35   NM $60   MIP $90

All Star Football, 1950, Gardner
EX $20   NM $45   MIP $65

All The King's Men, 1979, Parker Brothers
EX $6   NM $10   MIP $15

All Time Greats Baseball Game, 1971, Midwest Research
EX $15   NM $35   MIP $50

Alumni Fun, 1964, Milton Bradley
EX $8   NM $20   MIP $30

Amazing Dunninger Mind Reading Game, 1967, Hasbro
EX $12   NM $20   MIP $25

American Derby, The, 1951, Cadaco-Ellis
EX $15   NM $20   MIP $30

American Dream, The, 1979, Milton Bradley
EX $10   NM $25   MIP $35

Animal Crackers, 1970s, Milton Bradley
EX $4   NM $7   MIP $11

Annette's Secret Passage, 1958, Parker Brothers
EX $20   NM $25   MIP $35

Annie Oakley (larger), 1955, Milton Bradley
EX $35   NM $50   MIP $75

Annie Oakley (smaller game), 1950s, Milton Bradley
EX $12   NM $30   MIP $40

Annie, The Movie Game, 1981, Parker Brothers
EX $4   NM $6   MIP $10

Anti-Monopoly, 1973, Anti-Monopoly
EX $8   NM $20   MIP $30

APBA "Pro" League Football, 1980s, APBA
EX $12   NM $20   MIP $30

APBA Baseball Master Game, 1975, APBA
EX $20   NM $75   MIP $100

APBA Pro League Football, 1964, APBA
EX $25   NM $60   MIP $85

APBA Saddle Racing Game, 1970s, APBA
EX $15   NM $25   MIP $40

Apollo: A Voyage to the Moon, 1969, Tracianne
EX $12   NM $30   MIP $40

Apple's Way, 1974, Milton Bradley
EX $12   NM $20   MIP $30

Archies, The, 1969, Whitman
EX $15   NM $20   MIP $40

Arena, 1962, Lakeside
EX $6   NM $15   MIP $25

Arnold Palmer's Inside Golf, 1961, D.B. Remson
EX $30   NM $45   MIP $75

Around the World, 1962, Milton Bradley
EX $10   NM $25   MIP $35

Around The World in 80 Days, 1957, Transogram
EX $10   NM $20   MIP $30

Art Lewis Football Game, 1955, Morgantown Game
EX $70   NM $115   MIP $175

Art Linkletter's House Party, 1968, Whitman
EX $8   NM $20   MIP $30

As The World Turns, 1966, Parker Brothers
EX $12   NM $20   MIP $30

ASG Baseball, 1989, 3W (World Wide Wargames)
EX $15   NM $35   MIP $50

ASG Major League Baseball, 1973, Gerney Games
EX $35   NM $75   MIP $125

Assembly Line, 1953, Selchow & Righter
EX $18   NM $25   MIP $50

Astro Launch, 1963, Ohio Art
EX $18   NM $40   MIP $60

Astron, 1955, Parker Prothers
EX $25   NM $35   MIP $60

(KP Photo)

A-Team, 1984, Parker Brothers
EX $5   NM $10   MIP $15

Atom Ant Game, 1966, Transogram
EX $25   NM $60   MIP $90

Aurora Pursuit! Game, 1973, Aurora
EX $8   NM $25   MIP $40

Auto Dome, 1967, Transogram
EX $18   NM $40   MIP $60

Autograph Baseball Game, 1948, Philadelphia Inquirer
EX $110   NM $180   MIP $275

B.T.O. (Big Time Operator), 1956, Bettye-B
EX $20   NM $30   MIP $40

B-17 Queen of The Skies, 1983, Avalon Hill
EX $6   NM $10   MIP $15

(KP Photo)

Babes in Toyland, 1961, Whitman
EX $15   NM $25   MIP $35

Ballplayer's Baseball Game, 1955, Jon Weber
EX $30   NM $50   MIP $75

Bamboozle, 1962, Milton Bradley
EX $15   NM $20   MIP $30

Banana Tree, 1977, Marx
EX $10   NM $15   MIP $25

Bang, A Game of the Old West, 1956, Selchow & Righter
EX $35   NM $75   MIP $100

Bantu, 1955, Parker Brothers
EX $15   NM $20   MIP $30

Barbapapa Takes A Trip, 1977, Selchow & Righter
EX $3   NM $5   MIP $8

Barbie, Queen of The Prom, 1960, Mattel
EX $30   NM $60   MIP $85

Barbie's Little Sister Skipper Game, 1964, Mattel
EX $15   NM $40   MIP $60

(KP Photo)

Baretta, 1976, Milton Bradley
EX $30   NM $50   MIP $75

Bargain Hunter, 1981, Milton Bradley
EX $6   NM $15   MIP $25

(KP Photo)

Barnabas Collins Game, 1969, Milton Bradley
EX $20   NM $45   MIP $70

(KP Photo)

Barney Miller, 1977, Parker Brothers
EX $10   NM $15   MIP $25

Barnstormer, 1970s, Marx
EX $20   NM $35   MIP $55

Bart Starr Quarterback Game, 1960s
EX $175   NM $295   MIP $450

Bar-Teen Ranch Game, 1950s, Warren Built-Rite
EX $10   NM $25   MIP $35

Baseball Challenge, 1980, Tri-Valley Games
EX $15   NM $35   MIP $50

Baseball Game, Official, 1969, Milton Bradley
EX $50   NM $75   MIP $100

Baseball Game, The, 1988, Horatio
EX $12   NM $20   MIP $30

Baseball Strategy, 1973, Avalon Hill
EX $6   NM $15   MIP $25

Baseball, A Sports Illustrated Game, 1971-73, Time
EX $60   NM $150   MIP $200

Baseball, Football & Checkers, 1957, Parker Brothers
EX $20   NM $30   MIP $50

Basketball Strategy, 1974, Avalon Hill
EX $10   NM $15   MIP $25

(KP Photo)

Bat Masterson, 1958, Lowell
EX $45   NM $60   MIP $75

Batman, 1978, Hasbro
EX $15   NM $30   MIP $50

Batman and Robin Game, 1965, Hasbro
EX $30   NM $65   MIP $95

Batman Game, 1966, Milton Bradley
EX $25   NM $60   MIP $90

Batter Up, 1946, M. Hopper
EX $30   NM $50   MIP $75

Batter-Rou Baseball Game (Dizzy Dean), 1950s, Memphis Plastic
EX $100   NM $165   MIP $250

Battle Cry, 1962, Milton Bradley
EX $25   NM $50   MIP $85

(KP Photo)

Battle Line, 1964, Ideal
EX $25   NM $50   MIP $75

Battle Masters, 1992, Milton Bradley
EX $15   NM $40   MIP $60

(KP Photo)

Battle of the Planets, 1970s, Milton Bradley
EX $15   NM $25   MIP $35

Battleboard, 1972, Ideal
EX $10   NM $25   MIP $35

(KP Photo)

Battleship, 1965, Milton Bradley
EX $10   NM $15   MIP $20

(KP Photo)

Battlestar Galactica, 1978, Parker Brothers
EX $10   NM $15   MIP $25

Battling Tops Game, 1968, Ideal
EX $30   NM $50   MIP $80

Bazaar, 1967, 3M
EX $12   NM $30   MIP $40

Bazaar, 1987, Discovery Toys
EX $8   NM $20   MIP $30

Beany & Cecil Match It, 1960s, Mattel
EX $30   NM $50   MIP $80

Beat Inflation, 1975, Avalon Hill
EX $8   NM $20   MIP $30

Beat the 8 Ball, 1975, Ideal
EX $10   NM $15   MIP $25

Beat The Buzz, 1958, Kenner
EX $10   NM $15   MIP $25

Beat The Clock, 1954, Lowell
EX $15   NM $30   MIP $50

Beat The Clock, 1960s, Milton Bradley
EX $6   NM $10   MIP $16

(KP Photo)

Beatles Flip Your Wig Game, 1964, Milton Bradley
EX $100   NM $150   MIP $275

Beetle Bailey, The Old Army Game, 1963, Milton Bradley
EX $30   NM $50   MIP $65

Behind the 8 Ball Game, 1969, Selchow & Righter
EX $8   NM $15   MIP $20

(KP Photo)

Ben Casey MD Game, 1961, Transogram
EX $15   NM $20   MIP $35

Bermuda Triangle, 1976, Milton Bradley
EX $10   NM $15   MIP $20

GAMES

Betsy Ross and the Flag, 1950s, Transogram
 EX $18   NM $45   MIP $70

(Toy Shop File Photo)

Beverly Hillbillies Game, 1963, Standard Toykraft, "If you like the T.V. show… you'll love the game…"
 EX $25   NM $50   MIP $70

Bewitched, 1965
 EX $50   NM $75   MIP $100

Beyond the Stars, 1964, Game Partners
 EX $20   NM $45   MIP $65

Bible Baseball, 1950s, Standard
 EX $50   NM $75   MIP $150

Big Boggle, 1979, Parker Brothers
 EX $15   NM $20   MIP $25

Big Foot, 1977, Milton Bradley
 EX $5   NM $12   MIP $20

Big League Baseball, 1959, Saalfield
 EX $20   NM $45   MIP $65

Big League Baseball Game, 1966, 3M
 EX $15   NM $25   MIP $40

Big League Manager Football, 1965, BLM
 EX $30   NM $75   MIP $100

Big Payoff, 1984, Payoff Enterprises
 EX $6   NM $10   MIP $15

Big Six Sports Game, 1950s, Gardner
 EX $125   NM $295   MIP $450

Big Time Colorado Football, 1983, B.J. Tall
 EX $6   NM $10   MIP $15

Big Town, 1954, Lowell
 EX $20   NM $30   MIP $50

Billionaire, 1973, Parker Brothers
 EX $5   NM $10   MIP $15

Bing Crosby's Game, Call Me Lucky, 1954, Parker Brothers
 EX $15   NM $35   MIP $50

Bingo-Matic, 1954, Transogram
 EX $5   NM $10   MIP $15

(KP Photo)

Bionic Crisis, 1975, Parker Brothers
 EX $6   NM $15   MIP $20

(KP Photo)

Bionic Woman, 1976, Parker Brothers
 EX $6   NM $15   MIP $20

Bird Brain, 1966, Milton Bradley
 EX $10   NM $25   MIP $40

Bird Watcher, 1958, Parker Brothers
 EX $15   NM $35   MIP $50

Birdie Golf, 1964, Barris
 EX $15   NM $35   MIP $50

Black Ball Express, 1957, Schaper
 EX $8   NM $25   MIP $40

Black Beauty, 1957, Transogram
 EX $15   NM $25   MIP $25

Black Box, 1978, Parker Brothers
 EX $5   NM $10   MIP $15

Blade Runner, 1982
 EX $25   NM $60   MIP $85

Blast Off, 1953, Selchow & Righter
 EX $50   NM $75   MIP $125

Blast, The Game of, 1973, Ideal
 EX $8   NM $20   MIP $35

Blitzkrieg, 1965, Avalon Hill
 EX $4   NM $10   MIP $16

Blockhead, 1954, Russell
 EX $10   NM $15   MIP $25

Blondie, 1970s, Parker Brothers
 EX $6   NM $10   MIP $15

Blondie and Dagwood's Race for the Office, 1950, Jaymar
 EX $20   NM $45   MIP $70

Blue Line Hockey, 1968, 3M
 EX $10   NM $25   MIP $40

Bluff, 1964, Saalfield
 EX $10   NM $25   MIP $40

BMX Cross Challenge Action Game, 1988, Cross Challenge
 EX $6   NM $10   MIP $15

Bob Feller's Big League Baseball, 1949, Saalfield
 EX $75   NM $100   MIP $150

Bobbsey Twins, 1957, Milton Bradley
 EX $8   NM $15   MIP $20

Bobby Shantz Baseball Game, 1955, Realistic Games
 EX $80   NM $150   MIP $225

Body Language, 1975, Milton Bradley
 EX $2   NM $5   MIP $10

Boggle, 1976, Parker Brothers
 EX $3   NM $8   MIP $12

(KP Photo)

Bonanza Michigan Rummy Game, 1964, Parker Brothers
 EX $20   NM $35   MIP $50

Bonkers!, This Game is, 1978, Parker Brothers
 EX $3   NM $10   MIP $15

Boom or Bust, 1951, Parker Brothers
 EX $75   NM $150   MIP $225

Booth's Pro Conference Football, 1977, Sher-Co
 EX $10   NM $15   MIP $25

(KP Photo)

Boots and Saddles, 1960, Chad Valley
 EX $35   NM $65   MIP $100

Boris Karloff's Monster Game, 1965, Gems
 EX $100   NM $150   MIP $250

Boston Marathon Game, Official, 1978, Perl Products
 EX $15   NM $25   MIP $35

Bottoms Up, 1970s
 EX $3   NM $5   MIP $8

Boundary, 1970, Mattel
 EX $8   NM $20   MIP $30

Bowl & Score, 1974, Lowe
 EX $6   NM $8   MIP $10

Bowl And Score, 1962, Lowe
 EX $6   NM $10   MIP $15

Bowl Bound!, 1973, Sports Illustrated
 EX $15   NM $25   MIP $40

Brain Waves, 1977, Milton Bradley
 EX $6   NM $15   MIP $25

(KP Photo)

Branded, 1966, Milton Bradley
  EX $20   NM $50   MIP $75

Brass Monkey Game, The, 1973, U.S. Game Systems
  EX $6   NM $10   MIP $15

Break Par Golf Game, 1950s, Warren/Built-Rite
  EX $8   NM $20   MIP $30

Break The Bank, 1955, Bettye-B
  EX $12   NM $30   MIP $45

Breaker 1-9, 1976, Milton Bradley
  EX $5   NM $10   MIP $15

Breakthru, 1965, 3M
  EX $8   NM $20   MIP $30

Brett Ball, 1981, 9th Inning
  EX $15   NM $20   MIP $30

Bride Bingo, 1957, Leister Game
  EX $2   NM $5   MIP $8

Bride Game, The, 1971, Selchow & Righter
  EX $12   NM $25   MIP $50

Broadside, 1962, Milton Bradley
  EX $35   NM $75   MIP $100

Broadsides & Board Gameing Parties, 1984, Milton Bradley
  EX $50   NM $125   MIP $175

Bruce Jenner Decathlon Game, 1979, Parker Brothers
  EX $4   NM $7   MIP $11

Buck Fever, 1984, L & D Robton
  EX $12   NM $20   MIP $30

Buck Rogers Game, 1979, Milton Bradley
  EX $10   NM $25   MIP $50

Buck Rogers: Battle for the 25th Century, 1988, TSR
  EX $18   NM $45   MIP $65

Buckaroo, 1947, Milton Bradley
  EX $20   NM $35   MIP $45

Bucket Ball, 1972, Marx
  EX $10   NM $15   MIP $25

Bug-A-Boo, 1968, Whitman
  EX $6   NM $15   MIP $20

(KP Photo)

Bugaloos, 1971, Milton Bradley
  EX $15   NM $35   MIP $60

Bugs Bunny Under the Cawit Game, 1972, Whitman
  EX $15   NM $25   MIP $40

Building Boom, 1950s, Kohner
  EX $10   NM $20   MIP $35

Built-Rite Swish Basketball Game, 1950s, Warren/Built-Rite
  EX $10   NM $20   MIP $35

(KP Photo)

Bullwinkle Hide & Seek Game, 1961, Milton Bradley
  EX $20   NM $45   MIP $100

Bullwinkle's Super Market Game, 1970s, Whitman
  EX $15   NM $50   MIP $75

Buster Brown Game and Play Box, 1950s, Buster Brown Shoes
  EX $40   NM $75   MIP $125

Buy and Sell, 1953, Whitman
  EX $8   NM $15   MIP $20

Buy or Sell, 1967, KMS Industries
  EX $5   NM $12   MIP $18

C&O/B&O, 1969, Avalon Hill
  EX $20   NM $50   MIP $95

Cabbage Patch Kids, 1984, Parker Brothers
  EX $5   NM $10   MIP $15

California Raisins Board Game, 1987, Decipher
  EX $4   NM $16   MIP $25

Call it Golf, 1966, Strauss
  EX $15   NM $25   MIP $40

Call My Bluff, 1965, Milton Bradley
  EX $15   NM $20   MIP $30

Calling All Cars, 1930s-40s, Parker Brothers
  EX $50   NM $75   MIP $100

Calling All Cars, 1950s, Parker Brothers
  EX $15   NM $25   MIP $35

Calling Superman, 1955, Transogram
  EX $45   NM $85   MIP $125

Calvin & The Colonel High Spirits, 1962, Milton Bradley
  EX $12   NM $25   MIP $35

Camelot, 1955, Parker Brothers
  EX $15   NM $25   MIP $30

Camouflage, 1961, Milton Bradley
  EX $5   NM $20   MIP $35

Camp Granada Game, Allan Sherman's, 1965, Milton Bradley
  EX $40   NM $70   MIP $125

Camp Runamuck, 1965, Ideal
  EX $25   NM $45   MIP $65

Campaign, 1966, Campaign Game
  EX $8   NM $25   MIP $40

Campaign, 1971, Waddington
  EX $10   NM $30   MIP $45

Campaign: The American "Go" Game, 1961, Saalfield
  EX $15   NM $45   MIP $65

Can You Catch It Charlie Brown?, 1976, Ideal
  EX $10   NM $25   MIP $35

Candid Camera Game, 1963, Lowell
  EX $15   NM $25   MIP $40

Candyland, 1949, Milton Bradley
  EX $25   NM $50   MIP $75

Candyland, 1955, Milton Bradley
  EX $20   NM $35   MIP $50

Cannonball Run, The, 1981, Cadaco
  EX $4   NM $16   MIP $25

Can't Stop, 1980, Parker Brothers
  EX $5   NM $12   MIP $20

Caper, 1970, Parker Brothers
  EX $30   NM $70   MIP $100

Capital Punishment, 1981, Hammerhead
  EX $20   NM $35   MIP $75

Captain America, 1966, Milton Bradley
  EX $25   NM $50   MIP $75

Captain America, 1977, Milton Bradley
  EX $10   NM $15   MIP $25

Captain Caveman and the Teen Angels, 1981, Milton Bradley
  EX $8   NM $20   MIP $30

(KP Photo)

Captain Gallant Desert Fort Game, 1956, Transogram
  EX $20   NM $40   MIP $65

(KP Photo)

Captain Kangaroo, 1956, Milton Bradley
  EX $35   NM $45   MIP $100

(KP Photo)

Captain Video Game, 1952, Milton Bradley
EX $50   NM $75   MIP $125

Car Travel Game, 1958, Milton Bradley
EX $5   NM $16   MIP $20

Carapace, 1970, Plan B Corp.
EX $5   NM $16   MIP $25

Cardino, 1970, Milton Bradley
EX $10   NM $15   MIP $25

Careers, 1957, Parker Brothers
EX $8   NM $20   MIP $30

Careers, 1965, Parker Brothers
EX $15   NM $20   MIP $33

Cargoes, 1958, Selchow & Righter
EX $10   NM $25   MIP $50

Carl Hubbell Mechanical Baseball, 1950, Gotham
   NM $100   MIP $150

Carl Yastrzemski's Action Baseball, 1968, Pressman
EX $50   NM $75   MIP $125

Carrier Strike, 1977, Milton Bradley
EX $15   NM $25   MIP $45

Cars 'n Trucks Build-A-Game, 1961, Ideal
EX $15   NM $45   MIP $80

Cartel, 1974, Gamut of Games
EX $18   NM $45   MIP $65

Case of the Elusive Assassin, The, 1967, Ideal
EX $20   NM $30   MIP $50

Casey Jones, 1959, Saalfield
EX $20   NM $45   MIP $65

(KP Photo)

Casper the Friendly Ghost Game, 1959, Milton Bradley
EX $5   NM $10   MIP $15

Casper the Friendly Ghost Game, 1974, Schaper
EX $8   NM $18   MIP $30

Castle Risk, 1986, Parker Brothers
EX $15   NM $35   MIP $50

Cat & Mouse, 1964, Parker Brothers
EX $7   NM $15   MIP $20

Catchword, 1954, Whitman
EX $3   NM $10   MIP $15

Catfish Bend Storybook Game, 1978, Selchow & Righter
EX $15   NM $20   MIP $35

Cathedral, 1986, Mattel
EX $10   NM $25   MIP $35

Cattlemen, The, 1977, Selchow & Righter
EX $10   NM $15   MIP $25

Cavalcade, 1953, Selchow & Righter
EX $15   NM $25   MIP $45

Caveat Emptor, 1971, Plan B
EX $5   NM $16   MIP $25

Centipede, 1983, Milton Bradley
EX $6   NM $10   MIP $15

Century of Great Fights, 1969, Research Games
EX $40   NM $75   MIP $110

Challenge Golf at Pebble Beach, 1972, 3M
EX $6   NM $15   MIP $25

Challenge the Yankees, 1960s, Hasbro
EX $500   NM $1000   MIP $1800

Challenge Yahtzee, 1974, Milton Bradley
EX $7   NM $15   MIP $20

Championship Baseball, 1966, Championship Games
EX $8   NM $20   MIP $30

Championship Basketball, 1966, Championship Games
EX $8   NM $20   MIP $30

Championship Golf, 1966, Championship Games
EX $8   NM $20   MIP $30

Changeover: The Metric Game, 1976, John Ladell
EX $8   NM $20   MIP $30

Changing Society, 1981, Phil Carter
EX $5   NM $16   MIP $25

Chaos, 1965, Amsco Toys
EX $5   NM $16   MIP $25

Chaos, 1971, Lakeside
EX $8   NM $20   MIP $30

Charlie Brown's All Star Baseball Game, 1965, Parker Brothers
EX $18   NM $23   MIP $50

Charlie's Angels, 1977, Milton Bradley
EX $6   NM $10   MIP $20

(KP Photo)

Charlie's Angels (Farrah Fawcett box), 1977, Milton Bradley, Notice the price difference between this version and the non-Farrah edition? Star power really brings up the price on this game
EX $10   NM $20   MIP $45

Charlotte's Web Game, 1974, Hasbro
EX $10   NM $25   MIP $35

Chase, The, 1966, Cadaco
EX $12   NM $30   MIP $45

Chaseback, 1962, Milton Bradley
EX $5   NM $16   MIP $25

Checkpoint: Danger!, 1978, Ideal
EX $5   NM $16   MIP $25

Cherry Ames' Nursing Game, 1959, Parker Brothers
EX $50   NM $90   MIP $135

Chess, 1977, Milton Bradley
EX $3   NM $5   MIP $8

Chevyland Sweepstakes, 1968, Milton Bradley
EX $25   NM $50   MIP $100

Chex Ches Football, 1971, Chex Ches Games
EX $15   NM $25   MIP $40

Cheyenne, 1958, Milton Bradley
EX $25   NM $50   MIP $75

Chicago Sports Trivia Game, 1984, Sports Trivia
EX $6   NM $10   MIP $15

Chicken In Every Pot, A, 1980s, Animal Town Game
EX $20   NM $30   MIP $50

Children's Hour, The, 1946, Parker Brothers
EX $10   NM $15   MIP $20

CHiPs, 1981, Ideal
EX $7   NM $10   MIP $20

(KP Photo)

CHiPs Game, 1977, Milton Bradley
EX $4   NM $7   MIP $10

Chit Chat Game, 1963, Milton Bradley
EX $6   NM $10   MIP $15

Chopper Strike, 1976, Milton Bradley
EX $10   NM $15   MIP $20

Chug-A-Lug, 1969, Dynamic
EX $5   NM $16   MIP $25

Chute-5, 1973, Lowe
EX $5   NM $12   MIP $20

Chutes & Ladders, 1956, Milton Bradley
EX $10   NM $15   MIP $25

Chutzpah, 1967, Middle Earth
EX $15   NM $35   MIP $50

Chutzpah, 1967, Cadaco
EX $10   NM $25   MIP $40

Cimarron Strip, 1967, Ideal
EX $35   NM $75   MIP $100

Circle Racer Board Game, 1988, Sport Games USA
EX $6   NM $10   MIP $15

Cities Game, The, 1970, Psychology Today
EX $5   NM $16   MIP $25

Civil War, 1961, Avalon Hill
EX $15   NM $45   MIP $65

Civilization, 1982, Avalon Hill
EX $7   NM $10   MIP $20

Clash of the Titans, 1981, Whitman
EX $10   NM $25   MIP $45

Class Struggle, 1978, Bernard Ollman
EX $15   NM $25   MIP $50

(KP Photo)

Clean Sweep, 1960s, Schaper
EX $15   NM $20   MIP $45

Clean Water, 1972, Urban Systems
EX $8   NM $25   MIP $40

Cloak & Dagger, 1984, Ideal
EX $8   NM $25   MIP $40

(KP Photo)

Close Encounters of the Third Kind, 1977, Parker Brothers
EX $7   NM $15   MIP $20

Clue, 1949, Parker Brothers
EX $35   NM $50   MIP $85

Clue, 1972, Parker Brothers
EX $4   NM $7   MIP $11

Clue Master Detective, 1988, Parker Brothers
EX $20   NM $55   MIP $75

Clue: The Great Museum Caper, 1991, Parker Brothers
EX $8   NM $20   MIP $30

Code Name: Sector, 1977, Parker Brothers
EX $10   NM $30   MIP $45

Collector, The, 1977, Avalon Hill
EX $5   NM $16   MIP $25

College Basketball, 1954, Cadaco-Ellis
EX $10   NM $25   MIP $35

(KP Photo)

Columbo, 1973, Milton Bradley
EX $6   NM $10   MIP $15

Combat, 1963, Ideal
EX $25   NM $45   MIP $70

Comin' Round The Mountain, 1954, Einson-Freeman
EX $30   NM $50   MIP $80

Computer Baseball, 1966, Epoch Playtime
EX $25   NM $40   MIP $65

Computer Basketball, 1969, Electric Data
EX $10   NM $25   MIP $35

Computerized Pro Football, 1971, Data Prog.
EX $15   NM $25   MIP $40

Concentration (25th Anniversary Ed.), 1982, Milton Bradley
EX $6   NM $10   MIP $16

Concentration (3rd Ed.), 1960, Milton Bradley
EX $12   NM $20   MIP $35

Conestoga, 1964, Washburne Research
EX $25   NM $65   MIP $95

Coney Island, The Game of, 1956, Selchow & Righter
EX $20   NM $35   MIP $60

Conflict, 1960, Parker Brothers
EX $25   NM $35   MIP $60

Confucius Say, 1960s, Pressman
EX $10   NM $20   MIP $30

Conquer, 1979, Whitman
EX $8   NM $17   MIP $25

Conquest of the Empire, 1984, Milton Bradley
EX $50   NM $105   MIP $150

Consetta and Her Wheel of Fate, 1946, Selchow & Righter
EX $20   NM $50   MIP $65

Conspiracy, 1982, Milton Bradley
EX $4   NM $9   MIP $11

Containment, 1979, Shamus Gamus
EX $10   NM $25   MIP $35

Contigo, 1974, 3M
EX $7   NM $20   MIP $35

Cootie, 1949, Schaper
EX $10   NM $25   MIP $35

Count Coup, 1979, Marcian Chronicles
EX $10   NM $30   MIP $45

Count Down Space Game, 1960, Transogram
EX $15   NM $25   MIP $43

Countdown, 1967, Lowe
EX $15   NM $40   MIP $60

Counter Point, 1976, Hallmark
EX $10   NM $15   MIP $25

Cowboy Roundup, 1952, Parker Brothers
EX $10   NM $20   MIP $30

Cracker Jack Game, 1976, Milton Bradley
EX $5   NM $16   MIP $25

Creature Castle, 1975, Whitman
EX $12   NM $30   MIP $40

Creature Features, 1975, Athol
EX $20   NM $50   MIP $75

Creature From the Black Lagoon, 1963, Hasbro
EX $150   NM $410   MIP $750

Cribb Golf, 1980s
EX $10   NM $22   MIP $40

Crosby Derby, The, 1947, Fishlove
EX $25   NM $75   MIP $100

Cross Up, 1974, Milton Bradley
EX $2   NM $5   MIP $10

Crosswords, 1954, National Games
EX $12   NM $20   MIP $32

(KP Photo)

Crusader Rabbit TV Game, 1960s, Tryne
EX $50   NM $100   MIP $175

Cub Scouting, The Game of, 1987, Cadaco
EX $5   NM $16   MIP $25

Curious George Game, 1977, Parker Brothers
EX $4   NM $6   MIP $10

Curse of the Cobras Game, 1982, Ideal
EX $10   NM $25   MIP $35

Cut Up Shopping Spree Game, 1968, Milton Bradley
EX $8   NM $15   MIP $20

Dallas, 1980, Yaquinto
EX $10   NM $15   MIP $20

Dallas, 1985, Maruca Industries
EX $17   NM $35   MIP $55

Dallas (TV Role Playing), 1980, SPI
EX $4   NM $7   MIP $11

Danger Pass, 1964, Game Partners
EX $15   NM $45   MIP $65

Daniel Boone Trail Blazer, 1964
EX $20   NM $50   MIP $75

Dark Crystal Game, The, 1982, Milton Bradley
EX $7   NM $20   MIP $35

Dark Shadows Game, 1968, Whitman
EX $20   NM $40   MIP $75

Dark Tower, 1981, Milton Bradley
EX $125   NM $175   MIP $400

Dark World, 1992, Mattel
EX $12   NM $25   MIP $35

Dastardly and Muttley, 1969, Milton Bradley
EX $15   NM $25   MIP $40

Dating Game, The, 1967, Hasbro
EX $10   NM $20   MIP $30

Davy Crockett Adventure Game, 1956, Gardner
EX $45   NM $75   MIP $100

Davy Crockett Frontierland Game, 1955, Parker Brothers
EX $20   NM $50   MIP $75

Davy Crockett Radar Action Game, 1955, Ewing Mfg. & Sales
EX $40   NM $100   MIP $150

Davy Crockett Rescue Race Game, 1950s, Gabriel
EX $20   NM $50   MIP $75

Dawn of the Dead, 1978, SPI
EX $45   NM $95   MIP $135

Daytona 500 Race Game, 1989, Milton Bradley
EX $10   NM $25   MIP $35

Dead Pan, 1956, Selchow & Righter
EX $8   NM $10   MIP $15

Deadlock, 1972, American Greetings
EX $8   NM $20   MIP $30

Dealer's Choice, 1972, Parker Brothers
EX $10   NM $20   MIP $35

Dealer's Choice, 1974, Gamut of Games
EX $18   NM $45   MIP $65

Dear Abby, 1972, Ideal
EX $7   NM $20   MIP $35

Decathalon, 1972, Sports Illustrated
EX $10   NM $25   MIP $35

Decoy, 1956, Selchow & Righter
EX $12   NM $25   MIP $45

Deduction, 1976, Ideal
EX $5   NM $9   MIP $12

Deluxe Wheel of Fortune, 1986, Pressman
EX $5   NM $8   MIP $13

Dennis The Menace Baseball Game, 1960
EX $22   NM $50   MIP $70

Denny McLain Magnetik Baseball Game, 1968, Gotham
EX $115   NM $195   MIP $295

Deputy Dawg TV Lotto, 1961, Ideal
EX $15   NM $35   MIP $60

(Toy Shop File Photo)

Deputy Game, The, 1960, Bell, "Starring Henry Fonda as Simon Fry"
EX $20   NM $50   MIP $85

Derby Day, 1959, Parker Brothers
EX $18   NM $35   MIP $50

Derby Downs, 1973, Great Games
EX $10   NM $30   MIP $45

(KP Photo)

Detectives Game, The, 1961, Transogram
EX $15   NM $30   MIP $50

Dick Tracy Crime Stopper, 1963, Ideal
EX $20   NM $30   MIP $50

(KP Photo)

Dick Tracy The Master Detective Game, 1961, Selchow & Righter
EX $25   NM $65   MIP $90

Dick Van Dyke Board Game, 1964, Standard Toykraft
EX $75   NM $150   MIP $200

Diet, 1972, Dynamic
EX $5   NM $16   MIP $25

Diner's Club Credit Card Game, The, 1961, Ideal
EX $15   NM $25   MIP $45

Dinosaur Island, 1980, Parker Brothers
EX $5   NM $16   MIP $25

Diplomacy, 1961, Games Research
EX $15   NM $35   MIP $50

Diplomacy, 1976, Avalon Hill
EX $15   NM $25   MIP $40

Direct Hit, 1950s, Northwestern Products
EX $40   NM $70   MIP $110

Dirty Water—The Water Pollution Game, 1970, Urban Systems
EX $8   NM $20   MIP $30

Disney Mouseketeer, 1964, Parker Brothers
EX $40   NM $65   MIP $100

(KP Photo)

Disneyland Game, 1965, Transogram
EX $25   NM $60   MIP $85

Dispatcher, 1958, Avalon Hill
EX $45   NM $70   MIP $125

Dobbin Derby, 1950, Cadaco-Ellis
EX $8   NM $25   MIP $40

(KP Photo)

Doctor Who, 1980s, Denys Fisher
EX $35   NM $75   MIP $100

Doctor, Doctor! Game, 1978, Ideal
EX $8   NM $20   MIP $30

(KP Photo)

Dogfight, 1962, Milton Bradley
EX $35   NM $50   MIP $75

Dollar A Second, 1955, Lowell
EX $12   NM $20   MIP $30

Dollars & Sense, 1946, Sidney Rogers
EX $100   NM $150   MIP $200

Domain, 1983, Parker Brothers
EX $2   NM $3   MIP $5

Domination, 1982, Milton Bradley
EX $8   NM $20   MIP $30

Don Carter's Strike Bowling Game, 1964, Saalfield
EX $20   NM $55   MIP $75

Donald Duck Big Game Box, 1979, Whitman
EX $10   NM $15   MIP $20

Donald Duck Pins & Bowling Game, 1955s, Pressman
EX $35   NM $50   MIP $70

Donald Duck Tiddley Winks Game, 1950s
EX $6   NM $10   MIP $15

Donald Duck's Party Game, 1950s, Parker Brothers
EX $10   NM $35   MIP $50

Dondi Potato Race Game, 1950s, Hasbro
EX $10   NM $20   MIP $35

Donkey Party Game, 1950, Saalfield
EX $4   NM $10   MIP $15

Donny & Marie Osmond TV Show Game, 1977, Mattel
EX $8   NM $25   MIP $40

Don't Miss the Boat, 1965, Parker Brothers
EX $12   NM $30   MIP $40

Doorways to Adventure VCR Game, 1986, Pressman
EX $6   NM $15   MIP $25

Doorways to Horror VCR Game, 1986, Pressman
EX $10   NM $25   MIP $35

Double Cross, 1974, Lakeside
  EX $5   **NM** $16   **MIP** $25

Double Crossing, 1988, Lionel Games
  EX $10   **NM** $25   **MIP** $35

Double Trouble, 1987, Milton Bradley
  EX $3   **NM** $5   **MIP** $8

Doubletrack, 1981, Milton Bradley
  EX $2   **NM** $7   **MIP** $12

(KP Photo)

Dr. Kildare, 1962, Ideal
  EX $20   **NM** $30   **MIP** $40

(KP Photo)

Dracula Mystery Game, 1960s, Hasbro
  EX $80   **NM** $160   **MIP** $250

Dracula's "I Vant To Bite Your Finger" Game, 1981, Hasbro
  EX $10   **NM** $20   **MIP** $30

Dragnet, 1955, Transogram
  EX $20   **NM** $40   **MIP** $80

Dragonlance, 1988, TSR
  EX $15   **NM** $35   **MIP** $50

Dragon's Lair, 1983, Milton Bradley
  EX $7   **NM** $10   **MIP** $20

Dream House, 1968, Milton Bradley
  EX $15   **NM** $35   **MIP** $50

Driver Ed, 1973, Cadaco
  EX $6   **NM** $10   **MIP** $20

Duell, 1976, Lakeside
  EX $5   **NM** $16   **MIP** $25

(KP Photo)

Dukes of Hazzard, 1981, Ideal
  EX $6   **NM** $15   **MIP** $25

Dunce, 1955, Schaper
  EX $7   **NM** $20   **MIP** $35

Dune, 1984, Parker Brothers
  EX $10   **NM** $25   **MIP** $35

Dune, Frank Herbert's, 1979, Avalon Hill
  EX $20   **NM** $50   **MIP** $75

Dungeon Dice, 1977, Parker Brothers
  EX $5   **NM** $8   **MIP** $15

Dungeon!, 1981, TSR
  EX $10   **NM** $25   **MIP** $35

Dungeons & Dragons, Electronic, 1980, Mattel
  EX $12   **NM** $30   **MIP** $40

Duplicate Ad-Lib, 1976, Lowe
  EX $5   **NM** $10   **MIP** $15

Duran Duran Game, 1985, Milton Bradley
  EX $45   **NM** $80   **MIP** $125

Dynomutt, 1977, Milton Bradley
  EX $10   **NM** $15   **MIP** $25

E.T. The Extra-Terrestrial, 1982, Parker Brothers
  EX $6   **NM** $10   **MIP** $15

Earl Gillespie Baseball Game, 1961, Wei-Gill
  EX $25   **NM** $40   **MIP** $50

Earth Satellite Game, 1956, Gabriel
  EX $30   **NM** $70   **MIP** $100

Easy Money, 1956, Milton Bradley
  EX $10   **NM** $15   **MIP** $25

Ecology, 1970, Urban Systems
  EX $7   **NM** $20   **MIP** $35

Egg and I, The, 1947, Capex
  EX $30   **NM** $50   **MIP** $80

El Dorado, 1977, Invicta
  EX $7   **NM** $20   **MIP** $35

Electra Woman and Dyna Girl, 1977, Ideal
  EX $10   **NM** $25   **MIP** $45

Electric Sports Car Race, 1959, Tudor
  EX $35   **NM** $60   **MIP** $90

(KP Photo)

Electronic Detective Game, 1970s, Ideal
  EX $12   **NM** $30   **MIP** $40

Electronic Lightfight, 1981, Milton Bradley
  EX $8   **NM** $20   **MIP** $30

Electronic Radar Search, 1967, Ideal
  EX $10   **NM** $15   **MIP** $25

Eliot Ness and the Untouchables, 1961, Transogram
  EX $30   **NM** $50   **MIP** $85

Ellsworth Elephant Game, 1960, Selchow & Righter
  EX $30   **NM** $45   **MIP** $70

Elmer Wheeler's Fat Boys Game, 1951, Parker Brothers
  EX $18   **NM** $30   **MIP** $40

Elvis Presley Game, 1957, Teen Age Games
  EX $1000   **NM** $2000   **MIP** $4000

Emenee Chocolate Factory, 1966
  EX $6   **NM** $10   **MIP** $15

Emergency, 1974, Milton Bradley
  EX $15   **NM** $35   **MIP** $50

Emily Post Popularity Game, 1970, Selchow & Righter
  EX $10   **NM** $25   **MIP** $40

Emperor of China, 1972, Dynamic
  EX $10   **NM** $25   **MIP** $40

Empire Auto Races, 1950s, Empire Plastics
  EX $20   **NM** $30   **MIP** $50

Empire Builder (1sy edition), 1982, Mayfair Games
  EX $20   **NM** $50   **MIP** $75

(KP Photo)

Empire Strikes Back, Hoth Ice World, 1977, Kenner
  EX $10   **NM** $20   **MIP** $30

Encore, 1989, Parker Brothers
  EX $8   **NM** $20   **MIP** $30

Enemy Agent, 1976, Milton Bradley
  EX $8   **NM** $20   **MIP** $30

Energy Quest, 1977, Weldon
  EX $5   **NM** $16   **MIP** $25

Engineer, 1957, Selchow & Righter
  EX $8   **NM** $25   **MIP** $40

Entertainment Trivia Game, 1984, Lakeside
  EX $5   **NM** $10   **MIP** $15

Entre's Fun & Games In Accounting, 1988, Entrepreneurial Games
  EX $4   **NM** $7   **MIP** $12

Ergo, 1977, Invicta
  EX $5   **NM** $16   **MIP** $25

(KP Photo)

Escape From New York, 1980, TSR
EX $12   NM $20   MIP $30

Escape from the Casbah, 1975, Selchow & Righter
EX $7   NM $20   MIP $35

Escape From the Death Star, 1977, Kenner
EX $10   NM $20   MIP $30

Escort: Game of Guys and Gals, 1955, Parker Brothers
EX $15   NM $20   MIP $30

Espionage, 1973, MPH
EX $6   NM $18   MIP $30

Events, 1974, 3M
EX $6   NM $15   MIP $25

Everybody's Talking!, 1967, Watkins-Strathmore
EX $8   NM $25   MIP $40

Executive Decision, 1971, 3M
EX $5   NM $16   MIP $25

Exit, 1983, Milton Bradley
EX $2   NM $6   MIP $10

Expanse, 1949, Milton Bradley
EX $15   NM $20   MIP $30

Extra Innings, 1975, J. Kavanaugh
EX $30   NM $50   MIP $75

(KP Photo)

Eye Guess, 1960s, Milton Bradley
EX $15   NM $20   MIP $35

F.B.I., 1958, Transogram
EX $35   NM $55   MIP $90

F.B.I. Crime Resistance Game, 1975, Milton Bradley
EX $12   NM $30   MIP $40

F/11 Armchair Quarterback, 1964, James R. Hock
EX $15   NM $25   MIP $40

Fact Finder Fun, 1963, Milton Bradley
EX $10   NM $15   MIP $25

Fall Guy, The, 1981, Milton Bradley
EX $10   NM $15   MIP $25

(KP Photo)

Family Affair, 1967, Whitman
EX $25   NM $40   MIP $65

Family Feud, 1977, Milton Bradley
EX $4   NM $12   MIP $20

Family Ties Game, The, 1986, Apple Street
EX $10   NM $20   MIP $25

Famous 500 Mile Race, 1988
EX $8   NM $13   MIP $20

Fang Bang, 1966, Milton Bradley
EX $12   NM $25   MIP $35

Fangface, 1979, Parker Brothers
EX $5   NM $8   MIP $13

Fantastic Voyage Game, 1968, Milton Bradley
EX $15   NM $25   MIP $40

Fantasy Island Game, 1978, Ideal
EX $7   NM $20   MIP $35

Farming Game, The, 1979, Weekend Farmer Co.
EX $8   NM $20   MIP $30

Fast 111s, 1981, Parker Brothers
EX $5   NM $16   MIP $25

Fastest Gun, The, 1974, Milton Bradley
EX $10   NM $35   MIP $50

Fat Albert, 1973, Milton Bradley
EX $15   NM $25   MIP $40

Fearless Fireman, 1957, Hasbro
EX $45   NM $70   MIP $150

(KP Photo)

Felix the Cat Dandy Candy Game, 1957, Warren/Built-Rite
EX $10   NM $20   MIP $45

Felix the Cat Game, 1960, Milton Bradley
EX $15   NM $25   MIP $45

Felix the Cat Game, 1968, Milton Bradley
EX $8   NM $20   MIP $30

Feudal, 1967, 3M
EX $8   NM $20   MIP $30

Fighter Bomber, 1977, Cadaco
EX $15   NM $25   MIP $40

Finance, 1962, Parker Brothers
EX $10   NM $15   MIP $20

Finger Dinger Man, 1969, Mattel
EX $10   NM $25   MIP $35

Fingers Harry, 1967, Topper Toys
EX $20   NM $50   MIP $75

Fire Chief, 1957, Selchow & Righter
EX $10   NM $25   MIP $40

Fire Fighters!, 1957, Russell
EX $15   NM $25   MIP $40

Fire House Mouse Game, 1967, Transogram
EX $10   NM $35   MIP $50

(KP Photo)

Fireball XL-5, 1963, Milton Bradley
EX $40   NM $75   MIP $100

First Class Farmer, 1965, F & W Publishing
EX $7   NM $20   MIP $35

First Down, 1970, TGP Games
EX $50   NM $80   MIP $125

Fish Bait, 1965, Ideal
EX $20   NM $50   MIP $75

Fish Pond, 1950s, National Games
EX $10   NM $15   MIP $20

Flagship Airfreight: The Airplane Cargo Game, 1946, Milton Bradley
EX $40   NM $70   MIP $115

Flash Gordon, 1977, Waddington/House Of Games
EX $10   NM $25   MIP $35

Flash: The Press Photographer Game, 1956, Selchow & Righter
EX $35   NM $60   MIP $125

Flight Captain, 1972, Lowe
EX $5   NM $16   MIP $25

Flintstones, 1971, Milton Bradley
EX $6   NM $15   MIP $25

Flintstones, 1980, Milton Bradley
EX $15   NM $20   MIP $35

Flintstones Dino The Dinosaur Game, 1961, Transogram
EX $45   NM $75   MIP $100

Flintstones Hoppy The Hopperoo Game, 1964, Transogram
EX $45   NM $75   MIP $120

Flintstones Mitt-Full Game, 1962, Whitman
EX $25   NM $50   MIP $75

Flintstones Stone Age Game, 1961, Transogram
EX $20   NM $45   MIP $65

Flip Flop Go, 1962, Mattel
EX $6   NM $10   MIP $15

Flip 'N Skip, 1971, Little Kennys
EX $5   NM $10   MIP $15

(KP Photo)

Flipper Flips, 1960s, Mattel
 EX $30   NM $50   MIP $80

Flying Nun Game, The, 1968, Milton Bradley
 EX $15   NM $25   MIP $40

(KP Photo)

Fonz Game, The, 1976, Milton Bradley
 EX $15   NM $25   MIP $40

Fooba-Roo Football Game, 1955,
 Memphis Plastic
 EX $15   NM $35   MIP $50

Football Fever, 1985, Hansen
 EX $20   NM $35   MIP $50

Football Strategy, 1962, Avalon Hill
 EX $8   NM $25   MIP $40

Football Strategy, 1972, Avalon Hill
 EX $3   NM $10   MIP $15

Football, Baseball, & Checkers, 1948,
 Parker Brothers
 EX $15   NM $45   MIP $65

Fore, 1954, Artcraft Paper
 EX $20   NM $35   MIP $50

Forest Friends, 1956, Milton Bradley
 EX $5   NM $12   MIP $18

Formula One Car Race Game, 1968,
 Parker Brothers
 EX $25   NM $40   MIP $50

Fortress America, 1986, Milton Bradley, Part
 of a series of intricate strategy games
 developed by Milton Bradley in the 1980s.
 Two others in the series were "Axis &
 Allies" and "Conquest of the Empire"
 EX $35   NM $75   MIP $100

Fortune 500, 1979, Pressman
 EX $5   NM $16   MIP $25

Foto-Electric Baseball, 1951, Cadaco-Ellis
 EX $15   NM $25   MIP $40

(KP Photo)

Foto-Electric Football, 1965, Cadaco
 EX $10   NM $25   MIP $35

Four Lane Road Racing, 1963, Transogram
 EX $15   NM $45   MIP $65

Fox & Hounds, Game of, 1948, Parker
 Brothers
 EX $10   NM $20   MIP $30

Frank Cavanaugh's American Football,
 1955, F. Cavanaugh
 EX $25   NM $60   MIP $90

Frankenstein Game, 1962, Hasbro
 EX $80   NM $160   MIP $250

Frantic Frogs, 1965, Milton Bradley
 EX $10   NM $20   MIP $30

Frisky Flippers Slide Bar Game, 1950s,
 Warren/Built-Rite
 EX $5   NM $10   MIP $15

Frontier Fort Rescue Game, 1956, Gabriel
 EX $10   NM $35   MIP $50

Frontier-6, 1980, Rimbold
 EX $8   NM $25   MIP $40

F-Troop, 1965, Ideal
 EX $50   NM $100   MIP $125

Fu Manchu's Hidden Hoard, 1967, Ideal
 EX $23   NM $50   MIP $75

(KP Photo)

Fugitive, 1966, Ideal
 EX $30   NM $60   MIP $100

Fun City, 1987, Parker Brothers
 EX $8   NM $20   MIP $30

Funky Phantom Game, 1971, Milton Bradley
 EX $10   NM $15   MIP $25

G.I. Joe, 1982, International Games
 EX $15   NM $25   MIP $40

G.I. Joe Adventure, 1982, Hasbro
 EX $20   NM $30   MIP $50

G.I. Joe Card Game, 1965, Whitman
 EX $10   NM $15   MIP $25

G.I. Joe Marine Paratrooper, 1965, Hasbro
 EX $20   NM $30   MIP $50

G.I. Joe Navy Frogman, 1965, Hasbro
 EX $25   NM $60   MIP $75

Gambler, 1977, Parker Brothers
 EX $6   NM $15   MIP $20

Gambler's Golf, 1975, Gammon Games
 EX $4   NM $10   MIP $15

Games People Play Game, The, 1967,
 Alpsco
 EX $7   NM $20   MIP $35

Gammonball, 1980, Fun-Time Products
 EX $10   NM $16   MIP $25

Gang Way For Fun, 1964, Transogram
 EX $25   NM $40   MIP $65

Gardner's Championship Golf, 1950s,
 Gardner
 EX $10   NM $35   MIP $50

Garfield, 1981, Parker Brothers
 EX $4   NM $6   MIP $10

Garrison's Gorillas, 1967, Ideal
 EX $45   NM $75   MIP $120

Gay Puree, 1962
 EX $25   NM $40   MIP $65

Gene Autry's Dude Ranch Game, 1950s,
 Warren/Built-Rite
 EX $25   NM $35   MIP $65

General Hospital, 1974, Parker Brothers
 EX $7   NM $15   MIP $25

General Hospital, 1980s, Cardinal
 EX $15   NM $20   MIP $30

Generals, The, 1980, Ideal
 EX $7   NM $20   MIP $35

Gentle Ben Animal Hunt Game, 1967, Mattel
 EX $30   NM $70   MIP $100

Geo-Graphy, 1954, Cadaco-Ellis
 EX $5   NM $15   MIP $25

George of the Jungle Game, 1968, Parker
 Brothers
 EX $40   NM $80   MIP $100

Get Beep Beep: The Road Runner Game,
 1975, Whitman
 EX $15   NM $25   MIP $35

Get in That Tub, 1969, Hasbro
 EX $15   NM $35   MIP $50

(KP Photo)

Get Smart Game, 1966, Ideal
 EX $20   NM $30   MIP $50

Get That License, 1955, Selchow & Righter
 EX $10   NM $15   MIP $25

Get the Message, 1964, Milton Bradley
 EX $5   NM $15   MIP $25

Get the Picture, 1987, Worlds Of Wonder
 EX $6   NM $10   MIP $15

Gettysburg, 1960, Avalon Hill
 EX $5   NM $16   MIP $25

Ghosts, 1985, Milton Bradley
 EX $8   NM $20   MIP $35

Giant Wheel Thrills 'n Spills Horse Race, 1958, Remco
 EX $15   NM $20   MIP $30

Gil Hodges' Pennant Fever, 1970, Research Games
 EX $35   NM $75   MIP $100

(KP Photo)

Gilligan, The New Adventures of, 1974, Milton Bradley
 EX $15   NM $20   MIP $30

(KP Photo)

Gilligan's Island, 1965, Game Gems
 EX $125   NM $250   MIP $400

Gingerbread Man, 1964, Selchow & Righter
 EX $10   NM $35   MIP $50

Globetrotter Basketball, Official, 1950s, Meljak
 EX $60   NM $100   MIP $150

Globe-Trotters, 1950, Selchow & Righter
 EX $8   NM $25   MIP $40

Go For Broke, 1965, Selchow & Righter
 EX $5   NM $10   MIP $15

Go for the Green, 1973, Sports Illustrated
 EX $10   NM $25   MIP $40

Goal Line Stand, 1980, Game Shop
 EX $12   NM $20   MIP $30

Godfather Game, The (violin case box), 1971, Family Games
 EX $35   NM $50   MIP $75

Godfather, The (white box), 1971, Family Games
 EX $8   NM $20   MIP $30

Godzilla, 1960s, Ideal
 EX $100   NM $200   MIP $300

Godzilla, 1978, Mattel
 EX $30   NM $50   MIP $80

Going to Jerusalem, 1955, Parker Brothers
 EX $15   NM $20   MIP $40

Going, Going, Gone!, 1975, Milton Bradley
 EX $6   NM $15   MIP $25

Gold!, 1981, Avalon Hill
 EX $5   NM $16   MIP $25

Golden Trivia Game, 1984, Western
 EX $6   NM $10   MIP $15

Goldilocks, 1955, Cadaco-Ellis
 EX $8   NM $25   MIP $35

Goldilocks and the Three Bears, 1973, Cadaco
 EX $2   NM $6   MIP $10

Gomer Pyle Game, 1960s, Transogram
 EX $15   NM $30   MIP $40

Gong Show Game, 1975, Milton Bradley
 EX $15   NM $25   MIP $40

Gong Show Game, 1977, American Publishing
 EX $15   NM $25   MIP $40

Good Guys 'N Bad Guys, 1973, Cadaco
 EX $5   NM $16   MIP $25

Good Ol' Charlie Brown Game, 1971, Milton Bradley
 EX $8   NM $20   MIP $30

Goodbye Mr. Chips Game, 1969, Parker Brothers
 EX $8   NM $20   MIP $30

Goofy's Mad Maze, 1970s, Whitman
 EX $6   NM $10   MIP $15

Goonies, 1980s, Milton Bradley
 EX $12   NM $30   MIP $40

Gooses Wild, 1966, CO-5
 EX $2   NM $7   MIP $12

(KP Photo)

Gotham Professional Basketball, 1950s, Gotham
 EX $35   NM $50   MIP $70

Grand Master of Martial Arts, 1986, Hoyle
 EX $6   NM $10   MIP $15

Gray Ghost, The, 1958, Transogram
 EX $30   NM $50   MIP $75

Great Escape, The, 1967, Ideal
 EX $8   NM $25   MIP $40

Great Grape Ape Game, The, 1975, Milton Bradley
 EX $15   NM $25   MIP $40

(KP Photo)

Green Acres Game, The, 1960s, Standard Toykraft
 EX $73   NM $100   MIP $200

(KP Photo)

Green Ghost Game, 1965, Transogram
 EX $50   NM $90   MIP $125

Green Ghost Game (re-issue), 1997, Marx
 EX $15   NM $35   MIP $50

Green Hornet Quick Switch Game, 1966, Milton Bradley
 EX $90   NM $225   MIP $300

Gremlins, 1984, International Games
 EX $10   NM $15   MIP $25

Greyhound Pursuit, 1985, N/N Games
 EX $8   NM $13   MIP $20

(KP Photo)

Grizzly Adams, 1978, Waddington's House of Games
 EX $15   NM $25   MIP $40

(KP Photo)

Groucho's TV Quiz Game, 1954, Pressman
 EX $40   NM $50   MIP $75
(KP Photo)

Groucho's You Bet Your Life, 1955, Lowell
 EX $25   NM $35   MIP $55

Group Therapy, 1969, Group Therapy Assn.
 EX $3   NM $12   MIP $20

Guinness Book of World Records Game, The, 1979, Parker Brothers
 EX $5   NM $9   MIP $15

Gulf Strike, 1983, Victory Games
 EX $5   NM $16   MIP $25

(KP Photo)

Gunsmoke Game, 1950s, Lowell
 EX $40   NM $65   MIP $100

GAMES

Gusher, 1946, Carrom Industries
EX $50   **NM** $75   **MIP** $125

Half-Time Football, 1979, Lakeside
EX $5   **NM** $9   **MIP** $15

Handicap Harness Racing, 1978, Hall of Fame Games
EX $15   **NM** $25   **MIP** $35

Hang On Harvey, 1969, Ideal
EX $15   **NM** $20   **MIP** $30

Hangman, 1976, Milton Bradley
EX $5   **NM** $8   **MIP** $15

Hank Aaron Baseball Game, 1970s, Ideal
EX $50   **NM** $80   **MIP** $125

Hank Aaron Bases Loaded, 1976, Twentieth Century Enterprises
EX $45   **NM** $70   **MIP** $100

Hank Bauer's "Be a Manager", 1960s, Barco Games
EX $75   **NM** $125   **MIP** $175

Happiness, 1972, Milton Bradley
EX $12   **NM** $20   **MIP** $30

Happy Days, 1976, Parker Brothers
EX $8   **NM** $20   **MIP** $30

Happy Little Train Game, The, 1957, Milton Bradley
EX $3   **NM** $12   **MIP** $20

(KP Photo)

Hardy Boys Mystery Game, Secret of Thunder Mountain, 1978, Parker Brothers
EX $7   **NM** $15   **MIP** $25

Hardy Boys Mystery Game, The, 1968, Milton Bradley
EX $6   **NM** $15   **MIP** $25

Hardy Boys Treasure, 1960, Parker Brothers
EX $25   **NM** $40   **MIP** $60

Harlem Globetrotters Game, 1971, Milton Bradley
EX $12   **NM** $30   **MIP** $40

Harlem Globetrotters Official Edition Basketball, 1970s, Cadaco-Ellis
EX $45   **NM** $75   **MIP** $100

Harpoon, 1955, Gabriel
EX $20   **NM** $45   **MIP** $65

Harry Lorayne Memory Game, The, 1976, Reiss
EX $7   **NM** $20   **MIP** $35

Hashimoto San, 1963, Transogram
EX $20   **NM** $30   **MIP** $60

Haul the Freight, 1962, Bar-Zim
EX $25   **NM** $50   **MIP** $75

Haunted House Game, 1963, Ideal
EX $120   **NM** $250   **MIP** $400

Haunted Mansion, 1970s, Lakeside
EX $60   **NM** $150   **MIP** $200

Have Gun Will Travel Game, 1959, Parker Brothers
EX $45   **NM** $75   **MIP** $100

Hawaii Five-O, 1960s, Remco
EX $30   **NM** $90   **MIP** $120

Hawaiian Eye, 1960, Transogram
EX $50   **NM** $120   **MIP** $200

Hawaiian Punch Game, 1978, Mattel
EX $5   **NM** $10   **MIP** $15

Hector Heathcote, 1963, Transogram
EX $35   **NM** $50   **MIP** $75

Hex: The Zig-Zag Game, 1950, Parker Brothers
EX $10   **NM** $35   **MIP** $50

Hey Fatso, 1969, Hasbro
EX $15   **NM** $35   **MIP** $50

Hey Pa, There's a Goat on the Roof!, 1965, Parker Brothers
EX $40   **NM** $60   **MIP** $75

Hide 'N' Thief, 1965, Whitman
EX $7   **NM** $20   **MIP** $35

Hide-N-Seek, 1967, Ideal
EX $20   **NM** $50   **MIP** $75

High-Bid, 1965, 3M
EX $7   **NM** $20   **MIP** $35

Highway Traffic Game, 1957, John H Allison Jr.
EX $15   **NM** $35   **MIP** $50

Hi-Ho! Cherry-O, 1960, Whitman
EX $6   **NM** $10   **MIP** $15

Hijacked, 1973, Valley Games
EX $12   **NM** $30   **MIP** $40

Hip Flip, 1968, Parker Brothers
EX $6   **NM** $15   **MIP** $25

Hippety Hop, 1947, Corey Game
EX $20   **NM** $30   **MIP** $50

Hippopotamus, 1961, Remco
EX $8   **NM** $25   **MIP** $40

Hispaniola, The Game of, 1957, Schaper
EX $30   **NM** $70   **MIP** $100

Hit The Beach, 1965, Milton Bradley
EX $45   **NM** $50   **MIP** $75

Hobbit Game, The, 1978, Milton Bradley
EX $25   **NM** $60   **MIP** $85

Hock Shop, 1975, Whitman
EX $3   **NM** $12   **MIP** $20

Hocus Pocus, 1960s, Transogram
EX $40   **NM** $65   **MIP** $100

Hog Tied, 1981, Selchow & Righter
EX $3   **NM** $12   **MIP** $20

Hogan's Heroes Game, 1966, Transogram
EX $45   **NM** $85   **MIP** $120

Holiday, 1958, Replogle Globes
EX $40   **NM** $65   **MIP** $100

Holiday, 1973, RGI-Athol
EX $18   **NM** $40   **MIP** $60

Hollywood Awards Game, 1976, Milton Bradley
EX $8   **NM** $25   **MIP** $40

Hollywood Go, 1954, Parker Brothers
EX $10   **NM** $25   **MIP** $35

Hollywood Squares, 1974, Ideal
EX $6   **NM** $10   **MIP** $15

Hollywood Squares, 1980, Milton Bradley
EX $4   **NM** $6   **MIP** $10

Hollywood Stars, The Game of, 1955, Whitman
EX $8   **NM** $20   **MIP** $30

Home Court Basketball, 1954
EX $145   **NM** $250   **MIP** $375

Home Game, 1960s, Pressman
EX $30   **NM** $50   **MIP** $60

Home Stretch Harness Racing, 1967, Lowe
EX $15   **NM** $35   **MIP** $50

Home Team Baseball Game, 1957, Selchow & Righter
EX $18   **NM** $30   **MIP** $50

Honey West, 1965, Ideal
EX $35   **NM** $50   **MIP** $75

Honeymooners Game, The, 1986, TSR
EX $7   **NM** $12   **MIP** $20

Hoodoo, 1950, Tryne
EX $4   **NM** $10   **MIP** $15

Hookey Go Fishin', 1974, Cadaco
EX $8   **NM** $16   **MIP** $25

Hopalong Cassidy Chinese Checkers Game, 1950s
EX $20   **NM** $50   **MIP** $75

(KP Photo)

Hopalong Cassidy Game, 1950s, Milton Bradley
EX $50   **NM** $85   **MIP** $125

Horse Play, 1962, Schaper
EX $10   **NM** $35   **MIP** $50

Horseshoe Derby Game, 1950s, Built-Rite
EX $8   **NM** $20   **MIP** $30

Hot Property!, 1980s, Take One Games
EX $8   **NM** $25   **MIP** $40

Hot Rod, 1953, Harett-Gilmar
EX $15   **NM** $35   **MIP** $50

Hot Wheels Game, 1982, Whitman
EX $8   **NM** $13   **MIP** $20

Hot Wheels Wipe-Out Game, 1968, Mattel
EX $15   **NM** $35   **MIP** $60

Hotels, 1987, Milton Bradley
EX $20   **NM** $35   **MIP** $50

Houndcats Game, 1970s, Milton Bradley
EX $8   **NM** $15   **MIP** $25

House Party, 1968, Whitman
EX $10   **NM** $25   **MIP** $35

Houston Astros Baseball Challenge Game, 1980, Croque
EX $15   **NM** $25   **MIP** $35

How To Succeed In Business Without Really Trying, 1963, Milton Bradley
EX $6   **NM** $10   **MIP** $20

Howard Hughes Game, The, 1972, Family Games
EX $10   NM $35   MIP $50

Howdy Doody Adventure Game, 1950s, Milton Bradley
EX $35   NM $60   MIP $75

Howdy Doody Quiz Show, 1950s, Multiple Products
EX $20   NM $40   MIP $60

Howdy Doody's Electric Carnival Game, Harrett-Gilmar
EX $20   NM $30   MIP $50

Howdy Doody's Own Game, 1949, Parker Brothers
EX $50   NM $80   MIP $100

Howdy Doody's Three Ring Circus, 1950, Harett-Gilmar
EX $35   NM $50   MIP $75

(KP Photo)

Howdy Doody's TV Game, 1950s, Milton Bradley
EX $50   NM $50   MIP $100

Huckleberry Hound, 1981, Milton Bradley
EX $10   NM $20   MIP $35

Huckleberry Hound Bumps, 1960, Transogram
EX $20   NM $50   MIP $75

Huckleberry Hound Spin-O-Game, 1959
EX $45   NM $75   MIP $120

Huckleberry Hound Tiddly Winks, 1959, Milton Bradley
EX $15   NM $30   MIP $60

Huckleberry Hound Western Game, 1959, Milton Bradley
EX $25   NM $35   MIP $50

Huff 'N Puff Game, 1968, Schaper
EX $6   NM $15   MIP $25

Huggermugger, 1989, Huggermugger Co.
EX $8   NM $20   MIP $30

(KP Photo)

Hullabaloo, 1965, Remco
EX $25   NM $65   MIP $75

Humor Rumor, 1969, Whitman
EX $10   NM $20   MIP $30

Humpty Dumpty Game, 1950s, Lowell
EX $25   NM $50   MIP $60

Hunch, 1956, Happy Hour
EX $7   NM $20   MIP $35

Hungry Ant, The, 1978, Milton Bradley
EX $5   NM $16   MIP $25

Hunt For Red October, 1988, TSR
EX $5   NM $15   MIP $25

Hurry Up, 1971, Parker Brothers
EX $5   NM $16   MIP $25

Hurry Waiter! Game, 1969, Ideal
EX $8   NM $20   MIP $30

Husker Du, 1970, Regina Products
EX $10   NM $25   MIP $35

I Dream of Jeannie Game, 1965, Milton Bradley
EX $35   NM $50   MIP $75

I Spy, 1965, Ideal
EX $35   NM $75   MIP $100

I Vant to Bite Your Finger, 1981, Hasbro
EX $12   NM $20   MIP $30

I Wanna Be President, 1983, J.R. Mackey
EX $5   NM $16   MIP $25

Ice Cube Game, The, 1972, Milton Bradley
EX $50   NM $125   MIP $175

(KP Photo)

Identipops, 1969, Playvalue
EX $75   NM $175   MIP $250

I'm George Gobel, And Here's The Game, 1955, Schaper
EX $12   NM $20   MIP $30

Image, 1972, 3M
EX $3   NM $12   MIP $20

Incredible Hulk, 1978, Milton Bradley
EX $6   NM $10   MIP $15

Indiana Jones: Raiders of The Lost Ark, 1981, Kenner
EX $15   NM $20   MIP $30

Indianapolis 500 75th Running Race Game, 1991, International Games
EX $8   NM $13   MIP $20

Input, 1984, Milton Bradley
EX $4   NM $7   MIP $15

Inside Moves, 1985, Parker Brothers
EX $3   NM $12   MIP $20

Inspector Gadget, 1983, Milton Bradley
EX $15   NM $25   MIP $40

Instant Replay, 1987, Parker Brothers
EX $8   NM $13   MIP $20

Intercept, 1978, Lakeside
EX $7   NM $20   MIP $35

International Airport Game, 1964, Magic Wand
EX $8   NM $20   MIP $30

International Grand Prix, 1975, Cadaco
EX $8   NM $20   MIP $30

Interpretation of Dreams, 1969, Hasbro
EX $7   NM $15   MIP $25

Interstate Highway, 1963, Selchow & Righter
EX $15   NM $35   MIP $50

(KP Photo)

Intrigue, 1954, Milton Bradley
EX $12   NM $30   MIP $40

Inventors, The, 1974, Parker Brothers
EX $10   NM $20   MIP $30

Ipcress File, 1966, Milton Bradley
EX $15   NM $25   MIP $35

(KP Photo)

Ironside, 1976, Ideal
EX $55   NM $75   MIP $100

(KP Photo)

Is the Pope Catholic?!, 1986, Crowley Connections
EX $10   NM $25   MIP $50

Isolation, 1978, Lakeside
EX $2   NM $7   MIP $12

It Takes Two, 1970, NBC-Hasbro
EX $5   NM $12   MIP $18

Itinerary, 1980, Xanadu Leisure
EX $3   NM $12   MIP $20

Jace Pearson's Tales of The Texas Rangers, 1955, E.E. Fairchild
EX $40   NM $60   MIP $95

Jack and The Beanstalk, 1946, National Games
EX $25   NM $45   MIP $65

Jack and The Beanstalk Adventure Game, 1957, Transogram
EX $25   NM $40   MIP $50

GAMES

Jack Barry's Twenty One, 1956, Lowell
EX $20   NM $30   MIP $50

Jackie Gleason's and AW-A-A-A-Y We Go!, 1956, Transogram
EX $50   NM $75   MIP $125

Jackie Gleason's Story Stage Game, 1955, Utopia Enterprises
EX $50   NM $75   MIP $150

Jackpot, 1975, Milton Bradley
EX $7   NM $11   MIP $20

Jacmar Big League Electric Baseball, 1950s, Jacmar
EX $100   NM $175   MIP $250

James Bond 007 Goldfinger Game, 1966, Milton Bradley
EX $35   NM $60   MIP $85

James Bond 007 Thunderball Game, 1965, Milton Bradley
EX $35   NM $75   MIP $100

James Bond Message From M Game, 1966, Ideal
EX $1125   NM $250   MIP $400

James Bond Secret Agent 007 Game, 1964, Milton Bradley
EX $15   NM $35   MIP $45

James Bond You Only Live Twice, 1984, Victory Games
EX $5   NM $8   MIP $13

James Clavell's Noble House, 1987, FASA
EX $6   NM $15   MIP $25

James Clavell's Shogun, 1983, FASA
EX $6   NM $15   MIP $25

James Clavell's Tai-Pan, 1987, FASA
EX $6   NM $15   MIP $25

James Clavell's Whirlwind, 1986, FASA
EX $6   NM $15   MIP $25

Jan Murray's Charge Account, 1961, Lowell
EX $15   NM $20   MIP $30

Jan Murray's Treasure Hunt, 1950s, Gardner
EX $10   NM $25   MIP $35

JDK Baseball, 1982, JDK Baseball
EX $20   NM $45   MIP $65

Jeanne Dixon's Game of Destiny, 1968, Milton Bradley
EX $7   NM $10   MIP $15

Jeopardy, 1964, Milton Bradley
EX $10   NM $15   MIP $25

Jerry Kramer's Instant Replay, 1970, EMD Enterprises
EX $15   NM $25   MIP $40

Jet World, 1975, Milton Bradley
EX $5   NM $16   MIP $25

Jetsons Fun Pad Game, 1963, Milton Bradley
EX $30   NM $75   MIP $90

Jetsons Game, 1985, Milton Bradley
EX $5   NM $10   MIP $15

Jetsons Out of this World Game, 1963, Transogram
EX $40   NM $75   MIP $125

Jimmy the Greek Oddsmaker Football, 1974, Aurora
EX $10   NM $25   MIP $35

Jockette, 1950s, Jockette
EX $25   NM $40   MIP $60

Jockey, 1976, Hallmark Games
EX $10   NM $25   MIP $35

Joe Palooka Boxing Game, 1950s, Lowell
EX $75   NM $125   MIP $200

John Drake Secret Agent, 1966, Milton Bradley
EX $15   NM $20   MIP $35

Johnny Ringo, 1959, Transogram
EX $40   NM $90   MIP $135

Johnny Unitas Football Game, 1970, Pro Mentor
EX $15   NM $35   MIP $50

Joker's Wild, 1973, Milton Bradley
EX $5   NM $10   MIP $15

Jonathan Livingston Seagull, 1973, Mattel
EX $8   NM $20   MIP $30

(KP Photo)

Jonny Quest Game, 1964, Transogram
EX $250   NM $500   MIP $700

Jose Canseco's Perfect Baseball Game, 1991, Perfect Game
EX $8   NM $13   MIP $20

Jubilee, 1954, Cadaco-Ellis
EX $10   NM $25   MIP $35

Jumbo Jet, 1963, Jumbo
EX $18   NM $45   MIP $65

Jumpin', 1964, 3M
EX $7   NM $20   MIP $35

Jumping DJ, 1962, Mattel
EX $15   NM $50   MIP $75

Junior Bingo-Matic, 1968, Transogram
EX $6   NM $10   MIP $15

Junior Executive, 1963, Whitman
EX $7   NM $15   MIP $30

Junior Quarterback Football, 1950s, Warren/Built-Rite
EX $7   NM $20   MIP $35

Junk Yard Game, 1975, Ideal
EX $8   NM $20   MIP $30

Jurisprudence, 1974, James Vail
EX $8   NM $20   MIP $30

Justice, 1954, Lowell
EX $25   NM $55   MIP $75

Justice League of America, 1967, Hasbro
EX $70   NM $150   MIP $250

Ka Bala, 1965, Transogram
EX $40   NM $75   MIP $125

Karate, The Game of, 1964, Selchow & Righter
EX $7   NM $20   MIP $35

Karter Peanut Shell Game, 1978, Morey & Neely
EX $7   NM $20   MIP $35

Kar-Zoom, 1964, Whitman
EX $15   NM $20   MIP $35

Kennedys, The, 1962, Transogram
EX $35   NM $65   MIP $85

Kentucky Derby, 1960, Whitman
EX $25   NM $35   MIP $65

Kentucky Jones, 1964, T. Cohn
EX $20   NM $35   MIP $50

Keyword, 1954, Parker Brothers
EX $3   NM $6   MIP $10

Kick-Off Soccer, 1978, Camden Products
EX $7   NM $20   MIP $35

King Kong Game, 1963, Ideal
EX $100   NM $200   MIP $325

King Kong Game, 1966, Milton Bradley
EX $8   NM $20   MIP $30

King Kong Game, 1976, Ideal
EX $8   NM $30   MIP $45

King Leonardo and His Subjects Game, 1960, Milton Bradley
EX $18   NM $45   MIP $65

King of the Hill, 1965, Schaper
EX $35   NM $50   MIP $70

King of the Sea, 1975, Ideal
EX $8   NM $25   MIP $40

King Oil, 1974, Milton Bradley
EX $25   NM $55   MIP $85

King Tut's Game, 1978, Cadaco
EX $5   NM $16   MIP $25

(KP Photo)

King Zor, The Dinosaur Game, 1964, Ideal
EX $55   NM $85   MIP $120

Kismet, 1971, Lakeside
EX $6   NM $15   MIP $25

KISS On Tour Game, 1978, Aucoin
EX $25   NM $60   MIP $100

Klondike, 1975, Gamma Two
EX $12   NM $30   MIP $40

Knight Rider, 1983, Parker Brothers
EX $7   NM $12   MIP $20

(KP Photo)

Kojak, 1975, Milton Bradley
EX $7   NM $12   MIP $35

Kommisar, 1960s, Selchow & Righter
EX $12   NM $20   MIP $30

Koo Koo Choo Choo, 1960s, Ohio Art
EX $12   NM $30   MIP $40

Kooky Carnival, 1969, Milton Bradley
EX $10   NM $35   MIP $50

Korg 70,000 BC, 1974, Milton Bradley
EX $7   NM $15   MIP $25

(KP Photo)

Kreskin's ESP, 1966, Milton Bradley
EX $4   NM $10   MIP $15

Krull, 1983, Parker Brothers
EX $6   NM $10   MIP $15

KSP Baseball, 1983, Koch Sports Products
EX $25   NM $60   MIP $85

Kukla & Ollie, 1962, Parker Brothers
EX $20   NM $35   MIP $50

Labyrinth (movie game), 1986, Golden
EX $25   NM $60   MIP $85

Lancer, 1968, Remco
EX $40   NM $90   MIP $135

(KP Photo)

Land of The Giants, 1968, Ideal
EX $75   NM $125   MIP $175

Land of The Lost, 1975, Milton Bradley
EX $10   NM $25   MIP $35

Landmarks, The Game of, 1962, Selchow & Righter
EX $6   NM $15   MIP $25

Landslide, 1971, Parker Brothers
EX $5   NM $16   MIP $20

Laramie, 1960, Lowell
EX $50   NM $100   MIP $150

Las Vegas Baseball, 1987, Samar Enterprises
EX $8   NM $13   MIP $20

Laser Attack Game, 1978, Milton Bradley
EX $7   NM $20   MIP $35

Lassie Game, 1965, Game Gems
EX $20   NM $35   MIP $75

Last Straw, 1966, Schaper
EX $5   NM $10   MIP $15

(KP Photo)

Laugh-In's Squeeze Your Bippy Game, 1968, Hasbro
EX $35   NM $75   MIP $100

Laurel & Hardy Game, 1962, Transogram
EX $20   NM $30   MIP $40

(KP Photo)

Laverne & Shirley Game, 1977, Parker Brothers
EX $9   NM $15   MIP $25

Leave It To Beaver Ambush Game, 1959, Hasbro
EX $25   NM $45   MIP $70

Leave It To Beaver Money Maker, 1959, Hasbro
EX $25   NM $45   MIP $70

(KP Photo)

Leave It To Beaver Rocket To The Moon, 1959, Hasbro
EX $25   NM $45   MIP $70

Lee Vs Meade: Battle of Gettysburg, 1974, Gamut of Games
EX $7   NM $15   MIP $25

Legend of Jesse James Game, The, 1965, Milton Bradley
EX $30   NM $50   MIP $75

LeMans, 1961, Avalon Hill
EX $25   NM $60   MIP $85

Let's Bowl a Game, 1960, DMR
EX $5   NM $12   MIP $20

Let's Drive, 1969, Milton Bradley
EX $8   NM $20   MIP $30

Let's Go to the Races, 1987, Parker Brothers
EX $7   NM $20   MIP $35

Let's Make a Deal, 1964, Milton Bradley
EX $12   NM $30   MIP $40

Let's Make A Deal, 1970s, Ideal
EX $10   NM $15   MIP $25

Let's Play Golf "The Hawaiian Open", 1968, Burlu
EX $8   NM $20   MIP $30

(KP Photo)

Let's Play Safe Traffic Game, 1960s, X-Acto
EX $25   NM $50   MIP $90

Let's Play Tag, 1958, Milton Bradley
EX $5   NM $16   MIP $25

Let's Take a Trip, 1962, Milton Bradley
EX $8   NM $15   MIP $20

Leverage, 1982, Milton Bradley
EX $4   NM $6   MIP $10

LF Baseball, 1980, Len Feder
EX $18   NM $45   MIP $65

Lie Detector Game, 1961, Mattel
EX $25   NM $50   MIP $85

Lie Detector Game, 1987, Pressman
EX $8   NM $20   MIP $30

Lieutenant, The, 1963, Transogram
EX $20   NM $50   MIP $60

Life, The Game of, 1960, Milton Bradley
EX $8   NM $20   MIP $30

Limit Up, 1980, Willem
EX $6   NM $18   MIP $30

Line Drive, 1953, Lord & Freber
EX $18   NM $45   MIP $65

Linebacker Football, 1990, Linebacker
EX $12   NM $20   MIP $30

Linkup, 1972, American Greetings
EX $5   NM $16   MIP $25

Linus the Lionhearted Uproarious Game, 1965, Transogram
EX $50   NM $85   MIP $135

Linx, 1972, American Greetings
EX $6   NM $15   MIP $25

Lion and the White Witch, The, 1983, David Cook
EX $5   NM $16   MIP $25

(KP Photo)

GAMES

Lippy the Lion Game, 1963, Transogram
EX $30   NM $45   MIP $70

Little Black Sambo, 1952, Cadaco-Ellis
EX $85   NM $125   MIP $175

Little Boy Blue, 1955, Cadaco-Ellis
EX $6   NM $18   MIP $30

Little Creepies Monster Game, 1974, Toy Factory
EX $6   NM $10   MIP $15

Little House On The Prairie, 1978, Parker Brothers
EX $12   NM $30   MIP $40

Little League Baseball Game, 1950s, Standard Toykraft
EX $20   NM $35   MIP $60

Little Orphan Annie, 1981, Parker Brothers
EX $10   NM $15   MIP $20

Little Red Schoolhouse, 1952, Parker Brothers
EX $10   NM $25   MIP $35

Lobby, 1949, Milton Bradley
EX $8   NM $20   MIP $30

Long Shot, 1962, Parker Brothers
EX $45   NM $75   MIP $125

Longball, 1975, Ashburn Industries
EX $35   NM $75   MIP $100

Look All-Star Baseball Game, 1960, Progressive Research
EX $35   NM $60   MIP $90

Looney Tunes Game, 1968, Milton Bradley
EX $20   NM $40   MIP $50

Lord of the Rings, The, 1979, Milton Bradley
EX $40   NM $85   MIP $125

Los Angeles Dodgers Baseball Game, 1964, Ed-U-Cards
EX $10   NM $25   MIP $35

Lost Gold, 1975, Parker Brothers
EX $7   NM $20   MIP $35

(KP Photo)

Lost In Space Game, 1965, Milton Bradley
EX $35   NM $75   MIP $100

Lost Treasure, 1982, Parker Brothers
EX $7   NM $20   MIP $35

Lottery Game, 1972, Selchow & Righter
EX $6   NM $18   MIP $30

Louie the Electrician, ca. 1960, Hasbro
EX $20   NM $50   MIP $70

Love Boat World Cruise, 1980, Ungame
EX $5   NM $15   MIP $20

Loving Game, The, 1987, R.J.E. Enterprises
EX $4   NM $6   MIP $10

Lucan, The Wolf Boy, 1977, Milton Bradley
EX $5   NM $10   MIP $15

Lucky Break, 1975, Gabriel
EX $10   NM $20   MIP $30

Lucky Strike, 1972, International Toy
EX $5   NM $10   MIP $15

Lucky Town, 1946, Milton Bradley
EX $15   NM $40   MIP $50

Lucy Show Game, The, 1962, Transogram
EX $75   NM $100   MIP $150

Lucy's Tea Party Game, 1971, Milton Bradley
EX $20   NM $35   MIP $55

Ludwig Von Drake Ball Toss Game, 1960
EX $6   NM $10   MIP $15

Luftwaffe, 1971, Avalon Hill
EX $3   NM $8   MIP $15

(KP Photo)

M Squad, 1958, Bell Toys
EX $35   NM $75   MIP $125

M*A*S*H* Game, 1981, Milton Bradley
EX $15   NM $25   MIP $35

MacDonald's Farm, 1948, Selchow & Righter
EX $12   NM $20   MIP $30

(KP Photo)

MAD Magazine Game, The, 1979, Parker Brothers
EX $4   NM $12   MIP $20

MAD, What Me Worry?, 1987, Milton Bradley
EX $6   NM $10   MIP $15

Madame Planchette Horoscope Game, 1967, Selchow & Righter
EX $6   NM $18   MIP $30

Magic Miles, 1956, Hasbro
EX $10   NM $15   MIP $20

Magilla Gorilla, 1964, Ideal
EX $40   NM $65   MIP $100

Magnetic Flying Saucers, 1950s, Pressman
EX $21   NM $35   MIP $55

Magnificent Race, 1975, Parker Brothers
EX $10   NM $20   MIP $30

Mail Run, 1960, Quality Games
EX $35   NM $75   MIP $100

Main Street Baseball, 1989, Main St. Toy
EX $20   NM $35   MIP $55

Major League Baseball, 1965, Cadaco
EX $10   NM $20   MIP $30

Major League Baseball Magnetic Dart Game, 1958, Pressman
EX $20   NM $45   MIP $65

(KP Photo)

Man from U.N.C.L.E. Napoleon Solo Game, 1965, Ideal
EX $25   NM $45   MIP $60

Man from U.N.C.L.E. THRUSH Ray Gun Affair Game, 1966, Ideal
EX $50   NM $85   MIP $135

Manage Your Own Team, 1950s, Warren
EX $10   NM $30   MIP $40

Management, 1960, Avalon Hill
EX $10   NM $25   MIP $40

Mandinka, 1978, Lowe
EX $3   NM $12   MIP $20

Manhunt, 1972, Milton Bradley
EX $5   NM $16   MIP $20

Maniac, 1979, Ideal
EX $7   NM $15   MIP $20

Margie, The Game of Whoopie, 1961, Milton Bradley
EX $12   NM $20   MIP $30

Marlin Perkins' Zoo Parade, 1965, Cadaco-Ellis
EX $12   NM $30   MIP $40

Martin Luther King Jr., 1980, Cadaco
EX $6   NM $10   MIP $15

Mary Hartman, Mary Hartman, 1976, Reiss Games
EX $10   NM $25   MIP $35

(KP Photo)

Mary Poppins Carousel Game, 1964, Parker Brothers
EX $12   NM $20   MIP $30

Masquerade Party, 1955, Bettye-B
EX $30   NM $50   MIP $75

Mastermind, 1970s, Invicta
EX $5   NM $10   MIP $15

Masterpiece, The Art Auction Game, 1971, Parker Brothers
EX $8   NM $20   MIP $30

Match Game (3rd Ed.), The, 1963, Milton Bradley
EX $25   NM $50   MIP $75

Matchbox Traffic Game, 1960s, Bronner
EX $25   NM $45   MIP $70

(KP Photo)

McDonald's Game, The, 1975, Milton Bradley
EX $12   NM $30   MIP $40

(KP Photo)

McHale's Navy Game, 1962, Transogram
EX $30   NM $40   MIP $65

McMurtle Turtle, 1965, Cadaco-Ellis
EX $8   NM $25   MIP $40

Mechanic Mac, 1961, Selchow & Richter
EX $15   NM $35   MIP $50

Meet The Presidents, 1953, Selchow & Righter
EX $8   NM $15   MIP $20

Megiddo, 1985, Global Games
EX $8   NM $20   MIP $30

(KP Photo)

Melvin The Moon Man, 1960s, Remco
EX $30   NM $70   MIP $100

Men Into Space, 1960, Milton Bradley
EX $25   NM $60   MIP $90

Merger, 1965, Universal Games
EX $12   NM $30   MIP $40

(KP Photo)

Merry Milkman, 1955, Hasbro
EX $50   NM $85   MIP $125

Merv Griffin's Word For Word, 1963, Mattel
EX $5   NM $16   MIP $25

Miami Vice: The Game, 1984, Pepperlane
EX $10   NM $25   MIP $35

Mickey Mantle's Action Baseball, 1960, Pressman
EX $75   NM $125   MIP $200

(KP Photo)

Mickey Mantle's Big League Baseball, 1958, Gardner
EX $150   NM $225   MIP $325

Mickey Mouse, 1950, Jacmar
EX $35   NM $55   MIP $90

Mickey Mouse, 1976, Parker Brothers
EX $6   NM $10   MIP $15

Mickey Mouse Basketball, 1950s, Gardner
EX $55   NM $90   MIP $135

Mickey Mouse Lotto Game, 1950s, Jaymar
EX $10   NM $15   MIP $25

Mickey Mouse Pop Up Game, 1970s, Whitman
EX $7   NM $15   MIP $20

Mickey Mouse Slugaroo, 1950s
EX $20   NM $30   MIP $50

Mid Life Crisis, 1982, Gameworks
EX $5   NM $15   MIP $20

Mighty Comics Super Heroes Game, 1966, Transogram
EX $30   NM $70   MIP $100

Mighty Heroes on the Scene Game, 1960s, Transogram
EX $35   NM $75   MIP $120

Mighty Mouse, 1978, Milton Bradley
EX $15   NM $20   MIP $30

(KP Photo)

Mighty Mouse Rescue Game, 1960s, Harett-Gilmar
EX $25   NM $50   MIP $75

(KP Photo)

Milton The Monster, 1966, Milton Bradley
EX $25   NM $35   MIP $45

Mind Over Matter, 1968, Transogram
EX $10   NM $15   MIP $25

Miss America Pageant Game, 1974, Parker Brothers
EX $20   NM $30   MIP $40

Miss Popularity Game, 1961, Transogram
EX $20   NM $35   MIP $55

Missing Links, 1964, Milton Bradley
EX $6   NM $18   MIP $35

Mission: Impossible, 1967, Ideal
EX $40   NM $100   MIP $135

(KP Photo)

Mission: Impossible, 1975, Berwick
EX $10   NM $15   MIP $25

(KP Photo)

Mighty Hercules Game, 1963, Hasbro
EX $125   NM $300   MIP $500

Mister Ed Game, 1962, Parker Brothers
EX $25   **NM** $50   **MIP** $75

Mister Football, 1951, Alkay
EX $30   **NM** $75   **MIP** $100

Mob Strategy, 1969, NBC-Hasbro
EX $4   **NM** $10   **MIP** $15

Mod Squad game, 1960s, Remco
EX $45   **NM** $85   **MIP** $125

Monday Morning Quarterback, 1963, Zbinden
EX $8   **NM** $25   **MIP** $35

Money Card: Amer. Express Travel Game, 1972, Schaper
EX $8   **NM** $20   **MIP** $30

Money! Money! Money!, 1957, Whitman
EX $15   **NM** $20   **MIP** $30

(KP Photo)

Monkees Game, 1968, Transogram
EX $65   **NM** $100   **MIP** $150

Monkeys and Coconuts, 1965, Schaper
EX $6   **NM** $15   **MIP** $20

Monopoly (large maroon box), 1964, Parker Brothers
EX $25   **NM** $35   **MIP** $60

(KP Photo)

Monopoly (train cover), 1958, Parker Brothers
EX $50   **NM** $85   **MIP** $125

Monster Game, 1977, Ideal
EX $25   **NM** $60   **MIP** $85

Monster Game, The, 1965, Milton Bradley
EX $15   **NM** $25   **MIP** $40

Monster Mansion, 1981, Milton Bradley
EX $20   **NM** $50   **MIP** $75

Monster Squad, 1977, Milton Bradley
EX $10   **NM** $20   **MIP** $35

Monsters of the Deep, 1976, Whitman
EX $5   **NM** $16   **MIP** $25

Moon Blast-Off, 1970, Schaper
EX $12   **NM** $30   **MIP** $40

Moon Shot, 1960s, Cadaco
EX $15   **NM** $35   **MIP** $60

Moon Tag, Game of, 1957, Parker Brothers
EX $40   **NM** $75   **MIP** $100

(KP Photo)

Mork and Mindy, 1978, Milton Bradley
EX $6   **NM** $15   **MIP** $25

Mostly Ghostly, 1975, Cadaco
EX $8   **NM** $20   **MIP** $30

Movie Moguls, 1970, RGI
EX $15   **NM** $35   **MIP** $50

Movie Studio Mogul, 1981, International Mktg.
EX $8   **NM** $25   **MIP** $40

Mr. Bug Goes To Town, 1955, Milton Bradley
EX $15   **NM** $20   **MIP** $30

Mr. Doodle's Dog, 1940s, Selchow & Righter
EX $20   **NM** $30   **MIP** $40

Mr. Machine Game, 1961, Ideal
EX $60   **NM** $90   **MIP** $150

Mr. Magoo Maddening Misadventures Game, The, 1970, Transogram
EX $45   **NM** $75   **MIP** $120

Mr. Magoo Visits The Zoo, 1961, Lowell
EX $25   **NM** $45   **MIP** $70

Mr. President, 1967, 3M
EX $8   **NM** $25   **MIP** $40

Mr. Ree, 1957, Selchow & Righter
EX $25   **NM** $30   **MIP** $65

Mt. Everest, 1955, Gabriel
EX $18   **NM** $25   **MIP** $50

Mug Shots, 1975, Cadaco
EX $7   **NM** $12   **MIP** $20

Munsters Drag Race Game, 1965, Hasbro
EX $250   **NM** $600   **MIP** $1000

Munsters Masquerade Game, 1965, Hasbro
EX $250   **NM** $600   **MIP** $1000

Munsters Picnic Game, 1965, Hasbro
EX $200   **NM** $500   **MIP** $1000

(KP Photo)

Muppet Show, 1977, Parker Brothers
EX $6   **NM** $15   **MIP** $20

Murder on the Orient Express, 1967, Ideal
EX $20   **NM** $50   **MIP** $75

Murder She Wrote, 1985, Warren
EX $4   **NM** $6   **MIP** $10

Mushmouse & Punkin Puss, 1964, Ideal
EX $45   **NM** $75   **MIP** $120

MVP Baseball, The Sports Card Game, 1989, Ideal
EX $8   **NM** $13   **MIP** $20

My Fair Lady, 1960s, Standard Toykraft
EX $10   **NM** $15   **MIP** $20

(KP Photo)

My Favorite Martian, 1963, Transogram
EX $40   **NM** $60   **MIP** $90

(KP Photo)

My First (Walt Disney Character) Game, 1963, Gabriel
EX $20   **NM** $35   **MIP** $60

Mystery Checkers, 1950s, Creative Designs
EX $15   **NM** $20   **MIP** $30

Mystery Date, 1965, Milton Bradley
EX $75   **NM** $125   **MIP** $300

Mystery Date Game, 1972, Milton Bradley
EX $50   **NM** $70   **MIP** $125

Mystery Mansion, 1984, Milton Bradley
EX $10   **NM** $25   **MIP** $35

Mystic Skull The Game of Voodoo, 1965, Ideal
EX $15   **NM** $30   **MIP** $50

Mystic Wheel of Knowledge, 1950s, Novel Toy
EX $15   **NM** $20   **MIP** $30

Name That Tune, 1959, Milton Bradley
EX $12   **NM** $20   **MIP** $30

Names and Faces, 1960, Pressman
EX $6   **NM** $15   **MIP** $25

Nancy Drew Mystery Game, 1957, Parker Brothers
EX $35   **NM** $100   **MIP** $150

NASCAR Daytona 500, 1990, Milton Bradley
EX $10   **NM** $25   **MIP** $35

National Football League Quarterback, Official, 1965, Standard Toykraft
EX $12   **NM** $30   **MIP** $40

National Inquirer, 1991, Tyco
EX $10   **NM** $15   **MIP** $20

National Lampoon's Sellout, 1970s, Cardinal
EX $6   **NM** $15   **MIP** $25

National Pro Football Hall of Fame Game, 1965, Cadaco
EX $15   NM $25   MIP $40

National Pro Hockey, 1985, Sports Action
EX $15   NM $25   MIP $40

(KP Photo)

National Velvet Game, 1950s, Transogram
EX $15   NM $25   MIP $40

Naval Battle, 1954, Coronet Products
EX $25   NM $60   MIP $85

NBA Basketball Game, Official, 1970s, Gerney Games
EX $35   NM $75   MIP $100

NBC Game of the Week, 1969, Hasbro
EX $10   NM $25   MIP $35

NBC Peacock, 1966, Selchow & Righter
EX $20   NM $50   MIP $75

NBC Pro Playoff, 1969, Hasbro
EX $10   NM $25   MIP $35

NBC TV News, 1960, Dadan
EX $15   NM $35   MIP $50

Nebula, 1976, Nebula
EX $4   NM $6   MIP $10

Neck & Neck, 1981, Yaquinto
EX $8   NM $13   MIP $20

Negamco Basketball, 1975, Nemadji Game
EX $10   NM $16   MIP $25

New Avengers Shooting Game, 1976, Denys Fisher
EX $165   NM $275   MIP $440

New Frontier, 1962, Colorful Products
EX $30   NM $50   MIP $80

New York World's Fair, 1964, Milton Bradley
EX $20   NM $35   MIP $55

Newlywed Game (1st Ed.), 1967, Hasbro
EX $15   NM $20   MIP $30

(KP Photo)

Newlywed Game (2nd Ed.), 1967, Hasbro
EX $11   NM $22   MIP $35

Newtown, 1972, Harwell Associates
EX $15   NM $35   MIP $50

Next President, The, 1971, Reiss
EX $15   NM $35   MIP $50

NFL Armchair Quarterback, 1986, Trade Wind
EX $8   NM $13   MIP $20

NFL Franchise, 1982, Rohrwood
EX $10   NM $16   MIP $25

NFL Game Plan, 1980, Tudor
EX $6   NM $10   MIP $15

NFL Quarterback, 1977, Tudor
EX $8   NM $20   MIP $30

NFL Strategy, 1970, Tudor
EX $10   NM $20   MIP n/a

NFL Strategy, 1976, Tudor
EX $15   NM $35   MIP $65

NHL All-Pro Hockey, 1969, Ideal
EX $12   NM $30   MIP $40

NHL Strategy, 1976, Tudor
EX $10   NM $35   MIP $50

Nieuchess, 1961, Avalon Hill
EX $12   NM $40   MIP $60

Nightmare, 1991, Chieftain Products
EX $8   NM $20   MIP $30

Nightmare II, III, IV (add-ons, each), mid-1990s, Chieftain Products
EX $15   NM $35   MIP $50

Nightmare On Elm Street, 1989, Cardinal
EX $20   NM $30   MIP $45

Nile, 1967, Lowe
EX $6   NM $18   MIP $30

Nirtz, The Game is, 1961, Ideal
EX $8   NM $20   MIP $30

No Respect, The Rodney Dangerfield Game, 1985, Milton Bradley
EX $2   NM $6   MIP $8

No Time for Sergeants Game, 1964, Ideal
EX $12   NM $20   MIP $30

Noah's Ark, 1953, Cadaco-Ellis
EX $8   NM $25   MIP $40

Nok-Hockey, 1947, Carrom
EX $20   NM $35   MIP $55

Noma Party Quiz, 1947, Noma Electric
EX $15   NM $20   MIP $25

Northwest Passage, 1969, Impact
EX $8   NM $15   MIP $20

Number Please TV Quiz, 1961, Parker Brothers
EX $15   NM $20   MIP $30

Numble, 1968, Selchow & Righter
EX $4   NM $10   MIP $15

Numeralogic, 1973, American Greetings
EX $6   NM $18   MIP $30

Nurses, The, 1963, Ideal
EX $15   NM $50   MIP $60

Nuts to You, 1969, Hasbro
EX $15   NM $35   MIP $50

O.J. Simpson See-Action Football, 1974, Kenner
EX $50   NM $125   MIP $175

Obsession, 1978, Mego
EX $5   NM $10   MIP $15

Obstruction, 1979, Whitman
EX $4   NM $10   MIP $15

Octopus, 1954, Norton Games
EX $12   NM $40   MIP $60

Off To See The Wizard, 1968, Cadaco
EX $10   NM $15   MIP $25

Oh Magoo Game, 1960s, Warren
EX $10   NM $20   MIP $30

Oh What a Mountain, 1980, Milton Bradley
EX $5   NM $16   MIP $25

Oh, Nuts! Game, 1968, Ideal
EX $10   NM $25   MIP $35

Oh-Wah-Ree, 1966, 3M
EX $8   NM $20   MIP $30

Oil Power, 1980s, Antfamco
EX $20   NM $45   MIP $65

Old Shell Game, The, 1974, Selchow & Righter
EX $7   NM $20   MIP $35

Oldies But Goodies, 1987, Orig. Sound Record
EX $6   NM $18   MIP $30

On Guard, 1967, Parker Brothers
EX $6   NM $10   MIP $15

Oodles, 1992, Milton Bradley
EX $8   NM $20   MIP $30

(KP Photo)

Operation, 1965, Milton Bradley
EX $5   NM $20   MIP $25

Opinion, 1970, Selchow & Righter
EX $6   NM $15   MIP $25

Option, 1983, Parker Brothers
EX $2   NM $7   MIP $12

Orbit, 1959, Parker Brothers
EX $10   NM $20   MIP $30

Organized Crime, 1974, Koplow Games
EX $6   NM $18   MIP $30

Orient Express, 1985, Just Games
EX $5   NM $16   MIP $25

Original Home Jai-Alai Game, The, 1984, Design Origin
EX $15   NM $25   MIP $35

GAMES

(KP Photo)

Oscar Robertson's Pro Basketball Strategy, 1964, Research Games
EX $50   NM $72   MIP $100

Our Gang Bingo, 1958
EX $50   NM $85   MIP $100

Outdoor Survival, 1972, Avalon Hill
EX $2   NM $6   MIP $10

Outer Limits, 1964, Milton Bradley
EX $80   NM $180   MIP $250

Outlaw & Posse, 1978, Milton Bradley
EX $8   NM $20   MIP $30

Outlaw Trail, 1972, Dynamic
EX $6   NM $18   MIP $30

Outwit, 1978, Parker Brothers
EX $5   NM $10   MIP $15

Over the Rainbow See-Saw, 1949, Milton Bradley
EX $12   NM $20   MIP $30

Overboard, 1978, Lakeside
EX $3   NM $12   MIP $18

Overland Trail Board Game, 1960, Transogram
EX $45   NM $75   MIP $90

Ozark Ike's Complete 3 Game Set, 1956, Warren Built-Rite
EX $45   NM $80   MIP $110

P.T. Boat 109 Game, 1963, Ideal
EX $25   NM $35   MIP $50

Pac-Man, 1980, Milton Bradley
EX $5   NM $15   MIP $20

Pan American World Jet Flight Game, 1960, Hasbro
EX $10   NM $20   MIP $35

Panic Button, 1978, Mego
EX $7   NM $15   MIP $20

Panzer Blitz, 1970, Avalon Hill
EX $6   NM $12   MIP $20

Panzer Leader, 1974, Avalon Hill
EX $8   NM $15   MIP $25

Par '73, 1961, Big Top Games
EX $15   NM $25   MIP $40

Par Golf, 1950s, National Games
EX $35   NM $40   MIP $60

Parcheesi (Gold Seal Ed.), 1964, Selchow & Righter
EX $7   NM $10   MIP $15

Pari Horse Race Card Game, 1959, Pari Sales
EX $20   NM $35   MIP $50

Paris Metro, 1981, Infinity Games
EX $10   NM $16   MIP $25

Park and Shop, 1952, Traffic Game
EX $50   NM $75   MIP $100

Park and Shop Game, 1960, Milton Bradley
EX $75   NM $100   MIP $225

Parker Brothers Baseball Game, 1955, Parker Brothers
EX $25   NM $60   MIP $75

Parollette, 1946, Selchow & Righter
EX $18   NM $40   MIP $60

(KP Photo)

Partridge Family, 1974, Milton Bradley
EX $20   NM $25   MIP $50

Pass It On, 1978, Selchow & Righter
EX $3   NM $12   MIP $20

Pass the Buck, 1964, Transco Adult Games
EX $12   NM $30   MIP $40

(KP Photo)

Password, 1963, Milton Bradley
EX $6   NM $15   MIP $20

Pathfinder, 1977, Milton Bradley
EX $5   NM $15   MIP $20

Patty Duke Game, 1963, Milton Bradley
EX $18   NM $30   MIP $50

Paul Brown's Football Game, 1947, Trikilis
EX $110   NM $180   MIP $275

Payday, 1975, Parker Brothers
EX $5   NM $10   MIP $20

Payday: The People's Game, 1975, Payday Game Co/Barker
EX $12   NM $30   MIP $40

Paydirt, 1979, Avalon Hill
EX $12   NM $30   MIP $40

Paydirt!, 1973, Time, Inc., (Sports Illustrated)
EX $10   NM $25   MIP $35

Payoff Machine Game, 1978, Ideal
EX $5   NM $16   MIP $25

Pazaz, 1978, E.S.Lowe
EX $4   NM $10   MIP $15

Peanut Butter & Jelly Game, 1971, Parker Brothers
EX $12   NM $30   MIP $40

(KP Photo)

Peanuts: The Game of Charlie Brown And His Pals, 1959, Selchow & Righter
EX $20   NM $30   MIP $50

Pebbles Flintstone Game, 1962, Transogram
EX $20   NM $35   MIP $55

Pee Wee Reese Marble Game, 1956, Pee Wee Enterprises
EX $175   NM $295   MIP $450

Penetration, 1968, Crea-Tek
EX $8   NM $20   MIP $30

Pennant Chasers Baseball Game, 1946, Craig Hopkins
EX $25   NM $45   MIP $70

Pennant Drive, 1980, Accu-Stat Game
EX $8   NM $13   MIP $20

People Trivia Game, 1984, Parker Brothers
EX $7   NM $11   MIP $20

People's Court, The, 1986, Pressman
EX $4   NM $10   MIP $15

Per Plexus, 1976, Aladdin
EX $10   NM $25   MIP $35

Perils of Pauline, 1964, Marx
EX $40   NM $90   MIP $135

Perquackey, 1970, Lakeside
EX $4   NM $9   MIP $12

Perry Mason Case of The Missing Suspect Game, 1959, Transogram
EX $20   NM $30   MIP $45

Personalysis, 1957, Lowell
EX $15   NM $25   MIP $40

Pete the Plumber, c. 1960, Hasbro
EX $20   NM $50   MIP $75

Peter Gunn Dectective Game, 1960, Lowell
EX $25   NM $35   MIP $50

Peter Pan, 1953, Transogram
EX $10   NM $15   MIP $20

Peter Potamus Game, 1964, Ideal
EX $30   NM $50   MIP $80

Peter Principle Game, 1973, Skor-Mor
EX $6   NM $18   MIP $30

Peter Principle Game, 1981, Avalon Hill
EX $5   NM $16   MIP $25

Petropolis, 1976, Pressman
EX $10   NM $25   MIP $40

Petticoat Junction, 1963, Standard Toykraft
EX $45   NM $65   MIP $85

Phalanx, 1964, Whitman
EX $10   NM $30   MIP $45

Phantom Game, The, 1965, Transogram
EX $75   NM $160   MIP $200

GAMES

Phantom's Complete Three Game Set, The, 1955, Built-Rite
EX $30   NM $75   MIP $125

Phil Silvers' You'll Never Get Rich Game, 1955, Gardner
EX $25   NM $50   MIP $60

(KP Photo)

Philip Marlowe, 1960, Transogram
EX $20   NM $30   MIP $50

Phlounder, 1962, 3M
EX $6   NM $18   MIP $30

Pig in the Garden, 1960, Schaper
EX $20   NM $30   MIP $50

Pigskin Vegas, 1980, Jokari/US
EX $6   NM $10   MIP $15

Pilgrimage, 1984, Whitehall Games
EX $8   NM $20   MIP $30

Pinbo Sport-o-Rama, 1950s
EX $35   NM $60   MIP $90

Pinhead, 1959, Remco
EX $10   NM $35   MIP $50

Pink Panther Game, 1977, Warren
EX $10   NM $20   MIP $30

Pink Panther Game, 1981, Cadaco
EX $4   NM $7   MIP $12

Pinky Lee and the Runaway Frankfurters, 1950s, Lisbeth Whiting
EX $30   NM $50   MIP $60

Pinocchio, 1977, Parker Brothers
EX $5   NM $8   MIP $15

Pinocchio Board Game, Disney's, 1960, Parker Brothers
EX $10   NM $15   MIP $25

Pinocchio, The New Adventures of, 1961, Lowell
EX $25   NM $45   MIP $70

(KP Photo)

Pirate and Traveller, 1953, Milton Bradley
EX $10   NM $25   MIP $40

Pirate Raid, 1956, Cadaco-Ellis
EX $8   NM $25   MIP $40

Pirate's Cove, 1956, Gabriel
EX $15   NM $35   MIP $65

Pizza Pie Game, 1974, Milton Bradley
EX $5   NM $16   MIP $25

Plane Parade, 1950s, Harett-Gilmar Inc.
EX $25   NM $60   MIP $85

Planet of the Apes, 1974, Milton Bradley
EX $20   NM $45   MIP $65

Play Ball! A Baseball Game of Skill, 1940s, Rosebud Art
EX $50   NM $75   MIP $150

Play Basketball with Bob Cousy, 1950s, National Games
EX $60   NM $100   MIP $200

Play Your Hunch, 1960, Transogram
EX $8   NM $25   MIP $40

Playoff Football, 1970s, Crestline
EX $20   NM $35   MIP $50

Plaza, 1947, Parker Brothers
EX $7   NM $20   MIP $35

Plot!, 1968, Cadaco
EX $10   NM $25   MIP $35

Ploy, 1970, 3M
EX $5   NM $16   MIP $25

Plus One, 1980, Milton Bradley
EX $6   NM $18   MIP $30

Pocket Size Bowling Card Game, 1950s, Warren/Built-Rite
EX $15   NM $25   MIP $40

Pocket Whoozit, 1985, Trivia
EX $4   NM $7   MIP $10

Point of Law, 1972, 3M
EX $4   NM $14   MIP $20

Pole Position, 1983, Parker Brothers
EX $8   NM $13   MIP $20

Police Patrol, 1955, Hasbro
EX $50   NM $100   MIP $125

Police State, 1974, Gameophiles Unltd.
EX $25   NM $60   MIP $85

Politics, Game of, 1952, Parker Brothers
EX $20   NM $35   MIP $50

Ponents, 1974, Dynamic
EX $6   NM $15   MIP $25

Pony Express, Game of, 1947, Polygon
EX $12   NM $40   MIP $60

Pooch, 1956, Hasbro
EX $10   NM $20   MIP $30

Pop Yer Top!, 1968, Milton Bradley
EX $15   NM $35   MIP $50

Popeye Spinach Flip, 1969, Whitman
EX $10   NM $25   MIP $35

Popeye, Adventures of, 1957, Transogram
EX $35   NM $75   MIP $100

Poppin Hoppies, 1968, Ideal
EX $10   NM $25   MIP $35

Population, 1970, Urban Systems
EX $6   NM $18   MIP $30

Pop-Up Store Game, 1950s, Milton Bradley
EX $25   NM $40   MIP $75

Post Office, 1968, Hasbro
EX $8   NM $20   MIP $30

Postman, 1957, Selchow & Righter
EX $8   NM $15   MIP $30

Pothole Game, The, 1979, Cadaco
EX $10   NM $25   MIP $40

Pow, The Frontier Game, 1955, Selchow & Righter
EX $12   NM $40   MIP $60

Power 4 Car Racing Game, 1960s, Manning
EX $15   NM $50   MIP $75

Power Play Hockey, 1970, Romac
EX $12   NM $35   MIP $50

Power: The Game, 1981, Power Games
EX $10   NM $25   MIP $35

Prediction Rod, 1970, Parker Brothers
EX $5   NM $16   MIP $25

Presidential Campaign, 1979, John Hansen
EX $6   NM $18   MIP $30

Prince Caspian, 1983, David Cook
EX $5   NM $16   MIP $25

Prince Valiant (Harold Foster's), 1950s, Transogram
EX $20   NM $40   MIP $75

Prize Property, 1974, Milton Bradley
EX $8   NM $15   MIP $30

Pro Draft, 1974, Parker Brothers
EX $15   NM $35   MIP $45

Pro Football, 1980s, Strat-O-Matic
EX $10   NM $20   MIP $30

Pro Foto-Football, 1977, Cadaco
EX $6   NM $15   MIP $25

Pro Franchise Football, 1987, Rohrwood
EX $10   NM $16   MIP $25

Pro Golf, 1982, Avalon Hill
EX $7   NM $11   MIP $17

Pro Quarterback, 1964, Tod Lansing
EX $20   NM $40   MIP $50

Pro Soccer, 1968, Milton Bradley
EX $12   NM $30   MIP $40

Probe, 1964, Parker Brothers
EX $2   NM $7   MIP $12

Products and Resources, Game of, 1962, Selchow & Righter
EX $6   NM $18   MIP $30

Profit Farming, 1979, Foster Enterprises
EX $6   NM $18   MIP $30

Prospecting, 1953, Selchow & Righter
EX $20   NM $30   MIP $50

Prospector, The, 1980, McJay Game Co.
EX $8   NM $20   MIP $30

Public Assistance, 1980, Hammerhead
EX $20   NM $40   MIP $50

Pug-i-Lo, 1960, Pug-i-Lo Games
EX $55   NM $90   MIP $135

Pure Greed, 1971, Crea-Tek
EX $12   NM $30   MIP $40

Pursue the Pennant, 1984, Pursue the Pennant
EX $30   NM $70   MIP $100

Pursuit!, 1973, Aurora
EX $8   NM $25   MIP $40

Push Over, 1981, Parker Brothers
EX $3   NM $12   MIP $18

Put and Take, 1956, Schaper
EX $5   NM $16   MIP $25

Puzzling Pyramid, 1960, Schaper
EX $6   NM $18   MIP $30

Pyramid, 1978, Hasbro
EX $6   NM $15   MIP $25

Pyramid Power, 1978, Castle Toy
EX $8   NM $20   MIP $30

Q*Bert, 1983, Parker Brothers
EX $4   NM $10   MIP $15

Quad-Ominos, 1978, Pressman
EX $2   NM $6   MIP $10

Quarterback Football Game, 1969, Transogram
EX $25   NM $40   MIP $65

Qubic, 1965, Parker Brothers
EX $3   NM $10   MIP $15

Quest, 1962, Lakeside
EX $12   NM $30   MIP $40

Quest, 1978, Gametime/Heritage Models
EX $10   NM $25   MIP $35

Quick Draw McGraw Game, 1981, Milton Bradley
EX $5   NM $12   MIP $18

Quick Draw McGraw Private Eye Game, 1960
EX $15   NM $25   MIP $35

Quinto, 1964, 3M
EX $6   NM $18   MIP $30

Quiz Panel, 1954, Cadaco-Ellis
EX $6   NM $18   MIP $30

Race-A-Plane, 1947, Phon-O-Game
EX $12   NM $40   MIP $60

Race-O-Rama, 1960, Warren/Built-Rite
EX $10   NM $20   MIP $30

Raceway, 1950s, B & B Toy
EX $30   NM $50   MIP $75

Radaronics, 1946, ARC
EX $15   NM $40   MIP $50

Raggedy Ann, 1956, Milton Bradley
EX $10   NM $20   MIP $35

Raiders of the Lost Ark, 1981, Kenner
EX $8   NM $20   MIP $30

Rainy Day Golf, 1980, Bryad
EX $6   NM $18   MIP $30

Raise the Titanic, 1987, Hoyle
EX $12   NM $30   MIP $40

Rat Patrol Game, 1966, Transogram
EX $40   NM $70   MIP $100

Rawhide, 1959, Lowell
EX $125   NM $250   MIP $350

Raymar of The Jungle, 1952, Dexter Wayne
EX $30   NM $50   MIP $65

Razzle, 1981, Parker Brothers
EX $2   NM $6   MIP $10

Razzle Dazzle Football Game, 1954, Texantics Unlimited
EX $50   NM $80   MIP $125

React-Or, 1979
EX $15   NM $25   MIP $40

Real Action Baseball Game, 1966, Real-Action Games
EX $20   NM $35   MIP $50

Real Baseball Card Game, 1990, National Baseball
EX $110   NM $180   MIP $275

Real Ghostbusters, The, 1986, Milton Bradley
EX $6   NM $18   MIP $30

Real Life Basketball, 1974, Gamecraft
EX $20   NM $50   MIP $75

Realistic Football, 1976, Match Play
EX $15   NM $25   MIP $35

(KP Photo)

Rebel, The, 1961, Ideal
EX $65   NM $85   MIP $100

Rebound, 1971, Ideal
EX $5   NM $16   MIP $25

Record Game, The, 1984, The Record Game
EX $8   NM $25   MIP $40

Red Barber's Big League Baseball Game, 1950s, G & R Anthony
EX $450   NM $1200   MIP $1700

Red Herring, 1945, Cadaco-Ellis
EX $12   NM $40   MIP $60

Red Rover Game, The, 1963, Cadaco-Ellis
EX $5   NM $16   MIP $25

Reddy Clown 3-Ring Circus Game, 1952, Parker Brothers
EX $15   NM $35   MIP $55

Reese's Pieces Game, 1983, Ideal
EX $5   NM $8   MIP $15

Reflex, 1966, Lakeside
EX $5   NM $16   MIP $25

Regatta, 1946
EX $40   NM $70   MIP $110

Regatta, 1968, 3M
EX $10   NM $20   MIP $30

Replay Series Baseball, 1983, Bond Sports
EX $6   NM $10   MIP $15

Restless Gun, 1950s, Milton Bradley
EX $18   NM $40   MIP $60

Return To Oz Game, 1985, Western
EX $10   NM $15   MIP $25

Reward, 1958, Happy Hour
EX $10   NM $35   MIP $50

Rhyme Time, 1969, NBC-Hasbro
EX $6   NM $15   MIP $25

Rich Farmer, Poor Farmer, 1978, McJay Game
EX $5   NM $16   MIP $25

Rich Uncle The Stock Market Game, 1955, Parker Brothers
EX $20   NM $30   MIP $40

(KP Photo)

Rich Uncle, Game of, 1946, Parker Brothers
EX $20   NM $40   MIP $50

Richie Rich, 1982, Milton Bradley
EX $3   NM $5   MIP $10

Rickenbacker Ace Game, 1946, Milton Bradley
EX $50   NM $75   MIP $100

Ricochet Rabbit Game, 1965, Ideal
EX $45   NM $75   MIP $120

Rifleman Game, 1959, Milton Bradley
EX $30   NM $50   MIP $75

(KP Photo)

Rin Tin Tin Game, 1950s, Transogram
EX $30   NM $50   MIP $65

Ringmaster Circus Game, 1947, Cadaco-Ellis
EX $15   NM $20   MIP $30

Rio, The Game of, 1956, Parker Brothers
EX $10   NM $30   MIP $40

Ripley's Believe It Or Not, 1979, Whitman
EX $6   NM $10   MIP $15

Risk, 1959, Parker Brothers
EX $25   NM $40   MIP $60

Riverboat Game, 1950s, Parker Brothers/Disney
EX $20   NM $35   MIP $55

Road Runner Game, 1968, Milton Bradley
EX $10   NM $25   MIP $35

Road Runner Pop Up Game, 1982, Whitman
EX $20   NM $30   MIP $50

Robert Schuller's Possibility Thinkers Game, 1977, Selchow & Righter
EX $3   NM $5   MIP $10

GAMES

Robin Hood, 1955, Harett-Gilmar
EX $30 NM $40 MIP $60

Robin Hood Game, 1970s, Parker Brothers
EX $7 NM $15 MIP $30

Robin Hood, Adventures of, 1956, Bettye-B
EX $30 NM $50 MIP $70

Robin Roberts Sports Club Baseball Game, 1960, Dexter Wayne
EX $100 NM $165 MIP $250

Robocop VCR Game, 1988, Spinnaker
EX $7 NM $20 MIP $35

Robot Sam the Answer Man, 1950, Jacmar
EX $20 NM $30 MIP $40

Rock 'N' Roll Replay, 1984, Baron-Scott
EX $7 NM $20 MIP $35

Rock the Boat Game, 1978, Milton Bradley
EX $6 NM $18 MIP $30

Rock Trivia, 1984, Pressman
EX $5 NM $10 MIP $15

Rocket Race, 1958, Stone Craft
EX $30 NM $70 MIP $95

Rocket Race To Saturn, 1950s, Lido
EX $15 NM $20 MIP $35

Rodeo, The Wild West Game, 1957, Whitman
EX $12 NM $40 MIP $60

(KP Photo)

Roger Maris' Action Baseball, 1962, Pressman
EX $50 NM $80 MIP $100

Rol-A-Lite, 1947, Durable Toy & Novelty
EX $45 NM $75 MIP $120

Rol-It, 1954, Parker Brothers
EX $4 NM $12 MIP $20

Roll And Score Poker, 1977, Lowe
EX $3 NM $7 MIP $12

Roll-A-Par, 1964, Lowe
EX $8 NM $20 MIP $30

Roller Derby, 1974, Milton Bradley
EX $70 NM $150 MIP $225

Roman X, 1964, Selchow & Righter
EX $7 NM $20 MIP $35

Roscoe Turner Air Race Game, 1960, Southern Games
EX $40 NM $90 MIP $135

Rose Bowl, 1949, Keck Enterprises
EX $15 NM $35 MIP $50

Rose Bowl, 1966, E.S.Lowe
EX $15 NM $20 MIP $30

Roundup, 1952, Wales Game Systems
EX $15 NM $35 MIP $50

Route 66 Game, 1960, Transogram
EX $70 NM $100 MIP $160

Roy Rogers Game, 1950s
EX $20 NM $35 MIP $55

Rribit, Battle of the Frogs, 1982, Genesis Enterprises
EX $6 NM $18 MIP $30

Ruffhouse, 1980, Parker Brothers
EX $3 NM $10 MIP $15

Rules of the Road, 1977, Cadaco
EX $5 NM $16 MIP $25

Run to Win, 1980, Cabela
EX $6 NM $18 MIP $30

Russian Campaign, The, 1976, Avalon Hill
EX $3 NM $5 MIP $10

(KP Photo)

S.O.S., 1947, Durable Toy & Novelty
EX $65 NM $85 MIP $110

S.W.A.T, 1976, Milton Bradley
EX $5 NM $10 MIP $15

(KP Photo)

S.W.A.T. Game, 1970s, Milton Bradley
EX $10 NM $15 MIP $25

Sabotage, 1985, Lakeside
EX $2 NM $6 MIP $10

Saddle Racing Game, 1974, APBA
EX $20 NM $50 MIP $75

Safari, 1950, Selchow & Righter
EX $12 NM $40 MIP $50

Safecrack, 1982, Selchow & Righter
EX $4 NM $15 MIP $20

Sail Away, 1962, Howard Mullen
EX $12 NM $30 MIP $40

Salvo, 1961, Ideal
EX $15 NM $25 MIP $40

Samsonite Basketball, 1969, Samsonite
EX $15 NM $35 MIP $60

Samsonite Football, 1969, Samsonite
EX $12 NM $30 MIP $50

Sandlot Slugger, 1960s, Milton Bradley
EX $35 NM $60 MIP $75

Save the President, 1984, Jack Jaffe
EX $8 NM $20 MIP $30

Say When!, 1961, Parker Brothers
EX $6 NM $18 MIP $30

Scarne's Challenge, 1947, John Scarne Games
EX $10 NM $15 MIP $20

Scavenger Hunt, 1983, Milton Bradley
EX $3 NM $5 MIP $10

Scooby Doo and Scrappy Doo, 1983, Milton Bradley
EX $3 NM $8 MIP $16

Scooby-Doo, Where are You?, 1973, Milton Bradley
EX $20 NM $40 MIP $50

Scoop, 1956, Parker Brothers
EX $35 NM $50 MIP $60

Scoop: The Newspaper Game, 1976, Western Publishing
EX $18 NM $45 MIP $65

Score Four, 1968, Funtastic
EX $3 NM $10 MIP $15

Scotland Yard, 1985, Milton Bradley
EX $3 NM $10 MIP $15

Scrabble, 1953, Selchow & Righter
EX $5 NM $12 MIP $20

Scrabble for Juniors, 1968, Selchow & Righter
EX $2 NM $5 MIP $8

Scrabble RPM, 1971, Selchow & Righter
EX $8 NM $20 MIP $30

Screaming Eagles, 1987, Milton Bradley
EX $4 NM $15 MIP $20

Screwball The Mad Mad Mad Game, 1960, Transogram
EX $30 NM $50 MIP $75

Scribbage, 1963, Lowe
EX $3 NM $10 MIP $15

Scrimmage, 1973, SPI
EX $5 NM $15 MIP $25

Scruples, 1986, Milton Bradley
EX $5 NM $10 MIP $15

Scrutineyes, 1992, Hersch & Co/Mattel
EX $12 NM $30 MIP $40

Sea World Treasure Key, 1983, International Games
EX $4 NM $15 MIP $20

Sealab 2020 Game, 1973, Milton Bradley
EX $6 NM $10 MIP $15

Seance, 1972, Milton Bradley
EX $75 NM $100 MIP $225

Secrecy, 1965, Universal Games
EX $12 NM $30 MIP $40

Secret Agent Man, 1966, Milton Bradley
EX $25　　NM $40　　MIP $65

Secret of NIMH, 1982, Whitman
EX $15　　NM $20　　MIP $30

Secret Weapon, 1984, Selchow & Righter
EX $5　　NM $16　　MIP $25

Seduction, 1966, Createk
EX $10　　NM $25　　MIP $35

See New York 'Round the Town, 1964, Transogram
EX $50　　NM $75　　MIP $110

Sergeant Preston Game, 1950s, Milton Bradley
EX $15　　NM $35　　MIP $50

Set Point, 1971, XV Productions
EX $8　　NM $20　　MIP $30

Seven Keys, 1961, Ideal
EX $12　　NM $30　　MIP $40

(KP Photo)

Seven Seas, 1960, Cadaco-Ellis
EX $20　　NM $40　　MIP $60

(KP Photo)

Seven Up, 1960s, Transogram
EX $7　　NM $12　　MIP $20

Shadowlord!, 1983, Parker Brothers
EX $3　　NM $10　　MIP $15

Sha-ee, the Game of Destiny, 1963, Ideal
EX $20　　NM $65　　MIP $90

(KP Photo)

Shazam, Captian Marvel's Own Game, 1950s, Reed & Associates
EX $30　　NM $60　　MIP $95

Shenanigans, 1964, Milton Bradley
EX $15　　NM $40　　MIP $50

Sheriff of Dodge City, 1966, Parker Brothers
EX $8　　NM $25　　MIP $40

Sherlock Holmes, 1950s, National Games
EX $25　　NM $60　　MIP $75

Sherlock Holmes, 1980, Whitman
EX $5　　NM $16　　MIP $25

Sherlock Holmes Game, The, 1974, Cadaco
EX $6　　NM $18　　MIP $30

Shifty Checkers, 1973, Aurora
EX $8　　NM $25　　MIP $40

Shifty Gear Game, 1962, Schaper
EX $5　　NM $16　　MIP $25

Shindig, 1965, Remco
EX $30　　NM $50　　MIP $75

Shmo, 1960s, Remco
EX $10　　NM $30　　MIP $40

Shogun, 1976, Epoch Playthings
EX $6　　NM $15　　MIP $25

Shogun, 1986, Milton Bradley
EX $18　　NM $45　　MIP $75

Shopping, 1973, John Ladell
EX $5　　NM $16　　MIP $25

(KP Photo)

Shotgun Slade, 1960, Milton Bradley
EX $20　　NM $45　　MIP $65

Show-Biz, 1950s, Lowell
EX $15　　NM $50　　MIP $75

SI: The Sporting Word Game, 1961, Time
EX $10　　NM $16　　MIP $25

Siege Game, 1966, Milton Bradley
EX $20　　NM $50　　MIP $70

Silly Carnival, 1969, Whitman
EX $7　　NM $12　　MIP $20

Silly Safari, 1966, Topper
EX $30　　NM $70　　MIP $105

Silly Sidney, 1963, Transogram
EX $12　　NM $30　　MIP $40

Simpsons Mystery of Life, The, 1990, Cardinal
EX $5　　NM $7　　MIP $10

Sinbad, 1978, Cadaco
EX $20　　NM $30　　MIP $50

Sinking of The Titanic, The, 1976, Ideal
EX $35　　NM $50　　MIP $75

Sir Lancelot, Adventures of, 1960s, Lisbeth Whiting
EX $40　　NM $70　　MIP $110

Situation 4, 1968, Parker Brothers
EX $5　　NM $16　　MIP $20

Situation 7, 1969, Parker Brothers
EX $8　　NM $25　　MIP $40

Six Million Dollar Man, 1975, Parker Brothers
EX $10　　NM $15　　MIP $25

Skatebirds Game, 1978, Milton Bradley
EX $7　　NM $20　　MIP $35

Skatterbug, Game of, 1951, Parker Brothers
EX $30　　NM $50　　MIP $60

Skedaddle, 1965, Cadaco-Ellis
EX $8　　NM $25　　MIP $40

Ski Gammon, 1962, American Publishing
EX $8　　NM $20　　MIP $30

Skill-Drive, 1950s, Sidney Tarrson
EX $10　　NM $35　　MIP $40

Skins Golf Game, Official, 1985, O'Connor Hall
EX $12　　NM $20　　MIP $30

Skip-A-Cross, 1953, Cadaco
EX $3　　NM $7　　MIP $10

Skipper Race Sailing Game, 1949, Cadaco-Ellis
EX $25　　NM $60　　MIP $90

(KP Photo)

Skirmish, 1975, Milton Bradley
EX $30　　NM $50　　MIP $60

Skirrid, 1979, Kenner
EX $4　　NM $15　　MIP $20

Skudo, 1949, Parker Brothers
EX $8　　NM $25　　MIP $40

Skully, 1961, Ideal
EX $3　　NM $5　　MIP $10

Skunk, 1950s, Schaper
EX $7　　NM $12　　MIP $20

Sky Lanes, 1958, Parker Brothers
EX $20　　NM $50　　MIP $75

Sky's The Limit, The, 1955, Kohner
EX $15　　NM $25　　MIP $40

Sla-lom Ski Race Game, 1957, Cadaco-Ellis
EX $20　　NM $50　　MIP $75

Slap Trap, 1967, Ideal
EX $8　　NM $25　　MIP $40

Slapshot, 1982, Avalon Hill
EX $10　　NM $25　　MIP $35

Slip Disc, 1980, Milton Bradley
EX $5　　NM $16　　MIP $25

Smess, The Ninny's Chess, 1970, Parker Brothers
EX $35　　NM $50　　MIP $75

Smog, 1970, Urban Systems
EX $8　　NM $20　　MIP $30

Smokey: The Forest Fire Prevention Bear, 1961, Ideal
EX $30　　NM $65　　MIP $105

Smurf Game, 1984, Milton Bradley
EX $4　　NM $7　　MIP $12

Snafu, 1969, Gamescience
EX $7   NM $20   MIP $35

Snagglepuss Fun at the Picnic Game,
1961, Transogram
EX $40   NM $50   MIP $75

Snake Eyes, 1957, Selchow & Righter
EX $15   NM $30   MIP $40

Snakes & Ladders, 1974,
Summmerville/Canada
EX $4   NM $7   MIP $10

Snake's Alive, Game of, 1967, Ideal
EX $12   NM $30   MIP $40

Snakes In The Grass, 1960s, Kohner
EX $10   NM $15   MIP $25

**Snappet Catch Game with Harmon
Killebrew,** 1960, Killebrew
EX $55   NM $90   MIP $135

Sniggle!, 1980, Amway
EX $4   NM $10   MIP $15

Snob, A Fantasy Shopping Spree, 1983,
Helene Fox
EX $7   NM $20   MIP $35

Snoopy & The Red Baron, 1970, Milton
Bradley
EX $15   NM $35   MIP $50

Snoopy Come Home Game, 1973, Milton
Bradley
EX $10   NM $16   MIP $25

Snoopy Game, 1960, Selchow & Righter
EX $25   NM $45   MIP $60

Snoopy's Doghouse Game, 1977, Milton
Bradley
EX $5   NM $16   MIP $25

(KP Photo)

Snow White and the Seven Dwarfs,
1970s, Cadaco
EX $6   NM $10   MIP $15

Snuffy Smith Game, 1970s, Milton Bradley
EX $15   NM $20   MIP $30

Society Scandals, 1978, E.S.Lowe
EX $6   NM $15   MIP $25

Sod Buster, 1980, Santee
EX $10   NM $16   MIP $25

Solar Conquest, 1966, Atech Enterprises
EX $15   NM $35   MIP $50

Solarquest, 1986, Western
EX $6   NM $10   MIP $15

Solid Gold Music Trivia, 1984, Ideal
EX $6   NM $10   MIP $15

Solitaire (Lucille Ball), 1973, Milton Bradley
EX $2   NM $5   MIP $10

Sons of Hercules Game, The, 1966, Milton
Bradley
EX $30   NM $50   MIP $75

Soupy Sales Sez Go-Go-Go Game, 1960s,
Milton Bradley
EX $35   NM $50   MIP $80

Southern Fast Freight Game, 1970,
American Publishing
EX $8   NM $25   MIP $40

Space Angel Game, 1966, Transogram
EX $25   NM $65   MIP $85

Space Chase, 1967, United Nations
Constructors
EX $15   NM $35   MIP $50

Space Game, 1953, Parker Brothers
EX $25   NM $65   MIP $85

Space Pilot, 1951, Cadaco-Ellis
EX $20   NM $50   MIP $75

Space Shuttle 101, 1978, Media-Ungame
EX $8   NM $20   MIP $30

Space Shuttle, The, 1981, Ungame
EX $8   NM $20   MIP $30

(KP Photo)

Space: 1999 Game, 1975, Milton Bradley
EX $10   NM $15   MIP $25

Special Agent, 1966, Parker Brothers
EX $10   NM $25   MIP $40

Special Detective/Speedway, 1959,
Saalfield
EX $15   NM $40   MIP $60

Speedorama, 1950s, Jacmar
EX $30   NM $50   MIP $80

Speedway, Big Bopper Game, 1961, Ideal
EX $18   NM $40   MIP $60

Spider and the Fly, 1981, Marx
EX $12   NM $20   MIP $30

Spider-Man Game, The Amazing, 1967,
Milton Bradley
EX $20   NM $45   MIP $85

(KP Photo)

Spider-Man with The Fantastic Four,
1977, Milton Bradley
EX $10   NM $20   MIP $35

Spider's Web Game, The, 1969, Multiple
Plastics
EX $7   NM $12   MIP $20

Spin Cycle Baseball, 1965, Pressman
EX $25   NM $40   MIP $65

Spin The Bottle, 1968, Hasbro
EX $8   NM $20   MIP $30

Spin Welder, 1960s, Mattel
EX $7   NM $12   MIP $20

**Spiro T. Agnew American History
Challenge Game,** 1971, Gabriel
EX $20   NM $35   MIP $55

Splat!, 1990, Milton Bradley
EX $8   NM $20   MIP $30

Sporting News: Baseroll, 1986, Mundo
Games
EX $8   NM $13   MIP $20

Sports Arena No. 1, 1954, Rennoc Games
& Toys
EX $35   NM $60   MIP $90

**Sports Illustrated All Time All Star
Baseball,** 1973, Sports Illustrated
EX $75   NM $175   MIP $250

Sports Illustrated Baseball, 1972, Time,
Inc. (Sports Illustrated)
EX $60   NM $120   MIP $175

Sports Illustrated College Football, 1971,
Sports Illustrated
EX $8   NM $25   MIP $40

Sports Illustrated Decathlon, 1972, Time
EX $8   NM $25   MIP $40

Sports Illustrated Handicap Golf, 1971,
Sports Illustrated
EX $10   NM $25   MIP $35

Sports Illustrated Pro Football, 1970, Time
EX $15   NM $25   MIP $40

Sports Trivia Game, 1984, Hoyle
EX $6   NM $10   MIP $15

Sports Yesteryear, 1977, Skor-Mor
EX $15   NM $25   MIP $35

Spot Cash, 1959, Milton Bradley
EX $7   NM $15   MIP $20

Spy vs. Spy, 1986, Milton Bradley
EX $10   NM $15   MIP $25

Square Mile, 1962, Milton Bradley
EX $15   NM $25   MIP $30

Square Off, 1972, Parker Brothers
EX $8   NM $20   MIP $30

Square-It, 1961, Hasbro
EX $5   NM $16   MIP $25

Squares, 1950s, Schaper
EX $4   NM $15   MIP $20

Squatter: The Australian Wool Game,
1960s, John Sands/Australia
EX $15   NM $25   MIP $45

St. Louis Cardinals Baseball Card Game,
1964, Ed-U-Cards
EX $10   NM $25   MIP $35

Stadium Checkers, 1954, Schaper
EX $7   NM $12   MIP $20

Stagecoach West Game, 1961,
Transogram
EX $35   NM $50   MIP $75

Stampede, 1952, Wales Game Systems
EX $15   NM $35   MIP $40

Stampede, 1956, Gabriel
EX $8   NM $25   MIP $40

Star Reporter, 1950s, Parker Brothers
EX $85   NM $125   MIP $175

Star Team Battling Spaceships, 1977, Ideal
EX $8   NM $20   MIP $30

(Toy Shop File Photo)

Star Trek, 1979, Milton Bradley
EX $18   NM $40   MIP $50

Star Trek Adventure Game, 1985, West End Games
EX $8   NM $20   MIP $30

(KP Photo)

Star Trek Game, 1960s, Ideal
EX $35   NM $75   MIP $100

Star Trek: The Next Generation, 1993, Classic Games
EX $15   NM $25   MIP $50

Star Wars Adventures of R2D2 Game, 1977, Kenner
EX $12   NM $20   MIP $30

Star Wars Battle at Sarlacc's Pit, 1983, Parker Brothers
EX $10   NM $15   MIP $25

Star Wars Escape from Death Star, 1977, Kenner
EX $10   NM $15   MIP $25

Star Wars Monopoly, 1997, Parker Brothers
EX $15   NM $20   MIP $35

(KP Photo)

Star Wars ROTJ Ewoks Save The Trees, 1984, Parker Brothers
EX $10   NM $15   MIP $25

Star Wars Wicket the Ewok, 1983, Parker Brothers
EX $7   NM $12   MIP $20

Star Wars X-Wing Aces Target Game, 1978
EX $20   NM $30   MIP $50

Starship Troopers, 1976, Avalon Hill
EX $5   NM $16   MIP $25

Starsky & Hutch, 1977, Milton Bradley
EX $10   NM $16   MIP $25

State Capitals, Game of, 1952, Parker Brothers
EX $4   NM $10   MIP $15

States, Game of the, 1975, Milton Bradley
EX $4   NM $6   MIP $10

Statis Pro Football, 1970s, Statis-Pro
EX $25   NM $40   MIP $65

Stay Alive, 1971, Milton Bradley
EX $6   NM $15   MIP $25

Steps of Toyland, 1954, Parker Brothers
EX $20   NM $35   MIP $55

Steve Allen's Qubila, 1955, Lord & Freber
EX $8   NM $25   MIP $40

Steve Canyon, 1959, Lowell
EX $20   NM $40   MIP $75

Steve Scott Space Scout Game, 1952, Transogram
EX $30   NM $50   MIP $75

Stick the IRS!, 1981, Courtland Playthings
EX $10   NM $16   MIP $20

Sting, The, 1976, Ideal
EX $10   NM $20   MIP $25

Stock Car Race, 1950s, Gardner
EX $25   NM $50   MIP $75

Stock Car Racing Game, 1956, Whitman
EX $12   NM $30   MIP $40

Stock Car Racing Game (w/Petty/Yarborough), 1981, Ribbit Toy
EX $17   NM $30   MIP $45

Stock Car Speedway, Game of, 1965, Johnstone
EX $55   NM $90   MIP $135

Stock Market Game, 1955, Gabriel
EX $20   NM $30   MIP $50

Stock Market Game, 1963, 1968, Whitman
EX $25   NM $45   MIP $75

Stock Market Game, 1970, Avalon Hill
EX $7   NM $12   MIP $20

Stock Market Specialist, 1983, John Hansen
EX $6   NM $18   MIP $30

Stoney Burk, 1963, Transogram
EX $30   NM $70   MIP $90

Stop Thief, 1979, Parker Brothers
EX $15   NM $35   MIP $50

Straight Arrow, 1950, Selchow & Righter
EX $25   NM $45   MIP $70

Straightaway, 1961, Selchow & Righter
EX $45   NM $60   MIP $90

Strata 5, 1984, Milton Bradley
EX $5   NM $16   MIP $25

Strategic Command, 1950s, Transogram
EX $15   NM $35   MIP $50

Stratego (plastic pieces), 1962-on, Milton Bradley
EX $6   NM $15   MIP $25

Stratego (wood pieces), 1961, Milton Bradley
EX $50   NM $75   MIP $90

Strategy Manager Baseball, 1967, McGuffin-Ramsey
EX $2   NM $6   MIP $12

Strato Tac-tics, 1972, Strato-Various
EX $8   NM $25   MIP $40

Strat-O-Matic Baseball, 1961, Strat-O-Matic
EX $125   NM $165   MIP $300

Strat-O-Matic College Football, 1976, Strat-O-Matic
EX $25   NM $55   MIP $75

Strat-O-Matic Hockey, 1978, Strat-O-Matic
EX $12   NM $30   MIP $50

Strat-O-Matic Sports "Know-How", 1984, Strat-O-Matic
EX $6   NM $10   MIP $15

Strato-O-Matic Baseball, 1970, Strat-O-Matic
EX $25   NM $50   MIP $70

Strato-O-Matic Baseball, 1980, Strat-O-Matic
EX $20   NM $35   MIP $50

Strato-O-Matic Baseball (varies by season of cards), 1960s, Strat-O-Matic
EX $80   NM $150   MIP $225

Strato-O-Matic Football (varies by season of cards), 1967-74, Strat-O-Matic
EX $50   NM $125   MIP $175

Strato-O-Matic Football (varies by season of cards), 1975-85, Strat-O-Matic
EX $25   NM $60   MIP $85

Strato-O-Matic Football (varies by season of cards), 1986-90s, Strat-O-Matic
EX $12   NM $30   MIP $40

Stretch Call, 1986, Sevedeo A. Vigil
EX $12   NM $20   MIP $30

Strike Three (Carl Hubbell's), 1948, Tone Products
EX $75   NM $150   MIP $300

Stuff Yer Face, 1982, Milton Bradley
EX $6   NM $20   MIP $35

Stump the Stars, 1962, Ideal
EX $8   NM $25   MIP $40

Sub Attack Game, 1965, Milton Bradley
EX $7   NM $20   MIP $35

Sub Search, 1973, Milton Bradley
EX $8   NM $45   MIP $50

Sub Search, 1977, Milton Bradley
EX $6   NM $18   MIP $30

Sudden Death!, 1978, Gabriel
EX $5   NM $16   MIP $25

Suffolk Downs Racing Game, 1947, Corey Game
EX $40   NM $90   MIP $135

Sugar Bowl, 1950s, Transogram
EX $20   NM $40   MIP $50

GAMES

Summit, 1961, Milton Bradley
EX $15   NM $25   MIP $40

Sunken Treasure, 1948, Parker Brothers
EX $15   NM $25   MIP $45

Sunken Treasure, 1976, Milton Bradley
EX $7   NM $12   MIP $20

Super Coach TV Football, 1974, Coleco
EX $5   NM $12   MIP $20

Super Market, 1953, Selchow & Righter
EX $10   NM $35   MIP $50

Super Powers, 1984, Parker Brothers
EX $15   NM $25   MIP $40

Super Spy, 1971, Milton Bradley
EX $15   NM $25   MIP $40

(KP Photo)

Superboy Game, 1960s, Hasbro
EX $45   NM $75   MIP $135

Supercar Road Race, 1962, Standard Toykraft
EX $45   NM $100   MIP $140

(KP Photo)

Supercar to the Rescue Game, 1962, Milton Bradley
EX $25   NM $50   MIP $75

Superman & Superboy, 1967, Milton Bradley
EX $40   NM $65   MIP $105

Superman Game, 1965, Hasbro
EX $45   NM $75   MIP $120

Superman Game, 1966, Merry Manufacturing
EX $35   NM $55   MIP $90

Superman II, 1981, Milton Bradley
EX $10   NM $20   MIP $30

Superman III, 1982, Parker Brothers
EX $4   NM $12   MIP $20

Superman, Adventures of, 1940s, Milton Bradley
EX $125   NM $250   MIP $450

Superstar Baseball, 1966, Sports Illustrated
EX $30   NM $50   MIP $75

Superstar Pro Wrestling Game, 1984, Super Star Game
EX $8   NM $13   MIP $20

Superstar TV Sports, 1980, ARC
EX $6   NM $10   MIP $15

Superstition, 1977, Milton Bradley
EX $12   NM $30   MIP $40

Sure Shot Hockey, 1970, Ideal
EX $15   NM $25   MIP $40

(KP Photo)

Surfside 6, 1961, Lowell
EX $30   NM $50   MIP $75

Surprise Package, Your, 1961, Ideal
EX $25   NM $60   MIP $85

Survive!, 1982, Parker Brothers
EX $12   NM $30   MIP $40

Swahili Game, 1968, Milton Bradley
EX $8   NM $20   MIP $30

Swap, the Wheeler-Dealer Game, 1965, Ideal
EX $7   NM $20   MIP $35

Swat Baseball, 1948, Milton Bradley
EX $20   NM $35   MIP $50

(KP Photo)

Swayze, 1954, Milton Bradley
EX $12   NM $20   MIP $30

Swish, 1948, Jim Hawkers Games
EX $45   NM $75   MIP $115

Swoop, 1969, Whitman
EX $7   NM $12   MIP $20

Sword In The Stone Game, 1960s, Parker Brothers
EX $18   NM $40   MIP $60

Swords and Shields, 1970, Milton Bradley
EX $10   NM $35   MIP $50

Syncron-8, 1963, Transogram
EX $18   NM $40   MIP $60

T.V. Bingo, 1970, Selchow & Richter
EX $3   NM $5   MIP $10

Tabit, 1954, John Norton
EX $25   NM $35   MIP $75

Tactics II, 1984, Avalon Hill
EX $6   NM $10   MIP $15

Taffy's Party Game, 1960s, Transogram
EX $10   NM $15   MIP $25

Taffy's Shopping Spree Game, 1964, Transogram
EX $10   NM $25   MIP $35

Tagalong Joe, 1950, Wales Game Systems
EX $8   NM $15   MIP $20

Tales of Wells Fargo, 1959, Milton Bradley
EX $40   NM $65   MIP $105

Talking Baseball, 1971, Mattel
EX $35   NM $60   MIP $85

Talking Football, 1971, Mattel
EX $35   NM $50   MIP $75

Talking Monday Night Football, 1977, Mattel
EX $25   NM $30   MIP $50

Tally Ho!, 1950s, Whitman
EX $8   NM $20   MIP $30

Tangle, 1964, Selchow & Righter
EX $6   NM $18   MIP $30

Tank Battle, 1975, Milton Bradley
EX $15   NM $35   MIP $50

Tank Command, 1975, Ideal
EX $7   NM $20   MIP $35

Tantalizer, 1958, Northern Signal
EX $10   NM $20   MIP $30

Tarzan, 1984, Milton Bradley
EX $5   NM $10   MIP $15

(KP Photo)

Tarzan To The Rescue, 1976, Milton Bradley
EX $10   NM $15   MIP $25

Taxi!, 1960, Selchow & Righter
EX $20   NM $35   MIP $50

Tee Off by Sam Snead, 1973, Glenn Industries
EX $18   NM $40   MIP $60

Teed Off!, 1966, Cadaco
EX $6   NM $15   MIP $25

Teeko, 1948, John Scarne Games
EX $10   NM $15   MIP $20

Teen Time, 1960s, Warren-Built Rite
EX $6   NM $15   MIP $25

Telephone Game, The, 1982, Cadaco
EX $7   NM $20   MIP $35

Television, 1953, National Novelty
EX $35   NM $75   MIP $100

Tell It To The Judge, 1959, Parker Brothers
EX $20   NM $35   MIP $50

Temple of Fu Manchu Game, The, 1967, Pressman
EX $20   NM $30   MIP $50

Ten-Four, Good Buddy, 1976, Parker Brothers
EX $5   NM $7   MIP $12

Tennessee Tuxedo, 1963, Transogram
EX $75   NM $125   MIP $200

Tennis, 1975, Parker Brothers
EX $10   NM $16   MIP $25

Tension, 1970, Kohner
EX $7   NM $12   MIP $20

GAMES

(KP Photo)

Terrytoons Hide N' Seek Game, 1960, Transogram
EX $35   NM $60   MIP $80

Test Driver Game, The, 1956, Milton Bradley
EX $45   NM $80   MIP $100

Texas Millionaire, 1955, Texantics
EX $25   NM $55   MIP $75

Texas Rangers, Game of, 1950s, All-Fair
EX $25   NM $50   MIP $75

That's Truckin', 1976, Showker
EX $7   NM $20   MIP $35

They're at the Post, 1976, MAAS Marketing
EX $12   NM $30   MIP $40

Thing Ding Robot Game, 1961, Schaper
EX $35   NM $75   MIP $100

Think Twice, 1974, Dynamic
EX $4   NM $15   MIP $20

Thinking Man's Football, 1969, 3M
EX $6   NM $15   MIP $25

Thinking Man's Golf, 1966, 3M
EX $5   NM $15   MIP $25

Think-Thunk, 1973, Milton Bradley
EX $6   NM $18   MIP $30

Third Man, 1969, Saalfield
EX $6   NM $15   MIP $25

Third Reich, 1974, Avalon Hill
EX $3   NM $8   MIP $15

Thirteen, 1955, Cadaco-Ellis
EX $3   NM $7   MIP $10

(KP Photo)

This Is Your Life, 1954, Lowell
EX $20   NM $30   MIP $35

Three Little Pigs, 1959, Selchow & Righter
EX $7   NM $20   MIP $35

Three Musketeers, 1958, Milton Bradley
EX $35   NM $55   MIP $90

Three On a Match, 1972, Milton Bradley
EX $10   NM $25   MIP $35

(KP Photo)

Three Stooges Fun House Game, 1950s, Lowell
EX $125   NM $275   MIP $400

Thunder Road, 1986, Milton Bradley
EX $10   NM $16   MIP $25

(KP Photo)

Thunderbirds Game, 1965, Waddington/England
EX $45   NM $75   MIP $120

Tic-Tac Dough, 1957, Transogram
EX $12   NM $25   MIP $30

Tiddle Flip Baseball, 1949, Modern Craft
EX $20   NM $35   MIP $50

Tiddle-Tac-Toe, 1955, Schaper
EX $3   NM $10   MIP $15

Tilt Score, 1964, Schaper
EX $4   NM $15   MIP $20

Time Machine, 1961, American Toy
EX $100   NM $175   MIP $250

(KP Photo)

Time Tunnel Game, The, 1966, Ideal
EX $90   NM $150   MIP $240

Time: The Game, 1983, Time/John Hansen
EX $2   NM $5   MIP $8

Tiny Tim Game of Beautiful Things, The, 1970, Parker Brothers
EX $20   NM $30   MIP $50

(KP Photo)

Tom & Jerry, 1977, Milton Bradley
EX $15   NM $20   MIP $30

Tom & Jerry Adventure In Blunderland, 1965, Transogram
EX $25   NM $45   MIP $70

Tom Seaver Game Action Baseball, 1969, Pressman
EX $50   NM $125   MIP $175

Tomorrowland Rocket To Moon, 1956, Parker Brothers
EX $20   NM $50   MIP $75

Toot! Toot!, 1964, Selchow & Righter
EX $8   NM $25   MIP $40

(KP Photo)

Tootsie Roll Train Game, 1969, Hasbro
EX $20   NM $30   MIP $50

Top Cat Game, 1962, Transogram
EX $50   NM $100   MIP $125

Top Cop, 1961, Cadaco-Ellis
EX $35   NM $50   MIP $75

Top Pro Basketball Quiz Game, 1970, Ed-U-Cards
EX $6   NM $15   MIP $25

Top Pro Football Quiz Game, 1970, Ed-U-Cards
EX $6   NM $15   MIP $25

Top Scholar, 1957, Cadaco-Ellis
EX $5   NM $16   MIP $25

Top Ten College Basketball, 1980, Top Ten Game
EX $30   NM $70   MIP $100

Top-ography, 1951, Cadaco-Ellis
EX $10   NM $15   MIP $20

Topper, 1962, Lakeside
EX $15   NM $35   MIP $50

Topple, 1979, Kenner
EX $4   NM $15   MIP $20

Tornado Bowl, 1971, Ideal
EX $5   NM $16   MIP $25

Tornado Rex, 1991, Parker Brothers
EX $10   NM $25   MIP $35

Total Depth, 1984, Orc Productions
EX $12   NM $30   MIP $40

Touche Turtle Game, 1964, Ideal
EX $45   NM $100   MIP $175

Town & Country Traffic Game, 1950s, Ranger Steel
EX $50   NM $90   MIP $150

Track Meet, 1972, Sports Illustrated
EX $10   NM $25   MIP $35

Trade Winds: The Caribbean Sea Pirate Treasure Hunt, 1960, Parker Brothers
EX $65   NM $100   MIP $150

Traffic Game, 1968, Matchbox
EX $35   NM $55   MIP $90

Traffic Jam, 1954, Harett-Gilmar
EX $15   NM $35   MIP $50

(KP Photo)

Trail Blazers Game, 1964, Milton Bradley
EX $20   NM $35   MIP $50

Trails to Tremble By, 1971, Whitman
EX $6   NM $18   MIP $30

Trap Door, 1982, Milton Bradley
EX $3   NM $10   MIP $15

Trap-em!, 1957, Selchow & Righter
EX $8   NM $25   MIP $40

Trapped (Ellery Queen's), 1956, Bettye-B
EX $30   NM $70   MIP $100

Traps, The Game of, 1950s, Traps
EX $75   NM $125   MIP $200

Travel America, 1950, Jacmar
EX $15   NM $25   MIP $40

Travel-Lite, 1946, Saxon Toy
EX $45   NM $75   MIP $120

Treasure Island, 1954, Harett-Gilmar
EX $15   NM $40   MIP $60

Tribulation, The Game of, 1981, Whitman
EX $3   NM $10   MIP $15

Tri-Ominoes, Deluxe, 1978, Pressman
EX $3   NM $5   MIP $10

Triple Play, 1978, Milton Bradley
EX $5   NM $10   MIP $15

Triple Yahtzee, 1972, Lowe
EX $4   NM $6   MIP $10

Tripoley Junior, 1962, Cadaco-Ellis
EX $5   NM $16   MIP $25

Trivial Pursuit, 1981, Selchow & Righter
EX $10   NM $15   MIP $20

Troke (Castle Checkers), 1961, Selchow & Righter
EX $6   NM $18   MIP $25

Tru-Action Electric Baseball Game, 1955, Tudor
EX $12   NM $30   MIP $50

Tru-Action Electric Sports Car Race, 1959, Tudor
EX $20   NM $50   MIP $75

True Colors, 1990, Milton Bradley
EX $20   NM $50   MIP $70

Trump, the Game, 1989, Milton Bradley
EX $10   NM $16   MIP $25

Trust Me, 1981, Parker Brothers
EX $5   NM $8   MIP $13

Truth or Consequences, 1955, Gabriel
EX $12   NM $40   MIP $60

Truth or Consequences, 1962, Lowell
EX $10   NM $35   MIP $50

TSG I: Pro Football, 1971, TSG
EX $35   NM $55   MIP $85

Tumble Bug, 1950s, Schaper
EX $6   NM $18   MIP $30

Turbo, 1981, Milton Bradley
EX $4   NM $15   MIP $20

TV Guide Game, 1984, Trivia
EX $8   NM $13   MIP $15

Twelve O'Clock High, 1965, Ideal
EX $35   NM $60   MIP $85

Twiggy, Game of, 1967, Milton Bradley
EX $30   NM $50   MIP $100

(KP Photo)

Twilight Zone Game, 1960s, Ideal
EX $75   NM $100   MIP $200

Twinkles Trip to the Star Factory, 1960, Milton Bradley
EX $45   NM $75   MIP $120

Twister, 1966, Milton Bradley
EX $15   NM $20   MIP $35

Twixt, 1962, 3M
EX $5   NM $16   MIP $25

Two For The Money, 1950s, Lowell
EX $10   NM $25   MIP $40

Tycoon, 1966, Parker Brothers
EX $12   NM $30   MIP $40

Tycoon, 1981, Wattson Games
EX $4   NM $10   MIP $15

Tycoon: The Real Estate Game, 1986, Ram Innovations
EX $6   NM $15   MIP $20

U.N. Game of Flags, 1961, Parker Brothers
EX $12   NM $20   MIP $30

U.S. Air Force, Game of, 1950s, Transogram
EX $25   NM $45   MIP $70

Ubi, 1986, Selchow & Righter
EX $6   NM $18   MIP $30

Ultimate Golf, 1985, Ultimate Golf
EX $6   NM $18   MIP $25

Uncle Milton's Ant Farm Game, 1969, Uncle Milton Industries
EX $20   NM $35   MIP $50

Uncle Wiggly, 1979, Parker Brothers
EX $8   NM $20   MIP $30

(KP Photo)

Undercover: The Game of Secret Agents, 1960, Cadaco-Ellis
EX $20   NM $50   MIP $60

Underdog, 1964, Milton Bradley
EX $20   NM $50   MIP $75

Underdog Save Sweet Polly, 1972, Whitman
EX $25   NM $45   MIP $70

Undersea World of Jacques Cousteau, 1968, Parker Brothers
EX $20   NM $40   MIP $60

Ungame, 1975, Ungame
EX $4   NM $6   MIP $10

United Nations, A Game about the, 1961, Payton Products
EX $12   NM $30   MIP $40

Universe, 1966, Parker Brothers
EX $6   NM $18   MIP $30

Up for Grabs, 1978, Mattel
EX $6   NM $15   MIP $20

Up! Against Time, 1977, Ideal
EX $4   NM $10   MIP $15

Ur, Royal Game of Sumer, 1977, Selchow & Righter
EX $3   NM $10   MIP $15

Uranium, 1950s, Saalfield
EX $18   NM $40   MIP $60

(KP Photo)

Uranium Rush, 1955, Gardner
EX $45   NM $60   MIP $80

USAC Auto Racing, 1980, Avalon Hill
EX $18   NM $45   MIP $65

Vagabondo, 1979, Invicta
EX $5   NM $16   MIP $25

Vallco Pro Drag Racing Game, 1975, Zyla
EX $15   NM $25   MIP $35

Valvigi Downs, 1985, Valvigi
EX $6   NM $18   MIP $30

Vaquero, 1952, Wales Game Systems
EX $15   NM $20   MIP $35

Varsity, 1955, Cadaco-Ellis
EX $12   NM $30   MIP $50

VCR Basketball Game, 1987, Interactive VCR Games
EX $6   NM $10   MIP $15

VCR Quarterback Game, 1986, Interactive VCR Games
EX $8   NM $13   MIP $20

(KP Photo)

Veda, The Magic Answer Man, 1960s,
Pressman
EX $15   NM $20   MIP $30

Vegas, 1969, NBC-Hasbro
EX $6   NM $15   MIP $20

Vegas, 1974, Milton Bradley
EX $4   NM $15   MIP $20

Venture, 1970, 3M
EX $8   NM $20   MIP $30

Verbatim, 1985, Lakeside
EX $3   NM $10   MIP $15

Verdict, 1959, Avalon Hill
EX $15   NM $50   MIP $75

Verdict II, 1961, Avalon Hill
EX $12   NM $40   MIP $60

Verne Gagne World Champion Wrestling,
1950, Gardner
EX $40   NM $90   MIP $135

Vice Versa, 1976, Hallmark Games
EX $5   NM $16   MIP $25

Video Village, 1960, Milton Bradley
EX $15   NM $30   MIP $40

Vietnam, 1984, Victory Games
EX $10   NM $15   MIP $25

Vince Lombardi's Game, 1970, Research
Games
EX $35   NM $65   MIP $85

Virginian, The, 1962, Transogram
EX $45   NM $80   MIP $100

Visit To Walt Disney World Game, 1970,
Milton Bradley
EX $15   NM $20   MIP $35

Voice of The Mummy, 1960s, Milton Bradley
EX $75   NM $125   MIP $300

Voodoo Doll Game, 1967, Schaper
EX $12   NM $30   MIP $40

Voyage of the Dawn Treader, 1983, David
Cook
EX $5   NM $16   MIP $25

Voyage to Cipangu, 1979, Heise-Cipangu
EX $25   NM $55   MIP $75

Wackiest Ship In The Army, 1964, Ideal
EX $18   NM $25   MIP $50

Wacky Races Game, 1970s, Milton Bradley
EX $15   NM $25   MIP $40

(KP Photo)

Wagon Train, 1960, Milton Bradley
EX $25   NM $40   MIP $65

Wahoo, 1947, Zondine
EX $15   NM $20   MIP $30

Wally Gator Game, 1963, Transogram
EX $65   NM $85   MIP $130

Walt Disney's 101 Dalmatians, 1960,
Whitman
EX $20   NM $35   MIP $55

**Walt Disney's 20,000 Leagues Under The
Sea,** 1954, Jacmar
EX $45   NM $75   MIP $120

Walt Disney's Jungle Book, 1967, Parker
Brothers
EX $15   NM $25   MIP $45

(KP Photo)

Walt Disney's Official Frontierland,
1950s, Parker Brothers
EX $15   NM $35   MIP $50

Walt Disney's Sleeping Beauty Game,
1958, Whitman
EX $30   NM $50   MIP $80

Walt Disney's Swamp Fox Game, 1960,
Parker Brothers
EX $30   NM $50   MIP $80

(KP Photo)

Waltons, 1974, Milton Bradley
EX $15   NM $20   MIP $30

(KP Photo)

Wanted Dead or Alive, 1959, Lowell
EX $50   NM $75   MIP $125

War At Sea, 1976, Avalon Hill
EX $10   NM $20   MIP $30

War of the Networks, 1979, Hasbro
EX $6   NM $18   MIP $30

Watergate Scandal, The, 1973, American
Symbolic
EX $8   NM $20   MIP $30

Waterloo, 1962, Avalon Hill
EX $10   NM $20   MIP $45

(KP Photo)

Weird-Ohs Game, The, 1964, Ideal
EX $85   NM $145   MIP $230

(KP Photo)

Welcome Back, Kotter, 1977, Ideal
EX $10   NM $25   MIP $35

Welfare, 1978, Jedco
EX $12   NM $40   MIP $60

(KP Photo)

Wendy, The Good Little Witch, 1966,
Milton Bradley
EX $60   NM $100   MIP $125

West Point Story, The, 1950s, Transogram
EX $25   NM $50   MIP $75

What Shall I Be?, 1966, Selchow & Righter
EX $15   NM $35   MIP $45

What Shall I Wear?, 1969, Selchow &
Righter
EX $15   NM $35   MIP $45

What's My Line Game, 1950s, Lowell
EX $20   NM $30   MIP $40

What's Up, Doc?, 1978, Milton Bradley
EX $6   NM $15   MIP $20

Whatzit?, 1987, Milton Bradley
EX $5   NM $16   MIP $25

Wheel of Fortune, 1985, Pressman
EX $5   NM $8   MIP $13

Where's The Beef?, 1984, Milton Bradley
EX $6   NM $10   MIP $15

Which Witch?, 1970, Milton Bradley
EX $65   NM $100   MIP $125

Whirl Out Game, 1971, Milton Bradley
EX $6   NM $18   MIP $30

Whirl-A-Ball, 1978, Pressman
EX $10   NM $15   MIP $25

Whirligig, 1963, Milton Bradley
EX $8   NM $20   MIP $30

Whirly Bird Play Catch, 1960s, Innovation
Industries
EX $20   NM $35   MIP $50

White Shadow Basketball Game, The,
1980, Cadaco
EX $20   NM $30   MIP $40

Who Can Beat Nixon?, 1971, Dynamic
EX $10   NM $35   MIP $40

Who Framed Roger Rabbit?, 1987, Milton
Bradley
EX $20   NM $35   MIP $55

Who What Or Where?, 1970, Milton
Bradley
EX $5   NM $8   MIP $13

Who, Game of, 1951, Parker Brothers
EX $20   NM $30   MIP $40

Whodunit, 1972, Selchow & Righter
EX $10   NM $15   MIP $25

Whodunit?, 1959, Cadaco-Ellis
EX $8   NM $25   MIP $40

Whosit?, 1976, Parker Brothers
EX $6   NM $10   MIP $15

Wide World, 1957, 1962, Parker Brothers
EX $10   NM $20   MIP $30

Wide World of Sports Auto Racing, 1975, Milton Bradley
EX $12   NM $30   MIP $45

Wide World of Sports Golf, 1975, Milton Bradley
EX $12   NM $30   MIP $45

Wide World of Sports Tennis, 1975, Milton Bradley
EX $12   NM $30   MIP $45

Wide World Travel, 1957, Parker Brothers
EX $15   NM $35   MIP $50

Wil-Croft Baseball, 1971, Wil-Croft
EX $10   NM $16   MIP $25

(KP Photo)

Wild Bill Hickok, 1955, Built-Rite
EX $15   NM $25   MIP $40

Wild Kingdom Game, 1977, Teaching Concepts
EX $20   NM $35   MIP $50

Wild, Wild West, The, 1966, Transogram
EX $125   NM $350   MIP $500

Wildcatter, 1981, Kessler
EX $12   NM $30   MIP $40

Wildlife, 1971, Lowe
EX $15   NM $35   MIP $50

Willie Mays "Say Hey", 1954, Toy Development
EX $200   NM $350   MIP $700

Willie Mays "Say Hey" Baseball, 1958, Centennial Games
EX $190   NM $295   MIP $450

Willie Mays Push Button Baseball, 1965, Eldon
EX $175   NM $295   MIP $450

Willow, 1988, Parker Brothers
EX $10   NM $25   MIP $35

Win, Place & Show, 1966, 3M
EX $6   NM $20   MIP $30

Wine Cellar, 1971, Dynamic
EX $5   NM $16   MIP $25

Winko Baseball, 1940s, Milton Bradley
EX $35   NM $50   MIP $75

(KP Photo)

Winky Dink Official TV Game Kit, 1950s
EX $50   NM $100   MIP $150

Winnie The Pooh Game, 1959, Parker Brothers
EX $20   NM $40   MIP $60

Winnie The Pooh Game, 1979, Parker Brothers
EX $5   NM $8   MIP $13

Winning Ticket, The, 1977, Ideal
EX $6   NM $20   MIP $30

Wiry Dan's Electric Baseball Game, 1953, Harett-Gilmar
EX $8   NM $25   MIP $35

Wiry Dan's Electric Football Game, 1953, Harett-Gilmar
EX $8   NM $25   MIP $35

Wise Old Owl, 1950s, Novel Toy
EX $20   NM $35   MIP $45

Witch Pitch Game, 1970, Parker Brothers
EX $15   NM $25   MIP $40

Wit's End, Game of, 1948, Parker Brothers
EX $15   NM $35   MIP $50

Wizard of Oz Game, 1962, Lowe
EX $20   NM $30   MIP $50

(KP Photo)

Wizard of Oz Game, 1974, Cadaco
EX $15   NM $20   MIP $30

(KP Photo)

Wolfman Mystery Game, 1963, Hasbro
EX $80   NM $160   MIP $225

Woman & Man, 1971, Psychology Today
EX $4   NM $15   MIP $20

Women's Lib, 1970, Urban Systems
EX $12   NM $30   MIP $40

Wonder Woman Game, 1967, Hasbro
EX $20   NM $35   MIP $65

Wonderbug Game, 1977, Ideal
EX $8   NM $25   MIP $35

(KP Photo)

Woody Woodpecker Game, 1959, Milton Bradley
EX $15   NM $30   MIP $40

(KP Photo)

Woody Woodpecker, Travel With, 1950s, Cadaco-Ellis
EX $35   NM $65   MIP $100

Woody Woodpecker's Crazy Mixed Up Color Factory, 1972, Whitman
EX $12   NM $20   MIP $30

Woody Woodpecker's Moon Dash Game, 1976, Whitman
EX $12   NM $20   MIP $30

Word War, 1978, Mattel
EX $6   NM $15   MIP $20

World Bowling Tour, 1979, World Bowling Tour
EX $7   NM $20   MIP $35

World Champion Wrestling Official Slam O' Rama, 1990, International Games
EX $5   NM $8   MIP $12

World of Micronauts, 1978, Milton Bradley
EX $10   NM $15   MIP $25

World of Wall Street, 1969, NBC-Hasbro
EX $4   NM $10   MIP $15

World's Greatest Baseball Game, 1977, J. Woodlock
EX $35   NM $75   MIP $100

Wrestling Superstars, 1985, Milton Bradley
EX $8   NM $13   MIP $20

WWF Wrestling Game, 1991, Colorforms
EX $5   NM $8   MIP $12

GAMES

Wyatt Earp Game, 1958, Transogram
  EX $35   **NM** $60   **MIP** $85

Xaviera's Game, 1974, Dynamic
  EX $7   **NM** $20   **MIP** $35

X-Men Alert! Adventure Game, 1992, Pressman
  EX $5   **NM** $16   **MIP** $25

Yacht Race, 1961, Parker Brothers
  EX $35   **NM** $85   **MIP** $100

(KP Photo)

Yahtzee, 1956, Lowe
  EX $6   **NM** $10   **MIP** $15

(KP Photo)

Yertle, The Game of, 1960, Revell
  EX $55   **NM** $75   **MIP** $100

Yogi Bear Break A Plate Game, 1960s, Transogram
  EX $40   **NM** $60   **MIP** $80

Yogi Bear Cartoon Game, 1980, Milton Bradley
  EX $3   **NM** $5   **MIP** $10

Yogi Bear Game, 1971, Milton Bradley
  EX $8   **NM** $20   **MIP** $30

Yogi Bear Go Fly A Kite Game, 1961, Transogram
  EX $25   **NM** $50   **MIP** $75

Your America, 1970, Cadaco
  EX $2   **NM** $7   **MIP** $12

Yours For a Song, 1962, Lowell
  EX $20   **NM** $35   **MIP** $55

Zaxxon, 1982, Milton Bradley
  EX $6   **NM** $10   **MIP** $15

Zig Zag Zoom, 1970, Ideal
  EX $10   **NM** $20   **MIP** $30

Ziggy Game, A Day With, 1977, Milton Bradley
  EX $4   **NM** $10   **MIP** $15

Zingo, 1950s, Empire Plastics
  EX $15   **NM** $20   **MIP** $30

(KP Photo)

Zip Code Game, 1964, Lakeside
  EX $40   **NM** $90   **MIP** $100

Zomax, 1988, Zomax
  EX $8   **NM** $25   **MIP** $40

Zoography, 1972, Amway
  EX $5   **NM** $16   **MIP** $25

Zorro Game, Walt Disney's, 1966, Parker Brothers
  EX $25   **NM** $40   **MIP** $65

Zorro Target Game with Dart Gun, 1950s, Knickerbocker
  EX $20   **NM** $30   **MIP** $50

CARD GAMES

Addams Family, 1965, Milton Bradley
  EX $20   **NM** $30   **MIP** $60

(KP Photo)

Archie Bunker's Card Game, 1972, Milton Bradley
  EX $6   **NM** $15   **MIP** $20

Art Linkletter's People are Funny Party Game, 1954, Whitman
  EX $5   **NM** $16   **MIP** $20

Bali, 1954, I-S Unlimited
  EX $8   **NM** $20   **MIP** $30

Baseball Card All Star Game, 1987, Captoys
  EX $5   **NM** $12   **MIP** $15

Baseball Card Game, 1950s, Ed-U-Cards
  EX $8   **NM** $20   **MIP** $30

Baseball Card Game, Official, 1965, Milton Bradley
  EX $20   **NM** $40   **MIP** $50

Batman Card Game, 1966, Ideal
  EX $35   **NM** $75   **MIP** $95

Batter Up Card Game, 1949, Ed-U-Cards
  EX $8   **NM** $20   **MIP** $30

(KP Photo)

Beverly Hillbillies Game, "Set Back", 1963, Milton Bradley
  EX $10   **NM** $25   **MIP** $30

(KP Photo)

Bewitched Stymie Game, 1960s, Milton Bradley
  EX $20   **NM** $50   **MIP** $60

Bible Quiz Lotto, 1949, Jack Levitz
  EX $5   **NM** $12   **MIP** $20

Boston Red Sox Game, 1964, Ed-U-Cards
  EX $15   **NM** $35   **MIP** $55

Bullwinkle Card Game, 1962, Ed-U-Cards
  EX $10   **NM** $30   **MIP** $40

Charge It!, 1972, Whitman
  EX $5   **NM** $15   **MIP** $25

Combat, 1964, Milton Bradley
  EX $10   **NM** $20   **MIP** $30

Cowboys & Indians, 1949, Ed-U-Cards
  EX $8   **NM** $20   **MIP** $35

Dallas Game, 1980, Mego
  EX $3   **NM** $10   **MIP** $15

Daniel Boone Wilderness Trail, 1964, Transogram
  EX $10   **NM** $40   **MIP** $65

Dick Tracy Playing Card Game, 1934, Whitman
  EX $30   **NM** $60   **MIP** $75

Dick Tracy Playing Card Game, 1937, Whitman
  EX $20   **NM** $45   **MIP** $60

Dick Tracy Playing Card Game, 1939, Esquire Novelty
  EX $20   **NM** $45   **MIP** $60

Dragonmaster, 1981, Lowe
  EX $8   **NM** $20   **MIP** $30

Fast Golf, 1977, Whitman
  EX $8   **NM** $13   **MIP** $20

Flintstones Animal Rummy, 1960, Ed-U-Cards
  EX $7   **NM** $25   **MIP** $30

Flintstones Cut-Ups Game, 1963, Whitman
  EX $15   **NM** $45   **MIP** $60

Funny Bones Game, 1968, Parker Brothers
  EX $5   **NM** $7   **MIP** $11

GAMES

Gidget, 1966, Milton Bradley
EX $15   NM $35   MIP $50

Go Go Go, 1950s, Arco Playing Card
EX $6   NM $20   MIP $35

Gong Hee Fot Choy, 1948, Zondine Game
EX $20   NM $35   MIP $55

Grabitz, 1979, International Games
EX $2   NM $5   MIP $7

Harry's Glam Slam, 1962, Harry Obst
EX $35   NM $60   MIP $90

Howdy Doody Card Game, 1954, Russell
EX $10   NM $20   MIP $30

I Survived New York!, 1981, City Enterprises
EX $4   NM $7   MIP $12

James Bond Live and Let Die Tarot Game, 1973, US Games Systems
EX $25   NM $55   MIP $85

Kardball, 1946, Ajak
EX $20   NM $30   MIP $40

Know Your States, 1955, Garrard Press
EX $10   NM $25   MIP $45

Let's Play Basketball, 1965, D.M.R.
EX $12   NM $20   MIP $35

Li'l Abner's Spoof Game, 1950, Milton Bradley
EX $65   NM $95   MIP $135

Man from U.N.C.L.E. Illya Kuryakin Card Game, 1966, Milton Bradley
EX $15   NM $25   MIP $30

Match, 1953, Garrard Press
EX $10   NM $15   MIP $25

Mickey Mouse Canasta Jr., 1950, Russell
EX $20   NM $40   MIP $50

Mickey Mouse Jr. Royal Rummy, 1970s, Whitman
EX $5   NM $15   MIP $30

Mickey Mouse Library of Games, 1946, Russell
EX $30   NM $65   MIP $125

Mille Bornes, 1962, Parker Brothers
EX $10   NM $15   MIP $20

(KP Photo)

Monster Old Maid, 1964, Milton Bradley
EX $15   NM $40   MIP $55

Mr. T Game, 1983, Milton Bradley
EX $5   NM $15   MIP $25

Munsters Card Game, 1966, Milton Bradley
EX $20   NM $45   MIP $65

New York World's Fair Children's Game, 1964, Ed-U-Cards
EX $15   NM $35   MIP $55

Nuclear War, 1965, Douglas Malewicki
EX $25   NM $40   MIP $75

NY Mets Baseball Card Game, Official, 1961, Ed-U-Cards
EX $20   NM $45   MIP $65

Pro Baseball Card Game, 1980s, Just Games
EX $6   NM $10   MIP $15

Scan, 1970, Parker Brothers
EX $3   NM $10   MIP $15

Scott's Baseball Card Game, 1989, Scott's Baseball Cards
EX $12   NM $20   MIP $30

Skeeter, 1950s, Arco Playing Card
EX $6   NM $20   MIP $35

Strategy Poker Fine Edition, 1967, Milton Bradley
EX $5   NM $12   MIP $18

Superheroes Card Game, 1978, Milton Bradley
EX $15   NM $30   MIP $55

Superman Game, 1966, Whitman
EX $35   NM $75   MIP $110

Syllable, 1948, Garrard Press
EX $10   NM $15   MIP $25

Touch, 1970, Parker Brothers
EX $5   NM $16   MIP $25

Trail Drive, 1950s, Arco Playing Card
EX $15   NM $35   MIP $65

(KP Photo)

Twelve O'Clock High, 1966, Milton Bradley
EX $20   NM $30   MIP $40

Waterworks, 1972, Parker Brothers
EX $5   NM $12   MIP $20

Welcome Back, Kotter, 1976, Milton Bradley
EX $5   NM $16   MIP $25

SKILL GAMES

Call It!, 1978, Ideal
EX $5   NM $12   MIP $20

Chicken Lotto, 1965, Ideal
EX $8   NM $25   MIP $40

Chutes Away!, 1978, Gabriel
EX $15   NM $60   MIP $85

Clickety-Clak, 1950s, Milton Bradley
EX $10   NM $25   MIP $30

Clunk-A-Glunk, 1968, Whitman
EX $8   NM $25   MIP $40

Don't Break the Ice, 1960s, Schaper
EX $5   NM $16   MIP $25

Don't Spill the Beans, 1967, Schaper
EX $10   NM $16   MIP $25

Feed the Elephant!, 1952, Cadaco-Ellis
EX $10   NM $35   MIP $50

Gnip Gnop, 1971, Parker Brothers
EX $5   NM $16   MIP $20

Hoc-Key, 1958, Cadaco-Ellis
EX $10   NM $35   MIP $50

Hungry Henry, 1969, Ideal
EX $7   NM $20   MIP $35

Jack & Jill Target Game, 1948, Cadaco-Ellis
EX $7   NM $20   MIP $35

Jaws, The Game of, 1975, Ideal
EX $10   NM $16   MIP $20

Kick Back, 1965, Schaper
EX $5   NM $16   MIP $25

Leapin' Letters, 1969, Parker Brothers
EX $5   NM $16   MIP $25

Marblehead, 1969, Ideal
EX $5   NM $16   MIP $25

Mark "Three", 1972, Ideal
EX $6   NM $18   MIP $30

Mentor, 1960s, Hasbro
EX $18   NM $40   MIP $50

Mind Maze Game, 1970, Parker Brothers
EX $5   NM $16   MIP $25

Mr. Mad Game, 1970, Ideal
EX $12   NM $40   MIP $60

Nibbles 'N Bites, 1964, Schaper
EX $5   NM $16   MIP $25

On Target, 1973, Milton Bradley
EX $12   NM $40   MIP $60

Pitchin' Pal, 1952, Cadaco-Ellis
EX $7   NM $20   MIP $35

(KP Photo)

Poosh-em-up Slugger Bagatelle, 1946, Northwestern Products
EX $30   NM $50   MIP $75

Quick Shoot, 1970, Ideal
    EX $6   **NM** $18   **MIP** $30

Sharpshooter, 1962, Cadaco-Ellis
    EX $12   **NM** $20   **MIP** $30

Skip Bowl, 1955, Transogram
    EX $6   **NM** $18   **MIP** $30

Slap Stick, 1967, Milton Bradley
    EX $7   **NM** $20   **MIP** $35

Smack-A-Roo, 1964, Mattel
    EX $6   **NM** $18   **MIP** $30

(KP Photo)

Tight Squeeze, 1967, Mattel
    EX $7   **NM** $20   **MIP** $35

Tip-It, 1965, Ideal
    EX $5   **NM** $16   **MIP** $20

Topple Chairs, 1962, Eberhard Faber
    EX $6   **NM** $18   **MIP** $30

Wing-Ding, 1951, Cadaco-Ellis
    EX $8   **NM** $25   **MIP** $40

SKILL/ACTION GAMES

Airways, 1950s, Lindstrom Tool & Toy
    EX $25   **NM** $40   **MIP** $60

Angry Donald Duck Game, 1970s, Mexico
    EX $40   **NM** $65   **MIP** $100

Bandu, 1991, Milton Bradley
    EX $12   **NM** $30   **MIP** $40

Baseball, 1960s, Tudor
    EX $20   **NM** $30   **MIP** $50

(KP Photo)

Bash!, 1967, Milton Bradley
    EX $10   **NM** $15   **MIP** $25

Batman Batarang Toss, 1966, Pressman
    EX $150   **NM** $250   **MIP** $400

Batman Pin Ball, 1966, Marx
    EX $55   **NM** $95   **MIP** $150

Bats in the Belfry, 1964, Mattel
    EX $35   **NM** $75   **MIP** $100

(KP Photo)

Big 5 Poosh-M Up, 1950s, Knickerbocker
    EX $35   **NM** $40   **MIP** $50

Big Game Hunt, The, 1947, Carrom Industries
    EX $15   **NM** $25   **MIP** $30

Big Sneeze Game, The, 1968, Ideal
    EX $10   **NM** $25   **MIP** $40

Boob Tube Race, 1962, Milton Bradley
    EX $2   **NM** $15   **MIP** $20

Booby Trap, 1965, Parker Brothers
    EX $10   **NM** $15   **MIP** $20

Bop Bop 'N Rebop, 1979, Hasbro
    EX $12   **NM** $30   **MIP** $40

Bop The Beetle, 1963, Ideal
    EX $20   **NM** $30   **MIP** $40

Bowl-A-Matic, 1963, Eldon
    EX $100   **NM** $250   **MIP** $350

Bugs Bunny Game (Bagatelle), 1975, Ideal
    EX $15   **NM** $25   **MIP** $40

Candid Camera Target Shot, 1950s, Lindstrom Tool & Toy
    EX $35   **NM** $60   **MIP** $70

Careful: The Toppling Tower, 1967, Ideal
    EX $8   **NM** $20   **MIP** $30

Coney Island Penny Pitch, 1950s, Novel Toy
    EX $33   **NM** $55   **MIP** $88

(KP Photo)

Crazy Clock Game, 1964, Ideal
    EX $30   **NM** $45   **MIP** $60

Crazy Maze, 1966, 1975, Lakeside
    EX $8   **NM** $20   **MIP** $30

Deputy Dawg Hoss Toss, 1973
    EX $15   **NM** $25   **MIP** $40

(KP Photo)

Disney Dodgem Bagatelle, 1960s, Marx
    EX $30   **NM** $65   **MIP** $90

Don't Dump the Daisy, 1970, Ideal
    EX $10   **NM** $25   **MIP** $35

Dynamite Shack Game, 1968, Milton Bradley
    EX $10   **NM** $25   **MIP** $30

Facts In Five, 1967, 3M
    EX $3   **NM** $8   **MIP** $12

Fascination, 1962, Remco
    EX $20   **NM** $35   **MIP** $40

Fascination Pool, 1962, Remco
    EX $8   **NM** $20   **MIP** $30

Feeley Meeley Game, 1967, Milton Bradley
    EX $20   **NM** $50   **MIP** $75

Fireball XL-5 Magnetic Dart Game, 1963, Magic Wand
    EX $75   **NM** $125   **MIP** $200

Flea Circus Magnetic Action Game, 1968, Mattel
    EX $15   **NM** $25   **MIP** $40

Flintstones Brake Ball, 1962, Whitman
    EX $45   **NM** $75   **MIP** $90

Flintstones Mechanical Shooting Gallery, 1962, Marx
    EX $75   **NM** $125   **MIP** $200

Flying Nun Marble Maze Game, The, 1967, Hasbro
    EX $20   **NM** $30   **MIP** $50

(KP Photo)

G.I. Joe Bagatelle Gun Action Game,
1970s, Hasbro
EX $7   **NM** $12   **MIP** $15

(KP Photo)

Gotham's Ice Hockey, 1960s, Gotham
EX $35   **NM** $60   **MIP** $85

Grab A Loop, 1968, Milton Bradley
EX $7   **NM** $12   **MIP** $20

Grand Slam Game, 1969, Ideal
EX $8   **NM** $20   **MIP** $30

Hands Down, 1965, Ideal
EX $10   **NM** $15   **MIP** $25

Hi Pop, 1946, Advance Games
EX $20   **NM** $35   **MIP** $55

Hopalong Cassidy Bean Bag Toss Game,
1950s
EX $20   **NM** $40   **MIP** $60

Hoppity Hooper Pin Ball Game, 1965, Lido
EX $40   **NM** $75   **MIP** $115

Howdy Doody Dominoes Game, 1950s,
Ed-U-Cards
EX $50   **NM** $75   **MIP** $100

Huckleberry Hound's Huckle Chuck
Target Game, 1961, Transogram
EX $25   **NM** $50   **MIP** $100

(KP Photo)

Huggin' The Rail, 1948, Selchow & Righter
EX $40   **NM** $50   **MIP** $60

I-Qubes, 1948, Capex
EX $10   **NM** $15   **MIP** $25

Johnny Apollo Moon Landing Bagatelle,
1969, Marx
EX $20   **NM** $35   **MIP** $55

KaBoom!, 1965, Ideal
EX $10   **NM** $15   **MIP** $25

Ker-Plunk, 1967, Ideal
EX $5   **NM** $10   **MIP** $15

Kimbo, 1950s, Parker Brothers
EX $10   **NM** $25   **MIP** $70

King Arthur, 1950s, Northwestern Products
EX $25   **NM** $40   **MIP** $65

King Pin Deluxe Bowling Alley, 1947,
Baldwin Mfg.
EX $10   **NM** $20   **MIP** $30

(KP Photo)

Knockout, Electronic Boxing Game,
1950s, Northwestern Products
EX $75   **NM** $125   **MIP** $175

Krokay, 1955, Transogram
EX $4   **NM** $10   **MIP** $15

Land of The Lost Pinball, 1975, Larami
EX $10   **NM** $20   **MIP** $30

Lone Ranger and Tonto Spin Game, The,
1967, Pressman
EX $15   **NM** $25   **MIP** $40

Loopin' Louie, 1992, Milton Bradley
EX $10   **NM** $25   **MIP** $35

Magnetic Fish Pond, 1948, Milton Bradley
EX $10   **NM** $20   **MIP** $30

Man from U.N.C.L.E. Pinball Game, 1966
EX $80   **NM** $135   **MIP** $215

Man from U.N.C.L.E. Target Game, 1966,
Marx
EX $130   **NM** $275   **MIP** $550

Marathon Game, 1978, Sports Games
EX $10   **NM** $20   **MIP** $35

(KP Photo)

Marx-O-Matic All Star Basketball, 1950s,
Marx
EX $150   **NM** $250   **MIP** $400

(KP Photo)

Mechanical Shooting Gallery, 1950s,
Wyandotte
EX $95   **NM** $135   **MIP** $195

(KP Photo)

Mickey Mouse Haunted House Bagatelle,
1950s
EX $210   **NM** $350   **MIP** $550

(KP Photo)

Mighty Mouse Target Game, 1960s, Parks
EX $30   NM $60   MIP $90

(KP Photo)

Monster Lab, 1964, Ideal
EX $225   NM $275   MIP $500

Mouse Trap, 1963, Ideal
EX $20   NM $30   MIP $50

NFL Football Game, Official, 1968, Ideal
EX $12   NM $30   MIP $40

Nixon Ring Toss, 1970s
EX $20   NM $30   MIP $50

Nutty Mads Bagatelle, 1963, Marx
EX $25   NM $45   MIP $85

(KP Photo)

Nutty Mads Target Game, 1960s, Marx
EX $35   NM $70   MIP $125

Par-A-Shoot Game, 1947, Baldwin
EX $15   NM $25   MIP $40

(KP Photo)

Pony Polo, 1960s, Remco
EX $10   NM $20   MIP $35

(KP Photo)

Pro Bowl Live Action Football, 1960s,
Marx
EX $35   NM $65   MIP $95

Rat Patrol Spin Game, 1967, Pressman
EX $30   NM $65   MIP $85

(KP Photo)

Rocket Patrol Magnetic Target Game,
1950s, American Toy Products
EX $35   NM $65   MIP $100

(KP Photo)

Rocket Sock-It Rifle and Target Game,
1960s, Kenner
EX $20   NM $35   MIP $75

Saratoga: 1777, 1974, Gamut of Games
EX $10   NM $25   MIP $50

Simon, 1978, Milton Bradley
EX $6   NM $15   MIP $20

Space Strike, 1980, Ideal
EX $12   NM $30   MIP $40

Speed Circuit, 1971, 3M
EX $15   NM $30   MIP $45

Superman Spin Game, 1967, Pressman
EX $40   NM $65   MIP $105

Suspense, 1950s, Northwestern Products
EX $15   NM $20   MIP $30

Tickle Bee, 1956, Schaper
EX $15   NM $20   MIP $25

(KP Photo)

Time Bomb, 1965, Milton Bradley
EX $45   NM $75   MIP $100

Time Tunnel Spin-to-Win Game, 1967,
Pressman
EX $60   NM $100   MIP $160

Tipp Kick, 1970s, Top Set
EX $15   NM $25   MIP $40

Tournament Labyrinth, 1980s, Pressman
EX $10   NM $15   MIP $25

Tru-Action Electric Basketball, 1965,
Tudor
EX $25   NM $50   MIP $75

Tru-Action Electric Harness Race Game,
1950s, Tudor
EX $15   NM $40   MIP $65

Try-It Maze Puzzle Game, 1965, Milton
Bradley
EX $7   NM $12   MIP $20

Tug Boat, 1974, Parker Brothers
EX $10   NM $30   MIP $40

Untouchables, The, 1950s, Marx
EX $95   NM $160   MIP $250

Whiplash, 1966, Lakeside
EX $10   NM $25   MIP $35

Wow! Pillow Fight For Girls Game, 1964,
Milton Bradley
EX $12   NM $30   MIP $40

Yogi Berra Pitch Kit, 1963, Ross Products
EX $35   NM $50   MIP $100

Zowie Horseshoe Game, 1947, James L.
Decker
EX $20   NM $35   MIP $55

GAMES

G.I. Joe
By Karen O'Brien

"G.I. Joe, G.I. Joe. Fighting man from head to toe. On the land, on the sea, in the air . . ."

To children in the 1960s, this familiar phrase signaled the arrival of a G.I. Joe television commercial. It is one of the few advertising slogans to stand the test of time, and still brings smiles to the grown-ups who remember dashing to the television to see the latest G.I. Joe figures. G.I. Joe revolutionized the toy industry in the 1960s. A twelve-inch action figure made especially for boys had never been attempted, and Hasbro's secret project had to overcome several challenges. Would the public embrace G.I. Joe as a military action figure? Or would it be perceived as a doll for boys? Hasbro decided that G.I. Joe was worth the gamble and launched an extensive advertising campaign portraying G.I. Joe as "America's Movable Fighting Man."

Today, G.I. Joe is acknowledged as the first action figure, and its articulated design set the standard for all action toys following in its boot tracks. Hasbro shattered the potential stigma of "boys playing with dolls" by offering boys a fully articulated, movable man of action, not a doll. G.I. Joe accomplished for boys in 1964 what Barbie accomplished five years earlier for girls—it allowed boys to role-play any situation their imaginations could dream up.

THE 1960s

G.I. Joe rapidly moved through the development stages in 1963 at Hasbro's Pawtucket, Rhode Island, facility in preparation for its debut at the 1964 International Toy Fair. Round-the-clock efforts to assemble figures, produce equipment, and prepare the dioramas culminated on February 9, 1964 when G.I. Joe was presented to toy buyers and the media. Merrill Hassenfeld, president of Hasbro, convinced the toy buyers that G.I. Joe was an action figure and not a doll, and their orders were enough to test the market. New York City was chosen as an initial test market for G.I. Joe and the figures sold out in a week. The same happened in stores across the country—G.I. Joe was a hit.

Four figures were offered in 1964; Action Soldier, Action Sailor, Action Marine, and Action Pilot. Each figure was clothed in a branch-specific basic uniform with hat, boots, and dog tag. Uniform and equipment sets for all four branches were sold separately. Authenticity was one of Hasbro's goals with the line, and with 21 points of articulation and realistic equipment and uniforms, they produced a fighting man that was capable of real action poses and unlimited play value.

From its 1964 introduction through 1968, G.I. Joe was a military man of action. The Action Soldiers of the World were introduced in 1966, and the Talking G.I. Joe debuted in 1967. Dozens of uniform and equipment sets were added to the line so that G.I. Joe could participate in backyard battles through snow, desert, water, outer space, jungles, or anywhere the imagination lead. Vehicles scaled-to-size for the figures included the Jeep, Space Capsule, and Sea Sled. In 1967, Hasbro attempted to bring girls into the G.I. Joe market by introducing the G.I. Nurse. Instead of a warm reception, she gathered dust on store shelves. She couldn't compete with Mattel's Barbie and boys weren't interested in adding girls to their adventures. Because so few were sold, the G.I. Nurse is one of the most valuable and sought-after G.I. Joe action figures.

Due to the escalation of the Vietnam conflict, G.I. Joe saw his last year of military service in 1968. Many anti-war activists protested Hasbro's production of a military figure. As public sentiment turned against the military action in Southeast Asia, many parents didn't want their children playing with "war" toys of any kind. Hasbro recognized the need for a change.

G.I. Joe became a civilian man of adventure in 1969. He was an Adventurer, Aquanaut, and an Astronaut. He became a Frogman, an Underwater Diver, lead missions to Spy Island, searched for sunken treasure, and even drove a dog sled in the Fight for Survival. Referred to as the Adventures of G.I. Joe, each figure came with a generic uniform consisting of a white t-shirt, green pants, boots, hat, dog tags, a shoulder holster with six-shot revolver, and a booklet outlining possible adventures.

THE 1970s

The Adventure Team was the next step for the G.I. Joe line. Using the same articulated body, Hasbro added "Life-Like" hair and a beard through a special flocking process to create the distinctive look of the new figures. The basic figures included the Land Adventurer, Sea Adventurer, Air Adventurer, the Man of Action, and the Black Adventurer. Each figure came with a distinctive uniform that included either a jumpsuit (for the Air Adventurers) or a shirt/pants combination. They also had boots, an "AT" dog tag, and shoulder holster with revolver.

The success of the Adventure Team prompted Hasbro to release a series of themed equipment sets including, Danger of the Depths, Hidden Missile Discovery, Fantastic Freefall, White Tiger Hunt, Capture of the Pigmy Gorilla, and Secret of the Mummy's Tomb among many others. Diversification of the tasks produced a variety of uniform sets including Karate, Smoke Jumper, Demolition, Jungle Survival, Secret Agent, and dozens more. Talking figures were still featured.

THE TOP TEN
G.I. JOE TOYS *(In Mint Condition)*

1. G.I. Nurse, Hasbro, 1967	$5,000
2. Action Soldiers of the World Talking Adventure Pack, Hasbro, 1968	5,000
3. Canadian Mountie Set, Sears Exclusive, Hasbro, 1967	4,000
4. Flying Space Adventure Set, Hasbro, 1970	3,700
4. Army Adventure Pack, bivouac equipment set, Hasbro, 1968	3,500
5. Crash Crew Fire Truck Vehicle set, Hasbro, 1967	3,500
6. Talking Shore Patrol set, Hasbro, 1968	3,500
7. Dress Parade Adventure Pack, Hasbro, 1968	3,500
8. Talking Landing Signal Officer set, Hasbro, 1968	3,500
9. Shore Patrol equipment set, Hasbro, 1967	3,500
10. Military Police equipment set, Hasbro, 1967	3,500

KUNG-FU Grip was added in 1974 and the basic figures were packaged with rifles instead of the shoulder holster and revolver. Hasbro continued to add new equipment and vehicle sets for the popular lines.

The success of Kenner's Six Million Dollar Man action figures in 1975 prompted the expansion of the Adventure Team to include a part-man, part-machine character named Mike Powers: Atomic Man. Mike Powers featured an all-new body sculpt to accommodate his "Atomic" right arm and left leg, but retained a scar on his left cheek in homage to his military roots.

The G.I. Joe line began to fade in the mid-1970s prompted in part to the rising costs of plastic due to the OPEC oil shortage. A "New Life-Like" muscle-bodied G.I. Joe was introduced using only 15 points of articulation to keep the costs down. Eagle Eye Man of Action and Land Commander could move their eyes side to side, and talking versions were included. The Invaders were introduced to provide an intergalactic foe, and Bulletman was introduced to counter the popularity of super-hero toys throughout the decade.

The Defenders were the last twelve-inch figures produced, and in 1977, G.I. Joe was reduced to an eight-inch size and changed to the Super Joe Adventure Team. Super Joe fought for the safety of the universe and had interchangeable equipment sets, his own command center, and villains including Gor, Luminos, and Terron the Beast from Beyond. Super Joe was Steven Hassenfeld's last attempt to keep the line going, but G.I. Joe ceased production in 1978.

The 1980s

The phenomenal success of the 3-3/4" Star Wars figures in 1978 prompted Hasbro to re-introduce G.I. Joe in the small format as "G.I. Joe: A Real American Hero." The concept was changed to a team of individual characters assembled from all military ranks to combat the evil forces of Cobra. In 1982, G.I. Joe was reborn as a 3-3/4" action figure and no one could have predicted the amazing success of this new line. The figures were fully articulated in the arms, shoulders, waist, legs, and neck, and were the most poseable figures ever created in this scale. A swivel-arm feature added in 1983 enhanced their mobility and enabled the figures to achieve any pose with their equipment.

The G.I. Joe team consisted of nine members in 1982, while Cobra had just two figures. Each figure was packaged with individual accessories and a file card that provided detailed information on that character's personal background, military specialties, vital statistics, and code name. Many of the characters were sculpted from the likenesses of Hasbro employees. Vehicles, play sets, and expanded equipment sets accompanied the line.

More than 500 characters were produced for the 3-3/4" line by the time it came to an end in 1994. The success of the line was bolstered by the Marvel comic book series that ran for twelve years and two television cartoon series.

The 1990s

The 3-3/4" G.I. Joe: A Real American Hero figures continued until 1994. A few special sets were released with much success in 1997, and 1998, receiving approval from collectors and a new generation of children. This prompted the return of the line in 2000.

In 1991, Hasbro created an exclusive twelve-inch figure, Duke: Master Sergeant. Its success prompted the release of the Hall of Fame figures. This combined well-known characters from the 3-3/4" line with the larger twelve-inch format and included four characters, Duke, Stalker, Cobra Commander, and Snake Eyes. The success of this new series prompted Hasbro to release additional characters, vehicles, and equipment. Electronic Talking Battle Command Duke was introduced in 1993, continuing a line of talking G.I. Joe figures that began in 1967.

Hasbro celebrated G.I. Joe's 30th Anniversary in 1994 at New York's International Toy Fair by introducing a special line of 12- and 3-3/4-inch action figures. G.I. Joe Action Soldier, Action Sailor, Action Marine, Action Pilot, and an African-American Action Soldier were released to commemorate the anniversary and to honor the four branches of the military represented by the original G.I. Joe. The first G.I. Joe Collector's Convention was also held that year. Hasbro presented attendees and dealers with, among other items, limited-edition figures representing the entire G.I. Joe line.

The 1995 creation of the G.I. Joe Extreme, Sgt. Savage, and Mortal Kombat lines would never achieve the success of the 1996 Classic Collection. Hasbro released a nameless series of twelve-inch figures that, like their 1960s predecessors, focused on specific military branches, historical conflicts, and international military specialists. The Classic Collection enjoyed continued success through the late 1990s as the line expanded each year to include figures representing all service branches and virtually all U.S. military conflicts. Hasbro also released the Timeless Collection in 1998, a Target exclusive series featuring reproductions of 1960s figure favorites with an interesting assortment of reproduction equipment.

G.I. Joe turned 35-years-old in 1999 and the line expanded to include celebrity additions to the Classic Collections such as Ted Williams, Buzz Aldrin, and Lieutenant Col. Teddy Roosevelt. In 2000, the Adventures of G.I. Joe featured Save the Tiger and Peril of the Raging Inferno sets, and the Timeless Collection featured an Action Sailor and the popular Deep Sea Diver: Danger of the Depths set. Ever mindful that G.I. Joe is for kids, Hasbro also released two series at lower price-points, the G.I. Joe 2010 series featured futuristic equipment and the Alpha assortment offered military and paramilitary figures.

Today, both the 3 3/4- and 12-inch G.I. Joe lines enjoy considerable popularity. The 2000 release of the Collector's Special Edition new "waves" of 3 3/4" figure favorites lead to an additional release of eight sets of figure two-packs for 2001. 2002 saw the release of the G.I. Joe v. Cobra resculpted figures that provided more detail, though less mobility due to the removal of the "o-ring" that enabled previous figures to pivot at the waist. Repaints of these figures also released in 2002 will send collectors scrambling. A full line of vehicles accompanies the new 3-3/4" releases and is available in the Collector's Special Edition series and the G.I. Joe v. Cobra series. The o-ring returned in 2003 as the line expanded to new heights with the introduction of Spy Troops. New sculpts for some of your favorite characters were released in 2003 including The Crimson Guard Commanders, Tomax and Xamot. Valor v. Venom is the theme for 2004, with a host of new sculpts for some favorite characters. Of special note are the 3-pack figures based on classic G.I. Joe comic book covers. The line expanded in 2005 to include the Sigma Six line accompanied by a television cartoon in the fall.

The 12" series is enjoying considerable popularity among collectors and kids alike. The authentic military figures are complimented by the Navy Seals collection, World War II Liberators, Timeless Collection, Strategic Operations Forces figures, and Adventure Team figure sets, equipment sets, vehicles, and even 12" Valor v. Venom figures.

No matter which era is your collecting preference, there are G.I. Joe figures for every backyard mission or collector's shelf. This hobby has a vivid past and a bright future. Yo Joe!

Contributor: Karen O'Brien is the toy book editor for KP Books. She prefers to collect figures out of the package and recently found a mint 1984 Baroness. She may be reached at: karen.o'brien@fwpubs.com or KP Books, 700 E. State St., Iola, WI 54990. Rob Barilla contributed pricing to the Adventure Team section. He may be reached in care of Toys & Prices at the above address.

ORIGINAL SERIES AND ADVENTURE TEAM (1964-78)

ACTION GIRL SERIES

Figure Sets

G.I. Nurse, 1967, Hasbro, Red Cross hat and arm band, white dress, stockings, shoes, crutches, medic bag, stethoscope, plasma bottle, bandages and splints, Model No. 8060
EX $1750   NM $2000   MIP $5000

ACTION MARINE SERIES

Figure Sets

Action Marine, 1964, Hasbro, fatigues, green cap, boots, dog tags, insignias and manual, Model No. 7700
EX $125   NM $145   MIP $450

Marine Medic Series, 1967, Hasbro, Red Cross helmet, flag and arm bands, crutch, bandages, splints, first aid pouch, stethoscope, plasma bottle, stretcher, medic bag, belt with ammo pouches, Model No. 90711
EX $325   NM $425   MIP $1550

Talking Action Marine, 1967, Hasbro, Model No. 7790
EX $175   NM $200   MIP $850

Talking Adventure Pack, 1968, Hasbro, with Field Pack Equipment, Model No. 90712
EX $275   NM $325   MIP $1550

Talking Adventure Pack and Tent Set, 1968, Hasbro, Model No. 90711
EX $275   NM $325   MIP $1550

Uniform/Equipment Sets

Beachhead Assault Field Pack Set, 1964, Hasbro, M-1 rifle, bayonet, entrenching shovel and cover, canteen with cover, belt, mess kit with cover, field pack, flamethrower, first aid pouch, tent, pegs and poles, tent camo and camo, Model No. 7713
EX $100   NM $175   MIP $325

(ToyShop File Photo)

Beachhead Assault Tent Set, 1964, Hasbro, tent, flamethrower, pistol belt, first-aid pouch, mess kit with utensils and manual, Model No. 7711
EX $100   NM $200   MIP $425

Beachhead Fatigue Pants, 1964, Hasbro, Model No. 7715
EX $15   NM $30   MIP $200

Beachhead Fatigue Shirt, 1964, Hasbro, Model No. 7714
EX $20   NM $30   MIP $225

Beachhead Field Pack, 1964, Hasbro, cartridge belt, rifle, grenades, field pack, entrenching tool, canteen and manual, Model No. 7712
EX $40   NM $65   MIP $150

Beachhead Flamethrower Set, 1964, Hasbro, Model No. 7718
EX $15   NM $30   MIP $125

Beachhead Flamethrower Set, 1967, Hasbro, reissue, Model No. 7718
EX $15   NM $30   MIP $225

Beachhead Mess Kit Set, 1964, Hasbro, Model No. 7716
EX $25   NM $40   MIP $275

Beachhead Rifle Set, 1964, Hasbro, bayonet, cartridge belt, hand grenades and M-1 rifle, Model No. 7717
EX $30   NM $50   MIP $150

Beachhead Rifle Set, 1967, Hasbro, reissue, Model No. 7717
EX $30   NM $50   MIP $225

Communications Field Radio/Telephone Set, 1967, Hasbro, reissue, Model No. 7703
EX $35   NM $60   MIP $275

Communications Field Set, 1964, Hasbro, Model No. 7703
EX $35   NM $50   MIP $175

Communications Flag Set, 1964, Hasbro, flags for Army, Navy, Air Corps, Marines and United States, Model No. 7704
EX $200   NM $250   MIP $475

Communications Poncho, 1964, Hasbro, Model No. 7702
EX $35   NM $50   MIP $250

Communications Post and Poncho Set, 1964, Hasbro, field radio and telephone, wire roll, carbine, binoculars, map, case, manual, poncho, Model No. 7701
EX $125   NM $175   MIP $475

Dress Parade Set, 1964, Hasbro, Marine jacket, trousers, pistol belt, shoes, hat, M-1 rifle and manual, Model No. 7710
EX $125   NM $225   MIP $450

Dress Parade Set, 1968, Hasbro, reissue, Model No. 7710
EX $125   NM $225   MIP $750

Jungle Fighter Set, 1967, Hasbro, bush hat, jacket with emblems, pants, flamethrower, field telephone, knife and sheath, pistol belt, pistol, holster, canteen with cover and knuckle knife, Model No. 7732
EX $450   NM $700   MIP $1350

Jungle Fighter Set, 1968, Hasbro, reissue, Model No. 7732
EX $450   NM $700   MIP $1050

Marine Automatic M-60 Machine Gun Set, 1967, Hasbro, Model No. 7726
EX $35   NM $75   MIP $325

Marine Basics Set, 1966, Hasbro, Model No. 7722
EX $55   NM $85   MIP $275

Marine Bunk Bed Set, 1966, Hasbro, Model No. 7723
EX $55   NM $80   MIP $375

Marine Bunk Bed Set, 1967, Hasbro, reissue, Model No. 7723
EX $55   NM $175   MIP $350

(ToyShop File Photo)

Marine Demolition Set, 1966, Hasbro, mine detector and harness, land mine, Model No. 7730
EX $50   NM $100   MIP $350

Marine Demolition Set, 1968, Hasbro, reissue, Model No. 7730
EX $50   NM $145   MIP $400

Marine First Aid Set, 1964, Hasbro, first-aid pouch, arm band and helmet, Model No. 7721
EX $45   NM $85   MIP $125

Marine First Aid Set, 1967, Hasbro, reissue, Model No. 7721
EX $45   NM $85   MIP $225

Marine Medic Set, 1965, Hasbro, with crutch, etc., Model No. 7720
EX $25   NM $40   MIP $125

Marine Medic Set, 1967, Hasbro, reissue, Model No. 7720
EX $25   NM $40   MIP $225

Marine Medic Set with stretcher, 1964, Hasbro, first-aid shoulder pouch, stretcher, bandages, arm bands, plasma bottle, stethoscope, Red Cross flag, and manual, Model No. 7719
EX $175   NM $300   MIP $850

Marine Mortar Set, 1967, Hasbro, Model No. 7725
EX $60   NM $80   MIP $350

Marine Weapons Rack Set, 1967, Hasbro, Model No. 7727
EX $75   NM $145   MIP $625

Paratrooper Camouflage Set, 1964, Hasbro, netting and foliage, Model No. 7708
EX $20   NM $35   MIP $65

Paratrooper Helmet Set, 1964, Hasbro, Model No. 7707
EX $20   NM $40   MIP $85

Paratrooper Parachute Pack, 1964, Hasbro, Model No. 7709
EX $30   NM $80   MIP $125

Paratrooper Small Arms Set, 1967, Hasbro, reissue, Model No. 7706
EX $30   NM $75   MIP $225

Tank Commander Set, 1967, Hasbro, includes faux leather jacket, helmet and visor, insignia, radio with tripod, machine gun, ammo box, Model No. 7731
EX $325   NM $500   MIP $1350

Tank Commander Set, 1968, Hasbro, reissue, Model No. 7731
EX $325   NM $500   MIP $1200

ACTION PILOT SERIES

Figure Sets

Action Pilot, 1964, Hasbro, orange jumpsuit, blue cap, black boots, dog tags, insignias, manual, catalog and club application, Model No. 7800
EX $135   NM $165   MIP $600

Talking Action Pilot, 1967, Hasbro, Model No. 7890
EX $190   NM $245   MIP $1500

Uniform/Equipment Sets

Air Academy Cadet Set, 1967, Hasbro, deluxe set with figure, dress jacket, shoes, and pants, garrison cap, saber and scabbard, white M-1 rifle, chest sash and belt sash, Model No. 7822
EX $225   NM $450   MIP $1100

Air Academy Cadet Set, 1968, Hasbro, reissue, Model No. 7822
EX $225   NM $450   MIP $950

Air Force Basics Set, 1966, Hasbro, Model No. 7814
EX $30   NM $55   MIP $200

Air Force Basics Set, 1967, Hasbro, reissue, Model No. 7814
EX $30   NM $55   MIP $275

Air Force Mae West Air Vest & Equipment Set, 1967, Hasbro, Model No. 7816
EX $85   NM $125   MIP $325

Air Force Police Set, 1965, Hasbro, Model No. 7813
EX $70   NM $150   MIP $250

Air Force Police Set, 1967, Hasbro, reissue, Model No. 7813
EX $70   NM $150   MIP $325

Air Force Security Set, 1967, Hasbro, Air Security radio and helmet, cartridge belt, pistol and holster, Model No. 7815
EX $275   NM $350   MIP $590

Air/Sea Rescue Set, 1967, Hasbro, includes black air tanks, rescue ring, buoy, depth gauge, face mask, fins, orange scuba outfit, Model No. 7825
EX $325   NM $550   MIP $1600

Air/Sea Rescue Set, 1968, Hasbro, reissue, Model No. 7825
EX $325   NM $550   MIP $1600

Astronaut Set, 1967, Hasbro, helmet with visor, foil space suit, booties, gloves, space camera, propellant gun, tether cord, oxygen chest pack, silver boots, white jumpsuit and cloth cap, Model No. 7824
EX $100   NM $200   MIP $3000

Astronaut Set, 1968, Hasbro, reissue, Model No. 7824
EX $100   NM $250   MIP $850

Communications Set, 1964, Hasbro, Model No. 7812
EX $55   NM $100   MIP $225

Crash Crew Set, 1966, Hasbro, fire proof jacket, hood, pants and gloves, silver boots, belt, flashlight, axe, pliers, fire extinguisher, stretcher, strap cutter, Model No. 7820
EX $125   NM $250   MIP $450

Dress Uniform Jacket Set, 1964, Hasbro, Model No. 7804
EX $40   NM $65   MIP $250

Dress Uniform Pants, 1964, Hasbro, Model No. 7805
EX $20   NM $35   MIP $200

Dress Uniform Set, 1964, Hasbro, Air Force jacket, trousers, shirt, tie, cap and manual, Model No. 7803
EX $225   NM $550   MIP $1650

Dress Uniform Shirt & Equipment Set, 1964, Hasbro, Model No. 7806
EX $25   NM $40   MIP $200

Fighter Pilot Set, 1967, Hasbro, working parachute and pack, gold helmet, Mae West vest, green pants, flash light, orange jump suit, black boots, Model No. 7823
EX $400   NM $650   MIP $1550

Fighter Pilot Set, 1968, Hasbro, reissue, Model No. 7823
EX $400   NM $650   MIP $1600

Scramble Communications Set, 1965, Hasbro, poncho, field telephone and radio, map with case, binoculars and wire roll, Model No. 7812
EX $35   NM $75   MIP $175

Scramble Communications Set, 1967, Hasbro, reissue, Model No. 7812
EX $35   NM $75   MIP $250

Scramble Crash Helmet, 1964, Hasbro, helmet, face mask, hose, tinted visor, Model No. 7810
EX $65   NM $90   MIP $125

Scramble Crash Helmet, 1967, Hasbro, reissue, Model No. 7810
EX $65   NM $90   MIP $225

Scramble Flight Suit, 1964, Hasbro, gray flight suit, Model No. 7808
EX $50   NM $300   MIP $225

Scramble Flight Suit, 1967, Hasbro, Model No. 7808
EX $50   NM $75   MIP $400

Scramble Parachute Set, 1964, Hasbro, Model No. 7811
EX $20   NM $40   MIP $150

Scramble Parachute Set, 1967, Hasbro, reissue, Model No. 7809
EX $20   NM $40   MIP $250

Scramble Set, 1964, Hasbro, deluxe set, gray flight suit, orange air vest, white crash helmet, pistol belt with .45 pistol, holster, clipboard, flare gun and parachute with insert, Model No. 7807
EX $125   NM $225   MIP $950

Survival Life Raft Set, 1964, Hasbro, raft with oar, flare gun, knife, air vest, first-aid kit, sea anchor and manual, Model No. 7801
EX $75   NM $125   MIP $550

Survival Life Raft Set, 1964, Hasbro, raft with oar and sea anchor, Model No. 7802
EX $45   NM $90   MIP $325

Vehicle Sets

(ToyShop File Photo)

Crash Crew Fire Truck Set, 1967, Hasbro, Includes blue truck and fireproof silver suit. Truck has working firehose, Model No. 8040
EX $950   NM $1700   MIP $3500

Official Space Capsule Set, 1966, Hasbro, space capsule, record, space suit, cloth space boots, space gloves, helmet with visor, Model No. 8020
EX $175   NM $225   MIP $350

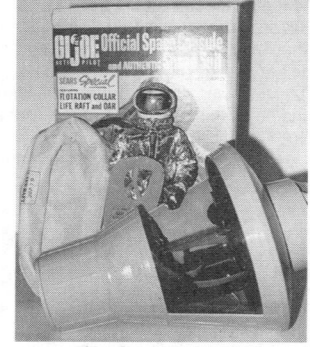

(ToyShop File Photo)

Official Space Capsule Set with flotation, 1966, Hasbro, Sears Exclusive with collar, life raft and oars, Model No. 5979
EX $200   NM $325   MIP $700

Spacewalk Mystery, 1969, Hasbro, Model No. 7981
EX $120   NM $265   MIP $450

G.I. JOE

ACTION SAILOR SERIES

Figure Sets

Action Sailor, 1964, Hasbro, white cap, denim shirt and pants, boots, dog tags, navy manual and insignias, Model No. 7600
EX $125   **NM** $225   **MIP** $450

Navy Scuba Set, 1968, Hasbro, Adventure Pack, Model No. 7643-83
EX $300   **NM** $450   **MIP** $3250

Talking Action Sailor, 1967, Hasbro, Model No. 7690
EX $200   **NM** $330   **MIP** $1250

Talking Landing Signal Officer Set, 1968, Hasbro, Talking Adventure Pack, Model No. 90621
EX $325   **NM** $350   **MIP** $3500

Talking Shore Patrol Set, 1968, Hasbro, Talking Adventure Pack, Model No. 90612
EX $200   **NM** $450   **MIP** $3500

Uniform/Equipment Sets

Annapolis Cadet, 1967, Hasbro, garrison cap, dress jacket, pants, shoes, sword, scabbard, belt and white M-1 rifle, Model No. 7624
EX $275   **NM** $375   **MIP** $1350

Annapolis Cadet, 1968, Hasbro, reissue, Model No. 7624
EX $275   **NM** $375   **MIP** $1350

Breeches Buoy, 1967, Hasbro, yellow jacket and pants, chair and pulley, flare gun, blinker light, Model No. 7625
EX $325   **NM** $425   **MIP** $1500

Breeches Buoy, 1968, Hasbro, reissue, Model No. 7625
EX $325   **NM** $425   **MIP** $1450

Deep Freeze, 1967, Hasbro, white boots, fur parka, pants, snow shoes, ice axe, snow sled with rope and flare gun, Model No. 7623
EX $250   **NM** $375   **MIP** $1600

Deep Freeze, 1968, Hasbro, reissue, Model No. 7623
EX $250   **NM** $375   **MIP** $1500

Deep Sea Diver Set, 1965, Hasbro, underwater uniform, helmet, upper and lower plate, sledge hammer, buoy with rope, gloves, compass, hoses, lead boots and weight belt, Model No. 7620
EX $325   **NM** $425   **MIP** $1850

Deep Sea Diver Set, 1968, Hasbro, reissue, Model No. 7620
EX $325   **NM** $425   **MIP** $1850

Frogman Scuba Bottoms, 1964, Hasbro, Model No. 7604
EX $20   **NM** $35   **MIP** $100

Frogman Scuba Tank Set, 1964, Hasbro, Model No. 7606
EX $25   **NM** $40   **MIP** $100

Frogman Scuba Top Set, 1964, Hasbro, Model No. 7603
EX $25   **NM** $45   **MIP** $125

Frogman Underwater Demolition Set, 1964, Hasbro, headpiece, face mask, swim fins, rubber suit, scuba tank, depth gauge, knife, dynamite and manual, Model No. 7602
EX $175   **NM** $250   **MIP** $1500

Landing Signal Officer, 1966, Hasbro, jumpsuit, signal paddles, goggles, cloth head gear, headphones, clipboard (complete), binoculars and flare gun., Model No. 7621
EX $225   **NM** $350   **MIP** $575

Navy Attack Helmet Set, 1964, shirt and pants, boots, yellow life vest, blue helmet, flare gun binoculars, signal flags, Model No. 7610
EX $35   **NM** $75   **MIP** $150

Navy Attack Life Jacket, 1964, Hasbro, Model No. 7611
EX $20   **NM** $45   **MIP** $120

Navy Attack Set, 1964, Hasbro, life jacket, field glasses, blinker light, signal flags, manual, Model No. 7607
EX $60   **NM** $125   **MIP** $425

Navy Attack Work Pants Set, 1964, Hasbro, Model No. 7609
EX $25   **NM** $40   **MIP** $150

Navy Attack Work Shirt Set, 1964, Hasbro, Model No. 7608
EX $25   **NM** $40   **MIP** $175

Navy Basics Set, 1966, Hasbro, Model No. 7628
EX $25   **NM** $55   **MIP** $125

Navy Dress Parade Rifle Set, 1965, Hasbro, Model No. 7619
EX $35   **NM** $65   **MIP** $125

Navy Dress Parade Set, 1964, Hasbro, billy club, cartridge belt, bayonet and white dress rifle, Model No. 7619
EX $45   **NM** $80   **MIP** $175

Navy L.S.O. Equipment Set, 1966, Hasbro, helmet, headphones, signal paddles, flare gun, Model No. 7626
EX $40   **NM** $80   **MIP** $150

Navy Life Ring Set, 1966, Hasbro, U.S.N. life ring, helmet sticker, Model No. 7627
EX $25   **NM** $45   **MIP** $150

Navy Machine Gun Set, 1965, Hasbro, MG and ammo box, Model No. 7618
EX $40   **NM** $80   **MIP** $175

Sea Rescue Set, 1964, Hasbro, life raft, oar, anchor, flare gun, first-aid kit, knife, scabbard, manual, Model No. 7601
EX $95   **NM** $135   **MIP** $500

(ToyShop File Photo)

Sea Rescue Set, 1966, Hasbro, reissued with life preserver, Model No. 7622
EX $95   **NM** $135   **MIP** $500

Shore Patrol, 1964, Hasbro, dress shirt, tie and pants, helmet, white belt, .45 and holster, billy club, boots, arm band, sea bag, Model No. 7612
EX $500   **NM** $1000   **MIP** $2000

Shore Patrol, 1967, Hasbro, reissued with radio and helmet and shoes, Model No. 7612
EX $1000   **NM** $2000   **MIP** $3500

Shore Patrol Dress Jumper Set, 1964, Hasbro, Model No. 7613
EX $75   **NM** $125   **MIP** $225

Shore Patrol Dress Pant Set, 1964, Hasbro, Model No. 7614
EX $40   **NM** $75   **MIP** $175

Shore Patrol Helmet and Small Arms Set, 1964, Hasbro, white belt, billy stick, white helmet, .45 pistol, Model No. 7616
EX $40   **NM** $75   **MIP** $150

Shore Patrol Sea Bag Set, 1964, Hasbro, Model No. 7615
EX $25   **NM** $50   **MIP** $125

Vehicle Sets

Official Sea Sled and Frogman Set, 1966, Hasbro, without cave, Model No. 8050
EX $150   **NM** $300   **MIP** $550

(ToyShop File Photo)

Official Sea Sled and Frogman Set, 1966, Hasbro, Sears, with figure and underwater cave, orange scuba suit, fins, mask, tanks, sea sled in orange and black, Model No. 5979
EX $175   **NM** $325   **MIP** $650

ACTION SOLDIER SERIES

Figure Sets

(ToyShop File Photo)

Action Soldier, 1964, Hasbro, fatigue cap, shirt, pants, boots, dog tags, army manual and insignias, helmet, belt with pouches, M-1 rifle, Model No. 7500
EX $100   NM $175   MIP $450

Black Action Soldier, 1965, Hasbro, Model No. 7900
EX $450   NM $800   MIP $2200

Canadian Mountie Set, 1967, Hasbro, Sears Exclusive, Model No. 5904
EX $850   NM $1500   MIP $4000

Desert Patrol Attack Jeep Set, 1967, Hasbro, Desert Fighter figure, jeep with steering wheel, spare tire, tan tripod, gun and gun mount and ring, black antenna, tan jacket and shorts, socks, goggles, Model No. 8030
EX $400   NM $1250   MIP $2000

Forward Observer Set, 1966, Hasbro, Sears Exclusive, Model No. 5969
EX $200   NM $375   MIP $750

Green Beret, 1966, Hasbro, field radio, bazooka rocket, bazooka, green beret, jacket, pants, M-16 rifle, grenades, camo scarf, belt pistol and holster, Model No. 7536
EX $275   NM $400   MIP $2800

Machine Gun Emplacement Set, 1965, Hasbro, Sears Exclusive, Model No. 7531
EX $150   NM $275   MIP $1250

Talking Action Soldier, 1967, Hasbro, Model No. 7590
EX $85   NM $135   MIP $825

Talking Adventure Pack, Bivouac Equipment, 1968, Hasbro, Model No. 90513
EX $275   NM $325   MIP $3000

Talking Adventure Pack, Command Post Equip., 1968, Hasbro, Model No. 90517
EX $275   NM $375   MIP $2750

Talking Adventure Pack, Mountain Troop Series, 1968, Hasbro, Model No. 7557-83
EX $375   NM $650   MIP $3150

Talking Adventure Pack, Special Forces Equip., 1968, Hasbro, Model No. 90532
EX $275   NM $500   MIP $3150

Uniform/Equipment Sets

Adventure Pack with fourteen pieces, 1968, Hasbro, Adventure Pack Footlocker, Model No. 8008.83
EX $75   NM $125   MIP $600

Adventure Pack with sixteen items, 1968, Hasbro, Adventure Pack Footlocker, Model No. 8007.83
EX $75   NM $125   MIP $600

Adventure Pack with twelve items, 1968, Hasbro, Adventure Pack Footlocker, Model No. 8005.83
EX $75   NM $125   MIP $600

Adventure Pack with twelve items, 1968, Hasbro, Adventure Pack Footlocker, Model No. 8006.83
EX $75   NM $125   MIP $600

Adventure Pack, Army Bivouac Series, 1968, Hasbro, Model No. 7549-83
EX $225   NM $450   MIP $3500

Air Police Equipment, 1964, Hasbro, gray field phone, carbine, white helmet and bayonet, Model No. 7813
EX $40   NM $95   MIP $200

Basic Footlocker, 1964, Hasbro, wood tray with cardboard wrapper, Model No. 8000
EX $35   NM $75   MIP $125

Bivouac Deluxe Pup Tent Set, 1964, Hasbro, M-1 rifle and bayonet, shovel and cover, canteen and cover, mess kit, cartridge belt, machine gun, tent, pegs, poles, camoflage, sleeping bag, netting, ammo box, Model No. 7513
EX $115   NM $225   MIP $450

Bivouac Machine Gun Set, 1964, Hasbro, machine gun set and ammo box, Model No. 7514
EX $25   NM $40   MIP $125

Bivouac Machine Gun Set, 1967, Hasbro, reissue, Model No. 7514
EX $25   NM $40   MIP $225

Bivouac Sleeping Bag, 1964, Hasbro, zippered bag, Model No. 7515
EX $20   NM $30   MIP $125

Bivouac Sleeping Bag Set, 1964, Hasbro, mess kit, canteen, bayonet, cartridge belt, M-1 rifle, manual, Model No. 7512
EX $25   NM $30   MIP $150

(ToyShop File Photo)

Combat Camouflaged Netting Set, 1964, Hasbro, foliage and posts, Model No. 7511
EX $25   NM $40   MIP $85

Combat Construction Set, 1967, Hasbro, orange safety helmet, work gloves, jack hammer, Model No. 7572
EX $325   NM $400   MIP $575

Combat Demolition Set, 1967, Hasbro, Model No. 7573
EX $65   NM $100   MIP $525

Combat Engineer Set, 1967, Hasbro, pick, shovel, detonator, dynamite, tripod and transit with grease gun, Model No. 7571
EX $125   NM $175   MIP $625

Combat Fatigue Pants Set, 1964, Hasbro, Model No. 7504
EX $15   NM $25   MIP $110

Combat Fatigue Shirt Set, 1964, Hasbro, Model No. 7503
EX $20   NM $30   MIP $125

Combat Field Jacket, 1964, Hasbro, Model No. 7505
EX $45   NM $65   MIP $325

Combat Field Jacket Set, 1964, Hasbro, jacket, bayonet, cartridge belt, hand grenades, M-1 rifle and manual, Model No. 7501
EX $65   NM $100   MIP $525

Combat Field Pack & Entrenching Tool, 1964, Hasbro, Model No. 7506
EX $25   NM $45   MIP $125

Combat Field Pack Deluxe Set, 1964, Hasbro, field jacket, pack, entrenching shovel with cover, mess kit, first-aid pouch, canteen with cover, Model No. 7502
EX $75   NM $125   MIP $325

Combat Helmet Set, 1964, Hasbro, with netting and foliage leaves, Model No. 7507
EX $20   NM $35   MIP $75

Combat Mess Kit, 1964, Hasbro, plate, fork, knife, spoon, canteen, etc., Model No. 7509
EX $20   NM $45   MIP $85

G.I. JOE

Combat Rifle Set, 1967, Hasbro, bayonet, M-1 rifle, belt and grenades, Model No. 7510
EX $55 NM $100 MIP $325

Combat Sandbags Set, 1964, Hasbro, three bags per set, Model No. 7508
EX $10 NM $40 MIP $85

Command Post Field Radio and Telephone Set, 1964, Hasbro, field radio, telephone with wire roll and map, Model No. 7520
EX $35 NM $70 MIP $135

Command Post Field Radio and Telephone Set, 1967, Hasbro, reissue, Model No. 7520
EX $35 NM $70 MIP $400

Command Post Poncho, 1964, Hasbro, on card, Model No. 7519
EX $30 NM $45 MIP $225

Command Post Poncho Set, 1964, Hasbro, poncho, field radio and telephone, wire roll, pistol, belt and holster, map and case and manual, Model No. 7517
EX $85 NM $125 MIP $400

Command Post Small Arms Set, 1964, Hasbro, holster and .45 pistol, belt, grenades, Model No. 7518
EX $30 NM $60 MIP $100

Dress Parade Adventure Pack, 1968, Hasbro, Adventure Pack with thirty-seven pieces, Model No. 8009.83
EX $750 NM $1250 MIP $3500

Green Beret and Small Arms Set, 1966, Hasbro, Model No. 7533
EX $85 NM $110 MIP $300

Green Beret and Small Arms Set, 1967, Hasbro, reissue, Model No. 7533
EX $85 NM $100 MIP $425

(ToyShop File Photo)

Green Beret Machine Gun Outpost Set, 1966, Hasbro, Sears Exclusive with two figures and equipment, Model No. 5978
EX $225 NM $450 MIP $1500

Heavy Weapons Set, 1967, Hasbro, mortar launcher and shells, M-60 machine gun, grenades, flak jacket, shirt and pants, Model No. 7538
EX $175 NM $325 MIP $1750

Heavy Weapons Set, 1968, Hasbro, reissue, Model No. 7538
EX $175 NM $325 MIP $1500

Military Police Duffle Bag Set, 1964, Hasbro, Model No. 7523
EX $25 NM $40 MIP $85

Military Police Helmet and Small Arms Set, 1964, Hasbro, Model No. 7526
EX $35 NM $75 MIP $125

Military Police Helmet and Small Arms Set, 1967, Hasbro, reissue, Model No. 7526
EX $35 NM $75 MIP $250

Military Police Ike Jacket, 1964, Hasbro, jacket with red scarf and arm band, Model No. 7524
EX $40 NM $60 MIP $125

(ToyShop File Photo)

Military Police Ike Pants, 1964, Hasbro, matches Ike jacket, Model No. 7525
EX $20 NM $30 MIP $100

Military Police Uniform Set, 1964, Hasbro, includes Ike jacket and pants, scarf, boots, helmet, belt with ammo pouches, .45 pistol and holster, billy club, armband, duffle bag, Model No. 7521
EX $450 NM $1650 MIP $3000

Military Police Uniform Set, 1967, Hasbro, includes green or tan uniform, black and gold MP Helmet, billy club, belt, pistol and holster, MP armband and red tunic, Model No. 7539
EX $450 NM $1650 MIP $3500

Military Police Uniform Set, 1968, Hasbro, reissue, Model No. 7539
EX $450 NM $900 MIP $3000

(ToyShop File Photo)

Mountain Troops Set, 1964, Hasbro, snow shoes, ice axe, ropes, grenades, camoflage pack, web belt, manual, Model No. 7530
EX $90 NM $175 MIP $350

Sabotage Set, 1967, Hasbro, dingy and oar, blinker light, detonator with strap, TNT, wool stocking cap, gas mask, binoculars, green radio and .45 pistol and holster, Model No. 7516
EX $125 NM $250 MIP $2000

Sabotage Set, 1968, Hasbro, reissued in photo box, Model No. 7516
EX $125 NM $250 MIP $1700

Ski Patrol Deluxe Set, 1964, Hasbro, White parka, boots, goggles, mittens, skis, poles and manual, Model No. 7531
EX $170 NM $350 MIP $1250

Ski Patrol Helmet and Small Arms Set, 1965, Hasbro, Model No. 7527
EX $35 NM $75 MIP $135

Ski Patrol Helmet and Small Arms Set, 1967, Hasbro, reissue, Model No. 7527
EX $75 NM $125 MIP $250

(ToyShop File Photo)

Snow Troop Set, 1966, Hasbro, snow shoes, goggles and ice pick, Model No. 7529
EX $20 NM $45 MIP $150

Snow Troop Set, 1967, Hasbro, reissue, Model No. 7529
EX $20 NM $45 MIP $225

Special Forces Bazooka Set, 1966, Hasbro, Model No. 7528
EX $35 NM $45 MIP $225

Special Forces Bazooka Set, 1967, Hasbro, reissue, Model No. 7528
EX $35   **NM** $45   **MIP** $325

Special Forces Uniform Set, 1966, Hasbro, Model No. 7532
EX $200   **NM** $375   **MIP** $1000

West Point Cadet Uniform Set, 1967, Hasbro, dress jacket, pants, shoes, chest and belt sash, parade hat with plume, saber, scabbard and white M-1 rifle, Model No. 7537
EX $250   **NM** $475   **MIP** $1500

West Point Cadet Uniform Set, 1968, Hasbro, reissue, Model No. 7537
EX $250   **NM** $375   **MIP** $1200

Vehicle Sets

Amphibious Duck, 1967, Irwin, 26" long, Model No. 5693
EX $175   **NM** $375   **MIP** $700

Armored Car, 1967, Irwin, friction powered, 20" long, Model No. 5397
EX $150   **NM** $300   **MIP** $500

Helicopter, 1967, Hasbro, Irwin, friction powered, 28" long, Model No. 5395
EX $150   **NM** $300   **MIP** $500

Jet Fighter Plane, 1967, Irwin, friction powered, 30" long, Model No. 5396
EX $225   **NM** $475   **MIP** $800

Military Staff Car, 1967, Irwin, friction powered, 24" long, Model No. 5652
EX $200   **NM** $400   **MIP** $750

Motorcycle and Sidecar, 1967, Irwin, 14" long, khaki, with decals, Model No. 5651
EX $75   **NM** $150   **MIP** $325

Official Combat Jeep Set, 1965, trailer, steering wheel, spare tire, windshield, cannon, search light, shell, flag, guard rails, tripod, tailgate and hood, without Moto-Rev Sound, Model No. 7000
EX $200   **NM** $375   **MIP** $550

Official Jeep Combat Set, 1965, With Moto-Rev sound, Model No. 7000
EX $225   **NM** $400   **MIP** $650

Personnel Carrier/Mine Sweeper, 1967, Irwin, 26" long, Model No. 5694
EX $300   **NM** $350   **MIP** $700

ACTION SOLDIERS OF THE WORLD

Figure Sets

Australian Jungle Fighter, 1966, Hasbro, action figure with jacket, shorts, socks, boots, bush hat, belt, "Victoria Cross" medal, knuckle knife, flamethrower, entrenching tool, bush knife and sheath, Model No. 8105
EX $250   **NM** $400   **MIP** $2500

Australian Jungle Fighter, 1966, standard set with action figure uniform, no equipment, Model No. 8205
EX $150   **NM** $275   **MIP** $1200

British Commando, 1966, Hasbro, deluxe set with action figure, helmet, night raid green jacket, pants, boots, canteen and cover, gas mask and cover, belt, Sten sub machine gun, gun clip and "Victoria Cross" medal, Model No. 8104
EX $300   **NM** $425   **MIP** $2500

British Commando, 1966, Hasbro, standard set with no equipment, Model No. 8204
EX $150   **NM** $275   **MIP** $1750

Foreign Soldiers of the World, 1968, Hasbro, Talking Adventure Pack, Model No. 8111-83
EX $750   **NM** $825   **MIP** $5000

French Resistance Fighter, 1966, Hasbro, Standard set with action figure and equipment, Model No. 8203
EX $125   **NM** $225   **MIP** $1250

French Resistance Fighter, 1966, Hasbro, deluxe set with figure, beret, short black boots, black sweater, denim pants, "Croix de Guerre" medal, knife, shoulder holster, pistol, radio, sub machine gun and grenades, Model No. 8103
EX $200   **NM** $250   **MIP** $2250

German Storm Trooper, 1966, Hasbro, deluxe set with figure, helmet, jacket, pants, boots, Luger pistol, holster, cartridge belt, cartridges, "Iron Cross" medal, stick grenades, 9MM Schmeisser, field pack, Model No. 8100
EX $275   **NM** $425   **MIP** $2500

German Storm Trooper, 1966, Hasbro, Standard set with no equipment, Model No. 8200
EX $275   **NM** $325   **MIP** $1300

Japanese Imperial Soldier, 1966, Hasbro, deluxe set with figure, Arisaka rifle, belt, cartridges, field pack, Nambu pistol, holster, bayonet, "Order of the Kite" medal, helmet, jacket, pants, short brown boots, Model No. 8101
EX $425   **NM** $675   **MIP** $2700

Japanese Imperial Soldier, 1966, Hasbro, Standard set with equipment, Model No. 8201
EX $300   **NM** $325   **MIP** $1425

Russian Infantry Man, 1966, Hasbro, standard set with no equipment, Model No. 8202
EX $315   **NM** $400   **MIP** $1250

Russian Infantry Man, 1966, Hasbro, deluxe set with action figure, fur cap, tunic, pants, boots, ammo box, ammo rounds, anti-tank grenades, belt, bipod, DP light machine gun, "Order of Lenin" medal, field glasses and case, Model No. 8102
EX $275   **NM** $400   **MIP** $2250

Uniforms of Six Nations, 1967, Hasbro, Model No. 5038
EX $750   **NM** $950   **MIP** $2500

Uniform/Equipment Sets

(ToyShop File Photo)

Australian Jungle Fighter Set, 1966, Hasbro, basic set with flamethrower, machete, grenades, Victoria Cross medal, shovel, bayonet, Model No. 8305
EX $25   **NM** $50   **MIP** $250

British Commando Set, 1966, Hasbro, Sten submachine gun, gas mask and carrier, canteen and cover, cartridge belt, rifle, "Victoria Cross" medal, manual, Model No. 8304
EX $125   **NM** $200   **MIP** $325

French Resistance Fighter Set, 1966, Hasbro, shoulder holster, Lebel pistol, knife, grenades, radio, 7.65 submachine gun, "Croix de Guerra" medal, counter-intelligence manual, Model No. 8303
EX $25   **NM** $50   **MIP** $275

German Storm Trooper, 1966, Hasbro, Model No. 8300
EX $125   **NM** $175   **MIP** $325

Japanese Imperial Soldier Set, 1966, Hasbro, field pack, Nambu pistol and holster, Arisaka rifle with bayonet, cartridge belt, "Order of the Kite" medal, counter-intelligence manual, Model No. 8301
EX $175   **NM** $275   **MIP** $625

Russian Infantry Man Set, 1966, Hasbro, DP light machine gun, bipod, field glasses and case, anti-tank grenades, ammo box, "Order of Lenin" medal, counter-intelligence medal, Model No. 8302
EX $175   **NM** $220   **MIP** $325

ADVENTURE TEAM

Figure Sets

Air Adventurer, 1970, Hasbro, includes figure with Kung Fu grip, orange flight suit, boots, insignia, dog tags, rifle, boots, warranty, club insert, Model No. 7403
EX $120   **NM** $375   **MIP** $400

Air Adventurer, 1974, Hasbro, with Kung Fu grip, Model No. 7282
EX $95   **NM** $160   **MIP** $325

Air Adventurer, 1976, Hasbro, life-like body figure, uniform and equipment, Model No. 7282

EX $75   NM $100   MIP $200

Black Adventurer, 1970, Hasbro, includes figure, shirt with insignia, pants, boots, dog tags, shoulder holster with pistol, Model No. 7404

EX $125   NM $150   MIP $375

Black Adventurer, 1976, Hasbro, with life-like body and Kung Fu grip, Model No. 7283

EX $85   NM $125   MIP $225

Bulletman, 1976, Hasbro, Model No. 8026

EX $60   NM $100   MIP $175

Eagle Eye Black Commando, 1976, Hasbro, Model No. 7278, Model No. 7278

EX $85   NM $125   MIP $250

Eagle Eye Land Commander, 1976, Hasbro, Model No. 7276, Model No. 7276

EX $65   NM $80   MIP $150

Eagle Eye Man of Action, 1976, Hasbro, Model No. 7277

EX $65   NM $80   MIP $165

Intruder Commander, 1976, Hasbro, Model No. 8050

EX $50   NM $60   MIP $135

Intruder Warrior, 1976, Hasbro, Model No. 8051

EX $50   NM $60   MIP $175

(ToyShop File Photo)

Land Adventurer, 1970, Hasbro, includes figure, camo shirt and pants, boots, insignia, shoulder holster and pistol, dog tags and team inserts, Model No. 7401

EX $45   NM $90   MIP $160

Land Adventurer, 1974, Hasbro, with life-like body and Kung Fu grip and uniform set, Model No. 7280

EX $50   NM $65   MIP $200

Land Adventurer, 1976, Hasbro, Model No. 7280, Model No. 7280

EX $35   NM $50   MIP $150

Land Adventurer, 1976, Hasbro, Model No. 7270, Model No. 7270

EX $20   NM $50   MIP $180

Man of Action, 1970, Hasbro, includes figure, shirt and pants, boots, insignia, dog tags, team inserts, Model No. 7500

EX $50   NM $75   MIP $225

Man of Action, 1974, Hasbro, figure with life-like body and Kung Fu grip, Model No. 7284

EX $45   NM $75   MIP $200

Man of Action, 1976, Hasbro, Model No. 7274, Model No. 7274

EX $25   NM $45   MIP $175

Mike Powers/Atomic Man, 1975, Hasbro, figure with "atomic" flashing eye, arm that spins hand-held helicopter, Model No. 8025

EX $20   NM $45   MIP $125

(ToyShop File Photo)

Sea Adventurer, 1970, Hasbro, includes figure, shirt, dungarees, insignia, boots, shoulder holster and pistol, Model No. 7402

EX $45   NM $95   MIP $250

Sea Adventurer, 1974, Hasbro, with life-like body and Kung Fu grip and uniform with equipment, Model No. 7281

EX $55   NM $135   MIP $295

Sea Adventurer, 1976, Hasbro, Model No. 7271, Model No. 7271

EX $40   NM $75   MIP $250

Sea Adventurer, 1976, Hasbro, Model No. 7281, Model No. 7281

EX $55   NM $85   MIP $200

Secret Mountain Outpost, 1975, Hasbro, Model No. 8040

EX $50   NM $85   MIP $200

Talking Adventure Team Black Commander, 1973, Hasbro, Model No. 7406

EX $150   NM $475   MIP $825

Talking Adventure Team Black Commander, 1974, Hasbro, with Kung Fu grip, Model No. 7291

EX $85   NM $350   MIP $750

(ToyShop File Photo)

Talking Adventure Team Commander, 1970, Hasbro, includes figure, two-pocket green shirt, pants, boots, insignia, instructions, dog tag, shoulder holster and pistol. With life-like hair and beard, Model No. 7400

EX $65   NM $140   MIP $400

Talking Adventure Team Commander, 1974, Hasbro, with Kung Fu grip, Model No. 7290

EX $75   NM $200   MIP $500

Talking Astronaut, 1970, Hasbro, Model No. 7590

EX $90   NM $175   MIP $430

Talking Black Commander, 1976, Hasbro, Model No. 7291

EX $125   NM $300   MIP $600

Talking Commander, 1976, Hasbro, Model No. 7290

EX $75   NM $115   MIP $500

Talking Man of Action, 1970, Hasbro, shirt, pants, boots, dog tags, rifle, insignia, instructions, Model No. 7590

EX $75   NM $125   MIP $350

Talking Man of Action, 1974, Hasbro, with life-like body and Kung Fu grip, Model No. 7292

EX $75   NM $200   MIP $650

Talking Man of Action, 1976, Hasbro, Model No. 7292

EX $75   NM $120   MIP $525

Uniform/Equipment Sets

(ToyShop File Photo)

G.I. JOE

Adventure Team Headquarters Set, 1972, Hasbro, Adventure Team playset, Model No. 7490
EX $50　　**NM** $125　　**MIP** $300

Adventure Team Training Center Set, 1973, Hasbro, rifle rack, logs, barrel, barber wire, rope ladder, three tires, two targets, escape slide, tent and poles, first aid kit, respirator and mask, snake, instructions, Model No. 7495
EX $75　　**NM** $125　　**MIP** $225

Aerial Reconnaissance Set, 1971, Hasbro, jumpsuit, helmet, aerial recon vehicle with built-in camera, Model No. 7345
EX $75　　**NM** $125　　**MIP** $242

Attack at Vulture Falls, 1975, Hasbro, super deluxe set, Model No. 7420
EX $75　　**NM** $150　　**MIP** $275

Black Widow Rendezvous, 1975, Hasbro, super deluxe set, Model No. 7414
EX $125　　**NM** $200　　**MIP** $350

Buried Bounty, 1975, Hasbro, deluxe set, Model No. 7328-5
EX $10　　**NM** $25　　**MIP** $85

Capture of the Pygmy Gorilla Set, 1970, Hasbro, Model No. 7437
EX $100　　**NM** $175　　**MIP** $485

Challenge of Savage River, 1975, Hasbro, deluxe set, Model No. 8032
EX $100　　**NM** $175　　**MIP** $350

Chest Winch Set, 1972, Hasbro, Model No. 7313
EX $10　　**NM** $15　　**MIP** $65

Chest Winch Set, 1974, Hasbro, reissue, Model No. 7313
EX $10　　**NM** $15　　**MIP** $75

Command Para Drop, 1975, Hasbro, deluxe set, Model No. 8033
EX $175　　**NM** $250　　**MIP** $550

Copter Rescue Set, 1973, Hasbro, blue jumpsuit, red binoculars, Model No. 7308-3
EX $15　　**NM** $20　　**MIP** $30

Danger of the Depths Set, 1970, Hasbro, Model No. 7412
EX $100　　**NM** $175　　**MIP** $325

Danger Ray Detection, 1975, Hasbro, magnetic ray detector, solar communicator with headphones, two-piece uniform, instructions and comic, Model No. 7338-1
EX $45　　**NM** $90　　**MIP** $225

Dangerous Climb Set, 1973, Hasbro, Model No. 7309-2
EX $20　　**NM** $35　　**MIP** $75

Dangerous Mission Set, 1973, Hasbro, green shirt, pants, hunting rifle, Model No. 7608-5
EX $20　　**NM** $35　　**MIP** $75

Demolition Set, 1971, Hasbro, armored suit, face shield, bomb, bomb disposal box, extension grips, Model No. 7370
EX $20　　**NM** $45　　**MIP** $125

Demolition Set, 1971, Hasbro, with land mines, mine detector and carrying case with metallic suit, Model No. 7371
EX $75　　**NM** $100　　**MIP** $250

Desert Explorer Set, 1973, Hasbro, Model No. 7309-5
EX $20　　**NM** $40　　**MIP** $80

Desert Survival Set, 1973, Hasbro, Model No. 7308-6
EX $20　　**NM** $40　　**MIP** $80

Dive to Danger, 1975, Hasbro, Mike Powers set, orange scuba suit, fins, mask, spear gun, shark, buoy, knife and scabbard, mini sled, air tanks, comic, Model No. 8031
EX $150　　**NM** $250　　**MIP** $450

Diver's Distress, 1975, Hasbro, Model No. 7328-6
EX $35　　**NM** $70　　**MIP** $125

Drag Bike Set, 1971, Hasbro, three-wheel motorcycle brakes down to backpack size, Model No. 7364
EX $25　　**NM** $65　　**MIP** $125

Eight Ropes of Danger Set, 1970, Hasbro, Model No. 7422
EX $125　　**NM** $225　　**MIP** $375

Emergency Rescue Set, 1971, Hasbro, shirt, pants, rope ladder and hook, walkie talkie, safety belt, flashlight, oxygen tank, axe, first aid kit, Model No. 7374
EX $45　　**NM** $75　　**MIP** $145

Equipment Tester Set, 1972, Hasbro, Model No. 7319-5
EX $15　　**NM** $75　　**MIP** $40

Escape Car Set, 1971, Hasbro, Model No. 7360
EX $30　　**NM** $60　　**MIP** $85

Escape Slide Set, 1972, Hasbro, Model No. 7319-1
EX $15　　**NM** $25　　**MIP** $40

Fangs of the Cobra, 1975, Hasbro, deluxe set, Model No. 8028-2
EX $125　　**NM** $175　　**MIP** $235

Fantastic Freefall Set, 1970, Hasbro, Model No. 7423
EX $125　　**NM** $200　　**MIP** $345

Fight For Survival Set, 1970, Hasbro, with blue parka, Model No. 7431
EX $300　　**NM** $550　　**MIP** $2500

Fight for Survival Set, 1973, Hasbro, brown shirt and pants, machete, Model No. 7308-2
EX $20　　**NM** $30　　**MIP** $70

Fight for Survival Set with Polar Explorer, 1969, Hasbro, Model No. 7982
EX $250　　**NM** $450　　**MIP** $850

Fire Fighter Set, 1971, Hasbro, Model No. 7351
EX $20　　**NM** $30　　**MIP** $55

Flying Rescue Set, 1971, Hasbro, Model No. 7361
EX $35　　**NM** $60　　**MIP** $85

Flying Space Adventure Set, 1970, Hasbro, Model No. 7425
EX $400　　**NM** $600　　**MIP** $3700

Footlocker, 1974, Hasbro, green plastic with cardboard wrapper, Model No. 8000
EX $35　　**NM** $45　　**MIP** $200

Green Danger, 1975, Hasbro, Model No. 7328-4
EX $30　　**NM** $75　　**MIP** $60

Hidden Missile Discovery Set, 1970, Hasbro, Model No. 7415
EX $100　　**NM** $225　　**MIP** $1750

Hidden Treasure Set, 1973, Hasbro, shirt, pants, pick axe, shovel, Model No. 7308-1
EX $15　　**NM** $25　　**MIP** $40

High Voltage Escape Set, 1971, Hasbro, net, jumpsuit, hat, wrist meter, wire cutters, wire, warning sign, Model No. 7342
EX $40　　**NM** $75　　**MIP** $110

Hurricane Spotter Set, 1971, Hasbro, slicker suit, rain measure, portable

G.I. JOE

radar, map and case, binoculars, Model No. 7343

EX $55   **NM** $110   **MIP** $220

Jaws of Death, 1975, Hasbro, super deluxe set, Model No. 7421

EX $325   **NM** $500   **MIP** $650

Jettison to Safety, 1975, Hasbro, infrared terrain scanner, mobile rocket pack, two-piece flight suit, instructions and comic, Model No. 7339-2

EX $85   **NM** $200   **MIP** $275

Jungle Ordeal Set, 1973, Hasbro, Model No. 7309-3

EX $15   **NM** $25   **MIP** $66

Jungle Survival Set, 1971, Hasbro, Model No. 7373

EX $15   **NM** $60   **MIP** $180

Karate Set, 1971, Hasbro, Model No. 7372

EX $35   **NM** $70   **MIP** $210

Laser Rescue Set, 1972, Hasbro, hand-held laser with backpack generator, Model No. 7311

EX $20   **NM** $35   **MIP** $45

Laser Rescue Set, 1974, Hasbro, reissue, Model No. 7311

EX $20   **NM** $35   **MIP** $100

Life-Line Catapult Set, 1971, Hasbro, Model No. 7353

EX $15   **NM** $25   **MIP** $85

Long Range Recon, 1975, Hasbro, deluxe set, Model No. 7328-3

EX $10   **NM** $20   **MIP** $35

Magnetic Flaw Detector Set, 1972, Hasbro, Model No. 7319-2

EX $10   **NM** $20   **MIP** $56

Mine Shaft Breakout, 1975, Hasbro, sonic rock blaster, chest winch, two-piece uniform, netting, instructions, comic, Model No. 7339-3

EX $70   **NM** $125   **MIP** $250

Missile Recovery Set, 1971, Hasbro, Model No. 7340

EX $100   **NM** $200   **MIP** $325

Mystery of the Boiling Lagoon, 1973, Hasbro, Sears, pontoon boat, diver's suit, diver's helmet, weighted belt and boots, depth gauge, air hose, buoy, nose cone, pincer arm, instructions

EX $150   **NM** $200   **MIP** $295

Night Surveillance, 1975, Hasbro, deluxe set, Model No. 7338-2

EX $65   **NM** $160   **MIP** $165

Peril of the Raging Inferno, 1975, Hasbro, fireproof suit, hood and boots, breathing apparatus, camera, fire extinguisher, detection meter, gaskets, Model No. 7416

EX $85   **NM** $150   **MIP** $275

Photo Reconnaissance Set, 1973, Hasbro, Model No. 7309-4

EX $20   **NM** $30   **MIP** $65

Race for Recovery, 1975, Hasbro, Model No. 8028-1

EX $20   **NM** $35   **MIP** $140

Radiation Detection Set, 1971, Hasbro, jumpsuit with belt, "uranium ore", goggles, container, pincer arm, Model No. 7341

EX $30   **NM** $50   **MIP** $160

Raging River Dam Up, 1975, Hasbro, Model No. 7339-1

EX $100   **NM** $225   **MIP** $450

Rescue Raft Set, 1971, Hasbro, Model No. 7350

EX $15   **NM** $45   **MIP** $65

Revenge of the Spy Shark, 1975, Hasbro, super deluxe set, Model No. 7413

EX $50   **NM** $175   **MIP** $400

Rock Blaster, 1972, Hasbro, sonic blaster with tripod, backpack generator, face shield, Model No. 7312

EX $10   **NM** $20   **MIP** $35

Rocket Pack Set, 1972, Hasbro, Model No. 7315

EX $10   **NM** $20   **MIP** $75

Rocket Pack Set, 1974, Hasbro, reissue, Model No. 7315

EX $10   **NM** $20   **MIP** $50

Sample Analyzer Set, 1972, Hasbro, Model No. 7319-3

EX $45   **NM** $145   **MIP** $255

Search for the Abominable Snowman Set, 1973, Hasbro, Sears, white suit, belt, goggles, gloves, rifle, skis and poles, show shoes, sled, rope, net, supply chest, binoculars, Abominable Snowman, comic book, Model No. 7439.16

EX $110   **NM** $175   **MIP** $290

Secret Agent Set, 1971, Hasbro, Model No. 7375

EX $30   **NM** $55   **MIP** $190

Secret Courier, 1975, Hasbro, Model No. 7328-1

EX $45   **NM** $80   **MIP** $135

Secret Mission Set, 1973, Hasbro, Model No. 7309-1

EX $45   **NM** $65   **MIP** $135

Secret Mission Set, 1975, Hasbro, deluxe set, Model No. 8030

EX $65   **NM** $95   **MIP** $200

Secret Mission to Spy Island Set, 1970, Hasbro, comic, inflatable raft with oar, binoculars, signal light, flare gun, TNT and detonator, wire roll, boots, pants, sweater, black cap, camera, radio with earphones, .45 submachine gun, Model No. 7411

EX $75   **NM** $125   **MIP** $400

Secret Rendezvous Set, 1973, Hasbro, parka, pants, flare gun, Model No. 7308-4

EX $10   **NM** $20   **MIP** $35

Seismograph Set, 1972, Hasbro, Model No. 7319-6

EX $10   **NM** $20   **MIP** $35

Shocking Escape, 1975, Hasbro, escape slide, chest pack climber, jumpsuit with gloves and belt, high voltage sign, instructions and comic, Model No. 7338-3

EX $125   **NM** $240   **MIP** $525

Signal Flasher Set, 1971, Hasbro, large back pack type signal flash unit, Model No. 7362

EX $20   **NM** $30   **MIP** $66

Sky Dive to Danger, 1975, Hasbro, super deluxe set, Model No. 7440

EX $90   **NM** $150   **MIP** $350

Solar Communicator Set, 1972, Hasbro, Model No. 7314

EX $10   **NM** $20   **MIP** $35

Solar Communicator Set, 1974, Hasbro, reissue, Model No. 7314

EX $10   **NM** $20   **MIP** $95

Sonic Rock Blaster Set, 1972, Hasbro, Model No. 7312

EX $10   **NM** $20   **MIP** $35

Sonic Rock Blaster Set, 1974, Hasbro, reissue, Model No. 7312

EX $10   **NM** $20   **MIP** $35

Special Assignment, 1975, Hasbro, deluxe set, Model No. 8028-3

EX $30   **NM** $55   **MIP** $135

Thermal Terrain Scanner Set, 1972, Hasbro, Model No. 7319-4

EX $25   **NM** $35   **MIP** $50

Three-in-One Super Adventure Set, 1971, Hasbro, cold of the Arctic, Heat of the Desert and Danger of the Jungle, Model No. 7480

EX $250   **NM** $400   **MIP** $750

Three-in-One Super Adventure Set, 1971, Hasbro, Danger of the Depths, Secret Mission to Spy Island and Flying Space Adventure Packs, Model No. 7480

EX $550   **NM** $975   **MIP** $1250

Thrust into Danger, 1975, Hasbro, deluxe set, Model No. 7328-2

EX $45   **NM** $55   **MIP** $175

Trouble at Vulture Pass, 1975, Hasbro, Sears Exclusive, super deluxe set, Model No. 59289

EX $75   **NM** $175   **MIP** $325

Turbo Copter Set, 1971, Hasbro, strap-on one man helicopter, Model No. 7363

EX $15   **NM** $35   **MIP** $65

Undercover Agent Set, 1973, Hasbro, trenchcoat and belt, walkie-talkie, Model No. 7309-6

EX $15   **NM** $30   **MIP** $45

Underwater Demolition Set, 1972, Hasbro, hand-held propulsion device, breathing apparatus, dynamite, Model No. 7310

EX $15   **NM** $20   **MIP** $40

Underwater Demolition Set, 1974, Hasbro, reissue, Model No. 7310

EX $10   **NM** $20   **MIP** $75

G.I. JOE

G.I. JOE

Underwater Explorer Set, 1971, Hasbro, self propelled underwater device, Model No. 7354
EX $15   NM $30   MIP $60

Volcano Jumper Set, 1971, Hasbro, jumpsuit with hood, belt, nylon rope, chest pack, TNT pack, Model No. 7344
EX $45   NM $80   MIP $250

White Tiger Hunt Set, 1970, Hasbro, hunter's jacket and pants, hat, rifle, tent, cage, chain, campfire, white tiger, comic, Model No. 7436
EX $80   NM $180   MIP $340

Windboat Set, 1971, Hasbro, back pack, sled with wheels, sail, Model No. 7353
EX $10   NM $25   MIP $65

Winter Rescue Set, 1973, Hasbro, Replaced Photo Reconnaissance Set, Model No. 7309-4
EX $40   NM $75   MIP $150

Vehicle Sets

Action Sea Sled, 1973, Hasbro, J.C. Penney, 13", Adventure Pack
EX $25   NM $40   MIP $85

Adventure Team Vehicle Set, 1970, Hasbro, Model No. 7005
EX $50   NM $75   MIP $225

All Terrain Vehicle, 1973, Hasbro, 14" vehicle, Model No. 23528
EX $50   NM $75   MIP $125

Amphicat, 1973, Hasbro, Irwin, scaled to fit two figures, Model No. 59158
EX $35   NM $55   MIP $125

Avenger Pursuit Craft, 1976, Hasbro, Sears Exclusive
EX $100   NM $175   MIP $275

Big Trapper, 1976, Hasbro, without action figure, Model No. 7498
EX $75   NM $245   MIP $600

Big Trapper Adventure with Intruder, 1976, Hasbro, with action figure, Model No. 7494
EX $100   NM $150   MIP $425

Capture Copter, 1976, Hasbro, without action figure, Model No. 7480
EX $80   NM $175   MIP $325

Capture Copter Adventure with Intruder, 1976, Hasbro, with action figure, Model No. 7481
EX $110   NM $200   MIP $350

Chopper Cycle, 1973, Hasbro, 15" vehicle, J.C. Penney's, Model No. 59114
EX $30   NM $50   MIP $100

Combat Action Jeep, 1973, Hasbro, 18" vehicle, J.C. Penney's, Model No. 59751
EX $50   NM $65   MIP $125

Combat Jeep and Trailer, 1976, Hasbro, Model No. 7000
EX $80   NM $135   MIP $550

Devil of the Deep, 1974, Hasbro, Model No. 7439
EX $80   NM $135   MIP $325

Fantastic Sea Wolf Submarine, 1975, Hasbro, Model No. 7460
EX $60   NM $100   MIP $175

(ToyShop File Photo)

Fate of the Troubleshooter, 1974, Hasbro, Includes vehicle, vulture, instructions and comic book, Model No. 7450
EX $85   NM $210   MIP $310

Giant Air-Sea Helicopter, 1973, Hasbro, 28" vehicle, J.C. Penney's, Model No. 59189
EX $50   NM $125   MIP $225

Helicopter, 1973, Hasbro, 14", yellow, with working winch, Model No. 7380
EX $50   NM $90   MIP $150

Helicopter, 1976, Hasbro, Model No. 7380
EX $50   NM $90   MIP $300

Mobile Support Vehicle Set, 1972, Hasbro, Model No. 7499
EX $125   NM $200   MIP $425

(ToyShop File Photo)

Recovery of the Lost Mummy Adventure Set, 1971, Hasbro, Sears Exclusive
EX $125   NM $250   MIP $575

Sandstorm Survival Adventure, 1974, Hasbro, Model No. 7493
EX $125   NM $200   MIP $335

Search for the Stolen Idol Set, 1971, Hasbro, Model No. 7418
EX $120   NM $225   MIP $400

Secret of the Mummy's Tomb Set, 1970, Hasbro, with Land Adventurer figure, shirt, pants, boots, insignia, pith helmet, pick, shovel, Mummy's tomb, net, gems, vehicle with winch, comic, Model No. 7441
EX $250   NM $600   MIP $1500

Sharks Surprise Set with Sea Adventurer, 1970, Hasbro, Model No. 7442
EX $250   NM $375   MIP $550

Signal All Terrain Vehicle, 1973, Hasbro, J.C. Penney's, 12" vehicle
EX $30   NM $65   MIP $125

Sky Hawk, 1975, Hasbro, 5-3/4-foot wingspan, Model No. 7470
EX $65   NM $100   MIP $175

Spacewalk Mystery Set with Astronaut, 1970, Hasbro, Model No. 7445
EX $225   NM $300   MIP $550

Trapped in the Coils of Doom, 1974, Hasbro, J.C. Penney's Exclusive, Model No. 79-59301
EX $250   NM $300   MIP $550

ADVENTURES OF G.I. JOE

Figure Sets

Aquanaut, 1969, Hasbro, Model No. 7910
EX $175   NM $550   MIP $3000

Negro Adventurer, 1969, Hasbro, Sears Exclusive, includes painted hair figure, blue jeans, pullover sweater, shoulder holster and pistol, plus product letter from Sears, Model No. 7905
EX $450   NM $750   MIP $2750

Sharks Surprise Set with Frogman, 1969, Hasbro, with figure, orange scuba suit, blue sea sled, air tanks, harpoon, face mask, treasure chest, shark, instructions and comic, Model No. 7980
EX $125   NM $300   MIP $750

Talking Astronaut, 1969, Hasbro, hard-hand figure with white coveralls with insignias, white boots, dog tags, Model No. 7615
EX $85   NM $275   MIP $1000

Uniform/Equipment Sets

Adventure Locker, 1969, Hasbro, Footlocker, Model No. 7940
EX $165   NM $400   MIP $450

Aqua Locker, 1969, Hasbro, Footlocker, Model No. 7941
EX $110   NM $180   MIP $325

Astro Locker, 1969, Hasbro, Footlocker, Model No. 7942
EX $90   NM $225   MIP $375

Danger of the Depths Underwater Diver Set, 1969, Hasbro, Model No. 7920
EX $140   NM $275   MIP $500

Eight Ropes of Danger Set, 1969, Hasbro, diving suit, treasure chest, octopus, Model No. 7950
EX $110   NM $225   MIP $525

Fantastic Freefall Set, 1969, Hasbro, includes figure with parachute and pack, blinker light, air vest, flash light, crash helmet with visor and oxygen mask, dog tags, orange jump suit, black boots, Model No. 7951
EX $150   NM $325   MIP $675

Flight for Survival Set with Polar Explorer, 1969, Hasbro, reissue, Model No. 7982.83
EX $150   NM $300   MIP $500

Hidden Missile Discovery Set, 1969, Hasbro, Model No. 7952
EX $70   NM $135   MIP $400

Mouth of Doom Set, 1969, Hasbro, Model No. 7953
EX $125   NM $250   MIP $550

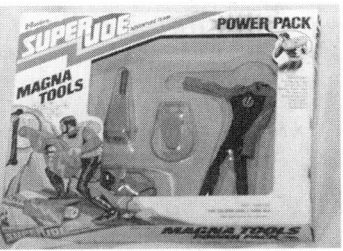

(ToyShop File Photo)

Mysterious Explosion Set, 1969, Hasbro, basic, Model No. 7921
EX $60   NM $180   MIP $425

Perilous Rescue Set, 1969, Hasbro, basic, Model No. 7923
EX $150   NM $300   MIP $500

Secret Mission to Spy Island Set, 1969, Hasbro, basic, Model No. 7922
EX $110   NM $225   MIP $545

Vehicle Sets

Sharks Surprise Set with Frogman, 1969, Hasbro, Model No. 7980
EX $175   NM $325   MIP $650

Sharks Surprise Set without Frogman, 1969, Hasbro, Model No. 7980.83
EX $150   NM $300   MIP $550

Spacewalk Mystery Set with Spaceman, 1969, Hasbro, Model No. 7981
EX $150   NM $375   MIP $650

Spacewalk Mystery Set without Spaceman, 1969, Hasbro, reissue, Model No. 7981.83
EX $125   NM $275   MIP $550

GI JOE ACTION SERIES, ARMY, NAVY, MARINE AND AIR FORCE

Uniform/Equipment Sets

Basic Footlocker, 1965, Hasbro, Model No. 8000
EX $50   NM $75   MIP $175

Footlocker Adventure Pack, 1968, Hasbro, 22 pieces, Model No. 8002.83
EX $70   NM $145   MIP $450

Footlocker Adventure Pack, 1968, Hasbro, 15 pieces, Model No. 8001.83
EX $65   NM $135   MIP $450

Footlocker Adventure Pack, 1968, Hasbro, 16 pieces, Model No. 8000.83
EX $65   NM $135   MIP $450

Footlocker Adventure Pack, 1968, Hasbro, 15 pieces, Model No. 8002.83
EX $65   NM $135   MIP $450

SUPER JOE

Figure Sets

Gor, 1977, Hasbro, Model No. 7510
EX $40   NM $70   MIP $130

Luminos, 1977, Hasbro, Model No. 7506
EX $45   NM $70   MIP $130

Super Joe, 1977, Hasbro, Model No. 7503
EX $20   NM $35   MIP $70

Super Joe (Black), 1977, Hasbro, Model No. 7504
EX $35   NM $50   MIP $100

Super Joe Commander, 1977, Hasbro, Model No. 7501
EX $25   NM $45   MIP $75

The Shield, 1977, Hasbro, Model No. 7505
EX $40   NM $65   MIP $125

Uniform/Equipment Sets

Aqua Laser, 1977, Hasbro, Model No. 7528-1
EX $10   NM $20   MIP $30

Edge of Adventure, 1977, Hasbro, Model No. 7518-2
EX $10   NM $20   MIP $35

Emergency Rescue, 1977, Hasbro, Model No. 7518-3
EX $10   NM $20   MIP $30

Fusion Bazooka, 1977, Hasbro, Model No. 7528-3
EX $10   NM $20   MIP $30

Helipak, 1977, Hasbro, Model No. 7538-2
EX $10   NM $20   MIP $30

Invisible Danger, 1977, Hasbro, Model No. 7518-1
EX $10   NM $20   MIP $35

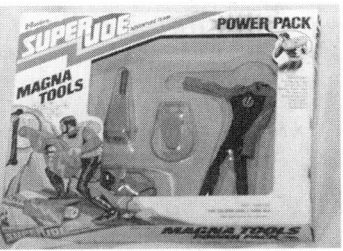

(ToyShop File Photo)

Magna Tools, 1977, Hasbro, With uniform and rock-cutting drill and saw, Model No. 7538-1
EX $10   NM $20   MIP $30

Path of Danger, 1977, Hasbro, Model No. 7518-4
EX $10   NM $20   MIP $30

Sonic Scanner, 1977, Hasbro, Model No. 7538-3
EX $10   NM $20   MIP $30

Treacherous Dive, 1977, Hasbro, Model No. 7528-2
EX $10   NM $20   MIP $30

Vehicle Sets

Rocket Command Center, 1977, Hasbro, Super Adventure Set including Gor, Model No. 7571
EX $60   NM $115   MIP $225

Rocket Command Center, 1977, Hasbro, Model No. 7570
EX $50   NM $100   MIP $200

3-3/4" FIGURES

SERIES 01, COBRA

Figure Sets

Cobra, 1982, Hasbro, Infantry Soldier, Model No. 6423
EX $25   NM $55   MIP $140

Cobra Commander, 1982, Hasbro, mail order; Commanding Leader
EX $25   NM $55   MIP $175

Cobra Officer, 1982, Hasbro, Infantry Officer, Model No. 6424
EX $25   NM $55   MIP $130

Major Bludd, 1982, Hasbro, mail order; Mercenary with card, Model No. 6426
EX $18   NM $30   MIP $110

SERIES 01, GI JOE

Figure Sets

Breaker, 1982, Hasbro, Communications Officer, Model No. 6403
EX $20   NM $35   MIP $85

Flash, 1982, Hasbro, Laser Rifle Trooper, Model No. 6406
EX $20   NM $35   MIP $85

Grunt, 1982, Hasbro, Infantry Trooper, Model No. 6409
EX $20   NM $35   MIP $85

Rock 'n Roll, 1982, Hasbro, Machine Gunner, Model No. 6408
EX $30   **NM** $50   **MIP** $95

Scarlett, 1982, Hasbro, Counter Intelligence, Model No. 6407
EX $40   **NM** $85   **MIP** $175

Short-Fuze, 1982, Hasbro, Mortar Soldier, Model No. 6402
EX $20   **NM** $35   **MIP** $75

Snake Eyes, 1982, Hasbro, Commando, Model No. 6404
EX $45   **NM** $85   **MIP** $180

Stalker, 1982, Hasbro, Ranger, Model No. 6401
EX $25   **NM** $40   **MIP** $125

Zap, 1982, Hasbro, Bazooka Soldier, Model No. 6405
EX $20   **NM** $35   **MIP** $85

Uniform/Equipment Sets

F.L.A.K., 1982, Hasbro, Attack Cannon, Model No. 6075
EX $20   **NM** $45   **MIP** $80

H.A.L., 1982, Hasbro, Heavy Artillery Laser with Grand Slam, Model No. 6052
EX $30   **NM** $55   **MIP** $125

J.U.M.P., 1982, Hasbro, Jet Pack with Platform, Model No. 6071
EX $20   **NM** $45   **MIP** $80

M.M.S., 1982, Hasbro, Mobile Missile System with Hawk, Model No. 6054
EX $20   **NM** $45   **MIP** $80

Vehicle Sets

M.O.B.A.T., 1982, Hasbro, Motorized Battle Tank with Steeler, Model No. 6000
EX $40   **NM** $75   **MIP** $140

R.A.M., 1982, Hasbro, Rapid Fire Motorcycle, Model No. 6073
EX $15   **NM** $25   **MIP** $55

V.A.M.P., 1982, Hasbro, Multi-Purpose Attack Vehicle with Clutch, Model No. 6050
EX $30   **NM** $65   **MIP** $90

SERIES 02, COBRA

Figure Sets

Cobra, 1983, Hasbro, Reissue, Model No. 6423
EX $25   **NM** $50   **MIP** $110

Cobra Commander, 1983, Hasbro, Reissue, Model No. 6425
EX $25   **NM** $50   **MIP** $110

Cobra Officer, 1983, Hasbro, Reissue, Model No. 6424
EX $25   **NM** $50   **MIP** $110

Destro, 1983, Hasbro, Enemy Weapons Supplier, Model No. 6427
EX $25   **NM** $50   **MIP** $75

Major Bludd, 1983, Hasbro, Model No. 6426
EX $15   **NM** $30   **MIP** $65

Uniform/Equipment Sets

Headquarters Missile-Command Center, 1983, Hasbro, with three figures, Model No. 6200
EX $65   **NM** $125   **MIP** $250

S.N.A.K.E., 1983, Hasbro, One-Man Battle Armor, Model No. 6083
EX $10   **NM** $25   **MIP** $50

Vehicle Sets

Cobra Glider, 1983, Hasbro, Attack Glider with Viper, Model No. 6097
EX $35   **NM** $75   **MIP** $150

F.A.N.G., 1983, Hasbro, Fully Armed Negator Gyro Copter, Model No. 6077
EX $10   **NM** $20   **MIP** $40

H.I.S.S., 1983, Hasbro, High Speed Sentry Tank with H.I.S.S., Model No. 6051
EX $35   **NM** $70   **MIP** $125

SERIES 02, GI JOE

Figure Sets

Airborne, 1983, Hasbro, Helicopter Assault Trooper, Model No. 6411
EX $15   **NM** $35   **MIP** $75

Breaker, 1983, Hasbro, Reissue, Model No. 6403
EX $15   **NM** $30   **MIP** $65

Doc, 1983, Hasbro, Medic, Model No. 6415
EX $20   **NM** $40   **MIP** $75

Duke, 1983, Hasbro, mail order; Master Sergeant
EX $20   **NM** $55   **MIP** $100

Flash, 1983, Hasbro, Reissue, Model No. 6406
EX $20   **NM** $35   **MIP** $85

Grunt, 1983, Hasbro, Reissue, Model No. 6409
EX $20   **NM** $35   **MIP** $85

Gung-Ho, 1983, Hasbro, Marine, Model No. 6414
EX $20   **NM** $40   **MIP** $85

Rock 'n Roll, 1983, Hasbro, Reissue, Model No. 6408
EX $30   **NM** $50   **MIP** $95

Scarlett, 1983, Hasbro, Reissue, Model No. 6407
EX $40   **NM** $85   **MIP** $175

Short-Fuze, 1983, Hasbro, Reissue, Model No. 6402
EX $20   **NM** $35   **MIP** $75

Snake Eyes, 1983, Hasbro, Reissue, Model No. 6404
EX $40   **NM** $80   **MIP** $180

Snow Job, 1983, Hasbro, Arctic Trooper, Model No. 6412
EX $15   **NM** $35   **MIP** $75

Stalker, 1983, Hasbro, Reissue, Model No. 6401
EX $25   **NM** $45   **MIP** $100

Torpedo, 1983, Hasbro, Navy S.E.A.L., Model No. 6413
EX $15   **NM** $35   **MIP** $75

Tripwire, 1983, Hasbro, Mine Detector, Model No. 6410
EX $15   **NM** $30   **MIP** $65

Zap, 1983, Hasbro, Reissue, Model No. 6405
EX $15   **NM** $30   **MIP** $65

Uniform/Equipment Sets

Battle Gear Accessory Pack #1, 1983, Hasbro, Model No. 6088
EX $10   **NM** $20   **MIP** $40

Headquarters Command Center, 1983, Hasbro, Model No. 6020
EX $50   **NM** $95   **MIP** $175

Jump, 1983, Hasbro, Jet Pack and Platform with Grand Slam, Model No. 6065
EX $25   **NM** $50   **MIP** $115

Pac/Rats Flamethrower, 1983, Hasbro, Remote Control Weapon, Model No. 6086-1
EX $10   **NM** $25   **MIP** $40

Pac/Rats Machine Gun, 1983, Hasbro, Remote Control Weapon, Model No. 6086-2
EX $10   **NM** $25   **MIP** $40

Pac/Rats Missile Launcher, 1983, Hasbro, Remote Control Weapon, Model No. 6086-3
EX $10   **NM** $25   **MIP** $40

Whirlwind, 1983, Hasbro, Twin Battle Gun, Model No. 6074
EX $10   **NM** $25   **MIP** $45

Vehicle Sets

A.P.C., 1983, Hasbro, Amphibious Personnel Carrier, Model No. 6093
EX $25   **NM** $55   **MIP** $90

Dragon Fly XH-1, 1983, Hasbro, Assault Copter with Wild Bill, Model No. 4025
EX $25   **NM** $65   **MIP** $125

Falcon, 1983, Hasbro, Attack Glider with Grunt, Model No. 6097
EX $30   **NM** $75   **MIP** $150

Polar Battle Bear, 1983, Hasbro, Sky Mobile, Model No. 6072
EX $15   **NM** $25   **MIP** $40

Sky Striker XP-14F, 1983, Hasbro, F-14 Jet and Parachute with Ace, Model No. 6010
EX $35   **NM** $75   **MIP** $150

Wolverine, 1983, Hasbro, Armored Missile Vehicle with Cover Girl, Model No. 6048
EX $25   **NM** $50   **MIP** $100

SERIES 03, COBRA

Figure Sets

Baroness, 1984, Hasbro, Intelligence Officer, Model No. 6428
EX $50   **NM** $85   **MIP** $175

Cobra Commander, 1984, Hasbro, mail order; Enemy Leader with Hood, Model No. 6425
EX $10   **NM** $20   **MIP** $40

Fire Fly, 1984, Hasbro, Saboteur, Model No. 6432
EX $45   **NM** $85   **MIP** $180

Scrap-Iron, 1984, Hasbro, Anti-Armor Specialist, Model No. 6431
EX $17   **NM** $30   **MIP** $60

Storm Shadow, 1984, Hasbro, Ninja, Model No. 6429
EX $40   **NM** $80   **MIP** $150

Uniform/Equipment Sets

A.S.P., 1984, Hasbro, Assault System Pod, Model No. 6070
EX $15   **NM** $30   **MIP** $50

C.L.A.W., 1984, Hasbro, Cobra Covert Light Aerial Weapons, Model No. 6081-1
EX $15   **NM** $30   **MIP** $50

S.N.A.K.E., 1984, Hasbro, One-Man Armored Suit (white), Model No. 6081-2
EX $10   **NM** $25   **MIP** $50

Vehicle Sets

Rattler, 1984, Hasbro, Ground Attack Jet with Wild Weasel, Model No. 6027
EX $25   **NM** $55   **MIP** $110

Stinger, 1984, Hasbro, Night Attack Jeep with Cobra Officer, Model No. 6055
EX $20   **NM** $40   **MIP** $80

Swamp Skier, 1984, Hasbro, Chameleon Vehicle with Zartan, Model No. 6064
EX $55   **NM** $95   **MIP** $145

Water Moccasin, 1984, Hasbro, Swamp Boat with Copperhead, Model No. 6058
EX $35   **NM** $65   **MIP** $95

SERIES 03, GI JOE

Figure Sets

Blow Torch, 1984, Hasbro, Flamethrower, Model No. 6421
EX $10   **NM** $20   **MIP** $50

Duke, 1984, Hasbro, First Sergeant, Model No. 6422
EX $15   **NM** $25   **MIP** $75

Mutt, 1984, Hasbro, Dog Handler with Dog, Model No. 6416
EX $15   **NM** $25   **MIP** $65

Recondo, 1984, Hasbro, Jungle Trooper, Model No. 6420
EX $15   **NM** $25   **MIP** $60

Rip Cord, 1984, Hasbro, H.A.L.O. Jumper, Model No. 6418
EX $15   **NM** $25   **MIP** $50

Roadblock, 1984, Hasbro, Heavy Machine Gunner, Model No. 6419
EX $25   **NM** $45   **MIP** $75

Spirit, 1984, Hasbro, Tracker with Eagle, Model No. 6417
EX $22   **NM** $45   **MIP** $75

Uniform/Equipment Sets

Battle Gear Accessory Pack #2, 1984, Hasbro, Model No. 6092
EX $10   **NM** $20   **MIP** $40

Bivouac, 1984, Hasbro, Battle Station, Model No. 6125-1
EX $10   **NM** $25   **MIP** $35

M.A.N.T.A., 1984, Hasbro, mail order; Marine Assault Nautical Air Driven Transport
EX $10   **NM** $20   **MIP** $35

Machine Gun Defense Unit, 1984, Hasbro, Model No. 6129-2
EX $10   **NM** $20   **MIP** $35

Missile Defense Unit, 1984, Hasbro, Model No. 6129-1
EX $10   **NM** $15   **MIP** $25

Mortar Defense Unit, 1984, Hasbro, Model No. 6129-3
EX $10   **NM** $15   **MIP** $25

Mountain Howitzer, 1984, Hasbro, Model No. 6125-3
EX $10   **NM** $15   **MIP** $25

Watchtower, 1984, Hasbro, Model No. 6125-2
EX $10   **NM** $15   **MIP** $25

Vehicle Sets

(ToyShop File Photo)

Hovercraft Killer W.H.A.L.E., 1984, Hasbro, Armored Hovercraft with Cutter driver, Model No. 6005
EX $40   **NM** $75   **MIP** $130

RAM, HAL & VAMP, 1984, Hasbro, three-piece, die-cast set, Model No. 74450
EX $10   **NM** $20   **MIP** $40

(KP Photo, Karen O'Brien collection)

S.H.A.R.C., 1984, Hasbro, Submersible High-Speed Attack & Recon Craft with Deep Six figure (shown), Model No. 6049
EX $25   **NM** $55   **MIP** $100

Sky Hawk, 1984, Hasbro, V.T.O.L. Jet, Model No. 6079
EX $15   **NM** $30   **MIP** $45

Slugger, 1984, Hasbro, Self-Propelled Cannon with Thunder, Model No. 6056
EX $15   **NM** $35   **MIP** $65

(ToyShop File Photo)

V.A.M.P. and H.A.L., 1984, Hasbro, Sears exclusive, no figures, Model No. 7444-2
EX $10   **NM** $15   **MIP** $25

V.A.M.P. Mark II, 1984, Hasbro, w/ Clutch (tan version) driver, Model No. 7444-1
EX $25   **NM** $40   **MIP** $85

SERIES 04, COBRA

Figure Sets

Buzzer, 1985, Hasbro, Mercenary, Model No. 6433
EX $15   **NM** $30   **MIP** $60

Crimson Guard, 1985, Hasbro, Elite Trooper, Model No. 6450
EX $25   **NM** $50   **MIP** $110

Eel, 1985, Hasbro, Frogman, Model No. 6448
EX $22   **NM** $30   **MIP** $60

Ripper, 1985, Hasbro, Mercenary, Model No. 6434
EX $15   **NM** $30   **MIP** $60

Snow Serpent, 1985, Hasbro, Polar Assault Trooper, Model No. 6449
EX $20   **NM** $40   **MIP** $70

Tele-Viper, 1985, Hasbro, Communications Trooper, Model No. 6447
EX $15   **NM** $30   **MIP** $60

Tomax and Xamot, 1985, Hasbro, Crimson Guard Commanders, Model No. 6063
EX $45   **NM** $75   **MIP** $165

Torch, 1985, Hasbro, Mercenary, Model No. 6435
EX $15   **NM** $30   **MIP** $60

Uniform/Equipment Sets

Cobra Bunker, 1985, Hasbro, Battle Station, Model No. 6125
EX $5   **NM** $15   **MIP** $25

Cobra Rifle Range Unit, 1985, Hasbro, Battlefield Accessories, Model No. 6129
EX $5   **NM** $15   **MIP** $25

Flight Pod, 1985, Hasbro, Trouble-Bubble, One-Man Bubble Pod, Model No. 6081
EX $12   **NM** $20   **MIP** $35

Night Landing, 1985, Hasbro, small boat, Model No. 6085
EX $5   **NM** $15   **MIP** $25

Vehicle Sets

C.A.T., 1985, Hasbro, Motorized Crimson Attack Tank, Sears exclusive
EX $25   **NM** $45   **MIP** $95

Ferret, 1985, Hasbro, All-Terrain Vehicle, Model No. 6069
EX $10   **NM** $15   **MIP** $35

Moray, 1985, Hasbro, Cobra Hydrofoil with Lamprey, Model No. 6024
EX $25   **NM** $45   **MIP** $80

Sentry and Missile System, S.M.S., 1985, Hasbro, Sears exclusive, with H.I.S.S. Tank, Model No. 6686
EX $75   **NM** $150   **MIP** $250

SERIES 04, GI JOE

Figure Sets

Airtight, 1985, Hasbro, Hostile Environment Trooper, Model No. 6439
EX $20   **NM** $40   **MIP** $60

Alpine, 1985, Hasbro, Mountain Trooper, Model No. 6443
EX $15   **NM** $25   **MIP** $55

Barbecue, 1985, Hasbro, Fire Fighter, Model No. 6445
EX $20   **NM** $30   **MIP** $60

Bazooka, 1985, Hasbro, Missile Specialist, Model No. 6438
EX $20   **NM** $30   **MIP** $65

Dusty, 1985, Hasbro, Desert Trooper, Model No. 6442
EX $15   **NM** $30   **MIP** $65

Flint, 1985, Hasbro, Warrant Officer, Model No. 6436
EX $22   **NM** $35   **MIP** $70

Footloose, 1985, Hasbro, Infantry Trooper, Model No. 6444
EX $15   **NM** $30   **MIP** $60

Lady Jaye, 1985, Hasbro, Covert Operations Officer, Model No. 6440
EX $30   **NM** $55   **MIP** $100

Quick Kick, 1985, Hasbro, Silent Weapons Martial Artist, Model No. 6441
EX $20   **NM** $40   **MIP** $85

Shipwreck, 1985, Hasbro, Sailor and Parrot, Model No. 6446
EX $22   **NM** $40   **MIP** $85

Snake Eyes, 1985, Hasbro, Commando and Wolf, Model No. 6437
EX $45   **NM** $75   **MIP** $145

Tripwire, 1985, Hasbro, Mine Detector, Model No. 6102
EX $20   **NM** $35   **MIP** $75

Uniform/Equipment Sets

Air Defense, 1985, Hasbro, Battle Station, Model No. 6125-2
EX $10   **NM** $15   **MIP** $25

Ammo Dump, 1985, Hasbro, Battlefield Accessories, Model No. 6129-1
EX $10   **NM** $15   **MIP** $25

Battle Gear Accessory Pack #3, 1985, Hasbro, Model No. 6092
EX $5   **NM** $10   **MIP** $15

Bomb Disposal, 1985, Hasbro, small vehicle, Model No. 6085-2
EX $10   **NM** $15   **MIP** $25

Check Point, 1985, Hasbro, Battle Station, Model No. 6125-1
EX $10   **NM** $15   **MIP** $25

Forward Observer Unit, 1985, Hasbro, Battlefield Accessories, Model No. 6129-2
EX $10   **NM** $15   **MIP** $25

Parachute Pack, 1985, Hasbro, mail order; HALO parachute pack with working parachute, available from 1985-89
EX $5   **NM** $10   **MIP** $20

(ToyShop File Photo)

Transportable Tactical Battle Platform, 1985, Hasbro, with crane, heli-pad, swivel guns and missile launcher, Model No. 6021
EX $15   **NM** $30   **MIP** $60

Weapon Transport, 1985, Hasbro, small vehicle, Model No. 6085-1
EX $10   **NM** $18   **MIP** $25

Vehicle Sets

A.W.E. Striker, 1985, Hasbro, All-Weather Environment Jeep with Crankcase driver, Model No. 6053
EX $30   **NM** $25   **MIP** $60

Armadillo Mini Tank, 1985, Hasbro, holds up to three figures, Model No. 6078
EX $17   **NM** $25   **MIP** $35

Bridge Layer Toss 'n Cross, 1985, Hasbro, Bridge Laying Trank with Toll Booth, Model No. 6023
EX $22   **NM** $25   **MIP** $55

Mauler M.B.T. Tank, 1985, Hasbro, Motorized Battle Tank w/ Heavy Metal driver, Model No. 6015
EX $25   **NM** $45   **MIP** $85

Silver Mirage, 1985, Hasbro, Motorcycle with Sidecar, Model No. 6076
EX $18   **NM** $30   **MIP** $50

Snow Cat, 1985, Hasbro, Snow Half-Track Vehicle with Frost-Bite, Model No. 6057
EX $25   **NM** $45   **MIP** $75

U.S.S. Flagg, 1985, Hasbro, Aircraft Carrier with Admiral Keel Haul, Model No. 6001
EX $145   **NM** $275   **MIP** $550

SERIES 05, COBRA

Figure Sets

B.A.T., 1986, Hasbro, Battle Android Trooper, Model No. 6456
EX $15   **NM** $20   **MIP** $35

Dr. Mindbender, 1986, Hasbro, Master of Mind Control, Model No. 6461
EX $10   **NM** $20   **MIP** $35

Monkeywrench, 1986, Hasbro, Mercenary, Model No. 6460
EX $10   **NM** $20   **MIP** $35

Viper, 1986, Hasbro, Infantry Trooper, Model No. 6473
EX $10   **NM** $20   **MIP** $35

Zandar, 1986, Hasbro, Zartan's Brother, Mercenary, Model No. 6457
EX $10   **NM** $20   **MIP** $35

Zarana, 1986, Hasbro, Zartan's Sister, Mercenary, without earrings, Model No. 6472
EX $10   **NM** $15   **MIP** $35

Zarana, 1986, Hasbro, Reissue with earrings, Model No. 6472
EX $30   **NM** $65   **MIP** $125

Uniform/Equipment Sets

Battle Gear Accessory Pack #4, 1986, Hasbro, Model No. 6096
EX $5   **NM** $10   **MIP** $15

Surveillance Port, 1986, Hasbro, Battle Station, Model No. 6130
EX $7   **NM** $14   **MIP** $25

Terrordrome, 1986, Hasbro, Armored Headquarters with Firebat Jet and A.V.A.C. pilot, Model No. 6003
EX $100   **NM** $165   **MIP** $310

Vehicle Sets

Air Chariot, 1986, Hasbro, w/ Serpentor "Cobra Emperor", Model No. 6062
EX $15   **NM** $20   **MIP** $55

Cobra Hydro Sled, 1986, Hasbro, small vehicle, Model No. 6099-2
EX $10   **NM** $15   **MIP** $25

Dreadnok Air Assault, 1986, Hasbro, Sears Exclusive, VTOL and Gyrocopter
EX $10   **NM** $15   **MIP** $25

Dreadnok Ground Assault, 1986, Hasbro, Sears Exclusive, motorcycle and 4WD vehicle
EX $10   **NM** $20   **MIP** $25

Dreadnok Swampfire, 1986, Hasbro, Air/Swamp Transforming Vehicle with Color-Change, Model No. 6068
EX $10   **NM** $20   **MIP** $30

Dreadnok Thunder Machine, 1986, Hasbro, Compilation vehicle of spare car and truck parts, designed by Destro, w/ Thrasher driver, Model No. 6042
EX $10   **NM** $20   **MIP** $35

Night Raven S-3P, 1986, Hasbro, Surveillance Jet with Drone Pod and Strato Viper pilot, Model No. 6014
EX $25   **NM** $45   **MIP** $75

Stun, 1986, Hasbro, Split Attack Vehicle with Motor Viper driver, Model No. 6041
EX $10   **NM** $20   **MIP** $35

SERIES 05, GI JOE

Figure Sets

Beach Head, 1986, Hasbro, Ranger, Model No. 6463
EX $15   **NM** $22   **MIP** $40

Dial-Tone, 1986, Hasbro, Communications Expert, Model No. 6471
EX $15   **NM** $22   **MIP** $40

Hawk, 1986, Hasbro, Commander, Model No. 6468
EX $15   **NM** $22   **MIP** $40

Iceberg, 1986, Hasbro, Snow Trooper, Model No. 6466
EX $15   **NM** $22   **MIP** $40

Leatherneck, 1986, Hasbro, Marine Gunner, Model No. 6458
EX $15   **NM** $22   **MIP** $40

Lifeline, 1986, Hasbro, Rescue Trooper, Model No. 6465
EX $15   **NM** $22   **MIP** $40

Low-Light, 1986, Hasbro, Night Spotter, Model No. 6459
EX $10   **NM** $15   **MIP** $30

Mainframe, 1986, Hasbro, Computer Specialist, Model No. 6462
EX $10   **NM** $15   **MIP** $30

Roadblock, 1986, Hasbro, Heavy Machine Gunner, Model No. 6467
EX $10   **NM** $15   **MIP** $30

Sci-Fi, 1986, Hasbro, Laser Trooper, Model No. 6469
EX $10   **NM** $15   **MIP** $30

Special Missions: Brazil, 1986, Hasbro, Toys R Us set with five figures: Dial-Tone, Mainframe, Wet-Suit, Leatherneck, and Claymore (this figure's only appearance)
EX $75   **NM** $150   **MIP** $300

The Fridge, 1986, Hasbro, Mail order, Physical Training Instructor
EX $10   **NM** $15   **MIP** $30

Wet-Suit, 1986, Hasbro, Navy S.E.A.L., Model No. 6470
EX $15   **NM** $20   **MIP** $40

Uniform/Equipment Sets

Outpost Defender, 1986, Hasbro, Battle Station, Model No. 6130
EX $5   **NM** $10   **MIP** $15

Vehicle Sets

Conquest X-30, 1986, Hasbro, Super-Sonic Jet with Slip-Stream pilot, Model No. 6031
EX $30   **NM** $65   **MIP** $110

Devilfish, 1986, Hasbro, High-Speed Attack Boat, Model No. 6066
EX $10   **NM** $15   **MIP** $25

H.A.V.O.C., 1986, Hasbro, Heavy Artillery Vehicle Ordinance Carrier with Cross-Country driver, Model No. 6030
EX $10   **NM** $20   **MIP** $45

L.V.C. Recon Sled, 1986, Hasbro, Low-Crawl Vehicle Cycle, Model No. 6067
EX $10   **NM** $15   **MIP** $25

Tomahawk, 1986, Hasbro, Troop Transit Helicopter with Lift-Ticket, Model No. 6022
EX $45   **NM** $90   **MIP** $135

Triple T (Tag Team Terminator), 1986, Hasbro, One-man tank with Sgt. Slaughter driver, Model No. 6061
EX $10   **NM** $25   **MIP** $50

SERIES 06, COBRA

Figure Sets

Big Boa, 1987, Hasbro, Troop Trainer, Model No. 6484
EX $8   **NM** $14   **MIP** $20

Cobra Commander, 1987, Hasbro, Cobra Leader with Battle Armor, Model No. 6474
EX $10   **NM** $15   **MIP** $30

Cobra-La Team, 1987, Hasbro, Three-figure set: Nemesis Enforcer, Royal Guard, Golobulus, Model No. 6154
EX $20   **NM** $40   **MIP** $75

Croc Master, 1987, Hasbro, Reptile Trainer, Model No. 6487
EX $10   **NM** $15   **MIP** $30

Crystal Ball, 1987, Hasbro, Hypnotist, Model No. 6479
EX $8   **NM** $14   **MIP** $20

Raptor, 1987, Hasbro, Falconer, Model No. 6485
EX $8   **NM** $14   **MIP** $20

Techno-Viper, 1987, Hasbro, Battlefield Technician, Model No. 6490
EX $8   **NM** $14   **MIP** $20

Uniform/Equipment Sets

Cobra Jet Pack, 1987, Hasbro, accessory for figures
EX $8   **NM** $14   **MIP** $15

Earth Borer, 1987, Hasbro, Motorized Action Packs, Model No. 6133-3
EX $8   **NM** $14   **MIP** $15

Mountain Climber, 1987, Hasbro, Motorized Action Packs, Model No. 6133-7
EX $8   **NM** $14   **MIP** $15

Pom-Pom Gun Pack, 1987, Hasbro, Motorized Action Packs, Model No. 6133-8
EX $8   **NM** $14   **MIP** $15

Rope Crosser, 1987, Hasbro, Motorized Action Packs, Model No. 6133-5
EX $8   **NM** $14   **MIP** $15

Vehicle Sets

Buzz Boar, 1987, Hasbro, Underground Attack Vehicle, Model No. 6087-3
EX $8   **NM** $14   **MIP** $15

Dreadnok Air Skiff, 1987, Hasbro, Mini-set with Zanzibar, Model No. 6070
EX $10   **NM** $20   **MIP** $30

Dreadnok Cycle, 1987, Hasbro, Compilation Cycle with Gunner Station, Model No. 6171
EX $8   **NM** $14   **MIP** $20

Maggot, 1987, Hasbro, three-in-one tank vehicle with W.O.R.M.S. driver, Model No. 6029
EX $10   **NM** $15   **MIP** $35

Mamba, 1987, Hasbro, Attack Copter with removable pods with Gyro-Viper, Model No. 6026
EX $10   **NM** $15   **MIP** $30

Pogo, 1987, Hasbro, Ballistic Battle Ball, Model No. 6170
EX $5   **NM** $10   **MIP** $20

Sea Ray, 1987, Hasbro, Combination Submarine/Jet with Sea Slug, Model No. 6040
EX $10   **NM** $20   **MIP** $40

Wolf, 1987, Hasbro, Arctic Terrain Vehicle with Ice Viper, Model No. 6039
EX $10   **NM** $20   **MIP** $45

SERIES 06, GI JOE

Figure Sets

Battleforce 2000 Avalanche, 1987, Hasbro, Dominator Snow Vehicle Driver
EX $10   **NM** $20   **MIP** $30

Battleforce 2000 Blaster, 1987, Hasbro, Vindicator Hovercraft pilot
EX $10   **NM** $20   **MIP** $30

Battleforce 2000 Blocker, 1987, Hasbro, 4-wheeled driver
EX $10   **NM** $20   **MIP** $30

Battleforce 2000 Dodger, 1987, Hasbro, Marauder Half-Track driver
EX $10   **NM** $20   **MIP** $30

Battleforce 2000 Knockdown, 1987, Hasbro, Sky Sweeper Anti-Aircraft operator
EX $10   **NM** $20   **MIP** $30

Battleforce 2000 Maverick, 1987, Hasbro, Jet Fighter Pilot
EX $10   **NM** $20   **MIP** $30

Chuckles, 1987, Hasbro, Undercover M.P., Model No. 6482
EX $10   **NM** $14   **MIP** $25

Crazy Legs, 1987, Hasbro, Air Assault Trooper, Model No. 6475
EX $10   **NM** $15   **MIP** $30

Falcon, 1987, Hasbro, Green Beret, Model No. 6476
EX $10   **NM** $15   **MIP** $30

Fast Draw, 1987, Hasbro, Mobile Missile Specialist, Model No. 6488
EX $10   **NM** $15   **MIP** $25

Gung-Ho, 1987, Hasbro, Marine in Dress Blues, Model No. 6486
EX $10   **NM** $15   **MIP** $25

Jinx, 1987, Hasbro, Ninja Intelligence Officer, Model No. 6480
EX $10   **NM** $15   **MIP** $25

Law & Order, 1987, Hasbro, M.P. with Dog, Model No. 6478
EX $10   **NM** $15   **MIP** $25

Outback, 1987, Hasbro, Survivalist, Model No. 6483
EX $10   **NM** $15   **MIP** $20

Psyche-Out, 1987, Hasbro, Deceptive Warfare Trooper, Model No. 6477
EX $10   **NM** $15   **MIP** $20

Sgt. Slaughter's Renegades, 1987, Hasbro, Three-figure set: Red Dog, Mercer, Taurus, Model No. 6153
EX $10   **NM** $25   **MIP** $50

Sneak Peek, 1987, Hasbro, Advanced Recon Trooper, Model No. 6491
EX $10   **NM** $15   **MIP** $30

Starduster, 1987, Hasbro, Jet Pack Trooper, mail-in figure through 1991
EX $10   **NM** $20   **MIP** $30

Steel Brigade, 1987, Hasbro, Special Forces trooper, mail-in figure through 1994, five versions were produced
EX $10   **NM** $25   **MIP** $40

Tunnel Rat, 1987, Hasbro, Underground Explosive Expert, Model No. 6481
EX $10   **NM** $25   **MIP** $30

Uniform/Equipment Sets

Battle Gear Accessory Pack #5, 1987, Hasbro, Model No. 6677
EX $5   **NM** $10   **MIP** $15

Mobile Command Center, 1987, Hasbro, w/ Steam-Roller driver, large crane play set, Model No. 6006
EX $25   **NM** $50   **MIP** $100

Vehicle Gear Accessory Pack #1, 1987, Hasbro, Model No. 6098
EX $5   **NM** $10   **MIP** $15

Vehicle Sets

Anti-Aircraft Gun, 1987, Hasbro, Motorized Action Pack, Model No. 6133-1
EX $5   **NM** $10   **MIP** $15

Coastal Defender, 1987, Hasbro, Mini-Vehicle with accessories, Model No. 6087-2
EX $5   **NM** $10   **MIP** $15

Crossfire-Alfa, 1987, Hasbro, Radio Control Vehicle with Rumbler, Model No. 6004-1
EX $25   **NM** $50   **MIP** $100

Crossfire-Delta, 1987, Hasbro, Radio Control Vehicle with Rumbler, Model No. 6004-2
EX $25   **NM** $50   **MIP** $100

Defiant Space Shuttle Complex, 1987, Hasbro, Space shuttle, space station, crawler, Model No. 6002
EX $85   **NM** $350   **MIP** $525

Dominator Snow Tank, 1988, Hasbro, Battleforce 2000
EX $10   **NM** $14   **MIP** $25

Eliminator 4WD, 1988, Hasbro, Battleforce 2000
EX $10   **NM** $14   **MIP** $25

Helicopter, 1987, Hasbro, Motorized Action Pack, Model No. 6133-2
EX $10   **NM** $14   **MIP** $25

Marauder Motorcycle-Tank, 1988, Hasbro, Battleforce 2000
EX $10   **NM** $14   **MIP** $25

Outpost Defender, 1987, Hasbro
EX $10   **NM** $14   **MIP** $25

Persuader, 1987, Hasbro, Laser Tank with Backstop, Model No. 6038
EX $10   **NM** $15   **MIP** $35

Radar Station, 1987, Hasbro, Motorized Action Pack, Model No. 6133-3
EX $10   **NM** $14   **MIP** $25

Road Toad, 1987, Hasbro, Tow Vehicle with accessories, Model No. 6087-1
EX $10   **NM** $14   **MIP** $25

Rope Walker, 1987, Hasbro, Motorized Action Pack, Model No. 6133-4
EX $10   **NM** $14   **MIP** $25

S.L.A.M., 1987, Hasbro, Strategic Long-Range Artillery Machine, Model No. 6172
EX $10   **NM** $15   **MIP** $30

Sky Sweeper Anti-Aircraft Tank, 1988, Hasbro, Battleforce 2000
EX $5   **NM** $12   **MIP** $20

Vector Jet, 1988, Hasbro, Battleforce 2000
EX $5   **NM** $12   **MIP** $20

Vindicator Hovercraft, 1988, Hasbro, Battleforce 2000
EX $5   **NM** $12   **MIP** $20

SERIES 07, COBRA

Figure Sets

Astro-Viper, 1988, Hasbro, Cobranaut
EX $7   **NM** $14   **MIP** $25

Hydro-Viper, 1988, Hasbro, Underwater Elite Trooper
EX $7   **NM** $14   **MIP** $25

Iron Grenadier, 1988, Hasbro, Destro's Elite Troops
EX $5   **NM** $10   **MIP** $15

Road Pig, 1988, Hasbro, Dreadnok
EX $5   **NM** $12   **MIP** $20

Toxo-Viper, 1988, Hasbro, Hostile Environment
EX $7   **NM** $14   **MIP** $25

Voltar, 1988, Hasbro, Destro's General
EX $5   **NM** $12   **MIP** $20

Uniform/Equipment Sets

Dreadnok Battle Axe, 1988, Hasbro, Motorized Action Packs
EX $4   **NM** $8   **MIP** $12

Machine Gun Nest, 1988, Hasbro, Motorized Action Packs
EX $4   **NM** $8   **MIP** $12

Twin Missile Launcher, 1988, Hasbro, Motorized Action Packs
EX $4   **NM** $8   **MIP** $12

Vehicle Sets

Cobra Adder, 1988, Hasbro, Twin Missile Launcher
EX $5   **NM** $12   **MIP** $20

Cobra B.U.G.G., 1988, Hasbro, w/ Secto-Viper driver
EX $35   **NM** $75   **MIP** $125

Cobra Battle Barge, 1988, Hasbro
EX $5   **NM** $12   **MIP** $20

Cobra IMP, 1988, Hasbro
EX $5   **NM** $12   **MIP** $20

Cobra Stellar Stiletto, 1988, Hasbro, w/ Star Viper
EX $20   **NM** $40   **MIP** $60

Gyrocoptor, 1988, Hasbro, Motorized Vehicle Packs
EX $4   **NM** $8   **MIP** $12

Iron Grenadiers A.G.P. (Anti-Gravity Pods), 1988, Hasbro, w/ Nullifier pilot
EX $10   **NM** $20   **MIP** $30

Iron Grenadiers D.E.M.O.N., 1988, Hasbro, w/ Ferret the driver
EX $15   **NM** $30   **MIP** $45

Iron Grenadiers Destro's Despoiler, 1988, Hasbro, w/ Destro, gold helmet, black outfit, gold sword
EX $15   **NM** $25   **MIP** $40

Rocket Sled, 1988, Hasbro, Motorized Vehicle Packs
EX $4   **NM** $8   **MIP** $12

SERIES 07, GI JOE

Figure Sets

Blizzard, 1988, Hasbro, Artic Attack
EX $5   **NM** $12   **MIP** $20

Budo, 1988, Hasbro, Samuri Warrior
EX $5   **NM** $12   **MIP** $20

Charbroil, 1988, Hasbro, Flamethrower
EX $5   **NM** $12   **MIP** $20

Hardball, 1988, Hasbro, Multi-Shot Grenadier
EX $5   **NM** $10   **MIP** $15

Hit 'N Run, 1988, Hasbro, Light Infantryman
EX $7   **NM** $14   **MIP** $25

Lightfoot, 1988, Hasbro, Explosives Expert
EX $5   **NM** $10   **MIP** $15

Muskrat, 1988, Hasbro, Swamp Fighter
EX $5   **NM** $12   **MIP** $20

Night Force (Toys R Us exclusive), 1988, Hasbro, 2-figure pack: Psyche-Out and Tunnel Rat
EX $30   **NM** $55   **MIP** $80

Night Force (Toys R Us exclusive), 1988, Hasbro, 2-figure pack: Outback and Crazylegs
EX $30   **NM** $55   **MIP** $80

Night Force (Toys R Us exclusive), 1988, Hasbro, 2-figure pack: Lt. Falcon and Sneak Peek
EX $30   **NM** $55   **MIP** $80

Repeater, 1988, Hasbro, Stedi-Cam Machine Gunner
EX $5   **NM** $12   **MIP** $20

Shockwave, 1988, Hasbro, S.W.A.T.
EX $5   **NM** $12   **MIP** $20

Spearhead & Max, 1988, Hasbro, Point Man & Bobcat
EX $5   **NM** $12   **MIP** $20

Storm Shadow, 1988, Hasbro, Ninja
EX $12   **NM** $25   **MIP** $40

Super Trooper, 1988, Hasbro, mail-in
EX $10   **NM** $20   **MIP** $30

Tiger Force Bazooka, 1988, Hasbro, Missile Specialist
EX $15   **NM** $25   **MIP** $45

Tiger Force Duke, 1988, Hasbro, First Sergeant
EX $15   **NM** $25   **MIP** $45

Tiger Force Dusty, 1988, Hasbro, Desert Trooper
EX $15   **NM** $25   **MIP** $45

Tiger Force Flint, 1988, Hasbro, Warrant Officer
EX $15   **NM** $25   **MIP** $45

Tiger Force Lifeline, 1988, Hasbro, Medic
EX $15   **NM** $25   **MIP** $45

Tiger Force Roadblock, 1988, Hasbro, Heavy Machine Gunner
EX $15   **NM** $25   **MIP** $45

Tiger Force Tripwire, 1988, Hasbro, Mine Detector
EX $15   **NM** $25   **MIP** $45

Uniform/Equipment Sets

Double Machine Gun, 1988, Hasbro, Motorized Action Packs
EX $4   **NM** $8   **MIP** $12

Mine Sweeper, 1988, Hasbro, Motorized Action Packs
EX $4   **NM** $8   **MIP** $12

Mortar Launcher, 1988, Hasbro, Motorized Action Packs
EX $4   **NM** $8   **MIP** $12

Vehicle Sets

A.T.V., 1988, Hasbro, Motorized Vehicle Packs
EX $4   **NM** $8   **MIP** $12

Desert Fox 6-Wheel Drive, 1988, Hasbro, w/ Skidmark driver
EX $15   **NM** $30   **MIP** $50

Mean Dog, 1988, Hasbro, w/ Wildcard driver
EX $20   **NM** $40   **MIP** $60

Phantom X-19 Stealth Fighter, 1988, Hasbro, w/ Ghostrider pilot
EX $30   **NM** $60   **MIP** $100

R.P.V. (Remote Piloted Vehicle), 1988, Hasbro
EX $5   **NM** $10   **MIP** $15

Rolling Thunder, 1988, Hasbro, w/ Armadillo driver
EX $35   **NM** $75   **MIP** $125

Scuba Pack, 1988, Hasbro, Motorized Vehicle Packs
EX $4   **NM** $8   **MIP** $12

Skystorm X-Wing Chopper, 1988, Hasbro, w/ Windmill pilot
EX $10   **NM** $20   **MIP** $30

Swampmasher, 1988, Hasbro
EX $5   **NM** $10   **MIP** $15

Tank Car, 1988, Hasbro, Motorized Vehicle Packs
EX $10   **NM** $18   **MIP** $25

Tiger Cat, 1988, Hasbro, Tiger Force snow vehicle w/ Frostbite driver
EX $15   **NM** $30   **MIP** $50

Tiger Fly, 1988, Hasbro, Tiger Force Helicopter w/ Recondo
EX $35   **NM** $65   **MIP** $100

Tiger Paw, 1988, Hasbro, Tiger Force 4WD vehicle
EX $10   **NM** $18   **MIP** $25

Tiger Rat, 1988, Hasbro, Tiger Force Airplane w/ Skystriker pilot
EX $40   **NM** $75   **MIP** $110

Tiger Shark, 1988, Hasbro, Tiger Force (Water Mocassin) boat
EX $10   **NM** $18   **MIP** $25

Warthog A.I.F.V (Amphibious Infantry Fighting Vehicle), 1988, Hasbro, w/ Sgt. Slaughter driver
EX $15   **NM** $30   **MIP** $50

SERIES 08, COBRA

Figure Sets

Alley Viper, 1989, Hasbro, Cobra Urban Assault
EX $5   **NM** $10   **MIP** $15

Frag-Viper, 1989, Hasbro, Cobra Grenade Thrower
EX $5   **NM** $10   **MIP** $15

Gnawgahyde, 1989, Hasbro, Dreadnok Poacher
EX $5   **NM** $10   **MIP** $15

H.E.A.T. Viper, 1989, Hasbro, Cobra Bazooka Man
EX $5   **NM** $10   **MIP** $15

Iron Grenadiers Annihilator, 1989, Hasbro, Destro's Elite Trooper
EX $5   **NM** $12   **MIP** $20

Iron Grenadiers T.A.R.G.A.T., 1989, Hasbro, Trans Atmospheric Rapid Global Assault Trooper
EX $5   **NM** $10   **MIP** $15

Night-Viper, 1989, Hasbro, Night Fighter
EX $5   **NM** $12   **MIP** $20

Python Patrol Copperhead, 1989, Hasbro, Swamp Fighter
EX $10   **NM** $18   **MIP** $25

Python Patrol Crimson Guard, 1989, Hasbro, Elite Trooper
EX $10   **NM** $18   **MIP** $25

Python Patrol Officer, 1989, Hasbro
EX $10   **NM** $18   **MIP** $25

Python Patrol Tele-Viper, 1989, Hasbro, Communications
EX $10   **NM** $18   **MIP** $25

Python Patrol Trooper, 1989, Hasbro, Infantry
EX $10   **NM** $18   **MIP** $25

Python Patrol Viper, 1989, Hasbro, Assault Trooper
EX $10   **NM** $18   **MIP** $25

Vehicle Sets

Condor Z25, 1989, Hasbro, w/ Aero-Viper pilot
EX $20   **NM** $40   **MIP** $65

Devastator, 1989, Hasbro, Battlefield Robot
EX $5   **NM** $10   **MIP** $15

F.A.N.G. II, 1989, Hasbro
EX $10   **NM** $20   **MIP** $30

G.I. JOE

H.I.S.S. II, 1989, Hasbro, Cobra tank w/ Track Viper
EX $30   NM $60   MIP $85

Hovercraft, 1989, Hasbro, Battlefield Robot
EX $5   NM $10   MIP $15

Iron Grenadiers Darklon's Evader, 1989, Hasbro, w/ Darklon
EX $10   NM $20   MIP $30

Iron Grenadiers Destro's Razorback, 1989, Hasbro, w/ Wild Boar
EX $15   NM $25   MIP $40

Python Patrol ASP, 1989, Hasbro, cannon
EX $10   NM $20   MIP $30

Python Patrol Conquest, 1989, Hasbro, plane
EX $15   NM $25   MIP $45

Python Patrol STUN, 1989, Hasbro, tri-wheel vehicle
EX $10   NM $20   MIP $30

SERIES 08, GI JOE

Figure Sets

Backblast, 1989, Hasbro, Anti-aircraft Soldier
EX $5   NM $10   MIP $15

Battleforce 2000 Dee Jay, 1989, Hasbro, Comm-Tech Trooper
EX $5   NM $10   MIP $15

Countdown, 1989, Hasbro, Astronaut
EX $5   NM $12   MIP $20

Deep Six, 1989, Hasbro, Deep Sea Diver
EX $5   NM $12   MIP $20

Downtown, 1989, Hasbro, Mortar Man
EX $5   NM $12   MIP $20

Night Force (Toys R Us exclusive), 1989, Hasbro, 2-figure pack: Muskrat and Spearhead & Max
EX $30   NM $50   MIP $85

Night Force (Toys R Us exclusive), 1989, Hasbro, 2-figure pack: Charbroil and Repeater
EX $30   NM $50   MIP $85

Night Force (Toys R Us exclusive), 1989, Hasbro, 2-figure pack: Lightfoot and Shockwave
EX $30   NM $50   MIP $85

Recoil, 1989, Hasbro, Long Range Recon Patrol
EX $5   NM $10   MIP $15

Rock & Roll, 1989, Hasbro, Gatling Gunner
EX $5   NM $10   MIP $15

Scoop, 1989, Hasbro, Information Specialist
EX $5   NM $10   MIP $15

Slaughter's Marauders Barbecue, 1989, Hasbro, Firefighter
EX $7   NM $14   MIP $25

Slaughter's Marauders Footloose, 1989, Hasbro, Infantry Trooper
EX $7   NM $14   MIP $25

Slaughter's Marauders Low Light, 1989, Hasbro, Night Spotter
EX $7   NM $14   MIP $25

Slaughter's Marauders Mutt & Junkyard, 1989, Hasbro, Animal Control
EX $7   NM $14   MIP $25

Slaughter's Marauders Sgt. Slaughter, 1989, Hasbro, Commander
EX $7   NM $14   MIP $25

Slaughter's Marauders Spirit & Freedom, 1989, Hasbro, Tracker
EX $7   NM $14   MIP $25

Snake Eyes, 1989, Hasbro, Commando
EX $15   NM $30   MIP $45

Stalker, 1989, Hasbro, Tundra Ranger
EX $5   NM $10   MIP $15

Vehicle Sets

Battleforce 2000 Pulverizer, 1989, Hasbro, mini-tank
EX $5   NM $10   MIP $15

Crusader Space Shuttle, 1989, Hasbro, w/ Avenger aircraft and Payload the pilot
EX $40   NM $75   MIP $100

Mudfighter, 1989, Hasbro, w/ Dogfight driver
EX $10   NM $20   MIP $30

Radar Rat, 1989, Hasbro, Battlefield Robot
EX $5   NM $10   MIP $15

Raider, 1989, Hasbro, w/ Hot Seat
EX $20   NM $40   MIP $60

Slaughter's Marauders Armadillo, 1989, Hasbro, tank w/ rocket launchers
EX $10   NM $20   MIP $30

Slaughter's Marauders Equalizer, 1989, Hasbro, tank w/ rocket launchers and two laser cannons
EX $10   NM $25   MIP $40

Slaughter's Marauders Lynx, 1989, Hasbro, tank w/ large cannon
EX $10   NM $20   MIP $30

Thunderclap, 1989, Hasbro, w/ Long Range driver
EX $40   NM $75   MIP $110

Tiger Fish, 1989, Hasbro, Tiger Force (Devil Fish) boat
EX $7   NM $14   MIP $25

Tiger Sting, 1989, Hasbro, Tiger Force (Vamp Mark II) jeep vehicle
EX $7   NM $14   MIP $25

Tri-Blaster, 1989, Hasbro, Battlefield Robot
EX $5   NM $10   MIP $15

SERIES 09, COBRA

Figure Sets

Iron Grenadiers Metal-Head, 1990, Hasbro, Destro's Anti-Tank Specialist and one crazy guy!
EX $5   NM $11   MIP $17

Iron Grenadiers Undertow, 1990, Hasbro, Destro's Frogman
EX $5   NM $11   MIP $17

Laser-Viper, 1990, Hasbro, Laser Trooper
EX $5   NM $10   MIP $15

Night Creeper, 1990, Hasbro, Ninja
EX $5   NM $10   MIP $15

Range-Viper, 1990, Hasbro, Wilderness Trooper
EX $5   NM $11   MIP $18

Rock-Viper, 1990, Hasbro, Mountain Trooper
EX $5   NM $11   MIP $18

S.A.W.-Viper, 1990, Hasbro, Heavy Machine Gunner
EX $5   NM $11   MIP $17

Sonic Fighters Lampreys, 1990, Hasbro, Amphibious Assault
EX $5   NM $12   MIP $20

Sonic Fighters Viper, 1990, Hasbro, Infantry
EX $5   NM $12   MIP $20

Vehicle Sets

Cobra Piranha, 1990, Hasbro, Depth Charge Firing Sea Marauder
EX $5   NM $10   MIP $16

Cobra Rage, 1990, Hasbro
EX $7   NM $14   MIP $21

Hammerhead, 1990, Hasbro, Submersible Sea Tank, 6 vehicles in one, w/ Decimator driver
EX $15   NM $30   MIP $50

Hurricane VTOL, 1990, Hasbro, Vertical Take-off and Landing plane w/ Vapor pilot
EX $25   NM $50   MIP $75

Iron Grenadiers Destro's Dominator, 1990, Hasbro, Tank converts to helicopter
EX $7   NM $14   MIP $21

Overlord's Dictator, 1990, Hasbro, w/ Overlord driver
EX $10   NM $20   MIP $30

SERIES 09, GI JOE

Figure Sets

Ambush, 1990, Hasbro, Concealment Specialist
EX $5   NM $10   MIP $15

Bullhorn, 1990, Hasbro, Intervention Specialist
EX $5   NM $10   MIP $15

Captain Grid Iron, 1990, Hasbro, Hand-to-Hand Combat
EX $5   NM $10   MIP $15

Freefall, 1990, Hasbro, Paratrooper
EX $5   NM $10   MIP $15

Pathfinder, 1990, Hasbro, Jungle Assault
EX $5   NM $10   MIP $15

Rampart, 1990, Hasbro, Shoreline Defender
EX $5   NM $10   MIP $15

Salvo, 1990, Hasbro, Anti-Armor Trooper
EX $5   NM $10   MIP $15

Sky Patrol Airborne, 1990, Hasbro, Parachute Assembler
EX $7   NM $14   MIP $25

Sky Patrol Airwave, 1990, Hasbro, Audible Frequency Specialist
EX $7   NM $14   MIP $25

Sky Patrol Altitude, 1990, Hasbro, Recon Scout
EX $7   NM $14   MIP $25

Sky Patrol Drop Zone, 1990, Hasbro, Weapons Specialist
EX $7   NM $14   MIP $25

Sky Patrol Sky Dive, 1990, Hasbro, Leader
EX $7   NM $14   MIP $25

Sky Patrol Static Line, 1990, Hasbro, Demolitions Expert
EX $7   NM $14   MIP $25

Sonic Fighters Dial-Tone, 1990, Hasbro, Communications w/ sonic backpack
EX $5   NM $12   MIP $20

Sonic Fighters Dodger, 1990, Hasbro, Heavy Ordinance Operator w/ sonic backpack
EX $5   NM $12   MIP $20

Sonic Fighters Law, 1990, Hasbro, M.P. w/ sonic backpack
EX $5   NM $12   MIP $20

Sonic Fighters Tunnel Rat, 1990, Hasbro, E.O.D. w/ sonic backpack
EX $5   NM $12   MIP $20

Stretcher, 1990, Hasbro, Medical Specialist
EX $5   NM $10   MIP $15

Sub-Zero, 1990, Hasbro, Winter Operations
EX $5   NM $10   MIP $15

Topside, 1990, Hasbro, Navy Assault Seaman
EX $5   NM $10   MIP $15

Vehicle Sets

Avalanche, 1990, Hasbro, w/ Cold Front driver
EX $10   NM $20   MIP $30

General, 1990, Hasbro, Mobile Strike Headquarters and Launch Pad w/ Major Storm driver
EX $20   NM $40   MIP $60

Hammer, 1990, Hasbro, High-Tech Attack Jeep
EX $5   NM $10   MIP $15

Locust, 1990, Hasbro, Bomb Dropping Assault Copter
EX $7   NM $14   MIP $25

Mobile Battle Bunker, 1990, Hasbro
EX $5   NM $10   MIP $15

Retaliator, 1990, Hasbro, Helicopter w/ Updraft the pilot
EX $11   NM $24   MIP $40

Sky Patrol Sky HAVOC, 1990, Hasbro, Heavy Armored Transport vehicle w/ hidden scout ship
EX $14   NM $28   MIP $45

Sky Patrol Sky Hawk, 1990, Hasbro, VTOL craft
EX $15   NM $25   MIP $40

Sky Patrol Sky Raven, 1990, Hasbro
EX $25   NM $55   MIP $80

Sky Patrol Sky SHARC, 1990, Hasbro
EX $15   NM $25   MIP $40

SERIES 10, COBRA

Figure Sets

B.A.T., 1991, Hasbro, Android Trooper
EX $5   NM $10   MIP $15

Cobra Commander w/ eybrows, 1991, Hasbro, Leader
EX $20   NM $40   MIP $60

Cobra Commander w/out eyebrows, 1991, Hasbro, Leader
EX $7   NM $14   MIP $25

Crimson Guard Immortal, 1991, Hasbro, Elite Trooper
EX $7   NM $14   MIP $22

Desert Scorpion, 1991, Hasbro, Desert Fighter
EX $7   NM $14   MIP $22

Eco Warriors Cesspool, 1991, Hasbro, Chief Environmental Operative
EX $4   NM $8   MIP $12

Eco Warriors Sludge-Viper, 1991, Hasbro, Hazardous Waste
EX $4   NM $8   MIP $12

Eco Warriors Toxo-Viper, 1991, Hasbro, Hostile Environment
EX $4   NM $8   MIP $12

Incinerators, 1991, Hasbro, Flamethrowers
EX $5   NM $10   MIP $15

Snow Serpent, 1991, Hasbro, Snow Trooper
EX $5   NM $10   MIP $15

Super Sonic Fighters Major Bludd, 1991, Hasbro, Mercenary
EX $5   NM $10   MIP $15

Super Sonic Fighters Road Pig, 1991, Hasbro, Dreadnok
EX $5   NM $10   MIP $15

Talking Battle Commanders Cobra Commander, 1991, Hasbro, Cobra Leader
EX $5   NM $10   MIP $15

Talking Battle Commanders Overkill, 1991, Hasbro, B.A.T. Leader
EX $5   NM $10   MIP $15

Vehicle Sets

Air Commandos w/ Night Vulture, 1991, Hasbro, Air Recon Trooper
EX $10   NM $20   MIP $30

Air Commandos w/ Sky Creeper, 1991, Hasbro, Air Recon Leader
EX $10   NM $20   MIP $30

Battle Copter, 1991, Hasbro, w/ Interrogator pilot
EX $10   NM $15   MIP $25

Eco Warriors Septic Tank, 1991, Hasbro
EX $10   NM $15   MIP $25

Ice Sabre, 1991, Hasbro
EX $5   NM $10   MIP $15

Paralyzer, 1991, Hasbro
EX $5   NM $10   MIP $15

SERIES 10, GI JOE

Figure Sets

Big Ben, 1991, Hasbro, S.A.S
EX $5   NM $10   MIP $15

Dusty & Sandstorm, 1991, Hasbro, Desert Trooper
EX $5   NM $10   MIP $15

Eco Warriors Clean-Sweep, 1991, Hasbro, Anit-Tox Trooper
EX $4   NM $8   MIP $12

Eco Warriors Flint, 1991, Hasbro, Commander
EX $4   NM $8   MIP $12

Eco Warriors Ozone, 1991, Hasbro, Ozone Replenisher
EX $4   NM $8   MIP $12

General Hawk, 1991, Hasbro, Commander
EX $7   NM $14   MIP $20

Grunt, 1991, Hasbro, Infantry Squad Leader
EX $6   NM $12   MIP $18

Heavy Duty, 1991, Hasbro, Heavy Ordinance Trooper
EX $5   NM $10   MIP $15

Lifeline, 1991, Hasbro, Kellog's mail in, no guns
EX $7   NM $14   MIP $22

Low-Light, 1991, Hasbro, Night Fighter
EX $6   NM $12   MIP $18

Mercer, 1991, Hasbro, Mercenary
EX $7   NM $14   MIP $22

Red Star, 1991, Hasbro, Oktober Guard
EX $7   NM $14   MIP $22

Sci-Fi, 1991, Hasbro, Directed Energy Expert
EX $6   NM $12   MIP $18

Snake Eyes, 1991, Hasbro, Commando
EX $7   NM $14   MIP $22

Super Sonic Fighters Lt. Falcon, 1991, Hasbro, Green Beret
EX $5   NM $10   MIP $15

Super Sonic Fighters Psyche-Out, 1991, Hasbro, Deceptive Warfare
EX $5   NM $10   MIP $15

Super Sonic Fighters Rock 'N Roll, 1991, Hasbro, Machine Gunner
EX $5   NM $10   MIP $15

Super Sonic Fighters Zap, 1991, Hasbro, Ground Artillery Soldier
EX $5   NM $10   MIP $15

Talking Battle Commanders General Hawk, 1991, Hasbro, Commander
EX $5   NM $10   MIP $15

Talking Battle Commanders Stalker, 1991, Hasbro, Ranger
EX $5   NM $10   MIP $15

Tracker, 1991, Hasbro, S.E.A.L.
EX $6   NM $12   MIP $18

Vehicle Sets

Air Commandos w/ Cloudburst, 1991, Hasbro, Glider Trooper
EX $10   **NM** $20   **MIP** $30

Air Commandos w/Skymate, 1991, Hasbro, Glider Trooper, Australian S.A.S.
EX $10   **NM** $20   **MIP** $30

Attack Cruiser, 1991, Hasbro, Mobile Attack Vehicle w/ Flying Glider Bomb
EX $10   **NM** $15   **MIP** $24

Badger, 1991, Hasbro, Attack Jeep
EX $5   **NM** $10   **MIP** $15

Battle Copter, 1991, Hasbro, w/ Major Altitude pilot
EX $10   **NM** $15   **MIP** $25

Brawler, 1991, Hasbro
EX $10   **NM** $15   **MIP** $24

Motorized Battle Wagon, 1991, Hasbro
EX $10   **NM** $15   **MIP** $24

SERIES 11, COBRA

Figure Sets

Cobra Ninja Viper, 1992, Hasbro, mail-in
EX $7   **NM** $14   **MIP** $25

Destro, 1992, Hasbro, Weapons Supplier
EX $4   **NM** $8   **MIP** $12

Eel, 1992, Hasbro, Underwater Demolitions
EX $4   **NM** $8   **MIP** $12

Evil Headhunters Headman, 1992, Hasbro, Drug Kingpin
EX $4   **NM** $8   **MIP** $12

Evil Headhunters, Headhunters, 1992, Hasbro, Narcotics Guards
EX $4   **NM** $8   **MIP** $12

Firefly, 1992, Hasbro, Saboteur
EX $4   **NM** $8   **MIP** $12

Flak-Viper, 1992, Hasbro, Anti-Aircraft Trooper
EX $4   **NM** $8   **MIP** $12

Ninja Force Dice, 1992, Hasbro, Cobra Ninja Bo Staff
EX $5   **NM** $10   **MIP** $15

Ninja Force Slice, 1992, Hasbro, Cobra Ninja Swordsman
EX $5   **NM** $10   **MIP** $15

Toxo-Zombie, 1992, Hasbro, Toxic Disaster Trooper
EX $4   **NM** $8   **MIP** $12

Uniform/Equipment Sets

Eco Warriors Toxo-Lab, 1992, Hasbro, Play set for Eco Warriors
EX $10   **NM** $20   **MIP** $30

Vehicle Sets

Air Commandos w/Cobra Air Devil, 1992, Hasbro, Aerobatic Arial Assault Trooper
EX $10   **NM** $20   **MIP** $30

Battle Copter w/Heli-Viper, 1992, Hasbro
EX $7   **NM** $13   **MIP** $20

Cobra Earthquake, 1992, Hasbro, Bulldozer
EX $5   **NM** $10   **MIP** $15

Cobra Parasite, 1992, Hasbro, Armored Personnel Carrier w/ Catapult launcher
EX $7   **NM** $14   **MIP** $25

Cobra Rat, 1992, Hasbro, High-Speed Attack Hovercraft
EX $7   **NM** $14   **MIP** $25

SERIES 11, GI JOE

Figure Sets

Barbecue, 1992, Hasbro, Firefighter
EX $3   **NM** $6   **MIP** $10

Barricade, 1992, Hasbro, Bunker Buster
EX $3   **NM** $6   **MIP** $10

Big Bear, 1992, Hasbro, Oktober Guard Anti-Armor Specialist
EX $3   **NM** $6   **MIP** $10

D.E.F. Bullet-Proof, 1992, Hasbro, Drug Elimination Force Leader
EX $4   **NM** $8   **MIP** $12

D.E.F. Cutter, 1992, Hasbro, Vehicle Operations Specialist
EX $4   **NM** $8   **MIP** $12

D.E.F. Mutt & Junkyard, 1992, Hasbro, K-9
EX $4   **NM** $8   **MIP** $12

D.E.F. Shockwave, 1992, Hasbro, S.W.A.T.
EX $4   **NM** $8   **MIP** $12

Duke, 1992, Hasbro, Master Sergeant
EX $4   **NM** $8   **MIP** $12

Eco Warriors Deep Six, 1992, Hasbro, Deep Water Specialist
EX $4   **NM** $8   **MIP** $12

General Flagg, 1992, Hasbro, General
EX $4   **NM** $8   **MIP** $12

Gung-Ho, 1992, Hasbro, Marine
EX $3   **NM** $6   **MIP** $10

Ninja Force Dojo, 1992, Hasbro, Silent Weapons
EX $7   **NM** $14   **MIP** $25

Ninja Force Nunchuk, 1992, Hasbro, Nunchaku Ninja
EX $7   **NM** $14   **MIP** $25

Ninja Force Storm Shadow, 1992, Hasbro, Leader
EX $7   **NM** $14   **MIP** $25

Ninja Force T'Jbang, 1992, Hasbro, Ninja Swordsman
EX $4   **NM** $8   **MIP** $12

Roadblock, 1992, Hasbro, Heavy Machine Gunner
EX $3   **NM** $6   **MIP** $10

Wet-Suit, 1992, Hasbro, S.E.A.L.
EX $4   **NM** $8   **MIP** $12

Wild Bill, 1992, Hasbro, Air Cavalry Scout
EX $4   **NM** $8   **MIP** $12

Uniform/Equipment Sets

G.I. Joe Headquarters, 1992, Hasbro, Play set w/ electronic battle sounds
EX $20   **NM** $40   **MIP** $65

Vehicle Sets

Air Commandos w/ Spirit, 1992, Hasbro, Air Commandos Leader
EX $7   **NM** $14   **MIP** $25

Barracuda, 1992, Hasbro, One-Man Attack Sub w/ Real Diving Action
EX $5   **NM** $10   **MIP** $15

Battle Copter w/ Ace, 1992, Hasbro
EX $7   **NM** $13   **MIP** $20

Eco Warriors Eco Striker, 1992, Hasbro, All-Terrain Environmental Assault Vehicle
EX $5   **NM** $10   **MIP** $15

Patriot, 1992, Hasbro, Armored Missile Launcher Transport
EX $10   **NM** $20   **MIP** $30

Storm Eagle Jet, 1992, Hasbro
EX $7   **NM** $14   **MIP** $25

Super Sonic Fort America, 1992, Hasbro, Fortress turns into tank
EX $10   **NM** $20   **MIP** $30

SERIES 12, COBRA

Battle Corps Figure Sets

Alley-Viper, #6, 1993, Hasbro, Urban Assault Trooper
EX $4   **NM** $8   **MIP** $12

Cobra Commander, #24, 1993, Hasbro, Supreme Leader
EX $5   **NM** $9   **MIP** $13

Cobra Eel, #27, 1993, Hasbro, Underwater Demolitions
EX $4   **NM** $8   **MIP** $12

Crimson Guard Commander, #23, 1993, Hasbro, Elite Trooper
EX $5   **NM** $9   **MIP** $13

Dr. Mindbender, #15, 1993, Hasbro, Master of Mind Control
EX $4   **NM** $8   **MIP** $12

Firefly, #18, 1993, Hasbro, Saboteur
EX $5   **NM** $9   **MIP** $13

Flak-Viper, #9, 1993, Hasbro, Anti-Aircraft Trooper
EX $5   **NM** $9   **MIP** $13

H.E.A.T. Viper, #5, 1993, Hasbro, Hi Explosive Anti-Tank Trooper
EX $5   **NM** $9   **MIP** $13

Headhunter Stormtrooper, #33, 1993, Hasbro, Elite Urban Crime Guard
EX $5   **NM** $9   **MIP** $13

Headhunters, #35, 1993, Hasbro, Cobra Street Troopers
EX $4   **NM** $8   **MIP** $12

Night Creeper Leader, #14, 1993, Hasbro, Ninja Supreme Master
EX $4   **NM** $8   **MIP** $12

Figure Sets

Ninja Force Night Creeper, 1993, Hasbro, Cobra Ninja
EX $4   **NM** $8   **MIP** $12

Ninja Force Slice, 1993, Hasbro, Cobra Ninja Swordsman
EX $4   **NM** $8   **MIP** $12

G.I. JOE

Ninja Force Zartan, 1993, Hasbro, Master of Disguise

EX $4   **NM** $8   **MIP** $15

Mail-In Figures

Name Your Own Cobra, 1993, Hasbro, "Create A Cobra"

EX $8   **NM** $15   **MIP** $25

Mega Marines/Mega Monsters

Bio-Viper, 1993, Hasbro, Genetically Enhanced Undersea Monster

EX $5   **NM** $10   **MIP** $15

Cyber-Viper, 1993, Hasbro, Cybernetic Officer

EX $5   **NM** $10   **MIP** $15

Mega-Viper, 1993, Hasbro, Mega-Monster Trainer

EX $5   **NM** $10   **MIP** $15

Monstro-Viper, 1993, Hasbro, Mega Monster

EX $5   **NM** $10   **MIP** $15

Star Brigade Figure Sets

Astro Viper, #11, 1993, Hasbro, Cobranaut

EX $4   **NM** $8   **MIP** $12

B.A.A.T., #6, 1993, Hasbro, Battle Armored Android Trooper

EX $5   **NM** $10   **MIP** $15

Destro, #5, 1993, Hasbro, Cobra-Tech Commander

EX $4   **NM** $8   **MIP** $12

T.A.R.G.A.T., 1993, Hasbro, Trans Asmospheric Rapid Global Assault Trooper

EX $4   **NM** $8   **MIP** $12

Vehicle Sets

Battle Corps Cobra Detonator, 1993, Hasbro, w/ Nitro-Viper

EX $15   **NM** $30   **MIP** $45

Battle Corps Ice Snake, 1993, Hasbro

EX $4   **NM** $8   **MIP** $12

Ninja Force Battle Ax, 1993, Hasbro, w/ Red Ninja driver

EX $5   **NM** $10   **MIP** $15

Star Brigade Cobra Invader, 1993, Hasbro

EX $3   **NM** $6   **MIP** $10

SERIES 12, GI JOE

Battle Corps Figure Sets

Backblast, #22, 1993, Hasbro, Anti-Aircraft Soldier

EX $5   **NM** $10   **MIP** $15

Barricade, #17, 1993, Hasbro, Bunker Buster

EX $5   **NM** $10   **MIP** $15

Bazooka, #1, 1993, Hasbro, Missile Specialist

EX $5   **NM** $10   **MIP** $15

Beach-Head, #4, 1993, Hasbro, Ranger

EX $5   **NM** $10   **MIP** $15

Bulletproof, #34, 1993, Hasbro, Urban Commander

EX $5   **NM** $10   **MIP** $15

Colonel Courage, #10, 1993, Hasbro, Strategic Commnader

EX $5   **NM** $10   **MIP** $15

Cross-Country, #2, 1993, Hasbro, Transport Expert

EX $5   **NM** $10   **MIP** $15

Duke, #19, 1993, Hasbro, Battle Commander

EX $5   **NM** $10   **MIP** $15

Frostbite, #20, 1993, Hasbro, Arctic Commander

EX $5   **NM** $10   **MIP** $15

General Flagg, #26, 1993, Hasbro, General

EX $5   **NM** $10   **MIP** $15

Gristle, #32, 1993, Hasbro, Urban Crime Commander

EX $5   **NM** $10   **MIP** $15

Gung-Ho, #16, 1993, Hasbro, Marine

EX $5   **NM** $10   **MIP** $15

Iceberg, #3, 1993, Hasbro, Arctic Assault Trooper

EX $5   **NM** $10   **MIP** $15

Keel-Haul, #21, 1993, Hasbro, Admiral, most have large logo on back, small logo is rare

EX $5   **NM** $10   **MIP** $15

Law, #28, 1993, Hasbro, M.P.

EX $5   **NM** $10   **MIP** $15

Leatherneck, #11, 1993, Hasbro, Infantry Training Specialist

EX $5   **NM** $10   **MIP** $15

Long Arm, #31, 1993, Hasbro, Fire Strike Specialist

EX $5   **NM** $10   **MIP** $15

Mace, #29, 1993, Hasbro, Undercover Operative

EX $5   **NM** $10   **MIP** $15

Muskrat, #30, 1993, Hasbro, Heavy Fire Specialist

EX $5   **NM** $10   **MIP** $15

Mutt & Junkyard, #36, 1993, Hasbro, K-9

EX $5   **NM** $10   **MIP** $15

Outback, #13a, 1993, Hasbro, Survival Specialist, Eco Warriors version released as Battle Corps instead

EX $4   **NM** $8   **MIP** $12

Outback, #13b, 1993, Hasbro, Survival Specialist, tan pants, green shirt

EX $4   **NM** $8   **MIP** $12

Road Block, #7a, 1993, Hasbro, Heavy Machine Gunner, yellow shirt

EX $4   **NM** $8   **MIP** $12

Road Block, #7b, 1993, Hasbro, Heavy Machine Gunner, blue shirt

EX $4   **NM** $8   **MIP** $12

Snow Storm, #12a, 1993, Hasbro, High-Tech Snow Trooper, white body w/ orange accents

EX $4   **NM** $8   **MIP** $12

Snow Storm, #12b, 1993, Hasbro, High-Tech Snow Trooper, white body w/ blue accents

EX $4   **NM** $8   **MIP** $12

Wet-Suit, #8, 1993, Hasbro, S.E.A.L.

EX $5   **NM** $9   **MIP** $13

Wild Bill, #25, 1993, Hasbro, Aero Scout

EX $4   **NM** $8   **MIP** $12

Figure Sets

Ninja Force Banzai, 1993, Hasbro, Rising Sun Ninja

EX $4   **NM** $8   **MIP** $12

Ninja Force Bushido, 1993, Hasbro, Snow Ninja

EX $4   **NM** $8   **MIP** $12

Ninja Force Scarlett, 1993, Hasbro, Counter Intellegence

EX $7   **NM** $14   **MIP** $25

Ninja Force Snake Eyes, 1993, Hasbro, Covert Mission Specialist

EX $5   **NM** $10   **MIP** $15

Mail-In Figures

Arctic Commandos, 1993, Hasbro, 4-figure pack: Dee-Jay, Snow Serpent, Stalker, Sub-Zero

EX $7   **NM** $14   **MIP** $25

Copter Pilots, 1993, Hasbro, 2-figure pack: Interrogator and Major Altitude

EX $5   **NM** $10   **MIP** $15

Deep Six, 1993, Hasbro, Deep Sea Diver

EX $3   **NM** $5   **MIP** $8

General Hawk, 1993, Hasbro, Commander

EX $3   **NM** $5   **MIP** $8

International Action Force, 1993, Hasbro, 4-figure pack: Big Bear, Big Ben, Budo, and Spirit

EX $7   **NM** $14   **MIP** $25

Rapid Deployment Force, 1993, Hasbro, 3-figure pack: Fast Draw, Night Force Repeater, Night Force Shockwave

EX $5   **NM** $12   **MIP** $20

Mega Marines/Mega Monsters

Blast-Off, 1993, Hasbro, Flame Thrower

EX $4   **NM** $8   **MIP** $12

Clutch, 1993, Hasbro, Monster Blaster A.P.C.

EX $4   **NM** $8   **MIP** $12

Gung-Ho, 1993, Hasbro, Commander

EX $4   **NM** $8   **MIP** $12

Mirage, 1993, Hasbro, Bio-Artillery Expert

EX $4   **NM** $8   **MIP** $12

Star Brigade Figure Sets

Countdown, #8, 1993, Hasbro, Combat Astronaut

EX $4   **NM** $8   **MIP** $12

Duke, #2, 1993, Hasbro, Commander

EX $4   **NM** $8   **MIP** $12

Heavy Duty, #4, 1993, Hasbro, Heavy Ordinance Specialist
| EX $4 | NM $8 | MIP $12 |

Ozone, #10a, 1993, Hasbro, Astro Infantry Trooper, tan suit
| EX $4 | NM $8 | MIP $12 |

Ozone, #10b, 1993, Hasbro, Astro Infantry Trooper, gray suit
| EX $4 | NM $8 | MIP $12 |

Payload, #7a, 1993, Hasbro, Astro Pilot, black suit, green and silver accents
| EX $4 | NM $8 | MIP $12 |

Payload, #7b, 1993, Hasbro, Astro Pilot, black suit, blue and gold accents
| EX $4 | NM $8 | MIP $12 |

Roadblock, #9, 1993, Hasbro, Space Gunner
| EX $4 | NM $8 | MIP $12 |

Robo-JOE, #1, 1993, Hasbro, Jet Tech Ops Expert
| EX $4 | NM $8 | MIP $12 |

Rock 'N Roll, #3, 1993, Hasbro, Robo-Gunner
| EX $4 | NM $8 | MIP $12 |

Street Fighter Figure Sets

Balrog, #11, 1993, Hasbro, Heavyweight Boxer
| EX $3 | NM $5 | MIP $8 |

Blanka, #5, 1993, Hasbro, Jungle Fighter
| EX $3 | NM $5 | MIP $8 |

Chun-Li, #4, 1993, Hasbro, Kung-Fu Fighter
| EX $3 | NM $5 | MIP $8 |

Dhalsim, #8, 1993, Hasbro, Yoga Fighter
| EX $3 | NM $5 | MIP $8 |

Edmond Honda, #7, 1993, Hasbro, Sumo Wrestler
| EX $3 | NM $5 | MIP $8 |

Guile, #3, 1993, Hasbro, Special Forces Fighter
| EX $3 | NM $5 | MIP $8 |

Ken Masters, #2, 1993, Hasbro, Shotokan Karate Fighter
| EX $3 | NM $5 | MIP $8 |

M. Bison, #6, 1993, Hasbro, Grand Master
| EX $3 | NM $5 | MIP $8 |

Ryu, #1, 1993, Hasbro, Kung-Fu Fighter
| EX $3 | NM $5 | MIP $8 |

Sagat, #12, 1993, Hasbro, Thai Fighter
| EX $3 | NM $5 | MIP $8 |

Vega, #10, 1993, Hasbro, Spanish Ninja
| EX $3 | NM $5 | MIP $8 |

Zangeif, #9, 1993, Hasbro, Russian Bear Wrestler
| EX $3 | NM $5 | MIP $8 |

Street Fighters Vehicle Sets

Beast Blaster, 1993, Hasbro, w/ Blanka and Chun-Li
| EX $5 | NM $12 | MIP $20 |

Crimson Cruiser, 1993, Hasbro, w/ M. Bison
| EX $4 | NM $8 | MIP $12 |

Dragon Fortress, 1993, Hasbro, w/ Ken Masters and Ryu
| EX $10 | NM $20 | MIP $30 |

Sonic Boom, 1993, Hasbro, w/ Guile
| EX $4 | NM $8 | MIP $12 |

Vehicle Sets

Battle Corps Ghoststriker X-16, 1993, Hasbro, w/ Ace pilot
| EX $15 | NM $25 | MIP $40 |

Battle Corps Mudbuster, 1993, Hasbro, All-terrain, 4x4 truck
| EX $4 | NM $8 | MIP $12 |

Battle Corps Shark 9000, 1993, Hasbro, w/ Cutter driver
| EX $10 | NM $20 | MIP $30 |

Mega Marines Monster Blaster, 1993, Hasbro, APC
| EX $5 | NM $10 | MIP $15 |

Ninja Force Ninja Lightning, 1993, Hasbro, Fast Attack Ninja Cycle w/ Detachable Sidecar
| EX $4 | NM $8 | MIP $12 |

Ninja Force Pile Driver, 1993, Hasbro, w/ T'Gin-Zu driver
| EX $5 | NM $10 | MIP $15 |

Star Brigade Armor-Bot, 1993, Hasbro, w/ Armor-Tech General Hawk
| EX $10 | NM $20 | MIP $30 |

Star Brigade Starfighter, 1993, Hasbro, w/ Sci-Fi
| EX $4 | NM $8 | MIP $12 |

SERIES 13, COBRA

Battle Corps Figure Sets

Alley Viper, #7, 1994, Hasbro, Urban Assault Trooper
| EX $5 | NM $10 | MIP $15 |

Major Bludd, #11, 1994, Hasbro, Mercenary
| EX $5 | NM $10 | MIP $15 |

Night Creeper Leader, #13, 1994, Hasbro, Cobra Ninja Supreme Leader
| EX $5 | NM $10 | MIP $15 |

Viper, #5, 1994, Hasbro, Cobra Infantry Trooper
| EX $5 | NM $10 | MIP $15 |

Shadow Ninjas Figure Sets

Night Creeper, #42, 1994, Hasbro, Cobra Ninja
| EX $5 | NM $10 | MIP $15 |

Slice, #40, 1994, Hasbro, Cobra Ninja Swordsman
| EX $5 | NM $10 | MIP $15 |

Star Brigade Figure Sets

Cobra Blackstar, #25, 1994, Hasbro, Cobra Elite Space Pilot
| EX $4 | NM $8 | MIP $12 |

Cobra Commander, #24, 1994, Hasbro, Cobra Supreme Leader
| EX $5 | NM $10 | MIP $15 |

Vehicle Sets

Battle Corps Scorpion, 1994, Hasbro, 4WD vehicle
| EX $5 | NM $10 | MIP $15 |

Star Brigade Cobra Power Fighter, 1994, Hasbro, w/ Techno-Viper driver
| EX $5 | NM $10 | MIP $15 |

Star Brigade Power Fighter, 1994, Hasbro, w/ Gears driver
| EX $5 | NM $10 | MIP $15 |

SERIES 13, GI JOE

30th Anniversary

Action Marine, 1994, Hasbro, #81047, Marine Corps Commando
| EX $5 | NM $10 | MIP $15 |

Action Pilot, 1994, Hasbro, #81046, Air Force Fighter Pilot
| EX $5 | NM $10 | MIP $15 |

Action Pilot Astronaut, 1994, Hasbro, Astronaut was available in the boxed gift set
| EX $7 | NM $13 | MIP $20 |

Action Sailor, 1994, Hasbro, #81048, Navy Frogman
| EX $5 | NM $10 | MIP $15 |

Action Soldier, 1994, Hasbro, #81045, U.S. Army Infantryman
| EX $5 | NM $10 | MIP $15 |

Battle Corps Figure Sets

Beach-Head, #6, 1994, Hasbro, Ranger
| EX $5 | NM $10 | MIP $15 |

Dial-Tone, #2, 1994, Hasbro, Communications Expert
| EX $5 | NM $10 | MIP $15 |

Flint, #1, 1994, Hasbro, Desert Paratrooper
| EX $5 | NM $10 | MIP $15 |

Ice Cream Soldier, #10, 1994, Hasbro, Flamethrower Commando
| EX $6 | NM $12 | MIP $17 |

Lifeline, #8, 1994, Hasbro, Rescue Trooper
| EX $5 | NM $10 | MIP $15 |

Metal-Head, #4, 1994, Hasbro, Anti-Tank Trooper
| EX $5 | NM $10 | MIP $15 |

Shipwreck, #3, 1994, Hasbro, Navy S.E.A.L.
| EX $5 | NM $10 | MIP $15 |

Snow Storm, #12, 1994, Hasbro, High Tech Snow Trooper
| EX $5 | NM $10 | MIP $15 |

Stalker, #9, 1994, Hasbro, Ranger
| EX $5 | NM $10 | MIP $15 |

Windchill, #14, 1994, Hasbro, Blockbuster Driver
| EX $5 | NM $10 | MIP $15 |

Mail-In Figures

Lt. Joseph Colton, G.I. Joe, 1994, Hasbro
- EX $4   NM $8   MIP $12

Shadow Ninjas Figure Sets

Bushido, #39, 1994, Hasbro, Shadow Ninja
- EX $5   NM $10   MIP $15

Nunchuk, #41, 1994, Hasbro, Nunchuku Ninja
- EX $5   NM $10   MIP $15

Snake Eyes, #37, 1994, Hasbro, Covert Mission Specialist
- EX $5   NM $10   MIP $15

Storm Shadow, #38, 1994, Hasbro, Shadow Ninja Leader
- EX $5   NM $10   MIP $15

Star Brigade Figure Sets

Carcass, #52, 1994, Hasbro, Alien Destroyer
- EX $4   NM $8   MIP $12

Countdown, #53, 1994, Hasbro, Combat Astronaut
- EX $4   NM $8   MIP $12

Duke, #21, 1994, Hasbro, Star Brigade Commander
- EX $5   NM $10   MIP $15

Effects, #49, 1994, Hasbro, Explosives Expert
- EX $4   NM $8   MIP $12

Lobotomax, #50, 1994, Hasbro, Stellar Explorer
- EX $4   NM $8   MIP $12

Ozone, #54, 1994, Hasbro, Astro-Infantry Trooper
- EX $4   NM $8   MIP $12

Payload, #26a, 1994, Hasbro, Astro Pilot, black suit, blue and gold accents
- EX $4   NM $8   MIP $12

Payload, #26b, 1994, Hasbro, Astro Pilot, white suit, red and silver accents
- EX $4   NM $8   MIP $12

Predacon, #51, 1994, Hasbro, Alien Bounty Hunter
- EX $4   NM $8   MIP $12

Roadblock, #27, 1994, Hasbro, Space Gunner
- EX $4   NM $8   MIP $12

Sci-Fi, #22, 1994, Hasbro, Star Brigade Pilot
- EX $4   NM $8   MIP $12

Space Shot, #23, 1994, Hasbro, Combat Freighter Pilot
- EX $4   NM $8   MIP $12

Vehicle Sets

Battle Corps Blockbuster, 1994, Hasbro, w/ Windmill driver
- EX $6   NM $12   MIP $18

Battle Corps Manta Ray, 1994, Hasbro, wind up propeller
- EX $5   NM $10   MIP $15

Battle Corps Razor-Blade, 1994, Hasbro, one-man copter
- EX $5   NM $10   MIP $15

COLLECTOR EDITIONS (1990s TO PRESENT)

12" HALL OF FAME

Figure Sets

Ace, Fighter Pilot, 1993, Hasbro, Model No. 6837
- EX $10   NM $15   MIP $25

Cobra Commander, Cobra Leader, 1992, Hasbro, Model No. 6827
- EX $15   NM $20   MIP $35

Destro, Weapons Manufacturer, 1993, Hasbro, Model No. 6839
- EX $10   NM $15   MIP $25

Duke, Combat Camo, 1994, Hasbro, Model No. 6044
- EX $10   NM $12   MIP $15

Duke, Master Sergeant, 1991, Hasbro, Target exclusive, Model No. 6019
- EX $15   NM $30   MIP $45

Duke, Master Sergeant, 1992, Hasbro, Model No. 6826
- EX $15   NM $25   MIP $35

Flint, Green Beret, 1994, Hasbro, Model No. 6127
- EX $10   NM $12   MIP $30

Grunt, Infantry Squad Leader, 1993, Hasbro, Model No. 6111
- EX $10   NM $20   MIP $25

Gung-Ho, Dress Marine, 1993, Hasbro, Model No. 6849
- EX $10   NM $20   MIP $25

Heavy Duty, Heavy Ordinance Specialist, 1993, Hasbro, Model No. 6114
- EX $10   NM $20   MIP $35

Major Budd, Battle-Pack, 1994, Hasbro, Model No. 6159
- EX $10   NM $15   MIP $30

Martial Arts Specialist, 1995, Hasbro, Kay Bee Exclusive
- EX $10   NM $20   MIP $30

Rapid Fire, Commando, 1993, Hasbro, Model No. 6924
- EX $20   NM $50   MIP $60

Red Beret Commando, 1995, Hasbro, Kay Bee Exclusive
- EX $15   NM $30   MIP $45

Roadblock, Combat Camo, 1994, Hasbro, Model No. 6049
- EX $10   NM $12   MIP $20

Rock n Roll, Gatlin' Blastin', 1994, Hasbro, Model No. 6128
- EX $10   NM $25   MIP $30

Rock 'n Roll, Heavy Weapons Gunner, 1993, Hasbro, Model No. 6128
- EX $10   NM $20   MIP $25

Snake Eyes, Commando, 1992, Hasbro, Model No. 6828
- EX $15   NM $30   MIP $35

Snake-Eyes, Karate Choppin', 1994, Hasbro, Model No. 6089
- EX $10   NM $25   MIP $30

Stalker, Ranger, 1992, Hasbro, Model No. 6829
- EX $15   NM $30   MIP $35

Storm Shadow, Ninja, 1993, Hasbro, Model No. 6848
- EX $10   NM $20   MIP $25

Surveillance Specialist, 1995, Hasbro, Kay Bee Exclusive
- EX $10   NM $20   MIP $30

Talking Duke, Talking Battle Commander, 1993, Hasbro, Model No. 6117
- EX $20   NM $40   MIP $60

Uniform/Equipment Sets

Air Force Flyer Gear, 1993, Hasbro
- EX $4   NM $8   MIP $12

Arctic Assault Mission Gear, 1993, Hasbro
- EX $4   NM $8   MIP $12

Army Boot Camp Gear, 1993, Hasbro
- EX $4   NM $8   MIP $12

Backpack Missile Blaster, 1993, Hasbro
- EX $3   NM $6   MIP $10

Cobra Helicopter Attack, 1993, Hasbro, Deluxe Mission Gear
- EX $5   NM $10   MIP $15

Cobra Infantry Uniform, 1993, Hasbro, mail-in
- EX $4   NM $8   MIP $12

Deep Water Salvage Mission Gear, 1995, Hasbro
- EX $4   NM $8   MIP $12

Desert Camo Mission Gear, 1993, Hasbro
- EX $4   NM $8   MIP $12

Footlocker, 1993, Hasbro, storage for Hall of Fame equipment
- EX $4   NM $8   MIP $12

GI Joe Infantry Uniform, 1993, Hasbro, mail-in
- EX $4   NM $8   MIP $12

Green Beret Weapons Arsenal, 1993, Hasbro
- EX $4   NM $8   MIP $12

High Caliber Weapons Arsenal, 1994, Hasbro, weapons pack
- EX $3   NM $6   MIP $10

Jungle Patrol Mission Gear, 1993, Hasbro
- EX $4   NM $8   MIP $12

Light Infantry Mission Gear, 1993, Hasbro
- EX $4   NM $8   MIP $12

Marine Paris Island Gear, 1993, Hasbro
- EX $4   NM $8   MIP $12

Mobile Artillery Assault Set, 1993, Hasbro
- EX $5   NM $10   MIP $15

Mountain Assault Mission Gear, 1993, Hasbro
- EX $4   NM $8   MIP $12

Navy SEAL Commando, 1993, Hasbro, Deluxe Mission Gear
- EX $5   NM $10   MIP $15

Navy Shore Patrol Gear, 1993, Hasbro
- EX $4   NM $8   MIP $12

Ocean Enforcer Mission Gear, 1994, Hasbro
EX $4   NM $8   MIP $12

Red Beret Weapons Arsenal, 1993, Hasbro
EX $4   NM $8   MIP $12

Red Ninja Mission Gear, 1993, Hasbro
EX $4   NM $8   MIP $12

S.W.A.T. Assault Mission Gear, 1993, Hasbro
EX $4   NM $8   MIP $12

Smart Gun Blaster, 1993, Hasbro
EX $3   NM $6   MIP $10

Star Brigade Astronaut Mission Gear, 1994, Hasbro
EX $4   NM $8   MIP $12

Swamp Fighter Mission Gear, 1994, Hasbro
EX $4   NM $8   MIP $12

The Ultimate Arsenal, 1993, Hasbro, more than 25 pieces
EX $7   NM $14   MIP $20

Underwater Attack Mission Gear, 1993, Hasbro
EX $4   NM $8   MIP $12

Urban S.W.A.T., 1994, Hasbro, weapons pack
EX $3   NM $6   MIP $10

Vehicle

Jet Pack, 1994, Hasbro
EX $4   NM $8   MIP $12

Strike Cycle, 1994, Hasbro
EX $4   NM $8   MIP $12

Vehicles

Rhino G.P.V., 1993, Hasbro, General Purpose Vehicle, 4WD
EX $8   NM $16   MIP $24

30TH SALUTE SERIES

30th Salute Black Action Soldier, 1994, Hasbro, Model No. 81271
EX $55   NM $100   MIP $150

35th Anniversary Gift Set, 1999, Hasbro, Then and Now, 1964 figure, 1999 figure, set of two, 1999
EX $25   NM $50   MIP $75

Action Marine, 1994, Hasbro, Model No. 81047
EX $45   NM $60   MIP $80

Action Pilot, 1994, Hasbro, Model No. 81046
EX $50   NM $75   MIP $125

Action Sailor, 1994, Hasbro, Model No. 81048
EX $60   NM $80   MIP $100

Action Soldier, 1994, Hasbro, Model No. 81045
EX $25   NM $50   MIP $95

Green Beret Lt. Joseph Colton, 1994, Hasbro, mail order
EX $75   NM $125   MIP $175

ACTION ASSORTMENT

Adventures of G.I. Joe: Peril of the Raging River, 1999, Hasbro
EX $7   NM $12   MIP $25

Delta Force, 1999, Hasbro
EX $7   NM $12   MIP $25

Salute to the Millennium Marine, 1999, Hasbro
EX $7   NM $12   MIP $25

ALPHA ASSORTMENT

Battle of the Bulge, 2000, Hasbro
EX n/a   NM n/a   MIP n/a

Demolitions Expert, 2000, Hasbro
EX n/a   NM n/a   MIP n/a

Navy Seal, 2000, Hasbro
EX $7   NM $12   MIP $25

WWII Pacific Marine, 2000, Hasbro
EX n/a   NM n/a   MIP n/a

ARMED FORCES ASSORTMENT

Army National Guard, 1998, Hasbro
EX $10   NM $12   MIP $25

U.S. Air Force Crew Chief, 1998, Hasbro
EX $10   NM $12   MIP $25

U.S. Marine Corps Korean Soldier, 1998, Hasbro
EX $10   NM $12   MIP $25

U.S. Marine Corps Recruit, 1998, Hasbro
EX $10   NM $12   MIP $25

U.S. Navy Serviceman, 1998, Hasbro
EX $10   NM $12   MIP $25

ARMED FORCES SERVICE COLLECTION

Police Officer, 1999, Hasbro
EX $5   NM $8   MIP $25

U.S. Army Infantry Desert Soldier, 1999, Hasbro
EX $5   NM $8   MIP $25

U.S. Army Pacific Forces, 1999, Hasbro
EX $5   NM $8   MIP $25

U.S. Army Vietnam Soldiers, 1998, Hasbro
EX $5   NM $8   MIP $20

U.S. Navy SEAL, 1999, Hasbro
EX $5   NM $8   MIP $20

USAF Fighter Pilot: Korean War, 1999, Hasbro
EX $5   NM $8   MIP $20

Vietnam Marine, 1999, Hasbro
EX $5   NM $10   MIP $15

ASTRONAUT ASSORTMENT

(Hasbro Photo)

Mercury Astronaut, 1997, Hasbro, In spacesuit and helmet
EX $15   NM $12   MIP $25

(Hasbro Photo)

Space Shuttle Astronaut, 1997, Hasbro, In orange spacesuit
EX $15   NM $12   MIP $25

BRAVO ASSORTMENT

Vietnam Combat Engineer, 2000, Hasbro
EX n/a   NM n/a   MIP n/a

Vietnam Jungle Recon Soldier, 2000, Hasbro
EX $5   NM $10   MIP $20

G.I. JOE

CORE FIGURE ASSORTMENT

Adventures of G.I. Joe: Save the Tiger, 1999, Hasbro
EX $5 NM $10 MIP $15

G.I. Joe: Challenge at Hawk River, 1999, Hasbro
EX $5 NM $10 MIP $15

U.S. Army Nurse: Vietnam, 1999, Hasbro
EX $5 NM $10 MIP $20

U.S. Coast Guard Boarding Party, 1999, Hasbro
EX $5 NM $10 MIP $20

DELTA ASSORTMENT

Navajo Code Talker, 2000, Hasbro
EX $7 NM $15 MIP $30

U.S. Marine Dog Unit, 2000, Hasbro
EX $7 NM $12 MIP $25

ECHO ASSORTMENT

John F. Kennedy, 2000, Hasbro
EX $8 NM $15 MIP $25

Vietnam Wall, 2000, Hasbro
EX n/a NM n/a MIP n/a

WWI Doughboy, 2000, Hasbro
EX $7 NM $12 MIP $20

WWII U.S. Army Airborne Normandy, 2000, Hasbro
EX $7 NM $15 MIP $30

FOREIGN ASSORTMENT

Japanese Zero pilot, 2000, Hasbro
EX n/a NM n/a MIP n/a

Red Infantry Pilot, 2000, Hasbro
EX n/a NM n/a MIP n/a

FOURTH OF JULY EDITION

(Hasbro Photo)

D-Day Salute, 1997, Hasbro, With M-1 rifle, pack and camo-net helmet
EX $7 NM $12 MIP $20

GREATEST HEROES

Buzz Aldrin, 1999, Hasbro
EX $10 NM $20 MIP $40

(KP Photo)

Lt. Colonel Theodore Roosevelt, 1999, Hasbro, In Spanish-American War uniform, dark blue shirt, tan coat and pants. Includes American flag, pistol and other accessories
EX $10 NM $20 MIP $30

Ted Williams, 1999, Hasbro
EX $10 NM $20 MIP $35

WWII Flame Thrower Soldier, 1999, Hasbro
EX $7 NM $12 MIP $25

HISTORICAL COMMANDERS ASSORTMENT

Colin Powell, 1998, Hasbro
EX $10 NM $20 MIP $45

Dwight Eisenhower, 1997, Hasbro
EX $7 NM $12 MIP $20

General Patton, 1997, Hasbro
EX $7 NM $12 MIP $20

Omar Bradley, 1998, Hasbro
EX $7 NM $12 MIP $20

HOLIDAY SALUTE

(Hasbro)

George Washington, 1998, Hasbro
EX $7 NM $12 MIP $20

HOLLYWOOD HEROES

Bob Hope, 1998, Hasbro
EX $15 NM $25 MIP $40

MILITARY SPORTS ASSORTMENT

Army Football, 1998, Hasbro
EX $5 NM $8 MIP $15

Navy Football, 1998, Hasbro
EX $5 NM $8 MIP $15

MODERN FORCES ASSORTMENT

82nd Airborne Division, female, 1998, Hasbro
EX $5 NM $8 MIP $15

Australian O.D.F., 1996, Hasbro
EX $5 NM $8 MIP $15

Battle of the Bulge, Toys R Us Exlcusive, 1996, Hasbro
EX $8 NM $12 MIP $20

Belgium Para Commando, 1997, Hasbro
EX $8 NM $12 MIP $20

(Hasbro Photo)

British SAS, 1996, Hasbro, Limited edition, with rifle, helmet and goggles
EX $8 NM $15 MIP $25

Dress Marine, Toys R Us Exclusive, 1996, Hasbro
EX $8 NM $15 MIP $25

French Foreign Legion Legionnaire, 1997, Hasbro
EX $8 NM $12 MIP $20

U.S. Airborne Ranger HALO Parachutist, 1996, Hasbro
EX $7 NM $15 MIP $25

U.S. Army Coldweather Soldier, 1998, Hasbro
EX $8 NM $12 MIP $20

U.S. Army Drill Sergeant, 1997, Hasbro
EX $5 NM $10 MIP $15

U.S. Army Helicopter Pilot, female, 1997, Hasbro
EX $10 NM $20 MIP $30

G.I. JOE

(Hasbro Photo)

U.S. Army Infantry Soldier, 1996, Hasbro, Limited edition, with goggles, machine and desert-pattern uniform
EX $8   **NM** $12   **MIP** $20

U.S. Army M-1 Tank Commander, 1997, Hasbro
EX $8   **NM** $12   **MIP** $20

U.S. Marine Corp Force Recon, 1998, Hasbro
EX $7   **NM** $10   **MIP** $15

(Hasbro Photo)

U.S. Marine Corps Sniper, 1996, Hasbro, Camouflaged rifle with scope, camo netting
EX $10   **NM** $20   **MIP** $40

U.S. Navy Blue Angel, 1998, Hasbro
EX $8   **NM** $12   **MIP** $20

U.S. Navy Flight Deck Fuel Handler, 1997, Hasbro
EX $7   **NM** $12   **MIP** $20

PEARL HARBOR COLLECTION

Army Defense Diorama Set, 2000, Hasbro
EX n/a   **NM** n/a   **MIP** n/a

Battleship Row Defender, 2000, Hasbro
EX n/a   **NM** n/a   **MIP** n/a

Diamond Head Lookout Invasion Alert, 2000, Hasbro
EX n/a   **NM** n/a   **MIP** n/a

Hickam Field Army Defender, 2000, Hasbro
EX n/a   **NM** n/a   **MIP** n/a

Vicker's Machine Gun, 2000, Hasbro
EX n/a   **NM** n/a   **MIP** n/a

Wheeler Field Army Air Corp, 2000, Hasbro
EX n/a   **NM** n/a   **MIP** n/a

WWII COMMEMORATIVE FIGURES, TARGET EXCLUSIVE

(Hasbro)

Action Marine, 1995, Hasbro, In camo uniform with cap, rifle, canteen, grenades and pack
EX $8   **NM** $15   **MIP** $25

(Hasbro)

Action Pilot, 1995, Hasbro, Khaki uniform, leather jacket and helmet, goggles, bayonet, .45 pistol, dog tags
EX $5   **NM** $10   **MIP** $15

(Hasbro)

Action Sailor, 1995, Hasbro, Blue uniform, Shore Patrol armband, M-1 rifle, duffle bag
EX $8   **NM** $15   **MIP** $20

Action Soldier, 1995, Hasbro
EX $8   **NM** $10   **MIP** $15

WWII FORCES ASSORTMENT

442nd Americans of Japanese Descent Combat Soldiers, 1998, Hasbro
EX $8   **NM** $15   **MIP** $25

Congressional Medal of Honor, Platoon Sgt. Mitchell Paige, 1998, Hasbro
EX $8   **NM** $12   **MIP** $20

Congressional Medal of Honor, Sgt. Francis S. Currey, 1997, Hasbro
EX $10   **NM** $20   **MIP** $40

Tuskegee B-25 Bomber Pilot, African American, 1997, Hasbro
EX $8   **NM** $10   **MIP** $15

Tuskegee Fighter Pilot, African American, 1997, Hasbro
EX $8   **NM** $10   **MIP** $15

U.S. Air Force B-17 Bomber Crewman, 1998, Hasbro
EX $8   **NM** $10   **MIP** $15

U.S. Navy PT-Boat Commander, 1998, Hasbro
EX $8   **NM** $10   **MIP** $20

G.I. JOE

Guns

By Karen O'Brien

I remember the toy guns I had as a kid. Considering the increasing popularity of toy guns at toy shows and auctions, it seems that plenty of other collectors have equally fond memories of backyard bag guys and the good guys who chased them. My plastic double holster rig came with six plastic, silver-colored bullets and six molded places just for them. Mom always made me take the bullets out of the holster when I played outside—didn't want to lose 'em after all. The silver twin cap pistols with white plastic handles never had caps in them, but they made a great sound when I pulled the triggers anyway. I bet you can describe your rig too.

The first cap gun patent dates back to 1860. Until World War II, the preferred material for cap guns was cast iron. Most early cap guns, exploders, and figural guns were made of cast iron, though variations of plastic, tin, and stamped metal also appear. Metal toy gun production ceased around 1940. The companies that survived after 1946 experimented with a variety of materials and methods of production, the most successful of which was die-casting. This involved injecting an alloy mixture into a mold, which resulted in fine detail, lower costs, and a much lighter gun.

Die-cast guns dominated the 1950s and '60s marketplace. Television brought little buckaroos daily installments of the thrilling adventures of cowboy heroes such as Roy Rogers, Gene Autry, and Hopalong Cassidy. Manufacturers such as the George Schmidt Company, Classy Products, Marx, Hubley, Nichols, Kilgore, and Wyandotte all scrambled to arm these cowpokes. The introduction of plastics changed the market as manufacturers lowered production costs.

While cap guns sold in the American market were largely produced by American manufacturers in both the prewar and postwar periods, other toy guns came from overseas producers. Tin lithography became an art form in postwar Japan. The same Japanese companies that produced the robots and tin cars so widely sought by today's collectors also produced space ray guns, cowboy, G-men, and military-style tin litho guns for the American market.

COLLECTING

Collectors of toy guns vary in scope and focus. While some prefer the guns of a favorite manufacturer, others collect those of a particular type. Space guns in particular, have gained in popularity the last few years.

Condition is a prime consideration. Mint guns in their mint packaging are worth more than well-loved guns that have exploded countless caps. It must be noted that the acidic nature of the paper used to make boxes for toy guns has damaged the pristine finish of many toy guns. Mattel's Fanner 50s have been prone to this problem.

Manufacturers often produced the same gun for several years with only minor changes, thus creating variations the collector should be aware of when valuing toy guns. Repaired or restored guns should always be represented as such to buyers.

2006 TRENDS

Toy guns, especially western cap pistols, will retain their value. Lesser-condition guns are appearing in greater numbers, as mint-quality examples are more difficult to obtain. Western guns from cowboy heroes like Hopalong Cassidy, Roy Rogers, and the Lone Ranger remain the most popular. Detective/Spy guns hold their value on the strength of The Man From U.N.C.L.E. and Dragnet tie-ins.

THE TOP TEN TOY GUNS (In Mint Condition)

1. Hopalong Cassidy Double Holster Set, Wyandotte, 1940s	$4,000
2. Man From U.N.C.L.E. THRUSH Rifle, Ideal, 1966	3,250
3. Hopalong Cassidy Holster/Gun Set, Schmidt, 1950s	3,000
4. Man From U.N.C.L.E. Attache Case, Ideal, 1965	1,650
5. Roy Rogers Double Gun & Holster Set, two 8-1/2" pistols, Classy, 1950s	1,600
6. Roy Rogers Double Holster Set, two 9" pistols, Classy, 1950s	1,550
7. Roy Rogers Double Holster Set, two 10" pistols, Classy, 1950s	1,500
8. Dale Evans D-26 cap pistol, Schmidt, 1950s	1,250
9. Popeye Pirate Click Pistol, tin litho, Marx, 1930s	1,000
10. Cap Gun Store Display, Nichols, 1950s	950

DETECTIVE/SPY

Agent Zero M Pocket-Shot, 1965-66, Mattel, cap gun and "knife"
EX $15 **NM** $25 **MIP** $45

Agent Zero M Potshot, 1965, Mattel, 3" die-cast potshot derringer, gold finish, has brown vinyl armband holster holds two Shootin' Shell cartridges, gold buckle w/Agent Zero W logo
EX $40 **NM** $85 **MIP** $125

Agent Zero M Radio Gun, 1964, Mattel, 8-1/2" closed, 22-1/2" open, looks like portable radio
EX $50 **NM** $100 **MIP** $150

Agent Zero M Snap-Shot Camera Pistol, 1964, Mattel, 7-1/2" extended, camera turns into pistol at press of a button
EX $35 **NM** $60 **MIP** $85

Detective Shell Firing Pistol, 1950s, Nichols, 5-1/2" snub-nose pistol chambers and fires six three-piece cap cartridges, cut-out badge, bullet cartridges, extra red plastic bullet heads
EX $100 **NM** $175 **MIP** $275

Dick Cap Pistol, 1930, Hubley, 4-1/8" cast iron automatic style, side loading, nickel finish, Dick oval in red paint
EX $75 **NM** $150 **MIP** $275

Dick Cap Pistol, 1950s, Hubley, die-cast, 4-1/4" automatic style, side loading w/nickel finish, Model 210A, eagles on grips
EX $25 **NM** $65 **MIP** $120

Dick Cap Pistol, 1950s, Benton Harbor Novelty, 4-3/4", automatic, side loading, black finish
EX $20 **NM** $40 **MIP** $85

Dragnet Badge 714 Detective Special Repeating Revolver, 1955, Knickerbocker, no. 639, plastic cap pistol
EX $45 **NM** $100 **MIP** $175

Dragnet Badge 714 Triple Fire Comb. Game, 1955, Knickerbocker, tin litho stand-up target has four plastic spinners, includes two 6" black plastic guns, one fires darts, the other cork gun, includes four plastic darts and three corks
EX $90 **NM** $150 **MIP** $275

Dragnet Snub Nose Cap Pistol, 1960s, Knickerbocker, plastic/die-cast works, 6-3/4", black plastic w/gold "Dragnet" and "714" badge on grip, on card
EX $35 **NM** $100 **MIP** $250

Dragnet Water Gun, 1960s, Knickerbocker, 6" black plastic, .38 Special-style w/gold "714" shield on grip
EX $25 **NM** $65 **MIP** $200

Girl From U.N.C.L.E. Garter Holster, 1966, Lone Star, "gang buster" metal gun fires plastic bullets from metal shells, checker design vinyl holster and bullet pouch, on card
EX $80 **NM** $145 **MIP** $225

G-Man Gun Wind-Up Machine Gun, 1948, Marx, 23" tin-litho, red, black, orange and gray litho, round drum magazine, wind-up mechanism makes sparks from muzzle, uses cigarette flint, wooden stock
EX $145 **NM** $285 **MIP** $450

Man From U.N.C.L.E. Attache Case, 1965, Ideal, 15" x 10" x 2-1/2", comes w/cap firing pistol and clip, ID card, wallet, cap grenade, badge, passport and secret message sender
EX $525 **NM** $1050 **MIP** $1650

Man From U.N.C.L.E. Attache Case, 1966, Lone Star, vinyl case w/pistol, holster, walkie talkie, cigarette box gun, badge, passport, invisible cartridge pen, handcuffs
EX $265 **NM** $530 **MIP** $775

Man From U.N.C.L.E. Attache Case, 1966, Lone Star, vinyl covered cardboard, 9mm automatic Luger, shoulder stock, sight, silencer, belt, holster, secret wrist holster and pistol, grenade, wallet, passport, money
EX $300 **NM** $600 **MIP** $800

Man From U.N.C.L.E. Attache Case, 1966, Lone Star, small cardboard briefcase, contains die-cast Mauser and parts to assemble U.N.C.L.E. Special
EX $140 **NM** $280 **MIP** $450

Man From U.N.C.L.E. Illya K. Special Lighter Gun, 1966, Ideal, cigarette lighter gun shoots caps, has radio compartment concealed behind fake cigs, in window box
EX $125 **NM** $225 **MIP** $350

Man From U.N.C.L.E. Illya Kuryakin Gun Set, 1966, Ideal, includes clip loading, cap firing plastic pistol, badge, wallet, ID card, in window box
EX $210 **NM** $420 **MIP** $650

Man From U.N.C.L.E. Napoleon Solo Gun Set, 1965, Ideal, clip loading, cap firing plastic pistol w/rifle attachments, badge, ID card, in window box
EX $280 **NM** $560 **MIP** $875

Man From U.N.C.L.E. Pistol and Holster, 1965, Ideal, 7" long pistol and plastic holster, both w/orange ID sticker
EX $45 **NM** $90 **MIP** $135

Man From U.N.C.L.E. Pistol Cane, 1966, Marx, 25" long, cap firing, bullet shooting aluminum cane w/eight bullets and one metal shell, on card
EX $175 **NM** $350 **MIP** $550

Man From U.N.C.L.E. Secret Service Pop Gun, 1960s, Unknown, bagged luger pop gun on header card w/unlicensed art of Napoleon and Illya
EX $4 **NM** $12 **MIP** $30

Man From U.N.C.L.E. Stash Away Guns, 1966, Ideal, three cap firing guns, holsters, two straps, ID card and badge, in window box
EX $210 **NM** $420 **MIP** $650

(KP Photo)

Man From U.N.C.L.E. THRUSH Rifle, 1966, Ideal, 36" long
EX $875 **NM** $1750 **MIP** $3250

Official Detective Shootin' Shell Snub-Nose .38, 1959, Mattel, .38 die-cast chrome w/brown plastic grips, black vinyl shoulder holster, wallet, badge, ID card, Pistol Range Target and bullets
EX $95 **NM** $175 **MIP** $250

Official Detective Shootin' Shell Snub-Nose .38, 1960, Mattel, .38 die-cast 7" chrome finish, gold cylinder, brown plastic grips, Private Detective badge and Shootin' Shell bullets
EX $60 **NM** $100 **MIP** $165

Official Dick Tracy Shootin' Shell Snub-Nose .38, 1961, Mattel, die-cast chrome .38 w/brown plastic grips, chrome finish w/Shootin' Shell bullets and Stick-m caps
EX $75 **NM** $150 **MIP** $250

Sharkmatic Cap Gun, 1980s, Edison, 6" automatic, style pistol, fires "Supermatic System" strip caps
EX $10 **NM** $15 **MIP** $20

The Saint Ruger, 1960s, Lone Star, die-cast w/telescopic sight and silencer
EX $50 **NM** $100 **MIP** $150

MILITARY/AUTOMATICS

7580 UZI Automatic, 1986, Esquire Novelty, 10-1/2", battery-operated, black plastic uses 250-shot roll caps, shoulder strap
EX $20 **NM** $45 **MIP** $60

9mm Z-Matic Uzi Cap Gun, 1984, Larami, 8" replica, removeable cap storage magazine, black finish, small orange plug in barrel
EX $5 **NM** $10 **MIP** $15

Anti Aircraft Gun, Marx, mechanical, sparks, tin litho, 16-1/2" long, 1941
EX $50 **NM** $135 **MIP** $275

Army .45 Cap Pistol, 1950s, Hubley, 6-1/2" automatic, dark gray finish, white plastic grips, pop-up cap
EX $50 **NM** $150 **MIP** $300

GUNS

Army 45 Automatic, 1959, Nichols, 4-1/4" all metal, side loading automatic, olive
EX $15   NM $25   MIP $50

Army Automatic Pistol, 1950s, Marx, 2-1/2" automatic, (ACP style), black w/white grips, small leather holster w/flaps (Marx Miniature)
EX $10   NM $20   MIP $40

Army Pistol with Revolving Cylinder, Marx, tin litho
EX $35   NM $60   MIP $125

Army Sparking Pop Gun, Marx, 1940-50
EX $45   NM $75   MIP $150

Automatic Cap Pistol, 1925, National, 4-1/4" automatic style, grip swivels to load, black finish
EX $45   NM $100   MIP $200

Automatic Cap Pistol, 1950s, National, 6-1/2" silver finish w/simulated walnut grip
EX $35   NM $65   MIP $90

Automatic Cap Pistol No. 290, Hubley, die-cast, 6-1/2", nickel finish, brown checkered grips, magazine pops up when slider is pulled back
EX $85   NM $170   MIP $310

Burp Gun, 1960s, Marx, 20" battery-operated, green and black plastic
EX $20   NM $35   MIP $75

Desert Patrol Machine Pistol, Marx, plastic, 11" long
EX $30   NM $45   MIP $75

Falcon Service Automatic, 1950s, Kilgore, Colt .45 cap pistol
EX $8   NM $16   MIP $25

Green Beret Tommy Gun, 1960s, Marx, sparkles, trigger action, on card
EX $35   NM $55   MIP $95

Johnny Seven One Man Army-OMA, 1964, Topper/Deluxe, 36" multi-purpose seven guns in one, removeable pistol fires caps, rifle fires white plastic bullets, bolt spring fired machine gun "tommy gun" sound, rear launcher fires grenades, forward diff. shell
EX $125   NM $225   MIP $350

M-1 Kadet Training Rifle, 1960s, Parris, 32" wood/metal M-1 carbine, clicker action, metal barrel, trigger guard, bolt
EX $20   NM $35   MIP $50

Matic 45 Cap Gun, 1980s, Edison, 24", plastic gun w/stock, fires "Supermatic System" strip caps
EX $10   NM $15   MIP $20

Mattel-O-Matic Air Cooled Machine Gun, 1955, Mattel, 16" machine gun fires

perforated roll caps by cranking handle, plastic w/die-cast, tripod-mounted, plastic/die-cast works, red and black plastic, box
EX $45   NM $85   MIP $125

Mini-M.A.G. Combat Gun, Marx, cap pistol, miniature scale, die-cast
EX $20   NM $30   MIP $40

MM Automatic Carbine, 1960s, Unknown, 24" recoil red slide in muzzle and flashing light, brown and black plastic
EX $15   NM $30   MIP $45

Model 12 SoftAir Gun, 1990, Daisy, machine gun style, loads "SoftAir" pellets in plastic cartridge, ten rounds, spring fired, can be cocked by barrel grip or bolt
EX $35   NM $50   MIP $75

Molotov Cocktail Tank Buster Cap Bomb, 1964, Maco, 6" plastic and die-cast, insert caps in head and throw
EX $10   NM $15   MIP $25

MP Holster Set, 1950s, Maco, plastic pistol has removeable magazine, loads and ejects bullets, white leather belt and holster
EX $65   NM $120   MIP $175

Mustang Toy Machine Gun, 1950s, Main Machine, 25" long chrome and hard plastic paper firing gun
EX $75   NM $125   MIP $175

Official James Bond 007 Thunderball Pistol, 1985, Coibel, 4-1/2" Walther PPK style, single shot fires plastic caps, Secret Agent ID
EX $15   NM $30   MIP $65

Paratrooper Carbine, 1950s, Maco, 24" carbine, removeable magazine, fires plastic bullets, bayonet and target
EX $75   NM $115   MIP $165

Revolver Mauser Cap Pistol, 1960s, Redondo, 6-1/4", Mauser style automatic pop-up magazine, silver finish, brown plastic grips
EX $4   NM $15   MIP $30

SA Automatic Burp Gun, 1970s, Daisy, 10" w/stock, black plastic, burp-gun style, removeable clip, loads and fires white plastic bullets
EX $20   NM $35   MIP $50

Siren Sparkling Airplane Pistol, Marx, heavy-gauge enamel steel, 9-1/2" wingspan, 7" long
EX $50   NM $75   MIP $100

Sparkling Siren Machine Gun, 1949, Marx, 26" long
EX $45   NM $90   MIP $175

Special Mission Tommy Gun, Marx
EX $20   NM $35   MIP $45

Spitfire Automatic Cap Pistol, 1940, Stevens, 4-5/8" cast iron, side loading, silver finish, "flying airplanes" white plastic grips
EX $65   NM $150   MIP $300

Spitfire Cap Firing Machine Gun, 1950, Buddy L, biped stand attached to muzzle, black plastic stock and grip w/cap or clicker firing
EX $80   NM $140   MIP $200

Tommy Burp Gun, 1957, Mattel, 17" plastic w/die-cast works, perforated roll caps fired by cranking the handle
EX $100   NM $200   MIP $350

Tommy Gun, 1939, Marx, sparks and makes noise
EX $65   NM $130   MIP $225

USA Machine Gun, 1950s, Maco, 12" tripod-mounted gun fires plastic bullets, red and yellow plastic
EX $65   NM $130   MIP $200

Wind-Up Burp Gun, 1955, Mattel, plastic/pressed steel, 24", "Grease Gun", fires perforated roll caps, fold-over wire stock, cap storage in magazine, boxed
EX $50   NM $90   MIP $150

MISCELLANEOUS

25 Jr. Cap Pistol, 1930, Stevens, 4-1/8" automatic, side loading, silver finish
EX $25   NM $75   MIP $150

6 Shot Cap Pistol, Stevens, 6-3/4", six separate triggers revolve to deliver caps to hammer, metal finish
EX $85   NM $150   MIP $300

Airplane Clicker Pistol, 1950s, Palmer Plastics, 4-1/2" yellow and black plane, red pilot and guns
EX $25   NM $45   MIP $65

Atomee Water Pistol, 1960s, Park Plastics, 4-1/4" black plastic
EX $10   NM $20   MIP $35

Automatic Repeater Paper Pop Pistol, Marx, 7-3/4" long
EX $35   NM $65   MIP $125

Automatic Sparkling Pistol, 1960s, EMU Rififi, 6-1/2", plastic/metal, uses cigarette lighter flints to make sparks, available in green-red, yellow-green, red or white colors
EX $15   NM $30   MIP $45

Blastaway Cap Gun, Marx, 50 shooter repeater
EX $25   NM $35   MIP $75

Buzz Barton Special, No. 195, 1930s, Daisy, blue metal finish, wood stock w/ring sight
EX $85   NM $125   MIP $200

Click Pistol, Marx, pressed steel, 7-3/4" long
EX $20   NM $50   MIP $100

Click Pistol, Marx, tin litho
EX $20   NM $50   MIP $100

Clip 50 Cap Pistol, 1940, Kilgore, 4-1/4", unusual automatic style, black Bakelite plastic frame, removeable cap magazine clip
EX $75   NM $110   MIP $200

Crack Shot Dart Pistol, 1950s, Wyandotte, black plastic, shoots darts at target
EX $10   NM $25   MIP $45

Double Holster Set, 1950s, Unknown, black leather, large size, steer head conches, lots of red jewels, fringe, holsters only, no guns
EX $75   NM $125   MIP $250

GUNS

Dynamic Automatic Repeating Bubble Gun, Atomic Industries, 8" black plastic pistol projects bubbles
EX $25   NM $40   MIP $65

Famous Firearms Deluxe Edition Collectors Album, 1959, Marx, set of four rifles, five pistols and four holsters miniature series, includes: Mare's Laig, Thompson machine gun, Sharps rifle, Winchester saddle rifle, Derringer, .38 snub-nose, Civil War pistol, six shooter/Flint
EX $50   NM $100   MIP $200

Hideaway Derringer, 1950s, Esquire Novelty, 3-1/2" single shot, loads solid metal bullet, grip is removeable to store two more bullets, gold finish, white plastic grips
EX $65   NM $90   MIP $110

Jack Armstrong Shooting Propeller Plane Gun, 1933, Daisy, 5-1/2" gun, shoots flying disk, pressed tin, in box
EX $100   NM $200   MIP $350

Johnny Tremain Flintlock Pistol, 1950s, Swansea Industries, cap gun based on Walt Disney character
EX $35   NM $70   MIP $110

Long Tom Dart Gun, 1950s, Midwest, 11" pressed steel
EX $35   NM $50   MIP $100

M240 Machine Pistol, 1970s, Marx, black plastic, no caps, pull trigger produces sound
EX $5   NM $12   MIP $20

Marx Miniatures Famous Gun Sets, 1958, Marx, set of four guns, features tommy gun, Civil War revolver, "Mare's Laig" and western saddle rifle
EX $25   NM $50   MIP $100

Marxman Target Pistol, Marx, plastic, 5-1/2" long
EX $35   NM $50   MIP $100

Midget Cap Pistol, 1950s, Hubley, 5-1/2" long, die-cast, all metal flintlock w/silver finish
EX $20   NM $35   MIP $50

Model 25-50, 1930, Stevens, 4-1/2" nickel finish
EX $35   NM $90   MIP $175

Model No. 25 Pump Action BB Gun, 1960s, Daisy, plastic stock
EX $35   NM $65   MIP $125

Mountie Automatic Cap Pistol, Kilgore, 6", double action, automatic style w/pop-up magazine, unusual nickel finish, black plastic grips
EX $20   NM $30   MIP $60

Nu-Matic Paper Popper Gun, 1940s, Langson, pressed steel, 7" squeeze grip trigger, mechanism pops roll of paper (reel at top of gun) to make loud noise, black finish
EX $30   NM $50   MIP $75

P-38 Clicker Pistol, 1950s, Meldon, 7-1/2" black finish, automatic style
EX $35   NM $50   MIP $100

Paper Cracker Rifle, 1940s, Buddy L, 26" steel and machined aluminum mechanism, barrel, trigger and operating lever, uses 1000 shot paper roll, brown plastic stock
EX $95   NM $190   MIP $250

Pirate Cap Pistol, 1940s, Hubley, 9-1/2" side-by-side flintlock style w/die-cast frame and cast double hammers and trigger, chrome finish, white plastic grips feature Pirate in red oval
EX $70   NM $250   MIP $500

Pluck Cap Pistol, 1930, Stevens, 3-1/2" cast iron, single shot single action
EX $30   NM $80   MIP $125

Popeye Pirate Click Pistol, Marx, tin litho, 10" long, 1930s, with box
EX $225   NM $600   MIP $1000

Potato Gun, 1991, Hong Kong, Spud Gun, plastic, pneumatic action fires potato pellet from muzzle
EX $3   NM $7   MIP $10

Presto Cap Pistol, 1940, Kilgore, 5-1/8", pop up cap magazine nickel finish brown plastic grips
EX $65   NM $120   MIP $225

Repeating Cap Pistol, Marx, aluminum
EX $20   NM $30   MIP $50

Revolver Aquila Pop Pistol, 1960s, Rosvi, 10" green finish, pop gun breaks to cock, fires cork from barrel, sparks from mechanism under barrel
EX $15   NM $30   MIP $60

Rex Automatic Cap Pistol, 1939, Kilgore, 3-7/8", blue metal finish cast iron, small size automatic style, side loading, white pearlized grips
EX $45   NM $100   MIP $200

Sparkling Machine Gun "Sure-Shot", 1950s, T. Cohn, tin litho in red, yellow and blue, turn handle and barrel sparks
EX $30   NM $60   MIP $110

Sparkling Pop Gun, Marx
EX $25   NM $50   MIP $100

Spud Gun, 1950s, Ambrit Industries, case aluminum, pneumatic all-metal gun shoots pellets
EX $15   NM $35   MIP $50

Spud Gun (Tira Papas), 1960s, Welco, 6" all-metal gun
EX $10   NM $20   MIP $35

Streamline Siren Sparkling Pistol, Marx, tin litho
EX $25   NM $50   MIP $100

Targeteer No. 18 Target Air Pistol, 1949, Daisy, 10" gun metal finish, push barrel to cock, Daisy BB tin w/special BBs, spinner target
EX $50   NM $90   MIP $135

Tiger Cap Pistol, 1935, Hubley, 6 7/8", single action, mammoth caps, metal finish
EX $35   NM $100   MIP $200

Trooper Cap Pistol, 1950, Hubley, 6-1/2" all metal, pop up cap magazine, nickel finish, black grips
EX $30   NM $85   MIP $175

Water Pistol No. 17, 1940, Daisy, 5-1/4" tin
EX $25   NM $50   MIP $75

Water Pistol No. 8, 1930s, Daisy, 5-1/4" tin
EX $30   NM $60   MIP $85

Winner Cap Pistol, 1940, Hubley, 4-3/8" automatic style, pop-up magazine release in front of trigger guard, nickel finish
EX $45   NM $100   MIP $200

POLICE

.38 Cap Pistol, Marx, w/caps, miniature scale, die-cast
EX $35   NM $75   MIP $125

Detective Snub-Nose Special, 1950s, Marx, die-cast, 5-3/4" top release break, unusual revolving cylinder, fires Kilgore style disc caps, chrome finish w/black plastic grips
EX $65   NM $100   MIP $150

Dick Tracy Click Pistol, Marx
EX $50   NM $125   MIP $200

Dick Tracy Jr. Click Pistol, 1930s, Marx, aluminum
EX $75   NM $150   MIP $275

Dick Tracy Siren Pistol, 1935, Marx, pressed steel, 8-1/2" long
EX $85   NM $150   MIP $350

Dick Tracy Sparkling Pop Pistol, Marx, tin litho
EX $50   NM $125   MIP $200

Gang Buster Crusade Against Crime Sub-Machine Gun, 1938, Marx, litho, metal w/wooden stock, 23" long
EX $110   NM $225   MIP $450

G-Boy Pistol, 1950s, Acme Novelty, 7" automatic (ACP) style entire left rear side of gun swings down to load
EX $15   NM $35   MIP $65

G-Man Automatic Silent Arm Pistol, Marx, tin
EX $35   NM $55   MIP $100

G-Man Automatic Sparkling Pistol, 1930s, Marx, pressed steel, 4" long
EX $45   NM $85   MIP $175

G-Man Machine Gun, 1940s, Marx, tin miniature, wind-up, wood stock, red and yellow litho
EX $25   NM $35   MIP $65

G-Man Sparkling Sub-Machine Gun, Marx
EX $50   NM $75   MIP $150

G-Man Tommy Gun, 1936, Marx, sparkles when wound

EX $65   NM $110   MIP $225

Machine Gun Cap Pistol, 1938, Kilgore, 5-1/8", long cast iron crank-fired gun

EX $125   NM $225   MIP $350

Marx Miniatures Detective Set, 1950s, Marx, miniature cap firing brown and gray tommy gun, chrome pistol and holster on card w/wood grain frame border

EX $25   NM $45   MIP $75

Mountie Automatic Cap Pistol, 1960s, Hubley, die-cast, 7-1/4" automatic style, pop up lever-release magazine, blue finish

EX $20   NM $35   MIP $65

Official Dick Tracy Tommy Burst Machine Gun, 1960s, Mattel, 25" Thompson style machine gun fire perforated roll caps, single shot or in full burst when bolt is pulled back, brown plastic stock and black plastic body, lift up rear sight, Dick Tracy decal on stock

EX $130   NM $275   MIP $450

Peter Gunn Private Eye Revolver & Holster Set, 1959, Pilgrim Leather, 36" die-cast Remington w/six two-piece bullets, badge and wallet, Peter Gunn business cards, black leather shoulder holster

EX $200   NM $325   MIP $450

Sheriff Signal Pistol, 1950, Marx, plastic, 5-1/2" long

EX $20   NM $30   MIP $60

Siren Sparkling Pistol, Marx, tin litho

EX $20   NM $30   MIP $60

Sparkling "Sure-Shot" Machine Gun, 1950s, T. Cohn, long body tin multicolored red/yellow/blue tin noise making gun, great box graphics show boy shooting sparks as pigtailed blond girl looks

EX $50   NM $75   MIP $150

WESTERN

2 Guns in 1 Cap Pistol, 1950s, Hubley, die-cast, 8" w/long barrel, twist-off barrels to change from long to short, side loading, white plastic grips

EX $75   NM $125   MIP $200

45 Smoker, 1950s, Product Engineering, 10" single cap, shoots talcum-like powder by use of bellows when trigger is pulled, aluminum finish

EX $50   NM $100   MIP $175

49er Cap Pistol, 1940, Stevens, cast iron, 9", unusual internal hammer w/revolving steel cylinder, nickel finish, white plastic figural grips

EX $125   NM $350   MIP $600

760 Rapid Fire Shotgun Air Rifle, 1960s, Daisy, 31" pump shotgun, gray metal one piece frame, brown plastic stock and slider grip, fires blast of air

EX $65   NM $95   MIP $150

Authentic Derringer, 1960, Esquire Novelty, classic miniature Series #10, 2" cap firing, copper finish, twin swivel barrel

EX $15   NM $25   MIP $60

Authentic Derringer, 1960, Esquire Novelty, die-cast, 2" cap firing, copper finish, twin swivel barrel

EX $15   NM $25   MIP $60

Big Horn Cap Pistol, 1950s, Kilgore, 7" all metal revolving cylinder, break-to-front, disk caps, silver finish

EX $100   NM $175   MIP $300

Billy The Kid Cap Pistol, Stevens, 8" long, cap pistol

EX $55   NM $110   MIP $225

Bobcat Saddle Gun, 1960s, USA, 5-1/2" black finish, imprinted w/"Official Wanted Dead or Alive" Mare's Laig logo, brown plastic stock, Model No. 57-G1025

EX $10   NM $25   MIP $50

Bonanza Guns Outfit, 1960s, Marx, 25" cap firing saddle rifle, magazine pulls down to load, 9-1/2" Western pistol fires two-piece Marx shooting bullets, wood plastic stocks and gun metal gray plastic body, tan vinyl holster

EX $75   NM $145   MIP $300

Bronco Cap Pistol, 1950s, Kilgore, 8-1/2", revolving swing-out cylinder fires Kilgore disc caps, silver finish, black plastic "Bronco" grips

EX $65   NM $125   MIP $250

Buck'n Bronc Marshal Cap Pistol, 1950s, Schmidt, 10" long barrel revolver style, lever release, break-to-front, plain silver finish, copper color metal grips

EX $125   NM $250   MIP $400

Buck'n Bronc Shoot'n Iron, 1950s, Schmidt, cap gun, 50-shot repeater

EX $100   NM $175   MIP $250

Buffalo, Marx, 50 shooter repeater

EX $70   NM $100   MIP $140

Buffalo Bill Cap Pistol, 1940, Stevens, 7-3/4", silver nickel finish, side loading magazine door, white "tenite" plastic horse and cowboy grips, red jewels

EX $65   NM $125   MIP $250

Cap Gun Store Display, 1950s, Nichols, 24" x 14" wood board, derringer and two strips of Nichols bullets

EX $300   NM $600   MIP $950

Centennial Rifle, Marx, w/big sound

EX $25   NM $35   MIP $65

Champion Quick Draw Timer Cap Pistol, 1959, Kilgore, silver finish, side loading, wind up mechanism in grip records elapsed time of draw, black plastic grips

EX $100   NM $200   MIP $375

Cheyenne Cap Pistol, 1974, Kilgore, 9-3/4" side loading, "Sure-K" plastic stag grips, silver finish

EX $10   NM $25   MIP $50

Cody Colt Paper Buster Gun, 1950s, Langson, 7-3/4", paper popper, nickel finish, white plastic steer grips fires Cody Colt ammunition

EX $40   NM $80   MIP $125

Colt .38 Detective Special, 1959, Hubley, 4-1/2" Colt .38 pistol single shot caps

and loads six play bullets w/suspenders chest holster

EX $35   NM $75   MIP $150

Colt .45 Cap Pistol, 1959, Hubley, die-cast, 13", revolving cylinder produced w/open or closed chamber ends, loads six two-piece cap-firing bullets, white plastic grips, red felt box

EX $110   NM $225   MIP $425

Colt Cap Pistol, 1935, Stevens, 6-1/2", revolver-style double action

EX $20   NM $55   MIP $110

Cork-Shooting Rifle, Marx

EX $25   NM $40   MIP $60

Cowboy Cap Pistol, 1935, Stevens, 3-1/2" cast iron, single shot single action, sold loose

EX $20   NM $55   MIP $110

Cowboy Cap Pistol, 1940, Hubley, 8" friction break-to-front nickel finish cast iron, rose swirl plastic grips w/Colt logo

EX $110   NM $225   MIP $350

Cowboy Cap Pistol, 1950s, Hubley, 12", die-cast, swing-out revolving cylinder, release on barrel, nickel finish, black plastic steer grips

EX $125   NM $250   MIP $400

Cowboy Cap Pistol, 1950s, Hubley, die-cast, 12" swing out revolving cyclinder, release on barrel, nickel or aluminum finish, white plastic steer grips w/black steer head

EX $115   NM $235   MIP $375

Cowboy Jr. Cap Pistol No. 225, 1950s, Hubley, 9" die-cast, revolving cylinder, side loading, release on barrel, silver finish, white plastic cow grips, lanyard ring and cord

EX $65   NM $130   MIP $275

Cowboy King Cap Pistol, 1940, Stevens, 9" break-to-front release, gold finish cast iron, black plastic grips, yellow jewels

EX $110   NM $275   MIP $450

Dagger Derringer, 1958, Hubley, 7", unusual over and under pistol has hidden red plastic dagger that slides out from between barrels, rotating barrels load and fire two-piece bullets

EX $55   NM $100   MIP $145

Dale Evans D-26, 1950s, Schmidt, initials in butterfly symbol

EX $450   NM $900   MIP $1250

Dale Evans Holster Set, Classy, brown and yellow leather, white fringe on holsters, stylized blue butterflies are also "DE" logo, if buckled in front, holsters are backwards; holsters only, no guns

EX $100   NM $200   MIP $375

Davy Crockett Buffalo Rifle, 1950s, Hubley, 25" die-cast and plastic, unusual flintlock style, fires single cap under pan cover, brown plastic stock, ammo storage door in stock

EX $75   NM $145   MIP $225

Davy Crockett Frontier Fighter Cork Gun, 1950s, Unknown, 21" pop gun shoots cork on string and has cigarette flint

mechanism at muzzle that makes sparks when fired, wood stock, leather sling
EX $75   **NM** $150   **MIP** $250

Deputy Cap Pistol, 1950s, Hubley, 10" die-cast, front breaking, release on barrel, ornate scroll work, nickel finish
EX $50   **NM** $100   **MIP** $200

Double Holster Set, 1950s, Classy, imitation alligator-texture brown leather, steer-head conches on holsters, lots of studs, yellow felt backing, holsters only, no guns
EX $150   **NM** $300   **MIP** $500

Double Holster Set, 1960, Marx, 10" two pistols similar to 1860s Remington, fires roll caps by use of a lanyard that is pulled from the bottom of the grip, internal hammer, white plastic horse and steer grips, silver, brown vinyl holster
EX $70   **NM** $120   **MIP** $300

Double-Barrel Pop Gun Rifle, 1935, Marx, 28" long
EX $50   **NM** $100   **MIP** $200

Double-Barrel Pop Gun Rifle, 1935, Marx, 22" long
EX $45   **NM** $85   **MIP** $175

Dyna-Mite Derringer, 1955, Nichols, 3-1/4" die-cast, loads single cap cartridge, silver finish, white plastic grips
EX $15   **NM** $30   **MIP** $45

Dyna-Mite Derringer in Clip, Nichols, 3-1/2" die-cast, fires single cap in Nichols cartridge, nickel finish, white plastic grips w/small leather holster
EX $25   **NM** $45   **MIP** $65

Fanner 50 "Swivelshot Trick Holster" Set, 1958, Mattel, die-cast bullet loading Fanner 50, leather swivel style holster, attaches to any belt, gun fires in holster when swiveled, string included for last ditch draw
EX $110   **NM** $225   **MIP** $375

Fanner 50 Cap Pistol, 1960s, Mattel, 11" fanner non-revolving cylinder, stag plastic grips, nickel finish, black vinyl "Durahyde" holster
EX $55   **NM** $110   **MIP** $225

Fanner 50 Cap Pistol, 1960s, Mattel, later version 11" fires perforated roll caps, black finish, white plastic antelope grips
EX $45   **NM** $90   **MIP** $175

Fanner 50 Smoking Cap Pistol, 1957, Mattel, 10-1/2" w/revolving cylinder, first version w/grapefruit cylinder does not chamber bullets
EX $100   **NM** $200   **MIP** $400

Fanner 50 Smoking Cap Pistol, 1958, Mattel, 10-1/2" w/revolving cylinder, chambers six metal play bullets, die-cast
EX $90   **NM** $180   **MIP** $400

Fastest Gun Electronic Draw Game, 1958, Kilgore, die-cast, wire plug into "Rangers" gun grips, gun that shoots first lights eye of plastic battery-operated steer head, red and blue plastic holsters w/matching cowboy gun grips, plastic belts
EX $90   **NM** $175   **MIP** $300

Flintlock Jr. Cap Pistol, 1955, Hubley, 7-1/2" single shot, double action, brown swirl plastic stock
EX $20   **NM** $45   **MIP** $85

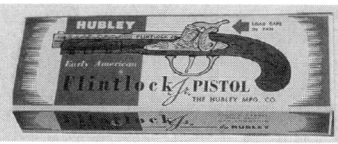

Flintlock Pistol, 1954, Hubley, 9-1/4", two shot cap shooting single action double barrel, over and under style, brown swirl plastic stock, nickel finish
EX $50   **NM** $110   **MIP** $175

Frontier Repeating Cap Rifle, 1950s, Hubley, 35-1/4" rifle nickel finish w/brown plastic stock and forestock, blue metal barrel, red plastic choke and front sight, pop down magazine, released by catch in front of trigger, scroll work
EX $75   **NM** $165   **MIP** $210

Frontier Six-Shooter cap pistol, Kilgore, black handle, Model No. 2048
EX $65   **NM** $110   **MIP** $155

Frontier Smoker, Product Engineering, 9-1/2" cap pistol, die-cast, pop up magazine shoots white powder from internal bellows, all metal, black grips, silver finish, gold magazine, hammer and trigger
EX $85   **NM** $150   **MIP** $225

Gene Autry 44 Cap Pistol, 1950s, Leslie-Henry, 11" lever release, side loading, long barrel, nickel finish, white plastic horse-head grips
EX $125   **NM** $300   **MIP** $550

Gene Autry 44 Cap Pistol, 1950s, Leslie-Henry, 11" lever release, side loading, long barrel, loads solid metal bullets, nickel finish, brown translucent plastic horse-head grips
EX $175   **NM** $500   **MIP** $800

Gene Autry Cap Pistol, 1939, Kenton, 8-3/8" cast iron, long barrel, dark gray gunmetal finish w/white plastic grips w/signature, (Best/Logan G3.1.1), Model No. 36-G1067
EX $200   **NM** $275   **MIP** $500

Gene Autry Cap Pistol, 1940, Kenton, 6-1/2" cast iron, nickel finish, red plastic grips w/etched signature (Best/Logan G3.2.1), Model No. 37-G1111
EX $125   **NM** $225   **MIP** $450

Gene Autry Cap Pistol, 1950s, Leslie-Henry, 9" break-to-front, lever release, nickel finish, black plastic horse-head grips
EX $115   **NM** $275   **MIP** $500

Gene Autry Cap Pistol, 1950s, Leslie-Henry, 7-3/4" die-cast, small size, lever release, break-to-front, nickel finish w/extension scroll work, black plastic horse-head grips
EX $115   **NM** $275   **MIP** $500

Gene Autry Cap Pistol, 1950s, Leslie-Henry, 9" break-to-front lever release, copper finish, white plastic horse-head grips
EX $115   **NM** $275   **MIP** $500

Gene Autry Cap Pistol, 1950s, Leslie-Henry, 9", break-to-front lever release, nickel finish, white plastic horse-head grips
EX $115   **NM** $275   **MIP** $500

Gene Autry Champion Single Holster Set, 1940s, Unknown, leather and cardboard, red, yellow and green "jewels," four white wooden bullets, silver buckle
EX $125   **NM** $250   **MIP** $400

Gene Autry Dummy Cap Pistol, 1939, Kenton, cast iron, 8-3/8", long barrel, dark gray, gunmetal finish, white plastic grips
EX $125   **NM** $225   **MIP** $450

Grizzly Cap Pistol, 1950s, Kilgore, 10" revolving cylinder fires disc caps, swing out cylinder, black plastic grips w/grizzly bear
EX $100   **NM** $200   **MIP** $375

Gunfighter Holster Set, 1960s, Lone Star, 9" Frontier Ace, lever release, break-to-front, silver finish, brown plastic grips, white and red leather "Laramie" single holster w/separate belt
EX $60   **NM** $125   **MIP** $250

Gunsmoke Double Holster Set, Leslie-Henry, w/copper clad grips
EX $250   **NM** $520   **MIP** $750

Hawkeye Cap Pistol, 1950s, Kilgore, 4-1/4" all metal, automatic style, side loading, silver finish
EX $20   **NM** $40   **MIP** $75

Historic Guns Derringer, 1974, Marx, Marx Historic Guns series, derringer w/plastic presentation case, 4-1/2" long, on card
EX $15   **NM** $25   **MIP** $30

Hi-Yo Silver Lone Ranger Pistol, Marx, tin gun
EX $60   **NM** $200   **MIP** $350

Hopalong Cassidy Cap Pistol, 1950, Schmidt, 9" pull hammer to release, scroll work, nickel finish w/black plastic grips w/white bust of Hopalong Cassidy, Model No. 80-G1140
EX $175   **NM** $400   **MIP** $750

Hopalong Cassidy Double Holster Set, 1940s, Wyandotte, w/two guns; gold guns w/black grips; holster has silver studs w/Hoppy's name in belt
EX $1250   **NM** $2500   **MIP** $4000

Hopalong Cassidy Holster/Gun Set, 1950s, Schmidt, black holster; black grips on gun w/bust of Hoppy
EX $1000   **NM** $2000   **MIP** $3000

How the West Was Won Gun Rifle, Marx, deep gray Winchester model w/tan stock, in box
EX $55   NM $85   MIP $145

Johnny Eagle Red River Bullet Firing, 1965, Topper/Deluxe, over 12" double action revolving cylinder pistol, die-cast hammer, trigger, blue plastic overall w/wood plastic grips w/gold horse, side loading, shell ejector, fires two-piece plastic bullets
EX $65   NM $95   MIP $175

Johnny Ringo Gun & Holster Set, 1960, Marx, die-cast gun, white plastic head grips, vinyl quick draw holster has rawhide tie, gun is fired by lanyard which passes through grip butt and attaches to belt, when pulled lanyard trips internal hammer
EX $100   NM $200   MIP $375

Johnny Ringo, Adventure of, Gun & Holster, 1960, Esquire Novelty, 10-3/4" long barrel Actoy, friction break, black/gold plastic stag grips, black leather two-gun holster, felt backing, loops hold four to six bullets, silver buckle
EX $250   NM $500   MIP $750

Johnty West Cowboy Rifled, 1950s, Marx, repeater cap action, winchester-style,
EX $35   NM $80   MIP $155

Johnty West, The Cowboy Rifle, 1960s, Marx, repeater cap action
EX $25   NM $50   MIP $85

Lawmaker Cap Pistol, 1941, Kenton, 8-3/8", break-to-front friction break, unusual dark gray gunmetal finish, white plastic raised grips
EX $125   NM $225   MIP $450

Lone Ranger 45 Flasher Flashlight Pistol, Marx, in box
EX $60   NM $125   MIP $200

Lone Ranger Cap Pistol, 1938, Kilgore, 8-1/4" cast iron, small hammer, nickel finish, friction break, purple plastic "Hi-Yo Silver" grips
EX $125   NM $300   MIP $500

Lone Ranger Cap Pistol, 1940, Kilgore, 8-1/2" cast iron, large hammer, nickel finish, spring release on side for break, red-brown, Hi-Yo Silver grips
EX $110   NM $275   MIP $450

Lone Ranger Carbine, 1950s, Marx, 26" gray plastic repeater-style rifle has pull down cap magazine, western trim and Lone Ranger signature on stock
EX $65   NM $100   MIP $165

Lone Ranger Clicker Pistol, 1938, Marx, 8", nickel finish, red jewels, inlaid white plastic grip w/the Lone Ranger, Hi-Yo Silver and LR head embossed, brown leather holster
EX $100   NM $300   MIP $400

Lone Ranger Double Target Set, 1939, Marx, 9-1/2" square stand up target, tin litho, wire frame holds target upright, backed w/bulls-eye target, 8" metal dart gun fires wooden shaft dart
EX $150   NM $325   MIP $450

Lone Ranger Holster, Unknown, 9", leather/pressboard, Hi-Yo Silver and Lone Ranger printed, red jewel, belt loop
EX $50   NM $100   MIP $200

Lone Ranger Rifle, 1973, Hubley, 29" long
EX $55   NM $100   MIP $150

Lone Rider Cap Pistol, 1950s, Buzz-Henry, 8" die-cast, white plastic inset rearing horse grips
EX $40   NM $100   MIP $175

Long Boy Cap Gun, Kilgore, 11-1/2" long, cast iron
EX $75   NM $1335   MIP $275

Longhorn Cap Pistol, 1950s, Leslie-Henry, 10" die-cast, release in front of trigger guard, scroll work, white plastic horse head grips, unusual pop-up cap magazine, Model No. 38-G927
EX $85   NM $125   MIP $225

Mare's Laig Rifle Pistol, Marx, 13-1/2" brown plastic, black plastic body, pull down magazine
EX $60   NM $95   MIP $135

Marshal Cap Pistol, 1950s, Leslie-Henry, 10" revolving cylinder chambers, Nichols-style bullets, white plastic grips w/star ovals
EX $35   NM $75   MIP $150

Marshal Cap Pistol, 1960, Hubley, 9-3/4" die-cast, side loading, nickel finish w/scrollwork, w/brown and white plastic stag grips w/a clip on left grip, Model No. 24-G1142
EX $35   NM $75   MIP $150

Marshal Matt Dillon "Gunsmoke" Cap Pistol, 1950s, Leslie-Henry, 10" pop-up cap magazine, release in front of trigger guard, scroll work, bronze steer-head grips
EX $60   NM $125   MIP $275

Matt Dillon Marshal Set, John Henry Products, gun and holster set w/jail keys, handcuffs and badge
EX $55   NM $100   MIP $200

Maverick Cap Pistol, 1960, Carnell, 9" break-to-front, lever release, nickel finish, Maverick on sides, cream and

brown swirl colored grips features notch bar w/extra set of black plastic grips
EX $60   NM $175   MIP $300

Maverick Derringer, 1958, Leslie-Henry, 3-1/4" w/removeable cap-shooting bullets, tan vinyl holster w/two bullets
EX $35   NM $55   MIP $85

Maverick Two Gun Holster Set, 1958, Leslie-Henry, 11x14" box picutres James Garner as Maverick, two six-shooters w/individual bullets
EX $400   NM $800   MIP $1200

Maverick Two Gun Holster Set, 1960, Carnell, 9" break-to-front, lever release, nickel finish, Maverick on sides, cream/brown swirl grips features notch bar, black leather dbl. holster set w/silver plates, studs and white trim, six loops, buckle
EX $225   NM $450   MIP $750

Model 1860 Cal .44 Cap Pistol, 1959, Hubley, 13", revolving cylinder w/closed chamber ends, six two-piece bullets, flat aluminum finish, white plastic grips, complete w/wooden display plaque
EX $130   NM $275   MIP $450

Model 95 Shell Firing Rifle, 1961, Nichols, 35-1/2" rifle uses shell firing cartridges, holds five in removeable magazine and one chamber, lever action ejects cartridges, open frame box holds six bullets and twelve additional red bullet heads
EX $200   NM $350   MIP $550

Mustang Cap Pistol, 1960s, Kilgore, 9-1/2" chrome finish w/"stag" plastic grips
EX $20   NM $35   MIP $75

Official Wanted Dead or Alive Mare's Laig Rifle, Marx, 19" bullet loading, cap firing saddle rifle-pistol ejects plastic bullets, w/holster
EX $110   NM $225   MIP $350

Official Wyatt Earp Buntline Clicker Pistol, Young Premiums, 18-1/2" plastic
EX $50   NM $125   MIP $200

Panther Pistol, 1958, Hubley, die-cast, 4" derringer style pistol snaps out from secret spring-loaded wrist holster
EX $85   NM $130   MIP $185

Pecos Kid Cap Pistol, 1970s, Lone Star, 9" silver chrome finish, brown plastic grips, lever release
EX $10   NM $15   MIP $50

Pepperbox Derringer Cap Pistol, 1960, Lone Star, die-cast, 6-1/4" rotating barrel holds four cap loads, silver finish w/black plastic grips
EX $75   NM $110   MIP $185

Pinto Cap Pistol, 1950s, Nichols, 3-1/2", chrome finish, black plastic grips, flip out cylinder, white plastic "Pinto" holster in leather holster clip
EX $20   NM $35   MIP $75

Pony Boy Double Holster Set, 1950s, Esquire Novelty, brown leather double holster w/bucking broncs and studs,

cuffs, spurs and spur leathers, guns are Actoy "Spitfires", die-cast 8-1/2" copper finish, white plastic grips
EX $200   **NM** $400   **MIP** $600

Pony Cap Pistol, 1950s, Actoy, single shot, all-metal, nickel finish w/eagle on grip
EX $25   **NM** $45   **MIP** $100

Ranch Rifle, Marx, plastic, repeater
EX $30   **NM** $45   **MIP** $60

Ranger Cap Pistol, 1950s, Leslie-Henry, 7-3/4" derringer w/removeable cap, shooting bullets, tan vinyl holster w/two bullets
EX $85   **NM** $110   **MIP** $150

Ranger Cap Pistol, 1950s, Kilgore, 8-1/2" nickel finish, brown swirl plastic grips, spring release on right side, break-to-front
EX $90   **NM** $125   **MIP** $200

Real Texan Outfit with Nichols Stallion .22, 1950s, Smart Style, brown/white leather double holsters have silver conches w/red reflectors, silver horses at top of holster, belt w/three bullet loops, guns are a pair of double action .22s
EX $110   **NM** $250   **MIP** $475

Rebel Holster & Pistol, 1960s, Classy, 12" die-cast long barrel pistol, brown plastic grips, black leather single holster left side, Rebel insignia on holster flap,
EX $225   **NM** $450   **MIP** $750

Red Ranger Jr. Cap Pistol, 1950s, Wyandotte, 7-1/2" lever release, break-to-front, silver finish, white plastic horse grips
EX $40   **NM** $85   **MIP** $150

Red Ryder BB Rifle, 1980, Daisy, carved wooden stock
EX $35   **NM** $75   **MIP** $125

Remington .36 Cap Pistol, 1950s, Hubley, 8" long, nickel finish, black plastic grips, revolving cylinder chambers two-piece bullets
EX $80   **NM** $160   **MIP** $275

Rex Trailer Two Gun & Holster Set, 1960, Hubley, 9-1/2" side loading, nickel finish, stag plastic grips, brown textured tooled leather w/white holsters and trim, six bullet loops w/plastic silver bullets, plain buckle
EX $110   **NM** $225   **MIP** $450

Ric-O-Shay .45 Cap Pistol, 1959, Hubley, 13" die-cast, nickel chrome finish, large frame, revolving cylinder, fires rolled caps, chambers brass bullets and fires caps, black plastic grips, makes a twang sound when fired, Model No. 28-G938
EX $85   **NM** $150   **MIP** $300

Ric-O-Shay .45 Cap Pistol Holster Set, Hubley, 13", die-cast, revolving cylinder

swings out to chamber six brass bullets, six loaded in gun and 12 on holster, 1" flake in nickel finish at heel, holster black leather w/separate belt, horse-head emblem, rawhide tiedown, Model No. 26-G1141
EX $250   **NM** $500   **MIP** $850

Rifleman Flip Special Cap Rifle, 1959, Hubley, 3' long rifle, resembles classic Winchester w/ring lever, brown plastic stock, pop down cap magazine
EX $160   **NM** $350   **MIP** $500

Rodeo Cap Pistol, 1950s, Hubley, 7-1/2" single shot, white plastic steer grips
EX $20   **NM** $50   **MIP** $100

Roy Rogers Cap Pistol, 1950s, Kilgore, 10" revolving cylinder swings out to load, fires disc caps, white plastic horse-head grips w/"RR" logo
EX $150   **NM** $300   **MIP** $550

Roy Rogers Carbine, 1950s, Marx, 26" gray plastic repeater-style rifle has pull down cap magazine, western trim and Roy Rogers signature on stock
EX $80   **NM** $150   **MIP** $300

Roy Rogers Double Gun & Holster Set, 1950s, Classy, die-cast two 8-1/2" nickel finish pistols w/copper figural grips, holster is brown and black leather w/raised detail, plastic play bullets and leather tie-downs
EX $550   **NM** $1100   **MIP** $1600

Roy Rogers Double Holster Set, Classy, 10" guns w/plain nickel finish and copper grips, lever release, brown and cream leather set, silver studs, gold fleck jewels and four wooden bullets
EX $500   **NM** $1000   **MIP** $1500

Roy Rogers Double Holster Set, 1950s, Classy, black and white leather set, silver studs and conches, 9" Roy Rogers pistols w/plain nickel finish and copper figural grips, friction release
EX $525   **NM** $1050   **MIP** $1550

Roy Rogers Tiny Tots Double Holster Set, Hubley
EX $55   **NM** $100   **MIP** $150

Ruff Rider Western Holster Set, Pilgrim Leather, brown leather double holster, variety of studs and red jewels, twelve plastic silver bullets, tie-downs
EX $110   **NM** $275   **MIP** $450

Sheriff's Derringer Pocket Pistol, 1960s, Ohio Art, 3-1/4" silver finish derringer chambers two-piece, Nichols-style cartridge, red plastic grips w/an "A" logo, on card
EX $10   **NM** $20   **MIP** $25

Shootin' Shell .45 Fanner Cap Pistol, 1959, Mattel, 11" revolving cylinder pistol shoots Mattel Shootin' Shell cartridges, shell ejector
EX $250   **NM** $400   **MIP** $650

Shootin' Shell Buckle Gun, 1958, Mattel, cap and bullet shooting copy of Remington Derringer pops out from belt buckle, two brass cartridges and six bullets
EX $45   **NM** $80   **MIP** $125

Shootin' Shell Fanner, 1958, Mattel, 9" die-cast chrome finish, revolving cylinder chambers six Shootin' Shell bullets
EX $100   **NM** $200   **MIP** $375

Shootin' Shell Fanner & Derringer Set, 1958, Mattel, small size Shooting Shell Fanner w/chrome finish, revolving cylinder, chambers six Shootin' Shell bullets, brown leather holster
EX $100   **NM** $200   **MIP** $375

Shootin' Shell Fanner Single Holster, 1959, Mattel, cowhide holster takes small size Shootin' Shell Fanner w/six brass play bullets and tie-downs
EX $105   **NM** $210   **MIP** $375

Shootin' Shell Indian Scout Rifle, 1958, Mattel, 29-1/2" plastic/metal Sharps rolling block rifle, chambers two-piece Shootin' Shell bullets, secret compartment in stock for ammo storage, plastic stock and metal barrel
EX $100   **NM** $175   **MIP** $300

Shootin' Shell Potshot Remington Derringer, 1959, Mattel, 3" derringer, on card
EX $35   **NM** $60   **MIP** $90

Shootin' Shell Winchester Rifle, Mattel, 26" long
EX $60   **NM** $125   **MIP** $175

Showdown Set with Three Shootin' Shell Guns, 1958, Mattel, 30" single shot rifle w/metal barrel, die-cast w/plastic stock, Shootin' Shell Fanner sm. size, revolving cylinder, chrome finish and imitation stag plastic grips, tan holster w/bullet loops
EX $300   **NM** $600   **MIP** $950

Side-By Double Barrel Pop Gun Rifle, Marx, 9" long
EX $20   **NM** $35   **MIP** $45

Silver Pony Cap Pistol, 1950s, Nichols, 7-1/2" single shot, silver metal grip and one replacement black plastic grip, silver finish
EX $30   **NM** $45   **MIP** $100

Spitfire Hip Gun No. 100, 1950s, Nichols, 9" cap cartridge loading mini rifle, chrome finish, tan plastic stock
EX $15   **NM** $20   **MIP** $35

Spitfire with Clip, 1950s, Nichols, 9" mini rifle, chrome finish, plastic stock, plastic holders w/two extra cartridges
EX $12   **NM** $25   **MIP** $35

Spittin Image Peacemaker BB Pistol, Daisy, 10-1/2" die-cast, spring fired, single action, BBs load into spring fed magazine under barrel

EX $25   **NM** $60   **MIP** $120

Stagecoach Pistol, 1950s, Marx, 5" pistol with plastic box marked "Stagecoach Pistol"

EX $40   **NM** $65   **MIP** $90

Stallion .22 Cap Pistol, 1950s, Nichols, 7" revolving cylinder chambers five two-piece cartridges, single action, black plastic stag grips, never came in box

EX $30   **NM** $75   **MIP** $150

Stallion .22 Double Action Cap Pistol, 1950s, Nichols, 7" double action, pull trigger to fire, white plastic grips, nickel finish, cylinder revolves

EX $50   **NM** $150   **MIP** $300

Stallion .38 Cap Pistol, 1950s, Nichols, 9-1/2", chambers six two-piece cap cartridges, nickel finish, white plastic grips

EX $85   **NM** $175   **MIP** $375

Stallion .45 MK I Cap Pistol, 1950, Nichols, die-cast, 12" chrome finish, revolving cylinder, chambers six two-piece bullets, shell ejector, white "pearlescent" plastic grips w/rearing stallion, red jewels and 6 bullets and Stallion caps

EX $1550   **NM** $300   **MIP** $500

Stallion .45 MK II Cap Pistol, 1956, Nichols, 12" pistol, chrome finish, revolving cylinder, chambers six two-piece, bullets, shell ejector, extra set of white grips to replace black grips on gun and box of Stallion caps

EX $100   **NM** $185   **MIP** $375

Stallion 32 Six Shooter, 1955, Nichols, 8" revolving cylinder chambers six two-piece cartridges, nickel finish, black plastic grips

EX $75   **NM** $150   **MIP** $300

Stallion 41-40 Cap Pistol, 1950s, Nichols, 10-1/2" revolving cylinder chrome finish pistol, swing out cylinder that chambers

six two-piece cap cartridges, shell ejector, scroll work on frame, cream-purple swirl colored plastic grips

EX $160   **NM** $375   **MIP** $500

Susanna 90 12 Shot Cap Pistol, 1980s, Edison, 9" uses ring caps, wind out cylinder, black finish, plastic wood grips

EX $10   **NM** $15   **MIP** $25

Tales of Wells Fargo Double Barrel Shotgun, 1950s, Marx, 26" long double barrel shotgun, two toy shotgun shells, decal on the butt of the gun, Model No. 44

EX $100   **NM** $210   **MIP** $350

Texan .38 Cap Pistol, 1950s, Hubley, 10" long, revolving cylinder gun chambers six solid brass bullets (caps go into cylinder first), top release front break automatically ejects shells, plastic steer grips

EX $100   **NM** $200   **MIP** $350

Texan Cap Pistol, 1940, Hubley, 9-1/4" cast iron revolving cylinder lever release, white plastic steer grips, nickel finish, Colt rearing horse logo on grips

EX $110   **NM** $225   **MIP** $400

Texan Cap Pistol, 1950s, Hubley, die-cast, nickel finish, white plastic steer grips, star logo on grips

EX $75   **NM** $150   **MIP** $300

Texan Cap Pistol No. 285, 1940, Hubley, 9-1/4", cast iron, revolving cylinder, lever release, white plastic steer grips, nickel finish w/star logo in grip

EX $120   **NM** $250   **MIP** $425

Texan Dummy Cap Pistol, 1940, Hubley, 9-1/4" revolving cylinder, lever release, white plastic steer grips, nickel finish, Colt rearing horse logo

EX $85   **NM** $150   **MIP** $300

Texan Dummy Cap Pistol, 1950s, Hubley, 9-1/4", revolving cylinder, lever release, white plastic steer grips, nickel finish, star logo on grip

EX $90   **NM** $165   **MIP** $350

Texan Jr. Cap Pistol, 1950s, Hubley, 10", spring button release on side of cylinder, break-to-front, nickel finish white plastic grips w/black steers

EX $85   **NM** $125   **MIP** $250

Texan Jr. Cap Pistol, 1954, Hubley, die-cast, release under cylinder, nickel finish, white plastic Longhorn grips

EX $65   **NM** $110   **MIP** $225

Texan Jr. Gold Plated Cap Pistol, 1950s, Hubley, 9", gold finish w/black longhorn steer grips, break-to-front release from cylinder

EX $95   **NM** $175   **MIP** $350

Texas Cap Pistol, 1950s, Long Island Die Casting, die-cast, 8-1/2" friction break, Circle "T" logo, scroll work on barrel

EX $50   **NM** $100   **MIP** $200

Texas Ranger Cap Pistol, Leslie-Henry, 8-1/4" die-cast, lever release break to front, nickel finish, scroll work, vasoline colored plastic grips

EX $65   **NM** $125   **MIP** $300

The Plainsman Cap Pistol, 1950s, National Metal & Plastic Toy, 10-1/2" revolving cylinder loads Kilgore-style disk caps, lever holds cylinder forward for loading, scroll work, white plastic grips, Model No. 62-G1101

EX $125   **NM** $225   **MIP** $350

Thundergun Cap Pistol, 1950s, Marx, 12-1/2" single action,"Thundercaps" perforated roll cap system, silver finish, brown plastic grips

EX $100   **NM** $200   **MIP** $300

Tom Mix Wooden Gun, 1930s, Ralston-Purina, three all-wood versions w/leather holster, came in mailer, each

EX $125   **NM** $275   **MIP** $375

Tophand 250 Cap Pistol, 1960, Nichols, 9-1/2" break-to-front, lever release, black finish, brown plastic grips w/a roll of "Tophand 250" caps

EX $45   **NM** $90   **MIP** $180

Wagon Train Complete Western Cowboy Outfit, 1960, Leslie-Henry, plastic flip ring lever rifle and wagon train pistol (late model L-H pistol) and leather holster

EX $110   **NM** $225   **MIP** $450

Wagon Train Gun & Holster Set, 1950s, Unknown, two 5" plastic guns, vinyl holster w/plastic bullets and metal badge, Model No. 45

EX $25   **NM** $50   **MIP** $100

Wanted Dead or Alive Miniature Mare's Laig, 1959, Marx, Marx Miniatures series miniature cap rifle on "wood frame" card

EX $20   **NM** $40   **MIP** $65

Wells Fargo Buntline Cap Pistol, 1950s, Actoy, 11" long barrel, break-to-front, cream plastic stag grips

EX $85   **NM** $160   **MIP** $350

Western Buntline Pistol, 1963, Haig, 13", pistol fires single caps and/or BBs, BBs are propelled down barrel sleeve by cap explosion

EX $75   **NM** $130   **MIP** $175

Western Cap Pistol, 1950s, Hubley, 9" die-cast, friction break, nickel finish w/white plastic steer grips w/black steer, Model No. 33-G1100

EX $40   **NM** $75   **MIP** $150

Wild Bill Hickok 44 Cap Pistol Set, 1950s, Leslie-Henry, 11" nickel finish, swing-out side loading action, revolving cylinder chambers six metal bullets, amber plastic horse-head grips, single holster black and brown leather w/silver studs, diamond conches

EX $200   **NM** $400   **MIP** $650

Wild Bill Hickok Cap Pistol, 1950s, Leslie-Henry, 10" pop-up cap magazine, release in front of trigger guard, scroll work, translucent brown plastic grips w/oval star inserts

EX $100   **NM** $200   **MIP** $350

Wild Bill Hickok Gun & Holster, Leslie-Henry, single gun and holster set

EX $150   **NM** $300   **MIP** $500

GUNS

Wild West Rifle, Marx, 30" long w/sight, cap rifle
EX $40   NM $75   MIP $125

Winchester Saddle Gun Rifle, 1959, Mattel, 33" die-cast and plastic, perforated roll caps and chambers eight play bullets loaded through side door
EX $50   NM $125   MIP $375

Wyatt Earp Buntline Special, 1950s, Actoy, 11" barrel, die-cast, friction break-to-front, white plastic grips, nickel finish
EX $100   NM $250   MIP $425

Wyatt Earp Double Holster Set, 1950s, Unknown, med. size, reflectors, black leather w/brown rawhide fringe, holsters only
EX $50   NM $80   MIP $125

Wyatt Earp Double Holster Set, 1950s, Hubley, black and white leather holster w/silk screened "Marshal Wyatt Earp" logo, two No. 247 Hubley Wyatt Earp Buntline Specials, 10-3/4" nickel finish, purple swirl grips
EX $250   NM $500   MIP $850

Yo Gun, 1960s, Ideal, 7-1/4" red plastic gun releases yellow plastic ball which snaps back when trigger is pulled, functions like a yo-yo
EX $30   NM $45   MIP $60

Young Buffalo Bill Cowboy Outfit, Leslie-Henry, black and white leather holster set w/pistol, white grip, holster bands read Texas Ranger
EX $100   NM $200   MIP $350

Zorro Flintock Pistol, Marx
EX $30   NM $65   MIP $125

Zorro Rifle, Marx
EX $60   NM $125   MIP $175

GUNS

Lunch Boxes

By Karen O'Brien

Lunch kits have been manufactured since the 1920s, but the boxes that are most collectible today are those bearing illustrations of popular licensed characters.

It took the power of television to launch the lunch box industry out of the domed steel domain of workmen and into the colorful art boxes generations of children carried to school each day.

As World War II ended, Aladdin Industries returned to providing millions of workmen with sturdy, if uninspired, lunch kits designed to take the beating of the workplace. Great change occurred in 1950 when Aladdin released a pair of rectangular steel boxes, one red and one blue, sporting scalloped color decals of the television Western hero of the day, Hopalong Cassidy. Soon thereafter, 600,000 Hoppy boxes were carried to school by proud young owners. Once discovered, the youth market would never be ignored again.

The envious classmates of those first Hoppy boxers would not be denied. American Thermos, Aladdin's chief competitor, went one up on Aladdin by introducing the 1953 Roy Rogers box in full-color lithography. Aladdin responded by issuing a new 1954 Hoppy box in full color litho, and the lunch box era officially began.

Throughout the later 1950s, the box wars were fought in earnest between Aladdin and American Thermos, with occasional challenges by Adco Liberty, Ohio Art, and Okay Industries.

The smaller firms produced some classic boxes, notably Mickey Mouse and Donald Duck (1954), Howdy Doody (1954), and Davy Crockett (1955) from Adco Liberty; and Captain Astro (1966), Bon XX (1967), Snow White (1980), and Pit Stop (1968) from Ohio Art. Okay Industries weighed in briefly later on with the now highly prized Wake Up America (1973) and Underdog (1974) boxes, but from the beginning it had always been a two-horse race.

The popular boxes of each year mirrored the stars, heroes, and interests of the times. From the Westerns and space explorations f the late 1950s through the 1960s, Americans enjoyed a golden age of cartoon and film heroes such as the Flintstones (1962), Dudley Do-Right (1962), Bullwinkle and Rocky (1962) and Mary Poppins (1965). As the decade progressed, America grew more aggressive, turning toward such violent heroes as the Man from U.N.C.L.E. (1966) and G.I. Joe (1967)

before Vietnam changed the national consciousness.

The early 1970s brought us such innocuous role models as H.R. Pufnstuf (1970), The Partridge Family (1971), and Bobby Sherman (1972). By decade's end, we were greeting both the promise and the threat from beyond in Close Encounters of the Third Kind (1978) and Star Wars (1978).

The metal box reigned supreme through the mid-1980s when parental groups began calling for a ban on metal boxes as "deadly weapons." The industry capitulated, and by 1986, both Aladdin and American Thermos were producing all of their boxes in plastic.

The switch to plastic was not nearly as abrupt as might be expected. Aladdin and Thermos had been making plastic and vinyl boxes since the late 1950s. These included many character boxes that had no counterparts in metal, which is presently their major saving grace in the collector market.

Vinyl boxes were made of lower-cost materials consisting basically of cardboard sheathed in thin vinyl. They were not as popular as metal boxes, and their poor construction combined with lower unit sales have resulted in a field with higher rarity factors than the metal box arena. Additionally, vinyl was more affordable to small companies that produced numerous limited-run boxes for sale or use as premiums.

Vinyl box collecting is an emerging field with few firmly established prices compared to the relative maturity of the metal box market, so any price guide such as this will be more open to debate. As the field matures, the pricing precedents of sales and time will build into a stronger body of knowledge. In this book, for ease of searching, boxes are listed alphabetically by box composition—plastic, steel, and vinyl.

TRENDS

Quality lunch boxes are still visible at toy and collectibles shows, but generalized dealers don't feature them quite as often as other items. Specialized dealers still exist, however, and deal in good numbers. Character-related boxes from Superman to Western heroes like Roy Rogers to television favorites like Lost in Space remain popular and are increasing in value.

Editor's Note: An "n/a" in the bottle column means the box did not come with a bottle.

Contributor: Joe Soucy of Seaside Toys specializes in pristine-condition lunch boxes. "Top-quality condition boxes bring top dollar all the time," Soucy said in an interview with *Toy Shop* magazine. He can be reached at the Seaside Toy Center, 179 Main St., Westerly, RI, 02891.

THE TOP TEN LUNCH BOXES *(In Mint Condition)*

1. Superman, Universal, 1954	$13,500
2. 240 Robert, Aladdin, 1978	4,200
3. Toppie Elephant, American Thermos, 1957	3,200
4. Underdog, Okay Industries, 1974	2,500
5. Dudley Do-Right, Universal, 1962	2,450
6. Bullwinkle & Rocky, Universal, 1962	1,600
7. Beatles, Aladdin, 1966	1,600
8. Jetsons Dome, Aladdin, 1963	1,650
9. Star Trek Dome, Aladdin, 1968	1,450
10. Gunsmoke, Double L version, Aladdin, 1959	1,350

PLASTIC

101 Dalmatians, 1990, Aladdin
    Box $25   **Bottle** $8

18 Wheeler, 1978, Aladdin
    Box $35   **Bottle** $10

ALF, 1987, Thermos, red plastic
    Box $35   **Bottle** n/a

Animalympics Dome, 1979, Thermos
    Box $40   **Bottle** $10

Astronauts, 1986, Thermos
    Box $35   **Bottle** $15

Atari Missile Command Dome, 1983, Aladdin
    Box $45   **Bottle** $10

Back to School, 1980, Aladdin
    Box $75   **Bottle** $20

Back to the Future, 1989, Thermos
    Box $35   **Bottle** $12

Bang Bang, 1982, Thermos
    Box $50   **Bottle** n/a

Barbie with Hologram Mirror, 1990, Thermos
    Box $30   **Bottle** $8

Batman (dark blue), 1989, Thermos
    Box $25   **Bottle** $10

Batman (light blue), 1989, Thermos
    Box $50   **Bottle** $10

Batman Returns, 1991, Thermos
    Box $25   **Bottle** $5

Beach Bronto, 1984, Aladdin, no bottle
    Box $45   **Bottle** n/a

Beach Party (blue/pink), 1988, Deka, with generic plastic bottle
    Box $20   **Bottle** $5

Bear with Heart (3-D), 1987, Servo
    Box $20   **Bottle** n/a

Beauty & the Beast, 1991, Aladdin
    Box $25   **Bottle** $5

Bee Gees, 1978, Thermos
    Box $45   **Bottle** $20

Beetlejuice, 1980, Thermos
    Box $20   **Bottle** $10

(KP Photo)

Big Jim, 1976, Thermos
    Box $80   **Bottle** $30

Bozostuffs, 1988, Deka
    Box $30   **Bottle** $10

C.B. Bears, 1977, Thermos
    Box $25   **Bottle** n/a

Care Bears, 1986, Aladdin
    Box $15   **Bottle** $5

Centurions, 1986, Thermos
    Box $20   **Bottle** $8

Chiclets, 1987, Thermos, no bottle
    Box $45   **Bottle** n/a

Chipmunks, Alvin and The, 1983, Thermos
    Box $25   **Bottle** $10

CHiPs, 1977, Thermos
    Box $55   **Bottle** $20

Cinderella, 1992, Aladdin
    Box $30   **Bottle** $10

Civil War, The, 1961, Universal, generic "Thermax" bottle
    Box $200   **Bottle** $25

Colonial Bread Van, 1984, Moldmark Industries
    Box $65   **Bottle** $20

Crestman Tubular!, 1980, Taiwan
    Box $55   **Bottle** $20

Days of Thunder, 1988, Thermos
    Box $35   **Bottle** $10

Deka 4 x 4, 1988, Deka, generic plastic bottle
    Box $35   **Bottle** $5

Dick Tracy, 1989, Aladdin
    Box $25   **Bottle** $10

Dino Riders, 1988, Aladdin
    Box $25   **Bottle** $10

Dinobeasties, 1988, Thermos
    Box $25   **Bottle** n/a

Dinorocker with Radio & Headset, 1986, Fundes
    Box $55   **Bottle** n/a

Disney on Parade, 1970, Aladdin, plastic bottle, glass liner
    Box $35   **Bottle** $15

Disney's Little Mermaid, 1989, Thermos, w/generic plastic bottle
    Box $20   **Bottle** $5

Duck Tales (4 X 4/Game), 1986, Aladdin
    Box $25   **Bottle** $5

Dukes of Hazzard, 1981, Aladdin
    Box $50   **Bottle** $10

Dukes of Hazzard Dome, 1981, Aladdin
    Box $50   **Bottle** $10

Dune, 1984, Aladdin
    Box $45   **Bottle** $20

Dunkin Munchkins, 1972, Thermos
    Box $30   **Bottle** $15

Ecology Dome, 1980, Thermos
    Box $45   **Bottle** $20

Ed Grimley, 1988, Aladdin
    Box $20   **Bottle** $5

Entenmann's, 1989, Thermos
    Box $20   **Bottle** n/a

Ewoks, 1983, Thermos, red box
    Box $25   **Bottle** $5

Fame, 1972, Thermos
    Box $35   **Bottle** $15

Fievel Goes West, 1991, Aladdin
    Box $15   **Bottle** $4

Fire Engine Co. 7, 1985, D.A.S., w/generic plastic bottle
    Box $30   **Bottle** $5

Fisher-Price Mini Lunch Box, 1962, Fisher-Price, red w/barnyard scenes, matching bottle
    Box $25   **Bottle** $5

Flash Gordon Dome, 1979, Aladdin
    Box $65   **Bottle** $20

Flintstones, unknown, premium, Denny's Restaurants
    Box $30   **Bottle** n/a

Flintstones Kids, 1987, Thermos
    Box $45   **Bottle** $10

Food Fighters, 1988, Aladdin
    Box $25   **Bottle** $10

Fraggle Rock, 1987, Thermos
    Box $25   **Bottle** $7

Frito Lay's, 1982, Thermos, no bottle
    Box $60   **Bottle** n/a

G.I. Joe (Space Mission), 1989, Aladdin
    Box $30   **Bottle** $10

G.I. Joe, Live the Adventure, 1986, Aladdin
    Box $25   **Bottle** $10

Garfield (food fight), 1979, Thermos
    Box $25   **Bottle** $10

Garfield (lunch), 1977, Thermos
    Box $20   **Bottle** $10

(KP Photo)

Geoffrey, 1981, Aladdin
    Box $35   **Bottle** $10

Get Along Gang, 1983, Aladdin
    Box $15   **Bottle** $5

Ghostbusters, 1986, Deka
    Box $25   **Bottle** $8

Go Bots, 1984, Thermos
    Box $25   **Bottle** $5

Golden Girls, 1984, Thermos
    Box $20   **Bottle** $5

Goonies, 1985, Aladdin
    Box $25   **Bottle** $8

Gumby, 1986, Thermos
    Box $65   **Bottle** $20

Hot Wheels, 1984, Thermos
    Box $50   **Bottle** $20

(KP Photo)

Howdy Doody Dome, 1977, Thermos
    Box $80   **Bottle** $35

Incredible Hulk Dome, 1980, Aladdin
    Box $35   **Bottle** $10

(KP Photo)

Incredible Hulk, The, 1978, Aladdin, plastic bottle
    Box $30   **Bottle** $10

Inspector Gadget, 1983, Thermos
    Box $25   **Bottle** $8

It's Not Just the Bus - Greyhound, 1980, Aladdin
    Box $60   **Bottle** $20

(KP Photo)

Jabber Jaw, 1977, Thermos
    Box $55   **Bottle** $20

Jetsons (3-D), 1987, Servo
    Box $75   **Bottle** $30

Jetsons (paper picture), 1987, Servo
    Box $125   **Bottle** $30

Jetsons, The Movie, 1990, Aladdin
    Box $30   **Bottle** $15

Kermit the Frog, Lunch With, 1988, Thermos
    Box $25   **Bottle** $5

Kermit's Frog Scout Van, 1989, Superseal, no bottle
    Box $15   **Bottle** n/a

Kool-Aid Man, 1986, Thermos
    Box $20   **Bottle** $10

Lisa Frank, 1980, Thermos
    Box $20   **Bottle** $5

Little Orphan Annie, 1973, Thermos
    Box $60   **Bottle** $20

Looney Tunes Birthday Party, 1989, Thermos, blue or red
    Box $25   **Bottle** $10

Looney Tunes Dancing, 1977, Thermos
    Box $20   **Bottle** $10

Looney Tunes Playing Drums, 1978, Thermos
    Box $30   **Bottle** $10

Looney Tunes Tasmanian Devil, 1988, Thermos, w/generic plastic bottle
    Box $20   **Bottle** $10

Los Angeles Olympics, 1984, Aladdin
    Box $40   **Bottle** $5

Lucy's Luncheonette, 1981, Thermos, Peanuts characters
    Box $25   **Bottle** $5

Lunch Man with Radio, 1986, Fun Design, w/built-in radio, no bottle
    Box $40   **Bottle** n/a

Lunch 'N Tunes Safari, 1986, Fun Design, w/built-in radio, no bottle
    Box $35   **Bottle** n/a

Lunch 'N Tunes Singing Sandwich, 1986, Fun Design, w/built-in radio, no bottle
    Box $40   **Bottle** n/a

Lunch Time with Snoopy Dome, 1981, Thermos
    Box $25   **Bottle** $5

Mad Balls, 1986, Aladdin
    Box $25   **Bottle** $10

Marvel Super Heroes, 1990, Thermos
    Box $30   **Bottle** $10

Max Headroom (Coca-Cola), 1985, Aladdin
    Box $55   **Bottle** $25

McDonald's Happy Meal, 1986, Fisher-Price
    Box $25   **Bottle** n/a

Menudo, 1984, Thermos
    Box $15   **Bottle** $5

Mickey & Minnie Mouse in Pink Car, 1988, Aladdin
    Box $20   **Bottle** $5

(ToyShop File Photo)

Mickey Mouse & Donald Duck, 1984, Aladdin, Dome-style lunchbox with image of Mickey, Minnie, Donald and Daisy having a picnic
    Box $25   **Bottle** $5

Mickey Mouse & Donald Duck See-Saw, 1986, Aladdin
    Box $15   **Bottle** $5

Mickey Mouse at City Zoo, 1985, Aladdin
    Box $10   **Bottle** $5

(KP Photo)

Mickey Mouse Head, 1989, Aladdin
    Box $25   **Bottle** $5

Mickey on Swinging Bridge, 1987, Aladdin
    Box $10   **Bottle** $5

Mickey Skateboarding, 1980, Aladdin
    Box $25   **Bottle** $5

Mighty Mouse, 1979, Thermos, light blue, Viacom Int'l
    Box $45   **Bottle** $15

Miss Piggy's Safari Van, 1989, Superseal, no bottle
    Box $18   **Bottle** n/a

Monster in My Pocket, 1990, Aladdin
    Box $30   **Bottle** $5

Movie Monsters, 1979, Universal
    Box $35   **Bottle** $12

Mr. T, 1984, Aladdin
    Box $25   **Bottle** $10

Munchie Tunes Bear with Radio, 1986, Fun Design, w/built-in radio
    Box $35   **Bottle** $5

Munchie Tunes Punchie Pup w/Radio, 1986, Fun Design, w/built-in radio
    Box $40   **Bottle** $5

Munchie Tunes Robot with Radio, 1986, Fun Design, w/built-in radio
    Box $35   **Bottle** $5

Muppets, 1982, Thermos, blue
    Box $18   **Bottle** $5

Muppets Dome, 1981, Thermos, plastic red box w/matching bottle
    Box $20   **Bottle** $5

New Kids on the Block, 1990, Thermos, pink/orange
    Box $15   **Bottle** $5

Nosy Bears, 1988, Aladdin
    Box $12   **Bottle** $5

Official Lunch Football, 1974, unknown, football shaped box, red or brown
    Box $100   **Bottle** n/a

Peanuts, Wienie Roast, 1985, Thermos
    Box $15   **Bottle** $4

Pee Wee's Playhouse, 1987, Thermos, w/generic plastic bottle
    Box $20   **Bottle** $5

Peter Pan Peanut Butter, 1984, Taiwan
    Box $90   **Bottle** $20

Pickle, 1972, Fesco, no bottle
    Box $140   **Bottle** n/a

Popeye & Son, 1987, Servo, plastic red box, flat paper label, w/matching bottle
    Box $65   **Bottle** $12

Popeye & Son (3-D), 1987, Servo, plastic box, red or yellow, w/matching bottle
    Box $50   **Bottle** $12

Popeye Dome, 1979, Aladdin, blue
    Box $35   **Bottle** $15

Popeye, Truant Officer, 1964, King Seeley Thermos, plastic red box, matching metal bottle (Canada)
    Box $150   **Bottle** $35

Punky Brewster, 1984, Deka
    Box $25   **Bottle** $10

Q-Bert, 1983, Thermos, bright yellow
    Box $18   **Bottle** $12

Race Cars, 1987, Servo
    Box $25   **Bottle** n/a

Raggedy Ann & Andy, 1988, Aladdin
    Box $45   **Bottle** $20

Rainbow Bread Van, 1984, Moldmark Industries
    Box $60   **Bottle** $20

Rainbow Brite, 1983, Thermos
    Box $25   **Bottle** $5

Robot Man and Friends, 1984, Thermos
    Box $25   **Bottle** $10

Rocketeer, 1990, Aladdin
    Box $15   **Bottle** $5

Rocky Roughneck, 1977, Thermos
    Box $25   **Bottle** $10

Roller Games, 1989, Thermos
    Box $30   **Bottle** $10

S.W.A.T. Dome, 1975, Thermos
    Box $45   **Bottle** $15

Scooby Doo, 1973, Thermos
    Box $35   **Bottle** $20

Scooby Doo, 1984, Aladdin
    Box $40   **Bottle** $20

Scooby-Doo, A Pup Named, 1988, Aladdin
    Box $25   **Bottle** $10

Sesame Street, 1985, Aladdin/Canada
    Box $15   **Bottle** $5

Shirt Tales, 1981, Thermos
    Box $18   **Bottle** $5

Sky Commanders, 1987, Thermos, generic plastic bottle
    Box $15   **Bottle** $5

Smurfette, 1984, Thermos
    Box $15   **Bottle** $7

Smurfs, 1984, Thermos
    Box $25   **Bottle** $15

Smurfs Dome, 1981, Thermos
    Box $35   **Bottle** $15

Smurfs Fishing, 1984, Thermos
    Box $20   **Bottle** $5

Snak Shot Camera, 1987, Hummer, camera-shaped box, blue or green, w/generic plastic bottle
    Box $30   **Bottle** $2

Snoopy Dome, 1978, Thermos
    Box $25   **Bottle** $5

Snorks, 1984, Thermos
    Box $12   **Bottle** $5

Snow White, 1980, Aladdin
    Box $40   **Bottle** $15

Spare Parts, 1982, Aladdin, w/generic plastic bottle
    Box $35   **Bottle** $10

Sport Billy, 1982, Thermos
    Box $20   **Bottle** $10

Sport Goofy, 1986, Aladdin
    Box $30   **Bottle** $10

Star Com. U.S. Space Force, 1987, Thermos
    Box $20   **Bottle** $10

Star Trek Next Generation, 1988, Thermos, blue box, group picture, matching bottle
    Box $60   **Bottle** $25

Star Trek Next Generation, 1989, Thermos, red box, Picard, Data, Wesley, matching bottle
    Box $75   **Bottle** $20

Star Wars, Droids, 1985, Thermos
    Box $60   **Bottle** $25

Strawberry Shortcake, 1980, Aladdin
    Box $10   **Bottle** $5

Superman II Dome, 1986, Aladdin
    Box $55   **Bottle** $25

Superman, This is a Job For, 1980, Aladdin, no bottle
    Box $25   **Bottle** n/a

Tail Spin, 1986, Aladdin
    Box $25   **Bottle** $10

Tang Trio, 1988, Thermos, red or yellow box w/generic plastic bottle
    Box $35   **Bottle** $5

Teenage Mutant Ninja Turtles, 1990, Thermos, w/generic plastic bottle
    Box $18   **Bottle** $5

Thundarr the Barbarian Dome, 1981, Aladdin, plastic dome box w/matching bottle
    Box $25   **Bottle** $10

Timeless Tales, 1989, Aladdin
    Box $10   **Bottle** $5

Tiny Toon Adventures, 1990, Thermos
    Box $10   **Bottle** $5

Tom & Jerry, 1989, Aladdin
    Box $30   **Bottle** $10

Transformers, 1985, Aladdin
    Box $45   **Bottle** $20

Transformers Dome, 1986, Aladdin/Canada, dome box, generic plastic bottle
    Box $75   **Bottle** $15

Tweety & Sylvester, 1986, Thermos
    Box $45   **Bottle** $20

(KP Photo)

Wayne Gretzky, 1980, Aladdin
    Box $100   **Bottle** $30

Wayne Gretzky Dome, 1980, Aladdin
    Box $120   **Bottle** $30

Where's Waldo, 1990, Thermos
    Box $10   **Bottle** $5

Who Framed Roger Rabbit, 1987, Thermos, red or yellow, w/matching bottle
    Box $25   **Bottle** $10

Wild Fire, 1986, Aladdin
    Box $15   **Bottle** $8

Wizard of Oz, 50th Anniversary, 1989, Aladdin
    Box $60   **Bottle** $20

Woody Woodpecker, 1972, Aladdin, yellow box, red bottle
    Box $50   **Bottle** $40

World Wrestling Federation, 1986, Thermos
    Box $25   **Bottle** $10

Wrinkles, 1984, Thermos
    Box $10   **Bottle** $5

Wuzzles, 1985, Aladdin
    Box $10   **Bottle** $5

Yogi's Treasure Hunt, 1987, Servo, flat paper label, w/matching bottle
    Box $25   **Bottle** $30

Yogi's Treasure Hunt (3-D), 1987, Servo, 3-D box, green or pink, w/matching bottle
    Box $65   **Bottle** $30

STEEL

240 Robert, 1978, Aladdin
    Box $4200   **Bottle** n/a

Action Jackson, 1973, Okay Industries, matching steel bottle
    Box $1350   **Bottle** $450

Adam-12, 1973, Aladdin, matching plastic bottle
    Box $375   **Bottle** $100

LUNCH BOXES

⬅**Action Figures,** Marvel Super Heroes, Fantastic Four Sue Storm, Toy Biz, 1990, $150

⬆**Action Figures,** Shogun Warriors, Gaiking, Mattel, 1979, $150

⬆**Action Figures,** World's Greatest Super Heroes Iron Man, boxed, Mego, 1974, $125

➡**Action Figures,** A-Team B.A. Baracus, Galoob, 1984, $35

⬆**Action Figures,** Zipline Batman, Mattel, 2003, $10

⬆**Action Figures,** Lord of the Rings Frodo the Hobbit, Toy Vault, 1998, $14

➡**Action Figures,** Moon McDare Action Spaceman Blinker Light in box, Gilbert, 1960s, $85

⬅**Action Figures,** Captain Action, boxed, with damaged arm, Ideal, 1966, $500

⤴ **Action Figures**, Donny Osmond and Osmond TV Show Playset, Mattel, 1970s, $45 and $55 respectively

⬆ **Action Figures**, Grizzly Adams figure, Mattel, 1979, $35

⬆ **Action Figures**, Super Powers, Flash, Kenner, 1984, $25

⬆ **Action Figures**, ST:TNG Lwaxana Troi, 7th Season, Playmates, 1995, $10

⬆ **Action Figures**, The Outer Space Men, Electron The Man From Pluto, Colorforms, 1968, $500

⬅ **Action Figures**, Best of the West, Johnny West, boxed, Marx, 1965, $150

➡ **Action Figures**, Robotech, Lynn Minmei, 3-3/4", Matchbox, 1986, $12

Advertising, Freddy Fast figure, Douglas Oil Co., 1976, $130

Advertising, Alka Seltzer Speedy figure, 1963, $350

Advertising, Mr. Peanut, Planter's Peanuts, $40

Barbie, Fashions, Barbie in Mexico Bubblecut, 1962, $250

Barbie, This is an American Girl Barbie in her original outfit. Doll dealer Barbara Blocker was sharing a table at the Santa's show with her sister, Dorla Thompson, and was also kind enough to let me photograph her vintage Barbie. Thanks!

Barbie, This is a Color Magic Barbie in her original outfit with the original pin in her hair. While attending the Santa's Toy Show in Portage, Ind., last spring, doll dealer Dorla Thompson brought in this outstanding Barbie so I could include it in this color section.

13th Edition

TOYS & PRICES 2006

⬆ **Battery-Operated**, Mew-Mew Walking Cat, MT, 1950s, $150

⬆ **Battery-Operated**, Maxwell Coffee-Loving Bear, TN, 1960s, $260

➡ **Character Toys**, Snoopy Pencil Sharpener, Kenner, 1974, $90

⬆ **Character Toys**, Batman Figure Set, Ideal, 1966, $175

⬆ **Character Toys**, Superman Colorforms set, 1964, $65

⬅ **Fisher-Price**, Little Snoopy, #693, 1966, $25

➡ **Fisher-Price**, Donald Duck Cart, #544, 1942, $485

⬆ **Fisher-Price**, Mickey Mouse Safety Patrol, #733, 1956, $575

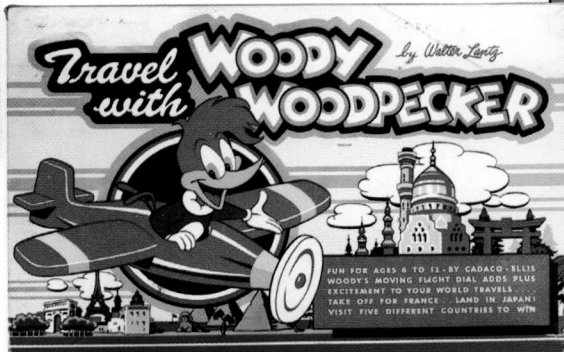

Games, Pro Bowl Live Action Football, Marx, 1960s, $95

Games, Travel With Woody Woodpecker, Cadaco-Ellis, 1950s, $100

Games, Walter Johnson Base Ball Game, 1930s, $325

Guns, Popeye Pirate Pistol, Marx, 1930s, $1000

Guns, Detective Shootin' Shell Snub-Nose .38, Mattel, 1960, $165

Guns, Potato Gun, Hong Kong, 1991, $10

Guns, Texan by Hubley, 1950s, $300

13th Edition
TOYS & PRICES 2006

➡️ **G.I. Joe**, Talking Astronaut in box, Hasbro, 1967, $450

↘️ **G.I. Joe**, Action Marine Medic set on card, Hasbro, $225

⬅️ **G.I. Joe**, Action Pilot Official Space Capsule and Space Suit set with Soundtrack recording, Hasbro, 1967, $350

⬆️ **G.I. Joe**, Action Soldier, Hasbro, 1960s, $100. Although this soldier is in need of a re-stringing, unbroken figures remain desirable.

➡️ **G.I. Joe**, Adventure Team Action Pack Underwater Explorer set in box, Hasbro, 1971, $60

⬆ **G.I. Joe**, Breaker, Hasbro, 1982, $85

⬆ **G.I. Joe**, Duke, Hasbro, 1984, $75

⬆ **G.I. Joe**, Cobra Stellar Stiletto, boxed, Hasbro, 1988, $40

⬆ **G.I. Joe**, Hawk, Hasbro, 1982, $15

⬅ **G.I. Joe** Bridge Layer, Toss N Cross, 1985, $55
(Mark Bellomo photo)

⬇ **G.I. Joe**, Headquarters Command Center, 1983, $175

⬆ **G.I. Joe**, Sci-Fi, Hasbro, 1986, $30

⬆ **Lunch Boxes**, Mickey Mouse School Days, Aladdin, 1968, $110

⬆ **Lunch Boxes**, The Munsters, King Seeley Thermos, 1965, $650

⬅**Lunch Boxes**, Mary Poppins, Aladdin, 1973, $175

⬆ **Lunch Boxes**, Zorro, Aladdin, 1966, $400

⬆ **Lunch Boxes**, The Flying Nun, Aladdin, 1968, $325

⬆ **Lunch Boxes**, Smurfs, King Seeley Thermos, 1983, $225

⬆ **Lunch Boxes**, Atom Ant/Secret Squirrel, King Seeley Thermos, 1966, $245

⬆ **Marx Play Sets**, Modern Farm Set, #3932, 1967, $310

⬆ **Marx Play Sets**, The Lone Ranger Ranch Set, Series 500, #3969, 1958, $435

⬆ **Marx Play Sets**, Ben-Hur, Series 2000, #4702, 1959, $1400

⬆ **Marx Play Sets**, Wards Service Center, #3488, 1959, $410

⬆ **Model Kits**, Mummy's Chariot, Aurora, 1965, $575

⬆ **Model Kits**, UFO from "The Invaders," Aurora, 1968, $110

⬆ **Model Kits**, Drag Nut, Revell, 1963, $75

⬆ **Model Kits**, Weird-Ohs "Daddy", Hawk, 1963, $99

TOYS & PRICES 2006
13th Edition

PEZ, Pilgrim, $150
(Courtesy Tracy Schmidt)

⬆ PEZ, Bozo the
Clown, $200
(Steve Warner photo)

⬆ PEZ, Asterix,
$1500
(Steve Warner photo)

➡ PEZ, Sheriff, $200
(Steve Warner photo)

➡ PEZ, Boy With
Cap, $100
(Steve Warner photo)

⬅ PEZ, Crazy Fruit
Lemon, $3000
(Steve Warner photo)

⬅ Restaurant Premiums, McDonald's Lego,
1999, $3 each

↪ Restaurant Premiums, Burger King, The
Great Gazoo's Close Encounter from Flintstone's
Viva Rock Vegas, $3

⬇ Restaurant Premiums, Burger King, Oliver &
Co., 1996, $4

➡️ **Robots**, Frankenstein Robot, Marx, 1968, $2000

⬅️ **Robots**, Mr. Atom The Electronic Walking Robot, Advance Toys, 1960s, $650

➡️ **Robots**, Radar-Scope Space Scout, S.H., 1964, $350

⬅️ **Robots**, Smoking Spaceman, Yonezawa, 1960, $3750

➡️ **Robots**, Mechanized Robot "Robby", TN, 1947, $4500

⬅️ **Rock and Roll**, The Monkees Punch-Out Model Book, $60

⬅️ **Rock and Roll**, Dick Clark American Bandstand Official Jewelry display, $85

⬆ **Star Wars**, POTF2 Darth Vader, carded, Hasbro, 1995, $20

⬆ **Star Wars**, Darth Vader Tie-Fighter, model kit, MPC, 1978, $30

⬆ **Star Wars**, Obi-Wan Kenobi Unleashed, Hasbro, 2004, $20

⬆ **Star Wars**, Patrol Dewback, Star Wars, boxed, Kenner, 1978, $75

⇨ **Star Wars**, ESB, Yoda Costume, Ben Cooper, $55

⇨ **Star Wars**, 12" Clone Trooper, Hasbro, 2002, $25

⇦ **Star Wars**, 12" Darth Vader, Kenner, 1978, $185

⇨ **Star Wars**, ESB, Princess Leia Organa in Boushh Disguise, Kenner, 1983, $43

13th Edition
TOYS & PRICES
2006

Sci-Fi, Space Patrol Drink Mixer, Sterilite, 1950s, $200

➪ **Sci-Fi**, Space Commander Walkie Talkies, Remco, 1960s, $125

⬅ **Sci-Fi**, Tom Corbett Space Cadet Polaris Ship, tin wind-up, Marx, 1950s, $600

➪ **TV Toys**, S.W.A.T. Clicker Gun and Handcuffs Set, Fleetwood Toys, Inc., 1975, $45

⬅ **Tin Toys**, Balky Mule, Marx, 1948, $250
(Scott Smiles photo)

↘ **Tin Toys**, Mechanical Drummer No. 109, Chein, $225
(Scott Smiles photo)

⬇ **TV Toys**, Soupy Sales Our Hero figure, 1950s, $150

⬇ **TV Toys**, McHale's Navy Signal Sender, Gabriel-Bell Inc., $75

⬆ **Vehicles**, Dinky Toys, Johnston Road Sweeper, No. 451, $85

⬆ **Vehicles**, Corgi Chipperfields Circus Land Rover Parade Vehicle, No. 487, $175

⬆ **Vehicles**, Dinky Toys, Airport Fire Tender, No. 276, $135

⬆ **Vehicles**, Johnny Lightning Topper, Frantic Ferrari, 1970, $110

⬆ **Vehicles**, Johnny Lightning Topper, Custom Turbine, unpainted interior, 1969, $125

⬆ **Vehicles**, Hot Wheels Redlines, Dune Daddy, 1973, $300

⬅ **Vehicles**, Buddy L Dump Truck, 1966, $125

➡ **Vehicles**, Corgi Chevrolet Impala, No. 220, $125

➡ **Vehicles**, Hot Wheels Redlines, Moving Van, 1970, $160

⬅ **Vehicles**, Japanese Tin, Agajanin Racer No. 98, friction, "Y" Co., 1950s, 18", $2800

➡ **Vehicles**, Japanese Tin, 1967 Chevrolet Camaro, TN, 14" long, $350

⬅ **Vehicles**, Marx, Gravel Mixer, 1930s, $250

⇐ **Vehicles**, Marx, Milton Berle Crazy Car, 1950s, $595

⬇ **Vehicles**, Matchbox Regular Wheels, No. 9 Merryweather Marquis Fire Engine, 1959, $70

⇒ **Vehicles**, Nylint, Elgin Street Sweeper, 1950-52, $175

⇐ **Vehicles**, Matchbox King Size, K17-1 Low Loader w/ Bulldozer, 1967, $150

⇒ **Vehicles**, Structo, Cattle Truck, #720, $195

⇐ **Vehicles**, Structo, Sanitation Department, 1963, $95

⇒ **Vehicles**, Tonka, Minute Maid Van, No. 725, 1954, $950

⇐ **Vehicles**, Tonka, Cement Mixer, No. 120, 1960, $300

⬆ **Vehicles**, Tootsietoy, Boattail Roadsters, $55

⬆ **Vehicles**, Tootsietoy, Insurance Patrol Fire Engines, $60

13th Edition
TOYS & PRICES 2006

⬆ **View-Master**, Godzilla, $15

⬆ **View-Master**, Donald Duck, $8

⬆ **View-Master**, The Flintstones, $12

⬆ **View-Master**, Dracula, $15

⬆ **View-Master**, 20,000 Leagues Under the Sea, $15

⬆ **View-Master**, Wild Animals of Africa, $11

⬆ **Western**, Quick Draw McGraw Battery-Operated Target, $60

⬆ **Western**, Daniel Boone Puzzle, Plas-Trix, no. 144, 1950s, $25

⬇ **Western**, Bonanza model kit, Revell, $45

(KP Photo)

Addams Family, 1974, King Seeley Thermos, matching plastic bottle
>Box $350   Bottle $75

Airline, 1969, Ohio Art, no bottle
>Box $175   Bottle n/a

All American, 1954, Universal, steel/glass bottle
>Box $525   Bottle $125

America on Parade, 1976, Aladdin, matching plastic bottle
>Box $95   Bottle $40

Americana, 1958, King Seeley Thermos, steel/glass bottle
>Box $425   Bottle $165

Animal Friends, 1978, Ohio Art, yellow or red background behind name
>Box $90   Bottle n/a

(KP Photo)

Annie Oakley & Tagg, 1955, Aladdin, matching steel bottle, shown with Dukes of Hazzard & Magic Kingdom lunch boxes
>Box $525   Bottle $175

Annie, The Movie, 1982, Aladdin, plastic bottle
>Box $80   Bottle $25

Apple's Way, 1975, King Seeley Thermos, plastic bottle
>Box $165   Bottle $40

Archies, 1969, Aladdin, matching plastic bottle
>Box $250   Bottle $75

Astronaut Dome, 1960, King Seeley Thermos, steel/glass bottle
>Box $300   Bottle $75

Astronauts, 1969, Aladdin, matching plastic bottle
>Box $195   Bottle $75

A-Team, 1985, King Seeley Thermos, plastic bottle
>Box $90   Bottle $35

Atom Ant/Secret Squirrel, 1966, King Seeley Thermos, matching steel bottle
>Box $245   Bottle $120

Auto Race, 1967, King Seeley Thermos, matching steel bottle
>Box $195   Bottle $75

Back in '76, 1975, Aladdin, plastic bottle
>Box $95   Bottle $40

Barbie Lunch Kit, 1962, King Seeley Thermos, steel/glass bottle
>Box $275   Bottle $90

Basketweave, 1968, Ohio Art, no bottle
>Box $75   Bottle n/a

Batman and Robin, 1966, Aladdin, matching steel bottle
>Box $475   Bottle $145

Battle Kit, 1965, King Seeley Thermos, matching steel bottle
>Box $200   Bottle $75

(KP Photo)

Battle of the Planets, 1979, King Seeley Thermos, matching plastic bottle,

shown with Chan Clan, The & Hot Wheels lunch boxes
>Box $120   Bottle $40

Battlestar Galactica, 1978, Aladdin, matching plastic bottle
>Box $175   Bottle $45

Beatles, 1966, Aladdin, blue, matching bottle
>Box $1850   Bottle $400

Bedknobs & Broomsticks, 1972, Aladdin, plastic bottle
>Box $150   Bottle $45

Bee Gees, 1978, King Seeley Thermos, Barry on back, matching plastic bottle
>Box $175   Bottle $45

Bee Gees, 1978, King Seeley Thermos, Maurice on back, matching plastic bottle
>Box $150   Bottle $45

Bee Gees, 1978, King Seeley Thermos, Robin on back, matching plastic bottle
>Box $150   Bottle $45

Berenstain Bears, 1983, American Thermos, matching plastic bottle
>Box $90   Bottle $40

Beverly Hillbillies, 1963, Aladdin, matching steel bottle
>Box $375   Bottle $95

Bionic Woman, with Car, 1977, Aladdin, plastic bottle
>Box $225   Bottle $50

Bionic Woman, with Dog, 1978, Aladdin, matching plastic bottle
>Box $250   Bottle $50

Black Hole, 1979, Aladdin, matching plastic bottle
>Box $95   Bottle $40

Blondie, 1969, King Seeley Thermos, matching steel bottle
>Box $300   Bottle $75

Boating, 1959, American Thermos, matching steel bottle
>Box $400   Bottle $125

Bobby Sherman, 1972, King Seeley Thermos, matching steel bottle
>Box $275   Bottle $75

Bonanza, 1963, Aladdin, green rim box, steel bottle
>Box $325   Bottle $95

Bonanza, 1965, Aladdin, brown rim box, steel bottle
>Box $275   Bottle $80

(KP Photo)

Bonanza, 1968, Aladdin, black rim box, steel bottle

 Box $375   Bottle $120

Bond XX, 1967, Ohio Art, no bottle

 Box $200   Bottle n/a

Boston Bruins, 1973, Okay Industries, steel/glass bottle

 Box $525   Bottle $250

Bozo the Clown Dome, Aladdin, steel bottle

 Box $375   Bottle $120

Brady Bunch, 1970, King Seeley Thermos, matching steel bottle

 Box $575   Bottle $150

Brave Eagle, 1957, American Thermos, red, blue, gray or green band, matching steel bottle

 Box $375   Bottle $150

Bread Box Dome, 1968, Aladdin, Campbell's Soup bottle

 Box $450   Bottle $125

(KP Photo)

Buccaneer Dome, 1957, Aladdin, matching bottle, shown with Julia lunch box

 Box $375   Bottle $125

Buck Rogers, 1979, Aladdin, matching plastic bottle

 Box $95   Bottle $35

Bugaloos, 1971, Aladdin, matching plastic bottle

 Box $250   Bottle $75

Bullwinkle & Rocky, 1962, Universal, blue box, steel bottle

 Box $1850   Bottle $500

Cabbage Patch Kids, 1984, King Seeley Thermos, matching plastic bottle

 Box $60   Bottle $20

Cable Car Dome, 1962, Aladdin, steel/glass bottle

 Box $600   Bottle $125

Campbell's Kids, 1973, Okay, matching steel bottle

 Box $265   Bottle $150

Campus Queen, 1967, King Seeley Thermos, matching steel bottle

 Box $200   Bottle $65

Canadian Pacific Railroad, 1970, Ohio Art, no bottle

 Box $45   Bottle n/a

Captain Astro, 1966, Ohio Art, no bottle

 Box $525   Bottle n/a

Care Bear Cousins, 1985, Aladdin, matching plastic bottle

 Box $50   Bottle $20

Care Bears, 1984, Aladdin, plastic bottle

 Box $55   Bottle $20

Carnival, 1959, Universal, matching steel bottle

 Box $750   Bottle $250

Cartoon Zoo Lunch Chest, 1962, Universal, steel/glass bottle

 Box $450   Bottle $125

Casey Jones, 1960, Universal, steel dome box, steel/glass bottle

 Box $650   Bottle $125

(KP Photo)

Chan Clan, The, 1973, King Seeley Thermos, plastic bottle, shown with Battle of the Planets & Hot Wheels lunch boxes

 Box $100   Bottle $40

Charlie's Angels, 1978, Aladdin, matching plastic bottle

 Box $225   Bottle $50

Chavo, 1979, Aladdin, matching plastic bottle

 Box $250   Bottle $50

Children, blue, 1974, Okay Industries, plastic bottle

 Box $175   Bottle $40

Children, yellow, 1974, Okay Industries, plastic bottle

 Box $250   Bottle $40

Children's, 1984, Ohio Art, no bottle

 Box $75   Bottle n/a

Chitty Chitty Bang Bang, 1969, King Seeley Thermos, matching steel bottle

 Box $400   Bottle $75

Chuck Wagon Dome, 1958, Aladdin, matching bottle

 Box $325   Bottle $90

Circus Wagon Dome, 1958, King Seeley Thermos, steel/glass bottle

 Box $350   Bottle $150

Clash of the Titans, 1981, King Seeley Thermos, matching plastic bottle

 Box $125   Bottle $40

Close Encounters of the Third Kind, 1978, King Seeley Thermos, plastic bottle

 Box $125   Bottle $40

Color Me Happy, 1984, Ohio Art, no bottle

 Box $260   Bottle n/a

Corsage, 1958, American Thermos, matching steel bottle

 Box $115   Bottle $60

(KP Photo)

Cowboy in Africa, Chuck Connors, 1968, King Seeley Thermos, matching steel bottle

 Box $300   Bottle $75

Cracker Jack, 1969, Aladdin, matching plastic bottle

 Box $150   Bottle $50

Curiosity Shop, 1972, King Seeley Thermos, matching steel bottle

 Box $150   Bottle $60

Cyclist Dirt Bike, 1979, Aladdin, plastic bottle

 Box $110   Bottle $45

Daniel Boone, 1955, Aladdin, matching steel bottle

 Box $450   Bottle $110

Daniel Boone, 1965, Aladdin, matching steel bottle

 Box $400   Bottle $90

Dark Crystal, 1982, King Seeley Thermos, matching plastic bottle

 Box $65   Bottle $25

(ToyShop File Photo)

LUNCH BOXES

Davy Crockett, 1955, Holtemp, matching steel bottle (shown)
      Box $375   **Bottle** $75

Davy Crockett, 1955, Kruger, no bottle
      Box $750   **Bottle** n/a

Davy Crockett/Kit Carson, 1955, Adco Liberty
      Box $350   **Bottle** n/a

Debutante, 1958, Aladdin, matching steel bottle
      Box $110   **Bottle** $75

Denim Diner Dome, 1975, Aladdin, matching plastic bottle
      Box $95   **Bottle** $30

(KP Photo)

Dick Tracy, 1967, Aladdin, matching steel bottle
      Box $450   **Bottle** $125

Disco, 1979, Aladdin, matching plastic bottle
      Box $90   **Bottle** $30

Disco Fever, 1980, Aladdin, matching plastic bottle
      Box $110   **Bottle** $35

(KP Photo)

Disney Express, 1979, Aladdin, matching plastic bottle, shown with Disney, Wonderful World & Mickey Mouse Club lunch boxes
      Box $75   **Bottle** $25

Disney Fire Fighters Dome, 1974, Aladdin, matching plastic bottle
      Box $195   **Bottle** $60

Disney School Bus Dome, 1968, Aladdin, steel/glass bottle
      Box $150   **Bottle** $40

Disney World, 1972, Aladdin, matching plastic bottle
      Box $75   **Bottle** $30

(KP Photo)

Disney, Wonderful World of Ice, 1982, Aladdin, plastic bottle, shown with Mickey Mouse Club & Disney Express lunch boxes
      Box $90   **Bottle** $30

Disneyland (Castle), 1957, Aladdin, matching steel bottle
      Box $350   **Bottle** $115

Disneyland (Monorail), 1968, Aladdin, matching steel bottle
      Box $400   **Bottle** $115

(KP Photo)

Disney's Magic Kingdom, 1980, Aladdin, plastic bottle
      Box $75   **Bottle** $40

Disney's Rescuers, The, 1977, Aladdin, plastic bottle
      Box $95   **Bottle** $35

Disney's Robin Hood, 1974, Aladdin, plastic bottle
      Box $75   **Bottle** $30

Donald Duck, 1980, Cheinco, no bottle
      Box $75   **Bottle** n/a

Double Decker, 1970, Aladdin, matching plastic bottle
      Box $175   **Bottle** $50

Dr. Dolittle, 1968, Aladdin, steel/glass bottle
      Box $350   **Bottle** $90

Dr. Seuss, 1970, Aladdin, matching plastic bottle
      Box $400   **Bottle** $75

(KP Photo)

Drag Strip, 1975, Aladdin, matching plastic bottle
      Box $175   **Bottle** $45

Dragon's Lair, 1983, Aladdin, matching plastic bottle
      Box $60   **Bottle** $25

Duchess, 1960, Aladdin, steel/glass bottle
      Box $125   **Bottle** $40

Dudley Do-Right, 1962, Universal, matching steel bottle
      Box $2450   **Bottle** $800

(KP Photo)

Dukes of Hazzard, 1983, Aladdin, matching plastic bottle, shown with Annie & Magic Kingdom lunch boxes
      Box $150   **Bottle** $50

Dutch Cottage Dome, 1958, King Seeley Thermos, steel/glass bottle
      Box $450   **Bottle** $150

Dyno Mutt, 1977, King Seeley Thermos, plastic bottle
      Box $110   **Bottle** $40

E.T., The Extra-Terrestrial, 1982, Aladdin, matching plastic bottle
      Box $95   **Bottle** $25

Early West Indian Territory, 1982, Ohio Art, no bottle
      Box $120   **Bottle** n/a

Early West Oregon Trail, 1982, Ohio Art, no bottle
      Box $120   **Bottle** n/a

Early West Pony Express, 1982, Ohio Art, no bottle
      Box $120   **Bottle** n/a

Emergency!, 1973, Aladdin, plastic bottle
      Box $350   **Bottle** $50

Emergency! Dome, 1977, Aladdin, plastic bottle
      Box $400   **Bottle** $50

Evel Knievel, 1974, Aladdin, plastic bottle
      Box $225   **Bottle** $45

Exciting World of Metrics, The, 1976, King Seeley Thermos, plastic bottle
      Box $80   **Bottle** $30

Fall Guy, 1981, Aladdin, matching plastic bottle
      Box $65   **Bottle** $30

Family Affair, 1969, King Seeley Thermos, matching steel bottle
      Box $260   **Bottle** $75

Fat Albert and the Cosby Kids, 1973, King Seeley Thermos, plastic bottle
      Box $120   **Bottle** $30

Fess Parker, 1965, King Seeley Thermos, matching steel bottle
      Box $325   **Bottle** $90

Fireball XL5, 1964, King Seeley Thermos, steel/glass bottle
      Box $360   **Bottle** $85

Firehouse Dome, 1959, American Thermos, steel/glass bottle
      Box $475   **Bottle** $150

Flag-O-Rama, 1954, Universal, steel/glass bottle
  Box $475   **Bottle** $110

Flintstones, 1962, Aladdin, orange, 1st issue, matching bottle
  Box $450   **Bottle** $110

Flintstones, 1964, Aladdin, yellow, 2nd issue, matching bottle
  Box $500   **Bottle** $110

Flintstones, 1973, Aladdin, matching plastic bottle
  Box $300   **Bottle** $50

(KP Photo)

Flipper, 1966, King Seeley Thermos, matching steel bottle
  Box $350   **Bottle** $75

Floral, 1970, Ohio Art, no bottle
  Box $40   **Bottle** n/a

Flying Nun, 1968, Aladdin, matching steel bottle
  Box $350   **Bottle** $95

Fonz, The, 1978, King Seeley Thermos, plastic bottle
  Box $250   **Bottle** $40

Fox and the Hound, 1981, Aladdin, plastic bottle
  Box $65   **Bottle** $30

Fraggle Rock, 1984, King Seeley Thermos, matching plastic bottle
  Box $75   **Bottle** $30

Fritos, 1975, King Seeley Thermos, generic bottle
  Box $300   **Bottle** n/a

Frontier Days, 1957, Ohio Art, no bottle
  Box $350   **Bottle** n/a

Frost Flowers, 1962, Ohio Art, no bottle
  Box $70   **Bottle** n/a

Fruit Basket, 1975, Ohio Art, no bottle
  Box $45   **Bottle** n/a

Funtastic World of Hanna-Barbera, 1977, King Seeley Thermos, Huck Hound, plastic bottle
  Box $250   **Bottle** $45

Funtastic World of Hanna-Barbera, 1978, King Seeley Thermos, Flintstones & Yogi, plastic bottle
  Box $275   **Bottle** $45

G.I. Joe, 1967, King Seeley Thermos, steel/glass bottle
  Box $425   **Bottle** $90

G.I. Joe, 1982, King Seeley Thermos, plastic bottle
  Box $100   **Bottle** $25

Gene Autry, 1954, Universal, steel/glass bottle
  Box $900   **Bottle** $225

(KP Photo)

Gentle Ben, 1968, Aladdin, plastic bottle, glass liner, shown here with Lance Link lunch box
  Box $225   **Bottle** $75

(KP Photo)

Get Smart, 1966, King Seeley Thermos, steel/glass bottle
  Box $450   **Bottle** $95

Ghostland, 1977, Ohio Art, spinner game, no bottle
  Box $80   **Bottle** n/a

(KP Photo)

Globe-Trotter Dome, 1959, Aladdin, steel dome box, matching steel/glass bottle
  Box $300   **Bottle** $120

Gomer Pyle USMC, 1966, Aladdin, matching steel bottle
  Box $450   **Bottle** $110

(KP Photo)

Goober and the Ghostchasers / Inch High, 1974, King Seeley Thermos, matching plastic bottle
  Box $120   **Bottle** $25

Great Wild West, 1959, Universal, matching steel bottle
  Box $625   **Bottle** $225

Green Hornet, 1967, King Seeley Thermos, matching steel bottle
  Box $550   **Bottle** $175

(KP Photo)

Gremlins, 1984, Aladdin, matching plastic bottle
  Box $75   **Bottle** $35

Grizzly Adams Dome, 1977, Aladdin, plastic bottle
  Box $200   **Bottle** $40

Guns of Will Sonnett, The, 1968, King Seeley Thermos, steel/glass bottle
  Box $300   **Bottle** $90

Gunsmoke, 1959, Aladdin, plastic bottle
  Box $375   **Bottle** $95

Gunsmoke, 1972, Aladdin, mule splashing box w/matching bottle
  Box $250   **Bottle** $65

Gunsmoke, 1973, Aladdin, stagecoach box, matching bottle
  Box $225   **Bottle** $65

Gunsmoke, Double L Version, 1959, Aladdin, double L error version, matching bottle
  Box $1350   **Bottle** $95

(KP Photo)

Gunsmoke, Marshal Matt Dillon, 1962, Aladdin, matching steel bottle
  Box $375   **Bottle** $95

(KP Photo)

H.R. Pufnstuf, 1970, Aladdin, matching plastic bottle
  Box $350   **Bottle** $70

Hair Bear Bunch, The, 1972, King Seeley Thermos, plastic bottle
Box $95 **Bottle** $35

Hansel and Gretel, 1982, Ohio Art, no bottle
Box $80 **Bottle** n/a

Happy Days, 1977, American Thermos, matching plastic bottle
Box $250 **Bottle** $40

Hardy Boys Mysteries, 1977, King Seeley Thermos, matching plastic bottle
Box $100 **Bottle** $30

Harlem Globetrotters, 1971, King Seeley Thermos, steel bottle, blue or purple uniforms
Box $175 **Bottle** $65

Have Gun, Will Travel, 1960, Aladdin, matching bottle, Paladin
Box $450 **Bottle** $150

Heathcliff, 1982, Aladdin, matching plastic bottle
Box $65 **Bottle** $20

Hector Heathcote, 1964, Aladdin, matching steel bottle
Box $325 **Bottle** $90

(KP Photo)

Hee Haw, 1971, King Seeley Thermos, matching steel bottle
Box $250 **Bottle** $65

He-Man & Masters of the Universe, 1984, Aladdin, matching plastic bottle
Box $95 **Bottle** $30

Highway Signs, 1972, Ohio Art, no bottle
Box $70 **Bottle** n/a

(KP Photo)

Hogan's Heroes Dome, 1966, Aladdin, steel/glass bottle
Box $525 **Bottle** $150

Holly Hobbie, 1968, Aladdin, red rim, matching plastic bottle
Box $65 **Bottle** $20

Holly Hobbie, 1973, Aladdin, matching plastic bottle
Box $65 **Bottle** $20

Holly Hobbie, 1979, Aladdin, matching plastic bottle
Box $65 **Bottle** $20

Home Town Airport Dome, 1960, King Seeley Thermos, steel/glass bottle
Box $1200 **Bottle** $275

(KP Photo)

Hong Kong Phooey, 1975, King Seeley Thermos, steel/glass bottle
Box $200 **Bottle** $40

(KP Photo)

Hopalong Cassidy, 1950, Aladdin, red or blue, steel/glass bottle
Box $400 **Bottle** $90

Hopalong Cassidy, 1952, Aladdin, steel bottle
Box $400 **Bottle** $90

Hopalong Cassidy, 1954, Aladdin, black rim, steel/glass bottle, full litho
Box $525 **Bottle** $150

(ToyShop File Photo)

Hot Wheels, 1969, King Seeley Thermos, matching steel bottle
Box $275 **Bottle** $75

How the West Was Won, 1979, King Seeley Thermos, matching plastic bottle
Box $125 **Bottle** $40

Howdy Doody, 1954, Adco Liberty
Box $750 **Bottle** n/a

Huckleberry Hound, 1961, Aladdin, steel/glass bottle
Box $300 **Bottle** $90

Indiana Jones, 1984, King Seeley Thermos, matching plastic bottle
Box $100 **Bottle** $30

Indiana Jones Temple of Doom, 1984, King Seeley Thermos, matching plastic bottle
Box $100 **Bottle** $30

It's About Time Dome, 1967, Aladdin, matching bottle
Box $350 **Bottle** $125

Jack and Jill, 1982, Ohio Art
Box $400 **Bottle** n/a

James Bond 007, 1966, Aladdin, matching steel bottle
Box $550 **Bottle** $150

Jet Patrol, 1957, Aladdin, matching steel bottle
Box $400 **Bottle** $150

Jetsons Dome, 1963, Aladdin, matching bottle
Box $1800 **Bottle** $350

Joe Palooka, 1949, Continental Can, no bottle
Box $90 **Bottle** n/a

(KP Photo)

Johnny Lightning, 1970, Aladdin, plastic bottle
Box $200 **Bottle** $60

Jonathan Livingston Seagull, 1973, Aladdin, matching plastic bottle
Box $150 **Bottle** $50

(KP Photo)

Julia, 1969, King Seeley Thermos, matching steel bottle, shown with Buccaneer Dome lunch box
Box $200 **Bottle** $75

Jungle Book, 1968, Aladdin, matching steel bottle
Box $225 **Bottle** $75

Junior Miss, 1978, Aladdin, matching plastic bottle
Box $85 **Bottle** $40

Kellogg's, 1969, Aladdin, plastic bottle
    Box $325   **Bottle** $75

King Kong, 1977, King Seeley Thermos, plastic bottle
    Box $200   **Bottle** $40

KISS, 1977, King Seeley Thermos, plastic bottle
    Box $300   **Bottle** $50

Knight in Armor, 1959, Universal, matching steel bottle
    Box $1250   **Bottle** $300

Knight Rider, 1984, King Seeley Thermos, matching plastic bottle
    Box $75   **Bottle** $25

Korg, 1975, King Seeley Thermos, matching plastic bottle
    Box $120   **Bottle** $45

Krofft Supershow, 1976, Aladdin, matching plastic bottle
    Box $225   **Bottle** $50

Kung Fu, 1974, King Seeley Thermos, matching plastic bottle
    Box $225   **Bottle** $40

(KP Photo)

Lance Link, Secret Chimp, 1971, King Seeley Thermos, matching steel bottle, shown here with Gentle Ben lunch box
    Box $225   **Bottle** $75

(KP Photo)

Land of the Giants, 1968, Aladdin, plastic bottle
    Box $325   **Bottle** $85

Land of the Lost, 1975, Aladdin, matching plastic bottle
    Box $250   **Bottle** $50

Laugh-In (Helmet), 1969, Aladdin, helmet on back, matching plastic bottle
    Box $250   **Bottle** $65

Laugh-In (Tricycle), 1969, Aladdin, trike on back, matching plastic bottle
    Box $275   **Bottle** $65

Lawman, 1961, King Seeley Thermos, generic bottle
    Box $250   **Bottle** $85

Legend of the Lone Ranger, 1980, Aladdin, plastic bottle
    Box $175   **Bottle** $45

Lidsville, 1971, Aladdin, matching plastic bottle
    Box $300   **Bottle** $65

Little Dutch Miss, 1959, Universal, matching steel bottle
    Box $185   **Bottle** $75

Little Friends, 1982, Aladdin, matching plastic bottle
    Box $850   **Bottle** $260

Little House on the Prairie, 1978, King Seeley Thermos, matching plastic bottle
    Box $250   **Bottle** $45

Little Red Riding Hood, 1982, Ohio Art, no bottle
    Box $50   **Bottle** n/a

Lone Ranger, 1955, Adco Liberty, blue band, no bottle
    Box $950   **Bottle** n/a

Lone Ranger, 1955, Adco Liberty, red rim, no bottle
    Box $750   **Bottle** n/a

Looney Tunes TV Set, 1959, King Seeley Thermos, steel/glass bottle
    Box $350   **Bottle** $95

Lost in Space Dome, 1967, King Seeley Thermos, steel/glass bottle
    Box $1350   **Bottle** $100

Ludwig Von Drake, 1962, Aladdin, steel/glass bottle
    Box $350   **Bottle** $90

Luggage Plaid, 1955, Adco Liberty, no bottle
    Box $75   **Bottle** n/a

Luggage Plaid, 1957, Ohio Art, no bottle
    Box $75   **Bottle** n/a

Magic of Lassie, 1978, King Seeley Thermos, matching plastic bottle
    Box $185   **Bottle** $40

Major League Baseball, 1968, King Seeley Thermos, matching bottle
    Box $225   **Bottle** $55

Man from U.N.C.L.E., 1966, King Seeley Thermos, matching steel bottle
    Box $675   **Bottle** $90

Marvel Super Heroes, 1976, Aladdin, black rim, matching plastic bottle
    Box $150   **Bottle** $45

Mary Poppins, 1965, Aladdin, steel/glass bottle
    Box $225   **Bottle** $75

Masters of the Universe, 1983, Aladdin, matching plastic bottle
    Box $75   **Bottle** $25

Mickey Mouse & Donald Duck, 1954, Adco Liberty, matching steel bottle
    Box $800 **Bottle** $1500

(KP Photo)

Mickey Mouse Club, 1963, Aladdin, yellow, steel/glass bottle, shown with Disney, Wonderful World & Mickey Mouse Club lunch boxes
    Box $225   **Bottle** $60

Mickey Mouse Club, 1976, Aladdin, white, matching steel bottle
    Box $175   **Bottle** $50

Mickey Mouse Club, 1977, Aladdin, red rim, sky boat, matching bottle
    Box $125   **Bottle** $40

Miss America, 1972, Aladdin, matching plastic bottle
    Box $200   **Bottle** $50

Mod Floral Dome, 1975, Okay Industries, matching steel bottle
    Box $400   **Bottle** n/a

Monroes, 1967, Aladdin, matching steel bottle
    Box $350   **Bottle** $110

(KP Photo)

Mork & Mindy, 1979, American Thermos, matching plastic bottle
Box $125   Bottle $45

Mr. Merlin, 1982, King Seeley Thermos, matching plastic bottle
Box $100   Bottle $35

Munsters, 1965, King Seeley Thermos, matching steel bottle
Box $650   Bottle $150

Muppet Babies, 1985, King Seeley Thermos, matching plastic bottle
Box $65   Bottle $20

Muppet Movie, 1979, King Seeley Thermos, plastic bottle
Box $150   Bottle $40

Muppet Show, 1978, King Seeley Thermos, plastic bottle
Box $95   Bottle $30

Muppets, 1979, King Seeley Thermos, back shows Animal, Fozzie or Kermit, matching plastic bottle
Box $95   Bottle $30

My Lunch, 1976, Ohio Art, no bottle
Box $65   Bottle n/a

Nancy Drew, 1978, King Seeley Thermos, plastic bottle
Box $150   Bottle $30

NFL, 1962, Okay, black rim, steel/glass bottle
Box $275   Bottle $130

NFL, 1975, King Seeley Thermos, yellow rim, plastic bottle
Box $95   Bottle $40

NFL, 1976, King Seeley Thermos, red rim, matching plastic bottle
Box $95   Bottle $40

NFL, 1978, King Seeley Thermos, blue rim, matching plastic bottle
Box $95   Bottle $40

NFL Quarterback, 1964, Aladdin, matching steel bottle
Box $325   Bottle $80

NHL, 1970, Okay Industries, plastic bottle
Box $525   Bottle $250

Orbit, 1963, King Seeley Thermos, matching steel bottle
Box $350   Bottle $90

Osmonds, The, 1973, Aladdin, matching plastic bottle
Box $185   Bottle $45

Our Friends, 1982, Aladdin, matching plastic bottle
Box $850   Bottle $350

Pac-Man, 1980, Aladdin, matching plastic bottle
Box $95   Bottle $25

Para-Medic, 1978, Ohio Art, no bottle
Box $65   Bottle n/a

Partridge Family, 1971, King Seeley Thermos, plastic or steel bottle
Box $200   Bottle $60

Pathfinder, 1959, Universal, matching steel bottle
Box $600   Bottle $200

Patriotic, 1974, Ohio Art, no bottle
Box $75   Bottle n/a

(KP Photo)

Peanuts, 1966, King Seeley Thermos, orange rim, matching steel bottle (shown)
Box $250   Bottle $50

Peanuts, 1973, King Seeley Thermos, red rim psychiatric box, plastic bottle
Box $125   Bottle $30

Peanuts, 1976, King Seeley Thermos, red pitching box, plastic bottle
Box $150   Bottle $35

Peanuts, 1980, King Seeley Thermos, pitching box, yellow face, green band, matching bottle
Box $125   Bottle $35

Pebbles & Bamm-Bamm, 1971, Aladdin, matching plastic bottle
Box $275   Bottle $60

Pele, 1975, King Seeley Thermos, matching plastic bottle
Box $180   Bottle $45

Pennant, 1950, Ohio Art, basket type box, no bottle
Box $50   Bottle n/a

Peter Pan, 1969, Aladdin, matching plastic bottle, Disney
Box $195   Bottle $50

Pete's Dragon, 1978, Aladdin, matching plastic bottle
Box $110   Bottle $35

Pets 'n Pals, 1961, King Seeley Thermos, matching steel bottle
Box $125   Bottle $55

Pigs In Space, 1977, King Seeley Thermos, matching plastic bottle
Box $75   Bottle $30

Pink Gingham, 1976, King Seeley Thermos, matching plastic bottle
Box $60   Bottle $20

Pink Panther & Sons, 1984, King Seeley Thermos, matching plastic bottle
Box $75   Bottle $30

Pinocchio, 1938, unknown, steel round tin w/handle
Box $250   Bottle n/a

Pinocchio, 1938, unknown, square
Box $200   Bottle n/a

Pinocchio, 1971, Aladdin, plastic bottle
Box $200   Bottle $50

Pit Stop, 1968, Ohio Art
Box $360   Bottle n/a

Planet of the Apes, 1974, Aladdin, matching plastic bottle
Box $350   Bottle $80

Play Ball, 1969, King Seeley Thermos, game on back, steel bottle
Box $225   Bottle $55

Police Patrol, 1978, Aladdin, plastic bottle
Box $300   Bottle $45

Polly Pal, 1975, King Seeley Thermos, matching plastic bottle
Box $60   Bottle $20

Pony Express, 1982, Ohio Art
Box $110   Bottle n/a

Popeye, 1962, Universal, "Popeye socks Bluto" box, matching bottle
Box $800   Bottle $450

Popeye, 1964, King Seeley Thermos, "Popeye in boat" box w/matching steel bottle
Box $325 Bottle $80

Popeye, 1980, Aladdin, "arm wrestling" box, plastic bottle
Box $150 Bottle $45

Popples, 1986, Aladdin, plastic bottle
Box $50 Bottle $20

Porky's Lunch Wagon Dome, 1959, King Seeley Thermos, steel/glass bottle
Box $550 Bottle $95

Pro Sports, 1974, Ohio Art, no bottle
Box $75 Bottle n/a

Psychedelic Dome, 1969, Aladdin, plastic bottle
Box $335 Bottle $85

Racing Wheels, 1977, King Seeley Thermos, plastic bottle
Box $100 Bottle $25

Raggedy Ann & Andy, 1973, Aladdin, plastic bottle
Box $150 Bottle $40

Rambo, 1985, King Seeley Thermos, matching plastic bottle
Box $75 Bottle $20

(KP Photo)

Rat Patrol, 1967, Aladdin, steel/glass bottle
Box $350 Bottle $90

Red Barn Dome, 1957, King Seeley Thermos, closed door version, plain Holtemp bottle
Box $150 Bottle $30

Red Barn Dome, 1958, King Seeley Thermos, open door version, matching steel bottle
Box $125 Bottle $50

Red Barn Dome, 1972, Thermos, matching steel/glass bottle
Box $175 Bottle $50

Rifleman, The, 1961, Aladdin, steel/glass bottle
Box $450 Bottle $165

Road Runner, 1970, King Seeley Thermos, lavender or purple rim, steel or plastic bottle
Box $150 Bottle $50

(KP Photo)

Robin Hood, 1956, Aladdin, matching bottle
Box $275 Bottle $120

Ronald McDonald, Sheriff, 1982, Aladdin, plastic bottle
Box $95 Bottle $20

Rose Petal Place, 1983, Aladdin, plastic bottle
Box $60 Bottle $15

Rough Rider, 1973, Aladdin, plastic bottle
Box $125 Bottle $40

Roy Rogers & Dale Double R Bar Ranch, 1953, King Seeley Thermos, steel/glass bottle
Box $300 Bottle $75

(KP Photo)

Roy Rogers & Dale Double R Bar Ranch, 1954, American Thermos, blue or red band, woodgrain tall bottle
Box $300 Bottle $85

(KP Photo)

Roy Rogers & Dale Double R Bar Ranch, 1955, American Thermos, cowhide back box, red or blue band, matching bottle
Box $325 Bottle $85

(KP Photo)

Roy Rogers & Dale Double R Bar Ranch, 1955, American Thermos, eight-scene box, red or blue band, matching bottle
Box $300 Bottle $85

Roy Rogers & Dale on Rail, 1957, American Thermos, red or blue band, matching bottle
Box $375 Bottle $85

(KP Photo)

Roy Rogers Chow Wagon Dome, 1958, King Seeley Thermos, steel/glass bottle
Box $475 Bottle $85

Saddlebag, 1977, King Seeley Thermos, generic plastic bottle
Box $150 Bottle $40

Satellite, 1958, American Thermos, matching bottle, narrow band
Box $250 Bottle $60

Satellite, 1960, King Seeley Thermos, steel bottle
Box $225 Bottle $60

Scooby Doo, 1973, King Seeley Thermos, yellow rim, plastic bottle
Box $425 Bottle $40

Scooby Doo, 1973, King Seeley Thermos, orange rim, plastic bottle
Box $500 Bottle $40

Secret Agent T, 1968, King Seeley Thermos, matching bottle
Box $250 Bottle $60

Secret of NIMH, 1982, Aladdin, plastic bottle
Box $75 Bottle $30

Secret Wars, 1984, Aladdin, plastic bottle
Box $120 Bottle $40

See America, 1972, Ohio Art, no bottle
Box $75 Bottle n/a

Sesame Street, 1983, Aladdin, yellow or green rim, plastic bottle
Box $95 Bottle $30

Sigmund and the Sea Monsters, 1974, Aladdin, plastic bottle
> Box $300   Bottle $60

Six Million Dollar Man, 1974, Aladdin, plastic bottle
> Box $150   Bottle $40

Six Million Dollar Man, 1978, Aladdin, plastic bottle
> Box $160   Bottle $40

Skateboarder, 1977, Aladdin, plastic bottle
> Box $125   Bottle $40

Sleeping Beauty, 1960, General Steel Ware/Canada, generic steel bottle
> Box $450   Bottle $55

Smokey Bear, 1975, Okay Industries, plastic bottle
> Box $550   Bottle $350

Smurfs, 1983, King Seeley Thermos, blue box, plastic bottle
> Box $225   Bottle $30

Snoopy Dome, 1968, King Seeley Thermos, yellow, "Have Lunch w/Snoopy", matching bottle
> Box $195   Bottle $50

Snow White, Disney, 1975, Aladdin, orange rim, plastic bottle
> Box $110   Bottle $30

Snow White, with Game, 1980, Ohio Art, no bottle
> Box $75   Bottle n/a

Space Explorer Ed McCauley, 1960, Aladdin, matching steel bottle
> Box $475   Bottle $150

Space Ship, 1950, unknown, Decoware, dark blue square
> Box $250   Bottle n/a

Space Shuttle Orbiter Enterprise, 1977, King Seeley Thermos, plastic bottle
> Box $200   Bottle $45

Space: 1999, 1976, King Seeley Thermos, plastic bottle
> Box $200   Bottle $35

Speed Buggy, 1974, King Seeley Thermos, red rim, plastic bottle
> Box $120   Bottle $25

Spider-Man & Hulk, 1980, Aladdin, Captain America on back, plastic bottle
> Box $150   Bottle $30

Sport Goofy, 1983, Aladdin, yellow rim, plastic bottle
> Box $75   Bottle $25

Sport Skwirts, 1982, Ohio Art, several variations
> Box $60   Bottle n/a

Sports Afield, 1957, Ohio Art, no bottle
> Box $220   Bottle n/a

(KP Photo)

Star Trek Dome, 1968, Aladdin, matching bottle
> Box $1600   Bottle $450

(ToyShop File Photo)

Star Trek, The Motion Picture, 1980, King Seeley Thermos, matching bottle
> Box $225   Bottle $60

Star Wars, 1978, King Seeley Thermos, cast or stars on band, matching plastic bottle
> Box $250   Bottle $40

Star Wars, Empire Strikes Back, 1980, King Seeley Thermos, swamp scene, plastic bottle
> Box $175   Bottle $30

Star Wars, Empire Strikes Back, 1980, King Seeley Thermos, ship scene, plastic bottle
> Box $125   Bottle $30

Star Wars, Return of the Jedi, 1983, King Seeley Thermos, plastic bottle
> Box $95   Bottle $30

Stars and Stripes Dome, 1970, King Seeley Thermos, matching plastic bottle
> Box $90   Bottle $40

Steve Canyon, 1959, Aladdin, steel/glass bottle
> Box $395   Bottle $150

Strawberry Land, 1985, Aladdin, no bottle
> Box $75   Bottle n/a

Strawberry Shortcake, 1980, Aladdin, plastic bottle
> Box $50   Bottle $15

Strawberry Shortcake, 1981, Aladdin, plastic bottle
> Box $50   Bottle $15

Street Hawk, 1985, Aladdin, plastic bottle
> Box $250   Bottle $90

Submarine, 1960, King Seeley Thermos, steel/glass bottle
> Box $250   Bottle $80

Super Friends, 1976, Aladdin, matching plastic bottle
> Box $125   Bottle $40

Super Powers, 1983, Aladdin, plastic bottle
> Box $120   Bottle $40

Supercar, 1962, Universal, steel/glass bottle
> Box $400   Bottle $150

Superman, 1954, Universal, blue rim
> Box $13500   Bottle n/a

Superman, 1967, King Seeley Thermos, red rim, "under fire" art on back, matching steel/glass bottle
> Box $550   Bottle $85

Superman, 1978, Aladdin, red rim, Daily Planet Office on back, matching bottle
> Box $250   Bottle $50

Tapestry, 1963, Ohio Art, no bottle
> Box $60   Bottle n/a

Tarzan, 1966, Aladdin, steel/glass bottle
> Box $250   Bottle $65

Teenager, 1957, King Seeley Thermos, generic bottle
> Box $110   Bottle $10

Teenager Dome, 1957, King Seeley Thermos, generic bottle
> Box $160   Bottle $10

Three Little Pigs, 1982, Ohio Art, red rim, generic/plastic bottle
> Box $95   Bottle n/a

Thundercats, 1985, Aladdin, plastic bottle
> Box $175   Bottle $25

(KP Photo)

Tom Corbett Space Cadet, 1952, Aladdin, blue or red paper decal box, steel/glass bottle
> Box $325   Bottle $95

Tom Corbett Space Cadet, 1954, Aladdin, full litho, matching bottle
> Box $585   Bottle $110

Toppie Elephant, 1957, American Thermos, yellow, matching bottle
    Box $3200   **Bottle** $800

Track King, 1975, Okay Industries, matching steel bottle
    Box $285   **Bottle** $275

Train, 1971, Ohio Art, no bottle
    Box $45   **Bottle** n/a

Transformers, 1986, Aladdin, red box, matching plastic bottle
    Box $75   **Bottle** $15

Traveler, 1962, Ohio Art, no bottle
    Box $85   **Bottle** n/a

Trigger, 1956, King Seeley Thermos, no bottle
    Box $550   **Bottle** n/a

U.S. Mail Dome, 1969, Aladdin, plastic bottle
    Box $125   **Bottle** $45

U.S. Space Corps, 1961, Universal, plastic rocket bottle
    Box $525   **Bottle** $150

UFO, 1973, King Seeley Thermos, plastic bottle
    Box $150   **Bottle** $40

Underdog, 1974, Okay Industries, plastic bottle
    Box $2500   **Bottle** $750

Universal's Movie Monsters, 1980, Aladdin, plastic bottle
    Box $225   **Bottle** $50

(KP Photo)

Voyage to the Bottom of the Sea, 1967, Aladdin, steel/glass bottle
    Box $750   **Bottle** $175

VW Bus Dome, 1960, Omni, plastic bottle
    Box $850   **Bottle** $220

Wagon Train, 1964, King Seeley Thermos, matching steel bottle
    Box $325   **Bottle** $75

Wags 'n Whiskers, 1978, King Seeley Thermos, matching plastic bottle
    Box $75   **Bottle** $15

Wake Up America, 1973, Okay Industries, matching steel bottle
    Box $700   **Bottle** $250

Waltons, The, 1973, Aladdin, plastic bottle
    Box $225   **Bottle** $40

Washington Redskins, 1970, Okay Industries, steel bottle
    Box $300   **Bottle** $140

Wee Pals Kid Power, 1974, American Thermos, matching plastic bottle
    Box $95   **Bottle** $25

Welcome Back Kotter, 1977, Aladdin, flat or embossed face, red rim, matching plastic bottle
    Box $250   **Bottle** $50

Western, 1963, King Seeley Thermos, tan band, steel/glass bottle
    Box $275   **Bottle** $75

Western, 1963, King Seeley Thermos, gear band, steel/glass bottle
    Box $225   **Bottle** $75

(KP Photo)

Wild Bill Hickok, 1955, Aladdin, steel/glass bottle
    Box $350   **Bottle** $110

Wild Frontier, 1977, Ohio Art, spinner game on back, no bottle
    Box $90   **Bottle** n/a

Wild, Wild West, 1969, Aladdin, plastic bottle
    Box $375   **Bottle** $120

Winnie the Pooh, 1976, Aladdin, blue rim, plastic bottle
    Box $325   **Bottle** $80

Yankee Doodles, 1975, King Seeley Thermos, plastic bottle
    Box $85   **Bottle** $25

(KP Photo)

Yellow Submarine, 1968, King Seeley Thermos, steel/glass bottle
    Box $1300   **Bottle** $350

Yogi Bear, 1974, Aladdin
    Box $225   **Bottle** $60

Yogi Bear & Friends, 1961, Aladdin, black rim, matching steel bottle
    Box $275   **Bottle** $80

Zorro, 1958, Aladdin, black band, steel/glass bottle
    Box $400   **Bottle** $120

Zorro, 1966, Aladdin, red band, steel/glass bottle
    Box $525   **Bottle** $180

VINYL

Alice in Wonderland, 1972, Aladdin, matching plastic bottle
    Box $200   **Bottle** $45

All American, 1976, Bayville, Styrofoam bottle
    Box $160   **Bottle** $20

All Dressed Up, 1970s, Bayville, Styrofoam bottle
    Box $90   **Bottle** $20

All Star, 1960, Aladdin
    Box $450   **Bottle** $95

Alvin and the Chipmunks, 1963, King Seeley Thermos, matching plastic bottle
    Box $400   **Bottle** $140

Annie 1, 1981, Aladdin, matching plastic bottle
    Box $75   **Bottle** $20

(KP Photo)

Bach's Lunch, 1975, Volkwein Bros., red Styrofoam bottle
    Box $130   **Bottle** $20

Ballerina, 1960s, Universal, black, Thermax bottle
    Box $800   **Bottle** $150

Ballerina, 1962, Aladdin, pink, steel/glass bottle
    Box $200   **Bottle** $60

Ballet, 1961, Universal, red, plastic generic bottle
    Box $500   **Bottle** $20

Banana Splits, 1969, King Seeley Thermos, matching steel/glass bottle
    Box $500   **Bottle** $150

(KP Photo)

Barbarino Brunch Bag, 1977, Aladdin, zippered bag, plastic bottle
Box $300   **Bottle** $60

Barbie & Francie, 1965, King Seeley Thermos, black, matching steel/glass bottle
Box $150   **Bottle** $65

(KP Photo)

Barbie & Midge, 1963, King Seeley Thermos, black, matching steel/glass bottle
Box $150   **Bottle** $65

Barbie & Midge Dome, 1964, King Seeley Thermos, matching glass/steel bottle
Box $530   **Bottle** $65

Barbie Softy, 1988, King Seeley Thermos, generic plastic bottle
Box $45   **Bottle** $15

Barbie, World of, 1971, King Seeley Thermos, pink box, matching steel/glass bottle
Box $100   **Bottle** $40

Barbie, World of, 1971, King Seeley Thermos, blue box, matching steel/glass bottle
Box $90   **Bottle** $25

Barnum's Animals, 1978, Adco Liberty, no bottle
Box $60   **Bottle** n/a

(KP Photo)

Beany & Cecil, 1963, King Seeley Thermos, steel/glass bottle
Box $850   **Bottle** $150

Beatles, 1965, Air Flite, no bottle
Box $950   **Bottle** n/a

Beatles Brunch Bag, 1966, Aladdin, zippered bag, matching bottle
Box $750   **Bottle** $300

Beatles Kaboodles Kit, 1965, Standard Plastic Products, no bottle
Box $950   **Bottle** n/a

Betsey Clark, 1977, King Seeley Thermos, yellow box, matching plastic bottle
Box $110   **Bottle** $15

Betsey Clark Munchies Bag, 1977, King Seeley Thermos, zippered bag, plastic bottle
Box $90   **Bottle** $10

Blue Gingham Brunch Bag, 1975, Aladdin, zippered box and plastic bottle
Box $45   **Bottle** $30

Bobby Soxer, 1959, Aladdin
Box $575   **Bottle** n/a

(KP Photo)

Boston Red Sox, 1960s, Universal
Box $90   **Bottle** $20

Boy on the Swing, Abeama Industries
Box $80   **Bottle** $20

Buick 1910, 1974, Bayville, Styrofoam bottle
Box $90   **Bottle** $20

Bullwinkle, 1963, King Seeley Thermos, blue steel/glass bottle
Box $800   **Bottle** $200

Bullwinkle, 1963, King Seeley Thermos, yellow, generic steel bottle
Box $575   **Bottle** $60

Calico Brunch Bag, 1980, Aladdin, zippered bag, plastic bottle
Box $70   **Bottle** $30

Captain Kangaroo, 1964, King Seeley Thermos, steel/glass bottle
Box $500   **Bottle** $150

Captain Marvel Brunch Bag, 1947, red rectangular vinyl w/strap handle
Box $425   **Bottle** $200

Carousel, 1962, Aladdin, matching steel/glass bottle
Box $425   **Bottle** $130

Cars, 1960, Universal
Box $150   **Bottle** n/a

Casper the Friendly Ghost, 1966, King Seeley Thermos, blue box, orange steel bottle
Box $550   **Bottle** $150

Challenger, Space Shuttle, 1986, Babcock, puffy box, no bottle
Box $225   **Bottle** n/a

(KP Photo)

Charlie's Angels Brunch Bag, 1978, Aladdin, zippered bag, plastic bottle
Box $250   **Bottle** $50

(KP Photo)

Coca-Cola, 1947, Aladdin, Styrofoam bottle
Box $160   **Bottle** $20

Coco the Clown, 1970s, Gary, Styrofoam bottle
Box $90   **Bottle** $20

Combo Brunch Bag, 1967, Aladdin, zippered bag, steel/glass bottle
Box $200   **Bottle** $80

Corsage, 1970, King Seeley Thermos, steel/glass bottle
Box $90   **Bottle** $30

Cottage, 1974, King Seeley Thermos
Box $95   **Bottle** n/a

Cowboy, 1960, Universal, plain plastic bottle
Box $170   **Bottle** $20

Dateline Lunch Kit, 1960, Hasbro, blue/pink, no bottle
Box $250   **Bottle** n/a

Dawn, 1971, Aladdin, matching plastic bottle
Box $140   **Bottle** $35

Dawn, 1972, Aladdin, matching plastic bottle
Box $140   **Bottle** $35

Dawn Brunch Bag, 1971, Aladdin, zippered bag, plastic bottle
Box $180   **Bottle** $35

Denim Brunch Bag, 1980, Aladdin, zippered bag, plastic bottle
Box $80   **Bottle** $15

Deputy Dawg, King Seeley Thermos, steel/glass bottle
Box $600   **Bottle** $50

Deputy Dawg, 1964, Thermos, no bottle
Box $550   **Bottle** n/a

Donny & Marie, 1977, Aladdin, long hair version, matching plastic bottle
    Box $125   **Bottle** $40

(KP Photo)

Donny & Marie, 1978, Aladdin, short hair version, matching plastic bottle
    Box $130   **Bottle** $40

Donny & Marie Brunch Bag, 1977, Aladdin, zippered bag, plastic bottle
    Box $125   **Bottle** $40

Dr. Seuss, 1970, Aladdin, plastic bottle
    Box $575   **Bottle** $95

Dream Boat, 1960, Feldco, dark brown, Styrofoam bottle
    Box $350   **Bottle** $20

Dream Boat, 1960, Feldco, white, Styrofoam bottle
    Box $500   **Bottle** $20

Dream Boat, 1960, Feldco, blue, Styrofoam bottle
    Box $700   **Bottle** $20

Eats 'n Treats, King Seeley Thermos, blue or pink steel/glass bottle
    Box $200   **Bottle** $40

Fess Parker Kaboodle Kit, 1960s, Aladdin, matching steel bottle
    Box $425   **Bottle** n/a

Fishing, 1970, Universal, Styrofoam bottle
    Box $90   **Bottle** $20

Frog Flutist, 1975, Aladdin, matching plastic bottle
    Box $75   **Bottle** $20

Fun to See'n Keep Tiger, 1960, unknown, no bottle
    Box $350   **Bottle** n/a

G.I. Joe, 1960s, Hasbro, styrofoam thermos, Hasbro license
    Box $350   **Bottle** $20

G.I. Joe, 1989, King Seeley Thermos, generic plastic bottle
    Box $55   **Bottle** $10

Gigi, 1962, Aladdin, matching steel/glass bottle
    Box $280   **Bottle** $80

Girl & Poodle, 1960, Universal, Styrofoam bottle
    Box $140   **Bottle** $20

Glamour Gal, 1960, Aladdin, steel/glass bottle
    Box $100   **Bottle** $35

Goat Butt Mountain, 1960, Universal, Styrofoam bottle
    Box $90   **Bottle** $20

Go-Go Brunch Bag, 1966, Aladdin, plastic bottle
    Box $245   **Bottle** $60

Happy Powwow, 1970s, Bayville, red, blue or yellow, w/Styrofoam bottle
    Box $90   **Bottle** $20

(KP Photo)

Highway Signs Snap Pack, 1988, Avon
    Box $50   **Bottle** n/a

Holly Hobbie, 1972, Aladdin, white bag, matching plastic bottle
    Box $110   **Bottle** $30

I Love a Parade, 1970, Universal, Styrofoam bottle
    Box $130   **Bottle** $20

Ice Cream Cone, 1975, Aladdin, matching plastic bottle
    Box $55   **Bottle** $20

It's a Small World, 1968, Aladdin, matching steel/glass bottle
    Box $250   **Bottle** $110

Jonathan Livingston Seagull, 1974, Aladdin, matching plastic bottle
    Box $160   **Bottle** $50

Junior Deb, 1960, Aladdin, steel/glass bottle
    Box $175   **Bottle** $50

Junior Miss Safari, 1962, Prepac, no bottle
    Box $150   **Bottle** n/a

Junior Nurse, 1963, King Seeley Thermos, steel/glass bottle
    Box $320   **Bottle** $90

Kaboodle Kit, 1960s, Aladdin, pink or white, no bottle
    Box $220   **Bottle** n/a

Kewtie Pie, Aladdin, steel/glass bottle
    Box $200   **Bottle** $60

Kodak Gold, 1970s, Aladdin
    Box $85   **Bottle** $20

Kodak II, 1970s, Aladdin
    Box $85   **Bottle** $20

Lassie, 1960s, Universal, Styrofoam bottle
    Box $120   **Bottle** $20

(KP Photo)

Laugh-In, 1960s, "Sock it to Me"
    Box $85   **Bottle** n/a

Liddle Kiddles, 1969, King Seeley Thermos, matching steel/glass bottle
    Box $450   **Bottle** $60

L'il Jodie (Puffy), 1985, Babcock
    Box $90   **Bottle** n/a

Linus the Lion-Hearted, 1965, Aladdin, steel/glass bottle
    Box $600   **Bottle** $125

Little Ballerina, 1975, Bayville, Styrofoam bottle
    Box $75   **Bottle** $20

Little Old Schoolhouse, 1974, Dart
    Box $80   **Bottle** n/a

Love, 1972, Aladdin, matching plastic bottle
    Box $160   **Bottle** $45

(KP Photo)

Lunch 'n Munch, 1959, American Thermos, boys on raft, tan, boating bottle
    Box $400   **Bottle** $125

Lunch 'n Munch, 1959, King Seeley Thermos, space theme, tan, satellite botle
    Box $450   **Bottle** $60

Lunch 'n Munch, 1959, King Seeley Thermos, space theme, red, satellite botle
    Box $450   **Bottle** $60

Lunch 'n Munch, 1959, American Thermos, boys on raft, red, boating bottle
    Box $450   **Bottle** $125

Mam'zelle, 1971, Aladdin, plastic bottle
    Box $180   **Bottle** $60

Mardi-Gras, 1971, Aladdin, matching plastic bottle
    Box $80   **Bottle** $20

Mary Ann, 1960, Aladdin, matching steel/glass bottle
    Box $75   **Bottle** $25

Mary Ann Lunch 'N Bag, 1960, Universal, no bottle
    Box $110   **Bottle** n/a

(KP Photo)

Mary Poppins, 1973, Aladdin, matching plastic bottle
    Box $175   **Bottle** $50

Mary Poppins Brunch Bag, 1966, Aladdin, steel/glass bottle
    Box $150   **Bottle** $50

Mod Miss Brunch Bag, 1969, Aladdin, plastic bottle
    Box $80   **Bottle** $30

(KP Photo)

Monkees, 1967, King Seeley Thermos, matching steel/glass bottle
    Box $525   **Bottle** $125

Moon Landing, 1960, Universal, Styrofoam bottle
    Box $250   **Bottle** $20

Mr. Peanut Snap Pack, 1979, Dart, snap close bag, no bottle
    Box $110   **Bottle** n/a

Mushrooms, 1972, Aladdin, matching plastic bottle
    Box $90   **Bottle** $45

(KP Photo)

New Zoo Revue, 1975, Aladdin, plastic bottle
    Box $250   **Bottle** $60

Pac-Man (Puffy), 1985, Aladdin
    Box $65   **Bottle** n/a

Peanuts, 1967, King Seeley Thermos, red "kite" box, steel/glass bottle
    Box $150   **Bottle** $50

Peanuts, 1969, King Seeley Thermos, red "baseball" box, steel bottle
    Box $150   **Bottle** $50

Peanuts, 1971, King Seeley Thermos, green "baseball" box, steel bottle
    Box $200   **Bottle** $50

Peanuts, 1973, King Seeley Thermos, white "piano" box, steel bottle
    Box $150   **Bottle** $50

Pebbles & Bamm-Bamm, 1973, Gary, matching plastic bottle
    Box $275   **Bottle** $55

Penelope & Penny, 1970s, Gary, yellow box w/Styrofoam bottle
    Box $80   **Bottle** $20

Peter Pan, 1969, Aladdin, white box, matching plastic bottle
    Box $210   **Bottle** $65

Pink Panther, 1980, Aladdin, matching plastic bottle
    Box $200   **Bottle** $50

Pony Tail, 1960s, Thermos, white box, original art w/gray border added, no bottle
    Box $200   **Bottle** n/a

Pony Tail, 1965, King Seeley Thermos, white box, fold over lid, steel/glass bottle
    Box $200   **Bottle** $30

Pony Tail Tid-Bit-Kit, 1962, King Seeley Thermos, steel/glass satellite bottle
    Box $200   **Bottle** $30

Ponytails Poodle Kit, 1960, King Seeley Thermos, steel/glass bottle
    Box $150   **Bottle** $20

Princess, 1963, Aladdin, steel/glass bottle
    Box $190   **Bottle** $55

Psychedelic, 1969, Aladdin, yellow, matching steel/glass bottle
    Box $150   **Bottle** $30

(KP Photo)

Pussycats, The, 1968, Aladdin, plastic bottle
    Box $220   **Bottle** $80

Ringling Bros. Circus, 1970, King Seeley Thermos, orange box w/matching steel/glass bottle
    Box $425   **Bottle** $140

Ringling Bros. Circus, 1971, King Seeley Thermos, puffy blue box, steel/glass bottle
    Box $250   **Bottle** $40

Robo Warriors, 1970, unknown, no bottle
    Box $35   **Bottle** n/a

Roy Rogers Saddlebag, 1960, King Seeley Thermos, brown, steel/glass bottle
    Box $400   **Bottle** $95

Roy Rogers Saddlebag, 1960, King Seeley Thermos, cream, steel/glass bottle
    Box $650   **Bottle** $95

Sabrina, 1972, Aladdin, yellow box w/matching plastic bottle
    Box $230   **Bottle** $85

Sesame Street, 1979, Aladdin, orange, matching plastic bottle
    Box $120   **Bottle** $30

Sesame Street, 1981, Aladdin, yellow, matching plastic bottle
    Box $150   **Bottle** $30

(KP Photo)

Shari Lewis, 1963, Aladdin, matching steel/glass bottle
    Box $470   **Bottle** $120

Sizzlers, Hot Wheels, 1971, King Seeley Thermos, matching steel/glass bottle
    Box $375   **Bottle** $60

Skipper, 1965, King Seeley Thermos, steel/glass bottle
    Box $220   **Bottle** $60

Sleeping Beauty, Disney, 1970, Aladdin, white box, matching plastic bottle
    Box $240   **Bottle** $80

Smokey the Bear, 1965, King Seeley Thermos, steel/glass bottle
    Box $450   **Bottle** $110

Snoopy Munchies Bag, 1977, King Seeley Thermos, plastic bottle
    Box $75   **Bottle** $20

Snoopy Softy, 1988, King Seeley Thermos, matching plastic bottle
    Box $45   **Bottle** $20

Snow White, 1975, Aladdin, white box w/matching plastic bottle
    Box $290   **Bottle** $45

Snow White, Disney, 1967, unknown, fold-over lid, tapered box, no bottle
    Box $400   **Bottle** n/a

Soupy Sales, 1966, King Seeley Thermos, blue box, no bottle
    Box $600   **Bottle** n/a

Spirit of '76, unknown, red
    Box $110   **Bottle** n/a

Sports Kit, 1960, Universal
    Box $350   **Bottle** $40

Stewardess, 1962, Aladdin, steel/glass bottle
    Box $650   **Bottle** $110

Strawberry Shortcake, 1980, Aladdin, matching plastic bottle
    Box $65   **Bottle** $15

Tammy, 1964, Aladdin, matching steel/glass bottle
    Box $240   **Bottle** $85

LUNCH BOXES

Tammy & Pepper, 1965, Aladdin, matching steel/glass bottle
Box $240   **Bottle** $85

Tinker Bell, Disney, 1969, Aladdin, plastic bottle
Box $260   **Bottle** $90

Twiggy, 1967, King Seeley Thermos, steel/glass bottle
Box $225   **Bottle** $80

Twiggy, 1967, Aladdin, matching steel/glass bottle
Box $225   **Bottle** $80

U.S. Mail Brunch Bag, 1971, Aladdin, zippered bag, plastic bottle
Box $160   **Bottle** $80

Winnie the Pooh, Aladdin, steel/glass bottle
Box $450   **Bottle** $110

Wonder Woman (blue), 1977, Aladdin, matching plastic bottle
Box $230   **Bottle** $50

Wonder Woman (yellow), 1978, Aladdin, matching plastic bottle
Box $255   **Bottle** $50

Wrangler, 1982, Aladdin, steel/glass bottle
Box $325   **Bottle** $95

Yosemite Sam, 1971, King Seeley Thermos, matching steel/glass bottle
Box $560   **Bottle** $140

Ziggy's Munch Box, 1979, Aladdin, plastic bottle
Box $140   **Bottle** $40

LUNCH BOXES

Marx Play Sets

For all practical purposes, play sets could have been invented by Louis Marx...at least as far as boys growing up in the 1950s and 1960s were concerned. The words "Marx" and "play set" just went together. And they still go together today for many dedicated collectors. A typical Marx play set included buildings, figures, and lots of realistic accessories that helped bring the miniature world to life. The Fort Apache Stockade, for example, came with a hard plastic log fort, a colorful lithographed tin cabin, and, of course, pioneers and Indians locked in deadly combat. It was no wonder millions of kids had a burning desire for these toys. The play scenarios were almost endless.

This modern version of an age-old toy was a tribute to the marketing and manufacturing talents and whimsical genius of Louis Marx, the modern-day king of toys.

Not only was he responsible for developing the play set, but he also popularized the yo-yo and produced some of the most innovative tin wind-ups, guns, dolls, trains, trikes, trucks, and other toys that were commercially feasible. In 1955, Marx sold more than $30 million worth of toys, easily making it the largest toy manufacturer in the world.

What makes Marx's domination even more impressive was the fact that he rose from humble beginnings. He was born in Brooklyn in 1896 and didn't learn to speak English until he started school. At age 16, Marx went to work for Ferdinand Strauss, a toy manufacturer who produced items for Abraham & Strauss department stores. By the age of 20, Marx was managing the company's New Jersey factory.

After being fired by Strauss, Marx contracted with manufacturers to produce toys he designed. By the mid-1920s, Marx had three plants in the United States. By 1955, there were more than 5,000 items in the Marx toy line with plants worldwide.

Mass production and mass marketing through stores such as Sears and Montgomery Ward allowed Marx to keep prices low and quality high. Marx was also a master at producing new toys from the same basic components. Existing elements could be modified slightly, and new lithography would produce a new building from standard stock.

Part of Marx's repackaging genius included using popular television or movie tie-ins to breathe new life into existing products. The Rifleman Rage, Roy Rogers' Ranch, Wyatt Earp, and Wagon Train play sets were examples of repackaging existing toys and parts to capture the fad of the day.

Marx sold his company to the Quaker Oats Company in 1972 for $31 million. Quaker Oats sold the company four years alter for $15 million after losing money every year of its ownership.

The Marx Toy Company is in existence once again and making favorite Marx toys from original molds.

With the passing of a few short decades, once affordable children's toys have become highly prized collectibles. Play sets are among the price leaders in today's market for childhood treasures. And the figures that accompanied the play sets are also highly desired for their craftsmanship and detail.

A play set listed as MIB (Mint in Box) should be untouched and unassembled in the original box. Excellent condition means a complete set, but the buildings are assembled and the box may be worn or damaged. Good condition means the play set shows wear and may be missing a few minor pieces.

2006 TRENDS

As it becomes increasingly difficult to find complete sets, individual pieces should continue to sell well. Play sets based on popular characters continue to be among the most desired sets on the market and can expect to hold their value. Service Station sets are becoming increasingly desirable due in part to the crossover collecting of toy car and truck enthusiasts, so look for their values to increase as demand increases and supplies decrease.

THE TOP TEN
MARX PLAY SETS (In Mint Condition)

1. Johnny Ringo Western Frontier, 1959	$4,500
2. Johnny Tremain Revolutionary War, 1957	2,750
3. Gunsmoke Dodge City, 1960	2,100
4. Fire House, 1960s	2,000
5. Ben Hur, Series 5000, 1959	1,900
6. Sears Store, 1961	1,850
7. Civil War Centennial, 1961	1,800
8. Custer's Last Stand, 1963	1,800
9. Sword in the Stone, 1960s	1,560
10. Untouchables, 1961	1,550

MINIATURE PLAY SETS

101 Dalmatians, 1961, "The Wedding Scene"
EX $75   NM $300   MIP $450

101 Dalmatians, 1961, "The Barn Scene"
EX $75   NM $300   MIP $450

(ToyShop File Photo)

20 Minutes to Berlin, 1964, 174 handpainted pieces
EX $110   NM $320   MIP $520

Alice in Wonderland, 1961, New series
EX $100   NM $225   MIP $350

Attack on Fort Apache, stable, cowboys, Indians, Model No. HK-8078
EX $85   NM $225   MIP $500

Babes In Toyland, six different scenes, each
EX $25   NM $65   MIP $125

Battleground, 1963, 170 pieces, Model No. HK-6111
EX $20   NM $60   MIP $200

(ToyShop File Photo)

Blue and Gray, 1960s, 101 individual pieces, "Featured on T.V.", Model No. HK-6109
EX $95   NM $180   MIP $350

(ToyShop File Photo)

Border Battle, Mexican-American War set with plastic Alamo, Mexican and Texan troops, horses and accessories
EX $150   NM $365   MIP $725

Charge of the Bengal Lancers, British/Turks
EX $125   NM $325   MIP $500

Charge of the Light Brigade, Sears, 216 pieces, Lancers/Cossacks
EX $175   NM $325   MIP $400

Charge of the Light Brigade, 2nd version, photo box art, Lancers/Turks
EX $110   NM $300   MIP $400

Charge of the Light Brigade, smaller version, Lancers/Russians
EX $75   NM $225   MIP $325

Cinderella, New series
EX $100   NM $225   MIP $350

Covered Wagon Attack
EX $95   NM $200   MIP $400

Custer's Last Stand, 1964, 181 pieces
EX $125   NM $325   MIP $600

Disney 3-in-1 Set, original series
EX $100   NM $225   MIP $365

Disney Circus Parade, Super Circus performers, Disneykins
EX $85   NM $225   MIP $350

(ToyShop File Photo)

Disney See and Play Castle, 1st and 2nd series Disneykins, Model No. 48-24388
EX $155   NM $360   MIP $465

Disney See and Play Doll House, 1st series Disneykins
EX $100   NM $265   MIP $350

Donald Duck, original series; Donald, Daisy, Louie, Goofy
EX $45   NM $100   MIP $150

Dumbo's Circus, original series
EX $50   NM $100   MIP $165

Fairykin, six different, each
EX $30   NM $80   MIP $125

Fairykin TV Scenes, 12 different, each
EX $8   NM $20   MIP $30

Fairykin TV Scenes Gift Set, two different, each w/six scenes, each
EX $65   NM $165   MIP $250

Fairykins 3-in-1 Diorama Set
EX $100   NM $265   MIP $400

Fairykins Gift Set, 34 in window box
EX $40   NM $175   MIP $250

Fairykins TV Scenes Boxed Set of Eight
EX $45   NM $200   MIP $250

Fort Apache, large set, HQ bldg., cavalry/cowboys/Indians
EX $115   NM $295   MIP $375

Fort Apache, 1963, 90 pieces, Indians, Model No. HK-7526
EX $55   NM $80   MIP $185

Guerrilla Warfare, 1960s, Viet Cong
EX $275   NM $350   MIP $450

Huckleberry Hound Presents, two different, each
EX $75   NM $115   MIP $175

(ToyShop File Photo)

Invasion Day, 1964, 304 pieces, miniature D-Day Invasion set
EX $70   NM $205   MIP $450

Jungle, smaller than Jungle Safari
EX $50   NM $85   MIP $175

Jungle Safari, 260 pieces, hunters/natives
EX $55   NM $100   MIP $225

Knights and Castle, 1963, 132 pieces, Model No. HK-7563
EX $130   NM $200   MIP $315

Knights and Castle, 1964, 64 pieces, Model No. HK-7562
EX $95   NM $175   MIP $275

Knights and Vikings, 1964, 143 pieces
EX $145   NM $275   MIP $425

Lady and the Tramp, 1961, New series
EX $100   NM $225   MIP $350

Lost Boys, New series
EX $100   NM $225   MIP $350

Lost Boys, 1961, second series
EX $40   NM $120   MIP $200

Ludwig Von Drake, RCA premium set
EX $65   NM $130   MIP $200

Ludwig Von Drake, 1962, "The Nearsighted Professor"
EX $50   NM $115   MIP $165

Ludwig Von Drake, 1962, "The Professor Misses"
EX $50   NM $100   MIP $150

Mickey Mouse and Friends, original series, display box
EX $50   NM $100   MIP $150

Munchville, vegetable characters
EX $65   NM $165   MIP $265

Noah's Ark, Ward's version, soft plastic figures
EX $20   NM $50   MIP $85

(ToyShop File Photo)

Noah's Ark, 1968, 100 pieces
EX $28   NM $70   MIP $110

Over The Top, WWI, Germans/Doughboys
EX $200   NM $600   MIP $950

Panchito Western, original series, display box
EX $50   NM $100   MIP $150

Pinocchio, six different sets, each original series, display box
EX $65   NM $165   MIP $280

Pinocchio 3-in-1 Set
EX $115   NM $295   MIP $450

Quick Draw McGraw, two different, each
EX $75   NM $115   MIP $200

Revolutionary War, British/Colonials
EX $95   NM $250   MIP $475

Sands of Iwo Jima, 1963, 205 pieces
EX $115   NM $210   MIP $325

Sands of Iwo Jima, 1963, 88 pieces
EX $75   NM $145   MIP $225

Sands of Iwo Jima, 1964, 296 pieces
EX $150   NM $295   MIP $425

See and Play Dollhouse, American Beauties/Campus Cuties
EX $75   NM $175   MIP $350

Sleeping Beauty, 1961, new series
EX $75   NM $175   MIP $275

Snow White and the Seven Dwarfs, original series, display box
EX $50   NM $100   MIP $185

Sunshine Farm Set, farmers and animals
EX $45   NM $115   MIP $175

(ToyShop File Photo)

Sword in the Stone, British only Disney release
EX $310   NM $1050   MIP $1560

Ten Commandments, Montgomery Ward
EX $150   NM $395   MIP $600

Three Little Pigs, new series
EX $100   NM $225   MIP $350

Tiger Town, 1960s, ENCO-like tigers
EX $75   NM $175   MIP $300

Top Cat, three different, each
EX $75   NM $115   MIP $200

(ToyShop File Photo)

Troll Village, Includes hillside, troll figures, ox cart, trees, fence sections and accessories
EX $85   NM $220   MIP $360

TV-Tinykins Gift Set, set of 34 figures
EX $115   NM $350   MIP $550

TV-Tinykins TV Scenes, 12 different, each
EX $12   NM $35   MIP $50

(ToyShop File Photo)

Western Town, over 170 pieces, hand painted buildings, stagecoach, fence sections, figures and accessories, Model No. 48-24398
EX $55   NM $160   MIP $265

Wooden Horse of Troy, British only issue
EX $175   NM $600   MIP $850

PLAY SETS

Adventures of Robin Hood, 1956, Richard Greene TV series, Model No. 4722
EX $250   NM $750   MIP $1250

Alamo, 1957, only two cannons, w/ metal Alamo, Model No. 3546
EX $100   NM $300   MIP $500

Alamo, 1960, Sears exclusive, Model No. 3543
EX $50   NM $140   MIP $265

Alamo, 1960, for 54mm figures, four cannons, Model No. 3534
EX $140   NM $250   MIP $400

(ToyShop File Photo)

Alaska, 1959, 100 pieces including: igloos, polar bears, kayak, dog sled team, litho storefront, prospectors. Just in time for Alaskan statehood, this is a neat set, Model No. 3707-8
EX $300   NM $625   MIP $1000

Alaska, 1960, Model No. 2755-6
EX $250   NM $550   MIP $800

American Airlines Astro Jet Port, 1961, Model No. 4821-2
EX $150   NM $250   MIP $450

American Airlines International Jet Port, 1960, 98 pieces, Model No. 4810
EX $150   NM $250   MIP $450

Arctic Explorer, 1958, Series 2000, Model No. 3702
EX $250   NM $450   MIP $700

Army Combat Set, 1963, Sears exclusive, 411 pieces, Model No. 4158
EX $100   NM $300   MIP $500

Army Combat Training Center, 1958, Model No. 4153
EX $40   NM $60   MIP $95

Army Combat Training Center, 1959, Model No. 2654
EX $35   NM $55   MIP $90

Babyland Nursery, 1955, Model No. 3379-80
EX $125   NM $225   MIP $375

Bar-M Ranch, 1957, Model No. 3956
EX $50   NM $100   MIP $150

Battle of Iwo Jima, 1964, 128 pieces, Sears exclusive, Model No. 4154
EX $35   NM $105   MIP $185

Battle of Iwo Jima, 1964, 247 pieces, U.S. and Japanese, Model No. 4147
EX $80   NM $240   MIP $410

(ToyShop File Photo)

Battle of Little Big Horn, 1972, includes cavalrymen, Indians, horses, wagons, totem pole (?), and tepees, Model No. 4679MO
EX $130   NM $260   MIP $410

Battle of the Blue & Gray, Series 2000, large set, Model No. 4658
EX $250   NM $700   MIP $1250

Battle of the Blue & Gray, 1959, Series 2000, 54mm, Model No. 4745-6
EX $175   NM $375   MIP $625

Battle of the Blue & Gray, 1960, Series 1000, small set, no house, Model No. 2645-6
EX $80   NM $240   MIP $425

Battle of the Blue & Gray, 1963, Centennial edition, Model No. 4744
EX $200   NM $700   MIP $1250

Battlefield, 1958, Series 5000, Model No. 4756
EX $25   NM $95   MIP $175

Battleground, 1958, largest of military sets, Model No. 4749-50
EX $130   NM $395   MIP $660

Battleground, 1959, 180 pieces, Model No. 4751
EX $40   NM $110   MIP $190

Battleground, 1960s, U.S. and Nazi troops, Model No. 4756
EX $40   NM $90   MIP $150

Battleground, 1962, 200 pieces, Model No. 4754
EX $40   NM $110   MIP $195

Battleground, 1965, Montgomery Ward, Model No. 4139
EX $80   NM $240   MIP $425

Battleground, 1965, Sears, 160 pieces, Model No. 4150
EX $70   NM $210   MIP $350

Battleground, 1971, Montgomery Ward Exclusive, Model No. 4752
EX $95   NM $285   MIP $465

Battleground Convoy, 1962, Model No. 3745-6
EX $40   NM $125   MIP $275

Beach Head Landing Set, U.S. and Nazi Troops, Model No. 4939
EX $25   NM $65   MIP $110

Ben Hur, blister card, Model No. 2648
EX $25   NM $95   MIP $150

(ToyShop File Photo)

Ben Hur, 1959, Series 5000, large set, Model No. 4701
EX $450   NM $1100   MIP $1900

(ToyShop File Photo)

Ben Hur, 1959, Series 2000, medium set, Model No. 4702
EX $255   NM $770   MIP $1450

Ben Hur, 1959, 132 pieces, Model No. 4696
EX $170   NM $510   MIP $160

Big Inch Pipeline, 1963, 200 pieces, Model No. 6008
EX $85   NM $250   MIP $400

Big Top Circus, 1952, Model No. 4310
EX $100   NM $325   MIP $525

(ToyShop File Photo)

Boot Camp, Carry-All, tin box set, with tank, half-track, jeep, artillery, figures and tents, Model No. 4645
EX $35   NM $135   MIP $215

Boy Scout
EX $115   NM $600   MIP $925

Boys Camp, 1956, Model No. 4103
EX $130   NM $395   MIP $650

Cape Canaveral, 1959, Sears set, Model No. 5963
EX $90   NM $325   MIP $510

Cape Canaveral, 1960, Series 2000, Model No. 4524
EX $85   NM $195   MIP $325

Cape Canaveral Missile Center, 1959, includes four-stage rocket, missile and launcher, flying saucer and launcher, scientists, and other accessories, Model No. 2656
EX $65   NM $160   MIP $265

Cape Canaveral Missile Center, 1959, Model No. 4528
EX $80   NM $240   MIP $400

Cape Canaveral Missile Center, 1961, Model No. 4525
EX $55   NM $195   MIP $310

Cape Canaveral Missile Set, 1958, Model No. 4526
EX $55   NM $225   MIP $350

Cape Kennedy Carry All, 1968, tin box set, Model No. 4625
EX $45   NM $65   MIP $105

(ToyShop File Photo)

Captain Gallant of the Foreign Legion, 1956, includes foreign legion soldiers,

sheiks, horses, camel and "Cuffy." A hard-to-find set, Model No. 4729/4730
EX $210   NM $620   MIP $1100

Captain Space Solar Academy, 1953, Model No. 7026
EX $80   NM $325   MIP $510

Captain Space Solar Port, 1954, Model No. 7018
EX $75   NM $250   MIP $410

Castle and Moat Set, Sears Exclusive, Model No. 4734
EX $65   NM $260   MIP $400

Cattle Drive, 1972-73, Model No. 3983
EX $70   NM $250   MIP $385

Civil War Centennial, 1961, Model No. 5929
EX $400   NM $1200   MIP $1800

Comanche Pass, 1976, Model No. 3416
EX $30   NM $130   MIP $225

Complete Happitime Dairy Farm, Sears, Model No. 5957
EX $80   NM $325   MIP $510

Complete U.S. Army Training Center, 1954, Model No. 4145
EX $70   NM $210   MIP $350

(ToyShop File Photo)

Construction Camp, 1954, includes trucks, figures, buildings and accessories, Model No. 4439
EX $100   NM $290   MIP $475

(ToyShop File Photo)

Construction Camp, 1956, 54mm, Series 1000, includes: field office building, workmen, heavy duty equipment (friction-power dozer, road roller, high-lift loader), Model No. 4442
EX $120   NM $330   MIP $600

Cowboy And Indian Camp, 1953, Model No. 3950
EX $95   NM $275   MIP $450

Custer's Last Stand, 1956, Series 500, Model No. 4779
EX $110   NM $325   MIP $550

Custer's Last Stand, 1963, Sears, 187 pieces, Model No. 4670
EX $195   **NM** $1200   **MIP** $1800

D.E.W. Defense Line Arctic Satellite Base, Model No. 4802
EX $125   **NM** $300   **MIP** $500

Daktari, Model No. 3718
EX $100   **NM** $325   **MIP** $500

Daktari, 1967, 140 pieces, Model No. 3720
EX $145   **NM** $395   **MIP** $660

Daktari, 1967, 110 pieces, Model No. 3717
EX $100   **NM** $300   **MIP** $525

(ToyShop File Photo)

Daniel Boone Frontier, 1958, includes covered wagon and horses with driver, Indians, Frontiersman, other accessories, Model No. 1393
EX $85   **NM** $235   **MIP** $375

Daniel Boone Wilderness Scout, 1964, Model No. 0631
EX $85   **NM** $225   **MIP** $400

Daniel Boone Wilderness Scout, 1964, Model No. 2640
EX $120   **NM** $360   **MIP** $650

Daniel Boone Wilderness Scout, 1964, Model No. 0670
EX $90   **NM** $225   **MIP** $385

Davy Crockett at the Alamo, Model No. 3442
EX $150   **NM** $360   **MIP** $650

Davy Crockett at the Alamo, 1955, official Walt Disney, biggest set, Model No. 3544
EX $160   **NM** $500   **MIP** $825

(ToyShop File Photo)

Davy Crockett at the Alamo, 1955, official Walt Disney, 100 pieces, first set, Model No. 3530
EX $80   **NM** $275   **MIP** $425

D-Day Army Set, U.S. and Nazi troops, Model No. 6027
EX $100   **NM** $300   **MIP** $525

Desert Fox, 1966, 244 pieces, Model No. 4177
EX $105   **NM** $275   **MIP** $450

Desert Patrol, 1967, U.S. and Nazi troops, Model No. 4174
EX $85   **NM** $185   **MIP** $325

Farm Set, Model No. 6006
EX $50   **NM** $195   **MIP** $300

Farm Set, Model No. 6050
EX $45   **NM** $180   **MIP** $275

Farm Set, 1958, 100 pieces, Series 2000, Model No. 3948
EX $80   **NM** $250   **MIP** $400

Farm Set, 1965, 1968-73, w/ 20" steel barn, 14 farm animals, 5 sections of fence, 4 rows of crops, plastic tractor w/ 7 attachments, farm tools, feed boxes, Model No. 5942
EX $40   **NM** $160   **MIP** $250

Farm Set, 1969, deluxe, Model No. 3953
EX $75   **NM** $225   **MIP** $375

(ToyShop File Photo)

Fighting Knights Carry All, 1966-68, includes litho walls, plastic towers, metallic and solid color knights, catapults and horses, Model No. 4635
EX $50   **NM** $140   **MIP** $200

Fire House, Model No. 4819
EX $225   **NM** $700   **MIP** $1100

Fire House, w/two friction vehicles, Model No. 4820
EX $500   **NM** $1500   **MIP** $2000

Flintstones, The, 1960s, Bedrock, stone fences, buildings, palm trees, play mat, vehicles, figures, dinosaurs, Model No. 4672
EX $150   **NM** $225   **MIP** $550

Fort Apache, Model No. 3616
EX $45   **NM** $90   **MIP** $150

Fort Apache, Model No. 6068
EX $40   **NM** $100   **MIP** $165

Fort Apache, Sears, Model No. 6059
EX $20   **NM** $35   **MIP** $75

Fort Apache, Model No. 3681A
EX $35   **NM** $90   **MIP** $150

Fort Apache, giant set, Model No. 3685
EX $140   **NM** $425   **MIP** $700

Fort Apache, Model No. 3682
EX $15   **NM** $50   **MIP** $85

Fort Apache, 1965, Sears, 335 pieces, Model No. 6063
EX $105   **NM** $315   **MIP** $550

Fort Apache, 1965, Sears, 147 pieces
EX $45   **NM** $120   **MIP** $225

Fort Apache, 1967, Model No. 3681
EX $55   **NM** $135   **MIP** $225

Fort Apache, 1970s, Model No. 4202
EX $25   **NM** $50   **MIP** $80

(ToyShop File Photo)

Fort Apache, 1972, Sears, over 100 pieces including: plastic fort, U.S. flag, Indians, tepee, horses, soldiers, cannon and accessories, Model No. 59093C
EX $45   **NM** $95   **MIP** $160

Fort Apache, 1976, Model No. 3681
EX $50   **NM** $120   **MIP** $210

(ToyShop File Photo)

Fort Apache Carry All, 1967, with plastic block houses, cowboys, horses and Indians, Model No. 4685
EX $35   **NM** $55   **MIP** $100

Fort Apache Rin Tin Tin, 1956, early, 60mm, Model No. 3627
EX $125   **NM** $300   **MIP** $450

Fort Apache Rin Tin Tin, 1957, 54mm, Model No. 3658
EX $100   **NM** $250   **MIP** $375

Fort Apache Rin Tin Tin, 1958, mixed scale set, Model No. 3957
EX $90   **NM** $275   **MIP** $350

Fort Apache Stockade, 1951, Model No. 3610
EX $70   **NM** $210   **MIP** $350

(ToyShop File Photo)

Fort Apache Stockade, 1953, includes stockade, block house, ladders, cowboys and Indians, Model No. 3612
EX $55   **NM** $160   **MIP** $260

MARX PLAY SETS

Fort Apache Stockade, 1960, Series 2000, 60mm figures, Model No. 3660
EX $85   **NM** $225   **MIP** $400

(ToyShop File Photo)

Fort Apache Stockade, 1961, Series 5000 includes: cavalry HQ building, stockade fence and gate blockhouses, cannon, cavarly men and horses, tepee, Indian figures, totem pole, canoe, horses and other accessories
EX $60   **NM** $170   **MIP** $285

Fort Apache with Famous Americans, Model No. 3636
EX $55   **NM** $165   **MIP** $270

Fort Dearborn, w/plastic walls, Model No. 3688
EX $80   **NM** $240   **MIP** $400

Fort Dearborn, larger set, Model No. 3514
EX $20   **NM** $60   **MIP** $100

Fort Dearborn, 1952, w/metal walls, Model No. 3510
EX $85   **NM** $255   **MIP** $375

Fort Mohawk, 1958, British, Colonials, Indians, 54mm, Model No. 3751-2
EX $80   **NM** $325   **MIP** $550

Fort Pitt, 1959, Series 750, 54mm, Model No. 3741
EX $65   **NM** $260   **MIP** $400

Fort Pitt, 1959, Series 1000, 54mm, Model No. 3742
EX $100   **NM** $300   **MIP** $475

Four-Level Allstate Service Station, 1962, Model No. 3499
EX $80   **NM** $325   **MIP** $500

Four-Level Parking Garage, Model No. 3511
EX $40   **NM** $200   **MIP** $300

Four-Level Parking Garage, Model No. 3502
EX $40   **NM** $120   **MIP** $200

Freight Trucking Terminal, 1950, plastic trucks, Model No. 5220
EX $30   **NM** $90   **MIP** $150

Freight Trucking Terminal, 1950, friction trucks, Model No. 5422
EX $30   **NM** $90   **MIP** $150

Galaxy Command, 1976, Model No. 4206
EX $20   **NM** $45   **MIP** $85

Gallant Men, official set from TV series, Model No. 4634
EX $70   **NM** $290   **MIP** $450

Gallant Men Army, 1963, U.S. troops, Model No. 4632
EX $65   **NM** $260   **MIP** $400

(ToyShop File Photo)

Gunsmoke Dodge City, 1960, official, Series 2000, 80 pieces including: Gunsmoke characters, town building, ranch house, gold mine, stagecoach, wagon, oxen, horses, cowboys, trees, steers and other accessories, Model No. 4268
EX $350   **NM** $1300   **MIP** $2100

Happi-time Army and Air Force Training Center, 1954, Sears, 147 pieces, Model No. 4159
EX $50   **NM** $150   **MIP** $250

Happi-time Civil War Centennial, 1962, Sears, Model No. 5929
EX $115   **NM** $455   **MIP** $700

Happi-Time Deluxe Farm Set, 1958, Sears, Series 2000, tin litho barn and silo, Model No. 3949
EX $50   **NM** $150   **MIP** $250

Happi-time Farm Set, Sears, Model No. 3480
EX $35   **NM** $95   **MIP** $150

Happi-Time Farm Set, 1953, Sears, barn, silo, no figures, 60mm animals and implements, Model No. 3940
EX $50   **NM** $150   **MIP** $250

Happi-Time Farm Set, 1958, Sears, Series 2000, 100 pieces, chicken shed, Model No. 3943
EX $65   **NM** $150   **MIP** $260

Happi-Time Farm Set, 1959-60, Sears, Deluxe Platform Farm, barn and 2 silos on raised platform, 2-wheel cart pictured on box never included, Model No. 5931
EX $100   **NM** $225   **MIP** $375

Happi-time Roy Rogers Rodeo Ranch, 1953, Sears, Model No. 3990
EX $85   **NM** $185   **MIP** $325

Heritage Battle of the Alamo, 1972, Heritage Series, Model No. 59091
EX $80   **NM** $240   **MIP** $400

History in the Pacific, 1972-73, Model No. 4164
EX $100   **NM** $285   **MIP** $450

Holiday Turnpike, battery-operated w/HO scale vehicles, Model No. 5230
EX $10   **NM** $30   **MIP** $45

(ToyShop File Photo)

I.G.Y. Arctic Satellite Base, 1959, Series 1000, with quonset hut, missiles, launchers, explorer figures, eskimo figures, igloos, sleds, animals, weather station, skis, etc. A true "cold war" play set, for sure, Model No. 4800
EX $250   **NM** $750   **MIP** $1250

Indian Warfare, Series 2000, Model No. 4778
EX $65   **NM** $260   **MIP** $400

International Airport, 1973, terminal, planes, cars, trucks, people, accessories, Model No. 4814
EX $35   **NM** $75   **MIP** $150

Irrigated Farm Set, working pump, Model No. 6021
EX $7   **NM** $20   **MIP** $35

Johnny Apollo Moon Launch Center, 1970, Model No. 4630
EX $75   **NM** $150   **MIP** $275

Johnny Ringo Western Frontier Set, 1959, Series 2000, Model No. 4784
EX $1400   **NM** $2750   **MIP** $4500

(ToyShop File Photo)

Johnny Tremain Revolutionary War, 1957, official Walt Disney, Series 1000, Model No. 3401-2
EX $635   **NM** $1400   **MIP** $2750

Jungle, metal trading post, Series 500, Model No. 3705
EX $110   **NM** $325   **MIP** $550

Jungle, 1960, 48 pieces, Sears, large animals, Model No. 3716
EX $25   **NM** $95   **MIP** $150

(ToyShop File Photo)

Jungle Jim, 1957, official, Series 1000, includes: HQ building, hunters, natives, wild animals, thatched huts, log fence and accessories, Model No. 3705-6
EX $290   **NM** $875   **MIP** $1450

King Arthur's Castle Medieval Play Set, 1960s, w/ 22 knights on horses, benches, working drawbridge, accessories, Model No. 4800
EX $100   **NM** $200   **MIP** $300

Knights and Vikings, Model No. 4773
EX $45   **NM** $90   **MIP** $150

Knights and Vikings, 1972, Model No. 4743
EX $60   **NM** $150   **MIP** $275

(ToyShop File Photo)

Knights and Vikings, 1973, includes plastic castle and mat with metallic silver knights fighting Vikings, Model No. 4733
EX $65   **NM** $175   **MIP** $285

Lazy Day Farm, 1951, Wards, barn, 60mm people, no silos, animals, Model No. 3931
EX $50   **NM** $150   **MIP** $250

Lazy Day Farm Set, 1958, Wards, Series 1000, no silo, 54mm people and animals, Model No. 3942
EX $50   **NM** $150   **MIP** $250

Lazy Day Farm Set, 1960, Wards, 100 pieces, Model No. 3945
EX $55   **NM** $165   **MIP** $275

Little Red School House, 1956, Model No. 3381-2
EX $90   **NM** $270   **MIP** $450

(ToyShop File Photo)

Lone Ranger Ranch, 1957, Series 500, includes: Lone Ranger, Tonto, cabin, gateway, cowboys, horses, saddles, Indians and accessories, Model No. 3969
EX $110   **NM** $260   **MIP** $465

Lone Ranger Rodeo Set, 1952-53, Model No. 3696
EX $60   **NM** $125   **MIP** $210

Medieval Castle, w/knights and Vikings, Model No. 4733
EX $60   **NM** $130   **MIP** $210

Medieval Castle, Sears, w/knights and Vikings, Model No. 4734
EX $100   **NM** $290   **MIP** $465

Medieval Castle, w/knights and Vikings, Model No. 4707
EX $45   **NM** $110   **MIP** $195

Medieval Castle, 1954, Model No. 4709
EX $35   **NM** $95   **MIP** $150

Medieval Castle, 1959, Sears, Series 2000, Model No. 4708
EX $120   **NM** $350   **MIP** $600

Medieval Castle, 1960, metallic knights, castle, horses, tree and catapult, Model No. 4700
EX $80   **NM** $295   **MIP** $460

Medieval Castle, 1964, gold knights, moat, Model No. 4704
EX $40   **NM** $90   **MIP** $150

Medieval Castle Fort, 1953, included: fortress, figures, horses, cannons and accessories, Model No. 4709-10
EX $55   **NM** $140   **MIP** $250

(ToyShop File Photo)

Midtown Service Station, 1960, electric elevator, pumps with canopy, attendants, cars and accessories, Model No. 3420
EX $52   **NM** $155   **MIP** $255

Midtown Shopping Center, Model No. 2644
EX $30   **NM** $90   **MIP** $150

Military Academy, 1954, w/ six generals, Model No. 4718
EX $100   **NM** $350   **MIP** $500

Modern Farm Set, 1951, 54mm, Model No. 3931
EX $50   **NM** $150   **MIP** $250

(ToyShop File Photo)

Modern Farm Set, 1967, Model No. 3932
EX $65   **NM** $185   **MIP** $310

Modern Farm Set, c.1951, metal barn, fence, tractor, animals, Model No. 3925
EX $50   **NM** $150   **MIP** $250

Modern Service Center, 1962, Model No. 3471
EX $70   **NM** $210   **MIP** $350

(ToyShop File Photo)

Modern Service Station, 1966, plastic building with gray metal base, plastic vehicles, gas pumps, mechanics and attendants, Model No. 6044
EX $40   **NM** $115   **MIP** $180

(ToyShop File Photo)

Navarone Mountain Battleground Set, 1976, included 5-level plastic mountain with two gun emplacements, German troops, ladders, communication and radio benches, tank, landing craft, halftrack, jeep, American soldiers, over 200 pieces, Model No. 3412
EX $45   **NM** $120   **MIP** $200

(ToyShop File Photo)

New Car Sales and Service, With battery powered light, Model No. 3466, 3465
EX $80   **NM** $295   **MIP** $460

One Million, B.C., 1970s
EX $40   **NM** $115   **MIP** $225

(ToyShop File Photo)

Operation Moon Base, 1962, includes vehicles, moon base structure, space

man, moon ship and accessories, Model
No. 4653-4
EX $95   **NM** $275   **MIP** $465

Pet Shop, Model No. 4209
EX $60   **NM** $230   **MIP** $350

(ToyShop File Photo)

Pet Shop, 1953, includes Shop building,
fence, tree, cages, crates, dogs,
monkees, rabbits, birds, aquarium and
accessories, Model No. 4209-10
EX $65   **NM** $240   **MIP** $365

Prehistoric, 1969, Model No. 3398
EX $35   **NM** $105   **MIP** $175

Prehistoric Dinosaur, 1978, Model
No. 4208
EX $35   **NM** $105   **MIP** $175

(ToyShop File Photo)

Prehistoric Times, Series 500, plain box
that reads, "Prehistoric Play Set
Complete with Animals in Natural
Setting", Model No. 3389
EX $50   **NM** $120   **MIP** $195

Prehistoric Times, Model No. 2650
EX $30   **NM** $130   **MIP** $200

Prehistoric Times, Model No. 3388
EX $25   **NM** $75   **MIP** $150

Prehistoric Times, Model No. 3391
EX $20   **NM** $55   **MIP** $95

Prehistoric Times, 1957, Series 1000, big
set, includes: molded terrain base,
cavemen, prehistoric animals, palm
trees, ferns, tree stumps and
accessories, Model No. 3390
EX $85   **NM** $230   **MIP** $400

(ToyShop File Photo)

Prince Valiant Castle, 1954, has figures,
Model No. 4706
EX $110   **NM** $320   **MIP** $550

Prince Valiant Castle, 1955, Model
No. 4705
EX $100   **NM** $270   **MIP** $475

Project Apollo Cape Kennedy, Model
No. 4523
EX $45   **NM** $75   **MIP** $125

Project Apollo Moon Landing, Model
No. 4646
EX $55   **NM** $150   **MIP** $250

Project Mercury Cape Canaveral, 1959,
Model No. 4524
EX $100   **NM** $270   **MIP** $450

Raytheon Missile Test Center, 1961,
Model No. 603-A
EX $70   **NM** $180   **MIP** $325

Real Life Western Wagon, Model
No. 4998
EX $15   **NM** $45   **MIP** $75

Red River Gang, 1970s, mini set
w/cowboys, Model No. 4104
EX $35   **NM** $105   **MIP** $175

(ToyShop File Photo)

Revolutionary War, 1950s, Series 1000,
includes British Redcoats, stone wall
section, shooting cannon, trees, litho
building, Revolutionary troops and
more, Model No. 3404
EX $125   **NM** $500   **MIP** $850

Revolutionary War, 1957, Series 500,
Model No. 3401
EX $225   **NM** $550   **MIP** $1150

Revolutionary War, 1959, No. 3408, 80
pieces, Sears, Model No. 3408
EX $100   **NM** $390   **MIP** $650

(ToyShop File Photo)

Rex Mars Planet Patrol, Model No. 7040
EX $125   **NM** $310   **MIP** $575

Rex Mars Space Drome, 1954, Model
No. 7016
EX $150   **NM** $395   **MIP** $700

Rifleman Ranch, The, 1959, Model
No. 3997-8
EX $130   **NM** $455   **MIP** $750

Rin Tin Tin at Fort Apache, 1956, Series
5000, Model No. 3686R
EX $240   **NM** $725   **MIP** $1250

Rin Tin Tin at Fort Apache, 1956, Series
500, 60mm, Model No. 3628
EX $160   **NM** $475   **MIP** $800

Robin Hood Castle, 1956, 60mm, Model
No. 4717
EX $150   **NM** $375   **MIP** $650

Robin Hood Castle, 1958, 54mm, Model
No. 4718
EX $120   **NM** $325   **MIP** $500

Robin Hood Castle Set, 1950s, Series
1000, 54mm, Model No. 4724
EX $100   **NM** $225   **MIP** $400

Roy Rogers Double R Bar Ranch, 1962,
Model No. 3982
EX $100   **NM** $300   **MIP** $525

Roy Rogers Mineral City, 1958, 95 pieces,
Model No. 4227
EX $110   **NM** $300   **MIP** $500

Roy Rogers Ranch, 1950s, w/ranch kids,
Model No. 3980
EX $200   **NM** $300   **MIP** $525

Roy Rogers Rodeo, 1952, w/ fence pieces,
Model No. 3689-90
EX $60   **NM** $80   **MIP** $150

Roy Rogers Rodeo Ranch, 54mm, Model
No. 3988
EX $90   **NM** $195   **MIP** $345

Roy Rogers Rodeo Ranch, Series 2000,
Model No. 3996
EX $130   **NM** $395   **MIP** $650

(ToyShop File Photo)

Roy Rogers Rodeo Ranch, 1952, 60mm,
includes: bunk house, rodeo chute,
cowboys, horses, steers, saddles,
bridles, fence and accessories, Model
No. 3985
EX $75   **NM** $140   **MIP** $235

Roy Rogers Rodeo Ranch, 1952, Model
No. 3979
EX $55   **NM** $165   **MIP** $275

Roy Rogers Rodeo Ranch, 1958, Model No. 3986R
EX $250   NM $750   MIP $1250

Roy Rogers Western Town, official, Series 5000, Model No. 4259
EX $95   NM $235   MIP $450

Roy Rogers Western Town, Model No. 4216
EX $80   NM $240   MIP $400

Roy Rogers Western Town, 1952, large set, Mineral City, Model No. 4257-8
EX $160   NM $475   MIP $800

Sears Store, 1961, Allstate box, Model No. 5490
EX $350   NM $1200   MIP $1850

Service Station, deluxe, Model No. 3501
EX $50   NM $150   MIP $250

Service Station, Model No. 5459
EX $15   NM $45   MIP $125

(ToyShop File Photo)

Service Station, with parking garage, includes: service station, cars, attendants, high-level parking garage, Model No. 3485
EX $115   NM $325   MIP $540

Service Station, w/elevator, Model No. 3495
EX $30   NM $90   MIP $150

Shopping Center, 1962, Model No. 3755-6
EX $40   NM $120   MIP $200

Silver City Frontier Town, 1555, Model No. 4219-20
EX $50   NM $150   MIP $250

Silver City Western Town, 1956, has Custer, Boone, Carson, Buffalo Bill, Sitting Bull, Model No. 4220
EX $50   NM $150   MIP $250

Silver City Western Town (Ward's), 1954, Montgomery Wards exclusive, Model No. 4256
EX $50   NM $150   MIP $275

Skyscraper, 1957, working elevator, Model No. 5449-50
EX $155   NM $800   MIP $1200

Skyscraper (Ward's), 1957, Montgomery Ward's exclusive, working elevator and light, Model No. 5450
EX $155   NM $800   MIP $1250

(ToyShop File Photo)

Sons of Liberty, 1972, Sears Exclusive set includes: litho building, plastic figures and accessories, flag and stand, historic booklet, Model No. 4170
EX $55   NM $155   MIP $260

Star Station Seven, 1978, 32 pieces
EX $10   NM $30   MIP $50

Strategic Air Command, Model No. 6013
EX $130   NM $520   MIP $800

(ToyShop File Photo)

Super Circus, 1952, over 70 pieces, including big top, Model No. 4319
EX $95   NM $245   MIP $435

Super Circus, 1952, w/character figures, Model No. 4320
EX $75   NM $290   MIP $450

Tactical Air Command, 1970s, Model No. 4106
EX $25   NM $50   MIP $85

Tales of Wells Fargo, Model No. 4263
EX $80   NM $240   MIP $450

(ToyShop File Photo)

Tales of Wells Fargo, Series 1000, play set includes Wells Fargo office, western town building, stagecoach, horses and cowboys, Indians and accessories, Model No. 4264
EX $155   NM $465   MIP $760

Tales of Wells Fargo, Model No. 4262
EX $150   NM $450   MIP $750

Tales of Wells Fargo Train Set, 1959, w/electric train, Model No. 54752
EX $240   NM $600   MIP $800

Tank Battle, 1964, Sears, U.S., Nazi troops, Model No. 6056
EX $40   NM $120   MIP $200

Tank Battle, 1964, U.S., Nazi troops, Model No. 6060
EX $60   NM $120   MIP $225

Tom Corbett Space Academy, 1952, No. 7099, 9 wall sections and gate,
EX $150   NM $375   MIP $710

Treasure Cove Pirate Set, 1962, Model No. 4597-8
EX $50   NM $125   MIP $210

Turnpike Service Center, 1961, Model No. 3459-60
EX $100   NM $300   MIP $500

U.S. Air Force, 1963, Model No. 4807
EX $30   NM $90   MIP $160

U.S. Armed Forces, Model No. 4151
EX $70   NM $210   MIP $350

U.S. Armed Forces Training Center, Model No. 4150
EX $50   NM $150   MIP $265

U.S. Armed Forces Training Center, Marines, soldiers, sailors, airmen, tin litho building, Model No. 4144
EX $40   NM $160   MIP $250

(ToyShop File Photo)

U.S. Armed Forces Training Center, 1955, Series 500, "Featuring Guided Missiles," and including: HQ building, flag, fence, jet plane, compass, helicopter, Air Force, Navy, Army and Marines figures, Model No. 4149-50
EX $90   NM $265   MIP $430

(ToyShop File Photo)

U.S. Armed Forces Training Center, 1956, includes barracks, tents, planes, soldiers, Marines, sailors, Air Force personnel, guns and accessories, Model No. 4158
EX $115   NM $340   MIP $600

(ToyShop File Photo)

U.S. Army Mobile Set, 1956, flat figures, includes vehicles, Model No. 3655
EX $22   NM $75   MIP $125

U.S. Army Training Center, Model No. 4122
EX $25   NM $60   MIP $100

U.S. Army Training Center, Model No. 3378
EX $30   NM $65   MIP $110

U.S. Army Training Center, Model No. 4153
EX $15   NM $55   MIP $95

MARX PLAY SETS

U.S. Army Training Center, Model No. 3146
    EX $30   **NM** $55   **MIP** $95

(ToyShop File Photo)

U.S. Army Training Center, 1954, 45mm, includes: HQ building, vehicle, soldiers and accessories, Model No. 4123
    EX $30   **NM** $80   **MIP** $130

(ToyShop File Photo)

Untouchables, 1961, 90 pieces including: buildings, figures, guns, street layout, furniture and accessories, Model No. 4676
    EX $300   **NM** $985   **MIP** $1550

Vikings and Knights, Model No. 6053
    EX $60   **NM** $180   **MIP** $300

Wagon Train, official, Series 2000, Model No. 4788
    EX $120   **NM** $360   **MIP** $600

Wagon Train, official, Series 5000, Model No. 4888
    EX $245   **NM** $975   **MIP** $1500

Wagon Train, 1960, Series 1000, X Team, Model No. 4805
    EX $160   **NM** $480   **MIP** $800

Walt Disney Television Playhouse, 1953, Model No. 4352
    EX $120   **NM** $360   **MIP** $600

Walt Disney Television Playhouse, 1953, Peter Pan figures, Model No. 4352
    EX $105   **NM** $420   **MIP** $750

Walt Disney Television Playhouse, 1953, Model No. 4350
    EX $100   **NM** $300   **MIP** $475

(ToyShop File Photo)

Walt Disney's Zorro, 1958, official, Series 1000, includes buildings, horses, figures and accessories, Model No. 3754
    EX $265   **NM** $780   **MIP** $1200

Walt Disney's Zorro, 1958, official, Model No. 3758
    EX $240   **NM** $725   **MIP** $1150

Walt Disney's Zorro, 1958, official, Series 500, Model No. 3753
    EX $230   **NM** $695   **MIP** $1100

Walt Disney's Zorro, 1972, official, Series 1000, Model No. 3758
    EX $160   **NM** $500   **MIP** $800

(ToyShop File Photo)

Ward's Service Station, 1959, included service station with elevator, water-filled gasoline pump, cars and attendents, Model No. 3488
    EX $82   **NM** $245   **MIP** $410

Western Frontier Set
    EX $90   **NM** $275   **MIP** $450

Western Mining Town, 1950s, 1950s, Model No. 4265
    EX $135   **NM** $400   **MIP** $675

Western Mining Town, 1950s, 1950s, Model No. 4266
    EX $135   **NM** $405   **MIP** $675

Western Ranch Set, Model No. 3954
    EX $50   **NM** $105   **MIP** $175

Western Ranch Set, Model No. 3980
    EX $50   **NM** $105   **MIP** $175

Western Stagecoach, 1965, Model No. 1395
    EX $45   **NM** $60   **MIP** $100

Western Town, single level, Model No. 2652
    EX $60   **NM** $180   **MIP** $400

Western Town, 1952, bi-level town, Model No. 4229
    EX $120   **NM** $490   **MIP** $650

(ToyShop File Photo)

Westgate Auto Center, 1968, nice-looking litho building and base, plastic accessories and "New, Fast Rolling Cars!"
    EX $45   **NM** $125   **MIP** $205

White House, house w/eight figures
    EX $20   **NM** $45   **MIP** $125

White House & Presidents, house & figures, Model No. 3921
    EX $25   **NM** $45   **MIP** $125

White House & Presidents, house & figures, 1/48 scale presidents, Model No. 3920
    EX $20   **NM** $45   **MIP** $150

Wild Animal Jungle, large animals, Model No. 3716
    EX $25   **NM** $45   **MIP** $85

(ToyShop File Photo)

World War II Battleground, 1966, with U.S. and German troops, halftrack, landing craft, barbed wire, barricades, gun emplacements, tank and jeep, Model No. 4204
    EX $35   **NM** $95   **MIP** $175

World War II European Theatre, rare big set, Model No. 5949
    EX $245   **NM** $1200   **MIP** $1500

World War II European Theatre, 1966, Sears, Model No. 5939
    EX $165   **NM** $470   **MIP** $780

World War II Set, U.S., Nazi troops, Model No. 5938
    EX $50   **NM** $80   **MIP** $150

Wyatt Earp Dodge City Western Town, 1957, Series 1000, Model No. 4228
    EX $165   **NM** $465   **MIP** $825

Yogi Bear at Jellystone National Park, 1962, w/ Ranger station, jeep, well, benches, Yogi and friends, Model No. 4363-4
    EX $125   **NM** $285   **MIP** $475

Model Kits
By Karen O'Brien

Building model kits has been a popular hobby since the 1960s, and in recent years, unbuilt model kits have found a loyal following among collectors seeking to recapture a part of their youth. Plastic model kits were first produced shortly before World War II, but it wasn't until after the war that plastic kit building really began to take off as a hobby. Automobiles, aircraft, and ships all became the subject matter for miniature replicas popularized by companies including Aurora, Revell, Monogram, and Lindberg.

Each type of model kit has its own enthusiastic following, but probably the most collectible kits today are the figure and character kits produced in the 1960s. These kits continue to increase in value despite the up and down fluctuations of the model kit market over the last twelve years.

The Aurora Company is responsible for popularizing figure model kits, with its early 1960s representations of the Universal Pictures monsters. Aurora went into business in August of 1950 and ventured into the hobby business in 1952 with two plastic model airplanes. Aurora expanded its line through the 1950s to include ships, modern and historic aircraft, and trucks before issuing its first figure kits, the knights, starting with the Silver Knight in 1956.

The vision and tenacity of Aurora employee Bill Silverstein in 1961 would change Aurora forever. The remarkable popularity of the 1930s Universal monster films at Saturday matinees and on television prompted the idea of producing a Frankenstein model. Repeated rejections by the Aurora staff almost killed the project, but Silverstein won enough support for the model pattern to be displayed at the January, 1962, HIAA show. No distributors placed orders and on the last day of the convention, two boys accompanying a wholesaler came to the table, ignored the popular Model Motoring layout and headed straight for Frankenstein. Orders trickled in, then poured in, and the rest is history. Frankenstein production began in earnest in 1962, followed by Dracula and the Wolfman. The Creature from the Black Lagoon, The Phantom of the Opera, and The Mummy were released in 1963. The Hunchback of Notre Dame, Godzilla, and King Kong followed in 1964, and Dr. Jekyll and Mr. Hyde joined the lineup in 1965. The Universal monster kits propelled Aurora to the top of the hobby and remain some of the most desired kits by collectors today.

During the 1960s, Aurora also produced kits of more general monstrosities, such as its famous working guillotine kit. These toys offended the sensibilities of some groups, who brought about the political pressure that spelled the end of these kits. Aurora also produced kits based on popular television shows, comic book characters, and sports celebrities. Monogram and Revell reissued some of the popular Aurora kits, and resin copies of the harder-to-find Aurora kits are still being produced and sold today by independent "garage kit" makers. Recently, Polar Lights (a division of the Playing Mantis company) has enjoyed tremendous success with its award-winning reissues of old Aurora favorites, as well as new releases of television and movie favorites.

Other popular monster kits continued the fad of the 1960s. These kits weren't of traditional movie monsters, rather, they were an assortment of strange characters that often came in wild hot rods. Among the most popular were the Revell kits based on Ed "Big Daddy" Roth's Rat Fink concept. (The modern reissues of those classic kits are certain to be collectibles of the future.) Other companies, notably Hawk, also produced kits with this monstrous hot rod theme. Hawk's Weird-Ohs kits are still popular with collectors today. Even popular celebrities became model kit subjects. Airfix produced a series of historical figures, and Revell issued figure kits for each of the four Beatles.

After a slow period in the late 1970s, (the OPEC oil shortage sent plastic costs soaring, which had a ripple-effect throughout the toy and hobby industry) figure kits enjoyed a renewed popularity in the 1980s as new large-scale kits of rather limited production runs were offered in vinyl and resin. Billiken, a Japanese company, produced vinyl kits of the classic movie monsters, some of which have become highly collectible. Screamin' and Horizon are two leaders in the burgeoning "garage kit" field of large-scale vinyl and resin kits of movie, monster, and comic book characters. This area continues to command collector's attention, as the limited runs of these "garage kits" will likely translate into future desirability.

The prices listed provide a general guideline as to the amount these kits would sell for today. MIB refers to a kit that is Mint in Box, in original condition in the original Mint condition box with instructions. The box may not be in the original factory seal, but if the kit pieces are contained within bags inside the box, those original bags have not been opened. Kits that remain in pristine condition and are still in their factory seals may command a slight premium over the MIB price. Near Mint (NM) refers to a kit that is like new, complete, and unassembled. The box may show some shelf wear and the interior bags may have been opened. B/U refers to a kit that has been assembled, or built up and assumes a neatly built, cleanly painted, complete kit.

2006 TRENDS

Kits based on popular characters continue to command collector interest and higher prices. Look for this to continue throughout the year.

REFERENCES

Graham, Thomas. *Greenberg's Guide To Aurora Model Kits*. (Waukesha, Wi: Kalmbach Publishing Co., 1998).

THE TOP TEN MODEL KITS *(In Mint Condition)*

1. Godzilla's Go-Cart, Aurora, 1966	$3,750
2. Lost in Space large kit w/Chariot, Aurora, 1966	1,600
3. Munsters Living Room, Aurora, 1964	1,450
4. Frankenstein Gigantic 1:5 scale, Aurora, 1964	1,430
5. King Kong's Thronester, Aurora, 1966	1,375
6. Lost in Space small kit, Aurora, 1966	1,100
7. Lost in Space Robot, Aurora, 1966	895
8. Addams Family Haunted House, Aurora, 1964	880
9. Bride of Frankenstein, Aurora, 1965	825
10. The Penguin, Aurora, 1967	625

MODEL KITS

ADDAR

Caesar, Planet of the Apes, 1974, Addar, Model No. 106
EX $15 **NM** $42 **MIP** $55

Cornelius, Planet of the Apes, 1974, Addar, Planet of the Apes, Model No. 101
EX $12 **NM** $33 **MIP** $55

Cornfield Roundup, Planet of the Apes, 1975, Addar, Planet of the Apes, Model No. 216
EX $15 **NM** $42 **MIP** $55

Dr. Zaius, Planet of the Apes, 1974, Addar, Planet of the Apes, Model No. 102
EX $10 **NM** $28 **MIP** $44

Dr. Zira, Planet of the Apes, 1974, Addar, Planet of the Apes, Model No. 105
EX $10 **NM** $28 **MIP** $44

Evil Knievel, 1974, Addar, w/cycle, Model No. 152
EX $12 **NM** $28 **MIP** $55

Evil Knievel's Sky Cycle, 1974, Addar, Model No. 154
EX $12 **NM** $28 **MIP** $85

Gen. Aldo, Planet of the Apes, 1974, Addar, Planet of the Apes, Model No. 104
EX $10 **NM** $28 **MIP** $55

Gen. Ursus, Planet of the Apes, 1974, Addar, Planet of the Apes, Model No. 103
EX $12 **NM** $34 **MIP** $50

Jail Wagon, Planet of the Apes, 1975, Addar, Planet of the Apes, Model No. 217
EX $15 **NM** $42 **MIP** $52

Jaws, 1975, Addar, Model No. 270
EX $35 **NM** $60 **MIP** $110

Jaws in a Bottle, 1975, Addar, Jaws, Model No. 270
EX $20 **NM** $55 **MIP** $75

Spirit in a Bottle, 1975, Addar, Model No. 227
EX $10 **NM** $21 **MIP** $55

Stallion & Soldier, Planet of the Apes, 1974, Addar, Model No. 107
EX $25 **NM** $75 **MIP** $125

Tree House, Planet of the Apes, 1975, Addar, Model No. 215
EX $15 **NM** $42 **MIP** $55

AIRFIX

10th British Hussar 1915, 1976, 1:32, Airfix, Model No. 2551
EX $10 **NM** $18 **MIP** $28

2001: A Space Odyssey Orion, 1970, Airfix, Model No. 701
EX $60 **NM** $80 **MIP** $110

2001: A Space Odyssey Orion, 1980, Airfix, Model No. 5175
EX $10 **NM** $20 **MIP** $40

Anne Boleyn, 1974, Airfix, Model No. 3542
EX $7 **NM** $16 **MIP** $25

Anne Boleyn, 1976, 1:32, Airfix, Model No. 3542
EX $10 **NM** $18 **MIP** $30

Black Prince, 1973, Airfix, Model No. 2502
EX $10 **NM** $26 **MIP** $35

Boy Scout, 1965, Airfix, Model No. 212
EX $7 **NM** $16 **MIP** $25

Charles I, 1965, Airfix, Model No. 211
EX $10 **NM** $21 **MIP** $40

Empire Strikes Back, Slave I, 1982, Airfix
EX $35 **NM** $45 **MIP** $60

English Musketeer 1642, 1976, Airfix, Model No. 1560
EX $12 **NM** $18 **MIP** $30

English Pikeman 1642, 1976, Airfix, Model No. 1559
EX $12 **NM** $18 **MIP** $30

Flying Saucer, 1981, Airfix, Model No. 7171
EX $12 **NM** $18 **MIP** $30

George Washington, 1980, 1:32, Airfix, Model No. 2554
EX $12 **NM** $18 **MIP** $30

Henry VIII, 1973, Airfix, Model No. 2501
EX $10 **NM** $15 **MIP** $20

James Bond and Odd Job, 1966, Airfix, Model No. M401F
EX $65 **NM** $135 **MIP** $225

James Bond Autogyro, 1996, 1:24, Airfix, Model No. 4401
EX $10 **NM** $18 **MIP** $50

James Bond's Aston Martin DB-5, 1965, Airfix, Model No. 823
EX $100 **NM** $185 **MIP** $275

Julius Caesar, 1973, Airfix, Model No. 2504
EX $10 **NM** $26 **MIP** $35

Napoleon, 1978, Airfix, Model No. 2508
EX $10 **NM** $15 **MIP** $20

Queen Elizabeth I, 1980, Airfix, Model No. 3546
EX $12 **NM** $22 **MIP** $35

Queen Victoria, 1976, Airfix, Model No. 3544
EX $12 **NM** $22 **MIP** $35

Richard I, 1965, Airfix, Model No. 203
EX $10 **NM** $27 **MIP** $33

(KP Photo)

Space: 1999 Eagle Transporter, 1979, 1:72, Airfix, Model No. 6174
EX $25 **NM** $45 **MIP** $60

Space: 1999 Hawk Spaceship, 1977, 1:72, Airfix, Model No. 5173
EX $80 **NM** $95 **MIP** $110

Yeoman of the Guard, 1978, Airfix, Model No. 2507
EX $4 **NM** $9 **MIP** $11

AMAZING FIGURE MODELER

London After Midnight, 1998, Amazing Figure Modeler, London After Midnight
EX $30 **NM** $60 **MIP** $90

AMT

B.J. and the Bear "Big Rig" set, 1980, 1:32, AMT, Model No. 7705
EX $30 **NM** $40 **MIP** $55

B.J. and the Bear Kenworth cap, 1980, 1:32, AMT, Snap-together, Model No. 5025
EX $17 **NM** $25 **MIP** $35

Bigfoot, 1978, AMT, Model No. 7701
EX $20 **NM** $63 **MIP** $83

Brute Farce, 1960s, AMT, Model No. 611
EX $5 **NM** $11 **MIP** $25

Cliff Hanger, 1960s, AMT, Model No. 610
EX $5 **NM** $11 **MIP** $25

Drag-U-La, Munsters, 1965, AMT, Munsters, Model No. 905
EX $40 **NM** $185 **MIP** $275

Farrah's Foxy Vette, 1977, 1:25, AMT, Model No. 3101
EX $40 **NM** $50 **MIP** $70

Fireball 500 Plymouth by George Barris, 1967, AMT, Model No. 911
EX $50 **NM** $65 **MIP** $80

Flintstones Rock Crusher, 1974, AMT, Flintstones, Model No. 497
EX $20 **NM** $53 **MIP** $75

Flintstones Sports Car, 1974, AMT, Model No. 495
EX $20 **NM** $58 **MIP** $73

Get Smart Sunbeam, 1967, 1:25, AMT, Model No. 925
EX $50 **NM** $65 **MIP** $85

Girl From U.N.C.L.E. Car, 1974, AMT, Model No. 913
EX $75 **NM** $265 **MIP** $375

Graveyard Ghoul Duo (Munsters cars), 1970, AMT, Graveyard Ghoul Duo, Model No. 309
EX $50 **NM** $105 **MIP** $175

Hero, 1966 Chrysler Imperial, 1966, 1:25, AMT, Model No. 914
EX $75 **NM** $105 **MIP** $145

KISS Custom Chevy Van, 1977, AMT, KISS, Model No. 2501
EX $20 **NM** $53 **MIP** $125

Laurel & Hardy '27 T Roadster, 1976, AMT, Model No. 462
EX $20 **NM** $55 **MIP** $66

Laurel & Hardy '27 T Touring Car, 1976, AMT, Model No. 461
EX $20 **NM** $60 **MIP** $75

Man From U.N.C.L.E. Car, 1966, AMT, Model No. 912
EX $75 **NM** $185 **MIP** $250

Matilda Custom Ford Van, 1978, 1:25, AMT, Model No. 2504
EX $25 **NM** $35 **MIP** $45

Mr. Spock, large box, 1973, AMT, Model No. 956
EX $15   NM $79   MIP $225

(KP Photo)

Mr. Spock, small box, 1973, AMT
EX $20   NM $105   MIP $175

Munster Koach, 1964, AMT, Munsters, Model No. 901
EX $80   NM $145   MIP $235

My Mother The Car, 1965, AMT, Model No. 904
EX $15   NM $30   MIP $45

Sonny & Cher Mustang, 1960s, AMT, Sonny & Cher, Model No. 907
EX $75   NM $265   MIP $350

Star Trek the Motion Picture, Klingon Cruiser, 1979, AMT, Model No. 971
EX $19   NM $28   MIP $40

Star Trek the Motion Picture, Mr. Spock, 1979, AMT, Model No. 973
EX $25   NM $38   MIP $55

Star Trek the Motion Picture, U.S.S. Enterprise, 1979, AMT, Model No. 970
EX $50   NM $85   MIP $150

Star Trek the Motion Picture, Vulcan Shuttle, 1979, AMT, Model No. 972
EX $25   NM $35   MIP $50

Star Trek, Command Bridge Model Kit, 1975, AMT, Model No. S950-601
EX $40   NM $50   MIP $85

Star Trek, Galileo Shuttle Model Kit, 1974, AMT, #S959-602, Model No. 959
EX $80   NM $95   MIP $175

Star Trek, K-7 Space Station, 1976, AMT, Model No. 955
EX $19   NM $60   MIP $160

Star Trek, Klingon Cruiser Model Kit, AMT, Model No. PK-5111
EX $45   NM $60   MIP $100

Star Trek, Klingon Cruiser Model Kit, 1968, AMT, Model No. S952-802
EX $135   NM $180   MIP $250

Star Trek, Romulan Bird of Prey Model Kit, 1975, AMT, Model No. S957-601
EX $100   NM $120   MIP $130

Star Trek, Space Ship Set, 1976, AMT, Snap-together, Model No. 953
EX $50   NM $65   MIP $85

T.h.e. Cat, 1967 Custom Corvette, 1967, 1:25, AMT, Model No. 915
EX $50   NM $60   MIP $75

Threw'd Dude, 1960s, AMT, Model No. 612
EX $10   NM $15   MIP $20

Touchdown?, 1960s, AMT, Model No. 614
EX $10   NM $18   MIP $25

UFO Mystery Ship, AMT, UFO
EX $15   NM $63   MIP $85

USS Enterprise Bridge, Star Trek, 1975, AMT, Model No. 950
EX $10   NM $27   MIP $55

(KP Photo)

USS Enterprise w/lights, Star Trek, 1967, AMT, Model No. 921-200
EX $40   NM $210   MIP $275

USS Enterprise, Star Trek, 1966, AMT, Model No. 951-250
EX $40   NM $132   MIP $165

Vega$, 1957 Thunderbird, 1979, 1:25, AMT, Model No. 3105
EX $35   NM $45   MIP $60

AURORA

Addams Family Haunted House, 1964, Aurora, Addams Family, Model No. 805
EX $300   NM $630   MIP $880

Alfred E. Neuman (MAD), 1965, Aurora, Model No. 802
EX $150   NM $175   MIP $200

(KP Photo)

American Astronaut, 1967, Aurora, Astronaut, Model No. 409
EX $25   NM $71   MIP $90

American Buffalo, 1964, Aurora, Model No. 402
EX $19   NM $37   MIP $52

American Buffalo, reissue, 1972, Aurora, Model No. 402
EX $10   NM $20   MIP $30

Apache Warrior on Horse, 1960, Aurora, Model No. 401
EX $180   NM $320   MIP $500

Aramis, Three Musketeers, 1958, Aurora, Three Musketeers, Model No. K-10
EX $25   NM $85   MIP $115

Archie's Car, 1969, Aurora, Model No. 582
EX $25   NM $90   MIP $110

Aston Martin Super Spy Car, 1965, Aurora, Model No. 819
EX $40   NM $158   MIP $220

(KP Photo)

Athos, Three Musketeers, 1958, Aurora, Three Musketeers, Model No. K-8
EX $20   NM $80   MIP $115

Banana Splits Banana Buggy, 1969, Aurora, Banana Splits, Model No. 832
EX $150   NM $420   MIP $550

(KP Photo)

Batboat, 1968, Aurora, Batman, Model No. 811
EX $150   NM $315   MIP $500

Batcycle, 1967, Aurora, Batman, Model No. 810
EX $125   NM $265   MIP $450

Batman, 1964, Aurora, Batman, Model No. 467
EX $20   NM $80   MIP $275

(KP Photo)

Batman, Comic Scenes, 1974, Aurora, Batman, Model No. 187

EX $20　　**NM** $42　　**MIP** $90

Batmobile, 1966, Aurora, Batman, Model No. 486

EX $100　　**NM** $225　　**MIP** $450

Batplane, 1967, Aurora, Batman, Model No. 487

EX $50　　**NM** $105　　**MIP** $285

Black Bear and Cubs, 1962, Aurora, Model No. 407

EX $15　　**NM** $30　　**MIP** $44

Black Bear and Cubs, reissue, 1969, Aurora, Model No. 407

EX $17　　**NM** $25　　**MIP** $35

Black Fury, 1958, Aurora, Black Fury, Model No. 400

EX $10　　**NM** $26　　**MIP** $33

Black Fury, reissue, 1969, Aurora, Black Fury, Model No. 400

EX $12　　**NM** $13　　**MIP** $17

Black Knight, 1956, Aurora, Black Knight, Model No. K-3

EX $12　　**NM** $55　　**MIP** $85

(KP Photo)

Black Knight, reissue, 1963, Aurora, Black Knight, Model No. 473

EX $12　　**NM** $30　　**MIP** $45

Blackbeard, 1965, Aurora, Blackbeard, Model No. 463

EX $75　　**NM** $210　　**MIP** $248

(KP Photo)

Blue Knight, 1956, Aurora, Blue Knight, Model No. K-2

EX $15　　**NM** $35　　**MIP** $55

Blue Knight, reissue, 1963, Aurora, Model No. 472

EX $15　　**NM** $25　　**MIP** $35

Bond, James, 1966, Aurora, James Bond, Model No. 414

EX $250　　**NM** $315　　**MIP** $525

(KP Photo)

Bride of Frankenstein, 1965, Aurora, Bride of Frankenstein, Model No. 482

EX $300　　**NM** $525　　**MIP** $825

Brown, Jimmy, 1965, Aurora, Brown, Jimmy, Model No. 863

EX $75　　**NM** $155　　**MIP** $200

(KP Photo)

Canyon, Steve, 1958, Aurora, Canyon, Steve, Model No. 409

EX $75　　**NM** $180　　**MIP** $275

(KP Photo)

Captain Action, 1966, Aurora, Captain Action, Model No. 480

EX $100　　**NM** $290　　**MIP** $330

(KP Photo)

Captain America, 1966, Aurora, Captain America, Model No. 476

EX $85　　**NM** $200　　**MIP** $330

Captain America, Comic Scenes, 1974, Aurora, Captain America, Model No. 192

EX $30　　**NM** $84　　**MIP** $145

Captain Kidd, 1965, Aurora, Captain Kidd, Model No. 464

EX $25　　**NM** $100　　**MIP** $150

(KP Photo)

Cave Bear, 1971, Aurora, Cave Bear, Model No. 738

EX $15　　**NM** $30　　**MIP** $45

MODEL KITS

Chinese Girl, 1957, Aurora, Chinese Girl, Model No. 416
EX $15   NM $27   MIP $50

Chinese Junk, 1962, Aurora, Model No. 430
EX $100   NM $125   MIP $150

Chinese Mandarin, 1957, Aurora, Chinese Mandarin, Model No. 415
EX $12   NM $25   MIP $50

(KP Photo)

Chinese Mandarin & Girl, 1957, Aurora, Model No. 213
EX $75   NM $105   MIP $330

Chitty Chitty Bang Bang, 1968, Aurora, Chitty Chitty Bang Bang, Model No. 828
EX $45   NM $90   MIP $175

(KP Photo)

Confederate Raider, 1959, Aurora, Model No. 402
EX $150   NM $210   MIP $385

Creature From the Black Lagoon, 1963, Aurora, Creature, Model No. 426
EX $125   NM $325   MIP $475

Creature From The Black Lagoon, Glow Kit, 1969, Aurora, Creature, Model No. 483
EX $65   NM $105   MIP $250

Creature From The Black Lagoon, Glow Kit, 1972, Aurora, Creature, Model No. 483
EX $85   NM $130   MIP $240

Creature, Monsters of Movies, 1975, Aurora, Creature, Model No. 653
EX $100   NM $145   MIP $265

Cro-Magnon Man, 1971, Aurora, Model No. 730
EX $10   NM $32   MIP $50

(KP Photo)

Cro-Magnon Woman, 1971, Aurora, Model No. 731
EX $7   NM $26   MIP $39

(KP Photo)

Crusader, 1959, Aurora, Model No. K-7
EX $75   NM $160   MIP $220

D'Artagnan, Three Musketeers, 1966, Aurora, Three Musketeers, Model No. 410
EX $50   NM $160   MIP $200

Dempsey vs Firpo, 1965, Aurora, Dempsey, Model No. 861
EX $40   NM $100   MIP $125

Dick Tracy in Action Model Kit, 1968, Aurora, plastic, Model No. 818
EX $85   NM $175   MIP $350

Dr. Deadly, 1971, Aurora, Dr. Deadly, Model No. 631
EX $25   NM $70   MIP $85

Dr. Deadly's Daughter, 1971, Aurora, Dr. Deadly's Daughter, Model No. 632
EX $25   NM $70   MIP $85

(KP Photo)

Dr. Jekyll as Mr. Hyde, 1964, Aurora, Dr. Jekyll, Model No. 460
EX $45   NM $250   MIP $385

Dr. Jekyll, Glow Kit, 1969, Aurora, Dr. Jekyll, Model No. 482
EX $45   NM $105   MIP $195

Dr. Jekyll, Glow Kit, 1972, Aurora, Dr. Jekyll, Model No. 482
EX $45   NM $65   MIP $85

Dr. Jekyll, Monster Scenes, 1971, Aurora, Dr. Jekyll, Model No. 462
EX $40   NM $90   MIP $125

(KP Photo)

Dr. Jekyll, Monsters of Movies, 1975, Aurora, Dr. Jekyll, Model No. 654
EX $25   NM $50   MIP $77

Dracula, 1962, Aurora, Dracula, Model No. 424
EX $25   NM $225   MIP $330

Dracula, Frightning Lightning, 1969, Aurora, Dracula, Model No. 454
EX $30   NM $315   MIP $550

Dracula, Glow Kit, 1969, Aurora, Dracula, Model No. 454
EX $20   NM $80   MIP $165

(KP Photo)

Dracula, Glow Kit, 1972, Aurora, Dracula, Model No. 454
EX $20   NM $63   MIP $83

Dracula, Monster Scenes, 1971, Aurora, Dracula, Model No. 641
EX $75   NM $105   MIP $220

Dracula, Monsters of Movies, 1975, Aurora, Dracula, Model No. 656
EX $75   NM $105   MIP $275

Dracula's Dragster, 1966, Aurora, Dracula, Model No. 466
EX $125   NM $315   MIP $450

(KP Photo)

Dutch Boy, 1957, Aurora, Dutch Boy, Model No. 413
EX $20 **NM** $45 **MIP** $80

Dutch Boy & Girl, 1957, Aurora, Model No. 209
EX $75 **NM** $210 **MIP** $330

(KP Photo)

Dutch Girl, 1957, Aurora, Dutch Girl, Model No. 414
EX $20 **NM** $40 **MIP** $60

Flying Sub, 1968, Aurora, Model No. 817
EX $35 **NM** $175 **MIP** $220

Flying Sub, reissue, 1975, Aurora, Model No. 254
EX $35 **NM** $85 **MIP** $110

Forgotten Prisoner, 1966, Aurora, Forgotten Prisoner, Model No. 422
EX $65 **NM** $325 **MIP** $440

Forgotten Prisoner, Frightning Lightning, 1969, Aurora, Forgotten Prisoner, Model No. 453
EX $65 **NM** $320 **MIP** $500

Forgotten Prisoner, Glow Kit, 1969, Aurora, Forgotten Prisoner, Model No. 453
EX $65 **NM** $180 **MIP** $220

Forgotten Prisoner, Glow Kit, 1972, Aurora, Forgotten Prisoner, Model No. 453
EX $65 **NM** $155 **MIP** $193

Frankenstein, 1961, Aurora, Frankenstein, Model No. 423
EX $30 **NM** $210 **MIP** $345

Frankenstein, Frightning Lightning, 1969, Aurora, Frankenstein, Model No. 449
EX $30 **NM** $315 **MIP** $440

(KP Photo)

Frankenstein, Gigantic 1:5 scale, 1964, Aurora, Frankenstein, Model No. 470
EX $300 **NM** $945 **MIP** $1430

Frankenstein, Glow Kit, 1969, Aurora, Frankenstein, Model No. 449
EX $20 **NM** $70 **MIP** $165

Frankenstein, Glow Kit, 1972, Aurora, Frankenstein, Model No. 449
EX $20 **NM** $50 **MIP** $90

Frankenstein, Monster Scenes, 1971, Aurora, Frankenstein, Model No. 633
EX $50 **NM** $80 **MIP** $120

(KP Photo)

Frankenstein, Monsters of Movies, 1975, Aurora, Frankenstein, Model No. 651
EX $100 **NM** $210 **MIP** $350

Frankie's Flivver, 1964, Aurora, Frankenstein, Model No. 465
EX $150 **NM** $375 **MIP** $500

(KP Photo)

Frog, Castle Creatures, 1966, Aurora, Frog, Model No. 451
EX $75 **NM** $210 **MIP** $275

Ghidrah, 1975, Aurora, Model No. 658
EX $95 **NM** $275 **MIP** $345

Giant Insect, Monster Scene, 1971, Aurora, Model No. 643
EX $95 **NM** $365 **MIP** $450

Gladiator, The, Aurora, w/ trident, Model No. 406
EX $50 **NM** $110 **MIP** $185

Godzilla, 1964, Aurora, Godzilla, Model No. 469
EX $85 **NM** $425 **MIP** $575

Godzilla, Glow Kit, 1969, Aurora, Godzilla, Model No. 466
EX $75 **NM** $225 **MIP** $360

Godzilla, Glow Kit, 1972, Aurora, Godzilla, Model No. 466
EX $75 **NM** $150 **MIP** $200

(KP Photo)

Godzilla's Go-Cart, 1966, Aurora, Godzilla, Model No. 485
EX $850 **NM** $2500 **MIP** $3750

Gold Knight of Nice, 1957, Aurora, Gold Knight, Model No. 475
EX $145 **NM** $280 **MIP** $350

Gold Knight of Nice, 1965, Aurora, Gold Knight, Model No. 475
EX $125   **NM** $260   **MIP** $310

Green Beret, 1966, Aurora, Green Beret, Model No. 413
EX $75   **NM** $160   **MIP** $200

(KP Photo)

Green Hornet Black Beauty, 1966, Aurora, Green Hornet, Model No. 489
EX $125   **NM** $365   **MIP** $550

Gruesome Goodies, 1971, Aurora, Model No. 634
EX $45   **NM** $85   **MIP** $115

Guillotine, 1964, Aurora, Guillotine, Model No. 800
EX $125   **NM** $350   **MIP** $440

Hanging Cage, 1971, Aurora, Model No. 637
EX $30   **NM** $80   **MIP** $110

Hercules, 1965, Aurora, Hercules, Model No. 481
EX $125   **NM** $235   **MIP** $375

(KP Photo)

Hulk, Comic Scenes, 1974, Aurora, Hulk, Model No. 184
EX $25   **NM** $75   **MIP** $110

Hulk, Original, 1966, Aurora, Hulk, Model No. 421
EX $75   **NM** $260   **MIP** $325

(KP Photo)

Hunchback of Notre Dame, 1964, Aurora, Hunchback, Model No. 460
EX $45   **NM** $210   **MIP** $330

Hunchback of Notre Dame, Glow Kit, 1969, Aurora, Hunchback, Model No. 481
EX $45   **NM** $95   **MIP** $165

Hunchback of Notre Dame, Glow Kit, 1972, Aurora, Hunchback, Model No. 481
EX $45   **NM** $85   **MIP** $125

Indian Chief, 1957, Aurora, Model No. 417
EX $35   **NM** $85   **MIP** $100

Indian Chief & Squaw, 1957, Aurora, Model No. 212
EX $60   **NM** $125   **MIP** $165

Indian Squaw, 1957, Aurora, Model No. 418
EX $15   **NM** $40   **MIP** $65

Infantryman, 1957, Aurora, Infantryman, Model No. 411
EX $20   **NM** $75   **MIP** $110

(KP Photo)

Invaders UFO, 1968, Aurora, Model No. 813
EX $35   **NM** $85   **MIP** $110

Invaders UFO, 1975, Aurora, Model No. 256
EX $30   **NM** $55   **MIP** $85

Iwo Jima, 1966, Aurora, Model No. 853
EX $75   **NM** $185   **MIP** $220

(KP Photo)

Jesse James, 1966, Aurora, Jesse James, Model No. 408
EX $60   **NM** $105   **MIP** $210

Kennedy, John F., 1965, Aurora, Kennedy, John F., Model No. 851
EX $50   **NM** $75   **MIP** $175

King Arthur, 1973, Aurora, Model No. 885
EX $65   **NM** $105   **MIP** $220

King Arthur of Camelot, 1967, Aurora, King Arthur, Model No. 825
EX $30   **NM** $70   **MIP** $85

King Kong, 1964, Aurora, King Kong, Model No. 468
EX $75   **NM** $315   **MIP** $495

King Kong, Glow Kit, 1969, Aurora, King Kong, Model No. 468
EX $75   **NM** $185   **MIP** $275

King Kong, Glow Kit, 1972, Aurora, King Kong, Model No. 468
EX $75   **NM** $132   **MIP** $195

King Kong's Thronester, 1966, Aurora, King Kong, Model No. 484
EX $370   **NM** $840   **MIP** $1375

Land of the Giants Space Ship, 1968, Aurora, Land of Giants, Model No. 830
EX $150   **NM** $308   **MIP** $440

Land of the Giants, Diorama, 1968, Aurora, Land of the Giants, Model No. 816
EX $150   **NM** $368   **MIP** $500

Lone Ranger, 1967, Aurora, Lone Ranger, Model No. 808
EX $75   **NM** $105   **MIP** $196

Lone Ranger, Comic Scenes, 1974, Aurora, Lone Ranger, Model No. 188
EX $20   **NM** $42   **MIP** $65

Lost In Space, Large kit w/chariot, 1966, Aurora, Lost in Space, Model No. 420
EX $450   **NM** $1100   **MIP** $1600

(KP Photo)

Lost In Space, Small kit, 1966, Aurora, Lost in Space, Model No. 419
EX $300   **NM** $735   **MIP** $1100

(KP Photo)

Lost In Space, The Robot, 1968, Aurora, Robot B-9, Model No. 418
EX $250   **NM** $630   **MIP** $895

Mad Barber, 1972, Aurora, Mad Barber, Model No. 455
EX $50   **NM** $105   **MIP** $165

Mad Dentist, 1972, Aurora, Model No. 457
EX $50   **NM** $105   **MIP** $165

Mad Doctor, 1972, Aurora, Model No. 456
EX $50   **NM** $105   **MIP** $165

Man From U.N.C.L.E., Illya Kuryakin, 1966, Aurora, Man From U.N.C.L.E., Model No. 412
EX $75   **NM** $105   **MIP** $220

(KP Photo)

Man From U.N.C.L.E., Napoleon Solo, 1966, Aurora, Man From U.N.C.L.E., Model No. 411
EX $75   **NM** $165   **MIP** $290

Marine, 1959, Aurora, Marine, Model No. 412
EX $30   **NM** $84   **MIP** $110

Mays, Willie, 1965, Aurora, Model No. 860
EX $100   **NM** $210   **MIP** $330

Mexican Caballero, 1957, Aurora, Model No. 421
EX $95   **NM** $100   **MIP** $175

Mexican Senorita, 1957, Aurora, Mexican Senorita, Model No. 422
EX $50   **NM** $96   **MIP** $170

Mod Squad Wagon, 1970, Aurora, Model No. 583
EX $50   **NM** $132   **MIP** $192

(KP Photo)

Monster Customizing Kit #1, 1964, Aurora, Model No. 463
EX $35   **NM** $117   **MIP** $140

Monster Customizing Kit #2, 1964, Aurora, Model No. 464
EX $65   **NM** $160   **MIP** $195

Moon Bus from 2001, 1968, Aurora, Model No. 828
EX $100   **NM** $250   **MIP** $330

(KP Photo)

Mr. Hyde, Monsters of the Movies, 1975, Aurora, Mr. Hyde, Model No. 655
EX $40   **NM** $110   **MIP** $150

Mr. Spock, 1972, Aurora, Star Trek, Model No. 922
EX $40   **NM** $125   **MIP** $175

Mummy, 1963, Aurora, Mummy, Model No. 427
EX $30   **NM** $160   **MIP** $350

Mummy, Frightning Lightning, 1969, Aurora, Mummy, Model No. 452
EX $30   **NM** $210   **MIP** $440

Mummy, Glow Kit, 1969, Aurora, Mummy, Model No. 452
EX $20   **NM** $80   **MIP** $190

(KP Photo)

Mummy, Glow Kit, 1972, Aurora, Mummy, Model No. 452
EX $20   **NM** $42   **MIP** $75

(KP Photo)

Mummy's Chariot, 1965, Aurora, Mummy, Model No. 459
EX $200   **NM** $350   **MIP** $600

Munsters, Living Room, 1964, Aurora, Munsters, Model No. 804
EX $400   **NM** $945   **MIP** $1450

(KP Photo)

Neanderthal Man, 1971, Aurora, Neanderthal Man, Model No. 729
EX $15   NM $42   MIP $75

Neuman, Alfred E., 1965, Aurora, Alfred E. Neuman, Model No. 802
EX $100   NM $289   MIP $440

(KP Photo)

Nutty Nose Nipper, 1965, Aurora, Nutty Nose Nipper, Model No. 806
EX $45   NM $185   MIP $220

(KP Photo)

Odd Job, 1966, Aurora, Odd Job, Model No. 415
EX $200   NM $360   MIP $495

Pain Parlor, 1971, Aurora, Model No. 635
EX $25   NM $105   MIP $140

Pendulum, 1971, Aurora, Model No. 636
EX $25   NM $55   MIP $90

Penguin, 1967, Aurora, Penguin, Model No. 416
EX $200   NM $420   MIP $625

Phantom of the Opera, 1963, Aurora, Phantom of the Opera, Model No. 428
EX $75   NM $250   MIP $330

Phantom of the Opera, Frightning Lightning, 1969, Aurora, Phantom of the Opera, Model No. 451
EX $65   NM $250   MIP $385

(KP Photo)

Phantom of the Opera, Glow Kit, 1969, Aurora, Phantom of the Opera, Model No. 451
EX $20   NM $75   MIP $165

Phantom of the Opera, Glow Kit, 1972, Aurora, Phantom of the Opera, Model No. 451
EX $20   NM $63   MIP $88

Pilot USAF, 1957, Aurora, Model No. 409
EX $75   NM $145   MIP $190

Porthos, Three Musketeers, 1958, Aurora, Three Musketeers, Model No. K-9
EX $25   NM $75   MIP $110

(KP Photo)

Pushmi-Pullyu, Dr. Dolittle, 1968, Aurora, Model No. 814
EX $60   NM $110   MIP $160

Rat Patrol, 1967, Aurora, Rat Patrol, Model No. 340
EX $30   NM $70   MIP $120

Red Knight, 1957, Aurora, Red Knight, Model No. K-4
EX $25   NM $55   MIP $110

Red Knight, 1963, Aurora, Red Knight, Model No. 474
EX $25   NM $85   MIP $150

(KP Photo)

Robin, 1966, Aurora, Robin, Model No. 488
EX $40   NM $75   MIP $150

Robin, Comic Scenes, 1974, Aurora, Robin, Model No. 193
EX $40   NM $70   MIP $120

Rodan, 1975, Aurora, Rodan, Model No. 657
EX $125   NM $210   MIP $400

Roman Gladiator with sword, 1959, Aurora, Model No. 405
EX $75   NM $130   MIP $200

Roman Gladiator with Trident, 1964, Aurora, Gladiator, Model No. 406
EX $75   NM $140   MIP $200

Roman Gladiators, 1959, Aurora, Model No. 216
EX $100   NM $210   MIP $275

Ruth, Babe, 1965, Aurora, Ruth, Babe, Model No. 862
EX $100   NM $240   MIP $360

(KP Photo)

Scotch Lad, 1957, Aurora, Scoth Lad, Model No. 419
EX $17   NM $38   MIP $55

Scotch Lad & Lassie, 1957, Aurora, Model No. 214
EX $60   NM $95   MIP $110

MODEL KITS

(KP Photo)

Scotch Lassie, 1957, Aurora, Scotch Lassie, Model No. 420
EX $17   **NM** $38   **MIP** $65

Seaview, Voyage to the Bottom of Sea, 1966, Aurora, Voyage to the Bottom, Model No. 707
EX $100   **NM** $210   **MIP** $330

Seaview, Voyage to the Bottom of Sea, 1975, Aurora, Model No. 253
EX $100   **NM** $168   **MIP** $209

Silver Knight, 1956, Aurora, Silver Knight, Model No. K-1
EX $15   **NM** $42   **MIP** $60

(KP Photo)

Silver Knight, 1963, Aurora, Silver Knight, Model No. 471
EX $15   **NM** $21   **MIP** $40

Sir Galahad, 1973, Aurora, Model No. 881
EX $15   **NM** $42   **MIP** $70

Sir Galahad of Camelot, 1967, Aurora, Galahad, Model No. 826
EX $25   **NM** $95   **MIP** $195

Sir Kay, 1973, Aurora, Model No. 882
EX $20   **NM** $42   **MIP** $55

Sir Lancelot, 1973, Aurora, Model No. 883
EX $20   **NM** $42   **MIP** $55

(KP Photo)

Sir Lancelot of Camelot, 1967, Aurora, Lancelot, Model No. 827
EX $25   **NM** $95   **MIP** $140

Sir Percival, 1973, Aurora, Model No. 884
EX $20   **NM** $30   **MIP** $75

(KP Photo)

Spartacus (Gladiator/sword reissue), 1964, Aurora, Spartacus, Model No. 405
EX $85   **NM** $150   **MIP** $275

Spider-Man, 1966, Aurora, Spider-Man, Model No. 477
EX $85   **NM** $210   **MIP** $400

Spider-Man, Comic Scenes, 1974, Aurora, Spider-Man, Model No. 182
EX $75   **NM** $100   **MIP** $150

Star Trek, Klingon Cruiser, 1972, Aurora, Model No. 923
EX $20   **NM** $50   **MIP** $90

Star Trek, U.S.S. Enterprise, 1972, Aurora, Model No. 921
EX $20   **NM** $65   **MIP** $130

Superboy, 1964, Aurora, Superboy, Model No. 478
EX $75   **NM** $210   **MIP** $275

Superboy, Comic Scenes, 1974, Aurora, Superboy, Model No. 186
EX $35   **NM** $75   **MIP** $110

Superman, 1963, Aurora, Superman, Model No. 462
EX $100   **NM** $180   **MIP** $425

(KP Photo)

Superman, Comic Scenes, 1974, Aurora, Superman, Model No. 185
EX $20   **NM** $42   **MIP** $66

Tarpit, 1972, Aurora, Model No. 735
EX $65   **NM** $110   **MIP** $150

(KP Photo)

Tarzan, 1967, Aurora, Tarzan, Model No. 820
EX $25   **NM** $105   **MIP** $220

(KP Photo)

Tarzan, Comic Scenes, 1974, Aurora, Tarzan, Model No. 181
EX $15   **NM** $45   **MIP** $65

Three Knights Set, 1959, Aurora, Model No. 207
EX $50   **NM** $105   **MIP** $190

Three Musketeers Set, 1958, Aurora, Model No. 398
EX $95   **NM** $210   **MIP** $385

Tonto, 1967, Aurora, Tonto, Model No. 809
EX $25   NM $150   MIP $220

Tonto, Comic Scenes, 1974, Aurora, Tonto, Model No. 183
EX $30   NM $60   MIP $100

Tracy, Dick, 1968, Aurora, Tracy, Dick, Model No. 818
EX $60   NM $105   MIP $275

Tracy, Dick, Space Coupe, 1968, Aurora, Tracy, Dick, Model No. 819
EX $50   NM $105   MIP $165

U.S. Marshal, 1958, Aurora, Model No. 408
EX $55   NM $78   MIP $115

Unitas, Johnny, 1965, Aurora, Unitas, Johnny, Model No. 864
EX $75   NM $132   MIP $195

(KP Photo)

United States Sailor, 1957, Aurora, Sailor, Model No. 410
EX $15   NM $31   MIP $45

Vampire, Castle Creatures, 1966, Aurora, Model No. 452
EX $60   NM $185   MIP $275

(KP Photo)

Vampirella, 1971, Aurora, Vampirella, Model No. 638
EX $75   NM $132   MIP $225

Victim, 1971, Aurora, Model No. 632
EX $20   NM $70   MIP $85

Viking, 1959, Aurora, Viking, Model No. K-6
EX $65   NM $105   MIP $275

Voyager, Fantastic Voyage, 1969, Aurora, Model No. 831
EX $125   NM $235   MIP $525

(KP Photo)

Wacky Back-Whacker, 1965, Aurora, Model No. 807
EX $50   NM $105   MIP $275

Washington, George, 1965, Aurora, Great American Presidents, Model No. 852
EX $25   NM $55   MIP $110

West, Jerry, 1965, Aurora, West, Jerry, Model No. 865
EX $50   NM $105   MIP $165

White Stallion, 1964, Aurora, Model No. 401
EX $12   NM $25   MIP $35

White Stallion, reissue, 1969, Aurora, Model No. 401
EX $12   NM $25   MIP $35

White-tailed Deer, 1962, Aurora, Model No. 403
EX $12   NM $25   MIP $35

White-tailed Deer, reissue, 1969, Aurora, Model No. 403
EX $12   NM $18   MIP $25

Whoozis, Alfalfa, 1966, Aurora, Whoozis, Model No. 204
EX $25   NM $50   MIP $83

Whoozis, Denty, 1966, Aurora, Whoozis, Model No. 203
EX $25   NM $50   MIP $83

Whoozis, Esmerelda, 1966, Aurora, Whoozis, Model No. 202
EX $25   NM $50   MIP $83

Whoozis, Kitty, 1966, Aurora, Whoozis, Model No. 205
EX $25   NM $50   MIP $83

Whoozis, Snuffy, 1966, Aurora, Whoozis, Model No. 206
EX $25   NM $50   MIP $83

Whoozis, Susie, 1966, Aurora, Whoozis, Model No. 201
EX $25   NM $50   MIP $83

Witch, 1965, Aurora, Witch, Model No. 483
EX $85   NM $210   MIP $330

Witch, Glow Kit, 1969, Aurora, Witch, Model No. 470
EX $55   NM $105   MIP $220

Witch, Glow Kit, 1972, Aurora, Witch, Model No. 470
EX $75   NM $105   MIP $138

Wolfman, 1962, Aurora, Wolfman, Model No. 425
EX $40   NM $210   MIP $330

Wolfman, Frightning Lightning, 1969, Aurora, Wolfman, Model No. 450
EX $40   NM $315   MIP $440

Wolfman, Glow Kit, 1969, Aurora, Wolfman, Model No. 450
EX $20   NM $55   MIP $165

Wolfman, Glow Kit, 1972, Aurora, Wolfman, Model No. 450
EX $25   NM $50   MIP $90

(KP Photo)

Wolfman, Monsters of the Movies, 1975, Aurora, Wolfman, Model No. 652
EX $100   NM $210   MIP $275

Wolfman's Wagon, 1965, Aurora, Wolfman, Model No. 458
EX $175   NM $315   MIP $468

(KP Photo)

Wonder Woman, 1965, Aurora, Wonder Woman, Model No. 479
EX $150   NM $315   MIP $575

Zorro, 1965, Aurora, Zorro, Model No. 801
EX $125   NM $210   MIP $340

BILLIKEN

Batman, type A, 1989, Billiken, Batman
EX $35   NM $90   MIP $110

Batman, type B, 1989, Billiken, Batman
EX $35   NM $95   MIP $140

Bride of Frankenstein, 1984, Billiken, Bride of Frankenstein
EX $75   NM $105   MIP $250

Colossal Beast, 1986, Billiken, Colossal Beast
EX $20   NM $32   MIP $44

Creature From the Black Lagoon, 1991, Billiken, Creature
EX $70   NM $100   MIP $160

Cyclops, 1984, Billiken
EX $75   NM $105   MIP $220

Dracula, 1989, Billiken, Dracula
EX $60   NM $105   MIP $165

Frankenstein, 1988, Billiken, Frankenstein
EX $60   NM $125   MIP $180

Joker, 1989, Billiken
EX $40   NM $95   MIP $165

Mummy, 1990, Billiken, Mummy
EX $60   NM $125   MIP $180

Phantom of the Opera, 1980s, Billiken, Phantom of the Opera
EX $100   NM $210   MIP $305

Predator, 1991, Billiken, Predator
EX $25   NM $53   MIP $75

Saucer Man, Billiken, Saucer Man
EX $20   NM $32   MIP $44

She-Creature, 1989, Billiken, She-Creature
EX $25   NM $42   MIP $55

Syngenor, 1984, Billiken, Syngenor
EX $100   NM $160   MIP $275

The Thing, 1984, Billiken, The Thing
EX $150   NM $210   MIP $330

Ultraman, 1987, Billiken, Ultraman
EX $25   NM $35   MIP $50

BOWEN DESIGNS

Kongzilla, 1998, Bowen Designs, Kongzilla
EX $15   NM $30   MIP $50

GEOMETRIC DESIGNS

Alien, Ripley, 1998, Geometric Designs
EX $35   NM $45   MIP $60

Aliens, Alien Warrior, 1996, Geometric Designs
EX $50   NM $65   MIP $80

Creature From the Black Lagoon, 1:8, Geometric Designs, vinyl kit, figure from original film, sculpted by Jim Gorman
EX $20   NM $40   MIP $60

Hunchback of Notre Dame, The, 1:8, Geometric Designs, vinyl kit, figure of Charles Laughton as the Hunchback
EX $20   NM $40   MIP $60

King Kong, 1:35, Geometric Designs, vinyl kit, figure from original King Kong film
EX $25   NM $50   MIP $100

Masters of the Universe, Talon Fighter, 1984, Geometric Designs, Model No. 6015
EX $20   NM $30   MIP $40

Mummy, The, 1:8, Geometric Designs, vinyl kit, figure of Boris Karloff from original Mummy film
EX $20   NM $40   MIP $60

Predator, 1:8, Geometric Designs, vinyl kit, figure from original Predator film
EX $20   NM $40   MIP $60

Shogun Warriors, Raider, 1978, Geometric Designs, Model No. 6023
EX $12   NM $18   MIP $25

Son of Frankenstein, 1998, 1:8, Geometric Designs, Frankenstein monster from Son of Frankenstein, sculpted by William Paquet
EX $10   NM $20   MIP $35

Wolfman, The, 1998, 1:8, Geometric Designs, vinyl kit, depicting Lon Chaney, Jr., sculpted by Mike Hill
EX $20   NM $40   MIP $60

HAWK

Beach Bunny, 1964, Hawk, Model No. 542
EX $25   NM $65   MIP $150

(KP Photo)

Daddy the Way-Out Suburbanite, 1963, Hawk, Daddy, Model No. 532
EX $30   NM $70   MIP $125

Davy the Way-Out Cyclist, 1963, Hawk, Davy, Model No. 531
EX $30   NM $70   MIP $125

Digger and Dragster, 1963, Hawk, Digger, Model No. 530
EX $30   NM $70   MIP $125

(KP Photo)

Drag Hag, 1963, Hawk, Drag Hag, Model No. 536
EX $30   NM $70   MIP $125

(KP Photo)

Endsville Eddie, 1963, Hawk, Endsville Eddie, Model No. 537
EX $20   NM $50   MIP $110

Francis The Foul, 1963, Hawk, Francis The Foul, Model No. 535
EX $20   NM $50   MIP $95

Frantic Banana, 1965, Hawk, Frantics, Model No. 548
EX $20   NM $84   MIP $175

Frantic Cats, 1965, Hawk, Frantics, Model No. 550
EX $20   NM $75   MIP $135

(KP Photo)

Frantics Steel Pluckers, 1965, Hawk, Frantics, Model No. 547
EX $20   NM $75   MIP $140

Frantics Totally Fab, 1965, Hawk, Frantics, Model No. 549
EX $20   NM $84   MIP $125

Freddy Flameout, 1963, Hawk, Freddy Flameout, Model No. 533
EX $20   NM $70   MIP $125

Hidad Silly Surfer, 1964, Hawk, Hidad Silly Surfer, Model No. 543
EX $20   NM $70   MIP $125

Hot Dogger Hangin' Ten, 1964, Hawk, Model No. 541
EX $20   NM $65   MIP $125

(KP Photo)

Huey's Hut Rod, 1963, Hawk, Huey's Hut Rod, Model No. 538
EX $20   NM $50   MIP $90

Killer McBash, 1963, Hawk, Killer McBash
EX $60   NM $125   MIP $185

(KP Photo)

Leaky Boat Louie, 1963, Hawk, Leaky Boat Louie, Model No. 534
EX $25   NM $84   MIP $135

Riding Tandem, Hawk
EX $25   NM $65   MIP $100

(KP Photo)

Sling Rave Curvette, 1964, Hawk, Sling Rave Curvette, Model No. 637
EX $20   **NM** $50   **MIP** $95

Steel Pluckers, 1965, Hawk, Frantics, Model No. 547
EX $20   **NM** $65   **MIP** $125

Totally Fab, 1965, Hawk, Frantics, Model No. 550
EX $25   **NM** $75   **MIP** $135

Wade A Minute, 1963, Hawk, Wade A Minute, Model No. 636
EX $45   **NM** $90   **MIP** $145

Weird-Oh Customizing Kit, 1964, Hawk, Weird-Oh
EX $100   **NM** $250   **MIP** $375

Weirdsville Customizing Kit, 1964, Hawk, plastic kit featuring multiple characters
EX $100   **NM** $200   **MIP** $325

Wild Woodie Car, Hawk, Wild Woodie, Model No. 545
EX $20   **NM** $55   **MIP** $85

Woodie on a Surfari, 1964, Hawk, Model No. 540
EX $45   **NM** $90   **MIP** $125

HORIZON

Bride of Frankenstein, 1990s, 1:6, Horizon, vinyl kit
EX $20   **NM** $40   **MIP** $75

Creature From the Black Lagoon, 1990s, 1:6, Horizon, vinyl kit, rare
EX $35   **NM** $75   **MIP** $110

Dracula, 1990s, 1:6, Horizon, vinyl kit, Model No. HM004
EX $25   **NM** $50   **MIP** $85

Frankenstein, 1990s, 1:6, Horizon, vinyl kit
EX $25   **NM** $50   **MIP** $85

Invisible Man, The, 1990s, 1:6, Horizon, vinyl kit
EX $20   **NM** $40   **MIP** $70

Mole People, The, 1990s, 1:6, Horizon, vinyl kit
EX $20   **NM** $40   **MIP** $70

Mummy, The, 1990s, 1:6, Horizon, vinyl kit
EX $20   **NM** $40   **MIP** $70

Phantom of the Opera, 1990s, 1:6, Horizon, vinyl kit
EX $20   **NM** $40   **MIP** $70

Wolfman, The, 1990s, 1:6, Horizon, vinyl kit
EX $20   **NM** $40   **MIP** $65

LINDBERG

Baywatch Pickup, 1995, Lindberg, Model No. 72598
EX $5   **NM** $10   **MIP** $15

Bert's Bucket, 1971, Lindberg, Model No. 6422
EX $30   **NM** $84   **MIP** $110

Big Wheeler, 1965, Lindberg, Lindberg Loony, Model No. 277
EX $30   **NM** $84   **MIP** $110

Blurp, 1964, Lindberg, Lindy Loony Repulsive, Model No. 280
EX $10   **NM** $21   **MIP** $50

Captain Kidd Pirate Ship, 1990, 14", Lindberg
EX $10   **NM** $15   **MIP** $45

Creeping Crusher, 1965, Lindberg, Model No. 273
EX $20   **NM** $42   **MIP** $60

Fat Max, 1971, Lindberg, Model No. 6420
EX $30   **NM** $84   **MIP** $99

Flintstones, Flintmobile, 1994, Lindberg, Model No. 72411
EX $10   **NM** $15   **MIP** $20

Flintstones, Le Sabertooth 5000, 1994, Lindberg, Model No. 72412
EX $5   **NM** $10   **MIP** $15

Giant American Bullfrog, 1973, Lindberg
EX $15   **NM** $30   **MIP** $50

Glob, 1964, Lindberg, Lindy Loony Repulsive, Model No. 281
EX $10   **NM** $21   **MIP** $55

Godzilla, 1995, Lindberg, Model No. 71344
EX $15   **NM** $22   **MIP** $40

Green Ghoul, 1965, Lindberg, Model No. 274
EX $20   **NM** $35   **MIP** $55

Independence Day, Alien Exskeleton, 1996, Lindberg, Model No. 77312
EX $5   **NM** $10   **MIP** $15

Independence Day, Capt. Hiller's F/A-18 Hornet, 1996, Lindberg, Model No. 77313
EX $20   **NM** $30   **MIP** $40

Independence Day, Captured Alien Attacker, 1996, Lindberg, Model No. 77311
EX $20   **NM** $30   **MIP** $40

Independence Day, Russell Casse's PT-17 Bi-Plane, 1996, Lindberg, Model No. 77314
EX $20   **NM** $30   **MIP** $40

Jurassic Park, Vilociraptor, 1993, 15", Lindberg
EX $10   **NM** $15   **MIP** $25

Krimson Terror, 1965, Lindberg, Model No. 272
EX $20   **NM** $42   **MIP** $65

Mad Mangler, 1965, Lindberg, Model No. 275
EX $20   **NM** $42   **MIP** $65

Road Hog, 1964, Lindberg, Lindberg Loony, Model No. 276
EX $30   **NM** $84   **MIP** $100

Satan's Crate, 1964, Lindberg, Lindberg Loony
EX $75   **NM** $130   **MIP** $165

Scuttle Bucket, 1964, Lindberg, Lindberg Loony, Model No. 278
EX $30   **NM** $84   **MIP** $100

Shrieker, Glo-Monster, 1971, Lindberg, Model No. 290
EX $35   **NM** $45   **MIP** $75

Sick Cycle, 1971, Lindberg, Model No. 6421
EX $30   **NM** $84   **MIP** $100

UFO, 1976, Lindberg, Model No. 1152
EX $35   **NM** $45   **MIP** $60

Voop, 1964, Lindberg, Lindy Loony Repulsive, Model No. 283
EX $10   **NM** $21   **MIP** $60

Zopp, 1964, Lindberg, Lindy Loony Repulsive, Model No. 282
EX $35   **NM** $65   **MIP** $110

MONOGRAM

Battlestar Galactica, 1979, Monogram, Model No. 6028
EX $20   **NM** $35   **MIP** $60

Battlestar Galactica, Colonial Viper, 1979, Monogram, Model No. 6027
EX $20   **NM** $35   **MIP** $65

Battlestar Galactica, Cylon Base Star Model Kit, 1979, Monogram, Model No. 6029
EX $20   **NM** $40   **MIP** $55

Battlestar Galactica, Cylon Raider, 1979, Monogram, Model No. 6026
EX $20   **NM** $35   **MIP** $55

Buck Rogers, Marauder, 1979, Monogram, Model No. 6031
EX $30   **NM** $50   **MIP** $75

Dracula, 1983, 1:8, Monogram, Dracula, Model No. 6008
EX $20   **NM** $30   **MIP** $40

Elvira Macabre Mobile, 1988, Monogram, Model No. 2783
EX $10   **NM** $20   **MIP** $30

Flip Out, 1965, Monogram, Fred Flypogger, Model No. 105
EX $50   **NM** $150   **MIP** $220

Flying Sub, Voyage to the Bottom of the Sea, 1979, Monogram, Model No. 6011
EX $25   **NM** $45   **MIP** $55

Frankenstein, 1983, 1:8, Monogram, Frankenstein, Model No. 6007
EX $20   **NM** $30   **MIP** $40

Godzilla, 1978, Monogram, Model No. 6300
EX $40   **NM** $65   **MIP** $100

Masters of the Universe, Roton Assault Vehicle, 1984, Monogram, Model No. 6016
EX $5   **NM** $10   **MIP** $15

Mummy, 1983, 1:8, Monogram, Mummy, Model No. 6010
EX $20   **NM** $30   **MIP** $40

Skull, Lizard & Rat, 1998, Monogram, Model No. 5020
EX $10   **NM** $15   **MIP** $30

Sleepy Hollow, Headless Horseman, 1999, Monogram, Model No. 5022
EX $15   **NM** $20   **MIP** $35

Snoopy & Motorcycle, 1971, Monogram, snap-tite, Model No. 5902
EX $30   **NM** $65   **MIP** $110

Snoopy & Sopwith Camel, 1971, Monogram, Model No. 6779
EX $20   **NM** $35   **MIP** $75

Snoopy as Joe Cool, 1971, Monogram, Model No. 7502
EX $25   **NM** $55   **MIP** $110

Speed Racer Mach 5, 2000, Monogram, Model No. 6700
EX $10   **NM** $15   **MIP** $35

Speed Shift, 1965, Monogram, Fred Flypogger, Model No. MM106
EX $70   **NM** $105   **MIP** $220

Super Fuzz, 1965, Monogram, Fred Flypogger
EX $80   **NM** $105   **MIP** $250

Superman, 1978, Monogram, Superman, Model No. 6301
EX $25   **NM** $35   **MIP** $50

Three Stooges, Curly, 1999, Monogram, Model No. 5063
EX $10   **NM** $20   **MIP** $30

Three Stooges, Larry, 1999, Monogram, Model No. 5061
EX $10   **NM** $15   **MIP** $20

Three Stooges, Moe, 1999, Monogram, Model No. 5062
EX $10   **NM** $15   **MIP** $20

UFO, The Invaders, 1979, Monogram, UFO, Model No. 6012
EX $15   **NM** $32   **MIP** $45

Undertaker Dragster, 1997, Monogram, Model No. 5014
EX $10   **NM** $15   **MIP** $20

Vulture, Customizing Monster kit, 1998, Monogram, Model No. 5021
EX $10   **NM** $15   **MIP** $20

Witch, 2000, Monogram, Model No. 5092
EX $15   **NM** $20   **MIP** $25

(KP Photo)

Wolfman, 1983, 1:8, Monogram, Wolfman, Model No. 6009
EX $20   **NM** $30   **MIP** $40

Wolfman's Wagon, 1997, Monogram, Model No. 5015
EX $10   **NM** $15   **MIP** $20

MPC

Alien, 1979, MPC, Alien, Model No. 1-1961
EX $25   **NM** $76   **MIP** $110

Ape Man Haunted Glow Head, 1975, MPC, Ape Man, Model No. 0303
EX $17   **NM** $38   **MIP** $60

AT-AT, Empire Strikes Back, 1980, MPC, Model No. 190218
EX $15   **NM** $35   **MIP** $60

(KP Photo)

Barnabas Vampire Van, 1969, MPC, Dark Shadows, Model No. 626
EX $75   **NM** $105   **MIP** $300

Barnabas, Dark Shadows, 1968, MPC, Dark Shadows, Model No. 1550
EX $100   **NM** $325   **MIP** $450

Batman, 1984, MPC, Super Powers, Model No. 1702
EX $20   **NM** $35   **MIP** $75

Beverly Hillbillies Truck, 1968, MPC, Beverly Hillbillies, Model No. 612
EX $60   **NM** $105   **MIP** $225

Bionic Bustout, Six Million Dollar Man, 1975, MPC, Model No. 0609
EX $15   **NM** $35   **MIP** $75

Bionic Repair, Bionic Woman, 1976, MPC, Bionic Woman, Model No. 0610
EX $15   **NM** $35   **MIP** $75

Black Hole, Cygnus, 1979, MPC, Model No. 1983
EX $75   **NM** $150   **MIP** $200

Black Hole, Maximillian, 1979, MPC, Model No. 1982
EX $65   **NM** $85   **MIP** $115

Black Hole, V.I.N.CENT., 1979, MPC, Model No. 1915
EX $65   **NM** $85   **MIP** $110

Bloody Mama, Ma Barker Getaway Special, 1970, MPC, Model No. 625
EX $30   **NM** $45   **MIP** $65

C-3PO, Structors Action Walker, 1984, MPC, Model No. 1901
EX $5   **NM** $10   **MIP** $15

Cannonball Run, "Hawaiian Tropic" Malibu, 1981, MPC, Model No. 681
EX $25   **NM** $38   **MIP** $65

Cannonball Run, Emergency Van, 1981, MPC, Model No. 447
EX $11   **NM** $16   **MIP** $30

Cannonball Run, Lamborghini Countach, 1981, MPC, Model No. 682
EX $18   **NM** $25   **MIP** $35

CB Freak, 1975, MPC, Model No. 778
EX $10   **NM** $17   **MIP** $30

Condemned to Chains Forever, 1974, MPC, Model No. 5003
EX $20   **NM** $42   **MIP** $65

Creepy T, 1970, MPC, Model No. 631
EX $20   **NM** $35   **MIP** $50

Curl's Gurl, 1960s, MPC, Model No. 103
EX $25   **NM** $65   **MIP** $100

Darth Vader Bust, 1977, MPC, Model No. 1921
EX $20   **NM** $42   **MIP** $60

(KP Photo)

Darth Vader with Light Saber, 1979, MPC, Model No. 1916
EX $15   **NM** $30   **MIP** $44

Dead Man's Raft, 1974, MPC, Model No. 5005
EX $20   **NM** $84   **MIP** $110

Dead Men Tell No Tales, 1972, MPC, Model No. 5001
EX $60   **NM** $100   **MIP** $125

Dukes of Hazzard, Cooter's Cruiser, 1980, MPC, Snap-together, Model No. 3220
EX $12   **NM** $17   **MIP** $25

Dukes of Hazzard, Cooter's Tow Truck, 1981, MPC, Model No. 441
EX $15   **NM** $20   **MIP** $25

Dukes of Hazzard, Daisy's Jeep CJ, 1980, MPC, Model No. 662
EX $17   **NM** $25   **MIP** $35

Dukes of Hazzard, Duke's Digger, 1980, MPC, Snap-together, Model No. 3219
EX $15   **NM** $20   **MIP** $25

Dukes of Hazzard, General Lee, 1979, 1:25, MPC, Model No. 661
EX $40   **NM** $65   **MIP** $90

Dukes of Hazzard, General Lee, 1981, 1:16, MPC, Model No. 3058
EX $20   **NM** $45   **MIP** $50

Dukes of Hazzard, Sheriff Rosco's Police Car, 1982, MPC, Model No. 663
EX $10   **NM** $17   **MIP** $25

Empire Strikes Back, Battle on Ice Planet Hoth, 1981, MPC, Snap-together, Model No. 1922
EX $10   **NM** $15   **MIP** $20

Empire Strikes Back, Luke Skywalker Snowspeeder, 1980, MPC, Model No. 1917
EX $20   **NM** $30   **MIP** $40

Empire Strikes Back, Rebel Base, 1981, MPC, Model No. 1924
EX $10   **NM** $15   **MIP** $20

Empire Strikes Back, Slave I, 1982, MPC, Model No. 1919
EX $20   **NM** $45   **MIP** $80

Empire Strikes Back, Snow Speeder, 1980, MPC
EX $10   **NM** $20   **MIP** $35

Empire Strikes Back, Star Destroyer, 1980, MPC, Model No. 1926
EX $10   **NM** $35   **MIP** $75

Encounter With Yoda Diorama, 1981, MPC, Model No. 1983
EX $20   **NM** $40   **MIP** $60

(KP Photo)

Escape From the Crypt, 1974, MPC, Disney's Haunted Mansion series, Model No. 5053
EX $60   **NM** $100   **MIP** $125

Evil Rider, Six Million Dollar Man, 1975, MPC, Model No. 604
EX $15   **NM** $21   **MIP** $44

Fate of the Mutineers, 1974, MPC, Model No. 5004
EX $20   **NM** $42   **MIP** $55

Fight for Survival, Six Million Dollar Man, 1975, MPC, Model No. 602
EX $15   **NM** $21   **MIP** $50

Fonzie & Dream Rod, 1976, MPC, Fonzie, Model No. 0635
EX $20   **NM** $35   **MIP** $50

Fonzie & Motorcycle, 1976, MPC, Fonzie, Model No. 0634
EX $20   **NM** $28   **MIP** $45

Freed in the Nick of Time, 1972, MPC, Model No. 5007
EX $20   **NM** $63   **MIP** $85

Ghost of America, Hot Rodder's, 1960s, MPC, Model No. 104
EX $50   **NM** $65   **MIP** $80

(KP Photo)

Ghost of the Treasure Guard, 1974, MPC, Disney's Pirates of the Caribbean, Model No. 5006
EX $35   **NM** $55   **MIP** $70

Grave Robber's Reward, 1974, MPC, Model No. 5051
EX $20   **NM** $42   **MIP** $55

Hardcastle & McCormick, GMC Truck, 1984, MPC, Model No. 450
EX $20   **NM** $32   **MIP** $45

Hogan's Heroes Jeep, 1968, MPC, Hogan's Heroes, Model No. 402
EX $30   **NM** $80   **MIP** $140

Hoist High the Jolly Roger, 1974, MPC, Disney's Pirates of the Caribbean, Model No. 5002
EX $35   **NM** $55   **MIP** $70

Hot Curl, 1960s, MPC, Hot Curl, Model No. 101
EX $20   **NM** $42   **MIP** $55

Hot Shot, MPC, Hot Shot
EX $20   **NM** $42   **MIP** $55

Hulk, 1978, MPC, Hulk, Model No. 1932
EX $20   **NM** $32   **MIP** $44

Jaws of Doom, Six Million Dollar Man, 1975, MPC, Model No. 603
EX $15   **NM** $21   **MIP** $44

Knight Rider, Knight 2000 "KITT", 1982, MPC, Model No. 675
EX $15   **NM** $22   **MIP** $30

Mannix Roadster, 1968, MPC, Model No. 609
EX $35   **NM** $45   **MIP** $60

Monkeemobile, 1967, MPC, Monkees, Model No. 605
EX $75   **NM** $165   **MIP** $250

Muldowney, Shirley, 1970s, MPC, Shirley "Cha Cha" Muldowney Funny Car Plymouth Hemi, Model No. 1-0702
EX $20   **NM** $45   **MIP** $65

Mummy Haunted Glow Head, 1975, MPC, Model No. 304
EX $20   **NM** $32   **MIP** $55

Mummy, Strange Changing, 1974, MPC, Model No. 902
EX $50   **NM** $75   **MIP** $100

Night Crawler Wolfman Car, 1971, MPC
EX $45   **NM** $80   **MIP** $140

Paul Revere & The Raiders Coach, 1970, MPC, Model No. 622
EX $55   **NM** $95   **MIP** $150

Play It Again Sam, 1974, MPC, Model No. 5052
EX $35   **NM** $84   **MIP** $110

Raiders of the Lost Ark Chase Scene, 1982, MPC, Model No. 1906
EX $15   **NM** $32   **MIP** $60

Raiders of the Lost Ark, Desert Chase, 1982, MPC, Snap-together, Model No. 1906
EX $15   **NM** $25   **MIP** $35

Return of the Jedi, AT-ST, 1984, MPC, Snap-together, Model No. 1903
EX $10   **NM** $15   **MIP** $22

Return of the Jedi, B-Wing Fighter, 1984, MPC, Snap-together, Model No. 1974
EX $15   **NM** $25   **MIP** $35

Return of the Jedi, C-3PO, 1983, MPC, Model No. 1935
EX $10   **NM** $20   **MIP** $50

Return of the Jedi, Jabba's Throne Room, 1983, MPC, Model No. 1928
EX $20   **NM** $32   **MIP** $50

Return of the Jedi, Millennium Falcon, 1983, MPC, Model No. 1933
EX $50   **NM** $65   **MIP** $90

Return of the Jedi, R2-D2, 1983, MPC, Model No. 1934
EX $15   **NM** $25   **MIP** $35

Return of the Jedi, Shuttle Tyridium, 1983, MPC, Model No. 1920
EX $15   **NM** $25   **MIP** $55

Return of the Jedi, Speeder Bike, 1983, MPC, Model No. 1927
EX $12   **NM** $17   **MIP** $25

Return of the Jedi, TIE Interceptor, 1983, MPC, Model No. 1972
EX $15   **NM** $25   **MIP** $35

Return of the Jedi, X-Wing Fighter, 1983, MPC, Snap-together, Model No. 1971
EX $11   **NM** $18   **MIP** $25

Return of the Jedi, X-Wing Fighter, 1983, MPC, Model No. 1930
EX $15   **NM** $22   **MIP** $30

Return of the Jedi, Y-Wing Fighter, 1983, MPC, Snap-together, Model No. 1975
EX $11   **NM** $18   **MIP** $25

Road Runner Beep Beep, MPC, Road Runner
EX $20   **NM** $50   **MIP** $85

Space: 1999 Hawk Spaceship, 1977, MPC, Model No. 1904
EX $30   **NM** $50   **MIP** $65

Space: 1999, Eagle One Model Kit, 1976, MPC
EX $50   NM $90   MIP $125

Space: 1999, Moon Base Alpha Model Kit, 1976, MPC
EX $20   NM $35   MIP $70

Space: 1999, The Alien vehicle, 1976, MPC, Model No. 1902
EX $30   NM $50   MIP $65

Spider-Man, 1978, MPC, Snap-together, clings to wall, Model No. 1931
EX $20   NM $30   MIP $40

Spider-Van, 1977, MPC, snap kit
EX $10   NM $17   MIP $22

Star Wars, C-3PO, 1978, MPC, Model No. 1913
EX $17   NM $30   MIP $45

Star Wars, Darth Vader TIE Fighter, 1978, MPC, Model No. 1915
EX $12   NM $20   MIP $30

Star Wars, Darth Vader Van, 1979, MPC, Snap-together, Model No. 3209
EX $10   NM $15   MIP $20

Star Wars, Luke Skywalker Van, 1977, MPC, Snap-together, Model No. 3210
EX $10   NM $15   MIP $20

Star Wars, Luke Skywalker's X-Wing Fighter, 1978, MPC, Model No. 1914
EX $15   NM $25   MIP $35

Star Wars, Millennium Falcon with Light, 1977, MPC, Model No. 1925
EX $35   NM $85   MIP $150

Star Wars, R2-D2, 1977, MPC, Model No. 1912
EX $20   NM $30   MIP $40

Star Wars, R2-D2 Van, 1977, MPC, Snap-together, Model No. 3211
EX $15   NM $25   MIP $35

Strange Changing Mummy, 1974, MPC, Model No. 0902
EX $15   NM $32   MIP $44

Strange Changing Time Machine, 1974, MPC, Model No. 0903
EX $20   NM $42   MIP $55

Strange Changing Vampire, 1974, MPC, Model No. 0901
EX $20   NM $42   MIP $55

Stroker McGurk & Surf Rod, 1960s, MPC, Stroker McGurk, Model No. 100
EX $30   NM $84   MIP $140

Stroker McGurk Tall T, 1964, MPC, Stroker McGurk, Model No. 102
EX $30   NM $84   MIP $140

Superman, 1984, MPC, Super Powers, Model No. 1701
EX $20   NM $35   MIP $55

(KP Photo)

Sweathog Dream Machine, 1976, MPC, Model No. 641
EX $15   NM $25   MIP $40

T.J. Hooker, Police Car, 1982, MPC, Model No. 676
EX $10   NM $20   MIP $30

The Fall Guy, GMC Pickup, 1982, MPC, Model No. 673
EX $15   NM $20   MIP $25

Time Machine, Strange Changing, 1974, MPC, Model No. 903
EX $50   NM $75   MIP $100

Vampire Haunted Glow Head, 1975, MPC, Model No. 301
EX $15   NM $21   MIP $50

Vampire, Strange Changin, 1974, MPC, Model No. 901
EX $50   NM $75   MIP $100

Vampire's Midnight Madness, 1974, MPC, Model No. 5050
EX $20   NM $45   MIP $55

Wacky Races, Compact Pussycat w/Penelope, 1969, MPC, Model No. 901
EX $125   NM $160   MIP $225

Wacky Races, Mean Machine, 1969, MPC, Model No. 900
EX $100   NM $145   MIP $175

Werewolf Haunted Glow Head, 1975, MPC, Model No. 302
EX $20   NM $35   MIP $50

Werewolf, Dark Shadows, 1969, MPC, Dark Shadows, Model No. 1552
EX $75   NM $200   MIP $325

Wile E. Coyote, MPC, Wile E. Coyote, Model No. 2651
EX $20   NM $50   MIP $75

Yellow Submarine, 1968, MPC, Beatles, Model No. 617
EX $75   NM $190   MIP $400

MULTIPLE TOYMAKERS

Automatic Baby Feeder, 1965, Multiple Toymakers, Rube Goldberg, Model No. 955
EX $25   NM $63   MIP $85

Back Scrubber, 1965, Multiple Toymakers, Rube Goldberg, Model No. 958
EX $25   NM $63   MIP $85

Iron Maiden, 1966, Multiple Toymakers, Model No. 981
EX $35   NM $105   MIP $165

Painless Tooth Extractor, 1965, Multiple Toymakers, Rube Goldberg, Model No. 956
EX $25   NM $63   MIP $85

Signal for Shipwrecked Sailors, 1965, Multiple Toymakers, Rube Goldberg, Model No. 957
EX $25   NM $63   MIP $85

Torture Chair, 1966, Multiple Toymakers, Model No. 980
EX $35   NM $95   MIP $165

Torture Wheel, 1966, Multiple Toymakers, Model No. 979
EX $35   NM $95   MIP $165

PARK

(KP Photo)

Castro, Born Losers, 1965, Park, Castro, Model No. 803
EX $35   NM $70   MIP $140

(KP Photo)

Hitler, Born Losers, 1965, Park, Hitler, Model No. 802
EX $35   NM $70   MIP $200

MODEL KITS

(KP Photo)

Napoleon, Born Losers, 1965, Park, Napoleon, Model No. 801
EX $35 **NM** $70 **MIP** $145

PLAYING MANTIS/ POLAR LIGHTS

Addams Family Haunted House, 1995, Playing Mantis/Polar Lights, Model No. 5002
EX $15 **NM** $30 **MIP** $40

Back to the Future Delorean, 2002, Playing Mantis/Polar Lights, movie version
EX $5 **NM** $10 **MIP** $15

Batcycle, 2002, Playing Mantis/Polar Lights, DC Comic Book 1960s version, Model No. 6902
EX $5 **NM** $10 **MIP** $15

(Playing Mantis)

Bates Mansion from Psycho, 1998, Playing Mantis/Polar Lights, Model No. 5028
EX $10 **NM** $20 **MIP** $30

Batplane, 2002, Playing Mantis/Polar Lights, DC Comic Book 1960s version, Model No. 6905
EX $5 **NM** $10 **MIP** $15

Beatles Yellow Submarine, George, 1999, Playing Mantis/Polar Lights, Model No. 5071
EX $10 **NM** $15 **MIP** $20

Beatles Yellow Submarine, John, 2000, Playing Mantis/Polar Lights, Model No. 5074
EX $10 **NM** $15 **MIP** $20

Beatles Yellow Submarine, Paul, 2000, Playing Mantis/Polar Lights, Model No. 5073
EX $10 **NM** $15 **MIP** $20

Beatles Yellow Submarine, Ringo, 1999, Playing Mantis/Polar Lights, Model No. 5072
EX $10 **NM** $15 **MIP** $20

Bellringer of Notre Dame, 2000, Playing Mantis/Polar Lights, Model No. 5090
EX $10 **NM** $20 **MIP** $30

Boris Karloff, The Mummy, 1998, Playing Mantis/Polar Lights
EX $35 **NM** $45 **MIP** $60

(Playing Mantis)

Bride of Frankenstein, 1997, Playing Mantis/Polar Lights, Model No. 5005
EX $10 **NM** $20 **MIP** $30

Cats, Bats, n' Rats, 1998, Playing Mantis/Polar Lights
EX $10 **NM** $20 **MIP** $30

Chamber of Horrors, Guillotine, 2000, Playing Mantis/Polar Lights, Model No. 5091
EX $15 **NM** $20 **MIP** $25

Clash of the Titans, Medusa, 1994, Playing Mantis/Polar Lights
EX $50 **NM** $65 **MIP** $80

Crash Bandicoot on Jet Board, 1999, Playing Mantis/Polar Lights, Model No. 6026
EX $10 **NM** $15 **MIP** $20

Creature From the Black Lagoon, 1998, Playing Mantis/Polar Lights, The Creature
EX $10 **NM** $20 **MIP** $35

Creature from the Black Lagoon, 1999, Playing Mantis/Polar Lights
EX $35 **NM** $45 **MIP** $60

Creepy Critters, 1998, Playing Mantis/Polar Lights
EX $10 **NM** $20 **MIP** $30

Cyclops, The 7th Voyage of Sinbad, 1990, Playing Mantis/Polar Lights
EX $34 **NM** $45 **MIP** $60

Demolition Man, Sandra Bullock, 1990s, Playing Mantis/Polar Lights
EX $25 **NM** $35 **MIP** $50

Dick Tracy, 2000, Playing Mantis/Polar Lights, on fire escape, Model No. 5093
EX $4 **NM** $8 **MIP** $12

(Playing Mantis)

Dick Tracy, Space Coupe, 2000, Playing Mantis/Polar Lights, Model No. 5097
EX $10 **NM** $15 **MIP** $20

Dracula, Aurora box reissue, 1999, Playing Mantis/Polar Lights, Model No. 424
EX $20 **NM** $30 **MIP** $40

Dracula's Dragster, 1999, Playing Mantis/Polar Lights, Model No. 5025
EX $10 **NM** $20 **MIP** $30

Forgotten Prisoner of Castel-Mare', 1999, Playing Mantis/Polar Lights, Model No. 7509
EX $10 **NM** $20 **MIP** $30

Frankenstein, 1999, Playing Mantis/Polar Lights, Model No. 423
EX $30 **NM** $45 **MIP** $60

Frankenstein's Flivver, 1997, Playing Mantis/Polar Lights, Model No. 5006
EX $10 **NM** $20 **MIP** $30

Fright Night, Amy, 1990, Playing Mantis/Polar Lights
EX $35 **NM** $45 **MIP** $60

Ghost of Frankenstein, bust, 1997, Playing Mantis/Polar Lights
EX $35 **NM** $45 **MIP** $60

Ghostbusters ECTO 1, 2002, Playing Mantis/Polar Lights, movie version, Model No. 6812
EX $4 **NM** $8 **MIP** $12

Godzilla, 2000, Playing Mantis/Polar Lights, Model No. 7502
EX $15 **NM** $20 **MIP** $25

Godzilla's Go-Cart, 1999, Playing Mantis/Polar Lights, Model No. 5029
EX $25 **NM** $35 **MIP** $60

Green Hornet Black Beauty, 1999, Playing Mantis/Polar Lights, Model No. 5017
EX $10 **NM** $20 **MIP** $30

H.P. Lovecraft's The UnNamable II, 1999, Playing Mantis/Polar Lights
EX $50 **NM** $60 **MIP** $70

(Playing Mantis)

James Bond 007, 1999, Playing Mantis/Polar Lights, Model No. 5035
EX $10 **NM** $15 **MIP** $20

King Ghidorah, 2000, Playing Mantis/Polar Lights, Model No. 6802
EX $10   **NM** $15   **MIP** $20

King Kong, 1990s, Playing Mantis/Polar Lights
EX $50   **NM** $65   **MIP** $80

King Kong, 2000, Playing Mantis/Polar Lights, Model No. 7507
EX $10   **NM** $15   **MIP** $20

King Kong's Thronester, 1998, Playing Mantis/Polar Lights, Model No. 5016
EX $10   **NM** $15   **MIP** $20

KISS, Ace Frehley, 1998, Playing Mantis/Polar Lights, Ace Frehley
EX $10   **NM** $20   **MIP** $30

KISS, Gene Simmons, 1998, Playing Mantis/Polar Lights, Gene Simmons, Model No. 5058
EX $10   **NM** $20   **MIP** $30

KISS, Paul Stanley, 1998, Playing Mantis/Polar Lights, Paul Stanley, Model No. 5055
EX $10   **NM** $20   **MIP** $30

KISS, Peter Criss, 1998, Playing Mantis/Polar Lights, Peter Criss, Model No. 5056
EX $10   **NM** $20   **MIP** $30

Land of the Giants Diorama, 2002, Playing Mantis/Polar Lights, Diorama w/ snake & crew, Model No. 7512
EX $7   **NM** $14   **MIP** $20

Land of the Giants, Spaceship Spindrift, 2000, Playing Mantis/Polar Lights, Model No. 7513
EX $7   **NM** $14   **MIP** $20

Lon Chaney, The Wolfman, 1999, Playing Mantis/Polar Lights
EX $35   **NM** $45   **MIP** $60

(KP Photo)

Lost in Space Cyclops w/Chariot, 1998, Playing Mantis/Polar Lights, Lost in Space Cyclops
EX $10   **NM** $20   **MIP** $30

(Playing Mantis)

Lost In Space, Cyclops, 1997, Playing Mantis/Polar Lights, Model No. 5031
EX $10   **NM** $15   **MIP** $20

Lost In Space, Cyclops w/ diorama and vehicle, 1998, Playing Mantis/Polar Lights, Model No. 5032
EX $10   **NM** $20   **MIP** $30

Lost In Space, Dr. Smith and Robot B-9, 1999, Playing Mantis/Polar Lights, Model No. 5019
EX $10   **NM** $20   **MIP** $30

Lost In Space, Jupiter 2, 1998, Playing Mantis/Polar Lights, Model No. 5033
EX $10   **NM** $20   **MIP** $30

(KP Photo)

Lost In Space, Jupiter 2 new box, 2000, Playing Mantis/Polar Lights, Model No. 5033
EX $15   **NM** $25   **MIP** $35

Lost In Space, Robot, 1997, Playing Mantis/Polar Lights, Model No. 5030
EX $10   **NM** $15   **MIP** $20

Michael Myers, Halloween, 2000, Playing Mantis/Polar Lights, Model No. 5095
EX $10   **NM** $20   **MIP** $30

Mummy, 1999, Playing Mantis/Polar Lights, Model No. 427
EX $30   **NM** $45   **MIP** $60

Mummy, 1999 movie version, 1999, Playing Mantis/Polar Lights, Model No. 5023
EX $15   **NM** $20   **MIP** $30

Mummy's Chariot, 1995, Playing Mantis/Polar Lights, Model No. 5003
EX $10   **NM** $15   **MIP** $20

Munsters Living Room diorama, 1997, Playing Mantis/Polar Lights, Model No. 5013
EX $10   **NM** $15   **MIP** $25

(Playing Mantis)

Mystery Machine, 2000, Playing Mantis/Polar Lights, Model No. 6808
EX $10   **NM** $15   **MIP** $20

Nosferatu, 1998, Playing Mantis/Polar Lights
EX $35   **NM** $45   **MIP** $60

Odd Job, 1999, Playing Mantis/Polar Lights, Model No. 5036
EX $10   **NM** $15   **MIP** $20

Phantom of the Opera, 2000, Playing Mantis/Polar Lights, Model No. 5027
EX $30   **NM** $45   **MIP** $60

Phantom of the Opera, bust, 1997, Playing Mantis/Polar Lights
EX $35   **NM** $45   **MIP** $60

Planet of the Apes, Cornelius, reissue, 2000, Playing Mantis/Polar Lights, Model No. 6803
EX $10   **NM** $15   **MIP** $20

Planet of the Apes, Dr. Zaius, 2000, Playing Mantis/Polar Lights, Model No. 6805
EX $10   **NM** $15   **MIP** $20

Planet of the Apes, Dr. Zira, 2000, Playing Mantis/Polar Lights, Model No. 6804
EX $10   **NM** $15   **MIP** $20

Planet of the Apes, General Ursus, 2000, Playing Mantis/Polar Lights, Model No. 6806
EX $10   **NM** $15   **MIP** $20

Predator, 1997, Playing Mantis/Polar Lights
EX $35   **NM** $45   **MIP** $60

Pumpkinhead the Metamorphosis, 1994, Playing Mantis/Polar Lights
EX $35   **NM** $45   **MIP** $60

(Playing Mantis)

Robby the Robot, Forbidden Planet, 1999, Playing Mantis/Polar Lights, Model No. 5025
EX $10   **NM** $20   **MIP** $30

Rodan, Aurora reissue, 2000, Playing Mantis/Polar Lights, Model No. 6801
EX $10   **NM** $15   **MIP** $20

Sleepy Hollow, Headless Horseman, 1999, Playing Mantis/Polar Lights, movie version, Model No. 5022
EX $5   **NM** $10   **MIP** $15

Son of Frankenstein, 1998, Playing Mantis/Polar Lights
EX $35   **NM** $45   **MIP** $60

Star Trek the Next Generation, Ambassador Spock, 1996, Playing Mantis/Polar Lights
EX $50   **NM** $65   **MIP** $75

Star Trek the Next Generation, Capt. Picard,
1992, Playing Mantis/Polar Lights
EX $25   **NM** $35   **MIP** $50

Star Trek the Next Generation, Commander Riker, 1993, Playing Mantis/Polar Lights
EX $25   **NM** $35   **MIP** $50

Star Trek the Next Generation, Counselor Troi, 1993, Playing Mantis/Polar Lights
EX $25   **NM** $35   **MIP** $50

Star Trek the Next Generation, Ferengi,
1995, Playing Mantis/Polar Lights
EX $25   **NM** $35   **MIP** $50

Star Trek the Next Generation, Geordi La Forge, 1993, Playing Mantis/Polar Lights
EX $25   **NM** $35   **MIP** $50

Star Trek the Next Generation, Gowron the Klingon, 1995, Playing Mantis/Polar Lights
EX $25   **NM** $35   **MIP** $50

Star Trek the Next Generation, Lieutenant Worf, 1992, Playing Mantis/Polar Lights
EX $25   **NM** $35   **MIP** $50

Star Trek the Next Generation, Locutus of Borg, 1994, Playing Mantis/Polar Lights
EX $25   **NM** $35   **MIP** $50

Star Trek the Next Generation, Lt. Comdr. Data, 1993, Playing Mantis/Polar Lights
EX $25   **NM** $35   **MIP** $50

Star Trek the Next Generation, Romulan,
1994, Playing Mantis/Polar Lights
EX $25   **NM** $35   **MIP** $50

The Wolf Man, 1998, Playing Mantis/Polar Lights, cold-cast resin, Model No. 5018
EX $50   **NM** $100   **MIP** $200

Titan A.E., Drej Alien, 2000, Playing Mantis/Polar Lights, Model No. 5094
EX $10   **NM** $15   **MIP** $20

Tremors, 1999, Playing Mantis/Polar Lights
EX $35   **NM** $45   **MIP** $60

Voyage to the Bottom of the Sea, Seaview Submarine, 2001, Playing Mantis/Polar Lights, Model No. 5099
EX $5   **NM** $10   **MIP** $15

Ymir, 20 Million Miles to Earth, 1990s, Playing Mantis/Polar Lights
EX $50   **NM** $60   **MIP** $70

PRECISION

Cap'n Kidd the Pirate, 1959, Precision, Captain Kidd, Model No. 402
EX $25   **NM** $63   **MIP** $125

Crucifix, Precision, Jesus Christ, Model No. 501
EX $20   **NM** $42   **MIP** $75

Fighting Blue Marlin, 1958, Precision, Model No. 101
EX $10   **NM** $20   **MIP** $35

PYRO

Der-Baron, 1958, Pyro, Model No. 166
EX $50   **NM** $80   **MIP** $125

Gladiator Show Cycle, Pyro, Gladiator, Model No. 175
EX $20   **NM** $42   **MIP** $75

Human Eye, Pyro
EX $15   **NM** $30   **MIP** $60

Indian Chief, Pyro, Model No. 281
EX $20   **NM** $45   **MIP** $80

Indian Medicine Man, 1960s, Pyro, Model No. 282
EX $20   **NM** $45   **MIP** $80

Indian Warrior, 1960, Pyro, Model No. 283
EX $20   **NM** $45   **MIP** $80

Li'l Corporal, 1970, Pyro, Li'l Corporal, Model No. 168
EX $25   **NM** $65   **MIP** $100

(KP Photo)

Rawhide, Gil Favor, 1958, Pyro, Rawhide, Model No. 276
EX $25   **NM** $53   **MIP** $100

(KP Photo)

Restless Gun Deputy, 1959, Pyro, Restless Gun, Model No. 277
EX $20   **NM** $45   **MIP** $66

Surf's Up, 1970, Pyro, Surf's Up, Model No. 176
EX $15   **NM** $32   **MIP** $44

U.S. Marshal, Pyro, Model No. 286
EX $40   **NM** $60   **MIP** $80

(KP Photo)

Wyatt Earp, 1958, Pyro, Hugh O'Brian, Model No. 278
EX $30   **NM** $75   **MIP** $110

REMCO

Flintstones Motorized Paddy Wagon,
1961, Remco, Model No. 452
EX $30   **NM** $105   **MIP** $220

Flintstones Motorized Sports Car & Trailer, 1961, Remco, Model No. 450
EX $30   **NM** $105   **MIP** $225

Flintstones Motorized Yacht, 1961, Remco, Model No. 451
EX $30   **NM** $105   **MIP** $220

REVELL

(KP Photo)

Angel Fink, 1965, Revell, Big Daddy Roth, Model No. 1307
EX $40   **NM** $105   **MIP** $175

Apollo Astronaut on the Moon, 1970, Revell, Model No. 1860
EX $115   **NM** $130   **MIP** $155

Apollo II Columbia and Eagle, 1969, Revell, Model No. 1862
EX $115   **NM** $130   **MIP** $165

Apollo II Tranquility Base, 1975, Revell, Model No. 714
EX $75   **NM** $100   **MIP** $125

Beatles, George Harrison, 1965, Revell, Beatles, Model No. 1353
EX $75   **NM** $150   **MIP** $275

Beatles, John Lennon, 1965, Revell, Beatles, Model No. 1352
EX $75   **NM** $150   **MIP** $275

Beatles, Paul McCartney, 1965, Revell, Beatles, Model No. 1350
EX $75   **NM** $150   **MIP** $250

Beatles, Ringo Starr, 1965, Revell, Beatles, Model No. 1351
EX $75　　NM $150　　MIP $250

(KP Photo)

Beatnik Bandit, 1963, Revell, Big Daddy Roth, Model No. 1279
EX $125　　NM $190　　MIP $250

Billy Carter's Pickup, 1978, Revell, Model No. 1385
EX $35　　NM $50　　MIP $65

Birthday Bird, 1959, Revell, Dr. Seuss
EX $40　　NM $150　　MIP $275

(Toy Shop File Photo)

Bonanza, 1965, Revell, Bonanza, Model No. 1931
EX $50　　NM $105　　MIP $165

(KP Photo)

Brother Rat Fink, 1963, Revell, Big Daddy Roth, Model No. 1304
EX $25　　NM $50　　MIP $75

Busby the Tasselated Afghan Spaniel Yak, 1960, Revell, Dr. Seuss
EX $50　　NM $125　　MIP $275

Cat in the Hat, 1960, Revell, Dr. Seuss, Model No. 2000
EX $45　　NM $105　　MIP $165

Cat in the Hat with Thing 1 and Thing 2, 1960s, Revell, Model No. 2050
EX $45　　NM $120　　MIP $250

Charlie's Angels Mobile Unit Van, 1977, 1:25, Revell, Model No. 1397
EX $30　　NM $40　　MIP $75

CHiPs Helicopter, 1980, Revell, Model No. 6102
EX $20　　NM $30　　MIP $40

CHiPs Kawasaki Motorcycle, 1980, Revell, Model No. 7800
EX $20　　NM $30　　MIP $40

CHiPs Z-28 Chase Car, 1980, Revell, Model No. 6228
EX $10　　NM $20　　MIP $30

Dallas Cowboys Cheerleaders Van, 1979, Revell, Snap-together, Model No. 6405
EX $10　　NM $20　　MIP $30

Dr. Seuss Zoo Kit #1, 1959, Revell, three kits: Gowdy, Tingo, Norval
EX $50　　NM $240　　MIP $440

Dr. Seuss Zoo Kit #2, 1960, Revell, three kits: Roscoe, Grickily, Busby
EX $50　　NM $350　　MIP $550

(KP Photo)

Drag Nut, 1963, Revell, Big Daddy Roth, Model No. 1303
EX $45　　NM $85　　MIP $150

Fink-Eliminator, 1965, Revell, Big Daddy Roth, Model No. 1310
EX $45　　NM $105　　MIP $225

Flash Gordon & Martian, 1965, Revell, Flash Gordon, Model No. 1450
EX $60　　NM $105　　MIP $165

Flipper, 1965, Revell, Flipper, Model No. 1930
EX $75　　NM $105　　MIP $165

G.I. Joe Attack Vehicle, 1982, Revell, Model No. 8901
EX $10　　NM $20　　MIP $30

G.I. Joe Rapid Fire Motorcycle, 1982, Revell, Model No. 8900
EX $10　　NM $20　　MIP $30

Gowdy the Dowdy Grackle, 1959, Revell, Dr. Seuss
EX $40　　NM $85　　MIP $190

Grickily the Gractus, 1960, Revell, Dr. Seuss
EX $50　　NM $135　　MIP $275

Hardy Boys Van, 1977, Revell, Model No. 1398
EX $10　　NM $20　　MIP $50

Horton the Elephant, 1960, Revell, Dr. Seuss
EX $150　　NM $210　　MIP $440

Jacques Cousteau Calypso, 1976, Revell, Model No. 575
EX $30　　NM $45　　MIP $60

Magnum P.I., 308 Ferrari GTS, 1981, Revell, Model No. 7378
EX $25　　NM $35　　MIP $50

Magnum P.I., T.C.'s Chopper, 1981, Revell, Model No. 4416
EX $25　　NM $35　　MIP $50

McHale's Navy PT-73, 1965, Revell, McHale's Navy, Model No. 323
EX $25　　NM $63　　MIP $83

Model Racer, Mr. Gasser, 1964, 1:25, Revell, Big Daddy Roth
EX $50　　NM $100　　MIP $175

Model Racer, Rat Fink, 1964, 1:25, Revell, Big Daddy Roth
EX $50　　NM $100　　MIP $175

Moonraker Space Shuttle, 1979, Revell, Model No. 4306
EX $10　　NM $20　　MIP $30

Mother's Worry, 1963, Revell, Big Daddy Roth, Model No. 1302
EX $50　　NM $100　　MIP $175

Mr. Gasser, 1963, Revell, Big Daddy Roth, Model No. 1301
EX $50　　NM $100　　MIP $175

(KP Photo)

Mr. Gasser BMR Racer, 1964, Revell, Big Daddy Roth, Model No. 3181
EX $50　　NM $100　　MIP $175

Mysterion, 1964, 1:25, Revell, Big Daddy Roth
EX $55　　NM $110　　MIP $185

(KP Photo)

Norval the Bashful Blinket, 1959, Revell, Dr. Seuss
EX $40　　NM $85　　MIP $193

Outlaw, 1962, 1:25, Revell, Big Daddy Roth
EX $50　　NM $100　　MIP $175

Outlaw w/ Robin Hood Fink, 1960s, 1:25, Revell, Big Daddy Roth
EX $50   NM $125   MIP $200

(KP Photo)

Peter Pan Pirate Ship, 1960, Revell, Model No. 377
EX $75   NM $85   MIP $110

Peter Pan, Pirate Ship, 1969, Revell, Model No. 364
EX $25   NM $60   MIP $100

Phantom & Voodoo Witch Doctor, 1965, Revell, Phantom, Model No. 1451
EX $50   NM $105   MIP $220

(KP Photo)

Rat Fink, 1963, Revell, Big Daddy Roth, Model No. 1305
EX $125   NM $200   MIP $250

Rat Fink Lotus Racer, 1964, Revell, Big Daddy Roth
EX $75   NM $125   MIP $175

Red October Submarine, 1990, Revell, Model No. 4006
EX $45   NM $60   MIP $75

Road Agent, 1960s, 1:25, Revell, Big Daddy Roth
EX $50   NM $100   MIP $175

Robbin' Hood Fink, 1965, Revell, Big Daddy Roth
EX $200   NM $325   MIP $475

Robotech Defenders Aqualo, 1984, Revell, Model No. 1148
EX $10   NM $15   MIP $20

Robotech Defenders Robot Revovery Unit, 1984, Revell, Model No. 1194
EX $25   NM $40   MIP $50

Robotech Defenders Thoren, 1984, Revell, Model No. 1150
EX $10   NM $20   MIP $30

Robotech Defenders Zoltek, 1984, Revell, Model No. 1151
EX $20   NM $30   MIP $50

Robotech Nebo, 1984, Revell, Model No. 1400
EX $10   NM $20   MIP $30

Robotech SDF1, 1985, Revell, Model No. 1143
EX $45   NM $80   MIP $125

Robotech Trigon, 1985, Revell, Model No. 1405
EX $10   NM $20   MIP $30

Robotech VF-1A Fighter, 1985, Revell, Model No. 1409
EX $30   NM $40   MIP $50

Robotech VF-1D Fighter, 1985, Revell, Model No. 1408
EX $30   NM $40   MIP $50

Robotech VF-1J Fighter, 1985, Revell, Model No. 1406
EX $30   NM $40   MIP $50

Robotech, Condar, 1984, Revell, Model No. 1152
EX $20   NM $30   MIP $45

Robotech, Decimax, 1985, Revell, Model No. 1148
EX $20   NM $30   MIP $50

Robotech, Recon Team 2 in 1, 1984, Revell, Model No. 1135
EX $20   NM $35   MIP $50

Robotech, Tactical Unit 2 in 1, 1984, Revell, Model No. 1136
EX $10   NM $15   MIP $20

Roscoe the Many-Footed Lion, 1960s, Revell, Dr. Seuss, Model No. 2004
EX $30   NM $85   MIP $190

Saint's Jaguar XJS, 1979, Revell, Model No. 6402
EX $25   NM $50   MIP $75

Scuz-Fink with Dingbat, 1965, Revell, Big Daddy Roth, Model No. 1309
EX $275   NM $350   MIP $500

Superfink, 1964, Revell, Big Daddy Roth
EX $150   NM $275   MIP $400

Surfink, 1965, Revell, Big Daddy Roth, Model No. 1306
EX $50   NM $100   MIP $175

Surfite w/ Tiki Hut, 1960s, 1:25, Revell, Big Daddy Roth
EX $50   NM $100   MIP $175

Tingo the Noodle-Topped Stroodle, 1960s, Revell, Dr. Seuss
EX $50   NM $75   MIP $185

Tweedy Pie with Boss-Fink, 1965, Revell, Big Daddy Roth, Model No. 1271
EX $200   NM $335   MIP $465

TOYBIZ

Beast, 1998, ToyBiz, Marvel Comics, Model No. 47782
EX $5   NM $10   MIP $15

Captain America, 1998, ToyBiz, Marvel Comics, Model No. 48622
EX $5   NM $10   MIP $15

Ghost Rider, 1996, ToyBiz, Model No. 48660
EX $7   NM $17   MIP $30

Hulk, 1996, ToyBiz, Model No. 48656
EX $5   NM $12   MIP $22

Onslaught, 1997, ToyBiz, Model No. 48640
EX $7   NM $12   MIP $28

Rhino, 1998, ToyBiz, Marvel Comics, Model No. 48886
EX $5   NM $10   MIP $15

Silver Surfer, 1996, ToyBiz, Model No. 48653
EX $5   NM $12   MIP $22

Spider-Man, 1996, ToyBiz, Model No. 48651
EX $5   NM $12   MIP $22

Spider-Man, with wall, 1996, ToyBiz, Model No. 48658
EX $5   NM $12   MIP $22

Storm, 1996, ToyBiz, Model No. 48659
EX $5   NM $12   MIP $22

Thing, 1996, ToyBiz, Model No. 48652
EX $5   NM $12   MIP $22

Thor, 1998, ToyBiz, Marvel Comics, Model No. 48621
EX $5   NM $10   MIP $15

Venom, 1996, ToyBiz, Model No. 48654
EX $5   NM $12   MIP $22

Wolverine, 1996, ToyBiz, Model No. 48657
EX $5   NM $12   MIP $22

MODEL KITS

PEZ

By Shawn Peterson

P EZ, thought to be the worlds first ever breath mint, got it's start well over 60 years ago in Vienna, Austria. But what is "pezzing" or better yet PEZ? The name was derived from the German word for peppermint, "pfefferminz". It was abbreviated using the first, middle, and last letter of the word, thus giving the unique and now very recognizable name of PEZ.

The candy was originally sold in small pocket size tins (much like Altoids of today) and marketed as an upscale, alternative to smoking for adults. The slogan was "smoking prohibited—pezzing allowed!" Some 20 years after the candy was invented, in 1948, a mechanical "box" was invented to dispense the candy. This invention, which looked much like a "Bic" lighter, now gave consumers a way to enjoy the candy in a "hygienic fashion."

Having moderate success in Europe with this new product, it was decided in 1952, to try and conquer the U.S. market. In less than 2 years, the company realized this was not going to be a worthwhile venture, and decided to re-invent the product, changing from an upscale adult item to a childs toy. Fruit flavors replaced the original peppermint candy and a three-dimensional cartoon head was added to the top of the dispenser. What a success this turned out to be! It combined two of kids' most favorite things; candy and a toy. This marketing shift proved to be a brilliant move, one that made PEZ a recognizable commercial brand name and an icon of pop culture.

It is hard to say how many different heads have graced the top of a PEZ dispenser. Conservative estimates put the number between 400-450 different character heads. Despite numerous requests for Elvis (among others) they have never (aside from Betsy Ross, Paul Revere, and Daniel Boone) depicted a real person, nor will they start. The company sites two main reasons: rarely do real people have interesting shaped heads; and the possibility of that person winding up in the middle of a front page controversy makes the thought less than appealing for a children's product. The company also tries to stay away from passing fads, using only characters that have stood the test of time. At any given time there are as many as 60-70 different dispensers available at local retailers not to mention the seasonal selection that appears for such holidays as Christmas, Easter, Halloween, and Valentines Day.

The dispenser itself has seen a few modest changes over the years. One of the biggest happened in the late 1980s when "feet" where added to the bottom of the

dispenser base to give it more stability when standing upright.

Although PEZ has a long history, only in the last decade has it become a hot collectable. PEZ collecting has been gathering steam since the early 1990s when the first book appeared depicting all of the known dispensers and their rarity. 1991 saw the first ever PEZ convention, with several others soon following. Today, these conventions are still going strong. Now with five annual events across the country, collectors have a chance to meet each other, buy and sell PEZ, and see rare and unusual dispensers on display. Conventions have quickly become a must-attend event for addicted collectors, drawing people from all over the United States and all over the world!

PEZ has done very little in the way of advertising, relying on impulse purchases and parents buying for

THE TOP TEN
PEZ *(Most expensive dispensers once sold at retail in the United States)*

1. Political Elephant	$5,000
2. Witch Regular	3,500
3. Pineapple	3,500
4. Make-A-Face, American card	3,400
5. Make-A-Face, German card	3,000
6. Mueslix	3,000
7. Lion's Club Lion	3,000
8. Space Trooper	2,000
9. Make-A-Face, no feet	2,000
10. Bride	1,500

their kids on a nostalgic whim. This doesn't seem like the best method but the company claims it can barely keep up with demand. No one can say for sure where this hobby will go or if the dispensers will continue to hold their value. Right now this hobby has two things in its favor: the collector demand is far surpassing the supply of vintage dispensers; and PEZ is still being produced today and can be found in almost any grocery or discount store making it available to a whole new generation of collectors. With new additions added regularly its continued success is almost assured.

TIPS

Generally a dispensers value is in the head. Age, country of origin, stem, and patent numbers can play a part but are commonly thought of as non-determining factors when assessing value. Exceptions to this regarding the stems are features such as die-cuts, advertising, or pictures, such as the witch regular. One or more of these features can actually increase the value of the dispenser. Other stem characteristics must be present in certain dispensers to complete the value and be considered correct.

And finally, resale is something you must consider. A complete, mint condition dispenser will always be easier to sell than one that has problems or is missing parts. Collectors be aware, some people have begun making and selling reproduction parts. Trust your instinct, if you think something is questionable it is better to pass than find out later you have been taken. Know what you are buying and be familiar with what a piece should look like.

Some dispensers such as Elvis and Kiss were never made by PEZ but can be found with relative ease. How can this be? When a character or person is in demand but does not exist collectors have resorted to making their own dispensers. These are known as "fan-made" or "fantasy" pieces. Most of these dispensers sell in the $25 or less range and are considered by some to be very collectable. Only knowledge, experience, and buying from a well known, reputable dealer will help to avoid having a repro or fake unknowingly passed on to you. Common reproduction parts include but are not limited to: Ringmasters mustache; goatee and earrings for the Mexican; hat badges for the Policeman and Fireman; Knight's plume; Doctor's reflector; and cape for Batman. Studying the pictures in collectors' books and going to PEZ conventions are your best sources for comparing dispensers.

2006 TRENDS

The current trend with PEZ is trends. In the fall of 2004, PEZ Candy Inc., pursued a new direction under new leadership. The idea is to follow what is current and offer dispensers that are in sync with movies and other licences of the time. The result is an exciting new direction that will see many new lines from what is arguably the best-known novelty candy maker of all time.

Currently, dispensers released in the last couple of years have seen little, if any, value beyond retail. With the addition of so many new lines and characters the "lie" of the license becomes significantly shorter and as a result, the window of opportunity to buy them at retail will also shorten. This theory leads me to speculate that some of the more recent offerings may have the potential to go up in value by becoming sought after in the secondary collectible market. Only time will tell what will become valuable.

The best advice I can give to collectors is to not buy as an investment. Buy what you like because you love it, and have FUN collecting!

Contributor: Shawn Peterson is the author of Collectors Guide to PEZ: Identification and Price Guide 2nd Edition (Krause Publications, 2003). Shawn is available upon request for book signings as well as PEZ speaking engagements in your area. He is always interested in adding to his collection; you may contact him by writing P.O. Box 571, Blue Springs, MO 64013-0571 or www.bookofpez.com

CONVENTION INFORMATION:

1. Southern California: Conventions have been held since 1994 in several different locations with different hosts. Usually meets sometime in the spring.

2. St.Louis, Mo.: First convention held in 1993 and still going strong. Meets in June. Your host is John "CoolPezman" Devlin, www.pezconvention.com, 24-hr. hotline: 314-416-0333

3. Bloomington, Mn.: First convention held in October 1996 across from the Mall of America. Now meets in August. Contact Dana and Julie Kraft at www.mnpezcon.com

4. Cleveland, Oh.: First ever PEZ convention, "Dispensor-O-Rama" held June, 1991 in Mentor, Oh. Continues to meet each July in the Cleveland area, hosted by John and Linda Gliha, www.pezamania.com

5. Stamford, Ct.: Called the "East Coast PEZ Convention," first met in April 1999 in Orange, Ct. (home of PEZ!) Now held in Stamford, Ct. Your host: Richie Belyski (editor of Pez Collectors News), www.pezcollectorsnews.com

NEWSLETTER

Published bi-monthly by Richard Belyski. For subscription rates and info write:

PEZ Collectors News
P.O. Box 14956
Surfside Beach, SC 29587

Or visit; www.pezcollectorsnews.com

BOOKS

Shawn Peterson, Collectors Guide to PEZ: Identification and Price Guide 2nd Edition (Krause Publications, 2003). Now in its second edition you can see over 600 full color photos ranging from the most common to ultra-rare dispensers and everything in between. Visit www.bookofpez.com to find out more.

PEZ

PEZ

Advertising Regular, PEZ, no feet, no head, advertising printed on side MUST be complete
NM $1000 MIP $1500

Air Spirit, PEZ, no feet, reddish triangular fish face
NM $200 MIP $250

Alpine, PEZ, 1972 Munich Olympics, no feet, green hat w/beige plume, black mustache
NM $2000 MIP $2500

Angel A, PEZ, no feet, hair and halo
NM $60 MIP $80

Arithmetic Regular, PEZ, no feet, headless dispenser w/white top, side of body has openings w/columns of numbers
NM $500 MIP $700

Arlene, PEZ, w/feet, pink head, Garfield's girlfriend
NM $2 MIP $5

Asterix, PEZ, no feet, blue hat w/wings, yellow mustache, European
NM $1000 MIP $1500

Asterix (1998 foreign issue), 1998, PEZ, head different than old
NM $3 MIP $5

Astronaut A, early 1960s, PEZ, no feet, helmet, yellow visor, small head
NM $500 MIP $600

Astronaut B, PEZ, no feet, green stem, white helmet, yellow visor, large head
NM $100 MIP $150

Baloo, PEZ, w/feet, Jungle Book
NM $12 MIP $25

Baloo, PEZ, no feet, Jungle Book
NM $20 MIP $40

Bambi, PEZ, w/feet
NM $30 MIP $50

Barney Bear, PEZ, w/feet, brown head, white cheeks and snout, black nose
NM $15 MIP $30

Barney Bear, PEZ, no feet, brown head, white cheeks and snout, black nose
NM $30 MIP $45

Barney Rubble, PEZ, Flintstones
NM $1 MIP $2

Baseball Dispenser Set, PEZ, no feet, baseball glove w/ball, bat, white home plate marked "PEZ"
NM $500 MIP $800

Baseball Glove, PEZ, no feet, brown baseball glove w/white ball
NM $125 MIP $150

Batgirl, PEZ, Soft Head Superhero, no feet, blue mask, black hair
NM $120 MIP $150

Batman, PEZ, w/feet, blue
NM $3 MIP $6

Batman, PEZ, no feet, blue cape, mask and hat
NM $75 MIP $100

Batman, PEZ, Soft Head Superhero, no feet, blue mask
NM $150 MIP $225

Betsy Ross, PEZ, no feet, dark hair and white hat, Bicentennial issue
NM $130 MIP $175

Big Top Elephant, PEZ, no feet, orange head w/blue pointed hat
NM $80 MIP $120

Big Top Elephant, PEZ, no feet, gray-green head, red flat hat
NM $90 MIP $125

Big Top Elephant With Hair, PEZ, no feet, yellow head and red hair
NM $125 MIP $250

Bob the Builder, 2002, PEZ, w/feet, four characters: Bob, Wendy, Pilchard, and Spud
NM $1 MIP $2

Bouncer Beagle, PEZ
NM $5 MIP $6

Boy, PEZ, no feet, brown hair
NM $20 MIP $35

Boy with Cap, PEZ, no feet, white hair, blue cap
NM $85 MIP $100

Bozo the Clown, PEZ, die-cut Bozo and Butch on stem, no feet, white face, red hair and nose
NM $150 MIP $200

Bride, PEZ, no feet, white veil, light brown, blond or red hair
NM $1500 MIP $2000

Bride, limited edition, 2000s, PEZ, w/feet, mail-order
NM $10 MIP $20

Brutus, PEZ, no feet, black beard and hair
NM $175 MIP $250

Bubbleman, 1990s, PEZ, w/feet, Neon, Crystal, and Glowing varieties
NM $5 MIP n/a

Bugs Bunny, PEZ, w/feet, gray head w/white cheeks
NM $2 MIP $4

Bugs Bunny, PEZ, no feet, gray head w/white cheeks
NM $5 MIP $10

Bugs Bunny, 1999, PEZ
NM $1 MIP $3

Bullwinkle, PEZ, no feet, brown head, yellow antlers
NM $200 MIP $250

Bunny, 1999, PEZ
NM $1 MIP $3

Bunny 1990, PEZ, w/feet, long ears, white face
NM $1 MIP $3

Bunny 1999, 1999, PEZ
NM $1 MIP $3

Bunny Original A, PEZ, no feet, narrow head and tall ears
NM $225 MIP $275

Bunny Original B, PEZ, no feet, tall ears and full face, smiling buck teeth
NM $275 MIP $375

Bunny with Fat Ears, PEZ, no feet, wide ear version, yellow
NM $20 MIP $25

Bunny with Fat Ears, PEZ, no feet, wide ear version, pink
NM $25 MIP $30

Camel, PEZ, w/feet, brown face w/red fez hat
NM $35 MIP $50

Candy Shooter, PEZ, red body, white grip, w/German license and double PEZ candy
NM $35 MIP $45

Candy Shooter, PEZ, black gun w/PEZ logo on stock
NM $85 MIP $135

Captain (Paul Revere), PEZ, no feet, blue hat, Bicentennial issue
NM $125 MIP $150

Captain America, PEZ, blue mask
NM $125 MIP $150

Captain America, PEZ, no feet, blue cowl, black mask w/white letter A
NM $150 MIP $175

Captain Hook, PEZ, no feet, black hair, flesh face winking w/right eye open
NM $75 MIP $100

Casper the Friendly Ghost, PEZ, die-cut
NM $165 MIP $225

Casper the Friendly Ghost, PEZ, no feet, white face
NM $125 MIP $200

Cat with Derby (Puzzy Cat), 1970s, PEZ, no feet, blue hat most valuable
NM $80 MIP $125

Charlie Brown, 1990s, PEZ, w/feet, blue cap, eyes closed
NM $45 MIP $75

Charlie Brown, 1990s, PEZ, w/feet, blue cap, smile w/red tongue at corner
NM $15 MIP $20

Charlie Brown, 1990s, PEZ, w/feet, crooked smile, blue cap
NM $1 MIP $2

Chick in Egg, PEZ, no feet, yellow chick in egg shell, red hat
NM $15 MIP $25

Chick in Egg, PEZ, no feet, yellow chick in egg shell, no hat
NM $80 MIP $125

Chip, PEZ, no feet, black top hat, tan head w/white sideburns, brown nose, foreign issue
NM $80 MIP $100

Clown, PEZ, w/feet, green hat, foreign issue (Merry Music Makers)
NM $5 MIP $10

Clown with Chin, 1970s, PEZ, no feet, long chin, hat and hair
NM $80 MIP $100

Clown with Collar, 1960s, PEZ, no feet, yellow collar, red hair, green hat
NM $60 MIP $80

Cockatoo, PEZ, no feet, yellow beak and green head, red head feathers
NM $45 MIP $75

Cocoa Marsh Spaceman, 1950s, PEZ, no feet, clear helmet on small male head, w/Cocoa Marsh embossed on side
NM $175 MIP $225

Cool Cat, PEZ, w/feet, orange head, blue snout, black ears
NM $35 MIP $60

Cow A, PEZ, no feet, cow head, separate nose
NM $75 MIP $95

Cow B, PEZ, no feet, blue head, separate snout, horns, ears and eyes
NM $60 MIP $90

Cowboy, PEZ, no feet, human head, brown hat
NM $225 MIP $275

Creature From Black Lagoon, PEZ, no feet, green head and matching stem, w/copyright
NM $225   MIP $275

Crocodile, PEZ, no feet, dark green head w/red eyes
NM $75   MIP $120

Daffy Duck, 1999, PEZ
NM $1   MIP $3

Daffy Duck A, PEZ, no feet, black head, yellow beak, removable white eyes
NM $10   MIP $15

Daffy Duck B, PEZ, w/feet, black head, yellow beak
NM $3   MIP $5

Dalmatian Pup, PEZ, w/feet, white head w/left ear cocked, foreign issue
NM $35   MIP $55

Daniel Boone, PEZ, no feet, light brown hair under dark brown hat, Bicentennial issue
NM $150   MIP $215

Dewey, PEZ, (Donald Duck's nephew) no feet, blue hat, white head, yellow beak, small black eyes
NM $20   MIP $35

Diabolic, PEZ, no feet, soft orange monster head
NM $200   MIP $250

Dino the Dinosaur, PEZ, (Flintstones)
NM $1   MIP $2

Dinosaurs, 1990s, PEZ, PEZasaurs line, four different dinosaurs, each
NM $1   MIP $2

Doctor, PEZ, no feet, white hair and mustache, gray reflector on white band, black stethoscope
NM $175   MIP $225

Donald Duck, PEZ, die-cut
NM $135   MIP $185

Donald Duck A, PEZ, no feet, blue hat, one-piece head and bill, open mouth
NM $12   MIP $25

Donald Duck B, PEZ, w/feet, blue hat, white head and hair w/large eyes, removable beak
NM $1   MIP $3

Donkey, PEZ, w/feet, gray head w/pink nose, whistlehead
NM $5   MIP $10

Donkey Kong Jr., PEZ, no feet, blond monkey face, dark hair, white cap w/"J" on it, w/box
NM $350   MIP $650

Dopey, PEZ, no feet, flesh colored die cut face w/wide ears, orange cap
NM $150   MIP $175

Dr. Skull B, PEZ, no feet, black collar
NM $10   MIP $15

Droopy Dog A, PEZ, w/feet, white face, flesh snout, black movable ears and red hair
NM $10   MIP $25

Droopy Dog B, 1992, PEZ, w/feet
NM $5   MIP $6

Duck, PEZ, no feet, brown head w/yellow beak, whistlehead
NM $30   MIP $55

Duck, PEZ, w/feet, brown head w/yellow beak, whistlehead
NM $25   MIP $50

Duckie with Flower, PEZ, no feet, flower, duck head w/beak
NM $75   MIP $125

Dumbo, PEZ, no feet, gray head w/large ears, red hat
NM $40   MIP $60

Dumbo, PEZ, w/feet, blue head w/large ears, yellow hat
NM $30   MIP $40

E.T., 2002, PEZ, w/feet
NM $2   MIP $4

Easter Bunny Die Cut, PEZ, no feet, die cut
NM $450   MIP $575

eBay, 2000, PEZ, crystal heard dispensers, set of 4
NM $40   MIP $60

Elephant, PEZ, gold or black, one-piece head
NM $3000   MIP $10000

Engineer, PEZ, no feet, blue hat
NM $100   MIP $175

Fireman, PEZ, no feet, red hat w/gray #1 insignia
NM $75   MIP $95

Foghorn Leghorn, PEZ, w/feet, brown head, yellow beak, red wattle
NM $60   MIP $85

Foghorn Leghorn, PEZ, no feet, brown head, yellow beak, red wattle
NM $75   MIP $95

Football Player, PEZ, no feet, white stem, red helmet w/white stripe
NM $100   MIP $150

Fozzie Bear, PEZ, w/feet, brown head, bow tie, small brown hat
NM $1   MIP $2

Frankenstein, PEZ, no feet, black hair, gray head
NM $180   MIP $300

Fred Flintstone, PEZ, Flintstones
NM $1   MIP $2

Frog, PEZ, no feet, yellow and green head w/black eyes, foreign issue
NM $40   MIP $50

Frog, PEZ, w/feet, yellow and green head w/black eyes, foreign issue
NM $35   MIP $45

Garfield, PEZ, w/feet, orange head
NM $1   MIP $2

Garfield w/teeth, PEZ, w/feet, orange head, wide painted toothy grin
NM $1   MIP $2

Garfield w/visor, PEZ, w/feet, orange face, green visor
NM $1   MIP $2

Giraffe, PEZ, no feet, orange head w/horns, black eyes
NM $125   MIP $200

Girl, PEZ, no feet, blond pigtails
NM $25   MIP $35

Girl, PEZ, w/feet, pigtails
NM $4   MIP $8

Golden Glow, PEZ, no feet, no head, gold stem and top
NM $80   MIP $150

Gonzo, PEZ, w/feet, blue head, yellow eyelids, bow tie
NM $1   MIP $2

Goofy B, PEZ, no feet, red hat, painted nose, removable white teeth
NM $35   MIP $50

Goofy C, PEZ, same as version B except teeth are part of head
NM $15   MIP $25

Goofy D, PEZ, w/feet, beige snout, green hat
NM $1   MIP $3

Gorilla, PEZ, no feet, black head w/red eyes and white teeth
NM $50   MIP $80

Green Hornet, PEZ, no feet, green mask and hat; two hat styles exist
NM $175   MIP $255

Groom, PEZ, no feet, black top hat, white bow tie
NM $350   MIP $500

Groom, limited edition, 2000s, PEZ, w/feet, mail-order
NM $15   MIP $25

Gyro Gearloose, 1990s, PEZ, w/feet
NM $5   MIP $8

Henry Hawk, PEZ, no feet, light brown head, yellow beak
NM $60   MIP $95

Henry Hawk, PEZ, w/feet
NM $55   MIP $80

Hippo, PEZ, no feet, green stem w/"Hippo" printed on side, foreign issue
NM $700   MIP $925

Huey, PEZ, (Donald Duck's nephew) no feet, red hat, white head, yellow beak, small black eyes
NM $20   MIP $35

Huey, Dewey, or Louie Duck, PEZ, w/feet, red, blue, or green stem and matching cap, white head and orange beak
NM $5   MIP $10

Hulk A, PEZ, no feet, dark green head, black hair
NM $30   MIP $60

Hulk B, PEZ, no feet, light green head, dark green hair
NM $25   MIP $30

Hulk B, PEZ, w/feet, light green head, tall dark green hair
NM $3   MIP $6

Hulk C, PEZ
NM $1   MIP $2

Indian, PEZ, w/feet, black hair and green headband w/feather, foreign issue (Merry Music Makers)
NM $15   MIP $25

Indian Brave, PEZ, no feet, small human head, Indian headband w/one feather, Bicentennial issue
NM $150   MIP $200

Indian Chief, PEZ, no feet, war bonnet, Bicentennial issue
NM $100   MIP $110

Indian Chief, PEZ, no feet, marbleized headress
NM $110   MIP $155

Indian Woman, PEZ, no feet, black hair in braids w/headband
NM $95   MIP $175

Jerry (Tom & Jerry), PEZ, no feet, rare variation w/brown face, pink lining in ears is removable
NM $75   MIP $125

Jerry (Tom & Jerry), PEZ, w/feet, brown face, multiple piece head
NM $8   MIP $10

Jiminy Cricket, PEZ, no feet, green hatband and collar, flesh face, black top hat
NM $180   MIP $225

Joker, PEZ, Soft Head Superhero, no feet, green painted hair
NM $125   MIP $175

Kermit the Frog, PEZ, w/feet, green head
NM $1   MIP $2

King Louie, PEZ, w/feet, brown hair and 'sideburns' over light brown head
NM $20   MIP $30

Knight, PEZ, no feet, gray helmet w/plume
NM $400   MIP $600

Koala, PEZ, w/feet, brown head w/a black nose, foreign issue, whistlehead
NM $5   MIP $10

Lamb, PEZ, no feet, white head w/a pink bow
NM $10   MIP $15

Lamb, PEZ, no feet, pink stem, white head, whistle
NM $10   MIP $25

Li'l Bad Wolf, PEZ, w/feet, black ears, white face, red tongue
NM $12   MIP $20

Li'l Bad Wolf, PEZ, no feet, black ears, white face, red tongue
NM $15   MIP $25

Lion with Crown, PEZ, no feet, black mane, green head w/yellow cheeks and red crown
NM $95   MIP $150

Lion's Club Lion, PEZ, no feet, stem imprinted "1962 Lion's Club Inter'l Convention," yellow roaring lion head
NM $2000   MIP $3000

Little Lion, PEZ, no feet, yellow head w/brown mane
NM $65   MIP $80

Little Orphan Annie, PEZ, no feet, light brown hair, flesh face w/black painted features
NM $100   MIP $160

Louie, PEZ, (Donald Duck's nephew) no feet, green hat, white head, yellow beak, small black eyes
NM $10   MIP $30

Lucy, PEZ, w/feet, black hair
NM $1   MIP $2

Maharajah, PEZ, no feet, green turban w/red inset
NM $40   MIP $60

Make-A-Face, PEZ, no card, feet, oversized head w/18 facial parts
NM $1700   MIP $2000

Make-A-Face, PEZ, American card
NM $2400   MIP $3400

Make-A-Face, PEZ, German "Super Spiel" card
NM $2000   MIP $3000

Mary Poppins, PEZ, no feet, flesh face, reddish hair, lavender hat
NM $300   MIP $500

Merlin Mouse, PEZ, no feet, gray head w/flesh cheeks, green hat
NM $20   MIP $30

Merlin Mouse, PEZ, w/feet, gray head w/flesh cheeks, green hat
NM $10   MIP $15

Mexican, PEZ, no feet, yellow sombrero, black beard and mustache, two earrings
NM $140   MIP $185

Mickey Mouse A, PEZ, no feet, black head and ears, pink face, mask w/cut out eyes and mouth, nose pokes through mask
NM $60   MIP $85

Mickey Mouse B, PEZ, no feet, painted face, non-painted black eyes and mouth
NM $85   MIP $140

Mickey Mouse C, PEZ, no feet, flesh face, removable nose, painted eyes
NM $10   MIP $15

Mickey Mouse D, PEZ, no feet, flesh face, mask embossed white and black eyes
NM $5   MIP $10

Mickey Mouse Die-Cut, PEZ, no feet, die-cut stem w/Minnie, die cut face mask
NM $120   MIP $175

Mickey Mouse Die-Cut, PEZ, no feet, die-cut stem w/Minnie, painted face
NM $200   MIP $350

Mickey Mouse E, PEZ, w/feet, flesh face, bulging black and white eyes, oval nose
NM $1   MIP $3

Mimic the Monkey, PEZ, no feet, wearing baseball cap, white eyes
NM $35   MIP $45

Miss Piggy, 1990s, PEZ, w/feet, pink face, yellow hair
NM $1   MIP $2

Miss Piggy, 1990s, PEZ, w/eyelashes
NM $10   MIP $15

Miss Piggy B, 1999, PEZ, w/feet, current version larger ears
NM $1   MIP $3

Monkey, PEZ, w/feet, tan monkey face in brown head, foreign issue
NM $10   MIP $25

Monkey, PEZ, whistle head
NM $10   MIP $25

Monkey Sailor, PEZ, no feet, cream face, brown hair, white sailor cap, whistlehead
NM $40   MIP $50

Mowgli, PEZ, no feet, black hair over brown head, Jungle Book
NM $20   MIP $35

Mowgli, PEZ, w/feet; black hair over brown head, Jungle Book
NM $5   MIP $20

Mr. Ugly, PEZ, no feet, black hair, many color variations
NM $45   MIP $60

Mueslix, PEZ, no feet, white beard, moustache and eyebrows, European
NM $2800   MIP $3000

Nermal, PEZ, w/feet, gray stem and head
NM $3   MIP $5

Nintendo, Diddy Dong, 1990s, PEZ, w/feet, yellow stem, red cap
NM $4   MIP $6

Nintendo, Koopa Trooper, 1990s, PEZ, w/feet, green stem, orange head
NM $4   MIP $6

Nintendo, Mario, 1990s, PEZ, w/feet, blue stem, red cap
NM $4   MIP $6

Nintendo, Yoshi, 1990s, PEZ, w/feet, red stem, green head
NM $4   MIP $6

Nurse, PEZ, no feet, hair color variations, white nurse's cap
NM $150   MIP $220

Obelix, PEZ, no feet, red mustache and hair, blue hat, European
NM $1500   MIP $2000

Obelix (1998 foreign issue), 1998, PEZ, head different than old
NM $3   MIP $5

Octopus, PEZ, no feet; black; orange or black head
NM $45   MIP $75

Octopus, PEZ, no feet, red head
NM $70   MIP $90

Olive Oyl, PEZ, no feet, black hair and flesh painted face
NM $175   MIP $250

One-Eyed Monster, PEZ, no feet, gorilla head w/one eye missing
NM $75   MIP $95

Orange, PEZ, no feet, orange (fruit) head w/face and leaves on top
NM $160   MIP $200

Panda A, PEZ, no feet, white head w/black eyes and ears
NM $20   MIP $25

Panda A, PEZ, no feet, yellow head w/black eyes and ears
NM $250   MIP $350

Panda B, PEZ, w/feet, white head w/black eyes and ears
NM $1   MIP $3

Panther, PEZ, no feet, blue head w/pink nose
NM $100   MIP $200

Papa Smurf, PEZ, reissue w/feet, red hat, white beard, blue face
NM $2   MIP $5

Parrot, PEZ, w/feet, red hair, yellow beak and green eyes, whistle head
NM $5   MIP $10

Pear, PEZ, no feet, yellow pear face, green visor
NM $800   MIP $1000

Pebbles Flintstone, PEZ, Flintstones
NM $1   MIP $2

Penguin, PEZ, w/feet, penguin head w/yellow beak and red hat, foreign issue, whistle head
NM $5   MIP $10

Penguin (Batman villain), PEZ, Soft Head Superhero, no feet, yellow top hat, black painted monocle, whistlehead
NM $130   MIP $175

Personalized Regular, PEZ, no feet, no head, paper label for monogramming
NM $175   MIP $250

Peter Pan, PEZ, no feet, green hat, flesh face, orange hair
NM $100   MIP $175

Peter PEZ, PEZ, no feet, blue top hat that says "PEZ," white face, yellow hair
NM $50   MIP $65

Peter PEZ, PEZ, 1990s remake w/feet
NM $1   MIP $2

Petunia Pig, PEZ, w/or without feet, black hair in pigtails
NM $25   MIP $35

Phone, PEZ
NM $2   MIP $5

Pig, PEZ, w/feet, pink head, whistlehead
NM $25   MIP $50

Pilgrim, PEZ, no feet, pilgrim hat, blond hair, hat band
NM $125   MIP $160

Pilot, PEZ, no feet, blue hat, gray headphones
NM $150   MIP $225

Pineapple, 1970s, PEZ, no feet, pineapple head w/greenery and sunglasses
NM $3000   MIP $3500

Pinocchio A, PEZ, no feet, red or yellow cap, pink face, black painted hair
NM $145   MIP $180

Pinocchio B, PEZ, no feet, black hair, red hat
NM $110   MIP $175

Pirate, PEZ, no feet, red cap, patch over right eye
NM $50   MIP $60

Pluto A, PEZ, no feet, yellow head, long black ears, small painted eyes
NM $10   MIP $20

Pluto C, PEZ, w/feet, yellow head, long painted black ears, large white and black decal eyes
NM $1   MIP $5

Pokemon, 2001, PEZ, w/feet, Pikachu, Meowth, Mew, Psyduck and Kofing
NM $1   MIP $4

Policeman, PEZ, no feet, blue hat w/gray badge
NM $60   MIP $75

Pony-Go-Round, PEZ, no feet, orange head, white harness, blue hair
NM $60   MIP $85

Popeye A, PEZ, no feet, yellow face, painted hat
NM $125   MIP $150

Popeye B, PEZ, no feet, removable white sailor cap
NM $65   MIP $100

Popeye C, PEZ, no feet, one eye painted, removeable pipe and red cap
NM $85   MIP $125

Practical Pig A, PEZ, no feet, rounded blue hat, round snout
NM $45   MIP $65

Practical Pig B, PEZ, no feet, crooked blue hat
NM $40   MIP $60

(KP Photo)

Psychedelic Eye, PEZ, no feet, decal design on stem, beige or black hands; many color variations, shown with Psychedelic Flower
NM $200   MIP $350

Psychedelic Eye (1998 limited-edition), 1998, PEZ, has 1967 copyright date
NM $10   MIP $20

Psychedelic Flower, PEZ, no feet, stem w/decal on side, many color variations
NM $225   MIP $400

Psychedelic Flower, PEZ, reproduction
NM $10   MIP $20

Pumpkin A, PEZ, no feet, green stem, carved face
NM $10   MIP $15

Pumpkin B, PEZ, black facial features
NM $1   MIP $3

Puzzy Cat, PEZ, no feet, cat head w/hat
NM $65   MIP $95

Raven, PEZ, no feet, black head, beak, and glasses
NM $60   MIP $85

Regular, PEZ, no feet, no head, stem w/top only; 1950s
NM $80   MIP $160

Regular, PEZ, no feet, no head, stem w/top only; assorted colors; 1990s issues
NM $2   MIP $3

Rhino, PEZ, w/feet, green head, red horn, foreign issue, whistle head
NM $5   MIP $10

Ringmaster, PEZ, no feet, white bow tie, white hat w/red hatband, and black handlebar moustache
NM $200   MIP $325

Road Runner A, PEZ, no feet, purple head, yellow beak
NM $25   MIP $35

Road Runner B, PEZ, w/feet, purple head, yellow beak
NM $15   MIP $20

Roman Soldier (1998 foreign issue), 1998, PEZ
NM $4   MIP $6

Rooster, PEZ, no feet, white head, comb
NM $40   MIP $65

Rooster, PEZ, no feet, yellow head, comb and wattle
NM $75   MIP $125

Rudolph, PEZ, no feet, brown deer head, red nose
NM $35   MIP $60

Sailor, PEZ, no feet, blue hat, white beard
NM $150   MIP $200

Santa, PEZ, full body stem w/painted Santa suit and hat
NM $135   MIP $200

Santa Claus A, PEZ, no feet, ivory head w/painted hat
NM $80   MIP $125

Santa Claus B, PEZ, no feet, small head w/flesh painted face, black eyes, red hat
NM $85   MIP $150

Santa Claus C, PEZ, w/feet, removable red hat, white beard
NM $2   MIP $4

Santa Claus C, PEZ, no feet, large head w/white beard, flesh face, red open mouth and hat
NM $7   MIP $12

Scarewolf, PEZ, no feet, soft head w/orange hair and ears
NM $200   MIP $250

Scrooge McDuck A, PEZ, no feet, white head, yellow beak, black top hat and glasses, white sideburns
NM $15   MIP $30

Scrooge McDuck B, PEZ, w/feet, white head, removable yellow beak, tall black top hat and glasses, large eyes
NM $5   MIP $10

Sheik, PEZ, no feet, white head drape, headband
NM $75   MIP $95

Sheriff, PEZ, no feet, brown hat w/badge
NM $125   MIP $175

Smiley, 2000s, PEZ, w/feet, Wal-Mart character exclusive
NM $1   MIP $3

Smurf, PEZ, no feet, blue face, white hat
NM $3   MIP $6

Smurf, PEZ, original, no feet, blue face, white hat
NM $10   MIP $20

Smurfette, PEZ, w/feet, blue face, yellow hair, white hat
NM $3   MIP $8

Smurfette, PEZ, original, no feet, blue face, white hat
NM $10   MIP $20

Snoopy, PEZ, w/feet, w/white head and black ears
NM $1   MIP $2

Snow White, PEZ, no feet, flesh face, black hair w/ribbon and matching collar
NM $170   MIP $220

Snowman, PEZ, no feet, black hat, white face
NM $10   MIP $15

Sourz, 2002, PEZ, w/feet, Pineapple, Blue Raspberry, Watermelon, Green Apple
NM $1   MIP $2

Space Gun 1950s, PEZ, various colors
NM $275   MIP $500

Space Gun 1980s, PEZ, red or silver, on blister pack
NM $150   MIP $200

Space Gun 1980s, PEZ, silver
NM $100   MIP $125

Space Gun 1980s, PEZ, red, loose
NM $55   MIP $85

Space Trooper, PEZ, gold
NM $1400   MIP $2000

Space Trooper, PEZ, full bodied robot w/backpack; blue, red, or yellow
NM $250   MIP $375

PEZ

Spaceman, PEZ, no feet, clear helmet over flesh-color head
NM $90   MIP $150

Sparefroh (foreign issue), PEZ, no feet, green stem, red triangle hat, coin glued on stem
NM $575   MIP $1200

Speedy Gonzales, PEZ, no feet, brown head, yellow sombrero
NM $25   MIP $35

Speedy Gonzales, PEZ, w/feet, brown head, yellow sombrero
NM $15   MIP $20

Spider-Man A, PEZ, no feet, red head w/black eyes
NM $10   MIP $15

Spider-Man B, PEZ, w/feet, bigger head
NM $1   MIP $2

Spider-Man C, PEZ
NM $1   MIP $2

Spike, PEZ, w/feet, brown face, pink snout
NM $5   MIP $6

Spook, PEZ, blue head w/horns, soft head
NM $200   MIP $250

Sports teams, 2000-present, PEZ, w/feet, professional baseball, basketball, soccer teams
NM $20   MIP $30

Stand By Me, PEZ, dispenser packed w/mini film poster and candy
NM $150   MIP $200

Stewardess, PEZ, no feet, light blue flight cap, blond hair
NM $150   MIP $225

Sylvester, PEZ, w/feet, black head, white whiskers, red nose
NM $1   MIP $2

Sylvester, PEZ, no feet, black head, white whiskers, red nose
NM $10   MIP $15

Sylvester, 1999, PEZ
NM $1   MIP $3

Taz, 1999, PEZ
NM $1   MIP $3

Teenage Mutant Ninja Turtles, PEZ, four different characters
NM $2   MIP $3

Thor, PEZ, no feet, yellow hair, gray winged helmet
NM $225   MIP $325

Thumper, PEZ, no feet, orange face, w/logo
NM $200   MIP $300

Thumper, PEZ, w/feet, no Disney logo
NM $30   MIP $50

Tiger, PEZ, w/feet, tiger head w/white snout, whistle head
NM $5   MIP $10

Tinkerbelle, PEZ, no feet, pale pink stem, white hair, flesh face w/blue and white eyes
NM $180   MIP $230

Tom A (Tom & Jerry), PEZ, no feet, gray cat head w/painted black features
NM $25   MIP $35

Tom B (Tom & Jerry), PEZ, w/feet, gray cat head w/removable facial features
NM $10   MIP $15

Truck A, PEZ, cab, stem body, single rear axle
NM $50   MIP $90

Truck B, PEZ, cab, stem body, dual rear axle and dual arch fenders
NM $40   MIP $65

Truck C, PEZ, cab, stem body, dual rear wheels w/single arch fender, movable wheels
NM $15   MIP $20

Truck D, PEZ, cab, stem body, dual rear wheels, single arch fender, nonmovable wheels
NM $1   MIP $2

Tweenies, 2002, PEZ, w/feet, 5 characters, Jake, Fuzz, Milo, Bella, and Doodles
NM $2   MIP $4

Tweety, 1999, PEZ
NM $1   MIP $3

Tweety Bird, PEZ, w/feet, yellow head
NM $1   MIP $2

Tweety Bird, PEZ, no feet, yellow head
NM $10   MIP $17

Tyke, PEZ, w/feet, brown head
NM $10   MIP $25

Uncle Sam, PEZ, no feet, stars and stripes on hat band, white hair and beard, Bicentennial issue
NM $150   MIP $200

Valentine Heart, PEZ, no feet, red stem
NM $1   MIP $2

Vamp, PEZ, no feet, light gray head on black collar, green hair and face, red teeth
NM $225   MIP $280

Vucko Wolf, 1984, PEZ, 1984 Sarajevo Olympics issue, w/feet, gray or brown face w/bobsled helmet
NM $300   MIP $500

Vucko Wolf, 1984, PEZ, 1984 Sarajevo Olympics issue, w/feet, gray or brown face w/ski hat
NM $300   MIP $500

Vucko Wolf, 1984, PEZ, 1984 Sarajevo Olympics issue, w/feet, gray or brown face
NM $200   MIP $350

Whistles, PEZ, no feet, police whistles on top
NM $25   MIP $40

Wile E. Coyote, PEZ, w/feet, brown head
NM $30   MIP $40

Wile E. Coyote, PEZ, no feet, brown head
NM $60   MIP $75

Winnie the Pooh, PEZ, w/feet, yellow head
NM $60   MIP $70

Winnie the Pooh, 2001, PEZ, w/feet, remakes of originals, Winnie, Piglet, Tigger, Eeyore
NM $1   MIP $2

Winter Olympics Snowman, 1976, PEZ, 1976 Innsbruck, red nose and hat, white head w/arms extended, black eyes, blue smile
NM $375   MIP $425

Witch 1 Piece, PEZ, no feet, black stem w/witch embossed on stem, orange one-piece head
NM $200   MIP $250

Witch 3-Piece A, PEZ, no feet, chartreuse face, black hair, orange hat
NM $70   MIP $120

Witch 3-Piece B, PEZ, w/feet, red head and hair, green mask, black hat
NM $3   MIP $7

Witch Regular, 1950s, PEZ, no feet, orange stem w/black witch graphics, no head
NM $2000   MIP $3500

Wolf Man, PEZ, no feet, black stem, gray head
NM $200   MIP $275

Wolverine, 1999, PEZ, w/feet
NM $1   MIP $2

Wonder Woman, PEZ, w/feet, red stem
NM $1   MIP $3

Wonder Woman, PEZ, no feet, black hair and yellow band w/red star
NM $5   MIP $10

Wonder Woman, PEZ, Soft Head Superhero, no feet, black hair and yellow band w/raised red star
NM $100   MIP $165

Woodstock, PEZ, w/painted feathers
NM $5   MIP $10

Woodstock, PEZ, w/feet, yellow head
NM $1   MIP $2

Wounded Soldier, PEZ, no feet, white bandage, brown hair, Bicentennial issue
NM $135   MIP $170

Yappy Dog, PEZ, no feet, black floppy ears and nose, green or orange head
NM $60   MIP $70

Zielpunkt, 1999, PEZ, w/feet, from Austrian grocery chain
NM $10   MIP $15

Zombie, PEZ, no feet, burgundy and black soft head
NM $175   MIP $250

Zorro, PEZ, no feet, black mask and hat
NM $55   MIP $65

Zorro with Logo, PEZ, no feet, black mask and hat, says "Zorro" on stem
NM $95   MIP $125

Restaurant Premiums

By Dan Stearns

Restaurant premiums or fast food toys are probably one of the easiest and genuinely most fun items to collect. Plus, because they show up at almost every garage sale or flea market, you don't even have to watch your waistline while you amass your collection.

Because so many of these toys are so common, condition is a big determiner of price. There are two price grades shown here—Excellent and Mint. Even "excellent" toys are rarely played with and have no scratches or imperfections.

Rarity is, as always, a big factor in determining price. A toy's age, popularity, and cross-collectibility play a crucial role here. A popular Disney tie-in, even a modern one, can be more valuable than older toys because of the strong Disneyana collector market.

Sometimes toys are only distributed in certain regions, making them instantly rare for the rest of us. Understandably, these toys command higher prices than the usual national campaigns.

Several years back some of these toys had to be recalled, resulting in the design of special one-piece toys for younger children, commonly called "under 3" or "U3" toys. (You'll see the "U3" designation scattered throughout the listings.) These toys are not produced for every campaign and aren't normally advertised in the in-store displays. The lower number of these toys results in prices that are typically twenty percent higher than regular toys of the same campaign.

International toys are a fun subset of restaurant premiums. Often a movie is released virtually everywhere, and there are no real differences to the toy other than some subtleties in packaging. However, every once in a while, there are items that just aren't released anywhere else. Right now, they can trade for a higher value than others, just because they're different. However, it'll take time to see if they hold value or not.

As you probably expect, McDonald's and Disney lead the way with restaurant premium toys. Although, the restaurant's most successful promotion, as you'll probably recall, was the Teeny Beanie Baby Happy Meal promotion.

2006 TRENDS

Some of the most desirable restaurant premiums are those associated with favorite movie and television characters. Also popular are those based on popular toy lines including Barbie, Beanie Babies, and Hot Wheels. Vintage premiums rule this hobby, and because of their limited quantities as compared with those available today, will likely remain on top.

Editor's Note: Unless otherwise noted, prices listed are for each piece in a set, not the entire set.

THE TOP TEN
RESTAURANT PREMIUMS *(In Mint Condition)*

1. Big Boy Nodder, Big Boy Restaurants, 1960s	$1,500
2. Black History Coloring Books, McDonald's, 1988	500
3. Big Boy Bank, large, Big Boy Restaurants, 1960s	300
4. Metrozoo Happy Meal, McDonald's, 1987	250
5. High Flying Kite Happy Meal, McDonald's, 1986	225
6. Big Boy Bank, medium, Big Boy Restaurants, 1960s	165
7. Colonel Sanders Nodder, KFC, 1960s	150
8. Big Boy Doll, Big Boy Restaurants, 1973	150
9. Transformers/My Little Pony set, McDonald's, 1985	140
10. Barbie/Hot Wheels set, McDonald's, 1990	125

ARBY'S

Babar's World Tour at the Beach Summer Sippers, 1991, Arby's, set of three squeeze bottles: orange, yellow or purple top
NM $1   MIP $5

Babar's World Tour Finger Puppets, 1990, Arby's, set of four: King Babar, Queen Celeste, Alexander & Zephyr, Pom
NM $3   MIP $5

Babar's World Tour License Plates, 1990, Arby's, set of four: Paris, Brazil, USA, North Pole
NM $1   MIP $2

Babar's World Tour Puzzles, 1990, Arby's, set of four: Cousin Arthur's New Camera, Babar's Gondola Ride, Babar, the Haunted Castle, Babar's Trip to Greece
NM $2   MIP $4

Babar's World Tour Racers, 1992, Arby's, set of three pull-back racers: King Babar, Cousin Arthur, Queen Celeste
NM $2   MIP $4

Babar's World Tour Squirters, Arby's, set of three
NM $1   MIP $3

Babar's World Tour Stampers, 1990, Arby's, set of three: Babar, Flora, Arthur
NM $2   MIP $4

Babar's World Tour Storybooks, 1991, Arby's, set of three: Read Get Ready, Set, Go, Calendar-Read and Have Fun-Read, Grow and Grow
NM $1   MIP $2

Babar's World Tour Vehicles, 1990, Arby's, set of three vehicles: Babar in helicopter, Arthur on trike, Zephyr in car
NM $2   MIP $4

Classic Fairy Tales, 1993, Arby's, set of three: Jack and the Beanstalk, The 3 Little Pigs, Hansel and Gretel
NM $4   MIP $5

Little Miss Figures, 1981, Arby's, set of eight: Little Miss Giggles, Little Miss Helpful, Little Miss Shy, Little Miss Splendid, Little Miss Late, Little Miss Naughty, Little Miss Star, Little Miss Sunshine
NM $3   MIP $10

Little Miss Stencil, 1985, Arby's
NM $2   MIP $4

Looney Tunes Car-Tunes, 1989, Arby's, set of six: Sylvester's Cat-illac, Daffy's Dragster, Yosemite Sam's Rackin Frackin Wagon, Taz's Slush Musher, Bugs' Buggy, Road Runner's Racer
NM $3   MIP $6

Looney Tunes Christmas Ornament, 1989, Arby's, set of three: Bugs as Santa, Porky Pig as toy soldier, Tweety as elf
NM $3   MIP $8

(Arby's Photo)

Looney Tunes Figures, 1987, Arby's, set of seven figures on oval base: Tasmanian Devil, Tweetie, Porky, Bugs Bunny, Yosemite Sam, Sylvester, Pepe Le Pew
NM $4   MIP $10

Looney Tunes Figures, 1988, Arby's, set of six free-standing figures: Bugs Bunny, Daffy Duck, Taz, Elmer Fudd, Road Runner, Wile E. Coyote
NM $3   MIP $6

Looney Tunes Flicker Rings, 1987, Arby's, set of four rings: Bugs Bunny, Yosemite Sam, Porky Pig, Daffy Duck
NM $20   MIP $40

Looney Tunes Fun Figures, 1989, Arby's, set of three: Tazmanian Devil as pilot, Daffy as student, Sylvester as fireman
NM $3   MIP $6

Looney Tunes Pencil Toppers, 1988, Arby's, set of six: Sylvester, Yosemite, Porky Pig, Bugs Bunny, Taz, Daffy Duck, Tweety Bird
NM $5   MIP $10

Megaphone, Minnesota Twins 25th Anniversary, 1986, Arby's
NM $1   MIP $2

Mr. Men Figures, 1981, Arby's, set of ten: Mr. Bounce, Mr. Bump, Mr. Daydream, Mr. Funny, Mr. Greedy, Mr. Mischeif, Mr. Nosey, Mr. Rush, Mr. Strong, Mr. Tickle
NM $3   MIP $10

Polar Swirl Penguins, 1987, Arby's, set of four: penguin with mask and snorkle, penguin with headphones, penguin with sunglasses, penguin with surfboard
NM $15   MIP $40

Yogi & Friends Fun Squirters, 1994, Arby's, set of three: Yogi, Cindy, Boo-Boo
NM $4   MIP $5

Yogi & Friends Mini-Disk, 1993, Arby's, set of four: Ranger Smith, Yogi, Cindy, Snagglepus
NM $1   MIP $2

Yogi & Friends Winter Wonderland Crazy Cruisers, 1995, Arby's, Yogi, Snagglepuss, Cindy
NM $4   MIP $5

BIG BOY

Action Figures, 1990, Big Boy, complete set of four: skater, pitcher, surfer, race driver
NM $2   MIP $4

Big Boy Bank, Large, 1960s, Big Boy, produced from 1966-1976, 18" tall, full color
NM $125   MIP $300

Big Boy Bank, Medium, 1960s, Big Boy, produced from 1966-1976, 9" tall, brown
NM $50   MIP $165

Big Boy Bank, Small, 1960s, Big Boy, produced from 1966-1976, 7" tall, painted red/white
NM $40   MIP $100

Big Boy Board Game, 1960s, Big Boy
NM $50   MIP $120

Big Boy Kite, 1960s, Big Boy, kite with image of Big Boy
NM $10   MIP $25

(Toy Shop File Photo)

Big Boy Nodder, 1960s, Big Boy, papier-mâché
NM $900   MIP $1500

Big Boy Playing Cards, 1960s, Big Boy, produced in four designs
NM $15   MIP $45

Big Boy Stuffed Dolls, 1960s, Big Boy, set of three: Big Boy, girlfriend Dolly, both 12" tall, and dog Nuggets, 7" tall
NM $40   MIP $80

Helicopters, 1991, Big Boy, set of plastic vehicles: Ambulance, Police, Fire Department
NM $1   MIP $3

Monster In My Pocket, 1991, Big Boy, various secret monster packs
NM $2   MIP $4

Racers, 1992, Big Boy, set of three cars: yellow, orange, purple
NM $2   MIP $5

Sport Poses, 1990, Big Boy, set of four: surfing, baseball, racing, roller skating
NM $3   MIP $5

BOB'S BIG BOY

Big Boy Doll, 1973, Bob's Big Boy, 8" plastic jointed doll holding a hamburger, made by Dakin, Model No. Dakin
NM $75   MIP $150

Big Boy Doll, 1978, Bob's Big Boy, 14" cloth boy doll wearing checkerboard outfit
NM $25　　**MIP** $30

Big Boy Lamp, 1960, Bob's Big Boy, 6-1/2" vinyl figural lamp
NM $60　　**MIP** $75

BURGER CHEF

Fun Village Funmeal Boxes, 1973-74, Burger Chef, set of 24 featuring Burger Chef characters
NM $25　　**MIP** $60

Funmeal Boxes, 1975, Burger Chef, set of 24 village buildings: Antique Shop, Bakery Shop, Barn, Beauty Shop, Bike Shop, Burger Chef, Cape Cod, Castle, Cottage (2), Colonial, Gas Station, Grocery Shop, Hardware Store, Haunted House, Pirate Ship, Ranch (2), Toy Shop, Two Story (2), Shoe Shop
NM $20　　**MIP** $30

Star Wars Funmeal Boxes, 1978, Burger Chef, set of seven: Darth Vader's Card Game, Tie Fighter, X-Wing Fighter, Land Speeder, R2D2 Droid Puppet, C3PO Droid Puppet, Flight Game
NM $25　　**MIP** $40

(Toy Shop File Photo)

Triple Play Funmeal Boxes, 1978, Burger Chef, set of 24 featuring Major League Baseball teams: Astros, A's, Braves, Brewers, Cubs, Cards, Dodgers, Expos, Giants, Indians, Orioles, Padres, Rangers, Reds, Red Sox, Tigers, Twins, White Sox, Mets, Yankees, Angels, Phillies, Pirates, Royals
NM $20　　**MIP** $90

Vacuform Race Cars, 1981, Burger Chef
NM $20　　**MIP** $30

BURGER KING

Adventure Kits, 1991, Burger King, set of four activity kits with crayons; Passport, African Adventure, European Escapades, Worldwide Treasure Hunt
NM $1　　**MIP** $3

(KP Photo)

Aladdin, 1992, Burger King, set of five figures: Jafar and Iago, Genie in lamp, Jasmine and Rajah, Abu, Aladdin and the Magic Carpet
NM $1　　**MIP** $3

Aladdin Hidden Treasures, 1994, Burger King, set of four: Jasmine, Aladdin, Abu, Iago
NM $2　　**MIP** $5

ALF, 1987, Burger King, set of four: joke and riddle disk, door knob card, sand mold, refrigerator magnet
NM $1　　**MIP** $2

ALF Puppets, 1987, Burger King, set of four puppets with records: Sporting with Alf, Cooking with Alf, Born to Rock, Surfing with Alf
NM $3　　**MIP** $8

Alvin and the Chipmunks, 1987, Burger King, set of three: super ball, stickers, pencil topper
NM $1　　**MIP** $2

Anastasia, 1997, Burger King, set of six: Bouncing Bartok, Fiendish Flyer, Fall-Apart Rasputin, Beanie Bat Bartok, Collision Course Dimitri, Anya & Pooka
NM $2　　**MIP** $5

Aquaman Tub Toy, 1987, Burger King, green
NM $3　　**MIP** $5

(KP Photo)

Archie Cars, 1991, Burger King, set of four: Archie in red car, Betty in aqua car, Jughead in green car, Veronica in purple car
NM $1　　**MIP** $3

Barnyard Commandos, 1991, Burger King, set of four: Major Legger Mutton in boat, Sgt. Shoat & Sweet in plane, Sgt. Wooley Pullover in sub, Pvt. Side O'Bacon in truck
NM $1　　**MIP** $2

Batman Toothbrush Holder, 1987, Burger King
NM $4　　**MIP** $10

(Toy Shop File Photo)

Beauty & the Beast, 1991, Burger King, set of four PVC figures: Belle, Beast, Chip, Cogsworth
NM $2　　**MIP** $5

(KP Photo)

Beetlejuice, 1990, Burger King, set of six figures: Uneasy Chair, Head Over Heels, Ghost to Ghost TV, Charmer, Ghost Post, Peek A Boo Doo
NM $1　　**MIP** $2

Bicycle Safety Fun Booklet, Burger King
NM $1　　**MIP** $2

BK Kids Club Action Figures, 1991, Burger King, set of four: Boomer, I.Q., Jaws, Kid Vid
NM $1　　**MIP** $3

BK Kids Club All-Stars, 1994, Burger King, set of five: All-Stars Boomer, All-Stars I/Q, All-Stars Jaws, All-Stars Kid Vid, All-Stars Snaps
NM $2　　**MIP** $5

BK Kids Club Bugs, 1998, Burger King, set of five: I/Q Caterpillar, Snaps Cricket, Lingo Spider, Boomer Fire Eye, Kid Vid Scorpian
NM $1　　**MIP** $3

(Burger King Photo)

BK Kids Club Coolers, 1995, Burger King, set of five: Kid Vid, blue; Jaws, turquoise; Snaps, yellow; I/Q, red; Boomer, purple
NM $2　　**MIP** $4

(Burger King Photo)

BK Kids Club Glo Force, 1996, Burger King, set of five glow-in-the-dark figures with costumes: Jaws as scubdiver, Snaps with safari gear, I/Q as surgeon, Kid Vid as astronaut, Boomer with ski gear
NM $1　　**MIP** $2

BK Kids Club Mini Sports Games, 1993, Burger King, set of four games: two catcher mitts with ball, football, basketball hoop with ball, inflatable soccer ball
NM $1　　**MIP** $2

BK Kids Club Planet Patrol, 1997, Burger King, Space Commander Jaws, I.Q.'s Planet Pacer, Boomer's Lightspeed Spacetop, Kid Vid's Glo Chopper, J.D. Shuttle Launch

NM $2　　　MIP $1

BK Kids Club Pranks, 1994, Burger King, set of five: Boomer's Joy Buzzer, Jaw's Spider, Kid Vid's Squirting Remote Control, Longo's Gumballs, I/Q's Whoopee Cushion

NM $3　　　MIP $5

BK Kids Club Transporters, 1990, Burger King, set of six: Snaps and her Camera Car, Boomer and her Super Shoe, I/Q and his World Book Mobile, Kid Vid and his SEGA Video Gamester

NM $4　　　MIP $6

BK Kids Club World Travel Adventure Kits, 1991, Burger King, set of four: Kid Vid's Mystery Treasure Map, Lingo's South American Quest, Jaw's African Adventure, Snap's Euprpoean Escapade

NM $3　　　MIP $5

Bone Age Skeleton Kit, 1989, Burger King, set of four dinos: T-Rex, Dimetron, Mastadon, Similodon

NM $3　　　MIP $6

Bonkers Crash-Apart Cars, 1993, Burger King, set of five: Toots, Jitters, Fall-apart Rabbit, Piquel, Bonkers

NM $1　　　MIP $2

Burger King Clubhouse, Burger King, full size for kids to play in

NM $15　　　MIP $35

Burger King Socks, Burger King, rhinestone accents

NM $2　　　MIP $5

Calendar "20 Magical Years" Walt Disney World, 1992, Burger King

NM $2　　　MIP $4

Capitol Critters, 1992, Burger King, set of four: Hemmet for Prez in White House, Max at Jefferson Memorial, Muggle at Lincoln Memorial, Presidential Cat

NM $1　　　MIP $2

Capitol Critters Cartons, 1992, Burger King, punch-out masks: dog, chicken, duck, panda, rabbit, tiger, turtle

NM $2　　　MIP $4

(KP Photo)

Captain Planet, 1991, Burger King, set of four flip-over vehicles: Captain Planet & Hoggish Greedily, Linka, Ma-Ti & Dr. Blight ecomobile, Verminous Skumm & Kwane helicopter, Wheeler and Duke Nukem snowmobile

NM $1　　　MIP $2

Captain Power, 1988, Burger King, set of four plastic vacuform boxes: Powerjet Xt-7, Bio-Dread Patroller, Power Base, Phantom Striker

NM $8　　　MIP $10

(Toy Shop File Photo)

Cartoon King Doll, 1972, Burger King, 16" tall; cloth

NM $20　　　MIP $30

Cartoon Network Racing Team, 1997, Burger King, set of five: Speeding Bomber, Jeff Gordon Car, Scooby Doo Car, Burger King Race Car, Stoneage Rocker

NM $1　　　MIP $2

CatDog, 1999, Burger King, set of five: Souped-up Skateboard, Crazy Catch Up, Gourmet Garbage Chaser, Key Catchin' Clock, Wacy Walker Upper

NM $1　　　MIP $3

Chicago Bull Bendies, 1994, Burger King, set of four figures: Stacey King #21, John Paxson #5, Scotti Pippen #33, BJ Armstrong #10

NM $3　　　MIP $6

(KP Photo)

Chicken Run, 2000, Burger King, set of four: Mac's Highwire Act, Ginger's Eggstream Eggscape, Rocky's Rooster Booster, Bunty Breaks Out

NM $1　　　MIP $3

Chipmunk Adventure, 1987, Burger King, set of four: bicycle licence plate; Alvin pencil topper, Alvin rubber ball, Sick 'Ems

NM $4　　　MIP $6

Christmas Crayola Bear, 1986, Burger King, set of four bears: blue, red, yellow, red

NM $5　　　MIP $8

Christmas Crayola Bear Plush Toys, 1986, Burger King, set of four: red, yellow, blue or purple

NM $3　　　MIP $6

Christmas Sing-A-Long Cassette Tapes, 1989, Burger King, set of three Christmas sing-a-long tapes: Joy to the World/Silent Night, We Three Kings/O Holy Night, Deck the Halls/Night Before Christmas

NM $2　　　MIP $4

Crayola Coloring Books, 1990, Burger King, set of six books: Boomer's Color Chase, I.Q.'s Computer Code, Kids Club Poster, Jaws' Colorful Clue, Snaps' Photo Power, Kid Vid's Video Vision

NM $2　　　MIP $4

Crayola World Travel Adventure Kits, 1991, Burger King, set of four: Kid Vid's Tresure Map, Lingo's South American Quest, Jaw's African Adventure, Snap's European Escape

NM $2　　　MIP $5

Dino Crawlers, 1994, Burger King, set of five: blue, red, yellow, green, purple

NM $1　　　MIP $2

Dino Meals, 1987, Burger King, punch-out sheets: Stegosaurus, Woolly Mammoth, T-Rex, Triceratops

NM $3　　　MIP $6

Disney 20th Anniversary Figures, 1992, Burger King, set of four wind-up vehicles with connecting track: Minnie, Donald, Roger Rabbit, Mickey

NM $3　　　MIP $5

Disney Afternoon, 1994, Burger King, set of four: Shovel, Treasure Chest, Sunshoes, Beach Balls

NM $2　　　MIP $5

Disney Collector Series Tumblers, 1994, Burger King, set of eight: Snow White, Jungle Book, Lion King, Peter Pan, Beauty and the Beast, Pinocchio, Dumbo, Aladdin

NM $2　　　MIP $4

(KP Photo)

Disney Parade Figures, 1991, Burger King, set of four: Mickey, Minnie, Donald, Roger Rabbit

NM $3　　　MIP $5

(Burger King Photo)

Dragonball Z, 2000, Burger King, set of seven: Goku, Gohan, Vegeta, Frieza, Krillin, Piccolo, Super Saiyan Goku

NM $1   MIP $3

Fairy Tale Cassette Tapes, 1989, Burger King, set of four fairy tale cassettes: Goldilocks, Jack and the Beanstalk, Three Little Pigs, Hansel and Gretel

NM $1   MIP $3

Food Miniatures, 1983, Burger King

NM $3   MIP $5

Freaky Fellas, 1992, Burger King, set of four: blue, green, red, yellow; each came with a roll of Life Savers candy

NM $2   MIP $4

Gargoyles I, 1995, Burger King, set of four: Spin to Life Goliath, Color Mutation Broadway, Gargoyles Pop-up book

NM $3   MIP $5

Gargoyles II, 1995, Burger King, set of five: Spectroscope, Sparkling Spinner, Mini-viewer, Spin-attack Broadway, Bronx Launcher

NM $4   MIP $5

Go-Go Gadget Gizmos, 1992, Burger King, set of four: Copter Gadget, Inflated Gadget, Scuba Gadget, Surfer Gadget

NM $4   MIP $6

Golden Junior Classic Books, Burger King, set of four: Roundabout Train, The Circus Train, Train to Timbucktoo, My Little Book of Trains

NM $1   MIP $2

Good Gobblin', 1989, Burger King, set of three: Frankie Steen, Zelda Zoombroom, Gordy Goblin

NM $4   MIP $6

(Burger King Photo)

Goof Troop Bowlers, 1992, Burger King, set of four total: Goofy, Pete, PJ, and Max

NM $3   MIP $4

Goofy and Max's Adventure Toys, 1995, Burger King, set of five: Water Raft, Water Skis, Goofy on Bucking Bronco, Row Boat, Runaway Car

NM $2   MIP $5

(Burger King Photo)

Hunchback of Notre Dame, 1996, Burger King, set of eight figures: Laverne, Clopin, Hugo, Frollo, Pheobus, Victor, Quasimodo, Esmerelda and Djali the Goat

NM $1   MIP $2

Hunchback of Notre Dame Puppets, 1996, Burger King, four finger: Quasimodo, Esmeralda, Gargoyle, Jester

NM $2   MIP $4

It's Magic, 1992, Burger King, set of four: Magic Trunk, Disappearing Food, Magic Frame, Remote Control

NM $1   MIP $2

Jet Age Meal, 1982, Burger King, set of three: Widebody Glider, X-2000 Gilder, Magellan Glider

NM $10   MIP $12

Kid's Choice Awards, 1999, Burger King, set of six: Slimed Again, Big Bold Blimp, Winning Wiggle Writer, Pop Goes the Rosie, Give the Winner a Hand, Heeeeere's Rosie

NM $1   MIP $3

Land Before Time, 1997, Burger King, set of six: Littlefoot, Spike, Perle, Chomper, Cera, Duckey

NM $3   MIP $6

Lickety Splits, 1990, Burger King, set of seven: Carbo Cooler, Carsan'which, Chicken Chassis, Expresstix, Flame Broiled Buggy, Indianapolis Racer, Spry Fries

NM $3   MIP $5

Lifesaver Funsters, 1992, Burger King, set of four: red, yellow, green, blue

NM $2   MIP $5

Lion King Collectible Kingdom, 1994, Burger King, set of seven figures: Mufasa, Young Nala, Young Simba, Scar, Rafiki, Ed the Hyena, Pumbaa and Timon

NM $2   MIP $3

Lion King Finger Puppets, 1995, Burger King, set of six: Mufasa, Simba, Rafiki, Pumbaa and Timon, Ed the Hyena, Scar

NM $1   MIP $2

Lion King's Timon & Pumbaa, 1996, Burger King, set of four: Timon, Pumbaa, Bug Munchin' Pumbaa, Super Secret Compass

NM $2   MIP $3

Little Mermaid Splash Collection, 1993, Burger King, set of four: Ariel wind-up, Flounder squirter, Sebastian wind-up, Urchin squirter

NM $2   MIP $4

(Burger King Photo)

M & M's, 1997, Burger King, set of five: red, orange, yellow, blue, green

NM $2   MIP $5

M & M's Minis, 1997, Burger King, set of five: Chomping Teeth Swarm, Giggle Stick, Crazy Pull-back Swarm, Secret Swarm Squirter, Scoop & Shoot Buggy

NM $1   MIP $2

Masters of the Universe Cups, 1985, Burger King, set of four: Thunder Punch He-Man Saves the Day, He-Man and Roboto to the Rescue, He-Man Takes on the Evil Horde, Spydor—Stalking Enemies of Skeletor

NM $3   MIP $5

Matchbox Cars, 1987, Burger King, set of four vehicles: blue Mountain Man 4x4, yellow Corvette, red Ferrari, Ford LTD police car

NM $5   MIP $7

Meal Bots, 1986, Burger King, paper masks with 3-D lenses: Broil Master, red; Winter Wizard, blue; Beta Burger, gray; Galactic Guardians, yellow

NM $4   MIP $8

Men in Black, 1998, Burger King, set of twelve: Squishy Worm Guy, Squirting Worm Guy, Globe Space Spinner, Building Space Spinner, Split Apart Light Up Zed, Split Apart Rotating Zed, Red Button Building Blaster, Red Button Loop Blaster, Slimed Out Kay, Slimed Out Jay, MIB Alien Detector, MIB Neitralyzer

NM $1   MIP $3

Mickey's Toontown, 1993, Burger King, set of four: Mickey and Minnie, Goofy, Donald, Chip 'n Dale; each comes with map section

NM $5   MIP $7

Mr. Potato Head, 1998, Burger King, set of five: Speedster, Hats Off, Fry Flyer, Spinning Spud, Basket Shoot

NM $1   MIP $3

Mr. Potato Head, 1999, Burger King, set of five: Fry Fighter, Gotta Get 'Em Mr. Potato Head, Fry Jumper, Smashed Potato, Light Up Mr. Potato Head
NM $1   MIP $3

Nerfuls, 1989, Burger King, set of four: Bitsy Ball, Fetch, Officer Bob, Scratch; rubber characters, interchangeable
NM $5   MIP $7

Nickel-O-Zone, 1998, Burger King, set of five: Action League Now, Hay Arnold Football, Alien Strange Pod, Cruising Skeeter, Thornberry Comvee
NM $1   MIP $3

Nightmare Before Christmas Wristwatches, Burger King, set of four different styles
NM $15   MIP $30

Oliver & Co., 1996, Burger King, set of four: Dashing Dodger, Desot Launcher, Skateway Tito, Oliver Viewer; the second Oliver & Co. set was released to coincide with home video release
NM $2   MIP $5

(Burger King Photo)

Oliver & Company, 1996, Burger King, set of four: Sneak-A-Peek Oliver, Dashing Dodger, Surprise Attack DeSoto, Skateaway Tito
NM $1   MIP $2

Pilot Paks, 1988, Burger King, set of four Styrofoam airplanes: two-seater, sunburst, lightning, one unknown example
NM $4   MIP $8

Pinocchio Inflatables, 1992, Burger King, set of four: Pinocchio, Jiminy Cricket, Monstro the Whale, Figaro
NM $3   MIP $5

Pocahontas Figures, 1995, Burger King, set of eight: Meeko, Governor Radcliffe, Pocahontas, Flit, Captain John Smith, Grandmother Willow, Chief Powhatan, Percy
NM $1   MIP $3

(Burger King Photo)

Pocahontas Pop-Up Puppets, 1996, Burger King, set of six: Peek-a-Boo

Pocahontas, Meeko's Hideout, Pampered Percy, Ruthless Radcliffe, John Smith's Lookout, Busy Body Flit
NM $1   MIP $2

Pocahontas Tumblers, 1995, Burger King, set of four: Chief Powhatan, Meeko, Governor Radcliffe, John Smith and Pocahontas
NM $3   MIP $5

(Burger King Photo)

Pokemon Mini Game Boys, 2000, Burger King, set of twelve Mini Game Boys, each with a different play function; included are over 100 removable gold or silver cartidges featuring different Pokemon Gold or Silver characters
NM $1   MIP $4

(Burger King Photo)

Pokemon: The First Movie, 1999, Burger King, set of fifty-seven toys with 151 cards; each toy came in in Pokeball with a card
NM $1   MIP $4

Pokemon: The First Movie, 1999, Burger King, set of six gold plated trading cards: No. 25 Pikachu, No. 151 Mewtwo, No. 39 Jigglypuff, No. 61 Poliwhirl, No. 06 Charizard, Togepi
NM $1   MIP $5

Pokemon: The Movie 2000, 2000, Burger King, set of twenty-four Power Cards. Each card features a a special power action
NM $1   MIP $3

Purrtenders, 1988, Burger King, set of four: Free Wheeling Cheese Rider, Flip-Top Car, Radio Bank, Storybook
NM $2   MIP $5

Purrtenders Plush, 1988, Burger King, set of four: Hop-purr, Flop-purr, Scamp-purr, Romp-purr
NM $2   MIP $4

Record Breakers, 1990, Burger King, set of six cars: Aero, Indy, Dominator, Accelerator, Fastland, Shockwave
NM $3   MIP $6

(Burger King Photo)

Road to El Dorado, The, 2000, Burger King, set of four: Swashbuckling Miguel and Prancing Altivo, Sabor Rattling Tulio and Headbutting Bull, Tzekel-Kan and Pouncing Jaguar, Bibo on the Go with Chel
NM $1   MIP $2

Rodney & Friends, 1986, Burger King, set of four plush toys: Rodney, Rhonda, Romona, Randy
NM $5   MIP $8

Rugrats, 1998, Burger King, set of five: Reptar Alive, Hero on the Move Tommy, Jumpin' Chuckle, Wind Blown Angelica, Tandem Phil & Lil
NM $1   MIP $3

(KP Photo)

Rugrats in Paris, 2000, Burger King, set of eight: Tumbling Kimi Volcano, Daktar's Descent with Lil, Susie's Super Spiral, Dil's Ooey Gooey Roller Ride, Rumbling Robot Buggy, Phil's Snail Spinner, Angelica's Princess Castle Ride
NM $1   MIP $3

Rugrats, The Movie, 1998, Burger King, set of twelve: Okeydokey Tommy; Reptar Wagon; Aqua Reptar; Monkey Mayhem; Phil & Lil: Reptar Mine!; Chuckie's Treasure Hunt; Spike to the Rescue; Shirley Lock Angelica; Dactar Glider; Scooting Susie; Baby Dil Awakened; Clip-On Tommy with Baby Dil
NM $1   MIP $3

Save the Animals, 1993, Burger King, set of four: Mammals, Birds, Reptiles and Amphibians, Fish
NM $3   MIP $5

(Burger King Photo)

Scooby Doo, 1996, Burger King, set of five: Scrappy-Doo, Scooby and Shaggy, Scooby Coffin, Scoby-Doo, Mystery Machine

NM $1   MIP $3

(KP Photo)

Scooby-Doo and the Alien Invaders, 2000, Burger King, set of eight: Roll-Around Alien, Clip n' Glow Scooby-Doo, Scared Silly Shaggy, Fright in Glowing Armor, Speakin' Scooby, Alien Attack Mystery Machine, Scooby-Doo and Shaggy's Alienship Adventure, Scramblin' Scooby-Doo

NM $1   MIP $3

Sea Creatures, 1989, Burger King, set of four terrycloth wash mitts: Stella Starfish, Dolly Dolphin, Sammy Seahorse, Ozzie Octopus

NM $2   MIP $3

Silverhawks, 1987, Burger King, set of four: Sticker, Name Plate, Decoder Ring, Pencil Topper

NM $5   MIP $10

Simpsons Cups, 1991, Burger King, set of four

NM $1   MIP $2

Simpsons Dolls, 1990, Burger King, set of five soft plastic dolls: Bart, Homer, Lisa, Marge, Maggie

NM $2   MIP $4

(Burger King Photo)

Simpsons Figures, 1991, Burger King, set of five: Bart with backpack, Homer with skunk, Lisa with saxaphone, Marge with birds, Maggie with turtle

NM $2   MIP $5

Small Soldiers, 1998, Burger King, set of twelve: Chip Hazard, Slamfist Soft 'n Cuddly, Rip Roarin' Kip Killigan, Butch's Battle, Bobbling Insaniac, Levitating Lens Ocula, Morning Brake Brick Bazooka, Nick Nitro, Freedom Firing Archer, Laughing

Insaniac, Boulder Blasting Punchit & Scratchit, Crawling Link Static

NM $1   MIP $3

Spacebase Racers, 1989, Burger King, set of five plastic vehicles: Moon Man Rover, Skylab Cruiser, Starship Viking, Super Shuttle, Cosmic Copter

NM $2   MIP $4

Spacebase Racers, 1989, Burger King, set of four: Super Shuttle, Moonman Rover, Starship Viking, Cosmic Copter

NM $5   MIP $10

Super Hero Cups, 1984, Burger King, set of four cups with figural handles: Batman, Wonder Woman, Darkseid, Superman

NM $4   MIP $8

Super Powers, 1987, Burger King, set of four: Superman coin, Batman toothbrush holder, Aquaman toy, Super Powers door nameplate

NM $7   MIP $15

(KP Photo)

Teenage Mutant Ninja Turtles Bike Gear, 1993, Burger King, set of eleven: pouch, horn, water bottle, four spike buttons, three license plates

NM $3   MIP $5

Teenage Mutant Ninja Turtles Poster, 1991, Burger King

NM $2   MIP $4

Teenage Mutant Ninja Turtles Rad Badges, 1990, Burger King, set of six: Michaelangelo, Leonardo, Raphael, Donatello, Heroes in a Half Shell, Shredder

NM $3   MIP $5

Teletubbies, 1999, Burger King, set of six: Laa-Laa, Tinky Winky, Dipsy, Po, Bunny, Noo-Noo

NM $1   MIP $3

Thundercats, 1986, Burger King, set of four: cup/bank, Snarf strawholder, light switch plate, secret message ring

NM $3   MIP $8

Toonsylvania, 1998, Burger King, set of five: Gurney Getaway, Phil's Teddy Cruiser, Vic's Walkaway Bride, Monster Maker, Screaming Screetch

NM $1   MIP $3

Top Kids, 1993, Burger King, set of four spinning tops with figural heads: Wheels, Kid Vid, Jaws, Boomer

NM $1   MIP $2

Toy Story, 1995, Burger King, set of six: Hopping Mr. Potato Head, Woody, Action Wing Buzz, Racing R.C. Car, Squash 'N Go Rex, Green Army Men Recon Squad

NM $2   MIP $4

(Burger King Photo)

Toy Story, 1996, Burger King, set of eight: Stroll 'n Scope Lenny, Jawbreaker Scud, Speedy Deposit Hamm, Round 'em Up Woody, Spin-Top Bo Peep, Blast-away Buzz, Spaced Out Alien, Slinky Dog

NM $2   MIP $3

(Burger King Photo)

Toy Story Puppets, 1995, Burger King, set of four: Woody, Buzz Lightyear, Rex, Hamm

NM $2   MIP $3

Toy Story Talking Puppets, 1995, Burger King, set of four: R.C. Racer, Talking Woody, Talking Buzz

NM $3   MIP $5

Tricky Treaters Boxes, 1989, Burger King, Monster Manor, Creepy Castle, Haunted House

NM $1   MIP $3

Tricky Treaters Figures, 1989, Burger King, set of three PVC figures: Frankie Steen, Gourdy Goblin, Zelda Zoom Broom

NM $3   MIP $10

Trolls Dolls, 1993, Burger King, set of four Kids Club characters with neon hair: Snaps, I.Q. Jaws, Kid Vid

NM $1   MIP $2

Universal Monsters, 1997, Burger King, set of four: Wolf Man, Frankenstein, Dracula, Creature

NM $2   MIP $4

(KP Photo)

Viva Rock Vegas, 2000, Burger King, set of four: Puppy Dino Breaks Out, The Great Gazoo's Close Encounter, Fred's Two-Heel Drive, Bronto King Dine & Drive

NM $1   MIP $2

Watermates, 1991, Burger King, set of four: Lingo's Jet Ski, Snaps in Boat, Wheels on raft, I.Q. on dolphin

NM $1   MIP $2

Wild Wild West, 1999, Burger King
    NM $1   **MIP** $3

Z-bots, 1994, Burger King, set of five: Bugeye, Buzzsaw, Jawbreaker, Skyviper, Turbine
    NM $2   **MIP** $5

CARL'S JR.

50th Anniversary, 1991, Carl's Jr., set of four: Happy Star baseball, Happy Star plastic puzzle, Cruisin booklet, Groovy 60's jigsaw puzzle
    NM $3   **MIP** $5

Addams Family Figure, 1993, Carl's Jr., set of five: Thing pencil topper, Lurch stamper, Cousin Itt Bubbles, The Addams Family Mansion and Stickers
    NM $2   **MIP** $5

Camp California, 1992, Carl's Jr., set of four: Bear Squirter, Lil' Bro Disk, Mini Volleyball, Spinner; similar to set issued by Hardee's
    NM $3   **MIP** $5

Camping with Woody Woodpecker, 1991, Carl's Jr., set of two: Andy Panda container, pen knife utensil kit
    NM $5   **MIP** $10

Fender Bender 500, 1990, Carl's Jr., set of five: Yogi and Boo Boo, Huckleberry Hound and Snagglepuss, Magilla Gorilla and Wally Gator, Quick Draw McGraw and Baba Looey, Dick Dasterdly and Muttley; also issued by Hardee's
    NM $3   **MIP** $5

Life Savers Roll 'Em, 1990, Carl's Jr., set of five: Pineapple, Cherry, Orange, Lemon, Lime
    NM $4   **MIP** $8

Life Savers Roll 'Em, 1995, Carl's Jr., set of five: Pineapple, Cherry, Orange, Lemon, Lime
    NM $1   **MIP** $2

Muppet Parade of Stars, 1995, Carl's Jr., set of four: Miss Piggy, Kermit Gonzo, Fozzy
    NM $4   **MIP** $6

Starnaments, 1990, Carl's Jr., set of seven: Yellow star, Reindeer star, Snowman star, Elf Star, Chimney Sweep star, Toy Soldier star
    NM $4   **MIP** $6

Starnaments, 1991, Carl's Jr., set of four: Anniversary star, Moose star, Holly star, Twinkle star
    NM $4   **MIP** $6

Starnaments, 1992, Carl's Jr., set of five: Angel star, Mouse star, Toy Soldier star, Caroler star, Snow star
    NM $4   **MIP** $6

CHICK-FIL-A

Adventures in Odyssey Books, 1991, Chick-Fil-A, set of seven: Mike Makes Right, The Treasure of La Monde, Isaac the Courageous, All's Well with Boswell, A Matter of Obedience, Last Great Adventure of Summer
    NM $2   **MIP** $4

Adventures in Odyssey Cassette Tapes, 1993, Chick-Fil-A, set of six: The Ill-Gotten Deed, This is Chad Pearson?, Wishful Thinking, A Test for Robin, Suspicious Minds, Father's Day
    NM $3   **MIP** $6

On the Go, 1993, Chick-Fil-A, set of six foam vehicles: car, airplane, train, truck, boat, helicopter
    NM $1   **MIP** $2

Wonderful World of Kids, 1995, Chick-Fil-A
    NM $2   **MIP** $5

DAIRY QUEEN

Circus Train, 1994, Dairy Queen
    NM $4   **MIP** $5

Dennis the Menace, 1993, Dairy Queen, set of four: Dennis in fire truck, Margaret in astronaut suit, Ruff in dinosaur costume, Joey in race car
    NM $4   **MIP** $6

Dennis the Menace, 1993, Dairy Queen, set of four: Dennis, Margaret, Joey, Ruff; each cup featured images of individual character and a 3-D molded plastic cup lid
    NM $4   **MIP** $6

Funbunch Flyer, Dairy Queen, each featured a different animal with the Dairy Queen logo
    NM $3   **MIP** $5

Holiday Bendies, 1993, Dairy Queen, set of four: Santa with open eyes, Santa with closed eyes, Reindeer with bell, Reindeer with scarf
    NM $3   **MIP** $5

Rock-A-Doodles, 1992, Dairy Queen, set of six: Chanticleer, Patou, Edmund, Peepers, Peepers, The Grand Duke of Owl
    NM $6   **MIP** $10

Rockin' Toppers, 1993, Dairy Queen, set of four pencil toppers: blue, yellow, green, red; rubber toppers with clingy surface allowing them to walk down walls
    NM $1   **MIP** $2

Supersaurus Puzzles, 1993, Dairy Queen, set of three
    NM $2   **MIP** $3

Tom and Jerry figures, 1993, Dairy Queen, set of six: Tom Squirter, Jerry Squirter, Tom Summer Cruiser, Jerry Summer Cruiser, Tom Stamper, Jerry Stamper
    NM $4   **MIP** $6

DENNY'S

Dino-Makers, 1991, Denny's, set of six: including blue dino, purple elephant, orange bird
    NM $1   **MIP** $2

(Denny's Photo)

Flintstones Dino Racers, 1991, Denny's, set of six: Fred, Bamm-Bamm, Dino, Pebbles, Barney, Wilma
    NM $3   **MIP** $6

(Denny's Photo)

Flintstones Fun Squirters, 1991, Denny's, set of six: Fred with telephone, Wilma with camera, Dino with flowers, Bam Bam with soda, Barney, Pebbles
    NM $2   **MIP** $4

Flintstones Glacier Gliders, 1990, Denny's, set of six: Bamm-Bamm, Barney, Fred, Dino, Hoppy, Pebbles
    NM $2   **MIP** $4

Flintstones Mini Plush, 1989, Denny's, set of four, in packages of two: Fred/Wilma, Betty/Barney, Dino/Hoppy, Pebbles/Bamm-Bamm
    NM $2   **MIP** $4

Flintstones Rock 'n Rollers, 1990, Denny's, set of six: Fred with guitar, Barney with sax, Bam Bam, Dino with piano, Elephant, Pebbles
    NM $3   **MIP** $6

Flintstones Stone-Age Cruisers, 1991, Denny's, set of six: Fred in green car, Wilma in red car, Dino in blue car, Pebbles in purple bird, Bam Bam in orange car, Barney in yellow car with sidecar
    NM $2   **MIP** $4

Flintstones Vehicles, 1990, Denny's, set of six: Fred, Wilma, Pebbles, Dino, Barney, Bamm-Bamm
    NM $2   **MIP** $4

Jetsons Crayon Fun Game, Denny's, set of six booklets with crayon game: George in Leisurly George, Jane in Jane Gets Decorated, Judy in Dream Date, Elroy What a Sport, Astro in Every Dog has his Daydream, Rosie in I Need Some Space
    NM $2   **MIP** $4

Jetsons Game Packs, 1992, Denny's, set of six: George, Elroy, Judy, Astro, Rosie, Jane
    NM $2   **MIP** $4

Jetsons Go Back to School, 1992, Denny's, set of six school tools: mini dictionary, folder, message board, pencil and topper, pencil box, triangle and curve
    NM $2   **MIP** $4

Jetsons Puzzle Ornaments, 1992, Denny's, set of six: Saturn with George, Earth with Jane, Jupiter with Judy, Mars with Elroy, Moon with Astro, Neptune with Rosie
    NM $2   **MIP** $4

Jetsons Space Balls (Planets), 1992, Denny's, set of six: Jupiter, Neptune, Earth, Saturn, Mars, glow-in-the-dark Moon
    NM $2   **MIP** $4

Jetsons Space Cards, 1992, Denny's, set of five: Spacecraft, Phenomenon, Astronomers, Constellations, Planets
NM $2   MIP $4

Jetsons Space Travel Coloring Books, 1992, Denny's, set of six books: each with four crayons
NM $2   MIP $4

DOMINO'S PIZZA

(KP Photo)

Noids, 1987, Domino's Pizza, set of seven figures: Boxer, Clown, He Man, Holding Bomb, Holding Jack Hammer, Hunchback, Magician
NM $2   MIP $4

Quarterback Challenge Cards, 1991, Domino's Pizza, pack of four cards
NM $1   MIP $2

HARDEE'S

Apollo 13, 1995, Hardee's
NM $2   MIP $5

Beach Bunnies, 1989, Hardee's, set of four: girl with ball, boy with skateboard, girl with skates, boy with frisbee
NM $2   MIP $4

California Raisins, 1987, Hardee's, set of four: dancer with blue and white shoes, singer with mike, sax player, raisin with sunglasses
NM $2   MIP $8

California Raisins, 1988, Hardee's, set of six: Waves Weaver, F.F. Strings, Captain Toonz, Rollin' Rollo, Trumpy Tru-Note, S.B. Stuntz
NM $2   MIP $4

California Raisins, 1991, Hardee's, third set: Alotta Stile in pink boots, Anita Break with package under her arm, Benny bowling, Buster with skateboard
NM $2   MIP $6

California Raisins, 1991, Hardee's, set of four: Berry, Anita Break, Alotta Stile, Buster
NM $3   MIP $5

California Raisins Plush, 1988, Hardee's, set of four: lady in yellow shoes, dancer in yellow hat, with mike in white shoes, in sunglasses with orange hat; each 6" tall
NM $3   MIP $6

Camp California, 1993, Hardee's, set of four: Bear Squirter, Lil' Bro Disk, Mini Volleyball, Spinner; similar to set issued by Carl's Jr.
NM $3   MIP $5

Days of Thunder Racers, 1990, Hardee's, set of four cars: Mello Yello #51, Hardee's #18 orange, City Chevrolet #46, Superflo #46 pink/white
NM $3   MIP $6

Dinosaur in My Pocket, 1993, Hardee's, set of four: Stegosaurus, Triceratops, Bronotsaurus, Tyrannosaurus
NM $2   MIP $5

Disney's Animated Classics Plush Toys, Hardee's, Pinocchio, Bambi
NM $3   MIP $5

Fender Bender 500, 1990, Hardee's, set of five: Yogi and Boo Boo, Huckleberry Hound and Snagglepuss, Magilla Gorilla and Wally Gator, Quick Draw McGraw and Baba Looey, Dick Dasterdly and Muttley; also issued by Carl's Jr.
NM $2   MIP $3

Finger Crayons, 1992, Hardee's, set of four: two Crayons included in each package; not marked Hardee's
NM $2   MIP $3

Flintstones First 30 Years, 1991, Hardee's, set of five: Fred with TV, Barney with grill, Pebbles with phone, Dino with jukebox, Bamm Bamm with pinball
NM $3   MIP $6

(KP Photo)

Food Squirters, 1990, Hardee's, set of four: cheeseburger, hot dog, shake, fries
NM $2   MIP $4

Ghostbuster Beepers, 1989, Hardee's, set of four: red, white, black, gray
NM $10   MIP $12

Gremlin Adventures, 1989, Hardee's, set of five book and record sets: Gift of the Mogwai, Gismo & the Gremlins, Escape from the Gremlins, Gremlins Trapped, The Late Gremlin
NM $2   MIP $4

Halloween Hideaways, 1989, Hardee's, set of four: goblin in blue cauldron, ghost in yellow bag, cat in pumpkin, bat in stump
NM $3   MIP $6

Hardee's Racer, Hardee's, blue or green
NM $4   MIP $6

Home Alone 2, 1992, Hardee's, set of four cups: Kevin, The Pigeo Lady, Marv, Harry
NM $1   MIP $2

Homeward Bound, Hardee's, set of five: Chance, Riley, Sassy, Delilah, Shadow
NM $2   MIP $5

Kazoo Crew Sailors, 1991, Hardee's, set of four: bear, monkey, rabbit, rhino
NM $1   MIP $2

Little Little Golden Books, 1987, Hardee's, set of four: The Poky Little Puppy, Little Red Riding Hood, The Three Little Pigs, The Little Red Hen
NM $5   MIP $7

Little Little Golden Books, 1988, Hardee's, set of four: The Little Red Caboose, The Three Bears, Old MacDonald Had a Farm, Three Little Kittens
NM $2   MIP $4

(KP Photo)

Marvel Super Heroes, 1990, Hardee's, set of three: She Hulk, Hulk, Captain America, Spider-Man
NM $3   MIP $6

Muppet Christmas Carol Finger Puppets, 1994, Hardee's, set of four: Miss Piggy, Kermit, Gonzo, Fozzy Bear
NM $3   MIP $5

Nicktoons, 1994, Hardee's, set of eight: Ren, Stimpy, Angelica Pickles, Tommy Pickles, Porkchop, Doug Funnie, Rocko, Spunky
NM $4   MIP $6

Pound Puppies, 1986, Hardee's, set of four: black, white with black, tan with black, gray with black
NM $5   MIP $10

Pound Puppies and Pur-r-ries, 1987, Hardee's, set of four: white cat with gray stripes, brown cat, gray bulldog, Damlatian
NM $5   MIP $10

Shirt Tales Plush Dolls, Hardee's, set of five: Bogey, Pammy, Tyg, Digger, Rick; each 7" tall
NM $3   MIP $6

Smurfin' Smurfs, 1990, Hardee's, set of four: Papa Smurf with red board, boy with orange board, girl with purple board, dog with blue board
NM $2   MIP $4

(KP Photo)

Smurfs figures, 1987, Hardee's, Hardee's issued over 100 Smurfs in this promotion
NM $3   MIP $5

Speed Bunnies, 1994, Hardee's, set of four: Cruiser, Dusty, Sunny, Stretch
NM $2   MIP $4

Super Bowl Cloisonné Pins, 1991, Hardee's, set of twenty-five NFL Super Bowl pins
NM $2   MIP $6

Swan Princess, 1994, Hardee's, set of four: Prince Derek, Princess Odette/Swan, Jean-Bob, Puffin, Rothbart
NM $3   MIP $5

Tang Mouth Figures, 1989, Hardee's, set of four: Lance, Tag, Flap, Awesome Annie
NM $2   MIP $4

Waldo and Friends Holiday Ornaments, 1991, Hardee's, in sets of three: Waldo with Woof, Waldo Watchers, Snowman; Waldo with camping gear, Wenda, Woof; Reindeer in sleigh, Wizard, Waldo with books
NM $3   MIP $5

Waldo's Straw Buddies, 1990, Hardee's, set of four: Waldo, Wenda, Wizard, Woof
NM $2   MIP $3

Waldo's Travel Adventure, 1992, Hardee's, set of four: Adventure Travel Journal, Postcards, Fold 'N Solve Travel Pictures, Space Puzzle
NM $2   MIP $3

X-Men, 1995, Hardee's, set of three, in sets of two: Cyclops vs. Commando; Phantasia vs. Storm; The Blob vs. Wolverine; Rogue vs. Wolverine
NM $3   MIP $6

INTERNATIONAL HOUSE OF PANCAKES

Pancake Kid dolls, 1992, International House of Pancakes, set of three cloth dolls: Bonnie Blueberry, Susie Strawberry, Chocolate Chip Charlie
NM $7   MIP $10

Pancake Kids, 1991, International House of Pancakes, set of ten: Cynthis Cinnamon Apple, Susie Strawberry, Bonnie Blueberry, Harvey Harvest, Betty Buttermilk, Frenchy, Rosana Banana Nut, Peter Potato, Von der Gus
NM $4   MIP $6

Pancake Kids Cruisers, 1993, International House of Pancakes, set of eight: Von der Gus, Bonnie Blueberry, Susie Strawberry, Harvey Harvest, Chocolate Chip Charlie, Frenchy, Cynthia Cinnamon Apple, Betty Buttermilk
NM $4   MIP $6

KENTUCKY FRIED CHICKEN

Alvin and the Chipmunks, 1991, Kentucky Fried Chicken, Canadian issues; Alvin and Theodore
NM $3   MIP $5

Alvin and the Chipmunks, 1992, Kentucky Fried Chicken, Canadian issues; Alvin and Simon
NM $2   MIP $4

(KP Photo)

Animorphs, 1998, Kentucky Fried Chicken, set of five: Animorphs Puzzle Cube, DNA Transfer Cards, Animorphing Box, Tobias Hawk Glider, Thought Speak Revealer
NM $2   MIP $3

(KP Photo)

Beakman's World, 1998, Kentucky Fried Chicken, set of six: Lester Reverser, Penguin TV, Optical Illusion Top, Diver Don, Beakman's Balancer, Dancing Liza
NM $2   MIP $3

Carmen Sandiego, 1997, Kentucky Fried Chicken, set of six: Jr. Sleuth Pocket Pack, Carmen's Mystery Decoder, Carmen's World Map Puzzle, Carmen's Breakaway Escape Care, Carmen's Undercover Case with Stickers, Magic Answer Globe
NM $2   MIP $3

Colonel Sanders Figure, 1960s, Kentucky Fried Chicken, 9" tall
NM $35   MIP $50

Colonel Sanders Nodder, 1960s, Kentucky Fried Chicken, 7" tall; papier-mâché
NM $50   MIP $150

Colonel Sanders Nodder, 1960s, Kentucky Fried Chicken, 7" tall; plastic
NM $15   MIP $40

Cool Summer Stuff featuring Chester Cheetah, 1996, Kentucky Fried Chicken, set of five: Fast Flyin' Disk, Spotted Summer Shades, Mini Wrist-Pack, Totally Fun Visor, Inflatable Wobble Ball
NM $2   MIP $3

(KP Photo)

Extreme Ghostbusters, 1997, Kentucky Fried Chicken, set of six: Haunted Cube, Ghost Trap Challenge, Screamin' Scrambler, Ecto1 Haunted Hauler, Ghostbusters Keychain Keeper, Slimer Squirter
NM $2   MIP $3

Garfield Catmobiles, 1996, Kentucky Fried Chicken, set of six: Arlene finger puppet, Pookie finger puppet, Nermal Freewheeler, Jon Freewheeler, Garfield Pullback, Odie Pullback
NM $2   MIP $3

Garfield Racers, 1996, Kentucky Fried Chicken, set of six
NM $2   MIP $4

Ghostly Glowing Squirters, 1996, Kentucky Fried Chicken, set of six: Casper, Spooky, Stretch, Fatso, Poil, Stinkie
NM $2   MIP $3

Giga Pets, 1997, Kentucky Fried Chicken, set of four: Digipooch, Cyberkitty, Micropup, Bitty Kitty; over the counter promotion
NM $2   MIP $3

Jim Henson's Scary Scary Monsters, 1999, Kentucky Fried Chicken, set of five: Flip-A-Mungo, Super Stretch Norbert, Zuzu Zoomer, Monster Shoelace Munchers, Scary Scary Stick-Ons
NM $2   MIP $3

Koosh, 1995, Kentucky Fried Chicken, set of three: Zipper Pull, Bookmark, Pencil Topper
NM $2   MIP $3

Linkbots, 1995, Kentucky Fried Chicken, set of six Transformers
NM $2   MIP $3

Marvel Super Heroes, 1997, Kentucky Fried Chicken, set of six: Spider-Man Symbol Clip, Invisible Woman Escape Launcher, Incredible Hulk Pencil Twirler, Spider-Man Wall Walker, Fantastic Four Terra Craft, Wolverine Press 'n Go
NM $2   MIP $3

Masked Rider to the Rescue, 1997, Kentucky Fried Chicken, set of six: Masked Rider Super Gold, Magno the Super Car, Press & Go Super Chopper, Glow-in-the-Dark X-Ray Cyclopter, Ecto Viewer Wrist Band, Bump & Go Ferbus
NM $2   MIP $3

Matchbox, 1995, Kentucky Fried Chicken, set of six: BMW, Ambulance, Fire Engine, Mustang, Jeep, Ferrari
NM $2   MIP $3

(KP Photo)

NCAA March Madness, 1999, Kentucky Fried Chicken, set of three: 2-Hoop Game, Wacky Wrist Toss, Final Four Basketball
NM $2   MIP $3

(KP Photo)

Pokémon, 1998, Kentucky Fried Chicken, set of six: Pokémon Monster Blocks, Go Pokémon Card Game, Pokémon Monster Matcher, Pokémon Tattoos, Ivysaur Squirter, Pikachu Treasure Keeper

NM $2   **MIP** $3

Pokémon Beanbags, 1998, Kentucky Fried Chicken, set of four: Seel, Vulpix, Dratini, Zubat; over-the-counter promotion

NM $2   **MIP** $5

(KP Photo)

Secret Files of the Spy Dogs, 1999, Kentucky Fried Chicken, set of five: The Evil Cat Astrophe, Fidgety Scribble, Mitzy Rolling Stamper, Eye Popping Space Slug, Agent Ralph's Marble Game

NM $2   **MIP** $3

(KP Photo)

SI for Kids, 1998, Kentucky Fried Chicken, set of four: Dunk It In Fun Book, Slam Dunk! Flipbook, Kick it in Fun Book, Kick! Flipbook

NM $2   **MIP** $3

(KP Photo)

Slimamander, 1998, Kentucky Fried Chicken, set of six: Slimamander Wrist Squirter, Slimamander's Glowing Goo, Slimamander and Leap the Frog Tattoos, Leap the Frog Launcher, Slimamander Bubble Wand, Slimamander Spraying Top

NM $2   **MIP** $3

Timon and Pumbaa's World of Bugs, 1997, Kentucky Fried Chicken, set of six: Snail Snackin' Timon, Bug Munchin' Pumbaa, Out-to-Lunch Timon,

Hawaiian Luau Pumbaa, Jungle River-Riding Timon, Bug Bath Pumbaa

NM $2   **MIP** $3

Treeples, 1999, Kentucky Fried Chicken, set of six: Dress-Up Rachel, Stevie's Acorn Searcher, Tangled Treeples, Othello Yo-Yo, Miranda's Banana-mated Theater, Linky Lurker

NM $2   **MIP** $3

Ultimate Eekstravaganza, 1996, Kentucky Fried Chicken, set of five: Eek! Balancing Act, Sharky's Dog House Launcher, Ka-Boooom! Annabelle, Cool Moves Doc, Kutler Copter

NM $2   **MIP** $3

(KP Photo)

Wallace & Gromit, 1998, Kentucky Fried Chicken, set of six: The Wrong Trousers, Gromit's Rollalong Sidecar, Wallace Bendable, Wallace & Gromit Character Card Set, Sheep-on-a-String, Blinking Feathers McGraw

NM $2   **MIP** $3

(KP Photo)

Winter Wonderpals, 1999, Kentucky Fried Chicken, set of five: Wallace the Walrus Paper Puncher, Roley Poley Polar Ball, Sippy the Penguin Play Straw, Slick the Sled Dog Igloo Launcher, Howl E. Wolf

NM $2   **MIP** $4

WWF Stampers, Kentucky Fried Chicken, set of four: Canadian issues

NM $2   **MIP** $4

LEE'S FRIED CHICKEN

Cartoon Viewers, 1980s, Lee's Fried Chicken, set of six: Mighty Mouse, Woody Woodpecker, Popeye, Superman, Bugs Bunny, Porky Pig

NM $20   **MIP** $50

LONG JOHN SILVER'S

Adventure on Volcano Island, 1991, Long John Silver's, paint with water activity book

NM $2   **MIP** $4

Berenstain Bear books, 1995, Long John Silver's

NM $2   **MIP** $5

Fish Cars, 1986, Long John Silver's, fish-shaped cars done in red, yellow and blue, each with different peel-off stickers and details

NM $8   **MIP** $12

Once Upon a Forest, 1993, Long John Silver's, set of five straw huggers: Abigail, Michelle, Cornelius, Edgar, Russell; done in two mold colors

NM $3   **MIP** $6

Sea Walkers, 1990, Long John Silver's, set of four packaged with string: Parrot, Penguin, Turtle, Sylvia

NM $3   **MIP** $8

Sea Watchers Kaleidoscopes, 1991, Long John Silver's, set of three: orange, yellow, pink

NM $2   **MIP** $4

Superstar Baseball Cards, 1990, Long John Silver's, eight sets of five cards: Don Mattingly, Mark McGwire, Mark Grace, Wade Boggs, Darryl Strawberry, Nolan Ryan, Bobby Bonilla, Bret Saberhagen

NM $10   **MIP** $15

Treasure Trolls, 1992, Long John Silver's, set of six: yellow hair, red hair, pink hair, blue hair, purple hair, green hair

NM $1   **MIP** $3

(KP Photo)

Water Blasters, 1990, Long John Silver's, set of four: Billy Bones, Captain Flint, Ophelia Octopus, Parrot

NM $3   **MIP** $5

McDONALD'S

(KP Photo)

101 Dalmatians, 1991, McDonald's, set of four: Lucky, Pongo, Sergeant Tibbs, Cruella

NM $1   **MIP** $2

101 Dalmatians, 1996, McDonald's, 101 different PVC dogs. Premiums were randomly distributed in opaque bag and were un-named. Values for each dog can vary due to the haphazzard distribution.

NM $3   **MIP** $10

101 Dalmatians Snow Globes, 1996, McDonald's, set of four: Snoman's Best Friend (snowman), Snow Furries (dome with red ribbon), Dog Sledding (sleigh), Dalmatian Celebration (number 101)

NM $2   **MIP** $5

101 Dalmatians the Series, 1997, McDonald's, set of eight flip cars: Perdita/Scorch, Two-Tone/Lt. Pug, Lucky/Cruella, Rolly/Ed Pig, Steven/Sydney, Tripod/Dumpling, Cadpig/Spot, Pongo/Swamprat

NM $1   **MIP** $2

102 Dalmatians, 2000, McDonald's, 102 different PVC dogs. Premiums were randomly distributed in opaque bag and were un-named. Values for each dog can vary due to the haphazzard distribution.

NM $3   **MIP** $8

3-D Happy Meal, 1981, McDonald's, set of four cartons with 3-D designs and 3-D glasses inside: Bugsville, High Jinx, Loco Motion, Space Follies

NM $20   **MIP** $40

A Bug's Life Figures, 1998, McDonald's, set of eight wind-ups: Dim, Rosie, Dot, Flik, Francis, Heimlich, Hopper, Atta

NM $1   **MIP** $2

A Bug's Life Watches, 1998, McDonald's, set of three: Leafy Ant-icks with 3-D face, Pop Topper with flip-top lid, Bug Eye Spy with two floating characters

NM $2   **MIP** $3

Adventures of Ronald McDonald, 1981, McDonald's, set of seven rubber figures: Ronald, Birdie, Big Mac, Captain Crook, Mayor McCheese, Hamburglar, Grimace

NM $5   **MIP** $10

Airport Happy Meal, 1986, McDonald's, set of five: Birdie Bentwing Blazer, Fry Guy Flyer, Grimace Bi-Plane, Big Mac Helicopter, Ronald Sea Plane

NM $5   **MIP** $10

Airport Happy Meal, 1986, McDonald's, set of two U3 toys: Fry Guy Friendly Flyer, Grimace Smiling Shuttle

NM $3   **MIP** $5

Aladdin and the King of Theives, 1996, McDonald's, one U3 toy: Abu squirter

NM $2   **MIP** $5

Aladdin and the King of Thieves, 1996, McDonald's, set of eight: Cassim, Abu, Jasmine, Iago, Genie, Sa'luk, Aladdin, Maitre d'Genie

NM $1   **MIP** $3

Alvin and The Chipmunks, 1991, McDonald's, set of four figures: Simon with movie camera, Theodore with rap machine, Brittany with juke box, Alvin with guitar

NM $3   **MIP** $6

Alvin and The Chipmunks, 1991, McDonald's, one U3 toy: Alvin leaning on jukebox

NM $10   **MIP** $20

Amazing Wildlife, 1995, McDonald's, set of eight plush animals: Asiatic Lion, Chimpanzee, Koala Bear, African Elephant, Dromedary Camel, Galapagos Tortoise, Siberian Tiger, Polar Bear

NM $2   **MIP** $3

American Trio Teenie Beanie Babies, 2000, McDonald's, set of three: Righty, Lefty, Libearty

NM $1   **MIP** $3

An American Tail, 1986, McDonald's, set of four books: Fievel and Tiger, Fievel's Friends, Fievel's Boat Trip, Tony and Fievel

NM $2   **MIP** $3

Animal Kingdom, 1998, McDonald's, set of thirteen: triceratops, toucan, gorilla and baby, elephant, dragon, iguanodon, lion, cheetah, zebra, rhino, crocodile, ringtail lemur, tortoise (only available at McDonald's in Wal-Mart stores); four special collector's cups were available with super sized combo meal

NM $1   **MIP** $2

Animal Pals, 1997, McDonald's, set of six plush toys: Panda, Rhinoceros, Yak, Moose, Brown Bear, Gorilla

NM $1   **MIP** $2

Animal Riddles, 1979, McDonald's, set of eight rubber figures: condor, snail, turtle, mouse, anteater, alligator, pelican, dragon, in various colors

NM $2   **MIP** $4

Animaniacs, 1994, McDonald's, set of eight: Bicycle Built for Trio, Goodskate Goodfeathers, Upside-Down Wakko, Slappy and Skipper's Chopper, Dot's Ice Cream Machine, Midy and Buttons Wild RideYakko Ridin' Ralph, Pink and the Brain Mobile,

NM $2   **MIP** $3

Animaniacs, 1995, McDonald's, set of eight: Pinky & the Brain, Goodfeathers, Dot & Ralph, Wacko & Yakko, Slappy & Skippy, Mindy & Buttons, Wakko, Yakko & Dot, Hip Hippos

NM $1   **MIP** $2

Animaniacs, 1995, McDonald's, set of four U3 toys: Bicycle Built for Trio, Goodskate Goodfeathers, Yakko Ridin' Ralph, Mindy and Buttons Wild Ride

NM $3   **MIP** $5

Astrosnick Spacemobile, 1984, McDonald's, 9-1/2" rocket ship available with four Happy Meal Cosmic Coupons

NM $30   **MIP** $60

(Toy Shop File Photo)

Astrosnicks I, 1983, McDonald's, set of eight: eight different 3" rubber space creatures: Scout, Thirsty, Robo-Robot, Laser, Snickapotamus, Sport, Skater, Astralia

NM $4   **MIP** $20

Astrosnicks II, 1984, McDonald's, set of six: Copter, Drill, Ski, Racing, Perfido, Commander

NM $5   **MIP** $20

Astrosnicks III, 1985, McDonald's, set of eleven figures: C.B., Banner, Commander, Junior, Jet, Laser, Perfido, Pyramido, Robo-Robot, Astralia, Snikapotamus; regionally distributed in the Oklahoma area, many are the same as other Astroniks but without "m" marking

NM $5   **MIP** $40

Attack Pack/Polly Pocket, 1995, McDonald's, set of four: Ruck, Battle Bird, Lunar Invader, Sea Creature; joint promotion with Polly Pocket

NM $1   **MIP** $2

Attack Pack/Polly Pocket, 1995, McDonald's, one U3 toy: Truck

NM $2   **MIP** $3

Babe, 1996, McDonald's, set of seven plush toys: Babe, Ferdinand, Fly, Maa, Cow, Mouse, Dutchess

NM $1   **MIP** $2

(KP Photo)

Back to the Future, 1992, McDonald's, set of four: Doc's DeLorean, Verne's Jukebox, Marty's Hoverboard, Einstein's Traveling Train

NM $1   **MIP** $2

Bambi, 1988, McDonald's, set of three U3 toys: Bambi with butterfly on tail, Bambi, Thumper

NM $5   **MIP** $10

(Copyright Museum of Science and Industry, Chicago)

Bambi, 1988, McDonald's, set of four figures: Owl, Flower, Thumper, Bambi

NM $2   **MIP** $4

Barbie and Friends/World of Hot Wheels, 1994, McDonald's, set of eleven: Bicyclin' Barbie, Jewel and Glitter Shani, Camp Barbie, Camp Teresa, Locket Surprise Ken, African-American or

Caucasian, Locket Surprise Barbie, African-American or Caucasian, Jewel and Glitter Barbie, Bridesmaid Skipper; joint promotion with Hot Wheels

NM $2   **MIP** $5

Barbie/Hot Wheels, 1990, McDonald's, set of four Barbie figures with dioramas: Movie Star with SuperStar Barbie; In Concert with Solo in the Spotlight Barbie; Tea Party with Enchanted Evening Barbie; Moonlight Ball with 1989 Happy Holiday Barbie. Test Market Happy Meal, regionally distributed in Savanah, Georgia; joint promotion with Hot Wheels

NM $90   **MIP** $125

Barbie/Hot Wheels, 1991, McDonald's, set of two U3 toys: Costume Ball Barbie, Wedding Day Midge; joint promotion with Hot Wheels

NM $2   **MIP** $4

Barbie/Hot Wheels, 1991, McDonald's, set of eight: Ice Capades, All American, Lights & Lace, Hawaiian Fun, Happy Birthday, Costume Ball, Wedding Day Midge, My First Barbie

NM $2   **MIP** $3

Barbie/Hot Wheels, 1993, McDonald's, set of eight: My First Ballerina, Birthday Party, Western Stamping, Romantic Bride, Hollywood Hair, Paint 'n Dazzle, Twinkle Lights, Secret Hearts; joint promotion with Hot Wheels

NM $2   **MIP** $3

Barbie/Hot Wheels, 1995, McDonald's, one U3 toy: figurine of blond girl wearing green dress

NM $2   **MIP** $3

Barbie/Hot Wheels, 1995, McDonald's, set of ten: Hot Skatin' Barbie, Dance Moves Barbie, Butterfly Princess Teresa, Cool Country Barbie, Caucasian Lifeguard Ken, African-American Ken, Caucasian Lifeguard Barbie, African-American Lifeguard Barbie, Bubble Angel Barbie, Ice Skatin' Barbie; joint promotion with Hot Wheels

NM $2   **MIP** $3

Barbie/Hot Wheels, 1996, McDonald's, set of five: Dutch Barbie, Kenyan Barbie, Japanese Barbie, Mexican Barbie, USA Barbie; joint promotion with Hot Wheels

NM $1   **MIP** $3

Barbie/Hot Wheels, 1996, McDonald's, one U3 toy: Barbie slide puzzle

NM $2   **MIP** $3

Barbie/Hot Wheels, 1997, McDonald's, set of five: Wedding Rapunzel Barbie, Rapunzel Barbie, Angel Princess Barbie, Blossom Beauty Barbie, Happy Holidays Barbie; joint promo with Hot Wheels

NM $1   **MIP** $3

Barbie/Hot Wheels, 1998, McDonald's, set of four: Barbie, Teen Skipper, Eating Fun Kelly, Bead Blast Christie; joint promo with NASCAR Hot Wheels

NM $1   **MIP** $3

Barbie/Hot Wheels, 1999, McDonald's, set of eight Barbies: Soccer Barbie,

---

Sleeping Beauty Barbie, Happening Hair Barbie, Totally Yo-Yo Barbie, Birthday Party Barbie, Giggles 'n' Swing Barbie, Pet Loving Barbie, Bowling Party Barbie; joint promotion with Hot Wheels

NM $1   **MIP** $4

Barbie/Hot Wheels, 2000, McDonald's, set of sixteen: Swimming Champion Barbie, Olympic Pin Barbie, Paralympic Barbie, Barbie Stopwatch, Rainbow Princess Barbie, Cool Clip Christie, Secret Message Teresa, Barbie Rainbow Horse, Birthday Party Barbie, Crew Barbie, Celebration Cake Barbie, Barbie Rock 'n Roll Radio, Cool Skating Barbie, Awesome Skateboard Stacie, Bicycling Barbie, Barbie Sports Water Bottle; joint promotion with Hot Wheels

NM $1   **MIP** $3

Barbie/Hot Wheels, 2000, McDonald's, set of eighteen: Millenium Princess Barbie, Barbie No. 1, Solo in the Spotlight, Hollywood Nails Barbie, Malibu Barbie, Gymnast Barbie, Totally Hair Barbie, Sit 'n Style Barbie, Working Woman Barbie, Chic Barbie; joint promotion with Hot Wheels

NM $1   **MIP** $3

Barbie/Hot Wheels Mini-Streex, 1992, McDonald's, one U3 toy: Sparkle Eyes Babie

NM $2   **MIP** $5

Barbie/Hot Wheels Mini-Streex, 1992, McDonald's, set of eight dolls: Sparkle Eyes, Roller Blade, Rappin' Rockin', My First Ballerina, Snap 'N PLay, Sun Sensation, Birthday Surprise, Rose Bride; joint promotion with Hot Wheels Mini-Streex

NM $1   **MIP** $2

(KP Photo)

Batman, 1992, McDonald's, set of four: Batmobile, Batmissle, Catwoman Cat Coupe, Penguin Roto-Roadster

NM $1   **MIP** $2

Batman Cups, 1992, McDonald's, set of six cups; offered in conjunction with Happy Meal

NM $1   **MIP** $2

Batman, The Animated Series, 1993, McDonald's, one U3 toy: Batman without removable cape

NM $2   **MIP** $5

Batman, The Animated Series, 1993, McDonald's, set of eight: Batman with removable cape, Robin, Batgirl, Two

---

Face, Poison Ivy, Joker, Catwoman with leopard, Riddler

NM $2   **MIP** $3

Beach Ball, 1986, McDonald's, set of three inflatables: Ronald waving, red; Birdie with sandcastle, blue; Grimace with beach umbrella, yellow. Regionally distributed in Washington, New York and Colorado

NM $10   **MIP** $15

Beach Ball Characters, 1985, McDonald's, set of three: Grimace in kayak, Ronald holding flag and beachball, Birdie in sailboat

NM $10   **MIP** $15

Beach Toy II, 1990, McDonald's, set of eight: Ronald and Grimace sand pail with yellow lid and shovel, Birdie Seaside Submarine, Fry Kid Super Sailor, Fry Kids Sand Castle Pail, Grimace Beach Ball, Birdie Shovel, Ronald Squirt Gun Rake, Ronald Fun Flyer

NM $2   **MIP** $3

Beach Toys I, 1989, McDonald's, set of four: Birdie Seaside Submarine, Grimace Bouncin' Beachball, Fry Kid Super Sailor, Ronald Fun Flyer; test market Happy Meal

NM $10   **MIP** $15

Beachcomber Happy Meal, 1986, McDonald's, set of three sand pails with shovels: Grimace, Mayor McCheese, Ronald

NM $5   **MIP** $10

Bedtime, 1989, McDonald's, set of four: Ronald toothbrush with tube of Crest toothpaste, Ronald bath mitt, Ronald Nite Stand Star Figure, Ronald cup

NM $4   **MIP** $8

BeetleBorgs Metallix, 1997, McDonald's, set of six: Stinger Drill, Beetle Bonder, Hunter Claw, Platinum Purple BeetleBorg Covert Compact, Chromuim Gold BeetleBorg Covert Compact, Titanium Silver BeetleBorg Covert Compact

NM $1   **MIP** $2

Behind the Scenes, 1992, McDonald's, set of four: Cartoon Wheel, Rainbow Viewer, Rub 'N' Draw, Balance Builder

NM $2   **MIP** $3

(KP Photo)

Berenstain Bears I, 1986, McDonald's, set of four figures: Papa with wheelbarrow, Mama with shopping cart, Brother with scooter, Sister with sled; test market set, distributed in Evansville, Indiana

NM $30   **MIP** $75

Berenstain Bears II, 1987, McDonald's, set of four figures with flocked heads:

Papa with wheelbarrow, Mama with shopping cart, Brother with scooter, Sister with wagon

NM $2   **MIP** $4

Berenstain Bears II, 1987, McDonald's, set of two U3 toys with paper punch outs: Mama, Papa

NM $5   **MIP** $10

Berenstain Bears Story Books, 1990, McDonald's, set of eight books: Attic Treasure Story Book, Attic Treasure Activity Book, Substitute Teacher Story Book, Substitute Activity Book, Eager Beavers Story Book, Eager Beavers Activity Book, Life with Papa Story Book, Life with Papa Activity Book

NM $2   **MIP** $4

Bigfoot, 1987, McDonald's, set of eight Ford trucks: Bronco, green or orange; Pickup, purple or orange; Ms. Pickup, turquoise or pink; Shuttle, red or black; without McDonald's "M" logo on back window

NM $5   **MIP** $10

Bigfoot, 1987, McDonald's, set of eight Ford trucks: Bronco, green or orange; Pickup purple or orange; Ms. Pickup, turquoise or pink; Shuttle, red or black; each had McDonald's "M" logo on back window

NM $3   **MIP** $5

Birdie Bike Horn, McDonald's, Japanese

NM $4   **MIP** $9

Birdie Magic Trick, McDonald's, green or orange

NM $2   **MIP** $5

Black History, 1988, McDonald's, two coloring books: Little Martin Jr. Coloring Book Volume One, Little Martin Jr. Coloring Book Volume Two; sold in six Detroit stores

NM $200   **MIP** $500

Boats 'n Floats, 1987, McDonald's, set of four vaccuform boats with stickers: Chicken McNugget lifeboat, Birdie float, Fry Guys raft, Grimace ski boat

NM $5   **MIP** $10

Bobby's World, 1994, McDonald's, one U3 toy: Bobby in intertube

NM $1   **MIP** $3

Bobby's World, 1994, McDonald's, one U3 toy: inner tube

NM $2   **MIP** $3

Bobby's World, 1994, McDonald's, set of four: Wagon-Race Car, Innertube-Submarine, Three Wheeler-Space Ship, Skates-Roller Coaster

NM $1   **MIP** $2

Breakfast Happy Meal, 1991, McDonald's, squeeze bottle with Minute Maid logo

NM $1   **MIP** $3

Buzz Lightyear of Star Command, 2001, McDonald's, set of six: Buzz Lightyear, Mira Nova, Booster, XR, The Evil Emperor Zurg, Commander Nebula

NM $1   **MIP** $3

Cabbage Patch, 1992, McDonald's, one U3 toy: Anne Louise "Ribbons & Bows"

NM $1   **MIP** $2

Cabbage Patch Kids/Tonka, 1992, McDonald's, set of five: Tiny Dancer, Holiday Pageant, Holiday Dreamer, Fun On Ice, All Dressed Up; joint promotion with Tonka

NM $2   **MIP** $3

Cabbage Patch Kids/Tonka, 1994, McDonald's, one U3 toy: SaraJane

NM $2   **MIP** $3

Cabbage Patch Kids/Tonka, 1994, McDonald's, set of four: Mimi Kristina, Abigail Lynn, Kimberly Katherine, Michelle Elyse; joint promotion with Tonka

NM $1   **MIP** $3

Camp McDonaldland, 1990, McDonald's, set of four: Grimace Canteen, Birdie Mess Kit, Fry Kid Utensils, Ronald Collapsible Cup (also U3 premium)

NM $2   **MIP** $3

Captain Crook Bike Reflector, 1988, McDonald's, blue plastic, Canada

NM $1   **MIP** $3

Castlemaker, 1987, McDonald's, set of four vacuuform molds: dome, square, cylinder, rectangle; regionally distributed in Michigan and Houston, Texas

NM $20   **MIP** $40

Changeables, 1987, McDonald's, set of six figures that change into robots: Big Mac, Milk Shake, Egg McMuffin, Quarter Pounder, French Fries, Chicken McNuggets

NM $4   **MIP** $8

Chip 'n Dale Rescue Rangers, 1989, McDonald's, set of four figures: Chip's Whirly-Cuptor, Dale's Roto-Roadster, Gadgets Rescue Racer, Monteray Jack's Propel-A-Phone

NM $2   **MIP** $4

Chip 'n Dale Rescue Rangers, 1989, McDonald's, set of two U3 toys: Gadget's Rockin', Chip's Rockin Racer

NM $2   **MIP** $4

Christmas Ornaments, 1987, McDonald's, Fry Guy and Fry Girl, cloth, 3-1/2" tall

NM $3   **MIP** $6

Christmas Stocking, 1981, McDonald's, plastic, "Merry Christmas to My Pal"

NM $3   **MIP** $6

Circus, 1983, McDonald's, set of nine: Fun House Mirror with Ronald; Fun House Mirror with Hamburglar; Acrobatic Ronald, French Fry Faller; Strong Gong with Grimace; Punchout Midway: The Ronald Midway; Punchout Midway: Fun House; Punchout Tent with Grimace; Punchout Tent with Birdie

NM $15   **MIP** $25

Circus Parade, 1991, McDonald's, set of four: Ringmaster Ronald McDonald, Bareback Rider Birdie, Grimace Playing Caliope, Elephant Trainer Fry Guy

NM $2   **MIP** $4

Circus Wagon, 1979, McDonald's, set of four rubber toys: poodle, chimp, clown, horse

NM $2   **MIP** $3

Colorforms Happy Meal, 1986, McDonald's, set of five: Beach set, Grimace; Farm set, Ronald; Camping set, Professor; Play set, Birdie; Picnic, Hamburglar

NM $10   **MIP** $15

Colorforms Happy Meal, 1986, McDonald's, two U3 sticker sets: Beach set, Grimace; Farm set, Ronald

NM $10   **MIP** $15

Colorful Puzzles-Japan, McDonald's, set of three: Dumbo, Mickey & Minnie, Dumbo & Train

NM $5   **MIP** $10

Coloring Stand-Ups, 1978, McDonald's, characters and backgrounds to color, punch out and stand

NM $4   **MIP** $8

Combs, 1988, McDonald's, set of four: Capt. Crook, red; Grimace, yellow; Ronald, yellow, blue or purple; Grimace Groomer, green

NM $1   **MIP** $2

Commandrons, 1985, McDonald's, set of four robots: Solardyn, Magna, Motron, Velocitor

NM $5   **MIP** $15

Connectables, 1991, McDonald's, set of four: Birdie on tricycle, Grimace in wagon, Hamburglar in airplane, Ronald in soapbox racer

NM $3   **MIP** $5

Construx, 1986, McDonald's, set of four: axle, wing, body cylinder, canopy; spaceship could be built from all four preiums

NM $10   **MIP** $25

CosMc Crayola, 1988, McDonald's, one U3 toy: two fluorescent crayons with coloring page

NM $5   **MIP** $10

CosMc Crayola, 1988, McDonald's, set of five coloring kits: four crayons with coloring page, thin red marker with coloring page, four chalk with chalkboard, washable thin marker with coloring page, three paints and brush with paint-by-number page

NM $5   **MIP** $10

Crayola Happy Meal, 1986, McDonald's, set of three kits: triangle stencil with green marker, rectangular stencil with four fluorescent crayons, triangle stencil with orange marker, traingle stencil with thin blue marker, triangle stencil with thin red marker

NM $10   **MIP** $15

Crayola II, 1987, McDonald's, one U3 stencil: Ronald on fire engine with four crayons

NM $5   **MIP** $10

Crayola II, 1987, McDonald's, set of four stencils: Grimace with four fluorescent crayons, Hamburglar with four crayons, Birdie with thick orange or green marker, Ronald with thin blue or red marker

NM $2   **MIP** $5

Crayola Squeeze Bottle, Kay Bee, McDonald's, set of four: regional promotion

NM $3   **MIP** $6

Crayon Squeeze Bottle, 1992, McDonald's, set of four: blue, green, yellow, red; regionally distributed in New York state and Connecticut

NM $3   **MIP** $5

Crazy Creatures with Popoids, 1985, McDonald's, set of four made up of two bellows and one connector: red and blue bellows with wheel joint; yellow and blue connectors with ball joint; yellow and red bellows with cube joint; red and yellow with seven-sided joint

NM $6   **MIP** $12

Crazy Vehicles, 1991, McDonald's, set of four: Ronald in red car, Hamburglar in yellow train engine, Grimace in green car, Birdie in pink airplane

NM $3   **MIP** $5

Design-O-Saurs, 1987, McDonald's, set of four: Ronald on Tyrannosaurus, Grimace on Pterodactyl, Fry Guy on Brontosaurus, Hamburglar on Triceratops

NM $5   **MIP** $10

Dink the Little Dinosaur, 1990, McDonald's, set of six figures with diorama and description: Dink, Flapper, Amber, Crusty, Scat, Shyler

NM $4   **MIP** $8

Dino-Motion Dinosaurs, 1993, McDonald's, set of six: Baby, Grandma, Robbie, Earl, Fran, Charlene

NM $1   **MIP** $2

Dino-Motion Dinosaurs, 1993, McDonald's, one U3 toy: Baby squirter

NM $2   **MIP** $4

Dinosaur Days, 1981, McDonald's, set of six plastic dinos: Pteranodon, Triceratops, Stegosaurus, Dimetrodon, T-Rex, Ankylosaurus

NM $1   **MIP** $2

Dinosaur Talking Storybook, 1989, McDonald's, set of four books and tape: The Dinosaur Baby Boom, Danger Under the Lake, The Creature in the Cave, The Amazing Birthday Adventure

NM $5   **MIP** $10

Dinosaurs, 2000, McDonald's, set of ten: Aladar Hand Puppet, Neera Hand Puppet, Carnotaur Hand Puppet, Kron Hand Puppet, Plio/Zini/Suri/Yar Talking Toy, Baylene Action Figure, Eema Action Figure, Bruton Action Figure

NM $1   **MIP** $3

Discover the Rain Forest, 1991, McDonald's, set of four activity books with punch out figures: Sticker Safari, Wonders in the Wild, Paint It Wild, Ronald and the Jewel of the Amazon Kingdom

NM $2   **MIP** $4

Disney Favorites, 1987, McDonald's, set of four activity books: Lady and the Tramp, Dumbo, Cinderella, The Sword in the Stone

NM $3   **MIP** $4

Disney Masterpiece Collection, 1996, McDonald's, figures in video-shaped box

NM $1   **MIP** $2

Disney Video Favorites, 1998, McDonald's, set of six: The Spirit of Mickey, Lady & the Tramp, Pocahontas: Journey to a New World, Mary Poppins, The Black Cauldron, Flubber

NM $1   **MIP** $3

Disney Video Showcase Collection, 2000, McDonald's, set of six boxes and eighteen toys: A Bug's Life, Dinosaur, Little Mermaid II, Mickey's Once Upon a Christmas, Winnie the Pooh Season of Giving, Toy Story II

NM $1   **MIP** $3

Disneyland 40th Anniversary Viewers, 1995, McDonald's, one U3 toy: Winnie the Pooh on Big Thunder Mountain without viewer (green cab)

NM $2   **MIP** $3

Disneyland 40th Anniversary Viewers, 1995, McDonald's, set of nine: Brer on Space Mountain; Aladdin & Jasmine at Aladdin's Castle; Roger Rabbit in Mickey's Toontown; Winnie the Pooh on Big Thunder Mountain with viewer, green cab; Winnie the Pooh on Big Thunder Mountain with viewer, black cab; Simba in The Lion King Celebration; Mickey Mouse on Space Mountain; Peter Pan in Fantasmic!; King Louie on the Jungle Cruise

NM $2   **MIP** $3

Disney's House of Mouse, 2001, McDonald's, set of six: Mickey Mouse, Minnie Mouse, Daisy Duck, Donald Duck, Goofy, Pluto

NM $1   **MIP** $3

Double Bell Alarm Clock, McDonald's, wind-up alarm clock with silver bells, hammer ringer, silver feet, image of Ronald on face with head tilted over folded hands, as if asleep

NM $20   **MIP** $40

Doug's First Movie, 1999, McDonald's, set of eight: Doug the Keychain, Doug the Pen Pal, Patti the Keychain Pal, Doug the Clip-on, Quilman the Bouncing Zipper Gripper, Skeeter the Keychain, Monster the Pocket Protector

NM $1   **MIP** $3

Duck Tales I, 1988, McDonald's, set of four toys: Telescope, Duck Code Quacker, Magnifying Glass, Wrist Decoder

NM $2   **MIP** $4

Duck Tales I, 1988, McDonald's, one U3 toy: Motion Magic Map

NM $2   **MIP** $5

Duck Tales II, 1988, McDonald's, set of four toys: Uncle Scrooge in red car; Launchpad in plane; Huey, Dewey and Louie on jet ski; Webby on blue trike

NM $3   **MIP** $6

Duck Tales II, 1988, McDonald's, one U3 toy: Huey on skates

NM $15   **MIP** $20

Dukes of Hazzard, 1982, McDonald's, set of five vaccuform container vehicles, Boss Hogg's Caddy, Daisy's Jeep, Sheriff Roscoe's Police Car, Uncle Jesse's Pickup, General Lee; each container came with sticker sheet; regionally distributed in Missouri

NM $20   **MIP** $50

Dukes of Hazzard, 1982, McDonald's, set of six white plastic cups: Luke, Boss Hogg, Bo, Sheriff Roscoe, Daisy, Uncle Jesse

NM $3   **MIP** $6

E.T., 1985, McDonald's, set of four posters: E.T. with boy and girl in front of spaceship, E.T. with boy and bike, E.T. with glowing finger, E.T. with radio

NM $8   **MIP** $12

Earth Days, 1994, McDonald's, one U3 toy: tool carrier with shovel

NM $1   **MIP** $2

Earth Days, 1994, McDonald's, one U3 toy: tool carrier with shovel

NM $1   **MIP** $2

Earth Days, 1994, McDonald's, set of four: birdfeeder, globe terrarium, binoculars, tool carrier with shovel

NM $1   **MIP** $2

Emporer's New Groove, The, 2000, McDonald's, set of six: Kuzco, Yzma the Kittycat, Kuzco as Llama, Kronk, Pacha, zma

NM $1   **MIP** $3

Eric Carle Finger Puppets, 1996, McDonald's, set of six puppets: The Very Quiet Crickett, The Very Lonely Firefly, A House for Hermit Crab, The Grouchy Ladybug, The Very Hungry Caterpillar, The Very Busy Spider

NM $1   **MIP** $2

Extremely Goofy Movie, An, 2000, McDonald's, set of eight: Goofy, Sylvia, Max, Bradley, PJ, Tank, Bobby, Slouch

NM $1   **MIP** $3

Fast Macs I, 1984, McDonald's, set of four pull-back action cars: Big Mac in white police car, Ronald in yellow Jeep, Hamburglar in red racer, Birdie in pink convertible

NM $3   **MIP** $5

Fast Macs II, 1985, McDonald's, set of four pull-back action cars: Big Mac in white police car, Ronald in yellow Jeep, Hamburglar in red racer, Birdie in pink convertible

NM $3   **MIP** $5

Favorite Friends, 1978, McDonald's, set of seven character punch-out cards

NM $2   **MIP** $5

Feeling Good, 1985, McDonald's, set of two U3 floating toys: Grimace in Tub, Fry Guys on Duck

NM $5   **MIP** $8

Feeling Good, 1985, McDonald's, set of six grooming toys: Grimace soap dish, Fry Guy sponge, Birdie mirror, Ronald toothbrush, Hamburglar toothbrush, Captain Crook comb

    NM $1   **MIP** $3

Field Trip, 1993, McDonald's, one U3 toy: Nature Viewer

    NM $1   **MIP** $2

Field Trip, 1993, McDonald's, set of four: Kaleidoscope, Leaf Printer, Nature Viewer, Explorer Bag

    NM $1   **MIP** $2

Fingerboard Pro Gear, 2000, McDonald's, set of eight: Fingerboard w/Blue Ramp, Fingerboard w/Yellow Ramp, Fingerboard w/Light Blue Ramp, Fingerboard w/Green Ramp, Fingerboard w/Orange Clip, Fingerboard w/Pink Clip, Fingerboard w/purple Clip, Fingerboard w/Blue Clip

    NM $1   **MIP** $2

Fisher-Price U3 Toys, 1996, McDonald's, set of twenty-four: Balls in ball, Barn Puzzle, Bear in Train, Birdie in Poppity-Pop Car, Bus, Clock, Corn Popper, Cow Book, Dog Squeek, Dog Roll-A-Rounds, Dog in House, Dog on Red Wheels, Grimace Roll-A-Rounds, Horse, Jeep, Key Ring, Man in Poppity-Pop Car, Truck, Fun Sounds Ball, Puzzle Maze, Ronald McDonald in Drive-thru, Pig in Barrel, Radio Rattle, Chatter Telephone; In 1996, McDonald's began offering generic Fisher-Price toys as the U3 premium for Happy Meals.

    NM $3   **MIP** $5

Flintstone Kids, 1988, McDonald's, set of four figures in animal vehicles: Betty, Barney, Fred, Wilma

    NM $4   **MIP** $8

Flintstone Kids, 1988, McDonald's, one U3 toy: Dino figure

    NM $10   **MIP** $15

Flintstones, 1994, McDonald's, one U3 toy: Rocking Dino

    NM $3   **MIP** $5

Flintstones, 1994, McDonald's, set of five: Fred at Bedrock Bowl-O-Rama, Betty and Bamm Bamm at Roc Donald's, Wilma at the Flinstone's house, Barney at the Fossil Fill-Up, Pebbles and Dino at Toy-S-Aurus

    NM $1   **MIP** $2

Florida Beach Ball, 1985, McDonald's, set of three with Florida logo: Grimace in kayak, Ronald holding flag and beachball, Birdie in sailboat

    NM $20   **MIP** $25

(Toy Shop Photo File)

Food Fundamentals, 1993, McDonald's, set of four: Slugger the steak; Otis the sandwhich, Milly the milk carton, Ruby the apple

    NM $1   **MIP** $2

Food Fundamentals, 1993, McDonald's, one U3 toy: Dunkan the ear of corn

    NM $1   **MIP** $2

Fraggle Rock I, 1987, McDonald's, set of four: Gobo Fraggle, Bulldoozer and Friends, Cotterpin Doozer and Friends, Cotterpin Doozer; test market Happy Meal, regionally distributed in West Virginia

    NM $20   **MIP** $30

(KP Photo)

Fraggle Rock II, 1988, McDonald's, set of four: Gobo in carrot car, Red in radish car, Mokey in eggplant car, Wembly and Boober in pickle car

    NM $1   **MIP** $2

Fraggle Rock II, 1988, McDonald's, set of two U3 toys: Gobo holding carrot, Red holding radish

    NM $4   **MIP** $6

French Fry Radio, 1977, McDonald's, large red fry container with fries

    NM $12   **MIP** $25

Friendly Skies, 1991, McDonald's, set of two: Ronald in white plane, Grimace in white plane

    NM $5   **MIP** $10

Friends of Barbie/World of Hot Wheels, 1994, McDonald's, one U3 toy: Barbie Ball

    NM $2   **MIP** $3

Fry Benders, 1990, McDonald's, set of four figures: Grand Slam with baseball glove, Froggy with scuba tanks, Roadie with bicycle, Freestyle with rollerskates

    NM $5   **MIP** $10

Fry Guy Cookie Cutter, 1987, McDonald's, Fry Guy on unicycle, green or orange

    NM $1   **MIP** $3

Fun Ruler, 1983, McDonald's, white platic ruler featuring Mayor McCheese, Fry Guys, Birdie, Ronald, Grimace, Hamburglar

    NM $3   **MIP** $5

Fun To Go, 1977, McDonald's, set of seven cartons with games and activities

    NM $2   **MIP** $4

Fun with Food, 1989, McDonald's, set of four: Hamburger Guy, Fry Guy, Soft Drink Guy, Chicken McNugget Guys

    NM $3   **MIP** $6

Funny Fry Friends, 1990, McDonald's, two U3 toys: Lil' Chief, Little Darling

    NM $3   **MIP** $5

(KP Photo)

Funny Fry Friends II, 1990, McDonald's, set of eight: Too Tall, Tracker, Rollin' Rocker, Sweet Cuddles, Zzz's, Gadzooks, Matey, Hoops

    NM $2   **MIP** $4

Funny Fry Guys, 1989, McDonald's, set of four: Gadzooks, Matey, Zzz's, Tracker; test market Happy Meal, regionally distributed in California, Pennsylvania, Maryland

    NM $15   **MIP** $25

Furby, 1999, McDonald's, eight different designs done in ten different color combinations; there are a total of eighty diffferent Furby toys available. Each toy comes packaged in opage bags so the collector doesn't know which Furby they have

    NM $5   **MIP** $10

Furby Keychains, 2000, McDonald's, set of twelve: Tiger, Elephant, Tree Frog, Raccoon, Giraffe, Monkey, Fox, Dinosaur, Snake, Lamb, Cow, Owl

    NM $1   **MIP** $3

Garfield, 1988, McDonald's, set of four: Garfield on skateboard, Garfield on tricycle, Garfield in car, Garfield on scooter; test market Happy Meal, regionally distributed in Erie, Pennsylvania and Charlston, South Carolina

    NM $20   **MIP** $50

Garfield II, 1989, McDonald's, set of two U3 toys: Garfield Skating, Garfield with Pooky

    NM $2   **MIP** $5

(KP Photo)

Garfield II, 1989, McDonald's, set of four: Garfield on Scooter, Garfield on

Skateboard, Garfield in Jeep, Garfield with Odie on Motorscooter

NM $3   **MIP** $6

Glo-Tron Spaceship, 1986, McDonald's, set of four vacuform spaceships: red, blue, green, gray; each spaceship came with set of glow-in-the-dark stickers

NM $25   **MIP** $50

Glow in the Dark Yo-Yo, 1978, McDonald's, no markings or dates

NM $2   **MIP** $5

Going Places/Hot Wheels, 1983, McDonald's, set of fourteen: Corvette Stingray, Jeep CJ-7, 3-Window '34, Baja Breaker, Chevy Citation, Firebird Funny Car, Land Lord, Malibu Grand Prix, 380-SEL, Minitrek, P-928, Sheriff Patrol, Split Window '63, Turismo

NM $12   **MIP** $15

Golf Ball, McDonald's, marked with McDonald's logo

NM $1   **MIP** $3

Good Morning, 1991, McDonald's, set of four: Ronald toothbrush, McDonaldland comb, Ronald clock, white plastic cup

NM $1   **MIP** $2

Good Sports, 1984, McDonald's, set of six puffy stickers: Hamburglar, Mayor McCheese, Ronald, Sam the Olympic Eagle, Birdie, Grimace

NM $8   **MIP** $12

Good Times Great Taste Record, McDonald's

NM $2   **MIP** $4

Gravedale High, 1991, McDonald's, set of four mechanical Halloween figures: Cleofatra, Frankentyke, Vinnie Stoker, Sid the Invisible Kid

NM $2   **MIP** $3

Gravedale High, 1991, McDonald's, one U3 toy: Cleofatra

NM $3   **MIP** $5

Grimace Bank, 1985, McDonald's, purple ceramic, 9" tall

NM $10   **MIP** $20

Grimace Pin, McDonald's, enamel

NM $6   **MIP** $12

Grimace Ring, 1970, McDonald's

NM $8   **MIP** $15

Grimace Sponge, McDonald's, Grimace, Grimace Car Wash

NM $2   **MIP** $4

Halloween, 1995, McDonald's, one U3 toy: pumpkin with pop-up Grimace

NM $2   **MIP** $3

Halloween, 1995, McDonald's, set of four figures: Hamburglar with witch costume, Grimace with ghost costume, Ronald with Frankenstein soctume, Birdie with pumpkin costume

NM $2   **MIP** $3

Halloween, 1995, McDonald's, set of four cassete tapes: Ronald Makes it Magic, Travel Tunes, Silly Sing-Along, Scary Sound Affects

NM $1   **MIP** $2

Halloween Buckets, 1986, McDonald's, set of three pumpkin-shaped pails: McGoblin, McPumpkin, McBoo

NM $2   **MIP** $4

Halloween Buckets, 1987, McDonald's, set of three pumpkin-shaped pails: McBoo, McGoblin, McPunk'n

NM $2   **MIP** $3

Halloween Buckets, 1989, McDonald's, set of three: Ghost, Witch, Pumpkin

NM $1   **MIP** $3

Halloween Buckets, 1990, McDonald's, set of threepumpkin-shaped pails: orange pumpkin, white glow-in-dark ghost, Green witch

NM $2   **MIP** $4

Halloween Buckets, 1992, McDonald's, set of three pumpkin-shaped pails with cut-out lids: Ghost, Witch, Pumpkin

NM $1   **MIP** $2

Halloween Buckets, 1994, McDonald's, set of three with cookie-cutter lids: Ghost, Whitch, Pumpkin

NM $1   **MIP** $3

Halloween Happy Meal, 1985, McDonald's, set of five pumpkin-shaped pails: McGoblin, McPunk'n, McPunky, McBoo, McBoo; regionally distributed in the northeast, marked with 1985 copyright

NM $12   **MIP** $15

Halloween McNugget Buddies, 1993, McDonald's, set of six: Pumpkin McNugget, McBoo McNugget, Monster McNugget, McNuggula McNugget, Witchie McNugget, Mummie McNugget

NM $1   **MIP** $3

Halloween McNugget Buddies, 1993, McDonald's, one U3 toy: McBoo McNugget

NM $3   **MIP** $5

Halloween McNugget Buddies, 1996, McDonald's, set of six: Dragon, Spider, Fairy Princess, Alien Monster, Rock Star, Ronald

NM $2   **MIP** $3

Halloween Pails, 1999, McDonald's, set of two: white bucket, orange bucket

NM $1   **MIP** $3

Halloween Pumpkin Ring, McDonald's, orange pumpkin face

NM $1   **MIP** $3

Hamburglar Doll, 1976, McDonald's, 7" stuffed doll by Remco; one of set of seven, sold on blister card

NM $12   **MIP** $25

Hamburglar Hockey, 1979, McDonald's

NM $2   **MIP** $4

Happy Holidays, 1984, McDonald's, set of two cards with stickers: Gingerbread House, Train

NM $15   **MIP** $20

Happy Meal From the Heart, 1990, McDonald's, set of two scratch-and-sniff Valentines: Grimace—Valentine

Your Shake Me Up!; Ronald—Valentine You Warm My Heart!

NM $2   **MIP** $3

Happy Pail, 1983, McDonald's, set of three: pink pail with purple shovel, shows Ronald and Mayor McCheese under umbrella with purple shovel; white pail with yellow shovel, shows Ronald in intertube; white pail with slotted yellow shovel, shows airplane pulling banner; distributed in the New York state and New England area only

NM $25   **MIP** $35

Happy Pail III, 1986, McDonald's, set of five sand pails with either yellow shovel or red rake: Beach with blue lid, Parade with orange lid, Treasure Hunt with red lid, Vacation with green lid, Picnic with yellow lid

NM $5   **MIP** $10

Happy Pails, Olympics, 1984, McDonald's, set of four with shovels: Swimming, blue; Cycling, yellow; Athletics, beige; Olympic Games, white

NM $1   **MIP** $3

Happy Teeth, 1983, McDonald's, set of two: Reach toothbrush, tube of toothpaste

NM $15   **MIP** $20

Hat Happy Meal, 1990, McDonald's, set of four: Birdie green derby, Fry Guy orange safari hat, Grimace yellow construction hat, Ronald red fireman hat

NM $10   **MIP** $15

(KP Photo)

Hello Kitty/Transformers, 2000, McDonald's, set of nine: Hello Kitty Crew Kid, Hello Kitty Charm Watch, Hello Kitty Sticker Art, Hello Kitty Pull String Toy, Helloe Kitty Wrap, Dear Daniel Stamp Mobile, Hello Kitty Kimono Clip, Hello Kitty Ballerina Scrunchy, Hello Kitty Apple Lock; joint promotion with Transformers

NM $1   **MIP** $4

Hercules, 1997, McDonald's, set of ten: Wind Titan & Hermes, Rock Titan & Zeus, Hydra & Hercules, Lava Titan & Baby Pegasus, Cyclops & Pain, Fates & Panic, Pegasus & Megara, Ice Tita & Calliope, Nessus & Phil, Cerberus & Hades

NM $1   **MIP** $2

Hercules Plates, 1997, McDonald's, set of six: Hercules, Megara, Pegasus, Zeus, Muses, Phil; offered by McDonald's for $1.99 with purchase and $2.99 without purchase

NM $3   **MIP** $5

Hercules Sports Toys, 1998, McDonald's, set of eight: Zeus football, Hades stopwatch, Hercules sport bottle, Eye of

Fates foot bag, Pain and Panic sound stick, Hercules medal, Phil megaphone, Whistling Discus

NM $1   MIP $2

High Flying Kite Happy Meal, 1986, McDonald's, set of three kites: Hamburglar, Birdie, Ronald; regionally distributed in New England area

NM $200   MIP $225

Hobby Box, 1985, McDonald's, set of four plastic boxes: yellow, green, red, blue; regionally distributed in the Southern United States

NM $10   MIP $15

Honey, I Shrunk the Kids Cups, 1988, McDonald's, set of three white 20 oz. plastic cups: Giant Bee, On the Dog's Nose, Riding the Ant

NM $1   MIP $2

(Toy Shop File Photo)

Hook Figures, 1991, McDonald's, set of four: Peter Pan, Mermaid, Rufio, Hook

NM $1   MIP $2

Hot Wheels Mini-Streex/Barbie, 1992, McDonald's, one U3 toy: Orange Arrow car

NM $3   MIP $6

Hot Wheels Mini-Streex/Barbie, 1992, McDonald's, set of eight: Flame-Out, Quick Flash, Turbo Flyer, Black Arrow, Hot Shock, Racer Tracer, Night Shadow, Blade Burner; joint promotion with Barbie

NM $2   MIP $4

Hot Wheels/Barbie, 1988, McDonald's, set of twelve: Streat Beast, silver or red; P-911, white or black; Split Window '63, silver or black; '57 T-Bird, turquoise or white; 80's Firebird, blue or black; Sheriff Patrol; Fire Patrol

NM $10   MIP $15

Hot Wheels/Barbie, 1990, McDonald's, set of four: Corvette, white; Ferrari, red; Hot Bird, silver; Camaro, turquoise; test market Happy Meal, regionally distributed in Savanah, Georgia; joint promotion with Barbie

NM $50   MIP $75

(Toy Shop File Photo)

Hot Wheels/Barbie, 1991, McDonald's, set of eight cars: '55 Chevy, white or yellow; '63 Corvette, green or black; Camaro Z-28, purple or orange; '57 T-Bird, turquoise or red; joint promotion with Barbie

NM $2   MIP $3

Hot Wheels/Barbie, 1991, McDonald's, one U3 tool set: yellow wrench and red hammer

NM $2   MIP $3

Hot Wheels/Barbie, 1993, McDonald's, one U3 tool set: blue wrench and yellow hammer

NM $3   MIP $6

Hot Wheels/Barbie, 1993, McDonald's, set of eight: Quaker State Racer #62, McDonald's Dragster, McDonald's Thunderbird #23, Hot Wheels Dragster, McDonald's Funny Car, Hot Wheels Funny Car, Hot Wheels Camaro #1, Duracell Racer #88; joint promotion with Barbie

NM $2   MIP $3

Hot Wheels/Barbie, 1995, McDonald's, one U3 toy: Key Force car

NM $2   MIP $3

Hot Wheels/Barbie, 1995, McDonald's, set of eight: Lightning Speed, Shock Force, Blue Bandit, Power Circuit, Twin Engine, Radar Racer, Back Burner, After Blast; joint promotion with Barbie

NM $2   MIP $3

Hot Wheels/Barbie, 1996, McDonald's, set of five: Flame Series, Roarin' Road Series, Dark Rider Series, Hot Hubs Series, Krakel Car Series; joint promotion with Barbie

NM $1   MIP $2

Hot Wheels/Barbie, 1996, McDonald's, one U3 toy: Hot Wheels squeek toy

NM $1   MIP $3

Hot Wheels/Barbie, 1997, McDonald's, set of five: Tow Truck, Taxi, Police Car, Ambulance, Fire Truck; joint promotion with Barbie

NM $1   MIP $2

Hot Wheels/Barbie, 1998, McDonald's, Ronald NASCAR, Mac Tonight NASCAR, Hot Wheels NASCAR, 50th Anniversary NASCAR; joint promo with Barbie

NM $1   MIP $2

Hot Wheels/Barbie, 1999, McDonald's, set of eight: Double Cross, Maximizer, Lead Sled, Surf Boarder, Street Raptor, Black Track, Trail Runner, Innovator; joint promotion with Barbie

NM $1   MIP $4

Hot Wheels/Barbie, 2000, McDonald's, set of sixteen: Lamborghini Diablo, Chevrolet Corvette, Lotus Elise, Key Clip Launcher, Jordan, Williamsf1 Car, Jaguar Racing, Hot Wheels Keychain, Motorcycle, BMX Bike, Sprint Car, Stop Watch, Helicopter, McDonald's Hot Rod, Airplane, Binocluars; joint promotion with Barbie

NM $1   MIP $3

Hot Wheels/Barbie, 2000, McDonald's, set of eighteen: McDonald's NASCAR (current), McDonald's NASCAR (future), Hot Wheels NASCAR (current), Hot Wheels NASCAR (future), McLaren Grand Prix (current), McLaren Grand Prix (future), Del Worsham Funny Car (current), Del Worsham Funny Car (future), Champ Car (current), Champ Car (future)

NM $1   MIP $3

Hunchback of Notre Dame, 1997, McDonald's, set of eight: Esmeralda Amulet, Scepter, Clopin Mask, Hugo Horn, Clopin Puppet Drum, Juggling Balls, Tambourine, Quasimodo Bird Catcher

NM $1   MIP $2

I Like Bikes, 1990, McDonald's, set of four bike accessories: Ronald Basket, Grimace mirror, Birdie spinner, Fry Guy Horn

NM $10   MIP $20

Inspector Gadget, 1999, McDonald's, set of eight: Navik 7 Sparker, Arm Squirter, Watch Belt, Leg Tool, Leg Circuit Signaler, Leg Tool, Secret Communicator, Siren Hat

NM $2   MIP $5

(Toy Shop File Photo)

Jungle Book, 1990, McDonald's, set of four wind-up figures: Baloo the bear, Shere Kahn the tiger, King Louie the orangutan, Kaa the snake

NM $1   MIP $3

Jungle Book, 1990, McDonald's, set of two U3 toys: Junior, Mowgli

NM $3   MIP $6

Jungle Book, 1997, McDonald's, set of six: Baloo, Junior, Bagheera, King Louie, Kaa, Mowgli
NM $1 **MIP** $2

Kissyfur, 1987, McDonald's, set of four non-flocked figures: Floyd, Gus, Kissyfur, Jolene; the flocked and non-flocked figres make up one complete set
NM $5 **MIP** $10

Kissyfur, 1987, McDonald's, set of four flocked figure: Beehonie, Duane, Toot, Lennie
NM $20 **MIP** $40

Lego, 1999, McDonald's, set of eight: Ronald Helicopter, Sundae Water Vehicle, Birdie Airplane, McNugget Buddy Race Car, Grimmace Snow Plow, Yellow Fry Guy Seaplane, Hamburglar Airplane, Blue Fry Guy Speedplane
NM $1 **MIP** $3

Lego Building Set III, 1986, McDonald's, four different sets: tanker boat, blue; airplane, green; roadster, red; helicopter, yellow
NM $3 **MIP** $5

Lego Building Sets, 1983, McDonald's, set of four Duplo U3 toys: blue blocks, Bird, red blocks, green Duplo blocks
NM $5 **MIP** $10

Lego Building Sets, 1983, McDonald's, set of four: ship, helicopter, truck, airplane
NM $25 **MIP** $40

Lego Building Sets II, 1984, McDonald's, set of four: ship, truck, helicopter, airplane
NM $3 **MIP** $5

Lego Building Sets II, 1984, McDonald's, set of two U3 toys: Duplo bird, Duplo boat with sailor
NM $4 **MIP** $8

Lego Building Sets III, 1986, McDonald's, set of two U3 toys: Duplo bird, Duplo boat
NM $3 **MIP** $5

Lego Motion IV, 1989, McDonald's, set of eight kits: Gyro Bird, Lightning Striker, Land Laser, Sea Eagle, Wind Whirler, Sea Skimmer, Turbo Force, Swamp Stinger
NM $3 **MIP** $6

Lego Motion IV, 1989, McDonald's, set of two U3 Duplo toys: Giddy the Gator, Tuttle the Turtle
NM $2 **MIP** $5

Linkables, 1993, McDonald's, set of four: Birdie on tricycle, Ronald in soap-box racer, Grimace in wagon, Hamburglar in airplane; regionally distributed in New England area
NM $2 **MIP** $4

Lion Circus, 1979, McDonald's, set of four rubber figures: bear, elephant, hippo, lion
NM $2 **MIP** $3

Little Engineer, 1987, McDonald's, set of five vacuform train engines: Birdie Sunshine Special, Fry Girl's Express, Fry Guy's Flyer, Grimace Streak, Ronald Railway
NM $4 **MIP** $8

Little Engineer, 1987, McDonald's, set of four floating toys: Grimace Happy Taxi, green or yellow; Birdie, green or yellow
NM $2 **MIP** $6

Little Gardener, 1989, McDonald's, one U3 toy: Birdie shovel
NM $5 **MIP** $10

Little Gardener, 1989, McDonald's, set of four: Ronald Water Can, Birdie Shovel with Marigold seeds, Grimace Rake with radish seeds, Fry Guy Planter
NM $1 **MIP** $2

Little Golden Books, 1982, McDonald's, set of five books: Country Mouse and City Mouse, Tom & Jerry, Pokey Little Puppy, Benji, Monster at the End of This Block
NM $2 **MIP** $4

Little Mermaid, 1989, McDonald's, set of four: Flounder, Ursula, Prince Eric, Ariel with Sebastian
NM $1 **MIP** $2

Little Mermaid, 1997, McDonald's, set of eight: Ursula, Flounder, Scuttle, Ariel, Max, Glut, Eric, Sebastian
NM $1 **MIP** $2

Little Mermaid, Gold, 1997, McDonald's, set of eight: Ursula, Flounder, Scuttle, Ariel, Max, Glut, Eric, Sebastian; one out of every ten toys distributed with Happy Meal was a gold toy; compete sets of gold Little Mermaid premiums could be ordered for $12.99 plus shipping with forms available at McDonald's
NM $5 **MIP** $10

Little Travelers with Lego Building Sets, 1985, McDonald's, set of four: airplane, boat, helicopter, car; regionally distributed in Oklahoma; similar to Lego Building Set Happy Meal
NM $20 **MIP** $30

Littlest Pet Shop/Transformers Beast Wars, 1996, McDonald's, one U3 toy: Hamster Wheel.
NM $1 **MIP** $2

Littlest Pet Shop/Transformers Beast Wars, 1996, McDonald's, set of four: Swan, Unicorn, Dragon, Tiger; joint promotion with Transformers Beast Wars
NM $1 **MIP** $2

Looney Tunes Christmas Dolls-Canada, McDonald's, set of four: Sylvester in nightgown and cap, Tasmanian Devil in Santa hat, Bugs in winter scarf , Tweetie dressed as Elf
NM $3 **MIP** $6

Looney Tunes Quack Up Cars, 1993, McDonald's, one U3 toy: Bugs Bunny Swingin' Sedan in red or orange
NM $3 **MIP** $5

(KP Photo)

Looney Tunes Quack Up Cars, 1993, McDonald's, set of five: Taz Tornado Tracker, Porky Ghost Catcher, Bugs Super Stretch Limo in red or orange, Daffy Splittin' Sportster
NM $3 **MIP** $5

Luggage Tags, 1988, McDonald's, set of four: Birdie, Hamburglar, Grimace, Ronald
NM $3 **MIP** $5

Lunch Box, 1987, McDonald's, set of four lunch boxes: Grimace at bat, Ronald playing football, Ronald on rainbow, Ronald flying spaceship
NM $5 **MIP** $10

(Toy Shop File Photo)

Mac Tonight, 1988, McDonald's, set of six: Mac in Jeep, Mac in sports car, Mac on Surf Ski (with or without wheels), Mac on Motorcycle (red or black), Mac in Airplane (wearing blue or black sunglasses), Mac on Scooter; given out from 1988 to 1990, Surf Ski with wheels and Airplane with dark sunglasses were distributed in 1990
NM $8 **MIP** $15

Mac Tonight Pin, 1988, McDonald's, Moonface and slogan enamel pin
NM $2 **MIP** $4

Mac Tonight Puppet, 1988, McDonald's, Fingertronic foam puppet
NM $6 **MIP** $15

Mac Tonight Sunglasses, 1988, McDonald's, adult size
NM $2 **MIP** $5

Magic School Bus, 1994, McDonald's, set of four: Collector Card Kit, Space Tracer, Geo Fossil Finder, Undersea Adventure Game with yellow tab
NM $1 **MIP** $2

Magic School Bus, 1994, McDonald's, one U3 toy: Undersea Adventure Game without yellow tab
NM $1 **MIP** $2

Magic Show, 1985, McDonald's, set of five tricks: String Trick, Disappearing Hamburger Patch, Magic Tablet, Magic Picture—Ronald, Magic Picture—Grimace
NM $3 **MIP** $6

Makin' Movies, 1994, McDonald's, one U3 toy: Sound Effects Machine
NM $1 **MIP** $2

Makin' Movies, 1994, McDonald's, set of four: Sound Effects Machine, Movie Camera, Clapboard with chalk, Megaphone

NM $1   **MIP** $2

Marvel Super Heroes, 1996, McDonald's, set of eight: Spider-Man, Storm, Wolverine, Jubilee, Color Change Invisible Woman, Thing, Hulk, Human Torch

NM $1   **MIP** $2

Marvel Super Heroes, 1996, McDonald's, one U3 Toy: Spider-Man Ball

NM $1   **MIP** $2

Matchbox Mini-Flexies, 1979, McDonald's, set of eight rubber cars: Cosmobile, Hairy Hustler, Planet Scout, Hi-Tailer, Datsun, Beach Hopper, Baja Buggy

NM $2   **MIP** $4

McBoo Bags, 1991, McDonald's, set of six: three McBoo bags: Witch, Ghost, Monster; three pails: McBoo, McGoblin, witch

NM $3   **MIP** $5

McBunny Easter Pails, 1989, McDonald's, set of three: Pinky, Fluffy, Whiskers

NM $3   **MIP** $6

McCharacters on Bikes, 1991, McDonald's, set of four: Ronald on red tricycle, Grimace on blue tricycle, Hamburglar on yellow tricycle, Birdie on pink tricycle

NM $3   **MIP** $5

(KP Photo)

McDino Changeables, 1991, McDonald's, set of eight: Happy Meal-o-don, Quarter Pounder Chees-o-saur, Big Mac-o-saurus Rex, McNugget-o-saurus, Hotcakes-o-dactyl, Large Fry-o-saur, Tri-shak-atops, McDino cone

NM $2   **MIP** $3

McDino Changeables, 1991, McDonald's, set of three U3 toys: Bronto Cheeseburger, Small Fry Ceratops with yellow arches, Small Fry Ceratops with red arches

NM $2   **MIP** $3

McDonald Sun Glasses, 1989, McDonald's, set of four: Grimace, Birdie, Ronald, Hamburglar; over-the-counter premium, sold for 99 cents, each

NM $5   **MIP** $7

McDonaldland Band, 1987, McDonald's, set of eight music toys: Grimace saxophone, Fry Guy trumpet, Fry Guy boat whistle, Ronald harmonica, Ronald train whistle, Ronald pan pipes, Birdie kazoo, Hamburglar whistle

NM $1   **MIP** $3

McDonaldland Carnival, 1990, McDonald's, set of four: Birdie on swing, Grimace in turn-around, Hamburglar on ferris wheel, Ronald on carousel

NM $3   **MIP** $5

McDonaldland Carnival, 1990, McDonald's, one U3 floaty toy: Grimace

NM $10   **MIP** $15

McDonaldland Dough, 1990, McDonald's, set of eight, each included can of modeling clay and mold: red with Ronald star mold, yellow with Ronald square mold, green with Fry Girl octagon mold, blue with Fry Guy hexagon mold, purple with Grimace square mold, orange with Grimace triangle mold, pink with Birdie heart mold, white with Birdie circle mold; sold in the Southern United States only

NM $3   **MIP** $5

McDonaldland Express, 1982, McDonald's, set of four train car containers: Ronald engine, caboose, freight car, coach car

NM $25   **MIP** $50

McDonaldland Junction, 1983, McDonald's, set of four snap-together train cars: red Ronald Engine, yellow Birdie Parlor car, green Hamburger Flat Car, purple Grimace caboose

NM $5   **MIP** $10

McDonaldland Junction, 1983, McDonald's, set of four regionally distributed cars: blue Ronald Engine, pink Birdie Parlor Car, white Hambuger Flat Car, orange Grimace Caboose

NM $20   **MIP** $30

McDonaldland Play-Doh, 1986, McDonald's, set of eight colors: white, orange, yellow, purple, pink, red, green, blue

NM $2   **MIP** $4

McDonaldland TV Lunch Box, 1987, McDonald's, set of four lunch boxes: blue, green, yellow, red; each box came with a sheet of stickers; regionally distributed in New England area

NM $5   **MIP** $10

McDonald's All-Star Race Team (MAXX) '91, 1991, McDonald's, complete set of cards

NM $4   **MIP** $5

McDonald's All-Star Race Team (MAXX) '92, 1992, McDonald's, complete set of 36 cards

NM $4   **MIP** $5

McDonald's Playing Cards, McDonald's, two decks to a set

NM $2   **MIP** $5

McDonald's Spinner Top-Holland, McDonald's

NM $2   **MIP** $4

McDrive Thru Crew, 1990, McDonald's, set of four: fries in potato roadster, shake in milk carton, McNugget in egg roadster, hamburger in ketchup bottle; regionally distributed in Ohio and Illinois

NM $20   **MIP** $40

(KP Photo)

McNugget Buddies, 1988, McDonald's, set of ten: Cowpoke, First-Class, Sarge, Drummer, Corny, Sparky, Boomerang, Volley, Snorkel, Rocker

NM $4   **MIP** $6

McNugget Buddies, 1989, McDonald's, set of two U3 toy: Slugger, Daisy

NM $1   **MIP** $2

McNugget Buddies, 1989, McDonald's, set of ten rubber figures and accessories: Sparky, Volley, Corny, Drummer, Cowpoke, Sarge, Snorkel, First Class, Rocker, Boomerang

NM $1   **MIP** $2

Metrozoo Happy Meal, 1987, McDonald's, set of four: Elephant, Chimp, Flamingo, Tiger; distributed only in South Florida area

NM $25   **MIP** $250

Michael Jordan Fitness, 1992, McDonald's, set of eight toys: soccer ball, squeeze bottle, stopwatch, basketball, football, baseball, jump rope, flying disc

NM $2   **MIP** $4

Michael Jordan Fitness Fun Challenge, 1992, McDonald's, set of eight: baseball, basketball, flying disc, football, jump rope, soccer ball, squeeze bottle, stop watch; all premiums are marked with Michael Jordan logo

NM $2   **MIP** $4

Mickey and Friends Epcot Center '94 Adventure, 1994, McDonald's, set of eight: Donald in Mexico, Daisy in Germany, Mickey in U.S.A., Minnie in Japan, Chip in China, Pluto in France, Dale in Moroco, Goofy in Norway

NM $2   **MIP** $3

Mickey and Friends Epcot Center '94 Adventure, 1994, McDonald's, one U3 toy: Mickey in U.S.A.

NM $2   **MIP** $3

Mickey's Birthdayland, 1989, McDonald's, set of four U3 vehicles: Mickey's Convertible, Goofy's Car, Minnie's Convertible, Donald's Jeep

NM $5   **MIP** $10

Mickey's Birthdayland, 1989, McDonald's, set of five characters in vehicles: Minnie's Convertible, Donald's Train, Goofy's Jalopy, Mickey's Roadster, Pluto's Rumbler
NM $1   MIP $3

Micro Machines/Sky Dancers, 1997, McDonald's, set of four: Evac Copter, Polar Explorer, Ocean Flyer, Deep Sea Hunter; joint promotion with Sky Dancers
NM $1   MIP $2

Mighty Duck Pucks, 1997, McDonald's, set of four: Wildwing, Nosedive, Mallory, Duke L'Orange
NM $1   MIP $2

Mighty Mini 4x4s, 1991, McDonald's, set of four: Cargo Climber, Dune Buster, L'il Classic, Pocket Pickup
NM $1   MIP $2

Mighty Mini 4x4s, 1991, McDonald's, one U3 toy: Pocket Pickup
NM $3   MIP $5

Mighty Morphin Power Rangers, 1995, McDonald's, one U3 toy: Power Flute
NM $1   MIP $2

Mighty Morphin Power Rangers, 1995, McDonald's, set of four: Power Com, Powermorpher Buckle, Alien Detector, Power Siren
NM $1   MIP $2

Minnesota Twins Baseball Glove, 1984, McDonald's, Twins logo on side, Coca-Cola inside glove, McDonald's satin logo on back, given to the first 100 kids at 1984 Twins game
NM $40   MIP $75

Mix 'em Up Monsters, 1989, McDonald's, set of four: Thuggle, Blibble, Corkle, Gropple; regionally distributed in St. Louis, Missouri and Northern California
NM $2   MIP $5

Moster Crazy Bones, 2000, McDonald's, set of twelve: Funny Bone, Howler, Sweetie, Webs, Cool Dude, Haggy, Eggy, Punky, Boo, Menace, Goodie Goodie, Tut, Chef, Drac, Raskall, Wow, Music, Scraps, Fangs, Speedy, Doc, Top Hat, Luckey, Smiley
NM $1   MIP $3

Moveables, 1988, McDonald's, set of six vinyl bendies: Birdie, Captain Crook, Fry Girl, Hamburglar, Professor, Ronald; regionally distributed in St Louis, Missouri area
NM $4   MIP $12

M-Squad, 1993, McDonald's, one U3 toy: Spytracker watch
NM $1   MIP $2

M-Squad, 1993, McDonald's, set of four: Spystamper, Spytracker, Spynocular, Spycoder
NM $2   MIP $4

Mulan, 1998, McDonald's, set of eight: Mulan, Kahn, Little Brother, Shan-Yu, Mushi, Shang-Li, Cri-Kee, Chien-Po, Ling, Yao
NM $1   MIP $2

Mulan on Video, 1999, McDonald's, set of eight: Ling, Mulan, Kahn, Mushu, Shan-Yu, Chien-Po, Shang, Yao
NM $1   MIP $3

Muppet Babies holiday promotion, 1988, McDonald's, set of four stuffed toys: Miss Piggy, Kermit, Fozzie; over-the-counter premium sold with food purchase for for $1.99
NM $2   MIP $5

Muppet Babies I, 1986, McDonald's, set of four: Kermit with skateboard, Miss Piggy with car and flat hair ribbon, Gonzo with tricycle and no shoes, Fozzie with horse; test market Happy Meal, regionally distributed in Savannah, Georgia
NM $25   MIP $50

Muppet Babies II, 1987, McDonald's, set of two U3 toys: Kermit on skates, Miss Piggy on Skates
NM $3   MIP $5

Muppet Babies II, 1987, McDonald's, set of four: Kermit with skateboard, Miss Piggy with pink car, Gonzo with tricycle and shoes, Fozzie with horse
NM $2   MIP $4

(KP Photo)

Muppet Babies III, 1991, McDonald's, set of four: Miss Piggy on tricycle, Gonzo in airplane, Fozzie in wagon, Kermit on soapbox racer
NM $2   MIP $4

Muppet Kids, 1989, McDonald's, set of four: Kermit with red tricycle, Miss Piggy with pink tricycle, Gonzo with yellow tricycle, Fozzie with green tricycle
NM $15   MIP $25

Muppet Treasure Island, 1996, McDonald's, set of four: Miss Piggy, Kermit, Gonzo, Fozzy Bear
NM $2   MIP $3

Muppet Treasure Island, 1996, McDonald's, one U3 toy: Bath Book "The Muppet Treasure Island"
NM $1   MIP $2

Muppet Workshop, 1995, McDonald's, one U3 toy: What-Not
NM $1   MIP $2

Muppet Workshop, 1995, McDonald's, set of four: Bird, Dog, What-Not, Monster
NM $1   MIP $2

Music Happy Meal, 1985, McDonald's, set of four 33-1/3 RPM records: If You're Happy/Little Bunny Foo Foo; Do the Hokey Pokey/Eensy Weensy Spider; Boom, Boom, Ain't it Great to Be Crazy;

She'll be Comin' 'Round the Mountain, Head, Shoulders, Knees and Toes
NM $3   MIP $5

My Little Pony (joint promotion w/Transformers), 1985, McDonald's, set of six: Minty, Snuzzle, Blossom, Cotton Candy, Blue Belle, Butterscotch; regionally distributed in St. Louis, Missouri area
NM $20   MIP $80

My Little Pony/Transformers, 1998, McDonald's, set of three: Ivy, Sundance, Light Heart; split promo with Transformers
NM $1   MIP $2

Mystery Happy Meal, 1983, McDonald's, set of five: Detective Kit, Crystal Ball, Ronald Magni-Finder, Birdie Mangi-Finder, Fry Guys Magni-Finder
NM $20   MIP $35

Mystery of the Lost Arches, 1992, McDonald's, set of four: mini-cassette, phone, telescope, camera
NM $1   MIP $2

Mystery of the Lost Arches, 1992, McDonald's, set of five: Phone/Periscope, Flashlight/Telescope in red and blue or red and yellow, Magic Lens Camera, Microcaste/Magnifier
NM $1   MIP $2

Mystic Knights of Tir na Nog, 1999, McDonald's, set of eight: Rohan, Queen Maeve, Angus. Tore, Deirdre, mider, Ivar, Lugad; a bonus toy can be built from Queen Maeve, Tore, Mider and Lugad
NM $1   MIP $3

NASCAR Hot Wheels/Barbie, 1998, McDonald's, set of four: Ronald Happy Meal NASCAR, Mac Tonight, Hot Wheels, 50th Anniversary NASCAR; split promo with Barbie;
NM $1   MIP $3

Nature's Helpers, 1991, McDonald's, set of five: Double Digger with cucumber seeds, Bird Feeder, Watering Can, Terrarium with coleus seeds, Rake with marigold seeds
NM $1   MIP $2

Nature's Watch, 1992, McDonald's, one U3 toy: double shovel-rake
NM $1   MIP $2

Nature's Watch, 1992, McDonald's, set of four: Bird Feeder, Double Shovel-Rake, Greenhouse, Sprinkler
NM $1   MIP $2

New Archies, 1988, McDonald's, set of six figures in bumper cars: Moose, Reggie, Archie, Veronica, Betty, Jughead; regionally distributed in St. Louis, Missouri area
NM $5   MIP $15

New Food Changeables, 1989, McDonald's, set of eight: Krypto Cup, Fry Bot, Turbo Cone, Macro Mac, Gallacta Burger, Robo Cakes, C2 Cheeseburger, Fry Force
NM $2   MIP $4

Nickelodeon, 1993, McDonald's, one U3 toy: Blimp squirter
NM $1   **MIP** $2

Nickelodeon, 1993, McDonald's, set of four: Blimp Game, Loud-Mouth Mike, Gotcha Gusher, Applause Paws
NM $1   **MIP** $2

Nickelodeon's Tangle Toy, 1997, McDonald's, set of eight Twist-a-zoids
NM $1   **MIP** $2

Norman Rockwell Brass Ornament, 1983, McDonald's, 50th Annivesary Norman Rockwell design, gift packaged with McDonald and Coca-Cola logos
NM $3   **MIP** $7

Norman Rockwell Ornament, 1978, McDonald's, clear acrylic, "Christmas Trio," gift boxed
NM $3   **MIP** $7

Old McDonald's Farm, 1986, McDonald's, set of six figures: farmer, wife, rooster, pig, sheep, cow; regionally distributed in Missouri and Tennessee
NM $10   **MIP** $15

Old West, 1981, McDonald's, set of six rubber figures: cowboy, frontiersman, lady, Indian, Indian woman, sheriff
NM $7   **MIP** $14

Oliver & Company, 1988, McDonald's, set of four finger puppets: Oliver, Georgette, Francis, Dodger
NM $3   **MIP** $5

Olympic Beach Ball, 1984, McDonald's, set of three: Grimace in kayak, green; Ronald holding flag and beachball, red; Birdie in sailboat, blue
NM $15   **MIP** $20

Olympic Sports, 1984, McDonald's, set of five Guess'n'Glow puzzles: Guess Which Guy Comes in Under the Wire (Grimace and Hamburglar), Guess Who Makes the Biggest Splash (Ronald, Birdie and Captain); Guess Who Finished Smiles Ahead (Hamburglar and Birdie); Who Do You Know That Can Help them Row? (Ronald and Fry Guy); Guess Who Stole the Winning Goal (Grimace); this promotion replaced the original Olympics Sports Happy Meal
NM $15   **MIP** $30

Olympic Sports, 1984, McDonald's, set of five zip-action toys: Ronald on bicycle, roller skating Birdie, Grimace, Birdie and Captain rowing, running Grimace; prototypes only. The Olympic sports Happy Meal was cancelled after the toys failed safety tests. It was replaced by Guess'n'Glow puzzles
NM $30   **MIP** $60

Olympic Sports II, 1988, McDonald's, set of six clip-on buttons: Birdie/gymnastics, Hamburglar/track and field, CosMc/basketball, Fry Girl/diving, Ronald/bicyclling, Grimace/soccer
NM $5   **MIP** $8

On the Go I, 1985, McDonald's, set of five: On the Go Bead Game, Stop & Go Bead Game, Ronald Magic Slate, Hamburglar Magic Slate, On the Go Transfers
NM $10   **MIP** $15

On the Go Lunch Box II, 1988, McDonald's, set of four: red lunch box with bulliten board and stickers, green lunch box with bulletin board and stickers, yellow lunch bag with Ronald, white lunch bag with Grimace
NM $2   **MIP** $4

Out of Fun Happy Meal, 1993, McDonald's, set of four: Balloon Ball, Ronald Bubble Shoe Wand, Sunglasses, Sand Pail
NM $1   **MIP** $2

Paint with Water, 1978, McDonald's, paintless coloring board with self contained frame and easel
NM $5   **MIP** $10

(Toy Shop File Photo)

Peanuts, 1990, McDonald's, set of four: Snoopy's Hay Hauler, Charlie Brown's Seed Bag 'N Tiller, Lucy's Apple Cart, Linus' Milk Mover
NM $2   **MIP** $4

Peanuts, 1990, McDonald's, set of two U3 toys: Charlie Brown's egg basket or Snoopy's potato sack
NM $2   **MIP** $4

Pencil Puppets, 1978, McDonald's, six different pencil toppers in shapes of McDonaldland characters
NM $2   **MIP** $4

Peter Pan, 1998, McDonald's, set of seven: Peter Pan Glider, Tic Tock Croc, Captain Hook Spyglass, Tinker Bell Lantern Clip, Smee Light, Wendy & Michael Magnifier, Activity Tool
NM $1   **MIP** $2

Peter Rabbit, 1988, McDonald's, set of four books: The Tale of Benjamin Bunny, The Tale of Peter Rabbit, The Tale of the Flopsy Bunnies, The Tale of Squirrel Nutkin; regionally distributed in Pennsylvania and New York
NM $10   **MIP** $25

Picture Perfect, 1985, McDonald's, set of four Crayola products: coloring (thin) marker, red or blue; drawing (thick) marker, orange or green; box of three fluorescent Cayons; box of six Crayons
NM $5   **MIP** $10

Piggsburg Pigs, 1991, McDonald's, set of four: Rembrandt, Huff & Puff, Piggy & Crackers, Portly & Pighead; regionally distributed in Florida, Colorado and Ohio
NM $3   **MIP** $5

Play-Doh, 1983, McDonald's, set of four containers of Play-Doh: blue, red, yellow, white; regionally distributed in the New England area; containers did not have any McDonald's markings
NM $15   **MIP** $20

Play-Doh II, 1985, McDonald's, set of two containers of Play-Doh: pink and green
NM $15   **MIP** $20

Play-Doh III, 1986, McDonald's, set of eight containers of Play-Doh: pink, blue, purple, green, red, yellow, white, orange
NM $5   **MIP** $8

Playmobile, 1982, McDonald's, set of five toys and accesories: farmer, sheriff, Indian, umbrella girl, horse and saddle
NM $10   **MIP** $20

Polly Pocket/Attack Pack, 1995, McDonald's, one U3 toy: watch
NM $2   **MIP** $3

Polly Pocket/Attack Pack, 1995, McDonald's, set of four: Ring, Locket, Watch, Bracelet; joint promotion with Attack Pack
NM $1   **MIP** $2

Popoids, 1984, McDonald's, set of six made up of two to three bellows and one joint piece: blue and dark blue bellows with one ball joint; blue and white bellows with cube joint; blue and dark blue bellows with one cube joint; red and yellow bellows with pentahedron joint; red and yellow bellows with wheel joint; blue, dark blue and yellow bellows without joint; regionally distributed in the St. Louis, Missouri area
NM $40   **MIP** $50

Potato Head Kids I, 1987, McDonald's, set of twelve: Lumpy, Potato Dumpling, Big Chip, Smarty Pants, Dimples, Spike, Potato Puff, Tulip, Spud, Lolly, Slugger, Slick; regionally distributed in Texas, Oklahoma and New Mexico
NM $5   **MIP** $25

Potato Head Kids II, 1992, McDonald's, set of eight: Dimples, Spike, Potato Dumpling, Slugger, Slick, Tulip, Potato Puff, Spud
NM $3   **MIP** $6

(KP Photo)

Power Rangers, 2000, McDonald's, set of eleven: Red Power Ranger, Yellow Power Ranger, Pink Power Ranger, Green Power Ranger, Blue Power Ranger, Silver Power Ranger, Yellow Rail Rescue, Blue Rail Rescue, Pink Rail Rescue, Green Rail Rescue

NM $1   **MIP** $3

Punkin' Makins, 1977, McDonald's, character cutouts to decorate pumpkins: Ronald, Goblin, Grimace

NM $7   **MIP** $15

Raggedy Ann and Andy, 1989, McDonald's, one U3 toy: Camel with Wrinkled Knees

NM $8   **MIP** $12

Raggedy Ann and Andy, 1989, McDonald's, set of four: Raggedy Andy with slide, Raggedy Ann with swing, Grouchy Bear merry-go-round, Camel with Wrinkled Knees with teeter totter

NM $5   **MIP** $10

Read Along with Ronald, 1989, McDonald's, set of four books and tapes: Grimace Goes to School, The Day Birdie the Early Bird Learned to Fly, The Mystery of the Missing French Fries, Dinosaur in McDonaldland

NM $5   **MIP** $10

Real Ghostbusters, 1987, McDonald's, set of five school tools: pencil case, notepad, ruler, pencil with pencil topper, pencil sharpener

NM $3   **MIP** $5

Real Ghostbusters II, 1992, McDonald's, one U3 toy: Slimer squirter

NM $3   **MIP** $5

Real Ghostbusters II, 1992, McDonald's, set of four: Ecto Siren, Egon Spinner, Slimer horn, water bottle; regionally distributed in Kansas City, Kansas

NM $3   **MIP** $5

Recess, 1998, McDonald's, set of seven: TJ, Spinelli, Vince, Mikey, Gretchen, Gus, School Teacher

NM $1   **MIP** $2

Records, 1985, McDonald's, set of four 45-RPM records in sleeves with different songs and colored labels

NM $3   **MIP** $6

Rescuers Down Under, 1990, McDonald's, One U3 toy: Bernard

NM $3   **MIP** $6

(KP Photo)

Rescuers Down Under, 1990, McDonald's, set of four slide-viewing movie camera toys: Jake, Wilbur, Bernard and Bianca, Cody

NM $2   **MIP** $4

Rescuers Down Under Christmas Ornament, 1990, McDonald's, set of two: Miss Bianca, Bernard

NM $3   **MIP** $6

Rings, 1977, McDonald's, set of five rings with character heads: Big Mac, Captain Crook, Grimace, Hamburglar, Ronald

NM $5   **MIP** $10

Robo-Chi Pets, 2001, McDonald's, set of eight, each in four different color schemes: Laydown Poo-Chi, Batting Meow-Chi, Dancing Poo-Chi, Lightup Meow-Chi, Predicting Poo-Chi, Singing Chirpy-Chi, Barking Poo-Chi, Flapping Chirpy-Chi

NM $1   **MIP** $3

Roger Rabbit Scarf-Japan, 1988, McDonald's, McDonald's logo, Japanese writing on scarf

NM $10   **MIP** $20

Ronald and Pals Haunted Halloween, 1998, McDonald's, set of six: Birdie, Gramace, Iam Hungry, Hamburglar, Ronald, McNugget Buddy

NM $1   **MIP** $2

Ronald McDonald Celebrates Happy Birthday, 1994, McDonald's, one U3 toy: Ronald McDonald

NM $3   **MIP** $5

Ronald McDonald Celebrates Happy Birthday, 1994, McDonald's, set of sixteen: Ronald McDonald, Barbie, Hot Wheels, E.T., Sonic the Hedgehog, Berenstain Bears, Tonka, Cabbage Patch Kids, 101 Dalmatians, Little Mermaid, Muppet Babies with white tie, Muppet Babies with or blue tie, Peanuts, The Little Mermaid, Tiny Toons, Happy Meal Guys

NM $3   **MIP** $5

Ronald McDonald Cookie Cutter, 1987, McDonald's, Ronald with balloons, green or orange

NM $1   **MIP** $3

Ronald McDonald Doll, McDonald's, 7" doll by Remco

NM $18   **MIP** $25

Ronald McDonald Doll, McDonald's, 14" vinyl head with a soft body by Dakin

NM $15   **MIP** $35

Ronald McDonald Maze, 1979, McDonald's, lift up mystery game

NM $4   **MIP** $10

Ronald McDonald Pin, McDonald's, enamel, Ronald in Christmas wreath

NM $6   **MIP** $12

Ronald McDonald Plastic Flyers, McDonald's, Ronald with legs and arms extended, red or yellow

NM $1   **MIP** $3

Ronald McDonald Shoe & Sock Game-Japan, McDonald's, plastic with ball and string, with Japanese writing

NM $5   **MIP** $10

Ronald McDonald Tote Bag-Japan, McDonald's, writing in Japanese

NM $5   **MIP** $10

Runaway Robots, 1987, McDonald's, set of six: Skull, Jab, Flame, Beak, bolt, Coil; regionally distributed in Nebraske, Maine, Massachusettes, Tenessee and Alabama

NM $15   **MIP** $20

Safari Adventure, 1980, McDonald's, six different rubber animals: alligator, monkey, gorilla, tiger, hippo, rhinoceros

NM $2   **MIP** $4

Sailors, 1988, McDonald's, set of four floating toys: Hamburglar Sailboat, Ronald Airboat, Grimace Submarine, Fry Kids Ferry

NM $5   **MIP** $10

Sailors, 1988, McDonald's, set of two U3 floating toys: Grimace in speedboat, Fry Guy on intertube

NM $4   **MIP** $8

Santa Claus: The Movie, 1985, McDonald's, set of four books: The Elves at the Top of the World, Sleighful of Surprises, Workshop of Surprises

NM $1   **MIP** $3

School Days, 1984, McDonald's, set of twelve: Ronald pencil, Grimace pencil, Hamburglar Pencil, Ronald eraser, Grimace eraser, Hamburglar eraser, Captain Crook eraser, Birdie eraser, Grimace pencil sharpener, Ronald pencil sharpener, Ronald and Birdie ruler, Ronald and Birdie pencil case

NM $5   **MIP** $10

Sea World of Ohio, 1988, McDonald's, set of three figures: Dolly Dolphin, Penny Penguin, Shamu the whale; regionally distributed in Cleveland, Ohio area

NM $20   **MIP** $40

Sea World of Texas, 1988, McDonald's, set of four stuffed toys: dolphin, penguin, walrus, whale; regionally distributed in San Antonio, Texas area

NM $20   **MIP** $30

Sea World of Texas II, 1989, McDonald's, set of five: sea otter stuffed toy, dolphin stuffed toy, whale stuffed toy, penguin sunglasses, whale sunglasses

NM $25   **MIP** $50

Serving Trays, McDonald's, set of six white plastic wedge-shaped trays: Ronald, Big Mac, Mayor McCheese, Hamburglar, Grimace, Captain Crook

NM $3   **MIP** $7

Ship Shape I, 1983, McDonald's, set of four vacuform boat containers with stickers: Tubby Tugger, Splash Dasher, Rub-a-Dub Sub, Riverboat

NM $10   **MIP** $15

Ship Shape II, 1985, McDonald's, set of two U3 floating toys: Grimace in Tub, Fry Guys on Duck

NM $5   **MIP** $8

Ship Shape II, 1985, McDonald's, set of four vacuform boat containers with stickers: Tubby Tugger, Splash Dasher,

Rub-a-Dub Sub, Riverboat; similar to 1983 Ship Shape Happy Meal but with redesigned stickers
NM $10 **MIP** $20

Sindy Doll, 1970, McDonald's, dressed in older McDonald's uniform
NM $4 **MIP** $8

Sky Dancers/Micro Machines, 1997, McDonald's, set of four dancing dolls: Rosemerry, Swan Shimmer, Princess Pegasus, Flutter Fly; split promo with Micro Machines
NM $1 **MIP** $2

Sky-Busters, 1982, McDonald's, set of six rubber airplanes: Skyhawk AAF, Phantom, Mirage F1, United DC-10, MIG-21, Tornado
NM $3 **MIP** $5

Sleeping Beauty, 1997, McDonald's, set of six: Sleeping Beauty, Maleficent, Prince Philip, Flora, Dragon, Raven
NM $1 **MIP** $2

Smart Duck, 1979, McDonald's, set of six rubber figures: duck, cat, donkey, chipmunk, two rabbits
NM $2 **MIP** $3

Snow White and the Seven Dwarfs, 1993, McDonald's, set of nine: Snow White with wishing well, Prince on horse with green base, Prince on horse without base, Queen/Witch, Bashful, Dopey and Sneezy, Doc, Happy and Grumpy, Sleepy
NM $3 **MIP** $6

Snow White and the Seven Dwarfs, 1993, McDonald's, one U3 toy: Dopey and Sleepy
NM $2 **MIP** $3

Sonic 3 The Hedgehog, 1994, McDonald's, set of four: Sonic the Hedgehog, Miles "Tails" Power, Knuckles & Dr. Ivo Robotnik
NM $2 **MIP** $4

Sonic 3 The Hedgehog, 1994, McDonald's, one U3 toy: Sonic Ball
NM $3 **MIP** $6

Space Aliens, 1979, McDonald's, set of eight rubber monsters: Lizard Man, Vampire Bat, Gill Face, Tree Monster, Winged Fish, Cyclops, Veined Brain, Insectman
NM $2 **MIP** $3

Space Jam, 1996, McDonald's, set of eight interlocking pieces: Lola Bunny, Bugs Bunny, Taz, Marvin the Martian, Daffy Duck, Monstar, Sylvester & Tweety, Nerdlucks
NM $2 **MIP** $4

Space Jam Plush, 1996, McDonald's, set of six: Lola Bunny, Bugs Bunny, Taz, Daffy Duck, Monstar, Nerdlucks
NM $3 **MIP** $5

Space Raiders, 1979, McDonald's, set of eight rubber aliens: Drak, Dard, flying saucer, Rocket Kryoo-5, Horta, Zama, Rocket Ceti-3, Rocket Altair-2
NM $2 **MIP** $3

(KP Photo)

Space Rescue, 1995, McDonald's, set of four: Astro Viewer, Tele-Communicator, Space Slate, Lunar Grabber
NM $1 **MIP** $2

Space Rescue, 1995, McDonald's, one U3 toy: Astro-Viewer
NM $1 **MIP** $2

Spider-Man, 1995, McDonald's, one U3 toy: The Amazing Spider-man
NM $3 **MIP** $5

Spider-Man, 1995, McDonald's, set of eight: The Amazing Spider-Man, Dr. Octopus with moving tentacles, Mary Jane Watson with clip-on costumes, Spider-Sense Peter Parker, Scorpion Stingstriker, Spider-Man Webrunner, Venom Transport, Hobgoblin Landglider
NM $3 **MIP** $5

Spinner Baseball Game, 1983, McDonald's, green plastic with four characters
NM $2 **MIP** $4

Spinner Bicycle Game, 1984, McDonald's, pink or green game with two bicyclists
NM $2 **MIP** $5

Sports Ball, 1991, McDonald's, set of gour: white baseball, brown football, orange basketball, red and yellow soccer ball; regionally distributed in Kansas City and Indiana
NM $2 **MIP** $5

Sports Balls, 1988, McDonald's, set of four: basketball, baseball, football and tennis ball; test market Happy Meal, regionally distributed in Springfield, Missouri
NM $20 **MIP** $40

Sports Balls, 1988, McDonald's, one U3 toy: hard plastic baseball
NM $30 **MIP** $40

Sports Balls, 1990, McDonald's, set of four: baseball, football, basketball, soccer
NM $2 **MIP** $4

Star Trek, 1979, McDonald's, set of four glitter iron-ons: Kirk, Spock, McCoy, Ilia; packaged in pairs
NM $10 **MIP** $20

Star Trek, 1979, McDonald's, rings: Kirk, Spock, Starfleet insignia, Enterprise
NM $15 **MIP** $20

Star Trek, 1979, McDonald's, Starfleet game
NM $10 **MIP** $15

Star Trek, 1979, McDonald's, set of five video viewers, each with different story
NM $15 **MIP** $30

Star Trek, 1979, McDonald's, navigation bracelet with decals
NM $10 **MIP** $25

Sticker Club, 1985, McDonald's, set of five different sticker sheets: shiny, scratch and sniff, action stickers, puffy stickers, paper
NM $5 **MIP** $10

Stomper Mini 4x4 I, 1985, McDonald's, set of six: Chevy S-10 Pick-Up, blue; Chevy S-10 Pick-up, white; Chevy Van; Dodge Rampage, white; Dodge Rampage, blue; Jeep Renegade
NM $5 **MIP** $10

Stomper Mini 4x4 I, 1985, McDonald's, set of six push toys: Jeep Renegade, Dodge Rampage, white; Dodge Rampage, blue; Chevy S-10 Pick-up, blue; Chevy S-10 Pick-up, yellow; Chevy Van
NM $5 **MIP** $10

Stomper Mini 4x4 II, 1986, McDonald's, set of sixteen: Toyota Tercel, blue or gray; AMC Eagle, black or orange; Chevy S-10 pickup, black or yellow; Chevy van, red or yellow; Chevy Blazer, yellow or red; Ford Ranger, orange or red; Jeep Renegade, maroon or orange; Dodge Rampage, blue or white
NM $5 **MIP** $10

Story of Texas, 1986, McDonald's, set of eight books: Austin series—The Beginning, Independence, The Frontier, The 20th Century; Houston series—The Beginning, Independence, The Frontier, The 20th Century; regionally distributed in Texas
NM $75 **MIP** $100

Storybook Muppet Babies, 1988, McDonald's, set of three books: Baby Piggy, the Living Doll; The Legend of Gimmee Gulch; Just Kermit and Me!
NM $2 **MIP** $5

Super Looney Tunes, 1991, McDonald's, set of four figures with costumes: Super Bugs, Bat Duck, Taz Flash, Wonder Pig
NM $2 **MIP** $4

Super Looney Tunes, 1991, McDonald's, one U3 toy: Bat Duck in rocking boat
NM $2 **MIP** $4

Super Mario Brothers, 1990, McDonald's, set of four action figures: Mario, Luigi, Little Goomba, Koopa
MIP $4

Super Mario Brothers, 1990, McDonald's, one U3 toy: Super Mario
NM $2   **MIP** $4

Super Sticker Squares, 1987, McDonald's, nine scenes and over 100 reusable stickers
NM $1   **MIP** $3

Super Summer, 1987, McDonald's, set of three: sailboat, watering can, beachball; test market Happy Meal, distributed in Fresno, California
NM $20   **MIP** $30

Super Summer II, 1988, McDonald's, set of six: sand castle pail with shovel, sand pail with rake, fish sand mold, inflatable sailboat, beach ball, watering can
NM $2   **MIP** $4

(KP Photo)

Tale Spin, 1990, McDonald's, set of four characters in airplanes: Wildcat's Flying Machine, Baloo's Seaplane, Molly's Biplane, Kit's Racing Plane
NM $2   **MIP** $4

Tale Spin, 1990, McDonald's, set of U3 toys: Baloo's seaplane, Wildcat's jet
NM $2   **MIP** $4

Tamagotchi Key Chains, 1998, McDonald's, set of nine: yellow, purple, green, red, blue with yellow figure inside, white with red figure inside, red/orange flip action, blue flashlight, purple #9 (only available at McDonald's in Wal-Mart stores)
NM $2   **MIP** $4

Tarzan, 1999, McDonald's, set of eight: Tarzan with Surf Branch, Terk, Jane, Tantor, Porter, Kala, Clayton, Sabor
NM $1   **MIP** $3

Tarzan on Video, 2000, McDonald's, set of eight: Tarzan, Sabor, Tantor, Young Tarzan, Terk, Kerchak, Kala & Baby Tarzan
NM $1   **MIP** $3

Teenie Beanie Babies, 1997, McDonald's, set of ten plush toys: Patti the Platypus, Pinky the Flamingo, Chops the Lamb, Chocolate the Moose, Goldie the Goldfish, Speed the Turtle, Seamore the Seal, Snort the Bull, Quack the Duck, Lizz the Lizard
NM $10   **MIP** $20

(KP Photo)

Teenie Beanie Babies, 1998, McDonald's, set of twelve plush toys: Doby the Doberman, Bongo the Monkey, Twigs the Giraffe, Inch the Worm, Pinchers the Lobster, Happy the Hippo, Mel the Koala, Scoop the Pelican, Bones the Dog, Zip the Cat, Waddle the Penguin, Peanut the Elephant
NM $4   **MIP** $8

Teenie Beanie Babies, 1999, McDonald's, set of twelve: Freckles the Leopard, Smoochy the Frog, Rocket the Blue Jay, Strut the Rooster, Claude the Crab, 'Nook the Husky, Antsy the Anteater, Spunk the Cocker Spaniel, Iggy the Iguana, Nuts the Squirrel, Stretchy the Ostrich, Chip the Cat
NM $2   **MIP** $4

(KP Photo)

Teenie Beanie Babies, 2000, McDonald's, set of twelve: Dotty the Fish, Lip the Fish, Slither the Snake, Flip the Cat, Tusk the Walrus, Blizz the White Tiger, Schweetheart the Orangutan, Spike the Rhino, Spinner the Spider, Bumble the Bee, Flitter the Butterfly, Lucky the Ladybug, Coral the Fish, Sting the Ray, Goochy the Jellyfish, Neon the Jellyfish
NM $1   **MIP** $3

Teenie Beanie Babies International Bears, 1999, McDonald's, set of four: Britania, Glory, Erin, Maple; over-the-counter promotion available for $1.99 with food purchase
NM $1   **MIP** $2

Teletubbies, 2000, McDonald's, set of four: Po, Laa-Laa, Tinky Winky, Dipsy
NM $1   **MIP** $3

The Busy World of Richard Scarry, 1995, McDonald's, one U3 toy: Lowly Worm, rubber
NM $1   **MIP** $2

The Busy World of Richard Scarry, 1995, McDonald's, set of four: Lowly Worm and Post Office, Huckle Cat and School, Mr. Fumble and Fire Station, Bananas Gorilla and Grocery Store
NM $1   **MIP** $2

The Legend of Mulan, 1998, McDonald's, set of ten figures: Mulan, Khan, Mushu, Shanyu, Shang, Chein Po, Ying, Yao, Little Brother, Cri-Kee
NM $1   **MIP** $2

The Lion King II Simba's Pride, 1998, McDonald's, set of eight: Kovu, Zazu, Timon, Simba, Kiara, Zira, Rafiki, Pumbaa
NM $1   **MIP** $2

Tic Toc Mac Game, 1981, McDonald's, yellow base, Grimace is X, Ronald is O
NM $2   **MIP** $5

Tigger Movie, The, 2000, McDonald's, set of six: Tigger, Roo, Pooh, Eeyore, Piglet, Owl
NM $1   **MIP** $3

Tinosaurs, 1986, McDonald's, set of eight figures: Link the Elf, Baby Jad, Merry Bones, Dinah, Time Traveller Fern, Tiny, Grumpy Spell, Kave Kolt Kobby; regionally distributed in St. Louis, Missouri
NM $5   **MIP** $10

Tiny Toon Adventures Flip Cars, 1991, McDonald's, set of two U3 toys: Gogo Dodo in bathtub, Plucky Duck in red boat
NM $3   **MIP** $5

(KP Photo)

Tiny Toon Adventures Flip Cars, 1991, McDonald's, set of four cars, each with two characters: Montana Max/Gobo Dodo, Babs/Plucky Duck, Hampton/Devil, Elmyra/Buster Bunny
NM $1   **MIP** $2

Tiny Toon Adventures Wacky Rollers, 1992, McDonald's, set of eight: Buster Bunny, Babs Bunny, Elmyra, Dizzy Devil, Gogo Dodo, Montana Max, Plucky Duck, Sweetie
NM $1   **MIP** $3

Tiny Toons Adventures Wacky Rollers, 1992, McDonald's, one U3 toy: Sweetie
NM $2   **MIP** $4

Tom & Jerry Band, 1990, McDonald's, one U3 toy: Droopy
NM $5   **MIP** $8

Tom & Jerry Band, 1990, McDonald's, set of four characters with musical instruments: Tom at keyboard, Jerry on drums, Spike on bass, Droopy at the mike
NM $4   **MIP** $8

Tonka/Cabbage Patch Kids, 1992, McDonald's, set of five: Fire Truck, Loader, Cement Mixer, Dump Truck, Backhoe; joint promotion with Cabbage Patch Kids
NM $1   **MIP** $2

Tonka/Cabbage Patch Kids, 1992, McDonald's, one U3 toy: Dump Truck
NM $1   **MIP** $2

Tonka/Cabbage Patch Kids, 1992, McDonald's, set of four: Crane, Loader, Grader, Bulldozer; joint promotion with Cabbage Patch Kids
NM $1   **MIP** $3

RESTAURANT PREMIUMS

Tonka/Cabbage Patch Kids, 1994, McDonald's, one U3 toy: Dump Truck
NM $2   **MIP** $3

Toothbrush Happy Meal, 1985, McDonald's, set of three Ronald toothbrushes: red, yellow, blue
NM $20   **MIP** $40

Tops, 1978, McDonald's, set of three: red, blue and green
NM $3   **MIP** $7

Totally Toy Holiday, 1993, McDonald's, set of three U3 toys: Keyforce Car, Magic Nursery Boy, Magic Nursery Boy
NM $2   **MIP** $3

Totally Toy Holiday, 1993, McDonald's, Holiday Barbie snow dome; recalled
NM $25   **MIP** $50

Totally Toy Holiday, 1993, McDonald's, set of eleven: Lil' Miss Candistripes, Magic Nursery Boy, Magic Nursery Girl, Polly Pocket, Key Force Truck, Key Force Car, Mighty Max, Tattoo Machines, Attack Pack Vehicles, Sally Secrets, Caucasian, Sally Sercets, African-American
NM $2   **MIP** $3

Totally Toy Holiday, 1995, McDonald's, set of two U3 toys: Magic Nursery Boy, Magic Nursery Girl, Key Force Car
NM $3   **MIP** $5

Totally Toy Holiday, 1995, McDonald's, set of eight: Great Adventures Knight figurine with green dragon, Holiday Barbie, Hot Wheels Vehicle with ramp (came with red or green vehicle), "Once Upon a Dream" Princess figurine, Polly Pocket Playset, Mighty Max Playset, Cabbage Patch Playset, South Pole Explorer Vehicle
NM $1   **MIP** $2

Toy Story 2, 1999, McDonald's, set of twenty: Woody, Mr. And Mrs. Potatoe Head, Robot, Slinky Dog, Little Green Alien, Bo Peep, Hamm, Jessy, Rex, Lenny, Zurg, Prospector Pete, Marionette Woody, Barrel of Monekys, Buzz, Bullseye, Remote-controlled Car, Green Army Man, Tour Guide Barbie
NM $2   **MIP** $5

Toy Story 2 Candy Dispensers, 1999, McDonald's, set of stx: Woody w/Nerds, Jesse w/Sprees, Rex w/Smarties, Mr./Mrs. Potato Head w/Tart n Tinys, Hamm, Buzz w/Nerds
NM $2   **MIP** $5

Transformers Beast Wars/Littlest Pet Shop, 1996, McDonald's, set of four Transformer Beast Wars: Manta Ray, Beetle, Panther, Rhino; joint promotion with Littlest Pet Shop
NM $1   **MIP** $2

Transformers Beast Wars/Littlest Pet Shop, 1996, McDonald's, one U3 toy: Lion's Head Transformer
NM $1   **MIP** $2

(KP Photo)

Transformers/Hello Kitty, 2000, McDonald's, set of nine: Cheetor, Optimus Primal, Megatron, Jetstorm, Rattrap, Blackarachnia, Thrust, Nightsream, Tankor; Joint promotion with Hello Kitty
NM $1   **MIP** $3

Transformers/My Little Pony, 1985, McDonald's, set of twenty-six: Brawn— green/blue, blue/yellow, red/green, red/blue, red/yellow, green/yellow; Cliffjumper—red/black, burgundy/black, yellow/black, black/green, violet/blue, teal/black, black/blue; Bumblebee—black/red, burgundy/black, teal/black, violet/blue, black/green, yellow/black; Gears— green/yellow, green/blue, red/yellow, red/green, blue/yellow, red/blue; joint promotion with My Little Pony; regionally distributed in St. Louis, Missouri area
NM $50   **MIP** $140

Transformers/My Little Pony, 1998, McDonald's, set of three: Scorponok, Dinobot, Blackarachnia; split promo with My Little Pony
NM $1   **MIP** $2

Turbo Macs I, 1988, McDonald's, set of four: Birdie in pink car, Hamburglar in yellow car, Grimace in white car, Ronald in red car; test market Happy Meal
NM $5   **MIP** $10

Turbo Macs I, 1988, McDonald's, one U3 toy: Ronald in red car with yellow wheels
NM $5   **MIP** $10

Turbo Macs II, 1990, McDonald's, set of four: Ronald in red car, Grimace in white car, Birdie in pink car, Hamburglar in yellow car
NM $3   **MIP** $6

Turbo Macs II, 1990, McDonald's, one U3 toy: Ronald in red car with yellow wheels
NM $5   **MIP** $10

Under Sea, 1980, McDonald's, set of six cartons with undersea art: Alligator, Dolphin, Hammerhead Shark, Sea Turtle, Seal, Walrus
NM $2   **MIP** $3

VR Troopers, 1996, McDonald's, one U3 toy: Sphere
NM $1   **MIP** $2

VR Troopers, 1996, McDonald's, set of four: Visor, Wrist Spinner, Virtualizer, Kaleidoscope
NM $1   **MIP** $2

Walt Disney Home Video Masterpiece Collection, 1996, McDonald's, one U3 toy: Dumbo water squirter
NM $3   **MIP** $5

Walt Disney Home Video Masterpiece Collection, 1996, McDonald's, set of eight: Cinderella, Robin Hood, Pocahontas, Return to Jafar, Snow White, Sword and the Stone, Alice in Wonderland, Aristocats
NM $1   **MIP** $2

Walt Disney Home Video Masterpiece Collection, 1997, McDonald's, set of eight video cases with figure: Bambi with Bambi figure, The Lion King with Simba figure, Pete's Dragon with Elliot figure, Oliver and Company with Dodger figure, Toy Story with Woody figure, Sleeping Beauty with Sleeping Beauty figure, The Three Caballeros with Donald Duck figure, Winnie the Pooh with Tigger figure
NM $2   **MIP** $3

Water Friends, 1992, McDonald's, one U3 toy: soft rubber Giant Panda
NM $3   **MIP** $5

Water Games, 1992, McDonald's, one U3 toy: Grimace with squirting camera
NM $15   **MIP** $20

(Toy Shop File Photo)

Water Games, 1992, McDonald's, set of four: Birdie sorts eggs, Grimace juggles shakes, Ronald catches fries, Hamburglar stacks burgers
NM $3   **MIP** $5

What is It?, 1979, McDonald's, set of six rubber animals: Skunk, Squirrel, Bear, Owl, Baboon, Snake
NM $1   **MIP** $3

Wild Friends, 1992, McDonald's, set of four animals on mini-comic books: Crocodile, Gorilla, Elephant, Panda; regionally distributed in Indiana and southern California
NM $3   **MIP** $5

Winnie the Pooh Sing a Song with Pooh Bear, 1999, McDonald's, set of eight: Eeyore, Owl, Winnie the Pooh, Rabbit, Roo, Piglet, Gopher, Tigger
NM $5   **MIP** $10

Winter World, 1983, McDonald's, set of five flat vinyl tree ornaments: Ronald, Hamburglar, Grimace, Mayor McCheese, Birdie
NM $5   **MIP** $10

World of Hot Wheels/Friends of Barbie, 1994, McDonald's, set of eight: Turbine 4-2, Flame Rider, 2-Cool, Bold Eagle, Black Cat, Gas Hog, X21J Cruiser, Street Shocker; joint promotion with Barbie
NM $2   **MIP** $3

World of Hot Wheels/Friends of Barbie, 1994, McDonald's, one U3 toy: Fast Forward
  NM $2   **MIP** $3

Wrist Wallets, 1977, McDonald's, set of four watch-type bands with coin-holding dial: Ronald, Captain Crook, Big Mac, Hamburglar
  NM $5   **MIP** $10

Yo Yogi, 1992, McDonald's, set of four: Yogi Bear on wave jumper, Cindy Bear on scooter, Huckleberry Hound in race car, Boo Boo Bear on skate board
  NM $3   **MIP** $5

Young Astronauts, 1986, McDonald's, set of four snap-together models: Apollo Command Module, Argo Land Shuttle, Space Shuttle, Cirrus Vtol
  NM $5   **MIP** $20

Young Astronauts, 1992, McDonald's, set of four vehicles: Space Shuttle & Space Walker, Command Module, Lunar Rover, Satalite Dish & Space Walker
  NM $2   **MIP** $4

Young Astronauts, 1992, McDonald's, one U3 toy: Ronald in lunar rover
  NM n/a   **MIP** n/a

Yo-Yo, 1979, McDonald's, half red, half yellow
  NM $2   **MIP** $5

Zoo Face I, 1987, McDonald's, set of four masks: Alligator, Monkey, Tiger, Toucan; test market Happy Meal, distributed in Evansville, Indiana
  NM $20   **MIP** $30

Zoo Face II, 1988, McDonald's, set of four rubber noses and makeup kits: Alligator, Monkey, Tiger, Toucan
  NM $5   **MIP** $10

PIZZA HUT

Air Garfield, 1993, Pizza Hut, figure of Garfield attached to either a parachute or suspended in a spaceball
  NM $2   **MIP** $4

Air Garfield Cups, 1993, Pizza Hut, set of two: each cup featured Garfield and Odie
  NM $1   **MIP** $4

Beauty & the Beast Puppets, 1992, Pizza Hut, set of four: Belle, Beast, Chip, Cogsworth
  NM $4   **MIP** $8

Color Your World, 1993, Pizza Hut, set includes erasable calendar board with four Crayons, poster with four Crayons; each meal came with plastic cup
  NM $4   **MIP** $6

Dinosaurs!, 1993, Pizza Hut, set of four 16 oz. cups with 3-D lids and sticker books: Brachiosaurus, Tyrannosaurus, Stegosaurus, Brachiosaurus
  NM $4   **MIP** $8

(KP Photo)

Eureeka's Castle Puppets, 1991, Pizza Hut, set of three: Batly, Eureeka, Magellan
  NM $3   **MIP** $6

Fievel Goes West cups, 1991, Pizza Hut, set of three: Fievel with cowboy hat, Cat R. Waul with red top hat, Wylie Burp with tan hat
  NM $4   **MIP** $6

(KP Photo)

Land Before Time Puppets, 1988, Pizza Hut, set of six: Spike, Sharptooth, Pteri, Little Foot, Cera, Ducky
  NM $4   **MIP** $8

Marsupilami Houba Douba, 1994, Pizza Hut, set of three: yo-yo, jump rope, glow ball
  NM $4   **MIP** $6

Universal Monster Cups, Pizza Hut, set of three: holographic cards with 3-D cups
  NM $10   **MIP** $20

Young Indiana Jones Chronicles, 1993, Pizza Hut
  NM $4   **MIP** $6

ROY ROGERS

Critters, 1990, Roy Rogers, set of eight: blue eyes-yellow; blue eyes-orange; blue eyes-purple; blue eyes-red; yellow eyes-orange; yellow eyes-yellow; pink eyes-orange; pink eyes-purple
  NM $1   **MIP** $2

Cup Critters, 1994, Roy Rogers, Elephant/Alligator/Frog/Bear/Pig/Beaver/Lion/Duck/Turtle
  NM $2   **MIP** $5

Gator Tales, 1989, Roy Rogers, set of four: AV Gator, Investi-Gator, Flora Gator, Skater Gator
  NM $4   **MIP** $6

Hide 'n Keep Dinos, 1989, Roy Rogers, set of three: Brontosaurus, Triceratops, Stegosaurus
  NM $3   **MIP** $5

Ickky Stickky Bugs, 1989, Roy Rogers, set of sixteen: Centipede, Grasshopper, Worm, Spider
  NM $2   **MIP** $3

Skateboard Kids Figures, 1989, Roy Rogers, set of four: Boy with red skateboard; Boy with orange skateboard, Boy with purple, Girl with blue skateboard
  NM $3   **MIP** $5

Snorks, 1988, Roy Rogers, set of thirty version of the four characters: Allstar, Case, Dimmy, Tooter
  NM $3   **MIP** $5

Star Searchers, 1990, Roy Rogers, set of four: Saucer, Robot, Vehicle, Shuttle
  NM $2   **MIP** $3

Tatoo Heads, 1995, Roy Rogers
  NM $2   **MIP** $5

SONIC DRIVE-IN

Bag-A-Wag, 1990, Sonic Drive-In, set of four: man with bag of burgers in hamburger car, man with bag of burgers walking, man with bag of burgers rollerblading, man with hamburger
  NM $3   **MIP** $6

Brown Bag Bowlers, 1994, Sonic Drive-In, set of four brown bag figures holding ball: yellow ball, red ball, blue ball, orange ball
  NM $3   **MIP** $5

Brown Bag Buddies, 1993, Sonic Drive-In, set of four brown bag figures with sports equipment: sled, skiis, surfboard, intertube
  NM $2   **MIP** $5

(KP Photo)

Brown Bag Juniors, 1989, Sonic Drive-In, set of four brown bag figures: Too Cool, Bookworm, Sure Shot, Marbles
  NM $4   **MIP** $6

Bump and Go, 1993, Sonic Drive-In, series of 2" metal cars
  NM $2   **MIP** $5

Custom Cruisers, 1993, Sonic Drive-In, set of four: Mercury, Chevy Convertible, Chevy Nomad, Cadillac Convertible
  NM $3   **MIP** $5

Dino Makers, 1994, Sonic Drive-In
  NM $2   **MIP** $5

Sonic Super Kids, 1989, Sonic Drive-In, set of four with comic book: Steve, Rick, Corky, Brin
  NM $5   **MIP** $8

Sonic Turbo Racers, 1993, Sonic Drive-In, set of four: pink, yellow, orange, green
  NM $2   **MIP** $5

Wacky Sackers, 1994, Sonic Drive-In, set of six: pink with bug-eyes, green with sunglasses, yelow, pink with three eyes, blue
  NM $3   **MIP** $5

TACO BELL

Chihuahua Plush, 1999, Taco Bell, set of four talking dogs:standing, says "Yo Quiero Toca Bell"; sitting with Free Tacos sign, says "Here Lizard, Lizard"; sitting wearing beret, says: "Viva Gorditas"; lying down wearing Santa hat, says: "Feliz Navidad Amigos"
    NM $3   MIP $7

Happy Talk Sprites, Taco Bell, set of two: Spark, yellow; Twink, white
    NM $2   MIP $4

Hugga Bunch Plush Dolls, Taco Bell
    NM $2   MIP $4

TASTEE FREEZE

Roy Campanella Figure, Tastee Freeze
    NM $20   MIP $35

WENDY'S

ALF Tales, 1990, Wendy's, set of six: Sleeping Alf, Alf Hood, Little Red Riding Alf, Alf of Arabia, Three Little Pigs, Sir Gordon of Melmac
    NM $2   MIP $4

Alien Mix-Ups, 1990, Wendy's, set of six: Crimsonoid, Bluezoid, Limetoid, Spotasoid, Yellowboid, Purpapoid
    NM $1   MIP $2

(KP Photo)

All Dogs Go To Heaven, 1989, Wendy's, set of six: Anne Marie, Carface, Charlie, Flo, Itchy, King Gator
    NM $2   MIP $4

Definitely Dinosaurs, 1988, Wendy's, set of four: blue Apatosaurus, gray T-Rex, yellow Anatosaurus, green Triceratops
    NM $3   MIP $6

Definitely Dinosaurs, 1989, Wendy's, set of five: green Ankylosaurus, blue Parasaurolophus, green Ceratosaurus, yellow Stegosaurus, pink Apatosaurus
    NM $2   MIP $4

(KP Photo)

Fast Food Racers, 1990, Wendy's, set of five: hamburger, fries, shake, salad, kid's meal
    NM $2   MIP $4

Felix the Cat, 1995, Wendy's
    NM $2   MIP $5

Fun Flyers, Wendy's, 3-1/2" wide in red, yellow or blue
    NM $1   MIP $3

Furskins Plush Dolls, 1988, Wendy's, set of three: Boone in plaid shirt and red pants, Farrell in plaid shirt and blue jeans, Hattie in pink and white dress; all 7" tall
    NM $4   MIP $8

Glass Hangers, Wendy's, set of four: yellow turtle, yellow frog, yellow penguin and purple gator
    NM $3   MIP $5

Glo Friends, 1988, Wendy's, set of twelve: Book Bug, Bop Bug, Butterfly, Clutter Bug, Cricket, Doodle Bug, Globug, Granny Bug, Skunk Bug, Snail Bug, Snug Bug
    NM $2   MIP $4

Good Stuff Gang, 1985, Wendy's, set of six: Cool Stuff, Cat, Hot Stuff, Overstuffed, Bear, Penguin
    NM $2   MIP $4

Jetsons Figures, 1989, Wendy's, set of six figures in spaceships: George, Judy, Jane, Elroy, Astro, Spacely
    NM $2   MIP $4

(KP Photo)

Jetsons: The Movie Space Gliders, 1990, Wendy's, set of six PVC figures on wheeled bases: Astro, Elroy, Judy, Fergie, Grunchee, George
    NM $2   MIP $4

Micro Machines Super Sky Carriers, 1990, Wendy's, set of six kits: connect to form Super Sky Carrier
    NM $2   MIP $4

Mighty Mouse, 1989, Wendy's, set of six: Bat Bat, Cow, Mighty Mouse, Pearl Pureheart, Petey, Scrappy
    NM $3   MIP $5

Play-Doh Fingles, 1989, Wendy's, set of three finger puppet molding kits: green dough with black mold, blue dough with green mold, yellow dough with white mold
    NM $3   MIP $6

Potato Head Kids, 1987, Wendy's, set of six: Captain Kid, Daisy, Nurse, Policeman, Slugger, Sparky
    NM $4   MIP $8

(KP Photo)

Speed Writers, 1991, Wendy's, set of six car-shaped pens: black, blue, fuchsia, green, orange, red
    NM $2   MIP $4

Summer Fun, 1991, Wendy's, float pouch, sky saucer
    NM $1   MIP $2

Teddy Ruxpin, 1987, Wendy's, set of five: Professor Newton Gimmick, Teddy, Wolly Whats-It, Fob, Grubby Worm
    NM $3   MIP $8

Too Kool for School, Wendy's, set of five
    NM $2   MIP $4

Tricky Tints, Wendy's, set of four
    NM $2   MIP $4

(KP Photo)

Wacky Wind-Ups, 1991, Wendy's, set of five: Milk Shake, Biggie French Fry, Stuff Potato, Hamburger, Hamburger in box
    NM $2   MIP $3

Where's the Beef Stickers, 1984, Wendy's, set of six
    NM $1   MIP $3

World Wildlife Foundation, 1988, Wendy's, set of four plush toys: Panda, Snow Leopard, Koala, Tiger
    NM $5   MIP $10

World Wildlife Foundation, 1988, Wendy's, set of four books: All About Koalas, All About Tigers, All About Snow Leopards, All About Pandas
    NM $2   MIP $4

(KP Photo)

Yogi Bear & Friends, 1990, Wendy's, set of six: Ranger Smith in kayak, Boo Boo on skateboard, Yogi on skates, Cindy on red scooter, Huckleberry in inner tube, Snagglepuss with surfboard
    NM $2   MIP $4

WHITE CASTLE

Ballerina's Tiara, White Castle
    NM $3   MIP $6

Bendy Pens, 1993, White Castle, set of five: Wilfred, Wobbles, Woofles, Woozy Wizard, Willis
    NM $3   MIP $6

Camp White Castle, White Castle
    NM $2   **MIP** $4

Camp White Castle Bowls, White Castle, orange plastic
    NM $3   **MIP** $6

Castle Creatures, White Castle
    NM $2   **MIP** $5

Castle Friends Bubble Makers, 1992, White Castle, set of four
    NM $3   **MIP** $5

(KP Photo)

Castle Meal Family, 1989, White Castle, set of six: Princess Wilhelmina, Wendell, Sir Wincelot, Willis, Woozy Wizard, Woofles
    NM $4   **MIP** $6

Castle Meal Family, 1992, White Castle, set of five: Wilfred, King Wooly and Queen Winnevere, Wally, Wobbles and Woody, Friar Wack
    NM $4   **MIP** $6

Castle Meal Friends, 1989-90, White Castle, set of six
    NM $4   **MIP** $10

Castleburger Dudes Figures, 1991, White Castle, set of four: Castleburger Dude, Castle Fry Dudette, Castle Drink Dude, Castle Cheeseburger Dude
    NM $3   **MIP** $6

Castleburger Dudes Wind-Up Toys, 1991, White Castle, set of four: Castleburger Dude, Castle Fry Dudette, Castle Drink Dude, Castle Cheeseburger Dude
    NM $2   **MIP** $4

Easter Pals, White Castle, set of two: rabbit with carrot, rabbit with purse
    NM $3   **MIP** $5

(Copyright Museum of Science and Industry, Chicago)

Fat Albert and the Cosby Kids, 1990, White Castle, set of four: Fat Albert, Dumb Donald, Russely, Weird Harold
    NM $8   **MIP** $15

Food Squirters, 1994, White Castle, set of three: Castle Fry Dudette, Castle Drink Dude, Castleburger Dude
    NM $2   **MIP** $4

Glow in the Dark Monsters, 1992, White Castle, set of three: Wolfman, Frankenstein, Mummy
    NM $3   **MIP** $6

Godzilla Squirter, White Castle
    NM $3   **MIP** $6

Halloween PEZ, 1990, White Castle, set of three PEZ dispensers: Pumpkin, Witch, Skull
    NM $3   **MIP** $6

Holiday Huggables, White Castle, Candy Canine, Kitty Lights, Holly Hog
    NM $2   **MIP** $5

Nestle's Quik Rabbit, 1990, White Castle, set of four: straw holder, spoon, cup, plush toy
    NM $2   **MIP** $4

Puppy in My Pocket, 1995, White Castle, set of twelve, two per package
    NM $2   **MIP** $3

Silly Putty, 1994, White Castle, set of three molds with Silly Putty: orange mold, yellow mold, green mold
    NM $2   **MIP** $4

Stunt Grip Geckos, 1992, White Castle, set of four figures: turquoise, pink, purple, blue
    NM $2   **MIP** $4

Super Balls, 1994, White Castle, set of four: Castleburger Dude, Castle Cheeseburger Dude, Castle Fry Dudette, Castle Drink Dude
    NM $2   **MIP** $3

Swat Kats, 1994, White Castle, set of three figures with launchers: Razor, T-Bone, Callie
    NM $2   **MIP** $3

Tootsie Roll Express, 1994, White Castle, set of four train cars: Engine, Gondola, Hopper, Caboose
    NM $3   **MIP** $5

Totally U Back To School, White Castle, set of two: pencil, pencil case
    NM $2   **MIP** $4

Triastic Take-a-Parta, 1994, White Castle, set of four: Megasaur, Spinasaur, Coolasaur, Sorasaur; also distributed by Carl's Jr.
    NM $2   **MIP** $3

Water Balls, 1993, White Castle, set of four: Castleburger Dude, Castle Cheeseburger Dude, Castle Fry Dudette, Castle Drink Dude
    NM $2   **MIP** $3

Willis the Dragon, White Castle, Christmas giveaway
    NM $3   **MIP** $6

Willis the Dragon Sunglasses, White Castle
    NM $2   **MIP** $4

Robots

By Karen O'Brien

The word "robot" is derived from the Czech world "robota" meaning forced labor or drudgery. The word quickly gained usage in English after 1920.

The style, look, composition, and purpose of robots has changed quite a bit throughout the past sixty years, since the time when the earliest toy robots were made. But collectors have remained enamored of the artistry, design, and function of these otherworldly pieces of pop culture.

Think of a toy robot, and it's likely you'll think of Japan. As early as the 1940s, Japan was making somewhat crude walking robots. Among the earliest is Atomic Robot Man, made in occupied Japan in the late 1940s. The small robot, a mere five inches tall, featured clunky red feet, a blank facial expression, and oversized gauges. Its value, like many early robots, can soar to four figures or more in Mint-in-Box condition.

The 1950s was the true golden age of robots and space toys. Science fiction exploded into the pop culture sensibilities with television shows and movies catering to space themes. The lithographed tin toymakers in Japan responded accordingly, setting the world awash in a sea of spacemen robots. One of the world's major Japanese makers of robots at the time was Alps.

Notable entries to the robot field in the 1950s included Ideal's Robert the Robot, unusual because it was made of plastic, unlike Japan's tin-litho giants. Louis Marx's Japanese subsidiary, Linemar, also brought many Japanese-made robots to the United States.

Easily the most popular robots ever made are known as the Gang of Five—a series of five skirted robots made in the mid-1950s by Masudaya of Japan. These stunningly colorful robots (the most familiar is the Lavender Robot) have easily commanded five to six figures when sold at top-of-the-line space auctions.

According to Jim Bunte's book, Vintage Toys (Krause Publications, 1999), "Japan had dominated the 1950s robot and space toy category with innovation, creativity, and perhaps most important, low price points.

"Yet their success was also their undoing, because as the Japanese saw their standard of living grow, the costs associated with their successful industries also rose, reducing their marketplace competitiveness…Most Japanese toymakers fought this losing battle well into the decade, but by the end of the 1960s, most had either vanished or constricted precipitously. In fact, as the 1970s dawned, it was becoming difficult to find playthings on American toy shelves marked 'Made in Japan.'"

By the mid-1970s, interest in robots and space toys had waned. Japan's reign in the space toys arena had fallen. Items made in Hong Kong and Taiwan were more readily available.

By the late 1970s, however, the space toy world would turn its focus from robots and space men to Star Wars and other licensed realms.

The exciting historic and artistic world of robot toys would be gone, but those toys remain valuable vintage icons.

THE TOP TEN
ROBOTS (In Mint Condition)

1. Machine Man, Masudaya, 1950s	$45,000
2. Robby Space Patrol, Nomura/TN, 1957	37,000
3. Musical Drummer Robot R-57, Nomura/TN, 1950s	20,000
4. Giant Sonic Robot (Train Robot), Masudaya, 1959	16,000
5. Deep-Sea Robot, Naito Shoten, 1956	16,000
6. Mr. Atomic, Cargstan, 1962	15,000
7. Eightman, Yonezawa, 1966	10,000
8. Thunder Robot, Asakusa-Japan, 1950s	9,000
9. Robot Lilliput, KTA-Japan, 1939	9,000
10. Radar Robot, ASC-Japan, 1950s	7,000

ADVANCE TOYS

Mr. Atom, 1960s, Advance Toys, 18", red and silver plastic, battery-operated. "The Electronic Walking Robot...Completely Harmless," according to the box
EX $125   NM $300   MIP $650

AHI

Lost in Space Robot, 1977, 12", AHI, battery-operated, different in design than the Robinson family's companion but desirable
EX $150   NM $300   MIP $500

ALPS

Cragstan Great Astronaut, 1960s, Alps, 11", red tin, battery-operated, w/video scene, key in head
EX $500   NM $1250   MIP $2000

Door Robot, 1958, Alps, 9 1/2", tin, battery-operated, remote cont, revolving head
EX $725   NM $1700   MIP $3500

Mechanical Television Spaceman, 1965, 7", Alps, wind-up, w/chest scene and antenna
EX $95   NM $185   MIP $500

Mr. Robot the Mechanical Brain, 1954, Alps, tin wind-up
EX $500   NM $1000   MIP $1500

Television Space Man, 1959, 11", Alps, battery-operated, chest video, key in head operates as antenna
EX $175   NM $350   MIP $800

AN-JAPAN

Astronaut Robot, 1950s, 8", AN-Japan, wind-up, tanks on back, gun in hand
EX $500   NM $1250   MIP $2000

ARCO

Ro-Gun "It's A Robot", 1984, Arco, robot changes into a rifle
EX $11   NM $16   MIP $25

ASAK

Space Guard Pilot, 1975, 8", Asak
EX $20   NM $30   MIP $45

ASAKUSA-JAPAN

Thunder Robot, 1950s, 11", Asakusa-Japan, battery-operated, w/antenna and guns in palms of hands
EX $1500   NM $5000   MIP $9000

ASC JAPAN

Radar Robot, 1950s, 11", ASC Japan, wind-up, orange body, rotating antenna, chest sparks
EX $1500   NM $4000   MIP $7000

BANDAI

Moon Explorer, 1958, 14", Bandai, battery-operated, chest-mounted clock, antenna on head
EX $600   NM $1300   MIP $2000

CDI

Star Robot, 1978, 11", CDI, battery-operated, knock-off Storm Trooper helmet, chest cannons behind a door, made in Hong Kong
EX $50   NM $150   MIP $225

CRAGSTAN

Astronaut, 1961, 11", Cragstan, battery-operated, head-mounted antenna spins, jackhammer gun, barrel chest
EX $300   NM $650   MIP $1200

Astronaut, 1962, 15", Cragstan, battery-operated, round chest, laster rifle in right hand, "Cragstan Astronaut" written on waist
EX $275   NM $550   MIP $900

Countdown-Y, 1960s, 9", Cragstan
EX $125   NM $175   MIP $275

Cragstan Robot, 1962, 12", Cragstan, battery-operated, bump-and-go action, silver body, skirted legs, plastic domed head
EX $500   NM $1100   MIP $1800

(ToyShop File Photo)

Cragstan's Mr. Robot, 1960s, 10-1/2", Cragstan, battery-operated, red or white body, clear dome head
EX $325   NM $525   MIP $925

Magnor, 1975, 9", Cragstan, 9", plastic
EX $23   NM $35   MIP $50

Mr. Atomic, 1962, 9", Cragstan, rare, battery-operated, bump-and-go action, built by Yonezawa, 16 lights under plastic dome
EX $5000   NM $10000   MIP $15000

Mr. LEM Astronaut Robot, 1970, 13", Cragstan, battery-operated, rotates
EX $150   NM $310   MIP $475

Mr. Robot, 1960, 12", Cragstan, battery-operated, skirted legs, "Cragstan Mr. Robot" on chest, red body (white body variation worth 25% more), black wrench arms,
EX $600   NM $1200   MIP $1700

Space Robot Patrol, 1959, 11" long, Cragstan, friction motor, robot driving red Mercedes convertible
EX $500   NM $1000   MIP $1500

(ToyShop File Photo)

Talking Robot, 1963, 12", Cragstan, battery-operated voice, friction-motor robot, three functions, says four messages, "Cragstan Talking Robot" on chest
EX $375   NM $650   MIP $1300

DAIYA

Astro Captain, 1970s, 6", Daiya, wind-up, red/white/blue sparker, NASA on helmet
EX $35   NM $65   MIP $125

DIAYA

Astronaut, 1963, 15", Diaya, battery-operated, identical to Cragstan Astronaut, different litho design, laser rifle
EX $600   NM $1300   MIP $2200

DURHAM

Robot 2500, 1970s, 10", Durham, battery-operated, "cyclops"
EX $25   NM $45   MIP $65

DUX

Astroman, 1962, 12", Dux, battery-operated w/ corded remote, green plastic allows view of inner workings, antenna on head
EX $500   NM $1100   MIP $1750

HAJI

Space Trooper, 1955, Haji, wind-up, human face in helmet, holding rifle across left arm, blue barrel chest, yellow arms and legs
EX $500   NM $1000   MIP $1750

HONG KONG

Action Robot, 1970s, 10", Hong-Kong, battery-operated, yellow/blue, multiple functions
EX $15   NM $35   MIP $55

ROBOTS

Radar Hunter, 1970s, 5", Hong-Kong, wind-up, red/silver or orange
EX $15   **NM** $35   **MIP** $55

Robbie Robot, 1970s, 9", Hong-Kong, battery-operated, blue/red/yellow, blinks
EX $25   **NM** $45   **MIP** $85

See-Thru Robot, 1970s, 10", Hong Kong, battery-operated, clear head and chest w/gears
EX $125   **NM** $325   **MIP** $600

Sounding Robot, 1970s, 8", Hong-Kong, battery-operated, three push buttons on head
EX $25   **NM** $50   **MIP** $75

Sparking Robot, 1970s, 6", Hong-Kong, wind-up, black body
EX $20   **NM** $35   **MIP** $50

Star Robot, 1970s, 10", Hong-Kong, battery-operated, Star Wars Storm Trooper head
EX $25   **NM** $45   **MIP** $70

HORIKAWA/SH

Astronaut, 1963, 11", Horikawa/SH, battery-operated, human face, opening chest doors w/firing guns
EX $200   **NM** $400   **MIP** $700

Attack Robot, 1962, 11", Horikawa/SH, battery-operated, block head w/mesh eyes, chest doors open and guns fire
EX $250   **NM** $450   **MIP** $650

Attacking Martian, 1964, 11", Horikawa/SH, battery-operated, guns in chest, red mesh eyes, black body
EX $100   **NM** $250   **MIP** $425

Battle Robot, 1962, 11", Horikawa/SH, battery-operated, silver body, round eyes, red lights on head
EX $200   **NM** $350   **MIP** $575

Cosmic Fighter Robot, 1970s, 11-1/2", Horikawa/SH, head opens to reveal gunner inside while body spins
EX $50   **NM** $85   **MIP** $130

Dino Robot, 1960s, 11", Horikawa/SH, battery-operated, head opens to reveal dinosaur
EX $450   **NM** $950   **MIP** $1600

Engine Robot, 1968, 9", Horikawa/SH, battery-operated, square chest w/four rotating chest gears
EX $150   **NM** $300   **MIP** $500

Engine Robot, 1970s, 10", Horikawa/SH, battery-operated
EX $75   **NM** $150   **MIP** $350

Excavator Robot, 1960s, 10", Horikawa/SH, battery-operated, w/drill type hands
EX $275   **NM** $550   **MIP** $875

Excavator Robot, 1970s, 10", Horikawa/SH, battery-operated, w/drill-type hands
EX $60   **NM** $125   **MIP** $250

Fighting Martian, 1960s, Horikawa/SH, battery-operated, single gun in chest, moving antennas in shoulders, sounds,
EX $150   **NM** $350   **MIP** $750

Fighting Robot, 1960s, 11", Horikawa/SH, battery-operated, single chest gun, flashing light on head. "Sounding and lighted rapid fire gun" on box
EX $150   **NM** $350   **MIP** $600

Fighting Space Man, 1962, 11", Horikawa/SH, battery-operated, same toy as Fighting Robot but head has a human face
EX $200   **NM** $400   **MIP** $650

Gear Robot, 1960s, 11-1/2", Horikawa/SH, battery-operated, plastic gears in chest, antennae on shoulders
EX $225   **NM** $500   **MIP** $850

Gear Robot, 1960s, 9", Horikawa/SH, wind-up, visible gears
EX $125   **NM** $275   **MIP** $450

Giant Robot, 1960s, 17", Horikawa/SH, battery-operated, yellow legs, red feet and head
EX $150   **NM** $300   **MIP** $450

Golden Gear Robot, 1960s, 9", Horikawa/SH, gold, battery-operated, w/chest gears and lit dome
EX $225   **NM** $500   **MIP** $850

Launching Robot, 1975, 10", Horikawa/SH
EX $25   **NM** $35   **MIP** $75

(ToyShop File Photo)

Mr. Zerox, 1968, 9-1/2", Horikawa/SH, battery-operated, w/blinking chest guns, uses parts from other SH robots
EX $100   **NM** $210   **MIP** $350

Piston Robot, 1972, 11", Horikawa/SH, battery-operated, lighted pistons in square head, black body
EX $200   **NM** $450   **MIP** $750

Radar Robot, 1970s, 6-1/2", Horikawa/SH, wind up, red body, yellow arms, radar rotates
EX $25   **NM** $50   **MIP** $75

Radar Scope Space Scout, 1964, 10", Horikawa/SH, battery-operated, TV screen w/noise
EX $85   **NM** $200   **MIP** $375

Robot, 1958, Horikawa/SH, battery-operated, early models tin, late models tin and plastic, square chest opens to reveal guns, mesh eyes
EX $250   **NM** $500   **MIP** $800

Silver Ray Secret Weapon Space Scout, 1962, 9", Horikawa/SH, battery-operated, chrome silver body, chest

doors open to expose spy camera that transforms to cannons
EX $275   **NM** $550   **MIP** $825

(ToyShop File Photo)

Sky Robot, 1970s, 8", Horikawa/SH, battery-operated, yellow and red
EX $20   **NM** $45   **MIP** $65

Smoking Engine Robot, 1970s, 10", Horikawa/SH, battery-operated, piston action, w/sound and smoke
EX $45   **NM** $85   **MIP** $135

Space Astronaut, 1969, Horikawa/SH, battery-operated, human face, doors open to show chest cannons
EX $85   **NM** $200   **MIP** $350

(ToyShop File Photo)

Space Capsule, 1963, Horikawa/SH, battery-operated, blinking nosecone on top, opening panels and spacewalking astronaut, rolling action
EX $220   **NM** $375   **MIP** $600

Space Commander Robot, 1960s, 10", Horikawa/SH, tank type base, bump-and-go motion, w/guns
EX $500   **NM** $1200   **MIP** $2000

Space Explorer Robot, 1960s, 11", Horikawa/SH, battery-operated, drop down chest cover reveals video
EX $100   **NM** $225   **MIP** $350

Space Fighter, 1960s, 9", Horikawa/SH, battery-operated, w/chest doors and guns
EX $100   **NM** $225   **MIP** $350

Space Station, 1959, Horikawa/SH, battery-operated, circular station w/5 animated bays, large satalite dish in center
EX $700   **NM** $1400   **MIP** $2250

(ToyShop File Photo)

Super Giant (Rotate-a-Matic) Robot,
1970s, 16", Horikawa/SH, battery-
operated, w/chest guns
EX $85   **NM** $150   **MIP** $250

Super Moon Explorer, 1969,
Horikawa/SH, battery-operated, torso
swivels, plastic arms and feet
EX $100   **NM** $200   **MIP** $300

Super Robot Tank, 1950s, 9" long,
Horikawa/SH, friction powered w/two
guns
EX $80   **NM** $175   **MIP** $400

Super Space Commander, 1970s, 10",
Horikawa/SH, battery-operated, blue
body, chest video
EX $20   **NM** $40   **MIP** $60

Swivel-O-Matic Astronaut, 1960s, 12",
Horikawa/SH, battery-operated, black
body
EX $75   **NM** $150   **MIP** $350

Video Robot, 1969, 9", Horikawa/SH,
battery-operated, blue body, red feet,
simple motion, w/chest video
EX $75   **NM** $175   **MIP** $350

IDEAL

Maxx Steele Robot, 1984, 30", Ideal,
programmable servant, w/charger
EX $100   **NM** $250   **MIP** $425

Mighty Zogg the Leader Zeroid, 1960s, 6",
Ideal, battery-operated, w/Motorific
motors
EX $60   **NM** $110   **MIP** $225

Mr. Machine, 1961, 18", Ideal, wind-up,
w/bell and key, disassembles
EX $100   **NM** $325   **MIP** $600

(ToyShop File Photo)

Mr. Machine, 1977, 18", Ideal, wind-up,
whistles, does not disassemble
EX $20   **NM** $40   **MIP** $75

(ToyShop File Photo)

Robert the Robot, 1954, 14", Ideal, battery-
operated, remote "laser gun" styled
control attached to toy
EX $100   **NM** $250   **MIP** $550

(Edwin Price, Jr.)

Robot Commando, 1961, 19", Ideal,
battery-operated, blue/red, remote
control, fires rockets and balls
EX $150   **NM** $450   **MIP** $800

(ToyShop File Photo)

Zerak the Blue Destroyer Zeroid, 1968, 6",
Ideal, battery-operated, w/Motorific
motors
EX $75   **NM** $125   **MIP** $200

Zeroid Alien, 1970, 6", Ideal,
battery-operated
EX $75   **NM** $125   **MIP** $175

ZEROIDS

Zintar the Silver Explorer Zeroid, 1960s,
6", Ideal, battery-operated, w/Motorific
motors
EX $75   **NM** $125   **MIP** $200

Zobor the Bronze Transporter Zeroid,
1960s, 6", Ideal, battery-operated,
w/Motorific motors
EX $50   **NM** $100   **MIP** $200

Zogg, Zeroid Commander-in-Chief, 1970,
6", Ideal, battery-operated
EX $50   **NM** $100   **MIP** $175

IRWIN

Man From Mars, 1950s, 11", Irwin, wind-up,
red w/yellow body, shooting "space boy"
EX $275   **NM** $750   **MIP** $1500

Man from Mars, 1950s, 11", Irwin, wind-
up, red body, "space boy"
EX $125   **NM** $275   **MIP** $500

JAPAN

Answer Game Machine, 1960s, 14", Japan,
battery-operated, performs math tricks
EX $350   **NM** $675   **MIP** $950

Apollo 2000 Robot, 1960s, 12", Japan,
battery-operated, red and blue, w/chest
guns
EX $95   **NM** $175   **MIP** $300

ROBOTS

Apollo 2000X, 1970s, 6", Japan, wind-up, blue and red, w/spark
EX $45   **NM** $95   **MIP** $165

Atomic Robot Man, 1948, 6", Japan, wind-up
EX $325   **NM** $900   **MIP** $1700

Blink-A-Gear Robot, 1960s, 14", Japan, battery-operated, black body, clear plastic front w/gears
EX $250   **NM** $600   **MIP** $1150

Construction Robot, 1960s, 12", Japan, battery-operated, yellow body with forklift
EX $450   **NM** $1000   **MIP** $1650

High-Wheel Robot, 1950s, 9", Japan, battery-operated, blue body, remote control
EX $325   **NM** $750   **MIP** $1250

High-Wheel Ronot, 1950s, 9", Japan, wind-up, black body w/chest gears
EX $175   **NM** $425   **MIP** $700

Machine Robot, 1960s, 11", Japan, battery-operated, w/shoulder antennae
EX $145   **NM** $325   **MIP** $600

Mars Explorer, 1950s, 9-1/2", Japan, battery-operated, red body, w/wheels, face doors open
EX $450   **NM** $1000   **MIP** $1750

Mars King, 1960s, 9", Japan, battery-operated, w/video, siren and treads
EX $125   **NM** $350   **MIP** $650

Mr. Chief, 1960s, 11-1/2", Japan, battery-operated, smoking action
EX $475   **NM** $1000   **MIP** $1950

Mr. Patrol, 1960s, 11", Japan, battery-operated, meter in chest
EX $150   **NM** $350   **MIP** $575

New Astronaut Robot, 1970s, 9", Japan, battery-operated, w/three firing chest guns
EX $45   **NM** $85   **MIP** $135

Piston Robot, 1970s, 10", Japan, 10", tin and plastic, battery-operated, lighted chest pistons
EX $60   **NM** $110   **MIP** $225

Piston Robot, 1980s, 10", Japan, battery-operated, lighted chest pistons
EX $35   **NM** $65   **MIP** $125

(ToyShop File Photo)

Robot Mighty 8, 1960s, Japan, Dark blue metal body, red feet, electric color display on chest
EX $100   **NM** $225   **MIP** $450

Robot Tank - Mini, 5-1/2", Japan, battery-operated, w/two guns
EX $85   **NM** $160   **MIP** $275

Roto-Robot, 1960s, 9", Japan, battery-operated, w/chest guns, rotates 360 degrees
EX $95   **NM** $185   **MIP** $325

RX-008 Robot, 1960s, 5", Japan, wind-up, w/sparking chest
EX $150   **NM** $400   **MIP** $700

Singing Robot, 1970s, 10", Japan, battery-operated, missiles in head
EX $35   **NM** $75   **MIP** $100

Space Explorer Robot, 1950s, 9", Japan, wind-up, w/O2 gauge on chest
EX $450   **NM** $1000   **MIP** $1650

Space Explorer Robot, 1960s, 12", Japan, battery-operated, rotating shoulder antenna
EX $450   **NM** $1000   **MIP** $1650

Space Ranger, 1970s, 10", Japan, battery-operated, R/C, fires balls from chest
EX $50   **NM** $110   **MIP** $165

(ToyShop File Photo)

Space Robot X-70, 1960s, 12", Japan, battery-operated, lights, noise, and "Tulip Head"
EX $450   **NM** $1000   **MIP** $1650

Sparky Robot, 1960s, 7", Japan, wind-up, green cylindrical body
EX $45   **NM** $65   **MIP** $150

Super Astronaut, 1960s, 10", Japan, battery-operated, man's face, w/chest guns
EX $100   **NM** $200   **MIP** $300

Zoomer Robot, 1950s, 7", Japan, battery-operated, blue or silver w/red, w/wrench
EX $295   **NM** $525   **MIP** $900

KTA-JAPAN

Robot Lilliput, 1939, 6", KTA-Japan, wind-up, one of the oldest, square "block" head w/yellow litho, "N.P. 5257" on chest
EX $1500   **NM** $5000   **MIP** $10000

LINEMAR

Golden Robot, 1958, 6-1/2", Linemar, battery-operated w/corded remote, gold color, smiling, "ROBOT" lights up in chest
EX $600   **NM** $1300   **MIP** $2000

Lantern Robot, 1955, 8", Linemar, battery-operated w/corded remote, holds illuminated lantern, blows smoke from mouth
EX $500   **NM** $1000   **MIP** $1500

Mechanical Walking Sparking Robot, 1950s, 6", Linemar, batttery-operated
EX $250   **NM** $550   **MIP** $1000

Spaceman, 1958, 8", Linemar, battery-operated, small face within helmet, lights up, has gun
EX $1000   **NM** $2000   **MIP** $3000

MARX

Big Loo, 1963, 36", Marx, battery-operated, water squirter, w/rockets and tools
EX $450   **NM** $1300   **MIP** $2600

Colonel Hap Hazard, 1968, 11", Marx, rotating antenna on head
EX $250   **NM** $575   **MIP** $1200

Electric Robot, 1950s, 15", Marx, battery-operated, blk and red, w/morse code
EX $125   **NM** $250   **MIP** $550

Frankenstein, 1960s, 6", Marx, wind-up walker
EX $100   **NM** $250   **MIP** $450

Frankenstein Robot, 1968, 14", Marx, battery-operated, wired remote control
EX $575   **NM** $1250   **MIP** $2000

Great Garloo, The, 1962, 23", Marx, battery-operated, remote control, monster features, 7 movements, popular
EX $100   **NM** $300   **MIP** $600

ROBOTS

Hi-Bouncer Moon Scout, 1968, 11-1/2",
Marx, battery-operated w/corded
remote, human face
EX $550   NM $1200   MIP $2000

Moon Creature, 1968, 5-1/2", Marx, Bug-
eyed, mechanical, wind-up
EX $95   NM $165   MIP $275

Moon Scout, 1968, 11", Marx, shoots balls
from chest
EX $500   NM $1050   MIP $2200

Mr. Mercury, 1962-64, 14", Marx, battery-
operated w/corded remote, bending
action, "Mr. Mercury" on chest
EX $275   NM $650   MIP $1200

Mr. Smash, 1970s, 6", Marx, wind-up, red
body, Martian Mashed Potato promo
EX $50   NM $95   MIP $150

Robot and Son, 1956, 15", Marx, battery-
operated, similar to Marx Robot toy but
comes with small plastic son holding a
bar overhead used by Robot to lift him
EX $125   NM $250   MIP $450

(ToyShop File Photo)

Rock 'Em, Sock 'Em Robots, 1970s, Marx,
Two plastic robots in boxing ring
controlled by handles, when one is
punched just right his head flies upward
on a spring. Just plain goofy fun
EX $60   NM $120   MIP $200

Son of Garloo, 1960s, 6", Marx, wind-up,
green body, monster walker
EX $100   NM $225   MIP $450

MASUDAYA

Forbidden Planet Robby, 1985, 5",
Masudaya, wind-up
EX $15   NM $25   MIP $40

Forbidden Planet Robby, 1985, 16",
Masudaya, battery-operated, talks
EX $65   NM $125   MIP $200

(ToyShop File Photo)

Giant Sonic Robot (Train Robot), 1959,
15", Masudaya, battery-operated, red
body, black arms and head, robot makes
"trainlike" sound as it rolls along. Very
hard to find, one of the "Gang of Five"
EX $4000   NM $7300   MIP $16000

(Sotheby's Photo)

Machine Man, 1950s, 15", Masudaya,
battery-operated, the rarest robot from
Masudaya's "Gang of Five" series, this
robot sold for $42,550 at the Sotheby's
auction of the Tin Toy Robot Collection
of Matt Wyse in 1996
EX n/a   NM n/a   MIP $45000

Non-Stop (Lavender) Robot, 1956,
Masudaya, battery-operated, part of the
skirted "Gang of Five"
EX $2000   NM $3500   MIP $6000

(ToyShop File Photo)

R-35 Robot, 1962, 8", Masudaya, battery-
operated, remote control - battery box
is red, eyes light up
EX $175   NM $400   MIP $650

Robot YM-3, 1985, 5", Masudaya, wind-
up, "Lost in Space B9" type
EX $10   NM $20   MIP $35

Space Commando, 1958, 7-1/2",
Masudaya, battery-operated w/corded
remote, one of a few astronauts
produced by Masudaya, poseable head
EX $600   NM $1300   MIP $2000

Target Robot, 1958, 15", Masudaya,
battery-operated, blue skirted robot
w/red target disk in chest, one of the
"Gang of Five"
EX $2000   NM $4000   MIP $6000

The Gang of Five, 1997, 5", Masudaya, five
mini-robots, Mini Sonic Robot, Mini Target
Robot, Mini Machine Man, Mini Non-Stop
Lavender Robot, Mini Radicon Robot
EX $50   NM $75   MIP $110

MEGO

Gigantor Robot, 1960s, 17", Mego,
battery-operated, silver w/ white "hands"
and red feet
EX $50   NM $100   MIP $200

MEGO-JAPAN

Krome-Dome Robot, 1960s, 11", Mego-
Japan, plastic, battery-operated, disk-
type head opes w/sound
EX $125   NM $295   MIP $525

MIKES TOY HOUSE

Mr. Atomic, 1990s, Mikes Toy House,
Limited reproduction
EX $95   NM $200   MIP $350

MISCELLANEOUS

Lightning Robot, 1980s, Miscellaneous,
battery-operated, looks like R2D2
w/ flashing lights
EX $20   NM $40   MIP $80

Lunar Spaceman, 1978, 12",
Miscellaneous, battery operated
EX $20   NM $30   MIP $45

Mechanical Interplanetary Explorer,
1950s, 8", Miscellaneous, wind-up
EX $180   NM $260   MIP $400

Mechanized Robot, 1950s, 13",
Miscellaneous, battery-operated, black
body, "Robby the Robot" type
EX $500   NM $1200   MIP $2100

Myrobo, 1970s, 9", Miscellaneous, battery
operated
EX $25   NM $35   MIP $55

Raid "Bug" Robot, Miscellaneous, Large,
battery-operated, remote control, ad
promo, Korea
EX $75   NM $150   MIP $250

Ranger Robot, 11", Miscellaneous,
battery-operated, clear body, w/smoke
and sound, Japan
EX $500   NM $1200   MIP $2250

Space Scout, 1950s, 10", Miscellaneous,
Rare, wind-up, w/radiation meter in chest
EX $1000   NM $2250   MIP $5000

Zero of Space, 1970s, 14", Miscellaneous,
battery-operated, red and yellow
w/visor, w/lights
EX $100   NM $225   MIP $350

MTU-KOREA

Captain the Robot, 1970s, 6", MTU-Korea,
gray wind-up, sparking
EX $15   NM $35   MIP $50

NAITO SHOTEN

Deep-Sea Robot, 1956, 8", Naito Shoten,
very rare
EX $4000   NM $9000   MIP $16000

ROBOTS

N-JAPAN

Mighty Robot, 1969, N-Japan, wind-up, paddle-feet rotate to move robot forward, sparks in chest
EX $50 **NM** $100 **MIP** $150

Robot-7, 1966, N-Japan, wind-up, paddle-feet forward motion
EX $65 **NM** $125 **MIP** $225

Wind-Up Walking Robot, 1960s, 7", N-Japan, wind-up sparker, plastic antenna on head
EX $100 **NM** $225 **MIP** $350

NOMURA/TN

Earth Man, 1957, 9", Nomura/TN, battery-operated w/corded remote, walks and fires his gun
EX $600 **NM** $1450 **MIP** $2500

Mechanized Robot, 1957, 14", Nomura/TN, battery-operated; the icon of the hobby, this is based on Robby the Robot from the 1956 film "The Forbidden Planet"
EX $1500 **NM** $3000 **MIP** $4500

Moon Space Ship, 1958, Nomura/TN, battery-operated, cousin of the cancelled Robby Space Patrol, this ship features blue litho and bump-and-go action
EX $600 **NM** $1300 **MIP** $2000

Musical Drummer Robot R 57, 1950s, Nomura/TN, From the Matt Wyse collection, this robot sold for $17,250 at a Sotheby's auction in 1996
EX n/a **NM** n/a **MIP** $20000

Piston Action Robot, 1958, 11", Nomura/TN, battery-operated w/corded remote, Robby-like w/pistons moving in clear dome
EX $500 **NM** $1200 **MIP** $2000

Radar Robot, 1955-58, 9", Nomura/TN, battery-operated w/corded remote, wrench in right hand, radar dish atop head, several color variations
EX $600 **NM** $1250 **MIP** $1900

Robby Space Patrol, 1957, Nomura/TN, battery-operated, bump-and-go motion. This is one of the most famous space toys, representing (in an

unlicensed way) the robot and his transport vehicle from the 1956 film, "The Forbidden Planet."
EX $7000 **NM** $17500 **MIP** $37000

Robot Tank-Z, 1960s, 10", Nomura/TN, battery-operated, bump-and-go motion
EX $200 **NM** $425 **MIP** $700

Space Command Robot, 1950s, 7-1/2", Nomura/TN, wind-up, w/gun in hand
EX $375 **NM** $1000 **MIP** $1650

Space Commando, 1956, 11", Nomura/TN, battery-operated, plastic helmet only part of face visible, laser rifle
EX $500 **NM** $1000 **MIP** $1550

Zoomer the Robot, 1954, Nomura/TN, battery-operated, holding wrench in right hand, eyes glow red, antenna spins, many color variations
EX $250 **NM** $500 **MIP** $750

ORIKAWA

Mr. Hustler, 1960s, 11-1/2", Orikawa, battery-operated, center chest light
EX $100 **NM** $225 **MIP** $400

PLAYING MANTIS

(ToyShop File Photo)

Robot B-9, Lost In Space, 1990s, 3", Playing Mantis, rolling wheels under base, sold individually, part of a series of four Lost-In-Space toys made by Playing Mantis Johnny Lightning
EX $4 **NM** $8 **MIP** $15

R.M.

Astronaut, 1960s, 7", R.M., wind up, arms move back and forth, red body, human face
EX $50 **NM** $85 **MIP** $125

REMCO

Big Max & His Electronic Conveyor, 1958, 8" x 7", Remco, battery-operated, w/truck and coins
EX $100 **NM** $185 **MIP** $300

Lost in Space Motorized Robot, 1966, 14", Remco, battery-operated, black and red body, lights up, arms move
EX $125 **NM** $250 **MIP** $450

Mr. Brain, 1970, 13", Remco, battery-operated, programmable memory
EX $75 **NM** $150 **MIP** $250

(ToyShop File Photo)

Rudy the Robot, 1967, 16", Remco, orange, battery-operated, "He Walks Like a Man!"
EX $75 **NM** $165 **MIP** $375

ROSKO

Astronaut, 1962, Rosko, battery-operated, blue or red litho, uses legs and torso of Nomura Robby series, human face
EX $550 **NM** $1300 **MIP** $2000

Space Conqueror, 1961, Rosko, battery-operated, blue and yellow litho, copy of Cragstan Astronaut, human face
EX $550 **NM** $1300 **MIP** $2000

S.J.M.

(ToyShop File Photo)

Super Astronaut, 1981, 10", S.J.M., battery-operated, man's face, w/chest guns
EX $12 **NM** $20 **MIP** $30

SAUNDERS

Marvelous Mike, 1955, 14" long, Saunders, battery-operated, plastic robot on yellow tin Caterpillar bulldozer, rubber treads
EX $110 **NM** $225 **MIP** $395

SCHAPER

Tobor, 1978, 7", Schaper, black, battery-operated, radio control
EX $15 **NM** $30 **MIP** $50

SNK

Flashy Jim, 1955, 7-1/2", SNK, battery-operated, square head, "R7" on chest, walks forward, eyes light up
EX $250   NM $500   MIP $800

Robbie the Roving Robot, 1956, 7", SNK, wind-up, antenna,
EX $450   NM $1000   MIP $1800

Sparkling Mike Robot, 1957, 7", SNK, wind-up, red diamonds in knees, hole in chest shoots sparks, antenna
EX $150   NM $300   MIP $550

SONSCO

Space Man, 1958, Sonsco, battery-operated, rifle in right hand, flashlight in left hand, antenna
EX $1000   NM $2000   MIP $3000

STRACO-JAPAN

Hysterical Robot, 1970s, 13", Straco-Japan, battery-operated, black body, bump-and-go and laughing actions
EX $100   NM $250   MIP $400

SY JAPAN

Mechanical Walking Space Man, 1962, 7-1/2", SY Japan, wind-up, black body, w/floppy arms and forward walking motion
EX $150   NM $400   MIP $700

Mechanical Walking Space Man w/Spark, 1970s, 7", SY Japan, wind-up, silver litho, this variation sparks from chest
EX $100   NM $175   MIP $275

Sparking Robot, 1965, 7", SY Japan, keywound, silver w/litho
EX $125   NM $275   MIP $450

TAIYO

Wheel-A-Gear Robot, 1950s, 15", Taiyo, battery-operated, black body, w/mutli-chest gears and pullies
EX $425   NM $1000   MIP $1850

TOMY

Chatbot, 1970s, 8", Tomy, battery-operated, tape recorder in head, serving tray, speaks, remote control
EX $30   NM $65   MIP $110

Omnibot 2000, 1980s, 24", Tomy, battery-operated, remote control, programmable servant
EX $175   NM $400   MIP $675

Verbot, 1984, 8", Tomy, battery-operated, radio control, programmable
EX $15   NM $35   MIP $60

TOPPER

Boxer Ding-A-Ling, 1970s, Topper, battery-operated, orange and blue body
EX $20   NM $40   MIP $60

Chef Ding-A-Ling, 1970s, Topper, battery-operated, red, white and blue body
EX $20   NM $40   MIP $60

(ToyShop File Photo)

King-Ding Robot, 1970, 12", Topper, battery-operated, separate brain robot goes in head
EX $110   NM $275   MIP $500

WACO-JAPAN

Laughing Robot, 1960s, 13", Waco-Japan, battery-operated, mouth opens, laughs loudly
EX $125   NM $275   MIP $500

YANOMAN

Rendezvous 7.8, 15", Yanoman
EX $170   NM $245   MIP $375

YONEZAWA

Conehead Robot, 1962, 8-1/2", Yonezawa, wind-up, Robby body and legs, cone-shaped head w/large eyes
EX $650   NM $1400   MIP $2300

Directional Robot, 1963, 10", Yonezawa, battery-operated, blue body, head rotates, bump-and-go action
EX $225   NM $650   MIP $1500

Eightman, 1966, 14", Yonezawa, battery-operated, based on the anime superhero cyborg, rare
EX $2500   NM $5500   MIP $10000

Lunar Robot, 1960s, 7", Yonezawa, wind-up, sparks, companion to Thunder Robot
EX $225   NM $550   MIP $800

Mechanic Robot, 1969, Yonezawa, battery-operated, phone dial in chest
EX $65   NM $135   MIP $250

Modern Robot, 1962, Yonezawa, battery-operated, copy of Cragstan Robot w/new litho, "Modern Robot" written on chest
EX $650   NM $1400   MIP $2000

Mr. Mercury, 1961, 13", Yonezawa, battery-operated, believed to be the first model in the series, "Mr. Mercury" across chest
EX $650   NM $1500   MIP $2100

Robby Robot, 1958, 8", Yonezawa, wind-up, wrenches for arms
EX $600   NM $1500   MIP $2400

Robot Captain, 1968, 5-1/2", Yonezawa, wind-up, wrenches for arms,
EX $50   NM $100   MIP $150

Roby Robot, 1960, 8", Yonezawa, wind-up, wrenches for arms, black body w/red feet
EX $800   NM $1750   MIP $2600

Scare Mighty Robot, 1960s, 10", Yonezawa, wind-up, red and white, sparking action
EX $175   NM $550   MIP $1000

(ToyShop File Photo)

Smoking Spaceman, 1960, 12", Yonezawa, battery-operated, dark gray metal body, smoke puffs from mouth as robot walks
EX $1250   NM $1900   MIP $3750

Space Explorer, 1959, 9-1/2", Yonezawa, wind-up, astronaut face, oxygen meter in chest, swings arms
EX $350   NM $700   MIP $1450

Space Explorer, 1959, Yonezawa, battery-operated, tv screen in chest, robot transforms into a tv
EX $350   NM $700   MIP $1300

Swinging Baby Robot, 1958, Yonezawa, wind-up, clockwork swings the square-head baby, counterweight often missing
EX $350   NM $700   MIP $1300

X-27 Explorer, 1958, Yonezawa, wind-up, barrel-chest, human face in helmet, two antennae
EX $600   NM $1350   MIP $2500

YOSHIYA/KO

Action Planet Robot, 1958, 8", Yoshiya/KO, wind-up, Robby look-alike, forward walking, grate over face, black body w/red feet
EX $175   NM $400   MIP $700

(ToyShop File Photo)

Chief Robotman, 1959, 12", Yoshiya/KO, battery-operated, bump-and-go motion, two spinning antennae, swinging arms, flashing lights, turning head
EX $450   NM $900   MIP $1550

Jupiter Robot, 1969, 7", Yoshiya/KO, wind-up, red body, w/two antennae, sparks
EX $85   **NM** $175   **MIP** $350

Mechanical Space Man Robot, 1950s, 6", Yoshiya/KO, wind-up, silver litho, full face showing in helmet, antenna moves as he walks
EX $100   **NM** $200   **MIP** $500

Moon Explorer, 1959, 7-1/2", Yoshiya/KO, wind-up, fixed legs, human-faced astronaut in dome helmet
EX $550   **NM** $1200   **MIP** $2000

Moon Explorer, 1960s, 12", Yoshiya/KO, battery-operated, w/clock in chest
EX $475   **NM** $1000   **MIP** $1850

Planet Robot, 1958, 8", Yoshiya/KO, battery-operated w/corded remote, just like Action Planet Robot, blue and other color variations
EX $250   **NM** $600   **MIP** $1000

Robby, 1958, 7", Yoshiya/KO, wind-up, fixed-legs, red body, plastic dome head
EX $200   **NM** $500   **MIP** $850

Robot Dog, 1956, 7" long, Yoshiya/KO, wind-up
EX $250   **NM** $600   **MIP** $1000

Space Whale, 1957, 7" long, Yoshiya/KO, wind-up, vehicle moves forward when antenna is raised, white and blue litho, google eyes,
EX $175   **NM** $285   **MIP** $600

(ToyShop File Photo)

Sparky Robot, 1954-59, 7", Yoshiya/KO, wind-up, silver and red, w/head spring antenna; earliest version all silver from 1954
EX $275   **NM** $650   **MIP** $1000

(ToyShop File Photo)

Venus Robot, 1960s, 8", Yoshiya/KO, battery-operated, blue/red, remote control
EX $95   **NM** $200   **MIP** $325

Rock and Roll

The beginnings of rock and roll took root with the rhythm and blues music popularized after World War II. In the 1950s, Elvis Presley revolutionized the rock sound. Elvis memorabilia and licensed products are highly sought by fans of the King. And nothing is more certain to cause a stir in the auction world than an Elvis memorabilia auction. The popularity of the King wasn't rivaled until Liverpool's four young men swept America in the early 1960s. In fact, the impact of the Beatles and Elvis was so strong that it resonated not only in the music world but also in the merchandising and collectibles arena.

It's not surprising that images of the Beatles were used to endorse products. What's surprising is so many toys were made to help kids re-create the frenzy at home. Toy guitars, drums, and dolls brought the Beatles to life to a younger audience. Today, collectors are thrilled to find such remnants of rock and roll history. And while Beatles collectibles aren't particularly difficult to find, those in the best condition are treasured.

After the success of marketing Beatles toys, rock and roll continued to be a booming business for merchandisers. Although their musical talent was scrutinized, both the Monkees and the Partridge Family enjoyed added exposure on television. That exposure created much interest in related memorabilia, especially for young fans.

In the 1970s, KISS stormed onto the rock scene in wild face makeup and costumes unlike anything previously seen. Armies of KISS fans rocked and rolled all night long, and in 1979, Mego made 12-inch dolls of band members Paul Stanley, Gene Simmons, Ace Frehley, and Peter Criss. Dozens of KISS toys followed to the delight of eager fans. McFarlane Toys continues the KISS craze today with new action figures. (See the Action Figure chapter for values.)

But KISS was one of the last rock and roll groups featured on numerous toys and memorabilia. While 1980s and 1990s icons like Michael Jackson and Madonna have been the subjects of some toys and collectibles, the trend died for a few years. Then with the teen pop craze phenomenon in the early part of the twenty-first century, toys related to stars again found an avid audience. At this point, however, the trend of pop-music figures seems to be waning again.

McFarlane Toys continues to enjoy success with new KISS figures marketed toward an older collector. The company has also released with figures of heavy metal rockers like Ozzy Osbourne, Metallica, and Rob Zombie along with figures of classic crooners such as Janis Joplin and Jim Morrison. And even Art Asylum joined the ranks with figures of iconic rap group Run DMC.

2006 TRENDS

Beatles toys lead the pack of rock and roll memorabilia. The market remains active with growth each year, particularly with renewed interest in the group since the release of a Beatles anthology, titled One, released in 2000 and the recent death of George Harrison.

Rock and roll licenses, although decades years old, haven't lost their power. In fact, many new limited-edition collectibles like plates, dolls, and Christmas ornaments have continued to satisfy the public's hunger for Beatles and Elvis items.

Collectors can't really go wrong picking up items featuring major players in rock and roll history. One caveat, however. Reproductions and unlicensed items run rampant, so collectors should educate themselves about items before making purchases, especially through online auction sites.

THE TOP TEN
ROCK AND ROLL TOYS *(In Mint Condition)*

1. Beatles Banjo, Mastro, 1964	$800
2. Beatles Bobbin' Head Dolls, set of four, 1960s	750
3. Beatles Guitar, Selcol, 1960s	550
4. Beatles Cartoon Kit, Colorforms, 1966	525
5. Beatles Magic Slate, Merit, 1960s	500
6. Beatles Costume, Ben Cooper, 1960s	425
7. Beatles Jr. Guitar, Mastro, 1960s	425
8. Paint Your Own Beatle Kit, Artistic Creations, 1960s	400
9. Yellow Submarine Costume, Collegeville, 1960s	375
10. Paul McCartney Doll, Remco, 1964	275

BEATLES

Beatles Banjo, 1964, Mastro
EX $200   **NM** $400   **MIP** $800

Beatles Cartoon Kit, 1966, Colorforms
EX $150   **NM** $300   **MIP** $525

Beatles Costume, 1960s, Ben Cooper, child's costume and mask; John, Paul, George, or Ringo, each
EX $100   **NM** $200   **MIP** $425

Beatles Forever Cloth Dolls, 1987, Applause, 22" tall, each
EX $55   **NM** $75   **MIP** $100

Beatles Guitar, 1960s, Selcol, 23", plastic
EX $200   **NM** $300   **MIP** $600

Beatles in Pepperland Puzzles, Jaymar, many variations and sizes, each
EX $35   **NM** $60   **MIP** $100

Beatles Jr. Guitar, 1960s, Mastro, 14" red/pink plastic guitar w/Beatles graphics
EX $100   **NM** $225   **MIP** $425

Beatles Magic Slate, Merit, British
EX $150   **NM** $300   **MIP** $500

Beatles Notebook Binder, 1960s, binder from Beatles Fan Club
EX $50   **NM** $75   **MIP** $135

Beatles Toy Watches, 1960s, four, tin w/plastic bands, on card
EX $30   **NM** $75   **MIP** $150

Beatles Wig, Lowell Toy
EX $65   **NM** $90   **MIP** $150

Bobbin' Head Dolls, 1960s, 8" tall, ceramic, four in set
EX $300   **NM** $500   **MIP** $750

Disk Go Case, 1966, Charter, 45 rpm carrying case; several colors
EX $100   **NM** $150   **MIP** $250

George Harrison Doll, 1964, Remco
EX $50   **NM** $100   **MIP** $250

Harmonica, Hohner, in Beatles box
EX $35   **NM** $50   **MIP** $85

Inflatable Dolls, 1966, Lux promotional; 13" tall; each
EX $25   **NM** $35   **MIP** $50

John Lennon Doll, 1964, Remco
EX $50   **NM** $100   **MIP** $250

Paint Your Own Beatle Kit, 1960s, Artistic Creations, oil painting kit; John, Paul, George, or Ringo, each
EX $150   **NM** $300   **MIP** $400

Paul McCartney Doll, 1964, Remco
EX $50   **NM** $100   **MIP** $275

Paul McCartney Soaky, 1965, Colgate, red plastic
EX $70   **NM** $125   **MIP** $250

Ringo Starr Doll, 1964, Remco
EX $50   **NM** $100   **MIP** $250

Ringo Starr Soaky, 1965, Colgate, blue plastic
EX $70   **NM** $125   **MIP** $275

Yellow Submarine Halloween Costume, 1960s, Collegeville, Blue Meanie costume and mask
EX $100   **NM** $200   **MIP** $375

Yellow Submarine Water Color Set, 1960s, Craft Master, pictures and paints
EX $40   **NM** $80   **MIP** $145

ELVIS PRESLEY

Elvis Presley Doll, 1984, World Dolls, 21" tall
EX $50   **NM** $100   **MIP** $200

Elvis Presley Doll, 1984, Eugene, 12" tall
EX $20   **NM** $40   **MIP** $80

Elvis Presley Wristwatch, 1983, Bradley, white plastic case, quartz, stainless back, face shows a young Elvis, white vinyl band
EX $25   **NM** $45   **MIP** $85

Jigsaw Puzzle, 1992, Milton Bradley, Elvis postage stamp
EX $5   **NM** $10   **MIP** $20

KISS

Jigsaw Puzzles, 1970s, Milton Bradley
EX $10   **NM** $20   **MIP** $35

KISS Rub n' Play Magic Transfer Set, 1979, Colorforms
EX $20   **NM** $40   **MIP** $80

KISS Van Model Kit, 1977, AMT
EX $35   **NM** $70   **MIP** $140

KISS Your Face Make-Up Kit, 1978, Remco
EX $30   **NM** $65   **MIP** $115

Trading Cards Set, 1978, Donruss, set of 132 cards
EX $25   **NM** $35   **MIP** $70

View-Master Set, 1978, GAF
EX $10   **NM** $20   **MIP** $35

Wastebasket, 1978, metal, cylindrical
EX $20   **NM** $45   **MIP** $70

MICHAEL JACKSON

Michael Jackson AM Radio, 1984, Ertl
EX $12   **NM** $25   **MIP** $45

Michael Jackson Doll, 1984, LJN, several styles
EX $12   **NM** $25   **MIP** $50

Michael Jackson Dress-Up Set, 1984, Colorforms
EX $10   **NM** $15   **MIP** $25

Michael Jackson Microphone, 1984, LJN, cordless, electronic
EX $10   **NM** $20   **MIP** $35

Michael's [Jackson] Pets, 1987, Ideal, plush animals, 10 kinds, each
EX $7   **NM** $15   **MIP** $25

MISCELLANEOUS

Andy Gibb Doll, 1979, Ideal, 7" tall
EX $15   **NM** $30   **MIP** $60

Boy George Doll, 1980s, LJN, 15", polka dot shirt
EX $20   **NM** $40   **MIP** $75

Boy George Doll, 1980s, LJN, 12", poseable in alphabet shirt
EX $30   **NM** $60   **MIP** $120

Cher Doll, 1976, Mego, 12", w/growing hair
EX $55   **NM** $125   **MIP** $175

Cher Doll, 1976, Mego, 12"
EX $50   **NM** $100   **MIP** $150

Debby Boone Doll, Mattel, 10" tall
EX $20   **NM** $40   **MIP** $80

Dolly Parton Doll, 1970s, Goldberger, 12" tall
EX $20   **NM** $40   **MIP** $80

Pat Boone Paper Dolls, 1959, Whitman, two cardboard dolls plus clothes
EX $20   **NM** $45   **MIP** $75

Pinky Lee Costume, 1950s, hat, pants, and shirt
EX $35   **NM** $75   **MIP** $145

Pinky Lee Xylophone, Emenee
EX $35   **NM** $70   **MIP** $120

Rick Nelson Paper Dolls, 1959, Whitman
EX $20   **NM** $45   **MIP** $80

Sonny & Cher Play Set, 1976, Mego
EX $25   **NM** $50   **MIP** $85

Toni Tennile Doll, 12" tall
EX $8   **NM** $15   **MIP** $30

OSMONDS

Donny & Marie TV Show Play Set, 1976, Mattel
EX $15   **NM** $35   **MIP** $55

Donny Osmond Doll, 1976, Mattel, 12" tall
EX $15   **NM** $25   **MIP** $45

Donny Osmond String Puppet, 1978, Madison
EX $20   **NM** $35   **MIP** $60

Marie Osmond Doll, 1976, Mattel, 12" tall
EX $10   **NM** $25   **MIP** $40

Marie Osmond Modeling Doll, 1976, Mattel, 30" tall
EX $20   **NM** $40   **MIP** $80

Marie Osmond String Puppet, 1978, Madison
EX $25   **NM** $35   **MIP** $65

Osmonds Colorforms Dress-Up Set, 1976, Colorforms
EX $10   **NM** $25   **MIP** $50

Sci-Fi & Space Toys

Some would trace the modern age of science fiction to 1956 and Forbidden Planet. Undoubtedly, the toy world would be poorer for the lack of the movie's Robby the Robot. But through one medium or another, science fiction has enthralled millions for many years, right back to Jonathan Swift's Gulliver's Travels.

The first universally acclaimed work of science fiction was Mary Shelley's Frankenstein or The Modern Prometheus, and her vision made way for Verne, Wells, Burroughs, Lovecraft, Heinlein, Asimov, Clarke, and a host of others whose collective imaginations led us up to today and through tomorrow.

Even with its classical pedigree, science fiction is almost exclusively a product of the twentieth century as the hard foundation of science had to exist before fiction writers could extrapolate upon it. In particular, science fiction is a phenomenon of the atomic age. World War II, more than any other event this century, opened our eyes to the wondrous and horrific potential of applied science.

Just as science fiction has captivated readers of all ages, so have toys. Buck Rogers made his first appearance in 1928. But in 1929, Buck Rogers went from pulp to newsprint, becoming the first science fiction comic strip. Flash Gordon followed Buck Rogers into print in 1934 and was an immediate success. Within two years, Flash was on the silver screen, portrayed by Buster Crabbe. Buck Rogers finally made it to the screen in 1939, also played by Crabbe.

During this period, Marx produced numerous toys in support of each character, including two ships that have become classics in the space toy field. Opinions vary as to which wind-up is better executed—Buck Rogers' 25th Century Rocket Ship or Flash Gordon's Rocket fighter. Both are considered superb examples of tin character space toys.

FROM RAY GUNS TO STAR WARS

No discussion of space toys would be complete without mention of ray guns. Here again Marx is a major player, producing numerous generic and character space guns. Daisy, Hubley, and Wyandotte, among others, all made memorable contributions as well.

Space toys have been made continuously for most of the twentieth century. The 1930s and 1940s saw Buck Rogers and Flash Gordon. The 1950s saw fiction become reality with the growth of television. Captain Video was the first space series on television, appearing in the summer of 1949. Buzz Correy and his Space Patrol and Tom Corbett, Space Cadet would feed the appetite for adventure until 1956 when the heavens took on a visual scale and grandeur never see before—in the panoramic wonder of Forbidden Planet.

In 1966, when the low-budget Star Trek went on the air, few dreamed that for millions of people, life would never be the same. Even though the original show ran only three seasons, its impact and legacy are undeniable. The phenomenon of Star Trek has grown far beyond cult status, and the extraordinary success of Star Trek: The Next Generation has only broadened its reach.

Star Trek may be big. But the king of space toys has to be Star Wars. The array of books, models, figures, play sets, and other items released since its debut in 1977 continued unabated until 1988. The license gained a new lease in 1987 with the opening of Star Tours at Disneyland and Disney World, generating still more new merchandise.

Today, store shelves are again featuring new Star Wars toys thanks to the phenomenal success of the Prequel trilogy that recently concluded with 2005's Episode III: Revenge of the Sith. Star Wars' longevity and international name recognition are excellent assurances of the continuing popularity of its toys. (See the Star Wars chapter for values.)

2006 TRENDS

Toys from older nostalgic series such as Lost in Space and Buck Rogers in the 25th Century continue to top lists of the most sought-after space/science fiction toys, and their values continue to soar, particularly at auction. Watch for vintage Battlestar Galactica items to increase this year, as the popular Sci-Fi Network show enters its second season and places the spotlight on the cult-favorite 1970s series that was also recently released on DVD.

Editor's Note: Several abbreviations are used in this section to denote Star Trek movies. Key is as follows: ST:TMP – Star Trek: The Motion Picture. ST:TNG – Star Trek: The Next Generation.

THE TOP TEN
SCI-FI & SPACE TOYS (In Mint Condition)

1. Buck Rogers Solar Scouts Patch, Cream of Wheat, 1936	$7,000
2. Lost in Space Doll Set, Marusan, 1960s	7,000
3. Buck Rogers Cut-Out Adventure Book, Cocomalt, 1933	6,500
4. Space Patrol Monorail Set, Toys of Tomorrow, 1950s	4,200
5. Buck Rogers Pocket Watch, Ingraham, 1935	3,750
6. Space Patrol Lunar Fleet Base, 1950s	3,200
7. Buck Rogers Rocket Skates, Marx, 1935	3,000
8. Lost in Space Roto-Jet Gun Set, Mattel, 1966	2,600
9. Space Patrol, Emergency Kit, 1950s	2,500
10. Buck Rogers Repeller Ray Ring, 1936	2,500

SPACE TOYS

ALIEN/ALIENS

Alien Blaster Target Game, 1979, H.G. Toys, set features large free standing cardboard Alien target and plastic dart shooting rifle, gun has large block letters "Alien" on side, based on the movie
EX $65   NM $135   MIP $225

Alien Blaster Target Set, HG Toys, larger set
EX $110   NM $220   MIP $325

Alien Chase Target Set, HG Toys, dart pistol, cardboard target
EX $80   NM $190   MIP $250

Alien Costume, Ben Cooper, black/white
EX $50   NM $65   MIP $110

Alien Model Kit, 1980s, Tsukuda, vinyl, 1/6 scale
EX $60   NM $225   MIP $350

Alien Warrior Model Kit, Halcyon, base and egg
EX $30   NM $40   MIP $60

Aliens Colorforms Set, Colorforms
EX $10   NM $20   MIP $45

Aliens Computer Game, 1985, Commodore
EX $5   NM $15   MIP $30

Glow Putty, Laramie, unlicensed art, carded
EX $10   NM $15   MIP $25

Movie Viewer, Kenner, "Alien Terror" film clip
EX $40   NM $75   MIP $125

BATTLESTAR GALACTICA

Colorforms Adventure Set, 1978, Colorforms
EX $12   NM $25   MIP $35

Cylon Helmet Radio, 1979, Vanity Fair
EX $25   NM $50   MIP $85

Cylon Warrior Costume, 1978, boxed
EX $10   NM $15   MIP $35

Galactic Cruiser, 1978, Larami, die-cast
EX $5   NM $10   MIP $25

Game of Starfighter Combat, 1978, FASA, role playing game
EX $10   NM $17   MIP $30

L.E.M. Lander, 1978, Larami, die-cast
EX $5   NM $10   MIP $15

Lasermatic Pistol, 1978, Mattel
EX $15   NM $35   MIP $60

Lasermatic Rifle, 1978, Mattel
EX $25   NM $50   MIP $75

Muffit the Daggit Halloween Costume, 1978, Collegeville
EX $10   NM $17   MIP $35

Poster Art Set, 1978, Craft Master
EX $10   NM $15   MIP $25

Puzzles, 1978, Parker Brothers, The Rag-Tag Fleet, Starbuck, Interstellar Battle, price for each
EX $10   NM $15   MIP $25

Space Alert Game, 1978, Mattel, hand-held electronic game
EX $10   NM $25   MIP $50

Viper Vertibird, 1979, Mattel
EX $60   NM $120   MIP $220

BUCK ROGERS

25th Century Police Patrol Rocket, 1939, Marx, tin wind-up, 12" long
EX $325   NM $950   MIP $1650

25th Century Scientific Laboratory, 1934, Porter Chemical, w/three manuals
EX $800   NM $1300   MIP $2200

Adventures of Buck Rogers Book, 1934, Whitman, All Pictures Comics edition, Big Big Book
EX $25   NM $100   MIP $200

Battle Cruiser Rocket, 1937, Tootsietoy, two grooved wheels to run on string
EX $75   NM $225   MIP $350

Buck and Wilma Masks, 1933, Einson-Freeman, paper litho, each
EX $120   NM $220   MIP $375

Buck Rogers 25th Century Rocket, 1934, Marx, Buck and Wilma in window, 12" long, tin wind-up
EX $250   NM $650   MIP $1200

Buck Rogers and the Children of Hopetown Book, 1979, Golden Press, Little Golden Book
EX $4   NM $7   MIP $15

Buck Rogers and the Depth Men of Jupiter Book, 1935, Whitman, Big Little Book
EX $50   NM $100   MIP $160

Buck Rogers and the Doom Comet Book, 1935, Whitman, Big Little Book
EX $50   NM $100   MIP $160

Buck Rogers and the Overturned World Book, 1941, Whitman, Big Little Book
EX $50   NM $85   MIP $130

Buck Rogers and the Planetoid Plot Book, 1936, Whitman, Big Little Book
EX $50   NM $100   MIP $160

Buck Rogers and the Super Dwarf of Space Book, 1943, Whitman, Big Little Book
EX $50   NM $85   MIP $130

Buck Rogers Battlecruiser, 1937, Tootsietoy, with wheels that run on string to simulate flying
EX $75   NM $110   MIP $165

Buck Rogers Figure, 1937, Tootsietoy, 1-3/4" tall, cast, gray
EX $100   NM $150   MIP $275

Buck Rogers Films, 1936, Irwin, set of six
EX $110   NM $190   MIP $285

Buck Rogers Flash Blast Attack Cruiser, 1937, Tootsietoy
EX $50   NM $90   MIP $165

Buck Rogers Holster for U-238 Atomic Pistol, 1946, Daisy, leather holster only
EX $40   NM $150   MIP $300

Buck Rogers Holster for XZ-35 Pop Gun, 1935, Daisy, embossed leather, attached to belt by two short riveted straps
EX $50   NM $175   MIP $350

Buck Rogers in the 25th Century Book, 1933, Whitman, Big Little Book, Cocomalt premium
EX $50   NM $90   MIP $160

Buck Rogers in the 25th Century Book, 1933, Whitman, Big Little Book
EX $75   NM $130   MIP $210

Buck Rogers in the 25th Century Button, 1935, pinback, color Buck bust profile on blue background, w/small ray gun and rocket ship at his shoulders
EX $30   NM $75   MIP $150

Buck Rogers in the 25th Century Pistol Set, 1934, Daisy, XA-32, holster is red, yellow and blue suede cloth, gun is 9-1/2" pressed steel pop gun
EX $210   NM $425   MIP $750

Buck Rogers in the 25th Century Star Fighter, 1979, Mego, vehicle for 3-3/4" figures
EX $20   NM $35   MIP $60

Buck Rogers in the 25th Century XZ-31 Rocket Pistol, 1934, Daisy, holster is red, yellow and blue leather, gun is 9-1/2" pressed steel Rocket Pistol w/single cooling fin at barrel base
EX $180   NM $400   MIP $725

Buck Rogers in the City Below the Sea Book, 1934, Whitman, Big Little Book
EX $75   NM $160   MIP $275

Buck Rogers in the City of Floating Globes Book, 1935, Whitman, Cocomalt premium, paperback Big Little Book
EX $125   NM $250   MIP $500

Buck Rogers in the War With the Planet Venus Book, 1938, Whitman, Big Little Book
EX $45   NM $80   MIP $130

Buck Rogers on the Moons of Saturn Book, 1934, Whitman, premium, paperback Big Little Book
EX $75   NM $160   MIP $260

Buck Rogers Rubber Band Gun, 1930s, Unknown, cut-out paper gun, on card, advertising premium item
EX $30   NM $75   MIP $150

Buck Rogers Sonic Ray Flashlight Gun, 1955, Norton-Honer, 7-1/4" black, green and yellow plastic w/code signal screw
EX $80   NM $150   MIP $325

Buck Rogers Starfighter, 1980, Corgi, white body w/yellow plastic wings, amber windows, blue jets, color decal, Buck and Wilma figures, 6-1/2", Model No. 647-A
EX $32   NM $48   MIP $100

Buck Rogers U-235 Atomic Pistol, 1945, Daisy, 9-1/2" long, pressed steel, makes pop noise and flash in window when trigger is pulled
EX $125   NM $275   MIP $575

Buck Rogers vs. The Fiend of Space Book, 1940, Whitman, Big Little Book
EX $45   NM $80   MIP $130

Buck Rogers Wristwatch, 1935, E. Ingraham
EX $400   NM $750   MIP $1500

Buck Rogers Wristwatch, 1971, Huckleberry Time
EX $50   NM $125   MIP $250

Buck Rogers XXVc Role Playing Game, 1990, TSR, numerous game modules, paperback books, comics and a board game sprang from this concept
EX $10   NM $20   MIP $30

Buck Rogers XZ-35 Space Gun, 1934, Daisy, 7-1/2" long, heavy blued metal ray gun, the grip pumps the action and the gun pops when trigger is pulled, single cooling fin at barrel base, also called "Wilma Gun"
EX $125   NM $275   MIP $575

Buck Rogers XZ-38 Disintegrator Pistol, 1935, Daisy, 10-1/2" long, polished copper finish, four flutes on barrel, spark is produced in the window on top of the gun when the trigger is pulled
EX $115   NM $400   MIP $625

Buck Rogers XZ-44 Liquid Helium Water Gun, 1936, Daisy, 7-1/4" long, red and yellow lightning bolt design stamped metal body w/a leather bladder to hold water; a later version was available in copper finish
EX $175   NM $500   MIP $850

Century of Progess Key Fob, 1934, metal, coin style, reverse shows Buck silhouette profile
EX $135   NM $275   MIP $500

Century of Progress Button, 1934, pinback, I Saw Buck Rogers 25th Century Show, color litho
EX $135   NM $250   MIP $500

Chemistry Set, 1937, Gropper, beginners
EX $325   NM $775   MIP $1350

Chemistry Set, 1937, Gropper, advanced
EX $350   NM $800   MIP $1600

Chief Explorer Badge, 1936, red enamel
EX $90   NM $215   MIP $385

Chief Explorer Badge, 1936, gold
EX $150   NM $350   MIP $750

Chief Explorer Folder, 1936
EX $70   NM $125   MIP $250

Clock, 1990s, Ingraham, wall clock
EX $15   NM $30   MIP $45

Colorforms Set, 1979, Colorforms
EX $10   NM $15   MIP $40

Comet Socker Paddle Ball, 1935, Lee-Tex
EX $35   NM $100   MIP $200

Communicator Set, 1979, w/silver Twiki figure
EX $10   NM $20   MIP $45

Costume, 1934, Sackman Bros.
EX $850   NM $1400   MIP $2500

Cut-Out Adventure Book, 1933, Cocomalt premium
EX $1250   NM $3500   MIP $6500

Electric Caster Rocket, 1934, Marx
EX $125   NM $210   MIP $350

Flash Blast Attack Ship Rocket, 1937, Tootsietoy, Flash Blast Attack Ship 4-1/2", Venus Duo-Destroyer w/two grooved wheels to run on string
EX $90   NM $150   MIP $250

Galactic Play Set, 1980s, HG Toys
EX $17   NM $30   MIP $55

Helmet and Rocket Pistol Set, 1933, Einson-Freeman, set of paper partial-face "helmet" mask and paper pop gun, in envelope
EX $115   NM $275   MIP $550

Helmet XZ-34, 1935, Daisy, leather
EX $285   NM $500   MIP $750

Interplanetary Games Set, 1934, three game boards in box: Cosmic Rocket Wars, Secrets of Atlantis, Siege of Gigantica, set
EX $235   NM $425   MIP $700

Interplanetary Space Fleet Model Kit, 1935, six different kits, including instructions and poster, in box, each
EX $100   NM $200   MIP $350

Lite-Blaster Flashlight, 1936
EX $155   NM $285   MIP $500

Martian Wars Game, 1990s, TSR, role playing game expansion set for the Buck Rogers XXVc game
EX $10   NM $20   MIP $35

Midget Caster, 1934, Rapaport Bros., mold and metal to cast lead figures
EX $150   NM $300   MIP $450

Official Utility Belt, 1979, Remco, in window box, w/decoder glasses, wristwatch, disk-shooting ray gun, intruder detection badge, city decoder map, secret message
EX $20   NM $40   MIP $85

Paint By Number Set, 1980s, Transogram
EX $15   NM $25   MIP $40

Pencil Box, 1930s, American Pencil
EX $75   NM $150   MIP $275

Pendant Watch, 1971, Huckleberry Time
EX $115   NM $200   MIP $300

Pocket Knife, 1935, Adolph Kastor, red, green, blue
EX $450   NM $900   MIP $2000

Pocket Watch, 1935, E. Ingraham, round, face shows Buck and Wilma, lightning bolt hands
EX $500   NM $1800   MIP $3750

Pocket Watch, 1971, Huckleberry Time
EX $90   NM $175   MIP $275

Punching Bag, 1942, Morton Salt, balloon w/characters
EX $50   NM $75   MIP $150

Puzzle, 1945, Puzzle Craft, Buck Rogers and His Atomic Bomber, three different each
EX $75   NM $150   MIP $300

Puzzle, 1979, Milton Bradley, four versions showing TV scenes, each
EX $6   NM $15   MIP $30

Puzzle with sleeve, 1952, Milton Bradley, space station scene, 14" x 10"
EX $75   NM $150   MIP $200

Repeller Ray Ring, 1936, brass w/inset green stone
EX $400   NM $1250   MIP $2500

Rocket Rangers Iron-On Transfers, 1944, set of three
EX $30   NM $50   MIP $100

Rocket Rangers Membership Card, 1939
EX $45   NM $75   MIP $150

Rocket Skates, 1935, 11-1/2", Marx, roller skates w/leather straps, red jeweled reflector on back
EX $1400   NM $200   MIP $3000

Satellite Pioneers Button, 1958, green or blue
EX $20   NM $50   MIP $125

Satellite Pioneers Map of Solar System, 1958
EX $20   NM $40   MIP $85

Satellite Pioneers Membership Card, 1958
EX $30   NM $60   MIP $110

Satellite Pioneers Starfinder, 1958, paper
EX $20   NM $50   MIP $75

Saturn Ring, 1946, Post Corn Toasties, red stone, glow-in-the-dark white plastic on crocodile base
EX $150   NM $300   MIP $650

School Bag, 1935, suede cloth
EX $60   NM $100   MIP $200

Solar Scouts Member Badge, 1936, gold color
EX $60   NM $100   MIP $160

Solar Scouts Patch, 1936, Cream of Wheat, three colors
EX $1500   NM $5000   MIP $7200

Solar Scouts Radio Club Manual, 1936
EX $125   NM $275   MIP $550

Space Glasses, 1955, Norton-Honer, No. 1440
EX $40   NM $75   MIP $200

Space Ranger Halolight Ring, 1953, Sylvania
EX $300   NM $750   MIP $1000

Space Ranger Kit, 1952, Sylvania, 11" x 15" premium, envelope w/six punch-out sheets
EX $50   NM $100   MIP $200

Spaceship Commander, 1936, stationery
EX $50   NM $100   MIP $200

Spaceship Commander Banner, 1936
EX $350   NM $1000   MIP $2000

Spaceship Commander Whistling Badge, 1936
EX $50   NM $110   MIP $225

SPACE TOYS

Strange Adventures in the Spider Ship Pop-Up Book, 1935
EX $110   NM $250   MIP $400

Strato-Kite, 1946, Aero-Kite
EX $20   NM $35   MIP $75

Super Foto Camera, 1955, Norton-Honer
EX $40   NM $70   MIP $150

Super Scope Telescope, 1955, Norton-Honer, No. 1430, 9" plastic telescope
EX $40   NM $70   MIP $150

Super Sonic Ray Gun, 1950, Norton-Honer, No. 1432, 6-1/4", black w/ red and green knobs on the side
EX $75   NM $150   MIP $225

Superdreadnought SD51X Model Kit, 1936, 6-1/2" long, balsa wood, one of Interplanetary Space Fleet kit set
EX $100   NM $200   MIP $350

Toy Watch, 1978, GLJ Toys
EX $15   NM $30   MIP $60

Two-Way Transceiver, 1948, DA Myco
EX $80   NM $130   MIP $200

View-Master Set, 1979, View-Master, three-reel set, in envelope or on blister card
EX $5   NM $10   MIP $20

Walkie Talkies, 1950s, Remco
EX $60   NM $150   MIP $200

Wilma Deering Figure, 1937, Tootsietoy, 1-3/4" tall, cast, gold color
EX $70   NM $125   MIP $225

CAPTAIN MIDNIGHT

Air Heroes Stamp Album, 1930s, twelve stamps
EX $35   NM $75   MIP $150

Captain Midnight Medal, 1930s, gold medal pin w/centered wings and words "Flight Commander"; Capt. is embossed on top w/medal dangling beneath
EX $65   NM $150   MIP $200

Cup, Ovaltine, plastic, 4" tall, "Ovaltine-The Heart of a Hearty Breakfast"
EX $15   NM $35   MIP $60

Key-O-Matic Code-O-Graph w/key, 1949, Secret Squadron brass decoder sets number and letter combinations
EX $80   NM $185   MIP $325

Membership Manual, 1930s, Secret Squadron official code and manual guide
EX $40   NM $60   MIP $110

CAPTAIN VIDEO

Captain Video and Ranger Photo, 1950s, premium
EX $25   NM $50   MIP $90

Captain Video Game, 1952, Milton Bradley
EX $75   NM $150   MIP $275

Captain Video Rite-O-Lite Flashlight Gun, 1950s, Power House Candy, 3" long, red plastic gun w/bulb, space map, paper, directions and order form, in mailing envelope
EX $20   NM $60   MIP $100

Captain Video Rocket Launcher, 1952, Lido
EX $65   NM $185   MIP $360

Comic Book, Captain Video No. 1, 1951, Fawcett
EX $100   NM $375   MIP $1000

Flying Saucer Ring, 1950s, w/two saucers and papers
EX $500   NM $1000   MIP $1500

Galaxy Spaceship Riding Toy, 1950s
EX $250   NM $425   MIP $675

Interplantary Space Men Figures, 1950s, in die-cut box
EX $55   NM $110   MIP $175

Kukla, Fran and Ollie Puppet Show, 1962, Milton Bradley, cardboard stage, puppets, props
EX $50   NM $200   MIP $375

Mysto-Coder, 1950s, w/photo
EX $65   NM $200   MIP $400

Rite-O-Lite Flashlight Gun, 1950s, Power House Candy
EX $40   NM $90   MIP $185

Rocket Tank, 1952, Lido
EX $55   NM $95   MIP $150

Secret Seal Ring, 1950s, w/initials CV, gold or copper
EX $250   NM $400   MIP $600

(ToyShop File Photo)

Space Port Play Set, 1950s, Superior, All tin set, including rocket (not shown)
EX $250   NM $430   MIP $660

Troop Transport Ship, 1950s, Lido, in box
EX $55   NM $95   MIP $155

DEFENDERS OF THE EARTH

Gripjaw Vehicle, 1985, Galoob
EX $11   NM $16   MIP $25

Mongor Figure, 1985, Galoob
EX $16   NM $23   MIP $35

Puzzle, 1985, frame tray
EX $9   NM $15   MIP $25

DEFENDERS OF THE UNIVERSE

Battling Black Lion Voltron Vehicle, 1986, LJN
EX $9   NM $13   MIP $20

Coffin of Darkness Voltron Vehicle, 1986, LJN
EX $7   NM $10   MIP $15

Doom Blaster Voltron Vehicle, 1986, LJN, mysterious flying machine
EX $9   NM $13   MIP $20

Doom Commander Figure, 1985, Matchbox
EX $5   NM $7   MIP $10

Green Lion Voltron Vehicle, 1986, LJN
EX $9   NM $13   MIP $20

Hagar Figure, 1985, Matchbox
EX $5   NM $7   MIP $15

Hunk Figure, 1985, Matchbox
EX $5   NM $7   MIP $15

Keith Figure, 1985, Matchbox
EX $5   NM $7   MIP $15

King Zarkon Figure, 1985, Matchbox
EX $5   NM $7   MIP $15

Lance Figure, 1985, Matchbox
EX $5   NM $7   MIP $15

Motorized Lion Force Voltron Vehicle Set, 1986, LJN, black lion w/blazing sound
EX $9   NM $13   MIP $20

Pidge Figure, 1985, Matchbox
EX $5   NM $7   MIP $12

Prince Lothar Figure, 1985, Matchbox
EX $5   NM $7   MIP $12

Princess Allura Figure, 1985, Matchbox
EX $5   NM $7   MIP $12

Robeast Mutilor Figure, 1985, Matchbox
EX $5   NM $7   MIP $12

Robeast Scorpious Figure, 1985, Matchbox
EX $5   NM $7   MIP $12

Skull Tank Voltron Vehicle, 1986, LJN
EX $9   NM $13   MIP $20

Vehicle Team Assembler, 1986, LJN, forms Voltron
EX $9   NM $13   MIP $20

Voltron Lion Force & Vehicle Team Assemblers Gift Set, 1986, LJN
EX $9   NM $13   MIP $20

Voltron Motorized Giant Commander, 1984, LJN, plastic 36", multicolor body w/movable head, arms and wings, wire remote control, battery operated
EX $15   NM $25   MIP $40

Zarkon Zapper Voltron Vehicle, 1986, LJN, w/galactic sound
EX $11   NM $16   MIP $25

DOCTOR WHO

Cyberman Robot Doll, 1970s, Denys Fisher, 10"
EX $250   NM $350   MIP $550

Dalek Bagatelle, 1976, Denys Fisher
EX $70   NM $110   MIP $175

Dalek Shooting Game, 1965, Marx, 8" x 20", four-color tin litho stand up target and generic cork rifle
EX $225   NM $325   MIP $525

Dalek's Oracle Question & Answer Board Game, 1965, magnetized Dalek that spins
EX $115   NM $165   MIP $250

Davros Figure, 1986, Dapol, villain w/left arm
EX $11   NM $16   MIP $45

Doctor Who Card Set, 1970s, 12 octagon cards
EX $14   NM $20   MIP $35

Doctor Who Card Set, 1976, Denys Fisher, 24 cards
EX $18   NM $26   MIP $45

Doctor Who Trump Card Game, 1970s
EX $9   NM $13   MIP $20

(ToyShop File Photo)

Doctor Who...Dodge the Daleks Board Game, 1965
EX $120   NM $175   MIP $280

FLASH GORDON

Adventure on the Moons of Mongo Game, 1977, House of Games
EX $15   NM $25   MIP $40

Arak Figure, 1979, Mattel, 3-3/4", carded
EX $17   NM $30   MIP $50

Battle Rocket with Space Probing Action, 1976
EX $6   NM $10   MIP $20

Beastman Figure, 1979, Mattel, 3-3/4", carded
EX $15   NM $25   MIP $45

Book Bag, 1950s, 12" wide, three-color art on flap
EX $17   NM $35   MIP $75

Candy Box, 1970s, eight illustrated boxes, each
EX $4   NM $10   MIP $20

Dr. Zarkov Figure, 1979, Mattel, 3-3/4" figure, on card
EX $15   NM $35   MIP $50

Flash and Ming Button, 1970s, shows Flash and Ming crossing swords
EX $4   NM $10   MIP $20

Flash Gordon Air Ray Gun, 1950s, Budson, 10" unusual air blaster, handle on top cocks mechanism, pressed steel
EX $215   NM $350   MIP $700

Flash Gordon and Martian, 1965, Revell, #1450
EX $60   NM $125   MIP $175

Flash Gordon and the Ape Men of Mor Book, 1942, Dell, 196 pages, Fast Action Story
EX $75   NM $150   MIP $250

Flash Gordon and the Fiery Desert of Mongo Book, 1948, Whitman, Big Little Book
EX $30   NM $60   MIP $90

Flash Gordon and the Monsters of Mongo Book, 1935, Whitman, hardback Big Little Book
EX $50   NM $90   MIP $135

Flash Gordon and the Perils of Mongo Book, 1940, Whitman, Big Little Book
EX $35   NM $70   MIP $100

Flash Gordon and the Power Men of Mongo Book, 1943, Whitman, Big Little Book
EX $35   NM $65   MIP $95

Flash Gordon and the Red Sword Invaders Book, 1945, Whitman, Big Little Book
EX $30   NM $60   MIP $90

Flash Gordon and the Tournaments of Mongo Book, 1935, Whitman, paperback Big Little Book
EX $45   NM $80   MIP $120

Flash Gordon and the Tyrant of Mongo Book, 1941, Whitman, Big Little Book, w/flip pictures
EX $35   NM $70   MIP $105

Flash Gordon and the Witch Queen of Mongo Book, 1936, Whitman, Big Little Book
EX $45   NM $80   MIP $120

Flash Gordon Arresting Ray Gun, 1939, Marx, picture of Flash on handle, 12" long
EX $200   NM $500   MIP $1250

Flash Gordon Costume, 1951, Esquire Novelty
EX $90   NM $145   MIP $250

Flash Gordon Figure, 1944, wood composition, 5" tall
EX $115   NM $195   MIP $300

Flash Gordon Game, 1970s, House of Games
EX $15   NM $30   MIP $40

Flash Gordon Hand Puppet, 1950s, rubber head
EX $90   NM $145   MIP $250

Flash Gordon in the Forest Kingdom of Mongo Book, 1938, Whitman, Big Little Book
EX $40   NM $75   MIP $110

Flash Gordon in the Ice World of Mongo Book, 1942, Whitman, Big Little Book, w/flip pictures
EX $35   NM $70   MIP $100

Flash Gordon in the Jungles of Mongo Book, 1947, Whitman, Big Little Book
EX $35   NM $65   MIP $95

Flash Gordon in the Water World of Mongo Book, 1937, Whitman, Big Little Book
EX $35   NM $70   MIP $105

Flash Gordon Kite, 1950s, 21" x 17", paper
EX $55   NM $90   MIP $135

Flash Gordon on the Planet Mongo Book, 1934, Whitman, Big Little Book
EX $55   NM $105   MIP $155

Flash Gordon Paint Book, 1930s
EX $60   NM $125   MIP $200

Flash Gordon Radio Repeater Clicker Pistol, Marx, 10" long, 1930s
EX $250   NM $750   MIP $1500

Flash Gordon Signal Pistol, 1930s, Marx, 7", siren sounds when trigger is pulled, tin/pressed steel, green w/red trim
EX $250   NM $600   MIP $1200

Flash Gordon Space Water Gun, 1976, Nasta, water ray gun on illustrated card
EX $10   NM $25   MIP $50

Flash Gordon Three Color Ray Gun, 1976, Nasta, battery-operated
EX $8   NM $35   MIP $80

Flash Gordon vs. the Emperor of Mongo Book, 1936, Dell, 244 pages, Fast Action Story
EX $70   NM $140   MIP $225

Flash Gordon Water Pistol, 1940s, Marx, plastic w/whistle in handle, 7-1/2" long
EX $80   NM $250   MIP $500

Flash Gordon Wristwatch, 1979, Bradley, medium chrome case, back and sweep seconds, Flash in foreground w/city behind
EX $70   NM $115   MIP $175

Flash Gordon, The Movie Buttons, 1980, set of five, each
EX $2   NM $4   MIP $8

Home Foundry Casting Set, 1935, lead casting set w/molds of Flash and other characters
EX $575   NM $975   MIP $1500

Lizard Woman Figure, 1979, Mattel, 3-3/4", carded
EX $15   NM $25   MIP $40

Medals and Insignia, 1978, Larami, set of five on blister card
EX $10   NM $25   MIP $50

Ming Figure, 1979, Mattel, 3-3/4", carded
EX $12   NM $20   MIP $35

Ming's Space Shuttle, Mattel
EX $15   NM $25   MIP $50

Pencil Box, 1951
EX $75   NM $150   MIP $225

Puzzle, 1930s, Featured Funnies
EX $55   NM $110   MIP $160

Puzzle, 1951, Milton Bradley, frame tray
EX $45   NM $80   MIP $125

Puzzles, 1951, Milton Bradley, set of three
EX $105   NM $200   MIP $300

Rocket Fighter, 1939, Marx, tin wind-up, 12" long
EX $175   NM $350   MIP $600

Rocket Ship, 1975, 3" die-cast metal
EX $10   NM $20   MIP $35

Rocket Ship, 1979, Mattel, inflatable, 3' long, w/plastic nose, rocket and gondola attachments
EX $20   NM $40   MIP $60

Solar Commando Set, 1950s, Premier Products
EX $65   NM $115   MIP $175

Space Compass, 1950s, ornately housed compass on illustrated watchband
EX $25   NM $40   MIP $75

Space Water Gun, 1976, Nasta, water ray gun on illustrated card
EX $6   NM $15   MIP $30

Sunglasses, 1981, Ja-Ru, plastic w/emblem on bridge, carded
EX $3   NM $5   MIP $10

SPACE TOYS

Three-Color Ray Gun, 1976, Nasta
EX $8   **NM** $15   **MIP** $30

Thun, Lion Man Figure, 1979, Mattel, 3-3/4", carded
EX $15   **NM** $25   **MIP** $45

Two-Way Telephone, 1940s, Marx
EX $60   **NM** $110   **MIP** $185

View-Master Set, 1963, View-Master, three reels in envelope
EX $20   **NM** $35   **MIP** $60

View-Master Set, 1976, View-Master, three reels, In the Planet Mongo
EX $6   **NM** $10   **MIP** $20

Vultan Figure, 1979, Mattel, 3-3/4", carded
EX $15   **NM** $30   **MIP** $50

Wallet, 1949, w/zipper
EX $70   **NM** $115   **MIP** $175

Water Pistol, 1950s, Marx, 7-1/2" plastic
EX $155   **NM** $275   **MIP** $500

LAND OF THE GIANTS

Annual Book, 1969, World Dist./UK, two volumes, set
EX $30   **NM** $50   **MIP** $75

Colorforms Set, 1968, Colorforms
EX $30   **NM** $50   **MIP** $75

Costumes, 1968, Ben Cooper, Steve Burton, Giant Witch, or Scientist, each
EX $35   **NM** $60   **MIP** $150

Deluxe Numbered Pencil Coloring Set, 1969, Hasbro
EX $60   **NM** $100   **MIP** $150

Double Action Bagatelle Game, 1969, Hasbro, pinball game, cardboard back
EX $35   **NM** $75   **MIP** $160

Flight of Fear Book, Whitman, hardcover
EX $8   **NM** $15   **MIP** $35

Flying Saucer, 1968, Remco, flying disk
EX $60   **NM** $100   **MIP** $150

Land of the Giants Book, Pyramid, paperback by Murray Leinster
EX $8   **NM** $13   **MIP** $25

Land of the Giants Comic Book #1, 1968, Gold Key
EX $10   **NM** $15   **MIP** $30

Land of the Giants Comic Books #2-#5, 1968, Gold Key, each
EX $8   **NM** $13   **MIP** $25

Motorized Flying Rocket, 1968, Remco, plastic airplane w/motor, LOTG logo on wings
EX $80   **NM** $130   **MIP** $200

Movie Viewer, 1968, Acme, film strip viewer, on card
EX $25   **NM** $45   **MIP** $65

Painting Set, 1969, Hasbro
EX $40   **NM** $65   **MIP** $100

Puzzle, 1968, Whitman, round floor puzzle w/cartoon illustration
EX $35   **NM** $55   **MIP** $85

Rub-Ons, 1969, Hasbro
EX $30   **NM** $50   **MIP** $75

Shoot & Stick Target Rifle Set, 1968, Remco, western rifle w/logo decals
EX $90   **NM** $145   **MIP** $225

Signal Ray Space Gun, 1968, Remco, ray gun w/logo decals
EX $70   **NM** $115   **MIP** $175

Space Sled, 1968, Remco, Supercar refitted w/LOTG decals—Mike Mercury still sits behind the wheel
EX $200   **NM** $350   **MIP** $525

Spaceship Control Panel, 1968, Remco, Firebird 99 dashboard w/a cardboard cut-out of logo on top
EX $200   **NM** $300   **MIP** $525

Spindrift Interior Model Kit, 1989, Lunar Models, #Sf029, interior for 16" model shell
EX $35   **NM** $55   **MIP** $85

Spindrift Toothpick Kit, 1968, Remco, box of toothpicks w/a few cardboard pieces to build ship
EX $35   **NM** $60   **MIP** $85

Target Set, 1969, Hasbro, small guns w/darts
EX $60   **NM** $100   **MIP** $160

The Hot Spot Book, Pyramid, paperback, #2 in series, by Leinster
EX $12   **NM** $20   **MIP** $35

Trading Card Wrapper, 1968, Topps/A & BC
EX $60   **NM** $100   **MIP** $160

Trading Cards, 1968, A & BC/England, 55 cards
EX $275   **NM** $450   **MIP** $710

Trading Cards, 1968, Topps USA, 55 cards
EX $275   **NM** $450   **MIP** $710

Trading Cards Box, 1968, Topps/A & BC, display box only
EX $395   **NM** $650   **MIP** $1000

Unknown Danger Book, Pyramid, paperback #3 by Leinster
EX $12   **NM** $20   **MIP** $35

View-Master Set, 1968, GAF, three reels, first episode
EX $20   **NM** $35   **MIP** $50

Walkie Talkies, 1968, Remco, generic walkie talkies w/LOTG decals added
EX $80   **NM** $130   **MIP** $210

Wrist Flashlight, 1968, Bantam Lite
EX $30   **NM** $50   **MIP** $80

LOST IN SPACE

Chariot Model Kit, Marusan/Japanese, figures and motor
EX $625   **NM** $975   **MIP** $1500

Chariot Model Kit, 1987, Lunar Models, #SF009, 1:35 scale, w/clear vacuform canopy and dome, plastic body, treads, roof rack
EX $35   **NM** $50   **MIP** $80

Costume, 1965, Ben Cooper, silver spacesuit w/logo
EX $85   **NM** $150   **MIP** $225

Doll Set, Marusan/Japanese, dressed in spacesuits w/their own freezing tubes

w/a cardboard insert w/color photos and description
EX $2900   **NM** $4500   **MIP** $7000

Fan Cards, 1960s, promo cards mailed to fans; color photo
EX $20   **NM** $35   **MIP** $60

Fan Cards, 1960s, promo cards mailed to fans; black/white photo
EX $15   **NM** $25   **MIP** $50

Helmet and Gun Set, 1967, Remco, child size helmet w/blue flashing light and logo decals, blue and red molded gun
EX $300   **NM** $530   **MIP** $880

Jupiter Model Kit, 1966, Marusan/Japanese, large version
EX $425   **NM** $650   **MIP** $1000

Jupiter-2 Model Kit, Comet/England, 2" diameter, solid metal
EX $8   **NM** $13   **MIP** $35

Jupiter-2 Model Kit, 1966, Marusan/Japanese, 6" molded in green plastic w/wheels and wind-up motor
EX $425   **NM** $650   **MIP** $1000

Laser Water Pistol, Unknown, 5" long, first season pistol style
EX $30   **NM** $50   **MIP** $80

(ToyShop File Photo)

Lost In Space 3-D Action Fun Game, 1966, Remco, three levels w/small cardboard figures
EX $530   **NM** $785   **MIP** $1250

Note Pad, June Lockhart on front
EX $25   **NM** $40   **MIP** $65

Puzzles, 1966, 10 x 14", Milton Bradley, frame tray; three poses w/Cyclops
EX $40   **NM** $65   **MIP** $100

Robot, 1966, Remco, 12" high, motorized w/blinking lights
EX $180   **NM** $365   **MIP** $700

Robot, 1968, Aurora, 6" high w/base
EX $150   **NM** $400   **MIP** $1100

Robot, 1977, K-mart/Ahi, 10", plastic w/green dome, battery-operated
EX $85   **NM** $200   **MIP** $325

Robot YM-3, 1985, Masudaya, 4" high, wind-up
EX $20   **NM** $30   **MIP** $50

Robot YM-3, 1986, Masudaya, 16" high, speaks English and Japanese
EX $85   **NM** $150   **MIP** $250

Roto-Jet Gun Set, 1966, Mattel, TV tie-in, modular gun can be reconfigured into different variations, shoots discs
EX $775   **NM** $1300   **MIP** $2600

Saucer Gun, 1977, Ahi, disk shooting gun
EX $30   NM $60   MIP $150

Space Family Robinson Comic Book,
1960s, Gold Key
EX $15   NM $25   MIP $45

Switch-and-Go Set, 1966, Mattel, figures,
Jupiter and chariot that ran around track
EX $975   NM $1500   MIP $2400

Trading Cards, 1966, Topps, 55 black and
white cards, no wrappers or box
EX $175   NM $300   MIP $525

Tru-Vue Magic Eyes Set, 1967, GAF,
rectangular reels
EX $30   NM $50   MIP $80

View-Master Set, 1967, GAF, Condemned
of Space
EX $25   NM $40   MIP $65

Walkie Talkies, 1977, AHI, small card
EX $30   NM $50   MIP $85

MISCELLANEOUS

Astro Base, 1960, Ideal, 22" tall, red/white
astronaut base, control panel opens lock
door, extends crane and lowers
astronaut in scout car
EX $225   NM $325   MIP $525

Astro Boy Mask/Glasses, 1960s, blue
glasses w/Astro boy hair on top
EX $25   NM $50   MIP $75

Astronaut Costume, 1960, Collegeville
EX $18   NM $25   MIP $50

Astronaut Costume, 1962, Ben Cooper
EX $18   NM $25   MIP $50

Astronaut Space Commander Play Suit,
1950s, Yankeeboy, green outfit and cap
(military style) w/gold piping on collar
and pants
EX $35   NM $50   MIP $85

Fireball XL-5 Space City Play Set, 1963,
MPC, includes ship, base and figures
EX $550   NM $1100   MIP $2200

Fireball XL-5 Spaceship, 1963, MPC,
plastic, 20" ship w/figures
EX $200   NM $500   MIP $1300

Martian Bobbing Head, 1960s, 7" tall, blue
vinyl martian w/bobbing eyes and
exposed brain
EX $23   NM $35   MIP $60

Men into Space Astronaut Space Helmet,
1960s, Ideal, plastic helmet w/visor
EX $35   NM $50   MIP $80

Puzzle, 1970, Selchow & Righter, 10" x 14",
picture of the moon's surface
EX $14   NM $20   MIP $35

Rex Mars Atomix Pistol Flashlight,
1950s, Marx, plastic
EX $50   NM $80   MIP $175

Space Safari Planetary Play Set, 1969,
four battery operated space vehicles, 3"
tall astronaut figures in silver plastic, 2"
hard plastic aliens
EX $45   NM $65   MIP $100

TV Space Riders Coloring Book, 1952,
Abbott, 14" X 15"
EX $7   NM $12   MIP $25

V-Enemy Visitor Doll, 1984, LJN, 12"
EX $16   NM $30   MIP $60

**Voyage to the Bottom of the Sea Scout
Play Set,** 1964, Remco, includes mini-
sub, sea crawler and divers
EX $250   NM $650   MIP $1300
(ToyShop File Photo)

**Voyage to the Bottom of the Sea Seaview
Play Set,** 1964, Remco, includes plastic
sub, sea monster and divers
EX $320   NM $675   MIP $1625

MONSTERS

**Creature From the Black Lagoon
Aquarium Figure,** 1950s, Japan, 3 1/2"
Lead figure
EX $85   NM $150   MIP n/a

**Creature from the Black Lagoon
Aquarium Figure,** 1971, Penn-Plax, 6"
Moving Figure
EX $150   NM $250   MIP $450

Creature From the Black Lagoon Figure,
1963, Marx, 5", hard plastic blue or orange
EX $10   NM $20   MIP $40

Creature From the Black Lagoon Figure,
1973, 74, AHI, 5", hard rubber like bendy
EX $40   NM $65   MIP $100

Creature From the Black Lagoon Figure,
1974, AHI, 8", plastic, bendable joints
EX $295   NM $425   MIP $700

**Creature From the Black Lagoon
Halloween Costume,** 1973, Ben
Cooper, Child's Mask and Costume
EX $35   NM $80   MIP $120

**Creature From the Black Lagoon
Motionette,** 1992, Telco, 24", Electric,
w/sound
EX $100   NM $200   MIP $350

**Creature From the Black Lagoon
Motionette,** 1992, Telco, 17", Batt op,
w/sound
EX $10   NM $15   MIP $30

Creature From the Black Lagoon Robot,
1991, Robot House, 9", tin/plastic, wind-up
EX $35   NM $65   MIP $110

Creature From the Black Lagoon Soaky,
1963, Colgate-Palmolive, 10", plastic,
bubble bath bottle
EX $35   NM $75   MIP $110

Creature From the Black Lagoon Sparky,
1970s, Hong Kong, 3 1/2", plastic, wind-up
EX $10   NM $20   MIP $35

**Creature From the Black Lagoon Wiggle
Ick Figure,** 1960s, Japan, 7", rubbery
plastic, bobbin' head
EX $50   NM $85   MIP $150

Deadly Grell Figure, 1983, LJN, bendable
EX $5   NM $7   MIP $10

Dracula Action Figure, AHI, w/Aurora head
EX $65   NM $125   MIP $200

Dracula Glow-in-the-Dark Mini Monsters,
Remco
EX $23   NM $30   MIP $45

**Dwarves of the Mountain Human/Monster
Figure,** 1983, LJN
EX $5   NM $7   MIP $10

Evil Monster Figure Bugbear & Goblin,
1983, LJN, Orcs of the Broken Bone
EX $5   NM $7   MIP $10

Frankenstein Figure, AHI, w/Aurora head
EX $65   NM $125   MIP $200

Frankenstein Figure, 1978, Remco,
poseable, glow-in-the-dark features and
removable cloth costumes
EX $23   NM $35   MIP $50

Godzilla Combat Joe Set, 1984, vinyl,
w/12" tall Combat Joe figure, poseable
EX $450   NM $650   MIP $1000

Godzilla Figure, 1977, Mattel, 19" tall
EX $20   NM $30   MIP $60

Godzilla Figure, 1985, Imperial, 6-1/2" tall,
arms, legs and tail movable
EX $5   NM $10   MIP $20

Godzilla Figure, 1985, Imperial, 13" tall,
arms, legs and tail movable
EX $15   NM $23   MIP $40

MOON MCDARE

Action Communication Set, 1966, Gilbert
EX $25   NM $35   MIP $60

Moon Explorer Set, 1966, Gilbert
EX $35   NM $50   MIP $85

Moon McDare Figure, 1966, Gilbert, 12"
tall astronaut w/blue jumpsuit
EX $55   NM $85   MIP $150

Moon McDare Space Gun Set, 1966, Gilbert
EX $25   NM $50   MIP $130

Space Accessory Pack, 1966, Gilbert
EX $25   NM $35   MIP $75

Space Gun Set, 1966, Gilbert
EX $40   NM $80   MIP $125

Space Mutt Set, 1966, Gilbert
EX $30   NM $45   MIP $75

OTHER WORLDS, THE

Castle Zendo, 1983, Arco
EX $20   NM $30   MIP $50

SPACE TOYS

Fighting Glowgons Figure Set, 1983, Arco
EX $18   NM $25   MIP $40

Fighting Terrans Figure Set, 1983, Arco
EX $20   NM $30   MIP $50

Kamaro Figure, 1983, Arco
EX $8   NM $12   MIP $18

Sharkoss Figure, 1983, Arco
EX $8   NM $12   MIP $18

PLANET OF THE APES

Cap Pistol, 1974, Mattel, Fanner 50
EX $30   NM $65   MIP $95

Color-Vue Set, 1970s, Hasbro, eight pencils and nine 12" x 13" pictures to color
EX $30   NM $45   MIP $70

Dr. Zaius Bank, 1967, Play Pal, figural, vinyl, 11"
EX $20   NM $30   MIP $60

Fun-Doh Modeling Molds, 1974, Chemtoy, molds of Zira, Cornelius, Zaius, and Aldo
EX $20   NM $30   MIP $50

Galen Bank, 1960s, Play Pal
EX $25   NM $35   MIP $60

Machine Gun, 1974, Mattel, "Planet of the Apes" sticker on stock, sub-machine gun
EX $40   NM $85   MIP $125

Planet of the Apes Activity Book, 1974, Saalfield, #C3031
EX $15   NM $30   MIP $45

Puzzle, 1974, Whitman, #7512, 224 pieces, 18-1/2 x 13",
EX $5   NM $10   MIP $15

Puzzle, Battle on Planet of the Apes, 1967, H.G. Toy Co., #486-01, 500 pieces, 16 x 20"
EX $7   NM $14   MIP $20

Puzzle, General Aldo, 1967, H.G. Toy Co., #485-05, 96 pieces, 10 x 14"
EX $5   NM $10   MIP $15

Puzzle, On Patrol, 1967, H.G. Toy Co., #486-06, 96 pieces, 10 x 14"
EX $5   NM $10   MIP $15

Puzzle, The Chase, 1967, H.G. Toy Co., #486-02, 500 pieces, 16 x 20"
EX $7   NM $14   MIP $20

Puzzles, H.G. Toys, 96-piece canister puzzles, each
EX $7   NM $12   MIP $25

Rapid Fire Rifle, 1974, Mattel, "Planet of the Apes" sticker on stock, Winchester mechanism
EX $40   NM $85   MIP $125

Wagon, AHI, friction powered prison wagon
EX $20   NM $45   MIP $70

Wastebasket, 1967, Chein, oval, tin
EX $25   NM $35   MIP $60

Zaius, Zera, or Cornelius Walkers, 1970s, Hong Kong, 3 1/2" plastic, wind-up
EX $20   NM $40   MIP $80

ROCKY JONES, SPACE RANGER

Pin, Silvercup Bread, 1950s, 1-1/2", photo, "Rocky Jones Space Ranger Silvercup Bread"
EX $10   NM $20   MIP $35

Rocky Jones, Space Ranger Coloring Book, 1951, Whitman, 14" x 16"
EX $25   NM $50   MIP $80

Space Ranger Button, 1954
EX $17   NM $35   MIP $75

Space Ranger Wings Pin, 1954, gold wings say "Space Ranger" silver ring w/spaceship around it
EX $17   NM $40   MIP $85

Wristwatch, 1954, in illustrated box
EX $80   NM $150   MIP $300

SPACE GUNS

4-Barrel Waist Space Dart Gun Belt, 1950s, Knickerbocker, 11" wide gun system on belt, designed to be worn on waist or chest and aimed w/periscope sight, red plastic belt
EX $30   NM $50   MIP $85

888 Space Gun, 1955, Japan, 3" long, tin, shoots caps, painted blue body and grip w/stars, planets and spaceship, red barrel w/"888" above grip
EX $30   NM $60   MIP $120

Astro Ray Gun, 1960s, Shudo/Japan, 5-7/8" long, silver finish body w/red, yellow and black detailing, friction sparkling action, single large spark window near muzzle, prominent "Astro Ray Gun" in center of body
EX $15   NM $30   MIP $60

Astro Ray Gun, 1968, Shudo/Japan, 9" long, friction spark action, tin litho body w/clear red plastic barrel, red on yellow "ASTRO RAY GUN" lettering
EX $25   NM $40   MIP $75

Astro Ray Laser Lite Beam Dart Gun, 1960s, Ohio Art, 10" red and white plastic flashlight lights target w/four darts
EX $70   NM $120   MIP $185

Astroray Gun, 1960s, MTU, 10", tin litho, blue w/ red and silver accents, red transparent plastic barrel, Korea, unusual triangular box
EX $20   NM $40   MIP $65

Astro-Ray Space Gun, 10"
EX $20   NM $30   MIP $50

Atom Bubble Gun, 1940s, Unknown, red tubular barrel w/handle attached, two sets of silver finish fins--at barrel base and muzzle, wire loop projects from muzzle for bubble blowing, handle embossed "Atom Trade Mark"
EX $75   NM $150   MIP $250

Atom Buster Mystery Gun, 1950s, Webb Electric, 11" long yellow plastic gun w/inner bladder, fires blast of air at tissue paper atomic mushroom target, w/instructions, atomic explosion cover art on box
EX $105   NM $200   MIP $300

Atom Ray Gun, 1949, Hiller, 5-1/2" long, sleek red body gun of aluminum and brass w/bulbous water reservoir on top of gun, reads "Atom Ray Gun" between two lightning bolts on reservoir
EX $135   NM $300   MIP $500

Atomee Water Pistol, 1960s, Park Plastics, 4-1/4" black plastic
EX $15   NM $25   MIP $40

Atomic Disintegrator Ray Gun, 1954, Hubley, 8" long, die-cast metal w/red handles, ornately embellished w/dials and other equipment outcroppings, shoots caps
EX $200   NM $500   MIP $850

Atomic Flash Gun, 1955, Chein, 7-1/2" long, tin, sparkling action seen through tinted elongated oval plastic muzzle, w/yellow and red on turquoise body w/red lettered "Atomic Flash" over trigger
EX $40   NM $70   MIP $135

Atomic Gun, 1960s, Japan, 5" long, gold, blue, white and red tin litho, friction sparkling action, "Atomic Gun" on body sides
EX $20   NM $40   MIP $75

Atomic Gun, 1969, Haji, 9" long, red, gray and yellow tin litho gun w/plastic muzzle, friction sparkling action, large hollow letter "ATOMIC GUN" on body
EX $15   NM $35   MIP $70

Atomic Jet Gun, 1954, Stevens, 8-1/2" long, gold chromed die-cast metal, cap shooting, "Atomic Jet" and large circular "S" logo on grip
EX $90   NM $160   MIP $275

Atomic Ray Gun, 1957, Marx, 30" long, "Captain Space Solar Scout," blue plastic w/oversized telescope sight flashlight and "electric buzzer" sound
EX $75   NM $175   MIP $300

Baby Space Gun, 1950s, Daiya/Japan, 6" friction siren and spark action
EX $35   NM $60   MIP $135

Batman Ray Gun, 1960s, Unknown, cap pistol w/bat symbol for the sight
EX $35   NM $65   MIP $140

Battlestar Galactica Lasermatic Pistol, 1978, Mattel
EX $15   NM $30   MIP $60

Battlestar Galactica Lasermatic Rifle, 1978, Mattel
EX $25   NM $40   MIP $80

Bee-Vo Bell Gun, 1950s, Beaver Toys, #204, 6-1/2" long, red plastic, fires trapped marble at bell in muzzle, in box
EX $25   NM $40   MIP $80

Bicycle Water Cannon Ray Gun, 1950s, Unknown, 10", red plastic, swivel mount attached to bicycle handles, fired by lever
EX $30   **NM** $75   **MIP** $125

Cherilea Space Gun, Marx, miniature scale, die-cast
EX $27   **NM** $40   **MIP** $65

Clicker Ray Gun, 1950s, Unknown, 5" red, blue or gray hard plastic, no boxes, sold loose
EX $15   **NM** $25   **MIP** $50

Clicker Ray Gun, 1960, Irwin, 9" long, red plastic w/deep blue cooling fins on barrel base
EX $30   **NM** $45   **MIP** $75

Clicker Whistle Ray Gun, 1950s, Unknown, 5" plastic, blue/green or olive/green swirl plastic, imprinted spacemen and rocket ships, back of gun is a whistle
EX $15   **NM** $25   **MIP** $50

Daisy Rocket Dart Pistol, 1954, Daisy, 7" long, red, blue and yellow sheet metal gun w/blue body, blue grips w/yellow trim, blue and yellow barrel stripes, same body as Zooka Pop Pistol but w/connecting rod from gun to barrel
EX $80   **NM** $175   **MIP** $350

Daisy Zooka Pop Pistol, 1954, Daisy, 7" long, colorful red, blue and yellow sheet metal gun w/blue body, red grips w/yellow trim and litho star reading "It's a Daisy Play Gun," yellow barrel w/red stripes, and wide red muzzle, handle cock
EX $80   **NM** $175   **MIP** $350

Dan Dare & the Aliens Ray Gun, 1950s, 21", tin litho gun
EX $105   **NM** $175   **MIP** $300

Dune Fremen Tarpel Gun, 1984, LJN, 8" long, battery-operated w/internal light, light beam and chirping sound, plastic
EX $25   **NM** $40   **MIP** $70

Dune Sardaukar Laser Gun, 1984, LJN, 7" black plastic w/flashing lights, battery-operated
EX $20   **NM** $35   **MIP** $55

Flash-O-Matic, The Safe Gun, 1950s, Royal Plastics, 7" long red and yellow plastic battery-operated light beam gun
EX $60   **NM** $100   **MIP** $160

Flashy Ray Gun, 1960s, TN, battery-operated, tin litho, machine gun by Nomura of Japan
EX $70   **NM** $140   **MIP** $200

Floating Satellite Target Game, 1958, S. Horikawa/Japan, 6-1/2" x 9", battery-operated, includes a pistol and three rubber tipped darts, a blower supports the styrofoam ball on a column of air and the players shoot darts to knock it down
EX $175   **NM** $300   **MIP** $475

Ideal Flash Gun, 1957, Ideal, 9" long, plastic three-color flashlight gun w/red or blue body and bulbous contrasting-color blue or red rimmed flash unit, trigger switch and tail battery compartment cover, w/color switch at top of flash unit
EX $80   **NM** $150   **MIP** $220

Jack Dan Space Gun, 1959, Metamol/Spain, 7-1/2" long, in black, red or blue painted die-cast metal cap gun w/"Jack Dan" over trigger
EX $105   **NM** $200   **MIP** $300

Jet Gun, 1957, Japan, 6" long, tin, sparkling action, red body w/three small red tinted spark windows near muzzle, grip shows silver-suited astronaut in modern helmet and wording "JET GUN" at top of grip near trigger
EX $35   **NM** $60   **MIP** $130

Jet Jr. Cap Gun, 1950s, Stevens, 6-1/2" long, fires roll caps, side loading door, silver finish, rear jet "Blast Off Fins"
EX $135   **NM** $250   **MIP** $375

Jet Plane Missile Gun, 1968, Hasbro, jet shaped handgun shoots darts, targets supplied on box back
EX $35   **NM** $60   **MIP** $100

Jupiter 4 Color Signal Gun, 1950s, Remco, 9" long black, red and yellow plastic gun that lights up in four colors, red telescoping sight
EX $35   **NM** $55   **MIP** $90

Over and Under Ray Gun, 1960s, Haji, 8-1/2" long, red, yellow, white and black tin litho gun w/two over and under reciprocating plastic muzzles, friction sparkling action
EX $30   **NM** $50   **MIP** $80

Planet Clicker Bubble Gun, 1953, Mercury Toys, 8" long, plastic, red body w/yellow accents, dip the barrel in bubble solution and pull trigger to make bubbles and produce click sound, in illustrated box
EX $40   **NM** $65   **MIP** $110

Planet Patrol Saucer Gun, 1950s, Unknown, w/spaceman motif
EX $40   **NM** $70   **MIP** $120

Pop Gun, 1967, Chemtoy, 4-1/2" long red hard plastic gun w/space designs on handle
EX $25   **NM** $35   **MIP** $80

Pop Ray Gun, 1930s, Wyandotte, red pressed steel body w/five widely spaced vertical round fins, unpainted trigger and muzzle w/large gunsight, rod connects body to pop mechanism in muzzle
EX $70   **NM** $125   **MIP** $200

Radar Gun, 1956, Unknown, 5-1/2" long, mauve or silver/gray swirl plastic body w/green or yellow spaceman sight and trigger, Saturn and star embossed above grip and "Radar Gun" embossed above that
EX $20   **NM** $35   **MIP** $60

Ranger Gun, 1960s, KO-Japan, 15", No. 2057, Double barreled, friction powered, tin litho, camo pattern, white barrels, spark action
EX $50   **NM** $100   **MIP** $150

Ratchet Sound Space Gun, 1950s, Ideal, 7" long, red plastic w/silver trim, flywheel ratchet on top of gun
EX $30   **NM** $50   **MIP** $80

Ratchet Water Pistol Ray Gun, 1960s, Hong Kong, 6-1/2" unusual pull back mechanism loads pistol, ratchet forces water out when trigger is pulled
EX $25   **NM** $40   **MIP** $70

Ray Dart Gun, 1968, Tarrson, 9-1/2" long, blue plastic body w/yellow muzzle, w/three darts, storage compartment in red handle base
EX $15   **NM** $27   **MIP** $55

Ray Gun, 1936, Wyandotte, 7" stamped metal pop gun that uses a captive cork to make the pop, red body, unpainted muzzle, w/connecting rod from body to barrel tip
EX $50   **NM** $100   **MIP** $175

Ray Gun, 1957, Japan, 6-1/2" long, tin, sparkling action w/two red tinted plastic tapered rectangle windows at muzzle, "Ray Gun" in red at top of body w/rocket exhaust encircling green/blue planet against deep blue star studded background
EX $32   **NM** $65   **MIP** $130

Ray Gun Water Pistol, 1950s, Palmer Plastics, 5-1/2" many color variations: green, orange, translucent blue, royal blue, black, yellow and red
EX $10   **NM** $15   **MIP** $30

Razer Ray Gun, 1972, H.Y. Mfg./Hong Kong, plastic bronze finish body w/five large cooling fins near red plastic barrel, friction sparkling action, chrome finish muzzle tip, "Razer Ray Gun" embossed on rear of barrel
EX $10   **NM** $15   **MIP** $30

Rex Mars Planet Patrol 45 Caliber Machine Gun, 1950s, Marx, 22" long, tin and plastic, wind-up
EX $60   **NM** $150   **MIP** $300

SPACE TOYS

Rex Mars Planet Patrol Space Pistol Arresting Ray, 1950, Marx, tin w/ red and yellow litho

EX $100   **NM** $200   **MIP** $300

Rex Mars Planet Patrol Super Beam Signal Ray Gun, 1950s, Marx, flashlight gun, red plastic, name in grip, clear plastic cap at end of barrel reveals battery compartment, blue trigger

EX $35   **NM** $75   **MIP** $110

Robot Raiders Space Signal Gun, 1980s, TNT/Hong Kong, 6" long flashlight gun w/interchangeable lenses and click sound

EX $6   **NM** $10   **MIP** $20

Robotech Water Pistol, 1985, Matchbox

EX $6   **NM** $10   **MIP** $20

Rocket Gun, 1958, Jak-Pak, 7" hard yellow/green plastic w/spring loaded plunger that shoots corks up to 50 feet

EX $10   **NM** $15   **MIP** $30

Rocket Jet Water Pistol, 1957, U.S. Plastics, 5" long, red, orange or yellow clear plastic body, fill plug at top of gun, large integral gunsight fin at rear, small sight fin at front

EX $12   **NM** $30   **MIP** $60

Rocket Pop Gun, 1955, Unknown, wood, green and red horizontal striped body w/black tri-fin pump base, cork and string stopper in nose, pump fins into body to make it pop

EX $25   **NM** $40   **MIP** $75

Rocket Signal Pistol, 1930s, Marx, same bulbous teardrop metal body as Flash Gordon Signal Pistol and Siren sparkling Airplane Pistol but without siren hole or wings; same rear fin, red w/litho of three horizontally stacked finned orange/yellow bombs

EX $135   **NM** $275   **MIP** $525

Ro-Gun "It's A Robot", 1984, Arco, Shogun-type robot transforms into a rifle, in window box

EX $8   **NM** $13   **MIP** $25

S-58 Space Gun, 1957, Japan, 12" long, tin litho, deep metallic blue body w/friction sparkling action, "S-58" on muzzle, w/ringed planet graphic on front sight

EX $35   **NM** $70   **MIP** $135

Satellite & Rocket Pistol, 1960s, Hong Kong, 5" long, green plastic gun fires either yellow plastic darts or saucers, on card

EX $12   **NM** $20   **MIP** $60

Secret Squirrel Ray Gun, 1960s, Unknown

EX $25   **NM** $50   **MIP** $100

Signal Flash Gun, 1957, Unknown, 6" long, plastic flashlight, black body w/translucent white plastic light housing at muzzle and pearl finish plastic grip plates, modern missile type sight on top of barrel, large "SIGNAL FLASH" above trigger

EX $20   **NM** $40   **MIP** $75

Smoke Ring Gun, 1950s, Nu-Age Products, large, sleek gray finished breakfront pistol w/red barrel and muzzle ring, used rocket shaped

matches to produce smoke, trigger fired smoke rings, small engraved "Smoke Ring Gun" logo on gunsight fin

EX $175   **NM** $295   **MIP** $450

Space Atomic Gun, 1955, Japan, 5-1/2" long, tin, sparkling action seen through red tinted plastic window, two-tone blue body w/red/white atomic symbol on grip, "Space Atomic Gun" letters around oval spaceship-and-stars logo above trigger

EX $32   **NM** $65   **MIP** $130

Space Atomic Gun, 1960, T/Japan, 4" long, tin litho, friction sparkling action, silver gray finish w/yellow and red trim, w/"SPACE" on body in white small all caps and large yellow lower caps "atomic gun", small "T/Made in JAPAN" logo above trigger

EX $25   **NM** $40   **MIP** $70

Space Atomic Gun, 1960s, Unknown, 4" silver, orange/red tin litho, sparkling action

EX $25   **NM** $40   **MIP** $70

Space Control Ray Gun, 1956, Unknown, 5-1/2" long, red plastic w/yellow trigger, clicks

EX $25   **NM** $42   **MIP** $85

Space Control Space Gun, 1954, Nomura/Japan, 3" long, tin sparkling gun w/green body, red sights, decorated all over w/stars and planets, red and yellow "Space Control" letters over trigger and spacemen firing gun and rocket flying overhead on grips

EX $30   **NM** $50   **MIP** $85

Space Dart Gun, 1950s, Unknown, 6" long, gun has one white side and one black side, both w/star and lightning motif, eight thin cooling fins on barrel

EX $30   **NM** $50   **MIP** $90

Space Dart Gun, 1950s, Arliss, 4" solid color plastic gun, shoots standard rubber tipped darts

EX $12   **NM** $35   **MIP** $70

Space Gun, 1955, San/Japan, 3-1/4" long, tin, sparkling action, aqua blue body w/red and yellow highlights and "Space" in script lettering over grip, grip shows rocket shooting toward planets, circular San/Japan logo behind trigger

EX $30   **NM** $50   **MIP** $85

Space Gun, 1957, Daiya/Japan, 6" long, tin, sparkling action, metallic teal finish w/red grooves and muzzle, green spaceship on body above "Space Gun," small Daiya logo inside red/yellow burst on grip w/"577001" at bottom of grip

EX $35   **NM** $75   **MIP** $150

Space Gun, 1957, Yoshiya/Japan, 7" long, tin w/sparkling action, shows a realistic white rocket blasting off over lunar terrain on side of body and atomic symbol on grip center w/diamond-shaped "SY" logo and "Made in Japan" at bottom of grip

EX $40   **NM** $65   **MIP** $120

Space Gun, 1957, Japan, 9" long, friction sparkling action w/three red tinted plastic spark windows and clear red

plastic barrel, body in metallic blue w/large red "SPACE GUN" letters on yellow background

EX $35   **NM** $65   **MIP** $140

Space Gun, 1960, Hero Toy/Japan, 7" long, tin litho, friction sparkling action, yellow body w/blue and red trim, small Hero Toy logo by trigger

EX $35   **NM** $60   **MIP** $95

Space Gun, 1960s, TN/Japan, 8" long, battery-operated, reciprocating barrel shaft has red and blue lenses that flash when fired, makes rat-a-tat noise, large circular "8" over handgrip, winged eagle over trigger, large block letter "SPACE GUN" on barrel

EX $70   **NM** $115   **MIP** $185

Space Gun, 1967, Shudo/Japan, 4" tin litho, friction sparkling action, red body w/blue inset and grips, yellow block letter "SPACE GUN," large yellow and white vertical painted fins, six red tinted plastic sparkling windows, oval Shudo logo by grip

EX $20   **NM** $35   **MIP** $70

Space Jet Gun, 1957, KO/Japan, 9" long, tin, sparkling action w/black body, orange "Space Jet" on body w/orange and red atomic symbol on grip, clear green plastic finned barrel base, clear blue plastic finned muzzle

EX $35   **NM** $60   **MIP** $120

Space Jet Water Pistol, 1957, Knickerbocker, 4" long, black plastic w/white "Space Jet" lettering and spaceship line art on sides, fill plug in gunsight

EX $15   **NM** $30   **MIP** $65

Space Navigator Gun, 1953, Asahitoy/Japan, 3-1/2" long, tin, looks like sawed off military .45, colorfully trimmed blue body w/smiling spaceman, blasting winged rocketship and "Space Navigator" logo on grips, planets and star on body

EX $35   **NM** $60   **MIP** $135

Space Outlaw Ray Gun, 1965, B.C.M., 10" long, chrome plated, die-cast metal, recoiling barrel action, "Cosmic", "Sonic" or "Gamma" power levels, large red clear plastic teardrop shaped window

EX $115   **NM** $250   **MIP** $450

Space Pilot Junior Jet Ray Gun, 1960s, Taiyo-Japan, friction powered, gold plastic w/silver and green accents

EX $45   **NM** $90   **MIP** $135

Space Pilot Super-Sonic Gun, 1953, J&C Randall Ltd., gun flashes red, white, and green light, battery-operated

EX $30   **NM** $60   **MIP** $95

Space Rocket Gun, 1950s, M & L Toy, 9" gray plastic, modern police-style pistol grip and shell chamber body w/oversized barrel and muzzle sights, spring loaded, shoots rocket projectiles, in box w/two "rockets"

EX $55   **NM** $95   **MIP** $185

Space Scout Spud Gun, 1960s, Mil Jo, 7"
black and white plastic
EX $15   **NM** $30   **MIP** $50

Space Ship Flashlight Gun, 1950s, Irwin,
7-1/4", blue plastic ray gun has cockpit
w/orange spaceman, nose unscrews for
AAA batteries, pulling trigger lights nose
and moves guns and spaceman
EX $60   **NM** $110   **MIP** $165

Space Target Game, 1952, T. Cohn, 24"
tall, metal target w/rubber tipped darts
and dartgun to shoot down all the jet
rockets and missiles
EX $40   **NM** $80   **MIP** $175

Space Water Gun, 1957, Palmer Plastics,
5-1/2" long, clear red plastic body
w/embossed Ringed planet and star,
four cooling fins at barrel base, hollow
telescope sight, yellow plastic trigger,
white plastic stopper attached by loop
to red knob at gun back
EX $15   **NM** $30   **MIP** $50

Space Water Gun, 1960, Park Plastics, 6"
long, red transparent plastic, stopper at
rear of gun, finned trigger guard,
zeppelin-shaped reservoir w/single
embossed lightning bolt running its
length, tiny "Park Plastics" imprinted
along lateral reservoir fin
EX $15   **NM** $25   **MIP** $40

Space Water Pistol, 1976, Nasta
EX $7   **NM** $10   **MIP** $20

Space X-Ray Gun, 1970s, Lido, #46598, 8-
1/2" long, plastic, friction sparkling action,
same Razer Ray Gun but w/more
futuristic handgrip and noisemaker at rear,
sold in bag w/header card
EX $15   **NM** $25   **MIP** $40

Sparking Atom Buster Pistol, Marx,
aluminum
EX $30   **NM** $50   **MIP** $85

Sparking Space Gun Rifle, Marx
EX $50   **NM** $100   **MIP** $175

Sparkling Ray Gun, 1976, Nasta
EX $6   **NM** $10   **MIP** $20

Star Team Ionization Nebulizer, 1969, Ideal,
9" water gun fires water mist, red, white,
blue and black plastic, Star Team decal
EX $30   **NM** $50   **MIP** $85

Strato Gun, 1950s, Futuristic Products, 9"
long, gray finish die-cast, cap firing,
internal hammer, top of gun lifts to load
EX $70   **NM** $125   **MIP** $200

Strato Gun, 1950s, Futuristic Products, 9"
long, chrome finish die-cast, red cooling
fins, cap firing, internal hammer, top of
gun lifts to load
EX $100   **NM** $175   **MIP** $325

Super Sonic Gun, 1957, Endoh/Japan, 9"
long, tin, sparkling action w/three red
plastic spark windows and clear red
plastic barrel, blue body w/red lightning
bolt beneath yellow "Super Sonic" on
rounded gun body, small ENDOH logo
printed above grips
EX $40   **NM** $80   **MIP** $160

Super Sonic Space Gun, 1957,
Daiya/Japan, 7-1/2" long, tin litho,
metallic gray body w/red gunsight fin,
friction siren and sparkling action, large
oval center art w/outstanding lunar
scene of rockets, mountains and Earth
in sky, red helmeted spaceman on grip
EX $40   **NM** $80   **MIP** $160

Super Space Gun, 1960, Japan, 6" long,
tin litho, friction sparkling action, blue
on blue body w/white/yellow/red
highlights, large red on white "SUPER
SPACE" lettering on side
EX $25   **NM** $50   **MIP** $100

Superior Rocket Gun, 1956, Unknown, 8"
long, dark gray plastic, embossed
"Superior Rocket Gun" on grip
EX $30   **NM** $50   **MIP** $85

Tom Corbett Space Cated Atomic Pistol,
1950s, Marx, Flashlight, battery-
operated, "Space Cadet" on handle
EX $50   **NM** $125   **MIP** $200

Tomi Space Gun, 1950s, Shawnee, solid
red plastic w/yellow barrel plug,
modelled after modern .45 caliber pistol
w/rounded reservoir lined w/two
horizontal fins over grip; embossed logo
and circular Shawnee logos on grip
EX $50   **NM** $90   **MIP** $135

Universe Gun, 1960s, T/Japan, 4" long,
blue, yellow and red tin litho gun
w/friction sparkling action, large all caps
italic "Universe" on body side, sold in
bag w/header card
EX $15   **NM** $25   **MIP** $40

Visible Sparkling Ray Gun, Hong Kong, 8-
1/2" long, plastic, mechanism visible,
bagged w/header card
EX $15   **NM** $32   **MIP** $65

Wham-O Air Blaster, 1960s, Wham-O, 10"
long plastic gun uses rubber diaphragm
to shoot air; styling is reminiscent of
Budson Flash Gordon Air Ray Gun
EX $70   **NM** $120   **MIP** $185

X100 Mystery Dart Gun, 1956, Arliss, 3-
3/4" long, yellow or gray plastic gun on
cardboard display card, w/two yellow
and blue talcum impregnated darts
which create a smoke effect when
striking any target
EX $25   **NM** $45   **MIP** $80

X-Ray Gun, 1950s, Daiya, Japan, red see-
through plastic, friction toy, sparks
EX $50   **NM** $85   **MIP** $125

SPACE PATROL

Atomic Pistol Flashlight Gun, 1950s,
Marx, plastic
EX $85   **NM** $160   **MIP** $275

Cosmic Cap, 1950s
EX $125   **NM** $200   **MIP** $400

Cosmic Gun, 1970, Nomura/Japan, 12" long,
plastic, battery-operated w/a small electric
motor that runs reciprocating light in clear
red plastic barrel, dark blue body, red and
orange lettered "COSMIC GUN" decal
EX $35   **NM** $55   **MIP** $90

Cosmic Ray Gun, 1954, Ranger Steel
Products, 9" long, tin body w/plastic
barrel, boldly painted in blue, yellow and
red lightning bolts
EX $50   **NM** $90   **MIP** $150

Cosmic Ray Gun #249, 1953, Ranger Steel
Products, 8" long, plastic, blue body,
yellow barrel, red tip, in box showing
two space kids in bubble helmets and
backpacks shooting at spaceships
EX $40   **NM** $75   **MIP** $135

Cosmic Rocket Launcher Set, 1950s
EX $300   **NM** $525   **MIP** $850

Cosmic Smoke Gun, 1950s, green
EX $120   **NM** $325   **MIP** $675

Cosmic Smoke Gun, 1950s, red
EX $110   **NM** $170   **MIP** $325

Drink Mixer, 1950s, boxed
EX $60   **NM** $100   **MIP** $200

Emergency Kit, 1950s, w/rations, plastic
w/yellow insert
EX $600   **NM** $1350   **MIP** $2500

Handbook, 1950s
EX $55   **NM** $125   **MIP** $200

**Interplanetary Space Patrol Credits
Coins,** different denominations and
colors: Terra, Moon and Saturn, each
EX $10   **NM** $16   **MIP** $35

Jet Glow Code Belt, 1950s, gold-finish
metal, spaceship-shaped buckle,
decoder ring behind buckle
EX $120   **NM** $200   **MIP** $375

Lunar Fleet Base, 1950s, premium punch-
outs in mailing envelope
EX $500   **NM** $1700   **MIP** $3200

Man From Mars Totem Head Mask,
1950s, paper, several styles
EX $65   **NM** $105   **MIP** $175

Monorail Set, 1950s, Toys of Tomorrow
EX $1650   **NM** $3000   **MIP** $4200

Non-Fall Space Patrol X-16, 1950s,
Masudaya
EX $50   **NM** $150   **MIP** $300

Outer Space Helmet Mask, 1950s, paper
helmet w/plastic one-way visor
EX $110   **NM** $170   **MIP** $300

Project-O-Scope, 1950s, rocket-shaped film viewer w/filmstrips
EX $175   NM $350   MIP $800

Puzzle, 1950s, Milton Bradley, frame tray w/sleeve
EX $40   NM $75   MIP $175

Rocket Gun and Holster Set, 1950s, w/darts
EX $200   NM $300   MIP $525

Rocket Gun Set, 1950s, w/darts, without holster
EX $110   NM $185   MIP $360

Rocket Lite Flashlight, 1950s, Rayovac, in box
EX $140   NM $250   MIP $375

Rocket Port Set, 1950s, Marx
EX $125   NM $200   MIP $375

Rocket-Shaped Pen, 1950s
EX $120   NM $185   MIP $350

Space Binoculars, 1950s, Ralston Purina, black plastic, logo on sides
EX $80   NM $125   MIP $200

Space Binoculars, 1950s, Ralston Purina, green plastic, large logo on top, premium
EX $120   NM $190   MIP $300

Space Holster with oval badge, 1950, w/unmarked blue gun
EX $200   NM $500   MIP $800

Space Patrol Atomic Flashlight Pistol, 1950s, Marx, gold/bronze finish pistol w/seven large cooling fins on barrel and three smaller ones at back of gun, large clear plastic diffuser on muzzle, white "Official Space Patrol" on handgrip
EX $135   NM $225   MIP $525

Space Patrol Badge, 1950s, plastic, w/ship and crest
EX $75   NM $150   MIP $300

Space Patrol Badge, 1950s, metal oval on card
EX $125   NM $400   MIP $800

Space Patrol Cadet Membership Card, 1950s
EX $25   NM $75   MIP $175

Space Patrol Cereal Box, 1953, Wheat Chex Magic Picture Offer
EX $125   NM $275   MIP $450

Space Patrol Commander Helmet, 1950s, plastic, in box
EX $140   NM $275   MIP $425

Space Patrol Cosmic Glow Ring, 1950s, red and blue
EX $450   NM $900   MIP $1800

Space Patrol Cosmic Smoke Gun, 1950s, Unknown, solid color red or green plastic w/"Space Patrol" on body above grip, TV show tie-in, shoots baking powder, on card
EX $135   NM $375   MIP $750

Space Patrol Hydrogen Ray Gun Ring, 1950s, Unknown, glow-in-the-dark ring
EX $80   NM $125   MIP $275

Space Patrol Mobile Store Display, Wheat Chex, 1953
EX $400   NM $1200   MIP $1600

Space Patrol Periscope, 1950s, paper w/mirrors
EX $75   NM $200   MIP $400

Space Patrol Printing Ring, 1950s
EX $200   NM $400   MIP $800

Space Patrol Wristwatch, 1950s, illustrated box w/"Terra" compass
EX $275   NM $500   MIP $750

Space-A-Phones, 1950s
EX $175   NM $500   MIP $750

SPACE:1999

Astro Popper Gun, 1976, Larami, on card
EX $6   NM $10   MIP $40

Colorforms Adventure Set, 1975, Colorforms
EX $10   NM $16   MIP $25

Cut and Color Book, 1975, Saalfield
EX $6   NM $12   MIP $25

Dr. Russell, 1976, Mattel
EX n/a   NM $30   MIP $60

Dr. Russell Figure, 1976, Mattel
EX $17   NM $30   MIP $45

Eagle Freighter, 1975, Dinky, No. 360, die-cast
EX $25   NM $80   MIP $160

Eagle One Spaceship, 1976, Mattel
EX $125   NM $325   MIP $525

Eagle Transport, 1975, Dinky, No. 359, die-cast
EX $25   NM $55   MIP $110

Eagle Transporter Model Kit, 1976, Airfix
EX $12   NM $20   MIP $80

Film Viewer TV Set, 1976, Larami
EX $8   NM $20   MIP $55

Galaxy Time Meter, 1976, Larami
EX $6   NM $10   MIP $20

Puzzle, 1976, HG Toys
EX $8   NM $15   MIP $30

Space Expedition Dart Set, 1976, Larami, carded
EX $6   NM $10   MIP $20

(ToyShop File Photo)

Space:1999 Adventure Play Set, 1976, Amsco/Milton Bradley, Paper color and cut-out construction, included two Eagle Spacecraft, Moonbase Alpha with moving antenna, six-wheeled moon buggy, complete cast
EX $40   NM $55   MIP $85

Space:1999 Astro Popper Gun, 1976, Mattel, on card
EX $6   NM $10   MIP $20

Space:1999 Utility Belt Set, 1976, Remco, w/disc shooting stun gun, watch and compass
EX $12   NM $30   MIP $60

Stamping Set, 1976, Larami
EX $8   NM $13   MIP $25

Superscope, 1976, Larami
EX $6   NM $10   MIP $18

Utility Belt Set, 1976, Remco
EX $12   NM $40   MIP $110

Walking Spaceman, 1975, Azrak Hamway
EX $50   NM $175   MIP $425

Zython Figure, 1976, Mattel
EX $40   NM $80   MIP $100

SPACESHIPS

Eagle Lunar Module, 1960s, 9"
EX $80   NM $115   MIP $185

Friendship 7, 9-1/2", friction
EX $35   NM $50   MIP $80

Inter-Planet Toy Rocketank Patrol, 1950, Macrey, 10"
EX $30   NM $45   MIP $75

Jupiter Space Station, 1960s, TN/Japan, 8"
EX $90   NM $135   MIP $225

Moon-Rider Spaceship, 1930s, Marx, tin wind-up
EX $125   NM $200   MIP $275

(ToyShop File Photo)

Mystery Spaceship, 1960s, Marx, 35mm astronauts and moonmen, rockets, launchers
EX $80   NM $165   MIP $260

Rocket Fighter, 1950s, Marx, w/tail fin and sparking action, tin wind-up
EX $250   NM $375   MIP $525

Rocket Fighter Spaceship, 1930s, Marx, celluloid window, tin wind-up, 12" long
EX $125   NM $225   MIP $300

Satellite X-107, 1965, Cragstan, 9"
EX $90   NM $130   MIP $200

Sky Patrol Jet, 1960s, TN/Japan, 5" x 13" x 5", battery operated, working taillights
EX $295   NM $425   MIP $650

Solar-X Space Rocket, TN/Japan, 15"
EX $45   NM $65   MIP $100

Space Bus, tin helicopter, battery operated w/wired remote
EX $350   NM $500   MIP $750

Space Pacer, 1978, 7", battery operated
EX $20   NM $29   MIP $50

Space Survey X-09, battery operated, tin and plastic flying saucer w/clear bubble
EX $175   NM $375   MIP $550

Space Train, 1950s, 9" long, engine and three metallic cars
EX $18   NM $26   MIP $50

Spaceship, Marx, bronze plastic
EX $40   NM $60   MIP $100

Super Space Capsule, 1960s, 9-1/2"
EX $70   NM $100   MIP $160

X-3 Rocket Gyro, 1950s
EX $25   NM $35   MIP $60

STAR TREK

Action Toy Book, 1976, Random House
EX $7   NM $10   MIP $20

Beanbag Chair, ST:TMP
EX $25   NM $35   MIP $55

Bowl, ST:TMP, 1979, Deka, plastic
EX $3   NM $7   MIP $15

Bridge Punch-Out Book, ST:TMP, 1979, Wanderer
EX $7   NM $10   MIP $25

Bulletin Board, ST:TMP, 1979, Milton Bradley, w/four pens
EX $6   NM $8   MIP $15

Clock, 1986, white wall clock, red 20th anniversary logo on face, Official Star Trek Fan Club
EX $14   NM $20   MIP $40

Clock, 1989, Enterprise orbiting planet, rectangular
EX $23   NM $33   MIP $60

Colorforms Set, 1975, Colorforms
EX $15   NM $20   MIP $40

Comb & Brush Set, 1977, 6" x 3", blue, oval brush
EX $14   NM $20   MIP $35

Communicators, 1976, Mego, blue plastic walkie talkies
EX $70   NM $125   MIP $200

Communicators, 1989, McNerney, black plastic walkie talkies
EX $35   NM $50   MIP $85

Communicators, ST:TMP, 1980, Mego, plastic wristband walkie talkies belt pack, battery operated
EX $90   NM $150   MIP $250

Controlled Space Flight, 1976, Remco, plastic Enterprise, battery operated
EX $80   NM $125   MIP $225

Digital Travel Alarm, Lincoln Enterprises
EX $15   NM $20   MIP $35

Dinnerware Set, ST:TMP, 1979, Deka, plate, bowl, glass and cup
EX $15   NM $25   MIP $40

Enterprise Make-A-Model, ST:TNG, 1990, Chatham River Press
EX $4   NM $5   MIP $10

Enterprise Model Kit, 1980, Mego/Grand Toys, #91232/B, Canadian issue, ST:TMP
EX $90   NM $100   MIP $150

Enterprise Punch-Out Book, ST:TMP, 1979, Wanderer
EX $9   NM $15   MIP $30

Enterprise Wristwatch, ST:TMP, Bradley
EX $20   NM $30   MIP $50

Enterprise Wristwatch, ST:TMP, 1989, Rarities Mint, gold-plated silver
EX $55   NM $80   MIP $125

Enterprise, ST:III, 1984, Ertl, 4" long, die-cast w/black plastic stand
EX $10   NM $15   MIP $30

Enterprise, ST:IV, 1986, Sterling, 24", silver plastic, inflatable
EX $20   NM $30   MIP $45

Enterprise, ST:TMP, 1979, South Bend, 20" long, white plastic, battery powered lights and sound w/stand
EX $80   NM $120   MIP $185

Excelsior, ST:III, 1984, Ertl, 4" long, die-cast w/black plastic stand
EX $7   NM $10   MIP $40

Ferengi Costume, ST:TNG, 1988, Ben Cooper
EX $7   NM $10   MIP $25

Figurine Paint Set, 1979, Milton Bradley
EX $14   NM $25   MIP $40

Flashlight, 1976, battery operated, small phaser shape
EX $6   NM $10   MIP $15

Flashlight, ST:TMP, 1979, Larami
EX $6   NM $10   MIP $15

Giant in the Universe Pop-Up Book, 1977, Random House
EX $14   NM $20   MIP $35

Golden Trivia Game, 1985, Western
EX $20   NM $30   MIP $50

Helmet, 1976, Remco, plastic, w/sound and red lights
EX $55   NM $80   MIP $130

Kirk & Spock Wristwatch, ST:TMP, Bradley, LCD rectangular face display, Enterprise on blue face w/Kirk and Spock
EX $25   NM $35   MIP $60

Kirk Bank, 1975, Play Pal, 12" plastic
EX $25   NM $35   MIP $60

Kirk Costume, 1975, Ben Cooper, plastic mask, one-piece jumpsuit
EX $9   NM $13   MIP $25

Kirk Doll, ST:TMP, 1979, Knickerbocker, 13" tall, soft body w/plastic head
EX $16   NM $23   MIP $50

Kirk or Spock Costumes, 1967, Ben Cooper, tie-on jumpsuit, mask
EX $11   NM $16   MIP $30

Kirk Puzzle, ST:TMP, 1979, Larami, fifteen-piece sliding puzzle
EX $5   NM $7   MIP $12

Kite, 1975, Hi-Flyer, TV Enterprise or Spock
EX $14   NM $20   MIP $35

Kite, ST:III, 1984, Lever Bros., pictures Enterprise
EX $14   NM $20   MIP $35

Kite, ST:TMP, 1976, Aviva, picture of Spock
EX $17   NM $22   MIP $38

Klingon Bird of Prey, ST:III, 1984, Ertl, 3-1/2", die-cast w/black plastic stand
EX $7   NM $10   MIP $30

Klingon Costume, 1975, Ben Cooper, plastic mask, one piece jumpsuit
EX $9   NM $13   MIP $30

Klingon Costume, ST:TNG, 1988, Ben Cooper
EX $7   NM $10   MIP $20

Light Switch Cover, 1985, American Tack & Hardware, ST:TMP
EX $6   NM $8   MIP $15

Magic Slates, 1979, Whitman, four designs: Spock, Kirk, Kirk and Spock
EX $7   NM $10   MIP $20

Make-a-Game Book, 1979, Wanderer
EX $7   NM $10   MIP $20

Metal Detector, 1976, Jetco, U.S.S. Enterprise decal
EX $100   NM $145   MIP $225

Mirror, 1966, 2" x 3" metal, w/black and white photo of crew
EX $2   NM $5   MIP $10

Mix 'N Mold, 1975, Kirk, Spock or McCoy, molding compound, paint and brush
EX $35   NM $50   MIP $75

Movie Viewer, 1967, Chemtoy, 3" red and black plastic
EX $10   NM $16   MIP $35

Needlepoint Kit, 1980, Arista, Kirk
EX $16   NM $23   MIP $35

Needlepoint Kit, 1980, Arista, 14" x 18", "Live Long and Prosper"
EX $16   NM $23   MIP $35

Paint-By-Numbers Set, 1972, Hasbro, small
EX $20   NM $35   MIP $55

Paint-By-Numbers Set, 1972, Hasbro, large
EX $35   NM $50   MIP $80

Pen & Poster Kit, 1976, Open Door, four versions; each
EX $11   NM $16   MIP $30

Pen & Poster Kit, ST:III, 1984, Placo, 3-D poster "Search for Spock" w/overlay, 3-D glasses and four felt tip pens
EX $10   NM $20   MIP $40

Pennant, 1982, Image Products, 12" x 30" triangular, black, yellow and red on white w/"Spock Lives"
EX $6   NM $10   MIP $15

Pennant, 1982, Image Products, 12" x 30" triangle, The Wrath of Khan
EX $6   NM $10   MIP $15

Pennant, 1988, Universal Studios, Paramount Pictures Adventure
EX $6   NM $10   MIP $15

Phaser, 1975, Remco, black plastic, shaped like pistol, electronic sound, flashlight projects target
EX $35   NM $100   MIP $200

Phaser Battle Game, 1976, Mego, black plastic, 13" high battery operated electronic target game, LED scoring lights, sound effects and adjustable controls
EX $195   NM $275   MIP $450

Phaser Gun, 1967, Remco, Astro Buzz-Ray Gun w/three-color flash beam
EX $80   NM $150   MIP $250

Phaser Gun, ST:III, 1984, Daisy, white and blue plastic gun w/light and sound effects
EX $35   NM $60   MIP $100

Phaser Gun, ST:TNG, 1988, Galoob, gray plastic light and sound hand phaser
EX $14   NM $20   MIP $40

Pinball Game, ST:TMP, Azrak-Hamway, 12", plastic, Kirk or Spock
EX $23   NM $35   MIP $80

Pinball Game, ST:TMP, 1979, Bally, electronic
EX $200   NM $350   MIP $650

Pocket Flix, 1978, Ideal, battery operated movie viewer and film cartridge
EX $18   NM $25   MIP $50

Pop-Up Book, ST:TMP, 1980, Wanderer
EX $10   NM $20   MIP $40

Puzzle, 1974, H.G. Toys, 150 pieces, Battle on the Planet Romulon
EX $5   NM $10   MIP $15

Puzzle, 1974, H.G. Toys, 150 pieces, Attempted Hijacking of U.S.S. Enterprise
EX $4   NM $8   MIP $15

Puzzle, 1974, H.G. Toys, 150 pieces, Kirk and officers beaming down
EX $3   NM $7   MIP $12

Puzzle, 1974, H.G. Toys, 150 pieces, Battle on the Planet Klingon
EX $3   NM $7   MIP $12

Puzzle, 1976, H.G. Toys, 150 pieces; Kirk, Spock, and McCoy
EX $4   NM $8   MIP $12

Puzzle, 1976, H.G. Toys, 150 pieces, "Force Field Capture"
EX $4   NM $8   MIP $15

Puzzle, 1978, Whitman, 8-1/2" x 11" tray, Spock in spacesuit
EX $2   NM $5   MIP $10

Puzzle, 1979, Milton Bradley, ST:TMP, 50 pieces
EX $3   NM $7   MIP $12

Puzzle, 1979, Larami, ST:TMP, 15-piece sliding puzzle
EX $3   NM $7   MIP $12

Puzzle, 1979, Aviva, 551 pieces
EX $8   NM $15   MIP $25

Puzzle, 1986, Mind's Eye Press, 551 pieces, ST:IV, "The Voyage Home"
EX $10   NM $20   MIP $30

Role Playing Game, 2001 Deluxe Edition, FASA, Star Trek Basic Set and the Star Trek III Combat Game
EX $20   NM $30   MIP $50

Role Playing Game, 2004 Basic Set, FASA, three books outlining Star Trek Universe
EX $7   NM $10   MIP $20

Role Playing Game, Second Deluxe Edition, FASA
EX $14   NM $20   MIP $35

Space Design Center, ST:TMP, 1979, Avalon, blue plastic tray, paints, pens, crayons, project book and crew member cut-outs
EX $70   NM $110   MIP $175

Spock & Enterprise Wristwatch, ST:TMP, 1986, Lewco, 20th anniversary, digital
EX $9   NM $20   MIP $40

Spock Bank, 1975, Play Pal, 12" plastic
EX $25   NM $35   MIP $60

Spock Bop Bag, 1975, plastic, inflatable
EX $55   NM $80   MIP $125

Spock Chair, ST:TMP, 1979, inflatable
EX $16   NM $23   MIP $40

Spock Costume, 1973, Ben Cooper, plastic mask, one-piece jumpsuit
EX $11   NM $16   MIP $30

Spock Doll, ST:TMP, 1979, Knickerbocker, 13" tall, soft body, plastic head
EX $16   NM $25   MIP $50

Spock Ears, ST:TMP, 1979, Aviva
EX $7   NM $10   MIP $20

Spock Tray, 1979, Aviva, 17-1/2" metal lap tray
EX $9   NM $13   MIP $20

Spock Wristwatch, Bradley, ST:TMP
EX $20   NM $30   MIP $50

Star Trek Cartoon Puzzle, 1978, Whitman
EX $4   NM $5   MIP $10

Star Trek Costume, 1979, Collegeville, one-piece outfit, Spock, Kirk, Ilia or Klingon, each
EX $11   NM $16   MIP $25

Star Trek II U.S.S. Enterprise Ship, 1982, Corgi, 3" die-cast
EX $9   NM $13   MIP $25

Star Trek Tracer Gun, 1966, Rayline, 6-1/2" plastic firing tracer gun
EX $40   NM $65   MIP $125

Star Trek Tracer Scope, 1968, Rayline, rifle w/disks
EX $50   NM $80   MIP $150

Star Trek Water Pistol, 1976, Azrak-Hamway, white plastic, shaped like U.S.S. Enterprise
EX $15   NM $30   MIP $60

Star Trek:TMP Water Pistol, 1979, Aviva, gray plastic, early pistol-grip phaser design
EX $10   NM $20   MIP $60

Telescreen, 1976, Mego, plastic, battery operated target game w/light and sound effects
EX $70   NM $100   MIP $160

Tracer Gun, 1966, Rayline, plastic pistol w/colored plastic discs
EX $45   NM $65   MIP $135

Tricorder, 1976, Mego, blue plastic tape recorder, battery operated w/shoulder strap
EX $70   NM $110   MIP $160

Trillions of Trilligs Pop-Up Book, 1977, Random House
EX $16   NM $25   MIP $40

Utility Belt, 1975, Remco, black plastic phaser miniature, tricorder, communicator and belt w/Star Trek buckle
EX $45   NM $85   MIP $150

Vulcan Shuttle Model Kit, 1980,
Mego/Grand Toy, #91231, ST:TMP
EX $100   **NM** $120   **MIP** $145

Vulcan Shuttle Model Kit, 1984, Ertl,
#6679, ST:III
EX $20   **NM** $25   **MIP** $50

Vulcan Shuttle Model Kit, 1984, Ertl,
#6679, ST:TMP
EX $18   **NM** $20   **MIP** $35

Wastebasket, 1977, Chein, black metal
EX $35   **NM** $50   **MIP** $80

Wastebasket, ST:TMP, 1979, Chein, 13"
high, metal rainbow painting
w/photograph of Enterprise surrounded
by smaller pictures
EX $11   **NM** $16   **MIP** $35

Water Pistol, 1976, Azrak-Hamway, white
plastic, shaped like U.S.S. Enterprise
EX $20   **NM** $30   **MIP** $50

Water Pistol, ST:TMP, 1979, Aviva, gray
plastic, early phaser
EX $11   **NM** $16   **MIP** $30

Writing Tablet, 1967, 8" x 10"
EX $11   **NM** $16   **MIP** $30

Yo-Yo, 1979, Aviva, ST:TMP, blue sparkle
plastic
EX $10   **NM** $20   **MIP** $40

TOM CORBETT

Binoculars
EX $60   **NM** $100   **MIP** $150

Flash X-1, 1967, Shudo/Japan, 4" long, tin
litho, friction sparkling action, red body
w/blue and yellow inset and grips, large
white "Flash X-1" on body, four red
tinted plastic sparkling windows
EX $15   **NM** $25   **MIP** $75

Flash X-1 Space Gun, 5" long
EX $55   **NM** $110   **MIP** $160

Model Craft Molding and Coloring Set,
1950s, Kay Standley, various characters
EX $150   **NM** $350   **MIP** $500

Official Sparking Space Gun, Marx, 21"
long, w/numerous apparatus on body
EX $80   **NM** $150   **MIP** $250

Polaris Wind-Up Spaceship, 1952, Marx,
12" long, blue litho w/yellow, Tom, Astro
and Roger visible in the litho cockpit
EX $200   **NM** $375   **MIP** $600

Push-Outs Book, 1952, Saalfield
EX $35   **NM** $65   **MIP** $100

Puzzles, 1950s, Saalfield, frame tray, three
versions, each
EX $17   **NM** $30   **MIP** $50

Rocket Scout Ring, 1950s
EX $10   **NM** $20   **MIP** $35

School Bag, 1950s, 15" long, 10" wide,
plastic vinyl w/ Tom's picture and
rocketships on front
EX $25   **NM** $55   **MIP** $85

Signal Siren Flashlight, 1950s, Usalite
EX $70   **NM** $115   **MIP** $200

Space Cadet Belt, 1950s
EX $65   **NM** $105   **MIP** $175

Space Gun, 1950s, 9-1/2" long light blue
and black sparking
EX $70   **NM** $130   **MIP** $250

Space Suit Ring, 1950s
EX $10   **NM** $16   **MIP** $35

Tom Corbett Coloring Book, 1950s,
Saalfield, two versions, each
EX $25   **NM** $40   **MIP** $80

Tom Corbett Official Space Cadet Gun,
1950s, Marx, poorly designed
composite rifle w/modern military
plastic stock and front grip at ends of
long tin litho gun body w/litho bombs
and "Ray Adjuster" scale
EX $135   **NM** $300   **MIP** $500

Tom Corbett Portrait Ring, 1950s,
premium
EX $20   **NM** $35   **MIP** $60

Tom Corbett Space Academy Play Set,
1950s, Marx, #7020
EX $195   **NM** $550   **MIP** $600

(ToyShop File Photo)

Tom Corbett Space Academy Play Set,
1952, Marx, #7010, 45mm figures
EX $205   **NM** $360   **MIP** $515

**Tom Corbett Space Cadet Atomic
Flashlight Pistol,** 1950s, Marx,
identical to Space Patrol Atomic
Flashlight Pistol except for body colors
and "Tom Corbett Space Cadet" printed
upside down on handgrip
EX $135   **NM** $300   **MIP** $500

Tom Corbett Space Cadet Gun, 1952,
Marx, 10-1/2" long, sheet metal clicker
based on Flash Gordon Radio repeater
molds, red body, blue barrel reads
"Space Cadet," handgrips show bust of
Tom in front of planet w/rocket ship
symbol above
EX $150   **NM** $400   **MIP** $725

Tom Corbett Wristwatch, 1950s,
Ingraham, round dial, embossed band
w/ship and planets, on illustrated rocket
shaped card
EX $250   **NM** $450   **MIP** $700

Star Wars

By Merry Dudley

"a long time ago in a galaxy far, far away…"

Heroes in space were commonplace by the late 1970s. Amazing Stories magazine had been around since the 1920s, Flash Gordon and Buck Rogers were immortalized by comic strips and radio broadcasts in the 1930s, and the film industry caught on after World War II by producing a variety of low-budget space-themed movies—but nothing produced before it could prepare movie-goers for Star Wars.

The success of George Lucas' 1973 film, American Graffiti, made him a rising star in the eyes of Twentieth Century Fox executive, Alan Ladd Jr., who agreed to take a risk on the young director's new science fiction project. Now we all know what a success Lucas' "space opera" turned out to be, and we all know that Star Wars changed the course of science fiction representations in film and on television. But not many know that George Lucas contracted to retain all sequel and merchandising rights for Star Wars as well.

It was his license with toy manufacturer, Kenner, to produce toys based on the characters, vehicles, and creatures of Star Wars that changed the face of toy collecting.

Kenner's line of Star Wars characters debuted in 1978, and were unlike anything else on the U.S. market save for the imported Micronauts line. At just 3-3/4" tall, the Star Wars characters were portable and practical to manufacture. The oil shortages of the 1970s increased the plastic production costs to levels where several toy lines, including Hasbro's G.I. Joe and Mego's World's Greatest Super Heroes, ceased production.

The pocket-sized Star Wars figures and their appropriately scaled vehicles and creatures became staples of the toy aisles and allowed children to recreate their favorite scenes from the film. Never before had a toy line possessed such an established backstory, and never before had a film been so successfully (and thoroughly) merchandised.

Once a sensation, the toys are now among the most coveted of modern collectibles. Beyond the popularity of the movies and the world-wide fame of the characters, the toys were the treasured playthings of a generation that is now actively seeking to remember its youth. Values for Star Wars toys still sealed in their original packaging are at an all-time high, and it's no wonder why. Kids lucky enough to have received those original figures ripped them from their packages and enacted the saga in their living rooms. Kids didn't dream of leaving the greatest heroes in the galaxy safely attached to their packaging, but collectors can be happy that some forward-thinking fans did.

2006 TRENDS

This is the year of Darth Vader. The final chapter in George Lucas' masterpiece finally revealed the events and choices that drove the galaxy's greatest hero to the dark side. And Hasbro has released a stunning array of toys in support of Episode III that are plentiful in number, but destined for collectible greatness. My advice it to buy one to open, and one to keep sealed in the original packaging, and one to sell or trade later on…

Demand for vintage Darth Vader toys is on the rise, as is the demand for Yoda. The Unleashed series continues to appeal to collectors of new and vintage figures.

Contributors: Chris Fawcett served as pricing consultant for "vintage" Star Wars collectibles, those from Star Wars through Power of the Force. He can be reached at www.12back.com. Stuart W. Wells III, served as the pricing consultant for "modern" Star Wars collectibles from Power of the Force II through Clone Wars. He is the author of A Universe of Star Wars Collectibles, (Krause Publications, 2002) and can be reached at Toys & Prices, Krause Publications, 700 E. State St., Iola, WI 54990.

THE TOP TEN
STAR WARS TOYS (In Mint Condition)

#	Toy	Price
1.	Luke w/Telescoping Lightsaber, SW, 3-3/4" figure, Kenner, 1977	$3,450
2.	Anakin Skywalker, POTF, 3-3/4" figure, Kenner, 1985	1,625
3.	Yak Face, POTF, 3-3/4" figure, Kenner, 1985	1,150
4.	Boba Fett, ESB, 12" figure, Kenner, 1979	875
5.	Nikto, POTF, 3-3/4" figure, Kenner, 1985	725
6.	Boba Fett, Droids, 3-3/4" figure, Kenner, 1985	650
7.	Boba Fett, SW, 3-3/4" figure, Kenner, 1978	650
8.	AT-AT Driver, POTF, 3-3/4" figure, Kenner, 1985	575
9.	Jawa Sandcrawler, SW, vehicle, Kenner, 1977	525
10.	Han Solo, small head, SW, Kenner, 1977	500

ACTION FIGURES, 03-3/4"

STAR WARS

Boba Fett, 1978

          MNP $19   **MIP** $650

(ToyShop File Photo)

C-3PO, 1977

          MNP $11   **MIP** $200

Chewbacca, 1977

          MNP $13   **MIP** $200

(ToyShop File Photo)

Darth Vader, 1977

          MNP $14   **MIP** $410

(ToyShop File Photo)

Death Squad Commander, 1977

          MNP $12   **MIP** $190

(ToyShop File Photo)

Death Star Droid, 1978

          MNP $12   **MIP** $165

Early Bird Figures — Luke, Leia, R2-D2, Chewbacca, 1977

          MNP $195   **MIP** $425

(ToyShop File Photo)

Greedo, 1978

          MNP $20   **MIP** $200

(KP Photo)

Hammerhead, 1978

          MNP $15   **MIP** $185

(ToyShop File Photo)

Han Solo, Large Head, 1977

          MNP $20   **MIP** $475

STAR WARS

STAR WARS

(ToyShop File Photo)

Han Solo, Small Head, 1977
      MNP $30   **MIP** $500

(ToyShop File Photo)

Jawa, Cloth Cape, 1977
      MNP $20   **MIP** $200

(ToyShop File Photo)

Jawa, Vinyl Cape, 1977
      MNP $250   **MIP** $2500

(ToyShop File Photo)

Luke as X-Wing Pilot, 1978
      MNP $15   **MIP** $185

Luke Skywalker, 1977
      MNP $30   **MIP** $480

(ToyShop File Photo)

Luke w/Telescoping Saber, 1977
      MNP $185   **MIP** $3500

Obi-Wan Kenobi, 1977
      MNP $21   **MIP** $300

(KP Photo)

Power Droid, 1978, Dark blue body with stocky legs. These robots are also called "Gonk" droids, based on the sound they make as seen in Star Wars Episode IV,

"A New Hope." Very reminiscent of the robots in the movie "Silent Running"
      MNP $11   **MIP** $135

Princess Leia Organa, 1977
      MNP $19   **MIP** $420

(ToyShop File Photo)

R2-D2, 1977
      MNP $18   **MIP** $175

R5-D4, 1978
      MNP $17   **MIP** $200

(ToyShop File Photo)

Sand People (Tusken Raider), 1977
      MNP $13   **MIP** $210

Snaggletooth, Blue Body, Sears Exclusive, 1978
      MNP $140   **MIP** n/a

(KP Photo)
Snaggletooth, Red Body, 1978
MNP $10 MIP $170

(ToyShop File Photo)
Stormtrooper, 1977
MNP $30 MIP $250

(ToyShop File Photo)
Walrus Man, 1978
MNP $15 MIP $110

EMPIRE STRIKES BACK

2-1B, 1981, The medical droid who assists Luke's recovery after his duel with Vader. In the movie, you actually never see his legs
MNP $9 MIP $95

4-LOM, 1982, Tan plastic cloak with brown belt worn over the top, unique blaster rifle
MNP $10 MIP $130

(KP Photo)
AT-AT Commander, 1982, Available with Sears Exclusive Hoth Rebel base set, or individually. Includes blaster pistol
MNP $8 MIP $95

AT-AT Driver, 1981, White and gray uniform, includes blaster rifle
MNP $7 MIP $80

(KP Photo)
Bespin Security Guard, black, 1982, Includes blaster pistol
MNP $10 MIP $50

Bespin Security Guard, white, 1980, With blaster pistol
MNP $11 MIP $60

Bossk, 1980, Includes blaster rifle with forward grip so rifle body rests against arm
MNP $10 MIP $85

(KP Photo)
C-3PO w/Removable Limbs, 1982, Included pouch for Chewbacca to carry the disassembled 3PO
MNP $10 MIP $55

Cloud Car Pilot, 1982, White uniform, orange and yellow helmet. Style of figure reminiscent of rebel troops
MNP $18 MIP $75

(KP Photo)
Dengar, 1980, One of the bounty hunters hired by Vader ("we don't need their scum…"). This figure originally came with a long rifle
MNP $7 MIP $80

FX-7, 1980, Also called the "medical droid," this model had a series of spindly arms that pivoted up from the cylindrical body
MNP $8 MIP $46

Han in Bespin Outfit, 1981, Includes blaster pistol
MNP $9 MIP $75

Han in Hoth Gear, 1980, In dark blue parka, khaki pants, includes small blaster pistol
MNP $8 MIP $95

(KP Photo)
Hoth Rebel Soldier, 1980, Light brown and off-white uniform, small blaster pistol looking a bit like a Star Trek phaser
MNP $6 MIP $49

IG-88, 1980, One of the most highly-collected ESB figures, very classic robot look. According to Star Wars lore, IG88's head was one of the props behind the bar in the Cantina scene from the first movie. Includes two blasters

MNP $25   **MIP** $135

Imperial Commander, 1981, The packaging showed General Veers in a green uniform, but the figure was an anonymous black-uniformed officer. Some variation in hair color paint exists. Included standard-issue Stormtrooper blaster

MNP $8   **MIP** $50

Imperial TIE Fighter Pilot, 1982, Black uniform, gray gloves and boots, included gray blaster pistol

MNP $13   **MIP** $85

Lando Calrissian, 1981, Two-tone blue clothing with gray plastic cloak and blaster pistol

MNP $12   **MIP** $75

Leia in Bespin Gown, 1980, Brown outfit with printed plastic cloak. Included blaster pistol

MNP $27   **MIP** $120

Leia in Hoth Gear, 1981, White uniform with light tan vest and brown boots, included small blaster pistol

MNP $18   **MIP** $75

(KP Photo)

Lobot, 1981, Includes blaster pistol

MNP $8   **MIP** $80

(ToyShop File Photo)

Luke in Bespin Fatigues, 1980, Included blaster pistol and stand-alone lightsaber (not part of the figure)

MNP $16   **MIP** $120

Luke in Hoth Gear, 1982, White uniform with brown vest and gray boots. Included blaster rifle

MNP $10   **MIP** $115

(ToyShop File Photo)

R2-D2 with Sensorscope, 1982, Available first with Sears Exclusive Hoth Rebel Base play set, or individually. Essentially the same as the standard R2, but with a blue plastic sensorscope that could be raised or lowered from his head

MNP $21   **MIP** $60

Rebel Commander, 1980, Off-white uniform, brown boots, blaster rifle

MNP $9   **MIP** $65

Snowtrooper, 1980, Plastic cloak along belt, included heavy laser rifle

MNP $14   **MIP** $95

Ugnaught, 1981, With blue cloth apron and white toolkit

MNP $9   **MIP** $55

(ToyShop File Photo)

Yoda, 1981, With cloth cloak, plastic belt, snake and walking stick. The plastic accessories were produced in varying colors

MNP $40   **MIP** $185

Zuckuss, 1982

MNP $10   **MIP** $95

RETURN OF THE JEDI

8D8, 1983

MNP $7   **MIP** $55

(KP Photo)

Admiral Ackbar, 1983

MNP $7   **MIP** $28

(KP Photo)

AT-ST Driver, 1983

MNP $9   **MIP** $55

(KP Photo)

Bib Fortuna, 1983, "Pay Jabba no bother..." This figure is the original sculpt of Jabba's major domo who apparently, was weak-minded enough to allow Luke's Jedi mind trick to work on him

MNP $8   **MIP** $34

Biker Scout, 1983

MNP $25   **MIP** $100

B-Wing Pilot, 1984

MNP $9   **MIP** $27

Chief Chirpa, 1983
     MNP $8   **MIP** $49

(KP Photo)

Emperor Palpatine, 1983
     MNP $10   **MIP** $46
Emperor's Royal Guard, 1984
     MNP $7   **MIP** $55

(KP Photo)

Gamorrean Guard, 1983
     MNP $4   **MIP** $27

General Madine, 1983
     MNP $10   **MIP** $50
Han in Trenchcoat, 1984
     MNP $12   **MIP** $40

Klaatu, 1983
     MNP $9   **MIP** $32

(KP Photo)

Klaatu in Skiff Guard Outfit, 1983
     MNP $8   **MIP** $35
Lando Calrissian, Skiff Guard Outfit, 1983
     MNP $8   **MIP** $47

(KP Photo)

Leia in Battle Poncho, 1984, Green camo
pattern cloth poncho, removeable
helmet, ammo belt and blaster pistol
     MNP $18   **MIP** $55

Leia in Boushh Disguise, 1983,
w/removable helmet and tall gun
     MNP $15   **MIP** $45
Logray, 1983
     MNP $7   **MIP** $42
Luke as Jedi Knight, Blue Saber, 1983
     MNP $23   **MIP** $110
Luke as Jedi Knight, Green Saber, 1983
     MNP $21   **MIP** $60
Lumat, 1983
     MNP $29   **MIP** $47
Nien Nunb, 1983
     MNP $4   **MIP** $55
Nikto, 1984
     MNP $7   **MIP** $30

(KP Photo)

Paploo, 1984

MNP $29   **MIP** $42

(ToyShop File Photo)

Ree-Yees, 1983

MNP $7   **MIP** $25

(ToyShop File Photo)

Teebo, 1984

MNP $13   **MIP** $34

(ToyShop File Photo)

Prune Face, 1984

MNP $7   **MIP** $43

Rancor Keeper, 1984

MNP $7   **MIP** $39

Rebel Commando, 1983

MNP $8   **MIP** $40

(ToyShop File Photo)

Squid Head, 1983

MNP $6   **MIP** $55

Sy Snootles and the Rebo Band, 1984, 3 figures

MNP $65   **MIP** $100

(ToyShop File Photo)

Weequay, 1984

MNP $6   **MIP** $49

Wicket, 1984

MNP $14   **MIP** $60

POTF

Amanaman, w/coin, 1985

MNP $90   **MIP** $170

Anakin Skywalker, w/coin, 1985

MNP $23   **MIP** $1625

AT-AT Driver, w/coin, 1985

MNP $9   **MIP** $575

(KP Photo)

AT-ST Driver, w/coin, 1985
      MNP $9   **MIP** $70

(KP Photo)

A-Wing Pilot, w/coin, 1985
      MNP $48   **MIP** $125

(KP Photo)

Barada, w/coin, 1985
      MNP $40   **MIP** $90
Biker Scout, w/coin, 1985
      MNP $12   **MIP** $150

(KP Photo)

B-Wing Pilot, w/coin, 1985
      MNP $9   **MIP** $65
C-3PO w/Removable Limbs, w/coin, 1985
      MNP $6   **MIP** $80
Chewbacca, w/coin, 1985
      MNP $9   **MIP** $85
Darth Vader, w/coin, 1985
      MNP $12   **MIP** $150
Emperor Palpatine, w/coin, 1985
      MNP $6   **MIP** $110

(KP Photo)

EV-9D9, w/coin, 1985
      MNP $65   **MIP** $130
Gamorrean Guard, w/coin, 1985
      MNP $5   **MIP** $250

(ToyShop File Photo)

Han in Carbonite, w/coin, 1985
      MNP $75   **MIP** $225
Han in Trenchcoat, w/coin, 1985
      MNP $50   **MIP** $350

(KP Photo)

Imperial Dignitary, w/coin, 1985
      MNP $45   **MIP** $105
Imperial Gunner, w/coin, 1985
      MNP $48   **MIP** $110
Jawa, w/coin, 1985
      MNP $11   **MIP** $110

(ToyShop File Photo)

Lando as General Pilot, w/coin, 1985
      MNP $55   MIP $95

Leia in Battle Poncho, 1985
      MNP $16   MIP $75

Luke as Jedi Knight w/Green Saber, w/coin, 1985
      MNP $30   MIP $165

Luke as X-Wing Pilot, w/coin, 1985
      MNP $12   MIP $85

Luke in Battle Poncho, w/coin, 1985
      MNP $60   MIP $115

(ToyShop File Photo)

Luke in Stormtrooper Disguise, w/coin, 1985
      MNP $80   MIP $260

Lumat, w/coin, 1985
      MNP $18   MIP $65

Nikto, w/coin, 1985
      MNP $10   MIP $725

Obi-Wan Kenobi, w/coin, 1985
      MNP $13   MIP $135

Paploo, w/coin, 1985
      MNP $16   MIP $60

R2-D2 with pop-up Lightsaber, w/coin, 1985
      MNP $85   MIP $140

(KP Photo)

Romba, w/coin, 1985
      MNP $35   MIP $70

Stormtrooper, w/coin, 1985
      MNP $35   MIP $140

Teebo, w/coin, 1985
      MNP $13   MIP $85

(KP Photo)

Warok, w/coin, 1985
      MNP $45   MIP $75

Wicket, w/coin, 1985
      MNP $10   MIP $105

Yak Face, w/coin, 1985
      MNP $175   MIP $1150

(ToyShop File Photo)

Yoda, w/coin, 1985
      MNP $25   MIP $350

DROIDS

(ToyShop File Photo)

A-Wing Pilot, 1985
      MNP $40   MIP $90

Boba Fett, 1985
      MNP $35   MIP $650

C-3PO, 1985, Solid, multicolored plastic body (not gold chromed) with painted eyes
      MNP $85   MIP $175

(KP Photo)

Jann Tosh, 1985
      MNP $18   MIP $50

Jord Dusat, 1985
      MNP $17   MIP $40

(KP Photo)

Kea Moll, 1985, Light tan and darker
brown clothing, includes blaster pistol
MNP $18   **MIP** $36

(KP Photo)

Kez-Iban, 1985, Purple body, tan clothing,
standard-issue blaster (same as early
Stormtroopers)
MNP $17   **MIP** $39

(KP Photo)

R2-D2, 1985, Simplified body markings
and head--same sculpt and legs as
regular (vintage) R2, though
MNP $55   **MIP** $125

Sise Fromm, 1985, Large-headed, green
skinned figure with purple cloth robe
MNP $55   **MIP** $250

(KP Photo)

Thall Joben, 1985
MNP $15   **MIP** $40

(KP Photo)

Tig Fromm, 1985, Blue and gray figure
MNP $50   **MIP** $115

Uncle Gundy, 1985, Short, portly figure
with white hair and mustache. Includes
blaster pistol
MNP $18   **MIP** $32

EWOKS

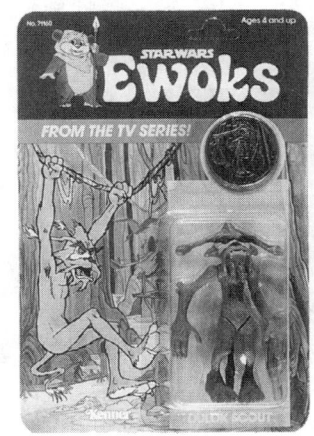

(KP Photo)

Dulok Scout, 1985, Medium-green figure
with club
MNP $14   **MIP** $28

(KP Photo)

Dulok Shaman, 1985, Bright green figure
with skull-topped staff
MNP $12   **MIP** $29

(KP Photo)

King Gorneesh, 1985, Fearsome bright
green figure with staff
MNP $12   **MIP** $27

STAR WARS

STAR WARS

(KP Photo)

Logray, 1985, With bright blue plastic robe and staff

  MNP $11 **MIP** $38

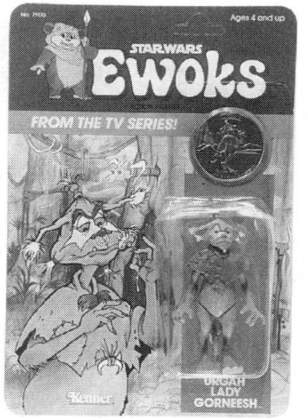

(KP Photo)

Urgah Lady Gorneesh, 1985, Green figure with red-brown poncho, blue highlights on head and face

  MNP $10 **MIP** $26

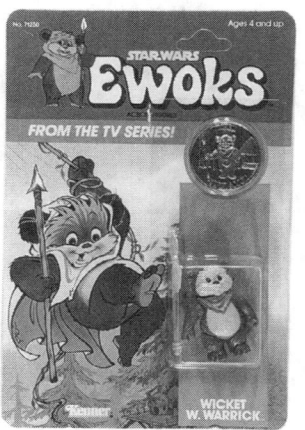

(KP Photo)

Wicket, 1985, Fittingly, a more "cartoony" simplified version of the Wicket from ROTJ. Included spear

  MNP $14 **MIP** $45

POTF2

(Hasbro Photo)

2-1B Medic Droid, 1997, Series 5
  MNP $2 **MIP** $10

4-LOM, 1997, Series 7
  MNP $3 **MIP** $12

8-D8 Droid, 1998, Series 14
  MNP $3 **MIP** $10

Admiral Ackbar, 1997, Series 7
  MNP $3 **MIP** $10

Admiral Motti, 1999, Series 20
  MNP $5 **MIP** $20

Anakin Skywalker, 1999, Series 17
  MNP $3 **MIP** $12

ASP-7 Droid, 1997, Series 7
  MNP $3 **MIP** $10

AT-ST Driver, 1997, Series 5
  MNP $3 **MIP** $12

Aunt Beru, 1999, Series 17
  MNP $3 **MIP** $12

Bib Fortuna, 1997, Series 6
  MNP $3 **MIP** $10

(Hasbro Photo)

Biggs Darklighter, 1998, Series 11
  MNP $3 **MIP** $20

Boba Fett, 1996, Series 2, Variation: half circle one hand, full circle on other hand, scarce $350

  MNP $4 **MIP** $50

(Hasbro Photo)

Bossk, 1997, Series 5
  MNP $3 **MIP** $12

C-3PO, 1995, Series 1
  MNP $3 **MIP** $10

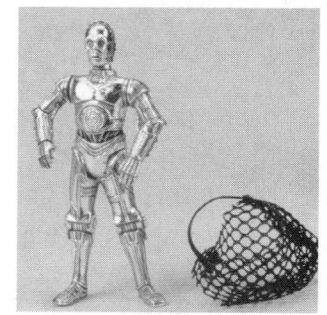

(Hasbro Photo)

C-3PO w/Removable Limbs and Backpack, 1998, Series 13
  MNP $3 **MIP** $15

C-3PO, Shop Worn, 1999, Series 17
  MNP $3 **MIP** $10

Cantina Greedo, 1999, Series 18
  MNP $3 **MIP** $8

Cantina Han Solo, 1999, Series 18
  MNP $3 **MIP** $8

Captain Piett, 1998, Series 12
  MNP $5 **MIP** $30

Chewbacca, 1995, Series 1
  MNP $3 **MIP** $15

Chewbacca (Hoth), 1998, Series 16, with painted "snow" on face
  MNP $3 **MIP** $10

Chewbacca as Boushh's Bounty, 1998, Series 15
  MNP $3 **MIP** $15

Darth Vader, 1995, Series 1, long lightsaber
  MNP $4 **MIP** $25

Darth Vader, 1998, Series 16, removable cape
  MNP $3 **MIP** $20

Darth Vader w/Interrogation Droid, 1999, Series 19, Commtech chip version
  MNP $5 **MIP** $12

(KP Photo)

Darth Vader w/Removable Helmet, 1998, Series 12

MNP $4		MIP $40	

Death Star Gunner, 1996, Series 3

MNP $3   MIP $25

Death Star Trooper, 1998, Series 15

MNP $3   MIP $25

Dengar, 1997, Series 7

MNP $3   MIP $12

Emperor Palpatine, 1997, Series 6, Collection 1

MNP $3   MIP $12

Emperor Palpatine, 1998, Series 16

MNP $3   MIP $10

Emperor's Royal Guard, 1997, Series 8

MNP $3   MIP $10

(Hasbro Photo)

Endor Rebel Soldier, 1998, Series 10

MNP $3   MIP $10

(Hasbro Photo)

EV-9D9, 1997, Series 9

MNP $3   MIP $12

(Hasbro Photo)

Gamorrean Guard, 1997, Series 9

MNP $3   MIP $10

Garindan (Long Snoot), 1997, Series 7

MNP $3   MIP $7

(KP Photo)

Grand Moff Tarkin, 1997, Series 7, Collection 2, surprisingly not produced until the re-release of the first three movies

MNP $3   MIP $40

Greedo, 1996, Series 3, Collection 1

MNP $3   MIP $25

Han in Bespin Outfit, 1997, Series 8

MNP $3   MIP $7

Han in Endor Gear, 1997, Series 6, blue pants

MNP $3   MIP $12

Han in Hoth Gear, 1996, Series 2

MNP $3   MIP $15

(KP Photo)

Han Solo, 1995, Series 1

MNP $3   MIP $15

(KP Photo, Karen O'Brien collection)

Han Solo in Carbonite, 1996, Han in Bespin outfit, frozen in carbonite, blaster

MNP $3   MIP $6

Hoth Rebel Soldier, 1997, Series 5

MNP $3   MIP $10

(Hasbro Photo)

Ishi Tib, 1998, Series 12
  MNP $3 **MIP** $20

Jawa & Gonk Droid, 1999, Series 18, Droid also known as "power droid," a walking generator. Called "Gonk" because of the noise it makes when walking around on the Jawas' Sandcrawler in Episode IV
  MNP $3 **MIP** $8

(Hasbro Photo)

Jawas, 1996, Series 4
  MNP $3 **MIP** $25

(Hasbro Photo)

Lak Sivrak, 1998, Series 11
  MNP $3 **MIP** $20

(Hasbro Photo)

Lando as General, 1998, Series 10
  MNP $3 **MIP** $20

Lando as Skiff Guard, 1997, Series 6
  MNP $3 **MIP** $10

(Hasbro Photo)

Lando Calrissian, 1996, Series 2
  MNP $3 **MIP** $10

Leia as Jabba's Prisoner, 1997, Series 8
  MNP $3 **MIP** $8

(Hasbro Photo)

Leia in Ewok Celebration Outfit, 1998, Series 10
  MNP $3 **MIP** $20

Leia w/All-New Likeness, 1998, Series 13, a much better sculpt than the first re-release
  MNP $3 **MIP** $10

Lobot, 1998, Series 15
  MNP $3 **MIP** $15

(Hasbro Photo)

Luke as X-Wing Pilot, 1996, Series 2, short lightsaber
  MNP $3 **MIP** $15

Luke in Bespin Outfit, 1998, Series 10, detachable hand
  MNP $3 **MIP** $10

Luke in Ceremonial Garb, 1997, Series 10, Collection 1
  MNP $3 **MIP** $8

Luke in Dagobah Fatigues, 1996, Series 3, short lightsaber
  MNP $3 **MIP** $20

(Hasbro Photo)

Luke in Hoth Gear, 1997, Series 5, Collection 1
  MNP $3 **MIP** $10

(KP Photo)

Luke in Stormtrooper Disguise, 1996, Series 4
    MNP $4   **MIP** $35

Luke Skywalker, 1995, Series 1, short lightsaber
    MNP $4   **MIP** $15

Luke Skywalker, 1998, Series 16, Flashback photo
    MNP $3   **MIP** $10

Luke Skywalker w/T16, 1999, Series 18
    MNP $3   **MIP** $8

Luke w/Blast Shield Helmet, 1998, Series 13
    MNP $3   **MIP** $15

(Hasbro Photo)

Malakili (Rancor Keeper), 1997, Series 9
    MNP $3   **MIP** $10

Momaw Nadon (Hammerhead), 1996, Series 4, Collection 2
    MNP $2   **MIP** $35

Mon Mothma, 1998, Series 15
    MNP $3   **MIP** $20

(Hasbro Photo)

Nien Nunb, 1997, Series 9
    MNP $3   **MIP** $10

Obi-Wan Kenobi, 1995, Series 1, short lightsaber
    MNP $4   **MIP** $15

Obi-Wan Kenobi, 1998, Series 16
    MNP $3   **MIP** $20

Orrimaarko (Prune Face), 1998, Series 15, with brown plastic cloak
    MNP $3   **MIP** $15

Ponda Baba, 1997, Series 7, Collection 3, Collection 2 issue $40
    MNP $3   **MIP** $7

Princess Leia, 1995, Series 1
    MNP $3   **MIP** $20

Princess Leia, 1998, Series 16
    MNP $3   **MIP** $10

Princess Leia Organa, 1997, Series 9
    MNP $5   **MIP** $10

R2-D2, 1995, Series 1
    MNP $3   **MIP** $15

R2-D2, 1998, Series 16
    MNP $3   **MIP** $10

R2-D2 w/Datalink and Sensorscope, 1998, Series 13
    MNP $3   **MIP** $15

R2-D2 w/Holographic Princess Leia, 1999, Series 20
    MNP $12   **MIP** $45

R5-D4, 1996, Series 4
    MNP $3   **MIP** $25

Rebel Fleet Trooper, 1997, Series 7, Collection 1
    MNP $3   **MIP** $10

Ree-Yees, 1998, Series 15
    MNP $3   **MIP** $25

(Hasbro Photo)

Saelt-Marae (Yak Face), 1997, Series 9
    MNP $3   **MIP** $12

(KP Photo)

Sandtrooper, 1996, Series 3, with blaster rifle and backpack
    MNP $3   **MIP** $15

(KP Photo)

Snowtrooper, 1997, Series 8, nicely detailed sculpt
    MNP $3   **MIP** $8

Stormtrooper, 1995, Series 1
    MNP $3   **MIP** $12

Stormtrooper, 1999, Series 19, Commtech Chip
    MNP $5   **MIP** $15

STAR WARS

(KP Photo)

TIE Fighter Pilot, 1996, Series 2, equipped with two blaster rifles
MNP $3   MIP $6

(KP Photo)

Tusken Raider, 1996, Series 4
MNP $3   MIP $25

Ugnaught, 1998, Series 13
MNP $3   MIP $12

Weequay Skiff Guard, 1997, Series 7, Collection 3
MNP $3   MIP $7

(Hasbro Photo)

Wicket and Logray, 1998, Series 11
MNP $3   MIP $18

Yoda, 1996, Series 2
MNP $3   MIP $12

Yoda, 1998, Series 16
MNP $3   MIP $12

Zuckuss, 1998, Series 12
MNP $3   MIP $30

Cantina Aliens—Labria, Nabrun Leids, Takeel, 1999
MNP $10   MIP $18

Cantina Showdown—Obi-Wan Kenobi, Ponda Baba, Dr. Evazan, 1997
MNP $10   MIP $20

Death Star Escape—Luke and Han in Stormtrooper Disguise, Chewbacca, 1997
MNP $10   MIP $45

Final Jedi Duel—Darth Vader, Luke, Emperor Palpatine, 1998
MNP $10   MIP $28

Jabba the Hutt's Dancers—Rystall, Greeata, Lyn Me, 1998
MNP $10   MIP $15

(KP Photo)

Jabba's Skiff Guards - Klaatu, Barada, Nikto, 1999, Well-detailed figures with stand. Keeping them in-pack, the box doubles as a diorama background
MNP $10   MIP $35

Jedi Spirits—Anakin Skywalker, Yoda, Obi-Wan Kenobi, 1999
MNP $10   MIP $18

Mynock Hunt—Han, Leia, Chewbacca, 1998
MNP $10   MIP $50

Purchase of the Droids—Luke, C-3PO, Uncle Owen, 1998
MNP $10   MIP $20

Rebel Pilots—Wedge Antilles, B-Wing Pilot (Ten Nunb), Y-Wing Pilot, 1999
MNP $10   MIP $15

Dagobah w/Yoda, 1998
MNP $10   MIP $12

Death Star w/Darth Vader, 1998
MNP $10   MIP $12

Endor w/Wicket, 1998
MNP $10   MIP $22

Tatooine w/Luke Skywalker, 1998
MNP $10   MIP $25

Clone Emperor, 1998
MNP $3   MIP $18

Darktrooper, 1998
MNP $3   MIP $30

Imperial Sentinel, 1998
MNP $3   MIP $18

Kyle Katarn, 1998
MNP $3   MIP $35

Luke Skywalker (Dark Empire), 1998
MNP $3   MIP $18

Princess Leia Organa Solo, 1998
MNP $3   MIP $18

Boba Fett, 1997
MNP $5   MIP $12

Crowd Control Stormtrooper, 1996
MNP $5   MIP $7

Han Solo w/Smuggler's Flight Pack, 1996
MNP $5   MIP $10

Imperial Probe Droid, 1997
MNP $5   MIP $10

Luke Skywalker's Desert Sport Skiff, 1996
MNP $5   MIP $10

Snowtrooper (Deluxe), 1997, With tripod laser cannon
MNP $5   MIP $10

Boba Fett vs. IG-88, 1996, Packaged with comic book
MNP $6   MIP $30

Droopy McCool and Barquin D'an, 1998
MNP $6   MIP $35

Leia and Han, 1998
MNP $6   MIP $10

(Hasbro Photo)

Leia and Luke, 1998
MNP $6   MIP $10

Leia and R2-D2, 1998
MNP $6   MIP $10

(Hasbro Photo)

Leia and Wicket the Ewok, 1998
MNP $6   MIP $10

Max Rebo and Doda Bodonawieedo, 1998
MNP $6   MIP $38

Prince Xizor vs. Darth Vader, 1996
MNP $6   MIP $25

Sy Snootles and Joh Yowza, 1998
MNP $6   MIP $35

Ben (Obi-Wan) Kenobi, 1997
MNP $5   MIP $10

Darth Vader, 1997
MNP $5   MIP $10

Emporer Palpatine, 1997
MNP $5   MIP $10

Jedi Knight Luke Skywalker, 1997
MNP $5   MIP $10

R2-D2, 1997
MNP $5   MIP $10

AT-AT Driver, 1998
MNP $3   MIP $20

Death Star Droid w/Mouse Droid, 1998
MNP $3   MIP $20

Leia in Hoth Gear, 1998
MNP $3   MIP $22

Pote Snitkin, 1998
MNP $3   MIP $20

Falcon w/Han Solo, 1998
MNP $6   MIP $10

Falcon w/Luke Skywalker, 1998
MNP $6   MIP $10

Tie Fighter w/Darth Vader, 1998
MNP $6   MIP $30

Grand Admiral Thrawn, 1998
MNP $3   MIP $20

Mara Jade, 1998
MNP $3   MIP $35

Spacetrooper, 1998
MNP $3   MIP $25

C-3PO, w/Millennium Minted Coin, 1998
MNP $5   MIP $12

Chewbacca, w/Millennium Minted Coin, 1998
MNP $5   MIP $12

Emperor Palpatine, w/Millennium Minted Coin, 1998
MNP $5   MIP $12

Han in Bespin Outfit, w/Millennium Minted Coin, 1998
MNP $5   MIP $12

Leia in Endor Gear, w/Millennium Minted Coin, 1998
MNP $5   MIP $12

Luke in Battle Poncho, w/Millennium Minted Coin, 1998
MNP $5   MIP $12

Snowtrooper, w/Millennium Minted Coin, 1998
MNP $5   MIP $12

B'omarr Monk, Internet exclusive offer. Moving spider-like legs and brain encased in plastic bubble
MNP $10   MIP $15

Figrin D'an (Cantina Band Member),
MNP $10   MIP $15

Han in Stormtrooper Disguise,
MNP $10   MIP $20

Mace Windu,
MNP $5   MIP $10

Muftak and Kabe,
MNP $10   MIP $16

(KP Photo)

Obi-Wan Kenobi Spirit, Figure was a mail-in offer from Frito Lay. Made of translucent blue plastic
MNP $10   MIP $10

Oola and Salacious Crumb,
MNP $10   MIP $14

(KP Photo)

STAP and Battle Droid,
MNP $10   MIP $12

Theater Edition Jedi Knight Luke Skywalker, 1996
MNP $10   MIP $65

Chewbacca in Bounty Hunter Disguise, 1996
MNP $3   MIP $10

Dash Rendar, 1996
MNP $3   MIP $20

Han in Carbonite, 1996
MNP $3   MIP $10

Leia in Boushh Disguise, 1996
MNP $3   MIP $10

Luke in Imperial Guard Disguise, 1996
MNP $3   MIP $20

Prince Xizor, 1996
MNP $3   MIP $10

POTJ

Aurra Sing, Bounty Hunter, 2001
MNP $3   MIP $15

Boba Fett,
MNP $3   MIP $8

Boss Nass, Gungan Sacred Place,
MNP $3   MIP $15

Chewbacca, Dejarik Champion, 2000
MNP $3   MIP $15

Coruscant Guard, 2001
MNP $3   MIP $15

Darth Maul w/Sith Attack Droid,
MNP $3   MIP $15

Darth Maul, Final Duel, 2000
MNP $5   MIP $20

Darth Maul, Sith Apprentice, 2001
MNP $3   MIP $25

Darth Vader, Dagobah,
MNP $3   MIP $15

Destroyer Droid, Battle Damaged, 2000
MNP $3   MIP $8

Eeth Koth,
MNP $3   MIP $8

(KP Photo)

Ellorrs Madak, Duros, 2001, Fan Choice Figure #1
MNP $3   MIP $8

Gungan Warrior,
MNP $3   MIP $10

(KP Photo)

Han Solo, Bespin Capture, 2002, Includes blaster pistol, cuffs and 8-page "Jedi Force File"
MNP n/a   MIP $20

Jar Jar Binks, Tatooine,
MNP $3   MIP $8

Ketwol, 2001
MNP $3   MIP $12

Mas Amedda, 2000
MNP $3   MIP $15

Obi-Wan Kenobi, Cold Weather Gear, 2001
MNP $3   MIP $15

Obi-Wan Kenobi, Jedi Training Gear,
MNP $3   MIP $15

Plo Koon, 2000
MNP $3   MIP $15

Queen Amidala, Decoy,
MNP $3   MIP $8

Qui-Gon Jinn, Mos Espa Disguise, Includes gray cloth poncho and lightsaber
MNP $5   MIP $12

R2-D2, Naboo Escape, 2000
MNP $3   MIP $12

Red Throne Queen, 2001
MNP $3   MIP $6

Sabe, 2001, With blaster pistol
MNP $3   MIP $12

Saesae Tiin, 2001
MNP $3   MIP $15

Sandtrooper, 2001, With binoculars and pistol
MNP $5   MIP $8

Sebulba, Includes removeable helmet and goggles
MNP $3   MIP $12

Shmi Skywalker,
MNP $3   MIP $8

Tusken Raider, Desert Sniper, 2000
MNP $3   MIP $15

THE PHANTOM MENACE

(KP Photo)

Adi Gallia, 1999, With removeable cloak and lightsaber
MNP $3   MIP $10

Anakin Skywalker, Mechanic, 2000, Includes pit droid figure
MNP $3   MIP $7

(KP Photo)

Anakin Skywalker, Naboo, 1999, With removable plastic cloak
MNP $3   MIP $7

Anakin Skywalker, Naboo Pilot, 2000, Includes helmet and ship controls
MNP $3   MIP $12

(KP Photo)

Anakin Skywalker, Tatooine, 1999, With backpack and blaster pistol
MNP $3   MIP $12

(KP Photo)

Battle Droid w/Federation Issue Blaster, 1999, These droids came in variety of paint finishes--some pristine, others with battle damage
MNP $3   MIP $7

(KP Photo)

Battle Droid, Battle Damage, 1999, Variations on this model include: "star" blast point on chest, silver lines on body, and lighter and darker sand marks
MNP $3   MIP $10

Battle Droid, Security, 2000, Fairly plain light tan with dark brown. Includes blaster rifle
MNP $3   MIP $8

(KP Photo)

Boss Nass, 1999, With staff
MNP $3   MIP $8

(KP Photo)

C-3PO, 1999, Skeletal-looking version of 3PO before he had metal "skin"
MNP $3   MIP $10

(KP Photo)

Captain Panaka, 2000, With blaster rifle
MNP $3   **MIP** $10

(KP Photo)

Captain Tarpals, 1999, With "electropole" staff
MNP $3   **MIP** $12

(KP Photo)

Chancellor Valorum, 1999, Includes staff
MNP $3   **MIP** $12

(KP Photo)

Darth Maul, 1999
MNP $5   **MIP** $9

Darth Maul, Jedi Duel, 1999, The first release of a 3-3/4" Darth Maul figure
MNP $5   **MIP** $20

(KP Photo)

Darth Maul, Sith Lord, 2000, With double-edged lightsaber, second stand-alone release of figure
MNP $3   **MIP** $12

Darth Maul, Tatooine, 1999, With black cloth cloak--the cloak and other weapons were also available in an accessory set
MNP $3   **MIP** $7

(KP Photo)

Darth Sidious, 1999, Black-robed figure with Commtech chip
MNP $3   **MIP** $12

Darth Sidious, Holograph, 2000, Translucent purple figure with Commtech chip
MNP $3   **MIP** $30

Destroyer Droid, 1999, Includes Commtech chip
MNP $3   **MIP** $7

(KP Photo)

Gasgano, w/pit droid, 1999, Mult-armed figure packaged with pit droid and Commtech chip
MNP $3   **MIP** $10

(KP Photo)

Jar Jar Binks, 1999, Figure included Gungan Battle Staff and comtech chip stand
MNP $3   **MIP** $20

Jar Jar Binks, Naboo Swamp, 2000, Specially made to be posed in swimming motion, includes fish
MNP $3   **MIP** $18

(KP Photo)

Ki-Adi-Mundi, 1999, With lightsaber
MNP $3   MIP $10

(KP Photo)

Mace Windu, 1999, With lightsaber and removeable plastic cloak
MNP $3   MIP $12

Mace Windu, Sneak Preview, 1998, Includes different cloak and has a more stoic, less active pose and expression than the regular-issue Mace Windu
MNP $3   MIP $30

Mos Espa Encounter - Sebulba, Jar Jar, Anakin, 1999
MNP $5   MIP $18

Naboo Royal Guard, 2000, Includes removeable helmet and blaster pistol
MNP $3   MIP $20

Naboo Royal Security, 2000, Included two blaster rifles
MNP $3   MIP $7

(KP Photo)

Nute Gunray, 1999, A good likeness-- includes Commtech chip
MNP $3   MIP $6

Obi-Wan Kenobi, 1999
MNP $5   MIP $9

(KP Photo)

Obi-Wan Kenobi, Jedi Duel, 1999, Includes lightsaber
MNP $3   MIP $10

Obi-Wan Kenobi, Jedi Knight, 2000, In plain white robe, much like the Jedi Duel figure, but includes extra belt and gear, along with lightsaber
MNP $3   MIP $20

Obi-Wan Kenobi, Naboo, 1999, In dark robe--has two lightsabers, one activated, the other not
MNP $3   MIP $7

Ody Mandrell w/Pit Droid, 1999, Another two-figure pack with Commtech chip
MNP $3   MIP $7

OOM-9, 1999, Yellow markings on head and body. This figure includes binoculars and blaster rifle
MNP $3   MIP $7

(KP Photo)

Padme Naberrie, 1999, Figure included viewscreen to watch the pod race
MNP $3   MIP $12

(KP Photo)

Pit Droids, 2000, Highly-detailed sculpts of the ubiquitous droids seen in Episode 1
MNP $3   MIP $25

Queen Amidala, Battle, 2000, In dark robe, includes blaster pistol and grappling hook crossbow
MNP $3   MIP $30

Queen Amidala, Coruscant, 1999, In full royal outfit and makeup
MNP $3   MIP $15

(KP Photo)

Queen Amidala, Naboo w/Blaster Pistols, 1999, Figure included two sleek blaster pistols and comtech chip stand
MNP $3   MIP $12

Qui-Gon Jinn, 1999
MNP $5   MIP $9

Qui-Gon Jinn, Jedi Duel, 1999, In plain-colored robe. Includes lightsaber
MNP $3   MIP $10

Qui-Gon Jinn, Jedi Master, 2000, With lightsaber and Commtech chip
MNP $3   MIP $20

Qui-Gon Jinn, Naboo, 1999, Includes two lightsabers: one activated, the other not
MNP $3   MIP $7

R2-B1 Astromech Droid, 2000, Dark blue with light green body, includes harness pod
MNP $3   MIP $25

(KP Photo)

R2-D2, 1999, With retractable middle "foot"
       MNP $3   **MIP** $7

(KP Photo)

Ric Olie, 1999, Removeable helmet and two blaster pistols
       MNP $3   **MIP** $8

Rune Haako, 1999, Includes Commtech chip
       MNP $3   **MIP** $6

(KP Photo)

Senator Palpatine, 1999, With cam droid and Commtech chip
       MNP $3   **MIP** $12

Sio Bibble, 2000, Includes blaster pistol and Commtech chip
       MNP $3   **MIP** $45

Tatooine Showdown - Darth Maul, Qui-Gon, Anakin, 1999
       MNP $5   **MIP** $18

TC-14, 2000, Silver-plated, includes serving tray and Commtech chip. Somewhat harder to find, almost exlusively available from dealers
       MNP $3   **MIP** $35

(KP Photo)

Watto, 1999, Highly-detailed figure
       MNP $3   **MIP** $10

Watto's Box - Watto, Graxol Kelvyyn, Shakka, 2000
       MNP $5   **MIP** $25

Yoda, w/Jedi Council Chair, 1999, Includes blue chair and Commtech chip
       MNP $3   **MIP** $8

SAGA

Aayla Secura, Jedi Knight, 2003, platform, blue lightsaber
       MNP $3   **MIP** $7

(KP Photo, Karen O'Brien collection)

Achk Med-Beq, Courscant Outlander Club, 2003
       MNP $3   **MIP** $7

Admiral Ozzel, 2004, Star Destroyer
       MNP $3   **MIP** $7

(KP Photo, Karen O'Brien collection)

Anakin Skywalker, Hangar Duel, 2002, Includes two lightsabers, has fighting action
       MNP n/a   **MIP** $13

(KP Photo)

Anakin Skywalker, Outland Peasant Disguise, 2002, Includes cloak, lightsaber, and cargo
       MNP n/a   **MIP** $6

Anakin Skywalker, Secret Ceremony, 2003, flowing robes, mechanical hand
       MNP $3   **MIP** $7

Anakin Skywalker, Tatooine Attack, 2002, mad Anakin, blue lightsaber, Tusken stand
       MNP $3   **MIP** $7

(KP Photo, Karen O'Brien collection)

Ashla & Jempa, Younglings, 2003, 2-pack, helmet and blue lightsaber for Ashla and helmet, green lightsaber for Jempa
       MNP $3   **MIP** $7

Ayy Vida, Outlander Nightclub Patron, 2003, barstool and drink
MNP $5   MIP $10

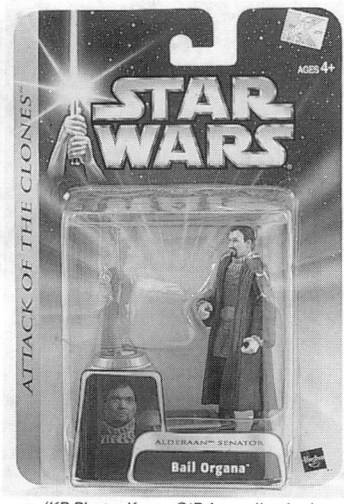

(KP Photo, Karen O'Brien collection)

Bail Organa, Alderaan Senator, 2003, holographic Jedi and projector
MNP $5   MIP $10

Barriss Offee, Luminara Unduli's Padawan, 2003, flowing robes, green lightsaber
MNP $3   MIP $7

(KP Photo)

Battle Droid, Arena Battle, 2002, With orange laser blast
MNP n/a   MIP $6

Boba Fett, Kamino Escape, 2002, Two blaster pistols, flame effect, missile pack
MNP n/a   MIP $12

Boba Fett, The Pit of Carkoon, 2003, molded engine flames and energy blast, laser rifle
MNP $5   MIP $10

Bossk, Executor Meeting, 2004
MNP $3   MIP $7

C-3PO, Hoth Evacuation, 2004
MNP $3   MIP $7

(KP Photo)

C-3PO, Protocol Droid, 2002, Comes with removeable outer plating and box for storage
MNP n/a   MIP $6

C-3PO, Tatooine Ambush, 2003, removable arm, serving tray
MNP $3   MIP $7

Captain Antilles, Tantive IV Invasion, Fan's Choice Figure #5, 2004
MNP $3   MIP $7

Captain Typho, 2002, With removeable helmet, blaster with blast effect
MNP n/a   MIP $18

Chewbacca, Cloud City, 2002, w/net and C3PO in pieces
MNP $3   MIP $7

(KP Photo, Karen O'Brien collection)

Chewbacca, Mynock Hunt, 2003, crossbow, red bolt, Mynock
MNP $3   MIP $7

(KP Photo)

Clone Trooper, 2002, With rifle and tripod-style gun. This figure also lacks the painted-on sand and grime that the preview model features
MNP n/a   MIP $9

Clone Trooper, Republic Gunship Pilot, 2002, white figure w/yellow stripe on helmet, gun turret attaches to Republic Gunship
MNP $3   MIP $7

Coleman Trebor, Battle of Geonosis, 2003, Jedi knight, green lightsaber
MNP $3   MIP $7

Count Dooku, 2002, Includes lightsaber and smaller Darth Sidious hologram figure
MNP n/a   MIP $18

Darth Maul, Sith Training, 2002, flowing black robes w/red accents, double-sided retractable lightsaber, training droid
MNP $3   MIP $7

Darth Maul, Theed Hangar Duel, 2003, two-ended red lightsaber
MNP $5   MIP $10

Darth Tyranus, Geonosian Escape, 2003, flowing robes, red lightsaber, jedi lightning
MNP $3   MIP $7

(KP Photo, Karen O'Brien collection)

Darth Vader, Bespin Duel, 2002, "Luke, I am your father…"
MNP $3   MIP $7

Darth Vader, Death Star Clash, 2003, cloth robe, red lightsaber
MNP $5   MIP $10

Darth Vader, Throne Room Duel, 2003, removable helmet, red lightsaber
MNP $5   MIP $10

Dengar, Executor Meeting, 2004
MNP $3   MIP $7

Destroyer Droid, Arena Battle, 2002, w/two energy beams
MNP $3   MIP $7

(KP Photo)

Dexter Jetster, 2002, Detailed sculpt with four moving arms. Includes cutlery
    MNP n/a   **MIP** $9

Djas Puhr, Alien Bounty Hunter, 2002, A New Hope, w/ two long pistols
    MNP $3   **MIP** $7

Dutch Vander: Gold Leader, Battle of Yavin, 2004
    MNP $3   **MIP** $7

Eeth Koth, Jedi Master, 2002, green lightsaber
    MNP $3   **MIP** $7

Elan Sleazebaggano, Outlander Nightclub Encounter, 2003, "I do not want to sell you death sticks", bar, death sticks, drink
    MNP $3   **MIP** $7

Emperor, Throne Room, 2003, cane, Jedi lightning
    MNP $3   **MIP** $7

Endor Rebel Soldier, 2002, Bearded or non-bearded versions
    MNP $3   **MIP** $7

Ephant Mon, Fan's Choice Figure #3, 2002, w/cane and axe head
    MNP $7   **MIP** $17

General Jan Dodonna, Battle of Yavin, 2004
    MNP $3   **MIP** $7

General Madine, Imperial Shuttle Capture, 2004
    MNP $3   **MIP** $7

(KP Photo)

Geonosian Warrior, 2002, Poseable wings
    MNP n/a   **MIP** $9

Han Solo, Endor Raid, 2002, w/two detonators and pistol
    MNP $3   **MIP** $7

Han Solo, Endor Strike, 2004, dressed as AT-ST driver
    MNP $3   **MIP** $7

Han Solo, Flight to Alderan, 2003, pistol
    MNP $3   **MIP** $7

(KP Photo, Karen O'Brien collection)

Han Solo, Hoth Rescue, 2003, two versions-blue or brown coat, snow mask, pistol, radio, blue lightsaber
    MNP $3   **MIP** $7

Holographic Luke Skywalker, Jabba's Palace, 2004
    MNP $3   **MIP** $7

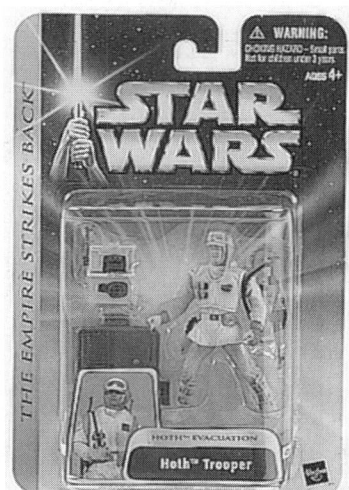

(KP Photo, Karen O'Brien collection)

Hoth Trooper, Hoth Evacuation, 2004
    MNP $3   **MIP** $7

Imperial Dignitary Janus Greejatus, Death Star Procession, 2003
    MNP $3   **MIP** $7

(KP Photo, Karen O'Brien collection)

Imperial Officer, 2002, Blonde or Brown hair version, w/laser rifle
    MNP $3   **MIP** $7

Jango Fett, Final Battle, 2002, Includes pack, two blasters, and plastic "flame"
    MNP n/a   **MIP** $18

(KP Photo)

Jango Fett, Kamino Escape, 2002, With two pistols, grappling hook, and firing missile pack
    MNP n/a   **MIP** $12

Jango Fett, Kamino Escape, 2003, removable helmet, two pistols, string from wrist w/hook, backpack missile
    MNP $3   **MIP** $7

Jango Fett, Slave 1 Pilot, 2002, two silver pistols, can see his face
    MNP $3   **MIP** $7

(KP Photo)

STAR WARS

Jar Jar Binks, Gungan Senator, 2002, With staff and blue energy bolts
MNP n/a   MIP $6

J'Quille, Jabba's Sail Barge, 2004
MNP $3   MIP $7

Ki-Adi Mundi, Jedi Master, 2002, blue lightsaber, deflected energy beam
MNP $3   MIP $7

(KP Photo)

Kit Fisto, Jedi Master, 2002, With "laser blast" attachment for lightsaber
MNP n/a   MIP $9

Klen Blista-Vanee, Imperial Dignitary, 2003
MNP $3   MIP $7

Lama Su with Clone Youth, 2003, 2-pack
MNP $3   MIP $7

Lando Calrissian, Death Star Attack, 2004
MNP $3   MIP $7

Lando Calrissian, Jabba's Sail Barge, 2004
MNP $3   MIP $7

Lott Dod, Neimoidian Senator, 2002, w/tall hat and small holographic Darth Sidious
MNP $3   MIP $7

Lt. Dannl Faytonni, Coruscant Outlander Club, 2003, table, drink, pistol
MNP $3   MIP $7

(KP Photo, Karen O'Brien collection)

Luke Skywalker, Bespin Duel, 2002, "Bloody Luke," right hand removable, comes with antenna
MNP $3   MIP $7

Luke Skywalker, Hoth Attack, 2004
MNP $3   MIP $7

Luke Skywalker, Jabba's Palace, 2004
MNP $3   MIP $7

Luke Skywalker, Tatooine Encounter, 2003, blue lightsaber
MNP $3   MIP $7

Luke Skywalker, Throne Room Duel, 2003, green lightsaber, slashing action, causeway breaks - error version has black glove on left hand rather than right
MNP $5   MIP $10

(KP Photo)

Luminara Unduli, Jedi Master, 2002, Extremely detailed sculpt. Figure includes lightsaber with blaster deflect attachement
MNP n/a   MIP $14

Mace Windu, Arena Confrontation, 2003, purple lightsaber, flowing robes
MNP $3   MIP $7

(KP Photo)

Mace Windu, Geonosian Rescue, 2002, Pushing a button on Mace's back moves arm with lightsaber in a "slashing attack." These newest Star Wars figures probably have the most detail and moving parts of any series yet--and this is just one example
MNP n/a   MIP $18

Massif w/ Geonosian Warrior, 2002
MNP $3   MIP $7

Massif with Geonosian Warrior, 2002, Includes Geonosian warrior with Massif on chain leash
MNP n/a   MIP $14

(KP Photo, Karen O'Brien collection)

McQuarrie Concept Stormtrooper, Fan Choice Figure #4, 2003, shield, blaster, lightsaber
MNP $5   MIP $10

(KP Photo)

Nikto, Jedi Knight, 2002, With lightsaber and "force blast effect"
MNP n/a   MIP $7

(KP Photo, Karen O'Brien collection)

Obi Wan Kenobi, Outlander Nightclub Encounter, 2003, bar and drink
MNP $3   MIP $7

Obi-Wan Kenobi, Acklay Battle, 2003, w/break-away column, handcuffs, spear, blue lightsaber

    MNP $3   **MIP** $7

(KP Photo)

Obi-Wan Kenobi, Coruscant Chase, 2002, With flying droid that magnetically attaches to Obi-Wan's hand

    MNP n/a   **MIP** $8

Obi-Wan Kenobi, Jedi Starfighter Pilot, 2002

    MNP $3   **MIP** $7

(KP Photo)

Orn Free Taa, 2002, With floating camera droid

    MNP n/a   **MIP** $14

(KP Photo)

Padme Amidala, Arena Escape, 2002, Swinging arm with blaster pistol and column

    MNP n/a   **MIP** $8

Padme Amidala, Coruscant Arrival, 2002, pilot outfit w/ helmet

    MNP $3   **MIP** $7

Padme Amidala, Droid Factory Chase, 2003, platform, white cape, pistol

    MNP $3   **MIP** $7

(KP Photo, Karen O'Brien collection)

Padme Amidala, Lars Homestead, 2003, cloak and platform

    MNP $3   **MIP** $7

Padme Amidala, Secret Ceremony, 2003, in wedding dress, ornate railing and flowers

    MNP $3   **MIP** $7

Plo Koon, Arena Battle, 2002, With lightsaber

    MNP n/a   **MIP** $13

Princess Leia, Imperial Captive, 2003, pistol and laser rifle

    MNP $3   **MIP** $7

Qui-Gon Jinn, Jedi Master, 2002, better robes

    MNP $3   **MIP** $7

R1-G4, Tatooine Transaction, 2004

    MNP $3   **MIP** $7

(KP Photo)

R2-D2, Coruscant Sentry, 2002, With two plastic assassin bugs. Probably the best R2 sculpt yet, with lights and sound, to boot

    MNP n/a   **MIP** $8

R2-D2, Droid Factory Flight, 2003, molded energy bolts, string, retractable side rockets

    MNP $5   **MIP** $10

R2-D2, Jabba's Sail Barge, 2004, w/drink tray

    MNP $3   **MIP** $7

Rappertunie, Jabba's Palace, 2004

    MNP $3   **MIP** $7

Rebel Fleet Trooper, 2002, Red or Black hair version, w/pistol

    MNP $3   **MIP** $7

(KP Photo)

Royal Guard, Coruscant Security, 2002, Red figure with staff and blue "energy bolts." Definitely the prototype for the Imperial Guard after the fall of the Republic

    MNP n/a   **MIP** $14

(KP Photo)

Saesee Tiin, Jedi Master, 2002, With lightsaber and force-repelled blast effect

    MNP n/a   **MIP** $8

(KP Photo)

Shaak Ti, Jedi Master, 2002, With "blast effect" lightsaber. Very well-detailed figure

    MNP n/a   **MIP** $12

(KP Photo, Karen O'Brien collection)

Snowtrooper, The Battle of Hoth, 2003, backpack, laser pistol, cannon w/missile
MNP $5   **MIP** $10

(KP Photo, Karen O'Brien collection)

SP-4 and JN-66, Research Droids, 2003, SP-4 has spiked head, JN-66 has flat head
MNP $3   **MIP** $7

(KP Photo)

Super Battle Droid, 2002, With laser blast battle damage and attachments
MNP n/a   **MIP** $6

(KP Photo, Karen O'Brien collection)

Supreme Chancellor Palpatine, 2002
MNP $3   **MIP** $7

Tanus Spijek, Jabba's Sail Barge, 2004
MNP $3   **MIP** $7

(KP Photo)

Taun We, Kamino Cloner, 2002, With cloning pod
MNP n/a   **MIP** $14

Teebo, Ewok, 2002, w/horn
MNP $3   **MIP** $7

Teemto Pagalies, Pod Racer, 2002, arms in the air, w/droid and engine part
MNP $3   **MIP** $7

TIE Fighter Pilot, Battle of Yavin, 2004
MNP $3   **MIP** $7

Tusken Raider w/Massiff, 2002
MNP $3   **MIP** $7

Tusken Raider, Female w/Tusken Child, 2002, Child figure can be freestanding or fit in pack
MNP n/a   **MIP** $11

Tusken Raider, Tatooine Camp Ambush, 2003, gaffi stick, platform
MNP $3   **MIP** $7

WA-7, Dexter's Diner, 2003, waitress w/ platform and tray
MNP $3   **MIP** $7

Wat Tambor, Geonosis War Room, 2003, mechanical console
MNP $3   **MIP** $7

Watto, Mos Espa Junk Dealer, 2002, wearing hat
MNP $3   **MIP** $7

Yoda & Chian, 2003, 2-pack, hoverchair, cane, green lightsaber for Yoda and helmet, blue lightsaber for Chian
MNP $3   **MIP** $7

(KP Photo, Karen O'Brien collection)

Yoda, Battle of Geonosis, 2004, Hall of Fame assortment
MNP $3   **MIP** $6

Yoda, Jedi High Council, 2002, w/elevated chair
MNP $5   **MIP** $12

Yoda, Jedi Master, 2002, Includes lightsaber, walking stick, and base
MNP $5   **MIP** $17

(KP Photo)

Zam Wessell, Bounty Hunter, 2002, Shorter blaster than preview edition, removable changeling face
MNP $5   **MIP** $11

Anakin Skywalker w/Lightsaber Slashing Action, 2002, Includes two lightsabers and an easily-sliced Geonosian warrior
MNP $5   **MIP** $19

Anakin Skywalker, Flipping, 2002, Force Flipping action, lands on his feet
MNP $5   **MIP** $10

C-3PO and Battle Droid, 2002, interchangable heads
MNP $5   **MIP** $10

Clone Trooper w/Speeder Bike, 2002, blaster, grenade, removable armor and helmet

    MNP $7 **MIP** $14

Darth Tyranus w/Force Flipping Attack, 2002, Like the Obi-Wan version, pushing a button on the launch pad makes Tyranus leap, flip and land on his feet

    MNP $5 **MIP** $11

Geonosian Warrior, 2002, w/ insect pod and energy weapon

    MNP $5 **MIP** $10

Jango Fett, Kamino Showdown, 2003, 2 pistols, jet pack w/ missile, column w/ flipping base

    MNP $5 **MIP** $10

(KP Photo)

Jango Fett, w/Electronic Attack and Snap-On Armor, 2002, Another incredibly detailed Jango figure

    MNP $5 **MIP** $11

(KP Photo)

Mace Windu w/Blast-Apart Battle Droid, 2002, Battle droid breaks apart as Mace stikes with saber

    MNP $5 **MIP** $11

Nexu w/Snapping Jaw and Attack Roar, 2002, Well detailed with snapping jaw and roaring sound

    MNP $5 **MIP** $19

(KP Photo)

Obi-Wan Kenobi w/Force Flipping Attack, 2002, Includes platform and launcher that makes Obi-Wan figure flip over and then land on his feet (after a few tries, usually). A neat idea that easily lends itself to "I betcha can't make him land this time" games

    MNP $5 **MIP** $9

Obi-Wan, Kamino Showdown, 2003, flowing robes, blue lightsaber, terrace pieces

    MNP $5 **MIP** $10

Spider Droid, 2003, creepy

    MNP $5 **MIP** $10

Super Battle Droid Builder, 2003, factory to "finish" the SBD

    MNP $5 **MIP** $10

Yoda and Super Battle Droid, 2002, w/Force powers

    MNP $5 **MIP** $10

Battle of Hoth, 2003, Chewbacca, Princess Leia, Luke Skywalker, R3-A2, Taun Taun, TRU exclusive

    MNP $7 **MIP** $15

Imperial Forces, 2003, AT-ST Driver, Darth Vader, R4-19, Stormtrooper, accessories, TRU exclusive

    MNP $7 **MIP** $15

Ultimate Bounty, 2003, Aurra Sing, Boba Fett, Bossk, IG-88, Swoop Bike, TRU exclusive

    MNP $7 **MIP** $15

Geonosian War Room No. 1, 2003, Poggle the Lesser, Count Dooku, San Hill

    MNP $7 **MIP** $15

Geonosian War Room No. 2, 2003, Nute Gunray, Passel Argente, Shu Mai

    MNP $7 **MIP** $15

Jedi High Council No. 1, 2003, Mace Windu, Oppo Rancisis, Even Piell

    MNP $7 **MIP** $15

Jedi High Council No. 2, 2003, Yarael Poof, Depa Billaba, Yaddle

    MNP $7 **MIP** $15

Trash Compactor No. 1, 2003, Han and Luke

    MNP $7 **MIP** $15

Trash Compactor No. 2, 2003, Leia and Chewbacca

    MNP $7 **MIP** $15

(KP Photo)

Clone Trooper, 2002, With laser rifle and blue "blast" attachment. This model shows painted-on battlefield "dirt" detail

    MNP n/a **MIP** $11

Jango Fett, 2002

    MNP n/a **MIP** $14

R3-T7, 2002, Detailed astromech droid with blue engergy bolts that wrap around body

    MNP n/a **MIP** $11

(KP Photo)

Zam Wessell, 2002, With long gun, human face partially covered by scarf

    MNP n/a **MIP** $11

CLONE WARS

(KP Photo, Karen O'Brien collection)

Anakin Skywalker, Army of the Republic, 2003, 2 armor pieces, headgear, belt, blue lightsaber

    MNP $3 **MIP** $7

STAR WARS

(KP Photo, Karen O'Brien collection)

ARC Trooper, Army of the Republic, 2003, laser rifle

> **MNP** $3   **MIP** $7

(KP Photo, Karen O'Brien collection)

Asajj Ventress, Sith Apprentice, 2003, 2 curved-handled red lightsabers, flowing black robes

> **MNP** $3   **MIP** $7

Clone Trooper Army (White), 2003, Kneeling Trooper, Prone Trooper, Standing Trooper

> **MNP** $9   **MIP** $15

Clone Trooper Army w/Clone Captain (Red), 2003, Prone Clone Captain (Red), Standing Clone Trooper (White), Kneeling Clone Trooper (White)

> **MNP** $9   **MIP** $15

Clone Trooper Army w/Clone Commander, 2003, Standing Clone Trooper w/Binoculars (Yellow), Standing Clone Trooper (White), Kneeling Clone Trooper (White)

> **MNP** $9   **MIP** $15

Clone Trooper Army w/Clone Lieutenant (Blue), 2003, Kneeling Trooper, Prone Trooper, Standing Lieutenant (Blue)

> **MNP** $9   **MIP** $15

Clone Trooper Army w/Clone Sergeant (Green), 2003, Standing Clone Trooper (White), Kneeling Clone Sergeant (Green), Standing Clone Trooper w/Binoculars (White)

> **MNP** $9   **MIP** $15

Clone Trooper w/ Speeder Bike, 2003

> **MNP** $5   **MIP** $10

Destroyer Droid w/Battle Launcher, 2003

> **MNP** $7   **MIP** $10

Droid Army, 2003, Battle Droid, Super Battle Droid, Destroyer Droid

> **MNP** $9   **MIP** $15

Durge w/Swoop Bike, 2003

> **MNP** $7   **MIP** $10

Durge, Commander of the Separatist Forces, 2003, laser rifle, pistol, rocket backpack, mace

> **MNP** $3   **MIP** $7

Jedi Knight Army, 2003, Human Jedi, Rodian Jedi, Twi'lek Jedi

> **MNP** $9   **MIP** $15

(KP Photo, Karen O'Brien collection)

Mace Windu, General of the Republic Army, 2003, 2 armor pieces, purple lightsaber

> **MNP** $3   **MIP** $7

Obi-Wan Kenobi, General of the Republic Army, 2003, belt, backpack, blue lightsaber

> **MNP** $3   **MIP** $7

(KP Photo, Karen O'Brien collection)

Yoda w/Hoverchair, 2003, green lightsaber

> **MNP** $3   **MIP** $7

ACTION FIGURES, 12"

STAR WARS

(ToyShop File Photo)

Boba Fett, 1979, Star Wars Box

> **MNP** $135   **MIP** $350

(ToyShop File Photo)

C-3PO, 1979

> **MNP** $30   **MIP** $130

Chewbacca, 1979

> **MNP** $50   **MIP** $185

COLLECTOR'S SERIES

Admiral Ackbar, 1997
    MNP $15   MIP $40

AT-AT Driver, 1998
    MNP $15   MIP $18

Barquin D'an, 1998
    MNP $7   MIP $15

Boba Fett, 1997
    MNP $15   MIP $75

C-3PO, 1997
    MNP $15   MIP $35

Cantina Band Aliens, six members, six different members
    MNP $15   MIP $35

Chewbacca, 1997
    MNP $15   MIP $85

Chewbacca (Chained), 1998
    MNP $15   MIP $35

Darth Vader, 1996
    MNP $15   MIP $30

Emperor Palpatine, 1998
    MNP $7   MIP $12

Grand Moff Tarkin and Imperial Gunner,
    MNP $45   MIP $80

Grand Moff Tarkin w/Interrogation Droid, 1998
    MNP $15   MIP $22

Greedo, 1998
    MNP $15   MIP $22

Han and Luke in Stormtrooper Disguise,
    MNP $30   MIP $55

Han in Carbonite, 1998
    MNP $10   MIP $15

Han in Hoth Gear, 1998
    MNP $10   MIP $15

Han in Hoth Gear w/Tauntaun,
    MNP $25   MIP $50

Han Solo, 1996
    MNP $15   MIP $35

Jawa, 1998
    MNP $15   MIP $12

Lando Calrissian, 1997
    MNP $5   MIP $12

Leia as Jabba's Prisoner and R2-D2,
    MNP $25   MIP $43

Leia in Hoth Gear, 1999
    MNP $15   MIP $22

Luke as Jedi Knight, 1998
    MNP $5   MIP $12

Luke as Jedi Knight and Bib Fortuna,
    MNP $30   MIP $60

(ToyShop File Photo)

Darth Vader, 1978
    MNP $50   MIP $185

Han Solo, 1979
    MNP $110   MIP $280

(ToyShop File Photo)

Jawa, 1979
    MNP $55   MIP $135

(ToyShop File Photo)

Luke Skywalker, 1979
    MNP $70   MIP $220

(ToyShop File Photo)

Obi-Wan Kenobi, 1979
    MNP $75   MIP $270

Princess Leia Organa, 1979
    MNP $85   MIP $220

R2-D2, 1979
    MNP $45   MIP $110

(ToyShop File Photo)

Stormtrooper, 1979
    MNP $50   MIP $160

EMPIRE STRIKES BACK

Boba Fett, 1979, Empire Strikes Back Box
    MNP $130   MIP $875

(ToyShop File Photo)

IG-88, 1980, Empire Strikes Back Box
    MNP $160   MIP $490

STAR WARS

(KP Photo)

Luke as X-Wing Pilot, 1997
  MNP $15 MIP $35

Luke in Bespin Outfit, 1997
  MNP $11 MIP $25

Luke in Ceremonial Garb, 1998
  MNP $15 MIP $15

Luke in Hoth Gear, 1998
  MNP $8 MIP $15

Luke in Hoth Gear w/Wampa,
  MNP $30 MIP $80

Luke Skywalker, 1996
  MNP $8 MIP $22

Luke w/Poncho (Tatooine), Han w/Flight Jacket, Leia in Boushh Disguise,
  MNP $20 MIP $50

Obi-Wan Kenobi, 1996
  MNP $10 MIP $50

Princess Leia, 1997
  MNP $10 MIP $45

Princess Leia in Ceremonial Gown, 1999
  MNP $10 MIP $25

R2-D2, 1998
  MNP $15 MIP $12

R2-D2 (Wal-Mart Exclusive), 1998
  MNP $10 MIP $15

R5-D4, 1998
  MNP $10 MIP $15

Sandtrooper, 1998
  MNP $15 MIP $15

Snowtrooper, 1998
  MNP $12 MIP $25

Stormtrooper, 1997
  MNP $10 MIP $40

TIE Fighter Pilot, 1997
  MNP $10 MIP $35

Tusken Raider, 1997
  MNP $10 MIP $35

Wedge Antilles and Biggs Darklighter,
  MNP $30 MIP $70

Wicket, 1998
  MNP $10 MIP $15

Yoda, 1998
  MNP $15 MIP $20

POWER OF THE JEDI

Luke Skywalker, 100th figure, 2001
  MNP n/a MIP $15

THE PHANTOM MENACE

Anakin Skywalker, 1999
  MNP $5 MIP $15

Anakin Skywalker, w/Theed Hangar Droid, 2000
  MNP $5 MIP $15

Aurra Sing, 2000
  MNP $5 MIP $15

Battle Droid, 1999
  MNP $5 MIP $20

Battle Droid Commander w/electrobinoculars, 1999
  MNP $5 MIP $15

Boss Nass, 2000
  MNP $5 MIP $15

(KP Photo)

Darth Maul, 1999
  MNP $5 MIP $35

(KP Photo)

Jar Jar Binks, 1999
  MNP $5 MIP $25

Mace Windu w/lightsaber, 1999
  MNP $5 MIP $15

Obi-Wan Kenobi, 1999
  MNP $5 MIP $25

Padme, Beautiful Braids, 2000
  MNP $5 MIP $15

Pit Droid, 1999
  MNP $5 MIP $15

(KP Photo)

Queen Amidala, Black Travel Dress, 1999
  MNP $5 MIP $20

(KP Photo)

Queen Amidala, Hidden Majesty, 1999
  MNP $5 MIP $10

Queen Amidala, Red Senate Gown, 1999
  MNP $5 MIP $20

Queen Amidala, Return to Naboo, 2000
  MNP $5 MIP $25

Queen Amidala, Royal Elegance, 1999
  MNP $5 MIP $10

Queen Amidala, Ultimate Hair, 1999
  MNP $5 MIP $10

Qui-Gon Jimm w/Tatooine Poncho, 1999
  MNP $5 MIP $15

(KP Photo)

Qui-Gon Jinn, 1999
MNP $5   MIP $30

Qui-Gon Jinn and Queen Amidala,
Entertainment Earth exclusive, 2000,
Entertainment Earth exclusive
MNP $5   MIP $100

R2-A6, 1999
MNP $5   MIP $15

R2-D2, 1998, Wal-Mart exclusive
MNP $5   MIP $15

Sebulba, with Chubas, 2000
MNP $10   MIP $35

TC-14 Protocol Droid, electronic, 1999,
KayBee exclusive
MNP $5   MIP $15

Watto, 1999
MNP $5   MIP $15

SAGA

(KP Photo)

Anakin Skywalker, 2002, In black robe,
includes lightsaber
MNP n/a   MIP $25

Anakin Skywalker, Removable Arm, 2003,
w/two lightsabers and robotic arm
MNP $10   MIP $20

AT-ST Driver, 2002
MNP $10   MIP $20

Ben Kenobi, A New Hope, 2003
MNP $10   MIP $20

Biker Scout, Battle of Endor, 2003
MNP $10   MIP $20

Clone Commander, Yellow, 2002, KB
Toys exclusive
MNP $12   MIP $25

Clone Trooper, 2002, Includes blaster rifle
MNP n/a   MIP $25

Clone Trooper, Red, 2002, KB Toys exclusive
MNP $12   MIP $25

Count Dooku, 2002
MNP $10   MIP $20

Dengar, 2003
MNP $10   MIP $20

Electronic Jango Fett, 2002
MNP $10   MIP $20

Electronic Obi-Wan Kenobi, 2002
MNP $10   MIP $20

(KP Photo, Karen O'Brien collection)

Gammorean Guard, 2003, KB Toys exclusive
MNP $15   MIP $30

Garindan, Long Snoot, 2003
MNP $15   MIP $35

Geonosian Warrior, 2002
MNP $10   MIP $20

Han Solo, 2003
MNP $10   MIP $20

Imperial Officer, 2003
MNP $10   MIP $20

Jango Fett, 2002, deluxe set with extra
accessories
MNP $15   MIP $30

Jawas, 2003, 2-pack
MNP $10   MIP $20

Ki-Adi-Mundi, 2002, Star Wars Fan Club
exclusive
MNP $15   MIP $30

Lando Calrissian, Skiff Guard, 2003
MNP $10   MIP $20

Leia as Boosh w/Han Solo in Carbonite,
2003, TRU exclusive
MNP $20   MIP $40

Logray & Paploo, Battle of Endor, 2003
MNP $10   MIP $20

Luke Skywalker w/Taun Taun, 2002, Hoth
scene, large scale, TRU exclusive
MNP $30   MIP $60

(KP Photo, Karen O'Brien collection)

Luke Skywalker, Jedi Knight, 2003,
w/handcuffs and green lightsaber
MNP $10   MIP $20

Mace Windu, Jedi Master, 2002, In light tan
cloak, includes lightsaber, TRU exclusive
MNP n/a   MIP $30

Max Rebo w/Organ, 2003, Wal-Mart
exclusive to be released
MNP $10   MIP $20

(KP Photo)

Obi-Wan Kenobi, 2002, Includes lightsaber
MNP n/a   MIP $25

(KP Photo, Karen O'Brien collection)

Padme Amidala, 2002
MNP $10   MIP $20

STAR WARS

Plo Koon, 2003, Star Wars Fan Club exclusive
  MNP $15   MIP $30

Super Battle Droid, 2002
  MNP $10   MIP $20

Sy Snoodles and Droopy McCool, 2003,
  Wal-Mart exclusive to be released
  MNP $10   MIP $20

Yoda, Jedi Master, 2003, w/hoverchair,
  green lightsaber, belt
  MNP $15   MIP $25

Zam Wessell, 2002
  MNP $10   MIP $20

(KP Photo, Karen O'Brien collection)

Zuckuss, 2003
  MNP $10   MIP $20

ACTION FIGURES, 6"

UNLEASHED

Aayla Secura, 2004
  MNP $10   MIP $16

Anakin Skywalker, 2002
  MNP $8   MIP $15

Boba Fett, 2003
  MNP $8   MIP $15

Bossk, 2004
  MNP $10   MIP $16

Chewbacca, 2004
  MNP $10   MIP $16

Clone Trooper, 2004, color variations exist
  MNP $10   MIP $16

(KP Photo, Brian Brogaard collection)

Darth Maul, 2002
  MNP $8   MIP $15

Darth Sidious w/Sith Lightning, 2003
  MNP $8   MIP $15

Darth Tyranus, 2002
  MNP $8   MIP $15

Darth Vader, with mask, 2002
  MNP $10   MIP $20

Darth Vader, with/out mask, 2003
  MNP $15   MIP $25

(KP Photo, Karen O'Brien collection)

Han Solo, 2003, running up ramp
  MNP $8   MIP $15

Jango and Boba Fett, 2002
  MNP $8   MIP $15

Luke Skywalker, 2003, RotJ outfit
  MNP $8   MIP $15

Luke Skywalker, 2004, X-Wing Pilot
  MNP $10   MIP $16

(KP Photo, Karen O'Brien collection)

Mace Windu, 2002
  MNP $8   MIP $15

Obi-Wan Kenobi, 2003
  MNP $8   MIP $15

Padme Amidala, 2002
  MNP $8   MIP $15

Princess Leia, 2003
  MNP $8   MIP $15

Tusken Raider, 2004
  MNP $10   MIP $16

(KP Photo, Brian Brogaard collection)

Yoda, 2003
  MNP $8   MIP $15

CARRYING CASES

EMPIRE STRIKES BACK

(KP Photo)

Darth Vader, 1982
  MNP $10   MIP $30

(KP Photo)

Mini Figure, 1980
  MNP $11   MIP $27

RETURN OF THE JEDI

(ToyShop File Photo)

C-3PO, 1983
	MNP $12	MIP $29	

Darth Vader (w/three figs.), 1983, w/three figures
	MNP $11	MIP $225	

Laser Rifle, 1984
	MNP $9	MIP $33	

STAR WARS

24-Figure, 1978
	MNP $14	MIP $27	

COINS

2-1B, 1985
MNP $105 MIP n/a

63rd Coin, lightsaber, 1985
MNP $1200 MIP n/a

Amanaman, 1985
MNP $4 MIP n/a

Anakin Skywalker, 1985
MNP $70 MIP n/a

AT-AT, 1985
MNP $55 MIP n/a

AT-ST Driver, 1985
MNP $9 MIP n/a

A-Wing Pilot, 1985
MNP $4 MIP n/a

Barada, 1985
MNP $4 MIP n/a

Bib Fortuna, 1985
MNP $105 MIP n/a

Biker Scout, 1985
MNP $9 MIP n/a

Boba Fett, 1985
MNP $225 MIP n/a

B-Wing Pilot, 1985
MNP $9 MIP n/a

C-3PO, 1985
MNP $9 MIP n/a

Chewbacca, 1985
MNP $9 MIP n/a

Chief Chirpa, 1985
MNP $35 MIP n/a

Creatures, 1985
MNP $55 MIP n/a

Darth Vader, 1985
MNP $18 MIP n/a

Droids, 1985
MNP $50 MIP n/a

Emperor, 1985
MNP $12 MIP n/a

Emperor's Royal Guard, 1985
MNP $50 MIP n/a

EV-9D9, 1985
MNP $4 MIP n/a

FX-7, 1985
MNP $165 MIP n/a

Gamorrean Guard, 1985
MNP $20 MIP n/a

Greedo, 1985
MNP $175 MIP n/a

Han Hoth, 1985
MNP $75 MIP n/a

Han in Carbonite, 1985
MNP $4 MIP n/a

Han Original, 1985
MNP $145 MIP n/a

Han Rebel (trenchcoat), 1985
MNP $9 MIP n/a

Hoth Stormtrooper, 1985
MNP $225 MIP n/a

Imperial Commander, 1985
MNP $65 MIP n/a

Imperial Dignitary, 1985
MNP $4 MIP n/a

Imperial Gunner, 1985
MNP $4 MIP n/a

Jawas, 1985
MNP $9 MIP n/a

Lando General, 1985
MNP $4 MIP n/a

Lando with Cloud City, 1985
MNP $70 MIP n/a

Logray, 1985
MNP $35 MIP n/a

Luke Jedi, 1985
MNP $16 MIP n/a

Luke on Dagobah, 1985
MNP $120 MIP n/a

Luke original, 1985
MNP $75 MIP n/a

Luke Poncho, 1985
MNP $4 MIP n/a

Luke Stormtrooper, 1985
MNP $4 MIP n/a

Luke with Taun Taun, 1985
MNP $75 MIP n/a

Luke X-Wing, 1985
MNP $5 MIP n/a

Luke X-Wing, small, 1985
MNP $45 MIP n/a

Lumat, 1985
MNP $9 MIP n/a

Millennium Falcon, 1985
MNP $65 MIP n/a

Millennium Falcon, 1994
MNP $5 MIP n/a

Obi-Wan Kenobi, 1985
MNP $16 MIP n/a

Paploo, 1985
MNP $9 MIP n/a

Princess Leia Rebel Leader (poncho), 1985
MNP $9 MIP n/a

Princess Leia, Boushh, 1985
MNP $145 MIP n/a

Princess Leia, Original, 1985
MNP $85 MIP n/a

R2-D2 Pop-Up Lightsaber, 1985
MNP $4 MIP n/a

Romba, 1985
MNP $4 MIP n/a

Sail Skiff, 1985
MNP $250 MIP n/a

Star Destroyer Commander, 1985
MNP $60 MIP n/a

Stormtrooper, 1985
MNP $16 MIP n/a

Teebo, 1985
MNP $18 MIP n/a

TIE Fighter, 1994
MNP $5 MIP n/a

TIE Fighter Pilot, 1985
MNP $50 MIP n/a

Tusken Raider, 1985
MNP $145 MIP n/a

Warok, 1985
MNP $4 MIP n/a

Wicket, 1985
MNP $9 MIP n/a

X-Wing, 1994
MNP $5 MIP n/a

Yak Face, 1985
MNP $85 MIP n/a

Yoda, 1985
MNP $16 MIP n/a

Zuckuss, 1985
MNP $145 MIP n/a

CREATURES

STAR WARS

(ToyShop File Photo)

Patrol Dewback, 1978
	MNP $20	MIP $85	

STAR WARS

EMPIRE STRIKES BACK

Hoth Wampa, 1980
MNP $17   MIP $37

(KP Photo)

Tauntaun, solid belly, 1980
MNP $15   MIP $40

Tauntaun, split belly, 1980
MNP $15   MIP $45

RETURN OF THE JEDI

(ToyShop File Photo)

Rancor, 1983
MNP $30   MIP $85

THE PHANTOM MENACE

(KP Photo)

Kaadu w/Jar Jar Binks, 1999
MNP $2   MIP $5

SAGA

Acklay, Arena Battle Beast, 2002
MNP $10   MIP $20

Reek, Arena Battle Beast, 2002
MNP $10   MIP $20

Reek, Arena Battle Beast w/Attack Sounds, 2002
MNP $4   MIP $18

LEGO SETS

ATTACK OF THE CLONES

Bounty Hunter Pursuit w/Obi-Wan Kenobi, Anakin Skywalker, Zam Wessell, 7133
MNP n/a   MIP $25

Jango Fett, 8011
MNP n/a   MIP $30

Jango Fett's Slave I w/Jango Fett, Boba Fett, 7153
MNP n/a   MIP $40

(KP Photo)

Jedi Duel w/Yoda, Count Dooku, 7103
MNP n/a   MIP $10

Jedi Starfighter w/Obi-Wan Kenobi, R4-P17, 7143
MNP n/a   MIP $15

Republic Gunship w/Jedi Clone Troopers, Battle Droids, Destroyer Droids, 7163
MNP n/a   MIP $75

Super Battle Droid, 8012
MNP n/a   MIP $30

Tusken Raider Encounter w/Anakin Skywalker, two Tusken Raiders, 7113
MNP n/a   MIP $10

EMPIRE STRIKES BACK

Boba Fett's Slave I, 7144
MNP n/a   MIP $20

Luke Skywalker, Han Solo, Boba Fett, 3341
MNP n/a   MIP $5

Twin-Pod Cloud Car w/Lobot, 7119
MNP n/a   MIP $10

Yoda, 7194
MNP n/a   MIP $100

RETURN OF THE JEDI

B-Wing at Rebel Control Center w/pilot, droid, mechanic, 7180
MNP n/a   MIP $30

Chewbacca, two Biker Scouts, 3342
MNP n/a   MIP $5

Desert Skiff w/Luke Skywalker, Han Solo, 7104
MNP n/a   MIP $6

Ewok Attack w/Biker Scout, Stormtrooper, two Ewoks, 7139
MNP n/a   MIP $13

Final Duel I w/Emperor, Darth Vader, 7200
MNP n/a   MIP $10

Final Duel II w/Luke Skywalker, Imperial Officer, Stormtrooper, 7201
MNP n/a   MIP $7

Imperial AT-ST w/Chewbacca, 7127
MNP n/a   MIP $10

Imperial Shuttle w/Emperor, Pilot, two Royal Guards, 7166
MNP n/a   MIP $35

STAR WARS

C-3PO, 8007
MNP n/a   MIP $35

Dark Side Developer, 9754
MNP n/a   MIP $100

Darth Vader, 8010
MNP n/a   MIP $40

Droid Escape w/R2-D2, C-3PO, 7106
MNP n/a   MIP $7

Emperor Palpatine, Darth Maul, Darth Vader, 3340
MNP n/a   MIP $5

(KP Photo)

Landspeeder w/Luke Skywalker, Obi-Wan Kenobi, 1999, 7110
MNP n/a   MIP $6

Millennium Falcon w/Han Solo, Leia, Luke, Chewbacca, R2-D2, C-3PO, 7190
MNP n/a   MIP $100

R2-D2, 8009
MNP n/a   MIP $20

Rebel Blockade Runner - Tantive IV Corellian Corvette, 10019
MNP n/a   MIP $150

Stormtrooper, 8008
MNP n/a   MIP $35

TIE Figher w/Pilot, Stormtrooper, 7146
MNP n/a   MIP $20

TIE Interceptor, 7181
MNP n/a   MIP $20

(LEGO Photo)

X-Wing Fighter, 7140
MNP n/a   MIP $45

THE PHANTOM MENACE

Battle Droid, 8001
MNP n/a   MIP $25

Command Officer, two Battle Droids, 3343
MNP $2   MIP $5

Darth Maul (bust), 10018
MNP n/a   MIP $125

Destroyer Droid, 8002
MNP n/a   MIP $45

Droid Fighter, 7111
MNP n/a   MIP $6

Flash Speeder w/Royal Naboo Security Force, 7121
MNP n/a   MIP $10

Gungan Patrol w/Jar Jar Binks, Gungan Warrior, 7115
MNP n/a   MIP $10

Gungan Sub w/Qui-Gon Jinn, Obi-Wan Kenobi, Jar Jar Binks, 1999, 7161
MNP n/a   MIP $45

Jedi Defense I w/Obi-Wan Kenobi, two Destroyer Droids, 7203
MNP n/a   MIP $7

Jedi Defense II w/Qui-Gon Jinn, two Battle Droids, 7204
MNP n/a   MIP $7

(KP Photo)

Lightsaber Duel w/Qui-Gon Jinn, Darth Maul, 1999, 7101
MNP n/a   MIP $5

Mos Espa Podrace w/Padme, Anakin, R2-D2, Qui-Gon, Jar Jar, Sebulba, Gasgano, 7171
MNP n/a   MIP $85

(KP Photo)

Naboo Fighter w/Anakin Skywalker, two Battle Droids, 1999, 7141
MNP n/a   MIP $25

(KP Photo)

Naboo Swamp w/Qui-Gon Jinn, Jar Jar Binks, two Battle Droids, 1999, 7121
MNP n/a   MIP $10

Pit Droid, 8000
MNP n/a   MIP $20

Podracer, 1999, 7131
MNP n/a   MIP $20

Sith Infiltrator w/Darth Maul, 7151
MNP n/a   MIP $30

Trade Federation MTT, 7184
MNP n/a   MIP $45

MICRO COLLECTION

Bespin Control Room, 1982
MNP $7   MIP $17

Bespin Freeze Chamber, 1982
MNP $12   MIP $44

Bespin Gantry, 1982
MNP $9   MIP $25

Bespin World, 1982
MNP $32   MIP $90

Death Star Compactor, 1982
MNP $27   MIP $50

Death Star Escape, 1982
MNP $25   MIP $42

Death Star World, 1982
MNP $48   MIP $100

Hoth Generator Attack, 1982
MNP $15   MIP $30

(ToyShop File Photo)

Hoth Ion Cannon, 1982
MNP $17   MIP $50

Hoth Turret Defense, 1982
MNP $19   MIP $32

Hoth Wampa Cave, 1982
MNP $12   MIP $23

(ToyShop File Photo)

Hoth World, 1982
MNP $30   MIP $105

Imperial TIE Fighter, 1982
MNP $20   MIP $47

(ToyShop File Photo)

Millennium Falcon, 1982
MNP $80   MIP $230

(ToyShop File Photo)

Snowspeeder, 1982
MNP $48   MIP $95

(ToyShop File Photo)

X-Wing Fighter, 1982
MNP $21   MIP $43

THE PHANTOM MENACE

(KP Photo)

Anakin Skywalker & Ratts Tyerell, 1999
MNP $3   MIP $8

Anakin Skywalker's Podracer w/figure, 1999
MNP $2   MIP $6

Arch Canyon Adventure, 1999
MNP $2   MIP $6

Battle Droid/Trade Federation Droid Control Ship, 1999
MNP $2   MIP $6

Beggar's Canyon Challenge, 1999
MNP $2   MIP $6

Boles Roor & Neva Kee, 1999
MNP $3   MIP $8

Boonta Eve Challenge Deluxe Podracing Track Set, 1999
MNP $2   MIP $6

Build Your Own Podracer Pack I, 1999
MNP $5   MIP $8

Destroyer Droid Ambush, 1999
MNP $3   MIP $8

Dud Bolt & Mars Guo, 1999
MNP $3   MIP $8

Fambaa, 1999
MNP $4   MIP $18

Flash Speeder w/figure, 1999
MNP $2   MIP $6

Galactic Dogfight, 1999
MNP $2   MIP $5

Galactic Senate, 1999
MNP $2   MIP $5

Generator Core Duel, 1999
MNP $3   MIP $8

(KP Photo)

Gian Speeder, 1999, A nicely detailed, heavy model with pivoting cannon and slide-open canopy
MNP $3   MIP $8

Gian Speeder & Theed Palace Sneak Preview Set, 1999
MNP $2   MIP $6

Gungan Sub (Bonto)/Otoh Gunga, 1999
MNP $3   MIP $8

Gungan Sub w/figure, 1999
MNP $2   MIP $6

(KP Photo)

Jar Jar Binks/Naboo, 1999
MNP $3   MIP $8

Mars Guo's Podracer w/figure, 1999
MNP $2   MIP $6

Naboo Fighter w/figure, 1999
MNP $2   MIP $6

Naboo Temple Ruins, 1999
MNP $2   MIP $5

Podrace Arena, 1999
MNP $2   MIP $5

Podracer Launchers, 1999
MNP $2   MIP $6

Republic Cruiser, 1999
MNP $3   MIP $8

Republic Cruiser w/figure, 1999
MNP $2   MIP $6

Royal Starship, 1999
MNP $3   MIP $8

Royal Starship Repair Deluxe Platform Action Set, 1999
MNP $2   MIP $5

Sebulba & Clegg Holdfast, 1999
MNP $3   MIP $8

Sebulba's Podracer, 1999
MNP $3   MIP $8

Sebulba's Podracer w/figure, 1999
MNP $2   MIP $6

Sith Infiltrator, 1999
MNP $3   MIP $8

Tatooine Desert, 1999
MNP $3   MIP $6

Theed Palace Assault, 1999
MNP $4   MIP $18

Theed Rapids, 1999
MNP $2   MIP $5

Trade Federation Battleship, 1999
MNP $3   MIP $8

Trade Federation Droid Fighter, 1999, The wings of this model slide open into "firing" mode
MNP $3   MIP $8

Trade Federation Droid Fighter w/figure, 1999
MNP $2   MIP $6

Trade Federation Landing Ship w/figure, 1999
MNP $2   MIP $6

Trade Federation MTT w/figure, 1999
MNP $2   MIP $6

Trade Federation MTT/Naboo Battlefield Mega Deluxe Action Set, 1999
MNP $3   MIP $8

Trade Federation Tank, 1999
MNP $4   MIP $18

Trade Federation Tank, 1999
MNP $3   MIP $8

Turbo Blast Podracers, 1999
MNP $2   MIP $6

MINI RIGS

AST-5, 1983
MNP $6   MIP $18

CAP-2 Captivator, 1982, Bubble-topped vehicle with room for one figure. Roller wheels on bottom with tank tread façade and two laser moveable laser cannon in front
MNP $6   MIP $21

Desert Sail Skiff, 1984
MNP $9   MIP $19

Endor Forest Ranger, 1984
MNP $12   MIP $26

INT-4 Interceptor, 1982
MNP $7   MIP $24

ISP-6 Imperial Shuttle Pod, 1983
MNP $10   MIP $21

MLC-3 Mobile Laser Cannon, 1981
MNP $8   MIP $22

(KP Photo)

MTV-7 Multi-Terrain Vehicle, 1981, Off-white with room for one 3-3/4" figure (most likely a snowtrooper, if the box is a guide). Features two spring-loaded roller wheels and a pivoting front blaster. The Mini Rigs were, in a way, the first "expanded universe" toys for Star Wars
MNP $9   MIP $25

PDT-8 Personal Deployment Transport, 1981
MNP $10   MIP $23

Radar Laser Cannon, 1982
MNP $7   MIP $24

Tri-Pod Laser Cannon, 1982, Cannon with "ammo box" and three folding legs
MNP $6   MIP $18

Vehicle Maintenance Energizer, 1982, Generator for vehicles
MNP $8 **MIP** $18

PLAY SETS

EMPIRE STRIKES BACK

(ToyShop File Photo)

Cloud City Play Set, Sears Exclusive, 1981
MNP $95 **MIP** $250

(ToyShop File Photo)

Dagobah, 1982
MNP $22 **MIP** $80

(ToyShop File Photo)

Darth Vader's Star Destroyer,
MNP $32 **MIP** $115

(ToyShop File Photo)

Hoth Ice Planet, 1980
MNP $25 **MIP** $80

(ToyShop File Photo)

Imperial Attack Base, 1980
MNP $20 **MIP** $60

(ToyShop File Photo)

Rebel Command Center, 1980
MNP $45 **MIP** $105

Turret and Probot, 1980
MNP $22 **MIP** $100

EWOKS

Ewoks Treehouse, 1985
MNP $18 **MIP** $50

RETURN OF THE JEDI

(ToyShop File Photo)

Ewok Village, 1983
MNP $38 **MIP** $80

(ToyShop File Photo)

Jabba the Hutt, 1983
MNP $17 **MIP** $60

(ToyShop File Photo)

Jabba the Hutt Dungeon, w/EV-9D9, Amanaman, Barada, 1983
MNP $175 **MIP** $250

Jabba the Hutt Dungeon, w/Nikto, 8D8, Klaatu, 1983
MNP $30 **MIP** $60

SAGA

Geonosian Arena, 2002
MNP $17 **MIP** $45

STAR WARS

Cantina Adventure Set, Sears Exclusive, 1977
MNP $150 **MIP** $420

(ToyShop File Photo)

Creature Cantina, 1977
MNP $25 **MIP** $100

(ToyShop File Photo)

Death Star Space Station, 1977
MNP $75 **MIP** $320

(ToyShop File Photo)

Droid Factory, 1977

        MNP $50   MIP $135

(ToyShop File Photo)

Land of the Jawas, 1977

        MNP $41   MIP $85

VEHICLES

DIE-CAST

Darth Vader's TIE Fighter, 1979

        MNP $14   MIP $50

Land Speeder, 1979

        MNP $14   MIP $65

Millennium Falcon, 1979

        MNP $20   MIP $105

Naboo Starfighter, 1999

        MNP $4   MIP $10

(ToyShop File Photo)

Slave I, 1979

        MNP $25   MIP $75

Snowspeeder, 1979

        MNP $17   MIP $65

Star Destroyer, 1979

        MNP $25   MIP $110

TIE Bomber, 1979

        MNP $150   MIP $410

TIE Fighter, 1979

        MNP $12   MIP $45

(ToyShop File Photo)

Twin-Pod Cloud Car, 1979

        MNP $17   MIP $70

X-Wing Fighter, 1979

        MNP $15   MIP $70

Y-Wing Fighter, 1979

        MNP $22   MIP $90

EXPANDED UNIVERSE

(KP Photo)

Speeder Bike, 1998, Based on previous concept drawing for speeder bike. Includes figure unique to vehicle, like other Expanded Universe vehicles. Fires missile, and outriggers move to sides when in "battle mode"

        MNP $3   MIP $11

STAR WARS

(ToyShop File Photo)

Darth Vader's TIE Fighter, 1977, Fly-apart panels, battery-powered laser cannon lights up in front

        MNP $30   MIP $125

(KP Photo)

Imperial Cruiser, 1982, Second version of this vehicle. What was once the compartment for a 9-volt battery was now a "weapons storage bin." This vehicle had no battery-powered sounds, but did have opening doors, rotating turret and antenna and opening tailgate

        MNP $20   MIP $45

Imperial TIE Fighter, 1977, Fly-apart panels

        MNP $27   MIP $100

Imperial Trooper Transport, 1977, First version was a Sears Exclusive, with battery-powered laser sounds. Later model released with "Empire Strikes Back" didn't include sounds or require battery power

        MNP $20   MIP $65

(ToyShop File Photo)

Jawa Sandcrawler, battery-operated, 1977, battery-operated

        MNP $220   MIP $525

(ToyShop File Photo)

Land Speeder, 1977, Retractable hovering wheels, opening hood

        MNP $13   MIP $47

Land Speeder, battery-operated, 1977, battery-operated

        MNP $16   MIP $50

Millennium Falcon, 1977

        MNP $80   MIP $350

Sonic Land Speeder, JC Penney Exclusive, 1977

        MNP $95   MIP $400

X-Wing Fighter, 1977, Pushing R2 head into vehicle would put foils in "X-wing"

position. Opening canopy, light-up laser cannon on front
     MNP $17   **MIP** $80

EMPIRE STRIKES BACK

AT-AT, 1980, All-Terrain Armored Transport
     MNP $85   **MIP** $160

(ToyShop File Photo)

Rebel Transport, 1980
     MNP $35   **MIP** $80

(KP Photo)

Scout Walker, 1982, Two-legged vehicle with "walking" legs operated by button behind cockpit. A lever allowed the legs to remain locked so the vehicle could stand in place. Opening flip-up top to place figures, and opening turret allowing stormtroopers to fire weapons
     MNP $22   **MIP** $42

Slave I, 1980
     MNP $50   **MIP** $125

(ToyShop File Photo)

Snowspeeder, 1980
     MNP $45   **MIP** $100

Twin-Pod Cloud Car, 1980
     MNP $35   **MIP** $80

RETURN OF THE JEDI

B-Wing Fighter, 1984
     MNP $60   **MIP** $150

Ewok Combat Glider, 1984
     MNP $10   **MIP** $30

(ToyShop File Photo)

Imperial Shuttle, 1984
     MNP $150   **MIP** $500

Speeder Bike, 1983
     MNP $20   **MIP** $65

TIE Interceptor, 1984
     MNP $42   **MIP** $90

(ToyShop File Photo)

Y-Wing Fighter, 1983
     MNP $55   **MIP** $150

POTF

(ToyShop File Photo)

Ewok Battle Wagon, 1985
     MNP $75   **MIP** $190

Imperial Sniper Vehicle, 1985
     MNP $35   **MIP** $55

One-Man Sand Skimmer, 1985
     MNP $20   **MIP** $45

Security Scout Vehicle, 1985
     MNP $32   **MIP** $75

(ToyShop File Photo)

Tatooine Skiff, 1985
     MNP $190   **MIP** $440

DROIDS

ATL Interceptor, 1985
     MNP $25   **MIP** $65

(ToyShop File Photo)

A-Wing Fighter, 1983
     MNP $165   **MIP** $360

(ToyShop File Photo)

Inperial Side Gunner, 1985
     MNP $14   **MIP** $55

EWOKS

Ewoks Fire Cart, 1985
     MNP $6   **MIP** $17

Ewoks Woodland Wagon, 1985
     MNP $7   **MIP** $30

DIE-CAST

Darth Vader's TIE Fighter, 1979
     MNP $14   **MIP** $50

Land Speeder, 1979
     MNP $14   **MIP** $65

Millennium Falcon, 1979
     MNP $20   **MIP** $105

Naboo Starfighter, 1999
     MNP $4   **MIP** $10

STAR WARS

(ToyShop File Photo)

Slave I, 1979

| | MNP $25 | MIP $75 |

Snowspeeder, 1979

| | MNP $17 | MIP $65 |

Star Destroyer, 1979

| | MNP $25 | MIP $110 |

TIE Bomber, 1979

| | MNP $150 | MIP $410 |

TIE Fighter, 1979

| | MNP $12 | MIP $45 |

(ToyShop File Photo)

Twin-Pod Cloud Car, 1979

| | MNP $17 | MIP $70 |

X-Wing Fighter, 1979

| | MNP $15 | MIP $70 |

Y-Wing Fighter, 1979

| | MNP $22 | MIP $90 |

POTF2

Speeder Bike, 1997, Includes Scout Trooper figure. Bike pieces and trooper fall off when "battle damage" button is pushed on bike

| | MNP $10 | MIP $25 |

POTJ

(KP Photo)

TIE Interceptor, 2002, Includes figure, wings pop off simulating battle damage. A Toys R Us exclusive, these toys are now exclusively found in the secondary market, doubling the price collectors pay to get their hands on one

| | MNP $15 | MIP $30 |

THE PHANTOM MENACE

Ammo Wagon and Falumpaset, 1999

| | MNP $5 | MIP $25 |

Anakin Skywalker's Podracer, 1999

| | MNP $10 | MIP $20 |

Armored Scout Tank w/Battle Droid, 1999

| | MNP $5 | MIP $25 |

(KP Photo)

Flash Speeder, 1999, Hovercraft much in the style of other Star Wars speeders. Shown here with unloaded gun turret, this model actually fires a missle (a pretty fair distance, too)

| | MNP $5 | MIP $15 |

Gungan Assault Cannon w/Jar Jar Binks, 1999

| | MNP $5 | MIP $15 |

Gungan Mini-Sub w/Obi-Wan Kenobi, 1999

| | MNP $5 | MIP $25 |

Naboo Starfighter, 1999

| | MNP $5 | MIP $25 |

Sebulba's Pod Racer w/Sebulba, 1999

| | MNP $10 | MIP $25 |

(KP Photo)

Sith Speeder w/Darth Maul, 1999

| | MNP $8 | MIP $25 |

STAP w/Battle Droid, 1999

| | MNP $5 | MIP $15 |

Trade Federation Droid Fighter, 1999

| | MNP $5 | MIP $20 |

Trade Federation Tank, 1999

| | MNP $5 | MIP $30 |

SAGA

(KP Photo)

Anakin Skywalker Speeder, 2002, With blast-off panels. Apparently, Lucas made a last-minute color change to this model (for the movie) making the speeder yellow as an homage to Bob Milner's '32 Ford Coupe in the movie "American Graffiti"

| | MNP $3 | MIP $16 |

Anakin Skywalker's Swoop Bike, 2003, w/Anakin figure (showing a lot of teeth)

| | MNP $10 | MIP $20 |

A-Wing Fighter, 2003, Target exclusive, w/pilot

| | MNP $25 | MIP $50 |

A-Wing Fighter w/Rebel Pilot, 2003, Target exclusive

| | MNP $10 | MIP $20 |

Darth Thranus' Geonosian Speeder Bike, 2003, w/Darth Tyranus figure

| | MNP $10 | MIP $20 |

Imperial Dogfight Tie Fighter w/Tie Pilot, 2003, KB Toys exclusive

| | MNP $10 | MIP $25 |

Imperial Shuttle, 2003, FAO Schwarz exclusive

| | MNP $75 | MIP $125 |

(KP Photo)

Jango Fett's Slave I, 2002, Launches four missiles, has more vibrant color as a new ship than it does by the time Boba inherits it
    MNP $10   **MIP** $25

Jedi Starfighter w/ Obi-Wan Kenobi, 2002, KB Toys exclusive
    MNP $10   **MIP** $25

Jedi Starfighter, Obi-Wan Kenobi, 2002, no figure
    MNP $10   **MIP** $25

Landspeeder, 2002, TRU exclusive
    MNP $10   **MIP** $20

Luke Skywalker's X-Wing Fighter, 2002, TRU exclusive, R2-D2
    MNP $10   **MIP** $25

Republic Gunship, 2002, Fits one pilot, carries troops in main body, pivoting laser cannon
    MNP $10   **MIP** $30

Tie Bomber, 2003, w/pilot
    MNP $10   **MIP** $25

(KP Photo)

Zam Wessell Coruscant Speeder, 2002, With flexible "crush zones" to emulate Zam's rough landing on Coruscant. A nice-looking vehicle
    MNP $3   **MIP** $17

CLONE WARS

Anakin Skywalker's Jedi Starfighter, 2003, 1 missile, red droid
    MNP $15   **MIP** $22

Arrmored Assault Tank (AAT), 2003, 4 missiles
    MNP $15   **MIP** $25

(KP Photo, Karen O'Brien collection)

Command Gunship, 2003
    MNP $15   **MIP** $40

(KP Photo, Karen O'Brien collection)

Geonosian Starfighter w/pilot, 2003, exclusive Geonosian pilot, 1 missile
    MNP $15   **MIP** $22

(KP Photo, Karen O'Brien collection)

Hailfire Droid, 2003, 32 red missiles
    MNP $15   **MIP** $22

(KP Photo, Karen O'Brien collection)

Jedi Starfighter, 2003, blue w/yellow droid
    MNP $15   **MIP** $22

WEAPONS

STAR WARS

Han Solo's Laser Pistol, 1977
    MNP $35   **MIP** $110

Inflatable Lightsaber, 1977
    MNP $25   **MIP** $120

Three-Position Laser Rifle, 1980
    MNP $65   **MIP** $250

EMPIRE STRIKES BACK

Laser Pistol, 1980
    MNP $18   **MIP** $65

Lightsaber, red or green, 1980, red or green
    MNP $30   **MIP** $60

RETURN OF THE JEDI

Biker Scout's Laser Pistol, 1984
    MNP $18   **MIP** $60

Lightsaber, red or green, red or green plastic
    MNP $20   **MIP** $30

DROIDS

Droids Lightsaber, 1985
    MNP $85   **MIP** $225

SAGA

Anakin Skywalker Lightsaber, 2002
    MNP $5   **MIP** $25

Count Dooku Lightsaber, 2002
    MNP $5   **MIP** $25

Lightsaber, blue, 2002
    MNP $3   **MIP** $9

Lightsaber, green, 2002
    MNP $3   **MIP** $9

Lightsaber, purple, 2002
    MNP $4   **MIP** $14

Lightsaber, red, 2002
    MNP $4   **MIP** $14

Obi-Wan Kenobi Lightsaber, 2002
    MNP $5   **MIP** $25

Tin Toys

Yesterday's tin creations are some of today's priciest collectible toys. Many of the metal toys produced before World War I can be considered true works of art, especially since tin toys were often painstakingly hand-painted.

The advent of chromolithography changed all that. The technology was actually developed late in the 19th century, but first applied to tin toys in the 1920s. The technique allowed multicolor illustrations to be printed on flat tin plates that were molded into toys. American manufacturers could produce these colorful toys more inexpensively than the classic European toys that had dominated to the toy market until this time.

With mass production came mass appeal, and these new tin mechanical toys were often based on popular characters and celebrities. Comic strip characters and Walt Disney movies provided most of the already-popular subject matter for toy marketers.

Among the most well-known makers of mechanical tin toys were Marx, Chein, Lehmann, and Strauss. Others included Courtland, Girard, Ohio Art, Schuco, Unique Art, and Wolverine.

Many of these manufacturers had business relationships with each other. Over the years, some would be found working together, producing or distributing other's toys, or being absorbed by other companies. Of course, there appeared to be some occasional pilfering and reproducing of others' ideas, as well.

One of the advantages of lithography was that it allowed old toys to be recycled in many ways. When a character's public appeal began to wane, a new image could be printed on the same body to produce a new toy. Or when a toy company was absorbed by another, older models could be dusted off and dressed up with new lithography. Many of the mechanical tin wind-up toys show up in surprisingly similar versions bearing another manufacturer's name.

Of the companies listed here, Marx was no doubt the most prolific. The company's founder, Louis Marx, at one time was employed by another leading toymaker, Ferdinand Strauss. Eventually Marx left Strauss in 1918 to start his own company. Some of his first successes were new versions of old Strauss toys like the still reproduced and quite famous Climbing Monkey.

Many of the popular Marx tin wind-ups were also based on popular characters. Not surprisingly, some of the other highly valued character toys are the Amos 'N Andy Walkers, the Donald Duck Duet, Popeye the Champ, Li'l Abner and his Dogpatch Band, and the Superman Rollover Airplane.

While Marx went on to produce many different kinds of toys, other companies such as Chein specialized in inexpensive lithographed tin. And like Marx, Chein also capitalized on popular cartoon characters, producing several Popeye toys, among others. J. Chein and Co., which was founded in 1903, was best known for its carnival-themed mechanical toys. Its Ferris Wheel is fairly well known among toy collectors and was made in several lithographed versions, including one with a Disneyland theme. Chein also produced a number of affordable tin banks.

Girard was founded shortly after Chein but didn't start producing toys until 1918. The company then subcontracted toys for Marx and Strauss in the 1920s. In fact, several Girard and Marx toys are identical, having been produced in the same plant with different names on them. Marx later took over Girard in the 1930s.

Unique Art, based in New Jersey, isn't known for an extensive line of toys, but it produced some items that are favorites among tin toy collectors. Unique Art was also reportedly acquired by Marx at some point.

There are many other companies that produced lithographed tin toys not included in this section, particularly German and Japanese companies. Lehmann and Schuco, both German firms, are the only non-American toymakers listed in this guide. More lithographed tin toys can be found in the vehicles section of this book.

Prices listed are for toys in Good, Excellent, and Mint conditions. Toys will usually command a premium over the listed price if they are found with their original boxes.

2006 TRENDS

Tin toys have held their values over the years, and the trade is still pretty healthy. Character-specific tin toys are among this year's strong performers.

There are a number of quality reproductions available for fairly low prices for the collector who just wants the toy without making a huge investment. Just make sure that you do your homework to know the difference between a reproduction and a vintage piece.

Contributor: Scott Smiles, 157 Yacht Club Way, Apt. 112, Hypoluxo, FL 33462, email: ssmiles@msn.com, phone: (561) 582-6016

THE TOP TEN TIN TOYS *(In Mint Condition)*

1. Popeye the Heavy Hitter, Chein	$6,500
2. Popeye Acrobat, Marx	5,000
3. Popeye the Champ, Marx, 1936	4,000
4. Red the Iceman, Marx	2,700
5. Popeye Express, Marx, 1936	2,500
6. Popeye with Punching Bag, Chein	2,500
7. KADI, Lehmann, 1917-27	2,400
8. Paddy and the Pig, Lehmann, 1903-35	2,300
9. Superman Holding Airplane, Marx, 1940	2,250
10. Superman Turnover Tank, Marx, 1940	2,000

BANKS

2nd National Duck Bank, 1954, 3-1/2" high, Chein, Disney characters
EX $90   NM $145   MIP $225

Cash Box, 1930, 2" high, Chein, round trap
EX $30   NM $50   MIP $75

Child's Safe Bank, 1900s, 5-1/2" high, Chein
EX $40   NM $65   MIP $100

Child's Safe Bank, 1910, 4" high, Chein, sailboat on front of door
EX $35   NM $60   MIP $90

Child's Safe Bank, 1910, 3" high, Chein, dog on front of door
EX $35   NM $60   MIP $95

Church, 1930s, 4" high, Chein
EX $35   NM $60   MIP $90

Church, 1954, 3-1/2" high, Chein
EX $70   NM $115   MIP $175

Clown, 1931, 5" high, Chein
EX $70   NM $115   MIP $175

(Toy Shop File Photo)

Clown, 1949, 5" high, Chein, says bank on front
EX $35   NM $60   MIP $95

Drum, 1930s, 2-1/2" high, Chein
EX $35   NM $60   MIP $95

(Toy Shop File Photo)

Elephant, 1950s, 5" high, Chein
EX $55   NM $90   MIP $135

God Bless America, 1930s, 2-1/2" high, Chein, drum shaped
EX $30   NM $50   MIP $75

Happy Days Cash Register, 1930s, 4" high, Chein
EX $45   NM $80   MIP $120

Humpty Dumpty, 1934, 5-1/4" high, Chein
EX $60   NM $100   MIP $150

Log Cabin, 1930s, 3" high, Chein
EX $80   NM $130   MIP $200

Mascot Safe, 1914, 5" high, Chein
EX $35   NM $60   MIP $95

Mascot Safe, 1914, 4" high, Chein
EX $35   NM $55   MIP $85

(Toy Shop File Photo)

Monkey, 1950s, 5-1/4" high, Chein
EX $55   NM $90   MIP $135

New Deal, 1930s, 3-1/4" high, Chein
EX $50   NM $80   MIP $125

Prosperity Bank, 1930s, 2-1/4" high, Chein, pail shaped, w/band
EX $35   NM $60   MIP $95

Prosperity Bank, 1930s, 2-1/4" high, Chein, pail shaped, without band
EX $30   NM $50   MIP $75

Roly Poly, 1940s, 6" high, Chein
EX $135   NM $230   MIP $350

Scout, 1931, 3-1/4" high, Chein, cylinder
EX $100   NM $165   MIP $250

Three Little Pigs, 1930s, 3" high, Chein
EX $60   NM $100   MIP $150

Treasure Chest, 1930s, 2" high, Chein
EX $35   NM $60   MIP $90

Uncle Sam, 1934, 4" high, Chein, hat shaped
EX $50   NM $75   MIP $100

Uncle Wiggly, 1950s, 5" high, Chein
EX $50   NM $75   MIP $100

BUILDINGS AND ROOMS

Airport, 1930s, Marx
EX $125   NM $200   MIP $300

Automatic Car Wash, Marx
EX $135   NM $225   MIP $350

Automatic Firehouse with Fire Chief Car, 1940s, Marx, friction car, firehouse w/plastic doors
EX $125   NM $200   MIP $300

Automatic Garage, Marx, family car
EX $150   NM $245   MIP $375

Blue Bird Garage, 1937, Marx
EX $150   NM $225   MIP $350

Brightlite Filling Station, 1930s, Marx, pump w/round top says "Fresh Air"
EX $250   NM $425   MIP $650

Brightlite Filling Station, 1930s, Marx, bottle-shaped gas pumps, battery-operated
EX $255   NM $425   MIP $650

Brightlite Filling Station, late 1930s, Marx, rectangular shaped pumps, battery-operated
EX $255   NM $425   MIP $650

Bus Terminal, 1937, Marx
EX $175   NM $295   MIP $450

Busy Airport Garage, 1936, Marx
EX $195   NM $325   MIP $500

Busy Parking Lot, 1937, Marx, five heavy gauge streamline autos
EX $235   NM $390   MIP $600

Busy Street, 1935, Marx, six vehicles
EX $150   NM $300   MIP $475

City Airport, 1938, Marx, w/two metal planes
EX $125   NM $200   MIP $300

Crossing Gate House, Marx
EX $125   NM $200   MIP $300

Crossover Speedway, 1938, Marx, litho buildings on bridge, two cars, litho drivers
EX $125   NM $200   MIP $295

Crossover Speedway, 1941, Marx
EX $100   NM $175   MIP $250

Dick Tracy Automatic Police Station, Marx, station and car
EX $375   NM $625   MIP $950

Gas Pump Island, Marx
EX $125   NM $200   MIP $300

General Alarm Fire House, 1938, Marx, wind-up alarm bell, steel chief car and patrol truck
EX $175   NM $295   MIP $450

Greyhound Bus Terminal, 1938, Marx
EX $125   NM $200   MIP $300

Gull Service Station, 1940s, Marx
EX $200   NM $300   MIP $475

Hollywood Bungalow House, 1935, Marx
EX $175   NM $275   MIP $425

Home Town Drug Store, 1930s, Marx
EX $175   NM $300   MIP $450

Home Town Favorite Store, 1930s, Marx
EX $175   NM $300   MIP $450

Home Town Fire House, 1930s, Marx
EX $175   NM $300   MIP $450

Home Town Grocery Store, 1930s, Marx
EX $165   NM $275   MIP $425

TIN TOYS

Home Town Meat Market, 1930s, Marx
 EX $180   NM $300   MIP $465

Home Town Movie Theatre, 1930s, Marx
 EX $150   NM $250   MIP $375

Home Town Police Station, 1930s, Marx
 EX $150   NM $250   MIP $375

Home Town Savings Bank, 1930s, Marx
 EX $150   NM $250   MIP $375

Honeymoon Garage, 1935, Marx
 EX $165   NM $275   MIP $425

Lincoln Highway Set, 1933, Marx, pumps, oil-grease rack, traffic light and car
 EX $350   NM $600   MIP $900

Loop-the-Loop Auto Racer, 1931, 1-3/4", Marx
 EX $150   NM $295   MIP $400

Magic Garage, 1934, Marx, w/friction town car
 EX $150   NM $250   MIP $375

Magic Garage, 1934, Marx, litho garage, wind-up car
 EX $150   NM $250   MIP $375

Main Street Station, Marx, litho garage, 4" wind-up steel vehicles
 EX $175   NM $275   MIP $425

Metal Service Station, 1949-1950, Marx
 EX $175   NM $275   MIP $425

Military Airport, Marx
 EX $100   NM $180   MIP $275

Model School House, 1960s, Marx
 EX $50   NM $80   MIP $125

Mot-O-Run 4 Lane Hi-Way, 1949, Marx, cars, trucks, buses move on 27" electric track
 EX $100   NM $180   MIP $275

New York World's Fair Speedway, 1939, Marx, litho track, two red cars
 EX $300   NM $500   MIP $750

Newlyweds' Bathroom, 1920s, Marx
 EX $100   NM $165   MIP $500

Newlyweds' Bedroom, 1920s, Marx
 EX $100   NM $165   MIP $500

Newlyweds' Dining Room, 1920s, Marx
 EX $100   NM $165   MIP $500

Newlyweds' Kitchen, 1920s, Marx
 EX $100   NM $165   MIP $500

Newlyweds' Library, 1920s, Marx
 EX $100   NM $165   MIP $500

Roadside Rest Service Station, 1935, Marx, Laurel and Hardy at counter, w/stools in front
 EX $625   NM $1050   MIP $1600

Roadside Rest Service Station, 1938, Marx, Laurel and Hardy at counter, no stool in front
 EX $550   NM $950   MIP $1450

Service Station, 1929, Marx, two pumps, two friction vehicles
 EX $300   NM $500   MIP $750

Service Station Gas Pumps, 9", Marx, wind-up
 EX $125   NM $200   MIP $325

Sky Hawk Flyer, 7-1/2" tall, Marx, wind-up, two planes, tower
 EX $125   NM $200   MIP $325

Stunt Auto Racer, 1931, Marx, two blue racers
 EX $135   NM $225   MIP $350

Sunnyside Garage, 1935, Marx
 EX $255   NM $425   MIP $650

TV and Radio Station, Marx
 EX $150   NM $225   MIP $350

Universal Motor Repair Shop, 1938, Marx, tin
 EX $250   NM $425   MIP $650

Used Car Market, 1939, Marx, base, several vehicles and signs
 EX $250   NM $425   MIP $650

Whee-Whiz Auto Racer, 1925, Marx, four 2" multicolored racers w/litho driver
 EX $300   NM $500   MIP $750

JACK IN THE BOXES

(Toy Shop File Photo)

Flipper, 1967, Mattel
 EX $45   NM $75   MIP $125

Mother Goose, Mattel
 EX $10   NM $15   MIP $25

(Toy Shop File Photo)

(Toy Shop File Photo)

Porky Pig, 1965, Mattel
 EX $40   NM $75   MIP $150

Super Chief, 1964, Mattel
 EX $50   NM $200   MIP $300

(Toy Shop File Photo)

Tom & Jerry, 1966, Mattel
 EX $25   NM $45   MIP $100

(Toy Shop File Photo)

Woody Woodpecker, 1965, Mattel
 EX $40   NM $75   MIP $150

MISCELLANEOUS TOYS

1917 Ford, Schuco
 EX $50   NM $80   MIP $125

Aha Truck, 1907-1935, 5-1/2", Lehmann, delivery van
 EX $500   NM $650   MIP $900

Airplane and Pilot, 1930s, Schuco, friction toy, oversized pilot
EX $135   NM $225   MIP $350

Airplane Carousel, 1930s, Wyandotte
EX $100   NM $200   MIP $375

Ajax Acrobat, 10" tall, Lehmann, does somersaults
EX $800   NM $1300   MIP $2000

(Toy Shop File Photo)

Alabama Jigger, 1920s, Lehmann, No. 685, wind-up tap dancer on square base
EX $500   NM $700   MIP $900

Arithmetic Quiz Toy, 1950s, Wolverine, math quiz machine
EX $35   NM $50   MIP $75

Army Code Sender, Marx, pressed steel
EX $20   NM $35   MIP $50

Army Drummer, 1930s, 7" high, Chein, plunger-activated
EX $125   NM $200   MIP $250

Artie the Clown in his Crazy Car, Unique Art
EX $350   NM $450   MIP $550

Automatic Airport, 1940s, 9" high, Ohio Art, two planes circle tower
EX $100   NM $150   MIP $200

Auton Boy & Cart, Lehmann
EX $200   NM $350   MIP $500

Baby Grand Piano, Marx, w/piano-shaped music books
EX $50   NM $100   MIP $250

Battleship, 1930s, 14" long, Wolverine
EX $75   NM $125   MIP $200

Bavarian Boy, 1950s, 5" tall, Schuco, tin and cloth boy w/beer mug
EX $100   NM $200   MIP $300

Bavarian Dancing Couple, 5" high, Schuco, tin and cloth
EX $125   NM $175   MIP $250

Big Shot, Marx
EX $75   NM $100   MIP $150

Black Man, 5" high, Schuco, tin and cloth
EX $250   NM $425   MIP $650

Bombo the Monk, 1930s, 9-1/2" tree, 5-1/2" monkey, Unique Art, two pieces, tree and monkey
EX $130   NM $180   MIP $230

Capitol Hill Racer, 1930s, 17-1/2" long, Unique Art
EX $125   NM $150   MIP $175

Captain of Kopenick, early 1900s, Lehmann
EX $625   NM $1050   MIP $1600

(Toy Shop File Photo)

Carnival Set, 1930s, Wyandotte, diorama w/several rides on tin base
EX $350   NM $550   MIP $950

Casey the Cop, Unique Art
EX $600   NM $800   MIP $1000

Cat Pushing Ball, 1938, Marx, lever action, wood ball
EX $75   NM $100   MIP $125

Circus Shooting Gallery, 1950s, 12" high, 17" long, Ohio Art, w/gun and darts
EX $60   NM $90   MIP $150

(Toy Shop File Photo)

Clown Playing Violin, 1950s, 4-1/2" tall, Schuco, tin and cloth
EX $135   NM $200   MIP $275

Coast Guard Plane, 1950s, 10" wingspan, Ohio Art
EX $75   NM $125   MIP $175

Combinato Convertible, 1950s, 7-1/2" long, Schuco
EX $100   NM $175   MIP $250

Coney Island Roller Coaster, 1950s, Ohio Art
EX $125   NM $175   MIP $250

Crane, 18" high, Wolverine, red and blue
EX $40   NM $65   MIP $100

Crocodile, 1940s, Lehmann, walks, mouth opens
EX $250   NM $350   MIP $475

Curvo Motorcycle, 1950s, 5" long, Schuco
EX $150   NM $225   MIP $350

Dancing Boy and Girl, 1930s, Schuco, tin and cloth
EX $125   NM $200   MIP $300

Dancing Mice, 1950s, Schuco, large and small mouse, tin and cloth
EX $135   NM $225   MIP $350

Dancing Monkey with Mouse, 1950s, Schuco, tin and cloth
EX $125   NM $210   MIP $325

(Toy Shop File Photo)

Dancing Sailor, 1904-1948, 7-1/2" high, Lehmann, No. 535
EX $600   NM $850   MIP $1000

(Toy Shop File Photo)

Dandy Jim Dancer, 1921, Unique Art
EX $450   NM $650   MIP $850

Daredevil Motor Cop, 1940s, 8-1/2" long, Unique Art
EX $300   NM $450   MIP $600

Delivery Van, Lehmann, "Huntley & Palmers Biscuits"
EX $650   **NM** $1000   **MIP** $1500

Disneyland Tea Set, 1954, Chein, fifteen-piece set featuring Disney characters
EX $100   **NM** $175   **MIP** $300

Doll Stroller, 1950s, Ohio Art, teddy bear design
EX $40   **NM** $60   **MIP** $80

Dolly's Washer, 1930s, Chein, washing machine
EX $65   **NM** $100   **MIP** $300

Donald Duck Carpet Sweeper, 1940s, Ohio Art, red w/Disney litho
EX $60   **NM** $100   **MIP** $250

Drum Major, 13", Wolverine, round base
EX $100   **NM** $175   **MIP** $225

Drum Major, 1950, 7-1/2", Wolverine
EX $125   **NM** $200   **MIP** $275

Drummer, 1930s, 5" tall, Schuco, tin and cloth
EX $125   **NM** $210   **MIP** $325

Easter Basket, Chein, nursery rhyme figures
EX $35   **NM** $55   **MIP** $100

Easter Egg, 1938, 5-1/2", Chein, tin, chicken on top, opens to hold candy
EX $35   **NM** $55   **MIP** $85

Examico 4001 Convertible, 5-1/2", Schuco, maroon tin wind-up
EX $175   **NM** $250   **MIP** $375

Express Bus, Wolverine
EX $125   **NM** $210   **MIP** $325

(Toy Shop File Photo)

Express Man & Cart, 1888-1918, 6" long, Lehmann, No. 140, porter pulls striped cart
EX $450   **NM** $600   **MIP** $700

Finnegan the Porter, 1930s, 14" long, Unique Art, w/cardboard luggage
EX $200   **NM** $300   **MIP** $400

Flic 4520, Schuco, traffic cop-type figure
EX $135   **NM** $225   **MIP** $350

Flying Bird, Lehmann
EX $300   **NM** $475   **MIP** $600

Flying Circus, Unique Art, elephant supports plane and clown
EX $450   **NM** $650   **MIP** $850

Fox And Goose, 1950s, 4-1/4" high, Schuco, tin and cloth, fox holding goose in cage
EX $800   **NM** $1200   **MIP** $1600

(Scott Smiles. Photo by Mike Adams)

G.I. Joe and His Jouncing Jeep, 1940s, 7", Unique Art, wind-up
EX $175   **NM** $225   **MIP** $275

(Scott Smiles)

G.I. Joe and His K-9 Pups, 1940s, Unique Art
EX $150   **NM** $200   **MIP** $250

Galop Race Car, 1920s, Lehmann
EX $250   **NM** $400   **MIP** $600

Gertie the Galloping Goose, 1930s, 9-1/2" long, Unique Art
EX $125   **NM** $175   **MIP** $225

Gustav The Climbing Miller, Lehmann
EX $375   **NM** $500   **MIP** $700

Hee Haw, 10" long, Unique Art, donkey pulling milk cart
EX $175   **NM** $250   **MIP** $325

Helicopter, Toy Town Airways, 1950s, 13" long, Chein, friction drive
EX $55   **NM** $90   **MIP** $135

(Toy Shop File Photo)

Hillbilly Express, 1930s, 18" long, Unique Art
EX $100   **NM** $150   **MIP** $200

(Toy Shop File Photo)

Hobo Train, 1920s, 8-1/2", Unique Art, dog biting pants of hobo atop train
EX $325   **NM** $450   **MIP** $650

(Scott Smiles)

Hoky Poky, 1930s, Wyandotte, clowns on railcar
EX $200   **NM** $275   **MIP** $325

Hopping Rabbit, 1950s, 4" tall, Marx, metal and plastic
EX $35   **NM** $60   **MIP** $95

Hott and Trott Musical Band, 1920s, Unique Art
EX $500   **NM** $750   **MIP** $1000

Indian in Headdress, 1930s, 5-1/2" high, Chein
EX $125   **NM** $175   **MIP** $225

Ito Sedan and Driver, 1914-1935, 6-1/2", Lehmann, No. 679
EX $500   **NM** $700   **MIP** $900

(Bill Bertoia Auctions)

Jazzbo Jim-The Dancer on the Roof, 1920s, 10" high, Unique Art
EX $300   **NM** $425   **MIP** $550

Jet Roller Coaster, 21" long, Wolverine
EX $200   **NM** $250   **MIP** $300

Juggling Clown, 4-1/2" tall, Schuco, tin and cloth
EX $135   NM $225   MIP $350

Jumping Frog, Marx
EX $40   NM $65   MIP $100

Jungle Eyes Shooting Gallery, 1950s, 14" high, 18" long, Ohio Art, w/gun and darts
EX $90   NM $135   MIP $180

Jungle Man Spear, Marx
EX $100   NM $150   MIP $200

(Bill Bertoia Auctions)

KADI, 1917-1927, Lehmann, No. 723, Chinese men carrying box
EX $1000   NM $1700   MIP $2400

Kiddy Go-Round, Unique Art
EX $175   NM $250   MIP $375

Kid-Go-Round, Unique Art, plastic horsemen and boat
EX $150   NM $225   MIP $300

King Kong, 6-1/2" tall, Marx, on wheels, w/spring-loaded arms
EX $35   NM $60   MIP $95

Krazy Kar, 1921, Unique Art
EX $275   NM $425   MIP $550

(Toy Shop File Photo)

Lehmann's Autobus, 1907-1945, Lehmann, No. 590
EX $1000   NM $1500   MIP $2000

(Scott Smiles)

Li'l Abner and His Dogpatch Band, Unique Art
EX $425   NM $675   MIP $1000

Li-La Car, 1903-1935, 5-1/2", Lehmann, driver in rear, women passengers
EX $1000   NM $1500   MIP $2000

(Toy Shop File Photo)

Lincoln Tunnel, 1935, 24" long, Unique Art
EX $225   NM $325   MIP $425

Little Red Riding Hood Tea Set, 1920s, Ohio Art, seven-piece set
EX $100   NM $200   MIP $350

Marine, 1950s, 6" high, Chein, hand on belt
EX $125   NM $150   MIP $175

Mauswagen, Schuco, tin and cloth mice and wagon
EX $200   NM $325   MIP $500

Melody Organ Player, Chein
EX $75   NM $125   MIP $175

Mercer Car No. 1225, 1950s, 7-1/2" long, Schuco
EX $100   NM $150   MIP $225

Merry-Go-Round, 1930s, 11" diameter, 12" high, Wolverine, No. 31
EX $275   NM $400   MIP $500

Mexican Boy Tea Set, 1940s, Ohio Art, nine-piece set
EX $75   NM $100   MIP $200

Mickey & Minnie Dancing, Schuco, tin and cloth
EX $700   NM $1200   MIP $1800

Mickey Mouse Tray, 1930s, Ohio Art
EX $50   NM $100   MIP $200

Mikado Family, 1894-1918, 6-1/2", Lehmann, No. 350
EX $650   NM $1000   MIP $1400

Minstrel Man, early 1900s, Lehmann
EX $350   NM $550   MIP $1000

Model Shooting Gallery, 1930s, Wyandotte
EX $100   NM $200   MIP $300

Monk Drinking Beer, 5" high, Schuco, tin and cloth
EX $125   NM $200   MIP $300

Monkey Drummer, 1950s, Schuco, tin and cloth
EX $125   NM $200   MIP $300

Monkey in Car, 1930s, Schuco
EX $335   NM $550   MIP $850

Monkey on Scooter, 1930s, Schuco, tin and cloth
EX $125   NM $200   MIP $300

Monkey Playing Violin, 1950s, Schuco, tin and cloth
EX $125   NM $225   MIP $325

Mother Duck with Baby Ducks, 1950s, Wyandotte, two baby ducks on wheels pulled behind mother ducks
EX $50   NM $100   MIP $125

Mother Goose Tea Set, 1931, Ohio Art, seven-piece set
EX $90   NM $150   MIP $250

Musical Sail-Way Carousel, 9" tall, Unique Art, three kids spin in plastic boats
EX $175   NM $250   MIP $350

Musical Top Clown, 1950s, 7" high, Chein, clown head handle
EX $75   NM $125   MIP $195

Mysterious Woodpecker, Marx
EX $50   NM $75   MIP $100

Mystery Car, Wolverine
EX $100   NM $175   MIP $250

(Scott Smiles)

Mystic Motorcycle Cop, 1930s, 9" long, Unique Art
EX $200   NM $300   MIP $400

New Century Cycle, 1895-1938, 5", Lehmann, No. 345, driver and black man w/umbrella
EX $400   NM $600   MIP $900

Ostrich Cart, Lehmann
EX $375   NM $650   MIP $950

Paddy and the Pig, 1903-1935, 6", Lehmann, No. 500
EX $1300   NM $1800   MIP $2300

Pathe Movie Camera, 1930s, 6" tall, Marx
EX $75   NM $100   MIP $125

Pecking Goose, Witch and Cat, Unique Art
EX $350   NM $525   MIP $700

Player Piano, Chein, eight rolls
EX $195   NM $325   MIP $500

Quack Quack, Lehmann, duck pulling babies
EX $325   NM $450   MIP $600

Rabbit in shirt and pants, 1938, Chein, red pants, yellow feet, hands in pockets
EX $50   NM $75   MIP $95

Rodeo Joe Crazy Car, 1950s, Unique Art
EX $200   NM $275   MIP $325

Rollover Motorcycle Cop, 1935, Unique Art
EX $275   **NM** $375   **MIP** $475

Rooster and Rabbit, Lehmann, rooster pulls rabbit on cart
EX $400   **NM** $600   **MIP** $900

(Toy Shop File Photo)

Rooster Pulling Wagon, 1930s, Marx
EX $60   **NM** $90   **MIP** $120

Sand Toy, 7" high, Chein, monkey bends and twists
EX $30   **NM** $50   **MIP** $75

Sand Toy Set, Chein, duck mold, sifter, frog on card
EX $30   **NM** $45   **MIP** $70

Sandy Andy Fullback, 8" tall, Wolverine, kicking fullback
EX $200   **NM** $250   **MIP** $325

Schuco Turn Monkey on Suitcase, 1950s, Schuco, tin and cloth
EX $125   **NM** $195   **MIP** $300

Scuba Diver, 10" long, Chein
EX $75   **NM** $125   **MIP** $175

Sea Lion, Lehmann
EX $150   **NM** $250   **MIP** $375

Searchlight, 3-1/2" tall, Marx
EX $40   **NM** $65   **MIP** $100

Sedan and Garage, Lehmann
EX $375   **NM** $575   **MIP** $775

(Toy Shop File Photo)

See-Saw Sand Toy, 1930s, Chein, bright colors, boy and girl on see-saw move
EX $75   **NM** $100   **MIP** $135

See-Saw Sand Toy, 1930s, Chein, pastel colors, boy and girl on see-saw move
EX $70   **NM** $120   **MIP** $185

Shenandoah Zeppelin, Lehmann
EX $155   **NM** $255   **MIP** $395

Skier, 1920s, Lehmann, wind-up
EX $500   **NM** $850   **MIP** $1200

(Toy Shop File Photo)

Sky Rangers, Unique Art, plane and zepplin
EX $325   **NM** $450   **MIP** $600

Snow White Stove, 1960s, Wolverine
EX $20   **NM** $35   **MIP** $50

Space Ride, 1940s, 9" high, Chein, tin litho, boxed, lever action w/music
EX $425   **NM** $650   **MIP** $850

Sparkler Toy, 5", Chein, on original card
EX $30   **NM** $50   **MIP** $75

Studio No. 1050 Race Car, 1950s, 5-1/2" long, Schuco
EX $125   **NM** $180   **MIP** $250

Submarine, 13" long, Wolverine
EX $100   **NM** $175   **MIP** $250

Sunny and Tank, 14-1/2" long, Wolverine, yellow and green
EX $75   **NM** $130   **MIP** $200

Sunny Suzy Deluxe Washing Machine, 1930s, Wolverine
EX $50   **NM** $95   **MIP** $200

Taxi, 1920s, 10" long, Lehmann
EX $450   **NM** $750   **MIP** $1150

Ten Little Indians Spinning Top, Ohio Art
EX $15   **NM** $25   **MIP** $35

Three Little Pigs Spinning Top, Ohio Art
EX $15   **NM** $25   **MIP** $35

Three Little Pigs Wind-Up Toy, 1930s, Schuco, 4-1/2" pigs playing fiddle, fife and drum
EX $300   **NM** $550   **MIP** $775

Toto the Acrobat, Marx
EX $100   **NM** $150   **MIP** $200

Trapeze Artist, 1930s, Wyandotte
EX $125   **NM** $200   **MIP** $325

Tumbling Boy, 1950s, Schuco, tin and cloth
EX $100   **NM** $165   **MIP** $250

Tut-Tut Car, 1903-1935, 6-3/4" long, Lehmann, No. 490, driver has horn
EX $1000   **NM** $1500   **MIP** $2000

Watering Cans, Ohio Art, many variations, value is for each
EX $25   **NM** $30   **MIP** $40

Wild West Bucking Bronco, Lehmann
EX $700   **NM** $1000   **MIP** $1500

Yellow Taxi, 1940s, 13" long, Wolverine
EX $150   **NM** $225   **MIP** $350

Yes-No Monkey, Schuco
EX $175   **NM** $275   **MIP** $425

Zebra Cart "Dare Devil", 1920s, Lehmann
EX $400   **NM** $600   **MIP** $800

Zig-Zag, 1910-1945, 5" long, Lehmann, handcar-type vehicle on oversized wheels
EX $1000   **NM** $1500   **MIP** $2000

(Toy Shop File Photo)

Zilotone, 1920s, Wolverine, clown on xylophone, w/three musical discs
EX $550   **NM** $800   **MIP** $1100

MUSICAL TOYS

Hickory Dickory Dock Clock, Mattel, crank; mouse climbs clock
EX $10   **NM** $25   **MIP** $40

Man on the Flying Trapeze, Mattel, tin base, two metal rods holding trapeze man on top
EX $75   **NM** $100   **MIP** $145

Sing a Song of Sixpence, Mattel, pie-shaped tin music box
EX $20   **NM** $35   **MIP** $65

TRAINS

Commodore Vanderbilt Train, Marx, track, wind-up
EX $75   **NM** $125   **MIP** $190

Crazy Express Train, 1960s, 12" long, Marx, plastic and litho, wind-up
EX $115   **NM** $195   **MIP** $300

Disneyland Express, 1950s, 21-1/2" long, Marx, locomotive and three tin cars, wind-up
EX $255   **NM** $425   **MIP** $650

Disneyland Express, Casey Jr. Circus Train, 12" long, Marx, wind-up
EX $100   **NM** $165   **MIP** $250

Disneyland Train, 1950, Marx, Goofy drives locomotive w/three tin cars, wind-up
EX $135   **NM** $225   **MIP** $350

Engine Train, 1960s, Marx, ten cars, no track, HO-scale
EX $65   **NM** $110   **MIP** $170

Flintstones Choo Choo Train "Bedrock Express", 1950s, 13" long, Marx, wind-up
EX $235   NM $390   MIP $600

Glendale Depot Railroad Station Train, 1930s, Marx
EX $235   NM $390   MIP $600

Mickey Mouse Express Train Set, 1952, Marx
EX $235   NM $390   MIP $900

Mickey Mouse Meteor Train, 1950s, Marx, four cars/engine, wind-up
EX $255   NM $425   MIP $650

Musical Choo-Choo, 1966, Marx
EX $75   NM $100   MIP $125

Mystery Tunnel, Marx, wind-up
EX $90   NM $145   MIP $225

New York Central Engine Train, Marx, four cars
EX $200   NM $325   MIP $500

New York Circular with Train, with airplane, 1928, 9-1/2", Marx, wind-up
EX $600   NM $900   MIP $1250

Popeye Express, 1936, Marx, version of Honeymoon Express, w/airplane
EX $925   NM $1550   MIP $2500

Railroad Watch Tower, 9" tall, Marx, electric light
EX $35   NM $60   MIP $90

Scenic Express Train Set, 1950s, Marx, wind-up
EX $100   NM $150   MIP $200

(Toy Shop File Photo)

Subway Express, 1954, 9-3/8", Marx, w/plastic tunnel
EX $125   NM $175   MIP $225

Train Set, 1950s, 6" long, Marx, plastic locomotive, tin cars, wind-up
EX $60   NM $100   MIP $150

Trolley No. 200, 1920s, 9" long, Marx, headlight, bell, tin wind-up
EX $195   NM $325   MIP $500

WAGONS AND CARTS

Busy Delivery, 1939, 9" long, Marx, open three-wheel cart, wind-up
EX $325   NM $475   MIP $600

Farm Wagon, 1940s, 10" long, Marx, horse pulling wagon
EX $75   NM $100   MIP $150

Horse and Cart, 1934, 7" long, Marx, wind-up
EX $75   NM $125   MIP $175

Horse and Cart, 1950s, 9-1/2" long, Marx, w/driver
EX $50   NM $75   MIP $125

Horse and Cart with Clown Driver, 1923, 7-5/8" long, Marx, wind-up
EX $150   NM $225   MIP $325

Pinocchio Busy Delivery, 1939, 7-3/4" long, Marx, on unicycle facing two-wheel cart, wind-up
EX $250   NM $425   MIP $650

Popeye Horse and Cart, Marx, wind-up
EX $325   NM $525   MIP $825

Rooster Pulling Wagon, 1930s, Marx
EX $150   NM $225   MIP $350

Toyland's Farm Products Milk Wagon, 1930s, 10-1/2" long, Marx, wind-up
EX $225   NM $350   MIP $225

Two Donkeys Pulling Cart, 1940s, 10-1/4" long, Marx, w/driver
EX $150   NM $225   MIP $325

Wagon with Two-Horse Team, late 1940s, Marx, wind-up
EX $90   NM $145   MIP $225

WIND-UP TOYS

(Don Hultzman)

Acrobatic Marvel Monkey, 1930s, Marx, balances on two chairs
EX $100   NM $150   MIP $225

Airplane, square-winged, 7" wingspan, Chein, early tin
EX $100   NM $150   MIP $225

Amos 'n Andy Fresh Air Taxi, 1930s, Marx, 5" x 8" long
EX $500   NM $900   MIP $1400

(Toy Shop File Photo)

Amos 'n Andy Walkers, 1930, 11" tall, Marx, values are for each
EX $600   NM $1000   MIP $1200

Army Cargo Truck, 1920s, 8" long, Chein
EX $235   NM $390   MIP $600

Army Plane, 11" wingspan, Chein
EX $135   NM $230   MIP $350

Army Sergeant, Chein
EX $75   NM $125   MIP $175

Army Truck, 8-1/2" long, Chein, open bed
EX $50   NM $75   MIP $100

Army Truck, 8-1/2" long, Chein, cannon on back
EX $50   NM $80   MIP $125

(Scott Smiles. Photo by Mike Adams)

Balky Mule, 1948, 8-3/4" long, Marx
EX $150   NM $200   MIP $250

Ballerina, 6" tall, Marx
EX $100   NM $150   MIP $225

(Christie's East)

Barnacle Bill, 1930s, Chein, looks like Popeye, waddles
EX $325   NM $425   MIP $525

Barney Rubble Riding Dino, 1960s, 8" long, Marx
EX $175   NM $275   MIP $425

TIN TOYS

(Scott Smiles)

Bear, 1938, Chein, w/hat, pants, shirt, bow tie
EX $50   NM $75   MIP $100

Bear Cyclist, 1934, 5-3/4" tall, Marx
EX $175   NM $250   MIP $325

Bear Waddler, 1960s, 4" tall, Marx
EX $50   NM $80   MIP $125

Beat It! The Komikal Kop, 1930s, Marx
EX $400   NM $625   MIP $700

Big Parade, 1928, 24" long, Marx
EX $250   NM $375   MIP $450

Big Three Aerial Acrobats, 1920, Marx
EX $200   NM $300   MIP $400

Bimbo Clown, Irwin, colorful outfit, umbrella
EX $30   NM $60   MIP $90

Blacksmith Teddy, TN, black fur, hammer and anvil
EX $30   NM $60   MIP $90

Boxing Monkey, MM, brown fur, red punching bag, blue trunks
EX $50   NM $75   MIP $100

Boy on Trapeze, Marx
EX $100   NM $125   MIP $175

Bunny, 1940s, Chein
EX $35   NM $60   MIP $100

Busy Bridge, 1937, 24" long, Marx, vehicles on bridge
EX $325   NM $425   MIP $500

(Toy Shop File Photo)

Busy Miners, 1930s, 16-1/2" long, Marx, with miner's car
EX $175   NM $250   MIP $325

(Scott Smiles)

Butter and Egg Man, 1930s, 8" tall, Marx, wind-up walker
EX $450   NM $650   MIP $850

Cabin Cruiser, 1940s, 9" long, Chein
EX $65   NM $95   MIP $85

Captain America Wind-up Toy, 1968, 5" tall, Marx, tin
EX $55   NM $90   MIP $140

Carter Climbing Monkey, 1921, 8-1/2" tall, Marx
EX $100   NM $175   MIP $250

(Toy Shop File Photo)

Cat, Chein, w/wood wheels
EX $50   NM $75   MIP $125

Charleston Trio, 1926, 9" tall, Marx, man, boy and dog dancers on roof
EX $550   NM $750   MIP $950

Charlie McCarthy Bass Drummer, 1939, Marx
EX $450   NM $750   MIP $1150

Charlie McCarthy Walker, 1930s, Marx
EX $350   NM $550   MIP $750

Chick, 4" high, Chein, bright colored clothes, polka dot bow tie
EX $50   NM $75   MIP $100

Chicken Pushing Wheelbarrow, 1930s, Chein
EX $50   NM $75   MIP $100

China Clipper, 10" long, Chein
EX $150   NM $250   MIP $350

Chipmunk, Marx
EX $50   NM $75   MIP $125

Chompy the Beetle, 1960s, 6" tall, Marx, w/action and sound
EX $60   NM $100   MIP $150

Clancy, 1931, 11" tall, Marx, walker
EX $195   NM $325   MIP $500

(Toy Shop File Photo)

Climbing Fireman, 1950s, Marx, tin and plastic
EX $125   NM $175   MIP $250

Clown Boxing, 8" tall, Chein
EX $325   NM $500   MIP $600

(Toy Shop File Photo)

Clown in Barrel, 1930s, 8" high, Chein, waddles
EX $250   NM $375   MIP $525

Clown with Parasol, 1920s, 8" tall, Chein
EX $100   NM $175   MIP $275

Coast Defense Revolving Airplane, 1929, Marx, circular w/three cannons
EX $500   NM $750   MIP $950

Cowboy on Horse, 1925, 6" tall, Marx
EX $75   NM $125   MIP $175

Cowboy Rider, 1930s, 7", Marx, black horse version
EX $175   NM $275   MIP $375

Cowboy Rider, 1941, Marx, w/lariat on black horse
EX $175   NM $250   MIP $350

Crazy Dora, Marx
EX $100   NM $150   MIP $200

Dan-Dee Dump Truck, Chein
EX $175   NM $300   MIP $400

(Toy Shop File Photo)

Dapper Dan Coon Jigger, 1922, 10" tall, Marx
EX $500   NM $700   MIP $950

Dippy Dumper, Marx
EX $135   NM $225   MIP $350

(Toy Shop File Photo)

Disneyland Ferris Wheel, 1940s, Chein
EX $400   NM $600   MIP $850

Disneyland Roller Coaster, 1950s, Chein
EX $375   NM $575   MIP $775

Donald Duck and Scooter, 1960s, Marx
EX $100   NM $150   MIP $225

(Toy Shop File Photo)

Donald Duck Duet, 1946, 10-1/2" tall, Marx, Donald and Goofy
EX $450   NM $650   MIP $850

Donald Duck Walker, Marx, w/three nephews
EX $100   NM $175   MIP $250

Donald the Skier, 1940s, 10-1/2" tall, Marx, plastic, metal skis
EX $175   NM $275   MIP $425

Dopey, 1938, 8" tall, Marx, walker
EX $300   NM $525   MIP $950

Doughboy, 1920s, 6" high, Chein, tin litho, WWI soldier w/rifle
EX $175   NM $250   MIP $325

Doughboy Walker, Marx
EX $225   NM $350   MIP $550

Drummer Boy, 1930s, 9" high, Chein, w/shako
EX $100   NM $150   MIP $225

Drummer Boy, 1939, Marx
EX $275   NM $375   MIP $650

Duck, 1930, 4" high, Chein, waddles
EX $75   NM $100   MIP $125

Duck, 1930, 6" high, Chein, waddles
EX $125   NM $175   MIP $225

Dumbo, 1941, 4" tall, Marx, flip-over action
EX $175   NM $275   MIP $375

Easter Rabbit, 5" tall, Marx, holds Easter basket
EX $75   NM $125   MIP $175

(Scott Smiles)

Ferris Wheel, 1930s, 16-1/2" high, Chein, six compartments, ringing bell
EX $250   NM $350   MIP $450

(Toy Shop File Photo)

Ferris Wheel, The Giant Ride, 16" high, Chein
EX $100   NM $250   MIP $500

Figaro (Pinocchio), 1940, 5" long, Marx, rollover action
EX $150   NM $225   MIP $350

Fireman on Ladder, 24" tall, Marx
EX $200   NM $300   MIP $400

Flipping Monkey, Marx
EX $100   NM $150   MIP $200

Flippo the Jumping Dog, 1940, 3" tall, Marx
EX $100   NM $150   MIP $200

Flutterfly, 1929, 3" long, Marx
EX $90   NM $145   MIP $225

(Scott Smiles)

George the Drummer Boy, 1930s, 9" tall, Marx, stationary eyes
EX $125   NM $175   MIP $250

George the Drummer Boy, 1930s, 9" tall, Marx, moving eyes
EX $150   NM $200   MIP $275

Gobbling Goose, 1940s, Marx, lays golden eggs
EX $125   NM $200   MIP $275

Golden Goose, 1929, 9-1/2" long, Marx
EX $100   NM $125   MIP $175

Goofy, 1950s, 9" tall, Marx, tail spins, plastic
EX $125   NM $200   MIP $300

Goofy the Walking Gardener, 1960, 9" tall, Marx, holds a wheelbarrow
EX $250   NM $350   MIP $525

Greyhound Bus, 6" long, Chein, wood tires
EX $90   NM $155   MIP $235

(Scott Smiles)

Handstand Clown, 1930s, 5" tall, Chein
EX $75   NM $125   MIP $175

Handstand Clown, 1940s, 6", Chein
EX $50   NM $100   MIP $125

Hap/Hop Ramp Walker, 1950s, 2-1/2" tall, Marx
EX $40   NM $65   MIP $100

Happy Hooligan, 1932, 6" high, Chein, tin litho
EX $200   NM $325   MIP $475

Harold Lloyd Funny Face, 1928, 11" tall, Marx, walker
EX $275   NM $475   MIP $600

Hercules Ferris Wheel, Chein
EX $150   NM $250   MIP $350

Hey Hey the Chicken Snatcher, 1926, 8-1/2", Marx, black man w/chicken and dog biting seat of his pants
EX $850   NM $1250   MIP $1750

(Toy Shop File Photo)

Hi-Yo Silver and the Lone Ranger, 1938, 8" tall, Marx
EX $200   NM $325   MIP $525

Honeymoon Cottage, Honeymoon Express 7, 1950s, Marx, square base
EX $100   NM $150   MIP $200

Honeymoon Express, 1927, Marx, old-fashioned train on circular track
EX $150   NM $200   MIP $250

Honeymoon Express, 1937, 9-3/8", Marx, circular train and plane
EX $125   NM $175   MIP $200

(Continental Hobby House)

Honeymoon Express, 1948, 9-3/8", Marx, streamlined train on circular track
EX $100   NM $150   MIP $200

(Toy Shop File Photo)

Hop-A-Long Cassidy Rocker, 1950s, Marx
EX $90   NM $150   MIP $325

Hoppo the Waltzing Monkey, 1925, 9-1/2", Marx, plays cymbals
EX $200   NM $300   MIP $400

Howdy Doody, 1950, 5" tall, Marx, plays banjo and moves head
EX $250   NM $425   MIP $650

(Scott Smiles)

Howdy Doody Band, 1950, 5-1/2" tall, Marx, does jig and Bob Smith sits at piano
EX $700   NM $950   MIP $1450

(Scott Smiles)

Indian in Headdress, 1930s, 4" high, Chein, red
EX $50   NM $100   MIP $150

Jazzbo Jim, 1920s, 9" tall, Marx
EX $250   NM $400   MIP $600

Jetsons Figure, 1960s, 4" tall, Marx
EX $75   NM $150   MIP $200

Jiminy Cricket Pushing Bass Fiddle, Marx, walker
EX $100   NM $175   MIP $225

(Toy Shop File Photo)

Jiving Jigger, 1950, Marx
EX $150   NM $225   MIP $350

(Scott Smiles)

Joe Penner and His Duck Goo-Goo, 1934, 7-1/2" tall, Marx
EX $375   NM $625   MIP $875

Jumbo The Climbing Monkey, 1923, 9-3/4" tall, Marx
EX $125   NM $225   MIP $350

Jumping Rabbit, 1925, 5", Chein
EX $100   NM $125   MIP $150

Junior Bus, 9" long, Chein, yellow
EX $70   NM $115   MIP $175

Knockout Champs Boxing Toy, 1930s, Marx
EX $175   NM $300   MIP $450

Leopard, 1950, Marx, growls and walks
EX $75   NM $125   MIP $175

Little King Walkers, 1963, Marx, 3" tall
EX $50   NM $75   MIP $125

Little Orphan Annie and Sandy, 1930s, Marx
EX $300   NM $475   MIP $600

Little Orphan Annie Skipping Rope, Marx
EX $200   NM $300   MIP $425

Mack Hercules Motor Express, 19-1/2" long, Chein, tin litho
EX $235   NM $385   MIP $595

Mack Hercules Truck, 7-1/2" long, Chein
EX $165   NM $275   MIP $425

Mad Russian Drummer, 7" tall, Marx
EX $200   NM $275   MIP $325

Main Street, 1929, Marx, street scene w/moving cars, traffic cop
EX $275   NM $375   MIP $475

Mammy's Boy, 1929, 11" tall, Marx, wind-up walker
EX $500   NM $750   MIP $1000

Mark 1 Cabin Cruiser, 1957, 9" long, Chein
EX $50   NM $75   MIP $100

Mechanical Aquaplane, No. 39, 1932, 8-1/2" long, Chein, boat-like pontoons
EX $200   NM $300   MIP $400

Mechanical Fish, 1940s, 11" long, Chein
EX $50   NM $75   MIP $100

Merry-Go-Round, Chein, 11" w/swan chairs
EX $475   NM $775   MIP $1200

(Scott Smiles)

Merrymakers Band, 1931, Marx, w/marquee, mouse band
EX $800   NM $1300   MIP $1600

Merrymakers Band, 1931, Marx, without marquee, mouse band w/violinist
EX $750   NM $1100   MIP $1400

Mickey Mouse, 7" tall, Marx
EX $200   NM $400   MIP $600

Minnie Mouse, 7" tall, Marx
EX $200   NM $400   MIP $600

Minnie Mouse in Rocker, 1950s, Marx
EX $275   NM $450   MIP $550

Minstrel Figure, 11" tall, Marx
EX $175   NM $295   MIP $450

Monkey Cyclist, 1923, 9-3/4" tall, Marx
EX $100   NM $175   MIP $250

Moon Creature, 1950s, 5-1/2" tall, Marx
EX $100   NM $175   MIP $250

Moon Mullins and Kayo on Handcar, 1930s, 6" long, Marx
EX $335   NM $550   MIP $700

Mortimer Snerd Bass Drummer, 1939, Marx
EX $750   NM $1250   MIP $1700

Mortimer Snerd Hometown Band, 1935, Marx
EX $700   NM $1100   MIP $1500

Mortimer Snerd Walker, 1939, Marx
EX $200   NM $300   MIP $450

Mother Goose, 1920s, 7-1/2" tall, Marx
EX $150   NM $250   MIP $400

Mother Penguin with Baby Penguin on Sled, 1950s, 3" long, Marx
EX $35   NM $55   MIP $85

Motorboat, 1950s, 9" long, Chein
EX $40   NM $65   MIP $100

Motorboat, 1950s, 7" long, Chein, crank action
EX $35   NM $60   MIP $90

(Toy Shop File Photo)

Musical Aero Swing, 1940s, 10" high, Chein
EX $250   NM $375   MIP $475

Musical Circus Horse, 1939, 10-1/2" long, Marx, pull toy, metal drum rolls w/chimes
EX $100   NM $150   MIP $200

Musical Merry-Go-Round, Chein, small version
EX $150   NM $250   MIP $375

Musical Toy Church, 1937, Chein, crank music box
EX $90   NM $145   MIP $225

Mystery Cat, 1931, 8-1/2" long, Marx
EX $100   NM $165   MIP $250

Mystery Pluto, 1948, 8" long, Marx
EX $100   NM $175   MIP $250

Nodding Goose, Marx
EX $75   NM $125   MIP $175

Pecos Bill, 1950s, 10" tall, Marx, twirls rope, plastic
EX $125   NM $225   MIP $325

Peggy Jane Speedboat, 13", Chein
EX $60   NM $90   MIP $120

Pelican, 1940s, Chein
EX $100   NM $150   MIP $200

Penguin in Tuxedo, 1940s, Chein
EX $75   NM $100   MIP $125

(Scott Smiles)

Pig, 1940s, 4-1/2", Chein
  EX $50   **NM** $75   **MIP** $125

Pikes Peak Mountain Climber, 1930s, 30" long, Marx, vehicle on track
  EX $300   **NM** $450   **MIP** $600

Pinched Roadster, 1927, 9-1/2", Marx, square based, open circular track
  EX $325   **NM** $500   **MIP** $650

Pinocchio, 1938, 9" tall, Marx
  EX $275   **NM** $450   **MIP** $700

Pinocchio, 1950s, 5" tall, Marx
  EX $250   **NM** $425   **MIP** $650

Pinocchio the Acrobat, 1939, 16" tall, Marx
  EX $350   **NM** $550   **MIP** $785

Pinocchio Walker, 1930s, 8-1/2" tall, Marx, animated eyes
  EX $275   **NM** $425   **MIP** $650

Pinocchio Walker, 1930s, Marx, stationary eyes
  EX $225   **NM** $400   **MIP** $600

(Toy Shop File Photo)

Playland Merry-Go-Round, 1930s, 9-1/2" high, Chein
  EX $375   **NM** $500   **MIP** $600

Playland Whip, No. 340, Chein, four bump cars, driver's head wobbles
  EX $425   **NM** $600   **MIP** $775

(Ed Hayes Antique Toys)

Pluto Drum Major, Marx
  EX $225   **NM** $350   **MIP** $500

Pluto Watch Me Roll-Over, 1939, 8" long, Marx
  EX $175   **NM** $275   **MIP** $375

Poor Fish, 1936, 8-1/2" long, Marx
  EX $75   **NM** $125   **MIP** $175

(Toy Shop File Photo)

Popeye Acrobat, Marx
  EX $2000   **NM** $3500   **MIP** $5000

Popeye and Olive Oyl Jiggers, 1936, 10" tall, Marx
  EX $700   **NM** $1200   **MIP** $1500

Popeye Express, 1932, Marx, w/trunk and wheelbarrow
  EX $300   **NM** $525   **MIP** $825

Popeye Handcar, 1935, Marx
  EX $775   **NM** $1300   **MIP** $1900

Popeye in Barrel, Chein
  EX $400   **NM** $650   **MIP** $1000

Popeye the Champ, 1936, 7" long, Marx, tin and celluloid
  EX $1800   **NM** $2800   **MIP** $4000

Popeye the Heavy Hitter, Chein, bell and mallet
  EX $2550   **NM** $4225   **MIP** $6500

(Toy Shop File Photo)

Popeye the Pilot, 1936, Marx
  EX $600   **NM** $800   **MIP** $1100

(Toy Shop File Photo)

Popeye with Punching Bag, Chein
  EX $1000   **NM** $1625   **MIP** $2500

Porky Pig Cowboy with Lariat, 1949, 8" tall, Marx
  EX $275   **NM** $400   **MIP** $650

Porky Pig with Rotating Umbrella, 1939, 8" tall, Marx, w/or without top hat
  EX $250   **NM** $400   **MIP** $600

Red Cap Porter, Marx
  EX $350   **NM** $550   **MIP** $725

(Toy Shop File Photo)

Red the Iceman, Marx
  EX $1350   **NM** $2000   **MIP** $2700

Ride 'Em Cowboy, Marx
  EX $125   **NM** $175   **MIP** $225

Ride-A-Rocket Carnival Ride, 1950s, 19" high, Chein, four rockets
  EX $300   **NM** $450   **MIP** $650

(Scott Smiles)

Ring-A-Ling Circus, 1925, 7-1/2" diameter pink base, Marx, green base, (pink base is $200 more)
  EX $1000   **NM** $1500   **MIP** $2000

Roadster, 1925, 8-1/2" long, Chein
EX $50   NM $80   MIP $125

Rodeo Joe, 1933, Marx
EX $200   NM $300   MIP $400

Roller Coaster, 1938, Chein, includes two cars
EX $275   NM $400   MIP $525

Roller Coaster, 1950s, Chein, includes two cars
EX $200   NM $300   MIP $400

Royal Blue Line Coast to Coast Service, Chein
EX $800   NM $685   MIP $1050

Running Scottie, 1938, 12-1/2" long, Marx
EX $100   NM $150   MIP $200

Sandmill, Chein, beach scene on side
EX $90   NM $145   MIP $225

Santa's Elf, 1925, 6" high, Chein, boxed
EX $225   NM $350   MIP $475

Sea Plane, 1930s, Chein, silver, red, and blue
EX $125   NM $200   MIP $325

Seal, Chein, balancing barbells
EX $100   NM $150   MIP $225

Ski-Boy, 1930s, 6" long, Chein
EX $150   NM $200   MIP $250

Smitty Riding a Scooter, 1932, 8" tall, Marx
EX $500   NM $850   MIP $1300

Smokey Joe the Climbing Fireman, 1930s, 7-1/2" tall, Marx
EX $325   NM $450   MIP $550

Smokey Sam the Wild Fireman, 1950s, 7" tall, Marx
EX $150   NM $225   MIP $300

Snappy the Miracle Dog, 1931, 3-1/2" long, Marx, w/dog house
EX $75   NM $125   MIP $175

Speedboat, 14" long, Chein
EX $90   NM $145   MIP $225

Spic and Span the Hams What Am, 1924, 10" tall, Marx, black drummer and dancer
EX $1000   NM $1500   MIP $2000

Stop, Look and Listen, 1927, Marx, circular track toy
EX $300   NM $500   MIP $750

Streamline Speedway, 1938, 31", Marx, two racers on track
EX $125   NM $175   MIP $250

Subway Express, 1954, 9-3/8", Marx
EX $125   NM $175   MIP $225

(Toy Shop File Photo)

Superman Holding Airplane, 1940, 6" wingspan on airplane, Marx
EX $875   NM $1450   MIP $2250

Superman Turnover Tank, 1940, Marx, 2-1/2 x 3" x 4" long tin wind-up
EX $500   NM $1200   MIP $2000

Telephone Monkey, 1960s, TN, brown fuzzy monkey on blue telephone
EX $150   NM $175   MIP $200

Tidy Tim Streetsweeper, 1933, 8" tall, Marx, pushes wagon
EX $350   NM $575   MIP $750

(Ed Hyers Antique Toys)

Tom Tom Jungle Boy, 7" tall, Marx
EX $100   NM $150   MIP $200

Touring Car, 7" long, Chein
EX $75   NM $100   MIP $150

(Scott Smiles)

Tumbling Monkey, 1942, 4-1/2" tall, Marx
EX $100   NM $175   MIP $225

Tumbling Monkey and Trapeze, 1932, 5-3/4" tall, Marx
EX $125   NM $225   MIP $275

Turtle with Native on Its Back, 1940s, Chein
EX $250   NM $375   MIP $500

Twist Dog, TN, brown fur, ball on head
EX $30   NM $60   MIP $90

Walking Popeye, 1932, 8-1/4" tall, Marx, carrying parrots in cages
EX $400   NM $600   MIP $800

Walking Porter, 1930s, 8" tall, Marx, carries two suitcases
EX $200   NM $350   MIP $500

Wee Running Scottie, 1930s, 5-1/2" long, Marx
EX $125   NM $175   MIP $250

Wee Running Scottie, 1952, 5-1/2" long, Marx
EX $100   NM $150   MIP $200

Wise Pluto, Marx
EX $100   NM $175   MIP $250

Woody Car, 1940s, 5" long, Chein, red
EX $100   NM $175   MIP $250

WWI Soldier, Marx, prone position w/rifle
EX $125   NM $150   MIP $175

Xylophonist, 5" long, Marx
EX $100   NM $150   MIP $200

(Toy Shop File Photo)

Yellow Cab, 7" long, Chein
EX $200   NM $300   MIP $400

Yellow Taxi, 6" long, Chein, orange and black
EX $125   NM $225   MIP $325

Zippo the Climbing Monkey, 1938, 9-1/2", Marx
EX $100   NM $125   MIP $175

TV Toys

What is your favorite television show of all time? Beany and Cecil? The Avengers? The Flintstones? Chips?

Whatever the decade, these television programs shared one important component—licensed merchandise. Licensed toys based on television shows have been around for more than sixty years, and collectors have been fond of them ever since. Among the earliest toys released from television licenses were those based on The Howdy Doody Show in the 1950s.

Making toys based on television characters was an effective way of marketing the program to a target audience. The popularity of the shows, for example, fueled interest in the toys—and often vice versa. For example, young aspiring cowpokes were thrilled to carry their lunches to school in a Rifleman or Bonanza lunch box. Young musicians perhaps sought the toys from Josie & the Pussycats and The Monkees. Space fans couldn't get their hands on enough Lost in Space of Land of the Giants toys.

Television-based toys transported yesterday's kids (and today's collectors) into the virtual worlds represented in the shows. They are one of the most popular crossover toy categories in this book. If you don't find a particular television toy in this chapter, be sure to check the Contents page and look through the Action Figures, Character Toys, Games, Guns, Lunch Boxes, Marx Play Sets, Model Kits, Sci-Fi and Space, View-Master, and Western Toys chapters.

2006 TRENDS

The continued popularity of television toys owes its success in part to the Internet. The proliferation of online auctions has brought out many television toys to collectors crossing over from other hobby areas.

Today, television toys still exist, but fewer 1990s shows has spawned successful toy lines or licensed merchandise. Recent examples of successful items have come from shows like The X-Files, Buffy the Vampire Slayer, The Simpsons, and Family Guy.

Children's diversified interests, like video and computer games, have somewhat replaced television shows. Toys based on the latest action-packed games are now sharing shelf space with the more popular licensed movie toys.

Will there be a return to licensed television toys? As tastes change and topics become more adult, it is unlikely many toy manufacturers will take expensive risks. And with the saturation of "reality" shows on television these days, what fun toys could we expect?

But collectors needn't worry. Their vintage favorites remain tangible memories of a simpler—and a more imaginative—time and place.

THE TOP TEN TV TOYS *(In Mint Condition)*

1. Green Hornet Dashboard, Remco, 1966	$2,000
2. Green Hornet Seal Ring, General Mills, 1940	1,800
3. Gilligan's Island Trading Cards, Topps, 1965	1,550
4. Man From U.N.C.L.E. Counterspy Outfit Store Display, Marx, 1966	1,250
5. Gilligan's Island Dip Dots Painting Set, Kenner, 1975	1,200
6. Green Hornet Fan Club Photos, Golden Jersey Milk, 1938	1,200
7. Man From U.N.C.L.E. Crime Buster Gift Set, Corgi, 1966	1,050
8. Howdy Doody Periscope, Wonder Bread, 1950s	1,000
9. Girl From U.N.C.L.E. Doll, Marx, 1967	1,000
10. Howdy Doody, Rice Crispies Cereal Box, Kellogg's, 1954	1,000

ADDAMS FAMILY

Gomez Hand Puppet, 1965, Ideal
  EX $50   NM $120   MIP $250

Lurch Figure, 1964, Remco
  EX $80   NM $185   MIP $360

Morticia Figure, 1964, Remco
  EX $100   NM $210   MIP $675

Morticia Halloween Costume, 1964, Ben Cooper, painted hair
  EX $40   NM $100   MIP $200

Morticia Halloween Costume, 1964, Ben Cooper, w/hair
  EX $60   NM $125   MIP $250

Morticia Hand Puppet, 1965, Ideal
  EX $50   NM $130   MIP $260

Thing Bank, 1964, plastic, battery-operated
  EX $40   NM $150   MIP $225

Uncle Fester Figure, 1964, Remco
  EX $100   NM $250   MIP $625

ALVIN SHOW

(Toy Shop File Photo)

Sliding Squares Game, 1960s, Roalex Co., Sliding squares form a variety of "possible" solutions
  EX $25   NM $45   MIP n/a

A-TEAM

(Toy Shop File Photo)

A-Team Combat Headquarters Set, 1980s, Galoob, Includes 3-3/4" figures of Hannibal, Face, B.A. Baracus, Murdock and gear, including inflatable raft, machine guns, flag and tent
  EX $40   NM $85   MIP $125

A-Team Rocket Ball Target Set, 1983, gumballs w/gun and target
  EX $5   NM $10   MIP $25

A-Team Shrinky Dinks Set, 1980s
  EX $5   NM $10   MIP $20

AVENGERS

(Toy Shop File Photo)

Shooting Game, 1960s, Merit
  EX $20   NM $45   MIP n/a

(Toy Shop File Photo)

Steed Sword Stick, 1960s, Lone Star, Toy of John Steed's secret cane/sword combo
  EX $35   NM $70   MIP n/a

BANANA SPLITS

(Toy Shop File Photo)

4 The Banana Splits Puzzle, 1969, Whitman, frame tray
  EX $25   NM $55   MIP $85

Banana Band, 1973, Larami, horn, sax, mouth harp
  EX $25   NM $60   MIP $120

Banana Buggy Model Kit, 1968, Aurora
  EX $60   NM $200   MIP $325

Banana Splits Bingo Costume, 1968, Ben Cooper
  EX $60   NM $175   MIP $300

(Toy Shop File Photo)

Banana Splits Doll, 1960s, Sutton, 12" tall, plush Drooper
  EX $45   NM $95   MIP $200

Banana Splits Kut-Up Kit, 1973, Larami
  EX $25   NM $40   MIP $75

Banana Splits Mug, 1969, plastic yellow dog mug
  EX $20   NM $40   MIP $65

Banana Splits Record, 1969, Kellogg's
  EX $20   NM $90   MIP $175

Paint-By-Number Set, 1969, Hasbro
  EX $45   NM $80   MIP $150

Talking Telephone, 1969, Hasbro
  EX $75   NM $175   MIP $350

BEANY AND CECIL

Beany and Cecil and Their Pals Record Player, 1961, Vanity Fair
  EX $80   NM $200   MIP $375

Beany and Cecil Carrying Case, 1960s, 9" diameter, w/strap, vinyl-covered cardboard
  EX $40   NM $85   MIP $100

Beany and Cecil Gun, 1961, Mattel, w/propeller disks
  EX $30   NM $150   MIP $200

Beany and Cecil Puzzle, 1961, Playskool, wooden frame tray
  EX $25   NM $65   MIP $100

Beany and Cecil Skill Ball, 1960s, colorful tin w/wood frame
  EX $30   NM $80   MIP $125

Beany and Cecil Travel Case, 1960s, 8" tall, round, red vinyl w/zipper and strap
  EX $25   NM $55   MIP $95

Beany and Cecil Travel Case, 1960s, square, 4-1/2" x 3-1/2" x 3" red vinyl, carrying strap, illustrated w/characters
  EX $30   NM $70   MIP $100

Beany and His Magic Set Book, 1953, Tell-a-Tale Book
  EX $10   NM $20   MIP $55

Beany Doll, 1963, Mattel, 15" tall, non-talking
  EX $45   NM $100   MIP $165

Beany Figure, 1984, Caltoy, 8" tall
  EX $10   NM $20   MIP $45

Beany Talking Doll, 1950s, Mattel, 17" tall, stuffed cloth, vinyl head w/pull string
  EX $90   NM $250   MIP $425

Bob Clampetts' Beany Coloring Book, 1960s, Whitman
  EX $15   NM $75   MIP $150

Captain Huffenpuff Puzzle, 1961, large
  EX $25   NM $85   MIP $120

Cecil and His Disguise Kit, 1962, Mattel, 17" tall plush Cecil w/disguise wigs, mustaches, etc.
  EX $30   NM $90   MIP $175

Cecil in the Music Box, 1961, Mattel, jack-in-the-box
  EX $90   NM $225   MIP $375

Cecil Soaky, 8-1/2" tall, plastic
EX $35   NM $85   MIP $150

Leakin' Lena Boat, 1962, Irwin, plastic and wood
EX $50   NM $115   MIP $225

Leakin' Lena Pound 'N Pull Toy, 1960s, Pressman, wood
EX $60   NM $125   MIP $250

BEN CASEY M.D.

Ben Casey Pencils, 1962, Hassenfeld Bros., ten red/white pencils on card
EX $15   NM $30   MIP $70

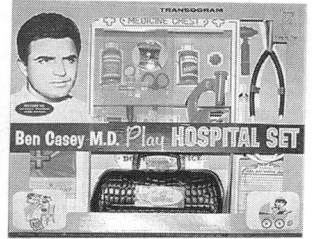

(Toy Shop File Photo)

Play Hosptial Set, 1960s, Transogram, Includes doctor bag, microscope, stethascope and more
EX $50   NM $100   MIP $175

BEVERLY HILLBILLIES

(Toy Shop File Photo)

Paper cut-outs, 1960s, Whitman, Includes Jed, Jethro, Granny and Elly May
EX $35   NM $80   MIP $125

BEWITCHED

(Toy Shop File Photo)

Bewitched Samantha Doll, 1967, Ideal, 12-1/2" tall
EX $180   NM $395   MIP $750

Bewitched Tabitha Paper Doll Set, 1966, Magic Wand, 11" cardboard doll, clothes
EX $30   NM $75   MIP $150

BIONIC WOMAN

(Toy Shop File Photo)

Play-Doh Action Play Set, 1970s, Kenner, Includes molds for making Play-Doh characters from the show, 3 containers of Play-Doh, plastic mat and six-wheeled vehicle
EX $25   NM $40   MIP n/a

BOZO

(Toy Shop File Photo)

Bozo Record Player
EX $45   NM $90   MIP n/a

Bozo the Clown Beach Towel, 1960s, 16" x 24"
EX $8   NM $15   MIP $35

Bozo the Clown Doll, 1970
EX $25   NM $50   MIP $85

Bozo the Clown Figure, 1970s, vinyl, 5" tall
EX $5   NM $15   MIP $30

Bozo the Clown Push Button Marionette, 1962, Knickerbocker
EX $25   NM $45   MIP $85

Bozo the Clown Puzzle, 1965, Whitman, #4516, Model No. 4516
EX $10   NM $25   MIP $50

Bozo the Clown Slide Puzzle, 1960s
EX $15   NM $40   MIP $75

Bozo the Clown Soaky, 1960s, Palmolive
EX $15   NM $45   MIP $85

Bozo Trick Trapeze, 1960s, red base
EX $15   NM $35   MIP $65

BRADY BUNCH

Brady Bunch Halloween Costume, 1970s, Collegeville, smock reads "One of The Brady Bunch"
EX $40   NM $90   MIP $150

Brady Bunch Kite Fun Book, 1976, Pacific Gas and Electric
EX $15   NM $35   MIP $75

Brady Bunch Paper Dolls Cut-Out Book, 1973, Whitman
EX $30   NM $85   MIP $150

Brady Bunch Puzzle, frame tray
EX $25   NM $45   MIP $80

Brady Bunch Trading Cards, 1971, Topps, 55 cards
EX $250   NM $525   MIP $775

Kitty Karry-All Doll, 1969, Remco
EX $90   NM $175   MIP $325

CAPTIAN KANGAROO

(Toy Shop File Photo)

Captain Kangaroo Duck Pin Game, 1950s, Gardner, With self returning ball
EX $35   NM $75   MIP n/a

(Toy Shop File Photo)

Captain Kangaroo Presto Slate, 1960s, Fairchild, slate on illustrated card, several versions
EX $12   NM $30   MIP $40

Captain Kangaroo Puzzle, 1960, Whitman, #4446, frame tray, Model No. 4446
EX $10   NM $30   MIP $60

CHARLIE'S ANGELS

Charlie's Angels Paper Dolls, 1977, Toy Factory, Farrah, Kate or Jaclyn sets, each
EX $20   NM $50   MIP $90

Charlie's Angels Pendant, 1977, Fleetwood Toys, 4" plastic figure of Farrah hangs from pendant
EX $10   NM $25   MIP $45

Farrah Fawcett Doll, 1977, Mattel, 12"
EX $50   NM $125   MIP $200

Farrah Travel Trunk, 1970s, Grand Toys, Canadian toy, box has french language
EX $10   NM $20   MIP $30

(Toy Shop File Photo)

Hide-A-Way House, 1970s, Hasbro, Revolving five-sided dollhouse for Charlie's Angels figures
EX $50   NM $100   MIP $150

Kate Jackson Doll, 1978, Mattel, 12"
EX $20   NM $45   MIP $90

Kelly Doll, 1977, Hasbro, 8"
EX $12   NM $35   MIP $80

Kris Doll, 1977, Hasbro, 8"
EX $10   NM $30   MIP $70

River Race Outfits, 1977, Palitoy
EX $15   NM $35   MIP $60

Sabrina Doll, 1977, Hasbro, 8"
EX $20   NM $70   MIP $120

Sabrina, Kelly, and Kris Gift Set, 1977, Hasbro
EX $30   NM $70   MIP $145

Slalom Caper Outfits, 1977, Palitoy
EX $10   NM $30   MIP $50

(Toy Shop File Photo)

Target Set, 1970s, Placo Toys, Includes 2 safety guns, 6 safety darts and a knockdown target
EX $40   NM $85   MIP n/a

(KP Photo)

Underwater Intrigue Outfits, 1977, Palitoy
EX $10   NM $30   MIP $50

CHiPs

(Toy Shop File Photo)

Colorforms Play Set, 1970s, Colorforms
EX $30   NM $55   MIP n/a

(Toy Shop File Photo)

Free Wheeling Motorcycle, 1970s, Mego, Made to fit Mego's 8" figures from the series
EX $35   NM $50   MIP n/a

(Toy Shop File Photo)

Police Set, 1970s, HG Toys, Includes snub-nose revolver, badge, sunglasses (of course!), handcuffs and holster
EX $27   NM $60   MIP n/a

COMBAT!

(Toy Shop File Photo)

Official Play Set, 1960s, Marx, Super-cool toy soldier set includes tanks, howitzers, army trucks, tanks, personnel carriers, soldiers and landing craft. This same set was re-packaged in the 1970s without the "Combat" TV-show name or tie-in
EX $40   NM $85   MIP n/a

DOBIE GILLIS

(Toy Shop File Photo)

Paint-N-Press Art Set, 1960s, Includes watercolors and instructions
EX $15   NM $25   MIP n/a

DR. KILDARE

Dr. Kildare Photo Scrapbook, 1962
EX $10   NM $25   MIP $50

DRAGNET

(Toy Shop File Photo File)

Dragnet Badge 714, 1955, Knickerbocker, 2-1/2" bronze finish badge in yellow box w/illustration of Jack Webb, box bottom has ID card
EX $45   NM $90   MIP $135

TV TOYS

(Toy Shop File Photo)

Dragnet Badge 714 Target Game, 1950s, Includes 3 guns, corks and darts and litho metal target. $2.98 original price!
EX $75   NM $150   MIP n/a

(Toy Shop File Photo)

Dragnet Crime Lab, 1950s, Transogram, "A complete crime detection outfit for the junior detective"
EX $120   NM $225   MIP n/a

DUKES OF HAZZARD

(Toy Shop File Photo)

Daisy's Jeep, 1970s, Includes "Dixie," a white and brown CJ5 Jeep and one Daisy Duke figure
EX $35   NM $50   MIP n/a

FAMILY AFFAIR

(Toy Shop File Photo File)

5 Family Affair Paper Dolls, Whitman
EX $30   NM $45   MIP $55

Buffy Halloween Costume, 1970, Ben Cooper
EX $20   NM $40   MIP $80

Buffy Make-Up and Hairstyling Set, 1971, Amsco
EX $20   NM $40   MIP $80

Buffy with Mrs. Beasley Dolls, 1967, Mattel, 6" Buffy w/smaller Mrs. Beasley
EX $30   NM $65   MIP $115

Family Affair Cartoon Kit, 1970, Colorforms
EX $12   NM $25   MIP $50

Family Affair Puzzle, 1970, Whitman
EX $12   NM $30   MIP $60

Mrs. Beasley Paper Dolls, 1970s, Whitman, several variations
EX $12   NM $30   MIP $60

Mrs. Beasley Rag Doll, 1973, Mattel, 14"
EX $12   NM $25   MIP $45

Talking Mrs. Beasley Doll, 1967, Mattel
EX $50   NM $100   MIP $225

FLINTSTONES

Baby Puss Figure, 1961, Knickerbocker, 10" tall, vinyl
EX $35   NM $75   MIP $135

Bamm-Bamm Bank, 1960s, 11" tall, hard plastic figure sitting on turtle
EX $20   NM $45   MIP $75

Bamm-Bamm Bubble Pipe, 1963, Transogram, figural pipe on illustrated card
EX $12   NM $25   MIP $50

Bamm-Bamm Doll, 1962, Ideal, 15" tall
EX $50   NM $115   MIP $225

Bamm-Bamm Figure, 1970, Dakin, 7" tall
EX $20   NM $40   MIP $75

Bamm-Bamm Finger Puppet, 1972, Knickerbocker
EX $5   NM $15   MIP $25

Bamm-Bamm Soaky, 1960s, Purex
EX $20   NM $40   MIP $75

Barney Bank, 1973, solid plastic, Barney holding a bowling ball
EX $15   NM $35   MIP $60

Barney Doll, 1962, 6" tall, soft vinyl doll, movable arms and head
EX $25   NM $45   MIP $80

Barney Figure, 1961, Knickerbocker, 10" tall, vinyl
EX $40   NM $55   MIP $160

Barney Figure, 1970, Dakin, 7-1/4" tall
EX $20   NM $40   MIP $75

Barney Figure, 1986, Flintoys
EX $5   NM $10   MIP $15

Barney Finger Puppet, 1972, Knickerbocker
EX $8   NM $15   MIP $25

Barney Night Light, 1979, Electricord, figural
EX $8   NM $15   MIP $25

Barney Policeman Figure, 1986, Flintoys
EX $4   NM $8   MIP $12

Barney Riding Dino Toy, 1960s, Marx, 8" long, metal and vinyl, wind-up
EX $110   NM $300   MIP $550

Barney Soaky, 1970s, Roclar
EX $10   NM $20   MIP $55

Barney Wind-Up Toy, 1960s, Marx, 3-1/2" tall figure, tin
EX $85   NM $190   MIP $375

Barney's Car, 1986, Flintoys
EX $8   NM $15   MIP $30

Betty Figure, 1961, Knickerbocker, 10" tall, vinyl
EX $50   NM $100   MIP $200

Betty Figure, 1986, Flintoys
EX $4   NM $7   MIP $10

Dino Bank, china, Dino carrying a golf bag
EX $45   NM $95   MIP $185

Dino Bank, 1973, hard vinyl, blue w/Pebbles on his back
EX $18   NM $35   MIP $75

Dino Bath Puppet Sponge, 1973, bath mitt
EX $10   NM $18   MIP $35

Dino Doll, movable head and arms
EX $15   NM $25   MIP $50

Dino Figure, 1970, Dakin, 7-3/4" tall
EX $25   NM $50   MIP $100

Dino Figure, 1986, Flintoys
EX $4   NM $7   MIP $15

Dino Wind-Up Toy, 1960s, Marx, 3-1/2" tall, tin
EX $90   NM $180   MIP $360

Fang Figure, 1970, Dakin, 7" tall
EX $25   NM $50   MIP $95

Flintmobile, 1986, Flintoys
EX $10   NM $18   MIP $40

Flintmobile with Fred Figure, 1986, Flintoys
EX $18   NM $33   MIP $60

Flintstones Ashtray, 1960, ceramic w/Wilma
EX $25   NM $70   MIP $100

Flintstones Bank, 1971, 19" tall w/Barney and Bamm Bamm
EX $25   NM $50   MIP $85

Flintstones Car, 1964, Remco, battery operated car w/Barney, Fred, Wilma and Betty
EX $85   NM $200   MIP $385

Flintstones Figure Set, 1981, Spoontiques, eight figures
EX $35   NM $50   MIP $90

Flintstones Figures, 1976, Empire, three-inch solid figures of Fred, Barney, Wilma and Betty
EX $10   NM $40   MIP $85

Flintstones Figures, 1976, Imperial, eight acrylic figures: Fred, Barney, Wilma, Betty, Pebbles, Bamm Bamm, Dino and Baby Puss
EX $15   NM $35   MIP $65

Flintstones House, 1986, Flintoys
EX $12   NM $25   MIP $35

Flintstones Lamp, 9-1/2" tall, plastic Fred w/lampshade picturing characters
EX $50   NM $120   MIP $210

Flintstones Paint Box, 1961, Transogram
EX $18   NM $35   MIP $60

Flintstones Party Place Set, 1969, Reed, tablecloth, napkins, plates, cups
EX $10   NM $20   MIP $40

Flintstones Roto Draw, 1969, British
EX $30   NM $70   MIP $100

Flintstones Tru-Vue Film Card, 1962, Tru-Vue, #T-37, w/strips of Fred
EX $30   NM $70   MIP $100

Fred Bubble Blowing Pipe, soft vinyl w/curved stem
EX $6   NM $12   MIP $20

Fred Doll, 1960, 13" soft vinyl doll w/movable head
EX $45   NM $100   MIP $225

Fred Doll, 1972, Perfection Plastic, 11" tall
EX $15   NM $35   MIP $60

Fred Figure, 1960, Knickerbocker, 15" tall
EX $40   NM $85   MIP $200

Fred Figure, 1961, Knickerbocker, 10" tall, vinyl
EX $32   NM $75   MIP $150

Fred Figure, 1970, Dakin, 8-1/4" tall
EX $22   NM $45   MIP $85

Fred Figure, 1986, Flintoys
EX $4   NM $8   MIP $12

Fred Finger Puppet, 1972, Knickerbocker
EX $8   NM $15   MIP $22

Fred Flintstone's Bedrock Bank, 1962, Alps, 9", tin and vinyl, battery operated
EX $175   NM $310   MIP $325

Fred Flintstone's Lithograph Wind-Up, 1960s, Marx, 3-1/2" tall figure, metal
EX $85   NM $170   MIP $385

Fred Gumball Machine, 1960s, plastic, shaped like Fred's head
EX $20   NM $32   MIP $60

Fred Loves Wilma Bank, ceramic
EX $50   NM $110   MIP $185

Fred Night Light, 1970, figural
EX $6   NM $12   MIP $25

Fred Policeman Figure, 1986, Flintoys
EX $4   NM $8   MIP $15

Fred Push Puppet, 1960s, Kohner
EX $10   NM $25   MIP $45

Fred Riding Dino, 1962, Marx, 18" long battery operated w/Fred in Howdah
EX $175   NM $350   MIP $675

Fred Riding Dino, 1962, Marx, 8" long, tin and vinyl, wind-up
EX $175   NM $350   MIP $675

Great Big Punch-Out Book, 1961, Whitman
EX $20   NM $50   MIP $125

Motorbike, 1986, Flintoys
EX $6   NM $12   MIP $20

Pebbles Bank, 9" tall vinyl w/Pebbles sitting in chair
EX $10   NM $25   MIP $50

Pebbles Doll, 1963, Ideal, 15" tall
EX $55   NM $115   MIP $225

Pebbles Doll, 1982, Mighty Star, vinyl head, arms and legs, cloth stuffed body 12" tall
EX $15   NM $25   MIP $45

Pebbles Figure, 1970, Dakin, 8" tall w/blonde hair and purple velvet shirt
EX $25   NM $45   MIP $85

Pebbles Finger Puppet, 1972, Knickerbocker
EX $5   NM $13   MIP $20

Pebbles Flintstone Cradle, 1963, Ideal, for a 15" doll
EX $40   NM $75   MIP $150

Pebbles Soaky, 1960s, Purex
EX $20   NM $35   MIP $70

Police Car, 1986, Flintoys
EX $8   NM $15   MIP $30

Wilma Figure, 1961, Knickerbocker, 10" tall, vinyl
EX $50   NM $100   MIP $190

Wilma Figure, 1986, Flintoys
EX $4   NM $7   MIP $15

Wilma Friction Car, 1962, Marx, metal
EX $90   NM $175   MIP $375

FLIPPER

(Toy Shop File Photo)

Flipper Game, 1970s, Koide, Japanese issue
EX $40   NM $65   MIP n/a

(Toy Shop File Photo)

Flipper Numbered Pencil Coloring Set, 1960s. Includes colored pencils, sharpener and pre-sketched pictures to color
EX $20   NM $40   MIP n/a

(Toy Shop File Photo)

Puncho, 1960s, Coleco, Inflatable 40" toy with weighted bottom, so he appears to be swimming upright in a pool or lake
EX $25   NM $45   MIP n/a

FLYING NUN

Flying Nun Chalkboard, 1967, Screen Gems
EX $22   NM $45   MIP $80

Flying Nun Doll, 1960s, Hasbro, 4"
EX $22   NM $125   MIP $200

Flying Nun Doll, 1967, Hasbro, 11"
EX $30   NM $85   MIP $175

Flying Nun Halloween Costume, 1967, Ben Cooper
EX $20   NM $60   MIP $100

(Toy Shop File Photo)

Flying Nun Paint-By-Number Set, 1960s, Hasbro, two scenes and 10 paint vials
EX $15　　**NM** $30　　**MIP** $60

Flying Nun Paper Doll Set, 1969, Saalfield, five dolls and costumes
EX $16　　**NM** $40　　**MIP** $80

GET SMART

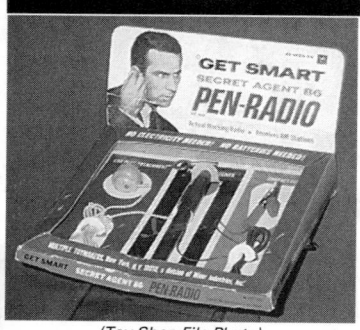

(Toy Shop File Photo)

Secret Agent 86 Pen Radio, 1960s, Miner Industries, Functioning crystal radio set in shape of pen, included earphone and contact clip. Received AM radio stations
EX $35　　**NM** $70　　**MIP** n/a

(Toy Shop File Photo)

Secret Agent 99 Spy Purse, 1960s, Miner Industries, Includes secret compartment, two-way mirror, secret micro-film holder (inside rose), ID card
EX $55　　**NM** $105　　**MIP** n/a

GILLIGAN'S ISLAND

Gilligan's Floating Island Play Set, 1977, Playskool
EX $75　　**NM** $190　　**MIP** $350

Gilligan's Island Notepad, 1965, Whitman, Gilligan and Skipper on cover
EX $12　　**NM** $30　　**MIP** $60

Gilligan's Island Trading Cards, 1965, Topps, set of 55 cards
EX $400　　**NM** $800　　**MIP** $1550

New Adventures of Gilligan Dip Dots Painting Set, 1975, Kenner, book w/paints and brush
EX $220　　**NM** $570　　**MIP** $1200

GIRL FROM U.N.C.L.E.

1967 British Annual Book, 1967, World Distributors, hardcover, 95 pages, photo cover
EX $10　　**NM** $30　　**MIP** $60

1968 British Annual Book, 1968, World Distributors, hardcover, 95 pages, photo cover
EX $10　　**NM** $30　　**MIP** $60

1969 British Annual Book, 1969, World Distributors, hardcover, 95 pages, photo cover
EX $10　　**NM** $30　　**MIP** $60

Costume, 1967, Halco, transparent or painted mask, dress-style costume has show logo and silhouette image of Girl spy holding smoking gun, in illustrated window box
EX $55　　**NM** $115　　**MIP** $250

Garter Holster, 1966, Lone Star, metal pistol fires small plastic bullets from metal shells, checker design vinyl holster and bullet pouch, on card
EX $80　　**NM** $175　　**MIP** $350

Girl From U.N.C.L.E. Doll, 1967, Marx, 11" tall w/30 accessories in illustrated box
EX $250　　**NM** $500　　**MIP** $1000

Music from the Television Series, 1966, M.G.M. Records, photo cover shows Stephanie against a wall
EX $9　　**NM** $20　　**MIP** $40

Secret Agent Wristwatch, 1966, Bradley, watch has pink face w/April Dancer image, in case
EX $85　　**NM** $200　　**MIP** $400

GREEN ACRES

(Toy Shop File Photo)

2 Magic Stay-On Dolls, 1960s, Includes Oliver and Lisa figures, plus complete wardrobes
EX $25　　**NM** $40　　**MIP** $75

GREEN HORNET

Assistant Badge, 1966, Don Howard Associates
EX $45　　**NM** $95　　**MIP** $200

Bike Badge, 1966, Burry Cookies, premium; w/Vari-Vue flasher
EX $85　　**NM** $175　　**MIP** $350

Black Beauty Balloon Toy, 1966, Oak Rubber
EX $70　　**NM** $145　　**MIP** $275

Black Beauty Slot Car, 1966, Aurora, clear box w/insert
EX $85　　**NM** $175　　**MIP** $400

Black Beauty Slot Car, 1966, BZ Industries, large scale
EX $160　　**NM** $380　　**MIP** $775

Captain Action Flasher Ring, 1966, Vari-Vue, blue
EX $10　　**NM** $18　　**MIP** $30

Captain Action Flasher Ring, 1966, Vari-Vue, chrome
EX $13　　**NM** $25　　**MIP** $40

Charm, 1966, Cracker Jack, hornet-shaped
EX $10　　**NM** $30　　**MIP** $50

Charms, 1966, Folz Vending, hornet-shaped
EX $10　　**NM** $15　　**MIP** $25

Comic Strip Stickers, 1966, Folz Vending, 7" long, from vending machines, each
EX $25　　**NM** $50　　**MIP** $100

Electric Drawing Set, 1966, Lakeside
EX $90　　**NM** $190　　**MIP** $275

Fan Club Photos, 1938, Golden Jersey Milk, set of four; radio premium
EX $400　　**NM** $800　　**MIP** $1200

Flasher Button, 1966, Vari-Vue, pinback, 3"
EX $15　　**NM** $30　　**MIP** $45

Flasher Button, 1966, Vari-Vue, no pinback, 3"
EX $10　　**NM** $20　　**MIP** $35

Flasher Button, 1966, Vari-Vue, no pinback, 7"
EX $25　　**NM** $45　　**MIP** $80

Flasher Rings, 1960s, Vari-Vue, chrome base, each
EX $10　　**NM** $20　　**MIP** $50

Flasher Rings, 1960s, Vari-Vue, blue plastic base, each
EX $5　　**NM** $10　　**MIP** $40

Flashlight Whistle, 1966, Bantamlight
EX $40　　**NM** $90　　**MIP** $175

Frame Tray Puzzles, 1966, Whitman, box of four
EX $40　　**NM** $90　　**MIP** $175

Green Hornet Bendy Figure, 1966, Lakeside
EX $40　　**NM** $80　　**MIP** $175

Green Hornet Bubble Gum Ring, Frito Lay, rubber ring, in cello pack
EX $25　　**NM** $45　　**MIP** $90

Green Hornet Candy/Toy Box, 1966, Phoenix Candy, several variations
EX $40　　**NM** $90　　**MIP** $150

Green Hornet Charm Bracelet, 1966, gold finish chain w/five charms: Hornet, Van, Kato, Pistol, Black Beauty, on 3" x 7-1/2" illustrated card
EX $50   NM $125   MIP $200

Green Hornet Colorforms Set, 1966, Colorforms
EX $60   NM $125   MIP $250

Green Hornet Dashboard, 1966, Remco
EX $300   NM $1000   MIP $2000

Green Hornet Mini Walkie Talkies, 1966, Remco
EX $75   NM $150   MIP $300

Green Hornet Print Putty, 1966, Colorforms
EX $20   NM $50   MIP $95

Green Hornet Seal Ring, 1940, General Mills, cereal premium
EX $225   NM $780   MIP $1800

Green Hornet Soundtrack Record, 1966, 20th Century Fox
EX $25   NM $100   MIP $200

Green Hornet Troll Figure, 1966, Uneeda Wishnik, 7" tall
EX $55   NM $100   MIP $250

Green Hornet Troll Figure, 1966, Damm, 3" tall
EX $45   NM $75   MIP $150

Green Hornet TV Guide, 1966, Cover features Van Williams and Bruce Lee
EX $50   NM $125   MIP $250

Green Hornet Utensils, 1966, Imperial Knife, fork and spoon
EX $30   NM $75   MIP $150

Green Hornet Walkie Talkies, 1966, Remco
EX $50   NM $100   MIP $175

Green Hornet Wallet, 1966, green vinyl, Hornet or Kato
EX $25   NM $50   MIP $100

Green Hornet Wrist Radios, 1966, Remco, battery-operated
EX $150   NM $250   MIP $525

Halloween Costume, 1966, Ben Cooper, several variations
EX $100   NM $200   MIP $375

Hand Puppet, 1966, Ideal, w/hat
EX $80   NM $175   MIP $300

Inflatable Raft, 1966, Ideal
EX $160   NM $350   MIP $700

Instant Squeeze Candy, 1966, Dre's Inc., toothpaste-type container w/hornet-shaped plug
EX $40   NM $90   MIP $175

Kato and Black Beauty Glass, 1938, Golden Jersey Milk, radio premium
EX $100   NM $300   MIP $500

Kite, 1966, Roalex
EX $30   NM $75   MIP $150

Magic Eyes Movie Viewer Slides, 1966, Sawyers
EX $75   NM $150   MIP $300

Magic Rub-On Set, 1966, Whitman
EX $70   NM $150   MIP $275

Magic Slate, 1966, Watkins-Strathmore, three variations
EX $35   NM $90   MIP $175

Mini Movie Viewer, 1966, Acme/Chemtoy, w/filmstrips
EX $50   NM $100   MIP $200

Mini Movie Viewer, 1971, Chemtoy, w/filmstrips
EX $25   NM $45   MIP $90

Numbered Pencil and Paint Set, 1966, Hasbro
EX $75   NM $160   MIP $300

Paint By Number Set, 1966, Hasbro
EX $65   NM $130   MIP $260

Pencil Case, 1966, Hasbro
EX $30   NM $65   MIP $120

Pencils, 1966, Empire Pencil, five on card
EX $30   NM $80   MIP $150

Pennant, 1966, RMS, blue or orange
EX $35   NM $100   MIP $175

Playing Cards, 1966, Ed-U-Cards
EX $10   NM $75   MIP $150

Postcard, 1936, Golden Jersey Milk, radio premium
EX $150   NM $300   MIP $400

Punch-Out Book, 1966, Whitman
EX $100   NM $200   MIP $375

Secret Agent Badge, 1966, Don Howard Associates
EX $20   NM $35   MIP $65

Stardust Craft Kit, 1966, Hasbro
EX $35   NM $75   MIP $150

The Case of the Disappearing Doctor Book, 1966, Whitman
EX $20   NM $30   MIP $45

The Green Hornet Cracks Down Book, 1942, Whitman, Better Little Books
EX $25   NM $60   MIP $120

The Green Hornet Returns Book, 1941, Whitman, Better Little Books
EX $25   NM $60   MIP $120

The Green Hornet Strikes Book, 1940, Whitman, Better Little Books
EX $25   NM $60   MIP $120

Thingmaker Mold and Accessories, 1966, Mattel
EX $100   NM $175   MIP $325

Trading Cards, 1966, Donruss, set of 44
EX $85   NM $100   MIP $325

Trading Cards Display Box, 1966, Donruss
EX $100   NM $250   MIP $500

Trading Cards Wrapper, 1966, Donruss
EX $15   NM $30   MIP $60

Trading Stickers, 1966, Topps, set of 44
EX $85   NM $160   MIP $325

Trading Stickers Display Box, 1966, Topps
EX $100   NM $250   MIP $500

Trading Stickers Wrapper, 1966, Topps
EX $10   NM $25   MIP $50

Wrist Signal Light, 1966, Bantamlight
EX $40   NM $80   MIP $175

GRIZZLY ADAMS

Grizzly Adams, 1979, Mattel, 9" figure, w/accessories, #2377
EX $15   NM $30   MIP $45

Nakoma, 1979, Mattel, 9" figure, w/accessories
EX $15   NM $30   MIP $45

HOGAN'S HEROES

(Toy Shop File Photo)

Peri-Peeper, 1977, Continental Plastics, Includes Periscope, ID card and pinback button
EX $15   NM $30   MIP n/a

HOWDY DOODY

Cereal Box, 1954, Kellogg's, Rice Krispies, Howdy Mask on back
EX $250   NM $650   MIP $1000

Clarabell Bank, 1976, Strauss, flocked plastic, 9"
EX $20   NM $65   MIP $120

Clarabell Jumping Toy, 1950s, Linemar, 7" tall tin litho, squeeze lever to make figure hop forward and squeak
EX $200   NM $450   MIP $825

Clarabell Marionette, 1950s, Peter Puppet
EX $100   NM $210   MIP $425

Flub-a-Dub Figure, 1950s, TeeVee Toys, 4" x 4" painted plastic, movable mouth
EX $40   NM $90   MIP $150

Flub-a-Dub Flip A Ring Game, 1950s, Flip-A-Ring, 9", ring toss game
EX $25   NM $45   MIP $75

Flub-a-Dub Marionette, 1950s, Peter Puppet
EX $100   NM $225   MIP $450

Flub-a-Dub Puppet, 1950s, Gund
EX $40   NM $75   MIP $150

Howdy Doody Acrobat, 1950s, Arnold, tin, plastic, Howdy swings on high bar
EX $15   NM $25   MIP $60

Howdy Doody Air Doodle Beanie, 1950s, Kellogg's, Rice Krispies premium
EX $75   NM $200   MIP $300

Howdy Doody Air-O-Doodle Circus Train, 1950s, Plasticraft/Kagran, red/yellow plastic train, boat and plane toy on card w/cut out character passengers
EX $40   NM $100   MIP $160

Howdy Doody and Clarabell Book, 1952, Simon and Schuster, Little Golden Book
EX $12   NM $22   MIP $50

Howdy Doody and Clarabell Coloring Book, 1955, Whitman, Model No. 1188
EX $15   NM $75   MIP $185

Howdy Doody and Clarabell Puppet Mitten Kit, 1950s, Connecticut Leather
EX $30   NM $75   MIP $110

Howdy Doody and his Magic Hat Book, 1953, Whitman, Little Golden Book
EX $12   NM $22   MIP $40

Howdy Doody and Mr. Bluster Book, 1954, Whitman, Little Golden Book
EX $10   NM $22   MIP $40

Howdy Doody and the Musical Forest Record, 1950s, RCA, 45 rpm
EX $20   NM $50   MIP $80

Howdy Doody and the Princess Book, 1952, Whitman, Little Golden Book
EX $10   NM $25   MIP $45

Howdy Doody and You Record, 1950s, RCA, 45 rpm
EX $18   NM $40   MIP $65

Howdy Doody Bank, Vandor, ceramic figural head
EX $25   NM $55   MIP $100

Howdy Doody Bank, 1950s, ceramic bank, all color, bust of Howdy
EX $300   NM $500   MIP $900

Howdy Doody Bank, 1950s, 7" tall, ceramic, Howdy riding a pig
EX $70   NM $160   MIP $300

Howdy Doody Bank, 1976, Strauss, flocked plastic, 9"
EX $20   NM $40   MIP $85

Howdy Doody Bubble Pipe, 1950s, Lido, 4" long, Howdy or Clarabell
EX $30   NM $160   MIP $285

Howdy Doody Button, 1949, New York Sunday News, reads "New Color Comic—Sunday News"
EX $30   NM $55   MIP $100

Howdy Doody Coin, 1950s, Kellogg's, plastic, silver, raised bust on Howdy on front
EX $20   NM $40   MIP $75

Howdy Doody Color TV Set, American Plastic, plastic, w/films
EX $130   NM $275   MIP $500

Howdy Doody Coloring Books, 1955, Whitman, boxed set of six
EX $42   NM $150   MIP $300

Howdy Doody Comic Book, 1950, Dell, Issue No. 1, January
EX $110   NM $275   MIP $425

Howdy Doody Cookbook, 1952, Welch's
EX $30   NM $110   MIP $225

Howdy Doody Cookie-Go-Round, 1950s, Luce/Krispy Kan, lithographed cookie tin
EX $75   NM $160   MIP $285

Howdy Doody Costume, 1950s, Collegeville
EX $50   NM $100   MIP $200

Howdy Doody Crayon Set, 1950, Milton Bradley, 16 crayons w/pictures
EX $45   NM $100   MIP $200

Howdy Doody Doll, 1950s, Ideal, eyes and mouth move
EX $40   NM $90   MIP $160

Howdy Doody Doll, 1950s, 7" tall vinyl squeeze toy, Howdy in blue pants and red shirt
EX $40   NM $90   MIP $170

Howdy Doody Doll, 1970s, Goldberger, 30", vinyl ventriloquist doll
EX $40   NM $90   MIP $160

Howdy Doody Doll, 1976, Goldberger, 12" vinyl ventriloquist doll
EX $25   NM $50   MIP $110

Howdy Doody Doll, 1988, Applause, 11" cloth doll
EX $10   NM $40   MIP $75

Howdy Doody Dominoes, 1950s
EX $20   NM $40   MIP $80

Howdy Doody Figure, Stahlwood, 5" x 7" rubber squeeze figure on airplane
EX $175   NM $360   MIP $725

Howdy Doody Fingertronic Puppet Theater, 1970s, Sutton
EX $25   NM $45   MIP $85

Howdy Doody Flasher Rings, 1950s, Nabisco, set of eight plastic character rings
EX $90   NM $175   MIP $400

Howdy Doody Flicker Ring, 1950s, Nabisco
EX $10   NM $20   MIP $50

Howdy Doody in Funland Book, 1953, Whitman, Little Golden Book
EX $10   NM $25   MIP $50

Howdy Doody Kiddie Pool, 1950s, Ideal, 40" diameter, yellow/blue vinyl
EX $80   NM $150   MIP $275

Howdy Doody Marionette, 1950s, Peter Puppet
EX $85   NM $190   MIP $375

Howdy Doody Mug, 1950s, Ovaltine, red plastic w/Howdy decal (Be Keen, Drink Chocolate Flavored Ovaltine)
EX $35   NM $50   MIP $100

Howdy Doody Music Box, Vandor, Howdy playing piano
EX $40   NM $55   MIP $90

Howdy Doody Newspaper #1, 1950, Poll Parrot, premium
EX $200   NM $400   MIP $500

Howdy Doody Night Light, 1950s, Leco, figural, Howdy's face
EX $35   NM $75   MIP $140

Howdy Doody Outdoor Sports Box, 1950s, tin litho box w/colorful graphics
EX $30   NM $60   MIP $110

Howdy Doody Paint Set, 1950s, Milton Bradley
EX $40   NM $80   MIP $160

Howdy Doody Paint Set, 1950s, Marx, plaster figures, paint
EX $35   NM $100   MIP $185

Howdy Doody Pencil Case, 1950s, vinyl; smiling Howdy on front
EX $20   NM $90   MIP $160

Howdy Doody Periscope, 1950s, Wonder Bread premium
EX $350   NM $700   MIP $1000

Howdy Doody Phono Doodle, Sharatone Products
EX $120   NM $260   MIP $350

Howdy Doody Pumpmobile, Nylint, tin vehicle
EX $110   NM $275   MIP $525

Howdy Doody Puppet Show Set, 1950s, includes plastic figures of Howdy, Clarabell, Mr. Bluster, Flub, Dilly Dally
EX $80   NM $170   MIP $325

Howdy Doody Puzzle, 1950s, Whitman, frame tray, Howdy Goes Fishing
EX $25   NM $45   MIP $90

Howdy Doody Puzzle Set, 1950s, Milton Bradley, set of three
EX $40   NM $75   MIP $150

Howdy Doody Ranch House Tool Box, 1950s, Liberty Steel, 14" x 6" x 3" illustrated steel box w/handle
EX $45   NM $110   MIP $185

Howdy Doody Salt and Pepper Shakers, 1950s, Peter Puppet, shape of Howdy's head; removable blue vinyl neckerchief
EX $75   NM $160   MIP $300

Howdy Doody Sand Forms, 1952, Ideal/Kagran, on card
EX $40   NM $80   MIP $150

Howdy Doody Songs Record, 1974, Take Two, record, cut-outs, coloring book
EX $20   NM $50   MIP $75

Howdy Doody Sticker Fun Book, 1952, Whitman
EX $15   NM $30   MIP $60

Howdy Doody Swim Ring, 1950s, Ideal, inflatable, 20" diameter
EX $20   NM $40   MIP $75

Howdy Doody Talking Alarm Clock, 1974, Janex
EX $30   NM $90   MIP $185

Howdy Doody Television, 1950s, Lido, filmstrips w/TV box
EX $25   NM $110   MIP $250

Howdy Doody Ukulele, 1950s, Emenee, plastic, white or yellow, 17"
EX $40   NM $65   MIP $110

Howdy Doody Umbrella, 1950s, Holllander, Howdy head for handle
EX $30   NM $80   MIP $160

Howdy Doody Wall Walker, Tigrett
　EX $25　　**NM** $50　　**MIP** $100

Howdy Doody Wristwatch, 1950s, Ever Tick/Kagran, glow-in-the-dark
　EX $100　　**NM** $300　　**MIP** $600

Howdy Doody Wristwatch, 1954, Ingraham, deep blue band w/blue and white dial showing character faces
　EX $140　　**NM** $350　　**MIP** $750

Howdy Doody Xylo-Doodle, 1950s, yellow plastic piano/xylophone w/colorful graphics
　EX $75　　**NM** $375　　**MIP** $675

Howdy Doody's Animal Friends Book, 1956, Whitman, Little Golden Book
　EX $10　　**NM** $20　　**MIP** $50

Howdy Doody's Circus Book, 1950, Whitman, Little Golden Book
　EX $10　　**NM** $20　　**MIP** $50

Howdy Doody's Electric Carnival Game, 1950s, Harett-Gilmar
　EX $60　　**NM** $120　　**MIP** $225

Howdy Doody's Laughing Circus Record Set, 1950s, RCA, two 78 rpm records
　EX $35　　**NM** $70　　**MIP** $135

Howdy Doody's Lucky Trip Book, 1953, Whitman, Little Golden Book
　EX $12　　**NM** $25　　**MIP** $50

Howdy Doody's One-Man Band, Trophy Products/Kagran, musical instruments
　EX $100　　**NM** $225　　**MIP** $500

Merchandise Manual, 1954, list of toys
　EX $150　　**NM** $450　　**MIP** $650

Merchandise Manual, 1955, list of toys
　EX $100　　**NM** $350　　**MIP** $600

Mr. Bluster Bank, 1976, Strauss, flocked plastic, 9"
　EX $20　　**NM** $35　　**MIP** $75

Princess Summerfall Winterspring Doll, 1950s, Beehler Arts, 8", hard plastic, braided black hair
　EX $100　　**NM** $190　　**MIP** $400

Princess Summerfall Winterspring Sewing Cards, 1950s, Milton Bradley, four cards, thread, plastic needle
　EX $30　　**NM** $65　　**MIP** $135

Puppets, 1950s, Gund, Howdy, Bluster, Clarabell, Dilly or Princess
　EX $20　　**NM** $50　　**MIP** $90

Sparkle Gun, 1987, Ja-Ru, plastic gun
　EX $6　　**NM** $20　　**MIP** $45

Spinning Top, 1970s, Lorenz Bolz, tin top w/characters
　EX $30　　**NM** $60　　**MIP** $110

I DREAM OF JEANNIE

I Dream of Jeannie Costume, 1970s, Ben Cooper
　EX $8　　**NM** $20　　**MIP** $50

I Dream of Jeannie Doll, 1965, Ideal, 18"
　EX $65　　**NM** $165　　**MIP** $300

I Dream of Jeannie Doll, 1977, Remco, 6"
　EX $25　　**NM** $50　　**MIP** $110

I Dream of Jeannie Play Set, 1977, Remco, w/6" doll
　EX $40　　**NM** $120　　**MIP** $250

I SPY

(Toy Shop File Photo)

Official Shoulder Holster Set, 1960s, Ray Line, Inc., Includes rapid fire pistol ("shoots more than 50 rounds in one loading"), shoulder holster and ammo
　EX $40　　**NM** $65　　**MIP** $95

JETSONS

Elroy Toy, 1963, Transogram
　EX $10　　**NM** $20　　**MIP** $40

Jetson Figures, 1990, Applause, 10" tall; Judy, George, Elroy, Rosie, each
　EX $50　　**NM** $100　　**MIP** $185

Jetsons Birthday Surprise Book, 1963, Whitman, Tell-A-Tale Book
　EX $12　　**NM** $25　　**MIP** $65

Jetsons Colorforms Kit, 1963, Colorforms
　EX $40　　**NM** $75　　**MIP** $150

Puzzle, 1962, Whitman, 70 pieces
　EX $25　　**NM** $95　　**MIP** $175

KNIGHT RIDER

Knight Rider Impossibles Stunt Set, 1982, LJN
　EX $45　　**NM** $95　　**MIP** $150

Knight Rider Wrist Communicator, 1982, Larami
　EX $10　　**NM** $20　　**MIP** $40

LASSIE

(Toy Shop File Photo)

Lassie's Pups, 1950s, Set including plastic toy dogs, blanket, tub and puppy bed
　EX $25　　**NM** $45　　**MIP** n/a

(Toy Shop File Photo)

Original Lassie Stuffed Toy, 1950s, Smile Novelty Toy Co., Reddish-brown and white stuffed toy with plastic face
　EX $80　　**NM** $120　　**MIP** n/a

LAUGH-IN

(Toy Shop File Photo)

"Sock It To Me" Plastic Purse, 1970s, Yellow with black lettering and strap
　EX $17　　**NM** $30　　**MIP** n/a

(Toy Shop File Photo)

Laugh-In Electric Drawing Set, 1960s, Lakeside Toys, Included an "electric" drawing set, color pencils, Laugh-In cartoon guides, drawing paper, eraser, sharpener and instructions
　EX $30　　**NM** $65　　**MIP** n/a

LOVE BOAT

(Toy Shop File Photo)

Love Boat Playset, 1970s, Boat-shaped dollhouse with figures of the cast, furniture and accessories. Over two feet long
　EX $45　　**NM** $90　　**MIP** n/a

MAN FROM U.N.C.L.E.

1966 British Annual, 1966, World Distributors, hardcover, 95 pages, photo cover
EX $20   NM $50   MIP $75

1967 British Annual Book, 1967, World Distributors, hardcover, 95 pages, photo cover
EX $15   NM $35   MIP $65

1968 British Annual Book, 1968, World Distributors, hardcover, 95 pages, photo cover
EX $15   NM $30   MIP $60

1969 British Annual, 1969, World Distributors, hardcover, 95 pages, photo cover
EX $15   NM $25   MIP $55

Action Figure Apparel Set, 1965, Gilbert, bullet proof vest, three targets, three shells, binoculars, and bazooka
EX $50   NM $100   MIP $210

Action Figure Armament Set, 1965, Gilbert, for 12" figures: jacket, cap firing pistol w/barrel extension, bipod stand, telescopic sight, grenade belt, binoculars, accessory pouch and beret
EX $50   NM $90   MIP $180

Action Figure Arsenal Set #1, 1965, Gilbert, tommy gun, bazooka, three shells, cap firing pistol and attachments, in shallow window box
EX $40   NM $80   MIP $175

Action Figure Arsenal Set #2, 1965, Gilbert, cap firing THRUSH rifle w/telescopic sight, grenade belt and four grenades, on wrapped header card
EX $40   NM $80   MIP $175

Action Figure Jumpsuit Set, 1965, Gilbert, for 12" figures: jumpsuit w/boots, helmet w/chin strap, 28" parachute and pack, cap firing tommy gun w/scope, instructions
EX $50   NM $100   MIP $225

Action Figure Pistol Conversion Kit, 1965, Gilbert, binoculars and pistol w/attachments, for 12" figures, on wrapped header card
EX $22   NM $45   MIP $90

Action Figure Scuba Set, 1965, Gilbert, for 12" Gilbert dolls: swim trunks, air tanks, tank bracket, tubes, scuba jacket and knife
EX $65   NM $130   MIP $260

Affair of the Gentle Saboteur Book, 1966, Whitman, hardcover
EX $8   NM $15   MIP $35

Affair of the Gunrunners' Gold Book, 1967, Whitman, hardcover
EX $8   NM $15   MIP $35

Alexander Waverly Figure, 1966, Marx, blue plastic, 5-3/4" tall, stamped w/character's name and U.N.C.L.E. logo on the bottom of base
EX $8   NM $15   MIP $30

Arcade Cards, 1960s, postcards w/b/w photo fronts, Napoleon or Illya
EX $5   NM $10   MIP $30

Attache Case, 1966, Lone Star, small cardboard briefcase, contains die-cast Mauser and parts to assemble U.N.C.L.E. Special
EX $130   NM $230   MIP $500

Attache Case, British, 1965, Lone Star, 15" x 8" x 2" vinyl case w/a pistol, holster, walkie talkie, cigarette box gun, U.N.C.L.E. badge, international passport, invisible cartridge pen and handcuffs
EX $225   NM $450   MIP $900

Attache Case, British, 1966, Lone Star, cardboard covered in vinyl, 9mm automatic luger, shoulder stock, sight, silencer, belt, holster, secret wrist holster and pistol that fires cap and cork, grenade, wallet w/passport, play money
EX $250   NM $500   MIP $950

Bagatelle Game, 1966, Hong Kong, 8" x 14" pinball game
EX $75   NM $155   MIP $325

Bicycle License Plates, 1967, Marx, four different, metal: Man from U.N.C.L.E., The Girl from U.N.C.L.E., Napoleon Solo, Illya Kuryakin, each
EX $15   NM $30   MIP $50

Calcutta Affair Book, 1967, Whitman, 254 pages, Big Little Book
EX $10   NM $20   MIP $45

Candy Cigarette Box, 1966, Cadet Sweets, candy and trading card, illustrated box
EX $25   NM $60   MIP $125

Candy Cigarette Counter Display Box, 1966, Cadet Sweets, holds 72 candy cigarette boxes, illustrated
EX $30   NM $90   MIP $200

Coin of El Diablo Affair Book, 1965, Wonder Books, softcover, 48 pages
EX $10   NM $20   MIP $40

Counter Spy Water Gun, 1960s, Hong Kong, luger water gun w/unlicensed Napoleon Solo illustration header card
EX $5   NM $15   MIP $40

Counterspy Outfit, 1966, Marx, contains trench coat w/secret pockets, pistol, shoulder holster, launcher barrel, silencer, scope sight, two pair of glasses, beards, eye patch, badge case, etc., in box
EX $125   NM $230   MIP $485

Counterspy Outfit Store Display, 1966, Marx, 35" x 36" wide cardboard display w/one piece of each item in Counterspy Outfit
EX $320   NM $650   MIP $1250

Crime Buster Gift Set, 1966, Corgi, set includes Man from U.N.C.L.E. car, James Bond Aston Martin and Batmobile w/Batboat on trailer, in window box
EX $275   NM $525   MIP $1050

Die-Cast Car, 1968, Playart, 2-3/4" long, die-cast metal, metallic purple
EX $90   NM $200   MIP $425

Die-Cast Metal Gun, 1965, Lone Star, die-cast automatic cap pistol w/plastic grips, plus cut-out badge, on card
EX $75   NM $150   MIP $325

Diving Dames Affair Book, 1967, Souvenir Press/England, #10 in series
EX $4   NM $8   MIP $20

Doomsday Affair Book, 1965, Souvenir Press, #2 in series
EX $4   NM $8   MIP $20

Fingerprint Kit, 1966, ink pad, roller, code book, magnifier, fingerprint records and pressure plate, in illustrated window box
EX $125   NM $250   MIP $500

Flicker Ring, 1965, silver plastic ring w/b/w photos, each
EX $10   NM $20   MIP $50

Flicker Ring, 1966, blue plastic w/"changing portrait" of Napoleon or Illya, each
EX $10   NM $20   MIP $40

Foto-Fantastiks Coloring Set, 1965, Eberhard Faber, six colored pencils, paint brush, and six 8" x 10" photos, came in four different versions, each
EX $40   NM $85   MIP $175

Generic Spies Figures, 1966, Marx, six different solid plastic, unpainted figures 5-3/4" tall, each
EX $8   NM $15   MIP $20

Handkerchief, 1966, England, U.N.C.L.E. logo, Illya and Napoleon
EX $30   NM $65   MIP $150

Headquarters Transmitter, 1965, Cragstan, molded gold colored plastic transmitter, amplifier and under cover case, silver ID card, 20-foot wire, in box
EX $80   NM $160   MIP $350

Illya Kuryakin Action Figure, 1965, Gilbert, 12" tall, plastic, black sweater, pants and shoes, spring loaded arm for firing cap pistol, folding badge, ID card and instruction sheet, in photo box
EX $80   NM $225   MIP $425

Illya Kuryakin Action Puppet, 1965, Gilbert, 13" tall, soft vinyl hand puppet of Illya holding a communicator, on 10" x 16" card
EX $80   NM $175   MIP $375

Illya Kuryakin Costume, 1967, Halco, painted mask, rayon costume in three colors showing Illya holding a gun, in illustrated window box
EX $45   NM $90   MIP $200

Illya Kuryakin Figure, 1966, Marx, blue or gray plastic figure, 5-3/4" tall, stamped w/character's name and U.N.C.L.E. logo on the bottom of base
EX $15   NM $40   MIP $80

Illya, That Man From U.N.C.L.E. Book, 1966, Pocket Books, 6" x 9" paperback, 100 pages of David McCallum
EX $10   NM $30   MIP $70

Invisible Writing Cartridge Pen, 1965, Platinum/England, pen, two vials of ink and two invisible ink vials
EX $125   NM $230   MIP $475

Magic Slates, 1965, Watkins-Strathmore, 9" x 14" slate w/two punch-out figures of either Napoleon or Illya, each
EX $45   NM $100   MIP $200

Man from the U.N.C.L.E. Record, 1965, Capitol Records, 45 rpm w/The Man from U.N.C.L.E. theme song and "The Vagabond"
EX $25   NM $60   MIP $120

Man from U.N.C.L.E. and other TV Themes Record, 1965, Metro Records, photo cover, has three songs from U.N.C.L.E. plus theme songs from Dr. Kildare, Mr. Novak, Bonanza and other shows
EX $8   NM $25   MIP $50

Man from U.N.C.L.E. Button, 1965, Button World, 3-1/2" diam. round button w/portrait of Napoleon or Illya, each
EX $10   NM $17   MIP $30

Man from U.N.C.L.E. Card Game, 1966, Japan, small artwork cards in illustrated box
EX $40   NM $75   MIP $160

Man from U.N.C.L.E. Code Board, 1966, chalkboard w/line art illustrations
EX $70   NM $150   MIP $300

Man from U.N.C.L.E. Finger Puppets, 1966, Dean, vinyl; THRUSH agent, Solo, Kuryakin, Waverly and two female agents; window box
EX $140   NM $300   MIP $600

Man from U.N.C.L.E. Playing Cards, 1965, Ed-U-Cards, standard 54-card deck w/action photo illustrations, on card
EX $20   NM $35   MIP $70

Man from U.N.C.L.E. Playing Cards Display Box, 1965, Ed-U-Cards, holds 12 packs
EX $130   NM $250   MIP $525

Man from U.N.C.L.E. Puzzles, 1965, Jaymar, frame tray; three versions; each
EX $25   NM $40   MIP $75

Man from U.N.C.L.E. Record, 1965, Crescendo Records, by the Challengers, cover shows blonde female spy w/gun
EX $5   NM $15   MIP $35

Man from U.N.C.L.E. Record, 1966, Union/Japan, 45 rpm w/photo sleeve
EX $35   NM $75   MIP $150

Man from U.N.C.L.E. Sheet Music, 1964, Hastings Music Corp., six pages, theme song and a brief description of the TV show
EX $15   NM $50   MIP $100

Man from U.N.C.L.E. Trading Cards, 1965, Topps, set of 55 b/w photo cards
EX $45   NM $95   MIP $175

Man from U.N.C.L.E. Trading Cards, 1966, Cadet Sweets, set of 50 cards, color photos, set
EX $22   NM $45   MIP $90

Man from U.N.C.L.E. Trading Cards, 1966, ABC/England, 25 cards
EX $22   NM $45   MIP $90

Mystery Jigsaw Series Puzzles, 1965, Milton Bradley, 14" x 24" puzzle, 250 pieces plus story booklet, The Loyal Groom, The Vital Observation, The Impossible Escape, The Micro-Film Affair, each
EX $25   NM $50   MIP $100

Napoleon Solo Costume, 1965, Halco, transparent plastic "mystery mask," costume has line art shirt, tie, shoulder holster and U.N.C.L.E. logo, in illustrated box
EX $50   NM $95   MIP $185

Napoleon Solo Credentials and Passport Set, 1965, Ideal, silver ID card, badge, identification wallet, slide window passport, on header card
EX $35   NM $65   MIP $150

Napoleon Solo Credentials and Secret Message Sender, 1965, Ideal, message sender, badge, and silver ID, on card
EX $40   NM $80   MIP $175

Napoleon Solo Doll, 1965, Gilbert, 11" tall, plastic, white shirt, black pants and shoes, spring loaded arm for firing cap pistol, folding badge, ID card and instruction sheet
EX $70   NM $145   MIP $350

Napoleon Solo Figure, 1966, Marx, blue or gray plastic figure, 5-3/4" tall stamped w/character's name and U.N.C.L.E. logo on the bottom of base
EX $15   NM $35   MIP $80

Pinball Affair Game, 1966, Marx, 12" x 24" tin litho pinball game
EX $75   NM $150   MIP $300

Pistol Cane Gun, 1966, Marx, 25" long, cap firing, bullet shooting aluminum cane w/eight bullets and one metal shell, on illustrated card
EX $125   NM $250   MIP $600

Power Cube Affair Book, 1968, Souvenir, #15 in series, British
EX $5   NM $10   MIP $25

Puzzle, 1966, Milton Bradley, 10" x 19", 100 pieces, Illya's Battle Below
EX $15   NM $35   MIP $70

Puzzle, 1966, Milton Bradley, 10" x 19", 100 pieces, Illya Crushes THRUSH
EX $15   NM $40   MIP $70

Puzzles, 1966, England, four 11" x 17" puzzles, each w/340 pieces: The Getaway, Solo in Trouble, The Frogman Affair, Secret Plans, each
EX $40   NM $80   MIP $165

Secret Agent Wristwatch, 1966, Bradley, gray watch face shows Solo holding a communicator, came w/either plain "leather" or "mod" watch band, in case
EX $115   NM $250   MIP $500

Secret Code Wheel Pinball, 1966, Marx, 10" x 22" x 6" tin litho pinball game
EX $80   NM $170   MIP $325

Secret Message Pen, 1966, American Character, 6-1/2" long double tipped pen for writing invisible messages, on header card
EX $100   NM $200   MIP $325

Secret Print Putty, 1965, Colorforms, putty in a gun shaped container, print paper, display cards of Kuryakin and Solo and a book of spy and weapons illustrations, on card
EX $20   NM $45   MIP $95

Secret Service Gun, 1965, Ideal, pistol, holster, badge and silver ID card, in window box
EX $160   NM $310   MIP $650

Secret Service Pop Gun, 1960s, bagged Luger pop gun on header card w/unlicensed illustration of Illya and Napoleon on header
EX $10   NM $15   MIP $50

Secret Weapon Set, 1965, Ideal, clip loading cap firing pistol, holster, ID wallet, silver ID card, U.N.C.L.E. badge, two demolition grenades and holster, in window box
EX $190   NM $400   MIP $775

Shirt, 1965, has secret pocket, glow-in-the-dark badge and ID, photo package
EX $190   NM $375   MIP $725

Shoot Out! Game, 1965, Milton Bradley, skill and action game for two players, plastic marble game in illustrated box
EX $80   NM $160   MIP $325

Shooting Arcade Game, 1966, Marx, tin litho arcade w/mechanical wind-up THRUSH agent targets for pellet shooting pistol, scope and stock attachments
EX $200   NM $400   MIP $850

Shooting Arcade Game, 1966, Marx, smaller version w/THRUSH spinner targets
EX $150   NM $275   MIP $525

Spy Magic Tricks, 1965, Gilbert, mystery gun, Illya playing cards, tricks
EX $125   NM $250   MIP $525

Television Picture Story Book, 1968, P.B.S. Limited, hardcover, 62 pages, Gold Key reprints
EX $15   NM $20   MIP $60

THRUSH Agent Figures, 1966, Marx, three different blue plastic figures, 5-3/4" tall stamped w/titles and U.N.C.L.E. logo on the bottom of each base, each
EX $10   NM $20   MIP $50

THRUSH Ray-Gun Affair Game, 1966, Ideal, four U.N.C.L.E. agent pieces, Area Decoder cards, 3-D THRUSH hideouts, THRUSH vehicles, crayons, dice and a rotating "ray gun," in illustrated box
EX $55   NM $110   MIP $225

THRUSH-Buster Display Box, 1966, Corgi, large display box w/graphics, holds 12 cars
EX $170   NM $330   MIP $700

U.N.C.L.E. Badges Store Display, 1965, Lone Star, illustrated card holds 12 triangular black plastic badges w/gold lettering, w/badges
EX $50   NM $120   MIP $225

McHALE'S NAVY

(Toy Shop File Photo)

McHale's Navy Signal Sender, 1960s, Gabriel-Bell, Inc., Megaphone sends amplifies voice, sends light signal and includes a Morse code button
EX $25   **NM** $55   **MIP** n/a

MONKEES

Flip Movies, 1967, Topps, each
EX $5   **NM** $10   **MIP** $30

Halloween Costumes, 1967, Bland Charnas, each
EX $60   **NM** $125   **MIP** $250

Jigsaw Puzzle, 1967, Fairchild
EX $15   **NM** $25   **MIP** $45

Monkees Dolls, 1967, Remco, 4", rubber, each
EX $35   **NM** $80   **MIP** $175

Monkees Finger Puppets, 1969, Remco
EX $15   **NM** $25   **MIP** $45

Talking Hand Puppet, 1966, Mattel, cloth w/heads of Monkees on fingertips
EX $50   **NM** $110   **MIP** $200

Tambourine, 1967, Raybert
EX $45   **NM** $100   **MIP** $200

Toy Guitar, 1966, Mattel, 20"
EX $60   **NM** $125   **MIP** $250

(Toy Shop File Photo)

Toy Guitar, 1966, Mattel, 14", wind-up crank
EX $40   **NM** $90   **MIP** $175

MORK AND MINDY

Mork and Mindy Colorforms, 1979, Colorforms
EX $10   **NM** $15   **MIP** $30

MR. ED

(Toy Shop File Photo)

Mr. Ed Talking Horse Puppet, 1962, Mattel
EX $40   **NM** $80   **MIP** $150

MUNSTERS, THE

Grandpa Doll, 1964, Remco
EX $150   **NM** $325   **MIP** $610

Herman Munster Doll, 1964, Remco
EX $155   **NM** $350   **MIP** $720

Lily Baby Doll, 1965, Ideal, unlicensed "monster baby"
EX $45   **NM** $85   **MIP** $170

Lily Doll, 1964, Remco
EX $150   **NM** $325   **MIP** $625

Puzzle, 1960s, Whitman, frame tray
EX $30   **NM** $50   **MIP** $100

Puzzle, 1965, Whitman, 100 pieces, boxed
EX $35   **NM** $60   **MIP** $150

The Last Resort Book, 1964, Whitman
EX $13   **NM** $30   **MIP** $50

PARTRIDGE FAMILY

David Cassidy Dress-Up Kit, 1972, Colorforms
EX $20   **NM** $40   **MIP** $75

Laurie Partridge Doll, 1973, Remco, 20" tall
EX $55   **NM** $120   **MIP** $225

Partridge Family Bus, 1973, Remco, plastic, 14" long
EX $65   **NM** $160   **MIP** $300

Partridge Family Guitar, 1970s, Carnival, 19" plastic, decal of David Cassidy on body
EX $35   **NM** $75   **MIP** $150

Partridge Family Paper Dolls, 1970s, Saalfield, several styles
EX $20   **NM** $40   **MIP** $75

Patti Partridge Doll, 1971, Ideal
EX $50   **NM** $110   **MIP** $200

PEE WEE HERMAN

Ball Dart Set
EX $5   **NM** $10   **MIP** $15

Billy Baloney Doll, 1988, Matchbox, 18" tall
EX $12   **NM** $20   **MIP** $75

Chairry Figure, Matchbox, 15" tall
EX $12   **NM** $20   **MIP** $45

Conky Wacky Wind-Up, 1988, Matchbox
EX $3   **NM** $5   **MIP** $10

Cowboy Curtis Figure, Matchbox
EX $8   **NM** $15   **MIP** $35

Globey with Randy, 1988, Matchbox
EX $8   **NM** $15   **MIP** $40

King of Cartoons Figure, 1988, Matchbox, 5" tall
EX $8   **NM** $15   **MIP** $35

Magic Screen Figure, 1988, Matchbox, 5" tall poseable
EX $8   **NM** $15   **MIP** $35

Magic Screen Wacky Wind-Up, 1988, Matchbox, 6" tall
EX $3   **NM** $5   **MIP** $10

Miss Yvonne Doll, 1988, Matchbox, poseable 5" tall
EX $8   **NM** $15   **MIP** $45

Pee Wee Herman Deluxe Colorforms, 1980s, Colorforms
EX $7   **NM** $10   **MIP** $35

Pee Wee Herman Doll, 1980s, Matchbox, 15" tall, non talking
EX $10   **NM** $35   **MIP** $75

Pee Wee Herman Doll, 1988, Matchbox, poseable 5" tall
EX $4   **NM** $10   **MIP** $25

Pee Wee Herman Play Set, 1989, Matchbox, 20" x 28" x 8" for use w/5" figures, Pee Wee's bike, folds into large carrying case
EX $12   **NM** $28   **MIP** $60

Pee Wee Herman Slumber Bag, 1988, Matchbox
EX $10   **NM** $20   **MIP** $35

Pee Wee Herman Ventriloquist Doll, 1980s, Matchbox
EX $30   **NM** $65   **MIP** $135

Pee Wee with Scooter and Helmet, 1988, Matchbox
EX $4   **NM** $7   **MIP** $15

Pee Wee Yo-Yo, 1980s
EX $3   **NM** $10   **MIP** $20

Pterri Doll, 1980s, Matchbox, 13" tall
EX $15   **NM** $25   **MIP** $45

Pterri Wacky Wind-Ups, 1988, Matchbox
EX $3   **NM** $5   **MIP** $10

Reba Figure, 1988, Matchbox, poseable
EX $5   **NM** $10   **MIP** $30

Ricardo Figure, 1988, Matchbox
EX $5   **NM** $10   **MIP** $30

Vance the Talking Pig Figure, 1987, Matchbox
EX $20   **NM** $40   **MIP** $85

PINKY LEE

Pinky Lee Paint Set, 1950s, Gabriel, 8 pictures to watercolor
EX $10   NM $20   MIP $33

Toy Medicine Chest, 1950s
EX $10   NM $20   MIP $50

Who Am I? Game, 1950s, based on the tv show
EX $5   NM $15   MIP $25

RAT PATROL

(Toy Shop File Photo)

Rat Patrol Diorama Kit, 1960s, Aurora, includes 15 figures, 2 Rat Patrol Jeeps, 1 German Panzer Tank, 1 German Panther Tank, dimensional battlefield with sandbags, bunkers, dunes and palm trees
EX $40   NM $65   MIP n/a

ROCKY AND BULLWINKLE

Bullwinkle and Rocky Clock Bank, 1969, Larami, 4-1/2" tall, plastic
EX $30   NM $60   MIP $120

Bullwinkle and Rocky Movie Viewer, 1960s, #225, red and white plastic viewer w/three movies
EX $25   NM $50   MIP $75

Bullwinkle and Rocky Wastebasket, 1961, 11" tall, metal w/Jay Ward cast pictured
EX $35   NM $65   MIP $135

Bullwinkle Bank, 1960s, 6" tall, glazed china
EX $75   NM $125   MIP $400

Bullwinkle Bank, 1972, Play Pal, 11-1/2", plastic
EX $35   NM $50   MIP $100

Bullwinkle Cartoon Kit, 1962, Colorforms
EX $35   NM $50   MIP $160

Bullwinkle Dinner Set, 1960s, Boonton Molding, plate and cup pictures Bullwinkle and the Cheerios Kid
EX $25   NM $50   MIP $85

Bullwinkle Figure, 1976, Dakin, Cartoon Theater, 7-1/2" tall, plastic
EX $25   NM $50   MIP $90

Bullwinkle Flexy Figure, 1970, Larami
EX $10   NM $35   MIP $75

Bullwinkle for President Bumper Sticker, 1972
EX $10   NM $16   MIP $40

Bullwinkle Jewelry Hanger, 1960s, 5" tall, suction cup on back
EX $15   NM $25   MIP $50

Bullwinkle Magic Slate, 1963
EX $15   NM $40   MIP $85

Bullwinkle Make Your Own Badge Set, 1960s, Larami
EX $20   NM $40   MIP $85

Bullwinkle Paintless Paint Book, 1960, Whitman
EX $15   NM $35   MIP $80

Bullwinkle Spell and Count Board, 1969
EX $12   NM $25   MIP $50

Bullwinkle Stamp Set, 1970, Larami
EX $12   NM $25   MIP $40

Bullwinkle Stickers, 1984, Bullwinkle, Sherman and Peabody, Snidely Whiplash
EX $5   NM $10   MIP $20

Bullwinkle Talking Doll, 1970, Mattel
EX $30   NM $75   MIP $150

Bullwinkle Travel Adventure Board Game, 1960s, Transogram
EX $30   NM $70   MIP $135

Bullwinkle Travel Game, 1971, Larami, magnetic
EX $15   NM $30   MIP $60

Bullwinkle's Circus Time Toy, 1969, Rocky on a circus horse
EX $20   NM $40   MIP $90

Bullwinkle's Circus Time Toy, 1969, Bullwinkle on a elephant
EX $20   NM $40   MIP $90

Bullwinkle's Double Boomerangs, 1969, Larami, set of two on illustrated card
EX $15   NM $25   MIP $50

Dudley Do-Right Figure, 1972, Wham-O, 5" tall, flexible
EX $12   NM $40   MIP $80

Dudley Do-Right Figure, 1976, Dakin, Cartoon Theater
EX $15   NM $40   MIP $85

Dudley Do-Right Puzzle, 1975, Whitman
EX $12   NM $30   MIP $60

Mr. Peabody Bank, 1960s, 6" tall, glazed china
EX $90   NM $190   MIP $385

Mr. Peabody Figure, 1972, Wham-O, 4" tall, flexible
EX $10   NM $30   MIP $70

Natasha Figure, 1972, Wham-O
EX $10   NM $30   MIP $70

Rocky and Bullwinkle Bank, 1960, 5" tall, glazed china
EX $90   NM $190   MIP $385

Rocky and Bullwinkle Presto Sparkle Painting Set, 1962, Kenner, six cartoon pictures and two comic strip panels
EX $30   NM $70   MIP $135

Rocky and Bullwinkle Puzzle, 1972, Whitman, boxed
EX $15   NM $30   MIP $75

Rocky and Bullwinkle Toothpaste Holder, 1960s, glazed china
EX $80   NM $190   MIP $375

Rocky and His Friends Book, 1960s, Whitman, Little Golden Book
EX $20   NM $50   MIP $80

Rocky Bank, 1950s, 5" tall, slot in large tail, glazed china
EX $80   NM $225   MIP $425

Rocky Figure, 1976, Dakin, Cartoon Theater, 6-1/2" tall, plastic
EX $30   NM $60   MIP $125

Rocky Flexy Figure, 1970, Larami
EX $10   NM $25   MIP $50

Rocky Soaky, Colgate-Palmolive, 10-1/2" tall, plastic
EX $15   NM $35   MIP $65

Rocky the Flying Squirrel Coloring Book, 1960, Whitman
EX $20   NM $40   MIP $85

Sherman Figure, 1972, Wham-O, 4" tall, flexible
EX $15   NM $35   MIP $70

Snidely Whiplash Figure, 1972, Wham-O, 5" tall, flexible
EX $15   NM $40   MIP $80

ROMPER ROOM

(Toy Shop File Photo)

Bop-A-Loop Toy (MIB), Hasbro, Shown here with Romper Room Rhythm set
EX n/a   NM $8   MIP $10

Build & Play Discs, Hasbro
EX n/a   NM $6   MIP $12

Can You Guess? Wonder Book, Hasbro
EX n/a   NM $4   MIP $8

Ceramic Mug – Jack-in-the-Box, Hasbro
EX n/a   NM $15   MIP $34

Chalkboard, Hasbro
EX n/a   NM $7   MIP $15

Digger the Dog (MIB), Hasbro
EX n/a   NM $15   MIP $32

Do Bee Dough Machine, Hasbro
EX n/a   NM $15   MIP $34

Do Bee Iron On Transfer, Hasbro
EX n/a   NM $3   MIP $5

Do Bee Rider, Hasbro
EX n/a   NM $20   MIP $55

Do Bees Little Golden Book of Manners, Hasbro
EX n/a   NM $9   MIP $18

Dump Truck (Do Bee hubcaps), Hasbro
EX n/a   NM $3   MIP $6

Fitness Fun 45 RPM, Hasbro
EX n/a   NM $2   MIP $4

Fun Time Puzzle Clock, Hasbro
EX n/a   NM $5   MIP $10

G.E. Show 'N Tell Phonoviewer, Hasbro
EX n/a   NM $14   MIP $28

G.E. Show 'N Tell Picturesound Refill Programs (each), Hasbro
EX n/a   NM $2   MIP $4

Happy Jack and Mr. Do Bee hand puppets, Hasbro
EX n/a   NM $20   MIP $40

Happy Jack Magnetic Puzzle, Hasbro
EX n/a   NM $8   MIP $16

Happy Jack Punching Clown, Hasbro
EX n/a   NM $9   MIP $18

Inchworm, Hasbro, green w/yellow saddle; yes, I still have mine!!
EX n/a   NM $30   MIP $65

Moe the Monkey Game, Hasbro
EX n/a   NM $5   MIP $10

Mr. Do Bee Bank, Hasbro
EX n/a   NM $15   MIP $35

Mr. Do Bee Miniature Poly-Blocks, Hasbro
EX n/a   NM $5   MIP $10

Mr. Stacking Man, Hasbro
EX n/a   NM $8   MIP $15

Musical Block Clock, Hasbro
EX n/a   NM $20   MIP $45

Musical Jack in the Box, Hasbro
EX n/a   NM $35   MIP $75

Official TV Bo Dee Dance Record, Hasbro
EX n/a   NM $8   MIP $20

Peg Town Railroad, Hasbro
EX n/a   NM $5   MIP $10

Preschool Super Fun Pad, Hasbro
EX n/a   NM $3   MIP $6

Rhythm Set, Hasbro
EX n/a   NM $9   MIP $22

Sew Easy Sewing Machine, Hasbro
EX n/a   NM $6   MIP $12

Snoopy Counting Camera, Hasbro
EX n/a   NM $10   MIP $20

Snoopy Play Telephone, Hasbro
EX n/a   NM $5   MIP $10

Squirt, Squirt, Squirt the Animals Tub Toy, Hasbro
EX n/a   NM $5   MIP $10

Super Mr. Potato Head, Hasbro
EX n/a   NM $7   MIP $14

Talk 'N Chalk Board, Hasbro
EX n/a   NM $15   MIP $30

Toy Ring – Gold Plated Plastic, Hasbro
EX n/a   NM $20   MIP $40

Weebles Playground, Hasbro
EX n/a   NM $55   MIP $110

Willie the Weather Man, Hasbro
EX n/a   NM $20   MIP $45

ROOKIES, THE

Rookie Chris figure, 1973, LJN, 8" tall
EX $10   NM $20   MIP $60

Rookie Mike figure, 1973, LJN, 8" tall
EX $10   NM $20   MIP $60

Rookie Terry figure, 1973, LJN, 8" tall
EX $10   NM $20   MIP $60

Rookie Willy figure, 1973, LJN, 8" tall
EX $10   NM $20   MIP $60

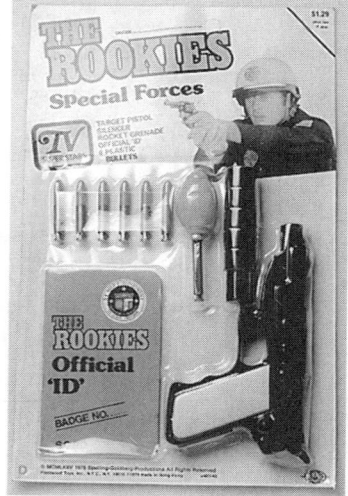
(Toy Shop File Photo)

Special Forces Set, 1975, Fleetwood Toys, Includes target pistol, silencer, rocket grenade, official ID and six plastic bullets
EX $15   NM $25   MIP $50

S.W.A.T.

Bullhorn, 1976
EX $15   NM $25   MIP $35

(Toy Shop File Photo)

Clicker Gun & Handcuffs Set, 1975, Fleetwood Toys
EX $12   NM $20   MIP n/a

Deacon, 1976, LJN, 8" figure
EX $5   NM $12   MIP $35

Hondo, 1976, LJN, 8" figure
EX $5   NM $12   MIP $35

Luca, 1976, LJN, 8" figure
EX $5   NM $12   MIP $35

McCabe, 1976, LJN, 8" figure
EX $5   NM $12   MIP $35

Officer Jim Street, 1976, LJN, 8" figure
EX $5   NM $12   MIP $35

T.J., 1976, LJN, 8" figure
EX $5   NM $12   MIP $35

Van, 1976, LJN, fits 8" figures
EX $15   NM $30   MIP $45

SCOOBY DOO

Scooby Doo and the Pirate Treasure Book, 1974, Golden, Little Golden Book
EX $5   NM $10   MIP $15

Scooby Doo Hand Puppet, 1970s, Ideal, vinyl head
EX $20   NM $40   MIP $75

Scooby Doo Paint with Water Book, 1984
EX $5   NM $10   MIP $20

Scooby Doo Squeak Toy, 1970s, Sanitoy, 6" tall
EX $20   NM $35   MIP $50

SGT. PRESTON

Sgt. Preston of the Yukon Punch-Out Cards, 1950s, Quaker, "Big Game Trophy" cardboard cut-outs, set of nine
EX $30   NM $100   MIP $175

SIX MILLION DOLLAR MAN

(Toy Shop File Photo)

Porta-Communicator, 1970s, Kenner, Walkie-talkie device that attaches to Colonel Austin like a backpack. You transmit your voice on one end, and it's broadcasted from the receiver on the other. Included a 10-foot cord
EX $20   NM $45   MIP $65

SOUPY SALES

Soupy Sales Card Game, 1960s, Jaymar, Slap Jack, Old Maid, Funny Rummy, or Hearts/Crazy 8s
EX $20   NM $40   MIP $60

Soupy Sales Doll, 1960s, Remco, 5" doll
EX $40   NM $150   MIP $250

Soupy Sales Doll, 1966, Knickerbocker, 12" plush, vinyl head
EX $25   NM $60   MIP $150

STARSKY & HUTCH

Deluxe Police Set, 1970s, HG Toys, Includes badges, service revolver, Colt .45, shoulder holster, cuffs, whistle and poster
EX $30 **NM** $60 **MIP** $75

Starsky and Hutch Puzzle, 1970s, HG Toys
EX $15 **NM** $30 **MIP** $50

Starsky and Hutch Shoot-Out Target Set, 1970s, Berwick
EX $25 **NM** $45 **MIP** $95

STINGRAY

(Toy Shop File Photo)

Puzzle, 1960s, Whitman
EX $15 **NM** $35 **MIP** n/a

(Toy Shop File Photo)

Stingray Atomic Submarine, Doyusha, With electonic lights and sounds
EX $40 **NM** $90 **MIP** n/a

(Toy Shop File Photo)

Stingray Hand Puppet, Titan, 1960s
EX $15 **NM** $30 **MIP** n/a

(Toy Shop File Photo)

Stingray Hand Puppet, Troy Tempest, 1960s
EX $15 **NM** $30 **MIP** n/a

(Toy Shop File Photo)

Stingray Hand Puppet, X2-Zero, 1960s
EX $17 **NM** $40 **MIP** n/a

(Toy Shop File Photo)

Stingray Underwater Maze Game, 1960s, Transogram
EX $35 **NM** $70 **MIP** n/a

THE FALL GUY

(Toy Shop File Photo)

Fall Guy Bounty Hunter HO Scale Race set, 1970s, Aurora, Includes Fall Guy truck, passenger car, figure 8 track
EX $50 **NM** $90 **MIP** n/a

Pickup Truck Model Kit, 1980s, MPC
EX $5 **NM** $12 **MIP** $25

TV TOYS

Target Shooting Game, 1980s, Arco, targets spin when hit

EX $5   **NM** $12   **MIP** $20

THUNDERBIRDS

(Toy Shop File Photo)

"The Mole" vehicle, Bandai, Tracked vehicle with rotating drill section, from the Gerry Anderson series "Thunderbirds"

EX $22   **NM** $45   **MIP** n/a

UNDERDOG

Kite Fun Book, 1970s, Pacific Gas and Electric

EX $10   **NM** $35   **MIP** $85

Puzzle, 1975, Whitman, 100 pieces

EX $10   **NM** $20   **MIP** $30

Underdog Costume, 1969, Ben Cooper

EX $55   **NM** $85   **MIP** $150

Underdog Dot Funnies Kit, 1974, Whitman

EX $10   **NM** $20   **MIP** $40

Underdog Figure, 1976, Dakin, plastic, Cartoon Theater

EX $35   **NM** $100   **MIP** $150

WELCOME BACK, KOTTER

Halloween Costume, 1976, Collegeville, several styles

EX $10   **NM** $20   **MIP** $25

Sweathogs Dolls, 1976, Mattel, Epstein, Washington, Barbarino, Kotter, Horshack; each

EX $10   **NM** $25   **MIP** $60

Sweathogs Grease Machine Cars, 1977, Ahi, 3" long, plastic cars; various styles, each

EX $15   **NM** $30   **MIP** $60

Welcome Back, Kotter Classroom, 1976, Mattel, play set

EX $25   **NM** $45   **MIP** $100

Welcome Back, Kotter Colorforms Set, 1976, Colorforms

EX $10   **NM** $20   **MIP** $50

WINKY DINK AND YOU

When Winky Winks at You Record, 1956, Decca

EX $45   **NM** $60   **MIP** $80

Winky Dink Book, 1956, Golden, Little Golden Book

EX $9   **NM** $16   **MIP** $30

Winky Dink Comic Book, 1950s, Dell, #663

EX $20   **NM** $40   **MIP** $90

Winky Dink Costume, 1950s, Halco, No. 642, cloth mask and jumper

EX $10   **NM** $20   **MIP** $40

Winky Dink Magic Crayons, 1960s

EX $20   **NM** $35   **MIP** $50

Winky Dink Official TV Game Kit, 1950s

EX $30   **NM** $50   **MIP** $100

Winky Dink Secret Message Game, 1950s, Lowell

EX $75   **NM** $130   **MIP** $225

Winky Dink Winko Magic Kit, 1950s

EX $20   **NM** $35   **MIP** $50

TV TOYS

Vehicles

By Merry Dudley, editor, *Toy Cars & Models* magazine

I'm always amazed by the way today's pugnacious "realism is king" collector reacts to the sight of a pressed steel truck, particularly a dump truck, tow truck, or car carrier.

First of all, they have to touch it, regardless of condition. The truck could be rusted through and full of dirt, but the person will still touch it with an astounding air of reverence. If it's a dump truck, the hand will go straight to the dump box, probably where it used to go many years before...because everyone knows that the best way to push a dump truck across the floor is to get on your knees, place your hand in the dump box and give it a good shove. Those who are still fairly agile may even have to fight the desire to scoot across the floor on those now-scarred knees to keep up with the rambling truck.

The phenomenon changes slightly with a tow truck or car carrier. The hook and pulley assembly gets the most attention on the tow truck, and deservedly so. How many times did we have to hook up that battered yet loved pickup or passenger car to haul it safely back to the garage or toy box? Car carriers serve a dual purpose. The nostalgia of the car carrier is only slightly eclipsed by the way it has become the perfect piece on which to display other cars of similar scale. (Although I've heard that a dump truck is the perfect holder for your remote controls.)

Perhaps it's a response to today's very different market. Stores are flooded with die-cast, a market driven by the flawed idea that licensing is imperative and increased realism is the only [feature/technological advancement] that matters. In smaller scales, the charm of opening features has been eclipsed by the desire for realistic shut lines. But how many times is the illusion of realism shattered when the toy is actually removed from the package and a cheap plastic base is revealed? Larger scales suffer from the licensing disease – if it's not licensed by a movie studio, manufacturers reason, why will it sell? And why should it be manufactured in the first place?

The old days may be gone, but the memories of a simpler time remain to come flooding back whenever we encounter those pressed-steel treasures. So while the debate rages over whether pressed steel is alive and well or dead and gone, those who attend toy shows and swap meets and actually see the objects of their youth's desire know the truth.

2006 Trends

The affect of Internet auction giant eBay on the toy vehicle hobby remains impossible to underestimate. Toys that were once reasonably hard to find at regional toy shows are now available to anyone with Internet access.

Die-cast continues to appeal to a wide audience. Mint-in-box/package prices for continue to hold their values and increase, while lesser-condition examples are finding a willing audience just happy to acquire certain favorites. Values for lesser-condition toys are increasing. The Hot Wheels Redlines chapter now includes values for lesser conditions. Hot Wheels Superfast cars are a good bargain and enjoying increased demand. Johnny Lightning Topper cars are findable in lesser conditions, but prices are increasing. Corgi and Dinky enjoy steady popularity. Matchbox cars are also experiencing an increase in demand and once-steady prices are on the rise. Vintage favorite Tootsietoy has seen a slow-down as prices have increased for mint examples, but lesser-condition models are plentiful.

Pressed steel continues to be a strong collecting category whether or not one can afford vintage Buddy "L." The market for affordable 1960s and 1970s trucks is increasing. More lesser-condition vehicles are featuring higher-condition prices, but are they selling? Structo and Nylint remain steady, and Tonka is plentiful at shows.

Tin vehicles remain good investments. Japanese Tin Cars are increasingly appreciated for their craftsmanship if not their accuracy. Marx vehicles are popular, especially those featuring specific characters.

Contributors: Corgi contributor Dr. Douglas Sadecky; Hot Wheels Numbered Packs contributor Michael Zarnock is the author of Warman's Hot Wheels Field Guide (Krause Publications, 2003) and The Ultimate Guide to Hot Wheels Variations (Krause Publications, 2004); Japanese Tin Cars contributor Ron Smith; Nylint contributor Jeff Hubbard; Structo contributor Randy Prasse; and Mark Rich, columnist for Toy Shop and Toy Cars & Models magazines for contributions to the Buddy L, Marx, Tonka, Tootsietoy, Gay Toys, Midgetoy, Processed Plastic, Remco, Deluxe Reading, and Eldon Industries chapters. *Toys & Prices* editor Karen O'Brien handled the rest and loved every minute of the research. Merry Dudley, editor of *Toy Cars & Models* magazine, is an avid collector of cars with great big fins, which is tough to believe since she was raised in a Ford family. She can be reached at Krause Publications, 700 E. State St., Iola, WI 54990 or by email at: merry.dudley@fwpubs.com

THE TOP TEN VEHICLES TOYS *(In Mint Condition)*

1. Coal Truck, Buddy "L," 1926	$11,500
2. Baggage Truck, Buddy "L," 1930-32	7,000
3. Express Truck, Buddy "L," 1930-32	6,000
4. Johnny Lightning Topper Custom Charger, 1968-69	6,000
5. Johnny Lightning Topper Custom Mustang, 1968-69	6,000
6. Johnny Lightning Topper Custom Camaro, 1968-69	6,000
7. Water Tower Truck, Buddy "L," 1929	5,500
8. Cement Mixer on Treads, Buddy "L,"	5,200
9. Johnny Lightning Topper Custom T-Bird, 1969	5,000
10. Trench Digger, Buddy "L," 1928-31	5,000

BUDDY L

AIRPLANES

5000 Monocoupe "The Lone Eagle", orange wing, black fuselage and tail w/tailskid, all steel high wind cabin monoplane, 9-7/8" wingspan, 1929
EX $250   **NM** $300   **MIP** $400

Army Tank Transport Plane, low-wing monoplane, two small four-wheel tanks that clip beneath wings, 27" wingspan; 1941
EX $250   **NM** $350   **MIP** $400

Catapult Airplane and Hangar, 5000 Monocoupe w/tailwheel, 9-7/8" wingspan, olive/gray hangar, black twin-spring catapult, 1930
EX $955   **NM** $1210   **MIP** $1520

Four Motor Air Cruiser, white, red engine cowlings, yellow fuselage and twin tails, four engine monoplane, 27" wingspan; 1952
EX $200   **NM** $310   **MIP** $350

Four-Engine Transport, green wings, white engine cowlings, yellow fuselage and twin tails, four engine monoplane, 27" wingspan; 1949
EX $205   **NM** $300   **MIP** $405

Hangar and Three 5000 Monocoupes, olive/gray hangar, windows outlined in red or orange, planes 9-7/8" wingspan, all steel high wing cabin monoplanes, 1930
EX $750   **NM** $1000   **MIP** $2000

Transport Airplane, white wings and engine cowlings, red fuselage and twin tails, four engine monoplane, 27" wingspan; 1946
EX $205   **NM** $310   **MIP** $410

BUSES

Greyhound Americruiser, made in Macau; marked 1979
EX $3   **NM** $7   **MIP** $10

Greyhound Americruiser, 7-1/2" long; made in Japan, "No. 4950"; 1979
EX $5   **NM** $10   **MIP** $15

School Bus, 9-3/4" long; yellow, open top; 1981
EX $3   **NM** $5   **MIP** $8

School Bus, 6-1/2" long; made in Macau; marked 1980.
EX $2   **NM** $4   **MIP** $7

School Bus, 6-1/2" long; yellow, black front fenders, made in Japan; 1980
EX $3   **NM** $6   **MIP** $9

CARS

Army Jeep, 5-1/2" long; metal base, plastic body, Army green with white star on hood and sides; 1979
EX $3   **NM** $5   **MIP** $5

Army Staff Car, olive drab body, 15-3/4" long; 1964
EX $100   **NM** $150   **MIP** $200

Big "H" Race Team, 17" long; hot Rod with two trailers and two Honda motorcycles; 1966-68
EX $35   **NM** $75   **MIP** $110

Bloomin' Bus (VW), 10-3/4" long; chartreuse body, white roof and supports; 1969
EX $25   **NM** $55   **MIP** $85

Brute Baby Buggy, 5" long; baby-carriage type vehicle; 1969-70
EX $3   **NM** $5   **MIP** $8

Brute Beach Buggy, 5" long; covered dune buggy; 1969-70
EX $3   **NM** $5   **MIP** $8

Brute Boss Bug, 5" long; muscle car style; 1970-71
EX $3   **NM** $5   **MIP** $8

Brute Fire Buggy, 5" long; ladder truck; 1969-71
EX $3   **NM** $5   **MIP** $8

Brute Road Buggy, 5" long; roadster; 1970-71
EX $3   **NM** $5   **MIP** $8

Brute Super Bug, 5" long; VW Beetle; 1970-71
EX $3   **NM** $7   **MIP** $8

Buddywagen (VW), 10-3/4" long; red body with white roof, opening side doors, folding seats, sliding sun roof; 1966
EX $30   **NM** $60   **MIP** $90

Buddywagen (VW), 10-3/4" long; red body with white roof, no chrome "V" on front; 1967
EX $30   **NM** $60   **MIP** $90

Buddywagon, red body w/white roof, 10-3/4" long; 1966
EX $100   **NM** $150   **MIP** $200

Camaro, 4-1/2" long; plastic, opaque windows, "Camaro" sitcker on sides; 1980
EX $2   **NM** $4   **MIP** $6

Colt Sportsliner, 10-1/4" long; red open body, white hardtop; off-white seats and interior; 1967
EX $20   **NM** $45   **MIP** $70

Colt Sportsliner, 10-1/4" long; light blue-green open body, white hardtop, pale tan seats and interior; 1968-69
EX $20   **NM** $40   **MIP** $65

Colt Utility Car, 10-1/4" long; red open body, white plastic seats, floor and luggage spade; 1967
EX $20   **NM** $45   **MIP** $70

Colt Utility Car, light orange body, tan interior, 10-1/4" long; 1968
EX $35   **NM** $45   **MIP** $65

Country Squire Wagon, off-white hood fenders, end gate and roof, brown woodgrain side panels, 15-1/2" long; 1963
EX $85   **NM** $140   **MIP** $175

Country Squire Wagon, red hood fenders, end gate and roof, brown woodgrain side panels, 15" long; 1965
EX $75   **NM** $115   **MIP** $150

Deluxe Convertible Coupe, metallic blue enamel front, sides and deck, cream top retracts into rumble seat, 19" long; 1949
EX $310   **NM** $455   **MIP** $605

Desert Rat Command Car, 10-1/4" long; tan body, beige interior, black machine gun between seats, whitewall tires; 1967
EX $30   **NM** $65   **MIP** $90

Desert Rat Command Car, 10-1/4" long; tan body, beige interior, blackwall tires; 1968
EX $30   **NM** $65   **MIP** $90

Flivver Coupe, black w/red eight-spoke wheels, black hubs, aluminum tires, flat, hardtop roof on enclosed glass-window-style body, 11" long, 1924
EX $700   **NM** $1100   **MIP** $1400

Flivver Roadster, black w/red eight-spoke wheels, black hubs, aluminum tires, simulated soft, folding top, 11" long, 1924
EX $700   **NM** $1200   **MIP** $1350

Gull Wing Vette, 4" long; "Pace Car" on sides; 1979
EX $6   **NM** $12   **MIP** $18

Hot Rod, whitewall tires, plastic roof, spare tire in rear, various colors; mid to late 1960s.
EX $13   **NM** $25   **MIP** $40

Hot Rod Woody Station Wagon, Ol' Buddys series, 10-1/2" long; made in Japan, opening driver door and back door, steering; late 1960s
EX $12   **NM** $25   **MIP** $35

Jr. Buggy Hauler, 12" long; Jeep, Sandpiper dune buggy on trailer; 1971
EX $17   **NM** $33   **MIP** $50

Jr. Camaro, 9" long; metallic blue body, white racing stripes on hood; 1968
EX $17   **NM** $35   **MIP** $50

Jr. Flower Power Sportster, purple hood, fenders and body, white roof and supports, white plastic seats, lavender and orange five-petal blossom decals on hood top, roof, and sides, 6" long; 1969
EX $23   **NM** $35   **MIP** $55

Jr. Mustang, 9" long; whitewall tires; 1971
EX $7   **NM** $13   **MIP** $20

Jr. Sportster, blue hood and open body, white hardtop and upper sides, 6" long; 1968
EX $23   **NM** $35   **MIP** $55

Mechanical Scarab Automobile, red radically streamlined body, bright metal front and rear bumpers, 10-1/2" long, 1936
EX $200   **NM** $300   **MIP** $500

Police Colt, 10-1/4" long; blue body, white hardtop, "Police 1" on sides; 1968-69
EX $17   **NM** $33   **MIP** $50

Ski Bus (VW), 10-3/4" long; white body and roof; 1967-68
EX $25   **NM** $50   **MIP** $75

Station Wagon, light blue/green body and roof, 15-1/2" long; 1963
EX $75   **NM** $115   **MIP** $150

Streamline Scarab, red, radically streamlined body, non-mechanical, 10-1/2" long; 1941
EX $145   **NM** $225   **MIP** $290

Suburban Wagon, powder blue or white body and roof, 15-1/2" long; 1963
EX $75   **NM** $115   **MIP** $150

Suburban Wagon, gray/green body and roof, 15-3/4" long; 1964
EX $70   **NM** $100   **MIP** $140

Town and Country Convertible, maroon front, hood, rear deck and fenders, gray top retracts into rumble seat, 19" long; 1947
EX $300   **NM** $450   **MIP** $600

(Toy Shop File Photo)

Travel Trailer and Station Wagon, red station wagon, two-wheel trailer w/red lower body and white steel camper-style upper body, 27-1/4" long; 1965
EX $155   **NM** $230   **MIP** $310

Yellow Taxi with Skyview, yellow hood, roof and body, red radiator front and fenders, 18-1/2" long; 1948
EX $200   **NM** $400   **MIP** $600

CONSTRUCTION AND FARM EQUIPMENT

Aerial Tower Tramway, two tapering dark green 33-1/2" tall towers and 12" square bases, black hand crank, 1928
EX $1000   **NM** $1300   **MIP** $2700

Big Derrick, red mast and 20" boom, black base, 24" tall, 1921
EX $600   **NM** $900   **MIP** $1200

Brute Articulated Scooper, 5-1/2" long; yellow, front-loading scoop, articulated frame; 1970
EX $6   **NM** $12   **MIP** $18

Brute Articulated Scooper, yellow front-loading scoop, cab, articulated frame and rear power unit, black radiator, exhaust, steering wheel and driver's seat, 5-1/2" long; 1970
EX $50   **NM** $75   **MIP** $100

Brute Double Dump Train, yellow hood, fenders and back on tractor unit, yellow coupled bottom-dumping earth carriers, 9-1/2" long; 1969
EX $50   **NM** $75   **MIP** $100

Brute Double Dump Train (tractor-trailer), 9-1/2" long; yellow, coupled bottom-dumping earth carriers; 1969
EX $8   **NM** $17   **MIP** $25

Brute Dumping Scraper, 7" long; yellow; 1970
EX $7   **NM** $13   **MIP** $20

Brute Dumping Scraper, yellow hood, fenders and back on two-wheel tractor unit, yellow scraper-dump unit, 7" long; 1970
EX $50   **NM** $75   **MIP** $100

Brute Farm Tractor-n-Cart, bright blue tractor body and rear fenders, green plastic radiator, engine, exhaust and driver's seat, bright blue detachable, square, two-wheel open cart, 6-1/4" long; 1969
EX $30   **NM** $45   **MIP** $60

Brute Farm Tractor-n-Cart, 6-1/4" long; blue tractor with green engine and driver's seat, blue two-wheel open car; 1969
EX $7   **NM** $13   **MIP** $20

Brute Road Grader, yellow hood, cab, frame and adjustable blade, black radiator, driver's seat and steering wheel, 6-1/2" long; 1970
EX $50   **NM** $75   **MIP** $100

Brute Road Grader, 6-1/2" long; yellow, adjustable blade; 1970
EX $6   **NM** $12   **MIP** $18

Cement Mixer on Treads, medium gray w/black treads and water tank, No. 280A, 16" tall, 1929-31
EX $2500   **NM** $3800   **MIP** $5200

Cement Mixer on Wheels, medium gray w/black cast steel wheels and water tank, 14-1/2" tall, 1926-29
EX $700   **NM** $900   **MIP** $1500

Concrete Mixer, medium gray w/black cast-steel wheels, black water tank, w/wood-handle, steel-blade scoop shovel, No. 280, 17-3/4" long w/tow bar up, 1926
EX $500   **NM** $750   **MIP** $1000

Concrete Mixer, green w/black cast-steel wheels, crank, gears, and band mixing drum, 10-1/2" long, 1930
EX $175   **NM** $265   **MIP** $350

Concrete Mixer, yellow/orange frame and base, red hopper and drum, black crank handle, 10-1/2" long, 1936
EX $110   **NM** $175   **MIP** $225

Concrete Mixer, red frame and base, cream/yellow hopper, drum and crank handle, 10-1/2" long; 1941
EX $135   **NM** $195   **MIP** $255

Concrete Mixer, green frame, base, crank, crank handle and bottom of mixing drum, gray hopper and top of drum, 9-5/8" long; 1949
EX $100   **NM** $150   **MIP** $200

Concrete Mixer with Motor Sound, green frame, base, crank, crank handle and bottom of mixing drum, gray hopper and top of drum, w/sound when crank rotates drum, 9 5/8" long; 1950
EX $75   **NM** $115   **MIP** $150

Dandy Digger, yellow main frame, operators, seat and boom, brown shovel, arm, under frame and twin skids, 27" long; 1941
EX $95   **NM** $145   **MIP** $195

Dandy Digger, yellow seat, lower control lever and main boom, black underframe, skids, shovel, arm and control lever, 38-1/2" long w/shovel arm extended; 1953
EX $75   **NM** $115   **MIP** $150

Dandy Digger, red main frame, operators, seat and boom, black shovel, arm, under frame and twin skids, 27" long, 1931
EX $100   **NM** $160   **MIP** $215

Dandy Digger, yellow seat lower control lever and main boom, black underframe, skids, shovel and arm, 38-1/2" long w/shovel arm extended; 1953
EX $75   **NM** $115   **MIP** $150

Dandy Digger, yellow main frame, operators, seat and boom, green shovel, arm, under frame and twin skids, 27" long, 1936
EX $85   **NM** $130   **MIP** $175

Digger, red main frame, operators, seat and boom, black shovel, arm, lower frame and twin skids, curved connecting rod, boom tilts down for digging, 11-1/2" long w/shovel arm extended, 1935
EX $100   **NM** $150   **MIP** $200

Dredge, red corrugated roof and base w/four wide black wheels, red hubs, black boiler, floor, frame boom and clamshell bucket, 19" long, 1924
EX $750   **NM** $1000   **MIP** $1500

Giant Digger, yellow main frame, operators, seat and boom, brown shovel, arm, lower frame and twin skids, boom tilts, 11-1/2" long w/shovel arm extended; 1941
EX $75   **NM** $115   **MIP** $155

Giant Digger, red main frame, operators, seat and boom, black shovel, arm, lower frame and twin skids, boom tilts down for digging, 42" long w/shovel arm extended; 1931
EX $275   **NM** $415   **MIP** $550

Giant Digger, red main frame, operators, seat and boom, black shovel, arm, lower frame and twin skids, curved connecting rod, boom tilts, 31" long w/shovel arm extended, 1933
EX $265   **NM** $395   **MIP** $525

Giant Digger, yellow main frame, operators, seat and boom, green shovel, arm, lower frame and twin skids, boom tilts, 11-1/2" long w/shovel arm extended, 1936
EX $85   **NM** $130   **MIP** $175

Gradall, bright yellow truck and superstructure, black plastic bumper and radiator, 32" long w/digging arm extended; 1965
EX $350   **NM** $750   **MIP** $1000

Hauling Rig with Construction Derrick, yellow tractor unit, green semi-trailer, winch on front of trailer makes sound, 36-3/4" long; 1954
EX $110   **NM** $175   **MIP** $225

Hauling Rig with Construction Derrick, duo-tone slant design tractor, yellow bumper, lower hood and cab sides, white upper hood and cab, white trailer w/yellow loading ramp, overall 38-1/2" long; 1953
EX $175   **NM** $250   **MIP** $400

Hoisting Tower, dark green, hoist tower and three distribution chutes, 29" tall, 1928-31
EX $1500   **NM** $2000   **MIP** $2500

Husky Tractor, 13" long; yellow body (blue body in 1969); 1966-70
EX $15   **NM** $30   **MIP** $45

Husky Tractor, bright yellow body, red large rear fenders and wheels, black engine block, exhaust, steering wheel and driver's seat, 13" long; 1970
EX $30   **NM** $45   **MIP** $65

Husky Tractor, bright blue body with white wheels and large rear fenders, black engine block, exhaust, steering wheel and driver's seat, 13" long; 1969
EX $40   **NM** $60   **MIP** $80

Husky Tractor, bright yellow body and large rear fenders, black engine block, exhaust, steering wheel and driver's seat, 13" long; 1966
EX $50   **NM** $80   **MIP** $105

Improved Steam Shovel, black w/red roof and base, 14" tall, 1927-29
EX $100   **NM** $150   **MIP** $200

Junior Excavator, red shovel, arm, underframe, control lever and twin skids, yellow boom, rear lever, frame and seat, 28" long; 1945
EX $75   **NM** $115   **MIP** $150

Mechanical Crane, orange removable roof, boom, yellow wheels in white rubber crawler treads, olive green enclosed cab and base, hand crank w/rat-tat motor noise, 20" tall; 1952
EX $150   **NM** $225   **MIP** $300

Mechanical Crane, orange removable roof, boom and wheels in black cleated rubber crawler treads, olive green enclosed cab and base, hand crank w/rat-tat motor noise, 20" tall; 1950
EX $175   **NM** $265   **MIP** $350

Mobile Construction Derrick, orange laticework main mast, swiveling base, yellow latticework boom, green clamshell bucket and main platform base, 25-1/2" long w/boom lowered; 1953
EX $155   **NM** $250   **MIP** $355

Mobile Construction Derrick, orange laticework main mast, swiveling base, yellow latticework boom, gray clamshell bucket, green main platform base, 25-1/2" long w/boom lowered; 1955
EX $160   **NM** $260   **MIP** $355

Mobile Construction Derrick, orange laticework main mast, swiveling base, yellow latticework boom, gray clamshell

bucket, orange main platform base, 25-1/2" long w/boom lowered; 1956
EX $150   **NM** $250   **MIP** $350

Mobile Power Digger Unit, clamshell dredge mounted on 10-wheel truck, orange truck, yellow dredge cab on swivel base, 31-3/4" long w/boom lowered; 1955
EX $125   **NM** $185   **MIP** $250

Mobile Power Digger Unit, clamshell dredge mounted on six-wheel truck, orange truck, yellow dredge cab on swivel base, 31-3/4" long w/boom lowered; 1956
EX $100   **NM** $150   **MIP** $250

Overhead Crane, black folding end frames and legs, braces, red crossbeams and platform, 46" long, 1924
EX $800   **NM** $1500   **MIP** $2300

Pile Driver on Wheels, black w/red roof and base, No. 260, 22-1/2" tall, 1924-27
EX $800   **NM** $1700   **MIP** $2500

Polysteel Farm Tractor, orange molded plastic four-wheel tractor, silver radiator front, headlights, and motor parts, 12" long; 1961
EX $80   **NM** $120   **MIP** $155

Pull-n-Ride Horse-Drawn Farm Wagon, red four-wheel steel hopper-body wagon, detailed litho horse, 22-3/4" long; 1952
EX $150   **NM** $225   **MIP** $300

Road Roller, dark green w/red roof and rollers, nickel plated steam cylinders, No. 290, 20" long, 1929-31
EX $1300   **NM** $2400   **MIP** $3500

Ruff-n-Tuff Tractor, yellow grille, hood and frame, black plastic engine block and driver's seat, 10-1/2" long; 1971
EX $50   **NM** $75   **MIP** $100

Sand Loader, warm gray w/twelve black buckets, 21" long, 18" high, 1924
EX $150   **NM** $210   **MIP** $450

Sand Loader, warm gray w/twelve black buckets, chain-tension adjusting device at bottom of elevator side frames, 21" long, 1929
EX $175   **NM** $305   **MIP** $500

Sand Loader, yellow w/twelve black buckets, chain-tension adjusting device at bottom of elevator side frames, 21" long, 1931
EX $200   **NM** $250   **MIP** $350

Scoop-n-Load Conveyor, cream body frame, green loading scoop, black circular crank operates black rubber cleated conveyor belt, 18" long; 1953
EX $75   **NM** $115   **MIP** $150

Scoop-n-Load Conveyor, cream body frame, green loading scoop, black circular crank operates black rubber cleated conveyor belt, "PORTABLE" decal in red, 18" long; 1954
EX $65   **NM** $105   **MIP** $140

Scoop-n-Load Conveyor, cream body frame, red loading scoop and chute, bright-plated circular crank operates black rubber cleated conveyor belt, "PORTABLE" decal in white, 18" long; 1955
EX $60   **NM** $95   **MIP** $125

Scoop-n-Load Conveyor, cream body frame, red loading scoop and chute, bright-plated circular crank operates black rubber cleated conveyor belt, "PORTABLE" decal in yellow, 18" long; 1956
EX $55   **NM** $85   **MIP** $115

Scoop-n-Load Conveyor, 1956-57, cram body frame, green loading scoop, black circular crank operates black rubber cleated conveyor belt, "PORTABLE" decal in green, 18" long; 1956-57
EX $50   **NM** $100   **MIP** $150

Side Conveyor Load-n-Dump, yellow plastic front end including cab, yellow steel bumper, green frame and dump body, red conveyor frame w/chute, 20-1/2" long; 1953
EX $80   **NM** $130   **MIP** $150

Side Conveyor Load-n-Dump, all steel yellow cab, hood, bumper and frame, white dump body and tailgate, red conveyor frame w/chute, 21-1/4" long; 1954
EX $65   **NM** $100   **MIP** $135

Side Conveyor Load-n-Dump, all steel yellow cab, hood, bumper and frame, deep blue dump body, white tailgate, red conveyor frame w/chute, 21-1/4" long; 1955
EX $60   **NM** $95   **MIP** $125

Small Derrick, red 20" movable boom and three angle-iron braces, black base and vertical mast, 21-1/2" tall, 1921
EX $500   **NM** $750   **MIP** $1000

Steam Shovel, black w/red roof and base, 25-1/2" tall, 1921-22
EX $125   **NM** $250   **MIP** $500

Traveling Crane, red crane, carriage, and long cross beams, hand wheel rotates crane boom, 46" long, 1928
EX $1275   **NM** $1900   **MIP** $2550

Trench Digger, yellow main frame, base, and motor housing, red elevator and conveyor frame and track frames, 20" tall, 1928-31
EX $2000   **NM** $3500   **MIP** $5000

EMERGENCY VEHICLES

Aerial Ladder and Emergency Truck, red w/white ladders, bumper and steel disc wheels, three eight-rung steel ladders, no rear step, no siren or SIREN decal, 22-1/4" long; 1953
EX $225   **NM** $345   **MIP** $450

Aerial Ladder and Emergency Truck, red w/white ladders, bumper and steel disc wheels, three eight-rung steel ladders, 22-1/4" long; 1952
EX $200   **NM** $300   **MIP** $400

Aerial Ladder Fire Engine, red tractor, wraparound bumper and semi-trailer, two aluminum thirteen-rung extension

ladders on sides, swivel-base aluminum central ladder, 26-1/2" long; 1960
EX $125   **NM** $185   **MIP** $250

Aerial Ladder Fire Engine, red tractor and semi-trailer, white plastic bumper w/integral grille guard, two aluminum thirteen-rung extension ladders on sides, swivel-base aluminum central ladder, 26-1/2" long; 1961
EX $125   **NM** $185   **MIP** $250

Aerial Ladder Fire Engine, red tractor and semi-trailer, chrome one-piece wraparound bumper, slotted grille, two aluminum thirteen-rung extension ladders on sides, swivel-base aluminum central ladder, 26-1/2" long; 1966
EX $125   **NM** $185   **MIP** $250

Aerial Ladder Fire Engine, red cabover-engine tractor and semi-trailer units, two thirteen-rung white sectional ladders and swivel-mounted aerial ladder w/side rails, 25-1/2" long; 1968
EX $100   **NM** $150   **MIP** $200

Aerial Ladder Fire Engine, snub-nose red tractor and semi-trailer, white swivel-mounted aerial ladder w/side rails, two white thirteen-rung sectional ladders, 27-1/2" long; 1970
EX $100   **NM** $150   **MIP** $200

Aerial Ladder Fire Engine (tractor-trailer), 27-1/2" long; snub-nose cab, white swivel-mounted aerial ladder with side rails, two white 13-rung sectional ladders; 1970
EX $25   **NM** $50   **MIP** $75

Aerial Ladder Fire Engine (tractor-trailer), 25-1/2" long; cabover, two 13-rung white sectional ladders, swivel-mounted aerial ladder with side rails; 1968
EX $35   **NM** $65   **MIP** $100

Aerial Ladder Fire Engine (tractor-trailer), 26-1/2" long; chrome one-piece wraparound bumper, slotted grille; 1966-67
EX $40   **NM** $85   **MIP** $125

Aerial Truck, red w/nickel ladders, black hand wheel, brass bell, and black hubs, 39" long w/ladder down, 1925
EX $850   **NM** $1300   **MIP** $1700

American LaFrance Aero-Chief Pumper, 25-1/2" long; cabover, white underbody, rear step and simulated hose reels, black extension ladders on right side; 1962
EX $22   **NM** $43   **MIP** $65

American LaFrance Aero-Chief Pumper, red cabover-engine and body, white underbody, rear step and simulated hose reels, black extension ladders on right side, 25-1/2" long; 1972
EX $90   **NM** $150   **MIP** $200

Brute Fire Pumper, 5-1/4" long; red cabover, two yellow 5-rung sectional ladders on sides; 1969
EX $4   **NM** $8   **MIP** $12

Brute Fire Pumper, red cabover-engine body and frame, two yellow five-rung

sectional ladders on sides of open body, 5-1/4" long; 1969
EX $35   **NM** $60   **MIP** $85

Brute Hook-N-Ladder, red cabover-engine tractor and detachable semi-trailer, white elevating, swveling aerial ladder w/side rails, 10" long; 1969
EX $30   **NM** $40   **MIP** $55

Brute Hook-N-Ladder (tractor-trailer), 10" long; cabover, detachable semi-trailer, white swiveling aerial ladder with side rails; 1969
EX $7   **NM** $13   **MIP** $20

Extension Ladder Fire Truck, red w/silver ladders and yellow removable rider seat, enclosed cab, 35" long; 1945
EX $200   **NM** $300   **MIP** $400

Extension Ladder Rider Fire Truck, duo-tone slant design, tractor has white front, lower hood sides and lower doors, red hood top, cab and frame, red semi-trailer, white ten-rung and eight-rung ladders, 32-1/2" long; 1949
EX $150   **NM** $225   **MIP** $300

Extension Ladder Trailer Fire Truck, red tractor unit and semi-trailer, enclosed cab, two white thirteen-rung side extension ladders on sides, white central ladder on swivel base, 29-1/2" long; 1956
EX $125   **NM** $185   **MIP** $250

Extension Ladder Trailer Fire Truck, red tractor w/enclosed cab, boxy fenders, red semi-trailer w/fenders, two white eight-rung side ladders, ten-rung central extension ladder, 29-1/2" long; 1955
EX $200   **NM** $300   **MIP** $400

Fire and Chemical Truck, duo-tone slant design, white front, lower hood sides and lower doors, rest is red, bright-metal or white eight-rung ladder on sides, 25" long; 1949
EX $125   **NM** $185   **MIP** $250

Fire Department Emergency Truck, red streamlined body, enclosed cab, chrome one-piece grille, bumper, and headlights, 12-3/4" long; 1953
EX $100   **NM** $150   **MIP** $200

Fire Engine, red w/nickel rim flywheels on dummy pump, brass bell, dim-or-bright electric headlights, 25-1/2" long, 1933
EX $500   **NM** $750   **MIP** $1500

Fire Engine, red w/nickel-plated upright broiler, nickel rims and flywheels on dummy water pump, brass bell, 23-1/4" long, 1925-29
EX $500   **NM** $800   **MIP** $1600

Fire Hose and Water Pumper, red w/two white five-rung ladders, two removable fire extinguishers, enclosed cab, 12-1/2" long; 1950
EX $105   **NM** $155   **MIP** $200

Fire Hose and Water Pumper, red w/two white five-rung ladders, one red/white removable fire extinguisher, enclosed cab, 12-1/2" long; 1952
EX $100   **NM** $150   **MIP** $200

Fire Pumper, No. 5311, station wagon design, "Buddy L No. 6" on cab door, siren light, ladder; 1964-65
EX $20   **NM** $40   **MIP** $60

Fire Pumper, 16-1/4" long; red cabover, 11-rung white 10" ladder on each side; 1968
EX $56   **NM** $85   **MIP** $100

Fire Pumper with Action Hydrant, red wraparound bumper, hood cab and cargo section, aluminum nine-rung ladders, white hose reel, 15" long; 1960
EX $75   **NM** $115   **MIP** $150

Fire Truck, red w/black solid-rubber Firestone tires on red seven-spoke embossed metal wheels, two 18-1/2" red steel sectional ladders, 26" long, 1930
EX $800   **NM** $1000   **MIP** $1600

Fire Truck, red w/two white ladders, enclosed cab, bright metal grille and headlights, 25" long; 1948
EX $125   **NM** $200   **MIP** $250

Fire Truck, duo-tone slant design, yellow front, bumper, hood sides and skirted fenders, rest is red, nickel ladders, 28-1/2" long, 1939
EX $500   **NM** $700   **MIP** $1000

Fire Truck, red w/nickel or white ladders, bright-metal radiator grille and black removable rider saddle, 25-1/2" long, 1935
EX $255   **NM** $385   **MIP** $510

Fire Truck, bright red, red floor, open driver's seat, 26" long, 1928
EX $450   **NM** $800   **MIP** $1200

Fire Truck, bright red w/black inverted L-shaped crane mounted in socket on seat back, red floor, open driver's seat, 26" long, 1925
EX $450   **NM** $800   **MIP** $1600

Fire Truck, bright red w/black inverted L-shaped crane mounted in socket on seat back, open driver's seat, 26" long, 1924
EX $500   **NM** $900   **MIP** $1850

Fire Truck, duo-tone slant design, tractor has white front, lower hood sides and lower doors, red hood top, cab and frame, red semi-trailer, rubber wheels w/black tires, 32-1/2" long; 1953
EX $200   **NM** $300   **MIP** $400

Fire Truck, red w/white ladders, black rubber wheels, enclosed cab, 12" long; 1945
EX $75   **NM** $115   **MIP** $150

Fire Truck, duo-tone slant design, yellow front, single-bar bumper, hood sides and removable rider seat, rest is red, 25-1/2" long, 1936
EX $170   **NM** $250   **MIP** $500

GMC Deluxe Aerial Ladder Fire Engine, white tractor and semi-trailer units, golden thirteen-rung extension ladder on sides, golden central aerial ladder, black and white DANGER battery case w/two flashing lights, 28" long; 1959
EX $225   **NM** $345   **MIP** $450

(Calvin L. Chaussee Photo)

GMC Extension Ladder Trailer Fire Engine, red tractor w/chrome GMC bar grille, red semi-trailer, white thirteen-rung extension ladders on sides, white swiveling central ladder w/side rails, 27-1/4" long; 1957
EX $110   NM $260   MIP $405

GMC Fire Pumper with Horn, red w/aluminum-finish eleven-rung side ladders and white reel of black plastic hose in open cargo section, chrome GMC bar grille, 15" long; 1958
EX $150   NM $200   MIP $300

GMC Hydraulic Aerial Ladder Fire Engine, red tractor unit w/chrome GMC bar grille, red semi-trailer, white thirteen-rung extension ladders on sides, white swiveling central ladder, 26-1/2" long; 1958
EX $125   NM $185   MIP $250

GMC Red Cross Ambulance, all white, removable fabric canopy w/a red cross and "Ambulance" in red, 14-1/2" long; 1960
EX $150   NM $250   MIP $400

Hook & Ladder Fire Truck, medium-dark red, w/black inverted L-shaped crane mounted in socket on seat back, open driver's seat, 26" long, 1923
EX $900   NM $1800   MIP $2800

(Joe & Sharon Freed Photo)

Hose Truck, red w/two white hose pipes, white cord hose on reel and brass nozzle, electric headlights w/red bulbs, 21 3/4" long, 1933
EX $495   NM $760   MIP $1100

Hydraulic Aerial Truck, red w/brass bell on cowl, nickel ladders mounted on 5-1/2" turntable rotated by black hand wheel, 39" long, 1927
EX $850   NM $1300   MIP $1700

Hydraulic Aerial Truck, duo-tone slant design, yellow front, single-bar bumper, chassis, radiator, front fender, lower sides and removable rider saddle, rest is red, 40" long w/ladders down, 1936
EX $550   NM $825   MIP $1100

Hydraulic Snorkel Fire Pumper, 21" long; red cabover, white 11-rung 10" ladder on each side; 1969
EX $32   NM $65   MIP $95

Hydraulic Snorkel Fire Pumper, red cabover-engine and open rear body, white eleven-rung 10" ladder on each side, snorkel pod w/solid sides, 21" long; 1969
EX $105   NM $155   MIP $210

Hydraulic Water Tower Truck, red w/nickel water tower, dim/bright electric headlights, brass bell, added-on bright-metal grille, 44-7/8" long w/tower down, 1935
EX $600   NM $900   MIP $1500

Hydraulic Water Tower Truck, duo-tone slant design, yellow bumper, hood sides, front fenders, rest is red, electric headlights, added-on bright-metal grille, 44-7/8" long w/tower down, 1936
EX $600   NM $1000   MIP $1500

Hydraulic Water Tower Truck, duo-tone slant design, yellow front, single-bar bumper and hood sides, red hood top, enclosed cab and water tank, brass bell, nickel water tower, 46" long w/tower down, 1939
EX $900   NM $1200   MIP $1700

Hydraulic Water Tower Truck, red w/nickel water tower, dim/bright electric headlights, brass bell, 44-7/8" long w/tower down, 1933
EX $800   NM $1000   MIP $1700

Jr. Fire Emergency Truck, 6-3/4" long; red cabover, wider bumper, 4-slot grille with two square plastic headlights; 1969
EX $8   NM $12   MIP $20

Jr. Fire Emergency Truck, 6-3/4" long; red cabover, one-piece chrome wraparound narrow bumper, 24-hole grille with plastic vertical-pair headlights; 1968
EX $8   NM $12   MIP $20

Jr. Fire Snorkel Truck, 11-1/2" long; red cabover, one-piece chrome wraparound narrow bumper, 24-hole grille with plastic vertical-pair headlights; 1968
EX $9   NM $14   MIP $22

Jr. Fire Snorkel Truck, 11-1/2" long; red cabover, wider bumper, 4-slot grille with two square plastic headlights; 1969
EX $9   NM $14   MIP $22

Jr. Hook-n-Ladder Aerial Truck, 17" long; red cabover, one-piece chrome wraparound narrow bumper, 24-hole grille with plastic vertical-pair headlights; 1968
EX $23   NM $35   MIP $48

Jr. Hook-n-Ladder Aerial Truck, 17" long; red cabover, wider bumper, 4-slot grille with two square plastic headlights; 1969
EX $17   NM $25   MIP $40

Ladder Fire Truck, red w/bright-metal V-nose radiator, headlights and ladder, black wooden wheels, 12" long; 1941
EX $125   NM $200   MIP $250

Ladder Truck, red w/yellow severely streamlined, skirted fenders and lower doors, white ladders, bright-metal grille, no bumper, 17-1/2" long; 1940
EX $200   NM $300   MIP $400

Ladder Truck, modified duo-tone slant design, white front, front fenders and lower doors, white ladders, bright-metal grille, no bumper, 17-1/2" long; 1941
EX $200   NM $300   MIP $400

Ladder Truck, red w/bright-metal grille and headlights, two white ladders, 24" long; 1939
EX $100   NM $200   MIP $300

Ladder Truck, duo-tone slant design, white front, hood sides, fenders and two ladders, rest is red, square enclosed cab w/sharply protruding visor, no headlights, 22-3/4" long, 1937
EX $135   NM $200   MIP $275

Ladder Truck, duo-tone slant design, white front, hood sides, fenders and two ladders, rest is red, square enclosed cab w/sharply protruding visor, 22-3/4" long, 1936
EX $150   NM $225   MIP $300

Ladder Truck, red w/two yellow ladders, enclosed square cab w/sharply protruding visor, bright-metal radiator front, 22-3/4" long, 1935
EX $255   NM $380   MIP $510

Ladder Truck, red w/two yellow ladders, enclosed square cab w/sharply protruding visor, 22-3/4" long, 1934
EX $200   NM $300   MIP $400

Ladder Truck, red w/two yellow sectional ladders, enclosed square cab, 22-3/4" long, 1933
EX $120   NM $250   MIP $500

Ladder Truck, red w/two white ladders, bright-metal radiator grille and headlights, 24" long; 1941
EX $125   NM $200   MIP $250

Police Squad Truck, yellow front and front fenders, dark blue-green body, yellow fire extinguisher, 21-1/2" long over ladders; 1947
EX $150   NM $300   MIP $550

Police Wrecker, 13-3/4" long; operating boom, front-wheel steering, whitewall tires; 1971
EX $8   NM $17   MIP $25

Police Wrecker, 5" long; bubble-window cabover; 1970s
EX $3   NM $7   MIP $10

Pumping Fire Engine, red w/nickel stack on boiler, nickel rims on pump flywheels, nickel-rim headlights and searchlight, 23-1/2" long, 1929
EX $2500   NM $3500   MIP $4000

Rear Steer Trailer Fire Truck, red w/two white ten-rung ladders, chrome one-piece grille, headlights and bumper, 20" long; 1952
EX $65   NM $100   MIP $200

Red Cross Ambulance, all white, removable fabric canopy w/a red cross and "Ambulance" in red, 14-1/2" long; 1958
EX $60   NM $95   MIP $125

Rescue Force Ambulance, 12" long; battery-operated, siren; 1993
EX $5   **NM** $10   **MIP** $15

Suburban Pumper, red station wagon body, white plastic wraparound bumpers, one-piece grille and double headlights, 15" long; 1964
EX $100   **NM** $150   **MIP** $175

Texaco Fire Chief American LaFrance Pumper, promotional piece, red rounded-front enclosed cab and body, white one-pice underbody, running boards and rear step, 25" long; 1962
EX $210   **NM** $305   **MIP** $410

Trailer Ladder Truck, all red w/cream removable rider saddle, three bright metal ten-rung ladders, 20" long over ladders; 1941
EX $150   **NM** $225   **MIP** $300

Trailer Ladder Truck, duo-tone slant design, tractor unit has yellow front, lower hood sides and lower doors, red hood top, enclosed cab and semi-trailer, nickel ten-rung ladders, 30" long w/ladders; 1940
EX $200   **NM** $300   **MIP** $400

Water Tower Truck, red w/nickel two-bar front bumper, red nickel-rim headlights plus searchlight on cowl, nickel latticework water tower, 45-1/2" long w/tower down, 1929
EX $2500   **NM** $4000   **MIP** $5500

MISCELLANEOUS

(Toy Shop File Photo)

49 LST, Gray landing craft with swivel guns on deck, opening ramp door, includes tank and army truck
EX $35   **NM** $75   **MIP** $95

Fill-R-Up gas pump, 7" high; battery operated, ringing bell, price "totals"; 1966-69
EX $6   **NM** $12   **MIP** $18

(Toy Shop File Photo)

Fill-R-Up Gas Pump, White plastic gas pump, 4" wide, 7" high, 2-3/4" deep. Magnetic pump holds to metal vehicles, two "C" batteries power the pump register and bell. According to the 1970

catalog, it "totals price automatically-- up to 39 gallons at $9.75."
EX $12   **NM** $25   **MIP** $40

Hydraulic Service Lift, 15" long; battery-operated service ramp, steel, push-button with bell and retractable air hoses; 1967-68
EX $8   **NM** $17   **MIP** $25

Jr. Animal Ark, 5" long; ten pairs of plastic animals; 1970
EX $5   **NM** $10   **MIP** $15

Traffic Light, 8" high; plastic, battery-operated, push-button, made in Japan; 1967-69
EX $3   **NM** $6   **MIP** $10

SETS

Army Combination, searchlight repair-it truck, transport truck and howitzer, ammunition conveyor, stake delivery truck, ammo, soldiers; 1956
EX $300   **NM** $400   **MIP** $500

Army Commando, 14-1/2" truck, searchlight unit, two-wheel howitzer, soldiers; 1957
EX $125   **NM** $185   **MIP** $250

Big Brute Freeway, scraper, grader, scooper and dump truck; 1971
EX $30   **NM** $60   **MIP** $90

Big Brute Hi-Way, bulldozer, dump truck, yellow four-wheel trailer; 1971
EX $20   **NM** $40   **MIP** $60

Big Brute Road, cement mixer truck, scooper, dump truck; 1971
EX $20   **NM** $40   **MIP** $60

Brute Fire Department, semi trailer aerial ladder, fire pumper, fire wrecker, tow truck; 1970
EX $17   **NM** $33   **MIP** $50

Brute Five-Piece Highway, bulldozer, grader, scraper, dumping scraper and double dump train; 1970
EX $50   **NM** $80   **MIP** $105

Brute Fleet, car carrier w/two plastic coupes, dump truck, pickup truck, cement mixer truck, tow truck; 1969
EX $85   **NM** $130   **MIP** $175

Brute Fleet, car carrier with two plastic coupes, dump truck, pickup truck, cement mixer truck, tow truck; 1970
EX $17   **NM** $56   **MIP** $50

Brute Hi-Way, bulldozer, grader, scraper, sumping scraper and double dump train; 1970
EX $17   **NM** $33   **MIP** $50

Coca-Cola, 10-1/2" trailer truck; three-vehicle set with tractor-trailer with clear plastic cover, five cases and hadtruck; deliver truck with two cases; and forklift truck with two extra cases; late 1970s
EX $20   **NM** $40   **MIP** $60

Delivery Set Combination, 16-1/2" long wrigley express truck, 15" long sand and stone dump truck, 14-1/4" long freight

conveyor and 14-1/4" long stake delivery truck; 1955
EX $175   **NM** $265   **MIP** $350

Deluxe Riding Academy, 18-1/2" long truck; Sears exclusive, red horse truck with bubbletop, "Riding Academy" on van sides, two horses and two colts, plastic six-piece fense; 1966-69
EX $40   **NM** $80   **MIP** $125

Family Camping, Camper/cruiser truck, 15-1/2" long maroon suburban wagon, and brown/light gray/beige folding teepee camping trailer; 1963
EX $60   **NM** $95   **MIP** $130

Family Camping, blue camping trailer and suburban wagon, blue camper-n-cruiser; 1964
EX $50   **NM** $75   **MIP** $100

Farm Combination, cattle transport stake truck w/six plastic steers, hydraulic farm supplies trailer dump truck, trailer and three farm machines and farm machinery trailer hauler truck; 1956
EX $100   **NM** $155   **MIP** $210

Fire Department, aerial ladder fire engine, fire pumper w/action hydrant that squirts water, two plastic hoses, two plastic firemen, fire chief's badge; 1960
EX $250   **NM** $375   **MIP** $505

Freight Conveyor and Stake Delivery Truck, blue frame 14-1/4" long conveyor, red, white and yellow body 14-3/4" long truck; 1955
EX $125   **NM** $185   **MIP** $250

Friendly Highway, 8-1/2" x 6-3/4" x 2-1/2" box; steel and plastic, includes Texacto Tanker truck; 1980s
EX $8   **NM** $17   **MIP** $25

GMC Air Defense, 15" long, GMC army searchlight truck, 15" long, GMC signal corps truck, two four-wheel trailers, plastic soliders; 1957
EX $300   **NM** $500   **MIP** $700

GMC Brinks Bank, silver gray, barred windows on sides and in double doors, coin slot and hole in roof, brass padlock w/two keys, pouch, play money, two gray plastic guard figures, 16" long; 1959
EX $305   **NM** $360   **MIP** $455

GMC Fire Department, red GMC extension ladder trailer and GMC pumper w/ladders and hose reel, four-wheel red electric searchlight trailer, warning barrier, red plastic helmet, firemen, policeman; 1958
EX $300   **NM** $500   **MIP** $750

GMC Highway Maintenance Fleet, orange maintenance truck w/trailer, sand and stone dump truck, scoop-n-load conveyor, sand hopper, steel scoop shovel, four white steel road barriers; 1957
EX $310   **NM** $505   **MIP** $710

GMC Livestock, red fenders, hood, cab and frame, white flatbed cargo section , six sections of brown plastic rail fencing, five black plastic steers, 14-1/2" long; 1958

EX $300   **NM** $400   **MIP** $500

GMC Western Roundup, blue fenders, hood, cab and frame, white flatbed cargo section, plastic six sections of rail fencing w/swinging gate, rearing and standing horse, cowboys, calf, steer; 1959

EX $300   **NM** $400   **MIP** $500

Highway Construction, orange and black bulldozer and driver, truck w/orange pickup body, orange dump truck; 1962

EX $200   **NM** $300   **MIP** $400

Highway Maintenance Mechanical Truck & Concrete Mixer, 20" truck plus movable ramp, w/duo-tone slant design, blue lower hood sides, yellow hood top and cab, 10-3/4" blue and yellow mixer, overall 36" long; 1949

EX $160   **NM** $245   **MIP** $325

Interstate Highway, orange, parks department dumper, landscape truck, telephone truck, accessories include trees, drums, workmen and traffic cones, scoop shovel; 1959

EX $260   **NM** $410   **MIP** $505

Interstate Highway, orange, husky dumper, contractor's truck and ladder, utility truck, plastic pickaxe, spade, shovel, nail keg; 1960

EX $250   **NM** $350   **MIP** $500

Jr. Animal Farm, Jr. Giraffe Truck, Jr. Kitty Kennel, Jr. Pony Trailer with Sportster; 1968

EX $32   **NM** $63   **MIP** $95

Jr. Animal Farm, 6-1/2" long Jr. Giraffe Truck, 6-1/4" long Jr. Kitty Kennel, 11-1/4" long Jr. Pony Trailer w/Sportster; 1968

EX $120   **NM** $185   **MIP** $250

Jr. Fire Department, 17" long Jr. hook-n-ladder aerial truck, 11-1/2" long Jr. fire snorkel, 6-3/4" long truck, all have twenty-four-hole chrome grilles; 1968

EX $32   **NM** $63   **MIP** $95

Jr. Fire Department, 17" long Jr. hook-n-ladder aerial truck, 11-1/2" long Jr. fire snorkel, 6-3/4" long truck, all have four-slot grilles and two square plastic headlights; 1969

EX $120   **NM** $185   **MIP** $250

Jr. Fire Department, Jr. Hook-n-Ladder Aerial, Jr. Fire Snorkel, Jr. Fire Emergency Truck with four-slot grilles and square plastic headlights; 1969

EX $32   **NM** $63   **MIP** $95

Jr. Hi-Way, Jr. Scooper Tractor, Jr. Cement Mixer, Jr. Dump Truck; 1969

EX $30   **NM** $60   **MIP** $90

Jr. Sportsman, Jr. camper pickup w/red cab and body and yellow camper, towing 6" plastic runabout on yellow two-wheel boat trailer; 1971

EX $50   **NM** $80   **MIP** $105

Jr. Sportsman, Jr. Camper Pickup, boat trailer and plastic runabout; 1971

EX $17   **NM** $33   **MIP** $50

Loader, Dump Truck, and Shovel, conveyor, blue body sand and gravel dump truck, 8-3/4" long blue-enameled steel scoop shovel; 1955

EX $85   **NM** $130   **MIP** $175

Loader, Dump Truck, and Shovel, conveyor, green body sand and gravel dump truck, 8-3/4" long green-enameled steel scoop shovel; 1954

EX $100   **NM** $150   **MIP** $200

Mechanical Hauling Truck and Concrete Mixer, truck w/duo-tone slant design, red-orange lower hood sides, dark green upper hood, cab, trailer and ramp, 9-5/8" green mixer, gray hopper, 38" long w/ramps; 1950

EX $160   **NM** $245   **MIP** $325

Mechanical Hauling Truck and Concrete Mixer, truck w/duo-tone slant design, red/orange lower hood sides, dark green upper hood, cab, ramp, yellow trailer, 9-5/8" green mixer, gray hopper, 38" long w/ramps; 1951

EX $150   **NM** $225   **MIP** $300

Polysteel Farm, blue milkman truck w/rack and nine milk bottles, red and gray milk tanker, orange farm tractor; 1961

EX $70   **NM** $115   **MIP** $160

Road Builder, green/white cement mixer truck, yellow/black bulldozer, red dump truck, husky dumper; 1963

EX $200   **NM** $300   **MIP** $400

Texaco Highway Truck Stop, 11" tractor-trailer; three-vehicle set with Texaco Tanker, red/white Jeep and red wrecker; also three attendant figures, two gas pumps with flexible hoses, made in Japan; late 1970s.

EX $18   **NM** $36   **MIP** $55

Truck with Concrete Mixer Trailer, 22" truck w/duo-tone slant design, green fenders and lower sides, yellow squarish cab and body, 10" mixer w/yellow frame and red hopper, overall 34-1/2" long, 1937

EX $175   **NM** $265   **MIP** $350

Truck with Concrete Mixer Trailer, 22" truck w/duo-tone slant design, green front and lower hood sides, yellow upper hood, cab and body, 10" mixer w/yellow frame and red hopper, overall 32-1/2" long, 1938

EX $165   **NM** $250   **MIP** $330

Warehouse, Coca-Cola truck, two hand trucks, eight cases Coke bottles, store-door delivery truck, lumber, sign, two barrels, forklift; 1958

EX $175   **NM** $265   **MIP** $350

Warehouse, Coca-Cola truck, two hand trucks, eight cases Coke bottles, store-door delivery truck, sign, two barrels, forklift; 1959

EX $150   **NM** $225   **MIP** $300

Western Roundup, turquoise fenders, hood, cab and frame, white flatbed cargo section, six sections of rail fencing w/swinging gate, rearing and standing horse, cowboys, calf, steer; 1960

EX $175   **NM** $250   **MIP** $400

TRUCKS

Air Force Supply Transport, blue w/blue removable fabric canopy, rubber wheels, decals on cab doors, 14-1/2" long; 1957

EX $125   **NM** $250   **MIP** $355

Air Mail Truck, black front, hood fenders, enclosed cab and opening doors, red enclosed body and chassis, 24" long, 1930

EX $675   **NM** $1000   **MIP** $1400

Allied Moving Van, tractor and semi-trailer van, duo-tone slant design, black front and lower sides, orange hood top, cab and van body, 29-1/2" long; 1941

EX $600   **NM** $900   **MIP** $1200

Army Electric Searchlight Unit, shiny olive drab flatbed truck, battery-operated searchlight, 14-3/4" long; 1957

EX $125   **NM** $230   **MIP** $330

Army Half-Track and Howitzer, olive drab w/olive drab carriage, 12-1/2" truck, 9-3/4" gun, overall 22-1/2" long; 1953

EX $105   **NM** $150   **MIP** $200

Army Half-Track with Howitzer, olive drab steel, red firing knob on gun, 17" truck, 9-3/4" gun, overall 27" long; 1955

EX $100   **NM** $150   **MIP** $200

Army Medical Corps Truck, white, black rubber tires on white steel disc wheels, 29-1/2" long; 1941

EX $125   **NM** $185   **MIP** $250

Army Searchlight Repair-It Truck, shiny olive drab truck and flatbed cargo section, 15" long; 1956

EX $125   **NM** $175   **MIP** $225

Army Spotlight Truck, 8" long; 1969

EX $5   **NM** $9   **MIP** $12

Army Supply Truck, shiny olive drab truck and removable fabric cover, 14-1/2" long; 1956

EX $100   **NM** $150   **MIP** $175

Army Transport, 5" long; bubble-window cabover, "T-415 Transport"; 1970s

EX $3   **NM** $6   **MIP** $9

Army Transport Truck and Trailer, olive drab truck, 20-1/2" long, trailer 34-1/2" long; 1940

EX $250   **NM** $350   **MIP** $450

Army Transport with Howitzer, olive drab, 12" truck, 9-3/4" gun, overall 28" long; 1953

EX $100   **NM** $150   **MIP** $200

Army Transport with Howitzer, olive drab steel, 17" truck, 9-3/4" gun, overall 27" long; 1955

EX $150   **NM** $250   **MIP** $350

Army Transport with Howitzer, olive drab steel, re-firing knob on gun, 17" truck, 9-3/4" gun, overall 27" long; 1954
EX $115   NM $175   MIP $230

Army Transport with Tank, olive drab, 15-1/2" long truck, 11-1/2" long detachable two-wheel trailer, overall 26-1/2" long, 7-1/2" long tank; 1959
EX $100   NM $150   MIP $200

Army Troop Transport with Howitzer, dark forest green truck and gun, canopy mixture of greens, 14" long truck, 12" long, gun, overall 25-3/4" long; 1965
EX $100   NM $150   MIP $200

Army Truck, olive drab, 17" long; 1940
EX $150   NM $200   MIP $250

Army Truck, olive drab, 20-1/2" long, 1939
EX $110   NM $175   MIP $225

Atlas Van Lines, green tractor unit, chrome one-piece toothed grille and headlights, green lower half of semi-trailer van body, cream upper half, silvery roof, 29" long; 1956
EX $200   NM $300   MIP $400

Auto Hauler, yellow cabover-engine tractor unit and double-deck semi-trailer, three 8" long vehicles, 25-1/2" long; 1968
EX $75   NM $115   MIP $150

Auto Hauler, 27-5/8" long; blue turbo cab, double-deck trailer, three plastic coupes, whitewall tires; 1970s
EX $35   NM $70   MIP $105

Baggage Rider, duo-tone horizontal design, green bumper, fenders and lower half of truck, white upper half, 28" long; 1950
EX $250   NM $175   MIP $500

Baggage Truck, green front, hood and fenders, non-open doors, yellow cargo section slat or solid sides, metal grille, 26-1/2" long, 1935
EX $350   NM $550   MIP $650

Baggage Truck, black front, hood, and fenders, doorless cab, yellow four-post stake sides, two chains across back, 26-1/2" long, 1927
EX $1000   NM $1500   MIP $2100

Baggage Truck, duo-tone slant design, yellow fenders, green hood top, cab, and removable rider seat, 26-1/2" long, 1936
EX $350   NM $750   MIP $1000

Baggage Truck, duo-tone slant design, yellow skirted fenders and cargo section, green hood top, enclosed cab, 27-3/4" long, 1938
EX $300   NM $600   MIP $1000

Baggage Truck, green hood, fenders, and cab, yellow cargo section, no bumper, 17-1/2" long; 1945
EX $175   NM $265   MIP $350

Baggage Truck, black front, hood, and fenders, enclosed cab w/opening doors, nickel-rim, red-shell headlights, yellow stake body, 26-1/2" long, 1930-32
EX $3000   NM $5000   MIP $7000

Big Brute Dumper, yellow cabover-engine, frame and tiltback dump section w/cab shield, striped black and yellow bumper, black grille, 8" long; 1971
EX $50   NM $75   MIP $100

Big Brute Mixer Truck, yellow cabover-engine, body and frame, white plastic mixing drum, white plastic seats, 7" long; 1971
EX $35   NM $50   MIP $70

Big Fella Hydraulic Rider Dumper, duo-tone slant design, yellow front and lower hood, red upper cab, dump body and upper hood, rider seat has large yellow sunburst-style decal, 26-1/2" long; 1950
EX $110   NM $175   MIP $225

Big Mack Dumper, yellow front, hood cab, chassis and tiltback dump section, black plastic bumper, single rear wheels, 20-1/2" long; 1968
EX $30   NM $45   MIP $60

Big Mack Dumper, yellow front, hood cab, chassis and tiltback dump section, black plastic bumper, heavy-duty black balloon tires on yellow plastic five-spoke wheels, 20-1/2" long; 1971
EX $26   NM $40   MIP $55

Big Mack Dumper, yellow front, hood cab, chassis and tiltback dump section, black plastic bumper, 20-1/2" long; 1967
EX $30   NM $45   MIP $60

Big Mack Dumper, off-white front, hood cab and chassis, blue-green tiltback dump section, white plastic bumper, 20-1/2" long; 1964
EX $30   NM $45   MIP $60

Big Mack Hydraulic Dumper, red hood, cab and tiltback dump section w/cab shield, white plastic bumper, short step ladder on each side, 20-1/2" long; 1968
EX $15   NM $30   MIP $45

Big Mack Hydraulic Dumper, white hood, cab and tiltback dump section w/cab shield, white plastic bumper, short step ladder on each side, 20-1/2" long; 1969
EX $15   NM $30   MIP $45

Big Mack Hydraulic Dumper, red hood, cab and tiltback dump section w/cab shield, dump body sides have a large circular back, white plastic bumper, short step ladder on each side, 20-1/2" long; 1970
EX $15   NM $30   MIP $45

Boat Transport, blue flatbed truck carrying 8" litho metal boat, boat deck white, hull red, truck 15" long; 1959
EX $200   NM $450   MIP $750

Borden's Milk Delivery Van, 11-1/2" long; white body, sliding side doors, opening rear doors, yellow tray with six white fillable polyethylene milk bottles with yellow caps; 1965-67
EX $90   NM $185   MIP $275

Brute Air Freight Truck, 5" long; blue cabover, "American Airlines Freight System" on doors. "Toys, Handle With

Pride" containers in rear, six wheels; 1960s
EX $5   NM $10   MIP $14

Brute Car Carrier (tractor-trailer), 10" long; blue cabover, double-deck trailer, two plastic cars; 1969
EX $7   NM $15   MIP $22

Brute Cement Mixer Truck, 5-1/4" long; blue cabover, white crank rotates drum; 1969
EX $5   NM $9   MIP $14

Brute Cement Mixer Truck, 5-1/4" long; beige cabover, white plastic mixing drum; 1968
EX $5   NM $9   MIP $14

Brute Coca-Cola Delivery Truck, 5" long; 1985
EX $3   NM $7   MIP $10

Brute Dumper, 5" long; red cabover; 1968-69
EX $3   NM $7   MIP $10

Brute Merry-Go-Round, 5" long; cabover, merry-go-round in rear; 1970s
EX $7   NM $15   MIP $22

Brute Monkey House, yellow cabover-engine body, red and white awning roof, cage on back, two plastic monkeys, 5" long; 1969
EX $6   NM $12   MIP $18

Brute Monkey House, yellow cabover-engine body, striped orange and white awning roof, cage on back, two plastic monkeys, 5" long; 1968
EX $6   NM $12   MIP $18

Brute Pick-Up, 4-3/4" long; 1968-70s
EX $3   NM $6   MIP $10

Brute Sanitation Truck, 5" long; lime-green cabover; 1968-69
EX $6   NM $12   MIP $18

Brute Vault Van, 5" long; bank vault truck; 1970s
EX $3   NM $5   MIP $8

Buddy L Milk Farms Truck, light cream body, red roof, nickel glide headlights, sliding doors, 13" long; 1949
EX $170   NM $300   MIP $500

Buddy L Milk Farms Truck, white body, black roof, short hood w/black wooden headlights, 13-1/2" long; 1945
EX $150   NM $300   MIP $450

Camper, bright medium blue steel truck and camper body, 14-1/2" long; 1964
EX $60   NM $95   MIP $125

Camper, medium blue truck and back door, white camper body, 14-1/2" long; 1965
EX $50   NM $75   MIP $100

Camper, 5" long; bubble-window cabover, green; 1970s
EX $3   NM $5   MIP $8

Camper-N-Cruiser, bright medium blue camper w/matching boat trailer and 8-1/2" long plastic sport cruiser, overall 27" long; 1964
EX $50   NM $75   MIP $100

Camper-N-Cruiser, powder blue pickup truck and trailer, pale blue camper body, 24-1/2" long; 1963
EX $60   **NM** $95   **MIP** $125

Campers Truck, turquoise pickup truck, pale turquoise plastic camper, 14-1/2" long; 1961
EX $55   **NM** $85   **MIP** $110

Campers Truck with Boat, green/turquoise pickup, no side mirror, lime green camper body w/red plastic runabout boat on top, 14-1/2" long; 1963
EX $50   **NM** $100   **MIP** $150

Campers Truck with Boat, green/turquoise pickup truck, lime green camper body, red plastic runabout boat on camper roof, 14-1/2" long; 1962
EX $50   **NM** $100   **MIP** $150

Camping Trailer and Wagon, bright medium blue suburban wagon, matching teepee trailer, overall 24-1/2" long; 1964
EX $60   **NM** $95   **MIP** $125

Canada Dry Delivery Truck, 9-1/2" long; two-tone green, high-window cabover, ten bottle cases, roll-up side doors, hand truck; 1968-69
EX $25   **NM** $35   **MIP** $50

Cattle Transport Truck, green and white w/white stake sides, 15" long; 1957
EX $75   **NM** $115   **MIP** $150

Cattle Transport Truck, red w/yellow stake sides, 15" long; 1956
EX $75   **NM** $115   **MIP** $150

Cement Mixer Truck, red body, tank ends, and chute, white water tank, mixing drum and loading hopper, whitewall tires, 15-1/2" long; 1968
EX $50   **NM** $75   **MIP** $100

Cement Mixer Truck, red body, tank ends, and chute, white water tank, mixing drum and loading hopper, blackwall tires, 15-1/2" long; 1967
EX $38   **NM** $76   **MIP** $115

Cement Mixer Truck, red body, tank ends, and chute, white side ladder, water tank, mixing drum and loading hopper, 15-1/2" long; 1965
EX $60   **NM** $95   **MIP** $125

Cement Mixer Truck, turquoise body, tank ends, and chute, white side ladder, water tank, mixing drum and loading hopper, 16-1/2" long; 1964
EX $60   **NM** $95   **MIP** $125

Cement Mixer Truck, snub-nosed yellow body, cab, frame and chute, white plastic mixing drum, loading hopper and water tank w/yellow ends, 16" long; 1970
EX $35   **NM** $50   **MIP** $70

Charles Chip Delivery Truck Van, beige body, potato-chip decal; 1966
EX $45   **NM** $90   **MIP** $135

City Baggage Dray, duo-tone slant design, green front and fenders, yellow hood top and cargo section, dummy headlights, 19" long, 1937
EX $400   **NM** $800   **MIP** $1200

City Baggage Dray, cream w/aluminum-finish grille, no bumper, black rubber wheels, 20-3/4" long; 1940
EX $100   **NM** $200   **MIP** $300

City Baggage Dray, light green w/aluminum-finish grille, no bumper, black rubber wheels, 20-3/4" long, 1939
EX $95   **NM** $250   **MIP** $300

City Baggage Dray, duo-tone slant design, green front and skirted fenders, yellow hood top, enclosed cab and cargo section, 20-3/4" long, 1938
EX $150   **NM** $200   **MIP** $350

City Baggage Dray, duo-tone slant design, green front and fenders, yellow hood top and cargo section, 19" long, 1936
EX $400   **NM** $800   **MIP** $1200

City Baggage Dray, green front, hood, and fenders, non-open doors, yellow stake-side cargo section, bright metal grille, 19" long, 1935
EX $150   **NM** $300   **MIP** $400

City Baggage Dray, green front, hood, and fenders, non-open doors, yellow stake-side cargo section, No. 839, 19" long, 1934
EX $400   **NM** $800   **MIP** $1200

Coal Truck, black front, hood, fenders, doorless cab, red chassis and disc wheels, No. 202, 25" long, 1926
EX $3700   **NM** $7500   **MIP** $11500

Coal Truck, black hopper body and fully enclosed cab w/opening doors, red wheels, 25" long, 1930
EX $900   **NM** $1500   **MIP** $2000

Coal Truck, black front, hood, fenders, sliding discharge door on each side of hopper body, red chassis and disc wheels, 25" long, 1927
EX $800   **NM** $1000   **MIP** $2000

Coca-Cola Bottling Route Truck, bright yellow, w/small metal hand truck, six or eight yellow cases of miniature green Coke bottles, 14-3/4" long; 1955
EX $125   **NM** $175   **MIP** $250

Coca-Cola Bottling Route Truck, bright yellow, w/two small metal hand trucks and eight yellow cases of miniature green Coke bottles, 14-3/4" long; 1957
EX $110   **NM** $175   **MIP** $225

Coca-Cola Delivery Truck, 9" long; red and white cabover and van body, left side lifts to show bottle cases, hand truck; 1970s
EX $9   **NM** $18   **MIP** $30

(KP Photo)

Coca-Cola Delivery Truck, red lower cabover-engine and van body, white upper cab, left side of van lifts to reveal 10 miniature bottle cases, 9-1/2" long; 1971
EX $30   **NM** $45   **MIP** $60

Coca-Cola Delivery Truck, orange/yellow cab and double-deck, open-side cargo, two small hand trucks, four red and four green cases of bottles, 15" long; 1960
EX $100   **NM** $150   **MIP** $200

Coca-Cola Delivery Truck, orange/yellow cab and double-deck, open-side cargo, two small hand trucks, four red and four green cases of bottles, 15" long; 1963
EX $75   **NM** $100   **MIP** $150

Coca-Cola Delivery Truck, orange/yellow cab and double-deck, open-side cargo, two small hand trucks, four red and four green cases of bottles, 15" long; 1964
EX $62   **NM** $100   **MIP** $130

Coca-Cola Delivery Truck (tractor-trailer), 10" long; five cases of bottles, handcart; 1980
EX $4   **NM** $8   **MIP** $12

Coca-Cola Delivery Truck (tractor-trailer), 14" long; load includes Coke machine and handtruck; 1980s
EX $7   **NM** $13   **MIP** $20

Coke Coffee Co. Delivery Truck Van, black lower half of body, orange upper half, roof and sliding side doors; 1966
EX $85   **NM** $130   **MIP** $175

Colt Vacationer, 22-1/2" long; blue and white Colt Sportsliner with trailer carrying red and white plastic 8-1/2" sport cruiser; 1967
EX $42   **NM** $85   **MIP** $125

Curtiss Candy Trailer Van, blue tractor and bumper, white semi-trailer van, blue roof, chrome one-piece toothed grille and headlights, white drop-down rear door, 32-3/4" long w/tailgate/ramp lowered; 1955
EX $250   **NM** $400   **MIP** $500

Dairy Transport Truck, duo-tone slant design, red front and lower hood sides, white hood top, cab and semi-trailer tank body, tank opens in back, 26" long, 1939
EX $150   **NM** $225   **MIP** $300

Deluxe Auto Carrier, turquoise tractor unit, aluminum loading ramps, three plastic cars, overall 34" long including; 1962
EX $100   **NM** $175   **MIP** $250

Deluxe Camping Outfit, turquoise pickup truck and camper, and 8-1/2" long

plastic boat on pale turquoise boat trailer, overall 24" long; 1961
EX $60   **NM** $95   **MIP** $125

Deluxe Hydraulic Rider Dump Truck, duo-tone slant design, red front and lower hood sides, white upper cab, dump body and chassis, red or black removable rider saddle, 26" long; 1948
EX $175   **NM** $265   **MIP** $350

Deluxe Motor Market, duo-tone slant design, red front, curved bumper, lower hood and cab sides, white hood top, body and cab, 22-1/4" long; 1950
EX $250   **NM** $350   **MIP** $500

(Joe and Sharon Freed Photo)

Deluxe Rider Delivery Truck, duo-tone horizontal design, gray lower half, blue upper half, red rubber disc wheels, black barrel skid, 22-3/4" long; 1945
EX $135   **NM** $200   **MIP** $270

Deluxe Rider Delivery Truck, duo-tone horizontal design, deep blue lower half, gray upper half, red rubber disc wheels, black barrel skid, 22-3/4" long; 1945
EX $135   **NM** $200   **MIP** $270

Deluxe Rider Dump Truck, various colors, dual rear wheels, no bumper, 25-1/2" long; 1945
EX $75   **NM** $115   **MIP** $150

Double Hydraulic Self-Loader-N-Dump, green front loading scoop w/yellow arms attached to cab sides, yellow hood and enclosed cab, orange frame and wide dump body, 29" long w/scoop lowered; 1956
EX $85   **NM** $130   **MIP** $175

Double Tandem Hydraulic Dump and Trailer, truck has red bumper, hood, cab and frame, four-wheel trailer w/red tow and frame, both w/white tiltback dump bodies, 38" long; 1957
EX $85   **NM** $130   **MIP** $175

Double-Deck Boat Transport, light blue steel flatbed truck carrying three 8" white plastic boats w/red decks, truck 15" long; 1960
EX $150   **NM** $250   **MIP** $400

Dr. Pepper Delivery Truck Van, white, red and blue; 1966
EX $45   **NM** $90   **MIP** $135

Dr. Pepper Delivery Truck Van (tractor-trailer), 6" long; bubble-window cabover; 1970s
EX $3   **NM** $7   **MIP** $10

Dump Body Truck, black front, hood, open driver's seat and dump section, red

chassis, crank windlass w/ratchet raises dump bed, 25" long, 1921
EX $800   **NM** $1400   **MIP** $2000

Dump Body Truck, black front, hood, open driver's seat and dump section, red chassis, chain drive dump mechanism, 25" long, 1923
EX $1200   **NM** $1800   **MIP** $2500

Dump Truck, duo-tone slant design, red front, fenders and dump body, yellow hood top, upper sides, upper cab and chassis, no bumper, 22-1/2" long; 1948
EX $125   **NM** $185   **MIP** $250

Dump Truck, red hood top and cab, white or cream dump body and frame, no bumper, 17-1/2" long; 1945
EX $75   **NM** $115   **MIP** $150

Dump Truck, white upper hood, enclosed cab, wide-skirt fenders and open-frame chassis, orange dump body, bright-metal grille, no bumper, 17-3/8" long; 1941
EX $85   **NM** $135   **MIP** $180

Dump Truck, green w/cream hood top and upper enclosed cab, no bumper, bright-metal headlights and grille, 22-1/4" long; 1941
EX $85   **NM** $130   **MIP** $175

Dump Truck, duo-tone slant design, red front, fenders and lower doors, white upper, bright radiator grille and headlights, no bumper, 22-1/4" long, 1939
EX $250   **NM** $375   **MIP** $500

Dump Truck, duo-tone slant design, red lower cab, lower hood, front and dump body, yellow upper hood, upper cab and chassis, no bumper, 22-1/4" long, 1939
EX $250   **NM** $375   **MIP** $500

Dump Truck, duo-tone slant design, yellow enclosed cab and hood, red front and dump body, no bumper, dummy headlights, 20" long, 1937
EX $250   **NM** $375   **MIP** $505

Dump Truck, duo-tone slant design, yellow enclosed cab and hood, red front and dump body, no bumper, bright-metal headlights, 20" long, 1936
EX $250   **NM** $375   **MIP** $500

Dump Truck, yellow enclosed cab, front and hood, red dump section, no bumper, bright-metal radiator, 20" long, 1935
EX $325   **NM** $485   **MIP** $650

Dump Truck, yellow enclosed cab, front and hood, red dump section, no bumper, 20" long, 1934
EX $275   **NM** $415   **MIP** $550

Dump Truck, black enclosed cab and opening doors, front and hood, red dump body and chassis, simple lever arrangement lifts dump bed, 24" long, 1930
EX $650   **NM** $975   **MIP** $1300

Dump Truck, various colors, black rubber wheels, 12" long; 1945
EX $50   **NM** $75   **MIP** $100

Dump Truck, black enclosed cab and opening doors, front and hood, red

dump body and chassis, crank handle lifts dump bed, 24" long, 1931
EX $750   **NM** $1125   **MIP** $1500

Dump Truck, 14-1/4" long; orange, turbine cabover, decal "It Steers" on driver's window; late 1960s
EX $6   **NM** $12   **MIP** $18

Dump Truck, yellow upper hood and enclosed cab, red wide-skirt fenders and open-frame chassis, blue dump body, no bumper, 17-1/4" long; 1940
EX $85   **NM** $130   **MIP** $175

Dump Truck-Economy Line, dark blue dump body, remainder is yellow, bright-metal grille and headlights, no bumper or running boards, 12" long; 1941
EX $75   **NM** $125   **MIP** $150

Dumper with Shovel, medium green body, frame and dump section, white one-piece bumper and grille guard, no side mirror, large white steel scoop shovel, 15" long; 1963
EX $75   **NM** $115   **MIP** $150

Dumper with Shovel, medium green body, frame and dump section, white one-piece bumper and grille guard, no side mirror, large white steel scoop shovel, spring suspension on front axle only, 15" long; 1964
EX $75   **NM** $115   **MIP** $150

Dumper with Shovel, orange body, frame and dump section, chrome one-piece grille, no bumper guard, no side mirror, large white steel scoop shovel, no spring suspension, 15-3/4" long; 1965
EX $75   **NM** $115   **MIP** $150

Dumper with Shovel, turquoise body, frame and dump section, white one-piece bumper and grille guard, large white steel scoop shovel, 15" long; 1962
EX $75   **NM** $115   **MIP** $150

Dump-n-Dozer, orange husky dumper truck and orange flatbed four-wheel trailer carrying orange bulldozer, 23" long including trailer; 1962
EX $75   **NM** $115   **MIP** $150

Express Trailer Truck, red tractor unit, hood, fenders and enclosed cab, green semi-trailer van w/removable roof and drop-down rear door, 23-3/4" long, 1933
EX $350   **NM** $525   **MIP** $700

Express Trailer Truck, red tractor unit, hood, fenders and enclosed cab, green semi-trailer van w/removable roof and drop-down rear door, bright-metal dummy headlights, 23-3/4" long, 1934
EX $350   **NM** $525   **MIP** $700

Express Truck, all black except red frame, enclosed cab w/opening doors, nickel-rim, red-shell headlights, six rubber tires, double bar front bumper, 24-1/2" long, 1930-32
EX $3000   **NM** $4500   **MIP** $6000

Farm Bureau Co-op Gas Tanker, 10" long; red tractor with chrome tanker trailer; 1980s

EX $3   **NM** $6   **MIP** $9

Farm Machinery Hauler Trailer Truck, blue tractor unit, yellow flatbed semi-trailer, 31-1/2" long; 1956

EX $125   **NM** $185   **MIP** $250

Farm Supplies Automatic Dump, duo-tone slant design, blue curved bumper, front, lower hood sides and cab, yellow upper hood, cab and rest of body, 22-1/2" long; 1950

EX $125   **NM** $190   **MIP** $250

Farm Supplies Dump Truck, duo-tone slant design, red front, fenders and lower hood sides, yellow upper hood, cab and body, 22-3/4" long; 1949

EX $125   **NM** $185   **MIP** $250

Farm Supplies Hydraulic Dump Trailer, green tractor unit, long cream body on semi-trailer, fourteen rubber wheels, 26-1/2" long; 1956

EX $100   **NM** $150   **MIP** $200

Fast Delivery Pickup, yellow hood and cab, red open cargo body, removable chain across open back, 13-1/2" long; 1949

EX $105   **NM** $155   **MIP** $200

Finger-Tip Steering Hydraulic Dumper, powder blue bumper, fenders, hood, cab and frame, white tiltback dump body, 22" long; 1959

EX $75   **NM** $115   **MIP** $150

Fisherman, light tan pickup truck w/tan steel trailer carrying plastic 8-1/2" long sport crusier, overall 24-1/4" long; 1962

EX $80   **NM** $120   **MIP** $160

Fisherman, pale blue/green station wagon w/four-wheel boat trailer carrying plastic 8-1/2" long boat, overall 27-1/2" long; 1963

EX $75   **NM** $115   **MIP** $150

Fisherman, metallic sage green pickup truck w/boat trailer carrying plastic 8-1/2" long sport cruiser, overall 25" long; 1964

EX $70   **NM** $100   **MIP** $140

Fisherman, sage gray/green and white pickup truck w/steel trailer carrying plastic 8-1/2" long sport cruiser, overall 25" long; 1965

EX $65   **NM** $100   **MIP** $135

Flat Tire Wrecker, 16" long; blue, battery-operated flasher on roof, spare tire, three polyethylene tools, boom and winch; 1965

EX $45   **NM** $125   **MIP** $200

Flivver Dump Truck, black w/red eight-spoke wheels, black hubs, aluminum tires, flat, open dump section w/squared-off back w/latching, drop-down endgate, 11" long, 1926

EX $700   **NM** $1000   **MIP** $1500

Flivver Scoop Dump Truck, black w/red eight-spoke wheels, 12-1/2" long, 1926-27, 1929-30

EX $1500   **NM** $2500   **MIP** $3500

Flivver Truck, black w/red eight-spoke wheels w/aluminum tires, black hubs, 12" long, 1924

EX $800   **NM** $1000   **MIP** $1500

Ford Flivver Dump Cart, black w/red eight-spoke wheels, black hubs, aluminum tires, flat, short open dump section tapers to point on each side, 12-1/2" long, 1926

EX $1500   **NM** $2500   **MIP** $3500

Frederick & Nelson Delivery Truck Van, medium green body, roof and sliding side doors; 1966

EX $125   **NM** $200   **MIP** $275

Freight Delivery Stake Truck, red hood, bumper, cab and frame, white cargo section, yellow three-post, three-slat removable stake sides, 14-3/4" long; 1955

EX $75   **NM** $125   **MIP** $150

Front Loader Hi-Lift Dump Truck, red scoop and arms attached to white truck at rear fenders, green dump body, 17-3/4" long w/scoop down and dump body raised; 1955

EX $85   **NM** $130   **MIP** $175

Giant Hydraulic Dumper, red bumper, frame, hood and cab, light tan tiltback dump body and cab shield 23-3/4" long; 1960

EX $125   **NM** $185   **MIP** $250

Giant Hydraulic Dumper, overall color turquoise, dump lever has a red plastic tip, 22-3/4" long; 1961

EX $135   **NM** $200   **MIP** $275

Giraffe Truck, 13-1/4" long; blue hood and white cab roof, open cargo section, two plastic giraffes; 1968

EX $35   **NM** $70   **MIP** $105

GMC Air Force Electric Searchlight Unit, all blue flatbed, off white battery-operated searchlight swivel mount, decals on cab doors, 14-3/4" long; 1958

EX $200   **NM** $300   **MIP** $410

GMC Airway Express Van, green hood, cab and van body, latching double rear doors, shiny metal drum coin bank and metal hand truck, 17-1/2" long w/rear doors open; 1957

EX $250   **NM** $350   **MIP** $450

GMC Anti-Aircraft Unit with Searchlight, 15" truck w/four-wheel trailer, battery-operated, over 25-1/4" long; 1957

EX $240   **NM** $345   **MIP** $460

GMC Army Hauler with Jeep, shiny olive drab tractor unit and flatbed trailer, 10" long jeep, overall 31-1/2" long; 1958

EX $200   **NM** $300   **MIP** $400

GMC Army Transport with Howitzer, shiny olive drab, 14-1/2" long, truck, overall w/gun 22-1/2" long; 1957

EX $200   **NM** $300   **MIP** $400

GMC Brinks Armored Truck Van, silver gray, barred windows on sides and in double doors, coin slot and hole in roof, brass padlock w/two keys, pouch, play money, three gray plastic guard figures, 16" long; 1958

EX $300   **NM** $350   **MIP** $450

GMC Coca-Cola Route Truck, orange/yellow, w/two small metal hand trucks and eight cases of miniature green Coke bottles, 14-1/8" long; 1958

EX $200   **NM** $300   **MIP** $400

GMC Coca-Cola Route Truck, lime/yellow, w/small metal hand truck and eight cases of miniature green Coke bottles, 14-1/8" long; 1957

EX $200   **NM** $305   **MIP** $410

GMC Construction Company Dumper, pastel blue including control lever on left and dump section w/cab shield, hinged tailgate, chrome GMC bar grille, six wheels, 16" long; 1958

EX $200   **NM** $305   **MIP** $410

GMC Construction Company Dumper, pastel blue including control lever on left and dump section w/cab shield, hinged tailgate, chrome GMC bar grille, four wheels, 16" long; 1959

EX $150   **NM** $250   **MIP** $350

GMC Highway Giant Trailer, blue tractor, blue and white van, chrome GMC bar grille and headlights, blue roof on semi-trailer, white tailgate doubles as loading ramp, eighteen-wheeler, 31-1/4" long; 1957

EX $250   **NM** $350   **MIP** $450

GMC Highway Giant Trailer Truck, blue tractor, blue and white van, chrome GMC bar grille and headlights, blue roof on semi-trailer, white tailgate doubles as loading ramp, fourteen-wheeler, 30-3/4" long; 1958

EX $200   **NM** $300   **MIP** $400

GMC Husky Dumper, red hood, bumper, cab and chassis, chrome GMC bar grille and nose emblem, white oversize dump body, red control lever on right side, 17-1/2" long; 1957

EX $150   **NM** $250   **MIP** $350

GMC Self-Loading Auto Carrier, yellow tractor and double-deck semi trailer, three plastic cars, overall 33-1/4" long; 1959

EX $200   **NM** $300   **MIP** $410

GMC Signal Corps Unit, both olive drab, 14-1/4" long truck w/removable fabric canopy, 8" long four-wheel trailer; 1957

EX $150   **NM** $200   **MIP** $255

Grocery Motor Market Truck, duo-tone slant design, yellow front, lower hood sides, fenders and lower doors, white hood top, enclosed cab and body, no bumper, 20-1/2" long, 1937

EX $275   **NM** $415   **MIP** $550

Grocery Motor Market Truck, duo-tone slant design, yellow front, lower hood sides, skirted fenders and lower doors,

white hood top, cab and body, no bumper, 21-1/2" long, 1938
EX $275   **NM** $420   **MIP** $560

Harley-Davidson Semi, 21" long; battery-operated sounds and lights, "Ten-four, good buddy" voice, pressed steel and plastic; 1992
EX $7   **NM** $13   **MIP** $20

Heavy Hauling Dumper, red hood, bumper, cab and frame, cream oversize dump body, hinged tailgate, 21-1/2" long; 1956
EX $75   **NM** $125   **MIP** $140

Heavy Hauling Dumper, red hood, bumper, cab and frame, cream tiltback dump body, 20-1/2" long; 1955
EX $75   **NM** $125   **MIP** $150

Heavy Hauling Hydraulic Dumper, green hood, cab and frame, cream tiltback dump body, and cab shield, raising dump body almost to vertical, 23" long; 1956
EX $70   **NM** $105   **MIP** $140

Hershey's Kiss Truck, 4-3/4" long; made in Japan; 1982
EX $3   **NM** $6   **MIP** $9

Hertz Auto Hauler, bright yellow tractor and double-deck semi-trailer, three plastic vehicles, 27" long; 1965
EX $100   **NM** $150   **MIP** $200

Hertz Auto Hauler (tractor-trailer), 27" long; yellow, double-deck trailer, three plastic vehicles; 1965
EX $67   **NM** $130   **MIP** $200

Highway Hawk Trailer Van, bronze cab tractor, chrome metallized plastic bumper, grille, air cleaner and exhaust, 19-3/4" long, 1985
EX $50   **NM** $80   **MIP** $100

Highway Maintenance Truck with Trailer, orange w/black rack of four simulated floodlights behind cab, 19-1/2" long including small two-wheel trailer; 1957
EX $100   **NM** $150   **MIP** $200

Hi-Lift Farm Supplies Dump, red plastic front end including hood and enclosed cab, yellow dump body, cab shield and hinged tailgate, 21-1/2" long; 1953
EX $100   **NM** $175   **MIP** $225

Hi-Lift Farm Supplies Dump, all steel, red front end including hood and enclosed cab, yellow dump body, cab shield and hinged tailgate, 23-1/2" long; 1954
EX $100   **NM** $175   **MIP** $225

Hi-Lift Scoop-n-Dump Truck, orange truck w/deeply fluted sides, dark green scoop on front rises to empty load into hi-lift light cream dump body, 16" long; 1953
EX $80   **NM** $125   **MIP** $175

Hi-Lift Scoop-n-Dump Truck, orange truck w/deeply fluted sides, dark green scoop on front rises to empty load into hi-lift cream/yellow dump body, 16" long; 1952
EX $85   **NM** $130   **MIP** $175

Hi-Lift Scoop-n-Dump Truck, orange hood, fenders and cab, yellow front loading scoop and arms attached to

fenders, white frame, dump body and cab shield, 17-3/4" long; 1956
EX $70   **NM** $135   **MIP** $145

Hi-Lift Scoop-n-Dump Truck, orange truck w/deeply fluted sides, dark green scoop on front rises to empty load into deep hi-lift slightly orange dump body, 16" long; 1955
EX $75   **NM** $115   **MIP** $155

Hi-Lift Scoop-n-Dump Truck, blue hood, fenders and cab, yellow front loading scoop and arms attached to fenders, white frame, dump body, cab shield, and running boards, 17-3/4" long; 1957
EX $65   **NM** $100   **MIP** $135

Hi-Tip Hydraulic Dumper, orange hood, cab and frame, cream tiltback dump body, and cab shield, raising dump body almost to vertical, 23" long; 1957
EX $70   **NM** $115   **MIP** $150

Horse Van, 17-1/2" long; maroon pickup cab with plastic horse van body, with side and rear ramps, two horses and one colt; 1965-66. See also Deluxe Riding Academy Set.
EX $23   **NM** $45   **MIP** $70

Horse Van (tractor-trailer), 14-1/2" long; high-window cabover tractor, brown with white roof, hauls white trailer, side and rear loading ramps, three horses; 1968-69
EX $12   **NM** $23   **MIP** $35

Horse Van (tractor-trailer), 10" long; red, paired circular windows on trailer; 1980
EX $3   **NM** $7   **MIP** $10

Horserack 400, 5" long; bubble-window cabover, red, stake truck back with two plastic horses; 1970s
EX $4   **NM** $8   **MIP** $12

Husky Dumper, red hood, cab, chassis and dump section, chrome one-piece bumper and slotted grille w/double headlights, 14-1/2" long; 1968
EX $20   **NM** $40   **MIP** $60

Husky Dumper, snub-nose red body, tiltback dump section and cab shield, full-width chrome bumperless grille, white-tipped dump-control lever on left, deep-tread whitewall tires, 14-1/2" long; 1971
EX $15   **NM** $30   **MIP** $45

Husky Dumper, orange wraparound bumper, body, frame and dump section, hinged tailgate, plated dump lever on left side, 15-1/4" long; 1960
EX $75   **NM** $115   **MIP** $150

Husky Dumper, yellow hood, cab, fram and tiltback dump section w/cab shield, crome one-piece wraparound bumper, 14-1/2" long; 1969
EX $17   **NM** $33   **MIP** $50

Husky Dumper, bright yellow, chrome one-piece bumper, slotted rectangular grille and double headlights, 14-1/2" long; 1966,
EX $25   **NM** $50   **MIP** $75

Husky Dumper, white plastic wraparound bumper, tan body, frame and dump section, hinged tailgate, plated dump lever on left side, 15-1/4" long; 1961
EX $75   **NM** $125   **MIP** $140

Husky Dumper, snub-nose red body, tiltback dump section, cab shield, full-width chrome bumperless grille, deep-tread whitewall tires, 14-1/2" long; 1970
EX $15   **NM** $30   **MIP** $45

Hydraulic Auto Hauler with Four GMC Cars, powder blue GMC tractor, 7" long plastic cars, overall 33-1/2" long including loading ramp; 1958
EX $250   **NM** $350   **MIP** $450

Hydraulic Construction Dumper, red front, cab and chassis, large green dump section w/cab shield, 15-1/4" long; 1962
EX $28   **NM** $56   **MIP** $85

Hydraulic Construction Dumper, tan/beige front, cab and chassis, large green dump section w/cab shield, 15-1/4" long; 1963
EX $28   **NM** $56   **MIP** $85

Hydraulic Construction Dumper, bright blue front, cab and chassis, large green dump section w/cab shield, 15-1/2" long; 1964
EX $23   **NM** $46   **MIP** $70

Hydraulic Construction Dumper, bright green front, cab and chassis, large green dump section w/cab shield, 14" long; 1965
EX $23   **NM** $46   **MIP** $70

Hydraulic Construction Dumper, medium blue front, cab and chassis, large green dump section w/cab shield, 15-1/4" long; 1967
EX $20   **NM** $40   **MIP** $60

Hydraulic Dump Truck, duo-tone slant design, red hood sides, dump body and chassis, white upper hood, cab and removable rider seat, electric headlights, 24-3/4" long, 1936
EX $300   **NM** $500   **MIP** $700

Hydraulic Dump Truck, black front, hood, fenders, dark reddish maroon dump body, red chassis and disc wheels w/seven embossed spokes, black hubs, 25" long, 1931
EX $665   **NM** $885   **MIP** $1300

Hydraulic Dump Truck, black front, hood, fenders and enclosed cab, red dump body, chassis and wheels w/six embossed spokes, bright hubs, 24-3/4" long, 1933
EX $325   **NM** $485   **MIP** $650

Hydraulic Dump Truck, black front, hood, fenders, open seat, and dump body, red chassis and disc wheels w/aluminum tires, 25" long, 1926
EX $700   **NM** $1400   **MIP** $2100

Hydraulic Dumper, green, plated dump lever on left side, large hooks on left side hold yellow or off-white steel scoop

shovel, white plastic side mirro and grille guard, 17" long; 1961
EX $125   **NM** $180   **MIP** $245

Hydraulic Dumper with Shovel, green, plated dump lever on left side, large hooks on left side hold yellow or off-white steel scoop shovel, 17" long; 1960
EX $120   **NM** $185   **MIP** $250

Hydraulic Highway Dumper, orange w/row of black square across scraper edges, one-piece chrome eight-hole grille and double headlights, no scraper blade, 17-3/4" long over blade and raised dump body; 1959
EX $55   **NM** $80   **MIP** $105

(Toy Shop File Photo)

Hydraulic Highway Dumper with Scraper Blade, orange w/row of black square across scraper edges, one-piece chrome eight-hole grille and double headlights, 17-3/4" long over blade and raised dump body; 1958
EX $75   **NM** $105   **MIP** $155

Hydraulic Hi-Lift Dumper, blue hood, fenders, cab, and dump-body supports, white dump body w/cab shield, 22-1/2" long; 1955
EX $75   **NM** $115   **MIP** $150

Hydraulic Hi-Lift Dumper, duo-tone slant design, green hood nose and lower cab sides, remainder white w/chrome grille, enclosed cab, 24" long; 1953
EX $75   **NM** $115   **MIP** $150

Hydraulic Hi-Lift Dumper, green hood, fenders, cab, and dump-body supports, white dump body w/cab shield, 22-1/2" long; 1954
EX $85   **NM** $130   **MIP** $175

Hydraulic Husky Dumper, red body, frame, dump section and cab shield, 15-1/4" long; 1962
EX $65   **NM** $100   **MIP** $135

Hydraulic Husky Dumper, red body, white one-piece bumper and grille guard, heavy side braces on dump section, 14" long; 1963
EX $50   **NM** $75   **MIP** $100

Hydraulic Rider Dumper, duo-tone slant design, yellow front and lower hood, red upper cab, dump body and upper hood, 26-1/2" long; 1949
EX $175   **NM** $265   **MIP** $360

Hydraulic Sturdy Dumper, 14-1/2" long; lime-green cab, green lever; 1969
EX $20   **NM** $40   **MIP** $60

Hydraulic Sturdy Dumper, 14-1/2" long; yellow cab; 1969
EX $20   **NM** $40   **MIP** $60

Hydraulic Sturdy Dumper, 14-1/2" long; snub-nose green-yellow body and cab; 1970
EX $7   **NM** $15   **MIP** $22

(Tim Oei Photo)

Hy-Way Maintenance Mechanical Truck and Concrete Mixer, Yellow and dark blue cab, silver wheels, yellow flatbed with dark blue and yellow mixer, 36" long; 1949
EX $345   **NM** $530   **MIP** $690

Ice Truck, black front, hood, fenders and enclosed cab, yellow open cargo section, canvas, ice cakes, miniature tongs, 26-1/2" long, 1930
EX $700   **NM** $900   **MIP** $1500

(Tim Oei Photo)

Ice Truck, black front, hood, fenders and doorless cab, yellow open cargo section, canvas sliding cover, 26-1/2" long, 1926
EX $600   **NM** $1200   **MIP** $1900

Ice Truck, black front, hood, fenders and enclosed cab, yellow ice compartment, canvas, ice cakes, tongs, 26-1/2" long, 1933-34
EX $700   **NM** $900   **MIP** $1300

Ice Truck, black front, hood, fenders and enclosed cab, yellow ice compartment, 26-1/2" long, 1933
EX $700   **NM** $900   **MIP** $1500

IHC "Red Baby" Express Truck, red w/black hubs and aluminum tires, 24-1/4" long, 1929
EX $800   **NM** $1300   **MIP** $1900

IHC "Red Baby" Express Truck, red doorless roofed cab, open pickup body, chassis and fenders, 24-1/4" long, 1928
EX $750   **NM** $1000   **MIP** $2000

Insurance Patrol, red w/open driver's seat and body, brass bell on cowl and full-length handrails, no CFD decal, 27" long, 1928
EX $625   **NM** $950   **MIP** $1250

Insurance Patrol, red w/open driver's seat and body, brass bell on cowl and full-length handrails, 27" long, 1925
EX $650   **NM** $1000   **MIP** $1300

International Delivery Truck, duo-tone slant design, red front, bumper and lower hood sides, yellow hood top, upper sides, cab and open cargo body, 24-1/2" long, 1936
EX $205   **NM** $320   **MIP** $410

International Delivery Truck, duo-tone slant design, red front, bumper and lower hood sides, yellow hood top, upper sides, cab and open cargo body, bright metal dummy headlights, 24-1/2" long, 1938
EX $150   **NM** $225   **MIP** $300

International Delivery Truck, red w/removable black rider saddle, black-edged yellow horizontal strip on cargo body, 24-1/2" long, 1935
EX $225   **NM** $350   **MIP** $450

International Dump Truck, red, w/red headlights on radiator, black removable rider saddle, 25-3/4" long, 1938
EX $125   **NM** $185   **MIP** $250

International Dump Truck, duo-tone slant design, yellow radiator, fenders, lower hood and detachable rider seat, rest of truck is red, 25-3/4" long, 1936
EX $315   **NM** $475   **MIP** $630

International Dump Truck, red w/bright-metal radiator grille, and black removable rider saddle, 25-3/4" long, 1935
EX $325   **NM** $485   **MIP** $650

International Railway Express Truck, duo-tone slant design, yellow front, lower hood sides and removable top, green hood top, enclosed cab and van body, dummy headlights, 25" long, 1938
EX $345   **NM** $525   **MIP** $690

International Railway Express Truck, duo-tone slant design, yellow front, lower hood sides and removable top, green hood top, enclosed cab and van body, electric headlights, 25" long, 1937
EX $350   **NM** $525   **MIP** $700

International Wrecker Truck, duo-tone slant design, yellow upper cab, hood, and boom, red lower cab, fenders, grille and body, rubber tires, removable rider seat, 32" long, 1938
EX $600   **NM** $900   **MIP** $1800

Jewel Home Service Truck Van, dark brown body, sliding side doors; 1967
EX $42   **NM** $83   **MIP** $125

Jewel Home Shopping Truck Van, pale mint green upper body, darker lower half, no sliding doors; 1968
EX $38   **NM** $76   **MIP** $115

Jolly Joe Ice Cream Truck, white w/black roof, black tires and wooden wheels, 17-1/2" long; 1947
EX $225   **NM** $350   **MIP** $455

Jolly Joe Popsicle Truck, white w/black roof, black tires and wooden wheels, 17-1/2" long; 1948
EX $275   **NM** $430   **MIP** $555

Jr. Animal Ark, fuschia lapstrake hull, four black tires, 10 pairs of plastic animals, 5" long; 1970
EX $40   **NM** $60   **MIP** $80

Jr. Auto Carrier, 15-1/2" long; yellow cabover, double-deck trailer, two red plastic cars; 1967
EX $17   **NM** $33   **MIP** $50

Jr. Auto Carrier, 17-1/2" long; blue cabover, double-deck trailer, two plastic cars; 1969
EX $17   **NM** $33   **MIP** $50

Jr. Beach Buggy, 6" long; yellow Jeep body, rollbar, white plastic surfboard; 1969
EX $5   **NM** $9   **MIP** $14

Jr. Beach Buggy, 6" long; lime-green Jeep body and surfboard; 1971
EX $5   **NM** $9   **MIP** $14

Jr. Buggy Hauler, 12" long; fuschia Jeep body, orange two-wheel trailer with Sandpiper beach buggy; 1970
EX $12   **NM** $23   **MIP** $35

Jr. Camper, 7" long; red pickup, yellow camper; 1971
EX $5   **NM** $9   **MIP** $14

Jr. Canada Dry Delivery Truck, 9-1/2" long; green and lime green cabover, hand truck, ten cases of green bottles; 1968-69
EX $27   **NM** $53   **MIP** $80

Jr. Cement Mixer Truck, 7-1/2" long; blue cabover, white mixing drum; 1968-69
EX $6   **NM** $12   **MIP** $18

Jr. Dump Truck, 7-1/2" long; red cabover, plastic vertical headlights, 1967
EX $4   **NM** $8   **MIP** $12

Jr. Dumper, 7-1/2" long; avocado cabover, four-slot grille; 1969
EX $4   **NM** $8   **MIP** $12

Jr. Giraffe Truck, 6-1/2" long; turquoise cabover, plastic giraffe; 1968-69
EX $7   **NM** $13   **MIP** $20

Jr. Kitty Kennel, 6-1/4" long; pink cabover, four white plastic cats; 1968-69
EX $7   **NM** $13   **MIP** $20

Jr. Sanitation Truck, 10" long ;yellow; 1969
EX $6   **NM** $12   **MIP** $18

Jr. Sanitation Truck, 10" long; blue cabover, white body; 1968
EX $6   **NM** $12   **MIP** $18

Jr. Tow Truck, No. 5107; red body, white winch; late 1960s or 1970s
EX $6   **NM** $12   **MIP** $18

Jr. Turbine Racer Transport, red truck, "Turbine Transport" on racer lift, with red racer; 1970s
EX $35   **NM** $65   **MIP** $100

Junior Line Air Mail Truck, black enclosed cab, red chassis and body, headlights and double bar bumper, six rubber tires, 24" long, 1930-32
EX $400   **NM** $650   **MIP** $1200

Kennel Truck, 13-1/4" long; bright blue, clear plastic 12-section kennel with 12 plastic dogs; 1966-67
EX $32   **NM** $63   **MIP** $95

Kennel Truck, 13-1/4" long; cream yellow; 1968
EX $27   **NM** $53   **MIP** $80

Kennel Truck, 13-1/4" long; red-orange, six-section kennel with six dogs; 1969
EX $22   **NM** $43   **MIP** $65

Kennel Truck, 13-1/4" long; snub-nosed red-orange cab, six-section kennel with six dogs; 1970
EX $20   **NM** $40   **MIP** $60

Kennel Truck, turquoise pickup body and cab, clear plastic twelve-section kennel w/twelve plastic dogs fits in cargo box, 13-1/2" long; 1965
EX $60   **NM** $95   **MIP** $125

Kennel Truck, medium blue pickup body and cab, clear plastic twelve-section kennel w/twelve plastic dogs fits in cargo box, 13-1/2" long; 1964
EX $60   **NM** $90   **MIP** $120

Lumber Truck, black front, hood, fenders, cabless open seat and low-sides cargo bed, red bumper, chassis and a pair of removable solid stake sides, load of lumber pieces, 24" long, 1924
EX $750   **NM** $1000   **MIP** $1500

Lumber Truck, black front, hood, fenders, doorless cab and low-sides cargo bed, red bumper, chassis and a pair of removable solid stake sides, load of lumber, 25-1/2" long, 1926
EX $650   **NM** $1300   **MIP** $2700

Mack Hydraulic Dumper, 20-1/2" long; red cab; 1965
EX $33   **NM** $65   **MIP** $100

Mack Hydraulic Dumper, 20-1/2" long; red cab, short step ladder on each side; 1967
EX $33   **NM** $65   **MIP** $100

Mack Quarry Dumper, 20-1/2" long, orange cab, blue-green tiltback dujmp; 1965
EX $50   **NM** $100   **MIP** $150

Mammoth Hydraulic Quarry Dumper, 23" long; green cab, red dump section, black bumper; 1962-63
EX $45   **NM** $89   **MIP** $135

Marshall Field's Delivery Truck Van, hunter green body, sliding doors; 1966
EX $42   **NM** $83   **MIP** $125

Merry-Go-Round, 1967, red truck w/ merry-go-round on flatbed, blackwall tires; 1967, Model No. 5429
EX $65   **NM** $140   **MIP** $230

Milkman Truck, light blue hood, cab and flatbed body, white side rails, 143"white plastic milk bottles, 14-1/4" long; 1963
EX $85   **NM** $130   **MIP** $175

Milkman Truck, light yellow hood, cab and flatbed body, white side rails, 143"white plastic milk bottles, 14-1/4" long; 1964
EX $75   **NM** $125   **MIP** $155

Milkman Truck, deep cream hood, cab and flatbed body, white side rails, fourteen 3" white plastic milk bottles w/red caps, 14-1/4" long; 1962
EX $50   **NM** $105   **MIP** $200

Milkman Truck, medium blue hood, cab and flatbed body, white side rails, eight 3" white plastic milk bottles, 14-1/4" long; 1961
EX $50   **NM** $100   **MIP** $200

Mister Buddy Ice Cream Truck, 11-1/2" long; red plastic underbody; 1966-67
EX $45   **NM** $89   **MIP** $135

Mister Buddy Ice Cream Truck, No. 5353, 11-1/2" long; white van, "Mister Buddy Ice Cream" and ice cream cone decoration, pale blue or off-white plastic underbody, spring suspension, window sides, whitewall tires; 1964-65
EX $45   **NM** $130   **MIP** $175

Model T Flivver Truck, black w/red eight-spoke wheels w/aluminum tires, black hubs, 12" long, 1924
EX $1000   **NM** $1500   **MIP** $2000

Motor Market Truck, duo-tone horizontal design, white hood top, upper cab and high partition in cargo section, yellow-orange grille, fenders, lower hood and cab sides, 21-1/2" long; 1941
EX $200   **NM** $350   **MIP** $800

Moving Van, black front, hood and seat, red chassis and disc wheels w/black hubs, green van body, roof extends forward above open driver's seat, 25" long, 1924
EX $1200   **NM** $2000   **MIP** $3000

NASA Lowboy and Shuttle, 10-1/2" long; tractor-trailer hauler with Shuttle Discovery, steel and plastic, made in Japan; 1979-80
EX $7   **NM** $13   **MIP** $20

Ole Buddy's Pie Wagon, old-fashioned delivery van; 1970
EX $12   **NM** $23   **MIP** $35

Overland Trailer Truck, duo-tone horizontal design, red and white tractor has red front, lower half chassis, chassis, enclosed cab, 40", 1939
EX $350   **NM** $560   **MIP** $710

Overland Trailer Truck, duo-tone slant design, green and yellow tractor unit w/yellow cab, red semi-trailer and four-wheel full trailer w/yellow removable roofs, 39-3/4" long, 1936
EX $325   **NM** $485   **MIP** $650

Overland Trailer Truck, yellow tractor, enclosed cab, red semi-trailer and four-

wheel full trailer w/removable roofs, 39-3/4" long, 1935
EX $350   **NM** $525   **MIP** $700

Overland Trailer Truck, duo-tone slant design, green and yellow semi-streamlined tractor and green hood sides, yellow hood, chassis, enclosed cab, 40", 1939
EX $350   **NM** $550   **MIP** $700

Pan-Am Clipper Cargo, tractor-trailer van truck, luggage truck, lift truck and cargo boxes; 1970s
EX $12   **NM** $23   **MIP** $35

Pepsi Delivery Truck, 15" long; blue hood and lower cab, white upper cab, double-deck cargo, two hand trucks, four blue cases of red bottles, four red cases of blue bottles; 1970
EX $42   **NM** $83   **MIP** $125

Pick-Up, 13" long; stepside, red body, white roof, whitewall tires; mid-1960s
EX $22   **NM** $43   **MIP** $65

Polysteel Boat Transport, medium blue soft plastic body, steel flatbed carrying 8" white plastic runabout boat w/red deck, truck 12-1/2" long; 1960
EX $75   **NM** $115   **MIP** $150

Polysteel Coca-Cola Delivery Truck, yellow plastic truck, slanted bottle racks, eight green Coke cases w/red bottles, small metal hand truck, 12-1/4" long; 1962
EX $60   **NM** $90   **MIP** $120

Polysteel Coca-Cola Delivery Truck, yellow plastic truck, slanted bottle racks, eight red Coke cases w/green bottles, small metal hand truck, 12-1/2" long; 1961
EX $50   **NM** $75   **MIP** $100

Polysteel Dumper, orange plastic body and tiltback dump section w/cab shield, no "Come-Back Motor," no door decals, 13-1/2" long; 1962
EX $60   **NM** $95   **MIP** $125

Polysteel Dumper, orange plastic body and tiltback dump section w/cab shield, "Come-Back Motor," 13" long; 1961
EX $75   **NM** $115   **MIP** $150

Polysteel Dumper, green soft molded plastic front, cab and frame, yellow steel dump body w/sides rounded at back, hinged tailgate, 13" long; 1959
EX $100   **NM** $150   **MIP** $200

Polysteel Dumper, medium blue soft molded plastic front, cab and frame, off-white steel dump body w/sides rounded at back, hinged tailgate, 13" long; 1960
EX $87   **NM** $130   **MIP** $175

Polysteel Highway Transport, red soft plastic tractor, cab roof lights, double horn, radio antenna and side fuel tanks, white steel semi-trailer van, 20-1/2" long; 1960
EX $100   **NM** $150   **MIP** $200

Polysteel Hydraulic Dumper, yellow soft plastic body, frame and tiltback ribbed dump section w/cab shield, 13" long; 1961
EX $75   **NM** $125   **MIP** $150

Polysteel Hydraulic Dumper, red soft plastic body, frame and tiltback ribbed dump section w/cab shield, 13" long; 1962
EX $65   **NM** $100   **MIP** $130

Polysteel Hydraulic Dumper, red soft molded-plastic front, cab and frame, light green steel dump section w/sides rounded at rear, 13" long; 1960
EX $80   **NM** $120   **MIP** $160

Polysteel Hydraulic Dumper, beige soft molded-plastic front, cab and frame, off-white steel dump section w/sides rounded at rear, 13" long; 1959
EX $60   **NM** $95   **MIP** $125

Polysteel Milk Tanker, turquoise soft plastic tractor unit, light blue/gray semi-trailer tank w/red ladders and five dooms, 22" long; 1961
EX $60   **NM** $95   **MIP** $125

Polysteel Milk Tanker, red soft plastic tractor unit, light blue/gray semi-trailer tank w/red ladders and five dooms, 22" long; 1961
EX $60   **NM** $95   **MIP** $125

Polysteel Milkman Truck, turquoise soft plastic front, cab and frame, light blue steel open cargo section w/nine oversized white plastic milk bottles w/red caps, 11-3/4" long; 1962
EX $35   **NM** $50   **MIP** $70

Polysteel Milkman Truck, light blue soft plastic front, cab and frame, light blue steel open cargo section w/nine oversized white plastic milk bottles, 11-3/4" long; 1961
EX $60   **NM** $95   **MIP** $125

Polysteel Milkman Truck, light blue soft plastic front, cab and frame, light yellow steel open cargo section w/nine oversized white plastic milk bottles, 11-3/4" long; 1960
EX $65   **NM** $100   **MIP** $130

Polysteel Supermarket Delivery, medium blue soft molded-plastic front, hood, cab and frame, steel off-white open cargo section, 13" long; 1959
EX $75   **NM** $115   **MIP** $150

Pull-N-Ride Baggage Truck, duo-tone horizontal design, light cream upper half, off-white lower half and bumper, 24-1/4" long; 1953
EX $150   **NM** $225   **MIP** $300

Racing Team, No. 5464; crossed-flag emblem on cab doors, double-deck racer carrier in rear, three racers; 1964-65
EX $30   **NM** $55   **MIP** $85

Raggedy Ann and Andy Camper, 11-1/2" long; van truck, blue with "Raggedy Ann and Andy Camper" panel decoration, pink interior, whitewall tires; with

Raggedy Ann and Andy figures, dog and boat; 1970s or 1980s
EX $30   **NM** $100   **MIP** $135

Railroad Transfer Rider Delivery Truck, duo-tone horizontal design, yellow upper half, hood top, cab and slatted caro sides, green lower half, small hand truck, two milk cans w/removable lids, 23-1/4" long; 1949
EX $70   **NM** $100   **MIP** $140

Railroad Transfer Store Door Delivery, duo-tone horizontal design, yellow hood top, cab and upper body, red lower half of hood and body, small hand truck, two metal drums w/coin slots, 23-1/4" long; 1950
EX $90   **NM** $135   **MIP** $180

Railway Express Truck, red tractor unit, enclosed square cab, green 12-1/4" long two-wheel semi-trailer van w/removable roof, "Wrigley's Spearmint Gum" poster on trailer sides, 23" long, 1935
EX $375   **NM** $565   **MIP** $750

Railway Express Truck, duo-tone horizontal design, tractor unit has yellow front, lower door and chassis, green hood top and enclosed upper cab, semi-trailer has yellow lower sides, 25" long; 1941
EX $325   **NM** $485   **MIP** $650

Railway Express Truck, duo-tone slant design, tractor unit has white skirted fenders and hood sides, green hood top, enclosed cab and chassis, green semi-trailer w/white removable roof, 25" long, 1939
EX $350   **NM** $475   **MIP** $700

Railway Express Truck, black front hood, fenders, seat and low body sides, dark green van body, red chassis, 25" long, 1926
EX $400   **NM** $800   **MIP** $1600

(Toy Shop File Photo)

Railway Express Truck, duo-tone slant design, tractor has silvery and hood sides, green hood top, enclosed cab, green semi-trailer, "Wrigley's Spearmint Gum" poster on trailer sides, 23" long, 1935
EX $400   **NM** $600   **MIP** $800

Railway Express Truck, yellow and green tractor unit has white skirted fenders and hood sides, green hood top, enclosed cab and chassis, green semi-trailer w/yellow removable roof, 25" long; 1940
EX $330   **NM** $495   **MIP** $660

Railway Express Truck, deep green plastic "Diamond T" hood and cab, deep green steel frame and van body w/removable silvery roof, small two-wheel hand truck, steel four-rung barrel skid, 21" long; 1952

EX $200   **NM** $300   **MIP** $400

Railway Express Truck, green plastic hood and cab, green steel high-sides open body, frame and bumper, small two-wheel hand truck, steel four-rung barrel skid, 20-3/4" long; 1953

EX $125   **NM** $185   **MIP** $250

Railway Express Truck, green all-steel hood, cab, frame and high-sides open bady, sides have three horizontal slots in upper back corners, 22" long; 1954

EX $75   **NM** $115   **MIP** $150

Railway Express Truck, dark green or light green screen body, double-bar nickel front bumper, brass radiator knob, red wheels, 25" long, 1930

EX $500   **NM** $1000   **MIP** $2000

Ranchero Stake Truck, medium green, white plastic one-piece bumper and grille guard, four-post, four-slat fixed stake sides and cargo section, 14" long; 1963

EX $50   **NM** $75   **MIP** $100

REA Express Van, 11-1/2" long; dark green, "REA Express" and pigeon decoration, sliding side doors, double rear doors, spring suspension; 1964-65

EX $45   **NM** $125   **MIP** $250

REA Express Van, 11-1/2" long; same as 1965 but with side doors embossed "Buddy L" and no suspension; 1966

EX $45   **NM** $90   **MIP** $200

Rider Dump Truck, duo-tone horizontal design, yellow hood top, upper cab and upper dump body, red front, hood sides, lower doors and lower dump body, no bumper, 21-1/2" long; 1945

EX $160   **NM** $245   **MIP** $325

Rider Dump Truck, duo-tone horizontal design, yellow hood top, upper cab and upper dump body, red front, hood sides, lower doors and lower dump body, no bumper, 23" long; 1947

EX $75   **NM** $115   **MIP** $150

(Thomas G. Nefos Photo)

Riding Acedemy Truck, Blue body, white roof over bed, side and rear opening ramps, three plastic horses, "Riding Acedemy" in white type along sides

EX $55   **NM** $78   **MIP** $125

Rival Dog Food Delivery Van, cream front, cab and boxy van body, metal drum coin bank w/"RIVAL DOG FOOD" label in blue, red, white and yellow, 16-1/2" long; 1956

EX $160   **NM** $245   **MIP** $325

Robotoy, black fenders and chassis, red hood and enclosed cab w/small visor,

green dump body's front and back are higher than sides, 21-5/8" long, 1932

EX $575   **NM** $900   **MIP** $1200

Rockin' Giraffe Truck, 13-1/4" long; blue cab, open cargo, two plastic giraffes; 1967

EX $30   **NM** $65   **MIP** $95

Ruff-n-Tuff Cement Mixer Truck, 16" long; yellow cabover, white plastic water tank; 1971

EX $22   **NM** $43   **MIP** $65

Ruff-n-Tuff Log Truck, 16" long; yellow cabover; 1971

EX $23   **NM** $46   **MIP** $70

Ryder City Special Delivery Truck Van, duo-tone horizontal design, yellow upper half including hood top and cab, brown removable van roof, warm brown front and lower half of van body, 24-1/2" long; 1949

EX $150   **NM** $225   **MIP** $300

Ryder Van Lines Trailer, duo-tone slant design, black front and lower hood sides and doors, deep red hood top, enclosed cab and chassis, 35-1/2" long; 1949

EX $350   **NM** $525   **MIP** $700

Saddle Dump Truck, duo-tone slant design, yellow front, fenders and removable rider seat, red enclosed square cab and dump body, no bumper, 19-1/2" long, 1937

EX $200   **NM** $300   **MIP** $400

Saddle Dump Truck, duo-tone horizontal design, deep blue hood top, upper cab and upper dump body, orange fenders radiator front lower two-thirds of cab and lower half of dump body, 21-1/2" long; 1941

EX $85   **NM** $130   **MIP** $175

Saddle Dump Truck, duo-tone slant design, yellow front, fenders, lower hood and cab, and removable rider seat, rest of body red, no bumper, 21-1/2" long, 1939

EX $125   **NM** $185   **MIP** $250

Sand and Gravel Rider Dump Truck, duo-tone horizontal design, blue lower half, yellow upper half including hoop top and enclosed cab, 24" long; 1950

EX $350   **NM** $525   **MIP** $700

Sand and Gravel Truck, black body, doorless roofed cab and steering wheel, red chassis and disc wheels w/black hubs, 25-1/2" long, 1926

EX $600   **NM** $1000   **MIP** $1200

Sand and Gravel Truck, dark or medium green hood, cab, roof lights and skirted body, white or cream dump section, 13-1/2" long; 1949

EX $100   **NM** $150   **MIP** $200

Sand and Gravel Truck, duo-tone horizontal design, red front, bumper, lower hood, cab sides, chassis and lower dump body sides, white hood top, enclosed cab and upper dump body, 23-3/4" long; 1949

EX $350   **NM** $525   **MIP** $700

Sand and Gravel Truck, black w/red chassis and wheels, nickel-rim, red-shell headlights, enclosed cab w/opening doors, 25-1/2" long, 1930-32

EX $2000   **NM** $3000   **MIP** $5000

Sand Loader and Dump Truck, duo-tone horizontal design, yellow hood top and upper dump blue cab sides, frame and lower dump body, red loader on dump w/black rubber conveyor belt, 24-1/2" long; 1950

EX $175   **NM** $265   **MIP** $350

Sand Loader and Dump Truck, duo-tone horizontal design, yellow hood top and upper dump blue cab sides, frame and lower dump body, red loader on dump w/black rubber conveyor belt, 24-1/2" long; 1952

EX $60   **NM** $95   **MIP** $125

Sanitation Service Truck, 17" long; blue cab, white body, two round plastic headlights; 1972

EX $17   **NM** $33   **MIP** $50

Sanitation Service Truck, 16-1/2" long; blue cab, white enclosed dump section, plastic windows in garbage section; 1967

EX $32   **NM** $63   **MIP** $95

Sanitation Service Truck, 16-1/2" long; blue cab, white enclosed dump section, no plastic windows in garbage section; 1968

EX $32   **NM** $63   **MIP** $95

Sanitation Truck, 6" long; white and blue; 1970s

EX $3   **NM** $5   **MIP** $8

Sears Roebuck Delivery Truck Van, gray/green and off-white, no side doors; 1967, Model No. *

EX $125   **NM** $200   **MIP** $280

Sears Service Van Truck, 11-1/2" long; gray/green, open side doors, swing-open rear doors; 1967-68

EX $42   **NM** $83   **MIP** $125

Self-Loading Auto Carrier, medium tan tractor unit, three plastic cars, overall 34" long including loading ramp; 1960

EX $85   **NM** $130   **MIP** $175

Self-Loading Boat Hauler, pastel blue tractor and semi-trailer w/three 8-1/2" long boats, no side mirror on truck, overall 26-1/2" long; 1963

EX $150   **NM** $225   **MIP** $350

Self-Loading Boat Hauler, pastel blue tractor and semi-trailer w/three 8-1/2" long boats, overall 26-1/2" long; 1962

EX $150   **NM** $225   **MIP** $350

Self-Loading Car Carrier, lime green tractor unit, three plastic cars, overall 33-1/2" long including; 1963

EX $75   **NM** $115   **MIP** $150

Self-Loading Car Carrier, beige/yellow tractor unit, three plastic cars, overall 33-1/2" long including; 1964

EX $60   **NM** $95   **MIP** $125

Service Wrecker, 14" long; red, black boom; mid-1960s
EX $50   **NM** $100   **MIP** $150

Shell Pickup and Delivery, reddish orange hood and body, open cargo section w/solid sides, chain across back, red coin-slot oil drum w/Shell emblem and lettering, 13-1/4" long; 1950
EX $135   **NM** $200   **MIP** $275

Shell Pickup and Delivery, yellow/orange hood and body, open cargo section w/three curved slots toward rear in sides, red coin-slot oil drum w/Shell emblem and lettering, 13-1/4" long; 1953
EX $110   **NM** $175   **MIP** $225

Shell Pickup and Delivery, yellow/orange hood and body, open cargo section, three curved slots toward rear in sides, chains across back, red coin-slot oil drum w/Shell emblem and lettering, 13-1/4" long; 1952
EX $125   **NM** $185   **MIP** $250

Sit-N-Ride Truck, 25" long; removable steel seat in dump bed, lever-action dump body; 1965
EX $38   **NM** $76   **MIP** $115

Smoke Patrol, 13-1/4" long; lemon-yellow body, six wheels, garden-hose attachment for water cannon; 1970
EX $22   **NM** $43   **MIP** $65

Sprinkler Truck, black front, hood, fenders and cabless open driver's seat, red bumper and chassis, bluish/gray/green water tank, 25" long, 1929
EX $800   **NM** $1500   **MIP** $2000

Stake Body Truck, black cabless open driver's seat, hood, front fenders and flatbed body, red chassis and five removable stake sections, cargo bed w/low sidesboards, drop-down tailgate, 25" long, 1924
EX $850   **NM** $1650   **MIP** $2500

Stake Body Truck, black cabless open driver's seat, hood, front fenders and flatbed body, red chassis and five removable stake sections, 25" long, 1921
EX $850   **NM** $1650   **MIP** $2500

Standard Coffee Co. Delivery Truck Van, 1966
EX $40   **NM** $79   **MIP** $120

Standard Oil Tank Truck, duo-tone slant design, white upper cab and hood, red lower cab, grille, fenders and tank, rubber wheels, electric headlights, 26" long, 1936-37
EX $350   **NM** $500   **MIP** $1000

Stor-Dor Delivery, red hood and body, open cargo body w/four horizontal slots in sides, plated chains across open back, 14-1/2" long; 1955
EX $65   **NM** $100   **MIP** $175

Street Sprinkler Truck, black front, hood, front fenders and cabless open driver's seat, red bumper and chassis, bluish/gray/green water tank, 25" long, 1929
EX $700   **NM** $900   **MIP** $1800

Street Sprinkler Truck, black front, hood, and fenders, open cab, nickel-rim, red-shell headlights, double bar front bumper, bluish/gray/green water tank, six rubber tires, 25" long, 1930-32
EX $800   **NM** $1000   **MIP** $1900

(Joe and Sharon Freed Photo)

Sunshine Biscuits Van, Dark yellow body, light gray chassis, whitewall tires, Sunshine chef decals along sides, with Sunshine Biscuits photo decal showing Krispy, Cheez-It crackers and Hydrox and HiHo cookies
EX $145   **NM** $260   **MIP** $330

Sunshine Biscuits Van Truck, 11-1/2" long; yellow cabover, sliding side doors, opening rear doors, "Sunshine Biscuits" on panels; 1967-68
EX $30   **NM** $59   **MIP** $90

Super Dog Truck, 6-1/2" long; high-windshield cabover, doghouse with Snoopy-like dog's head as load; 1970s
EX $6   **NM** $12   **MIP** $18

Super Motor Market, duo-tone horizontal design, white hood top, upper cab and high partition in cargo section, yellow/orange lower hood and cab sides, semi-trailer carrying supplies, 21-1/2" long, 1942
EX $300   **NM** $500   **MIP** $700

Supermarket Delivery, blue bumper, front, hood, cab and frame, one-piece chrome four-hole grille and headlights, 14-1/2" long; 1956
EX $75   **NM** $115   **MIP** $150

Supermarket Delivery, all white w/rubber wheels, enclosed cab, pointed nose, bright metal one-piece grille, 13-3/4" long; 1950
EX $125   **NM** $185   **MIP** $250

Tank and Sprinkler Truck, black front, hood, fenders, doorless cab and seat, dark green tank and side racks, black or dark green sprinkler attachment, 26-1/4" long w/sprinkler attachment, 1924
EX $700   **NM** $900   **MIP** $1700

Teepee Camping Trailer and Wagon, maroon suburban wagon, two-wheel teepee trailer and its beige plastic folding tent, overall 24-1/2" long; 1963
EX $75   **NM** $180   **MIP** $260

(Calvin L. Chaussee Photo)

Texaco Tank Truck, red steel GMC 550-series blunt-nose tractor and semi-trailer tank, 25" long; 1959
EX $175   **NM** $250   **MIP** $400

(Toy Shop File Photo)

Texaco Tanker, Promotional Piece, White rounded cabover with red tanker section, black plastic hose. "Texaco" logo stickers on cab, "Texaco" on tanker sides, 25" long
EX $78   **NM** $130   **MIP** $205

Tom's Toasted Peanuts Delivery Truck Van, 11-1/2" long; tan body , no sliding doors, blue underbody; 1973
EX $27   **NM** $53   **MIP** $80

Trail Boss, 7" long; red, white plastic seat; 1970
EX $4   **NM** $9   **MIP** $12

Trail Boss, 7" long; lime green, yellow seat; 1971
EX $4   **NM** $9   **MIP** $12

Trailer Dump Truck, cream tractor unit w/enclosed cab, dark blue semi-trailer dump body w/high sides and top-hinged opening endgate, no bumper, 20-3/4" long; 1941
EX $75   **NM** $115   **MIP** $155

Trailer Van Truck, red tractor and van roof, blue bumper, white semi-trailer van, chrome one-piece toothed grille and headlights, white drop-down rear door, 29" long w/tailgate/ramp lowered; 1956
EX $145   **NM** $225   **MIP** $300

Trailer Van with Tailgate Loader, green steel tractor, bumper, chrome one-piece toothed grille and headlights, cream van w/green roof and tailgate loader, 31-3/4" long, w/tailgate down; 1954
EX $125   **NM** $185   **MIP** $250

Trailer Van with Tailgate Loader, green high-impacted styrene plastic tractor on steel frame, cream steel detachable semi-trailer van w/green roof and crank operated tailgate, 33" long w/tailgate lowered; 1953
EX $125   **NM** $185   **MIP** $250

Traveling Zoo Truck, 14" long; red pickup, yellow six-copartment cage with six plastic jungle animals; 1965-67
EX $28   **NM** $56   **MIP** $85

Traveling Zoo Truck, 14" long; snub-nosed yellow cab, six red cages with six animals; 1970
EX $17   NM $33   MIP $50

Traveling Zoo Truck, 14" long; yellow pickup, six compartments with animals; 1969
EX $25   NM $50   MIP $75

U.S. Army Half-Track and Howitzer, olive drab, 12-1/2" truck, 9-3/4" gun, overall 22-1/2" long; 1952
EX $125   NM $200   MIP $275

U.S. Mail Delivery Truck, blue cab, hood, bumper, frame and removable roof on white van body, 23-1/4" long; 1956
EX $150   NM $300   MIP $510

U.S. Mail Delivery Van Truck, 11-1/2" long; sliding side doors, ear opening doors, whitewall tires, "U.S. Mail" and red, white and blue paint scheme; 1964-67
EX $32   NM $63   MIP $125

(Calvin L. Chaussee Photo)

U.S. Mail Truck, shiny olive green body and bumper, yellow-cream removable van roof, enclosed cab, 22-1/2" long; 1953
EX $215   NM $410   MIP $580

United Parcel Delivery Van, duo-tone horizontal design, deep cream upper half w/brown removable roof, chocolate brown front and lower half, 25" long; 1941
EX $250   NM $450   MIP $650

Utility Delivery Truck, duo-tone horizontal design, green upper half including hood top, dark cream lower half, green wheels, red and yellow horizontal stripe, 22-3/4" long; 1941
EX $125   NM $185   MIP $250

Utility Delivery Truck, duo-tone slant design, blue front and lower hood sides, gray hood top, cab and open body w/red and yellow horizontal stripe, 22-3/4" long; 1940
EX $250   NM $450   MIP $650

Utility Dump Truck, duo-tone slant design, red front, lower doord and fenders, gray chassis and enclosed upper cab, royal blue dump body, yellow removable rider seat, 25-1/2" long; 1940
EX $125   NM $185   MIP $250

Utility Dump Truck, duo-tone slant design, red front, lower door and fenders, gray chassis, red upper hood, upper enclosed cab and removable rider seat, yellow body, 25-1/2" long; 1941
EX $85   NM $130   MIP $175

Van Freight Carriers Trailer, bright blue streamlined tractor and enclosed cab, cream/yellow semi-trailer van, removable silvery roof, 22" long; 1949
EX $65   NM $100   MIP $135

Van Freight Carriers Trailer, red streamlined tractor, bright blue enclosed cab, light cream/white semi-trailer van w/removable white roof, 22" long; 1953
EX $125   NM $185   MIP $250

Van Freight Carriers Trailer, red streamlined tractor, bright blue enclosed cab, cream/yellow semi-trailer van, white removable van roof, 22" long; 1952
EX $55   NM $85   MIP $115

Wal-Mart Semi, 11" long; battery-operated voice, "Ten-four, good buddy"; 1990s
EX $7   NM $15   MIP $22

Wild Animal Circus (tractor-trailer), 26" long; red, with light-red cage doors; 1970
EX $50   NM $75   MIP $150

Wild Animal Circus (tractor-trailer), 26" long; red, three cages with plastic elephant, lion and tiger; 1966
EX $200   NM $300   MIP $400

Wild Animal Circus (tractor-trailer), 26" long; red, three cages with six plastic adult and baby animals; 1967
EX $75   NM $150   MIP $225

Wrecker, 5" long; made in Japan; 1980
EX $3   NM $6   MIP $9

Wrecker, 7-1/2" long; "AAA, 24 Hr. Service"; 1983
EX $2   NM $4   MIP $7

Wrecker Truck, black front, hood, and fenders, open cab, four rubber tires, red wrecker body, 26-1/2" long, 1930
EX $800   NM $1000   MIP $2500

Wrecker Truck, duo-tone slant design, red upper cab, hood, and boom, white lower cab, grille, fenders, body, rubber wheels, electric headlights, removable rider seat, 31" long, 1936
EX $250   NM $450   MIP $700

Wrecker Truck, black open cab, red chassis and bed, disc wheels, 26-1/2" long, 1928-29
EX $700   NM $1000   MIP $2000

Wrigley Express Truck, forest green w/chrome one-piece, three-bar grille and headlights, "Wrigley's Spearmint Gum" poster on sides, 16-1/2" long; 1955
EX $135   NM $215   MIP $295

Zoo-A-Rama, 20-3/4" long; lime green Colt Sportsliner with four-wheel trailer cage, with plastic tree, monkeys and bears; 1967
EX $50   NM $75   MIP $150

Zoo-A-Rama, 20-3/4" long; yellow; 1968
EX $50   NM $100   MIP $150

Zoo-A-Rama, 20-3/4" long; green-yellow; 1969
EX $50   NM $100   MIP $150

Zookeepr's Truck, 6-1/4" long; turbo cab, plastic giraffe; 1970
EX $7   NM $13   MIP $20

CORGI

AGRICULTURAL

Agricultural Set, 1962-66, Fordson, 1962-64 issue: No. 55 Fordson Tractor, No. 51 Tipping Trailer, No. 438 Land Rover, No. 101 Flat Trailer w/No. 1487 Milk Churns; 1965-66 issue: No. 60 Fordson Tractor, No. 62 Tipping Trailer, No. 438 Land Rover, red No. 100 Dropside Trailer w/No. 1487 Milk Churns, a difficult set to find, Model No. 22-A
EX $380   **NM** $900   **MIP** $1800

Agricultural Set, 1967-72, Massey-Ferguson, No. 69 Massey-Ferguson tractor, No. 62 trailer, No. 438 Land Rover, No. 484 Livestock Truck w/pigs, No. 71 harrow, No. 1490 skip and churns; w/accessories: four calves, farmhand, dog and six sacks, Model No. 5-B
EX $120   **NM** $180   **MIP** $400

Agricultural Set, 1978-80, No. 55 Tractor, No. 56 Tipping Trailer, Silo and mustard yellow conveyor, Model No. 42-A
EX $60   **NM** $90   **MIP** $130

Beast Carrier Trailer, 1965-71, red chassis, yellow body and tailgate, four plastic calves, red plastic wheels, black rubber tires, Model No. 58-A
EX $24   **NM** $36   **MIP** $60

Bedford Articulated Horse Box, 1973-76, Bedford, cast cab, lower body and three working ramps, yellow interior, plastic upper body, w/horse and Newmarket Racing Stables labels, dark metallic green or light green body w/orange or yellow upper, four horses, Model No. 1104-B
EX $32   **NM** $48   **MIP** $90

Berliet Articulated Horse Box, 1976-80, Berliet, bronze cab and lower semi body, cream chassis, white upper body, black interior, three working ramps, National Racing Stables decals, horse figures, chrome wheels, Model No. 1105-B
EX $30   **NM** $45   **MIP** $75

Combine, Tractor and Trailer, 1959-62, Massey-Ferguson, set of three: No. 1111 combine, No. 50 Massey-Ferguson tractor, and No. 51 trailer, Model No. 8-A
EX $110   **NM** $185   **MIP** $350

Country Farm Set, 1974-75, Massey-Ferguson, No. 50 Massey Ferguson tractor, red No. 62 hay trailer w/load, fences, figures, Model No. 4-B
EX $30   **NM** $45   **MIP** $75

Country Farm Set, 1976, Massey-Ferguson, same as 4-B but without hay load on trailer, Model No. 5-C
EX $30   **NM** $45   **MIP** $75

David Brown Combine, 1978-79, David Brown, No. 55 Tractor, red and yellow combines, white JF labels, Model No. 1112-B
EX $30   **NM** $45   **MIP** $75

David Brown Tractor, 1977-82, David Brown, white body w/black/white David Brown No. 1412 labels, red chassis and plastic engine, Model No. 55-B
EX $15   **NM** $25   **MIP** $45

David Brown Tractor & Trailer, 1976-79, David Brown, two-piece set; No. 55 tractor and No. 56 trailer, Model No. 34-A
EX $30   **NM** $45   **MIP** $75

Dodge Livestock Truck, 1967-72, Dodge, tan cab and hood, green body, working tailgate and ramp, five pigs, Model No. 484-A
EX $34   **NM** $51   **MIP** $85

Ford 5000 Super Major Tractor, 1967-73, Ford, blue body/chassis w/Ford Super Major 5000 decals, gray cast fenders and rear wheels, gray plastic front wheels, black plastic tires, driver, Model No. 67-A
EX $30   **NM** $45   **MIP** $75

Ford 5000 Tractor with Scoop, 1969-72, Ford, blue body/chassis, gray fenders, yellow scoop arm and controls, chrome scoop, black control lines, Model No. 74-A
EX $55   **NM** $80   **MIP** $130

(KP Photo by Dr. Douglas Sadecky)

Ford Tractor and Beast Carrier, 1966-72, Ford, Gift Set included No. 67 Ford 5000 tractor and No. 58 Beast Carrier, Model No. 1-B
EX $60   **NM** $90   **MIP** $150

Ford Tractor and Conveyor, 1966-69, Ford, No. 67 tractor, conveyor w/trailer, figures and accessories, Model No. 47-A
EX $60   **NM** $90   **MIP** $175

Ford Tractor with Trencher, 1970-74, Ford, blue body/chassis, gray fenders, cast yellow trencher arm and controls, chrome trencher, black control lines, Model No. 72-A
EX $50   **NM** $75   **MIP** $125

(KP Photo by Dr. Douglas Sadecky)

Fordson Power Major Halftrack Tractor, 1962-64, Fordson, blue body/chassis, silver steering wheel, seat and grille, three versions: orange cast wheels, gray treads, lights in radiator or on sides of

radiator. This bizarre little model can be quite difficult to find--especially with original tracks, Model No. 54-A
EX $90   **NM** $135   **MIP** $225

(KP Photo by Dr. Douglas Sadecky)

Fordson Power Major Tractor, 1961-63, Fordson, blue body/chassis w/Fordson Power Major decals, silver steering wheel, seat, exhaust, grille and lights. The 61-A Four Furrow Plough makes a nice companion piece to the model, Model No. 55-A
EX $45   **NM** $65   **MIP** $110

Fordson Power Major Tractor, 1964-66, Fordson, blue body w/Fordson Power Major decals, driver, blue chassis and steering wheel, silver seat, hitch, exhaust, Model No. 60-A
EX $50   **NM** $75   **MIP** $125

Fordson Tractor and Plow, 1961-64, Fordson, No. 55 Fordson Tractor and No. 56 Four Furrow plow, Model No. 18-A
EX $55   **NM** $85   **MIP** $140

Fordson Tractor and Plow, 1964-66, Fordson, No. 60 tractor and No. 61 four-furrow plow, Model No. 13-A
EX $55   **NM** $85   **MIP** $140

Four Furrow Plow, 1961-63, red frame, yellow plastic parts, Model No. 56-A
EX $15   **NM** $20   **MIP** $35

Four Furrow Plow, 1964-70, blue frame w/chrome plastic parts, Model No. 61-A
EX $15   **NM** $20   **MIP** $35

Jeep FC-150 Pickup with Conveyor Belt, 1965-69, Jeep, red body, yellow interior, orange grille, two black rubber belts, shaped wheels, black rubber tires; accessories include farmland figure and sacks, Model No. 64-A
EX $45   **NM** $65   **MIP** $130

Land Rover & Horse Box, 1968-77, Land Rover, blue/white Land Rover w/horse trailer in two versions: cast wheels (1968-74) and Whizz Wheels (1975-77); accessories include a mare and a foal; value is for each individual complete set, Model No. 15-B
EX $50   **NM** $75   **MIP** $125

Land Rover and Pony Trailer, 1958-62, Land Rover, two versions: green No. 438 Land Rover and a red and black No. 102 Pony trailer (1958-62); tan/cream No. 438 Land Rover and a pony trailer (1963-68); value given is for each individual complete set, Model No. 2-A
EX $50   **NM** $90   **MIP** $175

Massey-Ferguson 165 Tractor, 1966-72, Massey-Ferguson, gray engine and chassis, red hood and fenders w/black/white Massey Ferguson 165 decals, white grille, red cast wheels; makes engine sound, Model No. 66-A
EX $35   **NM** $55   **MIP** $90

(KP Photo by Dr. Douglas Sadecky)

Massey-Ferguson 165 Tractor with Saw, 1969-73, Massey-Ferguson, red hood and fenders, gray engine and seat, cast yellow arm and control, chrome circular saw, Model No. 73-A
EX $55   **NM** $85   **MIP** $140

(KP Photo by Dr. Douglas Sadecky)

Massey-Ferguson 165 Tractor with Shovel, 1967-73, Massey-Ferguson, gray chassis, red hood, fenders and shovel arms, unpainted shovel and cylinder, red cast wheels, black plastic tires, w/figure. This tractor even featured engine noises!, Model No. 69-A
EX $45   **NM** $65   **MIP** $120

Massey-Ferguson 50B Tractor, 1973-77, Massey-Ferguson, yellow body, black interior and roof, red plastic wheels w/black plastic tires, windows, Model No. 50-B
EX $15   **NM** $18   **MIP** $75

Massey-Ferguson 65 Tractor, 1959-66, Massey-Ferguson, silver metal or plastic steering wheel, seat and grille, red engine hood, red metal or plastic wheels w/black rubber tires, Model No. 50-A
EX $40   **NM** $60   **MIP** $100

Massey-Ferguson 65 Tractor And Shovel, 1960-66, Massey-Ferguson, two versions: red bonnet w/either cream or gray chassis, red metal or orange plastic wheels; value is for each, Model No. 53-A
EX $55   **NM** $85   **MIP** $140

Massey-Ferguson Combine, 1959-63, Massey-Ferguson, red body w/yellow metal blades, metal tines, black/white decals, yellow metal wheels, Model No. 1111-A
EX $70   **NM** $105   **MIP** $175

Massey-Ferguson Combine, 1968-73, Massey-Ferguson, red body, plastic yellow blades, red wheels, Model No. 1111-B
EX $60   **NM** $100   **MIP** $160

Massey-Ferguson Tipping Trailer, 1959-65, Massey-Ferguson, two versions: red chassis w/either yellow or gray tipper and tailgate, red metal or plastic wheels, value is for each, Model No. 51-A
EX $10   **NM** $18   **MIP** $35

Massey-Ferguson Tractor and Tipping Trailer, 1959-63, Massey-Ferguson, No. 50 tractor and No. 51 trailer, no driver, Model No. 7-A
EX $50   **NM** $75   **MIP** $125

Massey-Ferguson Tractor and Tipping Trailer, 1965, Massey-Ferguson, No. 50 Massey-Ferguson tractor w/driver, No. 51 trailer, Model No. 29-A
EX $50   **NM** $75   **MIP** $125

(KP Photo by Dr. Douglas Sadecky)

Massey-Ferguson Tractor with Fork, 1963-67, Massey-Ferguson, red cast body and shovel, arms, cream chassis, red plastic wheels, black rubber tires, Massey-Ferguson 65 decals, w/driver, Model No. 57-A
EX $60   **NM** $90   **MIP** $150

Massey-Ferguson Tractor with Shovel, 1974-81, Massey-Ferguson, two versions: either yellow and red or red and white body colors; value is for each, Model No. 54-A
EX $20   **NM** $30   **MIP** $50

Massey-Ferguson Tractor with Shovel & Trailer, 1965-66, Massey-Ferguson, No. 54 MF tractor w/driver and shovel, No. 62 trailer, Model No. 32-A
EX $30   **NM** $75   **MIP** $150

Pony Club Set, 1978-80, Land Rover, brown/white No. 421 Land Rover w/Corgi Pony Club labels, horse box, horse and rider, Model No. 47-B
EX $30   **NM** $45   **MIP** $75

Rice Beaufort Double Horse Box, 1969-72, long, blue body and working gates, white roof, brown plastic interior, two horses, cast wheels, plastic tires, Model No. 112-A
EX $15   **NM** $30   **MIP** $50

(KP Photo by Dr. Douglas Sadecky)

Rice Pony Trailer, 1958-65, cast body and chassis w/working tailgate, horse, in six variations, smooth or shaped hubs, cast or wire drawbar. Shown here is the harder-to-find two-tone cream/red variation, Model No. 102-A
EX $20   **NM** $30   **MIP** $50

Silo & Conveyor Belt, 1978-80, w/yellow conveyor and Corgi Harvesting Co. label on silo, Model No. 43-A
EX $35   **NM** $50   **MIP** $85

Tandem Disc Harrow, 1967-72, yellow main frame, red upper frame, working wheels linkage, unpainted linkage and cast discs, black plastic tires, Model No. 71-A
EX $15   **NM** $20   **MIP** $45

Tipping Farm Trailer, 1965-72, red working tipper and tailgates, yellow chassis, red plastic wheels, black tires, w/detachable raves, Model No. 62-A
EX $10   **NM** $15   **MIP** $30

Tipping Farm Trailer, 1977-80, cast chassis and tailgate, red plastic tipper and wheels, black tires, in two versions, Model No. 56-B
EX $10   **NM** $15   **MIP** $25

Tractor and Beast Carrier, 1965-66, Fordson, No. 55 Fordson tractor, figures and No. 58 beast carrier, Model No. 33-A
EX $65   **NM** $100   **MIP** $165

Tractor with Shovel and Trailer, 1968-73, Massey-Ferguson, standard colors, No. 69 Massey-Ferguson Tractor and No. 62 Tipping Trailer, Model No. 9-B
EX $65   **NM** $100   **MIP** $165

AIRCRAFT

(KP Photo by Dr. Douglas Sadecky)

Concorde-First Issues, 1969-72, Concorde, Japan Airlines decals. This rare model was probably an import issue. Ironically, the real Concorde was never part of the Japan Air Lines, Model No. 653-A
EX $280   **NM** $420   **MIP** $700

Concorde-First Issues, 1969-72, Concorde, Air Canada decals, Model No. 652-A
EX $80   **NM** $120   **MIP** $200

Concorde-First Issues, 1969-72, Concorde, Air France decals, Model No. 651-A
EX $20   **NM** $45   **MIP** $85

Concorde-First Issues, 1969-72, Concorde, BOAC decals, Model No. 650-A
EX $20   **NM** $40   **MIP** $70

Concorde-Second Issue, 1976-82, Concorde, Air France model on display stand, Model No. 651-B
EX $15   **NM** $20   **MIP** $35

Concorde-Second Issues, 1976-82, Concorde, BOAC model on display stand, Model No. 650-B
EX $15   **NM** $20   **MIP** $35

Corgi Flying Club Set, 1972-77, blue/orange No. 438 Land Rover w/red dome light, blue trailer w/either orange/yellow or orange/white plastic airplane, Model No. 19-B
EX $24   **NM** $50   **MIP** $100

Flying Club Set, 1978-80, Jeep, green and white No. 419 Jeep w/Corgi Flying Club labels, green trailer, blue/white airplane, Model No. 49-A
EX $36   **NM** $55   **MIP** $90

Glider Set, 1981-83, Honda, two versions: white No. 345 Honda, 1981-82; yellow Honda, 1983, value is for individual complete sets, Model No. 12-C
EX $30   **NM** $45   **MIP** $75

Lunar Bug, 1970-72, white body w/red roof, blue interior and wings, clear and amber windows, red working ramp, Lunar Bug labels, Model No. 806-A
EX $25   **NM** $40   **MIP** $95

NASA Space Shuttle, 1980, white body, two opening hatches, black plastic interior, jets and base, unpainted retracting gear castings, black plastic wheels, w/satalite, Model No. 648-A
EX $30   **NM** $45   **MIP** $75

Stromberg Jet Ranger Helicopter, 1978-79, black body w/yellow trim and interior, clear windows, black plastic rotors, white/blue labels, Model No. 926-A
EX $45   **NM** $65   **MIP** $125

AUTOMOBILE

AMC Pacer, 1977-78, AMC, metallic red body, white Pacer X decals, working hatch, clear windows, light yellow interior, chrome bumpers and wheels, Model No. 291-A
EX $15   **NM** $20   **MIP** $50

Aston Martin DB4, 1960-65, Aston Martin, red or yellow body w/working hood, detailed engine, clear windows, plastic interior, silver lights, grille, license plate and bumpers, red taillights, rubber tires, smooth or cast spoked wheels; working scoop on early models, Model No. 218-A
EX $45   **NM** $65   **MIP** $110

(KP Photo by Dr. Douglas Sadecky)

Austin A40, 1959-62, Austin, one-piece light blue body with dark blue roof or red body w/black roof and clear windows, smooth wheels, rubber tires, Model No. 216-A
EX $35   **NM** $50   **MIP** $100

Austin A40-Mechanical, 1959-60, Austin, friction motor, red body w/black roof, Model No. 216-M
EX $55   **NM** $75   **MIP** $170

(KP Photo by Dr. Douglas Sadecky)

Austin A60 Driving School, 1964-68, Austin, medium blue body w/silver trim, left-hand drive steering wheel, steering control on roof; came w/five language leaflet (US version of No. 236), Model No. 255-A
EX $45   **NM** $65   **MIP** $160

(KP Photo by Dr. Douglas Sadecky)

Austin A60 Motor School, 1964-69, Austin, light blue body w/silver trim, red interior, single body casting, right-hand drive steering wheel, two figures, steering control on roof; came w/Highway Patrol leaflet, Model No. 236-A
EX $45   **NM** $65   **MIP** $120

(KP Photo by Dr. Douglas Sadecky)

Austin Cambridge, 1956-61, Austin, available in gray, green/gray, silver/green, aqua, green/cream, two-tone green, smooth wheels, shown here with Austin Cambridge-Mechanical, Model No. 201-A
EX $40   **NM** $60   **MIP** $120

Austin Cambridge-Mechanical, 1956-59, Austin, fly-wheel motor, available in orange, cream, light or dark gray, or silver over metallic blue, smooth wheels, Model No. 201M
EX $50   **NM** $75   **MIP** $150

Austin Mini Countryman, 1965-69, Austin, turquoise body, jeweled headlights, opening rear doors, chrome roofrack w/two surfboards, shaped or cast wheels, w/surfer figure, Model No. 485-A
EX $55   **NM** $80   **MIP** $150

Austin Mini-Metro, 1981, Austin, blue or red body w/plastic interior, working rear hatch and doors, clear windows, folding seats, chrome headlights, orange taillights, black plastic base, grille, bumpers, Whizz Wheels, Model No. 275-B
EX $18   **NM** $27   **MIP** $45

Austin Seven Mini, 1961-67, Austin, primrose yellow, red interior, rare, Model No. 225-A2, second issue
EX $100   **NM** $200   **MIP** $325

Austin Seven Mini, 1961-67, Austin, red or yellow body, yellow interior, silver bumpers, grille and headlights, orange taillights, Model No. 225-A1
EX $50   **NM** $75   **MIP** $125

Bentley Continental, 1961-66, Bentley, two-tone green or black and silver bodies, w/red interior, clear windows, chrome grille and bumpers, jewel headlights, red jeweled taillights, suspension, shaped wheels, gray rubber tires, Model No. 224-A
EX $45   **NM** $65   **MIP** $110

Bentley T Series, 1970-72, Bentley, red body, cream interior, working hood, trunk and doors, clear windows, folding seats, chrome bumper/grille, jewel headlights, Whizz Wheels, Model No. 274-A
EX $36   **NM** $55   **MIP** $90

Buick and Cabin Cruiser, 1965-68, Buick, two versions: light blue or dark metallic blue, No. 245 Buick, red boat trailer, dolphin cabin cruiser w/two figures, Model No. 31-A
EX $80   **NM** $120   **MIP** $280

Buick Riviera, 1964-68, Buick, metallic gold, dark blue, pale blue or gold body, red interior, gray steering wheel, and tow hook, clear windshield, chrome grille and bumpers, suspension, Tan-o-lite headlights, spoked wheels and rubber tires, Model No. 245-A
EX $30   **NM** $45   **MIP** $75

Chevrolet Caprice Classic, 1981-82, Chevrolet, working doors and trunk, whitewall tires, two versions: light metallic green body w/green interior or silver on blue body w/brown interior, Model No. 325-B
EX $24   **NM** $36   **MIP** $60

(KP Photo by Dr. Douglas Sadecky)

Chevrolet Corvair, 1961-66, Chevrolet, either blue or pale-blue body w/yellow interior and working rear hood, detailed engine, clear windows, silver bumpers, headlights and trim, red taillights, rear window blind, shaped wheels, rubber tires, Model No. 229-A

EX $36   NM $55   MIP $90

(KP Photo by Dr. Douglas Sadecky)

Chevrolet Impala, 1960-62, Chevrolet, pink body, yellow plastic interior, clear windows, silver headlights, bumpers, grille and trim, suspension, die-cast base w/rubber tires; a second version has a blue body w/red or yellow interior and smooth or shaped hubs, Model No. 220-A

EX $50   NM $75   MIP $125

Chevrolet Impala, 1965-67, Chevrolet, tan body, cream interior, gray steering wheel, clear windshields, chrome bumpers, grille, headlights, suspension, red taillights, shaped wheels and rubber tires, Model No. 248-A

EX $50   NM $75   MIP $125

(KP Photo by Dr. Douglas Sadecky)

Chevrolet Kennel Club Van, 1967-69, Chevrolet, white upper, red lower body, working tailgate and rear windows, green interior, four dog figures, kennel club decals; shaped spun or detailed cast wheels, rubber tires, Model No. 486-A

EX $56   NM $90   MIP $160

Chrysler Imperial Convertible, 1965-66, Chrysler, red body w/gray base, working hood, trunk and doors, golf bag in trunk, detailed engine, clear windshield, aqua interior, driver, chrome bumpers, Model No. 246-A1

EX $45   NM $65   MIP $110

Chrysler Imperial Convertible, 1967-68, Chrysler, metallic blue body w/gray base, working hood, trunk and doors, golf bag in trunk, detailed engine, clear windshield, aqua interior, driver, chrome bumpers, Model No. 246-A2

EX $50   NM $90   MIP $160

Citroen 2CV Charleston, 1981, Citroen, yellow/black or maroon/black body versions w/opening hood, Model No. 346-A

EX $15   NM $18   MIP $30

Citroen DS19, 1957-65, Citroen, one-piece body in several colors, clear windows, silver lights, grille and bumpers, smooth wheels, rubber tires; colors: red, metallic green w/black roof, yellow w/red roof, Model No. 210-A

EX $56   NM $84   MIP $140

Citroen Dyane, 1974-78, Citroen, metallic yellow or green body, black roof and interior, working rear hatch, clear windows, black base and tow bar, silver bumpers, grille and headlights, red taillights, marching duck and French flag decals, suspension, chrome wheels, Model No. 287-A

EX $15   NM $18   MIP $30

Citroen ID-19 Safari, 1963-65, Citroen, orange body w/red/brown or red/green luggage on roof rack, green/brown interior, working hatch, two passengers, Wildlife Preservation decals, Model No. 436-A

EX $40   NM $70   MIP $120

Citroen Le Dandy Coupe, 1966, Citroen, metallic maroon body and base, yellow interior, working trunk and two doors, clear windows, plastic interior, folding seats, chrome grille and bumpers, jewel headlights, red taillights, suspension, spoked wheels, rubber tires, Model No. 259-A1

EX $50   NM $75   MIP $125

(KP Photo by Dr. Douglas Sadecky)

Citroen Le Dandy Coupe, 1967-69, Citroen, metallic dark blue hood, sides and base, plastic aqua interior, white roof and trunk lid, clear windows, folding seats, chrome grille and bumpers, jewel headlights, red taillights, suspension, spoked wheels, rubber tires, Model No. 259-A2

EX $70   NM $105   MIP $175

Citroen SM, 1971-75, Citroen, metallic lime gold w/chrome wheels or mauve body w/spoked wheels, pale blue interior and lifting hatch cover, working rear hatch and two doors, chrome inner drs., window frames, bumpers, grille, amber headlights, red taillights, Whizz Wheels, Model No. 284-A

EX $16   NM $24   MIP $40

Citroen Tour de France Car, 1970-72, Citroen, red body, yellow interior and rear bed, clear windshield and headlights, driver, black plastic rack w/four bicycle wheels, swiveling team manager figure w/megaphone in back of car, Paramount and Tour de France decals, Whizz Wheels, Model No. 510-A

EX $40   NM $70   MIP $120

Citroen Winter Olympics Car, 1967-69, Citroen, white body, blue roof and hatch, blue interior, red roof rack w/yellow skis, gold sled w/rider, skier, gold Grenoble Olympiade decals on car roof, Model No. 499-A

EX $70   NM $105   MIP $200

Citroen Winter Sports Safari, 1964-67, Citroen, white body in three versions: two w/Corgi Ski Club decals and either w/or without roof ski rack, or one w/1964 Winter Olympics decals, Model No. 475-A

EX $56   NM $84   MIP $140

(KP Photo by Dr. Douglas Sadecky)

Fiat 1800, 1960-63, Fiat, one-piece body in several colors, clear windows, plastic interior, silver lights, grille and bumpers, red taillights, smooth wheels, rubber tires, colors: blue body w/light or bright yellow interior, light tan, mustard, light blue or two-tone blue body, Model No. 217-A

EX $24   NM $40   MIP $80

Fiat 2100, 1961-64, Fiat, light two-tone mauve body, yellow interior, purple roof, clear windows w/rear blind, silver grille, license plates and bumpers, red taillights, shaped wheels, rubber tires, Model No. 232-A

EX $22   NM $33   MIP $75

(KP Photo by Dr. Douglas Sadecky)

Ford Consul, 1956-61, Ford, one-piece body in several colors, clear windows, silver grille, lights and bumpers, smooth wheels, rubber tires, Model No. 200-A

EX $45   NM $65   MIP $120

Ford Consul Classic, 1961-65, Ford, cream or gold body and base, yellow interior, pink roof, clear windows, gray steering wheel, silver bumpers, grille, opening hood, Model No. 234-A

EX $35   NM $55   MIP $90

Ford Consul-Mechanical, 1956-59, Ford, same as model 200-A but w/friction motor and blue or green body, Model No. 200-M

EX $55   NM $85   MIP $160

Ford Cortina Estate Car, 1966-68, Ford, 3-1/2" metallic dark blue body and base, brown and cream simulated wood panels, cream interior, chrome bumpers and grille, jewel headlights, Model No. 440-A

EX $35   **NM** $55   **MIP** $90

Ford Cortina Estate Car, 1966-69, Ford, red body and base or metallic charcoal gray body and base, cream interior, chrome bumpers and grille, jewel headlights, Model No. 491-A

EX $35   **NM** $55   **MIP** $90

Ford Escort 13 GL, 1980, Ford, red, blue or yellow body, opening doors, Model No. 334-B

EX $8   **NM** $15   **MIP** $25

Ford Torino Road Hog, 1981, Ford, orange-red body, yellow and gray chassis, gold lamps, chrome radiator shell, windows and bumpers, one-piece body, working horn, Model No. 1003-A

EX $15   **NM** $20   **MIP** $35

Ford Zephyr Estate Car, 1960-65, Ford, light blue one-piece body, dark blue hood and stripes, red interior, silver bumpers, grille and headlights, red taillights, Model No. 424-A

EX $30   **NM** $45   **MIP** $75

(KP Photo by Dr. Douglas Sadecky)

Ghia L64 Chrysler V8, 1963-69, metallic light blue, green, copper or yellow, plastic interior, hood, trunk and two doors working, detailed engine, clear windshield, shaped or detailed cast wheels, Model No. 241-A

EX $25   **NM** $40   **MIP** $75

Ghia-Fiat 600 Jolly, 1963-65, light or dark blue body, red and silver canopy, red seats, two figures, windshield, chrome dash, floor, steering wheels, Model No. 240-A

EX $45   **NM** $85   **MIP** $160

Golden Guinea Set, 1961-63, three vehicle set, gold plated No. 224 Bentley Continental, No. 229 Chevy Corvair and No. 234 Ford Consul, Model No. 20-A

EX $90   **NM** $150   **MIP** $325

(KP Photo by Dr. Douglas Sadecky)

Hillman Husky, 1956-60, Hillman, one-piece tan or metallic blue/silver body, clear windows, silver lights, grille and bumpers, smooth wheels. The car on the left is the more rare two-tone version, while the car on the right is the mechanical flywheel version that was only produced for one year in 1959, Model No. 206-A

EX $40   **NM** $70   **MIP** $125

Hillman Husky-Mechanical, 1956-59, Hillman, same as 206-A but w/friction motor, black base and dark blue, gray or cream body, Model No. 206-M

EX $50   **NM** $100   **MIP** $150

Hillman Imp, 1963-67, Hillman, metallic copper, blue, dark blue or gold one-piece bodies, w/white/yellow interior, silver bumpers, headlights, Model No. 251-A

EX $30   **NM** $45   **MIP** $85

Honda Ballade Driving School, 1982-83, Honda, red body/base, tan interior, clear windows, tow hook, mirrors, bumpers, Model No. 273-B

EX $10   **NM** $15   **MIP** $25

Honda Prelude, 1981-82, Honda, dark metallic blue body, tan interior, clear windows, folding seats, sunroof, chrome wheels, Model No. 345-B

EX $8   **NM** $15   **MIP** $20

Jaguar 2.4 Litre, 1957-63, Jaguar, one-piece white body w/no interior 1957-59, or yellow body w/red interior 1960-63, clear windows, smooth hubs, Model No. 208-A

EX $50   **NM** $80   **MIP** $130

(KP Photo by Dr. Douglas Sadecky)

Jaguar 2.4 Litre-Mechanical, 1957-59, Jaguar, same as 208-A but w/friction motor and metallic blue body, Model No. 208-M

EX $60   **NM** $90   **MIP** $180

(KP Photo by Dr. Douglas Sadecky)

Jaguar Mark X Saloon, 1962-67, Jaguar, several different color versions w/working front and rear hood castings, clear windshields, plastic interior, gray steering wheel. Shown here in silver and blue versions, pictured at the left are the two suitcases that were included with each car, Model No. 238-A

EX $35   **NM** $55   **MIP** $110

Lincoln Continental, 1967-69, Lincoln, metallic gold or light blue body, black roof, maroon plastic interior, working hood, trunk and doors, clear windows; accessories include TV w/picture strips for TV, Model No. 262-A

EX $60   **NM** $90   **MIP** $150

Mercedes-Benz 220SE Coupe, 1962-64, Mercedes-Benz, cream, black or dark red body, red plastic interior, clear windows, working trunk, silver bumpers, grille and plate, spare wheel in boot, Model No. 230-A

EX $40   **NM** $60   **MIP** $100

(KP Photo by Dr. Douglas Sadecky)

Mercedes-Benz 220SE Coupe, 1967-68, Mercedes-Benz, metallic maroon or blue body, cream plastic interior, medium gray base, clear windows, silver bumpers, headlights, grille and license; accessories include plastic luggage and spare wheel in boot. Except for different exterior colors and the inclusion of luggage, this was exactly the same car as the 230-A, Model No. 253-A

EX $40   **NM** $60   **MIP** $100

Mercedes-Benz 240D, 1975-81, Mercedes-Benz, silver, blue or copper/beige body, working trunk, two doors, clear windows, plastic interior, two hook, chrome bumpers, grille and headlights, Whizz Wheels, Model No. 285-A

EX $10   **NM** $15   **MIP** $25

Mercedes-Benz 600 Pullman, 1964-69, Mercedes-Benz, metallic maroon body, cream interior and steering wheel, clear windshields, chrome grille, trim and bumpers, working windshield operators; includes instruction sheet, Model No. 247-A

EX $40   **NM** $60   **MIP** $100

(KP Photo by Dr. Douglas Sadecky)

Morris Cowley, 1959-60, Morris, long, one-piece body in several colors, clear windows, silver lights, grille and bumper, smooth wheels, rubber tires. The model on the left is the rare blue version, and the car on the right is the 202-M mechanical flywheel version, Model No. 202-A

EX $45   **NM** $75   **MIP** $140

Morris Cowley-Mechanical, 1956-59, Morris, same as 202-A but w/friction motor, available in off-white or green body, Model No. 202-M
EX $55 **NM** $95 **MIP** $170

Oldsmobile Super 88, 1962-68, Oldsmobile, three versions: light blue, light or dark metallic blue body w/white stripes, red interior, single body casting, Model No. 235-A
EX $40 **NM** $60 **MIP** $100

Oldsmobile Toronado, 1967-68, Oldsmobile, metallic medium or dark blue body, cream interior, one-piece body, clear windshield, chrome bumpers, grille, headlight covers, shaped or cast spoked wheels, Model No. 264-A
EX $35 **NM** $55 **MIP** $90

Oldsmobile Toronado, 1968-70, Oldsmobile, metallic copper, metallic blue or red one-piece body, cream interior, Golden jacks, gray tow hook, clear windows, bumpers, grille, headlights, Model No. 276-A
EX $35 **NM** $55 **MIP** $90

Opel Senator Doctor's Car, 1980-81, Opel, Model No. 332-B
EX $10 **NM** $15 **MIP** $25

OSI DAF City Car, 1971-74, DAF, orange/red body, light cream interior, textured black roof, sliding left door, working hood, hatch and two right doors, Whizz Wheels, Model No. 283-A
EX $18 **NM** $25 **MIP** $45

Plymouth Sports Suburban, 1959-63, Plymouth, dark cream body, tan roof, red interior, die-cast base, red axle, silver bumpers, trim and grille and rubber tires, Model No. 219-A
EX $40 **NM** $60 **MIP** $100

(KP Photo by Dr. Douglas Sadecky)

Plymouth Sports Suburban, 1963-65, Plymouth, pale blue body w/silver trim, red roof, yellow interior, gray die-cast base without rear axle bulge, shaped wheels, Model No. 445-A
EX $40 **NM** $60 **MIP** $100

Plymouth Suburban Mail Car, 1963-66, Plymouth, white upper, blue lower body w/red stripes, gray die-cast base without rear axle bulge, silver bumpers and grille, U.S. Mail decals, Model No. 443-A
EX $55 **NM** $85 **MIP** $140

Rambler Marlin Fastback, 1966-69, Rambler, red body, black roof and trim, cream interior, clear windshield, folding seats, chrome bumpers, grille and headlights, opening doors, Model No. 263-A
EX $35 **NM** $55 **MIP** $90

Rambler Marlin with Kayak and Trailer, 1968-69, Rambler, blue No. 263 Marlin w/roof rack, blue/white trailer, w/two kayaks, Model No. 10-A
EX $100 **NM** $150 **MIP** $250

Renault 16, 1969, Renault, metallic maroon body, dark yellow interior, chrome base, grille and bumpers, clear windows, opening bonnet and hatch cover, Renault decal, Model No. 260-A
EX $25 **NM** $35 **MIP** $60

Renault 16TS, 1970-72, Renault, metallic blue body w/Renault decal on working hatch, clear windows, detailed engine, yellow interior, Model No. 202-B
EX $20 **NM** $25 **MIP** $50

Renault 5TS, 1980-81, Renault, light blue body, red plastic interior, dark blue roof, dome light, S.O.S. Medicine lettering, working hatch and two doors, French issue, Model No. 293-A
EX $20 **NM** $35 **MIP** $70

Renault Alpine 5TS, 1980, Renault, dark blue body, off white interior, red and chrome trim, clear windows and headlights, gray base and bumpers, black grille, opening doors and hatchback, Model No. 294-A
EX $15 **NM** $25 **MIP** $40

Renault Floride, 1959-65, Renault, one-piece dark red, maroon or lime green body, clear windows, silver bumper, grille, lights and plates, red taillights, smooth or shaped hubs, rubber tires, Model No. 222-A
EX $35 **NM** $55 **MIP** $95

(KP Photo by Dr. Douglas Sadecky)

Riley Pathfinder, 1956-61, Riley, red or dark blue one-piece body, clear windows, silver lights, grille and bumpers, smooth wheels, rubber tires, Model No. 205-A
EX $45 **NM** $65 **MIP** $125

Riley Pathfinder-Mechanical, 1956-59, Riley, w/friction motor and either red or blue body, Model No. 205-M
EX $60 **NM** $95 **MIP** $170

Rolls-Royce Corniche, 1979, Rolls-Royce, different color versions w/light brown interior, working hood, trunk and two doors, clear windows, folding seats, chrome bumpers, Model No. 279-A
EX $10 **NM** $20 **MIP** $40

Rolls-Royce Silver Shadow, 1970, Rolls-Royce, metallic white upper/dusty blue lower body, working hood, trunk and two doors, clear windows, folding seats, chrome bumpers, Golden Jacks wheels, Model No. 273-A
EX $30 **NM** $50 **MIP** $95

Rolls-Royce Silver Shadow, 1971-73, Rolls-Royce

Rolls-Royce, metallic silver upper and metallic blue lower body, light brown interior, may or may not include hole in trunk for spare tire, Whizz Wheels, Model No. 280-A1
EX $25 **NM** $40 **MIP** $65

Rolls-Royce Silver Shadow, 1974-78, Rolls-Royce, metallic blue or gold body, bright blue interior, working hood, trunk and two doors, clear windows, folding seats, spare wheel, Model No. 280-A2
EX $25 **NM** $40 **MIP** $65

Rover 2000, 1963-66, Rover, metallic blue w/red interior or maroon body w/yellow interior, gray steering wheel, clear windshields, Model No. 252-A
EX $30 **NM** $45 **MIP** $75

Rover 2000TC, 1968-70, Rover, metallic olive green or maroon one-piece body, light brown interior, chrome bumpers/grille, jewel headlights, red taillights, Golden Jacks wheels, Model No. 275-A
EX $30 **NM** $45 **MIP** $75

Rover 2000TC, 1971-73, Rover, metallic purple body, light orange interior, black grille, one-piece body, amber windows, chrome bumpers and headlights, Whizz Wheels, Model No. 281-A
EX $25 **NM** $35 **MIP** $60

Rover 3500, 1979, Rover, three different body and interior versions, plastic interior, opening hood, hatch and two doors, lifting hatch cover, Model No. 338-B
EX $8 **NM** $15 **MIP** $25

(KP Photo by Dr. Douglas Sadecky)

Rover 90, 1956-60, Rover, one-piece body, silver headlights, grille and bumpers, smooth wheels, rubber tires; multiple colors available. The car on the left is the rare two-tone color scheme and the vehicle on the right is the mechanical version in metallic green, Model No. 204-A
EX $50 **NM** $75 **MIP** $145

Rover 90-Mechanical, 1956-59, Rover, w/friction motor and red, green, gray or metallic green body, Model No. 204-M
EX $60 **NM** $90 **MIP** $170

(KP Photo by Dr. Douglas Sadecky)

Standard Vanguard, 1957-61, Standard, one-piece red and pale green body, clear windows, silver lights, grille and bumpers, smooth wheels, rubber tires. Pictured with the 207M, the attractive two-tone 207-A version is on the left, and the mechanical version is on the right, Model No. 207-A
EX $50   **NM** $75   **MIP** $125

Standard Vanguard-Mechanical, 1957-59, Standard, w/friction motor and yellow or off-white body w/black or gray base, or cream body w/red roof, Model No. 207-M
EX $55   **NM** $90   **MIP** $170

Studebaker Golden Hawk, 1958-60, Studebaker, one-piece body in blue and gold or white and gold, clear windows, silver lights, grille and bumpers, smooth wheels, rubber tires, Model No. 211-A
EX $55   **NM** $85   **MIP** $140

(KP Photo by Dr. Douglas Sadecky)

Studebaker Golden Hawk, 1960-65, Studebaker, second issue: gold painted body, shaped hubs. The "S" after the catalog number stood for "suspension" which was a new Corgi innovation at the time of the model's release, Model No. 211S2
EX $60   **NM** $180   **MIP** $180

Studebaker Golden Hawk, 1960-65, Studebaker, first issue: gold plated body, white flashing, shaped hubs, Model No. 211S1
EX $55   **NM** $85   **MIP** $140

Studebaker Golden Hawk-Mechanical, 1958-59, Studebaker, w/friction motor and white body w/gold trim, Model No. 211-M
EX $70   **NM** $105   **MIP** $175

Tour de France Set, 1968-72, Renault, white and black body, Renault w/Paramount Film roof sign, rear platform w/cameraman and black camera on tripod, plus bicycle and rider, Model No. 13-B
EX $60   **NM** $90   **MIP** $200

Tour de France Set, 1981-82, Peugeot, w/white No. 373 Peugeot, red and yellow Raleigh and Total logos, Racing cycles, includes manager figures, Model No. 13-C
EX $25   **NM** $45   **MIP** $90

Triumph Acclaim Driving School, 1982, Triumph, dark yellow body w/black trim, black roof mounted steering wheel steers front wheels, clear windows, mirrors, bumpers, Model No. 277-B
EX $15   **NM** $25   **MIP** $40

Triumph Acclaim Driving School, 1982-83, Triumph, yellow or red body/base, Corgi Motor School labels, black roof mounted steering wheel steers front wheels, clear windows, Model No. 278-B
EX $15   **NM** $25   **MIP** $50

Triumph Acclaim HLS, 1981-83, Triumph, metallic peacock blue body/base, black trim, light brown interior, clear windows, mirrors, bumpers, vents, tow hook, Model No. 276-B
EX $15   **NM** $18   **MIP** $30

Triumph Herald Coupe, 1961-66, Triumph, blue or gold top and lower body, white upper body, red interior, clear windows, silver bumpers, grille, headlights, shaped hubs, Model No. 231-A
EX $35   **NM** $65   **MIP** $110

(KP Photo by Dr. Douglas Sadecky)

Trojan Heinkel, 1962-72, Heinkel, issued in mauve, red, orange or lilac body, plastic interior, silver bumpers and headlights, red taillights, suspension, smooth, spun, or detailed cast wheels, Model No. 233-A
EX $35   **NM** $55   **MIP** $95

(KP Photo by Dr. Douglas Sadecky)

Vauxhall Velox, 1956-60, one-piece body in red, cream, yellow or yellow and red body, clear windows, silver lights, grille and bumpers, smooth wheels, rubber tires, Model No. 203-A
EX $50   **NM** $75   **MIP** $150

Vauxhall Velox-Mechanical, 1956-59, Vauxhall, w/friction motor; orange, red, yellow or cream body, Model No. 203-M
EX $60   **NM** $90   **MIP** $170

Volkswagen 1200 Driving School, 1974-75, Volkswagen, metallic red or blue body, yellow interior, gold roof mounted steering wheel that steers, silver headlights, red taillights, Model No. 400-A
EX $25   **NM** $35   **MIP** $60

Volkswagen 1500 Karmann-Ghia, 1963-68, Volkswagen, cream, red or gold body, plastic interior and taillights, front and rear working hoods, clear windshields, silver bumpers; includes spare wheel and plastic suitcase in trunk, Model No. 239-A
EX $35   **NM** $55   **MIP** $90

Volkswagen Driving School, 1975-77, Volkswagen, metallic blue body, yellow interior, gold roof mounted steering wheel that steers, silver headlights, red taillights, Model No. 401-A
EX $25   **NM** $40   **MIP** $70

Volkswagen Polo, 1976-79, Volkswagen, apple green or bright yellow body, black DBP and posthorn (German Post Office) labels, off white interior, black dash, Model No. 289-A
EX $25   **NM** $40   **MIP** $65

Volkswagen Polo, 1979-81, Volkswagen, metallic light brown body, off-white interior, black dash, clear windows, silver bumpers, grille and headlights, Model No. 302-C
EX $15   **NM** $18   **MIP** $30

Volkswagen Polo Auto Club Car, 1977-79, Volkswagen, yellow body, white roof, yellow dome light, ADAC Strassenwacht labels, Model No. 489-B
EX $15   **NM** $25   **MIP** $40

Volkswagen Polo German Auto Club Car, 1977-79, Volkswagen, yellow body, off-white interior, black dash, silver bumpers, grille and headlights, white roof, yellow dome light, Model No. 489-A2
EX $25   **NM** $35   **MIP** $60

Volkswagen Polo Mail Car, 1976-80, Volkswagen, bright yellow body, black DBP and Posthorn labels, German issue, Model No. 289-B
EX $25   **NM** $35   **MIP** $60

Volvo P-1800, 1962-65, Volvo, one-piece body light brown, dark red, pink or dark red body, clear windows, plastic interior, shaped wheels, rubber tires, Model No. 228-A
EX $40   **NM** $60   **MIP** $100

BOAT

(KP Photo by Dr. Douglas Sadecky)

Dolphin Cabin Cruiser, 1965-68, white hull, blue deck plastic boat w/red/white stripe labels, driver, blue motor w/white cover, gray prop, cast trailer w/smooth wheels, rubber tires, Model No. 104-A
EX $24   **NM** $40   **MIP** $80

Fiat X 1/9 & Powerboat, 1979-82, Fiat, green and white automobile, w/white and gold boat, Carlsberg labels, Model No. 37-B
EX $30   **NM** $45   **MIP** $75

HDL Hovercraft SR-N1, 1960-62, blue superstructure, gray base and deck, clear canopy, red seats, yellow SR-N1 decals, Model No. 1119-A
EX $60   **NM** $90   **MIP** $150

Olds Toronado and Speedboat, 1967-70, Oldsmobile, blue No. 276 Toronado, blue and yellow boat and chrome trailer, w/swordfish decals and three figures, Model No. 36-A
EX $60   **NM** $90   **MIP** $165

Powerboat Team, 1980-81, Jaguar, white/ed No. 319 Jaguar w/red/white boat on silver trailer, Team Corgi Carlsberg, Union Jack and #1 labels on boat, Model No. 38-C
EX $25   **NM** $35   **MIP** $60

BUS

Beep Beep London Bus, 1981, battery-operated working horn, red body, black windows, BTA decals, Model No. 1004-A
EX $26   **NM** $39   **MIP** $65

Green Line Bus, 1983, green body, white interior and stripe, TDK labels, six spoked wheels, Model No. 470-C
EX $10   **NM** $15   **MIP** $25

Inter-City Mini Bus, 1973-79, orange body w/brown interior, clear windows, green/yellow/black decals, Whizz Wheels, Model No. 701-A
EX $8   **NM** $15   **MIP** $25

(KP Photo by Dr. Douglas Sadecky)

London Set, 1964-68, Routemaster, No. 418 taxi and No. 468 bus w/policeman, in two versions: "Corgi Toys" on bus (1964-66); "Outspan Oranges" on bus (1967-68); values for each individual complete set, Model No. 35-A
EX $55   **NM** $95   **MIP** $170

London Set, 1971-75, Routemaster, orange No. 226 Mini, Policeman, No. 418 London Taxi and No. 468 Outspan Routemaster bus, Whizz Wheels, Model No. 11-B
EX $50   **NM** $75   **MIP** $125

London Set, 1980-82, Routemaster, No. 425 London Taxi and No. 469 Routemaster B.T.A. bus in two versions: w/mounted Policeman (1980-81); without Policeman, (1982-on); value is for each individual complete set, Model No. 11-C
EX $25   **NM** $35   **MIP** $60

(KP Photo by Dr. Douglas Sadecky)

London Transport Routemaster Bus, 1964-75, Routemaster, clear windows w/driver and conductor, released w/numerous advertiser logos, shaped or cast spoked wheels, Model No. 468-A
EX $35   **NM** $40   **MIP** $70

London Transport Routemaster Bus, 1975, Routemaster, long, clear windows, interior, some models have driver and conductor, released w/numerous advertiser logos, Whizz Wheels, Model No. 469-A
EX $25   **NM** $30   **MIP** $50

(KP Photo by Dr. Douglas Sadecky)

Midland Red Express Coach, 1961-62, red one-piece body, black roof w/shaped or smooth wheels, yellow interior, clear windows, silver grille and headlights. Two box variations shown in this photo, Model No. 1120-A
EX $70   **NM** $105   **MIP** $225

National Express Bus, 1983, variety of colors and label variations, Model No. 1168-A
EX $8   **NM** $15   **MIP** $25

Open Top Disneyland Bus, 1977-78, yellow body, red interior and stripe, Disneyland labels, eight-spoked wheels or orange body, white interior and stripe, Model No. 470-B
EX $30   **NM** $50   **MIP** $95

Routemaster Bus-Promotionals, 1977, Routemaster, different body and interior versions and promotional labels, Model No. 467-A
EX $15   **NM** $25   **MIP** $40

Silver Jubilee London Transport Bus, 1977, silver body w/red interior, no passengers, labels read "Woolworth Welcomes the World" and "The Queen's Silver," Model No. 471-B
EX $15   **NM** $18   **MIP** $30

CHARACTER

1927 Bentley "World of Wooster", 1967-69, Bentley, green body, metallic black chassis, cast spoked wheels, figures of Jeeves & Bertie Wooster, Model No. 9004-A
EX $50   **NM** $100   **MIP** $150

Avengers Set, 1966-69, white Lotus, red or green (rare) Bentley; Jonathan Steed and Emma Peel figures w/three umbrellas, Model No. 40-A
EX $260   **NM** $390   **MIP** $800

(KP Photo by Dr. Douglas Sadecky)

Basil Brush's Car, 1971-73, red body, dark yellow chassis, gold lamps and dash, Basil Brush figure, gold plastic wheels, plastic tires; w/"Laugh Tapes" and soundbox. Basil Brush could be heard laughing with the aid of laugh tapes and a soundbox that were included with the car, Model No. 808-A
EX $70   **NM** $105   **MIP** $200

Batbike, 1978-83, black body, one-piece body, black and red plastic parts, gold engine and exhaust pipes, clear windshield, chrome stand, black plastic five-spoked wheels, Batman figure and decals, Model No. 268-B
EX $40   **NM** $60   **MIP** $125

Batboat, 1967-72, black plastic boat, red seats, fin and jet, blue windshield, Batman and Robin figures, gold cast trailer, tinplate fin cover, cast wheels, plastic tires, w/plastic towhook for Batmobile, Model No. 107-A1
EX $60   **NM** $90   **MIP** $175

Batboat, 1976-80, black plastic boat w/Batman and Robin figures, small Bat logo labels on fin and on side of boat, chain link labels, Whizz Wheels on trailer, Model No. 107-A2
EX $30   **NM** $45   **MIP** $100

Batcopter, 1976-81, black body w/yellow/red/black decals, red rotors, Batman figure, operable winch, Model No. 925-A
EX $30   **NM** $50   **MIP** $100

Batman Set, 1976-81, three vehicle set: No. 267 Batmobile, No. 107 Batboat w/trailer and No. 925 Batcopter, Whizz Wheels on trailer, Model No. 40-B
EX $150   **NM** $300   **MIP** $800

(KP Photo by Dr. Douglas Sadecky)

Batmobile, 1966, matte black (rare) or gloss black body, gold hubs, bat logos on door and hubs, maroon interior, black body, plastic rockets, yellow headlights and gold rocket control, blue tinted canopy, working front chain cutter, no tow hook, rubber tires. Although it's difficult to tell from this photo, this is the rare first issue matte black finish with no towhook version of the famous Batmobile, Model No. 267-A1
EX $200   **NM** $300   **MIP** $550

Batmobile, 1967-72, same as first issue except for gloss black body, gold towhook, Model No. 267-A2
EX $200   **NM** $300   **MIP** $500

(KP Photo by Dr. Douglas Sadecky)

Batmobile, 1973, chrome hubs w/red bat logos on door, maroon interior, red plastic tires, gold tow hook, plastic rockets, yellow headlight and gold rocket control, tinted blue canopy w/chrome support, chain cutter. Made for only one year, this version featured red plastic tires and chrome wheels. Also pictured is the back of the rare first-issue window box for this model, Model No. 267-C1
EX $140   **NM** $200   **MIP** $400

Batmobile, 1974-79, chrome hubs w/black plastic tires, red bat logos on door, light red interior, gold tow hook, plastic rockets, yellow headlights and gold rocket control, tinted blue canopy w/chrome support, Model No. 267-C2
EX $80   **NM** $120   **MIP** $200

Batmobile, 1980-81, gloss black body, light red interior, gold towhook, Whizz-wheels with 8-spoke chrome hubs, Model No. 267-D
EX $80   **NM** $110   **MIP** $175

Batmobile, Batboat and Trailer, 1967-72, first and second versions: red bat hubs on wheels, 1967-72; red tires and chrome wheels 1972-73, Model No. 3-B1
EX $240   **NM** $360   **MIP** $650

Batmobile, Batboat and Trailer, 1973-81, third and fourth versions: 1973; black tires, labels on boat, 1974-76; chrome wheels, boat labels, Whizz Wheels on trailer, Model No. 3-B2
EX $120   **NM** $175   **MIP** $350

Beatles' Yellow Submarine, 1969, yellow and white hatches, red pinstripes, first issue, Model No. 803-A1
EX $200   **NM** $500   **MIP** $1000

Beatles' Yellow Submarine, 1969-70, second issue, yellow and white body, working red hatches w/two Beatles in each, Model No. 803-A2
EX $180   **NM** $270   **MIP** $700

Buck Rogers Starfighter, 1980, white body w/yellow plastic wings, amber windows, blue jets, color decal, Buck and Wilma figures, Model No. 647-A
EX $32   **NM** $48   **MIP** $90

Captain America Jetmobile, 1979-80, 6" white body, metallic blue chassis, black nose cone, red shield and jet, red-white-blue Captain America decals, light blue seats and driver, chrome wheels, red tires, Model No. 263-B
EX $24   **NM** $36   **MIP** $60

Captain Marvel Porsche, 1979-80, Porsche, white body, gold parts, red seat, driver, red/yellow/blue Captain Marvel decals, black plastic base, gold wheels, Model No. 262-B
EX $20   **NM** $30   **MIP** $60

Chevrolet Charlie's Angels Van, 1977-80, Chevrolet, light rose-mauve body w/Charlie's Angels decals, in two versions: either solid or spoked chrome wheels, Model No. 434-B
EX $15   **NM** $30   **MIP** $55

Chevrolet Spider-Van, 1978-80, Chevrolet, dark blue body w/Spider-Man decals, in two versions: w/either spoke or solid wheels, Model No. 436-B
EX $26   **NM** $39   **MIP** $65

Chitty Chitty Bang Bang, 1968-72, metallic copper body, dark red interior and spoked wheels, four figures, black chassis w/silver running boards, silver hood, horn, brake, dash, tail and headlights, gold radiator, red and orange wings, handbrake operates side wings, Model No. 266-A
EX $180   **NM** $270   **MIP** $425

Daily Planet Helicopter, 1979-81, red and white body, rocket launcher w/ten spare missiles, Model No. 929-A
EX $24   **NM** $36   **MIP** $60

Daktari Set, 1967-75, Land Rover, two versions: No. 438 Land Rover, green w/black stripes, spun or cast spoke wheels, 1968-73; Whizz Wheels, 1974-75, each set, Model No. 7-B
EX $50   **NM** $75   **MIP** $150

Dick Dastardly's Racing Car, 1973-76, dark blue body, yellow chassis, chrome engine, red wings, Dick and Muttley figures, Model No. 809-A
EX $40   **NM** $60   **MIP** $150

(KP Photo by Dr. Douglas Sadecky)

Dougal's Magic Roundabout Car, 1971-74, yellow body, red interior, clear windows, dog and snail figures, red wheels w/gold trim, Magic Roundabout labels, Model No. 807-A
EX $70   **NM** $105   **MIP** $175

Drax Jet Helicopter, 1979-81, white body, yellow rotors and fins, yellow/black Drax labels, Model No. 930-A
EX $35   **NM** $75   **MIP** $150

Giant Daktari Set, 1969-73, black and green No. 438 Land Rover, tan No. 503 Giraffe truck, blue and brown No. 484 Dodge Livestock truck, figures, Model No. 14-B
EX $225   **NM** $350   **MIP** $650

Green Hornet's Black Beauty, 1967-72, black body, green window/interior, two figures, working chrome grille and panels w/weapons, green headlights, red taillights, Model No. 268-A
EX $175   **NM** $275   **MIP** $550

Hardy Boys' Rolls-Royce, 1970, red body w/yellow hood, roof and window frames, band figures on roof on removable green base, Model No. 805-A
EX $70   **NM** $105   **MIP** $200

Incredible Hulk Mazda Pickup, 1979-80, Mazda, metallic light brown body, gray or red plastic cage, black interior, Hulk label on hood, chrome wheels; includes green and red Hulk figure, Model No. 264-B
EX $20   **NM** $30   **MIP** $75

(KP Photo by Dr. Douglas Sadecky)

James Bond Aston Martin, 1968-77, Aston Martin, metallic silver body, red interior, two figures, working roof hatch, ejector seat, bullet shield and guns, chrome bumpers, spoked wheels. Orginally issued in a rare bubble-pack, the subsequent issues were sold in window boxes. On the left, the rare first issue window box; on the right, the more commonly seen version, Model No. 270-A
EX $100   **NM** $150   **MIP** $325

James Bond Aston Martin, 1978, Aston Martin, metallic silver body and die-cast base, red interior, two figures, clear windows, passenger seat raises to eject, Model No. 271-B
EX $30   **NM** $45   **MIP** $90

James Bond Aston Martin DB5, 1965-68, Aston Martin, metallic gold body, red interior, working roof hatch, clear windows, two figures, left seat ejects, spoked wheels, accessory pack, Model No. 261-A
EX $70   **NM** $150   **MIP** $300

(KP Photo by Dr. Douglas Sadecky)

James Bond Citroen 2CV6, 1981-86, Citroen, dark yellow body and hood, red interior, clear windows, chrome headlights, red taillights, black plastic grille. This model was available in a window box, or the more difficult to find photo box shown here, Model No. 272-A

EX $15   **NM** $35   **MIP** $70

James Bond Lotus Esprit, 1977, white body and base, black windshield, grille and hood panel, white plastic roof device that triggers fins and tail, rockets, Model No. 269-B

EX $30   **NM** $45   **MIP** $95

James Bond Moon Buggy, 1972-73, white body w/blue chassis, amber canopy, yellow tanks, red radar dish, arms and jaws, yellow wheels, Model No. 811-A

EX $175   **NM** $275   **MIP** $525

(KP Photo by Dr. Douglas Sadecky)

James Bond Mustang Mach 1, 1972-73, Ford, red and white body w/black hood and opening doors. Because using this model as a Bond vehicle was a last-minute decision, a label was adhered to the right side of the window box. Without this label, no one would know this was a James Bond issue, Model No. 391-A

EX $100   **NM** $150   **MIP** $300

James Bond Set, 1979-81, set of three: No. 271 Lotus Esprit, No. 649 Space Shuttle and No. 269 Aston Martin, Model No. 22-B

EX $100   **NM** $200   **MIP** $400

James Bond Space Shuttle, 1979-81, white body w/yellow/black Moonraker labels, Model No. 649-A

EX $30   **NM** $50   **MIP** $95

James Bond Toyota 2000GT, 1967-69, Toyota, white body, black interior w/Bond and female driver, working trunk and gun rack, spoked wheels, plastic tires, accessory pack, Model No. 336-A

EX $115   **NM** $180   **MIP** $375

Kojak's Buick Regal, 1976-81, Buick, metallic bronze brown body, off-white interior, two opening doors, clear windows, chrome bumpers, grille and headlights, red taillights; accessories include Kojak and Crocker figures, Model No. 290-A

EX $25   **NM** $55   **MIP** $95

Lions of Longleat, 1968-74, Land Rover, black/white No. 438 Land Rover pickup w/lion cages and accessories, two versions: cast spoked wheels, 1969-73; Whizz Wheels, 1974, each, Model No. 8-B

EX $60   **NM** $90   **MIP** $200

Magic Roundabout Musical Carousel, 1973, plastic roundabout w/Swiss musical movement, w/Dylan, Rosalie, Paul, Florence and Basil figures, rare, Model No. 852-A

EX $275   **NM** $425   **MIP** $750

Magic Roundabout Playground, 1973, contains No. 851 Train, No. 852 Carousel, six figures, seesaw, park bench, shrubs and fowers, rare, Model No. 853-A

EX $295   **NM** $500   **MIP** $1000

Magic Roundabout Train, 1973, red and blue plastic three-piece train; accessories include figures of Mr. Rusty, Basil, Rosaile, Paul and Dougal, Model No. 851-A

EX $70   **NM** $195   **MIP** $350

Man From U.N.C.L.E. THRUSH-Buster, 1966-68, plastic interior, blue windows, two figures, two spotlights, dark metallic blue body, w/3-D Waverly ring, Model No. 497-A1

EX $80   **NM** $130   **MIP** $275

(KP Photo by Dr. Douglas Sadecky)

Man From U.N.C.L.E. THRUSH-Buster, 1968-69, plastic interior, blue windows, two figures, two spotlights, cream body, w/3-D Waverly ring, RARE, Model No. 497-A2

EX $100   **NM** $350   **MIP** $550

Monkeemobile, 1968-70, red body/base, white roof, yellow interior, clear windows, four figures, chrome grille, headlights, engine, orange taillights, Model No. 277-A

EX $145   **NM** $225   **MIP** $450

Mr. McHenry's Trike, 1972-74, red and yellow trike and trailer; accessories include Mr. McHenry and Zebedee figures, Model No. 859-A

EX $70   **NM** $105   **MIP** $175

Muppet Vehicles, Fozzie Bear's Truck, Model No. 2031-A

EX $15   **NM** $30   **MIP** $50

Muppet Vehicles, Animal's Percussionmobile, Model No. 2033-A

EX $15   **NM** $30   **MIP** $50

Muppet Vehicles, Miss Piggy's Sports Coupe, Model No. 2032-A

EX $15   **NM** $30   **MIP** $50

Muppet Vehicles, Kermit's Car, Model No. 2030-A

EX $15   **NM** $35   **MIP** $60

Noddy's Car, yellow body, red chassis, Noddy alone, closed trunk w/spare wheel, Model No. 804-A

EX $60   **NM** $90   **MIP** $175

Noddy's Car, 1969-71, first issue: yellow body, red chassis and fenders, figures of Noddy, Big-Ears, and black, gray, or light tan face Golliwog, Model No. 801-A1

EX $200   **NM** $400   **MIP** $600

Noddy's Car, 1972-73, second issue: same as first issue except Master Tubby is substituted for Golliwog, Model No. 801-A2

EX $100   **NM** $200   **MIP** $350

Penguinmobile, 1979-80, white body, black and white lettering on orange-yellow-blue labels, gold body panels, seats, air scoop, chrome engine, w/penguin figure, Model No. 259-B

EX $20   **NM** $30   **MIP** $65

(KP Photo by Dr. Douglas Sadecky)

Popeye's Paddle Wagon, 1969-72, yellow and white body, red chassis, blue rear fenders, bronze and yellow stacks, white plastic deck, blue lifeboat w/Swee' Pea; includes figures of Popeye, Olive Oyl, Bluto and Wimpey. Produced for a short period, the colorful Paddle-Wagon had multiple working features and contained all of the main characters, Model No. 802-A

EX $195   **NM** $300   **MIP** $525

Professionals Ford Capri, 1980-82, Ford, metallic silver body and base, red interior, black spoiler, grille, bumpers, tow hook and trim, blue windows, chrome wheels; includes figures of Cowley, Bodie and Doyle, Model No. 342-B

EX $30   **NM** $65   **MIP** $130

Saint's Jaguar XJS, 1978-81, Jaguar, white body, red interior, black trim, Saint figure hood label, opening doors, black grille, bumpers and tow hook, chrome headlights, Model No. 320-B

EX $30   **NM** $45   **MIP** $85

(KP Photo by Dr. Doug Sadecky)

Saint's Volvo P-1800, 1965-69, Volvo, three versions of white one-piece body w/silver trim and different colored Saint decals on hood, driver. Pictured here with the 201-B. Note the wheel and hood logo variation between the two cars, Model No. 258-A

EX $55   **NM** $85   **MIP** $175

Saint's Volvo P-1800, 1970-72, Volvo, one-piece white body w/red Saint decal on hood, gray base, clear windows, black interior w/driver, Whizz Wheels, Model No. 201-B

EX $55   **NM** $95   **MIP** $200

Silver Jubilee Landau, 1977-80, Landua w/four horses, two footmen, two riders, Queen and Prince figures, and Corgi dog, in two versions, Model No. 41-B

EX $15   **NM** $25   **MIP** $50

Spider-Bike, 1979-83, medium blue body, one-piece body, dark blue plastic front body and seat, blue and red Spider-Man figure, amber windshield, black or white wheels, Model No. 266-B

EX $40   **NM** $60   **MIP** $85

Spider-Buggy, 1979-81, red body, blue hood, clear windows, dark blue dash, seat and crane, chrome base w/bumper and steps, silver headlights; includes Spider-Man and Green Goblin figures, Model No. 261-B

EX $50   **NM** $75   **MIP** $150

Spider-Copter, 1979-81, blue body w/Spi-der-Man labels, red plastic legs, tongue and tail rotor, black windows and main rotor, Model No. 928-A

EX $30   **NM** $45   **MIP** $85

Spider-Man Set, 1980-81, set of three: No. 266 Spider-Bike, No. 928 Spider-Copter and No. 261Spider-Buggy, Model No. 23-B

EX $80   **NM** $160   **MIP** $350

Starsky and Hutch Ford Torino, 1977-81, Ford, red one-piece body, white trim, light yellow interior, clear windows, chrome bumpers, grille and headlights, orange taillights; includes Starsky, Hutch and Bandit figures, Model No. 292-A

EX $35   **NM** $55   **MIP** $100

Superman Set, 1979-81, set of three: No. 265 Supermobile, No. 925 Daily Planet Helicopter and No. 260 Metropolis Police Car, Model No. 21-C

EX $70   **NM** $120   **MIP** $225

Supermobile, 1979-81, blue body, red, chrome or gray fists, red interior, clear canopy, Superman figure, chrome arms w/removable "striking fists", Model No. 265-A

EX $30   **NM** $45   **MIP** $75

Supervan, 1978-81, silver van w/Super-man labels, working rear doors, chrome spoked wheels, Model No. 435-B

EX $15   **NM** $30   **MIP** $60

Tarzan Set, 1976-78, Land Rover, metallic green No. 421 Land Rover w/trailer and Dinghy; cage, five figures and other accessories, Model No. 36-B

EX $100   **NM** $150   **MIP** $285

Vegas Ford Thunderbird, 1980-81, Ford, orange/red body and base, black interior and grille, opening hood and trunk, amber windshield, white seats, driver, chrome bumper, Model No. 348-B

EX $25   **NM** $40   **MIP** $85

CIRCUS

Chipperfield Circus Bedford Giraffe Transporter, 1964-71, Bedford, red "TK" Bedford truck w/blue giraffe box w/Chipperfield decal, two giraffes, shaped, cast spoked or detailed wheels, Model No. 503-A

EX $60   **NM** $90   **MIP** $175

Chipperfield Circus Cage Wagon, 1961-68, red body, yellow chassis, smooth or spun hubs; includes lions, tigers or polar bears, Model No. 1123-A

EX $56   **NM** $84   **MIP** $140

Chipperfield Circus Chevrolet Performing Poodles Van, 1970-72, Chevrolet, blue upper body and tailgate, red lower body and base, clear windshield, pale blue interior w/poodles in back and ring of poodles and trainer, plastic tires, Model No. 511-A

EX $160   **NM** $240   **MIP** $550

Chipperfield Circus Crane and Cage, 1970-72, No. 1144 crane truck, cage w/rhinoceros, red and blue trailer w/three animal cages and animals; very rare gift set, Model No. 21-B

EX $400   **NM** $700   **MIP** $2000

Chipperfield Circus Crane and Cage Wagon, 1961-65, No. 1121 crane truck, No. 1123 cage wagon and accessories, Model No. 12-A

EX $150   **NM** $225   **MIP** $375

(KP Photo by Dr. Douglas Sadecky)

Chipperfield Circus Crane Truck, 1960-68, red body, embossed Chipperfield blue logo, tinplate boom, blue wheels. Pictured here with Chipperfield Circus Cage Wagon 1123-A, that included a set of polar bears or lions and their appro-priate label transfers, Model No. 1121-A

EX $80   **NM** $120   **MIP** $225

(KP Photo by Dr. Douglas Sadecky)

Chipperfield Circus Horse Transporter, 1962-72, Bedford, red Bedford "TK" cab, blue upper/red lower horse trailer, three wheel variations; includes six horses, Model No. 1130-A

EX $80   **NM** $120   **MIP** $235

(KP Photo by Dr. Douglas Sadecky)

Chipperfield Circus Karrier Booking Office, 1962-64, Karrier, red body, light blue roof, clear windows, tin lithographed interior, circus decals, smooth or shaped wheels, rubber tires, Model No. 426-A

EX $105   **NM** $165   **MIP** $325

Chipperfield Circus Land Rover and Ele-phant Cage, 1962-68, Land Rover, red No. 438 Range Rover w/blue canopy, Chipperfields Circus decal on canopy, burnt orange No. 607 elephant cage on red bed trailer, Model No. 19-A

EX $90   **NM** $135   **MIP** $275

(KP Photo by Dr. Douglas Sadecky)

Chipperfield Circus Land Rover Parade Vehicle, 1967-69, Land Rover, red body, yellow interior, blue rear and speakers, revolving clown, chimp figures, Chipper-field labels, Model No. 487-A

EX $60   **NM** $90   **MIP** $175

Chipperfield Circus Menagerie Trans-porter, 1968-72, Scammell, Scammell Handyman MKIII red/blue cab, blue trailer w/three animal cages, two lions, two tigers and two bears, Model No. 1139-A

EX $120   **NM** $180   **MIP** $375

Chipperfield Circus Scammell Crane Truck, 1969-72, Scammell, red upper cab and rear body, light blue lower cab, crane base and winch crank housing, red interior, tow hook, jewel headlights, Model No. 1144-A

EX $175   **NM** $275   **MIP** $450

Chipperfield Circus Set, 1st Version, 1963-65, vehicle and accessory set in two versions: w/No. 426 Booking Office, Model No. 23-A1

EX $380   **NM** $600   **MIP** $1300

Chipperfield Circus Set, 2nd Version, 1966, vehicle and accessory set w/#503 Giraffe Truck, Model No. 23-A2

EX $340   **NM** $500   **MIP** $1000

Circus Human Cannonball Truck, 1978-81, red and blue body; w/Marvo figure, Model No. 1163-A

EX $30   **NM** $45   **MIP** $75

Circus Land Rover and Trailer, 1978-81, Land Rover, yellow/red No. 421 Land Rover w/Pinder-Jean Richard decals; accessories include blue loudspeakers and figures, Model No. 30-B
EX $30   NM $50   MIP $90

Jean Richard Circus Set, 1978-81, Land Rover, yellow and red Land Rover and cage trailer w/Pinder-Jean Richard decals, No. 426 office van and trailer, No. 1163 Human Cannonball truck, ring and cut-out "Big Top" circus tent, Model No. 48-C
EX $90   NM $135   MIP $275

CLASSICS

1910 Renault 12/16, 1965-69, Renault, pale yellow body & spoked wheels, light black chassis, black ragtop, Model No. 9032-A
EX $25   NM $50   MIP $80

1910 Renault 12/16, 1965-69, Renault, light purple body & spoked wheels, light black chassis, Model No. 9031-A
EX $25   NM $50   MIP $80

(KP Photo by Dr. Douglas Sadecky)

1927 Bentley, 1964-69, Bentley, red body, metallic black chassis, brown interior, black ragtop, red spoked wheels, driver. The red Bentley is slightly harder to find than the green version, Model No. 9002-A
EX $30   NM $60   MIP $90

1927 Bentley, 1964-69, Bentley, green body, metallic black chassis, brown interior, black ragtop, spoked wheels, driver, Model No. 9001-A
EX $35   NM $50   MIP $75

(KP Photo by Dr. Douglas Sadecky)

Daimler 38 1910, 1964-69, Daimler, orange-red body, gray and yellow chassis, yellow spoked wheels; w/four figures, Model No. 9021-A
EX $20   NM $40   MIP $65

Model T Ford, 1964-69, Ford, blue body, black chassis, black ragtop, yellow wheels, one figure, Model No. 9013-A
EX $20   NM $40   MIP $65

Model T Ford, 1964-69, Ford, black body & chassis, spoked wheels, two figures, Model No. 9011-A
EX $20   NM $40   MIP $65

(KP Photo by Dr. Douglas Sadecky)

Model T Ford, 1964-69, Ford, yellow body & spoked wheels, black chassis, two figures, Model No. 9012-A
EX $20   NM $40   MIP $65

Rolls-Royce Silver Ghost, 1966-69, Rolls-Royce, silver body/hood, charcoal and silver chassis, bronze interior, gold lights, box and tank, clear windows, dash lights, radiator, Model No. 9041-A
EX $15   NM $30   MIP $60

CONSTRUCTION

Allis-Chalmers AFC 60 Fork Lift, 1981, Allis-Chalmers, yellow body, white engine hood, w/driver, tan pallets and red containers, Model No. 409-C
EX $15   NM $20   MIP $45

(KP Photo by Dr. Douglas Sadecky)

Bedford TK Tipper Truck, 1968-72, Bedford, red cab and chassis w/yellow or silver tipper, side mirrors, Model No. 494-A
EX $26   NM $39   MIP $65

Berliet Fruehauf Dumper, 1974-76, Berliet, yellow cab, fenders and dumper; black cab and semi chassis; plastic orange or dark orange dumper body; black interior, Model No. 1102-B
EX $30   NM $45   MIP $75

Caterpillar Tractor, 1960-64, Caterpillar, lime green body w/black or gray rubber treads, gray plastic seat, driver figure, controls, stacks, Model No. 1103-B
EX $70   NM $105   MIP $250

ERF 64G Earth Dumper, 1958-67, ERF, red cab, yellow tipper, clear windows, unpainted hydraulic cylinder, spare tire, smooth wheels, rubber tires, Model No. 458-A
EX $30   NM $45   MIP $85

Euclid Caterpillar Tractor, 1960-63, TC-12 lime green body w/black or pale gray rubber treads, gray plastic seat, driver figure, controls, stacks, silver grille, painted blue engine sides and Euclid decals, Model No. 1103-A
EX $50   NM $100   MIP $190

Euclid TC-12 Bulldozer, 1958-62, lime green body w/black or pale gray treads, silver blade surface, gray plastic seat, controls, and stacks; silver grille and lights, painted blue engine sides, black sheet metal base, rubber treads and Euclid decals, Model No. 1102-A
EX $80   NM $120   MIP $225

Euclid TC-12 Bulldozer, 1963-66, yellow or pale lime-green body, metal control rod, driver, black rubber treads, Model No. 1107-A
EX $80   NM $120   MIP $200

Ford Transit Tipper, 1983, Ford, orange cab and chassis, tan tipper, chrome wheels, Model No. 1121-B
EX $10   NM $15   MIP $25

Giant Tower Crane, 1981-82, white body, orange cab and chassis, Model No. 1154-B
EX $35   NM $50   MIP $85

Hyster 800 Stacatruck, 1977, Hyster, clear windows, black interior w/driver, Model No. 1113-B
EX $35   NM $50   MIP $85

JCB 110B Crawler Loader, 1976-80, white cab, yellow body, working red shovel, red interior w/driver, clear windows, black treads, JCB labels, Model No. 1110-B
EX $20   NM $30   MIP $50

Mack-Priestman Crane Truck, 1972-76, Mack, red truck, yellow crane cab, red interior, black engine, Hi Lift and Long Vehicle or Hi-Grab labels, Model No. 1154-A
EX $50   NM $75   MIP $125

Mercedes-Benz Unimog & Dumper, 1969-76, Mercedes-Benz, yellow cab and tipper, red fenders and tipper chassis, charcoal gray cab chassis, black plastic mirrors or without, Model No. 1145-A
EX $25   NM $35   MIP $60

Vehicles — Corgi

Priestman Cub Crane, 1972-74, orange body, red chassis and two-piece bucket, unpainted bucket arms, lower boom, knobs, gears and drum castings, clear window, Hi-Grab labels, Model No. 1153-A
EX $50   **NM** $75   **MIP** $125

(KP Photo by Dr. Douglas Sadecky)

Priestman Cub Power Shovel, 1963-76, orange upper body and panel, yellow lower body, lock rod and chassis, rubber or plastic treads, pulley panel, gray boom, w/figure of driver, Model No. 1128-A
EX $40   **NM** $60   **MIP** $100

Priestman Shovel and Carrier, 1963-72, No. 1128 cub shovel and No. 1131 low loader machinery carrier, Model No. 27-A
EX $90   **NM** $135   **MIP** $225

Raygo Rascal Roller, 1973-78, dark yellow body, base and mounting, green interior and engine, orange and silver roller mounting and castings, clear windshield, Model No. 459-B
EX $15   **NM** $25   **MIP** $45

Road Repair Unit, 1982, dark yellow Land Rover w/battery hatch and trailer w/red plastic interior w/sign and open panels, stripe and Roadwork labels, Model No. 1007-A
EX $15   **NM** $25   **MIP** $40

Scania Dump Truck, 1983, Scania, white cab w/green tipper, black/green Barratt labels, black exhaust and hydraulic cylinders, six-spoked Whizz Wheels, Model No. 1152-B
EX $7   **NM** $15   **MIP** $30

Scania Dump Truck, 1983, Scania, yellow truck and tipper w/black Wimpey labels, in two versions: either clear or green windows; six-spoked Whizz Wheels, Model No. 1153-B
EX $7   **NM** $15   **MIP** $30

Skyscraper Tower Crane, 1975-79, red body w/yellow chassis and booms, gold hook, gray loads of block, black/white Skyscraper labels, black tracks, Model No. 1155-A
EX $30   **NM** $45   **MIP** $75

Thwaites Tusker Skip Dumper, 1974-79, yellow body, chassis and tipper, driver and seat, hydraulic cylinder, red wheels, black tires two sizes, name labels, Whizz Wheels, Model No. 403-B
EX $10   **NM** $20   **MIP** $40

Unimog Dump Truck, 1971-73, Mercedes-Benz, first issue, blue cab, yellow tipper, fenders and bumpers, metallic charcoal gray chassis, red interior, black mirrors, gray tow hook, Model No. 409-B1
EX $20   **NM** $30   **MIP** $50

Unimog Dump Truck, 1976-77, Mercedes-Benz, second issue, yellow cab, chassis, rear frame and blue tipper, fenders and bumpers, red interior, no mirrors, gray tow hook, hydraulic cylinders, Model No. 409-B2
EX $20   **NM** $30   **MIP** $50

Unimog Dumper & Priestman Cub Shovel, 1971-73, Mercedes-Benz, standard colors, #1145 Mercedes-Benz unimog w/Dumper and 1128 Priestman Cub Shovel, Model No. 2-B
EX $70   **NM** $135   **MIP** $200

Volvo Concrete Mixer, 1977-81, Volvo, yellow or orange cab, red or white mixer w/yellow and black stripes, rear chassis, chrome chute and unpainted hitch casings, Model No. 1156-A
EX $30   **NM** $45   **MIP** $75

Warner & Swasey Crane, 1975-81, yellow cab and body, blue chassis, blue/yellow stripe labels, red interior, black steering wheel, silver knob, gold hook, Model No. 1101-B
EX $30   **NM** $45   **MIP** $75

EMERGENCY

AMC Pacer Rescue Car, 1978-80, AMC, chrome roll bars and red roof lights, white w/black engine hood; w/or without Secours decal, Model No. 484-B
EX $10   **NM** $15   **MIP** $30

(KP Photo by Dr. Douglas Sadecky)

American LaFrance Ladder Truck, 1968-81, American LaFrance, first issue: red cab, trailer, ladder rack and wheels; chrome decks and chassis, yellow plastic three-piece operable ladder, rubber tires, six firemen figures, issued 1968-70; second issue: same as first issue except for unpainted wheels, issued 1970-72; third issue: same as earlier issues except for white decks and chassis, silver wheels, plastic tires, issued 1973-81; later issues only had four firemen, Model No. 1143-A
EX $60   **NM** $90   **MIP** $150

(KP Photo by Dr. Douglas Sadecky)

Austin Police Mini Van, 1964-69, Austin, dark blue body w/policeman and dog figures, white police decals, opening rear doors, gray plastic antenna, Model No. 448-A
EX $50   **NM** $75   **MIP** $175

(KP Photo by Dr. Douglas Sadecky)

Bedford Fire Tender, 1956-61, Bedford, divided windshield, red or green body, each w/different decals, smooth or shaped hubs, Model No. 405-A
EX $60   **NM** $90   **MIP** $175

Bedford Fire Tender, 1960-62, Bedford, single windshield version, red body w/either black ladders and smooth wheels or unpainted ladders and shaped wheels, Model No. 423-A
EX $60   **NM** $90   **MIP** $150

Bedford Fire Tender-Mechanical, 1956-59, Bedford, friction motor, red body w/Fire Dept. decals, divided windshield, silver or black ladder, smooth or shaped hubs, Model No. 405M
EX $70   **NM** $115   **MIP** $185

(KP Photo by Dr. Douglas Sadecky)

Bedford Utilecon Ambulance, 1957-60, Bedford, divided windshield, cream body w/red/white/blue decals, smooth wheels, Model No. 412-A
EX $50   **NM** $75   **MIP** $125

Belgian Police Range Rover, 1976-77, white body, working doors, red interior, Belgian Police decal; includes policeman, Emergency signs, Model No. 483-B
EX $22   **NM** $33   **MIP** $55

Bell Rescue Helicopter, 1976-80, Bell, two-piece blue body w/working doors, red interior, yellow plastic floats, black rotors, white N428 decals, Model No. 924-A
EX $20   **NM** $30   **MIP** $50

Buick Police Car, 1977-78, Buick, metallic blue body w/white stripes and Police decals, chrome light bar w/red lights, orange taillights, chrome spoke wheels, w/two policemen, Model No. 416-B
EX $18   **NM** $27   **MIP** $45

610

(KP Photo by Dr. Douglas Sadecky)

Cadillac Superior Ambulance, 1962-68, Cadillac, battery-operated warning lights, red lower/cream upper body or white lower body/blue upper body, Model No. 437-A

EX $60　　**NM** $90　　**MIP** $150

Canadian Mounted Police Set, 1978-80, Land Rover, blue No. 421 Land Rover w/Police sign on roof and RCMP decals, No. 102 trailer; includes mounted Policeman, Model No. 45-B

EX $30　　**NM** $50　　**MIP** $100

Chevrolet Caprice Fire Chief Car, 1982, Chevrolet, red body, red-white-orange decals, chrome roof bar, opaque black windows, red dome light, chrome bumpers, grille and headlights, orange taillights, Fire Dept. and Fire Chief decals, chrome wheels; includes working siren and dome light, Model No. 1008-A

EX $28　　**NM** $42　　**MIP** $70

Chevrolet Caprice Police Car, 1980-81, Chevrolet, black body w/white roof, doors and trunk, red interior, silver light bar, Police decals, Model No. 326-A

EX $20　　**NM** $30　　**MIP** $50

Chevrolet Impala Fire Chief Car, 1963-65, Chevrolet, red body, yellow interior, w/four white doors, w/round either shield or rectangular decals on two doors; includes two fireman, Model No. 439-A

EX $55　　**NM** $80　　**MIP** $130

(KP Photo by Dr. Douglas Sadecky)

Chevrolet Impala Fire Chief Car, 1965-69, Chevrolet, w/Fire Chief decal on hood, yellow interior w/driver, red on white body w/either round or rectangular "Fire Chief" decals on doors, spun or cast spoked wheels, Model No. 482-A

EX $55　　**NM** $80　　**MIP** $130

(KP Photo by Dr. Douglas Sadecky)

Chevrolet Impala Police Car, 1965-69, Chevrolet, black lower body and roof, white upper body, yellow interior w/two policemen, Police and Police Patrol decals on doors and hood, Model No. 481-A

EX $55　　**NM** $80　　**MIP** $130

Chevrolet State Patrol Car, 1959-61, Chevrolet, black body, State Patrol decals, smooth wheels w/hexagonal panel or raised lines and shaped wheels, yellow plastic interior, gray antenna, clear windows, silver bumpers, grille, headlights and trim, rubber tires, Model No. 223-A

EX $50　　**NM** $75　　**MIP** $125

Chevrolet Superior Ambulance, 1978-80, Chevrolet, white body, orange roof and stripes, two working doors, clear windows, red interior w/patient on stretcher and attendant, Red Cross decals, Model No. 405-B

EX $30　　**NM** $45　　**MIP** $75

Chopper Squad Helicopter, 1978-79, blue and white body, Sure Rescue decals, Model No. 927-A

EX $20　　**NM** $30　　**MIP** $50

Chopper Squad Rescue Set, 1978-79, blue No. 919 Jeep w/Chopper Squad decal and red/white boat w/Surf Rescue decal, No. 927 Helicopter, Model No. 35-B

EX $40　　**NM** $60　　**MIP** $100

Chubb Pathfinder Crash Tender, 1981-83, red body, Emergency Unit decals, working water pump, Model No. 1118-B

EX $45　　**NM** $65　　**MIP** $110

Chubb Pathfinder Crash Truck, 1974-80, red body w/either "Airport Fire Brigade" or "New York Airport" decals, upper and lower body, gold water cannon unpainted and sirens, clear windshield, yellow interior, black steering wheel, chrome plastic deck, silver lights; w/working pump and siren, Model No. 1103-B

EX $60　　**NM** $90　　**MIP** $150

(KP Photo by Dr. Douglas Sadecky)

Citroen Alpine Rescue Safari, 1970-72, Citroen, white body, light blue interior, red roof and rear hatch, yellow roof rack and skis, clear windshield, man and dog, gold die-cast bobsled, Alpine Rescue decals, Model No. 513-A

EX $80　　**NM** $150　　**MIP** $375

Coast Guard Jaguar XJ12C, 1975-77, Jaguar, blue and white body, Coast Guard labels, Model No. 414-B

EX $18　　**NM** $27　　**MIP** $45

(KP Photo by Dr. Douglas Sadecky)

Commer 3/4 Ton Police Van, 1963-68, Commer, battery operated working dome light, in several color combinations of dark or light metallic blue or green bodies, various foreign issues. The van on the left has "County Police" labels, horizontal cast bars on the rear side windows, and a metallic blue paint finish. The van on the right has an embossed "Police" logo cast in the sides, vertical lines on the rear side windows, and a dark blue paint finish. Both models have a battery-operated flashing roof light, Model No. 464-A

EX $45　　**NM** $65　　**MIP** $120

(KP Photo by Dr. Douglas Sadecky)

Commer 3/4-Ton Ambulance, 1964-66, Commer, in either white or cream body, red interior, blue dome light, red Ambulance decals, shaped wheels, Model No. 463-A

EX $36　　**NM** $55　　**MIP** $90

Emergency Set, 1976-77, three-vehicle set w/figures and accessories, No. 402 Ford Cortina Police car, No. 921 Police Helicopter, No. 481 Range Rover Ambulance, Model No. 18-B

EX $40　　**NM** $60　　**MIP** $100

Emergency Set, 1979-81, No. 339 Land Rover Police Car and No. 921 Police Helicopter w/figures and accessories, Model No. 19-C

EX $30　　**NM** $50　　**MIP** $80

Fire Bug, 1972-73, orange body, Whizz Wheels, Model No. 395-A

EX $20　　**NM** $30　　**MIP** $50

Ford Cortina Police Car, 1972-76, Ford, white body, red or pink and black stripe labels, red interior, folding seats, blue dome light, clear windows, chrome bumpers, Police labels, opening doors, Model No. 402-A

EX $15　　**NM** $25　　**MIP** $45

Ford Escort Police Car, 1982, Ford, blue body and base, tan interior, white doors, blue dome lights, red Police labels, black grille and bumpers, Model No. 297-A

EX $8　　**NM** $15　　**MIP** $30

(KP Photo by Dr. Douglas Sadecky)

Ford Zephyr Patrol Car, 1960-65, Ford, white or cream body, blue and white Police red interior, blue dome light, silver bumpers. The car on the left has the common "Police" label, the car on the right, 419-A2, has the rare Dutch "Politie" label on the hood, Model No. 419-A1
| EX $35 | NM $50 | MIP $85 |

Ford Zephyr Patrol Car, 1960-65, Ford, white or cream body, blue and white Politie/Rijkspolitie decals, red interior, blue dome light, silver bumpers; import, rare, Model No. 419-A2
| EX $70 | NM $165 | MIP $275 |

German Life Saving Set, 1980-82, red/white No. 421 Land Rover and lifeboat, white trailer, German labels, Model No. 33-B
| EX $30 | NM $45 | MIP $75 |

HGB-Angus Firestreak, 1980, chrome plastic spotlight and ladders, black hose reel, red dome light, white water cannon, in two interior versions, electronic siren and lights, Model No. 1001-A
| EX $35 | NM $50 | MIP $85 |

Hi-Speed Fire Engine, 1975-78, red body, yellow plastic ladder, Model No. 703-A
| EX $16 | NM $24 | MIP $40 |

Hughes Police Helicopter, 1975-80, Hughes, red interior, dark blue rotors, in several international imprints, Netherlands, German, Swiss, in white or yellow, Model No. 921-A
| EX $20 | NM $30 | MIP $50 |

Jaguar 2.4 Litre Fire Chief's Car, 1959-61, Jaguar, red body w/unpainted roof signal/siren, red/white fire and shield decals on doors, in two versions, smooth or spun hubs, Model No. 213-A
| EX $60 | NM $90 | MIP $150 |

Jaguar XJ12C Police Car, 1978-80, Jaguar, white body w/blue and pink stripes, light bar w/blue dome light, tan interior, police labels, Model No. 429-A
| EX $15 | NM $28 | MIP $45 |

Jet Ranger Police Helicopter, 1980, white body w/chrome interior, red floats and rotors, amber windows, Police labels, Model No. 931-A
| EX $25 | NM $40 | MIP $65 |

Mercedes-Benz Ambulance, 1980-81, Mercedes-Benz, four different foreign versions, white interior, opening rear and two doors, blue windows and dome lights, chrome bumpers, grille and headlights, various labels; accessories include two attendant figures, Model No. 406-C
| EX $15 | NM $20 | MIP $35 |

Mercedes-Benz Ambulance, 1981, Mercedes-Benz, white body and base, red stripes and taillights, Red Cross and black and white ambulance labels, open rear door, white interior, no figures, Model No. 407-B
| EX $15 | NM $20 | MIP $35 |

Mercedes-Benz Fire Chief, 1982-83, Mercedes-Benz, light red body, black base, tan plastic interior, blue dome light, white Notruf 112 labels, red taillights, no tow hook, German export model, Model No. 284-B
| EX $15 | NM $25 | MIP $40 |

Mercedes-Benz Police Car, 1975-80, Mercedes-Benz, white body w/two different hood versions, brown interior, polizei or police lettering, blue dome light, Model No. 412-B
| EX $15 | NM $18 | MIP $30 |

Metropolis Police Car, 1979-81, metallic blue body, off white interior, white roof/stripes, two working doors, clear windows, chrome bumpers, grille and headlights, two roof light bars, City of Metropolis labels, Model No. 260-B
| EX $20 | NM $30 | MIP $50 |

Motorway Ambulance, 1973-79, white body, dark blue interior, red-white-black Accident and Red Cross labels, dark blue windows, clear headlights, red die-cast base and bumpers, Model No. 700-A
| EX $10 | NM $15 | MIP $30 |

(KP Photo by Dr. Douglas Sadecky)

Oldsmobile Sheriff's Car, 1962-66, Oldsmobile, black upper body w/white sides, red interior w/red dome light and County Sheriff decals on doors, single body casting, Model No. 237-A
| EX $50 | NM $75 | MIP $125 |

Police Land Rover, 1981, Land Rover, white body, red and blue police stripes, black lettering, open rear door, opaque black windows, blue dome light, working roof light and siren, Model No. 1005-A
| EX $15 | NM $25 | MIP $50 |

Police Land Rover and Horse Box, 1978-80, Land Rover, white No. 421 Land Rover w/police labels and mounted policeman, No. 112 Horse Box, Model No. 44-A
| EX $30 | NM $45 | MIP $75 |

Police Vigilant Range Rover, 1972-79, Land Rover, white body, red interior, black shutters, blue dome light, two chrome and amber spotlights, black grille, silver headlights, Police labels, w/police figure, Model No. 461-A
| EX $25 | NM $35 | MIP $60 |

Porsche 924 Police Car, 1978-80, Porsche, white body w/different hood and door color versions, blue and chrome light, Polizei white on green panels or Police labels, "1" or "20" labels, Model No. 430-B
| EX $15 | NM $25 | MIP $40 |

Porsche Targa Police Car, 1970-75, Porsche, white body and base, red doors and hood, black roof and plastic interior also comes w/an orange interior, unpainted siren, Polizei labels, Model No. 509-A
| EX $25 | NM $35 | MIP $60 |

Range Rover Ambulance, 1975-77, Land Rover, two different versions of body sides, red interior, raised roof, open upper and lower doors, black shutters, blue dome light, Ambulance label; includes stretcher and two ambulance attendants, Model No. 482-B
| EX $20 | NM $30 | MIP $50 |

Renault 5 Police Car, 1978-79, Renault, white body, red interior, blue dome light, black hood, hatch and doors w/white Police labels, orange taillights, aerial, Model No. 428-B
| EX $15 | NM $20 | MIP $35 |

Renault 5TS, 1977-80, Renault, metallic golden orange body, black trim, tan plastic interior, working hatch and two doors, clear windows and headlights, Model No. 293-A
| EX $15 | NM $18 | MIP $30 |

Renault 5TS Fire Chief, 1982, Renault, red body, tan interior, amber headlights, gray antenna, black/white Sapeurs Pompiers labels, blue dome light, French export issue, Model No. 295-A
| EX $15 | NM $25 | MIP $40 |

Riley Pathfinder Police Car, 1958-61, Riley, black body w/blue/white Police lettering, unpainted roof sign, gray antenna, Model No. 209-A
| EX $50 | NM $75 | MIP $135 |

Riot Police Quad Tractor, 1977-80, white body and chassis, brown interior, red roof w/white panel, gold water cannons, gold spotlight w/amber lens, Riot Police and No. 6 labels, Model No. 422-B
| EX $15 | NM $20 | MIP $35 |

Rover 3500 Police Car, 1980, Rover, white body, light red interior, red stripes, white plastic roof sign, blue dome light, red and blue Police and badge label, Model No. 339-B
| EX $8 | NM $15 | MIP $25 |

Sikorsky Skycrane Casualty Helicopter,
1975-78, Sikorsky, red and white body, black rotors and wheels, orange pipes, working rear hatch, Red Cross decals, Model No. 922-A
EX $15   **NM** $20   **MIP** $40

Simon Snorkel Fire Engine, 1964-76, red body w/yellow interior, two snorkel arms, rotating base, five firemen in cab and one in basket, three styles of wheels, Model No. 1127-A
EX $35   **NM** $55   **MIP** $100

Simon Snorkel Fire Engine, 1977-81, red body w/yellow interior, blue windows and dome lights, chrome deck, black hose reels and hydraulic cylinders, Model No. 1126-B
EX $30   **NM** $45   **MIP** $75

(KP Photo by Dr. Douglas Sadecky)

Sunbeam Imp Police Car, 1968-72, three versions, white or light blue body, tan interior, driver, black or white hood and lower doors, dome light, Police decals, cast spoked wheels. Shown here are two color and box variations, Model No. 506-A
EX $25   **NM** $45   **MIP** $85

Volkswagen 1200, 1970-76, Volkswagen, seven different color and label versions, plastic interior, one-piece body, silver headlights, red taillights, die-cast base and bumpers, Model No. 383-A2
EX $20   **NM** $45   **MIP** $85

Volkswagen 1200, 1970-76, Volkswagen, dark yellow body, white roof, red interior and dome light, unpainted base and bumpers, black and white ADAC Strassenwacht labels, Whizz Wheels, Model No. 383-A1
EX $60   **NM** $90   **MIP** $150

(KP Photo by Dr. Douglas Sadecky)

Volkswagen 1200 Police Car, 1966-69, Volkswagen, two different body versions made for Germany, Netherlands and Switzerland, blue dome light in chrome collar, Polizei or Politie decals. Note the opening hood and trunk on this attractive car. The front wheels turn via the roof warning light, Model No. 492-A
EX $40   **NM** $60   **MIP** $100

Volkswagen Police Car/Foreign Issues,
1970-76, Volkswagen, five different versions, one-piece body, red interior, dome light, silver headlights, red taillights, clear windows, Whizz Wheels, Model No. 373-A
EX $60   **NM** $90   **MIP** $150

Volkswagen Polo Police Car, 1976-80, Volkswagen, white body, green hood and doors, black dash, silver bumpers, grille and headlights, white roof, blue dome light, Model No. 489-A1
EX $15   **NM** $25   **MIP** $40

JEEP

Golden Eagle Jeep, 1979-82, Jeep, tan and brown or white and gold body, tan plastic top, chrome plastic base, bumpers and steps, chrome wheels, Model No. 441-B
EX $8   **NM** $15   **MIP** $25

Jeep & Horse Box, 1981-83, Jeep, metallic painted No. 441 Jeep and No. 112 trailer; accessories include girl on pony, three jumps and three hay bales, Model No. 29-C
EX $15   **NM** $30   **MIP** $50

Jeep and Motorcycle Trailer, 1982-83, Jeep, red working No. 441 Jeep w/two blue/ yellow bikes on trailer, Model No. 10-C
EX $15   **NM** $20   **MIP** $40

Jeep CJ-5, 1977-79, Jeep, dark metallic green body, removable white top, white plastic wheels, spare tire, Model No. 419-B
EX $8   **NM** $15   **MIP** $30

(KP Photo by Dr. Douglas Sadecky)

Jeep FC-150 Covered Truck, 1965-72, Jeep, four versions: blue body, rubber tires (1965-67); yellow/brown body; rubber tires w/spun hubs (1965-67); blue or yellow/brown body, plastic tires w/cast spoked hubs. The two major color and wheel variations are pictured here, Model No. 470-A
EX $30   **NM** $45   **MIP** $75

Jeep FC-150 Pickup, 1959-65, Jeep, blue body, clear windows, sheet metal tow hook, in two wheel versions: smooth or shaped wheels, Model No. 409-A
EX $35   **NM** $55   **MIP** $90

(KP Photo by Dr. Douglas Sadecky)

Jeep FC-150 Tower Wagon, 1965-69, Jeep, metallic green body, yellow interior and basket w/workman figure, clear windows, w/either rubber or plastic tires. This was the updated version of the previously released GS14-A which had a red Jeep, smooth wheels and a lamp post, Model No. 478-A
EX $40   **NM** $60   **MIP** $100

Off Road Set, 1983, Jeep, No. 5 label on No. 447 Jeep, blue boat, trailer, Model No. 36-C
EX $15   **NM** $20   **MIP** $45

Renegade Jeep, 1983, Jeep, dark blue body w/no top, white interior, base and bumper, white plastic wheels and rear mounted spare, Model No. 447-B
EX $8   **NM** $15   **MIP** $25

Renegade Jeep with Hood, 1983, Jeep, yellow body w/removable hood, red interior, base, bumper, white plastic wheels, side mounted spare, No. 8, Model No. 448-B
EX $8   **NM** $15   **MIP** $25

Tower Wagon and Lamp Standard, 1961-65, Jeep, red No. 409 Jeep Tower wagon w/yellow basket, workman figure and lamp post, Model No. 14-A
EX $40   **NM** $70   **MIP** $140

LAND ROVER

(KP Photo by Dr. Douglas Sadecky)

Land Rover 109 WB Pickup, 1957-62, Land Rover, yellow, green or metallic blue body, spare wheel on hood, clear windows, sheet metal tow hook, smooth hubs, rubber tires, Model No. 406-A
EX $45   **NM** $70   **MIP** $100

Land Rover 109WB, 1977-79, Land Rover, working rear doors, tan interior, spare wheel on hood, plastic tow hook, Model No. 421-B
EX $15   **NM** $18   **MIP** $30

Land Rover Breakdown Truck, 1960-65, Land Rover, red body w/silver boom and yellow canopy, revolving spotlight, Breakdown Service labels, Model No. 417-A
EX $35   **NM** $55   **MIP** $90

Land Rover Breakdown Truck, 1965-77, Land Rover, red body, yellow canopy, chrome revolving spotlight, Breakdown Service labels, shaped hubs or Whizz Wheels, Model No. 477-A
EX $25   **NM** $35   **MIP** $70

Land Rover with Canopy, 1963-77, Land Rover, long, one-piece body w/clear windows, plastic interior, spare wheel on hood, issued in numerous colors, Model No. 438-A

EX $35 **NM** $55 **MIP** $90

(KP Photo by Dr. Douglas Sadecky)

Public Address Land Rover, 1964-66, Land Rover, green No. 438 Land Rover body, yellow plastic rear body and loud-speakers, red interior, clear windows, silver bumper, grille and headlights; includes figure w/microphone and girl figure w/pamphlets, Model No. 472-A

EX $50 **NM** $75 **MIP** $145

(KP Photo by Dr. Douglas Sadecky)

RAC Land Rover, 1959-64, Land Rover, light or dark blue body, plastic interior and rear cover, gray antenna, RAC and Radio Rescue decals, Model No. 416-A

EX $60 **NM** $90 **MIP** $150

Safari Land Rover and Trailer, 1976-80, Land Rover, black and white No. 341 Land Rover in two versions: w/chrome wheels, 1976; w/red wheels, 1977-80; came w/Warden and Lion figures, Model No. 31-B

EX $20 **NM** $30 **MIP** $60

LARGE TRUCK

Bedford Car Transporter, 1957, first issue, Bedford, black die-cast cab base w/blue "S" cab, yellow semi trailer, blue letter-ing decals, RARE, Model No. 1101-A1

EX $100 **NM** $200 **MIP** $350

Bedford Car Transporter, 1957-62, sec-ond issue, Bedford, red cab, pale green upper and blue lower semi-trailer, white decals, working ramps, clear wind-shield, Model No. 1101-A2

EX $70 **NM** $105 **MIP** $175

Bedford Car Transporter, 1962-66, Bed-ford, red "TK" cab w/blue lower and light green upper trailer, working ramp, yel-low interior, clear windows, white letter-ing and Corgi dog decals, Model No. 1105-A

EX $60 **NM** $90 **MIP** $150

(KP Photo by Dr. Douglas Sadecky)

Bedford Carrimore Low Loader, 1958-62, Bedford, red or yellow "S" cab, metallic blue semi trailer and tailgate; smooth and/or shaped wheels, Model No. 1100-A

EX $60 **NM** $90 **MIP** $150

(KP Photo by Dr. Douglas Sadecky)

Bedford Carrimore Low Loader, 1963-65, Bedford, yellow "TK" cab, red trailer with working ramp, clear windows, red inte-rior, suspension, shaped wheels, rubber tires, Model No. 1132-A

EX $90 **NM** $225 **MIP** $350

(KP Photo by Dr. Douglas Sadecky)

Bedford Milk Tanker, 1962-65, Bedford, light blue "S" cab and lower semi, white upper tank, w/blue/white milk decals, shaped wheels, rubber tires, Model No. 1129-A

EX $100 **NM** $150 **MIP** $275

Bedford Milk Tanker, 1966-67, Bedford, light blue "TK" cab and lower semi, white upper tank w/blue/white milk decals, Model No. 1141-A

EX $110 **NM** $165 **MIP** $375

(KP Photo by Dr. Douglas Sadecky)

Bedford Mobilgas Tanker, 1959-65, Bed-ford, red "S" cab and tanker w/Mobilgas decals, shaped wheels, rubber tires, Model No. 1110-A

EX $100 **NM** $150 **MIP** $250

Bedford Mobilgas Tanker, 1965-66, Bed-ford, red "TK" cab and tanker w/red, white and blue Mobilgas decals, shaped wheels, rubber tires, Model No. 1140-A

EX $100 **NM** $175 **MIP** $350

Bedford Tanker, 1983, Bedford, red cab w/black chassis, plastic tank w/chrome catwalk, Corgi Chemco decals, Model No. 1130-B

EX $15 **NM** $20 **MIP** $35

Berliet Container Truck, 1978, Berliet, blue cab and semi fenders; white cab chassis and semi flatbed; each w/United States Lines label, Model No. 1107-B

EX $30 **NM** $45 **MIP** $75

Berliet Dolphinarium Truck, 1980-83, Berliet, yellow and blue cab and trailer, clear plastic tank; includes two dolphins and a girl trainer, Model No. 1164-A

EX $56 **NM** $84 **MIP** $175

Berliet Holmes Wrecker, 1975-78, Berliet, red cab and bed, blue rear body, white chassis, black interior, two gold booms and hooks, yellow dome light, driver, amber lenses and red/white/blue stripes, Model No. 1144-B

EX $30 **NM** $45 **MIP** $75

BL Roadtrain and Trailers, 1981, white and orange cab, dark blue freighter semi body w/Yorkie Chocolate labels and tanker semi body w/Gulf label; includes playmat, Model No. 1002-A

EX $16 **NM** $24 **MIP** $40

Car Transporter & Cars, 1970-73, Scam-mell, Scammell tri-deck transporter w/six cars: Ford Capri, the Saint's Volvo, Pontiac Firebird, Lancia Fulvia, MGC GT, Marcos 3 Litre, each w/Whizz Wheels; value is for complete set, Model No. 20-B

EX $200 **NM** $400 **MIP** $900

Car Transporter and Four Cars, 1963-66, two versions: No. 1105 Bedford TK Transporter w/Fiat 1800, Renault Floride, Mercedes 230SE and Ford Consul, 1963-65; No. 1105 Bedford TK Transporter w/Chevy Corvair, VW Ghia, Volvo P-1800 and Rover 2000, 1966 only; value is for each individual complete set, Model No. 28-A

EX $200 **NM** $300 **MIP** $700

Carrimore Car Transporter and Cars, 1966, Ford, Ford "H" series Transporter and six cars; there are several car variations; sold by mail order only, Model No. 41-A

EX $240 **NM** $360 **MIP** $700

Carrimore Car Transporter and Four Cars,
1957-62, Bedford, three versions: No.
1101 Bedford Carrimore Transporter
w/Riley, Jaguar, Austin Healey and Triumph, 1957-60; No. 1101 Bedford Carrimore Transporter w/four American
cars, 1959; No. 1101 Bedford Carrimore
Transporter w/Triumph, Mini, Citroen
and Plymouth, 1961-62; value is for
individual complete sets, Model No. 1-A
EX $300   **NM** $450   **MIP** $800

(KP Photo by Dr. Douglas Sadecky)

Ecurie Ecosse Transporter, 1961-65, in
dark blue body w/either blue or yellow
lettering, or light blue body w/red or yellow lettering, working tailgate and sliding door, yellow interior, shaped wheels,
rubber tires, Model No. 1126-A
EX $70   **NM** $105   **MIP** $225

Ford Aral Tank Truck, 1977-80, Ford, light
blue cab and chassis, white tanker body,
Aral labels, Model No. 1161-A
EX $20   **NM** $30   **MIP** $50

Ford Car Transporter, 1976-79, Ford,
metallic lime green or metallic cab and
semi, cream cab chassis, deck and
ramp, Model No. 1159-A
EX $20   **NM** $30   **MIP** $60

Ford Car Transporter, 1982, Ford, white
cab, red chassis and trailer, white labels
and ramps, Model No. 1170-A
EX $20   **NM** $30   **MIP** $50

Ford Covered Semi-Trailer, 1979-80,
Ford, blue cab and trailer, black cab
chassis and trailer fenders, yellow covers, Model No. 1109-B
EX $15   **NM** $25   **MIP** $50

Ford Esso Tank Truck, 1976-81, Ford,
white cab and tank, red tanker chassis
and fenders, chrome wheels, Esso
labels, Model No. 1157-A
EX $15   **NM** $30   **MIP** $60

Ford Express Semi-Trailer, 1965-70,
Ford, metallic blue cab and trailer, silver
roof on trailer, chrome doors marked
"Express Service," shaped or detailed
cast wheels, Model No. 1137-A
EX $60   **NM** $110   **MIP** $225

Ford Exxon Tank Truck, 1976-81, Ford,
white cab and tank, red tanker chassis
and fenders, chrome wheels, Exxon
labels, Model No. 1158-A
EX $15   **NM** $30   **MIP** $60

Ford Guinness Tanker, 1982, Ford,
orange, tan, black cab, tan tanker body,
Guinness labels, Model No. 1169-A
EX $20   **NM** $30   **MIP** $50

Ford Gulf Tank Truck, 1976-78, Ford,
white cab w/orange chassis, blue tanker
body, Gulf labels, chrome wheels,
Model No. 1160-A
EX $15   **NM** $25   **MIP** $40

Ford Holmes Wrecker, 1967-74, Ford,
white upper cab, black roof, red rear
body and lower cab, mirrors, unpainted
or gold booms, Model No. 1142-A
EX $60   **NM** $90   **MIP** $200

Ford Michelin Container Truck, 1981,
Ford, blue cab and trailer, white cab
chassis and trailer fenders, yellow
containers; includes Michelin Man
figure, Model No. 1108-B
EX $15   **NM** $25   **MIP** $50

Ford Transit Wrecker, 1981, Ford, white
cab and rear body, red roof, silver bed,
"24-hour Service" labels, Model
No. 1140-B
EX $25   **NM** $35   **MIP** $60

Mack Container Truck, 1972-78, Mack,
yellow cab, red interior, white engine,
red suspension, white ACL labels,
Model No. 1106-B
EX $30   **NM** $50   **MIP** $80

Mack Esso Tank Truck, 1971-75, Mack,
white cab and tank w/Esso labels, red
tank chassis and fenders, Model
No. 1152-A
EX $20   **NM** $40   **MIP** $80

Mack Exxon Tank Truck, 1974-75, Mack,
white cab and tank, red tank chassis and
fenders, red interior, chrome catwalk,
Exxon labels, Model No. 1151-B
EX $15   **NM** $35   **MIP** $75

Mack Trans Continental Semi, 1971-73,
Mack, orange cab body and semi chas-
sis and fenders, metallic light blue semi
body, unpainted trailer rests, Model
No. 1100-B
EX $35   **NM** $55   **MIP** $90

Mercedes-Benz Refrigerator, 1983, Mercedes-Benz, yellow cab and tailgate, red
semi-trailer, two-piece lowering tailgate
and yellow spare wheel base, red interior, clear window, Model No. 1131-B
EX $15   **NM** $18   **MIP** $30

Mercedes-Benz Semi-Trailer, 1983,
Mercedes-Benz, red cab and trailer,
black chassis, Model No. 1144-C
EX $15   **NM** $18   **MIP** $30

Mercedes-Benz Semi-Trailer Van, 1983,
Mercedes-Benz, black cab and plastic
semi trailer, white chassis and air-
screen, red doors, red-blue and yellow
stripes, white Corgi lettering, Model
No. 1129-B
EX $15   **NM** $18   **MIP** $30

Mercedes-Benz Tanker, 1983, Mercedes-
Benz, two different versions, white cab
and tank, green chassis, chrome or
black plastic catwalk, red/white/green 7-
Up labels or Corgi Chemo labels, Model
No. 1167-A
EX $15   **NM** $18   **MIP** $30

Mercedes-Benz Tanker, 1983, Mercedes-
Benz, tan cab, plastic tank body, black
chassis, black and red Guinness labels,
w/chrome or black plastic catwalk, clear
windows, Model No. 1166-A
EX $15   **NM** $18   **MIP** $30

**Scammell Carrimore Tri-deck Car Trans-
porter,** 1970-73, Scammell, orange lower
cab, chassis and lower deck, white upper
cab and middle deck, blue top deck, red
interior, black hydraulic cylinders, detachable rear ramp, Model No. 1146-A
EX $35   **NM** $60   **MIP** $130

Scammell Coop Semi-Trailer Truck,
1970, Scammell, white cab and trailer
fenders, light blue semi-trailer, red interior, gray bumper base, jewel headlights, black hitch lever, spare wheel,
Model No. 1151-A
EX $135   **NM** $210   **MIP** $350

**Scammell Ferrymasters Semi-Trailer
Truck,** 1969-72, Scammell, white cab,
red interior, yellow chassis, black fenders, clear windows, jewel headlights,
cast step-hub wheels, plastic tires,
Model No. 1147-A
EX $60   **NM** $90   **MIP** $150

Scania Bulk Carrier, 1983, Scania, white
cab, blue and white silos, ladders and catwalk, amber windows, blue British Sugar
labels, Whizz Wheels, Model No. 1150-B
EX $7   **NM** $15   **MIP** $30

Scania Bulk Carrier, 1983, Scania, white
cab, orange and white silos, clear win-
dows, orange screen, black/orange
Spillers Flour labels, Whizz Wheels,
Model No. 1151-C
EX $7   **NM** $15   **MIP** $30

Scania Container Truck, 1983, Scania,
yellow truck and box w/red Ryder Truck
rental labels, clear windows, black
exhaust stack, red rear doors, six-spoke
Whizz Wheels, Model No. 1147-B
EX $7   **NM** $15   **MIP** $30

Scania Container Truck, 1983, Scania,
blue cab w/blue and white box and rear
doors, white deck, Securicor Parcels
labels, in red or white rear door colors,
Model No. 1148-B
EX $7   **NM** $15   **MIP** $30

Scania Container Truck, 1983, Scania,
white cab and box w/BRS Truck Rental
labels, blue windows, red screen, roof
and rear doors, Model No. 1149-A
EX $7   **NM** $15   **MIP** $30

Transporter & Six Cars, 1970-73, Scam-
mell, Scammell transporter w/six cars:
No. 180 Mini DeLuxe, No. 204 Mini, No.
339 Mini Rally, No. 201 The Saint's
Volvo, No. 340 Sunbeam Imp, No. 378
MGC GT; includes bag of cones and
leaflet, Model No. 48-B
EX $250   **NM** $450   **MIP** $900

(KP Photo by Dr. Douglas Sadecky)

Transporter and Six Cars, 1966-69, Ford, first issue: No. 1138 Ford 'H' Series Transporter w/six cars, No. 252 Rover 2000, blue No. 251 Hillman Imp, No. 440 Ford Cortina Estate, No. 180 Mini w/'wickerwork', metallic maroon No. 204 Mini, and No. 321 Mini Rally ('1966 Monte Carlo Rally') racing No. 2; second issue: same as first issue except No. 251 Hillman is metallic gold, No. 204 Mini is blue, No. 321 Mini is substituted for No. 333 SUN/RAC Rally Mini w/autographs on roof. The Car Transporter gift sets were a good way for Corgi to get rid of their excess stock of automobile models, Model No. 48-A
EX $225　　**NM** $365　　**MIP** $700

MILITARY

AMX 30D Recovery Tank, 1976-80, olive body w/black plastic turret and gun, accessories and three figures, Model No. 908-A
EX $35　　**NM** $50　　**MIP** $80

Army Heavy Equipment Transporter, 1964-65, olive cab and trailer w/white U.S. Army decals w/red or yellow interior and driver, Model No. 1135-A
EX $70　　**NM** $105　　**MIP** $325

Army Troop Transporter, 1964-65, olive w/white U.S. Army decals, Model No. 1133-A
EX $70　　**NM** $105　　**MIP** $175

(KP Photo by Dr. Douglas Sadecky)

Bedford Army Fuel Tanker, 1964-65, Bedford, olive cab and tanker, w/white "U.S. Army" and "No Smoking" decals, Model No. 1134-A
EX $140　　**NM** $210　　**MIP** $375

Bedford Military Ambulance, 1961-64, Bedford, clear front and white rear windows, olive body w/Red Cross decals, w/or without suspension, Model No. 414-A
EX $56　　**NM** $84　　**MIP** $140

Bell Army Helicopter, 1975-80, Bell, two-piece olive/tan camouflage body, clear canopy, olive green rotors, U.S. Army decals, Model No. 920-A
EX $24　　**NM** $36　　**MIP** $60

Bloodhound Launching Ramp, 1959-62, military green ramp, Model No. 1116-A
EX $34　　**NM** $51　　**MIP** $85

Bloodhound Loading Trolley, 1959-62, military green working lift, red rubber nose cone, Model No. 1117-A
EX $40　　**NM** $60　　**MIP** $100

Bloodhound Missile, 1959-62, white and yellow missile, red rubber nose cone, Model No. 1115-A
EX $70　　**NM** $105　　**MIP** $175

(KP Photo by Dr. Douglas Sadecky)

Bloodhound Missile and Launching Platform, 1958-61, white and yellow missile, red rubber nose cone; military green ramp, Model No. 1108-A
EX $110　　**NM** $165　　**MIP** $275

Bloodhound Missile on Trolley, 1959-62, white and yellow missile, red rubber nose cone; military green trolley, rubber tires, Model No. 1109-A
EX $120　　**NM** $180　　**MIP** $300

Centurion Mark III Tank, 1974-78, tan and brown camouflage or olive drab body, rubber tracks; includes twelve shells, Model No. 901-A
EX $30　　**NM** $45　　**MIP** $75

Centurion Tank and Transporter, 1973-78, No. 901 olive tank and No. 1100 transporter, Model No. 10-B
EX $55　　**NM** $80　　**MIP** $130

Chieftain Medium Tank, 1974-80, olive drab body, black tracks, Union Jack labels; includes twelve shells, Model No. 903-A
EX $30　　**NM** $45　　**MIP** $75

Commer Military Ambulance, 1964-66, Commer, olive drab body, blue rear windows and dome light, driver, Red Cross decals, Model No. 354-A
EX $50　　**NM** $75　　**MIP** $125

Commer Military Police Van, 1964-65, Commer, olive drab body, barred rear windows, white MP decals, driver, Model No. 355-A
EX $55　　**NM** $80　　**MIP** $130

(KP Photo by Dr. Douglas Sadecky)

Corporal Missile & Erector Vehicle, 1959-62, white missile, red rubber-nose cone, olive green body on erector body, Model No. 1113-A
EX $240　　**NM** $360　　**MIP** $600

Corporal Missile Launching Ramp, 1960-61, sold in temporary pack, Model No. 1124-A
EX $36　　**NM** $55　　**MIP** $90

Corporal Missile on Launching Ramp, 1959-62, white missile, red rubber-nose cone, Model No. 1112-A
EX $80　　**NM** $120　　**MIP** $200

Corporal Missile Set, 1959-62, No. 1112 missile and No. 1113 ramp, erector vehicle and No. 1118 army truck, Model No. 9-A
EX $340　　**NM** $510　　**MIP** $850

Decca Airfield Radar Van, 1959-60, cream body w/four or five orange vertical bands, working rotating scanner and aerial, Model No. 1106-A
EX $120　　**NM** $180　　**MIP** $350

Decca Radar Scanner, 1959-60, w/either orange or custard colored scanner frame, silver scanner face, w/gear on base for turning scanner, Model No. 353-A
EX $34　　**NM** $51　　**MIP** $85

Half Track Rocket Launcher & Trailer, 1975-80, two rocket launchers and single trailer castings, gray plastic roll cage, man w/machine gun, front wheels and hubs, Model No. 907-A
EX $20　　**NM** $35　　**MIP** $55

International 6x6 Army Truck, 1959-63, International-Harvester, olive drab body w/clear windows, red/blue decals, six cast olive wheels w/rubber tires, Model No. 1118-A
EX $70　　**NM** $105　　**MIP** $225

(KP Photo by Dr. Douglas Sadecky)

Karrier Field Kitchen, 1964-66, Karrier, olive body, white decals, w/figure, Model No. 359-A
EX $60　　**NM** $90　　**MIP** $175

King Tiger Heavy Tank, 1974-78, tan and rust body, working turret and barrel, tan rollers and treads, German labels, Model No. 904-A
EX $30　　**NM** $45　　**MIP** $75

M60 A1 Medium Tank, 1974-80, green/tan camouflage body, working turret and barrel, green rollers, white decals, Model No. 902-A
EX $30   NM $45   MIP $75

Military Set, 1975-80, set of three, No. 904 Tiger tank, No. 920 Bell Helicopter, No. 906 Saladin Armored Car, Model No. 17-B
EX $60   NM $90   MIP $150

Oldsmobile 88 Staff Car, 1964-66, Oldsmobile, olive drab body, four figures, white decals, Model No. 358-A
EX $50   NM $75   MIP $125

RAF Land Rover, 1958-62, Land Rover, blue body and cover, sheet metal rear cover, RAF rondel label, w/or without suspension, silver bumper, Model No. 351-A
EX $60   NM $90   MIP $150

RAF Land Rover & Bloodhound, 1958-61, Land Rover, set of three standard colored, No, 351 RAF Land Rover, No. 1115 Bloodhound Missile, No. 1116 Ramp and No. 1117 Trolley, Model No. 4-A
EX $150   NM $300   MIP $600

RAF Land Rover and Thunderbird Missile, 1958-63, Standard colors, No. 350 Thunderbird Missile on Trolley and 351 RAF Land Rover, Model No. 3-A
EX $100   NM $150   MIP $300

Rocket Age Set, 1959-60, set of eight standard models including: No. 350 Thunderbird Missile on Trolley, No. 351 RAF Land Rover, No. 352 RAF Staff Car, No. 353 Radar Scanner, No. 1106 Decca Radar Van and No. 1108 Bloodhound missile w/ramp, Model No. 6-A
EX $325   NM $650   MIP $1400

Rocket Launcher and Trailer, 1975-80, steel blue and red launcher, fires rocket, Model No. 907-A
EX $25   NM $35   MIP $60

Saladin Armored Car, 1974-77, olive drab body, swiveling turret and raising barrel castings, black plastic barrel end and tires, olive cast wheels, w/twelve shells, fires shells, Model No. 906-A
EX $30   NM $45   MIP $75

Sikorsky Skycrane Army Helicopter, 1975-78, Sikorsky, olive drab and yellow body w/Red Cross and Army labels, Model No. 923-A
EX $15   NM $20   MIP $40

Standard Vanguard RAF Staff Car, 1958-62, Standard, blue body, RAF labels, Model No. 352-A
EX $55   NM $85   MIP $140

SU-100 Medium Tank, 1974-77, olive and cream camouflage upper body, gray lower, working hatch and barrel, black treads, red star and #103 labels; twelve shells included, fires shells, Model No. 905-A
EX $30   NM $50   MIP $80

Thunderbird Missile and Trolley, 1958-62, ice blue or silver missile, RAF blue trolley, red rubber nose cone, plastic tow bar, steering front and rear axles, Model No. 350-A
EX $55   NM $85   MIP $165

Tiger Mark I Tank, 1973-78, tan and green camouflage finish, German emblem, swiveling turret and raising barrel castings, black plastic barrel end, antenna; includes twelve shells, fires shells, Model No. 900-A
EX $30   NM $45   MIP $75

Tractor, Trailer and Field Gun, 1976-80, tan tractor body and chassis, trailer body, base and opening doors, gun chassis and raising barrel castings, brown plastic interior; twelve shells included, fires shells, Model No. 909-A
EX $30   NM $50   MIP $80

(KP Photo by Dr. Douglas Sadecky)

Volkswagen Military Personnel Carrier, 1964-66, Volkswagen, olive drab body, white decals, driver, Model No. 356-A
EX $55   NM $95   MIP $180

MISCELLANEOUS

Service Ramp, 1958-60, metallic blue and silver operable ramp, Model No. 1401-A
EX $30   NM $45   MIP $95

Shell or BP Garage Gift Set, 1963-65, gas station/garage w/pumps and other accessories including five different cars; in two versions: Shell or B.P., rare; value is for each set, Model No. 25-A
EX $295   NM $700   MIP $1500

Touring Caravan, 1975-79, white body w/blue trim, white plastic opening roof and door, pale blue interior, red plastic hitch and awning, Model No. 490-B
EX $15   NM $25   MIP $40

MOTORCYCLE

Cafe Racer Motorcycle, 1983, Model No. 173-A
EX $15   NM $18   MIP $30

Matra & Motorcycle Trailer, 1980-81, red No. 57 Talbot Matra Rancho w/two yellow and blue bikes on trailer, Model No. 25-C
EX $15   NM $20   MIP $35

Red Wheelie Motorcycle, 1982, red plastic body and fender w/black/white/yellow decals, black handlebars, kickstand and seat, chrome engine, pipes, flywheel-powered rear wheel, Model No. 171-A
EX $10   NM $15   MIP $25

Stunt Motorcycle, 1971-72, made for Corgi Rockets race track, gold cycle, blue rider w/yellow helmet, clear windshield, plastic tires, Model No. 681-A
EX $70   NM $105   MIP $175

White Wheelie Motorcycle, 1982, white body w/black/white police decals, Model No. 172-A
EX $15   NM $20   MIP $35

RACING

Adams Drag-Star, 1972-74, orange body, red nose, gold engines, chrome pipes and hood panels, Whizz Wheels, Model No. 165-A
EX $20   NM $30   MIP $45

Adams Probe 16, 1970-73, one-piece body, blue sliding canopy; metallic burgundy, or metallic lime/gold w/and without racing stripes, Whizz Wheels, Model No. 384-A
EX $15   NM $25   MIP $40

All Winners Set, 1966-69, first issue: No. 310 Corvette, No. 312 Jaguar XKE, No. 314 Ferrari 250LM, No. 324 Marcos, No. 325 Mustang; second issue: No. 312 Jaguar XKE, No. 314 Ferrari 250LM, No. 264 Toronado, No. 327 MGB, No. 337 Corvette, Model No. 46-A
EX $100   NM $240   MIP $450

(KP Photo by Dr. Douglas Sadecky)

Aston Martin DB4, 1962-65, Aston Martin, white top w/aqua green sides, yellow plastic interior, racing Nos. 1, 3 or 7, Model No. 309-A
EX $50   NM $75   MIP $125

Austin Mini-Metro Datapost, 1982-83, Austin, white body, blue roof, hood and trim, red plastic interior, hepolite and #77 decals, working hatch and doors, clear windows, folding seats, chrome headlights, orange taillights, Whizz Wheels, Model No. 281-B
EX $15   NM $18   MIP $30

Bertone Barchetta Runabout, 1971-73, yellow and black body, black interior, amber windows, die-cast air foil, suspension, red/yellow Runabout decals, Whizz Wheels, Model No. 386-A
EX $15   NM $22   MIP $45

BMC Mini-Cooper, 1971-74, BMC, white body, black working hood, trunk, two doors, red interior, clear windows, orange/black stripes and #177 decals, suspension, Whizz Wheels, Model No. 282-A
EX $30   NM $45   MIP $95

(KP Photo by Dr. Douglas Sadecky)

BMC Mini-Cooper S "Sun/RAC" Rally Car, 1967, BMC, red body, white roof w/six jewel headlights, RAC Rally and No. 21 decals, Model No. 333-A
EX $90   **NM** $180   **MIP** $350

BMC Mini-Cooper S Rally, 1967-72, BMC, red body, white roof, chrome roof rack w/two spare tires, Monte Carlo Rally and No. 177 decals, w/shaped wheels/rubber tires or cast detailed wheels/plastic tires, Model No. 339-A
EX $40   **NM** $90   **MIP** $180

(KP Photo by Dr. Douglas Sadecky)

BMC Mini-Cooper S Rally Car, 1965-66, BMC, red body, white roof, five jewel headlights, Monte Carlo Rally decals w/either No. 52 (1965) or No. 2 (1966); rare w/drivers' autographs on roof, Model No. 321-A
EX $100   **NM** $275   **MIP** $500

BMW M1, 1981, BMW, yellow body, black plastic base, rear panel and interior, white seats, clear windshield, multicolored stripes, lettering and #25 decal, Goodyear label, Model No. 308-B
EX $15   **NM** $20   **MIP** $35

BMW M1 BASF, 1983, BMW, red body, white trim w/black/white BASF and No. 80 decals, Model No. 380-B
EX $15   **NM** $18   **MIP** $30

British Leyland Mini 1000, 1978, Leyland, red interior, chrome lights, grille and bumper, #8 decal; three variations: silver body w/decals, 1978-82; silver body, no decals; orange body w/extra hood stripes, 1983, Model No. 201-C
EX $16   **NM** $24   **MIP** $40

British Racing Cars, 1959-63, set of three cars, three versions: blue No. 152 Lotus, green No. 151 BRM, green No. 150 Vanwall, all w/smooth wheels, 1959; same cars w/shaped wheels, 1960-61; red Vanwall, green BRM and blue Lotus, 1963, each set, Model No. 5-A
EX $140   **NM** $210   **MIP** $475

BRM Racing Car, 1958-65, BRM, silver seat, dash and pipes, smooth wheels, rubber tires, in three versions: dark

green body, 1958-60; light green body w/driver and various number decals 1961-65; light green body, no driver, Model No. 152-A
EX $50   **NM** $75   **MIP** $150

Campbell Bluebird, 1960-65, blue body, red exhaust, clear windshield, driver, in two versions: black plastic wheels, 1960; metal wheels and rubber tires, Model No. 153-A
EX $56   **NM** $84   **MIP** $175

Chevrolet Caprice Classic, 1981, Chevrolet, white upper body, red sides w/red/white/blue stripes and No. 43 decals, tan interior, STP labels, Model No. 341-B
EX $24   **NM** $36   **MIP** $60

(KP Photo by Dr. Douglas Sadecky)

Citroen DS 19 Rally, 1965-66, Citroen, light blue body, white roof, yellow interior, four jewel headlights, Monte Carlo Rally and No. 75 decals, w/antenna, Model No. 323-A
EX $70   **NM** $105   **MIP** $185

Commuter Dragster, 1971-73, Ford, maroon body w/Ford Commuter, Union Jack and #2 decals, cast silver engine, chrome plastic suspension and pipes, clear windshield, driver, spoke wheels, Model No. 161-A
EX $30   **NM** $45   **MIP** $75

Cooper-Maserati Racing Car, 1967-69, Cooper-Maserati, blue body w/red/white/blue Maserati and #7 decals, unpainted engine and suspension, chrome plastic steering wheel, roll bar, mirrors and pipes, driver, cast eight-spoke wheels, plastic tires, Model No. 156-A
EX $26   **NM** $39   **MIP** $65

Cooper-Maserati Racing Car, 1969-72, Cooper-Maserati, yellow/white body w/yellow/black stripe and #3 decals, driver tilts to steer car, Model No. 159-A
EX $18   **NM** $27   **MIP** $45

(KP Photo by Dr. Douglas Sadecky)

Corvette Sting Ray, 1967-69, Chevrolet, yellow body, red interior, suspension, No. 13 decals. This car's decorative appearance definitely places it in the 1960's, Model No. 337-A
EX $30   **NM** $55   **MIP** $95

Corvette Sting Ray, 1970-73, Chevrolet, metallic gray body w/black hood, Go-Go-Go labels, Whizz Wheels, Model No. 376-A
EX $40   **NM** $65   **MIP** $100

Datsun 240Z, 1973-76, Datsun, white body w/red hood and roof, No. 46 and John Morton labels, Whizz Wheels, Model No. 396-A
EX $15   **NM** $20   **MIP** $35

Datsun 240Z, 1973-76, Datsun, red body w/No. 11 and other labels, two working doors, white interior, orange roll bar and tire rack; one version also has East Africa Rally labels, Model No. 394-A
EX $15   **NM** $20   **MIP** $35

Ecurie Ecosse Racing Set, 1961-66, metallic dark or light blue No. 1126 transporter w/three cars in two versions: BRM, Vanwall and Lotus XI, 1961-64; BRM, Vanwall and Ferrari, 1964-66, value is for individual complete set, Model No. 16-A
EX $140   **NM** $210   **MIP** $450

Ferrari 206 Dino, 1969-73, Ferrari, black interior and fins, in either red body w/No. 30 label and gold hubs or Whizz Wheels, or yellow body w/No. 23 label and gold hubs or Whizz Wheels, Model No. 344-A
EX $24   **NM** $36   **MIP** $60

Ferrari 312 B2 Racing Car, 1973-75, Ferrari, red body, white fin, gold engine, chrome suspension, mirrors and wheels, Ferrari and #5 labels, Model No. 152-B
EX $16   **NM** $24   **MIP** $40

(KP Photo by Dr. Douglas Sadecky)

Ferrari Berlinetta 250LM, 1965-72, Ferrari, red body w/yellow stripe, blue windshields, chrome interior, grille and exhaust pipes, detailed engine, #4 Ferrari logo and yellow stripe decals, spoked wheels and spare, rubber tires, Model No. 314-A
EX $30   **NM** $45   **MIP** $75

Ferrari Daytona, 1973-78, Ferrari, white body w/red roof and trunk, black interior, two working doors, amber windows and headlights, No. 81 and other labels, Model No. 323-B
EX $15   **NM** $30   **MIP** $55

Ferrari Daytona, 1979, Ferrari, apple green body, black tow hook, red-yellow-silver-black Daytona #5 and other racing labels, amber windows, headlights, black plastic interior, base, four spoke chrome wheels, Model No. 300-C
EX $15   **NM** $20   **MIP** $35

Ferrari Daytona and Racing Car, 1975-77, Ferrari, blue/yellow No. 323 Ferrari and No. 150 Surtees on yellow trailer, Model No. 29-B
EX $25   **NM** $40   **MIP** $85

VEHICLES — CORGI

Ferrari Daytona JCB, 1973-74, Ferrari, orange body w/No. 33, Corgi and other labels, chrome spoked wheels, Model No. 324-B
EX $15   **NM** $25   **MIP** $50

Ferrari Racing Car, 1963-72, Ferrari, red body, chrome plastic engine, roll bar and dash, driver, silver cast base and exhaust, Ferrari and No. 36 decals, shaped or spoked wheels, Model No. 154-A
EX $24   **NM** $36   **MIP** $75

Fiat X1/9, 1980-81, Fiat, metallic blue body and base, white Fiat #3, multicolored lettering and stripe labels, black roof, trim, interior, rear panel, grille, bumpers and tow hook, chrome wheels and detailed engine, Model No. 306-B
EX $15   **NM** $20   **MIP** $35

Ford Capri 3 Litre GT, 1973-76, Ford, white and black body, racing number 5 label, Model No. 331-A
EX $15   **NM** $20   **MIP** $35

Ford Capri S, 1982, Ford, white body, red lower body and base, red interior, clear windshield, black bumpers, grille and tow hook, chrome headlights and wheels, red taillights, #6 and other racing labels, Model No. 312-C
EX $15   **NM** $20   **MIP** $35

Ford Capri Santa Pod Gloworm, 1971-76, Ford, white and blue body w/red, white and blue lettering and flag decals, red chassis, amber windows, gold-based black engine, gold scoop, pipes and front suspension, w/driver, plastic wheels, Model No. 163-A
EX $18   **NM** $27   **MIP** $45

Ford GT 70, 1972-73, Ford, green and black body, white interior, No. 32 label, Model No. 316-B
EX $10   **NM** $25   **MIP** $45

Grand Prix Racing Set, 1968-72, four vehicle set includes: No. 490 Volkswagen Breakdown Truck w/No. 330 Porsche (1969), Porsche No. 371 (1970-72), No. 155 Lotus, No. 156 Cooper-Maserati, red trailer, Model No. 12-B
EX $135   **NM** $210   **MIP** $425

Grand Prix Set, 1973, sold by mail order only; kit version of No. 151 Yardley, No. 154 JPS, No. 152 Surtees and No. 153 Surtees, Model No. 30-A
EX $60   **NM** $125   **MIP** $275

Hesketh-Ford Racing Car, 1975-78, white body w/red/white/blue Hesketh, stripe and #24 labels, chrome suspension, roll bar, mirrors and pipes, Model No. 160-A
EX $15   **NM** $18   **MIP** $30

Hillman Hunter, 1969-72, Hillman, blue body, gray interior, black hood, white roof, unpainted spotlights, clear windshield, red radiator screen, black equipment, Golden Jacks wheels; came w/Kangaroo figure, Model No. 302-B
EX $45   **NM** $70   **MIP** $140

(KP Photo by Dr. Douglas Sadecky)

Hillman Imp Rally, 1966, Hillman, in various metallic body colors, w/cream interior, Monte Carlo Rally and No. 107 decals, Model No. 328-A
EX $30   **NM** $65   **MIP** $110

Jaguar E Type Competition, 1964-68, Jaguar, gold or chrome plated body, black interior, blue and white stripes and black #2 decals, no top, clear windshield, headlights, w/driver, Model No. 312-A
EX $45   **NM** $65   **MIP** $130

Jaguar XJS Motul, 1983, Jaguar, black body w/red/white Motul and No. 4, chrome wheels, Model No. 318-B
EX $8   **NM** $15   **MIP** $25

JPS Lotus Racing Car, 1974-77, black body, scoop and wings w/gold John Player Special, Texaco and #1 labels, gold suspension, pipes and wheels, Model No. 190-A
EX $30   **NM** $45   **MIP** $75

Lamborghini Miura, 1973-74, Lamborghini, silver body, black interior, yellow/purple stripes and No. 7 label, Whizz Wheels, Model No. 319-B
EX $30   **NM** $45   **MIP** $75

Land Rover and Ferrari Racer, 1963-67, red and tan No. 438 Land Rover and red No. 154 Ferrari F1 on yellow trailer, Model No. 17-A
EX $60   **NM** $90   **MIP** $150

(KP Photo by Dr. Douglas Sadecky)

Lotus Elan S2 Roadster, 1965-67, Lotus, working hood, plastic interior w/folding seats, shaped wheels and rubber tires, issued in metallic blue, Exxon "I've got a Tiger in my tank" label on trunk. The ordinary model is powder blue, but shown here is the rare white version of the car, Model No. 318-A
EX $30   **NM** $50   **MIP** $110

(KP Photo by Dr. Douglas Sadecky)

Lotus Eleven, 1958-64, Lotus, red, silver, or light blue/green body, clear windshield and plastic headlights, smooth wheels, rubber tires, racing decals, Model No. 151-A
EX $60   **NM** $95   **MIP** $160

Lotus Racing Car, 1973-82, Lotus, black body and base, gold cast engine, roll bar, pipes, dash and mirrors, driver, gold cast wheels, in two versions, Model No. 154-B
EX $25   **NM** $35   **MIP** $60

Lotus Racing Set, 1976-79, Lotus, three versions: "3" on No. 301 Elite and "JPS" on No. 154 Lotus racer; "7" on No. 301 Elite and "JPS" on racer; "7" on No. 301 Elite and "Texaco" on No. 154 Lotus racer; value is for each individual complete set, Model No. 32-B
EX $30   **NM** $45   **MIP** $95

Lotus Racing Team Set, 1966-69, 490 VW Breakdown Truck, red trailer w/#318 Lotus Elan Open Top, #319 Lotus Elan Hard Top, #155 Lotus Climax; includes pack of cones, sheet of racing number labels, Model No. 37-A
EX $125   **NM** $200   **MIP** $375

Lotus-Climax Racing Car, 1964-69, Lotus, green body and base w/black/white #1 and yellow racing stripe labels, unpainted engine and suspension, w/driver, Model No. 155-A
EX $25   **NM** $35   **MIP** $65

Lotus-Climax Racing Car, 1969-72, Lotus, orange/white body w/black/white stripe and #8 labels, unpainted cast rear wing, cast eight-spoke wheels, w/driver, Model No. 158-A
EX $15   **NM** $25   **MIP** $50

Matra and Racing Car, 1983, black/yellow No. 457 Talbot Matra Rancho and No. 160 Hesketh yellow car w/Team Corgi trailer and labels, Model No. 26-B
EX $15   **NM** $35   **MIP** $65

McLaren M19A Racing Car, 1972-77, white body, orange stripes, chrome engine, exhaust and suspension, black mirrors, driver, Yardley McLaren #55 labels, Whizz Wheels, Model No. 151-B
EX $15   **NM** $25   **MIP** $40

McLaren M23 Racing Car, 1974-77, large 1:18-scale red and white body and wings w/red, white and black Texaco-Marlboro #5 labels, chrome pipes, suspension and mirrors, removable wheels, Model No. 191-A
EX $30   **NM** $60   **MIP** $110

Mercedes-Benz 240D Rally, 1982, Mercedes-Benz, cream or tan body, black, red and blue lettering, "dirt," red plastic interior, clear windows, black radiator guard and roof rack, opening doors, racing #5 label, Model No. 291-B
EX $10 **NM** $15 **MIP** $25

(KP Photo by Dr. Douglas Sadecky)

Mercedes-Benz 300SL Coupe, 1959-65, Mercedes-Benz, chrome body, red hardtop, red stripe, clear windows, 1959-60 smooth wheels no suspension, 1961-65 racing stripes, Model No. 304-A
EX $45 **NM** $65 **MIP** $130

Mercedes-Benz 300SL Roadster, 1958-66, Mercedes-Benz, blue or white body, yellow interior, plastic interior, smooth, shaped or cast wheels, racing stripes and number, driver, Model No. 303-A
EX $45 **NM** $75 **MIP** $140

Mini-Marcos GT850, 1972-73, white body, red-white-blue racing stripe and #7 labels, clear headlights, Whizz Wheels, opening doors and hood, Model No. 305-B
EX $20 **NM** $30 **MIP** $50

(KP Photo by Dr. Douglas Sadecky)

Monte Carlo Rally Set, 1965-67, three vehicle set, No. 326 Citroen, No. 318 Mini and No. 322 Land Rover rally cars, Model No. 38-A
EX $295 **NM** $450 **MIP** $900

(KP Photo by Dr. Douglas Sadecky)

Morris Mini-Cooper, 1962-65, Morris, yellow or blue body and base and/or hood, white roof and/or hood, two versions, red plastic interior, jewel headlights, flag, numbers decals. Even though there are various paint and decal versions of

this model, any one of them is valuable, Model No. 227-A
EX $80 **NM** $150 **MIP** $300

Morris Mini-Cooper, 1964-65, Morris, red body and base, white roof, yellow interior, chrome spotlight, No. 37 and Monte Carlo Rally decals, Model No. 317-A
EX $60 **NM** $125 **MIP** $250

Mustang Organ Grinder Dragster, 1971-74, Ford, yellow body w/green/yellow name, #39 and racing stripe labels, black base, green windshield, red interior, roll bar, w/driver, Model No. 166-A
EX $20 **NM** $30 **MIP** $50

Porsche 924, 1978-81, Porsche, red or metallic light brown or green body, dark red interior, opening two doors and rear window, chrome headlights, black plastic grille, racing No. 2, Model No. 321-B
EX $10 **NM** $25 **MIP** $50

Porsche Carrera 6, 1967-69, Porsche, white body, red or blue trim, blue or amber tinted engine covers, black interior, clear windshield and canopy, red jewel taillights, No. 1 or No. 20 decals, Model No. 330-A
EX $30 **NM** $45 **MIP** $75

Porsche Carrera 6, 1970-73, Porsche, white upper body, red front hood, doors, upper fins and base, black interior, purple rear window, tinted engine cover, racing No. 60 decals, Model No. 371-A
EX $25 **NM** $35 **MIP** $60

Porsche-Audi 917, 1973-78, Porsche, white body, red and black No. 6, L and M, Porsche Audi and stripe labels or orange body, orange, two-tone green, white No. 6, racing driver, Model No. 397-A
EX $15 **NM** $20 **MIP** $35

(KP Photo by Dr. Douglas Sadecky)

Psychedelic Ford Mustang, 1968, Ford, light blue body and base, aqua interior, red-orange-yellow No. 20 and flower decals, cast eight spoke wheels, plastic tire, Model No. 348-A
EX $30 **NM** $50 **MIP** $100

Quartermaster Dragster, 1971-73, long, dark metallic green upper body w/green/yellow/black #5 and Quartermaster labels, light green lower body, w/driver, Model No. 162-A
EX $30 **NM** $45 **MIP** $75

Radio Luxembourg Dragster, 1972-76, long, blue body w/yellow, white and blue John Wolfe Racing, Radio Luxembourg and #5 labels, silver engine, w/driver, Model No. 170-A
EX $30 **NM** $45 **MIP** $85

Renault 5 Turbo, 1981, Renault, bright yellow body, red plastic interior, black roof and hood, working hatch and two doors, black dash, chrome rear engine, racing #8 Cibie and other sponsor labels, Model No. 307-B
EX $15 **NM** $18 **MIP** $25

Renault 5 Turbo, 1983, Renault, white body, red roof, red and blue trim painted on, No. 5 lettering, blue and white label on windshield, facom decal, Model No. 381-B
EX $15 **NM** $18 **MIP** $25

Roger Clark's Capri, 1970-72, Ford, white body, black hood, grille and interior, open doors, folding seats, chrome bumpers, clear headlights, red taillights, Racing #73, label sheet, Whizz Wheels, Model No. 303-B
EX $15 **NM** $25 **MIP** $55

(KP Photo by Dr. Douglas Sadecky)

Rover 2000 Rally, 1965-66, Rover, white body, red interior, black bonnet, No. 21 decal, cast spoked wheels, Model No. 322-A2
EX $55 **NM** $135 **MIP** $225

Rover 2000 Rally, 1965-66, Rover, metallic dark red body, white roof, shaped wheels, No. 136 and Monte Carlo Rally decals, Model No. 322-A1
EX $50 **NM** $95 **MIP** $175

Rover 3500 Triplex, 1981, Rover, white sides and hatch, blue roof and hood, red plastic interior and trim, detailed engine, red-white-black No. 1 label, Model No. 340-B
EX $8 **NM** $15 **MIP** $20

Shadow-Ford Racing Car, 1974-76, Ford, black body and base w/white/black #17, UOP and American flag labels, cast chrome suspension and pipes, Embassy Racing label, Model No. 155-B
EX $10 **NM** $20 **MIP** $50

Shadow-Ford Racing Car, 1974-77, Ford, white body, red stripes, driver, chrome plastic pipes, mirrors and steering wheel, in two versions, Jackie Collins driver figure, Model No. 156-B
EX $10 **NM** $20 **MIP** $45

Silver Streak Jet Dragster, 1973-76, metallic blue body w/Firestone and flag labels on tank, silver engine, orange plastic jet and nose cone, Model No. 169-A
EX $15 **NM** $25 **MIP** $45

Silverstone Racing Layout, 1963-66, seven-vehicle set w/accessories; Vanwall, Lotus XI, Aston Martin, Mercedes 300SL, BRM, Ford Thunderbird, Land Rover Truck; second version has a No. 154 Ferrari substituted for Lotus XI, rare, Model No. 15-A
EX $400 **NM** $900 **MIP** $1700

(KP Photo by Dr. Douglas Sadecky)

Simca 1000, 1964-66, Simca, chrome plated body, No. 8 and red-white-blue stripe decals, one-piece body, clear windshield, red interior, Model No. 315-A
EX $30 **NM** $45 **MIP** $75

STP Patrick Eagle Racing Car, 1974-77, red body w/red, white and black STP and #20 labels, chrome lower engine and suspension, black plastic upper engine; includes Patrick Eagle driver figure, Model No. 159-B
EX $20 **NM** $30 **MIP** $50

Sunbeam Imp Rally, 1967-68, metallic blue body w/white stripes, Monte Carlo Rally and No. 77 decals, cast wheels, Model No. 340-A
EX $20 **NM** $45 **MIP** $85

Super Karts, 1982, two carts, orange and blue, Whizz Wheels in front, slicks on rear, silver and gold drivers, Model No. 46-B
EX $15 **NM** $18 **MIP** $30

Surtees TS9 Racing Car, 1972-74, black upper engine, chrome lower engine, pipes and exhaust, driver, Brook Bond Oxo-Rob Walker labels, eight-spoke Whizz Wheels, Model No. 150-B
EX $15 **NM** $20 **MIP** $40

Surtees TS9B Racing Car, 1972-74, red body w/white stripes and wing, black plastic lower engine, driver, chrome upper engine, pipes, suspension, eight-spoke wheels, Model No. 153-B
EX $15 **NM** $20 **MIP** $40

Tyrrell P34 Racing Car, 1977, dark blue body and wings w/yellow stripes, #4 and white Elf and Union Jack decals, chrome plastic engine, w/driver in red or blue helmet, Model No. 161-B
EX $20 **NM** $30 **MIP** $55

Tyrrell P34 Racing Car, 1978-79, without yellow stripes, First National Bank labels, w/driver in red or orange helmet, Model No. 162-B
EX $20 **NM** $30 **MIP** $55

Tyrrell-Ford Racing Car, 1974-78, dark blue body w/blue/black/white Elf and #1 labels, chrome suspension, pipes, mirrors, Jackie Stewart driver figure, Model No. 158-B
EX $18 **NM** $25 **MIP** $50

U.S. Racing Buggy, 1972-74, white body w/red/white/blue stars, stripes and USA #7 labels, red base, gold engine, red plastic panels, driver, Model No. 167-A
EX $18 **NM** $25 **MIP** $50

(KP Photo by Dr. Douglas Sadecky)

Vanwall Racing Car, 1957-65, clear windshield, unpainted dash, silver pipes and decals, smooth wheels, rubber tires, in three versions: green body or red body w/silver or yellow seats, Model No. 150-A
EX $35 **NM** $65 **MIP** $140

Volkswagen 1200 Rally, 1976-77, Volkswagen, light blue body, off-white plastic interior, silver headlights, red taillights, suspension, Whizz Wheels, Model No. 384-B
EX $20 **NM** $30 **MIP** $50

(KP Photo by Dr. Douglas Sadecky)

Volkswagen East African Safari, 1965-69, Volkswagen, light red body, brown interior, working front and rear hood, clear windows, spare wheel on roof steers front wheels, jewel headlights, w/rhinoceros figure. Although never issued as a gift set, this spectacular little toy could easily have been made into one. A rhinoceros was added as a charging menace to the racing VW, Model No. 256-A
EX $60 **NM** $130 **MIP** $285

Volkswagen Racing Tender and Cooper, 1967-69, Volkswagen, white No. 490 VW breakdown truck and No. 156 Cooper on trailer, Model No. 6-B
EX $50 **NM** $75 **MIP** $150

Volkswagen Racing Tender and Cooper Maserati, 1970-71, Volkswagen, two versions: tan or white No. 490 VW breakdown truck, and No. 159 Cooper-Maserati on trailer; value is for each set, Model No. 25-B
EX $50 **NM** $75 **MIP** $150

Wild Honey Dragster, 1971-73, yellow body w/red/yellow Wild Honey and Jaguar Powered labels, green windows and roof, black grille, driver, Whizz Wheels, Model No. 164-A
EX $25 **NM** $40 **MIP** $65

SMALL TRUCK

Breakdown Truck, 1975-79, red body, black plastic boom w/gold hook, yellow interior, amber windows, black/yellow decals, Whizz Wheels, Model No. 702-A
EX $15 **NM** $18 **MIP** $30

Commer 3/4-Ton Pickup, 1963-66, Commer, red cab w/orange canopy, yellow interior, Trans-o-Lites, Model No. 465-A
EX $30 **NM** $45 **MIP** $75

Commer 5-Ton Dropside Truck, 1956-62, Commer, either blue or red cab, both w/cream rear body, sheet metal tow hook, smooth or shaped wheels, rubber tires, Model No. 452-A
EX $40 **NM** $60 **MIP** $110

Commer 5-Ton Platform Truck, 1957-62, Commer, either yellow or metallic blue cab w/silver body, smooth or shaped wheels, Model No. 454-A
EX $40 **NM** $60 **MIP** $120

(KP Photo by Dr. Douglas Sadecky)

Commer Refrigerator Van, 1956-60, Commer, either light or dark blue cab (pictured here), both w/cream bodies and red/white/blue Wall's Ice Cream decals, smooth wheels, Model No. 453-A
EX $80 **NM** $120 **MIP** $225

(KP Photo by Dr. Douglas Sadecky)

Constructor Set, 1963-68, Commer, one red and one white cab bodies, w/four different interchangeable rear units; van, pickup, milk truck, and ambulance; various accessories include a milkman figure, Model No. 24-A
EX $48 **NM** $80 **MIP** $160

(KP Photo by Dr. Douglas Sadecky)

Dodge Kew Fargo Tipper, 1967-72, Dodge, white cab and working hood, blue tipper, red interior, clear windows, black hydraulic cylinders, cast spoked wheels, plastic tires, Model No. 483-A
EX $34 **NM** $51 **MIP** $85

ERF 44G Dropside Truck, 1961-64, ERF, yellow cab and chassis, metallic blue bed, smooth or shaped wheels, Model No. 456-A

EX $36   **NM** $55   **MIP** $110

(KP Photo by Dr. Douglas Sadecky)

ERF 44G Moorhouse Van, 1958-60, ERF, yellow cab, red body, Moorhouse Lemon Cheese decals, smooth wheels, rubber tires, Model No. 459-A

EX $100   **NM** $150   **MIP** $295

(KP Photo by Dr. Douglas Sadecky)

ERF 44G Platform Truck, 1958-64, ERF, light blue cab w/dark blue flatbed body or yellow cab and blue flatbed, smooth hubs, Model No. 457-A

EX $36   **NM** $55   **MIP** $110

ERF Dropside Truck and Trailer, 1960-64, ERF, No. 456 truck and No. 101 trailer w/No. 1488 cement sack load and No. 1485 plank load, Model No. 11-A

EX $60   **NM** $90   **MIP** $200

(KP Photo by Dr. Douglas Sadecky)

ERF Neville Cement Tipper, 1959-66, ERF, yellow cab, gray tipper, cement decal, plastic or metal filler caps, w/either smooth or shaped wheels, Model No. 460-A

EX $32   **NM** $48   **MIP** $85

Ford Transit Milk Float, 1982, Ford, white one-piece body, blue hood and roof, tan interior, chrome and red roof lights, open compartment door and milk cases, Model No. 405-C

EX $15   **NM** $25   **MIP** $40

Mazda 4X4 Open Truck, 1983, Mazda, blue body, white roof, black windows, no interior, white plastic wheels, Model No. 495-A

EX $15   **NM** $20   **MIP** $35

Mazda B-1600 Pickup Truck, 1975-78, Mazda, issued in either blue and white or blue and silver bodies w/working tailgate, black interior, chrome wheels, Model No. 493-A

EX $15   **NM** $20   **MIP** $35

Mazda Camper Pickup, 1976-78, Mazda, red truck and white camper w/red interior and folding supports, Model No. 415-A

EX $15   **NM** $25   **MIP** $451

Mazda Custom Pickup, 1979-80, Mazda, orange body w/red roof, United States flag label, Model No. 440-B

EX $15   **NM** $18   **MIP** $30

Mazda Motorway Maintenance Truck, 1976-78, Mazda, deep yellow body w/red base, black interior and hydraulic cylinder, yellow basket w/workman figure, Model No. 413-B

EX $18   **NM** $25   **MIP** $45

Mazda Pickup and Dinghy, 1975-78, Mazda, two versions: red No. 493 Mazda w/"Ford" labels; or w/"Sea Spray" labels, dinghy and trailer, Model No. 28-B

EX $25   **NM** $35   **MIP** $60

Mercedes-Benz and Caravan, 1975-81, Mercedes-Benz, truck and trailer in two versions: w/blue No. 285 Mercedes truck and No. 490 Caravan (1975-79); w/brown No. 285 Mercedes and No. 490 Caravan (1980-81); value is for each set, Model No. 24-B

EX $15   **NM** $30   **MIP** $50

Mercedes-Benz Unimog 406, 1970-76, Mercedes-Benz, yellow body, red and green front fenders and bumpers, metallic charcoal gray chassis w/olive or tan rear plastic covers, red interior, Model No. 406-B

EX $18   **NM** $25   **MIP** $45

Mercedes-Faun Street Sweeper, 1980, Mercedes-Benz, orange body w/light orange or brown figure, red interior, black chassis and unpainted brushing housing and arm castings, Model No. 1117-B

EX $15   **NM** $25   **MIP** $40

(KP Photo by Dr. Douglas Sadecky)

Milk Truck and Trailer, 1962-66, ERF, blue and white ERF No. 456 milk truck w/No. 101 trailer and milk churns, Model No. 21-A

EX $60   **NM** $130   **MIP** $250

Shelvoke and Drewry Garbage Truck, 1979, long, orange or red cab, silver body w/City Sanitation decals, black interior, grille and bumpers, clear windows, Model No. 1116-B

EX $15   **NM** $25   **MIP** $40

Unimog with Snowplow (Mercedes-Benz), 1971-76, Mercedes-Benz, 6" four different body versions, red interior, cab, rear body, fender-plow mounting, lower and charcoal upper chassis, rear fenders, Model No. 1150-A

EX $30   **NM** $45   **MIP** $75

Volkswagen Breakdown Truck, 1966-72, Volkswagen, tan or white body, red interior and equipment boxes, clear windshield, chrome tools, spare wheels, red VW emblem, no lettering, Model No. 490-A

EX $50   **NM** $75   **MIP** $125

Volkswagen Pickup, 1964-66, Volkswagen, dark yellow or gold body, red interior and rear plastic cover, silver bumpers and headlights, red VW emblem, shaped wheels, Model No. 431-A

EX $45   **NM** $65   **MIP** $110

SPORTS CAR

Alfa Romeo P33 Pininfarina, 1970-74, Alfa Romeo, white body, gold or black spoiler, red seats, Whizz Wheels, Model No. 380-A

EX $16   **NM** $24   **MIP** $45

Austin Healey, 1956-63, Austin, blue body w/cream seats, shaped hubs, rare, Model No. 300-A2

EX $100   **NM** $215   **MIP** $350

(KP Photo by Dr. Douglas Sadecky)

Austin-Healey, 1956-63, Austin, cream body w/red seats or red body w/cream seats, Model No. 300-A1

EX $50   **NM** $75   **MIP** $125

Beach Buggy & Sailboat, 1971-76, purple No. 381 buggy, yellow trailer and red/white boat, Model No. 26-A

EX $20   **NM** $30   **MIP** $55

Bertone Shake Buggy, 1972-74, clear windows, green interior, gold engine, four variations: yellow upper/white lower body or metallic mauve upper/white lower body w/spoked or solid chrome wheels, Model No. 392-A

EX $15   **NM** $22   **MIP** $45

BMC Mini-Cooper Magnifique, 1966-70, BMC, metallic blue or olive green body w/working doors, hood and trunk, clear windows and sunroof, cream interior w/folding seats, jewel headlights, cast detailed wheels, plastic tires, Model No. 334-A

EX $34   **NM** $65   **MIP** $115

BMC Mini-Cooper S, 1972-76, BMC, bright yellow body, red plastic interior, chrome plastic roof rack w/two spare wheels, clear windshield, one-piece body silver grille, bumpers, headlights, red taillights, suspension, Whizz Wheels, Model No. 308-A
EX $45   **NM** $65   **MIP** $110

British Leyland Mini 1000, 1976-78, Leyland, metallic blue body, working doors, black base, clear windows, white interior, silver lights, grille and bumper, Union Jack decal on roof, Whizz Wheels, Model No. 200-B
EX $18   **NM** $27   **MIP** $45

Chevrolet Astro I, 1969-74, Chevrolet, dark metallic green/blue body w/working rear door, cream interior w/two passengers, in two versions: gold wheels w/red plastic hubs or Whizz wheels, Model No. 347-A
EX $18   **NM** $40   **MIP** $85

Chevrolet Camaro SS, 1968-70, Chevrolet, metallic gold body w/two working doors, black roof and stripes, red interior, take-off wheels, Model No. 338-A
EX $30   **NM** $45   **MIP** $75

Chevrolet Camaro SS, 1972-73, Chevrolet, blue or turquoise body w/white stripe, cream interior, working doors, white plastic top, clear windshield, folding seats, silver air intakes, red taillights, black grille and headlights, suspension, Whizz Wheels, Model No. 304-B
EX $30   **NM** $45   **MIP** $95

(KP Photo by Dr. Douglas Sadecky)

Corvette Sting Ray, 1963-68, Chevrolet, metallic silver, bronze or red body, two working headlights, clear windshield, yellow interior, silver hood panels, four rotating jewel headlights, suspension, chrome bumpers, w/spoked or shaped wheels, rubber tires. The swivelling jeweled headlights and spoked wheels added real pizzaz to this cool toy, Model No. 310-A
EX $60   **NM** $90   **MIP** $175

Corvette Sting Ray, 1970-72, Chevrolet, metallic green or metallic red body, yellow interior, black working hood, working headlights, clear windshield, amber roof panel, gold dash, chrome grille and bumpers, decals, gray die-cast base, Golden jacks, cast wheels, plastic tires, Model No. 300-B
EX $40   **NM** $90   **MIP** $185

Corvette Sting Ray, 1972, Chevrolet, either dark metallic blue or metallic mauve-rose body, chrome dash, Whizz Wheels, Model No. 387-A
EX $40   **NM** $65   **MIP** $100

De Tomaso Mangusta, 1969, white upper/light blue lower body/base, black interior, clear windows, silver engine, black grille, amber headlights, red taillights, gray antenna, spare wheel, gold stripes and black logo decal on hood, suspension, removable gray chassis, Model No. 271-A
EX $32   **NM** $48   **MIP** $90

De Tomaso Mangusta, 1970-73, metallic dark green body w/gold stripes and logo on hood, silver lower body, clear front windows, cream interior, amber rear windows and headlights, gray antenna, spare wheel, Whizz Wheels, Model No. 203-B
EX $26   **NM** $39   **MIP** $65

Ferrari 308GTS, 1982, Ferrari, red or black body w/working rear hood, black interior w/tan seats, movable chrome headlights, detailed engine, Model No. 378-B
EX $15   **NM** $20   **MIP** $35

Ferrari 308GTS Magnum, 1982, Ferrari, red body w/solid chrome wheels, Model No. 298-A
EX $24   **NM** $36   **MIP** $60

Fiat X1/9, 1975-79, Fiat, metallic light green or silver body w/black roof, trim and interior, two working doors, rear panel, grille, tow hook and bumpers, detailed engine, suspension, chrome wheels, Model No. 314-B
EX $15   **NM** $20   **MIP** $35

Ford Capri, 1970-72, Ford, orange-red or dark red body, gold wheels w/red hubs or Whizz Wheels, two working doors, clear windshield and headlights, black interior, folding seats, black grille, silver bumpers, Model No. 311-A
EX $40   **NM** $80   **MIP** $145

Ford Capri 30 S, 1980-81, Ford, Silver or yellow body, black markings, opening doors and hatchback, Model No. 343-B
EX $15   **NM** $20   **MIP** $35

Ford Cobra Mustang, 1982, Ford, white, black, red and blue body and chassis, Mustang decal, Model No. 370-A
EX $15   **NM** $18   **MIP** $30

Ford Cortina GXL, 1970-73, Ford, tan or metallic silver blue body, black roof and stripes, red plastic interior, working doors, clear windshield, Model No. 313-A
EX $30   **NM** $45   **MIP** $75

Ford Mustang Fastback, 1965-66, Ford, metallic lilac, metallic dark blue, silver or light green body, spoked or detailed cast wheels, Model No. 320-A
EX $30   **NM** $45   **MIP** $95

(KP Photo by Dr. Douglas Sadecky)

Ford Mustang Fastback, 1965-69, Ford, white body w/double red stripe, blue interior, spun, detailed cast, wire or cast alloy wheels. Shown in the foreground of this photo is an unused number sheet to help jazz up the model, Model No. 325-A
EX $25   **NM** $45   **MIP** $85

Ford Mustang Mach 1, 1973-76, Ford, green upper body, white lower body and base, cream interior, folding seat backs, chrome headlights and rear bumper, Model No. 329-A
EX $25   **NM** $35   **MIP** $60

Ford Sierra, 1982, Ford, many body color versions w/plastic interior, working hatch and two doors, clear windows, folding seat back, lifting hatch cover, Model No. 299-A
EX $8   **NM** $15   **MIP** $25

Ford Sierra and Caravan Trailer, 1983, Ford, blue #299 Sierra, two-tone blue/white #490 Caravan, Model No. 1-C
EX $15   **NM** $20   **MIP** $35

Ford Thunderbird 1957, 1982, Ford, cream body, dark brown, black or orange plastic hardtop, black interior, open hood and trunk, chrome bumpers, Model No. 801-B
EX $10   **NM** $20   **MIP** $35

Ford Thunderbird 1957, 1983, Ford, white body, black interior and plastic top, amber windows, white seats, chrome bumpers, headlights and spare wheel cover, Model No. 810-B
EX $10   **NM** $20   **MIP** $35

(KP Photo by Dr. Douglas Sadecky)

Ford Thunderbird Hardtop, 1959-65, Ford, light green body, cream roof, clear windows, silver lights, grille and bumpers, red taillights, rubber tires, Model No. 214-A
EX $50   **NM** $80   **MIP** $130

(KP Photo by Dr. Douglas Sadecky)

Ford Thunderbird Hardtop-Mechanical, 1959, Ford, same as 214-A but w/friction motor and pink body and black roof. This model is fairly hard to find, Model No. 214-M
EX $70   **NM** $120   **MIP** $215

Ford Thunderbird Roadster, 1959-65, Ford, clear windshield, silver seats, lights, grille and bumpers, red taillights, rubber tires, white body, Model No. 215-A

EX $50   **NM** $75   **MIP** $125

(KP Photo by Dr. Douglas Sadecky)

Ghia-Fiat 600 Jolly, 1965-66, dark yellow body, red seats, two figures and a dog, clear windshield, silver bumpers and headlights, red taillights, rare, Model No. 242-A

EX $80   **NM** $175   **MIP** $325

GP Beach Buggy, 1970-76, metallic blue or orange-red body, two surfboards, flower label, Whizz Wheels, Model No. 381-A

EX $15   **NM** $20   **MIP** $35

Iso Grifo 7 Litre, 1970-73, metallic blue body, light blue interior, black hood and stripe, clear windshield, black dash, folding seats, chrome bumpers, Whizz Wheels, Model No. 301-B

EX $15   **NM** $18   **MIP** $30

Jaguar 1952 XK120 Rally, 1983, Jaguar, cream body w/black top and trim, red interior, Rally des Alps and #414 decals, Model No. 803-A

EX $8   **NM** $15   **MIP** $25

(KP Photo by Dr. Douglas Sadecky)

Jaguar E Type, 1962-64, Jaguar, maroon or metallic dark gray body, tan interior, red and clear plastic removable hardtop, clear windshield, folded top, spun hubs, Model No. 307-A

EX $45   **NM** $65   **MIP** $110

Jaguar E Type 2+2, 1968-69, Jaguar, red or blue body and chassis, working hood, doors and hatch, black interior w/folding seats, copper engine, pipes and suspension, spoked wheels, Model No. 335-A

EX $40   **NM** $60   **MIP** $120

Jaguar E Type 2+2, 1970-76, Jaguar, in five versions: red or yellow w/nonworking doors; or w/V-12 engine in yellow body or metallic yellow body, Whizz Wheels, Model No. 374-A

EX $35   **NM** $55   **MIP** $90

Jaguar XJ12C, 1974-79, Jaguar, five different metallic versions, working hood and two doors, clear windows, tow hook, chrome bumpers, grille and headlights, Model No. 286-A

EX $10   **NM** $15   **MIP** $35

Jaguar XJS, 1978-81, Jaguar, metallic burgundy body, tan interior, clear windows, working doors, spoked chrome wheels, Model No. 319-C

EX $10   **NM** $15   **MIP** $25

Jaguar XJS-HE Supercat, 1982-83, Jaguar, black body w/silver stripes and trim, red interior, dark red taillights, light gray antenna, no tow hook, clear windshield, Model No. 314-C

EX $8   **NM** $15   **MIP** $25

Jaguar XK120 Hardtop, 1983, Jaguar, red body, black hardtop, working hood and trunk, detailed engine, cream interior, clear windows, chrome wheels, Model No. 803-B

EX $8   **NM** $15   **MIP** $25

Lamborghini Miura P400, 1970-72, Lamborghini, w/red or yellow body, working hood, detailed engine, clear windows, jewel headlights, bull figure, Whizz Wheels, Model No. 342-A

EX $40   **NM** $60   **MIP** $100

Lancia Fulvia Zagato, 1967-69, Lancia, metallic blue body, metallic green or yellow and black body, light blue interior, working hood and doors, folding seats, amber lights, cast wheels, Model No. 332-A

EX $25   **NM** $35   **MIP** $70

Lancia Fulvia Zagato, 1970-72, Lancia, orange body, black working hood and interior, Whizz Wheels, Model No. 372-A

EX $15   **NM** $25   **MIP** $40

Lotus Elan S2 Hardtop, 1967-68, Lotus, cream interior w/folding seats and tan dash, working hood, separate chrome chassis, issued in blue body w/white top or red body w/white top, Model No. 319-A

EX $30   **NM** $45   **MIP** $75

Lotus Elite, 1976-78, Lotus, red body, white interior, two working doors, clear windshield, black dash, hood panel, grille, bumpers, base and tow hook, Model No. 315-C

EX $15   **NM** $18   **MIP** $35

Lotus Elite 22, 1970-75, Lotus, dark blue body w/silver trim, Whizz Wheels, Model No. 382-B

EX $15   **NM** $18   **MIP** $35

Marcos 3 Litre, 1970-73, working hood, detailed engine, black interior, Marcos label, Whizz Wheels, issued in orange or metallic blue-green, Model No. 377-A

EX $20   **NM** $30   **MIP** $55

Marcos Mantis, 1971-73, metallic red body, opening doors, cream interior and headlights, silver gray lower body base, bumpers, hood panel, spoked wheels, Model No. 312-B

EX $20   **NM** $35   **MIP** $55

(KP Photo by Dr. Douglas Sadecky)

Marcos Volvo 1800 GT, 1966-69, Volvo, issued w/either white body w/two green stripes or blue body w/two white stripes, plastic interior w/driver, spoked wheels, rubber tires. The blue version is shown here--the common version is white with racing stripes, Model No. 324-A

EX $25   **NM** $40   **MIP** $70

Mercedes-Benz 300SC Convertible, 1983, Mercedes-Benz, black body, black folded top, white interior, folding seat backs, detailed engine, chrome grille and wheels, lights, bumpers, Model No. 806-B

EX $8   **NM** $12   **MIP** $25

Mercedes-Benz 300SC Hardtop, 1983, Mercedes-Benz, maroon body, tan top and interior, open hood and trunk, clear windows, folding seat backs, top w/chrome side irons, Model No. 805-B

EX $8   **NM** $15   **MIP** $25

Mercedes-Benz 300SL, 1982, Mercedes-Benz, red body and base, tan interior, open hood and two gullwing doors, black dash, detailed engine, clear windows, chrome bumpers, Model No. 802-B

EX $8   **NM** $15   **MIP** $25

Mercedes-Benz 300SL, 1983, Mercedes-Benz, silver body, tan interior, black dash, clear windows, open hood and two gullwing doors, detailed engine, chrome bumpers, Model No. 811-B

EX $8   **NM** $15   **MIP** $25

Mercedes-Benz 350SL, 1972-79, Mercedes-Benz, white body, spoke wheels or metallic dark blue body solid wheels, pale blue interior, folding seats, detailed engine, Model No. 393-A

EX $15   **NM** $30   **MIP** $60

Mercedes-Benz C-111, 1971-74, Mercedes-Benz, orange main body w/black lower and base, black interior, vents, front and rear grilles, silver headlights, red taillights, Whizz Wheels, Model No. 388-A

EX $15   **NM** $20   **MIP** $45

MG Maestro, 1983, MG, yellow body, black trim, opaque black windows, black plastic grille, bumpers, spoiler, trim and battery hatch, clear headlights, AA Service label, Model No. 1009-A

EX $15   **NM** $20   **MIP** $35

MGA, 1957-65, red or metallic green body, cream seats, black dash, clear windshield, silver bumpers, grille and headlights, smooth or shaped wheels, Model No. 302-A

EX $60   **NM** $90   **MIP** $150

MGB GT, 1967-69, MG, dark red body, pale blue interior, opening hatch and two doors, jewel headlights, chrome grille and bumpers, orange taillights, spoked wheels, w/suitcase, Model No. 327-A

EX $50   **NM** $75   **MIP** $110

MGC GT, 1969, MG, bright yellow body and base, black interior, hood and hatch, folding seats, luggage, jewel headlights, red taillights, Model No. 345-A

EX $50   **NM** $75   **MIP** $125

MGC GT, 1970-73, MG, red body, black hood and base, black interior, opening hatch and two doors, folding seat backs, luggage, orange taillights, Whizz Wheels, Model No. 378-A

EX $50   **NM** $75   **MIP** $125

Mini Camping Set, 1977-78, cream Mini, w/red/blue tent, grille and two figures, Model No. 38-B

EX $25   **NM** $40   **MIP** $65

Mini-Marcos GT850, 1966-70, metallic maroon body, white name and trim decals, cream interior, open hood and doors, clear windows and headlights, Golden Jacks wheels, Model No. 341-A

EX $30   **NM** $45   **MIP** $75

Minissima, 1975-79, cream upper body, metallic lime green lower body w/black stripe centered, black interior, clear windows, headlights, Model No. 288-A

EX $15   **NM** $20   **MIP** $35

Morris Marina 1.8 Coupe, 1971-73, Morris, metallic dark red or lime green body, cream interior, working hood and two doors, clear windshield, chrome grille and bumpers, Whizz Wheels, Model No. 306-A

EX $15   **NM** $30   **MIP** $60

Morris Mini-Cooper Deluxe, 1965-68, Morris, black body/base, red roof, yellow and black wicker work decals on sides and rear, yellow interior, gray steering wheel, jewel headlights, Model No. 249-A

EX $45   **NM** $65   **MIP** $120

(KP Photo by Dr. Douglas Sadecky)

Morris Mini-Minor, 1960-71, Morris, light blue or red body w/shaped or smooth wheels, plastic interior, silver bumpers, grille and headlights, Model No. 226-A1

EX $40   **NM** $60   **MIP** $100

Morris Mini-Minor, 1960-71, Morris, sky blue body w/shaped and/or smooth wheels, plastic interior, silver bumpers, grille and headlights, rare, Model No. 226-A2

EX $100   **NM** $175   **MIP** $350

Morris Mini-Minor, 1972-73, Morris, one-piece body in dark or metallic blue or orange body, plastic interior, silver lights, grille and bumpers, red taillights, Whizz Wheels, Model No. 204-B

EX $30   **NM** $45   **MIP** $75

(KP Photo by Dr. Douglas Sadecky)

NSU Sport Prinz, 1963-66, metallic burgundy or maroon body, yellow interior, one-piece body, silver bumpers, headlights and trim, shaped wheels, Model No. 316-A

EX $30   **NM** $45   **MIP** $75

Pontiac Firebird, 1969-72, Pontiac, metallic silver body and base, red interior, black hood, stripes and convertible top, doors open, clear windows, folding seats, Golden Jacks wheels, Model No. 343-A

EX $50   **NM** $75   **MIP** $125

(KP Photo by Dr. Douglas Sadecky)

Pop Art Mini-Mostest, 1969, Morris, light red body and base, yellow interior, jewel headlights, orange taillights, yellow-blue-purple pop art and "Mostest" decals; very rare. This rare Mini is one of the Holy Grails of any Corgi collection. Very few of these cars were produced in 1969, possibly due to the fact that psychedelia had already passed its prime, Model No. 349-A

EX $1000   **NM** $1500   **MIP** $2700

Porsche 917, 1970-76, Porsche, red or metallic blue body, black or gray base, blue or amber tinted windows and headlights, opening rear hood, headlights, Whizz Wheels, Model No. 385-A

EX $15   **NM** $20   **MIP** $45

Porsche 92 Turbo, 1982, Porsche, black body w/gold trim, yellow interior, four chrome headlights, clear windshield, taillight-license plate decal, opening doors and hatchback, Model No. 310-B

EX $15   **NM** $20   **MIP** $35

Porsche 924, 1980-81, Porsche, bright orange body, dark red interior, black plastic grille, multicolored stripes, swivel roof spotlight, Model No. 303-C

EX $10   **NM** $15   **MIP** $25

Porsche Targa 911S, 1970-75, Porsche, metallic blue, silver-blue or green body, black roof w/or without stripe, orange interior, opening hood and two doors, chrome engine and bumpers, Whizz Wheels, Model No. 382-A

EX $25   **NM** $35   **MIP** $60

Reliant Bond Bug 700 E.S., 1971-74, bright orange or lime green body, off white seats, black trim, silver headlights, red taillights, Bug label, Model No. 389-A

EX $15   **NM** $25   **MIP** $50

Renault 11 GTL, 1983, Renault, light tan or maroon body and base, red interior, opening doors and rear hatch, lifting hatch cover, folding seats, grille, Model No. 384-C

EX $15   **NM** $25   **MIP** $40

Talbot-Matra Rancho, 1981-84, red and black, green and black or white and blue body, working tailgate and hatch, clear windows, plastic interior, black bumpers, grille and tow hook, Model No. 457-B

EX $10   **NM** $15   **MIP** $25

Toyota 2000 GT, 1970-72, Toyota, metallic dark blue or purple one-piece body, cream interior, red gear shift and antenna, two red and two amber taillights, Whizz Wheels, Model No. 375-A

EX $15   **NM** $30   **MIP** $55

Triumph TR2, 1956-59, Triumph, cream one-piece body w/red seats, light green body w/white or cream seats, clear windshield, silver grille, Model No. 301-A

EX $70   **NM** $105   **MIP** $175

(KP Photo by Dr. Douglas Sadecky)

Triumph TR3, 1960-62, Triumph, metallic olive or cream one-piece body, red seats, clear windshield, silver grille, bumpers and headlights, smooth or shaped hubs, Model No. 305-A

EX $60   **NM** $90   **MIP** $150

Volkswagen Polo Turbo, 1982, Volkswagen, cream body, red interior w/red and orange trim, working hatch and two door castings, clear windshield, black plastic dash, Model No. 309-B

EX $15   **NM** $18   **MIP** $30

TAXI

Austin London Taxi, 1960-65, Austin, black body w/yellow plastic interior, w/or without driver, shaped or smooth hubs or rubber tires, Model No. 418-A1

EX $36   **NM** $55   **MIP** $90

Austin London Taxi, 1978-83, Austin, black body w/two working doors, light brown interior, Whizz Wheels, Model No. 425-A

EX $15   **NM** $20   **MIP** $35

Austin London Taxi/Reissue, 1971-74, Austin, updated version w/Whizz Wheels, black or maroon body, Model No. 418-A2

EX $15   **NM** $20   **MIP** $35

Chevrolet Caprice Taxi, 1979-81, Chevrolet, orange body w/red interior, white roof sign, Taxi and TWA decals, Model No. 327-B
EX $20   **NM** $30   **MIP** $50

Chevrolet Impala Taxi, 1960-65, Chevrolet, light orange body, base w/hexagonal panel under rear axle and smooth wheels, or two raised lines and shaped wheels, one-piece body, clear windows, plastic interior, silver grille, headlights and bumpers; smooth or shaped spun wheels w/rubber tires, Model No. 221-A
EX $50   **NM** $75   **MIP** $125

(KP Photo by Dr. Douglas Sadecky)

Chevrolet Impala Yellow Cab, 1965-67, Chevrolet, red lower body, yellow upper, red interior w/driver, white roof sign, red decals, Model No. 480-A
EX $80   **NM** $120   **MIP** $200

Ford Sierra Taxi, 1983, Ford, cream body, Model No. 451-A
EX $8   **NM** $15   **MIP** $20

Mercedes-Benz 240D Taxi, 1975-80, Mercedes-Benz, orange body, orange interior, black roof sign w/red and white Taxi labels, black on door, Model No. 411-B
EX $15   **NM** $18   **MIP** $30

Peugeot 505 STI, 1981-82, Peugeot, red body and base, red interior, blue-red-white Taxi labels, black grille, bumpers, tow hook, chrome headlights and wheels, opening doors, Model No. 373-B
EX $8   **NM** $15   **MIP** $25

Peugeot 505 Taxi, 1983, Peugeot, cream body, red interior, red, white and blue taxi decals, Model No. 450-B
EX $8   **NM** $15   **MIP** $25

Thunderbird Bermuda Taxi, 1962-65, white body w/blue, yellow or green plastic canopy w/red fringe, yellow interior, driver, yellow and black labels, Model No. 430-A
EX $50   **NM** $75   **MIP** $135

TRAILER

Dropside Trailer, 1957-65, cream body, red chassis in five versions: smooth wheels 1957-61; shaped wheels, 1962-1965; white body, cream or blue chassis; or silver gray body, blue chassis, each, Model No. 100-A
EX $10   **NM** $21   **MIP** $45

Pennyburn Workmen's Trailer, 1968-69, blue body w/working lids, red plastic interior, three plastic tools, shaped wheels, plastic tires, Model No. 109-A
EX $15   **NM** $35   **MIP** $50

(KP Photo by Dr. Douglas Sadecky)

Platform Trailer, 1958-64, in five versions: silver body, blue chassis; silver body, yellow chassis; blue body, red chassis; blue body, yellow chassis, Model No. 101-A
EX $10   **NM** $20   **MIP** $45

VANS

(KP Photo by Dr. Douglas Sadecky)

Austin Mini Van, 1964-67, Austin, metallic deep green body w/two working rear doors, clear windows, Model No. 450-A
EX $40   **NM** $60   **MIP** $100

(KP Photo by Dr. Douglas Sadecky)

Bedford AA Road Service Van, 1957-62, Bedford, dark yellow body in two versions: first version with divided windshield, 1957-59 shown; single windshield, 1960-62, Model No. 408-A
EX $50   **NM** $75   **MIP** $125

(KP Photo by Dr. Douglas Sadecky)

Bedford Corgi Toys Van, 1960-62, Bedford, Corgi Toys decals, w/either yellow body/blue roof or blue body/yellow roof, Model No. 422-A2
EX $60   **NM** $105   **MIP** $200

Bedford Corgi Toys Van, 1962, Bedford, yellow upper/blue lower body, Corgi Toy decals, rare, Model No. 422-A1
EX $100   **NM** $225   **MIP** $400

Bedford Daily Express Van, 1956-59, Bedford, dark blue body w/white Daily Express decals, divided windshield, smooth wheels, rubber tires, Model No. 403-A
EX $60   **NM** $90   **MIP** $150

(KP Photo by Dr. Douglas Sadecky)

Bedford Dormobile, 1956-62, Bedford, two versions and several colors: divided windshield w/cream, green or metallic maroon body; or single windshield w/yellow body/blue roof w/shaped or smooth wheels. Pictured here; the 404-A on the left and the 404M on the right with a mechanical friction motor, Model No. 404-A
EX $50   **NM** $75   **MIP** $125

Bedford Dormobile-Mechanical, 1956-59, Bedford, friction motor, dark metallic red or turquoise body, smooth wheels, Model No. 404M
EX $60   **NM** $90   **MIP** $175

(KP Photo by Dr. Douglas Sadecky)

Bedford Evening Standard Van, 1960-62, Bedford, black body/silver roof or black lower body/silver upper body and roof, Evening Standard decals, smooth wheels, Model No. 421-A
EX $55   **NM** $80   **MIP** $130

Bedford KLG Van-Mechanical, 1956-59, Bedford, w/friction motor, red body w/KLG Spark Plugs decals, smooth hubs, Model No. 403M
EX $70   **NM** $125   **MIP** $285

Chevrolet Coca-Cola Van, 1978-80, Chevrolet, red body, white trim, w/Coca Cola logos, Model No. 437-B
EX $15   **NM** $20   **MIP** $35

Chevrolet Rough Rider Van, 1977-78, Chevrolet, yellow body w/working rear doors, cream interior, amber windows, Rough Rider decals, Model No. 423-B
EX $15   **NM** $18   **MIP** $30

Chevrolet Vantastic Van, 1977-80, Chevrolet, off white body w/Vantastic decals, Model No. 431-B
EX $10   **NM** $15   **MIP** $25

Chevrolet Vantastic Van, 1977-80, Chevrolet, black body w/Vantastic decals, Model No. 432-A
EX $10   **NM** $15   **MIP** $25

Commer 3/4-Ton Milk Float, 1964-65, Commer, white cab w/light blue body, Model No. 466-A1
EX $32   **NM** $48   **MIP** $80

Commer 3/4-Ton Milk Float, 1970, Commer, white cab w/light blue body, w/CO-OP decals, Model No. 466-A2
EX $40   **NM** $80   **MIP** $160

Commer 3/4-Ton Van, 1970-71, Commer, either dark blue body with green roof and Hammonds decals (1971) or white body with light blue roof and CO-OP labels (1970), both w/cast spoked wheels w/plastic tires, Model No. 462-A
EX $45   **NM** $90   **MIP** $180

Commer Holiday Mini Bus, 1968-69, Commer, white upper body w/orange lower body, white interior, clear windshield, silver bumpers, grille and headlights, Holiday Camp Special decal, roof rack, two working rear doors. With bathing suits packed in the roof luggage, a trip to the shore was inevitable in this mod van, Model No. 508-A
EX $30   **NM** $75   **MIP** $130

(KP Photo by Dr. Douglas Sadecky)

Commer Mobile Camera Van, 1967-72, Commer, metallic blue lower body and roof rack, white upper body, two working rear doors, black camera on gold tripod, cameraman, Model No. 479-A
EX $60   **NM** $105   **MIP** $195

(KP Photo by Dr. Douglas Sadecky)

Ford Thames Airborne Caravan, 1962-67, Ford, various color versions of body and plastic interior w/table, white blinds, silver bumpers, grille and headlights, two doors, Model No. 420-A
EX $35   **NM** $55   **MIP** $95

(KP Photo by Dr. Douglas Sadecky)

Ford Thames Wall's Ice Cream Van, 1965-68, Ford, light blue body, cream pillar, chimes, chrome bumpers and grille, no figures. This wonderful toy played the Wall's Ice Cream musical tune by turning the hand crank on the rear of the van, Model No. 474-A
EX $55   **NM** $110   **MIP** $225

Ford Wall's Ice Cream Van, 1965-67, Ford, light blue body, dark cream pillars, plastic striped rear canopy, white interior, silver bumpers, grille and headlights. A sidewalk/street display plus a salesman and small boy dress up this non-musical version of the van, Model No. 447-A
EX $80   **NM** $160   **MIP** $325

Karrier Bantam Two Ton Van, 1957-60, Karrier, blue body, red chassis and bed, clear windows, smooth wheels, rubber tires, Model No. 455-A
EX $35   **NM** $55   **MIP** $95

(KP Photo by Dr. Douglas Sadecky)

Karrier Butcher Shop, 1960-64, Karrier, white body, blue roof, butcher shop interior, Home Service labels, in two versions: w/or without suspension, smooth hubs. Note the meat hanging in the side windows, Model No. 413-A
EX $65   **NM** $100   **MIP** $165

Karrier Dairy Van, 1962-64, Karrier, light blue body w/Drive Safely on Milk decals, white roof, w/either smooth or shaped wheels, Model No. 435-A
EX $50   **NM** $75   **MIP** $145

Karrier Ice Cream Van, 1963-66, Karrier, cream upper, blue lower body and interior, clear windows, sliding side windows, Mister Softee decals, figure inside, Model No. 428-A
EX $90   **NM** $165   **MIP** $295

Karrier Lucozade Van, 1958-62, Karrier, yellow body w/gray rear door, Lucozade decals, rubber tires, w/either smooth or shaped wheels, Model No. 411-A
EX $70   **NM** $120   **MIP** $225

(KP Photo by Dr. Douglas Sadecky)

Karrier Mobile Canteen, 1965-66, Karrier, blue body, white interior, amber windows, roof knob rotates figure, working side panel counter, Joe's Diner label. In this photo, the model on the left has the common "Joe's Diner" label, while the van on the right (471-A2) features the rare Belgian-issued "patates frites" label, Model No. 471-A1
EX $60   **NM** $90   **MIP** $150

Karrier Mobile Canteen, 1965-66, Karrier, blue body, white interior, amber windows, roof knob rotates figure, working side panel counter, Patates Frites label, Belgium issue, Model No. 471-A2
EX $90   **NM** $150   **MIP** $325

Karrier Mobile Grocery, 1957-61, Karrier, light green body, grocery store interior, red/white Home Service labels, smooth hubs, rubber tires, Model No. 407-A
EX $70   **NM** $110   **MIP** $185

Radio Roadshow Van, 1982, white body, red plastic roof and rear interior, opaque black windows, red-white-black Radio Tele Luxembourg labels, gray plastic loudspeakers and working radio in van, Model No. 1006-A
EX $25   **NM** $35   **MIP** $60

Security Van, 1976-79, black body, blue mesh windows and dome light, yellow/black Security labels, Whizz Wheels, Model No. 424-B
EX $7   **NM** $15   **MIP** $25

Volkswagen Delivery Van, 1962-64, Volkswagen, white upper and red lower body, plastic red or yellow interior, silver bumpers and headlights, red VW emblem, shaped wheels, Model No. 433-A
EX $55   **NM** $85   **MIP** $140

Volkswagen Kombi Bus, 1962-66, Volkswagen, off-green upper and olive green lower body, red interior, silver bumpers and headlights, red VW emblem, shaped wheels, Model No. 434-A
EX $50   **NM** $75   **MIP** $125

Volkswagen Tobler Van, 1963-67, Volkswagen, light blue body, plastic interior, silver bumpers, Trans-o-lite headlights and roof panel, shaped wheels, rubber tires, Model No. 441-A
EX $55   **NM** $85   **MIP** $140

DELUXE READING

Crusader 101, 30" long; red plastic open convertible, chrome grille and accents, brown plastic driver, battery-operated remote control; 1964
EX $32   **NM** $63   **MIP** $95

Johnny Express Cargo Kit, cargo load for Johnny Express trucks, including four pallets, three barrels, one large crate, two mid-sized crates and eight small crates; 1965 and later
EX $4   **NM** $8   **MIP** $12

Johnny Express Conveyor, 17" long, 11" high; red conveyor-loader, hand-cranked belt, four wheels, for use with Johnny Express tractor-trailers; 1965 and later
EX $6   **NM** $12   **MIP** $18

Johnny Express Crane, 15" long, 9" high; yellow plastic boom, hand-crank action, sold individually or with Johnny Express Tractor Trailer; 1965-69
EX $6   **NM** $12   **MIP** $18

Johnny Express Dump Body, 24" long; dumping trailer to go on Johnny Express Tractor Trailer; 1965 and later
EX $25   **NM** $35   **MIP** $45

Johnny Express Fork Lift, 9" long, 7" high; red plastic, sold individually or with larger trucks; 1965 and later
EX $5   **NM** $9   **MIP** $14

Johnny Express Liquid Tanker, 26" long; tanker body, yellow plastic, for Johnny Express Tractor Trailer, with open top and valve underneath; 1965 and later
EX $35   **NM** $65   **MIP** $75

Johnny Express Pipe Kit, pipe load for Johnny Express Tractor Trailer; 1965 and later
EX $5   **NM** $9   **MIP** $14

Johnny Express Reefer Van, 24" long; van body with sliding door, yellow plastic, for Johnny express Tractor Trailer; 1965 and later
EX $18   **NM** $36   **MIP** $55

Johnny Express Tire Kit, set including spare tire, working jack, lug wrench, and tire rack for mounting on the Johnny Express Tractor Trailer; 1965 and later
EX $13   **NM** $26   **MIP** $40

Johnny Express Tractor & Trailer Combination, 33" long; motorized red cabover with yellow bumpers, black tires, gray wheel hubs, and yellow flat-bed trailer; 1965-69
EX $85   **NM** $152   **MIP** $230

Johnny Express Trooper Carrier, 24" long; trooper carrier with swiveling gun turret, canvas canopy; 1966-67
EX $18   **NM** $36   **MIP** $55

Johnny Seven Armored Battalion, No. 3018; includes Halftrack, Jeep, Cannon, Ammunition Trailer and six white plastic figures, originally in box 22" across; 1964-65
EX $32   **NM** $63   **MIP** $95

Johnny Seven Fire Brigade, No. 3034; includes Chief Car, Pumper Truck, Hook and Ladder Truck, and seven plastic firefighter figures, originally in box 24" across; 1964-65
EX $28   **NM** $56   **MIP** $85

Johnny Seven Service Station, No. 3042; includes Tow Truck, car with replaceable fender, Service Island, and four plastic service attendant figures, originally in box 31-1/8" across; 1964-65
EX $15   **NM** $36   **MIP** $45

Johnny Seven Service Station, gas station with wrecker, "Topper" gas pumps, battery display, tire display, oil can, Allstate lubricant dispenser, convertible car with replacement fender, dolly, three attendants, one policeman; 1960s
EX $50   **NM** $100   **MIP** $150

Johnny Seven Speed Set, No. 3050; red sports car, boat trailer and white speedboat, originally in box 31-5/8" across; 1964-65
EX $15   **NM** $30   **MIP** $45

Johnny Seven Task Force, boat set with PT 109 gun boat with rocket launcher, 12" long, D-109 Destroyer, U.S. Navy Target Float, 10 figures; 1960s
EX $50   **NM** $100   **MIP** $150

Johnny Speed, red plastic remote-control Corvette-type racer, with white plastic driver, 22" long; 1968-69
EX $18   **NM** $36   **MIP** $55

Tiger Joe, 3' long; remote-control plastic tank, three shells, rotating turret; 1965
EX $50   **NM** $100   **MIP** $150

DINKY

AIRCRAFT

A.W. Ensign, 1940, camouflaged, dark variation, Model No. 68a
EX $150   NM $300   MIP $450

A.W. Ensign, 1945-49, A.W. Airliner, silver, G-ADSV, Model No. 62P
EX $65   NM $145   MIP $175

A.W. Ensign, 1945-49, forty-seat airliner, olive/dark green, G-AZCA, Model No. 62x
EX $95   NM $275   MIP $350

Airspeed Envoy, 1938-40, King's Aeroplane, red, blue, and silver, G-AEXX, Model No. 62k
EX $80   NM $200   MIP $325

Airspeed Envoy, 1938-41, silver, G-ACVI, Model No. 62m
EX $55   NM $175   MIP $250

Airspeed Envoy, 1945-49, light transport, red, G-ATMH, Model No. 62m
EX $50   NM $125   MIP $200

Amiot 370, 1939-48, Model No. 64a
EX $70   NM $130   MIP $200

Arc-en-Ciel, 1935-40, Model No. 60a
EX $200   NM $375   MIP $450

Armstrong Whitworth Ensign, 1938-41, silver, G-ADSR, Model No. 62p
EX $90   NM $175   MIP $250

Atalanta, 1940, camouflaged, dark variation, Model No. 66a
EX $200   NM $450   MIP $650

Atalanta (Imperial Airways Liner), 1934-41, gold, G-ABTI, Model No. 60a
EX $150   NM $375   MIP $500

Autogyro, 1934-41, gold, blue rotor, w/pilot, Model No. 60f
EX $90   NM $180   MIP $250

Autogyro, 1940, Army cooperation, silver, RAF roundels, Model No. 66f
EX $125   NM $250   MIP $350

Avro Vulcan Delta Wing Bomber, 1955-56, Model No. 749/992
EX $800   NM $1500   MIP $4500

Avro York, 1946-59, silver, G-AGJC, Model No. 70a/704
EX $45   NM $155   MIP $200

Beechcraft C55 Baron, 1968-76, red or white w/yellow props, N555C, Model No. 715
EX $25   NM $60   MIP $90

Beechcraft S35 Bonanza, 1965-76, orange and yellow, Model No. 710
EX $20   NM $55   MIP $80

Beechcraft T42A, 1972-77, Model No. 712
EX $30   NM $75   MIP $110

Bell 47 Police Helicopter, 1974-80, Model No. 732
EX $15   NM $30   MIP $55

Bloch 220, 1939-48, Model No. 64b
EX $75   NM $150   MIP $250

Boeing 737, 1970-75, Model No. 717
EX $25   NM $50   MIP $95

Boeing Flying Fortress, 1939-41, silver, USAAC stars on wings, Model No. 62g
EX $100   NM $200   MIP $300

Boeing Flying Fortress, 1945-48, "Long Range Bomber" under wings, Model No. 62g
EX $70   NM $135   MIP $225

Breguet Corsair, 1935-40, red and green, Model No. 60d
EX $100   NM $200   MIP $325

Bristol 173 Helicopter, 1956-63, turquoise, red rotors, G-AUXR, Model No. 715
EX $40   NM $70   MIP $105

Bristol Blenheim, 1940-41, silver, roundels w/outer yellow ring, Model No. 62b/62d
EX $60   NM $140   MIP $175

Bristol Blenheim, 1945-48, medium bomber; silver, red, and blue roundels, Model No. 62B
EX $35   NM $95   MIP $150

Bristol Blenheim, 1946-49, Model No. 62B
EX $60   NM $85   MIP $160

(KP Photo by Dr. Douglas Sadecky)

Bristol Brittania, 1959-65, silver, blue line, CF-CZA. Canadian Pacific shown, Model No. 998
EX $50   NM $250   MIP $500

(KP Photo by Dr. Douglas Sadecky)

Caravelle S.E. 210, 1959-62, Model No. 60f/891
EX $45   NM $170   MIP $230

Cierva Autogyro, 1935-40, Model No. 60f
EX $100   NM $250   MIP $250

Clipper III Flying Boat, 1938-41, silver, NC16736, Model No. 60w
EX $150   NM $250   MIP $400

Clipper III Flying Boat, 1945-49, silver, no registration, Model No. 60w
EX $75   NM $175   MIP $250

D.H. Albatross, 1939-41, Frobisher Class Liner, silver, G-AFDI, Model No. 62w
EX $75   NM $275   MIP $400

D.H. Albatross, 1939-41, silver, G-AEVV, Model No. 62r
EX $75   NM $275   MIP $400

D.H. Albatross, 1940, camouflaged, dark variation, Model No. 68b
EX $150   NM $300   MIP $450

D.H. Albatross, 1945-49, four-engine liner; gray, G-ATPV, Model No. 62R
EX $75   NM $170   MIP $250

(KP Photo by Dr. Douglas Sadecky)

D.H. Comet Airliner, 1954-65, silver wings, G-ALYX, wingspan 7-1/8", Model No. 702/999
EX $45   NM $105   MIP $185

D.H. Comet Racer, 1935-40, silver, G-ACSR, Model No. 60g
EX $60   NM $125   MIP $225

D.H. Comet Racer, 1946-49, yellow, G-RACE, Model No. 60g
EX $50   NM $110   MIP $155

D.H. Sea Vixen, 1960-65, gray, white undersides, Model No. 738
EX $30   NM $65   MIP $110

Dewoitine 500, 1935-40, Model No. 60e
EX $100   NM $200   MIP $300

Dewoitine D338, 1937-46, Model No. 61a/64
EX $225   NM $350   MIP $500

Douglas DC3, 1938-41, silver, PH-ALI, Model No. 60t
EX $125   NM $300   MIP $650

Empire Flying Boat, 1937-41, MAIA, silver, G-AVKW, Model No. 700
EX $150   NM $275   MIP $350

Empire Flying Boat, 1937-41, silver, G-ADUV, solid front to hull, Model No. 60r
EX $150   NM $325   MIP $450

Empire Flying Boat, 1938-40, Atlantic Flying Boat, blue, cream wings, G-AZBP, Model No. 60x
EX $350   NM $600   MIP $1000

Empire Flying Boat, 1945-49, silver, G-ADUV, hollowed out front to hull, Model No. 60r
EX $90   NM $175   MIP $250

Fairy Battle, 1937-41, camouflaged, one roundel, light variation, Model No. 60s
EX $50   NM $125   MIP $200

Fairy Battle, 1937-41, silver, "Fairy Battle Bomber" under wing, Model No. 60n
EX $40   NM $100   MIP $140

General Monospar, 1934-41, silver, blue wing tips, Model No. 60e
EX $75   NM $225   MIP $300

General Monospar, 1940, camouflaged, dark, Model No. 66e
EX $90   NM $300   MIP $350

Gloster Gladiator, 1937-40, silver, RAF roundels, no words under wing, Model No. 60p
EX $90   **NM** $175   **MIP** $275

Gloster Javelin, 1956-65, green/gray camouflage, wingspan, 3-1/4", Model No. 735
EX $15   **NM** $50   **MIP** $90

(KP Photo)

Gloster Meteor, 1946-62, silver, RAF roundels, Model No. 70e/732
EX $10   **NM** $25   **MIP** $35

Hanriot 180M, 1937-40, Model No. 61e
EX $90   **NM** $150   **MIP** $225

Hawker Harrier, 1970-80, Model No. 722
EX $25   **NM** $65   **MIP** $95

Hawker Hunter, 1955-63, green/gray camouflage, Model No. 736
EX $15   **NM** $45   **MIP** $85

Hawker Hurricane, 1939-41, silver, no undercarriage, Model No. 62h
EX $30   **NM** $70   **MIP** $115

Hawker Hurricane, 1945-49, three-blade prop; red, white, and blue roundels, Model No. 62S
EX $40   **NM** $95   **MIP** $130

Hawker Hurricane IIc, 1972-75, Model No. 718
EX $50   **NM** $95   **MIP** $155

Hawker Siddeley HS 125, 1970-75, working landing gear, Model No. 723/728
EX $25   **NM** $50   **MIP** $80

Hawker Tempest II, 1946-55, silver, RAF roundels, flat spinner, Model No. 70b/730
EX $15   **NM** $45   **MIP** $75

Henriot 180T, 1935-40, Model No. 60c
EX $110   **NM** $170   **MIP** $225

Junkers JU87B Stuka, 1969-80, Model No. 721
EX $40   **NM** $75   **MIP** $145

Junkers JU89, 1938-41, high speed monoplane, green/dark green, D-AZBK, Model No. 62y
EX $100   **NM** $275   **MIP** $350

Junkers JU89, 1945-49, high speed monoplane, silver, G-ATBK, Model No. 62Y
EX $70   **NM** $160   **MIP** $225

Junkers JU89 Heavy Bomber, 1941, black, German cross, Model No. 67a
EX $100   **NM** $400   **MIP** $600

Junkers JU90 Airliner, 1938-40, silver, D-AIVI, Model No. 62n
EX $90   **NM** $250   **MIP** $325

Leopard Moth, 1934-41, light green, G-ACPT, Model No. 60b
EX $50   **NM** $140   **MIP** $180

Leopard Moth, 1940, camouflaged, dark, Model No. 66b
EX $70   **NM** $225   **MIP** $300

Lockheed P-80 Shooting Star, 1947-62, silver, USAF stars, Model No. 701/733
EX $10   **NM** $20   **MIP** $30

M.D. F-4 Phantom, 1972-77, Model No. 725/727/73
EX $70   **NM** $125   **MIP** $175

Mayo Composite, 1939-41, Model No. 63
EX $200   **NM** $450   **MIP** $750

ME BI 109, 1972-76, motorized, Model No. 726
EX $50   **NM** $100   **MIP** $175

Mercury Seaplane, 1939-41, silver, G-ADHJ, Model No. 63b
EX $50   **NM** $100   **MIP** $175

Mercury Seaplane, 1949-57, silver, G-AVKW, Model No. 700
EX $40   **NM** $80   **MIP** $120

Mitsubishi A65M Zero, 1975-78, motorized, Model No. 739
EX $75   **NM** $150   **MIP** $225

MRCA Tornado, 1974-76, Model No. 729
EX $35   **NM** $90   **MIP** $155

Mystere IV, 1957-63, Model No. 60a/800
EX $30   **NM** $75   **MIP** $110

Nord Noratlas, 1960-64, Model No. 804
EX $125   **NM** $250   **MIP** $400

P1B Lightning, 1959-69, silver, RAF roundels, Model No. 737
EX $20   **NM** $55   **MIP** $100

Percival Gull, 1934-41, white, blue wing tips, Model No. 60c
EX $70   **NM** $150   **MIP** $225

Percival Gull, 1940, camouflaged, dark, Model No. 66c
EX $100   **NM** $225   **MIP** $275

Percival Gull, 1945-48, Light Tourer, light green, Model No. 66c
EX $65   **NM** $125   **MIP** $150

Potez 56, 1937-40, Model No. 61b
EX $125   **NM** $200   **MIP** $270

Potez 58, 1935-40, Model No. 60b/61d
EX $100   **NM** $260   **MIP** $350

Potez 58 Sanitaire, 1937-40, Model No. 61d
EX $110   **NM** $175   **MIP** $250

Potez 63, 1939-48, Model No. 64c
EX $150   **NM** $250   **MIP** $400

Potez 662, 1939-40, Model No. 64d
EX $125   **NM** $250   **MIP** $400

Republic P47 Thunderbolt, 1975-78, motorized, Model No. 734
EX $75   **NM** $175   **MIP** $250

S.E. Caravelle Airliner, 1962-69, Air France, F-BGNY, starboard wing, Model No. 997
EX $70   **NM** $150   **MIP** $250

Sea King Helicopter, 1971-79, motorized, Model No. 724/736
EX $30   **NM** $60   **MIP** $100

SEPCAT Jaguar, 1973-76, Model No. 731
EX $25   **NM** $70   **MIP** $115

Short Shetland Flying Boat, 1947-49, silver, G-AGVD, Model No. 701
EX $200   **NM** $550   **MIP** $750

Sikorsky S58 Helicopter, 1957-61, Model No. 60d/802
EX $45   **NM** $135   **MIP** $190

Singapore Flying Boat, 1936-41, silver, RAF roundels, Model No. 60h
EX $100   **NM** $300   **MIP** $400

Singapore Flying Boat, 1936-41, four-engine, silver, G-EUTG, Model No. 60m
EX $125   **NM** $400   **MIP** $550

Spitfire, 1940-41, silver, small canopy, roundels red, white, and blue, Model No. 62e/62a
EX $35   **NM** $150   **MIP** $200

Spitfire, 1945-49, silver, large canopy, roundels red, white, and blue, Model No. 62A
EX $30   **NM** $75   **MIP** $125

Spitfire II, 1978-80, non-motorized, Model No. 741
EX $40   **NM** $80   **MIP** $135

Spitfire II, 1979, chrome, Model No. 700
EX $65   **NM** $165   **MIP** $250

(KP Photo by Dr. Douglas Sadecky)

Super G Constellation Lockheed, 1956-63, Wingspan, 7-3/4", Model No. 60c/892
EX $90   **NM** $200   **MIP** $350

Supermarine Spitfire II, 1969-78, motorized, Model No. 719
EX $60   **NM** $95   **MIP** $175

Supermarine Swift, 1955-63, green/gray camouflage, Model No. 734
EX $10   **NM** $45   **MIP** $85

Trident Star Fighter, French-made, Model No. 362
EX $15   **NM** $30   **MIP** $60

Trident Starfighter, Model No. 285
EX $30   **NM** $55   **MIP** $75

Twin Engined Fighter, 1946-55, silver, no registration, Model No. 70d/731
EX $10   **NM** $25   **MIP** $35

Vautour, 1957-63, Model No. 60b/801
EX $30   **NM** $80   **MIP** $125

Vickers Jockey, 1934-41, red, cream wing tips, Model No. 60d
EX $75   **NM** $110   **MIP** $150

Vickers Jockey, 1940, camouflaged, dark, Model No. 66d
EX $75   NM $175   MIP $225

Vickers Viking, 1947-63, silver, G-AGOL, flat spinners, Model No. 70c/705
EX $20   NM $45   MIP $70

(KP Photo by Dr. Douglas Sadecky)

Vickers Viscount, 1956-65, British European Airways, G-AOJA, wingspan 5-7/8", Model No. 708
EX $40   NM $125   MIP $200

Vickers Viscount, 1956-65, Air France, F-BGNL, Model No. 708
EX $40   NM $125   MIP $200

Viscount, 1957-60, Model No. 60e/803
EX $75   NM $125   MIP $175

Vulcan Bomber, 1955-56, silver, RAF roundels, Model No. 749/707/99
EX $500   NM $1500   MIP $4000

Westland Sikorsky Helicopter, 1957-63, red/cream, G-ATWX, Model No. 716
EX $30   NM $75   MIP $125

Whitley Bomber, 1937-41, silver, RAF roundels, Model No. 60v
EX $95   NM $150   MIP $225

Whitley Bomber, 1937-41, camouflaged, light variation, Model No. 62t
EX $95   NM $300   MIP $350

BUSES AND TAXIS

(KP Photo)

Austin Taxi with Driver, 1951-62, Pictured here with Robot Traffic Signal, 773 (which is 2-3/4" H and approx. $35 MIP), Model No. 40H/254
EX $70   NM $145   MIP $225

Austin/London Taxi, 1972-79, Model No. 284
EX $25   NM $35   MIP $75

Autobus Parisien, 1948-51, Model No. F29D
EX $80   NM $135   MIP $200

Autocar Chausson, 1956-60, Model No. F29F/571
EX $70   NM $120   MIP $200

(ToyShop File Photo)

B.O.A.C. Coach, 1956-63, Dark blue and white with "BOAC" lettering and symbol in yellow, Model No. 283
EX $55   NM $80   MIP $115

Continental Touring Coach, 1963-66, Model No. 953
EX $135   NM $200   MIP $350

Ford Vedette Taxi, 1956-59, Model No. F24XT
EX $60   NM $95   MIP $150

Observation Coach, 1954-60, Model No. 29F/280
EX $50   NM $75   MIP $100

Peugeot 404 Taxi, 1967-71, Model No. F1400
EX $50   NM $75   MIP $100

Plymouth Plaza Taxi, 1960-67, Model No. 266
EX $65   NM $100   MIP $155

(D. Klein Photo)

Plymouth USA Taxi, 1970s, Model No. 265
EX $15   NM $70   MIP $140

Routemaster Bus, 1964-80, Tern Shirts, Model No. 289
EX $75   NM $100   MIP $150

Silver Jubilee Bus, 1977, Model No. 297
EX $25   NM $35   MIP $70

CARS

Alfa Romeo Racing Car, 1954-64, open Grand Prix race car, white driver, red body, "8" on side, Model No. 23P/232
EX $40   NM $85   MIP $155

Armstrong Siddeley, 1937-40, blue or brown, Model No. 36A
EX $85   NM $130   MIP $225

Aston Martin DB3S, 1956-59, green or gray body, white driver, Model No. 104
EX $60   NM $120   MIP $180

Aston Martin DB5, Model No. 110
EX $25   NM $60   MIP $120

Austin 1800 Taxi, Model No. 282
EX $35   NM $70   MIP $100

Austin A105 Saloon, 1958-63, 4-door sedan, two-tone, Model No. 176
EX $75   NM $150   MIP $250

Austin Atlantic Convertible, 1954-58, blue, Model No. 106/140A
EX $70   NM $145   MIP $225

Austin Healey "100", 1956-59, Model No. 109
EX $30   NM $70   MIP $130

Austin Mini-Moke, 1967-75, Model No. 342
EX $20   NM $35   MIP $60

Austin Somerset, 1954-60, 4-door sedan, no interior, Model No. 161
EX $50   NM $100   MIP $150

Austin Somerset Saloon, 1954-60, red and yellow body, Model No. 161
EX $150   NM $325   MIP $550

Beach Buggy, Model No. 227
EX $5   NM $20   MIP $40

Big Cat Jaguar, Model No. 219
EX $5   NM $12   MIP $40

Bristol 450, 1956-60, racing car, green, #27 door decals, black tires, Model No. 163
EX $50   NM $100   MIP $165

Buick Roadmaster, French Dinky, Model No. 545
EX $70   NM $130   MIP $200

Cabriolet 404 Peugeot Pininfarina, Model No. 528
EX $25   NM $100   MIP $200

Cadillac 1962, 1962-69, blue, red interior, white tires, Model No. 147
EX $50   NM $95   MIP $150

Cadillac Eldorado, 1956-62, Model No. 131
EX $60   NM $95   MIP $135

Chrysler Airflow, 1935-40, Model No. 32/30A
EX $130   NM $250   MIP $450

Chrysler Royal Saloon, Note that some colors are worth more than values shown, Model No. 39e
EX $45   NM $150   MIP $300

Chrysler Saratoga, 1961-66, Model No. F550
EX $70   NM $100   MIP $190

Chrysler Simca 1308/GT, Model No. 11542
EX $25   NM $60   MIP $120

Citroen 2 CV, 1950, 1952-59, 1959-63, Model No. F535/24T
EX $50   NM $100   MIP $150

Citroen DS-19, 1959-68, Model No. F522/24C
EX $60   NM $90   MIP $135

Cooper-Bristol Racer, 1954-64, open cockpit, driver, green body, Model No. 233
EX $40   NM $90   MIP $175

Corvette Stingray, Model No. 221
EX $10   NM $25   MIP $50

Cunningham C-5R Racer, Model No. 133
EX $20   NM $50   MIP $100

Custom Land Rover, Model No. 202
EX $5   NM $15   MIP $60

Custom Stingray, Model No. 206
EX $5   NM $15   MIP $60

Customized Freeway Cruiser, Model No. 390
EX $5   **NM** $15   **MIP** $40

Customized Range Rover, Model No. 203
EX $5   **NM** $15   **MIP** $40

De Tomaso-Mangusta, Model No. 137
EX $5   **NM** $10   **MIP** $40

DeSoto Diplomat, 1960-63, orange, Model No. F545
EX $25   **NM** $85   **MIP** $160

DeSoto Diplomat, 1960-63, green, Model No. F545
EX $70   **NM** $130   **MIP** $200

DeSoto Fireflite Sedan, 1958-63, 4-door sedan; gray, green, or blue body, Model No. 192
EX $50   **NM** $105   **MIP** $175

(KP Photo)

Dodge Royal Sedan, 1959-64, available in various color schemes, Model No. 191
EX $80   **NM** $120   **MIP** $160

E Type Jaguar, Model No. 120
EX $20   **NM** $60   **MIP** $120

Estate Car, 1954-61, Model No. 27D/344
EX $45   **NM** $70   **MIP** $115

Ferrari Racer, Model No. 242
EX $15   **NM** $30   **MIP** $60

Fiat 1800 Familiale, 1960-63, silver/gray station wagon, red interior, Model No. 548
EX $45   **NM** $90   **MIP** $160

Ford Capri, 1969-74, Model No. 165
EX $40   **NM** $90   **MIP** $130

Ford Consul Corsair, 1963-69, 4-door sedan, white interior, black tires, Model No. 130
EX $50   **NM** $100   **MIP** $150

Ford Cortina Rally Car, 1967-69, Model No. 212
EX $35   **NM** $55   **MIP** $75

Ford Escort, Model No. 168
EX $30   **NM** $60   **MIP** $120

Ford Fairlane, Model No. 149
EX $25   **NM** $50   **MIP** $100

Ford Fairlane, 1962-66, pale green, Model No. 148
EX $60   **NM** $120   **MIP** $200

Ford Fairlane, 1962-66, South African Issue, bright blue, Model No. 148
EX $150   **NM** $300   **MIP** $700

Ford Fordor Sedan, 1954-59, 4-door sedan, pink and blue color combination rare, Model No. 170
EX $100   **NM** $200   **MIP** $300

Ford Thunderbird, South African Issue, blue, Model No. F565
EX $120   **NM** $250   **MIP** $600

Ford Thunderbird, 1965-67, (Hong Kong), Model No. 57/005
EX $50   **NM** $70   **MIP** $100

Ford Thunderbird Coupe, Model No. 1419
EX $25   **NM** $70   **MIP** $140

Ford Zephyr Saloon, 1956-60, 4-door sedan, two-tone, black tires, Model No. 162
EX $50   **NM** $100   **MIP** $150

Gabriel's Model T Ford, 1969-71, yellow and black, driver, "Gabriel" on doors, open cab, spoked wheels, Model No. 109
EX $25   **NM** $50   **MIP** $75

Hesketh 308E Racing Car, Model No. 222
EX $20   **NM** $40   **MIP** $75

Hillman Imp, Model No. 138
EX $50   **NM** $100   **MIP** $150

Hillman Minx, Model No. 40f
EX $40   **NM** $90   **MIP** $150

Hillman Minx, 1958-61, two-tone, black tires, Model No. 175
EX $50   **NM** $100   **MIP** $150

Hudson Commodore Sedan, Cream and blue body, Model No. 171
EX $25   **NM** $100   **MIP** $200

Hudson Commodore Sedan, Hi-Line, Model No. 171
EX $50   **NM** $200   **MIP** $400

(ToyShop File Photo)

Hudson Hornet Sedan, Yellow and brown, white tires, Model No. 174
EX $25   **NM** $80   **MIP** $160

Humber Hawk, 1959-63, two-tone, Model No. 165
EX $30   **NM** $80   **MIP** $150

HWM Racer, Model No. 235
EX $25   **NM** $70   **MIP** $140

Jaguar 3.4 Saloon, Model No. 195
EX $25   **NM** $80   **MIP** $160

Jaguar D-Type, 1957-65, light blue, white driver, racing car, Model No. 238
EX $60   **NM** $120   **MIP** $195

Jaguar Mark X, 1962-69, opening trunk, 2 pieces of luggage, Model No. 142
EX $65   **NM** $130   **MIP** $225

Jaguar SS 100 Sports Car, Model No. 38f
EX $30   **NM** $100   **MIP** $200

Jaguar XK 120, 1954-62, white, Model No. 157
EX $120   **NM** $200   **MIP** $400

Jaguar XK 120, 1954-62, yellow/gray, Model No. 157
EX $80   **NM** $125   **MIP** $275

Jaguar XK 120, 1954-62, turquoise, cerise, Model No. 157
EX $80   **NM** $125   **MIP** $275

(KP Photo by Dr. Douglas Sadecky)

Jaguar XK 120, 1959-62, gray-green, yellow or red, Model No. 157
EX $95   **NM** $210   **MIP** $375

Jensen FF, Model No. 188
EX $15   **NM** $50   **MIP** $100

Lamborghini Marzal, Model No. 189
EX $10   **NM** $20   **MIP** $60

Lotus F1 Racing Car, Model No. 225
EX $10   **NM** $20   **MIP** $40

Lotus Racing Car, 1963-70, Model No. 241
EX $20   **NM** $30   **MIP** $50

Maserati Race Car, 1954-64, red, green wheels, white driver, open Grand Prix racer, Model No. 231
EX $60   **NM** $135   **MIP** $200

Maserati Sport 2000, 1958, red open racer, white driver, black tires, Model No. 22A
EX $75   **NM** $150   **MIP** $215

McLaren M8A Can Am Racer, Model No. 223
EX $10   **NM** $20   **MIP** $40

Mercedes 190 SL, Model No. 526
EX $25   **NM** $100   **MIP** $200

Mercedes-Benz 250SE, 1968-72, metallic blue, white interior, Model No. 160
EX $20   **NM** $40   **MIP** $65

Mercedes-Benz C111, Model No. 224
EX $5   **NM** $20   **MIP** $50

MG Midget Sports, U.S. issue, Model No. 129
EX $250   **NM** $450   **MIP** $750

MG Midget Sports Car, Model No. 108
EX $25   **NM** $100   **MIP** $200

MGB Sports Car, Model No. 113
EX $25   **NM** $60   **MIP** $130

Morris Oxford, 1954-60, 4-door sedan, Model No. 159
EX $100   **NM** $200   **MIP** $300

Mustang Fastback, 1965-73, Model No. 161
EX $35   **NM** $55   **MIP** $75

Nash Rambler, Model No. 173
EX $20   **NM** $70   **MIP** $140

Packard Clipper Sedan, 1958-63, two-tone, white tires, Model No. 180
EX $50   **NM** $110   **MIP** $170

Packard Convertible, Model No. 132
EX $25   **NM** $80   **MIP** $160

Packard Super 8 Tourer, Model No. 39a
EX $25 **NM** $80 **MIP** $160

Panhard PL17, 1960-68, Model No. F547
EX $45 **NM** $80 **MIP** $120

Pathe News Camera Car, 1967-70, Model No. 281
EX $70 **NM** $105 **MIP** $180

Peugeot 203 Berline Saloon, Model No. 24r
EX $25 **NM** $100 **MIP** $200

Peugeot 403 Sedan, 1959-61, Model No. F521/24B
EX $60 **NM** $90 **MIP** $135

Peugeot 404, Model No. 553
EX $60 **NM** $120 **MIP** $200

Plymouth Belvedere, Model No. 24D
EX $35 **NM** $150 **MIP** $300

Plymouth Estate Car, Model No. 27F
EX $20 **NM** $70 **MIP** $140

Plymouth Fury Convertible, Model No. 137G
EX $20 **NM** $60 **MIP** $120

Plymouth Fury Sports, 1965-69, Model No. 115
EX $35 **NM** $55 **MIP** $80

Plymouth Plaza, 1959-63, white tires, Model No. 178
EX $25 **NM** $75 **MIP** $150

Plymouth Plaza, 1959-63, white roof, harder-to-find version, Model No. 178
EX $25 **NM** $150 **MIP** $300

Plymouth Stock Car, Model No. 201
EX $10 **NM** $20 **MIP** $40

Pontiac Parisienne, Model No. 173
EX $20 **NM** $50 **MIP** $100

Porsche 356A, 1958-66, cream, black tires, Model No. 182
EX $50 **NM** $100 **MIP** $150

Rambler Cross Country Station Wagon, Model No. 193
EX $20 **NM** $70 **MIP** $140

Range Rover, 1970-80, copper; opening doors, hood, and trunk, Model No. 192
EX $15 **NM** $35 **MIP** $65

Renault Dauphine, 1959-62, Model No. F524/24E
EX $50 **NM** $80 **MIP** $125

Rolls Royce Phantom V, Model No. 194
EX n/a **NM** n/a **MIP** n/a

Rolls Royce Silver Wraith, 1959-62, Model No. 150
EX $30 **NM** $65 **MIP** $125

Rolls-Royce, 1946-50, Model No. 30B
EX $65 **NM** $100 **MIP** $125

Rolls-Royce Phantom V, 1962-69, Model No. 198
EX $50 **NM** $75 **MIP** $100

Rover 3500, Model No. 180
EX $5 **NM** $20 **MIP** $60

Simca Chambord, 1959, 4-door sedan, two-tone, opening doors, Model No. 24K
EX $50 **NM** $100 **MIP** $150

Singer Gazel, 1959-63, 4-door sedan, two-tone, black tires, Model No. 168
EX $50 **NM** $100 **MIP** $150

Singer Vogue, 1962-67, Model No. 145
EX $50 **NM** $75 **MIP** $100

Standard Vanguard, 1954-60, Model No. 153
EX $60 **NM** $85 **MIP** $120

Streamline Racer, harder to find and subsequently, worth more, in red finish, Model No. 23s
EX $20 **NM** $40 **MIP** $80

(KP Photo)

Studebaker Commander, 1959-61, another in the line of French-made Dinky toys, Model No. F24Y/540
EX $75 **NM** $95 **MIP** $160

Studebaker Golden Hawk, 1958-63, green or tan body in two-tone, coupe, white tires, Model No. 169
EX $65 **NM** $115 **MIP** $185

Studebaker Land Cruiser, single color body, Model No. 172
EX $35 **NM** $85 **MIP** $160

Studebaker Land Cruiser, two-toned version, harder-to-find, Model No. 172
EX $25 **NM** $150 **MIP** $300

Studebaker President, Model No. 179
EX $25 **NM** $80 **MIP** $160

Sunbeam Alpine, Model No. 107
EX $30 **NM** $80 **MIP** $175

Sunbeam Rapier Saloon, 1958-63, two-tone, black tires, Model No. 166
EX $50 **NM** $100 **MIP** $150

Town Sedan, 1934-40, Model No. 24C
EX $85 **NM** $130 **MIP** $200

Triumph 1300, 1967-69, light blue body, red interior, Model No. 162
EX $30 **NM** $65 **MIP** $120

Triumph 1800 Saloon, 1954-60, 4-door sedan, baseplate changed in 1958, Model No. 40B/151
EX $65 **NM** $140 **MIP** $210

Triumph 2000, Model No. 135
EX $35 **NM** $60 **MIP** $100

Triumph Spitfire, Model No. 114
EX $20 **NM** $75 **MIP** $150

Triumph TR2, 1956-59, salmon/pink body, blue interior, white driver, Model No. 111
EX $100 **NM** $200 **MIP** $315

(KP Photo)

Triumph TR-2, 1957-60, yellow, pictured here with 773 Robot Traffic Signal, Model No. 105
EX $75 **NM** $120 **MIP** $200

Triumph TR-2, 1957-60, gray, Model No. 105
EX $60 **NM** $85 **MIP** $135

Universal Jeep, green or red body, Model No. 405
EX $25 **NM** $60 **MIP** $120

Vanguard, Model No. 40e
EX $25 **NM** $75 **MIP** $150

Vanwall Race Car, Model No. 239
EX $20 **NM** $60 **MIP** $130

Vauxhall, Model No. 151
EX $20 **NM** $50 **MIP** $100

Volkswagen 1300 Sedan, 1965-76, Model No. 129
EX $20 **NM** $35 **MIP** $75

Volkswagen Karmann-Ghia, 1959-64, red, green, or yellow body, Model No. 24M/187
EX $45 **NM** $80 **MIP** $125

Volkswagen VW 1600 TL, Model No. 163
EX $15 **NM** $40 **MIP** $100

Volkswagen VW Beetle, 1956-70, green, gray, white, or blue body, Model No. 181
EX $35 **NM** $70 **MIP** $130

Volvo 1800S, Model No. 116
EX $20 **NM** $60 **MIP** $120

(KP Photo)

Volvo 265 DL Estate, 1977-79, Blue, with opening rear hatch and brown plastic interior, black grille, Model No. 122
EX $12 **NM** $22 **MIP** $45

VW Porsche 914, Model No. 208
EX $15 **NM** $30 **MIP** $80

CHARACTER & TV RELATED

"Emergency" Rescue Paramedic Truck, Model No. 267
EX $10 **NM** $45 **MIP** $90

Captain Scarlett Spectrum Pursuit Vehicle, 1968-77, fantasy car from Captain Scarlett

and the Mysterons show, antenna, rocket, driver, Model No. 104
EX $150   **NM** $325   **MIP** $550

Gabriel's Model T, Model No. 109
EX $30   **NM** $60   **MIP** $100

Galactic War Chariot, 1979-80, Model No. 361
EX $30   **NM** $45   **MIP** $70

Joe's Car, 1969-75, from the tv show, "Joe 90", Model No. 102
EX $55   **NM** $90   **MIP** $140

Klingon Battle Cruiser, 1976-79, Model No. 357
EX $30   **NM** $45   **MIP** $70

Lady Penelope's Fab 1, 1966-76, shocking pink version, rocket and 4 missiles, Model No. 100
EX $125   **NM** $210   **MIP** $350

(ToyShop File Photo)

Lady Penelope's Fab 1, 1966-76, pink version, rocket and 4 missiles, Model No. 100
EX $90   **NM** $145   **MIP** $230

Maximum Security Vehicle, 1968-75, fantasy car from Captain Scarlett and the Mysterons show, white, gullwing doors, cargo, Model No. 105
EX $50   **NM** $100   **MIP** $160

(KP Photo by Dr. Douglas Sadecky)

Parsley's Car Morris Oxford, 1970-72, Cut-out stand-up figures of Parsley's friends were included for additional play, Model No. 477
EX $65   **NM** $115   **MIP** $145

Prisoner Mini-Moke, 1967-70, from the tv show, "The Prisoner", Model No. 106
EX $100   **NM** $195   **MIP** $325

Renault Sinpar, 1968-71, Model No. F1406
EX $80   **NM** $135   **MIP** $220

Santa Special Model T Ford, 1964-68, Model No. 485
EX $65   **NM** $100   **MIP** $150

Thunderbirds 2 & 4, 1967-73, space ship from Thunderbirds show, Model No. 101
EX $110   **NM** $275   **MIP** $400

Tiny's Mini-Moke, 1970-73, Model No. 350
EX $60   **NM** $85   **MIP** $120

(KP Photo)

U.S.S. Enterprise, 1980, Model No. 371/803
EX $40   **NM** $80   **MIP** $115

Zygon Marauder, Model No. 368
EX $20   **NM** $40   **MIP** $60

Zygon War Chariot, Model No. 368
EX $12   **NM** $24   **MIP** $45

CONSTRUCTION

Atlas Digger, Model No. 984
EX $30   **NM** $45   **MIP** $70

Aveling Barford Road Roller, 1954-63, green body, red rollers,, Model No. 25P/251
EX $30   **NM** $60   **MIP** $90

Bedford Tipper, orange, Model No. 410
EX $20   **NM** $75   **MIP** $150

Blaw Knox Bulldozer, Model No. 561
EX $45   **NM** $75   **MIP** $115

Coles Crane, Model No. 972
EX $10   **NM** $40   **MIP** $80

Coles Hydra Crane Truck 150T, Yellow with black chassis, swivel crane section with working boom and hook, working levellers. 210mm, Model No. 980
EX $10   **NM** $40   **MIP** $80

Coles Mobile Crane, 1955-66, Model No. 971
EX $40   **NM** $70   **MIP** $110

Conventry Climax Fork Lift, Model No. 401
EX $15   **NM** $40   **MIP** $80

Conveyancer Fork Lift Truck, Includes driver and pallet. Rear wheels turn, Model No. 404
EX $20   **NM** $40   **MIP** $60

Dinky Shovel Dozer, Yellow body, red-roofed cab, rolling treads, lifting and dumping bucket, Model No. 977
EX $10   **NM** $40   **MIP** $80

Dumper Truck, Model No. 382
EX $5   **NM** $10   **MIP** $20

Eaton Yale Articulated Tractor Shovel, Model No. 973
EX $10   **NM** $40   **MIP** $80

(KP Photo)

Euclid Dump Truck, 1955-69, with lever-operated tipping bed. Part of the "Dinky Supertoys" range, Model No. 965
EX $55   **NM** $80   **MIP** $125

Ford D800 Snow Plow Tipper, Blue cab with opening doors, silver tipping section with opening tailgate, yellow plow raises and lowers. 194mm, Model No. 439
EX $10   **NM** $40   **MIP** $80

Johnson 2-Ton Dumper, Yellow open-cab articulated body with driver, red tipper section, 106mm, Model No. 430
EX $5   **NM** $30   **MIP** $60

Lorry Mounted Concrete Mixer, Model No. 960
EX $10   **NM** $50   **MIP** $100

Michigan 180-111 Tractor Dozer, Yellow body, silver engine, red blade raises and lowers, cab is removeable, Model No. 976
EX $10   **NM** $40   **MIP** $80

Muir Hill Dumper Truck, Model No. 962
EX $15   **NM** $30   **MIP** $60

Muir Hill Loader & Trencher, Yellow tractor body with working loader and backhoe. 163mm, Model No. 967
EX $5   **NM** $30   **MIP** $60

Muir Hill Two-Wheel Loader, 1962-78, Model No. 437
EX $30   **NM** $40   **MIP** $60

Richier Road Roller, 1959-69, Model No. F830
EX $75   **NM** $100   **MIP** $150

(ToyShop File Photo)

Road Grader, 1973-75, Yellow and red with swivel blade, Model No. 963
EX $30   **NM** $45   **MIP** $70

Salev Crane, 1959-61, Model No. F595
EX $65   **NM** $100   **MIP** $175

Simca Tipper Dump Truck, French-made, Model No. 33
EX $30   **NM** $90   **MIP** $180

EMERGENCY VEHICLES

Airport Fire Engine, Model No. 263
EX $10   **NM** $40   **MIP** $80

(KP Photo by Dr. Douglas Sadecky)

Airport Fire Tender with Flashing Light, 1962-69, Model No. 276

EX $32   NM $65   MIP $100

Ambulance, Model No. 30F

EX $100   NM $160   MIP $275

Bedford Fire Escape, 1969-74, Model No. 956

EX $75   NM $110   MIP $175

(KP Photo by Dr. Douglas Sadecky)

Berliet Fire Pumper, Included two detachable hose reels as accessories. French-made Dinky toy, Model No. 32E

EX $75   NM $95   MIP $120

Citroen DS19 Police Car, 1967-70, Model No. F501

EX $75   NM $95   MIP $175

Citroen Fire Van, 1959-63, Model No. F25D/562

EX $80   NM $110   MIP $250

Commer Fire Engine, 1955-69, Model No. 955

EX $60   NM $85   MIP $135

Convoy Rescue Fire Truck, Model No. 384

EX $5   NM $20   MIP $40

Crash Squad set, With Bell Helicopter and Plymouth Police Car, Model No. 299

EX $10   NM $40   MIP $80

Daimler Ambulance, Model No. 254

EX $15   NM $60   MIP $120

Delahaye Fire Engine, Model No. 899

EX $150   NM $300   MIP $450

(KP Photo by Dr. Douglas Sadecky)

Delahaye Fire Truck, 1955-70, the white tires really enhance this French-made Dinky toy, Model No. F32D/899

EX $120   NM $190   MIP $375

DeSoto USA Police Car, Model No. 258

EX $10   NM $60   MIP $120

ERF Fire Tender, Red body, removable extending escape ladder with wheels, Model No. 266

EX $15   NM $50   MIP $100

Fire Chief Land Rover,

EX $35   NM $50   MIP $85

Fire Chief's Range Rover, Red body, opening hood, tailgate and doors, Model No. 195

EX $5   NM $30   MIP $60

Fire Engine, Model No. 555

EX $25   NM $65   MIP $130

Ford Escort Panda Police Car, Model No. 270

EX $5   NM $30   MIP $60

Ford Police Car, 1960s, Model No. F551

EX $50   NM $100   MIP $150

Ford Transit Ambulance, Model No. 274

EX $5   NM $25   MIP $50

(ToyShop File Photo)

Ford Transit Fire Appliance, Red with silver ladder and sliding door, Model No. 286

EX $5   NM $25   MIP $50

Ford Transit Police Accident Unit, Model No. 269

EX $5   NM $30   MIP $60

Merryweather Marquis Fire Tender, 1970s, Red body with removeable silver ladder and working fire pump, Model No. 285

EX $5   NM $50   MIP $100

(KP Photo)

Mersey Tunnel Police Land Rover, 1955-61, Model No. 255

EX $60   NM $85   MIP $135

Motorway Services Ford Transit Van, 1970s, Yellow body with "Motorway Services" on panel sides, Model No. 417

EX $5   NM $25   MIP $50

Nash Rambler Canadian Fire Chief's Car, Model No. 257

EX $10   NM $40   MIP $80

Plymouth Police Car, Model No. 244

EX $5   NM $30   MIP $60

Plymouth Police Car, 1977-80, Model No. 244

EX $25   NM $35   MIP $50

Police Accident Unit, Model No. 287

EX $5   NM $30   MIP $60

Police Land Rover, Model No. 277

EX $5   NM $30   MIP $60

Police Mini Clubman, 1976, Light blue with opening white doors and "Police" on sides, Model No. 255

EX $5   NM $30   MIP $60

Police Range Rover, White body, orange stripe on sides, opening hood, doors and tailgate. 109mm, Model No. 254

EX $5   NM $30   MIP $60

(ToyShop File Photo)

Range Rover Ambulance, 1974-78, With opening hood, doors and tailgate. Includes patient on stretcher, Model No. 268

EX $25   NM $35   MIP $50

RCMP Ford Fairlane, Model No. 264

EX $10   NM $60   MIP $120

Rover 3500 Police, Model No. 264

EX $5   NM $30   MIP $60

Streamlined Fire Engine, 1946-53, red, Merryweather fire engine, ladder, bell, Model No. 25H/25

EX $60   NM $85   MIP $160

Streamlined Fire Engine, 1954-62, red, Merryweather fire engine, ladder, bell, Model No. 250

EX $35   NM $65   MIP $125

(KP Photo)

Superior Cadillac Ambulance, 1971-79, opening rear hatch with plastic patient on stretcher, Model No. 288

EX $15   NM $28   MIP $60

Superior Criterion Ambulance, 1962-68, Model No. 263

EX $50   NM $75   MIP $100

(KP Photo by Dr. Douglas Sadecky)

Superior Criterion Ambulance, 1962-68, The roof beacon warning light actually flashed with the aid of a small battery, Model No. 277

EX $40   NM $75   MIP $110

USA Police Car (Pontiac), Model No. 251

EX $35   NM $50   MIP $85

Vauxhall Victor Ambulance, 1964-70, Model No. 278
EX $55   **NM** $85   **MIP** $115

Volvo Police Car, 1970s, Same body as 265 Estate, but in white with orange stripes, Model No. 243
EX $5   **NM** $30   **MIP** $60

FARM

Convoy Farm Truck, Model No. 381
EX $5   **NM** $15   **MIP** $30

David Brown Tractor, 1966-75, Model No. 305
EX $60   **NM** $120   **MIP** $200

Farm Tractor, 1933-40, Fordson-style; red, yellow, blue, Model No. 22E
EX $100   **NM** $225   **MIP** $450

Field Marshall Tractor, 1953, 1954-65, orange, driver, black tires, Model No. 27N/301
EX $60   **NM** $85   **MIP** $175

(KP Photo)

Garden Roller, 1948-54, Model No. 105A
EX $15   **NM** $25   **MIP** $35

Halesowen Harvest Trailer, 1949-53, 1954-70, Model No. 27B/320
EX $15   **NM** $35   **MIP** $75

Hayrake, 1954-71, Model No. 324
EX $30   **NM** $40   **MIP** $60

Leyland 384 Tractor, 1971-78, blue w/blue driver, Model No. 308
EX $45   **NM** $90   **MIP** $135

Massey-Harris Manure Spreader, 1949-53, 1954-71, red, Model No. 27C/321
EX $25   **NM** $50   **MIP** $75

Massey-Harris Tractor, 1948-53, 1954-71, red w/yellow wheels, brown driver to blue, Model No. 27A/300
EX $60   **NM** $135   **MIP** $225

Moto-Cart, 1954-60, Model No. 27G/342
EX $35   **NM** $50   **MIP** $75

Wheelbarrow, Model No. 382
EX $10   **NM** $20   **MIP** $40

MILITARY

1 Ton Cargo Truck, Model No. 641
EX $20   **NM** $40   **MIP** $80

10 Ton Army Truck, 1954-63, Model No. 622
EX $20   **NM** $40   **MIP** $80

105mm U.S. Howitzer with Crew, Model No. 609
EX $20   **NM** $40   **MIP** $80

155mm Mobile Gun, Model No. 654
EX $25   **NM** $50   **MIP** $100

155mm self-propelled gun, French-made toy, Model No. 813
EX $45   **NM** $90   **MIP** $180

25-pounder Field Gun, Model No. 686
EX $20   **NM** $40   **MIP** $85

25-pounder Field Gun with Tractor and Trailer, Model No. 697
EX $55   **NM** $110   **MIP** $220

25-pounder gun trailer, Model No. 687
EX $15   **NM** $30   **MIP** $60

(KP Photo)

5.5 Medium Gun, 1955, Model No. 692
EX $15   **NM** $30   **MIP** $50

6-pounder anti-tank gun, Model No. 625
EX $16   **NM** $32   **MIP** $65

7.2 Howitzer, Model No. 693
EX $25   **NM** $50   **MIP** $100

88mm gun, Model No. 656
EX $25   **NM** $50   **MIP** $100

AEC Arctic Transport with Helicopter, Model No. 618
EX $50   **NM** $85   **MIP** $125

Alvis Scorpion, 1970s, Turret fires plastic shells, includes camo netting. 1:40-scale, Model No. 690
EX $10   **NM** $40   **MIP** $80

AML Panhard Armored Car, French-made Dinky Toy, Model No. 814
EX $30   **NM** $60   **MIP** $120

AMX 13 T Tank, Model No. 801/80c
EX $35   **NM** $70   **MIP** $140

AMX Bridge Layer, Lever extends folding bridge set on AMX tank chassis, Model No. F883
EX $75   **NM** $110   **MIP** $200

(KP Photo)

AMX Tank, Model No. F80C/817
EX $50   **NM** $75   **MIP** $100

Armored Car, Model No. 670
EX $25   **NM** $50   **MIP** $100

Armored Personnel Carrier, Model No. 676
EX $25   **NM** $50   **MIP** $100

(KP Photo)

Armoured Command Vehicle, Squared, longer bodied six-wheeled vehicle. Shown here with #641 Cargo Truck, Model No. 677
EX $50   **NM** $85   **MIP** $125

Army Covered Wagon, Model No. 623
EX $40   **NM** $85   **MIP** $150

Army Field Kitchen Cuisine Roulante, Trailer with two boilers/kettles, stovepipe, spare tire, Model No. 823
EX $30   **NM** $60   **MIP** $120

Army Jeep, Model No. 669
EX $20   **NM** $40   **MIP** $80

Army Water Tanker, Model No. 643
EX $50   **NM** $75   **MIP** $120

Austin Champ, Model No. 674
EX $20   **NM** $40   **MIP** $80

Austin Champ, Model No. 674
EX $20   **NM** $40   **MIP** $80

Austin Covered Truck, Model No. 30SM/625
EX $85   **NM** $135   **MIP** $275

Austin Paramoke, Includes parachute, vehicle holder and vehicle, Model No. 601
EX $25   **NM** $35   **MIP** $50

Bedford Military Truck, Model No. 25WM/60
EX $80   **NM** $125   **MIP** $250

(ToyShop File Photo)

Berliet All Terrain 6x6 Truck, Green body with canopy top over bed. Shown here with 80E/819 Howitzer, Model No. 80D/818
EX $40   **NM** $80   **MIP** $150

(KP Photo)

Berliet Missile Launcher, Green six-wheeled truck with Nord R20 winged missile, Model No. 620
EX $75   NM $100   MIP $175

(ToyShop File Photo)

Berliet Tank Transporter, Another French-made Dinky Toy, shown here with Panhard Armored Car, #815, Model No. 890
EX $65   NM $130   MIP $250

(ToyShop File Photo)

Berliet Wrecker, Crane hook and swivel base, six-wheels, Model No. F826
EX $60   NM $120   MIP $240

Bren Gun Carrier, Green body, working treads. Two figures included, 1:32-scale, Model No. 622
EX $25   NM $45   MIP $85

Bren Gun Carrier and Anti-Tank Gun, Includes #622 Bren Gun Carrier with #625 6-pounder anti-tank gun that fires shells, Model No. 619
EX $35   NM $65   MIP $110

Centurian Tank, 1954-70, rubber or plastic treads, olive drab, Model No. 651
EX $60   NM $110   MIP $185

Centurion Tank, Rolling rubber treads, swivel turret, raising and lowering gun barrel, Model No. 683
EX $45   NM $90   MIP $180

Chieftain Tank, 1970s, With rolling treads, swivel turret, gun barrel that raises and lowers, white numbers on front, gold square emblem on turret. Fires shells, 1:50-scale, Model No. 683
EX $15   NM $50   MIP $100

Commando Jeep, Model No. 612
EX $25   NM $35   MIP $50

Commando Squad Gift Set, Model No. 303
EX $25   NM $70   MIP $140

Convoy Army Truck, Green body with removeable plastic canopy. "Available Later" in 1977 catalog, Model No. 687
EX $5   NM $20   MIP $40

Cooker Trailer, Model No. 151c
EX $25   NM $50   MIP $100

(ToyShop File Photo)

Covered Army Transport Wagon, 1937-41, Prewar toy, six-wheeled truck with black plastic tires. Molded driver, metal canopy, Model No. 151B
EX $50   NM $100   MIP $200

(KP Photo)

Daimler Ambulance, a popular casting available in military and civilian variations, Model No. 30HM/624
EX $80   NM $125   MIP $250

Dodge Command Car, Model No. F810
EX $40   NM $60   MIP $85

DUKW Amphibian, Green, open-topped body, 1:76-scale, Model No. 681
EX $10   NM $30   MIP $60

EBR Panhard Armored Car, 8-wheeled vehicle, 2 sets of road wheels, front and back, with two sets of floating all-terrain wheels in the center. Rotating turret, Model No. 80A/815
EX $30   NM $60   MIP $120

Ferret Armored Car, Green scout car with open turret, 1:48-scale, Model No. 680
EX $12   NM $30   MIP $50

Ferret Armoured Car, Model No. 630
EX $25   NM $35   MIP $50

Field Artillery Tractor, Model No. 688
EX $25   NM $50   MIP $90

Foden Army Truck, Model No. 668
EX $5   NM $30   MIP $60

Ford U.S. Army Staff Car, Model No. 170
EX $65   NM $130   MIP $250

GMC Military Truck, French-made, Model No. 809
EX $50   NM $100   MIP $200

GMC Tanker, Model No. F823
EX $125   NM $250   MIP $500

Hanomag Tank Destroyer, German Hanomag half-track with pivoting anti-tank gun that fires plastic shells. 1:35-scale, Model No. 694
EX $10   NM $40   MIP $80

(ToyShop File Photo)

Honest John Missile Launcher, Green truck with rubber-band powered plastic missile, Model No. 665
EX $45   NM $90   MIP $180

Jeep, Model No. F816
EX $50   NM $75   MIP $115

(ToyShop File Photo)

Jeep, Model No. 153a
EX $25   NM $50   MIP $100

Jeep, French-made, Model No. 80b
EX $30   NM $60   MIP $120

Jeep avec Canon de 106, French-made, Model No. 829
EX $25   NM $50   MIP $100

Jeep Hotchkiss-Willys, French-made, Model No. 816
EX $25   NM $50   MIP $100

Jeep with Rocket Launcher, French-made, Model No. 828
EX $35   NM $75   MIP $140

Land Rover Bomb Disposal Unit, 1976, Green Land-Rover Safari with orange quarter panels, blue dome light and "Explosive Disposal" sign on roof. Has opening doors and hood, and includes remote bomb-finding tank. 1:42-scale, Model No. 604
EX $20   NM $40   MIP $80

Leopard Recovery Tank, 1970s, Green with rolling treads, pivoting boom, raising and lowering blade, West German Bundeswehr markings. 1:50-scale, Model No. 699
EX $15   NM $50   MIP $100

Leopard Tank, Swivel turret, pivoting gun fires plastic shells, West German Army markings, Model No. 692
EX $15   NM $50   MIP $100

Light Dragon Field Gun Set, Model No. 162
EX $75   NM $150   MIP $300

Light Dragon Tractor, Model No. 162a
EX $40   **NM** $80   **MIP** $150

(ToyShop File Photo)

Light Tank, Green, metal treads, rolling tread wheels, Model No. 152A
EX $50   **NM** $100   **MIP** $200

Light Tank Set, Model No. 152
EX $125   **NM** $250   **MIP** $500

(ToyShop File Photo)

M3 Halftrack, Olive body, working treads, AA gun in turret, Model No. 822
EX $50   **NM** $100   **MIP** $200

(ToyShop File Photo)

Medium Artillery Tractor, Part of the Dinky Supertoys line, this model was 5-1/2" long. Shown here at bottom with #622 truck at top, Model No. 689
EX $25   **NM** $50   **MIP** $100

(ToyShop File Photo)

Mercedes-Benz Military Unimog, French-made toy, dark olive with canopy top over bed, shown here with 823 Field Kitchen trailer, Model No. 821
EX $30   **NM** $60   **MIP** $120

Military Ambulance, With Red Cross decals and opening rear doors, Model No. 626
EX $25   **NM** $45   **MIP** $75

Military Ambulance, Model No. F80F/820
EX $50   **NM** $75   **MIP** $100

(KP Photo by Dr. Douglas Sadecky)

Missile Erecting Vehicle, 1959, with Corporal Missile and Launching Platform, Model No. 666
EX $100   **NM** $155   **MIP** $240

(KP Photo by Dr. Douglas Sadecky)

Missile Servicing Platform, 1960, this vehicle made a nice companion to the 666 Missile Erecting Vehicle. A nicely detailed toy, it had a short production run, Model No. 667
EX $95   **NM** $130   **MIP** $270

Obusier 155mm Cannon, French Dinky toy, four-wheeled chassis under cannon, Model No. 80E/819
EX $40   **NM** $80   **MIP** $160

(ToyShop File Photo)

RAF Pressure Refueller, Dark gray body, part of the Dinky Supertoys line, 5-1/2" long. Shown here (top) in photo with #661 recovery tractor, Model No. 642
EX $40   **NM** $80   **MIP** $160

(KP Photo)

Reconnaisance Car, This model was produced in pre- and post-war periods, Model No. 152B
EX $40   **NM** $60   **MIP** $100

(KP Photo)

Recovery Tractor, 1957, Tow hook has working reel, Model No. 661
EX $60   **NM** $90   **MIP** $140

(ToyShop File Photo)

Scout Car, Open-turret scout car, shown here at right with Austin Para-Moke, #601. 2-5/8", Model No. 673
EX $5   **NM** $40   **MIP** $80

(ToyShop File Photo)

Searchlight, prewar, Model No. 161A
EX $125   **NM** $250   **MIP** $500

Sinpar 4x4 Military Police Vehicle, Model No. 815
EX $60   **NM** $120   **MIP** $200

Stalwart Load Carrier, Model No. 682
EX $10   **NM** $30   **MIP** $60

(ToyShop File Photo)

Static 88mm Gun with Crew, Includes shells and three soldiers, Model No. 662
EX $10   **NM** $40   **MIP** $80

Stiker Anti-Tank Vehicle, Angular armored vehicle with 5-missile launcher that fires all rockets individually or at once
EX n/a   **NM** n/a   **MIP** n/a

Tank Transporter, Model No. 660
EX $75   **NM** $100   **MIP** $175

(ToyShop File Photo)

Tank Transporter and Centurion Tank,
1956-64, Includes #660 Tank
Transporter with #651 Centurion Tank.
Shown here with single box for tank,
Model No. 698
EX $85   **NM** $165   **MIP** $250

Tank Transporter with Chieftain Tank,
Model No. 616
EX $20   **NM** $60   **MIP** $120

Task Force Set, Model No. 677
EX $20   **NM** $50   **MIP** $100

Three Ton Army Wagon, 1954-63, Model
No. 621
EX $50   **NM** $85   **MIP** $125

U.S. Jeep with 105mm Howitzer set,
Includes firing gun, Model No. 615
EX $20   **NM** $50   **MIP** $100

(ToyShop File Photo)

**VW KDF (Kubelwagen) and PAK Anti-Tank
gun,** Excellent two-piece set--the gun
actually fires plastic shells, Model No. 617
EX $20   **NM** $50   **MIP** $100

MISCELLANEOUS

(KP Photo by Dr. Douglas Sadecky)

Healey Sports Boat on Trailer, 1960-62,
Model No. 796
EX $25   **NM** $35   **MIP** $55

Land Rover, 1954-71, red, orange or green
open body, plastic driver, Model No. 340
EX $100   **NM** $200   **MIP** $300

Land Rover Trailer, Model No. 341
EX $15   **NM** $40   **MIP** $80

Large Trailer, Model No. 428
EX $15   **NM** $25   **MIP** $50

**Loading ramp for Pullmore Car
Transporter,** Model No. 994
EX $10   **NM** $20   **MIP** $40

MOTORCYCLES AND CARAVANS

4-Berth Caravan w/ Transparent Roof,
1963-69, Model No. 188
EX $25   **NM** $45   **MIP** $85

(KP Photo by Dr. Douglas Sadecky)

A.A. Motorcycle Patrol, 1946-64, the
decal on the sidecar changed depending
in which country the motorcycle was
sold, Model No. 270/44B
EX $30   **NM** $45   **MIP** $70

Caravan, postwar, Model No. 30G
EX $40   **NM** $60   **MIP** $85

Caravan, prewar, Model No. 30G
EX $55   **NM** $85   **MIP** $150

Caravan, 1956-64, Model No. 190
EX $30   **NM** $45   **MIP** $60

Caravane Caravelair,
EX $75   **NM** $150   **MIP** $250

Police Motorcycle Patrol, 1936-40, Model
No. 42B
EX $50   **NM** $75   **MIP** $125

Police Motorcycle Patrol, 1946-53, Model
No. 42B
EX $30   **NM** $45   **MIP** $70

Police Motorcyclist, 1938-40, Model
No. 37B
EX $50   **NM** $75   **MIP** $125

Police Motorcyclist, 1946-48, Model
No. 37B
EX $30   **NM** $45   **MIP** $70

Touring Secours Motorcycle Patrol,
1960s, Swiss version, Model No. 271
EX $70   **NM** $110   **MIP** $200

SHIPS

Coastguard Amphibious Missile Launch,
White-hulled amphibious vehicle
launches missiles from hood, 155mm,
Model No. 674
EX $5   **NM** $20   **MIP** $40

Cunard White-Star No 534 Queen Mary,
Model No. 52
EX $25   **NM** $50   **MIP** $100

MK 1 Corvette, White, black and gray camo
hull, gray conning tower, brown deck,
Model No. 671
EX $5   **NM** $20   **MIP** $40

Motor Patrol Boat, Model No. 1050
EX $5   **NM** $20   **MIP** $40

OSA Missile Boat, White and black, fires
four missiles, runs on concealed
wheels, Model No. 672
EX $5   **NM** $20   **MIP** $40

RAF Air/Sea Rescue Launch, Black hull,
orange cabin, silver deck. Includes
figure and raft, Model No. 678
EX $5   **NM** $20   **MIP** $40

Submarine Chaser, 1976, White and gray
with launching depth charges, Model
No. 673
EX $5   **NM** $20   **MIP** $40

TRUCKS

A.E.C. Hoynor Transporter, 1969-75,
Model No. 974
EX $60   **NM** $90   **MIP** $130

A.E.C. Shell Chemicals Tanker, Model
No. 991
EX $35   **NM** $80   **MIP** $160

B.E.V. Truck, 1954-60, Model No. 14A/400
EX $15   **NM** $30   **MIP** $70

Bedford Garbage Truck, brown, Model
No. 252
EX $15   **NM** $50   **MIP** $100

Berliet Flat Truck with Container, French-
made Dinky Toy truck, Model No. 34b
EX $30   **NM** $60   **MIP** $120

Berliet Transformer Carrier, 1961-65,
Model No. F898
EX $100   **NM** $200   **MIP** $450

Big Bedford, blue, yellow, Model No. 408/922
EX $90   **NM** $135   **MIP** $210

Big Bedford, maroon, fawn, Model
No. 408/922
EX $80   **NM** $120   **MIP** $200

Breakdown Lorry, 1954-64, "Dinky
Service," white cab, blue boom, Model
No. 25x/430
EX $80   **NM** $150   **MIP** $275

Chevrolet El Camino, 1961-68, Model
No. 449
EX $35   **NM** $65   **MIP** $100

Citroen Milk Truck, 1961-65, Model
No. F586
EX $145   **NM** $275   **MIP** $600

Citroen Wrecker, 1959-71, Model
No. F35A/582
EX $75   **NM** $120   **MIP** $250

Covered Wagon, Carter Paterson, Model
No. 25B
EX $150   **NM** $300   **MIP** $750

Covered Wagon, green, gray, Model No. 25B
EX $65   **NM** $115   **MIP** $160

Dodge Rear Tipping Wagon, Model No. 424
EX $30   **NM** $60   **MIP** $100

Electric Articulated Vehicle, Model
No. 30W/421
EX $60   **NM** $85   **MIP** $120

Esso Gas Tanker, Model No. 442
EX $40   **NM** $90   **MIP** $180

(KP Photo)

Foden Diesel 8-Wheel Wagon, 1948-52, Dark cab and bed, red fenders and chassis. Various color variations were available. Pictured here is the first-version cab, updated in 1952. Part of the Dinky Supertoy range, Model No. 501
EX $160   **NM** $220   **MIP** $435

Foden Flat Truck w/ Tailboard 1, red/black, Model No. 503/903
EX $140   **NM** $210   **MIP** $450

(ToyShop File Photo)

Foden Flat Truck w/Tailboard 2, blue/yellow, orange or blue, Model No. 503/903
EX $90   **NM** $150   **MIP** $275

Foden Flat Truck w/Tailboard 1, gray/blue, Model No. 503/903
EX $140   **NM** $210   **MIP** $450

Foden Mobilgas Tanker, 1954-57, Model No. 941
EX $145   **NM** $350   **MIP** $750

Foden Regent Tanker, Model No. 942
EX $135   **NM** $300   **MIP** $550

Fordson Thames Flat Truck, 1954-60, green or red body, flatbed truck, Model No. 422
EX $40   **NM** $80   **MIP** $135

Forward Control Wagon, 1948-53, Model No. 25R
EX $45   **NM** $65   **MIP** $90

Guy Flat Truck, common variations, Model No. 513
EX $80   **NM** $250   **MIP** $500

Guy Flat Truck w/Tailboard, 1956-58, blue cab and chassis, orange flatbed, Model No. 433
EX $75   **NM** $160   **MIP** $250

Guy Truck, "Eveready" decals, Model No. 918
EX $80   **NM** $200   **MIP** $400

Guy Warrior 4 Ton, 1958-64, Model No. 431
EX $150   **NM** $270   **MIP** $450

Guy Warrior Snow Plow, Model No. 958
EX $60   **NM** $150   **MIP** $300

Hindle Smart Helecs, Model No. 30w
EX $20   **NM** $50   **MIP** $100

Horse Box, Model No. 981
EX $30   **NM** $60   **MIP** $120

Johnson Road Sweeper, Opening doors on cab, moving brushes on sweeper section, Model No. 449
EX $15   **NM** $50   **MIP** $100

Johnston Road Sweeper, 1970s, as the toy was pushed forward, a spring coil turned the brushes in a sweeping motion, Model No. 449/451
EX $25   **NM** $50   **MIP** $75

Leland Tanker, Corn Products
EX $700   **NM** $1200   **MIP** $3000

Leland Tanker, 1963-69, Shell/BP, Model No. 944
EX $125   **NM** $215   **MIP** $450

(KP Photo)

Leyland Cement Wagon, 1956-59, one of Dinky's foreign vehicles, this toy was made in Argentina, Model No. 419/933
EX $90   **NM** $130   **MIP** $220

Leyland Comet Lorry, 1956-59, stake truck, gray tires, blue cab and chassis, yellow stakes, Model No. 417
EX $75   **NM** $190   **MIP** $300

Leyland Comet Truck, 1956-59, open hauler w/tailgate, gray tires, green cab and chassis, orange bed, Model No. 418
EX $75   **NM** $150   **MIP** $225

Leyland Eight-Wheeled Test Chassis, 1964-69, Model No. 936
EX $65   **NM** $125   **MIP** $175

Leyland Octapus Flat Truck w/ Chassis, 1964-66, Model No. 935
EX $500   **NM** $1000   **MIP** $1600

Leyland Octapus Esso Tanker, Model No. 943
EX $100   **NM** $300   **MIP** $600

Market Gardeners Wagon, yellow, Model No. 25F
EX $65   **NM** $115   **MIP** $160

(KP Photo by Dr. Douglas Sadecky)

McLean Tractor-Trailer, 1961-67, Model No. 948
EX $95   **NM** $190   **MIP** $280

Mechanical Horse, 1935-41, Model No. 33a
EX $35   **NM** $60   **MIP** $100

Midland Bank, 1966-68, Model No. 280
EX $60   **NM** $85   **MIP** $120

Mighty Antar With Propeller, 1959-64, the propeller included with this model is made of plastic, Model No. 986
EX $150   **NM** $300   **MIP** $425

Motor Truck, red, blue, Model No. 22C
EX $150   **NM** $350   **MIP** $650

Motor Truck, red, green, blue, Model No. 22C
EX $80   **NM** $120   **MIP** $200

National Benzole Tanker, Model No. 443
EX $30   **NM** $75   **MIP** $150

(KP Photo)

Panhard Esso Tanker, 1954-59, this toy was a French-made vehicle as part of the Dinky Supertoys line, Model No. F32C
EX $75   **NM** $120   **MIP** $170

Panhard Kodak Semi Trailer, 1952-54, Model No. F32AJ
EX $140   **NM** $250   **MIP** $450

Panhard SNCF Semi Trailer, 1954-59, Model No. F32AB
EX $100   **NM** $165   **MIP** $280

Petrol Wagon, Power, Model No. 25D
EX $150   **NM** $300   **MIP** $500

(KP Photo by Dr. Douglas Sadecky)

Pinder Circus Peugeot and Caravan, 1969-71, The Peugeot and Caravan are the only other vehicles produced in the Pinder Circus livery by Dinky. It would have been interesting to see what other circus vehicles would have been produced had sales been better. Again, this is a French-produced model, Model No. 882
EX $110   **NM** $240   **MIP** $380

Pinder Circus Truck and Wagon, 1969-71, A French-made Dinky toy. This photo shows the animals and decorative labels still in the package, Model No. 881
EX $110   **NM** $235   **MIP** $375

Pullmore Car Transporter, light blue, Model No. 583
EX $25   **NM** $70   **MIP** $140

(KP Photo by Dr. Douglas Sadecky)

Pullmore Car Transporter with 994 Loading Ramp, 1954-63, the 784 loading ramp cam separately packaged in the Transporter box and was used to unload the cars, Model No. 982
EX $85 NM $140 MIP $190

Renault Estafette, Model No. F561
EX $50 NM $85 MIP $150

Simca Glass Truck, gray, green, Model No. F33C/579
EX $75 NM $120 MIP $170

Simca Glass Truck, yellow, green, Model No. F33C/579
EX $100 NM $150 MIP $250

Studebaker Mobilgas Tanker, 1954-61, Model No. 440
EX $70 NM $100 MIP $175

Thames Flat Truck, 1951-60, Model No. 422/30R
EX $45 NM $75 MIP $110

(KP Photo by Dr. Douglas Sadecky)

Unic Auto Transporter, 1959-68, French-made Dinky toy, part of the Supertoys line. Ramp raises and lowers with a lever on the side of the trailer, Model No. F39A/984
EX $100 NM $200 MIP $300

Unic Bucket Truck, 1957-65, Model No. F38A/895
EX $75 NM $120 MIP $225

Willeme Log Truck, 1956-71, Model No. F36A/897
EX $75 NM $120 MIP $200

(KP Photo)

Willeme Semi Trailer Truck, 1959-71, another French-made Dinky toy, Model No. F36B/896
EX $95 NM $140 MIP $235

VANS

(KP Photo by Dr. Douglas Sadecky)

ABC-TV Mobile Control Room, 1962-69, A camera and cameraman was also included with this van, Model No. 987
EX $65 NM $130 MIP $210

ABC-TV Transmitter Van, 1962-69, this was the companion vehicle to the 987 ABC TV Mobile Control Room, Model No. 988
EX $80 NM $145 MIP $270

Atco Delivery Van, 1935-40, type 2, Model No. 28N
EX $200 NM $375 MIP $850

Atco Delivery Van, 1935-40, type 3, Model No. 28N
EX $135 NM $200 MIP $350

Austin Van, 1954-56, Shell/BP, Model No. 470
EX $60 NM $110 MIP $175

Austin Van, 1955-63, Nestle's, Model No. 471
EX $60 NM $110 MIP $175

Austin Van, 1957-60, Raleigh, Model No. 472
EX $60 NM $110 MIP $175

(KP Photo by Dr. Douglas Sadecky)

BBC-TV Camera Truck, 1959-64, Model No. 968
EX $60 NM $125 MIP $185

BBC-TV Control Room, 1959-64, Model No. 967
EX $60 NM $125 MIP $185

Bedford 10 cwt Van, Ovaltine, Model No. 481
EX $25 NM $100 MIP $200

Bedford 10 CWT. "Kodak" Van, 1954-56, yellow/orange body, "Kodak Cameras & Film" on sides, Model No. 480
EX $50 NM $125 MIP $180

Bedford AA Van, Model No. 412
EX $5 NM $30 MIP $60

Bedford CA Van, 1956-58, "Dinky Toys" on sides, orange and yellow, Model No. 482
EX $100 NM $275 MIP $425

Bedford Van, 1955-59, Heinz, Model No. 923
EX $100 NM $165 MIP $300

Citroen Breakdown Truck, Model No. 582
EX $100 NM $200 MIP $300

Citroen Cibie Delivery Van, 1960-63, Model No. F561
EX $90 NM $150 MIP $350

Citroen Police Van, Model No. 566
EX $120 NM $240 MIP $360

Electric Dairy Van, Model No. 490
EX $45 NM $90 MIP $120

Ensign Delivery Van, 1934, type 1, Model No. 28E
EX $300 NM $500 MIP $1000

Ford Transit Van, 1978-80, Model No. 417
EX $15 NM $20 MIP $30

Guy Van, Spratts, Model No. 514
EX $135 NM $300 MIP $575

Guy Van, Lyons, Model No. 514
EX $275 NM $550 MIP $1600

(KP Photo)

Guy Van, Slumberland, Model No. 514
EX $145 NM $315 MIP $590

Mini Minor Van, Joseph Mason Paints, Model No. 274
EX $150 NM $300 MIP $500

Mini Minor Van, 1960s, R.A.C., Model No. 273
EX $65 NM $115 MIP $150

Pickfords Delivery Van, 1934-35, type 2, Model No. 28B
EX $200 NM $375 MIP $600

Pickfords Delivery Van, 1934-35, type 1, Model No. 28B
EX $300 NM $500 MIP $1000

Royal Mail Bedford Van, Model No. 410
EX $5 NM $15 MIP $40

Royal Mail Van, 1955-61, Model No. 260
EX $50 NM $100 MIP $150

Saviem Race Horse Van, 1969-71, Model No. F571
EX $125 NM $225 MIP $400

Telephone Service Van, Model No. 261
EX $25 NM $75 MIP $150

Trojan Dunlop Van, 1952-57, Model No. 31B/451
EX $70 NM $110 MIoP $185

Trojan OXO Van, 1953, dark blue, Model No. 31D
EX $85 NM $210 MIP $320

DOEPKE

Adams Road Grader, 1948-56, Doepke, 26" long, yellow, #2006; 1948-56, Model No. 2006
EX $210   **NM** $295   **MIP** $395

Adams Road Grader, 1948-56, Doepke, 26" long, orange, #2006; 1948-56, Model No. 2006
EX $160   **NM** $255   **MIP** $355

American LaFrance Aerial Ladder Truck, 1950-52, Doepke, 33-1/2" long, red, #2008; 1950-52, Model No. 2008
EX $245   **NM** $325   **MIP** $400

American LaFrance Improved Aerial Ladder Truck, 1953-56, Doepke, 33-1/2" long, red, w/outriggers and cast aluminum ladder, #2014; 1953-56, Model No. 2014
EX $290   **NM** $375   **MIP** $450

American LaFrance Pumper, 1951-56, Doepke, 19" long, red, #2010; 1951-56, Model No. 2010
EX $255   **NM** $340   **MIP** $425

American LaFrance Searchlight Truck, 1955-56, Doepke, white w/battery-operated search light, #2023; 1955-56, Model No. 2023
EX $950   **NM** $1650   **MIP** $2100

Barber-Greene Bucket Loader, Doepke, on wheels, 22" long, green, #2013; Model No. 2013
EX $325   **NM** $400   **MIP** $525

Barber-Greene Bucket Loader, 1946-50, Doepke, on tracks, 18" tall, early model w/swivel chute, green, #2001; 1946-50, Model No. 2001
EX $430   **NM** $510   **MIP** $625

Barber-Greene Bucket Loader, 1946-50, Doepke, on tracks, 18" tall, later model w/out swivel chute, green, #2001; 1946-50, Model No. 2001
EX $300   **NM** $375   **MIP** $500

Barber-Greene Bucket Loader, 1946-50, Doepke, on tracks; 18" tall, later model w/out swivel chute, orange, #2001; 1946-50, Model No. 2001
EX $350   **NM** $425   **MIP** $550

Bulldozer, 1952-56, Doepke, 15" long, yellow, #2012; 1952-56, Model No. 2012
EX $425   **NM** $550   **MIP** $650

Clark Airport Tractor and Trailers Set, 1954-56, Doepke, 26-1/2" long; three pieces: red tractor, green trailer, yellow trailer, #2015; 1954-56, Model No. 2015
EX $375   **NM** $450   **MIP** $550

Euclid Truck, 1950-56, Doepke, 27" long, olive green, #2009; 1950-56, Model No. 2009
EX $250   **NM** $330   **MIP** $425

Euclid Truck, 1950-56, Doepke, 27" long, forest green, #2009; 1950-56, Model No. 2009
EX $250   **NM** $325   **MIP** $400

Euclid Truck, 1950-56, Doepke, 27" long, orange, #2009; 1950-56, Model No. 2009
EX $225   **NM** $300   **MIP** $375

Heiliner Scraper, 1951-56, Doepke, 29" long, red, #2011; 1951-56, Model No. 2011
EX $295   **NM** $300   **MIP** $375

Jaeger Concrete Mixer, 1947-49, Doepke, 15" long, yellow w/black drum, #2002; 1947-49, Model No. 2002
EX $225   **NM** $310   **MIP** $450

Jaguar, 1955-56, Doepke, 18" long, kit or built, light blue or red, #2018; 1955-56, Model No. 2018
EX $450   **NM** $550   **MIP** $650

MG Auto, 1954-56, Doepke, 15-1/2" long, kit, aluminum body; red, yellow, or gray primer, #2017; 1954-56, Model No. 2017
EX $325   **NM** $415   **MIP** $490

Unit Crane, 1949-54, Doepke, 11" long, without boom, orange, w/finger wheel, #2007; 1949-54, Model No. 2007
EX $250   **NM** $325   **MIP** $400

Unit Crane, 1949-54, Doepke, 11" long, without boom, orange, w/out finger wheel, #2007; 1949-54, Model No. 2007
EX $225   **NM** $300   **MIP** $375

Wooldridge Earth Hauler, 1946-49, Doepke, 25", yellow, #2000; 1946-49, Model No. 2000
EX $250   **NM** $325   **MIP** $450

ELDON INDUSTRIES

Clipper Ship, 21" long, 15" tall; three masts, two life boats, turning rudder; 1960s
EX $25   **NM** $40   **MIP** $60

Dump Truck, 18" long; Euclid-type dump truck, lever-activated dumping; 1960s
EX $10   **NM** $20   **MIP** $40

Dump Truck, 15-3/4" long; white and yellow plastic dump truck with red dumping body, whitewall tires; mid-1960s
EX $13   **NM** $18   **MIP** $30

Fire Pumper Truck, 13" long; red and silver plastic, water-squirting action; 1960s
EX $10   **NM** $15   **MIP** $22

Hot Rod, 14" long; red plastic body, black seats, chromed engine; early 1960s
EX $12   **NM** $23   **MIP** $35

House Trailer Hauler, 14-1/2" long; light blue tractor and house trailer with white roof and door; 1950s
EX $20   **NM** $30   **MIP** $45

Ladder Truck, 16" long; red and silver plastic, silver ladders on sides; 1960s
EX $10   **NM** $20   **MIP** $30

Pickup, large red plastic truck, black tires, chromed hubs and grille unit, issued individually or with white trailer to haul the Hot Rod; early 1960s
EX $15   **NM** $30   **MIP** $45

Ride 'Em Fire Engine, 27" long; red plastic riding truck, six wheels, red steering wheel emerging from cab roof, working siren, raising and extending ladder on swivel base, and two hoses; 1960
EX $42   **NM** $83   **MIP** $125

Service Panel Truck, 10" long; yellow plastic body, red opening rear gate and hood, removable ladder on roof; 1950s
EX $10   **NM** $18   **MIP** $28

Service Panel Truck, 10" long; opening rear gate and hood, removable ladder on roof; 1950s
EX $10   **NM** $18   **MIP** $28

Touch Command Car, 14" long; red plastic Corvette, battery-operated, remote-control with air pressure; 1968=69
EX $6   **NM** $12   **MIP** $18

Touch Command Corvette Sting Ray, 13-1/2" long; red car with darkened windows; battery-operated, six-way remote control; 1960s
EX $8   **NM** $14   **MIP** $25

Tow Truck, 21" long; white hard "Fortiflex" plastic, silver plastic winch and rails, red flasher on cab roof, silver grille unit and rear tow bar, six black tires, two metal cranks control boom height and hauling hood; 1960s
EX $25   **NM** $50   **MIP** $75

Truck Transport Set, truck hauler in red hard "Fortiflex" plastic, tractor-trailer,

black tires, load of small plastic dump, stake, pickup and wrecker trucks; 1960
EX $30   **NM** $60   **MIP** $90

USAF Missile Launcher Truck and Trailer, 20" long; "USAF" on cab doors, antenna on roof; flatbed with white and red platform with trigger for launching white missile with red nose cone, Air Force emblems on missile's wings; 1950s
EX $100   **NM** $225   **MIP** $300

Water Tanker Truck, 10" long; red soft plastic cab and chassis, white plastic tanker body and tire/axle units, opening at tank top for water and seven-hold trough in rear for dampening roads; 1960
EX $15   **NM** $30   **MIP** $45

GAY TOYS

AMC Pacer, 5" long; whitewall tires
EX $4   **NM** $6   **MIP** $10

Amphicat, 8-1/2" long; polyethylene, six-wheel all-terrain vehicle, snap-in interior, steering gear, chromed front, and rear lights; early 1970s
EX $3   **NM** $7   **MIP** $10

Back-Hoe Truck, 14" long; cabover with snap-in grille and steering wheel, oversize tires, lever-controlled hoe; early 1970s
EX $3   **NM** $7   **MIP** $10

Baha Jeep, polyethylene Jeepster with balloon tires, chromed hubs, hood decal; early 1970s
EX $2   **NM** $4   **MIP** $7

Beach Buggy, 8-1/2" long; polyethylene Jeep with striped canopy, flower decal on hood, chromed headlights, bumpers, and wheel hubs; early 1970s
EX $8   **NM** $18   **MIP** $25

Big Mac Earth Scraper, 14" long; two-piece yellow scraper with lever-controlled action, swiveling tractor with chromed grille; early 1970s
EX $6   **NM** $12   **MIP** $18

Camper Van, 7" long; red van, skylight roof, white interior, whitewall tires
EX $3   **NM** $6   **MIP** $9

Cement Mixer, 14" long; cabover with interior detail and snap-in grille and steering wheel, revolving and dumping mixing drum, oversize tires, polyethylene; early 1970s
EX $4   **NM** $8   **MIP** $12

Corvette, No. 7951; 18" long; T-roof, white interior, chrome hubs; 1970s
EX $5   **NM** $8   **MIP** $15

Dirt Demon, 18" long; pickup with rollbar; 1970s
EX $5   **NM** $8   **MIP** $15

Dukes of Hazzard's General Lee, Dodge Charger, 12" long; 180s
EX $12   **NM** $18   **MIP** $25

Dump Truck, 12" long; cabover with interior details, chromed hubs and grille, hinged dump, oversize tires, polyethylene; late 1960s-70s
EX $2   **NM** $4   **MIP** $7

Dump Truck, 20-1/2 long; Euclid-type, yellow body, black tires with white hubs; 1970s
EX $10   **NM** $15   **MIP** $20

Dune Buggy, polyethylene dune buggy, contrasting canopy, with chromed headlights, rear motor, and hub caps; early 1970s
EX $10   **NM** $18   **MIP** $22

Farm Tractor, 11" long; red and white body, white scoop, black tires; 1970s
EX $9   **NM** $14   **MIP** $20

Fire Ladder Truck, 9" long; red plastic with white ladder base and yellow ladder, black tires, cabover design, separate grille; 1960s
EX $4   **NM** $8   **MIP** $15

Fire Truck, 12" long; cabover design, oversized balloon tires, snap-in grille, steering wheel, hose reel and nozzle; late 1960s-70s
EX $3   **NM** $7   **MIP** $10

Ford Bronco, 12" long; black tires with white hubs, white grille and roof, tan/yellow body and interior; 1970s
EX $50   **NM** $100   **MIP** $225

Ford GT, 10" long; polyethylene, clear windshields, chromed motor visible through rear panel, gold lettering, chromed wheel details, early 1970s
EX $5   **NM** $10   **MIP** $15

Ford Pinto, 10-1/2" long; no decals, black tires with white hubs; 1970s
EX $7   **NM** $18   **MIP** $24

Ford Pinto, orange with "The Dukes of Hazzard" style Confederate flag; 1980s
EX $7   **NM** $13   **MIP** $20

Ford Ranchero, 4" long; 1960s
EX $2   **NM** $4   **MIP** $7

Maverick, race car with lift-off body, roll bars; early 1970s
EX $4   **NM** $8   **MIP** $12

Mercury Cougar, 11" long; chromed bumpers, clear windshields, chrome-detailed tires, in red, blue or green polyethylene; early 1970s
EX $5   **NM** $10   **MIP** $15

Puddle Jumper, polyethylene open-top dune buggy, "Puddle 77 Jumper" on hood, roll bar, chromed headlights, rear motor and wheel hubs; early 1970s
EX $3   **NM** $7   **MIP** $10

Pumper, 4" long; single-mold pumper truck, black plastic wheel-axle units; 1960s
EX $3   **NM** $5   **MIP** $8

Road Runner Camper, tan camper, white top and interior, black tires with white hubs; 1970s
EX $10   **NM** $17   **MIP** $25

Rough Riders Pickup Truck and Trailer, 11-1/2" truck, 7" trailer; "Rough Riders" stickers on truck and horse-trailer sides, truck tires black with white hubs, plastic horse
EX $10   **NM** $15   **MIP** $22

School Bus, 9" long" "School Bus" on sides, chrome grille, yellow body; 1960s
EX $8   **NM** $12   **MIP** $20

School Bus, 9" long; "Gay School Bus" on sides, chrome grille, yellow body; 1960s
EX $10   **NM** $18   **MIP** $25

School Bus Set, bus with "School Bus" on sides, chromed grille, issued with a child shelter, stop sign and three school figures; early 1970s
EX $10   **NM** $15   **MIP** $25

Street "T", polyethylene hot rod Model T coupe, chromed motor and wheel discs, headlights and front bumper; early 1970s
EX $4   **NM** $15   **MIP** $22

Texaco Star Racer, 17-3/4" long; white plstic open-cockpit racer, "Texaco Star" on sides and poiler; 1970s
EX $5   **NM** $10   **MIP** $15

Tractor Loader, farm tractor with lever-controlled front scoop and lifting and dumping action; early 1970s
EX $4   **NM** $8   **MIP** $12

U.S. Air Force Fighter, 13-1/2" long; 12" wingspan; Army-green single prop airplane, clear plastic cockpit cover
EX $3   **NM** $6   **MIP** $10

VW Camper, 6-1/2" long; "Gay Camper" decals on doors, opening side doors, interior plastic table and seats; early 1960s
EX $25   **NM** $35   **MIP** $45

Wrecker, cabover with interior design, snap-in grille, working crane with tow rope, oversize tires, polyethylene; early 1970s
EX $3   **NM** $7   **MIP** $10

Yard Tractor, 6-1/4" long tractor alone; polyethylene tractor, plow, mower, wagon, with snap-in hood, steering wheel, seats and wheel hubs; early 1970s
EX $2   **NM** $4   **MIP** $8

1995 SERIES

RACE TEAM

275 Lumina Stocker, lt. met. blue, wht. int., clr. win., metal M, uh
MIP $5

276 Hot Wheels 500, lt. met. blue, gray int., metal M, bw
MIP $5

277 Side Splitter, lt. met. blue, metal int., clr. win., metal M, bw
MIP $8

278 Dragster, lt. met. blue, wht. int., metal M, bw
MIP $5

KRACLE CAR

280 Sharkruiser, lime/blue, lime int., metal M, uh
MIP $5

281 Turboa, purp./red, red int., silv. metal M, uh
MIP $5

282 '63 Split Window, aqua/org., wht. int., org. win., chr. 1 rivet M, bw
MIP $7

284 Flashfire, purp./yel., yel. int., yel. win., blk. pl. M, uh
MIP $5

STEEL STAMP

285 Steel Passion, blk./rose, red int., tinted win., chr. M, ww
MIP $8

287 Zender Fact 4, blk., wht. int., smoked win., blk. pl. M, uh
MIP $5

289 '56 Flashsider, burgundy, chr. win., chr. M, uh
MIP $6

290 '57 Chevy, blue, blue int., blue win., chr. M, uh
MIP $6

PEARL DRIVER

292 Pearl Passion, pearl lavender, yel. int., tinted win., chr. M, ww
MIP $8

293 VW Bug, pearl pink, gray int., clr. win., metal M, bw
MIP $7

295 Talbot Lago, pearl blue, blue int., blue win., metal M, ww
MIP $8

296 Jaguar XJ220, pearl wht., tan int., smoked win., blk. pl. M, uh
MIP $5

DARK RIDER

297 Splittin Image, blk., dk. chr. int., dk. chr. win., blk. pl. M, 6sp
MIP $10

298 Twin Mill II, blk., blk. int., blk. pl. M, 6sp
MIP $10

299 Silhouette II, blk., blk. int., clr. win., blk. chr. M, 6sp
MIP $10

300 Rigor Motor, blk., chr. int., clr. win., blk. metal M, 5sp
MIP $10

ROARIN RODS

302 Mini Truck, tan, tan int., smoked win., tan pl. M, uh
MIP $5

303 Street Roader, org./blk., blk. int., smoked win., metal M, ct
MIP $25

304 Roll Patrol, wht./blk., blk. int., smoked win., blk. metal M, yct
MIP $4

305 Classic Cobra, neon yel., olive int., smoked win., metal M, 7sp
MIP $10

HOT HUBS

307 Cyber Cruiser, burgundy flake, purp. chr. int., metal M, blue/hh-org. tire
MIP $7

308 Vampyra, purp., gold int., blk. metal M, g/hh-blue tire
MIP $9

310 Shadow Jet, grn., grn. int., yel. win., metal M, y/hh-purp. tire
MIP $9

311 Suzuki Quadracer, yel. pl., purp. int., blk. metal M, alw-y/hh-blk. tire
MIP $10

SPEED GLEAMER

312 3-Window '34, grn. chr., aqua int., blue win., metal M, 7sp
MIP $4

313 T-Bucket, purp., wht. int., clr. win., blk. metal M, 5sp
MIP $35

315 Ratmobile, blk., chr. int., gray metal M, uh
MIP $3

316 Limozeen, gold, wht. int., smoked win., gold chr. M, ww
MIP $15

REAL RIDER

317 Dump Truck, neon yel., blk. int., blk. win., metal M, yel. hub rr
MIP $30

318 Mercedes Unimog, org./gray, org. int., tinted win., metal M, org. hub knobby/rr
MIP $25

320 '59 Caddy Convertible, red, wht. int., clr. win., chr. M, chr. hub ww/rr
MIP $45

321 Corvette Stingray, grn., clr. int., clr. win., metal M, gray hub rr
MIP $75

SILVER SERIES

322 Fire Eater, chr./blue insert, blue int., blue win., chr. M, bw
MIP $15

323 Rodzilla, chr., metal M, uh
MIP $4

325 Propper Chopper, chr., blk. int., blue win., blk. pl. M
MIP $3

328 School Bus, chr., wht. int., clr. win., blk. pl. M, bw
MIP $10

PHOTO FINISH

331 Aerostar, wht., silv. window win., metal M, 7sp
MIP $7

332 Flying Aces Blimp, gray, blk. win.
MIP $7

333 Tank Truck, blue, chr. win., chr. M, 7sp
MIP $7

335 Hiway Hauler, grn., blk. win., chr. M, 7sp
MIP $7

RACING METALS

336 Race Truck, chr., red int., smoked win., blk. metal M, ct
MIP $5

337 Ramp Truck, purp. chr., blk. win., metal M, 7sp
MIP $5

338 Camaro Racer, lt. blue chr. w/Baldwin, wht. int., clr. win., gray pl. M, 5sp
MIP $8

340 Dragster, lt. blue chr., wht. int., metal M, 5sp
MIP $5

1995 MODEL SERIES

341 58 Corvette, pink, chr. int., clr. win., pink pl. M, bw
MIP $5

342 Mercedes SL, red, tan int., clr. win., red pl. M, uh
MIP $5

343 Speed Blaster, blue, chr. win., chr. M, uh
MIP $10

344 Camaro Convertible, met. grn., gray int., clr. win., blk. pl. M, uh
MIP $7

345 Speed-a-Saurus, grn., metal M, bw
MIP $3

346 Hydroplane, blue/wht., chr. int., clr. win., wht. pl. M
MIP $3

347 Power Pistons, burgundy pl., gray int., blue win., metal M, 3sp
MIP $4

347 Power Rocket, bronze pl., gray int., blue win., metal M, uh
MIP $30

348 Dodge Ram, met. grn., chr. int., smoked win., gray pl. M, 5sp
MIP $4

349 Power Pipes, dk. blue pl., chr. int int., purp. win., silv. metal M, 3sp
MIP $3

350 Ferrari 355, yel., blk. int., clr. win., metal M, 3sp
MIP $3

351 Power Rocket, purp. flake pl., chr. int., metal M, 5sp
MIP $7

352 Big Chill, wht., chr. win., blk. pl. M, pink ski
MIP $12

1995 TREASURE HUNTS

353 Olds 442, met. blue, wht. int., clr. win., chr. M, redline/rr
MIP $70

354 Gold Passion, gold met., wht. int., clr. win., gold chr. M, gold hub/rr
MIP $75

355 '67 Camaro, wht. w/org. stripes, org. int., clr. win., metal M, chr. hub/rr
MIP $400

356 '57 T-Bird, dk. purp. met., clr. int., clr. win., chr. M, redline/rr
MIP $65

357 VW Bug, day-glo grn., purp. int., clr. win., metal M, purp. swirl
MIP $125

358 '63 Split Window, met. blue, wht. int., clr. win., chr. M, ww/rr
MIP $75

359 Stutz Blackhawk, blk. met., red int., clr. win., metal M, redline/rr
MIP $50

360 Rolls-Royce, dk. red met., red int., clr. win., metal M, red 6sp
MIP $50

361 Classic Caddy, lt. grn. met./olive fenders, tan int., clr. win., metal M, gold 6sp
MIP $50

362 Classic Nomad, met. teal, wht. int., clr. win., metal M, chr. swirl
MIP $60

363 Classic Cobra, dk. grn. met., tan int., clr. win., metal M, gold chr. 6sp
MIP $70

364 '31 Doozie, yel. w/blk. fenders, blk. int., clr. win., metal M, yel. 6sp
MIP $50

1996 First Editions

367 Chevy 1500 Pickup, silv. met., gray int., smoked win., metal M, alw-b7sp
MIP $12

369 Road Rocket, lt. grn./blue, metal M, gbbs
MIP $2

369 Sizzlers (Turbo Flame), wht. pearl pl., org. win., metal M, 5sp
MIP $3

369 Turbo Flame, wht. pearl pl., org. win., metal M, 5sp
MIP $6

370 Rail Rodder, blk. pl., metal M, sm. rear b5sp
MIP $8

371 Road Rocket, lt. grn./blue w/blue HW logo on side/red HW logo o, metal M, gbbs
MIP $10

372 VW Bus Funny Car, met. blue, org. int., clr. win., metal C, 5sp/front
MIP $65

373 Street Cleaver, yel., yel. metal M, 5sp
MIP $4

374 Radio Flyer Wagon, red, blk. int., metal M, 5sp
MIP $4

375 Dog Fighter, red met., chr. int., blk. pl. M, 5sp
MIP $3

376 Twang Thang, silv. met., chr. int., clr. win., pearl pl., 5sp
MIP $2

377 Ferrari F50, red, blk. int., clr. win., gray pl. M, bbs
MIP $3

377 Ferrari F50 (new casting), dk. red, blk. int., clr. win., gray pl. C, bbs
MIP $2

378 '96 Mustang, red met., tan int., clr. win., metal M, 3sp
MIP $7

382 '70 Dodge Daytona, red, tan int., clr. win., chr. M, gbbs
MIP $3

1996 Treasure Hunts

428 '40's Woodie, yel., blk. int., smoked win., metal M, yel. hub/yel. wall rr
MIP $40

429 Lamborghini Countach, day-glo org., tan int., clr. win., day-glo org. metal M, chr. 6sp
MIP $30

430 Ferrari 250, met. gray, red int., clr. win., gray pl. M, chr. hub/rr
MIP $35

431 Jaguar XJ 220, met. grn., blk. int., blk. win., blk. pl. M, gold 6sp
MIP $30

432 '59 Caddy, red, tan int., clr. win., chr. M, chr. hub ww/rr
MIP $50

433 Dodge Viper RT/10, wht., blk. int., clr. win., blk. pl. M, wht. 6sp
MIP $60

434 '57 Chevy, purp. met., purp. int., purp. win., chr. M, chr. hub/rr
MIP $60

435 Ferrari 355, wht. pearl, tan int., clr. win., metal M, gold star
MIP $30

436 '58 Corvette, silv. met., red int., clr. win., gray pl. M, chr. hub/rr
MIP $60

437 Auburn 852, olive met./gold fenders, gold int., clr. win., metal M, gold hub ww/rr
MIP $35

438 Dodge Ram 1500, maroon met., gray int., clr. win., dk. gray pl. M, chr. hub/rr
MIP $35

439 '37 Bugatti, blue met., red int., clr. win., metal M, chr. 6sp
MIP $25

1996 Series

RACE TRUCK

380 Dodge Ram 1500, red, red int., clr. win., red pl. M, yel. ltr. b7sp
MIP $3

381 Ford LTL (Kenworth T600), silv. met., blue win., red pl. M, yel. ltr. b7sp
MIP $10

381 Kenworth T600, silv. met., blue win., red pl. M, yel. ltr. b7sp
MIP $5

382 '56 Flashsider, blk. met. w/HW rear logo, chr. win., chr. M, b7sp
MIP $9

383 Nissan Truck, dk. blue met., yel. int., clr. win., chr. M, ct
MIP $125

FLAMETHROWER

384 '57 T-Bird, wht./copper flames/5 flame trunk/gold HW logo in r, clr. int., clr. win., chr. M, 7sp
MIP $8

385 Hydroplane, yel., chr. int., smoked win., blk. pl. M
MIP $3

386 Range Rover, red w/HW logo in side window, tan int., clr. win., chr. M, ct
MIP $5

387 Oshkosh Snowplow, blk., blk. int., metal M, ct
MIP $4

SPACE

388 Radar Ranger, wht. pearl/HW logo on top, org. int., clr. win., blk. metal M, ct
MIP $3

389 GM Lean Machine, wht. pearl, blk. win., metal M, 5sp
MIP $3

390 Alien, wht. pearl/HW logo on top, blk. win., metal M, 5sp
MIP $3

391 Treadator, lt. blue pearl/HW logo right front wing, blue chr. win., blk. pl. M
MIP $4

RACE TEAM II

392 Ramp Truck, blue/wht., clr. win., metal M, 5sp
MIP $3

393 Baja Bug, met. blue, wht. int., metal M, 5sp
MIP $5

394 '57 Chevy, met. blue, blue int., blue win., chr. M, 5sp
MIP $4

395 Bywayman, met. blue/wht., wht. int., clr. win., metal M, ct
MIP $4

MOD BOD

396 Hummer, pink pl., grn. win., purp. met. metal M, ct
MIP $4

397 School Bus, purp. met., org. int., clr. win., yel. pl. M, 7sp
MIP $4

398 VW Bug, blue, grn. int., clr. win., metal M, 7sp
MIP $5

399 '67 Camaro, bright grn., red/open steering wheel int., clr. win., metal M, 5sp
MIP $7

DARK RIDER II

400 Big Chill, blk. met., dk. chr. win., blk. pl. M, blk. ski
MIP $3

401 Street Beast, blk. met., blk. int., clr. win., blk. metal M, blk. tint 7sp
MIP $3

402 Thunderstreak, blk. met./dk. chr., blk. int., blk. metal M, blk. tint 7sp
MIP $3

403 Power Pistons, dk. chr., blk. int., clr. win., blk. metal M, blk. tint 7sp
MIP $3

SPORTS CAR

404 Porsche 930, silv. met., blk. int., smoked win., metal M, 7sp
MIP $3

405 Custom Corvette, purp. w/logo on windshield, gray int., smoked win., blk. pl. M, 5sp
MIP $45

406 Cobra 427 S/C, pearl wht., blk. int., clr. win., metal M, 5sp
MIP $55

407 '59 Caddy, blk. met., wht. int., clr. win., chr. M, 7sp
MIP $3

SPLATTER PAINT

408 Rescue Ranger, org., blue int., blue win., org. pl. M, t/b
MIP $7

409 Side Splitter Funny Car, wht., metal int., clr. win., metal M, 5sp
MIP $5

410 '55 Chevy, yel., magenta win., red pl. M, t/b
MIP $7

411 '80's Camaro, wht., wht. int., clr. win., metal M, 5sp
MIP $2

STREET EATERS

412 Speed Machine, lt. grn. pearl, red int., red win., metal M, 7sp
MIP $10

413 Silhouette II, purp. w/HW logo on rear, red int., org. win., red pl. M, 5sp
MIP $4

414 Propper Chopper, blue, org. int., clr. win., org. pl. M
MIP $15

415 Roll Patrol, lt. brn., lt. org. int., clr. win., org. metal M, yct
MIP $10

FAST FOOD

416 Pizza Vette, wht. pl., blk. win., blk. metal M, 3sp
MIP $3

417 Pasta Pipes, wht. pl., chr. int int., blue win., blk. metal M, 3sp
MIP $3

418 Sweet Stocker, wht., yel. int., yel. win., blk. metal M, 3sp
MIP $20

419 Crunch Chief, wht., yel. win., blk. metal M, 3sp
MIP $4

SILVER SERIES II

420 Dump Truck, chr. w/chr. box, metal M, ct/b
MIP $20

421 '40's Woodie/logo in rear window, chr., blk. int., clr. win., metal M, 5sp
MIP $5

421 '40's Woodie/logo in side window, chr., blk. int., clr. win., metal M, 5sp
MIP $5

422 '57 Chevy, chr., org. win., metal M, 5sp
MIP $5

423 Oscar Mayer Wienermobile, chr., smoked win., chr. M, b5sp
MIP $5

FIRE RESCUE

424 Ambulance, bright grn./smooth rear step, wht. int., blue win., chr. M, 5sp
MIP $8

425 Rescue Ranger, yel., blk. int., smoked win., chr. M, 5sp
MIP $3

426 Flame Stopper, yel., blk. win., blk. pl. M, yct
MIP $50

427 Fire Eater, red, blue int., blue win., chr. M, 5sp
MIP $4

440 Monte Carlo Stocker, blue met., wht. int., clr. win., gray pl. M, b7sp
MIP $3

377 Ferrari F50, dk. red, blk. int., clr. win., gray pl. lnd., bbs
MIP $2

441 Chevy Stocker, blk., red int., clr. win., metal M, 7sp
MIP $5

442 Ferrari F40, wht. pearl, tan int., smoked win., metal M, 5sp
MIP $3

443 Ferrari 348, blk. met., red int., clr. win., blk. pl. M, 5sp
MIP $8

444 Aeroflash, wht., org. int., org. win., day-glo org. metal M, g7sp
MIP $2

445 Jaguar, met. grn., gray int., clr. win., gray pl. M, 5sp
MIP $3

446 '32 Ford Delivery, dk. blue, blk. int., clr. win., metal M, 3sp
MIP $20

447 '63 Split Window, met. grn., tan int., clr. win., chr. M, 3sp
MIP $4

448 '67 Camaro, yel., blk. int., smoked win., metal no origin, 5sp
MIP $7

449 Camaro Z-28, org., blk. int., smoked win., blk. metal M, 3sp
MIP $5

450 Corvette Stingray, pearl wht., blue int., blue win., metal M, 3sp
MIP $3

451 3-Window '34, pink, pink int int., rose win., metal M, 3sp
MIP $15

452 Ferrari 250, met. grn., tan int., clr. win., grn. pl. M, 5sp
MIP $15

453 Audi Avus, red, tan int., smoked win., blk. pl. M, 5sp
MIP $10

453 Avus Quattro, red, tan int., smoked win., blk. pl. M, 5sp
MIP $3

454 Zender Fact 4, pearl wht., gray int., blue win., gray pl. M, 5sp
MIP $3

455 65 Mustang Convertible, gold flake, wht. int., smoked win., metal M, 5sp
MIP $5

455 '65 Mustang Convertible, gold flake, wht. int., smoked win., metal M, 3sp
MIP $4

457 Pontiac Banshee, blk. met., yel. int., clr. win., metal C, 5sp
MIP $3

458 Speed Shark, met. lavender, purp. int., purp. win., chr. C, 5sp
MIP $3

460 Zombot, blk. over silv., day-glo org. metal C, 5sp
MIP $3

461 Enforcer, candy purp., silv. win., metal C, 5sp
MIP $3

462 '80's Firebird, met. blue, wht. int., clr. win., blue pl. C, 5sp
MIP $3

463 Fiero 2M4, yel., blk. int., clr. win., metal C, 5sp
MIP $3

464 Blazer 4X4, met. blue, yel. int., blue win., metal C, ct
MIP $3

467 Peugeot 405, dk. grn. met., wht. int., clr. win., grn. pl. C, 5sp
MIP $4

468 GT Racer, dayglo org., blk. win., metal C, 5sp
MIP $5

469 Hot Bird, gold, wht. int., tinted win., metal C, 5sp
MIP $5

470 Turbo Streak, wht./blue, wht. int., wht. metal C, 5sp
MIP $4

471 Velocitor, met. blue, red int., clr. win., wht. metal C, 5sp
MIP $4

472 Buick Stocker, yel., blk. int., clr. win., blk. metal C, 5sp
MIP $3

473 BMW M1, silv./gray, blk. int., clr. win., gray metal C, 5sp
MIP $3

473 Street Beast, pearl teal, gray int., tinted win., teal metal C, 5sp
MIP $3

474 VW Golf, blk., red int., clr. win., blk. pl. C, 5sp
MIP $5

475 Forklift, yel., blk. int., metal C, lrg. bw front/5sp rear
MIP $5

477 Double Demon, grn./purp. chr., blk. metal C, 5sp
MIP $3

478 Dragon Wagon, yel., teal metal C, 5sp
MIP $3

479 Computer Warrior, blk. over blue, org. metal C, 5sp
MIP $3

481 Tall Ryder, grn. met., chr. win., metal C, cts
MIP $4

482 Earth mover, yel., blk. int., yel. metal C, cts
MIP $5

483 Thunder Roller, maroon met., tan int., clr. win., chr. C, lrg.bw rear/5sp front
MIP $5

484 Grizzlor, wht. pl., metal C, 5sp
MIP $3

485 Evil Weevil, lt. org. pl., org. metal C, 5sp
MIP $3

486 Command Tank, blk./purp., blk. pl. C
MIP $5

487 Troop Convoy, met. gray/org., gray int., blk. metal C, 5sp
MIP $15

488 Sting Rod, dk. met. gray, blk. win., org. metal C, cts
MIP $3

489 Big Bertha, met. dk. gray/org., gray pl. C
MIP $12

489 Tough Customer, blk./lt. purp., blk. pl. C
MIP $4

491 Rocket Shot, met. gray/org., gray pl. C
MIP $10

492 Swingfire, org., gray int., gray pl. C, 5sp
MIP $10

493 Porsche 911 Targa, yel., blk. int., clr. win., blk. pl. C, alw-5sp
MIP $8

494 Mercedes 500SL, met. gray, red int., clr. win., blk. metal C, 5sp
MIP $2

496 Ferrari 308GT, red, blk. int., tinted win., blk. pl. C, 5sp
MIP $3

497 Ferrari Testarossa, pearl wht., blk. int., clr. win., blk. pl. C, 5sp
MIP $3

498 BMW 850i, silv. met., red int., clr. win., blk. pl. C, 5sp
MIP $3

499 Corvette Coupe, dk. grn. met., red int., clr. win., blk. pl. C, 5sp
MIP $6

502 Chevy Nomad, red met., tan int/open wheel int., clr. win., metal M, g7sp
MIP $7

503 '80's Corvette, red met., gray int., clr. win., metal M, 3sp
MIP $3

504 Camaro Z28, pearl wht., blue win., blk. metal M, 3sp
MIP $3

505 1993 Camaro, blk. met., tan int., clr. win., blk. pl. M, 5sp
MIP $3

506 Nissan 300ZX, purp. met., purp. int., clr. win., purp. metal C, 5sp
MIP $3

507 Peugeot 205 Rallye, blk./blue/purp., blk. int., clr. win., org. metal C, 5sp
MIP $30

1997 FIRST EDITIONS

509 Firebird funny car, dk. met. blue, metal int., clr. win., metal M, 5sp
MIP $5

510 25th. Countach, pearl yel., blk. int., clr. win., blk. pl. M, 5dot
MIP $3

512 Excavator, wht., blk. pl. M, blk. treads
MIP $25

513 Ford 150 pickup truck, red, chr. int., smoked win., gray pl. M, 5sp
MIP $3

514 Way 2 Fast, org., chr. int., metal M "no tm", 5sp
MIP $5

515 '97 Corvette, met. grn., tan int., smoked win., blk. pl. M, bbs
MIP $3

516 10-Mercedes C-Class, blk., gray int., clr. win., gray pl. M, gbbs
MIP $3

517 '59 Chevy Impala, purp. pearl, wht. int., clr. win., chr. M, g7sp
MIP $35

518 BMW M Roadster, met. silv., red int., clr. win., metal M, 5sp
MIP $3

518 BMW Z3 Roadster, met. silv., red int., clr. win., metal M, 5sp
MIP $6

519 Scorchin' Scooter, candy purp., metal M, blk. spoke
MIP $5

520 Saltflat Racer, lt. red pl., chr. int., silv. metal M, 5sp
MIP $4

1997 TREASURE HUNTS

578 '56 Flashsider, met. grn., chr. win., chr. M, 5sp
MIP $25

579 Silhouette II, wht., wht. int., blue win., wht. pl. M, w3sp
MIP $15

580 Mercedes 500SL, blk., wht. int., clr. win., blk. pl. M, 5sp
MIP $15

581 Street Cleaver, blk. pl., gold metal M, 5sp
MIP $20

582 GM Lean Machine, burgundy met./chr., chr. win., blk. metal M, 5sp
MIP $12

583 Hot Rod Wagon, yel., blk. int., metal M, y5sp
MIP $35

584 Olds Aurora, purp., gray int., clr. win., chr. M, 5sp
MIP $11

585 Dogfighter, met. grn., yel. pl. M, 5sp
MIP $20

586 Buick Wildcat, silv. flake, blk. win., gray pl. M, 3sp
MIP $15

587 Blimp, blue, wht. Gondola
MIP $12

588 Avus Quattro, gold met., wht. int., smoked win., blk. pl. M, t/b
MIP $12

589 Rail Rodder, wht. pl., metal M, b5sp
MIP $25

1997 SERIES

PHANTOM RACERS

529 Power Rocket, transparent grn. pl., chr. int., pink win., metal M, 3sp
MIP $10

530 Power Pistons, transparent red pl., gray int., clr. win., metal M, 3sp
MIP $3

531 Power Pipes, transparent blue, chr. int., purp. win., metal M, 3sp
MIP $3

532 Road Rocket, transparent org., lime win., metal M, 3sp
MIP $4

RACE TEAM III

533 Hummer, blue pl., sm. antenna, gray win., metal M, t/b
MIP $3

534 Chevy 1500 pickup, met. blue, wht. int., smoked win., metal M, 3sp
MIP $9

535 3-Window '34, met. blue, blue int., smoked win., metal M, 7sp
MIP $130

536 '80s Corvette, met. blue, wht. int., trsp.blue roof win., metal M, 5sp
MIP $3

HEET FLEET

537 Police Cruiser, grn., purp. int., clr. win., purp. pl. M, 3sp
MIP $10

538 Peterbilt Tank Truck, met. maroon, chr. win., chr. M, 5sp
MIP $5

538 School Bus, dk. grn., wht. int., clr. win., blk. pl. M, 3sp
MIP $5

538 School Bus (China), dk. grn., wht. int., clr. win., blk. pl. M, 7sp
MIP $5

539 Peterbilt Fuel Tanker, met. maroon, chr. win., chr. M, t/b
MIP $3

539 Peterbilt Tank Truck, met. maroon, chr. win., chr. M, 7sp
MIP $3

540 Ramblin' Wrecker, blk., chr. int., smoked win., chr. M, 7sp
MIP $5

BIFF! BAM! BOOM!

541 Mini Truck, red, blk. int., smoked win., blk. pl. M, 3sp
MIP $3

542 Limozeen, lt. blue pearl, wht. int., smoked win., chr. M, 5dot
MIP $30

543 VW Bug, met. grn., blk. int., clr. win., metal M, 5sp
MIP $5

544 Range Rover, pearl purp., gray int., clr. win., chr. M, t/b
MIP $3

QUICKSILVER

545 Chevy Stocker, red, blk. win., metal M, 3sp
MIP $2

546 Aeroflash, purp. pl., wht. win., wht. metal M, 3sp
MIP $2

547 Ferrari 308, pearl wht. pl., blk. win., blk. metal M, 5dot
MIP $2

548 T-Bird Stock Car, blue pl., blk. win., metal M, 5sp
MIP $2

SPEED SPRAY

549 Hydroplane, wht., chr. int., clr. win., blue pl. M
MIP $3

550 Street Roader, wht., red int., clr. win., metal M, ct/b
MIP $3

551 XT-3, blue, org. win., wht. metal M, 5sp
MIP $3

552 Funny Car, pearl magenta, metal int., clr. win., metal M, 5sp
MIP $4

SPY PRINT

553 Stealth, purp. pl., chr. int., purp. win., metal M, 3sp

MIP $3

554 Alien, blue/wht., wht./blue int., smoked win., metal M, 3sp

MIP $3

555 Sol-Aire CX4, met. maroon, blk. win., blk. pl. M, 3sp

MIP $3

556 Custom Corvette, blk., gray int., smoked win., blk. pl. M, 3sp

MIP $2

STREET BEAST

557 Mercedes-Benz Unimog, red/blk., red int., clr. win., metal M, ct/b

MIP $2

558 Jaguar XJ220, org., blk. int., clr. win., blk. pl. M, yt/b

MIP $2

559 Blown Camaro, yel., blk. int., clr. win., metal M, ot/b

MIP $3

560 Corvette Stingray, wht., blue int., blue win., metal M, yt/b

MIP $3

WHITE ICE

561 Speed Machine, pearl wht., wht. int., red win., metal M, 3sp

MIP $2

562 Shadow Jet, pearl wht./gold tint chr., wht. int., yel. win., metal M, 5sp

MIP $2

563 Splittin' Image II, pearl wht., blue win., wht. pl. M, 3sp

MIP $2

564 Twin Mill II, pearl wht., wht. int., red win., wht. pl. M, 5sp

MIP $2

DEALER'S CHOICE

565 Silhouette II, pearl blue, gold int., clr. win., blk. pl. M, 5dot

MIP $2

566 Street Beast, wht./gold, gold int., clr. win., metal M, 5dot

MIP $2

567 Baja Bug, met. red, wht. int., metal M, 5sp

MIP $5

568 '63 Corvette, blk., red int., clr. win., red pl. "'63 Corvette" M, 5dot

MIP $3

ROCKIN' RODS

569 Twang Thang, dk. red met., chr. int., clr. win., blk. pl. M, 5sp

MIP $2

570 Ferrari 355, blk., purp. int., clr. win., metal M, 3sp

MIP $3

571 Turbo Flame, purp. pl., chr. int., yel. win., blk. metal M, 5sp

MIP $5

572 Porsche 930, met. grn., blk. int., smoked win., metal M, 3sp

MIP $50

BLUE STREAK

573 Olds 442, dk. candy blue, blk. int., blue win., chr. M, 3sp

MIP $5

574 Nissan Truck, candy blue, blk. int., blue win., blk. pl. M, ct/b

MIP $20

575 '55 Chevy, candy blue, blk. win., chr. M, 3sp

MIP $5

576 Speed Blaster, candy blue, chr. win., chr. M, 3sp

MIP $20

577 Police Cruiser, blk., tan int., smoked win., blk. pl. M, b7sp

MIP $4

1997 BASIC LINE

300 Rigor Motor, blk., red chr. int., red win., metal C, bbs

MIP $3

323 Rodzilla, chr., metal C, 5sp

MIP $3

341 58 Corvette, candy purp. met., chr. int., clr. win., purp. pl. M, 5dot

MIP $3

342 Mercedes SL, blk./gray, red int., clr. win., gray pl. M, bbs

MIP $3

343 Speed Blaster, grn., chr. win., chr. M, 5dot

MIP $3

344 Camaro Convertible, red, blk. int., clr. win., blk. pl. C, 5sp

MIP $3

345 Speed-a-Saurus, purp., metal M, 5sp

MIP $3

347 Power Pistons, burgundy pl., gray int., blue win., silv. metal M, t/b

MIP $2

348 Dodge Ram, met. grn., chr. int., smoked win., gray pl. M, 5dot

MIP $3

349 Power Pipes, dk. blue pl., chr. int int., purp. win., silv. metal M, 5sp

MIP $2

352 Big Chill, wht. w/blk. tampo, chr. win., blk. pl. M, org. ski

MIP $4

523 1970 Plymouth Barracuda, sublime, blk. int., tinted win., chr. C, 5sp

MIP $7

524 GMC Motorhome, blue met., wht. int., clr. win., gray pl. Ind., bw

MIP $25

525 Trail Buster Jeep, blk., blk. int., clr. win., metal Ind., bw

MIP $4

526 Neet Streater, yel., blk. int., metal Ind., bw

MIP $5

527 Second Wind, wht., blue int., blue win., blue pl. Ind., bw

MIP $3

528 Beach Blaster, wht., red int., clr. win., gray Ind., bw

MIP $2

590 Porsche 911, red, blk. int., smoked win., metal M, t/b

MIP $3

591 Porsche 959, silv. blue pearl, blk. int., smoked win., metal M, t/b

MIP $3

592 Porsche 930, blue pearl, blk. int., smoked win., metal M, t/b

MIP $3

593 Skullrider, dk. pink chr., blk. int., metal, 5sp

MIP $4

594 GM Ultralite, wht./blk. "Police", blk. win., blk. pl. "Warner" M, 7sp

MIP $10

594 Police Car, wht./blk., no tampo, blk. win., blk. pl. M, 3sp

MIP $3

595 Corvette Sting Ray III, met. purp., gray int., clr. win., purp. pl. M, 5sp

MIP $5

596 Pontiac Salsa, org., gray int., silv. win., chr. M, 3sp

MIP $25

597 Buick Wildcat, candy red, blk. win., blk. pl. M, 7sp

MIP $20

598 Turboa, butterscotch, gold int., metal C, 5sp

MIP $2

599 Camaro Wind, wht., pink chr. win., metal C, bbs

MIP $4

600 Nissan Custom "Z", lt. blue, blk. int., clr. win., metal C, bbs

MIP $4

601 Commando, bronze, blk. int., clr. win., metal C, cts

MIP $6

602 Sharkruiser, blk., gray metal C, bbs

MIP $3

603 BMW 325i, yel., blk. int., clr. win., gray ptd. C, bbs

MIP $2

604 Ferrari 308 GTS, yel./blk., blk. int., clr. win., blk. pl. C, 5sp

MIP $6

605 Mercedes 2.6, met. gold, blk. int., clr. win., blk. pl. C, bbs

MIP $2

606 Mercedes 300TD, dk. grn. met., gray int., clr. win., gray pl. C, 5sp

MIP $3

607 Fat Fendered '40, aqua, blk. int., clr. win., metal C, 5sp

MIP $12

608 Porsche 911, met. silv., blk. int., clr. win., blk. pl. C, 5sp

MIP $2

609 Jaguar XJ40, dk. blue met., wht. int., blue win., blk. pl. C, bbs

MIP $3

610 Land Rover Mk II, org., blk. int., clr. win., blk. pl. C, 5sp

MIP $10

611 Fire Eater II, red, blue win., gray pl. C, 5sp

MIP $2

612 '57 T-Bird, aqua, wht. int., clr. win., metal C, bw

MIP $10

613 London Bus, red, blk. win., blk. pl. C, 5sp

MIP $9

615 Ford XR4Ti, met. silv., red int., clr. win., blk. pl. C, 5sp

MIP $2

616 **'80's Corvette,** wht., blue int., clr. win., blk. pl. C, bbs
MIP $4

617 **Flame Stopper II,** red, blk. int., smoked win., gray pl. C, 5sp
MIP $2

618 **Chevy Stocker,** wht., purp. int., clr. win., metal C, 5sp
MIP $20

619 **London Taxi,** yel., blk. int., clr. win., metal C, 5sp
MIP $7

620 **Ford Transit Wrecker,** lt. blue, blk. win., wht. pl. C, 5sp
MIP $5

622 **City Police,** blk./wht., gray int., clr. win., blk. pl. C, b5sp
MIP $3

623 **Mustang Cobra,** pearl pink, blk. int., clr. win., blk. pl. C, bbs
MIP $2

624 **Assault Crawler,** olive, olive pl. C
MIP $5

625 **Classic Packard,** blk., blk. int int., clr. win., metal C, 5sp
MIP $5

641 **Wheel Loader,** org./wht. HW logo, gray int., metal C, cts
MIP $4

642 **Forklift,** wht., sm. blue HW logo, metal C, rear 5sp/front bw
MIP $5

643 **Digger,** yel., yel. C, no HW logo, 5sp
MIP $5

1998 First Editions

633 **Dodge Caravan,** dk. burgundy met., wht. int., smoked win., gray pl. M, t/b
MIP $5

634 **Dodge Sidewinder,** day-glo org./wht. HW logo, purp. int., smoked win., gray pl. M, 5sp
MIP $3

635 **'65 Impala,** candy purp., tan int., clr. win., chr. M, gbbs
MIP $4

636 **'32 Ford (no post),** blk. w/yel./red flames, red int., clr. win., blk. pl. M, 5sp
MIP $10

636 **'32 Ford (with post),** blk. w/mostly red flames, red int., clr. win., blk. pl. M, 5sp
MIP $15

637 **Escort Rally,** wht. pearl, red int., smoked win., gray pl. M "Escort Rally", bbs
MIP $2

637 **Escort Rally (Ford),** wht. pearl, red int., smoked win., gray pl. M "Ford Rally", bbs
MIP $10

638 **Jaguar D-Type,** dk. blue met., gray int., clr. win., dk. blue met. metal M, t/b
MIP $2

639 **Jaguar XK8,** pearl grn. met., wht. int., clr. win., gray pl. M, bbs
MIP $100

640 **Slideout,** candy purp., gray pl. M, 5sp
MIP $5

644 **'63 T-Bird,** teal met., wht. int., clr. win., metal M, 5dot
MIP $3

645 **Dairy Delivery,** wht. pearl/dk. pink curved top stripe, aqua int., clr. win., gray pl. M, 5sp
MIP $4

646 **Mercedes SLK,** yel. enamel w/wht. side paint, blk. int., smoked win., metal M, 5dot
MIP $12

647 **Lakester,** red, chr. int int., clr. win., red metal M, 5sp
MIP $3

648 **Hot Seat,** wht. pl., blk. int., metal M or T, 5sp
MIP $2

650 **Solar Eagle III,** yel., int., blk. win., blk. flake M
MIP $2

651 **Go Kart,** day-glo grn., blk. int., day-glo grn. metal M, 5sp
MIP $5

652 **Pikes Peak Celica,** yel. w/purp. tampo, red int., smoked win., blk. pl. M, gbbs
MIP $7

653 **IROC Firebird,** gold met., lt. gray int int., tinted win., gray pl. C, b5sp
MIP $2

654 **40 Ford Pickup,** candy blue met., gray int., blue win., chr. M, 5sp
MIP $3

654 **'40 Ford Pickup,** blue pearl, gray int., blue win., chr. M, 5sp
MIP $20

655 **Super Comp Dragster,** blk. w/3 decals, gray int., chr. M, 5sp
MIP $8

657 **Panoz GTR-1,** wht., dk. red stripes, lg. HW logo, blue int., clr. win., blk. pl. C, bbs
MIP $5

658 **Tow Jam,** red w/lg. HW logo on roof, blk. win., chr. M, 3sp
MIP $50

659 **Tail Dragger,** candy purp. met., wht. int., clr. win., metal M, bbs
MIP $4

661 **'70 Roadrunner,** lt. Hemi org. w/short trunk stripe, blk. int., clr. win., chr. M, 5sp
MIP $5

662 **Bad Mudder,** wht. w/roof tampo/dk. red tampos, blk. int., blk. pl. M, ct/b
MIP $5

663 **Customized C3500,** teal w/long thin stripe, gray int., smoked win., gray pl. M, 5dot
MIP $15

664 **Super Modified,** blk., pink int., metal M, bbs/2
MIP $3

665 **Mustang Cobra,** blk. w/no Cosen, gray int., clr. win., gray pl. M, gbbs
MIP $10

667 **At-A-Tude,** blue met., chr. int., org. win., blk. pl. M, lg. rear/bbs/bbs
MIP $4

668 **Ford GT-90,** wht., blue int., smoked win., metal M, 3sp
MIP $2

669 **Chaparral 2,** wht., blk. int., clr. win., blk. metal M, bbs/2
MIP $3

670 **Mustang Mach I,** day-glo org., blk. int., blue win., blk. pl. M, 5sp
MIP $40

671 **Chrysler Thunderbolt,** silv., wht. int., purp. win., blk. pl. M, 5dot
MIP $2

672 **Dodge Concept Car,** org. pearl, purp. int., smoked win., metal M, 5sp
MIP $300

673 **Whatta Drag,** met. red, chr. int., org. win., metal M, 3sp
MIP $3

674 **Sweet 16 II,** dk. purp. met., chr. int., purp. win., dk. purp. met. metal M, 5sp
MIP $3

677 **Callaway C-7,** silv. w/blk. ptd. headlt.s, blk. int., clr. win., blk. pl. M, 5sp
MIP $4

678 **Express Lane,** red pl., blk. int., metal M, 5sp
MIP $3

681 **Cat-A-Pult,** red w/red HW logo, blk. int., org. win., metal M, 5sp
MIP $25

682 **Fathom This,** wht. w/logo, tampo on top, org. win.
MIP $4

684 **Double Vision,** red met., gray int., clr. win., gray pl. M, gbbs
MIP $2

1998 Treasure Hunts

749 **Twang Thang,** blk. w/blue chr. guitars, chr. int., clr. win., blk. pl. M, 5sp
MIP $15

750 **Scorchin' Scooter,** met. red, metal M, chr./blk.
MIP $40

751 **Kenworth T600A,** dk. candy purp., blk. win., chr. M, 3sp
MIP $25

752 **3-Window '34,** org., chr. int int., clr. win., metal M, 5dot
MIP $35

753 **Turbo Flame,** chr./grn., chr. int., grn. win., blk. metal M, 5sp
MIP $15

754 **Saltflat Racer,** blk. pl., gold chr. int., red win., gold met. metal T, 5sp
MIP $15

755 **Street Beast,** red/wht., wht. int., red win., metal M, gbbs
MIP $15

756 **Road Rocket,** chr. body, metal M, 3sp
MIP $15

757 **Sol-Aire CX4,** wht., blue int., clr. win., blue pl. M, wbbs
MIP $15

758 **'57 Chevy,** met. grn., yel. int., yel. win., gold chr. T, 3sp
MIP $35

759 **Stingray III,** met. silv., red int., smoked win., blk. pl. M, 3sp
MIP $25

760 **Way 2 Fast,** olive flake, chr. int int., metal T, 5sp
MIP $20

1998 Series

TATTOO MACHINES

685 **'57 T-Bird,** lt. blue pearl, blue int., blue win., chr. M, 3sp
MIP $2

686 '93 Camaro, day-glo grn., wht. int., smoked win., blk. pl. M, 3sp
MIP $2

687 Stutz Blackhawk, met. red, wht. int., tinted win., metal M, 3sp
MIP $2

688 Corvette Stingray, org., blk. int., smoked win., metal M, 3sp
MIP $2

TECHNO BITS

689 Shadow Jet II, blk. w/org. side tampo, chr. int., grn. win., metal M, b5sp
MIP $3

690 Power Pistons, purp. pl., gold int., yel. win., metal M, 3sp
MIP $2

691 Shadow Jet, met. blue, blk. int., smoked win., metal M, 5sp
MIP $6

692 Radar Ranger, day-glo grn., purp. int., red win., blk. metal M, ct/b
MIP $2

TROPICOOL

693 Ice Cream Truck, wht. w/wht. HW logo, grn. int., clr. win., blk. pl. M, 5sp
MIP $10

694 Baja Bug, wht./dk. red, red int., metal M, lg. rear 5sp
MIP $7

695 Classic Caddy, red/blk. fenders, lt. gray int., smoked win., metal M, bbs
MIP $3

696 Corvette Convertible, day-glo grn., blue int., smoked win., blk. pl. M, 3sp
MIP $6

LOW 'N COOL

697 Mini Truck, day-glo yel., blk. int., smoked win., blk. pl. M, g3sp
MIP $2

698 '59 Impala, grn. pearl/dk. purp. tampo, wht. int., smoked win., chr. M, gbbs
MIP $4

699 '59 Caddy, pearl rose, wht. int., smoked win., chr. T, gbbs
MIP $3

716 Limozeen, blk. flake, wht. int., smoked win., gold chr. M, gbbs
MIP $4

BIOHAZARD

717 Hydroplane, dk. day-glo grn., chr. int., clr. win., blk. pl. T
MIP $25

718 Flame Stopper, day-glo pink, blk. win., blk. pl. T, yt/b
MIP $3

719 Recycling Truck, day-glo yel. w/blk. tampo, blk. win., blk. pl. M, t/b
MIP $5

720 Rescue Ranger, blk., yel. int., yel. win., chr. M, 5sp
MIP $4

DASH 4 CASH

721 Jaguar XJ220, silv., lt. purp. int., clr. win., blk. pl. M, bbs
MIP $5

722 Ferrari F40, lt. gold met., tan int., tinted win., metal M, gbbs
MIP $4

723 Audi Avus, blk., wht. int., smoked win., blk. pl. T, gbbs
MIP $3

724 Dodge Viper, wht. pearl, red int., smoked win., blk. pl. T, t/b
MIP $3

RACE TEAM IV

725 '67 Camaro, met. blue, wht. int., tinted win., no origin metal, 5sp
MIP $5

726 Mercedes C-Class, met. blue, wht. int., smoked win., blk. pl. T, 5sp
MIP $3

727 Shelby Cobra 427 S/C, met. blue, wht. int., smoked win., metal M, 5sp
MIP $3

728 '63 Corvette, met. blue, wht. int., tinted win., chr. M, 5sp
MIP $8

ARTISTIC LICENSE

729 Alien, wht. enamel, wht. int., tinted win., metal T, 3sp
MIP $8

730 '57 Chevy, gray pl., dk. smoked win., metal M, t/b
MIP $3

731 VW Bug, wht. pearl, blk. int., blue win., metal M, 5dot
MIP $4

732 1970 Barracuda, blk. w/org. HW logo, dk. day-glo org. int., smoked win., chr. M, 3sp
MIP $3

MIXED SIGNALS

733 Street Roader, wht. pearl, yel. int., smoked win., metal M, ct/b
MIP $2

734 '80's Corvette, met. grn., blk. int., smoked win., metal M, bbs
MIP $2

735 Nissan Truck, org. pearl, blk. int., clr. win., blk. pl. M, ct/b
MIP $2

736 School Bus, yel. w/HW logo on rear door, blk. int., clr. win., blk. pl. M, 5dot
MIP $3

FLYN' ACES

737 '70 Dodge Daytona, met. grn., blk. int., clr. win., tan M, 5dot
MIP $3

738 Dogfighter, blk., chr. int., yel. pl. M, 5dot
MIP $3

739 Sol-Aire CX4, yel. w/gray stripes, blk. int., clr. win., blk. pl. M, 5sp
MIP $3

740 XT-3, met. gray, blk. win., org. metal M, 5sp
MIP $2

SUGAR RUSH

741 Mazda MX-5 Miata, org. w/bright yel. headlights, blk. int., smoked win., org. metal T, 5sp
MIP $5

742 Funny Car, wht., metal int., blk. window win., metal M, 5sp
MIP $5

743 '95 Camaro, dk. met. blue, blk. int., clr. win., blk. pl. M, 5sp
MIP $4

744 '96 Mustang Convertible, yel., blk. int., clr. win., metal C, 5sp
MIP $5

TECH TONES

745 Buick Wildcat, blk./grn., silv. win., lt. grn. pl. M, 3sp
MIP $3

746 Silhouette II, blk./purp. w/wht. HW logo, wht. int., clr. win., purp. pl. M, 5dot
MIP $5

747 Speed Machine, blk./gold, gold int., clr. win., metal M, t/b
MIP $3

748 Avus Quattro, blk./red, wht. int., clr. win., dk. red pl. M, gbbs
MIP $3

1998 BASIC LINE

700 Shock Factor, yel./blue, blue int., metal C, alw-bw
MIP $3

702 Lumina Van, dk. grn. met., tan int., smoked win., blk. pl. C, bbs
MIP $4

712 Tipper, blue, blk. int., smoked win., blk. pl. C, 5sp
MIP $2

714 Talbot Lago, blue/blk., blue win., blk. metal C, bbs
MIP $255

715 1996 Mustang GT, wht., red int., clr. win., metal C, 5sp
MIP $30

761 Flame Stopper, red, blk. window win., blk. pl. M, ct/b
MIP $2

765 Oshkosh P-Series, lt. met. blue/wht., blue int., metal M, ct/b
MIP $4

767 Mercedes 380SEL, wht. pearl, tan int., clr. win., met. gold metal M, t/b
MIP $2

768 Lamborghini Countach, blk., red int., clr. win., blk. pl. M, 5dot
MIP $2

770 Lexus SC400, met. blue, wht. int., smoked win., blk. pl. M, bbs
MIP $5

771 '56 Flashsider, yel. pearl, blk. win., chr. M, 5dot
MIP $3

773 Hot Wheels 500, day-glo yel., blk. int., metal M, b7sp
MIP $3

774 Ramp Truck, dk. grn. met./gray, smoked win., metal C, 5sp
MIP $3

778 Speed Blaster, met. blue, chr. win., blk. pl. M, 3sp
MIP $4

779 Big Chill, blue, chr. int., wht. pl. T, blk.
MIP $8

780 '58 Corvette, aqua w/engine, chr. int., smoked win., aqua pl. M, 5dot
MIP $6

781 Lamborghini Diablo, dk. red met., tan int., tinted win., blk. metal M, 5sp
MIP $3

782 Radar Ranger, gold met., blk. int., clr. win., metal M, ct/b
MIP $3

783 Twin Mill II, met. silv., blk. win., blk. pl. M, all alw-bbs
MIP $3

784 Ferrari F512M, met. silv., blk. int., clr. win., blk. ptd. M, 5dot
MIP $3

784 Ferrari Testarossa, met. silv., blk. int., clr. win., blk. ptd. M, 5dot
MIP $5

787 '57 Chevy, met. purp., blk. int., smoked win., chr. T, t/b
MIP $4

788 Mercedes 540K, purp. met./blue, blk. int., clr. win., metal M, asw-bbs
MIP $4

791 Treadator, met. blue, chr. win., blk. pl. T, blk. treads
MIP $3

792 Camaro Race Car, wht. pearl, blk. int., clr. win., blk. pl. M, 5sp
MIP $3

793 Auburn 852, blk. w/gold fenders, gold int., tinted win., metal M, gbbs
MIP $6

795 Tractor, silv. met./blk., silv. int., blk. pl. M, c/tt rear-ct/b front
MIP $3

796 '96 Camaro Convertible, wht., org. int., smoked win., gray pl. Ind., w5sp
MIP $3

797 Dodge Ram 1500, red, yel. int., smoked win., wht. pl. M, 5dot
MIP $4

798 Propper Chopper, blue, blk. int., blue win., blk. pl. M
MIP $3

802 Flashfire, gold met./no logo, blk. int., smoked win., gold pl. M, 5dot
MIP $5

803 '40's Woodie, wht. pearl/tan, blk. int., smoked win., metal M, 5sp
MIP $8

808 Driven To The Max, wht. pearl, hot pink int., metal T, 5sp
MIP $3

812 GM Lean Machine, grn./gold met., gold int., smoked win., metal M, t/b
MIP $3

813 Ferrari 355, blk., yel. int., yel. win., metal M, 3sp
MIP $90

814 Speed-A-Saurus, glossy teal pl., org. metal M, lg. rear 5sp
MIP $3

815 Mercedes 500SL, dk. grn. met., tan int., smoked win., blk. pl. T, 3sp
MIP $3

816 Ferrari 308, met. bronze, tan int., smoked win., blk. metal M, 5dot
MIP $3

817 Porsche 928, wht. pearl, blk. win., metal M, bbs
MIP $3

818 Porsche Carrera, red met., tan int., smoked win., metal M, g5sp
MIP $3

820 Zender Fact 4, met. grn., blk. int., clr. win., blk. pl. C, bbs
MIP $3

821 '96 Mustang Convertible, wht., red int., clr. win., metal C, 5sp
MIP $4

822 Camaro Z-28, teal met., gray int., clr. win., metal no origin, 3sp
MIP $5

823 Sol-Aire CX4, blue met., wht. int., clr. win., wht. pl. M, gbbs
MIP $4

827 Radio Flyer Wagon, red, blk. int., metal M, 5sp
MIP $5

829 Porsche Carrera, silv. met., red int., clr. win., metal M, t/b
MIP $3

834 Ferrari Testarossa, blk., tan/blk. int., clr. win., gloss blk. metal Ind., bw
MIP $3

835 Baja Bug, dk. met. blue, wht. int int., metal Ind., amw-bw
MIP $5

837 Radio Flyer Wagon, met. blue, wht. int., metal C, 5sp
MIP $4

850 Rail Rodder, gray pl., metal M, b5sp
MIP $3

851 Treadator, lt. blue pearl, chr. win., day-glo grn. pl. T
MIP $5

852 Rigor Motor, candy purp. met., chr. int., yel. win., metal M, amw-g5sp
MIP $7

853 Camaro Z28, day-glo yel. pl., blk. win., metal M, 5dot
MIP $5

854 Porsche 959, wht. w/pink tampo, blk. int., smoked win., metal M, t/b
MIP $5

855 Ferrari F50, candy purp. met., blk. int., smoked win., blk. pl. M, t/b
MIP $3

856 Porsche 930, met. red, blk. int., smoked win., metal T, 3sp
MIP $4

857 T-Bird Stocker, org. pl., blk. win., blk. metal T, 5dot
MIP $3

858 Hummer, wht. pl./org. tampo, red win., blk. metal M, ct/b
MIP $6

859 Bronco, red/wht., blk. int., smoked win., metal T, ct/b
MIP $5

860 Road Rocket, wht./dk. blue, wht. int., metal T, 3sp
MIP $3

861 Twin Mill II, met. gold, blk. window win., blk. pl. M, bbs
MIP $3

862 Pontiac Salsa, red met., blk. win., chr. M, 5dot
MIP $3

863 Oshkosh Cement Mixer, day-glo yel. w/silv. fenders, yel. int., blk. pl. M, 3sp
MIP $4

864 Tank Truck, dk. burgundy met./chr., chr. win., blk. pl. M, 5dot
MIP $5

865 Ford F150, wht., chr. int., smoked win., blk. pl. M, 3sp
MIP $3

866 Ferrari 250, gold met., blk. int., smoked win., blk. pl. T, bbs
MIP $4

867 '97 Corvette, met. blue, wht. int., smoked win., red pl. T, 5sp
MIP $4

868 Range Rover, grn. met., tan int., smoked win., chr. T, ct/b
MIP $4

869 Power Pipes, blk. pl., chr. int., org. win., org. metal T, ot/b
MIP $3

870 Chevy Stocker, purp. pl., blk. win., blk. metal M, gt/b
MIP $3

871 Olds 442, met. blue, wht. int., smoked win., chr. T, 5sp
MIP $4

872 Rig Wrecker, wht., chr. int., smoked win., blk. pl. T, 5dot
MIP $5

873 Hydroplane, wht., blk. int., smoked win., blk. pl. M
MIP $3

874 Pit Crew Truck, candy gray, red int., blue win., red pl. T, 5dot
MIP $3

875 Police Car, blk., gray int., tinted win., blk. pl. T, 5sp
MIP $5

876 Bywayman, red, wht. int., tinted win., metal T, ct/b
MIP $3

877 Chevy 1500, gray pl., blk. int., clr. win., blk. metal Ind., t/b
MIP $3

881 '95 Camaro, blk., red int., smoked win., blk. pl. Ind., 3sp
MIP $3

884 Gulch Stepper, yel. pearl, blk. win., metal T, ct/b
MIP $3

889 Mercedes 380SEL, blk., tan int., tinted win., gold met. metal M, gbbs
MIP $3

890 BMW Roadster, wht., red int., smoked win., metal M, 3sp
MIP $3

894 Toyota MR2, wht., wht. int., smoked win., blk. pl. T, bbs
MIP $3

899 '56 Flashsider, candy gray/dk. red tampo, blk. win., chr. T, 5sp
MIP $7

908 Ford F Series "CNG" P/U, candy purp. met., chr. int., smoked win., blk. pl. M, 3sp
MIP $15

1999 FIRST EDITIONS

649 1936 Cord, dk. red met. w/casting peg, purp. int., clr. win., chr. M, bbs
MIP $10

656 '38 Phantom Corsair, blk. w/gray HW logo, gray int., clr. win., metal M, ww5sp
MIP $15

675 Pontiac Rageous, met. red, gray int., smoked/blk. win., blk. pl. M, 3sp
MIP $3

676 Porsche 911 GT1-98, wht., blk. int., clr. win., blk. pl. M, bbs
MIP $2

680 Baby Boomer, candy blue, metal M, 5sp
MIP $2

683 Tee'd Off, candy blue, wht. pearl int., metal M, 5sp
MIP $4

683 Tee'd Off, wht. pearl, gray int., metal M, 5sp
MIP $15

909 '99 Mustang, dk. candy purp. met., red int., clr. win., blk. pl. M, 5sp
MIP $31

910 Monte Carlo Concept Car, red, gray int., smoked win., silv. met. metal M, 5sp
MIP $3

911 Olds Aurora GT3, wht./met. blue, blk. int., clr. win., blk. pl. M, gbbs
MIP $20

911 Olds Aurora GTS-1, wht./met. blue, blk. int., clr. win., blk. pl. M, gbbs
MIP $15

912 Porsche 911 GT3 Cup, candy gray/yel. wing/wht. logo, org. int., blue win., blk. pl. M, bbs
MIP $10

913 Popcycle, burgundy met./org. stripe, metal int., org. win., metal M, 3sp
MIP $15

914 Semi Fast, red w/red grill, gray int., smoked win., metal M, 5sp
MIP $8

915 1970 Chevelle SS, met. gold, blk. int., blue win., metal M, 5sp
MIP $16

916 Phaeton, teal met., tan int., tinted win., metal M, 5sp
MIP $3

917 Track T, blk., tan cover int., metal M, 5sp
MIP $4

918 Screamin' Hauler, purp. met., metal int., blue win., metal M, 5sp
MIP $3

919 Fiat 500C, candy purp. met., gray int., chr. win., metal M, 5sp
MIP $5

921 Ford GT-40, blue met., gray int., blue win., gray pl. M, narrow rear 5sp
MIP $5

922 Jeepster, red/blk., blk. int., smoked win., metal M, 5sp
MIP $3

923 Turbolence, blk., gold chr. int., metal M, g5dot
MIP $2

924 Pikes Peak Tacoma, yel., blk. int., clr. win., blk. pl. M, gbbs
MIP $3

925 Shadow Mk IIa, blk., gray int., gray pl. M, 5sp
MIP $3

926 Mercedes CLK-LM, candy gray, blk. int., clr. win., blk. pl. M, gbbs
MIP $3

927 '56 Ford Truck, lt. blue pearl, chr. int., blue win., gray pl. M, 5sp
MIP $5

928 Chrysler Pronto, yel. pearl, gray int., smoked win., blk. pl. M, 5sp
MIP $3

1113 360 Modena, red/no HW logo, blk. int., clr. win., blk. pl. M, 5sp
MIP $10

1113 Ferrari 360 Modena, red/yel. HW logo, blk. int., clr. win., blk. pl. M, 5sp
MIP $4

1999 TREASURE HUNTS

929 Mercedes 540K, red, blk. int., clr. win., metal M, 5sp
MIP $25

930 T-Bird Stocker, blue enamel, yel. int., clr. win., gray pl. M, 5sp
MIP $10

931 '97 Corvette, pearl lavender, yel. int., smoked win., blk. pl. T, 5dot
MIP $25

932 Rigor Motor, day-glo yel., chr. int., yel. win., blk. metal M, g5sp
MIP $15

933 Ferrari F512M, yel., blk. int., clr. win., metal M, chr. star
MIP $20

934 '59 Impala, met. purp., wht. int., smoked win., gold chr. M, gbbs
MIP $20

935 Hot Wheels 500, blk., blk. int., metal M, org. ltr. b7sp
MIP $15

936 Jaguar D-Type, blk. met., gold int., clr. win., blk. met. M, 5sp
MIP $15

937 '32 Ford Delivery, met. gold w/purp. fenders, purp. int., clr. win., metal M, g5sp
MIP $15

938 Hot Seat, clr. pl., blk. seat int., metal M, 5sp
MIP $15

939 Mustang Mach I, grn. met., blk. int., clr. win., blk. pl. M, 5sp
MIP $25

940 Express Lane, purp., blk. seat int., metal M, g5sp
MIP $20

1999 SERIES

BUGGIN' OUT

941 Treadator, red/chr., chr. win., blk. pl. T, blk. treads
MIP $3

942 Shadow Jet II, gray pl., yel. int., grn. win., metal M, 5sp
MIP $3

943 Radar Ranger, purp. met., blue int., blue win., metal M, ct/b
MIP $3

944 Baja Bug, lt. blue met., org. int., metal M, 5sp
MIP $6

X-RAY CRUISER

945 Mercedes C-Class, blk. met., wht. int., yel. int., blk. pl. M, gbbs
MIP $8

946 Lamborghini Diablo, met. teal, gray int., smoked win., blk. metal M, 5sp
MIP $3

947 '67 Camaro, blue, wht. int., tinted win., metal M, 5sp
MIP $7

948 Jaguar XJ220, yel., blue int., clr. win., blk. pl. M, 3sp
MIP $3

1114 '63 Corvette, blk. met., tan int., clr. win., gold chr. M, g5sp
MIP $6

STREET ART

850 Propper Chopper, pearl grn., blk. int., yel. win., blk. pl. M
MIP $4

949 Mini truck, met. blk., blk. int., clr. win., blk. pl. M, t/b
MIP $3

951 Ambulance, candy purp. met., purp. int., org. win., chr. M, 5sp
MIP $4

952 School Bus, yel./no rear door, yel. int., red win., blk. pl. M, 5dot
MIP $8

PINSTRIPE POWER

953 3-Window '34, dk. purp. met., blk. int., blue win., metal M, 5sp
MIP $5

954 Tail Dragger, blk., tan int., clr. win., metal M, bbs
MIP $4

955 '65 Impala, lt. grn. met., tan int., smoked win., gold chr. M, gbbs
MIP $4

956 Auburn 852, blk./silv., wht. int., clr. win., metal M, bbs
MIP $3

GAME OVER

957 Lean Machine, purp./blk., blk. win., metal M, 5sp
MIP $3

958 Shadow Jet, yel., yel. int., smoked win., metal M, 5sp
MIP $3

959 Speed Blaster, lt. grn., gold chr. win., yel. pl. M, gt/b
MIP $2

960 Twin Mill II, pink pearl, blk. win., blk. pl. M, bbs
MIP $3

SURF 'N FUN

961 '40s Woodie, pearl purp. w/tan body, blk. int., blue win., metal M, 5sp
MIP $4

962 VW Bug, lt. blue pearl, wht. int., smoked win., metal M, 5sp
MIP $5

963 '55 Chevy, met. red, blk. win., chr. M, 3sp
MIP $4

964 Chevy Nomad, wht. pearl/long hood stripe, wht. int., smoked win., metal M, g5sp
MIP $8

X-TREEME SPEED

965 Dodge Sidewinder, wht., purp. int., smoked win., blk. pl. M, 5sp
MIP $3

966 Callaway C7, grn., blk. int., clr. win., blk. pl. M, t/b
MIP $3

967 Porsche Carrera, silv., wht. int., tinted win., metal M, g5sp
MIP $3

968 Mazda MX-5 Miata, blue, grn. int., clr. win., blue metal M, bbs
MIP $3

SUGAR RUSH

969 '70 Road Runner, yel., blk. int., clr. win., chr. M, 5dot
MIP $4

970 Jaguar XK8, red, tan int., smoked win., blk. pl. M, gbbs
MIP $3

971 Pikes Peak Celica, wht., blk. int., clr. win., blk. pl. M, bbs
MIP $3

972 Dodge Concept Car, wht., blue int., clr. win., metal M, 5dot
MIP $3

MEGA GRAPHICS

973 Funny Car, yel., metal int., yel. win., metal M, 5sp
MIP $5

974 Mustang Cobra, wht. pearl, blk. int., clr. win., blk. pl. M, t/b
MIP $3

975 Turbo Flame, blk. pl., blk. int., yel. win., red metal M, g5sp
MIP $3

976 Firebird Funny Car, dk. purp. met., metal int., smoked win., metal M, b5sp
MIP $5

TERRORIFIC

977 At-A-Tude, met. grn., chr. int., grn. win., blk. pl. M, b5sp
MIP $3

978 Cat-A-Pult, org., blk. int., smoked win., metal M, 5sp
MIP $3

979 Sweet Sixteen II, blk., yel. win., metal M, 5sp
MIP $4

980 Splittin' Image II, met. gold, pink chr. win., blk. pl. M, 3sp
MIP $3

CLASSIC GAMES

981 Super Modified, lt. blue pearl, blk. int., metal M, gbbs/2
MIP $3

982 Silhouette II, silv.-blue pearl, wht. int., blue win., blk. pl. M, 5dot
MIP $2

983 Sol-Aire CX4, wht., blk. int., blue win., blk. pl. M, 3sp
MIP $2

984 Escort Rally, red, blk. int., clr. win., gray pl. M, bbs
MIP $8

CAR-TOON FRIENDS

985 Saltflat Racer, purp. pl., chr. int., clr. win., silv. ptd. metal M, 5sp
MIP $3

986 XT-3, org., blk. win., blk. ptd. metal M, g5sp
MIP $3

987 Double Vision, blk., gray int., clr. win., blk. pl. M, gbbs
MIP $3

988 Lakester, wht./blk., chr. int., red win., blk. metal M, 5sp
MIP $2

1999 BASIC LINE

991 Rodzilla, chr., metal C, gbbs
MIP $3

992 Ferrari F512M, red, tan int., smoked win., blk. metal M, 5sp
MIP $3

993 Ferrari 348, yel., blk./yel. int., smoked win., blk. pl. M, 5sp
MIP $3

994 Way 2 Fast, blk. met., chr. int., met. gold ptd. metal, g5sp
MIP $3

995 Porsche 911, yel. enamel, blk. int., smoked win., metal M, 5sp
MIP $3

996 '32 Ford Delivery, lt. blue pearl, blk. int., blue win., metal M, bbs
MIP $3

997 Jaguar D-Type, red enamel w/grn. tint stripe, gray int., smoked win., red metal M, bbs
MIP $5

998 Firebird Funny Car, met. red, metal int., smoked win., metal M, g5sp
MIP $5

999 Hot Seat, chr. w/gold logo, red seat int., metal M, 5sp
MIP $5

1000 '59 Impala, wht. pearl, blk. int., smoked win., gold chr. M, gbbs
MIP $3

1001 Slideout, met. blue, wht. pl. M, 5sp
MIP $3

1003 Ferrari F40, blk., red int., smoked win., metal M, 5sp
MIP $4

1004 Dairy Delivery, wht. w/blk. spots, blk. int., clr. win., chr. M or C, 5sp
MIP $3

1005 Mercedes-Benz Unimog, red/blk., blk. int., clr. win., metal M, ct/b
MIP $3

1006 Dodge Viper RT/10, met. blue, blk. int., smoked win., blk. pl. M, 5sp
MIP $4

1007 Tow Jam, met. grn., blk. window win., chr. M, 3sp
MIP $3

1008 Chaparral 2, red, blk. int., clr. win., wht. metal M, bbs/2
MIP $3

1009 Peterbilt Dump Truck, blue w/wht. box, blue int., blue win., metal M, 5sp
MIP $4

1010 Ford Stake Bed Truck, teal w/gray stake bed, chr. int., blue win., chr. M, 5dot
MIP $4

1011 Oshkosh Cement Truck, blk./burgundy, blk. pl. M, t/b
MIP $4

1012 Flame Stopper, wht., blk. win., blk. pl. M, ct/b
MIP $3

1013 Mercedes 500SL, silv., blk. int., smoked win., blk. pl. M, bbs
MIP $3

1014 '67 Camaro, candy gray, blk. int., blue win., metal M, 5sp
MIP $5

1015 Mercedes C-Class, yel., red int., clr. win., blk. pl. M, bbs
MIP $2

1018 '32 Ford Coupe, wht. w/maroon in logo & flame, blk. int., clr. win., blk. pl. C, 5sp
MIP $4

1022 '63 T-Bird, met. gold, wht. int., tinted win., metal T, bbs
MIP $3

1024 Shelby Cobra 427 S/C, wht., blk. int., smoked win., metal T, 5sp
MIP $4

1025 Mercedes SLK, dk. blue flake, wht. int., tinted win., metal Ind., t/b
MIP $4

1026 Dodge Caravan, org. pearl, wht. int., smoked win., blk. pl. M, 5sp
MIP $9

1027 Customized C3500, magenta pearl, blk. int., blue win., blk. pl. T, 5sp
MIP $7

1028 '56 Flashsider, yel., blk. win., chr. T, 3sp
MIP $5

1029 '40's Ford Truck, red, wht. int., yel. win., chr. C, 5sp
MIP $4

1030 Porsche 959, gray pearl, blk. int., blue win., metal C, 5dot
MIP $3

1031 Aeroflash, grn. pl., blk. int., clr. win., blk. metal M, 3sp
MIP $4

1032 Ford GT-90, yel., blk. int., clr. win., metal C, 3sp
MIP $2

1035 1970 Plymouth Barracuda, purp. met., blk. int., smoked win., chr. C, 3sp
MIP $3

1037 Roll Patrol Jeep, yel., tan int., tinted win., metal T, ct/b
MIP $25

1038 Dodge Viper RT/10, silv. flake, blk. int., clr. win., blk. pl. C, 3sp
MIP $3

1040 Panoz GTR-1, pearl grn., blk. int., clr. win., blk. pl. C, 3sp
MIP $3

1041 Super Comp Dragster, candy gray w/blk. fenders, blk. int., chr. T, 5sp
MIP $3

1042 Twang Thang, met. grn., chr. int., grn. win., blk. pl. C, 5sp
MIP $3

1043 Rail Rodder, wht. pl., metal M, b5sp
MIP $4

1044 Whatta Drag, blk., red win., gray metal C, 5dot
MIP $3

1045 Dodge Ram 1500, blk., lt. gray int., clr. win., lt. gray pl. C, 5sp
MIP $5

1046 Police Cruiser, wht., blk. int., blue win., blk. pl. T, 3sp
MIP $5

1047 Olds Aurora, blk./wht., tan int., clr. win., blk. pl. T, 5dot
MIP $5

1048 Rescue Ranger, wht. "no Explosive Materials on fender", blue int., blue win., chr. C, 5sp
MIP $15

1049 Treadator, blk., chr. win., blue pl. T
MIP $3

1051 '65 Mustang, blk., tan int., tinted win., metal C, g5sp
MIP $4

1052 Rigor Motor, red, chr. int., smoked win., metal C, 5sp
MIP $3

1053 Hydroplane, blk., chr. int., yel. win., blk. pl. C
MIP $3

1054 Porsche 959, blk., wht. int., clr. win., metal C, bbs
MIP $2

1055 School Bus, blk., blk. int., red tint win., blk. pl. C, 5dot
MIP $2

1056 Corvette Stingray, tan pl., smoked int., smoked win., metal C, gbbs
MIP $3

1057 Thunderstreak, met. red/blue, blue int., metal C, yel. ltr. b5sp
MIP $3

1058 '96 Mustang, dk. red met., blk. int., smoked win., metal C, gbbs
MIP $3

1059 Dodge Ram 1500, met. grn., chr. int., tinted win., gray pl. C, 5dot
MIP $4

1060 Ramp Truck, blk./yel., blk. win., metal C, 5dot
MIP $4

1061 Rescue Ranger, wht., red int., red win., red pl. C, 5dot
MIP $4

1062 Rail Rodder, dk. blue pl., metal M, b5sp
MIP $3

1063 1970 Plymouth Barracuda, org., blk. int., tinted win., chr. C, 3sp
MIP $4

1064 Lakester, silv. met., chr. int., grn. win., silv. met. metal C, 5sp
MIP $2

1065 Firebird, wht., blk. int., smoked win., gray pl. C, b5sp
MIP $4

1066 Mustang Cobra, met. gold, blk. int., clr. win., blk. pl. Ind., 5sp
MIP $3

1067 Express Lane, org. pl., red int., metal C, 5sp
MIP $3

1068 Dodge Concept Car, met. silv., blk. int., tinted win., metal C, gbbs
MIP $2

1069 '40s Ford (Pickup), yel. w/red roof tampo, blk. int., smoked win., blk. pl. C, 5dot
MIP $10

1070 '32 Ford Coupe, dk. red met., blk. int., clr. win., gray pl. C, 5dot
MIP $4

1071 Panoz GTR-1, blk., red int., clr. win., blk. pl. C, 3sp
MIP $2

1073 Ford GT-90, red, blk. int., smoked win., metal C, t/b
MIP $2

1074 Blimp, blk. w/red tail, red metal M
MIP $3

1075 Scorchin' Scooter, red, metal M, chr./blk.
MIP $5

1076 '59 Eldorado, met. blue/wht. w/silv. logo & stripe, wht. int., blue win., chr. M, bbs
MIP $9

1077 '57 Chevy, red, blk. int., blk. win., chr. M, g/bbs
MIP $4

1078 Camaro Z/28, met. blue, blk. win., metal M, 3sp
MIP $3

1079 '63 Corvette, candy gray, blk. int., clr. win., blk. pl. M, 5dot
MIP $3

1080 Hummvee, grn. pl./rear "HUMMVEE", gray win., metal M, ct/b
MIP $3

1081 Power Plower, met. grn., lt. grn. int., yel. win., metal T, ct/b
MIP $3

1082 Jaguar XJ220, met. gold, gold int., smoked win., blk. pl. M, g3sp
MIP $2

1083 Blown Camaro, met. teal w/side hood stripes, blk. int., smoked win., metal M, bbs
MIP $3

1084 Mazda MX-5 Miata, wht., blk. int., smoked win., blk. metal M, 3sp
MIP $2

1085 Porsche 928, gold pearl, blk. win., metal M, 5dot
MIP $2

1086 Toyota MR2, candy purp., gray int., clr. win., metal M, 3sp
MIP $2

1087 Rig Wrecker, yel./blue, blk. int., clr. win., chr. M, 5dot
MIP $5

1088 Speed Machine, blk., wht. int., yel. win., metal M, g5dot
MIP $3

1089 25th Anniversary Lamborghini Countach, candy gray, blk. int., clr. win., blk. pl. M, 5dot
MIP $3

1090 '97 Corvette, blk., wht. int., blue win., blk. pl. M, 3sp
MIP $3

1091 X-Ploder, blk. pl. w/logo in front of wheel, chr. int., red win., metal M, t/b
MIP $7

1092 '58 Corvette, blk. w/aqua motor, chr. int., smoked win., blk. pl. M, bbs
MIP $15

1093 BMW 850i, met. gold, blk. int., smoked win., gold pl. M, bbs
MIP $2

1094 Ferrari F355 Berlinetta, red enamel, blk. int., clr. win., metal M, 5sp
MIP $4

1095 Mercedes SLK, gray met., blk. int., smoked win., blk. metal Ind., t/b
MIP $2

1096 Avus Quattro, chr., blk. int., smoked win., blk. pl. M, 5sp
MIP $2

1097 '31 Doozie, met. red/blk., blk. int., clr. win., metal M, bbs
MIP $3

1098 '37 Bugatti, blk./yel., chr. int., clr. win., metal M, bbs
MIP $3

1099 Road Rocket, red/blk., red int., metal M, bbs
MIP $2

1100 Power Pipes, wht. pl., gold chr. int., red win., red metal M, 5dot
MIP $2

1101 Radar Ranger, teal, wht. int., clr. win., metal M, ct/b
MIP $3

1102 Mini Truck, blk., red int., smoked win., blk. pl. M, gbbs
MIP $2

1103 1980 Corvette, met. gold, blk. int., smoked win., metal M, bbs
MIP $4

1104 Twang Thang, org. pearl, gold chr. int., smoked win., purp. pl. M, g5sp
MIP $3

1105 Mustang Mach I, met. blue, blk. int., clr. win., blk. pl. M, bbs
MIP $4

1106 Go Kart, org., blk. int., org. metal M, 5dot
MIP $8

1107 Chrysler Thunderbolt, dk. blue met., wht. int., smoked win., blk. pl. M, 3sp
MIP $5

1115 Ferrari F335 Challenge, silv., blk. int., smoked win., metal M, 5sp
MIP $3

1118 Ferrari 456M, red, tan int., clr. win., metal M, 5sp
MIP $3

1119 Ferrari F355 Spider, red, tan int., clr. win., metal M, 5sp
MIP $5

1120 Ferrari F50, red, blk. int., clr. win., blk. metal M "Ferrari F50", 5sp
MIP $5

1121 Chevy 1500, org. pl., blk. int., tinted win., silv. metal Ind., 5dot
MIP $3

2000 SERIES

FUTURE FLEET

1 Ford GT-90, blk., wht. int., grn. win., metal M, bbs
MIP $3

2 Pontiac Rageous, blk., red int., red win., gray pl. M, 3sp
MIP $3

3 Jeepster, blk., blk. int., blue win., metal M, 5sp
MIP $40

4 Chrysler Thunderbolt, blk., yel. int., yel. win., gray pl. M, 3sp
MIP $2

HOT ROD MAGAZINE

5 Phaeton, met. red/tan top, dk. gray int., smoked win., metal M, gbbs
MIP $3

6 Track T, yel., wht. int., metal M, t/b
MIP $3

7 Tail Dragger, pearl wht., blk. int., org. win., silv. metal M, gbbs
MIP $3

8 '33 Ford Roadster, met. grn., blk. int., clr. win., metal M, 5sp
MIP $5

SEEIN' 3-D

9 Propper Chopper, red, blk. int., yel. win., blk. pl. M
MIP $2

10 1970 Dodge Daytona, blue enamel w/org. stripe, org. int., clr. win., chr. M, 5sp
MIP $4

11 Lexus SC400, yel., wht. int., smoked win., blk. pl. M, 3sp
MIP $2

12 Olds 442, met. grn., wht. int., smoked win., chr. M, 3sp
MIP $2

SNACK TIME

13 Callaway C7, met. grn., org. int., clr. win., blk. pl. M, 5dot
MIP $2

14 Firebird, org. enamel, wht. int., clr. win., blk. pl. C, 5sp
MIP $2

15 Monte Carlo Concept Car, met. blue, lt. gray int., clr. win., red enamel M, bbs
MIP $2

16 Dodge Sidewinder, butterscotch, red int., red win., gray pl. M, t/b
MIP $3

MAD MANIAX

17 Hot Wheels 500, blue, blk. pl. driver int., metal M, yel. ltr. b7sp
MIP $2

18 Camaro Z/28, met. silv., blk. window win., blk. metal M, bbs
MIP $3

19 Slideout, blk., red pl. M, 5sp
MIP $2

20 Twin Mill II, org. pearl, blk. window win., gray pl. M, g5dot
MIP $2

ATTACK PACK

21 Nissan Truck, met. brn., gray int., clr. win., blk. pl. M, ct/b
MIP $2

22 Power Plower, pearl purp., org. int., clr. win., metal M, ct/b
MIP $3

23 '79 Ford F-150, blk., blk. int., clr. win., chr. M, 5sp
MIP $4

24 Dodge Ram 1500, dk. met. red, blk. int., clr. win., blk. pl. C, 5sp
MIP $3

CIRCUS ON WHEELS

25 '56 Flashsider, met. red, blk. window win., gold chr. M, g5dot
MIP $3

26 '32 Ford Delivery, blk. w/grn. fenders, grn. int., clr. win., metal M, bbs
MIP $3

27 Fat Fendered 40, blue, tan int., clr. win., metal M, bbs
MIP $4

28 Dairy Delivery, met. purp., yel. int., yel. win., met. purp./gray C, g5sp
MIP $3

CD CUSTOMS

29 Chrysler Pronto, met. grn., blk. int., clr. win., blk. pl. M, 3sp
MIP $2

30 Pikes Peak Tacoma, blk. w/blk. ptd. vent, red int., clr. win., blk. pl. M, gbbs
MIP $2

31 Shadow Mk IIa, wht., gray int., gray pl. M, 5sp
MIP $45

32 Pontiac Banshee, pearl org., blk. int., clr. win., metal M, 5dot
MIP $2

KUNG FU FORCE

33 Toyota MR2, blk. w/org. in tampo, red int., clr. win., blk. pl. M, 3sp
MIP $2

34 '99 Mustang, red, blk. int., clr. win., red enamel/blk. T Base, 3sp
MIP $2

35 Shadow Jet II, blue, chr. int., red win., metal M, 3sp
MIP $2

36 Mini Truck, met. grn., blk. int., blk. pl. M, asw-t/b
MIP $15

SPEED BLASTER

37 Firebird Funny Car, pearl org., metal int., clr. win., metal M, 5sp
MIP $3

38 At-A-Tude, pearl silv., chr. int., org. win., blk. pl. M, 5sp
MIP $2

39 Mustang Cobra, blue pearl, gray int., clr. win., blk. pl. M, 5sp
MIP $3

40 Shelby Cobra, wht., blue int., blue win., metal T, 5sp
MIP $3

SKATE

41 Rigor Motor, candy blue, chr. int., blue win., metal M, 5sp
MIP $8

42 Sol-Aire CX4, wht. pearl/blk. w/"6" tampo, blk. int., yel. win., blk. pl. M, 3sp
MIP $65

43 Speed Blaster, org., blk. window win., blk. pl. M, 3sp
MIP $2

44 Combat Medic, silv., blk. int., red win., blk. pl. T, 5sp
MIP $5

SECRET CODE

45 Fiat 500C, red/wht., blk. int., chr. win., metal M, 5sp
MIP $5

46 Baby Boomer, lt. blue pearl, metal M, 5sp
MIP $3

47 Tee'd Off, blk., wht. int., metal M, 5sp
MIP $3

48 Screamin' Hauler, lt. yel., metal seat int., smoked win., metal M, 5sp
MIP $4

VIRTUAL COLLECTION

97 1936 Cord, met. grn., tan int., clr. win., chr. C, bw
MIP $3

101 Hot Seat, blue, wht. seat int., metal M, 5sp
MIP $2

103 Tractor, dayglo yel., blk. metal M, ct/b
MIP $2

104 Speed-A-Saurus, lt. grn., mustard metal M, g5sp
MIP $2

109 Monte Carlo Concept Car, pearl pink/gold stripes, blk. int., clr. win., gray metal C, t/b
MIP $2

110 Fork Lift, org., blk. cage int., metal C, 5sp
MIP $3

111 Wheel Loader, red/wht., blk. int int., metal C, t/b
MIP $3

112 Turbo Flame, transparent red pl., org. win., metal M, g5sp
MIP $2

113 Flame Stopper, dk. org., blk. win., blk. pl. C, t/b
MIP $3

114 Lamborghini Countach, met. blue, wht. int., clr. win., met. blue metal M, 5dot
MIP $2

115 Way 2 Fast, dk. red met., chr. int., chr. int win., metal M, 5sp
MIP $2

117 Tee'd Off, red/wht., blue int., metal C, 5sp
MIP $2

118 Semi-Fast, blue pl./wht., gray int., clr. win., metal M, 5sp
MIP $4

123 Oshkosh Cement Truck, grn./blk., grn. int., lt. grn. metal M, 5dot
MIP $2

126 Rodzilla, lt. grn./gold tint chr., metal C, g3sp
MIP $2

127 Track T, wht., blk. int., metal M, t/b
MIP $2

129 Turbolence, candy gray met., chr. int., metal M, 5dot
MIP $2

133 Mercedes-Benz Unimog, met. dk. red/blk., blk. int., smoked win., metal M, ct/b
MIP $2

135 Thunderstreak, purp., purp. driver int., metal C, bbs
MIP $2

137 Dogfighter, yel., gold chr. int., blk. pl. C, g5sp
MIP $2

138 Skullrider, red, chr. int., gray metal C, 5sp
MIP $2

142 Blimp, wht./red
MIP $2

143 Recycling Truck, dk. blue, blk. win., gray pl. M, t/b
MIP $2

144 Ice Cream Truck, butterscotch, red int., clr. win., blk. metal M, 5dot
MIP $3

145 Fire Eater, wht., red int., red win., chr. M, 3sp
MIP $3

VEHICLES — HOT WHEELS NUMBERED PACKS

151 Go Kart, candy purp., gray seat int., pearl purp. metal M, 5dot
MIP $5

152 Fathom This, wht./org., org. window win.
MIP $2

153 Shadow Jet II, red pl./gray lower stripe, chr. int., smoked win., silv. metal M, b5dot
MIP $5

155 Splittin' Image II, candy gray, blk. win., blk. metal M, g3sp
MIP $2

156 Screamin' Hauler, met. red, silv. int., smoked win., silv. metal C, 5sp
MIP $2

157 Popcycle, met. grn., gold chr. int., yel. win., metal M, g3sp
MIP $2

158 Super Modified, red, wht. int., metal M, gbbs/2
MIP $2

164 Phaeton, blk., purp. int., clr. win., silv. metal C, 5sp
MIP $2

168 Lakester, blk., gold chr. int., yel. win., blk. metal C, 5sp
MIP $2

173 Baby Boomer, red/gold tint chr., metal C, 5sp
MIP $2

2000 TREASURE HUNTS

49 Double Vision, purp., gray int., clr. win., chr. M, chr. RR
MIP $14

50 Tow Jam, yel., blk. win., chr. M, chr. RR
MIP $15

51 1936 Cord, met. silv., wht. int., org. win., chr. M, chr. hub ww/RR
MIP $25

52 Sweet Sixteen II, red, wht. int., org. win., metal M, chr. RR
MIP $12

53 Lakester, met. grn., gold chr. int., yel. win., blk. metal M, g5sp
MIP $10

54 Go Kart, wht., gold frame, gold RR
MIP $25

55 Chaparral 2, dk. blue, gray int., blue win., wht. metal M, chr. RR
MIP $15

56 '57 T-Bird, pearl grn., yel. int., yel. win., chr. M, chr. RR
MIP $14

57 Pikes Peak Celica, met. blue, blk. int., clr. win., blk. pl. M, gold RR
MIP $14

58 '67 Pontiac GTO, pearl wht., blk. int., smoked win., gold chr. M, gold RR
MIP $40

59 Ford GT-90, gold flake, blk. int., clr. win., blk. pl. T, chr. RR
MIP $12

60 1970 Chevelle, blk., wht. int., tinted win., chr. C, chr. RR
MIP $20

2000 FIRST EDITIONS

61 Ferrari 365 GTB/4, red, tan int., clr. win., metal M, 5sp
MIP $3

62 Ferrari 550 Maranello, red enamel, tan int/clr. window int., clr. win., metal M, 5sp
MIP $3

63 1964 Lincoln Continental, wht. enamel w/chr. base, red int., clr. win., , bbs
MIP $2

64 Pro Stock Firebird, mustard yel., gray int., smoked win., metal M, wide rear 5sp
MIP $4

65 Deora II, silv., chr. int., smoked win., blk. pl. M, 5dot
MIP $2

66 Deuce Roadster, blue tint chr., blk. int., clr. win., metal M, 5sp
MIP $2

67 Chevy Pro Stock Truck, dayglo org., gray int., purp. win., chr. M, 5sp
MIP $3

68 '68 El Camino, pearl wht., gray int., blue win., metal M, 5sp
MIP $2

69 Phantastique, candy blue, tan int., clr. win., chr. M, gbbs
MIP $2

70 Thomassima 3, met. red w/rear logo, blk. int., clr. win., chr. M, 5sp
MIP $5

71 Ferrari 333sp, red, blk. int., blk. int & wing win., blk. pl. M, bbs
MIP $2

72 Dodge Charger R/T, met. red, gray int., smoked win., gray pl. M, 5sp
MIP $2

73 Surf Crate, met. blue w/dk. brn. wood, blk. int., metal M, 5sp
MIP $15

74 '41 Willys, pearl org. w/org. lettering, chr. int., smoked win., gray pl. M, 5sp
MIP $4

75 Lotus Elise 340R, silv. flake, blk. int., clr. win., silv. metal M, 5sp
MIP $30

76 1999 Isuzu VehiCross, met. silv./blk., blk. int., smoked win., metal M, pr5
MIP $2

77 Anglia Panel Truck, candy purp., chr. int., org. win., gray pl. M, 5sp
MIP $4

78 So Fine, blk., red int., clr. win., chr. M, bbs
MIP $3

79 '65 Vette, met. blk., red int., clr. win., gray pl. M, 5sp
MIP $3

80 MX-48 Turbo, purp., gray int., blue win., silv. metal M, 5sp
MIP $40

81 Holden, silv./transparent rear wing, yel. int., smoked win., blk. pl. M, 5sp
MIP $75

82 Cabbin' Fever, blk. w/lg. tampo, chr. window win., gray pl. M, pr5
MIP $8

83 Metrorail, aqua/wht., chr. int., smoked win., chr. M, sm. front 5sp
MIP $10

84 Muscle Tone, lt. org. pearl, blk. int., smoked win., gray pl. M, 5sp
MIP $10

85 Dodge Power Wagon, silv. met./sm. bumpers, blk. int., smoked win., gray pl. M, ct/b
MIP $4

86 Shoe Box, yel. w/purp. flames & logo, chr. int., purp. win., blk. pl. M, bbs/2
MIP $10

87 Sho-Stopper, pearl yel., blk. window win., gray pl. M, 3sp
MIP $4

88 '67 Dodge Charger, pearl silv., red int., clr. win., chr. M, pr5
MIP $3

89 Vulture, blk., chr./org. int., clr. win., transparent smoked M, 5sp
MIP $3

90 Mini Cooper, yel., blue int., blue win., metal M, bbs
MIP $4

91 Roll Cage, yel., blk. seats int., silv. metal M, ct/b
MIP $20

92 Austin Healey, blk./gray, red int., smoked win., chr./metal M, 5sp
MIP $10

93 Hammered Coupe, purp., chr. int., clr. win., metal M, 5sp
MIP $2

94 Arachnorod, met. Red, yel. int., smoked win., gray pl. M, pr5
MIP $2

95 Greased Lightnin', silv. pearl, purp. win., metal M, 5sp
MIP $7

96 Blast Lane, pearl tangerine/red flames, metal M, chr./blk.
MIP $5

2000 BASIC LINE

98 '99 Mustang, met red, blk. int., clr. win., blk. pl. C, 3sp
MIP $2

99 Phantom Corsair, met dk. red, wht. int., clr. win., metal C, bbs
MIP $2

100 BMW M Roadster, red, blk. int., clr. win., blk. metal M, 5sp
MIP $2

102 '90 T-Bird, chr., blk. win., metal M, gbbs
MIP $2

105 '57 Chevy, aqua w/girl tampo, blk. win., metal M, 5dot
MIP $4

106 Ferrari 348, blk. w/shield, tan & blk. int., smoked win., blk. metal M, 3sp
MIP $5

107 '70 Chevelle, met. gold, blk. int., clr. win., chr. C, 5sp
MIP $5

108 Olds Aurora, lt. yel., gray int., clr. win., yel. pl. C, t/b
MIP $2

116 '59 Chevy Impala, met. silv., gray int., smoked win., chr. M, t/b
MIP $2

119 Pontiac Rageous, met. blue, wht. int., tinted win., blk. ptd. M, 3sp
MIP $3

120 Mercedes SLK, met. teal, blk. int., clr. win., blk. metal Ind., 3sp
MIP $2

121 Mustang Cobra, met. red, wht. int., tinted win., met. red pl. Ind., t/b
MIP $2

122 Ferrari F40, yel. w/wht./grn. stripes over emblem, blk. int., clr. win., metal M, 5sp
MIP $2

124 Camaro Z/28, blk., blk. win., blk. ptd. M, gbbs
MIP $2

125 Porsche 930, wht., blk. int., smoked win., metal M, 3sp
MIP $2

128 Porsche 911 GT3 Cup, wht., red int., clr. win., blk. pl. Ind., 3sp
MIP $2

130 '63 T-Bird, charcoal flake/wht., wht. int., clr. win., metal T, bbs
MIP $2

131 Mercedes C Class, red, blk. int., clr. win., blk. pl. M, 5dot
MIP $2

132 3-Window '34, met. grn./grn. fenders, wht. int., yel. win., metal M, 3sp
MIP $2

134 Mercedes 500SL, met. blue, blk. int., smoked win., lt. blue pl. M, 5dot
MIP $10

135 Thunderstreak, purp., purp. driver int., metal C, bbs
MIP $2

136 Ferrari Testarossa, wht., blk. int., clr. win., blk. metal M, 5sp
MIP $2

139 Ford GT-40, red, blk. int., clr. win., blk. pl. C, 5sp
MIP $2

140 Jeepster, grn./blk. fenders, blk. int., smoked win., silv. metal C, 5dot
MIP $2

141 '95 Camaro Convertible, yel., blk. int., clr. win., blk. pl. M, g3sp
MIP $2

142 Blimp, wht./red
MIP $2

146 Porsche Carrera, met. blue, blk. int., clr. win., metal M, 3sp
MIP $2

148 Pikes Peak Tacoma, red/red ptd. vent, yel. int., clr. win., gray pl. M, 3sp
MIP $2

149 Shadow Mk IIa, red, gray int., gray pl. M, g5sp
MIP $2

150 Chrysler Pronto, purp., blk. int., clr. win., blk. pl. C, 3sp
MIP $2

154 Corvette Stingray, blue pl. body, blk. window win., metal C, 3sp
MIP $3

159 BMW 850i, lt. blue, blk. int., clr. win., dk. blue pl. M, 3sp
MIP $2

160 Jaguar XJ220, red, blk. int., blue win., blk. metal M, gbbs
MIP $2

161 Ferrari F50, yel. w/wht./grn. stripe over emblem, blk. int., clr. win., blk. metal M, 5sp
MIP $4

162 Ferrari 355 Challenge, yel., gray int., smoked win., metal M, 5sp
MIP $2

163 Mercedes CLK-LM, red, blk. int., clr. win., blk. pl. C, bbs
MIP $2

165 Jaguar XK8, gray pearl, blue int., smoked win., blk. metal M, 5dot
MIP $2

166 Pikes Peak Celica, wht., blk. int., clr. win., blk. metal M, 3sp
MIP $2

167 Dodge Concept Car, wht. pearl, gold int., clr. win., metal M, g3sp
MIP $4

169 Panoz GTR-1, met. blue, wht. int., clr. win., blk. pl. C, 3sp
MIP $2

171 '56 Ford Truck, pearl wht., gold chr. int., yel. win., gold pl. C, g5sp
MIP $2

172 Porsche 911 GT1-98, dk. purp./pink tampo, wht. int., smoked win., blk. pl. M, bbs
MIP $2

173 Baby Boomer, red/gold tint chr., metal C, 5sp
MIP $2

174 '63 Vette, blk. flake, wht. int., clr. win., blk. pl. M, bbs
MIP $2

175 Olds Aurora, pearl bronze, blk. int., blue win., blk. pl. C, bbs
MIP $2

176 Solar Eagle III, red, blk. canopy win., met. blk. metal M
MIP $2

177 Flashfire, wht., gray int., clr. win., blk. T, 3sp
MIP $2

178 Dodge Viper RT/10, met. silv., blk. int., blue win., blk. pl. C, 3sp
MIP $2

179 '95 Camaro Convertible, wht. enamel, blk. int., smoked win., blk. Ind., t/b
MIP $2

180 Jaguar D-Type, dk. maroon, gray int., smoked win., blk. pl. C, bbs
MIP $2

183 Buick Wildcat, bright grn., blk. win., blk. pl. T, 3sp
MIP $2

187 Panoz GTR-1, yel., blk. int., clr. win., blk. pl. C, 3sp
MIP $2

188 '97 Corvette, red, blk. int., clr. win., blk. metal M, gbbs
MIP $2

189 Semi Fast, grn. pl./wht., gray int., smoked win., silv. metal C, 5sp
MIP $2

190 Peterbilt Dump Truck, teal/blue, silv. int., smoked win., silv. metal C, 3sp
MIP $3

191 Ford Stake Bed Truck, met. red/blk., chr. int., smoked win., chr. M, 3sp
MIP $3

192 '40 Ford, silv., blue int., clr. win., blk. pl. C, t/b
MIP $2

193 '40s Woodie, pearl bronze, blk. int., clr. win., silv. metal C, bbs
MIP $2

194 T-Bird Stocker, met. blue, red int., clr. win., gray pl. C, 3sp
MIP $2

195 '32 Ford Coupe, pearl purp., blk. int., clr. win., chr. C, bbs
MIP $2

196 Chevy Nomad, org., wht. int., clr. win., silv. metal C, g3sp
MIP $2

197 '65 Impala, met. grn., yel. int., yel. win., gold chr. C, 3sp
MIP $2

198 Ford Bronco, pearl wht./grn., purp. int., clr. win., metal T, ct/b
MIP $3

199 Roll Patrol Jeep, red, tan int., smoked win., metal T, ct/b
MIP $4

200 Purple Passion, pearl wht., red int., clr. win., chr. T, gbbs
MIP $4

201 '65 Mustang, grn., yel. int., yel. win., metal T, t/b
MIP $4

202 Hydroplane, wht., chr. int., org. win., lt. org. pl. C
MIP $2

203 Surf Patrol, gray, purp. int., purp. win., metal T, ct/b
MIP $2

204 Saltflat Racer, blk., chr. int., org. win., silv. metal T, g5sp
MIP $2

205 Pikes Peak Celica, wht., blue int., clr. win., blk. pl. T, bbs
MIP $2

206 Rig Wrecker, blk., gold chr. int., clr. win., gold chr. T, g3sp
MIP $3

207 Police Car, lt. blue pearl, gray int., smoked win., blk. pl. T, t/b
MIP $2

208 Zender Fact 4, red, gray int., org. win., gray pl. T, t/b
MIP $4

209 Customized C3500, yel., blk. int., clr. win., blk. pl. C, t/b
MIP $7

210 Lexus SC400, met. blue, wht. int., smoked win., blk. metal M, bbs
MIP $2

211 Tow Jam, met. blue, blk. win., chr. M, 5sp
MIP $2

212 Double Vision, lt. grn. pearl, gray int., clr. win., gray pl. M, 3sp
MIP $2

213 Whatta Drag, org., chr. int., smoked win., metal M, 5sp
MIP $2

214 Super Comp Dragster, yel./blk., blk. cage int., chr. T, 5sp
MIP $2

215 XT-3, red flake, blk. win., yel. metal M, 5sp
MIP $2

VEHICLES — HOT WHEELS NUMBERED PACKS

216 School Bus, red, wht. int., blue win., blk. pl. T, 5dot
MIP $2

217 '57 T-Bird, met. purp., blue int., blue win., chr. M, bbs
MIP $2

218 Rescue Ranger, silv. met., smoked int., smoked win., chr. C, 3sp
MIP $3

219 Side Kick, gold met., metal int., red win., metal M, 5sp
MIP $4

220 Sweet Sixteen, blk., red int., metal M, bbs
MIP $2

221 Rail Rodder, blk./gold chr., silv. metal C, b5sp rear/gold mini L330 front
MIP $2

222 Dogfighter, silv. met., blk. pl. C, bbs
MIP $2

223 Twang Thang, met. blue/wht. guitar chr. strings, chr. int., smoked win., blue pl. C, 5sp
MIP $2

224 Ford GT-90, pearl grn./blk., wht. int., clr. win., metal C, 5dot
MIP $2

225 Chrysler Thunderbolt, red/dk. red top, blk. int., clr. win., blk. pl. M, 5sp
MIP $3

226 '67 Pontiac GTO, org., blk. int., clr. win., chr. T, 5sp
MIP $5

227 Skullrider, blk., chr. int., metal C, 5sp
MIP $2

228 '57 Chevy, pearl org. met., blk. int., smoked win., chr. M, 5sp
MIP $2

229 Blown Camaro, red, blk. int., smoked win., metal M, t/b
MIP $2

230 Ferrari F355 Spider, gray met./old HW logo, blk. int., smoked win., metal M, 5sp
MIP $4

231 Treadator, met. gold, chr. win., blk. pl. T
MIP $2

232 Porsche 959, blk., blk. int., clr. win., metal C, 5dot
MIP $2

233 Oshkosh Snowplow, pearl mustard yel./blk., mustard int., metal M, ct/b
MIP $5

234 '33 Ford Roadster, blk., blk. int., tinted win., metal M, pr5
MIP $2

235 Ferrari 550 Maranello, met. gray, red int., clr. win., metal M, 5sp
MIP $2

236 Ferrari 365 GTB/4, yel., blk. int., clr. win., metal M, 5sp
MIP $2

237 '64 Lincoln Continental, blk./wht. HW logo on trunk, red int., clr. win., chr. M, red HW logo on plate, 5dot
MIP $35

238 Deuce Roadster, met. gold, blk. int., red win., metal M, g5sp
MIP $2

239 Tail Dragger, met blue, silv. int., blue win., metal T, 3sp
MIP $2

240 Scorchin' Scooter, candy bronze/blk. forks, metal M, chr./blk.
MIP $4

241 Propper Chopper, blk., maroon int., blue win., maroon pl. M
MIP $2

242 Olds 442, wht., gold int., clr. win., chr. M, pr5
MIP $3

243 Deora II, candy blue, chr. int., clr. win., blk. pl. C, pr5
MIP $2

244 Chevy Pro Stock Truck, purp., org. int., clr. win., chr. C, 5sp
MIP $2

245 Phantastique, met. red, cream int., clr. win., chr. C, bbs
MIP $2

246 '68 El Camino, candy bronze, gray int., clr. win., metal C, 5sp
MIP $2

247 Ford F-150, blk., chr. int., yel. win., blk. pl. T, 3sp
MIP $2

248 Way 2 Fast, candy gray, chr. int., blk. metal T, pr5
MIP $50

249 '59 Impala, blk., red int., smoked win., gold chr. M, gbbs
MIP $2

250 Porsche 911 GTI-98, wht. w/aqua in tampo, gray int., clr. win., blk. pl. C, bbs
MIP $3

2001 TREASURE HUNTS

1 '65 Corvette, red, wht. int., clr. win., gray pl. M, chr. hub RR
MIP $15

2 Roll Cage, org., blk. int., smoked win., wht. metal M, chr. hub knobby RR
MIP $15

3 So Fine, met. grn., wht. int., smoked win., chr. M, chr. hub ww/RR
MIP $15

4 Rodger Dodger, blk., red int., smoked win., chr. M, chr. hub ww/RR
MIP $15

5 Blast Lane, met. gold, metal M, gold rim/blk. spoke
MIP $20

6 Hammered Coupe, gray/blk., chr. int., org. win., metal M, pr5
MIP $10

7 Vulture, wht. pearl, chr. int., red win., transparent org. M, pr5
MIP $10

8 Dodge Charger, yel., blk. int., clr. win., chr. M, chr. hub RR
MIP $12

9 Olds 442, lt. blue flake, wht. int., clr. win., chr. M, chr. hub RR
MIP $15

10 Rageous, met. brn., gray int., smoke w/blk. roof win., gray pl. M, chr. hub RR
MIP $12

11 Deora, blue met., blue int., blue win., metal T, redline bw
MIP $10

12 Cabbin' Fever, wht. pearl, gold chr. win., gold chr. M, pr5
MIP $15

2001 FIRST EDITIONS

13 Cadillac LMP, silv. met., blk. int., blk. pl. M, bbs
MIP $3

13 Cadillac LMP/no side tampo, silv. met., blk. int., blk. pl. M, bbs
MIP $26

14 Surfin' Scool Bus, yel., purp. win., gray pl. M, 5sp
MIP $2

15 La Troca, met. red, blk. win., gold chr. M, gbbs
MIP $3

16 Sooo Fast, wht. pearl, chr. int., clr. win., met. red metal M, 5sp
MIP $3

17 Super Tuned, candy blue met., red int., smoked win., gray pl. M, pr5
MIP $2

17 Super Tuned/open rear wing, candy blue met., red int., smoked win., gray pl. M, pr5
MIP $10

18 Hooligan, flat blk./no chr. on motor, red int., metal M, 5sp
MIP $15

19 Krazy 8s, dk. candy blue, int., smoked win., metal M, pr5
MIP $2

20 MS-T Suzuka, lime pearl, blk. int., tinted win., blk. pl. M, pr5
MIP $2

21 Panoz LMP-1 Roadster S, red, blk. int., blk. pl. M, bbs
MIP $2

22 Shredster, tangerine/mustard/blk., blk. int., smoked win., gray pl. M, wide rear pr5
MIP $2

23 Dodge Viper GTS-R, red/silv. stripes, blk. int., clr. win., blk. pl. M, 5sp
MIP $5

24 Maelstrom, dk. blue met., blk. int., smoked win., chr. M, 3sp
MIP $2

25 Lotus M250, silv. met./"LOTUS" ptd. on rear, red int., smoked win., blk. pl. "Lotus M250" M, 5sp
MIP $75

25 Lotus Project M250, silv. met., red int., smoked win., blk. pl. "Lotus Project M250" M, 5sp
MIP $4

26 1971 Plymouth GTX, Sub-Lime, blk. int., blue win., chr. M, 5sp
MIP $4

27 Honda Civic SI, red, wht. int., smoked win., blk. pl. M, pr5
MIP $2

28 Evil Twin, dk. met. purp./purp. HW logo, tan int., clr. win., blk. pl. M, bbs
MIP $15

29 Hyper Mite, lime pearl/lavender checks, chr. int., purp. win., blk. pl. M, 5sp rear/old mini front
MIP $10

30 Outsider, org. pearl/"VJ", metal M
MIP $8

31 Monoposto, org. pearl, chr. int., blk. pl. M, pr5
MIP $2

32 Vulture Roadster, candy purp., chr. int., org. win., org. transparent M, 5sp
MIP $2

33 Fright Bike, purp. transparent body, blk. win., metal M, chr./blk.
MIP $4

34 Jet Threat, silv. pearl met., chr. int., smoked win., silv. pearl met. metal M, 5dot
MIP $4

35 Montezooma, org.-yel. pearl, gold int., smoked win., chr. M, bbs
MIP $2

36 Toyota Celica, yel., wht. int., yel. win., blk. pl. M, pr5
MIP $2

37 Ford Focus, blk., blk. int., clr. win., blk. pl. M, 5dot
MIP $2

38 Mega Duty, candy gray, blk. int., red win., metal M, pr5
MIP $2

39 Riley & Scott MkIII, candy blue, wht. int., blk. pl. M, asw-bbs
MIP $2

40 XS-IVE, red, blk. win., metal M, ct/b
MIP $3

45 Mo' Scoot, org. transparent body/raised logo, metal M
MIP $35

46 Ford Thunderbolt, blk., red int., smoked win., chr. M, 5sp
MIP $3

47 Morris Wagon, blk./tan, chr. int., yel. win., metal M, ex. lg. rear 5sp
MIP $2

48 Fandango, pearl tangerine met., blk. int., org. win., gray pl. M, pr5
MIP $2

49 Old #3, red, blk. int., blk. metal M, 5sp
MIP $2

50 Ferrari 156, red, metal int., clr. win., metal M, bbs
MIP $2

51 Cunningham C4R, wht./pearl blue stripes, blue int., clr. win., charcoal flake pl. M, 5sp
MIP $2

52 '57 Roadster, red, pink int., smoked win., metal M, 5sp rear/old mini front
MIP $4

2001 SERIES

FOSSIL FUEL

41 School Bus, grn., wht. int., yel. win., blk. pl. M, 5dot
MIP $2

42 Ambulance, dk. purp. met., wht. int., blue win., gray pl. M, t/b
MIP $2

43 Firebird Funny Car, silv. met., metal int., org. win., metal M, 5sp
MIP $4

44 Camaro Z-28, red, blk. win., blk. metal M, 3sp
MIP $2

TURBO TAXI

53 '57 Chevy, blk., blk. int., smoked win., chr. M, 3sp
MIP $3

54 Limozeen, grn. met., wht. int., smoked win., gold chr. T, g5sp
MIP $8

55 '57 T-Bird, yel./org. in tampo, org. int., org. win., chr. M, 3sp
MIP $3

55 '57 T-Bird/no port hole, yel./org. in tampo, org. int., org. win., chr. M, 3sp
MIP $87

56 '70 Chevelle, met. blue, wht. int., blue win., chr. C, 5sp
MIP $3

RAT RODS

57 Track T, flat blk./brn. tampo, blk. int., metal M, ww/bw
MIP $5

58 '33 Roadster, flat blk., red int., clr. win., brn. primer metal M, ww/bw
MIP $3

59 Phaeton, brn. primer, blk. int., clr. win., blk. metal C, ww/bw
MIP $3

60 Shoe Box, flat lavender, chr. int., blue win., chr. M, ww/bw
MIP $3

60 Shoe Box/no HW logo, flat lavender, chr. int., blue win., chr. M, ww/bw
MIP $10

ANIME

61 Muscle Tone, met. grn./silv. in tampo, wht. int., yel. win., blk. pl. M, t/b
MIP $2

62 Ford GT-90, wht., gray int., blue win., metal C, pr5
MIP $2

63 Dodge Charger R/T, pearl mustard, blk. int., grn. win., blk. pl. M, 3sp
MIP $2

64 Olds Aurora GTS-1, lt. blue pearl, blk. int., clr. win., blk. pl. C, pr5
MIP $2

ROD SQUADRON

65 Dodge Daytona Charger, met. silv., blk. int., clr. win., blk. pl. M, bbs
MIP $2

66 Lakester, olive/blown, chr. int., clr. win., silv. pearl met. metal M, bbs
MIP $2

67 Greased Lightnin', blk., blk. int., yel. win., yel. metal M, 5sp
MIP $8

68 Propper Chopper, blue/yel., blk. int., clr. win., blk. pl. M
MIP $3

SKULL & CROSSBONES

69 Rigor Motor, org., gold chr. int., red win., blk. metal M, g5sp
MIP $2

70 Blast Lane, blk., metal M, magenta chr./blk.
MIP $5

71 Deuce Roadster, dk. purp. met., red int., clr. win., metal T, 5sp
MIP $2

72 Screamin' Hauler, gray pearl, silv. met. int., grn. win., silv. met. metal C, 5sp
MIP $2

LOGO-MOTIVE

73 Phantastique, red, blk. int., smoked win., chr. C, bbs
MIP $2

74 Pontiac Banshee, candy blue, gray int., blue win., metal M, 5sp
MIP $2

75 Turbolence, blk./chr. engine, chr. int., chr. win., blk. metal M, 5dot
MIP $2

76 Metrorail, wht., chr. int., org. win., chr. M, 5sp
MIP $2

MONSTERS

77 '59 Impala, blk., wht. int., grn. win., gray pl. M, bbs
MIP $2

78 Tail Dragger, blue pearl, wht. int., red win., metal M, bbs
MIP $2

79 Cadillac 1959, met. grn., gray int., yel. win., chr. T, g5sp
MIP $6

80 Purple Passion, red, wht. int., clr. win., chr. M, g5sp
MIP $10

EXTREME SPORTS

81 MX-48, silv. met., blk. int., org. win., blk. metal C, 3sp
MIP $2

82 Double Vision, backward blowers, met. grn., gray int., clr win., blk. pl. M, gbbs
MIP $5

83 Twin Mill II, red flake, blk. win., blk. pl. M, bbs
MIP $2

84 Funny Car, yel., metal int., clr. win., metal M, 5sp
MIP $3

COMPANY CARS

85 Jaguar XJ 220, blk., tan int., yel. win., blk. pl. M, g3sp
MIP $2

86 '99 Mustang, wht., wht. int., tinted win., blk. pl. C, 3sp
MIP $3

87 Monte Carlo Concept Car, mustard yel., blk. int., clr. win., blk. metal C, 5sp
MIP $3

88 Dodge Sidewinder, maroon met., blk. int., smoked win., blk. pl. M, pr5
MIP $4

HIPPIE MOBILES

89 '68 Mustang, pearl gray/gray peace signs, blk. int., blue win., metal M, 5sp
MIP $10

90 '63 Corvette, met. grn., wht. int., yel. win., chr. M, 5sp
MIP $3

91 '64 Lincoln Continental, met. lt. blue, wht. int., blue win., chr. C, bbs
MIP $2

92 '67 Pontiac GTO, yel., blk. int., smoked win., chr. M, 5sp
MIP $4

SKIN DEEP

93 Super Comp Dragster, met. gold/blk., blk. int., chr. M, 5sp
MIP $2

94 Jeep Willys Coupe, met. silv., chr. int., red win., chr. M, 5sp
MIP $3

95 Chevy Pro Stock Truck, yel., blk. int., clr. win., blk. pl. C, pr5
MIP $3

96 Pro Stock Firebird, blk., wht. int., smoked win., met. silv. metal C, pr5
MIP $2

2001 BASIC LINE

97 Anglia Panel, yel., chr. int., blue win., gray pl. C, 5sp
MIP $4

98 Thomassima III, candy blue met., blk. int., clr. win., chr. C, pr5
MIP $2

99 Pro Stock Firebird, wht., blk. int., clr. win., silv. metal C, pr5
MIP $2

100 '70 Road Runner, red, blk. int., clr. win., chr. M, 5sp
MIP $4

101 Chevy Pick-up, yel., blk. int., clr. win., metal M, 3sp
MIP $3

102 Road Rocket, lt. gold chr., gold chr. int., clr. win., metal M, pr5
MIP $3

103 Porsche 928/brown in tampo, met. grn., blk. win., silv. metal C, 5dot
MIP $2

103 Porsche 928/red in tampo, met. grn., blk. win., silv. metal C, 5dot
MIP $4

104 Audi Avus, candy+H179 pearl, wht. int., smoked win., blk. pl. M, 5dot
MIP $2

105 Demon, met. blk., red int., clr. win., metal T, 3sp
MIP $6

106 Power Pipes, chr., blue win., blk. metal M, 3sp
MIP $2

107 Surf Crate, gold flake, blk. int., metal "no origin", 5sp
MIP $3

108 Dodge Charger R/T, met. purp., blk. int., clr. win., blk. pl. M, pr5
MIP $40

109 '65 Corvette, wht., blk. int., clr. win., blk. pl. M, 5sp
MIP $3

110 '41 Willys, blk., chr. int., red win., gray pl. M, 5sp
MIP $3

111 Express Lane, org., tan int., metal C, 5sp
MIP $2

112 Mustang Mach I, silv. met., blk. int., clr. win., blk. pl. M, pr5
MIP $3

113 BMW Z3 Roadster, teal, blk. int., clr. win., blk. metal M, pr5
MIP $7

114 '96 Mustang, wht. pearl, blk. int., smoked win., metal M, 3sp
MIP $5

115 1935 Cadillac, gold flake, wht. int., clr. win., metal M, bbs
MIP $3

116 Auburn 852, wht./blk., blk. int., clr. win., metal M, bbs
MIP $2

117 Shoe Box, wht. pearl, chr. int., smoked win., blk. pl. M, pr5
MIP $2

118 Muscle Tone, blk./old HW logo, red int., clr. win., gray pl. M, pr5
MIP $5

119 Sho-Stopper, red/old HW logo, blk. int., clr. win., gray pl. C, pr5
MIP $5

120 Hammered Coupe, dk. candy blue, chr. int., smoked win., metal M, pr5
MIP $2

121 Firebird, silv. flake, blk. int., tinted win., blk. pl. C, wht. ltr. b5sp
MIP $2

122 Fork Lift, red/blk., blk. int., metal C, 5sp
MIP $3

123 Wheel Loader, candy gray/dk. blue, gray int., metal C, ct/b
MIP $3

124 Lamborghini Diablo, dk. purp. met., blk. int., smoked win., metal M, 3sp
MIP $3

125 '32 Ford Vicky, flat blk., org. int., tinted win., metal M, pr5
MIP $2

126 '68 Mustang, candy red, blk. int., clr. win., metal T, 5sp
MIP $8

127 Roll Cage, red, blk. int., metal M, ct/b
MIP $3

128 Lotus Elise 340R, dk. red pearl, gray int., tinted win., silv. metal C, pr5
MIP $3

129 Slide Out, yel., blue pl. M, 3sp
MIP $2

130 25th. ann. Lambo Countach, dk. candy blue, wht. int., clr. win., blk. pl. M, 5dot
MIP $15

131 Greased Lightnin', org. pearl, chr. int., smoked win., blk. metal M, 5sp
MIP $10

132 MX-48 Turbo, silv. met., blk. int., smoked win., blk. metal M, 3sp
MIP $2

133 '97 Corvette, silv. met./pearl blue in ribbon, wht. int., clr. win., blk. pl. M, bbs
MIP $4

134 Oshkosh Cement Truck, yel./silv., silv. int., blk. pl. M, 3sp
MIP $2

135 Corvette Stingray, blk., blk. int., smoked win., metal M, 5sp
MIP $3

136 Ice Cream Truck, wht. pearl, blue int., clr. win., blk. pl. M, 3sp
MIP $2

137 Arachnorod, blk., gray int., org. win., chr. C, 5sp
MIP $2

138 Vulture, met. blue pearl, chr. int., grn. win., transparent grn. C, 5sp
MIP $2

139 Ford GT-40, candy purp., wht. int., clr. win., blk. pl. C, bbs/2
MIP $2

140 Hot Seat, org./purp., purp. int., metal M, 5sp
MIP $2

141 Go Kart, org., blk. int., org. metal M, 5sp rear/old mini front
MIP $4

142 '63 T-Bird, red flake/wht. cove/silv. in pinstripe, wht. int., clr. win., metal M, bbs
MIP $4

143 SS Commodore (VT), lt. yel., blue int., blue win., blk. pl. C, pr5
MIP $2

144 Isuzu VehiCross, yel., blk. int., smoked win., metal C, pr5
MIP $2

145 Toyota MR-2, red, wht. int., smoked win., blk. pl. M, 3sp
MIP $2

146 Camaro Z-28, purp. met./silv. in tampo, blk. win., silv. metal M, 5sp
MIP $7

147 Sharkruiser, org., chr. int., org. metal T, gt/b
MIP $3

148 Speed Shark, red, gray int., chr. win., chr. T, 3sp
MIP $2

149 Police Car, wht., blk. int., clr. win., blk. pl. T, 5sp
MIP $4

150 Enforcer, met. grn., blk. win., blk. metal T, 5sp
MIP $3

151 Surf Crate, silv. flake, blk. int., metal "no origin", 5sp
MIP $3

152 Deora II, met. red, chr. int., clr. win., blk. pl. C, 5sp
MIP $3

153 Chevy Stocker, wht., blk. win., metal T, gt/b
MIP $4

154 Power Pistons, transparent org., gray int., clr. win., metal T, 3sp
MIP $2

155 '56 Ford, pearl gray, chr. int., clr. win., blk. pl. C, 5sp
MIP $2

156 '40 Ford Truck, wht./blk., org. int., clr. win., blk. pl. C, 5sp
MIP $4

157 Ferrari 333SP, blk., yel. int., blk. pl. C, pr5
MIP $2

158 Mini Cooper, dk. candy blue, org. int., org. win., metal M, bbs
MIP $3

159 Cabbin' Fever, met. grn., chr. win., gray pl. M, pr5
MIP $4

160 Metrorail, red/wht., chr. int., purp. win., chr. C, 5sp
MIP $3

161 Jaguar XK8, dk. met. red, tan int., clr. win., blk. pl. C, pr5
MIP $2

162 Hummer, yel., gray win., blk. metal M, ct/b
MIP $2

163 '37 Bugatti, wht. pearl/blk., gold chr. int., clr. win., metal M, 5dot
MIP $2

164 Dragster, candy purp. met./wht., wht. int., metal M, 5sp rear/old mini front
MIP $4

165 Flashfire, candy gray, org. int., tinted win., blk. pl. M, bbs
MIP $3

166 Ferrari 456M, met. blue, tan int., clr. win., silv. metal C, pr5
MIP $2

167 Austin Healey, red/wht., blk. int., tinted win., chr. C, bbs/2
MIP $2

168 So Fine, met. grn., wht. int., clr. win., chr. M, bbs
MIP $2

169 Blast Lane, dk. candy blue, metal M, chr./blk.
MIP $4

170 Solar Eagle, org., blk. win., blk. metal M
MIP $3

171 Mercedes C-Class, lt. blue pearl, blk. int., smoked win., blk. pl. M, bbs
MIP $2

172 Radio Flyer Wagon, candy purp., blk. int., metal M, 5sp
MIP $2

173 Talbot Lago, red, chr. int., clr. win., metal M, bbs
MIP $3

174 Baja Bug, silv. flake, blk. int., metal M, ct/b
MIP $3

175 VW Bug, brn. primer, blk. int., tinted win., silv. metal C, 5dot
MIP $3

176 1931 Duesenberg Model J, red flake/wht. HW logo, blk. int., smoked win., metal M, 5sp
MIP $2

177 Dodge Viper RT/10, yel., blk. int., smoked win., blk. pl. C, pr5
MIP $2

178 Chaparral II, met. grn., blk. int., clr. win., blk. metal C, pr5
MIP $2

179 Krazy 8s, yel., chr. int., grn. win., metal M, pr5
MIP $3

180 Corvette Stingray, silv. flake, milky wht. int., smoked win., blk. pl. M, bbs
MIP $3

181 Surfin' School Bus, dk. candy blue, gray int., org. win., gray pl. M, pr5
MIP $2

182 Sooo Fast, flat blk., chr. int., smoked win., metal M, 5sp
MIP $2

183 Super Modified, org., blk. int., metal M, bbs/2
MIP $2

184 Jaguar D-Type, met. silv., gray int., clr. win., silv. metal C, 5sp
MIP $2

185 Amored Car, blk., gray int., org. win., metal M, sm. front 5sp
MIP $15

186 Rodger Dodger, mustard yel., blk. int., smoked win., chr. M, 5sp
MIP $3

187 Bywayman, charcoal met., gray int., smoked win., silv. metal M, ct/b
MIP $2

188 Flame Stopper, brn. primer, blk. win., blk. pl. C, yct/b
MIP $7

189 Dodge Power Wagon, met. blk., gray int., tinted win., gray pl. M, ct/b
MIP $3

190 Ferrari 308, candy gray, blk. int., smoked win., blk. metal M, 5sp
MIP $2

191 Ferrari F355, yel., wht. int., smoked win., metal M, pr5
MIP $2

192 Ford Escort Rally, candy gray, blk. int., smoked win., blk. pl. "Escort Rally" base, 5dot
MIP $3

193 Rescue Ranger, red, blk. int., smoked win., chr. C, 5dot
MIP $3

194 Roll Patrol, blue, red int., smoked win., metal T, ct/b
MIP $4

195 Deuce Roadster, candy purp., wht. int., smoked win., metal T, 5sp
MIP $2

196 3-Window '34, grn./blk., chr. int., clr. win., blk. metal T, 5sp
MIP $3

197 Austin Healey, lt. candy blue, red int., clr. win., chr. C, 5sp
MIP $2

198 Side Kick, silv.-blue met., metal int., red win., blk. pl. T, 5dot
MIP $2

199 Dairy Delivery, yel., red int., tinted win., blk. pl. C, pr5
MIP $3

200 '68 El Camino, lt. org./purp. X's, yel. int., tinted win., metal C, pr5
MIP $7

201 Super Tuned, yel., red int., smoked win., gray pl. M, wide rear pr5
MIP $2

202 La Troca, flat lavender, blk. win., chr. C, bbs
MIP $2

203 Hooligan, dk. maroon met./no chr. motor, red int., silv. metal C, 5sp
MIP $15

204 Ferrari 360 Modena, blk. flake, pink int., clr. win., blk. flake metal M, pr5
MIP $4

205 '38 Phantom Corsair, rootbeer met., gray int., clr. win., metal C, ww/5sp
MIP $2

206 Panoz GTR-1, dk. candy red, lt. blue int., clr. win., blk. pl. C, pr5
MIP $3

207 Power Rocket, transparent red, chr. int., smoked win., metal T, 5dot
MIP $2

208 Cadillac LMP, flat blk., gold int., gold pl. M, gbbs
MIP $2

209 Ferrari F40, candy blue, blk. int., clr. win., metal M, pr5
MIP $2

210 Blimp, gold/org., M
MIP $2

211 Krazy 8s, flat blk., gold chr. int., yel. win., gloss blk. metal C, gpr5
MIP $2

212 Shreadster, dayglo lime/blk./purp., blk. int., smoked win., chr. C, pr5
MIP $2

213 MS-T Susuka, red, blk. int., clr. win., blk. pl. C, pr5
MIP $2

214 Porsche 911 GT3, tangerine pearl, blue int., smoked win., blk. pl. M, pr5
MIP $4

215 Popcycle, candy purp., chr. int., purp. win., metal C, 5dot
MIP $2

216 '32 Ford, flat blk., org. int., clr. win., blk. pl. C, 5sp
MIP $3

217 Shadow Jet, met. silv., silv. int., smoked win., metal M, 5sp
MIP $2

218 Ferrari 250, candy gray met., blk. int., clr. win., blk. pl. C, bbs
MIP $2

219 Corvette, tangerine pearl met., gray int., smoked win., metal M, pr5
MIP $4

220 GT Racer, dk. blue, metal int., yel. win., metal M, 5dot
MIP $2

221 Riley & Scott MkIII, red, blue int., blk. pl. M, bbs
MIP $2

222 Outsider, dayglo lime, metal M
MIP $2

223 Pikes Peak Tacoma, blk./old HW logo, red int., clr. win., gray pl. M, 5dot
MIP $5

224 Shadow Mk IIA, blk., gray int., blk. pl. M, pr5
MIP $2

225 Mercedes-Benz SLK, silv. flake, blk. int., blue win., metal M, 5dot
MIP $2

226 '65 Impala Lowrider, wht. pearl, gray int., purp. win., chr. C, gbbs
MIP $2

227 Mini Truck, burnt org. met., blk. int., clr. win., blk. pl. C, 5sp
MIP $2

228 Ford Stake Bed, candy blue met./gray, chr. int., clr. win., chr. M, 5dot
MIP $3

229 Silver Bullet, blk., burgundy met. int., red win., burgundy met. metal T, t/b
MIP $2

230 Oldsmobile Aurora, yel., red int., clr. win., blk. pl. C, bbs
MIP $2

231 Lotus Project M250, yel./ptd. rear "LOTUS", blk. int., smoked win., blk. pl. C, pr5
MIP $2

232 Panoz LMP-1 Roadster, grn./no blue in flag, blk. int., blk. pl. M, 5dot
MIP $3

233 Maelstrom, dayglo yel., blk. win., blk. pl. M, 5dot
MIP $2

234 1936 Cord, blk., red int., tinted win., chr. C, bbs
MIP $2

235 Semi-Fast, transparent red/blk., gray int., yel. win., silv. metal C, 5sp
MIP $2

236 Submarine, dayglo org., blk. win., gray pl. M

MIP $2

237 Fire Eater, dayglo lime, blk. int., smoked win., chr. M, 5dot

MIP $3

238 Ferrari F50, purp. met., blk. int., clr. win., metal M, 5dot

MIP $2

239 T-Bird Stocker, red, chr. win., metal M, 5dot

MIP $2

240 Shelby Cobra 427 S/C, red flake, tan int., clr. win., metal M, bbs

MIP $2

2002 TREASURE HUNTS

1 La Troca, yel., blk. win., gold chr. M, RR

MIP $11

2 '71 Plymouth GTX, dk. blue met., blk. int., clr. win., chr. M, RR

MIP $13

3 '57 Roadster, grn. met., blk. int., smoked win., metal M, RR

MIP $12

4 Lotus Project M250, burgundy met., blk. int., smoked win., blk. pl. M, RR

MIP $10

5 Ford Thunderbolt, silv. met., wht. int., blue win., chr. M, RR

MIP $10

6 Panoz LMP-1 Roadster S, wht./lt. blue, blk. int., blk. pl. M, RR

MIP $15

7 Phaeton, wht., blk. int., clr. win., metal M, RR

MIP $10

8 Fat Fendered '40, flat blk., wht. int., yel. win., metal T, RR

MIP $11

9 '40 Ford, aqua/pearl wht., gray int., clr. win., blk. pl. T, RR

MIP $13

10 Tail Dragger, purp./blk., wht. int., blue win., metal M, RR

MIP $13

11 Mini Cooper, blk. w/ptd. headlights, org. int., clr. win., metal M, redline RR

MIP $12

12 Anglia Panel, red met., chr. int., clr. win., lt. gray pl. T, RR

MIP $15

2002 FIRST EDITIONS

13 Midnight Otto, wht., blk. win., metal M, pr5

MIP $1

14 Hyperliner, yel., red int., smoked win., blk. pl. M, b5sp

MIP $1

15 Tantrum, lime/silv. HW logo, chr./blk. int., blue win., blk. pl. M, pr5

MIP $1

16 Overboard 454, blue met., chr. int., blue win., blk. pl. M, pr5

MIP $1

17 Jester, purp., metal int., grn. win., blk. pl. M, pr5

MIP $1

18 Alterd State, purp., blk. int., metal M, 5sp rear/pr5 front

MIP $20

19 Nissan Skyline, blue, blk. int., clr. win., blk. pl. M, pr5

MIP $20

20 Honda Spocket, red/blk., wht. int., smoked win., blk. pl. M, pr5

MIP $1

21 Corvette SR-2, red/blk., gray int., clr. win., chr. M, 5sp

MIP $2

22 NoMadder What, org., chr. int., smoked win., transparent org. M, pr5

MIP $2

23 Super Smooth, blue, blk. int., clr. win., blk. pl. M, pr5

MIP $2

24 '40 Ford Coupe, red, gray int., smoked win., chr. M, 5sp

MIP $2

25 Ferrari P4, red, blk. int., clr. win., blk. pl. M, g5sp

MIP $2

26 Saleen S7, silv., blk. int., smoked win., blk. pl. M, pr5

MIP $4

27 Backdraft, silv. blue, chr. int., smoked win., metal M, 3sp

MIP $3

28 Custom Cougar, blk., purp. int., org. win., blk. pl. M, pc/pr5

MIP $2

29 '68 Cougar, grn./gloss blk. roof, blk. int., smoked win., chr. M, 5sp

MIP $2

30 Torpedo Jones, red, chr. int., red metal M, bbs

MIP $2

31 Custom '69 Chevy, red, gray int., smoked win., blk. pl. M, pr5

MIP $2

32 Custom '59 Cadillac, lt. purp., wht. int., clr. win., chr. M, gbbs

MIP $2

33 Open Road-ster, mustard, chr. int., grn. win., metal M, pr5

MIP $1

34 Jaded, purp. met., chr. int., purp. win., gray pl. M, 5sp

MIP $2

35 '57 Cadillac Eldorado Brougham, blk./silv. met. HW logo, lt. gray int., clr. win., chr. M, bbs

MIP $2

36 HW Prototype, bronze met., gray int., dk. purp. win., metal M, pr5

MIP $2

37 Lancia Stratos, red, blk. int., clr. win., blk. pl. M, 5sp

MIP $15

38 Nissan Z, silv. met., blk. int., smoked win., blk. pl. M, pr5

MIP $1

39 Toyota RSC, gray met., blk. int., smoked win., blk. pl. M, or5

MIP $1

40 2001 Mini Cooper, mustard, blk. int., clr. win., metal M, pr5

MIP $15

41 Super Tsunami, gold met., gray int., blue win., blk. pl. M, pr5

MIP $2

42 '64 Riviera, bronze/grn./pink stripes, wht. int., purp. win., chr. M, pr5

MIP $5

43 Moto-Crossed, red, gray int., smoked win., metal M, 5sp

MIP $3

44 Lotus Esprit, blk., tan int., clr. win., blk. pl. M, 5sp

MIP $2

45 Volkswagen New Beetle Cup, yel./long stripe, gray int., blue win., gray pl. M, pr5

MIP $8

46 Pony-Up, bronze/pearl blue flames, blk. int., smoked win., metal M, pr5

MIP $3

47 I Candy, lime/purp., purp. int., org. win., metal M, 5sp

MIP $10

48 Rocket Oil Special, purp. met., chr. int., smoked win., metal M, 5sp

MIP $2

49 Hyundai Spyder Concept, gold met., blk. int., smoked win., blk. pl. M, pr5

MIP $2

50 Sling Shot, blue met., chr. int., smoked win., metal M, pr5

MIP $3

51 40 Something, yel., gray int., smoked win., blk. pl. M, pr5

MIP $2

52 Side Draft, bronze met./gray "7", blk. int., smoked win., blk. pl. M, pr5

MIP $4

53 Ballistic, grn./closed scoop, chr. int., blue win., blk. pl. M, y5

MIP $5

54 Syd Mead's Sentinel 400 Limo, dk. aqua/flat blk., gray int., smoked win., chr. M, 5sp

MIP $4

2002 SERIES

WILD FRONTIER

55 '59 Chevy Impala, bronze met., wht. int., smoked win., gold chr. M, g5sp

MIP $2

56 '32 Ford Delivery, blk./tan, tan int., tinted win., metal T, 3sp

MIP $2

57 Grillionaire, org., wht. int., smoked win., blk. pl. M, g5sp

MIP $2

57 Ice Cream Truck, org., wht. int., smoked win., blk. pl. M, g5sp

MIP $4

58 Power Plower, dk. red flake, gray int., yel. win., metal M, ct/b

MIP $4

SPARES & STRIKES

59 Surfin' School Bus, silv./blk., yel. win., gold chr. M, g5sp

MIP $2

60 So Fine, aqua/wht., wht. int., clr. win., chr. M, 5sp

MIP $2

61 Rodger Dodger, grn. met., gold int., clr. win., chr. M, 5sp

MIP $2

62 Sooo Fast, red, chr. int., clr. win., metal C, 5sp

MIP $3

TUNERS

63 Ford Focus, wht., red int., clr. win., blk. pl. M, bbs
MIP $2

64 Honda Civic, blue, blk. int., clr. win., blk. pl. M, 3sp
MIP $2

65 MS-T Suzuka, yel., blk. int., smoked win., blk. pl. M, 3sp
MIP $2

66 Toyota Celica, red, blk. int., smoked win., blk. pl. M, bbs
MIP $2

CORVETTE

67 '65 Corvette, blue/silv., blk. int., clr. win., gray pl. M, 5sp
MIP $3

68 '97 Corvette, purp./gray, gray int., clr. win., blk. pl. M, bbs
MIP $58

69 '58 Corvette, yel./wht. cove, chr. int., clr. win., blk. pl. C, 3sp
MIP $3

70 '63 Corvette, red, wht. int., tinted win., chr. M, 3sp
MIP $2

TRUMP CARS

71 Dodge Charger R/T, blk./silv. side panel, gray int., red win., gray pl. M, 5dot
MIP $5

72 Hammered Coupe, red flake, chr. int., clr. win., blk. metal M, g5sp
MIP $2

73 Montezooma, gold met., blk. int., red win., blk. pl. M, 5dot
MIP $1

74 '33 Ford, wht./maroon, blk. int., clr. win., metal M, 5sp
MIP $2

COLD BLOODED

75 Firebird Funny Car, blk., metal int., red win., metal M, r5sp
MIP $3

76 Speed Shark, bronze met., lt. gray int., chr. win., chr. M, 5sp
MIP $2

77 Vulture, yel., chr. int., smoked win., transparent smoked C, 5sp
MIP $2

78 Phaeton, teal met., blk. int., red win., silv. metal C, gt/b
MIP $1

STAR SPANGLED

79 Chrysler Pronto, red met., gray int., clr. win., blk. pl. C, bbs
MIP $2

80 3-Window '34, blue met., wht. int., blue win., metal T, t/b
MIP $3

81 Deora II, silv. met., chr. int., clr. win., chr. C, 5dot
MIP $2

82 '68 El Camino, wht., red int., clr. win., metal C, 5sp
MIP $1

YU-GI-OH

83 Power Pistons, blk., wht. int., red win., metal T, r5sp
MIP $1

84 Seared Tuner, red met., blk. int., yel. win., blk. pl. M, g5dot
MIP $2

85 Fandango, candy blue met., blk. int., grn. win., gray pl. M, magenta chr. 5sp
MIP $2

86 Super Tuned, candy lime met., blk. int., yel. win., gray pl. C, blue chr. 5sp
MIP $2

SPECTRAFLAME II

87 Monoposto, candy lime met., chr. int., purp. win., blk. pl. M, pr5
MIP $1

88 Muscle Tone, candy goldV, wht. int., smoked win., blk. pl. M, gpr5
MIP $2

89 Jet Threat 3.0, candy lt. blue, chr. int., yel. win., metal M, bbs
MIP $1

90 Screamin' Hauler, candy lt. purp. met., metal int., smoked win., blk. metal M, 5sp
MIP $4

SPECTROFLAME II

90 Screamin' Hauler, candy lt. purp. met., metal int., smoked win., blk. metal M, 5sp
MIP $13

MASTERS OF THE UNIVERSE HE-MAN

91 '41 Willys Coupe, blk., chr. int., red win., dk. gray pl. C, 5sp
MIP $2

92 Twin Mill, wht., gold int., yel. win., gold pl. M, g5sp
MIP $2

93 Double Vision, grn. met., gray int., clr. win., gray pl. C, 5sp
MIP $2

94 Phantastique, blue met./red eyes, blk. int., red win., blk. pl. M, t/b
MIP $1

SWEET RIDES

95 Chevy Pro Stock Truck, wht., red int., smoked win., blk. pl. M, red chr. 5sp
MIP $3

96 Pro Stock Firebird, silv.-blue, blk. int., blue win., metal M, 5sp
MIP $2

97 Mustang Cobra, candy gray/blue, orange tampo, blk. int., blue win., blk. pl. M, bbs
MIP $4

98 '70 Chevelle, yel., wht. int., blue win., chr. C, g5sp
MIP $3

GRAVE RAVE

99 Evil Twin, wht., red int., red win., blk. pl. C, 5sp
MIP $2

100 Krazy 8s, red met., chr. int., tinted win., metal C, pr5
MIP $2

101 Rigor Motor, silv. met., chr. int., org. win., flat blk. metal M, 5sp
MIP $1

102 Grave Rave Wagon, flat blk., gray int., org. win., chr. T, 5sp
MIP $3

RED LINES

103 The Demon, silv. met., wht. int., tinted win., metal M, RL5sp
MIP $2

104 Vicky, purp. met., wht. int., clr. win., metal M, RL5sp
MIP $3

105 Side Kick, lt. blue, metal int., blue win., chr. M, RL5sp
MIP $2

106 Chevy Nomad, org., blk. int., smoked win., metal M, RL5sp
MIP $2

HOT ROD MAGAZINE

107 Purple Passion, flat lavender, wht. int., tinted win., chr. M, ww5sp
MIP $3

108 Hooligan, lime/blk., gray int., metal C, 5sp
MIP $2

109 Deuce Roadster, brn. primer, blk. int., clr. win., metal C, 5sp
MIP $2

110 '70 Plymouth Roadrunner, yel., blk. int., clr. win., chr. T, 5sp
MIP $3

FED FLEET

111 Proper Chopper, flat blk., blk. int., org. win., blk. pl. M
MIP $2

111 Propper Chopper, flat blk. w/silv. tampo, blk. int., org. win., blk. pl. M
MIP $3

112 Armored Truck, blk., wht. int., red win., metal M, g5sp
MIP $3

113 Hydroplane, wht., chr. int., grn. win., blk. pl. C
MIP $3

114 Dodge Power Wagon, wht., blk. int., tinted win., gray pl. C, or5
MIP $3

2002 BASIC LINE

115 Honda Civic, blk., wht. int., grn. win., blk. pl. M, 5dot
MIP $2

116 '71 Plymouth GTX, yel., blk. int., smoked win., chr. C, 5sp
MIP $2

117 '67 Dodge Charger, mustard/no "Charger", blk. int., smoked win., chr. M, 3sp
MIP $8

118 Mercedes CLK-LM, burgundy met., blk. int., smoked win., blk. pl. C, bbs
MIP $1

119 Pontiac Rageous, silv. met., gray int., smoked win., blk. pl. M, bbs
MIP $2

120 Dodge Concept Car, lime, blk. int., tinted win., metal C, 3sp
MIP $1

121 Shock Factor, yel./blk., blk. int., metal M, ct/b
MIP $4

122 Deora, red met., wht. int., clr. win., metal M, t/b

MIP $3

123 Evil Twin, pearl yel., wht. int., smoked win., blk. pl. M, gbbs

MIP $15

124 Monoposto, red, wht. int., smoked win., blk. pl. M, 3sp

MIP $3

125 Hyper Mite, purp./wht. HW logo, gold chr. int., red win., blk. pl. M, g5sp/old mini g5sp

MIP $20

126 Surf Crate, red met., blk. int., dk. gold metal M.I., g5sp

MIP $2

127 Fore Wheeler, gold met., wht. int., metal C, g5sp

MIP $2

128 Tow Jam, flat blk., silv. win., chr. M, 3sp

MIP $3

129 Sweet Sixteen, wht. pearl, gold int., metal M, bbs

MIP $2

130 Porsche 911 Carrera, blue met., wht. int., tinted win., silv. metal C, 3sp

MIP $1

131 Thunderstreak, dk. blue met., blk. int., metal C, bbs

MIP $3

132 Vulture Roadster, blue, chr. int., red win., transparent red T, 5sp

MIP $2

133 Fright Bike, transparent red, blk. win., metal M, blk./chr.

MIP $4

134 Old # 3, org., silv. int., silv. metal C, 5sp

MIP $2

135 Porsche 911 GTI-98, candy bronze, gray int., clr. win., blk. pl. M, bbs

MIP $1

136 Chrysler Thunderbolt, dk. red flake, blk. int., yel. win., blk. pl. M, g5dot

MIP $2

137 Ferrari 348, yel., blk. int., smoked win., blk. pl. T, 3sp

MIP $1

138 Buick Wildcat, candy purp., blk. win., blk. pl. C, 3sp

MIP $2

139 '67 Camaro, dull met. blue, gray int., clr. win., blk. metal C, 3sp

MIP $4

140 XS-IVE, off wht., blk. int., yel. win., metal M, ct/b

MIP $4

141 Ferrari 156, red, metal int., clr. win., metal M, bbs

MIP $2

142 Ford Thunderbolt, dk. red, wht. int., smoked win., chr. M, 5sp

MIP $2

143 Anglia Panel, silv.-blue met., gray int., clr. win., blk. pl. C, 5sp

MIP $4

144 Jeepster, yel., gray int., smoked win., metal M, 5sp

MIP $2

145 Whatta Drag, pearl mustard, chr. int., clr. win., metal M, 5sp

MIP $2

146 Dogfighter, flat blk., chr. int., blk. pl. C, g3sp

MIP $1

147 '65 Mustang, silv. met., wht. int., tinted win., metal T, 5sp

MIP $2

148 Porsche 959, red, wht. int., smoked win., metal T, 5sp

MIP $2

149 Jet Threat 3.0, silv.-blue pearl, chr. int., smoked win., silv.-blue metal T, 5dot

MIP $2

150 Mega-Duty, org., blk. win., metal M, pr5

MIP $4

151 Toyota Celica, purp. met., wht. int., yel. win., gray pl. M, bbs

MIP $1

152 Silhouette II, candy lime, wht. int., smoked win., chr. T, 3sp

MIP $1

153 Sol-Aire CX4, blue met./dk. blue side panel, gray int., clr. win., gray pl. M, 3sp

MIP $3

154 Olds 442, dk. red flake, blk. int., smoked win., chr. M, 3sp

MIP $2

155 T-Bird Stocker, blue met., gray int., clr. win., blk. pl. C, 5sp

MIP $2

156 Cunningham C4R, dk. blue met., blk. int., clr. win., blk. pl. M, 5sp

MIP $1

157 Mo' Scoot, transparent blue, metal M

MIP $2

158 Fandango, yel., blk. int., smoked win., blk. pl. M, gpr5

MIP $2

159 Thomassima III, teal met., blk. int., clr. win., chr. C, pr5

MIP $2

160 Pikes Peak Celica, dk. met. blue, gray int., smoked win., blk. pl. T, bbs

MIP $2

161 M Roadster, champagne, blk. int., smoked win., blk. metal M, 5dot

MIP $20

162 Ferrari F512M, dk. gray met., blk. int., clr. win., blk. metal M, 5sp

MIP $2

163 Lexus SC400, gold met., wht. int., smoked win., blk. pl. M, gbbs

MIP $1

164 Ferrari F355 Spyder, dull met. blue, blk. int., smoked win., blk. metal C, 5sp

MIP $2

165 '57 T-Bird, dk. met. blue, blue int., blue win., chr. M, 5sp

MIP $2

166 Ferrari 308, blk., blk. int., smoked win., blk. metal M, bbs

MIP $2

167 Rodzilla, teal, teal metal C, t/b

MIP $2

168 Speed Blaster, candy blue met./red tampos, chr. win., chr. M, 3sp

MIP $8

169 Enforcer, met. gold, blk. win., silv. metal C, 5sp

MIP $3

170 Splittin' Image, candy lime-gold, wht. int., blue win., metal M, 5sp

MIP $1

171 Oshkosh Snowplow, pearl yel., yel. int., gray pl. T, or5

MIP $5

172 Ferrari F355, silv. met., blk. int., clr. win., metal M, 5sp

MIP $2

173 '70 Plymouth Barracuda, red/silv. trim, lt. red int., tinted win., chr. M, 5sp

MIP $5

174 Dodge Viper GTS-R, silv. tint champagne, blk. int., clr. win., blk. pl. C, 5sp

MIP $2

175 Auburn 852, silv./maroon, maroon int., clr. win., metal M, bbs

MIP $1

176 Cat-A-Pult, red, blk. int., smoked win., metal M, 5sp

MIP $2

177 '95 Camaro, wht., blk. int., smoked win., blk. pl. M, 5sp

MIP $3

178 1996 Chevy 1500, org., blk. int., clr. win., metal M, pr5

MIP $2

179 Mustang Mach I, blk./Burmudez and Bermudez, gray int., tinted win., blk. pl. M, 5sp

MIP $51

180 Shoe Box, flat blk., chr. int., clr. win., blk. pl. M, 5sp

MIP $3

181 '79 Ford, wht., gray int., purp. win., chr. M, 5sp

MIP $3

182 Morris Wagon, met. grn., chr. int., clr. win., metal C, 5sp

MIP $3

183 Montezooma, purp. flake, gold int., tinted win., gold chr. C, gbbs

MIP $2

184 Ford Focus, wht., gray int., yel. win., blk. pl. M, 5dot

MIP $2

185 '40s Woodie, blk./tan, blk. int., clr. win., metal M, bbs

MIP $2

186 Wheel Loader, dk. candy red, gray int., blk. pl. C, or5

MIP $4

186 Wheel Loader, backward bucket, dk. candy red, gray int., blk. pl. C, or5

187 Corvette Stingray III, wht., blk. int., blue win., blk. pl. M, 3sp

MIP $3

188 Slideout, grn., blk. int., blk. pl. M, 5sp

MIP $2

189 Express Lane, lt. grn., blk. int., metal C, 5sp

MIP $2

190 Pontiac Firebird, silv.-blue, blk. int., clr. win., blk. pl. 1997 M.I., 5sp

MIP $2

191 '56 Ford, flat blk., chr. int., clr. win., red pl. C, 5sp

MIP $3

192 Nomadder What, candy lime met., chr. int., smoked win., blk. pl. M, pr5

MIP $3

193 Cabbin' Fever, dk. blue met., blk. int., blue win., blk. pl. C, pr5

MIP $7

194 Altered State, pearl yel., blk. int., metal M, 5sp
MIP $8

195 Flashfire, wht., blk. int., smoked win., wht. pl. M, y5
MIP $2

196 Lamborghini Countach, candy tangerine, blk. int., clr. win., blk. pl. M, 5sp
MIP $2

197 Scorchin' Scooter, met. gold/blk. handlebars, metal engine, metal, blk./chr.
MIP $5

198 Go Kart, yel., lt. blue seat int., metal M, 5sp
MIP $7

199 Turbolance, lt. candy blue, chr. int., metal M, 3sp
MIP $2

200 Mini Cooper, dk. grn., .com tampo, grn. int., blue. win., metal M, bbs
MIP $81

201 Lotus Elise 340R, satin candy blue metalic, gray int., clr. win., metal C, y5
MIP $2

202 Midnight Otto, purp. met., blk. win., metal C, pr5
MIP $2

203 Honda Spocket, candy bronze/blk., wht. int., smoked win., blk. pl. M, pr5
MIP $2

204 '40 Ford Coupe, flat blk., pink int., yel. win., chr. M, 5sp
MIP $3

205 1932 Bugatti Type 50, dk. candy blue/blk., chr. int., clr. win., metal M, g5dot
MIP $2

206 Metrorail Nash Metropolitan, silv. met., chr. int., blue win., C, 5sp
MIP $2

207 Baja Bug, flat blk., red int., metal M, r5sp
MIP $3

208 '59 Cadillac, flat blk., gray int., blue win., chr. M, bbs
MIP $2

209 Jaguar D-Type, candy purp., gray int., org. win., candy purp. metal C, 5dot
MIP $2

210 Dodge Sidewinder, dk. met. blue, gray int., clr. win., blk. pl. M, y5
MIP $3

211 Super Modified, dk. blue met., gray int., metal M, bbs/2
MIP $3

212 Sweet Sixteen II, candy red, int., org. win., metal M, 5sp
MIP $1

213 Ferrari 456M, dk. blue met., lt. gray int., tinted win., blk. metal C, 5sp
MIP $2

214 Overbored 454, rust met., chr. int., tinted win., blk. pl. C, pr5
MIP $2

215 '68 Cougar, silv.-blue, blk. int., clr. win., chr. C, 5sp
MIP $3

216 Corvette SR-2, silv.-blue, blk. int., clr. win., chr. M, 5sp
MIP $2

217 Mustang Cobra, candy purp. met./Birthday, gray int., red win., blk. pl. C, bbs
MIP $4

218 Baby Boomer, dk. blue/Stork Express, silv. metal C, 5sp
MIP $4

219 Dodge Ram 1500, yel., chr. int., blue win., blk. pl. C, 3sp
MIP $3

220 Ford F-150, lt. purp., chr. int., org. win., blk. pl. T, 3sp
MIP $3

221 Maelstrom, silv. met., chr. int., red win., red chr. T, pr5
MIP $11

222 Ford GT40, silv.-blue met., gray int., blue win., blk. pl. T, 5sp
MIP $25

223 SS Commodore VT, grn., blk. int., clr. win., blk. pl. T, bbs
MIP $4

224 Dodge Caravan, pearl org., tan int., clr. win., gray pl. T, 5sp
MIP $11

225 '57 Chevy, red, blk. int., smoked win., gold chr. T, r5sp
MIP $281

226 Fiat 500C, grn., blk. int., gold chr. win., metal T, g5sp
MIP $20

227 Police Cruiser, dk. blue, gray int., clr. win., gray pl. T, 3sp
MIP $9

228 Oldsmobile Aurora, dk. red met., wht. int., org. win., blk. pl. T, 5dot
MIP $2

229 Roll Patrol, flat blk., tan int., org. win., metal T, or5
MIP $5

230 Surf Patrol, champagne, blue int., clr. win., metal T, or5
MIP $5

231 Chevy Stocker, yel., blk. win., metal C, 3sp
MIP $19

232 Jeepster, purp./wht., wht. int., grn. win., wht. metal C, 5sp
MIP $5

233 Hyper Mite, pearl wht. met., chr. int., org. win., blk. pl. M, pr5
MIP $8

234 Shredster, yel. pearl/flat blk., gray int., smoked win., gray M, pr5
MIP $2

235 Phantom Corsair, met. grn., yel. int., smoked win., metal T, g5dot
MIP $16

236 Hiway Hauler, blk. met., red win., blk. pl. T, g5sp
MIP $31

237 At-A-Tude, aqua, chr. int., smoked win., blk. pl. T, 5sp
MIP $2

238 Ford GT-40, silv.-blue met., gray int., blue win., blk. pl. C, 5sp
MIP $2

238 Saltflat Racer, burgundy pearl, chr. int., org. win., blk. metal T, 5sp
MIP $2

239 Greased Lightnin', silv. top/blue bottom, chr. int., blue win., blue metal M, pr5
MIP $18

240 Ford GT-90, silv.-lime met., blk. int., clr. win., metal M, 3sp
MIP $14

2003 TREASURE HUNTS

1 Hooligan, wht./blue w/silv. HW logo, blk. int., metal M, chr. wl/RR
MIP $12

2 '56 Ford, gold, gold chr. int., clr. win., blk. pl. M, gold chr. RR
MIP $15

3 Shoe Box, dk. purp., chr. int., smoked win., chr. M, chr. ww/RR
MIP $15

4 '68 Cougar, blk., blk. int., yel. win., chr. M, chr. RR
MIP $15

5 '68 El Camino, red/blk., unpainted headlights, blk. int., clr. win., metal M, chr. RR
MIP $25

6 Porsche 959, silv. met., blk. win., metal M, chr. RR
MIP $15

7 Midnight Otto, flat wht./org. stripes, red win., blk. metal M, chr. RR
MIP $15

8 Riley & Scott, gold/wht., blk. int., blue pl. M, chr. RR
MIP $15

9 '57 Cadillac Eldorado Brougham, champagne met., wht. int., smoked win., gold chr. M, wht. co-mold
MIP $20

10 Muscle Tone, blk., tan int., yel. win., gold chr. T, gold chr. RR
MIP $15

11 Super Tsunami, lime-gold met., gray int., smoked win., blk. pl. M, chr. RR
MIP $12

12 1971 Plymouth GTX ('Cuda), met. gray, blk. int., clr. win., blk. pl. M, gray co-mold
MIP $150

12 '70 Plymouth Barracuda, red, blk. int., clr. win., blk. pl. M, blk. co-mold
MIP $15

2003 FIRST EDITIONS

13 Bonneville 1965, candy blue met., blk. int., clr. win., chr. M, bbs
MIP $2

14 Steel Flame, dk. candy blue met., blue int., clr. win., blk. pl. M, pr5
MIP $2

15 Corvette Stingray, silv. flake, gray int., smoked win., metal M, 5sp
MIP $2

16 Fish'd & Chip'd, dk. met. blue/silv. met., pink int., lt. HW logo, clr. win., chr. M, 10sp
MIP $5

17 Switchback, candy tangerine met., chr. int., blue win., blk. pl. M, pr5
MIP $3

18 Wild Thing, candy tangerine met., chr. int., clr. win., org. pl. M, sm. thin blk.
MIP $2

19 1/4 Mile Coupe, candy purp. met., chr. int., clr. win., candy purp. M, 5sp
MIP $3

20 Zotic, dk. candy tangerine met., chr. int., smoked win., blk. pl. T, pr5
MIP $2

21 Chaparral 2D, wht., no "7" on nose, blk. int., clr. win., blk. pl. M, bbs/2
MIP $24

22 8 Crate, dk. gray met./blk. enamel, chr. int., purp. win., gray pl. M, 5sp
MIP $2

23 Vairy 8, silv. met., gray int., clr. win., metal M, asw-5sp
MIP $20

24 24/Seven, candy lime met., gray int., smoked win., blk. pl. M, pr5
MIP $2

25 Swoop Coupe, candy red met., blk. win., chr. M, 5sp
MIP $50

26 Whip Creamer II, pearl lavender met., chr. int., yel. win., chr. M, 10sp
MIP $2

27 Cadillac Cien, silv. met./flat blk., chr. int., red win., blk. pl. M, pr5
MIP $2

28 Sinistra, met. gold, chr. int., clr. win., blk. pl. M, chr. magenta pr5
MIP $2

29 Golden Arrow, dk. candy rose, yel. stripe, silv. roof, blk. int., clr. win., metal M, pr5 rear/10sp front
MIP $10

30 Bugatti Veyron, red enamel/blk. enamel/unptd. headlights, cream int., clr. win., blk. pl. M, 10sp
MIP $10

31 Flight '03, wht., red pl. trim, red int., smoked win., metal M, alw-10sp
MIP $15

32 Hyundai Tiburon, blk., yel. and org. flames, no "Troy Lee", wht. int., org. win., blk. pl. M, 10sp
MIP $10

33 GT-03, candy rose, blk. int., smoked win., chr. M, bbs
MIP $3

34 Tire Fryer, dk. candy blue met., chr. int., metal M, 5sp rear, skinny front
MIP $2

35 Boom Box, blue met., gold chr. int., smoked win., blk. pl. M, pr5
MIP $3

36 Enzo Ferrari, red, blk. int., clr. win., blk. pl. M, pr5
MIP $3

37 Dodge M80, yel. met., org. tampos, mostly org. door logo, blk. int., org. win., blk. pl. M, pr5
MIP $3

38 Sand Stinger, lime, blk. seat int., metal M, or5 rear-5sp front
MIP $3

39 Honda Civic, met. silv., red int., smoked win., chr. M, 10sp
MIP $3

40 HKS Alteeza, flat blk./wht. tampo, chr. int., purp. win., blk. pl. M, pr5
MIP $5

41 Power Panel, candy bronze met., gray int., yel. win., blk. pl. M, alw-or5
MIP $3

42 1970 Dodge Charger, brn. met., gold in tampo, chr. int., smoked win., blk. pl. M, 5sp
MIP $3

43 Lamborghini Murcielago, yel. pearl, blk. int., clr. win., blk. pl. M, pr5
MIP $3

44 Audacious, blk., gray int., org. win., blk. pl. M, y5
MIP $3

45 1969 Pontiac GTO Judge, org., blk. win., chr. M, 5sp
MIP $3

46 1968 Mustang, dk. blue met., chr. int., smoked win., blk. pl. M w/Boss Hoss, 5sp
MIP $103

46 1968 Mustang/Boss Hoss, dk. blue met., chr. int., smoked win., blk. pl. M w/Boss Hoss, 5sp
MIP $20

47 2002 Autonomy Concept, silv. met., blk. under blue logo, blue win., candy blue metal M, skinny
MIP $8

48 Da' Kar, mustard pearl, blk. int., smoked win., metal M, or5
MIP $3

49 Ground FX, dk. blue met., chr. int., org. win., blk. pl. M, sw
MIP $3

50 Ford F-150, red, blk. int., blk. pl. M, pr5
MIP $4

51 Meyers Manx, purp. met., yel. int., smoked win., metal M, 5sp
MIP $2

52 Cadillac Escalade, dk. met. gray, blk. win., chr. M, pr5
MIP $4

53 1941 Ford Pickup, yel./gloss blk., org. tampo, chr. int., smoked win., yel. pl. M, 5sp
MIP $5

54 Mitsubishi Eclipse, red, chr. int., smoked win., blk. pl. M, pr5
MIP $4

2003 SERIES

WILD WAVE

55 '69 El Camino, yel. met., blk. int., yel. win., chr. M, 5sp
MIP $2

56 Surf Crate, lt. blue pearl met., wht. int., metal "no origin", 5sp
MIP $2

57 '40 Woody, blk./blue, yel. int., blue win., metal M, 5sp
MIP $2

58 Deora II, lt. pearl lime, chr. int., yel. win., chr. C, 5dot
MIP $2

59 Backdraft, red, chr. int., smoked win., blk. metal T, pr5
MIP $2

FLAMIN' HOT WHEELS

60 Ford Thunderbolt, grn. met., yel. int., yel. win., chr. C, 5sp
MIP $3

61 Callaway C7, copper met., blk. int., smoked win., blk. pl. M, g3sp
MIP $4

62 Pony-Up, silv. met., blue int., blue win., metal M, pr5
MIP $2

63 '95 Camaro, candy purp., wht. int., smoked win., blk. pl. M, 5sp
MIP $2

64 Ford Escort, gold met., wht. int., smoked wing, blk. win., blk. pl. M, gpr5
MIP $25

DRAGON WAGONS

65 Dragster, lt. pearl blue met., blk. int., metal M, 5sp
MIP $2

66 Pontiac GTO, purp. met., wht. int., clr. win., chr. M, 5sp
MIP $2

67 Lincoln Continental, gold met., blk. int., clr. win., chr. C, bbs
MIP $2

68 Toyota Celica, red met., gray int., yel. win., gray pl. M, pr5
MIP $2

69 Lexus SC400, blk., wht. int., grn. win., grn. pl. M, t/b
MIP $2

ANIME

70 Seared Tuner, flat gray, blue int., grn. win., chr. C, red pr5
MIP $2

71 Jaguar D-Type, flat blk., gray int., grn. win., candy red met. metal C, grn. chr. pr5
MIP $2

72 '68 Cougar, bronze, wht. int., blue win., gold chr. M, g5dot
MIP $3

73 Olds Aurora GTS-1, flat olive, red int., grn. win., blk. pl. C, blue chr. pr5
MIP $2

74 Olds 442, blue met., wht. int., red win., gold chr. M, g5dot
MIP $3

FLYING ACES II

75 '32 Ford, blk., wht. int., red win., blk. pl. M, red 5sp
MIP $2

76 Track T, yel. pearl, metal int., blk. metal C, g5sp
MIP $2

77 Deuce Roadster, olive, wht. int., tinted win., metal C, 5sp
MIP $2

78 '33 Ford Roadster, red, blk. int., clr. win., blk. metal C, red chr. 5sp
MIP $2

79 Midnight Otto, gray met., red win., blk. metal C, b5sp
MIP $2

BOULEVARD BUCCANEERS

80 Shoe Box, wht., chr. int., red win., chr. M, 5sp
MIP $2

81 Anglia Panel, gold, blk. int., smoked win., blk. pl. C, 5sp
MIP $2

82 Phantom Corsair, blk. met., blue int., blue win., metal M, t/b
MIP $2

83 Nomadder What, brn. met., chr. int., org. win., org. C, pr5
MIP $2

84 Super Smooth, gray, red win., blk. pl. M, 10sp
MIP $2

CARBONATED CRUISERS

85 Chevelle SS 1970, candy bronze met., wht. int., tinted win., blk. pl. M, g5sp
MIP $2

86 MX48 Turbo, blk. enamel, red hood, lt. red int., tinted win., red metal C, pr5
MIP $2

87 SS Commodore (VT), candy red, blk. int., clr. win., blk. pl. M, bbs
MIP $2

88 Monoposto, wht. pearl, chr. int., grn. win., blk. pl. M, grn. chr. 5dot
MIP $3

RADICAL WRESTLERS

90 '56 Flashsider, wht., chr. win., chr. M, 5dot
MIP $2

91 Chevy 1969, grn., tan int., yel. win., chr. C, pr5
MIP $2

92 Cadillac 1959, yel., blk. int., clr. win., chr. M, bbs
MIP $10

93 Ford 1934, red, wht. int., clr. win., metal M, t/b
MIP $2

94 Mazda MX-5 Miata, blk., red int., clr. win., blk. metal M, 5sp
MIP $2

CRAZED CLOWNS

95 Steel Passion, blue met., gray int., red win., teal pl. C, grn. chr. 5sp
MIP $2

96 Morris Mini, red, yel. int., grn. win., blk. meta. C, y5dot
MIP $3

97 Nash Metropolitan, purp. met., gold chr. int., blue win., gold chr. M, red chr. 5sp
MIP $3

98 Side-Splitter, yel., metal int., smoked win., metal M, red chr. 5sp
MIP $3

99 Tropicool, candy lime, wht. int., blue win., blue pl. M, blue chr. pr5
MIP $3

TECH TUNERS

100 Super Tsunami, candy red, pink in tampo, wht. int., clr. win., chr. M, pr5
MIP $2

101 MS-T Suzuka, wht. pearl, blk. int., cmoked win., chr. M, 3sp
MIP $2

102 Super Tuned, blk. enamel, lt. grn. int., clr. win., dk. gray pl. M, pr5
MIP $2

103 Tantrum, lt. gold met., blk. int., smoked win., blk. pl. M, pr5
MIP $2

104 Ford Focus, silv. met., blk. int., smoked win., blk. pl. M, 5sp
MIP $3

SPECTRAFLAME II

105 Sweet 16 II, candy lt. purp., chr. int., purp. win., blk. metal M, 5sp
MIP $2

106 Double Vision, candy gold, gold chr. int., yel. win., blk. pl. M, gpr5
MIP $2

107 Ballistik, candy blue, chr. int., blue win., blk. pl. M, y5
MIP $2

108 Side Draft, candy lime, blk. int., grn. win., blk. pl. T, pr5
MIP $3

109 Silhouette II, candy burnt org., wht. int., smoked win., blk. pl. M, g/y5
MIP $2

SEGA

110 Fandango, silv.-blue met./wht. satin, blk. int., tinted win., blk. pl. C, pr5
MIP $2

111 Phaeton, semi-gloss blk., grn. int., clr. win., metal C, 5dsp
MIP $5

112 Lotus Esprit, dk. red met., blk. int., clr. win., blk. pl. M, pr5
MIP $3

113 GT Racer, met. grn., blk. int., smoked win., metal M, 5sp
MIP $3

114 Custom Cougar, pearl yel. met., blk. tint chr./blk. int., clr. win., chr. M, pr5
MIP $5

TRACK ACES

125 Turbo Flame, grn., grn. win., grn. M, g5sp
MIP $2

143 HW Prototype 12, org., gray int., clr. win., metal M, pr5
MIP $2

146 I Candy, silv./grn., grn. int., grn. win., gold metal M, g5sp
MIP $2

155 Speed Shark, blue satin, org. int., gold chr. win., org. C, g5sp
MIP $2

161 Hooligan, lt. blue satin/wht., blk. int., metal M, 5sp
MIP $2

167 Splittin' Image, candy lime satin, gold chr. win., blk. pl. M, g5dot
MIP $2

173 Buick Wildcat, blk. enamel, org. win., blk. pl. C, g3sp
MIP $3

176 Ford GT-40, met. gray, gray int., blue win., blk. pl. T, 5sp
MIP $2

185 Flashfire, met. grn. satin, yel. int., yel. win., blk. pl. M, gbbs
MIP $2

192 Speed Blaster, day-glo org., n/a int., gold chr. win., gold chr. M, g/y5
MIP $2

WASTELANDERS

130 Sooo Fast, flat blk., gold chr. int., red win., blk. pl. M, g5sp
MIP $2

144 1967 Dodge Charger, dk. org. met., blk. int., smoked win., blk. pl. M, 5sp
MIP $2

151 1958 Corvette, cnady purp. met., chr. int., smoked win., blk. pl. M, pr5
MIP $2

156 Fat Fendered '40, flat gray, org. side tampo, blk. int., red win., gold metal M, g5sp
MIP $3

162 Fright Bike, clr. pl. body, blk. win., metal M, red chr. rim
MIP $4

168 Camaro 1967, yel. enamel, blk. int., smoked win., metal C, blue chr. 5sp
MIP $3

174 Chevy 1957, candy lime, gray int., smoked win., metal C, 5sp
MIP $3

180 Chevy Impala, drk. candy gray met., blk. int., yel. win., gold chr. C, gbbs
MIP $2

188 Evil Twin, dk. red met., wht. int., clr. win., blk. pl. M, bbs
MIP $2

193 Mustang Mach I, flat blk., blk. int., yel. win., blk. pl. M, 5sp
MIP $3

213 1/4 Mile Coupe, blk. enamel, chr. int., red win., candy red metal C, red chr. 5 sp/chr. 5sp
MIP $2

PRIDE RIDES

133 1964 Buick Riviera, silv.-blue met., blk. int., blue win., chr. M, y5
MIP $2

140 1959 Cadillac, pearl org., yel. int., yel. win., gold chr. M, gt/b
MIP $2

148 1957 Cadillac Eldorado, purp. met., wht. int., smoked win., chr. w/blk. M tampo, bbs
MIP $8

152 Austin Healey, blk., red int., clr. win., metal C, 5sp
MIP $2

158 Mercedes CLK-LM, candy blue, blk/win., blk. pl. M, red chr. y5
MIP $2

164 Dodge Concept, burnt org. met., tan int., clr. win., metal C, gpr5
MIP $2

172 40 Somethin', wht./blk., blk. int., smoked win., blk. pl. M, pr5
MIP $2

179 1959 Chevy Bel Air, dk. red met., blk. int., clr. win., chr. M, bbs
MIP $10

182 Custom Chevrolet C3500, met. grn., chr. int., tinted win., blk. pl. C, pr5
MIP $4

183 La Troca, flat blue, blk. win., chr. C, 5sp
MIP $3

184 Honda Civic, candy blue, blk. int., clr. win., blk. pl. M, pr5
MIP $2

207 Sonic Special, burnt org. met., blk. int., clr. win., blk. pl. M, pr5
MIP $3

ALT TERRAIN

137 Salt Flat Racer, lt. grn., chr. int., blue win., blk. metal M, 5sp
MIP $2

141 Pikes Peak Tacoma, yel. w/wht. "Magnaflo", blk. int., clr. win., blk. pl. M, y5

MIP $8

150 Big Chill, wht., chr. int., blue pl. M, blue ski

MIP $2

154 Shock Factor, red/blk., red int., metal C, or5

MIP $2

160 Moto-Crossed, grn./yel., blk. int., smoked win., metal M, pr5

MIP $2

166 Treadator, met. grn., chr. win., blk. pl. M

MIP $3

171 Jeepster, met. copper, blk. int., smoked win., metal C, w5sp

MIP $2

178 Lakester, yel. enamel, chr. int., clr. win., semi-gloss blk. metal C, pr5

MIP $3

187 Go Kart, blk. enamel, wht. int., blk. metal M, 5sp

MIP $4

191 Roll Cage, flat olive, tan int., blk. metal M, or5

MIP $2

WORK CREWSERS

138 Dodge Ram 1500, dk. candy blue met., blk. win., wht. pl. M, 5dot

MIP $2

145 1956 Ford, dk. gray met., chr. int., clr. win., gray pl. M w/red rivets, 5sp

MIP $8

149 Bus, lt. candy blue/wht. fenders, red win., gray pl. M, 5sp

MIP $2

153 Tow Jam, pearl wht., blue tampo w/ "Lightin", blk. win., chr. M, blue chr. y5

MIP $5

159 Peterbilt, candy rose, smoked int., smoked win., metal C, 5sp

MIP $4

165 Limozeen, dk. blue pearl, tan int., smoked win., shiny smoked chr. M, bbs

MIP $3

170 Hiway Hauler, wht. pearl met., blk. win., chr. C, 5dot

MIP $4

177 1940 Ford, flat olive, blk. int., clr. win., blk. pl. C, 5sp

MIP $3

186 Cabbin' Fever, blk. enamel/org., frosted logo on base, clr. win., chr. C, pr5

MIP $2

190 Fire-Eater, candy red, yel. int., yel. win., chr. M, red chr. pr5

MIP $58

ROLL PATROL

142 Firebird Funny Car, blk., metal int., clr. win., metal M, b5sp

MIP $2

147 Syd Mead's Sentinel 400, lt. blue/gold HW logo, blk. int., smoked win., chr. M, 5sp

MIP $15

157 Saleen S7, blk., wht. int., red win., red pl. M, red chr. pr5

MIP $2

163 Police, flat blk., dk. blue enamel in tampos, blk. int., clr. win., dk. silv. pl. M, 10sp

MIP $3

169 Dodge Caravan, wht. Enamel, blk. int., red win., gray pl. M, 5sp

MIP $3

175 Jaded, blk. enamel, chr. int., clr. win., gray pl. C, 5sp

MIP $3

179 1959 Chevy Bel Air, dk. red met., blk. int., clr. win., chr. M, bbs

MIP $4

181 Phantom Corsair, silv./blue met., blk. int., blue win., metal C, 5dot

MIP $2

189 Fore Wheeler, blk. enamel/blue/wht., blue int., metal C, g5sp

MIP $2

194 Fish'd & Chip'd, dk. blue met., wht. int., red win., chr. M, bbs

MIP $2

208 Hyperliner, met. silv., blk./red int., smoked win., gray T, pr5

MIP $3

FINAL RUN

85 Chevelle SS 1970, candy bronze met., wht. int., tinted win., blk. pl. M, g5sp

MIP $2

87 SS Commodore (VT), candy red, blk. int., clr. win., blk. pl. M, bbs

MIP $2

89 Combat Ambulance, candy gray met., blue int., blue win., blue pl. M, blue chr. 5sp

MIP $3

195 Rig Wrecker/2002 on door, candy red met., gold int., clr. win., gold chr. M, gY5

MIP $5

195 Rig Wrecker/2003 on door, candy red met., gold int., clr. win., gold chr. M, gY5

MIP $3

196 Ambulance, yel./silv., red int., org. win., chr. M, 5sp

MIP $3

197 Mustang GT 1996, gray met., blk. int., smoked win., metal M, pr5

MIP $3

198 1970 Dodge Charger Daytona, red, wht. int., smoked win., chr. M, 5sp

MIP $3

199 Twang Thang, silv. met., gold chr. int., yel. win., blk. pl. C, gpr5

MIP $3

200 Ford Bronco, candy blue, uncolored pl. int., yel. win., metal M, or5

MIP $4

201 Bywayman, lt. brn. primer, blk. int., yel. win., blk. metal M, or5

MIP $5

202 Duesenberg Model J 1931, met. gray/blk., blk. int., yel. win., candy gold metal M, g5sp

MIP $3

203 Lamborghini Diablo, red enamel, blk. int., smoked win., blk. metal M, pr5

MIP $3

204 Porsche 911 Carrera, wht. pearl, blk. int., smoked win., metal M, red chr. 5sp

MIP $3

205 Auburn 852, gold/brn./chr., chr. int., clr. win., metal M, bbs

MIP $2

206 GM Lean Machine, candy satin blue, blk. win., metal T, pr5

MIP $3

2003 BASIC LINE

115 Jester, transparent red/blk., metal int., smoked win., blk. pl. M, pr5

MIP $2

116 Open Road-Ster, candy bronze met., chr. int., smoked win., metal M, pr5

MIP $2

117 Outsider, silv. met., metal C

MIP $2

118 Hot Seat, lt. gold chr., blk. seat int., metal M, g5sp

MIP $2

119 '63 Thunderbird, silv.-blue met., blk. int., clr. win., metal C, 10sp

MIP $2

120 Arachnorod, copper met., wht. int., red win., blk. pl. C, pr5

MIP $2

121 Rail Rodder, lt. blue, metal C, 5sp

MIP $2

122 1935 Cadillac, dk. grn. met., blk. int., clr. win., metal M, bbs

MIP $2

123 Mercedes 500SL, red met., tan int., tinted win., dk. red pl. C, pr5

MIP $2

124 Custom '69 Chevy, candy purp. met., blue bumper, wht. int., tinted win., blk. pl. T, pr5

MIP $2

126 Cadillac LMP, candy gray, blk. int., blk. pl. C, bbs

MIP $2

127 ISUZU Vehicross, dk. candy red, blk. int., clr. win., metal C, pr5

MIP $2

128 Porsche 911 GT3 Cup, silv.-blue met., gray in tampo, wht. int., gold lettering on smoked win., blk. pl. M, pr5

MIP $12

129 Mercedes C-Class, met. burgundy, gray int., smoked win., blk. pl. M, 10sp

MIP $2

131 Sharkruiser, wht. pearl, gold chr. int., gold met. metal M, gbbs

MIP $2

132 Zender Fact 4, purp. met., wht. int., org. win., blk. pl. C, 10sp

MIP $2

134 Lancia Stratos, yel., wht. int., tinted win., blk. pl. C, gpr5

MIP $3

135 Panoz LMP-1 Roadster S, dk. candy blue met., blk. int., blk. pl. C, pr5

MIP $2

136 Blast Lane, gold met./blk. handlebars, metal T, gold rim/blk. spoke

MIP $8

139 Panoz GTR-1, day-glo yel., blk. int., smoked win., dk. blue pl. T, blue chr. 3sp

MIP $3

209 Cat-A-Pult, blue pearl emt., blk. int., clear win., silv. ptd. metal C, 5sp

MIP $3

210 Splittin' Image, candy blue met., wht. int., org. win., metal M, 5sp

MIP $2

211 Switchback, burnt org. met., chr. int., smoked win., blk. pl. M, 10sp
MIP $2

212 Surf Patrol, blue flake, bright red int., tinted win., metal T, or5
MIP $2

214 Vary 8, burnt org. met., chr. int., blue win., metal T, 5sp
MIP $2

215 Bonneville, lt. gold met., blk. int., smoked win., chr. M, 10sp
MIP $3

216 Chevy 1500 1996, org. pl, blk. int., smoked win., blk. ptd. metal M, 5sp
MIP $2

217 Ford F150 1079, blk. met., blk. int., yel. win., chr. T, 5sp
MIP $3

218 Dodge Power Wagon, met. brn., blk. int., smoked win., chr. C, or5
MIP $2

219 Fiat 500C, flat blue, metal/blk. int., blk. win., metal T, g5sp
MIP $2

220 Nissan Z, flat gray, wht. "004" on side, blk. int., blue win., blk. pl. M, pr5
MIP $2

2004 TREASURE HUNTS

101 Pontiac Bonneville 1965, flat lavender, blk. int., smoked win., chr. M, chr. RR
MIP $5

102 GT-03, red/blk., red int., smoked win., blk. chr. M, chr. RR
MIP $5

103 Cadillac Cien, blk., tan int., smoked win., chr. M, redline RR
MIP $5

104 The Demon, met. gold, org. int., org. win., metal M, chr. WW/RR
MIP $8

105 Super Smooth, met. brn./champagne, blk. int., smoked win., blk. pl. M, gold chr. RR
MIP $5

106 Splittin' Image II, wht., chr. int., purp. win., metal M, chr. RR
MIP $9

107 Altered State, pearl yel., semi-gloss blk. int., semi-gloss blk., chr. RR
MIP $6

108 Morris Wagon, gold/blk., chr. int., clr. win., metal M, chrome RR
MIP $50

109 Whip Creamer II, candy lime met., chr. int., smoked win., chr. M, chr. WW/RR
MIP $25

110 Tantrum, red met., chr./blk. int., smoked win., blk. pl. M, chr. 5sp RR
MIP $10

111 Audacious, wht. pearl met., purp. tampo, tan int., org. win., chr. M, chr. RR
MIP $10

112 Meyers Manx, candy blue met., wht. int., blue win., blue metal M, chr. RR
MIP $10

2004 FIRST EDITIONS

BASIC

1 Batmobile, candy purp./blk., no bat logo on card, chr. int., clr. win., chr. M, pr5
MIP $6

2 Dodge Charger 1969, blk., org. stripe, gray int., blue win., chr. M, 5sp
MIP $4

3 Swoopy Do, copper met., chr. int., smoked win., metal M, 5sp
MIP $2

4 Chevy Impala 1964, silv./blue met., wht. int., blue win., chr. M, bbs
MIP $3

5 Nova 1968, dk. silv./blue met., wht. int., blue win., chr. M, 5sp
MIP $3

21 The Gov'ner, flat blk. pl., red taillight, chr. win., metal M, b5sp/ww
MIP $5

22 Mustang Funny Car, candy blue met., metal int., blk. win., metal M, 5sp
MIP $4

23 Rockster, yel. pearl met., chr. int., clr. win., gray pl. M, or5
MIP $15

27 Bedlam, lt. purp. pearl pl., chr. int., red win., metal M, pr5
MIP $15

28 Chevy Fleetline 1947, lt. lavender met., wht. int., smoked win., chr. M, bbs
MIP $3

29 Maserati Quattroporte, silv.-blue met., silv. grille emblem, tan int., smoked win., chr. M, 10sp
MIP $2

30 F-Racer, flat blk., blue chr., chr. int., metal M, pr5
MIP $3

31 Batmobile, blk. pl., blk. win., metal M, 5sp
MIP $3

32 Hi I.Q., lime satin, gray int., smoked win., frosted chr. M, skinny
MIP $3

35 16 Angles, candy purp. met., metal int., org. win., metal M, pr5
MIP $3

36 Lotus Sport Elise, met. gold, chr. int., tinted win., blk. pl. M, g10sp
MIP $2

37 Rapid Transit, lime, wht. int., purp. win., met. charcoal pl. M, pr5
MIP $3

38 Toyota MR2, met. grn., flat blk. hood, blk. int., grn. win., blk. pl. M, grn. chr. pr5
MIP $3

48 Ford Mustang Concept, silv. met., short T top, red int., tinted win., blk. pl. M, "Mustang Concept" on base, pr5
MIP $3

57 Cadillac V-16, blk., tan int., tinted win., chr. M, blings
MIP $10

58 C6 Corvette, red, tan int., tinted win., blk. pl. M, pr5
MIP $3

60 Hummer H3T, blk., cream int., blue win., frosted chr. M, or5
MIP $3

61 Suzuki GSX-R/4, met. red, flat blk., chr. int., clr. win., chr. M, 5dot
MIP $3

65 Dodge Neon, blk./wht., blk. win., gray pl. M, 5sp
MIP $3

70 CUL8R, silv.-blue met., maroon stripe, candy tangerine met. int., red win., maroon met. metal M, pr5
MIP $3

72 Trak-Tune, transparent blue, chr. int., org. win., org. metal M, 10sp
MIP $3

73 Asphalt Assault, pearl mustard met., chr. int., org. win., blk. pl. M, 10sp
MIP $5

74 2001 B Engineering Edonis, met. gold, gray int., smoked win., blk. pl. M, pr5
MIP $2

76 Madd Propz, candy cinnamon met., chr. int., smoked win., gray met. metal M, mini 5sp
MIP $5

80 Dodge Tomahawk, silv., blk. painted seat int., blue metal M, chr. rim, blk. tires
MIP $5

81 What-4-2, transparent org., chr. int., smoked win., metal M, pr5
MIP $2

82 Xtreemster, dk. red candy met., chr. int., smoked win., blk. pl. M, pr5
MIP $3

83 Torque Screw, silv.-blue met., chr. int., blue win., blk. pl. M, pr5
MIP $2

84 Off Track, blk. pl., chr. int., yel. win., metal M, 5sp
MIP $3

86 Brutalistic, candy purp. met., chr. int., yel. win., candy gold ptd. M, pr5
MIP $2

87 Shredded, red/met. gray, met. gray int., tinted win., blk. pl. M, pr5
MIP $2

88 Super Gnat, lt. or dk. candy tangerine met., chr. int., smoked win., metal M, 10sp
MIP $5

90 Mitsubishi Eclipse, met. gold, gray int., smoked win., blk. pl. M, y5
MIP $2

91 Buzz Off, candy purp./grn., chr. int., grn. win., metal M, 10sp
MIP $2

92 Jacknabitt Special, ZAMAC, blk. int., blue win., metal M, 5sp
MIP $10

94 Phantom Racer, org. pearl met. or candy tangerine met., chr. int., smoked win., blk. pl. M, pr5
MIP $3

100 Cool One, wht., org. tampo, wht. int., org. win., chr. M, pr5
MIP $3

BLINGS

11 Lotus Esprit, met. lt. gold, blk. int., smoked win., blk. pl. M, xlpr5
MIP $10

12 Dairy Delivery, wht. pearl, red win., metal M, xl5sp
MIP $2

VEHICLES — HOT WHEELS NUMBERED PACKS

13 Hyperliner, candy burnt org., blk. int., smoked win., metal M, blings
MIP $2

14 Cadillac Escalade, candy blue met., HW logo on win. and tailgate, smoked win., chr. M, blings
MIP $10

15 Dodge Ram Pickup, red, blk. win., chr. M, xl5sp
MIP $7

26 Chevy Avalanche, candy blue/gray pl., blk. win., blue metal M, blings
MIP $4

34 Hummer H2, yel., blk. win., blk. pl. M, blings
MIP $4

40 Out-A-Line, met. purp., blk. win., chr. M, xlpr5
MIP $10

53 Plymouth Barracuda 1972, org., gloss blk. hood, blk. win., chr. M, xlpr5
MIP $3

55 Brick Cutter, dk. blue met., red win., chr. M, blings
MIP $3

BLING2

12 Dairy Delivery, wht. pearl, red win., metal M, xl5sp
MIP $4

13 Hyperliner, candy burnt org., blk. int., smoked win., metal M, blings
MIP $3

CROOZE

44 Ozz Coupe, red met., blk. win., chr. M, skinny/sm. 5sp rear
MIP $5

46 W-Oozie, candy tangerine met., blue metal M, blk. spoke
MIP $5

49 Low Flow, silv. met./blk. met., red win., chr. M, 5sp
MIP $4

50 Slikt Back, blk., lt. purp. flames, chr. int., purp. win., blk. pl. M, 5sp
MIP $5

51 LeMelt, met. grn., chr. int., tinted win., flat blk. pl. M, 5sp
MIP $3

52 Bedtime, wht. pearl, chr. int., blue win., gloss blk. pl. M, 5sp
MIP $2

64 Fast Fuse, silv. met., chr. int., blue win., blk. pl. M, 5sp or b5sp
MIP $3

69 Batmobile, flat or semi-gloss blk., chr. int., org. win., blk. pl. M, 5sp
MIP $3

75 Ozznberg, org./brn. fenders, chr. int., clr. win., metal M, bbs
MIP $3

77 Wail Tale, wht. pearl met., short hood tampo, chr. int., blue win., blk. pl. M, g5sp
MIP $5

FATBAX

41 Mustang GT 2004, yel. pearl met., blk. win., metal M, fb5sp
MIP $5

45 Plymouth Barracuda, lt. yel., gray win., blue metal M, 5sp
MIP $10

62 Silhouette, candy lime, taillight on bumper, chr. int., org. win., candy lime metal M, 5sp
MIP $5

66 Shelby Cobra 427 S/C, silv. met., blk. int., clr. win., metal M, 5sp
MIP $4

67 Duplified, semi-gloss blk., chr. int., blk. win., metal M, 5sp
MIP $10

78 Toyota Supra, dk. or lt. candy purp. met., smoked win., blue metal M, 5sp
MIP $3

85 Exhausted, lt. purp. met., chr. win., blue metal M, 5sp
MIP $3

92 Jacknabitt Special, wht., one or two blk. stripes, blk. int., blue win., metal M, 5sp
MIP $3

95 2005 Corvette, candy blue, silv. headlights, red taillights, blk. win., metal M, 5sp
MIP $3

97 B-Machine, candy tangerine met., blk. win., blue metal M, 5sp
MIP $3

98 Power Sander, candy tangerine met., metal int., metal M, or5 rear, 5sp front
MIP $3

HARDNOZE

16 2 Cool, candy purp. met., chr. int., smoked win., chr. M, xl5sp
MIP $3

17 Grandy Lusion, dk. blue met., dk. red cove, chr. int., clr. win., metal M, xl5sp
MIP $3

18 Dodge Neon, wht. pearl, uncolored int., smoked win., chr. M, xl5sp
MIP $3

19 Merc 1949, grn./candy lime, blk. int., smoked win., blk. pl. M, xl5sp
MIP $4

20 Twin Mill, flat blk., red win., gray pl. M, xl5sp
MIP $3

24 Chevy 1959, met. gray, tan int., smoked win., chr. M, xl5sp
MIP $2

39 Chevy Monte Carlo 1974, gold met., wht. int., org. win., chr. M, xlg5sp
MIP $2

42 Batmobile, flat blk., blk. win., chr. M, xl5sp
MIP $3

47 Cadillac V-16 Concept, met. silv., chr. int., smoked win., chr. M, pr5
MIP $3

56 Toyota Celica, candy tangerine met./flat or semi-gloss black, wht. int., tinted win., chr. M, 5sp
MIP $2

'TOONED

6 Two 2 Go, wht./purp., chr. int., clr. win., blk. pl. M, pr5
MIP $3

7 360 Modena, yel., silv. tampo, blk. win., blk. pl. M, xlpr5
MIP $2

8 Toyota Supra, met. silv., blk. win., chr. M, xlgpr5
MIP $5

9 Enzo Ferrari, red, chr. int., smoked win., blk. pl. M, xlpr5
MIP $3

10 Shift Kicker, purp. pearl/blk., blk. int., chr. M, 5sp
MIP $2

25 Deora, met. gold, w/surfboards, chr. int., clr. win., blk. pl. M, 5sp
MIP $3

33 Chevy Impala 1964, flat lt. or dk. brn., chr. int., smoked win., frosted chr. M, 5sp
MIP $3

38 Toyota MR2, wht., semi-gloss blk. hood, blk. int., red win., blk. pl. M, pr5
MIP $3

43 Splittin' Image, purp. pl., wht. int., grn. win., metal M, pr5
MIP $3

54 Mitsubishi Pajero Evolution, lt. red, blk. int., smoked win., chr. M, xl5sp
MIP $2

59 Sir Ominous, purp. met., sm. tampo, chr. int., red win., gray pl. M, pr5
MIP $10

63 Furiosity, lt. candy blue met., chr. int., smoked win., blk. pl. M, pr5
MIP $2

68 Mercy Breaker, silv.-blue met., lt. or dk. gray tampo, chr. int., smoked win., blk. pl. M, pr5
MIP $3

71 Camaro Z28 1969, met. maroon, silv. vents, chr. int., tinted win., blk. pl. M, 5sp
MIP $10

79 Lamborghini Countach, org., flat blk. or semi-gloss blk. tailpipes, blk. int., smoked win., org. pl. M, pr5
MIP $3

89 Chevy S-10, met. grn., blk. win., frosted chr. M, blings
MIP $3

93 1963 Corvette, met. gray, red win., lt. gray pl. M, 5sp
MIP $3

96 Sixy Beast, lt. purp. pearl, wht. int., grn. win., chr. M, 5sp
MIP $3

99 2005 Corvette, yel. pearl met., four names, "Tscherne," blk./gray, chr. int., smoked win., blk. pl. M, pr5
MIP $15

2004 SERIES

CEREAL CRUNCHERS

113 Camaro 1995, blk., red int., smoked win., blk. pl. M, 10sp
MIP $2

114 8 Crate, wht. pearl met., chr. int., red win., chr. T, pr5
MIP $3

115 Lincoln Continental 1964, candy tangerine met., wht. int., clr. win., chr. M, 10sp
MIP $2

116 Plymouth GTX 1971, yel. or mustard met., blk. int., smoked win., chr. T, 5sp
MIP $3

117 Pontiac GTO 1967, brn. met., blk. int., org. win., chr. T, 5sp
MIP $3

TAT RODS

118 Sooo Fast, flat brn., chr. int., org. win., flat blk. ptd. metal C, extra lg. rear 5sp
MIP $2

119 Ford Vicky, lt. olive met., blk. int., smoked win., metal M, 3sp or 5sp
MIP $2

120 Deuce Roadster, blk., blue int., clr. win., metal C, 5sp
MIP $2

121 Ford 1932, candy blue, wht. int., smoked win., metal T, 5sp
MIP $10

122 Hooligan, gray, red pl., blk. int., metal C, 5dot
MIP $3

STAR SPANGLED 2

123 Mustang 1965, silv. met., wht. int., clr. win., metal T, 5sp
MIP $3

124 T-Bird 1957, wht. w/porthole, red int., red win., chr. T, red chr. 5sp
MIP $3

125 Chevy 1957, flat blue, lt. blue hood, red int., red win., metal M, 5sp
MIP $7

126 Purple Passion, candy red met., blk. int., smoked win., chr. C, blue chr. co-mold
MIP $5

127 Corvette 1963, blk., pearl blue int., clr. win., frosted chr. T, y5
MIP $3

FERRARI HEAT

128 Ferrari 360 Modena, yel., blk. int., smoked win., metal M, pr5
MIP $10

129 Ferrari F355 Challenge, red, blk. int., smoked win., metal M, 5sp
MIP $2

130 Ferrari 456M, grn., lt. brn. flame outline, no HW logo, cream int., clr. win., metal M, 5sp
MIP $10

131 Ferrari 550 Maranello, blk., blk. int., blue win., metal M, 5sp
MIP $2

132 Ferrari 333 SP, pearl wht. met., blk. int., blue win., blk. pl. M, 5sp
MIP $2

TAG RIDES

138 Boom Box, lt. candy purp. met., chr. int., tinted win., blk. pl. C, pr5
MIP $3

139 1968 Cougar, gold met., blk. int., blue win., blk. pl. T, 3sp
MIP $2

140 Surfin' S'cool Bus, yel. pearl met., blk. int., smoked win., blk. pl. T, 5sp
MIP $3

141 Fandango, candy lime met., yel. or grn. roof tampo, blk. int., smoked win., blk. pl. M, gpr5
MIP $2

142 Tropicool, candy tangerine met., blk. int., yel. win., blk. pl. T, 5dot
MIP $3

CRANK ITZ

143 Custom '59 Cadillac, lt. purp. pearl met., wht. int., org. win., gold chr. T, gy5
MIP $2

144 Steel Flame, brn. met., wht. int., smoked win., blk. pl. M, w/tb
MIP $3

145 Cadillac Escalade, blk., chr. int., blue win., chr. T, pr5
MIP $2

146 '40s Woody, lt. blue met., tan int., smoked win., silv. metal T, 5sp
MIP $7

147 Swoop Coupe, red, smoked win., frosted chr. M, 5sp rear, skinny front
MIP $2

DEMONITION

148 Evil Twin, dk. blue met., red int., smoked win., dk. blue pl. T, g5dot
MIP $2

149 1/4 Mile Coupe, met. grn., gold chr. int., smoked win., blk. metal T or M, g5sp
MIP $2

150 Jaded, blk., blue chr. int., blue win., blue chr. C, 5sp
MIP $2

151 Wild Thing, burgundy met., gold chr. int., blue win., blk. pl. M, thin blk.
MIP $2

152 Dairy Delivery, met. gold, narrow rear windows, blk. int., red win., blk. pl. M, red chr. pr5
MIP $2

SCRAPHEADS

153 Mega-Duty, met. bronze, blue win., metal C, blue chr. y5
MIP $3

154 Shadow Jet II, wht. pl., chr. int., ted win., blue metal M, 5sp
MIP $2

155 Humvee, yel. pl., lg or sm. antenna, red win., metal T, or5
MIP $3

156 Enforcer, met. grn., blk. win., metal T, 5sp
MIP $2

157 Nash Metropolitan, met. blk., chr. int., red win., frosted chr. T, 5sp
MIP $2

AUTONOMICALS

158 1969 Pontiac GTO Judge, blk., blue win., chr. T or C, 5sp
MIP $2

159 Zotic, blk., chr. int., grn win., blk. pl. T or M, gt/b
MIP $2

160 Sol-Aire CX4, blk., tan or org. tampo, org. int., org. win., org. pl. T, o10sp
MIP $3

161 Ground FX, blk., yel. win., blk. pl. T, gold skinny
MIP $2

162 Hammered Coupe, blk., chr. int., red win., candy red T, red chr. pr5
MIP $2

ROLL PATROL

163 Whatta Drag, blk./wht., chr. int., blue win., blk. metal T, 5sp
MIP $2

170 Whip Creamer II, dk. blue met., chr. int., blue win., chr. T, 5sp
MIP $2

174 Pikes Peak Celica, flat blue, blk. int., blk. win., blk. pl. M, gbbs
MIP $2

179 Hyundai Spyder Concept, flat tan, blk. int., smoked win., blk. pl. M, g10sp
MIP $2

184 Mitsubishi Eclipse, silv. met., chr. int., blue win., blk. pl. M, blue chr. pr5
MIP $2

189 Super Modified, semi-gloss blk., lt. red int., metal T, red chr. bbs2
MIP $2

194 Scorchin' Scooter, aqua, wht. int., metal T, blk. spoke, chr. rim
MIP $3

199 Deora, no boards, blk./wht./blue, blk. int., blue win., metal T, 3sp
MIP $2

204 Lamborghini Murcielago, silv. met., blk. int., smoked win., blk. pl. M, pr5
MIP $2

209 Surf Crate, candy blue/pale yel., blk. int., blue metal M, 5sp
MIP $3

WASTELANDERS

164 Rocket Oil Special, flat olive, chr. int., smoked win., flat blk. ptd. metal M, 5sp
MIP $2

169 1970 Plymouth Road Runner, yel. pearl met., blk. int., smoked win., chr. T, 5sp
MIP $5

175 Tire Fryer, met. grn., chr. int., metal T, pr5
MIP $2

180 Screamin' Hauler, flat gray, semi-gloss blk. int., red win., semi-gloss blk. ptd. metal C, pr5
MIP $2

185 Big Thunder, met. gray, chr. int., blk. pl. C, red chr. 10sp
MIP $2

190 Blast Lane, met. cinnamon, blk. seat int., metal T, blk. spoke, chr. rim
MIP $3

195 Plymouth Barracuda, flat blk., blk. int., dk. blue win., blk. chr. M, 10sp
MIP $4

200 Sand Stinger, candy tangerine met., black int., metal M, or5 rear, 5sp front
MIP $3

205 Altered State, wht. pearl met., blk. int., semi-gloss blk. T, 5sp
MIP $2

210 Slideout, brown primer, blk. int., yel. pl. T, gpr5
MIP $2

PRIDE RIDES

165 Mustang 1968, lime met., blue int., clr. win., metal T, 5sp
MIP $5

173 Corvette Sting Ray, pearl lime met., blk. int., smoked win., metal C, 5sp
MIP $3

176 Cunningham C4R, champagne met., blk. int., smoked win., blk. pl. M, g3sp
MIP $2

VEHICLES — HOT WHEELS NUMBERED PACKS

181 1936 Cord, blk., tan int., clr. win., chr. C, bbs

MIP $2

186 Shelby Cobra 427 S/C, silv.-blue met., blk. int., clr. win., metal M, 3sp

MIP $2

191 1935 Cadillac, flat lavender, gray int., smoked win., metal T, 3sp

MIP $2

196 1997 Corvette, pearl wht. met., wht. int., purp. win., blk. pl. T, 3sp

MIP $3

201 1957 Cadillac Eldorado Brougham, flat olive, lt. gray int., yel. win., chr. T, 5sp

MIP $3

206 1940 Ford Coupe, met. silv., blk. int., smoked win., chr. T, 5sp

MIP $4

211 1963 T-Bird, met. silv., blk. int., smoked win., blue metal M, 3sp

MIP $3

WORK CREWSERS

166 Sling Shot, wht. pearl met., chr. int., org. win., candy burnt org. met. metal T, chr. co-mold

MIP $5

171 Chevy, blue met. pl., blk. win., semi-gloss blk. ptd. metal T, 5sp

MIP $5

TRACK ACES

166 Sling Shot, wht. pearl met., chr. int., org. win., candy burnt org. met. metal T, pr5

MIP $5

167 Pontiac Rageous, candy red, gray int., blue win., dk. blue pl. T, red chr. co-mold

MIP $5

168 Corvette Stingray II, wht. pearl met., gray int., org. win., chr. T, 3sp

MIP $2

171 Chevy, blue met. pl., blk. win., semi-gloss blk. ptd. metal T, 5sp

MIP $2

172 Jester, dk. red pl., dk. blue met. met. blue int., blue win., red pl. T, red chr. pr5

MIP $3

177 Power Pipes, red pl., blue int., blue win., metal T, pr5

MIP $2

178 Road Rocket, blue, org. pl., blue int., org. win., metal T, red chr. pr5

MIP $3

182 I Candy, pearl wht. met., org. int., org. win., metal M, lg. rear chr. co-mold

MIP $2

183 Vulture, candy blue, chr. int., yel. win., smoked T, pr5

MIP $2

187 Open Road-Ster, dk. blue met., chr. int., org. win., metal M, red chr. pr5

MIP $2

188 Hyundai Tiburon, pearl wht. met., gray int., org. win., blk. pl. M, pr5

MIP $2

192 HW Prototype 12, wht. pearl met., org. int., clr. win., metal M, bbs

MIP $8

193 Backdraft, blue flake pl., chr. int., org. win., metal T, red chr. pr5

MIP $2

197 Krazy 8s, candy red, gold chr. int., blue win., candy red T, red chr. pr5

MIP $2

198 Sharkruiser, candy blue met., gold chr. int., candy blue met. T, red chr. 5dot

MIP $3

202 Turbo Flame, wht. pearl pl., wht. pearl int., org. win., candy tangerine met. metal M, knobby pr5

MIP $2

203 Speed Blaster, candy red met., blue win., blue pl. M, red chr. co-mold or 3sp

MIP $2

207 Roll Cage, blue met./candy red, red int., candy red T, g/or5

MIP $2

208 Aeroflash, wht. pl., chr. int., org. win., candy tangerine met. metal M, 10sp

MIP $2

212 Zender Fact 4, dk. blue met., chr. int., org. win., blk. pl. T, red chr. 3sp

MIP $3

FINAL RUN

133 Hot Seat, lt. or dk. blue chr., blk. int., metal M, 5sp

MIP $3

134 Ferrari 308, dk. blue met., blk. int., smoked win., metal M, 10sp

MIP $3

135 Semi Fast, purp. pl., gray int., smoked win., metal M, 5sp

MIP $2

135 Semi-Fast, purp. pl., gray int., smoked win., metal T, 5sp

MIP $4

136 Cat-A-Pult, pearl wht. met., maroon int., smoked win., metal M, 5sp or chr. co-mold

MIP $3

137 Sonic Special, candy tangerine met., wht. int., yel. win., blk. pl. C, g10sp

MIP $3

2005 TREASURE HUNTS

BASIC

121 Purple Passion, w/out chest, semi-gloss blk., org. int., org. win., chr. C, chr. RR

MIP $10

122 1967 Camaro, red, red motor, blk. int., smoked win., metal T, chr. hub, black-wall RR

MIP $181

123 1958 Corvette, wht. pearl met., chr. int., blue win., chr. M, chr. hub, redline RR

MIP $45

124 1957 Chevy, flat blk., blk. int., smoked win., chr. M, blk. hub RR

MIP $15

125 '56 Flashsider, gloss blk./flat gray, unptd. headlights, blk. int., smoked win., chr. T, red hub/ww RR

MIP $30

126 '34 3-Window, semi-gloss brn./gray met., blk. int., clr. win., meal C, blk. hub/ww RR

MIP $15

127 Mustang Mach I, met. blue, blk. int., blue win., chr. M, 5sp/RR

MIP $15

128 1967 Pontiac GTO, dk. blue met., blk. int., smoked win., chr. M, chr. hub RR

MIP $20

129 Rodger Dodger, red/blk., blk. int., clr. win., chr. M, chr. hub RR

MIP $30

2005 FIRST EDITIONS

REALISTIX

1 Ford Shelby Cobra Concept, candy gray met., short stripe, lt. blue int., clr. win., blk. pl. M, pr5

MIP $2

2 Mitsubishi Eclipse Concept Car, org. pearl, gray int., smoked win., dk. gray pl. M, pr5 or 10sp

MIP $2

3 Ferrari 575 GTC, red, gray int., clr. win., blk. ptd. metal M, pr5

MIP $2

4 Airy 8, met. silv., blue metal M, blk. spoke/red chr. rim

MIP $2

5 1969 Pontiac Firebird T/A, wht., chr. int., blue win., wht. pl., 5sp

MIP $2

6 2005 Ford Mustang GT, candy red met., blk. int., smoked win., chr. M, pr5

MIP $5

7 1971 Buick Riviera, met. teal, chr. int., clr. win., blk. pl. M, 10sp

MIP $2

8 Pocket Bikester, candy blue met., chr. int., clr. win., blue metal M, pr5

MIP $2

9 Firestorm, flat blk. or semi-gloss blk. rear, chr. int., org. win., candy met. gray metal M, 5sp

MIP $2

10 Acura HSC Concept, candy gray, blk. int., smoked win., blk. pl. M, 5sp

MIP $3

11 Aston Martin V8 Vantage, yel. pearl met., blk. int., smoked win., chr. M, pr5

MIP $2

12 Symbolic, met. silv./blk., blk. int., red win., blk. pl. M, pr5

MIP $2

13 Formul8r, candy purp. or dk. candy met., metal int., yel. win., blk. pl. M, g/10sp

MIP $2

15 Split Decision, transparent red/silv., blk. int., red win., semi-gloss blk. metal M, pr5

MIP $2

17 Cockney Cab II, blk., chr. win., metal M, 5sp

MIP $2

DROP TOPS

21 Low C-GT, candy blue met., chr. int., smoked win., blk. ptd. metal M, 10sp or pr5

MIP $2

22 '57 Nomad, candy red met., chr. int., yel. win., blue metal M, pr5

MIP $2

23 Curb Side, yel. pearl met., chr. int., blue win., blue metal M, pr5

MIP $2

24 **Low Carb,** flat blk., gold HW logo, chr. int., red win., blue metal M, 5sp
MIP $2

25 **1963 Corvette Stingray,** silv. met., blk. win., chr. M, 5sp
MIP $2

26 **Flattery,** candy purp. met., transparent org., metal int., org win., metal M, 5sp rear/skinny front
MIP $2

27 **Mid Drift,** met. silv./blk., red int., red win., blue metal M, 10sp
MIP $2

28 **Drop Top,** silv.-blue met., chr. int., tinted win., blue metal M, 5sp
MIP $2

29 **Speed Bump,** teal met., blk. win., blue metal M, pr5
MIP $2

30 **Dodge Super 8 Hemi,** met. sillv., chr. int., blue win., blk. pl. M, pr5
MIP $2

BLINGS

31 **Chrysler 300C,** gray met., red win., chr. M, bling
MIP $2

32 **Ford Bronco Concept,** gray met., chr. int., purp. win., gray pl. M, bling
MIP $2

33 **L'Bling,** candy tangerine met., pointed stripe, chr. int., tinted win., candy tangerine met. M, pr5
MIP $2

34 **Mercedes-Benz G500,** magenta/silv. met., blk. win., chr. M, bling
MIP $2

35 **Quadra-Sound,** red, yel. or mustard stripes, blk. win., chr. M, blings
MIP $2

36 **Rocket Box,** flat wht., gray panel #15, org. win., metal M, 5sp or pr5
MIP $5

39 **Dodge Magnum R/T,** pearl mustard met., blk. win., chr. "DDC 2005" M, pr5
MIP $3

TORPEDOES

41 **Tor-Speedo,** candy purp. met., blue metal int., blk. pl. M, blings
MIP $15

42 **1971 Dodge Charger,** org., chr. int., tinted win., blue metal M, pr5
MIP $2

43 **Bullet Nose,** mustard pearl, chr. int., tinted win., blue metal M, 5sp
MIP $2

44 **Itso-Skeenie,** candy tangerine/blk., blk. win., metal M, pr5
MIP $2

45 **Blastous,** wht./met. gray, wht. int., org win., metal M, 5sp
MIP $2

46 **Subaru WRX,** flat blk., gray int., yel. win., blue metal M, g/pr5
MIP $2

47 **Slider,** candy lime met., chr. int., clr. win., meal M, 5sp
MIP $2

48 **Overbored 454,** blue met., wht./blue or wht./silv. logo, chr. int., blue win., blue metal M, pr5
MIP $2

49 **Trim TRK,** candy red met., chr. int., tinted win., blk. pl. M, pr5
MIP $2

50 **Willys Coupe,** met. purp., gray int., clr. win., metal M, 5sp/skinny
MIP $2

X-RAYCERS

51 **Ferrari 360 Modena,** transparent red, chr. int., clr. win., blue metal M, pr5
MIP $2

52 **Paradigm Shift,** transparent org., chr. int., clr. win., met. silv. ptd. metal M, pr5
MIP $2

53 **'69 Chevelle,** transparent yel., gray logo, chr. int., tinted win., metal M, pr5
MIP $5

53 **Scion xB,** transparent blue, chr. int., tinted win., blue metal M, pr5
MIP $3

54 **'69 Chevelle,** transparent yel., chr. int., tinted win., blue metal M, pr5
MIP $2

55 **Horseplay,** transparent blue, chr. int., clr. win., blue metal M, pr5
MIP $2

56 **Stocker,** transparent yel., chr. int., clr. win., metal M, b5sp
MIP $2

57 **Phantasm,** transparent org., chr. int., smoked win., blk. ptd. metal M, 5sp
MIP $2

58 **Vandetta,** transparent blue, chr. int., purp. win., metal M, pr5
MIP $2

59 **Poison Arrow,** transparent green, chr. win., silv. met. ptd. metal M
MIP $3

60 **Burl-Esque,** transparent purp., chr. int., clr. win., metal M, 5sp/skinny
MIP $2

2005 SERIES

TRACK ACES

61 **Trak-Tune,** maroon pl., chr./blue int., blue win., candy blue met. metal T, 5sp
MIP $2

62 **Backdraft,** red pl., chr. int., blue win., blue met. ptd. metal T, pr5
MIP $2

63 **Flashfire,** wht. pearl met., blk. int., org. win., gray pl. M, 10sp
MIP $2

64 **Power Pipes,** transparent blue, blk. int., org. win., metal T, 5sp
MIP $2

65 **Vulture,** wht. pearl met., blk. win., blk. pl. T, pr5
MIP $2

66 **Open Road-Ster,** candy red met., 2-flame wing, red int., blue win., blue metal M, g/pr5
MIP $4

67 **Chevy Stocker,** red pl., blue win., met. blue ptd. metal T or M, g/y5
MIP $2

68 **Power Pistons,** pearl wht. pl., blk. int., red win., blue metal M, 5dot
MIP $2

FINAL RUN

71 **Thomassima III,** blk., chr. int., red win., chr. C, 5sp
MIP $2

72 **Treadator,** candy lime, chr. win., blk. pl. M
MIP $2

73 **Buick Wildcat,** candy red, chr. or blk. win., chr. T, 10sp
MIP $2

74 **Hydrojet,** wht. pearl met., chr. int., org. win., org. pl. T
MIP $2

75 **Big Chill,** wht. pearl met., chr. int., chr. win., blk. pl. T, blk. skis
MIP $2

REBEL RIDES

76 **Outsider,** dk. candy red met., metal int., blue metal M, chr. rim
MIP $2

77 **Blast Lane,** yel. pearl met., metal T, blk. rim/blk. spoke
MIP $3

78 **W-OOZIE,** wht. pearl met./gray, blue metal M, chr. rim/blk. spoke
MIP $3

79 **Scorchin' Scooter,** flat blk., metal T, blk. rim/blk. spoke
MIP $3

80 **Fright Bike,** transparent grn., metal T, chr. rim/blk. spoke
MIP $3

ASPHALT JUNGLE

81 **Combat Ambulance,** candy purp. met., blk. int., org. win., gray pl. M, 5sp or pr5
MIP $2

82 **Low Flow,** met. blk./met. gray, red win., blk. pl. M, 5sp
MIP $2

83 **Dodge Neon,** candy red met., blk. int., smoked win., chr. M, 5sp
MIP $2

84 **Deora,** met. grn., chr. int., clr. win., gray pl. C, 5sp
MIP $2

85 **Anglia Panel,** yel. pearl met., blk. int., clr. win., blk. pl. M, wide rear 5sp
MIP $5

HOT WHEELS RACERS

86 **Mustang Cobra,** dk. blue met., blk. int., clr. win., blk. pl. M, bbs
MIP $5

87 **Shadow Mk II a,** dk. blue met./burnt org., gray int., gray pl. M, pr5
MIP $2

88 **Pikes Peak Celica,** dk. blue met./burnt org., blk. int., smoked win., blk. pl. M, bbs
MIP $2

89 **Ford Escort,** dk. blue met., rear fender tampo, burnt org. tampo, red int., smoked win., gray pl. M, knobby pr5
MIP $2

90 **F-Racer,** dk. blue met., chr. int., dk. blue met. ptd. metal M, pr5
MIP $2

PIN HEDZ

91 **1959 Cadillac,** pearl magenta met., blk. int., clr. win., chr. T, bbs
MIP $2

92 '40s Woody, met. gold/blk. pl., cream int., smoked win., metal T, 5sp
MIP $3

93 1964 Chevy Impala, brn. met., wht. int., tinted win., gold chr. M, g/bbs
MIP $2

94 Way 2 Fast, candy red met., chr. engines, chr. int., blue metal M, 5sp
MIP $4

95 1956 Ford, flat cream, gray int., blue win., blk. pl. T, g/5sp
MIP $2

REDLINES

96 Surfin' S'cool Bus, candy red met., blk. win., gray pl. M, redline 5sp
MIP $2

97 Ford Delivery 1932, candy lt. lime-gold met., blk. int., clr. win., metal T, redline 5sp
MIP $2

98 8 Crate, candy gray met., chr. int., blk. win., blk. pl. M, redline 5sp
MIP $2

99 Pontiac Bonneville, candy lime met., blk. int., clr. win., chr. C, redline 5sp
MIP $2

100 Tail Dragger, pearl purp. met., blk. int., smoked win., metal C, redline 5sp
MIP $2

MUSCLE MANIA

101 1971 Plymouth GTX, yel., blk. int., smoked win., blk. pl. T, 5sp
MIP $2

102 1963 T-Bird, dk. maroon met., blk. int., clr. win., metal T, 5sp
MIP $10

103 1964 Buick Riviera, dk. gold met., blk. int., smoked win., blk. pl. T, pr5
MIP $5

104 1969 Charger, dk. blue met., gray int., blue win., chr. M, 5sp
MIP $2

105 1965 Chevy Impala, blk./blue, pink int., clr. win., chr. M, pr5
MIP $2

WHITE HEAT

106 16 Angles, pearl wht. met., gold chr. int., yel. win., blue metal M, g/pr5
MIP $2

2005 BASIC LINE

134 Phaeton, flat blk., red top, blk. int., clr. win., blue metal M, g/pr5
MIP $2

135 Fish'd & Chip'd, semi-gloss gray, blk. int., tinted win., uncured chr. C, 3sp
MIP $2

136 Vairy 8, flat lavender, gray int., smoked win., metal M, b5sp
MIP $2

137 Pikes Peak Tacoma, pearl wht. met., blk. int., smoked win., blk. pl. M, pr5
MIP $2

139 Meyers Manx, candy gold met., pink int., tinted win., blue metal M, gray 5sp co-mold
MIP $2

140 2001 Mini Cooper, blk., blk. int., clr. win., metal T or M, pr5
MIP $2

141 Ooz Coupe, candy blue met., blk. win., chr. M, 5sp rear/skinny front
MIP $2

142 Volkswagen New Beetle Cup, candy gray met., red int., red win., blk. pl. M, red chr. 5sp
MIP $2

143 Steel Flame, flat blk., blk. int., red win., blk. pl. M, pr5
MIP $2

144 Rocket Oil Special, wht. pearl met., chr. int., blue win., flat blk. metal M, 5sp
MIP $2

145 1932 Ford Vicky, candy gray met., blk. int., blue win., metal M, 10sp
MIP $2

146 Dodge Viper GTS-R, flat or semi-gloss blk., gray int., red win., dk. red met. pl. M, pr5
MIP $2

149 Maelstrom, blk., chr. int., red win., red pl. T, 5sp
MIP $2

151 Evil Twin, copper met., gray int., clr. win., blk. pl. M, bbs
MIP $2

154 1947 Chevy Fleetline, met. blk., gray int., clr. win., chr. M, bbs
MIP $2

156 1936 Cord, maroon/silv., dk. gray int., clr. win., chr. M, bbs
MIP $2

159 Off Track, olive pl. body, org. pearl int., tinted win., blue metal M, 5sp
MIP $2

160 Shelby Cobra S/C, candy red met., blk. int., clr. win., blue metal M, bbs
MIP $2

161 Baja Bug, pearl blue met., gray int., blue metal M, or5
MIP $2

164 Da' Kar, brown met., chr. int., org. win., metal M, or5
MIP $2

165 Power Sander, candy gold met., blue int., blue metal M, or5/5sp
MIP $2

166 Sand Stinger, candy blue, blk. seat int., blue metal M, or5/5sp
MIP $2

167 ATV, dk. olive pl., blk. seat int., blk. metal M, or5
MIP $2

169 La Troca, wht., blk. win., dk. red met. pl. M, 5sp
MIP $2

174 Mitsubishi Eclipse, pearl wht. met., chr. int., clr. win., blk. pl. M, pr5
MIP $2

175 Corvette C6, lt. yel., blk. int., clr. win., blk. pl. M, pr5
MIP $2

HOT WHEELS

REDLINES

'31 Doozie, 1977, orange, tan top, brown fenders, Model No. 9649
EX $25 **NM** $40 **MIP** $55

'56 Hi Tail Hauler, 1977, orange, redline, 2 black plastic motorcycles, Model No. 9647
EX $30 **NM** $50 **MIP** $70

'57 Chevy, 1977, red, yellow & white tampo, "57 Chevy", Model No. 9638
EX $40 **NM** $60 **MIP** $85

Alive '55, 1973, assorted, Model No. 6968
EX $135 **NM** $275 **MIP** $550

Alive '55, 1974, blue, Model No. 6968
EX $65 **NM** $150 **MIP** $350

Alive '55, 1974, green, Model No. 6968
EX $20 **NM** $50 **MIP** $110

Alive '55, 1977, chrome, redlines, green & yellow tampo, Model No. 9210
EX $20 **NM** $35 **MIP** $50

Ambulance, 1970, met. blue, white back with red cross & blue light on top, "Heavyweights" series, Model No. 6451
EX $30 **NM** $70 **MIP** $150

American Hauler, 1976, blue cab, white plastic box, American-flag-style tampo, "American Hauler", Model No. 9118
EX $20 **NM** $40 **MIP** $70

American Tipper, 1976, red metal cab, white plastic tipper bed, American flag tampo, "American Tipper", Model No. 9089
EX $20 **NM** $35 **MIP** $65

American Victory, 1975, light blue, American flag tampo, "9" on sides, silver interior, exposed silver engine, Model No. 7662
EX $10 **NM** $20 **MIP** $45

AMX/2, 1971, dark met. red, rear engine covers lift up, metal chassis, Model No. 6460
EX $40 **NM** $75 **MIP** $150

Aw Shoot, 1976, tank, olive drab, Model No. 9243
EX $10 **NM** $20 **MIP** $45

Backwoods Bomb, 1975, blue body with green & yellow tampo on sides, plastic camper shell on bed, "Keep On Camping," silver base, Model No. 7670
EX $30 **NM** $65 **MIP** $110

Baja Bruiser, 1974, orange, stars & stripes side tampo, "Firestone," "Cragar," and "Ford", Model No. 8258
EX $20 **NM** $45 **MIP** $90

Baja Bruiser, 1974, yellow, magenta in tampo, Model No. 8258
EX $175 **NM** $450 **MIP** $1200

Baja Bruiser, 1974, yellow, blue in tampo, Model No. 8258
EX $175 **NM** $450 **MIP** $1200

Baja Bruiser, 1976, light green, Model No. 8258
EX $100 **NM** $400 **MIP** $1300

Baja Bruiser, 1977, blue, redline or blackwall, Model No. 8258
EX $35 **NM** $60 **MIP** $85

Beatnik Bandit, 1968, met. blue, tan interior, clear bubble, exposed engine, Model No. 6217
EX $35 **NM** $60 **MIP** $150

Boss Hoss, 1970, chrome, black stripes on top, Club Kit, black number "9" in white circle on side, Model No. 6499
EX $80 **NM** $150 **MIP** $250

Boss Hoss, 1971, met. green, black "8" in white circle on side, exposed engine, Model No. 6406
EX $65 **NM** $125 **MIP** $300

Brabham-Repco F1, 1969, met. green, long tailpipes on silver engine, black "1" in white circle on side, blue-tinted windows, Model No. 6264
EX $20 **NM** $50 **MIP** $100

Breakaway Bucket, 1974, dark blue, orange tampo w/ yellow designs, Model No. 8262
EX $35 **NM** $85 **MIP** $145

Bugeye, 1971, red, black interior, hood lifts to expose engine, Model No. 6178
EX $25 **NM** $60 **MIP** $140

Bugeye, 1971, magenta, white interior, Model No. 6178
EX $25 **NM** $55 **MIP** $120

Buzz Off, 1973, assorted, Model No. 6976
EX $115 **NM** $250 **MIP** $500

Buzz Off, 1974, blue, Model No. 6976
EX $30 **NM** $75 **MIP** $115

Buzz Off, 1977, gold plated, redline or blackwall, Model No. 6976
EX $10 **NM** $20 **MIP** $30

Bye-Focal, 1971, met. green, opening hood, bifocals & "Bye Focal" on side, Model No. 6187
EX $50 **NM** $200 **MIP** $550

Carabo, 1970, assorted metallic colors, opening doors, black painted chassis,, Model No. 6420
EX $25 **NM** $60 **MIP** $150

Carabo, 1974, yellow, Model No. 7617
EX $275 **NM** $600 **MIP** $1400

Carabo, 1974, light green with blue and red stripes, opening gull-wing style doors, Model No. 7617
EX $30 **NM** $60 **MIP** $100

Cement Mixer, 1970, "Heavyweights" series, met. green, orange plastic cement mixer, Hot Wheels logo, Model No. 6452
EX $20 **NM** $65 **MIP** $125

Chaparral 2G, 1969, white, back opens to expose metal engine, Model No. 6256
EX $40 **NM** $80 **MIP** $160

Chevy Monza, 1977, chrome, yellow & black tampo, Model No. 9202
EX $15 **NM** $30 **MIP** $40

Chevy Monza 2+2, 1975, light green enamel with "Monza" rally stripes on hood and roof, black plastic interior, Model No. 7671
EX $125 **NM** $300 **MIP** $800

Chevy Monza 2+2, 1975, orange enamel finish, "Monza" rally stripes on hood and roof, Model No. 7671
EX $25 **NM** $50 **MIP** $110

Chief's Special Cruiser, 1975, red, redline, Model No. 7665
EX $15 **NM** $35 **MIP** $65

Classic '31 Ford Woody, 1969, met. red, metal engine, Model No. 6251
EX $25 **NM** $65 **MIP** $125

Classic '32 Ford Vicky, 1969, met. gold, metal engine, black roof, Model No. 6250
EX $25 **NM** $55 **MIP** $115

Classic '36 Ford Coupe, 1969, blue, Model No. 6253
EX $35 **NM** $70 **MIP** $125

Classic '36 Ford Coupe, 1969, red, opening back reveals rumble seat, black roof, Model No. 6253
EX $35 **NM** $70 **MIP** $125

Classic '57 T-Bird, 1969, met. orange, hood opens to reveal engine, Model No. 6252
EX $25 **NM** $55 **MIP** $140

Classic Cord, 1971, met. green, opening hood, detachable plastic soft-top roof (often missing), Model No. 6472
EX $65 **NM** $175 **MIP** $350

(KP Photo)

Classic Nomad, 1970, met. aqua, opening hood, metal engine, Model No. 6404
EX $30 **NM** $75 **MIP** $150

(KP Photo)

Cockney Cab, 1971, blue, British flag tampo on rear, "Cockney Cab", Model No. 6466
EX $50 **NM** $110 **MIP** $210

(KP Photo)

Cool One, 1976, Magenta body, "Cool One" letting on front, lightning tampo on body. Available as blackwalls variation, Model No. 9120
EX $20   **NM** $40   **MIP** $60

Corvette Stingray, 1976, red body, red, white, yellow & blue tampo, Model No. 9241
EX $15   **NM** $35   **MIP** $50

(KP Photo)

Custom AMX, 1969, met. green, hood lifts to expose engine, Model No. 6267
EX $45   **NM** $100   **MIP** $225

(KP Photo)

Custom Barracuda, 1968, met. green, hood opens to reveal metal engine, Model No. 6211
EX $40   **NM** $150   **MIP** $400

Custom Camaro, 1968, white enamel--an almost mythical car, and apparently none "in-pack", Model No. 6208
EX $500   **NM** $750   **MIP** $1000

(KP Photo)

Custom Camaro, 1968, met. orange, black roof, opening hood, Model No. 6208
EX $50   **NM** $125   **MIP** $750

(KP Photo)

Custom Charger, 1969, Assorted body colors, white plastic interior, opening hood, Model No. 6268
EX $50   **NM** $130   **MIP** $300

(KP Photo)

Custom Continental Mark III, 1969, met. pink, opening hood, metal engine, Model No. 6266
EX $35   **NM** $85   **MIP** $375

(KP Photo)

Custom Corvette, 1968, met. orange, opening hood, assorted interior color, Model No. 6215
EX $35   **NM** $125   **MIP** $400

(KP Photo)

Custom Cougar, 1968, met. green, opening hood, black interior, Model No. 6205
EX $35   **NM** $125   **MIP** $400

(KP Photo)

Custom El Dorado, 1968, met. green, black interior, black top, opening hood, Model No. 6218
EX $25   **NM** $65   **MIP** $180

(KP Photo)

Custom Firebird, 1968, met. orange, metal engine, opening hood, Model No. 6212
EX $30   **NM** $80   **MIP** $280

(KP Photo)

Custom Fleetside, 1968, met. purple, black roof, opening bed cover, Model No. 6213
EX $25   **NM** $75   **MIP** $250

(KP Photo)

Custom Mustang, 1968, assorted, Model No. 6206
EX $35   **NM** $150   **MIP** $450

(KP Photo)

Custom Mustang, 1968, assorted w/open hood scoops or louvered windows, Model No. 6206
EX $200   **NM** $450   **MIP** $1400

(KP Photo)

Custom Police Cruiser, 1969, Black and white paint scheme on a Plymouth with "Police" and star tampos, red dome light. A nice companion car to the the 6469 Fire Chief Cruiser, Model No. 6269
EX $30　　**NM** $90　　**MIP** $200

(KP Photo)

Custom T-Bird, 1968, met. brown, opening hood, metal engine, Model No. 6207
EX $30　　**NM** $115　　**MIP** $250

(KP Photo)

Custom VW Bug, 1968, met. aqua, oversized engine, sunroof, Model No. 6220
EX $20　　**NM** $55　　**MIP** $125

(KP Photo)

Demon, 1970, blue, exposed engine, called "Prowler" in 1973, Model No. 6401
EX $25　　**NM** $55　　**MIP** $110

(KP Photo)

Deora, 1968, assorted, Model No. 6210
EX $25　　**NM** $80　　**MIP** $375

(KP Photo)

Double Header, 1973, green, blue-tinted windshield, Model No. 5880
EX $120　　**NM** $250　　**MIP** $500

Double Vision, 1973, orange, white interior, blue-tinted windows, Model No. 6975
EX $70　　**NM** $175　　**MIP** $400

(KP Photo)

Double Vision, 1973, met. green, flip-up plastic canopy over the seats, rear engine, Model No. 6975
EX $70　　**NM** $175　　**MIP** $400

(KP Photo)

Dump Truck, 1970, metal cab & chassis, unpainted base, plastic dump truck bed, "Heavyweights" series, 1970-72, Model No. 6453
EX $30　　**NM** $65　　**MIP** $110

(KP Photo)

Dune Daddy, 1973, green, blue-tinted windshield, white interior, Model No. 6967
EX $50　　**NM** $110　　**MIP** $400

Dune Daddy, 1975, orange body with sixties-style flowers on hood, Model No. 6967
EX $85　　**NM** $200　　**MIP** $475

Dune Daddy, 1975, light green with sixties-style daisy tampos on hood, Model No. 6967
EX $25　　**NM** $50　　**MIP** $75

El Rey Special, 1974, light green, Model No. 8273
EX $30　　**NM** $75　　**MIP** $175

(KP Photo)

El Rey Special, 1974, green, yellow & red "Dunlop," number "1" tampos, silver metal base, Model No. 8273
EX $25　　**NM** $60　　**MIP** $120

El Rey Special, 1974, light blue with orange tampos, unpainted metal base, Model No. 8273
EX $175　　**NM** $400　　**MIP** $1100

El Rey Special, 1974, dark blue, Model No. 8273
EX $100　　**NM** $225　　**MIP** $700

Emergency Squad, 1975, red body, yellow & white side tampos, silver plastic base, very much in the mold of the paramedic vehicle used on the TV show, "Emergency!", Model No. 7650
EX $20　　**NM** $50　　**MIP** $75

(KP Photo)

Evil Weevil, 1971, met. blue, black "8" inside white circle, sunroof, blue-tinted windows, Model No. 6471
EX $60　　**NM** $100　　**MIP** $200

(KP Photo)

Ferrari 312P, 1970, gold chrome, back opens to expose metal engine, black "60" in white circles, Model No. 6417
EX $30　　**NM** $75　　**MIP** $140

Ferrari 312P, 1973, red, back opens to expose metal engine, black "60" in white circles, Model No. 6973
EX $140   **NM** $300   **MIP** $600

(KP Photo)

Ferrari 512S, 1972, met. magenta, opening rear hood & cockpit, Model No. 6021
EX $40   **NM** $95   **MIP** $250

Ferrari 512S, 1972, blue, opening rear hood & cockpit, Model No. 6022
EX $40   **NM** $95   **MIP** $250

(KP Photo)

Fire Chief Cruiser, 1970, red Plymouth Fury, matches Custom Police Cruiser, #6269, Model No. 6469
EX $20   **NM** $40   **MIP** $85

(KP Photo)

Fire Engine, 1970, met. red cab, black ladder, rear is red plastic, white hoses, "Heavyweights" series, Model No. 6454
EX $25   **NM** $75   **MIP** $165

Fire-Eater, 1977, blue-tinted window, blue plastic hoses, Model No. 9640
EX $20   **NM** $30   **MIP** $40

(KP Photo)

Ford J-Car, 1968, met. aqua, back opens to reveal metal engine, Model No. 6214
EX $20   **NM** $45   **MIP** $90

Ford MK IV, 1969, red, back opens to reveal metal engine, Model No. 6257
EX $25   **NM** $75   **MIP** $150

Formula 5000, 1976, white race car, metal chassis, Model No. 9119
EX $20   **NM** $35   **MIP** $50

Formula P.A.C.K., 1976, black race car, Model No. 9037
EX $15   **NM** $30   **MIP** $50

(KP Photo)

Fuel Tanker, 1971, white cab & chassis, plastic fuel tanker section, removable fuel hoses, "Heavyweights" series, Model No. 6018
EX $30   **NM** $75   **MIP** $200

(KP Photo)

Funny Money, 1972, gray armored car body on funny car chassis, orange plastic bumper (usually missing), "Funny Money" labels, Model No. 6005
EX $80   **NM** $165   **MIP** $335

Funny Money, 1974, plum w/floral tampo, Model No. 7621
EX $25   **NM** $50   **MIP** $85

Funny Money, 1977, gray body, white "Brink's" on sides, body lifts open, Model No. 7621
EX $25   **NM** $40   **MIP** $60

GMC Motor Home, 1977, orange, blue-tinted windows, Model No. 9645
EX $100   **NM** $250   **MIP** n/a

(KP Photo)

Grass Hopper, 1971, met. red, shown without white plastic canopy, Model No. 6461
EX $20   **NM** $60   **MIP** $125

(KP Photo)

Grass Hopper, 1974, light green, engine, orange & blue side tampo, blue-tinted windshield, Model No. 7622
EX $25   **NM** $50   **MIP** $100

Grass Hopper, 1975, light green, no engine, Model No. 7622
EX $45   **NM** $100   **MIP** $200

Gremlin Grinder, 1975, green, blue-tinted windows, yellow, orange & black tampo, exposed engine, Model No. 7652
EX $20   **NM** $45   **MIP** $85

(KP Photo)

Gremlin Grinder, 1976, chrome, orange, black & green tampo, exposed engine, Model No. 9201
EX $20   **NM** $40   **MIP** $60

(KP Photo)

Gun Bucket, 1976, olive-green body, white "Army" star & number tampos on hood,

black plastic anti-aircraft gun & treads, Model No. 9090
EX $20   **NM** $40   **MIP** $60

Gun Slinger, 1975, olive, Model No. 7664
EX $15   **NM** $30   **MIP** $50

(KP Photo)

Hairy Hauler, 1971, assorted, with lifting front canopy, exposed engine, Model No. 6458
EX $25   **NM** $65   **MIP** $110

(KP Photo)

Heavy Chevy, 1970, chrome, Club Kit, black stripes, Model No. 6189
EX $70   **NM** $135   **MIP** $210

Heavy Chevy, 1970, assorted, exposed engine, Model No. 6408
EX $55   **NM** $120   **MIP** $200

Heavy Chevy, 1974, light green, Model No. 7619
EX $95   **NM** $200   **MIP** $750

Heavy Chevy, 1974, yellow, exposed engine, orange & red side tampo, "7", Model No. 7619
EX $45   **NM** $90   **MIP** $200

Heavy Chevy, 1977, chrome, redline or blackwall, Model No. 9212
EX $35   **NM** $75   **MIP** $115

(KP Photo)

Hiway Robber, 1973, red, black interior, exposed engine, Model No. 6979
EX $75   **NM** $150   **MIP** $400

(KP Photo)

Hood, The, 1971, met. light green, exposed engine, black interior, Model No. 6175
EX $40   **NM** $85   **MIP** $150

(KP Photo)

Hot Heap, 1968, met. yellow, white interior, exposed engine, Model No. 6219
EX $20   **NM** $55   **MIP** $110

(KP Photo)

Ice T, 1971, yellow, with "Ice T" on plastic roof, Model No. 6184
EX $30   **NM** $75   **MIP** $200

(KP Photo)

Ice T, 1973, Body in assorted colors, black plastic interior, plastic roof (mostly in white), silver base. Blackwall wheels variations also produced at the same time, Model No. 6980
EX $95   **NM** $200   **MIP** $650

Ice T, 1974, yellow with hood tampo, Model No. 6980
EX $85   **NM** $200   **MIP** $500

Ice T, 1974, light green, Model No. 6980
EX $25   **NM** $50   **MIP** $75

Indy Eagle, 1969, gold, Model No. 6263
EX $75   **NM** $150   **MIP** $250

(KP Photo)

Indy Eagle, 1969, assorted colors with tinted plastic windshield and silver rear engine and tailpipes, Model No. 6263
EX $30   **NM** $75   **MIP** $125

Inferno, 1976, yellow drag racer, exposed engine, Model No. 9186
EX $30   **NM** $55   **MIP** $80

(KP Photo)

Jack Rabbit Special, 1970, white, blue stripe, clear windshield, Model No. 6421
EX $20   **NM** $60   **MIP** $90

Jack-in-the-Box Promotion, 1970, white, Jack Rabbit w/decals, Model No. 6421
EX $150   **NM** $300   **MIP** n/a

(KP Photo)

Jet Threat, 1971, met. yellow, blue-tinted windshield, Model No. 6179
EX $40   **NM** $95   **MIP** $225

Jet Threat, 1973, light blue, blue-tinted windshield
EX $30   **NM** $85   **MIP** $160

Jet Threat II, 1976, plum w/yellow flames, blue-tinted windshield, exposed engine, Model No. 8235
EX $20   **NM** $35   **MIP** $55

Khaki Kooler, 1976, khaki body, "Military Police", black interior, smoke-colored windshield, Model No. 9183
EX $15   **NM** $30   **MIP** $45

King Kuda, 1970, chrome, Club Kit, exposed engine, Model No. 6411
EX $70   **NM** $150   **MIP** $300

(KP Photo)

King 'Kuda, 1970, met. green, exposed
engine, blue-tinted windshield, Model
No. 6411
EX $45   **NM** $100   **MIP** $200

(KP Photo)

Large Charge, 1975, green, red & yellow
tampos, blue-tinted windows, Model
No. 8272
EX $20   **NM** $40   **MIP** $80

Letter Getter, 1977, U.S. Mail truck, white,
Model No. 9643
EX $125   **NM** $250   **MIP** n/a

(KP Photo)

Light My Firebird, 1970, Convertible in
assorted finishes, decal number on
doors, exposed silver engine in front,
brown plastic interior, Model No. 6412
EX $20   **NM** $55   **MIP** $110

(KP Photo)

Lola GT 70, 1969, dark green, opening
rear, clear windows, Model No. 6254
EX $30   **NM** $75   **MIP** $125

(KP Photo)

Lotus Turbine, 1969, met. brown, blue-
tinted windshield, Model No. 6262
EX $20   **NM** $45   **MIP** $90

Lowdown, 1976, light blue, "Flyin' Low",
Model No. 9185
EX $30   **NM** $50   **MIP** $75

Mantis, 1970, assorted, exposed engines,
Model No. 6423
EX $25   **NM** $65   **MIP** $100

Maserati Mistral, 1969, assorted, Model
No. 6277
EX $50   **NM** $100   **MIP** $200

(KP Photo)

Maxi Taxi, 1976, Oldsmobile 442 body,
yellow w/checkboard & "Maxi Taxi" tampo,
black plastic interior, Model No. 9184
EX $30   **NM** $45   **MIP** $60

(KP Photo)

McClaren M6A, 1969, orange, blue-tinted
windshield, Model No. 6255
EX $20   **NM** $45   **MIP** $90

(KP Photo)

Mercedes 280SL, 1969, red, opening
hood, metal engine, blue-tinted
windows, Model No. 6275
EX $25   **NM** $60   **MIP** $110

Mercedes 280SL, 1973, assorted, Model
No. 6962
EX $90   **NM** $200   **MIP** $450

Mercedes C-111, 1972, assorted, Model
No. 6169
EX $60   **NM** $145   **MIP** $280

Mercedes C-111, 1973, assorted, Model
No. 6978
EX $175   **NM** $400   **MIP** $900

(KP Photo)

Mercedes C-111, 1974, red, with stars and
stripes tampo, Model No. 6978
EX $20   **NM** $45   **MIP** $90

Mercedes-Benz 280SL, 1969, met. blue,
blue-tinted windows, opening hood,
metal engine, Model No. 6275
EX $30   **NM** $65   **MIP** $110

(KW6414)

Mighty Maverick, 1970, assorted, opening
hood, black plastic spoiler, Model
No. 6414
EX $40   **NM** $85   **MIP** $175

Mighty Maverick, 1975, blue, orange,
yellow & white tampo, blue-tinted
windows, Model No. 7653
EX $25   **NM** $60   **MIP** $100

(KP Photo)

Mighty Maverick, 1976, chrome, yellow &
blue tampo, blue-tinted windows, "Super
Chromes" series, Model No. 9209
EX $20   **NM** $35   **MIP** $50

(KP Photo)

Mod-Quad, 1970, met. red, black interior, four metal engines, top opens, Model No. 6456
EX $35 **NM** $80 **MIP** $170

Mongoose, 1973, blue w/red stickers, Model No. 6970
EX $275 **NM** $600 **MIP** $1400

(KP Photo)

Mongoose Funny Car, 1970, red, opening body, white, blue & yellow tampo, Model No. 6410
EX $65 **NM** $125 **MIP** $210

(KP Photo)

Mongoose II, 1971, met. blue, opening body, Model No. 5954
EX $55 **NM** $125 **MIP** $350

Mongoose Rail Dragster, 1971, blue, two pack, w/Snake Rail, Model No. 5952
EX $75 **NM** $165 **MIP** $1250

Monte Carlo Stocker, 1975, yellow, blue-tinted windows, black interior, Model No. 7660
EX $30 **NM** $65 **MIP** $110

(KP Photo)

Motocross I, 1975, red plastic seat and tank, unpainted gray die-cast body, Model No. 7668
EX $45 **NM** $100 **MIP** $200

(KP Photo)

Moving Van, 1970, met. blue, white trailer, "Heavyweights" series, Model No. 6455
EX $40 **NM** $90 **MIP** $150

Mustang Stocker, 1975, yellow w/red in tampo, Model No. 9203
EX $90 **NM** $175 **MIP** $650

Mustang Stocker, 1975, yellow with magenta and orange tampo with "Ford" and "450 HP", Model No. 7664
EX $50 **NM** $125 **MIP** $200

Mustang Stocker, 1975, white, Model No. 7664
EX $175 **NM** $400 **MIP** $1000

Mustang Stocker, 1976, chrome, Model No. 9203
EX $45 **NM** $65 **MIP** $90

Mustang Stocker, 1977, chrome, redline or blackwall, Model No. 9203
EX $25 **NM** $55 **MIP** $80

(KP Photo)

Mutt Mobile, 1971, met. red, dogs in back, Model No. 6185
EX $60 **NM** $125 **MIP** $300

Neet Streeter, 1976, blue, red & white roof stripes, Model No. 9244
EX $25 **NM** $45 **MIP** $75

(KP Photo)

Nitty Gritty Kitty, 1970, gold chrome, metal engine, blue-tinted windows, Model No. 6405
EX $50 **NM** $100 **MIP** $200

(KP Photo)

Noodle Head, 1971, assorted, opening headlight cover, Model No. 6000
EX $50 **NM** $100 **MIP** $200

Odd Job, 1973, red, white topper, exposed engine, Model No. 6981
EX $95 **NM** $200 **MIP** $600

(KP Photo)

Odd Rod, 1977, yellow plastic bucket around seats, clear plastic hood with flame graphics, Model No. 9642
EX $25 **NM** $55 **MIP** $80

Odd Rod, 1977, plum, blackwall or redline, Model No. 9642
EX $95 **NM** $200 **MIP** $400

Olds 442, 1971, assorted, Model No. 6467
EX $125 **NM** $400 **MIP** $800

(KP Photo)

Open Fire, 1972, met. red, modified AMC Gremilin, oversized engine & six wheels, Model No. 5881
EX $80 **NM** $185 **MIP** $450

(KP Photo)

Paddy Wagon, 1970, blue, with plastic covering over bed, Model No. 6402
EX $35 **NM** $80 **MIP** $125

Paddy Wagon, 1973, blue, Model No. 6966
EX $30 **NM** $65 **MIP** $120

(KP Photo)

Paramedic, 1975, white with yellow and red stripes and "Paramedic" lettering, Model No. 7661

EX $20 **NM** $40 **MIP** $75

(KP Photo)

Peepin' Bomb, 1970, met. yellow, clear windshield, exposed engine, Model No. 6419

EX $30 **NM** $70 **MIP** $110

Peepin' Bomb, 1973, red, exposed engine, blue-tinted windshield

EX $45 **NM** $90 **MIP** $150

(KP Photo)

Pit Crew Car, 1971, white, opening trunk w/tool box, Model No. 6183

EX $70 **NM** $150 **MIP** $350

(KP Photo)

Poison Pinto, 1976, light green body, skull & crossbones, "Poison Pinto" tampo, late-era redlines, Model No. 9240

EX $25 **NM** $50 **MIP** $75

Police Cruiser, 1973, white Olds 442, "Police" labels on doors, opening hood & red dome light on roof, Model No. 6963

EX $35 **NM** $80 **MIP** $150

Police Cruiser, 1974, white, "State Police, Law Enforcement" decal on doors, Model No. 6963

EX $25 **NM** $60 **MIP** $125

Police Cruiser, 1977, white Olds 442 with black doors, yellow police tampos on doors, non-opening hood, blue light, Model No. 6963

EX $15 **NM** $30 **MIP** $50

(KP Photo)

Porsche 911, 1975, yellow, with blue and red stripes on hood and roof, Model No. 7648

EX $40 **NM** $95 **MIP** $150

Porsche 911, 1976, chrome, red & green tampo, black interior, Model No. 9206

EX $20 **NM** $40 **MIP** $60

Porsche 917, 1970, silver, clear windshield, opening back, Model No. 6416

EX $40 **NM** $80 **MIP** $140

Porsche 917, 1973, red, opening back, blue-tinted windshield, Model No. 6972

EX $100 **NM** $250 **MIP** $600

Porsche 917, 1974, red, Model No. 6972

EX $85 **NM** $175 **MIP** $500

Porsche 917, 1974, orange, Model No. 6972

EX $20 **NM** $40 **MIP** $75

(KP Photo)

Power Pad, 1970, met. red, clear windshield, black interior, exposed engine, shown w/o camper, Model No. 6459

EX $30 **NM** $75 **MIP** $125

Prowler, 1973, assorted, Model No. 6965

EX $185 **NM** $400 **MIP** $1000

Prowler, 1974, orange with demon flame tampo on roof (which makes sense, considering this car was known as "The Demon" in its previous incarnation in 1970. Unpainted metal base, Model No. 6965

EX $15 **NM** $35 **MIP** $75

Prowler, 1974, light green, Model No. 6965

EX $175 **NM** $400 **MIP** $800

Prowler, 1976, chrome, yellow & red flames, devil tampo, exposed engine, Model No. 9207

EX $40 **NM** $65 **MIP** $85

(KP Photo)

Python, 1968, met. red, black top, exposed engine, Model No. 6216

EX $20 **NM** $45 **MIP** $80

(KP Photo)

Racer Rig, 1971, red/white, "Heavyweights" series, Model No. 6194

EX $70 **NM** $150 **MIP** $375

Ramblin' Wrecker, 1975, white, "Larry's 24 Hour Towing", blue lift, Model No. 7659

EX $25 **NM** $55 **MIP** $80

(KP Photo)

Ranger Rig, 1975, medium green w/yellow lettering & design, Model No. 7666

EX $20 **NM** $45 **MIP** $75

Rash 1, 1974, green, blue-tinted windshield, yellow & white tampo, exposed engine, Model No. 7616

EX $30 **NM** $65 **MIP** $140

Rash I, 1974, blue, Model No. 7616

EX $125 **NM** $300 **MIP** $800

Rear Engine Mongoose, 1972, red, Model No. 5699

EX $90 **NM** $200 **MIP** $600

(KP Photo)

Rear Engine Snake, 1972, yellow, blue w/red stars tampo, Model No. 5856
EX $90   **NM** $200   **MIP** $600

(KP Photo)

Red Baron, 1970, red, cross on helmet, Model No. 6400
EX $20   **NM** $45   **MIP** $80

(KP Photo)

Red Baron, 1973, red, note no Iron Cross on the helmet, Model No. 6964
EX $30   **NM** $80   **MIP** $150

Road King Truck, 1974, yellow cab and trailer with metal chassis, tilting dumper section, availabe in set only, Model No. 7615
EX $600   **NM** $1200   **MIP** n/a

Rock Buster, 1976, chrome dune buggy with black plastic rollcage and interior, racing graphics on hood and sides, Model No. 9507
EX $25   **NM** $40   **MIP** $55

Rock Buster, 1976, yellow, Model No. 9088
EX $20   **NM** $30   **MIP** $40

(KP Photo)

Rocket-Bye-Baby, 1971, met. yellow, metal rocket on top, Model No. 6186
EX $60   **NM** $120   **MIP** $280

Rodger Dodger, 1974, blue, Model No. 8259
EX $85   **NM** $200   **MIP** $550

(KP Photo)

Rodger Dodger, 1974, magenta Dodge Charger, flame tampos on hood & roof, exposed silver engine, red plastic exhaust pipes, Model No. 8259
EX $30   **NM** $60   **MIP** $125

Rodger Dodger, 1977, gold plated, blackwall or redline, Model No. 8259
EX $20   **NM** $45   **MIP** $80

(KP Photo)

Rolls-Royce Silver Shadow, 1969, silver, opening hood shows detailed engine, Model No. 6276
EX $25   **NM** $60   **MIP** $145

(KP Photo)

Sand Crab, 1970, red, black interior, clear windshield, Model No. 6403
EX $20   **NM** $50   **MIP** $90

Sand Drifter, 1975, green, Model No. 7651
EX $75   **NM** $150   **MIP** $425

(KP Photo)

Sand Drifter, 1975, yellow, flame tampo on hood, black plastic interior & covering over bed, Model No. 7651
EX $25   **NM** $45   **MIP** $85

(KP Photo)

Sand Witch, 1973, green, blue-tinted windshield, opening rear hood, Model No. 6974
EX $75   **NM** $175   **MIP** $450

(KP Photo)

S'Cool Bus, 1971, yellow, lift-up funny car body, silver chassis, "Heavyweights" series, Model No. 6468
EX $145   **NM** $250   **MIP** $750

(KP Photo)

Scooper, 1971, met. green, yellow scoop & rear, Model No. 6193
EX $50   **NM** $100   **MIP** $220

(KP Photo)

Seasider, 1970, met. light green, exposed engine, plastic boat, Model No. 6413
EX $60   **NM** $110   **MIP** $200

VEHICLES — HOT WHEELS REDLINES

(KP Photo)

Second Wind, 1977, white w/yellow & red striping, number "5" on hood, Model No. 9644
EX $30   **NM** $60   **MIP** $90

(KP Photo)

Shelby Turbine, 1969, met. Purple, Model No. 6265
EX $25   **NM** $60   **MIP** $110

(KP Photo)

Short Order, 1971, blue, extending plastic tailgate, exposed engine, Model No. 6176
EX $35   **NM** $75   **MIP** $230

(KP Photo)

Show Hoss II, 1977, yellow funny car Mustang II body lifts up over silver base, black plastic rollcage, redline or blackwalls versions available, Model No. 9646
EX $125   **NM** $300   **MIP** $600

Show-Off, 1973, orange, exposed engine, blue-tinted windows, Model No. 6982
EX $75   **NM** $175   **MIP** $450

Side Kick, 1972, met. green, exposed engine, Model No. 6022
EX $75   **NM** $145   **MIP** $300

(KP Photo)

Silhouette, 1968, Body in assorted colors, plastic dome canopy over seats, exposed front engine, Model No. 6209
EX $25   **NM** $50   **MIP** $100

(KP Photo)

Sir Sidney Roadster, 1974, Orange body with brown plastic roof and exposed silver engine. Red flame tampos, silver metal base, Model No. 8261
EX $180   **NM** $300   **MIP** $575

Sir Sidney Roadster, 1974, yellow, red flames, exposed engine, brown top, Model No. 8261
EX $25   **NM** $50   **MIP** $90

Sir Sidney Roadster, 1974, light green, Model No. 8261
EX $200   **NM** $325   **MIP** $625

(KP Photo)

Six Shooter, 1971, met. blue, exposed engines, blue-tinted windshield, six wheels, Model No. 6003
EX $35   **NM** $85   **MIP** $225

(KP Photo)

Sky Show Fleetside (Aero Launcher), 1970, met. blue, orange plastic ramp, Model No. 6436
EX $200   **NM** $400   **MIP** $850

Snake, 1973, white/yellow, Model No. 6969
EX $300   **NM** $700   **MIP** $1500

(KP Photo)

Snake Funny Car, 1970, yellow, body opens, metal engine, Model No. 6409
EX $35   **NM** $90   **MIP** $300

Snake II, 1971, white, Model No. 5953
EX $60   **NM** $100   **MIP** $275

(KP Photo)

Snake Rail Dragster, 1971, white, exposed engine, part of a two-pack with blue Mongoose Rail, Model No. 5951
EX $75   **NM** $150   **MIP** $1250

(KP Photo)

Snorkel, 1971, assorted, Model No. 6020
EX $30   **NM** $90   **MIP** $200

(KP Photo)

Special Delivery, 1971, blue, exposed engines, U.S. Mail tampo, Model No. 6006
EX $50   **NM** $100   **MIP** $250

(KP Photo)

Splittin' Image, 1969, met. orange, clear windows, exposed engine, Model No. 6261
EX $25   **NM** $65   **MIP** $115

(KP Photo)

Spoiler Sport, 1977, light green van, tropical island scene on side panels, Model No. 9641
EX $25   **NM** $45   **MIP** $70

Staff Car, 1976, Olsd 442 casting in olive drab, "Staff Car U.S. Army" on doors, Model No. 9521
EX $200   **NM** $400   **MIP** $600

(KP Photo)

Steam Roller, 1974, white body, stars & stripes tampo, three stars reversed out of red stripe on hood; the more common model, Model No. 8260
EX $25   **NM** $50   **MIP** $70

Steam Roller, 1974, white body with red white and blue graphics, seven stars on front, Model No. 8260
EX $70   **NM** $160   **MIP** $350

Street Rodder, 1976, black, flames, exposed engine, clear windshield, Model No. 9242
EX $40   **NM** $75   **MIP** $100

Street Snorter, 1973, assorted, Model No. 6971
EX $90   **NM** $180   **MIP** $500

Street Snorter, 1973, light green, blue-tinted windows, Model No. 6971
EX $95   **NM** $200   **MIP** $500

(KP Photo)

Strip Teaser, 1971, blue, opeing back, exposed engine, Model No. 6188
EX $45   **NM** $105   **MIP** $275

Strip Teaser, 1973, blue, exposed engine, driver area opens to reveal black interior
EX $25   **NM** $75   **MIP** $140

Sugar Caddy, 1971, assorted, exposed engine, Model No. 6418
EX $30   **NM** $75   **MIP** $150

(KP Photo)

Super Van, 1975, blue body, yellow flames, Model No. 7649
EX $100   **NM** $300   **MIP** $600

Super Van, 1975, black body, chrome plastic base, red & yellow flames, Model No. 7649
EX $30   **NM** $60   **MIP** $90

Superfine Turbine, 1973, red, exposed engine, black interior, Model No. 6004
EX $180   **NM** $425   **MIP** $850

Sweet 16, 1973, red, exposed engine, trunk opens to expose spare, Model No. 6007
EX $165   **NM** $275   **MIP** $650

(KP Photo)

Swingin' Wing, 1970, met. red, blue-tinted windows, Model No. 6422
EX $25   **NM** $60   **MIP** $125

(KP Photo)

T-4-2, 1971, met. yellow, black top, exposed metal engines, blue-tinted windows, Model No. 6177
EX $40   **NM** $80   **MIP** $175

(KP Photo)

Team Trailer, 1971, white/red, detailed plastic interior & opening door on trailer, "Heavyweights" series, Model No. 6019
EX $75   **NM** $150   **MIP** $275

(KP Photo)

TNT-Bird, 1970, met. green, white stripe, blue-tinted windshield, exposed engine, Model No. 6407
EX $35   **NM** $80   **MIP** $145

(KP Photo)

Top Eliminator, 1974, blue lift-up funny car body on silver chassis, green, light tan, and orange "Hot Wheels" tampo w/stripes on sides, Model No. 7630
EX $30   **NM** $80   **MIP** $145

(KP Photo)

Torero, 1969, gold chrome, opening hood, clear windows, white interior, Model No. 6260

EX $25   **NM** $55   **MIP** $125

(KP Photo)

Torino Stocker, 1975, red, blue-tinted windshield, black interior, Model No. 7647

EX $30   **NM** $65   **MIP** $110

(KP Photo)

Tough Customer, 1975, olive, with rotating turret and white numbering tampos, Model No. 7655

EX $15   **NM** $30   **MIP** $60

(KP Photo)

Tow Truck, 1970, assorted, "Heavyweights" series, Model No. 6450

EX $30   **NM** $70   **MIP** $120

Tri-Baby, 1970, blue, interesting engine casting under opening rear hood, Model No. 6424

EX $20   **NM** $55   **MIP** $85

T-Totaller, 1977, black, redlines, six-pack only, red body common $25, Model No. 9648

EX $200   **NM** $700   **MIP** n/a

Turbofire, 1969, met. yellow, opening rear, clear windshield, Model No. 6259

EX $20   **NM** $60   **MIP** $110

(KP Photo)

Twin Mill, 1969, met. aqua, clear windows, two exposed engines, Model No. 6258

EX $25   **NM** $65   **MIP** $150

Twin Mill, 1973, met. red, blue-tinted windshield, two exposed engines

EX $40   **NM** $90   **MIP** $165

Twin Mill II, 1976, orange, two engines, blue-tinted windows, blue, white & red tampo, Model No. 8240

EX $20   **NM** $30   **MIP** $45

Vega Bomb, 1975, green, Model No. 7658

EX $175   **NM** $400   **MIP** $950

Vega Bomb, 1975, orange, this model is right on the cusp of the Redlines era-- blackwall versions (like this one as #7654) were becoming a more common sight, Model No. 7658

EX $35   **NM** $65   **MIP** $120

(KP Photo)

Volkswagen, 1974, orange enamel, bug graphic on roof, Model No. 7620

EX $25   **NM** $75   **MIP** $125

Volkswagen, 1974, orange w/stripes on roof, Model No. 7620

EX $80   **NM** $175   **MIP** $500

(KP Photo)

Volkswagen Beach Bomb, 1969, surf boards on side raised panels, Model No. 6274

EX $85   **NM** $175   **MIP** $425

Volkswagen Beach Bomb, 1969, surf boards in rear window, Model No. 6274

EX n/a   **NM** $7000   **MIP** n/a

(KP Photo)

Warpath, 1975, white, stars & stripes tampo, opening plastic engine covers, Model No. 7654

EX $30   **NM** $75   **MIP** $115

(KP Photo)

Waste Wagon, 1971, met. yellow, orange receptacle, "Heavyweights" series, Model No. 6192

EX $65   **NM** $130   **MIP** $250

(KP Photo)

What-4, 1971, met. green, blue-tinted windshield, Model No. 6001

EX $70   **NM** $145   **MIP** $275

Whip Creamer, 1970, met. yellow, clear slide-back plastic canopy, Model No. 6457

EX $25   **NM** $65   **MIP** $120

Winnipeg, 1974, yellow body, orange spoiler, blue & orange tampo, Model No. 7618

EX $50   **NM** $100   **MIP** $210

Xploder, 1973, red, black interior, blue-tinted windows, Model No. 6977

EX $135   **NM** $225   **MIP** $500

Z Whiz, 1977, gray body, orange & yellow tampo, Model No. 9639

EX $30   **NM** $50   **MIP** $70

Z Whiz, 1977, white, redline, Model No. 9639

EX $200   **NM** $1500   **MIP** n/a

JAPANESE TIN CARS

(Ron Smith)

Agajanian Racer No.98, 1950s, friction, "Y" Co., 18" (J286)
EX $900   NM $1800   MIP $2800

(Ron Smith)

Aston-Martin DB5, 1960s, (James Bond), friction, Gilbert, 11-1/2" (J1)
EX $90   NM $175   MIP $400

(Ron Smith)

Aston-Martin DB6, 1960s, friction, Asahi Toy Co., 11" (J2)
EX $200   NM $400   MIP $600

(Ron Smith)

Atom Car, 1950s, Yonezawa, 17" (J284)
EX $400   NM $800   MIP $1600

BMW Coupe, 1960s, Yonezawa, 11" tan, battery-operated
EX $50   NM $105   MIP $150

(Ron Smith)

Buick, 1959, friction, T.N., 11" (J8)
EX $90   NM $150   MIP $350

(Ron Smith)

Buick Century, 1958, friction, Bandai, 8" (J7)
EX $80   NM $100   MIP $200

(Ron Smith)

Buick Century, 1958, friction, Yonezawa, 12" (J6)
EX $400   NM $800   MIP $1800

Buick Convertible, 1959, 11", orange/yellow, friction, dog and driver figures
EX $100   NM $275   MIP $350

Buick Fire Department Car, 1961, 16", red, friction, working wipers, revolving emergency light
EX $80   NM $150   MIP $265

(Ron Smith)

Buick Futuristic LeSabre, 1950s, friction, Yonezawa, 7-1/2" (J276)
EX $200   NM $400   MIP $750

Buick HT Convertible, 1959, Linemar, 9-1/2" red/white, friction
EX $50   NM $105   MIP $150

(Ron Smith)

Buick Roadmaster, 1955, friction, Yoshiya, 11" (J5)
EX $125   NM $250   MIP $500

Buick Special, 1955, 8-1/2", two-tone blue, battery-operated, working headlights
EX $55   NM $122   MIP $175

Buick Station Wagon, 1959, Yonezawa, 9", two-tone green, friction, HT or Conv.
EX $50   NM $105   MIP $150

(Ron Smith)

Buick Wildcat, 1963, friction, Ichiko, 15" (J13)
EX $300   NM $600   MIP $1200

(Ron Smith)

Cadillac, 1950, battery-op, Marusan, 11" (J18)
EX $400   NM $800   MIP $1800

(Ron Smith)

Cadillac, 1952, friction, Alps, 11-1/2" (J20)
EX $250   NM $400   MIP $800

Cadillac, 1954, battery-op, Joustra, 12" (J23)
EX $150   NM $300   MIP $550

Cadillac, 1960, 12", Maursan, black, Marusan, 12" (J27A), Model No. J27A
EX $250   NM $450   MIP $650

(Ron Smith)

Cadillac, 1967, friction, K.O., 10-1/2" (J34)
EX $65   NM $120   MIP $185

(Ron Smith)

Cadillac Convertible, 1960, friction, Bandai, 12" (J25)
EX $60   NM $110   MIP $220

(Ron Smith)

Cadillac Fleetwood, 1961, friction, SSS, 17-1/2" (J29)
EX $200   NM $400   MIP $750

Cadillac Four-Door Sedan, 1935, 8",
maroon, black, gold, friction
EX $30   **NM** $65   **MIP** $90

Cadillac Four-Door Sedan, 1951, Marusan, 12-1/2", gray, battery-operated,
remote control, working headlights
EX $480   **NM** $1120   **MIP** $1600

Cadillac Four-Door Sedan, 1951, Marusan, 12-1/2", gray, black, white, or red,
friction
EX $300   **NM** $700   **MIP** $1000

(Ron Smith)

Cadillac Four-Door Sedan & Convertible,
1960, Yonezawa, 18" black or maroon,
friction,
EX $300   **NM** $630   **MIP** $900

Cadillac Police Car, 1962, Ichiko, 6-1/2"
black/white, friction w/siren
EX $30   **NM** $65   **MIP** $90

(Ron Smith)

Champion No.15 Racer, 1950, friction,
German, 18" (J289)
EX $600   **NM** $900   **MIP** $1800

(Ron Smith)

Champion No.42 Racer, 1950, friction,
Gem France, 18" (J288)
EX $600   **NM** $900   **MIP** $1800

(Ron Smith)

Champion No.98 Racer, 1950s, friction,
"Y" Co., 18" (J287)
EX $600   **NM** $900   **MIP** $1850

(Ron Smith)

Chevrolet, 1954, friction, Marusan, 11" (J49)
EX $250   **NM** $500   **MIP** $1100

(Ron Smith)

Chevrolet, 1955, battery-op, Marusan,
10-3/4" (J50)
EX $300   **NM** $800   **MIP** $1500

(Ron Smith)

Chevrolet, 1960, friction, Marusan,
11-1/2" (J60)
EX $200   **NM** $400   **MIP** $800

(Ron Smith)

Chevrolet, 1962, friction, unknown manufacturer, 11" (J65)
EX $200   **NM** $300   **MIP** $600

Chevrolet Bel Air, 1954, Marusan and
Linemar, 11", gray/black, friction
EX $400   **NM** $600   **MIP** $1000

Chevrolet Bel Air, 1954, Marusan and Linemar, 11", rare orange/yellow, friction
EX $400   **NM** $600   **MIP** $1000

Chevrolet Bel Air, 1955, Asahi Toy, 7" light
green, friction
EX $50   **NM** $105   **MIP** $130

(Toy Shop File Photo)

Chevrolet Camaro, 1967, battery-op, T.N.,
14" (J46)
EX $125   **NM** $175   **MIP** $350

(Ron Smith)

Chevrolet Camaro Rusher, 1971, battery-
op, Taiyo, 9-1/2" (J48)
EX $10   **NM** $20   **MIP** $25

(Ron Smith)

Chevrolet Corvette, 1953, friction, Bandai,
7" (J37)
EX $125   **NM** $225   **MIP** $400

(Ron Smith)

Chevrolet Corvette, 1958, friction,
Yonezawa, 9-1/2" (J38)
EX $200   **NM** $300   **MIP** $500

(Ron Smith)

Chevrolet Corvette, 1964, battery-op,
Ichida, 12" (J41)
EX $150   **NM** $225   **MIP** $400

(Ron Smith)

Chevrolet Corvette, 1968, battery-op,
Taiyo, 9-1/2" (J42)
EX $20   **NM** $40   **MIP** $60

Chevrolet Corvette Coupe, 1963, 12",
metallic red or white, battery-operated,
working headlights
EX $180   **NM** $420   **MIP** $600

Chevrolet hardtop, 1959, 10", ASC, red
w/white top; 1960s, Model No. J59A
EX $90   **NM** $150   **MIP** $300

Chevrolet Highway Patrol Car, 1959, ASC, 10", black/white, friction
EX $55   **NM** $125   **MIP** $175

Chevrolet HT, 1959, 7", green, friction
EX $30   **NM** $70   **MIP** $100

(Ron Smith)

Chevrolet Impala, 1963, friction, T.N., 18" (J66)
EX $200   **NM** $300   **MIP** $500

(Ron Smith)

Chevrolet Impala Convertible, 1961, friction, Bandai, 11" (J63)
EX $100   **NM** $150   **MIP** $300

Chevrolet Impala HT, 1960, Alps, 9", red/white, friction
EX $105   **NM** $200   **MIP** $300

(Ron Smith)

Chevrolet Impala Sedan, 1961, friction, Bandai, 11" (J62)
EX $100   **NM** $150   **MIP** $300

(Ron Smith)

Chevrolet Secret Agent, 1962, battery-op, unknown manufacturer, 14" (J64)
EX $50   **NM** $75   **MIP** $150

(Ron Smith)

Chevrolet Sedan/Convertible/Wagon, 1959, friction, SY, 11-1/2" (J59)
EX $200   **NM** $400   **MIP** $800

(Toy Shop File Photo)

Chevrolet Station Wagon/Sedan/Convertible, 1958, friction, Bandai, 8" (J57)
EX $50   **NM** $65   **MIP** $125

(Ron Smith)

Chrysler Imperial Convertible or Sedan, 1959, friction, Bandai, 8" (J74)
EX $50   **NM** $100   **MIP** $150

(Ron Smith)

Chrysler, 1955, friction, Yonezawa, 8" (J71)
EX $100   **NM** $200   **MIP** $300

(Ron Smith)

Chrysler, 1958, battery-op, unknown manufacturer, 13" (J73)
EX $300   **NM** $400   **MIP** $800

(Ron Smith)

Chrysler Imperial, 1962, 16", friction, black, red (white: add 20% to value)
EX $600   **NM** $1200   **MIP** $2200

(Toy Shop File Photo)

Chrysler New Yorker, 1957, friction, Alps, 14" (J72)
EX $600   **NM** $1200   **MIP** $1800

Chrysler New Yorker, 1957, 6-1/2", red/black, friction
EX $25   **NM** $60   **MIP** $85

Chrysler Orion Convertible, 1953, 6-1/2", blue/green, friction
EX $25   **NM** $60   **MIP** $85

(Toy Shop File Photo)

Citroen 2 CV, 1960, friction, Daiya, 8" (J269A)
EX $100   **NM** $150   **MIP** $225

(Toy Shop File Photo)

Citroen DS 19 Sedan/Wagon/Convertible, 1960, friction, Bandai, 12" (J68)
EX $200   **NM** $400   **MIP** $600

Cunningham Roadster, 1950s, 7-1/2", light blue, friction
EX $40   **NM** $90   **MIP** $125

DeSoto, 1950s, 6", green, friction
EX $20   **NM** $45   **MIP** $65

DeSoto, 1950s, Asahi Toy, 8", green, friction
EX $40   **NM** $90   **MIP** $125

Dodge Charger Sonic Car, 1966, 16", red, battery-operated
EX $145   **NM** $250   **MIP** $350

Dodge Four-Door HT, 1958, 8-1/2", orange/white, friction
EX $55   **NM** $125   **MIP** $175

(Ron Smith)

Dodge Pickup, 1959, friction, unknown manufacturer, 18-1/2" (J84)
EX $300   **NM** $500   **MIP** $1000

(Ron Smith)

Dodge Sedan, 1958, friction, T.N., 11" (J82)
EX $300   NM $400   MIP $800

Dodge Two-Door HT, 1959, 9", blue/white, friction
EX $135   NM $315   MIP $450

(Toy Shop File Photo)

Dream Car, friction, "Y" Co., 17" (J278A)
EX $400   NM $600   MIP $1200

(Ron Smith)

Edsel Convertible/Sedan, 1958, friction, Haji, 10-1/2" (J86)
EX $300   NM $500   MIP $1000

(Ron Smith)

Edsel Hardtop, 1958, friction, Asahi, 10-3/4" (J91)
EX $100   NM $200   MIP $350

(Ron Smith)

Edsel Station Wagon, 1958, friction, T.N., 11" (J89)
EX $150   NM $200   MIP $300

(Ron Smith)

Edsel Wagon, 1958, friction, Haji, 10-1/2" (J87)
EX $200   NM $300   MIP $400

(Toy Shop File Photo)

Electrospecial No. 21, battery-op, "Y" Co., 10" (J290)
EX $300   NM $600   MIP $1200

(Toy Shop File Photo)

Ferrari Berlinetta 250 LeMans, 1960s, Asahi Toy, 11", red, friction
EX $115   NM $265   MIP $375

(Ron Smith)

Ford, 1960, friction, Haji, 11" (J119)
EX $85   NM $150   MIP $225

(Ron Smith)

Ford Ambulance, 1955, friction, Bandai, 12" (J98)
EX $150   NM $200   MIP $250

(Ron Smith)

Ford Convertible, 1955, friction, Bandai, 12" (J100)
EX $200   NM $400   MIP $600

Ford Convertible, 1955, Haji, 6-1/2", two-tone blue or red/white, friction
EX $60   NM $140   MIP $200

(Ron Smith)

Ford Convertible, 1956, friction, Haji, 11-1/2" (J102)
EX $400   NM $600   MIP $900

Ford Convertible, 1957, HTC, 12", orange/pink, friction
EX $115   NM $225   MIP $300

(Ron Smith)

Ford Country Sedan, 1961, friction, Bandai, 10-1/2" (J120)
EX $100   NM $160   MIP $225

(Ron Smith)

Ford Country Sedan, 1962, friction, Asahi, 12" (J121)
EX $200   NM $350   MIP $800

Ford Country Squire Wagon, 1965, 9", white, friction
EX $30   NM $70   MIP $100

Ford Fairlane 500 HT, 1957, ToyMaster, 9-1/2", green/yellow, friction
EX $45   NM $100   MIP $140

(Toy Shop File Photo)

Ford Fairlane Hardtop/Convertible, 1958, friction, Sankei Gangu, 9" (J114)
EX $90   NM $115   MIP $125

(Ron Smith)

Ford Fairlane Sedan, 1957, friction, Ichiko, 10" (J105)
EX $100   NM $200   MIP $300

Ford Falcon, 1960s, Marusan, 9",
red/white, friction
EX $20   **NM** $40   **MIP** $90

Ford Fire Chief Car, 1963, Taiyo, 12-1/2",
red, battery-operated
EX $23   **NM** $55   **MIP** $75

(Ron Smith)

Ford Galaxie Hardtop, 1965, friction, MT,
11" (J125)
EX $125   **NM** $150   **MIP** $300

Ford Gyron, 1960, Ichida, red/black,
friction
EX $45   **NM** $100   **MIP** $170

Ford Gyron, 1960, Ichida, 11", red/black,
remote control, battery-operated
EX $85   **NM** $195   **MIP** $275

Ford Gyron, 1960, Ichida, 11", red/white,
battery-operated
EX $135   **NM** $315   **MIP** $450

(Ron Smith)

Ford Hardtop, 1957, friction, T.N., 12"
(J106)
EX $100   **NM** $200   **MIP** $300

(Ron Smith)

Ford Hardtop, 1964, friction, Ichiko, 13"
(J122)
EX $200   **NM** $300   **MIP** $500

Ford HT Convertible, 1958, 11",
orange/white, battery-operated
EX $60   **NM** $140   **MIP** $200

Ford HT Convertible, 1958, 9-1/2",
blue/white, battery-operated
EX $85   **NM** $195   **MIP** $275

Ford HT Convertible, 1959, 11",
blue/white, red/white, or green/white,
battery-operated
EX $70   **NM** $160   **MIP** $225

Ford Model-T, 9", red, hard top, friction
EX $25   **NM** $55   **MIP** $75

Ford Model-T, 9", black, open top, friction
EX $25   **NM** $55   **MIP** $75

(Ron Smith)

Ford Mustang Fastback, 1965, friction,
Bandai, 11" (J139)
EX $45   **NM** $65   **MIP** $90

(Ron Smith)

Ford Mustang Fastback, 1966, friction,
T.N., 17" (J143)
EX $120   **NM** $200   **MIP** $300

Ford Mustang GT, 1965, 15-1/2", red, friction
EX $85   **NM** $195   **MIP** $275

(Ron Smith)

Ford Mustang Hardtop/Convertible,
1965, friction/battery-op, Bandai, 11"
(J140)
EX $75   **NM** $125   **MIP** $150

(Ron Smith)

Ford Panel Truck, 1955, "Flowers,"
friction, Bandai, 12" (J99)
EX $200   **NM** $400   **MIP** $800

(Ron Smith)

Ford Pickup, 1955, friction, Bandai, 12" (J96)
EX $150   **NM** $250   **MIP** $300

(Ron Smith)

Ford Retractable, 1959, friction, T.N., 11"
(J117)
EX $80   **NM** $100   **MIP** $150

(Ron Smith)

Ford Sedan, 1949, wind-up, Guntherman,
11" (J93)
EX $150   **NM** $300   **MIP** $400

Ford Sedan, 1951, 7", tan, battery-operated
EX $30   **NM** $70   **MIP** $100

(Ron Smith)

Ford Sedan, 1956, friction, Marusan, 13"
(J103)
EX $800   **NM** $1500   **MIP** $3000

(Ron Smith)

Ford Sedan/Convertible/Wagon/Pickup,
1957, friction, Joustra, 12" (J107)
EX $150   **NM** $200   **MIP** $275

(Ron Smith)

Ford Station Wagon, 1955, friction, Bandai, 12" (J97)
EX $150   **NM** $250   **MIP** $300

(Ron Smith)

Ford Station Wagon, 1959, friction, T.N.,
12" (J116)
EX $100   **NM** $150   **MIP** $200

Ford Station Wagon, 1959, 10-1/2",
green/white, friction
EX $40   **NM** $90   **MIP** $125

Ford Stock Car, 1963, Taiyo, 10-1/2",
red/silver/blue, friction
EX $25   **NM** $60   **MIP** $85

(Toy Shop File Photo)

Ford Taunus 17M, 1960s, friction, Bandai, 8" (J145)
EX $20   **NM** $40   **MIP** $80

(Toy Shop File Photo)

Ford Thunderbird, 1955, friction, Bandai, 7" (J126A)
EX $75   **NM** $100   **MIP** $150

(Ron Smith)

Ford Thunderbird, 1956, friction, T.N., 11" (J127)
EX $200   **NM** $300   **MIP** $400

(Ron Smith)

Ford Thunderbird, 1956, battery-op, T.N., 11" (J129)
EX $200   **NM** $300   **MIP** $400

(Ron Smith)

Ford Thunderbird, 1963, battery-op, Yonezawa, 11" (J134)
EX $80   **NM** $150   **MIP** $200

Ford Thunderbird Convertible, 1955, 8", orange, friction
EX $45   **NM** $100   **MIP** $140

(Ron Smith)

Ford Thunderbird Hardtop, 1964, friction, Asahi, 12" (J136)
EX $150   **NM** $200   **MIP** $400

(Ron Smith)

Ford Thunderbird Hardtop, 1965, friction, Bandai, 10-3/4" (J138)
EX $60   **NM** $90   **MIP** $160

Ford Thunderbird HT Convertible, 1962, Yonezawa, 11-1/2", red, battery-operated
EX $105   **NM** $245   **MIP** $350

(Ron Smith)

Ford Thunderbird HT Convertible, 1964, Ichiko, 15-1/2", red, working side windows, friction
EX $120   **NM** $280   **MIP** $400

(Ron Smith)

Ford Thunderbird Retractable, 1963, battery-op, Yonezawa, 11" (J134)
EX $80   **NM** $150   **MIP** $200

(Ron Smith)

Ford Torino, 1968, friction, S.T., 16" (J126)
EX $200   **NM** $350   **MIP** $800

Ford Two-Door HT, 1956, Ichiko, 10", two-tone blue or orange/white, friction
EX $165   **NM** $385   **MIP** $550

Ford Two-Door Sedan, 1956, Marusan, 13", orange/white or blue/white
EX $1050   **NM** $2450   **MIP** $3500

(Ron Smith)

Ford Wagon, 1956, friction, Nomura, 10-1/2" (J104)
EX $125   **NM** $225   **MIP** $300

(Toy Shop File Photo)

Ford Yellow Cab, 1952, Marusan, 10-1/2", yellow, friction, working money meter
EX $165   **NM** $385   **MIP** $550

Futuristic Buick LeSabre, 1951, Yonezawa, 7-1/2", black, friction
EX $240   **NM** $560   **MIP** $800

GM Gas Turbine Firebird II, 1956, Ashahi, 8-1/2", red, friction (J281)
EX $125   **NM** $200   **MIP** $350

Jaguar XKE Convertible, 1950s, Tomiyama, 12", white, friction
EX $195   **NM** $455   **MIP** $650

(Toy Shop File Photo)

Jaguar XKE Convertible, 1960s, friction, T.T., 10-1/2" (J155)
EX $75   **NM** $150   **MIP** $250

Jaguar XKE Coupe, 1960s, 10-1/2", red, friction
EX $50   **NM** $75   **MIP** $120

Jeep Station Wagon, 1950s, Yonezawa, 7-1/2", two-tone brown, friction
EX $100   **NM** $210   **MIP** $300

Kaiser Darren Convertible, 1950s, 6-1/2", red, friction
EX $30   **NM** $70   **MIP** $100

(Ron Smith)

Lincoln, 1956, friction, Ichiko, 16-1/2" (J165)
EX $150   **NM** $250   **MIP** $375

(Ron Smith)

Lincoln, 1964, friction, unknown manufacturer, 10-1/2" (J169)
EX $90   **NM** $175   **MIP** $275

(Ron Smith)

Lincoln Continental Mark II, 1956, friction, Linemar, 12" (J164)
EX $600   **NM** $1200   **MIP** $2500

(Ron Smith)

Lincoln Continental Mark III Convertible, 1959, friction, Bandai, 12" (J166)
EX $90   **NM** $125   **MIP** $200

(Ron Smith)

Lincoln Continental Mark III Sedan, 1959, friction, Bandai, 12" (J167)
EX $90   **NM** $125   **MIP** $175

(Ron Smith)

Lincoln Hardtop/Convertible, 1960, friction, Yonezawa, 11" (J168)
EX $100   **NM** $150   **MIP** $300

Lincoln Premiere Two-Door HT, 1956, 7-1/2", orange, friction
EX $30   **NM** $70   **MIP** $90

(Ron Smith)

Lincoln Sedan, 1955, friction, Yonezawa, 12" (J163)
EX $250   **NM** $600   **MIP** $1200

(Ron Smith)

Mazda Auto Tricycle, 1950s, friction, Bandai, 8" (J274)
EX $100   **NM** $200   **MIP** $400

Mercedes 220-S, 1961, 12", black, jack-up feature, friction
EX $75   **NM** $175   **MIP** $250

Mercedes 300 SL Coupe, 1955, 9", metallic red, opening gull-wing doors, battery-operated
EX $105   **NM** $245   **MIP** $350

Mercedes Convertible, 1950s, Alps, 9", red, friction
EX $105   **NM** $245   **MIP** $350

Mercedes Convertible, 1960s, HTC, 8", red, opening door w/swing-out driver, friction
EX $45   **NM** $105   **MIP** $150

(Ron Smith)

Mercedes-Benz 219 Convertible, 1960s, friction, Bandai, 8" (J177)
EX $50   **NM** $80   **MIP** $120

(Ron Smith)

Mercedes-Benz 219 Sedan, 1960s, friction, Bandai, 8" (J176)
EX $50   **NM** $70   **MIP** $110

(Ron Smith)

Mercury Cougar Hardtop, 1967, friction, Asakusa Toys, 15" (J197)
EX $200   **NM** $400   **MIP** $800

(Ron Smith)

Mercury Hardtop, 1956, friction, Alps, 9-1/2" (J193)
EX $800   **NM** $1200   **MIP** $2200

(Ron Smith)

Mercury Hardtop, 1958, friction, Yonezawa, 11-1/2" (J195)
EX $250   **NM** $325   **MIP** $400

(Toy Shop File Photo)

Midget Special No. 6, friction, "Y" Co., 7" (J291)
EX $100   **NM** $200   **MIP** $350

(Toy Shop File Photo)

Oldsmobile, 1952, friction, "Y" Co., 11" (J207A)
EX $150   **NM** $350   **MIP** $500

Oldsmobile, 1958, Asahi Toy, 12", gold/black, friction
EX $540   **NM** $1260   **MIP** $1800

(Ron Smith)

Oldsmobile Convertible/Sedan/Wagon, 1961, friction, Yonezawa, 12" (J214)
EX $100   **NM** $200   **MIP** $300

(Toy Shop File Photo)

Oldsmobile Highway Patrol Car, 1959, Ichiko, 12-1/2", black/white, friction, working speed meter on trunk
EX $75   **NM** $175   **MIP** $250

Oldsmobile Rally Car, 1961, Asahi Toy, 15", red, friction
EX $55   **NM** $125   **MIP** $175

(Ron Smith)

Oldsmobile Sedan, 1956, friction, Ichiko/Kanto, 10-1/2" (J208)
EX $200   **NM** $400   **MIP** $800

(Ron Smith)

Oldsmobile Sedan, 1958, friction, A.T.C., 12" (J210)
EX $200   **NM** $300   **MIP** $600

Oldsmobile Station Wagon, 1958, 7-1/2", red/black, friction
EX $30   **NM** $60   **MIP** $90

Oldsmobile Super 88, 1956, Modern Toys, 14", orange, battery-operated, working headlights and signal lights
EX $200   **NM** $400   **MIP** $600

(Ron Smith)

Oldsmobile Super 88 Sedan, 1956, friction, Masudaya, 16" (J209)
EX $200   **NM** $300   **MIP** $500

(Ron Smith)

Oldsmobile Toronado, 1966, battery-op, Bandai, 11" (J215)
EX $65   **NM** $110   **MIP** $150

(Ron Smith)

Oldsmobile Toronado, 1968, friction, Ichiko, 17-1/2" (J216)
EX $300   **NM** $400   **MIP** $500

(Ron Smith)

Oldsmobile Two-Door HT, 1959, Ichiko, 12-1/2", two-tone blue, two-tone green, or brown/white, friction
EX $135   **NM** $315   **MIP** $450

Packard Convertible/Sedan, 1953, friction, Alps, 16" (J222)
EX $500   **NM** $800   **MIP** $1600

(Ron Smith)

Packard Hawk Convertible, 1957, battery-op, Schuco, 10-3/4" (J223)
EX $300   **NM** $400   **MIP** $800

Plymouth Convertible, 1959, Asahi Toy, 11", red/white, friction
EX $330   **NM** $770   **MIP** $1100

(Ron Smith)

Plymouth Fury Hardtop, 1957, friction, "Y" Co., 11-1/2" (J226)
EX $300   **NM** $400   **MIP** $600

(Ron Smith)

Plymouth Fury/Sedan/Wagon/Conv., 1958, friction, Bandai, 8" (J227)
EX $75   **NM** $90   **MIP** $165

(Ron Smith)

Plymouth Hardtop, 1956, battery-op, Alps, 12" (J225)
EX $300   **NM** $400   **MIP** $600

(Ron Smith)

Plymouth Hardtop, 1956, friction, unknown manufacturer, 8-1/2" (J224)
EX $100   **NM** $200   **MIP** $300

(Ron Smith)

Plymouth Hardtop, 1959, friction, A.T.C., 10-1/2" (J228)
EX $200   **NM** $400   **MIP** $600

Plymouth HT, 1956, Alps, 8-1/2", two-tone green, friction
EX $165   **NM** $385   **MIP** $550

(Ron Smith)

Plymouth Sedan, 1961, friction, Ichiko, 12" (J230)
EX $150   **NM** $300   **MIP** $550

(Ron Smith)

VEHICLES — JAPANESE TIN CARS

Plymouth Station Wagon, 1961, friction, Ichiko, 12" (J231)
  EX $150   **NM** $250   **MIP** $500

(Ron Smith)

Plymouth T.V. Car, 1961, battery-op, Ichiko, 12" (J232)
  EX $100   **NM** $150   **MIP** $300

(Ron Smith)

Pontiac, 1954, Minister, friction, Minister, 11" (J218A)
  EX $10   **NM** $20   **MIP** $30

(Ron Smith)

Pontiac Firebird, 1967, friction, Akasura, 15-1/2" (J219)
  EX $200   **NM** $400   **MIP** $900

(Ron Smith)

Pontiac Firebird, 1967, friction, Bandai, 10" (J220)
  EX $30   **NM** $55   **MIP** $100

Pontiac Four-Door HT, 1958, Asahi Toy, 8", green/pink, friction
  EX $45   **NM** $105   **MIP** $150

(Toy Shop File Photo)

Porsche 911 Rally, 1960s, 11", red, friction
  EX $70   **NM** $160   **MIP** $225

Porsche 914 Rally, 1960s, Daiya, 9", blue, battery-operated
  EX $25   **NM** $55   **MIP** $75

(Ron Smith)

Porsche Speedster, 1950s, battery-op, Distler, 10-1/2" (J235)
  EX $200   **NM** $300   **MIP** $600

(Toy Shop File Photo)

Porsche Speedster, 1950s, battery-op, Distler, 10-1/2" (J235)
  EX $200   **NM** $300   **MIP** $600

(Ron Smith)

Ramgler Rebel Station Wagon, 1960s, friction, Bandai, 12" (J240)
  EX $60   **NM** $90   **MIP** $150

(Toy Shop File Photo)

Renault, 1960, friction, Bandai, 7-1/2" (J241)
  EX $60   **NM** $90   **MIP** $120

(Toy Shop File Photo)

Rolls Royce, 1960, friction, T.N., 10-1/2" (J239)
  EX $200   **NM** $300   **MIP** $500

(Ron Smith)

Rolls Royce Silver Coupe Convertible, 1960, friction, Bandai, 12" (J236)
  EX $100   **NM** $150   **MIP** $300

(Ron Smith)

Rolls Royce Silver Sedan Coupe, 1960s, friction, Bandai, 12" (J237)
  EX $100   **NM** $150   **MIP** $250

(Ron Smith)

Studebaker, 1954, friction, Yoshiya, 9" (J243)
  EX $150   **NM** $200   **MIP** $450

(Ron Smith)

Studebaker Avanti, 1960s, friction, Bandai, 8" (J242)
  EX $90   **NM** $150   **MIP** $225

Studebaker Coupe, 1953, 9", yellow, friction, working wipers
  EX $45   **NM** $100   **MIP** $140

Studebaker Lark, 1950s, 5-1/2", blue, friction
  EX $20   **NM** $45   **MIP** $65

(Ron Smith)

Volkswagen, 1960s, battery-op, Bandai, 11" (J264)
  EX $75   **NM** $125   **MIP** $200

(Ron Smith)

Volkswagen Convertible, 1950, friction, T.N., 9-1/2" (J258)

EX $100   **NM** $200   **MIP** $375

(Ron Smith)

Volkswagen Convertible, 1960s, battery-op, Bandai, 11" (J260)

EX $110   **NM** $145   **MIP** $200

(Ron Smith)

Volkswagen Karmann-Ghia, 1960, friction, Bandai, 7" (J252), add $50 for convertible

EX $100   **NM** $150   **MIP** $300

Volkswagen Micro-Bus, 1960s, 9-1/2", Bandai, orange w/white top; 1960s (J256), Model No. J256

EX $70   **NM** $145   **MIP** $200

(Ron Smith)

Volkswagen with or without Sun Roof, 1960s, friction, Bandai, 15" (J265)

EX $90   **NM** $120   **MIP** $250

(Toy Shop File Photo)

Volvo, 1950s, wind-up, Sweden, 11" (J265A)

EX $600   **NM** $1000   **MIP** $2000

Volvo, 1950s, 5-1/2", red, friction

EX $20   **NM** $38   **MIP** $55

Volvo PV-544, 1950s, HoKu, 7-1/2", black, friction

EX $200   **NM** $400   **MIP** $800

VW Convertible, 1950s, 9-1/2", dark blue, maroon, or light metallic blue, friction w/battery-operated engine light

EX $85   **NM** $195   **MIP** $275

VW Rabbit Rally Team Car, 1970s, Asahi Toy, 8", yellow, battery-operated

EX $20   **NM** $45   **MIP** $65

VW Sedan, 1950s, 7-1/2", gray, oval window, friction

EX $45   **NM** $105   **MIP** $150

Zephyr Deluxe Convertible, 1950s, 11", maroon/yellow/blue, friction

EX $120   **NM** $280   **MIP** $400

JOHNNY LIGHTNING / TOPPER

(KP Photo)

'32 Roadster, 1969, Varied chromed color body, rumble seat in back flips up. This model has missing windshield, common to play worn examples

| EX $25 | NM $60 | MIP $125 |

A.J. Foyt Indy Special, 1970, blackwall tires

| EX $40 | NM $60 | MIP $250 |

(KP Photo, Tom Michael collection)

Al Unser Indy Special, 1970, Chrome blue finish, Lightning number "2" decal, black wall tires

| EX $100 | NM $200 | MIP $500 |

Baja, 1970

| EX $45 | NM $125 | MIP $200 |

(KP Photo, Tom Michael collection)

Big Rig, 1971, Originally included add on extras called "Customs;" prices reflect fully accessorized car. Called the "Track Bac" in the 1970 Topper Toys catalog

| EX $65 | NM $150 | MIP $275 |

Bubble, 1970, Jet Powered

| EX $45 | NM $75 | MIP $150 |

(Photo courtesy Dennis Seleman)

Bug Bomb, 1970, Various chromed color schemes, two silver engines, blackwall tires. This example is missing the rear engine

| EX $40 | NM $90 | MIP $240 |

Condor, 1970, blackwall tires

| EX $150 | NM $200 | MIP $1200 |

Custom Camaro, 1968-69, Prototype, only one known to exist

| EX n/a | NM $6000 | MIP n/a |

Custom Charger, 1968-69, Prototype, only one known to exist. A Version of this car is now available by Playing Mantis as part of the "Lost Toppers" series

| EX n/a | NM $6000 | MIP n/a |

Custom Continental, 1968-69, Prototype, only six known to exist. Another casting re-released by Playing Mantis

| EX n/a | NM $4000 | MIP n/a |

Custom Dragster, 1969, Without canopy

| EX $35 | NM $75 | MIP $125 |

Custom Dragster, 1969, Mirror finish

| EX $150 | NM $250 | MIP $1000 |

(KP Photo)

Custom Dragster, 1969, Version with a plastic canopy, Topper-style redlines wheels, unpainted base. While versions were made without a canopy, the example here is simply missing one

| EX $60 | NM $150 | MIP $200 |

Custom El Camino, 1969, With sealed doors

| EX $110 | NM $300 | MIP $500 |

(Photo courtesy Dennis Seleman)

Custom El Camino, 1969, With opening doors, surfboards on back, Topper-style redlines wheels

| EX $150 | NM $275 | MIP $475 |

Custom El Camino, 1969, Mirror finish

| EX $200 | NM $350 | MIP $1125 |

Custom Eldorado, 1969, With sealed doors

| EX $150 | NM $300 | MIP $1000 |

Custom Eldorado, 1969, With opening doors

| EX $150 | NM $275 | MIP $350 |

Custom Ferrari, 1969, With opening doors, mirror finish

| EX $300 | NM $450 | MIP $1000 |

(KP Photo)

Custom Ferrari, 1969, With sealed doors

| EX $40 | NM $80 | MIP $130 |

Custom Ferrari, 1969, With opening doors

| EX $150 | NM $275 | MIP $500 |

Custom GTO, 1969, Mirror finish

| EX $200 | NM $475 | MIP $1200 |

Custom GTO, 1969, With sealed doors

| EX $200 | NM $450 | MIP $1700 |

Custom GTO, 1969, With opening doors

| EX $200 | NM $450 | MIP $1500 |

Custom Mako Shark, 1969, With sealed doors

| EX $40 | NM $75 | MIP $225 |

(Photo Courtesy Dennis Seleman)

Custom Mako Shark, 1969, With opening doors, mirror finish

| EX $200 | NM $500 | MIP $2000 |

Custom Mako Shark, 1969, With opening doors

| EX $125 | NM $350 | MIP $500 |

Custom Mustang, 1968-69, Prototype, only one known to exist

| EX n/a | NM $6000 | MIP n/a |

Custom Spoiler, 1970, Blackwall tires

| EX $35 | NM $75 | MIP $160 |

Custom T-Bird, 1969, With opening doors

| EX $100 | NM $250 | MIP $475 |

Custom T-Bird, 1969, Mirror finish

| EX $200 | NM $450 | MIP $5000 |

Custom T-Bird, 1969, With sealed doors

| EX $150 | NM $300 | MIP $700 |

Custom Toronado, 1969, With opening doors

| EX $225 | NM $400 | MIP $1000 |

Custom Toronado, 1969, Mirror finish

| EX $450 | NM $650 | MIP $2000 |

Custom Toronado, 1969, With sealed doors

| EX $300 | NM $500 | MIP $1500 |

Custom Turbine, 1969, Red, black, white painted interior

| EX $50 | NM $150 | MIP $200 |

(KP Photo, Tom Michael collection)

Custom Turbine, 1969, With unpainted interior, Topper redline-style wheels
EX $30   NM $60   MIP $125

Custom Turbine, 1969, Mirror finish
EX $150   NM $225   MIP $550

Custom XKE, 1969, With opening doors, mirror finish
EX $300   NM $450   MIP $800

(KP Photo, Tom Michael collection)

Custom XKE, 1969, With sealed doors, unpainted base, full window plastic all-around, opening hood, blackwalls tires
EX $35   NM $80   MIP $110

(KP Photo, Tom Michael collection)

Custom XKE, 1969, With opening doors, unpainted base, opening hood, black-walls tires
EX $150   NM $275   MIP $500

Double Trouble, 1970, Blackwall tires
EX $75   NM $180   MIP $1500

Flame Out, 1970, Black wall tires
EX $60   NM $150   MIP $350

Flying Needle, 1970, Jet Powered
EX $45   NM $125   MIP $225

(KP Photo)

Frantic Ferrari, 1970, Unpainted base, silver exposed engine, various finishes
EX $35   NM $55   MIP $110

Glasser, 1970, Jet Powered
EX $40   NM $85   MIP $150

Hairy Hauler, 1971, Came with add-on extras called "Customs;" prices reflect fully accessorized cars
EX $65   NM $150   MIP $275

Jumpin' Jag, 1970, Blackwall tires
EX $35   NM $80   MIP $175

(KP Photo)

Leapin' Limo, 1970, Blackwall tires, large silver and black plastic engine. Example here shows Topper packaging, duplicated to an extent by Playing Mantis with the Commemorative series
EX $50   NM $125   MIP $400

Mad Maverick, 1970, Blackwall tires
EX $75   NM $150   MIP $450

Monster, 1970, Jet Powered
EX $40   NM $74   MIP $150

Movin' Van, 1970, Blackwall tires
EX $35   NM $65   MIP $90

(KP Photo, Tom Michael collection)

Nucleon, 1970, Blackwall tires
EX $35   NM $75   MIP $220

Parnelli Jones Indy Special, 1970, Blackwall tires
EX $40   NM $85   MIP $250

Pipe Dream, 1971, Came with add-on extras called "Customs;" prices reflect fully accessorized cars
EX $65   NM $150   MIP $275

(KP Photo, Tom Michael collection)

Sand Stormer, 1970, Blackwall tires
EX $20   NM $35   MIP $90

Sand Stormer, 1970, Black roof, blackwall tires
EX $50   NM $100   MIP $200

Screamer, 1970, Jet Powered
EX $45   NM $75   MIP $200

Sling Shot, 1970, Blackwall tires
EX $50   NM $95   MIP $250

Smuggler, 1970, Blackwall tires
EX $35   NM $75   MIP $150

(KP Photo)

Stiletto, 1970, Blackwall tires, various paint schemes. The example shown is pretty rough. The casting was re-released by Playing Mantis as part of the "Topper Series"
EX $60   NM $85   MIP $300

TNT, 1970, Blackwall tires
EX $40   NM $75   MIP $175

Triple Threat, 1970, Blackwall tires
EX $40   NM $90   MIP $200

Twin Blaster, 1971, Came with add-on extras called "Customs;" prices reflect fully accessorized cars
EX $65   NM $150   MIP $275

(KP Photo)

Vicious Vette, 1970, Blackwall tires
EX $35   NM $80   MIP $225

Vulture w/wing, 1970, Blackwall tires
EX $75   NM $130   MIP $500

Wasp, 1970, Blackwall tires
EX $80   NM $100   MIP $400

Wedge, 1970, Jet Powered
EX $45   NM $75   MIP $200

Whistler, 1970, Blackwall tires
EX $75   NM $125   MIP $300

Wild Winner, 1971, Came w/add on extras called "Customs;" prices reflect fully accessorized cars
EX $60   NM $125   MIP $250

VEHICLES — JOHNNY LIGHTNING TOPPER

MARX

AIRPLANES

727 Riding Jet, jet engine sound
EX $150   NM $225   MIP $300

Airmail Biplane, four engines, tin wind-up, 18" wingspan, 1936
EX $225   NM $325   MIP $450

Airmail Monoplane, two engines, tin wind-up, 1930
EX $100   NM $150   MIP $225

Airplane, mail biplane, tin wind-up, 9-3/4" wingspan, 1926
EX $150   NM $225   MIP $300

Airplane, monoplane, pressed steel, 9" wingspan, 1942
EX $110   NM $165   MIP $300

Airplane, no engines, tin wind-up, 9-1/2" wingspan
EX $135   NM $200   MIP $300

Airplane, two propellers, tin wind-up, 9 7/8" wingspan, 1927
EX $200   NM $300   MIP $400

Airplane, tin wind-up, 9-1/4" wingspan, 1926
EX $150   NM $225   MIP $300

Airplane, adjustable rudder, tin wind-up, 10" wingspan, 1926
EX $150   NM $225   MIP $300

Airplane, monoplane, adjustable rudder, tin wind-up, 9-1/4" wingspan
EX $150   NM $225   MIP $300

Airplane, medium fuselage, tin wind-up
EX $125   NM $150   MIP $250

Airplane, light fuselage, tin wind-up
EX $125   NM $175   MIP $250

Airplane, twin engine, tin wind-up, 9-1/2" wingspan
EX $100   NM $150   MIP $200

Airplane #90, tin wind-up, 5" wingspan, 1930
EX $240   NM $360   MIP $480

Airplane with Parachute, monoplane, tin wind-up, 13" wingspan, 1929
EX $115   NM $170   MIP $325

Air-Sea Power Bombing Set, 12" wingspan; 1940s
EX $325   NM $450   MIP $650

Airways Express Plane, tin wind-up, 13" wingspan, 1929
EX $200   NM $300   MIP $400

American Airlines Airplane, passenger plane, tin wind-up, 27" wingspan; 1940
EX $130   NM $190   MIP $400

American Airlines Flagship, pressed steel, wood wheels, 27" wingspan; 1940
EX $200   NM $300   MIP $500

Army Airplane, biplane, tin wind-up, 25-3/4" wingspan, 1930
EX $225   NM $340   MIP $450

Army Airplane, 18" wingspan; 1951
EX $150   NM $225   MIP $300

Army Airplane, two engines, tin wind-up, 18" wingspan, 1938
EX $125   NM $190   MIP $250

Army Airplane, tin, mechanical fighter, 7" wingspan
EX $125   NM $170   MIP $230

Army Bomber, two engines, tin wind-up, 18" wingspan; 1940s
EX $250   NM $375   MIP $500

Army Bomber, monoplane, litho machine gun and pilot, 25-1/2" wingspan, 1935
EX $300   NM $450   MIP $600

Army Bomber, tri-motor, 25-1/2" wingspan, 1935
EX $250   NM $375   MIP $500

Army Bomber with Bombs, camouflage pattern, metal, wind-up, 12" wingspan, 1930s
EX $100   NM $150   MIP $250

Army Fighter Plane, tin wind-up, 5" wingspan; 1940s
EX $100   NM $150   MIP $250

Autogyro, tin wind-up, 27" wingspan; 1940s
EX $150   NM $225   MIP $375

Blue and Silver Bomber, two engines, tin wind-up, 18" wingspan; 1940
EX $190   NM $280   MIP $375

Bomber, four propellers, metal, wind-up, 14-1/2" wingspan
EX $100   NM $150   MIP $300

Bomber with Tricycle Landing Gear, four engine, tin wind-up, 18" wingspan; 1940
EX $225   NM $325   MIP $425

Camouflage Airplane, four engines, 18" wingspan, 1942
EX $125   NM $200   MIP $295

China Clipper, four engines, tin wind-up, 18-1/4" wingspan, 1938
EX $100   NM $150   MIP $250

City Airport, extra tower and planes, 1930s
EX $125   NM $190   MIP $250

Crash-Proof Airplane, monoplane, tin wind-up, 11-3/4" wingspan, 1933
EX $100   NM $150   MIP $200

Cross Country Flyer, 19" tall, 1929
EX $375   NM $550   MIP $725

Dagwood's Solo Flight Airplane, wind-up, 9" wingspan, 1935
EX $200   NM $300   MIP $950

Daredevil Flyer, tin wind-up, 1929
EX $115   NM $170   MIP $325

Daredevil Flyer, Zeppelin-shaped, 1928
EX $225   NM $350   MIP $475

DC-3 Airplane, aluminum, wind-up, 9-1/2" wingspan, 1930s
EX $125   NM $190   MIP $300

Eagle Air Scout, monoplane, tin wind-up, 26-1/2" wingspan, 1929
EX $200   NM $300   MIP $400

Fighter Jet, USAF, battery-operated, 7" wingspan
EX $90   NM $135   MIP $250

Fighter Plane, battery-operated, remote controlled; 1950s
EX $90   NM $135   MIP $250

Fix All Helicopter, Marx
EX $275   NM $400   MIP $600

Flip-Over Airplane, tin wind-up
EX $200   NM $300   MIP $450

Floor Zeppelin, 9-1/2" long, 1931
EX $225   NM $340   MIP $500

Floor Zeppelin, 16-1/2" long, 1931
EX $350   NM $525   MIP $750

Flying Fortress 2095, sparking, four engines; 1940
EX $150   NM $245   MIP $400

Flying Zeppelin, wind-up, 9" long, 1930
EX $225   NM $340   MIP $475

Flying Zeppelin, wind-up, 17" long, 1930
EX $350   NM $525   MIP $750

Flying Zeppelin, wind-up, 10" long
EX $275   NM $400   MIP $600

Four-Motor Transport Plane, friction, tin litho
EX $120   NM $180   MIP $325

Golden Tricky Airplane, Marx
EX $75   NM $115   MIP $225

Hangar with One Plane, 1940s
EX $150   NM $225   MIP $500

International Airline Express, monoplane, tin wind-up, 17-1/2" wingspan, 1931
EX $200   NM $300   MIP $425

Jet Plane, friction, 6" wingspan; 1950s
EX $65   NM $90   MIP $195

Little Lindy Airplane, friction, 2-1/4" wingspan, 1930
EX $200   NM $300   MIP $500

Looping Plane, silver version, tin wind-up, 7" wingspan; 1941
EX $225   NM $325   MIP $525

Lucky Stunt Flyer, tin wind-up, 6" long, 1928
EX $150   NM $225   MIP $350

Mammoth Zeppelin, 1st Mammoth, pull toy, 28" long, 1930
EX $400   NM $600   MIP $900

Mammoth Zeppelin, 2nd Mammoth, pull toy, 28" long, 1930
EX $375   NM $575   MIP $775

Municipal Airport Hangar, 1929
EX $100   NM $150   MIP $425

Overseas Biplane, three propellers, tin wind-up, 9-7/8" wingspan, 1928
EX $150   NM $275   MIP $395

PAA Clipper Plane, pressed steel, 27" wingspan; 1952
EX $125   NM $175   MIP $525

(Toy Shop File Photo)

PAA Passenger Plane, tin litho, 14" wingspan; 1950s
EX $120   NM $175   MIP $275

Pan American, pressed steel, four motors, 27" wingspan; 1940
EX $90   NM $150   MIP $525

Piggy Back Plane, tin wind-up, 9" wingspan, 1939
EX $100   NM $150   MIP $350

Pioneer Air Express Monoplane, tin litho, pull toy, 25-1/2" wingspan
EX $150   NM $300   MIP $400

Popeye Flyer, Popeye and Olive Oyl in plane, tin litho tower, wind-up, 1936
EX $475   NM $700   MIP $1250

Popeye Flyer, Wimpy and Swee'Pea litho on tower, 1936
EX $600   NM $900   MIP $1600

Pursuit Planes, one propeller, 8" wingspan, 1930s
EX $125   NM $200   MIP $300

Rollover Airplane, tin wind-up, forward and reverse, 6" wingspan; 1947
EX $200   NM $300   MIP $575

(Toy Shop File Photo)

Rollover Airplane, tin wind-up, 1920s
EX $200   NM $300   MIP $575

Rookie Pilot, tin litho, wind-up, 7" long, 1930s
EX $225   NM $340   MIP $550

Seversky P-35, single-engine plane, 16" wingspan; 1940s
EX $125   NM $200   MIP $350

Sky Bird Flyer, two planes, 9-1/2" tower; 1947
EX $275   NM $400   MIP $550

Sky Cruiser Two-Motored Transport Plane, 18" wingspan; 1940s
EX $125   NM $175   MIP $325

Sky Flyer, biplane and Zeppelin, 8-1/2" tall tower, 1927
EX $225   NM $340   MIP $450

Sky Flyer, 9" tall tower, 1937
EX $150   NM $225   MIP $375

Spirit of America, monoplane, tin wind-up, 17-1/2" wingspan, 1930
EX $325   NM $500   MIP $650

Spirit of St. Louis, tin wind-up, 9-1/4" wingspan, 1929
EX $150   NM $225   MIP $595

Stunt Pilot, tin wind-up
EX $175   NM $250   MIP $425

Tower Flyers, 1926
EX $175   NM $250   MIP $350

TP-816 USAF, twin engine, tin, made in Japan, 3-3/4" wingspan; 1960s
EX $5   NM $10   MIP $15

Trans-Atlantic Zeppelin, wind-up, 10" long, 1930
EX $225   NM $350   MIP $450

TWA Biplane, four-engine, 18" wingspan
EX $225   NM $350   MIP $450

U.S. Marines Plane, monoplane, tin wind-up, 17-7/8" wingspan, 1930
EX $200   NM $300   MIP $400

Zeppelin, friction pull toy, steel, 6" long
EX $100   NM $200   MIP $250

Zeppelin, flies in circles, wind-up, 17" long, 1930
EX $350   NM $525   MIP $700

Zeppelin, all metal, pull toy, 28" long, 1929
EX $400   NM $600   MIP $800

BOATS AND SHIPS

Battleship USS Washington, friction, 14" long; 1950s
EX $50   NM $75   MIP $225

Caribbean Luxury Liner, sparkling, friction, 15" long
EX $50   NM $75   MIP $225

Luxury Liner Boat, tin, friction
EX $100   NM $150   MIP $250

Mosquito Fleet Putt Putt Boat, Marx
EX $40   NM $55   MIP $95

River Queen Paddle Wheel Station, plastic
EX $50   NM $75   MIP $150

Sparkling Warship, tin friction motor, 14" long
EX $50   NM $75   MIP $195

(Toy Shop File Photo)

Tugboat, plastic, battery-operated, 6" long; 1966
EX $50   NM $75   MIP $195

BUSES

American Van Lines Bus, cream and red, tin wind-up, 13-1/2" long
EX $65   NM $100   MIP $130

Blue Line Tours Bus, tin litho, wind-up, 9-1/2" long, 1930s
EX $150   NM $225   MIP $425

(RLM MacNary Collection)

Bus, red, 4" long; 1940
EX $35   NM $50   MIP $95

(RLM MacNary Collection)

Coast to Coast Bus, tin litho, wind-up, 10" long, 1930s
EX $125   NM $200   MIP $325

Greyhound Bus, tin litho, wind-up, 6" long, 1930s
EX $100   NM $150   MIP $200

Liberty Bus, tin litho, wind-up, 5" long, 1931
EX $75   NM $125   MIP $200

Mystery Speedway Bus, tin litho, wind-up, 14" long, 1938
EX $200   NM $300   MIP $550

Royal Bus Lines Bus, tin litho, wind-up, 10-1/4" long, 1930s
EX $135   NM $200   MIP $450

(David W Mapes Inc)

Royal Van Co. Truck "We Haul Anywhere", tin wind-up, 9" long, 1920s-30's
  EX $140   **NM** $225   **MIP** $500

School Bus, steel body, wooden wheels, pull toy, 11-1/2" long
  EX $125   **NM** $200   **MIP** $325

Tricky Action Greyhound Bus, 6" long; plastic, battery-operated
  EX $10   **NM** $20   **MIP** $30

CARS

Anti-Aircraft Gun on Car, 5-1/4" long
  EX $50   **NM** $75   **MIP** $225

Archie Jalopy, No. 9009HK, yellow and orange plastic convertible, "Riverdale High" sticker on doors, made in Hong Kong, accessory for "Archies" plastic figures; 1975
  EX $15   **NM** $30   **MIP** $45

Army Car, battery-operated
  EX $65   **NM** $100   **MIP** $200

Army Staff Car, litho steel, tin wind-up, 1930s
  EX $125   **NM** $200   **MIP** $425

Army Staff Car, w/flasher and siren, tin wind-up, 11" long; 1940s
  EX $75   **NM** $125   **MIP** $400

Astro Buggy, 9-1/4" long; Johnny and Jane Apollo vehicle, oversize balloon tries, green-tinted windows; 1968
  EX $8   **NM** $17   **MIP** $25

(Toy Shop File Photo)

Automatic Brake Car, plastic w/tin litho base, 8-1/2" long
  EX $20   **NM** $30   **MIP** $60

Big Lizzie Car, tin wind-up, 7-1/4" long, 1930s
  EX $75   **NM** $125   **MIP** $235

(Bill Bertoia Auctions)

Blondie's Jalopy, tin litho, 16" long; 1941
  EX $325   **NM** $500   **MIP** $850

Boat Tail Racer #2, litho, 13" long; 1948
  EX $125   **NM** $200   **MIP** $425

Boat Tail Racer #3, tin wind-up, 5" long, 1930s
  EX $40   **NM** $55   **MIP** $200

Bouncing Benny Car, pull toy, 7" long, 1939
  EX $325   **NM** $500   **MIP** $750

Bumper Auto, large bumpers front and rear, tin wind-up, 1939
  EX $60   **NM** $100   **MIP** $225

Cadillac, Mini-Marx Blazers die-cast series; 1968
  EX $3   **NM** $7   **MIP** $10

Cadillac Coupe, trunk w/tools on luggage carrier, tin wind-up, 11" long, 1931
  EX $200   **NM** $300   **MIP** $525

Cadillac Coupe, 8-1/2" long, 1931
  EX $175   **NM** $275   **MIP** $400

Camera Car, heavy gauge steel car, 9-1/2" long, 1939
  EX $850   **NM** $1300   **MIP** $1900

Careful Johnnie, plastic driver, 6-1/2" long; 1950s
  EX $100   **NM** $150   **MIP** $350

Chaparral, Mini-Marx Blazers die-cast series; 1968
  EX $5   **NM** $10   **MIP** $15

Charlie McCarthy "Benzine Buggy" Car, w/red wheels, tin wind-up, 7" long, 1938
  EX $600   **NM** $900   **MIP** $1450

(Bill Bertoia Auctions)

Charlie McCarthy "Benzine Buggy" Car, w/white wheels, tin wind-up, 7" long, 1938
  EX $450   **NM** $625   **MIP** $950

(Bill Bertoia Auctions)

Charlie McCarthy and Mortimer Snerd Private Car, tin wind-up, 16" long, 1939
  EX $600   **NM** $900   **MIP** $1500

Charlie McCarthy Private Car, wind-up, 1935
  EX $1450   **NM** $2200   **MIP** $3500

Convertible Roadster, nickel-plated tin, 11" long, 1930s
  EX $175   **NM** $275   **MIP** $395

(Don Hultzmann)

Coo Coo Car, 8" long, tin wind-up, 1931
  EX $375   **NM** $575   **MIP** $825

Crazy Dan Car, tin wind-up, 6" long, 1930s
  EX $140   **NM** $225   **MIP** $395

Dagwood the Driver, 8" long, tin wind-up; 1941
  EX $200   **NM** $300   **MIP** $900

Dan Dipsy Car, nodder, tin wind-up, 5-3/4" long; 1950s
  EX $250   **NM** $375   **MIP** $450

Dick Tracy Police Car, 9" long
  EX $80   **NM** $200   **MIP** $350

Dick Tracy Police Station Riot Car, friction, sparkling, 7-1/2" long; 1946
  EX $60   **NM** $120   **MIP** $375

(The Toy Collector News)

Dick Tracy Squad Car, friction, 20" long; 1948
  EX $125   **NM** $170   **MIP** $300

(Toy Shop File Photo)

Dick Tracy Squad Car, battery-operated, tin litho, 11-1/4" long; 1949
  EX $170   **NM** $275   **MIP** $475

Dick Tracy Squad Car, yellow flashing light, tin litho, wind-up, 11" long; 1940s
  EX $250   **NM** $375   **MIP** $525

(Toy Shop File Photo)

Dippy Dumper, Brutus or Popeye, celluloid figure, tin wind-up, 9", 1930s
EX $350　　NM $525　　MIP $900

(Toy Shop File Photo)

Disney Parade Roadster, tin litho, wind-up; 1950s
EX $100　　NM $150　　MIP $900

(Toy Shop File Photo)

Donald Duck Disney Dipsy Car, plastic Donald, tin wind-up, 5-3/4" long; 1953
EX $425　　NM $650　　MIP $895

Donald Duck Go-Kart, plastic and metal, friction, rubber tires; 1960s
EX $75　　NM $130　　MIP $325

Donald the Driver, plastic Donald, tin car, wind-up, 6-1/2" long; 1950s
EX $200　　NM $300　　MIP $595

Dora Dipsy Car, nodder, tin wind-up, 5-3/4" long; 1953
EX $400　　NM $600　　MIP $725

Dottie the Driver, nodder, tin wind-up, 6-1/2" long; 1950s
EX $150　　NM $225　　MIP $450

Driver Training Car, tin wind-up; 1950s, "Safe Driving School"
EX $80　　NM $120　　MIP $225

(Bill Bertoia Auctions)

Drive-Up Self Car, turns left, right or straight; 1940
EX $100　　NM $150　　MIP $225

Electric Convertible, tin and plastic, 20" long
EX $65　　NM $100　　MIP $295

Falcon, plastic bubble top, black rubber tires
EX $85　　NM $165　　MIP $250

Ford GT, 2-1/2" long; Mini-Marx Blazers die-cast series; 1968
EX $3　　NM $7　　MIP $10

Funny Fire Fighters, 7" long, tin wind-up; 1941
EX $800　　NM $1200　　MIP $1600

(Bill Bertoia Auctions)

Funny Flivver Car, tin litho, wind-up, 7" long, 1926
EX $275　　NM $425　　MIP $675

Gang Buster Car, tin wind-up, 14-1/2" long, 1938
EX $200　　NM $300　　MIP $800

Giant King Racer, dark blue, tin wind-up, 12-1/4" long, 1928
EX $250　　NM $375　　MIP $725

G-Man Pursuit Car, sparks, 14-1/2" long, 1935
EX $190　　NM $285　　MIP $750

Go-Go Car, 36" long, 14" wide; No. 4820, riding toy, plastic yellow body, opening trunk, "Go-Go Car" sticker on sides; 1968-69
EX $53　　NM $110　　MIP $160

Hot Rod #23, friction motor, tin, 8" long; 1967
EX $45　　NM $75　　MIP $90

Huckleberry Hound Car, friction
EX $125　　NM $200　　MIP $250

Indy Racer, 1-3/4" long; plastic, black tires; 1960s
EX $3　　NM $5　　MIP $8

Instant Speedway Action Set, plastic track, hanging hook, die-cast car; 1968-69
EX $10　　NM $20　　MIP $45

International Agent Car, tin wind-up
EX $30　　NM $55　　MIP $125

International Agent Car, friction, tin litho; 1966
EX $60　　NM $100　　MIP $195

Jaguar, 8" long; blue plastic, plastic driver, made in Hong Kong
EX $5　　NM $10　　MIP $15

Jaguar, battery-operated, 13" long
EX $225　　NM $325　　MIP $450

Jalopy, tin driver, friction; 1950s
EX $125　　NM $200　　MIP $250

Jalopy Car, tin driver, motor sparks, crank, wind-up
EX $140　　NM $225　　MIP $280

Jolly Joe Jeep, tin litho, 5-3/4" long; 1950s
EX $150　　NM $225　　MIP $375

Joy Riders Crazy Car, tin litho, wind-up, 8" long, 1928
EX $340　　NM $500　　MIP $675

Jumping Jeep, tin litho, 5-3/4" long; 1947
EX $150　　NM $225　　MIP $425

King Racer, yellow w/black outlines, 8-1/2" long, 1925
EX $250　　NM $430　　MIP $575

King Racer, yellow body, red trim, tin wind-up, 8-1/2" long, 1925
EX $375　　NM $575　　MIP $750

(Bill Bertoia Auctions)

Komical Kop, black car, tin litho, wind-up, 7-1/2" long, 1930s
EX $450　　NM $675　　MIP $900

Leaping Lizzie Car, tin wind-up, 7" long, 1927
EX $250　　NM $375　　MIP $500

Learn To Drive Car, wind-up
EX $110　　NM $165　　MIP $225

Lola Climax Racer, plastic, make in Hong Kong, 6-1/2" long; 1960s
EX $8　　NM $12　　MIP $18

Lola GT, Super Speed Blazers die-cast series, 1969
EX $4　　NM $8　　MIP $12

(Bill Bertoia Auctions)

VEHICLES — MARX

Lonesome Pine Trailer and Convertible Sedan, 22" long, 1936
EX $375   NM $600   MIP $795

Machine Gun on Car, hand crank activation on gun, 3" long
EX $75   NM $130   MIP $225

Magic George and Car, litho; 1940s
EX $170   NM $250   MIP $350

Mechanical Speed Racer, tin wind-up, 12" long; 1948
EX $125   NM $200   MIP $275

Mechanical Speedway Racer, 4-1/2" long; red or blue plastic Porsche-type racer, metal key
EX $5   NM $17   MIP $25

Mercury, Mini-Marx Blazers die-cast series; 1968
EX $3   NM $7   MIP $10

(Toy Shop File Photo)

Mickey Mouse Disney Dipsy Car, plastic Mickey, tin wind-up, 5-3/4" long; 1953
EX $425   NM $655   MIP $875

Mickey the Driver, plastic Mickey, tin car, wind-up, 6-1/2" long; 1950s
EX $170   NM $250   MIP $450

(RLM MacNary Collection)

Midget Racer "Midget Special" #2, miniature car, clockwork-powered, 5" long, 1930s
EX $125   NM $200   MIP $250

(RLM MacNary Collection)

Midget Racer "Midget Special" #7, miniature car, tin wind-up, 5" long, 1930s
EX $125   NM $200   MIP $250

(Toy Shop File Photo)

Milton Berle Crazy Car, tin litho, wind-up, 6" long; 1950s
EX $250   NM $375   MIP $595

Mini Marx Super Speed Car, various models, die-cast racing cars, late 1960s
EX $5   NM $10   MIP $15

Miniature Sports Cars, set of 8, 4" long, hard plastic with metal tires, five plastic service station attendants; 1950s
EX $20   NM $50   MIP $80

(Toy Shop File Photo)

Mortimer Snerd's Tricky Auto, tin litho, wind-up, 7-1/2" long, 1939
EX $400   NM $600   MIP $750

Mystery Car, press down activation, 9" long, 1936
EX $125   NM $200   MIP $275

Mystery Taxi, press down activation, steel, 9" long, 1938
EX $160   NM $250   MIP $375

(Toy Shop File Photo)

Nutty Mad Car, red tin car, vinyl driver, friction, 4" long; 1960s
EX $100   NM $150   MIP $225

(Toy Shop File Photo)

Nutty Mad Car, w/driver, battery-operated; 1960s
EX $100   NM $300   MIP $400

(Toy Shop File Photo)

Nutty Mad Car, blue car w/goggled driver, friction, hard plastic; 1960s
EX $75   NM $130   MIP $200

(Toy Shop File Photo)

Old Jalopy, tin wind-up, driver, "Old Jalopy" on hood, 7" long; 1950
EX $150   NM $200   MIP $350

Old Jalopy, blue car w/yellow trim, college boys, hood reads "Queen of the Campus," tin wind-up, 8" long, 1930s
EX $300   NM $450   MIP $525

Parade Roadster, w/Disney characters, tin litho, wind-up, 11" long; 1950
EX $225   NM $325   MIP $900

Peter Rabbit Eccentric Car, tin wind-up, 5-1/2" long; 1950s
EX $250   NM $375   MIP $500

Porsche, Mini-Marx Blazers series, 1968
EX $3   NM $7   MIP $10

(Toy Shop File Photo)

Queen of the Campus, w/four college students' heads; 1950
EX $250   NM $400   MIP $525

Race 'N Road Speedway, HO scale racing set; 1950s
EX $60   NM $100   MIP $125

Racer #12, tin litho, wind-up, 16" long, 1942
EX $225   NM $325   MIP $625

(RLM MacNary Collection)

Racer #3, miniature car, tin wind-up, 5" long
EX $75   NM $125   MIP $195

(RLM MacNary Collection)

Racer #4, miniature car, tin wind-up, 5" long
EX $75   NM $125   MIP $195

(RLM MacNary Collection)

Racer #5, miniature car, tin wind-up, 5" long; 1948
EX $75   NM $125   MIP $195

Racer #61, miniature car, tin wind-up, 4-3/4" long, 1930
EX $75   NM $125   MIP $195

(RLM MacNary Collection)

Racer #7, miniature car, tin wind-up, 5" long; 1948
EX $75   NM $125   MIP $195

Racing Car, two man team, tin litho, wind-up, 12" long; 1940
EX $125   NM $200   MIP $425

Racing Car, plastic driver, tin wind-up, 27" long; 1950
EX $100   NM $175   MIP $450

Roadster, 11-1/2" long; 1949
EX $100   NM $150   MIP $225

Roadster and Cannon Ball Keeper, wind-up, 9" long
EX $175   NM $250   MIP $350

Roadster Convertible with Trailer and Racer, mechanical; 1950
EX $125   NM $200   MIP $275

Rocket Racer, tin litho, 1935
EX $275   NM $425   MIP $550

Rolls-Royce, black plastic, friction, 6" long; 1955
EX $40   NM $60   MIP $80

Royal Coupe, tin litho, wind-up, 9" long, 1930
EX $175   NM $275   MIP $375

Scooting Tooting Button Hot Rod, 14" long; battery operated hot rod convertible with nine control levers in rumble seat; 1964-65
EX $28   NM $56   MIP $85

Secret Sam Agent 012 Car, tin litho, friction, 5" long; 1960s
EX $40   NM $65   MIP $165

Sedan, battery-operated, plastic, 9-1/2" long
EX $175   NM $275   MIP $350

Sheriff Sam and His Whoopee Car, plastic, tin wind-up, 5-3/4" long; 1949
EX $200   NM $300   MIP $475

(Toy Shop File Photo)

Siren Police Car, 15" long, 1930s
EX $75   NM $125   MIP $395

Smokey Sam the Wild Fireman Car, 6-1/2" long; 1950
EX $125   NM $200   MIP $395

Smokey Stover Whoopee Car, 1940s
EX $175   NM $275   MIP $525

Snoopy Gus Wild Fireman, 7" long, 1926
EX $500   NM $750   MIP $1150

Space Car, gray plastic w/clear cockpit cover, 5-3/4" long, sold with play sets; 1950s
EX $30   NM $60   MIP $80

(Toy Shop File Photo)

Speed Cop, two 4" all tin wind-up cars, track, 1930s
EX $175   NM $275   MIP $795

Speed King Racer, tin litho, wind-up, 16" long, 1929
EX $325   NM $500   MIP $650

Speed Racer, 13" long, 1937
EX $250   NM $375   MIP $500

Speedway Coupe, tin wind-up, battery-operated headlights, 8" long, 1938
EX $200   NM $300   MIP $400

Speedway Set, two wind-up sedans, figure eight track, 1937
EX $250   NM $375   MIP $500

Sports Coupe, tin, 15" long, 1930s
EX $125   NM $200   MIP $250

(Toy Shop File Photo)

Sportster, 20" long; 1950s
EX $65   NM $110   MIP $150

Station Wagon, light purple w/woodgrain pattern, wind-up, 7-1/2" long
EX $60   NM $100   MIP $275

Station Wagon, friction, 11" long; 1950
EX $125   NM $200   MIP $325

Station Wagon, green w/woodgrain pattern, wind-up, 7" long; 1950
EX $50   NM $75   MIP $250

Station Wagon, litho family of four w/dogs on back windows, 6-3/4" long
EX $60   NM $100   MIP $275

Streamline Speedway, two tin wind-up racing cars, 1936
EX $175   NM $275   MIP $395

Stutz Roadster, driver, 15" long, wind-up, 1928
EX $325   NM $500   MIP $750

Super Hot Rod, "777" on rear door, 11" long; 1940s
EX $200   NM $300   MIP $400

Super Streamlined Racer, tin wind-up, 17" long; 1950s
EX $125   NM $200   MIP $400

Talk 'N' Do Mobile, No. 5242, talking toy, removable wheels, movable windshield wipers, made in Japan; mid-1960s
EX $7   NM $15   MIP $22

The Marvel Car, Reversible Coupe, tin wind-up, 1938
EX $125   NM $200   MIP $400

Tricky Safety Car, 6-1/2" long; 1950
EX $100   NM $150   MIP $200

(Toy Shop File Photo)

Tricky Taxi, black/white version, tin wind-up, 4-1/2" long, 1935
EX $160   **NM** $250   **MIP** $375

(Toy Shop File Photo)

Tricky Taxi, red, black, and white, tin wind-up, 4-1/2" long; 1940s
EX $175   **NM** $275   **MIP** $375

Uncle Wiggly, He Goes A Ridin' Car, rabbit driving, tin wind-up, 7-1/2" long, 1935
EX $425   **NM** $650   **MIP** $850

Uno Ferrari, Super Speed Blazers die-cast series, 1969
EX $4   **NM** $8   **MIP** $12

Walt Disney Television Car, friction, 7-1/2" long; 1950s
EX $125   **NM** $200   **MIP** $425

Western Auto Track, steel, 24" long
EX $75   **NM** $125   **MIP** $225

(Bill Bertoia Auctions)

Whoopee Car, witty slogans, tin litho, wind-up, 7-1/2" long, 1930s
EX $375   **NM** $580   **MIP** $775

(Bill Bertoia Auctions)

Whoopee Cowboy Car, bucking car, cowboy driver, tin wind-up, 7-1/2" long, 1930s
EX $400   **NM** $600   **MIP** $800

Woody Sedan, tin friction, 7-1/2" long
EX $60   **NM** $100   **MIP** $225

(Toy Shop File Photo)

Yellow Taxi, wind-up, 7" long, 1927
EX $275   **NM** $425   **MIP** $575

Yogi Bear Car, friction; 1962
EX $50   **NM** $85   **MIP** $195

Za Zoom Friction Racer, No. 7800; 1960s
EX $7   **NM** $15   **MIP** $22

Zoom-A-Car, set of six die-cast racers and two launchers; late 1960s
EX $25   **NM** $50   **MIP** $75

EMERGENCY VEHICLES

Ambulance, 13-1/2" long, 1937
EX $225   **NM** $350   **MIP** $650

Ambulance, tin litho, 11" long
EX $125   **NM** $175   **MIP** $375

(David W Mapes Inc)

Ambulance with Siren, tin wind-up
EX $100   **NM** $150   **MIP** $400

Army Ambulance, 13-1/2" long, 1930s
EX $250   **NM** $375   **MIP** $750

Chief-Fire Department No. 1 Truck, friction; 1948
EX $60   **NM** $90   **MIP** $195

Chrome Racer, miniature racer, 5" long, 1937
EX $85   **NM** $125   **MIP** $250

City Hospital Mack Ambulance, tin litho, wind-up, 10" long, 1927
EX $190   **NM** $280   **MIP** $500

Electric Car, runs on electric power, license #A7132, 1933
EX $225   **NM** $325   **MIP** $500

Electric Car, wind-up, 1933
EX $175   **NM** $250   **MIP** $475

Fire Chief Car, wind-up, 6-1/2" long; 1949
EX $75   **NM** $125   **MIP** $275

Fire Chief Car, battery-operated headlights, wind-up, 11" long; 1950
EX $75   **NM** $125   **MIP** $325

Fire Chief Car, friction, loud fire siren, 8" long, 1936
EX $150   **NM** $250   **MIP** $425

Fire Chief Car, working lights, 16" long
EX $125   **NM** $200   **MIP** $295

Fire Chief Car with Bell, 10-1/2" long; 1940
EX $175   **NM** $250   **MIP** $450

Fire Engine, 12" long; battery-operated plastic aerial ladder truck; 1968-69
EX $15   **NM** $30   **MIP** $45

Fire Engine, sheet iron, 9" long, 1920s
EX $100   **NM** $175   **MIP** $335

Fire Truck, friction, all metal, 14" long; 1945
EX $90   **NM** $135   **MIP** $295

Fire Truck, battery-operated, two celluloid firemen, 12" long
EX $50   **NM** $75   **MIP** $300

Giant King Racer, red, 13" long; 1941
EX $200   **NM** $300   **MIP** $550

Giant King Racer, pale yellow, tin wind-up, 12-1/2" long, 1928
EX $225   **NM** $325   **MIP** $575

Giant Mechanical Racer, tin litho, 12-3/4" long; 1948
EX $100   **NM** $175   **MIP** $350

H.Q. - Staff Car, 14-1/2" long, 1930s
EX $325   **NM** $500   **MIP** $750

Hook and Ladder Fire Truck, three tin litho firemen, 13-1/2" long
EX $90   **NM** $135   **MIP** $225

(Toy Shop File Photo)

Hook and Ladder Fire Truck, plastic ladder on top, 24" long; 1950
EX $90   **NM** $135   **MIP** $225

Plastic Racer, 6" long; 1948
EX $50   **NM** $75   **MIP** $150

Racer with Plastic Driver, tin litho car, 16" long; 1950
EX $150   **NM** $225   **MIP** $375

Rocket-Shaped Racer #12, 1930s
EX $275   **NM** $425   **MIP** $600

(Toy Shop File Photo)

Siren Fire Chief Car, red car w/siren, 1934
EX $225   **NM** $325   **MIP** $495

Siren Fire Chief Truck, battery-operated, 15" long, 1930s
EX $100   **NM** $175   **MIP** $325

Tricky Fire Chief Car, 4-1/2" long, 1930s
EX $250   **NM** $375   **MIP** $625

V.F.D. Emergency Squad, w/ladder, metal, electrically powered, 14" long; 1940s
EX $70   NM $125   MIP $200

V.F.D. Fire Engine, w/hoses and siren, 14" long; 1940s
EX $120   NM $180   MIP $295

V.F.D. Hook and Ladder Fire Truck, 33" long; 1950
EX $140   NM $225   MIP $325

War Department Ambulance, 1930s
EX $100   NM $150   MIP $695

FARM AND CONSTRUCTION EQUIPMENT

Aluminum Bulldog Tractor Set, tin wind-up, 9-1/2" long tractor; 1940
EX $250   NM $375   MIP $500

American Tractor, w/accessories, tin wind-up, 8" long, 1926
EX $150   NM $225   MIP $300

Army Design Climbing Tractor, tin wind-up, 7-1/2" long, 1932
EX $80   NM $120   MIP $300

Automatic Steel Barn and Mechanical Plastic Tractor, tin wind-up, 7" long red tractor; 1950
EX $85   NM $125   MIP $475

(Toy Shop File Photo)

Bulldozer Climbing Tractor, caterpillar type, tin wind-up, 10-1/2" long; 1950s
EX $45   NM $75   MIP $295

Bulldozer Climbing Tractor, bumper auto, large bumpers, tin wind-up, 1939
EX $50   NM $75   MIP $325

Caterpillar Climbing Tractor, yellow tractor, tin wind-up, 9-1/2" long, 1942
EX $75   NM $125   MIP $300

Caterpillar Climbing Tractor, orange tractor, tin wind-up, 9-1/2" long, 1942
EX $100   NM $175   MIP $325

Caterpillar Tractor and Hydraulic Lift, tin wind-up; 1948
EX $50   NM $75   MIP $295

Climbing Sparking Tractor, No. 904, 8-1/2" long; lithographed steel with rubber treads, plastic driver, wind-up; 1960s and 1970s
EX $15   NM $30   MIP $45

Climbing Tractor, w/driver, tin wind-up, 1920s
EX $50   NM $100   MIP $275

Climbing Tractor, tin wind-up, 8-1/4" long, 1930
EX $100   NM $150   MIP $325

Climbing Tractor, 5-1/2" long; wind-up, plastic and metal, plastic driver; 1960s
EX $12   NM $23   MIP $35

Climbing Tractor with Chain Pull, tin wind-up, 7-1/2" long, 1929
EX $150   NM $225   MIP $350

Construction Tractor, reversing, tin wind-up, 14" long; 1950s
EX $100   NM $150   MIP $465

Co-Op Combine, tin friction, 6"
EX $30   NM $45   MIP $95

Covered Wagon, friction, tin litho, 9" long
EX $20   NM $30   MIP $195

Crawler, w/or without blades and drivers, litho, 1/25 scale; 1950
EX $75   NM $125   MIP $150

Crawler with Stake Bed, litho, 1/25 scale; 1950
EX $75   NM $130   MIP $175

Farm Tractor and Implement Set, tin wind-up, tractor mower, hayrake, three-gang plow; 1948
EX $200   NM $300   MIP $400

Farm Tractor Set, 40 pieces, tin wind-up, 1939
EX $325   NM $500   MIP $650

Farm Tractor Set and Power Plant, 32 pieces, tin wind-up, 1938
EX $200   NM $300   MIP $400

Hill Climbing Dump Truck, tin wind-up, 13-1/2" long, 1932
EX $140   NM $210   MIP $375

Industrial Tractor Set, orange and red heavy gauge plate tractor, 7-1/2" long, 1930
EX $145   NM $225   MIP $395

International Harvester Tractor, diesel, driver and set of tools, 1/12 scale; 1954
EX $75   NM $125   MIP $150

(Toy Shop File Photo)

Magic Barn and Tractor, plastic tractor, tin litho barn; 1950s
EX $70   NM $100   MIP $375

Mechanical Tractor, tin wind-up, 5-1/2" long, 1942
EX $125   NM $200   MIP $275

Midget Climbing Tractor, tin wind-up, 5-1/4" long, 1935
EX $125   NM $200   MIP $250

Midget Road Building Set, tin wind-up, 5-1/2" long tractor, 1939
EX $200   NM $300   MIP $400

Midget Tractor, copper color metal, tin wind-up, 5-1/4" long; 1940
EX $40   NM $60   MIP $125

Midget Tractor, red metal, tin wind-up, 5-1/4" long; 1940
EX $30   NM $45   MIP $125

Midget Tractor and Plow, tin wind-up, 1937
EX $70   NM $100   MIP $225

Midget Tractor with Driver, red metal, tin wind-up, 5-1/4" long; 1940
EX $40   NM $60   MIP $220

No. 2 Tractor, red w/black wheels, tin wind-up, 8-1/2" long; 1940
EX $95   NM $150   MIP $225

Plastic Sparkling Tractor Set, tin wind-up, 6-1/2" long tractor w/10-1/2" long wagon; 1950
EX $40   NM $60   MIP $195

Plastic Tractor with Scraper, tin wind-up, 8" long w/road scraper; 1949
EX $50   NM $75   MIP $195

(Toy Shop File Photo)

Power Grader, black or white wheels, 17-1/2" long
EX $50   NM $100   MIP $125

(Toy Shop File Photo)

Power Shovel, Marx
EX $50   NM $75   MIP $100

Reversible Six-Wheel Farm Tractor-Truck, tin wind-up, 13-3/4" steel tractor, 7-1/2" stake truck; 1950
EX $80   NM $125   MIP $425

(Toy Shop File Photo)

Reversible Six-Wheel Tractor, red steel tractor, tin wind-up, 11-3/4" long; 1940
EX $200   **NM** $300   **MIP** $475

(Toy Shop File Photo)

Self-Reversing Tractor, tin wind-up, 10" long, 1936
EX $125   **NM** $200   **MIP** $350

(Toy Shop File Photo)

Sparkling Climbing Tractor, tin wind-up, 10" long; 1940s
EX $175   **NM** $275   **MIP** $350

(Toy Shop File Photo)

Sparkling Climbing Tractor, tin wind-up, 8-1/2" long; 1950s
EX $100   **NM** $150   **MIP** $300

Sparkling Heavy Duty Bulldog Tractor, w/road scraper, tin wind-up, 11" long; 1950s
EX $40   **NM** $60   **MIP** $225

Sparkling Hi-Boy Climbing Tractor, 10-1/2" long; 1950s
EX $25   **NM** $40   **MIP** $195

Sparkling Tractor, w/driver and trailer, tin wind-up, 16" long; 1950s
EX $60   **NM** $90   **MIP** $295

Sparkling Tractor, w/plow blade, tin wind-up, 1939
EX $50   **NM** $75   **MIP** $235

Sparkling Tractor and Trailer Set, "Marborook Farms," tin wind-up, 21" long; 1950s
EX $55   **NM** $75   **MIP** $255

Steel Farm Tractor and Implements, tin wind-up, 15" long steel bulldozer tractor; 1947
EX $160   **NM** $240   **MIP** $325

Super Power Reversing Tractor, tin wind-up, 12" long, 1931
EX $100   **NM** $150   **MIP** $325

Super Power Tractor and Trailer Set, tin wind-up, 8-1/2" tractor, 1937
EX $125   **NM** $200   **MIP** $375

Super-Power Bulldog Tractor with V-Shaped Plow, aluminum finish, tin wind-up, 1938
EX $75   **NM** $130   **MIP** $200

Super-Power Climbing Tractor and Nine-Piece Set, tin wind-up, 9-1/2" long tractor, 1942
EX $160   **NM** $240   **MIP** $395

Super-Power Giant Climbing Tractor, tin wind-up, 13" long, 1939
EX $180   **NM** $270   **MIP** $450

Tractor, tin wind-up, 8-1/2" long; 1941
EX $100   **NM** $175   **MIP** $315

Tractor, red tractor, tin wind-up, 8-1/2" long; 1941
EX $100   **NM** $175   **MIP** $300

Tractor and Equipment Set, five pieces, tin wind-up, 16" long tractor; 1949
EX $160   **NM** $240   **MIP** $320

Tractor and Mower, tin wind-up, 5" long litho steel tractor; 1948
EX $50   **NM** $75   **MIP** $215

Tractor and Six Implement Set, tin wind-up, 8-1/2" long aluminum tractor; 1948
EX $160   **NM** $240   **MIP** $425

Tractor and Trailer, tin wind-up, 16-1/2" long; 1950s
EX $40   **NM** $60   **MIP** $115

Tractor Road Construction Set, thirty-six pieces, tin wind-up, 8-1/2" long tractor, 1938
EX $200   **NM** $325   **MIP** $595

Tractor Set, forty pieces, tin wind-up, 8-1/2" long, 1942
EX $300   **NM** $450   **MIP** $800

Tractor Set, two-pieces, tin wind-up, 19" long steel tractor; 1950
EX $65   **NM** $100   **MIP** $215

Tractor Set, seven pieces, tin wind-up, 8-1/2" long tractor, 1932
EX $125   **NM** $200   **MIP** $400

Tractor Set, thirty-two pieces, tin wind-up, 1937
EX $180   **NM** $270   **MIP** $450

Tractor Set, five pieces, tin wind-up, 8-1/2" long tractor, 1935
EX $70   **NM** $100   **MIP** $220

Tractor Set, five pieces, tin wind-up, 8-1/2" tractor, 1938
EX $90   **NM** $135   **MIP** $295

Tractor Set, four pieces, tin wind-up, 8-1/2" long, 1936
EX $100   **NM** $150   **MIP** $325

Tractor Trailer and Scraper, tin wind-up, 8-1/2" long tractor; 1946
EX $80   **NM** $120   **MIP** $200

Tractor Train with Tractor Shed, tin wind-up, 8-1/2" long, 1936
EX $100   **NM** $150   **MIP** $220

Tractor with Airplane, wind-up, 5-1/2" long tractor, 27" wingspan on airplane; 1941
EX $250   **NM** $375   **MIP** $675

Tractor with Driver, wind-up; 1940s
EX $100   **NM** $150   **MIP** $300

Tractor with Earth Grader, tin wind-up, mechanical, 21-1/2" long; 1950s
EX $40   **NM** $60   **MIP** $190

Tractor with Plow and Scraper, aluminum tractor, tin wind-up, 1938
EX $70   **NM** $125   **MIP** $295

Tractor with Plow and Wagon, tin wind-up, 1934
EX $70   **NM** $125   **MIP** $295

Tractor with Road Scraper, tin wind-up, 8-1/2" long climbing tractor, 1937
EX $90   **NM** $125   **MIP** $325

Tractor with Scraper, tin wind-up, 8-1/2" long, 1933
EX $70   **NM** $125   **MIP** $295

Tractor with Trailer and Plow, tin wind-up, 8-1/2" long; 1940
EX $80   **NM** $120   **MIP** $295

Tractor, Trailer, and V-Shaped Plow, tin wind-up, 8-1/2" steel tractor, 1939
EX $85   **NM** $125   **MIP** $325

Tractor-Trailer Set, tin wind-up, 8-1/2" long copper-colored tractor, 1939
EX $70   **NM** $125   **MIP** $295

Yellow and Green Tractor, tin wind-up, 8-1/2" long, 1930
EX $90   **NM** $135   **MIP** $335

MOTORCYCLES

Motorcycle Cop, tin litho, mechanical, siren, 8-1/4" long
EX $75   **NM** $125   **MIP** $235

Motorcycle Delivery Toy, "Speedy Boy Delivery Toy" on rear of cart, tin wind-up, 1932
EX $175   **NM** $275   **MIP** $500

Motorcycle Delivery Toy, "Speedy Boy Delivery Toy" on side of cart, tin wind-up, 1930s
EX $175   **NM** $280   **MIP** $525

Motorcycle Police, red uniform on cop, tin wind-up, 8" long, 1930s
EX $125   **NM** $200   **MIP** $275

Motorcycle Police #3, tin wind-up, 8-1/2" long
EX $100   **NM** $150   **MIP** $250

Motorcycle Policeman, orange/blue, tin wind-up, 8" long, 1920s
EX $100   **NM** $150   **MIP** $325

VEHICLES — MARX

Motorcycle Trooper, tin litho, wind-up, 1935
EX $80　　NM $120　　MIP $275

Mystery Police Cycle, yellow, tin wind-up, 4-1/2" long, 1930s
EX $75　　NM $125　　MIP $225

Mystic Motorcycle, tin litho, wind-up, 4-1/4" long, 1936
EX $75　　NM $130　　MIP $235

P.D. Motorcyclist, tin wind-up, 4" long
EX $40　　NM $60　　MIP $195

Pinched Roadster Motorcycle Cop, in circular track, tin wind-up, 1927
EX $125　　NM $200　　MIP $365

Pluto Motorcycle with Siren, 1930s
EX $150　　NM $225　　MIP $550

Police Motorcycle with Sidecar, tin wind-up, 3-1/2" long, 1930s
EX $300　　NM $450　　MIP $750

Police Motorcycle with Sidecar, tin litho, wind-up, 8" long; 1950
EX $175　　NM $280　　MIP $425

Police Motorcycle with Sidecar, tin wind-up, 8" long, 1930s
EX $425　　NM $650　　MIP $950

Police Patrol Motorcycle with Sidecar, tin wind-up, 1935
EX $110　　NM $165　　MIP $400

Police Siren Motorcycle, tin litho, wind-up, 8" long, 1938
EX $150　　NM $225　　MIP $350

Police Squad Motorcycle Sidecar, tin litho, wind-up, 8" long; 1950
EX $100　　NM $150　　MIP $375

Police Tipover Motorcycle, tin litho, wind-up, 8" long, 1933
EX $200　　NM $300　　MIP $525

Rookie Cop, yellow w/driver, tin litho, wind-up, 8" long; 1940
EX $175　　NM $275　　MIP $425

Sparkling Soldier Motorcycle, tin litho, wind-up, 8" long; 1940
EX $175　　NM $275　　MIP $425

Speeding Car and Motorcycle Policeman, tin litho, wind-up, 1939
EX $90　　NM $150　　MIP $350

Tricky Motorcycle, tin wind-up, 4-1/2" long, 1930s
EX $100　　NM $150　　MIP $250

TANKS

Anti-Aircraft Tank Outfit, three cardboard tanks
EX $150　　NM $225　　MIP $350

Anti-Aircraft Tank Outfit, four flat metal soldiers, tank, anti-aircraft gun; 1941
EX $90　　NM $135　　MIP $300

Army Tank, sparking climbing tank, tin wind-up; 1940s
EX $150　　NM $225　　MIP $375

Climbing Fighting Tank, tin wind-up
EX $90　　NM $135　　MIP $250

Climbing Tank, tin wind-up, 9-1/2" long, 1930
EX $125　　NM $200　　MIP $325

Doughboy Tank, doughboy pops out, tin litho, wind-up, 9-1/2" long, 1930
EX $150　　NM $225　　MIP $425

Doughboy Tank, sparking tank, tin wind-up, 10" long, 1937
EX $125　　NM $200　　MIP $400

Doughboy Tank, tin wind-up, 10" long, 1942
EX $150　　NM $225　　MIP $450

E12 Tank, makes rat-a-tat-tat or rumbling noise, tin wind-up, 1942
EX $100　　NM $150　　MIP $375

(Bill Holt)

E12 Tank, green tank, 9-1/2" long, tin wind-up, 1942
EX $150　　NM $225　　MIP $375

M48T Tank, battery-operated; 1960s
EX $50　　NM $100　　MIP $225

Midget Climbing Fighting Tank, 5-1/2" long, 1937
EX $100　　NM $175　　MIP $375

Midget Climbing Fighting Tank, tin litho, wind-up, 5-1/4" long, 1931
EX $90　　NM $135　　MIP $235

(Harvey K Rainess)

Midget Climbing Fighting Tank, wide plastic wheels, supergrid tread, 5-1/4" long; 1951
EX $100　　NM $150　　MIP $300

Refrew Tank, tin wind-up
EX $75　　NM $125　　MIP $200

Rex Mars Planet Patrol Tank, tin wind-up, 10" long; 1950s
EX $150　　NM $225　　MIP $375

Sparkling Army Tank, tan or khaki hull, tin litho, wind-up, 1938
EX $95　　NM $150　　MIP $235

Sparkling Army Tank, yellow hull, E12 Tank, tin litho, wind-up, 1942,
EX $100　　NM $150　　MIP $300

Sparkling Army Tank, camouflage hull, two olive guns, tin wind-up, 5-1/2" long
EX $100　　NM $150　　MIP $275

Sparkling Army Tank, camouflage hull, two khaki guns, tin wind-up, 5-1/2" long
EX $125　　NM $200　　MIP $325

Sparkling Climbing Tank, tin wind-up, 10" long, 1939
EX $110　　NM $165　　MIP $310

Sparkling Space Tank, tin wind-up; 1950s
EX $250　　NM $375　　MIP $600

Sparkling Super Power Tank, tin wind-up, 9-1/2" long; 1950s
EX $75　　NM $125　　MIP $250

(Toy Shop File Photo)

Sparkling Tank, tin wind-up, 4" long; 1948
EX $75　　NM $130　　MIP $195

Superman Turnover Tank, Superman lifts tank, 4" long, tin wind-up; 1940
EX $250　　NM $375　　MIP $600

Tank, pop-up army man shooting
EX $150　　NM $225　　MIP $400

Turnover Army Tank, camouflage, tan or khaki hull, tin wind-up, 1938
EX $175　　NM $275　　MIP $450

Turnover Army Tank, tin wind-up, 9" long, 1930
EX $150　　NM $225　　MIP $375

Turnover Tank, tin litho, wind-up, 4" long, 1942
EX $100　　NM $150　　MIP $275

TRUCKS

(Toy Shop File Photo)

A & P Supermarket Truck, pressed steel, rubber tires, litho, 19" long
EX $50   NM $100   MIP $340

(Bob Smith)

Aero Oil Co. Mack Truck, tin litho, friction, 5-1/2" long, 1930
EX $125   NM $200   MIP $350

Air Force Truck, 32" long, No. 3290
EX $125   NM $190   MIP $250

American Railroad Express Agency Inc. Truck, open cab, 7" long, 1930s
EX $150   NM $300   MIP $450

American Truck Co. Mack Truck, friction, 5" long
EX $100   NM $150   MIP $225

Armored Trucking Co. Mack Truck, black cab, yellow printing, wind-up, 9-3/4" long
EX $200   NM $300   MIP $400

Armored Trucking Co. Truck, tin litho, wind-up, 10" long, 1927
EX $100   NM $150   MIP $325

Army Transport Truck, 19" long; 1960s
EX $30   NM $50   MIP $65

Army Truck, olive drab truck, 4-1/2" long, 1930s
EX $125   NM $200   MIP $350

Army Truck, canvas top, 20" long; 1940s
EX $150   NM $225   MIP $325

Army Truck, 20" long
EX $50   NM $75   MIP $125

Army Truck, tin, 12" long; 1950
EX $60   NM $90   MIP $150

Army Truck with Rear Benches and Canopy, olive drab paint, 10" long
EX $75   NM $125   MIP $225

Artillery Set, three-piece set, 1930
EX $100   NM $150   MIP $225

Auto Carrier, two yellow plastic cars, two ramp tracks, 14" long; 1950
EX $125   NM $200   MIP $295

Auto Hauler, hard plastic, 14: long; 1950
EX $25   NM $50   MIP $75

Auto Mack Truck, yellow/red, 12" long; 1950
EX $50   NM $75   MIP $175

Auto Transport Mack Truck and Trailer, dark blue cab, dark green trailer, wind-up, 11-1/2" long, 1932
EX $150   NM $225   MIP $375

Auto Transport Mack Truck and Trailer, medium blue cab, friction, 11-1/2" long, 1932
EX $150   NM $225   MIP $425

Auto Transport Mack Truck and Trailer, dark blue cab, wind-up, 11-1/2" long, 1932
EX $150   NM $225   MIP $400

Auto Transport Truck, w/three racing coupes, 22" long, 1933
EX $250   NM $375   MIP $525

Auto Transport Truck, pressed steel, w/two plastic cars, 14" long; 1940
EX $75   NM $125   MIP $225

Auto Transport Truck, w/three wind-up cars, 22-3/4" long, 1931
EX $250   NM $375   MIP $525

Auto Transport Truck, w/two tin litho cars, 34" long; 1950s
EX $60   NM $90   MIP $200

Auto Transport Truck, double decker transport truck, 24-1/2" long, 1935
EX $275   NM $425   MIP $575

Auto Transport Truck, w/dump truck, roadster and coupe, 30 1/2" long, 1938
EX $275   NM $425   MIP $575

Auto Transport Truck, w/three cars, 21" long; 1940
EX $250   NM $375   MIP $575

Auto Transport Truck, 21" long; 1947
EX $175   NM $250   MIP $400

Auto Transport Truck, w/two plastic sedans, wooden wheels, 13-3/4" long; 1950
EX $75   NM $130   MIP $225

Auto Transport Truck, w/three cars, 1930s
EX $175   NM $250   MIP $395

Bakery Van, plastic, clear top, "Bakery," 10" long; 1950s
EX $20   NM $30   MIP $45

Bamberger Mack Truck, dark green, wind-up, 5" long, 1920s
EX $200   NM $300   MIP $525

Big Blade, 18" long; battery-operated, remote-control plastic bulldozer with driver; 1966-68
EX $32   NM $63   MIP $95

Big Boss Car Carrier, plastic, battery-operated; 1963
EX $50   NM $80   MIP $125

Big Bruiser, 25" long; white plastic wrecker truck, battery-operated light and siren, jack, tool kit, pickup truck with spare parts; 1962-65
EX $42   NM $83   MIP $125

Big Bruiser Highway Service Truck, plastic, 24: long, battery-operated, w/large plastic pickup to tow; 1964
EX $35   NM $55   MIP $85

Big Job Dump Truck, plastic; 1970s
EX $15   NM $25   MIP $35

Big Job Dump Truck, No. 5214, 29" long; battery-operated plastic and steel dump truck, power steering and brakes; 1964-65
EX $18   NM $79   MIP $55

Big Load Van Co. Hauler and Trailer, w/little cartons of products, 12-3/4" long, 1927
EX $200   NM $300   MIP $525

Big Load Van Co. Mack Truck, wind-up, 13" long, 1928
EX $225   NM $350   MIP $600

Big Shot, 23" long; battery-operated plastic mobile artillery, radar on cab roof, six wheels, three rubber-tipped missiles; 1965-66
EX $38   NM $56   MIP $115

Big Shot Cannon Truck, battery-operated, 23" long; 1960s
EX $150   NM $250   MIP $325

Bruiser Jr., 12" long; white plastic remote-control wrecker truck, manual winch, jack, blue plastic 8" car with replacement car fender; 1968-69
EX $28   NM $36   MIP $85

Cannon Army Mack Truck, 9" long, 1930s
EX $175   NM $250   MIP $325

Carousel Truck, 7-1/2" long; metal, friction-powered, blue truck with merry-go-round load; 1967-68
EX $15   NM $30   MIP $45

Carpenter's Truck, stake bed truck, pressed steel, 14" long; 1940s
EX $175   NM $250   MIP $350

Carrier with Three Racers, tin litho, wind-up, 22-3/4" long, 1930
EX $150   NM $225   MIP $425

Cement Mixer Truck, red cab, tin finish mixing barrel, 6" long, 1930s
EX $100   NM $150   MIP $300

City Coal Co. Mack Dump Truck, 14" long, 1934
EX $225   NM $350   MIP $525

City Delivery Van, yellow steel truck, 11" long
EX $140   NM $210   MIP $280

(Calvin L Chaussee)

City Sanitation Dept. "Help Keep Your City Clean" Truck, 12-3/4" long; 1940
EX $60   NM $90   MIP $250

Coal Truck, 3rd version, Lumar Co. truck, 10" long, 1939
EX $150   NM $250   MIP $310

Coal Truck, battery-operated, automatic dump, forward and reverse, tin
EX $75   NM $125   MIP $175

Coal Truck, 1st version, red cab, litho blue and yellow dumper, 12" long
EX $140   **NM** $225   **MIP** $280

Coal Truck, 2nd version, light blue truck, 12" long
EX $140   **NM** $225   **MIP** $280

Coca-Cola Beverage Truck, No. 829, 12-5/8" long; yellow, double shelves in load area, six bottle cases, hand truck; 1960s
EX $67   **NM** $132   **MIP** $200

Coca-Cola Truck, yellow, 20" long; 1950
EX $150   **NM** $225   **MIP** $300

(Toy Shop File Photo)

Coca-Cola Truck, stamped steel, 20" long; 1940s, Sprite boy, stake body
EX $280   **NM** $570   **MIP** $880

Coca-Cola Truck, red steel, 11-1/2" long; 1940s
EX $100   **NM** $175   **MIP** $250

Coca-Cola Truck, tin, 17" long; 1940s
EX $125   **NM** $200   **MIP** $250

Concrete Company Truck, 6" long; gray hard plastic, black tires, "Lumar Concrete Company"
EX $3   **NM** $6   **MIP** $9

Construction Set, 3-piece set of mini trucks, 7" long, futuristic cabover style, electric headlights; cement, tow and dump trucks; 1968
EX $25   **NM** $35   **MIP** $55

Contractors and Builders Truck, 10" long
EX $125   **NM** $200   **MIP** $250

(Taylor's Toys John Taylor)

Cunningham's Drug Store Truck, plastic; 1950s
EX $40   **NM** $60   **MIP** $80

(Toy Shop File Photo)

Curtiss Candy Truck, red plastic truck, 10" long; 1950
EX $25   **NM** $55   **MIP** $75

Dairy Farm Pickup Truck, 22" long
EX $60   **NM** $100   **MIP** $150

Delivery Truck, blue truck, 4" long; 1940
EX $100   **NM** $175   **MIP** $225

Deluxe Delivery Stake Truck, plastic cab, metal bed, 12" long; 1950s
EX $40   **NM** $60   **MIP** $90

(Toy Shop File Photo)

Deluxe Delivery Truck, w/six delivery boxes, stamped steel, 13-1/4" long; 1948
EX $100   **NM** $150   **MIP** $200

Deluxe Fire Truck, red plastic ladder truck, open cab, keywind motor, 13-1/2" long
EX $30   **NM** $50   **MIP** $75

(Taylor's Toys John Taylor)

Deluxe Trailer Truck, tin and plastic, 14" long; 1950s
EX $70   **NM** $100   **MIP** $145

Diesel Power Shovel, No. 1782; 18" long; crank-controlled boom and shovel; 1960s-70s
EX $28   **NM** $56   **MIP** $85

Dodge Salerno Engineering Department Truck, Marx
EX $600   **NM** $900   **MIP** $1200

Dump Truck, 21" long; plastic and steel dump truck, battery-powered, three switches, battery-operated "Za-zoom" motor noise; 1964-68
EX $13   **NM** $26   **MIP** $40

Dump Truck, red cab, green dump bed, 12" long; 1940s
EX $50   **NM** $90   **MIP** $150

Dump Truck, 8" long; battery-operated toy, forward and back lever, dump lever, with plastic driver
EX $7   **NM** $13   **MIP** $20

Dump Truck, motor, tin friction, 12" long; 1950s
EX $50   **NM** $75   **MIP** $100

Dump Truck, red cab, gray bumper, yellow bed, 18" long; 1950
EX $100   **NM** $150   **MIP** $200

Dump Truck, 6" long, 1930s
EX $100   **NM** $150   **MIP** $250

Dump Truck, red cab, green body, 6-1/4" long
EX $50   **NM** $75   **MIP** $100

Dump Truck, various colors, 18" long; 1950s
EX $100   **NM** $150   **MIP** $200

(Toy Shop File Photo)

Dump Truck, 4-1/2" long, 1930s
EX $100   **NM** $175   **MIP** $325

Emergency Service Truck, friction, tin
EX $125   **NM** $200   **MIP** $275

(Toy Shop File Photo)

Emergency Service Truck, friction, tin, searchlight behind car and siren
EX $150   **NM** $225   **MIP** $300

Farm Stake Truck, No. 1010, 17-3/4" long; "Lazy Day Farms," lithographed stake body, polyethylene tires; 1959 to 1970s
EX $28   **NM** $65   **MIP** $85

Farm Truck, red plastic, chicken cage on stake bed, battery-operated, 11-1/2" long; 1960s
EX $10   **NM** $18   **MIP** $25

Firestone Truck, metal, 14" long; 1950s
EX $90   **NM** $150   **MIP** $200

Ford Heavy Duty Express Truck, cab w/canopy; 1950s
EX $60   **NM** $100   **MIP** $175

Gas Truck, green truck, 4" long; 1940
EX $60   **NM** $90   **MIP** $165

Giant Reversing Tractor Truck, w/tools, tin wind-up, 14" long; 1950s
EX $75   **NM** $130   **MIP** $350

Go-Cart, "Letters", Magic Marxie vehicle with mailbox figure, plastic w/rubber tires, 5-1/2" long; 1969
EX $20   **NM** $30   **MIP** $45

Gravel Truck, 1st version, pressed steel cab, red tin dumper, 10" long, 1930
EX $100   **NM** $150   **MIP** $250

(Taylor's Toys John Taylor)

Gravel Truck, 3rd version, metal w/"Gravel Mixer" drum, 10" long, 1930s
EX $100   **NM** $150   **MIP** $250

Gravel Truck, 2nd version, metal, 8-1/2" long; 1940s
EX $75   NM $125   MIP $200

Grocery Truck, cardboard boxes, tinplate and plastic, 14-1/2" long
EX $90   NM $150   MIP $225

Guided Missile Truck, blue, red and yellow body, friction, 16" long; 1958
EX $75   NM $125   MIP $225

Heavy Gauge Dump Truck, No. 978; 17-3/4" long; "Lumar Contractors," 11" dump body, polyethylene tires; 1960s
EX $25   NM $50   MIP $75

Hi Way Express Truck, "Nationwide Delivery," 1950s
EX $100   NM $150   MIP $225

Hi Way Express Truck, metal, 15-1/2" long; 1940s
EX $100   NM $150   MIP $225

Hi Way Express Truck, tin, tin tires, 16" long; 1940s
EX $65   NM $125   MIP $190

Hi Way Express Truck, pressed steel
EX $95   NM $150   MIP $185

High Lift Loader with scoop, No. 1756, 13-1/2" long; lever-cont4rolled front bucket, steering wheel controls rear wheels; 1960s
EX $22   NM $43   MIP $65

Hydraulic Dump Truck, steel, made "motor noise," hydraulic lift, 20-14" long, early 1970s
EX $20   NM $30   MIP $50

Jalopy Pickup Truck, tin wind-up, 7" long
EX $60   NM $90   MIP $175

Jeep, Mini-Marx Blazer die-cast series, 1968
EX $3   NM $7   MIP $10

Jeep, 11" long; 1946-50
EX $75   NM $130   MIP $200

Jeep, 4-1/2" long; gray plastic, white plastic tires, "Willys" on hood
EX $3   NM $5   MIP $8

Jeep, 6" long; white metal body, metal hub caps; late 1960s
EX $4   NM $8   MIP $12

Jeep with Canvas Tarp and Driver, No. 868, 11-1/2" long; opening hood, collapsing windshield, removable camouflage canvas roof, polyethylene driver, plastic wheels with tin hubs; mid-1960s
EX $18   NM $36   MIP $55

Jeepster, mechanical, plastic
EX $110   NM $165   MIP $250

Johnny West Jeep, No. 4560, yellow plastic Jeep with black hood, black balloon tires, issued in Johnny West Camping Set with pup tent, campfire, cot and other accessories; 1973
EX $47   NM $92   MIP $140

Johnny West Jeep and Horse Trailer, 3' long; No. 4543, red plastic Jeep, black windshield and steering wheel, spare tire, white plastic horse trailer with lowering rear gate; 1966-68
EX $75   NM $150   MIP $225

Lazy Day Dairy Farm Pickup Truck and Trailer, 22" long
EX $50   NM $75   MIP $150

Lincoln Transfer and Storage Co. Mack Truck, wheels have cut-out spokes, tin litho, wind-up, 13" long, 1928
EX $350   NM $525   MIP $750

Lone Eagle Oil Co. Mack Truck, bright blue cab, green tank, wind-up, 12" long, 1930
EX $225   NM $350   MIP $550

Lumar concrete Co. Truck, plastic, 5-1/2" long; 1950s
EX $10   NM $16   MIP $22

Lumar Contractors Scoop/Dump Truck, 17-1/2" long; 1940s
EX $75   NM $125   MIP $200

Lumar Hydraulic Dump Truck, "Mechanical Action Hydraulic Dump Truck," 19" long; 1950s
EX $50   NM $80   MIP $125

Lumar Lines and Gasoline Set, 1948
EX $250   NM $375   MIP $725

Lumar Lines Truck, red cab, aluminum finished trailer, 14" long
EX $125   NM $200   MIP $300

Lumar Log Truck, die-cast tractor-trailer, made in England, 7" long
EX $20   NM $30   MIP $40

Lumar Motor Transport Truck, litho, 13" long, 1942
EX $75   NM $130   MIP $250

Lumar Stake Truck, die-cast tractor-trailer, made in England, 7" long
EX $20   NM $30   MIP $40

(Bob Smith)

Lumar Van Lines Coast to Coast, red/white cab; blue, red and white trailer; 15" long; 1950s
EX $50   NM $90   MIP $150

(Taylor's Toys John Taylor)

Lumar Wrecker Truck, black and white, "Nite-Day Service," 18" long; 1950s
EX $50   NM $90   MIP $150

Machinery Moving Truck, Marx
EX $60   NM $90   MIP $200

Mack Army Truck, pressed steel, wind-up, 7-1/2" long
EX $70   NM $100   MIP $250

Mack Army Truck, 13-1/2" long, 1929
EX $225   NM $350   MIP $600

Mack Army Truck, khaki brown body, wind-up, 10-1/2" long
EX $125   NM $225   MIP $400

Mack Army Truck, friction, 5" long, 1930
EX $125   NM $200   MIP $350

Mack Dump Truck, silver cab, medium blue dump, wind-up, 12-3/4" long, 1936
EX $225   NM $355   MIP $525

Mack Dump Truck, no driver, 19" long, 1930
EX $300   NM $450   MIP $650

Mack Dump Truck, tin litho, wind-up, 13-1/2" long, 1926
EX $225   NM $350   MIP $575

Mack Dump Truck, medium blue truck, wind-up, 13" long, 1934
EX $200   NM $350   MIP $525

Mack Dump Truck, dark red cab, medium blue bed, wind-up, 10" long, 1928
EX $150   NM $225   MIP $475

Mack Railroad Express Truck #7, tin, 1930s
EX $75   NM $125   MIP $450

Mack Towing Truck, dark green cab, wind-up, 8" long, 1926
EX $175   NM $275   MIP $450

Mack U.S. Mail Truck, black body, wind-up, 9-1/2" long
EX $250   NM $375   MIP $500

(Bob Smith)

Magnetic Crane and Truck, 1950
EX $100   NM $150   MIP $275

Mammoth Truck Train, truck w/five trailers, 1930s
EX $175   NM $262   MIP $350

Marx-A-Power, 18" long; giant bulldozer; 1960s
EX $18   NM $36   MIP $55

Meadowbrook Dairy Truck, 14" long; 1940
EX $150   NM $275   MIP $375

Mechanical Climbing Army Tank, No. 461, 5-7/8" long; wind-up plastic and steel; 1960s
EX $8   NM $17   MIP $25

Mechanical Sand Dump Truck, steel; 1940s
EX $100   NM $150   MIP $275

VEHICLES — MARX

Medical Corps Ambulance Truck, olive drab paint; 1940s
EX $100   **NM** $150   **MIP** $275

(Bob Smith)

Merchants Transfer Mack Truck, 13-1/3" long, 1928
EX $250   **NM** $375   **MIP** $600

Merchants Transfer Mack Truck, red open-stake truck, 10" long
EX $225   **NM** $350   **MIP** $450

Midget Cement Mixer Truck, 4" long; steel, cabover; 1969-70s
EX $4   **NM** $8   **MIP** $12

Midget Pickup Truck, 4" long; steel, cabover; 1969070s
EX $3   **NM** $5   **MIP** $8

Midget Sanitation Truck, 4" long; steel, cabover, dump action; 1969-70s
EX $3   **NM** $7   **MIP** $10

Midget Stake Truck, 4" long; steel, cabover; 1969070s
EX $3   **NM** $7   **MIP** $10

Midget Wrecker Truck, 4" long; steel, cabover, winch action; 1969-70s
EX $3   **NM** $7   **MIP** $10

Mighty Concrete Mixer Truck, 7" long; cabover, turning mixer; 1968-70s
EX $5   **NM** $11   **MIP** $16

Mighty Dump Truck, 7" long; cabover, dumping body; 1968-70s
EX $5   **NM** $9   **MIP** $14

Mighty Fire Rescue Truck, 6" long; red, with plastic ladders; 1968-70s
EX $5   **NM** $10   **MIP** $15

Mighty Pickup Truck, 7" long; cabover style; 1968-70s
EX $5   **NM** $9   **MIP** $14

Mighty Sanitation Truck, 7" long; cabover, loader bucket; 1969-70s
EX $5   **NM** $11   **MIP** $16

Military Cannon Truck, olive drab paint, cannon shoots marbles, 10" long, 1939
EX $125   **NM** $200   **MIP** $250

Milk Truck, white truck, 4" long; 1940
EX $60   **NM** $90   **MIP** $120

Miniature Mayflower Moving Van, operating lights
EX $60   **NM** $90   **MIP** $125

Mini-Marx Auto Transport, plastic auto hauler for "Mini-Marx Blazers" for "Super Speed Blazers" die-cast cars; late 1960s
EX $15   **NM** $30   **MIP** $45

Moon Crawler, 11" long; No. 1738, Johnny and Jane Apollo vehicle, wheels with five

"legs," flip-open green-tinted bubble over cockpit, battery-operated; 1968
EX $27   **NM** $53   **MIP** $80

Motor Market Delivery, 14" long; 1940s-1950s
EX $50   **NM** $90   **MIP** $150

Motor Market Truck, 10" long, 1939
EX $100   **NM** $175   **MIP** $225

Navy Jeep, wind-up
EX $50   **NM** $75   **MIP** $100

North American Van Lines Tractor Trailer, wind-up, 13" long; 1940s
EX $100   **NM** $175   **MIP** $225

Panel Wagon Truck, Marx
EX $30   **NM** $55   **MIP** $75

(Toy Shop File Photo)

Pet Shop Truck, plastic, six compartments w/six vinyl dogs, 11" long
EX $125   **NM** $200   **MIP** $250

Pickup, large pickup truck from "Big Bruiser" sets; mid-1960s
EX $10   **NM** $20   **MIP** $30

Pickup Truck, blue/yellow w/wood tires, 9" long; 1940s
EX $50   **NM** $75   **MIP** $150

(Toy Shop File Photo)

Polar Ice Co. Ice Truck, 13" long; 1940s, stake body, picture of polar bear
EX $100   **NM** $175   **MIP** $275

Police Patrol Mack Truck, wind-up, 10" long
EX $200   **NM** $300   **MIP** $475

Popeye Dippy Dumper Truck, Popeye is celluloid, tin wind-up
EX $325   **NM** $500   **MIP** $800

Powerhouse Dump Truck, pressed steel, plastic windshield, 19" long; 1960s
EX $25   **NM** $35   **MIP** $55

Pure Milk Dairy Truck, glass bottles, pressed steel; 1940
EX $100   **NM** $200   **MIP** $300

Railway Express Agency Truck, green closed van truck; 1940s
EX $90   **NM** $135   **MIP** $300

Range Rider, tin wind-up, 1930s
EX $250   **NM** $375   **MIP** $500

Rapid Express Pickup, wind-up, 9" long; 1940s
EX $125   **NM** $180   **MIP** $225

Rat Patrol, No. 1545, large plastic Jeep packaged with Jack Moffitt and Sam Troy plastic dolls, and numerous accessories; 1967
EX $28   **NM** $56   **MIP** $85

(Taylor's Toys John Taylor)

RCA Television Service Truck, plastic Ford panel truck, 8-1/2" long; 1948-50
EX $150   **NM** $225   **MIP** $300

Reversing Road Roller, tin wind-up
EX $60   **NM** $100   **MIP** $125

Road Builder Tank, 1950
EX $125   **NM** $200   **MIP** $250

Road Grader, 17" long; No. 1760, enclosed cab, adjustable scraper, 1960s-70s
EX $15   **NM** $28   **MIP** $55

Road Grader, 6-1/2" long; orange hard plastic
EX $7   **NM** $15   **MIP** $22

Rocker Dump Truck, 17-1/2" long
EX $60   **NM** $90   **MIP** $120

Rocker Dump Truck, No. 1751, 17-1/2" long; rocker dumping unit swivel-mounted to two-wheel tractor; 1960s
EX $20   **NM** $48   **MIP** $75

Roy Rogers and Trigger Cattle Truck, metal, 15" long; 1950s
EX $60   **NM** $100   **MIP** $225

Royal Oil Co. Mack Truck, dark red cab, medium green tank, wind-up, 8-1/4" long, 1927
EX $200   **NM** $300   **MIP** $500

Royal Van Co. Mack Truck, 1927
EX $250   **NM** $375   **MIP** $600

(Toy Shop File Photo)

Royal Van Co. Mack Truck, red cab, tin litho and paint, wind-up, 9" long, 1928
EX $210   **NM** $315   **MIP** $550

Run Right To Read's Truck, 14" long; 1940
EX $125   **NM** $200   **MIP** $250

Safari Adventure Jeep, 14" long; tan Jeep with zebra-stripe hood, accessories including movie camera, spare tire, and radio; 1975-78
EX $23   **NM** $46   **MIP** $70

Safari Adventure Pursuit Truck, No. 2190, tan or off-white plastic stake-bed truck, black winch on hood; 1975-78
EX $15   **NM** $30   **MIP** $45

Sand and Gravel Truck, "Builder's Supply Co.," tin wind-up, 1920
EX $150   **NM** $275   **MIP** $350

Sand Truck, tin litho, 12-1/2" long; 1940s
EX $125   **NM** $200   **MIP** $275

Sand Truck, 9" long; 1948
EX $100   **NM** $150   **MIP** $200

Sand-Gravel Dump Truck, tin litho, 12" long; 1950
EX $150   **NM** $225   **MIP** $300

Sand-Gravel Dump Truck, blue cab, yellow dump w/"Gravel" on side, tin, 1930s
EX $140   **NM** $225   **MIP** $285

Sanitation Truck, 1940s
EX $135   **NM** $200   **MIP** $270

Scoop & Dump Truck, 17" long; 1940s
EX $50   **NM** $90   **MIP** $150

Searchlight Truck, pressed steel, 9-3/4" long, 1930s
EX $160   **NM** $250   **MIP** $325

Shop-Rite (tractor-trailer), 24" long; No. 3640, red cabover, silver van trailer; 1966-67
EX $25   **NM** $50   **MIP** $75

Side Dump Truck, 10" long, 1930s
EX $140   **NM** $225   **MIP** $280

Side Dump Truck, 1940
EX $90   **NM** $130   **MIP** $275

Side Dump Truck and Trailer, 15" long, 1935
EX $150   **NM** $225   **MIP** $300

Sinclair Tanker, tin, 14" long; 1940s
EX $150   **NM** $225   **MIP** $300

Stake Bed Truck, rubber stamped chicken on one side of truck, bunny on other
EX $100   **NM** $150   **MIP** $200

Stake Bed Truck, red cab, blue stake bed, 6" long, 1930s
EX $75   **NM** $125   **MIP** $150

Stake Bed Truck, red cab, yellow and red trailer, 14" long
EX $100   **NM** $150   **MIP** $200

Stake Bed Truck, medium blue cab, red stake bed, 10" long; 1940
EX $75   **NM** $130   **MIP** $185

Stake Bed Truck, pressed steel, wooden wheels, 7" long, 1936
EX $60   **NM** $90   **MIP** $200

Stake Bed Truck, red cab, green stake bed, 20" long; 1947
EX $100   **NM** $150   **MIP** $200

Stake Bed Truck and Trailer, red truck, silver or blue stake bed, 18" long
EX $125   **NM** $200   **MIP** $250

Stony Smith Jeep, 21-1/4" long; No. 4540, green hard plastic, for Stony plastic doll, with or without star on hood; 1966-68
EX $15   **NM** $30   **MIP** $45

Stony Smith Jeep and Trailer, No. 4544, Jeep with green plastic Search Light Trailer, 1968
EX $30   **NM** $60   **MIP** $90

Streamline Mechanical Hauler, Van, and Tank Truck Combo, heavy gauge steel, 10 3/8" long, 1936
EX $170   **NM** $275   **MIP** $350

Sunshine Fruit Growers Truck, red cab, yellow/white trailer w/blue roof, 14" long
EX $125   **NM** $175   **MIP** $250

Super Crane, 2' long; battery-operated and hand-crank operation, plastic truck with swiveling "Super Crane" body, boom with clamshell, drag bucket, and sky hook, rolling on six tires; 1964-65
EX $25   **NM** $50   **MIP** $75

Super Crane, plastic and metal, battery-operated, 18" long truck body; 1960s
EX $100   **NM** $150   **MIP** $200

Tipper Dump Truck, wind-up, 9-3/4" long; 1950
EX $75   **NM** $130   **MIP** $175

Tow Truck, aluminum finish, wind-up, 6-1/4" long
EX $95   **NM** $150   **MIP** $190

Tow Truck, aluminum finsih, tin litho wind-up, 6-1/4" long
EX $75   **NM** $125   **MIP** $150

Tow Truck, 10" long, 1935
EX $125   **NM** $200   **MIP** $250

Tow Truck, red cab, yellow towing unit, 6" long, 1930s
EX $137   **NM** $200   **MIP** $275

Toyland Dairy Truck, 10" long
EX $140   **NM** $210   **MIP** $280

(Bob Smith)

Toyland's Farm Products Mack Milk Truck, w/12 wooden milk bottles, 10-1/4" long, 1931
EX $200   **NM** $300   **MIP** $400

Toytown Express Truck, plastic cab
EX $45   **NM** $70   **MIP** $95

Tractor Trailer with Dumpster, blue/yellow hauler, tan dumpster
EX $125   **NM** $200   **MIP** $250

Truck Train, stake hauler and four trailers, 41" long, 1938
EX $350   **NM** $550   **MIP** $725

Truck Train, stake hauler and five trailers, 41" long, 1933
EX $250   **NM** $400   **MIP** $525

Truck with Electric Lights, battery-operated lights, 10" long, 1935
EX $125   **NM** $200   **MIP** $375

Truck with Electric Lights, 15" long, 1930s
EX $110   **NM** $165   **MIP** $300

Truck with Searchlight, toolbox behind cab, 10" long, 1930s
EX $150   **NM** $225   **MIP** $400

U.S. Air Force Willy's Jeep, tin body, plastic figures
EX $70   **NM** $100   **MIP** $140

U.S. Army Jeep with Trailer, Marx
EX $100   **NM** $150   **MIP** $200

(Toy Shop File Photo)

U.S. Mail Truck, metal, 14" long; 1950s
EX $225   **NM** $350   **MIP** $450

U.S. Trucking Co. Mack Truck, dark maroon cab, friction, 5-1/2" long, 1930
EX $100   **NM** $150   **MIP** $200

Van Truck, plastic, 10" long; 1950s
EX $40   **NM** $60   **MIP** $80

Western Auto (tractor-trailer), 25" long; red cabover, "Western Auto" silver van trailer with dual tandems; 1967-68
EX $42   **NM** $83   **MIP** $125

Western Auto Truck, steel, 25" long
EX $60   **NM** $90   **MIP** $125

(Richard Jansen)

Willy's Jeep, steel, 12" long, 1938
EX $125   **NM** $200   **MIP** $250

Willy's Jeep and Trailer, 1940s
EX $100   **NM** $160   **MIP** $215

(RLM MacNary Collection)

Wrecker Truck, 1930s
EX $145   **NM** $225   **MIP** $290

MATCHBOX

KING-SIZE

K1-1, Hydraulic Shovel, 1960, Yellow body and front loader, no plastic windows, no interior, gray plastic wheels

EX $30   **NM** $65   **MIP** $95

(KP Photo by Dr. Douglas Sadecky)

K1-2, Foden Tipper Truck, 1964, Red cab and chassis, orange dumper bed with "Hoveringham" decals or labels on sides, red plastic wheels with removable black plastic tires, blue plastic windows, no interior, axle suspension system to roll over bumps, silver metal horns on cab, 4-1/2"

EX $25   **NM** $45   **MIP** $70

K1-3, O & K Excavator, 1970, Red body with silver excavator arm, red hubs with eight black plastic removable tires, "MH6", "O&K" and white stripe labels on sides, 4-15/16"

EX $15   **NM** $25   **MIP** $35

K2-1, Dumper Truck, 1960, Blocky red body and chassis with open cab, gray or black plastic tires on green metal hubs, "Muir-Hill" decals

EX $25   **NM** $45   **MIP** $75

(KP Photo by Dr. Douglas Sadecky)

K2-2, KW-Dart Dump Truck, 1964, Yellow articulated body with silver trim on engine and hood. Red hubs with removable black plastic tires, "KW-Dart" decals with arrow graphic, no window plastic, 5-5/8"

EX $30   **NM** $65   **MIP** $95

K2-3, Scammell Heavy Wreck Truck, 1969, White or gold body with red plastic hubs and black removable wheels, silver metal hooks, red towing arm, silver horns on cab roof, "Esso" labels on doors, 4-3/4"

EX $22   **NM** $45   **MIP** $70

(KP Photo by Dr. Douglas Sadecky)

K3-1, Caterpillar Bulldozer, 1960, Yellow body with green rubber treads and unpainted metal or yellow or red plastic roller wheels, cast tow hook, red-painted engine

EX $25   **NM** $50   **MIP** $85

(KP Photo by Dr. Douglas Sadecky)

K3-2, Hatra Tractor Shovel, 1965, Orange-red body with articulating center and lifting loader. Blue-tinted plastic windows, "Hatra" decals on sides of cab, red hubs with black plastic removable tires, 6"

EX $36   **NM** $65   **MIP** $110

K3-3, Massey-Ferguson Tractor and Trailer, 1970, Red cab and hood with gray engine and base, yellow hubs with removable black plastic tires, white grille, green plastic windows. Trailer with yellow chassis, red dumper bed, yellow hubs with black removable tires. Set measures 8"

EX $17   **NM** $28   **MIP** $55

(KP Photo)

K4-1, International Tractor, 1960, Red body with "McCormick International" and "B-250" decals, green, red or orange hubs with black plastic removable tires, 2-7/8". Early versions with green metal hubs have approx. $80 MIP value

EX $25   **NM** $40   **MIP** $65

(KP Photo by Dr. Douglas Sadecky)

K4-2, GMC Tractor with Hopper Train, 1967, Red tractor with two silver hopper trailers, red plastic hubs with black plastic removable wheels, opening chutes, "Fruehauf" decals on each trailer, set measures 11-1/4"

EX $55   **NM** $90   **MIP** $145

(KP Photo)

K4-3, Leyland Tipper, 1969, Red cab and chassis, silver dumper bed, red hubs with black plastic removable tires, (duals in rear), "Wates" and "LE Transport" labels most common. Amber plastic windows, yellow plastic interior, 4-1/2". Some hard-to-find models with green cabs exist, but have approx. $300 MIP values. Other models include orange cabs with green dumper beds

EX $12   **NM** $20   **MIP** $45

(KP Photo by Dr. Douglas Sadecky)

K5-1, Tipper Truck, 1961, Yellow body, silver-painted grille, silver metal or red plastic hubs with black tires, "Foden" decal on sides of hood, 4-1/4". First-version siver-hub models about $80 MIP

EX $25   **NM** $50   **MIP** $80

(KP Photo)

K5-2, Racing Car Transporter, 1967, Medium-green body, cream plastic interior, clear plastic windows and skylights, red plastic hubs with black removable tires, decals on sides show racing car graphic with "Racing Transporter," "BP," and "LeMans, Sebring, Silverstone, Nurburgring." Silver metal base. Opening tailgate reveals tilting ramp and space for two racing cars, 5". This model entered the King-Size line, after being number M-6 in the Major Packs series

EX $25   **NM** $50   **MIP** $80

K6-1, Allis-Chalmers Earth Scraper, 1961, Orange scraper with silver metal or red plastic hubs and black plastic tires. Adjustable scraper bed with springs (sometimes missing) "Allis-Chalmers" decals, 5-7/8"

EX $45   **NM** $80   **MIP** $130

(KP Photo)

K6-2, Mercedes-Benz "Binz" Ambulance, 1967, White body with blue plastic windows and dome light, black base, red cross decal on hood and shield decals on opening doors, opening rear hatch with white plastic patient and red plastic blanket, silver hubs with black plastic tires, silver metal grille and bumpers, "True Guide" steering, 4-1/8"

EX $12   **NM** $25   **MIP** $55

(KP Photo by Dr. Douglas Sadecky)

K7-1, Curtiss-Wright Rear Dumper, 1961, Yellow articulated body with silver metal hubs and black plastic tires, tilting dumper bed, "Curtiss-Wright" decals, red-painted engine block, 5-3/4"

EX $40   **NM** $85   **MIP** $135

K7-2, SD Refuse Truck, 1967, Red cab & chassis, silver rear refuse unit, "Cleansing Service" decals or labels, red plastic wheels with black plastic tires, cream-colored plastic interior, clear plastic windows, 4-5/8"

EX $15   **NM** $25   **MIP** $45

(KP Photo by Dr. Douglas Sadecky)

K8-1, Prime Mover and Transporter with Caterpillar Tractor, 1962, Orange body

& trailer, yellow "Laing" decals, metal towhook, unpainted metal or red plastic wheels with black plastic tires, yellow tractor with green treads and no blade, set measures 12-1/2"

EX $125   **NM** $180   **MIP** $275

K8-2, Car Transporter, 1967, Green or yellow cab, orange or yellow trailer, orange or red plastic wheels with black plastic tires, "Car Auction Collection" and "Farnborough Meashan" decals on trailer, 8-1/2"

EX $25   **NM** $45   **MIP** $80

K8-3, Caterpillar Traxcavator, 1970, Various versions of shades of yellow cab, orange shovel & arms, figure, yellow or black wheels with green or black treads, "available mid-1970" in catalog, 4-1/4"

EX $15   **NM** $25   **MIP** $40

K9-1, Diesel Road Roller, 1962, Green body, red metal rollers, gray or red driver, red "Aveling Barford" decals on sides with white reversed type, 3-3/4"

EX $35   **NM** $65   **MIP** $95

(KP Photo)

K9-2, Claas Combine Harvester, 1967, Green or red body, red or yellow reels, "Claas" decals or labels, yellow plastic wheels with black plastic tires, 5-1/2"

EX $20   **NM** $40   **MIP** $75

K10-1, Aveling-Barford Tractor Shovel, 1963, Light-blue body & shovel, red seat, with or without air filter, unpainted metal or red plastic wheels with black plastic tires, 4-1/8"

EX $30   **NM** $60   **MIP** $90

K10-2, Pipe Truck, 1967, Yellow cab & trailer chassis, black house-shaped decal on cab doors, gray plastic pipes, red plastic wheels with black plastic tires, later issues had Superfast wheels and pink cab and chassis, 8"

EX $20   **NM** $40   **MIP** $75

(KP Photo)

K11-1, Fordson Tractor and Trailer, 1963, Blue tractor body & trailer chassis, light-gray trailer bed, orange metal or plastic wheels with black plastic tires, 6-1/4"

EX $25   **NM** $45   **MIP** $80

K11-2, DAF Car Transporter, 1969, Metallic blue cab with gold trailer or yellow cab with orange & yellow trailer, DAF

labels, red plastic wheels with black plastic tires or Superfast Wheels, 9"

EX $20   **NM** $50   **MIP** $85

(KP Photo by Dr. Douglas Sadecky)

K12-1, Heavy Breakdown Wreck Truck, 1963, Green body, yellow boom, with or without roof lights, unpainted metal or red plastic wheels with black plastic tires, 4-3/4"

EX $25   **NM** $50   **MIP** $75

(KP Photo)

K12-2, Scammell Crane Truck, 1970, Yellow cab & crane, red plastic wheels with black plastic tires or orange body & crane with Superfast wheels, 6"

EX $20   **NM** $35   **MIP** $50

(KP Photo by Dr. Douglas Sadecky)

K13-1, Ready-Mix Concrete Truck, 1963, Orange body & mixer with unpainted metal or red plastic wheels with black plastic tires, green plastic windows, no interior, "Readymix" or "RMC" decals on mixer barrel, 4-1/2"

EX $25   **NM** $50   **MIP** $75

(KP Photo by Dr. Douglas Sadecky)

K14-1, Taylor Jumbo Crane, 1964, Yellow body & crane, green windows, red or

yellow weight box, red plastic wheels with black plastic tires, 5-1/4"
EX $25   **NM** $50   **MIP** $75

(KP Photo)

K15-1, Merryweather Fire Engine, 1964, Red body, gray extending ladder, red plastic wheels with black plastic tires or Superfast wheels, 6-1/8"
EX $25   **NM** $45   **MIP** $65

(KP Photo by Dr. Douglas Sadecky)

K16-1, Dodge Tractor with Twin Tippers, 1966, Green cab & trailer chassis, yellow dumps, Dodge Trucks decals, red plastic wheels with black plastic tires; later issues had yellow cab with blue dump & Superfast wheels, 11-7/8"
EX $65   **NM** $135   **MIP** $185

(KP Photo by Dr. Douglas Sadecky)

K17-1, Low Loader with Bulldozer, 1967, Green Ford cab & trailer, red plastic wheels with black plastic tires, red Case bulldozer body, yellow roof & blade, green treads, "Laing" or "Taylor Woodrow" decals or labels, later issues had Superfast wheels and lime-green cab and trailer, 9-1/2"
EX $60   **NM** $90   **MIP** $135

K18-1, Articulated Horse Box, 1967, Red Dodge cab with tan trailer, clear windows on trailer, gray ramp, four white horses, red plastic wheels with black plastic tires, later issues had Superfast wheels , 6-5/8"
EX $35   **NM** $55   **MIP** $90

K19-1, Scammell Tipper Truck, 1967, Red cab & yellow dump, red plastic wheels with black plastic tires or Superfast wheels, 4-3/4"
EX $20   **NM** $35   **MIP** $50

K20-1, Tractor Transporter, 1968, Red Ford cab & trailer, red plastic wheels with black plastic tires, green plastic windows, 3 blue tractors with yellow wheels, later issues had Superfast wheels, 9"
EX $65   **NM** $100   **MIP** $150

K21-1, Mercury Cougar, 1968, Gold body, red or white interior, unpainted metal wheels with black plastic tires, 4-1/8". Shown in blue in 1968 catalog, announcing model would be available mid-year
EX $25   **NM** $50   **MIP** $75

K22-1, Dodge Charger, 1969, Dark-blue body, light-blue interior, unpainted metal wheels with black plastic tires with "True Guide" steering, 4-1/2". Shown in 1969 catalog, announcing available mid-year
EX $25   **NM** $50   **MIP** $75

(KP Photo)

K23-1, Mercury Police Car, 1969, White body, red interior, blue dome lights, police labels, unpainted metal wheels with black plastic tires with "True Guide" steering or Superfast wheels, 4-3/8". Introduced in 1969 catalog as being available mid-year
EX $20   **NM** $35   **MIP** $50

K24-1, Lamborghini Miura, 1969, Red body, white interior, unpainted metal wheels with black plastic tires and "True Guide" steering, many color & wheel variations exist, 4"
EX $20   **NM** $35   **MIP** $50

MATCHBOX

REGULAR WHEELS

1-1RW, Road Roller, 1953, One of the first Matchbox offerings, this model had a "steamroller"-style large-roofed cab that matched the large toy produced by Lesney. Green paint on body can vary in shade, red metal wheels and rollers
EX $40   **NM** $75   **MIP** $125

1-2RW, Diesel Road Roller, 1955, Second in the series, but first with a smaller cab, roller attachment a little more snug than the first version, red metal wheels and roller, driver available in light and dark tan variations, gold-painted upright tow hook, 2-1/4"
EX $30   **NM** $60   **MIP** $110

1-3RW, Road Roller, 1958, Third in the series, this casting kept the driver, but changed the tow hook at rear of the tractor. It still featured red metal wheels and rollers, 2-1/4"
EX $45   **NM** $70   **MIP** $95

(KP Photo)

1-4RW, Diesel Road Roller, 1962, Green with orange/red plastic wheels, open window on cab behind driver, tow hook on back. 2-5/8", "Aveling Barford Road Roller" on base near rear wheels
EX $12   **NM** $35   **MIP** $70

(KP Photo, George Cuhaj collection)

1-5RW, Mercedes-Benz Truck, 1968, Light pea-green, with orange or yellow plastic canopy, truck could be hitched to a matching trailer, released the same year, 3"
EX $5   **NM** $12   **MIP** $20

2-1RW, Dumper, 1953, This first version featured a gold-painted front grille on a green body with red dump bed, 1-1/2"
EX $25   **NM** $60   **MIP** $100

(KP Photo by Dr. Douglas Sadecky)

2-2RW, Dumper, 1957, Second casting is larger than first, with less painted detail. First issue with metal wheels, second with gray plastic wheels. Green body, red dumper bed, 2". Pictured here 2-3RW Muir-Hill Dumper
EX $25   **NM** $60   **MIP** $90

(KP Photo, George Cuhaj collection)

2-3RW, Dumper, 1961, Short, blocky cab with "Laing" or "Muir-Hill" decal on right-hand door. Red cab with pea-green dumper bed, black plastic wheels, 2-1/8". Although the cab is different, this model is very similar to the K-2 dumper released one year earlier. "Muir-Hill" decal versions can have about $100 MIP value
EX $12   **NM** $22   **MIP** $40

(KP Photo, George Cuhaj collection)

2-3RW, Dumper, 1961, Another view of 2-3RW, also simply called "Dumper" in Matchbox 1966 catalog
EX $7   **NM** $12   **MIP** $30

(KP Photo, George Cuhaj collection)

2-4RW, Mercedes-Benz Trailer, 1968, Pea-green trailer released same year as Mercedes-Benz Truck, 1-5RW. Also came with orange or yellow canopy, 3-1/2"
EX $5   **NM** $10   **MIP** $20

(KP Photo by Dr. Douglas Sadecky)

3-1RW, Cement Mixer, 1953, Another early Matchbox, this model mirrors one of Lesney's first larger die-cast toys. Variations seem to exist in castings, earlier models measure slightly larger at 1-3/4" length than the later ones, coming in at 1-1/2" length. Orange metal or gray plastic wheels
EX $25   **NM** $60   **MIP** $120

(KP Photo, Tom Michael collection)

3-2RW, Bedford Tipper Truck, 1961, Available in red and maroon dumper variations, as well as gray and black plastic wheels, 2-1/2". Gray plastic wheeled version harder to find, about $120 MIP
EX $10   **NM** $25   **MIP** $60

(KP Photo)

3-3RW, Mercedes-Benz "Binz" Ambulance, 1968, White or cream body with Red Cross label or decal and plastic patient on stretcher. This was a smaller version of the K-6 ambulance released one year earlier, 2-7/8". Unpainted base with textured surface along sides and near back tailgate
EX $10   **NM** $18   **MIP** $30

(KP Photo)

3-3RW, Mercedes-Benz "Binz" Ambulance, 1968, Variation photo showing

cream paint and decal version of Mercedes ambulance
EX $10   **NM** $18   **MIP** $30

4-1RW, Tractor, 1954, Red Massey-Harris tractor body and fenders; a small version of larger Lesney Massey-Harris toy tractor
EX $35   **NM** $65   **MIP** $125

4-2RW, Massey-Harris Tractor, 1957, Red with no fenders. An update on the previous model, this tractor was re-released painted green in 1994 as an anniversary issue. Metal wheel and gray plastic wheel variations, some casting variations with 1-1/2" and 1-3/4" lengths
EX $40   **NM** $75   **MIP** $135

(KP Photo, George Cuhaj collection)

4-3RW, Triumph Motorcycle w/Sidecar, 1960, Light metallic blue with 24-spoke silver wheels and black tires, 2-1/8"
EX $17   **NM** $30   **MIP** $85

(KP Photo, George Cuhaj collection)

4-4RW, Dodge Stake Truck, 1967, Yellow cab and body with green plastic stakes. A popular model, Matchbox made many toy trucks with this Dodge cab style, 2-7/8". Models with blue-green stakes, a very slight color difference, can have about $150 MIP value
EX $8   **NM** $16   **MIP** $25

5-1RW, Double Decker Bus, 1954, First of Matchbox's London Buses, this one featured decals that read "Buy Matchbox Series" on the side, 2"
EX $15   **NM** $45   **MIP** $80

(KP Photo, Tom Michael collection)

5-2RW, Double Decker Bus, 1958, Second London Bus, casting slightly larger, at 2-1/4" length. "No. 5" cast into front of bus, no interior. Available with metal

and gray plastic wheels, with a variety of decals
EX $40   **NM** $80   **MIP** $130

5-3RW, Routemaster London Bus, 1961, Red, with gray or black plastic wheels, "Visco-Static" decal most common. No interior in bus, major change from last model: a wider front grille, with cast headlights on front fenders
EX $20   **NM** $45   **MIP** $80

(KP Photo)

5-4RW, Routemaster London Bus, 1965, Red body, white plastic interior-first Matchbox model bus to feature one. Like 5-3RW, the "Visco-Static" decals and labels are the most common, 2-3/4"
EX $6   **NM** $12   **MIP** $25

6-1RW, Quarry Truck, 1954, Orange body with gray dumper bed. No interior. Most commonly seen with metal wheels, crimped or rounded axles, 2-1/4"
EX $20   **NM** $45   **MIP** $85

6-2RW, Quarry Truck, 1959, Yellow body, black plastic wheels most common, red, white and black decal on cab doors, cab extends the full width of the front of truck, appears first in 1959 catalog with black plastic wheels
EX $15   **NM** $35   **MIP** $75

(KP Photo)

6-3RW, Euclid 10-Wheel Quarry Truck, 1964, Yellow body, no decals, exposed engine shows on casting, partial cab does not extend across body of truck, 2-5/8"
EX $7   **NM** $15   **MIP** $30

(KP Photo, George Cuhaj collection)

6-4RW, Ford Pickup, 1969, Red, with white plastic camper top and white or silver plastic front grille. Featured "Autosteer," a

Matchbox innovation making its appearance in the 1969 catalog, that "turns the front wheels in either direction by simple pressure." 2-3/4"
EX $10   **NM** $20   **MIP** $30

(KP Photo by Dr. Douglas Sadecky)

7-1RW, Horse-Drawn Milk Float, 1954, Orange wagon body, white painted driver, brown horse. Available with metal spoked or gray solid plastic wheels, 2-1/4". Quite a detailed little model
EX $45   **NM** $75   **MIP** $125

(KP Photo, George Cuhaj collection)

7-2RW, Ford Anglia, 1961, Light blue body, no interior, gray, silver or black plastic wheels, silver painted grille, bumper and headlights, 2-5/8", black painted baseplate, tow hook. Gray plastic wheel versions, about $90 MIP; silver plastic wheel versions, about $55 MIP
EX $25   **NM** $50   **MIP** $80

(KP Photo by Dr. Douglas Sadecky)

7-2RW, Ford Anglia, 1961, A view of a gray-plastic-wheel version of the Ford Anglia, a harder-to-find variation
EX $30   **NM** $60   **MIP** $110

(KP Photo, Tom Michael collection)

7-3RW, Ford Refuse Truck, 1967, Red body, gray and silver dumper section, tilts together when dumped, no interior, black plastic wheels, green window plastic, 3"

EX $10   **NM** $18   **MIP** $30

8-1RW, Caterpillar Tractor, 1955, Yellow or orange with cast driver, silver painted grille. Unpainted roller wheels for treads, 1-1/2". Fully exposed engine under hood. Note: Orange variation harder to find, MIP value can reach over $200; yellow versions with painted drivers also about $200 MIP

EX $20   **NM** $40   **MIP** $85

8-2RW, Caterpillar Tractor, 1959, Yellow, different casting with engine partially covered by hood, and cast "roller wheels" between two actual turning metal wheels. Driver cast with toy, 1-3/4", green or gray rubber treads

EX $25   **NM** $65   **MIP** $90

8-3RW, Caterpillar Crawler Tractor, 1961, Yellow body with cast driver, metal or plastic tread wheels, very similar to previous casting, models with silver plastic roller wheels about $90 MIP

EX $20   **NM** $40   **MIP** $65

(KP Photo, Tom Michael collection)

8-4RW, Caterpillar Crawler Tractor, 1965, Yellow, cast without driver, black plastic roller wheels, 2", gray or black rubber treads

EX $12   **NM** $22   **MIP** $35

(KP Photo, George Cuhaj collection)

8-5RW, Ford Mustang Fastback, 1966, White, with red interior and tow hook. Black plastic tires on silver wheels. Unique steering lever on driver's side allows front wheels to turn left or right, 2-7/8", orange versions are quite rare, about $300 MIP

EX $12   **NM** $25   **MIP** $45

9-1RW, Fire Escape, 1955, Red with cast driver, metal wheels, gold-painted trim, 2-1/4", no front bumper in casting

EX $20   **NM** $45   **MIP** $80

9-2RW, Fire Escape, 1957, Red, cast with driver, metal wheels most common, versions with gray plastic wheels about $400 MIP, front bumper included in casting, 2-1/4"

EX $20   **NM** $45   **MIP** $80

(KP Photo)

9-3RW, Merryweather Marquis Fire Engine, 1959, Red body with cab, gold ladder, black plastic wheels (first versions had gray plastic wheels), ladder colors can vary, 2-5/8", simply called "Fire Truck" in 1966 catalog

EX $20   **NM** $55   **MIP** $70

(KP Photo, Tom Michael collection)

9-4RW, Boat and Trailer, 1967, Plastic blue and white boat with blue die-cast trailer, black plastic wheels. First time a stand-alone trailer makes appearance in regular wheels line

EX $10   **NM** $20   **MIP** $35

10-1RW, Mechanical Horse and Trailer, 1955, Red, three-wheeled cab and gray stake-style trailer, metal wheels, 3"

EX $55   **NM** $70   **MIP** $95

(KP Photo by Dr. Douglas Sadecky)

10-2RW, Mechanical Horse and Trailer, 1957, Second casting of Scammell Scarab, red three-wheeled cab and light-tan stake-style trailer with fenders. Grille can be painted or unpainted, metal wheels, 3". Appears first in 1957 catalog/flyer

EX $40   **NM** $60   **MIP** $95

(KP Photo, George Cuhaj collection)

10-3RW, Sugar Container Truck, 1962, Blue Foden truck body with "Tate & Lyle" decal, with silver, gray, or black plastic wheels (shown). Popular Foden cab design, 2-5/8". Gray-wheeled models tend to have higher MIP values, up to $200

EX $25   **NM** $50   **MIP** $80

(KP Photo, John Brown Sr. collection)

10-4RW, Pipe Truck, 1967, Red Leyland die-cast body, silver grille and baseplate, gray plastic pipes. "Ergomatic Cab" written on baseplate, 3". The Ergomatic cab was a new feature on large British trucks, including Leyland and AEC, beginning in the mid-sixties, so this model reflected the latest advance at time of release

EX $8   **NM** $12   **MIP** $25

11-1RW, Road Tanker, 1955, Yellow or red ERF truck body, metal wheels, "Esso" decal on rear of tank, 2", painted side gas tanks, crimped axles

EX $40   **NM** $75   **MIP** $115

11-2RW, Road Tanker, 1959, Red ERF truck body, metal wheels, gray or black plastic wheels, variations include silver painted side gas tanks and grilles, slightly larger casting, 2-1/2"

EX $35   **NM** $60   **MIP** $100

(KP Photo by Dr. Douglas Sadecky)

11-3RW, Jumbo Crane, 1965, Yellow, red plastic hook, large black plastic wheels in front near cab, small in back-1966 catalog illustration looks more like King Size version, K-14, with what appears to be a die-cast hook. Some with red counterweights, 3". Shown here with 42-3RW Iron Fairy Crane

EX $8   **NM** $15   **MIP** $30

(KP Photo, John Brown Sr. collection)

11-4RW, Scaffold Truck, mid-1969, Mercedes-Benz truck, silver body with yellow plastic scaffold sections in stake-style bed. "Builders Supply Company" decal on side, 2-5/8", released late in 1969, just before transition to Superfast

EX $8   **NM** $12   **MIP** $25

(KP Photo, John Brown Sr. collection)

12-1RW, Land Rover, 1957, Dark green body with tan driver, metal wheels. No real windshield, just a low flat piece of the casting appearing where the base of a windshield would be. Slight casting variations, some 1-5/8" length, later editions, 1-3/4" length. Silver-painted grille

EX $15 **NM** $40 **MIP** $85

(KP Photo, George Cuhaj collection)

12-2RW, Land Rover, 1960, Dark green, black or gray plastic wheels (black more common). Open cab, model shown has bent windshield. "Land-Rover Series II" on black baseplate

EX $15 **NM** $40 **MIP** $75

(KP Photo)

12-3RW, Safari Land Rover, 1965, Dark green body, dark brown plastic luggage on top, white interior, white tow hook, black plastic baseplate. First issue of the Safari Land Rover, says "Land Rover Safari" on base, 2-3/4"

EX $8 **NM** $15 **MIP** $25

(KP Photo)

12-3RW, Safari Land Rover, 1967, Medium-blue body, light reddish-brown plastic luggage, white plastic interior and tow hook, black plastic baseplate with "Land Rover Safari." Second issue of same casting in blue

EX $8 **NM** $15 **MIP** $25

(KP Photo, Tom Michael collection)

13-1RW, Wreck Truck, 1955, Tan Bedford truck with red tow hook and scaffold, metal wheels, silver-painted grille and bumper, 2-1/4"

EX $35 **NM** $50 **MIP** $75

13-2RW, Wreck Truck, 1958, Tan Bedford body, red boom section, metal or gray plastic wheels, no interior, slightly smaller than previous casting at 2"

EX $40 **NM** $60 **MIP** $90

(KP Photo, George Cuhaj collection)

13-3RW, Wreck Truck, 1961, Red body with metal or plastic tow hook, and gray or black plastic wheels, decal on side of truck says "A.A. & R.A.C. Matchbox Garages Breakdown Service," silver trim on front grille

EX $18 **NM** $45 **MIP** $110

(KP Photo, George Cuhaj collection)

13-4RW, Wreck Truck, 1966, Dodge Wreck Truck with yellow cab, green tow bed, red plastic hook, clear red plastic cab light, BP decals or labels, 3", black plastic wheels. Variations with colors reversed, (green cab and yellow body) are extremely rare. "Dodge Wreck Truck" on green base near rear wheels

EX $7 **NM** $12 **MIP** $30

14-1RW, Ambulance, 1956, Cream painted body, metal wheels, Red Cross decal, word "Ambulance" cast in raised letters along side of vehicle, 2"

EX $20 **NM** $45 **MIP** $85

(KP Photo, John Brown Sr. collection)

14-2RW, Ambulance, 1958, Daimler with cream or off-white body with metal or gray plastic wheels, Red Cross decal, slightly larger casting at 2-1/4", word "Ambulance" cast in raised letters

EX $18 **NM** $60 **MIP** $90

(KP Photo, George Cuhaj collection)

14-3RW, Lomas Ambulance, 1962, White body with black plastic wheels and "LCC Ambulance" decals, 2-5/8", referred to simply as "Ambulance" in catalog. "LCC" is an abbreviation for the "London County Council," responsible for designing and building ambulances in the 1950s and 1960s to its own specifications, later adapted by Daimler and other companies

EX $10 **NM** $20 **MIP** $45

(KP Photo, George Cuhaj collection)

14-4RW, Iso Grifo, 1968, Dark blue, almost purple body, light blue plastic interior and tow hook, opening doors, 3", in 1968 catalog, "available in early 1968," steering wheel on right-hand side, black tires on silver wheels, textured baseplate

EX $18 **NM** $34 **MIP** $60

(KP Photo, George Cuhaj collection)

15-1RW, Prime Mover Truck, 1956, Orange body, silver grille and trim, metal wheels. Harder to find editions: yellow body with metal wheels and orange with gray plastic wheels

EX $22 **NM** $45 **MIP** $70

15-2RW, Atlantic Prime Mover, 1959, Orange body, black plastic wheels, spare tire in bed of truck, no interior
EX $25   **NM** $45   **MIP** $80

(KP Photo, George Cuhaj collection)

15-3RW, Dennis Refuse Truck, 1963, Blue body, gray dumper section, red and white decals or labels say "Cleansing Service," and have cross-in-shield design at center. Black plastic knobby wheels, no interior, 2-1/2"
EX $7   **NM** $14   **MIP** $30

(KP Photo, George Cuhaj collection)

15-4RW, Volkswagen 1500 Saloon, 1968, White Volkswagen Beetle body with "137" decals or labels, black plastic tires on silver wheels, 2-7/8"
EX $7   **NM** $12   **MIP** $25

16-1RW, Transporter Trailer, 1956, Tan, flat bodied trailer with ramp and non-skid surface for vehicles, one axle and metal wheels in front near towbar, two axles with metal wheels on back near ramp, 3", ramp fold up onto trailer body
EX $17   **NM** $30   **MIP** $60

(KP Photo by Dr. Douglas Sadecky)

16-2RW, Atlantic Transporter, 1960, Orange trailer body, black plastic wheels, 4 axles; two at front near drawbar, two at back near ramp, non-skid tire tracks on trailer, pictured here with 15-2RW Atlantic Prime Mover
EX $17   **NM** $40   **MIP** $75

(KP Photo, George Cuhaj collection)

16-3RW, "Mountaineer" Dump Truck w/Snowplough, 1964, Gray cab and body with orange dumper section, snowplow on front with orange and white striped decal, black plastic wheels, 3", gray plastic wheel version about twice MIP value
EX $18   **NM** $30   **MIP** $50

(KP Photo, John Brown Sr. collection)

16-4RW, Case Bulldozer, 1969, Red body with yellow blade and cab, "Available mid-1969" in 1969 1st issue catalog, 2-1/2"
EX $9   **NM** $18   **MIP** $32

17-1RW, Removals Van, 1956, Green, blue or dark red body, metal wheels, "Matchbox Removals Service" decal, green more common color
EX $15   **NM** $60   **MIP** $100

(KP Photo by Dr. Douglas Sadecky)

17-2RW, Removals Van, 1958, Green body, with "Matchbox Removals Service" decal on sides, metal or gray plastic wheels
EX $35   **NM** $75   **MIP** $125

17-3RW, Metropolitan Taxi, 1960, Dark red with gray or silver plastic wheels, gray more common, silver can have $130+ MIP value, gray-wheel values shown
EX $25   **NM** $40   **MIP** $75

(KP Photo)

17-4RW, 8-Wheel Tipper, 1963, Red Foden body, orange dumper section, black plastic wheels, no interior, 3", "Hoveringham" decal on tipper. A "little brother" to the 8-Wheel Tipper K-1 in the King Size line
EX $9   **NM** $18   **MIP** $37

(KP Photo)

17-4RW, 8-Wheel Tipper, 1963, Another view of Foden 8-Wheel Tipper, with hinged gate at back opening when dumper section is tilted up
EX $9   **NM** $18   **MIP** $37

18-1RW, Bulldozer, 1956, Yellow body, tow hook, red blade, metal roller wheels, driver in hat cast as part of toy
EX $18   **NM** $35   **MIP** $85

18-2RW, Bulldozer, 1958, Yellow body, tow hook, yellow blade, driver cast into body, metal roller wheels. Engine partially covered on side
EX $25   **NM** $78   **MIP** $110

(KP Photo, John Brown Sr. collection)

18-3RW, Caterpillar Bulldozer, 1961, Yellow body, tow hook, yellow blade, driver cast into body, metal or black plastic rollers. Driver shown is painted, but normally they were the same color as casting
EX $18   **NM** $40   **MIP** $80

18-4RW, Caterpillar Crawler Bulldozer, 1964, Yellow body, curving tow hook, no driver, black plastic roller wheels. Casting essentially the same as 18-3, but with flatter blade and no driver
EX $7   **NM** $18   **MIP** $40

(KP Photo, George Cuhaj collection)

18-5RW, Field Car, 1969, Yellow body, white plastic interior, generally red wheels with black plastic tires. Many collectors consider this vehicle to be an International Scout model, and in fact the side view bears close resemblance. However, the front grille also looks a bit like a French SINPAR Renault military vehicle (although they were produced in

the 1970s). "Available mid-1969" in catalog. Auto-Steer model. 2-5/8"
EX $7   **NM** $11   **MIP** $18

19-1RW, Sports Car, 1956, White or
cream body with metal wheels, painted
driver, silver grille
EX $45   **NM** $70   **MIP** $150

19-2RW, MG "A" Sports Car, 1958, White
body, metal or gray plastic wheels,
painted driver, can have rounded or
crimped axles, silver- painted grille and
headlights, 2-1/4"
EX $58   **NM** $85   **MIP** $150

19-3RW, Aston Martin Racer, 1961,
Green body, white or gray driver, 24-
spoke wheels with black plastic tires.
Variable number decals on body
EX $45   **NM** $80   **MIP** $165

(KP Photo, Tom Michael collection)

19-4RW, Lotus Racing Car, 1966, Green
or orange body, white plastic driver, yellow wheels with black plastic tires, No.
"3" decal or label, 2-3/4". Green pictured
in 1966 catalog, but orange variation
included in G-4 Racetrack Set that same
year. Driver missing in this photo
EX $11   **NM** $22   **MIP** $50

20-1RW, Heavy Lorry, 1956, Dark red ERF
truck body, metal or gray plastic wheels,
no interior, dropside stake bed appearance with fuel tanks along sides. Can
have silver-painted grille, some casting
variations, 2-1/4" and 2-5/8"
EX $18   **NM** $40   **MIP** $100

20-2RW, Transport Truck, 1959, ERF
dropside truck with dark blue body, gray
or black plastic wheels, "Ever Ready For
Life" decal along stake sides, model also
called "Heavy Lorry" in 1959 catalog
EX $18   **NM** $45   **MIP** $90

(KP Photo by Dr. Douglas Sadecky)

20-3RW, Taxi Cab, 1965, Chevrolet
Impala Taxi Cab with yellow body, red
or white plastic interior, (red is harder
to find) black plastic wheels, 3"
EX $11   **NM** $18   **MIP** $30

(KP Photo, Colin Bruce collection)

21-1RW, Bedford Coach, 1956, Light pea-
green body with red and yellow "London
to Glasgow" decals above windows,
metal wheels
EX $22   **NM** $40   **MIP** $68

(KP Photo, George Cuhaj collection)

21-2RW, Bedford Coach, 1958, Light pea-
green body with red and yellow "London
to Glasgow" decal above windows,
metal or gray plastic wheels, "Bedford
Duple Luxury Coach" on black base,
2-1/2", silver painted grille and front
bumper, no interior
EX $25   **NM** $60   **MIP** $95

(KP Photo by Dr. Douglas Sadecky)

21-3RW, Milk Delivery Truck, 1961, Commer truck with light green body, white or
cream plastic cargo and gray or black plastic wheels, 2-1/4", cow or milk bottle decal
on cab doors. Both variations shown here
EX $20   **NM** $35   **MIP** $70

(KP Photo, George Cuhaj collection)

21-4RW, Foden Concrete Truck, 1969,
Yellow Foden cab and plastic mixer with
orange body, dark green plastic windows, eight black plastic wheels, 3".
Worm-gear under second set of wheels
turns mixer as truck rolls forward
EX $5   **NM** $9   **MIP** $22

22-1RW, Vauxhall Cresta, 1956, Red
body with white roof, no interior, metal
wheels, silver painted grille and
bumpers, tow hook
EX $30   **NM** $60   **MIP** $100

(KP Photo by Dr. Douglas Sadecky)

22-2RW, Vauxhall Cresta, 1958, Different
casting than previous version. Longer,
more "Chevy-like" body with low tailfins
and wraparound front and rear windshields. Many paint variations exist,
some pushing MIP price well into the
hundreds of dollars. Can have gray or
black plastic wheels or metal wheels
EX $30   **NM** $72   **MIP** $150

(KP Photo, George Cuhaj collection)

22-3RW, Pontiac Grand Prix, 1964, Red
body, black plastic wheels, gray plastic
interior & tow hook, 3", opening doors,
"Pontiac G.P. Sports Coupe" on black
painted baseplate
EX $12   **NM** $22   **MIP** $45

23-1RW, Caravan, 1956, Pale blue body,
metal wheels, 2-1/2"
EX $17   **NM** $30   **MIP** $75

23-2RW, Trailer, 1958, Pale blue-green or
lime-green body, metal or gray plastic
wheels
EX $22   **NM** $40   **MIP** $75

(KP Photo by Dr. Douglas Sadecky)

23-3RW, Bluebird Dauphine Trailer,
1960, Metallic tan or green body, opening door, no interior or plastic windows,
black or gray plastic wheels. Variations
with green bodies are hard to find, and
can be quite valuable. More common tan
variation prices given below
EX $25   **NM** $40   **MIP** $85

23-4RW, Trailer Caravan, 1966, Yellow or
pink body, black plastic wheels, white
plastic interior, 3", pink more common

beginning in 1968 and after. Yellow version about $45 MIP value

EX $9 **NM** $17 **MIP** $30

24-1RW, Hydraulic Excavator, 1956, Yellow or orange body with metal wheels; larger two at rear and smaller at front, figure cast as part of body, front dumping bucket

EX $18 **NM** $40 **MIP** $75

24-2RW, Hydraulic Excavator, 1959, Yellow body, black or gray plastic wheels, larger at rear or cab, smaller in front near dumper bucket. Figure cast in piece, 2-5/8"

EX $17 **NM** $28 **MIP** $45

(KP Photo, George Cuhaj collection)

24-3RW, Rolls-Royce Silver Shadow, 1967, Deep red sedan body, white plastic interior, opening trunk, silver wheels with black plastic tires, clear plastic windshield and windows, unpainted silver metal grille, headlights and front bumper, 3". Black baseplate with "A" near front axle

EX $7 **NM** $11 **MIP** $25

25-1RW, Bedford Dunlop Van, 1956, Dark blue Bedford panel van, with yellow "Dunlop" decals on sides, no interior or plastic windows

EX $18 **NM** $40 **MIP** $80

(KP Photo by Dr. Douglas Sadecky)

25-2RW, Volkswagen Sedan, 1960, Volkswagen 1200 Sedan, blue-silver body, gray plastic wheels, opening rear engine hood, green or clear plastic windows, black base

EX $45 **NM** $65 **MIP** $100

(KP Photo, George Cuhaj collection)

25-3RW, Petrol Tanker, 1964, Yellow Bedford cab, green body, white tanker with "BP" decal. Cab tilts to reveal white plastic interior. Black plastic wheels, 3". Called

"B.P. Tanker" in 1966 catalog. Blue versions with "Aral" decals on tanker section harder to find, about $200 MIP

EX $8 **NM** $14 **MIP** $25

(KP Photo)

25-4RW, Ford Cortina, 1968, Light brown body, cream-colored plastic interior and tow hook, black plastic wheels, "Auto-Steer," textured pattern on unpainted baseplate near front and rear axles, opening doors, 2-5/8". Interesting to note that its first catalog appearance in 1968 showed a blue car with the subhead "Available in mid-1968." The blue color wouldn't be used until the 1970 Superfast version was released. Yellow roof rack included in 1969 G-4 Race'n Rally Gift Set

EX $6 **NM** $9 **MIP** $17

(KP Photo, Tom Michael collection)

26-1RW, Ready Mixed Concrete Lorry, 1957, Orange ERF cab and body with silver-painted grille and side gas tanks, metal or gray plastic wheels, 1-3/4", metal mixer section, four wheels

EX $18 **NM** $45 **MIP** $88

(KP Photo, George Cuhaj collection)

26-2RW, Ready-Mix Concrete Truck, 1961, Orange die-cast Foden cab and body with plastic orange mixer section. Gray or black plastic wheels, 2-1/2". Six wheels, says "Foden Cement Mixer" on base

EX $9 **NM** $19 **MIP** $40

(KP Photo, George Cuhaj collection)

26-3RW, GMC Tipper Truck, 1968, Red cab with green plastic windows, silver-gray tipper bed, green chassis, black plastic wheels with duals at rear, 2-5/8", 1968 catalog shows subhead "Available early 1968" and model with yellow tipper bed

EX $6 **NM** $10 **MIP** $18

27-1RW, Bedford Low Loader, 1956, Green Bedford cab with silver trim, tan trailer, metal wheels, 3", no windows or interior

EX $28 **NM** $48 **MIP** $90

27-2RW, Bedford Low Loader, 1958, Green Bedford cab with silver trim, tan trailer, metal or gray plastic knobby wheels, slightly larger casting at 3-3/4" length. No windows or interior

EX $30 **NM** $75 **MIP** $140

(KP Photo, John Brown Sr. collection)

27-3RW, Cadillac Sixty Special, 1960, Silver-gray or silver-purple Cadillac body with cream or pink colored roof, plastic windows, no interior and gray or black plastic wheels, red base, tow hook, red-painted taillights and silver-painted trim

EX $28 **NM** $45 **MIP** $90

(KP Photo, George Cuhaj collection)

27-4RW, Mercedes 230SL, 1966, White Mercedes convertible with red plastic interior, opening doors, black plastic wheels, tow hook, 2-3/4", "Available early 1966" in catalog

EX $7 **NM** $13 **MIP** $25

(KP Photo by Dr. Douglas Sadecky)

28-1RW, Bedford Compressor Lorry, 1956, Orange or yellow Bedford cab and chassis with Caterpillar-type compressor engine on back, painted-silver grille and trim, 1-3/4", metal wheels. Pictured here with 28-2RW Thames Compressor Truck

EX $30 **NM** $60 **MIP** $90

(KP Photo, John Brown Sr. collection)

28-2RW, Ford Thames Compressor Lorry, 1959, Yellow Ford Thames truck cab and chassis with black plastic wheels, no interior or window plastic, silver headlights and grille

EX $25   **NM** $40   **MIP** $75

(KP Photo, George Cuhaj collection)

28-3RW, Mark Ten Jaguar, 1964, Light metallic brown body with opening hood, black plastic wheels, black-painted base. Engine can be painted the same as body color or left unpainted, 2-3/4". White plastic interior, clear window plastic, tow hook

EX $12   **NM** $20   **MIP** $30

(KP Photo, George Cuhaj collection)

28-4RW, Mack Dump Truck, 1969, Orange Mack truck body with orange dumper bed, black plastic tires on orange or yellow wheels, 2-5/8", green window plastic, unpainted base

EX $7   **NM** $18   **MIP** $25

29-1RW, Bedford Milk Delivery Van, 1956, Tan body with white plastic milk bottles and boxes, silver trim, metal or gray plastic wheels, no interior or window plastic, 2-1/4"

EX $20   **NM** $40   **MIP** $80

(KP Photo, George Cuhaj collection)

29-2RW, Austin A55 Cambridge, 1961, Medium green body with light green roof, gray or black plastic wheels, green

---

window plastic, no interior, black-painted base with tow hook, 2-1/2"

EX $17   **NM** $30   **MIP** $72

(KP Photo, John Brown Sr. collection)

29-3RW, Fire Pumper, 1966, Red LaFrance fire engine body, white plastic ladders along sides, unpainted base and trim, green window plastic, no interior, blue dome light, black plastic wheels, 3". With or without "Denver" decal

EX $6   **NM** $11   **MIP** $22

(KP Photo, George Cuhaj collection)

30-1RW, Ford Prefect, 1956, Light sage-green or light brown body with metal or gray plastic wheels, (light blue harder to find, $200 or more MIP). No window plastic or interior, silver-painted grille, headlights and bumpers, red-painted taillights. Tow hook, black-painted base, 2-3/8"

EX $15   **NM** $40   **MIP** $80

(KP Photo, George Cuhaj collection)

30-2RW, Magirus-Deutz Crane Truck, 1961, Silver cab and truck body with orange boom section and gray or black plastic wheels. Hook can be metal or plastic. Black-painted baseplate under front cab section, 2-3/8"

EX $17   **NM** $30   **MIP** $72

(KP Photo, George Cuhaj collection)

30-3RW, 8-Wheel Crane, 1965, Medium-dark green body with 8 black plastic wheels, orange crane section, yellow plastic hook, 3"

EX $5   **NM** $11   **MIP** $25

31-1RW, American Ford Station Wagon, 1957, Yellow body with metal or gray plastic wheels, silver painted bumpers and headlights, no interior or window plastic, 2-5/8". Appears brown in 1957 leaflet catalog

EX $15   **NM** $40   **MIP** $78

(Photo by Dr. Douglas Sadecky)

31-2RW, Ford Fairlane Station Wagon, 1960, Mint green with pink-white roof, gray or black plastic wheels, silver-painted trim, tow hook. Yellow-painted versions are harder to find, and can bring higher MIP values (up to $300). Two box variations shown

EX $22   **NM** $55   **MIP** $78

(KP Photo)

31-3RW, Lincoln Continental, 1964, Dark blue or mint-green body, white plastic interior, clear window glass, opening trunk, 3". Metallic tan versions rare, over $1000 MIP at auction

EX $10   **NM** $25   **MIP** $40

(KP Photo by Dr. Douglas Sadecky)

32-1RW, Jaguar XK140 Coupe, 1957, Cream body with metal or gray plastic wheels, 2-3/8", called "Fixed Head Coupe" in 1957 catalog/flyer. Silver-painted grille, red-painted taillights

EX $30   **NM** $45   **MIP** $70

(KP Photo, John Brown Sr. collection)

32-2RW, E-Type Jaguar, 1962, Metallic red body, spoked wheels with gray or

---

black tires, green or clear window plastic, 2-5/8", white plastic interior
EX $20   **NM** $40   **MIP** $80

32-2RW, Leyland Petrol Tanker, 1968, Medium-green Ergomatic cab and chassis, eight black plastic wheels, white tanker section, "BP" decals or labels, silver or white plastic grille and bumper, 3". A blue and white version with "Aral" labels is harder to find, and can have $120 or more MIP value. "Available early 1968" in catalog
EX $5   **NM** $12   **MIP** $22

(KP Photo by Dr. Douglas Sadecky)

33-1RW, Ford Zodiac, 1957, A variety of body colors exist for this model: blue, dark green, blue-green, silver, tan & orange and turquoise. Dark green and tan and orange models more common, with around $80-$90 MIP values. 2-5/8"
EX $20   **NM** $40   **MIP** $80

(KP Photo, George Cuhaj collection)

33-2RW, Ford Zephyr 6, 1962, Blue-green body, white plastic interior, gray or black plastic wheels, silver front grille and headlights, slight tailfins, black painted base, 2-1/2". Some models with black wheels have a lighter blue-green color than earlier versions
EX $10   **NM** $15   **MIP** $30

(KP Photo, George Cuhaj collection)

33-3RW, Lamborghini Miura, 1969, Yellow or gold body with red or cream plastic interior, 2-3/4", silver wheels with black plastic tires, opening doors. Gold cars with cream interiors (as shown in 1969 catalog) have high MIP values, around $200
EX $4   **NM** $12   **MIP** $25

(KP Photo, John Brown Sr. collection)

34-1RW, Volkswagen Microvan, 1957, Blue panel van body, no interior, "Matchbox International Express" yellow type decal on sides, with silver-painted bumper and headlights, 2-1/4". Mostly found with metal or gray plastic wheels, decal on side with "Matchbox International Express" in yellow lettering
EX $30   **NM** $50   **MIP** $95

(KP Photo)

34-2RW, Volkswagen Camping Car, 1962, Light sea-green body, gray or black plastic wheels, opening side doors, top window plastic, camper section interior, 2-5/8"
EX $20   **NM** $40   **MIP** $90

(KP Photo)

34-3RW, Volkswagen Camper, 1967, Silver body with opening camper section doors, orange plastic interior, yellow window plastic, raised roof with windows and top window plastic, black plastic wheels, 2-5/8"
EX $10   **NM** $18   **MIP** $45

(KP Photo)

34-3RW, Volkswagen Camper, 1967, Another view of the Volkswagen Camper
EX $10   **NM** $18   **MIP** $45

(KP Photo)

34-4RW, Volkswagen Camper, 1969, Silver body, opening doors to camper section, slightly raised roof with window plastic on top but no windows, orange plastic interior, black plastic wheels. Interestingly, the size of this vehicle remained the same since the 1962 release at 2-5/8". Makes first appearance in 1969 catalog
EX $11   **NM** $17   **MIP** $35

(Photo by Dr. Douglas Sadecky)

35-1RW, Marshall Horse Box, 1957, Red ERF cab with silver-painted grille and headlights, brown horse box with opening side door, metal and gray plastic wheels most common, 2-1/8". Silver plastic wheel version, about $180 MIP; black plastic wheel version, about $135 MIP
EX $15   **NM** $30   **MIP** $80

(Photo by Dr. Douglas Sadecky)

35-2RW, Snow-Trac Tractor, 1964, Red body with unpainted base, six black tread roller wheels, green window plastic, 2-1/4". White or gray treads, some versions have "Snow-Trac" cast in side of tractor, (as seen in 1968 and 1969 catalogs) others have decal, and some variations have neither, (as seen in the 1966 catalog). Gray-tread models may have slightly higher MIP values, although decal models (based on the tenuous nature of decals) may start to become more desirable
EX $9   **NM** $17   **MIP** $40

(KP Photo, George Cuhaj collection)

36-1RW, Austin A 50, 1957, Blue-green body, no interior, metal or gray plastic wheels, silver-painted grille, headlights and bumper, tow bar, 2-3/8"

EX $20   **NM** $35   **MIP** $75

(KP Photo, George Cuhaj collection)

36-3RW, Opel Diplomat, 1966, Gold body, black-painted metal base, white plastic interior and tow hook, opening hood, silver or gray plastic motor, 2-3/4". Pictured in elusive sea-green in 1966 catalog with caption "Available mid 1966." These (possibly) first versions are rarely seen

EX $5   **NM** $10   **MIP** $25

37-1RW, Coca-Cola Lorry, 1956, Yellow-orange truck with Coca-Cola decals on sides and back of truck, metal or gray plastic wheels, 2-1/4", no step on the running board on cab, silver-painted trim on running boards, grille. Some versions have "uneven" loads of cast Coca-Cola cases (as seen in 1957 flyer) in the bed of the truck. These typically run about $150 MIP. "Even" load versions in gray plastic wheels comparable MIP price. Even-load metal wheel version prices shown below

EX $30   **NM** $55   **MIP** $110

(KP Photo by Dr. Douglas Sadecky)

37-2RW, Coca-Cola Lorry, 1960, Yellow body, black baseplate, "even" cast crate load on bed, Coca-Cola decals on sides and back, 2-1/4", gray or black plastic wheels. Gray plastic wheel versions tend toward higher MIP values, about $110

EX $25   **NM** $40   **MIP** $95

(KP Photo, John Brown Sr. collection)

37-3RW, Cattle Truck, 1966, Yellow Dodge cab and chassis, gray plastic cattle box, originally included two white plastic steers, 2-1/2". Introduced in 1966 catalog as a new model, but hadn't yet replaced the #37 Coca-Cola truck in the line-up

EX $5   **NM** $10   **MIP** $20

38-1RW, Refuse Wagon, 1957, Silver-gray or dark-gray cab and almost tanker-truck shaped rounded-top bed and "Cleansing Department" decals. Metal or gray plastic wheels. 1957 flyer shows model painted green and without the decals. Casting variations must account for size difference: 2-1/8" and 2-1/2" lengths

EX $18   **NM** $45   **MIP** $85

38-2RW, Vauxhall Victor Estate Car, 1963, Yellow station wagon with opening rear hatch, gray, silver or black plastic tires, red or green plastic interiors, clear plastic windows. 2-1/2"

EX $18   **NM** $32   **MIP** $60

(KP Photo, George Cuhaj collection)

38-3RW, Honda Motorcycle with Trailer, 1967, Blue-silver Honda motorcycle with kickstand and orange or yellow trailer. Trailer may or may not included labels or decals. 3". As with many motorcycle-related toys, these fairly common models are increasing in value

EX $12   **NM** $25   **MIP** $40

(KP Photo, John Brown Sr. collection)

39-1RW, "Zodiac" Convertible, 1957, Pink body, turquoise interior, driver, tow hook. Metal, gray or silver plastic wheels. Casting variations: Model can measure 2-5/8" or 2-1/2". Silver-painted grille, gray-painted headlights, red-painted taillights, light green baseplate

EX $27   **NM** $68   **MIP** $95

(KP Photo by Dr. Douglas Sadecky)

39-2RW, Pontiac Convertible, 1962, Purple Pontiac convertible body with gray or silver plastic wheels; yellow body with gray, silver or black plastic wheels. Yellow with black plastic wheels is most common, around $55 MIP. Purple version with silver plastic wheels is hard to find (pictured above and in color section). 2-3/4". Yellow with gray or silver wheels prices shown below

EX $28   **NM** $55   **MIP** $95

(KP Photo)

39-3RW, Ford Tractor, 1967, Blue Ford tractor body with yellow die-cast hood, yellow wheels with black plastic tires, 2-1/8", tow hook. Versions of this tractor exist in all-blue, being part of the King Size K-20 set

EX $10   **NM** $20   **MIP** $30

(KP Photo, John Brown Sr. collection)

40-1RW, Bedford 7-Ton Tipper, 1957, Red Bedford cab and chassis, tan dumper bed, metal or gray plastic wheels, silver painted trim. Casting variations: Size varies between 2-1/8" and 2-1/4". Shown in all-green color in 1957 flyer

EX $15   **NM** $40   **MIP** $80

(KP Photo, Tom Michael collection)

40-2RW, Long Distance Bus, 1961, Blue-silver coach body with tailfins at rear, 3", green window plastic, silver-painted grille. With gray, silver or black plastic wheels. (Gray or silver-wheel versions about $55 MIP value.) Black-wheel version values given below

EX $7   **NM** $15   **MIP** $28

(KP Photo)

40-3RW, Hay Trailer, 1967, Blue die-cast trailer body with yellow die-cast stake-ends, often missing. Yellow plastic wheels with black plastic tires, 3-3/8"
EX $3   **NM** $8   **MIP** $15

(KP Photo by Dr. Douglas Sadecky)

41-1RW, "D" Type Jaguar, 1957, Green D-type body, metal driver in later catalogs, but not in 1957 flyer, "41" decal, metal or gray plastic tires, 2-1/4". Photo shows 41-1RW and second release with a larger casting, 41-2R
EX $25   **NM** $60   **MIP** $100

41-2RW, Jaguar Racing Car ("D"-Type), 1961, Second issue of car featured a green body and tan driver, but came in a variety of wheel types, from more common gray and silver plastic wheels to rare spoked versions and black plastic wheels
EX $30   **NM** $75   **MIP** $150

(KP Photo, George Cuhaj collection)

41-3RW, Ford G.T., 1966, Generally white Ford G.T. bodies with yellow plastic wheels and black plastic tires. Clear window plastic, blue rally stripe on hood with "6" or "9" reversed in white. Visible rear engine, 2-5/8". "Available early 1966" in 1966 catalog. Black base, red plastic interior. Versions with differently-colored wheels or bodies are hard to find
EX $15   **NM** $30   **MIP** $50

(KP Photo by Dr. Douglas Sadecky)

42-1RW, Bedford "Evening News" Van, 1957, Mustard-yellow Bedford panel van body with die-cast billboard on roof and red decal "First With The News" in white type. "Evening News" on panel side of van and "Football Results" in red type decals on each door. Metal, gray or black plastic wheels, (gray and black shown). 2-1/4"
EX $17   **NM** $40   **MIP** $95

(KP Photo, George Cuhaj collection)

42-2RW, Studebaker Station Wagon, 1965, Blue body with blue or light blue sliding roof, white plastic interior and tow hook, clear window plastic, white plastic dog and hunter figure included with original (often missing), 3"
EX $15   **NM** $30   **MIP** $65

(KP Photo, George Cuhaj collection)

42-3RW, Iron Fairy Crane, 1969-70, Red body, yellow crane arm, yellow plastic hook and seat, black plastic wheels, 3". Introduced in 1970 catalog, as a "non-Superfast" toy
EX $5   **NM** $11   **MIP** $20

(KP Photo, George Cuhaj collection)

43-1RW, Hillman "Minx", 1958, Blue body, light gray roof, no window plastic or interior, silver-painted grille, metal or gray plastic wheels, 2-1/2", first appears in 1958 catalog
EX $12   **NM** $40   **MIP** $75

(KP Photo, John Brown Sr. collection)

43-2RW, Aveling-Barford Tractor Shovel, 1962, Yellow tractor body with cast yel-low or red driver and yellow or red bucket, black wheels, 2-5/8". All yellow versions can have $140 MIP value. Model prices for yellow with red bucket and yellow with red driver shown
EX $15   **NM** $30   **MIP** $55

(KP Photo, George Cuhaj collection)

43-3RW, Pony Trailer, 1968, Yellow body with clear window plastic on sides and top, gray/brown plastic door, black plastic wheels, 2 white plastic horses, 2-5/8"
EX $8   **NM** $11   **MIP** $30

(KP Photo, John Brown Sr. collection)

44-1RW, Rolls Royce Silver Cloud, 1958, Blue metallic Rolls Royce body, metal, gray or silver plastic wheels, crimped axles, no interior, no window plastic, silver-painted grille and bumpers, 2-5/8"
EX $18   **NM** $35   **MIP** $80

(KP Photo, George Cuhaj collection)

44-2RW, Rolls Royce, 1962, Metallic tan or metallic silver/gray body, opening trunk, black plastic wheels, white plastic interior, clear window plastic, black base, silver-painted grille, 2-7/8"
EX $12   **NM** $20   **MIP** $40

(KP Photo, George Cuhaj collection)

44-3RW, Refrigerator Truck, 1967, Red GMC cab and chassis, green refrigerator box, green window plastic, black plastic wheels, opening rear door on box, 3"
EX $5   **NM** $12   **MIP** $20

(KP Photo, George Cuhaj collection)

45-1RW, Vauxhall "Victor", 1958, Yellow body, silver-painted headlights and grille, can have no windows, clear or green plastic windows. No interior. Metal, gray, silver or black plastic wheels, 2-3/8".
EX $18   **NM** $40   **MIP** $85

(KP Photo by Dr. Douglas Sadecky)

45-1RW, Vauxhall "Victor", 1958, Vauxhall Victor models can include green or clear plastic windows, as this one does

(KP Photo, George Cuhaj collection)

45-2RW, Ford Corsair, 1965, Cream-yellow body, red plastic interior and tow hook, gray or black plastic wheels, silver-painted grille and headlights, green plastic roof rack and boat (not shown), 2-5/8". Gray-wheeled versions may have higher MIP values
EX $6   **NM** $12   **MIP** $30

(KP Photo, George Cuhaj collection)

46-1RW, Morris Minor 1000, 1958, Dark blue or dark green body, metal or gray plastic wheels, black base, no interior, no plastic windows, 2". Dark blue with gray plastic wheels harder to find, with higher MIP values
EX $45   **NM** $65   **MIP** $125

(KP Photo by Dr. Douglas Sadecky)

46-2RW, Pickford's Removal Van, 1960, Dark blue or green body, silver-painted grille, no interior, no plastic windows, gray, silver or black plastic wheels, 2-5/8". Decals can have 2 or 3 lines. Many variations of this model exist, although versions with 2-line decals seem hard to find, bumping up the MIP price from what is shown here
EX $30   **NM** $80   **MIP** $150

(KP Photo, George Cuhaj collection)

46-3RW, Mercedes 300SE, 1968, Medium blue or green body, white plastic interior, opening doors and trunk, black plastic wheels, unpainted base extends to bumpers and front grille, 2-7/8"
EX $9   **NM** $18   **MIP** $25

(KP Photo by Dr. Douglas Sadecky)

47-1RW, Trojan "Brooke Bond" Van, 1958, Red body, metal or gray plastic wheels, decals on van box read "Brooke Bond Tea," tea leaf decal on each door, silver-painted headlights, 2-1/4"
EX $20   **NM** $45   **MIP** $95

(KP Photo, John Brown Sr. collection)

47-2RW, Commer Ice Cream Van, 1963, Blue, cream or metallic blue body with white plastic interior, clear plastic windows and black plastic wheels, 2-1/4".

Color and decal variations change MIP values considerably. Metallic blue versions with square roof decals are more rare than cream-colored models with plain (non-striped) side decals (see color section)
EX $20   **NM** $45   **MIP** $75

(KP Photo, George Cuhaj collection)

47-3RW, DAF Tipper Container Truck, 1969, Green or silver-gray cab and chassis, yellow tipper bed with removable gray top. Red plastic grille and baseplate under cab, black plastic wheels, 3". Makes first appearance in 1969 catalog. Green version higher MIP value, about $40
EX $5   **NM** $12   **MIP** $20

(KP Photo, Tom Michael collection)

48-1RW, "Meteor" Sports Boat on Trailer, 1958, Blue and yellow plastic boat with slight rise for windshield, black die-cast trailer, metal or gray plastic wheels, 2-3/4"
EX $25   **NM** $40   **MIP** $70

(KP Photo, George Cuhaj collection)

48-2RW, Sports-Boat and Trailer, 1961, Plastic red and white boat with gold or silver outboard motor, blue die-cast trailer, gray or black plastic wheels, 3-1/2". Boat can come with red deck and white hull or white deck and red hull
EX $12   **NM** $25   **MIP** $60

(KP Photo, John Brown Sr. collection)

48-3RW, Dumper Truck, 1967, Red Dodge cab, chassis and dumper bed, silver plastic baseplate, bumper and front grille, black plastic wheels, 3"

EX $3   **NM** $8   **MIP** $18

(KP Photo, George Cuhaj collection)

49-1RW, Army Half-Track, 1958, Dark olive-green with star-in-circle U.S. insignia on hood, no interior, metal, gray or black plastic wheels and rollers, gray treads (often missing as they are here) 2-1/2". Known as Army Half-Track and Military Personnel Carrier, this toy stayed in the 1-75 lineup for many years

EX $18   **NM** $30   **MIP** $55

(KP Photo, George Cuhaj collection)

49-2RW, Mercedes Unimog, 1967, Two color variations, one tan and blue and the other blue and red, green plastic windows, yellow plastic wheels with black plastic tires, silver-painted grille, tow hook cast, 2-1/2"

EX $8   **NM** $12   **MIP** $25

(KP Photo, John Brown Sr. collection)

50-1RW, Commer Pickup, 1958, Tan or red and gray body, with metal, gray or black plastic wheels, 2-1/2", silver-painted grille and headlights

EX $25   **NM** $45   **MIP** $665

(KP Photo by Dr. Douglas Sadecky)

50-1RW, Commer Pickup, 1958, A view of the red and gray variation of the Commer Pickup with black plastic wheels

EX $40   **NM** $75   **MIP** $150

(KP Photo)

50-2RW, John Deere-Lanz Tractor, 1964, Green body, yellow plastic wheels, gray or black plastic tires, cast tow hook, 2-1/8". After John Deere acquired the German manufacturer Lanz in the 1950s, a variety of toy manufacturers, including Matchbox, produced models of this tractor. Photo shows black-tire version tractor with 51-2RW Tipping Trailer. Note: Gray-tire versions have slightly higher MIP value, about $55

EX $14   **NM** $20   **MIP** $35

(KP Photo, John Brown Sr. collection)

50-2RW, John Deere-Lanz Tractor, 1964, A view of the gray-tire version of the John Deere-Lanz tractor-a very detailed model

50-3RW, Kennel Truck, 1969, Dark green die-cast body, white or silver plastic grille, green window plastic, truck bed partitioned into four sections, to hold one plastic dog each (included), clear plastic canopy over truck bed, "Auto-Steer" front wheels, black plastic wheels, 2-3/4"

EX $12   **NM** $30   **MIP** $50

51-1RW, Albion "Portland Cement" Lorry, 1958, Yellow Albion truck cab and chassis, two decal variations: "Portland Cement" and "Blue Circle Portland Cement." Metal, gray, silver or black plastic wheels, silver-painted trim, tan-painted cement bag load on flatbed, no interior, no window plastic, 2-1/2". Silver plastic wheel versions have about $150 MIP values

EX $18   **NM** $40   **MIP** $80

(KP Photo, George Cuhaj collection)

51-2RW, Tipping Trailer, 1964, Green body, yellow wheels, tilting bed, black or gray plastic tires, three yellow barrels, 2-5/8"

EX $8   **NM** $12   **MIP** $25

(KP Photo, George Cuhaj collection)

51-3RW, 8-Wheel Tipper, 1969, Orange or yellow Ergomatic AEC cab and chassis with silver-gray tipper bed, 8 black plastic wheels, green plastic windows, no interior, "Douglas" or "Pointer" labels on the sides of tipper bed, 3". Orange models with "Douglas" appear to have higher MIP values, about $40

EX $9   **NM** $16   **MIP** $28

(KP Photo by Dr. Douglas Sadecky)

52-1RW, Maserati 4CLT Racecar, 1958, Yellow or red body with spoked wheels and black tires or solid black plastic wheels. Open cockpit with driver, mostly seen with "52" decal, 2-3/8", silver-painted grille

EX $25   **NM** $50   **MIP** $100

(KP Photo, George Cuhaj collection)

52-2RW, BRM Racing Car, 1965, Blue or red body, white plastic driver, yellow wheels, black plastic tires, 2-3/4". Generally carries no. "5" decals on hood and sides

EX $10   **NM** $20   **MIP** $40

53-1RW, Aston Martin, 1958, Light green, metal or gray plastic wheels, no interior, no plastic windows, 2-1/2", silver-painted grille

EX $18   **NM** $35   **MIP** $70

(KP Photo, George Cuhaj collection)

53-2RW, Mercedes-Benz 220SE, 1963, Red or maroon body, opening doors, white plastic interior, clear plastic windows, 2-3/4", silver, gray or black plastic wheels

EX $10   **NM** $30   **MIP** $55

(KP Photo, Tom Michael collection)

53-3RW, Ford Zodiac Mk. IV, 1968, Blue-silver body, opening hood, white plastic interior, clear plastic windows, black plastic wheels, 2-3/4"

EX $3   **NM** $6   **MIP** $12

(KP Photo, George Cuhaj collection)

54-1RW, Army Saracen Carrier, 1958, Olive-green "turtle-shaped" body, six black plastic wheels, rotating turret on top, 2-1/4". One of Matchbox's first military vehicle releases. Like rescue and construction vehicles, military toys tend to be in rough shape, so finding mint or MIP examples can be a little tough

EX $8   **NM** $18   **MIP** $40

(KP Photo, George Cuhaj collection)

54-2RW, S&S Cadillac Ambulance, 1965, White Cadillac ambulance body with red cross decal or label, blue plastic windows, detailed white plastic interior, black plastic wheels, silver-painted grille, red plastic dome lights, 2-7/8"

EX $15   **NM** $30   **MIP** $60

(KP Photo)

55-1RW, D.U.K.W. Amphibian, 1958, Olive-green body, metal, gray or black plastic wheels, 2-3/4", another in the early military grouping of Matchbox vehicles

EX $15   **NM** $35   **MIP** $60

(KP Photo by Dr. Douglas Sadecky)

55-2RW, Ford Fairlane Police Car, 1963, Dark or light blue Ford Fairlane with white plastic interior, clear plastic windows, red dome light, silver-painted grille, black plastic wheels. Dark blue version is harder to find; about $300 MIP. Light blue values shown

EX $22   **NM** $40   **MIP** $85

(KP Photo, George Cuhaj collection)

55-3RW, Ford Galaxie Police Car, 1966, White body, white plastic interior with molded figure, black plastic wheels, red, white and blue stars-in-shield decals, unpainted base, red dome light

EX $20   **NM** $35   **MIP** $60

(KP Photo)

55-4RW, Mercury Police Car, 1969, White Mercury sedan with white plastic interior, featuring two officers, silver hubs with black plastic tires, blue dome light, clear plastic windows, unpainted base, "Auto-Steer" front wheels, 3-1/16". A new model, this police car was released at the same time as a Mercury station wagon, #73. Both share auto-steer feature and a baseplate, reading "55 or 73"

EX $20   **NM** $40   **MIP** $75

56-1RW, Trolley Bus, 1958, Red double-decker body with sloped front, no interior; six metal, gray, or black plastic wheels, "Drink Peardrax" decals on sides, flat trolley poles on roof, "OXO" decal on front, 2-5/8". Note that MIP metal wheel versions have sold for $250. Common prices for gray and black wheel versions shown

EX $20   **NM** $45   **MIP** $70

(KP Photo, George Cuhaj collection)

56-2RW, Fiat 1500, 1965, Pea-green Fiat 1500 sedan with dark or light brown plastic luggage on roof, red plastic interior, silver-painted grille and headlight details, black plastic wheels, 2-5/8", black plastic base. Red versions of this car were included with the G-1 Service Station Gift Set, and are tough to find, usually over $100 mint value. Standard green values shown

EX $4   **NM** $9   **MIP** $15

(KP Photo, George Cuhaj collection)

57-1RW, Wolseley 1500, 1958, Pale green body, no plastic windows, no interior, silver-painted grille, bumpers and headlights, red-painted taillights, black-painted base, 2-1/8"

EX $20   **NM** $35   **MIP** $70

(KP Photo by Dr. Douglas Sadecky)

57-2RW, Chevrolet Impala, 1961, Medium-blue body with light-blue top, cast tow hook, clear plastic windows, no interior, silver, gray or black plastic wheels

EX $25   **NM** $50   **MIP** $110

(KP Photo, George Cuhaj collection)

57-3RW, Land Rover Fire Truck, 1966, Red Land Rover body with "Kent Fire Brigade" and fire dept. insignia decals on sides, blue plastic windows and dome light, white plastic ladder (removable) on top, black plastic wheels, 2-1/2"

EX $6   **NM** $11   **MIP** $25

58-1RW, British European Airways Coach, 1958, Rounded metal blue bus body, no plastic windows, no interior, gray plastic wheels, "British European Airways" decals, 2-1/2"

EX $30   **NM** $50   **MIP** $85

(KP Photo, John Brown Sr. collection)

58-2RW, Drott Excavator, 1962, Red or orange body, silver-painted motors on some red variations, orange motor on some orange models, 2-5/8"

EX $15   **NM** $35   **MIP** $60

(KP Photo, John Brown Sr. collection)

58-3RW, DAF Girder Truck, 1968, Cream-colored cab and chassis, red plastic grille, green plastic windows, no interior, "Available mid-1968" in 1968 catalog, black plastic wheels, 12 red plastic girders, 3"

EX $4   **NM** $9   **MIP** $20

(KP Photo, John Brown Sr. collection)

59-1RW, Ford "Singer" Van, 1958, Light green Ford Thames van with "Singer" decals on panel sides and "S" logo decals on doors. No plastic windows, no interior, silver-painted grille, gray plastic wheels, 2-1/8". Dark green models seem hard to find, about $250 MIP

EX $35   **NM** $55   **MIP** $100

59-2RW, Ford Fairlane Fire Chief Car, Red Ford Fairlane casting (same as 55-2RW Ford Fairlane police car) black plastic wheels, white plastic interior, clear plastic windows

EX $25   **NM** $45   **MIP** $80

(KP Photo, Tom Michael collection)

59-3RW, Ford Galaxie Fire Chief Car, 1966, Red Ford Galaxie body, white plastic interior with figure cast as part of interior (like police car version) unpainted base and metal grille and headlight section, fire chief decals or labels on side doors and hood, clear plastic windows, white plastic tow hook, blue plastic dome light, 2-7/8"

EX $12   **NM** $30   **MIP** $50

(KP Photo, George Cuhaj collection)

60-1RW, Morris J2 Pick-Up Truck, 1958, Blue pick-up body, gray, silver or black plastic tires, "Builders Supply Company" decals on sides, silver-painted grille, no plastic windows, no interior, 2-1/4"

EX $18   **NM** $35   **MIP** $60

(KP Photo, George Cuhaj collection)

60-2RW, Site Hut Truck, 1967, Blue Leyland Ergomatic cab and flatbed chassis, silver plastic grille and headlights, blue plastic windows, no interior, black plastic wheels, plastic yellow hut on back with green roof, 2-1/2"

EX $5   **NM** $12   **MIP** $20

(KP Photo, George Cuhaj collection)

61-1RW, Ferret Scout Car, 1959, Olive-green, open-cockpit armored car body, tan-colored driver, four black plastic wheels, (one spare on side), 2-1/4"

EX $9   **NM** $12   **MIP** $30

(KP Photo, George Cuhaj collection)

61-2, Alvis Stalwart, 1967, White body with green plastic windows and green or yellow wheels with black plastic tires. Plastic canopy over bed (not shown), no interior, 2-5/8". Yellow wheels are less common and have approx. $75 MIP values

EX $9   **NM** $17   **MIP** $30

(KP Photo, George Cuhaj collection)

62-1RW, General Service Lorry, 1959, Olive green body with six black plastic wheels, no plastic windows, no interior

EX $20   **NM** $32   **MIP** $60

(KP photo by Dr. Douglas Sadecky)

62-2RW, TV Service Van, 1963, Cream colored body with "Rentaset" or "Radio Rentals" decals on sides, red plastic accessories: antenna, 3 TV sets and ladder. No interior, 2-1/2"

EX $20   **NM** $50   **MIP** $110

(KP Photo)

62-3RW, Mercury Cougar, 1969, Lime-green Mercury Cougar body with unpainted base, silver wheels with removable black plastic tires (like other Mercury models in the line), opening doors, red plastic interior, "auto-steer" front wheels, tow hook, 3"

EX $5   **NM** $8   **MIP** $15

(KP Photo, George Cuhaj collection)

63-2RW, Fire Fighting Crash Tender, 1964, Block-shaped red body with white plastic ladder (missing in this photo) and white plastic lettering on sides. No plastic windows, no interior, black plastic wheels, 2-3/8"
EX $12   **NM** $30   **MIP** $50

(KP Photo, George Cuhaj collection)

63-3RW, Service Ambulance, 1959, Olive green truck-ambulance chassis, black plastic wheels, no interior, no plastic windows, red cross decals on sides
EX $8   **NM** $22   **MIP** $50

(KP Photo, George Cuhaj collection)

63-3RW, Dodge Crane Truck, 1969, Yellow Dodge cab and chassis, red or yellow plastic hook, black grille and headlights, green plastic windows, no interior, six black plastic wheels, swivelling crane section, 3"
EX $6   **NM** $10   **MIP** $18

(KP Photo, George Cuhaj collection)

64-1RW, Scammell Breakdown Lorry, 1959, Olive green body, box cab, green, silver or gray hook, six black plastic wheels
EX $25   **NM** $45   **MIP** $75

(KP Photo, George Cuhaj collection)

64-2RW, M.G. 1100, 1966, Green car body, white plastic interior with driver in front and dog peeking out of rear window, clear plastic windows, black plastic wheels, unpainted base, white plastic tow hook, 2-5/8"
EX $5   **NM** $10   **MIP** $15

(KP Photo by Dr. Douglas Sadecky)

65-RW, Jaguar 3.4 Litre, 1959, Blue body, no interior, no plastic windows, gray plastic wheels, silver-painted grille. Shown here with 65-2RW Jaguar 3.8 Litre Sedan
EX $18   **NM** $35   **MIP** $65

(KP Photo, George Cuhaj collection)

65-2RW, Jaguar 3.8 Litre Sedan, 1962, Red body, opening hood, silver-painted grille and headlights, gray, silver or black plastic wheels, green plastic windows, no interior, 2-5/8"
EX $11   **NM** $25   **MIP** $50

(KP Photo)

65-3RW, Combine Harvester, 1967, Red Claas combine with yellow plastic grain reel and yellow wheels with removable black plastic tires, 3". A popular casting for Matchbox, matching the King-Size model (K-9) version
EX $10   **NM** $20   **MIP** $33

(KP Photo by Dr. Douglas Sadecky)

66-1RW, Citroen DS19, 1959, Yellow body, silver-painted grille, no window plastic, no interior, gray plastic wheels
EX $15   **NM** $32   **MIP** $60

(KP Photo by Dr. Douglas Sadecky)

66-2RW, Harley-Davidson Motorcycle with Sidecar, 1962, Gold metallic body with spoked wheels, 2-5/8". This piece has escalated in value due to Matchbox and Harley-Davidson collector cross-over
EX $65   **NM** $95   **MIP** $160

(KP Photo, George Cuhaj collection)

66-3RW, Greyhound Bus, 1967, Silver-gray body, "Greyhound" decals or labels, yellow plastic windows, white plastic interior, black plastic wheels, 3"
EX $10   **NM** $15   **MIP** $30

(KP Photo, George Cuhaj collection)

67-1RW, Saladin Armoured Car, 1959, Olive-green body, rotating turret (gun barrel in photo is broken, a common occurrence with these models) six black plastic wheels, 2-1/4"
EX $11   **NM** $18   **MIP** $30

(KP Photo, George Cuhaj collection)

67-2RW, Volkswagen 1600 TL, 1967, Red body, white interior, unpainted base running up into headlights, clear window plastic, opening doors, 2-11/16". One version with snap-on plastic roof rack was included with Race'n Rally G-4 gift set, harder to find
EX $11 **NM** $17 **MIP** $25

(KP Photo, George Cuhaj collection)

68-1RW, Austin Mark II Radio Truck, 1959, Olive-green body, no window plastic, no interior, black plastic wheels
EX $18 **NM** $35 **MIP** $65

(KP Photo, George Cuhaj collection)

68-2RW, Mercedes Coach, 1966, White and blue-green or white and orange body, clear window plastic, white plastic interior, black plastic wheels, 2-7/8". Blue-green version harder-to-find with approx. $130 MIP values. More common orange-version values shown
EX $7 **NM** $11 **MIP** $15

(KP Photo by Dr. Douglas Sadecky)

69-1RW, Commer 30 CWT Nestlé's Van, 1959, Dark red or red van with Nestlé's decals on panel sides, sliding doors, no window plastic, no interior, silver-painted grille, gray plastic wheels
EX $22 **NM** $40 **MIP** $90

(KP Photo, George Cuhaj collection)

69-2RW, Hatra Tractor Shovel, 1965, Yellow or orange body with black plastic removable tires. Hubs can be yellow or red, 3-1/8". Models with red hubs seem to have higher MIP values, about $90-$125
EX $11 **NM** $17 **MIP** $30

(KP Photo, George Cuhaj collection)

70-1RW, Ford Thames Estate Car, 1959, Pale blue and yellow van-shaped body with clear or green plastic windows, no interior, silver-painted grille. Gray, silver or black plastic wheels
EX $25 **NM** $40 **MIP** $70

(KP Photo, John Brown Sr. collection)

70-2RW, Grit Spreader, 1966, Red Ford cab and chassis, yellow hopper section, green plastic windows, no interior, black plastic wheels, silver metal grille, gray or black plastic "pulls" that open bottom chute, 2-5/8"
EX $7 **NM** $9 **MIP** $20

71-1RW, Service Water Truck, 1959, Olive-green truck chassis with water tank on back, black plastic wheels, spare black plastic tire behind cab, no plastic windows, no interior
EX $28 **NM** $40 **MIP** $75

(KP Photo, George Cuhaj collection)

71-2RW, Jeep Pick-Up Truck, 1964, Red body, opening doors, black partial base, black plastic wheels, clear plastic windows, silver-painted grille, 2-5/8". Early models came with green plastic interior (shown in 1964 catalog) and are hard to find, about $175 MIP. White plastic interior more common; prices shown
EX $12 **NM** $22 **MIP** $40

(KP Photo, George Cuhaj collection)

71-3RW, Ford Heavy Wreck Truck, 1969, Red cab, green plastic windows and dome light, red plastic hook, black plastic wheels, "Esso" label, white grille extending from white base with "1968" date, 3". A nice, hefty model
EX $12 **NM** $20 **MIP** $40

(KP Photo by Dr. Douglas Sadecky)

72-1RW, Fordson Major Tractor, 1959, Blue tractor with gray or black tires, and orange hubs in rear and in variations, on front. Silver-painted grille, 2". Gray-tire version and black-tire version with box variations shown
EX $18 **NM** $30 **MIP** $75

(KP Photo, George Cuhaj collection)

72-1RW, Fordson Major Tractor, 1959, Another variation of the Fordson tractor with orange hubs and black tires, front and rear. This is the version of the tractor that appeared in its last catalog appearance in 1966
EX $18 **NM** $30 **MIP** $75

(KP Photo, George Cuhaj collection)

72-2RW, Standard Jeep, 1967, Yellow body with upright windshield, black base, red plastic interior and tow hook, black plastic removable tires over yellow hubs, spare tire on back, 2-3/8"
EX $12   **NM** $20   **MIP** $40

73-1RW, RAF Refueller Truck, 1960, Blue body with RAF decal on top of truck behind cab, no plastic windows, no interior, gray plastic wheels
EX $20   **NM** $45   **MIP** $75

(KP Photo)

73-2RW, Ferrari Racing Car, 1962, Red racing car body with "73" and Ferrari decals on sides, spoked wheels, white or gray plastic driver, 2-5/8"
EX $20   **NM** $35   **MIP** $80

(KP Photo)

73-3RW, Mercury Commuter, 1969, Lime green body with clear plastic windows, white plastic interior (including two dogs peeking out of the back), black plastic removable tires with silver hubs, "Auto-Steer" front steering, 3-1/16"
EX $9   **NM** $12   **MIP** $25

(KP Photo)

73-3RW, Mercury Commuter, 1969, Another view of the Mercury station wagon, showing the two dogs peeking out of the back window

74-1, Mobile Refreshment Bar, 1960, Silver trailer body with opening sides and plastic interior, "Refreshments" decals below side openings, silver or gray plastic wheels, medium-blue baseplate models about $190 MIP, 2-5/8". Common prices with lighter blue bases shown below
EX $28   **NM** $45   **MIP** $95

(KP Photo, George Cuhaj collection)

74-2RW, Daimler Bus, 1966, Cream, green or red bodies with white plastic interior, black plastic wheels, "Esso Extra Petrol" decals or labels, 3". First appears in 1966 catalog as new model, "Available mid 1966" with no series number
EX $7   **NM** $14   **MIP** $25

(KP Photo, John Brown Sr. collection)

74-2RW, Daimler Bus, 1966, A view of the green variation of the 74-2RW Daimler Bus

(KP Photo by Dr. Douglas Sadecky)

75-1RW, Ford Thunderbird, 1960, Pink and cream 1959 Ford Thunderbird body, green plastic windows, no interior, silver, gray or black plastic wheels
EX $20   **NM** $50   **MIP** $90

(KP Photo)

75-2RW, Ferrari Berlinetta, 1965, Dark or light green body with white plastic interior and tow hook, clear plastic windows, spoked wheels or silver hubs, (with black plastic removable tires), 2-7/8". Red-colored versions of this model are very rare, about $750 MIP. Common prices shown below
EX $12   **NM** $25   **MIP** $50

MATCHBOX

SUPERFAST

(KP Photo, George Cuhaj collection)

1-1SF, Mercedes Truck, 1970, Gold-colored body, orange plastic tarp cover, green window plastic, narrow transitional Superfast wheels, silver plastic grille and half-baseplate, tow hook cast with body, 3"
EX $4   **NM** $8   **MIP** $18

(KP Photo, Tom Michael collection)

1-2SF, Mod Rod, 1972, Yellow body, amber window plastic, exposed silver-plastic engine in back, red or black Superfast wheels, "wildcat" label on hood, 2-7/8"
EX $6   **NM** $12   **MIP** $25

(KP Photo)

1-3SF, Dodge Challenger, 1976, Red or blue body, white or red plastic interior, black wheels, plastic air scoops on hood, blue-tinted windshield plastic, white plastic roof, 2-7/8"
EX $6   **NM** $12   **MIP** $25

1-4SF, Dodge Challenger, 1982, Yellow body, gray base, "Toyman" tampos, black plastic roof
EX $3   **NM** $6   **MIP** $9

2-1SF, Mercedes Trailer, 1970, Gold-colored body with orange plastic canopy, thin transitional wheels, 3-1/2"
EX $5   **NM** $9   **MIP** $20

2-2SF, Hot Rod Jeep, 1972, Pink body, exposed silver plastic engine with black plastic exhaust pipes, white plastic seats, lime-green base and bumpers, 2-5/16"
EX $5   **NM** $9   **MIP** $14

(KP Photo)

2-3SF, Hovercraft, 1976, Metallic-green hovercraft body with light brown plastic base and thin "hidden wheels" beneath, 3-1/6"
EX $2   **NM** $4   **MIP** $8

(KP Photo)

3-1SF, Mercedes-Benz "Binz" Ambulance, 1970, White body with opening hatch and patient on stretcher, red cross labels, blue window plastic, white plastic interior, thin transitional wheels, (later issued with thicker wheels as part of TP-10 Two-Pack), 2-7/8"
EX $7   **NM** $11   **MIP** $25

(KP Photo)

3-1SF, Mercedes-Benz "Binz" Ambulance, View of wider-wheel version without opening rear hatch, included as part of TP-10

(KP Photo)

3-2SF, Monterverdi Hai, 1974, Orange body with number "3" label on hood, blue

window plastic, thick black wheels, opening doors, 3"
EX $5   **NM** $7   **MIP** $15

(KP Photo, Tom Michael collection)

3-3SF, Porsche Turbo, 1979, Charcoal-gray, red or white exterior with rally number "14," plastic interior can be yellow, tan or brown, plastic tow hook, opening doors
EX $1   **NM** $2   **MIP** $5

4-1SF, Stake Truck, 1970, Yellow, or orange-yellow cab and chassis with green window plastic, no interior, green plastic stake-side cargo area, silver metal base, grille and headlights, 2-7/8"
EX $5   **NM** $10   **MIP** $17

(KP Photo, Tom Michael collection)

4-2SF, Gruesome Twosome, 1972, Gold with cream interiors and pink or purple window plastic. Two exposed engines, unpainted base, 2-7/8"
EX $4   **NM** $8   **MIP** $15

(KP Photo, Tom Michael collection)

4-3SF, Pontiac Firebird, 1976, Blue body with silver plastic interior, amber window plastic, unpainted base and bumpers, 2-7/8"
EX $1   **NM** $3   **MIP** $5

(KP Photo)

4-4SF, '57 Chevy, 1981, Red or light purple with unpainted or black base, opening hood with silver plastic engine underneath
EX $1   **NM** $3   **MIP** $5

(KP Photo)

5-1SF, Lotus Europa, 1970, Pink or blue body, white plastic interior, opening doors, 2-7/8", thin or thick Superfast wheels. Blue model shown in 1970 catalog, but pink was advertised afterward until model removed from lineup

EX $5   **NM** $10   **MIP** $20

(KP Photo, Tom Michael collection)

5-1SF, Lotus Europa, 1970, The pink version of the Lotus Europa, here with thin wheels. This color variation also comes with wide wheels, and generally seems more common

(KP Photo, John Brown Sr. collection)

5-2SF, Seafire, 1976, White body with "Seafire" label on front, blue base, blue or orange driver, exposed silver plastic engine with red plastic exhaust pipes. This casting has been used many times by Matchbox, returning in 5-Packs in the 1990s

EX $1   **NM** $3   **MIP** $5

(KP Photo)

6-1SF, Ford Pick-Up Truck, 1970, Red body, white plastic camper top, silver or white plastic grille, 2-3/4", black or charcoal base

EX $8   **NM** $15   **MIP** $25

(KP Photo, Tom Michael collection)

6-2SF, Mercedes Tourer, 1973, Orange or yellow 350SL body with black plastic top, amber windows, light yellow or cream plastic interior, 3", unpainted base. Later models in light or dark red with white plastic roof, or red or metallic blue with no roof

EX $3   **NM** $7   **MIP** $14

7-1SF, Ford Refuse Truck, 1970, Red-orange cab with gray plastic and silver metal garbage dumper bed, 3". The same model as the old regular-wheels version, just with thin or thick Superfast wheels

EX $4   **NM** $8   **MIP** $12

(KP Photo, Tom Michael collection)

7-2SF, Hairy Hustler, 1973, Bronze body, with amber windows, number "5" racing labels on front and side, or white body with checkered labels on hood and roof, and red stripes on fenders, black metal base

EX $5   **NM** $10   **MIP** $15

(KP Photo, John Brown Sr. collection)

7-3SF, Volkswagen Golf, 1977, Lime green, dark green, yellow or red body, amber window plastic, black plastic, detachable surf boards on roof rack, yellow plastic interior, black or charcoal base, tow hook

EX $4   **NM** $7   **MIP** $12

8-1SF, Ford Mustang Fastback, 1970, White, red or orange-red body, white or red plastic interior (red is harder-to-find), tow hook, 2-7/8". Red models with red plastic interiors are the most rare, selling for around $400 MIB

EX $65   **NM** $80   **MIP** $120

8-2SF, Wildcat Dragster, 1971, Orange or pink body with silver engine protruding from hood, and "Wild Cat" labels on sides, tow hook, 2-7/8". This is the same casting used on the Mustang Fastback model 8-1SF

EX $3   **NM** $5   **MIP** $11

(KP Photo)

8-3SF, De Tomasa Pantera, 1975, White body with "8" labels, blue base, red plastic interior, or blue body, tempo "17", black base, 3"

EX $2   **NM** $4   **MIP** $7

(KP Photo)

8-3SF, De Tomasa Pantera, 1975, A view of the blue version of the Pantera with the "17" tempo

9-1SF, Boat and Trailer, 1970, Blue die-cast boat trailer with thin Superfast wheels and plastic blue and white boat, 3-1/2"

EX $4   **NM** $9   **MIP** $20

9-2SF, AMX Javelin, 1972, Lime-green or blue body (blue included with Twin-Pack #3, Javelin and Pony Trailer), black or silver plastic air scoop, light yellow or white plastic interior, opening doors, tow hook, 3-1/16"

EX $3   **NM** $6   **MIP** $10

(KP Photo, Tom Michael collection)

9-3SF, Ford Escort RS 2000, 1979, White body with Ford and Shell rally labels, clear window plastic, black base, tan plastic interior

EX $3   **NM** $5   **MIP** $8

10-1SF, Pipe Truck, 1970, Red or orange cab and chassis, gray or yellow plastic pipes, thin or wide Superfast wheels, silver grille, green window plastic, 3". Red models about $35 MIB, orange model values shown below

EX $10   **NM** $16   **MIP** $25

(KP Photo, Tom Michael collection)

10-2SF, Piston Popper, 1973, Blue or yellow Mustang Mach I body with silver Rola-Matic engine with red plastic pistons that move as car is rolled along. Yellow plastic interior, unpainted base, 2-7/8"

EX n/a   **NM** $5   **MIP** $10

(KP Photo)

10-3SF, Plymouth Gran Fury Police Car, 1979, Black and white with "Metro Police" on doors and hood, blue police lights on roof, amber or blue window plastic, unpainted or silver base. Introduced in 1979/80 catalog, it hadn't yet replaced Piston Popper in the lineup

EX $1   **NM** $4   **MIP** $7

(KP Photo, George Cuhaj collection)

11-3SF, Scaffold Truck, 1970, Silver Mercedes-Benz truck with red plastic base and grille, yellow plastic scaffold sections in back, "Builders Supply Company" labels on sides of truck, green window plastic, no interior, 2-5/8"

EX $4   **NM** $8   **MIP** $12

11-2SF, Flying Bug, 1973, Red metallic Volkswagen Beetle with Iron Cross label on hood, oversized face with silver helmet peeking up from car, opaque windows, tailwing and yellow plastic jet engine section on back. Silver or unpainted base, 2-7/8"

EX $4   **NM** $9   **MIP** $16

(KP Photo)

11-3SF, Car Transporter, 1978, Orange body with black base and light tan/cream car carrying section with red, yellow and blue plastic cars. Dark blue window plastic, no interior

EX $4   **NM** $8   **MIP** $12

(KP Photo, Tom Michael collection)

11-4SF, Cobra Mustang, 1982, Orange body with opening hood, chrome interior, yellow windows, "The Boss" in white lettering on sides, number "5" on roof. Another in the many variations of the old "Boss Mustang" casting

EX $2   **NM** $4   **MIP** $6

(KP Photo)

12-1SF, Safari Land Rover, 1970, Gold body with white plastic interior, red-brown plastic luggage, tow hook, thin Superfast wheels, 2-3/4". Blue versions of this model exist as Superfasts, but are extremely rare, so prices shown are for gold models only

EX $8   **NM** $14   **MIP** $25

(KP Photo, John Brown Sr. collection)

12-2SF, Setra Coach, 1971, Metallic yellow and white or burgundy and white with clear or green window plastic, white plastic interior, unpainted base, 3"

EX $3   **NM** $6   **MIP** $14

(KP Photo, John Brown Sr. collection)

12-3SF, Big Bull, 1975, Orange bulldozer body and rollers, green base and blade, silver plastic engine and trim, 2-1/2"

EX $1   **NM** $3   **MIP** $5

(KP Photo)

66-2SF, Citroen CX Station Wagon, 1980, Blue body with cream or light yellow plastic interior, clear or blue window plastic, unpainted or silver base

EX $2   **NM** $5   **MIP** $10

13-1SF, Wreck Truck, 1970, Yellow Dodge cab and tow boom with green bed. "BP" labels on sides, thin Superfast wheels, red window plastic and dome light, no interior, red plastic tow hook, 3". This is another transitional model that is becoming hard to find

EX $17   **NM** $30   **MIP** $48

(KP Photo, Tom Michael collection)

13-2SF, Baja Buggy, 1972, Lime green body, orange plastic interior, no window plastic, thick Superfast wheels, flower label on hood, silver plastic engine with orange plastic exhaust pipes, 2-5/8"

EX $4   **NM** $8   **MIP** $12

(KP Photo)

13-3SF, Snorkel Fire Engine, 1977, Red body with blue or amber window plastic, yellow or white snorkel section, unpainted metal base. Models with amber-colored window plastic tend to have higher MIP prices, about $15. This fire engine first appeared in the 1977 catalog with a white snorkel as a new model to watch for, not yet replacing Baha Buggy in the lineup

EX $1   **NM** $4   **MIP** $7

(KP Photo)

14-1SF, Iso Grifo, 1970, Dark or medium blue with thin Superfast wheels, light blue or white plastic interior, unpainted base, 3"
EX $6   **NM** $12   **MIP** $25

14-2SF, Mini-Ha-Ha, 1976, Red body with blue opaque window plastic, silver plastic rotary engine protruding through hood, large rear wheels, head with pilot's helmet showing through roof, circular British RAF side labels on doors
EX $3   **NM** $8   **MIP** $17

15-1SF, Volkswagen 1500, 1970, White, cream or red body with white plastic interior, tow hook, unpainted base, "137" labels on doors, 2-7/8"
EX $7   **NM** $12   **MIP** $20

(KP Photo)

15-2SF, Fork Lift Truck, 1973, Red body with larger wheels at front, gray or yellow plastic lifting forks on yellow metal or unpainted track, "Lansing Bagnall" or "Hi-Lift" side labels, unpainted, black or green base, 2-3/4"
EX $3   **NM** $6   **MIP** $9

(KP Photo)

15-3SF, Hi Ho Silver, 1981, Silver Volkswagen Beetle (same casting as "Volks Dragon") with "Hi Ho Silver" and "31" tempo. Black base, clear window plastic, red plastic interior, 2-5/8". Having "31" on the roof is an interesting choice of graphic, considering it was the same vehicle casting as the 31-2SF
EX $4   **NM** $7   **MIP** $12

(KP Photo by Dr. Douglas Sadecky)

16-1SF, Case Bulldozer, 1970, Red with yellow engine, cab and blade and green or black rubber tracks, 2-1/2". This model

was released at the same time as the Superfast line-notice that the box has "speed lines" just like the other models
EX $5   **NM** $8   **MIP** $15

16-2SF, Badger, 1974, Block, metallic bronze-red body with surface detail tools, ladders, etc., and plastic "Rola-Matic" radar. Green window plastic, no interior, six thick wheels, 2-3/4". Later editions in olive green were included as part of TP-14 Two-Pack
EX $4   **NM** $7   **MIP** $12

(KP Photo, Tom Michael collection)

16-3SF, Pontiac Firebird, 1981, Metallic light or dark tan, Firebird tempo on hood, light tan plastic interior
EX n/a   **NM** $2   **MIP** $5

17-1SF, Horse Box, 1971, Red or orange AEC Ergomatic cab with green or gray plastic horse box, gray or mustard door, and two white plastic horses, 2-7/8"
EX $3   **NM** $7   **MIP** $12

(KP Photo, John Brown Sr. collection)

17-2SF, The Londoner, 1973, Red body with "Berger Paints" or "Swinging London Carnaby Street" side labels (most common). White plastic interior, no window plastic, 3". There are many color and label variations of this model, some limited runs that command MIP values over $200. However, prices shown are for the common red-colored "Berger" and "Swinging London" versions
EX $1   **NM** $3   **MIP** $5

(KP Photo, Tom Michael collection)

17-2SF, The Londoner, 1973, The "Swinging London" version of the The Londoner bus

(KP Photo, Tom Michael collection)

18-1SF, Field Car, 1970, Yellow body with tan plastic roof, white plastic interior, no window plastic, unpainted base, spare tire, tow hook, thin or thick wheels, 2-7/8". Other variations as part of Two-Packs in the 1970s, included orange with checked hood label and black plastic roof, olive green with light-tan plastic roof and hood label, red with light-tan plastic roof and "44" hood label-almost all with black plastic interiors. White editions are harder to find, about $250-300 in MIP condition. Prices shown reflect the more common models listed
EX $7   **NM** $12   **MIP** $25

(KP Photo, Tom Michael collection)

18-1SF, Field Car, Variation with dark yellow-orange body, black interior, base and roof. Part of Two Pack (TP-8), with Honda motorcycle

18-2SF, Hondarora, 1975, Red or orange body with silver or black forks and black seat are the most common, some with gas-tank labels, some without. Olive-drab military models were part of the TP-11 set with the olive-drab field car. 2-1/2"
EX n/a   **NM** $2   **MIP** $5

19-1SF, Lotus Racing Car, 1970, Dark metallic purple, white plastic driver, wide Superfast wheels, "3" decal on sides, 2-3/4"
EX $9   **NM** $20   **MIP** $48

(KP Photo, Tom Michael collection)

19-2SF, Road Dragster, 1971, Red or metallic pink body with unpainted base, exposed silver plastic engine, white plastic interior, wide wheels, clear window plastic, "8" labels on hood and roof, 3". Some models have "Wynns" or scorpion labels and are pink or orange-red and harder to find, about $80 MIP
EX $2   **NM** $5   **MIP** $10

(KP Photo)

19-3SF, Cement Truck, 1977, Red cab and chassis, unpainted metal base, green window plastic, no interior, yellow plastic mixer, with or without black or red stripes, 3"
EX $1   **NM** $3   **MIP** $6

(KP Photo)

20-1SF, Lamborghini Marzal, 1970, Pink or dark red with amber window plastic, white plastic interior and thin wheels; or pink or orange-pink with thick wheels, 2-3/4"
EX $8   **NM** $15   **MIP** $25

(KP Photo)

20-2SF, Police Patrol, 1975, White Range Rover with orange stripe "Police" label, frosted window plastic and blue or orange revolving police light (part of the Rola-Matics series). 2-7/8". Other models include orange Site Engineer from Gift Pack #13, olive-drab military ambulance model, and orange Paris-Dakar model, each with approx. $25-$35 MIP value. Common white model values given below
EX $1   **NM** $4   **MIP** $8

(KP Photo, Tom Michael collection)

20-2SF, Police Patrol: Site Engineer, 1977, Orange body with rotating orange

dome light, "Site Engineer" labels on doors, plain metal base. Part of #13 Construction Gift Pack
EX $5   **NM** $8   **MIP** $14

(KP Photo)

20-2SF, Police Patrol: Paris-Dakar Rallye, 1983, Gold body with black and white checkered label and "Securitie-Rallye Paris Dakar 83" on sides, black base, red rotating dome light
EX $5   **NM** $9   **MIP** $13

(KP Photo)

20-2SF, Police Patrol: County Sheriff, 1982, White body with blue doors and roof, star design on hood and doors, "County Sheriff" in blue type on sides, blue rotating dome light
EX $3   **NM** $5   **MIP** $8
(KP Photo)

20-2SF, Police Patrol: British Police, 1983, White body with yellow and black/white checkered "Police" labels on sides. Blue rotating dome light, black base
EX $4   **NM** $8   **MIP** $12

21-1SF, Foden Concrete Truck, 1971, Yellow cab, orange truck bed with yellow plastic mixer, eight thin wheels, 3"
EX $8   **NM** $12   **MIP** $25

(KP Photo)

21-2SF, Rod Roller, 1973, Yellow body with red plastic seat, star and flames label on hood, (later editions without black plastic roller wheels, some with red or metallic red hubs on rear, black plastic steering lever, 2-1/2". Prices for metallic red hub versions about $45 MIP
EX $3   **NM** $8   **MIP** $17

(KP Photo)

21-3SF, Renault 5TL, 1979, Yellow, blue, white or silver-gray body, clear or amber window plastic, tan or red plastic interior, tow hook, 2-1/2". Some yellow models have "Le Car" tempo
EX $2   **NM** $6   **MIP** $10

22-1SF, Pontiac Grand Prix, 1970, Purple body, thin wheels, silver grille and black base, 3"
EX $12   **NM** $22   **MIP** $55

(KP Photo, Tom Michael collection)

22-2SF, Freeman Inter-City Commuter, 1971, Purple-red body with white plastic interior, clear window plastic, unpainted base, some with side labels, 3"
EX $2   **NM** $4   **MIP** $8

(KP Photo)

22-3SF, Blaze Buster, 1976, Red body with yellow or black plastic ladder, silver plastic interior, amber window plastic, black or silver base, 3-1/16". Black-ladder versions about $25 MIP value
EX $2   **NM** $4   **MIP** $7

(KP Photo)

22-4SF, 4 x 4 Big Foot, 1982, Silver body, white plastic camper top, blue window plastic, black base, "Big Foot" and "26" tempos on sides and hood
EX $2   **NM** $5   **MIP** $12

23-1SF, Volkswagen Camper, 1970, Blue or orange body with plastic orange lift-up top reveals white plastic interior, amber or clear window plastic. Some models with sailboat labels on sides, 2-5/8". Military olive-drab versions without lift-up camper top were included as ambulances with TP-12 Two-Pack

EX $9   **NM** $22   **MIP** $45

(KP Photo)

23-2SF, Atlas Tipper, 1976, Blue body with orange or silver tipper section, wide wheels, amber or clear window plastic, silver or gray plastic interior, 2-3/4". Later versions available with red body

EX $1   **NM** $3   **MIP** $7

(KP Photo, Tom Michael collection)

23-3SF, Ford Mustang GT-350, 1981, White body, blue Shelby stripes, exposed engine in front, "GT 350" on sides

EX $5   **NM** $12   **MIP** $20

(KP Photo)

24-1SF, Rolls-Royce Silver Shadow, 1970, Metallic-red body, white plastic interior, clear window plastic, opening trunk, silver metal grille and headlights, black or silver base, 3"

EX $5   **NM** $9   **MIP** $20

(KP Photo, Tom Michael collection)

24-2SF, Team Matchbox, 1973, Metallic green, red or orange body, "8" or "44" label (included with TP-9, Field Car and Racing Car Two-Pack), white plastic driver, 2-7/8". Metallic green version, about $35 MIP, orange version about $85 MIP. Values for red shown

EX $1   **NM** $4   **MIP** $9

(KP Photo, John Brown Sr. collection)

24-3SF, Diesel Shunter, 1979, Dark green and red or yellow and red body, no window plastic, labels read "Rail Freight" or "D1496-RF"

EX n/a   **NM** $2   **MIP** $5

(KP Photo)

25-1SF, Ford Cortina GT, 1970, Metallic tan or blue body, white plastic interior, opening doors, tow hook, 2-5/8". Metallic tan versions, the first of the transitional Superfast models, are harder-to-find and have approx. $70-$80 MIP values

EX $8   **NM** $12   **MIP** $25

(KP Photo)

25-2SF, Mod Tractor, 1973, Metallic purple body, black base, some with "V" cast on fenders, some without, silver plastic exposed engine, yellow plastic seat, 2-1/4". Harder to find editions have headlights cast in rear fender, about $60 MIP

EX $1   **NM** $3   **MIP** $7

(KP Photo, John Brown Sr. collection)

25-3SF, Flat Car and Container, 1979, Black or charcoal flat car with tan or red plastic container with "NYK Worldwide Service" labels

EX $1   **NM** $3   **MIP** $5

26-1SF, GMC Tipper Truck, 1970, Red tipping cab, green engine and base, silver dump bed, green window plastic, no interior, 2-5/8"

EX $5   **NM** $9   **MIP** $20

(KP Photo, Tom Michael collection)

26-2SF, Big Banger, 1973, Red with dark-blue window plastic, no interior, large silver plastic engine and exhaust pipes, "Big Banger" side labels, 3". Later versions were brown with "Brown Sugar" side labels or white with "Cosmic Blues" tempo

EX $4   **NM** $9   **MIP** $18

(KP Photo, Tom Michael collection)

26-2SF, Brown Sugar, 1973, The "Brown Sugar" version of the Big Banger with brown body, large silver engine with black scoop and yellow and red "Brown Sugar" labels

26-3SF, Site Dumper, 1977, Yellow body with yellow or red dumper bed, or orange body with silver-gray dumper bed, no window plastic, black or brown base, black plastic interior

EX $2   **NM** $4   **MIP** $7

(KP Photo)

27-1SF, Mercedes 230SL, 1970, Yellow convertible body with black plastic interior, or white body with red plastic interior, clear window plastic, silver base, thin wheels, 2-3/4"

EX $8   **NM** $12   **MIP** $25

(KP Photo, Tom Michael collection)

27-2SF, Lamborghini Countach, 1973, Pale-orange body with "3" label on hood, or red-orange with "8" tempo and stripes, silver or gray plastic interior, amber or blue window plastic, opening rear hood, 3"

EX $3   **NM** $7   **MIP** $12

(KP Photo, John Brown Sr. collection)

28-1SF, Mack Dump Truck, 1970, Light-green body and dumper bed, silver base, wide wheels, no interior, amber window plastic, 2-5/8". Olive-drab versions were released with Case bulldozer in TP-16 Two-Pack

EX $6   **NM** $10   **MIP** $22

(KP Photo)

28-2SF, Stoat, 1973, Metallic bronze-tan body with rotating (Rola-Matic) soldier holding binoculars. Black base, wide wheels, 2-5/8". Olive-green versions with all-black wheels were included in TP-13 Two-Pack along with an olive version of 73-2SF Weasel armored vehicle

EX $2   **NM** $6   **MIP** $12

(KP Photo, Tom Michael collection)

28-3SF, Lincoln Continental Mk V, 1979, Red body, white plastic roof, light-yellow or gray interior, silver base. First introduced in the 1979/80 catalog, this model had not yet replaced the Stoat in the lineup, but was due to be "available in your shops later this year"

EX $3   **NM** $6   **MIP** $12

29-1SF, Fire Pumper, 1970, Red body, blue window plastic and dome light, white plastic ladders and reels, silver base, thin wheels, 3"

EX $12   **NM** $32   **MIP** $70

(KP Photo, Tom Michael collection)

29-2SF, Racing Mini, 1971, Orange-red body with yellow "29" labels, clear window plastic, white plastic interior, unpainted silver-gray base and grille, 2-1/4". Also included with TP-6 Two-Pack

EX $5   **NM** $8   **MIP** $16

(KP Photo)

29-3SF, Shovel-Nose Tractor, 1977, Yellow body with silver or black plastic engine and interior, shovel can be red or black plastic, 2-7/8". Lime green models with yellow plastic shovels are harder to find, about $65 MIP value. Models with yellow body, black plastic and stripes (as shown) were included in the G-5 Giftset in the 1979/80 catalog. Orange models with red plastic shovels, also about $65 MIP value

EX $5   **NM** $8   **MIP** $16

(KP Photo)

30-1SF, 8-Wheel Crane, 1970, Red with gold crane section, red plastic hook, no window plastic, yellow plastic hook, 3"

EX $10   **NM** $20   **MIP** $45

(KP Photo, Tom Michael collection)

30-2SF, Beach Buggy, 1971, Pink body with yellow "spatter paint," white or yellow plastic interior and side tanks, no window plastic, 2-9/16". White interior versions have approx. $20 MIP value

EX $4   **NM** $7   **MIP** $12

(KP Photo)

30-3SF, Swamp Rat, 1977, Squared-boat body with olive-green deck, tan plastic hull, rotating striped army gunner (Rola-Matic), "Swamp Rat" labels, 3-1/16"

EX $3   **NM** $7   **MIP** $9

31-1SF, Lincoln Continental, 1970, Lime-green body with thin wheels, opening trunk, clear window plastic, white plastic interior, 3"

EX $12   **NM** $21   **MIP** $38

31-2SF, Volksdragon, 1972, Red Volkswagen Beetle body with clear window plastic, white or yellow plastic interior, silver plastic engine, "eyes" label, unpainted base, 2-5/8"

EX $6   **NM** $10   **MIP** $16

(KP Photo, John Brown Sr. collection)

31-3SF, Caravan, 1978, White body with amber or blue window plastic, some with orange stripe with white reversed bird graphic label, unpainted base, light-yellow plastic interior, 2-3/4"

EX $1   **NM** $3   **MIP** $6

(KP Photo)

32-1SF, Leyland Petrol Tanker, 1970, Green cab and chassis, white tank, "BP" labels, thin wheels, blue or amber window plastic, no interior, chrome plastic base, 3"

EX $8   **NM** $14   **MIP** $22

(KP Photo, Tom Michael collection)

32-2SF, Maserati Bora, 1973, Magenta body with yellow plastic interior, clear window plastic, opening doors, "8" stripe label on hood, lime green, dark green or unpainted base, 3"

EX $3   **NM** $7   **MIP** $13

(KP Photo)

32-3SF, Field Gun, 1978, Olive-green with black plastic barrel that fired shells attached to sprue on tan plastic base with soldiers, 3". An interesting piece, in that it included a diorama with the toy. Field Gun was removable from base
EX $3   NM $6   MIP $11

(KP Photo, George Cuhaj collection)

33-1SF, Lamborghini Miura, 1970, Gold body, opening doors, white plastic interior, thin wheels, unpainted base, 2-3/4"
EX $7   NM $12   MIP $22

33-2SF, Datsun 126X, 1973, Yellow body with silver plastic interior, orange base, opening rear hood, amber window plastic, 3". Some versions have black and red flame tempo detail on hood and roof
EX $1   NM $4   MIP $8

33-3SF, Police Motorcycle, 1978, White motorcycle with blue plastic policeman rider, silver plastic engine, "Police" on saddlebags, silver or black wire spoked wheels, 2-7/8". Models included with the K-71 Porsche Polizei set had green plastic riders and detailing
EX $1   NM $4   MIP $7

34-1SF, Formula 1 Racing Car, 1970, Magenta or yellow body, white plastic driver, silver plastic engine, wide wheels, "16" striped label on hood, clear windshield plastic, 2-7/8"
EX $5   NM $8   MIP $14

(KP Photo, Tom Michael collection)

34-2SF, Vantastic, 1976, Modified orange Ford Mustang body, white plastic interior, blue window plastic, early models with large silver plastic engine, later models with closed hood, white base, 2-7/8"
EX $2   NM $6   MIP $12

(KP Photo, Tom Michael collection)

34-2SF, Vantastic, 1976, Earlier and harder-to-find release without the exposed engine. Number "34" appears on hood

(KP Photo, George Cuhaj collection)

35-1SF, Merryweather Marquis Fire Engine, 1970, Red body, blue window plastic, gray plastic reels and instrument panel, white plastic ladder, blue dome lights, "London Fire Service" labels, narrow or wide tires, 3". This model was also included with TP-2 Two-Pack (900 Range). A modified casting was later used for 63-5SF Snorkel Fire Engine
EX $4   NM $7   MIP $12

(KP Photo, Tom Michael collection)

35-2SF, Fandango, 1975, White body with red plastic interior, "35" label with stripe on hood, rotating (Rola-Matic) fan behind driver, clear window plastic, 3". Also red body with red or white plastic interiors, a later release. Versions with white body and red interior and a number "6" label are harder to find, and about $40 MIP
EX $3   NM $6   MIP $10

(KP Photo, Tom Michael collection)

36-1SF, Opel Diplomat, 1970, Metallic green-gold color, opening hood, thin wheels, 2-3/4"
EX $6   NM $11   MIP $20

(KP Photo, Tom Michael collection)

36-2SF, Hot Rod Draguar, 1971, Metallic pink or purple body with white or light yellow plastic interior, clear bubble window plastic, large silver engine, wide wheels, 2-7/8"
EX $5   NM $8   MIP $18

(KP Photo, Tom Michael collection)

36-3SF, Formula 5000, 1977, Orange with blue label number "3" and blue plastic driver, or red with "Texaco" and "Champion" labels and yellow plastic driver, 2-7/8"
EX $1   NM $4   MIP $8

37-1SF, Cattle Truck, 1970, Yellow Dodge cab and chassis, green plastic windows, no interior, gray-brown plastic stake-side bed with two white plastic cows, 2-1/2"
EX $6   NM $11   MIP $20

(KP Photo, Tom Michael collection)

37-2SF, Scoopa Coopa, 1973, Blue or pink body with yellow plastic interior, amber plastic windshield, unpainted base, 2-7/8". Pink models have a daisy-shaped sticker on the roof section, and were shown first in the 1976 catalog
EX $1   NM $3   MIP $8

(KP Photo)

37-3SF, Skip Truck, 1977, Red cab and chassis, clear or amber plastic windows, yellow bucket, white plastic interior, 2-3/4"
EX $2   NM $4   MIP $6

38-1SF, Honda Motorcycle with Trailer, 1970, Yellow motorcycle trailer with thin wheels and "Honda" labels. Green or pink motorcycle, silver spokes, 3"
EX $7　　**NM** $11　　**MIP** $19

38-2SF, Stingeroo, 1973, Purple chopper-style bike with cream-colored plastic horse head on seat, two wide wheels in rear, one solid wheel in front, purple plastic forks, silver plastic engine, 3-1/8"
EX $6　　**NM** $10　　**MIP** $22

38-3SF, Armored Jeep, 1977, Dark olive-drab with white star emblem on hood, black base and grille, black plastic gun on back (swivels), all-black wide wheels
EX $4　　**NM** $7　　**MIP** $10

(KP Photo)

39-1SF, Ford Tractor, 1970, Blue body with yellow hood and wheels or all-blue body (included with K-20 Tractor Transporter), 2-1/8". This was another regular-wheels holdover into the Superfast era
EX $7　　**NM** $16　　**MIP** $25

(KP Photo)

39-2SF, Clipper, 1973, Metallic magenta body with light metallic green base, yellow plastic interior, flip-up cockpit, and "clicking" exhaust pipes that moved up and down as the car rolled along. One of the first in the Rola-Matics series, 3"
EX $1　　**NM** $4　　**MIP** $9

(KP Photo)

39-4SF, Rolls-Royce Mark II, 1979, Silver body with red plastic interior or metallic red body with yellow plastic interior. Clear window plastic, opening doors, unpainted base, silver grille and headlights. Introduced in the 1979/80 catalog, but had not replaced Clipper in the 1-75 lineup
EX $2　　**NM** $5　　**MIP** $9

(KP Photo)

40-1SF, Hay Trailer, 1970, Blue with yellow wheels and stakeside attachments, 3-3/8". Another holdover from the regular wheels series, this model was replaced in 1972 with the Superfast Guildsman
EX $3　　**NM** $8　　**MIP** $12

(KP Photo, Tom Michael collection)

40-2SF, Guildsman, 1972, Pink with white plastic interior and light-green window plastic, star and flames label on hood; or, red body with white plastic interior with amber window plastic and "40" label on hood (first appears in 1976 catalog), 3"
EX $4　　**NM** $8　　**MIP** $16

(KP Photo, John Brown Sr. collection)

40-3SF, Horse Box, 1978, Orange cab and chassis, no interior, green window plastic, cream-colored plastic box with light-brown door, two white plastic horses, 2-7/8". This model was reissued in the 1990s with green and blue color variations
EX $2　　**NM** $6　　**MIP** $10

41-1SF, Ford GT, 1970, White or red with red plastic interior, blue stripe and number "6" label on hood, thin or wide wheels
EX $8　　**NM** $15　　**MIP** $28

(KP Photo, Tom Michael collection)

41-2SF, Siva Spyder, 1973, Red body with cream-colored plastic interior, black segment wraps behind cabin, wide wheels, clear window plastic, 3". Blue versions with stars and stripes label motif available in 1976 catalog
EX $3　　**NM** $7　　**MIP** $12

(KP Photo, John Brown Sr. collection)

41-3SF, Ambulance, 1979, White body, blue window plastic and dome lights, opening rear doors, unpainted base, white plastic interior, "Emergency Medical Service" or "Ambulance" with red cross labels, 2-1/2"
EX $3　　**NM** $6　　**MIP** $12

42-1SF, Iron Fairy Crane, 1971, Red with open cab (no window plastic) yellow plastic interior, yellow crane section with yellow plastic hook, wide wheels, 3". Continued as a regular wheels model, but only for the 1970 catalog, then converted to Superfast
EX $15　　**NM** $25　　**MIP** $45

(KP Photo, Tom Michael collection)

42-2SF, Tyre Fryer, 1973, Light or dark-blue body, open cockpit, yellow plastic seat, large silver plastic engine behind driver, large Superfast wheels in rear, wide wheels in front, 3"
EX $2　　**NM** $6　　**MIP** $12

(KP Photo, John Brown Sr. collection)

42-3SF, Mercedes Container Truck, 1978, Red cab and chassis, blue window plastic, no interior, unpainted or black base, plastic container with "SeaLand," "NYK" or "Matchbox" labels, 3"
EX $1　　**NM** $3　　**MIP** $6

(KP Photo)

42-4SF, '57 T-Bird, 1981, Red body, white interior, clear windshield, silver metal base
EX $1   **NM** $3   **MIP** $6

(KP Photo)

42-4SF, '57 T-Bird, 1982, Later version with black body, red interior, yellow windshield, plain base
EX $1   **NM** $3   **MIP** $7

(KP Photo)

43-1SF, Pony Trailer, 1970, Yellow body with green base, clear window plastic, two white plastic horses, narrow wheels, brown plastic door, 2-5/8". Orange version with horse label included with TP-3 Two-Pack
EX $5   **NM** $8   **MIP** $15

(KP Photo, Tom Michael collection)

43-2SF, Dragon Wheels, 1973, Green Volkswagen Beetle funny-car body hinged to silver plastic and metal base, "Dragon Wheels" labels on sides, 2-7/8"
EX $4   **NM** $7   **MIP** $14

(KP Photo, John Brown Sr. collection)

43-3SF, Steam Loco, 1979, Red and black body, red base, "4345" labels on sides, 2-11/16"
EX $1   **NM** $3   **MIP** $6

(KP Photo, Tom Michael collection)

44-1SF, Refrigerator Truck, 1970, Yellow GMC cab and chassis with red refrigeration box, green window plastic, 3". The first release in 1970 was painted like the regular wheels version with red cab and chassis and green refrigeration box. These are hard to find and command approx. $145 MIP values
EX $7   **NM** $14   **MIP** $21

44-2SF, Boss Mustang, 1973, Yellow body with opening black hood, silver plastic interior, amber plastic window, unpainted base, 3"
EX $5   **NM** $10   **MIP** $15

(KP Photo, John Brown Sr. collection)

44-3SF, Passenger Coach, 1979, Red body, cream-colored plastic top, green window plastic, black base, "431 & 432" or "GWR" labels, 2-7/8"

(KP Photo, Tom Michael collection)

45-1SF, Ford Group Six, 1970, Metallic green body with white plastic interior, silver plastic engine, clear window plastic and number "7" label; or red body with amber-colored windows and number "45" labels, (a later version, first appearing in 1973), 3"
EX $4   **NM** $10   **MIP** $22

(KP Photo)

45-2SF, B.M.W. 3.0 CSL, 1975, Orange body with opening doors, yellow plastic interior, amber or blue plastic windows, silver base, "BMW" label on hood, 2-7/8"
EX $3   **NM** $7   **MIP** $15

(KP Photo)

46-1SF, Mercedes 300SE, 1970, Gold or blue body, white plastic interior, opening trunk, (some early models with opening doors, too) thin wheels, unpainted base, grille and headlights, 2-7/8". Blue models are hard to find and may command MIP values of $100 or more. Olive-drab staff car versions as part of TP-14 Two-Pack set, about $15 in NM condition
EX $4   **NM** $8   **MIP** $16

(KP Photo, Tom Michael collection)

46-2SF, Stretcha Fetcha, 1973, White with blue windows, white plastic interior, red base, "Ambulance" red cross labels, wide wheels, opening rear hatch, 2-3/4"
EX $2   **NM** $4   **MIP** $8

(KP Photo)

46-3SF, Ford Tractor & Harrow, 1979, Blue Ford tractor with cab, no window plastic, gray engine block and base, black wheels with or without orange-yellow painted

hubs, yellow plastic disk or harrow included (not shown). Also included with hay trailer in TP-11 Two-Pack
EX $1 **NM** $6 **MIP** $14

(KP Photo)

46-4SF, Hot Chocolate, 1982, Metallic brown and black funny car body with white stripe. This car was an update on the "Dragon Wheels" funny car
EX $2 **NM** $5 **MIP** $8

47-1SF, DAF Tipper Container Truck, 1970, Silver-green cab and chassis, plastic tipping box with removable top, red plastic grille and partial base, green plastic windows, no interior, 3". A Superfast update of the regular wheels model
EX $6 **NM** $10 **MIP** $22

(KP Photo, Tom Michael collection)

47-2SF, Beach Hopper, 1973, Blue with pink "spatter" paint, brown plastic interior, tan plastic driver that "hops" as car moves along (a Rola-Matic model), wide wheels, sun label on hood, 2-5/8"
EX $2 **NM** $5 **MIP** $9

(KP Photo)

47-3SF, Pannier Locomotive, 1979, Green body, "GWR" labels, metallic brown base. This model had not yet replaced the Beach Hopper in the 1-75 catalog lineup, but was introduced as being available later in the year
EX $2 **NM** $5 **MIP** $8

(KP Photo)

47-4SF, Jaguar SS, 1982, Red body, silver grille, headlights and windshield, light-brown plastic interior, wide wheels
EX $2 **NM** $4 **MIP** $8

48-1SF, Dumper Truck, 1970, Blue Dodge cab and chassis, yellow dumper bed, green plastic windows, no interior, silver plastic grille, bumper and partial base, 3". A Superfast version of the 48-3RW regular wheels model
EX $10 **NM** $18 **MIP** $32

(KP Photo, John Brown Sr. collection)

48-2SF, Pi-Eyed Piper, 1973, Blue body, oversized plastic engine on hood, number "8" label on roof, silver exhaust pipes along sides, no interior, blue plastic windows, 2-1/2"
EX $5 **NM** $8 **MIP** $20

48-3SF, Sambron Jack Lift, 1978, Yellow body with yellow plastic lifting forks, no window plastic, 3-1/16"
EX $2 **NM** $4 **MIP** $7

49-3SF, Crane Truck, 1977, Yellow body with swiveling crane section, extendable crane arm, red plastic hook, six wide wheels, 3"
EX $3 **NM** $6 **MIP** $12

50-1SF, Kennel Truck, 1970, Dark-green Ford truck body, with four white plastic dogs and clear plastic canopy over bed. Green plastic window, no interior, thin wheels, 2-3/4"
EX $12 **NM** $25 **MIP** $40

(KP Photo, Tom Michael collection)

50-2SF, Articulated Truck, 1973, Short yellow cab with green plastic windows and blue trailer with yellow plastic chassis, wide wheels, 3". Some have arrow labels, some do not. Notice the difference in the wheels on the trailer.
EX $1 **NM** $4 **MIP** $7

(KP Photo, George Cuhaj collection)

51-1SF, 8-Wheel Tipper, 1971, Yellow AEC cab and chassis, silver tipper bed, green plastic windows, no interior, "Pointer" labels, silver grille and headlights and partial base, 3"
EX $8 **NM** $18 **MIP** $40

(KP Photo)

51-2SF, Citroen SM, 1973, Dark red metallic body, opening doors, unpainted base, white plastic interior and tow hook, clear plastic windows, 2-7/8". In 1976, the paint scheme changed to blue with a red stripe and number "8" on roof
EX $4 **NM** $7 **MIP** $12

(KP Photo)

51-3SF, Combine Harvester, 1979, Red with yellow reel and auger, black Superfast wheels, Superfast wheels with yellow hubs or regular wheels, 2-7/8"
EX $1 **NM** $3 **MIP** $7

(KP Photo)

52-1SF, Dodge Charger Mk III, 1970, Metallic red or metallic lime-green body with black plastic interior, lift-up canopy, wide wheels, 3". Early red models also featured "hood scoop" labels
EX $4 **NM** $7 **MIP** $18

(KP Photo)

52-2SF, Police Launch, 1977, White body with blue plastic base and two blue plastic officers, labels on sides read "Police," silver metal horns on cabin roof, dark-blue plastic windows, thin wheels, 3-1/16"

EX $1   **NM** $4   **MIP** $7

(KP Photo, Tom Michael collection)

53-1SF, Ford Zodiac Mk IV, 1970, Metallic green body, opening hood, silver engine with spare tire, white plastic interior, clear plastic windows, 2-3/4"

EX $7   **NM** $10   **MIP** $22

(KP Photo, Tom Michael collection)

53-2SF, Tanzara, 1973, Orange body, amber plastic windows, opening rear hood shows silver plastic engine, wide wheels, silver plastic interior, unpainted base, 3". Models in 1976 had a bicentennial color scheme; white with red and blue stripes and number "53" on hood

EX $2   **NM** $4   **MIP** $7

(KP Photo)

53-3SF, CJ6 Jeep, 1978, Red body, tan plastic roof, yellow plastic interior, unpainted metal base

EX $3   **NM** $7   **MIP** $12

(KP Photo by Dr. Douglas Sadecky)

54-1SF, Cadillac Ambulance, 1970, White body, blue plastic windows, white plastic interior, red cross labels, white or silver-painted grille, narrow wheels, 2-7/8". Shown here with its regular wheels predecessor

EX $12   **NM** $22   **MIP** $40

(KP Photo, Tom Michael collection)

54-2SF, Ford Capri, 1971, Red with black hood or all pink with white plastic interior, unpainted base, opening hood, wide wheels, 2-7/8". All-red models were included with boat and trailer in TP-5 Two-Pack starting in 1977

EX $2   **NM** $5   **MIP** $11

(KP Photo)

54-3SF, Personnel Carrier, 1978, Olive-green with tan plastic troops and gun, black base, wide wheels, 3"

EX $3   **NM** $7   **MIP** $12

(KP Photo, Tom Michael collection)

55-1SF, Police Car, 1970, White Mercury sedan, clear windows, white plastic interior with molded figures, police label on hood, shield labels on doors, blue or red dome light, thin wheels, 3-1/16"

EX $8   **NM** $17   **MIP** $30

(KP Photo, Tom Michael collection)

55-2SF, Mercury Police Car, 1971, White station wagon body with blue or red dome lights, thin or wide wheels, unpainted base and grille, clear plastic windows, 3-1/16". Early versions had shield labels on doors and "Police" label on hood. Versions from 1973 to 1975 had only arrow-shaped red "Police" label. This car was a minor casting variation of the Mercury Commuter 73-1SF

EX $7   **NM** $15   **MIP** $27

(KP Photo, Tom Michael collection)

55-3SF, Hellraiser, 1976, White body with red plastic interior, silver plastic rear engine, clear windshield, wide wheels, stars and stripes label on hood. Or, blue body and white plastic interior, stars and stripes label, 3"

EX $2   **NM** $5   **MIP** $12

(KP Photo, Tom Michael collection)

55-4SF, Ford Cortina 1600 GL, 1979, Metallic gold with clear plastic windows, opening doors, unpainted base, red plastic interior. Introduced in 1979/80 catalog, but not yet part of the 1-75 lineup

EX $2   **NM** $6   **MIP** $12

(KP Photo, George Cuhaj collection)

56-1SF, BMC 1800 Pininfarina, 1970, Metallic gold or orange body, thin or wide wheels, opening doors, clear plastic windows, unpainted base, white plastic interior, 2-3/4". Later models modified the casting of the rear wheel wells to accommodate the wider Superfast wheels that became standard by 1973. This was a new model in the 1-75 lineup, not an adapted regular wheels casting like many others in 1970. Orange body versions about $16 MIP

EX $4   **NM** $7   **MIP** $12

(KP Photo)

56-2SF, Hi-Tailer, 1975, White body with yellow or blue plastic driver, silver plastic rear engine, red, white and blue striped label with "5, Team Matchbox and MB," 3"

EX $2   **NM** $4   **MIP** $9

56-3SF, Mercedes 450 SEL, 1979, Blue body, opening doors, light-yellow plastic interior, clear plastic windows, unpainted base. Introduced in 1979/80 catalog, had not yet replaced Hi-Tailer in the 1-75 lineup

EX $1   **NM** $3   **MIP** $6

57-1SF, Eccles Caravan, 1970, Cream or light-yellow trailer body with four thin wheels, stripe and flower label on sides, red or orange plastic roof, green or light-yellow plastic interior, 3-1/16". Like many models, the Eccles Caravan continued on in a Two-Pack set, the TP-4 Holiday Set

EX $4   **NM** $7   **MIP** $16

57-2SF, Wild Life Truck, 1973, Yellow body, red plastic windows, "Ranger" label on hood with elephant illustration, silver plastic grille, wide wheels, red plastic lion circles in truck bed as it is pushed along (Rola-Matic), no interior, clear plastic canopy over truck bed

EX $4   **NM** $7   **MIP** $14

58-1SF, DAF Girder Truck, 1970, Off-white or lime-green cab and chassis, red plastic girders, red plastic grille and partial base, green window plastic, no interior, 3". Off-white versions aren't real common and have approx. $65 MIP value

EX $6   **NM** $11   **MIP** $20

(KP Photo, Tom Michael collection)

58-2SF, Woosh-N-Push, 1973, Yellow body with open cockpit, red plastic interior, silver plastic exhaust, number "2" label on back of roof; or metallic red body, cream plastic interior, number "8" label with stars and stripes on roof (1976 version), 3"

EX $2   **NM** $4   **MIP** $8

(KP Photo)

58-3SF, Faun Dumper, 1977, Yellow body and dumper bed, black base, red plastic windows, 2-3/4"

EX $1   **NM** $3   **MIP** $5

(KP Photo, Tom Michael collection)

59-1SF, Ford Galaxie Fire Chief Car, 1970, Red body, white plastic interior and tow hook, clear plastic windows, thin wheels, shield labels on doors, blue dome light, 2-7/8". Oddly, this model dropped from the lineup for one year and returned, briefly, for 1972

EX $12   **NM** $22   **MIP** $45

59-1SF, Mercury Fire Chief Car, 1971, Red sedan body with white plastic interior (early versions with two figures), unpainted base, blue dome light, thin or wide wheels, shield and fire chief labels or fire helmet labels, also included in TP-10 Two-Pack with a dual dome light arrangement

EX $4   **NM** $8   **MIP** $16

(KP Photo, Tom Michael collection)

59-3SF, Planet Scout, 1976, Metallic green with lime-green or red with yellow body, silver plastic interior, yellow plastic windows, wide wheels, 2-3/4"

EX $2   **NM** $4   **MIP** $8

60-1SF, Truck with Site Office, 1970, Blue Leyland truck with Ergomatic cab, yellow plastic hut with green plastic roof, thin wheels, green plastic windows, silver plastic grille and partial base, 2-1/2"

EX $6   **NM** $10   **MIP** $22

(KP Photo, Tom Michael collection)

60-2SF, Lotus Super Seven, 1972, Orange or yellow body with unpainted base, black plastic interior, clear plastic windshield, ghost and flame label on hood, or checker pattern with "60" along length of car, 2-7/8"

EX $5   **NM** $9   **MIP** $16

60-3SF, Holden Pick-Up, 1978, Red with yellow plastic motorcycles in bed and yellow plastic interior, unpainted base, checkered label with "500" on hood, 3-1/16"

EX $4   **NM** $7   **MIP** $14

(KP Photo, Tom Michael collection)

60-4SF, Piston Popper, 1982, Yellow body with "Piston Popper" on hood and number "60" on sides. Unpainted metal base, red Rola-Matic pistons like the earlier version

EX $2   **NM** $4   **MIP** $6

(KP Photo, George Cuhaj collection)

61-1SF, Alvis Stalwart, 1970, White body, with yellow plastic canopy (not shown) green plastic wheels with removable black tires, "BP Exploration" labels on sides, 2-5/8". Olive-green versions were included with TP-16 Two-Pack in 1979

EX $9   **NM** $17   **MIP** $30

(KP Photo)

61-2SF, Blue Shark, 1972, Blue body with unpainted base, white plastic driver, silver plastic rear engine, black plastic exhaust pipes, clear plastic windshield, "86" or Scorpion label (harder to find, about $50 MIP), 3"

EX $3   **NM** $8   **MIP** $15

61-3SF, Wreck Truck, 1979, Red truck body, black base, red plastic windows and dome lights, no interior, white towing arms with red plastic hooks

EX $3   **NM** $6   **MIP** $10

(KP Photo)

62-1SF, Mercury Cougar, 1970, Lime-green body with red plastic interior and tow hook, opening doors, 3"

EX $9   **NM** $16   **MIP** $30

(KP Photo, Tom Michael collection)

62-2SF, Renault 17TL, 1974, Red body with opening doors, white plastic interior, blue plastic windows, some with stripe and number "6" label, some without, 3". A version with "Fire" labels was included in the G-12 Rescue Gift Set in the 1977 catalog

EX $2   **NM** $5   **MIP** $12

62-2SF, Rat Rod Dragster, 1971, Light-green body, clear plastic windows, red plastic interior, exposed engine through hood, "Rat Rod" labels on sides, 3". A reworking of the Mercury Cougar casting

EX $5   **NM** $8   **MIP** $18

(KP Photo, Tom Michael collection)

62-3SF, Chevy Corvette, 1982, Black body with yellow and orange stripes running from hood to trunk, white plastic interior, plain base with side-pipes

EX $2   **NM** $5   **MIP** $8

62-1SF, Dodge Crane Truck, 1970, Yellow body with rotating crane section, yellow plastic hook, black base, green plastic windows, no interior, 3"

EX $6   **NM** $11   **MIP** $20

(KP Photo)

63-2SF, Freeway Gas Tanker, 1974, Short red cab with black base and wide wheels, white plastic tanker trailer with red chassis, "Burmah" labels on tanker section, 3-1/8". Also available in yellow and white Shell versions, blue and white Aral versions and red and white Chevron version (part of TP-17 Two-Pack). As with regular wheels editions, the German-issue Aral version is harder to find, about $25 MIP. There is also an olive-green version with TP-14 with "High Octane" labels on the sides

EX $2   **NM** $4   **MIP** $8

(KP Photo, Tom Michael collection)

63-2SF, Freeway Gas Tanker, 1974, A view showing the more popular edition with the "Burmah" labels and red cab

64-1SF, MG 1100, 1970, Blue body, white plastic interior with dog and driver, tow hook, thin wheels, silver base, 2-5/8"

EX $9   **NM** $22   **MIP** $40

(KP Photo, Tom Michael collection)

64-2SF, Slingshot Dragster, 1972, Pink or blue body with dual silver plastic engines and red exhaust pipes, label on hood with number "9" and flames, white plastic driver, 3"

EX $4   **NM** $7   **MIP** $15

(KP Photo, Tom Michael collection)

64-3SF, Fire Chief Car, 1976, Red body with blue plastic windows, silver air scoops on hood, silver base, "Fire Chief" labels with shield on sides, 3"

EX $3   **NM** $5   **MIP** $12

(KP Photo)

64-4SF, Caterpillar Bulldozer, 1981, Yellow die-cast body with yellow plastic blade and unpainted base and engine. Cab can be tan or black, and later models have "CAT" and "C" logos on sides near cab

EX $2   **NM** $4   **MIP** $7

(KP Photo, John Brown Sr. collection)

64-4SF, Caterpillar Bulldozer, The black cab and "CAT" logos appeared on later versions of the bulldozer

(KP Photo)

65-1SF, Combine Harvester, Red with yellow plastic reel and front wheels with removable black plastic tires, 3". This model was another holdover from the regular wheels lineup, first introduced in 1967, but remaining until 1973

EX $3   **NM** $7   **MIP** $12

65-2SF, Saab Sonnet, 1974, Blue body with plastic lift-up rear hatch, light-yellow plastic interior, wide wheels, unpainted base, 2-7/8"

EX $4   **NM** $7   **MIP** $15

(KP Photo, Tom Michael collection)

65-3SF, Airport Coach, 1978, Metallic blue body, white roof, yellow plastic windows, off-white interior, "British Airways," "American Airlines" or "Lufthansa" labels on sides are most common, 3-1/16". German versions with "Schulbus" labels are harder to find, about $45 MIP. Other variations include: Red body, white top with "TWA" or "Qantas" labels

EX $4   **NM** $6   **MIP** $9

(KP Photo, Tom Michael collection)

65-3SF, Airport Coach, 1978, Version with red body, white top and "TWA" labels

(KP Photo, Tom Michael collection)

65-3SF, Airport Coach, 1978, Version with red body, white top and "Qantas" labels

(KP Photo by Dr. Douglas Sadecky)

66-1SF, Greyhound Bus, 1971, Silver with yellow plastic windows, thin wheels, blue and white Greyhound labels on sides, 3". Shown here in an interesting blister-pack/box combo that Matchbox tried out in the late 1960s and early 1970s. MIP value approx $60 for this combo, regular MIP values shown
EX $9   **NM** $16   **MIP** $30

(KP Photo, Tom Michael collection)

66-2SF, Mazda RX 500, 1972, Early releases were orange with white base, opening rear engine hood, silver plastic interior with purple windows, 2-7/8". Later versions were red with white base and racing tempo "77" on hood with yellow windows
EX $3   **NM** $5   **MIP** $9

(KP Photo)

66-3SF, Ford Transit, 1978, Orange truck with dropside bed and plastic cargo crates, unpainted base, blue/green plastic windows, light-yellow plastic interior, 2-3/4"
EX $4   **NM** $7   **MIP** $12

(KP Photo)

67-1SF, Volkswagen 1600 TL, 1970, Pink or purple body, opening doors, white plastic interior, clear windows, unpainted base, thin or wide wheels (wide wheels version included in G-2 Transporter Gift Set), 2-11/16"
EX $8   **NM** $17   **MIP** $32

(KP Photo, Tom Michael collection)

67-2SF, Hot Rocker, 1973, Ford Capri body with open hood and oversized "hopping" engine (part of Rola-Matics series). Wide wheels, unpainted base. Available in lime-green and red paint variations, 3"
EX $3   **NM** $5   **MIP** $9

(KP Photo, Tom Michael collection)

67-3SF, Datsun 260Z, 1979, Pinkish-red or silver body with yellow plastic or red interior, opening doors, black base, 3". Silver model has red and black stripes on sides and hood with "Datsun 2+2" in black type
EX $3   **NM** $6   **MIP** $10

(KP Photo, Tom Michael collection)

68-1SF, Porsche 910, 1970, Red body with thin or wide wheels, cream or light-yellow plastic interior, clear windows, number "68" label on hood, 3"
EX $4   **NM** $8   **MIP** $17

(KP Photo)

68-2SF, Cosmobile, 1976, Blue or red body, silver plastic trim and interior, yellow base, wide wheels, 2-7/8"
EX $2   **NM** $5   **MIP** $8

68-3SF, Chevy Van, 1979, Orange with blue and red stripes along sides, blue plastic windows, silver base. Introduced in the 1979/80 catalog, but hadn't yet replaced the Cosmobile in the 1-75 lineup
EX $1   **NM** $4   **MIP** $7

(KP Photo, George Cuhaj collection)

69-1SF, Rolls-Royce Coupe, 1970, Blue body, clear windshield, brown plastic interior, thin wheels, opening trunk, tow hook, 3-1/16"
EX $6   **NM** $11   **MIP** $20

(KP Photo, Tom Michael collection)

69-2SF, Turbo Fury, 1973, Red body, clear windshield, number "69" label on hood, white plastic driver, fans on rear of car rotate when pushed (Rola-Matics series), and front of vehicle same style as Blue Shark, 3"
EX $1   **NM** $4   **MIP** $7

(KP Photo, Tom Michael collection)

69-3SF, Security Truck, 1979, Red armored truck with white "Wells Fargo"

type on sides, blue windows and dome light, unpainted base, wide wheels, white roof, 2-7/8"

EX $5   **NM** $9   **MIP** $14

70-1SF, Grit Spreader, 1971, Red Ford cab and chassis, yellow hopper section, no interior, thin wheels, green windows, 2-5/8"

EX $5   **NM** $10   **MIP** $18

(KP Photo)

70-2SF, Dodge Dragster, 1972, Pink funny-car Dodge Charger body, silver engine, black or unpainted base, red plastic struts to hold body, snake labels along sides, 3". A preview drawing of this model is seen in the 1971 catalog under the heading "watch out for these 4 new models"

EX $6   **NM** $11   **MIP** $20

70-3SF, Self-Propelled Gun, 1977, Green with black plastic gun that fires and recoils while rolled along (Rola-Matics series). Tan treads, black roller wheels, 2-5/8"

EX n/a   **NM** n/a   **MIP** $8

(KP Photo, Tom Michael collection)

70-4SF, Ferrari 308 GTB, 1981, Red, may or may not have "Ferrari" on sides and emblem on hood, black base

71-1SF, Ford Heavy Wreck Truck, 1970, Red cab and towing crane, red plastic hook, white bed with "Esso" labels on sides, green windows and dome light, white grille, 3". Olive-green versions with all-black wheels were included in 1978's TP-16 Two-Pack

EX $11   **NM** $17   **MIP** $32

71-2SF, Jumbo Jet, 1973, Motorcycle with blue seat and handlebars, black roller-style wheels, silver plastic engine, red elephant head on handlebars, 2-3/4"

EX $6   **NM** $9   **MIP** $18

(KP Photo, Tom Michael collection)

71-3SF, Cattle Truck, 1978, Red or metallic gold with plastic yellow or cream stake bed, black plastic cattle, blue or green windows, 2-7/8". Also included in the 1979 TP-19 Two-Pack in red with a matching trailer and plastic cattle

EX $2   **NM** $5   **MIP** $8

72-1SF, Standard Jeep, 1970, Yellow body with red plastic seats, black bumpers, spare tire on back, 2-3/8". An update of the 72-2RW Standard Jeep, but in this case the spare couldn't actually be used

EX $10   **NM** $20   **MIP** $30

(KP Photo)

72-2SF, SRN Hovercraft, 1972, White top with black plastic base and "SRN6" with British flag labels on sides, red plastic propeller, thin wheels in underside of hull, blue plastic windows, 3-1/16"

EX $1   **NM** $2   **MIP** $5

72-3SF, Bomag Road Roller, 1979, Yellow body with red plastic interior and engine, black plastic roller, silver or yellow hubs. Introduced in 1979/80 catalog, but hadn't yet replaced the SRN Hovercraft in the 1-75 lineup

EX $1   **NM** $4   **MIP** $7

(KP Photo)

72-4SF, Maxi Taxi, 1982, Yellow Ford Capri body with Rola-Matic engine that hops when car is moved, an update of the Hot Rocker model. Checkered taxi tampos and rates on sides, "Maxi Taxi" on roof, black base

(KP Photo)

73-1SF, Mercury Commuter, 1970, Metallic lime-green body with thin wheels, clear windows, white plastic interior with dogs looking out the back, unpainted base, 3-1/16". By 1972, this car had changed to red with a bull's head label on the hood and luggage rack grooves on the roof, with approx. $16 MIP value. Prices for green model shown

EX $6   **NM** $14   **MIP** $25

73-2SF, Weasel, 1973, Medium metallic-green armored vehicle with black turret that turns as the car is rolled (Rola-Matics series), wide wheels, all-black or with silver hubs, 2-7/8". Olive-green versions were issued as part of TP-13 Two-Pack

EX $2   **NM** $5   **MIP** $8

74-1SF, Daimler Bus, 1970, Red or pink body, white plastic interior, thin or wide wheels, "Esso Extra Petrol" and Esso logo labels on sides, 3"

EX $5   **NM** $11   **MIP** $20

(KP Photo, Tom Michael collection)

74-2SF, Toe Joe, 1974, Metallic lime-green body with green plastic towing arms and red plastic hooks, yellow windows, unpainted base, 3". Versions with yellow bodies and red towing arms with black plastic hooks were included with the Racing Mini in TP-6 Two-Pack

EX $3   **NM** $6   **MIP** $12

(KP Photo, Tom Michael collection)

74-3SF, Mercury Cougar Villager, 1979, Lime-green or blue body, pale yellow interior, unpainted base, opening tailgate, 3-1/16"

EX $2   **NM** $5   **MIP** $11

75-2SF, Alfa Carabo, 1971, Pink with yellow or white base, models in 1976 had yellow stripes running across top of car. White plastic interior, clear windows, 3"

EX $2   **NM** $5   **MIP** $11

(KP Photo)

75-3SF, Seasprite Helicopter, 1977, White body, red base, blue windows, regular wheels landing gear, black plastic rotor, "Rescue" labels on tail section, 2-7/8"

EX $4   **NM** $6   **MIP** $9

MIDGETOY

JUMBO SERIES, 6" VEHICLES

American LaFrance Pumper Truck, red with silver detailing and decals; 1970s-80s
EX $5   NM $10   MIP $15

Mobile Artillery, Army green, with silver detailing, 1970s-80s
EX $6   NM $12   MIP $18

Oil Tanker, white-green, "Midgetoy Oil Co.," painted details; 1970s-80s
EX $12   NM $25   MIP $37

Scenicruiser Bus, two-tone paint, "Midgetoy Bus Line"; 1970s-80s
EX $10   NM $20   MIP $30

JUNIOR SERIES, 2-1/2" TO 3" VEHICLES

Army Jeep, Army green, black plastic tires; 1960s-70s
EX $3   NM $6   MIP $9

Camper, Ford pickup with die-cast camper body; 1970s-80s
EX $4   NM $8   MIP $12

Corvette Stingray, various colors but often orange; 1971-80s
EX $1   NM $2   MIP $4

Ford Mustang, 1970s-80s
EX $1   NM $2   MIP $4

Ford Pickup, 1971 Ford model, white or other color; 19702-80s
EX $2   NM $3   MIP $5

Ford Torino, various colors but often orange; 1971-80s
EX $1   NM $2   MIP $4

Ford Torino Fire Chief Car, red, cast-in flasher lights; 1970s-80s
EX $4   NM $9   MIP $12

Hot Rod, Ford V-8 design, open cockpit, black plastic tires, decals and/or painted headlights; 1970s-80s
EX $2   NM $4   MIP $6

Hot Rod, Ford V-8 design, open cockpit, black plastic tires, single-color paint; 1960s
EX $3   NM $4   MIP $8

Indy Race Car, open cockpit, Kurtis Kraft race car, black plastic tires, decals and/or painted highlights; 1970s-80s
EX $3   NM $4   MIP $8

Indy Race Car, open cockpit, Kurtis Kraft design race car, black plastic tires, single-color paint; 1960s
EX $6   NM $9   MIP $13

MG Sports Roadster, open-top sports car, black plastic tires, single-color paint; 1960s
EX $6   NM $9   MIP $13

MG Sports Roadster, open-top sports car, black plastic tires, decals and/or painted highlights; 1960s-80s
EX $3   NM $6   MIP $9

Sunbeam Racer, land-speed race car, black plastic tires, decals and/or painted highlights; 1960s-80s
EX $3   NM $8   MIP $9

Volkswagen Beetle, black plastic tires, no decals or masking; 1960s
EX $8   NM $15   MIP $20

Volkswagen Beetle, various colors, black plastic tires, decals and/or painted detailing; 1970s-80s
EX $8   NM $15   MIP $20

Wrecker Truck, cabover, metal boom with hook, black plastic tires; 1960s-70s
EX $4   NM $8   MIP $12

PEE-WEE SERIES, 2" VEHICLES

American LaFrance Fire Truck, 1969-80s
EX $1   NM $1   MIP $2

Ford GT, 1969-80s
EX $1   NM $1   MIP $2

Hot Rod, 1969-80s
EX $1   NM $1   MIP $2

Jeep, 1969-80s
EX $1   NM $1   MIP $2

MG Sports Roadster, 1969-80s
EX $1   NM $1   MIP $2

VEHICLES — MATCHBOX SUPERFAST

NYLINT

No. 1000, Deliverall, 1946-51, wind-up; three-wheeled scooter with large cargo box; white, yellow, red, blue and black; rare
EX $100   **NM** $300   **MIP** $600

No. 1100, Big Dig, regular version
EX $50   **NM** $115   **MIP** $225

No. 1100, Elgin Street Sweeper, 1950-52, wind-up; yellow with red and black highlights, white plastic driver; bottom and side brooms rotate
EX $50   **NM** $175   **MIP** $350

No. 1101, Big Dig, 1967-70, re-design of No. SR1100 to look like Tonka's Mighty Cranes; orange, yellow and black with yellow plastic track wheels
EX $50   **NM** $100   **MIP** $200

No. 1200, Lawn and Garden Set, 1965, new number; same as No. 7000
EX $50   **NM** $125   **MIP** $250

No. 1200, Pumpmobile, 1950-52, wind-up; Howdy Doody cowboy-like figure (unlicensed), yellow, red and blue
EX $100   **NM** $300   **MIP** $600

No. 1210, Aerial Ladder Fire Truck, 1968-74, red with white ladders and black handwheels; Nylint's first large fire truck
EX $75   **NM** $140   **MIP** $275

No. 1211, Aerial Ladder Fire Truck, 1975, second version of No. 1210 (less steel)
EX $50   **NM** $100   **MIP** $200

No. 1300, Tournarocker, 1951-52, first version; open tractor w/driver; orange (1951) or mustard yellow (1952); scale model of a machine by R. G. Letourneau
EX $50   **NM** $150   **MIP** $300

No. 1300, Tournarocker, 1953-54, second version; closed cab, no driver, grille plate on front, larger 3-3/4" wheels; all yellow; also by R.G. Letourneau
EX $75   **NM** $125   **MIP** $250

No. 1300, Tournarocker, 1955-57, third version; embossed grille details, larger 3-3/4" wheels; all yellow (1955), orange and yellow (1956-57); also by R.G. Letourneau
EX $75   **NM** $125   **MIP** $250

No. 1310, Backhoe, 1968-73, yellow backhoe on rubber crawler tracks with black base
EX $75   **NM** $140   **MIP** $275

No. 1400, Road Grader, 1951, first version; small wheels and steel grille plate; orange
EX $75   **NM** $125   **MIP** $250

No. 1400, Road Grader, 1952-53, second version; larger 3-3/4" wheels and grille plate; orange
EX $50   **NM** $175   **MIP** $350

No. 1400, Road Grader, 1954-58, third version; embossed grille, large 3-3/4" wheels; orange (1954-55), yellow (1956-58)
EX $50   **NM** $175   **MIP** $350

No. 1410, Hopper Dump, 1968-69, regular single-trailer version; yellow with black dump doors
EX $75   **NM** $150   **MIP** $300

No. 1420, Twin Hopper Dump Truck, 1967, Sears exclusive; yellow semi tractor pulling two hopper dump trailers, black dump doors and operating levers
EX $125   **NM** $225   **MIP** $450

No. 1500, Tournahopper, 1952-53, first version; grille plate on front of closed tractor; yellow with black decals; replica of a R.G. Letourneau machine
EX $75   **NM** $175   **MIP** $350

No. 1500, Tournahopper, 1954-56, second version; embossed front, 3-3/4" wheels; yellow (1954-55), orange (1956). After 1953, these are replicas of Letourneau-Westinghouse machines
EX $75   **NM** $175   **MIP** $350

No. 1600, Payloader, 1951, tan
EX $50   **NM** $175   **MIP** $350

No. 1600, Payloader, 1951-55, red and yellow
EX $50   **NM** $175   **MIP** $350

No. 1600, Payloader, 1956-58, light green and yellow
EX $50   **NM** $175   **MIP** $350

No. 1600, Payloader, 1958, dark green
EX $50   **NM** $175   **MIP** $350

No. 1600, Payloader, 1958, yellow
EX $50   **NM** $175   **MIP** $350

No. 1610, Bronco Police Car, 1968, white Ford Bronco with lights and black trim
EX $35   **NM** $75   **MIP** $150

No. 1700, Tournahauler, 1953, first version; yellow
EX $100   **NM** $200   **MIP** $400

No. 1700, Tournahauler, 1953-54, second version dark green with grille plate
EX $50   **NM** $125   **MIP** $250

No. 1700, Tournahauler, 1954-55, third version; dark green embossed grille
EX $50   **NM** $125   **MIP** $250

No. 1700, Tournahauler, 1956, fourth version; light green
EX $50   **NM** $125   **MIP** $250

No. 1710, Bronco Petmobile, 1968-70s, dark blue Ford Bronco, white plastic cage for dogs
EX $40   **NM** $115   **MIP** $225

No. 1800, Traveloader, 1953-55, first version with smaller blades on front feeder belt (1953); second version with larger blades (1954-55); both versions orange with black decals, black belts on front feeder, black rear conveyor belt
EX $75   **NM** $125   **MIP** $250

No. 1810, Twister Exploration Car, 1969-73, yellow and black; Nylint's version of Tonka's Crater Crawler
EX $25   **NM** $100   **MIP** $200

No. 1900, Tournaractor, 1954-55, yellow and black with 4-7/16" wheels; by J.D. Adams
EX $50   **NM** $175   **MIP** $350

No. 1910, Hot Rod, 1969-72
EX $25   **NM** $40   **MIP** $75

No. 2000, Speed Swing Loader, 1955-58, orange or yellow; by Pettibone-Mulliken Co. orange and black (1955), yellow and black (1956-58)
EX $50   **NM** $125   **MIP** $250

No. 2010, Elevating Scraper, 1969-73, two-wheel tractor with large earthmover with rubber belt, pan scraper trailer (looked like a Caterpillar earthmover)
EX $50   **NM** $200   **MIP** $400

No. 2050, Jumbo Street Roller, 1971-77, roller in front, wheels in back; large red roller in front and red operator's cab (1971); yellow and black (1972-77)
EX $50   **NM** $100   **MIP** $200

No. 2070, Bobcat Loader, 1970-, yellow and black trim
EX $35   **NM** $65   **MIP** $125

No. 2100, Tournadozer, 1956-59, orange with black seat and motor; first version with larger 4-7/16" wheels (1956)
EX $75   **NM** $175   **MIP** $300

No. 2200, Michigan Shovel (crane), 1955-65, 10 wheels, clamshell bucket, single headlights, grille plate, steering (1955-56); six wheels, single or dual headlights, embossed front grille or grille plate (1956-60); no steering, grille sticker (1961-63); magnet added to bucket but only drop-down outriggers (1964-65); only Nylint toy to have real rubber tires through its first 10 years
EX $50   **NM** $150   **MIP** $400

No. 2201, Michigan Shovel (crane), 1966-73, redesigned version (made to look like Tonka mobile crane); clamshell bucket; this toy continued with number changes until the mid-1980s
EX $50   **NM** $150   **MIP** $300

No. 2300, Elgin Street Sweeper, 1956-57, battery-operated version, closed cab; yellow cab roof, red/yellow body (1956); red cab roof, yellow body (1957)
EX $50   **NM** $175   **MIP** $350

No. 2310, Beach Buggy, 1969-72
EX $25   **NM** $40   **MIP** $75

No. 2400, Electronic Cannon Truck, 1956, no radar antenna; four red/black-tipped rockets; Nylint's second battery-operated toy
EX $75   **NM** $150   **MIP** $300

No. 2400, Electronic Cannon Truck, 1957-59, with yellow radar antenna and four rockets
EX $75   **NM** $150   **MIP** $300

No. 2410, Bronco Bobcat, 1969-72, dark red Bronco with white top and larger wheels
EX $35   **NM** $85   **MIP** $175

No. 2500, Telescopic Crane, 1957-60, red with yellow boom, four-wheel steering, extendable boom
EX $100   **NM** $150   **MIP** $300

No. 2500, Telescopic Crane, 1957-60, green with white boom for 1959 NY Toy Fair (won award for toy of the year); rare
EX $150   **NM** $225   **MIP** $450

No. 2600, Missile Launcher, 1957-60, blue-gray, white radar antenna, white missiles with black tips
EX $50   **NM** $125   **MIP** $250

No. 2600, Missile Launcher, 1959, orange, white radar antenna, white missiles with black tips
EX $100   **NM** $175   **MIP** $350

No. 2700, Uranium Hauler, 1958-59, olive drab hydraulic bumper, yellow/black front guard
EX $50   **NM** $125   **MIP** $250

No. 2800, Guided Missile Carrier, 1958-59, first version (1958), non-firing missiles
EX $75   **NM** $125   **MIP** $250

No. 2800, Guided Missile Carrier, 1958-59, later version (through 1960), firing cone of missiles, side-mounted forklift with red/yellow pallet, white missile with red fins and red nose cone
EX $75   **NM** $125   **MIP** $250

No. 2900, Junior Jack Hammer, 1958-59, with air compressor package that connected to toy with 4' rubber hose; Nylint's first plastic toy; red/black jackhammer, yellow/red/black compressor box
EX $50   **NM** $125   **MIP** $250

No. 3000, Grader-Loader, 1959-62, first version with remote bucket release (1959 only); yellow, black bucket; first Nylint construction toy to have plastic tractor wheels (to keep shipping weight low)
EX $75   **NM** $150   **MIP** $300

No. 3100, Payloader Tractor-Shovel, 1959-62, first version yellow with levers in cab (1959 only); red/yellow with levers in cab (1959-60); without levers (1961-62); less than 1,300 made, replica of Hough machine; all toys had steel track base and rubber tracks
EX $75   **NM** $175   **MIP** $350

No. 3200, Power & Light Lineman Truck, 1959-61, yellow cab and flasher light, orange trailer, black rear hoist with tools, rope, yellow spool of wire, two stained poles; orange with yellow cab and flasher light, orange trailer, yellow wire spool
EX $75   **NM** $175   **MIP** $350

No. 3300, Power & Light Posthole Digger Truck, 1959-61, orange, yellow cab roof, orange trailer, yellow posthole assembly and tool box cover, plastic tools, four wooden phone poles
EX $75   **NM** $175   **MIP** $350

No. 3400, Highway Emergency Unit Truck, 1959-63, large cabover Ford wrecker, white with red cab roof, red dolly and wrecker boom; later versions

without boom hoist (only hook hoist); with whitewall tires and tilt cab with motor (1963 only)
EX $50   **NM** $150   **MIP** $300

No. 3500, Countdown Rocket Launcher, 1959-61, three rockets (Atlas, Jupiter, Thor) in various colors; gray gantry crane, dark blue base with yellow, black, or red countdown dial; last Nylint toy from the 1950s and second plastic toy
EX $50   **NM** $125   **MIP** $250

No. 3600, Ford Rapid Delivery Truck, 1960-62, dark blue cabover Ford truck with white stake racks and working lift gate, tilt cab with motor; first Nylint toy of 1960s
EX $75   **NM** $175   **MIP** $300

No. 3700, Street Sprinkler Truck, 1960-61, white tank truck, operating nozzles on front bumper, tilt cab
EX $75   **NM** $175   **MIP** $350

No. 3800, Ford Sales & Service, 1960-61, aqua green with utility rack and ladder
EX $50   **NM** $175   **MIP** $350

No. 3900, Ford Platform Tilt Truck, 1960, metallic blue, white cab roof with tilt cab, narrow side panels on rear bed
EX $75   **NM** $175   **MIP** $350

No. 3900, Platform Dump Truck, 1961, yellow, white cab roof, narrow side panels on rear bed; last truck to feature tilt cab
EX $75   **NM** $175   **MIP** $350

No. 4000, Ford Speedway Truck with Racer, 1960-63, dark tan pickup with white top and trailer and race car
EX $75   **NM** $140   **MIP** $275

No. 4100, Ford Pickup & U-Haul Box Trailer, 1961-66, orange pickup, white cab roof, orange trailer with white/cream top and opening rear door; trucks made before 1965 have two-piece front grille (trucks from 1965-66 with one-piece front grille/bumper and I-beam suspension)
EX $75   **NM** $175   **MIP** $350

No. 4200, Bulldozer, 1961-70, all yellow with rear chain winch (1961-65); yellow with orange winch (1967-70); black plastic motor
EX $50   **NM** $150   **MIP** $300

No. 4200, Bulldozer, 1967-72, orange with towbar instead of winch (1967-70); yellow with towbar (1971-72)
EX $50   **NM** $125   **MIP** $250

No. 4300, Ford U-Haul Rental Fleet, 1960s, includes orange Ford pickup, orange U-Haul van and orange U-Haul open trailer; pickup has two-piece front grille bumper (1961-64), one-piece bumper and I-beam suspension (1965)
EX $75   **NM** $225   **MIP** $450

No. 4400, Camper Pickup, 1961-63, red Ford pickup truck with two-piece front grille/bumper, white topper camper, two green air mattresses
EX $50   **NM** $125   **MIP** $250

No. 4500, Ranch Truck, 1961-64, light blue Ford stake truck, two-piece front grille/bumper, white stake racks, round decals on doors
EX $50   **NM** $100   **MIP** $200

No. 4501, Chase and Sanborne Stake Truck, 1964, same as No. 4500 but with coffee boxes (add 75 percent premium if present)
EX $75   **NM** $175   **MIP** $350

No. 4502, Boysen Paints Stake Truck, 1964, same as No. 4500
EX $75   **NM** $200   **MIP** $400

No. 4600, Construction Four-Wheel Platform Dump
EX $100   **NM** $150   **MIP** $225

No. 4600, Hydraulic Dump, 1961-66, same as No. 2700 but orange with yellow/black decals, front grille guard in yellow/black, hollow plastic wheels
EX $50   **NM** $125   **MIP** $250

No. 4700, Happy Acres Truck with Horses, 1961-63, same as No. 4500 but red truck with white stakes, large picture decal on doors
EX $75   **NM** $150   **MIP** $300

No. 4800, U-Haul Van, 1961, closed trailer, orange and cream, U-Haul decals
EX $50   **NM** $100   **MIP** $200

No. 4900, U-Haul Van, 1961, open trailer, orange and cream, U-Haul decals
EX $50   **NM** $100   **MIP** $200

No. 5000, Dump Truck with Cement Mixer, 1962-66, yellow truck with round decal on doors and two-piece front grille/bumper (1962-64); yellow/green truck with special decal on mixer (1965); yellow body, green dump box, large N logo decal on doors (1966); cement mixer is always yellow
EX $75   **NM** $200   **MIP** $400

No. 5100, Dump Truck, 1962-66, red truck, yellow dump box, two-piece grille/bumper (1962-64); red/yellow truck, one-piece grille/bumper (1965); light green truck, white dump box, one-piece grille/bumper (1966)
EX $50   **NM** $140   **MIP** $275

No. 5200, Econoline Pickup Truck, 1962-72, dual headlights (1962); teardrop headlights (1963-72); red/white truck (1962-65); yellow with black roof (1966-72)
EX $50   **NM** $125   **MIP** $250

No. 5201, Western Auto Econoline Pickup, 1964, rare
EX $75   **NM** $225   **MIP** $450

No. 5300, Custom Camper Econoline Pickup Truck, 1962-66, aqua green truck and plastic camper with opening windows and rear door, slide-out steps under rear door
EX $50   **NM** $125   **MIP** $250

No. 5301, Trailblazer Camper, 1969-72, green and white Econoline camper
EX $35   **NM** $65   **MIP** $125

No. 5302, Philco Radio Camper
EX $75   NM $325   MIP $650

No. 5400, Custom Camper on Pickup Truck with Boat, 1962-65, with red and green sailboat on trailer
EX $75   NM $175   MIP $350

No. 5500, Pepsi Delivery Truck, 1962-67, red, white and blue Ford C-600 truck with decals, six cases of Pepsi and hand truck
EX $50   NM $225   MIP $450

No. 5600, Farm Set, 1962-64, with light blue/white No. 4500 Stake Truck, light blue/white No. 5200 Econoline Pickup Truck and other assorted pieces
EX $75   NM $175   MIP $350

No. 5700, Construction Set, 1962-64, orange No. 5000 Dump and Cement Mixer with yellow drum, Econoline Pickup Truck and Open Stake Trailer; rare
EX $100   NM $300   MIP $600

No. 5800, Ford Econoline Van, 1963-64, purple with white decals; dark pink or maroon (1964 only)
EX $50   NM $175   MIP $350

No. 5801, U-Haul Van, 1966-67, orange Ford Econoline, white U-Haul decals
EX $50   NM $200   MIP $400

No. 5802, Admiral TV Van, 1966, Ford Econoline with decals on both sides and all doors; special premium available through Admiral TV delaers, very rare
EX $75   NM $325   MIP $650

No. 5803, Culligan Water Van, 1966, dark blue Ford Econoline with white top and Culligan decals on sides and doors; very rare
EX $75   NM $275   MIP $550

No. 5900, Race Team, 1963-66, Ford Econoline with race car (white and other colors) and red trailer
EX $50   NM $175   MIP $350

No. 600, Amazing Car, 1946-49, wind-up; green or blue; box commands a premium (contains operating instructions)
EX $75   NM $150   MIP $300

No. 600, Amazing Car, 1946-49, wind-up; red; box commands a premium (contains operating instructions)
EX $50   NM $125   MIP $250

No. 6000, American Oil Emergency Truck, 1963-69, red Ford Econoline Wrecker, white boom, with or without American Oil decals
EX $50   NM $150   MIP $300

No. 6001, JC Penney Wrecker, 1966, light blue Ford Econoline Wrecker with white boom; available only form the JC Penney's wishbook
EX $75   NM $250   MIP $500

No. 6100, Hydraulic Dump Truck, 1963-70, beige truck with red dump box; two-piece grille/bumper (1963-64); one-piece grille bumper (1965-70)
EX $75   NM $150   MIP $300

No. 6200, Kennel Truck, 1963-69, pink Ford Econoline, plastic dog cage in back, 12 dogs (12 different breeds); paper band around cage featuring the dog breeds on it (1964 only)
EX $175   NM $265   MIP $525

No. 6300, Horse Van Semi Truck, 1963-67, brownish-gold truck, white doors, decals, four horses and ponies; two-piece grille/bumper on front (1963-64); one-piece grille/bumper (1965-67); light blue and white truck (1967 only)
EX $50   NM $175   MIP $350

No. 6500, Payloader, 1963-66, red and yellow
EX $50   NM $100   MIP $200

No. 6600, Mobile Home Semi Truck, 1964, aqua blue cab with white or light tan roof, nine pieces of furniture, two-piece grille/bumper on front, round "6600" decal on cab doors
EX $75   NM $300   MIP $600

No. 6601, Mobile Home Trailer, 1965, aqua blue or turquoise with white or light tan top, 27 pieces of furniture, one-piece grille/bumper on front, round "6601" decal on cab doors
EX $75   NM $300   MIP $600

No. 6602, Mobile Home Trailer, 1966, dark blue cab with white top, no extras, large "N" logo on cab doors
EX $75   NM $325   MIP $650

No. 6603, Mobile Home Trailer, 1964-66, American Transit Mobile Home Movers and other variations
EX $100   NM $350   MIP $700

No. 6700, Ambulance, 1964-67, white Ford Econoline Van with red crosses on sides and doors; included stretcher, interior seats, red flasher light
EX $50   NM $150   MIP $300

No. 6800, Jalopy, 1964-78, Ford hot rod in red with white top or light blue with white top (1964); also No. 6801 with seats, available in same colors as 1964 version (1965-68); No. 6802 purple and white (1969-71); No. 6803 neon green top and purple body (1972-78)
EX $25   NM $150   MIP $300

No. 6900, Airport Courtesy Van, 1964, Ford Econoline Van, yellow with Holiday Inn decals on sides and doors; rare
EX $75   NM $350   MIP $700

No. 700, Lift Truck (fork lift), 1946-49, red and yellow; box commands a premium (contains operating instructions)
EX $75   NM $125   MIP $250

No. 700, Lift Truck (fork lift), 1946-49, green and yellow; box commands a premium (contains operating instructions)
EX $75   NM $140   MIP $275

No. 7000, Lawn and Garden Set, 1964, dark green Econoline Pickup with white roof; included lawn mower and other garden equipment
EX $50   NM $150   MIP $300

No. 7100, Fun on Farm Econoline Truck Set, 1964-65, 29 piecesFord Econoline Pickup with farm family, farming items, plus small cans of paint to customize your farm family
EX $50   NM $175   MIP $350

No. 7200, Happy Ranchers Set, 1964, Stake Truck with Open Stake Trailer, both light blue and white
EX $75   NM $175   MIP $350

No. 7300, Army Ambulance, 1965, olive drab Ford Econoline Van, stretcher, red cross decals on sides and doors, red flasher light on top
EX $50   NM $175   MIP $350

No. 7408, Suburban Fire Department Set, 1966-70, red Ford Econoline Pumper Fire Truck, Fire Rescue Econoline Van, Fire Chief's Econoline; Rescue Van and Fire Chief's Bronco available only in this set
EX $75   NM $225   MIP $450

No. 7800, Race Team, 1965-69, white Econoline Pickup, red trailer, white race car
EX $50   NM $150   MIP $300

No. 7900, Road Grader, 1965-68, yellow and black
EX $25   NM $100   MIP $200

No. 7910, Road Grader, 1969, yellow with larger wheels
EX $40   NM $65   MIP $125

No. 800, Scootscycle/Servicecycle, 1946-51, wind-up; red, blue, yellow or black; rare
EX $75   NM $225   MIP $450

No. 8000, Pony Farm Van Set, white Ford Econoline Pick,up, green cab top, large green/white Pony Farm decal on sides, four ponies
EX $75   NM $175   MIP $350

No. 8001, Gambles Stores Pickup, 1966, white Ford Econoline with green top
EX $75   NM $175   MIP $350

No. 8100, Suburban Fire Pumper, 1965-70, Ford Econoline Pumper fire Truck with water cannon; a garden hose could be connected to the cannon to shoot water; hard to find in good condition since the pressure from the garden hose usually blew up the truck
EX $50   NM $150   MIP $300

No. 8200, Ford Bronco, 1965-69, listed in the 1965 catalog as a Roustabout but was changed to a Bornco right after the catalog was printed
EX $50   NM $140   MIP $275

No. 8300, Texaco Service Van, 1965, red Ford Econoline Van, white decals, red flasher light
EX $50   NM $200   MIP $400

No. 8400, U-Haul Cube Van, 1966-67, five-ton cube van
EX $75   NM $175   MIP $350

No. 8401, Hertz Rental Truck, 1967, same as No. 8400 but exclusive to Sears; yel-

low cab, black base, silver cargo box, Hertz decals; rare
    EX $85   **NM** $250   **MIP** $500

No. 8410, U-Haul Truck & Trailer, 1974
    EX $100   **NM** $150   **MIP** $200

No. 8411, U-Haul Truck, 1975, Chevy
    EX $100   **NM** $125   **MIP** $175

No. 8600, Vacationer Set, 1966-70, blue and white Ford Bronco and camper trailer
    EX $50   **NM** $150   **MIP** $300

No. 8700, Truck and Horse Trailer, 1966-70, Ford Bronco, two-axle horse trailer with yellow top
    EX $50   **NM** $145   **MIP** $285

No. 8800, Safari Hunt Set, 1966-71, Ford Bronco with white top, cage trailer with wild animals; cage has door, trailer has slide-out ramp and winch for loading
    EX $75   **NM** $200   **MIP** $400

No. 8900, Car Carrier, 1967-77, yellow car carrier; three cars (1967-68); two cars (1969-77); several color variations for cars
    EX $50   **NM** $150   **MIP** $300

No. 900, Power Pony, 1949, light tan, black, yellow; three-wheeled pony performed tricks; rare
    EX $100   **NM** $250   **MIP** $500

No. 9000, Jungle Wagon, 1966-72, two-tone green Ford Econoline with cages to transport wild animals
    EX $45   **NM** $140   **MIP** $275

No. 9100, Stake Pickup Truck, 1966-69, light blue and white Ford Econoline stake truck
    EX $35   **NM** $125   **MIP** $250

No. 9200, Big Haul Dump, 1966-68, yellow and black, reminiscent of Tonka's Mighty Dump Truck
    EX $45   **NM** $125   **MIP** $250

No. 9201, Big Haul Dump, 1969-72, same as No. 9200 but larger wheels
    EX $45   **NM** $125   **MIP** $250

No. 9300, Tin Lizzy Hot Rod Pickup, 1967-72, red and other colors
    EX $35   **NM** $100   **MIP** $200

No. 9400, Truck and U-Haul Trailer, 1967-68, Ford Econoline Pickup and open trailer, orange and white
    EX $50   **NM** $140   **MIP** $275

No. 9401, Truck and Haul-It Trailer, 1969, rare; knock-off of U-Haul Trailer with similar decals
    EX $50   **NM** $175   **MIP** $350

No. 9500, Sportster, 1967-69, pink Ford Bronco
    EX $45   **NM** $140   **MIP** $275

No. 9600, Race Team, 1967-69, Ford Econline Pikup and trailer with race car, red and white
    EX $40   **NM** $140   **MIP** $275

No. 9700, Sportsman Set, 1967-69, truck with boat and trailer; white and other colors
    EX $50   **NM** $140   **MIP** $275

No. 9800, Hydraulic Big Haul Dump Truck, 1967-68, orange and black
    EX $35   **NM** $140   **MIP** $275

No. 9801, Hydraulic Big Haul Dump Truck, 1969-73, orange and black, new tires
    EX $35   **NM** $140   **MIP** $275

No. 9900, Farm Set, 1968-71, one of four farm sets made by Nylint; included light blue and white Ford Bronco, Ford Econoline Pickup, Stake Truck and trailer
    EX $75   **NM** $175   **MIP** $350

No. SR1000/5465, U-Haul Van Set, 1962, Sears exclusive; orange and white Ford Pickup, U-Haul Van (closed type), and trailer with race car
    EX $75   **NM** $200   **MIP** $400

No. SR1100, Big Dig Shovel, 1964-65, Sears exclusive; orange and black, all steel except for rubber tracks; later versions (non-exclusives) available in orange yellow and black while track wheels were yellow plastic
    EX $50   **NM** $140   **MIP** $275

No. SR1200/5439, Lawn and Garden Set, 1964-65, Sears exclusive
    EX $50   **NM** $175   **MIP** $350

VEHICLES — NYLINT

PROCESSED PLASTIC/ TIM-MEE TOYS

"Soupercharged" Airplane, 12" wing-span; four free-turning props, "Soupercharged" sticker, cast in beef, ham, and soup; 1960s
EX $7   NM $12   MIP $18

ABCD TV Blimp, 9" long; white blimp, "ABCD TV" on sides, on hauling platform
EX $10   NM $18   MIP $25

Armored Car, 5-1/2" long; center-mounted turret, light Army green, four black-rubber tires
EX $20   NM $35   MIP $40

Armored Car, 7" long; rear-mounted swiveling cannon atop Army green armored vehicle, black plastic tires
EX $5   NM $8   MIP $15

Army Jeep and Howitzer, 9-1/2" long; "Tim-Mee Toys" Army green Jeep, 5-1/4" long; with snugly fitting driver, snap-in steering wheel, towing cannon, 4-1/4" long, both toys with black rubber tires; 1960s
EX $6   NM $12   MIP $18

Army Jeep and Howitzer, 9-1/2" long; "Tim-Mee Toys," with black plastic tires
EX $1   NM $3   MIP $5

Boat and Trailer Set, plastic station wagon, 7-1/4" long, separate top and bottom moldings, black plastic tires on metal axles, "Bear Lake Lodge" stickers, hauling plastic trailer with motor boat; early 1970s
EX $20   NM $40   MIP $60

Chevy Camaro, 10-1/4" long; T-top, popped engine, flames on hood, chrome hubs on black wheels
EX $8   NM $12   MIP $20

Chevy Flatbed Truck, 4" long; 1950s-style, blue plastic with windows not cut out, simple rolling toy; 1960s
EX $3   NM $6   MIP $9

Chevy Hi-Rider, 9" long; yellow pickup truck, chromed grille and rear bumper, orange rollbar and interior, opening rear gate with "Chevrolet," "Hi-Rider 4WD" stickers on doors, oversize tires; 1980s
EX $5   NM $9   MIP $15

Chevy Nomad Station Wagon, 4" long; 1950s-style, blue plastic with windows not cut out, simple rolling toy; 1960s
EX $3   NM $6   MIP $9

Clipper Sailing Ship, 21" long, 15" tall; brown ship, three masts, white sails, two lifeboats, turning rudder, weighted keel; 1960s
EX $30   NM $45   MIP $60

Convertible, 4" long; 1950s-style red Cadillac with finned fenders, open top, simple rolling toy; 1960s
EX $3   NM $6   MIP $9

Dump Truck, 12-1/4" long; chrome grille, clear windshield, whitewall tires; 1950s to early 1960s
EX $10   NM $18   MIP $30

Dump Truck, 7" long; rounded-top cabover, tilting heavy-duty dump body; 1950s or 1960s
EX $3   NM $7   MIP $10

Eureka Hauler, 22" long; tractor-trailer, orange cab with white interior and chromed grille, white trailer with "Eureka Vacuum Cleaners" panels; 1980s
EX $12   NM $25   MIP $30

Ford Car, 8-1/2" long; red plastic with "The Dukes of Hazzard" style Confederate flag stickers; 1980s
EX $15   NM $30   MIP $40

Honda ATC Three-Wheeler, 9" long; red and white plastic, "ATC" on tank, black balloon tires
EX $20   NM $45   MIP $60

Honda Trail Bike, 8-1/2" long; "Honda" sticker, various colors, chromed engine, black plastic tires
EX $8   NM $15   MIP $25

Hot Rod, 5" long; green plastic body with red plastic driver, chrome engine and dual exhaust pipes
EX $15   NM $25   MIP $35

Indy Race Car, 9" long; open-cockpit racer, tail fin, red plastic with yellow steering wheel and chrome pipes, "98" on decal
EX $6   NM $12   MIP $20

Indy Race Car, 12-1/2" long; moveable front air fins and rear spoiler; 1970s
EX $5   NM $11   MIP $16

Motorboat, 7-1/4" long; snap-together open-top motorboat with plastic motor clear windshield; 1960s or 1970s
EX $7   NM $10   MIP $18

Pontiac Firebird, 17-1/2" long; red plastic, interior details; 1970s
EX $3   NM $7   MIP $10

Racer, 7-3/4" long; open cockpit race car with separately-cast driver, "7" cast into long nose, "700 Special" sticker; 1960s or 1970s
EX $9   NM $18   MIP $27

Renault Sedan, 4-1/4" long; simple rolling toy, modeled on 1950s Renault; 1960s or 1970s
EX $5   NM $10   MIP $15

Seaplane, 8" long; red and white plastic seaplane, wheels under pontoons, propeller
EX $5   NM $9   MIP $14

Space Shuttle Columbia, 9" long; white and red Space Shuttle, "NASA" on wings, "Columbia, United States" sticker on sides; 1980s
EX $3   NM $8   MIP $12

Station Wagon, 4" long; 1950s-style Chevy station wagon, simple rolling toy; 1960s or 1970s
EX $3   NM $5   MIP $8

Submarine, 10" long; hard plastic, "X-13 USN," with plastic on base, two red missiles, periscope, radar dish
EX $25   NM $40   MIP $60

Thunderhauler, 22" long; black tractor-trailer, batter-operated horn; 1980s
EX $8   NM $20   MIP $25

Troop Hauler, 7" long; Army-green plastic truck with "canvas" cover, three axles, six plastic tires
EX $10   NM $20   MIP $25

VW Bug, VW hot rod with popped and chromed engine, oversize rear tires; 1970s
EX $6   NM $10   MIP $18

VW Pickup, 4-1/4" long; Army-green body, black plastic tires, "1234" license plates; 1960s
EX $9   NM $15   MIP $25

REMCO

Bulldog Tank, 16" long; plastic tank, metal underside, four shells, remote-control firing; 1960s
EX $15   NM $30   MIP $65

Caterpillar Tractor, 8" long; 1986
EX $5   NM $8   MIP $11

Coca-Cola Set, window box set with pickup, car, tractor-trailer, Coca-Cola cases; 1989
EX $7   NM $12   MIP $20

Duffy's Daredevils, play set featuring plastic red convertible, car launcher, ramp, hoops of "fire" and barrels for auto thrill show; 1965
EX $7   NM $13   MIP $20

Fighting Lady Battleship, 36" long; depth charges, 5" plane, 7-1/2" small boat
EX $25   NM $55   MIP $110

Firebird "99", 13" across; battery-operated steering wheel and dashboard, with windshield, speedometer, ignition key; 1963-64
EX $22   NM $43   MIP $65

Flying Dutchman Antique Car, battery-operated "U-Control"
EX $20   NM $50   MIP $125

Midget Motors Mighty Mike Jeep, 5-1/2" long; battery-operated Jeep, white with black tires and exposed engine, sold individually and with Midget Motors Mighty Mike Action Sets; late 1960s
EX $15   NM $30   MIP $120

Mighty Mike Dump Truck Skyway Set, 1960s
EX $10   NM $20   MIP $30

Mighty Mike Motorized Truck, six-wheel truck with interchangeable, snap-on bodies; late 1960s
EX $10   NM $20   MIP $30

Mr. Kelly's Automatic Car Wash, 27" long; battery-operated working car wash with see-through roof, two cars, wax cans, towels, sponges and free-standing sign; 1963-64
EX $28   NM $56   MIP $85

Sanitation Truck, 13" long; "Save Our Planet," metal and plastic; early 1990s
EX $5   NM $10   MIP $15

Shark, 19" long; plastic, billed as "Battery Driven U-Control Racing Car," orange plastic body, white side pipes, chromed grille, black tires with chromed hubs; 1961 and later
EX $10   NM $20   MIP $90

Stubby Camper, 23" long; plastic, blue cab, white camper with rear slide-up door; 1973
EX $7   NM $13   MIP $20

Swamp Buggy, 12" long; battery-operated plastic pontoon, yellow and red with white plastic rider; 1968
EX $4   NM $15   MIP $22

Tru-Smoke Diesel Cement Truck, 12" long; battery-operated, smoking action; 1969
EX $15   NM $25   MIP $50

Tru-Smoke Diesel Dump Truck, 12" long; battery-operated, smoking action, working dump; 1969
EX $15   NM $25   MIP $50

Tru-Smoke Diesel Wrecker Truck, 12" long; battery-operated, smoking action, twin booms; 1969
EX $15   NM $25   MIP $60

Tuff Boy 6 (tractor-trailer), 38" long; yellow plastic, motorized cab powering forward or reverse, stake-side trailer with canopy, designed for taking other trailer bodies in the manner of Deluxe Reading's Johnny Express Tractor and Trailer Combination; 1965-70s
EX $15   NM $30   MIP $45

SMITH-MILLER

EMERGENCY VEHICLES

"L" Mack Aerial Ladder, Smith-Miller, red w/gold lettering; polished aluminum surface, SMFD decals on hood and trailer sides, six-wheeler; 1950
EX $375   **NM** $475   **MIP** $795

TRUCKS

"B" Mack Associated Truck Lines, Smith-Miller, red cab, polished aluminum trailer, decals on trailer sides, six-wheel tractor, eight-wheel trailer; 1954
EX $500   **NM** $850   **MIP** $1200

"B" Mack Blue Diamond Dump, Smith-Miller, all white truck w/blue decals, hydraulic piston, ten-wheeler; 1954
EX $600   **NM** $950   **MIP** $1300

"B" Mack Lumber Truck, Smith-Miller, yellow cab and timber deck, three rollers, loading bar and two chains, six-wheeler, load of nine timbers; 1954
EX $450   **NM** $650   **MIP** $1000

"B" Mack Orange Dump Truck, Smith-Miller, construction orange all over, no decals, hydraulic piston, ten-wheeler; 1954
EX $650   **NM** $1150   **MIP** $1650

"B" Mack P.I.E., Smith-Miller, red cab, polished trailer, six-wheel tractor, eight-wheel trailer; 1954
EX $375   **NM** $600   **MIP** $850

"B" Mack Searchlight, Smith-Miller, dark red paint schemes, fully rotating and elevating searchlight, battery-operated; 1954
EX $500   **NM** $775   **MIP** $1100

"B" Mack Silver Streak, Smith-Miller, yellow cab, unpainted, unpolished trailer sides, "Silver Streak" decal on both sides, six-wheel tractor, eight-wheel trailer; 1954
EX $450   **NM** $775   **MIP** $1050

"B" Mack Watson Bros., Smith-Miller, yellow cab, polished aluminum trailer, decals on trailer sides and cab doors, 10-wheel tractor, eight-wheel trailer; 1954
EX $650   **NM** $1100   **MIP** $1500

"L" Mack Army Materials Truck, Smith-Miller, Army green, flatbed w/dark green canvas, ten-wheeler, load of three wood barrels, two boards, large and small crate; 1952
EX $375   **NM** $500   **MIP** $750

"L" Mack Army Personnel Carrier, Smith-Miller, all Army green, wood sides, Army seal on door panels, military star on roof, ten-wheeler; 1952
EX $375   **NM** $500   **MIP** $750

"L" Mack Bekins Van, Smith-Miller, white, covered w/"Bekins" decals, six-wheel tractor, four-wheel trailer; 1953
EX $1000   **NM** $1650   **MIP** $2000

"L" Mack Blue Diamond Dump, Smith-Miller, white cab, white dump bed, blue fenders and chassis, hydraulically operated, ten-wheeler; 1952
EX $425   **NM** $750   **MIP** $1050

"L" Mack International Paper Co., Smith-Miller, white tractor cab, "International Paper Co." decals, six wheel tractor, four wheel trailer; 1952
EX $375   **NM** $650   **MIP** $900

"L" Mack Lyon Van, Smith-Miller, silver gray cab, dark blue fenders and frame, silver gray van box w/blue "Lyon" decal, six-wheeler; 1950
EX $425   **NM** $800   **MIP** $1100

"L" Mack Material Truck, Smith-Miller, light metallic green cab, dark green fenders and frame, wood flatbed, six-wheeler, load of two barrels and six timbers; 1950
EX $400   **NM** $600   **MIP** $875

"L" Mack Merchandise Van, Smith-Miller, red cab, black fenders and frame, "Smith-Miller" decals on both sides of van box, double rear doors, six-wheeler; 1951
EX $425   **NM** $695   **MIP** $1000

"L" Mack Mobil Tandem Tanker, Smith-Miller, all red cab, "Mobilgas" and "Mobiloil" decals on tank sides, six-wheel tractor, six-wheel trailer; 1952
EX $450   **NM** $725   **MIP** $1000

"L" Mack Orange Hydraulic Dump, Smith-Miller, orange cab, orange dump bed, hydraulic, ten-wheeler, may or may not have "Blue Diamond" decals; 1952
EX $850   **NM** $1500   **MIP** $1950

"L" Mack Orange Materials Truck, Smith-Miller, all orange, flatbed w/canvas, ten-wheeler, load of three barrels, two boards, large and small crate; 1952
EX $400   **NM** $650   **MIP** $900

"L" Mack P.I.E., Smith-Miller, all red tractor, polished aluminum trailer, "P.I.E." decals on sides and front, six wheel tractor, eight-wheel trailer; 1950
EX $395   **NM** $550   **MIP** $850

"L" Mack Sibley Van, Smith-Miller, dark green cab, black fenders and frame, dark green van box w/"Sibley's" decal in yellow on both sides, six-wheeler; 1950
EX $850   **NM** $1375   **MIP** $1850

"L" Mack Tandem Timber, Smith-Miller, red/black cab, six-wheeler, load of six wood lumber rollers, two loading bars, four chains and eighteen or twenty-four boards; 1950
EX $400   **NM** $600   **MIP** $725

"L" Mack Tandem Timber, Smith-Miller, two-tone green cab, six-wheeler, load of six wood lumber rollers, two loading bars, four chains, and 18 timbers; 1953
EX $400   **NM** $550   **MIP** $725

"L" Mack Telephone Truck, Smith-Miller, all dark or two-tone green truck, "Bell Telephone System" decals on truck sides, six-wheeler; 1952
EX $475   **NM** $750   **MIP** $975

"L" Mack West Coast Fast Freight, Smith-Miller, silver w/red/black or silver cab and chassis, "West Coast-Fast Freight" decals on sides of box, six-wheeler; 1952
EX $475   **NM** $775   **MIP** $1000

Chevrolet Arden Milk Truck, Smith-Miller, red cab, white wood body, four-wheeler; 1945
EX $275   **NM** $465   **MIP** $800

Chevrolet Bekins Van, Smith-Miller, blue die-cast cab, all white trailer, fourteen-wheeler; 1945
EX $275   **NM** $350   **MIP** $750

Chevrolet Coca-Cola Truck, Smith-Miller, red cab, wood body painted red, four-wheeler; 1945
EX $300   **NM** $600   **MIP** $850

Chevrolet Flatbed Tractor-Trailer, Smith-Miller, unpainted wood trailer, unpainted polished cab, fourteen-wheeler; 1945
EX $250   **NM** $300   **MIP** $500

Chevrolet Heinz Grocery Truck, Smith-Miller, yellow cab, load of four waxed cases; 1946
EX $225   **NM** $325   **MIP** $475

Chevrolet Livestock Truck, Smith-Miller, polished, unpainted tractor cab and trailer; 1946
EX $175   **NM** $275   **MIP** $375

Chevrolet Lumber, Smith-Miller, green cab, load of 60 polished boards and two chains; 1946
EX $150   **NM** $195   **MIP** $275

Chevrolet Lyons Van, Smith-Miller, blue cab, silver trailer; 1946
EX $165   **NM** $325   **MIP** $500

Chevrolet Material Truck, Smith-Miller, green cab, no side rails, load of three barrels, two cases and eighteen boards; 1946
EX $135   **NM** $185   **MIP** $225

Chevrolet Stake, Smith-Miller, yellow tractor cab
EX $185   **NM** $250   **MIP** $425

Chevrolet Transcontinental Vanliner, Smith-Miller, blue tractor cab, white trailer, "Bekins" logos and decals on trailer sides; 1946
EX $200   **NM** $350   **MIP** $495

Chevrolet Union Ice Truck, Smith-Miller, blue cab, white body, load of eight waxed blocks of ice; 1946
EX $300   **NM** $495   **MIP** $800

Ford Bekins Van, Smith-Miller, red sand-cast tractor, gray sheet metal trailer, fourteen-wheeler; 1944
EX $275   **NM** $500   **MIP** $750

Ford Coca-Cola Truck, Smith-Miller, red sandcast cab, wood body painted red, four-wheeler; 1944
EX $400   **NM** $650   **MIP** $900

GMC Arden Milk Truck, Smith-Miller, red cab, white painted wood body w/red stakes, four-wheeler; 1947
EX $200   **NM** $425   **MIP** $650

GMC Bank of America Truck, Smith-Miller, dark brownish green cab and box, 'Bank of America' decal on box sides, four-wheeler; 1949
EX $150   **NM** $325   **MIP** $500

GMC Be Mac Tractor-Trailer, Smith-Miller, red cab, plain aluminum frame,

"Be Mac Transport Co." in white letters on door panels, fourteen-wheeler; 1949
EX $250   **NM** $350   **MIP** $700

GMC Bekins Vanliner, Smith-Miller, blue cab, metal trailer painted white, fourteen-wheeler; 1947
EX $175   **NM** $275   **MIP** $425

GMC Coca-Cola Truck, Smith-Miller, red cab, yellow wood body, four-wheeler, load of 16 Coca-Cola cases; 1947
EX $400   **NM** $675   **MIP** $895

GMC Coca-Cola Truck, Smith-Miller, all yellow truck, red Coca-Cola decals, five spoke hubs, four-wheeler, load of six cases each w/24 plastic bottles; 1954
EX $275   **NM** $450   **MIP** $750

GMC Drive-O, Smith-Miller, red cab, red dump body, runs forward and backward w/handturned control at end of 5-1/2 ft. cable, six-wheeler; 1949
EX $175   **NM** $300   **MIP** $450

GMC Dump Truck, Smith-Miller, all red truck, six-wheeler; 1950
EX $150   **NM** $200   **MIP** $285

GMC Emergency Tow Truck, Smith-Miller, white cab, red body and boom, 'Emergency Towing Service' on body side panels, four-wheeler; 1953
EX $185   **NM** $250   **MIP** $400

GMC Furniture Mart, Smith-Miller, blue cab, off-white body, "Furniture Mart, Complete Home Furnishings" markings on body sides, four-wheeler; 1953
EX $275   **NM** $325   **MIP** $400

GMC Heinz Grocery Truck, Smith-Miller, yellow cab, wood body, six-wheeler; 1947
EX $250   **NM** $325   **MIP** $450

GMC Highway Freighter Tractor-Trailer, Smith-Miller, red tractor cab, hardwood bed on trailer w/full length wood fences, "Fruehauf" decal on trailer, fourteen-wheeler; 1948
EX $150   **NM** $210   **MIP** $325

GMC Kraft Foods, Smith-Miller, yellow cab, yellow steel box, large "Kraft" decal on both sides, four-wheeler; 1948
EX $300   **NM** $500   **MIP** $600

GMC Lumber Tractor-Trailer, Smith-Miller, metallic blue cab and trailer, three rollers and two chains, fourteen-wheeler; 1949
EX $185   **NM** $250   **MIP** $350

GMC Lumber Truck, Smith-Miller, green cab, six-wheeler; 1947
EX $165   **NM** $215   **MIP** $300

GMC Lyons Van Tractor-Trailer, Smith-Miller, blue tractor cab, "Lyons Van" decals on both sides, fold down rear door, fourteen-wheeler; 1948
EX $200   **NM** $350   **MIP** $400

GMC Machinery Hauler, Smith-Miller, construction orange, two loading ramps, ten-wheeler; 1953
EX $200   **NM** $325   **MIP** $425

GMC Machinery Hauler, Smith-Miller, construction orange cab and lowboy trailer, "Fruehauf" decal on gooseneck, thirteen-wheeler; 1949
EX $150   **NM** $225   **MIP** $335

GMC Machinery Hauler, Smith-Miller, construction orange cab and lowboy trailer, "Fruehauf" decal on gooseneck, thirteen-wheeler; 1949
EX $150   **NM** $225   **MIP** $335

GMC Marshall Field's & Company Tractor-Trailer, Smith-Miller, dark green cab and trailer, double rear doors, never had Smith-Miller decals, ten-wheeler; 1949
EX $295   **NM** $395   **MIP** $500

GMC Material Truck, Smith-Miller, green cab, wood body, six-wheeler, load of three barrels, three cases and eighteen boards; 1947
EX $115   **NM** $150   **MIP** $250

GMC Material Truck, Smith-Miller, yellow cab, natural finish hardwood bed and sides, four-wheeler, load of four barrels and two timbers; 1949
EX $125   **NM** $175   **MIP** $265

GMC Mobilgas Tanker, Smith-Miller, red cab and tanker trailer, large "Mobilgas", "Mobiloil" emblems on sides and rear panel of tanker, fourteen-wheeler; 1949
EX $200   **NM** $300   **MIP** $500

GMC Oil Truck, Smith-Miller, orange cab, rear body unpainted, six-wheeler, load of three barrels; 1947
EX $115   **NM** $220   **MIP** $375

GMC P.I.E., Smith-Miller, red cab, polished aluminum box trailer, double rear doors, "P.I.E." decals on sides and front panels, fourteen-wheeler; 1949
EX $150   **NM** $350   **MIP** $475

GMC People's First National Bank and Trust Company, Smith-Miller, dark brownish green cab and box, "People's First National Bank and Trust Co." decals on box sides; 1951
EX $165   **NM** $250   **MIP** $385

GMC Rack Truck, Smith-Miller, red or yellow cab, natural finish wood deck, red stake sides, six-wheeler; 1948
EX $135   **NM** $200   **MIP** $325

GMC Redwood Logger Tractor-Trailer, Smith-Miller, green or maroon cab, unpainted aluminum trailer w/four hardwood stakes, load of three cardboard logs; 1948
EX $365   **NM** $585   **MIP** $700

GMC Rexall Drug Truck, Smith-Miller, orange cab and closed steel box body, "Rexall" logo on both sides and on front panel of box, four-wheeler; 1948
EX $500   **NM** $750   **MIP** $1000

GMC Scoop Dump, Smith-Miller, rack and pinion dump w/a scoop, five spoke wheels, six-wheeler; 1954
EX $400   **NM** $800   **MIP** $1000

GMC Searchlight Truck, Smith-Miller, four wheel truck pulling four wheel trailer, color schemes vary, "Hollywood Film Ad" on truck body side panels; 1953
EX $300   **NM** $415   **MIP** $695

GMC Silver Streak, Smith-Miller, unpainted polished cab and trailer, wrap around sides and shield, some had tail gate; 1950
EX $200   **NM** $350   **MIP** $600

GMC Sunkist Special Tractor-Trailer, Smith-Miller, cherry/maroon tractor cab, natural mahogany trailer bed, fourteen-wheeler; 1947
EX $165   **NM** $275   **MIP** $475

GMC Super Cargo Tractor-Trailer, Smith-Miller, silver gray tractor cab, hardwood bed on trailer w/red wraparound side rails, fourteen-wheeler, load of ten barrels; 1948
EX $150   **NM** $225   **MIP** $395

GMC Timber Giant, Smith-Miller, green or maroon cab, unpainted aluminum trailer w/four hardwood stakes, load of three cardboard logs; 1948
EX $175   **NM** $285   **MIP** $495

GMC Tow Truck, Smith-Miller, white cab, red body and boom, five spoke cast hubs, "Emergency Towing Service" on body side panels, four-wheeler; 1954
EX $95   **NM** $135   **MIP** $200

GMC Transcontinental Tractor-Trailer, Smith-Miller, red tractor cab, hardwood bed on trailer w/full length wood fences, "Fruehauf" decal on trailer, fourteen-wheeler; 1948
EX $150   **NM** $210   **MIP** $325

GMC Triton Oil Truck, Smith-Miller, blue cab, mahogany body unpainted, six-wheeler, load of three Triton Oil drums (banks) and side chains; 1947
EX $115   **NM** $185   **MIP** $265

GMC U.S. Treasury Truck, Smith-Miller, gray cab and box, "U.S. Treasury" insignia and markings on box sides, four-wheeler; 1952
EX $235   **NM** $325   **MIP** $475

STRUCTO

Standard Steam Shovel, 1948, Orange, 20.5L x 6.25W x 7.75H, wooden wheels without tracks, Model No. 100
EX $55   **NM** $115   **MIP** $175

Heavy Duty Steam Shovel, 1948, Blue, 21.5L x 6.25W x 7.75H, rubber tracks, Model No. 105
EX $75   **NM** $135   **MIP** $195

Dump Truck, 1948, Red, 20L x 6.75W x 6.25H, long bullet headlights, Model No. 200
EX $95   **NM** $155   **MIP** $225

Aerial Fire Truck, 1948, Red, 24L x 6.75W x 6.25H, 1 raising/2 side ladders & bell on hood, Model No. 250
EX $115   **NM** $175   **MIP** $255

Machinery Truck & Steam Shovel, 1948, Orange and blue, 21.5L x 6.75 W x 6.25H, comes 2/#105 steam shovel & loading ramp, Model No. 402
EX $115   **NM** $175   **MIP** $245

Standard Steam Shovel, 1949, Orange, 20.5L x 6.25W x 7.75H, wooden wheels w/o tracks, Model No. 100
EX $55   **NM** $115   **MIP** $175

Heavy Duty Steam Shovel, 1949, Blue, 21.5L x 6.25W x 7.75H, rubber tracks, Model No. 105
EX $75   **NM** $135   **MIP** $195

Dump Truck, 1949, Red, 20L x 6.75W x 6.25H, long bullet headlights, Model No. 200
EX $95   **NM** $155   **MIP** $225

Aerial Fire Truck, 1949, Red, 24L x 6.75W x 6.25H, 1 raising, 2 side ladders & bell on hood, Model No. 250
EX $115   **NM** $175   **MIP** $255

Machinery Truck & Steam Shovel, 1949, Orange and blue, 21.5L x 6.75W x 6.25H, comes w/#105 steam shovel & loading ramp, Model No. 402
EX $115   **NM** $175   **MIP** $245

Standard Steam Shovel, 1950, Orange, 20.5L x 6.25W x 7.75H, wooden wheels w/o tracks, Model No. 100
EX $55   **NM** $115   **MIP** $175

Heavy Duty Steam Shovel, 1950, Blue, 21.5L x 6.25W x 7.75H, rubber tracks, Model No. 105
EX $75   **NM** $135   **MIP** $195

Dump Truck, 1950, Red, 20L x 6.75W x 6.25H, long bullet headlights, Model No. 200
EX $95   **NM** $155   **MIP** $225

Aerial Fire Truck, 1950, Red, 24L x 6.75W x 6.25H, 1 raising/2 side ladders & bell on hood, Model No. 250
EX $115   **NM** $175   **MIP** $255

Machinery Truck & Steam Shovel, 1950, Orange and blue, 21.5L x 6.75W x 6.25H, comes w/#105 steam shovel & loading ramp, Model No. 402
EX $115   **NM** $175   **MIP** $245

Heavy Duty Steam Shovel, 1951, Blue, 21.5L x 6.25W x 7.75H, Model No. 105
EX $65   **NM** $125   **MIP** $175

Dump Truck, 1951, Red, 20L x 6.75W x 6.25H, with plastic fireball motor under the hood, Model No. 200
EX $75   **NM** $135   **MIP** $195

Aerial Fire Truck, 1951, Red, 24L x 6.75W x 6.25H, with plastic fireball motor under the hood, Model No. 250
EX $115   **NM** $175   **MIP** $255

Road Grader, 1951, Orange, 18L x 7W x 7.5H, with plastic fireball motor under the hood, Model No. 300
EX $55   **NM** $85   **MIP** $105

Machinery Truck & Steam Shovel, 1951, Orange and blue, 21.5L x 6.75W x 6.25H, with plastic fireball motor under the hood, Model No. 402
EX $100   **NM** $155   **MIP** $195

Utility (Garbage) Truck, 1951, Red and blue, 21.5L x 6.5W x 7.5H, with plastic fireball motor under the hood, Model No. 500
EX $95   **NM** $155   **MIP** $205

(Randy Prasse Photo)

Motor Express Truck, 1951, Grey and orange, 12.75L x 5.5W x 5H, cast cab "Freeport Motor Express" decals, Model No. 601
EX $75   **NM** $125   **MIP** $195

(Calvin Chaussee Photo)

Package Delivery Truck, 1951, Orange and green, 13L x 5.5W x 5H, cast cab, tail gate with chain, Model No. 603
EX $75   **NM** $125   **MIP** $195

Shovel Dump Truck, 1951, Orange and blue, 12.75L x 5.5W x 5H, cast cab, dump box, Model No. 605
EX $75   **NM** $125   **MIP** $195

(Randy Prasse Photo)

Machinery Truck, 1951, orange and blue, 12.75L x 5.5W x 5H, with loading ramp and chain winch, Model No. 607
EX $95   **NM** $155   **MIP** $205

Transport Trailer, 1951, Blue and red, 21.5L x 5.5W x 7.5H, blue cast cab with red trailer, no hubcaps, Model No. 700
EX $95   **NM** $135   **MIP** $205

Steel Cargo Trailer, 1951, Blue and red, 20.75L x 5.5W x 5.5H, blue cast cab with red trailer, no hubcaps, Model No. 702
EX $95   **NM** $135   **MIP** $195

Overland Freight Trailer, 1951, Blue and orange, 20.75L x 5.5W x 5.5H, blue cast cab with orange stake trailer, Model No. 704
EX $115   **NM** $175   **MIP** $225

Combination With Two Trailers, 1951, Blue cast cab with #702 and 704 trailers, Model No. 706
EX $155   **NM** $215   **MIP** $275

Barrel Truck, 1951, Red and blue, 12.75L x 5.5W x 5H, wind-up motor and two oil can banks, Model No. 811
EX $135   **NM** $195   **MIP** $255

Wrecker Truck, 1951, Red and grey, 12.25L x 5.5W x 5.25H, wind-up motor and chain winch, Model No. 822
EX $95   **NM** $125   **MIP** $175

Hi-Lift Dump Truck, 1951, Red and blue, 12.5L x 5.5W x 5.25H, wind-up motor with scissors lift box, Model No. 844
EX $105   **NM** $155   **MIP** $215

Gasoline Truck, 1951, Red and red, 13.5L x 5.5W x 5H, wind-up motor, Model No. 866
EX $135   **NM** $195   **MIP** $255

Heavy Duty Steam Shovel, 1952, Blue, 21.5L x 6.25W x 7.75H,, Model No. 105
EX $65   **NM** $125   **MIP** $175

Dump Truck, 1952, Red, 20L x 6.75W x 6.25H, with plastic fireball motor under the hood, Model No. 200
EX $75   **NM** $135   **MIP** $195

Aerial Fire Truck, 1952, Red, 24L x 6.75W x 6.25H, with plastic fireball motor under the hood, Model No. 250
EX $115   **NM** $175   **MIP** $255

Road Grader, 1952, Orange, 18L x 7W x 7.5H, with plastic fireball motor under the hood, Model No. 300
EX $55   **NM** $85   **MIP** $105

Machinery Truck & Steam Shovel, 1952, Orange and blue, 21.5L x 6.75W x 6.25H, with plastic fireball motor under the hood, Model No. 402
EX $100   **NM** $155   **MIP** $195

Utility (Garbage) Truck, 1952, Red and blue, 21.5L x 6.5W x 7.5H, with plastic fireball motor under the hood, Model No. 500
EX $95   **NM** $155   **MIP** $205

(Randy Prasse Photo)

Motor Express Truck, 1952, Grey and orange, 12.75L x 5.5W x 5H, cast cab

"Freeport Motor Express" decals, Model No. 601
EX $75   NM $125   MIP $195

Package Delivery Truck, 1952, Orange and green, 13L x 5.5W x 5H, cast cab, tail gate with chain, Model No. 603
EX $75   NM $125   MIP $195

Shovel Dump Truck, 1952, Orange and blue, 12.75L x 5.5W x 5H, cast cab, dump box, Model No. 605
EX $75   NM $125   MIP $195

Machinery Truck, 1952, Orange and blue, 12.75L x 5.5W x 5H, with loading ramp and chain winch, Model No. 607
EX $95   NM $155   MIP $205

Transport Trailer, 1952, Blue and red, 21.5L x 5.5W x 7.5H, blue cast cab with red trailer, no hubcaps, Model No. 700
EX $95   NM $135   MIP $205

(Randy Prasse Photo)

Steel Cargo Trailer, 1952, Blue and red, 20.75L x 5.5W x 5.5H, blue cast cab with red trailer, no hubcaps, Model No. 702
EX $95   NM $135   MIP $195

(Randy Prasse Photo)

Overland Freight Trailer, 1952, Blue and orange, 20.75L x 5.5W x 5.5H, blue cast cab with orange stake trailer, Model No. 704
EX $115   NM $175   MIP $225

Combination With Two Trailers, 1952, Blue cast cab with #702 and 704 trailers, Model No. 706
EX $155   NM $215   MIP $275

Barrel Truck, 1952, Red and blue, 12.75L x 5.5W x 5H, wind-up motor and two oil can banks, Model No. 811
EX $135   NM $195   MIP $255

Wrecker Truck, 1952, Red and grey, 12.25L x 5.5W x 5.25H, wind-up motor and chain winch, Model No. 822
EX $95   NM $125   MIP $175

(Randy Prasse Photo)

Hi-Lift Dump Truck, 1952, Red and blue, 12.5L x 5.5W x 5.25H, wind-up motor with scissors lift box, Model No. 844
EX $105   NM $155   MIP $215

Gasoline Truck, 1952, Red and red, 13.5L x 5.5W x 5H, wind-up motor, Model No. 866
EX $135   NM $195   MIP $255

Steam Shovel (New Design), 1953, Blue, 26.5L x 6.5W x 8H, new design, 2 cranks, Model No. 105
EX $55   NM $95   MIP $125

Dump Truck, 1953, Red, 20L x 6.75W x 6.25H, with plastic fireball motor under the hood, Model No. 200
EX $65   NM $105   MIP $155

Road Grader, 1953, Orange, 18L x 7W x 7.5H, with plastic fireball motor under the hood, Model No. 300
EX $55   NM $85   MIP $105

Rocker, 1953, Red, 20L x 6.25W x 6.5H, with plastic fireball motor under the hood, Model No. 310
EX $75   NM $105   MIP $155

Bottom Dump, 1953, Orange, 21.5L x 6.5W x 6.5H, with plastic fireball motor under the hood, Model No. 320
EX $75   NM $105   MIP $155

Scraper, 1953, Red, 22L x 7W x 6.5H, with plastic fireball motor under the hood, Model No. 330
EX $75   NM $105   MIP $155

End Loader, 1953, Orange, 15.25L x 6.25W x 6.75H, with plastic fireball motor under the hood, Model No. 340
EX $65   NM $95   MIP $145

Machinery Truck & Steam Shovel, 1953, Orange and blue, 21.5L x 6.75W x 6.25H, comes w/#105 steam shovel & loading ramp, Model No. 402
EX $95   NM $155   MIP $195

Utility (Garbage) Truck, 1953, Red and white, 21.5L x 6.5W x 7.5H, with plastic fireball motor under the hood, Model No. 500
EX $95   NM $155   MIP $205

(Randy Prasse Photo)

Motor Express Truck, 1953, White and red, 12.75L x 5.5W x 5H, cast cab "Freeport Motor Express" decals, Model No. 601
EX $75   NM $125   MIP $195

Package Delivery Truck, 1953, White and orange, 13L x 5.5W x 5H, cast cab, tail gate with chain, w/hubcaps, Model No. 603
EX $75   NM $125   MIP $195

Shovel Dump Truck, 1953, White and blue, 12.75L x 5.5W x 5H, cast cab, dump box, w/hubcaps, Model No. 605
EX $75   NM $125   MIP $195

Transport Trailer, 1953, White and red, 21.5L x 5.5W x 7.5H, w/hubcaps, Model No. 700
EX $75   NM $125   MIP $195

Steel Cargo Trailer, 1953, White and red, 20.75L x 5.5W x 5.5H, w/hubcaps & loading ramp, Model No. 702
EX $75   NM $125   MIP $175

Grain Trailer, 1953, White and orange, 20.75L x 5.5W x 5.5H, replaced freight trailer, sliding rear door, Model No. 704
EX $95   NM $155   MIP $205

Cattle Trailer, 1953, White and red, 21.5L x 5.5W x 7.5H, no loading ramp or animals, Model No. 708
EX $95   NM $155   MIP $205

(Randy Prasse Photo)

Barrel Truck, 1953, Red and blue, 12.75L x 5.5W x 5H, wind-up motor and oil can bank, Model No. 811
EX $135   NM $195   MIP $255

Wrecker Truck, 1953, White and orange, 12.25L x 5.5W x 5.25H, wind-up motor and chain winch, Model No. 822
EX $115   NM $155   MIP $195

Hi-Lift Dump Truck, 1953, White and red, 12.5L x 5.5W x 5.25H, wind-up motor with scissors lift box, Model No. 844
EX $105   NM $155   MIP $215

Gasoline Truck, 1953, Red and red, 13.5L x 5.5W x 5H, wind-up motor, Model No. 866
EX $135   NM $195   MIP $255

Steam Shovel, 1953, Blue, 26.5L x 6.5W x 8H, 2 cranks and rubber tracks, Model No. 105
EX $55   NM $95   MIP $125

Dump Truck, 1953, Red, 20L x 6.75W x 6.25H, with plastic fireball motor under the hood, Model No. 200
EX $65   NM $105   MIP $155

Road Grader, 1953, Orange, 18L x 7W x 7.5H, with plastic fireball motor under the hood, Model No. 300
EX $55   NM $85   MIP $105

Rocker, 1953, Red, 20L x 6.25W x .6.5H, with plastic fireball motor under the hood, Model No. 310
EX $75   NM $105   MIP $155

Bottom Dump, 1953, Orange, 21.5L x 6.5W x 6.5H, with plastic fireball motor under the hood, Model No. 320
EX $75   NM $105   MIP $155

Scraper, 1953, Red, 22L x 7W x 6.5H, with plastic fireball motor under the hood, Model No. 330
EX $75   NM $105   MIP $155

End Loader, 1954, Orange, 15.25L x 6.25W x 6.75H, with plastic fireball motor under the hood, Model No. 340
EX $65   NM $95   MIP $145

Machinery Truck & Steam Shovel, 1954, Orange and blue, 26.5L x 6.75W x 14.25H, comes w/#105 steam shovel & loading ramp, Model No. 402
EX $95   **NM** $155   **MIP** $195

Utility (Garbage) Truck, 1954, Red and white, 21.5L x 6.5W x 7.5H, with plastic fireball motor under the hood, Model No. 500
EX $95   **NM** $155   **MIP** $205

(Randy Prasse Photo)

Package Delivery Truck, 1954, White and orange, 13L x 5.5W x 5H, cast cab, tail gate with chain, w/hubcaps, Model No. 603
EX $75   **NM** $125   **MIP** $195

Shovel Dump Truck, 1954, White and blue, 12.75L x 5.5W x 5H, cast cab, dump box, w/hubcaps, Model No. 605
EX $75   **NM** $125   **MIP** $195

Machinery Truck, 1954, White and blue, 12.75L x 5.5W x 5H, rare, made only in 1954. Hubcaps, loading ramp, Model No. 607
EX $95   **NM** $155   **MIP** $205

Barrel Truck, 1954, White and red, 12.75L x 5.5W x 5H, rare, made only in 1954. Replaced #811, no wind-up, Model No. 609
EX $115   **NM** $175   **MIP** $205

Transport Trailer, 1954, White and red, 21.5L x 5.5W x 7.5H, w/hubcaps, Model No. 700
EX $75   **NM** $125   **MIP** $195

Steel Cargo Trailer, 1954, White and red, 20.75L x 5.5W x 5.5H, w/hubcaps & loading ramp, Model No. 702
EX $75   **NM** $125   **MIP** $175

Grain Trailer, 1954, White and orange, 20.75L x 5.5W x 5.5H, sliding rear door, Model No. 704
EX $95   **NM** $155   **MIP** $205

Auto Transport, 1954, White and red, 27L x 5.5W x 6.75H, with 4 die cast cars and loading ramp, Model No. 706
EX $95   **NM** $155   **MIP** $205

Cattle Trailer, 1954, White and red, 21.5L x 5.5W x 7.5H, no loading ramp or animals, Model No. 708
EX $95   **NM** $155   **MIP** $205

Wrecker Truck, 1954, White and orange, 12.25L x 5.5W x 5.25H, wind-up motor and chain winch, Model No. 822
EX $115   **NM** $155   **MIP** $195

(Randy Prasse Photo)

Hi-Lift Dump Truck, 1954, White and red, 12.5L x 5.5W x 5.25H, wind-up motor with scissors lift box, Model No. 844
EX $105   **NM** $155   **MIP** $215

(Randy Prasse Photo)

Gasoline Truck, 1954, Red and red, 13.5L x 5.5W x 5H, wind-up motor, Model No. 866
EX $135   **NM** $195   **MIP** $255

Tow Truck (Fix-It), 1954, Red and red, 11.75L x 5.5W x 6H, with mini tool set. New pressed steel cab design, Model No. 910
EX $75   **NM** $105   **MIP** $155

Telephone Truck (Fix-It), 1954, Green, 12L x 5.5W x 5.25H, with mini tool set, new pressed steel cab design, Model No. 920
EX $75   **NM** $105   **MIP** $155

Freight Trailer, 1954, Red and red, 17.75L x 5W x 4.5H, new pressed steel cab design, Model No. 930
EX $115   **NM** $155   **MIP** $195

Log Trailer, 1954, Orange and orange, 17.75L x 5W x 4.5H, with five wooden logs, Model No. 940
EX $115   **NM** $155   **MIP** $195

Caddy Sedan, 1954, Various, 6.25L x 2.5W x 2H, same scale as appear on auto transport set, Model No. 20
EX $15   **NM** $25   **MIP** $35

Pick-Up Truck, 1954, Various, 6.5L x 2.5W x 2.25H, same scale as appear on auto transport set, Model No. 21
EX $15   **NM** $25   **MIP** $35

Wrecker Truck, 1954, Various, 7.5L x 2.5W x 2.25H, same scale #21 pick-up but with cast tow boom arm, Model No. 30
EX $25   **NM** $55   **MIP** $75

8-Wheel Transport Truck, 1954, Orange, 7.25L x 2.5W x 2.25H, also in 1957 as 6 wheeled, red version in farm set, Model No. 40
EX $25   **NM** $55   **MIP** $75

Dump Truck, 1954, Green and orange, 8.25L x 2.5W x 2.5H, spring dump action, Model No. 50
EX $35   **NM** $65   **MIP** $95

4 Pc. Truck Assortment, 1954, One each: #21, #30, #40, #50, Model No. 90
EX $95   **NM** $125   **MIP** $175

Dump Truck, 1954, Green and orange, 10.25L x 3.25W x 3.5H, spring dump action, Model No. 75
EX $35   **NM** $55   **MIP** $75

Stake Truck, 1954, Green and orange, 9.25L x 3.25W x 3.25H, removable stake panels, Model No. 76
EX $35   **NM** $55   **MIP** $75

Lumber Truck, 1954, Red and blue, 10.5L x 3.5W x 3.25H, with five wooden logs, Model No. 77
EX $35   **NM** $55   **MIP** $75

3 Pc. Truck Assortment, 1954, One each: #75, #76, #77, Model No. 91
EX $125   **NM** $175   **MIP** $255

Motor Express Truck, 1954, Yellow and blue, 12.5L x 5.25W x 4.5H, stake truck with "S" grill cab, Model No. 150
EX $75   **NM** $125   **MIP** $155

Machinery Hauling Truck, 1954, Red and yellow, 12.5L x 5.5W x 4H, flatbed with winch and "S" grill cab, Model No. 151
EX $75   **NM** $125   **MIP** $155

Semi Trailer Freight Truck, 1955, Yellow and red, 17L x 4.5W x 4.5H, same trailer as #930 with "S" grill cab, Model No. 155
EX $95   **NM** $155   **MIP** $175

Semi Trailer Lumber Truck, 1955, Green and orange, 17L x 4.5W x 4.5H, with three wooden logs and "S" grill cab, Model No. 156
EX $95   **NM** $155   **MIP** $175

Auto Haulaway, 1955, Blue and orange, 25L x 4.5W x 6.5H, with two cars, loading ramp and "S" grill cab, Model No. 175
EX $105   **NM** $175   **MIP** $195

Steam Shovel, 1955, Orange, 26.5L x 6.5W x 8H, 2 cranks and rubber tracks, Model No. 105
EX $55   **NM** $75   **MIP** $115

Dump Truck, 1955, Yellow and red, 20L x 6.75W x 6.25H, spring dump action, Model No. 201
EX $55   **NM** $95   **MIP** $125

Hydraulic Lift Dump Truck, 1955, Green and orange, 21L x 8W x 7H, hydraulic dump lift arm on dump box, Model No. 250
EX $95   **NM** $155   **MIP** $205

Hook and Ladder Truck, 1955, Red, 33.25L x 6.75W x 7H, with raising & two ladders, cast metal siren on roof, Model No. 260
EX $95   **NM** $155   **MIP** $205

Road Grader, 1955, Orange, 18L x 7W x 7.5H, with plastic fireball motor under the hood, Model No. 300
EX $55   **NM** $85   **MIP** $105

Rocker, 1955, Green, 20L x 6.25W x 6.5H, with plastic fireball motor under the hood, Model No. 310
EX $75   **NM** $105   **MIP** $155

Earth Mover, 1955, Orange, 21.5L x 6.5W x 6.5H, with plastic fireball motor under the hood, Model No. 320
EX $75   **NM** $105   **MIP** $155

VEHICLES — STRUCTO

Scraper, 1955, Red, 22L x 7W x 6.5H, with plastic fireball motor under the hood, Model No. 330
EX $75   **NM** $105   **MIP** $155

End Loader, 1955, Orange, 15.25L x 6.25W x 6.75H, with plastic fireball motor under the hood, Model No. 340
EX $65   **NM** $95   **MIP** $145

3 Pc. Truck Assortment, 1955, One each: #105, #201, $300, Model No. 325
EX $175   **NM** $225   **MIP** $345

Steam Shovel & Machinery Truck, 1955, Green and orange, 26.5L x 6.5W x 14.25H, with plastic fireball motor under the hood, Model No. 403
EX $95   **NM** $155   **MIP** $195

Utility (Garbage) Truck, 1955, Blue and grey, 21.5L x 6.5W x 7.5H, with plastic fireball motor under the hood, Model No. 500
EX $95   **NM** $155   **MIP** $205

Shovel Dump Truck, 1955, Chrome and orange, 12.75L x 6W x 6.25H, same as #605 from past years. Mag wheels, Model No. 606
EX $105   **NM** $175   **MIP** $205

Hi-Lift Dump Truck, 1955, Chrome and green, 12.5L x 6W x 5H, same as #844 from past years. Mag wheels, Model No. 644
EX $115   **NM** $195   **MIP** $225

Steel Cargo Trailer, 1955, White and red, 25.5L x 5.5W x 5.5H, shown in catalog with yellow cab but have not seen, Model No. 702
EX $75   **NM** $125   **MIP** $175

Grain Trailer, 1955, White and orange, 20.75L x 5.5W x 5.5H, shown in catalog with green cab but have not seen, Model No. 704
EX $95   **NM** $155   **MIP** $205

Deluxe Auto Transport, 1955, Chrome and yellow, 27L x 6W x 6.75H, with 4 die cast cars and loading ramp, Model No. 706
EX $75   **NM** $135   **MIP** $195

(Randy Prasse Photo)

Deluxe Moving Van, 1955, Chrome and yellow, 24L x 6W x 8.5H, with loading ramp, Model No. 710
EX $105   **NM** $175   **MIP** $205

Deluxe Cattle Transport, 1955, Chrome and green, 24L x 6W x 8.5H, with loading ramp and metal farm animals, Model No. 712
EX $75   **NM** $155   **MIP** $195

Timber Toter, 1955, Chrome and green, 21L x 6W x 6H, with six wooden logs and chains, Model No. 714
EX $65   **NM** $135   **MIP** $175

10 Pc. Truck Assortment, 1955, 2 cabs plus one each #702, #706, #714, cattle trailer, Model No. 725
EX $225   **NM** $495   **MIP** $695

Wrecker Truck, 1955, White and orange, 12L x 5.5W x 5.25H, shown in catalog with green cab but have not seen, Model No. 822
EX $115   **NM** $155   **MIP** $195

Tow Truck (Fix-It), 1955, Red and red, 11.75L x 5.5W x 6H, with mini tool set, Model No. 910
EX $75   **NM** $105   **MIP** $155

Telephone Truck (Fix-It), 1955, Green, 12L x 5.5W x 5.25H, with mini tool set, Model No. 920
EX $75   **NM** $105   **MIP** $155

Freight Trailer, 1955, Yellow and red, 17.75L x 5W x 4.5H, Model No. 930
EX $115   **NM** $155   **MIP** $195

Log Trailer, 1955, Green and orange, 17.75L x 5W x 4.5H, with five wooden logs, Model No. 940
EX $115   **NM** $155   **MIP** $195

Package Delivery Truck, 1955, Yellow and green, 13L x 5.5W x 4.75H, with tailgate and chains, Model No. 911
EX $55   **NM** $95   **MIP** $155

Gasoline Truck, 1955, Red and yellow, 13.5L x 5W x 4.5H, non-wind-up model, Model No. 912
EX $75   **NM** $115   **MIP** $175

Barrel Truck, 1955, Yellow and red, 12.75L x 5.5W x 5H, non-wind-up model, no oil can bank, Model No. 913
EX $75   **NM** $115   **MIP** $175

Transport Trailer, 1955, Yellow and red, 21L x 5W x 7.75H, new pressed steel cab design, Model No. 950
EX $75   **NM** $135   **MIP** $195

Cattle Trailer, 1955, Green and orange, 21L x 5W x 7.75H, new pressed steel cab design, Model No. 960
EX $75   **NM** $135   **MIP** $195

Dump Truck, 1956-57, Gold and blue, 10.25L x 3.25W x 3.5H, spring dump action, Model No. 75
EX $35   **NM** $55   **MIP** $75

Stake Truck, 1956-57, Gold and green, 9.25L x 3.25W x 3.25H, removable stake panels, Model No. 76
EX $35   **NM** $55   **MIP** $75

Lumber Truck, 1956-57, Red and blue, 10.5L x 3.5W x 3.25H, with five wooden logs, Model No. 77
EX $35   **NM** $55   **MIP** $75

3 Pc. Truck Assortment W/Garage, 1956-57, One each: #75, #76, #77 with garage storage box, Model No. 92
EX $155   **NM** $195   **MIP** $295

Motor Express Truck, 1956-57, Yellow and blue, 12.5L x 5.25W x 4.5H, stake truck with "S" grill cab, Model No. 150
EX $75   **NM** $125   **MIP** $155

Machinery Hauling Truck, 1956-57, Red and yellow, 12.5L x 5.5W x 4H, flatbed with winch and "S" grill cab, Model No. 151
EX $75   **NM** $125   **MIP** $155

Semi Trailer Freight Truck, 1956-57, Yellow and red, 17L x 4.5W x 4.5H, same trailer as #930 with "S" grill cab, Model No. 155
EX $95   **NM** $155   **MIP** $175

Auto Haulaway, 1956-57, Blue and orange, 25L x 4.5W x 6.5H, with two cars, loading ramp and "S" grill cab, Model No. 175
EX $105   **NM** $175   **MIP** $195

Clam Bucket, 1956-57, Yellow and green, 16.75L x 7W x 7.25H, Model No. 101
EX $75   **NM** $105   **MIP** $125

Heavy Duty Steam Shovel, 1956-57, Green and orange, 26.5L x 7W x 6.75H, 2 cranks and rubber tracks, Model No. 106
EX $55   **NM** $95   **MIP** $125

Dump Truck, 1956-57, Green and orange, 20L x 6.75W x 6.25H, spring dump action, Model No. 201
EX $55   **NM** $95   **MIP** $125

Hydraulic Lift Dump Truck, 1956-57, Yellow and green, 21L x 8W x 7H, hydraulic dump lift arm on dump box, Model No. 250
EX $95   **NM** $155   **MIP** $205

Hook and Ladder Truck, 1956-57, Red, 33.25L x 6.75W x 7H, with raising & two ladders, cast metal siren on roof, Model No. 260
EX $95   **NM** $155   **MIP** $205

Ready Mix Concrete Truck, 1956-57, Red and yellow, 21.5L x 7.5W x 9.25H, with gear on barrel, driven by axle, Model No. 271
EX $75   **NM** $105   **MIP** $155

Mobile Steam Shovel Unit, 1956-57, Green and yellow, 32.5L x 6.75W x 8H, half-track truck with steam shovel on back, Model No. 272
EX $95   **NM** $155   **MIP** $205

Road Grader, 1956-57, Green, 18L x 7W x 7.5H, with plastic fireball motor under the hood, Model No. 300
EX $55   **NM** $85   **MIP** $105

Rocker Dump, 1956-57, Green, 20L x 6W x 6.5H, rubber tracks on tractor, dumps to the rear, Model No. 311
EX $95   **NM** $125   **MIP** $155

Earth Mover, 1956-57, Orange, 22L x 6.5W x 6.5H, same tractor as #311, bottom panels open to dump, Model No. 321
EX $95   **NM** $125   **MIP** $155

Scraper, 1956-57, Orange, 22L x 7W x 6.5H, with plastic fireball motor under the hood, Model No. 330
EX $75   **NM** $105   **MIP** $155

End Loader, 1956-57, Green, 15.25L x 6W x 6.75H, with plastic fireball motor under the hood, Model No. 340
EX $65   **NM** $95   **MIP** $145

Clam Bucket and Machinery Truck, 1956-57, Yellow and green, 32L x 7.25W x 13.75H, with plastic fireball motor under the hood, Model No. 404
EX $105   **NM** $175   **MIP** $205

Utility (Garbage) Truck, 1956-57, Blue and grey, 21.5L x 6.5W x 7.5H, with plastic fireball motor under the hood, Model No. 500

EX $95   **NM** $155   **MIP** $205

Shovel Dump Truck, 1956-57, Green and yellow, 12.75L x 6W x 5H, with mag wheels, Model No. 606

EX $75   **NM** $155   **MIP** $195

Hi-Lift Dump Truck, 1956-57, Chrome and blue, 12.5L x 6W x 5H, same as #644 from 1955 only blue dump box, Model No. 644

EX $115   **NM** $195   **MIP** $225

Trailer Truck, 1956-57, Chrome and red, 24.5L x 6W x 5.5H, same as #702 but with chrome cab and lift gate, Model No. 705

EX $95   **NM** $155   **MIP** $205

Deluxe Auto Transport, 1956-57, Chrome and yellow, 27L x 6W x 6.75H, with 4 die cast cars and loading ramp, Model No. 706

EX $75   **NM** $135   **MIP** $195

Deluxe Moving Van, 1956-57, Chrome and blue, 24L x 6W x 8.5H, with loading ramp and mini grocery freight, Model No. 710

EX $105   **NM** $165   **MIP** $205

Western Auto Moving Van, 1956-57, Chrome and white, 24L x 6W x 8.5H, private label. Same body as #710 deluxe moving van. Red doors, Model No. 711

EX $125   **NM** $185   **MIP** $225

(Randy Prasse Photo)

Deluxe Cattle Transport, 1956-57, Chrome and green, 24L x 6W x 8.5H, with loading ramp and metal farm animals, Model No. 712

EX $75   **NM** $155   **MIP** $195

(Randy Prasse Photo)

Timber Toter, 1956-57, Chrome and green, 21L x 6W x 6H, with six wooden logs and chains, Model No. 714

EX $65   **NM** $135   **MIP** $175

Wrecker Truck, 1956-57, White and orange, 12L x 5.5W x 5.25H, wind-up, Model No. 822

EX $115   **NM** $155   **MIP** $195

Freight Hauler, 1956-57, Blue and yellow, 20.5L x 5.25W x 5.5H, with grocery freight, Model No. 935

EX $75   **NM** $105   **MIP** $155

Transport Truck, 1956-57, Red and yellow, 21L x 5W x 7.5H, Model No. 950

EX $75   **NM** $105   **MIP** $135

Cattle Transport, 1956-57, Green and orange, 21L x 5W x 7.75H, Model No. 960

EX $75   **NM** $135   **MIP** $195

Tow Truck (Fix-It), 1956-57, Blue and blue, 11.75L x 5.5W x 6H, with mini tool set, Model No. 910

EX $75   **NM** $105   **MIP** $155

Package Delivery Truck, 1956-57, Blue and yellow, 13L x 5.5W x 4.75H, with tailgate and chains, Model No. 911

EX $55   **NM** $95   **MIP** $155

Gasoline Truck, 1956-57, Blue and yellow, 13.5L x 5W x 4.5H, Model No. 912

EX $75   **NM** $115   **MIP** $175

Barrel Truck, 1956-57, Yellow and red, 12.75L x 5.5W x 5H, non-wind-up model, no oil can bank, Model No. 913

EX $75   **NM** $115   **MIP** $175

Telephone Truck (Fix-It), 1956-57, Blue, 12L x 5.5W x 5.25H, with mini tool set, Model No. 920

EX $75   **NM** $105   **MIP** $155

3 Pc. Truck Assortment, 1956-57, Various, one each: #106, #201, #300, Model No. 326

EX $175   **NM** $225   **MIP** $345

5 Pc. Turnpike Builder Set, 1956-57, Various, one each: #321, #340, #404 combo, Model No. 327

EX $195   **NM** $275   **MIP** $395

32 Pc. Big Job Transcontinental Set, 1956-57, Various, 2 cabs plus one each #702, #706, #714, cattle trailer, Model No. 726

EX $225   **NM** $495   **MIP** $695

17 Pc. Coast To Coast Fleet, 1956-57, Various, 2 cars plus lumber trailer, #175, #935, #950; 2 cars, Model No. 925

EX $175   **NM** $295   **MIP** $495

15 Pc. Farm Set, 1958, Various, caddy, dump, pick-up/horse trailer, 6 wheel transport, Model No. 93

EX $125   **NM** $175   **MIP** $225

3 Pc. Truck Assortment W/Garage, 1958, Various, one each; dump, log and stake truck, Model No. 94

EX $155   **NM** $195   **MIP** $295

Pick-Up Truck With Horse Van, 1958, Blue and yellow, 10.5L x 2.5W x 3H, includes 2 plastic horses, Model No. 100

EX $55   **NM** $85   **MIP** $105

Power Shovel, 1958, Orange, 26.5L x 7W x 6.75H, 2 cranks and rubber tracks, Model No. 106

EX $55   **NM** $95   **MIP** $115

Heavy Duty Dump Truck, 1958, Blue and orange, 20L x 6.75W x 6.25H, spring dump action plus red light on roof, Model No. 200

EX $75   **NM** $105   **MIP** $135

Dump With Front-End Loader, 1958, Yellow and blue, 23L x 6.75W x 6.25H, spring loaded dump with front loader bucket, Model No. 202

EX $105   **NM** $135   **MIP** $175

Pick-Up Truck, 1958, Red and yellow, 19.25L x 6.5W x 6H, includes mini grocery freight, Model No. 210

EX $95   **NM** $125   **MIP** $155

Air Force Truck, 1958, Blue and red, 17.25L x 7.25W x 8H, includes soldiers and canvas top, spare tires on side, Model No. 212

EX $115   **NM** $155   **MIP** $195

Farm Truck & Trailer, 1958, Blue and yellow, 28L x 6W x 6.25H, pick-up with pick-up box trailer & plastic farm animals, Model No. 213

EX $115   **NM** $155   **MIP** $195

Towing & Service Truck, 1958, Green and orange, 17.5L x 6W x 7.5H, same as #210 but with tow set-up and red light on roof, Model No. 214

EX $105   **NM** $135   **MIP** $175

Hydraulic Lift Dump Truck, 1958, Orange and green, 21L x 8W x 7H, hydraulic dump lift arm on dump box, Model No. 250

EX $125   **NM** $165   **MIP** $205

Double Hydraulic Load & Dump, 1958, Black and yellow, 24.5L x 7.75W x 7H, hydraulic dump lift arm on dump box & front bucket, Model No. 252

EX $125   **NM** $165   **MIP** $205

Hook and Ladder Truck, 1958, Red, 33.5L x 6W x 7H, with raising & two ladders, cast metal siren on roof, Model No. 261

EX $95   **NM** $155   **MIP** $205

Pumper Fire Truck W/Light, 1958, Red, 22.75L x 7.25W x 7H, pumps water through truck & hydrant, flashing light, Model No. 262

EX $105   **NM** $165   **MIP** $205

Hydraulic Hook & Ladder Truck, 1958, Red, 33.25L x 6.75W x 7H, with raising & two ladders, red flashing light on roof, Model No. 266

EX $95   **NM** $175   **MIP** $215

Mobile Communications Center, 1958, Red and blue, 20L x 6.25W x 6.25H, includes antenna tower & morse code buttons, Model No. 270

EX $115   **NM** $155   **MIP** $195

Ready Mix Concrete Truck, 1958, Green and orange, 21.5L x 7.5W x 9.25H, with gear on barrel, driven by axle, Model No. 271

EX $75   **NM** $105   **MIP** $175

Mobile Power Shovel Unit, 1958, Green and yellow, 32.5L x 6.75W x 8H, half-track truck with steam shovel on back, Model No. 272

EX $95   **NM** $155   **MIP** $205

Deluxe Cattle Transport, 1958, Yellow and brown, 25.75L x 6.25W x 8.5H, includes plastic farm animals, Model No. 275

EX $95   **NM** $155   **MIP** $205

Deluxe Road Grader, 1958, Orange, 18.75L x 7.25W x 7.5H, with plastic fireball motor under the hood, Model No. 301

EX $55   **NM** $95   **MIP** $115

Deluxe Rocker Dump, 1958, Orange, 20.25L x 6.25W x 6.5H, with plastic fireball motor under the hood, Model No. 312

EX $65   **NM** $105   **MIP** $125

Deluxe Earth Mover, 1958, Orange, 22L x 6.5W x 6.5H, with plastic fireball motor under the hood, Model No. 322
EX $65   **NM** $105   **MIP** $125

Combination, 1958, Green and orange, 32L x 7.5W x 6.75H, #106 power shovel and machinery hauling low-boy, Model No. 405
EX $75   **NM** $135   **MIP** $195

5 Pc. Highway Builder Set, 1958, Various, one each: #106, #201, #300 plus 2 metal road signs, Model No. 510
EX $175   **NM** $225   **MIP** $395

17 Pc. USA Combat Convoy Set, 1958, Green, transport, searchlight and missle trucks w/soldiers, Model No. 520
EX $155   **NM** $205   **MIP** $375

Big Job Transcontinental Fleet, 1958, Various, 2 cabs plus 1 each trailers: steel, auto, freight, cattle, Model No. 540
EX $225   **NM** $495   **MIP** $695

12 Pc. US Highway Set, 1958, Orange, dump, grader, maintenance, pick-up plus 8 road signs, Model No. 550
EX $195   **NM** $245   **MIP** $425

6 Pc. Fire Department, 1958, Red and white, pumper, hook & ladder, ambulance, road signs, Model No. 570
EX $175   **NM** $225   **MIP** $395

Deluxe Auto Transport, 1958, Chrome and yellow, 27L x 6W x 6.75H, with 2 cars, 1 truck and loading ramp, Model No. 707
EX $75   **NM** $135   **MIP** $195

(Randy Prasse Photo)

Gold Plated Cadillac, 1958, Gold, 6.75L x 2.25W x 2H, same as used on car carriers. 50th Anniversary decal on roof
EX $125   **NM** $175   **MIP** $225

Deluxe Moving Van, 1958, Chrome and blue, 31L x 6W x 8.5H, with loading ramp and mini grocery freight, Model No. 710
EX $105   **NM** $165   **MIP** $205

Timber Toter, 1958, Chrome and blue, 21L x 6W x 6.25H, with six wooden logs and chains, Model No. 714
EX $65   **NM** $135   **MIP** $175

USA Transport Truck, 1958, Green, 12.5L x 5.25W x 7.5H, with canvas top, Model No. 905
EX $55   **NM** $95   **MIP** $135

USA Guided Missile Launcher, 1958, Green, 12.75L x 5.25W x 6H, with 2 plastic missiles, Model No. 906
EX $65   **NM** $105   **MIP** $155

USA Searchlight Truck, 1958, Green, 12.75L x 5.25W x 7.25H, with battery operated searchlight, Model No. 907
EX $75   **NM** $115   **MIP** $175

Gasoline Truck, 1958, Blue and yellow, 13.5L x 5W x 4.5H, Model No. 912
EX $75   **NM** $115   **MIP** $175

Hi-Lift Dump Truck, 1958, Blue and yellow, 12L x 5.25W x 5.75H, with scissors lift mechanism, Model No. 914
EX $65   **NM** $95   **MIP** $125

Trailer W/Mechanical Lift, 1958, Blue and yellow, 50.75L x 5.5W x 5.75H, mechanical lift gate with mini grocery freight, Model No. 936
EX $95   **NM** $155   **MIP** $195

Farm Truck, 1958, Green and red, 13L x 5.75W x 4.5H, with plastic farm animals, Model No. 938
EX $65   **NM** $95   **MIP** $125

(Randy Prasse Photo)

Highway Maintenance Service, 1958, Orange and green, 12L x 4.5W x 7H, with lift/swivel boom arm, Model No. 939
EX $65   **NM** $95   **MIP** $125

Hydraulic Dump Trailer, 1958, Yellow and green, 20.5L x 5.5W x 5.75H, with hydraulic lift arm on trailer dump, Model No. 941
EX $115   **NM** $155   **MIP** $195

Parcel Service Truck, 1958, Yellow and green, 12.25L x 5.25W x 7H, with mini grocery freight, Model No. 942
EX $75   **NM** $115   **MIP** $155

US Main Truck, 1958, Blue and red, 12.25L x 5.25W x 6.5H, Model No. 943
EX $95   **NM** $125   **MIP** $175

Farm Trailer Truck, 1958, Blue and red, 20.5L x 5.5W x 5.5H, with plastic animals and loading ramp, Model No. 945
EX $75   **NM** $115   **MIP** $155

Auto Haulaway, 1958, Yellow and red, 21.5L x 4.5W x 6.5H, smaller model with 2 cars and loading ramp, Model No. 946
EX $75   **NM** $115   **MIP** $155

Refrigerated Express Truck, 1958, Yellow and brown, 21L x 5W x 7.5H, transport trailer with refrigerator unit on front, Model No. 951
EX $95   **NM** $155   **MIP** $195

Cattle Transport, 1958, Green and orange, 21L x 5W x 7.5H, with plastic farm animals, Model No. 961
EX $75   **NM** $115   **MIP** $155

Ride 'Em Dump Truck, 1958, Blue and yellow, 20.5L x 7.75W x 10.25H, with seat and steering wheel, Model No. 990
EX $95   **NM** $155   **MIP** $195

Ride 'Em Air Force Jeep, 1958, Blue and red, 25.5L x 11W x 14.5H, with steering wheel and fold-down windshield, Model No. 995
EX $105   **NM** $175   **MIP** $215

Kitchen-Laundry Ensemble, 1959, Pink and grey, 9 piece 1/4 scale set, Model No. 50
EX $95   **NM** $155   **MIP** $195

Counter-Top Cabinet, 1959, Pink and grey, 7L x 7.75W x 13H, cabinet doors open, includes pots and pans, Model No. 2
EX $15   **NM** $35   **MIP** $55

Built-In Cooking Range, 1959, Pink and grey, 7L x 7.75W x 13H, plastic burners on top, cabinets open, pots and pans, Model No. 4
EX $15   **NM** $35   **MIP** $55

Corner Counter-Top Cabinet, 1959, Pink and grey, 12L x 9.75W x 13H, 2 lazy susan shelves, drawer opens, pots and pans, Model No. 6
EX $15   **NM** $35   **MIP** $55

Built-In Double Sink, 1959, Pink and grey, 7L x 7.75W x 13H, works with water, battery operated, Model No. 8
EX $15   **NM** $55   **MIP** $75

Automatic Under Counter Dishwasher, 1959, Pink and grey, 7L x 7.75W x 13H, works with water, battery operated, Model No. 10
EX $15   **NM** $55   **MIP** $75

Combination Refrigerator/Freezer, 1959, Pink and grey, 7.25L x 7.75W x 13H, swing out shelves, freezer drawer, plastic food, Model No. 12
EX $15   **NM** $35   **MIP** $55

Built-In Double Oven, 1959, Pink and grey, 7.25L x 7.75W x 13H, battery operated, rotisserie in top oven unit, Model No. 14
EX $15   **NM** $35   **MIP** $55

Washer-Dryer Combination, 1959, Pink and grey, 7.25L x 8W x 10H, washes & spins, battery operated, Model No. 16
EX $15   **NM** $55   **MIP** $75

Dump Truck, 1959, Copper and cream, 10.75L x 4.5W x 4.5H, Model No. 70
EX $55   **NM** $75   **MIP** $95

Dump Truck, 1959, Blue and yellow, 9L x 3.5W x 3.5H, Model No. 75
EX $35   **NM** $55   **MIP** $75

Stake Truck, 1959, Copper and cream, 9.25L x 3.25W x 3H, Model No. 76
EX $35   **NM** $55   **MIP** $75

Air Force Radar Truck, 1959, Blue and red, 12L x 5.25W x 12.5H, scarce, radar dish on roof of box, 2 plastic soldiers, Model No. 102
EX $55   **NM** $95   **MIP** $125

Dump Truck, 1959, Black and yellow, 15.75L x 6.75W x 6.75H, red roof and plastic "S" grille, no windshield, Model No. 201
EX $55   **NM** $95   **MIP** $115

Fleetside Pick-Up, 1959, Copper and cream, 14.5L x 6W x 6H, 6 mini grocery box play freight, Model No. 202
EX $45   **NM** $75   **MIP** $95

Guided Missile Launcher, 1959, Red and silver, 12.25L x 5.25W x 10.25H, plastic missile launcher on bed, metal "S" grille, Model No. 203
EX $75   **NM** $95   **MIP** $125

Mechanical Hydraulic Dump, 1959, Red and white, 12.25L x 5.25W x 5.5H, scarce, hydraulic cylinder controls dump box, Model No. 204
EX $75   **NM** $115   **MIP** $135

Bulldozer, 1959, Copper and cream, 11.75L x 7W x 6.75H, cream blade, yellow wheels and motor, also on #502 set, Model No. 205
EX $35   **NM** $55   **MIP** $75

The Camper, 1959, Red and white, 21.75L x 4.5W x 6.75H, canvas cover on truck, convertible boat & trailer, Model No. 206
EX $55   **NM** $95   **MIP** $125

Farm Pick-Up And Trailer, 1959, Yellow and blue, 27.5L x 6.25W x 6H, 7 plastic animals included, Model No. 213
EX $55   **NM** $95   **MIP** $125

Double Hydraulic Load & Dump, 1959, Copper and yellow, 23.75L x 7.75W x 6.75H, yellow bucket dumps over top into dump box, Model No. 252
EX $55   **NM** $75   **MIP** $95

Deluxe Road Grader, 1959, Copper and yellow, 18.75L x 7.25W x 7.5H, copper with yellow wheels and engine, Model No. 301
EX $35   **NM** $55   **MIP** $75

Power Shovel, 1959, Copper, 26.5L x 7W x 6.75H, rubber tracks, Model No. 302
EX $35   **NM** $55   **MIP** $75

Emergency Fire Patrol Searchlight Unit, 1959, White and red, 19.5L x 5.75W x 7.5H, white trailer with red battery operated searchlight unit, Model No. 303
EX $55   **NM** $95   **MIP** $125

Cattle Transport, 1959, Red and white, 21.25L x 5.25W x 7.5H, farms decals on white trailer, Model No. 304
EX $45   **NM** $65   **MIP** $85

Deluxe Rocker Dump, 1959, Copper and cream, 20.25L x 6.25W x 6.5H, bronze dump, cream tractor with yellow wheels & motor, Model No. 312
EX $45   **NM** $75   **MIP** $95

Highway Truck Assortment, 1959, Varies, 13 pc. set, includes #70, #76 plus 6-wheel truck, log truck & signs, Model No. 400
EX $115   **NM** $155   **MIP** $195

Deluxe Auto Transport, 1959, Green and yellow, 31.5L x 5.5W x 6.75H, two cars, one truck with loading ramp, plastic "S" grille, Model No. 401
EX $65   **NM** $95   **MIP** $125

Army Troop Transport, 1959, Green, 18.75L x 6.75W x 9H, canvas top with "USA" printed. 4 plastic soldiers, Model No. 412
EX $55   **NM** $75   **MIP** $95

Hydraulic Sanitation Truck, 1959, Blue and white, 18L x 6W x 7.5H, hydraulic cylinder controls dump box, Model No. 454
EX $65   **NM** $95   **MIP** $125

Deluxe Hydraulic Dumper, 1959, Copper and yellow, 20.5L x 8W x 7H, hydraulic cylinder controls dump box, Model No. 500
EX $65   **NM** $95   **MIP** $125

Stock Farm Set, 1959, Red and white, 15L x 6W x 7.25H, stake truck with cattle loading ramp and 4 plastic horses, Model No. 501
EX $55   **NM** $85   **MIP** $115

Tilt-Top Trailer Truck With Dozer, 1959, Yellow and green, 20.25L x 7.5W x 6H, dozer is copper with yellow plastic wheels and engine, Model No. 502
EX $55   **NM** $75   **MIP** $95

Mobile Outer Space Launcher, 1959, Red and blue, 19.5L x 6W x 12.75H, scarce, 2 plastic missiles launch. Launcher swivels, Model No. 503
EX $95   **NM** $135   **MIP** $195

Deluxe Moving Van, 1959, Yellow and red, 26.25L x 6W x 8.5H, red cab with bulb horn on roof, Model No. 504
EX $55   **NM** $95   **MIP** $125

Ride-er Dump Truck, 1959, Blue and yellow, 20L x 7.75W x 10H, metal seat in dump box, bulb horn on steering wheel, Model No. 505
EX $55   **NM** $95   **MIP** $125

Air Force Anti-Aircraft Set, 1959, Red and blue, scarce, canvas covered truck, missile launcher, searchlight, Model No. 506
EX $115   **NM** $195   **MIP** $245

Duluxe Camper With Boat & Trailer, 1959, Red and white, 29L x 6W x 6H, red truck with white roof, battery op boat motor, Model No. 601
EX $75   **NM** $125   **MIP** $175

Mobile Anti-Missile Unit, 1959, Blue and yellow, 27L x 7.5W x 11.25H, scarce, battery op spotlight & missile launcher on trailer, Model No. 620
EX $85   **NM** $115   **MIP** $175

Ready-Mix Concrete Truck, 1959, Copper and cream, 20.75L x 7.5W x 9.25H, gear powered barrel, runs off axle, Model No. 700
EX $55   **NM** $85   **MIP** $125

Pumper Fire Truck, 1959, Red and red, 20L x 7.25W x 6H, open cab, plastic "S" grille, sprays water through hose, Model No. 701
EX $55   **NM** $95   **MIP** $155

Deluxe Power Wrecker, 1959, Blue and white, 23L x 7W x 9.25H, battery operated winch & lights, Model No. 702
EX $75   **NM** $125   **MIP** $175

Timber Toter, 1959, Red and blue, 21.5L x 4.75W x 5.25H, 5 wooden logs and load chains, Model No. 714
EX $55   **NM** $75   **MIP** $95

Explorer Vanguard Tracking Station, 1959, Red, 7.75L x 4.5W x 10H, scarce, various buttons, globe revolves in TV screen, Model No. 801
EX $95   **NM** $155   **MIP** $195

Boat With Play Motor, 1959, Red and white, 9.5L x 3W x 2.5H, boat only, from #206 set, convertible boat and motor, Model No. 802
EX $35   **NM** $55   **MIP** $75

Boat With Outboard Motor, 1959, Red and white, 13.25L x 4W x 3.25H, boat only,

from #601 set, convertible boat and motor, Model No. 803
EX $55   **NM** $75   **MIP** $95

Highway Builder Set, 1959, Varies, 11 pc. set includes #201, #205, #302, road signs, plastic workers, Model No. 900
EX $95   **NM** $155   **MIP** $195

Hydraulic Hook & Ladder, 1959, Red and red, 31L x 6.25W x 7.25H, open cab, plastic "S" grille, metal ladders, Model No. 901
EX $75   **NM** $115   **MIP** $135

Mobile Crane, 1959, Green and yellow, 19.25L x 6.25W x 7.25H, battery operated boom and cab, Model No. 902
EX $85   **NM** $135   **MIP** $195

Ride-er Fire Truck, 1959, Red and white, 25.5L x 10.5W x 12.75H, crank siren on hood, trunk opens, Model No. 925
EX $75   **NM** $115   **MIP** $155

Tree Trimming Truck, 1959, Copper and green, 12L x 4.25W x 12.5H, green boom arm and basket, Model No. 939
EX $35   **NM** $55   **MIP** $75

Ride-er Air Force Jeep, 1959, Blue and red, 25.75L x 10.25W x 18H, missile launcher and missiles on hood, trunk opens, Model No. 950
EX $75   **NM** $115   **MIP** $175

Fire Department Set, 1959, Red and white, 3 piece set, includes #701, #901, #303 (minus searchlight unit), Model No. 975
EX $125   **NM** $195   **MIP** $275

Kitchen Ensemble, 1960, Pink and grey, individual appliances still available, see 1959 for values
EX $15   **NM** $35   **MIP** $55

Kitchen Ensemble, 1960, Pink and grey, 3 pc. set, includes #8, #12, #4- 1959 models, Model No. 23
EX $75   **NM** $125   **MIP** $155

Kitchen-Laundry Ensemble, 1960, Pink and grey, 5 pc. set, includes #8, #12, #4, #10, #16- 1959 models, Model No. 25
EX $95   **NM** $155   **MIP** $175

Deluxe Kitchen-Laundry Ensemble, 1960, Pink and grey, 7 pc. set, includes #8, #12, #4, #10, #14, #16, #2- 1959 models, Model No. 27
EX $115   **NM** $155   **MIP** $195

All-In-One Wild Animal Set, 1960, Pink, blue, yellow, 5.5L x 4W x 2H, smaller animals fit inside larger animals, Model No. 105
EX $15   **NM** $25   **MIP** $35

Hammer Tower, 1960, Yellow and red, 6.5L x 4.75W x 9H, scarce, hammer button and marbles shoot up through tower, Model No. 110
EX $35   **NM** $55   **MIP** $75

Auto Elevator, 1960, Red and yellow, 9L x 3.5W x 9H, scarce, plastic parking garage, crank release car down ramp, Model No. 111
EX $75   **NM** $95   **MIP** $115

Jack And Jill Pump, 1960, Copper and yellow, 8L x 4.25W x 11.25H, scarce, plastic marble toy, pre-school series, Model No. 112

EX $75 **NM** $95 **MIP** $115

Concrete Mixer, 1960, Copper and yellow, 6.25L x 5.5W x 13.25H, scarce, plastic cement mixer with clear barrel w/marbels, Model No. 114

EX $75 **NM** $95 **MIP** $115

School Bus, 1960, Yellow, 5.5L x 4W x 12H, scarce, plastic, hinged school bus with blocks. Pull toy, Model No. 115

EX $75 **NM** $95 **MIP** $115

Pickup And Delivery, 1960, Met. green, 14L x 5.75W x 6.5H, whitewall tires, plastic horn on roof, Model No. 207

EX $45 **NM** $75 **MIP** $95

Dumper, 1960, Copper, 11.5L x 5.5W x 6H, whitewall tires, plastic horn on roof, Model No. 209

EX $45 **NM** $75 **MIP** $95

Bulldozer, 1960, Yellow, 11.75L x 7W x 6.75H, black tires and motor, blade tips up, Model No. 210

EX $35 **NM** $55 **MIP** $75

Camper, 1960, Teal and red, 23.25L x 4.5W x 6.5H, red and white canvas over truck bed, boat and trailer, Model No. 211

EX $55 **NM** $95 **MIP** $125

Cabin Cruiser, 1960, Red and white, 12L x 4W x 3H, plastic hull, wooden deck and cabin, battery op motor, Model No. 212

EX $55 **NM** $95 **MIP** $125

Road Grader, 1960, Yellow, 18.75L x 7.25W x 7.5H, black tires and motor, scraper blade lifts with levers, Model No. 301

EX $35 **NM** $55 **MIP** $75

Power Shovel, 1960, Yellow, 26.5L x 7W x 6.75H, black rubber tracks, Model No. 305

EX $35 **NM** $55 **MIP** $75

Livestock Truck, 1960, Red and white, 14.75L x 6W x 7.25H, white plastic stake panels and 2 plastic animals, Model No. 306

EX $35 **NM** $55 **MIP** $75

Earth Mover, 1960, Yellow, 21.5L x 6.5W x 6H, black tires and motor, Model No. 322

EX $35 **NM** $55 **MIP** $75

Timber Toter, 1960, Copper, 20.75L x 5.5W x 5.5H, plastic mirrors and horn, 5 wooden logs and chains, Model No. 323

EX $45 **NM** $65 **MIP** $85

Auto Transport, 1960, Met. green, 22L x 5.5W x 6.5H, 4 metal cars plus loading ramp, Model No. 402

EX $55 **NM** $75 **MIP** $95

Cattle Transport, 1960, Red and white, 21.25L x 5.5W x 7.5H, plastic mirrors, windshield wipers and horn, Model No. 403

EX $45 **NM** $65 **MIP** $85

Hydraulic Dumper, 1960, Met. green, 14.75L x 6.25W x 6.5H, plastic mirrors, windshield wipers and horn, Model No. 404

EX $35 **NM** $55 **MIP** $75

Machinery Hauler, 1960, Copper, 19.5L x 7.5W x 6.5H, includes #210 dozer, Model No. 509

EX $55 **NM** $75 **MIP** $95

Stock Farm Set, 1960, Red and white, 14.75L x 6W x 7.25H, stake truck with cattle loading ramp and 4 plastic horses, Model No. 510

EX $55 **NM** $85 **MIP** $115

Deluxe Camper, 1960, Gold, 27.5L x 6W x 6.5H, #207 truck plus #212 boat on trailer, Model No. 602

EX $55 **NM** $95 **MIP** $125

Pumper, 1960, White, 19.75L x 7.25W x 6H, scarce, open cab, operating water tank and hose, Model No. 603

EX $95 **NM** $125 **MIP** $175

Ready Mix Concrete Truck, 1960, Teal and white, 16L x 7.5W x 9H, axle driven gear operates barrel, Model No. 604

EX $55 **NM** $75 **MIP** $95

Ride-er Dump Truck, 1960, Blue and white, 20L x 7.75W x 10H, metal seat in dump box and bulb horn on steering wheel, Model No. 605

EX $55 **NM** $75 **MIP** $95

Mobile Crane, 1960, Copper and yellow, 19.25L x 6.25W x 7.25H, half-track with single-driver cab, Model No. 800

EX $75 **NM** $115 **MIP** $135

Power Wrecker, 1960, Blue and white, 23L x 7W x 9.25H, battery operated winch & lights, Model No. 802

EX $75 **NM** $125 **MIP** $175

Hydraulic Hook & Ladder, 1960, Red and red, 31L x 6.25W x 7.25H, open cab, two metal ladders, hydraulic lift ladder, Model No. 901

EX $75 **NM** $125 **MIP** $175

Highway Builder Set, 1960, Copper, includes #209, #210, #305 plus road barricade, Model No. 903

EX $95 **NM** $135 **MIP** $175

Transcontinental Express Fleet, 1960, Varies, 20 pc. set includes auto transport, express, steel trailer, Model No. 904

EX $115 **NM** $155 **MIP** $195

Transcontinental Express Semi, 1960, Blue and silver, 26L x 6W x 8.5H, unpainted aluminum trailer with blue decals, Model No. 905

EX $55 **NM** $95 **MIP** $125

Ride-er Fire Truck, 1960, Red and white, 25.5L x 10.5W x 12.75H, crank siren on hood, trunk opens, Model No. 925

EX $75 **NM** $115 **MIP** $155

Die-Cast Dump Truck, 1961, Varies, 7.25L x 2.5W x 2.25H, packaged on bubble pack for in-store display, Model No. 79

EX $35 **NM** $55 **MIP** $75

Rampside Pick-Up, 1961, Copper, 10.5L x 4.5W x 5H, plastic bed liner and drop-down door in side of bed, Model No. 195

EX $35 **NM** $55 **MIP** $75

Camper, 1961, Met. green, 21.5L x 4.5W x 5H, rampside truck towing boat and trailer, Model No. 202

EX $45 **NM** $65 **MIP** $85

Bulldozer, 1961, Yellow, 11L x 6.5W x 6.5H, rubber tracks, Model No. 206

EX $35 **NM** $75 **MIP** $95

Dispatch Truck, 1961, Met. green, 13L x 5.25W x 5H, similar to 1950's barrel truck, plastic mirrors, wipers & horns, Model No. 208

EX $55 **NM** $75 **MIP** $95

Road Grader, 1961, Yellow, 18.75L x 7W x 7.5H, plastic tires, Model No. 301

EX $25 **NM** $45 **MIP** $65

Wrecker, 1961, White, 12L x 5.75W x 6.5H, crank operated winch, plastic mirrors, wipers & horns, Model No. 302

EX $55 **NM** $75 **MIP** $95

Airlines Lift Truck, 1961, Copper and white, 12.5L x 5.25W x 7H, lever lifts cargo box with scissors lift mechanism, Model No. 303

EX $55 **NM** $75 **MIP** $95

Power Shovel, 1961, Yellow, 26.5L x 7.5W x 7H, rubber tracks, Model No. 305

EX $35 **NM** $55 **MIP** $75

Livestock Truck, 1961, Red and white, 14.5L x 6.25W x 7.5H, stake truck with 2 plastic animals, Model No. 306

EX $35 **NM** $65 **MIP** $85

Fire Rescue Truck, 1961, Red, 12L x 5.75W x 5.25H, plastic hose reel with braided hose, two ladders, Model No. 307

EX $35 **NM** $65 **MIP** $95

Deluxe Dump Truck, 1961, Met. green, 11.75L x 5.5W x 5.75H, lever operates dump box, Model No. 309

EX $35 **NM** $65 **MIP** $85

Timber Toter, 1961, Met. green, 23L x 5.5W x 6H, six wooden logs and chains, Model No. 406

EX $55 **NM** $75 **MIP** $95

Hydraulic Dumper, 1961, Met. green, 13.75L x 5.5W x 6.25H, hydraulic cylinder controls dump box, Model No. 407

EX $35 **NM** $65 **MIP** $85

Auto Transport, 1961, Copper, 22L x 5.5W x 7H, includes one car and one truck plus loading ramp, Model No. 502

EX $35 **NM** $65 **MIP** $95

Cattle Transport, 1961, Green and white, 23.5L x 6.5W x 8H, white trailer with green doors, Model No. 503

EX $35 **NM** $65 **MIP** $95

Deluxe Transport, 1961, Red and white, 23.5L x 6.5W x 8H, North American Vanlines decals on trailer, Model No. 504

EX $55 **NM** $95 **MIP** $155

Hydraulic Sanitation Truck, 1961, White, 18L x 6W x 8H, all white design, Model No. 606

EX $55 **NM** $95 **MIP** $115

Ride-er Wrecker Truck, 1961, Copper and white, 23.5L x 7.75W x 10.25H, metal

seat and crank operated boom in box, Model No. 607
EX $55   **NM** $95   **MIP** $125

Ready-Mix Concrete Truck, 1961, Red and white, 15.5L x 7.75W x 9H, axle driven gear operates barrel, Model No. 609
EX $55   **NM** $95   **MIP** $115

Mobile Crane, 1961, Yellow, 15.5L x 6.5W x 7.25H, double cranks control crane arm and clam bucket, Model No. 700
EX $55   **NM** $95   **MIP** $115

Pumper, 1961, Red, 19.5L x 7.25W x 6.5H, operating water tank and hose, two ladders, Model No. 708
EX $55   **NM** $95   **MIP** $125

Aerial Hook & Ladder, 1961, Red, 30.75L x 6.25W x 6.25H, two metal ladders, crank operated lift ladder, Model No. 902
EX $65   **NM** $115   **MIP** $145

Highway Builder Set, 1961, Copper, includes #206, #305, #309 plus road barricade, Model No. 905
EX $95   **NM** $135   **MIP** $175

Transcontinental Express Fleet, 1961, Varies, 25 pc. set includes auto transport, express, cattle trailers, Model No. 906
EX $125   **NM** $155   **MIP** $195

Construction And Paving Set, 1961, Varies, 4 pc. set includes #309, #609, #700 plus barricade, Model No. 907
EX $95   **NM** $135   **MIP** $175

Ride-er Fire Truck, 1961, Red and white, 25.5L x 10.5W x 12.75H, crank siren on hood, trunk opens, Model No. 925
EX $75   **NM** $105   **MIP** $135

Little Miss Washer/Dryer, 1962, Teal, 7.25L x 8W x 10H, washes & spins, battery operated, Model No. 16
EX $15   **NM** $25   **MIP** $55

Rampside Pick-Up, 1962, Red, 10.5L x 4.5W x 5H, plastic bed liner and drop-down door in side of bed, Model No. 195
EX $35   **NM** $55   **MIP** $75

School Bus, 1962, Yellow, 10.5L x 4.75W x 5H, steel body, plastic mirrors, wipers and horn, Model No. 196
EX $55   **NM** $75   **MIP** $95

Fisherman, 1962, Blue, 21.5L x 4.5W x 5H, rampside truck towing boat and trailer, Model No. 202
EX $45   **NM** $65   **MIP** $85

Camper, 1962, Green and yellow, 10.5L x 4.5W x 6.5H, rampside truck with plastic camper in bed of truck, Model No. 203
EX $55   **NM** $75   **MIP** $95

Hi-Lift Bulldozer, 1962, Yellow, 11.25L x 5.75W x 3.75H, rubber tracks, lever controls bucket, Model No. 207
EX $25   **NM** $55   **MIP** $75

Wrecker, 1962, White, 12L x 5.75W x 6.5H, crank operated winch, plastic mirrors, wipers & horns, Model No. 302
EX $55   **NM** $75   **MIP** $95

American Airlines Sky Chef, 1962, Blue and white, 12.5L x 5.25W x 7H, lever

lifts cargo box with scissors lift mechanism, Model No. 303
EX $75   **NM** $95   **MIP** $125

Deluxe Camper, 1962, Green and yellow, 21.5L x 4.5W x 6.5H, #203 plus boat and trailer, Model No. 304
EX $75   **NM** $105   **MIP** $135

Power Shovel, 1962, Yellow, 26.5L x 7.5W x 7H, rubber tracks, Model No. 305
EX $35   **NM** $55   **MIP** $75

Fire Rescue Truck, 1962, Red, 12L x 5.75W x 5.25H, plastic hose reel with braided hose, two ladders, Model No. 307
EX $35   **NM** $65   **MIP** $95

Deluxe Dump Truck, 1962, Yellow and red, 11.75L x 5.5W x 5.75H, lever operates dump box, Model No. 309
EX $35   **NM** $65   **MIP** $85

Sportsman, 1962, Red and white, 13.25L x 5.25W x 5.5H, scarce, white plastic "Sportsman" camper top, Model No. 311
EX $75   **NM** $115   **MIP** $155

Livestock Truck, 1962, Red and white, 14.75L x 6.25W x 5.5H, white metal stake panels, Model No. 312
EX $55   **NM** $75   **MIP** $95

Road Grader, 1962, Yellow, 19L x 7.5W x 8H, covered cab, plated blade, black plastic tires, Model No. 400
EX $55   **NM** $75   **MIP** $95

Giant Bulldozer, 1962, Orange, 11.5L x 7W x 5H, levers operate blade, rubber tracks, Model No. 405
EX $55   **NM** $75   **MIP** $95

Timber Toter, 1962, Red, 23L x 5.5W x 6H, six wooden logs and chains, Model No. 406
EX $55   **NM** $75   **MIP** $95

Hydraulic Dumper, 1962, Green, 13.75L x 5.5W x 6.25H, hydraulic cylinder controls dump box, Model No. 407
EX $35   **NM** $55   **MIP** $75

Ready Mix Concrete Truck, 1962, Red and white, 15.5L x 6.75W x 7.25H, axle driven gear operates barrel, Model No. 408
EX $35   **NM** $55   **MIP** $75

Nationwide Rental Truck & Trailer, 1962, Green and yellow, 21L x 5.75W x 5.5H, scarce, same design as #311 plus tow behind trailer, Model No. 500
EX $75   **NM** $125   **MIP** $155

Dump Truck and Sandloader, 1962, Yellow and red, 21.5L x 5.5W x 8.25H, crank operated conveyer belt takes sand up to truck, Model No. 501
EX $55   **NM** $85   **MIP** $115

Auto Transport, 1962, Yellow and green, 22L x 5.5W x 7H, two metal cars, one metal truck plus loading ramp, Model No. 502
EX $75   **NM** $115   **MIP** $155

Cattle Transport, 1962, Yellow and green, 23.5L x 5.5W x 8H, green trailer with yellow doors, Model No. 503
EX $55   **NM** $75   **MIP** $95

Farm Stake Truck & Horse Trailer, 1962, Red and white, 23.25L x 6.25W x 6H,

same as #312 plus tow behind trailer and 4 animals, Model No. 507
EX $75   **NM** $95   **MIP** $125

Deluxe Van Truck, 1962, Blue and white, 25.5L x 6.5W x 8.5H, express with rocketship on decals, Model No. 600
EX $75   **NM** $115   **MIP** $135

Hydraulic Sanitation Truck, 1962, Grey and white, 18L x 6W x 8H, with manual lift arm that dumps into body, Model No. 606
EX $75   **NM** $105   **MIP** $125

Ride-er Wrecker Truck, 1962, Red and yellow, 23.5L x 7.5W x 10.25H, metal seat and crank operated tow boom in box, Model No. 607
EX $55   **NM** $95   **MIP** $125

Grading Service Set, 1962, Yellow and red, 25L x 6W x 5.75H, same truck as in #501 set plus #207 bulldozer on trailer, Model No. 701
EX $75   **NM** $105   **MIP** $135

Pumper, 1962, Red, 19.5L x 7.25W x 6.5H, operating water tank and hose, two ladders, Model No. 708
EX $55   **NM** $95   **MIP** $125

Mobile Crane, 1962, Yellow, 15.5L x 6.5W x 7.25H, double cranks control crane arm and clam bucket, Model No. 800
EX $55   **NM** $95   **MIP** $115

Giant Bulldozer Truck & Trailer, 1962, Orange, 29L x 7.25W x 6.25H, construction company on decals, Model No. 850
EX $95   **NM** $135   **MIP** $175

Aerial Hook & Ladder, 1962, Red, 30.75L x 6.25W x 6.25H, two metal ladders, crank operated lift ladder, Model No. 902
EX $65   **NM** $115   **MIP** $155

Ride-er Fire Truck, 1962, Red and white, 25.5L x 10.5W x 12.75H, crank siren on hood, trunk opens, Model No. 925
EX $75   **NM** $105   **MIP** $135

Nationwide Rental Truck & Trailer Set, 1962, Green and yellow, scarce, same as #500 set plus larger open trailer, Model No. 904
EX $115   **NM** $155   **MIP** $195

Air Terminal Service Set, 1962, Red and white, includes #195, #303, #307, Model No. 908
EX $115   **NM** $135   **MIP** $175

Highway Builder Set, 1962, Varies, includes #207, #501 plus sand hopper and one barricade, Model No. 913
EX $115   **NM** $135   **MIP** $175

Farm Set, 1962, Varies, includes #507, pick-up and trailer similar to nationwide set, Model No. 914
EX $115   **NM** $135   **MIP** $175

Road Builder Set, 1962, Red and yellow, same as #913 set plus #400, Model No. 915
EX $125   **NM** $155   **MIP** $195

Paving Department, 1962, Varies, same as #913 but #408 replaces sand loader trailer, Model No. 916
EX $125   **NM** $155   **MIP** $195

Little Miss Washer/Dryer, 1963, Teal, 7.25L x 8W x 10H, washes & spins, battery operated, Model No. 16
EX $15   **NM** $25   **MIP** $55

Sand Hopper, 1963, Chartreuse, 8.25L x 6W x 12H, goes with construction sets, Model No. 190
EX $15   **NM** $25   **MIP** $35

Rampside Pick-Up, 1963, Red, 10.5L x 4.5W x 5H, plastic bed liner and drop-down door in side of bed, Model No. 194
EX $35   **NM** $55   **MIP** $75

School Bus, 1963, Yellow, 10.5L x 4.75W x 5H, steel body, plastic mirrors, wipers and horn, Model No. 196
EX $55   **NM** $75   **MIP** $95

The Army Cub, 1963, Army green, 10.75L x 5W x 4.75H, windshield and tailgate raise & lower, yellow seat, no doors, Model No. 200
EX $25   **NM** $55   **MIP** $75

Camper, 1963, Teal, 10.5L x 4.5W x 6.5H, rampside truck with plastic camper in bed of truck, Model No. 203
EX $55   **NM** $75   **MIP** $95

Fisherman, 1963, Teal, 21.5L x 4.5W x 5H, rampside truck towing boat and trailer, Model No. 204
EX $45   **NM** $65   **MIP** $85

Hi-Lift Bulldozer, 1963, Chartreuse, 11.25L x 5.75W x 4H, scarce chartreuse color - only used in 1963 production year, Model No. 207
EX $55   **NM** $75   **MIP** $95

Cub Pick-Up, 1963, Lt. blue, 10.75L x 5W x 5H, white plastic convertible roof, doors open, Model No. 250
EX $35   **NM** $55   **MIP** $75

Dump Truck, 1963, Green, 11.75L x 5.5W x 5.75H, new cab - over design, plus steering wheel and seat detail, Model No. 300
EX $35   **NM** $65   **MIP** $85

Wrecker, 1963, White, 13L x 5.25W x 5.5H, door windows and interior detail, black metal boom arm, Model No. 301
EX $55   **NM** $75   **MIP** $95

Power Shovel, 1963, Chartreuse, 26.5L x 7.25W x 7H, scarce chartreuse color - only used in 1963 production year, Model No. 305
EX $55   **NM** $75   **MIP** $95

Fire Rescue Truck, 1963, Red, 12L x 5.75W x 5.25H, plastic hose reel with braided hose, two ladders, Model No. 307
EX $35   **NM** $65   **MIP** $95

Pick-Up Truck, 1963, Red, 13.25L x 5.25W x 5.5H, Model No. 311
EX $35   **NM** $65   **MIP** $85

Livestock Truck, 1963, Blue and white, 14.75L x 6.25W x 5.5H, white metal stake panels, Model No. 314
EX $55   **NM** $75   **MIP** $95

Cub Station Wagon, 1963, Teal and white, 10.75L x 5W x 5H, same body as #250 but white plastic roof cover whole body, Model No. 325
EX $55   **NM** $75   **MIP** $95

The Cub Set, 1963, Teal and white, 10.75L x 5W x 5H, converts to three variations with #250 and #325 roofs, Model No. 350
EX $55   **NM** $75   **MIP** $95

Road Grader, 1963, Chartreuse, 19L x 7.5W x 8H, scarce chartreuse color - only used in 1963 production year, Model No. 400
EX $55   **NM** $75   **MIP** $95

(Randy Prasse Photo)

Hydraulic Dumper, 1963, Red, 13.75L x 5.5W x 6.25H, hydraulic cylinder controls dump box, Model No. 401
EX $35   **NM** $55   **MIP** $75

Auto Transport, 1963, Met. gold, 22L x 5.5W x 7H, one metal car, one metal truck plus loading ramp, Model No. 402
EX $35   **NM** $55   **MIP** $75

Cub Station Wagon & Horse Trailer, 1963, Teal and white, 20.5L x 5.25W x 6H, same as #190 plus 2 wheel horse trailer and 2 horses, Model No. 403
EX $75   **NM** $95   **MIP** $115

Deluxe Camper, 1963, Blue and white, 20L x 5W x 5H, same as #190 plus boat and trailer, Model No. 404
EX $65   **NM** $95   **MIP** $125

Giant Bulldozer, 1963, Chartreuse, 11.5L x 7W x 5H, scarce chartreuse color - only used in 1963 production year, Model No. 405
EX $55   **NM** $75   **MIP** $95

Timber Toter, 1963, Red, 23L x 5.5W x 6H, six wooden logs and chains, Model No. 406
EX $55   **NM** $75   **MIP** $95

Ready-Mix Concrete Truck, 1963, Green and chartreuse, 15.5L x 6.75W x 7.25H, axle driven gear operates barrel, Model No. 408
EX $35   **NM** $55   **MIP** $75

Dump Truck and Sandloader, 1963, Green and chartreuse, 21.5L x 5.5W x 8.25H, crank operated conveyer belt takes sand up to truck, Model No. 409
EX $55   **NM** $85   **MIP** $115

Nationwide Rental Truck & Trailer, 1963, Green and yellow, 21L x 5.75W x 5.5H, scarce, same design as #311 plus tow behind trailer, Model No. 500
EX $75   **NM** $125   **MIP** $155

Cattle Transport, 1963, Red and red, 22.25L x 6.5W x 8H, new cab - over design, plus steering wheel and seat detail, Model No. 503
EX $35   **NM** $65   **MIP** $95

Deluxe Van Truck, 1963, Red and white, 25.5L x 6.5W x 8.5H, white trailer with red doors, Model No. 601
EX $55   **NM** $85   **MIP** $105

(ToyShop File Photo)

Hydraulic Sanitation Truck, 1963, Blue and white, 18L x 6W x 8H, with manual lift arm that dumps into body, Model No. 602
EX $75   **NM** $105   **MIP** $125

Hydraulic Trailer Dump, 1963, Chartreuse, 20.75L x 6.25W x 5.75H, scarce chartreuse color - only used in 1963 production year, Model No. 603
EX $65   **NM** $95   **MIP** $125

Ride-er Dump Truck, 1963, Red and white, 20L x 7.75W x 10.25H, metal seat in dump box, Model No. 605
EX $75   **NM** $105   **MIP** $135

Mobile Crane, 1963, Chartreuse, 15.5L x 6.5W x 7.25H, scarce chartreuse color - only used in 1963 production year, Model No. 801
EX $75   **NM** $105   **MIP** $155

Aerial Hook & Ladder, 1963, Red and red, 30.75L x 6.25W x 6.25H, two metal ladders, crank operated lift ladder, Model No. 902
EX $65   **NM** $105   **MIP** $145

Nationwide Rental Truck & Trailer Set, 1963, Green and yellow, scarce, same as #500 set plus larger open trailer, Model No. 904
EX $115   **NM** $155   **MIP** $195

Highway Builder Set, 1963, Varies, includes #190 and #409, Model No. 913
EX $115   **NM** $135   **MIP** $175

Farm Set, 1963, Teal and white, includes #314 with trailer and #403, Model No. 914
EX $115   **NM** $135   **MIP** $175

Army Engineer's Set, 1963, Army green, includes #190, #400, #409, all in army green, Model No. 915
EX $115   **NM** $135   **MIP** $175

Paving Department, 1963, Varies, includes #190, #305, #400, #401, #408, Model No. 916
EX $115   **NM** $135   **MIP** $175

Ride-er Doodle Bug, 1963, Yellow, 25.5L x 10.25W x 12.75H, same as ride-er fire truck from 1962, Model No. 925
EX $75   **NM** $105   **MIP** $135

Pickup, 1964, Red and yellow, 8.75L x 3.5W x 3.5H, metal with rubber tires, Model No. 100
EX $15   **NM** $25   **MIP** $55

Fire Rescue Truck, 1964, Red, 8.75L x 3.5W x 3.5H, 2 plastic ladders, Model No. 105
EX $15   **NM** $35   **MIP** $65

Wrecker Truck, 1964, White and grey, 9.25L x 3.5W x 3.5H, with metal tow boom and hook, Model No. 110

EX $15   **NM** $25   **MIP** $55

Vista Dome Army Truck, 1964, Army green, 8.75L x 3.5W x 4H, clear plastic cover over bed, 2 plastic soldiers, Model No. 115

EX $15   **NM** $25   **MIP** $55

Vista Dome Livestock Truck, 1964, Blue and yellow, 8.75L x 3.5W x 4H, clear plastic cover over bed, 2 plastic animals, Model No. 120

EX $15   **NM** $35   **MIP** $65

Automatic Dump Truck, 1964, Copper, 8.75L x 3.5W x 4H, spring dump mechanism, Model No. 125

EX $15   **NM** $25   **MIP** $55

Vista Dome Kennel Truck, 1964, Teal and yellow, 8.75L x 3.5W x 4H, clear plastic cover over bed, 6 plastic dogs, Model No. 130

EX $15   **NM** $35   **MIP** $65

Rampside Pick-Up, 1964, Copper, 10.5L x 4.5W x 5H, plastic bed liner and dropdown door in side of bed, Model No. 194

EX $25   **NM** $55   **MIP** $75

The Army Cub, 1964, Army green, 10.75L x 5W x 4.75H, tailgate and windshield raises and lowers, Model No. 200

EX $25   **NM** $55   **MIP** $75

Camper, 1964, Teal and teal, 10.5L x 4.5W x 6.5H, plastic camper in truck bed, Model No. 203

EX $35   **NM** $65   **MIP** $85

Fisherman, 1964, Teal and red, 20L x 4.5W x 6H, rampside pick-up towing plastic boat on trailer, Model No. 204

EX $35   **NM** $65   **MIP** $85

Hi-Lift Bulldozer, 1964, Yellow and black, 11.25L x 5.75W x 4H, metal levers operate the bucket, Model No. 207

EX $25   **NM** $45   **MIP** $75

Cub Pick-Up, 1964, Blue and white, 20.75L x 5W x 6H, white plastic convertible roof covers cab, doors open, Model No. 250

EX $25   **NM** $55   **MIP** $75

Dump Truck, 1964, Green, 11.75L x 5.5W x 5.75H, cab-over design, plus steering wheel and seat detail, Model No. 300

EX $35   **NM** $65   **MIP** $85

Wrecker, 1964, White and black, 13.25L x 5.25W x 5.5H, door windows and interior detail, black metal boom arm, Model No. 301

EX $55   **NM** $75   **MIP** $95

Power Shovel, 1964, Yellow, 26.5L x 7.25W x 7H, rubber tracks, 2 cranks operate boom and bucket, Model No. 305

EX $35   **NM** $65   **MIP** $85

Fire Rescue Truck, 1964, Red, 12L x 5.75W x 5.25H, plastic hose reel with braided hose, two ladders, Model No. 307

EX $35   **NM** $65   **MIP** $95

Pick-Up Truck, 1964, Red, 13.25L x 5.25W x 5.5H, plastic window, yellow interior, whitewall tires, Model No. 311

EX $55   **NM** $75   **MIP** $95

Livestock Truck, 1964, Blue and white, 14.75L x 6.25W x 5.5H, white metal stake panels, 2 plastic cows, Model No. 314

EX $55   **NM** $75   **MIP** $95

Vista Dome Troop Carrier, 1964, Army green, 13.25L x 5.25W x 5.5H, clear plastic cover over bed, 8 plastic soldiers, Model No. 315

EX $55   **NM** $75   **MIP** $95

Cub Station Wagon, 1964, Teal and white, 10.75L x 5W x 5H, white plastic convertible roof cover body, doors open, Model No. 325

EX $25   **NM** $55   **MIP** $75

The Cub Set, 1964, Teal and white, 10.75L x 5W x 5H, converts to three variations with #250 and #325 roofs, Model No. 350

EX $55   **NM** $75   **MIP** $95

Road Grader, 1964, Orange, 19L x 7.5W x 8.25H, plated scraper blade, black plastic wheels & engine, Model No. 400

EX $45   **NM** $65   **MIP** $85

Hydraulic Dumper, 1964, Copper, 13.75L x 5.5W x 6.25H, hydraulic cylinder controls dump box, Model No. 401

EX $35   **NM** $55   **MIP** $75

Auto Transport, 1964, Red and yellow, 22L x 5.5W x 7H, includes 1 metal car and 1 metal truck & loading ramp, Model No. 402

EX $55   **NM** $75   **MIP** $95

Cub Station Wagon With Horse Trailer, 1964, Teal and white, 20.5L x 5.25W x 6H, #325 cub station wagon & trailer, 2 plastic horses, Model No. 403

EX $45   **NM** $75   **MIP** $95

Station Wagon With Boat & Trailer, 1964, Blue and red, 20L x 5W x 5H, cub station wagon (#325) towing plastic boat on trailer, Model No. 404

EX $35   **NM** $65   **MIP** $85

Giant Bulldozer, 1964, Orange and black, 11.5L x 7W x 5H, blade raises and lowers with lever controls, Model No. 405

EX $45   **NM** $65   **MIP** $85

Ready-Mix Concrete Truck, 1964, Red and yellow, 15.5L x 6.75W x 7.25H, axle driven gear operates barrel, Model No. 408

EX $35   **NM** $55   **MIP** $75

U.S. Army Missile Launcher, 1964, Army green, 17.25L x 6.5W x 7H, missile launcher on back, 3 missiles, 2 outriggers, Model No. 410

EX $45   **NM** $65   **MIP** $95

Army Engineers Dump & Sand Loader, 1964, Army green, 21.5L x 5.5W x 8.25H, includes 4 plastic soldiers, Model No. 411

EX $55   **NM** $75   **MIP** $95

Vista Dome Horse Van, 1964, Met. gold, 21.75L x 5.5W x 6H, ramp on side and back of trailer, 4 plastic horses, Model No. 412

EX $45   **NM** $65   **MIP** $85

Cattle Transport, 1964, Red and red, 22.25L x 6.5W x 8H, Model No. 503

EX $45   **NM** $75   **MIP** $95

Deluxe Van Truck, 1964, Red and white, 25.5L x 6.5W x 8.5H, white trailer with red doors, Model No. 601

EX $55   **NM** $85   **MIP** $105

Hydraulic Sanitation Truck, 1964, Grey and white, 18L x 6W x 8H, with manual lift arm that dumps into body, Model No. 602

EX $75   **NM** $105   **MIP** $125

Hydraulic Trailer Dump Truck, 1964, Grey and orange, 20.75L x 6.25W x 5.75H, also available as "Scotch-O-Lass" private label-add $50, Model No. 603

EX $55   **NM** $75   **MIP** $95

Ride-er Dump Truck, 1964, Red and white, 20L x 7W x 10.25H, metal seat in dump box, Model No. 605

EX $75   **NM** $105   **MIP** $135

Mobile Crane, 1964, Orange, 15.5L x 6.5W x 7.25H, cranks control the boom and clam bucket, swivels, Model No. 801

EX $75   **NM** $95   **MIP** $125

Aerial Hook & Ladder, 1964, Red and red, 30.75L x 6.25W x 6.25H, two metal ladders, crank operated lift ladder, Model No. 902

EX $55   **NM** $95   **MIP** $135

Highway Builder Set, 1964, Varies, includes #207, #300, sand hopper, sand loader & barricade, Model No. 913

EX $95   **NM** $125   **MIP** $155

Farm Set, 1964, Teal and white, 5 pc. set includes #314 & trailer, #250 cub pick-up & trailer, Model No. 914

EX $95   **NM** $125   **MIP** $155

U.S. Army Combat Set, 1964, Army green, includes #315 & searchlight, #410, 8 plastic soldiers, Model No. 920

EX $105   **NM** $155   **MIP** $195

Ride-er Doodle Bug, 1964, Yellow, 25.5L x 10.25W x 12.75H, Model No. 925

EX $75   **NM** $105   **MIP** $135

Pick-Up Truck, 1965, Teal and white, 8.75L x 3.5W x 3.5H, metal with rubber tires, Model No. 100

EX $15   **NM** $25   **MIP** $55

Fire Rescue Truck, 1965, Red, 8.75L x 3.5W x 3.5H, 2 plastic ladders, Model No. 105

EX $25   **NM** $45   **MIP** $65

Wrecker Truck, 1965, Red and white, 9.25L x 3.5W x 3.5H, with metal tow boom and hook, Model No. 110

EX $15   **NM** $25   **MIP** $55

Vista Dome Army Truck, 1965, Army green, 8.75L x 3.5W x 4H, clear plastic cover over bed, 2 plastic soldiers, Model No. 115

EX $15   **NM** $25   **MIP** $55

Automatic Dump Truck, 1965, Green and yellow, 8.75L x 3.5W x 4H, spring dump mechanism, Model No. 125

EX $15   **NM** $25   **MIP** $55

Vista Dome Kennel Truck, 1965, Blue and white, 8.75L x 3.5W x 4H, clear plastic cover over bed, 6 plastic dogs, Model No. 130

EX $15   **NM** $35   **MIP** $65

Cement Mixer, 1965, Red and white, 8.75L x 3.5W x 5H, axle driven gear operates barrel, Model No. 136
EX $15   **NM** $35   **MIP** $65

Road Grader, 1965, Orange and black, 11.75L x 4W x 4H, new z-z-z sound when unit rolls, no batteries, Model No. 140
EX $15   **NM** $35   **MIP** $65

Van Truck, 1965, Red and white, 16.5L x 4W x 5H, red van line decals on side, Model No. 145
EX $25   **NM** $45   **MIP** $65

Cattle Truck, 1965, Green and white, 16.5L x 4W x 5H, white plastic insert panels in side of trailer, Model No. 150
EX $25   **NM** $45   **MIP** $75

Kompak Assortment, 1965, Varies, 3 pc. set includes #100, #105, #110, Model No. 170
EX $55   **NM** $85   **MIP** $125

Contractor Set, 1965, Varies, 3 pc. set includes #125, #136, #140, Model No. 180
EX $55   **NM** $85   **MIP** $125

Rampside Pick-Up, 1965, Copper, 10.5L x 4.5W x 5H, plastic bed liner and drop-down door in side of bed, Model No. 194
EX $25   **NM** $55   **MIP** $75

The Army Cub, 1965, Army green, 10.75L x 5W x 4.75H, tailgate and windshield raises and lowers, Model No. 200
EX $25   **NM** $55   **MIP** $75

Camper, 1965, Teal and white, 10.5L x 4.5W x 6.5H, plastic camper in truck bed, Model No. 203
EX $35   **NM** $65   **MIP** $85

Fisherman, 1965, Teal and red, 20L x 4.5W x 5H, rampside pick-up towing plastic boat on trailer, Model No. 204
EX $35   **NM** $65   **MIP** $85

Hi-Lift Bulldozer, 1965, Yellow and black, 11.25L x 5.75W x 4H, metal levers operate the bucket, Model No. 207
EX $25   **NM** $45   **MIP** $75

Cub Pick-Up, 1965, Blue and white, 20.75L x 5W x 6H, white plastic convertible roof covers cab, doors open, Model No. 250
EX $25   **NM** $55   **MIP** $75

Wrecker Truck, 1965, White and red, 10.75L x 4.75W x 5.75H, red convertible roof, seats and metal boom arm, Model No. 251
EX $55   **NM** $75   **MIP** $95

Riding Academy, 1965, Teal and teal, 20L x 4.75W x 6H, #250 cub pick-up plus horse trailer, 2 plastic horses, Model No. 252
EX $55   **NM** $75   **MIP** $95

Dump Truck, 1965, Met. green, 11.75L x 5.5W x 5.75H, cab - over design, plus steering wheel and seat detail, Model No. 300
EX $35   **NM** $65   **MIP** $85

Wrecker Truck, 1965, White and red, 12.5L x 5.25W x 6.25H, red light on roof (non-operable), red metal boom arm, Model No. 302
EX $55   **NM** $75   **MIP** $95

Camper With Boat & Trailer, 1965, Teal and red, 20L x 4.5W x 6.5H, #203 with plastic boat on trailer, Model No. 304
EX $45   **NM** $85   **MIP** $105

Power Shovel, 1965, Orange, 26.5L x 7.25W x 7H, rubber tracks, 2 cranks operate boom and bucket, Model No. 305
EX $35   **NM** $55   **MIP** $75

Fire Rescue Truck, 1965, Red, 13.25L x 5.75W x 5.75H, red light on roof (non-operable), 2 metal ladders, Model No. 308
EX $45   **NM** $75   **MIP** $105

Livestock Truck, 1965, Blue and white, 14.75L x 6.25W x 5.5H, white stakes, 5 pc. plastic fence, 4 animals, Model No. 310
EX $55   **NM** $75   **MIP** $95

Vista Dome Troop Carrier, 1965, Army green, 13.25L x 5.25W x 5.75H, clear plastic cover over bed, 8 plastic soldiers, Model No. 315
EX $55   **NM** $75   **MIP** $95

Cub Station Wagon, 1965, Teal and white, 10.75L x 5W x 5H, white plastic convertible roof cover body, doors open, Model No. 325
EX $25   **NM** $45   **MIP** $65

Road Grader, 1965, Orange, 19L x 7.5W x 8.25H, plated scraper blade, black plastic wheels & engine, Model No. 400
EX $45   **NM** $65   **MIP** $85

Hydraulic Dump Truck, 1965, Red, 14L x 5.5W x 6.25H, hydraulic cylinder controls dump box, Model No. 401
EX $35   **NM** $55   **MIP** $75

Station Wagon With Boat & Trailer, 1965, Blue and red, 20L x 5W x 5H, cub station wagon (#325) towing plastic boat on trailer, Model No. 404
EX $35   **NM** $65   **MIP** $85

Giant Bulldozer, 1965, Orange and black, 11.5L x 7W x 5H, blade raises and lowers with lever controls, Model No. 405
EX $45   **NM** $65   **MIP** $85

Timber Toter, 1965, Red and red, 23L x 6W x 5H, 5 wooden logs plus chains, Model No. 406
EX $55   **NM** $75   **MIP** $95

U.S. Army Missile Launcher, 1965, Army green, 17.25L x 6.5W x 7H, missile launcher on back, 3 missiles, 2 outriggers, Model No. 410
EX $45   **NM** $65   **MIP** $95

Vista Dome Horse Van, 1965, Teal and teal, 21.75L x 5.5W x 6H, ramp on side and back of trailer, 4 pc. fence, 4 plastic horses, Model No. 412
EX $45   **NM** $65   **MIP** $85

Car Carrier, 1965, Teal and teal, 22L x 6W x 7H, new, 2 plastic cars (T-Birds) and loading ramp, Model No. 413
EX $55   **NM** $75   **MIP** $95

Hydraulic Dump Truck, 1965, Grey and orange, 14L x 5.5W x 6.25H, hydraulic cylinder controls dump box, Model No. 425
EX $45   **NM** $65   **MIP** $85

Cement Mixer, 1965, Grey and orange, 14L x 6.75W x 5.25H, axle driven gear operates barrel, Model No. 450
EX $45   **NM** $65   **MIP** $85

Livestock Set, 1965, Teal and white, 22.25L x 6.5W x 8H, white insert panels in side of trailer, 5 pc. fence & 4 animals, Model No. 505
EX $45   **NM** $65   **MIP** $85

Van Truck, 1965, Red and white, 22L x 6.5W x 8H, red van line decals on side, Model No. 506
EX $45   **NM** $65   **MIP** $85

Deluxe Van Truck, 1965, Red and white, 25.5L x 6W x 8.75H, white trailer with red doors, Model No. 601
EX $55   **NM** $85   **MIP** $105

Hydraulic Trailer Dump Truck, 1965, Grey and orange, 20.75L x 5.75W x 5.75H, also available as "Scotch-O-Lass" private label - add $50, Model No. 603
EX $55   **NM** $75   **MIP** $95

Hydraulic Sanitation Truck, 1965, Grey and white, 18L x 6W x 8H, with manual lift arm that dumps into body, Model No. 604
EX $55   **NM** $75   **MIP** $95

Ride-er Dump Truck, 1965, Teal and white, 20L x 7W x 10.25H, metal seat in dump box, Model No. 605
EX $75   **NM** $105   **MIP** $135

Weekender, 1965, Teal and white, 12L x 5.75W x 7H, canvas awning, white plastic interior, Model No. 700
EX $55   **NM** $75   **MIP** $95

U.S. Mail Van, 1965, White and blue, 12L x 5.75W x 6.5H, includes 2 plastic mail bags, Model No. 710
EX $65   **NM** $85   **MIP** $105

Mobile Crane, 1965, Orange, 16.5L x 5.5W x 7H, cranks control the boom and clam bucket, swivels, Model No. 801
EX $75   **NM** $95   **MIP** $125

Aerial Hook & Ladder, 1965, Red and red, 30.75L x 6.25W x 6.25H, two metal ladders, crank operated lift ladder, Model No. 900
EX $55   **NM** $95   **MIP** $135

Highway Builder Set, 1965, Varies, includes #207, #300, sand hopper, sand loader & barricade, Model No. 913
EX $95   **NM** $125   **MIP** $155

Highway Builder Set Showcase Display, 1965, Rare, boxed set for dealer trade show & store display, Model No. 9130
EX $155   **NM** $195   **MIP** $245

Farm Set, 1965, Teal and white, 5 pc. set includes #310 & trailer, #250 cub pick-up & trailer, Model No. 914
EX $95   **NM** $125   **MIP** $155

Farm Set Showcase Display, 1965, Rare, boxed set for dealer trade show & store display, Model No. 9140
EX $155   **NM** $195   **MIP** $245

U.S. Army Combat Set, 1965, Army green, includes #315 & searchlight, #410, 8 plastic soldiers, Model No. 920
EX $105   **NM** $155   **MIP** $195

U.S. Army Combat Set Showcase Display, 1965, Rare, boxed set for dealer trade show & store display, Model No. 9201
EX $175   NM $215   MIP $275

Ride-er Doodle Bug, 1965, Teal and white, 25.5L x 10.25W x 12.75H, Model No. 925
EX $75   NM $105   MIP $135

Pickup Truck, 1966, Teal, 8.75L x 3.5W x 3.5H, Kom-pak design, Model No. 100
EX $15   NM $25   MIP $45

Fire Rescue Truck, 1966, Red, 8.75L x 3.5W x 3.5H, Kom-pak design with 2 ladders, Model No. 105
EX $25   NM $45   MIP $65

Wrecker Truck, 1966, Yellow and red, 9.25L x 3.5W x 3.5H, Kom-pak design with red boom arm, Model No. 110
EX $15   NM $25   MIP $45

Army Troop Carrier, 1966, Army green, 8.75L x 3.5W x 4H, Kom-pak design with clear plastic cover $2 soldiers, Model No. 115
EX $15   NM $25   MIP $45

All Steel Dump Truck, 1966, Grey and orange, 8.75L x 3.5W x 4H, Kom-pak design, Model No. 125
EX $15   NM $25   MIP $45

Kennel Truck, 1966, Teal and white, 8.75L x 3.5W x 4H, Kom-pak design with clear cover and 6 dogs, Model No. 130
EX $15   NM $35   MIP $55

Cement Mixer, 1966, Grey and orange, 9.75L x 4W x 4.5H, Kom-pak design with dumping barrel, Model No. 136
EX $15   NM $25   MIP $45

Road Grader, 1966, Orange, 11.75L x 5W x 4.75H, Kom-pak design, Model No. 140
EX $15   NM $25   MIP $45

Van Truck, 1966, Red and white, 16.5L x 4W x 5.25H, Kom-pak design, Model No. 145
EX $25   NM $45   MIP $65

Cattle Truck, 1966, Teal and white, 16.5L x 4W x 5.25H, Kom-pak design white insert panels in side of trailer, Model No. 150
EX $25   NM $45   MIP $75

Contractor Set, 1966, Grey and orange, 3 pc. Kom-pak set includes #125, #136, #140, Model No. 180
EX $55   NM $85   MIP $125

Rampside Pick-Up, 1966, Red, 10.5L x 4.5W x 5H, plastic bed liner and drop-down door in side of bed, Model No. 194
EX $25   NM $45   MIP $65

The Army Cub, 1966, Army green, 10.75L x 5W x 4.75H, tailgate and windshield raises and lowers, Model No. 200
EX $25   NM $45   MIP $65

Camper, 1966, Lt. blue and white, 10.5L x 4.5W x 6.5H, plastic camper in truck bed, Model No. 203
EX $25   NM $55   MIP $75

Fisherman, 1966, Lt. blue and red, 20L x 4.5W x 5H, rampside pick-up towing plastic boat on trailer, Model No. 204
EX $35   NM $65   MIP $85

Hi-Lift Bulldozer, 1966, Orange and black, 11.25L x 5.75W x 4H, metal levers operate the bucket, Model No. 207
EX $25   NM $45   MIP $75

Wrecker Truck, 1966, White and black, 10.75L x 4.75W x 5.75H, black convertible roof and boom, red seat, Model No. 251
EX $35   NM $55   MIP $75

Riding Academy, 1966, Teal and teal, 18L x 4.75W x 6H, #194 rampside pick-up plus horse trailer, 2 plastic horses, Model No. 254
EX $55   NM $75   MIP $95

Dump Truck, 1966, Red, 11.75L x 5.5W x 5.75H, spring dump mechanism, Model No. 300
EX $25   NM $45   MIP $65

Power Shovel, 1966, Orange, 26.5L x 7.25W x 7H, rubber tracks, 2 cranks operate boom and bucket, Model No. 305
EX $35   NM $55   MIP $75

Livestock Truck Set, 1966, Teal and white, 14.75L x 6.25W x 5.5H, white stakes, 5 pc. plastic fence, 2 plastic cows, Model No. 310
EX $35   NM $65   MIP $85

Wrecker, 1966, White and red, 12.5L x 5.25W x 6.25H, red light on roof (non-operable), red interior & boom, Model No. 312
EX $45   NM $65   MIP $95

Fire Rescue Truck, 1966, Red, 12.75L x 5.75W x 5.75H, red light on roof (non-operable) 3 ladders, sim. hose reel, Model No. 313
EX $45   NM $65   MIP $95

Vista Dome Troop Carrier, 1966, Army green, 13.25L x 5.25W x 5.75H, clear plastic cover over bed, 6 plastic soldiers, Model No. 315
EX $55   NM $75   MIP $95

Dump Truck, 1966, Green and yellow, 13.5L x 5.5W x 5.75H, lever action dump box, Model No. 316
EX $25   NM $45   MIP $65

Station Wagon, 1966, Teal and white, 10.75L x 5W x 5H, white plastic convertible roof cover body, doors open, Model No. 325
EX $25   NM $45   MIP $65

Road Grader, 1966, Orange, 19L x 7.5W x 8.25H, plated scraper blade, black plastic wheels & engine, Model No. 400
EX $35   NM $55   MIP $75

Giant Bulldozer, 1966, Orange and black, 11.5L x 7W x 5H, blade raises and lowers with lever controls, Model No. 405
EX $45   NM $65   MIP $85

Timber Toter, 1966, Red and red, 23L x 6W x 5H, 6 wooden logs & chains, Model No. 406
EX $55   NM $75   MIP $95

Vista Dome Horse Van, 1966, Met. blue and met. blue, 21.75L x 6W x 6H, 2 ramp doors and 2 horses, 2 colts, Model No. 417
EX $45   NM $65   MIP $85

Car Carrier, 1966, Grey and yellow, 22.25L x 6W x 7H, 3 plastic cars (Mustangs & T-Birds) loading ramp, Model No. 418
EX $45   NM $65   MIP $85

(ToyShop File Photo)

Hydraulic Dump Truck, 1966, Met. blue, 13.75L x 5.5W x 6.25H, same body style as #316 but with hydraulic dump control, Model No. 419
EX $35   NM $55   MIP $75

Hydraulic Dump Truck, 1966, Grey and orange, 13.75L x 5.5W x 6.25H, hydraulic cylinder dumps box, POW-R-R-R sound, Model No. 425
EX $45   NM $65   MIP $85

Cement Mixer, 1966, Grey and orange, 15.5L x 6.75W x 5.25H, axle driven gear operates barrel, POW-R-R-R sound, Model No. 450
EX $45   NM $65   MIP $85

Bulldozer & Earth Mover, 1966, Green and yellow, 25.5L x 7.5W x 7H, combination bulldozer towing bottom dump earth mover unit, Model No. 460
EX $55   NM $75   MIP $95

Bulldozer & Scraper, 1966, Green and yellow, 25.5L x 7.5W x 7H, combination bulldozer towing scraper unit, Model No. 461
EX $55   NM $75   MIP $95

Livestock Van, 1966, Teal and white, 22.25L x 6.5W x 8H, white insert panels in side of trailer, 5 pc. fence & 4 animals, Model No. 505
EX $45   NM $65   MIP $85

Van Truck, 1966, Dk. blue and lt. blue, 22L x 6.5W x 8H, scarce 2 tone blue color combination, Model No. 506
EX $55   NM $75   MIP $95

Hydraulic Sanitation Truck, 1966, Grey and white, 18L x 6W x 8H, manual lift bucket dumps into body, POW-R-R-R sound, Model No. 604
EX $55   NM $75   MIP $95

Ride-er Dump Truck, 1966, White and green, 20L x 7W x 10.25H, metal seat in dump box, Model No. 605
EX $55   NM $85   MIP $115

Deluxe Van Truck, 1966, Red and silver, 24L x 6W x 8.75H, unpainted steel trailer with "Freught Lines" decal, Model No. 609
EX $45   NM $65   MIP $85

Hydraulic Trailer Dump Truck, 1966, Grey and orange, 21.5L x 5.75W x 5.75H, turbine cab, hydraulic controlled dump, Model No. 610
EX $45   NM $65   MIP $85

Weekender, 1966, Teal and white, 12L x 5.75W x 7H, canvas awning, white plastic interior, Model No. 700
EX $55   **NM** $75   **MIP** $95

U.S. Mail Van, 1966, Blue and white, 12L x 5.75W x 6.5H, includes 2 cloth mail bags, Model No. 710
EX $65   **NM** $85   **MIP** $105

Ice Cream Truck, 1966, White and teal, 12L x 6W x 6.5H, scarce, bell rings as truck moves, built-in coolers & detail, Model No. 712
EX $75   **NM** $115   **MIP** $155

Police Emergency Truck, 1966, Blue and white, 12L x 6W x 7.5H, bell rings as truck moves, 3 ladders, hose reel, Model No. 716
EX $55   **NM** $95   **MIP** $125

Mobile Crane, 1966, Orange, 16.5L x 5.5W x 7H, cranks control the boom and clam bucket, swivels, Model No. 801
EX $75   **NM** $95   **MIP** $125

Aerial Hook & Ladder, 1966, Red and white, 29.25L x 6.25W x 6.25H, two metal ladders, crank operated lift ladder, Model No. 901
EX $55   **NM** $85   **MIP** $125

Highway Builder Set, 1966, Green and yellow, 4 pc. set, includes #207, #316, sand hopper & sand loader, Model No. 910
EX $95   **NM** $125   **MIP** $155

Display For Highway Set, 1966, Rare, boxed set for dealer trade show & store display, Model No. 9101
EX $155   **NM** $195   **MIP** $245

Ride-er Chief's Car, 1966, Red and white, 25.5L x 10.25W x 12.75H, bell rings when string is pulled, Model No. 921
EX $75   **NM** $105   **MIP** $155

Farm Set, 1966, Green and yellow, 5 pc. set includes #194 & trailer, #310 & trailer, 4 animals, Model No. 937
EX $95   **NM** $125   **MIP** $155

Display For Farm Set, 1966, Rare, boxed set for dealer trade show & store display, Model No. 9371
EX $155   **NM** $195   **MIP** $245

State Fair Set, 1966, Met. blue, 4 pc. set includes #203, #310, #417, 6 animals, Model No. 952
EX $95   **NM** $125   **MIP** $155

Display For State Fair Set, 1966, Rare, boxed set for dealer trade show & store display, Model No. 9521
EX $155   **NM** $195   **MIP** $245

Pickup, 1967, Green, 8.75L x 3.5W x 3.5H, Kom-pak design, Model No. 101
EX $15   **NM** $25   **MIP** $45

Wrecker Truck, 1967, White and grey, 9.25L x 3.5W x 3.5H, Kom-pak design with red boom arm, Model No. 112
EX $15   **NM** $25   **MIP** $45

Fire Rescue Truck, 1967, Red, 8.75L x 3.5W x 3.5H, Kom-pak design with 2 ladders, Model No. 121
EX $25   **NM** $45   **MIP** $65

Green Beret Truck, 1967, Green, 8.75L x 3.5W x 4H, Kom-pak design with clear plastic cover $2 soldiers, Model No. 126
EX $15   **NM** $25   **MIP** $45

Kennel Truck, 1967, Yellow, 8.75L x 3.5W x 4H, Kom-pak design with clear cover and 6 dogs, Model No. 137
EX $15   **NM** $35   **MIP** $55

Steel Dump Truck, 1967, Grey and orange, 8.75L x 3.5W x 4H, Kom-pak design, Model No. 141
EX $15   **NM** $25   **MIP** $45

Cement Mixer, 1967, Grey and orange, 9.75L x 4W x 4.5H, Kom-pak design with dumping barrel, Model No. 153
EX $15   **NM** $25   **MIP** $45

Tractor Trailer Truck, 1967, Red and silver, 16.5L x 4W x 5.25H, Kom-pak design, no decals on trailer, Model No. 160
EX $25   **NM** $45   **MIP** $65

Mobile Merry-Go-Round Truck, 1967, Yellow and red, 9.25L x 4.25W x 5.75H, scarce, Kom-pak design, circus carousel spins when truck moves, Model No. 174
EX $55   **NM** $85   **MIP** $125

Kenya Karryall, 1967, Green and yellow, 9.25L x 4.25W x 4.25H, scarce, Kom-pak design, 4 cages with 4 hand-painted wild animals, Model No. 176
EX $45   **NM** $75   **MIP** $115

Sanitation Truck, 1967, Grey and white, 11.5L x 3.5W x 5H, Kom-pak design, bucket dumps into body, Model No. 178
EX $25   **NM** $45   **MIP** $65

Road Grader, 1967, Orange, 11.75L x 5W x 4.75H, Kom-pak design, Model No. 183
EX $15   **NM** $25   **MIP** $45

Contractor Set, 1967, Grey and orange, 3 pc. set includes #141, #153, #183, Model No. 192
EX $55   **NM** $85   **MIP** $125

Highway Department Set, 1967, Red and yellow, 4 pc. set includes emergency, dump, wrecker & pickup trucks, Model No. 197
EX $75   **NM** $105   **MIP** $155

Wrecker Truck, 1967, White and black, 10.75L x 4.75W x 5.75H, black convertible roof and boom, red seat, Model No. 205
EX $45   **NM** $65   **MIP** $85

Fisherman, 1967, White and red, 20L x 5W x 4.75H, jeep towing plastic boat & trailer, no doors on jeep, Model No. 210
EX $45   **NM** $65   **MIP** $85

Rampside Pick-Up, 1967, Red, 10.5L x 4.5W x 5H, plastic bed liner and drop-down door in side of bed, Model No. 230
EX $25   **NM** $45   **MIP** $65

Camper Truck, 1967, Lt. blue and dk. blue, 10.5L x 4.5W x 6.5H, dk. blue rampside truck with lt blue plastic cover, Model No. 235
EX $25   **NM** $55   **MIP** $75

Livestock Truck, 1967, Red and yellow, 14.75L x 3.25W x 5.5H, yellow metal panels, Model No. 260
EX $25   **NM** $45   **MIP** $65

Sanitation Truck, 1967, Green and white, 18L x 6W x 8H, lever action trash bucket dumps into box, Model No. 266
EX $45   **NM** $65   **MIP** $85

Dump Truck, 1967, Red, 13.5L x 5.5W x 5.75H, lever controls dump action, Model No. 303
EX $25   **NM** $45   **MIP** $65

Hydraulic Dump Truck, 1967, Red and yellow, 13.5L x 5.5W x 6.25H, hydraulic controlled dump box, Model No. 309
EX $35   **NM** $55   **MIP** $75

Hydraulic Dump Truck, 1967, Yellow and green, 12L x 6W x 6H, turbine cab. hydraulic controlled dump, Model No. 319
EX $35   **NM** $55   **MIP** $75

Vista Dome Horse Van, 1967, Met. gold, 21.75L x 6W x 6H, 2 ramp doors and 2 horses, 2 colts, Model No. 322
EX $45   **NM** $65   **MIP** $85

Car Carrier, 1967, Red and yellow, 22.25L x 6W x 7H, 3 plastic cars (Mustangs & T-Birds) loading ramp, Model No. 331
EX $45   **NM** $65   **MIP** $85

Livestock Van, 1967, Teal and white, 21.25L x 7.75W x 5.75H, turbine cab, white panels on side of trailer, Model No. 344
EX $55   **NM** $75   **MIP** $95

Timber Toter, 1967, Red and red, 20.75L x 6.5W x 5.5H, turbine cab., 5 wooden logs and chains, Model No. 360
EX $55   **NM** $75   **MIP** $95

Snorkel Utility Truck, 1967, Green and yellow, 21L x 6.5W x 5.5H, hydraulic snorkel book and plastic bucket, outriggers, Model No. 380
EX $65   **NM** $95   **MIP** $125

Aerial Hook & Ladder, 1967, Red and red, 29.25L x 6.25W x 6.25H, two metal ladders, crank operated lift ladder, Model No. 381
EX $55   **NM** $85   **MIP** $125

Wrecker Truck, 1967, White, 12.5L x 5.25W x 6.25H, red light (non-operable) on roof, POW-R-R-R sound, Model No. 415
EX $45   **NM** $65   **MIP** $95

Hydraulic Dump Truck, 1967, Grey and yellow, 12.75L x 6W x 6H, hydraulic dump box, POW-R-R-R sound, Model No. 423
EX $45   **NM** $65   **MIP** $85

Cement Mixer, 1967, Grey and orange, 16.5L x 6.5W x 7.5H, axle driven gear operates barrel, POW-R-R-R sound, Model No. 432
EX $45   **NM** $65   **MIP** $85

Fire Rescue Truck, 1967, Red, 12.75L x 5.75W x 5.75H, turbine cab. lever operated ladder, Model No. 453
EX $55   **NM** $75   **MIP** $95

Snorkel Fire Truck, 1967, Red, 21L x 6.5W x 8H, same design as #380, Model No. 466
EX $65   **NM** $95   **MIP** $125

Hydraulic Sanitation Truck, 1967, Grey and white, 16.5L x 5.75W x 7.75H, manual lift bucket dumps into body, POW-R-R-R sound, Model No. 474
EX $55   **NM** $75   **MIP** $95

Tractor Trailer Truck, 1967, Red and red, 21.25L x 7.75W x 5.75H, turbine cab. red, white & blue "" decal on trailer, Model No. 483

EX $55   **NM** $75   **MIP** $95

Auto Transporter, 1967, Red and yellow, 28.25L x 5.75W x 5.5H, large, open car carrier, ramps adjust, 3 plastic cars, Model No. 492

EX $85   **NM** $125   **MIP** $155

Hi-Lift Bulldozer, 1967, Orange and black, 11.25L x 5.75W x 4H, metal levers operate the bucket, Model No. 501

EX $25   **NM** $45   **MIP** $75

Giant Bulldozer, 1967, Orange and black, 11.5L x 7W x 5H, blade raises and lowers with lever controls, Model No. 514

EX $45   **NM** $65   **MIP** $85

Road Grader, 1967, Orange, 19L x 7.5W x 8H, plated scraper blade, black plastic wheels & engine, Model No. 527

EX $35   **NM** $55   **MIP** $75

Bulldozer & Earth Mover, 1967, Green and yellow, 24.5L x 6.5W x 5.75H, combination bulldozer towing bottom dump earth mover unit, Model No. 574

EX $45   **NM** $65   **MIP** $85

Weekender, 1967, Teal, 12L x 5.75W x 6.5H, molded built-in refrigerator & sink detail, Model No. 708

EX $55   **NM** $75   **MIP** $95

Police Emergency Truck, 1967, Blue and white, 12L x 6W x 7.5H, bell rings as truck moves, 3 ladders, hosse reel, Model No. 727

EX $55   **NM** $95   **MIP** $125

Highway Builder Set, 1967, Green and yellow, 4 pc. set includes #183, #303, #501 and sand hopper, Model No. 909

EX $65   **NM** $85   **MIP** $115

Heavy Construction Set, 1967, Red and yellow, 4 pc. set includes #303, #432, #514 and barricade, Model No. 941

EX $65   **NM** $95   **MIP** $135

Pickup, 1968, Teal, 8.75L x 3.5W x 3.5H, Kom-pak design, Model No. 101

EX $15   **NM** $25   **MIP** $45

Wrecker Truck, 1968, White and red, 9.25L x 3.5W x 3.5H, Kom-pak design with red boom arm, Model No. 112

EX $15   **NM** $25   **MIP** $45

Fire Rescue Truck, 1968, Red, 8.75L x 3.5W x 3.5H, Kom-pak design with 2 ladders, Model No. 121

EX $25   **NM** $45   **MIP** $65

Kennel Truck, 1968, Yellow, 8.75L x 3.5W x 4H, Kom-pak design with clear cover and 6 dogs, Model No. 137

EX $15   **NM** $35   **MIP** $55

Steel Dump Truck, 1968, Red and yellow, 8.75L x 3.5W x 4H, Kom-pak design, Model No. 141

EX $15   **NM** $25   **MIP** $45

Cement Mixer, 1968, Grey and orange, 9.75L x 4W x 4.5H, Kom-pak design with dumping barrel, Model No. 153

EX $15   **NM** $25   **MIP** $45

Tractor Trailer Truck, 1968, Red and silver, 16.5L x 4W x 5.25H, Kom-pak design, with "National Freight Lines" decal on trailer, Model No. 160

EX $25   **NM** $45   **MIP** $65

Kom-pak Pony Van, 1968, Teal and teal, 16.5L x 3.5W x 4.5H, clear roof on trailer with coral & 3 ponies, Model No. 163

EX $35   **NM** $55   **MIP** $75

Mobile Merry-Go-Round Truck, 1968, Yellow and red, 9.25L x 4.25W x 5.75H, scarce, Kom-pak design, circus carousel spins when truck moves, Model No. 174

EX $55   **NM** $85   **MIP** $125

Air Force Truck, 1968, Blue, 8.75L x 3.5W x 4H, scarce, Kom-pak design with clear cover on bed, 4 blue soldiers, Model No. 175

EX $45   **NM** $75   **MIP** $115

Kenya Karryall, 1968, Green and yellow, 9.25L x 4.25W x 4.25H, scarce, Kom-pak design, 4 cages with 4 hand-painted wild animals, Model No. 176

EX $45   **NM** $75   **MIP** $105

Sanitation Truck, 1968, Grey and white, 11.5L x 3.5W x 5H, Kom-pak design, bucket dumps into body, Model No. 178

EX $25   **NM** $45   **MIP** $65

Kom-pak Sandy, 1968, Green and yellow, 8.75L x 3.5W x 3.5H, Kom-pak design with plastic sand hopper, Model No. 184

EX $25   **NM** $45   **MIP** $65

Kom-pak Contractor Set, 1968, Green and yellow, 4 pc. set includes #153, #183, #184, Model No. 193

EX $55   **NM** $85   **MIP** $115

Kom-pak Animal Set, 1968, Teal and white, 4 pc. set includes #137, #163, 6 dogs, 4 ponies & fence coral, Model No. 196

EX $55   **NM** $85   **MIP** $115

Wrecker Truck, 1968, White and black, 10.75L x 4.75W x 5.75H, black convertible roof and boom, red seat, Model No. 205

EX $45   **NM** $65   **MIP** $85

Sea Sprite, 1968, White and red, 23.5L x 5W x 5.25H, jeep towing "Johnson Reveler" model boat on trailer, Model No. 211

EX $45   **NM** $65   **MIP** $85

Rampside Pick-Up, 1968, Red, 10.5L x 4.5W x 5H, plastic bed liner and drop-down door in side of bed, Model No. 230

EX $25   **NM** $45   **MIP** $65

Camper Truck, 1968, Lt. blue and Dk. blue, 10.5L x 4.5W x 6.5H, Dk. blue rampside truck with Lt. blue plastic camper, Model No. 235

EX $25   **NM** $55   **MIP** $75

Livestock Truck, 1968, Red and yellow, 14.75L x 3.25W x 5.5H, yellow metal panels, Model No. 260

EX $25   **NM** $45   **MIP** $65

Wrecker Truck, 1968, Red, 15L x 5.5W x 6.25H, white boom arm, red light (non-operable) on roof, Model No. 264

EX $45   **NM** $65   **MIP** $85

Sanitation Truck, 1968, Green and white, 18L x 6W x 8H, lever action trash bucket dumps into box, Model No. 266

EX $45   **NM** $65   **MIP** $85

Hydraulic Sanitation Truck, 1968, Grey and white, 16.5L x 5.75W x 7.75H, manual lift bucket dumps into body, Model No. 268

EX $45   **NM** $65   **MIP** $85

Cement Mixer, 1968, Red and yellow, 16.5L x 6.5W x 7.5H, axle driven gear operates barrel, Model No. 270

EX $35   **NM** $55   **MIP** $75

Hydraulic Cement Mixer, 1968, Green and yellow, 16.5L x 6.5W x 7.5H, same as #270 but with hydraulic dump action on barrel, Model No. 271

EX $45   **NM** $65   **MIP** $85

Dump Truck, 1968, Red, 13.5L x 5.5W x 5.75H, lever controls dump action, Model No. 303

EX $25   **NM** $45   **MIP** $65

Super Sandy Set, 1968, Yellow and green, 13.5L x 5.5W x 5.75H, dump truck and large plastic sand hopper, Model No. 306

EX $55   **NM** $75   **MIP** $95

Hydraulic Dump Truck, 1968, Red and yellow, 13.5L x 5.5W x 6.25H, hydraulic controlled dump box, Model No. 309

EX $35   **NM** $55   **MIP** $75

Hydraulic Dump Truck, 1968, Yellow and green, 12L x 6W x 6H, turbine cab. hydraulic controlled dump, Model No. 319

EX $35   **NM** $55   **MIP** $75

Vista Dome Horse Van, 1968, Met. gold, 21.75L x 6W x 6H, 2 ramp doors and 2 horses, 2 colts, Model No. 322

EX $45   **NM** $65   **MIP** $85

Car Carrier, 1968, Red and yellow, 22.25L x 6W x 7H, 3 plastic cars (Mustangs & T-Birds) loading ramp, Model No. 331

EX $45   **NM** $65   **MIP** $85

Livestock Van, 1968, Teal and white, 21.25L x 7.75W x 5.75H, turbine cab. white panels on side of trailer, Model No. 344

EX $55   **NM** $75   **MIP** $95

Timber Toter, 1968, Blue and blue, 20.75L x 6.5W x 5.5H, turbine cab, 5 wooden logs and chains, Model No. 360

EX $45   **NM** $65   **MIP** $85

Snorkel Utility Truck, 1968, Green and yellow, 21L x 6.5W x 5.5H, hydraulic snorkel book and plastic bucket, outriggers, Model No. 380

EX $65   **NM** $95   **MIP** $125

Aerial Hook & Ladder, 1968, Red and red, 29.25L x 6.25W x 6.25H, two metal ladders, crank lift ladder "9" decal on side, Model No. 381

EX $55   **NM** $85   **MIP** $115

Police Emergency Truck, 1968, Blue and white, 12L x 6W x 7.5H, bell rings as truck moves, 3 ladders, hose reel, Model No. 727

EX $55   **NM** $95   **MIP** $125

Wrecker Truck, 1968, White, 12.5L x 5.25W x 6.25H, red light (non-operable) on roof, POW-R-R-R sound, Model No. 415

EX $45   **NM** $65   **MIP** $95

Hydraulic Dump Truck, 1968, Grey and orange, 12.75L x 6W x 6H, hydraulic dump box, POW-R-R-R sound, Model No. 423

EX $45   **NM** $65   **MIP** $85

Fire Rescue Truck, 1968, Red, 12.75L x 5.75W x 5.75H, turbine cab. lever operated ladder, Model No. 453

EX $55   **NM** $75   **MIP** $95

Snorkel Fire Truck, 1968, Red, 21L x 6.5W x 8H, same design as #380, Model No. 466

EX $65   **NM** $95   **MIP** $125

Tractor Trailer Truck, 1968, Red and red, 21.25L x 7.75W x 5.75H, turbine cab. red, white & blue "" decal on trailer, Model No. 483

EX $55   **NM** $75   **MIP** $95

Auto Transporter, 1968, Red and yellow, 28.25L x 5.75W x 5.5H, large, open car carrier, ramps adjust, 3 plastic cars, Model No. 492

EX $85   **NM** $125   **MIP** $155

Road Grader, 1968, Orange, 11.75L x 5W x 4.75H, Kom-pak design, Model No. 183

EX $15   **NM** $25   **MIP** $45

Hi-Lift Bulldozer, 1968, Orange and black, 11.25L x 5.75W x 4H, metal levers operate the bucket, Model No. 501

EX $25   **NM** $45   **MIP** $75

Giant Bulldozer, 1968, Orange and black, 11.5L x 7W x 5H, blade raises and lowers with lever controls, Model No. 514

EX $45   **NM** $65   **MIP** $85

Road Grader, 1968, Orange, 19L x 7.5W x 8H, plated scraper blade, black plastic wheels & engine, Model No. 527

EX $35   **NM** $55   **MIP** $75

Bulldozer & Earth Mover, 1968, Green and yellow, 24.5L x 6.5W x 5.75H, combination bulldozer towing bottom dump earth mover unit, Model No. 574

EX $45   **NM** $65   **MIP** $85

Sand Master Set, 1968, Yellow, 17.5L x 9W x 15H, plastic sand hopper with rubber conveyor belt, Model No. 580

EX $15   **NM** $25   **MIP** $35

Roadbuilder Set, 1968, Yellow and green, #580 set and #303 dump truck, Model No. 905

EX $55   **NM** $75   **MIP** $95

Highway Builder Set, 1968, Yellow and green, 4 pc. set includes #183, #306 set, #501, Model No. 932

EX $65   **NM** $85   **MIP** $115

Heavy Construction Set, 1968, Red and yellow, 4 pc. set includes #270, #303, #514 and barricade, Model No. 941

EX $65   **NM** $95   **MIP** $135

Rough Rider Pick-Up Truck, 1969, Yellow, 9.25L x 4W x 4H, hurricanes design with open bed, Model No. 801

EX $15   **NM** $25   **MIP** $35

Minuteman Tow Truck, 1969, Dk. orange, 9.25L x 4W x 4H, hurricanes design with crank operated tow rope, Model No. 812

EX $15   **NM** $25   **MIP** $35

Waggin' Wagon Kennel Truck, 1969, Yellow, 9.25L x 4W x 4H, hurricanes design with clear kennel and 6 dogs, Model No. 837

EX $15   **NM** $25   **MIP** $35

Dump Truck, 1969, Dk. orange and white, 10.5L x 4W x 4.25H, hurricanes design, Model No. 841

EX $15   **NM** $25   **MIP** $35

Cement Mixer, 1969, Dk. orange and white, 9.5L x 4W x 4.25H, hurricanes design with axle driven barrel, Model No. 853

EX $15   **NM** $25   **MIP** $35

Livestock Truck, 1969, Teal and white, 9.5L x 4.25W x 4H, hurricanes design with white stake panels and 5 animals, Model No. 870

EX $15   **NM** $25   **MIP** $35

Merry-Go-Round, 1969, Yellow and red, 9.5L x 4.25W x 5.75H, hurricanes design with carousel, Model No. 874

EX $25   **NM** $35   **MIP** $45

Snorkel Fire Truck, 1969, Red and white, 9.5L x 4W x 5.25H, hurricanes design with white plastic snorkel arm & bucket, Model No. 878

EX $15   **NM** $25   **MIP** $35

Hydraulic Dump Truck, 1969, Dk. orange and white, 12.25L x 5.5W x 6.25H, thunderbolt design with steer-o-matic front wheels, Model No. 626

EX $25   **NM** $35   **MIP** $45

Cement Mixer, 1969, Dk. orange and white, 12.25L x 7W x 7H, thunderbolt design with steer-o-matic front wheels, Model No. 632

EX $25   **NM** $35   **MIP** $45

Fire Rescue Truck, 1969, Red and white, 12.5L x 6W x 6.5H, thunderbolt design with steer-o-matic front wheels, Model No. 653

EX $25   **NM** $35   **MIP** $45

Scamp, 1969, Gold and white, 9.5L x 4.5W x 5.25H, sport model design with 5" blond doll, Model No. 744

EX $25   **NM** $35   **MIP** $45

Sea Sprite, 1969, Blue and red, 23L x 5.5W x 5.25H, sport model design with "Johnson Reveler" boat in tow, Model No. 755

EX $25   **NM** $35   **MIP** $45

Boog-A-Loo, 1969, Pink and white, 9.5L x 4.5W x 5H, sport model design with 5" blond doll, Model No. 766

EX $25   **NM** $35   **MIP** $45

Tractor Trailer Truck, 1969, White and red, 16.5L x 4.25W x 5.5H, Kom-pak design with red trailer & white doors, Model No. 160

EX $25   **NM** $35   **MIP** $45

Pony Van, 1969, Lime green, 16.5L x 3.25W x 5H, Kom-pak design with clear roof on trailer and 3 colts, Model No. 163

EX $25   **NM** $35   **MIP** $45

Kom-pak Sandy, 1969, Green and yellow, 9L x 5.25W x 8.5H, Kom-pak design, Model No. 184

EX $25   **NM** $35   **MIP** $45

Rampside Pick-Up, 1969, Gold and white, 10.5L x 4.75W5.25H, typhoons design with white plastic bed liner, Model No. 230

EX $25   **NM** $35   **MIP** $45

Camper Truck, 1969, Gold and white, 10.5L x 5W x 6.5H, typhoons design with white plastic camper in bed, Model No. 235

EX $25   **NM** $35   **MIP** $45

Sanitation Truck, 1969, Grey and white, 16.5L x 6W x 7.5H, typhoons design with lever action, Model No. 269

EX $25   **NM** $35   **MIP** $45

Cement Mixer, 1969, Red and yellow, 14.5L x 7W x 7.5H, typhoons design with axle driven barrel, Model No. 270

EX $25   **NM** $35   **MIP** $45

Wrecker Truck, 1969, Yellow and red, 12.5L x 6W x 6.25H, typhoons design with red tow boom & crank winch, Model No. 277

EX $25   **NM** $35   **MIP** $45

Dump Truck, 1969, Red, 13.5L x 6W x 5.5H, typhoons design with lever action dump box, Model No. 303

EX $25   **NM** $35   **MIP** $45

Dump Truck, 1969, Grey and orange, 13L x 5.5W x 6H, typhoons design with spring action dump box, Model No. 311

EX $25   **NM** $35   **MIP** $45

Hydraulic Dump Truck, 1969, Yellow and green, 13L x 6W x 6H, typhoons design with hydraulic dump box, Model No. 319

EX $25   **NM** $35   **MIP** $45

Vista Dome Horse Van, 1969, Met. gold, 22L x 5.5W x 6.5H, typhoons design with 4 horses, Model No. 322

EX $35   **NM** $45   **MIP** $55

Car Carrier, 1969, Red and yellow, 22.5L x 5.5W x 5.5H, typhoons design with 3 plastic cars (Mustangs/T-Birds) ramp, Model No. 331

EX $35   **NM** $45   **MIP** $55

Livestock Van, 1969, Teal and white, 21.75L x 5.5W x 7.5H, typhoons design with fifth wheel detail, Model No. 344

EX $25   **NM** $35   **MIP** $45

Timber Toter, 1969, Red and red, 21.75L x 5.5W x 6.5H, typhoons design with 6 wooden logs and chain, Model No. 361

EX $25   **NM** $35   **MIP** $45

Tractor Trailer Truck, 1969, Red and red, 22L x 5.5W x 8H, typhoons design, Model No. 373

EX $25   **NM** $35   **MIP** $45

Snorkel Utility Truck, 1969, Green and yellow, 17.5L x 6W x 9H, typhoons design with white boom and plastic bucket, Model No. 380

EX $35   **NM** $45   **MIP** $55

Aerial Hook & Ladder, 1969, Red and red, 30.25L x 5.5W x 7H, typhoons design with crank operated extension ladder, Model No. 381

EX $35   **NM** $45   **MIP** $55

Snorkel Fire Truck, 1969, Red, 17.5L x 5.75W x 9H, typhoons design, Model No. 385

EX $35   **NM** $45   **MIP** $55

VEHICLES — STRUCTO

Road Grader, 1969, Orange, 11.75L x 5W x 6H, black plastic wheels and motor, Model No. 183
EX $15   NM $25   MIP $45

Super Sandy Set, 1969, Green and yellow, 13.5L x 9.5W x 13H, #303 dump truck plus plastic sand hopper, Model No. 306
EX $25   NM $35   MIP $45

Hi-Lift Bulldozer, 1969, Orange and black, 12L x 6W x 6.5H, metal levers operate the bucket, Model No. 501
EX $25   NM $35   MIP $55

Giant Bulldozer, 1969, Red and yellow, 12L x 6.75W x 7H, blade raises and lowers with lever controls, Model No. 514
EX $25   NM $35   MIP $55

Road Grader, 1969, Orange, 19L x 7.5W x 8H, plated scraper blade, black plastic wheels & engine, Model No. 527
EX $25   NM $35   MIP $55

Sand Master Set, 1969, Yellow, 17.5L x 9W x 15H, plastic sand hopper with rubber conveyor belt, Model No. 580
EX $15   NM $25   MIP $35

Roadbuilder Set, 1969, Yellow and green, #580 set and #303 dump truck, Model No. 905
EX $45   NM $65   MIP $85

Highway Builder Set, 1969, Green and yellow, 4 pc. set includes #183, #306 set, #501, Model No. 932
EX $55   NM $75   MIP $105

Animal Set, 1969, Yellow and green, 2 pc. set contains #837 and #870, Model No. 961
EX $35   NM $55   MIP $75

Hurricane Contractor Set, 1969, Dk orange and white, 2 pc. set contains #841 and #853 plus sand hopper and signs, Model No. 965
EX $35   NM $55   MIP $75

Typhoon Construction Set, 1969, Grey and orange, 3 pc. set including #270, #311, #501, Model No. 966
EX $65   NM $85   MIP $105

Dig 'N Dump Set, 1970, Orange and white, 20L x 3.25W x 4.25H, road tow'ds design with shovel & dual dump boxes in tow, Model No. 280
EX $15   NM $25   MIP $35

Pipe-Layer Set, 1970, Blue and white, 20L x 3.25W x 4.25H, road tow'ds design with grab bucket & dual trailers in tow, Model No. 285
EX $15   NM $25   MIP $35

Bridge Set, 1970, Yellow and white, 22.25L x 3.5W x 5.5H, road tow'ds design with stake truck, 2 trailers & 4 pc. Bridge, Model No. 290
EX $15   NM $25   MIP $35

Steerable Rough Rider Pickup, 1970, Blue and white, 9.25L x 4W x 4H, steerable stormers design, Model No. 420
EX $15   NM $25   MIP $35

Steerable Minuteman Wrecker, 1970, Lime green and white, 9.25L x 4W x 4H, steerable stormers design with white metal boom, Model No. 428
EX $15   NM $25   MIP $35

Steerable Waggin' Wagon, 1970, Blue and white, 9.25L x 4W x 4H, steerable stormers design with clear kennel & 6 dogs, Model No. 437
EX $15   NM $25   MIP $35

Steerable Dump Truck, 1970, Gold and white, 10.5L x 4W x 4.25H, steerable stormers design, Model No. 441
EX $15   NM $25   MIP $35

Steerable Livestock Truck, 1970, Gold and white, 9.5L x 4.25W x 4.25H, steerable stormers design with stake sides & 4 animals, Model No. 471
EX $15   NM $25   MIP $35

Steerable Snorkel Truck, 1970, Red and white, 9.5L x 4W x 5.5H, steerable stormers design with white plastic snorkel, Model No. 478
EX $15   NM $25   MIP $35

(ToyShop File Photo)

Steerable Stubby Wrecker, 1970, Gold and white, 11L x 5.5W x 7H, steerable thunderbolt design with "Road Tug" decal on side, Model No. 615
EX $15   NM $35   MIP $55

Steerable Hydraulic Dump Truck, 1970, Orange and white, 13.25L x 5.5W x 6.25H, steerable thunderbolt design, Model No. 626
EX $15   NM $25   MIP $35

Steerable Cement Mixer, 1970, Orange and white, 12.25L x 7W x 7.5H, steerable thunderbolt design, Model No. 632
EX $15   NM $25   MIP $35

Steerable Hydraulic Dump Truck, 1970, Blue and white, 13.25L x 5.5W x 6.25H, steerable thunderbolt design, Model No. 640
EX $15   NM $25   MIP $35

Steerable Fire Rescue Truck, 1970, Red, 12.5L x 6W x 6.5H, steerable thunderbolt design, Model No. 653
EX $15   NM $25   MIP $35

Steerable Timber Toter, 1970, Lime green and white, 21.75L x 5.5W x 6.5H, steerable thunderbolt design with 6 wooden logs & chains, Model No. 661
EX $25   NM $45   MIP $55

Steerable Tractor Trailer, 1970, Orange and orange, 22L x 5.5W x 8H, steerable thunderbolt design, Model No. 673
EX $25   NM $45   MIP $55

Steerable Hook & Ladder Truck, 1970, Red and red, 17.5L x 6W x 7.25H, steerable thunderbolt design, Model No. 681
EX $25   NM $45   MIP $55

Scamp Sportster, 1970, Gold and white, 9.5L x 4.5W x 5.25H, sport model design with 5" blond female doll, Model No. 744
EX $25   NM $35   MIP $45

Sea Sprite, 1970, Blue and red, 23L x 5.5W x 5.25H, sport model design with "Johnson Reveler" boat in tow, Model No. 755
EX $25   NM $35   MIP $45

Race-A-Roo, 1970, Gold and white, 9.5L x 4.5W x 5H, sport model design with 5" white male doll, Model No. 760
EX $25   NM $35   MIP $45

Boog-A-Loo, 1970, Pink and white, 9.5L x 4.5W x 5H, sport model design with 5" blond doll, Model No. 766
EX $25   NM $35   MIP $45

Lad-A-Bout, 1970, Lime green and white, 9.5L x 4.5W x 5.25H, sport model design with 5" black male doll, Model No. 769
EX $35   NM $45   MIP $55

Sand-Grenade Dune Buggy, 1970, Red and black, 9.5L x 4.5W x 5H, sport model design with dual rear mag wheels, Model No. 777
EX $25   NM $35   MIP $45

Rough Rider Pickup, 1970, Yellow, 9.25L x 4W x 4H, hurricanes design with open bed, Model No. 801
EX $15   NM $25   MIP $35

Minuteman Tow Truck, 1970, Dk. orange, 9.25L x 4W x 4H, hurricanes design with crank operated tow rope, Model No. 812
EX $15   NM $25   MIP $35

Camper Truck, 1970, Lime green and white, 9.25L x 4.25W x 5H, hurricane design with white plastic camper, Model No. 835
EX $15   NM $25   MIP $35

Waggin' Wagon Kennel Truck, 1970, Yellow, 9.25L x 4W x 4H, hurricanes design with clear kennel and 6 dogs, Model No. 837
EX $15   NM $25   MIP $35

Dump Truck, 1970, Dk. orange and white, 10.5L x 4W x 4.25H, hurricanes design, Model No. 841
EX $15   NM $25   MIP $35

Cement Mixer, 1970, Dk. orange and white, 9.5L x 4W x 4.25H, hurricanes design with axle driven barrel, Model No. 853
EX $15   NM $25   MIP $35

Livestock Truck, 1970, Green and white, 9.5L x 4.25W x 4H, hurricanes design with white stake panels and 5 animals, Model No. 870
EX $15   NM $25   MIP $35

Snorkel Fire Truck, 1970, Red and white, 9.5L x 4W x 5.25H, hurricanes design with white plastic snorkel arm & bucket, Model No. 878
EX $15   NM $25   MIP $35

Cement Mixer, 1970, Red and yellow, 14.5L x 7W x 7.5H, typhoons design with axle driven barrel, Model No. 270
EX $25   NM $35   MIP $45

Dump Truck, 1970, Red, 13.5L x 6W x 5.5H, typhoons design with lever action dump box, Model No. 303

EX $25   **NM** $35   **MIP** $45

Hydraulic Dump Truck, 1970, Yellow and green, 13L x 6W x 6H, typhoons design with hydraulic dump box, Model No. 319

EX $25   **NM** $35   **MIP** $45

Vista Dome Horse Van, 1970, Met. gold, 22L x 5.5W x 6.5H, typhoons design with 4 horses, Model No. 322

EX $35   **NM** $45   **MIP** $55

Car Carrier, 1970, Red and yellow, 22.5L x 5.5W x 5.5H, typhoons design with 3 plastic cars (Mustangs/T-Birds) ramp, Model No. 331

EX $35   **NM** $45   **MIP** $55

Snorkel Utility Truck, 1970, Green and yellow, 17.5L x 6W x 9H, typhoons design with white boom and plastic bucket, Model No. 380

EX $35   **NM** $45   **MIP** $55

Snorkel Fire Truck, 1970, Red, 17.5L x 5.75W x 9H, typhoons design, Model No. 385

EX $35   **NM** $45   **MIP** $55

Tractor Trailer Truck, 1970, White and red, 16.5L x 4.25W x 5.5H, Kom-pak design with red trailer & white doors, Model No. 160

EX $25   **NM** $35   **MIP** $45

Pony Van, 1970, Lime green, 16.5L x 3.25W x 5H, Kom-pak design with clear roof on trailer and 3 colts, Model No. 163

EX $25   **NM** $35   **MIP** $45

Road Grader, 1970, Lime green and yellow, 11.75L x 5W x 6H, black plastic wheels and motor, Model No. 183

EX $15   **NM** $25   **MIP** $35

Hi-Lift Bulldozer, 1970, Lime green and yellow, 12L x 6W x 6.5H, metal levers operate the bucket, Model No. 501

EX $25   **NM** $35   **MIP** $55

Giant Bulldozer, 1970, Lime green and yellow, 12L x 6.75W x 7H, blade raises and lowers with lever controls, Model No. 514

EX $25   **NM** $35   **MIP** $55

Kom-pak Sandy, 1970, Green and yellow, 9L x 5.25W x 8.5H, Kom-pak design, Model No. 184

EX $25   **NM** $35   **MIP** $45

Super Sandy Set, 1970, Green and yellow, 13.5L x 9.5W x 13H, #303 dump truck plus plastic sand hopper, Model No. 306

EX $25   **NM** $35   **MIP** $45

Sand Master Set, 1970, Yellow, 17.5L x 9W x 15H, plastic sand hopper with rubber conveyor belt, Model No. 580

EX $15   **NM** $25   **MIP** $35

Highway Builder Set, 1970, Green and yellow, 4 pc. set includes #183, #306 set, #501, Model No. 932

EX $55   **NM** $75   **MIP** $105

Steerable Stormer Construction Set, 1970, Yellow, #441 steer-o-matic dump, sand hopper & 10 pc. road sign set, Model No. 955

EX $35   **NM** $45   **MIP** $55

Hurricane Construction Set, 1970, Orange and white, 3 pc. set including #841, sand hopper & 10 pc. Road sign set, Model No. 965

EX $65   **NM** $85   **MIP** $105

Monster Machine, 1971, Green, 2.75L x 3.5W x 3H, 2 wheeled design with exposed "Chrome" engine, Model No. 215

EX $10   **NM** $15   **MIP** $20

Panic Panel, 1971, Orange, 2.75L x 3.5W x 3H, 2 wheeled design with panel wagon sides, Model No. 216

EX $10   **NM** $15   **MIP** $20

Weird Wagon, 1971, Red, 2.75L x 3.5W x 3H, 2 wheeled design with WV bug style, Model No. 217

EX $10   **NM** $15   **MIP** $20

Buzzin' Buggy, 1971, Yellow, 2.75L x 3.5W x 3H, 2 wheeled design with open dune buggy style, Model No. 218

EX $10   **NM** $15   **MIP** $20

Monster Machine, 1972, Green, 2.75L x 3.5W x 3H, 2 wheeled design with exposed "Chrome" engine, Model No. 215

EX $10   **NM** $15   **MIP** $20

Panic Panel, 1972, Orange, 2.75L x 3.5W x 3H, 2 wheeled design with panel wagon sides, Model No. 216

EX $10   **NM** $15   **MIP** $20

Weird Wagon, 1972, Red, 2.75L x 3.5W x 3H, 2 wheeled design with WV bug style, Model No. 217

EX $10   **NM** $15   **MIP** $20

Buzzin' Bugggy, 1972, Yellow, 2.75L x 3.5W x 3H, 2 wheeled design with open dune buggy style, Model No. 218

EX $10   **NM** $15   **MIP** $20

Giant 24-Pack Assortment, 1972, 17.75L x 16.5W x 16.5H, all 4 weird wheels designs in a store display - 24 cars total, Model No. 219

EX n/a   **NM** n/a   **MIP** $250

Triple Terrific 3 Pack, 1972, 14L x 5W x 5H, one each #215, #216, #217 in a 3 pack store display box, Model No. 220

EX n/a   **NM** n/a   **MIP** $150

Brain Barrel, 1972, Brown, 2.75L x 3.5W x 3H, 2 wheeled design with brown "Wooden" barrel & bald driver, Model No. 250

EX $10   **NM** $15   **MIP** $20

Loonie Looper, 1972, Yellow and orange, 2.75L x 3.5W x 3H, 2 wheeled design with airplane styling including propeller, Model No. 251

EX $10   **NM** $15   **MIP** $20

Litter Picker, 1972, Chrome and orange, 2.75L x 3.5W x 3H, 2 wheeled design with trash can style, Model No. 252

EX $10   **NM** $15   **MIP** $20

Triple Terrific 3 Pack, 1972, 14L x 5W x 5H, one each #250, #251, #252 in a 3 pack store display box, Model No. 262

EX n/a   **NM** n/a   **MIP** $150

Big 2-Dozen Assortment, 1972, 17.75L x 14.75W x 16.5H, all 3 weird wheels designs in a store display - 24 cars total, Model No. 265

EX n/a   **NM** n/a   **MIP** $250

Giant Gantry Crane, 1972, Yellow, 32.5L x 12.25W x 14H, hand crank pulley system with crane mechanism, Model No. 555

EX $25   **NM** $35   **MIP** $45

Kom-pak Sandy, 1972, Yellow, 9L x 5.25W x 8.5H, sand hopper and dump truck, Model No. 184

EX $15   **NM** $25   **MIP** $35

Sand Loader, 1972, Yellow, 9.5L x 5W x 9.5H, small sand hopper with conveyor, Model No. 560

EX $10   **NM** $15   **MIP** $20

Sand Set, 1972, Yellow, 9.75L x 5W x 9.5H, #560 unit plus sand hopper unit, Model No. 579

EX $15   **NM** $25   **MIP** $35

Sand Master Set, 1972, Yellow, 14.5L x 4.5W x 15H, plastic sand hopper with rubber conveyor belt, Model No. 580

EX $15   **NM** $25   **MIP** $35

Contractor Set, 1972, Yellow, combination of #579 set and #184 set plus 10 street signs, Model No. 967

EX $35   **NM** $55   **MIP** $75

Boon Dock'r, 1972, Red and green, 23L x 5.5W x 5.25H, sport model design with buggy towing boat & trailer, Model No. 758

EX $25   **NM** $35   **MIP** $45

Dirt Tracker, 1972, White and black, 10L x 4.5W x 5H, sport model design with dual wheels #1 logo & flags on doors, Model No. 770

EX $25   **NM** $35   **MIP** $45

American Rev-O-Lution, 1972, White and black, 10L x 4.5W x 5H, sport model design with american flag on doors, Model No. 775

EX $25   **NM** $35   **MIP** $45

Sand-Grenade Dune Buggy, 1972, Red and black, 9.5L x 4.5W x 5H, sport model design with dual rear mag wheels, Model No. 777

EX $25   **NM** $35   **MIP** $45

Blacktop Bandit, 1972, Plum and black, 10L x 4.5W x 5H, sport model design with dragster styling, Model No. 780

EX $25   **NM** $35   **MIP** $45

Speedway Series Wrecker, 1972, Purple, 9.25L x 4W x 4H, same as hurricane design #428 with speedway decals, Model No. 845

EX $25   **NM** $35   **MIP** $45

Speedway Series Ambulance, 1972, White, 9.25L x 4W x 4H, similar to hurricane design with first aid decals, Model No. 855

EX $25   **NM** $35   **MIP** $45

Speedway Series Pacer, 1972, Green, 9.25L x 4W x 4H, same as hurricane design #801 with speedway decals, Model No. 865

EX $25   **NM** $35   **MIP** $45

Road Boss Vista Dome Horse Van, 1972, Orange, 22L x 5.5W x 6H, with chrome stacks and air horn detail plus 4 black horses, Model No. 324

EX $35   **NM** $45   **MIP** $55

Road Boss Hydraulic Dump, 1972, Orange, 13.25L x 5.25W x 6.25H, with chrome stacks and air horn detail, Model No. 327

EX $25   **NM** $35   **MIP** $45

Road Boss Timber Toter, 1972, Orange, 21.75L x 5.5W x 6.5H, with chrome stacks and air horn detail, Model No. 328

EX $35   **NM** $45   **MIP** $55

Road Boss Tractor Trailer Truck, 1972, Orange, 22L x 5.5W x 8H, with chrome stacks and air horn detail, Model No. 329

EX $35   **NM** $45   **MIP** $55

Road Boss Car Carrier, 1972, Orange, 22.5L x 5.5W x 5.5H, with chrome stacks and air horn detail plus 3 cars, Model No. 335

EX $35   **NM** $45   **MIP** $55

Steerable Stubby Wrecker, 1972, Gold and white, 11L x 5.5W x 7H, thunderbolt design, with black tow boom, Model No. 615

EX $15   **NM** $25   **MIP** $35

Steerable Cement Mixer Truck, 1972, Gold and white, 12.25L x 7W x 7.5H, thunderbolt design, axle drives barrel, Model No. 634

EX $15   **NM** $25   **MIP** $35

Steerable Hydraulic Dump Truck, 1972, Blue and white, 13.25L x 5.5W x 6.25H, thunderbolt design, Model No. 640

EX $15   **NM** $25   **MIP** $35

Steerable Fire Rescue Truck, 1972, Red, 12.5L x 6W x 6.5H, thunderbolt design, with 2 ladders and extension ladder, Model No. 653

EX $15   **NM** $25   **MIP** $35

Dump Truck, 1972, Yellow, 13.5L x 6W x 5.5H, typhoon design, Model No. 303

EX $15   **NM** $25   **MIP** $35

Vista Dome Horse Van, 1972, Met. gold, 22L x 5.5W x 6H, typhoon design with 4 plastic horses, Model No. 320

EX $35   **NM** $45   **MIP** $55

Car Carrier, 1972, Red and yellow, 22.5L x 5.5W x 6H, typhoon design with 3 plastic cars and ramp, Model No. 330

EX $45   **NM** $55   **MIP** $65

Aerial Hook & Ladder, 1972, Red and red, 17.5L x 6W x 7.25H, typhoon design with 2 ladders and extension ladder, Model No. 381

EX $35   **NM** $45   **MIP** $55

Dig'n Dump, 1972, Orange and white, 20L x 3.25W x 4.25H, road tow'ds design with shovel & dual dump boxes in tow, Model No. 280

EX $15   **NM** $25   **MIP** $35

Pipe-Layer Set, 1972, Blue and white, 20L x 3.25W x 4.25H, road tow'ds design with grab bucket & dual trailers in tow, Model No. 285

EX $15   **NM** $25   **MIP** $35

Bridge Set, 1972, Yellow and white, 22.25L x 3.5W x 5.5H, road tow'ds design with stake truck, 2 trailers & 4 pc. Bridge, Model No. 290

EX $15   **NM** $25   **MIP** $35

Road Grader, 1972, Yellow, 11.75L x 5W x 6H, black plastic wheels and motor, Model No. 183

EX $15   **NM** $25   **MIP** $35

Hi-Lift Bulldozer, 1972, Yellow, 12L x 6W x 6.5H, metal levers operate the bucket, Model No. 501

EX $25   **NM** $35   **MIP** $55

Giant Bulldozer, 1972, Yellow, 12L x 6.75W x 7H, blade raises and lowers with lever controls, Model No. 514

EX $25   **NM** $35   **MIP** $55

Steerable Rough Rider Pickup, 1972, Blue and white, 9.25L x 4W x 4H, steerable stormers design, Model No. 420

EX $15   **NM** $25   **MIP** $35

Steerable Minuteman Wrecker, 1972, Lime green and white, 9.25L x 4W x 4H, steerable stormers design with white metal boom, Model No. 428

EX $15   **NM** $25   **MIP** $35

Steerable Camper Truck, 1972, Red and white, 9.25L x 4.25W x 5H, steerable stormers design with white plastic camper, Model No. 435

EX $15   **NM** $25   **MIP** $35

Steerable Waggin' Wagon, 1972, Blue and white, 9.25L x 4W x 4H, steerable stormers design with waggin' wagon treatment, Model No. 437

EX $15   **NM** $25   **MIP** $35

Steerable Dump Truck, 1972, Gold and white, 10.5L x 4W x 4.25H, steerable stormers design, Model No. 441

EX $15   **NM** $25   **MIP** $35

Rough Rider Pickup, 1972, Yellow, 9.25L x 4W x 4H, hurricanes design, Model No. 801

EX $10   **NM** $20   **MIP** $30

Camper Truck, 1972, Orange and white, 9.25L x 4.25W x 5H, hurricanes design, Model No. 835

EX $10   **NM** $20   **MIP** $30

Waggin' Wagon, 1972, Lime green and white, 9.25L x 4W x 4H, hurricanes design with clear cover & 6 dogs, Model No. 837

EX $10   **NM** $20   **MIP** $30

Tractor-Trailer Truck, 1972, Blue and silver, 16.5L x 4.25W x 5.5H, hurricanes design with van lines on trailer, Model No. 861

EX $15   **NM** $25   **MIP** $35

Livestock Truck, 1972, Blue and white, 9.5L x 4.25W x 4H, hurricanes design with white panels and 5 animals, Model No. 870

EX $10   **NM** $20   **MIP** $30

Kom-pak Sandy, 1973, Yellow and orange, 8.5L x 5.5W x 9.5H, sand hopper and dump truck, Model No. 184

EX $15   **NM** $25   **MIP** $35

Sand Master Set, 1973, Yellow and orange, 14.5L x 4.5W x 15H, plastic sand hopper with rubber conveyor belt, Model No. 580

EX $15   **NM** $25   **MIP** $35

Vacation Set, 1973, Orange and green, 22L x 5.75W x 10H, includes #758 and #835, Model No. 962

EX $25   **NM** $35   **MIP** $45

Contractor Set, 1973, Yellow and orange, combination of #580 set and #184 set plus 10 street signs, Model No. 967

EX $35   **NM** $55   **MIP** $75

Speedway Midget Race Hauler, 1973, Red and black, 10.5L x 4W x 4H, flatbed with race car, Model No. 842

EX $25   **NM** $35   **MIP** $45

Speedway Wrecker, 1973, Purple, 9.25L x 4W x 4H, same as hurricane design #428 with speedway decals, Model No. 845

EX $25   **NM** $35   **MIP** $45

Speedway Ambulance, 1973, White, 9.25L x 4W x 4H, similar to hurricane design with first aid decals, Model No. 855

EX $25   **NM** $35   **MIP** $45

Speedway Pacer, 1973, Green, 9.25L x 4W x 4H, same as hurricane design #801 with speedway decals, Model No. 865

EX $25   **NM** $35   **MIP** $45

Speedway Water Tanker, 1973, Blue and white, 9.25L x 4W x 4.5H, white plastic water tank on back, Model No. 868

EX $25   **NM** $35   **MIP** $45

Boon Dock'r, 1973, Orange and green, 23L x 5.5W x 5.25H, sport model design with buggy towing boat & trailer, Model No. 758

EX $25   **NM** $35   **MIP** $45

Scorpion, 1973, Pink and white, 10L x 4.5W x 5.75H, new design for 1973, Model No. 763

EX $25   **NM** $35   **MIP** $45

Top Chopper, 1973, Lime green and orange, 10L x 4.5W x 5.75H, new design for 1973, Model No. 765

EX $25   **NM** $35   **MIP** $45

Propur-T, 1973, Blue and white, 10L x 4.5W x 5.75H, new design for 1973, Model No. 768

EX $25   **NM** $35   **MIP** $45

Dirt Tracker, 1973, Yellow and black, 10L x 4.5W x 5H, sport model design with dual wheels #1 logo & flags on doors, Model No. 770

EX $25   **NM** $35   **MIP** $45

American Rev-O-Lution, 1973, White and black, 10L x 4.5W x 5H, sport model design with american flag on doors, Model No. 775

EX $25   **NM** $35   **MIP** $45

Blacktop Bandit, 1973, Yellow and black, 10L x 4.5W x 5H, sport model design with dragster styling, Model No. 780

EX $25   **NM** $35   **MIP** $45

Road Boss Pipeline Transport, 1973, Blue and yellow, 21.75L x 5.5W x 6.5H, with chrome stacks and air horn detail, same as #328, Model No. 323

EX $25 **NM** $35 **MIP** $45

Road Boss Vista-Dome Horse Van, 1973, Blue and yellow, 22L x 5.5W x 6H, with chrome stacks and air horn detail, 4 black horses, Model No. 324

EX $25 **NM** $35 **MIP** $45

Road Boss Hydraulic Dump, 1973, Blue and yellow, 13.25L x 5.5W x 6.25H, with chrome stacks and air horn detail, Model No. 327

EX $25 **NM** $35 **MIP** $45

Road Boss Timber Toter, 1973, Blue and yellow, 21.75L x 5.5W x 6.5H, with chrome stacks and air horn detail, same as #323, Model No. 328

EX $35 **NM** $45 **MIP** $55

Road Boss Tractor Trailer Truck, 1973, Blue and yellow, 22L x 5.5W x 8H, with chrome stacks and air horn detail, Model No. 329

EX $35 **NM** $45 **MIP** $55

Road Boss Car Carrier, 1973, Blue and yellow, 22.5L x 5.5W x 5.5H, with chrome stacks and air horn detail plus 3 cars, Model No. 335

EX $35 **NM** $45 **MIP** $55

Typhoon Dump Truck, 1973, Yellow, 13.5L x 6W x 5.5H, typhoon design, Model No. 303

EX $15 **NM** $25 **MIP** $35

Typhoon Hydraulic Dump, 1973, Blue and white, 13L x 6W x 6H, typhoon design with turbine cab, Model No. 311

EX $15 **NM** $25 **MIP** $35

Vista Dome Horse Van, 1973, Met. gold, 22L x 5.5W x 6H, typhoon design with 4 plastic horses, Model No. 320

EX $35 **NM** $45 **MIP** $55

Typhoon Cement Mixer, 1973, Blue and white, 13.5L x 6.75W x 7.5H, typhoon design with turbine cab, Model No. 325

EX $15 **NM** $25 **MIP** $35

Typhoon Car Carrier, 1973, Red and yellow, 22.5L x 5.5W x 6H, typhoon design with 3 plastic cars and ramp, Model No. 330

EX $45 **NM** $55 **MIP** $65

Typhoon Fire Rescue Truck, 1973, Red, 12.5L x 6W x 6.5H, typhoon design with 3 ladders, Model No. 353

EX $25 **NM** $35 **MIP** $45

Typhoon Emergency Truck, 1973, White, 12.5L x 6W x 6.5H, typhoon design with 1 red ladder on top, Model No. 358

EX $25 **NM** $35 **MIP** $45

Steerable Stubby Wrecker, 1973, Gold and white, 11L x 5.5W x 7H, thunderbolt design, with black tow boom, Model No. 615

EX $15 **NM** $25 **MIP** $35

Road Grader, 1973, Yellow, 11.75L x 5W x 6H, " 11" stencilled in black on blade, Model No. 183

EX $15 **NM** $25 **MIP** $35

Hi-Lift Bulldozer, 1973, Yellow, 12L x 6W x 6.5H, "11" stencilled in black on blade, Model No. 501

EX $25 **NM** $35 **MIP** $55

Giant Bulldozer, 1973, Yellow, 12L x 6.75W x 7H, " 11" stencilled in black on blade, Model No. 514

EX $25 **NM** $35 **MIP** $55

Rough Rider Pickup, 1973, Yellow, 9.25L x 4W x 4H, hurricanes design, Model No. 801

EX $10 **NM** $20 **MIP** $30

Camper Truck, 1973, Orange and white, 9.25L x 4.25W x 5H, hurricanes design, Model No. 835

EX $10 **NM** $20 **MIP** $30

Waggin' Wagon, 1973, Lime green and white, 9.25L x 4W x 4H, hurricanes design with clear cover & 6 dogs, Model No. 837

EX $10 **NM** $20 **MIP** $30

Dump Truck, 1973, Gold and white, 10.75L x 4W x 4.25H, " 841" stencilled on side of dump box, Model No. 841

EX $10 **NM** $20 **MIP** $30

Tractor-Trailer Truck, 1973, Blue and silver, 16.5L x 4.25W x 5.5H, hurricanes design with van lines on trailer, Model No. 861

EX $15 **NM** $25 **MIP** $35

Livestock Truck, 1973, Blue and white, 9.5L x 4.25W x 4H, hurricanes design with white panels and 5 animals, Model No. 870

EX $10 **NM** $20 **MIP** $30

Monster Machine, 1973, Green, 2.75L x 3.5W x 3H, 2 wheeled design with exposed "Chrome" engine, Model No. 215

EX $10 **NM** $15 **MIP** $20

Panic Panel, 1973, Orange, 2.75L x 3.5W x 3H, 2 wheeled design with panel wagon sides, Model No. 216

EX $10 **NM** $15 **MIP** $20

Weird Wagon, 1973, Red, 2.75L x 3.5W x 3H, 2 wheeled design with WV bug style, Model No. 217

EX $10 **NM** $15 **MIP** $20

Buzzin' Buggy, 1973, Yellow, 2.75L x 3.5W x 3H, 2 wheeled design with open dune buggy style, Model No. 218

EX $10 **NM** $15 **MIP** $20

Giant 24-Pack Assortment, 1973, 17.75L x 16.5W x 16.5H, all 4 weird wheels designs in a store display - 24 cars total, Model No. 219

EX n/a **NM** n/a **MIP** $250

Triple Terrific 3 Pack, 1973, 14L x 5W x 5H, one each #215, #216, #217 in a 3 pack store display box, Model No. 220

EX n/a **NM** n/a **MIP** $150

Brain Barrel, 1973, Brown, 2.75L x 3.5W x 3H, 2 wheeled design with brown "Wooden" brrel & bald driver, Model No. 250

EX $10 **NM** $15 **MIP** $20

Loonie Looper, 1973, Yellow and orange, 2.75L x 3.5W x 3H, 2 wheeled design with airplane styling including propeller, Model No. 251

EX $10 **NM** $15 **MIP** $20

Litter Picker, 1973, White and orange, 2.75L x 3.5W x 3H, 2 wheeled design with trash can style with propeller, Model No. 252

EX $10 **NM** $15 **MIP** $20

Triple Terrific 3 Pack, 1973, 14L x 5W x 5H, one each #250, #251, #252 in a 3 pack store display box, Model No. 262

EX n/a **NM** n/a **MIP** $150

Big 2-Dozen Assortment, 1973, 17.75L x 14.75W x 16.5H, all 3 weird wheels designs in a store display - 24 cars total, Model No. 265

EX n/a **NM** n/a **MIP** $250

Giant Gantry Crane, 1973, Yellow, 32.5L x 12.25W x 14H, hand crank pulley system with crane mechanism, Model No. 555

EX $25 **NM** $35 **MIP** $45

Motorized Giant Gantry Crane, 1973, Blue and yellow, 32.5L x 12.25W x 14H, motor operates all action, battery operated, Model No. 558

EX $35 **NM** $45 **MIP** $55

VEHICLES — TONKA

TONKA

MIGHTY-TONKA TOYS

Backhoe, 1968-70s, 21" long; swiveling body, rubber treads, yellow hoe
EX $25   NM $50   MIP $150

Bottom Dump, 1971, 34" long; No. 3938, green tractor-trailer; 1971 and later
EX $40   NM $85   MIP $260

Bulldozer, 1968-70s, 12-3/8" long; No. 3906, lever-adjusted blade, sun umbrella over seat
EX $10   NM $22   MIP $65

Bulldozer, 1970s, 17" long; yellow, "Turbo-Diesel," cage over seat
EX $8   NM $17   MIP $50

Car Carrier, 1967-69, 34-1/4" long; No. 3990, carries Mini-Tonka load of two Jeep Pickups and one Wagoneer
EX $30   NM $70   MIP $210

Car Carrier, 1970, 34-1/4" long; No. 2990, in 1968 changes to No. 3990, carries Mini-Tonka load of one Jeep Pickup and two Volkswagens
EX $30   NM $65   MIP $195

Car Carrier, 1971, 21-1/8" long; No. 3950, green, six wheels, 1971 and later
EX $30   NM $65   MIP $195

Cement Mixer, 1968-70s, 19" long; "Turbo-Diesel," yellow, white drums
EX $20   NM $45   MIP $75

Cement Mixer, 1971, 21-1/8" long; No. 3950, green, six wheels, 1971 and later
EX $25   NM $73   MIP $220

Clam, 1965, 25" long, 18" high; No. 2905, yellow
EX $12   NM $28   MIP $85

Crane, 1965-70s, 30" long, 20" high; No. 2940, yellow, black boom w/clam, also called Mobile Crane, in 1968 becomes No. 3940
EX $5   NM $12   MIP $35

Custom Van, 1970s, open top, sliding door; late 1970s
EX $3   NM $7   MIP $20

Dump, 1964-70s, 18-1/2" long; No. 900, becomes No. 2900 in 1965, then No. 3900 in 1968
EX $5   NM $10   MIP $30

Grader, 1972, 24-3/4" long; No. 3945, orange; 1972 and later
EX $10   NM $30   MIP $50

Hard Hat, 1960s, No. 4999; plastic hard hat, sold individually or w/sets of Mighty-Tonka toys; late 1960s
EX $5   NM $10   MIP $15

Hydraulic Dump, 1971, 18-1/2" long; No. 3902, orange; 1971 and later
EX $85   NM $175   MIP $260

Loader, 1967-70s, 1907/8" long; No. 2920, later 3920, lever-operated bucket
EX $12   NM $23   MIP $35

Loadmaster, 1971, 18" high; No. 4002, sand loader for dump trucks, green and black; 1971 and later
EX $10   NM $20   MIP $30

Lowboy (tractor-trailer), 1968-70s, "Mighty Diesel," yellow
EX $15   NM $30   MIP $45

Mobile Shovel, 1967-70, 23" long; box-shaped cab, rubber treads, handgrip on shovel handle
EX $20   NM $40   MIP $60

Motor Home, 1973, 22-3/4" long; No. 3885, Winnebago recreational vehicle, swiveling seats, shock-absorbing bumpers, fold-back top, two 6" dolls and dog; 1973 and later
EX $25   NM $50   MIP $75

Off-Road Adventure Buggy, 1970s, changeable tires, jack; late 1970s
EX $7   NM $13   MIP $20

Rescue Vehicle, 1974-79, 18" long; also Rescue Van, white van w/orange top, removable stretcher, driver, nurse and patient
EX $20   NM $40   MIP $60

Roller, 1971, 16" long; No. 3910, road-roller; 1971 and later
EX $22   NM $50   MIP $100

School Bus, 1970s, 19" long; yellow, van design, white plastic hubs, open top
EX $7   NM $15   MIP $22

Scraper, 1967-70s, 27-1/4" long; No. 2935, becomes No. 3935 in 1968, fills, hauls, dumps
EX $130   NM $260   MIP $400

Scraper-Dozer, 1967-69, 30" long; dozer w/swivel-attached scraper end
EX $40   NM $79   MIP $120

Shovel, 1965-69, 29" long; No. 2930, yellow, handgrip on shovel lever, becomes No. 3930 in 1968
EX $42   NM $83   MIP $125

Shovel, 1970, 29" long; No. 3930, lime green; 1970 and later
EX $15   NM $30   MIP $45

Wrecker, 1969-70, 17-1/4" long; No. 3915, white, dual hoists
EX $32   NM $63   MIP $95

Wrecker, 1971, 17-1/4" long; No. 3915, orange body, white cab and hoists; 1971 and later
EX $28   NM $56   MIP $85

MINI-TONKA TOYS

Allied Van (tractor-trailer), 1965-69, 16" long; No. 98, orange, high-window cabover, "Allied Van Lines," rear doors open, becomes No. 1098 in 1968
EX $35   NM $69   MIP $105

Apple Peeler, 1971, No. 1335, 7" long; hot rod panel truck
EX $6   NM $12   MIP $18

Beach Buggy, 1965-66, 6-1/2" long; No. 42, tan Jeep, balloon tires
EX $3   NM $7   MIP $10

Beach Buggy, 1967, 6-1/2" long; No. 42, brown Jeep, balloon tires, white canopy
EX $3   NM $7   MIP $10

Beach Buggy (Jeep), 1969-70, No. 1042, 6-1/2" long; purple w/white canopy, wide balloon tires
EX $3   NM $6   MIP $9

Beach Buggy (Jeep), 1971, No. 1042, 6-1/2" long; purple w/yellow canopy, wide balloon tires; 1971 and later
EX $3   NM $6   MIP $9

Bell System Truck, 1970s-80s, 5-1/2" long; boom lift, white cab, six wheels, No. 55010 on bottom
EX $5   NM $10   MIP $15

Bell System Van, 1979, 5" long; white van, w/blue-yellow side panels
EX $2   NM $4   MIP $6

Bone Bruzzer, 1972, No. 1020, orange Jeep w/roll bars
EX $3   NM $6   MIP $9

Camper, 1963-64, 9-1/2" long; No. 70, red-pink Jeep pickup w/white camper
EX $6   NM $12   MIP $18

Camper, 1965, 9-1/2" long; No. 70, tan pickup, white camper
EX $5   NM $10   MIP $15

Camper, 1967, 9-1/2" long; No. 70, brown body, white camper
EX $5   NM $10   MIP $15

Camper, 1968-70, 9-1/2" long; No. 1070, purple pickup w/camper
EX $10   NM $15   MIP $15

Car Carrier (tractor-trailer), 1964-70, 18-1/2" long; No. 96, green tall windshield cabover, green trailer, two plastic Sting Rays, becomes No. 1096 in 1968
EX $28   NM $56   MIP $85

Car Carrier (tractor-trailer), 1978, 20" long; white and orange
EX $7   NM $13   MIP $20

Cement Truck or Cement Mixer, 1964-70, 9-1/2" long; No. 77, originally called simply Mixer, red Jeep tuck w/white, crank-turned mixer assembly, lever-tilting body, becomes No. 1077 in 1968
EX $13   NM $26   MIP $40

Crane Truck, 1973, 12" long; No. 1099, mobile crane w/hook
EX $4   NM $8   MIP $12

Datsun, 1974, No. 1029
EX $9   NM $19   MIP $28

Dump, 1963, 9-1/2" long; No. 60, all red Jeep truck, lever-operated dump bed;
EX $9   NM $19   MIP $28

Dump, 1964, 9-1/2" long, No. 60, green body, yellow dump bed
EX $9   NM $19   MIP $29

Dump, 1965-70, 9-1/2" long; No. 60, red w/yellow dump bed, becomes No. 1060 in 1968
EX $8   NM $17   MIP $25

Farmer Charmer, 1971, 8-1/2" long; No. 1225, "super Thrust" in 1971, turbo cab, purple pickup; 1971 and later
EX $5   **NM** $10   **MIP** $15

Fire Chief, 1967-69, 9-1/8" long; No. 66, Jeep Wagoneer, all red, "Fire Chief" on door, flasher, becomes No. 1066 in 1968
EX $8   **NM** $17   **MIP** $25

Fire Chief, 1970, 9-1/8" long; No. 1066, Jeep Wagoneer, red body and white roof, "fire Chief" on door, flasher; 1970 and later
EX $7   **NM** $13   **MIP** $20

Fire Fighter, 1966-70, 9-3/4" long; No. 72, red and white, detachable ladders, flasher, becomes No. 1072 in 1968
EX $7   **NM** $13   **MIP** $20

Fire Fighter, 1971, 8-7/8" long; No. 1255, "Super Thrust" in 1971, turbo cab, removable ladders; 1971 and later
EX $5   **NM** $10   **MIP** $15

Fixer Mixer, 1971, 8-7/8" long; No. 1249, "Super Thrust" in 1971, turbo cab, yellow cement mixer; 1971 and later
EX $5   **NM** $11   **MIP** $16

Fun Buggy, 1969-70s, No. 1010, 7" long; roll bar, issued w/removable top in at least 1969, various colors
EX $3   **NM** $6   **MIP** $9

Grader, 1964-69, 10-3/4" long; No. 76, yellow, originally had black stripes on blade, open cab, yellow hubs, becomes No. 1076 in 1968
EX $5   **NM** $9   **MIP** $14

Grader, 1970, No. 1076, lime green, metal hubs; 1970 and later; 10-3/4" long
EX $5   **NM** $9   **MIP** $14

Hi-Way Patrol, 1965-70, No. 64, black and white police Jeep Wagoneer w/flasher, becomes No. 1064 in 1968; 9-1/8" long
EX $15   **NM** $30   **MIP** $45

Honey Bucket, 1972, No. 1025, yellow jeep, blue top
EX $3   **NM** $6   **MIP** $9

Hoot 'N Hauler, 1971, No. 1230, "Super Thrust" in 1971; turbo cabover, dump truck; 1971 and later; 8-7/8" long
EX $5   **NM** $9   **MIP** $14

Hot Hauler, 1971, No. 1330, yellow, hot rod pickup, 7" long
EX $5   **NM** $15   **MIP** $20

Jeep Commander, 1965-69, No. 40, Army green, w/canopy, becomes No. 1040 in 1968; 6-1/2" long
EX $7   **NM** $13   **MIP** $20

Jeep Dispatcher, 1965, No. 30, green, open top; 6-1/8" long
EX $7   **NM** $13   **MIP** $20

Jeep Dispatcher, 1965-70, No. 30, blue, becomes No. 1030 in 1968; 6-1/8" long
EX $5   **NM** $10   **MIP** $15

Jeep Wagoneer, 1965-66, No. 62, turquoise station wagon; 9-1/2" long
EX $12   **NM** $23   **MIP** $35

Lightning Bugs, 1972, No. 1165, Volkswagen, yellow hubs, chromed rear engines; 1972 and later
EX $6   **NM** $12   **MIP** $18

Litter Bug, 1971, No. 1260, "Super Thrust" in 1971, turbo cab, garbage truck; 9-1/2" long
EX $5   **NM** $11   **MIP** $16

Livestock Van (tractor-trailer), 1964-66, No. 90, red w/white trailer sides; high-window cabover, opening rear doors, 16" long
EX $15   **NM** $30   **MIP** $45

Loader, 1969-70s, No. 1087, yellow, movable scoop, metal hubs; 10-1/2" long
EX $6   **NM** $8   **MIP** $12

Luv Bug, 1971, No. 1160, Volkswagen; 8-5/8" long;
EX $6   **NM** $12   **MIP** $18

Mini-Bucket, 1971, No. 1349, hot rod, single bucket seat; 7" long;
EX $5   **NM** $11   **MIP** $16

Mixer, 1964, No. 1977, Jeep truck cab, rotating plastic mixer section and hopper, tilting bed; 9-5/8" long
EX $10   **NM** $20   **MIP** $30

Motor Mover (tractor-trailer), 1971, No. 1275, "Super Thrust" in 1971, turbo cab car carrier, two plastic Corvettes; 1971 and later; 18-5/8" long
EX $7   **NM** $15   **MIP** $22

Pacer Police Car, 1970s, white, flasher bar on roof, chromed bumpers, white plastic hubs; 9" long
EX $9   **NM** $19   **MIP** $28

Pickup, 1963-70, introduced as No. 50 in 1963, becomes No. 1050 in 1968, all red Jeep truck, snap-open tailgate; 9-1/8" long;
EX $8   **NM** $16   **MIP** $24

Pickup and Horse Trailer, 1967-70, No. 82, blue Jeep Pickup, white horse trailer, horses, becomes No. 1082 in 1968; 14-3/4" long
EX $17   **NM** $33   **MIP** $50

Pony Puller, 1972, No. 1265, pink bubble-window Pickup w/white horse trailer; 1972 and later; 14-1/8" long
EX $7   **NM** $13   **MIP** $20

Road Paver, 1973, No. 1095, green paver w/plastic "asphalt" road; 1973 and later; 9-1/2" long
EX $23   **NM** $46   **MIP** $75

Road Roller, 1972, No. 1083, 1972 and later
EX $5   **NM** $10   **MIP** $15

Rollin' On (tractor-trailer), 1970s, blue bubble-window cab, white van trailer w/large "Rollin' On" panels; 16" long
EX $5   **NM** $10   **MIP** $15

Ruff Rider, 1970, No. 1045, green, open top, six wheels; 6-1/8" long
EX $4   **NM** $8   **MIP** $12

Sanitary Service, 1968-70, No. 1084, blue tall-windshield cabover, lever-controlled white dump body; 9-1/2" long
EX $15   **NM** $30   **MIP** $45

Scamper Camper, 1971, No. 1250, "Super Thrust" in 1971, green bubble-window cabover, green camper w/opening white door; 1971 and later; 8-5/8" long
EX $5   **NM** $9   **MIP** $14

Scotts Pick-Up, 1979, green and white pickup, "Scotts" in oval; 8-1/2" long;
EX $3   **NM** $6   **MIP** $9

Scraper, 1969-70s, No. 1091, yellow, metal hubs; 14" long;
EX $7   **NM** $13   **MIP** $20

Side Winder (Volkswagen), 1970, wind-up key decal
EX $6   **NM** $12   **MIP** $18

Snow Seekers, 1970, No. 1081, originally called "Wagoneer and Snowmobile," yellow Wagoneer w/trailer and snowmobile; 1970, 1974 and later; 16-7/8" long
EX $17   **NM** $33   **MIP** $50

Snowmobile, 1970s, from Wagoneer set; 7" long
EX $7   **NM** $13   **MIP** $20

Stake Crate, 1971, No. 1245, "Super Thrust" in 1971, turbo cab, stake truck; 1971 and later; 8-7/8" long
EX $4   **NM** $8   **MIP** $12

Stake Truck, 1963, No. 56, blue Jeep body and stakes, lever-raised dump stake body; 9-3/4" long
EX $13   **NM** $26   **MIP** $40

Stake Truck, 1964-70, No. 56, blue Jeep truck, white stakes, became No. 1056 in 1968; 9-3/4" long
EX $8   **NM** $20   **MIP** $25

Stanley Home Products Truck (tractor-trailer), 1970s-80s, white van body w/opening rear doors, bubble-window cabover, "Stanhome" stickers; 16" long
EX $5   **NM** $11   **MIP** $16

Start Cart, 1971, No. 1235, "Super Thrust" in 1971, turbo cab, wrecker; 1971 and later; 9" long
EX $4   **NM** $8   **MIP** $12

Sun Seeker, 1972, No. 1079; Bone Bruzzer w/orange trailer and Tiny-Tonka dune buggy; 1972 and later.
EX $7   **NM** $13   **MIP** $20

Thunder Hubs, 1971, No. 1325, 7" long; hot rod convertible coupe
EX $5   **NM** $10   **MIP** $15

Track Duster, 1972, No. 1345, blue and orange, Mack-type hot rod truck w/rear water tank; 1972
EX $6   **NM** $12   **MIP** $18

Trencher, 1969, No. 1089, yellow w/black backhoe, metal hubs; 18" long
EX $7   **NM** $13   **MIP** $20

Trencher, 1970, No. 1089, lime green w/black backhoe, metal hubs; 1970 and later; 18" long
EX $5   **NM** $10   **MIP** $15

Twinkle Toes, 1970, Volkswagen, foot-shaped yellow "Twinkle Toes" decal on doors; 8-5/8" long
EX $5   **NM** $11   **MIP** $16

Van (tractor-trailer), 1964, No. 86, blue tall-windshield cabover, white van trailer w/"Tonka;" 16" long
EX $17   **NM** $33   **MIP** $50

Van (tractor-trailer), 1965-66, No. 86, blue cabover, white van trailer w/"Mini-Tonka;" 16" long
EX $12   **NM** $23   **MIP** $35

Volkswagen, 1970, No. 1158, assorted colors, previously grouped as Regular Tonka by Tonka Corp.; 1970 and later; 8-5/8" long
EX $8   **NM** $16   **MIP** $24

Wagoneer and Trailer, 1965-70s, No. 80, red Jeep Wagoneer w/trailer, yellow plastic Sting Ray, becomes No. 1080 in 1968; 17-1/2" long
EX $48   **NM** $96   **MIP** $145

Wrecker, 1963-70, No. 68, white Jeep truck, red boom, lever-operated winch, becomes No. 1068 in 1968; 9-1/2" long
EX $12   **NM** $23   **MIP** $35

REGULAR TONKA

"V" Blade Snow Plow, 1957, No. AC-308, orange Hi-Way blade w/mounting bracket, large "V" shape; 9" wide
EX n/a   **NM** n/a   **MIP** n/a

3-in-1 Hi-Way Service Truck, 1957, No. 44, orange, w/two snowblades, 13" long
EX $275   **NM** $400   **MIP** $700

5th Wheel Trailer, 1974-75, 14" pickup w/19" trailer; open-top trailer attaches to bed of white Styleside pickup; camper, Model No. 2100
EX $23   **NM** $46   **MIP** $70

Aerial Ladder, 1955, No. 700-4, red w/aluminum ladder, "MFD" decals; 32-1/2" long
EX $100   **NM** $300   **MIP** $450

Aerial Ladder, 1956, No. 700, red, 36" fully extendable aluminum ladder, rotating base, "TFD" decals, 2 extra ladders; 32-1/2" long
EX $150   **NM** $300   **MIP** $450

Aerial Ladder, 1960-61, No. 48, red w/aluminum ladder, "TFD" decals, 32-1/2" long
EX $125   **NM** $250   **MIP** $450

Aerial Ladder, 1962, No. 1348
EX $100   **NM** $150   **MIP** $350

Aerial Ladder, 1964, No. 998, two auxiliary ladders
EX $50   **NM** $75   **MIP** $100

Aerial Ladder, 1972, No. 2960, not tractor-trailer, open cab; 1972 and later, Model No. 2960
EX $12   **NM** $23   **MIP** $35

Aerial Ladder (tractor-trailer), 1965-70s, No. 998 in 1965, red, "glassed-in" cabover, "T.F.D." on sides, becomes No.

2998 in 1968; 1965-70s; 28-3/4" long, Model No. 998
EX $25   **NM** $50   **MIP** $75

(Harvey K Rainess)

Aerial Ladder Semi Fire Truck, 1954, No. 700, 32-1/2" long
EX $175   **NM** $260   **MIP** $450

Aerial Ladder Truck, 1963, No. 1348
EX $100   **NM** $150   **MIP** $200

(KP Photo)

Aerial Sand Loader Set, 1955, No. 825-5, Loader and Dump Truck; 25-1/2" long
EX $275   **NM** $425   **MIP** $875

Air Express Truck, 1959, No. 16, dark blue body, square box bed, whitewall tires, "Air Express" decals on sides, plastic windshield, opening rear doors
EX $350   **NM** $425   **MIP** $700

(ToyShop File Photo)

Air Force Ambulance, 1965, No. 402, Dark blue w/"troop carrier" canopy over bed, red cross decal on hood, "U.S.A.F." decals on doors. 14" long
EX $160   **NM** $325   **MIP** $650

Air Force Ambulance, 1965-66, No. 402, blue pickup w/"USAF" on doors, red cross on hood, canopy over bed; 14" long, Model No. 402
EX $45   **NM** $89   **MIP** $135

Air Force Jeep, 1965-68, No. 252 in 1965, blue w/"USAF," becomes No. 2252 in 1968; 10-1/2" long, Model No. 252
EX $10   **NM** $20   **MIP** $30

Airlines Luggage Service, 1962, No. 420, 16-5/8 long
EX $100   **NM** $250   **MIP** $400

Airport Service Set, 1963, No. 2100
EX $150   **NM** $225   **MIP** $300

Alley Gater, 1972, No. 2310, red and white open boat w/wheels, Model No. 2310
EX $7   **NM** $13   **MIP** $20

Allied Moving Van, 1957, No. 38, orange cab and box trailer, "Allied Van Lines" decals; 24" long
EX n/a   **NM** n/a   **MIP** n/a

(KP Photo)

Allied Van, 1961, No. 39, orange cab and trailer w/"Allied Van Lines" decals. Black bumper on cab, blackwall tires on cab and trailer; 21-1/4" long
EX $120   **NM** $250   **MIP** $450

Allied Van, 1962, No. 739
EX $125   **NM** $250   **MIP** $350

Allied Van, 1963, No. 739
EX $118   **NM** $175   **MIP** $235

Allied Van Lines, 1955, No. 400-5, orange tractor/trailer, 23-3/4" long
EX $100   **NM** $200   **MIP** $300

Allied Van Lines, 1964, No. 739, black knob on door
EX $75   **NM** $125   **MIP** $175

Allied Van Lines Semi, 1950, No. 400, 23-1/2" long
EX $175   **NM** $260   **MIP** $400

Back Hoe, 1963, No. 422, 17-1/8" long
EX $100   **NM** $175   **MIP** $350

Backhoe, 1963-65, No. 422, yellow truck cab, body, and backhoe, w/red rear seat; 17" long, Model No. 422
EX $28   **NM** $56   **MIP** $85

Backhoe, 1970s, yellow swivel body, black boom and scoop, six wheels, Model No. 2730
EX $17   **NM** $33   **MIP** $50

Backhoe, 1971, green; 1971 and later, Model No. 2730
EX $17   **NM** $33   **MIP** $50

Bell System Truck, 1978, lift truck, white cab roof
EX $7   **NM** $13   **MIP** $20

Big Mike Dual Hydraulic Dump Truck, 1957, No. 43, twin hydraulic mechanisms lift dump bed, 14" long
EX $325   **NM** $595   **MIP** $1000

Big Mike Dual Hydraulic Dump Truck, 1958 Next Generation Cars, No. 45, orange Hi-Way dump w/"V" snow plow, and "twin hydraulic action"
EX $375   **NM** $675   **MIP** $1000

Boat Service Truck, 1961, No. 117, 1961 only, included blue fleetside pickup truck w/white cab roof, silver hubs, whitewall

tires, blue trailer w/three plastic boats stacked horizontally, 23-1/2" long
EX $100   **NM** $250   **MIP** $450

(KP Photo)

Boat Transport, 1960, No. 41, blue truck w/semi-trailer, four plastic boats stacked virtually upright, w/a bar at the front for two outboard motors; 28" long
EX $250   **NM** $450   **MIP** $850

Boat Transport Truck, 1961, No. 41, blue truck w/semi-trailer, four plastic boats stacked virtually upright, w/a bar at the front for two outboard motors; 28" long
EX $150   **NM** $300   **MIP** $650

Bottom Dump (tractor-trailer), 1965-69, No. 910 in 1965, yellow, "glassed-in" cabover, five-position dump action, became No. 2910 in 1968, Model No. 910
EX $38   **NM** $76   **MIP** $115

Bulldozer, 1960, No. 10, plated roller wheels only in 1960. Black rubber treads, 3-position blade, 8-7/8" long
EX $75   **NM** $125   **MIP** $200

Bulldozer, 1962, Tonka
EX $50   **NM** $75   **MIP** $100

Bulldozer, 1962-70s, No. 300 in 1962, yellow, adjustable blade, becomes No. 2300 in 1968; 8-7/8" long, Model No. 300
EX $13   **NM** $26   **MIP** $40

Bulldozer, 1963, No. 300
EX $55   **NM** $82   **MIP** $110

Bulldozer, 1970s, "Tonka Trax," plastic rollover cage
EX $7   **NM** $13   **MIP** $20

Camper, 1962, No. 530, 14" long
EX $75   **NM** $150   **MIP** $250

Camper, 1962-65, No. 530, blue/turquoise Styleside Pickup w/white camper; 14-5/8" long
EX $60   **NM** $120   **MIP** $180

Camper, 1963, No. 530
EX $25   **NM** $38   **MIP** $50

Camper, 1965-66, No. 530, black pickup, white camper; 14-5/8" long;
EX $42   **NM** $83   **MIP** $125

(KP Photo)

Camper, 1968, No. 1070, Jeep Gladiator truck body, magenta, w/white camper top. The pattern for these trucks is the same as the No. 70 models dating from 1963, but color changes and line expansion forced Tonka to add more two more digits to the stock number
EX $15   **NM** $30   **MIP** $50

Camper, 1972, No. 255, red truck, white camper
EX $8   **NM** $17   **MIP** $25

Canadian Tire Jeep, 1972, red and white Jeep, oversized tires, "To Years of Service, 1922-1972" on hood
EX $10   **NM** $20   **MIP** $30

Car Carrier, 1960, No. 40, yellow cab w/trailer includes three plastic 1960 Ford Falcon cars. Moveable ramp for loading and unloading; 29" long
EX $100   **NM** $225   **MIP** $450

Car Carrier, 1961, No. 40, yellow cab and trailer includes three plastic cars; 29" long
EX $100   **NM** $250   **MIP** $450

Car Carrier, 1962, No. 840
EX $100   **NM** $150   **MIP** $300

Car Carrier, 1963, No. 840
EX $42   **NM** $63   **MIP** $85

(ToyShop File Photo)

Car Carrier, 1965, No. 840, Yellow cabover truck and trailer w/three plastic vehicles, 27" long. Makes first appearance in 1965 catalog
EX $80   **NM** $170   **MIP** $365

Car Carrier, 1965-68, No. 840, "glassed-in" cabover, yellow, trailer w/circular openings on sides, lever-operated loading ramp, three plastic cars, becomes No. 2840 in 1968; 27" long
EX $42   **NM** $83   **MIP** $125

Car Carrier (tractor-trailer), 1969-70s, No. 2850, yellow, trailer sides w/four larger openings, lever-operated ramp, two plastic cars; 27-1/2" long
EX $22   **NM** $43   **MIP** $65

Car Quest Pickup, 1970s, white Styleside, "Car Quest Auto Parts Stores" red and blue decals; 14-1/2" long
EX $8   **NM** $17   **MIP** $25

Cargo King Truck, 1957, No. 30, red cab, open aluminum box, "Cargo King" decals; 23-1/2" long
EX n/a   **NM** n/a   **MIP** n/a

(Mark McManus)

Carnation Milk Step Van, 1954, No. 750, 11-3/4" long
EX $200   **NM** $400   **MIP** $600

Carnation Milk Truck, 1955, No. 750-5, white Divco-style delivery truck w/Carnation Milk decals on panel sides, sliding front door, opening rear door; 11-3/4" long
EX $200   **NM** $400   **MIP** $600

(KP Photo)

Cement Mixer, 1960, No. 120, red body, plastic mixer and hopper, tilting bed, blackwall tires, 15-1/2" long
EX $100   **NM** $150   **MIP** $300

Cement Mixer, 1961, No. 120, red body, plastic mixer and hopper, tilting bed, adjustable chute for cement. Mixer geared to turn as truck moves, 15-1/2" long
EX $100   **NM** $150   **MIP** $300

Cement Mixer, 1962, No. 620
EX $85   **NM** $150   **MIP** $300

Cement Mixer, 1963, No. 620
EX $75   **NM** $125   **MIP** $250

Cement Mixer, 1965-70, No. 6320, red "glassed-in" cabover and chassis, white drum, becomes No. 2620 in 1968; 14" long
EX $15   **NM** $30   **MIP** $45

Cement Mixer, 1971, No. 2620, yellow-orange, w/white drum; 1971 and later; 14" long
EX $12   **NM** $23   **MIP** $35

Crane and Clam, 1947, No. 150, 24" long
EX $135   **NM** $200   **MIP** $350

Crater Crawler, 1970-71, No. 2546, metallic blue and white, bubble top, oversize tires; 1970-71; 11-7/16" long
EX $8   **NM** $17   **MIP** $25

Deluxe Fisherman, 1960, No. 130, new boat and trailer for this year (trailer stayed in lineup until the 1970s). Blue "Fisherman" pickup w/white cab roof and white topper, larger white and red plastic boat on blue trailer w/working winch
EX $150   **NM** $350   **MIP** $550

Deluxe Fisherman, 1961, No. 130, same as previous year's model, that is, a fleet-

side pickup w/topper, but this time in red and white rather than blue and white, 27-5/8" long in total
EX $150   **NM** $350   **MIP** $550

Deluxe Sportman, 1959, No. 22, blue pickup truck w/white cab roof, whitewall tires, silver rims, boat trailer w/plastic boat
EX $150   **NM** $325   **MIP** $500

Deluxe Sportman, 1960, No. 22, blue pickup truck w/white cab roof, whitewall tires, silver rims, boat trailer w/plastic boat
EX $100   **NM** $250   **MIP** $400

Deluxe Sportman, 1961, No. 22, blue pickup truck w/white cab roof, whitewall tires, silver rims, boat trailer w/plastic boat; 22-3/4" long
EX $100   **NM** $200   **MIP** $450

Deluxe Sportsman with Boat Trailer, 1958 Next Generation Cars, No. 34, red truck w/white cab roof, red trailer w/plastic fishing boat and attachable motor; 22-3/4" long
EX $150   **NM** $325   **MIP** $750

Dozer Packer, 1962, No. 524, 18-1/4" long total, Packer has eleven tires, sold only in 1962
EX $100   **NM** $250   **MIP** $400

Dozer Packer, 1963, No. 524, yellow
EX $200   **NM** $300   **MIP** $400

Drag, 1963, No. 514
EX $60   **NM** $90   **MIP** $120

Dragline, 1959, No. 14, yellow, rolling treads, working scoop that rotates on base, bucket actually scoops. Black nylon cord "cables" control bucket; 20" long
EX $100   **NM** $175   **MIP** $375

Dragline, 1961, No. 14, yellow, black bucked, rubber treads, 18" high, 18" long
EX $100   **NM** $150   **MIP** $250

Dragline, 1962, No. 514
EX $150   **NM** $225   **MIP** $300

Dragline, 1966, No. 514, yellow, "Dragline" in large letters, oval Tonka emblem, swivel body, rubber treads, black boom and dragging scoop, becomes No. 612 in 1966; 20-1/2" long
EX $48   **NM** $96   **MIP** $145

Dragline & Trailer, 1959, No. 44, lime-green cab and loboy trailer, lime-green dragline, 26-1/4" long
EX $150   **NM** $275   **MIP** $400

Dump (tailgate), 1965, No. 406, light orange, white cab roof, reinforced dump body w/opening tailgate; 13-3/8" long
EX $40   **NM** $80   **MIP** $120

Dump (tailgate), 1966, No. 406, tan, white cab roof, reinforced dump body w/opening tailgate; 13-3/8" long
EX $35   **NM** $65   **MIP** $100

Dump (tailgate), 1967, No. 406, red w/green-blue dump body; 13-3/8" long
EX $28   **NM** $56   **MIP** $85

Dump (tailgate), 1968, No. 406, red w/green dump, new cab w/slanted roof; 13-3/8" long
EX $20   **NM** $40   **MIP** $60

Dump (tailgate), 1969-70s, No. 2465, red "glassed-in" cabover w/yellow dump body; 13-1/2" long
EX $7   **NM** $15   **MIP** $22

Dump and Sand Loader, 1965, No. 616, all red w/yellow dump body, tailgate Dump w/conveyor; 23-3/4" long
EX $50   **NM** $100   **MIP** $150

Dump and Sand Loader, 1965-68, No. 616, Dump No. 315 w/conveyor, all red w/yellow dump body; 24-1/8" long
EX $40   **NM** $79   **MIP** $120

Dump and Sand Loader, 1968-70, No. 2315 Dump w/conveyor, all red except yellow dump body, new cab
EX $32   **NM** $63   **MIP** $95

(KP Photo)

Dump Truck, 1949, No. 180, 12" long
EX $100   **NM** $175   **MIP** $375

Dump Truck, 1955, No. 180-5, red cab, green dump body; 13" long
EX $100   **NM** $150   **MIP** $350

Dump Truck, 1956, No. 180-6, red cab, green dump bed, 13" long
EX $100   **NM** $150   **MIP** $350

Dump Truck, 1957, No. 06, red cab w/green dump bed; 13" long
EX n/a   **NM** n/a   **MIP** n/a

Dump Truck, 1958 Next Generation Cars, No. 06, red cab w/green dump bed, two-position tailgate, 13-1/2" long
EX $100   **NM** $150   **MIP** $300

Dump Truck, 1960, No. 06, silver five-spoke hubs, red cab, plastic windshield, opening tailgate on dumper bed, 13-1/2" long
EX $75   **NM** $125   **MIP** $290

Dump Truck, 1961, No. 06, red truck w/blue-green dump bed, plastic windshield; 13-1/2" long
EX $75   **NM** $100   **MIP** $250

Dump Truck, 1962, No. 406, 1962
EX $75   **NM** $150   **MIP** $275

Dump Truck, 1963, No. 406
EX $45   **NM** $68   **MIP** $90

Dump Truck, 1964, No. 315, 13-1/2" long
EX $40   **NM** $60   **MIP** $90

Dump Truck, 1964-65, No. 315, orange-red, dump body without tailgate; 13-5/16" long
EX $15   **NM** $30   **MIP** $45

Dump Truck, 1966-67, No. 315, red cab, yellow dump body, dump body without tailgate; 13-5/16" long
EX $15   **NM** $30   **MIP** $45

Dump Truck, 1968-69, No. 2315, red and yellow, new cab w/slanted windshield, lever operated; 13-7/8" long
EX $12   **NM** $23   **MIP** $35

Dump Truck, 1970, No. 2315, orange; 1970 and later; 13-7/8" long
EX $10   **NM** $20   **MIP** $30

Dump Truck & Sand Loader, 1963, No. 616, yellow
EX $100   **NM** $150   **MIP** $235

Dump Truck & Sandloader, 1964, No. 616, orange and yellow
EX $75   **NM** $125   **MIP** $175

Dump Truck and Sand Loader, 1962, No. 616
EX $100   **NM** $200   **MIP** $300

Dump Truck with Sandloader, 1961, No. 116, 23-1/4" long
EX $100   **NM** $175   **MIP** $395

(KP Photo)

Dune Buggy, 1968, No. 2445, Red body, white interior, removable white plastic top, fold-down windshield. Originally came w/chain for towing, expeditions, etc. 10-7/8" long
EX $22   **NM** $38   **MIP** $60

Dune Buggy, 1968-70s, No. 2445, red Jeep w/white canopy, folding windshield, removable top, oversize tires, "Dune Buggy" on front fenders; 10-7/8" long, 8-1/4" wide
EX $10   **NM** $20   **MIP** $30

Dune Buggy, 1970s, No. 2445, yellow Jeep w/white canopy; 10-7/8" long
EX $8   **NM** $16   **MIP** $24

Express Truck, 1950, No. 185, 13-1/2" long
EX $200   **NM** $450   **MIP** $900

Falcon, 1960s, plastic, sold separately and w/car carriers; 8" long
EX $4   **NM** $8   **MIP** $12

Farm Stake and Horse Trailer, 1959-61, No. 35, tan farm stake truck w/white stakes, white two-horse trailer, two plastic horses; 21-3/4" long
EX $125   **NM** $180   **MIP** $350

Farm Stake and Horse Trailer, 1962, No. 735
EX $75   **NM** $125   **MIP** $225

Farm Stake Truck, 1956, No. 925-6, white cab and flatbed section w/six blue removeable stake sections; 13-1/2" long
EX $125   **NM** $260   **MIP** $410

Farm Stake Truck, 1957, No. 04, white truck w/six removable blue stake panels, 13-1/2" long
EX $190   NM $375   MIP $480

Farm Stake Truck, 1958 Next Generation Cars, No. 04, "Tonka Farms" bull decal on sides, green truck w/white removeable stake panels
EX $100 NM $150 MIP $300

Farm Stake Truck, 1960, No. 04, turquoise truck w/six white removeable rack sections, whitewall tires, five-spoke silver hubs, plastic windshield, 14" long
EX $100   NM $200   MIP $325

Farm Stake Truck, 1961, No. 04, blue truck w/six white removeable rack sections, whitewall tires, five-spoke silver hubs, plastic windshield, 14" long
EX $85   NM $175   MIP $370

Farm Stake Truck, 1962, No. 404
EX $50   NM $95   MIP $150

Farm Stake Truck, 1963, No. 404
EX $60   NM $90   MIP $150

(KP Photo)

Farm Stake w/Two Horse Trailer, 1958 Next Generation Cars, No. 35, green farm stake truck w/white stakes, white two-horse trailer, two plastic horses; 21-3/4" long
EX $125   NM $250   MIP $450

Fisherman Pick-up, 1960, No. 110, blue and white two-tone body and topper. Opening tailgate, topper w/"Fisherman" decal, 14" long
EX $100   NM $175   MIP $375

Forklift with Container, 1970s, w/pallet and box; mid-1970s; 12-1/2" long
EX $10   NM $20   MIP $30

Gasoline Truck, 1957, No. 16, red tanker truck w/"Gasoline" decals, 15" long
EX $350   NM $525   MIP $1000

Gasoline Truck, 1958 Next Generation Cars, No. 33, hinged back door, "Gasoline" decals, hose and nozzle
EX $350   NM $500   MIP $900

Giant Dozer, 1961, No. 118, a king-sized version of the regular dozer, 12-1/2" long
EX $70   NM $100   MIP $250

Giant Dozer, 1962, No. 618
EX $100   NM $150   MIP $200

Giant Dozer, 1963, No. 536
EX $110   NM $160   MIP $225

Giant Dozer, 1964-65, No. 536, Army green; 12-3/8" long
EX $25   NM $50   MIP $75

Giant Dozer, 1965-67, No. 537, yellow; 12-3/8" long
EX $20   NM $40   MIP $60

Grader, 1955, No. 600-5, orange, blade adjustable, working steering; 17" long
EX $75   NM $125   MIP $200

Grader, 1965-66, No. 510, yellow, metal hubs; 17-1/8" long
EX $22   NM $43   MIP $65

Grader, 1967-70s, No. 510, yellow, lever steering, yellow plastic hubs, becomes No. 2510 in 1968; 17-1/2" long
EX $13   NM $26   MIP $40

Grading Service Truck, 1962, No. 834
EX $125   NM $250   MIP $350

Grading Service Truck, Trailer and Bulldozer, 1961, No. 134, includes yellow dump truck w/red dumper bed, yellow trailer and bulldozer w/3-position blade, 25-1/2" long total
EX $100   NM $150   MIP $350

Grain Hauler, 1955, No. 550-5, red cab w/silver steel box, decals; 23-1/2" long
EX $90   NM $135   MIP $280

Grain Hauler Semi, 1952, No. 550, 22-1/4" long
EX $125   NM $180   MIP $350

Green Giant Transport, 1956, No. 650-6, white tractor/trailer, refrigerated, "Green Giant" decals; 23-1/2" long
EX $155   NM $350   MIP $600

Green Giant Transport Semi, 1953, No. 650, White cab and trailer w/Green Giant logo decals; 22-1/4" long
EX $150   NM $300   MIP $500

(KP Photo)

Hi-Way Hydraulic Dump Truck, 1956, No. 980-6, orange w/yellow decals, 13" long
EX $130   NM $280   MIP $395

(KP Photo)

Hi-Way Patrol, 1965-70, No. 64, Jeep Wagoneer body, black w/white roof, red dome light, opening tailgate, "Hi-Way Patrol" decals on doors, 9-1/8" long, becomes No. 1964 in 1968
EX $20   NM $40   MIP $80

Hi-Way Service Truck, 1958 Next Generation Cars, No. 41, orange dump truck w/two-position tailgate, drop side bed, scraper blade and plastic road signs
EX $100   NM $200   MIP $400

Horse Van, 1965-67, No. 430, green truck w/horse-carrier body, two horses, ramp gate; 12-3/4" long
EX $17   NM $33   MIP $50

Horse Van, 1968-70, No. 2430, new cab w/slanted windshield, green, open-top horse compartment, two plastic horses; 13-1/4" long
EX $15   NM $30   MIP $45

Houseboat Set, 1961, No. 136, includes red and white "Fisherman" pickup w/red tilt-bed boat trailer and plastic (floating) houseboat, 29" long total
EX $200   NM $400   MIP $800

Hydraulic Aerial Ladder, 1958 Next Generation Cars, No. 48, bright red cab and trailer w/extending ladder to 36"
EX $125   NM $250   MIP $450

Hydraulic Aerial Ladder Truck, 1957, No. 48, red w/aluminum ladder, "TFD" decals, 32" long
EX $200   NM $300   MIP $500

Hydraulic Dump, 1962, No. 520
EX $75   NM $100   MIP $220

Hydraulic Dump, 1965-67, No. 520, blue w/white cab roof, "Hydraulic" decals on doors; 13-3/8" long
EX $25   NM $50   MIP $75

Hydraulic Dump, 1968-70s, No. 2520, becomes No. 2480 in 1969, blue, white roof, new cab w/slanting windshield; 13-7/8" long
EX $23   NM $46   MIP $70

Hydraulic Dump (tailgate), 1969, No. 2585, "glassed-in" cabover, orange cab and dumping body, hydraulic action, tailgate; 13-1/2" long
EX $30   NM $56   MIP $85

Hydraulic Dump (tailgate), 1970, No. 2585, "glassed-in" cabover, lime-green cab and dumping body, hydraulic action, tailgate; 1970 and later; 13-1/2" long
EX $32   NM $46   MIP $70

Hydraulic Dump Truck, 1957, No. 20, two-position tailgate, hydraulic cylinder controls dump bed; 13" long
EX n/a   NM n/a   MIP n/a

Hydraulic Dump Truck, 1958 Next Generation Cars, No. 20, dark gold body, workind dumper w/lever and hydraulic lifter, plastic windshield
EX $125   NM $175   MIP $275

Hydraulic Dump Truck, 1960, No. 20, dark gold body, working dumper w/lever and hydraulic lifter, two-position tailgate on dumper;
EX $75   NM $150   MIP $300

(KP Photo)

Hydraulic Dump Truck, 1961, No. 20, dark gold body, working dumper w/lever and hydraulic lifter, two-position tailgate on dumper; 13-1/2" long
EX $75   **NM** $110   **MIP** $250

Hydraulic Dump Truck, 1963, No. 520
EX $45   **NM** $68   **MIP** $90

(ToyShop File Photo)

Hydraulic Dump Truck, 1965, No. 520, Blue cab w/white roof, blue dumper bed, 13-3/8" long
EX $35   **NM** $60   **MIP** $82

Jeep & Horse Trailer, 1964, No. 525, 19-1/4" long total, two horses
EX $45   **NM** $68   **MIP** $135

Jeep Commander, 1964, No. 304, canvas top, 10-1/2" long
EX $30   **NM** $50   **MIP** $75

Jeep Commander, 1964-69, No. 304, Army green, "canvas" canopy top, becomes No. 2304 in 1968; 10-1/2 long
EX $7   **NM** $13   **MIP** $20

Jeep Dispatcher, 1962, No. 200, light blue w/white plastic interior, folding windshield, 9-3/4" long
EX $20   **NM** $40   **MIP** $60

Jeep Dispatcher, 1963, No. 200
EX $30   **NM** $50   **MIP** $75

Jeep Dispatcher, 1963-65, No. 200, turquoise; 9-3/4" long
EX $9   **NM** $19   **MIP** $28

Jeep Dispatcher, 1970, No. 2200, lime green; 9-3/4" long
EX $5   **NM** $10   **MIP** $15

Jeep Pumper, 1963, No. 425, 10-3/4" long
EX $100   **NM** $175   **MIP** $400

Jeep Pumper, 1963-65, No. 425, red, hose connector, removable ladder; 10-3/4" long
EX $67   **NM** $132   **MIP** $200

Jeep Pumper, 1964, No. 425, black steering wheel
EX $100   **NM** $150   **MIP** $275

Jeep Runabout, 1962-68, No. 516, blue Jeep Dispatcher w/boat trailer and red/white motorboat, becomes No. 2516 in 1968; 24-1/4" long
EX $17   **NM** $33   **MIP** $50

Jeep Runabout, 1963, No. 516, trailer and boat
EX $75   **NM** $150   **MIP** $300

(ToyShop File Photo)

Jeep Runabout, trailer, boat, 1962, No. 516, 25-5/8" long total. Jeep shown here, missing removeable canopy, and obviously, the boat and trailer
EX $75   **NM** $175   **MIP** $350

Jeep Surrey, 1963, No. 350
EX $50   **NM** $75   **MIP** $100

Jeep Surrey, fringe top, 1962, No. 350, 10-1/2" long
EX $42   **NM** $83   **MIP** $175

(KP Photo)

Jeep Universal, 1962, No. 249
EX $75   **NM** $125   **MIP** $175

Jeep Wrecker, 1964, No. 375, 11" long
EX $40   **NM** $85   **MIP** $125

Jeep Wrecker, 1965, No. 375, white, black boom; 11" long
EX $25   **NM** $50   **MIP** $75

Jeep Wrecker with Plow, 1965-69, No. 435, white jeep, flasher, black winch and snow plow, becomes No. 2435 in 1968; 12-3/8" long
EX $25   **NM** $50   **MIP** $75

Jeep Wrecker with Plow, 1970, No. 2435, blue w/orange plow and winch; 12-3/8" long
EX $20   **NM** $30   **MIP** $60

Jeepster Convertible Sedan, 1969-70s, No. 2245, red, removable top; 14" long
EX $12   **NM** $23   **MIP** $35

Jeepster Pickup, 1969-70, No. 2230, light green w/black roof; 13" long
EX $15   **NM** $30   **MIP** $45

Jeepster Runabout, 1969-70, No. 2460, yellow Jeepster and boat trailer w/red and white boat; 27-1/4" long
EX $17   **NM** $33   **MIP** $50

Jeepster Sport Convertible, 1969, No. 2240, blue, removable top; 13" long
EX $12   **NM** $23   **MIP** $35

(ToyShop File Photo)

Jeepster with Boat & Trailer, 1974, No. 2460, Blue jeep body w/white interior, blue trailer, blue and white plastic boat
EX $40   **NM** $75   **MIP** $92

Jet Delivery Truck, 1962, No. 410, 14" long; 1962 only
EX $200   **NM** $350   **MIP** $850

Jolly Green Giant Special, 1960-61, white w/green stake racks, "Green Giant Company" decal on doors, 14" long
EX $150   **NM** $300   **MIP** $450

Life Guard Jeep, 1968, No. 2306, orange, flasher, rescue raft on top; 9-3/4" long
EX $15   **NM** $30   **MIP** $45

Life Guard Jeep, 1969, No. 2306, red, yellow rescue raft on top; 9-3/4" long
EX $15   **NM** $30   **MIP** $45

Lift Truck and Trailer, 1948, No. 200
EX $200   **NM** $350   **MIP** $600

(KP Photo)

Livestock Hauler Semi, 1952, No. 500, 22-1/4" long
EX $100   **NM** $150   **MIP** $350

Livestock Van, 1955, No. 500-5, red, tractor/trailer has slits, 24" long
EX $110   **NM** $200   **MIP** $350

Livestock Van, 1957, No. 36, red cab and trailer w/slits, tailgate loading ramp; 24" long
EX n/a   **NM** n/a   **MIP** n/a

Livestock Van, 1958 Next Generation Cars, No. 36, red cab and trailer w/opening rear ramp and floating suspension
EX $175   **NM** $250   **MIP** $450

Loader, 1962, No. 402, yellow and green
EX $40   **NM** $60   **MIP** $80

Loader, 1963, No. 352
EX $40   **NM** $60   **MIP** $80

Loader, 1963-69, No. 352, yellow, rubber treads, lever-tripped dumping action, becomes No. 2352 in 1968; 11-3/4" long
EX $15   **NM** $30   **MIP** $45

Loader, 1970, No. 2352, lime green; 1970 and later; 11-3/4" long
EX $9   **NM** $19   **MIP** $28

Loading Tractor, 1949, No. 190, 10-1/2" long
EX n/a   **NM** n/a   **MIP** n/a

Logger, 1957, No. 14, red cab, aluminum frame, 9 round logs, chains; 23-3/4" long
EX n/a   **NM** n/a   **MIP** n/a

Logger [Tonka Logger], 1956, No. 575-6, red cab, logging trailer includes 9 sanded dowel logs. Silver five-hole hubs; 23-1/2" long
EX $130   **NM** $240   **MIP** $360

Logger Semi, 1953, No. 575, 22-1/4" long
EX $125   **NM** $180   **MIP** $350

Logger Semi, 1953, No. 575, wood flat bed
EX $125   **NM** $180   **MIP** $350

Lowboy and Bulldozer, 1960, No. 125, light green cab, trailer, and bulldozer. Solid rubber tires without hubs on rear of trailer. Bulldozer w/3-position blade, 26-1/4" long
EX $190   **NM** $375   **MIP** $675

Lowboy and Dozer, 1974, No. 2831, red tractor and lowboy w/orange dozer
EX $17   **NM** $33   **MIP** $50

Lumber Truck, 1955, No. 850-5, red cab, aluminum flatbed, six-wheel, square lumber pieces; 18-3/4" long
EX $175   **NM** $260   **MIP** $400

Lumber Truck, 1956, No. 850-6, red cab, aluminum flatbed, square lumber pieces;18-3/4" long
EX $130   **NM** $225   **MIP** $360

Lumber Truck, 1957, No. 22, bronze cab, aluminum flat bed, square lumber pieces; 18" long
EX n/a   **NM** n/a   **MIP** n/a

Mighty Tonka Dump Truck, 1964, No. 900, one of the most popular Tonka vehicles ever made; there were 9,655,000 sold between 1964 and 1983
EX $20   **NM** $40   **MIP** $60

Military Jeep & Box Trailer, 1964, No. 384, 19-3/8" overall
EX $50   **NM** $75   **MIP** $150

Military Jeep Universal, 1963, No. 251, 10-1/2" long
EX $25   **NM** $38   **MIP** $50

Military Jeep Universal, 1963-65, No. 251, Army green, no canopy; 10-1/2" long
EX $8   **NM** $16   **MIP** $24

Military Jeep Universal, 1964, No. 251
EX $35   **NM** $55   **MIP** $75

Military Tractor, 1964, No. 250, black seat
EX $55   **NM** $70   **MIP** $100

(KP Photo)

Minute Maid Van, 1955, No. 725-5, white truck w/Minute Maid Orange Juice graphics and opening rear doors; 14-1/2" long
EX $275   **NM** $650   **MIP** $950

Mobile Clam, 1961, No. 142, orange cab, flatbed section and crane cab. Floating rear wheels, operating "clam" style bucket (still in use on later "Mighty Tonka" models), that tripped open when pulled to top of crane boom, 27-1/4" long
EX $100   **NM** $250   **MIP** $450

Mobile Clam, 1962, No. 942
EX $100   **NM** $150   **MIP** $320

Mobile Clam, 1963, No. 942
EX $75   **NM** $112   **MIP** $150

Mobile Clam, 1964, No. 942, yellow
EX $50   **NM** $75   **MIP** $100

Mobile Dragline, 1960, No. 135, orange cab, flatbed section and crane cab w/black boom and bucket. Bucket operates w/cords and levers, and swivels on base attached to truck
EX $100   **NM** $250   **MIP** $450

Motor Boat, 1960s, plastic, sold separately and w/boat carriers and trailers; 13" long
EX $5   **NM** $10   **MIP** $15

Nationwide Moving Van, 1958 Next Generation Cars, No. 39, long white cab and trailer w/full-width doors; 24-1/4" long
EX $250   **NM** $475   **MIP** $800

No. 0250 Tractor, 1963, No. 250, yellow w/red seat
EX $75   **NM** $112   **MIP** $150

Parcel Delivery Truck, 1957, No. 10, bronze, Divco-style delivery van, "Parcel Delivery" decals; 12" long
EX $200   **NM** $350   **MIP** $500

Parcel Delivery Van, 1954, No. 750, 11-3/4" long
EX $200   **NM** $300   **MIP** $500

(ToyShop File Photo)

Pickup, 1962, No. 302, red body w/silver hubs, white cab roof, opening tailgate
EX $95   **NM** $150   **MIP** $250

Pickup, 1963, No. 302
EX $35   **NM** $52   **MIP** $70

(KP Photo)

Pickup, 1967, No. 302, all red body, opening tailgate, five-spoke silver hubcaps, 12-3/4" long
EX $35   **NM** $55   **MIP** $76

Pickup & Trailer, 1962, No. 528
EX $50   **NM** $75   **MIP** $150

(KP Photo)

Pickup and Horse Trailer, 1965, No. 82, Blue Jeep Gladiator truck w/white horse trailer w/clear plastic dome roof. Includes two plastic horses. 14-3/4" long
EX $30   **NM** $55   **MIP** $110

(ToyShop File Photo)

Pickup and Trailer, 1960, No. 28, bronze pickup towing stakeside trailer w/white plastic steer in back. End panel in trailer lifts out
EX $100   **NM** $150   **MIP** $300

Pickup Truck, 1955, No. 880-5, red pickup; 12-3/4" long
EX $125   **NM** $280   **MIP** $450

(KP Photo)

Pickup Truck, 1956, No. 880-6, dark blue body, opening tailgate w/securing chain; 13-3/4" long
EX $150   **NM** $350   **MIP** $650

Pickup Truck, 1957, No. 02, dark blue, opening tailgate w/chains; 12-1/2" long
EX n/a   **NM** n/a   **MIP** n/a

Pickup Truck, 1958 Next Generation Cars, No. 02, dark blue body, opening tailgate, trailer hitch, plastic windshield; 12-3/4" long
EX $100   **NM** $240   **MIP** $300

(ToyShop File Photo)

Pickup Truck, 1960, No. 02, bronze body, whitewall tires, solid silver hubs, opening tailgate, trailer hitch, plastic windshield
EX $100   **NM** $200   **MIP** $375

Pickup Truck, 1961, No. 02, bronze body, whitewall tires, solid silver hubs, opening tailgate, plastic windshield; 12-3/4" long
EX $100   **NM** $190   **MIP** $320

Pickup Truck, 1962-66, 12-3/4" long; No. 302, stepside, red body, white cab roof
EX $20   **NM** $40   **MIP** $60

Pickup Truck, 1967, 12-3/4" long; No. 302, all red
EX $20   **NM** $40   **MIP** $60

Pickup Truck, 1968-69, 13-1/2" long; No. 2302, all red, stepside w/rounded rear fenders, spoked metal hubs, new cab w/slanted windshield
EX $17   **NM** $33   **MIP** $50

Pickup w/Box Trailer, 1957, No. 26, dark blue No. 02 pickup, dark blue No. AC-310 box trailer; 20-1/2" long
EX n/a   **NM** n/a   **MIP** n/a

Pickup with Stake Trailer and Animal, 1957, No. 28, blue No. 02 Pickup and red No. AC-312 stake trailer, plastic animal; 20-1/2" long
EX $150   **NM** $250   **MIP** $400

Pickup with Stake Trailer and Animal, 1958 Next Generation Cars, No. 28, dark blue pickup, red stake trailer, plastic livestock animal, stake tailgate on trailer lifts out
EX $125   **NM** $175   **MIP** $350

Police Jeep, 1965, 10-1/2" long; No. 325, white Jeep, black and white canopy, flasher on hood, originally called Jeep Police Car
EX $28   **NM** $56   **MIP** $85

Police Jeep, 1966, 10-1/2" long; No. 325, white Jeep, all black canopy, flasher on hood
EX $28   **NM** $56   **MIP** $85

Power Boom Loader, 1960, No. 115, 1960 only, blue flatbed truck w/working clamp and winch to pick up logs, pipe, etc. Whitewall tires, plastic windshield, 18-1/2" long
EX $300   **NM** $650   **MIP** $1000

Pumper, 1963, No. 926
EX $60   **NM** $90   **MIP** $120

Pumper, 1965-68, 15-1/2" long; No. 926, "glassed-in" cabover, red, hydrant, becomes No. 2926 in 1968
EX $23   **NM** $46   **MIP** $70

Pumper, 1969-70s, 17-1/8" long; No. 2820, long LaFrance-style cab, hydrant, shoots water stream
EX $15   **NM** $30   **MIP** $45

Pumper Truck, 1962, No. 926
EX $100   **NM** $150   **MIP** $300

Ramp Hoist, 1963, No. 640, 19-1/4" long, red and white
EX $175   **NM** $350   **MIP** $550

Ramp Hoist, 1964, No. 640, park green and white, very rare
EX $300   **NM** $650   **MIP** $900

Ranchero, 1960s, 8" long; plastic, sold separately and w/car carriers
EX $5   **NM** $10   **MIP** $15

Rescue Squad, 1960, No. 105, white truck body w/square box bed. Silver siren on driver's side of hood, red dome light, Civil Defence "CD" decals on doors, "Rescue Squad" w/red cross decals on back, red plastic boat attached w/rubber straps on top, removeable ladder, 13-3/4" long
EX $100   **NM** $250   **MIP** $450

Rescue Squad Truck, 1956, Included with Tonka Fire Department Set, 11-3/4" long
EX $120   **NM** $260   **MIP** $400

Rescue Squad Truck, 1957, No. 24, white Divco-style van, "Rescue Squad" decals, sliding side door, opening rear doors; 12" long
EX n/a   **NM** n/a   **MIP** n/a

Rescue Van, 1955, Tonka
EX $200   **NM** $450   **MIP** $800

Road Builder Set, 1954, No. 775, Road Grader, Semi T&T Crane and Dump Truck, five pieces
EX $350   **NM** $525   **MIP** $900

Road Grader, 1953, No. 600, 17" long
EX $50   **NM** $75   **MIP** $100

Road Grader, 1956, No. 600-6, orange, steerable front wheels, tilting and rotating blade, floating rear wheels; 17" long
EX $75   **NM** $125   **MIP** $200

(KP Photo)

Road Grader, 1958 Next Generation Cars, No. 12, orange body w/rotating and tilting blade, working steering, floating rear wheels
EX $75   **NM** $112   **MIP** $150

Road Grader, 1961, No. 12, yellow cab and body w/steerable front wheels, tilting and rotating scraper blade, and floating rear wheels, 17" long
EX $75   **NM** $100   **MIP** $200

Road Grader, 1962, No. 512
EX $45   **NM** $68   **MIP** $90

Road Grader, 1963, No. 512, red clearance lights
EX $80   **NM** $120   **MIP** $160

Road Grader [All-Weather], 1957, No. 12, orange, yellow Hi-Way decals; 13" long
EX n/a   **NM** n/a   **MIP** n/a

Sanitary Service, 1967-70s, 16" long; No. 690, "glassed-in" cabover, blue cab, white garbage dump body, becomes No. 2690 in 1968
EX $23   **NM** $46   **MIP** $70

Sanitary Truck, 1959, square back
EX $450   **NM** $700   **MIP** $1000

(KP Photo)

Sanitary Truck, 1960, No. 140, hydraulic
EX $350   **NM** $550   **MIP** $900

(Patrick O'Neil)

Sanitary Truck, 1961, No. 140, white cab and rounded garbage section. Swinging rear door, hopper bucket raises up to drop garbage in truck, 19-1/2" long
EX $400   **NM** $700   **MIP** $1500

Scraper Blade, 1957, No. AC-306, orange Hi-Way blade w/mounting bracket; 7" wide
EX n/a   **NM** n/a   **MIP** n/a

Serv-I-Car, 1962, No. 201, 3-wheeled cart w/small dump bed, white, 9-1/8" long
EX $75   **NM** $125   **MIP** $200

(KP Photo)

Service Truck, 1959-60, No. 01, blue body, square box bed w/"Tonka Service" decals, whitewall tires, solid silver hubs, removable aluminum ladder, plastic windshield; 12-3/4" long
EX $100   **NM** $150   **MIP** $350

Servi-I-Car, 1963, No. 201
EX $55   **NM** $82   **MIP** $110

Shovel, 1957, No. 08, orange, rubber treads; 15" long
EX n/a   **NM** n/a   **MIP** n/a

Shovel, 1965-68, 20" long, 15" high; No. 526, yellow, lever-scoop w/handgrip, becomes No. 2536 in 1968
EX $25   **NM** $50   **MIP** $75

Shovel, 1970, 24-1/2" long, No. 2720, yellow swivel body, six tires; 1970 and later
EX $15   **NM** $30   **MIP** $45

Shovel and Carry-All (Loboy), 1955, No. 120-5, red tractor, blue loboy, red shovel w/rubber treads; 33" long
EX $150   **NM** $300   **MIP** $450

Shovel and Carry-All (Loboy), 1956, No. 120-6, red cab, blue loboy, red shovel w/rubber treads; 33" long
EX $188   **NM** $280   **MIP** $475

Shovel and Carry-All Trailer, 1957, No. 40, orange cab and loboy, orange shovel, yellow decals; 32" long
EX n/a   **NM** n/a   **MIP** n/a

Shovel and Carry-All Trailer, 1958 Next Generation Cars, No. 43, orange cab and loboy trailer, orange steam shovel w/black rubber treads
EX $200   **NM** $300   **MIP** $500

Snorkel Pumper, 1969-70s, 17-1/8" long; No. 2950, hand-operated aerial platform rising to 28", hydrant, 14" hose, long LaFrance-type cab
EX $12   **NM** $27   **MIP** $35

Sportsman, 1958 Next Generation Cars, No. 05, dark blue body, box camper top, opening tailgate, trailer hitch; 12-3/4" long
EX $150   **NM** $225   **MIP** $450

(KP Photo)

Sportsman, 1959, No. 05, tan body, box camper top, whitewall tires, solid silver hubs, white plastic boat attaches to topper w/rubber straps
EX $100   **NM** $175   **MIP** $350

Sportsman, 1960-61, No. 05, tan box pickup w/white boat strapped to top, silver disk wheels, whitewall tires; 12-3/4" long
EX $100   **NM** $275   **MIP** $400

Sportsman, 1962, No. 405
EX $75   **NM** $100   **MIP** $200

Sportsman w/Box Trailer, 1958 Next Generation Cars, No. 29, dark blue Sportsman, dark blue trailer w/opening tailgate
EX $150   **NM** $225   **MIP** $400

Stake Jumper, 1971, 13" long; No. 2447, lime green Jeepster w/oversized tires; 1971 and later
EX $12   **NM** $25   **MIP** $35

Stake Pickup, 1962, No. 308, 12-5/8" long
EX $40   **NM** $80   **MIP** $120

Stake Pickup, 1963, No. 308
EX $50   **NM** $95   **MIP** $150

Stake Pickup, 1964-65, 12-3/4" long, No. 308, light blue, white roof
EX $25   **NM** $50   **MIP** $75

Stake Pickup & Horse Trailer, 1963, No. 625, 21-3/4" long overall
EX $75   **NM** $125   **MIP** $175

Stake Pickup & Trailer, 1964, No. 504, 21-5/8" long
EX $50   **NM** $75   **MIP** $185

Stake Pickup and Trailer, 1965-66, 21-5/8" long; No. 504, Stake pickup w/stake trailer, light blue, white cab roof, animals
EX $32   **NM** $63   **MIP** $95

Stake Trailer, 1957, No. AC-312, red stake trailer, sold as accessory, originally retailed for $1.98; 5-1/2" long
EX $15   **NM** $30   **MIP** $45

Stake Truck, 1955, No. 860-5, red truck w/8 green stakes, six-wheel; 16-1/2" long
EX $175   **NM** $360   **MIP** $500

Stake Truck, 1956, No. 991, red w/8 removeable stake sides, 13" long
EX $150   **NM** $250   **MIP** $460

Stake Truck, 1964, No. 404, red
EX $70   **NM** $120   **MIP** $170

Standard Oil Company Wrecker Special, 1960, Tonka
EX $200   **NM** $400   **MIP** $600

Star Kist Van, 1954, No. 725, 14-1/2" long
EX $250   **NM** $575   **MIP** $950

Steam Shovel, 1947, No. 100, 20-3/4" long
EX $135   **NM** $200   **MIP** $350

Stearn Shovel Deluxe, 1949, No. 100, 22" long
EX $100   **NM** $250   **MIP** $400

Steel Carrier Semi, 1950, No. 145, 22" long
EX $125   **NM** $200   **MIP** $350

(KP Photo)

Steel Carrier Truck, 1954, No. 145, orange cab, green open box trailer, yellow "Steel Carrier" decals
EX $100   **NM** $185   **MIP** $380

Sting Ray, 1960s, 6-1/2" long; plastic, sold separately and w/car carriers
EX $4   **NM** $8   **MIP** $12

Stock Farm, 1957, No. B-202, No. 32 Stock Rack truck, 6 farm animals, wooden corral
EX n/a   **NM** n/a   **MIP** n/a

Stock Rack Truck, 1958 Next Generation Cars, No. 32, white cab and chassis, tall, removeable red stake sections
EX $100   **NM** $225   **MIP** $300

Stock Rack Truck with Animals, 1957, No. 32, blue truck w/red stock rack, 3 plastic animals; 16-1/4" long
EX $175   **NM** $365   **MIP** $650

Stump Jumper, 1970s, 13" long; No. 2447, red, "Stump Jumper" sticker; green in 1972, purple in 1973
EX $10   **NM** $20   **MIP** $30

Styleside Pickup, 1967, 14-1/8" long; No. 360, brown, white cab roof
EX $17   **NM** $33   **MIP** $50

Styleside Pickup, 1968, 14-9/16" long; No. 2360, maroon w/white cab roof, new cab w/slanted windshield
EX $13   **NM** $26   **MIP** $40

Styleside Pickup, 1969-70, 14-9/16" long; No. 2360, purple w/white cab roof
EX $13   **NM** $26   **MIP** $40

Styleside Pickup, 1971, 14-9/16" long; No. 2360, orange, white black cab roof; 1971 and later
EX $9   **NM** $18   **MIP** $26

Style-Side Pickup, 1963, No. 354, 14" long
EX $40   **NM** $60   **MIP** $125

Style-Side Pickup & Stake Trailer, 1963, No. 522, 22-3/4" long total
EX $75   **NM** $125   **MIP** $250

(Mark McManus)

Suburban Pumper, 1956, No. 950-6, includes toy hydrant that attaches to garden hose, two 6" black hoses, removeable ladder; 17" long
EX $120   **NM** $230   **MIP** $350

Suburban Pumper, 1957, No. 46, red pumper, hydrant attaches to garden hose, two black hoses, one 36" hose, ladder; 17" long
EX n/a   **NM** n/a   **MIP** n/a

(Harvey K Rainess)

Suburban Pumper, 1958 Next Generation Cars, No. 46, red truck w/hydrant that connects to garden hose, black hoses, whitewall tires
EX $175   **NM** $225   **MIP** $450

(Harvey K Rainess)

Suburban Pumper, 1960, No. 46, red, hydrant connects to garden hose, black hoses, whitewall tires
EX $100   NM $250   MIP $350

Tandem No. 36 Tandem Air Express, 1959, w/trailer, 24" long
EX $325   NM $650   MIP $1000

Tandem No. 40 Car Carrier, 1959, Tonka
EX $100   NM $300   MIP $500

Tandem No. 41 Boat Transport, 1959, 38" long
EX $250   NM $350   MIP $700

Tandem No. 42 Hydraulic Land Rover, 1959, 15" long
EX $550   NM $825   MIP $1700

Tandem Platform Stake, 1959, No. 30, bronze, whitewall tires on truck and trailer, 28-1/4" long
EX $240   NM $450   MIP $800

Tanker, 1960, No. 145, first Tonka w/major use of plastic, 28" long
EX $100   NM $250   MIP $450

(Harvey K Rainess)

Tanker, 1961, No. 145, red w/"Texaco" decals, dual rear wheels, 28" long
EX $100   NM $250   MIP $350

Terminal Train, 1963, No. 720, 33-5/8" long, total, fifteen suitcases
EX $105   NM $175   MIP $300

Thunderbird Express, 1957, No. 34, white semi tractor/trailer w/Thunderbird decal; 24" long
EX $150   NM $400   MIP $600

Thunderbird Express, 1958 Next Generation Cars, No. 37, white cab and freight trailer w/fold-down wheels and opening rear doors
EX $150   NM $300   MIP $600

Thunderbird Express, 1960, No. 37, red cab w/white roof, red trailer w/white stripe and "Thunderbird" decal. Floating tandem dual wheels on trailer
EX $150   NM $350   MIP $550

Timber (Logger) Truck, 1960, No. 08, red cab, aluminum bed, includes square and round sanded "logs"
EX $150   NM $225   MIP $300

Tonka "Cargo King", 1956, No. 550-6, red cab, open-top silver trailer, opening rear door; 23-1/2" long
EX $145   NM $230   MIP $355

(KP Photo)

Tonka Toy Transport Van, 1949, No. 140, 22-1/4" long
EX $150   NM $300   MIP $500

Tractor, 1962, No. 250, 8-5/8" long
EX $50   NM $75   MIP $100

Tractor and Carry-All Trailer, 1949, No. 170, w/No. 150 Crane and Clam
EX $200   NM $300   MIP $525

Tractor and Carry-All Trailer, 1949, No. 125, w/No. 100 Steam Shovel
EX $150   NM $250   MIP $550

Tractor and Carry-All Trailer, 1949, No. 120, w/No. 50 Steam Shovel
EX $155   NM $280   MIP $475

Tractor and Wagon, 1973, 21" No. 2710, green tractor, four-wheel wagon, yellow hubs
EX $8   NM $16   MIP $24

Tractor with Trencher, 1975, No. 2525, farm tractor w/scoop and backhoe; 21" long
EX $5   NM $17   MIP $25

Tractor-Carry-All Trailer, 1949, No. 130, 30-1/2" long
EX $100   NM $150   MIP $350

Trailer, 1955, No. 65, stake side
EX $30   NM $45   MIP $60

Trailer Fleet Set, 1953, No. 675, two tractors (five interchangeable trailers), per set
EX $450   NM $680   MIP $975

(KP Photo)

Trencher, 1963, No. 534, 18-1/4" long
EX $40   NM $75   MIP $150

Trencher, 1963-70s, No. 534, yellow, rubber tread, lever-operated front bucket, pivoting hoe, becomes No. 2534 in 1968; 18-1/4" long
EX $9   NM $18   MIP $26

Trencher & LoBoy, 1963, No. 1001, 28-1/2" long total
EX $75   NM $112   MIP $150

Troop Carrier, 1964, No. 380, 14" long
EX $70   NM $100   MIP $150

Troop Carrier, 1965, 14" long; No. 380, Army green Styleside pickup w/"canvas" cover
EX $18   NM $36   MIP $55

Utility Dump, 1961, No. 301, revised Golf Club Tractor; 1961 only, 12-1/2" long
EX $100   NM $150   MIP $300

Utility Hauler, 1950, No. 175, 12" long
EX $100   NM $150   MIP $300

Utility Truck, 1954, No. 175, orange cab w/green utility (slit) bed
EX $110   NM $275   MIP $425

Utility Truck, 1958 Next Generation Cars, No. 03, red cab, aluminum flatbed
EX $100   NM $150   MIP $300

Volkswagen, 1965-75, 8-5/8" long; No. 150 yellow, No 152 blue, No. 153 green, No 156 red, VW "beetle"
EX $8   NM $16   MIP $24

Volkswagen, 1967, 8-5/8" long; No. 150 black, No. 152 blue, No. 154 green, and No. 156 maroon
EX $8   NM $16   MIP $24

Volkswagen, 1969, No. 1158, 8-5/8" long; various colors, reclassified by Tonka Corp. in 1970, see Mini-Tonka listing
EX $8   NM $16   MIP $24

Wrecker, 1949, No. 250, 12-1/2" long
EX $125   NM $250   MIP $375

Wrecker, 1953, blue w/red boom, chain, hook
EX $125   NM $200   MIP $350

Wrecker, 1954, red cab, white bed, red boom, chain and hook
EX $100   NM $300   MIP $500

Wrecker, 1956, No. 960-6, white body, silver five-hole hubs, red dome light, "AAA" decal on sides, working winch, rare; 12" long
EX $390   NM $525   MIP $800

Wrecker, 1956, No. 996, white body, silver five-hole hubs, red dome light, "MM" decal on sides, working winch; 12" long
EX $100   NM $300   MIP $500

Wrecker, 1957, No. 18, white w/black boom, "AA" decals; 12-1/2" long
EX $100   NM $200   MIP $300

Wrecker, 1958-61, No. 18, white, "AA" decals, black boom w/chain and hook, red dome light, whitewall tires, plastic windshield; 13-1/4" long
EX $100   NM $250   MIP $400

Wrecker, 1962, No. 518, black boom
EX $50   NM $120   MIP $150

Wrecker, 1962-67, 14-1/4" long; No. 518, white, red boom, flasher light
EX $42   NM $83   MIP $125

(KP Photo)

Wrecker, 1963-64, No. 518, red boom
EX $45   NM $85   MIP $150

Wrecker, 1968-70, 14-5/8" long; No. 2518, white, new cab w/slanted windshield, "24 Hr. Service"
EX $30   NM $59   MIP $90

Wrecker, 1970s, 14" long; 4x4 "24 Hr. Towing" truck, green, oversize tires; 1970s or 1980s
EX $12   NM $23   MIP $35

Wrecker, 1971, 14-5/8" long; No. 2518, orange w/white winch, new cab w/slanted windshield; 1971 and later
EX $27   NM $55   MIP $80

TINY-TONKA TOYS

Aerial Ladder (fire truck, tractor-trailer), 1968-70s, ladder raises, swivels, also removable ladders, Model No. 675
EX $12   NM $23   MIP $35

Ambulance, 1970s, white van, "Ambulance," Fire Department set
EX $5   NM $9   MIP $14

Banana Wheeler, 1973, yellow hot rod, oversize tires, Model No. 788
EX $3   NM $7   MIP $10

Bottom Dump (tractor-trailer), 1969-70s, dumps, spreads;, Model No. 655
EX $5   NM $9   MIP $14

Car Carrier (tractor-trailer), 1968-70s, steel body, plastic cars, Model No. 635
EX $7   NM $15   MIP $22

Carnation Milk Tanker, 1970s, six-wheel tanker, red w/silver tank, "Milk is a Natural"
EX $7   NM $13   MIP $20

Cement Mixer, 1968-70s, yellow w/red rotating and tilting drum, Model No. 575
EX $4   NM $8   MIP $12

Dozer, 1969-70s, yellow, black treads, blade raises, Model No. 495
EX $3   NM $5   MIP $8

Draggin' Wagon, 1970-71, "Crazy A's" hot rod, purple convertible sedan, Model No. 452
EX $5   NM $10   MIP $15

Dump, 1968-70s, red cab, yellow dump box raises, Model No. 535
EX $5   NM $10   MIP $15

Dump Stake, 1969-70, blue cab, white stake box raises, Model No. 527
EX $3   NM $7   MIP $10

Dump Stake, 1971, blue cab, yellow stake box, Model No. 527
EX $3   NM $7   MIP $10

Fire Chief, 1970s, red van w/window sides, Fire Department set
EX $4   NM $8   MIP $12

Frantic Flivver, 1970, "Crazy A's" hot rod, black body w/orange-red running boards/fenders, Model No. 458
EX $5   NM $10   MIP $15

Fun-Buggy, 1969, orange dune buggy, roll bar, Model No. 500
EX $3   NM $5   MIP $8

Fun-Buggy, 1969, purple dune buggy, removable white top, Model No. 503
EX $3   NM $5   MIP $8

Fun-Buggy, 1970, orange dune buggy, removable white top; 1970 and later, Model No. 500
EX $2   NM $4   MIP $7

Fun-Buggy, 1973, yellow w/white top, Model No. 503
EX $2   NM $4   MIP $7

Hot Trike, 1972, red and blue three-wheeler, Model No. 750
EX $2   NM $4   MIP $6

Lemon Wheeler, 1970s, yellow hot rod, oversize tires
EX $3   NM $7   MIP $10

Loader, 1969, rubber treads, lever-operated scoop, yellow, Model No. 521
EX $3   NM $6   MIP $9

Loader, 1970, rubber treads, lever-operated scoop, lime green; 1970 and later, Model No. 521
EX $3   NM $5   MIP $8

Lowboy and Dozer (tractor-trailer), 1969-70s, hauls Tiny-Tonka Dozer, Model No. 695
EX $4   NM $8   MIP $12

Minnie Winnie, 1973, pickup w/white Winnebago camper body, Model No. 800
EX $5   NM $10   MIP $15

Mod Rod, 1970-71, "Crazy A's" hot rod, yellow convertible coupe, Model No. 450
EX $3   NM $7   MIP $10

Pickup, 1968-70, red w/white interior, Model No. 515
EX $9   NM $18   MIP $26

Pickup, 1971, orange, Model No. 515
EX $4   NM $8   MIP $12

Pumper, 1968-70s, red fire truck, removable white ladders, Model No. 595
EX $7   NM $13   MIP $20

Rat-a-Tat-Tat, 1971, black hot rod sedan, Model No. 434
EX $4   NM $8   MIP $12

Rumble Bee, 1971, hot rod coupe w/rumble seat, Model No. 436
EX $4   NM $8   MIP $12

Sand Piper, 1972, green and yellow three-wheeler, Model No. 755
EX $2   NM $4   MIP $6

Sand Roamer, 1972, pink dune buggy w/white canopy, oversize tires, Model No. 765
EX $2   NM $4   MIP $7

Sanitary Service (garbage truck), 1968-70s, blue cab, white body, Model No. 615
EX $5   NM $10   MIP $15

School Bus, 1970, yellow van, "Tonka School District;" 1970 and later, Model No. 580
EX $4   NM $8   MIP $12

Scorcher, 1970-71, "Crazy A's" hot rod pickup, Model No. 454
EX $3   NM $7   MIP $10

Shell Oil Truck, 1970s, yellow, "Shell" on tanker body
EX $3   NM $6   MIP $9

Smart Cart, 1971, blue hot rod coupe, orange fenders, Model No. 432
EX $3   NM $7   MIP $10

Snap Dragon (van), 1970, green, "Snap Dragon" decal; early 1970 and later, Model No. 585
EX $5   NM $11   MIP $16

Station Wagon, 1969, blue van w/window sides, Model No. 529
EX $5   NM $10   MIP $15

Stinger, 1970, "Crazy A's" hot rod, green convertible sedan, Model No. 456
EX $3   NM $7   MIP $10

Sun Buggy, 1972, blue dune buggy w/over-sized tires, Model No. 760
EX $2   NM $4   MIP $7

Taxi, 1971, orange hot rod sedan, Model No. 438
EX $3   NM $7   MIP $10

Van, 1969, "Tiny Van," orange, Model No. 531
EX $5   NM $11   MIP $16

Wrecker, 1969-70s, blue w/red lever-operated winch, Model No. 555
EX $5   NM $10   MIP $15

YKK Zipper Van (tractor-trailer), 1960s, white, van trailer w/"YKK World's Largest Zipper Manufacturer."
EX $25   NM $50   MIP $75

TONKA-TOTES

Beach Buzzer, 1971, 2-1/4" long; No. 169, pink hot rod
EX $2   NM $3   MIP $5

Bug Blaster, 1970, 2-1/2" long; No. 175, VW; 1970 and later
EX $2   NM $3   MIP $5

Construction Helmet, 1970s, No. 4999, early 1970s
EX $3   NM $6   MIP $9

Double Deuce, 1970, 3" long; No. 181, hot rod; 1970 and later
EX $2   NM $3   MIP $5

Dune Duster, 1970, 2-13/16" long; No. 179, rear-engine buggy; 1970 and later
EX $2   NM $3   MIP $5

Gremlin, 1972, No. 160, green
EX $2   NM $3   MIP $5

Hemi-Hauler, 1970, No. 110, 3-1/4" long; yellow, rear-engine; 1970 and later
EX $2   NM $3   MIP $5

Launcher and Turn-Around Ramp, 1970
EX $2   NM $3   MIP $5

Pocket Rocket Launcher, 1971, 5-1/4" long
EX $2   NM $3   MIP $5

Quicker-Mixer, 1970, 3-1/8" long; No. 114, cement mixer, six-wheel; 1970 and later
EX $2   NM $3   MIP $5

Racing Helmet, 1970s, No. 4950, early 1970s
EX $2   NM $3   MIP $5

Salt Flat Racer, 1972, No. 162, racer w/streamlined fenders
EX $2   NM $3   MIP $5

Scream'n Demon, 1970, No. 117, race car; 1970 and later
EX $2   NM $3   MIP $5

Strip Whip, 1971, 3-1/4" long; No. 165, thin-bodied racer; 1971 and later
EX $2   NM $3   MIP $5

Super Snoot, 1971, 2-3/4" long; No. 167, wedge-bodied; 1971 and later
EX $2   NM $3   MIP $5

Thumper Dumper, 1970, 3-1/16" long; No. 112, dump truck, six-wheel; 1970 and later
EX $2   NM $3   MIP $5

Tonka-Bronc, 1971, 2-7/8" long; No. 171, hot rod, blue
EX $2   NM $3   MIP $5

Wicked Wrecker, 1970, 3-9/16" long; No. 116, wreck truck, six-wheel; 1970 and later
EX $2   NM $3   MIP $5

TOOTSIETOY

AIRPLANES

Aero-Dawn, Tootsietoy, 1928, Model No. 4660
EX $30   NM $60   MIP $80

Atlantic Clipper, Tootsietoy, 2" long
EX $5   NM $10   MIP $20

Autogyro, Tootsietoy, white, 1934, Model No. 4659
EX $25   NM $40   MIP $90

Beechcraft Bonanza, Tootsietoy, orange, front propeller
EX $15   NM $25   MIP $35

Bi-Wing Seaplane, Tootsietoy, 1926, yellow, Model No. 4650
EX $30   NM $40   MIP $85

Bleriot Plane, Tootsietoy, 1910, Model No. 4482
EX $25   NM $50   MIP $100

Crusader, Tootsietoy, Model No. 719
EX $25   NM $50   MIP $75

Curtis P-40, Tootsietoy, light green, Model No. 721
EX $120   NM $250   MIP $525

Dirigible U.S.N. Los Angeles, Tootsietoy, silver, Model No. 1030
EX $40   NM $60   MIP $90

Douglas D-C 2 TWA, Tootsietoy, 1935, Model No. 717
EX $20   NM $45   MIP $85

F-94 Starfire, Tootsietoy, green, four engines; 1970s
EX $10   NM $15   MIP $35

Fly-N-Gyro, Tootsietoy, 1938
EX $50   NM $100   MIP $310

Helicopter, Tootsietoy, Die-cast and plastic, three blades 6" long; 1970s
EX $6   NM $9   MIP $12

KOP-1 USN, Tootsietoy
EX $20   NM $30   MIP $60

Low Wing Plane, Tootsietoy, miniature Piper Cub, Model No. 106
EX $20   NM $30   MIP $50

Navion, Tootsietoy, red, front propellor
EX $10   NM $15   MIP $35

Navy Jet, Tootsietoy, red; 1970s
EX $5   NM $10   MIP $30

Navy Jet Cutlass, Tootsietoy, red w/silver wings
EX $10   NM $15   MIP $30

Northrop F5A, Tootsietoy, U.S. fighter Jet; 1970s
EX $2   NM $4   MIP $5

P-38 Fighter Plane, Tootsietoy, 9-3/4" wingspan; 1950
EX $40   NM $60   MIP $110

P80 Panther Shooting Star, Tootsietoy
EX $25   NM $35   MIP $70

Piper Cub, Tootsietoy, blue, front propellor
EX $10   NM $15   MIP $30

S-58 Sikorsky Helicopter, Tootsietoy, 1970s
EX $15   NM $30   MIP $50

Snow Skids Airplane, Tootsietoy, rotating prop, 4" wingspan
EX $40   NM $60   MIP $85

Stratocruiser, Tootsietoy
EX $30   NM $50   MIP $110

Supermainliner, Tootsietoy
EX $20   NM $30   MIP $50

Top Wing Plane, Tootsietoy, miniature, Model No. 107
EX $20   NM $30   MIP $50

Transport Plane, Tootsietoy, 1941, orange, Model No. 722
EX $40   NM $75   MIP $110

Tri-Motor Plane, Tootsietoy, three propellors, Model No. 04649
EX $30   NM $85   MIP $150

TWA Electra, Tootsietoy, two engines, propellors, Model No. 125
EX $10   NM $20   MIP $45

Twin Engine Airliner, Tootsietoy, 10 windows, DC4
EX $20   NM $40   MIP $50

U.S. Army Plane, Tootsietoy, 1936, Model No. 119
EX $15   NM $25   MIP $50

UX214 Monoplane, Tootsietoy, 4", 1930s
EX $30   NM $60   MIP $90

Waco Bomber, Tootsietoy, blue base/silver top or silver base, Model No. 718
EX $50   NM $80   MIP $150

BOATS AND SHIPS

Battleship, Tootsietoy, silver w/some red on top, 6" long, 1939, Model No. 1034
EX $10   NM $20   MIP $35

Carrier, Tootsietoy, silver, Model No. 1036
EX $15   NM $25   MIP $40

Cruiser, Tootsietoy, silver; some red on top, 6" long, 1939, Model No. 1035
EX $10   NM $15   MIP $25

Destroyer, Tootsietoy, 4" long, 1939, Model No. 127
EX $10   NM $20   MIP $40

Freighter, Tootsietoy, 6" long; 1940, Model No. 1038
EX $10   NM $20   MIP $45

Submarine, Tootsietoy, 4" long, 1939, Model No. 128
EX $10   NM $15   MIP $30

Tanker, Tootsietoy, black, 6" long; 1940, Model No. 1039
EX $10   NM $20   MIP $25

Tender, Tootsietoy, 4" long; 1940, Model No. 129
EX $10   NM $15   MIP $25

Transport, Tootsietoy, 6" long, 1939, Model No. 1037
EX $15   NM $20   MIP $30

Yacht, Tootsietoy, 4" long; 1940, Model No. 130
EX $10   NM $15   MIP $30

BUSES

Cross Country Bus, Tootsietoy
EX $30   NM $45   MIP $65

Fageol Bus, Tootsietoy, 1927-33, Model No. 4651
EX $20   NM $40   MIP $65

GMC Greyhound Bus, Tootsietoy, blue/silver, 6"; 1948-55, Model No. 3571
EX $20   NM $35   MIP $55

Greyhound Bus, Tootsietoy, blue, 1937-41, Model No. 1045
EX $25   NM $60   MIP $80

Greyhound Scenicruiser Bus, Tootsietoy, 6" bus, raised upper deck, lower body painted silver, middle section and lower roof painted blue, roof top painted cream, 1955-69
EX $17   NM $33   MIP $50

Overland Bus, Tootsietoy, 1929-33, Model No. 4680
EX $45   NM $65   MIP $125

School Bus, Tootsietoy, "Buzy Bee Bus," white hub tires; 1970s
EX $2   NM $5   MIP $7

Twin Coach Bus, Tootsietoy, red w/black tires, 3" long; 1950
EX $20   NM $35   MIP $55

CANNONS AND TANKS

Army Tank, Tootsietoy, miniature
EX $5   NM $10   MIP $25

Army Tank, Tootsietoy, 1931-41, Model No. 4647
EX $35   NM $50   MIP $100

Four Wheel Cannon, Tootsietoy, 4" long; 1950s
EX $10   NM $20   MIP $45

Long Range Cannon, Tootsietoy, Model No. 4642
EX $7   NM $10   MIP $30

Six-Wheel Army Cannon, Tootsietoy, 1950s
EX $10   NM $20   MIP $50

CARS

Andy Gump Car, Tootsietoy, 1932; Funnies series, Model No. 5101X
EX $75   NM $300   MIP $500

Armored Car, Tootsietoy, "U.S. Army" on sides, camouflage, black tires, 1938-41, Model No. 4635
EX $25   NM $35   MIP $65

Auburn Roadster, Tootsietoy, red, white rubber wheels, Model No. 1016
EX $15   NM $30   MIP $45

Austin-Healey, Tootsietoy, light brown roadster; 6" long; 1956
EX $20   NM $30   MIP $60

Baggage Car, Tootsietoy, Model No. 1101
EX $10   NM $15   MIP $30

Baja Runabout, Tootsietoy, Midget, 2-1/4"; 1960s-70s
EX $1   NM $2   MIP $3

Bandito, Super Slicks series, 4-1/4" long, gold hardtop hot rod, side-panel stickers, chrome-hub wheels, 1971-76
EX $3   **NM** $5   **MIP** $8

Bluebird Daytona Race Car, Tootsietoy
EX $20   **NM** $35   **MIP** $65

Boat Tail Roadster, Tootsietoy, red roadster, 6" long, Model No. 233
EX $20   **NM** $35   **MIP** $55

Buckin' Bronco, Hitch-Up series, Ford Bronco, white hub tires, 1970s
EX $6   **NM** $14   **MIP** $28

Buick Brougham, Tootsietoy, tan/black, Model No. 6003
EX $20   **NM** $35   **MIP** $70

Buick Coupe, Tootsietoy, blue w/white wheels, 1924, Model No. 4636
EX $30   **NM** $42   **MIP** $65

Buick Coupe, Tootsietoy, 4" long, Model No. 6002
EX $20   **NM** $35   **MIP** $50

Buick Estate Wagon, Tootsietoy, yellow and maroon w/black wheels, 6" long; 1948
EX $20   **NM** $35   **MIP** $50

Buick Experimental Car, Tootsietoy, blue w/black wheels, detailed tin bottom, 6" long; 1954
EX $25   **NM** $50   **MIP** $85

Buick LaSabre, Tootsietoy, red open top, black wheels, 6" long; 1951
EX $25   **NM** $45   **MIP** $70

Buick Roadmaster, Tootsietoy, blue w/black wheels, four-door; 1949
EX $25   **NM** $40   **MIP** $65

Buick Roadster, Tootsietoy, yellow open top, black wheels, 4" long, 1938
EX $25   **NM** $45   **MIP** $65

Buick Sedan, Tootsietoy, 6" long, Model No. 6004
EX $25   **NM** $35   **MIP** $55

Buick Special, Tootsietoy, 4" long; 1947, Model No. 103
EX $15   **NM** $25   **MIP** $50

Buick Station Wagon, Tootsietoy, green w/yellow top, black wheels, 6" long; 1954
EX $20   **NM** $30   **MIP** $45

Buick Tourer, Tootsietoy, red w/white wheels, 1925, Model No. 4641
EX $25   **NM** $45   **MIP** $70

Buick Touring Car, Tootsietoy, Model No. 6005
EX $50   **NM** $75   **MIP** $110

Cadillac, Tootsietoy, HO series, blue car/white top, 2" long; 1960
EX $10   **NM** $20   **MIP** $30

Cadillac 60, Tootsietoy, red-orange w/black wheels, four-door; 1948
EX $20   **NM** $40   **MIP** $60

Cadillac 62, Tootsietoy, red-orange w/white top, black wheels, four-door, 6" long; 1954
EX $20   **NM** $35   **MIP** $120

Cadillac and Cabin Cruiser, Midget series combination, 5-1/2" long, Cadillac Eldorado hauls trailer with plastic Cabin Cruiser, 1969
EX $4   **NM** $8   **MIP** $12

Cadillac Brougham, Tootsietoy, Model No. 6103
EX $40   **NM** $60   **MIP** $85

Cadillac Coupe, Tootsietoy, blue/tan, black wheels, Model No. 6102
EX $40   **NM** $60   **MIP** $85

Cadillac Eldorado, Midget series, 2-5/8" long, 1960s
EX $2   **NM** $3   **MIP** n/a

Cadillac Sedan, Tootsietoy, white rubber wheels, Model No. 6104
EX $40   **NM** $60   **MIP** $85

Cadillac Touring Car, Tootsietoy, 1926, Model No. 6105
EX $50   **NM** $90   **MIP** $120

Cheetah, Midget series, 2" long, different numbers on hood, 1960s
EX $2   **NM** $3   **MIP** n/a

Chevrolet Ambulance, Tootsietoy, 4" long
EX $15   **NM** $20   **MIP** $35

Chevrolet Bel Air, Tootsietoy, yellow w/black wheels, 3" long; 1955
EX $15   **NM** $30   **MIP** $50

Chevrolet Brougham, Tootsietoy, Model No. 6203
EX $40   **NM** $60   **MIP** $85

Chevrolet Coupe, Tootsietoy, Model No. 6202
EX $20   **NM** $35   **MIP** $90

Chevrolet Coupe, Tootsietoy, green w/black wheels, 3", Model No. 231
EX $20   **NM** $35   **MIP** $55

Chevrolet Fastback, Tootsietoy, blue w/black wheels, 3" long; 1950
EX $15   **NM** $20   **MIP** $35

Chevrolet Roadster, Tootsietoy, Model No. 6201
EX $20   **NM** $35   **MIP** $90

Chevrolet Sedan, Tootsietoy, Model No. 6204
EX $20   **NM** $35   **MIP** $75

Chevrolet Touring Car, Tootsietoy, Model No. 6205
EX $60   **NM** $150   **MIP** $200

Chrysler Convertible, Tootsietoy, blue-green w/black wheels, 4" long; 1960
EX $15   **NM** $25   **MIP** $35

Chrysler Experimental Roadster, Tootsietoy, orange open top, black wheels
EX $13   **NM** $26   **MIP** $40

Chrysler New Yorker, Tootsietoy, blue w/black wheels, four-door, 6" long; 1953
EX $25   **NM** $35   **MIP** $55

Chrysler Windsor Convertible, Tootsietoy, black wheels, 6" long; 1950
EX $50   **NM** $90   **MIP** $120

Chrysler Windsor Convertible, Tootsietoy, green w/black wheels, 4" long; 1941
EX $20   **NM** $30   **MIP** $45

Classic Series 1906 Cadillac or Studebaker, Tootsietoy, green and black, spoke wheels
EX $5   **NM** $10   **MIP** $15

Classic Series 1907 Stanley Steamer, Tootsietoy, yellow and black, spoke wheels; 1960-65
EX $5   **NM** $10   **MIP** $15

Classic Series 1912 Ford Model T, Tootsietoy, black w/red seats, spoke wheels
EX $5   **NM** $10   **MIP** $15

Classic Series 1919 Stutz Bearcat, Tootsietoy, black and red, solid wheels
EX $5   **NM** $10   **MIP** $15

Classic Series 1929 Ford Model A, Tootsietoy, blue and black, black tread wheels; 1960-65
EX $5   **NM** $10   **MIP** $15

Corvair, Tootsietoy, red, 4" long; 1960s
EX $30   **NM** $55   **MIP** $75

Corvette Roadster, Tootsietoy, blue open top, black wheels, 4" long; 1954-55
EX $15   **NM** $25   **MIP** $35

Coupe, Tootsietoy, miniature, Model No. 101
EX $20   **NM** $25   **MIP** $40

Desert Fox, Super Slicks series, 4-1/4" long; purple open-top hot rod, side panel stickers, chrome-hub tires, 1971-76
EX $3   **NM** $5   **MIP** $8

DeSoto Airflow, Tootsietoy, green w/white wheels, Model No. 0118
EX $20   **NM** $35   **MIP** $60

Doodlebug, Tootsietoy, same as Buick Special
EX $50   **NM** $75   **MIP** $100

Dune Buggy, Hitch-Up series, red dune buggy, 3-3/4" long; with white plastic top and surfboards, white hub tires, front hitch for hauling, 1970s
EX $2   **NM** $4   **MIP** $6

Dune Buggy, Tootsietoy, White plastic top, white hub tires, 3-1/4" long; 1970s
EX $2   **NM** $4   **MIP** $6

Dune Buster, Super Slicks series, 4-14" long, green hot rod, roof sticker, chrome-hub tires, 1971-76
EX $3   **NM** $5   **MIP** $8

Ferrari Lancia Race Car, red or dark green racer, 5" long, with silver grille, no racing number, plastic driver's head, plastic tires, 1964-67
EX $10   **NM** $20   **MIP** $30

Ferrari Racer, Tootsietoy, red w/gold driver, black wheels, 6" long; 1956
EX $30   **NM** $40   **MIP** $65

Ford, Tootsietoy, red w/open top, black wheels, 6" long; 1940
EX $15   **NM** $25   **MIP** $40

Ford B Hot Rod, Tootsietoy, 1960s
EX $5   **NM** $10   **MIP** $20

Ford Convertible Coupe, Tootsietoy, 1934
EX $30   **NM** $50   **MIP** $70

Ford Convertible Sedan, Tootsietoy, red w/black wheels, 3" long; 1949
EX $10   **NM** $20   **MIP** $35

Ford Coupe, Tootsietoy, powder blue w/tan top, white wheels, 1934
EX $30   NM $50   MIP $75

Ford Coupe, Midget series, 2-3/4" long, model of 1940 Ford coupe, 1960s
EX $1   NM $2   MIP n/a

Ford Coupe, Tootsietoy, blue or red w/white wheels, 1935, Model No. 0112
EX $25   NM $35   MIP $45

Ford Customline, Tootsietoy, blue w/black wheels; 1955
EX $15   NM $20   MIP $30

Ford Fairlane 500 Convertible, two-door 1957 convertible, 3" long, painted red, blue or green, molded front windshield, open wheel wells, patterned plastic tires
EX $6   NM $12   MIP $18

Ford Falcon, two-door 1960 sedan, 3" long, painted red, blue or orange, open wheel wells, patterned plastic tires, 1961-69
EX $4   NM $8   MIP $12

Ford GT, Tootsietoy, Midget, 2-1/8"; 1960s-70s
EX $1   NM $2   MIP n/a

Ford LTD, Tootsietoy, blue w/black wheels, 4" long; 1969
EX $15   NM $20   MIP $35

Ford Mainliner, Tootsietoy, red w/black wheels, four-door, 3" long; 1952
EX $10   NM $20   MIP $30

Ford Model A Coupe, Tootsietoy, blue w/white wheels, Model No. 4655
EX $25   NM $35   MIP $50

Ford Model A Sedan, Tootsietoy, green w/black wheels, Model No. 6665
EX $25   NM $35   MIP $50

Ford Mustang, Midget series, 2-1/8" long, 1960s-70s
EX $1   NM $2   MIP n/a

Ford Mustang with Boat Trailer, Midget series combination, 4-1/2" long; Mustang hauling trailer with Chris-Craft Boat, 1966
EX $6   NM $10   MIP $15

Ford Ranch Wagon, Tootsietoy, red w/yellow top, four-door, 3" long; 1954
EX $15   NM $20   MIP $35

Ford Ranch Wagon, Tootsietoy, green w/yellow top, four-door, 4" long; 1954
EX $15   NM $25   MIP $35

Ford Ranch Wagon, four-door 1960 station wagon, 3" long, painted blue, open wheel wells, patterned plastic tires, 1962-67
EX $3   NM $6   MIP $9

Ford Roadster, Tootsietoy, powder blue w/open top, white wheels, Model No. 0116
EX $25   NM $40   MIP $60

Ford Sedan, Tootsietoy, 1934, Model No. 0111
EX $35   NM $50   MIP $70

Ford Sedan, Tootsietoy, lime green w/black wheels, four-door, 3" long; 1949
EX $15   NM $20   MIP $35

Ford Sedan, Tootsietoy, powder blue w/white solid wheels, 1935, Model No. 0111
EX $25   NM $35   MIP $50

Ford Station Wagon, Tootsietoy, red w/white top, black wheels, four-door, 6" long; 1962
EX $25   NM $40   MIP $55

Ford Station Wagon, Tootsietoy, powder blue w/white top, black wheels, 6" long; 1959
EX $15   NM $20   MIP $35

Ford Station Wagon, Tootsietoy, blue w/black wheels, 3" long; 1960
EX $20   NM $40   MIP $60

Ford Thunderbird, two-door 1955 coupe, 4" long; open wheel wells, fin-style rear fenders, open wheel wells, patterned plastic tires, 1960-67
EX $6   NM $12   MIP $18

Ford Thunderbird (1967), Tootsietoy, Midget, 2-3/8"; 1960s
EX $1   NM $2   MIP n/a

Ford Tourer, Tootsietoy, open top, red w/silver spoke wheels, Model No. 4570
EX $20   NM $30   MIP $45

Ford V-8 Hotrod, Tootsietoy, red w/open top, black wheels, open silver motor, 6" long; 1940
EX $15   NM $25   MIP $35

Ford w/Trailer, Tootsietoy, blue sedan, white rubber wheels, Model No. 1043
EX $50   NM $75   MIP $130

Graham Convertible Coupe, Tootsietoy, side spare tire, rubber wheels, 1933-35, Model No. 0614
EX $50   NM $125   MIP $175

Graham Convertible Coupe, Tootsietoy, rear spare tire, rubber wheels, 1933-35, Model No. 0514
EX $50   NM $125   MIP $175

Graham Convertible Sedan, Tootsietoy, side spare tire, rubber wheels, 1933-35, Model No. 0615
EX $50   NM $125   MIP $175

Graham Convertible Sedan, Tootsietoy, rear spare tire, rubber wheels, 1933-35, Model No. 0515
EX $50   NM $125   MIP $175

Graham Coupe, Tootsietoy, side spare tire, rubber wheels, 1933-35, Model No. 0612
EX $50   NM $115   MIP $150

Graham Coupe, Tootsietoy, rear spare tire, rubber wheels, 1933-35, Model No. 0512
EX $50   NM $115   MIP $150

Graham Roadster, Tootsietoy, rear spare tire, rubber wheels, 1933-35, Model No. 0511
EX $50   NM $115   MIP $150

Graham Roadster, Tootsietoy, side spare tire, rubber wheels, 1933-35, Model No. 0611
EX $50   NM $115   MIP $150

Graham Sedan, Tootsietoy, side spare tire, rubber wheels, 1933-35, Model No. 0613
EX $50   NM $115   MIP $150

Graham Sedan, Tootsietoy, rear spare tire, rubber wheels, 1933-35, Model No. 0513
EX $50   NM $115   MIP $150

Graham Towncar, Tootsietoy, rear spare tire, rubber wheels, 1933-35, Model No. 0516
EX $50   NM $115   MIP $150

Graham Towncar, Tootsietoy, side spare tire, 1933-35, Model No. 0616
EX $50   NM $115   MIP $140

Gremlin, Hitch-Up series, 4" long, "Gremlin" decal, 1970s
EX $3   NM $5   MIP $8

Hot Rod, Midget series, 2" long; 1960s
EX $1   NM $2   MIP $4

Hot Rod Model B, single-seat Ford hot rod, 3" long, painted red, blue or green, detailed engine, exposed plastic tires, 1961-69
EX $4   NM $8   MIP $12

Hot Rod Wagon, Hitch-Up series, "Bimini Buggy," white hub tires, 1970s
EX $2   NM $4   MIP $6

Indy Race Car, Midget series, 2-3/8" long, 1960s
EX $1   NM $2   MIP n/a

Insurance Patrol, Tootsietoy, miniature, Model No. 104
EX $15   NM $25   MIP $35

International Station Wagon, Tootsietoy, red/yellow, 3" long, Model No. 239
EX $15   NM $25   MIP $50

International Station Wagon, Tootsietoy, red/yellow, white wheels, 1939-41, Model No. 1046
EX $15   NM $25   MIP $50

International Station Wagon, Tootsietoy, 4" long, rubber wheels; 1940s
EX $25   NM $50   MIP $50

Jaguar Formula D, Midget series, 2-1/2" long, 1960s
EX $2   NM $3   MIP n/a

Jaguar Type D, Tootsietoy, green w/black wheels, 3" long; 1957
EX $10   NM $15   MIP $25

Jaguar XK 120 Roadster, Tootsietoy, green open top, black wheels, 3" long
EX $10   NM $15   MIP $25

Jaguar XK 140 Coupe, Tootsietoy, blue w/black wheels, 6" long
EX $8   NM $17   MIP $25

Kaiser Sedan, Tootsietoy, blue w/black wheels, 6" long; 1947
EX $25   NM $45   MIP $55

KO Ice, Tootsietoy, 1932; Funnies series, Model No. 5105X
EX $100   NM $325   MIP $425

Lancia Racer, Tootsietoy, dark green w/black wheels, 6" long; 1956
EX $30   NM $50   MIP $75

Large Bluebird Racer, Tootsietoy, green w/yellow solid wheels, Model No. 4666
EX $20   NM $40   MIP $60

LaSalle Convertible, Tootsietoy, rubber wheels, Model No. 0714
EX $80   NM $200   MIP $300

LaSalle Convertible Sedan, Tootsietoy, rubber wheels, Model No. 0715
EX $80   NM $200   MIP $300

LaSalle Coupe, Tootsietoy, rubber wheels, Model No. 0712
EX $150   NM $300   MIP $350

LaSalle Sedan, Tootsietoy, red w/black rubber wheels, 3" long, Model No. 230
EX $15   NM $20   MIP $30

LaSalle Sedan, Tootsietoy, rubber wheels, Model No. 0713
EX $140   NM $200   MIP $275

Limousine, Tootsietoy, blue w/silver spoke wheels; prewar, Model No. 4528
EX $20   NM $40   MIP $65

Lincoln, Tootsietoy, prewar; red w/white rubber wheels, four-door
EX $110   NM $400   MIP $500

Lincoln Capri, Tootsietoy, red w/yellow top, black wheels, two-door, 6" long
EX $20   NM $35   MIP $50

Maserati Race Car, Dark green or red race car, 5" long, with silver grille and black racing number on white background, driver's head of plastic, 1962-67
EX $10   NM $20   MIP $30

Mercedes 190 SL Coupe, Tootsietoy, powder blue w/black wheels, 6" long; 1956
EX $15   NM $25   MIP $40

Mercedes Convertible, Midget series, 2-3/8" long; 1960s
EX $1   NM $2   MIP n/a

Mercury, Tootsietoy, red w/black wheels, four-door, 4" long; 1952
EX $15   NM $20   MIP $40

Mercury Custom, Tootsietoy, blue w/black wheels, four-door, 4" long; 1949
EX $15   NM $30   MIP $40

Mercury Fire Chief Car, Tootsietoy, red w/black wheels, 4" long; 1949
EX $25   NM $35   MIP $50

MG, Midget series, 2-1/4" long, 1960s
EX $2   NM $4   MIP $18

MG TF Roadster, Tootsietoy, red open top, black wheels, 6" long; 1954
EX $15   NM $25   MIP $45

MG TF Roadster, Tootsietoy, blue open top, black wheels, 3" long; 1954
EX $10   NM $15   MIP $30

Monza, Midget series, 2-1/4" long; 1970s
EX $1   NM $2   MIP n/a

Moon Mullins Police Car, Tootsietoy, 1932; Funnies series, Model No. 5104X
EX $130   NM $200   MIP $425

Nash Metropolitan Convertible, Tootsietoy, red w/black tires; 1954
EX $25   NM $35   MIP $60

Observation Car, Tootsietoy, Model No. 1103
EX $10   NM $15   MIP $30

Offenhauser Racer, Tootsietoy, dark blue w/black wheels, 4" long; 1947
EX $10   NM $20   MIP $35

Oldsmobile 88 Convertible, Tootsietoy, bright green w/black wheels, 6" long; 1959
EX $20   NM $25   MIP $40

Oldsmobile 88 Convertible, Tootsietoy, yellow w/black wheels, 4" long; 1949
EX $15   NM $25   MIP $35

Oldsmobile 98, Tootsietoy, white body w/blue top, skirted fenders, black wheels, 4" long; 1955
EX $20   NM $25   MIP $40

Oldsmobile 98, Tootsietoy, red body w/yellow top, open fenders, black wheels, 4" long; 1955
EX $20   NM $25   MIP $45

Oldsmobile 98 Staff Car, Tootsietoy
EX $20   NM $25   MIP $45

Oldsmobile Brougham, Tootsietoy, Model No. 6303
EX $25   NM $35   MIP $50

Oldsmobile Coupe, Tootsietoy, Model No. 6302
EX $25   NM $35   MIP $50

Oldsmobile Roadster, Tootsietoy, orange/black, white wheels, 1924, Model No. 6301
EX $25   NM $45   MIP $75

Oldsmobile Sedan, Tootsietoy, Model No. 6304
EX $25   NM $35   MIP $50

Oldsmobile Touring, Tootsietoy, Model No. 6305
EX $25   NM $35   MIP $50

Open Touring, Tootsietoy, green convertible, white wheels, 3", Model No. 232
EX $25   NM $35   MIP $45

Packard, Tootsietoy, white body w/blue top, black wheels, four-door, 6" long; 1956
EX $12   NM $25   MIP $35

Panzer Wagon, Super Slicks series, 4-1/4" long, red hot rod with rear engine, hood sticker, chrome-hub tires, 1971-76
EX $3   NM $5   MIP $8

Pie Wagon, Super Slicks series, 4-1/4" long, pink hardtop hot rod, roof sticker, chrome-hub tires, 1971-76
EX $3   NM $5   MIP $8

Plymouth, Tootsietoy, dark blue w/black wheels, two-door, 3" long; 1957
EX $10   NM $15   MIP $20

Plymouth Belvedere, Plymouth 1957 model, 3" long; two-door hardtop, blue or red, open wheel wells, patterned plastic tires, 1959-69
EX $6   NM $12   MIP $18

Plymouth Sedan, Tootsietoy, blue w/black wheels, four-door, 3" long; 1950
EX $15   NM $20   MIP $30

Pontiac, Midget series, 2-3/8" long; 1970s
EX $1   NM $2   MIP n/a

Pontiac Fire Chief, Tootsietoy, red w/black wheels, 4" long; 1950
EX $20   NM $35   MIP $50

Pontiac Sedan, Tootsietoy, green w/black wheels, two-door, 4" long; 1950
EX $15   NM $25   MIP $45

Pontiac Star Chief, Tootsietoy, red w/black wheels, four-door, 4" long; 1959
EX $15   NM $25   MIP $40

Porsche, Midget series, 2-3/8" long; 1960s
EX $1   NM $2   MIP n/a

Porsche Roadster, Tootsietoy, red w/open top, black wheels, two-door, 6" long; 1956
EX $20   NM $25   MIP $40

Racer, Tootsietoy, orange w/black wheels, 3" long; 1950s
EX $10   NM $15   MIP $30

Racer, Tootsietoy, miniature, Model No. 1110
EX $25   NM $40   MIP $50

Rambler Wagon, Tootsietoy, blue w/black wheels, 4" long; 1960
EX $15   NM $25   MIP $35

Rambler Wagon, Tootsietoy, dark green w/yellow top, black wheels, yellow interior; 1960s
EX $15   NM $25   MIP $35

Roadster, Tootsietoy, miniature, Model No. 102
EX $15   NM $25   MIP $40

Roadster, Tootsietoy, Model No. 6001
EX $50   NM $100   MIP $140

Roadster, Midget series, 2-1/8" long; 1960s
EX $1   NM $2   MIP n/a

Sedan, Tootsietoy, Model No. 6-04
EX $50   NM $100   MIP $135

Sedan, Tootsietoy, miniature, Model No. 103
EX $20   NM $25   MIP $40

Small Racer, Tootsietoy, blue w/driver, white wheels, 1927, Model No. 23
EX $50   NM $110   MIP $175

Smitty, Tootsietoy, 1932; Funnies series, Model No. 5103X
EX $170   NM $250   MIP $500

Station Wagon, Tootsietoy, red w/tan upper, 3", Model No. 239
EX $15   NM $35   MIP $55

Stingin' Bug, VW Beetle, white plastic interior, "Stingin' Bug" sticker on doors, white-hub tires, 1970s
EX $3   **NM** $5   **MIP** $7

Studebaker Coupe, Tootsietoy, green w/black wheels, 3" long; 1947
EX $25   **NM** $35   **MIP** $50

Studebaker Lark Convertible, two-door 1960 convertible, 3" long; painted teal green, green, yellow, blue or red, molded front windshield, open wheel wells, patterned plastic tires, 1960-69
EX $4   **NM** $8   **MIP** $25

Tank Car, Tootsietoy, miniature, Model No. 105
EX $20   **NM** $25   **MIP** $40

Thunderbird Coupe, Tootsietoy, blue w/black wheels, 3" long; 1955
EX $15   **NM** $20   **MIP** $30

Thunderbird Coupe, Tootsietoy, powder blue w/black wheels, 4" long; 1955
EX $15   **NM** $30   **MIP** $40

Toronado, Midget series, 2-3/4" long, 1970s
EX $1   **NM** $2   **MIP** n/a

Torpedo Coupe, Tootsietoy, gray; prewar, Model No. 1017
EX $20   **NM** $25   **MIP** $45

Torpedo Sedan, Tootsietoy, red, Model No. 1018
EX $20   **NM** $30   **MIP** $50

Triumph, two-seat 1956 sports car, 3" long; painted green, red, blue, yellow or orange, bucket seats, oval grille, plastic tires, 1963-69
EX $4   **NM** $8   **MIP** $12

Triumph TR 3 Roadster, Tootsietoy, black wheels, 3" long; 1956
EX $4   **NM** $8   **MIP** $12

Twin Shaft, Super Slicks series, 4-1/4" long; blue bubble-top hot rod, side-panel stickers, chrome-hub tires, 1971-76
EX $3   **NM** $5   **MIP** $8

Uncle Walt, Tootsietoy, 1932; Funnies series, Model No. 5103X
EX $150   **NM** $300   **MIP** $450

Uncle Willie, Tootsietoy, 1932; Funnies series, Model No. 5106X
EX $150   **NM** $300   **MIP** $450

Volkswagen, two-door 1954 VW, 3" long, painted copper, red, yellow or green, open wheel wells, plastic tires, 1960-69
EX $5   **NM** $10   **MIP** $15

Volkswagen Rabbit, 4-3/4" long; opening rear gate, hood and side decals, 1970s
EX $3   **NM** $6   **MIP** $10

Volkswagen Rabbit, Midget series, 2-1/4" long, 1970s
EX $2   **NM** $3   **MIP** n/a

VW Bug, Tootsietoy, metallic gold w/black tread wheels, 6" long; 1960
EX $15   **NM** $25   **MIP** $30

VW Bug, Tootsietoy, "Stingin' Bug," white hub tires; 1970s
EX $3   **NM** $5   **MIP** $7

VW Bug, Tootsietoy, lime green w/black tread wheels, 3" long; 1960
EX $10   **NM** $20   **MIP** $35

VW Rabbit, Tootsietoy, Opening rear gate, hood and side decals, 4-3/4"; 1970s
EX $3   **NM** $6   **MIP** $10

Wedge Dragster, Midget series, 2-5/8" long, 1960s-70s
EX $1   **NM** $3   **MIP** n/a

Wheelie Wagon, blue pickup, 3-7/8" long; white plastic interior, "Wheelie Wagon" stickers, white hub tires, 1970s
EX $2   **NM** $3   **MIP** $5

Yellow Cab Sedan, Tootsietoy, green w/white wheels, 1921, Model No. 4629
EX $10   **NM** $20   **MIP** $30

EMERGENCY VEHICLES

Ambulance Van, white, "Ambulance" decal, white hub tires, 1970s
EX $2   **NM** $4   **MIP** $7

American LaFrance Ladder Truck, Collector series, 4-1/8" long; chromed plastic ladder, 1967-69
EX $3   **NM** $5   **MIP** $89

American LaFrance Pumper, Tootsietoy, red, 3" long; 1954
EX $15   **NM** $20   **MIP** $35

American LaFrance Snorkel Fire Truck, Collector Series, 4-1/8" long; red, 1967-60
EX $3   **NM** $6   **MIP** $9

Chevrolet Ambulance, Tootsietoy, army green, red cross on roof top, army star on top of hood, 4" long; 1950
EX $15   **NM** $25   **MIP** $50

Chevrolet Ambulance, Tootsietoy, yellow, red cross on top, 4" long; 1950
EX $15   **NM** $25   **MIP** $40

Fire Chief Pickup, Hitch-Up series scale, 3-3/4" long; pickup truck, white hub tires, "Fire Chief" decal, 1970s
EX $2   **NM** $4   **MIP** $6

Fire Hook and Ladder, Tootsietoy, red/blue w/side ladders, Model No. 4652
EX $25   **NM** $40   **MIP** $50

Fire Water Tower Truck, Tootsietoy, blue/orange, red water tower, Model No. 4653
EX $30   **NM** $60   **MIP** $80

Ford Wrecker, Tootsietoy, 3" long, 1935, brown, white rubber wheels, Model No. 0133
EX $30   **NM** $50   **MIP** $65

Graham Ambulance, Tootsietoy, white w/red cross on sides, Model No. 0809
EX $40   **NM** $95   **MIP** $125

Graham Wrecker, Tootsietoy, red/black; rubber wheels, Model No. 0806
EX $50   **NM** $110   **MIP** $150

Hook and Ladder, Tootsietoy, w/driver; white rubber wheels, 1937-41, Model No. 1040
EX $40   **NM** $60   **MIP** $75

Hook and Ladder, Tootsietoy, red and silver; white rubber wheels, Model No. 236
EX $15   **NM** $30   **MIP** $45

Hook and Ladder, Tootsietoy, #1040, Model No. 1040
EX $20   **NM** $25   **MIP** $40

Hook and Ladder, Road Haulers series, 7-1/4" long, red die-cast body, white plastic interior and ladder assembly, white-hub tires, 1970s
EX $5   **NM** $10   **MIP** $15

Hose Car, Tootsietoy, w/driver and figure standing by water gun; 1937-41, Model No. 1041
EX $35   **NM** $50   **MIP** $80

Hose Wagon, Tootsietoy, red, black rubber wheels, postwar, Model No. 238
EX $20   **NM** $25   **MIP** $40

Hose Wagon, Tootsietoy, red w/silver hose, white rubber wheels, 3" long, prewar, Model No. 238
EX $25   **NM** $30   **MIP** $45

Insurance Patrol, Tootsietoy, w/driver, Model No. 1042
EX $25   **NM** $40   **MIP** $60

Insurance Patrol, Tootsietoy, red, black rubber wheels, postwar, Model No. 237
EX $20   **NM** $25   **MIP** $40

Insurance Patrol, Tootsietoy, red, white wheels, prewar, Model No. 237
EX $25   **NM** $30   **MIP** $45

Jumbo Wrecker, Tootsietoy, 6" long; 1941, Model No. 1027
EX $25   **NM** $40   **MIP** $60

Ladder Fire Truck, Tootsietoy, Midget scale, swiveling ladder, 3-1/2" long; 1960s
EX $4   **NM** $8   **MIP** $12

Ladder Fire Truck, Tootsietoy, Swiveling white plastic ladder, 7-1/4"; 1970s
EX $8   **NM** $12   **MIP** $15

Lincoln Wrecker, Tootsietoy, sedan w/wrecker hook
EX $200   **NM** $425   **MIP** $600

Mack L-Line Fire Pumper, Tootsietoy, red w/ladders on sides
EX $35   **NM** $65   **MIP** $75

Mack L-Line Hook and Ladder, Tootsietoy, red w/silver ladder
EX $35   **NM** $65   **MIP** $75

Pumper Fire Truck, Hitch-Up series scale, 3-3/4" long; two removable plastic ladders, white hub tires, 1970s
EX $3   **NM** $5   **MIP** $7

Rescue Truck, Hitch-Up series scale, 3-5/8" long, die-cast and plastic, white hub tires, "Emergency" decal, 1970s
EX $2   **NM** $4   **MIP** $7

FARM AND CONSTRUCTION EQUIPMENT

Caterpillar Bulldozer, Tootsietoy, yellow, 6" long

EX $25   NM $45   MIP $55

Caterpillar Scraper, Tootsietoy, yellow w/black wheels, silver blade, 6" long; 1956

EX $15   NM $25   MIP $40

Caterpillar Tractor, Tootsietoy, miniature, Model No. 108

EX $15   NM $25   MIP $35

Caterpillar Tractor, Tootsietoy, 1931, Model No. 4646

EX $20   NM $30   MIP $50

Cement Truck, Road Haulers series, 6" long; die-cast cab, two-color plastic drum assembly, white plastic interior, white-hub tires; 1970s

EX $5   NM $9   MIP $14

D7 Crawler with Blade, Tootsietoy, 1:50 scale, die-cast; 1956

EX $20   NM $35   MIP $55

D8 Crawler with Blade, Tootsietoy, 1:87 scale, die-cast

EX $20   NM $30   MIP $45

Dozer, Construction Rigs series, 5-1/2" long, yellow die-cast tractor, black treads, plastic blade, 1970s

EX $1   NM $2   MIP $5

Earth Mover, Midget series, 2-1/2" long, 1960s

EX $2   NM $3   MIP n/a

Farm Tractor, Tootsietoy, w/driver, Model No. 4654

EX $60   NM $100   MIP $145

Farm Tractor and Utility Wagon, die-cast tractor with hay trailer, 4-1/4" long, 1968-69

EX $3   NM $7   MIP $10

Ford Tractor, Tootsietoy, red w/loader, die-cast, 1/32 scale

EX $30   NM $40   MIP $65

Grader, Tootsietoy, 1:50 scale; 1956, 6"

EX $20   NM $30   MIP $50

Heavy Duty Hydraulic Crane, Mobile crane, 4" long, with telescoping boom and rotating cab, 1968-69

EX $4   NM $8   MIP $12

Heavy Duty Power Shovel, Mobile shovel, operating boom and rotating cab, 1968-69

EX $4   NM $8   MIP $12

International Tractor, Tootsietoy

EX $10   NM $15   MIP $25

Loader, Construction Rigs series, 5-1/2" long, yellow tractor with plastic front scoop, black plastic tires, 1970s

EX $15   NM $2   MIP $12

Road Builder, tractor-trailer, 5" long, long-nose truck hauls flatbed trailer and Michigan Earth Mover, 1969

EX $2   NM $4   MIP $8

Roller, Construction Rigs series, 5" long, yellow die-cast body, yellow plastic front roller, 1970s

EX $1   NM $2   MIP $5

Steamroller, Tootsietoy, 1931-34, Model No. 4648

EX $75   NM $150   MIP $200

Super Tractor, Super Tootsietoys series, 6-3/4" long; 1966-68

EX $5   NM $10   MIP $15

SETS

Box Trailer and Road Scraper Set, Tootsietoy, w/driver on road scraper

EX $75   NM $130   MIP $250

Car Fleet, blister card 8-piece set, cars, racer trailer, boat trailer, Midget series scale, 1967

EX $16   NM $20   MIP $27

Car Fleet, blister card 8-piece set, cars and boat trailers in Midget series scale, 1969

EX $16   NM $20   MIP $25

Cheerios Tootsietoy Box, 1950s cereal box, Tootsietoy offer on side, 1950s

EX $80   NM $100   MIP $120

Contractor Set, Tootsietoy, pickup truck w/three wagons, Model No. 0191

EX $50   NM $100   MIP $130

Farm Set, blister card 4-piece set, tractor, trailer and implements, 1969

EX $8   NM $10   MIP $14

Fire Station Set, Midget series scale pumper, jeep, fire chief car and badge, 1967

EX $10   NM $14   MIP $18

Four-Car Transport Set, Tootsietoy, flatbed trailer carries cars, Model No. 0190X

EX $50   NM $90   MIP $135

Freight Train, Tootsietoy, five-piece set, Model No. 0194

EX $35   NM $60   MIP $80

Grand Prix #1687 Set, Tootsietoy, seven vehicles; 1969

EX $50   NM $95   MIP $150

Jam Pac, Midget series 10-car sets, 1966

EX $20   NM $23   MIP $27

Jam Pac, boxed 10-car Midget series set, 1969

EX $20   NM $22   MIP $35

Jam Pac, blister card 6-car Midget series set, late 1970s

EX $12   NM $13   MIP $15

Jam Pac, blister card 5-car Midget series set, 1981

EX $10   NM $11   MIP $12

Jam Pac, 12-piece Midget series set; 1967

EX $24   NM $27   MIP $30

Midget Series, Tootsietoy, yellow stake truck, red limo, green doodlebug, yellow railcar, blue racer, red fire truck, 1" long, 1936-41

EX $20   NM $40   MIP $60

Midget Series, Tootsietoy, single engine plane, St. Louis, bomber, Atlantic Clipper, 1" long, 1936-41

EX $10   NM $15   MIP $25

Midget Series, Tootsietoy, assorted ships, 1" long, 1936-41

EX $20   NM $40   MIP $60

Midget Series, Tootsietoy, green cannon, blue tank, green armored car, green tow truck, green camelback van, 1" long, 1936-41

EX $20   NM $40   MIP $60

Milk Trailer Set, Tootsietoy, tractor w/three milk tankers, Model No. 0192

EX $50   NM $100   MIP $200

Model "A" Collector Series, set of four cars, 1974

EX $16   NM $20   MIP $25

Model "A" Collector Series, Tootsietoy, Set of four cars

EX $16   NM $20   MIP $25

Passenger Train, Tootsietoy, five-piece set, Model No. 0193

EX $40   NM $60   MIP $100

Playtime Set, Tootsietoy, six cars, two trucks, two planes

EX $200   NM $500   MIP $850

Tractor with Scoop Shovel and Wagon, Tootsietoy, red w/silver scoop, flatbed trailer; 1946-52

EX $125   NM $185   MIP $250

SPACESHIPS

Buck Rogers Venus Duo-Destroyer, 1937

EX $75   NM $110   MIP $150

Flash Gordon Spaceship, 1970s

EX $3   NM $8   MIP $12

TRAILERS

Boat Trailer, Tootsietoy, two-wheel

EX $10   NM $15   MIP $20

Horse Trailer, Tootsietoy, red w/white top, two-wheel, black tread wheels

EX $10   NM $15   MIP $20

House Trailer, Tootsietoy, powder blue w/black wheels, two-wheel, door opens, 6" long

EX $10   NM $17   MIP $20

Restaurant Trailer, Tootsietoy, yellow w/black tread wheels, two-wheel, open sides

EX $30   NM $40   MIP $65

Small House Trailer, Tootsietoy, two-wheel, three side windows, 1935

EX $30   NM $45   MIP $65

U-Haul Trailer, Tootsietoy, red w/black tread wheels, two-wheel, U-Haul logo on sides

EX $10   NM $15   MIP $30

TRAINS

Borden's Milk Tank Car, Tootsietoy, yellow; red base, Model No. 1093

EX $15   NM $20   MIP n/a

Box Car, Tootsietoy, "Southern", Model No. 1089

EX $15   NM $20   MIP n/a

Caboose, Tootsietoy, red, Model No. 1095

EX $10   NM $15   MIP n/a

VEHICLES — TOOTSIETOY

Coal Car, Tootsietoy, red, Model No. 1090
EX $10   **NM** $15   **MIP** n/a

Cracker Jack Railroad Car, Tootsietoy, embossed white metal, painted orange, black rubber tires, 3" long, 1930s
EX $60   **NM** $150   **MIP** n/a

Diesel Train, Midget series scale, 13" long; complete with engine, three box cars, one caboose, early 1970s
EX $10   **NM** $15   **MIP** $25

Fast Freight Set, Tootsietoy, five-piece set; 1940, Model No. 186
EX $35   **NM** $60   **MIP** $80

Log Car, Tootsietoy, silver w/red wheels; logs chained on, Model No. 1092
EX $10   **NM** $15   **MIP** n/a

Oil Tank Car, Tootsietoy, silver top, red base, "Sinclair", Model No. 1094
EX $15   **NM** $20   **MIP** n/a

Passenger Train Set, Tootsietoy, four-piece set, 1925, Model No. 4625
EX $50   **NM** $125   **MIP** n/a

Pennsylvania Engine, Tootsietoy, red/silver
EX $20   **NM** $30   **MIP** n/a

Refrigerator Car, Tootsietoy, yellow ochre, red base, black roof, Model No. 1088
EX $10   **NM** $15   **MIP** n/a

Santa Fe Engine, Tootsietoy, black/silver
EX $15   **NM** $20   **MIP** n/a

Stock Car, Tootsietoy, red, Model No. 1091
EX $10   **NM** $15   **MIP** n/a

Tootsietoy Flyer, Tootsietoy, silver; three-piece set, 1937, Model No. 196
EX $35   **NM** $60   **MIP** $90

Wrecking Crane, Tootsietoy, green crane on silver flatbed car w/red wheels, Model No. 1087
EX $20   **NM** $30   **MIP** n/a

Zephyr Railcar, Tootsietoy, dark green, 4" long, 1935, Model No. 117
EX $35   **NM** $60   **MIP** n/a

TRUCKS

Army Half Truck, Tootsietoy, 1941
EX $30   **NM** $55   **MIP** $75

Army Jeep, Tootsietoy, windshield up, 6" long; 1950s
EX $15   **NM** $25   **MIP** $40

Army Jeep CJ3, Tootsietoy, extended back, windshield down, 4" long; 1950
EX $10   **NM** $15   **MIP** $35

Army Jeep CJ3, Tootsietoy, no windshield, 3" long; 1950
EX $10   **NM** $15   **MIP** $40

Army Rocket Launcher, Tootsietoy, Tractor-trailer, plastic rocket; late 1950s
EX $50   **NM** $75   **MIP** $100

Army Supply Truck, Tootsietoy, w/driver, Model No. 4634
EX $25   **NM** $40   **MIP** $55

Auto Transport, Collector Series tractor-trailer, 5" long; red Ford or Chevy tractor with yellow two-level hauler, with two Triumphs, 1967
EX $5   **NM** $9   **MIP** $21

Auto Transport, Road Haulers series tractor-trailer, 8-1/2" long, die-cast cab with white plastic interior and grille hauls yellow plastic hauler for Midget series cars, white-hub tires, 1970s
EX $4   **NM** $8   **MIP** $12

Auto Transport, Tractor-trailer, 8-3/4" long, Hendrickson tractor pulls polypropylene hauler with lowering ramp, and three Midget series cars, 1969
EX $6   **NM** $12   **MIP** $18

Bimini Buggy, hot rod bus, white plastic interior and exposed engine, "Bimini Buggy" stickers on sides, white-hub tires, 1970s
EX $2   **NM** $4   **MIP** $6

Box Truck, Tootsietoy, red w/white wheels, 3" long, Model No. 234
EX $15   **NM** $20   **MIP** $30

Buick Delivery Van, Tootsietoy, Model No. 6006
EX $25   **NM** $35   **MIP** $50

Cadillac Delivery Van, Tootsietoy, Model No. 6106
EX $25   **NM** $35   **MIP** $50

Carousel and Transport Unit, tractor-trailer, 4-1/2" long, Chevy or Ford truck hauls flatbed trailer with plastic carousel, 1968
EX $5   **NM** $9   **MIP** $14

Cherry Picker, Super Tootsietoys series, 8" long; Ford Pickup truck with cherry-picker snorkel mounted in truck bed, 1966
EX $7   **NM** $15   **MIP** $22

Chevrolet Cameo Pickup, Tootsietoy, green w/black wheels, 4" long; 1956
EX $15   **NM** $25   **MIP** $40

Chevrolet Delivery Van, Tootsietoy, Model No. 6206
EX $25   **NM** $35   **MIP** $50

Chevrolet El Camino, Tootsietoy, red
EX $20   **NM** $25   **MIP** $40

Chevrolet El Camino Camper and Boat, Tootsietoy, blue body w/red camper, black/white boat on top of camper
EX $25   **NM** $35   **MIP** $85

Chevrolet Panel Truck, Tootsietoy, green, 3" long; 1950
EX $10   **NM** $20   **MIP** $30

Chevrolet Panel Truck, Tootsietoy, green, front fenders opened, 3" long; 1950s
EX $8   **NM** $17   **MIP** $25

Chevrolet Panel Truck, Tootsietoy, light green w/black wheels, 4" long; 1950
EX $15   **NM** $30   **MIP** $40

Chevy El Camino, Midget series, 2-5/8" long, 1960s
EX $2   **NM** $4   **MIP** n/a

Civilian Jeep, Tootsietoy, red, open top, black wheels, 4" long; 1950
EX $15   **NM** $20   **MIP** $35

Civilian Jeep, Tootsietoy, blue w/black tread wheels, 6" long; 1960
EX $15   **NM** $20   **MIP** $35

Civilian Jeep, Tootsietoy, burnt orange, open top, black wheels, 3" long; 1950
EX $10   **NM** $15   **MIP** $30

CJ3 Army Jeep, Tootsietoy, open top, no steering wheel cast on dashboard, 3" long; 1950
EX $10   **NM** $15   **MIP** $30

CJ5 Jeep, Tootsietoy, red w/black tread wheels, windshield up, 6" long; 1960s
EX $15   **NM** $20   **MIP** $30

CJ5 Jeep, Tootsietoy, red w/black tread wheels, windshield up, 6" long; 1950s
EX $15   **NM** $25   **MIP** $35

Coast to Coast Van, Tootsietoy, 9" long
EX $40   **NM** $75   **MIP** $125

Commercial Tire Van, Tootsietoy, "Commercial Tire and Supply Co."; white rubber wheels; prewar
EX $70   **NM** $150   **MIP** $200

Dean Van Lines, Tootsietoy, Tractor-trailer; 1950-56
EX $35   **NM** $75   **MIP** $100

Delivery Van, Tootsietoy, "Wild Wagon," white hub tires, 3-7/8" long; 1970s
EX $3   **NM** $4   **MIP** $5

Diamond T K5 Dump Truck, Tootsietoy, yellow cab and chassis, green dump body, 6" long
EX $25   **NM** $35   **MIP** $50

Diamond T K5 Semi, Tootsietoy, red tractor and light green closed trailer
EX $25   **NM** $45   **MIP** $55

Diamond T K5 Stake Truck, Tootsietoy, orange, closed sides, 6" long; 1940
EX $25   **NM** $35   **MIP** $55

Diamond T K5 Stake Truck, Tootsietoy, orange, open sides, 6" long; 1940
EX $25   **NM** $35   **MIP** $55

Diamond T Metro Van, Tootsietoy, powder blue, 6" long
EX $35   **NM** $75   **MIP** $100

Diamond T Tow Truck, Tootsietoy, red w/silver tow bar
EX $25   **NM** $35   **MIP** $55

Dodge D100 Panel, Tootsietoy, green and yellow, 6" long
EX $18   **NM** $36   **MIP** $55

Dodge Pickup, Tootsietoy, lime green, 4" long
EX $20   **NM** $30   **MIP** $40

Double Bottom-Dumper Truck, tractor-trailer, 8-1/4" long, Hendrickson truck pulls two die-cast bottom-dumper transport units, with three-position lever for dumping, 1969
EX $5   **NM** $11   **MIP** $30

Dump Truck, Road Haulers series, 6-1/4" long; die-cast cab and chassis, white plastic interior, plastic dump body, white hub tires; 1970s
EX $4   **NM** $8   **MIP** $12

Federal Bakery Van, Tootsietoy, black w/cream wheels, 1924, Model No. 4631
EX $50   **NM** $85   **MIP** $110

Federal Florist Van, Tootsietoy, black w/cream wheels, 1924, Model No. 4635
EX $75   **NM** $175   **MIP** $220

Federal Grocery Van, Tootsietoy, black w/cream wheels, 1924, Model No. 4630
EX $45 **NM** $70 **MIP** $100

Federal Laundry Van, Tootsietoy, black w/cream wheels, 1924, Model No. 4633
EX $50 **NM** $85 **MIP** $110

Federal Market Van, Tootsietoy, black w/cream wheels, 1924, Model No. 4632
EX $55 **NM** $85 **MIP** $110

Federal Milk Van, Tootsietoy, black w/cream wheels, 1924, Model No. 4634
EX $55 **NM** $85 **MIP** $110

Ford Bronco, Tootsietoy, "Buckin' Bronco," white hub tires; 1969-70s
EX $6 **NM** $14 **MIP** $28

Ford C600 Oil Tanker, Tootsietoy, red, 6" long; 1962
EX $15 **NM** $30 **MIP** $40

Ford C600 Oil Tanker, Tootsietoy, bright yellow, 3" long
EX $10 **NM** $15 **MIP** $20

Ford Econoline Pickup, Tootsietoy, red; 1962
EX $15 **NM** $25 **MIP** $35

Ford Econoline Pickup Truck, cabover pickup 6" long; hidden axles, plastic "Tootsietoy" tires, 1962-69
EX $7 **NM** $18 **MIP** $25

Ford F1 Pickup, Tootsietoy, orange, open tailgate, 3" long; 1949
EX $15 **NM** $20 **MIP** $35

Ford F1 Pickup, Tootsietoy, orange, closed tailgate, 3" long; 1949
EX $15 **NM** $20 **MIP** $35

Ford F6 Oil, Tootsietoy, orange, 4" long; 1949
EX $10 **NM** $15 **MIP** $25

Ford F6 Oil Tanker, Tootsietoy, red w/Texaco, Sinclair, Shell or Standard on sides, 6" long; 1949
EX $25 **NM** $50 **MIP** $100

Ford F6 Pickup, Tootsietoy, red, 4" long; 1949
EX $15 **NM** $25 **MIP** $40

Ford F600 Army Anti-Aircraft Gun, Tootsietoy, tractor-trailer flatbed, guns on flatbed
EX $20 **NM** $30 **MIP** $45

Ford F600 Army Radar, Tootsietoy, tractor-trailer flatbed, yellow radar unit on flatbed, 6" long; 1955
EX $20 **NM** $30 **MIP** $45

Ford F600 Army Stake Truck, Tootsietoy, tractor-trailer box, army star on top of trailer box roof and "U.S. Army" on sides, 6" long; 1955
EX $25 **NM** $40 **MIP** $55

Ford F600 Stake Truck, Tootsietoy, light green, 6" long; 1955
EX $15 **NM** $25 **MIP** $35

Ford Pickup, Tootsietoy, 3", beige; 1935; white rubber wheels, Model No. 0121
EX $25 **NM** $40 **MIP** $55

Ford Pickup Truck, Ford 1957 model truck, 3" long; covered-over rear window, patterned plastic tires, 1968-69
EX $4 **NM** $8 **MIP** $12

Ford Shell Oil Truck, Tootsietoy, Model No. 1008
EX $45 **NM** $60 **MIP** $85

Ford Styleside Pickup, Tootsietoy, orange, 3" long; 1957
EX $10 **NM** $15 **MIP** $30

Ford Tanker Truck, Midget series, 2-1/2" long; 1960s-70s
EX $2 **NM** $3 **MIP** n/a

Ford Texaco Oil Truck, Tootsietoy, Model No. 1008
EX $45 **NM** $60 **MIP** $85

Ford Tow Truck, Midget series, 2-3/8" long; 1960s
EX $1 **NM** $2 **MIP** n/a

Hendrickson Cement Truck, Collector series, 3" long; red body and chassis, silver tank, yellow plastic drum, 1967-69
EX $4 **NM** $8 **MIP** $12

Hendrickson Dump Truck, Collector series, 3" long; red cab and chassis, green heavy-duty dump body, 1967-69
EX $4 **NM** $8 **MIP** $12

Horse Trailer, Road Haulers series tractor-trailer, 8-1/4" long, die-cast cab with white plastic interior and grille, orange plastic horse trailer with lowering gate, six plastic horses, white hub tires, 1970s
EX $5 **NM** $10 **MIP** $15

Hot Rod Truck, Midget series, 1-7/8" long; 1960s
EX $2 **NM** $3 **MIP** n/a

Houseboat and Transporter, tractor-trailer, 4-1/4" long; Ford or Chevy truck hauls flatbed trailer with House Boat, 1969
EX $5 **NM** $11 **MIP** $16

Hudson Pickup, Tootsietoy, red, 4" long; 1947
EX $25 **NM** $40 **MIP** $55

International Bottle Truck, Tootsietoy, lime green
EX $30 **NM** $45 **MIP** $65

International Car Transport Truck, Tootsietoy, red tractor, orange double-deck trailer w/cars
EX $35 **NM** $50 **MIP** $70

International Gooseneck Trailer, Tootsietoy, orange tractor and flatbed trailer
EX $30 **NM** $40 **MIP** $55

International K1 Oil Truck, Tootsietoy, green, comes w/oil brands on sides, 6" long
EX $12 **NM** $23 **MIP** $35

International K1 Panel Truck, Tootsietoy, blue, 4" long
EX $20 **NM** $30 **MIP** $55

International RC180 Grain Semi, Tootsietoy, green tractor and red trailer
EX $30 **NM** $50 **MIP** $70

International Sinclair Oil Truck, Tootsietoy, 6" long, Model No. 1006
EX $35 **NM** $75 **MIP** $100

International Standard Oil Truck, Tootsietoy, 6" long, Model No. 1006
EX $35 **NM** $75 **MIP** $100

Jeep and Racer, Midget series combination, 4-1/2" long, Jeep with trailer and Midget Racer, 1968-69
EX $2 **NM** $4 **MIP** $8

Jeep CJ5, Midget series, 2-1/8" long, 1960s-70s
EX $1 **NM** $2 **MIP** $35

Jeep Delivery Truck, Midget series, trailer hitch, 1960s
EX $1 **NM** $2 **MIP** $4

Jeep Panel Truck/Land Rover, Tootsietoy, Midget series, 2-3/8"; 1960s
EX $2 **NM** $4 **MIP** n/a

Jeep Pickup, Midget series, 2-1/8" long; late 1960s
EX $2 **NM** $3 **MIP** n/a

Jeep Pickup, Hitch-Up series, 3-5/8" long; die-cast and plastic, white hub tires, 1970s
EX $2 **NM** $3 **MIP** $5

Jeep Pickup, Tootsietoy, Die-cast and plastic, white hub tires, 3-5/8" long; 1970s
EX n/a **NM** n/a **MIP** $35

Jeep Pickup Truck, Midget series, 2-1/4" long; 1960s
EX $2 **NM** $3 **MIP** n/a

Jeep Pickup with U-Haul Trailer, Midget series combination, 4-1/2" long, 1967
EX $2 **NM** $3 **MIP** n/a

Jeep Truck with Honda Motorcycle, Midget series combination, 4-1/2" long; Jeep truck with trailer, chromed motorcycle, 1968-69
EX $3 **NM** $7 **MIP** n/a

Jeepster, Hitch-Up series, 3-7/8" long, "Jumpin Jeeper," white hub tires, 1970s
EX $2 **NM** $5 **MIP** $15

Jeepster, Tootsietoy, bright yellow w/open top, black wheels, 3" long; 1947
EX $10 **NM** $15 **MIP** $35

Jumbo Pickup, Tootsietoy, 6" long, green w/black wheels, 1936-41, Model No. 1019
EX $25 **NM** $35 **MIP** $50

Kennel Truck, Super Tootsietoy series, 8" long; Ford Pickup with clear plastic dome over truck bed, partitioned to hold four dogs, 1967
EX $8 **NM** $17 **MIP** $25

Livestock Transporter, tractor-trailer, 4-1/4" long; Ford or Chevy tractor hauls trailer with two horses and two cattle, 1969
EX $7 **NM** $13 **MIP** $20

Log Truck, tractor-trailer, 4-1/4" long; Ford or Chevy truck with logger trailer, three natural-finish logs, 1967-69
EX $10 **NM** $20 **MIP** $30

Logger, Road Haulers series tractor-trailer, 7-1/2" long; die-cast cab with white plastic interior, die-cast trailer with three wood logs, white-hub tires, 1970s
EX $5 **NM** $10 **MIP** $15

Mack Anti-Aircraft Gun, Tootsietoy, Model No. 4643
EX $25   **NM** $40   **MIP** $55

Mack B-Line Cement Truck, Tootsietoy, red truck w/yellow cement mixer; 1955
EX $20   **NM** $35   **MIP** $55

Mack B-Line Oil Tanker, Tootsietoy, red tractor and trailer, "Mobil"
EX $20   **NM** $35   **MIP** $75

Mack B-Line Stake Trailer, Tootsietoy, red tractor, orange closed trailer; 1955
EX $20   **NM** $35   **MIP** $55

Mack Coal Truck, Tootsietoy, "City Fuel Company," 10 wheels, Model No. 0804
EX $60   **NM** $120   **MIP** $175

Mack Coal Truck, Tootsietoy, orange cab w/blue bed, four wheels, 1925, Model No. 4639
EX $90   **NM** $100   **MIP** $250

Mack Coal Truck, Tootsietoy, red cab w/black bed, 1928, Model No. 4639
EX $60   **NM** $120   **MIP** $160

Mack Dairy Tanker, Tootsietoy, 1930s; two-piece cab; Tootsietoy Dairies
EX $75   **NM** $100   **MIP** $225

Mack L-Line Dump Truck, Tootsietoy, yellow cab and chassis, light green dump body, 6" long; 1947
EX $20   **NM** $35   **MIP** $55

Mack L-Line Semi and Stake Trailer, Tootsietoy, red tractor and trailer
EX $50   **NM** $95   **MIP** $125

Mack L-Line Semi-Trailer, Tootsietoy, red tractor cab, silver semi-trailer, "Gerard Motor Express" on sides
EX $60   **NM** $115   **MIP** $145

Mack L-Line Stake Truck, Tootsietoy, red w/silver bed inside
EX $25   **NM** $35   **MIP** $55

Mack L-Line Tow Truck, Tootsietoy, red w/silver tow bar
EX $25   **NM** $35   **MIP** $55

Mack Log Hauler, Tootsietoy, red cab, trailer w/load of logs; 1940s
EX $50   **NM** $95   **MIP** $135

Mack Mail Truck, Tootsietoy, red cab w/light brown box, "U.S. Mail Airmail Service" on sides, 3" long, 1920s, Model No. 4645
EX $40   **NM** $70   **MIP** $100

Mack Milk Truck, Tootsietoy, "Tootsietoy Dairy," one-piece cab, Model No. 0805
EX $50   **NM** $110   **MIP** $175

Mack Oil Tanker, Tootsietoy, "DOMACO" on side of tanker, Model No. 0802
EX $60   **NM** $100   **MIP** $155

Mack Oil Truck, Tootsietoy, red cab w/orange tanker, 1925, Model No. 4640
EX $25   **NM** $40   **MIP** $55

Mack Railway Express, Tootsietoy, 1930s; Wrigley's Gum
EX $55   **NM** $115   **MIP** $165

Mack Searchlight Truck, Tootsietoy, 1931-41, Model No. 4644
EX $25   **NM** $40   **MIP** $55

Mack Stake Trailer-Truck, Tootsietoy, enclosed cab, open stake trailer, 'Express' on sides of trailer, Model No. 0801
EX $50   **NM** $90   **MIP** $120

Mack Stake Truck, Tootsietoy, orange cab w/red stake bed, 1925, Model No. 4638
EX $25   **NM** $40   **MIP** $60

Mack Trailer-Truck, Tootsietoy, open cab, Model No. 4670
EX $50   **NM** $85   **MIP** $110

Mack Transport, Tootsietoy, red, open cab w/flatbed trailer, Model No. 190
EX $60   **NM** $150   **MIP** $200

Mack Transport, Tootsietoy, yellow; 1941, w/three cars at angle, Model No. 187
EX $150   **NM** $500   **MIP** $700

Mack Van Trailer-Truck, Tootsietoy, enclosed cab and box trailer, Model No. 0803
EX $50   **NM** $100   **MIP** $140

Mack Wrigley's Spearmint Gum Truck, Tootsietoy, 4", green w/white rubber wheels, red hubs, Model No. 0810
EX $70   **NM** $150   **MIP** $225

Mobil Gas Tanker, tractor-trailer, 4-1/4" long; Ford or Chevy tractor hauling red tanker body with "Mobil" sticker on sides, 1960s-70s
EX $8   **NM** $17   **MIP** $25

Mobile Gas Tanker, Tootsietoy, Midget scale; 1960s-70s
EX $10   **NM** $17   **MIP** $25

Model T Pickup, Tootsietoy, 3" long, 1914, Model No. 4610
EX $30   **NM** $50   **MIP** $75

Model T Pick-up, Tootsietoy, 3", black, spoked metal wheels, Model No. 4610
EX $25   **NM** $40   **MIP** $50

Oil Tanker, Tootsietoy, blue and silver, two caps on top of tanker, 3" long, Model No. 235
EX $13   **NM** $26   **MIP** $40

Oil Tanker, Tootsietoy, orange, four caps on top of tanker, 3" long, postwar, Model No. 235
EX $10   **NM** $15   **MIP** $25

Oil Tanker, Tootsietoy, blue, three caps on top, 2" long, 1932, Model No. 105
EX $20   **NM** $25   **MIP** $50

Oil Tanker, Tootsietoy, green w/white wheels; prewar, Model No. 0120
EX $15   **NM** $25   **MIP** $35

Oldsmobile Delivery Van, Tootsietoy, Model No. 6306
EX $25   **NM** $35   **MIP** $50

Pickup, Tootsietoy, "wheelie Wagon," white hub tires, 3-7/8" long; 1970s
EX $3   **NM** $4   **MIP** $5

Safari Hunt, Midget series combination, 5-1/4" long, Jeep Panel Truck hauls plastic animal cage trailer with giraffe, elephant, and hippo, 1968-69
EX $5   **NM** $9   **MIP** $14

Sanitation Truck, Road haulers series, 6-1/2" long, die-cast cab and chassis, white plastic interior and dumping body, white-hub tires, 1970s
EX $4   **NM** $8   **MIP** $12

Shell Oil Truck, Tootsietoy, yellow/silver, 6", white rubber wheels, Model No. 1009
EX $25   **NM** $50   **MIP** $75

Shell Oil Truck, Hitch-Up scale, "Shell" decal, white hub tires, 1970
EX $3   **NM** $5   **MIP** $7

Shuttle Truck, Midget series, 2-1/4" long; 1960s
EX $1   **NM** $2   **MIP** n/a

Sinclair Oil Truck, Tootsietoy, 6" long; green/silver, Model No. 1007
EX $30   **NM** $50   **MIP** $75

Special Delivery, Tootsietoy, 1936, Model No. 0123
EX $20   **NM** $25   **MIP** $40

Stake Truck, Tootsietoy, miniature, Model No. 109
EX $25   **NM** $40   **MIP** $55

Standard Oil Truck, Tootsietoy, red/silver; 6", white rubber wheels, Model No. 1006
EX $25   **NM** $50   **MIP** $75

Super Camper, Super Tootsietoy series, 8-1/2" long; Ford Pickup truck with removable camper
EX $7   **NM** $15   **MIP** $11

Super Dump Truck, Super Tootsietoy series, 9-3/8" long, blue Ford or GMC truck with yellow operating dump, 1966-68
EX $5   **NM** $10   **MIP** $15

Super Tow Truck, Super Tootsietoy series, 8-1/2" long, Ford or GMC truck with red cab, white rear tow assembly with windup winch and tow hook, 1966-68
EX $7   **NM** $15   **MIP** $22

Super U-Haul Truck, Super Tootsietoy series, 8-1/2" long; Ford truck with U-Haul body, 1966
EX $8   **NM** $17   **MIP** $25

Texaco Oil Truck, Tootsietoy, red/silver; 6", white rubber wheels, Model No. 1008
EX $25   **NM** $50   **MIP** $75

Tootsietoy Dairy, Tootsietoy, semi trailer truck, Model No. 0805
EX $75   **NM** $110   **MIP** $140

Tootsietoy Oil Tanker, Tootsietoy, red cab, silver tanker, "Tootsietoy Line" on side; 1950s
EX $60   **NM** $95   **MIP** $125

Turnpike Auto Transport, Tootsietoy, Midget scale, two cars, 5" long; 1960s-70s
EX n/a   **NM** n/a   **MIP** n/a

Van Transport, tractor-trailer, 4-1/4" long; Ford or Chevy truck with van trailer, 1967-69
EX $4   **NM** $8   **MIP** $12

Wild Wagon, green van, 3-7/8" long, white plastic interior, white hub tires, "Wild Wagon" sticker with Indian motif; 1970s
EX $2   **NM** $4   **MIP** $7

Wrigley's Box Van, Tootsietoy, w/or without decal; 1940s, Model No. 1010
EX $45   **NM** $60   **MIP** $75

VEHICLES — TOOTSIETOY

View-Master

7More Wonders of the World—this was one of the earliest advertising slogans for View-Master. Initially designed to be sold in camera, drug, and gift stores, the product has been in continuous production since 1939. View-Master reels were introduced at the 1939 New York World's Fair and at the 1940 Golden Gate Exposition in San Francisco. From there, the titles spread out to include a host of scenic attractions featuring everything from Crater Lake, Oregon, to Miami Beach, Florida.

In the early 1940s, film and paper were scarce and View-Master production all but halted due to the onset of World War II. However, a large contract to produce airplane and ship identification and range estimation reels saved the product from potential oblivion. Millions of reels were produced and used by GIs, along with thousands of Model B (round) View-Master viewers.

Although scenic reels were View-Master's forte, the company decided to spread out a bit in the late 1940s and produced a series of children's fairy-tale reels. These single-sleeved reels were identified with the prefix "FT". Clay figure models were initially produced by Lee Green Studios in Hollywood and later at the View-Master art studios in Portland, Oregon. Dozens of reel titles were produced using the great diorama effect created by tabletop photography.

Keeping ahead of the competition, View-Master purchased the assets of its main rival, Tru-Vue, in 1951. This acquisition resulted in obtaining the license to use Disney characters, previously held by Tru-Vue. Since that time, the company has produced many Disney and other cartoon/character favorites. Some of these were produced as clay figures, others were drawn as stereo cells, and still others were created using actual products in the reel set up, as was the case with Barbie and G.I. Joe.

From 1946 until 2002, the fundamental design of the View-Master viewer had remained the same. The basic principal is that you insert a View-Master reel vertically into the slot at the top of the viewer and pull a lever to advance the scene. All reels produced—from 1939 through today—can be viewed in any viewer. In 2003, Fisher-Price, the current manufacturer of View-Master, introduced a new viewer where the reel is now inserted horizontally, rather than vertically.

In the late 1980s and early 1990s, View-Master developed character viewers (Mickey Mouse, Big Bird, Batman, Casper, etc), but these were short-lived and abandoned in favor of colorful versions of regular production viewers. New viewers come in a wide variety of colors and many gift sets feature viewers with colorful graphics and logos. New titles are always being added to the line and a special line of educational titles is made under the Discovery Kids banner.

PRICING

Condition determines value. As with any other paper collectible, it is important that View-Master reels be free of mold, mildew, brown foxing spots, etc. Reels missing scenes are virtually worthless. Those reels with paper blisters (caused by heat/moisture) are valued at less than 1/4 of mint reels. Three-reel packets need to be complete with outer color envelope, three reels, and inner story booklet, if indicated. Any part of the packet or booklet that is torn or damaged drops the value of the set. Adjust prices accordingly. Prices shown here are for MIP—Mint in Package—examples. Those in excellent condition command about 85 percent of the MIP price.

2006 TRENDS

Prices have leveled off as the excess of material available on the Internet reveals which reels are truly rare. Crossover collecting is impacting the View-Master reel hobby. Scenic and travel collectors are adding View-Master as part of their inventory. Comic, TV/movie, world's fair, cowboy, and other specialty collectors are enamored of View-Master reels related to their collecting field.

Collector Groups: At present, there are no collector groups solely dedicated to View-Master; however, there is a national organization devoted to 3-D collectibles. This is the National Stereoscopic Association and can be found on the Web at www.stereoview.org.

Contributor: This information is developed and written by View-Master collector/historian Mary Ann Sell. She may be reached in care of the editor at the address on p. 2.

Other on-line resources:

The View-Master Homepage, featuring historic View-Master information. Web site: http://www.cinti.net:/~vmmasell/

The Lewis & Clark Trail—Custom View-Master reels in honor of the 200th anniversary of the trail. Web site: http://www.charleyvanpelt3d.com/index.html

Fisher-Price—official corporate View-Master page: Web site: http://www.fisher-price.com/us/view-master/

THE TOP TEN VIEW-MASTER REELS (In Mint Condition)

1. House of Wax (Movie Preview Reel)	$250
2. It Came From Outer Space (Movie Preview Reel)	250
3. The Maze (Movie Preview Reel)	150
4. Son of Sinbad (Movie Preview Reel)	150
5. Taza, Son of Cochise (Movie Preview Reel)	150
6. Wings of the Hawk (Movie Preview Reel)	150
7. They Called Him Hondo (Movie Preview Reel)	150
8. Jesse James v. The Daltons (Movie Preview Reel)	130
9. Addams Family,	125
10. Glass Web (Movie Preview Reel)	100

VIEW-MASTER

$1,000,000 Duck, Model No. B506
NM $7   MIP $10

101 Dalmatians, Model No. B532
NM $3   MIP $5

101 Dalmatians, Model No. 3014
NM $3   MIP $5

1939 New York World's Fair (single reel), Model No. 87
NM $10   MIP $25

1939 New York World's Fair (single reel), Model No. 86
NM $10   MIP $25

1939 New York World's Fair (single reel), Model No. 88
NM $5   MIP $10

1939 New York World's Fair (single reel), Model No. 89
NM $5   MIP $10

1940 Golden Gate International Expo (single reel), Model No. 58
NM $5   MIP $15

1940 Golden Gate International Expo (single reel), Model No. 59
NM $5   MIP $15

1940 Golden Gate International Expo (single reel), Model No. 57
NM $12   MIP $35

1940 Golden Gate International Expo (single reel), Model No. 56
NM $12   MIP $35

1962 Seattle World's Fair (four reels), Model No. A272
NM $20   MIP $50

1962 Seattle World's Fair (single reel), Model No. A2726
NM $7   MIP $15

1962 Space Needle U.S.A. (single reel), Model No. A2725
NM $7   MIP $15

1970s America's Cup (ABC's WW/Sports), Model No. B937
NM $45   MIP $40

(KP Photo)

20,000 Leagues Under the Sea, 1954, Model No. B370
NM $7   MIP $15

Adam & the Ants, Model No. BD199
NM $15   MIP $20

Adam-12, Model No. B593
NM $10   MIP $12

Addams Family, Model No. B486
NM $75   MIP $125

Adventures of Morph, Model No. BD205
NM $7   MIP $8

Aesop's Fables, clay figure, Model No. B309
NM $8   MIP $15

Aladdin, Model No. 3088
NM $3   MIP $4

Alex, Model No. BD265
NM $9   MIP $10

ALF, Model No. 4082
NM $5   MIP $10

Alice in Wonderland, Model No. B360
NM $8   MIP $12

An American Tail II, Model No. 4111
NM $5   MIP $6

Annie, Model No. N3
NM $5   MIP $6

Annie Oakley, Model No. B470
NM $12   MIP $25

Apple's Way, Model No. B558
NM $12   MIP $14

Arabian Nights, clay figure, Model No. B335
NM $8   MIP $15

Archie, Model No. B574
NM $7   MIP $8

Arena (Movie Preview Reel)
NM $50   MIP $75

Aristocats, The, 1970s, Model No. B365
NM $5   MIP $6

Astrix & Cleopatra, Model No. B457
NM $16   MIP $25

A-Team, Model No. 4045
NM $6   MIP $12

Auto Racing, Phoenix 200 (ABC's WW/Sports), Model No. B948
NM $25   MIP $35

Babar the Elephant, Model No. B419
NM $10   MIP $18

Babes in Toyland, Model No. B375
NM $21   MIP $25

Bad News Bears in "Breaking Training", 1977, Model No. H77
NM $7   MIP $8

Bambi, clay figure, Model No. B400
NM $5   MIP $8

Banana Splits, Model No. B502
NM $10   MIP $20

Bananaman, Model No. BD239
NM $9   MIP $10

Barbie and the Rockers, Model No. 4071
NM $7   MIP $10

Barbie Dolls of the World, Model No. 36338
NM $2   MIP $5

Barbie Prom Date, Model No. 35428
NM $3   MIP $5

Barbie Special Pink Viewer set; regular viewer in Barbie pink, Model No. 1998
NM $7   MIP $10

Barbie Special Pink Viewer set; Super-show viewer in Barbie pink; Target Exc, Model No. 1998
NM $12   MIP $20

Barbie's Around the World Trip, Model No. B500
NM $20   MIP $25

Barbie's Great American Photo Race, Model No. B576
NM $20   MIP $35

Batman - The Animated Series (blister pack), blister pack, three reel, Model No. 3086
NM $2   MIP $4

Batman (Adam West), original envelope package, three reel, Model No. B492
NM $9   MIP $10

Batman (Adam West), (blister pack), blister pack, three reel, Model No. BB492
NM $13   MIP $15

Batman (blister pack), Model No. 1086
NM $5   MIP $8

Batman Returns (blister pack), blister pack, three reel, Model No. 4137
NM $7   MIP $8

Batman, The Perfect Crime (blister pack), 1976, blister pack, three reel, Model No. 4011
NM $7   MIP $8

Battle Beyond the Stars, original envelope package, three reel, Model No. L16
NM $12   MIP $20

Battle of the Planets (blister pack), blister pack, three reel, Model No. BD185
NM $13   MIP $15

Beauty & the Beast (blister pack), blister pack, three reel, Model No. 3079
NM $2   MIP $4

Bedknobs & Broomsticks, original envelope package, three reel, Model No. B366
NM $5   MIP $10

Beetlejuice, Model No. 1074
NM $5   MIP $11

Beetlejuice (blister pack), blister pack, three reel, Model No. 1074
NM $5   MIP $6

Benji, Superstar (blister pack), blister pack, three reel, Model No. 4018
NM $5   MIP $6

Benji's Very Own Christmas, original envelope package, three reel, Model No. J51
NM $7   MIP $8

Bertha, blister pack, three reel, Model No. BD259
NM $7   MIP $8

Beverly Hillbillies, 1963, original envelope package, three reel, Model No. B570
NM $12   MIP $25

Big Blue Marble, original envelope package, three reel, Model No. B587
NM $10   **MIP** $12

Black Beauty, original envelope package, three reel, Model No. D135
NM $9   **MIP** $10

Black Hole, blister pack, three reel, Model No. BK035
NM $7   **MIP** $12

Black Hole, 1979, original envelope package, three reel, Model No. K35
NM $15   **MIP** $18

Blue's Clues, Model No. 73059
NM $2   **MIP** $6

Bollie & Billie, blister pack, three reel, Model No. BD207
NM $7   **MIP** $8

Bonanza, original envelope package, three reel, Model No. B471
NM $10   **MIP** $20

Bonanza, blister pack, three reel, Model No. BB487
NM $10   **MIP** $20

Bonanza (w/o Pernell Roberts), original envelope package, three reel, Model No. B487
NM $30   **MIP** $35

Bozo, blister pack, three reel, Model No. BD1484
NM $13   **MIP** $15

Brady Bunch, original envelope package, three reel, Model No. B568
NM $17   **MIP** $22

Brave Eagle, original envelope package, three reel, Model No. B466
NM $21   **MIP** $25

Bravestar, blister pack, three reel, Model No. BD272
NM $9   **MIP** $10

Buck Rogers, 1979, original envelope package, three reel, Model No. L15
NM $7   **MIP** $10

Buckaroo Banzai, blister pack, three reel, Model No. 4056
NM $8   **MIP** $10

Buffalo Bill, Jr., original envelope package, three reel, Model No. B464
NM $18   **MIP** $25

Buffalo Bill, Jr., 1955, original envelope package, three reel, Model No. 965abc
NM $21   **MIP** $25

Bugs Bunny, 1959, original envelope package, three reel, Model No. B531
NM $9   **MIP** $10

Bugs Bunny & Tweety, blister pack, three reel, Model No. 1077
NM $2   **MIP** $3

Bugs Bunny and Elmer Fudd (single reel), 1951, original envelope package, one reel, Model No. 800
NM $7   **MIP** $8

Bugs Bunny, Big Top Bunny, original envelope package, three reel, Model No. B549
NM $5   **MIP** $6

Bugs Bunny/Road Runner Show, original envelope package, three reel, Model No. M10
NM $3   **MIP** $4

(KP Photo)

Bullwinkle, original envelope package, three reel, Model No. B515
NM $12   **MIP** $20

Button Moon, blister pack, three reel, Model No. BD212
NM $7   **MIP** $8

Can't Stop the Music, original envelope package, three reel, Model No. L1
NM $17   **MIP** $20

Captain America, original envelope package, three reel, Model No. H43
NM $4   **MIP** $5

Captain Kangaroo, original envelope package, three reel, Model No. B560
NM $10   **MIP** $12

Captain Kangaroo, original envelope package, three reel, Model No. 755abc
NM $14   **MIP** $16

Captain Kangaroo Show, original envelope package, three reel, Model No. B565
NM $10   **MIP** $12

Care Bears, blister pack, three reel, Model No. BD264
NM $5   **MIP** $10

Cartoon Carnival with Supercar, original envelope package, three reel, Model No. B521
NM $40   **MIP** $60

Casimir Costureiro, blister pack, three reel, Model No. BD171
NM $7   **MIP** $8

Casper the Friendly Ghost, original envelope package, three reel, Model No. B533
NM $5   **MIP** $6

Casper the Friendly Ghost, 1988, blister pack, three reel, Model No. BB533
NM $5   **MIP** $6

Cat from Outer Space, 1970s, original envelope package, three reel, Model No. J22
NM $7   **MIP** $8

Centurions, blister pack, three reel, Model No. 1057
NM $3   **MIP** $4

Charge at Feather River, The (Movie Preview Reel), Movie Preview Reel
NM $75   **MIP** $100

Charlie Brown, Bon Voyage, original envelope package, three reel, Model No. L2
NM $4   **MIP** $6

Charlie Brown, It's a Bird, original envelope package, three reel, Model No. B556
NM $4   **MIP** $5

Charlie Brown, It's Your First Kiss, 1980s, blister pack, three reel, Model No. 1039
NM $9   **MIP** $10

Charlotte's Web, original envelope package, three reel, Model No. B321
NM $5   **MIP** $6

Chip 'n Dale Rescue Rangers, blister pack, three reel, Model No. 3075
NM $4   **MIP** $5

CHiPs, 1980, original envelope package, three reel, Model No. L14
NM $13   **MIP** $15

Cinderella, Model No. B318
NM $5   **MIP** $8

Cinderella (single reel), 1953, original envelope package, one reel, Model No. FT5
NM $1   **MIP** $2

Cisco Kid (single reel), original envelope package, one reel, Model No. 960
NM $2   **MIP** $4

City Beneath the Sea, original envelope package, three reel, Model No. B496
NM $15   **MIP** $25

Close Encounters of the Third Kind, original envelope package, three reel, Model No. J47
NM $10   **MIP** $12

(Toy Shop File Photo)

Cowboy Stars, original envelope package, three reel, Model No. B461
NM $21   **MIP** $25

Curiosity Shop, original envelope package, three reel, Model No. B564
NM $10   **MIP** $12

Curious George, Model No. 2015
NM $6   **MIP** $12

Daktari, original envelope package, three reel, Model No. B498
NM $10   **MIP** $13

Dale Evans, original envelope package, three reel, Model No. B463
NM $23   **MIP** $30

Dale Evans, original envelope package, three reel, Model No. 944abc
NM $26   **MIP** $33

Danger Mouse, blister pack, three reel, Model No. BD214
NM $15   **MIP** $18

Dangerous Mission (Movie Preview Reel), Movie Preview Reel
NM $75   **MIP** $100

Daniel Boone, original envelope package, three reel, Model No. B479
NM $15   **MIP** $20

Dark Crystal, blister pack, three reel, Model No. 4036
NM $7   **MIP** $10

Dark Shadows, original envelope package, three reel, Model No. B503
NM $30   **MIP** $75

Davy Crockett, original envelope package, three reel, Model No. 935abc
NM $64   **MIP** $75

Dempsey & Makepeace, blister pack, three reel, Model No. BD244
NM $7   **MIP** $8

Dennis the Menace, blister pack, three reel, Model No. 1065
NM $2   **MIP** $3

Dennis the Menace, original envelope package, three reel, Model No. B539
NM $3   **MIP** $4

Deputy Dawg, original envelope package, three reel, Model No. B519
NM $30   **MIP** $50

Devil's Canyon (Movie Preview Reel), Movie Preview Reel
NM $75   **MIP** $100

Dick Tracy, 1990, blister pack, three reel, Model No. 4105
NM $7   **MIP** $8

Dick Turpin, blister pack, three reel, Model No. BD188
NM $9   **MIP** $10

Dinosaurs (Disney TV show), blister pack, three reel, Model No. 4138
NM $4   **MIP** $7

(KP Photo)

Discovery Channel Space Images, 1997, In plastic case/envelope with relief of Shuttle and planet Saturn
NM $3   **MIP** $7

Disneyland, Adventureland, Model No. A177
NM $6   **MIP** $20

Disneyland, Fantasyland, Model No. A178
NM $6   **MIP** $20

Disneyland, Frontierland, Model No. A176
NM $6   **MIP** $20

Disneyland, Main Street U.S.A., Model No. A175
NM $6   **MIP** $20

Disneyland, New Orleans Square, Model No. A180
NM $6   **MIP** $20

Disneyland, Tomorrowland, Model No. A179
NM $6   **MIP** $20

Donald Duck, 1973, original envelope package, three reel, Model No. B525
NM $7   **MIP** $8

Dr. Shrinker & Wonderbug, original envelope package, three reel, Model No. H2
NM $10   **MIP** $14

Dr. Who, blister pack, three reel, Model No. BD216
NM $35   **MIP** $50

Dr. Who, blister pack, three reel, Model No. BD187
NM $35   **MIP** $50

Dracula, 1976, original envelope package, three reel, Model No. B324
NM $13   **MIP** $15

Drums of Tahiti (Movie Preview Reel), Movie Preview Reel
NM $75   **MIP** $100

Duck Tales, blister pack, three reel, Model No. 3055
NM $4   **MIP** $5

Dukes of Hazzard, original envelope package, three reel, Model No. L17
NM $7   **MIP** $8

Dukes of Hazzard #2, original envelope package, three reel, Model No. M19
NM $6   **MIP** $7

Dukes of Hazzard 2, blister pack, three reel, Model No. 4000
NM $6   **MIP** $7

Dumbo, blister pack, three reel, Model No. BD1474
NM $9   **MIP** $10

Dumbo, original envelope package, three reel, Model No. J60
NM $7   **MIP** $8

Dune, blister pack, three reel, Model No. 4058
NM $7   **MIP** $12

E.T. (reissued), blister pack, three reel, Model No. 4117
NM $3   **MIP** $6

E.T. The Extra-Terrestrial, 1982, original envelope package, three reel, Model No. N7
NM $15   **MIP** $18

E.T., More Scenes from, blister pack, three reel, Model No. 4001
NM $15   **MIP** $18

Eight is Enough, original envelope package, three reel, Model No. K76
NM $13   **MIP** $15

Electra Woman & Dyna Girl, 1977, original envelope package, three reel, Model No. H3
NM $7   **MIP** $10

Elmo Wants to Play, blister pack, three reel, Model No. 4125
NM $2   **MIP** $3

Emergency, original envelope package, three reel, Model No. B597
NM $10   **MIP** $12

Emil, blister pack, three reel, Model No. BD122
NM $10   **MIP** $12

Expo 67 Montreal, Model No. A074
NM $12   **MIP** $20

Expo 67 Montreal, Model No. A071
NM $12   **MIP** $20

Expo 67 Montreal, Model No. A073
NM $12   **MIP** $20

Expo 70 Osaka
NM $20   **MIP** $40

Expo 74 Spokane, single reel 1-6, each
NM $5   **MIP** $10

Fabeltjes Krant, blister pack, three reel, Model No. BD251
NM $10   **MIP** $12

Family Affair, original envelope package, three reel, Model No. B571
NM $21   **MIP** $25

Family Matters, blister pack, three reel, Model No. 4118
NM $4   **MIP** $8

Fang Face, original envelope package, three reel, Model No. K66
NM $5   **MIP** $6

Fantastic Four, 1979, blister pack, three reel, Model No. K36
NM $9   **MIP** $10

Fantastic Voyage, 1968, original envelope package, three reel, Model No. B546
NM $10   **MIP** $20

Fat Albert & Cosby Kids, original envelope package, three reel, Model No. B554
NM $5   **MIP** $6

Ferdy, blister pack, three reel, Model No. BD269
NM $9   **MIP** $10

Fiddler on the Roof, original envelope package, three reel, Model No. B390
NM $21   **MIP** $25

Flash Gordon in the Planet Mongo, 1963, original envelope package, three reel
NM $21   **MIP** $25

Flight to Tangier (Movie Preview Reel), Movie Preview Reel
NM $75   **MIP** $100

Flintstone Kids, blister pack, three reel, Model No. 1066
NM $2   MIP $4

Flintstones, blister pack, three reel, Model No. 1080
NM $2   MIP $3

(KP Photo)

Flintstones, 1962, original envelope package, three reel, Model No. L6
NM $10   MIP $12

(KP Photo)

Flintstones: Pebbles and Bamm-Bamm, 1964, Original picture envelope, three reel
NM $7   MIP $14

Flipper, blister pack, three reel, Model No. BB480
NM $10   MIP $12

Flipper, original envelope package, three reel, Model No. B485
NM $10   MIP $12

Flying Kiwi, blister pack, three reel, Model No. BD189
NM $10   MIP $12

Flying Nun, original envelope package, three reel, Model No. B495
NM $21   MIP $25

Fonz, The, blister pack, three reel, Model No. BJ013
NM $7   MIP $8

For the Love of Benji, original envelope package, three reel, Model No. H54
NM $7   MIP $8

Fort Ti (Movie Preview Reel), Movie Preview Reel
NM $75   MIP $100

Fox & Hound, original envelope package, three reel, Model No. L29
NM $7   MIP $8

Fox & the Hound, The (Disney), 1980, blister pack, three reel, Model No. 3000
NM $4   MIP $5

Fraggle Rock, blister pack, three reel, Model No. 1067
NM $4   MIP $5

Fraggle Rock, blister pack, three reel, Model No. 4053
NM $4   MIP $5

Frankenstein, 1976, original envelope package, three reel, Model No. B323
NM $13   MIP $15

French Line, The (Movie Preview Reel), Movie Preview Reel
NM $75   MIP $100

Full House, blister pack, three reel, Model No. 4119
NM $3   MIP $6

G.I. Joe, 1974, original envelope package, three reel, Model No. B585
NM $13   MIP $25

Garfield, original envelope package, three reel, Model No. L28
NM $3   MIP $4

Gene Autry (single reel), original envelope package, one reel, Model No. 950
NM $2   MIP $3

Gene Autry, "The Kidnapping" (single reel), 1953, original envelope package, one reel, Model No. 951
NM $2   MIP $3

Ghostbusters, The Real, blister pack, three reel, Model No. 1062
NM $4   MIP $6

Gil & Julie, blister pack, three reel, Model No. BD225
NM $7   MIP $8

Glass Web (Movie Preview Reel), Movie Preview Reel
NM $75   MIP $100

Godzilla, 1978, blister pack, three reel, Model No. J23
NM $13   MIP $15

Gold Cup Hydroplane Races (ABC's WW/Sports), original envelope package, three reel, Model No. B945
NM $34   MIP $40

Goldilocks, Model No. B317
NM $7   MIP $10

Goldilocks and the Three Bears (single reel), 1946, original envelope package, one reel, Model No. FT6
NM $1   MIP $2

Goonies, blister pack, three reel, Model No. 4064
NM $7   MIP $50

Great Muppet Caper, original envelope package, three reel, Model No. M7
NM $4   MIP $5

Green Hornet, original envelope package, three reel, Model No. B488
NM $30   MIP $60

Gremlins, blister pack, three reel, Model No. 4055
NM $7   MIP $12

Grimm's Fairy Tales, clay figure, Model No. B312
NM $7   MIP $12

Grizzly Adams, original envelope package, three reel, Model No. J10
NM $9   MIP $10

Gulliver's Travels, Model No. B374
NM $10   MIP $15

Gun Fury (Movie Preview Reel), Movie Preview Reel
NM $75   MIP $100

Gunsmoke, original envelope package, three reel, Model No. B589
NM $21   MIP $25

Hair Bear Bunch, original envelope package, three reel, Model No. B552
NM $7   MIP $8

Hammerman, blister pack, three reel, Model No. 1081
NM $3   MIP $6

Hammerman, MC Hammer, Model No. 1061
NM $6   MIP $12

Hannah Lee (Movie Preview Reel), Movie Preview Reel
NM $75   MIP $100

Hans Christian Andersen Fairy Tales, clay figure, Model No. B305
NM $7   MIP $9

Happy Birthday Bugs Bunny, Model No. 1072
NM $2   MIP $4

Happy Days, original envelope package, three reel, Model No. J13
NM $7   MIP $8

Happy Days, 1974, original envelope package, three reel, Model No. B586
NM $9   MIP $10

Happy Days, 1981, blister pack, three reel, Model No. BB586
NM $7   MIP $8

Hardy Boys, original envelope package, three reel, Model No. B547
NM $9   MIP $12

Harry Potter - Belgium Version, Model No. 73999
NM $12   MIP $25

Harry Potter Sorcerer's Stone Part 1, Model No. 73632
NM $4   MIP $8

Harry Potter Sorcerer's Stone Part 2, Model No. 73633
NM $4   MIP $8

Harry Potter Sorcerer's Stone Part 3, Model No. 73634
NM $4   MIP $8

Hawaii Five-O, 1972, original envelope package, three reel, Model No. B590
NM $17   MIP $20

Heidi, Model No. B425
NM $6   MIP $10

Herbie Rides Again, original envelope package, three reel, Model No. B578
NM $7   MIP $8

Here's Lucy, original envelope package, three reel, Model No. B588
NM $43   MIP $50

(KP Photo)

Holly Hobbie, 1976, "Classic Tales" series, picture envelope and booklet, three reels
NM $6   MIP $13

Hopalong Cassidy (single reel), original envelope package, one reel, Model No. 956
NM $2   MIP $3

Hopalong Cassidy (single reel), original envelope package, one reel, Model No. 955
NM $2   MIP $3

House of Wax (Movie Preview Reel), Movie Preview Reel
NM $150   MIP $250

Howard the Duck, blister pack, three reel, Model No. 4073
NM $7   MIP $10

Huckleberry Finn, original envelope package, three reel, Model No. B343
NM $5   MIP $8

Huckleberry Hound & Yogi Bear, 1960, original envelope package, three reel, Model No. B512
NM $4   MIP $5

I Go Pogo, original envelope package, three reel, Model No. L32
NM $7   MIP $15

Inferno (Movie Preview Reel), Movie Preview Reel
NM $75   MIP $100

Inspector Gadget, blister pack, three reel, Model No. BD232
NM $7   MIP $10

International Moto-Cross (ABC's WW/Sports), original envelope package, three reel, Model No. B946
NM $15   MIP $30

International Swimming & Diving Meet (ABC's WW/Sports), original envelope package, three reel, Model No. B936
NM $60   MIP $70

Ironman, original envelope package, three reel, Model No. H44
NM $3   MIP $5

Isis, 1976, original envelope package, three reel, Model No. T100
NM $10   MIP $12

Island at Top of the World, original envelope package, three reel, Model No. B367
NM $21   MIP $25

It Came From Outer Space (Movie Preview Reel), Movie Preview Reel
NM $220   MIP $250

Jack & the Beanstalk, clay figure, Model No. B314
NM $7   MIP $9

Jack and the Beanstalk (single reel), 1951, original envelope package, one reel, Model No. FT3
NM $1   MIP $2

James Bond, Live & Let Die, original envelope package, three reel, Model No. B393
NM $12   MIP $20

James Bond, Live & Let Die, 1973, blister pack, three reel, Model No. BB393
NM $17   MIP $20

James Bond, Moonraker, 1979, original envelope package, three reel, Model No. K68
NM $13   MIP $15

Jaws 3-D, blister pack, three reel, Model No. 4041
NM $4   MIP $6

Jem, 1986, blister pack, three reel, Model No. 1059
NM $6   MIP $7

Jesse James vs. The Daltons (Movie Preview Reel), Movie Preview Reel
NM $100   MIP $130

Jetsons, original envelope package, three reel, Model No. L27
NM $5   MIP $6

Jim Henson's Muppet Movie, original envelope package, three reel, Model No. K27
NM $4   MIP $7

Jimbo and the Jet Set, blister pack, three reel, Model No. BD261
NM $7   MIP $8

Joe 90, original envelope package, three reel, Model No. B456
NM $50   MIP $70

Joe Forrester, original envelope package, three reel, Model No. BB454
NM $9   MIP $10

Johnny Mocassin, original envelope package, three reel, Model No. B468
NM $21   MIP $25

Johnny Mocassin, 1960s, original envelope package, three reel, Model No. 937abc
NM $21   MIP $25

Julia, original envelope package, three reel, Model No. B572
NM $15   MIP $25

Jungle Book, Model No. B363
NM $7   MIP $11

Jurassic Park, blister pack, three reel, Model No. 4150
NM $7   MIP $10

King Kong, original envelope package, three reel, Model No. B392
NM $7   MIP $8

Kiss Me Kate (Movie Preview Reel), Movie Preview Reel
NM $75   MIP $100

Knight Rider, blister pack, three reel, Model No. 4054
NM $5   MIP $6

Korg 70,000 B.C., original envelope package, three reel, Model No. B557
NM $10   MIP $15

Kung Fu, original envelope package, three reel, Model No. B598
NM $13   MIP $15

Lancelot Link Secret Chimp, original envelope package, three reel, Model No. B504
NM $21   MIP $25

Land of the Giants, original envelope package, three reel, Model No. B494
NM $20   MIP $30

Land of the Lost, 1977, original envelope package, three reel, Model No. B579
NM $9   MIP $15

Land of the Lost 2, original envelope package, three reel, Model No. H1
NM $9   MIP $15

Larry the Lamb, blister pack, three reel, Model No. BD190
NM $7   MIP $8

Lassie & Timmy, original envelope package, three reel, Model No. B472
NM $13   MIP $15

Lassie Look Homeward, original envelope package, three reel, Model No. B480
NM $9   MIP $10

Lassie Rides the Log Flume, original envelope package, three reel, Model No. B489
NM $13   MIP $15

Last Starfighter, The, blister pack, three reel, Model No. 4057
NM $5   MIP $10

Laugh-In, original envelope package, three reel, Model No. B497
NM $13   MIP $20

Laverne & Shirley, original envelope package, three reel, Model No. J20
NM $5   MIP $6

Legend of Indiana Jones, blister pack, three reel, Model No. 4092
NM $5   MIP $6

Legend of the Lone Ranger, original envelope package, three reel, Model No. L26
NM $7   MIP $8

Legend of the Lone Ranger, blister pack, three reel, Model No. 4033
NM $6   **MIP** $8

Les Maitres Du Temps, blister pack, three reel, Model No. BD203
NM $7   **MIP** $8

Little League World Series (ABC's WW/Sports), original envelope package, three reel, Model No. B940
NM $43   **MIP** $50

Little Mermaid, blister pack, three reel, Model No. 3078
NM $2   **MIP** $3

Little Mermaid - TV Show, blister pack, three reel, Model No. 3089
NM $2   **MIP** $3

Little Red Hen/Thumbelina/Pied Piper, 1957, original envelope package, three reel, Model No. B319
NM $7   **MIP** $8

Little Red Riding Hood, clay figure, Model No. B310
NM $5   **MIP** $7

(KP Photo)

Little Yellow Dinosaur, The, 1971, Original picture envelope, three reel
NM $6   **MIP** $11

Lone Ranger, original envelope package, three reel, Model No. B465
NM $21   **MIP** $25

Lone Ranger, The, original envelope package, three reel, Model No. 962abc
NM $21   **MIP** $25

(KP Photo)

Lone Ranger, The Legend, Tie-in with the movie, original picture envelope, three reels
NM $10   **MIP** $17

Lost in Space, original envelope package, three reel, Model No. B482
NM $40   **MIP** $60

Lost Treasures of the Amazon (Movie Preview Reel), Movie Preview Reel
NM $75   **MIP** $100

Love Bug, The, 1968, original envelope package, three reel, Model No. B501
NM $9   **MIP** $12

Lucky Luke vs. The Daltons, original envelope package, three reel, Model No. B455
NM $21   **MIP** $25

M*A*S*H, original envelope package, three reel, Model No. J11
NM $9   **MIP** $10

M*A*S*H, blister pack, three reel, Model No. BJ011
NM $9   **MIP** $10

Magic Roundabout, The, original envelope package, three reel, Model No. B441
NM $13   **MIP** $15

Maja the Bee, blister pack, three reel, Model No. BD182
NM $7   **MIP** $8

Man from U.N.C.L.E., original envelope package, three reel, Model No. B484
NM $20   **MIP** $25

Mannix, original envelope package, three reel, Model No. BB450
NM $21   **MIP** $25

Mary Poppins, blister pack, three reel, Model No. BB372
NM $7   **MIP** $8

Mary Poppins, 1964, original envelope package, three reel, Model No. B376
NM $7   **MIP** $8

Mask, blister pack, three reel, Model No. 1056
NM $4   **MIP** $5

Maze, The (Movie Preview Reel), Movie Preview Reel
NM $128   **MIP** $150

Metal Mickey, blister pack, three reel, Model No. BD217
NM $7   **MIP** $8

Meteor, original envelope package, three reel, Model No. K46
NM $9   **MIP** $10

Michael, original envelope package, three reel, Model No. D122
NM $20   **MIP** $25

Michael Jackson's Thriller, blister pack, three reel, Model No. 4047
NM $6   **MIP** $18

Mickey Mouse, 1958, original envelope package, three reel, Model No. B528
NM $5   **MIP** $10

Mickey Mouse - Clock Cleaners, original envelope package, three reel, Model No. B551
NM $9   **MIP** $30

Mickey Mouse Club, original envelope package, three reel, Model No. 865abc
NM $21   **MIP** $25

Mickey Mouse Club Mouseketeers, 1956, original envelope package, three reel, Model No. B524
NM $21   **MIP** $25

Mickey Mouse Jubilee, 1980s, blister pack, three reel, Model No. J29
NM $9   **MIP** $10

Mighty Mouse, 1958, original envelope package, three reel, Model No. B526
NM $17   **MIP** $20

Mighty Mouse, 1970s, blister pack, three reel, Model No. BB526
NM $4   **MIP** $5

Miss Sadie Thompson (Movie Preview Reel), Movie Preview Reel
NM $75   **MIP** $100

Mission Impossible, original envelope package, three reel, Model No. B505
NM $15   **MIP** $18

Mod Squad, original envelope package, three reel, Model No. B478
NM $16   **MIP** $20

Money From Home (Movie Preview Reel), Movie Preview Reel
NM $75   **MIP** $100

Monkees, original envelope package, three reel, Model No. B493
NM $12   **MIP** $25

Mork & Mindy, 1978, original envelope package, three reel, Model No. K67
NM $7   **MIP** $8

Movie Stars I (single reel), original envelope package, one reel, Model No. 740
NM $13   **MIP** $15

Movie Stars II (single reel), original envelope package, one reel, Model No. 741
NM $13   **MIP** $15

Movie Stars III (single reel), original envelope package, one reel, Model No. 742
NM $13   **MIP** $15

Mr. Magoo, 1977, original envelope package, three reel, Model No. H56
NM $6   **MIP** $10

Munch Bunch, blister pack, three reel, Model No. BD197
NM $7   **MIP** $8

Munsters, original envelope package, three reel, Model No. B481
NM $75   **MIP** $100

Muppet Movie, Scenes From The, blister pack, three reel, Model No. 4005
NM $4   **MIP** $8

Muppets Go Hawaiian, The, original envelope package, three reel, Model No. L25
NM $4   **MIP** $8

Muppets, Meet Jim Henson's, original envelope package, three reel, Model No. K26
NM $4   **MIP** $8

Muppets, The, blister pack, three reel, Model No. BK026
NM $4   **MIP** $8

Nanny & The Professor, original envelope package, three reel, Model No. B573
NM $30   **MIP** $35

NCAA Track & Field Championships (ABC's WW/Sports), original envelope package, three reel, Model No. B935
NM $40   MIP $60

Nebraskan, The (Movie Preview Reel), Movie Preview Reel
NM $75   MIP $100

New Mickey Mouse Club, original envelope package, three reel, Model No. H9
NM $5   MIP $6

New Zoo Revue, original envelope package, three reel, Model No. B566
NM $13   MIP $15

New Zoo Revue 2, original envelope package, three reel, Model No. B567
NM $13   MIP $15

Old Surehand, original envelope package, three reel, Model No. B443
NM $30   MIP $40

One of Our Dinosaurs Is Missing, original envelope package, three reel, Model No. B377
NM $10   MIP $12

Oregon Centennial Exposition (1959), Model No. A0250
NM $30   MIP $50

Orm & Cheap, blister pack, three reel, Model No. BD266
NM $10   MIP $12

Partridge Family, blister pack, three reel, Model No. BB5924
NM $17   MIP $20

(KP Photo)

Partridge Family, 1971, Talking View-Master reels, original envelope package, three reel
NM $22   MIP $27

Partridge Family, 1971, original envelope package, three reel, Model No. B569
NM $17   MIP $20

Pee-Wee's Playhouse, 1988, blister pack, three reel, Model No. 4074
NM $9   MIP $10

Pendelton Round-Up (ABC's WW/Sports), original envelope package, three reel, Model No. B943
NM $30   MIP $35

Perishers, The, blister pack, three reel, Model No. BD184
NM $6   MIP $8

Peter Pan, Disney's, original envelope package, three reel
NM $5   MIP $6

Pete's Dragon, original envelope package, three reel, Model No. H38
NM $7   MIP $8

Pink Panther, original envelope package, three reel, Model No. J12
NM $5   MIP $6

Pink Panther, 1970s, blister pack, three reel, Model No. BJ012
NM $4   MIP $5

Pinky Lee's 7 Days (single reel), original envelope package, one reel, Model No. 750
NM $21   MIP $25

Pinocchio, clay figure, Model No. B311
NM $8   MIP $12

Pippi Longstocking, original envelope package, three reel, Model No. D113
NM $13   MIP $15

Pippi Longstocking, original envelope package, three reel, Model No. B322
NM $13   MIP $15

Planet of the Apes, blister pack, three reel, Model No. BB507
NM $30   MIP $35

Planet of the Apes, 1967, original envelope package, three reel, Model No. B507
NM $30   MIP $35

Pluto, original envelope package, three reel, Model No. B529
NM $9   MIP $10

Pluto, blister pack, three reel, Model No. 3013
NM $4   MIP $7

Pluto, blister pack, three reel, Model No. BB529
NM $4   MIP $7

Polly in Portugal, original envelope package, three reel, Model No. B442
NM $26   MIP $30

Polly in Venice, original envelope package, three reel, Model No. D100
NM $17   MIP $20

Popeye, 1962, original envelope package, three reel, Model No. B516
NM $6   MIP $8

Popeye Talking View-Master Set, 1983, original envelope package, three reel
NM $9   MIP $10

Popeye's Fun, original envelope package, three reel, Model No. B527
NM $7   MIP $8

Portland Bill, blister pack, three reel, Model No. BD226
NM $10   MIP $12

Poseidon Adventure, original envelope package, three reel, Model No. B391
NM $21   MIP $25

Postman Pat, blister pack, three reel, Model No. BD218
NM $7   MIP $8

Power Rangers, Model No. 36870
NM $2   MIP $4

Pumcki, blister pack, three reel, Model No. BD220
NM $7   MIP $8

Punky Brewster, 1984, blister pack, three reel, Model No. 4068
NM $7   MIP $8

Puppets Audition Night, blister pack, three reel, Model No. 4003
NM $4   MIP $5

Puppets Audition Night, The, original envelope package, three reel, Model No. L9
NM $4   MIP $5

Raggedy Ann & Andy, Model No. B406
NM $9   MIP $15

Red Riding Hood (single reel), 1950, original envelope package, one reel, Model No. FT1
NM $2   MIP $3

Rescuers, The, blister pack, three reel, Model No. BH026
NM $5   MIP $6

Rescuers, The, original envelope package, three reel, Model No. H26
NM $5   MIP $6

Return to Witch Mountain, original envelope package, three reel, Model No. J25
NM $5   MIP $6

(Toy Shop File Photo)

Rin-Tin-Tin, original envelope package, three reel, Model No. B467
NM $13   MIP $15

Rin-Tin-Tin, 1955, original envelope package, three reel, Model No. 930abc
NM $13   MIP $15

Robin Hood, 1954, original envelope package, three reel
NM $21   MIP $25

Robin Hood Meets Friar Tuck, 1956, original envelope package, three reel, Model No. B373
NM $17   MIP $20

Rocketeer, The, blister pack, three reel, Model No. 4115
NM $7   MIP $8

Roland Rat Superstar, blister pack, three reel, Model No. BD240
NM $7   MIP $8

Romper Room, original envelope package, three reel, Model No. K20
NM $7   MIP $8

Rookies, The, 1975, original envelope package, three reel, Model No. BB452
NM $13   MIP $15

(KP Photo)

Roy Rogers, original envelope package, three reel, Model No. B475
NM $21   MIP $25

Roy Rogers, original envelope package, three reel, Model No. 948abc
NM $21   MIP $25

Roy Rogers, original envelope package, three reel, Model No. B462
NM $21   MIP $25

Roy Rogers (single reel), original envelope package, one reel, Model No. 945
NM $2   MIP $3

(KP Photo)

Rudolph the Red-Nosed Reindeer, 1955, Definitely based on the Golden Book, the puppets even look like the illustrations. Interesting, considering these reels were created about ten years before the Rankin/Bass animated special. Includes picture envelope and three reels
NM $10   MIP $17

Rugrats, Model No. 36343
NM $2   MIP $4

Run Joe Run, 1974, original envelope package, three reel, Model No. B594
NM $13   MIP $15

Rupert the Bear, blister pack, three reel, Model No. BD109
NM $12   MIP $15

S.W.A.T., 1975, original envelope package, three reel, Model No. BB453
NM $10   MIP $12

Sangaree (Movie Preview Reel), Movie Preview Reel
NM $75   MIP $100

Scooby Doo, blister pack, three reel, Model No. 1079
NM $2   MIP $5

Scooby Doo, original envelope package, three reel, Model No. B553
NM $4   MIP $5

Search, original envelope package, three reel, Model No. B591
NM $17   MIP $20

Sebastian, original envelope package, three reel, Model No. D101
NM $26   MIP $30

Sebastian, original envelope package, three reel, Model No. B452
NM $26   MIP $30

Second Chance (Movie Preview Reel), Movie Preview Reel
NM $75   MIP $100

Secret Squirrel & Atom Ant, original envelope package, three reel, Model No. B535
NM $9   MIP $12

Secret Valley, blister pack, three reel, Model No. BD208
NM $10   MIP $12

Sesame Street - Follow That Bird, blister pack, three reel, Model No. 4066
NM $4   MIP $5

Sesame Street - People in Your Neighborhood, original envelope package, three reel, Model No. M12
NM $4   MIP $5

Sesame Street - People in Your Neighborhood, blister pack, three reel, Model No. 4049
NM $4   MIP $5

Sesame Street Alphabet, blister pack, three reel, Model No. 4051
NM $2   MIP $3

Sesame Street Baby Animals, blister pack, three reel, Model No. 4072
NM $4   MIP $5

Sesame Street Circus Fun, blister pack, three reel, Model No. 4097
NM $4   MIP $5

Sesame Street Counting, blister pack, three reel, Model No. 4050
NM $4   MIP $5

Sesame Street Goes on Vacation, blister pack, three reel, Model No. 4077
NM $4   MIP $5

Sesame Street Goes Western, blister pack, three reel, Model No. 4085
NM $4   MIP $5

Sesame Street Nursery Rhymes, blister pack, three reel, Model No. 4083
NM $4   MIP $5

Sesame Street Shapes, Colors, blister pack, three reel, Model No. 4052
NM $4   MIP $5

Sesame Street Visits the Zoo, blister pack, three reel, Model No. 4017
NM $4   MIP $5

Shaggy D.A., original envelope package, three reel, Model No. b368
NM $10   MIP $12

Shazam, original envelope package, three reel, Model No. B550
NM $5   MIP $7

Shoe People, The, blister pack, three reel, Model No. BD270
NM $10   MIP $12

Siegfried & Roy, Model No. 73930
NM $6   MIP $12

Sigmund & the Sea Monsters (correct issue numbers), original envelope package, three reel, Model No. B595
NM $15   MIP $18

Sigmund & the Sea Monsters (wrong issue number), original envelope package, three reel, Model No. B559
NM $15   MIP $18

Silverhawks, blister pack, three reel, Model No. 1058
NM $4   MIP $5

Six Million Dollar Man, 1974, original envelope package, three reel, Model No. B556
NM $13   MIP $15

Sleeping Beauty, clay figure, Model No. B308
NM $5   MIP $7

Sleeping Beauty, Disney's, original envelope package, three reel, Model No. B308
NM $4   MIP $5

Smith Family, The, original envelope package, three reel, Model No. B490
NM $10   MIP $30

Smokey Bear, Model No. B404
NM $10   MIP $20

Smuggler, blister pack, three reel, Model No. BD194
NM $7   MIP $8

Smurf, Baby, blister pack, three reel, Model No. BD246
NM $7   MIP $8

Smurf, Flying, original envelope package, three reel, Model No. N1
NM $4   MIP $5

Smurf, Traveling, original envelope package, three reel, Model No. N2
NM $4   MIP $5

Smurfs, blister pack, three reel, Model No. BD172
NM $5   MIP $6

Snoopy and the Red Baron, 1980s, blister pack, three reel, Model No. B544
NM $7   MIP $8

Snorkes, blister pack, three reel, Model No. BD250
NM $8   MIP $10

Snow White, clay figure, Model No. B300
NM $7   MIP $9

Snow White & the Seven Dwarfs, original envelope package, three reel, Model No. K69

  NM $7   **MIP** $8

Snow White (single reel), 1946, original envelope package, one reel, Model No. FT4

  NM $3   **MIP** $4

Snowman, blister pack, three reel, Model No. BD262

  NM $7   **MIP** $8

Son of Sinbad (Movie Preview Reel), Movie Preview Reel

  NM $128   **MIP** $150

Space Mouse, original envelope package, three reel, Model No. B509

  NM $10   **MIP** $20

Space:1999, blister pack, three reel, Model No. BD150

  NM $21   **MIP** $20

Space: 1999, 1975, original envelope package, three reel, Model No. BB451

  NM $21   **MIP** $20

Spider-Man, original envelope package, three reel, Model No. K31

  NM $9   **MIP** $10

Spider-Man, 1978, original envelope package, three reel, Model No. H11

  NM $10   **MIP** $12

Spider-Man, 1980s, blister pack, three reel, Model No. BH011

  NM $7   **MIP** $8

Star Trek - The Motion Picture, original envelope package, three reel, Model No. K57

  NM $10   **MIP** $12

Star Trek - The Next Generation, blister pack, three reel, Model No. 4095

  NM $7   **MIP** $8

Star Trek - Wrath of Khan, original envelope package, three reel, Model No. M38

  NM $10   **MIP** $12

Star Trek (Cartoon Series), original envelope package, three reel, Model No. B555

  NM $9   **MIP** $10

(KP Photo)

Star Trek (TV Series), "Omega Glory", 1968, original envelope package, three reel, Model No. B499

  NM $17   **MIP** $20

Steve Canyon, 1959, original envelope package, three reel, Model No. B582

  NM $64   **MIP** $75

Stranger Wore a Gun, The (Movie Preview Reel), Movie Preview Reel

  NM $75   **MIP** $100

Superman, blister pack, three reel, Model No. 1064

  NM $4   **MIP** $5

Superman, blister pack, three reel, Model No. BJ78

  NM $5   **MIP** $6

Superman - The Movie, original envelope package, three reel, Model No. J78

  NM $10   **MIP** $20

Superman (cartoon), original envelope package, three reel, Model No. B584

  NM $4   **MIP** $5

Superman II, original envelope package, three reel, Model No. L46

  NM $17   **MIP** $25

Superman III, blister pack, three reel, Model No. 4044

  NM $7   **MIP** $15

Superstar Barbie, Model No. J070

  NM $7   **MIP** $15

Tailspin, blister pack, three reel, Model No. 3081

  NM $4   **MIP** $5

Tarzan, original envelope package, three reel, Model No. B580

  NM $9   **MIP** $10

Tarzan (single reel), original envelope package, one reel, Model No. 975

  NM $4   **MIP** $5

Tarzan Finds a Son (single reel), 1955, original envelope package, one reel, Model No. 976A

  NM $3   **MIP** $4

Tarzan of the Apes, 1955, original envelope package, three reel, Model No. 976abc

  NM $21   **MIP** $25

Taza, Son of Cochise (Movie Preview Reel), Movie Preview Reel

  NM $128   **MIP** $150

Teenage Mutant Ninja Turtles, blister pack, three reel, Model No. 1073

  NM $2   **MIP** $5

Teenage Mutant Ninja Turtles - Movie II, blister pack, three reel, Model No. 4114

  NM $3   **MIP** $7

Teenage Mutant Ninja Turtles - Movie III, blister pack, three reel, Model No. 4149

  NM $2   **MIP** $5

Teenage Mutant Ninja Turtles - The Movie, blister pack, three reel, Model No. 4109

  NM $3   **MIP** $5

Telecat, blister pack, three reel, Model No. BD243

  NM $7   **MIP** $8

Terrahawks, blister pack, three reel, Model No. BD230

  NM $10   **MIP** $20

They Called Him Hondo (Movie Preview Reel), Movie Preview Reel

  NM $128   **MIP** $150

Thomas the Tank Engine, blister pack, three reel, Model No. BD238

  NM $6   **MIP** $10

Thor, original envelope package, three reel, Model No. H39

  NM $2   **MIP** $5

Those Redheads from Seattle (Movie Preview Reel), Movie Preview Reel

  NM $75   **MIP** $100

Three Little Pigs, clay figure, Model No. B307

  NM $7   **MIP** $9

Thunderbirds, original envelope package, three reel, Model No. B453

  NM $43   **MIP** $50

Time Tunnel, 1966, original envelope package, three reel, Model No. B491

  NM $20   **MIP** $35

Tiny Toon Adventures, blister pack, three reel, Model No. 1076

  NM $2   **MIP** $3

Tiswas, blister pack, three reel, Model No. BD205

  NM $7   **MIP** $8

(KP Photo)

Toby Tyler, original envelope package, three reel, Model No. B476

  NM $30   **MIP** $35

Tom & Jerry (single reel), 1956, original envelope package, three reel, Model No. 810

  NM $2   **MIP** $3

Tom & Jerry, Two Musketeers, 1956, original envelope package, three reel, Model No. B511

  NM $9   **MIP** $10

Tom Corbett, Secret from Space, original envelope package, three reel, Model No. B581

  NM $21   **MIP** $25

Tom Corbett, Space Cadet, 1954, original envelope package, three reel, Model No. 970abc

  NM $21   **MIP** $25

Tom Sawyer, original envelope package, three reel, Model No. B340
 NM $7   MIP $8

Tom Thumb, original envelope package, three reel, Model No. D123
 NM $13   MIP $15

Top Cat, original envelope package, three reel, Model No. B513
 NM $13   MIP $15

Top Cat, blister pack, three reel, Model No. BB513
 NM $13   MIP $15

Tournament of Thrills (ABC's WW/Sports), original envelope package, three reel, Model No. B947
 NM $30   MIP $35

Tripods, The, blister pack, three reel, Model No. BD242
 NM $10   MIP $12

Tron, original envelope package, three reel, Model No. M37
 NM $8   MIP $10

TV Shows at Universal Studios, original envelope package, three reel, Model No. B477
 NM $26   MIP $30

TV Stars I (single reel), original envelope package, one reel, Model No. 745
 NM $15   MIP $18

TV Stars II (single reel), original envelope package, one reel, Model No. 746
 NM $15   MIP $18

TV Stars III (single reel), original envelope package, one reel, Model No. 747
 NM $15   MIP $18

Tweety & Sylvester, original envelope package, three reel, Model No. J28
 NM $3   MIP $4

Tweety & Sylvester, blister pack, three reel, Model No. BD1161
 NM $7   MIP $8

Twice Upon a Time, blister pack, three reel, Model No. 4043
 NM $3   MIP $4

U.F.O., original envelope package, three reel, Model No. B417
 NM $38   MIP $45

Ulysses 31, blister pack, three reel, Model No. BD198
 NM $7   MIP $8

Veggie Tales - Madame Blueberry, Model No. 73992
 NM $6   MIP $12

Victor & Maria, blister pack, three reel, Model No. BD224
 NM $7   MIP $10

Voyage to the Bottom of the Sea, original envelope package, three reel, Model No. B483
 NM $10   MIP $12

Walt Disney Presents, Model No. B315
 NM $7   MIP $10

Waltons, The, blister pack, three reel, Model No. BB596
 NM $10   MIP $12

Waltons, The, 1972, original envelope package, three reel, Model No. B596
 NM $10   MIP $12

Welcome Back Kotter, original envelope package, three reel, Model No. J19
 NM $10   MIP $12

Who Framed Roger Rabbit, blister pack, three reel, Model No. 4086
 NM $8   MIP $16

(KP Photo)

Wild Animals of Africa, 1960, Original picture envelope showing giraffes, three reel set
 NM $5   MIP $11

Wild Bill Hickcock & Jingles, original envelope package, three reel, Model No. B473
 NM $26   MIP $30

Willo the Wisp, blister pack, three reel, Model No. BD215
 NM $7   MIP $8

Wind in the Willows, blister pack, three reel, Model No. 4084
 NM $7   MIP $10

Wind in the Willows, blister pack, three reel, Model No. BD231
 NM $7   MIP $8

Wings of the Hawk (Movie Preview Reel), Movie Preview Reel
 NM $128   MIP $150

Winnetou, original envelope package, three reel, Model No. B728
 NM $26   MIP $30

Winnetou, blister pack, three reel, Model No. BB7284
 NM $21   MIP $25

Winnetou, blister pack, three reel, Model No. BB731
 NM $21   MIP $25

Winnetou & Halfblood Apache, original envelope package, three reel, Model No. B728
 NM $26   MIP $30

Winnie the Pooh & The Blustery Day, original envelope package, three reel, Model No. K37
 NM $7   MIP $8

Wiz, The, 1978, original envelope package, three reel, Model No. J14
 NM $17   MIP $20

Wizard of Oz, blister pack, three reel, Model No. BD267
 NM $7   MIP $8

Wizard of Oz, 1957, original envelope package, three reel, Model No. FT45abc
 NM $13   MIP $15

Wombles, The, original envelope package, three reel, Model No. D131
 NM $13   MIP $15

Wombles, The, blister pack, three reel, Model No. BD131
 NM $7   MIP $8

(KP Photo)

Wonderful World of Disney, Includes three reels: Pinocchio, Lady & The Tramp, Snow White
 NM $8   MIP $15

Woody Woodpecker, 1955, original envelope package, three reel, Model No. B522
 NM $13   MIP $15

Woody Woodpecker Pony Express Ride (single reel), 1951, original envelope package, one reel, Model No. 820
 NM $3   MIP $4

World Bobsled Championships (ABC's WW/Sports), original envelope package, three reel, Model No. B949
 NM $60   MIP $80

Worzel Gummidge, blister pack, three reel, Model No. BD185
 NM $7   MIP $8

Wrestling Superstars, blister pack, three reel, Model No. 4067
 NM $8   MIP $10

Young Indiana Jones Chronicles, blister pack, three reel, Model No. 4140
 NM $6   MIP $8

(KP Photo)

Zorro, 1958, original envelope package, three reel, Model No. B469
 NM $34   MIP $40

Western Toys

Remember when Saturday afternoon at the movies for two kids with popcorn cost 25 cents? A quarter sure doesn't buy what it used to. In the 1940s and 1950s, American cowgirls and cowboys also plunked down their hard-earned silver for genuine articles endorsed (or at least bearing the names of) their favorite Western stars.

Heroes were aplenty, and included the likes of Gene Autry, Hopalong Cassidy, the Lone Ranger, and, of course, Roy Rogers, Zorro, and many others.

Today, grownup cowpokes drive hard bargains to get their hands on well-preserved toys that evoke well-preserved memories. That's because they don't make toys, or heroes, like they used to.

In the 1940s, straight shooters like Buck Jones, Red Ryder, and Tom Mix were everywhere. Not only were they peering down from the movie screen—their images also graced cereal boxes, comic books, clothing, clocks, furniture, and toy guns.

By the time Hopalong Cassidy, Gene Autry, and Roy Rogers became household names, cowboy toys and merchandise were everywhere. Soon every child could wear, eat, play with, read, or decorate his room with cowboy memorabilia.

The heyday of cowboy fever blossomed in the 1940s and 1950s. Sears Roebuck devoted entire sections to cowboy-related merchandise. At the time, toys ranged from 25 cents to $5. Six-guns of every size, were sold individually and in holstered sets. Generic guns, hats, and other pieces can still be widely found at reasonable prices today. Toys featuring the "Big Four" ("Hoppy," Lone Ranger, Gene, and Roy) command higher values. But other cowboy heroes enjoyed successful merchandising as well, including Wyatt Earp, Rex Allen, Wild Bill Hickok, Tom Mix, The Cisco Kid, and Tex Ritter.

2006 TRENDS

The recent releases of western films and television shows on DVD have increased the interest for pre- and post-World War II western toys. Paper ephemera, such as lobby cards, advertisements, food wrappers, or club membership items continue to be valuable because they were often discarded and are difficult to find today.

Premium rings were often sold bearing the likeness of a cowboy hero and continue to be among the most valuable western collectibles. Other premiums, offered by companies like Ovaltine, Kellogg's, and Ralston, were available only by mail, which adds to their scarcity. Condition is everything, and those rare pieces that are truly mint will command higher prices.

And as always, beware of reproductions.

For more information on Roy Rogers memorabilia, check out *The Ultimate Roy Rogers Collection Identification & Price Guide* by Ron Lenius. This 208-page softcover book was released in 2001 and features more than 1,000 color photos. To order, call 800-258-0929 or visit www.collect.com.

THE TOP TEN
WESTERN TOYS (In Mint Condition)

1. Zorro Target Shoot, 1950s	$1,510
2. Hopalong Cassidy Roller Skates, Rollfast,	1,000
3. Hopalong Cassidy Cap Gun, Wyandotte, 1950s	650
4. Hopalong Cassidy Radio, Arvin, 1950s	600
5. Roy Rogers Toy Chest, 1950s	550
6. Hartland Figures, Bill Longley – The Texan, 1959	525
7. Buck Jones Rangers Cowboy Suit, Yankiboy, 1930s	500
8. Hopalong Cassidy, metal figures, 1950s, Timpo	475
9. Lone Ranger Record Player, 1940s, Dekka	450
10. Roy Rogers Play Set, 1950s, Amsco	440

ANNIE OAKLEY

Annie Oakley Cut-Out Dolls, 1956, Watkins-Strathmore, paper dolls, Model No. 1822
EX $20   NM $45   MIP $80

Annie Oakley Cut-Out Dolls, 1958, Whitman, paper dolls
EX $20   NM $35   MIP $50

Annie Oakley Sewing Set, 1950s, Pressman
EX $20   NM $35   MIP $55

Annie Oakley Sharpshooter Book, 1956, Golden, Little Golden Books
EX $3   NM $5   MIP $10

Annie Oakley Sparkle Picture Craft, 1950s, Gabriel
EX $20   NM $30   MIP $45

Annie Oakley with Tagg and Lofty Cut-Out Dolls, 1955, Whitman, paper dolls
EX $20   NM $35   MIP $50

Girl's Outfit, 1950s, Pla-Master, red w/yellow fringe and four pictures (Gail Davis?)
EX $40   NM $85   MIP $140

Holster Set, 1950s, Daisy, leather holsters and cap pistols
EX $75   NM $150   MIP $225

Puzzle, 1955, Milton Bradley, boxed jigsaw puzzle
EX $5   NM $10   MIP $30

BONANZA

Ben Cartwright and his Horse, 1966, American Character, plastic figures
EX $60   NM $140   MIP $275

Bonanza Four-in-One Wagon, 1960s, American Character
EX $75   NM $150   MIP $300

Foto Fantastiks Photo Coloring Set, 1960s, Eberhard Faber
EX $40   NM $75   MIP $150

Hoss Cartwright and his Horse, 1966, American Character, plastic figures
EX $60   NM $140   MIP $275

Hoss Range Pistol, 1960s, Marx, carded plastic gun
EX $35   NM $65   MIP $125

Little Joe Cartwright Figure, 1966, American Character, 6" figure
EX $60   NM $140   MIP $275

Mustang, American Character, the outlaw's horse
EX $25   NM $50   MIP $100

Outlaw Figure, 1966, American Character
EX $40   NM $80   MIP $160

Palomino, American Character, Ben's horse
EX $25   NM $50   MIP $100

Pinto, American Character, Little Joe's horse
EX $25   NM $50   MIP $100

Puzzle, 1960s, Saalfield, frame tray
EX $20   NM $40   MIP $75

Puzzle, 1964, Milton Bradley
EX $10   NM $20   MIP $40

Stallion, American Character, Hoss's horse
EX $25   NM $50   MIP $100

Woodburning Set, 1960s, ATF Toys
EX $65   NM $125   MIP $250

DANIEL BOONE

Daniel Boone Card Game, 1965, Ed-U-Cards
EX $7   NM $10   MIP $15

Daniel Boone Figure, 1964, Remco, 5" tall, hard plastic body, vinyl head, cloth coonskin cap and long rifle
EX $35   NM $75   MIP $160

Daniel Boone Film Viewer, 1964, Acme, w/two arms
EX $7   NM $10   MIP $20

Daniel Boone Inflatable Toy, 1965, Multiple Toymakers
EX $25   NM $50   MIP $75

DAVY CROCKETT

3-D Moving Picture and Viewer, 1950s, Armour-Cloverbloom Margarine, premium cardboard viewer w/3-D cards
EX $40   NM $80   MIP $150

Alamo Construction Set, 1950s, Practi-Cole
EX $40   NM $75   MIP $150

Auto-Magic Picture Gun, 1950s, Stephens, projection gun w/films
EX $40   NM $75   MIP $150

Baby Davy Crockett Doll, 1950s, Spunky, 8" tall vinyl squeeze toy
EX $20   NM $40   MIP $75

Davy Crockett and His Horse Figures, 1950s, Ideal, plastic
EX $30   NM $50   MIP $150

Davy Crockett Doll, 1950s, 8", hard plastic, sleepy eyes, leather clothes, two rifles, hat
EX $60   NM $130   MIP $250

Davy Crockett Doll, 1973, Exel, Legends of the West series, 9-1/2"
EX $30   NM $55   MIP $95

Davy Crockett Frontier Target Game, American Toys, tin litho dartboard
EX $35   NM $75   MIP $130

Davy Crockett Guitar, 1950s, Peter Puppet Playthings, 24" long, wood
EX $80   NM $175   MIP $350

Davy Crockett Push Puppet, 1950s, Kohner Bros.
EX $30   NM $65   MIP $100

Davy Crockett Ring, 1950s, bronze-colored
EX $40   NM $50   MIP $60

Dispatch Case, 1950s, Neptune Plastics, vinyl pouch, yellow graphics
EX $15   NM $30   MIP $65

Frontier Rifle, 1950s, Marx, 32" rifle
EX $40   NM $75   MIP $150

Frontierland Pencil Case, 1950s, Hassenfeld Bros., cardboard
EX $45   NM $75   MIP $100

Frontierland Pioneer Scout Outfit, 1950s, Eddy, costume set
EX $50   NM $100   MIP $250

Iron-Ons, 1950s, Vogart, three transfers on sheet
EX $15   NM $35   MIP $50

Magic Paint with Water Pictures, 1950s, Artcraft, construction and art set set w/Frontierland fort
EX $75   NM $150   MIP $275

Offical Davy Crockett Color TV Set, 1950s, Lido, plastic viewer, four films
EX $75   NM $150   MIP $275

Official Davy Crockett Belt, 1950s, on card
EX $35   NM $80   MIP $150

Official Davy Crockett Tool Kit, 1950s, Liberty Steel Chest, w/tools
EX $75   NM $175   MIP $250

Pocket Knife, 1950s, Disney, single blade, 2", yellow
EX $20   NM $40   MIP $75

Pony Express Bank, 1950s, Randing, bown and white cloth pouch w/lock and key
EX $15   NM $30   MIP $50

Puzzle, 1950s, Marx, Seige on the Fort
EX $15   NM $40   MIP $60

Puzzle, 1955, Whitman, 11-1/4" x 15"
EX $15   NM $40   MIP $60

Ride-On Bouncing Horse, 1950s, Rich Toys, 37" x 31", white plastic w/black and yellow saddle
EX $75   NM $150   MIP $275

Sand Pail, 1950s, Ohio Art, tin litho
EX $20   NM $35   MIP $85

Suspenders, 1950s, tan w/Crockett graphics
EX $25   NM $50   MIP $90

Travel Bag, 1950s, Neevel, 6-1/2" x 12" x 10" heavy cardboard w/brass hinges and plastic handle
EX $30   NM $75   MIP $130

Wallet, 1950s, Walt Disney, red vinyl w/faux fur
EX $20   NM $45   MIP $80

Wood burning set, 1950s, American Toy & Furniture
EX $10   NM $25   MIP $50

GENE AUTRY

Frame Tray Puzzle, 1950s, Whitman, wood
EX $15   NM $21   MIP $40

Gene Autry Drum Set, 1940s, Colmor
EX $75   NM $160   MIP $275

Gene Autry Guitar, 1950s, Emenee, plastic
EX $65   NM $125   MIP $225

Gene Autry Jump-Up Book, 1955, Adprint Limited London
EX $30   NM $52   MIP $82

Gene Autry Ranch Outfit, 1940s, Henry, dress-up kit w/holster and gun
EX $56   NM $105   MIP $220

Gene Autry's Champion Slate, 1950s, Lowe
EX $15   NM $26   MIP $55

Gene Autry's Stencil Book, 1950s
EX $15   NM $31   MIP $55

Spurs, 1960s, Leslie-Henry, metal spur w/leather back "Gene Autry" signature burned into the leather
EX $40   NM $100   MIP $185

WESTERN TOYS

Stringless Marionette, 1950s, National Mask & Puppet, 14-1/2" tall
EX $45   **NM** $78   **MIP** $165

GUNSMOKE

Coloring Book, 1950s, Whitman
EX $10   **NM** $20   **MIP** $40

Gunsmoke Puzzle, 1950s, Whitman, boxed
EX $18   **NM** $33   **MIP** $55

Gunsmoke Puzzle, 1958, Whitman, frame tray
EX $19   **NM** $34   **MIP** $60

Marshall Matt Dillon's Gunsmoke Play-set, 1958, Multiple, red, yellow, and blue plastic characters, jailhouse, wagon, guns, hats and accessories
EX $40   **NM** $85   **MIP** $125

HARTLAND FIGURES

Annie Oakley and Target, 1950s, 9", Hartland, 9" plastic rider w/horse, #823, tan horse, white hat, black pistol, black saddle,
EX $70   **NM** $140   **MIP** $250

Bill Longley - The Texan, 1959, 9", Hartland, #827, 9" plastic rider w/horse
EX $125   **NM** $300   **MIP** $525

Brave Eagle and White Cloud, 1950s, 9", Hartland, 9" plastic rider w/horse
EX $75   **NM** $150   **MIP** $200

Bret Maverick, 1950s, 9", Hartland, #762, 9" plastic figure, long light blue jacket, light blue hat, two pistols
EX $65   **NM** $135   **MIP** $275

Bret Maverick, 1960s, 9", Hartland, #862, 9" plastic rider w/horse
EX $65   **NM** $130   **MIP** $225

Buffalo Bill, 1950s, 9", Hartland, #819, 9" plastic rider w/horse, hat, 2 pistols
EX $70   **NM** $140   **MIP** $250

Cheyenne, 1950s, 9", Hartland, #818, 9" plastic rider w/horse
EX $40   **NM** $80   **MIP** $150

Cheyenne, 1960s, 9", Hartland, 9" plastic rider w/horse
EX $30   **NM** $50   **MIP** $115

Chief Brave Eagle, 1950s, 9", Hartland, #812, white horse, headdress, saddle blanket, bow, knife
EX $50   **NM** $110   **MIP** $175

Chief Thunderbird and horse, 1950s, 9", Hartland, #813, black/white horse, saddle blanket, tomahawk, spear, knife, headdress
EX $50   **NM** $100   **MIP** $150

Clay Holister Gunfighter, 1950s, 9", Hartland, #763, figure only, two guns, black hat
EX $60   **NM** $125   **MIP** $200

Cochise, 1950s, 9", Hartland, 9" plastic rider w/horse, saddle blanket, rifle
EX $50   **NM** $110   **MIP** $175

Col. Ronald Mackenzie, 1959, 9", Hartland, #829, 9" plastic rider w/horse
EX $40   **NM** $80   **MIP** $150

Cowgirl, 1960s, 9", Hartland, #802, 9" plastic rider w/horse, jade green w/tan pants or red shirt w/white pants
EX $40   **NM** $80   **MIP** $150

Dale Evans, 1950s, 9", Hartland, 9" plastic rider w/horse
EX $40   **NM** $80   **MIP** $200

Davy Crockett, 1950s, 9", Hartland, 9" plastic rider w/horse
EX $45   **NM** $90   **MIP** $150

General Robert E. Lee, 1950s, 9", Hartland, #808, w/ horse (Traveller), confederate flag, saddle, and sword
EX $50   **NM** $110   **MIP** $175

George Washington and Ajax, 1950s, 9", Hartland, plastic rider w/horse, flag, hat
EX $40   **NM** $80   **MIP** $120

Gil Favor from Rawhide, 1950s, 9", Hartland, #831, w/ horse, saddle, hat, gun; 9" figure has dark blue pants, light blue shirt and yellow vest
EX $100   **NM** $200   **MIP** $300

Hoby Gilman, 1960s, 9", Hartland, #825, 9" plastic rider w/horse
EX $40   **NM** $80   **MIP** $150

Jim Bowie and Blaze, 1950s, 9", Hartland, #817, 9" plastic rider w/horse, long rifle, knife
EX $70   **NM** $200   **MIP** $375

Jim Hardie, 1950s, 9", Hartland, #864, 9" plastic rider w/horse
EX $40   **NM** $80   **MIP** $150

Johnny Yuma - The Rebel, 1961, 9", Hartland, #832, 9" plastic rider w/horse
EX $40   **NM** $80   **MIP** $150

Josh Randall, 1959, 9", Hartland, #828, 9" plastic rider w/horse
EX $40   **NM** $80   **MIP** $150

Lone Ranger, 1950s, 9", Hartland, #801, 9" plastic rider w/horse, hat
EX $45   **NM** $90   **MIP** $150

Lone Ranger, 1960s, 9", Hartland, 9" plastic rider w/horse, hat
EX $35   **NM** $70   **MIP** $110

Lucas McCain, 1960s, 9", Hartland, #826, 9" plastic rider w/horse
EX n/a   **NM** n/a   **MIP** $100

Major Seth Adams of Wagon Train and horse, 1950s, 9", Hartland, #824, horse and rider, red shirt, grey vest, yellow pants
EX $75   **NM** $145   **MIP** $225

Marshal Matt Dillon, 1950s, Hartland, 9" plastic rider w/horse
EX $15   **NM** $30   **MIP** $60

Marshal Matt Dillon, 1960s, Hartland, 9" plastic rider w/horse
EX $50   **NM** $100   **MIP** $175

Paladin, 1950s, 9", Hartland, #822, 9" plastic rider w/horse
EX $45   **NM** $90   **MIP** $150

Paladin, 1960s, 9", Hartland, 9" plastic rider w/horse
EX $15   **NM** $30   **MIP** $60

Roy Rogers and Trigger, 1950s, 9", Hartland, #806, 9" plastic rider w/horse, hat, 2 pistols
EX $50   **NM** $100   **MIP** $175

Roy Rogers and Trigger, 1960s, 9", Hartland, 9" plastic rider w/horse, hat, 2 pistols
EX $50   **NM** $100   **MIP** $200

Tom Jeffords, 1950s, 9", Hartland, #821, 9" plastic rider w/horse, hat, rifle
EX $70   **NM** $140   **MIP** $250

Tonto, 1950s, 9", Hartland, 9" plastic rider w/horse, knife
EX $30   **NM** $60   **MIP** $120

Tonto, 1960s, 9", Hartland, 9" plastic rider w/horse, knife
EX $45   **NM** $90   **MIP** $150

Ward Bond, 1960s, 9", Hartland, #824, 9" plastic rider w/horse
EX n/a   **NM** n/a   **MIP** n/a

Wyatt Earp, 1950s, 9", Hartland, #809, 9" plastic rider w/horse
EX $45   **NM** $90   **MIP** $150

(Toy Shop File Photo)

Wyatt Earp, 1960s, 9", Hartland, 9" plastic rider w/horse
EX $15   **NM** $30   **MIP** $75

Zorro and Tempest, 1960s, Hartland, 9" plastic figure with horse, saddle, sword, hat
EX $75   **NM** $150   **MIP** $225

HAVE GUN, WILL TRAVEL

Have Gun, Will Travel Play Set, 1958, Prestige
EX $50   **NM** $100   **MIP** $20

Have Gun, Will Travel Slate, 1960s
EX $10   **NM** $25   **MIP** $50

Holster Set, 1960s, Halco, holsters, belt, canteen
EX $40   **NM** $100   **MIP** $200

Paladin Checkers, 1960s, Ideal, carded
EX $25   **NM** $50   **MIP** $75

Paladin Western Outfit, 1959, Ben Cooper, mask, vest
EX n/a   **NM** $65   **MIP** $150

HOPALONG CASSIDY

Automatic Television Set, 1950s, Automatic Toy
EX $60   NM $100   MIP $200

Bar 20 Ranch Badge, 1950s
EX $25   NM $50   MIP $75

Bar Twenty Shooting Game, 1950s, Chad Valley
EX $50   NM $100   MIP $250

Bread Wrapper, 1950s, Butternut, 14" x 23"
EX $50   NM $70   MIP $95

Canvas School Bag, 1950s
EX $25   NM $50   MIP $150

Cap Gun, 1950s, Wyandotte, 7", silver metal w/white handles, Hoppy pictured on sides
EX $150   NM $300   MIP $600

(Toy Shop File Photo)

Coloring Outfit, 1950s, Transogram
EX $35   NM $75   MIP $150

Compass Hat Ring, 1950s, brass, features "HC" on one side and "20" on other; compass on top
EX $195   NM $250   MIP $300

Crayon and Stencil Set, 1950s, Transogram
EX $35   NM $75   MIP $150

(Toy Shop File Photo)

Frame Tray Puzzle, 1950s, Whitman
EX $10   NM $20   MIP $35

Hopalong Canasta, 1950s, Pacific Playing Card
EX $55   NM $100   MIP $250

Hopalong Cassidy Chinese Checkers, 1950, Milton Bradley
EX $60   NM $130   MIP $225

Hopalong Cassidy Figure, 1950s, Ideal, plastic figure of Hoppy w/Topper
EX $40   NM $65   MIP $150

Hopalong Cassidy Lasso Game, 1950s, Transogram
EX $35   NM $75   MIP $150

Hopalong Cassidy Western Series, 1950s, Timpo, British set of seven metal figures
EX $100   NM $250   MIP $475

(Toy Shop File Photo)

Mechanical Shooting Gallery, 1950s, Automatic Toy
EX $75   NM $150   MIP $350

Original Hopalong Pogo Stick, 1950s
EX $50   NM $100   MIP $225

Picture Gun and Theatre, 1950s, Stephens Products, projects film, Hoppy decals on sides, includes film, gun, cardboard stage
EX $75   NM $150   MIP $225

Pony Express Toss Game, 1950s, Transogram
EX $30   NM $45   MIP $70

Puzzles, 1950s, Milton Bradley, boxed set of three
EX $30   NM $50   MIP $100

Radio, 1950s, Arvin, red metal case, embossed image of Hoppy and topper on front
EX $200   NM $450   MIP $600

Roller Skates, Rollfast
EX $200   NM $500   MIP $1000

Stationary, 1950s, Whitman
EX $20   NM $50   MIP $100

Topper Rocking Horse, 1950s, Rich Toys, plastic/wood
EX $65   NM $125   MIP $250

Wrist Cuffs, 1950s
EX $55   NM $100   MIP $250

HOW THE WEST WAS WON

Dakota Figure, 1978, Mattel
EX $10   NM $20   MIP $35

How the West Was Won Action Play Set, 1977, Timpo
EX $10   NM $25   MIP $40

Lone Wolf Figure, 1978, Mattel
EX $10   NM $20   MIP $35

Puzzle, 1978, HG Toys, boxed jigsaw puzzle
EX $5   NM $7   MIP $15

Zeb Macahan Figure, 1978, Mattel
EX $10   NM $20   MIP $35

LONE RANGER

Electric Drawing Set, 1960s, Lakeside
EX $5   NM $10   MIP $20

Flashlight Ring, 1948, premium
EX $45   NM $90   MIP $175

Hand Puppet, 1940s, cloth body, blue and white polka-dot shirt w/bells in both hands
EX $40   NM $90   MIP $160

Lone Ranger and Tonto Target Set, 1970s, Multiple Toymakers, 3" figures w/horses, guns, darts
EX $15   NM $35   MIP $65

Lone Ranger Coloring Book, 1975, Whitman, #1010
EX $8   NM $15   MIP $25

(Toy Shop File Photo)

Lone Ranger Record Player, 1940s, Dekka, 12" x 10" x 6" wooden box w/burned in illustrations, leather strap
EX $100   NM $225   MIP $450

(Toy Shop File Photo)

Lone Ranger Sheriff Jail Keys, 1945, Esquire Novelty, 5", on ring, came on card w/cut-out Sheriff card
EX $30   NM $63   MIP $125

Pencil Box, 1940s, 8-1/2" long, American Pencil, snap close, 8-1/2" long
EX $20   NM $40   MIP $75

Tonto Indian Outfit, 1950s, Esquire, costume set
EX $50   NM $100   MIP $350

WESTERN TOYS

WESTERN TOYS

Toothbrush Holder, 19384" tall, red shirt, Silver rearing up, 4" tall
EX $40   **NM** $80   **MIP** $125

MISCELLANEOUS CHARACTERS

Bat Masterson Holster Set, 1950s, Carnell, holster, belt, cane, yellow and black vest
EX $75   **NM** $200   **MIP** $300

Buck Jones Rangers Cowboy Suit, 1930s, Yankiboy, costume set
EX $60   **NM** $200   **MIP** $500

Buffalo Bill Puzzle, 1956, Built-Rite, frame tray
EX $10   **NM** $20   **MIP** $35

Cheyenne Book, 1958, Whitman, Little Golden Book
EX $6   **NM** $13   **MIP** $24

Cheyenne Little Golden Record, 1950s, 45 rpm
EX $7   **NM** $15   **MIP** $25

Cheyenne Puzzle, 1957, Milton Bradley, frame tray
EX $12   **NM** $25   **MIP** $45

Cisco Kid Puzzle Set, 1950s, Saalfield, set of three puzzles
EX $30   **NM** $50   **MIP** $70

Johnny Moccasin View-Master Reels, 1957, Sawyers, set of three reelse, booklet
EX $20   **NM** $45   **MIP** $60

Johnny Ringo Hand Puppet, 1950s, Tops in Toys, 15" full body puppet, vinyl head
EX $65   **NM** $100   **MIP** $200

Laramie Cowboy Holster Set, 1960s, Clarke Bros.
EX $65   **NM** $100   **MIP** $225

Maverick Oil Painting by Numbers set, 1960s, Hassenfeld Bros.
EX $20   **NM** $40   **MIP** $60

Red Ranger Ride 'Em Cowboy, 1950s, Wyandotte, mechanical bucking horse and rider on half-circle base
EX $75   **NM** $140   **MIP** $220

Rin Tin Tin Magic Slate, 1950s, Whitman
EX $10   **NM** $20   **MIP** $30

Rin Tin Tin Ring, 1955, Nabisco, plastic, Nabisco Rice Honeys premium
EX $8   **NM** $15   **MIP** $24

Rin Tin Tin Rusty Costume, 1950s, Ben Cooper
EX $25   **NM** $40   **MIP** $85

Straight Arrow Target Game, 1949, Novel Novelties, tin litho target w/crossbow
EX $40   **NM** $75   **MIP** $150

Wild Bill Hickok and Jingles Puzzle Set, 1950s, Built-Rite, set of four
EX $25   **NM** $50   **MIP** $75

Wild Bill Hickok Treasure Map/Guide, 1950s, Kellogg's, cereal premium
EX $40   **NM** $65   **MIP** $90

RED RYDER

Frame Tray Puzzle, 1951, Jaymar, Red Ryder or Little Beaver
EX $5   **NM** $10   **MIP** $20

Little Beaver Archery Set, 1951, cardboard target
EX $10   **NM** $20   **MIP** $30

Little Beaver Coloring Book, 1956, Whitman
EX $5   **NM** $10   **MIP** $25

Red Ryder Corral Bagatelle Game, 1940s, Gotham
EX $25   **NM** $45   **MIP** $75

Red Ryder Pop-Um Shooting Game, 1940s, Daisy
EX $30   **NM** $50   **MIP** $150

Red Ryder Target Game, 1939, Whitman
EX $25   **NM** $50   **MIP** $100

Red Ryder Whirli-Crow Game, 1940s, Daisy
EX $30   **NM** $50   **MIP** $100

ROY ROGERS

Dale Evans Wristwatch, 1951, Ingraham, dale inside upright horseshoe, tan background, chrome case, black leather band
EX $61   **NM** $157   **MIP** $325

Deputy Badge, 1950s
EX $25   **NM** $50   **MIP** $75

Give-A-Show Projector, 1960s, Kenner, projector w/slides
EX $25   **NM** $52   **MIP** $82

Horsedrawn Wagon Pull Toy, 1950s, Hill, 18", wood w/paper litho
EX $56   **NM** $105   **MIP** $275

Ranch Lantern, 1950s, Ohio Art, tin litho, battery-operated
EX $56   **NM** $135   **MIP** $275

Roy Rogers & Dale Evans Coloring Book, 1975, Whitman
EX $10   **NM** $21   **MIP** $33

Roy Rogers & Dale Evans Paper Dolls, 1954, Whitman
EX $35   **NM** $57   **MIP** $88

(Toy Shop File Photo)

Roy Rogers & Dale Evans Western Dinner Set, 1950s, Ideal, utensils in 14" x 24" box
EX $35   **NM** $68   **MIP** $104

Roy Rogers Alarm Clock, 1950s, Ingraham, 4", square ivory-color case, full-color graphics
EX $153   **NM** $315   **MIP** $440

Roy Rogers Crayon Set, 1950s, Standard Toykraft
EX $35   **NM** $52   **MIP** $110

(Toy Shop File Photo)

Roy Rogers Fix-It Chuck Wagon and Jeep, 1950s, Ideal, set w/two horses, four figures, Nellybelle, accessories
EX $71   **NM** $157   **MIP** $330

Roy Rogers Horeshoe Set, Ohio Art, tin litho
EX $40   **NM** $105   **MIP** $275

Roy Rogers Horseshoe Set, 1950s, rubber horseshoes and pegs
EX $30   **NM** $52   **MIP** $143

Roy Rogers Nodder, Japanese, composition, blue shirt, white hat and pants and red bandana and boots
EX $10   **NM** $25   **MIP** $50

Roy Rogers Play Set, 1950s, Amsco, cardboard w/magnetic figures
EX $51   **NM** $210   **MIP** $440

Roy Rogers Puzzle, 1950s, frame tray
EX $20   **NM** $36   **MIP** $50

Roy Rogers Rodeo Board Game, 1949, Rogden, four games in one
EX $102   **NM** $147   **MIP** $220

Roy Rogers Rodeo Sticker Fun Book, 1953, Whitman
EX $35   **NM** $57   **MIP** $121

Roy Rogers Stagecoach, 1950s, Ideal, 14", plastic w/two harnessed horses, Roy, and accessories
EX $25   **NM** $70   **MIP** $135

Roy Rogers Toy Chest, 1950s, 17" x 17" x 12" w/Roy and Bullet graphics
EX $178   **NM** $315   **MIP** $550

Roy Rogers Toy Football, 1950s, white vinyl w/logo
EX $20   **NM** $42   **MIP** $66

Roy Rogers Trigger Trotter, 1950s, pogo stick
EX $153   **NM** $236   **MIP** $330

Roy Rogers Truck, 1950s, Marx, 14", tin litho, red, yellow and blue
EX $95   **NM** $175   **MIP** $300

Trigger Rocking Horse, 1950s, Bell Toys, wood w/metal seat
EX $51   **NM** $105   **MIP** $220

TOM MIX

Big Little Book Picture Puzzles, 1930s, boxed set of two
EX $100   **NM** $225   **MIP** $425

Bullet Flashlight, 1930s, 3" long
EX $50   **NM** $75   **MIP** $130

Magnet Ring, 1947, Ralston, Ralston cereal premium, brass w/silver magnet
EX $12   **NM** $25   **MIP** $65

Riding Horse, 1930s, Mengel, wood
EX $75   **NM** $150   **MIP** $365

Siren Ring, 1944, Ralston, Ralston cereal premium, whistles
 EX $15 **NM** $30 **MIP** $65

Tom Mix Rodeorope, 1930s, Mordt
 EX $75 **NM** $250 **MIP** $425

Tom Mix Shooting Gallery, 1935, Parker Brothers
 EX $75 **NM** $150 **MIP** $320

ZORRO

Dart Rifle Target Set, 1960s
 EX $40 **NM** $70 **MIP** $175

Dominoes, 1950s, Halsam
 EX $25 **NM** $45 **MIP** $65

Fencing Set, 1950s, swords, masks, face guards
 EX $45 **NM** $75 **MIP** $165

Gloves (Children's), 1950s, Walt Disney, black gloves w/white gauntlets that have Zorro image and logo, 8-1/2" long
 EX $15 **NM** $30 **MIP** $60

Hand Puppet, 1958, Gund, vinyl and fabric, 9-1/4" tall
 EX $25 **NM** $50 **MIP** $75

Official Zorro Action Set, 1950s, Marx, costume and weapons set
 EX $75 **NM** $150 **MIP** $350

Paint by Number Set, Hasbro, canvas and paints
 EX $35 **NM** $60 **MIP** $80

Pencil by Number Set, 1960s
 EX $35 **NM** $60 **MIP** $80

Puzzle, 1960s, Jaymar, boxed jigsaw puzzle
 EX $7 **NM** $20 **MIP** $40

Spring Action Target, 1950s, Knickerbocker
 EX $45 **NM** $75 **MIP** $150

Target Shoot, 1950s, gun w/soldier targets
 EX $40 **NM** $75 **MIP** $1510

Walt Disney's The Adventures of Zorro, 1958, Golden, Big golden Book
 EX $10 **NM** $20 **MIP** $30

Walt Disney's Zorro, 1958, Little Golden Book
 EX $5 **NM** $7 **MIP** $15

Walt Disney's Zorro, 1958, Golden, Golden Book
 EX $5 **NM** $10 **MIP** $25

Watch, 1960s, U.S. Time, "Zorro" on face
 EX $12 **NM** $25 **MIP** $75

WESTERN TOYS